Advanced Accountancy

Advanced Accountancy

Volume-I

PRINCIPLES OF ACCOUNTING (INCLUDING GST)

S.P. JAIN
Ex-Associate Professor in Commerce
Shaheed Bhagat Singh College
(University of Delhi)
Sheikh Sarai, Phase II, **New Delhi**

K.L. NARANG
Formerly Head
Department of Commerce
Government College, Chandigarh and
Principal, Government College **Kapurthala** (Punjab)

SIMMI AGRAWAL
Ph.D. FCA, ACMA
Director
Institute of Financial Education & Learning
Ghaziabad (U.P.)

MONIKA SEHGAL
Formerly Head
Department of Commerce Post-Graduate Govt.
College for Girls Sector 42, **Chandigarh** (U.T.) and
Principal, Jawahar Lal Nehru Government College
Mandi Gobindgarh (Punjab)

KALYANI PUBLISHERS
LUDHIANA • NEW DELHI • NOIDA (U.P.) • HYDERABAD • CHENNAI
KOLKATA • CUTTACK • GUWAHATI • KOCHI • BENGALURU

KALYANI PUBLISHERS

Head Office

3251/B, Street No. 5, Near Sandhu Tower, Gurdev Nagar, **Ludhiana**-141 001 • Ph : 0161-2760031
E-mail : kalyanibooks@yahoo.co.in **Website :** www.kalyanipublishers.co.in

Administrative Office

4779/23, Ansari Road, Daryaganj, **New Delhi**-110 002 • Ph : 011-23271469, 23274393
E-mail : kalyani_delhi@kalyanipublishers.in

Works

B-16, Sector-8, **NOIDA** (U.P.)

Branches

1, Mahalakshmi Street, T. Nagar, **Chennai**-600 017 • M : 9444117261
Gopabandhu Lane, Behind Govt. Bus Stand, Badambadi, **Cuttack**-753 012 (Odisha) • Ph : 0671-2311391
4-3-65/2/A, Behind HVS Public School, Raghunath Bagh
Sultan Bazar, **Hyderabad**-500 095 • Ph : 040-24750368
10/2B, Ramanath Mazumdar Street, **Kolkata**-700 009 • Ph : 033-35571565
Arunalaya, 1st Floor, Saraswati Road, Pan Bazar, **Guwahati**-781 001 • Ph : 0361-2731274
Koratti Parambil House, Convent Road, **Kochi**-682 035 • Ph : 0484-2367189
No. 24 & 25, 1st Floor, Hameed Shah Complex, Cubbonpet Main Road, **Bengaluru**-560 002

V 43732 2 8 + 1560 = 1568 Pages 20" x 30" 196 Forms

Twenty Second Revised Edition, 2025

Typesetting at
Times Printographic

ISBN 978-93-272-9608-2

PRINTED IN INDIA

Printed at: Yash Printographics

Preface

Twenty Second Revised Edition

We are pleased to present **Twenty-Second thoroughly revised and enlarged edition** of this book, made available to readers within a remarkably short span of time since the last reprint. The continued demand for this title is a source of great encouragement and responsibility for us.

In preparing this edition, we have taken into careful consideration the valuable suggestions and feedback received from our esteemed readers, teachers, and students across the country. The entire text has undergone a **comprehensive revision**, with every chapter updated to reflect the latest academic developments and practical applications as per the **prescribed syllabi of various universities and professional institutions.**

Salient Features of the Revised Edition

- **Comprehensive Coverage**: Designed to meet the academic and examination needs of students pursuing B.Com. (Pass and Hons.), M.Com., M.B.A., MCA, IPCC/ATC, C.A. (Final), I.C.M.A. (Stage II), Company Secretaries (Foundation and Intermediate), and CAIIB (Part-I).
- **Latest GST Provisions**: Incorporates updated provisions and **accounting treatment of Goods and Services Tax (GST)**, supported by practical illustrations in relevant chapters.
- **Updated Accounting Standards**: The edition reflects the latest changes and developments in **Accounting Standards (AS)** and **Indian Accounting Standards (Ind AS)**, along with their **practical implications** and **disclosures** across various topics. Relevant updates have been integrated into the content with clarity.
- **Rich Practice Material**: Includes a wide range of **solved illustrations** and **practical problems** drawn from recent university and professional examination papers. These are logically graded and edited for enhanced clarity.
- **Chapter-end Assessments**: Each chapter concludes with **Objective Type Questions**, **Short Answer Questions**, and **Long Answer Questions** to facilitate concept reinforcement and exam readiness.
- **Separate Volume for Problem-Solutions**: A companion book titled **"Practical Problems in Advanced Accountancy"** provides detailed solutions to all numerical problems for the convenience of learners and educators.

- **Pedagogically Structured Content**: Each topic is presented in a structured, easy-to-follow manner, supported by **working notes**, **diagrams**, and **tabular summaries**, to promote better conceptual understanding.

We are confident that this revised edition will serve as a reliable, up-to-date, and student-friendly guide for learners and educators alike.

We gratefully acknowledge the continued support of **M/s Kalyani Publishers**, whose commitment has ensured the timely publication of this edition. We also wish to express our sincere thanks to **Times Printographics** for their excellent printing services and keen attention to production quality.

Every effort has been made to ensure accuracy and remove errors. Nonetheless, readers are encouraged to bring any discrepancies to our notice. We welcome suggestions and feedback for further enhancement, which may be shared with us at **spjain73@gmail.com**.

We thank our readers for their trust and encouragement and dedicate this edition to the spirit of academic excellence in the field of Accountancy.

2025

S.P. Jain
K.L. Narang
Simmi Agrawal
Monika Sehgal

Contents

CHAPTER

1

Introduction to Accounting

Origin and Growth of Accounting

Accounting is as old as money itself. However, the act of accounting was not as developed as it is today because in the early stages of civilisation, the number of transactions to be recorded was so small that each businessman was able to record and check for himself all his transactions. Accounting was practised in India twenty-three centuries ago as is clear from the book named 'Arthashastra' written by Kautilya, King Chandragupta's minister. This book not only relates to politics and economics, but also explains the art of proper keeping of accounts. The chapter 'The Business of Keeping up Accounts in the Office of Accountants' describes records of accounts to be maintained in accountant's office and methods of checking accounts. However, the modern system of accounting based on the principles of Double Entry System owes its origin to Luco Pacioli who first published the principles of Double Entry System in 1494 at Venice in Italy. Thus, the art of accounting has been practised for centuries but it is only in the late thirties of 20th century that the study of the subject 'Accounting' has been taken up seriously.

In the recent years large scale production, cut throat competition, widening of the market and changes in the technology have brought remarkable changes in the field of accounting. In the words of ***Gordon* and *Gordon Shillinglaw*** "It has come to be recognised as a tool for mastering the various economic problems which a business organisation may have to face. It systematically writes the economic history of the organisation. It provides information that can be drawn upon by those responsible for decisions affecting the organisation's future. This history is written mostly in quantitative terms. It consists partly of files of data, partly of reports summarising various portions of these data, and partly of the plan established by management, to guide its operations."

Need for Accounting

The main aim of a business is to earn profit. For earning profit, a businessman will either purchase the goods in one market at a certain price and sell it in another market at higher price or will convert the raw materials into finished products and sell it to the different customers at a price which will give him some percentage of profit on cost of production. But this may not be true in all cases. Sometimes it may happen that the goods purchased or produced may go out of fashion and may be unsaleable simply because of depression in the market, or keen competition. He may be able to sell the goods either at a loss or at a very small margin of profit. However, he will be anxious at the end of the year to find out whether his goods taken together have been sold at a profit or at a loss and what is financial position on a particular date. Moreover, in a big business information is required for planning, control, evaluation of performance and decision making. This information can be provided only when business transactions are recorded, classified and summarised properly. In order to achieve these purposes it would be necessary to record business transactions according to a well devised system. Book-keeping (in elementary stage) and Accounting (in advanced stage) is the name given to such a system.

Meaning of Book-keeping

Book-keeping is the art and science of recording, classifying and summarizing business transactions in money or money's worth accurately and systematically so that the businessman may be able to know his profit or loss during a specified period and also his financial position on a particular date. Book-keeping is thus the recording of business transactions in a systematic manner. In the words of ***Carter*** **"Book-keeping is the science and art of correctly recording in books of accounts all those transactions that result in the transfer of money or money's worth."**

Definition of Accounting

Important purposes of accounting are to ascertain profit or loss during a specified period, to show financial position of the business on a particular date and to have control over the firm's property. Such accounting records are required to be maintained to measure the income of the business and communicate the information so that it may be used by managers, owners and other parties. Accounting is a discipline which records, classifies, summarises and interprets financial information about the activities of a concern so that intelligent decisions can be made about the concern.

"Financial Accounting is "the art of recording, classifying and summarising in a significant manner in terms of money transactions and events which are in part, at least of a financial character and interpreting the results thereof."
—American Institute of Certified Public Accountants

Accounting is "the process of identifying, measuring, and communicating economic information to permit informed judgements and decisions by users of the information". **— American Accounting Association**

Accounting is a service activity. Its function is to provide quantitative information, primarily financial in nature, about economic activities that is useful in making economic decision in making reasoned choices among alternative course of action. **—Accounting Principles Board (APB)**

Accounting may be defined "as the identifying, measuring, recording and communicating of financial information." **—H. Bierman and AR Drebin**

"Accounting is the science of recording and classifying business transactions and events, primarily of a financial character and the act of making significant summaries analysis and interpretation of these transactions and events and communicating the results to persons who must make decisions or form judgements." **—Smith & Ashburne**

From the above the following attributes of accounting emerge :

***(i)* Identifying the transactions and events.** Accounting identifies transactions and events of a separate entity. A transactions is a particular type of external event which can be expressed in terms of money and bring change in the financial position of a business unit. An event (whether internal or external) is a happening of consequence to an entity (*e.g.* use of raw material for production). An entity means an economic unit that performs economic activities (*e.g.* Reliance Industries Ltd., TISCO).

***(ii)* It is the art of recording business transactions.** First of all financial transactions should be recorded in the journal or in the books of original entry known as subsidiary books as and when they take place so that a complete record of financial transactions is available.

***(iii)* It is the art of classifying business transactions.** All entries in the journal or subsidiary books should be classified by posting them to the appropriate ledger accounts to find out at a glance the total effect of all such transactions in a particular account. For example, all transactions relating to Shyam Sunder in the journal or various subsidiary books will be posted to Shyam Sunder's Account. It may be noted that business transactions are recorded and classified in such a way so that it may be possible to determine profit or loss made by the business and its financial position on a specified date.

***(iv)* The transactions or events of a business must be recorded in monetary terms.** If there are certain events which cannot be measured in terms of money, they will not be recorded in financial accounting. For example, a quarrel between production manager and finance manager may be affecting the business but it cannot be measured in terms of money and thus will not be recorded in the books of accounts.

***(v)* It is the art of summarising financial transactions.** After recording and classifying financial transactions next stage is to prepare the trial balance and final accounts with a view to ascertaining the profit or loss made during a trading period and the financial position of the business on a particular date.

***(vi)* It is an art of analysis and interpretation of these transactions.** The accounting information must be analysed and interpreted by calculating various ratios and percentages or other relationship in order to evaluate the past performance of the business and to make sound plans for the future.

***(vii)* The results of such analysis must be communicated to the persons who are to make decisions or form judgements.** All information must be provided in time and presented to the different categories of the persons so that appropriate decisions may be taken at the right time.

Distinction Between Book-Keeping and Accountancy

Book-keeping is recording of the financial transactions of a business in a methodical manner so that information on any point in relation to them may be quickly obtained. A book-keeper may be responsible for keeping all the financial records of a business or only a minor segment such as maintenance of the customers' accounts in a departmental store. Much of the work of a book-keeper is clerical in nature and can be accomplished through the use of mechanical and electronic equipment.

On the other hand, Accounting is primarily concerned with the design of the system of records, the preparation of reports based on the recorded data, the interpretation of the reports and finally communicating the results of the interpretation to persons who are interested in such results. Accountants often direct and review the work of book-keepers. The work of accountants at the beginning may include some book-keeping but accountants must possess a much higher level of knowledge, conceptual understanding and analytical skill than is required of the book-keepers.

Welsch and Anthony have beautifully given the distinction between book-keeping and accounting as follows :

"Some people naively confuse a book-keeper with an accountant and book-keeping with accounting. In effect they confuse one of the minor parts with the whole of accounting. It is tantamount to comparing the simple administration of first aid with the complex practice of medicine by the physician. Book-keeping is the routine and clerical side of accounting and requires only minimal knowledge of the accounting model. A book-keeper records the repetitive and uncomplicated transactions in most businesses and may maintain the simple records of a very small business. In contrast, the accountant is a professional competent in the design of information systems, analysis of complex economic events, interpretative and analytical processes, reporting, financial advising, and management consulting."

Main differences between Book-keeping and Accounting are as follows :

Points of Distinction	*Book-keeping*	*Accounting*
1. Object	The object of book-keeping is to prepare original books of accounts, trial balance and final accounts and to maintain systematic records of financial results.	The object of accounting is to record, classify, summarise, analyse and interpret the business transactions and to ascertain operating results & financial position and to communicate to various users.
2. Scope	It has limited scope and is concerned with recording, classifying, and summarising of business transactions.	It has a wide scope and covers book-keeping plus analysis and interpretation.
3. Level of Work	It is restricted to clerical work and is done by lower levels of management.	It is concerned with all levels of management. Lower level clerks prepare the accounts, medium level report it and top level interpret it.

4. Mutual Dependence	It has to depend on accounting for making the accounting records more useful.	It has to depend on book-keeping for getting the required information from accounting records and for making them useful for planning, control and decision making.
5. Results of the Business	It shows the net result and financial position of the business as the scope extends to the preparation of final accounts.	It analyses the operating results and financial position of the business.
6. Stages	Bookkeeping is a primary stage.	Accounting is the secondary stage. It begins where book-keeping ends.
7. Nature of Job	The job of book-keeper is often routine and clerical in nature.	The job of an accountant is analytical in nature.
8. Knowledge Required	The book-keeper is not required to have higher level of knowledge than that of an accountant.	The accountant must have higher level of knowledge than that of bookkeeper.
9. Staff for Performing Work	Book keeping work is performed by junior staff.	Accounting work is performed by senior staff.

Accounting as an Information System (Or Users of Accounting Information)

Accounting is fundamentally an information system. It plays a critical role in identifying, recording, processing, and communicating financial data about an organisation to a variety of users. These users rely on the information generated by the accounting process to make informed economic decisions. The accounting cycle starts with the identification and recording of business transactions and concludes with the preparation of financial statements. Every step in this process generates useful information. However, the mere generation of data is not the final objective. The real value lies in how effectively this data is communicated to relevant users to support planning, control, and decision-making.

Accounting is often called the **"language of business"** because it facilitates communication of an organisation's economic affairs. Just as language enables us to share ideas, accounting enables stakeholders to understand a business's performance and financial health. According to Slavin and Reynolds, Professors of Accounting : *"Conceptually, accounting is the discipline that provides information on which external and internal users of the information may base decisions that result in the allocation of economic resources in society."*

Accounting information is used by two major groups: **external users** and **internal users**.

(*i*) External Users of Accounting Information

External users are individuals or entities outside the organisation who have an interest in its financial information, though they are not directly involved in the daily operations of the business. Their decisions often rely on the information provided in published financial statements.

1. **Investors:** Investors—both existing and potential—require accounting information to assess the financial health, profitability, and long-term viability of a business. They are concerned about the safety and return on their investments. By reviewing financial statements, investors can evaluate the past performance and future prospects of the business, helping them decide whether to invest more, hold, or withdraw their investment.
2. **Creditors:** Creditors such as suppliers, banks, and financial institutions provide goods, services, or money on credit. Before extending credit, they must assess the liquidity and repayment capacity of the organisation. Accounting records, especially the balance sheet and cash flow statements, provide insights into current assets, liabilities, and overall financial position, helping creditors make informed decisions.

3. **Members of Not-for-Profit Organisations :** Contributors and members of non-profit organisations—like educational institutions, hospitals, and charitable societies—use accounting information to understand how effectively their donations or subscriptions are being utilised. Since profitability is not the main goal in these organisations, accounting information helps assess service efficiency, cost control, and financial sustainability.
4. **Government:** Central and state governments depend on accounting information for a variety of purposes such as taxation, policy formulation, economic planning, and regulation. Income tax returns, GST filings, and other regulatory submissions are based on accounting data. Governments also use financial records to compile macroeconomic indicators like GDP and national income.
5. **Consumers :** Consumers indirectly benefit from accounting information through cost control and fair pricing mechanisms. For instance, when the government regulates the price of essential goods, it relies on accounting data to determine the cost structures and ensure that prices are fair to both producers and consumers. Sound accounting helps in cost reduction, leading to lower prices for consumers without compromising product quality.
6. **Research Scholars:** For academic or analytical purposes, researchers and scholars use accounting information to study business trends, financial behavior, and organisational efficiency. A detailed examination of income, expenditure, assets, and liabilities over time allows them to draw meaningful conclusions about industry performance, operational practices, and financial management techniques.

(*ii*) Internal Users of Accounting Information

Internal users are individuals within the organisation who use accounting information to manage operations, assess performance, and make strategic decisions. Their needs are more specific, detailed, and frequent compared to external users.

1. **Owners:** Owners or proprietors are the primary financial stakeholders in a business. They use accounting reports to determine whether their capital is being employed efficiently. Profit and loss accounts and balance sheets provide crucial insights into the returns on their investments, helping them assess business success and plan future strategies.
2. **Management:** Managers at all levels depend heavily on accounting data to perform key functions such as planning, directing, controlling, and decision-making. Budgetary control, cost analysis, profit analysis, and resource allocation are based on reliable accounting information. It allows managers to compare actual performance with targets, identify variances, and take corrective action when needed. Accounting acts as the eyes and ears of management, enabling strategic oversight and operational efficiency.
3. **Employees:** Employees may not directly engage with the accounting system, but they are often impacted by the outcomes it reveals. Bonus calculations, performance incentives, profit-sharing schemes, and even job security are influenced by the financial health of the organisation. Employees seek assurance that their contributions are valued and fairly rewarded. In unionised environments, financial statements often serve as a basis for collective bargaining and wage negotiations.

Objectives of Accounting

The starting point for any area of study is to set forth its boundaries and determine its objectives. Developments in the field of science and mathematics have brought about a significant change in the field of accounting. The whole concept of accounting has changed. Accounting has to be a versatile system serving a large number of goals of modern business and industry simultaneously. The type of accounting information useful to management in taking decisions is not necessarily the same as is needed by shareholders, prospective investors and creditors. Different accounting principles may be required to meet the several objectives of accounting.

Objectives of accounting (as given by American Accounting Association) are to provide information for the following purposes :

(*i*) Making decisions concerning the use of limited resources including identification of crucial decision areas and determination of objectives and goals.

(*ii*) Effectively directing and controlling the organisation's human and materials resources.

(*iii*) Maintaining systematic records and reporting on the custodianship of resources.

(*iv*) Facilitating special functions and control.

From the above, three main objectives of accounting can be given as follows :

1. To ascertain whether the business operations have been profitable or not. Accounting helps us to know whether a business has earned profit or suffered loss during the accounting period. It will give us an idea of efficiency of the business. To determine profit or loss of the accounting period, a Trading and Profit and Loss Account or an Income Statement is prepared by matching revenues and expired costs (*i.e.* revenue expenditures) incurred for earning the revenues. In the process of determination of profit or loss, it is expense or cost that is matched with revenue and not vice versa. Thus, first of all revenue is determined and then expenses incurred for earning the revenue are matched with the revenue for calculating the difference known as net profit or net loss.

2. To ascertain the financial position of the business. Balance Sheet or Position Statement is prepared to give an idea of the financial position of the business on a particular date. The financial position of an enterprise is indicated by its assets on a given date and its liabilities on that date. Excess of assets over liabilities represent the capital and is indicative of the financial soundness of an enterprise. A properly drawn up balance sheet gives information relating to (*i*) the nature and value of assets, (*ii*) the nature and extent of liabilities, (*iii*) whether the enterprise is solvent, (*iv*) whether the business concern is over trading.

3. To generate information. Accounting records generate information which may be helpful to various persons in planning, control, evaluation of performance and decision making.

Functions of Accounting

Functions refer to the specific activities or tasks performed by accounting to fulfill its objectives. These functions are the practical and operational aspects of accounting. The key functions of accounting include :

(*i*) **Recording Transactions :** Accounting functions involve systematically recording and documenting all financial transactions of an organisation. This includes the collection and organisation of financial data to create a complete and accurate record of business activities.

(*ii*) **Classifying and Categorising Transactions :** Accounting functions involve classifying financial transactions into different categories based on their nature and purpose. This classification helps in organising financial data and simplifies the retrieval and analysis of information.

(*iii*) **Summarising Financial Information :** Accounting functions include summarising financial transactions and preparing financial statements. This involves consolidating and presenting the financial data in a concise and structured format, such as income statements, balance sheets, and cash flow statements.

(*iv*) **Analysing and Interpreting Financial Data :** Accounting functions involve analysing and interpreting financial data to derive meaningful insights. This includes calculating financial ratios, comparing performance indicators, and assessing the financial health and efficiency of the organisation.

(*v*) **Reporting and Communication :** Accounting functions involve reporting financial information to stakeholders through various reports, statements, and disclosures. This includes preparing financial reports that comply with accounting standards and regulations and effectively communicating the results to users of financial information.

While objectives represent the broader goals and purposes of accounting, functions represent the specific activities and tasks performed to achieve those objectives. The functions of accounting support the attainment of the objectives by providing the necessary tools and processes for recording, analysing, interpreting, and communicating financial information.

Advantages of Accounting

Following are the main advantages of accounting :

1. Replacement of memory. In a large business it is very difficult for a businessman to remember all the transactions. Accounting provides records which will furnish information as and when desired and thus it replaces human memory.

2. Evidence in court. Properly maintained accounts are often treated as a good evidence in the court to settle a dispute.

3. Settlement of taxation liability. If accounts are properly maintained, it will be of great assistance to the businessman in settling the income tax and sale tax liability otherwise tax authorities may impose any amount of tax which the businessman will have to pay.

4. Comparative study. It provides the facility of comparative study of the various aspects of the business such as profits, sales, expenses etc. with that of previous year and helps the businessman to locate significant factor leading to the change, if any.

5. Sale of business. If accounts are properly maintained, it helps to ascertain the proper purchase price in case the businessman is interested to sell his business.

6. Assistance to the insolvent person. If a person is maintaining proper accounts and unfortunately he becomes insolvent (*i.e.* when he is unable to pay to his creditors), he can explain many things about the past with the help of accounts and can start a fresh life.

7. Assistance to various parties. It provides information to various parties, *i.e.,* owners, creditors, investors, government, managers, research scholars, public and employees and financial position of a business enterprise from their own view point.

8. Facilitates in raising loans. Accounting facilitates raising loans from lenders by providing them the required financial information.

9. Assistance to the management. Accounting assists the management in taking managerial decisions. For example, Projected Cash Flow Statement facilitates the management to know the future receipts and payments and to take decisions regarding anticipated surplus or shortage of funds.

10. Facilitate control over assets. Accounting facilitates control over assets by providing information regarding Cash Balance, Bank Balance, Stock, Debtors, Fixed Assets, etc.

Limitations of Accounting

Following are the main limitations of accounting :

1. Records only monetary transactions. Accounting records only those transactions which can be measured in monetary terms. Those transactions which cannot be measured in monetary terms as conflict between production and marketing managers, efficient management etc., may be very important for a concern but not recorded in the business books.

2. Effect of price level changes not considered. Accounting transactions are recorded at cost in the books. The effect of price level changes is not brought into the books with the result that comparison of the various years becomes difficult. For example, the sale to total assets in 2021 would be much higher than in 2017 due to rising prices, fixed assets being shown at cost and not at market price.

3. No realistic information. Accounting information may not be realistic as accounting statements are prepared by following basic concepts and conventions. For example, going concern concept gives us an idea that the business will continue and assets are to be recorded at cost but the book value which the asset is showing may not be actually realisable. Similarly, by following the principle of conservatism the financial statements will not reflect the true position of the business.

4. Personal Bias of Accountant affects the accounting statements. Accounting statements are influenced by the personal judgement of the accountant. He may select any method of depreciation, valuation of stock, amortisation of fixed assets and treatment of deferred revenue expenditure. Such judgement if based on integrity and competency of the accountant will affect the preparation of accounting statements.

5. Permits alternative treatments. Accounting permits alternative treatments within generally accepted accounting concepts and conventions. For example, method of charging depreciation may be straight line method or diminishing balance method or some other method. Similarly, closing stock may be valued by FIFO (First-in-First-Out) or LIFO (Last-in-First-out) or average price method. Application of different methods may give different results and results may not be comparable. **Hence accounting can be manipulated.**

6. Profit no real test of managerial performance. Profit earned during an accounting period is the test of managerial performance. Profit may be shown in excess by manipulation of accounts by suppressing such costs as depreciation, advertisement and research and development or taking excess value of closing stock. Consequently real idea of managerial performance may not be available by manipulated profit.

7. Historical in nature. Usually accounting supplies information in the form of Statement of Profit and Loss and Balance Sheet at the end of the year. Thus, the information provided is of historical interest and only gives post-mortem analysis of the past accounting information. For control and planning purposes management is interested in quick and timely information which is not provided by financial accounting.

8. Window Dressing in Balance Sheet. When an accountant resorts to window dressing in the Balance Sheet, then Balance Sheet cannot exhibit the true and fair view of the state of affairs of the business.

Accounting : The Fusion of Science and Art

Accounting is often described as both a science and an art due to its unique characteristics and functions within the business world. To fully appreciate its dual nature, let's try to understand the aspects that highlight its scientific and artistic elements.

Scientific Aspects of Accounting :

1. **Systematised Knowledge :** Accounting is built upon a structured framework of principles and rules, such as the double-entry system, which guide the recording, classification, and summarisation of financial transactions. This systematic approach creates a foundation for consistent and reliable financial reporting.
2. **Universal Application :** The fundamental principles of accounting, such as the matching principle, revenue recognition, and the accrual basis, have widespread applicability across various industries and sectors. These principles provide a basis for standardised financial reporting and analysis.
3. **Data Analysis :** Like a science, accounting involves the analysis of data to draw meaningful conclusions. Financial statements are scrutinised to interpret the financial health and performance of an organisation, allowing stakeholders to make informed decisions.

Artistic Aspects of Accounting :

1. **Application of Knowledge :** While accounting is grounded in principles, its practical application requires interpretation, judgment, and adaptability. Accountants apply their knowledge to unique business scenarios, making decisions on how to classify transactions, estimate values, and address uncertainties.
2. **Subjectivity and Judgment :** The use of estimates, assumptions, and professional judgment is inherent in accounting. Different accountants might approach the same transaction or event differently based on their interpretation and judgment, similar to how artists bring their creativity to their work.
3. **Customisation and Creativity :** In certain situations, accountants need to tailor their methods to suit the specific needs of a business or industry. This customisation requires creativity and adaptability, similar to how artists apply their skills in unique ways to achieve desired outcomes.

4. **Improvement with Practice :** Just as artists refine their craft through practice and experience, accountants become more proficient by consistently applying their knowledge and adapting to changing accounting standards and regulations.

In essence, accounting's scientific foundation provides a structured framework for recording and reporting financial information, while its artistic elements involve the application of knowledge, judgment, and customisation to meet diverse business needs. This combination of scientific principles and artistic interpretation makes accounting a dynamic and versatile discipline that plays a vital role in the functioning of modern organisations.

Classification or Sub-fields of Accounting

Accounting can be classified into the following categories :

(*i*) Financial Accounting. The main purpose of this type of accounting is to record business transactions in the books of accounts in such a way that operating results for a particular period and financial position on a particular date can be known for the information of the various groups of persons.

(*ii*) Cost Accounting. It relates to the collection, classification, ascertainment of cost and its accounting and cost control relating to the various elements of cost *i.e.* materials, labour and overheads.

(*iii*) Management Accounting. It relates to the use of accounting data collected with the help of financial accounting and cost accounting for the purpose of policy formulation, planning, control and decision-making by the management.

(*iv*) Tax Accounting. Different types of taxes have to be paid by an enterprise on behalf of itself or on behalf of others, such as, employees, shareholders etc. Tax Accounting is helpful in complying with the provisions of complex tax laws governing income-tax, sales tax, excise duties, custom duties and estate duties.

(*v*) Social Responsibility Accounting. It is concerned with social responsibility aspects of a business. Management is held responsible for what it contributes to the social well being and progress. It is the process of identifying, measuring and communicating the social effects of the business decisions to permit informed judgements and decisions by the users of information.

RELATIONSHIP OF ACCOUNTING WITH OTHER SUBJECTS

Accounting and Economics

Economics is the study of human behaviour related to the consumption, production, exchange, and distribution of wealth to maximise human satisfaction. It focuses on the problem of choice due to scarcity of resources and limits its scope to activities measurable in monetary terms. Similarly, accounting records only those transactions which can be expressed in monetary terms and are inherently economic. Accounting serves as applied economics by measuring economic variables and providing data essential for economic decision-making. Economists use accounting data to analyse alternative uses of resources, while accountants must understand economic concepts like value and wealth to ensure meaningful reporting. A sound understanding of both disciplines is crucial, particularly in fields like national accounting and the exchange of goods and services.

Accounting and Statistics

Both accounting and statistics deal with the systematic collection, classification, summarisation, analysis, and interpretation of data. However, accounting restricts itself to monetary data, while statistics handles both quantitative and non-monetary data.

Statistical techniques enhance the analytical power of accounting by facilitating comparisons over time, identifying trends, and forecasting the impact of seasonal fluctuations, economic cycles, and other business conditions. Thus, statistics supports decision-making based on accounting data.

Accounting and Law

Accounting and law are interlinked, as financial transactions are governed by legal requirements. While sole proprietorships and partnerships in India have no statutory obligation to prepare final accounts, companies are legally bound under the Companies Act, 2013 to present financial statements in prescribed formats. Compliance with legal provisions such as Schedule III of the Companies Act is essential. Additionally, laws specific to sectors like banking, insurance, and electricity mandate the preparation of financial statements. Accountants must therefore be well-versed in legal requirements, and lawmakers often rely on accounting data when drafting or amending legislation. Similarly, advocates, especially in fields like taxation, benefit from a good understanding of accounting.

Accounting and Engineering

In engineering projects, accounting plays a vital role by providing reliable cost data and profitability analysis. Due to limited funds, engineers must evaluate alternative capital projects, and accounting helps in selecting the most financially viable option. Collaboration between engineers and accountants ensures that both technical feasibility and financial feasibility are taken into account. This partnership is also beneficial in implementing cost reduction programs and improving overall efficiency.

Accounting and Management

Management aims to plan, organise, direct, and control business activities efficiently. Accounting supports these functions by providing timely, relevant, and accurate financial information. Accounting is often termed the language of business, as it communicates financial results and operational insights that help in policy formulation, decision-making, and performance evaluation. Managers rely on accounting data for budgeting, planning, controlling operations, and resource allocation.

Accounting and Sociology

Sociology studies the behaviour of individuals and groups in society to improve collective well-being. It emphasises the better utilisation of resources and the functioning of social institutions. Accounting contributes to this goal by offering insights into how economic resources are utilised within institutions. It also supports transparency and accountability, which are critical in a democratic society. Accurate and understandable financial information is essential for decisions related to public policy, budgeting, labour negotiations, education programs, and more.

As Welsch and Anthony observe: *"An open society demands adequate, understandable, and dependable financial information from institutions that affect citizens' lives. Informed decisions about taxation, public spending, environmental and economic policies depend on the availability of reliable accounting information."*

Role of an Accountant in Society

The role of an accountant is no longer confined to traditional bookkeeping. Accountants today are pivotal figures in shaping economic, social, and industrial settings. They contribute not only to the financial stability of organisations but also to the integrity of markets and the efficient functioning of governments. Their relevance can be studied through the following perspectives:

Accounting as a Profession

One of the most significant aspects is accounting as a profession. Over time, accounting has emerged as a prestigious and regulated profession comparable with law, medicine, engineering, and architecture. Though the basic principles of accounting were first documented by Luca Pacioli in 1494, it was the Industrial Revolution that catalysed the development of accountancy as a profession. The expansion of large-scale enterprises and the separation of ownership from management created a growing need for accurate and independent financial reporting. This, in turn, led to the establishment of professional bodies such as the American Accounting Association (AAA), the Institute of Chartered Accountants in England and Wales (ICAEW), the Canadian Institute of Chartered Accountants (CICA), and the Institute of

Chartered Accountants of India (ICAI). These institutions introduced strict ethical codes, academic standards, and licensing procedures to ensure high levels of professional competence. As Welsch and Anthony aptly noted, "Since 1900, accountancy has attained the stature of a profession similar to law, medicine, engineering, and architecture. Like these professions, it is licensed, governed by ethics, and committed to public service."

Accountants can be categorised based on their employment sector. Public accountants offer auditing, tax consultancy, and advisory services on a fee basis and are often certified professionals such as Chartered Accountants in India. Private accountants are employed by corporations and are responsible for internal accounting, budgeting, cost control, and financial analysis. Government accountants work at the central, state, or local levels, maintaining public accounts, monitoring the use of funds, and aiding policy formulation through reliable financial data.

Within organisations, accounting functions as a central system that integrates all other departments—such as operations, personnel, finance, and marketing—by translating their activities into financial terms. This integration allows management to evaluate performance and align business activities with organisational goals. Accounting provides a holistic view of the enterprise's financial health, making it indispensable for internal control and strategic planning.

The Accounting Principles Board (APB) of the American Institute of Certified Public Accountants (AICPA) defines accounting as "a service activity" that provides quantitative, primarily financial information about economic entities, enabling informed decision-making. As a service function, accounting encompasses multiple branches. Financial accounting focuses on external reporting, managerial accounting supports internal management decisions, and government accounting ensures accountability in public finance. This multi-dimensional role highlights accounting's adaptability and its centrality in decision-making across sectors.

Moreover, the relevance of accounting extends far beyond corporate boardrooms. Public administrators, school principals, hospital managers, and non-profit leaders rely on accounting information for operational efficiency and financial transparency. According to Horngren, accounting serves three key purposes: helping managers with internal reporting and control, supporting strategic decision-making, and enabling external reporting to shareholders, regulators, and creditors. These functions make accounting a universal tool for planning, control, and communication.

Accounting as an Aid in Resource Management

As an enterprise grows in size and complexity, so does the volume and variety of resources it controls. Effective management of these resources is critical to maintaining operational efficiency and long-term sustainability. Without systematic oversight, mismanagement becomes inevitable, potentially leading to financial instability and even liquidation. In this context, accounting plays a vital role in the **identification, classification, valuation, and monitoring of resources**. It provides a structured framework for recording what resources are held, who owns them, and how they change over time.

Accountants are responsible for maintaining accurate and up-to-date records of both tangible and intangible resources. By measuring the operational efficiency of resource utilisation, they provide meaningful insights to management. These insights can help in identifying underutilised assets, inefficient practices, or potential misappropriation by employees. Furthermore, accountants help assess whether resources are being allocated in alignment with organisational goals. Thus, accounting not only safeguards assets but also informs decision-making and performance evaluation.

Accounting as a Tool of Social Welfare

In the past, the success of a business was measured mainly by its profits. Today, businesses are expected to play a more responsible role in society. While earning profit is still important, companies must now also consider the social and environmental impact of their actions. A business uses society's resources and affects the lives of many people—through jobs, products, services, and its influence on the environment. Therefore, it must act as a responsible member of society.

Modern businesses function within complex economic, social, and political environments. Governments, investors, and the public increasingly demand that companies act ethically and contribute to the well-being of society. This broader role is captured in the global concept of **Environmental, Social, and Governance (ESG)**.

- **Environmental factors** include a company's impact on nature—like pollution, carbon emissions, and use of natural resources.
- **Social factors** cover employee welfare, community development, and customer rights.
- **Governance factors** include business ethics, transparency, and compliance with laws and regulations.

In India, the focus on ESG has grown significantly. The Securities and Exchange Board of India (SEBI) has made it mandatory for the top 1000 listed companies (by market capitalisation) to include a Business Responsibility and Sustainability Report (BRSR) as part of their annual filings. This report requires companies to disclose how they are performing in areas such as sustainability, environmental responsibility, social impact, and corporate governance. Accounting plays a vital role in collecting, analysing, and reporting this information in a reliable and standardised format.

To support this trend, the concept of *Social Accounting*—also called *Social Responsibility Accounting*—has emerged. It involves systematically assessing and reporting the social and environmental impact of a company's activities. Although not all Indian companies are legally required to provide social accounting data, many progressive companies—such as **Tata Steel**, **Infosys**, and **ITC**—voluntarily disclose their social and environmental contributions in their sustainability or ESG reports.

Role of Accountants in Achieving Cost Control and Budgeting

Accountants play a vital role in helping businesses achieve the key objectives of cost accounting, such as determining costs, presenting them clearly, and controlling expenses. By providing accurate historical cost information, accountants enable managers to compare current costs with past data and identify areas where costs have increased or decreased. This information is crucial for preparing budgets, which serve as important tools for monitoring and controlling costs effectively.

Role of Accountants as Management Consultants and Financial Advisors

Beyond cost accounting, accountants also serve as trusted management consultants, offering expert advice to improve overall business performance. One important area where accountants contribute is the design and rationalisation of Management Information Systems (MIS). They develop systems that deliver timely, accurate, and relevant information to managers at different levels, supporting effective planning, organisation, and control of business activities. This helps organisations run more efficiently and respond quickly to changing conditions.

Accountants also guide management in making sound investment decisions by analysing different options and recommending investments that offer the best returns with manageable risks, while ensuring that the company's liquidity remains stable. Additionally, they play a crucial role in managing working capital, advising businesses on how to efficiently handle cash, inventory, receivables, and payables to maintain smooth operations and profitability.

In the area of human resources, accountants evaluate personnel policies and suggest improvements that benefit both the organisation and its employees. When a company plans to start a new project, accountants prepare detailed feasibility studies and project reports, helping management decide whether the project is viable and worth pursuing.

Accountants also assist in designing efficient inventory management systems to prevent excess stock and unnecessary capital lock-up. Their role extends to company formation and legal compliance, where they help with registering shares, handling secretarial work, and ensuring that companies meet regulatory requirements.

Furthermore, accountants provide valuable financial advice on matters such as business sales, mergers, restructuring, and assessing a company's financial health. They also help design pension schemes that protect the interests of both employers and employees by ensuring secure retirement benefits.

In all these ways, accountants act as key advisors and problem-solvers who support better decision-making, promote financial discipline, and contribute to the long-term success and sustainability of businesses, which ultimately benefits society.

Role of Accountants in Capital Markets

Accountants play a crucial role in the smooth functioning and development of capital markets. Capital markets are platforms where companies raise funds by issuing shares, debentures, or bonds to the public and investors trade these financial instruments. In such a system, transparency, accuracy, and trustworthiness of financial information are essential for investors and other stakeholders to make informed decisions.

Accountants ensure that companies prepare their financial statements in accordance with established accounting standards and regulatory requirements. By doing so, they provide reliable and truthful information about a company's financial health, performance, and risks. This transparency helps investors assess the value of securities and make investment decisions based on accurate data.

Moreover, auditors—who are specialised accountants—examine and verify financial reports to assure stakeholders that the information presented is free from material misstatements or fraud. This independent verification builds investor confidence and enhances the credibility of companies in the capital markets.

Accountants also help companies comply with disclosure requirements mandated by securities regulators and stock exchanges. These disclosures include periodic financial reports, management discussions, and notes on significant business events, which are essential for maintaining fairness and efficiency in the market.

In addition, accountants assist in initial public offerings (IPOs), mergers and acquisitions, and other complex financial transactions by providing financial analysis, valuation, and due diligence services. Their expertise helps in accurate pricing of securities and reduces the risk of financial misrepresentation.

Accountants act as guardians of financial integrity in capital markets. They protect investors' interests by ensuring transparency, reliability, and accountability in corporate financial reporting. Their role supports the growth of capital markets and contributes to the overall economic development of the country.

Role of Accountants in Corporate Governance

Corporate governance refers to the system of rules, practices, and processes by which a company is directed and controlled. It ensures that the interests of shareholders, management, and other stakeholders are balanced, promoting transparency, accountability, and ethical business conduct.

Accounting plays a vital role in supporting effective corporate governance. It provides the financial information needed by boards of directors, shareholders, regulators, and other stakeholders to make informed decisions. Through accurate and timely financial reporting, accountants help ensure that the company's performance and position are clearly communicated.

One key aspect of accounting in corporate governance is financial transparency. Reliable accounting systems and audits help prevent fraud, mismanagement, and financial irregularities by presenting an honest picture of the company's finances. This transparency builds trust among investors and stakeholders, which is essential for attracting investment and maintaining a company's reputation.

Accountants also assist in internal controls and risk management by designing systems that monitor financial activities and ensure compliance with laws and policies. These controls safeguard company assets and promote responsible management. Moreover, accounting supports the board of directors and audit committees by providing them with detailed financial analysis, reports, and insights necessary to oversee management and make strategic decisions.

Bases of Accounting

For recording business transactions, there are three approaches to accounting which are widely accepted : (*a*) Cash basis (*b*) Accrual basis (*c*) Hybrid or Mixed basis. As you know, all business transactions ultimately result into realisation of revenue or incurring of expense. Truly speaking, the approaches to accounting which are to be discussed here tell how revenues and expenses are to be recognised.

Cash Basis of Accounting

Under cash basis of accounting actual cash receipts and actual cash payments are recorded. Credit transactions are not recorded at all and are ignored till the cash is actually received or paid. Income is merely the difference between the cash receipts and cash payments. The Receipts and Payments Account prepared in case of not-for-profit organisations such as a charitable institution, a club, a school, a college etc. and professional men like lawyer, doctor, chartered accountant etc. can be cited as the best example of cash basis.

Advantages

Main advantages of cash basis of accounting are :

(1) Cash basis of accounting has considerable appeal to many people because it is so simple, appears to be so realistic, is verifiable and satisfies the conservative instinct.

(2) This approach is more objective as very few estimates and judgements are required.

(3) This basis of accounting is suitable for those enterprises where most of the transactions are on cash basis.

Disadvantages

Main disadvantages of cash basis of accounting are :

(1) Cash basis of accounting does not give a true and fair view of profit and loss and financial position of the enterprise because it ignores outstanding and prepaid expenses and accrued income and income received in advance.

(2) This approach does not follow matching principle of accounting.

(3) Cash basis of accounting does not distinguish between capital and revenue items and as a result there is no consistency in the profits of the two years.

(4) In this approach actual cash inflows and outflows are considered, there is a great possibility of profit manipulation *e.g.*, payments may be delayed or prepaid, similarly incomes may be postponed or collected early.

(5) The basis of accounting does not follow Companies Act.

ILLUSTRATION 1. During the financial year 2024-25, Rajan had cash sales of ₹ 90,000 and credit sales of ₹ 60,000. His expenses for the year were ₹ 70,000 out of which ₹ 30,000 expenses are still to be paid. Find out Rajan's income for 2024-25 following cash basis of accounting.

SOLUTION

	₹
Revenues (Inflows of Cash)	90,000
Less: Expenses (Outflows of Cash)	40,000
Profit	50,000

Note: Credit sales and expenses outstanding will not be considered in cash basis of accounting.

Accrual Basis of Accounting

Keeping in view the disadvantages of cash basis of accounting, the accrual basis of accounting has been developed by accountants. In accounting every cash receipt cannot be treated income for determining the true profit of the accounting entity of the period. Accrual basis of accounting rejects the circumstances of receipt or payment of cash as criteria for associating either income or expense with a period. Rather this basis of accounting is based on concept of realisation and expiration and follows two basic accounting principles *viz.* the revenue recognition and the matching principle. In the accrual basis of accounting, the income whether received or not but has been earned or accrued during the period forms part of the total income of that period *e.g.*, sales made on credit will be included in the total sales of the period irrespective of the fact when cash is actually realised. Similarly, if the firm has taken benefit of a particular service, but has not paid within that period, the expense will relate to the period in which the service has been utilised and not to the period in which the payment for it is made, *e.g.*, rent due to the landlord but not paid will be taken as an expense for the period when it is due and not in the period when it is paid. Thus, under accrual basis of accounting net income for a period is the result of matching of revenue realised in the period and costs expired during the period.

Advantages

Main advantages of accrual basis of accounting are :

(1) Accrual basis of accounting is preferred by accountants as it is more scientific as compared to cash basis of accounting.

(2) This basis of accounting gives a complete picture of the financial transactions of the business as it makes a record of all transactions relating to a period and takes into account adjustments like outstanding expenses, prepaid expenses, income received in advance and income earned but not received etc.

(3) This system discloses correct profit or loss for a particular period and also exhibit true financial position of the business on a particular day.

(4) Accrual basis of accounting has wide acceptability as the Companies Act requiring all companies to maintain their accounts on accrual basis of accounting so that fairest possible periodic net income and financial position may be reported to the public.

Disadvantages

Main disadvantages of accrual basis of accounting are :

(1) This system is not as simple as cash basis of accounting.

(2) A quick appraisal of the profit or loss is not possible as a lot of adjustments are required for finding the true financial position of the business.

(3) This basis of accounting is too elaborate.

ILLUSTRATION 2. Taking the figures given in Illustration 1, find out net income according to accrual basis of accounting.

SOLUTION

		₹
Total Sales	= Cash Sales (₹ 90,000) + Credit Sales (₹ 60,000)	= 1,50,000
Less: Total Expenses for the year		70,000
Profit		80,000

Note : ₹ 30,000 expenses still to be paid belong to this year and hence are to be charged to the revenue of this year. Similarly credit sales of ₹ 60,000 are taken in the year in which transactions of credit sales are done.

Difference Between Accrual Basis of Accounting and Cash Basis of Accounting

Following are the main differences between Accrual Basis of Accounting and Cash Basis of Accounting :

Accrual Basis of Accounting	*Cash Basis of Accounting*
(1) Under this basis there may be outstanding expenses, prepaid expenses, accrued income and income received in advance in the Balance Sheet	Under this basis there is no outstanding or prepaid expenses and income accrued or received in advance in the Balance Sheet.

(2) Income statement will show relatively higher income if there are items of prepaid expenses and accrual income.	Income statement will show lower income in case there are items of prepaid expenses and accrued income.
(3) Income statement will show relatively lower income if there are items of outstanding expenses and income received in advance.	Income statement will show relatively higher income if there are items of outstanding expenses and income received in advance.
(4) This basis is recognised under the Companies Act, 1956.	This basis is not recognised under the Companies Act, 1956.
(5) Under this basis the accountant has the option of following alternative method of depreciation (*i.e.* SLM or DBM) or method of valuation of inventory (*i.e* LIFO or FIFO etc.)	Under this method the accountant has no such option to follow alternative method of depreciation or valuation of inventory.
(6) Enterprises with cash and credit transactions prefer this basis.	Enterprises with mostly cash transactions prefer this basis of accounting.
(7) Business enterprises with profit motive ascertain their profit or loss under accrual basis of accounting.	Professional people like doctors, lawyers, etc. and small non-trading concerns ascertain their profit or loss under cash basis.
(8) It is a reliable basis of accounting because it makes a complete record of all cash and credit transactions. It ascertains correct profit or loss.	It is not a reliable basis of accounting because accurate profit or loss can not be ascertained under this basis.
(9) This basis of accounting is technical because it involves the adjustments of accounts for preparing the final accounts.	This basis of accounting is simple because it does not require technical knowledge.
(10) This basis of accounting being based on a complete record of the financial transactions gives a true and fair view of profit or loss for particular period and also exhibits true financial position of the business on a particular day.	This basis does not give true and fair view of profit or loss and the financial position of the business because it does not take into consideration outstanding transactions.

Hybrid or Mixed Basis of Accounting

Cash basis of accounting is by far the simplest system whereas accrual basis of accounting is scientific and reliable. So accountants have tried to club the advantages of the two systems and have come up with mixed or hybrid basis of accounting. **Under mixed basis of accounting both cash basis and accrual basis are followed. Incomes are recorded on cash basis whereas expenses are taken on accrual basis**. The net income is ascertained by matching expenses on accrual basis with income on cash basis. This is the most conservative basis of ascertaining income because all possible expenses relating to the period whether actually paid or not are considered whereas income only received in cash is taken into consideration. When all the expenses are taken into account, there is reduction in taxable income and hence this system is popular among professionals like doctors, lawyers, chartered accountants etc.

ILLUSTRATION 3. Rajat supplies you the following information about his income and expenses for the financial year 2024-25.

	₹		₹
Expenses paid	80,000	Income received	1,20,000
Expenses paid in advance	20,000	Income received in advance	15,000
Expenses not paid yet	10,000	Income not received yet	12,000

Find out the net income or profit of Rajat if he adopts (*a*) Cash basis (*b*) Accrual basis (*c*) Hybrid basis of accounting.

SOLUTION

(*a*) ***Cash Basis***

	₹
Revenues :	
Income received	1,20,000
Less: Expenses :	
Expenses paid	80,000
Profit	40,000

(*b*) ***Accrual Basis***

		₹
Revenues :		
Income received		1,20,000
+ Income not received yet		12,000
– Income received in advance		15,000
	(*A*)	1,17,000

		₹
Expenses :		
Expenses paid		80,000
+ Expenses not paid yet		10,000
– Expenses paid in advance		20,000
	(*B*)	70,000

Profit = (*A*) – (*B*)
= ₹ 1,17,000 – ₹ 70,000 = ₹ 47,000

(*c*) ***Hybrid Basis***

	₹
Revenues :	
Income received	1,20,000
Expenses :	
Expenses paid	80,000
+ Expenses not paid yet	10,000
	90,000
–Expenses paid in advance	20,000
	70,000

Profit = Revenues – Expenses
= ₹ 1,20,000 – ₹ 70,000
= ₹ 50,000.

Factors Common to Every Business

To have a clear understanding of the Double Entry System, it is necessary to keep in mind the following factors which are common to every business :

1. The business has to enter into business dealings with a number of persons or firms. Therefore, an account of each person or firm, with whom the business has business dealings, is opened. Such accounts are known as **Personal Accounts.**
2. The business must necessarily have some assets such as stock, cash, furniture etc., with the help of which the business may be carried on. Therefore, an account of each asset in the business is opened. Such accounts are classified as **Real or Property Accounts.**

3. There must be certain sources from which the income of the business is derived. Similarly certain expenses must be incurred to earn the income. Therefore, an account of each expense and income is opened in the books. Such accounts are known as **Nominal or Fictitious Accounts.**

Classification of Acounts

From the above, it is clear that there are three types of accounts, namely, Personal Accounts, Real or Property Accounts and Nominal or Fictitious Accounts which are opened to keep a complete record of all the financial transactions of the business.

Systems of Accounting

Following are the two systems of accounting :

1. Single Entry System. Under this system, only personal accounts with or without subsidiary books are maintained. This system has no complete record of business transactions done during the year. Hence, neither the trial balance nor final accounts can be prepared due to non-availability of nominal and real accounts. This system is simple and less costly and is adopted by small concerns where business transactions are few. In fact, this is an unscientific, incomplete and defective system.

2. Double Entry System. Every business transaction has two aspects. *i.e.*, when we receive something, we give something else in return. For example, when we purchase goods for cash, we receive goods and give cash in return ; similarly in a credit sale of goods, goods are given to the customer and the customer becomes debtor for the amount of goods sold to him. This method of writing every transaction in two accounts is known as Double Entry System of Accounting. Of the two accounts, one account is given debit while the other account is given credit with an equal amount. Thus, on any date, the total of all debits must be equal to the total of all credits because every debit has a corresponding credit.

Rules of The Double Entry System

There are two approaches for understanding the rules of double entry system—Traditional and Modern approach. Both are discussed in detail in this chapter.

There are separate rules of the double entry system in respect of personal, real and nominal accounts which are discussed below :

1. Personal Accounts. These accounts record a business's dealings with persons or firms. The person receiving something is given debit and the person giving something is given credit. For example, if Vijay sells goods to Viney on credit, Viney's Account will be given debit (in Vijay's books) as he is the receiver of goods and Vijay's Account will be credited (in Viney's books) as he is the giver of goods. When Viney makes the payment for these goods, Vijay's Account will be debited in Viney's books as he is the receiver of cash and Viney's Account will be given credit in Vijay's books as he is the giver of cash. So, the rule is : debit the receiver and credit the giver.

2. Real Accounts. These are the accounts of assets. Asset entering the business is given debit and asset leaving the business is given credit. For example, when goods are sold for cash, Cash Account will be given debit as cash comes in and Sales Account will be credited as goods go out. So, the rule is : debit what comes in and credit what goes out.

3. Nominal Accounts. These accounts deal with expenses, incomes, profits and losses. Accounts of expenses and losses are debited and accounts of incomes and gains are credited. For example, when rent is paid to the landlord, Rent Account will be debited as it is an expense and Cash Account (real account) will be credited as it goes out. Similarly when commission is received, Cash Account will be debited as cash is received and Commission Account will be credited as it is an income. Thus, the rule is : debit all expenses and losses and credit all incomes and gains.

The rules of double entry system are shown in the following chart :

RULES OF THE DOUBLE ENTRY

Personal Accounts		Real Accounts		Nominal Accounts	
Debit	Credit	Debit	Credit	Debit	Credit
Receiver	Giver	What Comes In	What Goes Out	Expenses and Losses	Incomes and Gains

Analysis of Transactions

To make a correct record of the transactions, each transaction must be analysed. Following questions may be asked in this respect :

(*i*) Which are the two accounts involved in the transaction to be recorded ?

(*ii*) Whether the two accounts involved in the transaction are personal, real or nominal ?

(*iii*) What rules of debit and credit are applicable to the accounts involved ?

(*iv*) Which account should be debited or credited ?

The above method will make the recording of transactions more simple and easy. The chart given on the next page explains the procedure of analysing the transactions.

Few Basic Terms

(*i*) Business Transactions. Any exchange of money or money's worth as goods and services between two parties is called a business transaction. It may relate to purchase and sale of goods, receipt and payment of cash and rendering of service by one party to another.

(*ii*) Debtor. A debtor is a person who owes money. The amount due from him is called debt. The amount due from a person as per the books of account is called a book debt.

(*iii*) Creditor. A person to whom money is owing or payable is called a creditor.

(*iv*) Capital. This is the owner's financial interest or holding in the business and is represented by the value of net assets (*i.e.*, total assets less liabilities).

(*v*) Goods. This includes all articles, commodities or merchandise in which the business deals. Thus, cloth would be goods for a dealer in cloth, furniture would be goods for a dealer in furniture and so on.

(*vi*) Assets. Any physical thing or right owned that has a money value is an asset. In other words, an asset is that expenditure which results in acquiring of some property or benefit of a lasting nature.

(*vii*) Equity. A claim which can be enforced against the assets of the firm is called equity. In other words, the rights to properties are called equities. Equities are of two types ; the right of creditors and the right of owners. The equities of creditors represent debts of the business and are called *liabilities*. The equity of the owners is called capital, proprietorship or owner's equity. Thus,

$$\text{Assets} = \text{Liabilities} + \text{Capital}$$

(*viii*) Income. It is the favourable change in owner's equity which results from business operations. In other words, income in an inflow of assets which results in an increase in the owner's equity.

(*ix*) Expenditure. An expenditure takes place when asset or service is acquired.

(*x*) Expense. It means an expenditure whose benefit is finished or enjoyed immediately such as salaries, rent etc.

ANALYSIS OF TRANSACTIONS

Transactions	*Two Accounts Involved*	*Classification of Accounts*	*Rule of Debit and Credit*	*Explanation*	*Account to be debited with ₹*	*Account to be credited with ₹*
Started business with ₹ 50,000	Cash	Real	Debit what comes in	Cash enters the business	Cash 50,000	—
	Capital	Personal	Credit the giver	Proprietor is giver of cash	—	Capital 50,000
Purchased furniture for ₹ 1,000 on credit from Pankaj	Furniture	Real	Debit what comes in	Furniture comes in	Furniture 1,000	—
	Pankaj	Personal	Credit the giver	Pankaj is a giver of Furniture	—	Pankaj 1,000
Goods purchased for cash ₹ 20,000	Purchases	Real	Debit what comes in	Goods come in the business	Purchases 20,000	—
	Cash	Real	Credit what goes out	Cash goes out of the business	—	Cash 20,000
Goods sold to Ram Niwas for ₹ 5,000 on credit	Ram Niwas	Personal	Debit the receiver	Ram Niwas is a receiver of goods	Ram Niwas 5,000	
	Sales	Real	Credit what goes out	Goods go out of the business	—	Sales 5,000
Paid salaries to staff ₹ 1,800	Salaries	Nominal	Debit the expenses and losses	Salaries are expenses	Salaries 1,800	—
	Cash	Real	Credit what goes out	Cash goes out of the business	—	Cash 1,800
Goods worth ₹ 500 returned by Ram Niwas	Sales Retutrns	Real	Debit what comes in	Goods come in the business	Sales Returns 500	—
	Ram Niwas	Personal	Credit the giver	Ram Niwas is the giver of goods	—	Ram Niwas 500
₹ 1,000 Commission received	Cash	Real	Debit what comes in	Cash comes in the business	Cash 1,000	—
	Commission	Nominal	Credit all incomes & gains	Commission is income	—	Commission 1,000

The purchase of goods is an expenditure whereas cost of goods sold is an expense. Similarly, if an asset is acquired during the year, it is an expenditure, if it is consumed during the same year, it is also an expense of the year.

(*xi*) **Drawings.** Any amount or goods withdrawn by the owner of a business for personal use is called drawings.

(*xii*) **Loss.** A loss is an expenditure without any benefit to the concern. On the other hand, expense is incurred to result in some benefits.

(*xiii*) **Voucher.** Any written document in support of a business transaction is called a voucher.

(*xiv*) **Turnover.** It means total trading income from cash sales and credit sales.

(*xvi*) **Insolvent.** A person who cannot pay his debts is called insolvent. His liabilities are more than his assets.

(*xv*) **Net Worth.** It means assets minus outside liabilities. Profits of a business increase the net worth whereas losses reduce net worth of a business.

ACCOUNTING EQUATION (MODERN APPROACH)

Accounting equation is the basis of double entry system. It is a mathematical expression to show that assets and liabilities of a firm are always equal.

American accountants have derived the rules of debit and credit through accounting equation which is given below :

Assets = Equities

The equation is based on the principle that accounting deals with property and rights to property and the sum of the properties owned is equal to the sum of the rights to the properties. The properties owned by a business are called assets and the rights to properties are known as liabilities or equities of the business.

Equities may be divided into equities of creditors representing debts of the business known as liabilities and equity of the owners known as capital. Keeping in view the two types of equities the equation given above can be stated as below :

Assets = Liabilities + Capital

The equation given above is the basic accounting equation on which the double entry accounting is built up.

It is also called fundamental accounting equation. It is based on dual concept that every debit has equal credit. *It holds good for each transaction. Any transaction can change accounting equation but cannot break it.*

Rules of Accounting Equation (Modern Approach)

1. *Regarding assets.*
   Increases in assets are debits and decreases in assets are credits.
2. *Regarding Liabilities* :
   Increases in liabilities are credits and decreases in liabilities are debits.
3. *Regarding Capital* :
   Increases in capital are credits and decreases in capital are debits.
4. *Regarding Expenses* :
   Increases in expenses are debits and decreases in expenses are credits.
5. *Regarding Incomes or Profits* :
   Increases in incomes or profits are credits and decreases in incomes or profits are debits.

ILLUSTRATION 4. Give Accounting Equation for the following transactions of Hitesh for January 2025.

(*a*) Started business with cash ₹ 18,000.
(*b*) Paid rent in advance ₹ 400.
(*c*) Purchased goods for cash ₹ 5,000
(*f*) Bought motor cycle for personal use ₹ 8,000.
(*g*) Purchased equipments for cash ₹ 500.

and on credit ₹ 2,000.

(*d*) Sold goods for cash ₹ 4,000 (costing ₹ 2,400).

(*e*) Rent paid ₹ 1,000 and rent outstanding ₹ 200.

(*h*) Paid to creditors ₹ 600.

(*i*) Depreciation on equipment ₹ 25.

(*j*) Business expenses ₹ 400.

SOLUTION

Sl.	Equities			Assets			
No.	Rent Outstanding	Creditors	Capital	Cash	Rent in Advance	Stock of Goods	Equipments
	₹	₹	₹	₹	₹	₹	₹
(*a*)			18,000	18,000			
(*b*)				−400	+400		
			18,000	17,600	400		
(*c*)		+2,000		−5,000		+7,000	
		2,000	18,000	12,600	400	7,000	
(*d*)			+1,600	+4,000		−2,400	
		2,000	19,600	16,600	400	4,600	
(*e*)	+200	—	−1,200	−1,000		—	
	200	2,000	18,400	15,600	400	4,600	
(*f*)			−8,000	−8,000	—	—	
	200	2,000	10,400	7,600	400	4,600	
(*g*)			—	−500	—	—	+500
	200	2,000	10,400	7,100	400	4,600	500
(*h*)	—	−600	—	−600	—	—	—
	200	1,400	10,400	6,500	400	4,600	500
(*i*)			−25	—	—	—	−25
	200	1,400	10,375	6,500	400	4,600	475
(*j*)		—	−400	−400	—	—	—
	200	1,400	9,975	6,100	400	4,600	475
Total	200 + 1,400 + 9,975 = 11,575			6,100 + 400 + 4,600 + 475 = 11,575			

Advantages of Double Entry System

Following are the main advantages which can be derived from the use of this system:

1. It provides a *complete record* of every transaction whether it relates to the personal or impersonal accounts.
2. It provides an *arithmetical check* on the records as the total of debit entries must be equal to the total of all credit entries.
3. The *amount owing* to outsiders and the amount due to the business can be ascertained with the help of personal accounts.
4. The profit and loss account can be prepared with the help of nominal accounts which is helpful to the businessman to *ascertain the operating results* of the business.
5. It helps to prepare the balance sheet of the business which is helpful to ascertain the *financial position* of the business on a particular day.
6. It helps to *reduce the occurrence of the errors and frauds* and when occurred can be detected easily. It can work well with the help of internal check system.

Disadvantages of Double Entry System

Following are the main disadvantages of this system :

1. This system requires the *maintenance of a number of books of accounts* which is not practical in small concerns.
2. The system is *costly* because a number of records are to be maintained.
3. There is *no guarantee of absolute accuracy of the books of accounts* inspite of the agreement of the trial balance.

Accounting Cycle

It refers to a complete sequence of accounting procedures which are required to be repeated in the same order during such each accounting period. Accounting cycle includes :

(*a*) **Recording**. First, all transactions should be recorded in the Journal or Books of Original Entry known as subsidiary books as and when they take place.

(*b*) **Classifying.** All entries in the Journal or Books of Original Entry should be posted to the appropriate ledger accounts to find out at a glance the total effect of all such transactions in a particular account.

(*c*) **Summarising.** Last stage is to prepare the trial balance and final accounts with a view to ascertain the profit or loss made during a trading period and the financial position of the business on a particular date.

Thus sequential steps involved in an accounting cycle are : (*i*) Journalising, (*ii*) Posting, (*iii*) Balancing, (*iv*) Trial Balance, (*v*) Income Statement (*i.e.,* Trading and Profit & Loss Account), and (*vi*) Position Statement (*i.e.,* Balance Sheet).

All these successive stages will be discussed in detail one by one in the subsequent pages.

Ethics in Accounting

Ethics in accounting refers to the set of moral principles and professional standards that guide the behavior of accountants in their work. These principles include honesty, integrity, objectivity, confidentiality, and responsibility. Ethical conduct is fundamental in accounting because:

- *Ensures Accuracy and Reliability*: Ethics compel accountants to present financial information truthfully and accurately, preventing data manipulation and misrepresentation.
- *Builds Trust and Credibility*: Stakeholders such as investors, creditors, and regulators rely on ethical accounting for fair and transparent financial reporting. This trust underpins the stability and credibility of financial markets and organisations.
- *Prevents Fraud and Legal Risks*: Adherence to ethical standards deters fraudulent activities like embezzlement or data falsification, and helps organisations avoid legal penalties and reputational damage.
- *Promotes Accountability*: Ethical practices foster a culture of accountability, as financial statements prepared with integrity enable stakeholders to make informed decisions3.
- *Supports Long-term Success*: Ethical accounting enhances an organisation's reputation, employee morale, and sustainability by promoting lawful and responsible financial management.

Role of Accountants in Upholding Ethical Standards

Accountants are central to upholding ethical standards in the profession:

- *Guardians of Integrity*: Accountants must maintain uncompromising integrity, resisting pressures to manipulate figures or conceal important information.

- *Uphold Confidentiality*: They are entrusted with sensitive financial data and must protect it from unauthorised disclosure, unless legally required.
- *Ensure Transparency*: Accountants are responsible for transparent financial disclosures, enabling stakeholders to trust the information provided.
- *Apply Professional Judgment*: They must adhere to established accounting principles and exercise sound judgment in unique or ambiguous situations.
- *Follow Regulatory Guidelines*: Accountants must comply with laws, standards, and codes of conduct set by professional bodies and regulatory authorities.
- *Promote Ethical Culture*: By modeling ethical behavior, accountants help foster a culture of ethics within their organisations, deterring unethical conduct among colleagues and management.

Qualitative Characteristics of Accounting Information

Accounting information must possess certain qualitative characteristics to be considered useful for decision-making by stakeholders such as investors, managers, and creditors. The most critical attributes are reliability, relevance, comparability, and understandability. Each plays a distinct role in ensuring that financial data truly supports informed economic decisions.

Relevance: Relevance means that the information can influence users' economic decisions by helping them evaluate past, present, or future events, or confirm or correct prior expectations. Relevant information should have both predictive value (helping users forecast future outcomes) and confirmatory value (helping users assess past decisions). For example, current financial performance data is relevant for investors considering buying shares, as it helps predict future profitability.

Reliability (Faithful Representation): Reliability, also called faithful representation, means that the information faithfully reflects the actual transactions and events it purports to represent, without bias or error. Reliable information must be complete (nothing significant omitted), neutral (free from bias), and free from error. This ensures users can trust the accuracy of the financial data when making decisions, such as lending money or investing in a company.

Comparability: Comparability allows users to identify similarities and differences between two sets of economic phenomena, such as financial statements from different periods or different companies. This requires consistent application of accounting policies over time and across entities, or full disclosure when changes occur. Comparability enables stakeholders to analyse trends, benchmark against competitors, and assess performance over time.

Understandability: Understandability means that accounting information is presented clearly and concisely, so users with a reasonable knowledge of business and economic activities can comprehend its meaning. Financial reports should avoid unnecessary complexity and use explanatory notes where needed, making them accessible even to non-accountants involved in decision-making. This attribute ensures that information is not just available, but also usable by its intended audience.

Additional Enhancing Attributes: While the above are the primary attributes, several additional characteristics further enhance the usefulness of accounting information:

- **Timeliness:** Information should be available to users before it loses its capacity to influence decisions.
- **Verifiability:** Different independent observers should be able to reach consensus that the information faithfully represents what it purports to depict.
- **Consistency:** The same accounting methods should be applied from period to period within the same entity, supporting comparability over time.
- **Materiality:** Only information that could influence users' decisions should be included, avoiding unnecessary detail that could obscure important facts.

QUESTIONS

OBJECTIVE TYPE

1. Which of the following statements are correct ?

(a) Capital + Liabilities – Assets = Zero

(b) Capital = Assets + Liabilities

(c) Withdrawals by the owner would reduce both assets and owner's equity.

(d) Under accrual basis of accounting, actual cash receipts and actual cash payments are recorded.

(e) Nominal accounts are the accounts of assets.

(f) Both assets and owner's equity would increase by purchase of furniture on credit.

(g) For nominal accounts, the rules of the double entry system is : debit all expenses and losses and credit all incomes and gains.

(h) Capital = Net Assets

(i) Capital + Long Term Liabilities = Fixed Assets + Current Assets + Cash – Current Liabilities

(j) Accounting is the language of the business.

(k) Patent right is in the nature of nominal account.

(l) Under accrual basis of accounting, actual cash receipts and actual cash payments are recorded.

(m) Cash basis of accounting satisfies the conservative instinct.

(n) Cash basis of accounting follows matching principle of accounting.

(o) Cash basis of accounting is more scientific as compared to accrual basis of accounting.

(p) Accrual basis of accounting gives a complete picture of the financial transactions of the business.

(q) Cash basis of accounting discloses correct profit and loss for a particular period.

(r) Under hybrid basis of accounting, incomes are recorded on cash basis whereas expenses are taken on accrual basis.

Ans. [(a), (c), (g), (h), (j), (m) ; (p) ; (r)].

2. State under what heading (Personal, Real or Nominal) would you classify each of the following accounts:

(a) Bank Account

(b) Machinery Account

(c) Wages Outstanding Account

(d) Patents Account

(e) Bad Debts Account

(f) Expenses Paid in Advance Account

(g) Oswal Spinning Mills Ltd.

Ans. [(a) Personal ; (b) Real ; (c) Personal : (d) Real ; (e) Nominal ; (f) Personal ; (g) Personal].

3. Choose the correct answer :

(a) Recording of transactions and events as & when they occur and classifying them into suitable account heading is the subject matter of—

(i) Financial Accounting (ii) Cost Accounting

(iii) Management Accounting (iv) Book-keeping.

(b) Book-keeping is mainly concerned with the recording of financial data relating to the .... in significant and orderly manner.

(i) Business (ii) Personal

(iii) Company (iv) Monetary.

(*c*) Basic function of accounting is to
(*i*) Record all business transactions of monetary nature
(*ii*) Interpret the financial data
(*iii*) Assist the management in performing functions effectively.
(*iv*) Summarise the data.

(*d*) There are two systems of accounting *i.e.* cash basis system of accounting and .... basis system of accounting
(*i*) Double entry (*ii*) Accrual
(*iii*) Dual Aspect (*iv*) Single Entry.

(*e*) The alternative to cash basis of accounting is called .... basis of accounting
(*i*) Receipt (*ii*) Due
(*iii*) Credit (*iv*) Accrual.

(*f*) The system of recording transactions based on dual aspect concept is called
(*i*) Double Account System (*ii*) Double Entry System
(*iii*) Single Entry System (*iv*) Accrual Basis of Accounting.

(*g*) As per dual aspect concept
(*i*) Assets = Liabilities + Capital (*ii*) Assets = Liabilities – Capital
(*iii*) Assets + Liabilities = Capital (*iv*) Assets + Capital = Liabilities.

(*h*) Liabilities of a firm are ₹ 6,00,000 and capital of the proprietor is ₹ 4,00,000. Then total assets are :
(*i*) ₹ 6,00,000 (*ii*) ₹ 10,00,000
(*iii*) ₹ 2,00,000 (*iv*) ₹ 4,00,000.

(*i*) Assets are ₹ 10,00,000 and liabilities are ₹ 2,00,000. His capital would be —
(*i*) ₹ 10,00,000 (*ii*) ₹ 12,00,000
(*iii*) ₹ 8,00,000 (*iv*) ₹ 2,00,000.

(*j*) Capital + Liabilities =
(*i*) Total Assets (*ii*) Losses
(*iii*) Current Assets (*iv*) Fixed Assets.

(*k*) Which of the following will be goods for a business run by a furniture merchant :
(*i*) Electrical Appliances (*ii*) Shoes
(*iii*) Tables and Chairs (*iv*) Pens and Pencils.

(*l*) Which of the following is not a business transaction ?
(*i*) Rent paid to Landlord 5,000
(*ii*) Goods purchased from Z ₹ 20,000
(*iii*) Placed an order to Chandra & Co. for purchasing the goods for ₹ 35,000
(*iv*) Received interest from Bank ₹ 2,000.

(*m*) Which of the following item is not financial in nature :
(*i*) Purchase of a car on credit
(*ii*) Dismissing an employee from job
(*iii*) Withdrawal of cash by proprietor for his personal use
(*iv*) Purchase of building for cash.

(*n*) Total assets of a trader are ₹ 4,25,000 and outside liabilities are ₹ 1,75,000 ; owner's equity will be :
(*i*) ₹ 6,00,000 (*ii*) ₹ 2,50,000
(*iii*) ₹ 4,25,000 (*iv*) None of the above.

Ans. **[(*a*) (*iv*); (*b*) (*i*); (*c*) (*i*); (*d*) (*ii*); (*e*) (*iv*); (*f*) (*ii*); (*g*) (*i*); (*h*) (*ii*); (*i*) (*iii*); (*j*) (*i*); (*k*) (*iii*); (*l*) (*iii*); (*m*) (*ii*); (*n*) (*ii*)]**

SHORT ANSWER TYPE

1. Define Book-keeping.
2. Define Accounting.
3. Distinguish Book-keeping and Accounting.
4. Name the users of Accounting information.
5. State the main objectives of Accounting.
6. Give four functions of Accounting.
7. State four limitations of Accounting.
8. Name three divisions of Accounting.
9. Give two bases of Accounting.
10. How does a business transaction differ from an event ?
11. Distinguish between assets and liabilities.
12. Distinguish between revenue and expense.
13. Distinguish between Accrual basis of accounting vs. Cash basis of accounting.
14. Discuss briefly the role of Accountant in Society.
15. Which is correct ? Capital = Assets + Liabilities ; Liabilities = Capital – Assets ; Capital = Net Assets.
16. The profit made by a concern during the past one year would be, when the capital increased by ₹ 40,000 and drawings amounted to ₹ 10,000 (*i*) ₹ 50,000, or (*ii*) 30,000, or (*iii*) ₹ 40,000.
17. Which accounts should be debited or credited for cash of the following transactions ?

(*a*) Purchased goods for cash. (*b*) Withdrew from office cash for rent of proprietor's residential flat. (*c*) Started business with cash. (*d*) Amount withdrawn from bank for office use. (*e*) Cash received from A in settlement of his account.

Ans. **[(*a*) Debit to Purchases Account ; (*b*) Debit to Drawings Account ; (*c*) Credit to Capital Account ; (*d*) Credit to Bank Account ; (*e*) Credit to A's Account]**

18. Prepare accounting equation on the basis of the following :

(*i*) Rahim started business with cash ₹ 20,000. (*ii*) Rahim purchased furniture for cash ₹ 2,000. (*iii*) Rahim paid rent ₹ 200. (*iv*) Rahim purchased goods on credit ₹ 3,000. (*v*) Rahim sold goods (cost price ₹ 2,000) for ₹ 3,000 on cash.

Ans. **[₹ 23,800]**

19. What is owner's equity ? Give an equation for calculating owner's equity. Calculate total equity if—

(*i*) Owner's equity is ₹ 60,000 ; (*ii*) Equity of creditors is ₹ 50,000 ; (*iii*) Revenue during the period is ₹ 70,000 ; (*iv*) Expenses during the same period are ₹ 65,000. Also calculate revised amount of owner's equity.

Ans. **[₹ 1,10,000 ; Revised Owner's Equity ₹ 65,000.]**

20. Prove that the Accounting Equation is satisfied in all the following transactions of Suresh :

(*i*) Commenced business with cash ₹ 60,000. (*ii*) Rent paid in advance ₹ 500. (*iii*) Purchased goods for cash ₹ 30,000 and credit ₹ 20,000. (*iv*) Sold goods for cash ₹ 30,000 ; costing ₹ 20,000. (*v*) Paid salary ₹ 500 and salary outstanding ₹ 100. (*vi*) Bought motor cycle for personal use ₹ 5,000.

Ans. **[₹ 84,000]**

LONG ANSWER TYPE

1. Define Bookkeeping. How is it different from Accounting?
2. What is Accounting? Discuss its objectives and limitations.
3. Describe Accounting as an Information System.

4. Explain the Role of an Accountant in Society.
5. *"Accounting is often referred to as the language of business."* Explain how accounting performs this communicative role by highlighting how it helps various stakeholders such as owners, investors, creditors, employees, and government agencies in making informed decisions.
6. Distinguish between the following: (*a*) *Cash Basis of Accounting and Accrual Basis of Accounting* (*b*) *Single Entry System and Double Entry System*
7. What is the Double Entry System of Accounting?
8. What is the Accounting Equation?
9. What do you understand by the term Accounting Cycle?
10. Explain the interrelationship of accounting with subjects like economics, law, statistics, mathematics, management, and information technology.
11. Discuss the Role of Accountants in the following areas: (*a*) *Society* (*b*) *Capital Market* (*c*) *Corporate Governance*.
12. Explain the qualitative characteristics that make accounting information useful for decision-making. Discuss with suitable examples.
13. "Accounting information must be relevant, reliable, comparable, and understandable to be useful." Critically examine this statement by explaining each of these attributes in detail.
14. Explain the concept and importance of ethics in accounting. What role do accountants play in upholding ethical standards?

PRACTICAL PROBLEMS

1. Solve the Accounting Equation on the basis of the following transactions and present a Balance Sheet of the last new equation balances.

		₹			₹
(*i*)	Mohan commenced business with	70,000	(*vi*)	Paid to creditors	10,000
(*ii*)	Withdrew for private use	1,700	(*vii*)	Sold goods on credit for	15,000
(*iii*)	Purchased goods on credit	14,000	(*viii*)	Sold goods for cash	
(*iv*)	Purchased goods for cash	10,000		(cost price was ₹ 3,000)	4,000
(*v*)	Paid wages	300	(*ix*)	Purchased furniture for	500

Ans. [B/S Total ₹ 73,000]

2. Arvind had the following transactions. Use accounting equation to show their effect on his assets, liabilities and capital.
   (*a*) Brought ₹ 45,000 in cash to start business.
   (*b*) Purchased securities for cash ₹ 22,500.
   (*c*) Purchased an office building for ₹ 45,000 giving ₹ 15,000 in cash and the balance through a loan.
   (*d*) Sold securities costing ₹ 3,000 for ₹ 4,500.
   (*e*) Purchased an old car for ₹ 8,400 cash.
   (*f*) Received cash for rent ₹ 10,800.
   (*g*) Paid cash ₹ 1,500 for loan and ₹ 900 for interest.
   (*h*) Paid cash for office building expenses ₹ 900.
   (*i*) Received cash for dividend on securities ₹ 600.

Ans. [₹ 84,600]

3. Ram starts a real estate agency business with a cash investment of ₹ 70,000. Following business transactions have been recorded :
   (*a*) Paid three months advance rent for office accommodation ₹ 4,200.
   (*b*) Bought office car ₹ 42,000.

(c) Purchased office furniture ₹ 14,000.

(d) Bought office type-writer from Standard Supply Company ₹ 6,000.

(e) Sold extra office furniture at Cost to Amar for ₹ 2,000. Amar paid ₹ 1,200 in cash and accepted a bill at three months for the balance.

(f) Amar paid the amount of the bill at maturity and Ram paid half the amount he owned to Standard Supply Company.

(g) Collected ₹ 12,000 as commission.

(h) Paid telephone bill amounting to ₹ 300.

Work out the effect of the foregoing transactions on the equity of Ram through the Accounting Equation.

Ans. **[₹ 84,700]**

CHAPTER 2

Accounting Principles and Policies

Accounting is the language of business. To make the language convey the same meaning to all people, accountants all over the world have developed certain rules, procedures and conventions, which represent a consensus view by the profession of good accounting practices and procedures and are generally referred to as *Generally Accepted Accounting Principle (GAAP)*. The Phrase 'Generally Accepted Accounting Principles' (GAAP) is a technical accounting term that encompasses the conventions, rules and procedures necessary to define accepted accounting practices at a particular time. It includes not only broad guidelines of general applications but also detailed practices and procedures. These conventions, rules and procedures provide a standard by which to measure financial presentations.

Thus, GAAPs are common set of accounting principles, standards and procedures that companies use while preparing their financial statements. GAAPs are a combination of authoritative standards (set by policy boards) and simply the commonly accepted ways of recording and reporting accounting information. GAAPs recognise the importance of reporting transactions and events in accordance with their substance. They originate from a combination of tradition, experience and official decree and require authoritative support and some means of enforcement.

GAAPs are imposed on companies so that investors have a maximum level of consistency in the financial statements they use when analysing companies for investment purposes. Companies are expected to follow GAAPs rules when reporting their financial data through financial statements.

GAAPs are only a set of standards. There is plenty of room within GAAPs for accountants to distort figures. So even when a company uses GAAP, still there is need to scrutinize its financial statements. Accounting statements are prepared in confirmity with these principles in order to place more reliance on them. The need for the common accounting principles becomes more apparent when we contemplate the chaotic conditions that would prevail if every accountant could follow his own principles about the measurement of revenue and expenses.

Sources of Indian Gaap

Principal sources of Indian GAPPs are : (*i*) Company law. (*ii*) Accounting standards and related documents of the ICAI. (*iii*) SEBI requirements. (*iv*) Established conventions.

Meaning of Accounting Principles

The term 'Principle' refers to fundamental belief or a general truth which once established does not change. It is incorrect to apply the term with respect to accounting which is merely an art involving adaption for the attainment of some useful results by its applications. Application implies changing nature and hence is contradictory to the meaning of fundamental truth implied by the term 'principle'.To others, the term 'Principle' means rule of action or conduct and hence can be aptly applied to rules in accounting. AICPA defined the term 'Principle' **"as a guide to action, a settled ground or basis of conduct or practice**." Some Accountants prefer to use the term 'Standard' instead of using the word 'Principle' but accounting principles and accounting standards are not one and the same thing. ***Accounting principles* are guidelines to establish standards for sound accounting practices and procedures in reporting the financial status and periodic performance of a business. *Accounting standards* are written/policy documents issued by the government or professional institutes or other regulatory body covering various aspects of recognition, measurement, treatment, presentation and disclosure of accounting transactions in the financial statements.**

Characteristics of Accounting Principles

Following are the main characteristics of accounting principles :

1. Accounting principles are man made so they do not have the authoritativeness as universal principle like the principle of physics, chemistry and other natural sciences. They represent the best possible guidelines based on reasons and observations and have been developed by accountants to enhance the usefulness of accounting data in an ever changing society. Accounting is a social science and is the natural result of economic phenomena.

2. The science of accounting is not in a finished form, it is in the process of evolution. Consequently, accounting principles are fast developing. These are influenced by business practices and customs, government agencies and other business groups.

3. The general acceptance of an accounting principle usually depends on how well it meets *three criteria : relevance, objectivity and feasibility*. A principle is *relevant* to the extent that it results in information that is useful to those who want to know something about certain business. A principle is *objective* to the extent that the accounting information is not influenced by the personal bias of those who furnish the information. The accounting information given in the financial statements should be free from the personal bias of the persons who have taken part in the preparation of such statements. A principle is *feasible* to the extent that it can be applied without undue complexity or cost.

Accounting principles can be classified into two categories: (*i*) Accounting concepts, and (*ii*) Accounting conventions.

Accounting Concepts

Accounting concepts may be considered as postulates *i.e.*, basic assumptions or conditions upon which the science of accounting is based. There is no authoritative list of these concepts but most of the concepts have fairly general support.

Accounting Conventions

The term 'conventions' denote circumstances or traditions which guide the accountants while preparing the accounting statements.

Concepts and conventions are often used interchangeably. The basic difference between them is that concepts are concerned with maintenance of accounts whereas conventions are applicable while preparing financial statements *i.e.,* Profit and Loss Account and Balance Sheet.

Concepts and conventions can be put in the form of a chart as given on next page:

Accounting Principles

- Accounting Concepts
  - (i) Business Entity
  - (ii) Money Measurement
  - (iii) Going Concern
  - (iv) Cost
  - (v) Dual Aspect
  - (vi) Accounting Period
  - (vii) Matching
  - (viii) Realisation
  - (ix) Objective Evidence
  - (x) Accrual
  - (xi) Timeliness
- Accounting Conventions
  - (i) Consistency
  - (ii) Full Disclosure
  - (iii) Conservatism
  - (iv) Materiality

ACCOUNTING CONCEPTS

(*i*) Business Entity Concept

This concept implies that a business unit is separate and distinct from the person who supply capital to it. Irrespective of the form of organisation, a business unit has got its own individuality as distinguished from the person who own or control it. The accounting equation (*i.e.* Assets = Liabilities + Capital) is an expression of the entity concept because it shows that the business itself owns the assets and in turn owes to the various claimants. Business is kept separate from the proprietor so that transactions of the business may also be recorded with him. In case this concept is not followed, affairs of the business will be mixed up with the private affairs of the proprietor and the true picture of the business will not be available. Thus, in the books of a sole trader, a firm or a limited company, only business transactions are recorded and no note is taken of the personal transactions of a sole proprietor, the partners of the firms and the shareholders of the company. But their transactions with the business, (*e.g.,* capital provided to the business, goods and amount withdrawn from the business for the personal use of the sole trader and the partners of the firm, income tax or life insurance premium paid from the business on the taxable income or life of the proprietor etc.) are recorded so that true financial position and profitability of the business may be disclosed. For example, if the proprietor of the business invests ₹ 25,000 into the business, it will be deemed that he has given that much of money to the business as a loan which will be shown as a liability in the books of the firm. On receipt of the amount, Cash Account will be debited and the Proprietor's Capital Account will be credited. Similarly, on withdrawal of the amount from the business for personal use of the proprietor, the Proprietor's Capital or Drawings Account will be debited and Cash Account will be credited.

It may be mentioned that the business entity concept employed in accounting for a sole proprietorship is distinct from the legal concept of a sole proprietorship. The non-business expenses, incomes, assets and liabilities of a sole proprietor are excluded from the business accounts. Legally, however, a sole proprietor is personally liable for his business debts and may be required to use non-business assets (*i.e.* his private assets) to make the payment to his business creditors. Conversely, business assets are not immune from claims of the sole proprietor's personal creditors. In the eyes of law business and non-business assets and liabilities are treated alike in case of a sole proprietor. Similarly, in case of a partnership firm, business assets of the firm are used first for paying business liabilities of the firm and if a surplus remains after paying the firm's liabilities, a partner can use his share of the surplus for the payment of his private liabilities. In the same way, private assets of the individual partners are first utilised for the payment of their individual private liabilities and if there is a surplus in any partner's private estate, it shall be treated as part of partnership property and can be utilised for the payment of firm's liabilities.

In case of joint stock companies, there is a legal distinction between the owners (*i.e.* shareholders) and the business. Shareholders are not liable for the debts of their company beyond the amount of capital they have agreed to subscribe. The accounting treatment of capital contributed by shareholders is the same as it is in the case of sole trader and partnership, except of course that the capital of a joint stock company is divided into a number of shares. Thus, the effect of the business entity concept in case of a joint stock company is to recognise its separate identity from that of its shareholders.

(*ii*) Money Measurement Concept

Money is the only practical unit of measurement that can be employed to achieve homogeneity of financial data. Therefore, **accounting records only those transactions which can be expressed in terms of money though quantitative records are also kept.** The advantages of expressing business transactions in terms of money is that money serves a common denominator by means of which heterogeneous facts about a business can be expressed in terms of numbers (*i.e.* money) which are capable of additions and subtractions. It can better, be illustrated by taking the following example. A business unit has the following assets on March, 31, 2025.

Cash in hand and at bank ₹ 25,000, Sundry Debtors ₹ 48,500, Bills Receivable ₹ 6,500, Motor Cars 5, Stock 6,000 tons, Furniture 100 chairs and 20 tables, Machines 7, Building space 5,000 sq. metres, Land 10 acres

The items given in different units of measurement cannot be added together to get an idea of the total value of the assets owned by the business. To get an idea of the total value of the assets, all items should be expressed in terms of money as given below:

Cash in hand and at bank ₹ 25,000, Sundry Debtors ₹ 48,500, Bills Receivable ₹ 6,500, Motor Cars ₹ 1,15,000, Stock ₹ 4,00,000, Furniture ₹ 5,000, Machines ₹ 2,50,000, Building ₹ 4,40,000, Land ₹ 1,00,000, **Total = ₹ 13,90,000**

The money measurement concept restricts the scope of accounting as it does not record the fact that there is a strike in the factory or the sales manager is not on speaking terms with the production manager. Accounting, therefore, does not give a complete account of the happenings in a business unit. Money provides a common denominator for measuring, but it does not take care of inflation which takes place with the passage of time. Money is expressed in terms of value at the time a financial transaction is recorded in the books. Subsequent changes in the purchasing power of money due to inflation do not affect this amount. In the example given above, cash in hand and at bank is expressed at the value of 31st March, 2025, but the amounts of cars, furniture, machines, land and building are in terms of rupees of five years back when they were acquired. The value of rupee of five years back was much more than value on 31st March, 2025 because the purchasing power of the rupees has decreased due to inflation. Thus, money measurement concept of accounting has two major limitations as given below:

(*i*) It restricts the scope of accounting because it is not capable of recording transactions which cannot be expressed in terms of money.

(*ii*) It does not take care of the effects of inflation because it assumes a stability of the money measurement unit.

Generally business entity concept and money measurement concept are called fundamental accounting concepts.

(*iii*) Going Concern Concept

It is assumed that a business unit has a reasonable expectation of continuing business at a profit for an indefinite period of time. A business unit is deemed to be a going concern and not a gone concern. It will continue to operate in the future. Transactions are recorded in the books keeping in view the going concern aspect of the business unit. It is because of this concept that suppliers supply goods and services and other business firms enter into business transactions with the business unit. Suppliers will not supply goods and services and other person will not have business dealings with the business entity if they have the feelings that the concern will be liquidated. This assumption provides much of the justification for recording fixed assets at original cost (*i.e.* acquisition cost) and depreciating them in a systematic manner without reference to their current realisable value. It is useless to show fixed asset in the Balance Sheet at their estimated realisable values if there is no immediate expectation of selling them. Fixed assets are acquired for use in the business for earning revenues and are not meant for resale, so they are shown at their book values and not at their current realisable values. But when the concern is not a going concern and is to be liquidated, current realisable values of fixed assets become relevant.

Similarly, the going concern concept supports the treatment of prepaid expenses as assets even though they may be virtually unsaleable. Prepaid expenses are made assets on the assumption that the business entity will continue in future and the benefit of prepaid expenses will be utilised in future. A less direct effect of the going concern concept is that it lays emphasis on the determination of net income rather than on the valuation of assets. The earning capacity of the business entity is more significant that the market value of its individual assets in judging the overall worth of a business. Because of this emphasis on the earnings, the accountant directs his attention to the proper allocation of incomes and expenses to the current period and does not bother about the market value of fixed assets which will not be sold.

Following are the cases where going concern concept is not valid :

1. When an enterprise was set up for a particular purpose which has been achieved or to be achieved shortly.
2. When a company is declared sick by BIFR.
3. When an enterprise has been in the grip of severe financial crisis and is expected to wind up shortly.
4. When a receiver or liquidator has been appointed in case of a company which is to be liquidated.

(*iv*) Cost Concept

A fundamental concept of accounting closely related to the going concern concept, is that an asset is recorded in the books at the price paid to acquire it and that this cost is the basis for all subsequent accounting for the asset. This concept does not mean that the asset will always be shown at cost but it means that cost becomes basis for all future accounting for the asset. Asset is recorded at cost at the time of its purchase but is systematically reduced in its value by charging depreciation. The market value of an asset may change with the passage of time, but for accounting purpose it continues to be shown in the books at its book value *i.e.,* the cost at which it was purchased minus depreciation provided up to date.

The cost concept has the advantages of bringing objectivity in the accounts. Information given in the financial statements is not influenced by the personal bias or judgement of those who furnish such statement. In the absence of cost concept assets will be shown at their market values which will depend on the subjective views of persons who furnish financial statements. However, on account of high degree of inflation in the economy in the recent past, the preparation of financial statements on the basis of cost concept has become irrelevant for judging the financial position and ascertaining the profitability of the business entity. To overcome the drawback of cost concept, inflation accounting is advocated which makes a provision for recording all items regularly in the financial statements at their current values. But keeping in view the practical difficulties and absence of legal provisions for inflation accounting historical cost accounting based on cost concept still serves as a fair and adequate basis for reporting business performance.

According to this concept, it is possible to remove the cost of fixed assets from the accounts altogether by writing off their cost as depreciation against income even though assets are still in good condition and are being used in the business. As a result of this drawback, secret reserves are created and the auditor may overlook the verification of assets showing zero book value because their accounts will no longer appear in the books.

The cost concept raises another problem. There are some assets which earn income for a concern but are not shown in the books of account on account of this concept because no cost has been incurred to acquire such assets. According to *Glauier and Underdown*, "Often the major asset of a highly successful firm is the knowledge and the skill created as a result of teamwork and good organisation. This asset will not appear in the accounts, since the firm has paid nothing for it, excepts in terms of salaries which have been written off against yearly profits. Allied to this problem is the failure in making any mention in the balance sheet of the value of the human assets of the firm..... Other important assets of which no mention is made in financial accounting statements are for example, the value to the firm of its hold on the market, which may be a very valuable asset if the firm enjoys a monopoly position, and the value of the firm's own information system, which will affect the quality of its decisions."

(*v*) Dual Aspect Concept

This is the basic concept of accounting. According to this concept, every financial transaction involves a two-fold aspect, (*a*) yielding of a benefit and (*b*) the giving of that benefit. For example, if a business has acquired an asset, it must have given up some other asset such as cash or the obligation to pay for it in future. Thus, a giver necessarily implies a receiver and a receiver necessarily implies a giver. There must be a double entry to have a complete record of each business transaction, an entry being made in the receiving account and an entry of the same amount in the giving account. The receiving account is termed as debtor and the given account is called creditor. Thus, every debit must have a corresponding credit and vice versa and upon this dual aspect has been raised the whole superstructure of Double Entry System of Accounting. The Accounting Equation [*i.e.* Assets = Equities (or Liabilities + Capital)] is based on dual-aspect concept. The term 'Assets' denotes the resources owned by the business while the term 'Equities' denotes the claims of various claimants including the proprietors of the business against the assets. For example, if the business purchases machinery and furniture worth ₹ 25,000 and ₹ 5,000 respectively out of ₹ 40,000 provided by A (the proprietor) of the business, the situation will be as follows:

Assets = Equities

Machinery ₹ 25,000 + Furniture ₹ 5,000 + Cash ₹ 10,000 = Capital ₹ 40,000.

Subsequently, if the business purchases stock worth ₹ 8,000 on credit, the position will be as follows:

Machinery ₹ 25,000 + Furniture ₹ 5,000 + Cash ₹ 10,000 + Stock ₹ 8,000 = Creditors ₹ 8,000+Capital ₹ 40,000

Thus, accounting equation demonstrates the fact that for every debit there is an equivalent credit.

(*vi*) Accounting Period Concept

Truly speaking, the measurement of income or loss of a business entity is relatively simple on a whole-life basis. A complete and accurate picture of the degree of success achieved by a business unit cannot be obtained until it is liquidated, converts its assets into cash and pays off its debts. On liquidation, it is possible to determine with finality its net income. But the owners, the investors and overall the Government, all are impatient and do not want to wait, until the dissolution of the concern, to know what has been the result of the business activities. All these persons are interested in regular reports and accounts at proper intervals to know "how things are going?" This means that the final accounts must be prepared on a periodic basis rather than waiting till the business is terminated.

Under the going concern concept it is assumed that a business entity has a reasonable expectation of continuing business for an indefinite period of time. This assumption provides much of the justification that the business will not be terminated, so it is reasonable to divide the life of the business into accounting periods so as to be able to know the profit or loss of each such period and the financial position at the end of such a period. **Normally accounting period adopted is one year as it helps to take any corrective action, to pay income tax, to absorb the seasonal fluctuations and for reporting to the outsiders. A period of more than one year reduces the utility of accounting data.**

The principle of segregating capital expenditure from revenue expenditure is based on the accounting period concept. The revenue expenditure for a particular period is transferred to the Profit and Loss Account of that period whereas capital expenditure is carried forward to the extent its benefit will be utilised in future accounting periods. Thus, the accounting period concept plays a very important role in determining the income of a particular accounting period. It is also helpful in ascertaining the true and fair view of the financial position of a business entity on a particular data at a particular point of time.

(vii) Matching Concept

This concept is based on the accounting period concept. The most important objective of running a business is to ascertain profit periodically. **The determination of profit of a particular accounting period is essentially a process of matching the revenue recognised during the period and the costs to be allocated to the period to obtain the revenue. It is, thus, a problem of matching revenues and expired costs, the residual amount being the net profit or net loss for the period.** Revenue is considered to be earned on the date at which it is realised *i.e.* on the data when the goods are delivered or services rendered to the customer even though payment may be received at some future date. Revenue may also be considered to be earned at the time the cash is collected, regardless when the sale is made or service is rendered as is the practice with physicians, attorney and other enterprises in which professional services are source of revenue. It has little theoretical justification but has the practical advantages of simplicity of operation and avoidance of the problem of estimating losses on account of bad debts. It is also advantageous from income tax point of view because income tax is paid only on cash income.

Like revenue, all costs incurred during the period are not taken, but only costs related to the accounting period are taken. The purchase price of fixed assets is not taken but only depreciation on fixed assets related to the accounting period is taken. Expenses paid in advance are excluded from the total costs and expenses outstanding are added to the total costs to arrive at the costs attached to the period.

Let us take an example to make the matching concept clear.

A businessman purchases 100 table fans at a cost of ₹ 30,000. He paid ₹ 1,000 as freight and insurance, ₹ 200 as octroi and carriage and rent outstanding was ₹ 2,000. He sells all table fans at a price of ₹ 40,000 against which should be matched cost of table fans ₹ 30,000, freight and insurance ₹ 1,000, octroi and carriage ₹ 200 and outstanding rent ₹ 2,000. The net profit of the period would be ₹ 6,800 (*i.e.*, ₹ 40,000 – ₹ 33,200), though some of the above expenses incurred are not paid for and sale price of some of table fans may not have been realised as yet on account of being sold on credit.

It may be remembered that profit and cash are not synonymous because their nature is different. For example, if a business has made a profit of ₹ 1,00,000, it does not mean that it has the same amount of cash or cash is increased by the same amount. It is because there are outstanding expenses and creditors and outstanding debtors. The profit earned will increase the capital of the business on the liabilities side and a corresponding increase in the assets of the business will be made. Similarly, an increase in cash does not mean increase in profit. Cash may have increased because of issue of shares or sale of a fixed asset. Thus, income is tied to increase in owner's equity and has no direct link to changes in cash.

Application of matching concept in practice, however, is beset with certain difficulties. There are some expenses like preliminary expenses, share issue expenses, advertisement expenses etc. which are not readily identifiable against the revenue of a particular period. Similarly, how much of the capital expenditure should be written off by way of depreciation during the particular period poses the question of finding out the expected life of the asset. Likewise, in case of long term contracts when amount is not received in proportion to the work executed , the expenditure to be carried forward not related to the income received may present some difficulties. In spite of these practical difficulties, the matching concept stands on firm footing and should be followed while preparing financial statements to have a true and fair view of the profitability and financial position of a business entity.

(viii) Realisation Concept

According to this concept, revenue is considered as being earned on the date at which it is realised *i.e.* on the data when the property in goods passes to the buyer and he becomes legally liable to pay. This can be made clear by taking the following example:

A customer at Ranchi places an order with a manufacturer at Delhi on 1st January. On receipt of order, the manufacturer manufactures goods and delivers them to the customer at Ranchi on 1st February who makes payment of goods on March 1 after enjoying the credit period of one month. In this case, revenue was realised not on January 1, when order was received nor on March 1, when cash was realised but on February 1, when goods were delivered to the customer.

However, in case of hire-purchase sales, the ownership of goods sold on hire-purchase does not pass to the purchaser when the goods are delivered but it passes when the last instalment is paid. But sales are presumed to have been made to the extent of down payment, instalments received and instalments due but not received.

The realisation concept is criticised by economists on the ground that if an asset has increased in value then it is irrelevant because it has not yet been sold. In other words, unrealised gains are not considered in accounting. As a result of this concept, distinction is made between holding gains and operating gains. Holding gains arise as a result of increases in value from holding an asset and operating gains are realised as a result of selling assets. Holding gains are not recorded because property in goods has not yet transferred but operating gains are reported because they have resulted as a result of sale.

(*ix*) Objective Evidence Concept

Objectivity connotes reliability, trustworthiness and verifiability, which means that there is some evidence in ascertaining the correctness of the information reported. Entries in accounting records and data reported in financial statements must be based on objectively determined evidence. Without close adherence to this principle, the confidence of many users of the financial statements could not be maintained. Invoices and vouchers for purchases and sales, bank statements for amount of cash at bank, physical checking of stock in hand etc. are examples, of objective evidence which are capable of verification. **As far as possible, every entry in accounting records should be supported by some objective evidence. Evidence should be such which will minimise the possibility of error and intentional bias or fraud.** Evidence is not always conclusively objective for there are numerous occasions in accounting where judgements and other subjective factors play part. In such situation, it should be seen that most objective evidence available should be used. For example, the Provision for Doubtful Debts Account is an estimate of the losses expected from failure to collect sales made on credit. Estimation of this account should be made on such objective factors as past experience in collecting debtors and reliable forecasts of future business activities.

(*x*) Accrual Concept

The essence of the accrual concept is that revenue is recognised when it is realised, that is when sale is complete or services are given and it is immaterial whether cash is received or not. Similarly, according to this concept, expenses are recognised in the accounting period in which they help in earning the revenue whether cash is paid or not. Thus, to ascertain correct profit or loss for an accounting period and to show the true and fair financial position of the business at the end of the accounting period, we make record of all expenses and incomes relating to the accounting period whether actual cash has been paid or received or not. Therefore, as a result of the accrual concept, outstanding expenses and outstanding incomes are taken into consideration while preparing final accounts of a business entity.

ACCOUNTING CONVENTIONS

(*i*) Convention of Consistency

Accounting rules, practices and conventions should be continuously observed and applied *i.e.* these should not change from one year to another. The results of different years will be comparable only when accounting rules are continuously adhered to from year to year. For example, the principle of "valuing stock at cost or net realisable value, whichever is less" should be followed "year after year to get comparable results." Similarly, if depreciation on fixed assets is provided on straight line method, it should be done year after year. Consistency serves to eliminate personal bias because the accountant will have to follow consistent rules, practices and conventions year after year. The rationale behind this concept is that frequent changes in accounting treatment would make the financial statements unreliable to the persons who use them.

Consistency also implies external consistency, *i.e.,* the financial statements of one enterprise should be comparable with another. It means that every enterprise should follow same accounting methods and procedures of recording and reporting business transactions. The development of international and national accounting standards is due to the convention of consistency.

In relation to consistency, some other terms known as "vertical consistency", "horizontal consistency" and "third dimensional consistency" are used. Vertical consistency is achieved when the same accounting rules, policies, practices and conventions are adopted while preparing interrelated financial statements of the same date. Horizontal consistency is achieved when the same firm adopts the same accounting practice, policies and methods from year to year. By third dimensional consistency we mean when all units in the same industry follow the same accounting policies, methods and practices.

This convention does not completely prohibit changes. It does not debar from introducing improved accounting techniques. However, if a change becomes desirable, the change and its effect on profits and financial position as compared to the previous year should be clearly stated in the financial statements. In the words of *Yorston, Smith and Brown,* "Consistency serves to eliminate personal bias and to even out personal judgement but it must not become a fetish so as to ignore changed conditions or need for improvements in technique".

The rationale for following the convention of consistency is made clear in the following example:

A company purchased a fixed asset for ₹ 1,00,000 and it charges depreciation @ 20% on straight line method. At the end of the second year, the book value of the assets will be ₹ 60,000.

But if the method is changed to reducing balance method in the second year, the book value of the asset at the end of 2nd year will be ₹ 64,000.

The effect of change will be that depreciation of ₹ 20,000 will be reduced to ₹ 16,000 in the second year making in increase of ₹ 4,000 in profits and asset will be shown in the Balance Sheet at ₹ 64,000 and not at ₹ 60,000. This example brings into light the importance of consistency convention. The auditor should, therefore, refuse to certify the accounts of a company if the accounting procedures have not been consistently followed or if there is any departure in the consistency principle, it must be clearly disclosed in the financial statements along with its effects.

(*ii*) Convention of Full Disclosure

According to this convention, all accounting statements should be honestly prepared and to that end full disclosure of all significant information should be made. All information which is of material interest to proprietors, creditors and investors should be disclosed in accounting statements. An obligation is placed on the accounting profession to see that the books of accounts prepared on behalf of others are as reliable and informative as circumstances permit. This convention is becoming popular these days because most of big business units are in the form of joint stock companies where ownership is divorced from management. The Companies Act, 2013 has prescribed the forms in which financial statements are to be prepared. The Act makes ample provisions for the disclosure of essential information so that there is no chance of any material information being left out. For example, the basis of valuation of fixed assets, investments and stock should be clearly stated in the Balance Sheet because it is of material interest to the proprietors, creditors and prospective investors. In 1945, the Cohen Committee enquiring into company practices in England made the following observations regarding the convention of full disclosure:

"We are in favour of as much disclosure as practicable. It is also important in our opinion to ensure that there should be adequate disclosure and publication of the results of the companies so as to dissipate any suggestion that hidden profits are being accumulated by industrial concerns to the detriment of consumers and those who work for industry.

On the other hand, if there is no detailed disclosure in the statement of profit and loss, undisclosed reserves accumulated in the past periods may be used to swell the profits in years when the company is failing badly and the shareholders may be misled into thinking that company is making profits."

Generally disclosure is required when—(*i*) alternative policies are available (LIFO, FIFO, Average Cost etc. for inventory valuation) (*ii*) principle peculiar to a particular industry (revenue is recognised before completion of a job, in case of long-term contracts); and (*iii*) unusual or innovative application of accounting principles (valuation of live stock on herd basis in case of dairy firm).

(*iii*) Convention of Conservatism or Prudence

Literally speaking, conservatism means taking the gloomy view of a situation. It is a policy of caution or playing safe and had its origin as a safeguard against possible losses in a world of uncertainty. It compels the businessman to wear a "risk-proof" jacket, for the working rule is : ***anticipate no-profits but provide for all possible losses.*** " For example, closing stock is valued at cost or net realisable value, whichever is less. If market price is higher than the cost, the higher amount is ignored in the accounts and closing stock will be valued at cost which is lower than the net realisable value. But if the net realisable value is lower than the cost, the higher amount of cost will be ignored and stock will be valued at net realisable value which is less than the cost. Thus, the principle of conservatism is inherent in the valuation of stock. Other applications of the conservatism concept can be as follows:

(*a*) Research and development expenses are usually charged as expenses of the period in which they are incurred but benefits of research and development will be realised in future.

(*b*) Under the completed contract method, revenue from long term construction contract is recognised only when the contract is completed substantially.

(*c*) In case of "cash or delivery sales" revenue is recognised when cash is received by the seller or his agent and not on delivery of goods to the buyer.

(*d*) As per AS 4, "The amount of a contingent loss should be provided for by a charge in the statement of profit and loss if :

- (*a*) it is probable that at the date of the financial statements events subsequent thereto will confirm that (after taking into account any related probable recovery) an asset has been impaired or a liability has been incurred as at that date, and
- (*b*) a reasonable estimate of the amount of the resulting loss can be made.

Contingent gains and benefits from contracts to the extent not executed should not be accounted for in financial statements."

Overoptimism in reporting results in more undersirable results than overpessimism in reporting results because it shows position better than what actual financial position is. But the excessive application of the convention of conservatism could result in the creation of secret reserves, a practice which is contrary to the convention of full disclosure. Conservatism carried beyond what is warranted by reasonable doubts distorts earnings in as much as net profit in one period may be understated than what actual profit is. Keeping in view this, current accounting thought has shifted somewhat from the principle of conservatism. The concepts of consistency, full disclosure, materiality and objectivity take precedence over conservatism and the latter should be a factor only when the others do not play a significant part.

(*iv*) Convention of Materiality

An accounting concept according to which all *relatively important and relevant items*, (*i.e.*, items, the knowledge of which might influence the decisions of the user of the financial statements) are disclosed in the financial statements.

Whether something should be disclosed or not in the financial statements will depend on whether it is material or not. Materiality depends on the amount involved in the transaction. For example, minor expenditure of ₹ 10 for the purchase of waste basket may be treated as an expense of the period rather than an asset.

Customs also influence materiality. For example, only round figures (to the nearest rupee) may be shown in the financial statements to make the figures manageable without affecting the accounting data. Similarly, for income tax purpose the income has to be rounded to nearest ten rupees.

The term "materiality" is a subjective term. The accountant should record an item as material even though it is of small amount if its knowledge seems to influence the decision of the proprietors or auditors or investors. For example, commission paid to sole selling agents should be disclosed separately in the Statement of Profit and Loss. Similarly, amount due to directors or other officers of the bank should be disclosed separately in the Balance Sheet of a bank to know the amount of advances due from the directors or officers who are managing the affairs of the bank. The Companies Act, 2013 also lays emphasis on separate disclosure of material items. Any item of income or expenditure which exceeds 1% of the revenue from operations of the company or ₹ 1,00,000, whichever in higher should be shown as a separate and distinct item against an appropriate head in the Statement of Profit and Loss. Financial statements should disclose all material items the knowledge of which might influence the decisions of the user of the financial statements.

Accounting Principles Relating to Statement of Profit and Loss

Following are the main principles which are related to the preparation of statement of profit and loss account :

(*i*) Accounting period concept (*ii*) Accrual concept, (*iii*) Realisation concept, (*iv*) Materiality concept, (*v*) Matching concept. All these have been discussed in the previous pages of this chapter.

Accounting Principles Relating to Balance Sheet

Following are the main principles which are related to the preparation of balance sheet :

(*i*) Entity concept, (*ii*) Money Measurement Concept, (*iii*) Going Concern Concept, (*iv*) Cost Concept, (*v*) Conservatism Concept, (*vi*) Dual aspect concept. All these have already been discussed in the previous pages of this chapter.

Fundamental Accounting Assumptions

Following are recognised by the International Accounting Standards Committee and the Institute of Chartered Accountants of India as fundamental accounting assumptions as per International Accounting Standard 1 and Indian Accounting Standard 1. They are reproduced below:

(*a*) Going Concern. The enterprise is normally viewed as a going concern, that is, as continuing in operation for the forseeable future. It is assumed that the enterprise has neither the intention nor the necessity of liquidation or of curtailing materially the scale of its operations.

(*b*) Consistency. It is assumed that the accounting policies are consistent from one period to another.

(*c*) Accrual. Revenues and costs are accrued, that is, recognised as they are earned or incurred (and not as money is received or paid) and recorded in the financial statements of the periods to which they relate.

If fundamental accounting assumptions are not followed in the preparation and presentation of financial statements, the fact should be disclosed. If these are followed, no specific disclosure is necessary. These are called fundamental because these are to be followed and their disclosure in the financial statements is required if these are not followed. Otherwise there is no conflict between accounting concepts and fundamental accounting assumptions. In fact, fundamental accounting assumptions are part of the basic accounting concepts.

ACCOUNTING POLICIES

Accounting policies are the specific accounting principles and the methods of applying those principles that are considered by a business concern to be the most appropriate in the circumstances to present financial statements. *Accounting policies represent choices among different accounting methods that can be used in recording financial transactions and preparing financial statements.* To quote International Accounting Standards Committee, "Accounting policies encompass many principles, bases, conventions, rules and procedures adopted by managements in preparing and presenting financial statements. There are many different accounting policies in use even in relation to the same subject and judgement is required in selecting and applying those which are appropriate to the circumstances of the enterprises and are best suited to present properly its financial position and the results of its operation".

Accounting policies may be suitable for a particular period. As times change and views change on the appropriate method to record financial transactions, accounting policies also change. An accounting method that was once generally accepted may be rejected with change in circumstances.

In spite of too much emphasis on accounting standards by the International Accounting Standard Committee and the Institute of Chartered Accountants of India, the management of the entity has alternative choices out of a number of accounting policies, mainly in regard to the method of depreciation, valuation of inventory, provision for doubtful debts, treatment of research and development, provision for gratuity etc. The adoption of different accounting policies by different concerns destroys comparability of one concern with another. Figures of one year with another year of the same concern may not be comparable when the management makes a change in accounting policies in the other year. To get comparable results of different years, consistent accounting policies should be adhered to. If change in accounting policies is made because of compelling circumstances, (*i.e.* change in law, for compliance with an accounting standard) the fact should be mentioned in the financial statements of the year in which change is made so that use of the financial statements may not be misled.

Three considerations should govern the selection and application by management of the appropriate accounting policies and the preparation of financial statements.

***(a)* Prudence**. Uncertainties inevitably surround many transactions. This should be recognised by exercising prudence in preparing financial statements. Prudence does not, however, justify the creation of secret or hidden reserves.

***(b)* Substance Over Form.** Transactions and other events should be accounted for and presented in accordance with their substance and financial reality and not merely with their legal form.

***(c)* Materiality.** Financial statements should disclose all items which are material enough to affect evaluations or decisions.

Financial statements must be clear and understandable. They are based on accounting policies which vary from enterprise to enterprise, both within a single country and among countries. Disclosure of the significant accounting policies on which the financial statements are based is, therefore, necessary so that they may be properly understood. The disclosure of these policies should be an intergrated part of the financial statements; it is helpful to users if they are all disclosed in one place. Sometimes a wrong or inappropriate treatment adopted for items in balance sheets, income statements or statement of profit and loss, or other statements. Disclosure of the treatment adopted is necessary in any case,but disclosure cannot rectify a wrong or inappropriate treatment.

Financial statements give information which is used by a variety of users, especially shareholders and creditors (present and potential) and employees, Other important categories of users include suppliers, customers, trade unions, financial analysts, statisticians, economists, and taxing and regulatory authorities. The users of financial statements required them as part of the information needed among other purposes, for making evaluations and financial decisions. They cannot make reliable judgments on these matters unless the financial statements clearly disclose the significant accounting policies which have been adopted in preparing them.

Variations in Accounting Policies and their Disclosure

The task of interpreting financial statements is complicated by the adoption of diverse policies in many areas of accounting. There is no single list of accepted policies to which users may refer and the diverse accounting policies that are presently available for adoption can produce significantly different sets of financial statements based on the same events and conditions. Following are examples of areas in which differing accounting policies exists and which therefore require disclosure of the treatment selected :

General

(*i*) Consolidation policy ; (*ii*) Conversion of translation of foreign currencies including the disposition of exchange gain and losses ; (*iii*) Overall valuation policy (*e.g.* historical cost, general purchasing power, replacement value) ; (*iv*) Events subsequent to the balance sheet date ; (*v*) Leases, hire purchase, or instalments transactions and related interest ; (*vi*) Taxes ; (*vii*) Long term contracts ; (*viii*) Franchises

Assets

(*i*) Receivables ; (*ii*) Inventories (stock and work-in-progress) and related cost of goods sold ; (*iii*) Depreciable assets and depreciation ; (*iv*) Growing crops ; (*v*) Land held for development and related development costs ; (*vi*) Investments : subsidiary companies, associated companies and other investments ; (*vii*) Research and development ; (*viii*) Patents and trademarks ; (*ix*) Goodwill

Liabilities and Provisions

(*i*) Warranties ; (*ii*) Commitments and contingencies ; (*iii*) Pension costs and retirement plans ; (*iv*) Severance and redundancy payments.

Profits and Losses

(*i*) Methods of revenue recognition ; (*ii*) Maintenance, repairs and improvements ; (*iii*) Gains and losses on disposals of property ; (*iv*) Reserve accounting, statutory or otherwise, including direct charges and credits to surplus accounts.

Distinction Between Fundamental Accounting Assumptions and Accounting Policies

Following are the main distinctions between fundamental accounting assumptions and accounting policies :

(*i*) Number. There are only three accounting assumptions (*i.e.* Going Concern, Consistency and Accrual) but there is no such list of accounting policies which may be applied in all concerns. Different accounting policies may be adopted by different concerns according to their suitability and convenience.

(*ii*) Disclosure. There is no need of any disclosure of fundamental accounting assumptions which are followed but in case of accounting policies the disclosure is a must. If due to some reasons fundamental accounting assumptions are not followed, this fact must be disclosed in the financial statements alongwith reasons.

(*iii*) Choice. In case of fundamental accounting assumptions, one has to follow all. There is no choice but in case of accounting policies, there is a choice to select a particular policy.

QUESTIONS

OBJECTIVE TYPE

1. **Fill in the blanks :**

(*a*) A principle is ...... to the extent that the accounting information is not influenced by the personal bias of those who furnish the information.

(*b*) A principle is ...... to the extent that it can be applied without undue complexity or cost.

(*c*) Accounting concepts may be considered as ...... upon which the science of accounting is based.

(*d*) The term 'conventions' denotes ...... which guide the accountant while preparing the accounting statements.

(*e*) The business entity concept implies that a business unit is......from the persons who supply capital to it.

(*f*) According to the ...... concept, it is possible to remove the cost of fixed assets from the accounts altogether by charging depreciation.

(*g*) According to the ...... concept, revenue is considered as being raised on the date at which it is realised.

Ans. [(*a*) objective ; (*b*) feasible ; (*c*) basic conditions ; (*d*) customs or traditions ; (*e*) separate ; (*f*) cost ; (*g*) realisation]

2. Explain the principles of Accounting on which these comments are based :

(*a*) Balance Sheet is not a valuation statement.

(*b*) Calibre or Quality of management team is not directly disclosed on the Balance Sheet.

(*c*) Debentures are marked at the same amount in rupees which the Company borrowed though purchasing power of money may have changed substantially.

(*d*) Goods sold to a worker at cost are adjusted in Purchases Account.

(*e*) Unrealised appreciation in the value of fixed assets cannot be used for the payment of Dividends.

(*f*) Advance received from a Supplier is not taken as Income or Sales.

Ans. [(*a*) Going Concern Concept ; (*b*) Money Measurement Concept ; (*c*) Money Measurement Concept ; (*d*) Cost Concept ; (*e*) Realisation Concept ; (*f*) Matching Principle Concept]

3. Select the correct answer :

(*a*) According to the going concern concept, a business entity is assumed to have :
(*i*) a long life (*ii*) a very short life (*iii*) an indefinite life.

(*b*) Contingent liability is shown in the balance sheet because of :
(*i*) Convention of consistency (*ii*)Convention of materiality
(*iii*) Convention of disclosure.

(*c*) Revenue is considered as being earned when :
(*i*) Cash is received (*ii*) Production is done (*iii*) Sale is effected.

(*d*) Accounting does not record non-financial transactions because of
(*i*) Entity concept (*ii*) accrual concept (*iii*) measurement concept.

(*e*) According to which of the following concepts even the owner of the business who provides capital is treated as a creditor of the business ?
(*i*) Entity concept (*ii*) Cost concept (*iii*) Money measurement concept.

(*f*) Appending notes to the financial statements as per ...... convention
(*i*) Materiality (*ii*) Disclosure
(*iii*) Consistency (*iv*) Convertism.

(*g*) Accounting of a small calculator as an expense and not as an asset is due to .... convention
(*i*) Disclosure (*ii*) Materiality
(*iii*) Consistency (*iv*) Conservatism.

(*h*) Following the written down value method of depreciation on particular asset year after year is because of .... convention
(*i*) Disclosure (*ii*) Consistency
(*ii*) Conservatism (*iv*) Materiality.

(*i*) Valuation of stock is done at lower of cost or market value because of .... convention
(*i*) Disclosure (*ii*) Consistency
(*iii*) Conservatism (*iv*) Materiality.

(*j*) Making provision for doubtful debts is as per ...... convention
(*i*) Disclosure (*ii*) Consistency
(*iii*) Conservatism (*iv*) Materiality.

(*k*) Contingent liability shown in the balance sheet, arises due to the accounting convertion of
(*i*) Consistency (*ii*) Conservatism
(*iii*) Disclosure (*iv*) Materiality.

(*l*) Accounting principles are generally based on
(*i*) Practicability (*ii*) Subjectivity
(*iii*) Convenience in Recording (*iv*) Objectivity.

(*m*) According to money measurement concept the following will be recorded in the books of accounts of the business :
(*i*) Health of Director (*ii*) Quality of Company Goods
(*iii*) Value of Plant and Machinery (*iv*) Utility of Managers.

(*n*) The convention of conservatism when applied to the balance sheet results in
(*i*) Understatement of Assets (*ii*) Overstatement of Assets
(*iii*) Understatement of Liability (*iv*) Overstatement of Liabilities.

(*o*) Accounting concepts include those assumptions upon which the science of .... is based.
(*i*) Accounting (*ii*) Recording
(*iii*) Book-keeping (*iv*) Double Entry System.

(*p*) A firm follows the straight line method of depreciating fixed assets year after year due to :
(*i*) Convenience (*ii*) Comparability
(*iii*) Consistency (*iv*) None of the above.

(*q*) A change in accounting policy is justified :
(*i*) To comply with law
(*ii*) To comply with accounting standard
(*iii*) To ensure better presentation of the financial statements of the firm
(*iv*) All of the above.

(*r*) Which of the following is fundamental accounting assumption ?
(*i*) Full disclosure (*ii*) Materiality
(*iii*) Going Concern (*iv*) Accounting period.

(*s*) Revenue is generally recognised at the point of sale. Which principle is applied ?
(*i*) Consistency (*ii*) Marketing
(*iii*) Realisation (*iv*) Cost Realisation.

(*t*) The assumption that a business enterprise will not be sold or liquidated in the near future is known as ....
(*i*) Separate Entity (*ii*) Going Concern
(*iii*) Periodic (*iv*) Conservatism.

(*u*) Companies must prepare financial statements at least yearly due to the .... concept
(*i*) Business Entity (*ii*) Going Concern
(*iii*) Period (*iv*) Accrual.

(*v*) The .... principle requires that same accounting methods should be used from one accounting period to the next.
(*i*) Accounting period (*ii*) Consistency
(*iii*) Conservatism (*iv*) Materiality.

(*w*) Expenses not yet paid but belonging to the same accounting period are recorded as per .... concept
(*i*) Accrual (*ii*) Realisation
(*ii*) Conservatism (*iv*) Money Measurement.

(*x*) Classification of assets as current assets and fixed assets is as per .... concept
(*i*) Money Measurement (*ii*) Going Concern
(*iii*) Dual aspect (*iv*) Cost.

(*y*) The convention that sates that the accounting practice should be followed consistently over the years.

(*i*) Consistency (*ii*) Conservation,

(*iii*) Materiality (*iv*) Disclosure.

(*z*) General reserve is created on the basis of convention of—

(*i*) Conservatism (*ii*) Uniformity,

(*iii*) Materiality (*iv*) Full disclosure.

Ans. [(*a*) (i) ; (*b*) (*iii*) ; (*c*) (*iii*) ; (*d*) (*iii*) ; (*e*) (*i*) ; (*f*) (*ii*); (*g*) (*ii*); (*h*) (*ii*); (*i*) (*iii*); (*j*) (*iii*); (*k*) (*iii*); (*l*) (*i*); (*m*) (*iii*); (*n*) (*i*); (*o*) (*i*); (*p*) (*iii*) ; (*q*) (*iv*) ; (*r*) (*iii*) ; (*s*) (*iii*) ; (*t*) (*ii*) ; (*u*) (*iii*) ; (*v*) (*ii*) ; (*w*) (*i*) ; (*x*) (*ii*); (*y*) (*i*); (*z*) (*i*)].

4. Indicate if each of the following statements is correct or incorrect :

(*i*) Revenue is generally recognised at the point of sale.

(*ii*) A business and its proprietor are separate entities.

(*iii*) The going concern concept assumes that a business concern will go on for an indefinite period.

(*iv*) Accounting principles are formulated by the Government.

(*v*) Closing Stock is always valued at market price.

Ans. [Correct : (*i*), (*ii*), (*iii*) Incorrect : (*iv*), (*v*)].

5. A machine was purchased for ₹ 2,00,000 on 1-4-2024 and on 31-3-2025 its net realisable value was ₹ 2,50,000. Do you prefer to count this profit ? If you count which of the following conventions will be violated and why ?

(*i*) Disclosure, (*ii*) Consistency, (*iii*) Conservatism.

Hint : Convention of conservatism will be violated.

6. Recognising that the values of land have been increasing in the recent years. Mr. A owner of A & Co., increased the balance sheet amount of land from ₹ 50,000 to ₹ 70,000. Explain the accounting concept which has been violated.

Hint : Cost concept violated.

7. D & Company purchased a machine on 1st January, 2024 for ₹ 50,000. Depreciation at the rate of 20% was charged on machine for two years. From 1st January, 2025 the rate of depreciation was reduced to 10%. No mention of this change was made in the financial statements or notes thereto. Explain the accounting convention which has been violated.

Hint : Convention of full disclosure violated.

8. Give one example wherein the convention of consistency is followed and another example wherein it is violated.

Hint : An example where the convention of consistency is followed may be cited as valuation of inventory. Inventory is consistently valued from year to year either at cost or market price whichever of the two is lower. Whereas, an example where it is violated may be with regard to depreciation of Fixed Asset. If, in the current year, the method of providing depreciation is changed from Straight Line Method to Diminishing Balance Method, the convention of consistency will be violated.

9. What accounting principle is violated and what are the implications for the periodic operating results and on financial condition in each of the following cases ?

(*i*) A firm shows all purchases including fixed assets below ₹ 2,500 even when they have a useful life extending over many years in the Trading Account.

(*ii*) A motor car was fully depreciated in the first five years of its life, but it is still giving useful service to the firm.

Hint : (*i*) The practice of showing all purchases including fixed assets below ₹ 2,500 even when they have a useful life extending over many years to Trading A/c will result in understatement of profit and also under-valuation of assets in the Balance Sheet due to improper matching of cost with revenue. This will have an implication on the periodic operating result and also on the financial health or condition. The accounting concept violated in this case is the **principle of matching and also of full disclosure.**

(*ii*) The car which is available with the firm does not exist in the books since the same have been fully depreciated in the first five years of its life but the motor car is still giving useful service to the firm. It seems that due to over depreciation in the past, the asset is reduced to nil. Here too, the firm has violated the concept of **'matching' & full disclosure'.** Due to mismatch of depreciation cost with revenue, there has been understatement of profit and undervaluation of asset. The remedy lies in revaluing the motor car having regard to its remaining useful life by appreciating the asset and adjusting the difference to Capital A/c or P/L Appro. A/c as the case may be. Then the asset should be suitably depreciated in such a way so that it is reduced to nil by the end of its useful extended life.

SHORT ANSWER TYPE

1. What are Generally Accepted Accounting Principles (GAAP)?
2. Why is consistency an important accounting principle?
3. Name any two accounting concepts under GAAP.
4. State the principle that ensures expenses are recorded in the same period as the related revenues.
5. Which GAAP principle requires businesses to report all relevant financial information?
6. Explain the going concern concept in brief.
7. What is the matching principle in accounting?
8. State the conservatism principle in accounting.
9. Give two differences between accounting concepts and accounting conventions.
10. Which principle guides the recording of assets at their original cost?
11. A company purchased a machine for ₹ 10,00,000, but its market value dropped to ₹ 8,00,000. The accountant still recorded it at ₹ 10,00,000 in the books. Which accounting principle is followed here and why?
12. A business received an advance of ₹ 50,000 for services to be provided next month, but the amount was not recorded as revenue this month. Which GAAP concept applies here?
13. An accountant has been using the straight-line method for depreciation for many years. He decides to shift to written-down value method without any valid reason or disclosure. Which principle is being violated?
14. A company does not record the value of free office space provided by the owner in its books. Which accounting concept justifies this?
15. A firm anticipates a probable loss in a lawsuit and makes provisions for it, but does not record a potential gain from another pending case. Which principle is being applied?
16. A company paid ₹ 1,20,000 for a 12-month insurance policy starting from 1st Jan, but it records only ₹ 30,000 as an expense in the current quarter. Which accounting principle is applied here?
17. A business owner uses the same bank account for personal and business transactions, and the accountant refuses to record personal expenses in the business books. Which principle is the accountant following?
18. Even though the economy is in recession, a company continues preparing its financial statements assuming it will operate in the foreseeable future. Which accounting assumption supports this?
19. A company does not disclose a small calculator worth ₹ 800 as an asset and charges it off as an expense. Which concept is applied here and why?
20. In preparing final accounts, the accountant ensured that all expenses and incomes related to the current year were included, even if not paid or received in cash. Which accounting principle is being followed?

LONG ANSWER TYPE

1. What are basic accounting concepts? Explain their implications in accounting.
2. What are accounting concepts and conventions? Name them and explain any four accounting concepts in detail.
3. Briefly discuss the basic accounting concepts and fundamental accounting assumptions. Is there a conflict between the two?

   [Hint. There is no conflict between the two]
4. What are fundamental accounting assumptions? Are these different from accounting policies? Explain.
5. Explain the following accounting concepts and conventions:

   (*i*) Business Entity Concept (*ii*) Money Measurement Concept
   (*iii*) Dual Aspect Concept (*iv*) Cost Concept
   (*v*) Convention of Consistency (*vi*) Convention of Materiality
   (*vii*) Convention of Disclosure (*viii*) Revenue Matching Concept
   (*ix*) Going Concern Concept (*x*) Accounting Period (or Periodicity) Concept
   (*xi*) Accrual Concept (*xii*) Concept of Conservatism
   (*xiii*) Timeliness Principle
6. Examine the accounting concepts of conservatism and materiality and their significance in the preparation of financial statements.
7. 'Entity' and 'Continuity' concepts are inter-related. Comment.
8. 'Without accounting concepts and conventions objective, reliable, consistent and comparable accounts cannot be maintained.' Comment.
9. 'The focus of accounting is business enterprise for which the accounts are maintained and not its proprietors.' Do you agree? Explain.
10. 'The ascertainment of correct profit depends upon proper matching of costs and revenues.' Examine this statement in light of the Matching Concept.
11. Name the various accounting concepts and conventions. Explain the Realisation Concept and Business Entity Concept in detail.
12. Explain in detail the convention of materiality. Why is it considered so significant in accounting? Give examples.
13. Distinguish between:

    (*a*) Realisation Concept and Accrual Concept

    (*b*) Consistency and Conservatism in Accounting
14. Recognising that the values of land have been increasing in the recent years, Anil, owner of Anil Constructions Ltd., increased the balance sheet amount of land from ₹ 50 lakh to ₹ 6 crore. Identify and explain the accounting concept which has been violated.

    [Hint. Cost Concept]
15. 'Transactions and events are guided by generally accepted accounting principles subject to laws of land.' Explain this statement.

CHAPTER 3

Goods and Service Tax (GST)

Introduction

A number of countries around the globe have already implemented GST. For instance, Australia introduced GST in 2000, replacing the Federal Wholesale Tax. Canada replaced the Manufacturer's Sales Tax with GST in 1991. New Zealand implemented the reform in 1986, while Singapore did so in 1994. GST in Malaysia was introduced in 2015, and India has also implemented GST to provide benefits to the consumers, the industry, and the government.

GST is one indirect tax for the whole nation, which will make India one unified common market. GST is a single tax which shall be levied on the supply of goods and services, right from the manufacturer to the consumer. GST has replaced indirect taxes such as Service Tax, VAT, Excise, CST etc. and shall simplify business and accounting processes. GST is applicable on ***both*** Goods and Services.

The Goods and Service Tax Act was passed in the Parliament on 29th March, 2017. The Act came into effect on 1st July 2017.

India has adopted **DUAL MODEL OF GST** wherein GST shall be levied by both Central and the state. All traders who earn turnovers in excess of ₹ 20 lakh in a financial year will have to register under the Goods and Services Tax. They shall be called **Registered Dealers.**

Taxes to be Subsumed

GST has replaced under mentioned indirect taxes.

Central Taxes	State Taxes
• Central Excise Duty [including additional excise duties, excise duty under the Medicinal and Toilet Preparations (Excise Duties) Act, 1955] • Service tax • Additional Customs Duty (CVD) • Special Additional Duty of Customs (SAD) • Central Sales Tax (levied by the Central and collected by the States) • Central surcharges and cesses (relating to supply of goods and services)	• Value Added Tax • Octroi and Entry Tax • Purchase Tax • Luxury Tax • Taxes on lottery, betting & gambling • State cesses and surcharges • Entertainment tax (other than the tax levied by the local bodies) • Central Sales Tax (levied by the Central and collected by the States)

Goods and Services Tax is

- a comprehensive value added tax on supply of goods or services or both
- levied at every stage of production -distribution chain
- Ensures seamless input tax credit throughout the supply chain
- At all stages of production and distribution, taxes are a pass through and tax is borne by the final consumer
- No differentiation between Goods and Services as GST is levied at each stage in the supply chain

Administration of GST in India

India is a federal country where both the Central and the States have been assigned the powers to levy and collect taxes. Both the Governments have distinct responsibilities to perform, as per the Constitution, for which they need to raise tax revenue.

There are three components of GST – Central GST (CGST), State GST (SGST) and Integrated GST(IGST). Both Central and States will simultaneously levy GST across the value chain. Tax will be levied on every supply of goods and services. Central Government would levy and collect Central Goods and Services Tax (CGST), and States would levy and collect the State Goods and Services Tax (SGST) on all transactions within a State. IGST is a tax levied on all Inter-State supplies of goods and/or services and Central Government will levy and collect IGST.

GST comprises of

- Central Goods and Services Tax (CGST),
- State Goods and Services Tax (SGST) or Union Territory GST (UTGST),
- Integrated Goods and Services Tax (IGST).

Model of GST in India

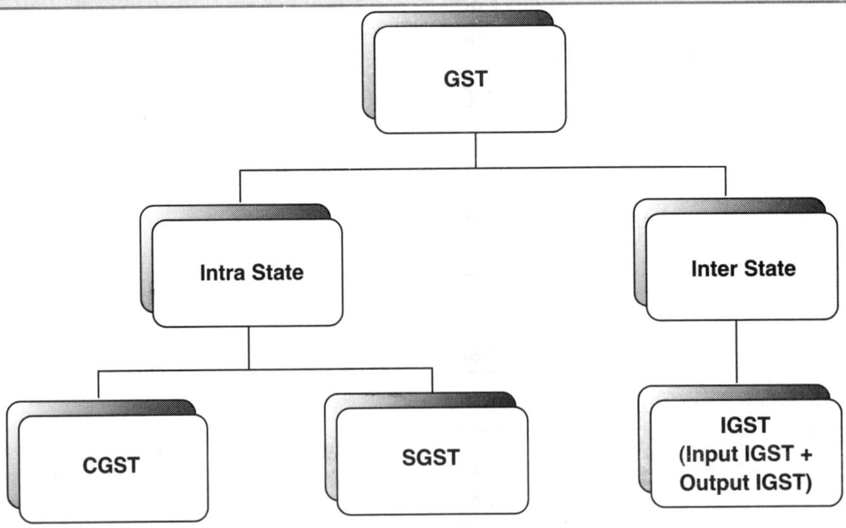

Determination of applicability of CGST, SGST or IGST

To determine whether Central Goods & Services Tax (CGST), State Goods & Services Tax (SGST) or Integrated Goods & Services Tax (IGST) will be applicable in a taxable transaction, it is important to first know if the transaction is an Intra State or an Inter-State supply.

- **Intra-State supply of goods or services** is when the location of the supplier and the place of supply i.e., location of the buyer are in the same state. In Intra-State transactions, a seller has to collect **both CGST and SGST** from the buyer. The CGST gets deposited with Central Government and SGST gets deposited with State Government.

- **Inter-State supply of goods or services** is when the location of the supplier and the place of supply are in different states. Also, in cases of export or import of goods or services or when the supply of goods or services is made to or by a SEZ unit, the transaction is assumed to be Inter-State. In an Inter-State transaction, a seller has to collect **IGST** from the buyer.

Central Goods and Services Tax (CGST)

Under GST, CGST is a tax levied on Intra State supplies of both goods and services by the Central Government and will be governed by the CGST Act. SGST will also be levied on the same Intra State supply but will be governed by the State Government.

State Goods and Services Tax (SGST)or Union Territory GST (UTGST)

Under GST, SGST (or UTGST) is a tax levied on Intra State/ Union Territory supplies of both goods and services by the State Government and will be governed by the SGST Act. As explained above, CGST will also be levied on the same Intra State supply but will be governed by the Central Government.

Note:

1. Any tax liability obtained under SGST can be set off against SGST or IGST input tax credit only.
2. For discussion purposes, SGST and UGST are referred as SGST.

Example for CGST and SGST

Let's suppose Rajendra is a dealer in Gujarat who sold goods to Ashish in Gujarat worth ₹ 20,000. The GST rate is 18% comprising of CGST rate of 9% and SGST rate of 9%. In such case, the dealer collects ₹ 3,600 of which ₹ 1,800 will go to the Central Government and ₹ 1,800 will go to the Gujarat Government.

Integrated Goods and Services Tax (IGST)

Under GST, IGST is a tax levied on all Inter-State supplies of goods and/or services and will be governed by the IGST Act. IGST will be applicable on any supply of goods and/or services or both in cases of import into India and export from India also.Central Government shall levy and collect IGST instead of CGST and SGST . IGST will be shared between the Central Government and State Government.

Note: Under IGST,

- Exports would be zero-rated.
- Tax will be shared between the Central and State Government.

Example for IGST:

Consider that a businessman Rajendra from Gujarat had sold goods to Ashish from Maharashtra worth ₹ 2,00,000. The GST rate is 18% comprised of 18% IGST. In such case, the dealer has to charge ₹ 36,000 as IGST. This IGST will be collected by the Central Government and later on shared with the State Government.

Reverse Charge

Normally, the supplier of goods or services pays the tax on supply. In the case of Reverse Charge, the receiver becomes liable to pay the tax, i.e., the chargeability gets reversed. Refer to figure 1 to understand the difference between Normal GST payment process and GST payment process under reverse charge.

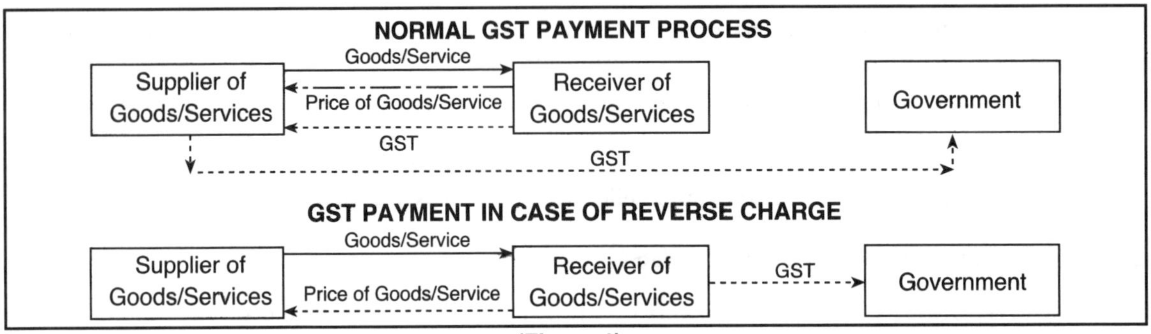

(Figure 1)

Reverse Charge Applicability (RCM)

A. Supply from an unregistered dealer to a registered dealer

If a vendor who is not registered under GST, supplies goods to a person who is registered under GST, then Reverse Charge would apply. This means that the GST will have to be paid directly by the receiver to the Government instead of the supplier.

The registered dealer who has to pay GST under reverse charge has to do self-invoicing for the purchases made.

For Inter-state purchases the buyer has to pay IGST. For Intra-state purchased CGST and SGST has to be paid under RCM by the purchaser.

B. Services through an e-commerce operator

If an e-commerce operator supplies services then reverse charge will be applicable to the e-commerce operator. He will be liable to pay GST.

For example, UrbanClap provides services of plumbers, electricians, teachers, beauticians etc. UrbanClap is liable to collect GST from the customers instead of the registered service providers and pay to Government.

If the e-commerce operator does not have a physical presence in the taxable territory, then a person representing such electronic commerce operator for any purpose will be liable to pay tax. If there is no representative, the operator will appoint a representative who will be held liable to pay GST.

C. Supply of certain goods and services specified by CBEC

CBEC has issued a list of goods and a list of services on which reverse charge is applicable.

Salient Features of GST

The salient features of GST are

1. It is a Dual GST model where both Central and state levy the taxes .
2. It is a multiple rate structure and at present most of the commodities and services that are subject to GST have been categorised under four tax slabs, viz. 5%, 12%, 18%, and 28%. However, GST Rates are not applicable to some goods and services, such as jute, fish, eggs, fresh meat, milk and other essential items.
3. Taxation is on destination based consumption principles
4. Taxable event of 'supply' as against manufacture (excise), sales (VAT) and services (service tax)
5. Dual GST (Central GST and State GST) to apply concurrently on supply of all goods and services
6. Integrated GST (IGST) on inter-State transactions including stock transfers
7. Exports zero rated;
8. Imports subject to IGST

Note:

1. Alcoholic beverages for human consumption are proposed to be kept out of the purview of GST
2. GST on petroleum products would be levied from a notified date recommended by the GST Council

Advantages of GST

GST has been envisaged as a more efficient tax system, neutral in its application and attractive in distribution. The advantages of GST are:

- **For business and industry**

1. **Easy compliance**: A robust and comprehensive IT system would be the foundation of the GST regime in India. Therefore, all tax payer services such as registrations, returns, payments, etc. would be available to the taxpayers online, which would make compliance easy and transparent.
2. **Uniformity of tax rates and structures**: GST will ensure that indirect tax rates and structures are common across the country, thereby increasing certainty and ease of doing business. In other words, GST would make doing business in the country tax neutral, irrespective of the choice of place of doing business.
3. **Removal of cascading of taxes**: A system of seamless tax-credits throughout the value-chain, and across boundaries of States, would ensure that there is minimal cascading of taxes. This would reduce hidden costs of doing business. Cascading of taxes means tax on tax.
4. **Improved competitiveness:** Reduction in transaction costs of doing business would eventually lead to an improved competitiveness for the trade and industry.
5. **Gain to manufacturers and exporters**: The subsuming of major Central and State taxes in GST, complete and comprehensive set-off of input goods and services and removal of Central Sales Tax (CST) would reduce the cost of locally manufactured goods and services. This will increase the competitiveness of Indian goods and services in the international market and give boost to Indian exports. The uniformity in tax rates and procedures across the country will also go a long way in reducing the compliance cost.

- **For Central Government and State Governments**

6. **Simple and easy to administer**: Multiple indirect taxes at the Central and State levels are being replaced by GST. Backed with a robust end-to-end IT system, GST would be simpler and easier to administer than all other indirect taxes of the Central and State levied so far.
7. **Better control on leakage:** GST will result in better tax compliance due to a robust GST infrastructure. Due to the seamless transfer of input tax credit from one stage to another in the chain of value addition, there is an in-built mechanism in the design of GST that would incentivize tax compliance by traders.
8. **Higher revenue efficiency:** GST is expected to decrease the cost of collection of tax revenues of the Government, and will therefore, lead to higher revenue efficiency.

- **For the consumer**

9. **Single and transparent tax proportionate to the value of goods and services:** Due to multiple indirect taxes being levied by the Central Government and State Government with incomplete or no input tax credits available at progressive stages of value addition, the cost of most goods and services in the country today are laden with many hidden taxes. Under GST, there would be only one tax from the manufacturer to the consumer, leading to transparency of taxes paid to the final consumer.
10. **Relief in overall tax burden:** Because of efficiency gains and prevention of leakages, the overall tax burden on most commodities will come down, which will benefit consumers.

Disadvantages of GST

1. There will be dual control on every business by the Central Government and State Government. So compliance cost may go up for smaller businesses.
2. All credit will be available on online connectivity with GST Network. Hence, small businesses may find it difficult to use the system.
3. GST on some products may become higher than the levels of VAT & Service Tax.

4. States may lose autonomy to change their tax rates.
5. Manufacturing states would lose big revenue.
6. Service sector may oppose because they have to register in every state with Central Government and State Government. So every business at all India level will have around 60 registrations while they were having just one in previous regime. Moreover their rates will also go up.

Implementation of GST

For the implementation of GST in the country, the Central and State Governments have jointly registered Goods and Services Tax Network (GSTN) as a not-for-profit, non-Government Company to provide shared IT infrastructure and services to Central and State Governments, tax payers and other stakeholders. The key objectives of GST are to provide a standard and uniform interface to the taxpayers, and shared infrastructure and services to Central and State/UT governments.

GST has developed a state-of-the-art comprehensive IT infrastructure including the common GST portal providing front end services of registration, returns and payments to all taxpayers, as well as the back end IT modules, for certain services that include processing of returns, registrations, audits, assessments, appeals, etc.

There would no manual filing of returns. All taxes are to be paid online.

Accounting and Records under GST

Every registered person is required to keep and maintain all records at his principal place of business.

It is the responsibility of the following persons to maintain specified records—

- The owner
- Operator of warehouse or godown or any other place used for storage of goods
- Every transporter

Every registered person whose turnover during a financial year exceeds the prescribed limit (2 crore) will get his accounts audited by a chartered accountant or a cost accountant.

Records Required to be maintained under GST

Every registered person must maintain records of—

- Production or manufacture of goods
- Inward and outward supply of goods or services or both
- Stock of goods
- Input tax credit availed
- Output tax payable and paid and
- Other particulars as may be prescribed

Accounts which must be maintained under GST

In GST Act, the GST paid is called Input GST and GST collected is called Output GST. Whatever GST is paid is set off against GST collected in a specified order.

That is, Input CGST, SGST and IGST is setoff against Output CGST, SGST and IGST individually in a prescribed order. Therefore, for accounting purposes, it becomes necessary that separate accounts for Input GST as well as output GST should be maintained. This helps the taxpayer in setting off each category of GST and finally arriving at the net figure of GST payable or excess paid, to be adjusted in next cycle.

Following GST accounts are required to be maintained :

1. Input CGST. Input CGST is CGST paid on intra state purchase of goods and/or services or both. Input CGST can be set-off against output IGST and output CGST in that order. If taxpayer pays CGST in Government account that is called as ***Input CGST***.

2. Input SGST. Input SGST is SGST paid on intra-state purchases of goods and/or services or both. Input SGST can be set-off against output IGST and Output SGST in that order. Any SGST paid by taxpayer in Government Account is called as ***Input SGST***.

> **Note :** It may be remembered that both CGST and SGST are levied at 50% of the specified rate. That is revenue is collected equally by Central Government and State Government. If the rate of GST is 18%, then CGST levied shall be 9% and SGST levied shall also be 9%.

3. Input IGST. Input IGST is the IGST paid on inter-state purchase of goods and/or services. IGST paid can be set-off against IGST collected, then CGST collected, and then SGST collected, in this order only. If goods and/or services are imported from other country, then also IGST is to paid. If tax payer pays IGST in Government Account, that is called as ***Input IGST***.

4. Output CGST. CGST collected on intra-state sale (supply) of goods and/or services is referred to as ***Output CGST***.

5. Output SGST. SGST collected on intra-state sale (supply) of goods and/or services is referred to as ***Output SGST***.

6. Output IGST. IGST collected on inter-state sales (supply) of goods and/or services is referred to as ***Output IGST***.

> **Note :** In case of inter-state purchase/sale, only IGST is levied. It is not divided into CGST and SGST like in case of intra-state purchase/sale. For example, if purchases are made from Delhi by a taxpayer in Punjab, it will be subject to IGST only.

ACCOUNTING TREATMENT OF GST

(1) Input GST (GST paid)

Input GST (paid) is to be set-off against output GST (GST collected). However, there are certain cases where GST paid is not allowed to be set-off as per GST Act.

The Accounting treatment of GST paid on purchase shall differ on whether GST paid can be set-off against GST collected or not.

(*a*) In case where GST paid on purchase can be set-off against GST collected. In cases, where GST paid on purchases of goods and/or services *can be set-off* against GST collected on sale of goods and/or services, the GST shall be debited to a separate account head *i.e.,* Input CGST/Input SGST/Input IGST as may be the case. *Till the time, it is set-off against GST collected, it shall be shown as an asset in the books of accounts.*

(*b*) In case where GST paid on purchase of goods and/or services cannot be set-off against GST collected. Where GST paid on purchase *cannot be set-off* against GST collected, it shall be debited to the asset head or expense head on which it has been paid. That implies that the GST paid shall be added to the cost of asset or expense made. For example, Sandeep pays a membership fee of ₹ 15,500 of the club inclusive of ₹ 1000 of CGST and ₹ 1,000 of SGST. GST paid on membership fee of the club is not allowed to be set-off against GST collected. It means that Sandeep should debit Business Promotion Account by ₹ 15,500.

Example of Supply (Purchase) of Goods and/or Services on which GST paid is not allowed to be set-off against GST collected.

(*i*) Membership fees of club, gyms, or any other health services.
(*ii*) Food and beverages bills.
(*iii*) Motor vehicles and conveyances except in certain cases
(*iv*) Free gifts to staff.
(*v*) Travel expenses on personal account.
(*vi*) Goods and services for personal consumption.
(*vii*) Goods and/or services purchased for sale which are exempt from levy of GST.

Any GST paid on items like above shall add to the cost of that asset or expense.

2. Output GST (GST collected)

Whatever GST is collected on sale of goods and/or services shall be set-off against Input GST (GST paid) and then if the balance remains, it is to be paid to government. *Therefore, it is a treated to be a liability and accordingly credited* to output GST as per applicable category, *i.e.,* Output CGST Account, Output SGST Account or Output IGST Account.

Input Tax Credit (ITC)

Throughout the chapter till now, we have been using the term 'setting off against'. GST paid is to be set-off against GST collected. As per GST Act, this means *Input Tax Credit* when you buy a product/service from a dealer you pay GST on purchase and on sales made by you, you collect GST. The Act allows you to adjust taxes paid at the time of purchase with the amount of taxes collected and balance of liability of tax (GST collected minus GST paid) has to paid to the Government. The mechanism is called utilisation of *Input Tax Credit.*

For Example

A businessman dealing in items of stationery made following business transactions.

Purchases			*Sales*		
Item	*Cost (₹)*	*GST Paid (₹)*	*Item*	*Sale (₹)*	*GST Collected*
Pens	1,000	150	Pens	1,500	180
paper	2,000	200	Paper	2,300	230
Staplers	1,500	180	Staplers	2,000	220
Total GST on Input		530	Total GST on Output		630

Tax to be paid by businessman = GST on Input *less* GST on Output = ₹ 630 – ₹ 530 = ₹ 100

Input tax Credit = ₹ 530 = Input GST

In other words, ITC is Input GST (GST paid). Businessman can claim ITC of ₹ 530.

ITC can be claimed in a prescribed order only as per GST Act. The order is presented below :

Input Credit Mechanism Order

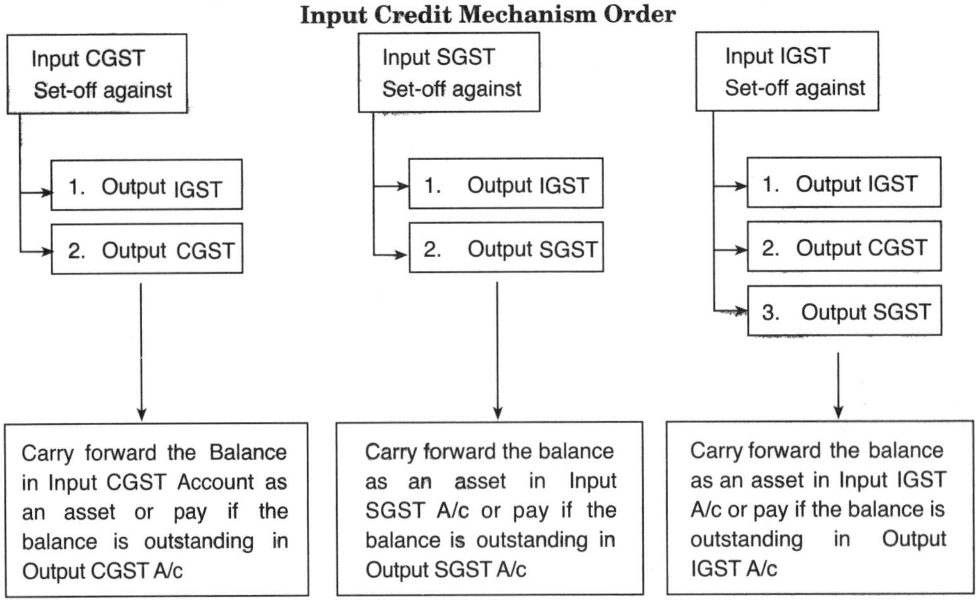

Note : ITC can be claimed only in the order mentioned above and only for business purposes. If they are made for non-business (personal) purpose or for making exempt supplies, ITC cannot be claimed.

Reversal of ITC (Input GST)

ITC may be reversed in the following cases :

(*i*) Non payment of invoices within 180 days
(*ii*) Goods destroyed, lost, stolen or written off.
(*iii*) Goods given as free samples, gifts, charity or used for personal purposes.
(*iv*) Goods and services as may be prescribed.

List of goods and/or services exempt from levy of GST:

(*i*) Supply of services to UNO;
(*ii*) Electricity and water bills;
(*iii*) Payment of salaries and wages;
(*iv*) Supply to Embassies of other countries;
(*v*) Health services given by doctors as consultancy (not medicines);
(*vi*) Educational services; and
(*vii*) Supply of services to the Government.
(*viii*) Royalty of copyright.

Accounting Treatment of GST while passing Journal Entries

Whenever a transaction happens where GST is to be paid or collected, it will have an impact on the Journal Entry also. GST paid shall be debited and GST collected shall be credited. That is, Input GST is debited and Output GST is credited.

Following are the examples of Journal Entries to be passed when GST is paid or collected.

(*i*) Purchase of Goods

Purchases A/c Dr.
Input CGST A/c Dr.
Input SGST A/c Dr.
To Creditor's A/c
(Being Intra-state purchases made)

Note : In case purchases are made inter-state, then instead of CGST and SGST A/c, IGST A/c shall be debited.

(*ii*) Sale of Goods

Debtor's A/c Dr.
To Sales A/c
To Output CGST A/c
To Output SGST A/c
(Being intra-state sales made).

Note : In case of sales are made inter-state, then instead of CGST and SGST A/c, IGST A/c shall be credited.

(*iii*) Purchases Return

Creditor's A/c Dr.
To Purchases Return A/c
To Input CGST A/c
To Input SGST A/c
or (To IGST A/c)
(Being the purchases return)

(*iv*) Sales Return

	Sales Return A/c	Dr.
	Output CGST A/c	Dr.
	Output SGST A/c	Dr.
or	(Output IGST A/c)	Dr.
	To Debtor's A/c	
	(Being the Sales Return)	

(*v*) Purchase of Fixed Asset

	Fixed Asset A/c	Dr.
	Input CGST A/c	Dr.
	Input SGST A/c	Dr.
or	(Input IGST A/c)	Dr.
	To Vendor's A/c	
	(Being Fixed Asset purchased)	

(*vi*) Expenses Made

	Rent A/c	Dr.
	Input CGST A/c	Dr.
	Input SGST A/c	Dr.
	To Cash/Bank A/c	
	(Being Rent and GST paid)	

(*vii*) Journal Entry for free samples distributed, goods stolen, goods destroyed by fire, drawn for personal use by proprietor

	Advertisement A/c	Dr.
	Loss of Goods in Fire A/c	Dr.
	Loss of Goods by Theft A/c	Dr.
	Capital A/c (Goods drawn for personal use)	
	To Purchases A/c	
	To Input CGST A/c	
	To Input SGST A/c	
or	(To Input IGST A/c)	
	(Beings goods distributed as samples, destroyed in fire, by theft and drawings)	

(*viii*) Journal Entry for Setting off Input CGST against Output CGST

Output CGST A/c	Dr.
To Input CGST	
(Being the input GST set-off against Output GST)	

(*ix*) Set-off Entry of Input CGST against Output IGST

Output IGST A/c	Dr.
To Input CGST A/c	
(Being the input CGST set-off against Output IGST	

(*x*) Set-off Entry for Input SGST against Output SGST

Output SGST A/c	Dr.
To Input SGST A/c	
(Being the input SGST set-off against Output SGST)	

(*xi*) Set-off Entry for Input SGST against Output IGST

Output IGST A/c Dr.
To Input SGST A/c
(Being the input SGST set-off against output IGST)

(*xii*) Set-off Entry for Input IGST against Output IGST

Output IGST A/c Dr.
To Input IGST A/c
(Being the input IGST set-off against Output IGST)

(*xiii*) Payment of GST to Government

Input CGST A/c Dr.
Input SGST A/c Dr.
Input IGST A/c Dr.
To bank A/c
(Being the GST payable deposited)

ILLUSTRATION 1. Journalise the following transactions :

(*i*) Bought goods for ₹ 50,000. CGST and SGST paid @ 6% each.
(*ii*) Bought goods from Rajeev for ₹ 30,000 plus CGST and SGST @ 6% each.
(*iii*) Purchased goods from Manoj for ₹ 40,000 plus CGST and SGST @ 6% each and payment made through cheque.
(*iv*) Sold goods to Manish for ₹ 1,50,000, charged CGST @ 6% and SGST @ 6%.
(*v*) Sold goods for ₹ 16,000, charged CGST and SGST @ 6% each.
(*vi*) Sold goods for ₹ 50,000 to Anita, charged IGST @ 12% and payment received through cheque.
(*vii*) Laptop purchased for ₹ 60,000 by Raj & Co. for office use, charged IGST @ 12% and made payment through cheque.
(*viii*) Free samples were given from purchases costing ₹ 5,000 on which CGST and SGST @ 6% each had been paid.
(*ix*) Telephone bill paid ₹ 4,000 plus CGST and SGST @ 6% each.
(*x*) Purchases costing ₹ 10,000 on which CGST and SGST @ 6% was also paid were given as donation in Old Age Home.
(*xi*) Goods costing ₹ 30,000 on which IGST @ 12% had been paid were destroyed by floods. These goods were insured and the Insurance Company admitted the claim for only ₹ 20,000.
(*xii*) An old machinery was sold for ₹ 15,000, received cheque and charged CGST and SGST @ 6% each.

SOLUTION **JOURNAL**

			L.F.	Dr. (₹)	Cr. (₹)
(*i*)	Purchases A/c	Dr.		50,000	
	Input CGST A/c	Dr.		3,000	
	Input SGST A/c	Dr.		3,000	
	To Cash A/c				56,000
	(Being the goods purchased for cash, paid CGST and SGST @ 6% each)				
(*ii*)	Purchases A/c	Dr.		30,000	
	Input CGST A/c	Dr.		1,800	
	Input SGST A/c	Dr.		1,800	
	To Rajeev				33,600
	(Being the goods purchased from Rajeev CGST and SGST payable @ 6% each)				

	Particulars		Dr. (₹)	Cr. (₹)
(*iii*)	Purchases A/c	Dr.	40,000	
	Input CGST A/c	Dr.	2,400	
	Input SGST A/c	Dr.	2,400	
	To Bank A/c			44,800
	(Being the goods purchased from Manoj and payment made through cheque)			
(*iv*)	Manish	Dr.	1,68,000	
	To Sales A/c			1,50,000
	To Output CGST A/c			9,000
	To Output SGST A/c			9,000
	(Being the goods sold to Manish, charged CGST and SGST @ 6% each)			
(*v*)	Cash A/c	Dr.	17,920	
	To Sales A/c			16,000
	To Output CGST A/c			960
	To Output SGST A/c			960
	(Being the goods sold for cash, charged CGST and SGST @ 6% each)			
(*vi*)	Bank A/c	Dr.	56,000	
	To Sales A/c			50,000
	To Output IGST A/c			6,000
	(Being the goods sold to Anita, charged IGST @ 12%)			
(*vii*)	Laptop A/c	Dr.	60,000	
	Input IGST A/c	Dr.	7,200	
	To Bank A/c			67,200
	(Being the Laptop purchased, paid IGST)			
(*viii*)	Advertisement A/c	Dr.	5,600	
	To Purchases A/c			5,000
	To Input CGST A/c			300
	To Input SGST A/c			300
	(Being the goods given as sample, Input CGST and Input SGST debited at the time of purchases is now reversed)			
(*ix*)	Telephone Expenses A/c	Dr.	4,000	
	Input CGST A/c	Dr.	240	
	Input SGST A/c	Dr.	240	
	To Cash/Bank A/c			4,480
	(Being the telephone bill paid along with CGST and SGST)			
(*x*)	Donation/Charity A/c	Dr.	11,200	
	To Purchases A/c			10,000
	To Input CGST A/c			600
	To Input SGST A/c			600
	(Being the goods given as donation, Input CGST and Input SGST debited at the time of purchases reversed)			

(*xi*)	Insurance Co. Dr.		20,000	
	Loss of Stock by Flood A/c Dr.		13,600	
	To Purchases A/c			30,000
	To Input IGST A/c			3,600
	(Being the goods destroyed by flood, Input IGST reversed. Insurance company admitted claim of ₹ 20,000)			
(*xii*)	Bank A/c Dr.		16,800	
	To Machinery A/c			15,000
	To Output CGST A/c			900
	To Output SGST A/c			900
	(Being the old machinery sold for ₹ 15,000 and charged CGST and SGST @ 6% each)			

Accounting Treatment of GST while preparing Ledger Accounts

We have discussed the accounting treatment of GST in journal entries. These journal entries remain the source for preparing ledger accounts. Posting of various GST accounts will create additional ledger accounts of

(*i*) Input CGST
(*ii*) Input SGST
(*iii*) Input IGST
(*iv*) Output CGST
(*v*) Output SGST
(*vi*) Output IGST

ILLUSTRATION 2. (With GST) Journalise the following transactions of Deepak, Delhi for April, 2025, post them in Ledger Accounts and balance them :

2025			₹
April	1	Deepak started business with cash*	3,00,000
April	2	Bought goods for cash	80,000
April	3	Opened Bank Account with cash*	60,000
April	4	Sold goods for cash	70,000
April	7	Bought goods from Agra (UP) on credit	50,000
April	10	Sold goods to Ravi, Delhi on credit	25,000
April	15	Purchased Machinery costing ₹ 20,000 from Sahil & Co. Gurugram (Haryana) and payment is made by cheque	
April	19	Paid to Vikas in cash on account*	30,000
April	21	Received loan from Rajesh and deposited the same into bank*	38,000
April	23	Goods returned to Vikas	5,000
April	26	Withdrew from bank for personal use*	5,000
April	27	Paid to Vikas by cheuqe in full settlement*	19,900
April	29	Received cash from Ravi	10,000
April	30	Purchased stationery for cash	5,000
April	30	Paid wages and salaries*	20,000

CGST and SGST is levied @ 6% each on intra-state transactions and IGST @ 12% on inter-state transactions. GST is not levied on transactions marked (*).

SOLUTION

In the Book of Deepak

JOURNAL

Date	Particulars		L.F.	Dr. (₹)	Cr. (₹)
2025					
April 1	Cash A/c	Dr.		3,00,000	
	To Capital A/c				3,00,000
	(Being the business started with capital of ₹ 3,00,000 brought in cash)				
April 2	Purchases A/c	Dr.		80,000	
	Input CGST A/c	Dr.		4,800	
	Input SGST A/c	Dr.		4,800	
	To Cash A/c				89,600
	(Being the intra-state purchase of goods for cash, paid CGST and SGST @6% each)				
April 3	Bank A/c	Dr.		60,000	
	To Cash A/c				60,000
	(Being the bank account opened by depositing cash into bank)				
April 4	Cash A/c			78,400	
	To Sales A/c				70,000
	To Output CGST A/c				4,200
	To Output SGST A/c				4,200
	(Being the intra-state sale of goods, charged CGST and SGST @6% each)				
April 7	Purchases A/c	Dr.		50,000	
	Input IGST A/c	Dr.		6,000	
	To Vikas				56,000
	(Being the inter-state purchase of goods on credit from Vikas, plus IGST @12%)				
April 10	Ravi	Dr.		28,000	
	To Sales A/c				25,000
	To Output CGST A/c				1,500
	To Output IGST A/c				1,500
	(Being the intra-state sale of goods on credit to Ravi, charged CGST and SGST @6% each)				
April 15	Machinery A/c	Dr.		60,000	
	Input IGST A/c	Dr.		7,200	
	To Bank A/c				67,200
	(Being the machinery purchased, *plus* IGST @12% and payment made by cheque)				
April 19	Vikas	Dr.		30,000	
	To Cash A/c				30,000
	(Being the amount paid to vikas in cash)				

April 21	Bank A/c Dr.		38,000	
	To Rajesh's Loan A/c			38,000
	(Being the loan from Rajesh received and deposited into bank)			
April 23	Vikas Dr.		5,600	
	To Returns Outward A/c			5,000
	To Input IGST A/c			600
	(Being the goods returned to Vikas, Input IGST reversed)			
April 26	Drawings A/c Dr.		5,000	
	To Bank A/c			5,000
	(Being the amount withdrawn from bank for personal use)			
April 27	Vikas Dr.		20,400	
	To Bank A/c			19,900
	To Discount Received A/c			500
	(Being the amount paid to Vikas by cheque and discount received)			
April 29	Cash A/c Dr.		10,000	
	To Ravi			10,000
	(Being the cash received from Rakesh)			
April 30	Stationery A/c Dr.		5000	
	Input CGST A/c Dr.		300	
	Input SGST A/c Dr.		300	
	To Cash A/c			5600
	(Being the stationery purchased for cash, paid CGST and SGST @6% each)			
April 30	Wages and Salaries A/c Dr.		20,000	
	To Cash A/c			20,000
	(Being the wages and salaries paid in cash)			

Ledger

Dr. **CASH ACCOUNT** Cr.

Date	*Particulars*	*J.F.*	₹	*Date*	*Particulars*	*J.F.*	₹
2025				2025			
April 1	To Capital A/c		3,00,000	April 2	By Purchases A/c		89,600
April 4	To Sales A/c		70,000	April 2	By Input CGST A/c		4,800
April 4	To Output CGST A/c		4,200	April 2	By Input SGST A/c		4,800
April 4	To Output SGST A/c		4,200	April 3	By Bank A/c		60,000
April 29	To Ravi		10,000	April 19	By Vikas		30,000
				April 30	By Stationery A/c		5000
				April 30	By Input CGST A/c		300
				April 30	By Input SGST A/c		300
				April 30	By Wages and Salaries A/c		20,000
				April 30	By Balance c/d		1,73,600
			3,88,400				3,88,400
May 1	To Balance b/d		1,73,600				

Dr. **CAPITAL ACCOUNT** Cr.

Date	Particulars	J.F.	₹	Date	Particulars	J.F.	₹
2025				2025			
April 30	To Balance c/d		3,00,000	April 1	By Cash A/c		3,00,000
			3,00,000				3,00,000
				May 1	By Balance b/d		3,00,000

Dr. **PURCHASES ACCOUNT** Cr.

Date	Particulars	J.F.	₹	Date	Particulars	J.F.	₹
2025				2025			
April 2	To Cash A/c		80,000	April 30	By Balance c/d		1,30,000
April 7	To Vikas		50,000				
			1,30,000				1,30,000
May 1	To Balance b/d		1,30,000				

Dr. **BANK ACCOUNT** Cr.

Date	Particulars	J.F.	₹	Date	Particulars	J.F.	₹
2025				2025			
April 3	To Cash A/c		60,000	April 15	By Machinery A/c		60,000
April 21	To Rajesh's Loan A/c		38,000	April 15	By Input IGST A/c		7,200
				April 26	By Drawings A/c		5,000
				April 27	By Vikas		19,900
				April 30	By Balance c/d		5,900
			98,000				98,000
May 1	To Balance b/d		5,900				

Dr. **SALES ACCOUNT** Cr.

Date	Particulars	J.F.	₹	Date	Particulars	J.F.	₹
2025				2025			
April 30	To Balance c/d		95,000	April 4	By Cash A/c		70,000
				April 10	By Ravi		25,000
			95,000				95,000
				May 1	By Balance b/d		95,000

Dr. **VIKAS** Cr.

Date	Particulars	J.F.	₹	Date	Particulars	J.F.	₹
2025				2025			
April 19	To Cash A/c		30,000	April 7	By Purchases A/c		50,000
April 23	To Returns Outward A/c		5,000	April 7	By Input IGST A/c		6,000
April 23	To Input IGST A/c		600				
April 27	To Bank A/c		19,900				
April 27	To Discount Received A/c		500				
			56,000				56,000

Dr. **RAVI** Cr.

Date	Particulars	J.F.	₹	Date	Particulars	J.F.	₹
2025				2025			
April 10	To Sales A/c		25,000	April 29	By Cash A/c		10,000
April 10	To Output CGST A/c		1,500	April 30	By Balance c/d		18,000
April 10	To Output SGST A/c		1,500				
			28,000				28,000
May 1	To Balance b/d		18,000				

Dr. **MACHINERY ACCOUNT** Cr.

Date	Particulars	J.F.	₹	Date	Particulars	J.F.	₹
2025				2025			
April 15	To Bank A/c		60,000	April 30	By Balance c/d		60,000
			60,000				60,000
May 1	To Balance b/d		60,000				

Dr. **RAJESH'S LOAN ACCOUNT** Cr.

Date	Particulars	J.F.	₹	Date	Particulars	J.F.	₹
2025				2025			
April 30	To Balance c/d		38,000	April 21	By Bank A/c		38,000
			38,000				38,000
				May 1	By Balance b/d		38,000

Dr. **RETURNS OUTWARD ACCOUNT** Cr.

Date	Particulars	J.F.	₹	Date	Particulars	J.F.	₹
2025				2025			
April 30	To Balance c/d		5,000	April 23	By Vikas		5,000
			5,000				5,000
				May 1	By Balance b/d		5,000

Dr. **DRAWINGS ACCOUNT** Cr.

Date	Particulars	J.F.	₹	Date	Particulars	J.F.	₹
2025				2025			
April 26	To Bank A/c		5,000	April 30	By Balance c/d		5,000
			5,000				5,000
May 1	To Balance b/d		5,000				

Dr. **STATIONERY ACCOUNT** Cr.

Date	Particulars	J.F.	₹	Date	Particulars	J.F.	₹
2025				2025			
April 30	To Cash A/c		5,000	April 30	By Balance c/d		5,000
			5,000				5,000
May 1	To Balance b/d		5,000				

Dr. **WAGES AND SALARIES ACCOUNT** Cr.

Date	Particulars	J.F.	₹	Date	Particulars	J.F.	₹
2025				2025			
April 30	To Cash A/c		20,000	April 30	By Balance c/d		20,000
			20,000				20,000
May 1	To Balance b/d		20,000				

Dr. **INPUT CGST ACCOUNT** Cr.

Date	Particulars	J.F.	₹	Date	Particulars	J.F.	₹
2025				2025			
April 2	To Cash A/c (Purchases)		4,800	April 30	By Balance c/d		5,100
April 30	To Cash A/c (Stationery)		300				
			5,100				5,100

Dr. **INPUT SGST ACCOUNT** Cr.

Date	Particulars	J.F.	₹	Date	Particulars	J.F.	₹
2025				2025			
April 2	To Cash A/c (Purchases)		4,800	April 30	By Balance c/d		5,100
April 30	To Cash A/c (Stationery)		300				
			5,100				5,100

Dr. **OUTPUT CGST ACCOUNT** Cr.

Date	Particulars	J.F.	₹	Date	Particulars	J.F.	₹
2025				2025			
April 30	To Balance c/d		5,700	April 4	By Cash A/c (Sales)		4,200
				April 10	By Ravi (Sales)		1,500
			5,700				5,700

Dr. **OUTPUT SGST ACCOUNT** Cr.

Date	Particulars	J.F.	₹	Date	Particulars	J.F.	₹
2025				2025			
April 30	To Balance c/d		5,700	April 4	By Cash A/c (Sales)		4,200
				April 10	By Ravi (Sales)		1,500
			5,700				5,700

Dr. **INPUT IGST ACCOUNT** Cr.

Date	Particulars	J.F.	₹	Date	Particulars	J.F.	₹
2025				2025			
April 7	To Vikas (Purchases)		6,000	April 23	By Vikas (Returns Outward)		600
April 15	To Bank A/c (Machinery)		7,200	April 30	By Balance c/d		12,600
			13,200				13,200

Dr. **DISCOUNT RECEIVED ACCOUNT** Cr.

Date	Particulars	J.F.	₹	Date	Particulars	J.F.	₹
2025				2025			
April 30	To Balance c/d		500	April 27	By Vikas		500

ILLUSTRATION 3. (With GST) From the following transactions, pass necessary Journal Entries in the books of Tarun & Co. and post them in Ledger and prepare a Trial Balance :

Date	Particulars	₹
2025		
Jan. 1	Tarun started business with Cash	1,00,000
2	Purchased Goods for ₹ 40,000 *plus* CGST and SGST @ 6% each	
5	Sold goods for ₹ 50,000 *plus* CGST and SGST @ 6% each	
6	Purchased goods from Prateek for ₹ 25,000 *plus* IGST @ 12%	
8	Sold goods to Ravi for ₹ 30,000 *plus* CGST and SGST @ 6% each	
10	Cash paid to Prateek	28,000
14	Cash received from Ravi	33,600
20	Purchased goods for Cash from Prateek for ₹ 20,000 *plus* CGST and SGST @ 6% each	
20	Withdrew cash for personal use	2,000
24	Purchased goods from Deepak for ₹ 22,000 *plus* IGST @ 12%	24,000
28	Cash paid to Deepak, Discount allowed by him	640
31	Paid Salaries	12,000

SOLUTION

In the Books of Tarun & Co.

JOURNAL

Date	Particulars		L.F.	Dr. (₹)	Cr. (₹)
2025					
Jan. 1	Cash A/c	Dr.		1,00,000	
	To Capital A/c				1,00,000
	(Being Cash brought in as capital)				
Jan. 2	Purchases A/c	Dr.		40,000	
	Input CGST A/c	Dr.		2,400	
	Input SGST A/c	Dr.		2,400	
	To Cash				44,800
	(Being purchases made for cash)				
Jan. 5	Cash A/c	Dr.		56,000	
	To Sales A/c				50,000
	To Output CGST A/c				3,000
	To Output SGST a/c				3,000
	(Being goods sold for cash)				

Jan. 6	Purchases A/c Dr.		25,000	
	Input IGST A/c Dr.		3,000	
	To Prateek			28,000
	(Being the purchases made from Sohan) (Outside the state)			
Jan. 8	Ravi A/c Dr.		33,600	
	To Sales A/c			30,000
	To Output CGST A/c			1,800
	To Output SGST A/c			1,800
	(Being the sales made to Ravi)			
Jan. 10	Prateek A/c Dr.		28,000	
	To Cash A/c			28,000
	(Being cash paid to Prateek)			
Jan. 14	Cash A/c Dr.		33,600	
	To Ravi A/c			33,600
	(Being cash received from Ravi)			
Jan. 20	Purchases A/c Dr.		20,000	
	Input CGST a/c Dr.		1,200	
	Input SGST A/c Dr.		1,200	
	To Cash A/c			22,400
	(Being goods purchases made for cash)			
Jan. 20	Drawings A/c Dr.		2,000	
	To Cash A/c			2,000
Jan. 24	Purchases A/c Dr.		22,000	
	Input IGST A/c		2,640	
	To Deepak A/c			24,640
	(Being purchases made from Deepak)			
Jan. 28	Deepak A/c Dr.		24,640	
	To Cash			24,000
	To Discount Received A/c			640
	(Being cash paid to Deepak and he allowed a discount of ₹ 640)			
Jan. 31	Salaries A/c Dr.		12,000	
	To Cash A/c			12,000

Dr. **CASH ACCOUNT** Cr.

Date	*Particulars*	*J.F.*	*₹*	*Date*	*Particulars*	*J.F.*	*₹*
2025				2025			
Jan. 1	To Capital A/c		1,00,000	Jan. 2	By Purchases A/c		40,000
Jan. 5	To Sales A/c		50,000	Jan. 2	By Input CGST A/c		2,400
Jan. 5	To Output CGST		3,000	Jan. 2	By Input SGST A/c		2,400
Jan. 5	To Output SGST		3,000	Jan. 10	By Prateek A/c		28,000
Jan. 14	To Ravi A/c		33,600	Jan. 20	By Purchases A/c		20,000
				Jan. 20	By Input CGST A/c		1,200
				Jan. 20	By Input SGST A/c		1,200

Date	Particulars	J.F.	₹	Date	Particulars	J.F.	₹
				Jan. 20	By Drawings		2,000
				Jan. 28	By Deepak A/c		24,000
				Jan. 31	By Salaries		12,000
				Jan. 31	By Balance c/d		56,400
			1,89,600				1,89,600

Dr. **CAPITAL ACCOUNT** Cr.

Date	Particulars	J.F.	₹	Date	Particulars	J.F.	₹
2025				2025			
Jan. 31	To Balance c/d		1,00,000	Jan. 1	By Cash A/c		1,00,000
				2025			
				Feb. 1	By Balance b/d		1,00,000

Dr. **PURCHASES ACCOUNT** Cr.

Date	Particulars	J.F.	₹	Date	Particulars	J.F.	₹
2025				2025			
Jan. 2	To cash A/c		40,000	Jan. 31	By Balance c/d		1,07,000
Jan. 6	To Prateek A/c		25,000				
Jan. 20	To Cash A/c		20,000				
Jan. 24	To Deepak		22,000				
			1,07,000				1,07,000

Dr. **SALES ACCOUNT** Cr.

Date	Particulars	J.F.	₹	Date	Particulars	J.F.	₹
2025				2025			
Jan. 31	To Balance b/d		80,000	Jan. 5	By Cash		50,000
				Jan. 8	By Ravi		30,000
			80,000				80,000

Dr. **PRATEEK ACCOUNT** Cr.

Date	Particulars	J.F.	₹	Date	Particulars	J.F.	₹
2025				2025			
Jan. 10	To Cash A/c		28,000	Jan. 6	By Purchases A/c		25,000
					By Input IGST A/c		3,000
			28,000				28,000

Dr. **RAVI ACCOUNT** Cr.

Date	Particulars	J.F.	₹	Date	Particulars	J.F.	₹
2025				2025			
Jan. 8	To Sales		30,000	Jan. 14	By Cash A/c		33,600
Jan. 8	To Output CGST A/c		1,800				
Jan. 8	To Output SGST A/c		1,800				
			33,600				33,600

Dr. **DRAWINGS ACCOUNT** Cr.

Date	Particulars	J.F.	₹	Date	Particulars	J.F.	₹
2025				2025			
Jan. 20	To Cash		2,000	Jan. 31	By Balance c/d		2,000
			2,000				2,000

Dr. **DEEPAK ACCOUNT** Cr.

Date	Particulars	J.F.	₹	Date	Particulars	J.F.	₹
2025				2025			
Jan. 28	To Cash A/c		24,000	Jan. 24	By Purchases A/c		22,000
Jan. 28	To Discount Received A/c		640	Jan. 24	By Input IGST A/c		2,640
			24,640				24,640

Dr. **DISCOUNT RECEIVED ACCOUNT** Cr.

Date	Particulars	J.F.	₹	Date	Particulars	J.F.	₹
2025				2025			
Jan. 31	To Balance c/d		640	Jan. 28	By Deepak A/c		640

Dr. **SALARIES ACCOUNT** Cr.

Date	Particulars	J.F.	₹	Date	Particulars	J.F.	₹
2025				2025			
Jan. 31	To Cash A/c		12,000	Jan. 31	By Balance c/d		12,000

Dr. **INPUT CGST ACCOUNT** Cr.

Date	Particulars	J.F.	₹	Date	Particulars	J.F.	₹
2025				2025			
Jan. 2	To Cash A/c (Purchases)		2,400	Jan. 31	By Balance c/d		3,600
Jan. 20	To Cash A/c (Purchases)		1,200				
			3,600				3,600

Dr. **INPUT SGST ACCOUNT** Cr.

Date	Particulars	J.F.	₹	Date	Particulars	J.F.	₹
2025				2025			
Jan. 2	To Cash A/c (Purchases)		2,400	Jan. 31	By Balance c/d		3,600
Jan. 20	To Cash A/c (Purchases)		1,200				
			3,600				3,600

Dr. **INPUT IGST ACCOUNT** Cr.

Date	Particulars	J.F.	₹	Date	Particulars	J.F.	₹
2025				2025			
Jan. 6	To Prateek A/c		3,000	Jan. 31	By Balance c/d		5,640
Jan. 24	To Deepak A/c		2,640				
			5,640				5,640

Dr. **OUTPUT CGST ACCOUNT** Cr.

Date	Particulars	J.F.	₹	Date	Particulars	J.F.	₹
2025				2025			
Jan. 31	To Balance c/d		4,800	Jan. 5	By Cash A/c (Sales)		3,000
				Jan. 8	By Ravi A/c (Sales)		1,800
			4,800				4,800

Dr. **OUTPUT SGST ACCOUNT** Cr.

Date	Particulars	J.F.	₹	Date	Particulars	J.F.	₹
2025				2025			
Jan. 31	To Balance c/d		4,800	Jan. 5	By Cash (Sales)		3,000
				Jan. 8	By Ravi (Sales)		1,800
			4,800				4,800

TRIAL BALANCE OF TARUN & CO.

as on 31st January, 2025

Amount Head	L.F.	Debit (₹)	Credit (₹)
Capital A/c			1,00,000
Cash A/c		56,400	
Purchases A/c		1,07,000	
Sales A/c			80,000
Drawings A/c		2,000	
Discount Received A/c			640
Salaries A/c		12,000	
Input CGST A/c		3,600	
Input SGST A/c		3,600	
Input IGST A/c		5640	
Output CGST A/c			4,800
Output SGST A/c			4,800
Total		1,90,240	1,90,240

Note : Input GST (CGST, SGST and IGST) are set off against output GST (CGST, SGST and IGST) as the case may be. The same has been discussed in Chapter 1 and Chapter 5 : Financial Statements also.

QUESTIONS

SHORT/LONG ANSWER TYPE

1. What is Goods and Service Tax?
2. Is it necessary for all traders to register under the Goods and Services Tax?
3. What are the taxes that got replaced by GST?
4. How would GST be administered in India?
5. What is Central Goods and Services Tax (CGST)?
6. What is State Goods and Services Tax (SGST)?
7. What is Integrated Goods and Services Tax (IGST)?
8. Explain what is Reverse Charge? When is Reverse Charge Applicable?
9. What are the benefits of GST?
10. What are the disadvantages of GST?
11. Who is responsible for maintaining accounts under GST?
12. Which Accounts must be maintained under GST?

PRACTICAL PROBLEMS

1. **(With GST)** Journalise the following transactions in the books of Pradeep, Delhi :
   (*i*) He started business contributing ₹ 10,000 in cash, ₹ 5,00,000 in cheque and a building valued at ₹ 5,00,000.
   (*ii*) Purchased goods from Fair deals, Moradabad for ₹ 2,00,000 out of which cheque was issued for ₹ 60,000.
   (*iii*) Sold goods on credit to Sandeep, Delhi for ₹ 2,60,000.
   (*iv*) Received ₹ 2,86,700 by cheque from Sandeep in full settlement of his account.
   (*v*) Paid ₹ 1,60,000 to Fair deals in full settlement of amount due to them.
   (*vi*) A new machine of ₹ 3,00,000 was purchased from Pristine Tools Ltd., Meerut in exchange of an old machine valued at ₹ 50,000. He gave a cheque of ₹ 1,20,000 from his savings account and balance from firm's account.
   (*vii*) Purchased machinery from Raj Shyama & Co., Delhi for ₹ 1,50,000 on credit.
   (*viii*) Depreciation of ₹ 15,000 was provided on machinery at the end of the year.
   (*ix*) Pradeep issued a cheque for ₹ 80,000 from his savings account in firm's name.
   (*x*) Paid ₹ 8,000 as income tax.
   (*xi*) A cheque amounting to ₹ 50,000 deposited in the bank from his savings account returned dishonoured for insufficient funds.

   CGST and SGST @ 6% each is to be levied on intra-state (within the state purchase and sale) while IGST is to be levied @ 12% on inter-state transactions.
2. **(With GST)** Record the following transactions of Shweta, Kerala in a Three-column Cash Book and balance the book on 31st January, 2025:

Date	Particulars	₹	Date	Particulars	₹
2025			2025		
Jan 1	Cash Balance	21,000	Jan 16	Bought goods, including IGST @ 12%	17,920
Jan 1	Bank Balance	34,500	Jan 19	Paid Rajan by cheque	18,700
Jan 1	Cash received from sale of shares	80,000		Discount received from him	300
Jan 2	Paid into Bank	1,50,000	Jan 20	Drew from Bank	3,000
Jan 3	Purchased goods from M/s. Bansal & Co. ₹ 30,000 plus CGST and SGST @ 6% each and paid by cheque ₹ 33,000 in full settlement		Jan 22	Cash Drawn from bank for personal use	22,000
			Jan 24	Cash Sales, including CGST and SGST @ 6% each	5,600
Jan 4	Paid Wages	12,500	Jan 27	Received from Varun	28,000
Jan 5	Received from Meenu a cheque for ₹ 19,600 against dues of ₹ 20,000 in full settlement of her account			Discount Allowed	500
			Jan 28	Deposited cash into Bank	25,000
Jan 8	Meenu's cheque deposited into Bank		Jan 28	Gave cheque for cash purchases including IGST @ 12%	22,400
Jan 14	Paid for stationery plus CGST and SGST @ 6% each	2,500	Jan 30	Paid rent by cheque plus CGST and SGST @ 6% each	13,440

*GST is not levied on purchases and sale of securities.

Ans. [Cash Balance ₹ 64,380 ; Bank Balance ₹ 1,16,560 ; Discount (Dr.) ₹ 900 ; Discount (Cr.) ₹ 860].

3. M/s Sood has following balances in the GST account as at 31st March, 2025.

Particulars	Dr. (₹)	Particulars	Cr. (₹)
Input IGST	3,80,000	Output IGST	2,40,000
Input CGST	2,50,000	Output CGST	3,60,000
Input SGST	3,70,000	Output SGST	4,30,000

Pass journal entries for setting off input GST against output GST. Also show extract of Balance Sheet showing balances. Show your workings clearly.

Ans. [Balance payable after set off ₹ 30,000 to be shown as liability in Balance Sheet].

CHAPTER 4

Accounting Process : Journal, Ledger, Trial Balance and Subsidiary Books

Accounting Cycle

The accounting cycle is a series of sequential steps that businesses follow to record, process, and summarise their financial transactions over a specific accounting period, typically one year. It is a fundamental process in accounting that ensures accurate and reliable financial information is captured and reported for decision-making purposes. The accounting cycle involves several key steps, each building upon the other, to create a complete set of financial statements. The steps of the accounting cycle can vary slightly depending on the specific accounting framework or software used, but the general process typically includes the following steps:

1. **Analysing Transactions :** The accounting cycle begins with the analysis of business transactions. These transactions include sales, purchases, expenses, investments, loans, and other financial activities. Each transaction must be examined to determine its impact on the financial statements.
2. **Recording Journal Entries :** After analysing transactions, accountants record them in the general journal. Journal entries are recorded in a chronological order, and each entry includes the date, accounts affected, amounts debited, and amounts credited.
3. **Posting to the General Ledger :** In this step, the amounts from the journal entries are transferred to the respective accounts in the general ledger. The general ledger is a collection of all the accounts used by a company, such as cash, accounts receivable, accounts payable, inventory, etc.
4. **Creating an Unadjusted Trial Balance :** Once all the journal entries are posted to the general ledger, an unadjusted trial balance is prepared. The trial balance lists all the accounts and their respective debit and credit balances. It serves as a preliminary check to ensure that debits and credits are equal and the books are in balance.
5. **Adjusting Entries :** Adjusting entries are made to record transactions or events that have occurred during the accounting period but were not yet entered into the accounting records. These entries ensure that revenues and expenses are recognised in the correct period and that the financial statements reflect the accurate financial position of the business.
6. **Creating an Adjusted Trial Balance :** After making the adjusting entries, an adjusted trial balance is prepared. This trial balance reflects all the adjustments made to the accounts and is used to verify that the books are in balance before generating the financial statements.
7. **Generating Financial Statements :** Using the adjusted trial balance, the company prepares the financial statements. The primary financial statements include the income statement (also known

as the profit and loss statement), the balance sheet, and the cash flow statement. These statements provide an overview of the company's financial performance and position during the accounting period.

The accounting cycle is a continuous and repetitive process that businesses follow at the end of each accounting period to maintain accurate financial records. By completing the accounting cycle, companies can produce reliable financial information that assists in making informed decisions, meeting regulatory requirements, and communicating the financial performance of the business to various stakeholders.

Source Documents

In order to record the transactions in the books of account, source documents must be there. These documents provide evidence of business transactions. These documents include cash memo, invoice, receipt, pay in slip, cheque, debit note and credit note, etc. These documents must be preserved till the accounts and tax assessment for the current period are completed. A source document also serves as a legal evidence in case of dispute. Accounts are debited or credited on the basis of these documents. The most common source documents are given as under :

1. Cash Memo. When goods are sold or purchased for cash, the firm receives or gives cash memos which provide details regarding cash transactions. These documents (which result from cash transactions) become the basis for recording these transactions in the books of accounts.

2. Invoice or Bill. This document is prepared when goods are sold or purchased on credit. A sale invoice is prepared to record credit sales. It contains information such as name of the party to whom goods are sold, the description of goods sold and the total amount of sales. The original copy is sent to the buyer and the duplicate copy is kept as evidence of sales for future reference. Purchases, made from various suppliers are supported by credit bills. One makes an invoice but receives a bill. Invoice and bill are interchargeable and mean the same thing.

3. Receipt. When a firm receives cash from customers it issues a receipt which is a proof for receiving cash. It is prepared in duplicate, the original copy is handed over to the party making payment and the duplicate is kept as record for future reference. This document contains the details such as date, amount, name of the party and the nature of payment.

4. Pay in Slip. This form is available from a bank for depositing cash or cheque in a bank account. The counterfoil is returned to the depositer by the cashier after his signatures. Separate slips for depositing cash and cheques are used in some banks. Generally firms get these slips bound in a book so that counterfoil remain in place and are not lost.

5. Cheque. It is document in writing drawn upon a specified banker and payable on demand. The name of the party to whom the payment is to be made is to be written after the words 'pay to'. The date of the cheque, the amount both in figures and words, signature of the drawer must be filled in or done properly. The drawer must fill in the details also on the counterfoil for future record. The counterfoil forms the source document for entries to be made in the account books.

6. Debit and Credit Notes. These notes are prepared when goods are returned to supplier or when an additional amount is recoverable from a customer. For the party from whom the money is recoverable this document becomes debit note and for the party who is to recover the amount the document becomes credit note (usually in red ink). When goods are returned by a customer, a proper credit note should be sent to him.

The decision as to which account is to be debited and which is to be credited is very important in accounting and is generally taken by some responsible person, usually the Chief Accountant. Transactions are recorded in the books of accounts on the basis of vouchers *i.e.* written documents in support of business transactions. Though the transactions can be directly recorded in the Ledger but in small businesses, the transactions are firstly recorded in the journal and then these are posted to the ledger.

JOURNAL

The **Journal** is the **primary book of accounts** where every financial transaction is recorded for the **first time**, in **chronological order**. It forms the basis of the accounting process by ensuring that **each**

transaction's dual aspect (debit and credit) is properly documented, in accordance with the principles of **double-entry bookkeeping**.

The word **'Journal'** is derived from the French word **'Jour'**, meaning **'day'**. Hence, a journal refers to the **daily recording** of business transactions. Each entry made in this book is known as a **Journal Entry**, and the act of recording it is referred to as **Journalising**.

As all transactions are first recorded in the Journal before being posted to the Ledger, it is also called the **Book of Original Entry**.

Ruling of Journal

The specimen ruling of journal is given below :

JOURNAL

Date (1)		*Particulars* (2)	*L.F.* (3)	*Dr. Amount* (4)	*Cr. Amount* (5)
Year		Name of Account to be debited		₹	₹
Month	Date	Name of Account to be credited (Narration or explanation)			

The columns have been numbered only to make these clear to the reader otherwise in practice they are never numbered.

***Column* (1).** The date of transactions is written in the first column after writing the year on the top, the column is subdivided into two sub-columns one for month and the second for date.

***Column* (2).** In this column the account to be debited and credited are written in such a way so that it may start leaving few spaces from the date line and the word Dr. is written against it near the line L.F. In the next line the account to be credited is written preceded by the word 'To' leaving few space from the line of debit entry. Narration or explanation is given in the brackets.

***Column* (3).** It indicates the page number of the ledger where the account is opened and posting from the journal is made.

***Columns* (4 & 5).** In these columns, the amount to be debited and credited is written separately mentioning the nature of currency.

Note: In manual journals, if entries span multiple pages, totals at the end of a page are 'carried forward' to the next. This ensures continuity and accuracy in tallying debit and credit totals. 'C/f' means carried forward, and 'B/f' means brought forward.

Rules of Journalising

Rules of debit and credit have already been discussed in the previous chapter but in order to recaptulate, these are given again :

Based on Accounting Equation

1. Increases in assets are debits, decreases in assets are credits.
2. Increases in liabilities are credits, decreases in liabilities are debits.
3. Increases in capital are credits, decreases in capital are debits.
4. Increases in profits are credits, decreases in profits are debits.
5. Increases in expenses are debits, decreases in expenses are credits.

Based on Traditional Approach

1. Debit the receiver, credit the giver.
2. Debit what comes in, credit what goes out.
3. Debit all expenses and losses, credit all incomes and gains.

Types of Journal Entries

***(i)* Simple Journal Entry:** A **simple journal entry** is one in which **only one account is debited and one account is credited**. This entry follows the basic **double-entry system**—where for every debit, there is an equal and corresponding credit.

EXAMPLE: *Paid rent ₹5,000 in cash.*

Rent A/c	Dr.	₹ 5,000	
To Cash A/c			₹ 5,000

(Being rent paid in cash)

***(ii)* Compound Journal Entry:** A **compound journal entry** is one in which **more than one account is debited or more than one account is credited** in a single entry. It is used to record multiple related transactions occurring at the same time or of the same nature.

EXAMPLE: *Paid ₹5,000 to Mohan, ₹3,000 to Sohan.*

Mohan A/c	Dr.	₹ 5,000	
Sohan A/c	Dr.	₹ 3,000	
To Cash A/c			₹ 8,000

(Being cash paid to Mohan and Sohan)

***(iii)* Opening Entry:** Opening Entry is the **first journal entry** made at the beginning of an accounting year to bring forward the **closing balances** of assets, liabilities, and capital from the **previous year's balance sheet**. It helps in continuing the books of accounts from where they were left off last year. The format of the journal entry is:

[All Asset Accounts] Dr.

To [All Liability Accounts]

To Capital Account

(Being opening balances brought forward)

EXAMPLE: Assets: Cash ₹ 10,000; Furniture ₹ 15,000. Liabilities: Creditors ₹ 5,000.

Cash A/c	Dr.	₹ 10,000	
Furniture A/c	Dr.	₹ 15,000	
To Creditors A/c			₹ 5,000
To Capital A/c			₹ 20,000

(Being balances brought forward)

Treatment of GST in Opening Entry

- GST balances are treated carefully:

  Input GST balances (CGST/SGST/IGST) remaining after set-off against output GST are treated as **debit balances** and shown as **current assets**.

- **Output GST balances (CGST/SGST/IGST)** remaining after adjusting input GST are treated as **credit balances** and shown as **current liabilities**.

This ensures that only the net receivable or payable GST is reflected in the books. Journal Entry is:

Dr. Individual Asset A/cs (incl. Input GST balances, if any)

Cr. Capital A/c, Liabilities A/cs (incl. Output GST balances, if any)

ILLUSTRATION 1. Pass the Opening Entry on 1st April 2025, on the basis of the following information available from the books of Mr. Jitendra.

	₹		₹
Cash in hand	30,000	Plant	1,00,000
Sundry Debtors	50,000	Land & Building	2,50,000
Closing Stock	60,000	Sundry Creditors	2,00,000
Input IGST Account	10,000		
Input CGST A/c	5,000		
Input SGST A/c	5,000		

SOLUTION

In the books of Mr. Jitendera

JOURNAL

Date	Particulars	L.F.	Dr. (₹)	Cr. (₹)
2025				
April 1	Cash A/c Dr.		30,000	
	Sundry Debtors		50,000	
	Opening Stock		60,000	
	Input IGST A/c		10,000	
	Input CGST A/c		5,000	
	Input SGST A/c		5,000	
	Plant		1,00,000	
	Land and Building		2,50,000	
	To Sundry Creditors			2,00,000
	To Capital (Note)			3,10,000
	(Being the last year's balances brought forward)			

Note : The excess of balance of assets over liabilities is capital. Capital has been calculated as balancing figure.

***(iv)* Adjusting Entry:** Made at the end of the accounting year for expenses incurred or incomes earned but not recorded.

EXAMPLE:

Outstanding salary ₹ 3,000.

Salary A/c Dr. ₹ 3,000

To Outstanding Salary A/c ₹ 3,000

(Being salary due but not paid)

***(v)* Closing Entry:**

Closing entries are passed at the **end of the accounting year** to:

1. Transfer **income and gains** to **Profit and Loss Account**
2. Transfer **expenses and losses** to **Profit and Loss Account**
3. Close all **nominal accounts** (*i.e.,* income and expense accounts)

This helps in determining the **net profit or loss** of the year.

Steps for Closing Entries:

1. **Transfer all expenses & losses to Profit & Loss A/c:**

Profit & Loss A/c Dr.
To Expenses A/c
To Losses A/c

2. **Transfer all incomes & gains to Profit & Loss A/c:**
Incomes A/c Dr.
Gains A/c Dr.
To Profit & Loss A/c

3. **Transfer net profit or loss to Capital A/c:**

If **profit**	If **loss**
Profit & Loss A/c Dr. To Capital A/c	Capital A/c Dr. To Profit & Loss A/c

Cash and Trade Discount

Cash Discount - A cash discount is a concession allowed by a seller (creditor) to a buyer (debtor) for prompt or early payment of the dues. It is given as an incentive for timely settlement of accounts, usually within a specified credit period. Unlike trade discount, **cash discount is recorded in the books of accounts** as it affects the actual amount received or paid. Being a **nominal account**, **discount allowed** (by the seller) is treated as an **expense** and debited, whereas **discount received** (by the buyer) is treated as an **income** and credited.

EXAMPLE 1: Cash received from Mahesh ₹ 1,900 and a discount of ₹ 100 was allowed to him.

Journal Entry in the books of the seller:

Cash A/c	Dr.	₹ 1,900	
Discount A/c	Dr.	₹ 100	
To Mahesh's A/c			₹ 2,000

(Being cash received and discount allowed)

EXAMPLE 2: Paid to Suresh ₹ 20,000 less 2% cash discount.

Journal Entry in the books of the buyer:

Suresh's A/c	Dr.	₹ 20,000	
To Cash A/c			₹ 19,600
To Discount A/c			₹ 400

(Being cash paid to Suresh after availing 2% cash discount)

If partial payment is made, cash discount is calculated only on the amount actually paid and not on the total value of the transaction.

Trade Discount: A trade discount is a reduction granted by a manufacturer or wholesaler to retailers or bulk buyers on the catalogue or list price of goods. It is provided to facilitate resale and to allow dealers their margin of profit. It is generally a marketing strategy to encourage bulk purchases or to promote new products.

Key Features:

- It is **not recorded** in the books of accounts.
- It is **deducted directly** on the invoice or bill from the gross amount.
- Journal entries are passed **only for the net amount** payable after deducting the trade discount.

EXAMPLE: Bought goods worth ₹ 6,000 from Ram at 20% trade discount. So, Trade Discount = ₹ 1,200 and Net Amount = ₹ 4,800. **Journal Entry will be**

Purchases A/c	Dr.	₹ 4,800	
To Ram's A/c			₹ 4,800

(For goods purchased from Ram at net price)

Combined Treatment of Trade and Cash Discount

Sometimes, both trade and cash discounts are offered on the same transaction. In such cases:

1. **Trade Discount is calculated first** on the gross value of goods.
2. **Cash Discount is then calculated** on the amount payable after trade discount.

EXAMPLE: Bought goods worth ₹ 6,000 from Ram less 20% trade discount and paid the entire amount in cash availing 2% cash discount. So, Trade Discount = ₹ 1,200 and Net Value = ₹ 4,800 ; Cash Discount = 2% of ₹ 4,800 = ₹ 96 and Amount Paid = ₹ 4,704.

Journal Entry will be —

Purchases A/c Dr. ₹ 4,800

To Cash A/c ₹ 4,704

To Discount A/c ₹ 96

(For goods purchased for cash after both discounts)

GST Treatment in Trade Discount

Under GST provisions, **if trade discount is pre-agreed and reflected on the invoice**, GST is levied **only on the net value of goods** after trade discount. This means:

Gross Sale Price – Trade Discount = Taxable Value for GST

If the discount is not mentioned on the invoice or not in terms of prior agreement, GST is levied on the full value **before trade discount**, which may lead to higher tax liability.

Note: Cash discount has no effect on GST calculation as it is applied after the sale has taken place.

ILLUSTRATION 2. Naresh sells goods to Arun of ₹ 1,20,000 and allows him trade discount of 20% CGST and SGST to be charged @ 6% each. Pass the journal entry in the books of both Naresh and Arun.

SOLUTION

In the books of Naresh, following Journal Entry will be passed :

JOURNAL

Date	Particulars		L.F.	Dr. (₹)	Cr. (₹)
	Arun A/c	Dr.		1,07,520	
	To Sales A/c				96,000
	To Output CGST A/c				5,760
	To Output SGST A/c				5,760
	(Being the goods sold to Arun)				

In the books of Arun, following Journal Entry will be passed.

JOURNAL

Date	Particulars		L.F.	Dr. (₹)	Cr. (₹)
	Purchases A/c	Dr.		96,000	
	Input CGST A/c	Dr.		5,760	
	Input SGST A/c	Dr.		5,760	
	To Naresh A/c				1,07,520
	(Being goods purchased from Naresh)				

GST in Case of Cash Discount. Cash Discount is given by seller to encourage the buyer to make an early payment. Cash discount is given on net price, *i.e.*, the invoice price minus the trade discount. Therefore, when cash discount is allowed or received, no GST is charged. The Journal Entries for cash discount allowed or received remain the same.

***(i)* When Cash Discount is received :**

Creditors' A/c	Dr.
To Cash or Bank A/c	
To Discount Received A/c	

***(ii)* When Cash Discount is allowed :**

Cash or Bank A/c	Dr.
Discount Allowed A/c	Dr.
To Debtors' A/c	

ILLUSTRATION 3. On 5th February, 2025 Vineeta sells goods to Parul for ₹ 1,00,000 plus CGST and SGST @ 6% each. Cash discount to be allowed @ 2% if the payment is made within 10 days. Parul makes the payment by cheque on 10th February, 2025. Journalise these transactions in the books of Vineeta.

SOLUTION

The Journal Entries would be made in the books of Vineeta.

JOURNAL

Date	*Particulars*		*L.F.*	*Dr. (₹)*	*Cr. (₹)*
2025					
Feb. 5	Parul A/c	Dr.		1,12,000	
	To Sales A/c				1,00,000
	To Output CGST A/c				6,000
	To Output SGST A/c				6,000
	(Being goods sold to Parul)				
Feb. 10	Bank A/c	Dr.		1,09,760	
	Discount Allowed	Dr.		2,240	
	To Parul A/c				1,12,000
	(Being payment received from Parul after cash discount of 2% on 1,12,000)				

Difference Between Cash Discount and Trade Discount

Basis of Difference	Cash Discount	Trade Discount
Meaning	A concession allowed to the buyer for making early or prompt payment.	A reduction in the list price of goods to encourage bulk purchase or resale.
Purpose	To encourage timely payment by the debtor.	To promote sales in bulk or to offer profit margin to traders.
Time of Allowance	Allowed **at the time of payment.**	Allowed **at the time of purchase or sale,** before invoicing.
Recording in Books	**Recorded** in the books of accounts (Nominal A/c).	**Not recorded** in the books; it is deducted directly in the invoice.
Impact on Accounts	Affects actual cash received or paid;	Only affects invoice value; purchase/sales recorded at net amount.

Important Considerations Before Journalising—Conceptual Clarifications & Special Cases

	Aspect	Explanation	Accounting Treatment
1	**Capital Account**	When the proprietor introduces cash, goods, or property into the business, it increases the owner's capital. According to the business entity concept, the owner and business are treated as separate entities. Hence, capital introduced is not an income but a liability of the business towards the owner.	**Dr.** Cash/Stock/Asset A/c **Cr.** Capital A/c
2	**Drawings Account**	When the proprietor withdraws cash, goods, or assets from the business for personal use, it is considered drawings. These are not business expenses and are deducted from the proprietor's capital.	**Dr.** Drawings A/c **Cr.** Cash/Stock A/c
3	**Cash/Credit Transactions**	A cash transaction occurs when payment is made immediately. A credit transaction involves deferred payment. If the nature is not specified, assume it is a credit transaction. For example, "Sold goods to X" implies a credit sale unless stated otherwise.	**Dr.** Purchases A/c **Cr.** Supplier's A/c (for credit purchase)
4	**Goods Given as Charity**	If goods from stock are given away as charity, it is treated as a business expense. Purchases A/c is credited to reduce stock, and Charity A/c is debited. If Input GST was earlier claimed on such goods, it must be reversed as no sale occurs.	**Dr.** Charity A/c **Cr.** Purchases A/c **Cr.** Input CGST/SGST/IGST A/c (if applicable)
5	**Purchase of Shares/Securities**	Shares/securities are recorded at actual cost, not at face value. Cost includes market price, and any brokerage paid. For instance, ₹ 50,000 shares bought at 90% = ₹ 45,000 + ₹ 200 brokerage = ₹ 45,200. This ensures true investment value is recorded.	**Dr.** Investment A/c ₹ 45,200 **Cr.** Cash/Bank A/c ₹ 45,200
6	**Sale of Shares/Securities**	Securities sold are recorded at net selling price (sale value less brokerage). If ₹ 50,000 shares sold at 95% with 2% brokerage, effective rate = 93%. Profit/loss is transferred to P&L A/c.	**Dr.** Cash A/c ₹ 46,500 **Cr.** Investment A/c ₹ 46,500
7	**Expenses on Purchase of Fixed Assets**	Any expenditure on purchasing and installing fixed assets (*e.g.*, freight, installation) is capitalised — added to asset cost — rather than treated as revenue expense. This reflects accurate asset valuation in Balance Sheet.	**Dr.** Asset A/c (*e.g.*, Machinery) **Cr.** Cash/Bank A/c
8	**Premium on Proprietor's Life Insurance**	Premium on life policy of the proprietor is a personal expense. Since it doesn't relate to the business operation, it is treated as drawings, not as insurance expense. This maintains accuracy in expense classification.	**Dr.** Drawings A/c **Cr.** Bank/Cash A/c

9	**Carriage Paid on Buyer's Behalf**	If carriage is paid by seller on behalf of buyer (*e.g.,* FOB origin), it is recoverable. Hence, it is added to buyer's account and not treated as seller's expense.	**Dr.** Buyer's A/c **Cr.** Cash/Bank A/c
10	**Goods Distributed as Free Samples**	Giving goods as free samples is a promotional expense. It is not a sale, so Purchases A/c is credited to reduce inventory. Advertisement A/c is debited. If Input GST was claimed earlier, it must be reversed.	**Dr.** Advertisement A/c **Cr.** Purchases A/c **Cr.** Input CGST/SGST/IGST A/c (if ITC reversal required)
11	**Bad Debts**	When a debtor cannot pay due to insolvency or other reasons, it is a loss for the business. The amount is written off by debiting Bad Debts A/c and crediting Debtor's A/c.	**Dr.** Bad Debts A/c **Cr.** Debtor's A/c
12	**Interest Due on Loan**	If interest on a loan becomes due but is not yet paid, it is recorded as an expense and a liability. The interest expense is debited, and the loan account is credited to reflect outstanding interest.	**Dr.** Interest A/c **Cr.** Loan A/c (or Interest Payable A/c)
13	**Loss of Stock by Fire**	Abnormal losses like fire are recorded separately. Purchases A/c is credited to reduce stock. If insured, claim receivable is debited. Unrecoverable loss is debited to P&L or Loss by Fire A/c.	**Dr.** Loss by Fire A/c **Cr.** Purchases A/c **If insured:** **Dr.** Insurance Co. A/c **Cr.** Loss by Fire A/c
14	**Commission (Paid/Received)**	Commission is payment to agents/brokers for services rendered. It is a revenue item — shown in accounts. **Commission paid** is expense; **commission received** is income.	**Dr.** Commission A/c (if paid) **Cr.** Cash/Bank A/c **OR** **Dr.** Cash A/c **Cr.** Commission A/c (if received)

ILLUSTRATION 4. Journalise the following transactions in the books of Ram Naresh.

October 1, 2025.

Assets : Furniture ₹ 5,000 ; Machinery ₹ 10,000 ; Stock ₹ 4,000 ; Cash in hand ₹ 550 ; Cash at bank ₹ 7,450 ; Amount due from Ramesh ₹ 1,000 ; and amount due from Suresh ₹ 2,000.

Liabilities : Amount due to Ram & Co. ₹ 4,500 ; Amount due to Ranjeet & Co. ₹ 2,000 ; and amount due to Shyam Sunder ₹ 1,500.

2025 Oct.		₹	2025 Oct.		₹
1	Purchased goods from Ajay Kumar	4,500	27	Goods worth ₹ 500 were damaged in transit ; a claim was made on the railway authorities for the same	
3	Sold goods for cash	1,500			
5	Paid to Himanshu by cheque	5,500			
10	Deposited in bank	2,800	28	Suresh is declared insolvent and a dividend of 50 paise in the rupee is received from him in full settlement	
13	Sold goods on credit to Mukesh	1,700			
15	Paid for Postage	100			
16	Received cash from Rakesh	2,200			
17	Paid telephone charges	250	28	Bought a horse for ₹ 2,600 and a carriage	
18	Cash Sales	1,500			

20	Purchased government securities	5,000		for ₹ 1,200 for delivering goods to customers.	
22	Purchased goods worth ₹ 16,000, less 20% trade discount and 5% cash discount from Malhotra & Co. for cash and supplied them to Ramesh & Co. at list price less 10% trade discount		30	The horse bought on	
			28	died, and its carcase was sold for ₹ 100	
			31	Allowed interest on capital @ 10% p.a. for one year	
			31	Paid for : Salaries ₹ 1,500, Rent ₹ 600.	
25	Cash purchases	16,500			

SOLUTION

RAM NARESH'S JOURNAL

Date	Particulars		Debit Amount	Credit Amount
2025 Oct.			₹	₹
1	Furniture Account	Dr.	5,000	
	Machinery Account	Dr.	10,000	
	Stock Account	Dr.	4,000	
	Cash Account	Dr.	550	
	Cash at Bank Account	Dr.	7,450	
	Ramesh	Dr.	1,000	
	Suresh	Dr.	2,000	
	To Ram & Co.			4,500
	To Ranjeet & Co.			2,000
	To Shyam Sunder			1,500
	To Capital Account (Balancing figure)			22,000
	(Being balances brought in from previous month)			
1	Purchases Account	Dr.	4,500	
	To Ajay Kumar			4,500
	(Being purchase of goods on credit)			
3	Cash Account	Dr.	1,500	
	To Sales Account			1,500
	(Being goods sold for cash)			
5	Himanshu	Dr.	5,500	
	To Bank Account			5,500
	(Being payment made to Himanshu by cheque)			
10	Bank Account	Dr.	2,800	
	To Cash Account			2,800
	(Being amount deposited in bank)			
13	Mukesh	Dr.	1,700	
	To Sales Account			1,700
	(Being goods sold on credit to Mukesh)			

Date	Particulars		Dr.	Cr.
15	Postage Account	Dr.	100	
	To Cash Account			100
	(Being amount paid for postage)			
16	Cash Account	Dr.	2,200	
	To Rakesh Account			2,200
	(Being receipt of cash from Rakesh)			
17	Telephone Charges Account	Dr.	250	
	To Cash Account			250
	(Being payment of telephone charges)			
18	Cash Account	Dr.	1,500	
	To Sales Account			1,500
	(Being entry for cash sales)			
20	Investment in Government Securities A/c	Dr.	5,000	
	To Cash Account			5,000
	(Being purchase of government securities)			
22	Purchases Account	Dr.	12,800	
	To Cash Account			12,160
	To Discount Account			640
	(Being goods bought for cash and cash discount allowed by the suppliers)			
22	Ramesh & Co.	Dr.	14,400	
	To Sales Account			14,400
	(Being goods having list price of ₹ 16,000 sold to Ramesh & Co. less 10% trade discount. Trade discount is not shown in the books, it is deducted from the sales or purchases as the case may be)			
25	Purchases Account	Dr.	16,500	
	To Cash Account			16,500
	(Being entry for cash purchases)			
27	Railway Claim Account	Dr.	500	
	To Purchases Account			500
	(Being claim sent to railway for goods damaged in transit)			
28	Cash Account	Dr.	1,000	
	Bad Debts Account	Dr.	1,000	
	To Suresh			2,000
	(Being half the dues received from Suresh on his becoming insolvent and balance written off as bad debts)			
28	Livestock Account	Dr.	2,600	
	Carriage Account	Dr.	1,200	
	To Cash Account			3,800
	(Being horse and carriage purchased to effect deliveries to customers)			
30	Cash Account	Dr.	100	
	Profit and Loss Account	Dr.	2,500	
	To Livestock Account			2,600
	(Being horse's carriage sold for cash and balance of cost written off as loss)			

31	Interest Account	Dr.	2,200	
	To Capital Account			2,200
	(Being interest charged on ₹ 22,000 capital @ 10% p.a.)			
31	Salaries Account	Dr.	1,500	
	Rent Account	Dr.	600	
	To Cash Account			2,100
	(Being salaries and rent paid)			
		Grand Total	1,11,950	1,11,950

Note : Rates of GST are not given in the problem, therefore GST has not been taken into consideration.

Advantages of Journal

(*i*) **Chronological Record of Transactions**—The journal maintains a date-wise (chronological) record of all financial transactions, ensuring that no entry is missed and each event is traceable to its exact date.

(*ii*) **Complete and Detailed Entry** —Each journal entry includes both the debit and credit aspects of a transaction, along with a narration. This provides clarity and helps in understanding the nature and purpose of the transaction.

(*iii*) **Minimises the Possibility of Errors**—Since both aspects of a transaction are recorded simultaneously in one place, the chance of recording errors (like omission or misposting) is significantly reduced.

(*iv*) **Reduces Dependence on Memory**—The journal serves as a written record of all transactions, reducing reliance on the memory of the accountant. This is especially useful for complex or infrequent transactions.

(*v*) **Foundation for Ledger Posting** —Journal entries form the basis for posting into the ledger. It ensures systematic and accurate classification of accounts for the preparation of trial balance and final accounts.

(*vi*) **Records Complex and Non-Routine Transactions**—Transactions that cannot be directly recorded in subsidiary books—such as depreciation, bad debts, accruals, adjustments, opening and closing entries—are recorded in the journal, making it essential for complete accounting.

(*vii*) **Evidence for Audit and Legal Purposes**—As the journal is the primary book of original entry, it serves as reliable documentary evidence during audits, inspections, and legal proceedings.

Limitations of Journal

Despite its usefulness, the journal has some inherent limitations:

(*i*) **Cumbersome for Large Volumes of Transactions**—Recording every transaction in a single journal can make the book excessively lengthy and unmanageable, especially in large organisations with high transaction volumes.

(*ii*) **Cannot Track Daily Cash Balance**—The journal does not facilitate daily cash balance tracking. Hence, cash transactions are directly recorded in a separate Cash Book that allows daily monitoring of cash inflows and outflows.

(*iii*) **Limited Scope for Special Transactions**— For recurring and specialised transactions (like bills of exchange, promissory notes, etc.), separate books are often required, limiting the journal's role in such cases.

(*iv*) **Requires Segregation through Subsidiary Books**—To maintain accuracy and speed, businesses need to classify transactions into different subsidiary books like Sales Book, Purchase Book, etc. Relying solely on the journal for all entries is impractical.

LEDGER

In the process of accounting, once transactions are recorded in the **Journal**, they need to be grouped according to the accounts they affect—such as individuals, expenses, incomes, assets, or liabilities. The **Journal**, being a chronological record, does not present a consolidated view of transactions affecting a particular account. To fulfill this purpose, all journal entries are subsequently transferred to the **Ledger**, which is the **second step in the accounting cycle**.

The **Ledger** serves as the **principal book of accounts** and is essential for preparing financial statements. It accumulates information account-wise, providing clarity on the impact of each transaction on a particular account over a specific period.

Definition of Ledger

A **Ledger** is a book or digital record containing individual accounts derived from journal entries. Each account presents a summary of all the transactions affecting that account.

"A Ledger Account is a summary statement of all transactions relating to a particular person, asset, liability, income, or expense, which have occurred during a particular period and shows the net effect thereof."

According to **Encyclopedia Britannica:** *"A group of accounts is known as a Ledger. The general ledger is the main book of accounts: it contains an account for each asset, liability, proprietorship, revenue, and expense account. The ledger includes all the basic accounts needed for the preparation of the financial statements."*

Purpose of Ledger

The **main purpose** of maintaining a ledger is to classify and group similar transactions under appropriate heads. It provides a **consolidated view** of each account, which is essential for:

- Determining account balances.
- Preparing the **Trial Balance**.
- Finalising accounts like **Trading Account**, **Profit & Loss Account**, and **Balance Sheet**.

Features of Ledger

The Ledger plays a pivotal role in the accounting process. Below are its key features that highlight its importance:

(*i*) **Principal Book of Accounts:** The ledger is often referred to as the principal or final book of entry, as all transactions recorded initially in the journal are ultimately transferred here. It serves as the central repository for all financial data. It offers answers to key accounting questions such as: How much is owed by or to a specific party? What is the total income or expenditure under a head? What is the closing balance of each asset or liability? What is the profit or loss of the business? What is the financial position on a particular date? Due to this summarising and organising role, the **Ledger** is rightly called the **Principal Book of Accounts**.

(*ii*) **Account-wise Classification:** Transactions are sorted and grouped under specific heads such as cash, capital, rent, sales, creditors, etc. This classification helps in viewing the entire history and impact of transactions related to one particular account in one place.

(*iii*) **Helps in Summarisation:** Each ledger account summarises the effects of all debit and credit entries, thus showing the net balance. This summarisation assists in understanding whether an account has a debit or credit surplus at any given time.

(*iv*) **Basis for Preparation of Financial Statements:** The balances derived from various ledger accounts are used to prepare key accounting statements like the Trial Balance, Trading Account, Profit and Loss Account, and Balance Sheet. Thus, it is the foundation for financial reporting.

(*v*) **Permanent and Systematic Record:** The ledger maintains a chronological and permanent record of all financial transactions, systematically categorised by accounts. This makes it easier to refer for future analysis, audits, or legal scrutiny.

Structure of Ledger Account: Ledger accounts are usually prepared in a **T-shape format:**

Name of Account

Debit Side (Dr.)				Credit Side (Cr.)			
Date	Particulars	J.F	Amount (₹)	Date	Particulars	J.F	Amount (₹)

The **left-hand side** records all **debit entries**. The **right-hand side** records all **credit entries**. Each account starts with the title of the account, and transactions are recorded as per the date and nature of the entry. The **balance** is computed periodically—either daily, weekly, or monthly.

Types of Ledgers

There are primarily **three types of ledgers** in business:

1. **General Ledger:** Contains all the accounts—assets, liabilities, income, expenses, and equity.
2. **Debtors Ledger (Sales Ledger):** Contains accounts of all credit customers.
3. **Creditors Ledger (Purchase Ledger):** Contains accounts of all credit suppliers.

Posting in Ledger

The process of transferring the debit and credit items from the journal to their respective accounts in the ledger is called **Posting**. Every debit in the journal is posted to the **debit side** of the respective ledger account. Every credit is posted to the **credit side** of the respective account.

Following example will make clear the process of posting:

2025, April 1. Goods sold for cash ₹ 2,500.

JOURNAL ENTRY

2025			*Dr.* ₹	*Cr.* ₹
April 1	Cash Account Dr. To Sales Account (Being goods sold for cash)		2,500	2,500

Posting is as follows :

Ledger

CASH ACCOUNT

Date	*Particulars*	*F.*	*Amount*	*Date*	*Particulars*	*F.*	*Amount*
2025			₹				₹
Apr. 1	To Sales Account		2,500				

SALES ACCOUNT

Date	*Particulars*	*F.*	*Amount*	*Date*	*Particulars*	*F.*	*Amount*
			₹	2025			₹
				Apr. 1	By Cash Account		2,500

From the above we see that while posting from the journal, the Dr. Account is debited and Cr. Account is credited and the entry in each account indicates the account in which the corresponding entry appears.

Ledger **posting of compound journal entry** is as follows :

2025, April 30 Paid for : Charity ₹ 101 ; Salaries ₹ 2,000 ; Stationery ₹ 199.

JOURNAL ENTRY

				Dr. ₹	Cr. ₹
2025 Apr. 30	Charity Account	Dr.		101	
	Salaries Account	Dr.		2,000	
	Stationery Account	Dr.		199	
	To Cash Account				2,300
	(Being amount paid for charity, salaries and stationery)				

Posting is as follows :

Ledger

CHARITY ACCOUNT

			₹				₹
2025 Apr. 30	To Cash Account		101				

SALARIES ACCOUNT

			₹				₹
2025 Apr. 30	To Cash Account		2,000				

STATIONERY ACCOUNT

			₹				₹
2025 Apr. 30	To Cash Account		199				

CASH ACCOUNT

			₹				₹
				2025 Apr. 30	By Charity A/c		101
				" 30	By Salaries A/c		2,000
				" 30	By Stationery A/c		199

Balancing of Accounts

Various accounts in the ledger are balanced with a view to preparing the final accounts. The procedure of balancing accounts is as follows :

1. Take the total of the two sides of the account concerned.
2. Ascertain the difference between the totals of two sides.
3. Enter the difference in the amount column of the side showing less total; writing against the difference in the particulars column "To Balance c/d" (c/d means carried down) on the debit side of the account and "By Balance c/d" on the credit side of the account. In this way, the totals of two sides will agree.
4. The balance is brought forward at the beginning of the next period. If "To Balance c/d" is written on the debit side before balancing, it is brought forward on the credit side and "By Balance b/d" (b/d means brought down) is written against the balance in the particulars column and vice versa.

An account is said to have a debit balance if the total of its debit side is more than the total of its credit side. On the other hand, an account is considered to have credit balance if the total of its credit side is more than the total of its debit side.

Difference Between Journal and Ledger

Basis of Difference	Journal	Ledger
Meaning	Journal is the book of original entry where all transactions are recorded first.	Ledger is the book of final entry where transactions are classified account-wise.
Purpose	To record all business transactions in a chronological order.	To group and summarise all transactions under respective accounts.
Nature of Record	Provides a complete record of each transaction in one place.	Shows the cumulative effect of all transactions related to a specific account.
Format Used	Uses a narrative format with date, particulars, ledger folio, debit, and credit.	Uses a T-account format with debit and credit sides.
Posting	Transactions recorded here are posted to ledger accounts.	Ledger receives entries from the journal and does not require reposting.
Balancing	Entries are not balanced in the journal.	Ledger accounts are balanced periodically to determine closing balances.
Financial Statements	Cannot be directly used to prepare financial statements.	Forms the basis for preparing the trial balance and final accounts.
Classification	Does not classify transactions by account.	Transactions are classified account-wise for clarity.
Duplication Check	Helps in identifying errors in recording transactions.	Helps in identifying errors in classification or balancing.
Frequency of Use	Used daily for recording transactions.	Used periodically to update and monitor account balances.

ILLUSTRATION 5. Prepare Ledger Accounts from the following transactions in the books of Imran dealing in essential items where GST is not charged :

2025 June		₹	2025 June		₹
1	Started business with cash	45,000	18	Cash received from Arvind Walia ₹ 3,760 and discount allowed to him	40
1	Paid into bank	25,000	21	Withdrew from bank for private use	1,000
2	Goods purchased for cash	15,000		Withdrew from bank for use in the business	5,000
3	Purchase of furniture and payment by cheque	5,000	25	Paid Wages	400
5	Sold goods for cash	8,500	28	Cash paid to Amrit Lal in full settlement of his account	5,940
8	Sold goods to Arvind Walia	4,000	30	Paid for Salaries	3,700
10	Goods purchased from Amrit Lal	7,000			
12	Goods returned to Amrit Lal	1,000			
15	Goods returned by Arvind Walia	200			

SOLUTION

JOURNAL OF IMRAN

Date	Particulars		L.F.	Dr. Amount	Cr. Amount
2025				₹	₹
June 1	Cash Account	Dr.		45,000	
	To Capital Account				45,000
	(Being cash brought in to start business)				
June 1	Bank Account	Dr.		25,000	
	To Cash Account				25,000
	(Being cash paid into bank)				
" 2	Purchases Account	Dr.		15,000	
	To Cash Account				15,000
	(Being goods purchased for cash)				
" 3	Furniture Account	Dr.		5,000	
	To Bank Account				5,000
	(Being purchase of furniture and payment made by cheque)				
June 5	Cash Account	Dr.		8,500	
	To Sales Account				8,500
	(Being goods sold for cash)				
" 8	Arvind Walia	Dr.		4,000	
	To Sales Account				4,000
	(Being goods sold to Arvind Walia on credit)				
" 10	Purchases Account	Dr.		7,000	
	To Amrit Lal				7,000
	(Being credit purchases from Amrit Lal)				
" 12	Amrit Lal	Dr.		1,000	
	To Returns Outwards Account				1,000
	(Being goods returned to Amrit Lal)				
" 15	Returns Inwards Account	Dr.		200	
	To Arvind Walia				200
	(Being goods returned by Arvind Walia)				
" 18	Cash Account	Dr.		3,760	
	Discount Account			40	
	To Arvind Walia				3,800
	(Being ₹ 3,760 received from Arvind Walia and ₹ 40 discount allowed to him)				
June 21	Drawings Account	Dr.		1,000	
	Cash Account	Dr.		5,000	
	To Bank Account				6,000
	(Being cash withdrawn from bank for personal use and for use in the business)				
" 25	Wages Account	Dr.		400	
	To Cash Account				400
	(Being payment of wages)				

June 28	Amrit Lal	Dr.	6,000	
	To Cash Account			5,940
	To Discount Account			60
	(Being cash paid to Amrit Lal and discount allowed by him)			
" 30	Salarties Account	Dr.	3,700	
	To Cash Account			3,700
	(Being salary paid)			
	Total		1,30,600	1,30,600

CASH ACCOUNT

2025			₹	2025			₹
June 1	To Capital A/c		45,000	June 1	By Bank A/c		25,000
" 5	To Sales A/c		8,500	" 2	By Purchases A/c		15,000
" 18	To Arvind Walia		3,760	" 25	By Wages A/c		400
" 21	To Bank A/c		5,000	" 28	By Amrit Lal		5,940
				" 30	By Salaries A/c		3,700
				" 30	By Balance c/d		12,220
			62,260				62,260
July 1	To Balance b/d		12,220				

CAPITAL ACCOUNT

2025			₹	2025			₹
June 30	To Balance c/d		45,000	June 1	By Cash A/c		45,000
				July 1	By Balance b/d		45,000

BANK ACCOUNT

2025			₹	2025			₹
June 1	To Cash A/c		25,000	June 3	By Furniture A/c		5,000
				June 21	By Drawings A/c		1,000
				June 21	By Cash A/c		5,000
				June 30	By Balance c/d		14,000
			25,000				25,000
July 1	To Balance b/d		14,000				

PURCHASES ACCOUNT

2025			₹	2025			₹
June 2	To Cash A/c		15,000	June 30	By Balance c/d		22,000
June 10	To Amrit Lal		7,000				
			22,000				22,000
July 1	To Balance b/d		22,000				

FURNITURE ACCOUNT

Date	Particulars	J.F.	₹	Date	Particulars	J.F.	₹
2025				2025			
June 3	To Bank A/c		5,000	June 30	By Balance c/d		5,000
July 1	To Balance b/d		5,000				

SALES ACCOUNT

Date	Particulars	J.F.	₹	Date	Particulars	J.F.	₹
2025				2025			
June 30	To Balance c/d		12,500	June 5	By Cash A/c		8,500
				June 8	By Arvind Walia		4,000
			12,500				12,500
				July 1	By Balance b/d		12,500

ARVIND WALIA

Date	Particulars	J.F.	₹	Date	Particulars	J.F.	₹
2025				2025			
June 8	To Sales A/c		4,000	June 15	By Returns InwardsA/c		200
				June 18	By Cash A/c		3,760
				June 18	By Discount A/c		40
			4,000				4,000

AMRIT LAL

Date	Particulars	J.F.	₹	Date	Particulars	J.F.	₹
2025				2025			
June 12	To Returns Outwards A/c		1,000	June 10	By Purchases A/c		7,000
June 28	To Cash A/c		5,940				
June 28	To Discount A/c		60				
			7,000				7,000

RETURNS INWARDS ACCOUNT

Date	Particulars	J.F.	₹	Date	Particulars	J.F.	₹
2025				2025			
June 15	To Arvind Walia		200	June 30	By Balance c/d		200
July 1	To Balance b/d		200				

RETURNS OUTWARDS ACCOUNT

Date	Particulars	J.F.	₹	Date	Particulars	J.F.	₹
2025				2025			
June 30	To Balance c/d		1,000	June 12	By Amrit Lal		1,000
				July 1	By Balance b/d		1,000

DISCOUNT ACCOUNT

Date	Particulars	J.F.	₹	Date	Particulars	J.F.	₹
2025				2025			
June 18	To Arvind Walia		40	June 28	By Amrit Lal		60
June 30	To Balance c/d		20				
			60				60
				July 1	By Balance b/d		20

DRAWINGS ACCOUNT

			₹				₹
2025				2025			
June 21	To Bank A/c		1,000	June 30	By Balance c/d		1,000
July 1	To Balance b/d		1,000				

WAGES ACCOUNT

			₹				₹
2025				2025			
June 25	To Cash A/c		400	June 30	By Balance c/d		400
July 1	To Balance b/d		400				

SALARIES ACCOUNT

			₹				₹
2025				2025			
June 30	To Cash A/c		3,700	June 30	By Balance c/d		3,700
July 1	To Balance b/d		3,700				

TRIAL BALANCE

In accounting, the Trial Balance is an essential step in the accounting process. It is prepared to verify the arithmetical accuracy of the ledger accounts and to serve as a foundation for the preparation of final accounts. The basic principle of the Double Entry System states that for every debit, there must be a corresponding credit of an equal amount. Consequently, at any point in time, the total of all debit balances must be equal to the total of all credit balances in the ledger if the records are mathematically accurate.

To confirm this, a statement is prepared by extracting the balances of all ledger accounts, known as the Trial Balance. It is a summary statement listing the debit and credit balances of all accounts to ensure that the books are in balance.

Definition: A Trial Balance is a statement of debit and credit totals or balances extracted from the various accounts in the ledger, prepared with a view to test the arithmetical accuracy of the books of accounts.

If the totals of the Trial Balance **agree**, it suggests that:

- Both aspects of each transaction have been recorded, and
- The accounts are free from **arithmetical errors**.

However, if the totals do not agree, it indicates that some errors exist which must be located and rectified before preparing the final accounts. Thus, the Trial Balance serves as a connecting link between the ledger accounts and the final accounts of a business.

Objectives of Preparing a Trial Balance

The key objectives of a Trial Balance are:

(*i*) **Summarisation of Account Balances:** To have the balances of all ledger accounts at one place to avoid scanning the entire ledger.

(*ii*) **Verification of Double Entry:** Its agreement assures that each transaction has been recorded in both debit and credit aspects, ensuring accuracy in double entry.

(*iii*) **Arithmetic Accuracy:** It helps to confirm the arithmetical accuracy of the accounting records.

(*iv*) **Preparation of Final Accounts:** It serves as a base document for preparing the Trading Account, Profit and Loss Account, and Balance Sheet.

Limitations of Trial Balance

Despite its usefulness, the Trial Balance has certain limitations:

(i) **Limited to Double Entry System:** It can only be prepared if the Double Entry System is followed. This system is costly and may not be feasible for small businesses.

(ii) **Not a Conclusive Proof of Accuracy:** Even if a trial balance agrees, certain types of errors (like omission, compensating errors, or errors of principle) are not disclosed.

(iii) **Dependent on Accuracy of Posting:** If any account is incorrectly balanced or omitted, the Trial Balance will not reflect the true position, and the final accounts may be misleading.

(iv) **Cannot Detect Fraud:** It cannot detect intentional frauds where equal debit and credit entries are made with wrong accounts.

Preparation of Trial Balance

There are **two primary methods** used to prepare a Trial Balance:

1. Total Method: In this method, the **total debits and credits** of each ledger account are shown in two separate columns. It is **less commonly used** in practice.

2. Balance Method (*Most Common*): Here, only the **net balance** (*i.e.,* the difference between total debits and credits of each account) is shown. If the **debit side exceeds** the credit, the **net balance** is shown on the **debit side** of the Trial Balance and vice versa. This method is preferred as it facilitates the preparation of **final accounts**.

The standard format of a Trial Balance is given below:

TRIAL BALANCE OF.................

as on ....

Serial No.	*Name of the Account*	*Dr. Balance (or Total)* ₹	*Cr. Balance (or Total)* ₹

Of the two methods of preparation, the second is usually used in practice because it facilitates the preparation of the final accounts.

ILLUSTRATION 6. From the following information, draw up a Trial balance in the books of Shri M as on 31st March, 2025 :

Particulars	*Amount (₹)*	*Particulars*	*Amount (₹)*
Capital	1,40,000	Purchases	36,000
Discount Allowed	1,200	Carriage Inward	8,700
Carriage Outwards	2,300	Sales	60,000
Return Inward	300	Return Outwards	700
Rent and Taxes	1,200	Plant and Machinery	80,700
Stock on 1st April 2024	15,500	Sundry Debtors	20,200
Sundry Creditors	12,000	Investments	3,600
Commission Received	1,800	Cash in Hand	100
Cash at Bank	10,100	Motor Cycle	34,600
Stock on 31st March, 2025	20,500		

(CA Foundation, Dec., 2021 Modified)

SOLUTION

TRIAL BALANCE OF SHRI M

as on 31st March, 2025

Particulars	Dr. Amount (₹)	Cr. Amount (₹)
Capital		1,40,000
Purchases	36,000	
Discount Allowed	1,200	
Carriage Inward	8,700	
Carriage Outwards	2,300	
Sales		60,000
Return Inward	300	
Return Outwards		700
Rent and Taxes	1,200	
Plant and Machinery	80,700	
Stock on 1st April, 2024	15,500	
Sundry Debtors	20,200	
Sundry Creditors		12,000
Investments	3,600	
Commission Received		1,800
Cash in Hand	100	
Cash at Bank	10,100	
Motor Cycle	34,600	
	2,14,500	2,14,500

Note: Stock as on 31st March, 2025 will not appear in trial balance.

ILLUSTRATION 7. Following Trial Balance has been prepared wrongly. You are asked to prepare the Trial Balance correctly.

Name of Account	*Debit Balance*	*Credit Balance*
	₹	₹
Cash in hand		2,000
Purchases Returns	4,000	
Wages	8,000	
Establishment Expenses	12,000	
Sales Returns		8,000
Capital	22,000	
Carriage Outward		2,000
Discount Received	1,200	
Commission Earned	800	
Machinery		20,000
Stock		10,000
Debtors	8,000	
Creditors		12,000
Sales		44,000
Purchases	28,000	
Bank Overdraft	8,000	

Input IGST A/c	6,000	
Manufacturing Expenses		10,000
Loan from Ashok	14,000	
Carriage Inward	1,000	
Interest on Investments		1,000
Output IGST A/c		4,000
	1,13,000	1,13,000

SOLUTION

CORRECT TRIAL BALANCE

as at.............

Name of Account	*Debit Balance*	*Credit Balance*
	₹	₹
Cash in hand	2,000	
Purchases Returns		4,000
Wages	8,000	
Establishment Expenses	12,000	
Sales Returns	8,000	
Capital		22,000
Carriage Outward	2,000	
Discount Received		1,200
Commission Earned		800
Machinery	20,000	
Stock	10,000	
Debtors	8,000	
Creditors		12,000
Sales		44,000
Purchases	28,000	
Bank Overdraft		10,000
Manufacturing Expenses	8,000	
Input IGST	6,000	
Loan from Ashok		14,000
Carriage Inward	1,000	
Interest on Investments		1,000
Output IGST		4,000
	1,13,000	1,13,000

Errors and Their Types

In accounting, maintaining accuracy in recording and summarising transactions is crucial. However, errors may still occur due to various reasons such as negligence, oversight, or misunderstanding. Some errors are easily detected when the Trial Balance does not tally, while others may go unnoticed even though the Trial Balance agrees. Therefore, it's important to understand the different types of errors and their implications.

The Trial Balance is a statement that checks the arithmetical accuracy of ledger accounts by ensuring that total debits equal total credits. However, even if the Trial Balance agrees, it does not guarantee the absence of errors. Many types of accounting mistakes remain undetected because they do not disturb the equality of debits and credits.

Classification of Errors

Accounting errors can be broadly classified into four categories:

1. Errors of Commission
2. Errors of Omission
3. Errors of Principle
4. Compensating Errors

Let us understand each of these in detail.

1. Errors of Commission

These errors are clerical mistakes made while recording, posting, or balancing entries in the books. They result from an act of commission by the person responsible for maintaining the books of account. Common examples include:

- *Wrong transfer to Trial Balance*: Transferring incorrect balances or omitting a ledger balance while preparing the Trial Balance.
- *Balancing mistake:* Errors in totaling the debit or credit side of an account.
- *Transposition of figures*: Writing ₹ 115 instead of ₹ 151, leading to a difference of ₹ 36.
- *Posting to the wrong side*: Crediting instead of debiting an account. A ₹ 500 error posted to the wrong side will result in a ₹ 1,000 discrepancy.
- *Errors in subsidiary book totals*: An incorrect total in the Purchases Book affects the Purchases Account, impacting the Trial Balance.

Note: These errors generally affect the Trial Balance, as they disturb the equality of debits and credits.

2. Errors of Omission

These errors occur due to negligence or oversight, not due to a lack of accounting knowledge. A transaction is either not recorded at all or partially recorded. There are two types of omission errors:

(*a*) **Complete Omission:** The transaction is entirely omitted from the books. Both debit and credit aspects are missing, so the Trial Balance remains unaffected. ***Example***: Failing to record a credit sale of ₹ 2,000 in the Sales Book.

(*b*) **Partial Omission:** The transaction is recorded in the original book but not posted to the ledger. This creates an imbalance in the Trial Balance. **Example:** Recording cash received in the Cash Book but omitting to post the corresponding amount in the debtor's ledger account.

3. Errors of Principle

These errors result from violating accounting principles, especially those related to classification of capital and revenue expenditure or income. The amount is entered on the correct side but in the wrong type of account, so the Trial Balance still agrees. **Example:** ₹ 6,550 spent on building extension is wrongly debited to Repairs Account instead of Building Account.

Note: These errors do not affect the Trial Balance, as the debit-credit rule is followed, but classification is incorrect. As a result, can misrepresent financial statements.

4. Compensating Errors

Compensating errors are those errors which occur in such a way that the effect of one error is offset or nullified by another error, resulting in no difference in the Trial Balance totals. These errors may occur independently and accidentally, but their combined impact cancels each other out, making them difficult to detect. **Example**: A debit posting of ₹ 500 is understated in the Wages Account (posted as ₹ 300 instead of

₹ 800). A credit posting of ₹ 500 is also understated in the Sales Account (posted as ₹ 2,500 instead of ₹ 3,000).

Note: These errors are not revealed by the Trial Balance, as they neutralise each other's effect.

ILLUSTRATION 8. A book-keeper, taking out a trial balance as on 30th June, 2025, found that it did not agree. He proceeded to check the entries and discovered the following errors:

1. A credit sale of ₹ 1,000 to Ajay had been correctly entered in the Sales Book but Ajay's Account had been debited with ₹ 100 only.
2. The total of the Bills Payable Book, ₹ 5,000 had been posted to the credit of Bills Receivable Account.
3. ₹ 2,500 paid to Ram had been wrongly posted to Shyam.
4. ₹ 100 owing by a customer had been omitted from the list of sundry debtors.
5. The discount column of the Cash Book representing discount allowed to customers has been over-added by ₹ 10.
6. Goods worth ₹ 100 taken by the proprietor omitted to be recorded in the books.
7. Depreciation on furniture, ₹ 100, had not been posted to Depreciation Account.
8. The total of Sales Book had been added ₹ 1,000 short.

Which of the above errors caused the totals of the Trial Balance to disagree and by how much did the totals differ ?

SOLUTION

The effect of the above noted errors on the Trial Balance will be as follows :

1. Ajay's Account has been given less debit for ₹ 900, so the debit side of the Trial Balance would be short by ₹ 900.
2. This error will not affect the agreement of the Trial Balance because the posting of the Bills Payable Book has been made to the correct side but in the wrong account. The credit given to Bills Receivable Account instead of Bills Payable Account does not affect the agreement of the Trial Balance.
3. This error will not affect the agreement of the Trial Balance because the amount paid has been posted to the right side though to a wrong account.
4. Sundry debtors have been shown in the Trial Balance with a less amount of ₹ 100, so debit side of the Trial Balance is short by ₹ 100.
5. Discount Account has been given an excess debit of ₹ 10 so debit side of the Trial Balance exceeds by ₹ 10.
6. This error will have no effect on the agreement of the Trial Balance because the dual aspect of the entry has been omitted, *i.e.,* neither of the two accounts involved in this transaction has been given debit or credit.
7. Depreciation on furniture has not been debited to Depreciation Account, so debit side of the Trial Balance will be ₹ 100 too short.
8. Sales Account has been given less credit for ₹ 1,000, so credit side of the Trial Balance would be short by ₹ 1,000.

The combined effect of all the errors is that the credit side of the Trial Balance would exceed the debit side by ₹ 90.

Location of Errors

When a Trial Balance does not agree, it indicates that there may be one or more errors in the books of account. The disagreement is a sign that the equality of total debits and total credits has not been maintained. However, it does not necessarily mean that all errors will be disclosed through the Trial Balance. The following systematic steps may be followed to locate the errors that result in such disagreement:

(*i*) **Recheck the Totals of the Trial Balance:** The first step is to verify the totals of the debit and credit columns of the Trial Balance. An error in totaling or omission of a balance may cause the disagreement. Ensure that all balances from the ledger have been correctly included.

(*ii*) **Divide the Difference by Two:** If the Trial Balance difference is divisible by two, examine whether a balance of that amount appears in the Trial Balance. It may be possible that such an amount has been recorded on the wrong side (*i.e.,* a debit balance shown as credit or vice versa), which would cause a difference double the amount of the error. ***Example:*** If an account with a debit balance of ₹ 750 is mistakenly recorded on the credit side, the Trial Balance will show a difference of ₹ 1,500.

(*iii*) **Divide the Difference by Nine:** If the difference is divisible by nine, the error may be due to **transposition** or **transplacement** of figures. **Transposition** occurs when digits within a number are reversed, such as writing ₹ 57 as ₹ 75, or ₹ 197 as ₹ 791. **Transplacement** involves shifting the digits to an incorrect place value, such as recording ₹ 5,694 as ₹ 569.40 or ₹ 56.94. If the difference is divisible by 9, the search for error may be narrowed to such figure-based mistakes.

(*iv*) **Verify Inclusion of All Ledger Balances:** Ensure that all balances, including cash, bank, and adjustment accounts, have been included in the Trial Balance. Omission of any account balance can result in a mismatch between the two sides.

(*v*) **Check Opening Balances:** Examine whether all opening balances from the previous accounting period have been correctly brought forward in the current year's books. Errors in transferring opening balances can impact the accuracy of the Trial Balance.

(*vi*) **Compare with Previous Year's Trial Balance:** If the error remains undetected and the difference is significant, compare the current year's Trial Balance with that of the previous year. Identify any unusual variations in account balances. Check whether the balances fall on the appropriate side (debit or credit) and investigate significant differences to find the possible source of error.

(*vii*) **Conduct a Detailed Review:** If the steps above do not help locate the error, a detailed review should be conducted:

(*a*) Recheck the totals of all subsidiary books (*e.g.,* Sales Book, Purchases Book), paying special attention to carry forwards and page totals.

(*b*) Check postings from the Journal and subsidiary books to the respective ledger accounts to ensure accuracy in amount and side (debit/credit).

(*c*) Verify the balancing of ledger accounts.

(*d*) Recast the list of balances prepared for the Trial Balance to ensure that no error has been made while compiling it.

(*viii*) **Recast the Books of Prime Entry (If Necessary):** If the error still cannot be found, the last resort is to thoroughly recheck all **books of prime entry**, such as the Journal and subsidiary books. This includes verifying the correctness of entries and cross-checking all postings to the ledger.

Subsidiary Books

In the earlier sections, we understood that all transactions are initially recorded in the Journal and subsequently posted to the ledger. However, entering every transaction in the Journal and then transferring it individually to the ledger can be a time-consuming and labor-intensive process. Each transaction requires dual entries—one on the debit side and another on the credit side—which can quickly become cumbersome when dealing with a large volume of transactions.

To streamline this process and improve efficiency, accountants use **Subsidiary Books**. These are specialised books that record transactions of a similar nature. The use of such books allows for the **division of the Journal into smaller, manageable parts**, thereby simplifying the recording and posting processes.

These **Subsidiary Books**, also referred to as **Books of Original Entry**, serve as the first point of record for financial transactions before they are transferred to the ledger. By categorising transactions, these books reduce redundancy, improve accuracy, and allow for easier analysis.

Advantages of Maintaining Subsidiary Books

The use of subsidiary books offers several distinct advantages:

(*i*) **Economy in Labour:** Recording transactions directly into categorised books is faster and reduces clerical effort, as compared to the traditional method of entering each transaction in the journal and then posting it to the ledger.

(*ii*) **Improved Accuracy:** Since similar transactions are recorded collectively and totals are posted periodically, the risk of errors is minimised, enhancing the overall accuracy of the accounting system.

(*iii*) **Helpful in Statistical Analysis:** Subsidiary books can be customised to capture additional data for internal analysis—for example, a Sales Book can include area-wise or salesman-wise data, aiding in business decision-making.

(*iv*) **Simplified Account Maintenance:** Subsidiary books may eliminate the need for maintaining multiple minor accounts. For instance, recording cheque numbers or payment dates in the Purchases Book can reduce the need to maintain such details separately in creditor accounts.

(*v*) **Effective Division of Work:** The accounting process can be divided among staff based on the type of book. This specialisation not only facilitates smooth workflow but also ensures timely recording.

(*vi*) **Increased Efficiency through Specialisation:** When clerical staff focus on one type of book regularly, they develop expertise in that specific area, which leads to greater speed and fewer errors.

(*vii*) **Ease in Error Detection:** The separation of transactions into different books allows quicker and more effective identification of errors or frauds, especially when a Trial Balance does not agree.

Classification of Subsidiary Books

The following is a classification of the commonly used subsidiary books along with the types of transactions they record:

(*i*) **Cash Book:** Records all cash and bank transactions, including receipts and payments. It may also include details of discount allowed or received. The Cash Book itself acts as both a book of original entry and a ledger account for cash and bank balances.

(*ii*) **Purchases Book:** Used to record all **credit purchases** of goods meant for resale or of raw materials and supplies used in production. Cash purchases are not recorded here.

(*iii*) **Sales Book:** Maintains a record of all **credit sales** of goods or services that the business normally deals in. Cash sales are excluded from this book.

(*iv*) **Purchases Returns Book (or Returns Outwards Book):** This book records goods returned to suppliers that were earlier purchased on credit, due to defects, damage, or excess quantity.

(*v*) **Sales Returns Book (or Returns Inwards Book):** Used to record goods returned by customers, which were originally sold to them on credit. It helps track reductions in revenue and stock.

(*vi*) **Bills Receivable Book:** Maintains details of bills of exchange received from customers. It helps track due dates and the total value of bills to be collected in the future.

(*vii*) **Bills Payable Book:** Records details of all bills of exchange accepted by the business. It provides information about future payment obligations and helps with cash flow planning.

(*viii*) **Journal Proper (or General Journal):** All transactions that do not fit into any of the above subsidiary books are recorded in the Journal Proper. These may include Opening and closing entries, Adjustment entries, Transfer entries, Rectification of errors, Depreciation entries, Other non-routine or one-off entries.

Cash Book

In the course of business, cash transactions occur frequently and in large volumes. Every enterprise engages in numerous receipts and payments of cash on a daily basis. To manage and record these transactions efficiently, a specialised book called the Cash Book is maintained.

The primary objective of the Cash Book is to keep a chronological and detailed record of all cash and bank transactions — including both receipts and payments. If each of these cash transactions were to be recorded in the general journal and then posted to the Cash Account in the ledger, the volume of work would become unmanageable. The Cash Book simplifies this process by acting as both a journal and a ledger.

Nature of Cash Book: Journal or Ledger

The Cash Book is unique in accounting because it serves a **dual purpose**—it functions both as a **book of original entry** and as a **ledger account**.

(*i*) **As a Book of Original Entry (Journal Function):** Like other subsidiary books, all cash transactions are first recorded in the Cash Book in the order of their occurrence. This makes the Cash Book a book of original entry, just like the Journal.

(*ii*) **As a Ledger Account:** The format of the Cash Book resembles that of a ledger account. All cash receipts are recorded on the debit side, and all cash payments are recorded on the credit side—just as they would be in a Cash Account in the ledger. Since all entries related to cash are already recorded here, there is no need to maintain a separate Cash Account in the ledger.

Simple Cash Book

The Simple Cash Book, also known as the Single Column Cash Book, is the most basic form of recording cash transactions. *It is used to record only cash receipts and payments made by a business.*

Format of Simple Cash Book

The Simple Cash Book is structured with two sides: the left-hand side (Debit side) records cash receipts and the right-hand side (Credit side) records cash payments.

Receipts **SIMPLE CASH BOOK** *Payments*

Date	Particulars	R.N.	L.F.	Amount	Date	Particulars	V.N.	L.F.	Amount
				₹					₹

- **Date:** Date of transaction.
- **Particulars:** Name of the party or description of the transaction.
- **R.N. (Receipt Number):** Used for referencing the number of receipt slips issued for incoming cash.
- **V.N. (Voucher Number):** Indicates the supporting document for cash payments.
- **L.F. (Ledger Folio):** Refers to the page number in the ledger where the entry is posted.
- **Amount:** Shows the value of cash received (on the debit side) or paid (on the credit side).

Recording in the Simple Cash Book

Cash Receipts: Whenever cash is received, the amount is recorded on the **debit side** along with the name of the party from whom cash is received and the receipt number.

Cash Payments: Whenever cash is paid, the amount is recorded on the **credit side**, along with the name of the party to whom cash is paid and the voucher number supporting the payment.

Posting from the Simple Cash Book

The opening balance shown on the debit side of the Cash Book is not posted to any ledger account; it originates from the journal proper. Other entries on the debit side (receipts) are posted to the credit side of the respective personal or nominal accounts in the ledger. Entries on the credit side (payments) are posted to the debit side of the corresponding accounts in the ledger. This method eliminates the need for a separate Cash Account in the ledger, as the Cash Book itself performs its function.

Balancing the Simple Cash Book

At regular intervals—preferably daily—the Cash Book is balanced to determine the cash in hand. The procedure involves totaling both sides of the Cash Book. The difference (debit minus credit) is the **closing cash balance**. This balance is carried forward as the opening balance for the next day.

Important Rule: A Cash Book **always shows a debit balance**, because total payments cannot exceed the opening balance plus receipts. If the credit side exceeds the debit, it indicates an error or fraud.

ILLUSTRATION 9. Record the following transactions in a Simple Cash Book:

Jan 01: Commenced business with cash ₹ 50,000

Jan 03: Purchased goods for cash ₹ 20,000.

Jan 05: Sold goods for cash ₹ 30,000

Jan 10: Paid rent ₹ 5,000

Jan 12: Purchased stationery ₹ 1,000

Jan 15: Paid salaries ₹ 8,000.

Jan 18: Received commission ₹ 3,000.

Jan 20: Paid electricity bill ₹ 2,000.

Jan 25: Purchased furniture for cash ₹ 7,000.

Jan 28: Paid telephone bill ₹ 1,200.

Jan 30: Cash withdrawn by owner for personal use ₹ 4,000.

SOLUTION

SIMPLE CASH BOOK

Date	Particulars	L.F.	Amount (₹)	Date	Particulars	L.F.	Amount (₹)
2025				2025			
Jan 01	To Capital Introduced		50,000	Jan 03	By Purchases		20,000
Jan 05	To Sales		30,000	Jan 10	By Rent		5,000
Jan 18	To Commission Received		3,000	Jan 12	By Stationery		1,000
				Jan 15	By Salaries		8,000
				Jan 20	By Electricity Bill		2,000
				Jan 25	By Furniture		7,000
				Jan 28	By Telephone Bill		1,200
				Jan 30	By Drawings		4,000
				Jan 31	By Balance c/d		34,800
Total			83,000	Total			83,000

Double Column Cash Book

The Double Column Cash Book is a practical extension of the Simple Cash Book and is used when a business needs to record additional information along with cash transactions. A Double Column Cash Book is used to record cash transactions along with one additional detail — either bank transactions or discounts.

1. Cash and Bank Columns Format: This format includes:

- **Cash Column**: Records all cash receipts and payments.
- **Bank Column**: Records all transactions made through the bank, such as cheque deposits, bank transfers, withdrawals, etc.

DOUBLE COLUMN CASH BOOK (CASH AND BANK FORMAT)

Date	Particulars	L.F.	Cash (₹)	Bank (₹)	Date	Particulars	L.F.	Cash (₹)	Bank (₹)
			Dr.	Dr.				Cr.	Cr

Key Points:

- **Contra Entries:** Transactions affecting both cash and bank accounts simultaneously (*e.g.,* cash deposited into the bank or cash withdrawn from the bank) are termed contra entries. These are denoted by writing 'C' in the L.F. (Ledger Folio) column and are not posted to the ledger, as they balance each other out within the cash book itself.
- **Posting to the Ledger:** Transactions recorded in the Double Column Cash Book are posted to respective ledger accounts. However, **contra entries** are not posted to the ledger, as they self-balance within the cash book. For other transactions, the corresponding accounts (*e.g.,* Sales, Purchases) are updated in the ledger to reflect these cash or bank movements.
- **Bank Overdrafts:** Unlike the cash column, which typically shows a debit balance (indicating cash on hand), the bank column can exhibit a credit balance. A credit balance in the bank column signifies a **bank overdraft**, meaning the business has withdrawn more money than is available in its bank account.

This format is ideal for businesses that operate both **cash and bank accounts** and frequently conduct transactions through both channels. It provides an integrated view of both cash and bank balances. Allows **contra entries**, *i.e.,* transactions involving both cash and bank (*e.g.,* depositing cash into bank or withdrawing cash from bank). These are marked with a "C" in the ledger folio column.

2. Cash and Discount Columns Format: When the additional column is meant for recording **discounts**, the Cash Book is called a **Double Column Cash Book (Cash and Discount)**. This format is useful for businesses that allow or receive trade discounts while dealing in cash. It allows for systematic recording of both **cash** and **discounts** on the same page.

DOUBLE COLUMN CASH BOOK (CASH AND DISCOUNT FORMAT)

Date	Particulars	R.N. / V.N.	L.F.	Discount Allowed (₹)	Cash (₹)	Date	Particulars	R.N. / V.N.	L.F.	Discount Received (₹)	Cash (₹)

Key Points:

- Two Functional Columns on Each Side:

  Debit Side (Receipts): Discount Allowed (to customers) – not balanced and Cash Received.

  Credit Side (Payments): Discount Received (from suppliers) – not balanced and Cash Paid.

- The discount columns are **memorandum columns only**, meaning they are not part of the double-entry system and are not balanced. Instead, the totals are posted periodically to separate ledger accounts for discount allowed and discount received.

- The cash columns are treated just like in a Simple Cash Book. They are **balanced periodically**, and the balance always appears on the **debit side** (as cash cannot be negative).
- The use of discount columns allows the business to maintain clear and separate records of **Discounts Allowed** to customers, and **Discounts Received** from suppliers, which is useful for **analysis and control**.

This format is useful for businesses that offer or receive frequent **cash discounts** and want to keep a track of them directly in the cash book. It is generally used by **smaller businesses or retail traders** where transactions are mostly in cash and discounts are commonly involved.

The choice between the **Cash + Bank** or **Cash + Discount** format depends on:

Criteria	**Cash + Bank Format**	**Cash + Discount Format**
Nature of transactions	Frequent bank dealings	Regular discounts involved
Size of business	Medium to large enterprises	Small traders or retailers
Volume of entries	High cash and bank volume	More focus on cash transactions
Need for contra entries	Yes	No
Accounting requirement	Recording dual medium (cash & bank)	Monitoring trade discounts

Advantages of the Double Column Cash Book:

- Simultaneously tracks cash and bank transactions, reducing errors and omissions.
- In accounting, a Double Column Cash Book is used to record cash transactions along with one additional detail — either **bank** transactions or **discounts**. Facilitates easy monitoring of cash flow and bank balances.
- Aids in reconciling bank statements by providing a clear record of all bank-related transactions.

ILLUSTRATION 10. Record the following transactions of AVR Technologies in Two Column Cash Book:

2024		₹	2024		₹
Oct. 1	Opening Balance:		Oct. 25	Credit Purchases from Aatmaj	25,470
	Cash in Hand	75,450	Oct. 26	Cash withdrew from Bank for office	12,450
	Cash at Bank (Overdraft)	25,500	Oct. 27	Office stationary purchased	3,500
Oct. 4	Cash Deposited in Bank	24,500	Oct. 29	Cheque paid to Aatmaj in full settlement	25,400
Oct. 5	Cash Purchases	13,400	Oct. 30	Rent paid in cash	7,500
Oct. 12	Cash Received from Abhay and half amount deposited in Bank	45,500	Oct. 30	Bank Charges	3,570
Oct. 17	Salaries paid to staff by cheque	14,750	Oct. 31	Postage and Stamp Charges paid in cash	150
Oct. 19	Cash Sales	26,750		Deposited in Bank all cash in excess of	2,710
Oct. 21	Interest charged by Bank	2,150			
Oct. 22	Cash deposited in Bank	10,500			
Oct. 23	Withdrew from Bank for personal use	4,570			

SOLUTION *(Please see next page)*

SOLUTION (ILLUSTRATION 10)

In the Books of AVR Technologies
Two Column Cash Book

Date	Particular	L.F.	Cash (₹)	Bank (₹)	Date	Particular	L.F.	Cash (₹)	Bank (₹)
2024					2024				
Oct. 1	To Balance b/d		75,450	—	Oct. 1	By Balance b/d		—	**25,500**
Oct. 4	To Cash A/c **(C)**		—	24,500	Oct. 4	By Bank A/c **(C)**		24,500	—
Oct. 5	To Purchase A/c		—	45,500	Oct. 5	By Purchase A/c		13,400	—
Oct. 12	To Abhay		45,500	—	Oct. 12	By Bank A/c **(C)**		22,750	—
Oct. 12	To Cash A/c **(C)**		—	22,750	Oct. 17	By Salary A/c		—	14,750
Oct. 19	To Sales A/c		26,750	—	Oct. 21	By Interest Expenses		—	2,150
Oct. 22	To Cash A/c **(C)**		—	10,500	Oct. 22	By Bank A/c **(C)**		10,500	—
Oct. 26	To Bank A/c **(C)**		12,450	—	Oct. 23	By Drawings A/c		—	4570
Oct. 31	To Cash A/c **(C)**		—	75,140	Oct. 26	By Cash A/c **(C)**		—	12,450
					Oct. 27	By Office Stationary		3,500	—
					Oct. 29	By Aatmaj		—	25,400
					Oct. 30	By Rent A/c		7,500	—
					Oct. 30	By Bank Charges		—	3,570
					Oct. 30	By Postage Stamps Charges		150	—
					Oct. 31	By Bank A/c **(C)**		75,140	—
					Oct. 31	By Balance c/d		2,710	90,000
			1,60,150	1,78,390				1,60,150	1,78,390

Three Column Cash Book (Cash Book with Discount, Cash, and Bank Columns)

In modern business practices, most financial transactions—especially receipts and payments—are conducted through banking instruments like cheques and online transfers rather than physical cash. Consequently, maintaining a simple cash book may not be sufficient for keeping comprehensive records. To address this, businesses maintain a Three Column Cash Book, which enables them to simultaneously record Cash transactions, Bank transactions, Discounts allowed and received.

Thus, it combines the functions of a Cash Book, a Bank Book, a Discount Register.

Dr. **CASH BOOK (THREE COLUMN)** **Cr.**

Date	Particulars	L.F.	Discount (₹)	Cash (₹)	Bank (₹)	Date	Particulars	L.F.	Discount (₹)	Cash (₹)	Bank (₹)

Posting Rules for Three Column Cash Book

1. Opening Balances: The opening balances of cash and bank are brought forward from the previous accounting period and entered directly on the debit side (To Balance b/d). These balances are not posted again into the ledger accounts.

2. Contra Entries: When cash is deposited into the bank or withdrawn from the bank for office use, the transaction affects both cash and bank accounts. These are recorded on both sides of the Cash Book and marked with a "C" in the L.F. column. No separate posting is required in the ledger because the double-entry is completed within the Cash Book itself.

3. Discount Columns: The discount allowed and discount received are not recorded for every transaction but only when such discounts are part of the transaction. The total of the Discount Allowed column (debit side) is posted to the debit of the Discount Allowed Account in the ledger. The total of the Discount Received column (credit side) is posted to the credit of the Discount Received Account in the ledger.

4. Other Transactions: All receipts are recorded on the debit side. All payments are recorded on the credit side. Except contra entries, each transaction is posted to the respective ledger accounts.

Purpose and Advantages

- Avoids duplication of work by combining three books into one.
- Provides a complete picture of the company's liquidity (cash + bank).
- Facilitates efficient management and control over cash and bank balances.
- Helps in quick reconciliation of cash and bank balances.
- Ensures proper recording of discounts allowed to customers and received from creditors.

ILLUSTRATION 11. Prepare a Triple Column Cash Book from the following transactions of G. Enterprises for the month of Jan. 2025.

Date	*Particulars*	*Amount*
1-1-2025	Cash in hand	14,500
	Cash in Bank	1,95,000
3-1-2025	Received from K	
	— Cash	7,300
	— Cheque	15,000
	Discount allowed to him	400

6-1-2025	Goods sold for Cash	9,100
7-1-2025	Withdrew from Bank by Self Cheque	3,000
12-1-2025	Issued a Cheque to B	10,590
	Discount received	410
14-1-2025	Received a Cheque from R (in full settlement of her account ₹ 6,500) by cheque	6,350
17-1-2025	Withdrew from Bank for personal use	15,000
18-1-2025	Paid Electricity Bill by Cheque	5,000
20-1-2025	Cash purchases of Stationery	1,200
31-1-2025	Deposit the entire Cash in Bank in excess of ₹ 10,000	

SOLUTION

TRIPLE COLUMN CASH BOOK

Date 2025	Particulars	Dis-count	Cash	Bank	Date 2025	Particulars	Dis-count	Cash	Bank
Jan. 1	To Balance b/d		14,500	1,95,000	Jan. 7	By Cash (C)			3,000
Jan. 3	To K	400	7,300	15,000	Jan. 12	By B A/c	410		10,590
Jan. 6	To Sales A/c		9,100		Jan. 17	By Drawings A/c			15,000
Jan. 7	To Bank (C)		3,000		Jan. 18	By Electricity Charges			5,000
Jan. 14	To R	150		6,350	Jan. 20	By Stationery		1,200	
Jan. 31	To Bank (C)			22,700	Jan. 31	By Bank (C)		22,700	
					Jan. 31	By Balance c/d		10,000	2,05,460
		550	33,900	2,39,050			410	33,900	2,39,050
Feb. 1	To Balance b/d		10,000	2,05,460					

Note: **Discount allowed and discount received ₹ 550 and ₹ 410 respectively should be posted in respective Accounts in the ledger.**

Petty Cash Book

In most business organisations, there are frequent small payments for expenses such as carriage, cartage, postage, stationery, refreshments, etc. Recording each of these minor payments in the main Cash Book would not only make it bulky but also cumbersome to handle. To resolve this issue, businesses maintain a separate book called the **Petty Cash Book**.

A Petty Cash Book is a subsidiary book maintained to record small day-to-day cash expenses. These minor transactions are recorded by a designated person known as the **Petty Cashier**. This book simplifies accounting by categorising routine payments under specific heads, making it easier to summarise and control.

Systems of Petty Cash

There are two commonly followed systems:

1. Ordinary System: A fixed sum is given to the petty cashier from time to time without any structured method.

2. Imprest System: Under this more efficient method, a fixed amount called *imprest* is given to the petty cashier. At the end of a set period (say, weekly or monthly), the amount spent is reimbursed so that the imprest is restored to its original level.

Columnar (Analytical) Petty Cash Book

Most organisations use a columnar or analytical Petty Cash Book where:

- The **left-hand side** records the receipt of cash from the main cashier.

- The **right-hand side** consists of columns for various common expense heads like Postage, Stationery, Cartage, Conveyance, Refreshments, etc.
- Each petty payment is first entered in the **Total Column** and then in the relevant **analysis column** corresponding to the nature of the expense.

This format reduces ledger posting work as only the **total of each column** is posted to its respective ledger account periodically.

SPECIMEN FORMAT OF PETTY CASH BOOK

Dr.		PETTY CASH BOOK							Cr.
Cash Recei-ved	*Date*	*Particulars*	*Vr. No.*	*Total*	*Statio-nery & Printing*	*Cart-age*	*Conve-yance*	*Postage and Tele-gram*	*Sundry Expe-nses*

Posting of Petty Cash Book

1. **Cash Received** from the main cashier is recorded on the **debit side** and is not posted to any ledger.

2. Each **payment** is entered on the **credit side** of the petty cash book under both total column and relevant expense column.

3. At the end of the period, totals of each analysis column are posted to the **debit** side of respective **expense accounts** in the ledger.

4. The balance left is carried forward as the closing balance or restored to the original imprest level.

Balancing the Petty Cash Book

At the end of a specified period—weekly, fortnightly, or monthly—the Petty Cash Book must be balanced to determine the amount of unspent cash remaining with the petty cashier.

The steps to balance the Petty Cash Book are as follows:

(*i*) The Total Payments column (usually the first column on the credit side) is added to determine the aggregate of all petty payments made during the period.

(*ii*) The total of all payments is subtracted from the cash received at the beginning of the period (imprest amount or opening balance).

Closing Balance = Opening Balance (Cash Received) – Total Payments

(*iii*) The resulting closing balance represents the cash still available with the petty cashier. This amount is carried forward to the next accounting period and is recorded as the opening balance for the next period in the Petty Cash Book.

(*iv*) If the business follows the Imprest System, the petty cashier is reimbursed for the exact amount spent during the period, restoring the petty cash to its original imprest amount. The reimbursement is recorded in the Petty Cash Book as a fresh receipt on the debit side.

Advantages of Petty Cash Book

Maintaining a Petty Cash Book offers several practical and managerial advantages. It plays a vital role in streamlining the accounting process, especially for small, frequent payments that would otherwise clutter the main Cash Book. The key advantages are as follows:

(*i*) The main Cash Book is spared from recording numerous small payments, making it more concise and easier to manage.

(*ii*) Since minor payments are handled by the petty cashier, the head cashier can focus on larger transactions and more important financial matters.

(*iii*) The analytical format of the Petty Cash Book provides clear categorisation of expenses, making it easier to monitor, control, and verify petty expenditures.

(*iv*) The columnar structure allows for totals of each expense head to be posted periodically, instead of recording each transaction separately in the ledger. This reduces workload and chances of errors.

(*v*) With distinct columns for various heads of expenditure, the Petty Cash Book offers a transparent view of how small cash amounts are being utilised within the business.

ILLUSTRATION 12. Prepare Petty Cash Book on imprest system from the following particulars and post it to the ledger :

2025 June		₹	2025 June		₹
1	Received for petty cash payments	500	20	Paid for conveyance	22
2	Paid for postage	40	25	Paid for travelling expenses	80
5	Paid for stationery	25	27	Paid for postage	50
8	Paid for advertisement	50	28	Wages to office cleaner	10
12	Paid for wages	20	30	Paid for telegrams	20
16	Paid for carriage	15	30	Sent registered notice to landlord	3

SOLUTION (*For Petty Cash Book please see next page*)

Ledger Accounts

POSTAGE AND TELEGRAMS ACCOUNT

2025			₹				
June 30	To Petty Cash A/c		113				

CARTAGE AND CARRIAGE ACCOUNT

2025			₹				
June 30	To Petty Cash A/c		15				

PRINTING AND ADVERTISEMENT ACCOUNT

2025			₹				
June 30	To Petty Cash A/c		50				

TRAVELLING EXPENSES ACCOUNT

2025			₹				
June 30	To Petty Cash A/c		80				

WAGES ACCOUNT

2025			₹				
June 30	To Petty Cash A/c		30				

STATIONERY ACCOUNT

2025			₹				
June 30	To Petty Cash A/c		25				

SUNDRIES ACCOUNT

2025			₹				
June 30	To Petty Cash A/c		22				

SOLUTION (*ILLUSTRATION 12*)

PETTY CASH BOOK

Cash Recei-ved	Date	Particulars	L.F.	Total Payments	Analysis of Payments						
					Postage & Telegrams	Cartage & Carriage	Printing & Adverti-sement	Travelling Expenses	Wages	Stationery	Sundries
₹	2025			₹	₹	₹	₹	₹	₹	₹	₹
500	June 1	To Cash									
	June 2	By Postage		40	40						
	June 5	By Stationery		25						25	
	June 8	By Advertisement		50			50				
	June 12	By Wages		20					20		
	June 16	By Carriage		15		15					
	June 20	By Conveyance		22							22
	June 25	By Travelling Expenses		80				80			
	June 27	By Postage		50	50						
	June 28	By Wages		10					10		
	June 30	By Telegrams		20	20						
	June 30	By Registered Notice to Landlord		3	3						
				335	113	15	50	80	30	25	22
	June 30	By Balance c/d		165							
500				500							
165	July 1	To Balance b/d									
335	July 1	To Cash Account									

PETTY CASH ACCOUNT

2025			₹	2025			₹
June 1	To Cash A/c		500	June 30	By Postage & Telegrams A/c		113
				June 30	By Cartage & Carriage A/c		15
				June 30	By Printing & Advertisement A/c		50
				June 30	By Travelling Expenses A/c		80
				June 30	By Wages A/c		30
				June 30	By Stationery A/c		25
				June 30	By Sundries A/c		22
				June 30	By Balance c/d		165
			500				500
July 1	To Balance b/d		165				
" 1	To Cash A/c		335				

Purchases Book

The Purchases Book is a subsidiary book maintained specifically to record all credit purchases of goods that are intended for resale. It is important to note that only purchases of goods on credit are recorded in this book. Purchases made for cash are recorded in the Cash Book, while purchases of assets (such as furniture or machinery) are recorded in the Journal Proper, not in the Purchases Book. This book is also referred to as the Invoice Book, since transactions are supported by purchase invoices received from suppliers.

SPECIMEN FORMAT OF PURCHASES BOOK

Date	*Particulars*	*Invoice No.*	*L.F.*	*Details*	*Amount*
					₹

Posting of Purchases Book

Each supplier (creditor) mentioned in the Purchases Book is credited in the Ledger with the amount of goods purchased from him. This reflects the liability of the business to the supplier. At the end of a specific period (daily, weekly, or monthly), the total of the Purchases Book is posted to the debit side of the Purchases Account in the Ledger with the narration: "To Sundries as per Purchases Book".

Sales Book

The Sales Book, also referred to as the **Sales Day Book**, is a subsidiary book used to record **only credit sales of goods** dealt in by the business. **Cash sales** and sales of **assets or non-trade items** are not recorded in this book—they are instead entered in the **Cash Book** or **Journal Proper**, respectively.

A specimen ruling of sales book is given below :

SALES BOOK

Date	*Particulars*	*Invoice No.*	*L.F.*	*Details* ₹	*Amount* ₹

Posting of Sales Book

Each customer's account is **debited individually** in the Ledger with the sales amount as the customer is the **receiver of goods**.The **total of the Sales Book at the end of the period** is posted to the **credit of the Sales Account** with the narration "By Sundries as per Sales Book".

Purchases Returns Book

Also known as the **Returns Outwards Book**, this book is used to record **goods returned to suppliers** that were previously purchased on credit. Such returns may be due to poor quality, excess quantity, or any other reason agreed upon by both parties.

Note: Cash purchases returned are not recorded here but adjusted directly in the Cash Book.

When goods are returned to the supplier, a **Debit Note** is sent to the supplier indicating that his account is being debited for the returned goods.

Posting of Purchases Returns Book

Each supplier's account is **debited individually** in the Ledger with the return amount. The **total of the Purchases Returns Book** is **credited to the Purchases Returns Account** with the narration "By Sundries as per Purchases Returns Book".

Sales Returns Book

Sales Returns Book, also **known as Returns Inwards Book, is kept for recording returns inwards, that is, returns of goods sold by us.** The trader sends a credit note to the customer informing him that he has credited the latter's account with the value of goods returned.

Posting of Sales Returns Book

Each customer's account is credited with the value of goods returned by him. The periodical total of the book is debited to Returns Inwards Account or Sales Returns Account as returned goods enter the business.

Debit Note and Credit Note

A debit note is prepared when goods are returned by the purchaser due to some reason. Two copies of this note are prepared. The original copy is sent to the party (*i.e.*, seller of goods) to whom goods are returned and the duplicate copy is kept in the office for office record. It is called a debit note because the party's account is debited with the amount written in this note for the goods returned. The same debit note becomes credit note from the receiving party's point of view because he credits the account of the party from whom he receives the note along with the goods.

A credit note, as stated above, is like a debit note. It is sent by the seller to the purchaser for the goods returned by the latter to the former. It is called a credit note because the party's account is credited with the amount written in this note for the goods returned by the party. The same credit note becomes debit note for the party who has returned the goods because that party gives debit to the party sending this note for the goods received.

Bills Receivable and Bills Payable Books

Where the number of acceptances received or given is large, it is advisable to record them in separate subsidiary books, instead of journalising each receipt of bill or issue of bill. For this purpose two books known as Bills Receivable and Bills Payable Book are used. Bills Receivable Book is used to record full particulars of bills receivable drawn by us and accepted by drawees and those endorsed to us by our debtors. Bills Payable Book is used for recording all bills accepted by us. The rulings for the two books are given in the next illustration.

Posting of Bills Receivable Book. Each bill appearing in this book is posted to the credit of the Drawee's or Endorsee's Account from whom the bill has been received. The book, like other subsidiary books, is periodically summed up and the periodical total of the book is posted to the debit of Bills Receivable Account with words, "To Sundries as per Bills Receivable Book".

Posting of Bills Payable Book. Each bill recorded in the Bills Payable Book is posted to the debit of the Drawer's Account to whom the acceptance has been given. The periodical total of this book is posted to the credit of Bills Payable Account with the words "By Sundries as per Bills Payable Book".

Journal Proper (General Journal)

Journal proper is used for recording only those transactions as cannot be recorded in any of the other subsidiary books. Examples of such transactions are :

1. Opening entries.
2. Transfer entries (transfer from one account to another).
3. Adjusting entries.
4. Closing entries.
5. Entries relating to rectification of errors.
6. Entries relating to dishonour of bills or promissory notes.
7. Withdrawal of goods by the proprietor for personal use or loss of goods by theft, fire, etc.
8. Credit purchase or sale of assets.
9. Bad debts.

All these entries have been discussed in detail in Subsequent Chapters.

Distinction between Special Journal and Journal Proper

Basis	Special Journal (Subsidiary books)	Journal Proper
1. Type of Transactions Recorded	Transactions of similar nature are recorded e.g. Purchase book, Sales book	Transactions recorded are not of similar nature, e.g. Opening Entries, Adjustment Entries.
2. Presentation	The format of special Journal is in the form of statement.	The format is in the form of a Journal.
3. Requirement	The organisation may not require to maintain Special Journal.	The organisation must maintain Journal Proper.
5. Rectification of Error	An error in the Journal Proper is not rectified in Special Journal.	An error in Special Journal is rectified by the Journal Proper.

ILLUSTRATION 13. Enter the following transactions in various subsidiary books and post them into Ledger and prepare a Trial Balance.

2025
June

1	Cash in hand, ₹ 15,700, Cash at Bank ₹ 25,400 and Capital Account ₹ 41,100.
3	Bought goods for cash for ₹ 4,100.
4	Purchased goods from Meera & Co. for ₹ 5,800 less 10% trade discount.
7	Sold goods to Bedi & Co. for ₹ 8,900 less 20% trade discount.
9	Withdrew ₹ 500 from bank for private use.
12	Sold goods to Amjadkhan for ₹ 6,400.
15	₹ 5,000 paid to Meera & Co. in full settlement of their account.
18	Goods worth ₹ 400 returned by Amjadkhan.
20	Received ₹ 4,000 from Amjadkhan.
21	Purchased goods from Shiv Dayal & Co. for ₹ 8,700.

23 ₹ 6,000 paid to Shiv Dayal & Co. by cheque ; discount allowed ₹ 300.
24 Purchased furniture for ₹ 800 from Manjeet Furniture House on credit.
26 Paid into bank ₹ 2,200.
28 Amjadkhan declared insolvent ; a first and final dividend of 50 paise in a rupee is received from him.
29 Goods worth ₹ 600 returned to Shiv Dayal & Co.
30 Interest on capital provided ₹ 411.
30 Goods worth ₹ 400 taken by the proprietor for his personal use.
30 Paid ₹ 500 for advertisement by cheque.
30 Paid salaries to staff ₹ 1,800.
30 Cash sales ₹ 21,800.
30 Paid into bank ₹ 20,000.
30 Bought 100 shares in Hind Mill Ltd. at ₹ 11 per share brokerage paid ₹ 25.
30 Received ₹ 5,900 from Bedi & Co., discount allowed ₹ 100.

SOLUTION (*For Cash Book please see next page*)

JOURNAL

Date	Particulars		L.F.	Debit Amount	Credit Amount
2025				₹	₹
June 24	Furniture Account	Dr.		800	
	To Manjeet Furniture House				800
	(Being furniture purchased on credit)				
June 28	Bad Debts Account	Dr.		1,000	
	To Amjadkhan				1,000
	(Being 50% amount due written off as bad debt on Amjadkhan becoming insolvent)				
June 30	Interest on Capital Account	Dr.		411	
	To Capital Account				411
	(Being interest on capital provided)				
June 30	Drawings Account	Dr.		400	
	To Purchases Account				400
	(Being goods taken for personal use of the proprietor)				
June 30	Capital Account	Dr.		900	
	To Drawings Account				900
	(Being transfer of balance of Drawings Account)				
				3,511	3,511

SALES BOOK

Date	Particulars	L.F.	Details	Amount
2025			₹	₹
June 7	Bedi & Co. Goods Sold		8,900	
	Less : 20% Trade Discount		1,780	7,120
June 12	Amjadkhan			6,400
June 30	Sales Account Cr.			13,520

CASH BOOK

Receipts | *Payments*

Date	Particulars	L.F.	Discount	Cash	Bank	Date	Particulars	L.F.	Discount	Cash	Bank
2025			₹	₹	₹	2025			₹	₹	₹
June 1	To Balance b/d			15,700	25,400	June 3	By Purchases A/c			4,100	
" 20	To Amjad Khan			4,000		" 9	By Drawings A/c				500
" 26	To Cash	C			2,200	" 15	By Meera & Co.		220	5,000	
" 28	To Amjad Khan			1,000		" 23	By Shiv Dayal & Co.		300		6,000
" 30	To Sales A/c			21,800		" 26	By Bank	C		2,200	
" 30	To Cash	C			20,000	" 30	By Advertisement A/c				500
" 30	To Bedi & Co.		100	5,900		" 30	By Salaries A/c			1,800	
						" 30	By Bank	C		20,000	
						" 30	By Investment in Shares A/c			1,125	
						" 30	By Balance c/d			14,175	40,600
	Discount Account Dr.		100	48,400	47,600		Discount Account Cr.		520	48,400	47,600
July 1	To Balance b/d			14,175	40,600						

PURCHASES BOOK

Date	Particulars	L.F.	Details	Amount
2025			₹	₹
June 4	Meera & Co. Goods Purchased		5,800	
	Less : 10% Trade Discount		580	5,220
June 21	Shiv Dayal & Co.			8,700
June 30	Purchases Account Dr.			13,920

SALES RETURNS BOOK

Date	Particulars	L.F.	Details	Amount
2025			₹	₹
June 18	Amjadkhan			400
June 30	Sales Returns Account Dr.			400

PURCHASES RETURNS BOOK

Date	Particulars	L.F.	Details	Amount
2025			₹	₹
June 29	Shiv Dayal & Co.			600
June 30	Purchases Returns Account Cr.			600

Ledger

CAPITAL ACCOUNT

Date	Particulars	L.F.	Amount	Date	Particulars	L.F.	Amount
2025			₹	2025			₹
June 30	To Drawings A/c		900	June 1	By Balance b/d		41,100
June 30	To Balance c/d		40,611	June 30	By Interest on Capital		411
			41,511				41,511
				July 1	By Balance b/d		40,611

FURNITURE ACCOUNT

Date	Particulars	L.F.	Amount	Date	Particulars	L.F.	Amount
2025			₹	2025			₹
June 30	To Manjeet Furniture House		800	June 30	By Balance c/d		800
July 1	To Balance b/d		800				

MANJEET FURNITURE HOUSE

Date	Particulars	L.F.	Amount	Date	Particulars	L.F.	Amount
2025			₹	2025			₹
June 30	To Balance c/d		800	June 24	By Furniture A/c		800
					By Balance b/d		800

BAD DEBTS ACCOUNT

Date	Particulars	L.F.	Amount	Date	Particulars	L.F.	Amount
2025			₹	2025			₹
June 28	To Amjadkhan		1,000	June 30	By Balance c/d		1,000
July 1	To Balance b/d		1,000				

AMJAD KHAN

2025			₹	2025			₹
June 12	To Sales A/c		6,400	June 18	By Sales Returns A/c		400
				June 20	By Cash A/c		4,000
				June 28	By Cash A/c		1,000
				June 28	By Bad Debts A/c		1,000
			6,400				6,400

INTEREST ON CAPITAL ACCOUNT

2025			₹	2025			₹
June 30	To Capital A/c		411	June 30	By Balance c/d		411
July 1	To Balance b/d		411				

DRAWINGS ACCOUNT

2025			₹	2025			₹
June 9	To Bank A/c		500	June 30	By Capital A/c		900
June 30	To Purchases A/c		400				
			900				900

PURCHASES ACCOUNT

2025			₹	2025			₹
June 4	To Cash A/c		4,100	June 30	By Drawings		400
June 30	To Amount as per Purchases Book		13,920	June 30	By Balance c/d		17,620
			18,020				18,020
July 1	To Balance b/d		17,620				

BEDI & CO.

2025			₹	2025			₹
June 7	To Sales A/c		7,120	June 30	By Cash A/c		5,900
				June 30	By Discount A/c		100
				June 30	By Balance c/d		1,120
			7,120				7,120
July 1	To Balance b/d		1,120				

SALES ACCOUNT

2025			₹	2025			₹
June 30	To Balance c/d		35,320	June 30	By Amount as per Sales Book		13,520
				June 30	By Cash A/c		21,800
			35,320				35,320
				July 1	By Balance b/d		35,320

MEERA & CO.

Date	Particulars	J.F.	₹	Date	Particulars	J.F.	₹
2025				2025			
June 4	To Purchases A/c		5,220	June 15	By Cash A/c		5,000
				June 15	By Discount A/c		220
			5,220				5,220

SHIV DAYAL & CO.

Date	Particulars	J.F.	₹	Date	Particulars	J.F.	₹
2025				2025			
June 23	To Bank A/c		6,000	June 21	By Purchases A/c		8,700
June 23	To Discount A/c		300				
June 29	To Purchases Returns A/c		600				
June 30	To Balance c/d		1,800				
			8,700				8,700
				July 1	By Balance b/d		1,800

SALES RETURNS ACCOUNT

Date	Particulars	J.F.	₹	Date	Particulars	J.F.	₹
2025				2025			
June 30	To Amount as per Sales Returns Book		400	June 30	By Balance c/d		400
July 1	To Balance b/d		400				

PURCHASES RETURNS ACCOUNT

Date	Particulars	J.F.	₹	Date	Particulars	J.F.	₹
2025				2025			
June 30	To Balance c/d		600	June 30	By Amount as per Purchases Returns Book		600
				July 1	By Balance b/d		600

ADVERTISEMENT ACCOUNT

Date	Particulars	J.F.	₹	Date	Particulars	J.F.	₹
2025				2025			
June 30	To Bank A/c		500	June 30	By Balance c/d		500
July 1	To Balance b/d		500				

SALARIES ACCOUNT

Date	Particulars	J.F.	₹	Date	Particulars	J.F.	₹
2025				2025			
June 30	To Cash Account		1,800	June 30	By Balance c/d		1,800
July 1	To Balance b/d		1,800				

INVESTMENT IN SHARES ACCOUNT

Date	Particulars	J.F.	₹	Date	Particulars	J.F.	₹
2025				2025			
June 30	To Cash Account		1,125	June 30	By Balance c/d		1,125
July 1	To Balance b/d		1,125				

DISCOUNT ACCOUNT

2025			₹	2025			₹
June 30	To Amount as per Cash Book		100	June 30	By Amount as per Cash Book		520
June 30	To Balance c/d		420				
			520				520
				July 1	By Balance b/d		420

Trial Balance
as at June 30, 2025

Serial No.	*Name of the Account*	*L.F.*	*Debit Balance*	*Credit Balance*
			₹	₹
1.	Capital Account			40,611
2.	Furniture Account		800	
3.	Manjeet Furniture House			800
4.	Bad Debts Account		1,000	
5.	Interest on Capital Account		411	
6.	Purchases Account		17,620	
7.	Bedi & Co.		1,120	
8.	Sales Account			35,320
9.	Shiv Dayal & Co.			1,800
10.	Sales Returns Account		400	
11.	Purchases Returns Account			600
12.	Advertisement Account		500	
13.	Salaries Account		1,800	
14.	Investment in Shares Account		1,125	
15.	Discount Account			420
16.	Cash in hand (as per Cash Book)		14,175	
17.	Cash at Bank (as per Cash Book)		40,600	
			79,551	79,551

QUESTIONS

OBJECTIVE TYPE

1. Indicate whether the following statements are TRUE or FALSE :

(*a*) Transactions are recorded datewise in journal.
(*b*) While recording transactions in the journal, principles of double entry are not followed.
(*c*) When more than one accounts are debited and credited, the entry is said to be simple.
(*d*) In order to bring balances of the last year, no entry is passed at the beginning of the year.
(*e*) When cash is received before the time from a party cash discount is allowed to the party.
(*f*) The difference of all debit balances and credit balances in the beginning of the year is called beginning capital.
(*g*) The total of one page of journal is carried forward to the next page.
(*h*) Total of all journal entries is not written at the end of the period say a month.

(*i*) The agreement of Trial Balance is a conclusive proof of the accuracy of a book-keeper.

(*j*) The credit balance of Bank Account indicates amount payable to the bank.

(*k*) The balance of Cash Account indicates total cash received.

(*l*) Compensating errors are those errors which compensate themselves in the net result.

(*m*) The Sales Day Book is a part of the Ledger.

Ans. [TRUE : (*a*), (*e*), (*f*), (*g*), (*j*), (*l*) ; FALSE : (*b*), (*c*), (*d*), (*h*), (*i*), (*k*), (*m*)].

2. In each of the following cases indicate the alternative you consider to be correct:

(*a*) In book-keeping posting means

(*i*) to record the transactions from the journal to the ledger.

(*ii*) to record the transactions in the journal.

(*b*) The basic rule of book-keeping, "debit the receiver and credit the giver" is applicable to;

(*i*) Nominal Accounts. (*ii*) Real Accounts. (*iii*) Personal Accounts.

(*c*) Goods of the value of ₹ 1,500 taken by the proprietor for his personal use should be debited to:

(*i*) Drawings Account. (*ii*) Sales Account. (*iii*) Purchases Account.

(*d*) Goods destroyed by fire should be credited to :

(*i*) Purchases Account. (*ii*) Sales Account. (*iii*) Loss of Goods by Fire Account.

(*e*) The credit balance of Bank Account indicates ;

(*i*) Amount payable by the bank. (*ii*) Amount payable to the bank.

(*iii*) Cash at bank.

Ans.[(*a*) (*i*) ; (*b*) (*iii*) ; (*c*) (*i*) ; (*d*) (*i*) ; (*e*) (*ii*)].

3. (*a*) Which of the following accounts will invariably have a debit balance ?

(*i*) Bank Account. (*ii*) Accounts Receivable Account.

(*iii*) Accounts Payable Account. (*iv*) Loan Account.

(*b*) Which of the following accounts will invariably have a credit balance ?

(*i*) Discount Account. (*ii*) Accounts Payable Account.

(*iii*) Cash Account.

(*c*) Which of the following accounts have only credit balance ?

(*i*) Accounts Payable Account. (*ii*) Salaries Outstanding Account.

(*iii*) Reserve Fund Account. (*iv*) All of the above accounts.

(*d*) Which of the following accounts may have a debit or credit balance ?

(*i*) Discount Received Account. (*ii*) Sales Account.

(*iii*) Trade Expenses Account. (*iv*) Loan Account.

Ans. [(*a*) (*ii*) ; (*b*) (*ii*) ; (*c*) (*iv*) ; (*d*) (*iv*)].

4. Select the correct answer :

(*a*) The .... records daily transactions of a business in the order in which they occur

(*i*) Journal (*ii*) Ledger

(*iii*) Account (*iv*) Trial Balance.

(*b*) Debit the receiver and credit the giver is the rule for .... account

(*i*) Personal (*ii*) Real

(*iii*) Nominal (*iv*) All of these.

(*c*) The various debit and credit balances of the different accounts are taken down in a statement which is known as ....

(*i*) Journal (*ii*) Final Account

(*iii*) Trial Balance (*iv*) Ledger.

(*d*) As a rule, the closing balance in any account ends with suffix......... and the opening balance with suffix ....

(*i*) c/d, a/c (*ii*) c/d, b/d

(*iii*) b/d, c/d (*iv*) b/d, a/c.

(*e*) Identify the correct golden rules for journalisation

(*i*) Income and Gains = Debit (*ii*) Expenses + Losses = Debit

(*iii*) Increase in Equity and Increase in Liability = Debit

(*iv*) Increase in Assets and Decrease in Liability = Credit.

(*f*) .... occurs if a transaction is not recorded whereas .... occurs when one error is set off against another error.

(*i*) Compensating error, Error of principle

(*ii*) Error of principle, Compensating error

(*iii*) Compensation error, Error of omission

(*iv*) Error of omission, compensating error.

(*g*) Journal is the book of—

(*i*) Original Entry (*ii*) Secondary Entry

(*iii*) All Cash Transactions (*iv*) All Non-cash Transactions.

(*h*) The process of recording a transaction in the journal is called ....

(*i*) Balancing (*ii*) Posting

(*iii*) Recording (*iv*) Journalising.

(*i*) Which of the following is a credit-transaction

(*i*) Sold Goods (*ii*) Sold Goods for Cash

(*iii*) Sold Goods to Ram (*iv*) Sold Goods to Ram for Cash.

(*j*) An account is a summary of .... at one place relating to a particular head

(*i*) All transactions (*ii*) Some Transactions

(*iii*) Journal (*iv*) None.

Ans. [(*a*) (*i*); (*b*) (*i*); (*c*) (*iii*); (*d*) (*ii*); (*e*) (*ii*); (*f*) (*iv*); (*g*) (*i*); (*h*) (*iv*); (*i*) (*iii*); (*j*) (*i*)]

5. Choose the correct answer :

(*a*) In how many types of accounts can be classified :

(*i*) 4 (*ii*) 3

(*iii*) 2 (*iv*) 5.

(*b*) If credit side is more than the debit side the balance is shown as ......

(*i*) To Balance c/d (on Credit Side) (*ii*) To Balance c/d (on Debit Side)

(*iii*) By Balance c/d (on Credit Side) (*iv*) By Balance c/d (on the Debit Side)

(*c*) The tallied trial balance means that there are ...... in the books of accounts.

(*i*) No Error (*ii*) No Frauds

(*iii*) No Casting Errors (*iv*) No Omission Errors.

(*d*) L.F. stands for—

(*i*) Left Forward (*ii*) Ledger Folio

(*iii*) Ledger Final (*iv*) Ledger Forward.

(*e*) *X* sold goods worth ₹ 10,000 at a trade discount of 10% and further a cash discount of 5% was provided. What amount will be debited to cash a/c—

(*i*) ₹ 10,000 (*ii*) ₹ 9,000

(*iii*) ₹ 8,550 (*iv*) ₹ 9,500.

(*f*) Following account has a credit balance

(*i*) Carriage Inward (*ii*) Carriage Outward
(*iii*) Return Inward (*iv*) Return Outward.

(*g*) Patent registered is a—

(*i*) Personal A/c (*ii*) Real A/c
(*iii*) Nominal A/c (*iv*) Expenses A/c.

(*h*) The golden rule for Nominal Account is—

(*i*) Debit the Receiver and Credit the Giver
(*ii*) Debit All Expenses and Credit All Incomes
(*iii*) Debit What Comes In and Credit What Goes Out
(*iv*) None of these.

Ans. [(*a*) (*ii*); (*b*) (*ii*); (*c*) (*iii*); (*d*) (*ii*); (*e*) (*iii*); (*f*) (*iv*); (*g*) (*ii*); (*h*) (*ii*)]

6. State whether the following statements are TRUE or FALSE :

(*a*) Cash Book is kept for recording the cash transactions.
(*b*) All the entries in the three column Cash Book are posted in the ledger.
(*c*) The Cash Account and the Bank Account are not posted in the ledger.
(*d*) The balance in the Cash columns of the Cash Book is always a debit balance whereas in the Bank column is sometimes credit also.
(*e*) Cash Book is a subsidiary book as well as a ledger.
(*f*) A contra entry in the Cash Book does not require posting to the ledger.
(*g*) Cash discount is provided on prompt payment and is recorded in the books.
(*h*) The balance of Petty Cash Book is a liability.

Ans. [TRUE: (*a*), (*c*), (*d*), (*e*), (*f*), (*g*) ; FALSE : (*b*), (*h*)].

7. State which of the following correctly complete the sentences given below :

(*i*) The Cash Book records (*a*) all cash receipts, (*b*) all cash payments, (*c*) all cash receipts and payments, (*d*) cash and credit sale of goods.
(*ii*) The balance in the petty cash book is (*a*) an expense, (*b*) a profit, (*c*) an asset.
(*iii*) If goods are sold for cash, the entry will be recorded (*a*) in the Cash Book , (*b*) in the Sales Book, (*c*) in the proper Journal.
(*iv*) In a triple column cash book the column other than discount and cash is used for recording .... transactions

(*a*) Discount (*b*) Payment
(*c*) Receipt (*d*) Bank.

(*v*) Returns inward book is called as .... and records ....

(*a*) Purchases Return Book, Goods Sent Back to Supporters
(*b*) Sales Return Book, Goods Returned by Customers
(*c*) Sales Return Book, Goods Sent to Customers
(*d*) Purchase Return Book, goods sent by suppliers.

(*vi*) Returns outward book is used to record transactions related to ....

(*a*) Goods Returned to Suppliers (*b*) Goods Returned from Customers
(*c*) Goods Returned to Customers (*d*) Goods Returned from Suppliers.

Ans. [(*i*) (*c*) ; (*ii*) (*c*) ; (*iii*) (*a*) ; (*iv*) (*d*); (*v*) (*b*); (*vi*) (*a*)]].

8. Select the correct answer :

(*a*) Cash Book Records.

(*i*) All receipts & payments of cash (*ii*) All cash and credit sale of goods
(*iii*) All cash and credit sale of goods.

(*b*) Cash Account will show

(*i*) Debit or credit balance (*ii*) Credit balance (*iii*) Debit balance.

(c) Cash discount is provided on :
(i) Sale (ii) Purchase (iii) Prompt payment

(d) Cash Book is a
(i) Ledger Account (ii) Subsidiary journal and ledger account
(iii) Subsidiary journal

(e) A columnar cash book records :
(i) All cash transactions only
(ii) Both cash and bank transactions except discounts
(iii) Both cash and bank transactions including discounts.

Ans. [(a) (i); (b) (iii); (c) (iii); (d) (ii); (e) (iii)].

9. Mention whether the following statements are right or wrong :

(a) Purchases Book makes a record of all purchases.
(b) Trade discount is not recorded in the books.
(c) Sales Book makes a record of all sales.
(d) Total of Returns Inwards Book is credited to Returns Inwards Account.
(e) Bills Receivable Book makes a record of the acceptances given whereas Bills Payable Book makes a record of the bills drawn.
(f) The sale of an asset is recorded in the Sales Book.
(g) Total of Returns Outward Book is debited to Returns Outward Account.
(h) Credit note is the basis for making entry in the Purchases Returns Book.
(i) Purchases of merchandise on credit are recorded in the Purchases Book.

Ans. [(a) Wrong, only credit purchases meant for resale are recorded (b) Right (c) Wrong, only credit sales are recorded (d) Wrong, debited not credited (e) Wrong, Bills Receivable Book should be substituted by Bills Payable Book to make statement correct (f) Wrong (g) Wrong (h) Wrong (i) Right].

10. Fill in the blanks :

(a) Total of the Sales Book is .... to Sales Account.
(b) Total of the Bills Payable Book is .... to Bills Payable Account.
(c) Total of the column of total payments in the Petty Cash Book is .... to Petty Cash Account.
(d) Journal Proper is used for recording only those transactions as cannot be recorded in any of the other .... books.

Ans. [(a) Credited (b) Credited (c) Credited (d) Subsidiary].

11. In each of the following cases indicate the alternative which you consider to be correct :

(a) A Purchases Book is kept to record
(i) all purchases of goods. (ii) all cash purchases,
(iii) all credit purchases, (iv) all credit purchases of goods,

(b) A Returns Inwards Book is kept to record
(i) returns of goods purchased, (ii) returns of any thing purchased,
(iii) returns of goods sold, (iv) returns of anything sold.

(c) The total of the Sales Book is posted periodically to the
(i) Credit of Sales Account, (ii) Debit of Purchases Account,
(iii) Credit of Capital Account,

(d) Sales Book is kept to record
(i) All sales of goods for cash, (ii) All credit sales,
(iii) All credit sales of goods, (iv) Returns of goods.

(e) Sales Returns Book is kept to record

(i) Returns of goods sold,

(ii) Returns of goods purchased by the proprietor for his personal use.

(iii) Return of machinery purchased.

(f) Which of the following is not a source document

(i) Cash Memo (ii) Invoice & bill

(iii) Pay-in Slip (iv) Cash Book

(g) Which of the following books should be used to record purchase of furniture on credit?

(i) Cash Book (ii) Journal Proper

(iii) Purchases Book.

(h) Which of the following accounts is increased by debit entries ?

(i) Machinery Account (ii) Purchases Return Account

(iii) Discount Received Account.

(i) The credit balance in the Bank Account is

(i) An asset (ii) A liability

(iii) An expense.

(j) Returns Outward Book makes a record of

(i) Goods returned to the suppliers (ii) Goods returned by the customers

(iii) Goods returned by the proprietor.

Ans. [(a), (iv), (b) (iii), (c) (i), (d) (iii), (e) (i) ; (f) (iv) ; (g) (ii) ; (h) (i) ; (i)(ii); (j) (i)].

12. In which subsidiary books the following transactions will be entered :

1. Purchased goods from Ram on cash payment of ₹ 600
2. Bought furniture for ₹ 200 from Jai Furniture House.
3. Sold goods to Shyam & Sons for ₹ 200.
4. Purchased goods from Ramesh & Co. for ₹ 300.
5. Returned goods to Ramesh & Co. for ₹ 20.
6. Withdrew from Bank for personal use ₹ 100.
7. Goods stolen by some employee ₹ 70.
8. Sold an old machinery for ₹ 2,000.
9. Acceptance given on the draft of A for three months for ₹ 150.
10. Received an acceptance from C for three months for ₹ 100.

Ans. [(1) Cash Book, (2) Journal Proper (3) Sales book, (4) Purchases Book, (5) Purchases Returns Book, (6) Cash Book, (7) Journal Proper, (8) Cash Book, (9) B/P Book, (10) B/R Book]

SHORT ANSWER TYPE

1. What is mean by Journal ?

2. What do you mean by narration ?

3. What are compound journal entries ? Give an example.

4. What is an opening entry ? Give one example.

5. State three advantages of journal.

6. State two limitations of journal.

7. Is the journal a book of original entry ?
8. What is Ledger ?
9. What do you mean by posting ?
10. What is Trial Balance ?
11. State the two objectives of Trial Balance.
12. What do you mean by subsidiary books ?
13. What are the two methods of preparing a Trial Balance ?
14. What do you mean by compensating errors ?
15. Give two examples of errors of principles.
16. What do you mean by imprest system of petty cash book ?
17. What do you mean by Journal Proper ? Give any two examples of entries to be recorded in this book.
18. What types of transactions are recorded in the Sales Book and the Purchases Book ?

LONG ANSWER TYPE

1. What do you mean by Journal ? Why is it called the book of original entry ? Give the rules and advantages of journalising.
2. Define a Ledger. Why is it known as the principal book of accounts ? Also give its ruling.
3. What do you mean by a posting ? How is posting made from the Journal in the Ledger ? Explain with suitable examples.
4. What do you mean by a Trial Balance ? Discuss the main objects, limitations and methods of preparing a Trial Balance.
5. 'Is the agreement of Trial Balance a conclusive proof of the accuracy of a book keeper ? If not, what are the errors, which remain undetected by the Trial Balance ?
6. Explain the errors which are disclosed by the Trial Balance.
7. In case of disagreement of the Trial Balance, in what order you would follow the procedure to locate the errors ?
8. What do you understand by 'Subsidiary Books' ? Describe the objects of preparing such books.
9. Define a Cash Book. Is it a subsidiary book or a principal book of accounts ? Give reasons.
10. What do you mean by Three Column Cash Book ? Give a specimen of it. Also explain the meaning of contra entry by giving examples.
11. Define a Purchases Book and a Sales Book. Give a proforma of these books and enter five imaginary transactions in them. Also show how these transactions will be posted to the ledger.
12. What is a Journal Proper ? What entries are recorded in it ?
13. Explain the 'Imprest System of Petty Cash Book'. What is the relation of Petty Cash Book to Cash Book?
14. Explain :

   (*i*) Petty Cash Book ; (*ii*) Subsidiary Books of Account ; (*iii*) Cash Book.
15. Distinguish :

   (*i*) Real and Nominal Accounts ; (*ii*) Commission and Discount ; (*iii*) Personal and Impersonal Accounts ; (*iv*) Errors of Principle and Errors of Omission.

PRACTICAL PROBLEMS

1. Journalise the following transactions, post them into Ledger and prepare a Trial Balance.

2024

September

1	Started business with ₹ 50,000, paid into Bank ₹ 20,000.
2	Bought furniture for ₹ 5,000 and machinery for ₹ 10,000.
3	Purchased goods for ₹ 14,000.
6	Sold goods for ₹ 8,000.
8	Purchased goods from Malhotra & Co. ₹ 11,000.
10	Paid telephone rent for the year by cheque ₹ 500.
11	Bought one typewriter for ₹ 2,100 from Universal Typewriter Co. on credit.
15	Sold goods to Keshav Ram for ₹ 12,000.
17	Sold goods to Rajesh Kumar for ₹ 2,000 for cash.
19	Amount withdrawn from bank for personal use ₹ 1,500.
20	Withdrew from bank for business use ₹ 3,500.
21	Received cash from Keshav Ram ₹ 11,900, discount allowed ₹ 100.
22	Paid into bank ₹ 5,800.
23	Bought 50 shares in XY and Co. Ltd. at ₹ 60 per share, brokerage paid ₹ 20.
25	Goods worth ₹ 1,000 found defective were returned to Malhotra & Co. and the balance of the amount due to them was settled by issuing a cheque in their favour.
28	Sold 20 shares of XY and Co. Ltd. at ₹ 65 per share, brokerage paid ₹ 20.
28	Bought goods worth ₹ 2,100 from Ramesh and supplied them to Suresh at ₹ 3,000.
30	Suresh returned goods worth ₹ 100, which in turn were sent to Ramesh.
30	Issued a cheque for ₹ 1,000 in favour of the landlord for rent for .
30	Paid salaries to staff ₹ 1,500 and received from travelling salesman ₹ 2,000 for goods sold by him, after deducting his travelling expenses ₹ 100.
30	Paid for ; Charity ₹ 101 ; Stationery ₹ 450 ; Postage ₹ 249

Ans. [Journal Total ₹ 1,83,370 ; Trial Balance Total ₹ 55,100].

2. Pass journal entries for the following transactions in the books of Mr. Kapil:

(*i*) Purchased goods from Sonu for ₹ 1,50,000 at a trade discount of 10% plus CGST and SGST @ 6% each.

(*ii*) Sold goods to Mohit for ₹ 50,000 and charged CGST and SGST @ 5% each. Out of the amount due 40% is received by cheque immediately.

(*iii*) Goods costing ₹ 25,000 withdrawn for personal use. Such Goods were purchased by paying CGST and SGST @ 6% each.

(*iv*) Machinery purchased from M/s Bright industries for ₹ 2,00,000 plus CGST and SGST @ 9% each. Paid ₹ 1,00,000 immediately by cheque and balance to be paid after two months.

3. Pass necessary entries to make the following adjustments at 31st Dec. 2024 :

(*a*) Depreciation at 5% on Office Furniture valued at ₹ 8,000, at 10% on Plant and Machinery of ₹ 80,000 ; at 5% on Factory Building of ₹ 2,00,000.

(*b*) The insurance premium has been paid for the year ending on 31st March next, ₹ 2,400.

(*c*) The telephone rent for one year was paid on last 30th April ₹ 300.

(*d*) Interest on capital at 6% p.a. is to be allowed. Capital in the beginning was ₹ 3,00,000.

(*e*) Following outstanding liabilities for expenses are to be provided for *viz.* wages ₹ 300, salaries ₹ 305, trade expenses ₹ 215.

(f) An unsold machinery appearing in the books at ₹ 5,000 is exchanged for a new machinery of ₹ 5,000. The old machinery has been valued at ₹ 800 for exchange purpose.

4. Pass one Journal Entry for each of the following items :

(a) Acquired the running business of X & Co. for cash ₹ 40,000, by taking over the following assets and liabilities at values stated against them :
Stock of Goods ₹ 15,000. Furniture ₹ 10,000. Debtors ₹ 7,000. Machinery ₹ 8,000. Creditors ₹ 12,000.
Out of ₹ 40,000 payable to X & Co. ₹ 10,000 were borrowed from B.

(b) Approached M for loan of ₹ 10,000, but he paid the amount after deducting interest in advance for one year at 6% p.a.

(c) Bought essential goods from D & Co. goods worth ₹ 6,000 at 15% trade discount and 2% cash discount terms, and paid them half the amount in cash.

(d) Sold to L essential goods worth ₹ 600 less $2\frac{1}{2}$% cash discount, and received from him ₹ 585 net on account by cheque.

(e) L's cheque is returned unpaid by Bank, marked 'Insufficient Funds'.

(f) Paid to D & Co. ₹ 2,500 in full settlement of their account.

(g) Withdrew cash ₹ 500 and goods worth ₹ 200 gross out of those bought from D & Co. for personal use.

(h) Cashed a cross cheque of ₹ 3,000 for T charging him ₹ 10 commission.

(i) L is declared insolvent and only 40 paise in the rupee is received from his estate.

(j) Out of the goods worth ₹ 5,000 insured for ₹ 4,000, a part is burnt by fire, the loss amounting to ₹ 400. The insurers admitted the claim for a proportionate loss and paid cash.

(k) Goods worth ₹ 600 were shop-soiled and sold to M for ₹ 300 only.

(l) Payment made to Krishna ₹ 5,000. He allowed a cash discount of ₹ 250.

(m) Cash received from Suresh ₹ 8,000 and allowed him ₹ 500 as discount.

(n) A running business was purchased by Mohan with following assets and liabilities :

Cash ₹ 2,000, Land ₹ 4,000, Furniture ₹ 1,000 ; Stock ₹ 2,000 ; Creditors ₹ 1,000, Bank Overdraft ₹ 2,000.

5. A book-keeper submitted to you the following Trial Balance, which he has not been able to agree. Rewrite the Trial Balance, correcting the mistakes committed by him.

	Dr. ₹	*Cr.* ₹
Capital		14,000
Drawings	3,250	
Stock (1-1-2024)	17,445	
Returns Inwards		554
Carriage Inwards	1,240	
Deposit with Anand Gupta		1,375
Returns Outwards	840	
Carriage Outwards		725
Loan to Ashok @ 5% given on 1-1-2024		1,000
Interest on the above		25
Rent	820	
Rent Outstanding	130	
Stock (31-12-2024)		18,792
Purchases	12,970	

Debtors	4,000	
Goodwill	1,730	
Creditors		2,000
Advertisement Expenses	954	
SGST Payable		1,000
CGST Payable		1,000
Provision for Doubtful Debts		1,200
Bad Debts	400	
Patents and Patterns	500	
Cash	62	
Sales		27,914
Discount allowed		330
Wages	754	
	45,095	69,915

Ans. [Correct T.B. Total ₹ 48,109].

6. One of your clients Mr. X asked you to finalised his account for the year ended 31st March, 2025. As a basis for audit. Mr. X furnished you with the following statement :

	Dr.	*Cr.*
X's Capital		4,668
X's Drawings	1,692	
Leasehold Premises	2,250	
Sales		8,250
Due from Customers		1,590
Purchases	3,777	
Purchase Return	792	
Loan from Bank		768
Trade Expenses	2,100	
Trade Payable	1,584	
Bills Payable	300	
Salaries and Wages	1,800	
Cash at Bank	678	
Opening Inventory		792
Rent and Rates	1,389	
Sales Return		294
	16,362	16,362

The closing inventory was ₹ 1,722. Mr. X claims that he has recorded every transaction correctly as the trial balance is tallied. Check the accuracy of the above trial balance and give reasons for the errors, if any. ***(Foundation Examination, May, 2022 Modified)***

7. Enter the following transactions in a **Three Column** Cash Book.

2025

Jan.

1 Cash in hand ₹ 14,000 ; Balance at Bank ₹ 5,000.

3 Cash sales ₹ 6,000 and received CGST ₹ 150 and SGST ₹ 150

5	Paid ₹ 7,000 into bank.
6	Received a cheque for ₹ 700 from Suraj.
8	Paid into bank Suraj's cheque of ₹ 700.
10	Paid to Anurag by cheque ₹ 980 in full settlement of his account of ₹ 1,000.
11	Withdrew from bank for office ₹ 4,000.
12	Cash sales ₹ 8,000 and received CGST 2.5% and SGST 2.5%.
13	Received a cheque from John for ₹ 10,000 and lodged it into the bank for clearance.
14	Paid commission to Ram by cheque ₹ 500.
15	John's cheque dishonoured.
29	Drew a cheque for ₹ 800 for personal use.
31	Paid salaries by cheque ₹ 1,500 and by cash ₹ 500.
31	Paid salaries by cheque ₹ 540.

Ans. [Cash Balance ₹ 25,200 ; Bank Balance ₹ 4,380; Discount Cr. ₹ 20].

8. Write up the **Triple Column Cash Book** of Ram from the following transactions :
On January 1, 2025 Ram dealing in essential goods exempted from GST had ₹ 450 in hand and ₹ 6,500 in bank.

2025 Jan.		₹	2025 Jan.		₹
2	Received cheque from Ali (in full settlement of debt of ₹ 650)	620	8	Received cheque from Mehta Bros. (Discount allowed ₹ 20)	800
3	Cash sales	250			
	Paid for advertisement by cheque	350	10	Sale of machinery, payment received in cheque	2,500
	Paid salaries and wages	435	12	Bank returns cheque of Metha Bros. dishonoured	
4	Amount withdrawn from bank for use in office	600			
5	Drawn cash for domestic use by Ram	200	15	New machinery purchased and cheque issued	10,000
6	Issued cheque in favour of Rao & Sons	1,000	15	Paid installation expenses in cash	500
				Bank charges as per pass book	10

Ans. [Cash (Dr.) ₹ 165 ; Bank overdraft ₹ 2,340 ; Discount Dr. ₹ 50 ; Cr. ₹ 40]

9. Shri Ramaswamy maintains a Columnar **Petty Cash book** on the Imprest System. The imprest amount is ₹ 500. From the following information show how his Petty Cash Book would appear for the week ended 12th September, 2024 :

2024 Sept.		₹	2024 Sept.		₹
7	Balance in hand	134.90	9	Repairs	156.70
	Received cash re-imbursement to make up the imprest		10	Postage	17.40
				Entertainment	12.70
	Postage	12.30		Travelling	38.40
	Stationery	32.10	11	Stationery	67.30
	Entertainment	5.40		Entertainment	4.10
8	Travelling and Conveyance	12.60	12	Miscellaneous	1.20
	Miscellaneous Expenses	1.10		Postage	5.10
	Entertainment	7.20		Repairs	48.30

Ans. [Balance ₹ 78.10]

10. Enter the following transactions in a **Single Column Cash Book**. No Journal is maintained.

(*i*) ₹ 5,750 cash received from Mr. A. Discount allowed ₹ 250.

(*ii*) Goods sold to Mr. B. on credit for ₹ 10,000.

(*iii*) Some old furniture (Book value ₹ 6,000) was sold for ₹ 4,000. A cheque of ₹ 3,000 was received and the balance remains outstanding.

(*iv*) A cheque received from Mr. D for ₹ 7,500 is returned dishonoured.

(*v*) A cheque of ₹ 9,500 paid to Mr. P in full settlement of his claim for ₹ 10,000.

(*vi*) Goods returned to Mr. Z for ₹ 3,500

(*vii*) Cash deposited to Bank ₹ 5,000.

(*viii*) Withdrew ₹ 3,000 by cheque for household expenses.

Ans. [Cash Balance ₹ 750].

11. On Ist October 2024 H. Wood commenced business dealing in essential goods exempted from GST with a capital of ₹ 30,000, of which ₹ 25,000 were deposited in bank and the balance was retained in hand for business purposes. During the month of October his transactions were as follows :

2024 Oct.		₹	2024 Oct.		₹
1	Bought of A Smith goods by cheque	7,000	16	Received cash from W. Williams	500
2	Sold goods to W. Williams	510		Discount allowed	10
3	Bought furniture for cash	500	17	Received back goods from S. Hart	20
4	Purchased goods from W. See	580	18	Received S. Hart's acceptance for	110
7	Purchased goods from J. Car	230	20	Withdrew from bank for	
8	Returned goods to J. Car	30		private expenses	110
8	Paid W. See by cheque in full		31	Cash sales for the month	1,400
	settlement of his account	560		Paid Salaries in cash	170
11	Accepted B/E drawn by J. Car	200		Remitted to bank cash in	
12	Goods bought for Cash	150		hand this day excepting ₹ 100	
14	Goods sold to S. Hart	130		Stock on 31st October, 2024	6,370

Enter the above transactions in proper **Subsidiary Books,** post therefrom into Ledger, and then prepare a Trial Balance.

Ans. [Cash Balance (Dr.) ₹ 100 ; Bank ₹ 23,310 ; Discount Dr. ₹ 10 ; Cr. ₹ 20 ; S.B. ₹ 640 ; P.B. ₹ 810 ; P.R.B. ₹ 30 ; S.R.B. ₹ 20 ; T.B. Total ₹ 32,280].

12. Mr. Sadanand operates two Bank Accounts both of which are maintained in the Columnar Cash Book itself. You are required to draw up the Cash Book and show how the following transactions relating to 28th February, 2025 will appear therein and close Cash Book for the day :

(*a*) Opening Balance : Cash ₹ 150 ; National Bank ₹ 11,240 (O/D) ; Overseas Bank ₹ 35,460.

(*b*) Received cheque for ₹ 1,250 in respect of sales for realising which the National Bank charged ₹ 1.50 and credited the balance.

(*c*) Purchased goods for ₹ 13,210 and a cheque issued on the Overseas Bank. The Bank charged ₹ 3 for collection of the cheque to the concerned party.

(*d*) Paid office expenses : ₹ 45 and ₹ 15.50 for stationery.

(*e*) Out of cash sales of ₹ 13,265 a sum of ₹ 10,000 was deposited in the National Bank.

(*f*) Credit purchases of ₹ 15,000 were made from Mr. Smith, who sent the documents relating to the goods through the Overseas Bank for 90 per cent of their value. The bank charged ₹ 115 for releasing the document.

(*g*) Deposited ₹ 5,000 in National Bank.

(*h*) A "Bill Receivable" for ₹ 10,000 was discounted with the Overseas Bank, which charges 1 per cent towards discounting.

(*i*) Withdrew ₹ 5,000 from the Overseas Bank.

(*j*) A Demand Draft was purchased for ₹ 3,000 from a bank after paying ₹ 2 towards their charges and paid to the Electricity Department as deposit.

(*k*) Interest of ₹ 122 and ₹ 50 was credited and debited respectively by the Overseas Bank and National Bank.

(*l*) An amount of ₹ 1,500 was withdrawn from the Overseas Bank and salaries paid to that extent.

(*m*) Manager's salary of ₹ 1,000 was paid by cheque drawn on the National Bank.

(*n*) Overseas Bank collected dividends of ₹ 1,250 and sent a credit note.

(*o*) An amount of ₹ 1,500 was transferred from the Overseas Bank to the National Bank.

Ans. [Balances as on 28 Febuary, 2024 : Cash ₹ 352.50 ; National Bank ₹ 5,458.50 and Overseas Bank ₹ 11,097].

CHAPTER

5

Bank Reconciliation Statement

Need for Bank Reconciliation Statement

Many transactions involving receipts and payments of money take place every day in a business unit. The businessman can relieve himself from this botheration of receiving and making payment by opening a current account in the Bank. Every businessman who opens a current account in the bank is usually given a Pass Book which makes a record of the businessman's transactions with the bank. This Pass Book is written by the bank. On the other hand, the businessman who opens a current account with the bank also writes his transactions with the bank either in a bank account opened in the ledger or in bank column of his Columnar Cash Book (already discussed). The specimen of a Pass Book can be as follows :

Name..................... Account No...........

Address..................

CURRENT ACCOUNT WITH THE CENTRAL BANK

Date	Particulars	*Dr.* Withdrawals	*Cr.* Deposits	*Balance* Dr. or Cr.	Amount	*Accountant's* Initials
		₹	₹	₹	₹	

The Pass Book and the Cash Book must show the same balance with a difference that in Cash Book it is a debit balance whereas the same is a credit balance in the Pass Book. The balance as per Cash Book is always reverse of the balance as per Pass Book and amount of the balance will be the same if all entries have been correctly recorded in the two books. But it is usually not so because some of the entries might not have been recorded or incorrectly recorded in any of the two books. Therefore, it is desirable for the business house to check periodically (preferably every month) the entries in the Pass Book with the entries in the bank column of the Cash Book and point out to the bankers the mistakes it comes across so that those may be corrected. A statement known as Bank Reconciliation Statement is, therefore, prepared usually every month with a view to reconciling the two balances shown by the Cash Book and the Pass Book on a particular date. The other important purpose of the preparation of this statement is to know the exact balance with the bank so that cheques might be drawn upto that amount if there be a need of withdrawal.

Meaning of Bank Reconciliation Statement

Bank reconciliation statement is a statement prepared on a particular date to reconcile the balance as per Cash Book with the balance as per Pass Book and to know the exact balance with the bank.

Reasons for the Difference in Two Balances

The reasons for the difference in the balances shown by the two books may be following :

(*a*) **Cheques issued but not yet presented for payment.** As soon as a cheque is issued, it is entered on the credit side of the Cash Book, but the bank makes no entry for the cheque until it is actually presented for payment. This means that if the cheque is not presented for payment upto the date of the preparation of the Bank Reconciliation Statement, the balance as per Pass Book will be higher than the balance shown by the Cash Book by the amount of cheque not presented for payment.

(*b*) **Cheques paid into bank but not yet collected by the bank.** As soon as cheques are received they are entered on the debit side of the Cash Book increasing the balance at the bank, but the bank does not give credit for the cheque deposited in the bank until it is cleared and collected.

(*c*) **The bank usually makes charges for the collection of outstation cheques and for the various services rendered by it to the trader.** If there is an overdraft, the bank will charge interest for the overdrawn amount. As a result, the balance as per Pass Book is reduced by the amount of bank charges and interest whereas balance as per Cash Book may not be reduced due to lack of information of these charges upto the date of the preparation of the Bank Reconciliation Statement. The business man comes to know of the bank charges and interest only when he receives the Pass Book from the bank duly filled up.

(*d*) **Interest or dividend on investments and rent on property collected by the bank on behalf of the client.** The businessman may entrust the task of collection of interest or dividend on investments and rent on property to the banker. After the collection of this income, the bank will give credit to the businessman and increase his balance whereas there may be no entry for this income in the Cash Book for want of information. Hence the Pass Book's balance will have to be reduced or the Cash Book's balance will have to be increased by the amount of such income collected by the bank to make the two balances agree.

(*e*) **Insurance premium, subscriptions to periodicals and other payments made by the bank on behalf of the client.** The businessman may give standing instructions to his bank to make the payment of insurance premium and other payments on his behalf when they fall due and reduce his balance. But, balance as per Cash Book will not reduce because of the omission of the entry in the Cash Book for payments made by the Bank.

Similarly there can be certain *other reasons* of disagreement of two balances as given below:

(*f*) Cheques omitted to be banked.

(*g*) Cheques or bills of exchange dishonoured.

(*h*) Payment by customers direct into businessman's account with the banker.

(*i*) Wrong debit or credit given in the Pass Book or the Cash Book.

Importance (or Advantages) of Bank Reconciliation Statement

Banks are essential to a modern society, but for a business they serve as a necessary instrument in the commercial world. Most of the transactions of business are done through bank whether it is a receipt or payment. Rather it is legally necessary to operate the transactions through bank after a certain limit. All the transactions, which have been operated through bank, if not verified properly, the business may not be sure about its liquidity position in the bank on a particular date. There may be some cheques which have been issued, but not presented, as well as there may be some deposits which have been deposited in bank, but not collected so far and some expenses might have been debited or bills might have been dishonoured. If it is not known to business in time, it may lead to wrong conclusions. The errors committed by bank may not be known without preparing bank reconciliation statement.

Following are the main advantages of bank reconciliation statement :

1. It brings to notice the causes of difference between bank balance as per cash book and balance as per pass book. Therefore, necessary corrections can be made at an early date and cash book and pass book can be amended by preparing a bank reconciliation statement.

2. Reasons for delay in the clearance of cheques deposited would be known by preparing a bank reconciliation statement.

3. A regular preparation of a bank reconciliation statement would reduce the chance of fraud by the staff of the firm dealing in cash.

4. Bank balance as per cash book cannot be taken as a final balance unless it agrees with the bank balance as per pass book. In case there is difference in the two balances shown by cash book and pass book, a bank reconciliation statement is required to be prepared to ascertain the correct bank balance that can be shown in the balance sheet.

5. A regular preparation of a bank reconciliation statement would impose moral check on the staff of the enterprise to keep the cash records always up to date. In this way cash meant to be deposited in the bank cannot be used by the cashier for his personal use and deposited at a later date.

6. A regular preparation of bank reconciliation statement prevents the chances of embezzlement. It reduces the chance of fraud by the staff dealing in cash. Hence, bank reconciliation statement is very important and is necessary for an industrial unit as it plays a key role in the liquidity control of the business.

Procedure for Preparation of Bank Reconciliation Statement

Procedure for preparation of Bank Reconciliation Statement is as follows :

(*a*) Tick off all the items in the Pass Book with the entries in the bank column of the Cash Book and make a list of the entries as are found not ticked either in the Cash Book or the Pass Book. The unticked items are responsible for the difference in the balances shown by the Cash book and the Pass Book.

(*b*) Take balance as per Cash Book or Pass Book as the starting point.

(*c*) Adjust the starting point with the other balance by adding or subtracting the unticked items as located in (*a*) step. If balance as per Cash Book has been taken as the starting point, then balance as per Cash Book is to be adjusted according to entries passed in the Pass Book or vice versa.

Following table will help to prepare the Bank Reconciliation Statement :

	Starting with	
	Dr. Balance as per Cash Book or Overdraft as per Pass Book	*Cr. Balance as per Pass Book or Overdraft as per Cash Book*
I. Those items which affect the debit side of Cash Book: (*i*) Cheques deposited but not collected by bank (*ii*) Cheque though entered in Cash Book but omitted to be sent to the bank	−	+
II. Those items which affect the credit side of Cash Book : Cheques issued but not presented for payment	+	−
III. Those items which affect the Credit side of Pass Book (*i*) Interest/dividend credited by bank (*ii*) Amount deposited direct by a customer into bank account (*iii*) Cheques sent to the bank but omitted to be entered into the Cash Book	+	−

IV. Those items which affect the debit side of Pass Book : (*i*) Bank charges charged by bank (*ii*) Interest on overdraft (*iii*) Payments made by bank on standing instructions of the customer	—	+

ILLUSTRATION 1. (*Debit Balance as per Cash Book*) Prepare a bank reconciliation statement from the following particulars as on 31st March, 2025.

Particulars	(₹)
Debit Balance as per Bank Column of the Cash Book	18,60,000
Cheque Issued to creditors but not yet presented to the Bank for payment	3,60,000
Dividend received by the bank but not entered in the Cash book	2,50,000
Interest allowed by the Bank	6,250
Cheques deposited into bank for collection but not collected by Bank up to this date	7,70,000
Bank charges not entered in Cash Book	1,000
A cheque deposited into Bank was dishonoured, but no intimation received	1,60,000
Bank paid house tax on our behalf, but no intimation received from bank in this connection	1,75,000

SOLUTION

BANK RECONCILIATION STATEMENT

as on 31st March, 2025

Particulars		₹
Balance as per Pass Book (Cr.) (Favourable)		18,60,000
Add: Cheque Issued but not yet Presented	3,60,000	
Dividend Received by Bank	2,50,000	
Interest Allowed by Bank	6,250	6,16,250
		24,76,250
Less : Cheques Deposited but not yet Collected	7,70,000	
Bank Charges	1,000	
Cheque Dishonoured	1,60,000	
House Tax paid by Bank	1,75,000	11,06,000
Balance as per Pass Book (Cr.) (Favourable)		13,70,250

ILLUSTRATION 2. (*Credit Balance as per Pass Book*) Prepare a Bank Reconciliation Statement as on 30th September 2025 from the following particulars :

	₹
Bank balance as per the pass-book (credit)	10,000
Deposited into the bank, but no entry was passed in the Cash Book	500
Cheque received, but not sent to bank	1,200
Insurance Premium paid directly by the bank under the standing advice	600
Bank charges entered twice in the Cash book	20
Cheque issued, but not presented to the bank for payment	500
Cheque received, entered twice in the Cash Book	1,000
Bills discounted, dishonored, not recorded in the Cash Book	5,200

SOLUTION

BANK RECONCILIATION STATEMENT
as on 30th September 2025

Particulars		₹
Balance as per Pass Book (Cr.) (Favourable)		10,000
Add: Cheque received but not sent to Bank	1,200	
Insurance Premium paid directly by Bank	600	
Cheque received, entered twice in Cash Book	1,000	
Bill Discounted, Dishonoured not Recorded in Cash Book	5,200	8,000
		18,000
Less : Deposited into Bank, but no Entry in Cash Book	500	
Bank Charges entered twice in Cash Book	20	
Cheques Issued but not presented to the Bank	500	1,020
Balance as per Cash Book (Dr.) (Favourable)		16,980

Bank Overdraft

Uptill now we were assuming that Cash Book shows a debit balance or Pass Book a credit balance, *i.e.*, bank owes amount to the trader. But sometimes Cash Book may show a credit balance or Pass Book a debit balance. What does it mean ? By this we mean that the trader owes this amount to the bank, *i.e.*, he has drawn more amount than his balance in the bank. Such a balance is technically known as bank overdraft.

The easier method of preparing Bank Reconciliation Statement in case of bank overdraft is to treat such a balance as a minus balance because balance at bank is treated as a plus balance. The rest of the items causing difference in balances disclosed by the Cash Book and the Pass Book can be treated in the same way as we have done in case of favourable balance. Therefore, two separate columns are prepared; one for recording plus items and the other for minus items. If the total of minus items exceeds the total of plus items, the result is minus and is bank overdraft as per Cash Book or Pass Book as the case may be. On the other hand, if the total of plus items, exceeds that of minus items, the result is plus and is a balance in favour of the trader.

Alternatively by following the signs given in the table on page 4.9 for credit balance (overdraft) as per Cash Book or Debit balance (overdraft) as per Pass Book, Bank Reconciliation statement can be prepared. This method has been followed in working of the following illustrations.

ILLUSTRATION 3. (*Overdraft as per Cash Book*) On checking Ram's Cash Book with the Bank Statement of his Overdraft Current Account for the month of November, 2024, you find the following :

(*a*) Cash Book showed an overdraft of ₹ 4,500.

(*b*) The payment side of the Cash Book had been undercast by ₹ 150.

(*c*) A cheque for ₹ 750 drawn on his saving account has been shown as drawn on current account.

(*d*) Cheques amounting to ₹ 7,500 drawn and entered in the Cash Book had not yet been presented.

(*e*) Cheques amounting to ₹ 6,000 sent to the bank for collection, though entered in the Cash Book, had not been credited by the bank.

(*f*) Bank charges of ₹ 75 as per Bank statement of account had not been taken into the Cash Book.

(*g*) Dividends of the amount of ₹ 3,000 had been paid direct into the bank and not entered in the Cash Book.

(*h*) Under instructions from Ram the Bank has transferred interest ₹ 900 from his deposit account to his current account on 3rd December, 2024. This amount had however been taken in the Cash Book before 30th November, 2024.

You are requested to prepare the Bank Reconciliation Statement on 30th November, 2024.

SOLUTION

BANK RECONCILIATION STATEMENT

as at 30th November, 2024

		₹	₹
	Overdraft as per Cash Book		4,500
Add :	1. Payment side of the Cash Book had been undercast	150	
	2. Cheques sent to the bank for collection entered in the Cash Book but not credited by the bank	6,000	
	3. Bank charges as per Pass Book not taken into the Cash Book	75	
	4. Transfer of interest from deposit account to current account recorded in Cash Book on 30-11-2024 but entered in the Pass Book on 3-12-2024	900	
			7,125
			11,625
Less :	1. Cheque drawn on saving account has been shown as drawn on current account in Cash Book	750	
	2. Cheques drawn but not yet presented for payment	7,500	
	3. Dividend paid direct into the bank not entered in the Cash Book	3,000	
			11,250
	Overdraft as per Pass Book		375

ILLUSTRATION 4. (*Overdraft as per Pass Book*) From the following particulars, prepare a Bank Reconciliation Statement as on 31st December, 2025.

(*i*) Debit balance (overdraft) shown by the pass book ₹ 2,48,000.

(*ii*) Cheques of ₹ 2,10,000 were issued in the last week of December, but of these ₹ 1,40,000 only were presented for payment.

(*iii*) A Cheque for ₹ 19,200 drawn for the payment of telephone bill had been entered in the cash book as ₹ 29,200 but was shown correctly in the bank statement.

(*iv*) A Cheque received of ₹ 37,520 entered twice in the Cash Book.

(*v*) A Cheque for ₹ 1,17,000 was issued for purchase of merchandise and was paid by the bank but not recorded in cash book.

(*vi*) Interest on overdraft and bank charges amounting to ₹ 3,500 were not entered in the Cash Book.

(*vii*) A Cheque for ₹ 45,000 was credited in the Pass Book but was not recorded in the Cash Book.

(*viii*) A bill of exchange for ₹ 26,200 which was discounted with bank, returned dishonoured but no entry was made in the cash book.

(*ix*) Payment side of the Cash Book has been undercast by ₹ 12,000.

SOLUTION

BANK RECONCILIATION STATEMENT

as on 31st December, 2025

Particulars	*(₹)*	*Amount (₹)*
Debit Balance as per Passbook (Overdraft)		2,48,000
Add : (*i*) Cheques Issued, but not presented till BRS date (₹ 2,10,000 – ₹ 1,40,000)	70,000	
(*ii*) Cheque Drawn for Telephone Bill entered in the Cash Book wrongly (₹ 29,200 – ₹ 19,200)	10,000	
(*iii*) Cheques credited in the Pass Book but not Recorded in the Cash Book	45,000	1,25,000
Total		3,73,000

Less : (*i*) A Cheque received entered twice in the Cash Book	37,520	
(*ii*) Interest on Overdraft and Bank Charges were not Recorded in Cash Book	3,500	
(*iii*) Bills of Exchange which is Discounted with the Bank Dishonoured not Recorded in cash Book	26,200	
(*iv*) Cheques Issued for Purchases, not Recorded in Cash Book	1,17,000	
(*v*) Under Casting of Payment side of CB	12,000	1,96,200
Debit Balance as per Cash Book		1,76,780

When Cash Book is to be rewritten, then all items which should be posted on debit or credit side of the Cash Book be posted and then balance as per Cash Book is extracted. With this balance, bank reconciliation statement is then prepared by adjusting rest of the items which do not affect the Cash Book but given effect in the Pass Book.

ILLUSTRATION 5. (***When Cash Book is prepared first and then Bank Reconciliation Statement***) Following is the Cash Book (Bank columns only) of M/s B.R.S. Limited for the month of March, 2025 :

	₹		₹
To Balance b/d	14,070	By Payments	1,55,200
To Receipts	1,50,730	By Balance c/d	9,600
	1,64,800		1,64,800

On scrutiny of the bank statements you find that :

(*a*) The bank statement shows an overdrawn balance at ₹ 1,240.

(*b*) Bank charges of ₹ 350 shown on the bank statement have not been entered in the cash book.

(*c*) A cheque drawn for ₹ 470 has been entered as a receipt.

(*d*) A cheque for ₹ 180 has been returned by the bank but not written back in the cash book.

(*e*) The opening balance should have been carried down as ₹ 14,700.

(*f*) The cheques paid to supplier for ₹ 2,140, ₹ 3,700 and ₹ 300 have not yet been presented to the bank.

(*g*) The last pay-in-slip of the month showing deposit of ₹ 15,420 has not yet been credited by the bank.

(*h*) The bank has debited a cheque for ₹ 720 by mistake to the company's account.

You are required to :

(*i*) Rewrite the Cash Book for the month, March 2025, and

(*ii*) Prepare a statement reconciling the adjusted balance in the cash book with the balance as per the bank statement.

SOLUTION

CASH BOOK

		₹			₹
To	Balance b/d	14,700	By	Payments	1,5
"	Receipts	1,50,730	"	Bank Charges	350
			"	Party's A/c (Double of ₹ 470)	940
			By	Party's A/c (Cheque dishonoured)	180
			"	Balance c/d	8,760
		1,65,430			1,65,430

BANK RECONCILIATION STATEMENT
as on 31st March, 2025

		₹	₹
	Revised Balance as per Cash Book	8,760	
Add :	Cheques issued but not presented for payment (₹ 2,140 + ₹ 3,700 + ₹ 300)	6,140	
			14,900
Less :	Amount deposited but not credited by bank	15,420	
	Wrong debit in Pass Book	720	
			16,140
	Overdraft as per Pass Book		1,240

When adjusted Cash Book is to be prepared, then all those entries which affect the preparation of Cash Book as posting on wrong side, posting twice or omission of an entry in the Cash Book should be adjusted and new balance as per Cash Book is to be calculated. With this balance then bank reconciliation statement is to be prepared with reference to those items which create difference between the balance as per Cash Book and balance as per Pass Book.

ILLUSTRATION 6. (***When Adjusted Cash Book is prepared before Bank Reconciliation Statement***) On 30th June, 2025, D's Cash Book showed that he had an overdraft of ₹ 300 on his Current Account at the bank.

On checking the Cash Book with the bank statement you find the following :

(*a*) Cheques drawn amounting to ₹ 500 had been entered in the Cash Book but had not been presented ;

(*b*) Cheques received, amounting to ₹ 400, had been entered in the Cash Book but had not been credited by the bank ;

(*c*) On instructions from D the bank had transferred interest, ₹ 60, from his deposit account to his current account recording the transfer on 5th July 2025. This amount had, however, been credited in the Cash Book as on 30th June, 2025.

(*d*) Bank charges, ₹ 35, shown in the Bank statement had not been entered in the Cash Book;

(*e*) The payment side of the Cash Book had been undercast by ₹ 10 ;

(*f*) Dividends amounting to ₹ 200 had been paid direct to the Bank and not entered in the Cash Book ;

(*g*) A cheque of ₹ 50 drawn on deposit account had been shown in the Cash Book as drawn on current account ;

(*h*) A cheque issued to N for ₹ 25 was replaced when out of date. It was entered again in the Cash Book, no other entry made. Both cheques were included in the total of unpresented cheques shown above.

You are required :

(*a*) to indicate the appropriate adjustments in the Cash Book ; and

(*b*) to prepare a statement reconciling the amended balance with the balance shown in the bank statement.

SOLUTION

CASH BOOK
(With Bank Column Only)

2025		₹	2025		₹
June 30	To Interest on Deposit (Cancelled)	60	June 30	By Balance b/d	300
			June 30	By Bank Charges	35

			₹				₹
June 30	To	Dividend Account	200	June 30	By	Payment side of the Cash Book under-cast on—now corrected	10
June 30	To	Deposit Account	50				
June 30	"	N (Cheque replaced wrongly entered again, now corrected)	25				
June 30	"	Balance c/d	10				
			345				345
				July 1	By	Balance b/d	10

BANK RECONCILIATION STATEMENT

as at 30th June, 2025

		₹
	Overdraft as per Cash Book (Amended Balance)	10
Add :	Cheques paid in bank but not yet cleared and credited by bank	400
		410
Less :	Cheques drawn but not presented for payment (₹ 500 – ₹ 25) for cheque issued to N replaced entered twice)	475
	Cr. Balance as per Pass Book	65

ILLUSTRATION 7. ***(When Cash Book is prepared after preparing Bank Reconciliation Statement)*** From the following particulars ascertain the balance that would appear in the Cash Book of Roy & Co., as on 30th June, 2025 before and after making the necessary adjustments:

		₹
(1)	Overdraft as per Pass Book as on 30th June, 2025	540
(2)	Cheques drawn but not presented upto 30th June, 2025	2,800
(3)	Cheques paid into bank but not cleared upto 30th June, 2025	3,900
(4)	Interest on overdraft as per Pass Book, not entered in the Cash Book	20
(5)	Insurance premium paid by the bank not entered in the Cash Book	400
(6)	Interest on investments collected by the bank appeared in the Pass Book	500
(7)	In June, Roy & Co. has discounted with the bank a bill for ₹ 500 and had entered this amount in the Cash Book but the proceeds credited in the Pass Book amounted to ₹ 490.	

SOLUTION

BANK RECONCILIATION STATEMENT OF ROY & CO.

as on 30th June, 2025

		₹	₹
	Overdraft as per Pass Book		540
Add :	Cheques drawn but not presented for payment	2,800	
	Interest on investment collected by the bank appeared in the Pass Book but not recorded in the Cash Book	500	
			3,300
			3,840
Less :	Cheques paid into bank but not yet cleared but credited in the Cash Book	3,900	
	Interest on overdraft recorded in the Pass Book but not entered in the Cash Book	20	

Insurance premium paid by the bank not entered in the Cash Book	400	
Discount on bill not recorded in the Cash Book	10	
		4,330
Dr. Balance as per Cash Book		490

As the minus items exceed that of plus items, so there is a balance of ₹ 490 (not overdraft) as per Cash Book before making the necessary adjustments. We prepare the Cash Book with Bank Column to know the balance as per Cash Book after making the necessary adjustments. This balance is ₹ 560 calculated as follows:

CASH BOOK (Bank Column only)

		₹			₹
2025			2025		
June 30	To Balance b/d	490	June 30	By Interest on Overdraft	20
" 30	" Interest on Investments	500	" 30	" Insurance Premium	400
			" 30	" Discount on Bills Receivable	10
			" 30	" Balance c/d	560
		990			990
July 1	To Balance b/d	560			

ILLUSTRATION 8. Prepare a Bank Reconciliation Statement as on 30th September, 2024 from the following extracts from the Bank Pass Book and the Cash Book (Bank column only).

BANK PASS BOOK

Date	*Particulars*	*Withdrawals*	*Deposits*	*Dr. or Cr.*	*Balance*
2024		₹	₹	₹	₹
Sept. 1	By Balance b/d			Cr.	9,810
3	To Mahesh Chander	740		Cr.	9,070
7	To Balwant Garg	580		Cr.	8,490
8	By Salaria & Co.		200	Cr.	8,690
12	By Cash		1,000	Cr.	9,690
18	By Santosh Arora		500	Cr.	10,190
21	To Rameshwar Vohra	440		Cr.	9,750
26	To Insurance Premium	400		Cr.	9,350
30	To Bank charges	20		Cr.	9,330
30	To Cash	3,000		Cr.	6,330
30	To Interest		70	Cr.	6,400
30	By Interest on Investments		600	Cr.	7,000

CASH BOOK (Bank Column only)

Date	*Particulars*	*Amount*	*Date*	*Particulars*	*Amount*
2024		₹	2024		₹
Sept. 1	To Balance b/d	9,810	Sept. 2	By Mahesh Chander	740
6	To S.P. Roy	300	6	By Balwant Garg	580
10	To Salaria & Co.	200	11	By Jagan Nath	470
12	To Cash	1,000	15	By Ashok Sood	350
14	To Santosh Arora	500	18	By Rameshwar Vohra	440
19	To Baljeet Grewal	460	24	By Ashok Kamal	630
26	To Bharat Singh	780	30	By Cash	3,000
			30	By Balance c/d	6,840
		13,050			13,050
Oct. 1	To Balance b/d	6,840			

SOLUTION

BANK RECONCILIATION STATEMENT
as at 30-9-2024

		₹	₹
	Cr. Balance as per Pass Book		7,000
Add :	Cheques paid into bank but not yet cleared and credited ₹		
	S.P. Roy 300		
	Baljeet Grewal 460		
	Bharat Singh 780	1,540	
	Insurance premium debited in the Pass Book but not yet entered in the Cash Book	400	
	Bank charges debited in the Cash Book but not yet recorded in the Cash Book	20	1,960
			8,960
Less :	Cheques issued but not yet presented for payment		
	Jagan Nath 470		
	Ashok Sood 350		
	Ashok Kamal 630	1,450	
	Interest credited in the Pass Book but not yet given effect in the Cash Book	70	
	Interest on investments collected by the bank but not yet recorded in the Cash Book	600	2,120
	Dr. Balance as per Cash Book		6,840

QUESTIONS

OBJECTIVE TYPE

1. **Choose the correct answer :**
   (*a*) In Cash Book Debit Balance of ₹ 112 was brought forward as Credit Balance of ₹ 121. While preparing a Bank Reconciliation Statement taking the balance as per Cash Book as the starting point :
   (*i*) ₹ 112 to be added (*ii*) ₹ 233 to be added
   (*iii*) ₹ 121 to be added (*iv*) ₹ 112 to be subtracted.
   (*b*) In case of an 'Unpresented Cheque' :
   (*i*) Bank Balance in Cash Book is more than Bank Pass book
   (*ii*) Bank Balance in Cash Book is less than Bank Pass book
   (*iii*) Either (A) or (B)
   (*iv*) No effect in both the books.

Ans. [(*a*) (*ii*); (*b*) (*ii*)]

2. **Fill in the blanks :**
   (*a*) When Bank column of a Cash Book shows a credit balance, it means.........
   (*b*) When Pass Book shows a credit balance, it means......
   (*c*) When Bank column of a Cash Book shows a debit balance, it means......
   (*d*) When Pass Book shows a debit balance, it means......
   (*e*) If we start with balance as per Cash Book, cheques paid into bank but not yet cleared and credited are......from balance as per Cash Book to arrive at balance as per Pass Book and......if we start with balance as per Pass Book to arrive at balance as per Cash Book.

(*f*) While preparing Bank Reconciliation Statement, balance as per Pass Book will have to be......or balance as per Cash Book......by the amount of direct payment by customers into trader's account with the banker.

(*g*) Bank balance as per Cash Book is ₹ 18,500. ₹ 4,500 is entered in the Cash Book as paid into Bank, but not credited by the Bank. The Pass Book balance is ₹ ......

(*h*) Bank balance as per Pass Book is ₹ 20,000. Dividends of ₹ 1,000 collected by Bank but entered in the Cash Book as ₹ 100. The Cash Book Bank balance is ₹ ....

(*i*) Overdraft balance as per Pass Book is ₹ 8,500. A cheque of ₹ 3,450 issued but wrongly entered in the debit side of the Cash Book. The cheque is not yet presented for payment. Overdraft Bank balance as per Cash Book is ₹ ......

(*j*) Overdraft Bank balance as shown by the Cash Book is ₹ 6,000. A cheque for ₹ 10,400 was deposited to Bank but omitted to be entered in the Cash Book. In the Pass Book the amount is wrongly entered in the withdrawal column. Overdraft balance as per Pass Book is ₹ ......

(*k*) Bank balance as per Cash Book is ₹ 7,800. Bank charges of ₹ 75 debited by Bank but not recorded in Cash Book. The Pass Book balance is ₹ ......

(*l*) Bank balance as per Pass Book is ₹ 9,700. Cash withdrawn from Bank ₹ 3,000 but recorded as ₹ 300 in the Cash Book. Bank balance as per Cash Book is ₹......

(*m*) Overdraft balance as per Pass Book is ₹ 11,500. Interest on Overdraft ₹ 350 debited by Bank but not recorded in the Cash Book. Overdraft Bank balance as per Cash Book is ₹ ......

(*n*) Bank balance as per Cash Book is ₹ 570. Debit side of the Cash Book Bank Column is overadded to the extent of ₹ 10,000. Overdraft balance as per Pass Book is ₹ ......

(Your answer in each case must be supported by workings in the form of plus or minus in the bracket)

Ans. [(*a*) Overdraft *i.e.* amount due to the bank (*b*) balance as per Pass Book *i.e.* amount due from the bank (*c*) Balance as per Cash Book (*d*) Overdraft as per Pass Book ; (*e*) Deducted, and added (*f*) Decreased, Increased ; (*g*) ₹ 14,000 ; (*h*) ₹ 19,100 ; (*i*) ₹ 5,050 ; (*j*) ₹ 16,400 ; (*k*) ₹ 7,725 ; (*l*) ₹ 12,400 ; (*m*) ₹ 11,150 ; (*n*) ₹ 9,430]

SHORT ANSWER TYPE

1. What is Bank Reconciliation Statement ? Why is it prepared ?
2. What is the need of preparing Bank Reconciliation Statement ?
3. List the reasons for difference in bank balance in Cash Book and in Pass Book.
4. On 31st October 2024, the Cash Book of a trader showed a favourable balance of ₹ 3,600 but the pass book showed a favourable balance of ₹ 3,850. The difference was due to the following reasons :

   (*a*) Interest on investment of ₹ 75 was credited in pass book but no entry was passed in cash book.

   (*b*) Debit of ₹ 12·50 for bank charges appeared twice in Pass book but no entry was made in Cash book.

   (*c*) Mr. Govindan deposited a cheque of ₹ 250 directly into Trader's Bank Account for which there is no entry in Cash Book.

   (*d*) A cheque for ₹ 50 received from Mr. Gopalan and deposited into Bank was returned dishonoured by Bank on 31st October which the Trader returned on 2nd November 2024. Reconcile the Balances.

Ans. [Credit Balance as per Pass Book ₹ 3,850].

5. From the following transactions prepare bank reconciliation statement of Sirisha as on 31-3-2025.

   (*a*) Bank balance as per cash book on 31-3-2025 was ₹ 6,000.

   (*b*) Cheques issued, but not presented for payment ₹ 4,850.

   (*c*) Cheques deposited but not collected ₹ 12,650.

(*d*) Insurance premium ₹ 250 ; Dividends on shares ₹ 150 were not shown in the cash book.
(*e*) ₹ 13,450 being the payment on bills payable by the bank, appeared in the pass book only.

Ans. [Overdraft as per Pass Book ₹ 14,350].

6. From the following particulars, prepare a bank reconciliation statement as on 31-12- 2024 :

(*a*) Overdraft as per cash book ₹ 1,000.
(*b*) Cheques issued but not presented ₹ 2,000.
(*c*) Cheques deposited but not collected ₹ 5,000.
(*d*) Dividends collected and credited in the pass book only ₹ 1,200.

Ans. [Debit balance as per pass book ₹ 2,800].

7. Find out the balance as per pass book from the following particulars :

(*i*) Bank Overdraft as per cash book on 30th April, 2025 ₹ 2,000.
(*ii*) Cheques issued but not presented for payment ₹ 1,350.
(*iii*) Cheques deposited but not yet collected by the banker ₹ 560.
(*iv*) Bank charges ₹ 80 made by the bank not yet entered in the cash book.
(*v*) Interest on investments collected by the bankers and credited in the pass book amounted to ₹ 950.

Ans. [Overdraft as per Pass Book ₹ 340].

LONG ANSWER TYPE

1. What is Bank Reconciliation Statement ? Why and How is it prepared ? Give your answer with an illustration.

2. What do you mean by a Bank Reconciliation Statement ? Explain the reasons on account of which the balance as shown by the Pass Book does not agree with the balance as shown by the Bank Column of the Cash Book.

3. Discuss the importance (or advantages) of bank reconciliation statement.

4. What do you understand by Bank Reconciliation Statement ? Explain its utility as a control technique,

PRACTICAL PROBLEMS

Debit Balance as per Cash Book

1. The cash book of Mr. Karan shows ₹ 2,60,400 as the balance of bank as on 31st December, 2025 but you find that it does not agree with the balance as per the bank pass book. On analysis, you found the following discrepancies :

(*i*) On 15th December, 2025 the payment side of the cash book was overcast by ₹ 10,000.
(*ii*) A cheque for ₹ 1,18,000 issued on 6th December, 2025 was not taken in the bank Column.
(*iii*) On 20th December, 2025 the debit balance of ₹ 8,460 as on the previous day, was brought forward as credit balance in the cash book.
(*iv*) Of the total cheques amounting to ₹ 12,370 drawn in the last week of December 2025, cheques aggregating ₹ 9,360 were encashed in December, 2025.
(*v*) Dividends of ₹ 35,000, collected by the bank and fire insurance premium of ₹ 7,900 paid by the bank were not recorded in the cash book.
(*vi*) A Cheque issued to a creditor of ₹ 1,75,000 was recorded twice in the cash book.
(*vii*) Bill for collection amounting to ₹ 53,000 credited by the bank on 21st December, 2025 but no advice was received by Mr. Karan till 31st December, 2025.

(*viii*) A customer, who received a cash discount of 3% on his account of ₹ 60,000 paid a cheque on 10th December, 2025. The cashier erroneously entered the gross amount in the bank column of the cash book.

You are required to prepare the bank reconciliation statement as on 31st December, 2025.

Ans. [Balance as per Pass Book ₹ 4,25,630].

2. Prepare Bank Reconciliation Statement from the following particulars as on 31st December, 2024 :

Particulars	₹
Bank Balances as per Cash Book (Debit)	1,98,000
Bank Charges Debited by the Bank not Recorded in Cash Book	34,000
Received from Debtors vide RTGS on 31st December, 2024 not Recorded in Cash Book	1,00,000
Cheque Issued but not Presented for Payment	45,000
Cheque Deposited but not Cleared	25,000
Cheque Received and Deposited but Dishonoured. Entry for Dishonour not made in the Cash Book	5,000
Instruction for Payment given to the Bank on 31st December, 2024 but the same effected by the Bank on 1st January, 2025	4,000

Ans. [Balance as per Pass Book ₹ 2,83,000].

3. On 31st December, 2024, the Cash Book of a firm showed a bank balance of ₹ 3,000. From the following information, prepare a Bank Reconciliation Statement, showing the balance as per Pass Book.

(*i*) Cheques have been issued for ₹ 2,500 out of which cheques worth ₹ 2,000 only were presented for payment.

(*ii*) Cheques worth ₹ 700 were paid on 28th December but had not been credited by the Bank. One cheque for ₹ 250 was entered in the Cash Book on 30th December but was banked on 3rd January, 2025.

(*iii*) A cheque from Mohan for ₹ 200 was paid in on 26th December but was dishonoured and the advise was received on 2nd January, 2025.

(*iv*) Pass book showed bank charges ₹ 10 debited by the bank. It also showed ₹ 400 collected by the bank as interest.

(*v*) One of the debtors deposited a sum of ₹ 250 in the account of the firm on 20th December. Intimation in this respect was received from the bank on 2nd January, 2025.

Ans. [Balance as per Pass Book ₹ 2,990].

Credit Balance as per Cash Book

4. From the following particulars prepare a Bank Reconciliation Statement showing the balance as per Cash Book on 31st December, 2024. Following cheques were paid into bank in December, 2024 but were credited by the bank in January, 2025 :

Manohar ₹ 700 ; Kulwant ₹ 800 ; Rajinder ₹ 600.

Following cheques were issued by the firm in December, 2024 but were presented for payment in January, 2025.

Smith ₹ 500; Bharat ₹ 450.

Following charges were made by the bank which were not recorded in the Cash Book :

Incidental charges for the half year ended 31st December, 2024 ₹ 20.

Collection charges for outstation cheques ₹ 15.

Following payments made by the bank direct as per standing instructions were not entered in the Cash Book :

Insurance premium ₹ 350 ; Subscription for Commerce ₹ 75.

A cheque for ₹ 500 which was received from a customer was entered in the bank column of Cash Book in December, 2024 but was omitted to be banked in December 2024. A bill for ₹ 1,000 was retired by the bank under rebate of ₹ 20 but the full amount of the bill was credited in bank column of the Cash Book.

The bank balance as per Pass Book was ₹ 15,800 on 31st December, 2024.

Ans. [Balance as per Pass Book ₹ 17,890].

5. From the following particulars, prepare a Bank Reconciliation Statement as on 31st December, 2024:

On 31st December, 2024 ; a merchant's pass book showed a credit balance of ₹ 5,400. A comparison of entries with the cash book revealed that he had paid in cheques of the value of ₹ 600 on 30th December, 2024, out of which cheques amounting to ₹ 240 were credited in the pass book on 2nd January, 2025. He had issued cheques of ₹ 1,500 before 31st December, but cheques amounting to ₹ 515 were debited to his account after 1st January, 2025. There was a debit in the Pass Book of ₹ 30 in respect of bank charges and credit of ₹ 25 for interest on current account but these were not recorded in the Cash Book.

Ans. [Dr. Balance as per Cash Book ₹ 5,130]

6. From the following particulars, prepare a Bank Reconciliation Statement on 31st March, 2025 :

Particulars	*Amount (₹)*
Bank Balance as per Pass Book	25,00,000
Bills discounted dishonoured not Recorded in Cash Book	12,50,000
Cheque received entered twice in Cash Book	25,000
Bank Charges entered twice in Cash Book	5,000
Insurance Premium paid directly by Bank under standing instruction	1,50,000
Cheque Issued but not presented to Bank for Payment	12,50,000
Cheque received, but not sent to Bank	28,00,000
Cheque deposited in Bank, but no entry passed in the Cash Book	12,50,000
Credit side of the Bank Column cast short	5,000

Ans. [Balance as per Cash Book ₹ 42,25,000]

7. On 31-3-2025, Mahesh's Cash Book showed a Bank Overdraft of ₹ 98,700. On comparison he finds the following :

(1) Out of the total cheques of ₹ 8,900 issued on 27th March, one cheque of ₹ 7,400 was presented for payment on 4th April and the other cheque of ₹ 1,500 handed over to the customer, was returned by him and in lieu of that a new cheque of the same amount was issued to him on 1st April. No entry for the return was made.

(2) Out of total cash and cheques of ₹ 6,800 deposited in the Bank on 24th March, one cheque of ₹ 2,600 was cleared on 3rd April and the other cheque of ₹ 500 was returned dishonoured by the bank on 4th April.

(3) Bank charges ₹ 35 and Bank interest ₹ 2,860 charged by the bank appearing in the passbook are not yet recorded in the cash book.

(4) A cheque deposited in his another account of ₹ 1,550 wrongly credited to this account by the bank.

(5) A cheque of ₹ 800, drawn on this account was wrongly debited in another account by the bank.

(6) A debit of ₹ 3,500 appearing in the bank statement for an unpaid cheque returned for being 'out of date' had been re-dated and deposited in the bank account again on 5th April, 2025.

(7) The bank allowed interest on deposit ₹ 1,000.
(8) A customer who received a cash discount of 4% on his account of ₹ 1,00,000 paid a cheque on 20th March, 2025. The cashier erroneously entered the gross amount in the bank column of the Cash Book.

Prepare Bank Reconciliation Statement as on 31-3-2025.

Ans. [Overdraft as per Pass Book ₹ 99,945]

8. Prepare a Bank Reconciliation Statement from the following particulars :
Sunder Lal & Sons find the Bank Balance shown by their Cash Book on 31st December, 2024 as ₹ 10,500 (Credit), but the Pass Book shows a difference due to the following reasons :

(*a*) Cheque No. 51 for ₹ 540 in favour of A has not yet been presented.
(*b*) A post-dated cheque for ₹ 300 has been debited to the bank account in the Cash Book, but it could not be presented for payment.
(*c*) Four cheques totalling ₹ 1,200 sent to the bank for collection have not yet been credited, while a fifth cheque for ₹ 400 deposited in the account has been dishonoured.
(*d*) Fire insurance premium amounting to ₹ 50 paid by the bank under standing instructions has not been entered in the Cash Book.
(*e*) A bill for ₹ 1,000 was retired by the bank under a rebate of ₹ 15, but the full amount of the bill was credited in the bank account in the Cash Book.

Ans. [Overdraft as per Pass Book ₹ 11,895].

9. On checking Surendra's Cash Book with the Bank Statement of his account for the month of March, 2025 you find the following :

(*a*) Cash Book showed an overdraft of ₹ 4,500.
(*b*) The payment side of the Cash Book has been undercast by ₹ 150.
(*c*) A cheque for ₹ 750 drawn on his savings deposits above has been shown as drawn on current account.
(*d*) Under instructions from Surendra the Bank has transferred interest ₹ 900 from his deposit account to his current account on 3rd April, 2025. This amount had, however, been taken in the Cash Book before 31st March, 2025.
(*e*) Cheques amounting to ₹ 7,500 drawn and entered in the Cash Book had not been presented.
(*f*) Cheques amounting to ₹ 6,000 sent to the bank for collection, though entered in Cash Book had not been entered by the Bank.
(*g*) Bank charges of ₹ 75 as per Bank Statement of account had not been taken in the Cash Book.
(*h*) Dividends of the amount of ₹ 3,000 had been paid direct to the Bank but not entered in the Cash Book.
(*i*) A cheque issued to Rafiq for ₹ 200 was replaced when out of date. But it was entered in the Cash Book again, no other entry having been recorded. Both cheques issued but not presented as shown above.

You are required to arrive at the balance as it would appear in the Bank Statement as on 31st March, 2025.

Ans. [Overdraft as per Pass Book ₹ 375]

10. From the following information, prepare a Bank Reconciliation Statement as on 31st March, 2025 for A Ltd.

	₹
Bank Overdraft as per Cash Book as 31st March, 2025	15,50,750
1. Cheques Deposited on 15th February, 2025 credited on 5th April, 2025	12,50,000
2. Interest debited by Bank on 31st March, 2025	1,75,500
3. Cheques Issued before 31st March, 2025 but not yet presented	7,75,000

4.	On 10th March, 2025 Bank credited to A Ltd. in error	1,50,000
5.	Draft Deposited in Bank but not credited till 31st March, 2025	12,75,000
6.	Bill for Collection credited by Bank but no advice received by the Company	9,45,000
7.	Bank Charges charged by Bank not entered in Cash Book	2,85,000
8.	Transport Subsidy received from the State Government directly by the Bank not advised to the Company	17,50,000

Ans. [Overdraft as per Pass Book ₹ 9,16,250]

Overdraft as per Cash Book

11. From the following information, ascertain the Cash Book balance of Mr. Bajaj as on 31st March, 2025 :

(*i*) Debit balance as per Bank Pass Book ₹ 3,500.

(*ii*) A cheque amounting to ₹ 2,500 deposited on 15th March, but the same was returned by the Bank on 24th March for which no entry was passed in the Cash Book.

(*iii*) During March, two bills amounting to ₹ 2,500 and ₹ 500 were collected by the Bank but no entry was made in the Cash Book.

(*iv*) A bill for ₹ 5,000 due from Mr. Balaji previously discounted for ₹ 4,800 was dishonoured. The Bank debited the account, but no entry was passed in the Cash Book.

(*v*) A cheque for ₹ 1,500 was debited twice in the cash book.

Ans. [Overdraft Balance as per Cash Book ₹ 2,500]

12. Prepare the Bank Reconciliation Statement of M/s R.K. Brothers on 30th June 2025 from the particulars given below :

(*i*) The Bank Pass Book had a debit balance of ₹ 25,000 on 30th June, 2025.

(*ii*) A cheque worth ₹ 400 directly deposited into Bank by a customer but no entry was made in the Cash Book.

(*iii*) Out of cheques issued worth ₹ 34,000, cheques amounting to ₹ 20,000 only were presented for payment till 30th June, 2025.

(*iv*) A cheque for ₹ 4,000 received and entered in the Cash Book but it was not sent to the bank.

(*v*) Cheques worth ₹ 20,000 had been sent to Bank for collection but the collection was reported by the Bank as under :

(1) Cheques collected before 30th June, 2025, ₹ 14,000

(2) Cheques collected on 10th July, 2025, ₹ 4,000

(3) Cheques collected on 12th July, 2025, ₹ 2,000.

(*vi*) The Bank made a direct payment of ₹ 600 which was not recorded in the Cash Book.

(*vii*) Interest on Overdraft charged by the Bank ₹ 1,600 was not recorded the Cash Book.

(*viii*) Bank charges worth ₹ 80 have been entered twice in the cash book whereas insurance charges for ₹ 70 directly paid by Bank was not at all entered in the Cash Book.

(*ix*) The credit side of bank column of Cash Book was undercast ₹ 2,000.

Ans. [Overdraft Balance as per Cash Book ₹ 25,210]

13. The Bank Pass Book of a trader showed an overdraft for ₹ 4,500 on 31st March, 2025 and a difference was noted when compared with the balance as per Cash Book. On a careful scrutiny the following facts were noticed :

(*a*) Cheques deposited for ₹ 7,500 but were not credited by the Bank before 31st March, 2025.

(*b*) Cheques issued for ₹ 3,850 were presented for payment on 4th April, 2025.

(*c*) Bank column total of Debit side of the Cash Book folio 36 for ₹ 65,950 was carried forward to the next folio as ₹ 56,950.

(*d*) Withdrawal column of the Bank Pass Book was added ₹ 600 excess.

(*e*) A cheque for ₹ 3,500 withdrawn from Bank but recorded in the Cash Book as ₹ 5,300.

(*f*) Bank charges ₹ 150 debited by the Bank but not recorded in the Cash Book.

You are required to prepare a Bank Reconciliation Statement (without preparing amended Cash Book) as at 31st March, 2025 and ascertain the balance as shown by the Cash Book on that date.

Ans. [Overdraft as per Cash Book ₹ 10,900]

14. (*Overdraft as per Pass Book*) The bank pass book of Account No. 1 of Mr. Stone showed an overdraft of ₹ 33,575 on 31st March, 2025. On going through the pass book, the accountant found the following :

(*a*) A cheque of ₹ 1,080 credited in the pass book on the 28th March being dishonoured is debited again in the pass book on 1st April, 2025. There was no entry in the cash book about the dishonour of the cheque until 15th April.

(*b*) Bankers had credited his account with ₹ 2,800 for interest collected by them on his behalf, but the same had not been entered in his cash book.

(*c*) Out of ₹ 20,500 paid in by Mr. Stone in cash and by cheques on 31st March, cheques amounting to ₹ 7,500 were collected on 7th April.

(*d*) Out of cheques amounting to ₹ 7,800 drawn by him on 27th March a cheque for ₹ 2,500 was encashed on 3rd April.

(*e*) Bankers seem to have given him wrong credit for ₹ 500 paid in by him in account No. 2 and a wrong debit in respect of a cheque for ₹ 200 against his account No. 2.

(*f*) Bank charges ₹ 100 (dated 27-3-2025) not entered in cash book.

Prepare Bank Reconciliation Statement on 31st March, 2025.

Ans. [Overdraft as per Cash Book ₹ 31,575]

15. D's Cash Book shows an overdrawn position of ₹ 3,630 on 31st March, 2025, although the bank statement shows only ₹ 3,378 overdrawn. Detailed examination of two records revealed the following :

(*a*) A cheque for ₹ 1,560 in favour of Rath Associates had been omitted by the Bank from its statement, the cheque having been debited to another Customer's A/c.

(*b*) The debit side of own book had been undercast by ₹ 300.

(*c*) A cheque for ₹ 182 drawn in payment of Electric Account had been entered in the Cash Book as ₹ 128 and was shown correctly in Bank Statement.

(*d*) A cheque for ₹ 210 from S. Gupta, having been paid into the bank, was dishonoured and shown as such in bank statement, although no entry relating to dishonour had been made in the Cash Book.

(*e*) The bank had debited a cheque for ₹ 126 to D's Account in error. It should have been debited to Shukla's A/c.

(*f*) A dividend of ₹ 90 on D's holding of Equity Shares has been directly collected by bank, but no entry has been made in Cash Book.

(*g*) A lodgement of ₹ 1,080 on 31-3-2025 had not been credited by the bank.

(*h*) Interest of ₹ 228 had been directly debited by bank but not recorded in Cash Book.

You are required to prepare a Bank Reconciliation Statement after necessary amendment in Cash Book as on 31st March, 2025.

Ans. [Amended Cash Book Balance (Cr.) ₹ 3,732 ; Overdraft as per Pass Book ₹ 3,378].

16. On 30th June, 2025 the bank column of the cash book of M showed a credit balance of ₹ 11,810. On comparison of the cash book and bank statement you find that :

(*a*) Cheques issued amounting to ₹ 17,520 in June, 2025 had been entered in the cash book as ₹ 17,250. The cheques were not presented at the Bank for payment until July, 2025.

(*b*) A cheque for ₹ 350 paid into the Bank in May, 2025 had been debited by the Bank in error in June, 2025.

(*c*) Interest of ₹ 880 charged by the Bank was not recorded in the cash book.

(*d*) Cheque received and recorded in the cash book but not sent to Bank for collection ₹ 1,240.

(*e*) Payment received from a customer direct by the Bank ₹ 2,730 but no entry was made in the Cash Book.

(*f*) ₹ 4,490 was entered in the cash book as paid into Bank on 30th June, 2025 but credited by the Bank until the following day.

(*g*) The payment side of the cash book had been undercast by ₹ 100.

You are required to show the necessary corrections in the Cash Book and to prepare a statement reconciling the amended cash balance with that shown in the Bank Pass Book as on 30th June, 2025.

Ans. [Amended Cash Balance ₹ 10,330 (Credit); Bank Balance as per Pass Book ₹ 760].

17. The Cash Book of Mehta showed a balance of ₹ 5,380 on 31st December, 2024 at the Bank. This figure did not agree with the bank Pass Book. A comparison of the two revealed the following :

(*a*) The bank has debited Mehta with ₹ 960, the annual premium on his life policy according to his standing instructions and with ₹ 30 as bank charges.

(*b*) The bank has credited Mehta by ₹ 1,400, the proceeds of a bill.

(*c*) Mehta paid in cheques totalling ₹ 2,100 on December 26th, of which those for ₹ 1,560 were collected in December and one for ₹ 150 was returned as dishonoured on 31st December, which Mehta received on 2nd January, 2025. The cash collection on 31st December, 2024 totalling ₹ 610 was entered in the Cash Book in the Bank Column on the same day but it was banked on 2nd January 2025.

(*d*) In December, 2024 Mehta issued cheques totalling ₹ 2,870 of which those for ₹ 850 had not been presented by 31st December, 2024.

Mehta has not yet recorded in the Cash Book matters mentioned in (*a*) and (*b*) and the dishonoured cheque mentioned in (*c*) above.

Show the corrections to be made in the Cash Book so as to ascertain the balance to be shown in the Balance Sheet and then prepare the Bank Reconciliation Statement.

Ans. [Adjusted Cash Book Balance ₹ 5,640 ; Cr. Balance as per Pass Book ₹ 5,490].

18. From the following particulars, find out adjusted bank balance as per Cash Book and prepare thereafter Bank Reconciliation Statement as on 31-12-2024 of a sole-proprietor :

	₹		₹
Bank overdraft as per Cash Book	80,000	Customer's cheque returned as per Bank statement only	4,000
Cheques deposited as per bank statement but not entered in Cash Book	3,000	Cheques issued but dishonoured on technical grounds	3,000
Cheques recorded for collection but not sent to Bank	10,000	Bills collected by Bank directly	20,000
Credit side of Bank column cast short	1,000	Cheque for ₹ 50,000 deposited but collection as per Bank Statement	49,980
Premium on Proprietor's LIP paid on standing advice	5,000	Cheque received entered twice in Cash Book	5,000
Bank charges recorded twice in Cash Book	100		

Ans. [Dr. Balance as per Adjusted Cash Book ₹ 85,900 ; Overdraft as per Pass Book ₹ 78,920]

19. Prepare a Bank Reconciliation Statement as on 31st December, 2024 from the following extracts from the Cash Book (Bank column only) and the Bank Pass Book.

CASH BOOK
(BANK COLUMN)

Date	Particulars	₹	Date	Particulars	₹
2024		₹	2024		₹
Dec. 1	To Balance b/d	4,450	Dec 1	By Salaries	2,800
" 4	To Patel & Co.	700	" 5	By Cash	1,000
" 8	To Kumar Bros.	400	" 11	By Smith & Co.	600
" 10	To Rajesh Khanna	800	" 15	By Chatterjee Bros.	750
" 15	To Ashok Kumar	1,000	" 21	By Sohan Singh	250
Dec 20	To Sunil Dutt	900	Dec 25	By Cash	1,000
" 26	To Prashant & Co.	1,500	" 28	By Pradeep Kumar	3,800
" 28	To Satwant Singh	450	" 31	By Rent	650
" 31	To Balance c/d	1,450	" 31	By Prabhat Works Ltd.	500
			" 31	By Sunanda Verma	300
		11,650			11,650
			2025		
			Jan. 1	By Balance b/d	1,450

BANK PASS BOOK

Date	*Withdrawals*	*Amount*	*Date*	*Receipts*	*Amount*
2025		₹	2025		₹
Jan. 1	To Cash	2,000	Jan. 1	By Balance b/d	300
" 3	To Pradeep Kumar	3,800	" 2	By Sunil Dutt	900
" 5	To Prabhat Works Ltd.	500	" 3	By Kulwant Singh	400
" 7	To Sunanda Verma	200	" 5	By Arti Co.	650
" 8	To Pratap Studio	250	" 6	By Prashant & Co.	1,500
			" 7	By Smith & Co.	850
			" 8	By Satwant Singh	450

Ans. [Credit Balance as per Pass Book ₹ 300]

CHAPTER

6

Rectification of Errors

Every concern is interested in ascertaining its true profit and financial position at the close of the trading year. But in spite of the best efforts of the book-keeper and the accountant, certain errors are committed in the recording of the transactions which affect the final accounts of the concern. It, therefore, becomes utmost important for the book-keeper and the accountant to locate such errors and rectify them so that correct profit and financial position of the concern may be ascertained. Hence whenever errors in accounting records come to notice, they should be rectified without waiting till the end of the accounting year when Trial Balance is to be prepared.

Errors in accountancy are not rectified by striking off the wrong figures and replacing it by the correct one. It is better to pass an appropriate entry for rectification of mistake to neutralise the effect of error and to bring the correct position. Thus the objectives of rectification of errors are as follows :

(*a*) Preparing correct accounting records.

(*b*) Ascertaining correct profit or loss for the accounting period by preparing the Profit and Loss Account with the correct figures.

(*c*) Exhibiting a true financial position of the concern on a particular date by preparing the Balance Sheet with correct accounting data.

Types of Errors

From the point of view of rectification of errors, errors can be divided into two types:

(*i*) Errors affecting one account only.

(*ii*) Errors affecting two or more accounts.

Errors which affect only one account can be (*a*) errors of posting, (*b*) errors of casting, (*c*) errors of carry forward, and (*d*) errors of omission of balance of any account in the trial balance.

Errors affecting two or more accounts can be (*a*) errors of posting to wrong account, (*b*) errors of omission, and (*c*) errors of principle.

Errors in accounts may be discovered at different stages and require rectification. These can be discovered :

(*i*) before the preparation of the Trial Balance.

(*ii*) after the preparation of the Trial Balance but before the preparation of final accounts.

(*iii*) after the preparation of the Trial Balance and final accounts.

Methods of Rectification of Errors

Following methods may be used for the rectification of errors :

1. By striking off wrong figure and replacing it by a correct one. For example, the cashier pays

₹ 1,015 for the purchase of goods but by mistake he writes ₹ 1,510 in the Cash Book. This method will be rectified in the following way :

CASH BOOK

			₹
		By Purchases Account	1,015 ~~1,510~~

Erasing of figures should be discouraged as it gives the impression of fraud. Wrong figure should be struck off and correct figure should be written above the wrong figure by drawing a straight line over the wrong figure as it has been demonstrated above.

This method of rectification can be applied when the error is detected in the subsidiary book and the entry has not yet been posted in the ledger. This method should be avoided as far as possible because it gives chances of fraud.

2. By passing a Journal Entry. This method of rectification of errors is followed in case of those errors which take place in two accounts. From the point of view of rectification, we can divide such errors into three categories :

(*a*) An error which occurs simultaneously in two accounts causing a short debit in one and an excess debit in another or an excess credit in one and a short credit in another account. For example, ₹ 500 received on account of cash sales has been posted to Bankey Bihari, a customer. The effect of this error will be to give more credit to Bankey Bihari and less credit to Cash Sales Account. To correct this entry, the following entry will be passed :

Bankey Bihari	Dr. ₹ 500	
To Cash Sales Account		₹ 500

(For cash received on account of cash sales wrongly credited to Bankey Bihari instead of Cash Sales Account, now corrected)

In the above rectifying entry, Bankey Bihari has been given debit to cancel the effect of wrong credit given previously and the other account (Cash Sales Account) has been credited for the amount received on account of cash sales for which no credit was given previously.

(*b*) An error which occurs simultaneously in two accounts but on the opposite sides causing a more or less debit in one and a more or less credit in the other account. For example, a purchase of ₹ 501 from Naresh Trading Co. was written in the Purchases Book as ₹ 105. The effect of this error was that Naresh Trading Co. had been given less credit of ₹ 396 (₹ 501—₹ 105.) and Purchases Account had been given less debit of ₹ 396. The entry will be rectified as follows :

Purchases Account	Dr. ₹ 396	
To Naresh Trading Co.		₹ 396.

(Being a credit purchase of ₹ 501 written as
₹ 105 in the Purchases Book, now corrected)

ILLUSTRATION 1. Following errors were detected in the accounts of Asa Ram & Sons for the year ended 30th June, 2025 :

(*i*) A builder's bill for ₹ 2,700 for the erection of a small shed was debited to repairs account.

(*ii*) A cheque for ₹ 300 received from Rahim Bux and Co. was dishonoured and debited to allowances account.

(*iii*) Goods to the value of ₹ 150 returned by Chandmal Bros. were included in stock, but no entry was made in the books.

(*iv*) Repairs to plant amounting to ₹ 567 had been charged to Plant and Machinery Account.

(*v*) Wages paid to the firm's own workmen for making certain additions to machinery amounting to ₹ 550 were posted to wages account.

(*vi*) A cheque for ₹ 75 received from Lala Ram was credited to the account of Tika Ram and debited incorrectly to cash account.

(*vii*) A sum of ₹ 100 drawn by the proprietor for personal use was debited to travelling expenses account.

Give Journal Entries to correct these errors. Which of these errors, if any, will cause disagreement of the trial balance ? Give reasons for your answer.

SOLUTION

JOURNAL ENTRIES

			₹	₹
(*i*)	Building Account Dr. To Repairs Account (Being a builder's bill for the erection of a small shed wrongly debited to Repairs Account, now corrected)		2,700	2,700
(*ii*)	Rahim Bux & Co. Dr. To Allowances Account (Being a cheque received from Rahim Bux & Co. dishonoured was wrongly debited to Allowances Account, now rectified)		300	300
(*iii*)	Returns Inwards Account Dr. To Chandmal Bros. (Being goods returned by Chandmal Bros. omitted to be recorded, now recorded)		150	150
(*iv*)	Repairs Account Dr. To Plant and Machinery Account (Being repairs to plant and machinery wrongly debited to Repairs Account, now corrected)		567	567
(*v*)	Plant and Machinery Account Dr. To Wages Account (Being wages paid for making certain additions to machinery wrongly debited to Wages Account, now rectified)		550	550
(*vi*) (*a*)	Tika Ram Dr. To Lala Ram (Being cheque received from Lala Ram wrongly credited to Tika Ram instead of to Lala Ram, now corrected)		75	75
(*b*)	Bank Account Dr. To Cash Account (Being cheque received from Lala Ram wrongly debited to Cash Account instead of to Bank Account, now rectified)		75	75
(*vii*)	Drawings Account Dr. To Travelling Expenses Account (Being amount drawn by the proprietor wrongly debited to Travelling Expenses Account, now corrected)		100	100

(*c*) An error which occurs in two accounts due to omission of recording the transaction in a subsidiary book can be rectified by passing the journal entry for the transaction. For example, a purchase of ₹ 500 from A omitted to be recorded in the Purchases Book will be corrected as follows :

Purchases Account Dr. ₹ 500

To A ₹ 500

(Being a purchase of ₹ 500 from A omitted to be recorded, now recorded)

3. By making a further debit or credit entry in the account which is affected by the error to cancel the effect of the error. This method is used when the error affects the trial balance and when the books have not been closed by placing the difference of the trial balance to the Suspense Account. An error of such type cannot be rectified by passing a journal entry, so if an account is debited in excess, it should be credited with the amount of excess debit to cancel the previous excess debit and if an account is given less debit, it should be given a further debit to make up short debit given previously. For example, depreciation of ₹ 1,000 on machinery posted to Depreciation Account as ₹ 100 will be rectified as follows :

DEPRECIATION ACCOUNT

	₹		₹
To Wrong posting of depreciation of ₹1,000 as ₹ 100......, now stands corrected	900		

If such an error is detected after the closing of the books and the trial balance has been made to agree by placing the difference to the Suspense Account, then the error will be corrected by passing a journal entry. The account in which the error exists will be given a further debit or credit according to the principle as described just now and the other aspect of the journal entry will be covered by giving credit or debit to the Suspense Account. In this way, the balance of the Suspense Account will become nil when all errors are detected which are responsible for the disagreement of the trial balance. In the above cited example, the following journal entry will be passed to correct the error if the difference of the trial balance (due to this mistake) had been transferred to the Suspense Account.

Depreciation Account Dr. ₹ 900

To Suspense Account ₹ 900

(Being depreciation of ₹ 1,000 wrongly posted to Depreciation Account as ₹100, now corrected)

Similarly, an error of casting arising due to wrong totalling of a subsidiary book can be corrected. As we know, total of a subsidiary book is posted to one impersonal account, so it affects only one account. For example, overcasting of Sales Book for the month of March by ₹ 100 will give more credit to Sales Account, so it will be corrected by giving a debit of ₹ 100 to Sales Account to cancel the excess credit of ₹ 100. If the error is discovered after the agreement of the trial balance, the rectification will be done as follows :

Sales Account Dr. ₹ 100

To Suspense Account ₹ 100

(Being rectification of overcasting of Sales Book by ₹ 100)

ILLUSTRATION 2. The Trial Balance of a firm is out by ₹ 2,788 (excess debit). Following errors were found subsequently to have been committed. Pass Journal Entries to correct them and also prepare the Suspense Account :

(*a*) An amount of ₹ 100 was received from D. Dass on 31st December, 2024 but had been entered in the Cash Book on 3rd January, 2025.

(*b*) The Returns Inwards Book for December had been cast ₹ 100 short.

(*c*) A purchase of ₹ 671 had been posted on the debit of the creditor's account as ₹ 617. The creditor is P. & Co.

(*d*) A cheque for ₹ 200 received from P.C. Joshi had been dishonoured on maturity and was passed to the debit of Allowances Account.

(*e*) Goods amounting to ₹ 100 had been returned by customer and were taken into stock, but no entry in respect thereof was made in the books.

(*f*) ₹ 2,000 paid for the purchase of a motor cycle for Mr. Dutt (a partner) had been charged to Miscellaneous Expenses Account.

(*g*) A sale of ₹ 200 to Singhi and Co. was credited to their account.

(*h*) A sale of ₹ 1,000 has been passed through the Purchases Day Book. The customer's account has, however, been correctly debited.

(*i*) On scrutinising the accounts of a defaulting cashier it was discovered that he had received ₹ 1,000 from cash sales and ₹ 6,000 from customers and had paid ₹ 200 for cash purchases and ₹ 820 to a creditor (after deducting ₹ 80 for discount) ; but none of these transactions were recorded in the books of account.

(*j*) Bought goods for ₹ 1,000 for certain employees of the firm but the same was debited to Purchases Account. The employees were paid their salaries after deduction of the aforesaid sum and the net amount paid was posted to the Salaries Account.

SOLUTION **JOURNAL ENTRIES**

			₹	₹
(*a*)	Cash Account Dr. To D. Dass (Being the amount received from D. Dass omitted to be recorded on 31st December, now recorded. The entry passed on 3rd January, 2025 will be reversed)		100	100
(*b*)	Returns Inwards Account Dr. To Suspense Account (Being Returns Inwards Book undercast, now corrected)		100	100
(*c*)	Suspense Account Dr. To. P. & Co. (Being a purchase of ₹ 671 from P. & Co. debited to their account as ₹ 617 instead of being given a credit of ₹ 671, now corrected)		1,288	1,288
(*d*)	P. C. Joshi Dr. To Allowances Account (Being a cheque received from P.C. Joshi dishonoured wrongly debited to Allowances Account instead of P.C. Joshi, now corrected)		200	200
(*e*)	Returns Inwards Account Dr. To Customer's Account (Being entry for returns from customer omitted to be recorded, now recorded)		100	100
(*f*)	Dutt's Drawings Account Dr. To Miscellaneous Expenses Account (Being amount paid for the purchase of motor cycle for Mr. Dutt (a partner) wrongly debited to Miscellaneous Expenses A/c instead of Dutt's Drawings Account, now corrected)		2,000	2,000
(*g*)	Singhi & Co. Dr. To Suspense Account (Being a sale of ₹ 200 to Singhi and Co. credited to their account instead of being debited now corrected)		400	400
(*h*)	Suspense Account Dr. To Purchases Account To Sales Account (Being a sale of ₹ 1,000 wrongly debited to Purchases Account instead of being credited to Sales Account, now corrected)		2,000	1,000 1,000

(i)	Cash Account Dr.		7,000	
	To Customer's Account			6,000
	To Sales Account			1,000
	(Being cash received from debtors and cash sales omitted to be recorded, now corrected)			
	Purchases Account Dr.		200	
	To Cash Account			200
	(Being entry for cash purchases not passed, now passed)			
	Creditor's Account Dr.		900	
	To Cash Account			820
	To Discount Account			80
	(Being cash paid to a creditor and discount allowed by him omitted to be recorded, now recorded)			
	Cashier's Account Dr.		5,980	
	To Cash Account			5,980
	(Being cash defaulted by the cashier)			
(j)	Salaries Account Dr.		1,000	
	To Purchases Account			1,000
	(Being goods bought for certain employees of the firm wrongly debited to Purchases Account and the amount of goods deducted from salaries, now corrected)			

SUSPENSE ACCOUNT

	₹		₹
To P. & Co.	1,288	By Difference in Books as per Trial Balance	2,788
To Purchases Account	1,000	By Returns Inwards Account	100
To Sales Account	1,000	By Singhi & Co.	400
	3,288		3,288

Effect of Errors on the Disagreement of the Trial Balance

All the errors given in the question do not affect the agreement of the Trial Balance because these errors are errors of omission in a subsidiary book or errors of posting to the correct side but in the wrong account or compensating errors or errors of principle. These types of errors do not affect the agreement of the trial balance because figures of debit and credit remain the same by such errors.

ILLUSTRATION 3. The Trial Balance of Mr. Sarvesh Kumar as on 31st March, 2025 did not tally and the difference was posted to Suspense Account. On a scrutiny of the books; the following errors were detected:

(*i*) The total of Sales Returns Book for January 2025 has been casted short by ₹ 1,000.

(*ii*) Freight paid for installation of a Machine ₹ 6,500 was posted to the Freight Account as ₹ 5,600.

(*iii*) Goods of the value of ₹ 2,500 returned by a customer were entered in the Sales day Book and posted therefrom to the credit of his account.

(*iv*) ₹ 18,000 paid for purchase of old Motorcycle for personal use of Mr. Sarvesh Kumar was debited to conveyance account.

(*v*) A purchase of ₹ 6,700 had been posted to creditor's account as ₹ 6,000.

(*vi*) Receipt of cash ₹ 5,000 from Mr. Avinash was posted to the debit of his account.

(*vii*) A cheque for ₹ 2,500 received from Mr. Alok had been dishonoured and was posted to the debit of Mr. Ashok.

(*viii*) Sale of ₹ 8,500 to Mr. Deepak was recorded in the sales book correctly but while posting in ledger credited to his account.

(*ix*) The total of 'Discount Allowed" column in the cash for the month of December 2024 amounting to ₹ 3,800 was not posted.

(*x*) Sale of old office table for ₹ 2,200 treated as sale of goods.

You are required to pass necessary journal entries with narrations to rectify the above errors.

SOLUTION

JOURNAL ENTRIES IN THE BOOKS OF MR. SARVESH KUMAR

S. No.	Particulars		L.F.	Amount Dr. (₹)	Amount Cr. (₹)
(*i*)	Returns Inward/Sales Return A/c	Dr.		1,000	
	To Suspense A/c				1,000
	(Being the mistake in totalling the Returns Inward Book corrected)				
(*ii*)	Machinery A/c	Dr.		6,500	
	To Freight A/c				5,600
	To Suspense A/c				900
	(Being the freight paid for installation of machinery should have been capitalised and not to be charged to Freight Account)				
(*iii*)	Returns Inward/Sales Return A/c	Dr.		2,500	
	Sales A/c	Dr.		2,500	
	To Suspense A/c				5,000
	(Being value of goods returned by a customer wrongly posted to sales and omission of debit to sales returns account, now rectified)				
(*iv*)	Drawings A/c	Dr.		18,000	
	To Conveyance A/c				18,000
	(Being the motorcycle purchased for Mr. Suresh Kumar debited to his Drawings Account instead of Conveyance Account as previously done by mistake)				
(*v*)	Suspense A/c	Dr.		700	
	To Creditors (Personal) A/c				700
	(Being the mistake in crediting the creditors account less by ₹ 700, now corrected)				
(*vi*)	Suspense A/c	Dr.		10,000	
	To Mr. Avinash's A/c				10,000
	(Being cash received for ₹ 5,000 wrongly posted to the debit of his account now corrected)				
(*vii*)	Mr. Alok's A/c	Dr.		2,500	
	To Ashok's A/c				2,500
	(Being the cheque of Mr. Alok dishonoured, previously debited to Mr. Ashok)				

(*viii*)	Deepak A/c Dr. To Suspense A/c (Being the correction of mistake by which the account of Deepak A/c was credited instead of being debited)		17,000	17,000
(*ix*)	Discount A/c Dr. To Suspense A/c (Being the total of discount allowed during December not posted; error now rectified)		3,800	3,800
(*x*)	Sales A/c Dr. To Furniture A/c (Being the rectification of mistake by which sales of furniture was entered in sales book and hence now corrected by debiting the Sales A/c)		2,200	2,200

Effect of Errors on Final Accounts

In order to calculate the effect of errors on final accounts (*i.e.,* Trading and Profit and Loss Account and Balance Sheet), it is essential to know the nature of the accounts in which errors lie. If the error affects the nominal account/accounts, it will increase or decrease the profit because all nominal accounts are transferred to Trading and Profit and Loss Account. In this connection following points may be noted :

1. Profit will increase or loss will reduce if a transaction is omitted to be debited to a nominal account. On rectification of an error of such a type, profit will decrease or loss will increase. For example, depreciation on furniture is omitted to be posted to Depreciation Account. This error will increase profit because depreciation will not be debited to Profit and Loss Account. Depreciation Account will be debited on rectification of this error and as a result, profit will reduce.

2. Similarly, profit will reduce or loss will increase if a nominal account is wrongly debited. With the rectification of such an error, profit will increase or loss will reduce. For example, an amount of ₹ 1,000 spent on erection of machinery wrongly debited to Repairs Account instead of Machinery Account will reduce net profit by ₹ 1,000. On rectification of this error, Machinery Account will be given debit and Repairs Account will be credited and consequently, profit will increase because Repairs Account will be transferred to the credit side of Profit and Loss Account.

3. Profit will increase or loss will decrease if a nominal account is wrongly credited. With the rectification of this type of error, profit will decrease or loss will increase. For example, overcasting of the Sales Book by ₹ 100 will give more credit to Sales Account and consequently profit will increase. On rectification, Sales Account will be debited with ₹ 100 to cancel the excess credit given previously, so profit will reduce by ₹ 100.

4. Profit will decrease or loss will increase if a transaction is omitted to be credited to a nominal account. On rectification, the nominal account omitted to be credited will be credited and Profit will increase or loss will reduce.

Thus, profit is increased or decreased on account of errors in nominal accounts. Balance Sheet will also be affected by the errors in nominal accounts because profit is ultimately transferred to Capital Account which is a part of the Balance Sheet. So, it can be concluded that error in nominal account will affect both Profit and Loss Account and Balance Sheet.

Balances of personal and real accounts form part of a Balance Sheet, so errors in such types of accounts will affect Balance Sheet only and not Profit and Loss Account.

ILLUSTRATION 4. Trial Balance of a trader has, however, agreed, but the following mistakes are discovered after the preparation of final accounts :

(*a*) ₹ 100 discount allowed to a customer had been debited to his account.

(*b*) Purchases Book had been overcast by ₹ 1,000.

(*c*) ₹ 200 received in respect of a book debt had been credited to Sales Account.

(*d*) Machinery of the value of ₹ 5,400 was purchased on credit but journal entry was passed for ₹ 4,500.

(*e*) No adjustment entry was made for an amount of ₹ 2,000 relating to outstanding salary.

Show the effect of the above errors on final accounts.

SOLUTION

Error	*Effect on Trading and Profit and Loss A/c*	*Effect on Balance Sheet*
(*a*)	No effect as the error is in Customer's Account which is a personal Account.	Sundry debtors overstated by ₹ 200 (*i.e.*, double amount) because Customer's Account was debited instead of being credited.
(*b*)	Gross Profit and net profit understated by ₹ 1,000 because purchases with an excess amount of ₹ 1,000 were shown in the Trading Account.	Capital understated by ₹ 1,000 because of under stated net profit.
(*c*)	Gross profit and net profit overstated by ₹ 200 because sales with an excess amount of ₹ 200 were shown in the Trading Account.	Capital overstated by ₹ 200 because of overstated net profit. Debtors overstated by ₹ 200 because of omission of credit to the customer.
(*d*)	No effect because the error does not involve any nominal account. The error relates to a real account (Machinery A/c) and a personal account (Creditor's A/c).	Creditors understated by ₹ 900 (₹ 5,400 – ₹ 4,500) and Machinery also understated by ₹ 900.
(*e*)	Net profit overstated by ₹ 2,000 because outstanding salary was not brought into books.	Capital overstated by ₹ 2,000 because of overstated profit and outstanding creditors understated by ₹ 2,000.

ILLUSTRATION 5. The difference in Trial Balance is kept in Suspense Account. Before preparing the Final Accounts, the following errors were detected :

1. Purchase for ₹ 540 was written in Sales Day Book, but was posted to the correct side of Party's Account.

2. Salary Account Total ₹ 12,600 in one page, was carried over to the next page, as ₹ 1,260, on the wrong side.

3. Interest on overdraft ₹ 650 was not posted to ledger from Cash Book.

4. ₹ 600 collected from a Party, in respect of the old dues from him, which were written off as Bad Debt two years ago, was credited to the Party's Account.

Show Rectification Entries and Suspense Account. State, to what extent the Profit and Loss Account would have been affected, if the above errors would not have been detected and corrected and also the Profit and Loss Account, before rectification.

SOLUTION **JOURNAL ENTRIES**

				₹	₹
(1)	Purchases Account	Dr.		540	
	Sales Account	Dr.		540	
	To Suspense Account				1,080
	(Being purchases of ₹ 540 wrongly entered in sales book but correctly credited to Party's A/c and the difference kept in Suspense Account, now corrected)				
(2)	Salary Account	Dr.		13,860	
	To Suspense Account				13,860
	(Being Salary Account total wrongly carried over to next page, now corrected and difference kept in Suspense Account)				

(3)	Interest on Overdraft Account Dr. To Suspense Account (Being interest on overdraft not posted to ledger A/c from Cash Book, now rectified)		650	650
(4)	Party's Account Dr. To Bad Debts Recovered Account (Being bad debt recovered wrongly credited to party account, now rectified)		600	600

SUSPENSE ACCOUNT

	₹		₹
To Difference in Trial Balance		By Purchases A/c	540
(Balancing figure)	15,590	By Sales A/c	540
		By Salary A/c	13,860
		By Interest on Overdraft	650
	15,590		15,590

PROFIT & LOSS ADJUSTMENT ACCOUNT

	₹		₹
To Purchases	540	By Bad Debt Recovered	600
To Sales	540	By Capital Account	14,990
To Salary	13,860		
To Interest on Overdraft	650		
	15,590		15,590

The effect of rectified entries on current year's Profit & Loss A/c will be that profit will decrease by ₹ 14,990. From this we can conclude that profit of the last year must have been in excess by ₹ 14,990 because of not rectifying the errors.

ILLUSTRATION 6. Hari Krishnan has got his Trial Balance tallied as on 31-3-2025 with a difference of ₹ 41,016. On proper analysis you have found the following errors :

(1) Pass Journal entries; (2) Prepare a rectified Trial Balance.

TRIAL BALANCE

as on 31-3-2025

Particulars	Dr. ₹	Cr. ₹
Capital		10,00,256
Plant and Machinery	2,50,000	
Furniture	26,500	
Car	4,85,000	
Building	6,20,000	
Cash	69,000	
Bank	72,000	
Depreciation	46,500	
Opening Stock	45,800	

Purchases	6,90,000	
Wages	1,90,000	
Manufacturing Expenses	2,06,000	
Salary	1,20,000	
Rent	2,40,000	
Postage and Telephone	89,000	
Electricity	94,000	
General Expenses	12,500	
Sales		10,25,000
Interest		4,500
Fixed Deposits	2,50,000	
Outstanding Expenses		63,500
Sundry Debtors	96,000	
Sundry Creditors		2,00,060
Unsecured Loan		13,50,000
Suspense	41,016	
	36,43,316	36,43,316

Your observations :

(1) Sales return considered as Purchases ₹ 2,693 ; (2) Purchases returns considered as Sales ₹ 4,923 ; (3) Ramu who is a creditor considered as Debtor ₹ 22,500 ; (4) Sales register's total actually was ₹ 10,52,000; (5) Receipts side of the Bank Book for the month of March undercast by ₹ 80,000 ; (6) Salary advance wrongly considered as outstanding expenses ₹ 12,000 ; (7) Discount received not considered in Trial Balance ₹ 984 ; (8) Sundry Debtors undercast by ₹ 10,000.

SOLUTION

In the Books of Mr. Hari Krishnan

JOURNAL ENTRIES

Date	Particulars		LF	Dr. (₹)	Dr. (₹)
31-3-2025	Sales A/c	Dr.		2,693	
	To Purchases Returns A/c				2,693
	(Being purchases returns considered as sales now rectified)				
31-3-2025	Sales A/c	Dr.		4,923	
	To Purchases Returns A/c				4,923
	(Being purchases returns considered as sales now rectified)				
31-3-2025	Suspense A/c	Dr.		45,000	
	To Sundry Creditors A/c				22,500
	To Sundry Debtors A/c				22,500
	(Being creditor considered as debtor now rectified)				
31-3-2025	Suspense A/c	Dr.		27,000	
	To Sales A/c				27,000
	(Being sales undercast now adjusted)				
31-3-2025	Bank A/c	Dr.		80,000	
	To Suspense A/c				80,000
	(Being Bank book undercast now rectified)				

Date	Particulars		L.F.	Dr.	Cr.
31-3-2025	Salary Advanced A/c	Dr.		12,000	
	Outstanding Expenses A/c	Dr.		12,000	
	To Suspense A/c				24,000
	(Being salary advance considered as outstanding expenses now rectified)				
31-3-2025	Suspense A/c	Dr.		984	
	To Discount A/c				984
	(Being discount not shown now adjusted)				
31-3-2025	Sundry Debtors A/c	Dr.		10,000	
	To Suspense A/c				10,000
	(Being debtors undercast now adjusted)				

TRIAL BALANCE

as on 31-3-2025 (Rectified)

Particulars	Dr. ₹	Cr. ₹
Capital		10,00,256
Plant and Machinery	2,50,000	
Furniture	26,500	
Car	4,85,000	
Building	6,20,000	
Cash	69,000	
Bank	1,52,000	
Depreciation	46,500	
Opening Stock	45,800	
Purchases	6,87,307	
Sales Return	2,693	
Wages	1,90,000	
Manufacturing Expenses	2,06,000	
Salary	1,20,000	
Rent	2,40,000	
Postage and Telephone	89,000	
Electricity	94,000	
General Expenses	12,500	
Sales		10,47,077
Purchases Return		4,923
Interest		4,500
Fixed Deposit	2,50,000	
Outstanding Expenses		51,500
Salary Advance	12,000	
Sundry Debtors	83,500	
Sundry Creditors		2,22,560
Unsecured Loan		13,50,000
Discount		984
	36,81,800	36,81,800

Rectification of Errors After Preparation of Final Accounts

Every businessman wants to ascertain correct profit or loss of every year, so it becomes necessary for him to rectify the errors of the last year in such a way that profit or loss of the current year is not affected by the rectification of errors of the last year. For example, ₹ 1,000 paid to the landlord as rent was wrongly debited to Landlord Account in 2024. In 2025, the rectification of this error will give debit to Rent Account and credit to Landlord Account and as a result, the amount of rent will increase in 2025 by ₹ 1,000 and net profit of 2025 will decrease by ₹ 1,000. To see that profit or loss of the current year is not affected, a Profit and Loss Adjustment Account is opened and all nominal accounts affected by the rectification of errors of the last year are not debited or credited but Profit and Loss Adjustment is given debit or credit in place of nominal accounts. After the rectification of all errors of the last year, the balance of Profit and Loss Adjustment Account is transferred to Capital Account being the net profit or loss due to rectification of errors of the last year.

ILLUSTRATION 7. Following errors were committed by the accountant of Geeta Dye-Chem :

(*a*) Cash ₹ 350 paid to Triman Chemicals posted as ₹ 530.

(*b*) Purchase of Stationery worth ₹ 150 remained unposted from the Cash Book.

(*c*) ₹ 260 paid for purchase of new office furniture charged to office expenses account (Ignore depreciation).

(*d*) Credit sales to Trivedi & Co., of ₹ 400 was posted to the credit of their account.

(*e*) Purchase of ₹ 420 from Mantri & Co. was passed through the Sales Day Book as ₹ 240.

How would you rectify the errors assuming that ?

(*i*) They were detected before preparing trial balance.

(*ii*) They were detected after preparing trial balance, but before preparing final accounts (the difference being taken to suspense account).

(*iii*) They were detected after preparing final accounts.

(Narrations to Journal Entries not required)

SOLUTION

(*i*) *When errors are detected before preparing trial balance.*

(*a*) Journal entry is not required to rectify this error because error is only in one account *i.e.* Triman Chemical's Account. Triman Chemical's Account should be credited by ₹ 180 to correct the excess debit given previously.

(*b*) Journal entry is not required to rectify this error because error is only one account *i.e.* Stationery Account. Stationery Account should be debited by ₹ 150 to correct the effect of not posting from the Cash Book.

		₹	₹
(*c*) Office Furniture Account	Dr.	260	
To Office Expenses Account			260

(*d*) No entry is required to rectify this error because the error is only in Trivedi & Co's Account. This account has been credited with ₹ 400 instead of being debited. So, now this account should be debited with ₹ 800 (*i.e.* double amount) to correct the error.

(*e*) Purchases Account	Dr.	420	
Sales Account	Dr.	240	
To Mantri & Co.			660

(*ii*) *When errors are rectified after preparing the trial balance but before preparing final accounts.*

JOURNAL ENTRIES

				₹	₹
(*a*)	Suspense Account	Dr.		180	
	To Triman Chemicals				180

(*b*)	Stationery Account Dr.		150	
	To Suspense Account			150
(*c*)	Office Furniture Account Dr.		260	
	To Office Expenses Account			260
(*d*)	Trivedi & Co. Dr.		800	
	To Suspense Account			800
(*e*)	Purchases Account Dr.		420	
	Sales Account Dr.		240	
	To Mantri & Co.			660

(*iii*) *When errors are rectified after preparing final accounts.*

JOURNAL ENTRIES

			₹	₹
(*a*)	Suspense Account Dr.		180	
	To Trimam Chemicals			180
(*b*)	Profit and Loss Adjustment Account Dr.		150	
	To Suspense Account			150
(*c*)	Office Furniture Account Dr.		260	
	To Profit and Loss Adjustment Account			260
(*d*)	Trivedi & Co. Dr.		800	
	To Suspense Account			800
(*e*)	Profit and Loss Adjustment Account Dr.		660	
	To Mantri & Co.			660
	Capital Account Dr.		550	
	To Profit and Loss Adjustment Account			550

Note: Profit and Loss Adjustment Account has been given debit or credit in place of nominal accounts because errors have been discovered after the preparation of final accounts. The last entry relates to balance of Profit and Loss Adjustment Account transferred to Capital Account being loss due to rectification of all errors.

ILLUSTRATION 8. On preparing a Trial Balance on 31st December, 2024 a trader found that the credit balances exceeded debit balances and he transferred this difference to Suspense Account to tally the trial balance. Following errors were subsequently discovered :

(*a*) ₹ 120 owing by a customer had been omitted from the schedule of sundry debtors.

(*b*) The total of the Returns Inwards Book was added ₹ 10 too much.

(*c*) Wages outstanding ₹ 2,500 had not been taken into account.

(*d*) A sale of ₹ 501 had been entered in the Sales Book as ₹ 705 and posted to the credit of the customer.

(*e*) Goods costing ₹ 1,000 were sent to a customer on sale or return basis for ₹ 1,150. These had been recorded in the books as actual sales but no information regarding their acceptance by the customer was received upto 31-12-2024.

(*f*) Unexpired insurance ₹ 250 has not been taken into account while preparing Profit and Loss Account for the year 2024.

(*g*) On 20th December, 2024 a sum of ₹ 5,000 spent on extension of building had been wrongly debited to Repairs to Building Account.

(*h*) Cash ₹ 10,000 paid to N. Roy was credited to the account of M. Roy.

You are required to give journal entries to rectify the errors in a way so as to show the current year's profit or loss correctly.

SOLUTION JOURNAL ENTRIES

	Particulars		L.F.	₹	₹
(a)	Sundry Debtors	Dr.		120	
	To Suspense Account				120
	(Being the omission of a balance of a customer from the schedule of a sundry debtors, now added. It is a trial balance error, so it does not affect an account)				
(b)	Suspense Account	Dr.		10	
	To Profit and Loss Adjustment Account				10
	(Being overcasting of the Returns Inwards Book, now rectified. Last year profit was decreased by ₹ 10 because of the excess returns inwards, so Profit and Loss Adjustment Account has been credited)				
(c)	Profit and Loss Adjustment Account	Dr.		2,500	
	To Outstanding Wages Account				2,500
	(Being outstanding wages not recorded, now recorded. Last year profit was overstated by ₹ 2,500 because of not recording of outstanding wages, so Profit and Loss Adjustment Account has been given debit)				
(d)	Profit and Loss Adjustment Account	Dr.		204	
	Customer's Account	Dr.		1,206	
	To Suspense Account				1,410
	(Being a sale of ₹ 501 wrongly entered in the Sales Book as ₹ 705 and posted to the credit of the customer now corrected. Last year profit was increased by ₹ 204 because of excess sale of ₹ 204 (₹ 705 – ₹ 501), so Profit and Loss Adjustment Account has been debited with ₹ 204. Customer's Account has been debited with ₹ 1,206 (₹ 705 + ₹ 501) because Customer's Account was credited with ₹ 705 instead of being debited with ₹ 501)				
(e)	Stock Account	Dr.		1,000	
	Profit and Loss Adjustment Account	Dr.		150	
	To Customer's Account				1,150
	(Being goods costing ₹ 1,000 sent to a customer on sale or return basis wrongly treated as actual sales for ₹ 1,150, now rectified)				
(f)	Unexpired Insurance Account	Dr.		250	
	To Profit and Loss Adjustment Account				250
	(Being unexpired insurance not recorded, now recorded, Last year profit was understated by ₹ 250 because of the higher amount of insurance, so Profit and Loss Account has been credited)				
(g)	Building Account	Dr.		5,000	
	To Profit and Loss Adjustment Account				5,000
	(Being amount spent on extension of building wrongly debited to Repairs Account, now corrected)				
(h)	M. Roy	Dr.		1,000	
	N. Roy	Dr.		1,000	
	To Suspense Account				2,000
	(Being cash paid to N. Roy wrongly credited to M. Roy instead of being debited to N. Roy, now corrected)				
(i)	Profit and Loss Adjustment Account	Dr.		2,406	
	To Capital Account				2,406
	(Being profit due to rectification of all errors—balance of Profit and Loss Adjustment Account—transferred to Capital Account)				

ILLUSTRATION 9. Mr. Balaji tallies his Trial Balance placing the difference in the Suspense A/c. But he finds the following mistakes and needs your help in correcting Trial Balance. With the data given below you are asked to prepare

(*a*) Profit & Loss Adjustment A/c for the year ended 31-3-2025.
(*b*) Corrected Trial Balance as on 31-3-2025.

(1) Profit before the following correction—₹ 22,950. (2) Purchase of goods from Gayathri recorded as ₹ 5,900 instead of ₹ 9,500. (3) Payment to Padma posted to Priya's A/c—₹ 22,200. (4) Electricity bill of residence posted to Electricity Expenses A/c—₹ 18,000. (5) Cash Balance as on 31-3-2025 recorded as ₹ 90,000 instead of ₹ 9,000. (6) Cash sale ₹ 45,000 not recorded at all. (7) Salary to Pappu debited to his Personal A/c. (8) Depreciation on Car provided at 15% instead of 20%. (9) Credit card expenses of Balaji debited to Interest A/c—₹ 15,000. (10) Loan from Yamini shown as cash sale—₹ 12,500.

TRIAL BALANCE AS ON 31-3-2025

Particulars	*Debit Amount*	*Credit Amount*
	₹	₹
Profit & Loss A/c		22,950
Gayathri	3,600	
Padma		22,200
Priya	22,200	
Cash	90,000	
Pappu	24,000	
Car	42,500	
Suspense		81,000
Capital		56,150
	1,82,300	1,82,300

SOLUTION

In the Books of Balaji

(*a*) PROFIT & LOSS ADJUSTMENT ACCOUNT

for the year ended 31-3-2025

	₹		₹
To Gayathri's A/c (₹ 9,500 – ₹ 5,900)	3,600	By Balance b/d	22,950
To Pappu's A/c	24,000	By Capital A/c (Electricity Bill)	18,000
To Depreciation on Car (2)	2,500	By Cash A/c	45,000
To Loan from Yamini's A/c	12,500	By Capital—Credit Card Expenses	15,000
To Balance c/d to Balance Sheet	58,350		
	1,00,950		1,00,950

(*b*) TRIAL BALANCE

as on 31-3-2025 (after corrections)

	Debit	*Credit*
	₹	₹
Profit & Loss Account	—	58,350
Cash (1)	54,000	—
Loan from Yamini	—	12,500
Car	40,000	
Capital (3)		23,150
	94,000	94,000

Working Notes :

(1) ***Cash Balance as on 31-3-2025***

	₹
Balance as per the Trial Balance	90,000
Less : Suspense (₹ 90,000 – ₹ 9,000)	81,000
	9,000
Add : Cash Sales	45,000
	54,000

(2) ***Difference in Depreciation Charges***

	₹
Car as per Trial Balance	42,500
Value of car before depreciation @ 15% $\left(₹ 42{,}500 \times \frac{100}{85}\right)$	50,000
Depreciation at 20% on ₹ 50,000	10,000
Less : Depreciation at 15% on ₹ 50,000	7,500
Additional depreciation to be charged	2,500

(3) ***Capital Account***

	₹	₹
Balance as per Trial Balance		56,150
Less : Electricity Bill	18,000	
Credit Card Expenses	15,000	
		33,000
		23,150

QUESTIONS

OBJECTIVE TYPE

1. Choose the correct answer :

(*a*) Error of commission arises when :

(*i*) Any transaction is recorded in a fundamentally incorrect manner. (*ii*) Any transaction is incorrectly recorded, either wholly or partially. (*iii*) Any transaction is omitted to be recorded.

(*b*) Error of omission arises when :

(*i*) Any transaction is left to be recorded. (*ii*) Any transaction is recorded in a fundamentally incorrect manner. (*iii*) Any transaction is incorrectly recorded, either wholly or partially.

(*c*) Error of principle arises when :

(*i*) Any transaction is recorded in a fundamentally incorrect manner. (*ii*) Any transaction is left to be recorded either wholly or partially.

(*d*) Errors which affect one account can be :

(*i*) Errors of omission. (*ii*) Errors of principle. (*iii*) Errors of posting.

(*e*) Errors of carry forward from one year to another year affect :

(*i*) Personal Account. (*ii*) Real Account. (*iii*) Nominal Account. (*iv*) Both Personal & Real A/cs.

(*f*) Wages paid for installation of Machinery debited to Wages Account. This is an error of

(*i*) Omission (*ii*) Principle. (*iii*) Commission (*iv*) Duplication.

(*g*) A motorbike is purchased for the owner's son and Firm's Vehicles Account is debited with the amount paid by the firm. It is—

(*i*) An error of principle. (*ii*) An error of omission. (*iii*) An error of commission (*iv*) A compensating error.

(*h*) Error of omission means :
(*i*) That errors are compensating each other. (*ii*) That any entry is totally missed. (*iii*) That there is a wrong entry in the books of accounts. (*iv*) That a transaction is recorded twice.

Ans. **[(*a*) (*ii*), (*b*) (*i*), (*c*) (*i*), (*d*) (*iii*), (*e*) (*iv*), (*f*) (*ii*), (*g*) (*i*), (*h*) (*ii*)]**

2. **Fill in the blanks :**

(*a*) Errors which affect one account can be errors of ....

(*b*) Errors which affect Profit and Loss Account relate to ....Accounts.

(*c*) Errors of carry forward affect.........Accounts.

(*d*) Undercasting of sales book is an error of ......

(*e*) Error of balancing affects ...... account.

(*f*) Error of posting affects ...... account.

Ans. **[(*a*) Posting, (*b*) Nominal, (*c*) Impersonal, (*d*) casting, (*e*) one, (*f*) one]**

3. **Mention whether the following statements are right or wrong :**

(*a*) Repairs to machinery affect Machinery Account.

(*b*) Sales to Vikas ₹ 495 posted to his account as ₹ 459 affect Vikas Account.

(*c*) An amount of ₹ 1,000 spent on erection of machinery is a revenue expenditure.

(*d*) Purchases of ₹ 1,000 from Janta Trading Company omitted to be recorded will affect only Purchases Account.

(*e*) ₹ 200 discount allowed to a customer credited to discount account will reduce profit by ₹ 200.

(*f*) Errors of carry forward affect two accounts.

(*g*) Errors of casting affect personal accounts.

(*h*) Omission of a transaction from a subsidiary book affects two accounts.

(*i*) Sales book was undercast by ₹ 4,000. Rectification of this entry will decrease gross profit by ₹ 4,000.

Ans. **[(*a*) Wrong, (*b*) Right, (*c*) Wrong, (*d*) Wrong, (*e*) Wrong, (*f*) Wrong, (*g*) Wrong, (*h*) Right, (*i*) Wrong]**

SHORT ANSWER TYPE

1. What are the types into which errors can be divided from the point of view of their rectification ?
2. Give a list of three methods of rectification of errors.
3. What do you mean by suspense account ?
4. Write a short note on errors of principles in not more than 100 words.
5. Give four examples of one sided errors.
6. Give two examples of two sided errors and their rectification entries.
7. What is meant by rectification of errors ?

LONG ANSWER TYPE

1. Explain the various methods of rectification of errors by giving suitable examples.
2. What do you mean by the suspense account ? Why is it opened ?
3. How would you rectify the errors of the last year so that current year's profit may not be affected ?
4. What do you understand by "compensation errors" ? Give illustrations.
5. Briefly explain 'Suspense Account' appearing in Trial Balance.

PRACTICAL PROBLEMS

RECTIFICATION THROUGH JOURNAL ENTRIES

1. How will you rectify the following errors discovered before preparation of the Trial Balance?
   (*a*) ₹ 1,000 spent for repairs of buildings has been posted to Building Account.
   (*b*) A sale of ₹ 730 to Mohinder Singh has been entered in the Sales Book as ₹ 370.
   (*c*) Goods worth ₹ 500 purchased from Bankey Lal have been omitted to be recorded in the books.
   (*d*) ₹ 400 paid as salary to a clerk has been debited to his personal account.
   (*e*) ₹ 75 discount allowed by a creditor has been debited to Discount Account.
   (*f*) Bad Debts aggregating ₹ 450 were written off during the year but were not posted; and
   (*g*) The total of "Discount Allowed" column in the Cash Book for the month of September, 2024 amounting to ₹ 250 was not posted.

RECTIFICATION THROUGH SUSPENSE ACCOUNT

2. A book-keeper while balancing his books, found that there was difference in the trial balance. Being required to prepare the final accounts, he placed this difference to a newly opened Suspense Account which was carried forward to the next year when the following errors were discovered :
   (*a*) A dishonoured bill receivable for ₹ 400 returned by the bank had been credited to the Bank Account and debited to Bills Receivable Account.
   (*b*) Sundry items of plant sold for ₹ 500 had been entered in the Sales Book, the total of which had been posted to the Sales Account.
   (*c*) ₹ 100 discount received from a creditor had been duly entered in his account but not posted to Discount Account.
   (*d*) Goods worth ₹ 200 returned by Gawaskar were recorded in the Sales Book and were posted accordingly.
   (*e*) Goods purchased from a merchant for ₹ 545 had been posted to the credit of his account ₹ 454.
   (*f*) An item of ₹ 100 entered in the Sales Returns Book had been posted to the debit of the customer who returned the goods.
   (*g*) An entry of ₹ 145 representing the selling price of goods returned to Gauri Shanker had been made in Returns Outwards Book and posted. The amount should have been ₹ 130—the invoice value of the goods in question.
   (*h*) Goods worth ₹ 250 taken by the proprietor had been omitted to be recorded in the books.
   (*i*) Amount of ₹ 420 received from Hatinder Desai which was written off as bad debt last year has been credited to his account.
   (*j*) On scrutinising the accounts of a defaulting cashier it was discovered that he had received ₹ 2,000 from customers and ₹ 1,000 from cash sales and had paid ₹ 480 to a creditor (after deducting ₹ 20 for discount), but none of these transactions were recorded in the books of account.

   Give Journal Entries to correct the errors. Ascertain the total amount of difference in Trial Balance.

Ans. [Suspense A/c Total ₹ 391]

3. A book-keeper prepared a trial balance on 31st December, 2024 which showed a difference of ₹ 275.The difference was placed to the debit of a Suspense Account. The undermentioned errors were subsequently discovered :
   (*a*) The total of Sales Book page ₹ 6,068 was carried forward as ₹ 6,000.
   (*b*) An item in the Sales Returns Book of ₹ 204 relating to Z was posted to his account as ₹ 294.
   (*c*) A cheque of ₹ 500 entered as cash sale on 31st December was not posted to Sales Account.

(*d*) Depreciation of plant at 10% on ₹ 7,720 has been credited to plant account, there being no corresponding debit.

(*e*) An item of ₹ 9.50 appearing in the debit discount column to the Cash Book representing discount allowed to B had been posted to the debit of C.

Pass Journal entries to rectify the errors and give the Suspense Account.

Ans. [Suspense A/c Total ₹ 862]

4. You are presented with a Trial Balance showing a difference which has been carried to Suspense Account, and the following errors are revealed :

(*a*) ₹ 1,700 paid in cash for a Typewriter was charged to Office Expenses Account.

(*b*) A cash sale of ₹ 5,000 to Black, correctly entered in the Cash Book, was posted to the credit of Black's Account instead of Sales Account.

(*c*) Goods amounting to ₹ 800, returned by Blue, were entered in the Sales Book and posted thereform to the credit of Blue's Account.

(*d*) Bills Receivable from Brown for ₹ 3,000, posted to the credit of Bills Payable Account and credited to Brown's Account.

(*e*) Goods amounting to ₹ 10,000 sold to Red were correctly entered in the Sales Book but posted to Red's Account for ₹ 18,000.

(*f*) Sales Returns Book were overcast by ₹ 100.

Journalise the necessary corrections and prepare the Suspense Account.

Ans. [Suspense Account Total ₹ 8,100; Difference in Trial Balance before Corrections ₹ 500 (Excess Debit)].

5. Assuming a difference in figures to have been entered in a Suspense Account, set out the journal entries required to correct the following mistakes, and show what the amount of the difference was before the errors were discovered :

(*a*) Cash ₹ 184 paid by Brown (a customer) posted as ₹ 180.

(*b*) Sale to Smith ₹ 52 not posted to his account.

(*c*) The account of a creditor, Johnson, over added on the credit side by ₹ 10, the balance extracted being too great by that amount.

(*d*) The balance of Petty Cash in hand ₹ 50 placed on the credit side of the Trial Balance.

(*e*) A debit balance of ₹ 70 in Robinson's account omitted from the Trial Balance.

(*f*) Goods returned by Brown ₹ 35 credited to him, but not recorded in Sales Returns Book.

(*g*) Sales Book overcast by ₹ 100.

(*h*) The Discount column on the debit side of the Cash Book underadded by ₹ 10.

Ans. [Suspense Account showed a debit balance of ₹ 373 before the discovery of errors]

EFFECT OF RECTIFICATION ON PROFIT

6. The book- keeper of a firm having been unable to agree the Trial Balance raised a Suspense Account in which he entered the amount by which he was out of balance. Following errors were discovered:

(*a*) The addition of the analysis column in the tabular Purchases Journal posted to Goods Purchased for Resale Account was found to be ₹150 short, though the addition of the total column was correct.

(*b*) Goods bought from a supplier amounting to ₹ 77 had been posted to the credit of his account as ₹ 770.

(*c*) A dishonoured bill of exchange receivable for ₹ 1,600 returned to the firm's bank had been credited to the Bank Account and debited to Bills Receivable Account. A cheque was received later from the customer for ₹ 1,600 and duly paid.

(*d*) An item of ₹ 80 entered in the Sales Returns Book had been posted to the debit of the customers who returned the goods.

(*e*) Sundry items of plant sold, amounting to ₹ 3,000 had been entered in Sales Day Book, the total of which book had been posted to the credit of Sales Account.

(*f*) An amount of ₹ 800, owing by a customer, had been omitted from the list of Sundry Debtors.

(*g*) Discount amounting to ₹ 30, allowed to a customer, had been duly entered in his account, but not posted to the Discount Account.

(*h*) An amount of ₹ 100, being rates treated as paid in advance in the previous year, had not been brought forward as a balance on the Rates Account.

You are required to : (*i*) Show the Suspense Account as raised by the book-keeper with necessary adjustments. (*ii*) Explain what effect any of the corrections would have on the profit shown in the uncertified account.

Ans. [Suspense A/c Total ₹ 1,773; Profit will reduce by ₹ 3,280]

7. The Trial Balance prepared by a book-keeper showed a difference of ₹ 100.60 which was placed in a newly opened Suspense Account carried forward to the next year when the following errors were detected:

(*a*) Goods purchased for ₹ 9.90 had been posted to the supplier as ₹99.

(*b*) ₹ 7.50 received as discount from a creditor was duly entered in his account but it was omitted to be posted to Discount Account.

(*c*) Sale of furniture for ₹ 140 had been entered in the Sales Book.

(*d*) ₹ 90 due from a customer were omitted to be taken in the Schedule of Sundry Debtors.

(*e*) Goods of the value of ₹ 300 returned by a customer were taken into the stock but no entry was made in the books. and

(*f*) ₹ 35.50 entered in the Sales Returns Book had been posted to the debit of the customer who returned the goods.

Give Journal Entries necessary to rectify the above errors and prepare Suspense Account. Also state the effect of the errors on the last Year's Profit and Loss Account.

Ans. [Suspense Account Total ₹ 179.10; Profit was overstated by ₹ 432.50].

RECTIFICATION OF ERRORS IN NEXT PERIOD

8. Some mistakes were omitted in the books of Careless Brother for the year ended 31st December, 2024 and the final accounts were completed taking the difference in Suspense Account shown in the Balance Sheet.

Following mistakes were detected in March, 2025 on scrutiny of the books of the earlier year :

(1) Sales Day Book was undercast by ₹ 500;

(2) Credit sale of ₹ 450 was debited to party's account as ₹ 540;

(3) Credit purchases of ₹ 215 was wrongly debited to supplier's account as ₹250;

(4) An old furniture having a book value of ₹ 400 was taken over by the furniture supplier at an agreed value of ₹ 300 as part exchange for new furniture of ₹ 500 supplied. The bill for the net amount was passed through Return Inward Day Book;

(5) White-washing and repairing charges of Building amounting to ₹ 320 were charged to Building Account on which depreciation was charged @ $2\frac{1}{2}$ %.

You are required to pass the Journal Entries to rectify the above mistakes and to draw up the Suspense and Profit & Loss Adjustment Accounts.

Ans. [Difference in T.B. (Cr.) ₹ 1,063; ₹ 288 transferred from Profit and Loss A/c to Capital Account; Suspense A/c Total ₹1,063]

9. The books of accounts of A Co.Ltd. for the year ending 31st March, 2025 were closed with a difference in books carried forward. Following errors were detected subsequently;

(*a*) Returns Outward Book was undercast by ₹ 100;

(*b*) ₹ 1,500 being the total of the Discount column on the credit side of the Cash Book was not posted;

(*c*) ₹ 6,000 being the cost of purchase of office furniture was debited to the Purchases Account;

(*d*) A credit Sale of ₹760 wrongly posted as ₹ 670 to the customer's account in the Sales Ledger;

(*e*) The Sales Account was understated by ₹10,000 being the carry-over mistake in the Sales Day Book;

(*f*) Closing Stock was overstated by ₹10,000 being casting error in the schedule of inventory.

Pass Rectification entries in the next year. Prepare Suspense Account and state effect of the errors on determination of net profit of last year.

Ans. [Difference in T.B. (Cr.) ₹ 11,510,Total of Suspense A/c ₹ 11,600; ₹ 7,600 transferred from Profit and Loss A/c to Capital A/c]

10. The Book-keeper of a trading concern, having failed to agree the Trial Balance opened a Suspense Account and entered the difference in the Trial Balance therein. Following errors were then subsequently discovered :

(*a*) A cheque for ₹ 75 received from Jones and Co. having been dishonoured was wrongly debited to Allowances Account.

(*b*) The discount column of the Cash Book representing discount allowed to customers for the month of December was over added by ₹ 30.

(*c*) The total of the Purchases Book for December was undercast by ₹100.

(*d*) An item of ₹ 50 representing Returns Inwards from P. Basin & Co., was omitted to be credited to their account from the Returns Inwards Book.

(*e*) The credit side of R. Roy's Account in the Ledger had been overcast by ₹ 10.

(*f*) A sale of old furniture amounting to ₹ 75 had been credited to Sales Account.

(*g*) A Bill Receivable accepted by S. Sampat & Co. for ₹ 200 which had been sent to the bankers for collection, having been dishonoured and returned by the bank had been debited to Bill Receivable Account.

You are required to make Journal Entries and ascertain the total amount of difference in the Trial Balance. Show the Suspense Account as opened by the book-keeper and the subsequent adjusting entries made therein. You are further required to explain how the rectification of the above errors would affect the profit already disclosed by the accounts.

Ans. [Suspense A/c Total ₹ 110; Profit already disclosed by the accounts will decrease by ₹ 70]

11. On 30th September, 2024, a manufacturer's Profit and Loss Account showed a credit balance of ₹ 16,720. Next year you find that he has committed certain mistakes :

(*a*) Wages outstanding ₹ 2,100 had not been taken into account.

(*b*) An amount of ₹ 500 taken by the proprietor for his personal use has been debited to Trade Expenses Account.

(*c*) An invoice of ₹ 31,500 in respect of a motor car, debited to Motor Car Account, included the cost of licence of ₹ 100.

(*d*) Goods costing ₹ 1,000 were sent to a customer on sale or return (approval) basis for ₹ 1,200. These had been recorded in the books as actual sales, but no information regarding their acceptance by the customer was received upto 30th September, 2024.

(*e*) Whole of the amount of ₹ 3,000 paid on account of rent of the building for the year ending 31st December had been shown in the Profit and Loss Account.

(*f*) $5\frac{1}{2}\%$ G.P. notes of the face value of ₹ 10,000 purchased through Bhalla & Co. at 99% ex-interest, brokerage ₹ 50. Accrued interest to date of purchase ₹ 275. The total payment of ₹ 10,225 stands debited in the books in the name of broker Bhalla and Co.

Pass the necessary Journal Entries to correct the above errors and omission in such a way that current year's profit or loss is not affected.

12. The trial balance extracted from the books of Ram on 31st December 2024 had not agreed. In 2025, the following errors were discovered :

(i) The total of one page of the Sales Book was carried forward to the next page as ₹ 6,785 instead of ₹ 6,587.

(ii) The total of purchases Book was ₹ 1,000 short.

(iii) A sale of ₹ 350 to Dutta was entered in the Sales Book as ₹ 530.

(iv) Cash received ₹150, from M. Roy was debited to the account of N. Roy.

(v) ₹ 580 spent on repairs to the Delivery Van was debited to Motor Vehicles Account as ₹ 580.

(vi) The total of the discount column in the Cash Book on the debit side was ₹ 385 on one page but was carried forward to the next as ₹ 538.

(vii) Goods returned ₹ 200, by Mirza were not entered in the books at all.

You are required to give Journal Entries to rectify the errors in a way not to affect the profit or loss for 2025.

Ans. [Balance of P & L Adj. A/c transferred to Capital A/c ₹ 2,005]

13. Mr. Mehrotra closes his books on 31st March every year. In August 2025 he found that his books for the year 2024-25 contained some errors inspite of an agreed Trial Balance. The errors were :

(a) ₹ 800 paid for purchase of Office Furniture was posted to the Purchases Account.

(b) The Sales Book was overcast by ₹ 250.

(c) ₹ 275 paid for freight on machinery was debited to Freight Account with ₹ 525.

(d) Closing stock was overstand by ₹ 3,000 by a wrong casting in the Inventory.

(e) An amount of ₹ 700 was received in full settlement from a customer after he was allowed a discount of ₹ 70, but while writing the books, the amount received was entered in the discount column and the discount allowed was entered in the amount column.

(f) A cheque of ₹ 7,330 received from Mr. Rao, after allowing him a discount of ₹ 70 was endorsed to Mr. Ray in full settlement for ₹ 7,500. The cheque was finally dishonoured but no entries for dishonour were passed in the books.

Give Journal entries to rectify the above errors using Suspense Account where necessary in such a way so that current year's profit or loss may not be affected.

Ans. [Current year's profit will decrease by ₹ 1,395 and will be debited to Capital Account].

14. Prosperity Company has produced a Trial Balance as on 31st March, 2025 which does not balance, the difference of ₹ 1,760 being transferred to Suspense Account. An examination of the Company's books discloses the following errors :

(a) The Sales Day Book has been undercast by ₹ 800 and posted to the Debtors Control Account accordingly.

(b) Goods received from XYZ Limited on 31st March, 2025 costing ₹ 9,690 have been included in stock but the invoice has not been received.

(c) Sales account in the General Ledger has been credited with a credit note for ₹ 950 being trade-in allowance given on a company van. This amount had already been taken into account when dealing with the replacement in the motor van account.

(d) An invoice from Joseph & Co. amounting ₹ 4,450 for goods purchased, has been omitted from the Purchases Day Book and posted direct to Purchases A/c in the General Ledger and Joseph & Co. account in the Suppliers' Ledger but has not been included in the Suppliers' Ledger Control A/c in the trial balance.

(e) Discount allowed for the month of March amounting to ₹ 1,740 has not been posted to the General Ledger.

(f) A cheque for ₹ 1,920 received from Jolly Limited, a debtor, has been posted directly to the Sales A/c in the General Ledger.

You are required :

(*i*) to give Journal Entries necessary to correct these errors or if no journal entry is required, state how they will be corrected; and

(*ii*) to prepare a statement showing the effect the corrections would have on the company's profit for the year.

Ans. [(*a*) The profit will be reduced by ₹ 13,500 provided the value of the closing stock as per (*b*) is reduced by ₹ 9,690].

EFFECTS OF RECTIFICATION ON PROFITS AND BALANCE SHEET ITEMS

15. Give Journal Entries to correct the following errors and show clearly what would be effect of such rectifications on the Profit and Loss Account and the Balance Sheet of the firm.

(*i*) There were three compensating errors :

(*a*) Discount received was undercast by ₹ 40;

(*b*) The debit side of Mr. Bali (a customer) was overcast by ₹ 250;

(*c*) A payment of ₹ 290 for legal expenses was not posted from the Cash Book.

(*ii*) ₹ 55 the total of the Returns Inwards Book, was posted to the credit of the Returns Outwards Account.

(*iii*) A sum of ₹ 75 was received from Suraj Prasad, and was duly entered in the Cash Book but was posted to his account as ₹ 57.

(*iv*) A sum of ₹ 1,000 written off as depreciation of building was not posted to Depreciation Account.

(*v*) An item of ₹ 25 having entered in the Returns Inwards Book was debited to the account of customer who had returned the goods.

(*vi*) An item of sale for ₹ 49 was posted in the Sales Account as ₹ 94.

(*vii*) During the year Plant and Machinery was purchased for ₹ 790. It was entered in the Purchases Book.

(*viii*) A debit balance of ₹ 65 on Telephone Account was entered on the wrong side in the Trial Balance.

16. The Trial Balance of a trader has, however, agreed but the following mistakes discovered after the preparation of final accounts :

(*a*) No adjustment entry was passed for an amount of ₹ 1,000 relating to outstanding rent.

(*b*) Furniture of the value of ₹ 3,200 was purchased on credit but journal entry was passed for ₹ 2,300.

(*c*) Purchases Book was overcast by ₹ 100.

(*d*) ₹ 200 discount allowed to a customer had been debited to his account.

(*e*) ₹ 500 received in respect of a book debt had been credited to Sales Account.

(*f*) ₹ 2,000 depreciation of machinery had been omitted to be recorded in the books.

(*g*) ₹ 300 paid for purchases of stationery had been debited to Purchases Account.

(*h*) Sales Book was overcast by ₹ 500. Show the effect of the above errors on final account.

Ans. [Gross Profit Overstated by ₹ 600; Net Profit Overstated by ₹ 3900; Capital Overstated by ₹ 3,900. Creditors Understated by ₹ 1,900; Furniture Understated by ₹ 900; Debtors Overstated by ₹ 900; Machinery Overstated by ₹ 2,000]

CHAPTER 7

Bills of Exchange and Promissory Notes

Credit is a very powerful instrument to promote sales, so most of the transactions in most businesses are usually conducted on a credit basis. When a purchaser makes the purchases on credit, he undertakes to make the payment of the goods purchased to the seller at a future date. It is possible that the oral promise of making the payment in future may not be fulfilled by the purchaser, so the seller of the goods asks the purchaser to give the undertaking of future payment on a written paper known as a bill of exchange or a promissory note. In case of non-payment by the purchaser in future, the seller can go to the court for the recovery of the amount of goods sold on credit, because the proof of the amount due from the purchaser is in writing in the form of a bill of exchange or a promissory note.

Definition of Bill of Exchange

A bill of exchange has been defined by Section 5 of the Indian Negotiable Instrument Act, 1881 as "an instrument in writing containing an unconditional order signed by the maker, directing a certain person to pay a certain sum of money only to or to the order of a certain person or to the bearer of the instrument."

Essentials of Bill of Exchange

Following are the essentials of a bill of exchange :

1. It should be in writing.
2. It should contain an order by the seller to the purchaser to make the payment in future. A mere request by the seller to the purchaser to make the payment in future does not amount to a bill of exchange.
3. The order contained in the bill should be unconditional. A bill of exchange with a conditional order cannot be made payable.
4. The maker of the bill or the seller is known as "drawer" and the bill must be signed by him, otherwise it will be invalid.
5. The purchaser upon whom the bill is drawn is known as "drawee" and he must be a certain person.
6. Amount ordered to be paid by the drawer in a bill must be certain and it should be in money alone and not in goods, *i.e.,* a bill for ₹ 2,000.
7. The person to whom payment of the bill is to be made is known as "payee" and he must be a certain person or the bearer of the bill.

Specimen of Bill of Exchange

Following is the specimen of a bill of exchange :

₹ 50,800

Stamp

420, Sector 60A
Chandigarh,
August 4, 2025

Two months after date, pay to us or our order, the sum of Rupees fifty thousand and eight hundred only for value received.

For Ravi Bros.
Ravi Bhalla
Partner

To
Hitesh Jain & Co.
E–141 (Phase 1)
Ashok Vihar, Delhi-52

Following are the important points in a bill of exchange which need clarification:

1. **Parties to a Bill of Exchange.** There can be three parties attached to a bill of exchange:
   (*a*) ***The Drawer***. He is the creditor and writes a bill of exchange on the debtor. He puts his signature on the bill of exchange. In the specimen given above, the firm of Ravi Bros. in the drawer.
   (*b*) ***The Drawee or the Acceptor***. He is the debtor and a bill is written on him by the drawer ordering him to make a certain payment after a fixed period.
   (*c*) ***The Payee***. He is the person to whom payment of the bill is to be made on the maturity date. Sometimes, the drawer and the payee can be one party when payment is to be made to the drawer, in which case the number of parties will be reduced to two.

2. **Stamp**. The stamp is affixed on every bill of exchange except bill payable on demand. The value of the stamp affixed varies according to the amount of the bill of exchange.

3. **Amount.** Amount for which bill is drawn is written twice, once in figures and again in words to avoid the possibility of alteration.

4. **Date.** The date of the drawal of the bill must be given on the face of the bill because the period of the bill is to be counted from this date. In the specimen given above, two months will be counted from August 4, 2025. But it is a general practice to give to the drawee three days of grace over and above the period of the bill, so the above cited bill will become payable on October 7, 2025.

5. **Term.** It is the period after which the payment of the bill becomes payable. It should be clearly written on a bill of exchange so that no ambiguity may be left regarding the day on which payment is to be made.

6. **For Value Received.** The last words in the body of the bill of exchange "value received" indicate that the drawer is drawing the bill upon the drawee in consideration of the goods he has sold to the drawee on credit.

Acceptance of the Bill

A bill drawn by the drawer must be accepted by the drawee to make it a legal document. Acceptance of the bill will be a proof of the willingness of the drawee that he agrees with the terms and conditions of the bill. Acceptance is given across the face of the bill as follows :

Accepted
For Hitesh Jain & Co.
Hitesh Jain
Partner
Delhi-110052
August 7, 2025

A bill of exchange may be accepted by the drawee by any one of the following two types of acceptances :

(*i*) **General Acceptance**. Acceptance given by the drawee without any further condition is known as general acceptance *i.e.,* the drawee agrees with the full contents of the bill without any change in it. The specimen given above is an example of general acceptance.

(*ii*) **Qualified Acceptance**. Acceptance given with some further condition attached by the drawee is known as qualified acceptance. An acceptance may be qualified as to time, place, amount or parties. A specimen of this type of acceptance may be as follows :

Payable three months
after date of the bill
For Hitesh Jain & Co.
Hitesh Jain
Partner
Delhi-110052
August 7, 2025

The acceptance given above is qualified as to time because the drawee does not agree with the period of 2 months as stated in the bill drawn by the drawer.

Classification of Bills of Exchange

Bills can be divided into two classes given as below :

(*a*) Inland Bills. These bills are drawn in India and upon persons living in India or made payable in India. Both drawer and drawee should reside in India or when the drawee resides in another country he should make the bill payable in India. The specimen of a bill given earlier is a specimen of an inland bill because both the drawer and the drawee are residents of India.

(*b*) Foreign Bills. These bills are drawn outside India but made payable in or drawn upon persons residing in India or drawn in India but made payable in, or drawn upon persons living outside India. A foreign bill is usually drawn in a set of three, each of which is called via. These three different sets are sent by different mails so that at least one may reach its destination. The drawee is to accept and make the payment of only one set. After the acceptance of one set, the other two sets become inoperative. Each set should be numbered and should bear a reference to the other sets, otherwise the set which does not have reference to the other sets shall from a separate bill.

The specimen of a foreign bill of exchange is as follows :

$ 1,000 Englewood Cliiff, U.S.A.
August 5, 2025

Stamp

Ninety days after sight of this first set of bill of exchange (second and third of the same tenor and date unpaid) pay to the State Bank of India or order the sum of one thousand dollars only, value received.

For Van Horne & Co.
Van Horne
Partner

To
Hitesh Jain & Co.
E–211 (Phase 1)
Ashok Vihar, Delhi-52

It is evident from the above specimen that the period of the due date of the foreign bill is to be counted from the date when it is seen and accepted by the drawee whereas in case of an inland bill, it is to be counted from the date given in the bill.

Definition of Promissory Note

A promissory note has been defined by Section 4 of the Indian Negotiable Instruments Act, 1881 as follows :

"An instrument in writing (not being a bank note or a currency note) containing an unconditional undertaking, signed by the maker, to pay a certain sum of money only to, or the order of a certain person, or to the bearer of the instrument."

Essentials of Promissory Note

Following are the essentials of a promissory note :

1. It should be in writing; an oral promise to make the payment will not amount to a legal document.
2. It must contain a promise by the maker of the promissory note to make the payment in future.
3. The promise to pay must be unconditional.
4. It must be signed by the maker of the instrument, *i.e.,* the debtor and he must be a certain person.
5. The amount payable in a promissory note must be certain and it should be in money alone.
6. It should be properly stamped.

Difference Between Bill of Exchange and Promissory Note

Following are the main points of differences :

(*i*) A bill of exchange is an unconditional order to pay whereas a promissory note is an unconditional promise to pay.

(*ii*) A bill of exchange is drawn by the creditor and he makes an order on the debtor to make the payment while a promissory note is written by the debtor wherein he promises to make the payment in future.

(*iii*) A bill of exchange has usually three parties namely, the drawer, the drawee and the payee whereas a promissory note has only two parties, *i.e.,* the maker and the payee.

(*iv*) A bill of exchange is required to be accepted by the drawee (*i.e.,* debtor) if it is to be a legal document, whereas a promissory note needs no acceptance because the debtor himself makes the promise to make the payment.

(*v*) Bills of exchange payable on demand do not require any stamp duty whereas promissory notes payable on demand require *ad valorem* stamp duty.

(*vi*) The liability of the drawer of the bill of exchange is secondary because he is required to make the payment only when the drawee of the bill fails to make the payment. On the other hand, the liability of the maker of the promissory note is primary and absolute because a promissory note is written by him.

(*vii*) Foreign bills are usually drawn in a set of three whereas foreign promissory notes are drawn in one set only.

(*viii*) Foreign bills must be noted and protested on their being dishonoured but foreign promissory notes do not need any noting and protesting on their dishonour.

Advantages of Bills of Exchange and Promissory Notes

Following are some of the advantages of bills of exchange and promissory notes :

1. These are helpful in increasing the size of the business because they facilitate credit transactions.
2. A bill of exchange or a promissory note is a conclusive proof of the indebtedness of the purchaser of goods or services on credit.

3. A bill or a promissory note is a legal document and can be enforced in a court for its payment if its payment is refused by dishonour.
4. A bill or a promissory note fixes date of payment, so it provides a great facility to the creditor to know exactly when to expect payment and the debtor to know when to make the payment.
5. If the creditor cannot wait for the payment till the date of the maturity of the bill or the promissory note, he can get the bill discounted with the bank and get the payment before the maturity of the document.
6. Foreign trade is facilitated with the help of foreign bills of exchange.
7. Usually a bill of exchange is drawn to settle a trade debt but, sometimes, a bill of exchange can be accepted without consideration just to oblige a friend who is temporarily in need of money. Such type of bill is known as an accommodation bill. In accommodation bill businessmen by lending their names on bills can financially help each other without selling or purchasing goods or providing or getting services.
8. A bill or promissory note is a negotiable instrument and can be easily transferred from one person to another person in settlement of debts.

Hundis

The term 'Hundis' stands for all instruments of exchange written in indigenous (vernacular) languages. These are the oldest surviving form of credit instruments in India. The meaning of hundi may be derived from the Sanskrit root 'Hund' which means to collect. It means that the hundis are used as means for collection of debts. A hundi may be defined as "A written order usually unconditional, signed by the creditor, directing the debtor to pay a certain sum of money on demand or after a specified period, to a person named therein." So, a hundi is almost like a bill of exchange. The only difference is that a bill of exchange is always unconditional, but a hundi is sometimes conditional, *e.g.*, jokhami hundi. Following are three important types of hundis :

1. **Darshani Hundi.** The hundi payable at sight or demand is known as darshani hundi.

2. **Muddati Hundi.** This type of hundi is payable after the lapse of some time and not at sight or demand. These hundis serve as security for granting loans.

3. **Jokhami Hundi.** Such type of hundi contains a conditional order, that is, payment of the hundi will be made only if the condition given in the hundi is fulfilled. For example, a hundi drawn against goods shipped on the vessel may provide for the payment of money only when the goods arrive safely.

Accounting Treatment

Though a bill or hundi differs from a promissory note in certain respects, both are treated alike for the purpose of accounting treatment. For the purpose of accounting treatment, bills of exchange and promissory notes can be treated as bills receivable and bills payable.

Bills Receivable. A bill of exchange or a promissory note is treated as a bill receivable if payment is to be received against it on demand or after a lapse of time. So, a bill of exchange is a bill receivable for a drawer because he is to receive payment against it and a promissory note is a bill receivable for a promisee because he has been promised payment against it. A bill receivable is shown as an asset in the Balance Sheet.

Bills Payable. A bill of exchange or a promissory note is a bill payable for a party who has to pay it on the due date. Therefore, a bill of exchange is a bill payable for a drawee (*i.e.* acceptor) because he is to make the payment against it. Similarly, a promissory note is a bill payable for a promiser because he promises to make the payment against it.

Thus, a bill of exchange or a promissory note can be a bill receivable to one party and a bill payable to another party. Bills drawn by us and accepted by others or promissory notes given by others are our bills receivable and bills drawn by others but accepted by us or promissory notes given by us are our bills payable.

The drawer or the promisee receiving a bill receivable can treat it in any of the following four ways :

1. He can keep it in his possession till the maturity date and realise payment against it on the due date.

2. He can get the bill discounted with the bank at any time before its maturity if he is in need of money. The bank deducts interest known as discount from the amount of the bill for the period for which it has to wait to get the payment of the bill on the due date.

3. He may transfer a bill in favour of a creditor in payment of his account. This method of treatment of a bill is known as endorsing over a bill in favour of a creditor.

4. He can send the bill to the bank for collection treating the bank as agent for this work. The bank will give credit to the person sending the bill for collection only when the bill is collected on the due date.

Now, we shall discuss the accounting treatment in the four cases mentioned above one by one.

1. When the Bill is Received and Retained in Own Possession Till Due Date

Entries in Creditor's or Drawer's or Promisee's Books. The drawer records the following entries in his books :

(*i*) When the goods are sold on credit :

Debtor/Customer's A/c	Dr.	(Total Amount)
To Sales A/c		(With Sale Amount)
To Output CGST A/c		(in case of intra-state sale)
To Output SGST A/c		(in case of intra-state sale)
or To Output IGST A/c		(in case of inter-state sale)
(Being goods sold on credit)		

(*ii*) When bill is drawn and duly accepted by the customer

Bills Receivable A/c	Dr.
To Debtor/Customer's A/c	
(Being bill drawn by us & returned as duly accepted)	

(*iii*) When the bill is presented on the due date to the drawee for payment and drawee honours the bill by making the payment :

Cash Account or Bank Account	Dr.
To Bills Receivable Account	
(Being amount of the bill received on the due date)	

It may be noted that when cash is received, it is credited to Bills Receivable Account and not to Customer's Account because cash is received against the bill receivable. The rule 'debit what comes in and credit what goes out' is applied to a bill receivable because it is a real account.

Entries in Debtor's or Acceptor's or Promiser's Books

Following entries are recorded in the acceptor's books :

(*i*) When goods are purchased on credit :

Purchases A/c	Dr.
Input CGST A/c	Dr.
Input SGST A/c	Dr.
Input IGST A/c	Dr.
To Supplier's A/c	
(Being purchase of goods on credit)	

(*ii*) When a bill is accepted :
Supplier's Account Dr.
To Bills Payable Account
(Being bill accepted drawn by the supplier)

(*iii*) When payment of the bill is made on the due date :
Bills Payable Account Dr.
To Cash Account or Bank Account
(Being bill taken back on the due date and payment made)

2. When Bill is Discounted with the Bank

Drawer's Books. When a bill receivable is discounted at a bank, the bill is transferred to the bank and cash is received after deducting discount for the period of the bill which is yet to mature. For example, a bill for ₹ 500 drawn on 1st April, 2025 payable 4 months after date discounted at a bank at 12% p.a. on 1st May, 2025. The bank will deduct ₹ 15 $\left(i.e.\ ₹\ 500 \times \frac{12}{100} \times \frac{3}{12}\right)$ as discount for 3 months from the amount of the bill and will pay the drawer ₹ 485 only. It may be noted that discount has been charged for 3 months and not for 4 months because the bank will have to wait for 3 months to get the payment of the bill on the due date. Following entry will be recorded in the books of the drawer :

Cash or Bank Account	Dr.	485	
Discount Account	Dr.	15	
To Bills Receivable Account			500
(Being bill discounted with the bank @ 12% p.a., discount charged for 3 months)			

The drawer is not to pass any entry when the bill is met on the due date because payment of the bill is to be made to the holder of the bill *i.e.* the bank.

Discounting the Bill with Bank in GST Regime

The holder of the bill may take the amount from the bank before the due date. The bank charges an amount for making the payment against bill which is called *'Discounting Charges'*. These discounting charges are the income for bank for service rendered. The bank charges GST (CGST, SGST) on these discounting charges.

Accounting Entries in the books of Drawer

When bill is discounted and cash is received or credited by bank to his account shall be

Cash or Bank A/c	Dr.	(Net amount after discount charges)
Discounting Charges A/c	Dr.	(Charges by bank)
Input CGST A/c	Dr.	(CGST on discounting charges)
Input SGST A/c	Dr.	(SGST on discounting charges)
To Bills Receivable A/c		(Full amount of bill)

Drawee's Books. Drawee makes no entry relating to discounting of a bill because he is not affected by this transaction in any way. He will make the payment of the bill on the due date to the holder of the bill whosoever he may be. In this case, he will make the payment of the bill to the bank, because bank is the holder on the due date.

ILLUSTRATION 1. (Discounting a bill) Sandeep received an acceptance for bill of ₹ 50,000 on 1st July, 2024 at 3 months from Sudhir. Sandeep got this acceptance discounted @ 10% p.a. at his bank. On the due date, Sudhir paid the amount due. Pass the Journal Entries in the books of Sandeep and Sudhir. The bank charged 6% CGST and 6% SGST on discounting charges.

SOLUTION

JOURNAL OF SANDEEP

Date	Particulars		L.F.	Dr. (₹)	Cr. (₹)
2024					
July 1	Bills Receivable A/c	Dr.		50,000	
	To Sudhir A/c				50,000
	(Being the acceptance received from Sudhir)				
July 1	Bank A/c	Dr.		48,600	
	Discounting Charges	Dr.		1,250	
	(₹ 50,000 × 10/100 × 3/12)				
	Input CGST A/c	Dr.		75	
	Input SGST A/c	Dr.		75	
	To Bills receivable A/c				50,000
	(Being the bills discounted with the bank @ 10% p.a.)				

In the Books of Sudhir
JOURNAL

Date	Particulars		L.F.	Dr. (₹)	Cr. (₹)
2024					
July 1	Sandeep A/c	Dr.		50,000	
	To Bills Payable				50,000
	(Being the amount of acceptance given to Sandeep)				
Oct 4	Bills Payable	Dr.		50,000	
	To Bank A/c				50,000
	(Being the payment of the bill on due date)				

3. Endorsing Over a Bill in Favour of a Creditor

Drawer's Books. When the bill is endorsed by the drawer in favour of a creditor as a consideration of the debit he owes to him, the following Journal Entry is passed :

Creditor's Account Dr.
To Bills Receivable Account
(Being payment of the creditor made by endorsement of the bill)

Drawee's Books. Drawee does not make any entry relating to endorsement of the bill because he is not affected by this transaction. He will make the payment of the bill on the due date to the holder *i.e.* creditor in this case.

Endorsee's Books. Following entries will be recorded in the books of the endorsee :

(*i*) On receipt of a bill from the endorser :
Bills Receivable Account Dr.
To Endorser's Account
(Being bill received)

(*ii*) When the bill is met on the due date :
Cash or Bank Account Dr.
To Bills Receivable Account
(Being amount of the bill received on the due date)

4. Bills Sent to the Bank for Collection

When a firm receives several bills every day, it becomes difficult to trace the due date of different bills and present them for payment to different drawees. So, this job of collection of bills receivable is entrusted to the bank and the bank gives credit to the customer whenever a bill is collected from the drawee. In this connection, the following Journal Entries are recorded :

(*i*) When a bill is sent to the bank for collection :
Bills Sent for Collection Account Dr.
To Bills Receivable Account
(Being bill receivable sent to the bank for collection)

(*ii*) On receipt of information from the bank that the payment against the bills has been received :
Bank Account Dr.
To Bills Sent for Collection Account
(Being collection of bill receivable by the bank)

Drawee's Books. No entry is passed in the drawee's books for bill receivable sent to the bank for collection because drawee is not affected by this transaction. On the due date, the drawee will make the payment of the bill to the bank because the bill is in the possession of the bank.

To Pledge the Bills Receivable

Sometimes drawer may pledge the bill receivable as security against a loan from a third party. In such a case, the drawer will not make any entry for pledging the bill receivable because right of the payment of the bill is not exercisable by the third party who has given a loan. Right of payment of the bill will be exercised by the third party only if the repayment of the loan is not made.

ILLUSTRATION 2. On 1st January, 2025, X sells goods to Y for ₹ 8,000 charging CGST 9% and SGST 9% and draws four bills of exchange on him. The first for ₹ 1,500 for one month, the second for ₹ 1,000 for 2 months, the third for ₹ 2,000 for 3 months and the fourth for ₹ 4,780 for 4 months. Y accepts and returns these bills to X.

The second bill is discounted with the bank at 12% p.a. on 4th January, 2025 and on the same date the third bill is endorsed by X to his creditor Z. The fourth bill is sent to the bank for collection on 10th January, 2025.

Pass Journal Entries in the books of X and Y assuming that all bills are met on their due dates.

SOLUTION **X's JOURNAL**

Date	Particulars		₹	₹
2025				
Jan. 1	Y	Dr.	9,440	
	To Sales Account			8,000
	To CGST A/c			720
	To SGST A/c			720
	(Being goods sold to Y on credit)			
" 1	Bills Receivable Account		9,440	
	To Y			9,440
	(Being four bills for ₹ 1,500, ₹ 1,000, ₹ 2,000 and ₹ 4,940 accepted by Y payable 1 month, 2 months, 3 months and 4 months after date respectively)			
" 4	Bank Account	Dr.	976	
	Discount Account	Dr.	20	
	Input CGST Acoount	Dr.	2	
	Input SGST Acoount	Dr.	2	
	To Bills Receivable Account			1,000
	(Being second bill discounted at bank at 12% p.a. ; discount charged for 2 months)			

Jan. 4	Z	Dr.	2,000	
	To Bills Receivable Account			2,000
	(Being third bill endorsed over to Z)			
" 10	Bills Sent for Collection Account	Dr.	4,940	
	To Bills Receivable Account			4,940
	(Being fourth bill sent to the Bank for collection)			
Feb. 4	Cash Account		1,500	
	To Bills Receivable Account			1,500
	(Being payment of the first bill received on the due date)			
May 4	Bank Account	Dr.	4,780	
	To Bills Sent for Collection Account			4,780
	(Being fourth bill sent to the bank for collection collected)			

Y's JOURNAL

2025			₹	₹
Jan. 1	Purchases A/c	Dr.	8,000	
	CGST A/c	Dr.	720	
	SGST A/c	Dr.	720	
	To X			9,440
	(Being goods purchased on credit)			
Jan. 1	X	Dr.	9,440	
	To Bills Payable Account			9,440
	(Being four bills accepted for ₹ 1,500, ₹ 1,000, ₹ 2,000 and ₹ 4,940 payable 1 month, 2 months, 3 months and 4 months after date respectively)			
Feb. 4	Bills Payable Account	Dr.	1,500	
	To Cash Account			1,500
	(Being payment of the first bill on the due date)			
March 4	Bills Payabie Account	Dr.	1,000	
	To Cash Account			1,000
	(Being payment of the second bill on the due date)			
April 4	Bills Payable Account	Dr.	2,000	
	To Cash Account			2,000
	(Being third bill met on the due date)			
May 4	Bills Payable Account	Dr.	4,780	
	To Cash Account			4,780
	(Being payment of the fourth bill on the due date)			

Dishonour of Bill

Dishonour of a bill means the non-acceptance of the bill or non-payment of the bill by the drawee at the time when the bill is presented for acceptance or for payment. So, a bill can be dishonoured in two ways :

1. When the bill drawn by the drawer is not accepted by the drawee.
2. When the drawee does not make the payment of the bill on the due date when it is presented for payment.

The entry for dishonour of a bill in the books of a drawer will depend as to how he has made the use of that bill previously. When the bill is dishonoured, it may be with any one of the following parties :

(*a*) With the drawer, if the bill is retained by him till the maturity date.
(*b*) With the drawer's bank, if the bill has been discounted with the bank.
(*c*) With a creditor of the drawer, if he has endorsed the bill in favour of his creditor.
(*d*) With the drawer's bank, if the bill has been sent to the bank for collection.

When the bill is dishonoured on presentation for payment, immediate notice of dishonour must be given by the holder of the bill to the drawer as well as to every endorser in order to make him liable for the amount of the bill dishonoured. Moreover, the holder of the bill should get the bill noted with the help of an officer called Notary Public to prove the fact of dishonour by the drawee. The appointment of this officer is made by the Government under Gazette Notification to exercise the functions of noting bills within a particular area. He charges a fee for providing the service of noting a bill and this fee is known as noting charges. The payment of noting charges is made by the holder of the bill who gets the bill noted and can be recovered from the drawer who in turn, recovers it from the acceptor. Thus, loss on account of noting charges is that of the acceptor who has dishonoured the bill. It may be noted that foreign bills are to be noted compulsorily to confirm the fact of dishonour but noting of inland bills is optional.

Accounting Treatment in Case of Dishonour of Bill by Non-acceptance

In Drawer's Books. Bills Receivable Account is given debit and Acceptor's Account is given credit when the bill is drawn on the drawee. When the bill is dishonoured by non-acceptance, it is obvious that reverse entry should be passed to neutralise the effect of the entry passed at the time of drawing a bill. Therefore, following journal entry is passed :

Acceptor's Account Dr.
  To Bills Receivable Account
(Being bill dishonoured by non-acceptance by the drawee)

In Drawee's Books. The drawee has not passed any entry for the bill because he has not accepted the bill. Therefore, no cancellation entry is required for the dishonour of a bill.

Accounting Treatment in Case of Dishonour of Bill by Non-payment

In Drawer's Books

(1) When bill in the possession of a drawer is dishonoured :
  Acceptor's Account Dr.
(with the amount of the bill dishonoured and noting charges, if any)
  To Bills Receivable Account
(with the amount of the bill dishonoured)
  To Cash Account
(with the amount paid as noting charges)

(2) When the bill endorsed in favour of a creditor is dishonoured :
Acceptor's Account Dr.
  To Creditor's Account
(with the amount of the bill dishonoured and noting charges, if any, paid by the creditor)

(3) When the bill discounted with the bank is dishonoured :
Acceptor's Account Dr.
  To Bank Account
(with the amount of the bill dishonoured and noting charges, if any, paid by the bank)

(4) When the bill sent to the bank for collection is dishonoured :

Acceptor's Account Dr.

To Bills sent for Collection Account

(with the amount of the bill dishonoured)

To Bank Account

(with the amount of noting charges paid by the bank)

In all the cases mentioned above, Acceptor's Account has been debited to cancel the credit given to him at the time of the acceptance of the bill. Acceptor's Account has also been debited for noting charges because noting charges are paid on account of his fault of dishonour of the bill.

In Drawee's Books

Bills Payable Account Dr.

(with the amount of the bill dishonoured)

Trade Expenses or Noting Charges Account Dr.

(with the amount of noting charges)

To Drawer's Account

(with the amount of the bill dishonoured and noting charges)

ILLUSTRATION 3. A sold goods to B on 30th October, 2024 for ₹ 14,000 and received three bills for ₹ 2,000, ₹ 4,000 and ₹ 8,000 at 2, 3 and 4 month's duration respectively. He kept the first bill till maturity, endorsed the second bill in favour of his creditor C and discounted the third bill on 3rd December, 2024 at 6% p.a. The first and second bills were duly met on maturity but the third bill was dishonoured ; the bank paying ₹ 40 as noting charges. On 10th April, 2024 B paid ₹ 4,000 and the noting charges in cash and accepted a new bill at 2 months after date for the balance plus ₹ 80 as interest. The new bill was met on maturity. Give Journal Entries in the books of A and B both ignoring GST.

SOLUTION

A's JOURNAL

Date	Particulars		₹	₹
2024				
Oct 30	B	Dr.	14,000	
	To Sales Account			14,000
	(Being goods sold on credit)			
" 30	Bills Receivable Account	Dr.	14,000	
	To B			14,000
	(Being three bills for ₹ 2,000, ₹ 4,000, ₹ 8,000 accepted by B payable 2 months, 3 months and 4 months after date respectively)			
Oct. 30	C	Dr.	4,000	
	To Bills Receivable Account			4,000
	(Being second bill endorsed in favour of C)			
Dec. 3	Bank Account	Dr.	7,880	
	Discount Account	Dr.	120	
	To Bills Receivable Account			8,000
	(Being third bill discounted at 6% p.a. ; discount for 3 months deducted by bank)			
2025				
Jan. 2	Bank Account	Dr.	2,000	
	To Bills Receivable account			2,000
	(Being first bill met on the due date)			

Date	Particulars		Dr. ₹	Cr. ₹
March 3	B To Bank Account (Being third bill dishonoured including noting charges ₹ 40)	Dr.	8,040	8,040
April 10	Cash Account To B (Being cash received from B)	Dr.	4,040	4,040
April 10	B To Interest Account (Being interest charged for the extended period of credit)	Dr.	80	80
" 10	Bills Receivable Account To B (Being acceptance received from B for the balance of the amount due plus ₹ 80 as interest payable after 2 months)	Dr.	4,080	4,080
June 13	Bank Account To Bills Receivable Account (Being bill met on the due date)	Dr.	4,080	4,080

B's JOURNAL

Date	Particulars		₹	₹
2024 Oct 30	Purchases Account To A (Being goods purchased on credit)	Dr.	14,000	14,000
Oct. 30	A To Bills Payable Account (Being three acceptances for ₹ 2,000, ₹ 4,000 and ₹ 8,000 given payable after 2 months, 3 months and 4 months respectively)	Dr.	14,000	14,000
2025 Jan. 2	Bills Payable Account To Bank Account (Being payment of the bill on the due date)	Dr.	2,000	2,000
Feb. 2	Bills Payable Account To Bank Account (Being second bill met on the due date)	Dr.	4,000	4,000
March 3	Bills Payable Account Trade Expenses Account To A (Being third bill dishonoured including noting charges ₹ 40)	Dr. Dr.	8,000 40	8,040
April 10	A To Cash Account (Being cash paid to A)	Dr.	4,040	4040
April 10	Interest Account To A (Being interest payable to A for the extended period of credit)	Dr.	80	80

April 10	A Dr. To Bills Payable Account (Being acceptance given to A for the balance of the amount due plus ₹ 80 as interest payable after 2 months)	4,080	4,080
June 13	Bills Payable Account Dr. To Bank Account (Being bill met on the due date)	4,080	4,080

Renewal of Bill

When the acceptor of the bill is unable to meet the bill on the maturity date, he makes a request to the drawer to cancel the old bill and draw a new bill in its place. If the drawer agrees with the request of the acceptor, the old bill is cancelled and a new bill for the amount of the old bill plus interest for the period of the new bill is drawn on the acceptor. Cancellation of an old bill and drawing a new bill in its place to allow more time to the acceptor for the payment of the bill is known as renewal of a bill. A bill can be renewed in any of the following two ways :

1. The old bill is cancelled and a new bill is drawn in its place for the amount of the old bill plus interest for the period of the new bill.
2. When the acceptor of the bill wants to make a partial payment at the time of renewal of a bill, the old bill is cancelled and a new bill is drawn for the balance of the amount of the old bill plus interest on the balance of the amount of the old bill for the period of the new bill.

Entries in Drawer's Books

1. Acceptor's Account Dr.
   To Bills Receivable Account
   (Being old bill cancelled)

It may be noted that the entry is reverse of the entry which was recorded when the bill was received from the acceptor.

2. Acceptor's Account Dr.
   To Interest Account
   (Being Interest for the extended period of credit allowed by the new bill)

If interest is received in cash, entry is :

Cash Account Dr.
To Interest Account

3. If the acceptor wants to make a partial payment of the old bill, the entry is :
   Cash Account Dr.
   To Acceptor's Account
4. Bills Receivable Account Dr.
   To Acceptor's Account
   (Being a renewed bill received for the amount due as a result of the cancellation of the old bill)

Entries in Drawee's Books

1. Bills Payable Account Dr.
   To Drawer's Account
   (Being cancellation of the old bill)

The above entry is reverse of the entry which was passed when the bill was accepted.

2. Interest Account Dr.
   To Drawer's Account
   (Being interest payable to the drawer for the extended period of credit allowed by him)

If interest is paid in cash, the entry is :

Interest Account Dr.
To Cash Account
(Being interest paid in cash for the extended period of credit)

3. If a partial payment of the old bill is made in cash, the entry is :
Drawer's Account Dr.
To Cash Account

4. Drawer's Account Dr.
To Bills Payable Account
(Being new acceptance given for the amount due as a result of the cancellation of the old bill)

Insolvency

An insolvent is one who is in financial difficulties and is not in a position to pay the amount due by him. If the acceptor of a bill or the maker of a promissory note becomes insolvent, the bill of exchange or the promissory note should be treated as dishonoured because he is unable to make the payment of the bill and entry relating to dishonour should be recorded. It is possible that a partial payment may be made by the estate of the insolvent, the balance of the amount due from the insolvent not recovered should be written off as bad debt in the drawer's books. The amount which the insolvent cannot pay to the drawer should be credited to Unpaid or Deficiency or Profit or Loss Account and debited to Drawer's Account in the insolvent's books.

Retiring Bill under Rebate

Sometimes the acceptor of the bill desires to make its payment before its due date. He will do so if he is given some rebate or discount by the holder of the bill on earlier payment. This rebate is like discount and is calculated at agreed rate for the period between the date of earlier payment and the due date of the bill. Thus, if a bill is paid before its due date and some rebate or discount is allowed by the holder to the acceptor, it is said to be retired under rebate. Following are the accounting entries in connection with retiring a bill under rebate.

Entries in Holder's Books

Cash Account Dr. (with actual amount received)
Rebate or Discount Account Dr. (with amount of rebate)
To Bills Receivable Account (with amount of the bill)
(Being bill retired under rebate, rebate given for the unexpired period of bill debited being loss to the holder)

Entries in Acceptor's Books

Bills Payable Account Dr. (with amount of the bill)
To Cash Account (with actual amount paid)
To Rebate or Discount Account (with rebate earned)
(Being bill retired under rebate, rebate granted for the unexpired period credited being gain to the acceptor).

ILLUSTRATION 4. Journalise the following transactions :

(*a*) Our own acceptance to Basu & Co. for ₹ 500 dishonoured due to omission of necessary instructions to our bank. Basu & Co., claim ₹ 520 including noting charges which we settle by cheque.

(*b*) Patel's promissory note for ₹ 1,000 endorsed in favour of Wadekar was dishonoured. Wadekar paid ₹ 25 as noting charges. We paid Wadekar by cheque and accepted from Patel another bill for the amount due plus interest ₹ 30.

(*c*) Renewed our acceptance to Kaul & Bros. for ₹ 2,000, by cheque ₹ 800 and a new bill at 3 months at 10% p.a. interest.

(*d*) Viney Malhotra's acceptance for ₹ 1,500 renewed for 2 months at 12% p.a. interest.

(*e*) Our acceptance to Himanshu for ₹ 2,500 retired before the date, rebate allowed to us was ₹ 25.

(*f*) Our acceptance to Ajay Verma for ₹ 1,200 was discharged by Arun Thaman's acceptance to us for a similar amount.

(*g*) Roy's acceptance for ₹ 1,400 which we sent to the bank for collection was returned by the bank as being dishonoured. Bank paid ₹ 20 as noting charges.

(*h*) Surjeet renewed a bill for ₹ 1,300 drawn by us by paying us ₹ 500 and accepting a new bill for the balance for 2 months, interest at 12% p.a. being paid in cash forthwith.

SOLUTION **JOURNAL ENTRIES**

			₹	₹
(*a*)	Bills Payable Account	Dr.	500	
	Trade Expenses Account	Dr.	20	
	To Basu & Co.			520
	(Being our acceptance to Basu & Co. dishonoured and noting charges ₹ 20 paid by Basu & Co.)			
	Basu & Co.	Dr.	520	
	To Bank Account			520
	(Being payment made by cheque)			
(*b*)	Patel	Dr.	1,025	
	To Wadekar			1,025
	(Being Patel's promissory note for ₹ 1,000 endorsed in favour of Wadekar dishonoured and noting charges ₹ 25 paid by Wadekar)			
	Wadekar	Dr.	1,025	
	To Bank Account			1,025
	(Being payment made by cheque)			
	Patel	Dr.	30	
	To Interest Account			30
	(Being interest charged for the extended period of credit)			
	Bills Receivable Account	Dr.	1,055	
	To Patel			1,055
	(Being acceptance given by Patel for the amount due ₹ 1,025 plus interest ₹ 30)			
(*c*)	Bills Payable Account	Dr.	2,000	
	To Kaul & Bros.			2,000
	(Being old acceptance to Kaul & Bros. cancelled)			
	Kaul & Bros.	Dr.	800	
	To Bank Account			800
	(Being part payment of the old bill made by cheque)			
	Interest Account	Dr.	30	
	To Kaul & Bros.			30
	(Being interest @ 10% on ₹ 1,200—the balance of the old bill—for 3 months)			

	Particulars		Dr.	Cr.
	Kaul & Bros.	Dr.	1,230	
	To Bills Payable Account			1,230
	(Being new acceptance given for 3 months for the balance of the amount of old bill plus interest ₹ 30)			
(*d*)	Viney Malhotra	Dr.	1,500	
	To Bills Receivable Account			1,500
	(Being Viney Malhotra's acceptance cancelled)			
	Viney Malhotra	Dr.	30	
	To Interest Account			30
	(Being interest charged @ 12% p.a. for 2 months on ₹ 1,500)			
	Bills Receivable Account	Dr.	1,530	
	To Viney Malhotra			1,530
	(Being new acceptance for 2 months received including interest)			
(*e*)	Bills Payable Account	Dr.	2,500	
	To Bank Account			2,475
	To Rebate Account			25
	(Being our acceptance for ₹ 2,500 retired before due date for ₹ 2,475)			
(*f*)	Bills Payable Account	Dr.	1,200	
	To Bills Receivable Account			1,200
	(Being our acceptance to Ajay Verma discharged by endorsing Arun Thaman's acceptance in favour of Ajay Verma)			
(*g*)	Roy	Dr.	1,420	
	To Bills Sent for Collection Account			1,400
	To Bank Account			20
	(Being bills sent to the bank for collection dishonoured and noting charges paid by bank debited to Roy and credited to Bank)			
(*h*)	Surjeet	Dr.	1,300	
	To Bills Receivable Account			1,300
	(Being Surjeet's acceptance cancelled)			
	Cash Account	Dr.	500	
	To Surjeet			500
	(Being part payment of the old bill received)			
	Cash Account	Dr.	16	
	To Interest Account			16
	(Being interest on ₹ 800—balance of the old bill—for 2 months @ 12% p.a.)			
	Bills Receivable Account	Dr.	800	
	To Surjeet			800
	(Being new acceptance for 2 months received from Surjeet)			

Accommodation Bill

Usually a bill of exchange is drawn to settle a trade debt owing to the drawer by the drawee because the last words in the body of a bill of exchange are "for value received." These words represent that the drawer has drawn a bill for the goods or services he has supplied to the drawee. Such types of bills are known as trade bills because these are drawn to settle trade debts. But sometimes a bill of exchange can be accepted without consideration just to oblige a friend who is temporarily in need of money. Such a bill is discounted at the bank and cash is utilised by the friend in need of money (*i.e.*, drawer) for the period of the bill and he (*i.e.*, drawer) will give the amount of the bill on the due date to the acceptor to enable him to meet the bill on the due date. Such a bill is accommodation bill because the object of this bill is to accommodate a certain person with financial assistance for the period of the bill. Thus, an accommodation bill may be defined as "*a bill which is drawn, accepted or endorsed without consideration but simply to oblige and help to raise money by discounting or negotiating it.*" Such bills are also known as "*Kite Bills*". If the drawer fails to provide with funds and the bill is dishonoured the drawer and not the drawee shall be responsible for noting charges.

Distinction Between Trade Bill and Accommodation Bill

Point of Distinction	*Trade Bill*	*Accommodation Bill*
1. Need	It arises from an indebtedness arising from purchase of goods or taking a loan.	It is drawn and accepted only for providing fund to one of the parties or both the parties of the bill
2. Discount	The full amount of discount is borne by the drawer on discounting this bill.	The amount of discount is shared by the drawer and the drawee in an agreed ratio.
3. Purpose	It is drawn to settle a business transaction	It is drawn to meet the financial needs of one or all parties.
4. Consideration	It is accepted for a present consideration.	No consideration is necessary for accepting such bills.
5. Evidence	Trade bill acts as an evidence of indebtedness.	Accommodation bill is not evidence of indebtedness; it only acts as a source of finance.
6. Recovery in case of dishonour	The drawer can file a suit against the drawee as he is liable to pay on dishonour.	No suit can be filed against the drawee.

The entries to be made for an accommodation bill are the same as for a trade bill except the re-imbursement of the accommodating party by the accommodated party on the due date of the bill. These bills can be drawn in three different ways as follows :

(i) When it is drawn for the accommodation of the drawer only

A person in need of money draws a bill on his friend who accepts the bill and returns it to him. After acceptance, the bill is discounted with the bank and the total cash proceeds of the bill are used by the drawer alone for the period of the bill. On the due date of the bill, the drawer remits the amount of the bill to the acceptor who in turn makes repayment to the bank.

(ii) When the bill is drawn for the accommodation of the drawer and the drawee

The drawer draws a bill on another person who accepts it without any consideration. The drawer gets the bill discounted, the cash thus realised is shared by the drawer and the drawee in agreed proportions. They also share the discounting charges of the bill in the same proportions in which they share the cash proceeds of the bill. Before the due date of the bill, the drawer sends his proportion to the drawee to enable him to meet the bill by adding his share of money.

(iii) When two persons draw on each other for equal amounts for their own accommodation

In some cases where two persons are in need of funds, they draw on each other for equal amounts. After acceptance both discount the bills with their bankers and bear the discount charges of their respective bills. Both of them meet their own acceptance on the due date.

ILLUSTRATION 5. For mutual accommodation of themselves, Samaresh and Animesh draw bills on each other. On 2nd January, 2025, Samaresh draws a bill on Animesh for ₹ 2,000 payable after three months and on 3rd Jan., 2025, Animesh draws a bill on Samaresh for ₹ 1,000 payable after three months. As arranged, both the bills are immediately discounted at 5% per annum and the proceeds are shared equally. On maturity of the first bill Animesh becomes insolvent and is unable to honour the bill. A dividend of 50 paise in the rupee is realised from his estate on 30th June, 2025.

Show the relevant Accounts in the books of Samaresh who closes books on 30th June, 2025.

SOLUTION

In the Books of Samaresh

BILLS RECEIVABLE ACCOUNT

2025		₹	2025		₹
Jan. 2	To Animesh	2,000	Jan. 2	By Bank A/c	1,975
			"	By Discount A/c	25
		2,000			2,000

ANIMESH's ACCOUNT

2025		₹	P.	2025		₹	P.
Jan. 2	To Bank A/c	987	50	Jan. 2	By Bills Receivable A/c	2,000	00
" 2	To Discount A/c	12	50	" 3	By Discount A/c	6	25
" 3	To Bill Payable A/c	1,000	00	" 3	By Bank A/c	493	75
April 5	To Bank A/c	2,000	00	June 30	By Bank A/c	750	00
				" 30	By Bad Debts A/c	750	00
		4,000	00			4,000	00

DISCOUNT ACCOUNT

2025		₹	P.	2025		₹	P.
Jan 2	To Bill Receivable A/c	25	00	Jan. 2	By Animesh	12	50
" 3	To Animesh	6	25	June 30	By Profit & Loss A/c	18	75
		31	25			31	25

BANK ACCOUNT

2025		₹	P.	2025		₹	P.
Jan. 2	To Bills Receivable A/c	1,975	00	Jan. 2	By Animesh	987	50
" 3	To Animesh	493	75	April 5	By Animesh	2,000	00
June 30	To Animesh	750	00	" 6	By Bills Payable A/c	1,000	00
" 30	To Balance c/d	768	75				
		3,987	50			3,987	50

BAD DEBTS ACCOUNT

2025		₹	P.	2025		₹	P.
June 30	To Animesh	750	00	June 30	By Profit & Loss A/c	750	00

BILLS PAYABLE ACCOUNT

2025		₹	P	2025		₹	P
April 6	To Bank A/c	1,000	00	Jan. 3	By Animesh A/c	1,000	00

ILLUSTRATION 6. Vikas draws a bill for ₹ 6,000 and Vishal accepts the same for mutual accommodation of both of them to the extent of 2/3 and 1/3. Vikas discounts the same for ₹ 5,640 and remits 1/3 of the proceeds to Vishal. Before the due date, Vishal draws another bill for ₹ 8,400 on Vikas in order to provide funds to meet the first bill. The second bill is discounted for ₹ 8,160 with the help of which the first bill is met and ₹ 1,440 are remitted to Vikas. Before the due date of the second bill Vikas became insolvent and Vishal receives a dividend of 50 paise in the rupee in full satisfaction.

Pass the necessary Journal Entries in the books of Vikas and Vishal and prepare Vikas's Account in Vishal's ledger.

SOLUTION

VIKAS's JOURNAL

			₹	₹
	Bills Receivable Account	Dr.	6,000	
	To Vishal			6,000
	(Being bill accepted by Vishal)			
	Bank Account	Dr.	5,640	
	Discount Account	Dr.	360	
	To Bills Receivable Account			6,000
	(Being bill discounted with the bank)			
	Vishal	Dr.	2,000	
	To Bank Account			1,880
	To Discount Account			120
	(Being 1/3 of the proceeds of the bill remitted to Vishal and 1/3 of the discount charged)			
	Vishal	Dr.	8,400	
	To Bills Payable Account			8,400
	(Being acceptance given)			
	Bank Account	Dr.	1,440	
	Discount Account	Dr.	(1) 160	
	To Vishal			1,600
	(Being the amount received from Vishal on his discounting our acceptance and 2/3 discount debitable to us)			
	Bills Payable Account	Dr.	8,400	
	To Vishal			8,400
	(Being bill dishonoured)			
	Vishal	Dr.	5,600	
	To Bank Account			2,800
	To Unpaid Account			2,800
	(Being the payment of the amount due by paying 50 paise in a rupee in full satisfaction)			

Working Note (1) :

The amount of discount credited to Vishal is calculated as follows :

₹ 4,000	payable to Vishal on account of first bill not remitted to him
₹ 1,440	received from Vishal on discounting the second bill
₹ 5,440	Total Amount due to Vishal is 2/3 of the cash proceeds of the second bill, so Vishal should be credited with 2/3 of the discount of the second bill.

Total amount of discount on second bill (₹ 8,400—₹ 8,160)	₹	240
Therefore, amount of discount credited to Vishal (₹ 240 × 2/3)	₹	160

VISHAL'S JOURNAL

			₹	₹
	Vikas	Dr.	6,000	
	To Bills Payable Account			6,000
	(Being acceptance given)			
	Bank Account	Dr.	1,880	
	Discount Account	Dr.	120	
	To Vikas			2,000
	(Being 1/3 of the proceeds of the bill received from Vikas and 1/3 of the discount charged by him)			
	Bills Receivable Account	Dr.	8,400	
	To Vikas			8,400
	(Being bill accepted by Vikas)			
	Bank Account	Dr.	8,160	
	Discount Account	Dr.	240	
	To Bills Receivable Account			8,400
	(Being bill discounted)			
	Vikas	Dr.	1,600	
	To Bank Account			1,440
	To Discount Account			160
	(Being 1/3 of the proceeds of the bill remitted and 1/3 of the discount charged)			
	Bills Payable Account	Dr.	6,000	
	To Bank Account			6,000
	(Being acceptance met on the due date)			
	Vikas	Dr.	8,400	
	To Bank Account			8,400
	(Being Vikas acceptance's dishonoured on his insolvency)			
	Bank Account	Dr.	2,800	
	Bad Debts Account	Dr.	2,800	
	To Vikas			5,600
	(Being 50 paise in a rupee received and the balance of the amount due written off as bad debts)			

VIKAS'S ACCOUNT

	₹		₹
To Bills Payable Account	6,000	By Bank Account	1,880
To Bank Account	1,440	By Discount Account	120
To Discount Account	160	By Bills Receivable Account	8,400
To Bank Account	8,400	By Bank Account	2,800
		By Bad Debts Account	2,800
	16,000		16,000

ILLUSTRATION 7. A, B and C for mutual accommodation drew the following bills, all for three months :

A drew on B for ₹ 15,000 and on C ₹ 12,000. B drew on A for ₹ 18,000 and on C ₹ 30,000. C drew on A for ₹ 24,000 and on B ₹ 12,000.

All the bills were discounted at 10% p.a. and the proceeds were shared equally. On due date C became bankrupt. Show entries in the books of A assuming that A and B had sent the money due and paid their obligations.

SOLUTION

A's JOURNAL

			₹	₹
	Bills Receivable Account	Dr.	27,000	
	To B			15,000
	To C			12,000
	(Being acceptances given by B and C)			
	B	Dr.	18,000	
	C	Dr.	24,000	
	To Bills Payable Account			42,000
	(Being acceptances given to B and C)			
	B	Dr.	30,000	
	To C			30,000
	(Being entry for bill drawn by B on C)			
	C	Dr.	12,000	
	To B			12,000
	(Being entry for bill drawn by C on B)			
	Bank Account	Dr.	26,325	
	Discount Account	Dr.	675	
	To Bills Receivable Account			27,000
	(Being acceptances from B and C discounted at 10% p.a.)			
	Bank Account	Dr.	(1) 9,750	
	Discount Account	Dr.	(2) 250	
	To B			10,000
	(Being amount received from B to make proceeds and discount equal)			
	C	Dr.	1,000	
	To B			1,000
	(Being amount paid by B to C to make distribution equal)			
	Bills Payable Account	Dr.	42,000	
	To Bank Account			42,000
	(Being payment of A's own acceptances on the due date)			
	C	Dr.	42,000	
	To Bank Account			12,000
	To B			30,000
	(Being C's acceptances dishonoured)			

	B	Dr.	18,500	
	Bad Debts Account	Dr.	18,500	
	To C			37,000
	(Being 1/2 of loss on account of C's insolvency to be borne by B and balance written off as bad debt)			
	B	Dr.	1,500	
	To Bank Account			1,500
	(Being amount due to B paid to settle his account)			

Working Notes :

(1) **ADJUSTMENT FOR CASH**

	Total ₹	*A* ₹	*B* ₹	*C* ₹
Total bills received	1,11,000	27,000	48,000	36,000
Less : Discount @ 10% p.a.	2,775	675	1,200	900
Net proceeds	1,08,225	26,325	46,800	35,100
A ₹ 36,075 / B ₹ 36,075 / C ₹ 36,075 — 1/3 of ₹ 1,08,225				
Adjustment required in Cash to equalise proceeds of each		+ 9,750	– 10,725	+ 975
		36,075	36,075	36,075

(2) **ADJUSTMENT FOR DISCOUNT**

	Total Discount ₹	*A's Share* ₹	*B's Share* ₹	*C's Share* ₹
Each should bear 1/3 of total discount	2,775	925	925	925
Less : Discount already borne		– 675	– 1,200	– 900
		+ 250	– 275	+ 25

B's ACCOUNT

	₹		₹
To Bills Payable Account	18,000	By Bills Receivable Account	15,000
" C	30,000	" C	12,000
" C	18,500	" Bank Account	9,750
" Bank Account	1,500	" Discount Account	250
		" C	1,000
		" C	30,000
	68,000		68,000

C's ACCOUNT

	₹		₹
To Bills Payable Account	24,000	By Bills Receivable Account	12,000
" B	12,000	" B	30,000
" B	1,000	" B	18,500
" Bank Account	12,000	" Bad Debts Account	18,500
" B	30,000		
	79,000		79,000

BILLS RECEIVABLE ACCOUNT

	₹		₹
To B	15,000	By Bank Account	26,325
" C	12,000	" Discount Account	675
	27,000		27,000

BILLS PAYABLE ACCOUNT

	₹		₹
To Bank Account	42,000	By B	18,000
		By C	24,000
	42,000		42,000

QUESTIONS

OBJECTIVE TYPE

1. **Fills in the blanks :**

(*a*) When the bill is dishonoured, ... Account is debited in the books of the drawee.

(*b*) When the bill is dishonoured, ... Account is debited in the books of the drawer.

(*c*) When the endorsed bill is dishonoured, ... Account is credited in the books of the drawer.

(*d*) The drawer always debits......... Account for noting charges paid on dishonour of a bill.

(*e*) When a bill sent for collection is dishonoured, the drawer gives debit to......... Account and credits to......... Account.

(*f*) At the time of renewal of a bill, Interest Account is ....in the books of the drawer.

(*g*) When the drawee becomes insolvent, the bill accepted by him is treated as.........

(*h*) When the bill is met on the due date, ...Account is debited in the books of the drawee.

(*i*) When the bill discounted with the bank is dishonoured, ...Account is debited and ....Account is credited in the books of the drawer.

(*j*) The drawee always debits ....Account and credits ....Account for noting charges paid on dishonour of a bill.

(*k*) A four months bill drawn on 1st January, 2025 will mature for payment on .... 2025.

(*l*) Bills Receivable Account is a .... Account.

(*m*) Sandeep pays ₹ 4,000 to Mandeep on maturity of the bill he had accepted. The amount of ₹ 4,000 will be credited to Cash Account and debited to .... Account.

(*n*) A bill of exchange in drawn by a ....

(*o*) A promissory note is made by a ....

(*p*) A promissory note executed by Mr. X is due on 12-8-2025. The maturity date of the promissory note including grace days will be ....

Ans. **[(*a*) Bills Payable (*b*) Acceptor's (*c*) Creditor's (*d*) Acceptor's (*e*) Acceptor's ; Bills sent for Collection (*f*) Credited (*g*) Dishonoured (*h*) Bills Payable (*i*) Acceptor's ; Bank (*j*) Noting Charges or Trade Expenses, Drawer's (*k*) May 4 (*l*) Real (*m*) Bills Payable (*n*) Creditor (*o*) Debtor (*p*) 14-8-2025].**

2. **State whether the following entries are right or wrong :**

(*a*) Amount of noting charges paid by the drawer is a loss to the drawee.

(*b*) Interest on renewal of a bill is a gain to the drawer and loss to the drawee.

(*c*) A bill discounted with the bank or sent to the bank for collection is treated alike in the books of the drawer.

(*d*) No entry is passed in the books of the drawee when a bill receivable is discounted with the bank.

(*e*) The drawer debits Drawee's Account and credits Noting Charges Account for noting charges paid by the endorsee of the bill.

(*f*) Bill of exchange contains an unconditional order.

(*g*) Promissory note contains an unconditional order.

(*h*) Certificate of protest is issued by a Notary Public.

Ans. [(*a*) Right, (*b*) Right, (*c*) Wrong, (*d*) Right, (*e*) Wrong, (*f*) Right, (*g*) Wrong, (*h*) Right].

3. Choose the correct answer

(*a*) A bill of Exchange is :

(*i*) Drawn on a specific banker

(*ii*) Drawn by seller and accepted by banker

(*iii*) An unconditional undertaking signed by the maker

(*iv*) An unconditional order signed by the maker.

(*b*) A person who draws a bill of exchange is called its—

(*i*) Drawer (*ii*) Drawee

(*iii*) Promisor (*iv*) Endorsee.

(*c*) Noting charges are paid by

(*i*) Acceptor (*ii*) Payee

(*iii*) Drawee (*iv*) None of the above.

(*d*) On 1-4-2024 X drew a bill of ₹ 1,00,000 after sight for 3 months of Y who accepted the bill on 1-5-2024.

On 4-6-2024, the bill was discounted at 12% p.a. At maturity, the bill returned dishonoured, due to Y's insolvency, noting charges ₹ 500 and 40 paisa in a rupee is recovered from Y's estate. The amount of deficiency in Y's books will be :

(*i*) ₹ 60,000 (*ii*) ₹ 40,000

(*iii*) ₹ 60,300 (*iv*) ₹ 40,200.

(*e*) On 21st February 2025, Akash draws a bill of exchange on Bhupesh for ₹ 10,000 payable 30 days after date. Bhupesh immediately accepts the bill. The due date of the bills will be—

(*i*) 24th March, 2025 (*ii*) 22nd March, 2025

(*iii*) 26th March, 2025 (*iv*) 21st March, 2025.

(*g*) Bills Receivable Book is a part of—

(*i*) Journal (*ii*) Ledger

(*iii*) Trial Balance (*iv*) Profit and Loss Account.

Ans. [(*a*) (*iv*); (*b*) (*i*); (*c*) (*iii*); (*d*) (*iii*); (*e*) (*iii*); (*f*) (*i*)]

SHORT ANSWER TYPE

1. Define Bills of Exchange.

2. What are the advantages of a Bills of Exchange ?

3. Define P/N.

4. Explain the following : (*i*) Endorsement of a Bill (*ii*) Discounting a Bill (*iii*) Accommodation Bill (*iv*) Insolvency of a Party (*v*) Trade Bill.

5. Distinguish between Trade Bill and Accommodation Bill.

LONG ANSWER TYPE

1. Differentiate between a Bill of Exchange and a Promissory Note ? What is their importance in the modern business world ?
2. What do you mean by renewal of a bill ? Give the various journal entries which are recorded in the books of the drawer and the drawee on renewal of a bill.
3. Distinguish between : (a) Inland Bill and Foreign Bill. (*b*) Trade Bill and Accommodation Bill.
4. What do you mean by accommodation bills ? Explain the three different ways in which these bills can be drawn.
5. Define a bill of exchange. Give its essentials.
6. Define a holder and a holder in due course.
7. What do you mean by noting and protesting ? When are these needed ?
8. What is the difference between dishonour by non-acceptance and dishonour by non-payment ?
9. Write notes on the following : (*i*) Discounting of a bill. (*ii*) Dishonour of a bill. (*iii*) Retiring of a bill under Rebate. (*iv*) Noting of a bill. (*v*) Renewal of bill.

PRACTICAL PROBLEMS

1. (*i*) A Bill of Exchange for ₹ 600 is drawn by M/s Bhogi Lal and Co. on C. Naraindas and accepted by the latter payable at Central Bank of India. Show the Journal entries in the books of account of M/s Bhogi Lal & Co. under each of the following circumstances:

   (*a*) If they retained the bill till the due date and realised it on maturity.

   (*b*) If they got it discounted with their bankers for ₹ 580. Bank deducted CGST @ 6% and SGST @ 6%.

   (*c*) If they endorsed it over to their creditors M/s Cox & Co. in full settlement of their dues of ₹ 650.

   (*d*) If they sent the bill to the bank for collection.

   (*ii*) Show what further entries are passed in the books of M/s Bhogi Lal & Co. if the bill is dishonoured on the due date.

2. On 1st January, 2025, Julie supplied goods to Vikram of the value of ₹ 9,000 and settled the account by means of three bills of ₹ 3,000 each, due after two, three and four months respectively.

   A week later, Julie discounted the first bill at the discount of ₹ 60. The other two bills were held till maturity. The first two bills were duly met on maturity. On the maturity of the third bill, however, Vikram arranged to retire the bill paying ₹ 1,000 cash and giving Julie a fresh bill for four months to cover the balance together with 12% interest per annum. Julie discounted for ₹ 2,000.

   Pass the necessary Journal Entries in the books of Juile and Vikram.

3. On 15th June 2025, Saxena Bros. owed Kapoor & Co. ₹ 1,500. The latter drew upon the former two bills, one for Rs, 1,000 payable two months after date and the other for ₹ 500 payable three months after date. Kapoor & Co. discounted the first bill at 6% per annum and endorsed the second bill in favour of Sorabji & Co. The first was duly met on maturity but the second was dishonoured and Sorabji & Co. paid ₹ 4.50 as noting charges. On 1st October Sexena Bros. cleared their account by paying ₹ 506, which also included ₹ 1.50 as interest.

   Write up the Bills Receivable Book and Bills Payable Book and give Journal Entries in the books of Kapoor and Co. and Sexana Bros. Also prepare Sexana Bros.'s Account.

4. On 1st May, 2025, Ahmed sold goods to Bawa for ₹ 6,000 and also purchased goods from Charles for ₹ 5,900. On the same date Ahmed drew a bill on Bawa for ₹ 5,800 for 3 months after date in full settlement of the claim. On 5th May, 2025, Bawa accepted the same and returned to Ahmed. On 8th May, 2025, Ahmed endorsed the bill to Charles in full settlement of the amount.

On 11th May, 2025, Charles discounted the bill from his banker for ₹ 5,650. On the due date, the bill was dishonoured, the noting charges incurred by the banker amounting to ₹ 50.

Journalise the above transactions in the books of Ahmed, Bawa and Charles.

5. Draft Journal entries necessary to record the following transactions :

(*a*) Dutt's promissory note for ₹ 900 endorsed in favour of Chatterjee was dishonoured. Chartterjee paid ₹ 15 as noting charges. We paid Chatterjee by cheque and accepted from Dutt another bill for the amount due plus interest ₹ 20.

(*b*) We retired a bill for ₹ 1,500 drawn by Manjeet before due date for ₹ 1,490.

(*c*) Krishna accepted a bill for ₹ 2,000 drawn by us which Krishna discharged by paying up ₹ 700 and accepting a new bill for ₹ 1,320 including interest. We discounted the bill for ₹ 1,290. Subsequently the bill was dishonoured.

(*d*) Goswami retired his acceptance for ₹ 800 by cheque ₹ 300 and a new bill for 2 months, interest at 9% p.a. being paid in cash forthwith.

(*e*) Renewed our acceptance to Sampat for ₹ 1,000 by cheque ₹ 400 and a new bill at 3 months at 4% p.a. interest.

(*f*) Our acceptance to Dharam Paul for ₹ 850 was discharged by Verma Bros.'s acceptance to us for a similar amount.

(*g*) Our own acceptance to Sen & Co., for ₹ 320 dishonoured due to omission of necessary instructions to our bank. Sen & Co., claim ₹ 330 including noting charges which we settle by cheque.

(*h*) Patel's acceptance for ₹ 2,000 which we sent to the bank for collection was returned by the bank as dishonoured. Bank paid ₹ 10 as noting charges.

6. On 1st April, 2025 Surinder and Veerinder draw on one another at 3 months for ₹ 1,200 for their accommodation. On 3rd April, they discount each other's bill at the rate of 12% p.a. On the due date Surinder honours his acceptance but Veerinder's acceptance is dishonoured and Surinder pays ₹ 10 as noting charges. On 4th August, 2025, Veerinder settles his account by paying ₹ 1,222 which includes ₹ 12 as interest. Pass necessary Journal Entries in the books of Surinder and Veerinder.

7. On 1st July 2025, Ramesh sold goods to Suresh priced at ₹ 6,000 subject to a deduction of 16-2/3% trade discount and drew a bill on Suresh for 3 months. Suresh accepted the bill and returned it to Ramesh. Ramesh and Suresh mutually agreed that this bill should be discharged by cash payment of ₹ 2,000 and a new bill on such a date as would enable the latter to earn a rebate of ₹ 100 @ 10% p.a. The new bill would be accepted for 2 months at 10% p.a. interest. The new bill was met on the due date.

Pass Journal Entries in the books of both the parties.

8. For the mutual accommodation of A and B, A draws a bill on B for ₹ 6,000. B accepts the bill and returns it to A. A discounts the same with his bankers and receives ₹ 5,940. The proceeds are shared between A and B in proportion of 2/3 and 1/3 respectively. On the due date A remits B his proportion of money who meets the bill. Pass necessary Journal Entries in the books of A and B to record the above transactions.

9. P draws the following accommodation bills :

(*a*) On Q ₹ 20,000. This is discounted for ₹ 19,600 and half of the proceeds is sent to P. Before maturity P remits his share and the bill is honoured.

(*b*) On R, ₹ 24,000. This is discounted for ₹ 23,400 and one third of the proceeds is sent to R. R fails to pay on maturity and ₹ 60 noting charge is incurred. The bill is met by P. R becomes insolvent and 50 paise dividend in a rupee is realised from his estate.

Show Journal Entries in the Books of P.

Ans. [Bad Debts ₹ 12,030]

10. Jaggi owes to Kamath ₹ 2,400. The debt is discharged by Jaggi on 1st February, 2024 by accepting three bills of exchange drawn on him by Kamath—one for ₹ 600 at 2 months, another for ₹ 800 at 3 months and the third for ₹ 1,000 at 4 months. The first bill is endorsed by Kamath in favour of Dass, his creditor. The second bill is discounted at the bank at 12% p.a. All the three bills were dishonoured. The noting charges in each case were ₹ 5. On 5th June, Jaggi agreed to accept another bill for the total amount including interest at the rate 15% p.a. The bill was for 3 months. On 1st September, Jaggi became insolvent, having his bills unpaid. On 1st October, a first and final dividend of 40 paise in a rupee was received from Jaggi's estate. Give Journal Entries in the books of both Jaggi and Kamath.

Ans. [Bad Debts ₹ 1,504]

11. On 1st July, 2024 Mr. Verma for mutual accommodation of himself and Mr. Sharma drew on the latter a bill of ₹ 5,000 payable 90 days after sight (without grace). On the same date the bill was discounted with the Punjab National Bank @ $7\frac{1}{2}$% and half of the proceeds were remitted to Mr. Sharma on 2-7-2024.

    On 3-7-2024 Mr. Sharma drew a bill on Mr. Verma for ₹ 2,000 payable 90 days after sight (also without grace). He discounted the bill with the Central Bank of India at 10% and remitted half the proceeds to Mr. Verma on the same date.

    Mr. Sharma became bankrupt on 10-9-2024 and only 50% was received by Mr. Verma on 25-9-2024 as the first and final dividend from his estate.

    Pass the necessary Journal Entries and show the account of Mr. Sharma in the books of Mr. Verma.

Ans. [Bad Debts ₹ 1,750]

12. Lalji draws a bill for ₹ 4,500 on Palji on 2nd January 2025 for 3 months. Lalji gets it discounted with the Bank for ₹ 4,410 ; and on 3rd January remits one-third of the amount to Palji, which Palji receives on 5th January. On the due date, Lalji fails to remit the amount due to Palji ; but he accepts a bill for ₹ 6,300 for 3 months which Palji discounts for ₹ 6,165 and remits ₹ 1,110 to Lalji. Before the maturity of the renewed bill Lalji becomes insolvent and only 50% was realised from his estate on July 10. Pass Journal Entries, with full narration, in the books of Lalji.

Ans. [Bad Debts ₹ 2,100]

13. Short owes Slow ₹ 6,000 for which the former accepts a three months bill drawn by the latter. Slow immediately discounts the bill with his banker Strong Bank at 12% p.a. GST rate was 12% on the due date the bill is dishonoured and Strong Bank pays ₹ 20 as noting charges.

    Short pays ₹ 1,180 including interest of ₹ 200 and gives another bill at three months for the balance. Slow endorses the bill to his creditor Slim in full settlement of his debts for ₹ 5,100. Slim discounts the bill from his banker, Strong Bank, who charges ₹ 40 as discount. Before maturity Short becomes bankrupt and a first and final dividend of 20 paise in a rupee is realised from his estate.

    Show Journal Entries in the books of Slim and Strong Bank and the Ledger Account of Short in the books of Slow.

Ans. [₹ 4,032 transferred to Bad Debts]

14. On 1st January, 2024, Pandit, for mutual accommodation of himself and Thakur, drew upon the latter a three months bill for ₹ 12,000, which was duly accepted. Pandit discounted the bill at 6% p.a. on 4th January, 2024 and remitted half the proceeds to Thakur.

    On 1st February, 2024, Thakur drew and Pandit accepted a bill at three months for ₹ 4,800. On 4th February, 2024, Thakur discounted the bill at 6% p.a. and remitted half the proceeds to Pandit.

    At maturity Pandit met his acceptance, but Thakur failed to meet his and Pandit had to take it up. Pandit drew and Thakur accepted a new bill at two months on 4th May, 2024 for the amount due to Pandit plus ₹ 100 as interest. On 1st July, 2024. Thakur became insolvent and a first and final dividend of 50 paise in the rupee was received from his estate on 30th September, 2024.

    Pass necessary Journal Entries in the books of Pandit.

Ans. [Bad Debts ₹ 4,250]

15. P draws a bill of ₹ 10,000 and R accepts the same for mutual accommodation equally. P discounts the same for ₹ 9,900 and remits $\frac{1}{2}$ share to R.

Before due date, R draws a bill on P for ₹ 20,000 and discounts the same for ₹ 19,800. He honours the first bill and remits ₹ 4,900 to P.

Before due date of second bill, P becomes bankrupt, and R receives a final dividend of 50 paise per rupee.

Prepare Ledger Accounts in the books of P and R. Journal entries are not required.

Ans. [Bad Debts ₹ 5,000]

16. On 1st January, 2024 A owes B ₹ 6,000 for which B receives two acceptances from A, one for ₹ 2,000 payable in two months, the other for ₹ 4,000 payable in four months, in each case from 1st January. B duly discounts both these acceptances which his bankers on 3rd January, at 6% per annum. Before the 1st bill became due, A requested B to assist him in taking up by providing him with ₹ 1,000 cash and drawing a third bill on A for that amount at three months from the due date of the 1st bill plus interest at 6% per annum ; B agrees to this proposal and advances the money, discounting the bill with his bankers at 4% per annum. A week before the second bill for ₹ 4,000 falls due, A again asks B to assist him to the extent of ₹ 2,500. A, however is not in a position to do this and he arranges with A to draw on him (B) two bills for ₹ 1,110 and ₹ 1,420 at two months and three months respectively from the due date of the bill of ₹ 4,000. B accepts these two bills and remits them to A, who discounts them with his bankers at 5% per annum and assisted by the proceeds, duly meets the ₹ 4,000 bill. B also meets his two bills on maturity. On 7th June, A becomes bankrupt, leaving his third bill unpaid. On 1st October, 2024, a first and final dividend of 50 paise in the rupee was received from A's estate. Pass Journal Entries and prepare A's A/c in B's Books.

Ans. [Bad Debts ₹ 1,772.50]

17. X, Y and Z for mutual accommodation draw the following bills all for 3 months :
X drew on Y for ₹ 10,000 and on Z for ₹ 15,000.
Y drew on X for ₹ 20,000 and on Z for ₹ 10,000.
Z drew on X for ₹ 10,000 and on Y for ₹ 5,000.

All the bills were discounted at 10% p.a. and the proceeds were shared equally. On the due date Y became bankrupt and later, a dividend of 20 paise in a rupee was received from his estate. Show entries in the books of X assuming that X and Z had sent the money due and paid their obligations.

Ans. [Bad Debts ₹ 9,333]

CHAPTER

8

Capital and Revenue

The proper distinction between capital and revenue as regard to expenditure, payments, profits, receipts and losses, is one of the fundamental principles of correct accounting. It is very essential that in all cases this distinction should be rigidly observed and amounts rightly allocated between capital and revenue. Failure or neglect to discriminate between the two will falsify the whole of the results of accounting. For example, plant may be purchased and charged to the Purchases Account ; additions may be made to the premises and debited to Repairs Account : some of the fixed assets may be sold and the proceeds treated as profits. In each case both the Profit and Loss Account and Balance Sheet would be inaccurate and misleading. These and similar mistakes are very easily made and if undetected would soon render the accounting useless as a record of financial results. **As all revenue items go to the Trading and Profit and Loss Account and all capital items to the Balance Sheet, it is necessary that the proper distinction should be made between capital and revenue while preparing the final accounts of a business at the end of a trading period.**

It is very difficult to give a clear cut rule as to the distinction between the capital and revenue expenditure. However, the following rules may serve as a guide for making distinction between capital and revenue expenditure :

Capital Expenditure

It consists of expenditure the benefit of which is not fully consumed in one period but spread over periods. It includes assets acquired for the purpose of earning and not for resale, improving and extending fixed assets, increasing the earning capacity of the business and raising capital for the business. Purchase of new plant, additions to the building, cost of removing the business to more spacious and better suited premises, brokerage and commission paid for procuring long term loans are few examples of such expenditure. Such expenses are taken to Balance Sheet and are determined by the fact whether :

(*i*) the expenditure made is for the purpose of acquiring fixed assets and in placing the business in a position in which it can commence or continue operation ;

(*ii*) the expenditure results in some more or less long term benefit to the business ;

(*iii*) expenditure increases the earning capacity of the business or reduces working expenses. *Prima facie* it must be established whether the expenditure results in the acquisition of permanent asset and that the asset is to be used for the purpose of earning revenue. Suppose a permanent asset has been acquired for the business and that in addition to the cost of the asset, certain other expenditures were incurred on account of installation and erection etc., and travelling expenses for a trip abroad for the purchase of the asset. The cost of the asset is a capital expenditure, no doubt, but other expenditures are also capital expenditures as these are incurred direct in connection with the acquisition of a permanent asset.

Some Examples

(*i*) Purchase of land, building, plant and machinery, furniture, vehicles and any other fixed asset.

(*ii*) Cost of replacing a petrol driven engine to a diesel driven engine.

(*iii*) Expenditure incurred for increasing the sitting accommodation in a cinema hall or restaurant.

(*iv*) Amount spent on erection of plant and machinery.

(*v*) Expenditure incurred for acquiring some right to carry on business, *e.g.,* copyright, goodwill, trade mark, patent rights etc.

(*vi*) Expenditure incurred for reconditioning an old fixed asset.

(*vii*) Expenditure incurred on major repairs and replacement of plant and machinery or any other fixed asset which results in increased efficiency.

Revenue Expenditure

It consists of expenditure incurred in one period of account, the full benefit of which is consumed in that period. It includes purchasing assets required for resale at a profit or for being made into saleable goods, maintaining fixed assets in good working order, meeting the day-to-day expenses of carrying on business. Cost of goods, raw materials and stores, replacements, renewals, repairs, depreciation of the fixed assets, rent, rates and taxes, wages and salaries, carriage, insurance and other trade expenses are few examples of such expenditures. Such items appear in the Trading and Profit and Loss Account and may be determined from the test as to whether the expenditure made is incurred for the maintenance of the earning capacity or for the upkeep of fixed asset in an efficient condition. For example, the expenditure incurred for the purpose of purchasing goods for resale, in selling those goods and in connection with administering and carrying a business are revenue expenditures.

Distinction Between Capital Expenditure and Revenue Expenditure

Important differences between the two are given as under :

Basis of Distinction	*Capital Expenditure*	*Revenue Expenditure*
1. Acquisition of Assets	It results in acquisition of fixed assets which are meant for use and not for resale. The assets acquired are used for earning profit as long as they can serve the purpose of the business and sold only when they become unfit or obsolete for business.	It does not result in acquisition of any fixed asset. This expenditure is incurred for meeting the day-to-day expenses of carrying on operations of business i.e. acquisition of current assets.
2. Earning Capacity	It results in improving the earning capacity of the fixed assets, *e.g.,* overhauling the machinery for improving the business by increasing the earning capacity of the machinery.	It results in maintenance of business assets such as repairs and maintenance of machinery. It is helpful in maintaining the existing capacity of the asset.
3. Cost	It represents unexpired cost *i.e.,* cost of benefit to be taken in future.	It represents expired cost *i.e.,* benefit of cost has been taken.
4. Expenditure	It is a non-recurring expenditure.	It is a recurring expenditure.
5. Charge	The benefit of such expenditure will be for more than one year. Only a portion of such expenditure known as depreciation is charged to Profit and Loss Account	The benefit of such expenditure expires during the year and the amount is charged to Revenue Account, (*i.e.,* Trading and Profit and Loss Account) of the same year

	and balance amount of such expenditure unless it is written off is shown in the Balance Sheet as an asset.	
6. Shown in Balance Sheet	All items of capital expenditure which are not written off are shown in the Balance Sheet as assets and are carried forward to the next year.	All items of revenue expenditure the benefit of which has exhausted during the year are transferred to Trading and Profit and Loss Account and the accounts representing such items are closed by transferring them to Trading and Profit and Loss. Such items are not carried forward to the next year because their benefit has been taken during the year. Only a portion of the deferred revenue expenditure, (*i.e.,* heavy advertisement) the benefit of which has not yet expired during the year is carried forward to the next year.
7. Matching the Expenses	It is not matched against capital receipts.	It is matched against revenue receipts.
8. Incurrence of Expenditure	It may be incurred before the commencement of the business.	It is incurred only after the commencement of business.

Revenue Expenditure Becoming Capital Expenditure

Following are some of the examples of revenue expenditure becoming capital expenditure :

1. **Repairs.** They are usually a revenue charge, but if we purchase a second hand plant and pay for immediate repairs necessary to make it efficient for our purpose, then such repairs become capital expenditure and must be added to the plant as part of its cost.
2. **Wages.** They are revenue item, but the wages paid to workmen to erect and fit some new machinery, the firm has bought, must be considered as an addition to the cost of the machinery. Similarly wages of workmen employed in the construction of any fixed assets are capital expenditure and must be treated as part of the cost of the asset.
3. **Legal Expenses.**They are a revenue charge, but the legal expenses incurred in connection with the purchase of fixed asset must be treated as a part of the cost of the asset.
4. **Transport Expenses.** They are usually a revenue charge but payment made for transporting any plant and machinery is added on as part of the cost.
5. **Interest on Capital.** Such interest, if paid, during the construction of works or buildings or plant may be capitalised.
6. **Raw Materials and Stores.** They are usually a revenue charge but if consumed in making of a fixed asset, must be treated as a part of the cost of the asset.
7. **Carriage and Freight.** Such expenses in connection with the acquisition of a fixed asset are capital expenditure.
8. **Advertising.** The cost of special advertising undertaken for the purpose of introducing a new line of goods may be treated as capital expenditure as the benefit of such advertising will be available in future also.
9. **Development Expenditure.** Some concerns such as tea and rubber plantations, horticulture, collieries etc. require a very long period of development before they can begin to earn any income. All such expenditure incurred during the period of development is called as development expenditure and must be treated as capital expenditure. For example, in case of tea industry it

takes about 5 years for a tea plant to develop before tea can be manufactured. All expenditure incurred during the period of development of tea plants is capital expenditure. Once the tea plants begin to bear tea leaves, the expenditure incurred to maintain them will be revenue expenditure

10. **Preliminary or Formation Expenses.** All expenses incurred before incorporation of a company are called Preliminary or Formation Expenses and must be written off from the Statement of Profit & Loss of the year in which these are incurred.

Deferred Revenue Expenditure

It is expenditure which would normally be treated as revenue expenditure but it is not written off in one period as its benefit is not completely exhausted in the year in which it is incurred or is of a non-recurring and special nature and is large in amount. It may be spread over a number of years, a proportionate amount being charged to the Profit and Loss Account of each year and the balance is carried forward to subsequent years as deferred revenue expenditure and is shown as an asset in the balance sheet. Suppose for an advertisement campaign a sum of ₹ 20,000 has been spent and the benefit of this campaign does not exhaust in the year, the expenses made should be spread over the estimated years during which the benefit is to be derived. Such expenditures are called deferred revenue expenditures. The determining factor, therefore, is whether the particular revenue expenditure has the element of deriving benefit over some years and that the benefit does not exhaust within the particular accounting year.

The basis of charge should usually be proportionate to the benefit consumed/reaped. The deferred revenue expenditure not yet written off is shown on the assets side of the balance sheet.

Deferred revenue expenditure is revenue in character but :

(*i*) the benefit of which is not exhausted in the same year; or

(*ii*) is applicable either wholly or in part to the future years; or

(*iii*) is accidental and heavy and it is not prudent to charge against the profit of one year.

Deferred revenue expenditure may be classified into the following categories :

(*i*) Expenditure where a portion of the benefit has been derived within the accounting period, the balance yet being unused and therefore, shown in the balance sheet as an asset *e.g.* special advertising expenditure for a new product.

(*ii*) Expenditure in respect of service rendered which for any sound reason is considered as an asset or more properly not considered to be allocable to the accounting period *e.g.* cost of experiments, discount on issue of debentures etc.

(*iii*) Amounts representing loss of an exceptional nature *e.g.* property confiscated in a foreign country, loss on uninsured assets, etc.

Difference Between Revenue Expenditure and Deferred Revenue Expenditure

Revenue Expenditure	*Deferred Revenue Expenditure*
(*a*) Expenses whose benefit expires within the year of expenditure and which are incurred to maintain the earning capacity of existing assets are termed as revenue expenditures.	Expenses whose benefit is extending over a few years say 3 to 5 years are known as deferred revenue expenditures.
Example : wages, salary, carriage of goods, repairs, rent etc.	*Example* : Heavy advertising expenditure to introduce a new product.
(*b*) Revenue expenses are charged entirely in the year in which the expenses are incurred.	Deferred revenue expenses are spread proportionately over the years in which benefit is received.

Capital Profit and Revenue Profit

Capital profit is a profit made on the sale of a fixed asset or a profit earned on getting capital for the business. For example, if the shares having an original cost of ₹ 4,00,000 are sold for ₹ 5,00,000, the profit of ₹ 1,00,000 thus made is capital profit. Similarly, premium received on the issue of shares and debentures is capital profit. Capital profits should not be transferred to the Profit and Loss Account but should be transferred to Capital Reserve which would appear as a liability in the Balance Sheet. **Revenue profit, on the other hand, is a profit made by trading, *e.g.* profit on sale of goods, income from investments, discount received, commission earned, rent received, interest earned etc. Such profits are taken to Profit and Loss Account.**

Capital Receipts and Revenue Receipts

Capital receipts comprise of payments or contributions into the business by the proprietor, partners or other shareholders towards the capital of the firm and any sum received from debentureholders, any loans and the proceeds of sale of any fixed assets of a business enterprise. Whereas revenue receipts are the outcome of a firm's activity in the accounting period, it is a part of rewards for offering goods or services to the public *e.g.* sales, commission, fees received for services, interest on investment, etc. Revenue expenses must be set off against the revenue receipts in order to calculate the profit or loss of the business in an accounting period. Capital receipts and expenses have no bearing on the profit or loss for the accounting period.

Capital receipts in a business comprise capital invested in the business, loans and the proceeds of sale of the assets etc. On the other hand, revenue receipts in a business are cash from sales, discount received, commission, interest on investments, transfer fees etc. Revenue receipts are transferred to Profit and Loss Account while capital receipts affect the Balance Sheet.

Following are the main distinctions between the two :

	Capital Receipt	*Revenue Receipt*
1.	It is the amount realised by sale of fixed assets or by issue of shares or debentures.	It is the amount realised by sale of goods or rendering of services.
2.	It is a receipt in substitution of a source of income.	It is a receipt in substitution of an income.
3.	It is the amount received for surrender of certain rights under an agreement as a capital asset is being given up in the form of these rights.	It is the amount received as compensation under an agreement for the loss of future profits.

Capital Losses And Revenue Losses

Capital losses are those losses which occur at selling fixed assets or raising share capital. For example, if investments having an original cost of ₹ 2,00,000, are sold for ₹ 1,60,000 ; there will be a capital loss of ₹ 40,000. Similarly when the shares of the face value of ₹ 100 are issued for ₹ 90 (*i.e.* at a discount), the amount of discount, *i.e.*, ₹ 10 per share, will be a capital loss. Capital losses should not be debited to Profit and Loss Account but may be shown as an asset in the Balance Sheet. As and when capital profits arise, losses are met against them. If, however, the capital losses are large, they are spread over a few years, a proportionate amount being charged to Profit and Loss Account and the balance being carried forward as an asset to be written off in future years. But if the amount of such losses is negligible they are debited to the Profit and Loss Account of the year in which they occur.

Revenue losses are those losses which arise during the normal course of business, *i.e.*, in trading operations such as losses on the sale of goods. Such losses are debited to Profit and Loss Account.

ILLUSTRATION 1. Do you consider the following to be Capital or Revenue items ?

(*i*) Carriage paid on goods purchased. (*ii*) An amount of ₹ 1,10,000 spent on painting a new factory. (*iii*) Repairs to a motor truck purchased second hand, (*iv*) Expenditure on advertising campaign. (*v*) Freight and carriage on a new machine purchased and its erection charges. (*vi*) A motor car, whose book value is ₹ 80,000 was sold for ₹ 1,00,000. (*vii*) Spent ₹ 1,00,000 as legal expenses in connection with the abuse of trade mark. (*viii*) Received ₹ 2,00,000 from the sale of equity shares of a company and the expenses of issue amounted to 2,500. (*ix*) Got a college building constructed for the students at a cost of ₹ 80,00,000. (*x*) Land purchased for agricultural farms with ₹ 3,00,000 and its annual land revenue was ₹ 18,000. (*xi*) ₹ 4,50,000 paid to the Government as excise duty. (*xii*) Spent ₹ 16,00,000 on the construction of railway sidings. (*xiii*) The cost of registration of a newly formed limited company was ₹ 4,05,000. (*xiv*) ₹ 4,50,000 was paid as compensation to a discharged employee. (*xv*) Legal expenses incurred in raising a debenture loan. (*xvi*) Legal expenditure incurred in defending a suit for breach of contract to supply goods.

SOLUTION

(*i*) The carriage paid on purchases is a *revenue* expenditure because goods purchased are meant for resale.

(*ii*) An amount of ₹ 1,10,000 spent on painting a new factory is a *capital* expenditure and will be added to the cost of factory building as it is for the new factory constructed.

(*iii*) Repairs to a motor truck purchased second hand is a *capital* expenditure as it is incurred to make the motor truck in working position.

(*iv*) Expenditure on advertising campaign is a *revenue* expenditure as it is for the increase of sales. But if the amount is large, it can be treated as a *deferred revenue* expenditure.

(*v*) Freight and carriage paid and erection charges for the purchase of a new machine are *capital* expenditure as they are in connection with the acquisition of a new asset.

(*vi*) A motor car is a fixed asset as it can be used for many years and its utility does not diminish in one year. The profit made on sale of the motor car is a *capital gain* and will not be treated as business profit.

(*vii*) Legal expenses incurred in connection with the abuse of trade mark are of *revenue* expenditure type, as expenses are incurred for the maintenance of a fixed asset.

(*viii*) Received ₹ 2,00,000 from the sale of equity shares of a company is a *capital receipt* and amount spent on the above issue is a *capital expenditure* as it is incurred in securing capital for the business.

(*ix*) This type of expenditure is of *capital* nature as the amount is spent for the welfare of the students and will serve for more than the financial year.

(*x*) Land purchased is a *capital* expenditure but the land revenue paid annually will be *revenue* expenditure.

(*xi*) Expenses incurred in respect of purchase or sale are always *revenue* expenses. This expense is also of *revenue* nature as it is related to sales.

(*xii*) Amount spent on construction of railway sidings is of *capital* nature as the railway sidings will be used for a number of years.

(*xiii*) The registration cost of a company is a *revenue* expenditure of non-recurring and special nature. As the amount is large, it can be treated as *deferred revenue* expenditure and should be spread over a number of years. The balance of such expenditure will be carried forward to subsequent years and will appear in the Balance Sheet as an asset.

(*xiv*) Compensation paid to a discharged employee is a *revenue* expenditure as it is incurred in the ordinary course of a business.

(*xv*) Legal expenses in raising a debenture loan are of *capital* expenditure type as they are incurred for obtaining loan for the business. They would appear as an asset in the Balance Sheet. But as this asset is purely a fictitious one not representing any valuable thing, it is prudent to write it off over a few years.

(*xvi*) Legal expenditure incurred in defending a suit for breach of contract to supply goods is an item of *revenue* expenditure as such expenditure is incurred in the ordinary course of trading.

ILLUSTRATION 2. Raja Ram has removed his works to a more suitable site :

(*i*) A sum of ₹ 5,00,000 was spent on dismantling, removing and reinstalling plant, machinery and fixtures.

(*ii*) The removal of stock from old works to new works costed ₹ 50,000.

(*iii*) Plant and machinery which stood in books at ₹ 7,50,000 included a machine at a book value of ₹ 1,50,000. This being obsolete was sold off for ₹ 50,000 and was replaced by a new machine which costs ₹ 2,40,000.

(*iv*) The fixtures and furniture appeared in the books at ₹ 7,50,000. Of these some portion of the book value of ₹ 1,50,000 was discarded and sold off for ₹ 1,60,000, and new furniture of the value of ₹ 1,20,000 was acquired.

(*v*) A sum of ₹ 4,00,000 was spent on painting the new factory.

State which item of expenditure is chargeable to revenue and which to capital.

SOLUTION

(*i*) ₹ 5,00,000 expended on dismantling, removing and reinstalling plant, machinery and fixtures will have to be treated as *revenue* expenditure, It may be treated as *deferred revenue* expenditure item and spread over a term of years, say for three to five years, and a proportionate amount charged to revenue.

(*ii*) The cost of removal of stock firm the old works to the new works does not either add to the value or the profit earning capacity of the asset and as such it should be treated as an item of *revenue* expenditure and will be dealt within a similar manner as in (*i*) above.

(*iii*) ₹ 1,00,000, the difference between the book value of the machine sold and the amount realised on sale, will have to be charged off to revenue as depreciation. ₹ 2,40,000, the cost of new machine, will have to be capitalised.

(*iv*) ₹ 4,00,000 the difference between the book value of the fixtures and fittings discarded and the amount realised therefrom, will be treated as *capital profit* and, therefore, be credited to Capital Reserve Account. ₹ 1,20,000, the cost of new furniture, will be capitalised.

(*v*) A sum of ₹ 4,00,000 spent on painting a new factory is capital expenditure and will be added to the cost of factory building as it is all to the new factory.

ILLUSTRATION 3. In 2024, Brick Manufacturers Ltd., built a new kiln in their brickyard. The work was carried out with the company's own labour and materials and the expenditure thereon was included in Brickyard. Following is a summary of that account for the years ended 31st December, 2023 and 2024 in the company's books.

	2023		*2024*			*2023*		*2024*	
	Bricks	₹	*Bricks*	₹		*Bricks*	₹	*Bricks*	₹
Stock on 1st Jan.	2,00,000	3,500	1,00,000	1,750	Sales	25,50,000	51,000	20,50,000	43,050
Wages		25,000		42,550	Bricks spoiled	50,000	—	50,000	—
Stores, Fuel etc.		10,000		38,000					
Head Office and Sundry Expenses		4,750		7,300	Bricks used for new kiln	—	—	9,50,000	—
Profit		9,500		—	Stock 31st Dec.	1,00,000	1,750	1,50,000	2,700
					Balance	—	—	—	43,850
		52,750		89,600			52,750		89,600

Examination revealed the following :

(*i*) That no particulars had been kept of wages spent on building the kiln ; men had worked part of their time in digging clay and watering in the kilns, and part on the building of new kiln.

(*ii*) That the wages cost per 1,000 bricks (including bricks spoiled) was higher by 5 per cent, in 2024 than in 2023.

(*iii*) That, in 2024 ₹ 1,500 of the salaries (included in H.O. Expenses), ₹ 25,000 of the stores, fuel etc. and ₹ 2,500 of the head office expenses were attri' utable to the new kiln.

(*iv*) That Employers' Liability Insurance was at a premium of $\frac{1}{2}$% of wages included in Sundry Expenses.

Construct the Brickyard Account for 2024 duly adjusted and show the amounts chargeable to capital expenditure and/or elsewhere in respect of the new kiln.

SOLUTION

BRICKYARD ACCOUNT

	Nos.	Amount ₹		Nos.	Amount ₹
To Wages (1)		32,550	By Bricks spoiled	50,000	—
" Stores, Fuel etc. (₹ 38,000–₹ 25,000)		13,000	" Sales	20,50,000	43,050
To Head Office & Sundry Exp. ₹ (₹ 7,300– ₹ 1,500 – ₹ 2,500– ₹ 50)		3,250	" New kiln @ ₹ 16 per 1,000 (3)	9,50,000	15,200
			By Closing Stock @ ₹ 16 per 1,000 (3)	1,50,000	2,400
Cost of Production	31,00,000	48,800			
To Opening Stock	1,00,000	1,750			
" Profit		10,100			
	32,00,000	60,650		32,00,000	60,650

NEW KILN ACCOUNT

	₹		₹
To Brickyard A/c 9,50,000 bricks @ ₹ 16 per 1,000 bricks	15,200	By Balance c/d	54,250
" Wages (2)	10,000		
" W.M.C. Insurance $\frac{1}{2}$% on ₹ 10,000	50		
" Salaries	1,500		
" Stores etc.	25,000		
" Head Office Expenses	2,500		
	54,250		54,250
To Balance b/d	54,250		

Working Notes :

(1) Production in 2023

	Bricks
Sales	25,50,000
Closing Stock	1,00,000
Spoiled bricks	50,000
	27,00,000
Less Opening Stock	2,00,000
Total Bricks Produced in 2023	25,00,000

Wages cost per 1,000 bricks in 2023 was $\frac{₹\ 25,000}{25,00,000} \times 1,000 = ₹\ 10.$

Wages cost per 1,000 bricks was higher in 2024 than in 2023 by 5%.

So, wages cost per 1,000 in 2024 = ₹ $\frac{10 \times 105}{100} = ₹\ 10.50.$

Production in 2024 :	Bricks
Sales	20,50,000
Closing Stock	1,50,000
Spoiled Bricks	50,000
Used for New Kiln	9,50,000
	32,00,000
Less : Opening Stock	1,00,000
Total Bricks Produced in 2024	31,00,000

Wages for 31,00,000 bricks @ ₹ 10.50 per 1,000 bricks

Or, $\frac{31,00,000}{1,000} \times ₹\ 10.50 = ₹\ 32,550$

	₹
(2) Total Wages for 2024 (as given)	42,550
Less : Wages for Bricks	32,550
Wages for Kiln	10,000
(3) Cost of Production	₹ 48,800
Total bricks *less* spoiled	30,50,000

Total cost of production per 1,000 bricks = $\frac{₹\ 48,800}{30,50,000} \times 1,000 = ₹\ 16.$

QUESTIONS

OBJECTIVE TYPE

1. Choose the correct answer

(*a*) Which of the following is a Capital Expenditure ?
- (*i*) Freight and cartage on purchase of new machine
- (*ii*) Legal expenses in connection with defending a title to firm's property
- (*iii*) Expenditure on painting of factory shed
- (*iv*) Wages paid to machine operator.

(*b*) Festival advance of ₹ 25,000 was given to employees at the time of Deepawali. It is a
- (*i*) Revenue Expenditure
- (*ii*) Capital Expenditure
- (*iii*) Deferred Revenue Expenditure
- (*iv*) Not an Expense

(*c*) A real estate developer purchased land for ₹ 20 crore. The expenditure is—
- (*i*) Revenue
- (*ii*) Capital
- (*iii*) Deferred revenue
- (*iv*) None of the above.

(*d*) Which of the following is a deferred revenue expenditure—
- (*i*) Brokerage charges
- (*ii*) Commission on purchase of building
- (*iii*) Advertisement Campaign Expense
- (*iv*) Installation charges of a machine.

Ans. [(*a*) (*i*); (*b*) (*iv*); (*c*) (*i*); (*d*) (*iii*)]

2. **State whether the following statements are 'TRUE' or 'FALSE' :**
   (*i*) Preoperative expenses are revenue expenses.
   (*ii*) Heavy expenditure incurred an advertisement at the time of introducing a new product is a deferred revenue expenditure.
   (*iii*) Expenses incurred to keep the machine in working condition is a capital expenditure.
   (*iv*) An expenditure intended to benefit current period is a revenue expenditure.
   (*v*) Amount written off from the cost of Fixed Assets is Capital Expenditure.
   (*vi*) Wages paid to workers to produce a tool to be completely consumed is capital expenditure.
   (*vii*) Deferred Revenue Expenditure is current year's revenue expenditure to be paid in later years:
   (*viii*) Expenditure which results in acquisition of a permanent asset is capital expenditure.
   (*ix*) Amount paid for acquiring goodwill is deferred revenue expenditure.
   (*x*) Overhaul expenses of a second hand machinery purchased are revenue expenses.
   (*xi*) Major repair charges including replacement of certain worn out parts incurred before using a second hand car purchased recently is a capital expenditure.

Ans. [True : (*ii*), (*iv*), (*vi*), (*viii*), (*xi*), . False : (*i*), (*iii*), (*v*), (*vii*) (*ix*), (*x*)].

SHORT ANSWER TYPE

1. Why distinction between Capital and Revenue items is important ?
2. Distinguish between Capital Expenditure and Revenue Expenditure.
3. What is Deferred Revenue Expenditure ?
4. Distinguish between Capital Receipts and Revenue Receipts.
5. Distinguish between Capital Loss and Revenue Loss.

LONG ANSWER TYPE

1. Why is the distinction between capital and revenue of great importance in Accounting ? State the considerations which would guide you in deciding whether a particular item should be regarded as of capital or revenue nature.
2. Give some examples of revenue expenditure becoming, under certain circumstances, capital expenditure.
3. State the criteria you would use for distinguishing between Capital Expenditure, Revenue Expenditure and Deferred Revenue Expenditure ? Give suitable examples.
4. Briefly explain and illustrate the difference between (*a*) Capital receipts and Revenue receipts ; (*b*) Capital payments and Revenue payments ; (*c*) Capital profits and Revenue profits ; (*d*) Capital losses and Revenue losses and (*e*) Capital expenditure and Revenue Expenditure.
5. The line of distinction between capital expenditure and revenue expenditure is thin and in the final analysis all expenses-whether capital or revenue-get recovered from profits and hence no special effort need be taken to distinguish between the two. Do you agree to the above ? Discuss.
6. Explain deferred revenue expenditure with examples.
7. What is capital expenditure ? Illustrate your answer by giving five examples.
8. State the factors that you will taken into consideration in allocating the expenditure as Capital and Revenue.

PRACTICAL PROBLEMS

1. State with reasons whether the following items relating to a sugar mill company are capital or revenue :
   (*a*) A motor truck costing ₹ 15,000 and standing in the books at ₹ 7,250 was sold for ₹ 12,000.

(*b*) ₹ 20,000 received from an issue of further shares, the expenses of issue being ₹ 2,500.
(*c*) ₹ 75,000 being cost of land purchased for agricultural farm and ₹ 450 paid for land revenue.
(*d*) ₹ 1,50,000 paid for excise duty on sugar manufactured.
(*e*) ₹ 50,000 invested in Government Loan.
(*f*) ₹ 60,000 spent on the construction of railway siding.

Hints. [(*a*) Revenue Profit ₹ 4,750 ; (*b*) ₹ 20,000 Capital Receipt, ₹ 2,500 Deferred Revenue Expenditure; (*c*) ₹ 75,000 Capital Expenditure and ₹ 450 Revenue Expenditure; (*d*) Revenue Expenditure ; (*e*) Capital Expenditure, (*f*) Capital Expenditure].

2. Explain with reasons whether the undermentioned items appearing in the books of a manufacturing concern are 'capital' or 'revenue'.

(*i*) Legal expenses incurred in raising a debenture loan, (*ii*) Legal expenses incurred in an action for infringement of its trade mark. (*iii*) Profit realised on the sale of investments. (*iv*) Labour welfare expenses, (*v*) Subsidy received from State Government.

Ans. [Capital Expenditure : (*i*), Revenue Expenditure : (*ii*), (*iv*) ; Capital Receipt : (*iii*); Revenue Receipt : (*v*)].

3. Classify the following expenses between Capital and Revenue, stating reasons in each case:

(*i*) A petrol-driven engine of a passenger bus was replaced by a diesel engine. (*ii*) Expenses incurred on research for a particular product which ultimately did not result in success. (*iii*) Expense incurred for shifting the work to new premises having better facilities, (*iv*) Cost of re-painting the factory shed. (*v*) A sum of ₹ 15,000 was expended by a large factory for overhauling its entire machinery which resulted in adding three years to its working life. (*vi*) Legal expenses incurred to raise a loan. (*vii*) ₹ 1,500 embezzled by the accountant of a company and ₹ 50,000 embezzled by its Managing Director. (*viii*) ₹ 2,000 paid as compensation to an injured person in an accident with the motor of the company. (*ix*) ₹ 3,50,000 received from the sale of investments which were purchased for ₹ 2,50,000 a few years before. (*x*) ₹ 80,000 was the cost of constructing a school building meant for the children of employees for which ₹ 25,000 was received from Government as grant in aid. (*xi*) ₹ 15,700 was the book value of electric installation destroyed by lightning and it was rebuilt at a cost of ₹ 56,000. (*xii*) ₹ 25,000 was the amount of premium received on the issue of shares.

4. Mahi Pal and Mahinder Kumar own and operate a brickyard and the books show the following results for the year ended December 31, 2024.

BRICKYARD ACCOUNT

	₹		₹
To Stock on 1st January, 2024 (2,00,000 Bricks)	9,334	By Sales (40,25,000 Bricks)	2,46,867
To Wages	1,98,267	By Stock on 31st Dec. 2024 (3,00,000 Bricks)	16,000
To Stores	1,01,333	By Balance being loss	1,26,533
To Fuel	52,733		
To Salaries	11,333		
To Head Office	16,400		
	3,89,400		3,89,400

You are informed by the Management that the above figures are distorted by the inclusion of the costs of construction during the year of an additional kiln and you are required to make the necessary adjustments.

It is ascertained :

(*a*) that 10,00,000 of the bricks made during the year were used in the construction of the new kiln ;

(*b*) that no accurate records has been made of wages spent on the new kiln ; and workmen had worked part of their time on the building of the new kiln and part on the ordinary work of brick making ;

(*c*) that the wages cost for making 1,000 bricks (including spoilage) in the previous year was ₹ 30 and that the wages rates during the current year had gone up by 10 per cent ;

(*d*) that in the current year 5,000 bricks were spoiled in the course of manufacture ;

(*e*) that ₹ 3,330 of salaries, ₹ 74,000 of the cost of stores and ₹ 2,660 of the Head Office expenses were properly attributable to the new kiln, the balance of Head Office expenses being selling expenses :

(*f*) that the closing stock valuation is to be adjusted to brickyard cost.

Reconstruct the Brickyard Account for the year and show the amount chargeable to capital expenditure in respect of the new kiln.

Ans. [Cost of New Kiln ₹ 1,57,324 ; Profit on Sale of Bricks ₹ 29,991].

5. Following details of the working of Rajalakshmi Bricks Works for the year 2024 are given to you for purpose of ascertaining the profits from the manufacture of bricks :

	No. of Bricks	*Amount* ₹
Stock on 1st January, 2024	50,000	3,000
Wages	—	82,000
Salaries of office staff	—	10,000
Coke, Stores etc.	—	50,000
Royalty, Rates and other Expenses	—	12,500
Sales	8,00,000	1,20,000
Stock as on 31-12-2024	60,000	—
Bricks spoilt	40,000	—
Bricks used for construction of a new kiln	6,50,000	—

Wages cost for manufacture of bricks this year were higher by 10% as compared to the last year when they amounted to ₹ 48,000. Last year 13.5 lakh bricks were sold, 25,000 bricks were damaged and stock of bricks on 1-1-2023 was 2.25 lakh

₹ 20,000 out of stores, wages other than for the manufacture of bricks, salaries of ₹ 2,500 and expenses of ₹ 6,500 are all relatable to the construction of the new kiln. You are requested to ascertain the cost of the new kiln.

Ans. [₹ 93,750].

CHAPTER 9

Depreciation, Provisions and Reserves

DEPRECIATION

Concept of Depreciation

The economic benefits of assets are typically consumed as the items are used by the organisations. Companies must find an appropriate method for allocating the benefits because assets are used over multiple periods. It is not possible to determine exactly how long a long-lived asset will be used productively by the organisations. However, it is possible to make reasonable estimates to allocate the benefits of asset over the useful life of assets.

By allocating the cost of assets over its useful life, businesses are able to match the costs and benefits of the assets with the revenue reported in each period. This allocation also helps to ensure the proper recording of depreciation expense and assets are carried at an amount no higher than what is expected to be recoverable from the assets.

Meaning of Depreciation

Depreciation is the systematic allocation of the depreciable amount of fixed asset over its useful life. This refers to a permanent, continuing and gradual shrinkage in the book value of a fixed asset. The depreciation charge for each period should be recognised in Income Statement unless it is included in carrying amount of any other asset.

As per the latest accounting standard [AS–10 (Revised) and Ind AS–16], depreciation is defined as, "the systematic allocation of the depreciable amount of an asset over its useful life." This approach emphasis that depreciation is not merely a measure of physical wear and tear, but a process of allocating the cost of an asset over the periods benefiting from its use.

The Institute of Cost and Management Accountants (ICMA), London:

"Depreciation is the diminution in intrinsic value of the asset due to use and/or lapse of time."

According to International Accounting Standard Committee:

"Depreciation is the allocation of the depreciable amount of an asset over its estimated useful life. Depreciation for the accounting period is charged to income either directly or indirectly."

Accounting Standard (AS) 6 lays down the basic principles for charging depreciation on long lived assets. Although AS 6 for Depreciation, an old accounting standard stands withdrawn, is still considered very significant, as it affects the preparation and presentation of financial statements for all enterprises. Therefore, all enterprises still follow AS-6.

Significant Terms in Depreciation

(*a*) **Depreciable Assets.** These are assets which—

(*i*) are expected to be used during more than one accounting period ;

(*ii*) have a limited life ; and

(*iii*) are held by an enterprise for use in the production or supply of goods and services for rental to others, or for administrative purposes and not for the purpose of sale in the ordinary course of business.

Depreciation is not usually charged on land, as land is considered to have unlimited useful life. Therefore, it is not appropriate to charge depreciation on land.

Depreciation Accounting applies to all depreciable assets except the following items to which special considerations apply :

(*a*) Forest, plantation and other regenerative natural resources.

(*b*) Wasting assets including expenditure on the exploration for and extraction of minerals, oils, natural gas and similar non-regenerative resources.

(*c*) Expenditure on research and development.

(*d*) Goodwill.

(*e*) Livestock.

(*f*) Land, unless it has a limited useful life to the enterprise.

(*b*) **Useful Life.** This is either (*i*) the period over which a depreciable asset is expected to be used by the enterprise ; or (*ii*) the number of production of similar units expected to be obtained from the use of the asset by the enterprise.

Useful life of a depreciable asset is shorter than its physical life and is :

(*i*) pre-determined by legal or contractual limits such as the expiry dates of related lease ;

(*ii*) directly governed by extraction or consumption ;

(*iii*) dependent on the extent of use and physical deterioration on account of wear and tear which again depends on operational factors, such as, the number of shifts for which the asset is to be used, repairs and maintenance policy of the enterprise etc., and

(*iv*) reduced by obsolescence arising from such factors as technological changes, improvement in production methods, change in market demand for the product or service, output of the asset or legal or other restrictions.

Determination of the useful life of a depreciable asset is a matter of estimation and is normally based on various factors including experience with similar types of assets. Such estimation is more difficult for an asset using new technology or used in the production of a new product or in the provision of a new service but is nevertheless required on some reasonable basis. Any addition or extension to an existing asset which is of a capital nature and which becomes an integral part of the existing asset is depreciated over the remaining useful life of that asset.

(*c*) **Depreciable Amount.** The amount of depreciable asset is its historical cost, or other amount substituted for historical cost in financial statements, less the estimated residual value.

(*d*) **Residual Value.** Determination of residual value of an asset is normally a difficult matter. If such value is considered as insignificant, it is normally regarded as nil. On the contrary, if the residual value is likely to be significant, it is estimated at the time of acquisition/installation, or at the time of subsequent revaluation of the asset.

Causes of Depreciation

Following are the main causes of depreciation :

(*i*) Physical Deterioration. It is caused mainly from wear and tear when the asset is in use and from erosion, rust, rot and decay from being exposed to wind, rain, sun and other elements of nature.

(*ii*) **Economic Factors.** These may be said to be those that cause the asset to be put out of use even though it is in good physical condition. These arise due to obsolescence and inadequacy. *Obsolescence* means the process of becoming obsolete or out of date. An old machinery though in good physical condition may be rendered obsolete by the introduction of a new model which produces more than the old machinery. *Inadequacy* refers to the termination of the use of an asset because of growth and changes in the size of the firm. But obsolescence and inadequacy do not necessarily mean that the asset is scrapped. It is merely put out of use by the firm. Another firm will often buy it.

(*iii*) **Time factors.** There are certain assets with a fixed period of legal life such as lease, patents, and copyrights. For instance, a lease can be entered into for any period while a patent's legal life is for some years but on certain grounds this can be extended. Provision for the consumption of these assets is called amortisation rather than depreciation.

(*iv*) **Depletion.** Some assets are of a wasting character perhaps due to the extraction of raw materials from them. These materials are then either used by the firm to make something else or are sold in their raw state to other firms. Natural resources such as mines, quarries and oil wells come under this heading. To provide for the consumption of an asset of a wasting character is called provision for depletion.

(*v*) **Accident.** An asset may reduce in value because of meeting of an accident.

Factors Affecting the Measurement of Depreciation

The amount of depreciation is an expense for an entity and brings down the profit and performance of the entity. Therefore, it is important to make the correct and accurate calculation of the amount of depreciation to be charged in financial statements.

The main factors which impact the measurement of depreciation:

1. The Cost of Assets: Depreciation is charged on the book value of fixed assets and fixed assets are initially measured at cost (*e.g.,* Actual or Historical) or subsequently measured either at cost or at revaluation model. Therefore, the assets must be recorded as fixed assets in the books for charging depreciation.

Recognition criteria of an item as Fixed Assets:

(*a*) Future economic benefits of the asset must flow to the entity and;

(*b*) Cost of asset can be measured reliably.

Further, the actual cost or historical cost refers to the acquisition cost of the asset plus all the incidental expenses incurred on it from the time it is purchased till it is put to use. Such incidental expenses being in the nature of installation charges, freight inwards, and any other expenses of capital nature to bring improvement to the assets.

ILLUSTRATION 1. On 1st April, 2025, ABC acquired a machine under the following terms :

	₹
List price of machine	40,00,000
Import duty	2,50,000
Transport fees	50,000
Installation costs	5,00,000
Pre-production testing	2,00,000
Purchase of a five-year AMC contract with vendor	3,50,000

In addition to the above information ABC was granted a trade discount of 10% on the initial list price of the asset and a settlement discount of 5%, if payment for the machine was received within one month of purchase. ABC paid for the plant on 20th April, 2025. At what cost the asset will be recognised ?

SOLUTION

In accordance with Ind AS 16, all costs required to bring an asset to its present location and condition for its intended use should be capitalised. Therefore, the initial purchase price of the asset should be :

	₹
List Price	40,00,000
Less : Trade Discount (10%)	(4,00,000)
	36,00,000
Import Duty	2,50,000
Delivery Fees	50,000
Electrical Installation Costs	5,00,000
Pre-production Testing	2,00,000
Total Amount to be Capitalised at 1st April, 2025	46,00,000

AMC contract is a separate contract to get service, therefore, the maintenance contract cost of ₹ 3,50,000 should be taken as a prepaid expense and charged to the profit or loss over a period of 5 years.

In addition the settlement discount received of ₹ 1,80,000 (₹ 36,00,000 × 5%) is to be shown as other income in the profit or loss.

2. **Estimated Salvage Value (Residual Value) of Assets:** The residual value is defined as the estimated value that a company would received today, if it disposes off the asset, reduced by the related disposal costs, if the assets were at the same age and condition expected at the end of its useful life.

In many cases, the residual value may be so low as to be immaterial whereas long-lived assets have substantial net realisable value at the end of the useful life of assets.

3. **Depreciation Period:** In order to calculate the depreciation, we need to estimate the useful life of an asset. An asset's useful life is the period during which the asset is expected to be "Available for Use" by the entity based on the factors such as the asset's expected capacity.

Depreciation begins when the asset is available for use and ends when the asset is either derecognised (removed from the books of account) or when asset is classified as held for sale. Depreciation continues even if the asset is idle or has been taken out of the service, unless it is fully depreciated.

Accounting Estimates and Changes in Accounting Estimates

The depreciation is based on various estimates that may change or require constant revision during the useful life of any asset. Therefore, the reasonable estimates regarding the useful life and residual value of any asset are treated as accounting estimates in case of depreciation.

The effects of any change in estimates will also be incorporated in the financial statements of entity. However, this adjustment is allowed in prospective manner and no prior period changes are adjusted in previous financial statements.

ILLUSTRATION 2. A machinery which cost ₹ 25,000 was purchased and it was estimated that machinery have a useful life of 20 years and scrap value of ₹ 5,000. However, after two year of production the useful life was estimated to next 5 remaining years only. Calculate the depreciation expenses to be recorded for third year in Income Statement.

SOLUTION

Particulars	*Year I*	*Year II*	*Year III*
Cost	25,000	25,000	25,000
Less : Accumulated Depreciation	1,000	2,000	5,600
WDV at the year end	24,000	23,000	19,400
Depreciation Expenses for the year	(25,000 – 5,000)/20	(25,000 – 5,000)/20	(23,000 – 5,000)/5
	1,000	1,000	3,600

Note : The WDV at the end of Year-II will be treated as the cost of Asset and the changes in estimates are recorded on prospective basis.

Difference Between Depreciation, Depletion, Amortisation and Dilapidations

Depreciation applies to fixed assets, *depletion* to wasting assets, *amortisations* to intangible assets and *dilapidations* to damage due to a building or other property during tenancy. *AICPA* has given the difference between these terms in the following words :

"**Depreciation** can be distinguished from other terms, with specialised meaning used by accountants to describe assets cost allocation procedures. Depreciation is concerned with charging the cost of man-made fixed assets to operations (and not with determination of asset value for the balance sheet). *Depletion* refers to cost allocations for natural resources such as oil and mineral deposits. *Amortisation* relates to cost allocation for intangible assets such as patent and leaseholds. The use of the term depreciation should also be avoided in connection with the valuation procedures for securities and investments."

Methods of Allocation of Depreciation

Depreciation in total to be spread over the life of an asset can be calculated quite simply as cost less amount receivable when the asset is put out of use by the firm. If the item is bought and sold within one accounting period, then depreciation for the period is charged as a revenue expense in arriving at the period's net profit. The difficulties start when the asset is used for more than one accounting period and an attempt is made to charge depreciation to each period with the depreciation of that period. Depreciation is looked at from the point of view that most of fixed assets are used up over a period of time and the task is to determine how these costs should be apportioned to each accounting period that the asset is in use.

This, major issue in depreciation process is used to decide the appropriate method. The underlying principle to select the method is that the resulting depreciation should reflect the pattern in which asset's benefits are expected to be used up by the entity. This selection is based on the pattern in which the physical capacity, wear and tear, technical obsolescence, and legal life affect the asset that provides service to the entity.

Following are the possible patterns in which the asset's benefits are expected:

* **Uniform:** This pattern applies to an asset that provides roughly the same level of benefits over the useful life of an asset. This pattern leads to selection of straight line method of depreciation because it results in a constant depreciation expenses each year.
* **Decreasing:** This pattern applies to an asset where the expected benefits are decreasing over the useful life of an asset because the asset is older and the operating efficiency declines. This pattern leads to selection of written down method of depreciation because the depreciation expense should therefore decline each year.
* **Fluctuating:** This pattern applies to those assets where the use of asset may fluctuate considerably from period to period resulting in benefit pattern that varies or fluctuates. This pattern leads to sum of digit or unit of production method to record depreciation expenses based on the actual use of assets.
* **Increasing:** This pattern applies to assets that provide more service potential or generate higher value cash flow as they age. Therefore, the benefits are increasing gradually over the period of time. This pattern suggests such depreciation method in which accelerated depreciation expenses are recorded accordingly.

Because of the difficulty in some cases in identifying the pattern in which benefits are received, the simplicity of each method may be considered for selection of depreciation method. The selection of a depreciation method affects both the statement of financial position and the income statement of an entity.

Depreciation Accounting

Depreciation accounting is a system of accounting which aims to distribute the cost or other basic value of tangible capital assets less salvage (if any), over the estimated useful life of the unit (which may be a group of assets) in a systematic and rational manner. *It is a process of allocation, not of valuation.* Depreciation for the year is the portion of the total charge under such a system that is allocated to the year. Although the allocation may properly take into account occurrences during the year, it is not intended to be the measurement of the effect of all such occurrences. Thus the main objective of depreciation accounting is to absorb the cost of using the asset to different accounting periods in such a way so that profit and loss account may give true figure of profit or loss made by the business.

Need for Providing Depreciation

Need for depreciation arises because of following reasons :

(*i*) **To ascertain the true profits.** We have seen that depreciation is an expense and becomes an important element of the cost of production. Though it is not visible like other expenses and never paid to the outside party yet it is desirable to charge depreciation on fixed assets as these are used for earning purposes ; so their depreciation must be deducted out of the income earned from their use in order to calculate true net profit or loss.

(*ii*) **To present true financial position.** Financial position can be studied from the balance sheet and for the preparation of the balance sheet fixed assets are required to be shown at their true value. If assets are shown in the balance sheet without any charge made for their use or depreciation, then their value must have been overstated in the balance sheet and will not reflect the true financial position of the business. So, for the purpose of reflecting true financial position, it is necessary that depreciation must be deducted from the assets and then at such reduced value these may be shown in the balance sheet.

(*iii*) **To make provision for replacement of assets.** If depreciation is not provided, the profits of the concern will be overstated and can be distributed to the shareholders as dividend. After the end of the working life of the asset, there will be no provision or funds at the disposal of the concern and has to borrow for purchasing new assets. Provision for depreciation is a charge to profit and loss account though depreciation is not paid. The amount of depreciation accumulated during the working life of the asset provides additional working capital besides providing sum at the end of the working life of the asset for its replacement.

(*iv*) **To ensure uniform rate of return.** It becomes necessary that ideal matching of expired cost against the revenue and proper measurement of the depreciable asset at each accounting date must be made to ensure uniform rate of return.

(*v*) **To maintain the capital invested in the cost of asset intact in the business**, it is necessary to charge depreciation. Further it can be re-invested in the profit earning process.

(*vi*) **To ensure maximum tax benefit.** Depreciation is an allowable expense for tax purposes. Hence, it becomes necessary to charge depreciation in order to ensure maximum tax benefit.

(*vii*) To determine accurate cost of products.

(*viii*) To comply with techniques and legal requirements.

Depreciation under GST Regime

Depreciation is calculated on the *Historical Cost of the Asset* purchased. Historical cost is the cost incurred to acquire the asset plus all expenses incurred on it from the time it is purchased till it is put to use.

Historical Cost = Purchase Price of Asset + Freight + Other Expenses + Installation Expenses.

When fixed assets are purchased, GST is to be paid on them. Where fixed assets are purchased and used in the course of business, the GST paid can be set off against the GST collected. That means Input Tax Credit (ITC) can be availed. **In such cases where Input tax credit can be availed, Depreciation shall be charged on cost of asset excluding GST paid.** GST paid (Input GST) shall not be the part of cost of asset.

***For Example* :**

Cost of Machine	=	₹ 1,00,000
GST paid	=	₹ 12,000
Total	=	₹ 1,12,000

Depreciation is to be charged on ₹ 1,00,000 and Input tax credit of ₹ 12,000 can be availed under GST law.

ITC is available for all fixed assets used for business purpose except motor vehicles and construction of immovable property. However, if motor vehicle is purchased by a firm which is engaged in the business of transportation, ITC shall be available.

Methods of Recording Depreciation

Following are the two methods of recording depreciation in the books of accounts :

1. **When a provision for depreciation account is not maintained.** Under this method the amount of depreciation is charged to Depreciation Account and credited to the Asset Account. Asset Account appears in the balance sheet at a written down value (*i.e.*, the value remaining after deducting depreciation). Depreciation Account, being nominal account, is transferred to the Profit and Loss Account. Following journal entries are passed to give effect to the depreciation :

(*i*) *For providing depreciation*
Depreciation Account Dr.
To Asset Account

(*ii*) *For transfer of depreciation to Profit and Loss A/c*
Profit and Loss Account Dr.
To Depreciation Account

(*iii*) *When additional asset is purchased during the year*
Asset Account Dr.
To Bank Account

(*iv*) When the asset is sold, it is desirable to calculate its book value after charging even the current period's depreciation and this value is to be compared with the realisable value in order to calculate the profit or loss on the sale of an asset. The entries will be :

(*a*) *When the asset is sold*
Bank A/c Dr.
To Asset A/c

(*b*) *For the depreciation of the current period*
Depreciation A/c Dr.
To Asset A/c

(*c*) *For loss on sale of asset*
Profit and Loss A/c Dr.
To Asset A/c

Note. Reverse entry will be passed if there is profit on the sale of asset.

2. **When a Provision for Depreciation Account is Maintained.** Under this method the amount of depreciation to be provided in a particular year is debited to Profit and Loss Account and corresponding credit being given to Provision for Depreciation Account. Asset Account appears in the books at its original value and Provision for Depreciation Account appears on the liabilities side. In case the asset is sold, the provision for depreciation (relating to the asset sold) is transferred to Asset Account. Amount realised from the sale of asset is also credited to the Asset Account. The balance, if any, in the Asset Account (being profit or loss) is transferred to Profit and Loss Account. Following journal entries are passed under this method :

(*i*) *For providing depreciation out of Profit and Loss A/c*
Profit & Loss Account Dr.
To Provision for Depreciation Account

(*ii*) *On sale of an asset*
(*a*) Provision for Depreciation Account Dr. (relaing to asset sold)
To Asset Account

(*b*) Bank Account Dr.
    To Asset Account

(*c*) *For Profit*
Asset Account
    To Profit & Loss Account

For Loss
Profit & Loss Account
    To Asset Account

Methods of Depreciation

Different methods of calculating provision for depreciation are mainly accounting customs which may be used by different concerns taking into consideration their individual peculiarities. Following are the main methods of providing depreciation :

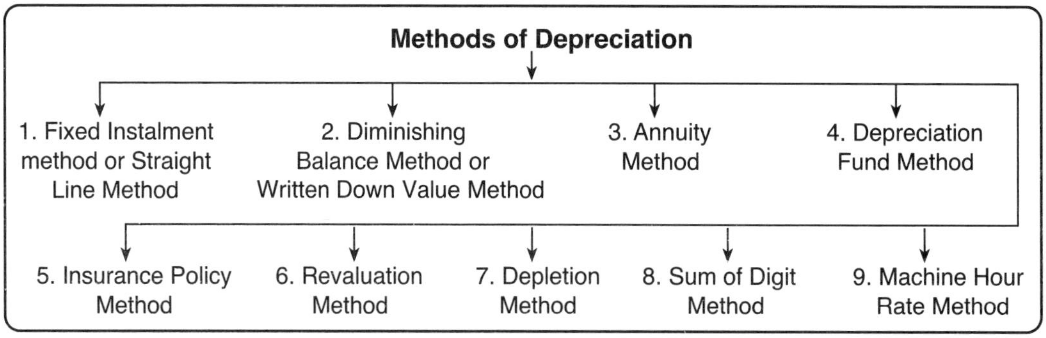

(*i*) **Fixed Instalment (or Fixed Percentage on Original Cost or Straight Line) Method.** Under this method a fixed percentage of the original value of the asset is written off every year so as to reduce the asset account to nil or to its scrap value at the end of the estimated life of the asset. To ascertain the annual charge under this method all that is necessary is to divide the original value of the asset (minus its residual value, if any) by the number of years of its estimated life *i.e.*,

$$\text{Depreciation} = \frac{\text{Cost price of asset} - \text{Scrap value}}{\text{Estimated life of asset}}$$

If, for example, a machine costing ₹ 11,000 is estimated to have a life of 10 years and the scrap value is estimated ₹ 1,000 at the end of its life, the amount of depreciation would be ₹ 11,000 – ₹ 1,000 ÷ 10 = ₹ 1,000

The amount of depreciation charged during each period of the asset's life is constant. If the charge of depreciation is plotted annually on a graph paper and the points joined together, then the graph will reveal a straight line, that is why it is also called as straight line method.

This method is suggested in case of assets where in the service value declines as a function of time and that too at a uniform rate. The repairs, maintenance and revenue also remain more or less constant.

It should be noted carefully that if depreciation is given as some percentage per annum and if the asset is purchased during the accounting year, say on July 1, then depreciation for six months is to be charged, if the accounting year closes on 31st December.

Merits

(1) This method is simple to understand and easy to apply.

(2) It can write down an asset to zero at the end of its working life, if so desired.

(3) This method is very suitable for those assets which have a fixed life *e.g.*, furniture, fixtures, short leases and other assets of small intrinsic value.

(4) Under this method, equal amount of depreciation is debited to P&L A/c of each year.

Demerits

(1) The charge for depreciation remains constant year after year. The expenses of repairs and maintenance are increasing as the asset grows older. The profit and loss account thus in the later years bears more than its share of valuation.
(2) It becomes difficult to calculate the depreciation on additions made during a year.
(3) Under this method the depreciation charge remains the same from year to year irrespective of the use of the asset. Thus it does not take into consideration the effective utilisation of the asset.
(4) It does not take into consideration the interest on capital invested in fixed assets.
(5) It does not provide funds for replacement of assets.
(6) This method tends to report an increasing rate of return on investment in the asset amount due to the fact that the original cost of the asset amount is taken.
(7) It is quite difficulty to assess the true scrap value of the assets after a long period *i.e.* from the day of installation.

Inspite of these drawbacks, this method is mostly used by firms in U.S.A., Canada, U.K. and some firms in India.

ILLUSTRATION 3. On 1st January, 2022, machinery was purchased by X for ₹ 50,000. On 1st July, 2023, additions were made to the extent of ₹ 10,000. On 1st April, 2024, further additions were made to the extent of ₹ 6,400.

On 30th June, 2025 machinery, the original value of which was ₹ 8,000 on 1st January, 2022, was sold for ₹ 6,000. Depreciation is charged at 10% p.a. on original cost.

Show Machinery Account for the years from 2022 to 2025 in the books of X. X Closes his books on 31st December.

SOLUTION

IN THE BOOKS OF X

MACHINERY ACCOUNT

Date	Particulars	₹	Date	Particulars	₹	₹
2022			2022			
Jan. 1	To Bank (Purchase)	50,000	Dec. 31	By Depreciation A/c		5,000
			Dec. 31	By Balance c/d		45,000
		50,000				50,000
2023			2023			
Jan. 1	To Balance b/d	45,000	Dec. 31	By Depreciation A/c		
July 1	To Bank (addition)	10,000		10% on ₹ 50,000 for one year	5,000	
				10% on ₹ 10,000 for 1/2 year	500	5,500
			"	By Balance c/d		49,500
		55,000				55,000
2024			2024			
Jan. 1	To Balance b/d	49,500	Dec. 31	By Depreciation A/c		
April 1	To Bank (addition)	6,400		10% on ₹ 50,000 For one year	5,000	
				10% on ₹ 10,000 for one year	1,000	
				10% on ₹ 6,400 for 9 months	480	6,480
			Dec. 31	By Balance c/d		49,420
		55,900				55,900

Date	Particulars	₹	Date	Particulars	₹	₹
2025 Jan.1	To Balance b/d	49,420	2025 June 30	By Bank		6,000
June 30	To Profit & Loss A/c (Profit on Sale) (1)	800	Dec. 31	By Depreciation A/c	₹	
				10% on ₹ 42,000 for one year	4,200	
				10% on ₹ 10,000 for one year	1,000	
				10% on ₹ 6,400 for one year	640	
				10% on ₹ 8,000 for 1/2 year	400	6,240
			"	By Balance c/d		37,980
		50,220				50,220
2026 Jan. 1	To Balance b/d	37,980				

Working Note :

(1) *Calculation of Profit on Sale of Machinery*

	₹
Original value of machinery on 1-1-23	8,000
Less : Depreciation for $3\frac{1}{2}$ years @ 10%	2,800
Written down value on 30-6-2025	5,200
Amount realised on sale	6,000
Profit on sale of machinery	800

ILLUSTRATION 4. On 1st April, 2022 a firm purchased a machinery for ₹ 2,00,000. On 1st October in the same accounting year, additional machinery costing ₹ 1,00,000 was purchased. On 1st October, 2023, the machinery purchased on 1st April, 2022, having become obsolete, was sold off for ₹ 90,000. On 1st October, 2024, new machinery was purchased for ₹ 2,50,000 while the machinery purchased on 1st October, 2022 was sold for ₹ 85,000 on the same day.

The firm provides depreciation on its machinery @ 10% per annum on *original cost* on 31st March every year.

Show Machinery Account, Provision for Depreciation Account and Depreciation Account for the period of three accounting years ending 31st March, 2025.

SOLUTION

MACHINERY ACCOUNT

Date	Particulars	₹	Date	Particulars	₹
1-4-2022	To Bank A/c	2,00,000	31-3-2023	By Balance c/d	3,00,000
1-10-2022	To Bank A/c	1,00,000			
		3,00,000			3,00,000
1-4-2023	To Balance b/d	3,00,000	1-10-2023	By Bank A/c	90,000
			"	By Provision for Dep. A/c	30,000
			"	By Profit & Loss A/c (Loss)	80,000
			31-3-2024	By Balance c/d	1,00,000
		3,00,000			3,00,000
1-4-2024	To Balance b/d	1,00,000	1-10-2024	By Bank A/c	85,000
1-10-2024	To Bank A/c	2,50,000	"	By Provision forDep. A/c	20,000
1-10-2024	To Profit & Loss A/c (Profit on Sale)	5,000	31-3-2025	By Balance c/d	2,50,000
		3,55,000			3,55,000

PROVISION FOR DEPRECIATION ACCOUNT

		₹			₹
31-3-2023	To Balance c/d	25,000	31-3-2023	By Depreciation A/c	25,000
1-10-2023	To Machinery A/c (₹ 20,000 + ₹ 10,000)	30,000	1-4-2023	By Balance b/d	25,000
			1-10-2023	By Depreciation A/c	10,000
			31-3-2024	By Depreciation A/c	10,000
31-3-2024	To Balance c/d	15,000			
		45,000			45,000
1-10-2024	To Machinery A/c (₹ 5,000 + ₹ 10,000 + 5,000)	20,000	1-4-2024	By Balance b/d	15,000
			1-10-2025	By Depreciation A/c	5,000
31-3-2025	To Balance c/d	12,500	31-3-2025	By Depreciation A/c	12,500
		32,500			32,500
			1-4-2025	By Balance b/d	12,500

DEPRECIATION ACCOUNT

		₹			₹
31-3-2023	To Provision for Dep. A/c	25,000	31-3-2023	By Profit& Loss A/c	25,000
1-10-2023	To Provision forDep. A/c	10,000	31-3-2024	By Profit & Loss A/c	20,000
31-3-2024	To Provision for Dep. A/c	10,000			
		20,000			20,000
1-10-2024	To Provision for Dep. A/c	5,000	31-3-2025	By Profit & Loss A/c	17,500
31-3-2025	To Provision for Dep. A/c	12,500			
		17,500			17,500

(*ii*) Diminishing Balance (or Reducing Instalment or Written Down Value) Method. Under this method, depreciation is calculated at a certain percentage each year on the balance of the asset which is brought forward from the previous year. The amount of depreciation charged in each period is not fixed but it goes on decreasing gradually as the beginning balance of the asset in each year will reduce. The charges in initial periods are higher than those in the later periods. Overall charge, *i.e.*, amount of depreciation, repairs and maintenance taken together remains equal throughout the life of the asset. This method is justified in the cases where (*i*) there is much uncertainty of revenue in later years and (*ii*) there is also increase in repairs and maintenance costs consequently decreasing efficiency and revenues in every succeeding period. It is usually adopted for plant and machinery.

Merits

(*i*) It tends to give a fairly even charge of depreciation against revenue each year. Depreciation is generally heavy during the first few years and is counterbalanced by the repairs being light and in the later years when repairs are heavy this is counterbalanced by the decreasing charge for depreciation.

(*ii*) Fresh calculations of depreciation are not necessary as and when additions are made.

(*iii*) This method is permissible and recognised by the income tax authorities in India.

(*iv*) This method is suitable for plant and machinery, building etc. where the amount of repairs and renewals increases as the asset grows older.

Demerits

(*i*) The original cost of the asset is altogether lost sight of in subsequent years and the asset can never be reduced to zero.

(*ii*) This method does not take into consideration the asset as an investment and interest is not taken into consideration.

(*iii*) As compared to the first method, it is difficult to determine the suitable rate of depreciation.

(*iv*) It does not provide for replacement of asset on the expiry of its useful life.

(*v*) It does not take into consideration the loss of interest on the amount invested in fixed assets.

Distinction Between Straight Line Method and Diminishing Balance Method

Points of Distinction	*Straight Line Method*	*Diminishing Balance Method*
1. Change of Depreciation.	Depreciation is charged on the original cost of asset.	Depreciation is charged on the written down value of the asset.
2. Change in Depreciation Amount	Throughout the life of the asset, the amount of depreciation remains to be equal.	Amount of depreciation is more during earlier years of the life of asset than later years and therefore amount is never equal.
3. Balance in Asset's A/c	Asset's A/c at the expiry of the expected life becomes nil.	The amount never becomes nil.
4. Overall Charge	The overall charge, *i.e.,* depreciation and repairs taken together go on increasing from year to year. In other words the amount of depreciation and repairs is relatively less during the earlier years of the life of the asset than later years because repairs go on increasing with use of asset.	Overall charge remains more or less same for every year throughout the life of the asset. Since depreciation goes on decreasing and amount of repairs goes on increasing.
5. Profits	Profits under this method are more during the earlier years of the life of the asset.	Profits are less during earlier years than the later years.
6. Suitability	It is suitable for assets having shorter life and lesser value.	It is suitable for assets having long life and requiring additions or extensions in its life and substantial repairs in later years.
7. Approval of Tax authority	This method is not approved by Income Tax authority	This method is approved by the Income Tax authority.
8. Rate of Depreciation	Rate of depreciation is low as comparison to written down value method.	One the other side rate of Depreciation is more as far as straight line method is considered.

ILLUSTRATION 5. A company charges depreciation on Plant and Machinery under *Reducing Balance System* @ 15% per annum. On 1st April, 2021 the balance in ledger stood at ₹ 4,60,000. Following particulars are given relating to Plant and Machinery during the four years ended 31st March, 2025 :

Date	
1-9-2021	A machine purchased for ₹ 20,000 (installation expenses ₹ 1,000) on 1.5.96 was fully destroyed in an accident.
1-7-2022	Purchased a new machine costing ₹ 50,000 (installation expenses ₹ 2,500). A sum of ₹ 30,000 was paid on the same date and the balance was paid in May, 2023.
31-8-2023	Plant purchased on 1st April, 2020 for ₹ 30,000 (installation expenses ₹ 1,500) was disposed off for ₹ 36,000.
1-11-2024	Some old machineries (Book value on 1-4-21—₹ 10,000) were sold for ₹ 4,000.

Show Plant & Machinery Account as would appear in the books of the company for the four years ended 31st March, 2025 assuming depreciation is charged proportionately even if the asset is sold or destroyed.

SOLUTION

PLANT & MACHINERY ACCOUNT

Date	Particulars	₹	Date	Particulars	₹
2021			2021		
April 1	To Balance b/d	4,60,000	Sept. 1	By Profit & Loss A/c (1)	14,434
			"	" Depreciation for 5 months (1)	962
			2022		
			March 31	By Depreciation A/c @ 15% on ₹ 4,44,604	66,691
			"	" Balance c/d	3,77,913
		4,60,000			4,60,000
2022			2023		
April 1	To Balance b/d	3,77,913	March 31	By Depreciation A/c [₹ 56,687 + ₹ 5,906]	62,593
July 1	To Bank	32,500	"	" Balance c/d	3,67,820
"	To Creditors	20,000			
		4,30,413			4,30,413
2023			2023		
April 1	To Balance b/d	3,67,820	Aug. 31	By Bank A/c (Sale)	36,000
Aug. 31	To P & L A/c (2) (Profit on sale of machinery)	17,864	"	" Depreciation (2)	1,209
			2024		
			March 31	By Depreciation A/c 15% on 3,48,475 (*i.e.*, ₹ 3,67,820 – ₹ 19,345)	52,271
			"	" Balance c/d	2,96,204
		3,85,684			3,85,684
2024			2024		
April 1	To Balance b/d	2,96,204	Nov. 1	By Bank A/c (Sale)	4,000
			"	By Depreciation (for 7 months on ₹ 6,141)	537
			"	" P & L A/c (3) (Loss)	1,604
			2025		
			March 31	" Depreciation A/c (15% of ₹ 2,90,063 full year)	43,509
				" Balance c/d	2,46,554
		2,96,204			2,96,204

Working Notes :

(1) *Calculation of loss on accident*

		₹
	Cost on 1-5-2019	21,000
Less :	Depreciation for 11 months in 2019-2020	2,887
	Value on 1-4-2020	18,113

Less :	Depreciation for 2020-21	2,717
	Value on 1-4-2021	15,396
Less :	Depreciation for 5 months	962
	Loss on accident	14,434

(2) *Calculation of profit on sale of machinery on 31-8-2023*

		₹
	Cost on 1-4-2020	31,500
Less :	Depreciation for 2020-21	4,725
	Value on 1-4-2021	26,775
Less :	Depreciation for 2021-22	4,016
	Value on 1-4-2022	22,759
Less :	Depreciation for 2022-2023	3,414
	Value on 1-4-2023	19,345
Less :	Depreciation for 5 months	1,209
	Value on 31-8-2023	18,136
Less :	Amount realised on sale	36,000
	Profit on sale of machinery	17,864

(3) *Calculation of loss on sale of machinery on 1-11-2024*

		₹
	Book value on 1-4-2021	10,000
Less :	Depreciation for 2021-22	1,500
	Value on 1-4-2022	8,500
Less :	Depreciation for 2022-2023	1,275
	Value on 1-4-2023	7,225
Less :	Depreciation for 2023-2024	1,084
	Value on 1-4-2024	6,141
Less :	Depreciation for 7 months	537
	Value on 1-11-2024	5,604
Less :	Amount realised on Sale	4,000
	Loss on sale of machinery	1,604

ILLUSTRATION 6. Hitesh maintains his fixed assets at cost. Provision for Depreciation Account is kept separately for each asset.

On 31st December 2023, position was as under :

	Cost	*Depreciation*
Plant and Machinery	₹ 1,50,710	₹ 62,350
Furniture and Fixtures	26,450	11,500

He purchased a machine for ₹ 10,000 on 1st April, 2024 and furniture for ₹ 3,000 on 1st June, 2024.

A machine costing ₹ 6,000 purchased on January 1, 2022 was sold for ₹ 5,500 on 30th June, 2024.

Depreciation is provided @ 10% on *written-down-value method*. Show the relevant accounts for the year ended 31st December, 2024.

SOLUTION

PLANT & MACHINERY ACCOUNT

		₹			₹
1-1-2024	To Balance b/d	1,50,710	30-6-2024	By Bank	5,500
1-4-2024	" Bank	10,000	30-6-2024	" Provision for Dep.	1,140
30-6-2024	" P. & L. A/c	883	"	" P. & L. A/c (Dep.)	243
			31-12-2024	" Balance c/d	1,54,710
		1,61,593			1,61,593

FURNITURE & FIXTURES ACCOUNT

		₹			₹
1-1-2024	To Balance b/d	26,450	31-12-2024	By Balance c/d	29,450
1-6-2024	" Bank	3,000			
		29,450			29,450

PROVISION FOR DEPRECIATION ACCOUNT

		on P. & M.	on F. & F.			on P. & M.	on F. & F.
		₹	₹			₹	₹
30-6-2024	To Machinery	1,140		1-1-2024	By Balance b/d	62,350	11,500
31-12-2024	" Balance c/d	70,310	13,170	31-12-2024	" P. & L. A/c (1)	9,100	1,670
		71,450	13,170			71,450	13,170

Working Note : (1) Calculation of Provision for Depreciation on Machinery and Furniture & Fittings for 2024

	₹	₹
Depreciation on Plant & Machinery for 2024		
Value of Plant & Machinery on 1-1-2024		1,50,710
Less : Depreciation provision on 1-1-2024	62,350	
Written down value on 1-1-2024 of plant sold	4,860	67,210
		83,500
∴ Depreciation @ 10% on ₹ 83,500 for one year		8,350
Add : Depreciation @ 10% on ₹ 10,000 for 9 months		750
Depreciation on Machinery for 2024		9,100
Depreciation on Furniture & Fixtures for 2024		
Book value on 1-1-2024 (₹ 26,450 – ₹ 11,500 Provision)		14,950
10% Depreciation on ₹ 14,950 for one year		1,495
Depreciation on addition of 1-6-2024 @ 10% p.a. for 7 months $\left(₹\ 3{,}000 \times \frac{10}{100} \times \frac{7}{12}\right)$		175
Total Depreciation		1,670

ILLUSTRATION 7. Shivaji Ltd. purchased fixed assets worth ₹ 90,00,000 on 1st April, 2021. The life of the assets is 10 years and they are to be depreciated on straight line basis. The assets were revalued on

1st April 2023 when 50% of the assets was assessed at 10% less than the book value, and the remaining assets were revalued at 15% higher than book value. The assets were ultimately sold on 1-4-2025 for ₹ 54,80,000. Excess depreciation on revaluation, if any, should be charged to Revenue Reserve.

Show Fixed Assets A/c, Depreciation A/c and *Revaluation Reserve* A/c, supported by workings wherever necessary.

SOLUTION

In the Books of Shivaji Ltd.

FIXED ASSETS ACCOUNT

		₹			₹
2021			2022		
April 1	To Bank	90,00,000	March 31	By Depreciation A/c	9,00,000
			" 31	By Balance c/d	81,00,000
		90,00,000			90,00,000
2022			2023		
April 1	To Balance b/d	81,00,000	March 31	By Depreciation A/c	9,00,000
			" 31	By Balance c/d	72,00,000
		81,00,000			81,00,000
2023		₹	2023		₹
April 1	To Balance b/d	72,00,000	April 1	By Revaluation Reserve A/c (1)	3,60,000
" 1	To Revaluation Reserve (1)	5,40,000	2024		
			March 31	By Depreciation A/c	9,22,500
			" 31	By Balance c/d	64,57,500
		77,40,000			77,40,000
2024			2025		
April 1	To Balance b/d	64,57,500	March 31	By Depreciation A/c	9,22,500
			" 31	By Balance c/d	55,35,000
		64,57,500			64,57,500
2025			2025		
April 1	To Balance b/d	55,35,000	April 1	By Bank	54,80,000
			" 1	By Revaluation Reserve A/c (Loss on Sale)	55,000
		55,35,000			55,35,000

DEPRECIATION ACCOUNT

		₹			₹
2022			2022		
March 31	To Fixed Assets A/c	9,00,000	March 31	By Profit & Loss A/c	9,00,000
2023			2023		
March 31	To Fixed Assets A/c	9,00,000	March 31	By Profit & Loss A/c	9,00,000

2024			2024		
March 31	To Fixed Assets A/c (3)	9,22,500	March 31	By Profit & Loss A/c	9,00,000
			March 31	By Revaluation Reserve A/c (4)	22,500
		9,22,500			9,22,500
2025			2025		
March 31	To Fixed Assets A/c (3)	9,22,500	March 31	By Profit & Loss A/c	9,00,000
			March 31	By Revaluation Reserve A/c (4)	22,500
		9,22,500			9,22,500

REVALUATION RESERVE ACCOUNT

		₹			₹
2023			2023		
April 1	To Fixed Assets A/c (Loss on Revaluation)	3,60,000	April 1	By Fixed Assets A/c (Profit on Revaluation)	5,40,000
2024					
March 31	To Depreciation A/c	22,500			
" 31	To Balance c/d	1,57,500			
		5,40,000			5,40,000
2025			2024		
March 31	To Depreciation A/c	22,500	April 1	By Balance b/d	1,57,500
" 31	To Balance c/d	1,35,0000			
		1,57,500			1,57,500
2025			2025		
March 31	To Fixed Assets A/c (Loss on Sale of Assets)	55,000	April 1	By Balance b/d	1,35,000
" 31	To General Reserve (Transfer)	80,000			
		1,35,000			1,35,000

Working Notes

(1) ***Calculation of Amount of Revaluation Reserve*** ₹

Downward revision of 50% of fixed assets book value ₹ 72,00,000 on 1-4-2023

$₹\ 72,00,000 \times \frac{50}{100} \times 10\%$ 3,60,000

Upward revision of remaining 50% of fixed assets $₹\ 72,00,000 \times \frac{50}{100} \times 15\%$ 5,40,000

(2) ***Value of Fixed Assets after Revaluation on 1-4-2023***

$₹\ 72,00,000 \times \frac{50}{100} - ₹\ 3,60,000$ 32,40,000

$₹\ 72,00,000 \times \frac{50}{100} + ₹\ 5,40,000$ 41,40,000

73,80,000

(3) ***Calculation of Depreciation per Annum for Remaining 8 years***

(*i.e.* 10 Years Life of the Assets – 2 Years Expired upto 1-4-2023 the Date of Revaluation)

Depreciation p.a. after 31-3-2023 = $\frac{₹\ 73,80,000}{8} = ₹\ 9,22,500$

(4) ***Calculation of Excess Depreciation to be Charged to Revaluation Reserve Account***

	₹
New Depreciation p.a.	9,22,500
Less : Depreciation p.a. charged previously	9,00,000
Excess Depreciation	22,500

ILLUSTRATION 8. (Where Provision for Depreciation alongwith Asset A/c is to be maintained) A firm writes off 95% of the cost of its machines over 10 years following the S.L. Method leaving the rest 5% as estimated scrap value (ESV). Full depreciation is provided even if an asset is used only for part of a year.

On 31-12-23, the original costs of the machines in possession were :

(*i*) those purchased in 2006 or earlier ₹ 2,40,000 ; (*ii*) those purchased in 2012 ₹ 80,000 ; (*iii*) those purchased in 2019 ₹ 60,000.

On 30-6-24, a machine purchased in 2006 for ₹ 20,000 was sold for ₹ 1,800. On 30-11-24, a machine purchased in 2019 for ₹ 30,000 was sold for ₹ 10,000 and on the same date a new machine was purchased for ₹ 90,000.

Show Machinery A/c, Provision for Depreciation A/c and Machinery Sold A/c for the year 2024.

SOLUTION

MACHINERY ACCOUNT

Date	Particulars	₹	Date	Particulars	₹
1-1-24	To Balance b/d [₹ 2,40,000 + ₹ 80,000 + ₹ 60,000]	3,80,000	30-6-24	By Machinery Sold A/c	20,000
30-11-24	To Bank	90,000	30-11-24	By Machinery Sold A/c	30,000
			31-12-24	By Balance c/d	4,20,000
		4,70,000			4,70,000

PROVISION FOR DEPRECIATION ACCOUNT

Date	Particulars	₹	Date	Particulars	₹	₹
30-6-24	To Machinery Sold A/c (2)	19,000	1-1-24	By Balance b/d (1)		3,24,900
30-11-24	To Machinery Sold A/c (3)	17,100	30-11-24	By Depreciation A/c (Mach. III) (3)		2,850
31-12-24	To Balance c/d	3,10,650	31-12-24	By Depreciation A/c (4)		
				II	7,600	
				III	2,850	
				IV	8,550	19,000
		3,46,750				3,46,750

MACHINERY SOLD ACCOUNT

Date	Particulars	₹	Date	Particulars	₹
30-6-24	To Machinery A/c	20,000	30-6-24	By Provision for Dep. A/c	19,000
"	To Profit & Loss A/c	800	"	By Bank	1,800
30-11-24	To Machinery A/c	30,000	30-11-24	By Provision for Dep. A/c	17,100
			"	By Bank	10,000
			"	By P/L A/c (Loss)	2,900
		50,800			50,800

Working Notes :

(1) *Calculation of Balance of Depreciation on 1-1-24*

	₹
(*a*) On Machinery purchased in 2006 or before 95% of ₹ 2,40,000	2,28,000
(*b*) On Machinery purchased in 2012	
Total dep. being 95% of ₹ 80,000 in 10 years ₹ 76,000	
∴ For 9 years ₹ 76,000 × $\frac{9}{10}$	68,400
(*c*) On Machinery purchased in 2019	
Total depreciation for 10 years *i.e.*, 95% of ₹ 60,000 = ₹ 57,000	
∴ Dep. for 5 years = ₹ 57,000 × $\frac{5}{10}$	28,500
	3,24,900

(2) *Calculation of Dep. on Machinery Sold on 30-6-24*

	₹
Original Cost	20,000
Total Depreciation @ 95% on ₹ 20,000	19,000

(3) *Calculation of Depreciation on Machinery sold on 30-11-24*

Original Cost	30,000
Total Depreciation in 10 years : 95% of ₹ 30,000	28,500
Dep. already charged upto 2023 $\left(\frac{5}{10} \times ₹\ 28{,}500\right)$	14,250
Dep. for 2024 (to be transferred to Provision for Dep. A/c) (1/10 of ₹ 28,500)	2,850
	17,100

(4) *Calculation of Depreciation for 2024*

On Machinery II (2012) $\left(\frac{1}{10} \times \frac{95}{100} \times ₹\ 80{,}000\right)$	7,600
On Machinery III (2019) $\left(\frac{1}{10} \times \frac{95}{100} \times ₹\ 30{,}000\right)$	2,850
On Machinery IV (2024) $\left(\frac{1}{10} \times \frac{95}{100} \times ₹\ 90{,}000\right)$	8,550
	19,000

ILLUSTRATION 9. (With GST) Subhash purchased a machine on 1st December, 2024 for 6,00,000 plus CGST and SGST @ 6% each. He paid ₹ 20,000 for loading/unloading and carriage expenses to bring the machine to factory. He further incurred ₹ 25,000 for installing the machine. Determine:

(*a*) How much amount did Subhash pay to the vendor of Machine?
(*b*) How much amount will be debited to Machinery Account?
(*c*) Pass the Journal entries giving effect to the transaction.

SOLUTION

(*a*) *Amount paid to Vendor of Machine:*

	₹
Value (Cost) of Machine	6,00,000
Add: CGST @ 6%	36,000
SGST @ 6%	36,000
	6,72,000

(*b*) *Amount to be debited to Machinery Account:*

	₹
Cost (Without CGST and SGST)	6,00,000
Loading/Unloading and Carriage Expenses	30,000
Installation Charges	25,000
	6,55,000

(*c*) **JOURNAL ENTRIES**

Date	Particulars		L.F.	Dr. (₹)	Cr. (₹)
2024					
Dec. 1	Machinery A/c	Dr.		6,00,000	
	Input CGST A/c	Dr.		36,000	
	Input SGST A/c	Dr.		36,000	
	To Cash/Bank A/c				6,72,000
	(Being the machinery purchased)				
	Machinery A/c	Dr.		55,000	
	To Cash/Bank A/c				55,000
	(Being loading/unloading carriage and installation charges paid)				

ILLUSTRATION 10. (With GST) Pankaj of Delhi purchased a machinery for ₹ 2,00,000 plus IGST @ 12% on Ist October, 2022 and payment was made by cheque. Another machine was purchased for ₹ 1,00,000 plus IGST @ 12%, payment made by cheque on 1st April 2024. Depreciation is charged @ 10% p.a. by Straight Line method. You are required to pass necessary Journal entries for years ended 31st Match 2023, 2024 and 2025. Show Machinery Account also. No Provision for Depreciation Account is maintained.

SOLUTION

In the books of Pankaj

JOURNAL

Date	Particulars		L.F.	Dr. (₹)	Cr. (₹)
2022					
Oct. 1	Machinery A/c	Dr.		2,00,000	
	Input IGST A/c	Dr.		24,000	
	To Cash/Bank A/c				2,24,000
	(Being the interstate purchase of machinery)				
2023					
March 31	Depreciation A/c (Note 1)	Dr.		10,000	
	To Machinery A/c				10,000
	(Being the depreciation charged on machinery for six months)				
March 31	Profit & Loss A/c	Dr.		10,000	
	To Depreciation A/c				10,000
	(Being the depreciation transferred to Profit & Loss A/c)				
2024					
March 31	Depreciation A/c	Dr.		20,000	
	To Machinery A/c				20,000
	(Being depreciation charged for one year)				
March 31	Profit & Loss A/c	Dr.		20,000	
	To Depreciation A/c				20,000
	(Being Depreciation transferred to Profit & Loss A/c)				

April 1	Machinery A/c	Dr.	1,00,000	
	Input IGST A/c	Dr.	12,000	
	To Bank			1,12,000
	(Being the inter-state purchase of Machinery)			
2025				
March 31	Depreciation A/c	Dr.	30,000	
	To Machinery A/c			30,000
	(Being the depreciation charged on machinery)			
March 31	Profit & Loss A/c	Dr.	30,000	
	To Depreciation A/c			30,000
	(Being depreciation transferred to P&L A/c)			

Notes 1. IGST Paid on machinery is not a cost of machinery as GST (CGST, SGST and IGST) paid on machinery can be set off against GST collected. Machinery Account will be debited with purchase price only. Depreciation shall also be calculated on cost of machinery excluding IGST paid.

2. Depreciation for 2025 is equal to depreciation for machinery bought in 2022 and 2024 for full one year that is ₹ 30,000 (₹ 20,000 + ₹ 10,000)

MACHINERY ACCOUNT

Date	Particulars	J.F.	₹	Date	Particulars	J.F.	₹
2022				2023			
Oct. 1	To Bank		2,00,000	March 31	By Depreciation A/c		10,000
				March 31	By Balance c/d		1,90,000
			2,00,000				2,00,000
2024				2024			
April 1	To Balance b/d		1,90,000	March 31	By Depreciation A/c (Machinery 1)		20,000
				March 31	By Balance c/d		1,70,000
			1,90,000				1,90,000
2025				2025			
April 1	To Balance b/d		1,70,000	March 31	By Depreciation A/c (₹ 20,000 + ₹ 10,000)		30,000
April 1	To Bank A/c		1,00,000				
				March 31	By Balance c/d (₹ 1,50,000 + 90,000)		2,40,000
			2,70,000				2,70,000

(iii) Sums of the Digits Method

This is a variant of the reducing instalment or diminishing balance method. Under this method depreciation is calculated by the following formula:

$$\text{Depreciation} = \text{Amount to be written off} \times \frac{\text{No. of years of the remaining life of the asset including the current year}}{\text{The total of all the digits representing the life of the asset (in years)}}$$

Suppose machinery was purchased for ₹ 60,000 on 1st January, 2022 and depreciation was charged following the sums of the digits method assuming its useful life to be 3 years. Depreciation for three years will be calculated as under :

Depreciation for the

First year = $\frac{3}{3+2+1}$ × ₹ 60,000 = ₹ 30,000 ; Second year = $\frac{2}{6}$ × ₹ 60,000 = ₹ 20,000 and Third year = $\frac{1}{6}$ × ₹ 60,000 = ₹ 10,000

(iv) Annuity Method

Under this method, amount spent on the purchase of an asset is regarded as an investment which is assumed to earn interest at a certain rate. Every year the asset account is debited with the amount of interest and credited with the amount of depreciation. This interest is calculated on the debit balance of the asset account at the beginning of the year.

The amount to be written off as depreciation is calculated from the Annuity Table, an extract of which is given below :

Years	*3%*	*$3\frac{1}{2}$%*	*4%*	*$4\frac{1}{2}$%*	*5%*
3	0.353530	0.359634	0.360349	0.363773	0.367209
4	0.269027	0.272251	0.275490	0.278744	0.282016
5	0.218355	0.221481	0.224627	0.227792	0.230975

The depreciation will be different according to the rate of interest and according to the period over which the asset is to be written off. The fixed amount of depreciation as well as the rate of interest is so adjusted that at the end of the working life of the asset its book value is reduced to zero or to its break up value, if any. It often happens that owing to a fraction of paise being neglected there often arises a slight difference at the end of the last year and it is, therefore, adjusted in the last instalment.

This method is to a great extent scientific as it treats the purchase of an asset as an investment in the business itself and charge interest on the same. But the chief defect is that the total charges of depreciation and repairs put together do not remain fairly uniform from year to year as in the diminishing balance method and again additions to the asset are sure to throw out calculations already made. The method is mainly used in the case of costly leases of long periods and other assets to which additions are not usually made and as such in case of machinery this method is not found suitable.

ILLUSTRATION 11. A firm purchases a 5 years' lease for ₹ 40,000 on 1st January. It decides to write off depreciation on the Annuity Method, presuming the rate of interest to be 5% per annum. The annuity tables show that a sum of ₹ 9,239 should be written off every year. Show the Lease Account for five years. Calculations are to be made to the nearest-rupee.

SOLUTION

LEASE ACCOUNT

		₹			₹
I Year			I Year		
Jan. 1	To Cash A/c	40,000	Dec. 31	By Depreciation A/c	9,239
Dec. 31	" Interest A/c	2,000	" "	" Balance c/d	32,761
		42,000			42,000
II Year		₹	II Year		₹
Jan. 1	To Balance b/d	32,761	Dec. 31	By Depreciation A/c	9,239
Dec. 31	" Interest A/c	1,638	" "	" Balance c/d	25,160
		34,399			34,399

III Year			III Year		
Jan. 1	To Balance b/d	25,160	Dec. 31	By Depreciation A/c	9,239
Dec. 31	To Interest A/c	1,258	Dec. 31	By Balance c/d	17,179
		26,418			26,418
IV Year			IV Year		
Jan. 1	To Balance b/d	17,179	Dec. 31	By Depreciation A/c	9,239
Dec. 31	" Interest A/c	859	" "	" Balance c/d	8,799
		18,038			18,038
V Year			V Year		
Jan. 1	To Balance b/d	8,799	Dec. 31	By Depreciation A/c	9,239
Dec. 31	" Interest A/c	440			
		9,239			9,239

(v) Depreciation Fund Method

Under all the methods discussed uptill now, ready cash may not be available when the time of replacement comes because the amount of depreciation is retained in the business itself in the form of assets not separate from other assets which cannot be readily sold.

The method (applied to long leases etc.) implies that the amount written off as depreciation should be kept aside and invested in readily saleable securities. The securities accumulate and when the life of the asset expires, the securities are sold and with the sale proceeds a new asset is purchased. Since the securities always earn interest, it is not necessary to provide for the full amount of depreciation, something less will do. How much amount is to be invested every year so that a given sum is available at the end of a given period depends on the rate of interest which is easily calculated from Sinking Fund Tables, an extract of which is given below :

Years	*3%*	*$3\frac{1}{2}$%*	*4%*	*$4\frac{1}{2}$%*	*5%*
3	0.323540	0.321934	0.320349	0.318773	0.317208
4	0.239027	0.237251	0.235490	0.233741	0.232023
5	0.188350	0.186481	0.184627	0.182792	0.180975

Instead of crediting the asset, another account is credited, which is known as Depreciation Fund Account together with any interest earned will be invested.

Journal Entries

First Year

(i) *For providing annual depreciation*

Depreciation A/c Dr.

To Depreciation Fund A/c

(ii) *For investing the amount of depreciation*

Depreciation Fund Investment A/c Dr.

To Bank A/c

(iii) *For transferring depreciation to Profit and Loss Account*

Profit and Loss A/c Dr.

To Depreciation A/c

Depreciation Fund Account appears on the liabilities side and the Depreciation Fund Investment Account on the assets side of the Balance Sheet.

Subsequent years

(*i*) *For interest received on investment out of depreciation fund*
Bank A/c Dr.
To Depreciation Fund A/c

(*ii*) *For annual instalment of Depreciation*
Depreciation A/c Dr.
To Depreciation Fund A/c

(*iii*) *For amount of depreciation and interest earned invested in securities.*
Depreciation Fund Investment A/c Dr.
To Bank A/c

(*iv*) *For transferring depreciation to Profit & Loss A/c*
Profit and Loss A/c Dr.
To Depreciation A/c

Last year

(*i*) *For interest received on investment*
Bank A/c Dr.
To Depreciation Fund A/c

(*ii*) *For annual instalment of depreciation*
Depreciation A/c Dr.
To Depreciation Fund A/c

(*iii*) *For transferring depreciation to Profit and Loss A/c*
Profit and Loss A/c Dr.
To Depreciation A/c

(*iv*) *For sale of investment*
Bank A/c Dr.
To Depreciation Fund Investment A/c

(*v*) *For profit on sale of securities*
Depreciation Fund Investment A/c Dr.
To Depreciation Fund A/c

Note : *If loss, reverse entry will be passed.*

(*v*) *For writing off the old asset*
Depreciation Fund A/c Dr.
To Asset A/c

(*vii*) *For transferring the balance of depreciation fund account (if credit balance)*
Depreciation Fund A/c Dr.
To Profit and Loss A/c

Note : *If debit balance, reverse entry will be passed*

(*viii*) *For purchase of the new asset*
New Asset A/c Dr.
To Bank A/c

ILLUSTRATION 12. A company purchased a 3 years' lease on January 1, 2022 for ₹ 25,000. It is decided to provide for the replacement of lease at the end of 3 years by setting up a depreciation fund. It is expected that the investments will fetch interest at 5%. Sinking fund tables show that to provide the requisite sum at 5% at the end of 3 years an investment of ₹ 7,932 is required every year. Investments are made to the nearest rupee.

On 31st December, 2024 the investments were sold for ₹ 15,250. On 1st January, 2025, the same lease was renewed for a further period of 3 years by payment of ₹ 30,000.

Show the journal entries and give the Lease Account, Depreciation Fund Account, Depreciation Fund Investment Account and the New Lease Account. Calculations are made to the nearest rupee.

SOLUTION

JOURNAL ENTRIES

Date	Particulars		₹	₹
2022 Jan. 1	Lease A/c	Dr.	25,000	
	To Bank A/c			25,000
	(Being purchase of lease)			
Dec. 31	Depreciation A/c	Dr.	7,932	
	To Depreciation Fund A/c			7,932
	(The annual depreciation as per sinking fund table)			
	Depreciation Fund Investment A/c	Dr.	7,932	
	To Bank A/c			7,932
	(Being investments purchased from Depreciation Fund)			
	Profit & Loss A/c	Dr.	7,932	
	To Depreciation A/c			7,932
	(Being depreciation charged from Profit & Loss A/c)			
2023 Dec. 31	Bank A/c	Dr.	397	
	To Depreciation Fund A/c			397
	(The interest received @ 5% on ₹ 7,932, credited to Depreciation Fund A/c)			
	Depreciation A/c	Dr.	7,932	
	To Depreciation Fund A/c			7,932
	(The annual depreciation as per sinking fund table)			
	Depreciation Fund Investment A/c	Dr.	8,329	
	To Bank A/c			8,329
	(Being the purchase of investment from Depreciation Fund A/c)			
	Profit & Loss A/c	Dr.	7,932	
	To Depreciation A/c			7,932
	(Being depreciation charged from P & L A/c)			
2024 Dec. 31	Bank A/c	Dr.	813	
	To Depreciation Fund A/c			813
	(Being the interest-received credited to Depreciation Fund A/c)			
	Depreciation A/c	Dr.	7,932	
	To Depreciation Fund A/c			7,932
	(Being the annual depreciation)			
	Bank A/c	Dr.	15,250	
	To Depreciation Fund Investment A/c			15,250
	(Being the sale of investments)			
	Depreciation Fund A/c	Dr.	1,011	
	To Depreciation Fund Investment A/c			1,011
	(Being the loss on the sale of investment transferred to Depreciation Fund A/c)			

Date	Particulars		Dr. ₹	Cr. ₹
	Depreciation Fund A/c	Dr.	25,000	
	To Lease A/c			25,000
	(Amount of Lease written off by transfer to Depreciation Fund A/c)			
	Profit & Loss A/c	Dr.	1,005	
	To Depreciation Fund A/c			1,005
	(Balance left in depreciation fund A/c transferred to P. & L. A/c)			
2025 Jan. 1	New Lease A/c	Dr.	30,000	
	To Bank A/c			30,000
	(Being the purchase of new lease)			

LEASE ACCOUNT

Date	Particulars	₹	Date	Particulars	₹
2022 Jan. 1	To Bank A/c	25,000	2022 Dec. 31	By Balance c/d	25,000
2023 Jan. 1	To Balance b/d	25,000	2023 Dec. 31	By Balance c/d	25,000
2024 Jan. 1	To Balance b/d	25,000	2024 Dec. 31	By Depreciation Fund A/c	25,000

DEPRECIATION FUND ACCOUNT

Date	Particulars	₹	Date	Particulars	₹
2022 Dec. 31	To Balance c/d	7,932	2022 Dec. 31	By Depreciation A/c	7,932
2023 Dec. 31	To Balance c/d	16,261	2023 Jan. 1	By Balance b/d	7,932
			Dec. 31	" Bank (Int.)	397
			" "	" Depreciation A/c	7,932
		16,261			16,261
2024 Dec. 31	To Depreciation Fund Investment A/c	1,011	2024 Jan. 1	By Balance b/d	16,261
" "	" Lease A/c	25,000	Dec. 31	" Bank (Int.)	813
			" "	" Depreciation A/c	7,932
			" "	" P. & L. A/c	1,005
		26,011			26,011

DEPRECIATION FUND INVESTMENT ACCOUNT

Date	Particulars	₹	Date	Particulars	₹
2022 Dec. 31	To Bank A/c	7,932	2022 Dec. 31	By Balance c/d	7,932
2023 Jan. 1	To Balance b/d	7,932	2023 Dec. 31	By Balance c/d	16,261
Dec. 31	To Bank A/c	8,329			
		16,261			16,261

2024 Jan. 1	To Balance b/d	16,261	2024 Dec. 31 " "	By Bank " Depreciation Fund A/c (Loss transferred)	15,250 1,011
		16,261			16,261

NEW LEASE ACCOUNT

		₹			₹
2025 Jan. 1	To Bank A/c	30,000			

Comparison of Sinking Find Method and Annuity Method

Points of Distinction	*Sinking Fund Method*	*Annuity Method*
1. Investment in Outside Securities	Depreciation charged is invested in outside securities at the end of the year.	Depreciation charged is not invested in outside securities.
2. Interest	First interest is earned during second year & the first entry for investment of interest is made at the end of second year.	Interest is earned from the first day of the first year. Hence, entry is made at the end of first year.
3. Receipt of Interest	Actual interest is received.	No interest is received ; only adjustment entries are made.
4. Calculation of Depreciation	Amount to be depreciated is calculated with the help of Sinking Fund Table.	Calculated with the help of Annuity Table.
5. Total Charge to P & L A/c for the Life of the Asset	Depreciation charged is cost of asset *minus* Interest.	Depreciation charged is cost of asset *plus* Interest.
6. Change in Interest	The amount of interest increases year after year.	It decreases year after year.
7. Value of Asset for Reporting Purposes	The value in the Asset Account remains same year after year and depreciation is charged to revenue account.	The depreciation is charged to the Asset Account every year so the value of asset decreases

However, inspite of the above distinctions between the two, both are similar in the following respects :

1. Under both methods the Asset Account shows nil balance after a given period of time.
2. The amount of depreciation provided year after year is fixed.
3. The net charge made against Profit and Loss Account is same under both the methods.

(*vi*) Insurance Policy Method

This method is similar to the depreciation fund method but instead of making investment, arrangements are made with an insurance company which will receive premiums annually and pay at the end of the fixed period the required amount. Premiums have to be paid at the beginning of each year. This method along with the previous two methods (*i.e.*, Annuity Method and Sinking Fund Method) can be adopted where (*i*) the repairs and maintenance costs are constant or decreasing over the life of the asset and (*ii*) the revenue and operating efficiency are constant or increasing over the life of the asset.

Journal Entries

First and Subsequent years

(*i*) *For payment of premium at the beginning of the year*

Depreciation Insurance Policy A/c Dr.
To Bank A/c

(*ii*) *For providing the amount of premium at the end of the year out of Profit and Loss Account in the form of depreciation reserve*

Profit and Loss A/c Dr.
To Depreciation Reserve A/c

(*iii*) *For interest on balance of the Policy together with the amount of premium.*

Depreciation Insurance Policy A/c Dr.
To Depreciation Reserve A/c

Note : This entry is to be passed only when it is desired to bring interest into account.

Last year

(*i*) *For the receipt of amount of policy on maturity*

Bank A/c Dr.
To Depreciation Insurance Policy A/c

(*ii*) *For writing off old asset*

Depreciation Reserve A/c Dr.
To Old Asset A/c

(*iii*) *For transferring the balance of Depreciation Insurance Policy Account to Depreciation Reserve Account.*

Depreciation Insurance Policy A/c Dr.
To Depreciation Reserve A/c

(*iv*) *For purchase of new asset*

New Asset A/c Dr.
To Bank A/c

ILLUSTRATION 13. On 1st Jan. 2021, a lease of premises is purchased for four years for ₹ 50,000 and it is decided to make provision for the replacement of the lease by means of an insurance policy purchased for an annual premium of ₹ 12,000.

Show the necessary ledger accounts for four years assuming that the renewal of the lease costs ₹ 50,000 on 1-1-2025.

SOLUTION

LEASE ACCOUNT

		₹			₹
2021 Jan. 1	To Bank	50,000	2021 Dec. 31	By Balance c/d	50,000
2022 Jan. 1	To Balance b/d	50,000	2022 Dec. 31	By Balance c/d	50,000

Date	Particulars	₹	Date	Particulars	₹
2023 Jan. 1	To Balance b/d	50,000	2023 Dec. 31	By Balance c/d	50,000
2024 Jan. 1	To Balance b/d	50,000	2024 Dec. 31	By Depreciation Reserve A/c	50,000

DEPRECIATION RESERVE ACCOUNT

Date	Particulars	₹	Date	Particulars	₹
2021 Dec. 31	To Balance c/d	12,000	2021 Dec. 31	By Profit and Loss A/c	12,000
2022 Dec. 31	To Balance c/d	24,000	2022 Jan. 1	By Balance b/d	12,000
			Dec. 31	" Profit and Loss A/c	12,000
		24,000			24,000
2023 Dec. 31	To Balance c/d	36,000	2023 Jan. 1	By Balance b/d	24,000
			Dec. 31	" Profit and Loss A/c	12,000
		36,000			36,000
2024 Dec. 31	To Lease Account	50,000	2024 Jan. 1	By Balance b/d	36,000
			Dec. 31	" Profit and Loss A/c	12,000
			Dec. 31	By Depreciation Insurance Policy A/c (Profit on the Realisation of Policy)	2,000
		50,000			50,000

DEPRECIATION INSURANCE POLICY ACCOUNT

Date	Particulars	₹	Date	Particulars	₹
2021 Jan. 1	To Bank	12,000	2021 Dec. 31	By Balance c/d	12,000
2022 Jan. 1	To Balance b/d	12,000	2022 Dec. 31	By Balance c/d	24,000
" "	" Bank	12,000			
		24,000			24,000
2023 Jan. 1	By Balance b/d	24,000	2023 Dec. 31	By Balance c/d	36,000
" "	" Bank	12,000			
		36,000			36,000
2024 Jan. 1	To Balance b/d	36,000	2024 Dec. 31	By Bank (Insurance Policy) matured	50,000
" "	" Bank	12,000			
Dec. 31	" Depreciation Reserve A/c (Profit on the Realisation of Policy)	2,000			
		50,000			50,000

NEW LEASE ACCOUNT

		₹			₹
2025 Jan. 1	To Bank A/c	50,000			

Comparison Between Sinking Fund and Insurance Policy Method

Though both methods' ultimate purpose is to accumulate the amount for the replacement of the asset when its useful life exhausts yet the following are the points of distinction between the two :

Points of Distinction	*Sinking Fund*	*Insurance Policy*
1. Use of depreciation amount	Depreciation amount is used to purchase securities at the end of the year.	It is used to pay premium to the insurance Co. at the beginning of the year.
2. Risk	There may be risk of loss when the securities are realised.	A fixed amount is received so there is no risk of loss.
3. Utilisation of amount received	New asset is purchased after selling the securities and adjusting the amount so received to buy new asset.	Even if the asset is destroyed during the year, we can realize full amount from insurance Co. and can replace the asset.

Irrespective of the above differences following are the similarities :

1. Under both methods amount is invested outside the business.
2. Amount of depreciation is not transferred to the Asset's A/c rather to Depreciation Fund Reserve A/c.
3. Interest or bonus is also received from outside.
4. At the end of the stipulated period cash is received from outside which is used to purchase new asset.

(vii) Revaluation Method

Under this method, the asset is revalued at the end of the accounting year and this value is compared with the value of the asset at the beginning of the year. The difference is treated as depreciation. Where purchase of asset is also made during the year then asset is valued at the start of the period ; the additions increase the value and then the asset is revalued at the end of the period. The amount of decrease in value shows the amount by which the asset is deemed to have depreciated. This method is used in case of bottles, corks, crates, loose tools, packages, patterns, trade marks, live stock etc.

(viii) Depletion Method

This method is mostly used in case of mines, quarries etc. from which a certain quantity of output is expected to be obtained. The value of mine depends only upon quantity of minerals that can be obtained. When the whole quantity is taken, the mine loses its value. The rate of depreciation is worked out only so much per tonne. It is obtained by simply dividing the cost of the mine by the total quantity of the minerals expected to be available. The use of this method is suggested in case of those assets where the value declines as a function of uses rather than of the passage of time and other service costs remain proportionate to use.

(ix) Machine Hour Rate Method

This method is useful in case of machines. The life of the machine is fixed in terms of hours. Hourly rate of depreciation is worked out by dividing the cost of the machine by the total number of hours for which the machine is expected to be used. Depreciation to be written off in a year will be ascertained by multiplying the hourly rate of depreciation by the number of hours that the machine actually runs in the year.

Asset Disposal Account

Sometimes a part of machinery is disposed off or discarded, then it is better to open a machinery disposal account. The book value less depreciation of the discarded portion should be debited to this account and credited to the asset account. But if the asset is maintained at original cost and a separate provision for depreciation account is maintained, then machinery disposal account should be debited with the cost of the discarded portion of the asset and credited with depreciation provision applicable to this asset. The amount realised or the estimated realisable value is credited to the machinery disposal account and the balance of this account will show profit or loss and is transferred to Profit and Loss Account. Following entries are passed in such a case on sale of an asset :

(*a*) Asset Disposal A/c
 To Asset A/c *[With original cost of asset]*

(*b*) Bank Account
 To Asset Disposal A/c *[With amount realised from the sale of asset]*

(*c*) Provision for Depreciation A/c
 To Asset Disposal A/c *[With accumulated depreciation on the asset sold]*

(*d*) Profit & Loss A/c
 To Asset Disposal A/c *[For transfer of loss on sale of asset]*

Note : Reverse entry in case there is profit.

ILLUSTRATION 14. The following balances appear in the books of Dheeraj Enterprises :

	₹
Machinery Account as on 1-4-2024	12,00,000
Provision for Depreciation Account as on 1-4-2024	4,65,000

On 1st October, 2024 the Machinery which was purchased on 1st April, 2021 for ₹ 2,00,000 was sold for ₹ 1,10,000 and on the same date another Machinery was purchased for ₹ 4,80,000. The firm has been charging depreciation at 10% p.a. on written down value of the Machinery every year. Prepare the Machinery Account, Provision for Depreciation Account and Machinery Disposal Account for the year ending 31st March, 2025. ***(Foundation Examination, June, 2023 Modified)***

SOLUTION

Dr. **MACHINERY ACCOUNT (AT ORIGINAL COST)** Cr.

Date	Particulars	Amount (₹)	Date	Particulars	Amount (₹)
1-4-24	To Balance b/d	12,00,000	1-10-24	By Disposed Machinery A/c	2,00,000
1-10-24	To Bank A/c	4,80,000	31-3-25	By Balance c/d	14,80,000
		16,80,000			16,80,000

Dr. **PROVISION FOR DEPRECIATION ACCOUNT** Cr.

Date	Particulars	Amount (₹)	Date	Particulars	Amount (₹)
1-10-24	To Disposed Machinery A/c	61,490	1-4-24	By Balance b/d	4,65,000
31-3-25	To Balance c/d	4,93,720	1-10-24	By Depreciation	7,290
			31-3-25	By Depreciation A/c	82,920
		5,55,210			5,55,210

Dr. **DISPOSED MACHINERY ACCOUNT** Cr.

Date	Particulars	Amount (₹)	Date	Particulars	Amount (₹)
1-10-24	To Machinery A/c	2,00,000	1-10-24	By Provision for Depreciation A/c	61,490
				By Bank A/c	1,10,000
				By Profit and Loss A/c	28,510
		2,00,000			2,00,000

Working Notes :

1. Calculation of Profit/Loss on Sale of Machinery

Particulars				₹
A. Original Cost				2,00,000
B. *Less* : Depreciation @ 10% WDV p.a. for $3\frac{1}{2}$ years				
Year	*Cost./WDV*	*Depreciation @ 10%*		
1	2,00,000	20,000		
2	1,80,000	18,000		
3	1,62,000	16,200		
4	1,45,800	7,290	(6 months)	61,490
C. Book Value as on Date of Sale (A – B)				1,38,510
D. *Less* : Sale Proceeds				1,10,000
E. Loss on Sale (C – D)				28,510

2. WDV of Remaining Machine

		₹
Cost of Machinery on 1-4-2024		12,00,000
Less : Cost of Machinery sold		2,00,000
		10,00,000
Less : Depreciation		
Provision for Depreciation	4,65,000	
Less : Depreciation on Machinery sold	54,200	4,10,800
WDV of remaining Machine		5,89,200

3. Calculation of Depreciation for Current Year on Machines

Particulars	₹
A. On WDV of Old Machines of ₹ 5,89,200 for 1 years (10% WDV)	58,920
B. On New Machine of ₹ 4,80,000 for 1/2 year	24,000
	82,920
C. Depreciation on Machinery sold (₹ 1,45,800 @ 10% for 6 months)	7,290
	90,210

Change of Method

Sometimes the method is changed either from straight line method to diminishing balance method or from diminishing balance method to straight line method with effect from the particular year or with retrospective effect. If the change is from the particular year, then there will be no problem but simply to change the method of depreciation. But if the change is to be effective with retrospective effect, then calculations are required to be made.

Steps in recording a change in the Method of Depreciation with retrospective effect :

Step 1 : Calculate the total depreciation already provided on the existing assets (*i.e.,* excluding the assets disposed off or discarded) from the back date (*i.e.,* from the date of the asset coming into use to the date of decision to change the method of charging depreciation) under the existing method.

Step 2 : Calculate the total depreciation on the existing asset from the back date under the new method and rate till date (*i.e.,* from the date of the asset coming into use to the date of decision to change the method).

Step 3 : Calculate the difference between the total depreciation under existing method (as per Step 1) and under the new method (Step 2).

Step 4 : Adjust the short depreciation (excess of Step 2 over Step 1) by debiting Profit & Loss Accounting and Crediting the Asset Account/Provision for Depreciation Account.

Or

Adjust the excess depreciation (Excess of Step 1 over Step 2) by debiting Asset Account/Provision for Depreciation Account and Crediting Profit & Loss Account)

Step 5 : Charge depreciation from the current accounting year and onwards by adopting new method.

The working of the change of the method will be more clear from the following 'illustrations'.

ILLUSTRATION 15. ***(Change from DBM to SLM with retrospective effect)*** P. Ltd. which depreciates its machinery @ 10% p.a. on written down value desires to change the basis to straight line method, the rate remaining the same. The decision is taken on 31st December, 2025 to be effective from 1st January, 2023.

On 1st January, 2025 the balance in the machinery account is ₹ 29,16,000.

On 1st July, 2025 a part of machinery purchased on 1st January, 2023 for ₹ 2,40,000 was sold for ₹ 1,35,000. On the same date a new machine is purchased for ₹ 4,50,000 and installed at a cost of ₹ 24,000.

Prepare Machinery Account for 2025.

SOLUTION **MACHINERY ACCOUNT**

2025		₹	2025		₹
Jan. 1	To Balance b/d	29,16,000	July 1	By Bank A/c	1,35,000
July 1	To Bank A/c		" "	" Depreciation A/c	12,000
	(₹ 4,50,000 +₹ 24,000)	4,74,000	" "	" P. & L. A/c (Loss on sale of Machine) (1)	45,000
			Dec. 31	By P. & L. A/c (Additional Depreciation to be charged (3)	36,000
			" "	By Depreciation A/c (4)	3,59,700
			" "	" Balance c/d	28,02,300
		33,90,000			33,90,000

Working Notes :

(1) ***Calculation of Loss on Machine Sold***

		₹
	Cost of Machine on 1-1-2023	2,40,000
Less :	Depreciation @ 10% for 2023	24,000
	W.D.V. on 1-1-2024	2,16,000
Less :	Depreciation @ 10% for 2024	24,000
	W.D.V. on 1-1-2025	1,92,000
Less :	Depreciation @ 10% for 1/2 year	12,000
	W.D.V. on 1-7-2025	1,80,000
Less :	Amount realised from the sale	1,35,000
Loss of sale of machine		45,000

(2) ***Calculation of Book Value of Unsold Machinery on 1-1-2023***

		₹
	W.D.V. on 1-1-2025	29,16,000
Add :	Depreciation for 2024 $\left(\frac{10}{90} \times ₹\ 29,16,000\right)$	3,24,000
		32,40,000
Add :	Depreciation for 2023 $\left(\frac{10}{90} \times ₹\ 32,40,000\right)$	3,60,000
	Book value of unsold machinery on 1-1-2023	36,00,000

(3) ***Calculation of Additional Depreciation because of Change in Method***

		₹	₹
	Depreciation to be charged under new method (*i.e.*, straight line method for 2023 and 2024) $\left(\frac{10}{100} \times ₹\ 36,00,000 \times 2\right)$		7,20,000
Less :	Depreciation already charged under the old method (*i.e.*, W.D. Value method)		
	2023	3,24,000	
	2024	3,60,000	6,84,000
	Additional Depreciation to be Charged		36,000

(4) ***Depreciation to be Charged for 2025***

Depreciation on ₹ 33,60,000 @ 10% for 2025	3,36,000
Depreciation on ₹ 4,74,000 @ 10% for half year	23,700
	3,59,700

ILLUSTRATION 16. (***Change from SLM to DBM with retrospective effect through disposal A/c***) A company purchased second hand machinery on 1st January, 2022 for ₹ 3,00,000, subsequent to which ₹ 60,000 and ₹ 40,000 were spent on its repairs and installation, respectively. On 1st July, 2023 another machinery was purchased for ₹ 2,60,000. On 1st July, 2024, the first machinery having become outdated was auctioned for ₹ 3,00,000 and on the same date, another machinery was purchased for ₹ 2,50,000.

On 1st July, 2025, the second machinery was also sold off and it fetched ₹ 2,30,000.

Depreciation was provided on machinery @ 10% on the original cost annually on 31st December, under the Fixed Instalment method. From 1st January, 2024, the method of providing depreciation was changed to Reducing Balance method from the date of asset coming into use, the rate being 15% p.a.

You are required to prepare the following accounts in the books of the company :

(*i*) Machinery Account for the years ending 2022 to 2025.

(*ii*) Machinery Disposal Account.

Note : *The figures may be rounded off to the nearest multiple of Rupees ten.*

SOLUTION

MACHINERY ACCOUNT

Date	Particulars	₹	Date	Particulars	₹
1-1-2022	To Bank A/c (A) (Cost ₹ 3,00,000 + Repairs ₹ 60,000 + Installation Charges ₹ 40,000)	4,00,000	31-12-2022	By Depreciation A/c (A)	40,000
			"	" Balance c/d (A)	3,60,000
		4,00,000			4,00,000
1-1-2023	To Balance b/d	3,60,000	31-12-2023	By Depreciation A/c (₹ 40,000 + B ₹ 13,000)	53,000
1-7-2023	To Bank A/c (B)	2,60,000	31-12-2023	By Balance c/d (A—₹ 3,20,000 + B—₹ 2,47,000)	5,67,000
		6,20,000			6,20,000
1-1-2024	To Balance b/d	5,67,000	1-7-2024	By Machinery Disposal A/c (A) (1)	2,67,320
1-7-2024	To Bank A/c (C)	2,50,000	31-12-2024	By Depreciation A/c ₹ A— 21,680; B— 36,080; C— 18,750 (1)	76,510
			31-12-2024	By Profit & Loss A/c (Short Depreciation) ₹ A— 31,000; B— 6,500 (2)	37,500
			31-12-2024	By Balance c/d : ₹ B— 2,04,420; C— 2,31,250	4,35,670
		8,17,000			8,17,000
1-1-2025	To Balance b/d	4,35,670	1-7-2025	By Machinery Disposal A/c (B)—(1)	1,89,090
			31-12-2025	By Depreciation A/c ₹ B— 15,330; C— 34,690	50,020
			"	By Balance c/d (C)	1,96,560
		4,35,670			4,35,670

MACHINERY DISPOSAL ACCOUNT

		₹			₹
1-7-2024	To Machinery A/c (A)	2,67,320	1-7-2024	By Bank A/c	3,00,000
"	To Profit & Loss A/c (Profit)	32,680			
		3,00,000			3,00,000
1-7-2025	To Machinery A/c (B)	1,89,090	1-7-2025	By Bank A/c	2,30,000
"	To Profit & Loss A/c (Profit)	40,910			
		2,30,000			2,30,000

Working Notes

	SL Method		W.D.V. Method	
	Depreciation @ 10% p.a.	Book Value	Depreciation @ 15% p.a.	Book Value
(A) Purchased for ₹ 4,00,000				
Year 2022	40,000	3,60,000	60,000	3,40,000
Year 2023	40,000	3,20,000	51,000	2,89,000
	80,000		1,11,000	
Year till July 2024			21,680	2,67,320
(B) Purchased for ₹ 2,60,000 : 1-7-23	13,000	2,47,000	19,500	2,40,500
Year 2024			36,080	2,04,420
Year till July 2025			15,330	1,89,090
(C) Purchased for ₹ 2,50,000				
on 1-7-2024 : Dep. for 2024			18,750	2,31,250
Year 2025			34,690	1,96,560

(2) *Adjusted Depreciation till 2023*

	SLM	*WDV*	₹	
Machinery A	₹ 80,000	₹ 1,11,000	31,000	(deficit to be charged to P/L A/c)
Machinery B	₹ 13,000	₹ 19,500	6,500	(deficit to be charged to P/L A/c)

Notes :

(1) When method of depreciation is changed, depreciation is recalculated in accordance with the new method from the date of the asset coming into use. The deficiency or surplus arising from retrospective recomputation of depreciation in accordance with the new method is adjusted in the accounts in the year to which the method of depreciation is changed. Therefore, in the above solution, the retrospective recomputation of depreciation as per new method has been considered.

(2) The method of depreciation was changed on 1st January, 2024. Since, machinery A existed on the date of change in method of depreciation, therefore, *retrospective effect* has also been given to it.

Depreciation on Replacement Cost

In all the methods of depreciation already discussed depreciation has been provided on historical cost basis. Though the objective of apportioning the total cost of the asset over the useful life is achieved but in times of rising prices the objective of retaining funds for the replacement of the asset at the end of its life cannot be achieved. For example, a machine costing ₹ 70,000 is depreciated on historical cost basis. At the end of its working life ₹ 70,000 will be available for replacement of the machine through depreciation charge to profit and loss account but it would be impossible to replace the machine if due to rise in prices, its cost has increased from ₹ 70,000 to ₹ 1,50,000. Some accountants have, therefore, suggested that depreciation should be charged to profit and loss account on the replacement cost rather than on historical cost basis as it will provide sufficient funds to replace the machine at the end of its working life and will not create any financial problem in the concern for its replacement.

Arguments in Favour of Replacement Cost

Accountants who favour charging of depreciation on replacement cost basis give the following arguments :

1. In order to maintain the capital assets properly, it is desirable that depreciation should be charged on replacement cost basis otherwise real earned profit will not be disclosed by the profit and loss account.

2. If depreciation is charged on historical cost basis, the charge for depreciation to profit and loss account will be less and it will show the inflated profit and can be paid away by means of dividend to the shareholders. This will prejudice the right of preference shareholders and debenture-holders and gradually undermines the capital structure of the business.

3. If depreciation is not provided on replacement cost basis, less charge of depreciation to profit and loss account, will provide insufficient funds to replace the asset at the end of its working life and the concern may have to resort to borrowing further capital.

4. Revenues are earned on current price basis. Hence, it will be logical to charge depreciation on replacement cost basis in order to give correct current price charge of depreciation to profit and loss account.

Arguments Against Replacement Cost Basis

Some accountants object the charging of depreciation on replacement cost basis because of certain practical difficulties, as given below :

1. The issue of replacement of an asset is distinct from writing it off by way of depreciation. For replacement of assets the managements should retain sufficient profits within the business. This issue, therefore, cannot be brought under depreciation.

2. Charging depreciation on replacement cost cannot guarantee that excessive dividend will not be paid. Higher dividends can be paid by an arbitrary accounting expedient of this kind.

3. Reserves can be made on regular basis to have business stability and future capital investment. It is of no use to inject fictitious charge into profit and loss account by way of adjustment of depreciation charge after the real cost has been written off.

4. The effect of depreciation based on replacement value on cost and financial accounts cannot be readily computed irrespective of the method of depreciation in operation.

5. It is very difficult to find out the replacement cost in the beginning of the asset's life. At the most an estimate, which is taken for the purpose of charging depreciation, may be more or less and may not provide correct amount of funds for the replacement of asset at the end of its working life.

6. The basis of charging depreciation on replacement cost is objected by the income tax authorities on the plea that depreciation charge to profit and loss account will be more which ultimately will reduce the profit for income tax purposes.

7. It is very difficult to replace the same asset at the end of its working life as asset always change in quality and type due to improvements. If estimate of the amount which is required for replacement of the asset is made on the latest model, then it will give an overcharge to profit and loss account which is not justified.

8. If depreciation is charged on replacement cost basis, *i.e.*, on the basis of some imaginary cost, it would defeat the basic accounting concept of objective evidence which of course, can be achieved if depreciation is provided on historical cost basis.

9. Businessmen and industrialists may prefer to charge depreciation on replacement cost as due to overcharge of depreciation to the profit and loss account, it will reduce the profit for income tax purposes but in time of depression when the prices of assets are falling, they may not agree to charge the depreciation on replacement cost as it will increase the profits due to less charge of depreciation to profit and loss account and ultimately their liability for income tax will increase.

Due to the practical difficulties discussed above, it is desirable to provide the depreciation on historical cost basis rather than on replacement cost but the following courses may be adopted to have more funds in the concern for replacement of the asset at the end of its working life :

(*i*) Difference between the depreciation according to replacement cost and historical cost should be appropriated out of surplus account and credited to a separate account called replacement reserve account. It will be shown on the liabilities side of Balance Sheet till it is required to be used for replacement purposes.

(*ii*) Provision for depreciation should be charged to profit and loss account at current rate of interest. The amount so provided will definitely be more than the original cost basis and may be sufficient to provide for its replacement.

Treatment of Depreciation under the Companies Act and Accounting Standards

Depreciation is an important accounting concept that ensures the systematic allocation of the cost of a tangible fixed asset over its useful life. The treatment of depreciation in India is governed by both the **Companies Act, 2013** and the relevant **Accounting Standards (AS and Ind AS)**.

(A) Under the Companies Act, 2013

The **Companies Act, 2013**, through **Schedule II**, lays down the legal framework for depreciation for companies registered under it.

1. **Useful Lives as per Schedule II:** Schedule II of the Act provides a **list of indicative useful lives** for various types of tangible fixed assets such as buildings, machinery, furniture, computers, vehicles, etc. These useful lives serve as the basis for calculating depreciation.
   - Companies are **not permitted to arbitrarily select useful lives**.
   - However, if a company believes the useful life of an asset differs from the one prescribed, it **must justify the change with proper technical advice** and disclose it in the notes to accounts.
2. **Methods of Charging Depreciation:** Companies may choose from the following methods to compute depreciation:
   - **Straight Line Method (SLM)** – where an equal amount of depreciation is charged each year.
   - **Written Down Value Method (WDV)** – where a fixed percentage is applied on the reduced book value of the asset each year.

   The method chosen must be applied **consistently**, and any change must be disclosed and justified.
3. **Component Accounting (Mandatory):** Schedule II mandates Component Accounting. If an asset has parts/components that have different useful lives or patterns of consumption, each significant part must be depreciated separately. This improves the accuracy of financial reporting and asset valuation.

(B) Under Accounting Standards

AS 10 (Revised) – Property, Plant and Equipment: Treatment of Depreciation

AS 10 (Revised) is the current Indian Accounting Standard that deals with the recognition, measurement, depreciation, and disposal of Property, Plant, and Equipment (PPE). It has replaced the older AS 10 (Accounting for Fixed Assets) and AS 6 (Depreciation Accounting), bringing depreciation and asset accounting in line with international norms.

1. **Depreciation – Meaning and Purpose**

   Under AS 10 (Revised), depreciation is defined as: *"The systematic allocation of the depreciable amount of an asset over its useful life."*

   Depreciation is not about estimating market value or wear and tear. Instead, it's about allocating the cost of a tangible fixed asset as an expense over the periods that benefit from its use.

2. **Depreciable Amount: The depreciable amount of an asset is calculated as:**

   Cost of the Asset – Residual Value

   - Cost of the asset includes: Purchase price , Import duties and taxes and Directly attributable costs (like installation, delivery)
   - Residual value is the estimated amount an enterprise expects to receive from disposing of the asset at the end of its useful life, after deducting the estimated costs of disposal.

   Only this net cost (*i.e.,* depreciable amount) is apportioned over the asset's useful life.

3. **Pattern of Consumption of Economic Benefits:** The method of depreciation must reflect the actual pattern in which the asset's future economic benefits are expected to be consumed by the enterprise. Common methods allowed:

   - Straight Line Method (SLM): Equal amount of depreciation each year
   - Written Down Value (WDV): Higher depreciation in earlier years, lower later
   - Units of Production Method: Based on actual usage/output

   The method selected must faithfully represent asset usage. If the pattern changes, the method should be changed prospectively (as a change in accounting estimate).

4. **Disclosure Requirements under AS 10 (Revised)**

   To ensure transparency and comparability in financial reporting, AS 10 (Revised) mandates detailed disclosures related to depreciation. The enterprise must disclose:

   (*a*) The depreciation method used (*e.g.,* SLM, WDV, Units of Production)

   (*b*) The useful life or depreciation rate used for each class of asset

   (*c*) The gross carrying amount of each class of asset

   (*d*) The accumulated depreciation and accumulated impairment losses at the beginning and end of the reporting period

   (*e*) A reconciliation of the carrying amount at the beginning and end of the period, showing additions, disposals, depreciation charges, impairment losses, other changes

5. **Review of Estimates and Method:** Although AS 10 (Revised) does not require an annual review, good accounting practice recommends periodically reviewing useful life, residual value and depreciation method. If there is a change in estimate, it must be dealt with prospectively, and not retrospectively, in accordance with AS 5 (Net Profit or Loss for the Period, Prior Period Items and Changes in Accounting Policies).

   Ind AS 16 – Property, Plant and Equipment (for Ind AS compliant entities):

   For companies required to follow Indian Accounting Standards (Ind AS), depreciation is dealt with under Ind AS 16. Key highlights:

   - Similar to AS 10 in terms of concept, but with stricter requirements:
     - Annual review of useful life, residual value, and depreciation method is mandatory.
     - Any change in estimate (life, method, value) must be accounted for prospectively, as per Ind AS 8.
   - The cost model and revaluation model are both permitted for asset valuation.
   - Disclosure requirements are more comprehensive, aligned with international standards (IFRS).

DEPRECIATION POLICY

The depreciation policy to be followed in an organisation is decided at the top level. Depreciation policy, in fact, relates to the choice of the method of depreciation and its suitability for the organisation. The decision regarding the method to be followed has far reaching consequences and that is why this problem is complex. It is the accountant who will analyse the implications of following a particular method and appraise the same to the management. The matter being policy decision is left for the final decision of the management. But various method can be evaluated in the light of the various factors, i.e., relationship between decline in market value and use, effect of obsolescence, repairs and maintenance, future operating efficiency of the asset in use, service cost of the asset to be charged against revenue and the degree of uncertainty regarding the latter period of the asset life. The method of depreciation many recover the original investment, provide uniform rate of return on investment, derive maximum tax benefit, to ascertain the profit or loss correctly and generate adequate funds to replace the assets.

Objectives of Depreciation Policy

Following are the main objectives of depreciation policy :

(i) **Determining income subject to income tax.** Depreciation being 'tax shield' is a deductible expense while computing the taxable income of a concern. The management should try to make this shield as effective as possible within the framework of the taxation laws. Depreciation is the allocation of the total cost of the asset over its effective life. This tax shield will be more effective, if more deductions for this are claimed in the beginning of the life of asset as present worth of tax savings in the beginning of life of asset will be more than they would be when depreciation is equally distributed over the effective life of the asset. It will also increase the financial flexibility because of greater funds in hand. That method which enables us to take depreciation as early as possible is considered as more suitable. Diminishing balance method of calculating depreciation results in greater tax saving in a balanced firm as compared to straight line method.

(ii) **Financial management considerations**. The main function of financial management is to keep intact the capital invested in depreciable assets and to make provision for the replacement, modernisation and expansion on most favourable terms. To achieve this objective, how far the management can depend on the method of depreciation will be clear from the effect of depreciation on the availability of the funds. Depreciation is a process of allocation and not that of generation. The provision of depreciation helps the management to retain this amount of profit in the business which otherwise would have gone to the government in the form of taxes or to the shareholders in the form of dividend or bonus to the employees. That method of depreciation which provides tax savings is most appropriate from the financial management point of view. Diminishing balance method is again better in this respect than straight line method because more depreciation is provided in the beginning of life of asset.

(iii) **Determining correct net income and financial condition for external reporting.** Depreciation expense arises from expiration of the capital cost spent on purchase of different assets with use and passage of time. In order to match the cost with revenue, it is necessary to measure the depreciation cost incurred during a given period. The charge of depreciation is also necessary to determine the correct net income and financial position of a concern so that financial statement may give true and fair view of the state of affairs of the business. From this angle any method, *i.e.*, Diminishing Balance or Straight Line (both are recognised by the income tax authorities in India) may be adopted. Generally that method of depreciation should be adopted which may help to keep the accounts in agreement with income tax rules.

(iv) **Measuring managerial performance.** Depreciation is an element of cost. Product costs are used to measure profitability of different products and guide the management in decisions regarding pricing and sales emphasis. The charge of depreciation is dependent on the method we adopt in a concern. The charge under straight line may be fix or varying under diminishing balance method. If diminishing method is adopted, it may give a wrong impression that operational efficiency is increasing as costs are declining with each successive period under this method. Thus differences in costs because of charge of depreciation under different methods, tend to mislead management in selecting their operational alternative which would be for more profitable for the company as a whole. Whether depreciation should be charged on historical cost or on replacement cost basis is again a controversial issue and will also affect the managerial decisions to be taken by the top level management.

(v) **Obsolescence.** It is a sudden loss arising in the value of an asset not due to wear and tear but because the asset may have to be discarded in favour of one better adopted to its purpose and giving better result. It is also called external depreciation as the asset has to be withdrawn before the end of its useful life owing to the external factors like technological improvements in the existing asset. It may also arise because an asset is not up to standard to cope with the increasing competition in the market. In such a case, depreciation method should be such that the asset should be depreciated quickly, otherwise profit and loss account will be over burdened with the amount of loss on account of obsolescence in the year in which the asset obsoletes.

(vi) **Convention of consistency.** Accounting rules, practices and conventions should be continuously observed and applied, *i.e.*, these should not change from one year to another. The results of different years will be comparable only when accounting rules, practices and conventions are continuously adhered to from year to year. Whatever method of depreciation is followed, it should be followed in future also to get comparable results, otherwise profit and loss account will not give a consistent view of the performance of the business. Consistency serves to eliminate personal bias because the accountant will have to follow a particular method of depreciation year after year. The rationale behind this concept is that frequent changes in accounting treatment (*i.e.*, method of depreciation) would make the financial statements unreliable to the persons who use them. The rationale for following the convention of consistency in respect of charging depreciation is made clear in the following example :

Suppose a company purchased a fixed asset for ₹ 5,00,000 and it charges depreciation @ 20% on straight line method. At the end of the second year, the book value of the asset will be :

	₹
Cost of the fixed asset	5,00,000
Less : 20% depreciation for 1st year	1,00,000
	4,00,000
Less : 20% depreciation for 2nd year	1,00,000
Book value at the end of 2nd year	3,00,000

Now, if the method of depreciation is changed from straight line method to reducing balance method in the second year, the book value of the asset at the end of second year will be :

	₹
Cost of the fixed asset	5,00,000
Less : 20% depreciation for 1st year	1,00,000
	4,00,000
Less: 20% depreciation for 2nd year $\left(i.e.\ ₹\ 4{,}00{,}000 \times \frac{20}{100}\right)$	80,000
Book value at the end of 2nd year	3,20,000

The effect of change will be that depreciation of ₹ 1,00,000 will be reduced to ₹ 80,000 in the second year making an increase of ₹ 20,000 in profit and asset will be shown in the Balance Sheet at ₹ 3,20,000 and not at ₹ 3,00,000.

(vii) **Availability of sufficient funds for replacement.** It is the objective of depreciation policy to see that sufficient funds are available when the asset is to be replaced. Though the objective of apportioning the total cost of the asset over its useful life is achieved by charging depreciation on historical cost basis but in times of rising prices the objective of retaining funds for the replacement of asset at the end of its working life cannot be achieved. For example, a machine costing ₹ 1,00,000 is depreciated on historical cost basis. At the end of its working life ₹ 1,00,000 will be available for replacement of the machine through depreciation charge to profit and loss account but it would be impossible to replace the machine if due to rise in prices its cost has increased from ₹ 1,00,000 to ₹ 2,00,000. Under such a situation, depreciation should be charged on replacement cost basis rather than on historical cost basis.

(viii) **Depreciation policy and investors.** The depreciation policy followed by a concern greatly affects the decisions of the investing public which primarily takes its decisions of investing the money or not in the concern on the basis of reported income. The income of the concern will be shown more if depreciation has not been provided or insufficient amount has been provided and thereby mislead the investing public to think that the concern is more profitable than it actually is. The objective of depreciation policy, therefore, should be to provide accurate amount of depreciation so that investing public may not be misled and correct investment decisions may be made by it.

In short, from tax saving and financial management point of view, diminishing balance method is better but for external reporting and managerial decisions, depreciation charge may better be computed by straight line method.

PROVISIONS AND RESERVES

There are many risks and uncertainties in business and in order to save the business from such untoward happenings and events, it is necessary to take provisions and reserves in every business. Provisions and reserves are used in different senses in accounting terminology.

Meaning of Provision

The term'provision' means any amount written off or retained by way of providing depreciation, renewals or diminution in the value of assets or retained by way of providing for any known liability the amount of which may not be determined with substantial accuracy. If the amount of such liability can be ascertained it will be a liability and not a provision. Provision for depreciation, provision for bad and doubtful debts, provision for taxation, provision for repairs and renewal and provision for contingencies are some examples of provisions. It is a charge to profit and loss account.

The main purpose of provision for repairs and renewals is to give a uniform charge to Profit and Loss Account in respect of machinery. This is all the more necessary as the usefulness of the machinery is also uniform from year to year. Under this method the total repairs over the life of the asset are estimated and then average is found. This amount is debited to the Profit and Loss Account of every year and credited to the provision for repairs and renewals account. The actual amount of repairs and renewals is debited to the provision for repairs and renewals account, the balance of the account appears on the liabilities side in the Balance Sheet. As soon as the life of the assets is over, the account is automatically closed.

Provision for Bad and Doubtful Debts has already been dealt with in the chapter of Final Accounts.

ILLUSTRATION 17. Shibalik Engineering Ltd. worked out an estimated expenditure of ₹ 1,20,000 over a period of 8 years on repairs of machinery. The company decided to raise a 'Provision for Repairs and Renewals Account' by debiting Profit & Loss Account with a uniform amount every year.

The actual expenditure on repairs during the first four years amounted to ₹ 5,200, ₹ 12,900; ₹ 10,700 and ₹ 16,800.

Prepare Provision for Repairs and Renewal Account stating in the footnote how the figures would appear in Balance Sheet and also for treatment in computing of managerial remuneration.

SOLUTION

Shibalik Engineering Ltd.

PROVISION FOR REPAIRS AND RENEWALS ACCOUNT

Year		₹	Year		₹
1st	To Bank A/c	5,200	1st	By Profit & Loss A/c	15,000
	To Balance c/d	9,800			
		15,000			15,000
2nd	To Bank A/c	12,900	2nd	By Balance b/d	9,800
	To Balance c/d	11,900		By Profit & Loss A/c	15,000
		24,800			24,800

3rd	To Bank A/c	10,700	3rd	By Balance b/d	11,900
	To Balance c/d	16,200		By Profit & Loss A/c	15,000
		26,900			26,900
4th	To Bank A/c	16,800	4th	By Balance b/d	16,200
	To Balance c/d	14,400		By Profit & Loss A/c	15,000
		31,200			31,200

Note : (1) The balance of this account will appear in the Balance Sheet as at the end of every year on the liabilities side under the head "Reserves and Surplus".

(2) The annual amount to be debited to Profit & Loss A/c every year will be ₹ $\frac{1,20,000}{8}$ = ₹ 15,000.

(3) Although the Profit & Loss A/c will be debited with provision of ₹ 15,000 each year, for the purpose of determining the net profit for computation of managerial remuneration excess provision over actual expenditure has to be added back to profits.

Meaning of Reserve

Any sum which is appropriated out of profit and loss appropriation account and is not meant to cover up liability, contingency, commitment, or reduction in the value of an asset is a reserve. It is provided for meeting prospective losses or liabilities, creation of reserves to increase the working capital in the business and strengthen its financial position. Sometimes the amount is not kept in the business as additional working capital but is invested in the purchase of outside securities, then it is called reserve fund and not a reserve. Reserve may be ***(i)* capital reserve** and ***(ii)* revenue reserve.**

***(i)* Capital Reserve.** Any reserve which is created out of capital profits and is not readily available for distribution as dividend among the shareholders is called capital reserve. Profits prior to incorporation, premium on the issue of shares or debentures, profit on the reissue of shares, profit on redemption of debentures, profit on the sale of undertaking or a part of it and any profit of exceptional or abnormal nature which is not meant for distribution as dividend to shareholders are examples of such reserves.

Some of the capital profits can be distributed as dividend among the shareholders under certain conditions whereas other capital profits can be disposed only in accordance with the provisions of the Companies Act, 2013. When a profit becomes available for dividend then it should be transferred to General Reserve. Premium on shares can be utilised only for the specified purposes as given in Section 52 of the Companies Act. If it is to be dealt in any other manner, sanction of the court will be necessary. Moreover amount utilised out of profits to redeem redeemable preference shares can be utilised for issuing bonus shares to the members of the company.

The profits prior to incorporation, premium on debentures and profit on redemption of debentures may be utilised to declare a dividend in absence of clear cut legal provisions regarding disposal of profit. The profit on the sale of fixed asset can be utilised to declare a dividend only if (*a*) the articles of the company do not prohibit such a distribution, (*b*) The profit has actually been realised in cash and (*c*) the profit exists after a revaluation of all assets and liabilities of the company). [*Vide decision in Lubbock* vs. *The British Bank of South America Ltd.*] But profit arising from revaluation of fixed assets cannot be distributed as dividend among shareholders. As far as possible, capital profits should not be distributed as dividend but should be retained in the business as reserve to strengthen the financial position of the concern.

***(ii)* Revenue Reserve.** Any reserve which is available for distribution as dividend to the shareholders is called revenue reserve. General reserve, dividend equalisation reserve, staff welfare reserve, debenture redemption reserve, investment fluctuation reserve and contingency reserve are some examples of such reserves.

Distinction Between Provision and Reserve

Following are the main points of distinction between a provision and a reserve :

1. The money which is kept aside for a known *event* is said to be *provision* whereas money which is kept aside for unknown event is said to be *reserve.*

2. Provision can be on a liability side or on the assets side but as a negative asset whereas reserve belongs to owners equity.

3. Provision is a charge to profit and loss account whereas reserve is an appropriation of profit. Thus provision must be charged to profit and loss account before calculating the net profit or loss but reserve can be made only when there is profit.

4. Provision is made because of legal necessity but creating a reserve is a matter of financial prudence and to save the concern from prospective losses and liabilities.

5. Provision is created for some specific object and must be utilised for the object for which it is created. Reserve is created for probable losses and can be used for any future liability or loss.

6. Provisions cannot be distributed as profits or transferred to any general reserve. Reserves can be distributed as profit if these remain unutilised for some period. Some amount out of reserves can be transferred to provisions, if needed.

7. Provisions reduce the net profit and are not invested in outside securities. Reserves reduce divisible profits and can be invested in outside securities.

8. Provision is *shown* by way of deduction from the amount of the item for which it is created but reserve is shown separately under Reserves and Surplus on the Liability side of the Balance Sheet.

9. **Examples of Provision** are : Provision for Depreciation, Provision for Repairs and Renewals, Provision for Doubtful Debts, Provision for Fluctuations in Investments, Provision for Contingent Liability, Provision for Taxation, Examples of Reserves are : Revenue Reserve, Capital Reserve, General Reserve and Specific Reserve.

Secret Reserve

A secret reserve is a reserve the existence and/or the amount of which cannot be disclosed in the Balance Sheet. Secret reserves are created in those concerns where public confidence is required for its working like banking companies, insurance companies and electricity companies. Such reserves are created by showing the assets at a lower figure and liabilities at a higher figure.

Some of the ways of creating secret reserves are given as under :

(*i*) by charging excessive depreciation,
(*ii*) by undervaluing stock in trade and goodwill,
(*iii*) by creating excessive or unnecessary provision for bad debts and other contingencies,
(*iv*) by charging capital expenditure to profit and loss account,
(*v*) by suppressing the sales,
(*vi*) by showing a contingent liability as a real liability,
(*vii*) by grouping free reserves as creditors,
(*viii*) showing an asset as a contingent asset.

Advantages of Secret Reserve. Following are the main advantages of secret reserve.

(*i*) It increases the working capital of the concern and also strengthens its financial position without disclosing this fact to the shareholders or the public.

(*ii*) It discourages competition by not disclosing the larger profit made by a concern in a particular line of business and industry.

(*iii*) It enables the directors to tide over unfavourable times. As and when there is less profit, the directors can maintain the rate of dividend by utilising the secret reserve and without disclosing this fact to the shareholders.

Disadvantages of Secret Reserve. Following are the main objections raised against the secret reserves :

(*i*) The balance sheet will not disclose a true and fair view of the state of affairs of the business.
(*ii*) Sometimes the directors make use of such reserves for their personal benefits.

(*iii*) The company's worst position can be concealed by the directors for some time by making the use of secret reserves.

(*iv*) When secret reserves are created the assets are shown at less value in the balance sheet. The concern will not get full claim for loss by fire of the assets as and when such assets are destroyed by fire.

The creation of secret reserve is not allowed under the Companies Act, 1956 as it requires a full disclosure of all material facts and financial position.

General and Specific Reserve

General reserves are those reserves which are not created for any specific purpose and are available for any future contingency or expansion of the business. These are created to provide additional working capital and strengthening the financial position of the concern.

Specific reserves are those reserves which are created for a specific purpose and can be utilised only for that purpose. Dividend equalisation reserve and debenture redemption reserve are good examples of such reserves.

Sinking Fund

Sinking Funds are created to have ready money after a particular period either for the replacement of an asset or for the repayment of a liability. Every year some amount is charged or appropriated from the profit and loss account and is invested in outside securities with the idea that at the end of the stipulated period money will be equal to the amount we need.

Difference Between a Sinking Fund to Replace a Wasting Asset and a Sinking Fund to Repay a Liability

Following are the main differences :

(*i*) The annual instalment in case of sinking fund to replace a wasting asset is really depreciation and is charge against Profit and Loss Account while in case of sinking fund to repay a liability, it is an appropriation of profit.

(*ii*) At the end of the working life when the asset is to be replaced, sinking fund is utilised for writing off Old Asset Account but in other case it is closed by transferring the balance to general reserve as the annual charge was an appropriation of profit.

(*iii*) A sinking fund to replace a wasting asset does not enhance the capital as it maintains the asset at its original value but in other case the assets are increased to the extent of redemption carried out.

Investment of Reserves

Whether reserves should be invested outside or not, there seems to be a controversy among the accountants. Some accountants are of the opinion that reserves should be invested in outside securities. Whenever the need arises, the amount can be realised by sale of securities. There are others who believe that there is no need of investing the reserves in outside securities ; it can be kept invested in the business. There is no doubt that the amount representing sinking funds should be invested in first class securities so that it may provide definite sums of money at a stipulated date. But it is not necessary to invest the amount of general reserves in outside securities. In fact, it will be folly on the part of management to buy outside securities when there is need of funds in the business itself. The main purpose of general reserve is to provide funds for the expansion of the business. The purpose will be defeated as soon as the funds are invested in outside securities. The outside investment is justified only when the business has no need of funds.

Nature of Reserves

Reserves are shown on the liabilities side of the Balance Sheet and by virtue of this, new students of accountancy understand reserve as a liability but this is wrong. Reserve is not a liability in real sense. It represents accumulated divisible profit which belongs to the shareholders just like capital and not have been distributed as dividend as yet ; that is why it is shown on the liabilities side of the Balance Sheet. Moreover, reserves represent a portion of the assets which is free to be utilised by the business as it likes *i.e.* assets equal to reserves are not meant to meet any liability of the business. Reserves also indicate surplus of assets over the amount of capital brought in as cash into the business by the proprietor and the sums owed to the outsiders. The surplus is really measured by the amount of reserves.

QUESTIONS

OBJECTIVE TYPE

1. In each of the following cases indicate the alternative which you consider to be correct :

(*a*) Depreciation is an accounting process of—(*i*) valuation (*ii*) allocation (*iii*) apportionment (*iv*) appropriation.

(*b*) The main objective of providing depreciation is : (*i*) to calculate true profit, (*ii*) to show the true financial position in the Balance Sheet, (*iii*) to reduce tax burden, (*iv*) to provide funds for replacement of fixed assets.

(*c*) Depreciation arises because of (*i*) fall in the market value of an asset, (*ii*) physical wear and tear, (*iii*) fall in the value of money.

(*d*) Under the straight line method of charging depreciation, depreciation (*i*) increases every year (*ii*) decreases every year, (*iii*) is constant every year.

(*e*) Under the Diminishing Balance Method depreciation is calculated on (*i*) original cost, (*ii*) written down value, (*iii*) the scrap value.

(*f*) A diminishing balance method of providing for depreciation is one according to which : (*i*) the amount of depreciation is reduced from year to year, (*ii*) the rate per cent declines from year to year at which the depreciation is charged, (*iii*) the rate per cent as well as the amount reduce every year.

(*g*) Depreciation on the diminishing balance method of ₹ 2,000 at the rate of 10% p.a. after three years will be (*i*) ₹ 1,400, (*ii*) ₹ 1,458, (*iii*) ₹ 542, (*iv*) none of the above.

(*h*) The amount of depreciation charged on a machinery will be debited to : (*i*) Machinery A/c, (*ii*) Depreciation A/c, (*iii*) Cash account.

(*i*) Loss on the sale of machinery should be written off against (*i*) Securities Premium Reserve Account, (*ii*) Sales Account, (*iii*) Depreciation Fund Account.

(*j*) Service hours method of providing depreciation is useful when : (*i*) Use of an asset can be measured in returns of time, (*ii*) Output can be measured, (*iii*) Use of an asset is dependent on sale, (*iv*) Name of the above.

(*k*) Depreciation is an expense resulting : (*i*) From the consumption of current asset, (*ii*) From the use of various services, (*iii*) From the use of fixed assets, (*iv*) None of the above.

(*l*) Under the annuity system, the amount of total depreciation is determined by adding to the cost of asset : (*i*) Interest thereon at an expected rate, (*ii*) Repair charges thereon during the life of the asset, (*iii*) Obsolescence cost, (*iv*) None of the above.

Ans. [(*a*) : (*ii*) ; (*b*) : (*i*) ; (*c*) : (*ii*) ; (*d*) : (*iii*) ; (*e*) : (*ii*) ; (*f*) : (*i*) ; (*g*) : (*ii*) ; (*h*) : (*ii*) ; (*i*) : (*iii*) ; (*j*) (*i*); (*k*) (*iii*) ; (*l*) (*i*)].

2. State with reasons whether the following statements are TRUE or FALSE :

(*i*) Depreciation is an amortised expenditure.

(*ii*) Providing depreciation ensures sufficient cash for asset replacement.

(*iii*) Depreciation cannot be provided in case of loss, in a financial year.

(*iv*) M/s. Ram and Co. did not provide any depreciation on Plant and Machinery as its market value is higher than the cost of purchases.

(*v*) The expressions-depreciation is to be charged at 10% and 10% p.a. on furniture and fittings-carry the same meaning.

(*vi*) Reducing Balance Method of Depreciation is followed to have a uniform charge for depreciation and repairs and maintenance together.

(*vii*) Providing depreciation in the accounts reduces the amount of profit available for dividend.

(*viii*) There exists difference between the Written Down Value method and Diminishing Balance method of depreciation.

(*ix*) Higher depreciation will not affect cash profits of the business.

(*x*) Depreciation is a cash expenditure like other normal expenses.

(*xi*) Depreciation is a process of allocation of cost of fixed assets.

(*xii*) Depreciation amount refers to the difference between historical cost and market value of an asset.

Ans. [TRUE : (*i*) ; (*ii*) ; (*vi*) ; (*vii*) ; (*ix*) ; (*xi*) ; FALSE : (*iii*) ; (*iv*) ; (*v*) ; (*viii*) ; (*x*) ; (*xii*)].

3. Fill in the blanks :

(*i*) Discarding of old machinery due to new invention is called ....

(*ii*) Machine hour rate method of depreciation is used in case of ....

(*iii*) Depletion method of charging depreciation is mostly used in case of ....

(*iv*) Amortisation relates to cost allocation for .... assets.

(*v*) Physical depreciation is caused mainly from .... when the asset is in use.

(*vi*) ....of providing depreciation is simple to understand and easy to apply.

(*vii*) Under .... of providing depreciation, amount spent on purchase of asset is regarded as an investment which is assumed to earn interest at a certain rate.

Ans. [(*i*) obsolescence; (*ii*) machines; (*iii*) mines, quarries etc.; (*iv*) intangible; (*v*) wear and tear; (*vi*) Fixed instalment method or straight line method; (*vii*) annuity method].

SHORT ANSWER TYPE

1. What do you mean by physical deterioration ?

2. What do you understand by depletion ?

3. What is obsolescence ?

4. Explain in brief the need for providing depreciation.

5. Give two important points of distinction between straight line method and diminishing balance method of providing depreciation.

6. How will you calculate depreciation under Sum of the Digits Method of providing depreciation ?

7. What is the basic idea of providing depreciation according to the annuity method ?

8. What is the basic purpose of providing depreciation according to depreciation fund method?

9. What do you mean by provision ?

10. Is there anv difference between provision and reserve ?

11. What are depreciable assets ? Explain why depreciation does not apply to land.

12. From the following particulars prepare truck account as on 31.12.2018. Cost of truck ₹ 30,000 ; Total depreciation provided upto 31.12.2017 ₹ 9,000. On 25th January 2018, the truck was damaged in an accident and was sold off as scrap for ₹ 3,000. A sum of ₹ 20,000 was received from the Insurance Company.

Ans. [Profit on Truck ₹ 2,000]

13. On 1st January, 2025 a lease was acquired for 5 years at a cost of ₹ 40,000. Write up the lease account assuming that depreciation is charged under **fixed instalment method.**

14. A machine was acquired on 1st April, 2025 at a cost of ₹ 15,000, the cost of installation being ₹ 1,000. It is expected that the scrap value at the end of the working life will be ₹ 2,000. Write up the machine account for the first two years under the **diminishing balance method** charging 10% depreciation. Assume that financial year is followed.

Ans. [Balance in Machinery Account ₹ 12,960]

LONG ANSWER TYPE

1. What do you understand by 'depreciation' and 'depreciable assets' ? Discuss the main causes of depreciation.
2. Define Depreciation, Depletion and Amortization. Why depreciation is provided for ?
3. 'Depreciation is an apportionment of cost'. Discuss and give the main problems which are faced in calculating the amount of depreciation.
4. **Discuss the merits and demerits of various** methods of calculating depreciation.
5. Distinguish between :
   (*i*) Straight line method and diminishing balance method. (*ii*) Annuity method and depreciation fund method. (*iii*) Straight line method and depletion method. (*iv*) Depreciation fund method and insurance policy method. (*v*) Depreciation, fluctuation and obsolescence.
6. Which method of depreciation will be suitable for the following and why ?
   (*i*) Machinery (to be replaced) (*ii*) Horses (*iii*) Trucks (not to be replaced) (*iv*) Office furniture (*v*) A mining lease (not to be renewed).
7. 'Depreciation Accounting is a process of allocation and not of valuation'. Comment.
8. Is it desirable to charge depreciation on replacement cost basis ? If not, why ?
9. Elucidate the objectives of Depreciation Policy. Why are accelerated methods preferred over other methods of depreciation ?
10. Explain the importance of a proper depreciation policy. What is its impact on the performance of business organisation ?
11. Is depreciation a source of fund ? Explain.
12. Distinguish between : (*i*) Provision and Reserve, (*ii*) Capital Reserve and Revenue Reserve, (*iii*) General and Specific Reserve. (*iv*) Reserve Account and Reserve Fund.
13. What is a secret reserve ? How is it created and what objections are raised against the creation of such reserves ?
14. Distinguish between a sinking fund to replace a wasting asset and a sinking fund to repay a liability.
15. Is reserve fund a liability in the real sense of the term ? If not, why is it shown on the liabilities side of the Balance Sheet ?
16. State the merits and demerits of Annuity Method of depreciation.

PRACTICAL PROBLEMS

1. A company, whose accounting year is the calendar year, purchased on 1st April, 2023 machinery costing ₹ 30,000.

   It purchased further machinery on 1st October, 2023 costing ₹ 20,000 and on 1st July, 2024 costing ₹ 10,000.

   On 1st January, 2025 one third of the machinery installed on 1st April, 2023 became obsolete and was sold for ₹ 3,000.

   Show how Machinery Account would appear in the books of the company, it being given that machinery was depreciated by ***Fixed Instalment Method*** at 10 p.c. per annum.

Ans. [Balance ₹ 38,500, Loss on Sale ₹ 5,250].

2. On 1st January, 2023 a limited company purchased machinery for ₹ 12,000 and on 30th June, 2024 it acquired additional machinery at a cost of ₹ 2,000. On 31st March, 2025 one of the original machines which had cost ₹ 500 was found to have become obsolete and was sold as scrap for ₹ 50. It was replaced on that date by a new machine costing ₹ 800.

   Depreciation is to be provided at the rate of 15 per cent per annum on the *written down value*. Show ledger accounts for the first three years.

Ans. [Balance in Machinery A/c ₹ 9,345 ; Loss on Sale ₹ 297].

3. A Transport company purchased 5 Trucks at ₹ 2,00,000 each on April 1, 2022. The company observes calendar year as its accounting year.

   On October 1, 2024 one of the Trucks is involved in an accident and is completely destroyed. Insurance company pays ₹ 90,000 in full settlement of the claim. On the same day the company purchases one used Truck for ₹ 1,00,000 and spends ₹ 20,000 on its overhauling.

   Prepare Trucks Account (in columnar form) for the three years ending on December 31, 2024 if the company writes off depreciation @ 20% per annum on

   (*i*) original cost method and

   (*ii*) diminishing balance method.

Ans. (*i*) ₹ 4,74,000 ; Loss on Sale of Machinery ₹ 10,000 ;
(*ii*) ₹ 5,49,200 ; Loss on Sale of Machinery ₹ 25,600].

4. A company has acquired a lease of a cinema building for a term of 5 years by payment of ₹ 4,00,000. It is proposed to depreciate the lease by the *annuity method*, charging 5 per cent per annum. Show the Ledger Account of the asset during the period of the lease.

   Reference to the Annuity Table shows that the amount for ₹ 1 for 5 years at 5 per cent is ₹ 0.230975. Calculations are made to the nearest rupee.

5. A company purchased a four years' lease on January 1, 2021 for ₹ 50,000. It is decided to provide for the renewal of the lease at the end of four years by setting up a *Depreciation Fund*. It is expected that investments will fetch interest at 4% p.a. Sinking Fund tables show that ₹ 0.235490 invested each year will produce ₹ 1 at the end of four years at 4% p.a. Investments are made in multiple of ₹ 5.

   On 31st December, 2024, the Depreciation Fund Investments are sold for ₹ 36,455. On 1st January, 2025 the same lease was renewed for a further period of four years by payment of ₹ 55,000. Prepare the necessary ledger accounts.

Ans. [Loss transferred to P & L A/c ₹ 300].

6. X purchases a 5 years' lease for ₹ 10,000 and arranges for its renewal by means of insurance policy the annual premium being ₹ 1,850. The value of the policy increases each year by 4%. Show the necessary accounts for 5 years, presuming that the renewal of the lease costs ₹ 9,500.

Ans. [Balance in Depreciation Reserve (*i.e.*, profit) transferred to Profit & Loss A/c ₹ 4,213].

7. A firm buys both loose tools and also makes some itself. Following data is available concerning the year 2025 :

		₹
Jan. 1	Stock of Loose Tools	6,680
	During the year :	
	Bought Loose Tools from suppliers	3,780
	Made own Loose Tools	
	The cost of wages of employees	580
	and the materials cost	290
	Received refund from a supplier for faulty tools returned to him	176
Dec. 31	Loose Tools valued at	7,360

   You are to draw up the Loose Tools Account for 2025 showing the amount transferred as an expense to the Manufacturing Account.

Ans. [₹ 3,794].

8. A mine was acquired at a cost of ₹ 5,00,000 on 1st June, 2023 ; it was expected it would yield 1,00,000 tonnes of minerals in all. The actual output was as follows :
2023—5,000 tonnes ; 2024—20,000 tonnes and 2025—16,000 tonnes.
Write up the Mine Account for the above years using *depletion method* of charging depreciation.

Ans. [Balance ₹ 2,95,000].

9. A machine was acquired on 1st April, 2024 at a cost of ₹ 9,000, the cost of installation being ₹ 1,000. It is expected that its total life will be 20,000 hours. During 2024 it worked for 1,600 hours and during 2025 for 2,400 hours. Write up the Machinery Account for 2024 and 2025.

Ans. [Balance ₹ 8,000].

10. Square Ltd., acquired the lease of a Cinema House on 1st April, 2022 for ₹ 50,000 for a period of three years ending on 31st March, 2025 with an option to renew the same for a further period of three years on the same terms.
With a view to accumulating sufficient funds for the purpose of renewal, it was decided to create a **sinking fund** to be credited/debited with annual contribution from profit, interest on sinking fund investments and any profit/loss arising out of realisation of the sinking fund investments. The sinking fund was represented by specific investments to be made for any sum available to the sinking fund except those credited at the termination of the fund.
Following transactions took place during three years ending :

			31-3-2023	*31-3-2024*	*31-3-2025*
			₹	₹	₹
1.	Contribution from Profit		16,000	16,000	Such amount as will make up the Fund to ₹ 50,000
2.	Interest received on investments		—	800	₹ 2,400
3.	Sale of investments' proceeds being immediately re-invested :		—		
	9-9-2023	Book value	—	9,000	
		Selling price		9,500	
	13-8-2024	Book value			₹ 10,500
		Selling price			₹ 11,500
4.	All Sinking Fund investments realised on 31-3-2025				₹ 33,000
	On 1st April, 2025 the lease was renewed on payment of				₹ 50,000

You are required to draw : (1) Sinking Fund Account, (2) Sinking Fund Investment Account, and (3) Leasehold Property Account for all the years.

Ans. [Profit on Sinking Fund ₹ 14,600].

TYPICAL

11. A company writes off depreciation 10% of the original cost of plant and machinery every year till the whole cost of a particular piece of machinery is wiped off. Full depreciation is written off even if the machinery is in use for part of a year. Accounts are made up to 31st December.
On 1st January, 2024 the balance in the Plant and Machinery Account was ₹ 1,95,150. The original cost of the various items in use was as follows :

	₹
Items bought in 2013 or earlier	58,000
" " " 2014	31,000
" " " 2015	17,000
" " " 2016 or later	2,52,000
	3,58,000

During 2024 new plant was bought at a cost of ₹ 29,500 and one machine which had cost ₹ 5,500 in 1990 was sold for ₹ 350. During 2025 there were additions costing ₹ 18,000 and a machine which had cost ₹ 7,000 in 2021 was sold on Jan. 1, 2025 for ₹ 3,500. Write up Plant and Machinery Account for 2024 and 2025.

Ans. **[₹ 1,79,350].**

12. A company writes off depreciation of 10% p.a. on the diminishing balance. On 1st January, 2025 the machinery account showed a balance of ₹ 1,49,000. It was discovered in 2025 that :

(*a*) Heavy repairs effected to plants and machinery (completed on 30th June, 2023) were debited to the machinery account. The amount was ₹ 15,000 ; and

(*b*) A machine costing ₹ 6,000 was entered in the purchases book on 1st October 2023.

The expenses on installation, ₹ 400, were debited to General Expenses Account.

Necessary corrections were to be made in 2025. On 30th June, 2025 a machine which had cost ₹ 20,000 on 1st January, 2023 was disposed off for ₹ 15,000 and a new machine costing ₹ 30,000 was installed on the same date, the expenses on installing the same being ₹ 500.

Show Machinery Account for the year ended 31st December, 2025, Please show your working in detail.

Ans. **[₹ 1,42,007].**

13. Depreciation has been charged for the years from 2022 to 2025 @ 10% on reducing balance method on opening balance of each item of Plant and Machinery in use. The balance of Plant and Machinery Account at the end of 31st December, 2025 was ₹ 54,000. There were no sales during these years ; purchases were ₹ 16,800 in Sept. 2022 and ₹ 11,400 in December, 2024.

The management decided that depreciation should be charged @ 20% on the same method but calculated on the closing balance of each item with retrospective effect from 2022.

You are required to pass Journal Entry for giving effect to the revised basis at the end of 2025.

Ans. **[Additional Depreciation Required ₹ 20,161].**

14. **(*With GST*)** Shiv Shakti Ltd. purchased on 1st April 2023, a plant for ₹ 2,00,000 plus CGST and SGST @ 6% each. On 1st October, 2023, an additional plant was purchased costing ₹ 1,00,000 plus CGST and SGST @ 6% each. On 1st October, 2024 and the plant purchased on 1st April 2023, having become obsolete, was sold for 80,000, charging CGST and SGST @ 6% each. Depreciation is provided @ 10% p.a. on cost on 31st March every year. Show the Machinery, Machinery Disposal and Provision for Depreciation Accounts for the years ended 31st March, 2024 and 2025. Also show CGST and SGST Accounts for the two years.

Ans. **[Machinery A/c Balance ₹ 1,00,000 ; Loss on Sale of Machinery ₹ 90,000].**

15. **(*With GST*)** On 1st January, 2023, the Dinesh Transport Company purchased a truck for 10,00,000. On 1st July, 2024, this truck was involved in an accident and was destroyed and ₹ 8,00,000 were received by a cheque from the Insurance company in full settlement on 1st Oct., 2024. On 1st July, 2024, another truck was purchased by the company for ₹ 12,00,000 plus CGST and SGST @ 6% each.

The company writes off depreciation @ 20% per annum under the Written Down Value Method. Prepare Truck Account and Depreciation Account for 2023 to 2025 when books are closed on 31st March every year.

Ans. **[Depreciation for 2025 : ₹ 2,18,000 ; Profit on Destroyed Truck ₹ 78,000 ; Book Value on accident date ₹ 7,22,000 ; Machinery A/c Balance ₹ 10,20,000].**

16. Bharat Cotton Mills Ltd. created a Repairs and Renewal Provision on and from 31st December, 2022 by charging ₹ 2,000 each year to Revenue. During the three years ended on 31-12-2023, 31-12-2024 and 31-12-2025 the total expenses under Repairs & Renewals were ₹ 1,360, ₹ 1,896 and ₹ 2,016 respectively.

You are required to show the Journal, Ledger and Balance Sheet entries relating to the above.

ASSETS DISPOSAL ACCOUNT

17. Shippers Concern has a flect of motor vessels. Depreciation is calculated thereon @ 20% on the *reducing balance method*, no amount being charged in the year of sale but full charge being made for the year during which addition is made. The concern closes its accounts annually on 31st December.

Following particulars are available :

(1) Motor Vessels at cost on 31-12-2024 ₹ 1,64,900
Less : Depreciation Provision 93,382

(2) Sales during 2025 :

Date	*Name of Vessel*	*Purchased on*	*Cost Price* ₹	*Selling Price* ₹
14-4-2025	MV-Cochin	15-2-2020	15,000	3,300
18-8-2025	MV-Kandla	20-7-2021	25,000	12,000

(3) Purchases during 2025 :

Date	*Name of vessel*	*Price* ₹
25-8-2025	MV-PRIDE OF INDIA	34,000
20-11-2025	MV-OKA	20,000

You are required to prepare : (*i*) The Motor Vessels A/c (*ii*) The Motor Vessels Depreciation Provision A/c and (*iii*) The Motor Vessels Disposal A/c.

Ans. **[(₹ 1,78,900 Balance in Motor Vessels Account : ₹ 89,823 Balance in Depreciation Provision Account ; Profit on Sale ₹ 1,760].**

CHANGE OF METHOD

18. On 1st April, 2024, LMP Co. which depreciates its machinery @ 10% p.a. on diminishing balance method, had ₹ 9,72,000 to the debit of Machinery Account. On 1st October, 2024, part of machinery purchased on 1st April, 2022 for ₹ 80,000 was sold for ₹ 45,000.

Also, a new machinery at a cost of ₹ 1,50,000 was purchased on 1st October, 2024 and installed on the same date and installation charges being ₹ 8,000.

The company changed the method of depreciation from diminishing balance method to straight line method with effect from 1st April, 2022 and adjusted the difference on 31st March, 2025. The rate of depreciation remains the same.

Show the Machinery Account and ascertain the amount chargeable to Profit and Loss Account as depreciation in the year 2024-25.

Ans. **[Machinery Account Balance ₹ 9,34,100 ; Amount chargeable ₹ 1,35,900 to Profit and Loss Account as depreciation in the year 2024-25]**

Hint. [Loss on sale of machinery ₹ 15,000; Difference of depreciation due to change in method ₹ 12,000]

Note: Change of method has been taken from retrospective effect

19. **(From DBM to SLM)** A firm purchased on 1st January, 2022 certain machinery for ₹ 58,200 and spent ₹ 1,800 on its erection. On 1st July, 2022 additional machinery costing ₹ 20,000 was purchased. On 1st July, 2024 the machinery purchased on 1st January, 2022 having become obsolete was auctioned for ₹ 28,600 and on the same date fresh machinery was purchased at a cost of ₹ 40,000.

Depreciation was provided for annually on 31st December at the rate of 10% p.a. on written down value. In 2025, however, the firm changed this method of providing depreciation and adopted the method of providing 5% per annum depreciation on the original cost of the machinery with retrospective effect *i.e.* 1st January, 2022.

Give Machinery Account as it would stand at the end of each year from 2022 to 2025.

Ans. **[Balance ₹ 53,500].**

Hint. ₹ 3,110 credited to Profit & Loss A/c being Excess Depreciation charged in the past. Loss on sale of machinery ₹ 17,570.

20. **(From DBM to SLM)** M/s Mill and Wright commenced business on 1st January, 2021 when they purchased plant and equipment of ₹ 7,00,000. They adopted a policy of (*i*) charging depreciation at

15% per annum on diminishing balance basis and (*ii*) charging full year's depreciation on additions.

Over the years, their purchases of plant have been :

Date	Amount
	₹
1-8-2022	1,50,000
30-9-2025	2,00,000

On 1-1-2025 it was decided to change the method and rate of depreciation to 10% on straight line basis with retrospective effect from 1-1-2021, the adjustment being made in the account for the year ending 31st December, 2025.

Calculate the difference in depreciation to be adjusted in the Plant and Equipment A/c on 1-1-2025, and show the ledger account for the year 2025.

Ans. [Balance ₹ 6,20,000].

Hint. Beginning Balance ₹ 4,57,522, Excess Depreciation charged in the past credited to P. & L. A/c ₹ 67,478. Depreciation for 2025 ₹ 1,05,000.

21. (SLM to DBM) A Limited Company was charging depreciation on Plant and Machinery on the Straight Line Method at 10 per cent per annum since 2021. The Directors decided in 2025 to change the method of providing depreciation to written down value keeping the rate at 10 per cent retrospectively. Following information in rupees were available from records :

	2021	*2022*	*2023*	*2024*	*2025*
	₹	₹	₹	₹	₹
Plant and Machinery purchased at cost	1,80,000	40,000	60,000	—	2,50,000
Plant and Machinery sold at cost price (as Purchased in 2021)	—	5,000	8,000	—	—
Depreciation charged to Profit and Loss Account	18,000	21,500	26,700	26,700	51,700
Actual sale proceeds of Plant and Machinery	—	4,000	7,200	—	—

Depreciation is not charged on assets sold during the year. You are required to compute the impact on profit of the company pursuant to the change in method of computing depreciation and also the profit/loss in assets sold on the two methods of depreciation.

Ans. [Profit will rise by ₹ 19,176 due to change in method of depreciation. Profit will fall by ₹ 80 because of profit or loss on sale of asset].

22. (SLM to DBM) On 1st April, 2021 a new plant was purchased for ₹ 40,000 and a further sum of ₹ 2,000 was spent on its installation.

On 1st October, 2023 another plant was acquired for ₹ 25,000.

Due to an accident on 3rd January, 2024 the first plant was totally destroyed and the remnants were sold for ₹ 1,000 only.

On 21st January, 2025 a second hand plant was purchased for ₹ 30,000 and a further sum of ₹ 5,000 was spent for bringing the same to use on and from 15th March, 2025.

Depreciation has been provided at 10 per cent on straight line basis. It was the practice to provide depreciation for full year on all acquisitions made at any time during any year and to ignore depreciation on any item sold or disposed of during the year. None of the assets were insured. The accounts are closed annually on 31st March.

It is now decided to follow the rate of 15 per cent on diminishing balance method with retrospective effect in respect of the existing items of plant and to make the necessary adjustment entry on 1st April, 2025.

Show the journal entries to be passed for the purpose and the Plant Account and the Accumulated Depreciation Provision Account for all the years.

Ans. [Balance in Plant A/c ₹ 60,000 and Depreciation Provision A/c ₹ 12,187 including additional depreciation of ₹ 3,687].

23. **(DBM to SLM)** Cure Ltd. started operations from 1st January, 2022. Following data are available regarding its plant and machinery :

Year	*Additional Plant put to use On 1st day of the year*	*Awaiting installation at the end of the year*	*Working*
2022	₹ 10 lakhs	₹ 97 lakhs	Double Shift
2023	₹ 137 lakhs	₹ 57 lakhs	" "
2024	₹ 66 lakhs	₹ 6 lakhs	" "

The company charges depreciation at reducing balance method, normal rate being 10 per cent. During 2025 the company has put to use on the first date, further machineries of ₹ 60 lakhs under double shift. Plant awaiting installation as on 31-12-2025 amount to ₹ 10 lakhs.

The company has decided to switch over to straight line method of depreciation as per section 205 (2) (*b*) of the Companies Act, 1956, with retrospective effect, the rate corresponding to 10 per cent being taken at 4 per cent.

(*a*) Show year wise plant account by, (*i*) old method, (*ii*) new method ; (*b*) Suggest a suitable note, complying with the minimum statutory requirement to be appended to 2025 accounts ; (*c*) Show journal entries to be passed in 2025 ; and (*d*) Create necessary development rebate reserve for 2025 only, rebate rate being 15 per cent. Compute all figures in lakhs of rupees only giving two decimal points.

Ans. **[Total Depreciation : *Old* Method ₹ 139.09 lakhs (1.5 + 36.37 + 49.36 + 51.86) and under *New* Method ₹ 63.24 lakhs (0.60 + 14.64 + 22.02 + 25.98)].**

Hint. For double shift, annual rate of depreciation will be one and a half times the given rate. Write back the excess depreciation of ₹ 75.85 lakhs. Compute Development Rebate Reserve on ₹ 60 lakhs @ 15%.

24. On 1-4-2021 a machine was acquired at ₹ 4,00,000. The machine was expected to have a useful life of 10 years. The residual value was estimated at 10% of the original cost. At the end of the 3rd year, an attachment was made to the machine at a cost of ₹ 1,80,000 to enhance its capacity. The attachment was expected to have a useful life of 10 years and zero terminal value. During the same time the original machine was revalued upwards by ₹ 90,000 and remaining useful life was reassessed at 9 years and residual value was reassessed at NIL.

Find depreciation for the year, if

(*i*) attachment retains its separate identity.

(*ii*) attachment becomes integral part of the machine. ***(CA—IPCE May, 2014 Modified)***

Ans. **[(*i*) Total Depreciation ₹ 60,444 (*i.e.* ₹ 42,444 + ₹ 18,000; (*ii*) Depreciation ₹ 62,444]**

CHAPTER 10

Inventory Valuation

Meaning of Inventory

Any stock that a firm keeps to meet its future requirements of production and sales is called 'inventory'. The basic reason for holding inventory is to keep up the production activities unhampered. It is neither physically possible nor economically justifiable to wait for the stocks to arrive at the time when they are actually required. Therefore, keeping of inventory is a must for the efficient working of a business unit. The Institute of Chartered Accountants of India defines inventories in Ind. AS–2 as follows :

"Inventories are assets :

(*a*) held for sale in the ordinary courses of business ;

(*b*) in the process of production for each sale ; or

(*c*) in the form of materials or supplies to be consumed in the production process or in the rendering of services."

The principal types of inventories are : (*i*) Raw materials and supplies, (*ii*) Goods in process *i.e.* work-in-progress, and (*iii*) Finished goods.

Raw Materials represent goods kept by a manufacturing firm prior to their being utilised in the production process. Supplies generally include tools and consumables which are consumed in the production of goods and services.

Goods in Process represent the semi-finished goods ; they include those materials that have been committed to production process but have not yet been converted into finished goods.

Finished Goods are completed goods awaiting sale. In a manufacturing concern, they are the final output of the production process.

The nature of inventory depends upon the type of activity carried on. In case of a *manufacturing unit,* inventory will generally include all types of inventories mentioned above, while in case of a *trading concern,* it will comprise only finished goods or stock-in-trade owned by it for sale to customers in the normal course of business. Inventory needs proper control as it is one of the largest assets of a business.

Effect of Wrong Inventory Valuation

Balance Sheet of a concern must show true and fair view of the financial position of the concern. For this purpose assets including inventory should be properly valued to exhibit a true and fair view. True profits cannot be calculated unless assets are properly valued. Only then, Balance Sheet will exhibit a true and fair view of the financial affairs of the business.

If inventory is valued at a value which is less than the actual value, the profits will be reduced and as a result, shareholders would get less dividend. On the other hand, if inventory is valued at a value which is more than the actual value, the profits would be inflated and the shareholders would receive more dividend, a part of which would, thus, be paid out of capital. Payment of dividend out of capital would exhaust the capital and the company would be insolvent. Moreover under- or over-valuation of inventory will not only affect the operating results and financial position of the current period but will also affect these for the next period because closing stock of the current period will become opening stock of the next period.

Objectives of Inventory Valuation

Following are some of the important objective of inventory valuation:

1. **Sufficient inventory for production sale process.** For practically all manufacturing and trading concerns, inventory represents a major current asset investment. Adequate inventory is essential for the 'production sale' process of an enterprise as insufficient inventory hampers production and fails to generate sufficient sales. Inventory represents type of business insurance which assures a business unit that it will not have to close down due to shortages of saleable goods. Inventory is not purchased as investment or to realise a gain from possession but rather to sell and realise a gain from resale. The fact of realising profit from resale of inventory makes it compulsory for a concern to follow a proper method of inventory valuation.

2. **Proper determination of profit.** The proper determination of profit depends upon the proper valuation. If the ending inventory is valued at a lower figure, profit is understated and if it is overvalued, profit is overstated. This shows that proper method of valuation of inventory should be followed. The American Production and Inventory Control Society (U.S.A.) has summarised the relationship between the measurement of income and inventory valuation as follows :

"A major objective of accounting for inventories is the proper determination of income through the process of matching appropriate costs against revenues."

The process of matching appropriate costs against revenues means ascertaining what portion of the cost of goods available for sale should be deducted from the revenue of the current period and what portion of the cost of goods should be carried as inventory to be matched against the revenue of the following period.

3. **True financial position.** Overvaluation of inventory amounts to window dressing which in turn gives wrong idea about the liquid position of the company. The proper valuation of inventory which constitutes a significant portion of current assets is essential so that short-term creditors may not be misled about the liquid position of the company. Balance sheet can exhibit a true and fair view of the financial position of a company if there is a proper valuation of inventory which constitutes a major portion of current assets.

METHODS OF TAKING INVENTORIES

There are two methods of ascertaining the value of stock. These are : (1) Periodic Inventory Method, (2) Perpetual Inventory Method.

1. Periodic Inventory Method

Under this method of taking inventories, value of stock is determined by physical counting of the stock on the accounting date, *i.e.,* the date of preparation of the final accounts. It is possible that stock taking may take a week or so in large enterprises and purchases and sales may have to be suspended for that period to get the correct figure of closing inventory. This method of ascertaining the value of stock at the end of the year is also known as annual stock taking. Thus this method is based on physical stock taking. It provides data once in a year. It is a simple and economical method of stock taking and can be adopted in small concerns. But it does not provide basis for control.

2. Perpetual Inventory Method

Perpetual inventory is defined as "a system of records maintained by the controlling department, which reflects the physical movements of stocks and their current balance." Under this method stock registers are maintained to make a record of the physical movements of stocks and their current balance. Stores ledger is maintained to keep a record of the various items of materials; it makes a record of the physical movements of the stock on the receipts and issues of the materials and also reflects the balance in the stores. Similarly, work-in-progress ledger is maintained to give the value of work-in-progress on hand and finished goods ledger is maintained to know the value of finished goods on hand. Thus, this system provides a running record of inventories on hand at any time. To ensure the accuracy of perpetual inventory records, physical verification of the inventory is made by a programme of continuous stock taking.

It is possible that the balance of stock shown by the perpetual inventory records may differ from the actual balance of stock as ascertained by physical verification. Any difference noted between actual stocks as disclosed by the physical verification and the stock shown by stock records should be investigated and rectification made then and there. If the physical verification reveals that actual balance of stock is more than the balance shown by the stores ledger or work-in-progress ledger or finished goods ledger, debit note is prepared and stock records are adjusted accordingly. Similarly, if there is a shortage of stock, a credit note is prepared and stock records are adjusted accordingly so that book balance may reconcile with actual balance. A Stock Adjustment Account is prepared and debited with the shortage of stock and credited with surplus.

Continuous stock taking is an essential feature of the perpetual inventory system. But the two terms, perpetual inventory and continuous stock taking, should not be taken as one; perpetual inventory means the system of stock records and continuous stock taking whereas continuous stock taking means only the physical verification of stock records with actual stocks.

After all what is done in continuous stock taking ? In continuous stock taking, physical verification is spread throughout the year. Every day 10 to 15 items are taken at random by rotation and checked so that surprise element in stock verification is maintained and each item is checked for a number of times during the year. On the other hand, surprise element is missing in case of periodical checking because checking is usually done at the end of the year. In short this method is based on records. It requires a lot of recording and is thus expensive. It can be adopted only in big concerns. It provides data on running basis and thus facilitates the preparation of financial statements at shorter intervals. It also provides bases for control by investigating the discrepancies arising from the comparison of physical stock with their book values.

Difference Between Periodic Inventory and Perpetual Inventory

Following are the main differences between the two methods of taking inventory.

	Periodic Inventory	*Perpetual Inventory*
1.	It is based on physical stock taking.	It is based on records.
2.	It provides information about stock and cost of sales periodically *i.e.* once in a year.	It provides the continuous information about stock and cost of sales.
3.	It directly determines stock and takes cost of goods sold as residual figure.	It directly determines cost of sales and takes stock as balancing figure.
4.	Under this system, cost of sales includes lost goods.	In this system, inventory includes lost goods.
5.	It requires closure of business for counting of stock.	Stock can be determined without affecting the operation of business.
6.	It does not provide basis for control.	It provides basis for control by investigating the discrepancies arising from the comparison of physical stock with book values.
7.	It is simple and economical method of taking inventory and can be adopted by small concerns.	It is expensive as it requires a lot of recording due to an elaborate method of taking inventory. It can be adopted by big concerns only.

Valuation of Inventory at Lower of Cost or Market Price (*i.e.* LCM Rule)

The general principle is that inventory should be valued at the cost at which it has been acquired. But there should be a departure from the cost basis of inventory valuation when the utility of the inventory is less than its cost. American Institute of Certified Public Accountants has rightly stated as follows :

"A departure from the cost basis of pricing the inventory is required when the utility of the goods is no longer as great as its cost. Where there is evidence that the utility of goods, in their disposal in the ordinary course of business, will be less than cost, whether due to physical deterioration, obsolescence, changes in price levels, or other causes, the difference should be recognised as a loss of the current period. This is generally accomplished by stating such goods at a lower level commonly designated as market."

As per Ind AS 2, "Inventories shall be measured at the lower of cost and net realisable value." Inventory is valued at cost or Net Realisable Value (NRV), whichever is lower. Inventory is valued at lower of cost or Net Realisable Value (NRV) to ensure that anticipated profits must not be accounted for until they have been realised and that full provision should be made for anticipated losses. This principle of valuation is based on the important accounting convention of conservatism. *Conservatism* means taking the gloomy view of a situation. It is a policy of caution or playing safe and had its origin as a safeguard against possible losses in a world of uncertainty. According to this principle of valuation based on convention of conservatism if market price of the inventory is higher than the cost of the inventory, the higher amount is ignored in the accounts because profit is not realised and the inventory will be valued at cost which is lower than the Net Realisable Value (NRV). If this is not done and inventory is valued at market value which is more than cost value, it is possible that dividends to shareholders may be distributed out of unrealised profits. It will not be a sound policy and in the future if the expected market price is not realised and there is a loss, unrealised profit distributed will amount to distribution of dividend out of capital. On the contrary, if the Net Realisable Value (NRV) of the inventory is lower than the cost, the higher amount of cost will be ignored and the inventory will be valued at Net Realisable Value (NRV) which is lower than the cost. In this way, anticipated loss is taken into consideration and even if a loss occurs in the future, the business will not be affected adversely because loss has already been provided by valuing the asset at a lower value and if there is no loss as expected, it is quite good for the business.

Cost in relation to inventory is outlay of cash or its equivalent in the acquisition or manufacturing of the inventory concerned. In other words, cost of inventory is the sum of the applicable expenditures and charges, directly or indirectly, incurred in bringing inventory to its existing condition and location. Market value in relation to inventory is the realisable value of the inventory in the market, *i.e.* the price at which it can be replaced.

As per Ind AS-2 'Valuation of Inventories' *certain costs are excluded from the cost of the inventories are the recognised as expenses in the period in which incurred*. Examples of such costs are :

(*a*) abnormal amount of wasted materials, labour, or other production costs;

(*b*) storage costs, unless those costs are necessary in the production process prior to a further production stage;

(*c*) administrative overheads that do not contribute to bringing the inventories to their present location and condition; and

(*d*) selling and distribution costs.

As per Ind AS 2, "The cost of inventories shall comprise all costs of purchase, cost of conversion and other costs incurred in bringing the inventories to their present location and condition." Costs of purchase of inventories as per Ind AS 2 comprise the purchase price, import duties and other taxes (other than those subsequently recoverable by the entity from the taxing authorities) and transport, handling and other costs directly attributable to the acquisition of finished goods, materials and services. Trade discounts, rebates and other similar items are deducting in determining the costs of purchase. Costs of conversion of inventories include costs directly related to the units of production, such as direct labour. They also include a systematic allocation of fixed and variable production overheads that are incurred in converting materials into finished goods. The allocation of fixed production overheads to the costs of conversion is based on the normal capacity of production facilities.

Criticism of LCM Rule

LCM rule violates the concept of consistency because it allows a change in inventory valuation from one period to another period. It treats value increases and value decreases in inventory differently because value increases in inventory are ignored and value decreases are depicted in financial statements. Because of this, LCM rule becomes a major cause of distortion of profit or loss of different periods.

Inventory to be valued at market price if it is less than cost gives rise to excessive subjectivity in the accounts because market value is more subjective than cost.

Inventory valuation according to LCM rule is conservative with respect to the current period but it is unconservative with respect to the income of future periods.

Inspite of the criticisms of LCM rule, inventory is valued according to this rule.

ILLUSTRATION 1. The company deals in three products, A, B & C which are neither similar nor interchangeable. At the time of closing of its accounts for the year 2024-25, the Historical Cost and Net Realisable Value of the items of closing stock are determined as follows :

Items	*Historical Cost* (₹ in lakhs)	*Net Realisable Value* (₹ in lakhs)
A	40	28
B	32	32
C	16	24

What will be the value of Closing Stock ?

SOLUTION

As per AS-2 on Valuation of Inventories, inventories should be valued at the lower of cost and net realisable value. Lower of cost or net realisable value is to be considered on an item-by-item basis as per para 5 of AS-2 as is shown below :

Items	*Historical Cost* *(₹ in lakhs)*	*Net Realisable Value* *(₹ in lakhs)*	*Valuation of Closing Stock* (₹ in lakhs)
A	40	28	28 (Lower of the two)
B	32	32	32
C	16	24	16 (lower of the two)
	88	84	76

Therefore, closing stock will be valued at ₹ 76 lakhs.

Methods of Valuation of Inventory

Valuation of inventory affects profit of the year. Therefore, method of valuation of inventory should not be changed from year to year to enable comparison of profits of different years.

Following are the various methods of the valuation of inventory.

(*i*) Specific Identification Method

Under this method, various items of inventory are valued at their purchase prices. This method requires a business enterprise to identify each unit of inventory with the unit cost and retain the identification until the inventory is sold or item is issued for use in production. Identification can be made by placing some distinguishing mark usually purchase price on every lot. This method provides satisfactory cost data for the closing inventory and the cost of goods sold because actual purchase prices can be easily seen from the price tags on various lots.

This method is simple in its mechanism and operation. This method does not create accounting complications as are associated with the working of FIFO, LIFO and base stock methods. This method provides an accurate matching of costs and revenues because purchase prices are specially identified with the sales prices. But this method is useful where items of inventory can be identified. Therefore, this method is impracticable for a large manufacturing company where inventory units lose their identity. It is suited to the needs of a small business enterprise where a small number of items are purchased and stored which can be easily identified. Further, the method can be used for manipulating profit of a particular year by issuing to production the lots with lower or higher acquisition costs because the method does not prescribe any particular order in which materials are to be issued.

(*ii*) First-in-First-out (FIFO)

This method of stock valuation is based on the assumption that the oldest items in the inventory are used first so that the inventories which remain unsold are the remains of more recent purchases, hence the costs should be charged to revenue in the order in which they were incurred. The materials issued are priced at the oldest cost price and consequently the inventory is valued at the price of latest purchases. The use of FIFO method does not necessarily mean that the units in the inventory which were oldest in stock are exhausted first but it means that the oldest costs are first used for accounting purposes. Thus, under this method, the physical flow of goods need not necessary coincide with the pattern of cost flow assumption. But in practice it is usually found that most firms issue oldest goods first as a protection against deterioration. The closing inventory does consist of the most recent or the latest acquisitions.

Advantages : (1) This method is simple to understand and easy to operate. (2) It is a logical method because it takes into consideration the normal procedure of utilising first those items of inventory which are received or manufactured first. (3) This method is very useful when prices are falling because cost of goods sold will be high on account of using earliest lots which are costly. (4) Closing stock is valued nearer the market price as it would consist of recent purchases of units. (5) This method is useful when transactions are not too many and prices are fairly steady. (6) This method is useful when inventory is subject to deterioration and obsolescence.

Disadvantages : (1) This method increases the possibility of clerical errors if the prices fluctuate considerably as every time an issue of material is made or goods sold, the store ledger clerk will have to go though his record to ascertain the price to be charged. (2) If the prices fluctuate, comparison between different jobs executed by the concern becomes difficult because one job started a few minutes later than another of the same nature may have consumed the supply of lower priced or higher priced stock. (3) When prices rise, the cost of goods sold does not reflect the market prices as it is calculated keeping in view the earliest lots which were purchased at lower rates.

ILLUSTRATION 2. HP is a leading distributor of petrol. A detail inventory of petrol in hand is taken when the books are closed at the end of each month. At the end of the month following information is available :

Sales	₹ 47,25,000	*Purchases*
General Overheads Cost	₹ 1,25,000	June 1 two lakh litres @ 14.25
Inventory at Beginning	1,00,000 litres	June 30 one lakh litres @ 15.15
	@ 15 per litre	Closing inventory 1.30 lakh litres

Compute the following by the FIFO as per AS 2

(*i*) Value of Inventory on June, 30.

(*ii*) Amount of cost of goods sold for June

(*iv*) Profit/Loss for the month of June. **(*CA—IPCE, Nov. 2016*)**

SOLUTION

	₹
(*i*) Cost of Closing Inventory of 1,30,000 litres as on 30th June	
1,00,000 litres @ ₹ 15.15	15,15,000
30,000 litres @ ₹ 14.25	4,27,500
Total	19,42,500

	₹
(ii) Calculation of Cost of Goods Sold	
Opening Inventories (1,00,000 litres @ ₹ 15)	15,00,000
Purchases June 1 (2,00,000 litres @ ₹ 14.25)	28,50,000
June 30 (1,00,000 litres @ ₹ 15.15)	15,15,000
	58,65,000
Less : Closing Inventories	19,42,500
Cost of Goods Sold	39,22,500
(iii) Calculation of Profit	
Sales (Given) (A)	47,25,000
Cost of Goods Sold	39,22,500
Add : General Overheads	1,25,000
Total Cost (B)	40,47,500
Profit (A – B)	6,77,500

(iii) Last-in-First-out (LIFO)

As against the first-in-first-out method, latest consignment of materials or goods manufactured are exhausted first under this method. Therefore, closing stock is valued at the cost of the earliest lot on hand and the cost of goods sold is based on the cost of recently purchased goods. This method is also sometimes known as the Replacement Cost Method because materials are charged to production at the current cost unless materials were purchased long ago. This method was first introduced in the U.S.A. during the second world war to get the advantages of rising prices.

Advantages : (1) Like FIFO method, LIFO method is simple to operate and is useful when transactions are not too many and the prices are fairly steady. (2) Production is charged at the recent prices because materials are issued from the latest consignment. Thus, effect of current market prices of materials is reflected in the cost of sales provided the materials are recently purchased. (3) In times of rising prices, the higher prices of recent lots are charged to the cost of goods sold. Closing stock is also valued at the lower cost of old purchases. The method thus helps in showing a lower profit and lower profit reduces burden of income tax. No unrealised profit or loss is usually made by using this method.

Disadvantages : (1) Like FIFO this method may lead to clerical errors as every time an issue is made, the store ledger clerk will have to go through his record to ascertain the price to be charged. (2) Like FIFO comparison between one job and the other job will become difficult because one job started a few minutes after another of the same type may bear a different charge for materials consumed, merely because the earlier job exhausted the supply of the lower priced or higher priced material in stock. (3) The stock in hand is valued at a price which does not reflect current market price. Consequently, closing stock will be understated or overstated in the balance sheet.

In 1938, LIFO Method of inventory valuation was permitted for limited classes of tax-payers in the U.S.A. and in 1939 the LIFO privilege was generalised for tax-payers because of inflation. As a result of this, LIFO method of inventory valuation got the world-wide general acceptance and is made use in a period of rising prices.

ILLUSTRATION 3. In computing costs, the owner of the filling station 'A' assumed that he was always pumping off the bottom of his tank. The owner of filling station 'B' assumed that he was always pumping off the top of his tank. On 31st March both had the same inventory of 6,000 litres which cost ₹ 1.10 per litre. In April, each owner bought an additional 6,000 litres at ₹ 1.15 per litre. Sales during April for each station amounted to 8,000 litres at ₹ 1.40 per litre. Determine for each station the net profit for the period, and the value of closing stock.

SOLUTION

Filling Station 'A' uses LIFO method of valuation of issues because petrol received latest is first pumped off. Filling station 'B' uses FIFO method of valuation of issues because petrol received first is pumped off first.

CALCULATION OF THE AMOUNT OF NET PROFIT AND THE VALUE OF CLOSING STOCK

	Filling Station A ₹	*Filling Station B* ₹
Opening stock : 6,000 litres @ ₹ 1.10	6,600	6,600
Add : Purchases: 6,000 litres @ ₹ 1.15	6,900	6,900
	13,500	13,500
Less : Closing stock : 4,000 litres	4,400 (@ ₹ 1.10 per litre as per LIFO Method)	4,600 (@ ₹ 1.15 per litre as per FIFO Method)
Cost of petrol sold	9,100	8,900
Sales: 8,000 litres @ ₹ 1.40	11,200	11,200
Less : Cost of petrol sold	9,100	8,900
Profit	2,100	2,300

ILLUSTRATION 4. From the following data, calculate the value of closing inventory according to Last-in-First-out method on March 31, 2025, using—

(*i*) Periodic inventory system, and

(*ii*) Perpetual inventory system :

March 1 Stock-in-Hand 400 units @ 7.50 each

Purchases :		Issues :	
March 5	600 units @ 8.00 each	March 3	300 units
March 15	500 units @ 9.00 each	March 10	500 units
March 25	400 units @ 8.50 each	March 17	400 units
March 30	300 units @ 9.50 each	March 26	500 units
		March 31	200 units

SOLUTION

(*i*) *Value of closing inventory according to LIFO method on March 31, 2025 using periodic inventory system.*

Total units = Opening stock + Purchases = 400 + 1,800	= 2,200
Less : Units issued	1,900
Balance in stock	300
∴ Value of stock = 300 × ₹ 7.50	₹ 2,250

(*ii*) *Value of closing inventory according to LIFO method on 31st March, 2025 using perpetual inventory system.*

Date	*Details*	*Units*			
March 1	Opening Stock	400			
" 3	Issued	300			
		100			

March 5	Purchases		600			
" 10	Issued		500			
			100			
March 15	Purchases			500		
" 17	Issued			400		
				100		
" 25	Purchases				400	
" 26	Issued			100	400	
				×	×	
" 30	Purchases					300
" 31	Issued					200
						100

		₹
∴ Value of stock =	100 × ₹ 7.50	= 750
	100 × ₹ 8.00	= 800
	100 × ₹ 9.50	= 950
Value of stock on 31-3-2025		2,500

(*iv*) Weighted Average Cost Method

The principle on which the average cost method is based is that all items in the stores are so mixed up that consumption of material or sale of finished goods cannot be made from any particular lot of purchases or manufactured goods. So, closing stock is valued at the weighted average cost of the various items on hand.

Weighted Arithmetic Average Price. Under weighted average cost formula, the cost of each item is determined from the weighted average cost of similar items purchased or produced during the period. The weighted average price is calculated by dividing the total cost of items of stocks by the total quantity of items in hand. The materials issued or goods sold are costed at this weighted price and the closing inventories are also valued at the same weighted price. The average may be calculated on a periodic basis, or at each additional shipment is received, depending upon the circumstances of the enterprise. The weighted average method is realistic in the sense that it represents the physical flow of goods when all goods available for sale (*i.e.* beginning inventory plus all the purchases) are mixed together with one another. This method is objective, consistent and does not permit profit manipulation. This approach provides the same cost for similar items of equal utility. This price is obtained by dividing the total cost of items in stock by the total quantity of items in hand. In the above example, the weighted average price is ₹ 11.33 per unit calculated as follows :

$$\frac{1{,}000 \times ₹\ 10 + 2{,}000 \times ₹\ 11 + 3{,}000 \times ₹\ 12}{1{,}000 + 2{,}000 + 3{,}000} = ₹\ 11.33$$

If average cost method of inventory valuation is to be used, weighted average price should be followed because it values inventory at cost. In the cited example, the total purchase price of the material in stock is ₹ 68,000 and the value of inventory at weighted average price is also ₹ 68,000 (*i.e.* 6,000 units @ ₹ 11.33).

Advantages of Weighted Average Method

(1) In case price of material in regular use fluctuates from time to time, the weighted average method irons out the fluctuations to a great extent, and as such cost of materials charged to jobs and of materials on hand reflects a greater uniformity than under the FIFO or Replacement price method.

(2) Prices of manufactured goods based on cost arrived at by using this method will be more competitive than under other methods.

(3) Clerical labour is much reduced as compared to that required under other methods.

Disadvantages of Weighted Average Method

(1) This method will not give current cost since it will always be influenced by price paid previously.

(2) Comparison of costs for the purpose of measuring efficiency is vitiated.

(3) This method is suitable only (*a*) when price fluctuates much, and (*b*) when the price of finished goods does not strictly depend on the market price of the input materials.

ILLUSTRATION 5. A company, started on 1st January, 2024, purchased raw material during 2024 as stated below :

January 2	800 kgs. @ ₹ 62 per kg.	July 10	3,000 kgs. @ ₹ 56 per kg.
February 26	1,200 kgs. @ ₹ 57 per kg.	September 18	1,500 kgs. @ ₹ 60 per kg.
April 13	2,500 kgs. @ ₹ 59 per kg.	November 29	1,000 kgs. @ ₹ 65 per kg.

While preparing its final accounts on 31st December, 2024, the company had 1,300 kgs. of raw material in its godowns.

Calculate the value of closing stock of raw material according to—

(*i*) 'First-in-First-out' basis

(*ii*) 'Last-in-First-out' basis

(*iii*) 'Weighted Average' basis.

SOLUTION

(i) Value of Stock according to FIFO Basis

	₹
1,000 × ₹ 65	= 65,000
300 × ₹ 60	= 18,000
	83,000

(ii) Value of Stock according to LIFO Basis

	₹
800 × ₹ 62	= 49,600
500 × ₹ 57	= 28,500
	78,100

(iii) Value of Stock as per Weighted Average Basis

Kgs.	*Rate* ₹	*Value* ₹
800	62	49,600
1,200	57	68,400
2,500	59	1,47,500
3,000	56	1,68,000
1,500	60	90,000
1,000	65	65,000
10,000		5,88,500

∴ Cost per kg. $= \dfrac{₹\,5,88,500}{10,000} = ₹\,58.85$

∴ Value of Stock = ₹ 58.85 × 1,300 = ₹ 76,505.

INDIAN ACCOUNTING STANDARD (IND AS)–2 DEALS WITH INVENTORIES

Objective

1. The objective of this Standard is to prescribe the accounting treatment for inventories. A primary issue in accounting for inventories is the amount of cost to be recognised as an asset and carried forward until the related revenues are recognised. This Standard deals with the determination of cost and its subsequent recognition as an expense, including any write-down to net realisable value. It also deals with the cost formulas that are used to assign costs to inventories.

Scope

2. This Standard applies to all inventories, except:

(*a*) work in progress arising under construction contracts, including directly related service contracts (as per Ind AS 11, Construction Contracts;

(*b*) financial instruments (as per Ind AS 39 , Financial Instruments: Recognition and Measurement and Ind AS 32, Financial Instruments: Presentation); and

(*c*) biological assets (i.e., living animals or plants) related to agricultural activity and agricultural produce at the point of harvest (as per Ind AS 41, Agriculture under formulation).

3. This Standard does not apply to the measurement of inventories held by:

(*a*) producers of agricultural and forest products, agricultural produce after harvest, and minerals and mineral products, to the extent that they are measured at net realisable value in accordance with well-established practices in those industries. When such inventories are measured at net realisable value, changes in that value are recognised in profit or loss in the period of the change.

(*b*) commodity broker-traders who measure their inventories at fair value less costs to sell. When such inventories are measured at fair value less costs to sell, changes in fair value less costs to sell are recognised in profit or loss in the period of the change.

4. The inventories referred to in paragraph 3(a) are measured at net realisable value at certain stages of production. This occurs, for example, when agricultural crops have been harvested or minerals have been extracted and sale is assured under a forward contract or a government guarantee, or when an active market exists and there is a negligible risk of failure to sell. These inventories are excluded from only the measurement requirements of this Standard.

5. Broker-traders are those who buy or sell commodities for others or on their own account. The inventories referred to in paragraph 3(b) are principally acquired with the purpose of selling in the near future and generating a profit from fluctuations in price or broker-traders' margin. When these inventories are measured at fair value less costs to sell, they are excluded from only the measurement requirements of this Standard.

Definitions

6. The following terms are used in this Standard with the meanings specified:

Inventories are assets:

(*a*) held for sale in the ordinary course of business;

(*b*) in the process of production for such sale; or

(*c*) in the form of materials or supplies to be consumed in the production process or in the rendering of services.

Net realisable value is the estimated selling price in the ordinary course of business less the estimated costs of completion and the estimated costs necessary to make the sale.

Fair value is the amount for which an asset could be exchanged, or a liability settled, between knowledgeable, willing parties in an arm's length transaction.

7. Net realisable value refers to the net amount that an entity expects to realise from the sale of inventory in the ordinary course of business. Fair value reflects the amount for which the same inventory could be exchanged between knowledgeable and willing buyers and sellers in the marketplace. The former is an entity-specific value; the latter is not. Net realisable value for inventories may not equal fair value less costs to sell.

8. Inventories encompass goods purchased and held for resale including, for example, merchandise purchased by a retailer and held for resale, or land and other property held for resale. Inventories also encompass finished goods produced, or work in progress being produced, by the entity and include materials and supplies awaiting use in the production process. In the case of a service provider, inventories include the costs of the service, as described in paragraph 19, for which the entity has not yet recognised the related revenue *(see* Ind AS 18, *Revenue)*.

Measurement of Inventories

9. Inventories shall be measured at the lower of cost and net realisable value.

Cost of Inventories

10. The cost of inventories shall comprise all costs of purchase, costs of conversion and other costs incurred in bringing the inventories to their present location and condition.

Costs of Purchase

11. The costs of purchase of inventories comprise the purchase price, import duties and other taxes (other than those subsequently recoverable by the entity from the taxing authorities), and transport, handling and other costs directly attributable to the acquisition of finished goods, materials and services. Trade discounts, rebates and other similar items are deducted in determining the costs of purchase.

Costs of Conversion

12. The costs of conversion of inventories include costs directly related to the units of production, such as direct labour. They also include a systematic allocation of fixed and variable production overheads that are incurred in converting materials into finished goods. Fixed production overheads are those indirect costs of production that remain relatively constant regardless of the volume of production, such as depreciation and maintenance of factory buildings and equipment, and the cost of factory management and administration. Variable production overheads are those indirect costs of production that vary directly, or nearly directly, with the volume of production, such as indirect materials and indirect labour.

13. The allocation of fixed production overheads to the costs of conversion is based on the normal capacity of the production facilities. Normal capacity is the production expected to be achieved on average over a number of periods or seasons under normal circumstances, taking into account the loss of capacity resulting from planned maintenance. The actual level of production may be used if it approximates normal capacity. The amount of fixed overhead allocated to each unit of production is not increased as a consequence of low production or idle plant. Unallocated overheads are recognised as an expense in the period in which they are incurred. In periods of abnormally high production, the amount of fixed overhead allocated to each unit of production is decreased so that inventories are not measured above cost. Variable production overheads are allocated to each unit of production on the basis of the actual use of the production facilities.

14. A production process may result in more than one product being produced simultaneously. This is the case, for example, when joint products are produced or when there is a main product and a by-product. When the costs of conversion of each product are not separately identifiable, they are allocated between the products on a rational and consistent basis. The allocation may be based, for example, on the relative sales value of each product either at the stage in the production process when the products become separately identifiable, or at the completion of production. Most by-products, by their nature, are immaterial. When this is the case, they are often measured at net realisable value and this value is deducted from the cost of the main product. As a result, the carrying amount of the main product is not materially different from its cost.

Other Costs

15. Other costs are included in the cost of inventories only to the extent that they are incurred in bringing the inventories to their present location and condition. For example, it may be appropriate to include non-production overheads or the costs of designing products for specific customers in the cost of inventories.

16. Examples of costs excluded from the cost of inventories and recognised as expenses in the period in which they are incurred are:

(a) abnormal amounts of wasted materials, labour or other production costs;

(b) storage costs, unless those costs are necessary in the production process before a further production stage;

(c) administrative overheads that do not contribute to bringing inventories to their present location and condition; and

(d) selling costs.

17. Ind AS 23, *Borrowing Costs,* identifies limited circumstances where borrowing costs are included in the cost of inventories.

18. An entity may purchase inventories on deferred settlement terms. When the arrangement effectively contains a financing element, that element, for example a difference between the purchase price for normal credit terms and the amount paid, is recognised as interest expense over the period of the financing.

Cost of Inventories of a Service Provider

19. To the extent that service providers have inventories, they measure them at the costs of their production. These costs consist primarily of the labour and other costs of personnel directly engaged in providing the service, including supervisory personnel, and attributable overheads. Labour and other costs relating to sales and general administrative personnel are not included but are recognised as expenses in the period in which they are incurred. The cost of inventories of a service provider does not include profit margins or non-attributable overheads that are often factored into prices charged by service providers.

Cost of Agricultural Produce Harvested from Biological Assets

20. In accordance with Ind AS 41, *Agriculture*, inventories comprising agricultural produce that an entity has harvested from its biological assets are measured on initial recognition at their fair value less costs to sell at the point of harvest. This is the cost of the inventories at that date for application of this Standard.

Techniques for the Measurement of Cost

21. Techniques for the measurement of the cost of inventories, such as the standard cost method or the retail method, may be used for convenience if the results approximate cost. Standard costs take into account normal levels of materials and supplies, labour, efficiency and capacity utilisation. They are regularly reviewed and, if necessary, revised in the light of current conditions.

22. The retail method is often used in the retail industry for measuring inventories of large numbers of rapidly changing items with similar margins for which it is impracticable to use other costing methods. The cost of the inventory is determined by reducing the sales value of the inventory by the appropriate percentage gross margin. The percentage used takes into consideration inventory that has been marked down to below its original selling price. An average percentage for each retail department is often used.

Cost Formulas

23. The cost of inventories of items that are not ordinarily interchangeable and goods or services produced and segregated for specific projects shall be assigned by using specific identification of their individual costs.

24. Specific identification of cost means that specific costs are attributed to identified items of inventory. This is the appropriate treatment for items that are segregated for a specific project, regardless of whether they have been bought or produced. However, specific identification of costs is inappropriate when there are large numbers of items of inventory that are ordinarily interchangeable. In such circumstances, the method of selecting those items that remain in inventories could be used to obtain predetermined effects on profit or loss.

25. The cost of inventories, other than those dealt with in paragraph 23, shall be assigned by using the first-in, first-out (FIFO) or weighted average cost formula. An entity shall use the same cost formula for all inventories having a similar nature and use to the entity. For inventories with a different nature or use, different cost formulas may be justified.

26. For example, inventories used in one operating segment may have a use to the entity different from the same type of inventories used in another operating segment. However, a difference in geographical location of inventories (or in the respective tax rules), by itself, is not sufficient to justify the use of different cost formulas.

27. The FIFO formula assumes that the items of inventory that were purchased or produced first are sold first, and consequently the items remaining in inventory at the end of the period are those most recently purchased or produced. Under the weighted average cost formula, the cost of each item is determined from the weighted average of the cost of similar items at the beginning of a period and the cost of similar items purchased or produced during the period. The average may be calculated on a periodic basis, or as each additional shipment is received, depending upon the circumstances of the entity.

Net Realisable Value

28. The cost of inventories may not be recoverable if those inventories are damaged, if they have become wholly or partially obsolete, or if their selling prices have declined. The cost of inventories may also not be recoverable if the estimated costs of completion or the estimated costs to be incurred to make the sale have increased. The practice of writing inventories down below cost to net realisable value is consistent with the view that assets should not be carried in excess of amounts expected to be realised from their sale or use.

29. Inventories are usually written down to net realisable value item by item. In some circumstances, however, it may be appropriate to group similar or related items. This may be the case with items of inventory relating to the same product line that have similar purposes or end uses, are produced and marketed in the same geographical area, and cannot be practicably evaluated separately from other items in that product line. It is not appropriate to write inventories down on the basis of a classification of inventory, for example, finished goods, or all the inventories in a particular operating segment. Service providers generally accumulate costs in respect of each service for which a separate selling price is charged. Therefore, each such service is treated as a separate item.

30. Estimates of net realisable value are based on the most reliable evidence available at the time the estimates are made, of the amount the inventories are expected to realise. These estimates take into consideration fluctuations of price or cost directly relating to events occurring after the end of the period to the extent that such events confirm conditions existing at the end of the period.

31. Estimates of net realisable value also take into consideration the purpose for which the inventory is held. For example, the net realisable value of the quantity of inventory held to satisfy firm sales or service contracts is based on the contract price. If the sales contracts are for less than the inventory quantities held, the net realisable value of the excess is based on general selling prices. Provisions may arise from firm sales contracts in excess of inventory quantities held or from firm purchase contracts. Such provisions are dealt with under Ind AS 37, *Provisions, Contingent Liabilities and Contingent Assets*.

32. Materials and other supplies held for use in the production of inventories are not written down below cost if the finished products in which they will be incorporated are expected to be sold at or above cost. However, when a decline in the price of materials indicates that the cost of the finished products exceeds net realisable value, the materials are written down to net realisable value. In such circumstances, the replacement cost of the materials may be the best available measure of their net realisable value.

33. A new assessment is made of net realisable value in each subsequent period. When the circumstances that previously caused inventories to be written down below cost no longer exist or when there is clear evidence of an increase in net realisable value because of changed economic circumstances, the amount of the write-down is reversed (*i.e.* the reversal is limited to the amount of the original write-down) so that the new carrying amount is the lower of the cost and the revised net realisable value. This occurs, for example, when an item of inventory that is carried at net realisable value, because its selling price has declined, is still on hand in a subsequent period and its selling price has increased.

Recognition as an Expense

34. When inventories are sold, the carrying amount of those inventories shall be recognised as an expense in the period in which the related revenue is recognised. The amount of any write-down of inventories to net realisable value and all losses of inventories shall be recognised as an expense in the period the write-down or loss occurs. The amount of any reversal of any write-down of inventories, arising from an increase in net realisable value, shall be recognised as a reduction in the amount of inventories recognised as an expense in the period in which the reversal occurs.

35. Some inventories may be allocated to other asset accounts, for example, inventory used as a component of self-constructed property, plant or equipment. Inventories allocated to another asset in this way are recognised as an expense during the useful life of that asset.

Disclosure

36. The financial statements shall disclose:

(*a*) the accounting policies adopted in measuring inventories, including the cost formula used;

(*b*) the total carrying amount of inventories and the carrying amount in classifications appropriate to the entity;

(*c*) the carrying amount of inventories carried at fair value less costs to sell;

(*d*) the amount of inventories recognised as an expense during the period;

(*e*) the amount of any write-down of inventories recognised as an expense in the period in accordance with paragraph 34;

(*f*) the amount of any reversal of any write-down that is recognised as a reduction in the amount of inventories recognised as expense in the period in accordance with paragraph 34;

(*g*) the circumstances or events that led to the reversal of a write-down of inventories in accordance with paragraph 34; and

(*h*) the carrying amount of inventories pledged as security for liabilities.

37. Information about the carrying amounts held in different classifications of inventories and the extent of the changes in these assets is useful to financial statement users. Common classifications of inventories are merchandise, production supplies, materials, work in progress and finished goods. The inventories of a service provider may be described as work in progress.

38. This paragraph 38 of IAS 2 dealing with recognition of inventories as an expense based on function-wise classification, has been deleted keeping in view the fact that option provided in IAS 1 to present an analysis of expenses recognised in profit or loss using a classification based on their function within the entity has been removed and Ind AS 1 requires only nature-wise classification of expenses. However, in order to maintain consistency with paragraph numbers of IAS 2, the paragraph number is retained in Ind AS 2.

39. An entity adopts a format for profit or loss that results in amounts being disclosed other than the cost of inventories recognised as an expense during the period. Under this format, the entity presents an analysis of expenses using a classification based on the nature of expenses. In this case, the entity discloses the costs recognised as an expense for raw materials and consumables, labour costs and other costs together with the amount of the net change in inventories for the period.

EXAMPLE 1. Toly Enterprise ordered 10,000 units of material X at ₹ 135 per unit. The purchase price includes excise duty @ ₹ 8 per unit, in respect of which full CENVAT Credit is admissible. Freight incurred amounted to ₹ 88,500. Normal transit loss is 5%. The enterprise actually received 9,400 units and consumed 8,500 units.

You are required to ascertain the *Value of Inventory* as per Ind. AS-2.

SOLUTION

Calculation of Normal Cost Per Unit :	₹
Purchase Price—10,000 Units @ ₹ 135	13,50,000
Less : CENVAT Credit—10,000 Units @ ₹ 8	80,000
	12,70,000
Add : Freight	88,500
Total Material Cost	13,58,500

No. of Units Normally Received : 100 – 5 = 95% of 10,000 = 9,500 Units

Normal Cost Per Unit = ₹ 13,58,500 ÷ 9,500 = ₹ 143

Valuation of Inventory : Units = 9,400 – 8,500 = 900 Units

Value of Inventory = 900 Units @ ₹ 143 = ₹ 1,28,700

EXAMPLE 2. The closing inventory at cost of a Company amounted to ₹ 9,56,700. The following items were included at cost in the total :

(*i*) 350 Shirts, which had cost ₹ 380 each and normally sold for ₹ 750 each. Owing to a defect in manufacture, they were all sold after the Balance Sheet date at 50% of their normal price. Selling expenses amounted to 5% of the proceeds.

(*ii*) 700 Trousers, which had cost ₹ 520 each. These too were found to be defective. Selling expenses for the batch totaled ₹ 3,800. They were sold for ₹ 950 each.

What should be the closing *inventory value*, after considering the above items ? ***(PCE)***

SOLUTION

CALCULATION OF VALUE OF CLOSING INVENTORY

	₹
Value of Closing Inventory (given)	9,56,700
Less : Adjustment to bring the stock of shirts at Net Realisable Value (1)	(8,313)
Revised Value of Closing Inventory as per Ind. AS 2 "Valuation of Inventories"	9,48,387

Working Notes :

(1) Valuation of Shirts

	₹
Total Cost of Shirts (₹ 380 × 350 Shirts)	1,33,000

NRV of Shirts		
Selling Price [(₹ 750 × 50%) × 350 Shirts)	₹ 1,31,250	
Less : Selling Expenses (5% of ₹ 1,31,250)	₹ 6,563	
NRV	₹ 1,24,687	
As per Ind. AS 2, Inventories are Valued at Cost or NRV, whichever is less		1,24,687
Therefore, Value of Inventory of Shirts is to be reduced by ₹ 8,313 (Difference of cost and NRV)		8,313

(2) Valuation of Trousers

		₹
Total Cost of Trousers (₹ 520 × 700 trousers)		3,64,000
NRV of Trousers		
Selling Price (₹ 950 × 700 trousers)	₹ 6,65,000	
Less : Selling Expenses	₹ 3,800	
NRV	₹ 6,61,200	
As per Ind. AS 2 inventories are valued at cost or NRV, whichever is less		3,64,000
Since, inventory of trousers is already carried at cost; no further adjustment is required in the total value of closing stock.		

EXAMPLE 3. The cost of production of Product X is ₹ 450 which includes per unit cost of material, labour and overheads of ₹ 250, ₹ 110 and ₹ 90 respectively. At the end of the accounting year on 31-3-2025 the replacement cost of raw material is ₹ 210 per unit.

There are 500 units of raw material in stock on 31-3-2025.

Calculate as per Ind. AS-2 the *Value of Closing Stock* of Raw Material when :

(*i*) Finished Product is sold at ₹ 420 per unit.

(*ii*) Finished Product is sold at ₹ 490 per unit.

SOLUTION

(*i*) In this situation net realisable value of the product is less than its total cost and cost of raw material is more than the replacement cost. Hence, raw material should be valued at replacement cost and the value of raw material stock will be—500 units × ₹ 210 = ₹ 1,05,000.

(*ii*) In this situation the net realisable value of the product is more than its total cost, then the raw material should be valued at actual cost and value of raw materials stock will be—500 units × ₹ 250 = ₹ 1,25,000.

EXAMPLE 4. Mr. Rakshit gives the following information relating to items forming part of inventory as on 31st March, 2025. His factory produces product X using raw material A.

(*i*) 800 units of raw material A (purchased @ ₹ 140 per unit). Replacement cost of raw material A as on 31st March, 2025 is ₹ 190 per unit.

(*ii*) 650 units of partly finished goods in the process of producing X and cost incurred till date ₹ 310 per unit. These units can be finished next year by incurring additional cost of ₹ 50 per unit.

(*iii*) 1,800 units of finished product X and total cost incurred ₹ 360 per unit.

Expected selling price of product X is ₹ 350 per unit.

In the context of AS-2, determine how each item of inventory will be valued as on 31st March, 2025. Also calculate the value of total inventory as on 31st March, 2025.

SOLUTION

As per AS 2 (Revised) "Valuation of Inventories", materials and other supplies held for use in the production of inventories are not written down below cost if the finished products in which they will be incorporated are expected to be sold at cost or above cost. However, when there has been a decline in the price of materials and it is estimated that the cost of the finished products will exceed net realisable value, the materials are written down to net realisable value. In such circumstances, the replacement cost of the materials may be the best available measure of their net realisable value. In the given case, selling price of product X is ₹ 350 and total cost per unit for production is ₹ 360.

Hence the valuation will be done as under :

(*i*) 800 units of raw material will be valued at cost 140.

(*ii*) 650 units of partly finished goods will be valued at 300 per unit* *i.e.* lower of cost (₹ 310) or Net realisable value ₹ 300 (Estimated selling price ₹ 350 per unit less additional cost of ₹ 50).

(*iii*) 1,800 units of finished product X will be valued NRV of ₹ 350 per unit since it is lower than cost ₹ 360 of product X.

VALUATION OF TOTAL INVENTORY

as on 31-3-2025

Particulars	*Units*	*Cost (₹)*	*NRV/Replacement cost (₹)*	*Value = Units × Cost or NRV whichever is less (₹)*	*₹*
Raw Material A	800	140	190	1,12,000	(800 × 140)
Partly Finished Goods	650	310	300	1,95,000	(650 × 300)
Finished Goods X	1,800	60	350	6,30,000	(1,800 × 350)
Value of Inventory				9,37,000	

*It has been assumed that the partly finished unit cannot be sold in semi-finished form and its NRV is zero without processing it further.

How to calculate the value of closing stock when it is not given ?

The value of closing stock is calculated as follows :

	Stock at the beginning of the period (*i.e.* opening stock)		× × ×
Add :	Purchases *less* purchases returns during the year		× × ×
	Value of goods that would have been in stock had there been no sales		× × ×
Less :	Cost of Sales : Sales *less* sales returns	× × ×	
Less :	Gross Profit	× × ×	
			× × ×
	Stock at the end of the period (*i.e.*, closing stock)		× × ×

If the value of closing stock is given but the value of the opening stock is not given, the procedure for the ascertainment of the value of the opening stock is the reverse of that followed above. It is as follows :

	Closing Stock		× × ×
Add :	Cost of Sales : Sales *less* sales returns	× × ×	
Less :	Gross Profit	× × ×	
			× × ×
	Value of total goods available for sale		× × ×
Less :	Purchases *less* purchases returns		× × ×
	Stock at the beginning of the period (*i.e.*, Opening Stock)		× × ×

ILLUSTRATION 6. Determine the value of stock to be taken for Balance Sheet as at 31st March, 2025 from the following information :

The stock was verified on 25th March, 2025 and was valued at ₹ 10,00,000. Following transactions took place between 25th March, 2025 and 31st March, 2025 :

(*a*) Out of goods sent on consignment goods worth ₹ 40,000 (at cost) were unsold.

(*b*) Sales were for ₹ 2,50,000. It includes goods worth ₹ 75,000 sent on approval basis. One-third of these were returned before 31st March, 2025. As regards remaining, no intimation is received.

(*c*) Purchases of ₹ 2,50,000, out of this, goods worth ₹ 50,000 were delivered after 31st March, 2025.

(*d*) The selling price is fixed by having a 20% margin on sales value. However, to one customer goods costing ₹ 20,000 were sold for ₹ 15,000.

SOLUTION

STATEMENT SHOWING THE VALUE OF STOCK

as on 31st March, 2025

			₹
Value of Stock on 25th March, 2025			10,00,000
Add : (1) Stock of unsold goods on consignment			40,000
(2) Goods on approval with customers :		₹	
Sales value		50,000	
Less : Profit 20% on Sales		10,000	
			40,000
(3) Purchases :			
(*a*) Goods received		2,00,000	
(*b*) Goods in Transit on 31-3-2025		50,000	
			2,50,000
			13,30,000
Less : (*i*) Cost of normal goods sold :	₹		
Sales	2,50,000		
Less : Sale of abnormal goods	15,000		
	2,35,000		
Less : Goods sent on approval but returned	25,000		
	2,10,000		
Less : Profit @ 20% on sales	42,000		
		1,68,000	
(*ii*) Cost of abnormal sale		20,000	
			1,88,000
Value of Stock on 31-3-2025			11,42,000

ILLUSTRATION 7. Mr. Stockist closed his books of accounts on 30th June, 2025, but for certain difficulties it was not possible for him to take stock on that date. Physical stock was taken on 7th July, 2025 and it was valued at ₹ 45,000.

An examination of the records of inventories from 1st to 7th July revealed the following :

(*a*) Sales during the period totalled ₹ 10,200. These goods were sold at the usual rate of gross profit of 25% on the cost except that goods which realised ₹ 1,200 had to be sold at a profit of only 20% on cost.

(*b*) Of the goods sold, certain goods valued ₹ 2,500 sold on 6th July, were delivered to the customer only on 9th July.

(*c*) Purchases during the period totalled ₹ 8,000, of which goods costing ₹ 7,000 were delivered on or before 7th July.

(*d*) During the period customers returned goods valued ₹ 800 which included goods of ₹ 600 sold during the year ending 30th June, 2025. All the returned goods were sold at a uniform profit of 25% on cost.

(*e*) On 25th July, the stockist received certain goods invoiced at ₹ 5,000 from Mr. Consignor to be sold on his behalf and at his risk. These goods were yet to be sold.

(*f*) Goods invoiced at ₹ 4,500 and despatched on 'sale or return' basis on 4th July were not included in the aforesaid sales.

You are required to prepare a statement showing clearly the value of the stock which Mr. Stockist should take into account for preparing his Trading and Profit and Loss Account for the year ending 30th June, 2025.

SOLUTION

STATEMENT SHOWING THE VALUE OF STOCK

as on 30th June, 2025

	₹	₹
Value of Stock on 7th July, 2025		45,000
Add : Cost of goods sold during 1st July, 2025 to 7th July, 2025 :		
Sales from 1-7-2025 to 7-7-2025	10,200	
Add : Sales not realising usual rate of gross profit	1,200	
	9,000	
Less : Goods sold on 6th July not delivered upto 9th July	2,500	
	6,500	
Less : 20% profit on sales which is equivalent to 25% of cost	1,300	
		5,200
Add : Cost of sales not realising usual rate of gross profit $\left(i.e., \frac{100}{120} \times ₹\ 1,200\right)$		1,000
Add : Cost of goods invoiced on 'sales or return' basis $\left(i.e., \frac{100}{125} \times ₹\ 4,500\right)$		3,600
		54,800
Less : Cost of goods purchased and delivered upto 7th July, 2025		7,000
		47,800
Less : Cost of goods returned sold during the year ending 30th, June, 2025 $\left(i.e., \frac{100}{125} \times ₹\ 600\right)$		480
		47,320
Less : Goods received on consignment basis (assuming that goods were valued at the same value at which these were consigned by the consignor while physical stock was taken)		5,000
Value of Stock on 30-6-2025		42,320

Mr. Stockist should take into account ₹ 42,320 as the value of the stock for preparing his Trading and Profit and Loss Account for the year ending 30th June, 2025.

ILLUSTRATION 8. Hans Ltd. keeps no running stock records but a physical inventory of stock is made at the end of each quarter and evaluated at cost. The company's year ends on 30th September, 2024 and draft accounts have been prepared to that date. The stock inventory taken on 30th September, 2024 was accidentally destroyed before the items had been evaluated, the closing stock figure used in the draft accounts being that shown by the inventory taken on 30th June, 2024. The gross margin earned by the company is 25% of cost.

During your audit you discovered the following :

(1) The cost of the stock on 30th June, 2024 as shown by the inventory was ₹ 40,525.

(2) On 30th June, 2024 stock sheets showed the following discrepancies.

(*a*) A page total of ₹ 5,059 had been carried to the summary as ₹ 5,509.

(*b*) A total of a page had been undercast by ₹ 98.

(*c*) 100 items which had cost ₹ 5 each had been taken at 25 paise each.

(3) Invoices for purchases entered in the Purchases Book during the month of July, August and September 2024 totalled ₹ 38,560. Of this total, ₹ 2,800 related to goods received on or prior to 30th June, 2024. Invoices entered in October 2024 relating to goods received in September 2024 totalled ₹ 3,700.

(4) Sales invoiced to customers in July, August and September 2024 totalled ₹ 51,073. Of this total, ₹ 3,824 related to goods despatched on or before 30th June, 2024. Goods despatched to customers before 30th September, 2024 but invoiced in October 2024 totalled ₹ 5,241.

(5) During the final quarter of the company's year, credit notes at invoiced value of ₹ 1,280 had been issued to customers in respect of goods returned during that period.

You are required to prepare a statement showing the amount of the stock at cost as on 30th September, 2024.

SOLUTION

STATEMENT SHOWING THE AMOUNT OF STOCK AT COST

as on 30-9-2024

Particulars		₹	₹
Cost of Stock on 30-6-2024 as shown in the draft accounts		40,525	
Less : Error in carry forward of page total (5,509 – 5,059)		450	
		40,075	
Add : Error in casting of page total		98	
Error in rate : 100 items @ ₹ 4.75 per item		475	
Actual cost of stock on 30-6-2024		40,648	
			40,648
Add :Adjusted Purchases during July-September, 2024 :			
Purchases as entered in the Purchases Book			38,560
Less : Goods received on or prior to 30-6-2024		2,800	
		35,760	
Add : Goods purchased and received before 30-9-2024 but entered in October, 2024		3,700	
			39,460
			80,108
Less : Cost of Goods sold during July-September, 2024 :			
Sales invoiced to customers during July-Sept.			51,073
Less : Goods despatched on or before 30-6-2024	₹	₹	
included in above sales	3,824		
Goods returned	1,280		
		5,104	
		45,969	

Add : Goods despatched before 30-9-2024 but invoiced in October	5,241	
Adjusted sales during July-Sept.	51,210	
Less : Gross profit 20% on sales (*i.e.* 25% on cost)	10,242	
Cost of goods sold		40,968
Cost of Stock on 30-9-2024		39,140

ILLUSTRATION 9. Profit and Loss Account of Sampat for the year ended 31st March, 2025 showed a net profit of ₹ 2,500 after taking into account the closing stock of ₹ 4,720.

On a scrutiny of the books the following information could be obtained :

(*i*) Purchases of the year included ₹ 500 spent on acquisition of a ceiling fan for his shop.

(*ii*) Sampat has taken goods valued at ₹ 1,800 for his personal use without making entry in the books.

(*iii*) Invoices for goods amounting to ₹ 4,000 have been entered on 29th Mach, 2025 but such goods were not included in stock.

(*iv*) Sale of goods amounting to ₹ 700 sold and delivered in March, 2025 had been entered in April, 2025 sales.

(*v*) ₹ 500 had been included in closing stock in respect of goods purchased and invoiced on 28th March, 2025 but included in purchases for April, 2025.

You are required to ascertain the correct amount of closing stock as on 31st March, 2025 and the adjusted Net Profit for the year ended on that date.

SOLUTION

Calculation of Correct Amount of Closing Stock

	₹
Stock on 31-3-2025 as already given	4,720
Add : Purchases entered on 29th March in the books but not included in closing stock on 31-3-2025	4,000
Correct Amount of Closing Stock as on 31-3-2025	8,720

PROFIT AND LOSS ADJUSTMENT ACCOUNT

	₹		₹
To Suppliers' A/c Goods Purchased on 28th March, 2025 included in Closing Stock but Recorded as Purchases in April, 2025)	500	By Profit (as already calculated)	2,500
To Net Profit (Balancing Figure)	9,000	By Furniture & Fittings (Acquisition of Ceiling Fan wrongly included in Purchases A/c)	500
		By Drawings (Goods for Personal Use not Recorded)	1,800
		By Closing Stock (Goods recorded as Purchases not included in Stock)	4,000
		By Customer's A/c (Sale of Goods in March, 2025 but entered in April, 2025 Sales)	700
	9,500		9,500

QUESTIONS

OBJECTIVE TYPE

1. **Fill in the blanks :**
   (*a*) First-in-first-out method of inventory valuation is suitable in times of ....
   (*b*) Last-in-first-out method is suitable in times of ....
   (*c*) Average cost method of inventory valuation is suitable when ....
   (*d*) Inflated price method of inventory valuation is followed to ....
   (*e*) Market price method of inventory valuation is followed when ....
   (*f*) Closing stock should be valued at cost or market price ....

Ans. [(*a*) falling prices; (*b*) rising prices; (*c*) there are fluctuations in prices; (*d*) provide for the normal loss; (*e*) the market price is lower than the cost; (*f*) whichever is lower].

2. **State which of the following statements are true or false :**
   (*a*) Stock should be valued at cost or market price whichever is lower.
   (*b*) Perpetual inventory system enables management to ascertain stock at any time without the expenses of physical verification.
   (*c*) Inventory valuation affects only the position statement.
   (*d*) Perpetual inventory system and continuous stock taking mean one and the same thing.
   (*e*) The inventory under Ind. AS-2 is valued on the basis of cost price or current replacement cost, whichever is less.
   (*f*) Damaged inventory should be valued at cost or market price, whichever is lower.

Ans. [True (*a*) and (*b*); False (*c*), (*d*), (*e*) and (*f*)].
Note. Damaged inventory should be valued at net realisable value.

3. **Indicate the correct answer :**
   (*a*) In perpetual inventory system, store balances are recorded
   (*i*) after every issue of stock
   (*ii*) after every issue and receipt of materials
   (*iii*) after every week
   (*iv*) None of the above.
   (*b*) LIFO method of pricing material issues is suitable
   (*i*) when material prices are rising
   (*ii*) when material prices are falling
   (*iii*) when there are too many fluctuations in prices of materials
   (*iv*) None of the above.
   (*c*) Methods of valuation of inventories as per Ind. AS-2 are
   (*i*) Specific Identification cost Method
   (*ii*) FIFO Method
   (*iii*) Weighted Average cost Method
   (*iv*) All of the above.
   (*d*) Under which method value of stock is determined by physical counting of stock ?
   (*i*) Periodic inventory system
   (*ii*) Perpetual inventory system
   (*iii*) Both of (*i*) and (*ii*)
   (*iv*) None of (*i*) and (*ii*).

Ans. [(*a*) (*ii*); (*b*) (*i*); (*c*) (*iv*); (*d*) (*i*)].

SHORT ANSWER TYPE

1. Give the meaning of inventory.
2. Why is valuation of inventory significant ? ***(B.Com. Hons. Delhi)***
3. Distinguish between periodic inventory and perpetual inventory method of stock valuation. ***(B.Com. Hons. Delhi)***
4. What is cost of inventory ?
5. "In determining the cost of inventories, it is appropriate to exclude certain costs and recognise them as expenses in the period in which they are incurred." Provide examples of such costs as per AS 2 '*Valuation of Inventories*'. ***(IPCE Nov. 2012)***
6. Distinguish between FIFO and LIFO methods of valuation of inventory. ***(B.Com. Hons. Delhi)***
7. Which of the following cost formulas is not allowed to be used for finding out cost of inventories as per Ind. AS-2—"Valuation of Inventories" ?
   (*i*) LIFO ; (*ii*) FIFO ; (*iii*) Weighted Average Cost ; State the possible reasons for such exclusion.
8. State the advantages and disadvantages of Weighted Average Method of Valuation of Inventory.

LONG ANSWER TYPE

1. "Closing inventory should be valued at cost or market price whichever is lower." Elaborate this statement.
2. Describe a system that would give you quickly the value of closing stock and work-in-progress at the end of the financial period with the least possible delay.
3. Discuss briefly perpetual and periodic methods of stock-taking.
4. Compare LIFO and FIFO methods of stock valuation with special reference to their effect on pricing of issue of goods, valuation of closing stock and profits during a period of rising prices. ***(B.Com. Hons. Delhi)***
5. Explain first in first out method and weighted average method of inventory valuation.
6. Describe in brief the various methods of inventory valuation. When do you advocate the inventory valuation at the inflated rate method ?
7. Your client seeks your advice in the matter of valuation of stocks. The market for the commodity is on the uprising and it is anticipated that such boom conditions will continue for the next two years. What method of valuation of stocks—cost or market value or any variation thereof will you suggest for adoption ? Discuss.

OR

8. State specific requirements of AS-2 issued by the Institute of Chartered Accountants of India regarding inventory valuation. ***(B.Com. Hons. Delhi)***

PRACTICAL PROBLEMS

1. Z Limited ordered 13,000 kgs. of chemicals at ₹ 90 per kg. after availing trade discount of ₹ 1 per kg. The purchase price includes GST of ₹ 5 per kg. in respect of which full input credit is admissible. Freight and other administrative expenses associated with purchases incurred accounted to ₹ 33,100. Normal transit loss is 5%. The company actually received 12,500 kgs. and consumed 10,000 kgs. 800 kgs. of chemical was stolen from factory. The chemicals were delivered in containers. The containers were not reusable, hence sold for ₹ 600. Compute the value of inventory, losses and allocate the material cost as per AS–2. Assume replacement cost of raw material is ₹ 88 and finished goods can be sold at a profit of 20% on cost.

Ans. [₹ 1,54,700 (*i.e.*, 1.700 kgs. @ ₹ 91].

2. Manish closed his books of account on 31st March, each year. Inventory taking for the year ended 31st March, 2025 was completed by 10th April, 2025 on which date value of the stock available in godown was of ₹ 4,50,000 at cost.

Following are the details of transactions that took place between 31st March, 2025 and 10th April, 2025 :

(i) Goods sold to customers ₹ 1,10,000.

(ii) Sales return ₹ 10,000.

(iii) Purchases ₹ 85,000 (including Cash Purchases ₹ 10,000).

(iv) Purchases return amounted to ₹ 2,500.

(v) Goods costing 15,000 received in March, for sale on consignment basis, out of which 60% of goods had been sold by 10th April. These sales are not included in above sales.

(vi) After the stock was taken, it was found that there was certain very old slow-moving items costing ₹ 14,850, which should be taken at ₹ 9,500 to ensure disposal to an interested customer.

Goods are sold at a profit margin of 25% on cost. Ascertain the value of inventory for inclusion in the final accounts for the year ended 31st March, 2025.

Ans. [₹ 4,36,150]

3. From the following receipts and issues of a material during the month of January, 2025, prepare **Stores Ledger Account** according to 'FIFO method' :

2025		*2025*	
January 1	Received 500 units @ ₹ 10 per unit.	January 13	Issued 250 units.
January 5	Received 250 units @ ₹ 11 per unit.	January 20	Received 100 units @ ₹ 11 per unit.
January 8	Issued 300 units.	January 28	Issued 400 units.
January 10	Received 400 units @ ₹ 12 per unit.		

On 1st January 2025, the stock in hand was 200 units @ ₹ 9 per unit.

Ans. [Value of Stock ₹ 5,900 (*i.e.,* 400 units @ ₹ 12 + 100 units @ ₹ 11].

4. Calculate the **cost of goods sold and the value of ending inventory** from the following data (i) FIFO & (ii) LIFO.

Dates			*Units*	*Price per unit*
Jan.	1	Opening Stock	1,500	₹ 20 each
Feb.	10	Purchases	750	₹ 25 each
March	15	Purchases	600	₹ 22 each
March	25	Sold	1,800	—
April	10	Sold	750	—
May	15	Purchases	600	₹ 25 each
June	10	Sold	750	—

Ans. [

	Cost of goods sold	**Value of ending inventory**
	₹	₹
(i)	**73,200**	**3,750**
(ii)	**73,950**	**3,000].**

5. A company purchased raw material during the month of March, 2025 as stated below :

March 2	1,600 units @ ₹ 60 per unit.	March 19	6,000 units @ ₹ 54 per unit.
March 8	2,400 units @ ₹ 55 per unit.	March 23	3,000 units @ ₹ 58 per unit.
March 11	5,000 units @ ₹ 57 per unit.	March 30	2,000 units @ ₹ 63 per unit.

While preparing the final accounts on 31st March, 2025, the company had 2,600 units of raw material in its godown.

You are required to calculate the **value of closing stock of raw materials** according to—
(*i*) First in first out method; (*ii*) Last in first out method; and (*iii*) Weighted average price method.

Ans. [(*i*) ₹ 1,60,800; (*ii*) ₹ 1,51,000; (*iii*) ₹ 1,47,810]

6. Oil India is a bulk distributor of high octane petrol. A periodic inventory of petrol on hand is taken when the books are closed at the end of each month. Following summary of information is available for the month of June, 2025 :

	₹	
Sales	9,45,000	Purchases (including freight in)
General administrative cost	25,000	June 1 2,00,000 litres @ ₹ 2.85 per litre
Opening stock : 1,00,000 litres @ ₹ 3 per litre	3,00,000	June 30 1,00,000 litres @ ₹ 3.03 per litre
		Closing stock June 30 : 1,30,000 litres

Compute the following data by first-in and first-out, weighted average and last-in and first-out method of inventory costing :

(*a*) Value of inventory on June 30.

(*b*) Amount of the cost of goods sold for June.

(*c*) Profit or loss for June.

Ans. [

	FIFO	**Weighted Average**	**LIFO**
	₹	₹	₹
(*a*)	**3,88,500**	**3,90,000**	**3,93,000**
(*b*)	**7,84,500**	**7,83,000**	**7,80,000**
(*c*)	**1,35,500**	**1,37,000**	**1,40,000].**

7. The Fairdeal Granary was not maintaining a perpetual inventory system for its stocks until recently. Only physical inventory was taken at the end of each month. The physical inventory at the end of December, 2024, showed 200 bags of fine rice at ₹ 212.25 per bag.

Following purchases were made in January, 2025 :

3rd	400 bags at ₹ 218.00 per bag.	28th	700 bags at ₹ 213.00 per bag
10th	900 bags at ₹ 223.50 per bag	30th	300 bags at ₹ 224.00 per bag
15th	400 bags at ₹ 220.00 per bag		

On 31st January, 2025 the physical stock was 1,200 bags. You are required to calculate **the value of stock** on 31st January, 2025 according to : (*a*) First-in-First-out, (*b*) Last-in-First-out, and (*c*) Average cost methods.

Ans. [Value of Closing Stock : (*a*) ₹ 2,60,300; (*b*) ₹ 2,63,750; (*c*) ₹ 2,60,832].

8. Ascertain the **value of stock** as on 30th June, 2025 from the following figures :

	₹
Stock of goods as on 1-7-2024	2,40,000
Purchases during the year ending 30-6-2025	9,85,000
Sales during the year ending 30-6-2025	12,50,000
Cost of goods taken for personal use of the proprietor	15,000
Purchases returns during the year	50,000
Sales returns during the year	12,500
Cost of goods destroyed by fire during the year	30,000
Cost of goods distributed as free samples during the year	10,000

Rate of gross profit on sales was 20%.

Ans. [₹ 1,30,000].

9. The annual accounts of a trading company are to be made up to December 31st but it was not possible to carry out a stock-taking until January 5 at which date the stock was valued at cost at ₹ 68,567.

Following transactions took place between 1st and 5th January :

	₹		₹
Goods received	4,600	Sales	10,500
Goods returned to supplier	200	Returns by customers	625

The rate of gross profit is 25% of cost

Prepare a statement to show the **valuation of stock** as at December 31.

Ans. [Value of Stock on 31st December : ₹ 72,067].

10. From the following information, ascertain the value of stock as on 31st March, 2025 :

	₹		₹
Stock as on 1-4-2024	35,000	Manufacturing Expenses	35,000
Purchases during the year	1,73,000	Sales during the year	2,61,000

At the time of valuing the stock as on 31st March, 2024, a sum of ₹ 3,000 was written off a particular item which was originally purchased for ₹ 10,000 and was sold during the year for ₹ 8,000. Barring the transaction relating to this item, the gross profit earned during the year was 25 per cent on cost.

Ans. [₹ 33,600].

11. From the following information, ascertain **the value of stock** as on 31st March, 2025 :

	₹
Stock as on 1-4-2024	28,500
Purchases	1,52,500
Manufacturing Expenses	30,000
Selling Expenses	12,100
Administration Expenses	6,000
Financial Expenses	4,300
Sales	2,49,000

At the time of valuing stock as on 31st March, 2024, a sum of ₹ 3,500 was written off on a particular item, which was originally purchased for ₹ 10,000 and was sold during the year for ₹ 9,000. Barring the transaction relating to this item, the gross profit earned during the year was 20% on sales. ***(CA IPCE Nov. 2012 Modified)***

Ans. [Value of Stock on 31-3-2025 ₹ 12,500]

12. X's financial year ends on March 31, but actual stock is not taken until the following 5th April when it is ascertained at ₹ 54,000. You find that :

(*i*) Sale between 31st March, and 5th April are ₹ 3,000;

(*ii*) Purchases between 31st March and 5th April are ₹ 1,400;

(*iii*) Sales Returns between 31st March and 5th April are ₹ 200;

(*iv*) Purchases return between 31st March and 5th April are ₹ 60.

All sales are made at 25% of Gross Profit on Cost.

You are required to calculate the **value of stock** on 31st March.

Ans. [₹ 54,900].

13. M/s Polypack and Company's financial year ends on 31st March, 2025. Their actual physical stock as on 31st March was ₹ 6,25,000 (net realizable value ₹ 6,40,000).

Following information regarding stock is also available :

(*i*) Goods costing ₹ 40,000 were damaged badly and it was expected that only ₹ 5,000 could be realized.

(*ii*) Goods costing ₹ 25,000 were sold on sale or return basis for which no confirmation has been received till 31st March, 2025. Invoice value of these goods was ₹ 30,000.

(*iii*) Goods were sent on consignment to Mr. B at invoice value (120% of cost) ₹ 1,50,000 on 31st March, 2025. He informed that half of the material remains unsold.

You are required to ascertain the **value of closing stock** as on 31st March, 2025 as per AS 2.

Ans. [₹ **6,77,500**].

14. A firm has to take complete stock on 21st June, 2025, because of a deal for sale of business which fell through only at the last stage. As a consequence, it decided not to carry out stock taking on 30th June, 2025 when accounts were closed for the year. The stock was on 21-6-2025 ₹ 67,460. Following information is supplied to you regarding transactions in stock between 21-6-2025 and 30-6-2025.

(*a*) Goods purchased from 21-6-2025 to 30-6-2025 amounted to ₹ 4,820, out of which goods worth ₹ 1,900 were received on 2-7-2025.

(*b*) Sales during the period from 21-6-2025 to 30-6-2025 amounted to ₹ 16,800 including ₹ 3,600 for goods sent on approval, half of which were still returnable on 30-6-2025. The firm sells goods at cost plus 25% but there was one lot of goods which had cost ₹ 2,800 but had to be sold for ₹ 1,200 due to damage. The stock as on 21-6-2025 included these goods at cost.

(*c*) Unsold goods in the hands of a consignee on 30-6-2025 were valued at ₹ 3,200.

Prepare a statement showing the **actual value of stocks** as on 30th June, 2025.

Ans. [₹ **59,740**].

15. Determine the **value of stock** to be taken for Balance Sheet as at 31st March, 2025 from the following information :

The stock was physically verified on 23rd March, 2025 and was valued at ₹ 6,00,000. Between 23rd March, 2025 and 31st March, 2025 the following transactions had taken place :

(1) Purchases ₹ 50,000 of this, goods worth ₹ 20,000 were delivered on 5th April, 2025.

(2) Out of goods sent on consignment, goods worth ₹ 30,000 (at cost) were unsold.

(3) Sales was of ₹ 1,70,000. This includes goods worth ₹ 40,000 sent on approval, $\frac{1}{2}$ of these were returned before 31st March. As regards remaining no intimation is received.

(4) Normally firm sells goods on cost + 25%. However, one lot of goods costing ₹ 30,000 was sold for ₹ 15,000.

Ans. [₹ **5,58,000**].

16. M/s XYZ's financial year ends on 31st March, 2025, but the actual physical stock is not taken until the following 10th April, 2025, when it is ascertained at ₹ 25,150. You find that :

(*i*) Sales are recorded in the Sales-book on the day of dispatch and returns inward on the day, when goods are received back.

(*ii*) Purchases are entered on the day, on which invoices are received.

(*iii*) Purchases between 1–14th April as per Purchases-book are ₹ 2,400, but out of these goods amounting to ₹ 800 are not received till 10th April.

(*iv*) Sales between 1–14th April, as per Sales-book and Cash-book are ₹ 40,800.

(*v*) Goods purchased and invoiced before 31st March amounting to ₹ 1,000 out of which ₹ 700 worth of goods received between 1–14th April and remaining goods after 10th April. Find out the **value of physical stock** as at 31st March, 2025 assuming that rate of profit is 1/3rd of cost.

Ans. [₹ **53,450**]

[**Hint :** Sales at cost ₹ 30,600]

17. Krishna Udyog Limited makes up its accounts to December 31 each year. The company was unable to take stock by physical inventory till 14th January, 2025 on which date the stock at cost was valued at ₹ 1,85,000. It was, therefore, necessary to estimate the value of stock in hand as on December 31, 2024.

You ascertain the following facts regarding the period, January 1 to January 14, 2025.

(1) Purchases totalled ₹ 48,000 and included (*i*) ₹ 5,000 in respect of goods received in December, 2024; (*ii*) ₹ 6,000 in respect of goods received on January 19, 2025; (*iii*) ₹ 2,000 in respect of goods received but returned to suppliers on January 7, 2025 for which no credit note has been received or passed through the books.

(2) Sales totalled ₹ 60,000 and included (*i*) ₹ 1,500 in respect of goods, which left the warehouse on December 28, 2024; (*ii*) ₹ 2,800 in respect of goods which were not despatched until January 16, 2025; (*iii*) ₹750 in respect of goods invoiced and despatched on January 10, 2025 but returned by the customers on January 12, for which no credit no te had been passed but which were, in fact, included in the stock taken on January 14, 2025.

(3) Other returns to suppliers totalled ₹ 1,400 and other returns by customers were ₹ 450.

(4) The rate of gross profit was 25% on the selling price with the exception of an isolated purchase on January 7, 2025 of 100 similar articles which had cost ₹ 11,000. Of these articles 50 were sold on January 7, 2025 for ₹ 6,500 and the remainder had been included at cost in the stock taken on January 14, 2025.

Prepare a statement showing the estimated **value of stock** held on December 31, 2024 at cost.

Ans. **[₹ 1,89,025].**

18. The financial year of Shri X ends on 31st March, 2025, but the stock in hand was physically verified only on 7th April, 2025. You are required to determine the **value of closing stock** (at cost) as on 31st March, 2025 from the following information.

(*i*) The stock (valued at cost) as verified on 7th April, 2025 was ₹ 15,000.

(*ii*) Sales have been entered in the sales day book only after the despatch of goods and sales returns only on receipt of goods.

(*iii*) Purchases have been entered in the purchase day book on receipt of the purchase invoice irrespective of the date of receipt of the goods.

(*iv*) Sales as per the sales day book for the period 1st April, 2025 to 7th April, 2025 (before the actual verification) amounted to ₹ 6,000 of which goods of a sale value of ₹ 1,000 had not been delivered at the time of verification.

(*v*) Purchases as per the purchases day book for the period 1st April, 2025 to 7th April, 2025 (before the actual verification) amounted to ₹ 6,000 of which goods for purchases of ₹ 1,500 had not been received at the date of verification and goods for purchases of ₹ 2,000 had been received prior to 31st March, 2025.

(*vi*) In respect of goods costing ₹ 5,000 received prior to 31st March, 2025 invoices had not been received up to the date of verification of stocks.

(*vii*) Rate of gross profit is 20% on sales.

Ans. **[₹ 9,500].**

19. Raja makes up his annual accounts to 31st December each year. He was unable to take stock of physical inventory till 9th January, 2025 on which date the physical stock at cost was valued at ₹ 75,200.

You are required to ascertain **the value of physical stock** at cost on 31st December, 2024, from the following information regarding the period from 1st January, 2025 to 9th January, 2025 :

(*a*) Purchases of goods amounted to ₹ 25,600 of which worth ₹ 4,700 had been received on 28-12-2024 and goods worth ₹ 5,900 had been received on 12-1-2025.

(*b*) Sales of goods amounted to ₹ 38,400 of which goods of a sale value of ₹ 3,600 had not been delivered at the time of verification and goods of a sale value of ₹ 6,000 had been delivered on 29-12-2024.

(*c*) Sales Returns amounted to ₹ 1,800 which included a return of ₹ 720 relating to the goods sold and delivered between 1-1-2025 to 9-1-2025.

(*d*) A sub-total of ₹ 12,000 on one of the stock sheets had been carried to the summary of stock sheets as ₹ 21,000.

(*e*) In respect of goods costing ₹ 4,000 received prior to 31st December, 2024, invoices had not been received up to the date of verification of stock.

(*f*) Rate of gross profit was 20% on the cost price.

Ans. [₹ 74,300].

20. A trader prepared his final accounts on 31st March, 2025. No stock taking could be possible till 14th April, 2025 on which date the cost of total goods in his godown came to ₹ 60,500. Following facts relating to the period between 1st April, 2025 and 15th April, 2025 were brought to your notice :

(*i*) Sales : ₹ 45,590 (including cash sales of ₹ 10,120). (*ii*) Purchases : ₹ 16,170 (including cash purchases of ₹ 5,990). (*iii*) Sales returns : ₹ 1,200. (*iv*) Collection from debtors : ₹ 14,600. (*v*) Payment to creditors : ₹ 7,816. (*vi*) On 15th March, 2025, goods of the sale value of ₹ 6,800 were sent on sale or return basis to a customer, the period of approval being four weeks. He returned 40% of goods on 10th April,. 2025 approving the rest. The customer was billed on 16th April, 2025. (*vii*) The trader had received goods costing ₹ 8,000 in March, 2025 for sale on consignment basis, 20% of which ad been sold by 31st March, 2025, another 40% by 15th April, 2025 and rest is unsold. These sales are not included in (*i*) above. Goods are sold by the trader at a gross profit of 20% on sales.

You are required to ascertain **the value of stock in hand** as on 31st March, 2025.

Ans. [₹ 79,906]

CHAPTER

11

Financial Statements—Nature and Preparation

Introduction

Every business, whether small or large, needs a clear understanding of its financial performance and position. This is accomplished through the preparation of financial statements, which represent the final phase of the accounting process. At the end of an accounting period, typically a year, financial transactions are summarised and presented in a structured format to provide insights into the profitability and financial health of the business. Financial statements serve two primary purposes: determining the profit or loss during a specific period and assessing the financial position on a particular date. These statements—such as the Trading or Manufacturing Account, Profit and Loss Account, and Balance Sheet—are essential for decision-making by a variety of stakeholders including owners, managers, investors, creditors, and regulatory bodies. In the case of companies, additional statements like the Cash Flow Statement and Notes to Accounts are also included. Together, these reports offer a comprehensive picture of the business's financial activities, making them critical tools for both internal management and external evaluation.

Definitions of Financial Statements

Financial statements are formal reports that summarise the financial activities and position of a business enterprise over a specific period. Various experts have defined financial statements from different perspectives:

According to **John N. Myer**, *"The Financial Statements provide a summary of the accounts of a business enterprise, the Balance Sheet reflecting the assets and liabilities and the Income Statement showing the results of operations during a certain period."*

This definition highlights two primary components—the **Balance Sheet**, which shows the financial position, and the **Income Statement** (or Statement of Profit and Loss), which shows the operational results.

In the words of **Smith and Ashburne**, *"The end product of financial accounting is a set of financial statements, that purports to reveal the financial position of the enterprise, the results of its recent activities, and an analysis of what has been done with earnings."*

This definition presents a broader view by recognising financial statements as the final output of the accounting process, revealing financial position, profitability, and use of earnings. They reflect not just figures, but how profits are earned and allocated within the business.

Nature of Financial Statements

Financial statements are the final outcome of the accounting process. They are formal records that provide a summary of the financial position and performance of a business over a specific period. As defined by experts, they not only show the assets and liabilities (Balance Sheet) and the results of operations (Profit and Loss Statement), but also reflect how the earnings have been utilised and offer insights into cash flows and equity movements. Thus, financial statements are not merely arithmetic summaries—they are a systematic presentation of financial data, influenced by various factors. The nature of financial statements can be understood through the following characteristics:

(*i*) **Combination of Recorded Facts, Conventions, and Judgements**: Financial statements are based on recorded transactions, but their preparation is also guided by accounting conventions (such as conservatism, consistency, and materiality) and personal judgements. For example, assets are recorded at historical cost, not at market value, and the choice of depreciation method or treatment of expenses often depends on the accountant's judgement.

(*ii*) **Historical in Nature**: These statements represent the past performance and position of the business. They do not account for unrecorded events or market fluctuations unless specifically required under accounting standards.

(*iii*) **Summarised and Periodical Reports**: Financial statements present a concise summary of the financial outcomes and status of the business for a given accounting period. They are typically prepared at the end of the financial year for review and decision-making.

(*iv*) **Governed by Accounting Principles**: The preparation of financial statements is done in accordance with generally accepted accounting principles (GAAP) or Ind AS in India. These principles ensure consistency, comparability, and standardisation across entities.

(*v*) **Limited Scope due to Non-Financial Factors**: Financial statements do not capture qualitative aspects of business such as customer satisfaction, employee efficiency, brand value, or market conditions. They also exclude any unrecorded liabilities or assets.

(*vi*) **Reliability Depends on Accuracy of Records**: The authenticity and usefulness of financial statements are directly dependent on the accuracy and integrity of underlying accounting records. Inaccurate or fraudulent entries compromise their reliability.

(*vii*) **Usefulness for Decision Making**: Despite limitations, financial statements serve as crucial tools for investors, creditors, management, and regulatory bodies to assess the performance and decide the future course of action.

Attributes of Financial Statements

To be useful and meaningful, financial statements should have certain key attributes. These qualities help ensure that the statements serve the needs of various users such as business owners, investors, creditors, and government authorities.

(*i*) **Relevance:** Financial statements should include only relevant and important information that helps users make decisions. Unnecessary or confusing details should be avoided.

(*ii*) **Accuracy and Objectivity:** The statements must be accurate and reflect the true financial position of the business. They should be prepared without personal bias or manipulation.

(*iii*) **Comparability**: Users should be able to compare the current statements with those of previous years or with other businesses. This helps in identifying trends and evaluating performance.

(*iv*) **Clear and Analytical Presentation:** Financial data should be presented in a well-organised and classified manner. This makes it easier to analyse the results, identify causes of profits or losses, and spot inefficiencies.

(*v*) **Timeliness**: Financial statements should be prepared and made available soon after the end of the accounting period. Delay in preparation can reduce their usefulness for decision-making.

(*vi*) **Compliance with Accounting Standards:** Statements should follow Generally Accepted Accounting Principles (GAAP) or applicable standards like Ind AS. This ensures consistency and acceptability.

(*vii*) **Consistency:** The same accounting methods and principles should be used from year to year unless there's a valid reason to change. This helps users make accurate comparisons over time.

(*viii*) **Reliability and Authenticity:** Financial statements should be verified and signed by qualified professionals, such as auditors. Audited statements are more trustworthy and credible.

(*ix*) **Legal Compliance**: The format, contents, and disclosures in the statements must follow legal requirements. In India, for example, company financial statements must comply with the Companies Act, 2013.

Objectives of Financial Statements

Financial statements are prepared to serve as key tools for conveying the financial performance and position of a business to various stakeholders. The main objectives of financial statements are as follows:

(*i*) The primary objective of financial statements is to ascertain the profit earned or loss incurred during an accounting period through the preparation of the Trading and Profit & Loss Account.

(*ii*) The Balance Sheet provides a snapshot of the business's financial position on a specific date, showing assets owned, liabilities owed, and the owner's equity in the business.

(*iii*) Financial statements offer valuable information to various users such as owners, investors, managers, creditors, and government authorities for making informed economic decisions.

(*iv*) These statements help determine how efficiently the resources of the business have been utilised by the management and whether they have fulfilled their responsibility to the stakeholders.

(*v*) By presenting results in a structured and consistent format, financial statements facilitate comparison with past performance, industry standards, and competitor data.

(*vi*) Analysis of trends and patterns in financial statements can help users forecast future earnings, cash flows, and growth prospects of the business.

(*vii*) Financial statements help fulfill legal obligations by presenting data in accordance with prescribed accounting standards and regulations.

(*viii*) They aim to present a true and fair view of the business's financial health, promoting transparency and building trust among users.

Importance (or Users) of Financial Statements

The information given in the financial statements is very useful to a number of parties. These are the following :

1. Owners. The owners provide funds for the operations of a business and they want to know whether their funds are being properly utilised or not. The financial statements prepared from time to time satisfy their curiosity.

2. Creditors. Creditors (*i.e.*, suppliers of goods and services on credit, bankers and other lenders of money) want to know the financial position of a concern before giving loans or granting credit. The financial statements help them in judging such position.

3. Investors. Prospective investors, who want to invest money in a firm, would like to make an analysis of the financial statements of that firm to know how safe the proposed investment will be.

4. Employees. Employees are interested in the financial position of a concern they serve, particularly when payment of bonus depends upon the size of the profits earned. They would like to know that the bonus being paid to them is correct; so they become interested in the preparation of correct Profit and Loss Account.

5. Government. Central and State Governments are interested in the financial statements because they reflect the earnings for a particular period for purposes of taxation. Moreover, these financial statements are used for compiling statistics concerning business which, in turn, help in compiling national accounts.

6. Research Scholars. The financial statements, being a mirror of the financial position of a firm, are of immense value to the research scholar who wants to make a study into financial operations of a particular firm.

7. Consumers. Consumers are interested in the establishment of good accounting control so that cost of production may be reduced with the resultant reduction of the prices of goods they buy.

8. Managers. Management is the art of getting things done through others. This requires that the subordinates are doing work properly. Financial statements are an aid in this respect because they serve the manager in appraising the performance of the subordinates. Actual results achieved by the employees can be measured against the budgeted performance they were expected to achieve and remedial action can be taken if the performance is not upto the mark.

Limitations of Financial Statements

Following are the main limitations of the financial statements :

(*i*) Interim and not final reports. Financial statements do not depict the exact position and are essentially interim reports. The exact position can be only known if the business is closed.

(*ii*) Lack of precision and definiteness. Financial statements may not be realistic because these are prepared by following certain basic concepts and conventions. For example, going concern concept gives us an idea that business will continue and assets are to be recorded at cost but the book value at which the asset is shown may not be actually realisable. Similarly, by following the principle of conservatism the financial statements will not reflect the true position of the business.

(*iii*) Lack of objective judgement. Financial statements are influenced by the personal judgement of the accountant. He may select any method for depreciation, valuation of stock, amortisation of fixed assets and treatment of deferred revenue expenditure. Such judgement if based on integrity and competency of the accountant will definitely affect the preparation of the financial statements.

(*iv*) Records only monetary facts. Financial statements disclose only monetary facts, *i.e.,* those transactions are recorded in the books of accounts which can be measured in monetary terms. Those transactions which cannot be measured in monetary terms such as, conflict between production manager and marketing manager may be very important for a business concern but not recorded in the business books.

(*v*) Historical in nature. These statements are drawn after the actual happening of the events. They attempt to present a view of the past performance and have nothing to do with the accounting for the future. Modern management is forward looking but these statements do not directly help them in making future estimates and taking decisions for the future.

(*vi*) Artificial view. These statements do not give a real and correct report about the worth of the assets and their loss of value as these are shown on historical cost basis. Thus, these statements provide artificial view as market or replacement value and the effect of the changes in the price level are completely ignored.

(*vii*) Scope of manipulations. These statements are sometimes prepared according to the needs of the situation or the whims of the management. A highly efficient concern may conceal its real profitability by disclosing loss or minimum profit whereas an inefficient concern may declare dividend by wrongly showing profit in the statement of profit and loss. For this under or over valuation of inventory, over or under charge of depreciation, excessive or inadequate provision for anticipated losses and other such manipulations may be resorted to. Window dressing may also be resorted to in order to show better financial position of a concern than its real position.

(*viii*) Inadequate information. There are many parties who are interested in the information given in the financial statements but their objectives and requirements differ. The financial statements as prepared under the provisions of the Companies Act, 2013, fail to meet the needs of all. These are mainly prepared to safeguard the interest of shareholders.

Financial Statements Across Different Forms of Business Organisation

The financial statements prepared by a business depend on its form of organisation. A **sole proprietorship**, being owned by a single individual, typically prepares a *Trading Account* (or *Manufacturing and Trading Account*), *Profit and Loss Account*, and *Balance Sheet* to determine profit and assess financial position. These statements are simple and primarily meant for internal use and tax reporting.

In the case of a **partnership firm**, the financial statements are similar but include an additional *Profit and Loss Appropriation Account*, which shows how the net profit is distributed among partners after accounting for interest on capital, drawings, partner salaries, etc. The final set includes the *Trading Account*, *Profit and Loss Account*, *P&L Appropriation Account*, and *Balance Sheet*.

For a **company**, financial statements are more formal and regulated under the Companies Act. They include the *Statement of Profit and Loss*, *Balance Sheet*, *Cash Flow Statement*, *Notes to Accounts*, and, where applicable, the *Statement of Changes in Equity*. These are prepared in a prescribed format as per Schedule III and in compliance with applicable Accounting Standards (Ind AS), making them suitable for statutory reporting and communication with investors and stakeholders.

Financial Statements of Sole Proprietor (Manufacturing and Non-Manufacturing Entities)

The nature of a business—whether it is engaged in manufacturing goods or merely trading them—affects the type and structure of financial statements it prepares.

1. Non-Manufacturing Entities: Non-manufacturing entities are those businesses which are engaged primarily in the purchase and resale of goods without any transformation or production process. These businesses prepare the Trading Account, Profit and Loss Account and Balance Sheet: These statements help a trading or service-based concern evaluate its profitability and financial stability.

2. Manufacturing Entities: Manufacturing entities are businesses involved in the conversion of raw materials into finished goods through a production process. To capture the cost of production and overall profitability, the financial statements which are prepared are Manufacturing Account, Trading Account, Profit and Loss Account and Balance Sheet.

Thus, while both types of entities prepare a Trading Account, Profit and Loss Account, and Balance Sheet, the Manufacturing Account is an additional statement unique to manufacturing entities, reflecting the cost structure involved in production.

In this section, we will focus on the basic structure and preparation of two key financial statements—**Trading Account, Profit and Loss Account and Balance Sheet**. These financial statements are crucial as they help us understand how a business has performed over a period (profit or loss) and what its financial position is at a given point in time (assets, liabilities, and capital).

Trading Account

This account is prepared to know the trading results or gross margin on trading of the business, *i.e.*, how much gross profit the business has earned from buying and selling during a particular period. The difference between the sales and cost of goods sold is gross profit. For the purpose of calculating cost of goods sold, we take into consideration opening stock, net purchases, direct expenses on purchasing or manufacturing the goods and closing stock. The balance of this account represents gross profit or loss and is transferred to the Profit and Loss Account. Thus, Trading Account shows the results of buying and selling of goods and in preparing this account indirect expenses (*i.e.* office and administrative expenses, selling and distribution expenses and financial expenses) are ignored. Only the transactions in goods and expenses related to purchase of goods and manufacturing of goods are included in this account.

In the form of Equation,

Gross Profit = Sales – Cost of Goods Sold

or = Sales – [Opening Stock + Net Purchases + Direct Expenses – Closing Stock]

or = Sales – Opening Stock – Net Purchases – Direct Expenses + Closing Stock

or Opening Stock + Net Purchases + Direct Expenses + Gross Profit = Sales + Closing Stock

TRADING ACCOUNT
for the year ended 31st March, 2025

Particulars	*Amount* ₹	*Particulars*	*Amount* ₹
To Opening Stock		By Sales	
To Purchases		*Less* : Sales Returns	
Less : Purchases Returns		By Closing Stock	
To Direct Expenses :		By Gross Loss c/d*	
Carriage Inward			
Wages			
Wages and Salaries			
Fuel and Power			
Manufacturing or Production Expenses			
Coal, Water and Gas			
Motive Power			
Factory Lighting			
Octroi			
Import Duty			
Custom Duty			
Excise Duty			
Consumable Stores			
Factory Rent, Rates and Taxes			
Foreman/ Works Manager's Salary			
Royalty on Manufactured Goods			
Other Direct Charges			
To Gross Profit c/d*			

*Balancing figure will be either Gross Profit or Gross Loss.

Detailed Study of the Items Posted to the Debit Side of Trading Account

1. Opening Stock. This is the amount of goods in hand at the beginning of the period for which the trading account is prepared. The figure is available from the Trial Balance. There will be no opening stock in case of a new business. Opening stock consists of Raw Materials, Work in Progress and Finished Goods.

2. Purchases. It includes both cash and credit purchases of goods which are for resale purposes. Purchases returns and discount on purchases, if any, should be deducted from purchases in the inner column and only net purchases are shown in the outer column.

Note : GST is to be paid whenever there is a purchase of goods or services. When purchase of goods is made within the state, CGST and SGST are to be paid. In case purchase of goods is from another state, then IGST is to be paid. The term used for GST paid is **'Input GST'**. While selling the goods, GST (CGST and SGST or IGST) shall be collected from the customer. The term used for GST collected is called **'Output GST'.** The net GST payable shall be Input GST *minus* Output GST. This mechanism of setting off Input GST against Output GST is known as **'Input Tax Credit' (ITC).**

GST (CGST and SGST or IGST) paid on purchases is not debited to Purchases Account because it is set off against GST (CGST and SGST or IGST) collected on sales. Hence, it is not cost of goods purchased.

Separate accounts is maintained for each type Input GST (CGST, SGST, IGST) as well as Output GST (CGST, SGST, IGST). In case of Purchase Returns, goods given as charity or samples, Input GST Account is credited, *i.e.,* reversed.

The worthnoting points in this respect are :

The *worthnoting points* in this respect are :

***(i)* Purchases include both credit and cash purchases of goods.**

***(ii)* GST is paid when purchases are made.** GST paid is **'Input GST'.** On Intra state purchases Input CGST and Input SGST is levied. On Inter state purchases of goods, Input IGST is levied.

The journal entry for say Cash Purchases shall be

Purchases A/c	Dr.	(Amount of purchases)
Input CGST A/c	Dr.	(CGST for intra state)
Input SGST A/c	Dr.	(SGST for intra state)
Input IGST A/c	Dr.	(IGST if purchases are inter state)
To Cash		(Amount of purchases *plus* GST)
(Being purchases made)		

***(iii)* Sometimes invoices of goods purchased are received in advance before the actual receipt of such goods.** For such goods neither the purchases account will be debited nor the goods will be included in the closing stock.

(iv) Purchases made *under future transactions* (*i.e.,* the goods will be delivered in future) and goods received on consignment or on behalf of third party, should not be included in purchases.

(v) Purchase of any asset such as furniture, machinery etc. should be kept separate.

***(vi)* Adjusted Purchases.** Some concerns, for comparison purposes, prefer to adjust the opening and closing stock through Purchases Account. Entries for this will be as under :

(*a*) For adjustment of opening stock

Purchases A/c	Dr.
To Opening Stock A/c	

(*b*) For adjustment of closing stock

Closing Stock A/c	Dr.
To Purchases A/c	

Due to these adjustments there will be no opening stock in the trial balance. Adjusted Purchases A/c is shown on the debit side of Trading Account and Closing Stock (having debit balance) appears as an asset in the Balance Sheet.

***(vii)* Goods purchased but in transit** will not affect Trading Account. It is better to debit the Goods in Transit Account and credit the Supplier's Account for such goods. Goods in Transit Account appears as an Asset and Supplier's Account as a liability in the Balance Sheet.

***(viii)* Goods withdrawn by the proprietor for personal use.** Goods withdrawn by the proprietor are not for sale but for personal use. Hence the Drawing Account of proprietor is debited with total amount, *i.e.,* purchase price plus GST (CGST, SGST or IGST) paid on these goods. Credit is given to Purchase Account and respective Input GST. The Journal; entry is

Drawings A/c Dr.
To Purchases A/c
To Input CGST A/c
To Input SGST A/c
or
To Input IGST A/c

(ix) Goods distributed as samples will be deducted from purchases and will be debited to Advertisement Account which ultimately will be shown on the debit side of Profit and Loss Account and credit is given to Purchases A/c and Input GST (CGST, SGST or IGST Account).

(x) Goods distributed as charity. If charity is given in the form of goods out of purchases made by the firm, the following entry will be passed :

Charity Account Dr.
To Purchases Account
To Input CGST A/c
To Input SGST A/c
or To Input IGST A/c

Goods distributed as charity will be deducted from purchases in Trading Account and Charity Account will be debited to Profit and Loss Account.

(*xi*) Following are deducted from purchases to calculate Net Purchases

(*a*) Purchase Returns

(*b*) Goods taken by proprietor for personal use

(*c*) Goods given as charity/donation/samples

3. Direct Expenses. These include all expenses which have been incurred before the goods become ready for sale and are shown on the debit side of Trading Account. The examples of direct expenses are given below :

(i) Wages (or Wages & Salaries). If wages have been incurred on manufacturing goods or making them more saleable, they become an item of direct expenses and are debited to Trading A/c but other wages (indirect) should be debited to Profit and Loss Account. If nothing is mentioned whether the wages are direct or indirect, they should be treated as direct and are shown on the debit side of Trading Account. Wages must include all wages outstanding but wages spent on constructing a building or manufacturing any other asset should be excluded while calculating the amount of wages. No GST is paid on wages and salaries, as they are exempt from GST levy.

(ii) Carriage, Cartage or Freight. These expenses when paid on bringing the goods purchased to the trading place or factory from the place of the supplier are taken to the debit side of Trading Account. Such expenses, if incurred on purchasing an asset should be capitalised by debiting the Asset Account and should not be taken to Trading Account. Outstanding carriage, cartage or freight should be added to these expenses and appears as a liability in the Balance Sheet.

(iii) Dock Charges. In case goods are imported from abroad, dock charges etc. have to be paid. As these relate to the goods purchased, they are shown on the debit side of Trading Account.

(iv) Motive Power, Coal, Gas and Fuel. These are direct expenses and are shown on the debit side of Trading A/c.

(v) Manufacturing Expenses. All expenses incurred in manufacturing the goods in the factory as Factory Rent, Factory Insurance, Depreciation on Factory Machinery, Factory Lighting etc. are debited to Trading A/c.

(vi) Consumable Stores. These are incurred to keep the machine in right condition and include engine oil, soft soap, cotton waste, oil, grease and waste consumed in a factory.

Expenses of consumable stores will be calculated as under :

	₹
Opening Balance of Stores	–
Add : Purchases of Stores during the year	–
	–
Less : Closing Balance of Stores	–
Stores Consumed during the year	–

The amount of such stores consumed during the year will be shown on the debit side of Trading Account.

(vii) Royalties. These are the payments made to a patentee, author or landlord for the right to use his patent, copyright or land. If royalty is paid on the basis of production, it is debited to Trading Account and if it is paid on the basis of sales, it is debited to Profit and Loss Account. There is no GST on royalties

(viii) Packing Charges. There may be *three types* of packing as given below :

(*a*) *Ordinary or primary packing* which is necessary for the handling of the product as tooth paste tube or bottle in case of ink. The cost of such packing is a direct expense and should be debited to Trading Account.

(*b*) If the packing is *required to transport the goods* from one place to another as boxes or containers etc. then such packing charges should be treated as distribution expenses and being indirect expenses should be debited to Profit and Loss Account.

(*c*) If the packing is *fancy to attract the customers* as in case of cosmetic goods then it should be treated as selling expenses and should be debited to Profit and Loss Account.

(ix) Subsidies. These are cash incentives provided by the Government on purchase of goods and are deducted from purchases to get the figure of net purchases.

(x) Duty Drawbacks and Modvatable Excise Duty. As per Accounting Standard 2, duty drawbacks should be deducted from the cost of purchases. Modvatable excise duty is refundable to a manufacturer and is deducted from the cost of purchases, whereas gross excise duty on finished goods is debited to Trading Account.

Detailed Study of the Items Posted to the Credit Side of Trading Account

1. Sales. Sales should include both cash and credit sales of those goods which were purchased for resale purposes. Some customers might return the goods sold to them (called sales return) which are deducted from the sales in the inner column and net amount is shown in the outer column.

Note : The firm shall charge GST when goods are sold by them. This GST (CGST and SGST or IGST) collected on sale is termed as Output GST (CGST, SGST, IGST). When sale is made in cash (for example) following journal entry shall be made.

Cash A/c	Dr.	(Sale Amount plus GST)
To Sales A/c		(Amount of Sales)
To Output CGST A/c		(Amount of CGST on Intra State Sales)
To Output SGST A/c		(Amount of SGST on Intra State Sales)
or		
To Output IGST A/c		(Amount of IGST on Inter State Sales)

This output GST Account is set off against Input GST (paid) Account GST (CGST and SGST or IGST) collected on sales is reversed and debited when goods are returned by the purchaser.

While ascertaining the amount of sales, the following *points* need attention :

(*a*) *If a fixed asset such as furniture, machinery etc., is sold,* it should not be included in sales. However, if the amount realised from the sale of an asset is included in sales, such amount should be separated by passing the following entry :

Sales A/c Dr.

To Asset A/c.

(*b*) Goods sold on Consignment or on Hire Purchase or on Sale or Return basis should be recorded separately. However, if their amount is included in the sales, that should be separated by passing the following entry :

Sales A/c Dr.

To Consignee's or Hire Purchaser's or Customer's A/c.

(*c*) If goods have been sold but not yet despatched, these should not be shown under sales but are included in closing stock.

(*d*) Sale of goods on behalf of others and forward sales should also be excluded from sales.

2. Closing Stock. It is the amount of unsold goods in hand at the end of the trading period. Generally closing stock is given outside the trial balance, but when purchases are adjusted through opening and closing stock, in that case closing stock will have a debit balance in the trial balance. *If given outside the trial balance, it will be credited to the Trading Account but if it is given in the trial balance, then it appears as asset in the Balance Sheet*. Closing Stock may be of Raw Materials, Work-in-Progress and Finished Goods. In order to ascertain the value of closing stock, a list of all goods in stock after physical checking is prepared, (known as stock taking). Stock includes only of those goods which are normally bought and sold by the trader. Goods unsold at branches and with agent should also be included in closing stock but stock of stationery and postage stamps will not be included in closing stock. *Closing stock is valued at cost or realisable price, whichever is less*. It is, hence, valued on conservative basis, *i.e.,* expected profit should be ignored but possible losses should be duly provided for.

Closing Entries

All accounts relating to expenses and revenues must be closed at the end of the year. For closing such accounts they are transferred either to trading account or profit and loss account. The journal entries required for transferring these accounts to trading account or profit and loss account are known as closing entries. Closing entries are passed at the end of each accounting period for the purpose of transferring the various revenue items to trading and profit and loss account and thus close the nominal accounts.

The process of framing closing entries is very simple. A debit balance in an account is credited and either trading account or profit and loss account is debited. Similarly, a credit balance in an account is debited and trading account or profit and loss account is credited. Closing entries in a journal may be divided into two categories, *i.e.,* simple and compound entries. A *simple closing entry* is one in which only two accounts are affected, one account to be debited and another account to be credited with an equal amount. In a *compound entry* there may be (*i*) several accounts to be debited and only one to be credited; or (*ii*) one account to be debited and several accounts to be credited, or (*iii*) several accounts to be debited and several accounts to be credited.

Closing Entries for Trading Account

The journal entries necessary to transfer Opening Stock, Purchases, Sales and Return to the Trading Account are called Closing Entries, as they serve to close these accounts. These are as follows:

1. For transfer of opening stock, net purchases and direct expenses to Trading A/c.

Trading A/c Dr.

To (Opening) Stock A/c

" Purchases (Net) A/c

" Direct Expenses A/c

2. For transfer of net sales and closing stock to Trading A/c.

Sales (Net) A/c Dr.

(Closing) Stock A/c Dr.

To Trading A/c

3. (*a*) For Gross Profit
   Trading A/c Dr.
   To Profit & Loss A/c

(*b*) For Gross Loss
   Profit & Loss A/c Dr.
   To Trading A/c

ILLUSTRATION 1. Prepare a Trading Account for the year ending 30th June, 2025 of Mr. Arun Sharma from the following balances :

	₹		₹
Stock on 1st July, 2024	4,80,000	Indirect Expenses incurred :	
Cash Purchases	3,60,000	Office Salaries	50,000
Credit Purchases	8,40,000	Office Lighting	5,000
Direct Expenses incurred :		Printing and Stationery	4,000
Freight	27,500	Goods destroyed by fire	10,000
Carriage	2,500	Subsidies on Purchase of Goods	30,000
Import Duty and Dock Charges	30,000	Excise Duty on Finished Goods	35,000
Clearing Charges	40,000	Duty Drawbacks	
Manufacturing Expenses	1,20,000	(Modvatable Excise Duty)	15,000
Cash Sales	7,60,000	Stock on 30th June, 2025 at Cost	
Credit Sales	14,20,000	(Market Value ₹ 3,00,000)	3,10,000

SOLUTION

TRADING ACCOUNT OF MR. ARUN SHARMA
for the year ending 30th June, 2025

		₹	₹			₹	₹
To Opening Stock			4,80,000	By Sales : Cash		7,60,000	
To Purchases :				Credit		14,20,000	
Cash		3,60,000					21,80,000
Credit		8,40,000		By Closing Stock			3,00,000
		12,00,000		By Stock Destroyed by Fire			10,000
Less : Subsidies on Purchase of Goods	₹ 30,000						
Duty Drawbacks	15,000	45,000	11,55,000				
To Freight			27,500				
To Carriage			2,500				
To Dock Charges			30,000				
To Clearing Charges			40,000				
To Manufacturing Expenses			1,20,000				
To Excise Duty on Finished Goods			35,000				
To Gross Profit c/d to Profit & Loss A/c			6,00,000				
			24,90,000				24,90,000

Notes :

(1) Office expenses being indirect expenses have not been debited to Trading Account. These expenses are debited to Profit and Loss Account.

(2) Closing stock has been valued on the principle of cost or market value, whichever is lower. Market value of ₹ 3,00,000 being lower than the cost of ₹ 3,10,000 has been considered for the valuation of closing stock.

(3) Stock destroyed by fire has been credited to Trading Account so that correct gross profit may be shown. If there had been no stock destroyed by fire, closing stock value would have been more.

Importance of Trading Account

Trading Account has the following advantages :

1. Information of Gross Profit or Gross Loss. Trading Account provides information regarding gross profit and sets the upper limit within which indirect expenses are to be incurred. Indirect expenses should be much less than the gross profit so that a good amount of profit may be earned. If Trading Account discloses gross loss, it is better to close the business rather than running at a gross loss because gross loss will further increase when indirect expenses are added to it.

2. Gross Profit Ratio. This ratio is calculated as follows :

$$\text{Gross Profit Ratio} = \frac{\text{Gross Profit}}{\text{Sales}} \times 100$$

Higher the ratio, the better it is. Gross profit ratio can be calculated with the help of the Trading Account year after year and comparison of performance of year after year can be made. A low ratio indicates unfavourable trend in the form of reduction in selling prices not accompanied by proportionate decrease in cost of goods purchased or increase in cost of production.

3. Comparison of Closing Stock with Opening Stock. Comparison of stock figures of one period with another period will be helpful in avoiding overstocking. Investment in stock should be reasonable so that production and sales go on smoothly.

4. Fixation of Selling Price. In case of a new product, the selling price can be easily fixed by adding in the cost of purchases or cost of goods manufactured the desired percentage of gross profit.

Profit and Loss Account

This account is prepared to calculate the net profit of the business. There are certain items of incomes and expenses of the business which must be taken into consideration for calculating net profit of the business. These are of indirect nature *i.e.* concerning the whole business and relating to various activities which are done by the business for the purpose of making the goods available to the consumers. Indirect expenses may be selling and distribution expenses, management expenses, financial expenses, extraordinary losses and expenses to maintain the assets into working order. This account is prepared from nominal accounts and its balance is transferred to capital account as the whole profit or loss will be that of the owner and it will increase or decrease his capital. The specimen proforma of this account is given below :

PROFIT AND LOSS ACCOUNT

for the year ended 31st March, 2025

	₹		₹
To Gross Loss b/d		By Gross Profit b/d	
" *Selling and Distribution Expenses* :		" Interest Received	
		" Discount	
Advertisement		" Commission	
Travellers' Salaries, Expenses & Commission		" Rent from Tenants	
		" Income from Investments	
Bad Debts		By Apprenticeship Premium	
Godown Rent		" Interest on Debentures	

Export Expenses		By Income from any Other Source	
Carriage Outwards		" Miscellaneous Revenue Receipts	
Bank Charges		" By Net Loss transferred to	
Agent's Commission		Capital A/c	
Upkeep of Motor Lorries			
To *Management Expenses* :			
Rent, Rates and Taxes			
Heating and Lighting			
Office Salaries			
Printing & Stationery			
Postage & Telegrams			
Telephone Charges			
Legal Charges			
Audit Fees			
Insurance			
General Expenses			
" *Depreciation and Maintenance* :			
Depreciation			
Repairs & Maintenance			
" *Financial Expenses* :			
Discount Allowed			
Interest on Capital			
Interest on Loans			
Discount on Bills			
" *Extraordinary Expenses* :			
Loss by Fire (not covered by Insurance)			
Cash Defalcations			
" Net Profit transferred to Capital A/c			

Important Points in Profit and Loss Account

***(i)* Salaries.** These include salaries paid to office, godown and warehouse staff and should be shown in Profit and Loss Account being indirect expenses.

Salaries to partners must be debited separately.

Salaries and wages are treated as unproductive and shown in Profit and Loss Account.

If salaries are paid after deduction of Income tax or Provident Fund then these should be added back to the salaries in order to have gross figure of salaries to be shown in Profit and Loss Account.

If salaries are paid in kind by providing certain facilities to the employees such as house free of rent, meals or cloth or washing facility free of charge, *e.g.*, in hospitals, hotels, farms etc., then the value of such facilities should be regarded as salaries.

***(ii)* Rent, Rates and Taxes.** These include offices and warehouse rent, municipal rates and taxes. Factory rent, rates and taxes should be debited to Trading Account and others to Profit and Loss Account. If any rent is received on sub-letting of the building, the same should be shown separately on the credit side of the Profit and Loss A/c. If rent is paid after deduction of some taxes, then these should be added back to know the correct amount of rent payable.

***(iii)* Interest**. Interest paid on loans, overdrafts and bills overdue is an expense and is taken to the debit side of Profit and Loss Account. Interest received on loans advanced by the firm, on deposits and on securities is a gain and is shown on the credit side of Profit and Loss A/c. Interest on capital should be shown separately on the debit side and interest on drawings on the credit side of Profit and Loss Account.

(iv) **Commission.** Commission received for doing the work of other firms may be credited to profit and loss as a gain and commission payable to the agents employed to sell the firm's goods is debited as an expense.

(v) **Repairs.** Repairs and small renewals or replacements relating to the plant and machinery, fixtures, fittings and utensils etc. are generally included under this heading and such expenditure, being as expense, is debited to profit and loss account.

(vi) **Depreciation.** It is an expense due to wear and tear, lapse of time and exhaustion of assets used in business. This is loss sustained by fixed assets and should be charged to Profit and Loss Account.

(vii) **Stable Expenses.** These are incurred for the fodder of the horse and wages paid to persons looking after stable. Being indirect expenses these should be debited to profit and loss account.

(viii) **Trade Expenses.** These are expenses of a varied nature for which it is not worthy to open separate accounts. They are amalgamated under trade or general or sundry or petty expenses. These are debited to profit and loss account being miscellaneous business expenses.

(ix) **Samples**. Samples of the goods manufactured by the business concerns are often distributed free of charge to push up sales. Being indirect expenses, these are debited to profit and loss account.

(x) **Advertisement.** All sums spent on advertising should be charged to Profit and Loss Account. If a large amount is paid under a contract covering two or three years, proportionate part should be charged to Profit and Loss Account and the balance appears as an asset in the Balance Sheet.

(xi) **Abnormal Losses**. Abnormal losses like cash defalcation, stock destroyed by fire not covered by insurance etc. are taken as extraordinary expenses and debited to the Profit and Loss Account.

(xii) **Apprentice Premium.** This is the amount charged from a person to whom training is given by the business. It is a gain and should be credited to Profit and Loss Account. If some amount of apprentice premium has been received in advance, due adjustment must be done in order to calculate the correct amount of income.

Expenses Not to be Shown in Profit and Loss A/c

Since final accounts are intended to show the profitability of the business and not that of its owners, it is essential to exclude personal income and expenditure from business income and expenditure. In this regard, the following items deserve mention :

(i) **Domestic and Household Expenses.** These expenses are not shown in Profit and Loss Account, as these are personal expenses of the proprietor and should be treated as drawings.

(ii) **Life Insurance Premium.** Premium paid on the life policy of the proprietor should be charged to the Drawings Account.

(iii) **Income on Private Investment.** If interest or dividend received on personal investment of the owner of the business is deposited in Bank Account of the business, it is not to be treated as business income but it is to be taken as addition to the capital of the owner.

Indirect expenses to be shown on the debit side of Profit and Loss Account can also be divided into two categories *i.e.* *(i)* operating expenses and *(ii)* Non-operating expenses.

Operating Expenses are those expenses which are incurred in a concern to run the business efficiently and smoothly. Expenses incurred on administration, selling and distribution come under this category.

Non-operating Expenses are those expenses which are not required to be incurred for efficient and smooth operation of the business but still shown on the debit side of profit and loss account. These include loss on the sale of fixed assets, writing off tangible assets and intangible assets, financial expenses etc.

Trading and Profit and Loss or Income Statement may be prepared in vertical form. Example of Vertical Trading and Profit & Loss or Income Statement is given below with imaginary figures.

TRADING AND PROFIT & LOSS OR INCOME STATEMENT

for the year ended 31st March, 2025 (*All figures in ₹ '000*)

Sales			16,000
Less :	Cost of Goods Sold :		
	Raw Materials Consumed	7,800	
	Consumables	800	
	Direct Labour	750	
	Other Direct Expenses	480	
			9,830
	Gross Profit		6,170
Less :	*Operating Expenses*		
	Administration Expenses	1,200	
	Selling Expenses	260	
	Depreciation	700	
			2,160
	Operating Profit		4,010
Add :	Non Operating Income		50
			4,060
Less :	Non Operating Expenses		100
	Net Profit before Interest & Tax		3,960
Less :	Interest Paid		360
	Net Profit before Tax		3,600
Less :	Income Tax @ 50%		1,800
	Net Profit after Tax		1,800

Closing Entries for Profit & Loss A/c

(*i*) For transfer of various expenses to Profit & Loss A/c

Profit and Loss A/c Dr.
 To Various Expenses A/c

(*ii*) For transfer of various incomes and gains to Profit & Loss A/c

Various Incomes & Gains A/c Dr.
 To Profit & Loss A/c

(*iii*) (*a*) For Net Profit
 Profit & Loss A/c Dr.
 To Capital A/c

(*b*) For Net Loss
 Capital A/c Dr.
 To Profit & Loss A/c

Notes :

1. Input GST (CGST and SGST or IGST) Accounts are not transferred to Profit and Loss Account as they are the items to be shown in Balance Sheet.
2. Output GST (CGST and SGST or IGST) Accounts are not transferred to Profit and Loss Account as they are the items to be shown in Balance Sheet.

Nature of Profit and Loss Account

1. It is a Periodic Account. It is prepared after a certain period usually a year for ascertaining profit or loss of that period, therefore, it is called a periodic account. Unlike other accounts, it is not operated throughout the accounting period.

2. It is an Interim Report. It is assumed that a business unit has a reasonable expectation of continuing business at a profit for an indefinite period of time unless otherwise stated. Truely speaking, ascertainment of profit or loss of a business entity is relatively simple on a whole-life basis when a business liquidates and converts its assets into cash and pays off its debts. But the owners, the investors and overall the Government all are impatient and do not want to wait, until the liquidation of the business entity, to know what has been the result of business activities. All these persons are interested in regular reports and accounts at proper intervals to know "how things are going ?" Therefore, Profit and Loss Account can be stated as an interim report for an unambiguous final report can be available only on the liquidation of a business entity.

3. It is an Absorbent Account. At the end of an accounting period all nominal accounts are absorbed in the Profit and Loss Account for ascertaining profit or loss.

4. It is an Allocation Statement. Receipts and payments should be allocated between present and future periods for ascertaining profit or loss of a specific period. Profit or losses, incomes and expenses of a particular accounting period are allocated to the Profit and Loss Account of that period and receipts and payments related to the future period are shown in the balance sheet. That is why Profit and Loss Account is called a statement of allocated income and expenditure.

Importance of Profit and Loss Account

1. Information of Net Profit or Net Loss. One of the important objectives of maintaining accounts is to see whether the business has earned profit or suffered loss during the accounting period. Profit and Loss Account provides information regarding this important objective because it gives information about the profitability or otherwise of the business.

2. Comparison of Current Profit with Past Profits. Profit and Loss Account affords comparison of the current year's net profit with those of the past years. With this comparison it can be ascertained whether net profit of the business is showing a rising trend or downward trend.

3. Comparison of Expenses. Comparison of the various expenses included in the Profit and Loss Account with the expenses of the previous period helps in taking effective steps for control of unnecessary expenses.

4. Helpful in Preparation of Balance Sheet. Net profit or net loss disclosed by the Profit and Loss Account is transferred to Capital Account and Capital Account appears on the liabilities side of the Balance Sheet. Without taking net profit or net loss, the Balance Sheet cannot be completed. Thus, Profit and Loss Account helps in the preparation of the Balance Sheet.

5. Helpful in Future Growth of the Business. On the basis of profit figures of the current period and the previous period, estimates about the profits in the years to come can be made and projections about the expansion of the business can be made.

6. Exceptional Items. 'Exceptional item' is yet another thing to be looked at in the P & L Account. These are infrequent items such as disposal of assets, winding up of operations, forex loss/gain, litigation settlements that may arise only in some particular years. But they can swing the profit numbers one way or the other.

Distinction Between Trading Account and Profit and Loss Account

Following are the points of distinction between trading account and profit and loss account :

	Trading Account	*Profit and Loss Account*
(*i*)	It is prepared to calculate gross profit or gross loss.	It is prepared to arrive at net profit or net loss.
(*ii*)	In this account, cost of goods sold, sales and direct expenses are recorded.	In this account, indirect expenses such as administrative, selling and distribution expenses are charged against gross profit and other revenues.
(*iii*)	Gross profit or loss is transferred to Profit and Loss Account.	Net profit or net loss is transferred to Capital Account which will be shown in the Balance Sheet.

MANUFACTURING ACCOUNT

Those concerns which convert raw materials into finished goods are required to find out the cost of goods manufactured besides gross and net profit of the concern. These are manufacturing cum trading concerns. In order to have full information about the cost of goods manufactured, these concerns firstly prepare Manufacturing Account and then prepare Trading and Profit and Loss Account.

Main object of Manufacturing Account is to show :

(*i*) cost of finished goods produced and

(*ii*) constituent items thereof such as cost of material consumed, productive wages, direct and indirect expenses.

Debit side of Manufacturing Account starts with the cost of materials consumed (*i.e.,* opening stock of raw materials plus net purchases less the closing stock of raw materials). Procurement cost *e.g.,* custom duty, landing charges, excise duty, carriage and freight inwards, insurance on incoming raw materials should also be included with the cost of raw materials.

Closing stock is taken and valued at lower of cost or net realisable value and is then deducted from the sum of opening stock and purchases to eliminate the charge to manufacturing account for stock of raw materials in hand on closing date. Next to raw materials are listed productive wages and direct expenses.

It is followed by debits relating to indirect factory expenses *e.g.,* rents, rates, salaries of supervising staff, power, light, heat and fuel, repairs and renewals, depreciation relating to factory property etc.

Total materials, productive wages, direct expenses and factory indirect expenses should be adjusted for opening and closing stock of partly finished goods or work-in-progress etc. Opening stock of these items should be added at its factory cost value, as current period's production has benefitted by drawing on the opening stock of partly finished goods. Closing stock of work in progress should be taken and valued at factory cost and deducted from the resulting total to eliminate the charge in respect thereof. After this adjustment, the net amount will represent cost of production. Sale of scrap, if any, will be deducted from cost of production.

Total of debit side will then represent the cost of production of finished goods which is credited to Manufacturing Account and debited to Trading Account.

Trading Account will show the cost of production of finished goods, opening and closing stock of finished goods, purchases and sales of finished goods and gross profit.

A specimen of Manufacturing and Trading Account and Profit and Loss Account is given below :

MANUFACTURING, TRADING AND PROFIT AND LOSS ACCOUNT

for the year ended 31st March, 2025

		₹		₹
To Raw Materials Consumed :			By Cost of Goods Manufactured	
(Opening Stock of Raw Materials + Purchases during the year – Closing Stock of Raw Materials)		×××	transferred to Trading A/c	×××
" Direct Wages		×××		
" Direct Expenses (as carriage on purchases)		×××		
Prime Cost				
" Factory Expenses :				
Factory Lighting	×××			
Factory Rent	×××			

Particulars			₹	Particulars	₹
Indirect Wages		×××			
Depreciation on Plant & Machinery		×××			
Factory Supervisor's Salary		×××			
Stores Consumed etc.		×××			
			×××		
			×××		
To Work-in-Progress Beginning		×××			
Less : Closing Work-in-Progress	××				
Sale of Scrap	××	×××			
			×××		
			×××		×××
To Opening Stock of Finished Goods			×××	By Sales	×××
" Cost of Goods Manufactured transferred from Trading A/c			×××	" Closing Stock of Finished Goods	×××
" Gross Profit c/d			×××		
			×××		×××
To Administration Expenses			×××	By Gross Profit b/d	×××
" Selling Expenses			×××	" All Items of Income and Gain	×××
" Distribution Expenses			×××		
" Financial Expenses			×××		
" Maintenance Expenses			×××		
" Net Profit transferred to Capital Account			×××		
			×××		×××

ILLUSTRATION 2. Following are the balances in the Ledger of Mr. Suresh for the year ended 31st March, 2025 :

	₹		₹
Discount (Dr.)	2,500	Advertisement	12,000
Carriage Inwards	10,200	Miscellaneous Expenses	3,300
Rent, Taxes & Rates	13,300	Interest paid	10,792
Printing & Stationery	2,600	Fuel and Coal	14,200
Purchase of Raw Materials	3,59,800	Factory Power	25,000
Sales (inclusive of Sales		Insurance (Fire)	1,760
Tax ₹ 20,000)	5,80,000	Staff Salaries	13,800
Opening Stock of Raw Materials	1,24,400	Electricity	2,500
Opening Stock of Finished Goods	63,800	Bad Debts	6,080
Factory Wages	59,700	Depreciation on Plant & Machinery	11,690
Cash Subsidy on Purchases	10,000	Depreciation on Furniture & Fixture	2,860
Carriage Outwards	12,400	Sale of Scrap	3,000
Life Insurance Premium	2,000	Income Tax paid	1,200

Prepare Manufacturing, Trading and Profit and Loss Account for the year ended 31st March, 2025. Stock as at 31-3-2025 was Raw Materials ₹ 46,900 and Finished Goods ₹ 1,52,300.

SOLUTION

MANUFACTURING, TRADING & PROFIT & LOSS A/C OF MR. SURESH

for the year ended 31st March, 2025

		₹		₹
To Raw Materials Used :	₹		By Cash Subsidy	10,000
Opening Stock	1,24,400		" Cost of Goods Manufactured transferred to Trading A/c	5,45,090
Add : Purchases	3,59,800			
	4,84,200			
Less : Closing Stock	46,900			
	4,37,300			
Less : Sale of Scrap	3,000			
		4,34,300		
" Carriage Inwards		10,200		
" Factory Wages		59,700		
" Fuel and Coal		14,200		
To Factory Power		25,000		
" Depreciation on Plant & Machinery		11,690		
		5,55,090		5,55,090
" Opening Stock of Finished Goods		63,800	By Sales (Less Sales Tax)	5,60,000
" Cost of Goods Manufactured		5,45,090	" Closing Stock of Finished Goods	1,52,300
" Gross Profit c/d		1,03,410		
		7,12,300		7,12,300
" Carriage Outwards		12,400	By Gross Profit b/d	1,03,410
" Advertisement		12,000		
" Discount		2,500		
" Rent, Rates & Taxes		13,300		
" Printing & Stationery		2,600		
" Bad Debts		6,080		
" Misc. Expenses		3,300		
" Interest		10,792		
" Insurance		1,760		
" Staff Salaries		13,800		
" Electricity		2,500		
" Dept. on Furniture & Fittings		2,860		
" Net Profit transferred to Capital A/c		19,518		
		1,03,410		1,03,410

Note : Life Insurance Premium and Income Tax being personal expenses of he proprietor have not been debited to Profit & Loss A/c. These are to be as drawings and should be deducted from Capital A/c.

BALANCE SHEET

A Balance Sheet is a statement prepared with a view to measure the financial position of a business on a certain fixed date. The financial position of a concern is indicated by its assets on

a given date and its liabilities on that date. Excess of assets over liabilities represents the capital and is indicative of the financial soundness of a company. A Balance Sheet is also described as a '*statement showing the sources and applications of capital*'. It is a statement and not an account and prepared from real and personal accounts. The left hand side of the balance sheet may be viewed as a description of the sources from which the business has obtained the capital with which it currently operates and the right hand side as a description of the form in which that capital is invested on a specified date.

On the left hand side of the balance sheet, the several liability items describe how much capital was obtained from trade creditors, from banks, from bill holders and other outside parties. The owner's equity section shows the capital supplied by the owner.

Capital obtained from various sources has been invested according to management's best judgement of the optimum mix or combination of assets for the business. A certain fraction is invested in buildings, another fraction in stock, another fraction is retained as cash for current need of the business and so on. The assets side of the balance sheet, therefore, shows the results of these management judgements as on the date of the balance sheet.

A properly drawn up balance sheet *gives information* relating to (*i*) the nature and value of assets, (*ii*) the nature and extent of liabilities, (*iii*) whether the firm is solvent, (*iv*) whether the firm is overtrading.

If assets exceed the liabilities, the firm is solvent, *i.e.*, able to pay its debts in full. A business is, therefore, solvent by the amount of ownership capital in it, as it is the excess of assets over liabilities. The last point, *i.e.*, (*iv*) concerns the stability of the business. If the total of the debts due to creditors (including bank overdraft) is greater than the liquid assets (*i.e.*, cash, investments, bills etc.) the position of the firm may be financially unsound. Where the debts are being incurred without sufficient means of payment, the firm is said to be over trading. For the position to be quite sound, there should be some working capital, *i.e.*, some spare liquid assets available for current expenditure. It is not a wise policy to lock up the capital in fixed assets. The concern may be solvent without being sound.

Characteristics of a Balance Sheet

Following are the main characteristics :

1. It is prepared on a particular date and not for a particular period.
2. It is prepared after the preparation of Trading and Profit & Loss Account.
3. As assets must be equal to total liabilities, the two sides of the balance must have the same total.
4. It shows the financial position of a business as a going concern.
5. It is a statement of assets (debit balances) and liabilities (credit balances) and not an account.

Information that Balance Sheet Conveys to Outsiders

Following are the main items of information that the Balance Sheet conveys to an outsider :

(1) The nature and the value of assets. (2) It shows the nature and extent of liabilities. (3) It shows the owners' equity (*i.e.*, assets – liabilities = capital) (4) It tells about creditworthiness and solvency of the firm. (5) It reflects the liquidity of a firm. (6) It reveals other information required to changes in economic reserves and obligations.

Classification of Assets and Liabilities

Assets. Assets are property and possession of a business. Stock, land and buildings, book debts, cash, bills receivable are some examples of assets. The classification of assets depends on their nature. The various types of assets are :

(*i*) **Fixed Assets.** Those assets which are acquired and held permanently in the business and are used for the purpose of earning profits are called fixed assets. Land and buildings, machinery, furniture and fixtures are some examples of these assets.

(*ii*) **Current Assets.** Those assets such as cash, debtors and stock that can be realised and readily available to discharge liabilities are called current assets.

(*iii*) **Tangible Assets.** These are definite assets which can be seen, touched and have volume such as machinery, cash, stock, etc.

(*iv*) **Fictitious Assets.** These assets are fictitious in nature, *i.e.*, they are virtually not assets. These are either the past accumulated losses or expenses which are incurred once in the life of a business and are capitalized for the time being. Profit and loss account (debit balance), organisation expenses, discount on the issue of shares, advertisement expenses capitalized for the time being are examples of such assets.

(*v*) **Intangible Assets.** Those assets which cannot be seen, touched and have no volume but have value are called intangible assets. Goodwill, patents and trade marks are examples of such assets but quite valuable to undertaking. An intangible asset may not be fictitious. If on account of the past goodwill purchased along with an existing concern, sales are readily effected and profit is readily earned, the asset is certainly not fictitious though it is intangible. However, if the amount of goodwill was paid in respect of a losing concern, the asset would be fictitious.

(*vi*) **Wasting Assets.** Those assets as mines, quarries etc. that become exhausted or reduce in value by their working are called wasting assets.

(*vii*) **Liquid Assets.** These are cash or such items as marketable securities which can be converted into cash quickly.

(*viii*) **Contingent Assets.** It is an asset the existence, value and ownership of which is dependent on the occurrence or non-occurrence of a specified act. Suppose a firm has filed a suit for some specified property now in possession of someone else. If the suit is decided in firm's favour, the firm will get the property. At the moment it is a contingent asset. Similar would be the position of a patent applied for arising of a firm's own research effort. Contingent liability in respect of a contract for capital expenditure already entered into will give rise to an asset on payment, at present it is only a contingent asset.

(*ix*) **Working Capital** is the difference between current assets and current liabilities.

(*x*) **Accounts Receivable** will include sundry debtors and bills receivable.

Liabilities. A liability is an amount which a business is legally bound to pay. It is a claim by an outsider on the assets of a business. Liabilities may be classified into four categories :

(*i*) **Fixed Liabilities.** These are those liabilities which are payable only on the termination of the business such as capital which is a liability to the owner.

(*ii*) **Long Term Liabilities.** Those liabilities which are not payable within the next accounting period but will be payable within next five to ten years are called long term liabilities such as debentures.

(*iii*) **Current Liabilities.** Those liabilities which are payable out of current assets within the next accounting period usually year or already due are called current liabilities. Sundry creditors, bills payable, short term bank overdraft are examples of such liabilities.

(*iv*) **Contingent Liabilities.** A contingent liability is one which is not an actual liability but which will become an actual one on the happening of some event which is uncertain. Thus such liabilities have two characteristics : (*a*) uncertainty as to whether the amount will be payable at all, and (*b*) uncertainty about the amount involved. It is sufficient if the amount of such liability is stated on the face of the Balance Sheet by way of a note unless there is a probability that a loss will materialise. In that event it is no more a contingent liability and a specific provision should be made therefor. Examples of such liabilities are :

(*a*) Claims against the companies not acknowledged as debts.

(*b*) Uncalled liability on partly paid up shares.

(*c*) Arrears of fixed cumulative dividend.

(*d*) Estimated amount of contracts remaining to be executed on capital account and not provided for.
(*e*) Liability of a case pending in the court.
(*f*) Bills of exchange, guarantees given against a particular firm or person.
(*g*) Income tax and sales tax demands under appeal.
(*h*) Other money for which the company is contingently liable.

A contingent liability should not be recognised, but is disclosed. Also contingent liability should be periodically reviewed by the enterprise.

Owners' Equity (or net worth) is the difference between assets and outside liabilities. It includes both capital and retained earnings.

Grouping and Marshalling of Assets & Liabilities

The arrangement of assets and liabilities in certain groups and in a particular order is called Grouping and Marshalling of the Balance Sheet of a business. Assets and liabilities can be arranged in the Balance Sheet into two ways : (*i*) In order of liquidity (*ii*) In order of permanence.

(*i*) In order of liquidity. When assets and liabilities are arranged according to their realisability and payment preferences, such an order is called liquidity order. Such arrangement is given in the Balance Sheet (I).

(*ii*) In order of permanence. When the order is reversed from that what is followed in case of liquidity, it is called order of permanence. This order is followed in case of joint stock companies compulsorily but can be followed in other concerns also. Fixed assets and liabilities are shown first on the assumption that these will be sold or paid only on the insolvency of a business. This order of Balance Sheet is given below in Balance Sheet (II).

BALANCE SHEET (I)

Liabilities	₹	*Assets*	₹
Current Liabilities :		*Liquid Assets* :	
Bills Payable		Cash in Hand	
Sundry Creditors		Cash at Bank	
Bank Overdraft		*Floating Assets* :	
GST Payable		Sundry Debtors	
Long Term Liabilities :		Investments	
Loan from Bank		Bills Receivable	
Debentures		Stock in Trade	
Fixed Liabilities :		Prepaid Expenses	
Capital		*Fixed Assets* :	
		Machinery	
		Building	
		Furniture & Fixtures	
		Motor Car	
		Fictitious Assets :	
		Advertisement	
		Misc. Expenses to the extent not written off	
		Profit & Loss A/c	
		Intangible Assets	
		Goodwill	
		Patents	
		Copyright	
Total		Total	

Note : For contingent liabilities, if any.

BALANCE SHEET (II)

Liabilities	₹	*Assets*	₹
1. Fixed Liabilities		1. Intangible Assets	
2. Long Term Liabilities		2. Fictitious Assets	
3. Current Liabilities		3. Fixed Assets	
		4. Floating Assets	
		5. Liquid Assets	

Note : For contingent liability if any.

BALANCE SHEET (in Vertical Format)

as on ....

		₹
Capital		—
Add : Reserves		—
		—
Less : Fictitious Assets (if any)		—
Proprietors' Fund		—
Add : Long-term Loans		—
Capital Employed		—
Represented by		
Fixed Asserts		—
Add : *Working Capital*		
Current Assets	—	
Less : Current Liabilities	—	
		—
		—

Note : Details of various heads have already been given in the above performa of Balance Sheet.

Distinction Between Profit and Loss Account and Balance Sheet

Important points of differences between a Profit and Loss Account and a Balance Sheet are as follows :

1. Profit and Loss Account is an account prepared with balances of nominal accounts whereas a Balance Sheet is a statement of assets and liabilities and prepared from real and personal accounts.

2. Profit and Loss Account discloses the profits earned or losses incurred for the accounting period usually a year whereas a Balance Sheet shows the financial position of the business on the last day of the accounting period.

3. Balances of nominal accounts are transferred to the Profit and Loss Account. Personal accounts and real accounts are shown in the Balance Sheet. Balance of Profit and Loss Account (*i.e.,* net profit) is also shown on the liabilities side of the Balance Sheet.

4. Nominal accounts are closed by transferring them to the Profit and Loss Account. But the accounts that are shown in the Balance Sheet do not close and become the opening balances for the next accounting period.

From the above discussion of the final accounts, it can be inferred that there is complementary relation between the Balance Sheet and the Profit and Loss Account which reflects vital distinction between capital and revenue items. Profit and Loss Account (including Trading Account) shows all revenue items pertaining to the accounting period whereas Balance Sheet shows all the items as may properly be capitalised, personal accounts' balances and profit or loss as disclosed by the Profit and Loss Account.

Distinction Between Trial Balance and Balance Sheet

Following are the main distinctions between Trial Balance and Balance Sheet.

Points of Distinction	*Trial Balance*	*Balance Sheet*
(*i*) Statement	It is a statement of debit and credit balances taken from the ledger.	It is a statement of assets and liabilities.
(*ii*) Purpose of Preparation	It is prepared to test the arithmetical accuracy of books of account.	It is prepared to ascertain the financial position of the organisation on a particular date.
(*iii*) Type of Balances	Balances of all types of accounts, *i.e.,* personal, real and nominal accounts are shown.	Balances of real and personal accounts only are shown.
(*iv*) When Prepared?	It is usually prepared at the end of each month, three months, six months or year before preparation of trading and profit and loss account.	It is usually prepared at the end of the year after the preparation of trading and profit and loss account.
(*v*) Closing Stock	Closing stock does not appear in the trial balance.	Closing stock is shown on the assets side of the balance sheet.
(*vi*) Use	It is prepared for internal use.	It is prepared for external use, *i.e.,* for outside parties such as creditors, shareholders, government authorities, etc.

REMEMBER

Set off of GST

Input GST (GST paid) on purchases of goods and/or services or both are set off against GST collected (Output GST) on sales of goods and/or services. The GST Act prescribes the order in which it can be set off. That order is :

Input CGST	**Input SGST**	**Input IGST**
↓	↓	↓
Set off Against Output IGST and if balance remains then Output CGST in this order only	Set off Against Output IGST and if balance remains then Output CGST in this order only	Set off Against Output IGST if balance remains then Output CGST and Output SGST in this order only

Ledger for each Input GST (Input CGST, Input SGST, Input IGST) and Output GST (Output CGST, Output SGST, Output IGST) are prepared and balance is shown in Trial Balance. When final accounts are prepared, the balances in GST accounts should be set off.

ILLUSTRATION 3. Following balances are extracted from the books of Kautilya & Co. dealing in essential goods exempted from GST on 31st March, 2025. You are required to make the necessary closing entries and to prepare Trading and Profit and Loss Account and a Balance Sheet as on that date :

	₹		₹
Opening Stock	500	Commission (Cr.)	200
B/R	2,250	Returns Outwards	250
Purchases	19,500	Trade Expenses	100
Wages	1,400	Office Fixtures	500
Insurance	550	Cash in Hand	250
Sundry Debtors	15,000	Cash at Bank	2,375
Carriage Inwards	400	Rent & Taxes	550
Commission (Dr.)	400	Carriage Outwards	725
Interest on Capital	350	Sales	25,000
Stationery	225	Bills Payable	1,500
Returns Inwards	650	Creditors	9,825
		Capital	8,950

Closing Stock was valued at ₹ 12,500.

SOLUTION

CLOSING ENTRIES

Date	Particulars		Dr. Amount	Cr. Amount
2025			₹	₹
March 31	Trading Account	Dr.	22,450	
	To Stock A/c			500
	To Purchases A/c			19,500
	To Wages A/c			1,400
	To Returns Inwards A/c			650
	To Carriage Inwards A/c			400
	(For balance transferred)			
March 31	Sales A/c	Dr.	25,000	
	Returns Outwards A/c	Dr.	250	
	To Trading Account			25,250
	(For balances transferred)			
"	Closing Stock A/c	Dr.	12,500	
	To Trading A/c			12,500
	(For value of closing stock)			
March 31	Trading Account	Dr.	15,300	
	To Profit and Loss A/c			15,300
	(For gross profit transferred)			
"	Profit and Loss Account	Dr.	2,900	
	To Insurance A/c			550
	To Commission A/c			400
	To Interest on Capital A/c			350
	To Stationery A/c			225
	To Trade Expenses A/c			100
	To Rent and Taxes A/c			550
	To Carriage Outwards A/c			725
	(For balances transferred)			

March 31	Commission A/c	Dr.	200	
	To Profit & Loss A/c			200
	(For balance transferred)			
"	Profit and Loss A/c	Dr.	12,600	
	To Capital A/c			12,600
	(For net profit transferred)			

TRADING & PROFIT AND LOSS A/c OF MESSRS KAUTILYA & CO.

for the year ended 31st March, 2025

	₹	₹		₹	₹
To Opening Stock		500	By Sales	25,000	
" Purchases	19,500		*Less* : Returns Inwards	650	
Less : Returns Outwards	250				24,350
		19,250	" Closing Stock		12,500
" Wages		1,400			
" Carriage Inwards		400			
" Gross Profit c/d		15,300			
		36,850			36,850
To Insurance		550	By Gross Profit b/d		15,300
" Commission		400	" Commission		200
" Interest on Capital		350			
" Stationery		225			
" Trade Expenses		100			
" Rent and Taxes		550			
" Carriage Outwards		725			
" Net Profit transferred to Capital A/c		12,600			
		15,500			15,500

BALANCE SHEET OF MESSRS KAUTILYA & CO.

as on 31st March, 2025

Liabilities		₹	*Assets*	₹
Creditors		9,825	Cash in Hand	250
Bills Payable		1,500	Cash at Bank	2,375
Capital	₹		Bills Receivable	2,250
April 1, 2024	8,950		Stock	12,500
Add : Net Profit	12,600		Sundry Debtors	15,000
		21,550	Office Fixtures	500
		32,875		32,875

ILLUSTRATION 4. **(*With GST*)** Following is the trial balance of Havells at 31st March, 2025 Draw the final accounts from the balances therefrom:

TRIAL BALANCE
As at 31st March, 2025

Particulars	*Dr. (₹)*	*Cr. (₹)*
Capital	—	7,50,000
Stock on 1st April, 2024	1,30,000	—
Cash at Bank	1,10,000	—
Cash in Hand	55,000	—
Machinery	2,00,000	—
Furniture	1,13,000	—
Purchases	2,50,000	—
Wages	50,000	—
Carriage	43,000	—
Salaries	60,000	—
Discount Allowed	4,000	—
Discount Received	—	5,000
Advertising	40,000	—
Office Expenses	50,000	—
Sales	—	5,00,000
Sundry Debtors	1,90,000	—
Sundry Creditors	—	47,000
Input CGST A/c	12,500	—
Input SGST A/c	12,500	—
Input IGST A/c	16,000	—
Output CGST A/c	—	10,000
Output SGST A/c	—	10,000
Output IGST A/c	—	14,000
Total	13,36,000	13,36,000

Value of Closing Stock on 31st March 2025 was ₹ 1,50,000.

SOLUTION

TRADING ACCOUNT OF HAVELLS
for the year ended 31st March, 2025

Dr. *Cr.*

Particulars	₹	*Particulars*	₹
To Opening Stock	1,30,000	By Sales A/c	5,00,000
To Purchases	2,50,000	By Closing Stock	1,50,000
To Wages	50,000		
To Carriage	43,000		
To Gross Profit c/d	1,77,000		
	6,50,000		6,50,000

PROFIT AND LOSS ACCOUNT OF HAVELLS

Dr. *or the year ended 31st March, 2025* Cr.

Particulars	₹	*Particulars*	₹
To Salaries	60,000	By Gross Profit b/d	1,77,000
To Discount Allowed	4,000	By Discount Received	5,000
To Advertising	40,000		
To Office Expenses	50,000		
To Net Profit transferred to Capital A/c	28,000		
	1,82,000		1,82,000

BALANCE SHEET OF HAVELLS

as at 31st March, 2025

Liabilities		₹	*Assets*	₹
Sundry Creditors		47,000	Cash in Hand	55,000
Capital:	₹		Cash at Bank	1,10,000
Opening Balance	7,50,000		Sundry Debtors	1,90,000
Add: Net Profit	28,000	7,78,000	Closing Stock	1,50,000
			Input CGST	2,500
			Input SGST	2,500
			Input IGST	2,000
			Furniture	1,13,000
			Machinery	2,00,000
		8,25,000		8,25,000

Note: *Setting-off GST:*

	Input (₹)	*Output (₹)*	*Balance (₹) Carried Forward*
IGST	16,000	14,000	2,000
CGST	12,500	10,000	2,500
SGST	12,500	10,000	2,500

ADJUSTMENTS

While preparing Trading and Profit and Loss Account one point that must be kept in mind is that expenses and incomes for the full trading period are to be taken into consideration. This means that if an expense has been incurred but not paid during that period, liability for the unpaid amount should be created before the accounts can be said to show the profit or loss. All expenses and incomes should properly be adjusted through entries. These entries which are passed at the end of the accounting period are called adjusting entries. Some important adjustments which are to be made at the end of the accounting year are discussed in the following pages one by one.

(*i*) Closing Stock

Unsold goods lying in stock at the end of the accounting period are called closing stock. Every concern prepares a list of items of stock which remains unsold and puts value against it. Stock is to be valued at cost or market price whichever is less. For the total value of closing stock, say ₹ 50,000, the following adjustment entry will be passed at the end of the year :

Stock Account	Dr.	₹ 50,000	
To Trading Account			₹ 50,000

The two accounts affected are

STOCK A/c

	₹		₹
To Trading A/c	50,000	By Balance c/d	50,000

TRADING A/c

			₹
		By Stock	50,000

The two fold effect of the above adjustment will be :

(*i*) Closing stock will be shown on the assets side of the Balance Sheet.

(*ii*) It will be shown on the credit side of the Trading Account.

Sometimes opening and closing stocks are adjusted through Purchases Account. In this case, there will be no opening stock in the Trial Balance. Adjusted purchases and closing stock (debit balance) will be given in the Trial Balance. Adjusted purchases will be taken on the debit side of the Trading Account and closing stock will be shown on the assets side of the Balance Sheet. It should be noted carefully that closing stock in this case will not be shown on the credit side of Trading Account as closing stock has already been adjusted through Purchases Account. At the beginning of the next accounting year, closing stock will become opening stock and will be brought into account by passing reverse entry as under :

Trading Account	Dr.
To Stock Account	

(*ii*) Outstanding Expenses

Those expenses which have been incurred and are due for payment *i.e.,* not paid as yet are called outstanding expenses.

The adjusting entry is

Expenses A/c (example salaries) Dr.

To Outstanding Expense (example Outstanding Salaries A/c)

(Being unpaid expenses booked)

If the expense provided is subject to levy of GST (CGST and SGST or IGST), GST payable is also provided along with that expense. It may be noted that wages and salaries are exempt from GST. No GST shall be levied upon payment of salaries or wages.

For example, ₹ 10,000 p.m. is paid as commission to an employee but during the year 2025, only ₹ 1,00,000 are paid as commission. Two months' commission *i.e.,* ₹ 20,000 which is due but not paid is outstanding commission. CGST & SGST is to be levied at 6% each in order to bring this fact into books of account, the following adjusting entry will be passed at the end of the year :

		₹	₹
Commission A/c	Dr.	20,000	
Input CGST A/c	Dr.	1,200	
Input SGST A/c	Dr.	1,200	
To Outstanding Commission			22,400

The effect of this entry on two accounts will be :

COMMISSION A/c

	₹		₹
To Cash A/c	1,00,000	By Profit & Loss A/c	1,20,000
" Outstanding Commission	20,000		
	1,20,000		1,20,000

OUTSTANDING COMMISSION A/c

	₹		₹
To Balance c/d	20,000	By Commission	20,000

The two fold effect of the above adjustment will be :

(*i*) outstanding expenses will be shown on the debit side of Trading or Profit and Loss Account by way of addition to the expenses and

(*ii*) outstanding expenses will be shown on the liabilities side of Balance Sheet.

If no adjustment was made for the outstanding commission then the net profit would be overstated by ₹ 20,000 and liabilities understated by ₹ 20,000.

In the beginning of the next year, a reverse entry will be passed to cancel the effect of the adjustment entry. Reverse entry will close Outstanding Commission Account and adjust the next year's Commission Account.

(*iii*) Unexpired or Prepaid Expenses

Those expenses which have been paid in advance *i.e.,* whose benefit will be available in future are called prepaid (or unexpired) expenses.

The adjusting entry is

Prepaid Expense (For example Prepaid Rent) A/c Dr.
  To Expense (For example Rent) A/c
(Being the prepaid expenses adjusted)

It may be noted that if that expense is subject to the levy of GST, then GST shall be paid at the time of making the payment of that expense. However, when the amount is transferred from Expense Account to Prepaid Expense A/c only the amount of Prepaid Expense is transferred and No GST is transferred.

For example, if a fire insurance policy is taken for a year paying ₹ 12,000 as insurance premium on along with CGST and SGST @ 6% 1st October, 2024 and will expire on 30th September, 2025. The position on 31st March 2025, when accounts are closed, will be that ₹ 5,000 *i.e.,* premium from 1st October, 2024 to 31st March, 2025 will be an expense but ₹ 3,000 *i.e.,* premium from 1st April, 2025 to 30th June, 2025 will be prepaid or unexpired expense. In order to bring this into account on 31st March, 2025, the following adjusting entry will be passed :

Prepaid Insurance Premium A/c	Dr.	₹ 3,000	
To Insurance Premium A/c			₹ 3,000

Two accounts affected will be :

PREPAID INS. PREMIUM A/c

	₹		₹
To Ins. Premium A/c	3,000	By Balance c/d	3,000

INSURANCE PREMIUM A/c

	₹		₹
To Bank A/c	12,000	By Prepaid Insurance Premium A/c	3,000
		" Profit & Loss A/c	9,000
	12,000		12,000

The two-fold effect of prepaid expenses will be :

(*i*) prepaid expenses will be shown in Profit and Loss Account by way of deduction from the expenses and

(*ii*) prepaid expenses being debit balance will be shown on the assets side of Balance Sheet.

In the beginning of the next year, a reverse entry will be passed to nullify the effect of the adjusting entry.

Note : No GST (CGST and SGST) paid shall be transferred when adjustment entry for prepaid insurance is made. When the premium was paid on 1st July 2024 following entry had been passed

		₹	₹
Insurance Premium A/c	Dr.	12,000	
Input CGST A/c	Dr.	720	
Input SGST A/c	Dr.	720	
To Bank/Cash A/c			13,440

(*iv*) Accrued Income

That income which has been earned but not received during the accounting year is called accrued income.

The adjustment entry is :

Accrued Income (Say Rent) A/c Dr.
  To Income (Say Rent) A/c
  To Output CGST A/c
  To Output SGST A/c
or To Output IGST A/c
(Being accrued income recorded in the books)

It may be noted that GST is levied on incomes like commission and Rent but not on interest)

For example (GST not levied), if the business has invested ₹ 1,00,000 in 5% gilt edged securities on 1st April, 2024 but during the year ₹ 3,500 has been received as interest on securities. Then ₹ 1,500 interest on securities earned upto 31st March, 2025 but not received, will be accrued interest for the year 2025. In order to bring accrued interest into books of account, the following adjusting entry will be passed :

Accrued Interest A/c	Dr.	₹ 1,500	
To Interest A/c			₹ 1,500

Two accounts affected will be :

ACCRUED INTEREST A/c

	₹		₹
To Interest A/c	1,500	By Balance c/d	1,500

INTEREST A/c

	₹		₹
To P. & L. A/c	5,000	By Bank A/c	3,500
		" Accrued Interest A/c	1,500
	5,000		5,000

The two-fold effect of accrued income will be :

(*i*) It will be shown on the credit side of Profit and Loss Account by way of addition to income, and

(*ii*) accrued income being debit balance, will be shown on the assets side of Balance Sheet.

Next year, in the beginning, a reverse entry will be passed in order to eliminate the effect of adjusting entry and to bring the same to the correct position.

Example (with GST). Rent of ₹ 70,000 is due for the month of March 2025 but has not been received. It is subject to levy of CGST and SGST @ 6% each. The journal entry for this adjustment shall be :

		₹	₹
Accrued Rent A/c	Dr.	78,400	
To Rent A/c			70,000
To Output CGST A/c			4,200
To Output SGST A/c			4,200
(Being accrued rent recorded in books with GST)			

(*v*) Income Received in Advance

Income received but not earned during the accounting year is called as income received in advance. For example, if building has been given to a tenant on ₹ 24,000 p.a. plus CGST & SGST @ 6% each but during the year ₹ 30,000 has been received, then ₹ 6,000 will be rent received in advance. In order to bring this into books of account, the following adjusting entry will be made at the end of the accounting year :

Rent A/c	Dr.	₹ 6,000	
To Rent Received in Advance Account			₹ 6,000

It may be noted that GST (CGST and SGST) A/cs shall not be debited when Rent (Income) Received in Advance A/c is credited.

GST (CGST and SGST or IGST) Accounts shall be credited when the payment is received. The journal entry at the time of receipt shall be :

		₹	₹
Bank/Cash A/c	Dr.	33,600	
To Rent A/c			30,000
To Output CGST A/c			1,800
To Output SGST A/c			1,800

Two affected accounts will be :

RENT RECEIVED IN ADVANCE A/c

	₹		₹
To Balance c/d	6,000	By Rent A/c	6,000

RENT ACCOUNT

	₹		₹
To Rent Received in Advance A/c	6,000	By Bank A/c	30,000
" Profit & Loss A/c	24,000		
	30,000		30,000

The two-fold effect of this adjustment will be :

(*i*) It is shown on the credit side of Profit and Loss Account by way of deduction from the income, and

(*ii*) income received in advance, being credit balance, is shown on the liabilities side of Balance Sheet.

(*vi*) Depreciation

Depreciation is the reduction in the value of fixed asset due to its use, wear and tear or obsolescence. When an asset is used for earning purposes, it is necessary that reduction due to its use, must be charged to the profit of that year in order to show correct profit or loss and to show the asset at its correct value in the Balance Sheet. Generally depreciation is charged at some percentage on the value of an asset. Suppose machinery for ₹ 1,00,000 is purchased on 1.4.2025, 20% p.a. is the rate of depreciation. Then ₹ 20,000 will be depreciation for the year 2025 and will be brought into account by passing the following adjusting entry :

Depreciation A/c	Dr.	₹ 20,000	
To Machinery A/c			₹ 20,000

Two accounts affected will be :

DEPRECIATION A/c

	₹		₹
To Machinery A/c	20,000	By P. & L. A/c	20,000

MACHINERY A/c

	₹		₹
To Bank	1,00,000	By Depreciation A/c	20,000
		" Balance c/d	80,000
	1,00,000		1,00,000

The two-fold effect of depreciation will be :

(*i*) Depreciation is shown on the debit side of Profit and Loss Account, and

(*ii*) it is shown on the assets side by way of deduction from the value of concerned asset.

Cost of asset affects the amount of Depreciation as depreciation is charged on cost of asset. It should be remembered that GST paid at the time of acquired asset is **not** a cost of asset as it may be set off against GST collected. The Depreciation is charged on cost of asset (excluding GST paid).

(*vii*) Interest on Capital

Sometimes in order to see whether the business is really earning profit or not, interest on capital at a certain rate is provided. For example, if A has invested ₹ 15,00,000 as capital and 10% interest is to be provided, then ₹ 1,50,000 as interest on capital is to be brought into the books by passing the following adjusting entry :

Interest on Capital A/c	Dr.	₹ 1,50,000	
To A's Capital A/c			₹ 1,50,000

Two affected accounts will be :

INTEREST ON CAPITAL A/c

	₹		₹
To Capital A/c	1,50,000	By P. & L. A/c	1,50,000

A'S CAPITAL A/c

	₹		₹
To Balance c/d	16,50,000	By Balance b/d	15,00,000
		" Interest on Capital A/c	1,50,000
	16,50,000		16,50,000

The two-fold effect of this adjusting entry will be :

(*i*) Interest on capital will be shown on the debit side of Profit and Loss Account.

(*ii*) It will be shown on the liabilities side of Balance Sheet by way of addition to the capital.

(*viii*) Interest on Drawings

If interest on capital is allowed, it is but natural that interest on drawings should be charged from the proprietor, as drawings reduce capital. Suppose during an accounting year, drawings are ₹ 1,00,000 and interest on drawings is ₹ 5,000. In order to bring this into account, the following entry will be passed :

Drawings A/c	Dr.	₹ 5,000	
To Interest on Drawings A/c			₹ 5,000

Two affected accounts will be :

INTEREST ON DRAWINGS A/c

	₹		₹
To P. & L. A/c	5,000	By Drawings	5,000

DRAWINGS A/c

	₹		₹
To Cash	1,00,000	By Capital A/c	1,05,000
To Interest on Drawings	5,000		
	1,05,000		1,05,000

The two-fold effect of interest on drawings will be :

(*i*) Interest on drawings will be shown on the credit side of Profit and Loss Account, and

(*ii*) Shown on the liabilities side of Balance Sheet by way of addition to the drawings which are ultimately deducted from the Capital.

(ix) Bad Debts

Debts which cannot be recovered or become irrecoverable are called bad debts. It is a loss for the business. For example, if sundry debtors on 31st March, 2025 are ₹ 5,20,000, bad debts on that date are ₹ 20,000. In order to bring this into account, an adjusting entry will be passed :

Bad Debts A/c	Dr.	₹ 20,000	
To Sundry Debtors A/c			₹ 20,000

Two affected accounts will be :

BAD DEBTS A/c

	₹		₹
To Sundry Debtors A/c	20,000	By P. & L. A/c	20,000

SUNDRY DEBTORS A/c

	₹		₹
To Balance b/d	5,20,000	By Bad Debts A/c	20,000
		" Balance c/d	5,00,000
	5,20,000		5,20,000

The two-fold effect of bad debts will be that bad debts will be :

(*i*) shown on the debit side of Profit and Loss Account, and

(*ii*) shown on the assets side of the Balance Sheet by way of deduction from sundry debtors.

(x) Provision for Doubtful Debts

Sometimes a merchant finds on the last day of the accounting year that certain debts are doubtful *i.e.,* the amount to be received may or may not be received. It is one of the golden principles of accountancy that *anticipated losses must be provided.* Therefore, provision for doubtful debts is generally made on the basis of some percentage (say 5%) which is fixed on the basis of past experience. Suppose sundry debtors on 31-3-2025 are ₹ 5,20,000. Further bad debts are ₹ 20,000. Provision of 5% is to be made on debtors. In order to bring the provision for doubtful debts of ₹ 25,000 *i.e.,* 5% on ₹ 5,00,000 (₹ 5,20,000 – ₹ 20,000), the following entry will be made :

Profit and Loss A/c	Dr.	₹ 25,000	
To Provision for Doubtful Debts A/c			₹ 25,000

Two affected accounts will be :

(*i*) It will be shown on the debit side of Profit and Loss Account or by way of addition to Bad Debts. (Old provision for doubtful debts at the beginning of the year will be deducted).

(*ii*) Provision for Doubtful Debts is shown on the assets side of Balance Sheet by way of deduction from Sundry Debtors (after deduction of further bad debts, if any.)

ILLUSTRATION 5. Following balances are given in the Trial Balance :

	Dr. (₹)	*Cr.* (₹)
Capital	—	1,00,000
Drawings	20,000	—
Bad Debts	1,200	—
Sundry Debtors	20,500	—
Provision for Doubtful Debts	—	2,000
Salaries Outstanding		1,000

Prepaid Insurance	200	—
Interest on Investment Account		500
Commission Received in Advance		400

Adjustments : (*i*) Further Bad Debts ₹ 500; (*ii*) Make Provision for Doubtful debts @ 5% on Sundry Debtors; (*iii*) Interest on Capital ₹ 10,000; (*iv*) Interest on Drawings ₹ 1,000.

Show how the above balances and adjustments will appear in the Final Accounts :

SOLUTION

PROFIT & LOSS ACCOUNT

	₹	₹		₹
To Interest on Capital		10,000	By Interest on Drawings	1,000
To Bad Debts	1,200			
Add : Further Bad Debts	500			
Add : New Provision	1,000			
	2,700			
Less : Old Provision	2,000	700		

BALANCE SHEET

as on ......

Liabilities		₹	₹	*Assets*	₹	₹
Salaries Outstanding			1,000	Prepaid Insurance		200
Commission Received in Advance			400	Interest Accrued		500
Capital		1,00,000		Sundry Debtors	20,500	
Add : Interest on Capital		10,000		*Less* : Further Bad Debts	500	
		1,10,000			20,000	
Less : Drawings	20,000			*Less* : Provision for Doubtful Debts	1,000	19,000
Interest on Drawings	1,000	21,000	89,000			

(*xi*) Provision for Discount on Debtors

If sales are made by the merchant on the condition that if the amount of sales is paid within a certain period, he will allow a certain percentage of discount. For example, if goods worth ₹ 10,000 are sold to X on 1st December, 2024 with the terms of $2\frac{1}{2}\%$ discount, if payment is made within 40 days. On 31st December, 2024 when accounts are to be closed, the position is that X may pay the amount of ₹ 10,000 upto 10th January, 2025 and earn a discount of ₹ 250. For such discount, provision is made generally on the basis of past experience and certain percentage $\left(\text{say } 2\frac{1}{2}\%\right)$ on debtors is determined to calculate such provision. In order to incorporate such provision for discount on debtors, an entry is made as given below :

	Profit and Loss A/c Dr.		₹ 250	
	To Provision for Discount on Debtors A/c			₹ 250

Note. *Such provision is made on debtors after deduction of further bad debts and provision for doubtful debts because discount is allowable to debtors who intend to make the payment.*

The two fold effect will be :

PROFIT & LOSS A/c

	₹		₹
To Provision for Discount on Debtors	250		

PROVISION FOR DISCOUNT ON DEBTORS A/c

	₹		₹
To Balance c/d	250	By P & L A/c	250

The two-fold effect of this entry will be :

(*i*) Such provision will be shown on the debit side of Profit and Loss Account.

(*ii*) It will be shown by way of deduction from Sundry Debtors (after deduction of further bad debts and provision for doubtful debts) on the assets side of Balance Sheet.

(*xii*) Reserve for Discount on Creditors

As the firm has to provide for discount on debtors, similarly, the firm may have chance to receive discount on the last date of the accounting year, if the payment is made within the scheduled period. Such discount on creditors is anticipated profit and, therefore, reserve for discount on creditors will be made instead of provision for discount on creditors. Such reserve will be calculated on the amount of creditors. Suppose on 31st December, 2024, the creditors are ₹ 10,000 and $2\frac{1}{2}\%$ Reserve is to be made for discount on creditors. In order to bring this into account, the following entry will be passed :

			Dr. (₹)	Cr. (₹)
Reserve for Discount on Creditors Account	Dr.		₹ 250	
To Profit & Loss Account				₹ 250

Two affected accounts will be :

PROFIT & LOSS A/c

	₹		₹
		By Res. for Dis. on Creditors	250

RESERVE FOR DISCOUNT ON CREDITORS A/c

	₹		₹
To P. & L. A/c	250	By Balance c/d	250

The two-fold effect of this reserve will be :

(*i*) It is shown on the credit side of Profit and Loss Account, and

(*ii*) Shown on the liabilities side of Balance Sheet by way of deduction from sundry creditors.

ILLUSTRATION 6. A trader maintained a Provision for Doubtful Debts @ 5%, a Provision for Discount @ 2% on Debtors and a Reserve for Discount @ 2% on Creditors which on 1st January, 2023 stood at ₹ 1,500, ₹ 500 and ₹ 400 respectively. His balances on 31st December, 2023 and 2024 were as follows :

	31st Dec. 2023	*31st Dec. 2024*
	₹	₹
Bad Debts written off	1,800	300
Discount allowed	600	200
Sundry Debtors	20,000	6,000
Discount received	300	50
Sundry Creditors	15,000	10,000

Show the necessary accounts in the ledger. Also show how the items would appear in the final accounts of each of the three years.

SOLUTION

BAD DEBTS ACCOUNT

Date	Particulars	₹	Date	Particulars	₹
2023			2023		
Dec. 31	To Sundry Debtors A/c	1,800	Dec. 31	By Provision for D/D A/c	1,800
2024			2024		
Dec. 31	To Sundry Debtors A/c	300	Dec. 31	By Provision for D/D A/c	300

PROVISION FOR DOUBTFUL DEBTS ACCOUNT

Date	Particulars	₹	Date	Particulars	₹
2023			2023		
Dec. 31	To Bad Debts A/c	1,800	Jan. 1	By Balance b/d	1,500
"	To Balance c/d	1,000	Dec. 31	" Profit and Loss A/c	1,300
		2,800			2,800
2024			2024		
Dec. 31	To Bad Debts	300	Jan. 1	By Balance b/d	1,000
"	To Profit and Loss A/c	400			
"	To Balance c/d	300			
		1,000			1,000

DISCOUNT ALLOWED ACCOUNT

Date	Particulars	₹	Date	Particulars	₹
2023			2023		
Dec. 31	To Sundry Debtors A/c	600	Dec. 31	By Provision for Discount on Debtors A/c	600
2024			2024		
Dec. 31	To Sundry Debtors A/c	200	Dec. 31	By Provision for Discount on Debtors A/c	200

PROVISION FOR DISCOUNT ON DEBTORS ACCOUNT

Date	Particulars	₹	Date	Particulars	₹
2023			2023		
Dec. 31	To Discount Allowed	600	Jan. 1	By Balance b/d	500
"	To Balance c/d (2% on ₹ 19,000)	380	Dec. 31	" Profit and Loss A/c	480
		980			980
2024			2024		
Dec. 31	To Discount Allowed	200	Jan. 1	By Balance b/d	380
"	To Profit and Loss A/c	66			
"	To Balance c/d (2% on ₹ 5,700)	114			
		380			380

DISCOUNT RECEIVED ACCOUNT

Date	Particulars	₹	Date	Particulars	₹
2023 Dec. 1	To Reserve for Discount on Creditors A/c	300	2023 Dec. 31	By Sundry Creditors A/c	300
2024 Dec. 31	To Reserve for Discount on Creditors A/c	50	2024 Dec. 31	By Sundry Creditors A/c	50

RESERVE FOR DISCOUNT ON CREDITORS ACCOUNT

Date	Particulars	₹	Date	Particulars	₹
2023 Jan. 31	To Balance b/d	400	2023 Dec. 31	By Discount Received	300
Dec. 31	To Profit and Loss A/c	200	"	" Balance c/d	300
		600			600
2024 Jan. 1	To Balance b/d	300	2024 Dec. 31	By Discount Received	50
			"	" Profit and Loss A/c	50
			"	" Balance c/d	200
		300			300

PROFIT AND LOSS ACCOUNT

Particulars	₹	₹	Particulars	₹	₹
2023			2023		
To Bad Debts	1,800		By Discount Received	300	
Add : Provision for Doubtful Debts	1,000		*Add* : New Reserve for Discount	300	
	2,800			600	
Less : Old Provision	1,500	1,300	*Less* : Old Reserve	400	200
To Discount Allowed	600				
Add : New Provision	380				
	980				
Less : Old Provision	500	480			
2024	₹		2024		
To Old Reserve for Discount	300		By Old Provision for Doubtful Debts ₹	1,000	
Less : Discount Received ₹ 50			*Less* : Bad Debts 300		
Less : New Reserve 200	250	50	New Provision 300	600	400
			By Old Provision for Discount	380	
			Less : Discount Allowed 200		
			New Provision 114	314	66

BALANCE SHEET

Liabilities	₹	₹	Assets	₹	₹
2023			2023		
Sundry Creditors	15,000		Sundry Debtors	20,000	
Less : Reserve for Discount on Creditors	300	14,700	*Less* : Provision for D.D.	1,000	
				19,000	
			Less : Provision for Discount on Debtors	380	18,620

2024			2024		
Sundry Creditors	10,000		Sundry Debtors	6,000	
Less : Reserve for Discount on Creditors	200		*Less* : Provision for D/D	300	
		9,800		5,700	
			Less : Provision for Discount on Debtors	114	
					5,586

ILLUSTRATION 7. (Without GST) Mr. A commenced business on 1st April, 2024 introducing the following as initial capital :

Bank Balance ₹ 8,000 ; Land ₹ 20,000 ; Building ₹ 11,200 ; Furniture ₹ 800 ; Motor Van ₹ 2,400.

In addition to the above, the following balances have been extracted from his books :

	₹		₹
Motor Expenses	6,400	Lights and Fans	1,472
Sundry Debtors	7,888	Telephone	816
Sales	3,88,000	Insurance	672
Purchases	3,54,560	Balance at Bank	16,000
Salaries	8,304	Cash in Hand	256
Discount Received	6,416	Sundry Creditors	20,000
Rates	1,104	Addition to Motor Van (as on 1-4-2024)	4,160
Addition to Buildings (as on 1-4-2024)	6,720	Sundry Expenses	3,863
Repairs to Buildings	944	Drawings	11,200
Rent Received	2,743	Income-tax advance	800

Prepare Trading and Profit and Loss Account for the year ending 31st March, 2025 and Balance Sheet as at that date after taking into consideration the following (*a*) Stock as on 31st March, 2025 ₹ 54,000. (*b*) Depreciate : Building 5% p.a., Furniture 6% p.a., Motor Vans 20% p.a. (*c*) Income Tax payable ₹ 5,200; Accountancy charges payable ₹ 400, Light and fans amount due ₹ 320, Telephone amount due ₹ 80. (*d*) Amount paid in advance for Insurance ₹ 240 ; Rates ₹ 160, Motor Expenses ₹ 480. (*e*) Income tax account be written off (*f*) Write off further bad debts ₹ 888. (*g*) Make Provision for Doubtful Debts @ 5%. (*h*) Discount of 2% on debtors and creditors are to be anticipated.

SOLUTION **TRADING AND PROFIT & LOSS ACCOUNT OF MR. A**

for the year ended 31st March, 2025

		₹		₹
To Purchases		3,54,560	By Sales	3,88,000
" Gross Profit c/d		87,440	" Closing Stock	54,000
	₹	4,42,000		4,42,000
" Motor Expenses	6,400		" Gross Profit b/d	87,440
Less : Prepaid	480		" Discount	6,416
		5,920	" Rent	2,743
" Salaries		8,304	" Reserve for Discount on Creditors	400
" Rates	1,104			
Less : Prepaid	160			
		944		

	₹	₹		₹	₹
To Repairs to Buildings		944			
" Light & Fans	1,472				
Add : Outstanding	320				
		1,792			
" Tolophone	816				
Add : Outstanding	80				
		896			
" Insurance	672				
Less : Prepaid	240				
		432			
" Sundry Expenses		3,863			
" Accountancy Charges		400			
To Depreciation on :					
Buildings	896				
Furniture	48				
Motor Car	1,104				
		2,048			
" Bad Debts	888				
Add : New Provision	350				
		1,238			
" Provision for Discount on Debtors		133			
" Net Profit transferred to Capital A/c		70,085			
		96,999			96,999

BALANCE SHEET

as on 31st March, 2025

	₹	₹		₹	₹
Sundry Creditors	20,000		Cash in Hand		256
Less : Reserve for Discount			Cash at Bank		16,000
on Creditors	400		Sundry Debtors	7,888	
		19,600	*Less* : Further Bad Debts	888	
Outstanding Expenses :					
Income Tax Payable	5,200			7,000	
Accountancy	400		*Less* : Provision for D/D	350	
Light & Fans	320			6,650	
Telephone	80		*Less* : Provision for Discount		
		6,000	on Debtors	133	
Capital on 1-4-2024	(1) 42,400				6,517
Add : Net Profit	70,085		Stock		54,000
	1,12,485		Prepaid Expenses :		
Less : Drawings	11,200		Insurance	240	
	1,01,285		Rates	160	
Less : Income Tax			Motor Expenses	480	
Advance & Payable	6,000				880
		95,285	Land		20,000
			Buildings (₹ 11,200+₹ 6,720)	17,920	
			Less : Depreciation	896	
					17,024

		Motor Van (₹ 2,400+₹ 4,160)	6,560	
		Less : Depreciation	1,104	
				5,456
		Furniture	800	
		Less : Depreciation	48	
				752
	1,20,885			1,20,885

(1) Capital is total of assets introduced at the commencement of the business (*i.e.*, ₹ 8,000 + ₹ 20,000 + ₹ 11,200 + ₹ 800 + ₹ 2,400) = ₹ 42,400.

(*xiii*) Deferred Revenue Expenditure

The expenditure done in the initial stage but the benefit of which will also be available in subsequent years is called deferred revenue expenditure. Part of such expenditure will be written off in each year and the rest will be capitalised. The entry for this expenditure (say advertisement ₹ 2,00,000 which will be spread over 5 years) will be:

Profit and Loss A/c	Dr.	₹ 40,000	
To Advertisement A/c			₹ 40,000

Two affected accounts will be :

PROFIT & LOSS A/c

	₹		₹
To Advertisement	40,000		

ADVERTISEMENT A/c

	₹		₹
To Bank	2,00,000	By P. & L. A/c	40,000
		" Balance c/d	1,60,000
	2,00,000		2,00,000

The two-fold effect of such expenditure will be :

(*i*) It is shown on the debit side of Profit and Loss Account, and

(*ii*) is shown on the assets side by way of deduction from capitalised expense.

(*xiv*) Loss of Stock by Fire

In business, the loss of stock may occur due to fire, theft, floods, earthquakes etc. In this case different possibilities may be :

(*a*) all the stock is fully insured.

(*b*) the stock is partly insured.

(*c*) the stock is not insured at all.

(a) If the stock is fully insured, the whole loss (say goods worth ₹ 2,00,000 plus CGST & SGST @ 6% each) will be claimed from the insurance company. Following entry will be passed :

Insurance Co. A/c	Dr.	₹ 2,24,000	
To Trading A/c			₹ 2,00,000
To Input CGST			₹ 12,000
To Input SGST			₹ 12,000

The double effect of this entry will be :

(*i*) It will be shown on the credit side of Trading Account, and

(*ii*) it is shown on the Assets side of Balance Sheet.

(b) *If the stock is partly insured,* the loss of stock covered by insurance policy (₹ 1,95,000) will be claimed from the insurance company and the rest of the amount (say ₹ 29,000) will be loss for the business. Following entry will be passed :

Insurance Co. A/c	Dr.	₹ 1,95,000	
Profit and Loss A/c	Dr.	₹ 29,000	
To Trading A/c			₹ 2,00,000
To Input CGST			₹ 12,000
To Input SGST			₹ 12,000

The two-fold effect of this entry will be :

(*i*) It will be shown on the credit side of Trading Account with the value of stock and shown on the debit side of Profit and Loss Account for that part of the stock which is not insured, and

(*ii*) Loss of Stock by Fire is shown on the Assets side of the Balance Sheet with the amount which is to be realised from the Insurance Co., *i.e.,* that part of the loss which is insured.

(c) *If the stock is not insured at all,* whole of the loss (say ₹ 2,24,000) will be borne by the firm. The entry for this will be :

Profit and Loss A/c	Dr.	₹ 2,24,000	
To Trading A/c			₹ 2,00,000
To Input CGST			₹ 12,000
To Input SGST			₹ 12,000

The double effect of this entry will be :

(*i*) It is shown on the credit side of Trading Account, and

(*ii*) it is shown on the debit side of Profit and Loss Account.

Instead of passing one entry in each case two entries can be passed as under in each case :

(*i*) Loss of Stock by Fire A/c

To Trading A/c

To Input CGST A/c

To Input SGST A/c Or

To Input IGST A/c

(*ii*) Profit & Loss A/c and/or Insurance Co. A/c Dr.

To Loss of Stock by Fire A/c

It may be noted that Input GST (CGST and SGST or IGST), *i.e.,* GST paid at the time when these goods were purchased is reversed and hence input CGST and Input SGST are credited. This is done so that Input GST on the goods which have destroyed cannot be set off against Output GST.

To ascertain the correct gross profit and net profit, it is important to make adjustment of the goods which have destroyed. Therefore, Trading Account is credited with the cost of goods destroyed.

In case goods destroyed are insured, the claim admitted by Insurance Co. is debited and balance, if any, is also debited to Profit and Loss Account.

(*xv*) Reserve Fund

Reserve is created out of the Profit and Loss Account and thus is an appropriation of net profit for strengthening the financial position of the business. Suppose ₹ 2,000 is to be transferred to Reserve Fund from the net profit, the entry will be :

Profit and Loss A/c	Dr.	₹ 2,000	
To Reserve Fund			₹ 2,000

The double effect of this entry will be :

(*i*) It is shown on the debit side of the Profit and Loss Account along with net profit in the inner column, and (*ii*) is shown on the liabilities side of the Balance Sheet. If reserve fund is already there, it will be shown by addition to the existing reserve fund on the liabilities side of the Balance Sheet.

(*xvi*) Goods Distributed as Free Samples

Sometimes in order to promote the sale of goods, some of the produced goods are distributed as free samples. For example, if goods worth ₹ 2,000 plust CGST & SGST @ 6% each are distributed as free samples then it will be an advertisement for the concern and on the other hand stock will be less by such goods. In order to bring this into books of account, the following entry is passed :

Advertisement A/c	Dr.	₹ 2,240	
To Purchases A/c			₹ 2,000
To Input CGST A/c			₹ 120
To Input SGST A/c			₹ 120

The two-fold effect of this entry will be :

(*i*) It is deducted from purchases, and

(*ii*) it is shown on the debit side of Profit and Loss A/c as advertisement expenses.

Input CGST and Input SGST or Input IGST (in case of inter state supply) is credited to respective Input GST account. GST paid on such goods is reversed because GST paid on these goods cannot be set off against GST (CGST and SGST or IGST) collected.

ILLUSTRATION 8. A. Pandit has prepared the following summary of assets and liabilities as on 31st March, 2025 :

Liabilities	₹	₹	*Assets*	₹
Self as on 1st April, 2024	4,070		Plant and Machinery	3,105
Add : Profit for the year	1,735	5,805	Debtors	6,100
Loan		3,000	Stock	4,250
Creditors		5,150	Balance at Bank	500
		13,955		13,955

Upon examination of the books, you ascertain that :

(1) Plant and Machinery cost ₹ 5,500 and should have a net book value of ₹ 3,005.

(2) Debtors were shown after deducting a doubtful debt of ₹ 75. It was agreed that this debt was bad and should be written off and that provision should be made for further debts amounting to ₹ 35, which were considered doubtful.

10 tons of raw material had been valued for stock purposes at cost, ₹ 15 per ton, but was damaged and unsuitable for production. It was considered to be worth ₹ 3 per ton as scrap.

(4) Goods sold for ₹ 300, which was 20% above stock valuation, had been included in sales. These goods awaited collection by the customers and had been included in stock valuation.

(5) Loan interest was outstanding for six months at 6% p.a.

(6) Rent ₹ 150 was due for the quarter ended 31st March, 2025.

(7) The balance at bank as shown by the Cash Book was not in accordance with the Bank statement on which the following debits had been made but not entered in the Cash Book :

	₹
Bank Charges	30
A. Pandit's drawings	520

You are required to prepare :

(*a*) a statement showing the adjustments to the profit for the year, and

(*b*) a Balance Sheet as at 31st March, 2025.

SOLUTION

(*a*) STATEMENT SHOWING ADJUSTMENTS TO THE PROFIT
for the year ending 31st March, 2025

	₹	₹
Profit for the year as per accounts		1,735
Less : Additional depreciation on plant and machinery	100	
Provision for doubtful debts	35	
Loss on revaluation of damaged and unsuitable raw material for production : 10 tons @ ₹ 12 (*i.e.*, ₹ 15—₹ 3) per ton	120	
Goods already sold to a customer wrongly included in closing stock : ₹ 300 × $\frac{100}{120}$	250	
Outstanding interest for 6 months on ₹ 3,000 loan @ 6% p.a. : ₹ 3,000 × $\frac{6}{100} \times \frac{6}{12}$	90	
Rent due for the quarter ending 31-3-2025	150	
Bank charges	30	
		775
Adjusted Profit for the year		960

(*b*) **BALANCE SHEET OF A PANDIT**
as at 31st March, 2025

Liabilities	₹	₹	*Assets*	₹	₹
A. Pandit's Capital Account			Plant & Machinery at Cost	5,500	
Balance on 1-4-2024	4,070		*Less* : Depreciation thereon	2,495	
Add : Profit for the year	960				3,005
	5,030		Stock (₹ 4,250 – ₹ 120 – ₹ 250)		3,880
Less : Drawings	520				
		4,510	Debtors	6,100	
Loan	3,000		*Less* : Provision for		
Add : Outstanding Interest	90		Doubtful Debts	35	
		3,090			6,065
Creditors		5,150			
Rent Due		150			
Bank Overdraft (Bank Balance ₹ 500 – ₹ 30 Bank Charges – ₹ 520 Drawings)		50			
		12,950			12,950

(*xvii*) Manager's Commission

Sometimes in order to increase the profits of the concern, manager is given some percentage of commission on profits of the concern. It can be given at a certain percentage (say 10%) on the net profits (say ₹ 33,000) but *before* charging such commission. In order to record commission payable, *i.e.* 10% of ₹ 33,000 or ₹ 3,300, the following entry will be passed :

Profit and Loss A/c	Dr.	₹ 3,300	
To Commission Payable A/c			₹ 3,300

But sometimes commission is allowed to the manager on the net profit *after* charging such commission. The commission in such a case will be calculated by the following formula :

$$\text{Commission Payable} = \frac{\%\text{ of Commission}}{100 + \text{Rate of Commission}} \times \text{Residual Profit}$$

In the above case, the commission payable will be ₹ 3,000 $\left(i.e., \frac{10}{110} \times ₹\ 33{,}000\right)$. For ₹ 3,000, the same entry will be passed in the books :

Profit and Loss A/c	Dr.	₹ 3,000	
To Commission Payable A/c			₹ 3,000

The two-fold effect of this entry will be :

(*i*) such commission will be shown on the debit side of Profit and Loss Account, and

(*ii*) is shown on the liabilities side of Balance Sheet as commission payable.

(*xviii*) Goods on Sale or Approval Basis

Sometimes the goods are sold to the customers on approval basis. If they approve, it will become sale. If such goods are lying with the customers on the last day of the accounting year and these can be yet returned, it should be treated as stock lying with the customers. In such a case, two entries will be passed.

(*i*) Sales Account Dr.] (with sale price)
To Debtors Account

(*ii*) Stock Account Dr.] (at cost price of goods)
To Trading Account

The two-fold effect of these entries will be :

(*i*) It will be shown on the credit side of Trading Account by way of deduction from the sales at sale price and added to the closing stock at cost price, and

(*ii*) is shown on the Assets side as a deduction from sundry debtors (sale price) and stock at cost on the Assets side of Balance Sheet.

(*xix*) Drawings

If the proprietor (owner) takes goods from the business for personal use, Drawing A/c is debited with cost of goods used for personal use and Purchase A/c is credited because withdrawal shall reduce the purchase meant for sales. It should be remembered that GST paid on goods withdrawn for personal use shall be reversed as this GST paid cannot be set off against the GST collected, the adjustment entry is as follows :

Drawings A/c Dr.
To Purchases A/c
To Input CGST A/c
To Input SGST A/c
(Being goods withdrawn by proprietor for personal use)

(*xx*) Hidden Adjustments

There are certain items given in the trial balance and require adjustment though specially no adjustment is given relating to such items. For example, in the Trial Balance, the following balances are given :

	Dr. ₹	Cr. ₹
6% Loan on (1-4-2024 *i.e.* beginning of the year)		10,000
Interest on Loan (paid during the year)	200	

Actually ₹ 600 interest on loan should have been paid but only ₹ 200 have been paid and the rest ₹ 400 is yet payable and outstanding. In order to bring this into account, the following entry will be passed :

Interest on Loan Account	Dr.	₹ 400	
To Loan Account			₹ 400

The two-fold effect of this entry will be :

(*i*) It will be shown on the debit side of Profit and Loss Account by way of addition to the interest on loan, and

(*ii*) is shown on the liabilities side of Balance Sheet by way of addition to the Loan Account.

Those adjustments which are given clearly after the trial balance are known as self evident adjustments and are opposite of hidden adjustments.

ILLUSTRATION 9. From the following Ledger Balances extracted at the close of trading year ended 31st March, 2025 prepare a Trading Account, Profit and Loss Account and Balance Sheet at that date, after giving effect to the undermentioned adjustments :

	₹		₹
Capital on 1-4-2024	50,000	Business Premises	55,000
Stock on 1-4-2024	8,000	Furniture and Fixtures	2,500
Purchases	20,000	Bills Receivable	3,500
Sales	80,000	Bills Payable	2,500
Returns Inwards	1,500	Sundry Debtors	20,000
Returns Outwards	400	Sundry Creditors	11,800
Wages	6,900	Packing Machinery	4,500
Advertisement	5,500	Smith's Loan (Dr.) @ 10% on 1-4-2024	5,000
Apprenticeship Premium	1,200	Investment	3,000
Interest on Smith's Loan	300	Cash in Hand	250
Proprietor's withdrawals	3,000	Cash at Bank	3,500
Office Expenses	8,050	Payable CGST	2,000
		Payable SGST	2,000

Adjustments to be made for the current period are :

(1) Stock in hand at 31st March, 2025 ₹ 7,000. (2) Apprenticeship Premium is for three years, paid in advance on 1st April, 2024. (3) Interest on Capital to be allowed at 5% for the year. (4) Interest on Drawings to be charged to him as ascertained for the year ₹ 80. (5) ₹ 4,000 out of the Advertisement Expenses are to be carried forward. (6) The Manager is entitled to a commission of 10% of the Net Profit calculated after charging such commission. (7) Included in sales is an amount of ₹ 10,000 representing goods on "sale or return", the customer still having the right to return the goods. The goods were invoiced charging a profit of 20% on sales. (8) Bill Receivable ₹ 5,000 not yet due was discounted on 31st March.

SOLUTION

TRADING AND PROFIT AND LOSS ACCOUNT

for the year ended 31st March, 2025

	₹	₹		₹	₹
To Opening Stock		8,000	By Sales	80,000	
To Purchases	20,000		*Less* : Sales Returns	1,500	
Less : Returns	400			78,500	
		19,600	*Less* : Goods sold		
To Wages		6,900	on return basis	10,000	
To Gross Profit c/d		49,000			68,500

			By Closing Stock	7,000	
			Add : Stock lying with customers sold on return basis	8,000	15,000
		83,500			83,500
To Interest on Capital		2,500	By Gross Profit b/d		49,000
To Advertisement	5,500		By Apprentice Premium	1,200	
Less : Carried Forward	4,000	1,500	*Less* : Received in Advance	800	400
To Loss of Stock by Fire		1,000			
To Office Expenses		8,050	By Interest on Drawings		80
		12,050	By Interest on Smith's Loan	300	
To Manager's Commission (*i.e.*, 1/11 of ₹ 37,930 ₹ 49,980 – ₹ 12,050)		3,448	*Add* : Accrued Interest	200	500
To Net Profit transferred to Capital Account		34,482			
		49,980			49,980

BALANCE SHEET
as on 31st March, 2025

Liabilities	₹	₹	*Assets*	₹	₹
Sundry Creditors		11,800	Cash in Hand		250
CGST Payble		2,000	Cash at Bank		3,500
SGST Payble		2,000	Investment		3,000
			Sundry Debtors	20,000	
Bills Payable		2,500	*Less* : Goods Sold on Return Basis	10,000	10,000
Apprentice Premium received in advance		800			
Manager's Commission Due		3,448	Closing Stock (₹ 7,000 + ₹ 8,000)		15,000
Capital	50,000		Bills Receivable		3,500
Add : Interest	2,500		Smith's Loan	5,000	
Add : Net Profit	34,482		*Add* : Accrued Interest	200	
	86,982				5,200
Less : Drawings & Interest	3,080		Packing Machinery		4,500
		83,902	Furniture & Fittings		2,500
			Business Premises		55,000
			Advertisement		4,000
		1,06,450			1,06,450

Note. There is a contingent liability of ₹ 5,000 on account of a bill receivable discounted but not yet due. GST has been ignored in the absence of information of rates of GST.

ILLUSTRATION 10. Following Trial Balance as at 31st March, 2025 is drawn from books of Raj Kumar a trader :

TRIAL BALANCE
as at 31st March, 2025

Particulars	*Dr.* (₹)	*Cr.* (₹)
Cash in Hand	70,000	
Cash at Bank	1,30,000	

Wages	1,50,000	
Sales		40,00,000
Machinery	19,20,000	
Bills receivable	3,00,000	
Opening Stock	6,40,000	
Creditors		3,00,000
Purchases	25,00,000	
Salaries Return	60,000	
Salaries	2,70,000	
Debtors	8,10,000	
Insurance	1,70,000	
Bad Debts	60,000	
Freight on Purchases	48,000	
Capital		28,00,000
Commission		38,000
Input CGST	5,000	
Input SGST	5,000	
Total	71,38,000	71,38,000

Taking into consideration the following adjustments, prepare Trading and Profit and Loss Account for the year ended 31st March, 2025 and a Balance Sheet as at that date. Also, pass Journal entries for the adjustments.

1. Using Stock ₹ 8,00,000
2. Outstanding salaries ₹ 32,000 and outstanding wages ₹ 20,000. Salaries and wages are not subject to levy of GST.
3. Prepaid Insurance ₹ 10,000 and Accrued commission ₹ 12,000. Prepaid Insurance and Accrued commission are subject to levy of GST @ 6% each.
4. Charge depreciation on Machinery @ 10% p.a.

SOLUTION

JOURNAL

Date	Particulars		L.F.	Dr. (₹)	Cr. (₹)
March 31	Closing Stock A/c	Dr.		8,00,000	
	To Trading A/c				8,00,000
	(Being the closing stock recorded)				
March 31	Salaries A/c	Dr.		32,000	
	Wages A/c	Dr.		20,000	
	To Outstanding Expenses A/c				50,000
	(Being the adjustments for Outstanding Salaries and wages)				
March 31	Prepaid Insurance Premium A/c	Dr.		10,000	
	To Insurance Premium A/c				10,000
	(Being the adjustment for Prepaid Insurance premium)				
	Note : Input CGST and SGST accounts will not be credited because GST is payable when premium is paid.				

March 31	Accrued Commission A/c Dr.		13,440	
	To Commission A/c			12,000
	To Output CGST A/c			720
	To Output SGST A/c			720
	(Being the adjustment for accrued commission)			
March 31	Depreciation A/c		1,92,000	
	To Machinery A/c			1,92,000
	(Being the depreciation charged on Machinery)			

TRADING AND PROFIT AND LOSS ACCOUNT

for the year ended 31st March, 2025

Dr. *Cr.*

Particulars	₹	₹	*Particulars*	₹	₹
To Opening Stock		6,40,000	By Sales	40,00,000	
To Purchases		25,00,000	*Less* : Sales Return	60,000	39,40,000
To Freight on Purchases		48,000	By Closing Stock		8,00,000
To Wages	1,50,000				
Add : Outstanding	20,000	1,70,000			
To Gross Profit c/d		13,82,000			
(Transferred to Profit & Loss A/c)					
		47,40,000			47,40,000
To Salaries	2,70,000		By Gross Profit b/d		13,82,000
Add : Outstanding	32,000	3,02,000	By Commission	38,000	
To Insurance	1,70,000		*Add* : Accrued	12,000	50,000
Less : Prepaid Insurance	10,000	1,60,000			
To Bad Debts		60,000			
To Depreciation on Machinery		1,92,000			
(₹ 19,20,000 × 10/100)					
To Net Profit transferred to Capital A/c		7,18,000			
		14,32,000			14,32,000

BALANCE SHEET OF RAJ KUMAR

as at 31st March, 2025

Liabilities		₹	*Assets*		₹
Capital	₹		**Fixed Assets**	₹	
Opening Balance	28,00,000		Machinery	19,20,000	
Add : Net Profit	7,18,000	35,18,000	*Less* : Depreciation	1,92,000	17,28,000
Current Liabilities			**Current Assets**		
Sundry Creditors		3,00,000	Cash in Hand		70,000
Outstanding Salaries		32,000	Cash at Bank		1,30,000
Outstanding Wages		20,000	Bills Receivable		3,00,000
			Debtors		8,10,000

		Input CGST	5,000	
		Less : Output CGST	720	4,280
		Input SGST	5,000	
		Less : Output CGST	720	4,280
		Prepaid Insurance		10,000
		Accrued Commission		13,440
		Closing Stock		8,00,000
	38,70,000			38,70,000

Some Typical Adjustments

Adjustment 1

Included in the creditors are the amounts owed by the proprietor for stationery ₹ 300 and coal ₹ 200. These items have been debited to advertisement and fuel accounts respectively. The available figures in the Trial Balance are :

Debit Balances	₹	*Credit Balances*	₹
Advertisements	3,300	Capital	50,000
Fuel	6,200	Creditors	10,500

Make adjustment entry and show its effect on final accounts.

SOLUTION

Adjustment Entry

Drawings A/c	Dr.	₹ 500	
To Advertisement A/c			₹ 300
To Fuel A/c			₹ 200

(Amount owed by the proprietor wrongly charged to advertisement and fuel but now adjusted.)

Drawings of ₹ 500 will reduce capital. Advertisement and fuel will be shown on the debit side of the Profit and Loss Account with reduced figures *i.e.*, advertisement ₹ 3,000 (*i.e.*, ₹ 3,300 – ₹ 300) and fuel ₹ 6,000 (*i.e.*, ₹ 6,200 – ₹ 200).

Adjustment 2

Private purchases amounting to ₹ 500 had been included in the purchases day book. Give adjusting entry and its effect on final accounts.

SOLUTION

Adjusting Entry

Drawings A/c	Dr.	₹ 500	
To Purchases A/c			₹ 500

(Private purchases wrongly debited to purchases, now adjusted).

The effect on final accounts will be that drawings of ₹ 500 will reduce capital and purchases will be reduced by ₹ 500 on the debit side of the Trading Account.

Adjustment 3

(*a*) Included in the stock in the beginning of ₹ 10,300, the stock of stationery of ₹ 300.

(*b*) Included in the general expenses account, the expenses on stationery purchased ₹ 500.

(*c*) Included in the stock at the end of ₹ 10,400, the stock of stationery ₹ 400.

How will you adjust the figures of opening and closing stock for final accounts purposes ? Show the amount of stationery used to be shown in the Profit and Loss Account.

SOLUTION

Opening stock will be shown with reduced figures, *i.e.*, ₹ 10,000 (₹ 10,300 – ₹ 300) on the debit side of the Trading Account. Stock at the end *i.e.*, ₹ 10,000 (₹ 10,400 – ₹ 400) will be shown on the credit side of the Trading Account and on the assets side of the Balance Sheet. The figure for stationery used to be shown on the debit side of the Profit and Loss Account is :

	₹
Stock of Stationery (Beginning)	300
Add : Stationery purchased during the year	500
	800
Less : Stationery in hand at the end of the period	400
Stationery used during the period	400

Adjustment 4

Following is the Trial Balance as on 31st March, 2025 :

	Dr.	Cr.
Loan at 10%		₹ 36,000
Interest on Loan	₹ 1,850	

Adjustment. Interest on loan is to be charged for full year having regard to the fact that ₹ 2,000 was paid back on 30th June and ₹ 2,000 on 30th September.

SOLUTION

Calculation of Outstanding Interest

		₹
Loan on 1st April, (₹ 36,000 + ₹ 4,000)	=	40,000
Interest on ₹ 40,000 at 10% p.a. for 3 months	=	1,000
Interest on ₹ 38,000 at 10% p.a. for 3 months	=	950
Interest on ₹ 36,000 at 10% p.a. for 6 months	=	1,800
		3,750
Less : Interest already paid as per T.B.		1,850
Interest outstanding		1,900

Adjustment Entry

Interest A/c	Dr.	₹ 1,900	
To Outstanding Interest A/c			₹ 1,900

Interest account will appear in the Profit and Loss A/c (Dr. side) at ₹ 3,750 (*i.e.*, ₹ 1,850 + ₹ 1,900) and ₹ 1,900 outstanding interest will be shown on the liabilities side of the Balance Sheet.

Adjustment 5

One machine whose value in books as at 1st April 2024 stood at ₹ 12,000 was disposed off on 31st December, 2024 for ₹ 8,750 in part exchange of a machine costing ₹ 19,000 and an invoice for the amount of ₹ 10,250 was entered in the purchases book. Give adjusting entry. No depreciation and GST.

SOLUTION

Adjusting Entry		₹	₹
New Plant A/c	Dr.	19,000	
Profit and Loss A/c	Dr.	3,250	
To Old Plant A/c			12,000
" Purchases A/c			10,250

Working Notes :

(1) *Loss on the Sale of Plant*

	₹
Book value of machine	12,000
Less : Adjustment in part exchange	8,750
Loss to be debited to Profit and Loss A/c	3,250

(2) New Asset is to be debited with ₹ 19,000.

(3) Old plant is to be credited with ₹ 12,000 as it is sold.

(4) Net Balance (₹ 19,000 – ₹ 8,750) ₹ 10,250 wrongly debited to Purchases Account now should be credited to Purchases Account.

Adjustment 6

Following figures are given in the Trial Balance :

	Dr.	Cr.
	₹	₹
Income tax	4,000	
Income tax advance payment	500	
Interest on advance payment of tax		20

Show how you will deal them.

SOLUTION

Income tax ₹ 4,000 and income tax advance payment ₹ 500 will be treated as paid on behalf of the proprietor and will be treated as drawings. So ₹ 4,500 will be deducted from capital on the liabilities side of the Balance Sheet. Interest on advance payment of tax, *i.e.*, ₹ 20 will be personal income of the proprietor and will be added to capital account on the liabilities side of the Balance Sheet.

Adjustment 7

A manufacturer of medicines used medicines for personal use worth ₹ 300, distributed as samples worth ₹ 2,500 and gave to his office staff worth ₹ 1,000 for their personal use. Give adjusting entry ignoring GST.

SOLUTION

		₹	₹
Drawings A/c	Dr.	300	
Advertisement A/c	Dr.	2,500	
Salaries A/c	Dr.	1,000	
To Purchases A/c			3,800

Notes :

(*i*) Medicines for personal use should be debited to Drawings A/c.

(*ii*) Medicines for distribution as samples should be charged to Profit and Loss A/c as Advertisement.

(*iii*) Medicines given to employees should be added to the salaries.

(*iv*) All medicines used for these purposes should be credited to Purchases Account as these are given at cost price.

Adjustment 8

Included in the trial balance are debtors of ₹ 61,000 including the amount of ₹ 2,000 in respect of a dishonoured bill of Tirath Ram.

Tirath Ram becomes insolvent and a dividend of 50% has been declared by the official receiver. Create provision for Doubtful Debts @ 5% on debtors.

SOLUTION

	₹
Total Debtors	61,000
Less : Bad Debts (on account of insolvency of Tirath Ram)	1,000
	60,000

Less : Amount surely recoverable	1,000
Remaining Debtors	59,000
Provision for Doubtful Debts	5% on ₹ 59,000 = ₹ 2,950

Note. Provision is to be created on doubtful debtors only, *i.e.*, out of total debtors bad debts and recoverable surely are to be deducted.

Adjustment 9

In the trial balance debtors appear at ₹ 12,000 and creditors ₹ 7,400. Make provision for doubtful debts at 5% on debtors and reserve for discount on creditors at $2\frac{1}{2}$% after considering the fact that included in the debtors is the amount of ₹ 2,000 due from X and included in creditors is the amount of ₹ 1,000 due to him.

SOLUTION

(*i*) Reduce debtors and creditors by ₹ 1,000.
(*ii*) Provision for doubtful debts will be 5% on ₹ 11,000, *i.e.*, (₹ 12,000 – ₹ 1,000) = ₹ 550.
(*iii*) Reserve for discount on creditors will be $2\frac{1}{2}$% on ₹ 6,400, *i.e.* (₹ 7,400 – ₹ 1,000) = ₹ 160.

Adjustment 10

On 1st April, 2024 Loose Tools Account showed the balance of ₹ 10,000 and on 31st March, 2025 loose tools were revalued at ₹ 12,500. During the year loose tools were purchased for ₹ 15,000 in respect of which carriage of ₹ 300 was paid. These items were charged to Purchases Account and Carriage Account respectively. Make adjusting entries. GST is to be ignored.

SOLUTION

			₹	₹
2025 March 31	Loose Tools A/c	Dr.	15,300	
	To Purchases A/c			15,000
	To Carriage A/c			300
	(Being purchases of loose tools and carriage paid on the same wrongly debited to Purchases and Carriage, now adjusted)			
"	Depreciation A/c	Dr.	12,800	
	To Loose Tools			12,800
	(Being depreciation ₹ 12,800 (*i.e.,* ₹ 10,000 + ₹ 15,300 – ₹ 12,500 value of loose tools on 31-3-2025)			

Adjustment 11

A manufacturer sells away a part of the plant for ₹ 5,500 on 30th September 2025 at a profit of 25% on book value as on 1st April, 2025. Depreciation is written off at 10% p.a. Give Plant Account along with working notes.

SOLUTION

PLANT A/c

	₹		₹
To Balance b/d (1)	4,400	By Depreciation (2)	220
" Profit & Loss A/c	1,320	" Bank	5,500
	5,720		5,720

Working Notes :

(*1*) ***Calculation of book value on 1-4-2025***

Profit on Sale of ₹ 5,500 = ₹ 5,500 $\times \frac{25}{125}$

= ₹ 1,100

∴ Book value on 1-4-2025 = ₹ 5,500 – ₹ 1,100

= ₹ 4,400

(*2*) ***Depreciation for six months from 1-4-2025 to 30-9-2025***

$$₹\,4{,}400 \times \frac{10}{100} \times \frac{6}{12} = ₹\ 220$$

(*3*) ***Calculation of profit on sale***

	₹
Book Value on 1-4-2025	4,400
Less : Depreciation for 6 months	220
Book value on 30-9-2025	4,180

Profit on Sale = ₹ 5,500 – ₹ 4,180 = ₹ 1,320

Treatment of Income Tax in Accounts

Income Tax. Income tax is a direct tax that Government imposes on financial income generated by the individual as well as all business entities like sole proprietorship firm, partnership firm, joint stock companies etc.

Income tax is neither an expense nor a loss for a business. It is an obligation of an entity to pay to the Government from the Income Earned during the financial year.

For a Sole Proprietorship, Income Tax is treated as drawings of the proprietor.

In such a case following Journal Entries should be passed :

(*i*) When income tax is paid :

Income Tax A/c Dr.

To Cash or Bank A/c

(Being the income tax paid)

(*ii*) Treating income tax as drawings of the proprietor :

Drawings A/c Dr.

To Income Tax A/c

(Being the income tax paid transferred to Drawings A/c)

Withholding Tax. Withholding tax is a government requirement for the payer of an item of income to withhold or deduct tax from the payment and pay that tax to the Government.

In India, Income Tax Act provides for deduction of tax at source on the payments made by any assessee. These provisions are also applicable in case of payment made to non-residents. For example, if the business entity makes payment to its employees for salaries, or pays interest to its investors, then its obligation of the business entity to deduct tax and make the balance payment. The tax deducted has to be deposited in the Government Account in due course of time.

Journal Entry for Tax Deducted at Source (TDS)

(*i*) When company pays the money and deducts the TDS

Expense A/c (Eg. Salary) Dr.

To Mr. Nikhil's A/c or Bank A/c

To TDS A/c

(Being payment made after deducting TDS)

(ii) When TDS is deposited to the Government A/c
TDS A/c
To Bank or Cash A/c
(Being TDS deposited to Government Account)

Note : TDS deducted while making the payment is the current liability and will be shown on the liabilities side of the Balance Sheet.

FINAL ACCOUNTS OF PARTNERSHIP

Final accounts of partnership firm are prepared on the same principles as is done in case of a sole trader. If there are no adjustments relating to partners, then distribution of profit is made in the profit & loss account and no profit and loss appropriation account is opened. But if there are certain adjustments relating to partners such as interest on capital, salary to any partner, interest on drawings etc. then these are not shown in the Profit and Loss Account and net profit before adjustments is transferred to Profit & Loss Appropriation A/c. In this account interest on partners capital, salary or commission to any partner is debited and interest on drawings is credited. Balance of this account represents profit or loss and is distributed among the partners in their profit sharing ratio.

ILLUSTRATION 11. From the following Trial Balance of a firm of P and Q as at 31st March, 2025, prepare final accounts :

	Dr.	*Cr.*
	₹	₹
P's Capital Account		41,000
Q's Capital Account		40,000
P's Drawings	4,000	
Q's Drawings	3,000	
Goodwill	40,000	
Sales		1,60,000
Sundry Creditors		14,500
Returns Outward		2,500
Bills Payable		8,900
Ouput CGST		12,000
Output SGST		12,000
Furniture	5,000	
Purchases	85,000	
Sundry Debtors	40,500	
Returns Inward	1,500	
Rent	3,750	
Postage and Telegrams	500	
Advertising	9,000	
Opening Stock	11,500	
Cash in hand	16,000	
Wages	14,000	
Telephone Charges	500	
Salaries	12,250	
Printing and Stationery	740	
Commission Paid	5,000	

Travelling Expenses	2,000	
Carriage Inward	5,800	
Motor Vans	20,860	
Plant & Machinery	10,000	
	2,90,900	2,90,900

***Adjustments* :**

(*a*) Write off ₹ 250 from Furniture; 10% on Plant and Machinery and 20% on Motor Vans.

(*b*) Create a provision of 5% on sundry debtors for doubtful debts.

(*c*) Write off one-fifth of advertising expenses.

(*d*) Provide for interest on capitals at 6% p.a.

(*e*) Q is entitled to a salary of ₹ 1,800 p.a.

(*f*) Stock on 31st March, 2025 ₹ 20,000.

(*g*) Provide for interest on drawings at 10% p.a.

(*h*) A case against the firm for ₹ 50,000 is pending in the court.

SOLUTION

TRADING AND PROFIT & LOSS ACCOUNT OF P AND Q

for the year ended 31st March, 2025

		₹			₹	₹
To Opening Stock	₹	11,500	By	Sales	1,60,000	
" Purchases	85,000			*Less* : Returns	1,500	
Less : Returns	2,500					1,58,500
		82,500	"	Closing Stock		20,000
" Wages		14,000				
" Carriage Inward		5,800				
" Gross Profit c/d		64,700				
		1,78,500				1,78,500
To Salaries		12,250	By	Gross Profit b/d		64,700
" Rent		3,750				
" Postage and Telegrams		500				
" Advertising $\left(\frac{1}{5}\text{ of ₹ }9,000\right)$		1,800				
" Telephone Charges		500				
" Printing & Stationery		740				
" Commission Paid		5,000				
" Travelling Expenses		2,000				
" Provision for D/D (5% of ₹ 40,500)		2,025				
" Depreciation	₹					
on Furniture	250					
on Plant & Machinery (10% of ₹ 10,000)	1,000					
on Motor Vans (20% of ₹ 20,860)	4,172					
		5,422				
" Net Profit c/d		30,713				
		64,700				64,700

Dr. **PROFIT & LOSS APPROPRIATION ACCOUNT** Cr.

for the year ended 31st March, 2025

		₹			₹
To Q's Salary		1,800	By Net Profit b/d		30,713
To Interest on Capital :			By Interest on Drawings :	₹	
P (6% on ₹ 65,000)		3,900	P (10% on ₹ 4,000 for 1/2 year)	200	
Q (6% on ₹ 40,000)		2,400	Q (10% on ₹ 3,000 for 1/2 year)	150	
To Profit to Capital A/cs	₹				350
P	11,482				
Q	11,481				
		22,963			
		31,063			31,063

BALANCE SHEET OF P & Q

as on 31st March, 2025

Liabilities		₹		*Assets*		₹
P's Capital Account :		₹		Goodwill	₹	40,000
Balance as at 1-4-2024		41,000		Furniture	5,000	
Add : Interest on Capital		3,900		*Less* : Depreciation	250	
Add : Net Profit		11.482				4,750
	₹	56,382		Plant & Machinery	10,000	
Less : Drawings	4,000			*Less* : Depreciation	1,000	
Int. on Drawings	200					9,000
		4,200		Motor Vans	20,860	
			52,182	*Less* : Depreciation	4,172	
Q's Capital Account :						16,688
Balance as at 1-4-2024		40,000		Sundry Debtors	40,500	
Add : Net Profit		11,481		*Less* : Provision	2,025	
Interest on Capital		2,400				38,475
Salary Payable		1,800		Cash in hand		16,000
	₹	55,681		Closing Stock		20,000
Less : Drawings	3,000			Advertising (to the extent not written off)		7,200
Int. on Drawings	150					
		3,150				
			52,531			
Sundry Creditors			14,500			
Bills Payable			8,900			
Output CGST			12,000			
Output SGST			12,000			
			1,52,113			1,52,113

Note : Contingent liability ₹ 50,000 for a case pending against the firm in the court not settled as yet.

MISCELLANEOUS ILLUSTRATIONS

ILLUSTRATION 12. From the following trial balance of G. Sahai and additional information as furnished prepare a Trading and Profit and Loss Account for the year ended 31st March, 2025 and a Balance Sheet as on that date :

Debit	₹	*Credit*	₹
Material consumed	7,50,000	Capital	2,00,000
Stock on 31-3-2025	1,00,000	Sales	10,00,000
Debtors	50,000	Creditors	20,000
Wages—productive	1,00,000	Commission	3,000
Wages—other	10,000	Discount	4,000
Salaries	12,000	Special Rebates	2,000
Rent, rates and taxes	3,000	Suspense Account of N.K. Sahai	40,000
Electric charges	2,000	Output CGST (after set off of Input CGST)	10,000
Telephone	1,000	Output SGST (after set off of Input SGST)	10,000
Delivery charges	2,000		
Freight and insurance on purchases	2,000		
Depreciation	5,000		
Commission	2,000		
Discount	6,000		
Special rebates	1,000		
Postage and telegram	2,000		
Travelling expenses	5,000		
Plant & machinery	57,000		
Furniture	14,000		
Land & building	98,000		
Suspense account of S.K. Sahai	15,000		
Drawings	9,000		
Insurance	2,000		
Books and library	5,000		
Cash in hand and at bank	26,000		
Loan to Ghanshyam	10,000		
	12,89,000		12,89,000

Additional Information :

(*a*) Salary includes proprietor's monthly drawings of ₹ 250 p.m.

(*b*) Divide rent, electricity and telephone between factory and office in the ratio of 3 : 2.

(*c*) An analysis of N.K. Sahai's account reveals that goods costing ₹ 60,000 were sent to him under consignment agreement. All the goods were sold (except 1/4th which were valued at cost) for ₹ 1,00,000 against which a cheque of ₹ 40,000 was received. No entry was passed except that for cash received. Commission at the rate of 10% is payable to N.K. Sahai.

(*d*) Similarly, a joint venture agreement was entered into with S.K. Sahai for which an advance of ₹ 15,000 was made. It is now ascertained that the venture earned a profit of ₹ 10,000 of which G. Sahai is entitled to get 3/5th share.

(*e*) Depreciation has been provided on the following assets :

	₹
(*i*) Plant and machinery (chargeable to factory)	3,000
(*ii*) Furniture and fittings	1,000
(*iii*) Land and building	1,000

(*f*) Insurance premium includes ₹ 500 for the life of G. Sahai.

(*g*) One year interest on loan to Ghanshyam has accrued @ 9%.

SOLUTION

TRADING AND PROFIT & LOSS ACCOUNT OF G. SAHAI
for the year ended 31st March, 2025

	₹	₹		₹	₹
To Material consumed	7,50,000		By Sales	10,00,000	
Less : Special rebates	2,000		*Less* : Special rebates	1,000	
	7,48,000				9,99,000
Less : Goods sent on consignment	60,000				
		6,88,000			
To Wages—Productive		1,00,000			
To Freight and insurance on purchases		2,000			
To Rent, rates & taxes		1,800			
To Electric charges		1,200			
To Telephone		600			
To Depreciation on plant & machinery		3,000			
To Gross Profit c/d		2,02,400			
		9,99,000			9,99,000
To Wages—other		10,000	By Gross Profit b/d		2,02,400
To Salaries	12,000		By Commission		3,000
Less : Proprietor's monthly drawings	3,000		By Discount		4,000
		9,000	By Profit on Consignment (1)		45,000
To Rent, rates and taxes		1,200	By Profit on Joint Venture (2)		6,000
To Electric charges		800	By Accrued interest on loan		
To Telephone		400	(9% for one year on ₹ 10,000)		900
To Delivery charges		2,000			
To Depreciation :					
Furniture & Fittings	1,000				
Land & Building	1,000				
		2,000			
To Commission		2,000			
To Discount		6,000			
To Postage & Telegrams		2,000			
To Travelling expenses		5,000			
To Insurance	2,000				
Less : For personal life paid	500				
		1,500			
To Net Profit transferred to Capital A/c		2,19,400			
		2,61,300			2,61,300

BALANCE SHEET OF MR. G. SAHAI
as on 31st March, 2025

Liabilities	₹	₹	*Assets*	₹	₹
Creditors		20,000	Cash in hand & at bank		26,000
CGST Payable		10,000	Sundry Debtors	₹	50,000
SGST Payable		10,000	Closing Stock	1,00,000	
Capital	2,00,000		Consignment Stock	15,000	
Add : Profit	2,19,400				1,15,000
	4,19,400		Loan to Ghanshyam	10,000	

Less : Drawings (₹ 9,000 + ₹ 3,000 + ₹ 500)	12,500		*Add* : Interest Accrued	900	10,900
		4,06,900	N.K. Sahai [₹ 1,00,000 – ₹ 40,000 – ₹ 10,000] (1)		50,000
			S.K. Sahai (₹ 15,000 + ₹ 6,000)		21,000
			Land & Buildings		98,000
			Furniture		14,000
			Plant & Machinery		57,000
			Books & Library		5,000
		4,46,900			4,46,900

Working Notes :

(1) **CONSIGNMENT ACCOUNT**

	₹		₹
To Goods sent on Consignment	60,000	By N.K. Sahai	1,00,000
To N.K. Sahai (Commission)	10,000	By Consignment Stock A/c	15,000
To Profit & Loss A/c	45,000		
	1,15,000		1,15,000

N.K. SAHAI'S ACCOUNT

	₹		₹
To Consignment A/c	1,00,000	By Balance b/d (as per T.B.)	40,000
		By Consignment A/c	10,000
		By Balance c/d	50,000
	1,00,000		1,00,000

(2) **S.K. SAHAI'S ACCOUNT**

	₹		₹
To Balance b/d	15,000	By Balance c/d	21,000
To Profit on Joint Venture	6,000		
	21,000		21,000

ILLUSTRATION 13. Mr. Reddy a retired Government Officer who started business in Kolkata in April, 2021 gives you the following balances relating to the year ending 31st March, 2025.

	₹		₹
Sundry Debtors	84,000	Salaries	18,910
Sundry Creditors	38,000	Suspense Account (*Dr.*)	3,000
Stock on Trade (1-4-2024)	40,000	Bad Debts	1,200
Machineries	56,000	Reserve for Doubtful Debts	3,200
Furniture	8,500	Purchases	4,95,000
Bills Receivable	4,900	Sales	6,76,000
Bills Payable	3,700	Printing Charges	2,300
Building Rent	9,600	Postage	1,500
Cash in hand	4,250	Travelling Expenses	7,900
Cash at Bank	17,394	Telephone	1,600
Drawings	12,000	Miscellaneous Expenses	41,806
Capital Account (*Cr.*)	90,000	Insurance	1,040

***Additional Information* :**

1. An old Furniture which stood at ₹ 1,200 in the books on 1st April, 2024 was disposed of at ₹ 580 on 30th September, 2024 in part exchange for a new furniture costing ₹ 1,040. A net invoice at ₹ 460 was passed through the Purchases Day Book.
2. Sales include ₹ 20,000 as Hire Purchase Sales. Hire Purchase Sales are determined after adding 33-1/3 per cent on cost price. 40 per cent of the instalments have not fallen due as yet (Profit or Loss on H.P. Sales is to be shown in P. & L. Account).
3. Suspense Account represents money advanced to Sales Manager who was sent to Delhi in August, 2024 for Sales promotion. On returning to Kolkata he submitted a statement disclosing that ₹ 1,200 was incurred for travelling, ₹ 500 for legal expenses and ₹ 900 for miscellaneous expenses. The balance lying with him is yet to be refunded.
4. Mr. Reddy desires to change the method of depreciation on machineries from straight line method (*i.e.*, on original cost) to diminishing balance method with retrospective effect from April, 2021 and adjust the difference in the accounting year 2024-25. The rate of depreciation will, however, remain unchanged.
5. Business is carried on in a rented house. The ground floor being 50 per cent of the accommodation is used for business. Mr. Reddy lives with his family on the first floor.
6. Total bad debts for the year amounted to ₹ 2,000. Provision for doubtful debts is to be maintained at 5 per cent on outstanding debtors.
7. Insurance premium covers a period of one month in advance.
8. Depreciation on time basis is to be provided on Machineries at 10 per cent p.a. as instructed and on Furniture at 5 per cent p.a. on diminishing balance method.
9. Closing Stock amounted to ₹ 50,000.

Prepare Mr. Reddy's Trading and Profit and Loss Account for the year ended 31st March, 2025 and a Balance Sheet as on that date after taking into consideration the above mentioned information. Ignore GST.

SOLUTION]

TRADING AND PROFIT & LOSS ACCOUNT OF MR. REDDY

for the year ended 31st March, 2025

	₹	₹		₹	₹
To Opening Stock		40,000	By Sales	6,76,000	
To Purchases	4,95,000		*Less* : H.P. Sales	20,000	
Less : Goods Sold on					6,56,000
H.P. (Cost)	15,000		By Closing Stock		50,000
	4,80,000				
Less : Purchases of Furniture	460				
		4,79,540			
To Gross Profit c/d		1,86,460			
		7,06,000			7,06,000
To Building Rent	9,600		By Gross Profit b/d		1,86,460
Less : For personal use	4,800		By Profit on Hire Purchase (*i.e.*,		
		4,800	₹ 20,000 – ₹ 15,000 –		
To Salaries		18,910	₹ 2,000) (1)		3,000
To Bad Debts	1,200		By Depreciation written back due to		
Add Further Bad Debts	800		change of method	(2)	2,320
	2,000				

Add : Provision for Doubtful Debts (5% on ₹ 75,200 (*i.e.* ₹ 84,000 – ₹ 8,000 – ₹ 800)	3,760			
	5,760			
Less : Old Provision	3,200			
		2,560		
To Printing Charges		2,300		
To Postage		1,500		
To Travelling Expenses (₹ 7,900 +₹ 1,200)		9,100		
To Telephone		1,600		
To Miscellaneous Expenses (₹ 41,806 + ₹ 900)		42,706		
To Legal Expenses		500		
Tc Insurance	1,040			
Less : Prepaid	80			
		960		
To Loss on Sale of Furniture (₹ 1,200 – ₹ 20 – ₹ 580)		590		
To Depreciation :				
Machinery (10% on ₹ 58,320)	5,832			
Furniture (5% on ₹ 7,300 for one year +5% on ₹ 1,200 for 6 months + 5% on ₹ 1,040 for 6 months *i.e.*, ₹ 365 + ₹ 30 +₹ 26)	421			
		6,253		
To Net Profit transferred to Capital Account		1,00,001		
		1,91,780		1,91,780

BALANCE SHEET OF MR. REDDY

as on 31st March, 2025

Liabilities		₹	*Assets*		₹
Sundry Creditors		38,000	Cash in hand		4,250
Bills Payable	₹	3,700	Cash at Bank		17,394
Capital	90,000		Bills Receivable		4,900
Add : Net Profit	1,00,001		Advance to Sales Manager		
			(₹ 3,000 – ₹ 2,600)		400
Less : Drawings	1,90,001		Closing Stock		50,000
(₹ 12,000 + ₹ 4,800)	16,800	1,73,201	Stock out on H.P.		
			(₹ 8,000– ₹ 2,000)	₹	6,000
			Sundry Debtors	84,000	
			Less : H.P. Debtors	8,000	
				76,000	
			Less : Further Bad Debts	800	
				75,200	
			Less : Provision for Doubtful Debts	3,760	
					71,440

	₹		₹	₹
		Prepaid Insurance		80
		Machinery at beginning of the year (2)	58,320	
		Less : Depreciation	5,832	
				52,488
		Furniture	8,500	
		Less : Sold during the year	1,200	
			7,300	
		Add : Purchased during the year	1,040	
			8,340	
		Less : Depreciation (₹ 365 + ₹ 26)	391	
				7,949
	2,14,901			2,14,901

Working Notes :

(1) ***Calculation of H.P. Profit***

H.P. TRADING ACCOUNT

	₹		₹
To Purchases	15,000	By Sales	20,000
To Stock Reserve (25% on ₹ 8,000)	2,000		
" Profit & Loss A/c	3,000		
	20,000		20,000

(2) ***Calculation of Depreciation Written Back***

Value of Machinery on 1-4-2021 = $\frac{₹\ 56,000 \times 100}{70}$ = ₹ 80,000

Depreciation for three years on Straight Line Method = ₹ 24,000

Depreciation for three years on Diminishing Balance Method [₹ 8,000 + ₹ 7,200 + ₹ 6,480] = ₹ 21,680

∴ Excess depreciation written back to profit & loss account = ₹ 24,000 – 21,680 = ₹ 2,320.

∴ Value of Machinery on 1-4-2024 according to Diminishing Balance Method = ₹ 80,000 – ₹ 8,000 – ₹ 7,200 – ₹ 6,480 = ₹ 58,320.

ILLUSTRATION 14. (*With GST*) Following Trial Balance is extracted from the books of a trader as at 31st March, 2025.

TRIAL BALANCE

as at 31st March, 2025

Particulars	*Dr. (₹)*	*Cr. (₹)*
Furniture and Fittings	1,64,000	
Motor Vehicles	7,25,000	
Building	8,50,000	
Capital A/c		14,00,000
Bad Debts	13,000	
Provision for Doubtful Debts		20,000
Sundry Debtors	4,00,000	

Sundry Creditors		3,00,000
Opening Stock	3,66,000	
Purchases	6,47,000	
Sales		18,45,000
Bank Loan		3,05,000
Sales Return	20,000	
Purchases Return		20,000
Advertising	55,000	
Interest	21,800	
Commission received		30,000
Cash	75,000	
Insurance	1,25,000	
General Expenses	88,200	
Salaries	3,50,000	
Input CGST	50,000	
Input SGST	50,000	
Output CGST		40,000
Output SGST		40,000
	40,00,000	40,00,000

The following adjustments are to be made :

1. Stock in hand on 31st March 2025 was ₹ 3,75,000.
2. Depreciate Building @ 5%, Furniture and Fittings @ 10% and Motor vehicles @ 20%.
3. ₹ 8,500 due for Interest on Bank loan.
4. Salaries ₹ 30,000 and Taxes ₹ 12,000 are outstanding.
5. Insurance amounted to ₹ 10,000 is prepaid. CGST and SGST is paid at 6% each.
6. One-third of the commission received in respect of work to be done next year. IGST is charged @ 12%.
7. Write off further ₹ 10,000 as bad debts and Provision for Doubtful Debts is to be made equal to 5% on Sundry Debtors.

Prepare Trading and Profit and Loss Account for the year ended 31st March 2025 and Balance Sheet as at that date.

SOLUTION

TRADING AND PROFIT & LOSS ACCOUNT

for the year ended 31st March, 2025

Particulars		₹	Particulars		₹
To Opening Stock		3,66,000	By Sales	18,45,000	
To Purchases	6,47,000		*Less* : Sale Return	20,000	18,25,000
Less : Purchase Return	20,000	6,27,000	By Closing Stock		3,75,000
To Gross Profit c/d		12,07,000			
(Transferred to Profit and Loss A/c)					
		22,00,000			22,00,000
To Salaries	3,50,000		By Gross Profit b/d		12,07,000
Add : Outstanding	30,000	3,80,000	By Commission Received	30,000	
To General Expenses		88,200	*Less* : Received in adv.	10,000	20,000

To Outstanding Taxes		12,000		
To Insurance	1,25,000			
Less : Prepaid Insurance	10,000	1,15,000		
To Interest	21,800			
Add : Outstanding Interest Bank Loan	8,500	30,300		
To Advertising		55,000		
To Bad Debts	13,000			
Add : Further Bad debts	10,000			
Provision for Doubtful debts	19,500			
	42,500			
Less : Existing Provision	20,000	22,500		
To Depreciation				
5% on Building	42,500			
10% on Furniture	16,400			
20% on Motor Vehicles	1,45,000	2,03,900		
To Net Profit transferred to Capital A/c		3,20,100		
		12,27,000		12,27,000

BALANCE SHEET

as at 31st March, 2025

Liabilities		₹	*Assets*		₹
Capital			**Fixed Assets**		
Opening Balance	14,00,000		Furniture and Fittings	1,64,000	
Add : Net Profit	3,20,100	17,20,000	*Less* : Depreciation	16,400	1,47,600
Current Liabilities			Motor Vehicles	7,25,000	
Sundry Creditors		3,00,000	*Less* : Depreciation	1,45,000	5,80,000
Bank Loan	3,05,000		Building	8,50,000	
Add : Outstanding Interest	8,500	3,13,500	*Less* : Depreciation	42,500	8,07,500
Outstanding Taxes		12,000	**Current Assets**		
Outstanding Salaries		30,000	Cash		75,000
Commission received in Advance		10,000	Sundry Debtors	4,00,000	
			Less : Further Bad Debts	10,000	
				3,90,000	
			Less : Provision for Doubtful Debts	19,500	3,70,500
			Prepaid Insurance		10,000
			Closing Stock		3,75,000
			Input CGST (₹ 50,000 – ₹ 40,000)		10,000
			Input SGST (₹ 50,000 – ₹ 40,000)		10,000
		23,85,600			23,85,600

Note : GST paid (Input GST) on Pre-paid Insurance is not to be adjusted. GST charged (Output GST) on commission received is not to be adjusted.

ILLUSTRATION 15. A retired from a Company and started a business at Chennai. On retirement he got ₹ 1,00,000 from his employers, which sum he invested in the business, on 1-6-2024. He got, from Life Insurance Corporation, ₹ 20,000 on the maturity of his policy. This was also invested by him in the business. He draws ₹ 1,000 for his personal expenses every month from 30-6-2024.

Following figures are extracted from his books as on 31-3-2025 :

	₹		₹
Purchases	3,10,000	Sundry Debtors	45,000
Cartage	5,000	Bills Receivable	30,000
Salaries	24,000	Cash on hand	7,997
Electricity Charges	4,500	Sales	3,00,000
Travelling	8,900	Income from Personal Investment	20,000
Telephone	4,300	Creditors	85,000
Advertisement	10,000	Bank Overdraft	80,000
Repairs and Renewals	3,303	Building (Cr.)	10,000
Plant and Machinery	1,50,000		
Bad Debts	2,000		

You are requested to prepare a Trading and Profit and Loss Account of the business for the period ended 31-3-2025 and also the Balance Sheet as on 31-3-2025, after taking into consideration the following further information :

1. 'Purchases' include ₹ 10,000 representing the value of furniture purchased.
2. ₹ 4,000 representing erection wages on plant and machinery are debited to salaries.
3. "Electricity Charges" include ₹ 2,500 paid as deposits. There were bills outstanding to the extent of ₹ 500.
4. Advertisement includes ₹ 4,000 representing the cost of *Neon sign*.
5. A dishonour of a bill for ₹ 5,000 stands debited to the debtor. 50% thereof is considered doubtful and has to be provided accordingly.
6. A debtor for ₹ 1,000 was declared insolvent on 30th March, 2025 and it is expected that nothing would be recovered from his estate.
7. Provide 5% discount on net realisable Debtors.
8. Mr. *A* received ₹ 25,000 in respect of a Joint Venture with Mr. *B*. The sum received stood credited to sundry creditors. It is noted that a sum of ₹ 5,000 was due to Mr. *A* as his share of profit in the Venture.
9. During the period, there was a fire, as a result of which stock costing ₹ 50,000 was damaged. The damaged goods were sold for ₹ 20,000. This sum of ₹ 20,000 is included in the sales. The Insurance Company paid ₹ 25,000 towards the loss of stock. The godown, containing the stock, was also damaged during the fire, the extent of damage being ₹ 15,000, which also the insurance company paid. The total amount received from the insurance company was credited to the building account.
10. Bank overdraft was given on the hypothecation of Stock-in-Trade. You are informed that the bank had a margin of $33\frac{1}{3}\%$ and the overdraft balance as on 31st March, 2025 was the maximum which could have been drawn on the basis of this margin.
11. The Manager of the business is entitled to a commission of 10% on the business profit after charging his commission.
12. Provide 10% depreciation on plant and machinery and on furniture and fittings and 5% on building. Depreciation is to be provided on the closing balances.

SOLUTION

TRADING AND PROFIT & LOSS ACCOUNT OF MR. A
for the year ended 31st March, 2025

	₹	₹		₹	₹
To Purchases	3,10,000		By Sales	3,00,000	
Less : for furniture purchased	10,000		*Less* : Sale of damaged stock	20,000	
		3,00,000			2,80,000
To Cartage		5,000	By Closing Stock (₹ 80,000 × 3/2)		1,20,000
" Gross Profit c/d		1,45,000	" Loss of Stock due to fire		50,000
		4,50,000			4,50,000
To Salaries	24,000		By Gross Profit b/d		1,45,000
Less : Erection Wages	4,000		" Income from Joint Venture		5,000
		20,000			
" Electric Charges	4,500				
Less : for Electricity Deposits	2,500				
	2,000				
Add : Outstanding	500				
		2,500			
" Travelling		8,900			
" Telephone		4,300			
" Advertisement	10,000				
Less : Cost of Neon Sign	4,000				
		6,000			
To Repairs & Renewals		3,303			
" Bad Debts (₹ 2,000 + ₹ 1,000)		3,000			
" Provision for Bad Debts		2,500			
" Provision for Discount (5% on ₹ 41,500)		2,075			
" Depreciation on :					
" Plant & Machinery @ 10% on ₹ 1,54,000		15,400			
" Furniture & Fixtures @ 10% of ₹ 14,000		1,400			
" Building @ 5% on ₹ 15,000		750			
" Loss of Stock by Fire	(1)	5,000			
" Commission to Manager (1/11 of ₹ 69,872)		6,352			
" Net Profit transferred to Capital A/c		68,520			
		1,50,000			1,50,000

BALANCE SHEET OF MR. A
as on 31-3-2025

Liabilities	₹	₹	*Assets*	₹	₹
Sundry Creditors	85,000		Cash in hand		7,997
Less : Income from Joint Venture			Electricity Deposit		2,500
(Amount not due to B) (4)	5,000		Bills Receivable		30,000
		80,000	Stock in Trade		1,20,000

Bank Overdraft (secured by hypothecation of stock)		80,000	Sundry Debtors	45,000	
			Less : Bad Debts	1,000	
Outstanding Electric Charges		500		44,000	
Outstanding Manager's Commission		6,352	*Less* : Provision for Bad Debts	2,500	
				41,500	
Capital	1,20,000		*Less* : Provision for Discount	2,075	
Add : Income from Private Investment	20,000				39,425
" Profit	68,520		Building	(2) 15,000	
			Less : Depreciation	750	
	2,08,520				14,250
Less : Drawings	10,000		Plant and Machinery	1,50,000	
		1,98,520	*Add* : Erection charges	4,000	
				1,54,000	
			Less : Depreciation	15,400	
					1,38,600
			Furniture & Fixtures (₹ 10,000 + ₹ 4,000)	14,000	
			Less : Depreciation	1,400	
					12,600
		3,65,372			3,65,372

Notes : (1) Loss of Stock by fire is ₹ 5,000 (*i.e.*, ₹ 30,000 – ₹ 25,000).

(2) Building has a credit balance of ₹ 10,000 after crediting it with ₹ 40,000. Therefore, opening balance must have been ₹ 30,000. Closing balance is ₹ 15,000 after deducting ₹ 15,000 value of godown destroyed by fire from the opening balance of ₹ 30,000.

(3) Depreciation has been calculated for full year.

(4) ₹ 5,000 is deducted from amount due to B and now he is creditor for ₹ 20,000.

(5) Figures are given for the financial year 2024-25. GST has been effective from Ist July, 2025. Hence, GST has been ignored.

QUESTIONS

OBJECTIVE TYPE

1. Tick the correct answer to each statement given below:

(*i*) The balance of the petty cash is : (*a*) an expense, (*b*) an income, (*c*) an asset.

(*ii*) Fixed assets are ; (*a*) kept in the business for use over a long time for earning income, (*b*) meant for resale, (*c*) meant for conversion into cash as quickly as possible.

(*iii*) Goodwill is : (*a*) a current asset, (*b*), intangible, (*c*) tangible.

(*iv*) Stock is : (*a*) included in the category of fixed assets; (*b*) part of current assets, (*c*) intangible.

(*v*) The profit and loss account shows : (*a*) financial position of the concern; (*b*) net profit earned, (*c*) the gross profit earned.

(*vi*) Closing stock is valued at (*a*) cost, (*b*) market value, (*c*) cost or market price whichever is lower.

(*vii*) The manufacturing account is prepared : (*a*) to ascertain the profit or loss on the goods purchased , (*b*) to ascertain the cost of the manufactured goods, (*c*) to show the sale proceeds from the goods produced during the year.

(*viii*) Unearned Income Account is : (*a*) Asset ; (*b*) Liability ; (*c*) Expense

Ans. [(*i*) (*c*); (*ii*) (*a*); (*iii*) (*b*); (*iv*) (*b*); (*v*) (*b*); (*vi*) (*c*); (*vii*) (*b*); (*viii*) (*b*)]

2. Choose the odd one :

(*i*) (*a*) Outstanding liability
(*b*) Sundry creditors
(*c*) Bills payable
(*d*) Capital

(*ii*) (*a*) Carriage inward
(*b*) Carriage outward
(*c*) Factory rent
(*d*) Direct wages

(*iii*) (*a*) Motor car
(*b*) Building
(*c*) Closing stock
(*d*) Furniture

(*iv*) (*a*) Bills receivable
(*b*) Cash in hand
(*c*) Factory expenses
(*d*) Sundry debtors

Ans. [(*i*) (*d*); (*ii*) (*b*); (*iii*) (*c*); (*iv*) (*c*)]

3. In each of the following cases, indicate the alternative which you consider to be correct :

(*a*) Assets are held for the purpose of :
(*i*) Earning revenue, (*ii*) Resale, (*iii*) Conversion into cash.

(*b*) Stock is valued at :
(*i*) Cost price, (*ii*) Market price, (*iii*) Cost or market price whichever is lower.

(*c*) Unearned Income Account is :
(*i*) Asset, (*ii*) Liability, (*iii*) Expense.

(*d*) Depreciation is provided on :
(*i*) Fixed assets, (*ii*) Outward charges, (*iii*) Current assets, (*iv*) Intangible assets.

(*e*) Heavy advertising to launch a new product is a :
(*i*) Capital expenditure, (*ii*) Revenue expenditure, (*iii*) Deferred revenue expenditure.

Ans. [(*a*) (*i*) ; (*b*) (*iii*) ; (*c*) (*ii*) ; (*d*) (*i*) ; (*e*) (*iii*)].

4. Mention whether the following statements are *right* or *wrong* :

(*i*) Sales – Gross Profit = Cost of Goods Sold.

(*ii*) The provision for doubtful debts is debited to bad debts account.

(*iii*) The provision for discount on creditors is generally not provided in the books of account in keeping with the principle of conservatism.

(*iv*) Closing stock generally appears outside the trial balance. In case it appears in the trial balance it is taken to the Trading Account.

(*v*) The bad debts previously written off, if recovered subsequently are credited to debtors account.

(*vi*) The adjustment entry in respect of outstanding expenses is
Debit—Outstanding Expenses A/c
Credit–Expenses account.

(*vii*) Income tax paid on behalf of the proprietor is debited to the profit and loss account.

(*viii*) Prepaid Rent appearing in the trial balance is taken only to the profit and loss account.

(*ix*) The expression depreciation at 5% and 5% p.a. convey the same meaning.

(*x*) Profit is always represented as a cash or bank balance.

Ans. [Right : (*i*), (*ii*); Wrong : (*iii*) to (*x*)]

5. Fill in the blanks :

(*i*) Gross Profit + Opening stock + Purchases + Direct expenses – Sales= ?

(*ii*) Income received in advance is debited to income account and credited to....... while making adjustment entries.

(*iii*) If outstanding salary appears in the trial balance, it is taken only to the.......

(*iv*) A claim of ₹ 600 was accepted in respect of stock worth ₹ 800 which was destroyed by fi₹ The amount of abnormal loss of ₹ 200 will be debited to........ and credited to.......

(*v*) The claim admitted in respect of stock destroyed by fire will be credited to...... and will go to the... side of Balance Sheet.

(*vi*) A commission of 10% on net profits after charging such commission will be calculated.......

(*vii*) If adjustment related to bad debts is given outside the trial balance then they are adjusted by debiting...... and crediting........

(*viii*) Medicines given to the office staff by a manufacturer of medicines will be debited to........

Ans. [(*i*) Closing Stock ; (*ii*) Income Received in Advance Account ; (*iii*) Balance Sheet (*iv*) Profit and Loss Account, Trading Account ; (*v*) Trading Account, assets ; (*vi*) 10/110 of residual profit, *i.e.*, crediting all incomes and gross profit and debiting all expenses except commission ; (*vii*) Bad Debts Account, Sundry Debtors Account ; (*viii*) Salaries Account].

6. Choose the correct answer :

(*a*) .... shown on the debit side of Trading Account

(*i*) Gross Profit b/d (*ii*) Closing stock
(*iii*) Sales (*iv*) Opening stock.

(*b*) .... is arrived at by deducting cost of goods sold from sales

(*i*) Net Loss (*ii*) Gross Profit
(*iii*) Net Profit (*iv*) Cost of Production.

(*c*) In .... excess of debit over credit is known as ....

(*i*) Profit & Loss A/c, Net Loss (*ii*) Profit & Loss A/c, Gross Profit
(*ii*) Trading A/c, Gross Profit (*iv*) Profit & Loss A/c, Net Profit.

(*d*) Closing stock balance given in the debit side of the trial balance will be written in financial statement in ....

(*i*) Trading A/c Debit Side (*ii*) Trading A/c Credit Side
(*iii*) Liabilities Side (*iv*) Asset Side.

(*e*) Goodwill is a ....

(*i*) Current Asset (*ii*) Fictitious Asset
(*iii*) Tangible Asset (*iv*) Intangible Asset.

(*f*) The properties owned by the business are called ....

(*i*) Assets (*ii*) Liabilities
(*iii*) Capital (*iv*) Accounting Equation.

(*g*) A debit means

(*i*) An increase in Asset (*ii*) Decrease in Assets
(*iii*) Increase in Liability (*iv*) Increase in Liability.

(*h*) A debit balance in which the following accounts would indicate a likely error

(*i*) Accounts Receivable (*ii*) Cash
(*iii*) Fees Earned (*iv*) Miscellaneous Expenses.

Ans. [(*a*) (*iv*); (*b*) (*ii*); (*c*) (*i*); (*d*) (*iv*); (*e*) (*iv*); (*f*) (*i*); (*g*) (*i*); (*h*) (*iii*)]

SHORT ANSWER TYPE

1. One of the characteristics of financial statements is neutrality. Do you agree with this statement ?
2. What are the main elements of financial statements ?
3. What is the purpose of preparing Trading Account ?
4. Why do business concerns prepare Profit and Loss Account ?
5. What is the difference between Trading Account and Manufacturing Account ?
6. Distinguish between Trading and Profit and Loss Account and Balance Sheet.
7. How do you show prepaid expenses in final accounts ?

8. Why is closing stock valued at cost or market price whichever is lower ?
9. What do you mean by cost of goods sold ?
10. Do we need a closing entry for carrying any account to a balance sheet ?
11. What do you mean by adjusting entries ? Name any four adjusting entries.
12. Distinguish between current assets and fixed assets.
13. The manager is entitled to a commission of 5% on net profit after charging his commission. Net profit before charging commission is ₹ 84,000. Find out the amount of commission payable to the manager.

Ans. **[₹ 4,000]**

14. What are contingent liabilities ? Give two examples of such liabilities.
15. Goods which cost ₹ 10,000 were in inventory on 1-4-2024. Purchases for the year ended 31-3-2025 amounted to ₹ 40,000 and the cost of inventory on that date was ₹ 15,000. The gross profit ratio was 20% on sales. Calculate the sales value for the year.

Ans. **[₹ 43,750]**

16. What is a Provision for Bad Debts, how is the amount of this provision arrived at and what is the object of making it ?
17. What is provision for bad and doubtful debts ? Why is it created ?
18. Ascertain cost of goods sold from the following figures :

	₹		₹
Opening stock	30,000	Closing stock	50,000
Purchases	5,10,000	Office expenses	40,000
Returns outward	10,000	Sales	7,00,000
Direct expenses	20,000		

Ans. **[₹ 5,00,000]**

19. Calculate net profit from the following :

	₹		₹
Purchases (1,000 units)	60,000	Indirect Expenses	12,000
Freight and Carriage Inward	3,000	Sales (800 units)	80,000

Ans. **[Net Profit ₹ 17,600].**

Hint. Closing Stock : $\frac{₹\ 63,000}{1,000 \text{ units}} \times 200 \text{ units} = ₹\ 12,600.$

20. Find out gross profit from the following figures :

	₹		₹
Opening stock	10,000	Sales	5,30,000
Purchases	3,20,000	Salaries	50,000
Wages	15,000	Closing stock	60,000
Carriage on purchases	20,000	Unproductive wages	7,000
Carriage on sales	12,000	Goods distributed as free samples	10,000
Returns inward	8,000	Goods withdrawn by the	
Returns outward	5,000	proprietor for personal use	6,000

Ans. **[₹ 2,38,000]**

LONG ANSWER TYPE

1. Distinguish between Trading Account and Profit and Loss Account. Give a specimen of Trading and Profit and Loss Account with imaginary figures.
2. What are closing entries ? Give the closing entries which are to be passed at the end of the accounting period.
3. What is a Balance Sheet ? Why is it prepared ? Give a specimen of the Balance Sheet.

4. (*a*) How various assets and liabilities are classified ?

(*b*) Write notes on : (*i*) Contingent assets, (*ii*) fictitious assets, (*iii*) contingent liability.

5. What do you understand by the terms 'Grouping' and 'Marshalling' used in connection with the Balance Sheet ? Illustrate the different forms of marshalling.

6. What are adjusting entries ? Why are these necessary for preparing final accounts ?

7. What adjusting entries would you pass in regard to (*i*) outstanding expenses, (*ii*) prepaid expenses, (*iii*) accrued income, (*iv*) income received in advance, and (*v*) depreciation.

8. How is the account relating to provision for doubtful debts kept ? What is the object of this account ? What is the influence of actual bad debts on it ? How is it shown in the Balance Sheet ?

9. What is meant for provision for discount on debtors ? How are the relevant accounts prepared ? How will you calculate the amount for provision for discount on debtors ?

10. Give the main limitations of financial statements. What safeguards can be provided against the preparation of false statements ?

11. Explain the following statements :

(*a*) "Balance Sheet is not an account, it is only the list of balances."

(*b*) "Balance Sheet and Profit and Loss are inter-dependent".

12. Explain the following adjustments and their treatment in final accounts :

(*i*) Loss of stock by fire (*ii*) Goods given away as charity (*iii*) Goods taken by the proprietor for personal use (*iv*) Contingent liability.

13. Bring out the points of resemblance and points of distinction between Trial Balance and Balance Sheet.

14. Define fixed, floating, fictitious, liquid and wasting assets. Give two examples of each.

15. What are the qualitative *characteristics of the financial statements* which improve the usefulness of the information furnished therein ?

16. Briefly explain the elements of financial statements. ***(C.A. Inter May, 2021)***

PRACTICAL PROBLEMS

1. Mr. Prakash runs a factory which produces Pressure Cookers. The following details were obtained about his manufacturing expenses for the year ended 31st March, 2025 :

	Amount (₹)
Opening Work-in-Progress	6,25,000
Closing Work-in-Progress	7,15,000
Opening Inventory of Raw Material	5,85,000
Closing Inventory of Raw Material	4,70,000
Purchases	18,74,000
Purchase Returns	95,000
Indirect Material	1,88,000
Direct Wages	3,97,000
Indirect Wages	82,000
Power & Electricity	1,76,000
Repairs and Maintenance	2,65,000
Depreciation on Factory Shed	1,44,000

Depreciation on Plant & Machinery	1,62,000
Sale of Scrap	36,000

You are required to prepare Manufacturing Account for the year ended 31st March, 2025.

Ans. [Cost of Finished Goods—₹ 31,82,000]

2. Following are balances appear in the books of Prasanna Polymers as at 31st March, 2025.

Particulars	*Dr. (₹)*	*Particulars*	*Cr. (₹)*
Debtors	2,00,000	Provision for Bad and Doubtful Debts	19,000
Bad Debts	15,000		

Additional information :

(*i*) Debtors include ₹ 20,000 receivable from Mohit who has become insolvent and will be able to pay 50% only.

(*ii*) Commission ₹ 50,000 paid to an agent has been wrongly debited to his personal account included in debtors.

(*iii*) During March 2025, goods valued at ₹ 40,000 were sent on approval basis. Approval was received on 30th March 2025. However, the transaction has not yet been recorded.

(*iv*) Create 10% provision for bad and doubtful debts.

Calculate the amount of bad debts and provision for bad and doubtful debts to be shown in Profit and Loss Account. Calculate the balance of Debtors to be shown in Balance Sheet.

Ans. [Amount of Bad Debts—₹ 23,000; Provision Closing Balance—₹ 17,000; Amount charged to Profit & Loss A/c ₹ 23,000; Debtors Closing Balance ₹ 1,63,000]

3. Following are the extracts of a Trial Balance as at 31st March, 2024 :

Particulars	*Dr. (₹)*	*Cr. (₹)*
Plant & Machinery on 1-4-2023	1,80,000	
Repairs	30,000	
Wages	40,000	

A Machinery costing ₹ 1,00,000 plus GST @ 18% was purchased on 1st July, 2023 by raising loan for ₹ 1,00,000 at an interest rate of 8% p.a. Wages 25,000 paid for its installation have been debited to Wages Account. The machine was ready for use on 1st August 2023 though it was put to use on 1st January 2025. Provide depreciation on Plant and Machinery @ 12% p.a. Show how these items will appear in the final accounts assuming the company intends to avail credit for GST paid.

Ans. [Closing balance of Machinery—₹ 2,73,706; Input GST to be shown as Current Asset in Balance Sheet]

Hint. Cost of machine to be capitalised ₹ 1,25,333

4. Prepare a Trading Account of a trader for the year ending 31st March, 2025 from the following data :

	₹		₹
Stock on 1-4-2024	2,40,000	Import duty	8,000
Cash purchases for the year	2,08,000	Clearing charges	12,000
Credit purchases for the year	4,00,000	Cost of goods distributed as free samples during the year	5,000
Cash sales for the year	3,50,000		
Credit sales for the year	6,00,000	Goods withdrawn by the trader for personal use	2,000
Purchases returns during the year	8,000		
Sales returns during the year	10,000	Stock damaged by fire during the year	13,000
Direct expenses incurred :		Output CGST (Payable)	10,000
Freight	10,000	Output SGST (Payable)	10,000
Carriage	2,000		

The cost of unsold stock on 31st March, 2025 was ₹ 1,20,000 but its market value was ₹ 1,50,000.

Ans. [Gross Profit ₹ 2,08,000].

Hint. GST payable will be shown in the Balance Sheet and not in Trading A/c.

5. Following Trading and Profit and Loss Account has been prepared by a junior accountant of a firm. Criticise it and redraft it correctly.

TRADING ACCOUNT

	₹		₹
To Opening stock of raw materials	7,352	By Closing stock of raw materials	9,368
" Purchases	63,681	" Sales	1,70,852
" Sundry creditors	25,375	" Sundry debtors	40,659
" Carriage inwards	2,654	" Gross loss c/d	8,182
" Carriage outwards	394		
To Salaries	24,370		
" Wages	51,963		
" Rent, Rates & Taxes	3,981		
" Repairs to factory	35,368		
" Insurance	13,923		
	2,29,061		2,29,061

PROFIT & LOSS ACCOUNT

	₹		₹
To Gross loss b/d	8,182	By Bank overdraft	17,681
To Interest on loans	6,180	By Interest on bank overdraft	123
To Dividend from investments	9,375	By Net loss transferred to B/S	39,691
To Furniture purchases	17,681		
To Telephone charges	985		
To Electric charges	2,756		
To Depreciation— Plant & machinery	663		
To Charges general	11,673		
	57,495		57,495

Ans. [Gross Profit ₹ 19,202 ; Net Loss ₹ 36,471].

6. Following is the Trial Balance of M/s Kasturi Agencies as on 31st March, 2025. Prepare Trading and Profit & Loss Account for the year ended 31st March, 2025 and a Balance Sheet on that date :

	Dr. ₹	*Cr.* ₹
Capital		1,00,000
Drawings	18,000	
Buildings	15,000	
Furniture & Fittings	7,500	
Motor Van	25,000	
Loan from Hari @ 12% interest		15,000
Interest paid on above	900	
Sales		1,00,000

Output CGST		2,000
Output SGST		2,000
Purchases	75,000	
Opening Stock	25,000	
Establishment Expenses	15,000	
Wages	2,000	
Insurance	1,000	
Commission received		7,500
Sundry Debtors	28,100	
Bank Balance	20,000	
Sundry Creditors		6,000
	2,32,500	2,32,500

Adjustments : (*a*) The value of stock on 31st March, 2025 was ₹ 32,000. (*b*) Outstanding Wages ₹ 500. (*c*) Prepaid Insurance ₹ 300. (*d*) Commission received in advance ₹ 800. (*e*) Allow interest on capital @ 10%. (*f*) Depreciate : Building $2\frac{1}{2}$%, Furniture & Fittings 10%, Motor Van 10%. (*g*) Charge interest on drawings ₹ 500.

Ans. [G.P. ₹ 29,500 ; N.P. ₹ 5,575 ; B/S Total ₹ 1,24,275].

7. Following are the balances in the Ledger of Mr. Suresh for the year ended 31st March, 2025 :

	₹		₹
Discount (Dr.)	2,500	Carriage Outwards	12,400
Carriage Inwards	10,200	Advertisement	12,000
Rent, Taxes & Rates	12,400	Miscellaneous Expenses	3,300
Printing & Stationery	2,600	Interest paid	10,792
Purchases of Raw Materials	3,49,800	Fuel and Coal	11,200
Sales	5,60,000	Factory Power	22,900
Opening Stock of Raw Materials	1,24,400	Insurance (Fire)	1,760
Opening Stock of Finished Goods	63,800	Staff Salaries	12,700
Factory Wages	59,700	Electricity (office)	2,300
		Bad Debts	6,080

Prepare Manufacturing, Trading and Profit and Loss Account for the year ended 31st March, 2025 after taking into consideration the following information :

1. Stock as at 31-3-2025 :
   Raw Materials ₹ 46,900 ; Finished Goods ₹ 1,52,300.
2. Depreciate Plant and Machinery by ₹ 11,690 and Furniture & Fixtures by ₹ 2,860.
3. Expenses outstanding and payable are : Salaries ₹ 2,000 ; Electricity ₹ 200 and Factory Power ₹ 2,100.

Ans. [Cost of Goods Manufactured ₹ 5,45,090 ; G.P. ₹ 1,03,410 ; N.P. ₹ 19,518].

8. From the following Trial Balance prepared from the books of Laxmi Narain on 31st March, 2025, prepare Trading and Profit and Loss Account and a Balance Sheet.

	Dr. ₹	*Cr.* ₹
Laxmi Narain's Capital and Drawings	10,550	1,19,400
Bills Receivable	7,500	
Purchases and Sales	2,56,590	3,56,430
Returns Inwards	2,780	
Opening Stock	89,680	

Commission		5,640
Input CGST	1,000	
Input SGST	1,000	
Plant and Machinery	28,800	
Salaries	11,000	
Travelling Expenses	1,880	
Debtors (including Mohan for dishonoured cheque ₹ 1,000)	62,000	
Stationery	2,000	
Telephone Charges	1,370	
Interest and Discount	5,870	
Bad Debts	3,620	
Fixtures and Fittings	8,970	
Creditors		59,630
6% Loan		20,000
Wages	40,970	
Cash in Hand	530	
Cash at Bank	18,970	
Insurance (including premium of ₹ 300 per annum paid up to 30-9-2025)	400	
Rent and Taxes	5,620	
	5,61,100	5,61,100

Stock in trade on 31st March, 2025 was ₹ 1,28,960. Write off half of Mohan's cheque. Create Provision of 5 per cent on Debtors. Manufacturing wages include ₹ 1,200 for erection of new machinery purchased last year. Depreciate Plant and Machinery by 5 per cent and Fixtures and Fittings by 10 per cent per annum. Commission accrued ₹ 600. Interest on loan for the last two months is not paid.

Ans. [G.P. ₹ 96,570 ; N.P. ₹ 65,028 ; B/S Total ₹ 2,53,708]

9. From the following balances extracted from the books of Mr. Rati Ram and the subjoined information, you are required to prepare Profit and Loss Account for the year ended on 31st March, 2025 and also the Balance Sheet as on that date :

	Dr. ₹	*Cr.* ₹
Stock on 1-4-2024	60,500	—
Purchases & Sales	90,300	1,37,200
Returns	2,200	1,300
Capital Account	—	30,000
Drawings Account	4,500	
Land & Buildings	30,000	
Furniture & Fittings	8,000	
Sundry Debtors & Creditors	25,000	45,000
Cash in Hand	3,500	
Investments	10,000	
Interest		500
Commission		3,000
Direct Expenditure	7,500	
Postages, Stationery & Phones	2,500	
Fire Insurance Premium	2,000	
Salaries	11,000	
Bank Overdraft		40,000
	2,57,000	2,57,000

(*a*) Closing Stock on 31st March, 2025 was valued at ₹ 65,000. Goods worth ₹ 500 are reported to have been taken away by the proprietor for his personal use at home during 2024-25. (*b*) Interest on Investments ₹ 500 is yet to be received while ₹ 1,000 of the commission received is yet to be earned in 2024-25. (*c*) ₹ 500 of the fire insurance premium paid is in respect of the quarter ending 30th June, 2025. (*d*) Salaries ₹ 1,000 for March, 2025 and Bank Overdraft interest estimated at ₹ 2,000 have to be recorded as outstanding charges. (*e*) Depreciation is to be provided on Land & Buildings @ 5% and on Furniture and Fittings @ 10%. (*f*) Make provision for doubtful debts @ 5% of Sundry Debtors.

Ans. [G.P. ₹ 43,500 ; N.P. ₹ 24,950 ; B/S Total ₹ 1,38,950]

10. Following balances were extracted from the books of Shri V. Balkrishna as on 31st March, 2025 :

Debit Balances :	₹		₹
Plant and Machinery	20,000	Purchases	1,02,000
Manufacturing Wages	34,500	Sales Returns	3,100
Salaries	15,850	Bad Debts	1,400
Furniture	10,000	Interest and Bank Charges	400
Freight on Purchases	1,860	Cash at Bank	4,200
Freight on Sales	2,140	Cash in Hand	1,120
Buildings	25,000		
Manufacturing Expenses	9,500	**Credit Balances :**	
Insurance and Tax	4,250	CGST Payable	5,000
Goodwill	25,000	SGST Payable	5,000
General Expenses	8,200	Capital Account	80,000
Factory Fuel and Power	1,280	Sundry Creditors	44,560
Sundry Debtors	78,200	Bank Loan	5,000
Factory Lighting	950	Purchases Returns	1,740
Opening Stock	34,200	Sales	2,50,850
Motor Car	12,000	Provisions for Bad Debts	2,000

Prepare Trading and Profit and Loss Account for the year ended 31st March, 2025 and the Balance Sheet as on that date after taking into consideration the following information :

(1) Stock on hand on 31st March, 2025 was valued at ₹ 30,500. (2) Depreciate Plant and Machinery by 10%, Furniture by 5% and Motor Car by ₹ 1,000. (3) Bring Provision for Bad Debts to 5% on Sundry Debtors. (4) A commission of 1% on the gross profit is to be provided for Works Manager. (5) A commission of 2% on net profit (after charging the Works Manager's commission) is to be credited to the General Manager.

Ans. [G.P. ₹ 95,700 ; N.P. ₹ 55,951 ; B/S Total ₹ 1,97,610]

11. Following is the Trial Balance of Ram Lal on March 31, 2025.

Debit Balances :	₹		₹
Bank	7,500	Input CGST	2,500
Purchases (adjusted)	34,96,000	Input SGST	2,500
Salaries	21,000		
Carriage on Sales	2,500	*Credit Balances* :	
Carriage on Purchases	2,000	Capital	2,00,000
Lighting	1,500	Bills Payable	50,000
Buildings	1,35,000	Loan	1,00,000
Rates and Taxes	2,000	Sales	36,00,000
Sundry Debtors	40,000	Discount	2,000
Furniture	30,000	Commission	500

Cash in Hand	1,250	Sundry Creditors	1,00,000
Bills Receivable	7,500	Output IGST	5,000
Stock (31st March, 2025)	3,06,250		

Rates have been prepaid to the extent of ₹ 600. During the year, bad debts amounted to ₹ 2,500. A provision @ 5% has to be made on debtors. Buildings have to be depreciated at 2% and Furniture at 10%. Prepare Trading and Profit & Loss A/c and Balance Sheet as on March 31, 2025.

Ans. [G.P. ₹ 1,02,000; N.P. ₹ 68,025; B/S Total ₹ 5,18,025].

12. (*a*) On 1st January, 2023, the provision for bad debts showed a credit balance of ₹ 3,600. During the year the bad debts amounted to ₹ 2,800. The debtors on 31st December, 2023 amounted to ₹ 96,000 and a Provision of 5% for Doubtful Debts was maintained.

In 2024, the bad debts amounted to ₹ 1,200 and the debtors at the end of the year amounted to ₹ 40,000, on which a provision of 5% for bad debts was to be maintained.

Make journal entries and prepare the Provision for Doubtful Debts Account. Also show how these items are to appear in the Profit & Loss Account and Balance Sheet of the respective years.

(*b*) On 1st January, 2024 the reserve for discount on creditors was ₹ 1,200. The discounts earned during the year amounted to ₹ 1,040. The creditors on 31st December, 2024 were ₹ 50,000 and a new reserve of $2\frac{1}{2}$% is required.

Show the Journal, Ledger, Profit & Loss A/c and Balance Sheet entries relating to discount.

(*c*) A Company maintains its Provision for Bad Debts @ 5% and a Provision for Discount @ 2%. You are given the following details :

	2023	*2024*
	₹	₹
Bad Debts	800	1,500
Discount allowed	1,200	500
Recovery of Bad Debts written off in earlier years.	500	300

Sundry Debtors (before writing off Bad Debts and Discounts) amounted to ₹ 60,000 on 31st December, 2023 and ₹ 42,000 on 31st December, 2024.

On January 1, 2023, Provision for Bad Debts and Provision for Discount on Debtors had balances of ₹ 4,550 and ₹ 800 respectively.

Show the Provision for Bad Debts Account and Provision for Discount on Debtors Account for 2023 and 2024.

13. A firm had the following Balances on 1st January, 2023

(*a*) Provision for Bad and Doubtful Debts ₹ 2,500 ; (*b*) Provision for Discounts on Debtors ₹ 1,200; (*c*) Reserve for Discounts on Creditors ₹ 1,000

During the year Bad Debts amounted to ₹ 2,000, discounts allowed were ₹ 100 and Discounts received were ₹ 200. During 2024, Bad Debts amounting to ₹ 1,000 were written off while Discounts allowed and received were ₹ 2,000 and ₹ 500 respectively.

Total Debtors on December 31, 2023 were ₹ 48,000 before writing off Bad Debts, but after allowing Discounts. On December 31, 2024 the amount was ₹ 19,000 after writing off the Bad Debts, but before allowing Discounts. Total creditors on these two dates were ₹ 20,000 and ₹ 25,000 respectively.

It is the firm's policy to maintain a provision of 5% against Bad and Doubtful Debts and 2% for Discount on Debtors and a reserve of 3% for Discount on Creditors.

Show the accounts relating to Provision on Debtors and Reserve on creditors for the years 2023 and 2024

14. From the following Balances of Shri Atma Ram, as at 31st March, 2025, you are required to prepare a Trading and Profit and Loss Account for the year ended 31st March, 2025 and a Balance Sheet as at that date, after making the necessary adjustments :

Debit Balances :	₹		₹
Drawings Account	6,000	Insurance Charges	700
Plant & Machinery (Balance on 1-4-2024)	20,000	Salaries & Wages	21,300
Plant & Machinery (addition on 1-10-2024)	5,000	Cash in Hand	6,200
Stock on 1-4-2024	15,000	Cash at Bank	25,500
Purchases	82,000	***Credit Balances :***	
Returns Inwards	2,000	Capital	80,000
Sundry Debtors	20,600	Sundry Creditors	10,000
Furniture & Fixtures	5,000	Sales	1,20,000
Freight	2,000	Returns Outwards	1,000
Carriage Outwards	500	Provision for Doubtful Debts	400
Rent, Rates & Taxes	4,600	Discounts	800
Printing & Stationery	800	Rent of Premises, sublet for the	
Trade Expenses	400	year to 30-9-2025	1,200
Postage & Telegrams	800	Reserve Fund	5,000

Adjustments :

(1) Stock on 31st March, 2025 was valued at ₹ 14,600. (2) Write off ₹ 600 as Bad Debts. (3) The Provision for Doubtful Debts is to be maintained at 5 per cent on Sundry Debtors. (4) Create a Provision for Discounts on Debtors and make Reserve on Creditors at 2%. (5) Provide for depreciation on Furniture and Fixtures at 5% per annum. (6) Insurance prepaid was ₹ 100. (7) A fire occurred on 25th March, 2025, in the godown and stock of the value of ₹ 5,000 was destroyed. It was fully insured and the Insurance Company admitted the claim in full. (8) ₹ 2,000 is to be transferred to Reserve Fund out of profits, if any.

Ans. [G.P. ₹ 39,600 ; N.P. ₹ 5,870 ; B/S Total ₹ 95,270]

15. From the following Trial Balance of Seth C.L. Gheewala of Baroda, prepare Trading and Profit & Loss Account for the year ending 31st March, 2025 and Balance Sheet as on that date after taking into consideration the adjustments given at the end of the Trial Balance.

TRIAL BALANCE

	Dr. ₹	*Cr.* ₹
Sales	—	7,40,000
Purchases	6,99,200	
Wages	900	
Capital Account		48,500
National Insurance	300	
Carriage in	400	
Carriage out	500	
Lighting	600	
Rates and Insurance (including Premium of ₹ 300 p.a. paid up to 30th September, 2025)	400	
Stock at 31-3-2025	61,250	
Cash in Hand and at Bank	1,750	

Discount earned		600
Buildings	30,000	
Discount allowed	100	
Debtors and Creditors	6,000	20,000
Furniture	8,000	
Dividends Received		300
	8,09,400	8,09,400

Adjustments :

(*i*) National Insurance Balance includes employees' contribution also ₹ 150. Wages are shown 'Net' after deducting National Insurance contribution borne by the employee. (*ii*) Owing to the nature of employment, some employees are housed in the building of the business. The rental value of such portion is assessed at ₹ 500 p.a. (*ii*) Sales as shown in the Trial Balance include the sale of old Furniture (effected half way through the yearly accounting period) realizing ₹ 200. The book value of the furniture at that period was ₹ 300 and in the past depreciation has been written off at 20% p.a. (*iv*) The manager is to get a commission of 1/5th on the net trading profits after charging his commission. (*v*) Depreciation Building by 5%.

Ans. [G.P. ₹ 38,650 ; N.P. ₹ 29,475 ; B/S Total ₹ 1,03,810]

16. From the following particulars extracted from the books of Rajesh prepare Trading and Profit and Loss Account and Balance Sheet as on 31st March, 2025 after making the necessary adjustments :

	₹		₹
Capital Account (Cr.)	54,050	Interest Received	725
Opening Stock	23,400	Cash with Trader Bank Ltd.	4,000
Sales	1,44,800	Discount Received	1,495
Sales Returns	4,300	Investment @ 5% as on 1-4-2024	2,500
Purchases	1,21,550	Furniture as on 1-4-2024	900
Purchases Returns	2,900	Discount Allowed	3,770
Carriage Inwards	9,300	General Expenses	1,960
Rent	2,850	Audit Fees	350
Salaries	4,650	Fire Insurance Premium	300
Sundry Debtors	12,000	Travelling Expenses	1,165
Sundry Creditors	7,400	Postage and Telegrams	435
Loan from Dena Bank Ltd. @ 12%	10,000	Cash in Hand	190
Interest paid	450	Deposits at 10% as on 1-4-2024 (Dr.)	15,000
Printing and Stationery	1,700	Drawings	5,000
Advertisement	5,600		

Adjustments :

(1) Value of stock as on 31st March, 2025 is ₹ 39,300. This includes goods returned by customers on 31st March, 2025 to the value of ₹ 1,500 for which no entry has been passed in the books. (2) Purchases include furniture purchased on 1st January, 2025 for ₹ 1,000. (3) Depreciation should be provided on furniture at 10% per annum. (4) The loan account from Dena Bank in the books of Rajesh appears as follows :

		₹			₹
31-3-2025	To Balance c/d	10,000	1-4-2024	By Balance	5,000
			31-3-2025	By Bank	5,000
		10,000			10,000

(5) Sundry Debtors include ₹ 2,000 due from X and Sundry Creditors include ₹ 1,000 due to him. (6) Interest paid includes ₹ 300 paid to Dena Bank. (7) Interest received represents ₹ 100 from the Sundry Debtors and the balance on investments and deposits. (8) Provide for interest payable to Dena Bank and for interest receivable on investments and deposits. (9) Provide for doubtful debts 5% on the balance under "Sundry Debtors". No reserve needed be credited for the deposits.

Ans. [G.P. ₹ 27,950 ; N.P. ₹ 7,050 ; B/S Total ₹ 72,800]

17. Following is the Trial Balance of Shri Om as on 31st March, 2025. You are requested to prepare the Trading and Profit and Loss Account for the year ended 31st March, 2025 and Balance Sheet as on that date after making the necessary adjustments.

	Debit ₹	*Credit* ₹
Sundry Debtors	5,00,000	—
Sundry Creditors	—	2,00,000
Outstanding Liability for Expenses	55,000	—
Wages	1,00,000	—
Carriage Outwards	1,10,000	—
Carriage Inwards	50,000	
General Expenses	70,000	—
Cash Discounts	20,000	—
Bad Debts	10,000	
Motor Car	2,40,000	
Printing and Stationery	15,000	
Furniture and Fittings	1,10,000	
Advertisement	85,000	
Insurance	45,000	
Salesmen's Commission	87,500	
Postage and Telephone	57,500	
Salaries	1,60,000	
Rates and Taxes	25,000	
Drawings	20,000	
Capital Accounts		14,43,000
Purchases	15,50,000	—
Sales	—	19,87,500
Stock on 1-4-2024	2,50,000	—
Cash at Bank	60,000	—
Cash in Hand	10,500	—
	36,30,500	36,30,500

Following adjustments are to be made :

1. Stock on 31st March, 2025 was valued at ₹ 7,25,000.
2. A Provision for Bad and Doubtful Debts is to be created to the extent of 5 per cent on Sundry Debtors.
3. Depreciate—Furniture and Fittings by 10%, Motor Car by 20%.
4. Shri Om had withdrawn goods worth ₹ 25,000 during the year.
5. Sales include goods worth ₹ 75,000 sent out to Shanti & Company on approval and remaining unsold on 31st March, 2025. The cost of the goods was ₹ 50,000.
6. The Salesmen are entitled to a Commission of 5% on total sales.
7. Debtors include ₹ 25,000 bad debts.

8. Printing and Stationery expenses of ₹ 55,000 relating to 2023-24 had not been provided in that year but was paid in this year by debiting outstanding liabilities.
9. Purchases include purchase of Furniture worth ₹ 50,000.

Ans. [Gross Profit ₹ 8,12,500 ; Net Profit ₹ 10,375, B/S Total ₹ 15,61,500].

18. From the following figures extracted from the books of Shri Govind, you are required to prepare a Trading and Profit & Loss Account for the year ended 31st March, 2025 and a Balance Sheet as on that date after making the necessary adjustments :

	₹		₹
Shri Govind's Capital	2,28,800	Stock 1-4-2024	38,500
Shri Govind's Drawings	13,200	Wages	35,200
Plant and Machinery	99,000	Sundry Creditors	44,000
Freehold Property	66,000	Postage and Telegrams	1,540
Purchases	1,10,000	Insurance	1,760
Returns Outwards	1,100	Gas and Fuel	2,970
Salaries	13,200	Bad Debts	660
Office Expenses	2,750	Office Rent	2,860
Office Furniture	5,500	Freight	9,900
Discount A/c (Dr.)	1,320	Loose Tools	2,200
Sundry Debtors	29,260	Factory Lighting	1,100
Loan to Shri Krishna @ 10%		Provision for D/D	880
p.a. balance on 1-4-2024	44,000	Interest on Loan to Shri Krishna	1,100
Cash at Bank	29,260	Cash in Hand	2,640
Bills Payable	5,500	Sales	2,31,440

Adjustments

1. Stock on 31st March, 2025 was valued at ₹ 72,600.
2. A new machine was installed during the year costing ₹ 15,400 but it was not recorded in the books as no payment was made for it. Wages ₹ 1,100 paid for its erection have been debited to wages account.
3. Depreciate Plant and Machinery by $33\frac{1}{3}\%$, Furniture by 10%, Freehold Property by 5%.
4. Loose tools were valued at ₹ 1,760 on 31-3-2025.
5. Of the Sundry Debtors ₹ 660 are bad and should be written off.
6. Maintain a provision of 5% on Sundry Debtors for doubtful debts.
7. The manager is entitled to a commission of 10% of the net profits after charging such commission.

Ans. [Gross Profit ₹ 1,08,570, Net Profit ₹ 40,800 ; B/S Total ₹ 3,25,380].

19. Following is the schedule of balances on 31st March, 2025 extracted from the books of Dinesh :

Particulars	*Debit* (₹)	*Credit* (₹)
Cash in hand	1,400	—
Cash at Bank	2,600	—
Sundry Debtors	86,000	—
Stock as on 1st April, 2024	62,000	—
Furniture and Fixtures	21,400	—
Office Equipments	16,000	—
Buildings	60,000	—
Motor Car	20,000	—
Sundry Creditors	—	83,000
Loan	—	30,000

Provision for Bad Debts	—	3,000
Purchases	1,40,000	—
Purchases Return	—	2,600
Sales	—	2,30,000
Sales Return	4,200	—
Salaries	11,000	—
Rent for Godown	5,500	—
Interest on Loan	2,700	—
Rate and Taxes	2,100	—
Discount Allowed to Debtors	2,400	—
Discount Received from Creditors	—	1,600
Freight on Purchases	1,200	—
Carriage Outwards	2,000	—
Drawings	12,000	—
Printing and Stationery	1,800	—
Electric Charges	2,200	—
Insurance Premium	5,500	—
General Office Expenses	3,000	—
Bad Debts	2,000	—
Bank Charges	1,600	—
Motor Car Expenses	3,600	—
Capital Account	—	1,62,000
Input CGST	60,000	
Input SGST	60,000	
Output CGST		40,000
Output SGST		40,000
	5,92,200	5,92,200

Prepare Trading and Profit and Loss Account for the year ended 31st March, 2025 and Balance Sheet as on that date after making the following adjustments :
(*i*) Provide depreciation on— (*a*) Building @ 5%; (*b*) Furniture and Fixture @ 10%; (*c*) Office Equipments @ 15%; and (*d*) Motor Car @ 20%. (*ii*) Value of stock at the close of the year was ₹ 44,000. (*iii*) Provision for bad debts is to be maintained at 5% of sundry debtors. (*iv*) Insurance premium includes ₹ 4,000 paid towards proprietor's life insurance policy and the balance of the insurance charges covers the period from 1st July, 2024 to 30th June, 2025.

Ans. [Gross Profit ₹ 69,200; Net Profit ₹ 16,935; Balance Sheet Total ₹, 2,75,935]

20. Following is the Trial Balance of Shri Arihant as on 31st March, 2025. You are required to prepare Trading and Profit & Loss Account for the year ended 31st March, 2025 and Balance Sheet as on that date after making the necessary adjustments :

	Debit ₹	*Credit* ₹
Stock on 1-4-2024	5,50,000	
Purchases	19,25,000	
Sales		29,35,000
Wages and Salaries	1,25,000	
Discount Received		2,000
Carriage Inwards	40,000	
Bills Payable		1,85,000
Insurance	35,000	

Creditors		9,32,500
Consignor's Balance 1-4-2024		4,00,000
Bills Receivable	2,25,000	
Debtors	15,00,000	
Capital		8,95,000
Commission	40,000	
Cash sent to Consigner	8,00,000	
Interest	35,000	
Trade Expenses	34,500	
Furniture on 1-4-2024	60,000	
Consignment Sales		6,40,000
Cash in hand and at Bank	4,22,500	
Rent and Taxes	1,27,500	
Sale of Furniture on 31-3-2025		10,000
Charges paid against consignment	80,000	
	59,99,500	59,99,500

Following adjustments are to be made :

1. Stock on 31st March—₹ 8,00,000 (including stock of stationery ₹ 800).
2. Bills receivable include a dishonoured bill of ₹ 8,000.
3. Trade expenses include payment of stationery of ₹ 22,500.
4. Stock in the beginning includes stock of stationery in the beginning ₹ 1,800.
5. Furniture sold was appearing in the Balance Sheet on 31st March, 2024 at ₹ 13,000.
6. Creditors at the end include creditors for stationery ₹ 3,000 for credit purchases.
7. Commission receivable on sale of Consignment is ₹ 40,000.
8. Stationery of ₹ 2,000 was consumed by Shri Arihant.
9. Included in the debtors is an amount of ₹ 2,000 in respect of a bankrupt debtor whose estate is expected to realise not more than 25 paise in the rupee and an item of ₹ 5,000 for goods supplied to Shri Arihant.
10. Make provision for bad and doubtful debts at 5% on debtors.
11. Depreciate furniture at 10% p.a.

Ignore GST

Ans. [Gross Profit ₹ 10,99,000 ; Net Profit ₹ 7,82,750 ; Balance Sheet Total ₹ 29,08,250].

Hint. Stationery Expenses ₹ 24,500 ; Provision for Doubtful Debts ₹ 76,550 (5% on ₹ 15,01,000 + 75% of ₹ 2,000). Loss on Sale of Furniture ₹ 1,700 ; Balance due to Consignor ₹ 1,20,000.

21. From the following Trial Balance of Kanti Lal Desai prepare Trading Account, Profit and Loss Account for the year ending 31st March, 2025, and Balance Sheet as on that date :

	Dr. ₹		*Cr.* ₹
Stock in the beginning	55,000	Discount Received	200
Purchases	1,92,500	Sale of Furniture	
Wages and Salaries	12,500	(on 31st March)	1,000
Carriage Outward	4,000	Sales	2,93,500
Insurance	3,500	Bills Payable	18,500
Bills Receivable	22,500	Creditors	93,250
Debtors	1,50,000	Capital	89,500
Commission	4,000	Consignor's Balance	
Interest	3,500	(1st April, 2024)	40,000
Trade Expenses	3,450	Sales—Re-consignment	64,000

Furniture (on 1st April, 2024)	6,000		
Cash in hand and at Bank	42,250		
Rent and Taxes	12,750		
Charges paid against consignment	8,000		
Cash sent to consigner	80,000		
	5,99,950		5,99,950

Adjustments :

(*i*) Stock in the shop on 31st March, 2025 ₹ 80,000 (including stationery stock ₹ 80). (*ii*) Trade Expenses include payment for stationery of ₹ 2,250. (*iii*) Stock in the beginning includes stock of stationery in the beginning ₹ 180. (*iv*) Creditors at the end include creditors for stationery ₹ 300. (*v*) Furniture sold was appearing in the Balance Sheet on 31st March, 2024 at ₹ 1,300. (*iv*) Stationery of ₹ 200 was consumed by the proprietor. (*vii*) Bills Receivable include a dishonoured bill of ₹ 800. Included in the debtors is an amount of ₹ 200 in respect of a bankrupt whose estate is expected to realise not more than 25 paise in the rupee and an item of ₹ 500 for goods supplied to the proprietor. (*ix*) Make Provision for Doubtful Debts at 5% on Debtors. (*x*) Commission on sale of consignment is ₹ 4,000.

Ans. [G.P. ₹ 1,09,900 ; N.P. ₹ 78,745 ; B/S Total ₹ 2,91,295]

22. Following figures have been extracted from the records of Fancy Stores, a proprietorship concern, as at 31st March, 2025 :

	₹		₹
Furniture	15,000	Insurance	6,000
Proprietor's Capital A/c	54,000	Rent	22,000
Cash in Hand	3,000	Sundry Debtors	60,000
Opening Stock	50,000	Sales	6,00,000
Fixed Deposit	1,34,600	Advertisements	10,000
Drawings	5,000	Postage and Telephone	3,400
Provision for Bad Debts	3,000	Bad Debts	2,000
Cash at Bank	10,000	Printing and Stationery	9,000
Purchases	3,00,000	General Charges	13,000
Salaries	19,000	Sundry Creditors	40,000
Carriage Inwards	41,000	Deposits from Customers	6,000

Prepare Trading, Profit and Loss A/c and Balance Sheet after taking into consideration the following further information :

(1) The closing stock as on 31st March, 2025 was ₹ 10,000. (2) A sale of ₹ 25,000 made for cash had been credited to the Purchases Account. (3) Salary of ₹ 2,000 paid to an employee had been entered in the Cash Book as ₹ 1,000. (4) Charge depreciation on furniture at 10%. (5) Furniture had been sold during the year for ₹ 10,000 and the proceeds had been credited to Furniture A/c. The written down value of furniture sold was ₹ 5,000. (6) A sum of ₹ 10,000 received from a party who had purchased some stocks belonging to a separate business of the proprietor was credited to Sundry Debtors Account. (7) The proceeds of a matured fixed deposit amounting to ₹ 25,400 has been credited to the Fixed Deposits Account. The original amount of the deposit was ₹ 20,000. (8) There was an outstanding liability for rent ₹ 2,000. (9) An advance of ₹ 1,000 paid to an employee against his salary of April, 2025 had been debited to the Salary Account. (10) The office Premises were sub-let from March, 2025 for a monthly rental of ₹ 1,000 but the rent for March has not yet been received.

Ans. [G.P. ₹ 2,19,000 ; N.P. ₹ 1,42,000 ; B/S Total ₹ 2,49,000]

23. Following are the closing balances as on 31-3-2025 extracted from the books of Sh. Mehta. Prepare Trading and Profit & Loss Account for the year ended 31-3-2025 and Balance Sheet as on that date after making the necessary adjustments :

	₹		₹
Sh. Mehta's Capital Account	1,65,000	Interest received from A.N. Sen	400
Opening Stock	70,200	Cash in Bank	12,000
Sales	4,34,400	Discounts received	6,300
Purchases	3,64,650	Investments	7,500
Carriage inwards	27,900	Furniture and Fittings	2,700
Rent and Taxes	8,550	Discount Paid	11,310
Sales Returns	12,900	General Expenses	6,000
Salaries	13,950	Audit Fees	1,050
Purchases Returns	8,700	Insurance	900
Sundry Debtors	36,000	Travelling Expenses	3,500
Sundry Creditors	22,200	Postage and Telegrams	4,070
Bank Loan at 6 per cent (1-4-2024)	30,000	Cash in Hand	570
Interest paid on above	1,350	Deposit with Sh. A.N. Sen (1-4-2024)	
Printing and Advertising	21,900	(Interest @ 9%)	45,000
		Drawings	15,000

***Adjustments* :**

(1) Stock as on 31st March, 2025 was ₹ 1,20,000. (2) Sundry Debtors included a sum of ₹ 3,000 due from Sh. Nair and Sundry Creditors included a sum of ₹ 4,000 due to Sh. Nair. (3) 25% of Printing and Advertisement was to be carried forward to the next year. (4) Provide 5% for bad debts and 2% on the balance for prompt payment. (5) Write off depreciation at 10% of Furniture and Fittings, depreciation in respect of items sold off during the year need not be provided. (6) As on the 31st March, 2025, salaries and carriage inwards that remain unpaid were ₹ 12,000 and ₹ 150 respectively. (7) Insurance paid in advance as on 31st March, 2025 was ₹ 120. (8) Furniture of the book value of ₹ 900 as on 1-4-2024 had been disposed off for ₹ 500 on 30-9-2024. The sale proceeds had been credited to Furniture Account, but the loss on sale of furniture had not been written off in books. (9) Furniture purchased for ₹ 1,000 on 1-4-2024 had been debited to Purchases Account. (10) Purchases to the value of ₹ 1,800 had been omitted to be entered in books. (11) Personal purchase of ₹ 700 made by Sh. Mehta had been included in the purchases. (12) Provide for interest on (*i*) the deposit with Sh. A.N. Sen, and (*ii*) Bank Loan.

Ans. [G.P. ₹ 87,200 ; N.P. 25,908 ; B/S Total ₹ 2,28,008]

24. Prepare Manufacturing, Trading and Profit and Loss Account from the following figures relating to the year 2024-25 :

	1-4-2024	*31-3-2025*
Stock :	₹	₹
Finished Goods	33,000	27,500
Raw Materials	16,000	18,300
Work-in progress (at Prime Cost)	11,000	9,400
Purchases of materials		1,50,900
Transactions during the year :		
Carriage on Purchases		4,100
Wages		65,000
Factory Salaries		26,000
Office Salaries		18,000
Repairs & Maintenance—Machinery		8,300
—Office Equipment		1,700

Depreciation & Maintenance—Machinery		25,000
" "	—Office Equipment	8,100
Sundry Expenses	—Factory	5,300
" "	Office	17,800
Sales		3,60,000

It is the firm's practice to transfer goods from the factory to the sales godown at cost plus 10%.

Ans. [Cost of goods produced ₹ 2,84,000 ; G.P. ₹ 42,100 ; Net Profit ₹ 25,400]

25. Prepare Manufacturing, Trading and Profit & Loss Account for the year ended 31st March, 2025 and Balance Sheet as at that date of Shri S. Singh, manufacturer, from the following Trial Balance and information.

Debit Balances :	₹		₹
Advertising	1,660	Salaries Office	7,380
Bad Debts	1,210	Stock 1-4-2024 :	
Bank Charges	240	Raw Materials	10,460
Drawings	16,000	Finished Goods	14,760
Factory Power	7,228	Work in Progress	3,340
Furniture	1,800	Wages Factory	41,400
General Expenses : Factory	410	Debtors	21,120
Office	692	Cash at Bank	7,852
Insurance	1,804	Cash in Hand	350
Light and Heat	964		
Plant and Machinery (1-4-2024)	30,000	*Credit Balances* :	
Plant & Machinery bought		Bad Debts Provision	2,000
on 30-6-2024	4,000	Capital	70,000
Purchases	67,336	Current Account	3,246
Packing & Transport	2,170	Discount	824
Rent & Rates	2,972	Sales	1,58,348
Repairs to Plant	1,570	Creditors	12,300

Stocks at 31st March, 2025 were : (*a*) Raw Materials ₹ 7,120 ; Work in Progress ₹ 3,480 ; Finished Goods ₹ 19,300 and Packing Materials ₹ 250. The liabilities to be provided for :(*b*) Factory Power ₹ 1,124 ; (*c*) Rent and Rates ₹ 772 ; (*d*) Light and Heat ₹ 320 ; (*e*) General Expenses—Factory : ₹ 50, Office ₹ 80. Insurance Prepaid ₹ 340. Provide Depreciation at 10% p.a. on plant & machinery and 5% p.a. on furnitu₹ Increase the Bad Debts Provision by ₹ 1,000. Five-Sixth of Rent and Rates, Light & Heat and Insurance are to be allotted to the Factory and one-sixth to the Office.

Ans. [Cost of goods manufactured ₹ 1,30,928 ; G.P. ₹ 31,960 ; N.P. ₹ 17,430 ; B/S Total ₹ 89,322]

26. Following is the Trial Balance of Shri Nanda as at 31st March, 2025. You are asked to prepare Trading and Profit and Loss Account and Balance Sheet as at that date :

	Dr.	*Cr.*
	₹	₹
Capital		1,08,090
Stock on 1-4-2024	46,800	
Sales and Sales Return	8,600	2,89,600
Purchases and Returns	2,43,100	5,800
Freight & Carriage	18,600	
Rent & Taxes	5,700	
Salaries and Wages	9,300	
Sundry Debtors and Creditors	24,000	14,800
Bank Loan at 6%		20,000
Bank Interest	900	

Printing & Advertisement	14,600	
Income from Investments		250
Cash at Bank	8,000	
Discount received		4,190
Investments	5,000	
Furniture and Fittings	1,800	
Discount paid	7,540	
General Expenses	3,910	
Audit Fees	700	
Insurance	600	
Travelling Expenses	2,330	
Postage & Telegrams	870	
Cash in hand	380	
Deposit with Mr. Ashok	30,000	
Drawings Account	10,000	
	4,42,730	4,42,730

Stock on 31st March, 2025 was ₹ 78,600. Make the following *adjustments* :

(*a*) Included amongst the Debtors is ₹ 3,000 from Anil and included amongst the creditors ₹ 1,000 due to him. (*b*) The effect of Advertising being not yet expired a quarter of the amount of "Printing and Advertisement" is to be carried forward to the next year. (*c*) Provide 2 per cent for discount on debtors and create provision for Doubtful Debts at 5 per cent. (*d*) A Depreciation of 10% is to be written off Furniture and Fittings. (*e*) Wages and Salaries owing on 31st March, 2025 is ₹ 800 and Carriage owing ₹ 100. (*f*) Insurance paid in advance on 31st March, 2025 is ₹ 80. (*g*) Furniture which stood at ₹ 600 in the books on 1-4-2024 was disposed of at ₹ 290 on 30-9-2024 in part exchange for new furniture costing ₹ 520. A net invoice at ₹ 230 was passed through the Purchases Day Book. (*h*) Purchase invoice amounting to ₹ 400 had been omitted from the books. (*i*) A new sign costing ₹ 100 is included in Advertising. (*j*) Two dishonoured cheques for ₹ 200 and ₹ 300 respectively have not been entered in the Cash Book. The first for ₹ 200 is known to be bad. In the case of the second cheque for ₹ 300 it is expected that the Debtor would be in a position to pay dividend of 75 p. in the Rupee. (*k*) Private Purchases amounting to ₹ 600 had been included in Purchases Day Book. (*l*) Charge full year's Interest on Deposit with Mr. Ashok at 7% p.a. (*m*) Provide for interest on Bank Loan for the amount due.

Ans. [Gross Profit ₹ 57,230 ; Net Profit ₹ 17,707 ; Balance Sheet Total ₹ 1,50,597].

27. From the following Ledger balances extracted at the close of a trading year ended 31st March, 2025, prepare a Trading Account, Profit & Loss Account and Balance Sheet as at that date, after giving effect to the undermentioned adjustments :

	₹		₹
Capital Account on 1-4-2024	50,000	Printing and Stationery Account	250
Stock Account on 1-4-2024	8,000	Rates and Taxes Account	350
Purchases Account	20,000	Travelling Expenses A/c	150
Sales Account	80,000	Sundry Trade Expenses Account	200
Returns Inwards A/c	1,500	Business Premises A/c	55,000
Returns Outwards A/c	400	Furniture and Fixtures Account	2,500
Carriage Inwards A/c	1,200	Bills Receivable Account	3,500
Carriage Outwards A/c	2,500	Bills Payable Account	2,500
Wages A/c	3,300	Sundry Debtors Account	20,000
Salaries A/c	5,500	Sundry Creditors A/c	15,800
Rent A/c	1,100	Packing Machinery A/c	4,500

Freight and Dock Charges	2,400	Smith's Loan A/c (Dr.)	5,000
Fire Insurance Premium Account	900	Investments Account	3,000
Bad Debts A/c	2,100	Cash in Hand	250
Discount Account (Dr.)	500	Cash at Bank	3,500
Apprenticeship Premium Account (Cr.)	1,500	Proprietor's Withdrawals	3,000

Adjustments to be made for the current period are :

(1) Stock in hand at 31st March, 2025, ₹ 7,000. (2) Wages to Labourers for the last month are outstanding ₹ 300. (3) Salaries to clerks for the month of March, 2025 are outstanding ₹ 500. (4) Rent of godowns for the last month is outstanding ₹ 100. (5) Fire Insurance Premium include ₹ 600 paid on 17th Oct, 2024 to run for one year from 1st October, 2024. (6) Apprenticeship premiums are for three years, paid in advance on 1-4-2024. (7) A Stationery bill for ₹ 30 remains unpaid and unrecorded (8) Depreciate : Business Premises by 5% ; Furniture and Fixtures by 10% ; and Packing Machinery by 10%. (9) Interest on Smith's Loan for one year has accrued at 7%. (10) Interest on Investments at 5% for the half year to 31st March, 2025 has accrued. (11) Interest on Capital to be allowed at 5% for the year. (12) Interest on Drawings to be charged to him, as ascertained for the year ₹ 80. (13) Create a provision on debtors for doubtful debts at 5% and discount at 3%. (14) Create a reserve for discount on creditors at 3%.

Ans. [G.P. ₹ 50,700 ; N.P. ₹ 30,779 ; B/S Total ₹ 99,955].

28. Following is the Trial Balance of X at 31st March, 2025 and it is desired to prepare final accounts showing the results of the transactions for the year :

Debit Balances :	₹		₹
Plant and Machinery	5,000	Salaries	1,330
Office Furniture & Fitting	260	Bad Debts	250
Opening Stock	4,800	Discount Allowed	650
Motors Vans	1,200	*Credit Balances* :	
Sundry Debtors	4,070	Capital	4,000
Cash in hand	40	Sales	48,000
Cash at bank	650	Bills Payable	560
Wages : Factory	15,000	Sundry Creditors	5,200
Office	1,400	Provision for Doubtful Debts	250
Purchases	21,350	Returns Outwards	550
Bills Receivable	720	Discount Received	370
Returns Inwards	930	Input CGST Receivable	250
Drawings	700	Input SGST Receivable	250
Factory Lighting & Heating	80		

Following adjustments are to be made :

(*i*) Stock 31st March, 2025—₹ 5,200. (*ii*) Salaries due but not paid 31st March, 2025, ₹ 200. (*iii*) 3 months factory lighting and heating due but not paid, ₹ 30, (*iv*) Insurance paid in advance, ₹ 10. (*v*) 10 per cent depreciation to be written off plant and machinery. (*vi*) 5 per cent depreciation to be written off furniture. (*vii*) 25 per cent depreciation to be written off motors vans (*vii*) Write off further bad debts ₹ 70. (*ix*) The provision for doubtful debts to be increased to ₹ 300. (*x*) Discounts of $2\frac{1}{2}$ per cent on debtors and creditors are to be anticipated. (*xi*) Bills Receivable ₹ 400, not yet due, were discounted on 31st March, 2025 :

Ans. [Gross Profit ₹ 11,560 ; Net Profit ₹ 7,202 ; B/S Total ₹ 16,362].

29. Mr. A, a shop-keeper, had prepared the following Trial Balance from his ledger as on 31st March, 2025 :

	₹	₹
Purchases	3,10,000	
Sales		4,15,000
Stock of Goods as on 1-4-2024	50,000	
Cash in hand	2,100	
Cash at Bank	12,000	
Mr. A's Capital		2,88,600
Drawings	4,000	
Rates and Taxes	5,000	
Salaries	32,000	
Postage and Telephone	11,500	
Salesmen's Commission	35,000	
Insurance	9,000	
Advertising	17,000	
Furniture and Fitting	22,000	
Printing and Stationery	3,000	
Motor Car	48,000	
Bad Debts	2,000	
Cash Discounts	4,000	
General Expenses	14,000	
Carriage Inwards	10,000	
Carriage Outwards	22,000	
Wages	20,000	
Outstanding Liability for Expenses	11,000	
Sundry Creditors		40,000
Sundry Debtors	1,00,000	
Total	7,43,600	7,43,600

You are requested to prepare Trading and Profit & Loss Account for the year ended on 31st March, 2025 and Balance Sheet as on that date.

You are also given the following further information :

(*a*) Cost of goods in stock as on 31st March, 2025—₹ 1,45,000. (*b*) Mr. A had withdrawn goods worth ₹ 5,000 during the year. (*c*) Printing and Stationery expenses of ₹ 11,000 relating to 2023-24 accounting year had not been provided in that year but was paid in this year by debiting outstanding liabilities. (*d*) Purchases include purchase of furniture worth ₹ 10,000. (*e*) Debtors include ₹ 5,000 bad debts. (*f*) Creditors include a balance of ₹ 4,000 to the credit of LM Corporation in respect of which it has been decided and settled with the party to pay only ₹ 1,000. (*g*) Sales include goods worth ₹ 15,000 sent out to SM & Co. on approval and remaining unsold as on 31st March, 2025. The cost of the goods was ₹ 10,000. (*h*) Provision for bad debts is to be created at 5% of Sundry Debtors. (*i*) Depreciate furniture and fittings by 10% and motor car by 20%. (*j*) The salesmen are entitled to a commission of 10% on total sales.

Ans. [Gross Profit ₹ 1,80,000 ; Net Profit ₹ 1,700 ; B/S Total ₹ 3,12,300]

30. Karuna decided to start business of fashion garments under the name of M/s. Designer Wear on 1st April, 2024. She had a saving of about ₹ 10,00,000. She invested ₹ 3,00,000 out of her savings and borrowed equal amount from bank. She purchased a commercial space for ₹ 5,00,000 and further spent ₹ 1,00,000 on its renovation to make it ready for business.

Loan and interest repaid by her in the first year are as follows :

30th June, 2024	—	₹ 15,000 principal + ₹ 9,000 interest
30th September, 2024	—	₹ 15,000 principal + ₹ 8,550 interest

31st December, 2024 — ₹ 15,000 principal + ₹ 8,100 interest

31st March, 2025 — ₹ 15,000 principal + ₹ 7,650 interest.

In view of further capital requirement, she transferred ₹ 2,00,000 from her saving bank account to the bank account of the business. She paid security deposit of ₹ 7,000 for telephone connection. Furniture of ₹ 10,000 was purchased, All payments were made by cheque and all receipts in cash were deposited in the bank.

At the end of the year, her business showed the following results :

Particulars	Amount (₹)	*Particulars*	Amount (₹)
Total Sales	20,00,000	Total Purchases	17,00,000
Electricity Expenses paid	40,000	Telephone Charge	50,000
Cartage Outwards	60,000	Travelling Expenses	45,000
Entertainment Expenses	5,000	Maintenance Expenses	25,000
Misc. Expenses	15,000	Electricity Expenses Payable	20,000

Other Information :

(*i*) She withdrew ₹ 5,000 by cheque each month for her personal expenses.

(*ii*) Depreciation on building @ 5% p.a. and oil furniture @ 10% p.a.

(*iii*) Closing stock in hand as on 31st March, 2025 : ₹ 5,50,000

Prepare trading account, profit and loss account for the year ended 31-3-2025 and Balance Sheet as on that date.

Ans. [Gross Profit ₹ 8,50,000 ; Net Profit ₹ 5,25,700 ; B/S Total ₹ 12,25,70]

CHAPTER 12

Measurement of Business Income

Concept of Income

The concept of income is the most important concept among all other accounting concepts. The computation of net income has been the central theme of financial accounting since the development of generally accepted accounting principles in the 1930s. One of the most important functions of accountants is to measure business income. Practically, income is the pivot around which the entire accounting process moves. The ultimate object of all accounting devices is to ascertain directly or indirectly, from beginning to end, the measurement of income. As a matter of fact, a business cannot have any income of its own. The income reported is actually that of the owners of the business. According to **Paton,** "Net income or profit is the amount accruing to the owners. "That is why, in accounting, profit is a credit item indicating a promise of the business in favour of ownership. Thus, business is rather a purveyor of income to its owners than a claimant for the same."

Objectives of Net Income Reporting

Following are the objectives of net income reporting :

1. Net income reporting gives an idea of the return on capital employed. Return on capital employed is a master ratio which gives an idea of overall efficiency of the business.

2. Profitability of the capital projects can be ascertained with the help of net income ; a project yielding higher return is favoured. Thus, net income reporting is a helpful tool for making capital budgeting decisions.

3. The future course of the business can be predicted on the basis of historical income figures.

4. The ascertainment of net income lays emphasis on the need to distinguish between invested capital and income. This distinction is helpful in paying dividends out of income only and not out of capital. If there is no reporting of net income, it is possible that dividends may be paid out of capital leading to erosion of capital which is not desirable. Dividends should always be paid out of revenue profits.

5. The ascertainment of income is a base for taxation because income tax is levied on the basis of income.

6. In evaluating the use of scarce resources, the use of income figure is a very helpful guide. The activities which give higher return on scarce resources are to be preferred to increase the wealth of the business.

7. For the purpose of giving a portion of the profit to the employees, the ascertainment of net income is a must. Trade unions feel satisfied when net income is reported to them because these unions can see that workers are not being exploited and their due share in profit is being given.

Definition of Income

To a layman income is what he earns in cash or its equivalent by producing or selling goods or rendering service like salary or wages, rent from property, interest earned on giving loan etc. According to **Hicks**, "We ought to define a man's income as the maximum value which he can consume during a week, and still expect to be as well off at the end of the week as he was at the beginning". In this definition of income the implicit assumption is that even if the whole of income is consumed by an individual, his financial position continues to be as good as before.

The income of an individual has been defined. But in accounting we are concerned with income of an entity because accounting is mainly concerned with an enterprise. Individuals create utilities by doing work and what they get in exchange is their income. Similarly a business unit generates utility through production or rendering service by using different factors of production and what it gets in exchange after deducting cost of various factors of production employed by it is its income.

Economists are of the view that income is the favourable change in wealth which takes place due to business operations. For the calculation of income as per this definition, determination of the amount of wealth at first and second point of time is made taking into consideration replacement values of various assets at those points of time. This definition does not give a clear picture of income because it suffers from the following defects :

1. It is difficult to determine the replacement values of the assets at two different points of time, which is a prerequisite for determining the amount of income.

2. Determining replacement values of assets is subjective and is subject to the whims of the persons who determine the replacement values.

3. It does not give an idea of the operating income as wealth may change mainly due to changes in prices of fixed assets.

4. It does not follow the going concern concept of accounting theory because it requires annual appraisal of assets for the determination of income. Assets are purchased for earning purposes and not for resale, so it is not sound to have the replacement value of assets every year.

Thus, the above definition is unsatisfactory, subjective and arbitrary.

Another definition of income as given by the American Accounting Association (AAA) Committee, is reproduced below :

"The realised net income of an enterprise measures effectiveness as an operating unit and is the change in its net assets arising out of (*a*) excess or deficiency of revenue compared with related expired cost, and (*b*) other gains and losses to the enterprise from sales, exchanges and other conversions of assets."

This definition is more satisfactory and scientific on account of the following reasons :

1. This definition adheres to the going concern concept of accounting as it does not take into consideration the replacement value of assets at two periods of time as the first definition takes. It realises the fact that assets are purchased for earning purposes and not for resale.

2. The former definition did not specify the type of changes to be taken into consideration for the measurement of income but this definition clearly states that the following changes should be taken into consideration for measuring the net realisable income :

(*a*) Change in net assets of an enterprise arising out of excess or deficiency of revenue compared with related expired cost. Revenue is measured by the amount charged to customers for goods delivered or services rendered to them and the expired cost is that cost which is incurred to earn the revenue. In other words, prepaid expenses are deducted from the cost incurred because they do not relate to the revenue of the current period. Similarly outstanding expenses are added to the cost actually paid because they relate to the revenue of the current period.

(*b*) Other gains and losses which arise as a result of sales, exchanges and other conversion of assets. Profit or loss on replacement value of assets is not taken into consideration as is done in the first definition but actual profit and loss which is realised on sales, exchanges and other conversion of assets is taken into consideration for the determination of income.

From the above definition, it is clear that net income is the difference between gains and losses or income and expenses or revenues and costs. **Backer** rightly summarises income as, "....from an accounting standpoint income is generally conceived to be a residuum which emerges out of matching expired costs against revenue." Various terms are used to express the business income. Organisations engaged in rendering services usually use the term "earnings" to convey the idea of income.

Organisations engaged in trading or manufacturing usually use the term "profit" to express the excess of revenue over cost and prepare profit and loss account to find out this income. American Accountants prefer to call profit and loss account as income statement. The term "income statement" seems to be justified because of its intimate relationship with income tax, where the term 'income' is more in use. According to **G. D. Roy**, the term 'income' may be preferable for another reason as well, namely, that accounting profit consists of both returns to organisation and remuneration for the use of capital. In this way, accounting profit includes much more than what economic profit does which is the return for the use of capital. In our discussion on the accounting concept of income we shall use both the terms, 'profit' and 'income' to convey the idea.

Accounting Concept of Income

Owners and investors take special interest in the profit or income of the entity. Only through participation in its income the owners can realise any return on their invested funds. Financial accounting is attuned to the measurement of business income or distributable income. Accountants and economists have different meanings of the word 'income' as we have seen in the definition of income. Accountants have not accepted economist's idea of real income because of the high degree of subjectivity of replacement value of the assets at two different points of time. Instead the procedures of financial accounting are designed to yield a measurement of monetary income which the accountants call net income for the period.

Net income for the period is defined as the excess of revenues realised during the period by a specific accounting entity over the costs expired (including losses) during the same period.

Accounting Period. A defined period of time is important for the determination of accounting income because income measurement concerns a span of time rather than a point of time. The problem of measuring monetary income is relatively simple on a whole-life basis. A complete and accurate picture of the degree of success achieved by an enterprise cannot be obtained until it discontinues operations, converts its assets into cash and pays off its debts. Then and only then, it is possible to determine finally its net income. But the owners, the creditors, the investors and overall the government, all are impatient and do not want to wait until the dissolution of the concern to know their trading results *i.e.*, what has been the result of their capital whether it has increased or decreased. All these persons demand regular reports and accounts at proper intervals. Reports may be prepared on the completion of a particular job or project but more often they are prepared at specified time intervals. The maximum interval between reports is one year as it helps the businessman to take any corrective action, to pay income tax, to absorb the seasonal fluctuations and for reporting to the outsiders.

Realisation concept and matching concept are strictly related to the accounting period concept with the result that no proper measurement of income is possible in the absence of any of them. The accountant should include the revenue items relevant to the accounting period (usually a year) on the basis of realisation concept in the Income Statement and expenses involved in obtaining the revenue should be determined and matched with the revenue in the accounting period and the result will be income or loss of the accounting period.

The principle of segregating capital expenditure from revenue expenditure is based on the accounting period concept. The revenue expenditure for a particular period is transferred to the Profit and Loss Account of that period whereas capital expenditure is carried forward to the extent its benefit will be utilised in future accounting periods. Thus, the accounting period concept plays a very important role in determining the income of a particular accounting period. It is also helpful in ascertaining the true and fair view of the financial position of a business entity on a particular date at a particular point of time.

Features of Accounting Income

From the above discussion, features of accounting income can be derived as follows :

1. Accounting income is a matter of matching revenue with the related cost or expense. Accounting income is, therefore, based on matching concept.
2. Accounting income is measured in relation to an accounting period and gives an idea of the operating performance of the business enterprise for the accounting period for which income has been ascertained. Accounting income is, therefore, based on the accounting period concept.
3. Expenses incurred to earn the revenue are measured in terms of historical cost to the enterprise. Determination of expenses is based on the cost concept.
4. Accounting income is based on the realisation principle. Revenue results from the sale of goods and the rendering of services. Revenue is earned only when it is realised and not necessarily when it is received.

Accounting Concepts and Income Measurement

Measurement of accounting income is influenced by various concepts. To understand the impact of these concepts on the measurement of income, a brief description is given below :

1. Conservatism. Under this approach, the income of one period may be shifted to another period in the measurement of income. The understatement of the income is more justified when it is compared with the dangers of its overstatement. The measurement of stock at cost or market price whichever is less, the principle of amortization of intangible assets, not recognising the increase in the value of assets are few examples as applied to measurement of income. But it must not understate the income by providing excessive depreciation or excessive reserves etc.

2. Consistency. According to this concept it is essential to follow the same basis from year to year in the measurement of income as it facilitates comparison of performance from one period to another. Thus the measurement of income in a particular year depends upon the bases which are followed in the previous year(s).

3. Entity Concept. According to this concept, the entity of the proprietor is totally different from the business. Thus the measurement of income is done from the business point of view and not from the owner's point of view. For example, interest on capital of owner, though income to the owner, is treated as an expense for measuring the income of the business.

4. The Accounting Period. Actually the income of a business can be determined precisely only on the termination of business. But the life of the business is uncertain and cannot be determined precisely. The business cannot wait indefinitely for knowing its operating results. Moreover, if the results are unfavourable, these will not be corrected in time. Thus it is desirable to adopt calendar year or natural business year to know the interim results of business and to correct these in time.

5. Accrual Concept. According to this concept revenue must be recognised in that period in which it was realised and costs must be matched with the revenue of that period in which the benefit of that cost has been utilised. Due to this concept the revenue from sales must be considered in that period in which the shipment took place rather than the receiving of payment. Similarly expenses paid in advance will be prorated between successive years according to the specific period covered by the prepayments.

6. Going Concern Concept. According to this concept life span of the business is indefinite and termination of the business at the end of accounting year is only a fiction. It is not proper to consider the asset appraisal for the determination of profit. If income is determined according to asset appraisal method based on market value, then it will be placing too much emphasis on liquidation rather than continuity.

COMPUTATION OF BUSINESS INCOME

The concept of income is used in all organisations and institutions inspite of the fact whether they exist to earn a profit or to render service to the members of society. In order to calculate income accounting will be essential in all types of organisations such as schools, hospitals, canteens, clubs, trading and industrial firms. Every organisation's main aim is to utilise its resources to the maximum extent and in such a way, so as to earn maximum income. The concept of income though applicable to all organisations is traditionally concerned with the business income. In order to discharge his duty faithfully, correctly, and sincerely, the accountant must be fully acquainted with his job of measuring of business income. There are two approaches of computation of business income as given below :

(1) Balance Sheet Approach

(2) Transaction Approach.

1. Balance Sheet Approach. The amount by which the figure of closing net assets (*i.e.* assets—outsiders' liabilities at the end of the accounting period) increases or decreases in comparison to that at the beginning of the accounting period is income or loss for the accounting period provided there is no addition to or withdrawal of capital during the accounting period. The amount so ascertained should be reduced by the addition to capital, if any, and increased by the amount of drawings, if any, during the accounting period for calculating the business income of the accounting period. This method of calculation of income is also known as capital maintenance approach or net worth method. This method is called balance sheet approach because income is calculated with the help of Balance Sheet at the beginning of the accounting period and Balance Sheet at the end of the accounting period. This method of computation of income is the same as is followed for the calculation of profit under the single entry system.

2. Transaction Approach. Most of the enterprises, which use double entry system adopt this method. In this method effect of each financial transaction is taken into consideration to measure the income of a business enterprise, so this method is called the transaction approach to income measurement. Transactions are mainly related to production or purchase of goods and sale of goods. All transactions are related directly or indirectly to revenue or to cost and the surplus of money collected by selling the goods over that spent for producing goods is the measure of income.

Measurement of Business Income

Before discussing measurement of business income, it is desirable to analyse and study the factors which have a direct bearing on the determination of income. Following are the two main factors which help in the estimation of income :

(*i*) Revenues, and (*ii*) Expenses or Expired costs.

***(i)* Revenues.** Revenue results from the sale of goods and the rendering of services and is measured by the charge made to the customers, clients or tenants for goods and services furnished to them. It also includes gains from sale or exchange of assets (other than stock in trade), interest/dividend earned on investments and other increases in the owners equity except those arising from capital contribution and capital adjustments. Revenue is thus the gross increase in capital attributable to business activities. It results from the sale of merchandise, the performance of services for a customer or a client, the rental of a property, the lending of money and other business and professional activities entered into for the purpose of earning income. If an enterprise has several types of revenue, a separate account should be maintained for each. Revenue tells us how assets are increased as a result of the services performed by the business. It can be defined as the consideration recovered by the business for rendering goods and services to its customers.

***(ii)* Expenses.** The costs assigned to a period are regarded as having expired and are designed as expenses. Thus, an expense is an expired cost. In other words, costs that have been consumed in the process of producing revenue are expired costs or expenses. The number of expense categories and individual expense accounts maintained in the ledger varies with the nature and the size of an enterprise. A large business with authority and responsibility spread among employees may use an elaborate classification and hundreds of accounts as an aid in controlling expenses. For a small service or business a modest number of expense accounts is satisfactory. Expenses tell us how assets are decreased as a result of services performed by the business. It may be defined as a measure of the assets given up in the process of rendering goods and services or in the process of producing revenue. Expense is different from loss.

Expense is incurred to result in some benefit whereas a loss is an expenditure without any benefit to the concern. Amount spent on purchase of stationery is an expense but loss due to fire or payment of damages to others is a loss.

The assigning of the cost to revenue is sometimes referred as maching cost with revenue as the accountant places together related costs and revenues relating to a particular period. At this stage, it is desirable to know how to measure the revenues and expenses accurately.

Measurement of Revenue

Revenues are measured in accordance with the accrual concept, *i.e.*, revenues accrue in the accounting period in which they are earned. This period is not necessarily same as the period in which it is received. Following are the two main considerations which affect the measurement of revenue.

(*i*) Revenue and receipt of cash are two different things.

(*ii*) Revenue is earned only when it is realised and not necessarily when received.

Sometimes business receives advance payment which cannot be treated as revenue and creates a liability to render a service on some future date. For example, the building owner who receives rent in advance and the magazine publisher who receives subscription revenue in advance will have such items as liabilities in their books and it cannot be treated as revenue because it has been received during the year. On the contrary, revenue may be earned this year even though payment is not received until the next, year, *i.e.*, accrued interest representing amounts due to the business for services rendered during the accounting period that have not been actually invoiced to the recipient. For example, interest on funds loaned by the business is revenue of the period during which the loan is outstanding and recognition of this revenue results in corresponding recognition of the amount of interest receivable from the borrower ; the latter amount is an asset.

The difference between revenue and receipts is illustrated in the following table which shows various types of sales transactions and classifies the effect of each on cash receipts and sales revenue for 2024.

	Amount	*2024* Cash Receipt	*2024* Sales Revenue
	₹	₹	₹
1. Cash Sales made during 2024	2,000	2,000	2,000
2. Credit Sales made during 2023	3,000	3,000	—
3. Credit Sales made during 2024 and Cash received during 2024	4,000	4,000	4,000
4. Credit Sales made during 2024 and Cash received during 2025	1,000	—	1,000
		9,000	7,000

From the afore-given, it is clear that the total cash receipts do not equal the total sales revenue for 2024. The total will be equal only if the company made all its sales for cash or if the amount of cash collected from credit customers in an accounting period happened to be equal to the amount of credit sales made during the period.

Revenue is considered as earned on that date at which it is realised, *i.e.*, on the date when goods or services are furnished to the customer in exchange for cash or some other valuable consideration. For example, a company manufactures a machine in March, ships and bills it to a customer in April and receives payment in May. The revenue from this transaction is realised neither in March, the month of manufacture, nor in May, the month in which the cash is received but in April, the month in which the exchange takes place. Thus, the revenue is recognised when the actual sales take place and the goods are despatched to the customers. It has nothing to do with the cash receipts.

Exceptions to the General Rule, following are the main exceptions to the general rule discussed above :

***(i)* Recognition of Revenue on Completion of Contract.** If revenue can objectively by measured earlier than the date of exchange between the buyer and the seller, then revenue is recognised on this earlier date. In case of gold mining, revenue is recognised in the accounting period in which the gold is mined rather than the period in which it is sold because gold has always a specified value and international market.

***(ii)* Recognition of Revenue Before Completion of Contract**. The sale basis of the recognition of revenue is not followed in case of long term contracts. If revenue is recognised on the completion of the contract, it will mean postponement of revenue and when revenue is recognised, it will be a very heavy amount. Such practice may discourage the shareholders and will attract high rate of taxation. Therefore, a proportion of the amount of revenue representing that part of the contract completed by the end of the year is treated as revenue even before the completion of the contract.

***(iii)* Non-recognition of Revenue in Case of Doubt.** Revenue may not be recognised in the period in which the goods are delivered if there is considerable doubt as to the amount of cash that is actually going to be received from the customer. In certain types of instalment selling or hire purchase, for example, a sizeable fraction of the customers default on their contracts and in view of the uncertainty of realising the full amount of sale, the seller may decide to recognise revenue only as the instalment payments are received.

Measurement of Expenses

For measurement of expenses we must know as to when an expense is recognised. Expense is given recognition in the period in which there is :

(a) a direct identification or association with the revenue of the period, as in the case of merchandise delivered to customers ;

(b) an indirect association with the revenue of the period as in the case of office salaries or rent ; or

(c) a measurable expiration of asset cost even though not associated with the production or revenue for the current period, as in case of losses from floods or fire.

The expenses of the current year, therefore, include the cost of the products sold during the year even though these products were purchased or manufactured in a prior year ; the wages and salaries earned by the employees whether or not they were paid during the year and the supplies, telephone, electricity and other assets or services consumed or used during the year in connection with the production of this revenue, whether or not the bills for these items were paid.

Four types of events need to be considered in distinguishing between amount that are properly considered as expenses of a given accounting period and the expenditures or cash payments made in connection with those items. These are :

(i) Expenditures this year that are also expenses of this year.

(ii) Expenditures made prior to this year that become expenses during this year. These appear as assets on the Balance Sheet at the beginning of the year such as opening stock, prepaid expenses and deferred charges, etc.

(iii) Expenditures made this year that will become expenses in future years. These will be shown assets in the balance sheet at the end of this year ; for example, purchase of assets this year and depreciation thereon will become expenditure in future

(iv) Expenses of this year, that will be paid in a future year. On the balance sheet at the end of the year, these will appear as liabilities such as outstanding expenses.

Thus, business income is the outcome of the excess of revenue over related expired cost and the result of other gains to the enterprise from sales, exchanges or other conversions of assets. It involves matching of cost with the revenues.

Matching Concept

The determination of periodic net income is a two fold problem involving the revenue recognised during the period and expired costs to be allocated to the period. It is thus a problem of matching revenues and expired costs, the residual amount being the provisional net income or net loss for the particular period. It may be mentioned here that in the process of determination of net income or profit, *it is expense or cost that is matched with revenue and not vice versa.* Thus, first of all revenue is determined and then expenses incurred for earning the revenue are matched with the revenue for calculating the difference known as net profit or net loss. Expenses and costs which do not relate to the current year are known as unexpired costs or prepaid expenses and are shown in the balance sheet as assets until the realisation of revenue. Once it becomes clear that benefit has been taken or revenue is realised, the unexpired costs of prepaid expenses are charged off as expenses and matched with the revenue they realise. It is because of this logic that expense is matched with revenue and not *vice versa*.

Recognition of Revenue. Revenue is measured by the amount charged to customers for goods delivered or services rendered to them. The problem created by periodicity is one of timing—at what point is the revenue realised ? For any particular accounting period, the question is whether revenue items should be recognised and reported as such in the current period or whether their recognition should be postponed to a future period. Various criteria are acceptable for determining when revenue is realised. In any case the criteria adopted should be reasonable in accordance with the terms of the contractual arrangements with the customer and based in so far as possible on objective evidence. The *criteria* most frequently used are described below :

(i) **Point of Sale.** It is customary to consider the revenue from the sale of commodities as being realised at the time title passes to the buyer. At this point the sale price has been agreed upon, the buyer acquires the right of ownership in the commodity and the seller has an enforceable claim against the buyer. The realisation of revenue from the sale of service may be determined in somewhat similar manner although there is frequently a time lag between the time of the initial agreement and the completion of the service. For example, assume that a contract provides that certain repair services be performed, either for a specific price or on a time and material basis. The price or terms agreed upon in the initial contract does not constitute revenue until the work has been performed. Theoretically, revenue from production and sale of commodities and services emerges continuously as effort is expanded. As a practical matter, however, it is ordinarily not possible to make an objective determination until the contract price has been agreed upon and the seller has completed his portion of the contract.

(ii) **Receipt of Payment.** The recognition of revenue may be postponed until payment is received. When this criterion is adopted, revenue is considered to be earned at the time the cash is collected, regardless when the sale is made. The cash basis is widely used by physicians, attorneys and other enterprises in which professional services are the source of revenue. It has little theoretical justification but has the practical advantages of simplicity of operation and avoidance of the problem of estimating losses from uncollectable debtors. Its acceptability as a fair method of timing, the recognition of revenue from personal services is influenced somewhat by the fact that it may be used in determining income subject to the income tax law. It is not an appropriate method of measuring revenue from the sale of commodities.

(iii) **Instalment Method.** In some businesses, especially in retail field it is common to make sales on the instalment plan. In such sales, the purchaser makes a down payment and agrees to pay the remainder in specified amounts at stated intervals over a period of time. The seller may retain technical title to the goods or may take other means to facilitate repossession in the event the purchaser defaults on his payment. Despite such provisions instalment sales should ordinarily be treated in the same manner as any other sale on credit, in which case the revenue is considered to be realised at the point of sale. In exceptional cases where the circumstances are such that collection of debts is not reasonably assured, an alternate method of determining the revenue may be used, *i.e.*, to consider each receipt of cash to be composed of a partial return of cost and gross profit.

(iv) **Degree of Contract Completion.** Enterprises engaged in large construction projects may devote several years to the completion of a particular contract. According to the point of sale criterion, neither the revenue nor the related costs would be recognised until the project is completed with the result that the entire net income from the contract would be reported in a single year. Whenever the total cost of a long term contract and the extent of progress can be reasonably estimated, it is preferable to consider the revenue as being earned over the entire life of the contract. The amount of revenue to be recognised in any particular period is then determined on the basis of the estimated percentage of the contract that has been completed during the period. The estimated percentage of completion can be developed by comparing incurred costs with the most recent estimates of total costs or by estimates of engineers, architects or other qualified personnel of the progress of the work performed. The costs actually incurred during the period are then matched against the revenue recognised. There is, of course, an element of subjectivity, and hence of possible error in the determination of the amount of revenue earned by the degree of contract completion method. The financial statements may, however, be more useful, inspite of estimates, than they would be if none of the revenue were recognised until the completion of the contract. Disclosure of this method used should be made in the financial statements.

***(v)* Gold Mines**. In cases where the revenue can be objectively measured earlier than the date of exchange between the buyer and seller, the revenue is recognised on this earlier date. In gold mining, for example, revenue is recognised in the accounting period in which the gold is mined, rather than the period in which it is sold because gold always has a specified value and a market exchange is not necessary to establish this value.

Effect of Uncertainties on Revenue Recognition

1. Recognition of revenue requires that revenue is measurable and that at the time of sale or the rendering of the service it would not be unreasonable to expect ultimate collection.
2. Where the ability to assess the ultimate collection with reasonable certainty is lacking at the time of raising any claim, *e.g.*, for escalation of price, export incentives, interest etc. revenue recognition is postponed to the extent of uncertainty involved. In such cases, it may be appropriate to recognise revenue only when it is reasonably certain that the ultimate collection will be made. When there is no uncertainty as to ultimate collection, revenue is recognised at the time of sale or rendering of service even though payments are made by instalments.
3. When the uncertainty relating to collectability arises subsequent to the time of sale or rendering of the service, it is more appropriate to make a separate provision to reflect the uncertainty rather than to adjust the amount of revenue originally recorded.
4. An essential criterion for the recognition of revenue is that the consideration receivable for the sale of goods, the rendering of services or from the use by others of enterprise resources is reasonably determinable. When such consideration is not determinable within reasonable limits, the recognition of revenue is postponed.
5. When recognition of revenue is postponed due to the effect of uncertainties, it is considered as revenue of the period in which it is properly recognised.

Allocation of Costs

Properties and services acquired by an enterprise are generally recorded at cost. Cost is the amount of cash or equivalent given to acquire the property or the service. If property other than cash is given to acquire properties or services, the cost is the cash equivalent of the property given. When the properties or the services acquired are sold or consumed, the costs are matched with the related revenues to determine the amount of net income or net loss. The costs of properties or services acquired that are on hand at any particular time represent assets. Such costs may also be referred to as "unexpired costs". As the assets are sold or consumed, they become the "expired costs" or expenses. Theoretically it is possible to assign all costs to each product sold or each service rendered. If this were done, the net income of an enterprise could be measured in terms of units of output. In practice, however, it would be difficult and costly to fragmentise cost allocations to such a degree. As stated earlier, the matching of expired revenue and expired costs on a periodic time basis is satisfactory.

There are two approaches to cost allocation : (1) compute the amount of the expired cost or (2) compute the amount of unexpired cost. For example, it is customary to determine the portion of plant assets that have expired cost. After recording the depreciation of the period, the balances of the plant assets accounts minus the balance of the related accumulated depreciation accounts represent unexpired cost of assets. The alternative approach must be employed for stock in hand. The cost of the stock in hand is ordinarily determined by taking a physical inventory and the remaining costs in the related accounts are assumed to be expired. It might appear that the first approach emphasises expired costs and the second method emphasises unexpired costs. This is not the case, however, as the selection of the method is based on convenience and practicability.

Many of the costs allocable to a period are treated as an expense at the time of incurrence because they will be wholly expired at the end of the period. For example, when a monthly rent is paid at the beginning of a month, the cost incurred is unexpired and hence it is an asset, but since the cost incurred will be wholly expired at the end of the month, it is customary to charge the rental directly to the appropriate expense account ; thus, avoiding the necessity for an additional entry later. The proper allocation of costs among periods is the paramount consideration ; any one of a variety of accounting techniques may be employed in achieving this objective.

Measurement of Cost

The second problem in matching cost with revenue is the measurement of the amount of cost to be matched with revenue. The cost may be historical cost and replacement cost.

***(i)* Historical Cost.** It is the cash equivalent outlay for goods and services actually acquired. The historical costs are recorded in the ledgers and others basic accounting records, the expired portions are reported as expenses in the income statement and the unexpired portions are reported as assets in the balance sheet. Historical costs are relevant in the determination of periodic net income and current financial status. They may be irrelevant, however, in planning for future.

***(ii)* Replacement Cost**. It is cost of replacing an asset at current market price. In many planning situations the cost of replacing an asset is of greater significance than its historical cost. For example, assume that an offer is received for goods to be manufactured at a specific price and there is a sufficient quantity of raw materials in stock that were acquired at a considerably higher cost than the current market price. In deciding, whether to accept the offer, it is the replacement cost of the material that is significant. It might be advisable to accept the offer even though on the basis of historical costs, a loss is likely to result. Replacement cost analysis is useful in planning the replacement of worn out or obsolete assets.

The difference between the replacement cost allocation against revenue and the historical cost of product and service factors given up should be designated in the income statement as *realised gains and losses from market fluctuations and price level changes*. This would help interested parties to evaluate the effectiveness of the management in so far as its buying efforts were concerned ; but more important, it would remove from the costs pertaining directly to operations those amounts realised simply as a result of market fluctuations.

The matching of cost and revenue under two approaches will be more clear from the following assumed data relating to an article :

(i) Cost of goods sold ₹ 150 ; *(ii)* Sale of goods ₹ 200 ; *(iii)* Replacement cost of goods sold ₹ 170 ; and *(iv)* Realised gains from the market fluctuations and price level changes ₹ 20.

Trading Account will be prepared as follows under the two approaches :

(*i*) Historical Cost Approach :

TRADING ACCOUNT

		₹			₹
To	Cost Goods Sold	150	By	Sales	200
"	Profit	50			
		200			200

(*ii*) **Replacement Cost Approach :**

TRADING ACCOUNT

	₹		₹
To Replacement Value of Goods Sold	170	By Sales	200
" Profit	50	By Realised Gains from Market Fluctuation and Price Level Changes	20
	220		220

From the above, it is clear that the profit is the same under both the approaches, but replacement cost approach also gives additional information regarding profit or loss due to market fluctuations and price level changes. This is why replacement cost approach is preferred as compared to the historical cost approach.

Bases of Measurement of Income

All schemes of income measurement start with the idea that the net income is the difference between gains and losses or incomes and expenses or revenues and costs. Net income may be measured by either of by Cash or Accrual basis or Hybrid basis. These have already been discussed in a previous chapter.

(*i*) Cash Basis. Under this concept, income is equivalent to cash received ; expense is equivalent to cash paid out. If cash is received within the accounting period, it is reported as income of the period. If cash has not been received as at the end of the accounting period, no income is reported. Exceptions are made of additional investments by owners and borrowed money ; these are recognized as non-income transactions even on the cash basis. The difference between the cash received and cash paid is termed as net income. It has considerable appeal to many people because it is so simple, appears to be so realistic, is verifiable and satisfies the conservative instinct. Although the basis is very simple and appealable to the general public, yet it is full of deficiencies and, therefore, the accrual basis is liked by the accountants as it is more scientific.

(*ii*) Accrual Basis. In accounting every cash receipt cannot be treated income for determining the true profit of the accounting entity of the period. This basis is not correct and, therefore, the accountant rejects the circumstances of receipt or payment of cash as criteria for associating either income or expense with a period. Instead he adopts the accrual basis, which rests on the concept of realisation and expiration. On the accrual basis of accounting, the income whether received or not but has been earned or accrued during the period forms part of the total income of that period. Similarly, if the firm has taken benefit of a particular service, but has not paid within that period, the expense will relate to the period in which the service has been utilised and not to the period in which payment for it is made. Thus net income for a period is the result of matching of revenue realised in the period and costs expired during the period, *i.e.*, matching concept already discussed.

Change in the Basis of Accounting

When the accounting records are changed from cash basis, to accrual basis the adjusting entries are to be made in respect of (*i*) Prepaid expenses, (*ii*) Outstanding expenses, (*iii*) Accrued income, (*iv*) Income received in advance, (*v*) Bad debts and provision for doubtful debts on sundry debtors, (*vi*) Provision for discount on debtors and creditors, (*vii*) Depreciation on fixed assets, (*viii*) Stock-in-trade etc.

How far the Concept of Income Follows the Accounting Conventions ?

We have already learnt the main accounting conventions. Now we will see how far the concept of income follows those accounting conventions :

(*i*) Convention of Full Disclosure, The convention of disclosure is followed by the concept of income, but not to the full extent. Many a time there is a change desirable on the part of accountants. The improved inventory accounting requires a change to a different method. Full disclosure is a matter of common honesty and is essential for professional integrity. But in practice it is not strictly followed. The concerns following the concept of income do not reveal the full information. They try to conceal their income to evade taxes and also they do not want to give a correct picture to their sister concerns because of competition. Hence this is not a drawback of the concept itself, but the drawback of the person who is using the concept.

***(ii)* Convention of Consistency.** The concept of income does not strictly follow the convention of consistency. Although this convention is very helpful in getting the useful results and enables comparison of one business with the other, yet improvements in the procedures lead the accountants to follow the change. Thus, the convention of consistency is not followed by this concept.

***(iii)* Convention of Conservatism.** Concept of income does not allow the accountants to follow the convention of conservatism in strict sense. For example, determination of income is more important than valuation of assets. Understatement of income is still favourably followed in comparison to overstatements. These two examples indicate that this concept many a time deviates from the convention of conservatism.

***(iv)* Convention of Reasonable Accuracy.** Income concept follows this convention ; that is why, round figures are adopted in published accounts. When comparison is made on the basis of ratio or percentages, exactness is sacrificed in favour of simplicity. But it does not mean that this convention is discarded at all. For correct ascertainment of income or profits, extractness or accuracy is not sacrified at all. But this concept does not follow the legal dictum in strict sense. For example, income-tax law does not treat some items of income for the purpose of taxable income. But they are the items of income and must be shown in the account books.

Thus it is clear that the concept of income does not strictly follow all the conventions of accounting.

QUESTIONS

OBJECTIVE TYPE

1. **State whether the following statements are *true* or *false* :**

   (*a*) Net income or profit is the amount accruing to the owners.
   (*b*) Determining replacement value is subjective.
   (*c*) In the process of determination of net income it is revenue that is matched with expense.
   (*d*) The concept of accounting income strictly follows all the conventions of accounting.
   (*e*) In gold mining, revenue is recognised in the accounting period in which the gold is mined.

Ans. [True : (*a*), (*b*) & (*e*) ; False : (*c*) & (*d*)].

SHORT/LONG ANSWER TYPE

1. What do you understand by the concept of matching cost with revenue ? When is revenue said to be 'realised' for accounting purposes ?
2. Explain the following :
   (*a*) Accounting Concept of Income.
   (*b*) Matching Principle.
3. Define "revenue-expense" matching. What are the criteria for the measurement of revenues and expenses for the matching process ?
4. "Measurement of business income requires matching costs with the revenues." Explain.
5. "Revenue earned and cost of earning revenue should be properly identified for a period." Elucidate this statement.
6. Will you prefer Replacement Cost as compared to Historical Cost approach for measurement of cost? If so, why ?
7. Discuss the importance of accounting period in determination of net income. Why 12 months accounting period is preferred ?

8. Explain the accounting concept of income and show how its determination is influenced by accounting conventions.
9. "Recognition of income presents two basic problems, namely, 'timing' and 'measurement'." Do you agree ? How would you solve these two basic problems ?
10. Discuss the principles behind the timing of revenue recognition.
11. Discuss critically the process of measurement of Income in Accounting.
12. Explain 'accounting income' and 'economic income'. Which concept is more useful and why ?

CHAPTER 13

Analysis of Changes in Income

A firm prepares Income Statement in order to calculate the net income or loss for a specified period. Motive is not only to analyse the net income or loss of a particular period but also changes in the net income or loss figure over the preceding period.

Income Statement is usually divided into two sections, *i.e.* Trading Account and Profit and Loss Account to show separately the amount of gross profit and net profit respectively. Net profit is mostly affected by the gross profit because most of the items shown in Profit and Loss Account are of fixed nature. If gross profit in one year is more, there are chances that net profit will also be more. Keeping this in view, we should analyse the changes in gross profit rather than net profit. In this connection, first we should understand the gross profit ratio and the reasons for an increase or decrease in such ratio before we take up the gross profit analysis.

Gross Profit Ratio

This ratio is of fundamental importance in the analysis of changes in the net income or loss over the preceding period. It is ratio of gross profit to the net sales and is usually expressed as a percentage. It is calculated as given below :

$$\textbf{Gross Profit Ratio} = \frac{\textbf{Gross Profit}}{\textbf{Net Sales}} \times 100$$

Here, gross profit represents the difference between the cost of goods sold and its selling price and by net sales we mean value of sales less value of returns inward. This ratio is useful in indicating losses due to theft, damage or bad management especially in those concerns where there is fixed mark up.

Higher the ratio, the better it is. A low ratio indicates unfavourable trends in the form of reduction in selling prices not accompanied by proportionate decrease in cost of goods or increase in cost of production. The gross profit should be adequate to cover fixed expenses, dividends and building up of reserves.

An increase in this ratio as compared with that for the previous year may indicate :

(*i*) An increase in the selling price of the goods sold without corresponding increase in costs.

(*ii*) A decrease in the cost of production per unit without corresponding decrease in the selling price of the goods sold or alternately a decrease in costs accompanied by a corresponding decrease in selling price but with the same amount of gross profit maintained as in the previous year.

(*iii*) Opening stock valued at a figure lower than it should have been.

(*iv*) Closing stock valued at prices which were too high.

(*v*) Sales figure inflated. For example, goods sent out on consignment or on approval basis may have been included in sales as well as stock on hand inadvertently or otherwise.

(*vi*) Invoices for purchases omitted from the accounts inadvertently or otherwise.

On the other hand, a decrease in the gross profit ratio as compared with that for the previous year may indicate :

(*i*) A decrease in the selling price of the goods sold without any corresponding decrease in cost of production per unit.

(*ii*) An increase in cost of production per unit without a corresponding increase in the sale price of the goods sold.

(*iii*) Misappropriation of goods.

(*iv*) Goods purchased for the private use of the proprietors recorded as purchases of the business.

(*v*) Goods omitted from the inventory at the end of the period.

(*vi*) Opening stock valued at a figure higher than it should have been.

(*vii*) Closing stock valued at prices which were too low.

Another factor which affects gross profit ratio is the practice of increasing or reducing the sale price of goods sold by "mark-ups" and "mark-downs". In case of such a practice, management should keep a record of mark-ups and mark-downs so that the gross profit ratio may be tested for regularity or otherwise after giving due considerations to such mark-ups and mark-downs.

A business should keep up its margin of profit, otherwise it may not cover its operating expenses and may not provide adequate return on capital employed.

Gross Profit Analysis

The determination of gross profit is usually the first step in the determination of net income; so the analysis of changes in income must be preceded by an analysis of the changes in the gross profit.

The changes in the amount of gross profit of the current year compared with that of the previous year may be caused by the following factors :

1. Increase or decrease in the amount of sales which may be due to the following factors :

(*a*) Increase or decrease in the selling price of the goods sold.

(*b*) Increase or decrease in the quantity of the goods sold without any change in the selling price.

(*c*) Simultaneous changes in the selling price and the quantity of the goods sold.

2. Increase or decrease in the amount of cost of goods sold which may be due to the following reasons :

(*a*) Increase or decrease in the cost of production of goods sold.

(*b*) Increase or decrease in the quantity of goods sold.

(*c*) Simultaneous changes in cost and the quantity thereof.

3. Changes in both, *i.e,* amount of sales and cost of goods sold.

ILLUSTRATION 1. From the following information, make an analysis of changes in total sales due to quantity and price.

	2024	*2025*	*Increase or Decrease*
	₹	₹	₹
Sales	5,00,000	6,60,000	1,60,000
Number of units sold	50,000	60,000	10,000
Selling price per unit	10	11	1

SOLUTION

Increase in amount of sales due to quantity

Increase in number of units sold × Price of previous year

10,000 × ₹ 10 = ₹ 1,00,000

Increase in amount of sales due to price

Increase in price per unit × Number of units sold in current year

₹ 1 × 60,000 = ₹ 60,000

Combined effect of change in quantity and price = ₹ 1,00,000 + ₹ 60,000 = ₹ 1,60,000 increase.

ILLUSTRATION 2. From the following data, analyse the changes in the cost of goods sold due to (*i*) quantity, (*ii*) price, and (*iii*) combined effect of quantity and cost.

	2024	*2025*	*Increase or Decrease*
	₹	₹	₹
Cost of goods sold	4,00,000	5,40,000	1,40,000
Number of units sold	50,000	60,000	10,000
Cost per unit	8	9	1

SOLUTION

(*i*) ***Increase in cost of goods sold due to quantity***

Increase in number of units sold × unit cost in previous year

₹ 10,000 × 8 = ₹ 80,000

(*ii*) ***Increase in cost of goods sold due to price***

Increase in cost per unit × Number of units sold in current year

₹ 1 × 60,000 = ₹ 60,000

(*iii*) ***Increase in cost of goods sold due to quantity and cost***

Increase in cost due to quantity + Increase in cost due to price

₹ 80,000 + ₹ 60,000 = Rs 1,40,000

ILLUSTRATION 3. From the following data, prepare a Statement of Analysis of Decrease in Gross Profit for the year ended 31st December, 2024 :

	2023	*2024*	*Increase or Decrease*
	₹	₹	₹
Sales	5,00,000	4,40,000	60,000
Less : Cost of goods sold	3,00,000	2,56,000	44,000
Gross Profit	2,00,000	1,84,000	16,000
Number of units sold	1,00,000	80,000	20,000
Unit sale price (₹)	5	5.50	0.50
Unit cost (₹)	3	3.20	0.20

SOLUTION

ANALYSIS OF DECREASE IN GROSS PROFIT

for the year ended 31st December, 2024

		₹	₹
Decrease in amount of sales due to :			
(*i*) Quantity factor :			
Decrease in number of units sold	20,000		
Unit sale price in 2023	× ₹ 5	1,00,000	
(*ii*) Price factor :			
Increase in unit sale price in 2024	₹ 0.50		
Number of units sold in 2024	× 80,000	40,000	
			60,000
Net decrease in amount of sales			
Decrease in cost of goods sold due to :			
(*i*) Quantity factor :			
Decrease in number of units sold	20,000		
Unit cost in 2023	× ₹ 3	60,000	
(*ii*) Price factor :			
Increase in unit cost in 2024	₹ 0.20		
Number of units sold in 2024	× 80,000	16,000	
Net decrease in cost of goods sold			44,000
Decrease in gross profit in 2024 (₹ 60,000 – ₹ 44,000)			16,000

The above analysis indicates that the increase in selling price of ₹ 0.50 per unit was offset by increase in cost of production of ₹ 0.20 per unit and decrease in number of units sold in 2024. Decrease in quantity of sales of 20,000 units in 2024 was the reason for the decrease in gross profit in 2024.

Use of Percents in Analysis of Changes in Income

So far analysis of changes in income was made when information relating to sales, cost of goods sold, number of units sold, unit cost and unit sale price was available.

In the following illustration use of per cents has been made in making an analysis of changes in income when the information relating to number of units sold, unit sale price and unit cost price is not given. For example, the per cent change in quantity is given, per cent change in other variables (*i.e.,* cost price and sale price) can be calculated and analysis of income can be made.

ILLUSTRATION 4. Following information is given.

	2024	*2025*
	₹	₹
Sales	75,000	1,50,000
Cost of goods sold	50,000	75,000
Gross profit on sales	25,000	75,000

During the year 2025, increase in quantity (or volume) was 20%. You are required to :

(*i*) calculate per cent change in selling price and cost of production.

(*ii*) prepare a reconciliation statement of gross profit earned in 2024 and 2025.

SOLUTION

The change due to quantity factor is given to be 20%. Other change in cost price and sales price is, therefore, due to price factor.

Calculation of per cent change in sale price

A 20% increase in quantity means that the units sold must be 120 in 2025 as against 100 in 2024. Therefore, if quantity factor is ignored, sales in 2025 would have been ₹ 1,25,000 $\left(i.e.\ ₹\ 1{,}50{,}000 \times \frac{100}{120}\right)$. The actual sale in 2024 was ₹ 75,000. Thus this increase in sale in 2025 over 2024 is due to price factor. The per cent change in sale due to price factor is as follows :

$$\frac{\text{Increase in sale price due to change in price}}{\text{Sales value in previous year (2024)}} = \frac{₹\ 1{,}25{,}000 - ₹\ 75{,}000}{₹\ 75{,}000} \times 100 = 66\tfrac{2}{3}\%$$

Thus, selling price increased by $66\frac{2}{3}\%$ in 2025 as compared to 2024.

Calculation of per cent change in cost of production

Cost of goods in 2025 without quantity increase

$$= \frac{100}{120} \times ₹\ 75{,}000 = ₹\ 62{,}500$$

Less : Cost of goods in 2024 = ₹ 50,000

Increase in cost = ₹ 12,500

Percentage change in cost price :

$$\frac{\text{Increase in Cost}}{\text{Cost of Goods in 2024}} \times 100 = \frac{₹\ 12{,}500}{₹\ 50{,}000} \times 100 = 25\%$$

Thus, cost of production increased by 25% in 2025 as compared to 2024.

RECONCILIATION STATEMENT OF GROSS PROFIT

Earned in 2024 and 2025

	₹
Gross profit earned during 2024	25,000
Add : 20% increase in gross profit due to 20% increase in quantity in 2025 $\left(i.e., \frac{20}{100} \times ₹\ 25{,}000\right)$	5,000
$\frac{66\frac{2}{3}}{166\frac{2}{3}}$ of ₹ 1,50,000 sales in 2025 *i.e.,* increase in gross profit due to increase in selling price	60,000
	90,000
Less : Decrease in gross profit due to 25% increase in cost of production	
i.e. $\frac{25}{125}$ of ₹ 75,000 cost of goods in 2025	15,000
Gross profit earned during 2025	75,000

ILLUSTRATION 5. From the following data prepare a reconciliation statement of gross profit earned in 2024 and 2025.

	2024	*2025*
	₹	₹
Sales	10,00,000	20,00,000
Less : Cost of goods sold	6,25,000	15,00,000
Gross profit	3,75,000	5,00,000

During the year 2025, cost increased by 25%.

SOLUTION

During the year 2025, cost increased by 25% so cost must be 125 in 2025 as against to 100 in 2024. Thus, the cost of goods sold in 2025 without taking into consideration 25% increase in cost should be :

	₹
$\frac{100}{125} \times ₹\ 15{,}00{,}000$	12,00,000
Cost of goods sold in 2024	6,25,000
Increase in cost without taking increase in price	5,75,000

Therefore, increase in quantity $= \frac{₹\ 5{,}75{,}000}{₹\ 6{,}25{,}000} \times 100 = 92\%$

Calculation of increase in selling price

Sales in 2025 after 92% increase in quantity	20,00,000
Sales in 2025 without taking 92% increase in quantity	
$₹\ 20{,}00{,}000 \times \frac{100}{192} =$	10,41,667
Less : Sales in 2024	10,00,000
Increase in sales without quantity factor	41,667

Therefore, increase in selling price

$$= \frac{₹\ 41{,}667}{₹\ 10{,}00{,}000} \times 100 = 4{\cdot}167\%$$

RECONCILIATION STATEMENT OF GROSS PROFIT

Earned in 2024 and 2025

	₹
Gross profit earned during 2024	3,75,000
Add : 92% increase in gross profit due to 92% increase in quantity in 2025 $\left[i.e., ₹\ 3,75,000 \times \frac{92}{100}\right]$	3,45,000
$\frac{4.167}{104.167}$ of ₹ 20,00,000 sales in 2025 *i.e.,* increase in gross profit due to increase in selling price	80,000
	8,00,000
Less : Decrease in gross profit due to 25% increase in cost of production, *i.e.,* $\frac{25}{125}$ of ₹ 15,00,000 cost of goods in 2025	3,00,000
Gross profit earned during 2025	5,00,000

ILLUSTRATION 6. The profits of 2024 and 2025 are given together with expenses :

		2024	*2025*
		₹	₹
Materials consumed		1,00,000	1,40,000
Wages		80,000	1,20,000
Overheads :	Fixed	30,000	32,000
	Variable	24,000	34,000
Net Profit		10,000	20,500

The wage rate was increased by 20% in 2025 than 2024. Similarly materials prices were higher by 10%. Sales prices were increased by 10% in 2025. Analyse the causes of increase in profits in 2025.

SOLUTION

RECONCILIATION STATEMENT OF PROFIT

Earned in 2024 and 2025

		₹	₹
Profit earned during 2024			10,000
Add : Increase in Profit in 2025 due to :			
(*i*) Increase in Sales Price	(1)	31,500	
(*ii*) Increase in Sales Volume	(2)	11,640	
(*iii*) Saving in Materials Used	(3)	1,827	
(*iv*) Saving in Wages Cost due to improvement in labour efficiency		(4)	3,280
			48,247
			58,247
Less : Decrease in Profit in 2025 due to :			
(*i*) Increase in Materials Price	(3)	12,727	
(*ii*) Increase in Wage Rate	(4)	20,000	
(*iii*) Increase (Disproportionate) in Variable Overheads	(5)	3,020	
(*iv*) Increase in Fixed Overheads	(6)	2,000	
			37,747
Net Profit earned during 2025			20,500

Working Notes :

Sales for 2024 are ₹ 1,00,000 + ₹ 80,000 + ₹ 30,000 + ₹ 24,000 + ₹ 10,000 = ₹ 2,44,000

Sales for 2025 are ₹ 1,40,000 + ₹ 1,20,000 + ₹ 32,000 + ₹ 34,000 + ₹ 20,500 = ₹3,46,500

Additional sales in 2025 have increased the profit in two ways :

(1) From increase in sale price, profit is increased by

$$₹\ 3,46,500 \times \frac{10}{110} = ₹\ 31,500$$

(2) From increase in sales volume, profit is increased by ₹ 11,640 calculated as follows :

	₹
Sales for the year 2025	3,46,500
Less : Increase in Sales Price	31,500
2025 sales at last year's prices	3,15,000
Less : 2024 Sales	2,44,000
Increase in Sales Volume	71,000

Increase in sales volume is 29.1% $\left(i.e.\ \frac{₹\ 71,000 \times 100}{₹\ 2,44,000}\right)$ of the last year's sales.

Increase in Profit = 29.1% of Contribution for 2024
= 29.1% of ₹ 40,000 (Fixed Expenses ₹ 30,000 + Profit ₹ 10,000) = ₹ 11,640

(3) Materials Consumed :

From increase in prices of materials, profit is decreased by

$$\frac{10}{110} \times ₹\ 1,40,000 = ₹\ 12,727$$

	₹
Materials consumed during the year 2025	1,40,000
Less : Increase in prices of materials	12,727
Materials consumed in 2025 at 2024 prices	1,27,273
Materials to be consumed on 2024 basis (₹ 1,00,000 + 29.1%)	1,29,100
Saving in Materials or Profit Increased	1,827

(4) Wages

From increase in wage rate, profit has decreased by ₹ 1,20,000 × $\frac{20}{120}$ = ₹ 20,000

	₹
Wages paid for the year 2025	1,20,000
Less : Increase in wage rate	20,000
Wages for the year 2025 at 2024 prices	1,00,000
Wages at 2024 efficiency should have been ₹ 80,000 + 29.1%	1,03,280
Saving resulting in increase in profit	3,280

(5) Variable Overheads

	₹
For 2025 Actual	34,000
For 2024	₹ 24,000
Add : 29.1% increase due to 29.1% increase in production in 2025	₹ 6,980
Variable Expenses for 2025 should have amounted to	30,980
Excess in Variable Expenses or Decrease in Profit (₹ 34,000 – ₹ 30,980)	3,020

(6) Fixed Overheads	₹
For 2025	32,000
For 2024	30,000
Excess resulting in decrease of profit in 2025	2,000

Fixed expenses should have remained constant (₹ 30,000) for 2025 because these do not change with the increase in production.

ILLUSTRATION 7. Revenue Account of Goodwill Co. Ltd. has been summarised as shown below :

	₹	₹
Sales		60,00,000
Direct Materials	18,00,000	
Direct Wages	12,00,000	
Variable Overheads	4,80,000	
Fixed Overheads	17,20,000	52,00,000
Profit		8,00,000

The licensed capacity of the company is ₹ 80,00,000 but the key factor is sales demand. It is proposed by the management that in order to utilise the existing capacity, the selling price of the product should be reduced by 5%.

You are required to prepare a forecast statement showing the effect of the proposed reduction in selling price after taking into account the following changes in costs :

(*i*) Sales forecast ₹ 76,00,000 (at reduced prices)
(*ii*) Direct wages rates and variable overheads are expected to increase by 5%.
(*iii*) Direct material prices are expected to increase by 2%.
(*iv*) Fixed overheads will increase by ₹ 80,000.

SOLUTION

GOODWILL CO. LTD.

Forecast Statement Showing the Effect of Changing Selling Price and Costs

		₹
Sales at full licensed capacity		80,00,000
Less : 5% Reduction in Selling Price $\left(₹\ 80{,}00{,}000 \times \frac{5}{100}\right)$		4,00,000
Sale Forecast	₹	76,00,000
Less : Direct Materials	24,48,000 (2)	
Direct Wages	16,80,000 (3)	
Variable Overheads	6,72,000 (4)	
Marginal Cost		48,00,000
Contribution		28,00,000
Less : Fixed Overheads	(5)	18,00,000
Estimated Profit		10,00,000

Working Notes :

(1) The sales volume has increased by $33\frac{1}{3}$%. It is calculated as follows :

	₹
Sales forecast at old prices	80,00,000
Less : Last year's sales	60,00,000
Increase in sales volume as compared to last year	20,00,000

$$\% \text{ increase in sales volume} = \frac{₹\ 20,00,000}{₹\ 60,00,000} \times 100 = 33\frac{1}{3}$$

Thus production is expected to increase by $33\frac{1}{3}$% because sales volume is increased by this percentage. Consequently, variable expenses will also increase by $33\frac{1}{3}$% if there is no change in prices.

(2) Direct Material Cost	₹
Last year	18,00,000
Add : $33\frac{1}{3}$% increase in production	6,00,000
	24,00,000
Add : 2% of ₹ 24,00,000 for increase in price of materials	48,000
	24,48,000

(3) Direct Wages	₹
Last year	12,00,000
Add : $33\frac{1}{3}$% increase due to increase in production	4,00,000
	16,00,000
Add : 5% of ₹ 16,00,000 due to increase in labour rates	80,000
	16,80,000

(4) Variable Overheads	₹
Last year	4,80,000
Add : $33\frac{1}{3}$% increase in production	1,60,000
	6,40,000
Add : 5% increase in rates :	32,000
	6,72,000

(5) Fixed Overheads	₹
Last year	17,20,000
Add : Increase	80,000
	18,00,000

QUESTIONS

OBJECTIVE TYPE

1. In each of the following cases, select the alternative which you consider to be correct:

(*a*) Gross profit ratio is ratio of gross profit to :
(*i*) Cost of goods produced (*ii*) net sales (*iii*) net profit.

(*b*) An increase in gross profit ratio as compared with that for previous year may indicate:
(*i*) An increase in the selling price. (*ii*) Opening stock valued at a higher figure (*iii*) Closing stock valued at a lower figure.

Ans. [(*a*) (*ii*); (*b*) (*i*)].

SHORT/LONG ANSWER TYPE

1. What do you mean by Gross Profit Ratio ? What are the indications given by this ratio when it increases or reduces ?

2. What may be the possible reasons for an increase in the size of gross profit of the current year as compared to that of the previous year ?
3. Analyse the factors which have direct bearing on the changes in income.
4. Discuss the two factors affecting both sales and cost of goods sold to which a change in gross profit can be attributed.
5. Give the various reasons of a change in gross profit and cost of goods sold.

PRACTICAL PROBLEMS

1. From the following information, analyse the changes in total sales due to.
(1) Quantity (2) Price, and (3) Joint effect of quantity and price.

	2024	*2025*
Sales	₹ 2,00,000	₹ 3,25,000
Number of units sold	50,000	65,000
Sale price per unit	4	5

Ans. **[(1) ₹ 60,000; (2) ₹ 65,000 ; (3) ₹ 1,25,000].**

2. From the following information, calculate :
(*i*) Per cent change in price.
(*ii*) Per cent change in cost of goods sold.

	2024	*2025*
	₹	₹
Sales	6,00,000	9,00,000
Cost of goods sold	4,00,000	4,50,000

Increase in quantity or volume is 20%.

Ans. **[(*i*) 25% ; (*ii*) 6.25%].**

3. Following information is given to you :

	2023	*2024*
	₹	₹
Sales	4,00,000	8,00,000
Less : Cost of goods sold	2,50,000	6,00,000
Gross profit on sales	1,50,000	2,00,000

During the year 2024, cost increased by 25%. You are required to calculate :
(*i*) Per cent change in quantity factor.
(*ii*) Per cent change in price factor.
(*iii*) Change in gross profit.

Ans. **[(*i*) 92% (*ii*) 4.167%; (*iii*) Increase in gross profit due to increase in quantity ₹ 1,38,000, increase in gross profit due to increase in selling price ₹ 32,000 and decrease in gross profit due to increase in cost ₹ 1,20,000].**

4. From the following information, prepare a Statement of Analysis of Increase in Gross Profit for the year ended 31st December, 2024.

		2024	*2023*	*Increase or (Decrease)*
		₹	₹	₹
	Sales	4,50,000	4,00,000	50,000
Less :	Cost of goods sold	3,25,000	2,80,000	45,000
	Gross profit on sale	1,25,000	1,20,000	5,000

Number of units sold	2,50,000	2,00,000	50,000
Unit sale price	1.80	2.00	(0.20)
Unit cost price	1.30	1.40	(0.10)

Ans. [Profit increased due to increase in amount of sales attributed to :

	₹	₹
Quantity factor	1,00,000	
Price factor (Loss)	50,000	50,000
Profit decreased due to increase in cost of goods sold attributed to :		
Quantity factor (Loss)	70,000	
Price factor (Profit)	25,000	45,000
Increase in Gross Profit in 2024		5,000].

5. The trading results of Jack to Jackson Limited for the year 2023 and 2024 were as follows :

	2023	*2024*
	₹	₹
Material Consumed	1,00,000	1,32,000
Wages	60,000	66,000
Variable Overheads	12,000	14,000
Fixed Overheads	20,000	24,000
Net Profit	8,000	17,000
Sale Value of Products	2,00,000	2,53,000

Material prices and wages rates were increased in 2024 by 10 per cent and sale prices were increased by 10 per cent.

Prepare a statement showing how much each factor has contributed to the variation of profit.

	₹
Ans. [Profit increased due to increase in sales price	**23,000**
Profit increased due to increase in sales volume	**4,200**
Profit increased due to increase in labour efficiency	**9,000**
Profit decreased due to increase in material prices	**12,000**
Profit decreased due to increase in use of materials	**5,000**
Profit decreased due to increase in labour rates	**6,000**
Profit decreased due to increase in variable overheads	**200**
Profit decreased due to increase in fixed overheads	**4,000].**

6. A manufacturing company had a loss in 2023-24. In order to improve the position the following steps were taken at the outset of the year 2024-25.

(*i*) Sale price was raised by 5%.

(*ii*) Special sales drive.

(*iii*) Improvement in production techniques.

(*iv*) General economy drive.

The comparative position of the two years were :

	2023-24	*2024-25*
	₹	₹
Sales	8,00,000	9,03,000
Less : Cost of sales	6,40,000	6,70,000
	1,60,000	2,33,000

Less : Overheads	1,80,000	1,70,000
Net Profit/(Net Loss)	(20,000)	63,000

Apportion the improvement over the different steps taken.

Ans. [Profit increased due to :

	₹
(*i*) Increase in selling price	**43,000**
(*ii*) Special sales drive	**12,000**
(*iii*) Improvement in production techniques	**18,000**
(*iv*) General economy drive	**10,000].**

CHAPTER 14

Accounting for Consignments

Need for Consignment

Now-a-days it is quite common that manufacturers or wholesale dealers despatch goods to their agents at home and abroad to increase their sales. *The knowledge of the agent of the local conditions* where he resides proves useful in increasing the sales. Moreover, it is *very expensive for the manufacturer to sell the goods directly* either in the home market or in the foreign market. Therefore, different agents are appointed for different places.

Meaning of Consignment

A shipment of goods by a manufacturer or wholesale dealer to an agent to be sold by him on commission basis, on the risk and account of the former, is known as *consignment.* The person who sends the goods to the agent to be sold by him on commission basis is called the *consignor.* The person to whom the goods are sent for sale on commission basis is called the *consignee.* To the consignor, the consignment of goods is known as *outward consignment* and to the consignee, it is known as *inward consignment*. The goods consigned to the agent (called *goods sent on consignment*) cannot be treated as sales at the time of the consignment; they are treated as sales only when these are sold by the consignee. Therefore, such goods require *special treatment* in accounts.

Distinction Between Consignment and Sale

Following are the main points of *difference between consignment and sale.*

(*i*) In case of sale, the *legal ownership of the goods* sold is transferred to the purchaser of goods; whereas in case of consignment of goods, the legal ownership of the goods is not transferred to the consignee but the ownership of the goods remains vested in the consignor till the goods consigned are sold by the consignee.

(*ii*) In case of sale of goods, the *relationship between the seller and the purchaser* of the goods is that of a creditor and a debtor whereas in case of consignment, the relationship between the consignor and the consignee is that of a principal and an agent because the consignee is to sell goods on behalf of the consignor.

(*iii*) In consignment, *expenses incurred by the consignee in connection with the goods consigned to him* are usually borne by the consignor whereas in case of sale, expenses incurred after sale of goods are borne by the purchaser.

(*iv*) In case of consignment, *risk attached to the goods sent* lies with the consignor till the goods consigned are sold by the consignee. But in case of sale, risk attached to the goods sold is transferred to the purchaser of goods.

(*v*) In case of consignment *return of goods is possible* if the goods are not sold by the consignee. But in case of sale, return of goods is not possible as goods once sold are not returnable.

(*vi*) In case of consignment, *account sale* is required to be submitted periodically by the consignee to the consignor. But in case of sale no account sale is required to be submitted by the purchaser to the seller.

(*vii*) In case of consignment, *unsold goods with the consignee will be treated as stock of the consignor.* But the seller has nothing to do with unsold goods of the buyer.

(*viii*) In consignment, *transactions are governed and regulated* by law of agency whereas in case of sale transactions are regulated by the Sale of Goods Act.

(*ix*) In case of sale if **goods are lost after delivery to the buyer,** it is the buyer who will bear the loss but in case of consignment if goods are lost, it is the consignor who will bear the loss.

Procedure to be Followed in Case of Consignment

The consignor sends goods to the consignee and incurs certain expenses in sending the goods to the consignee. Generally consignor receives advance against the goods from the consignee. Such goods can be sent by the consignor either at cost price or at invoice price for which the consignor will prepare a ***proforma invoice.*** Such invoice is exactly like invoice in appearence without being actually the invoice but it does not make the consignee responsible to pay the amount mentioned therein. It is in the nature of memorandum and is not a debit note so it is unlike a regular invoice. The consignee will incur some expenses for taking the delivery of goods and bringing these to the shop. He will try to sell the goods either for cash or on credit. He will get *commission* for the sales which he has made on behalf of the consignor besides getting reimbursement of actual expenses incurred by him on behalf of the consignor. When goods are sold by the consignee on credit, there is a possibility that the amount may not be realisable by the consignee from the consignment debtors. The consignee in order to increase the commission may sell the goods on credit without any responsibility for collection of debts. In order to check this tendency the consignor gives the consignee a commission (called ***Del Credere Commission).*** It is a commission which is paid by the consignor to the consignee for taking additional risks of recovery of debts on account of sales made on credit by the consignee on behalf of the consignor. *It is generally calculated on gross sales unless it is given to be calculated on credit sales.* **If a consignor allows del credere commission to the consignee, then bad debts will be borne by the consignee.** Moreover, it will also make the *consignee careful on choosing customers for credit sales.* Sometimes an extra commission (calculated on sales) is given by the consignor to the consignee for working hard to push a new line of product in the market. Such commission is called ***Over-riding Commission.***

After a particular fixed period or as and when the goods consigned are sold by the consignee, the consignee is required to send a statement known as an *Account Sales* which will show the quantity and quality of goods sold, the gross proceeds realised and the amount due to the consignor after deducting consignee's expenses on consignment of goods, commission payable to the consignee and advance (if any) paid by the consignee from the gross sale proceeds. Account sales is sent to the consignor with a view to enable him to note entries regarding sales of the goods consigned, expenses incurred and commission earned by the consignee. Following can be a *specimen* of an Account Sales :

Account sales of 100 table fans sold by Suresh & Co. of Delhi for the account and risk of Lakshmi Private Limited, Mumbai.

2025		₹	₹
June 30	Gross proceeds from sales :		
	100 table fans @ ₹ 1,000		1,00,000
	Less : Charges :		
	Freight and carriage	900	
	Insurance	650	
	Warehouse charges	800	

Commission @ 5% on ₹ 1,00,000	5,000	7,350
		92,650
Less : Advance		51,000
Balance sent by Bank Draft		41,650

E. & O.E.

Suresh & Co. Delhi
Consignee

Distinction Between Account Sales and Proforma Invoice

Point of Distinction	*Account Sales*	*Proforma Invoice*
1. **Preparation and Despatch**	It is prepared by the consignees and sent to the consignor.	It is prepared and despatched by consignor to all the consignees.
2. **Contents**	It contains details of goods sold by the consignee, expenses, commission and advance deducted showing net balance payable to the consignor.	It contains the particulars of goods despatched to the consignee.
3. **Nature**	It is a Statement or Account of Sales.	It is an advice note.
4. **Time**	It is prepared periodically or at the completion of sales.	It is prepared at the time of despatch of goods.
5. **Accountability of consignee**	It makes the consignee accountable to the consignor.	There is no responsibility on the part of the consignee.
6. **Basis for entries in books**	It serves as the basis for recording entries in the books by the consignor.	It does not serve as the basis of accounting entries. It is merely for advice and information of consignee.

Difference Between Invoice and Account Sales

Account sales differs from invoice. *Invoice is sent by a seller to a buyer*. It contains description of goods sold on credit and the price charged. The buyer is required to pay the amount of the invoice. Following are the *points of difference* between account sales and invoice :

(*i*) Account Sales is ***prepared by*** the consignee whereas invoice is sent by the seller.

(*ii*) All ***expenses and commission are deducted*** in Account Sales whereas in invoice expenses are added but trade discount is deducted.

(*iii*) ***All expenses incurred by the consignee are borne by the consignor*** but after sale, expenses are paid by the buyer.

(*iv*) The ***relationship*** between two parties in case of an invoice is that of a debtor and creditor but in case of account sales the relationship remains as principal and agent.

(*v*) In case of proforma invoice price, ***consignee is not to make payment*** on receiving the goods (but he will be liable only after sale) but in case of invoice the buyer is ***liable to make the payment*** on receiving the goods.

(*vi*) In case of proforma invoice *ownership* is not transferred while sending the goods but ownership is automatically transferred in case of invoice.

Consignment Sale in the VAT/CST Regime

In the previous regime, the consignor would send the goods to the consignee without any payment of VAT as there was no sale involved at this stage. Similarly, in the case of interstate transfer of goods for consignment, no CST or Form F procedure was involved. Taxation would come into the picture only when consignee would sell the goods to the end customer.

Consignment Sale under GST Regime

Before trying to understand the possible impact of GST on consignment sales, we need to be familiar with these two definitions, which have been introduced with respect to a consignment sales scenario :

- **Agent**—means a person, including a factor, broker, commission agent, arhatia, del credere agent, an auctioneer or any other mercantile agent, by whatever name called, who carries on the business of supply or receipt of goods or services or both on behalf of another—in other words, the consignee. Agents are required to get mandatorily registered irrespective of the threshold limit.
- **Principal**—means a person on which behalf an agent carries on the business of supply or receipt of goods or services or both. In other words, the consignor.

Now, as per the GST rules, both agent and principal, although part of the same organisational framework, will be considered as distinct persons as far as taxation is concerned. Thus, if there is a transfer of goods or services between the principal and the agent, GST will be applicable, even if there is no consideration between the two.

Valuation of Consignment Sales under GST. As per the CGST Act, supply of goods by a principal to his agent even without consideration, is treated as a supply and shall be liable to GST—and thus consignment sales have become taxable under GST. As per GST valuation rules, GST will need to be charged, either on :

- the open market value, Or
- 90% of the sales price charged by the agent to the end customer, at the option of the principal.

However, the agent/consignee can avail input credit of the GST charged by the principal/consignor.

GST on Consignment Sales. As discussed above, the principal/consignor will need to charge GST from the agent/consignee, which he will pass on the government while filing his returns. Similarly, while selling the goods to the end customer, the agent/consignee should charge GST from the customer, which he will pass to the government, while filing his returns. In addition, the agent/consignee has to charge GST at 18% on the commission, from the principal/consignor and pass that on to the government as well.

However the relief is, that while paying tax to the government, both principal and agent can adjust the same against their input tax credit and the remaining balance, if any, can be paid through cash.

Impact of GST. As consignment sales under GST has become a taxable supply, the following difficulties are bound to emerge :

- Working capital of the agent will be blocked as GST needs to be paid at the time of receiving goods from the principal on consignment basis.
- Working capital of the principal too will be impacted, as GST on the commission will need to be paid to the agent.

CONSIGNMENT ACCOUNTS

Consignment accounts record transactions relating to the goods sent on consignment by the consignor to the consignee. Accounting treatment in the books of consignor and consignee is discussed one by one.

Accounting Treatment in the Books of the Consignor

1. When goods are sent to the consignee

Consignment to__________A/c	Dr. (amount of goods)
Consignee A/c	Dr. (amount of GST)
To Goods Sent on Consignment A/c	(amount of goods)
To Output GST	(amount of GST)
(Being the cost of goods consigned to the consignee)	

It may be noted that *Consignee's Account is not to be debited* with the goods consigned as no sale takes place when the goods are sent on consignment. However, Consignee's A/c is debited for the amount of GST charged to be recovered from him.

If goods are *consigned to many consignees at different places*, a separate Consignment Account is opened for each consignment with a view to ascertain profit or loss on each consignment. Each consignment should be distinguished from the other by *adding the name of the place to which it is sent, e.g.,* Consignment to Surat Account. If there are more than one consignees at the same place, the name of the consignee may be added to the Consignment Account, *e.g.,* Consignment to Wadekar Account.

2. For Consignor's Expenses

Consignment to__________Account	Dr.	(Expense amount)
Input GST A/c (if any)	Dr.	(GST amount)
To Cash Account		(Total amount)

(Being expenses incurred on the consignment of goods to the consignee)

3. For Advance given by the Consignee. Usually the consignee is required to remit a certain sum of money as an advance by way of security against the goods received by him. The advance should not be credited to the Consignment Account but it should be credited to the Consignee's Account because the money has been received as an advance and not in lieu of the sale of the goods consigned. So, the journal entry is :

Bills Receivable or Bank Account	Dr.
To Consignee's Account	

(Being a bill or bank draft received from the consignee as an advance against the goods consigned).

If the bill is discounted by consignor, following entry will be passed :

Cash/Bank A/c	Dr.
Discount A/c	Dr.
Input GST (if any)	Dr.
To Bills Receivable A/c	

Note. Discount on bill receivable will not be a charge to Consignment Account as it is treated as financial activity or matter.

4. For Consignee's Expenses. The consignee is credited for the expenses incurred by him in connection with the goods received by him as he has incurred these expenses on behalf of the consignor. So, the journal entry is :

Consignment to__________Account	Dr.
Input GST A/c (if any)	Dr.
To Consignee's Account	

(Being expenses incurred by the consignee in connection with the goods consigned to him)

5. For Sales by the Consignee

Consignee's Account	Dr.
To Consignment to__________Account	

(Being the gross sale proceeds as per Account Sales)

6. For Consignee's Commission

Consignment to__________Account	Dr.
Input GST A/c (if any)	Dr.
To Consignee's Account	

(Being commission on sale of goods sent on consignment payable to the consignee)

7. For the Remittance from the Consignee in Settlement of Account

Bank Account or Bills Receivable Account Dr.

To Consignee's Account

(Being amount due from the consignee received)

8. For Profit or Loss on Consignment. The balance of the Consignment Account in the books of the consignor will show either profit or loss on consignment. The journal entry is :

(*i*) If there is a profit on consignment :

Consignment to__________Account Dr.

To Profit and Loss Account

(Being profit on consignment transferred)

(*ii*) If there is a loss on consignment :

Profit and Loss Account Dr.

To Consignment to__________Account

(Being loss on consignment transferred to Profit and Loss Account)

9. For Close of Goods sent on Consignment Account. This account is closed by transferring it to the credit of Purchases Account in case of a trading concern or Trading Account in case of a manufacturing concern. So the journal entry is :

Goods sent on Consignment Account Dr.

To Trading Account or Purchases Account

From the above discussion it becomes clear that the Consignment Account is, in fact, a special Trading and Profit and Loss Account while the Consignee's Account is a personal account.

10. For Payment of GST

Output GST Dr.

To Input GST

To Bank A/c

(Being Input GST Set off against Output GST and balance (if any) to be paid to the Government)

Accounting Treatment in the Books of the Consignee

1. On Receipt of Goods by the Consignee. The consignee *need not make any entry on receipt* of goods from the consignor but shall pass following entry to book GST credit.

Input GST Dr.

To Consignor A/c

(Being credit of GST taken on the goods consigned)

Any how, the consignee is liable to account for the goods he has received from the consignor, so *he keeps record of the receipt of the goods in Inwards Consignment Book* which is only a memorandum book and not a financial book.

2. For Expenses incurred by the Consignee

Consignor's Account Dr. (Expenses plus GST)

To Cash Account (Expenses plus GST)

(Being expenses incurred on goods received on consignment basis)

Consignor's Account is debited with amount including GST because expenses are incurred by the consignee on behalf of the consignor and the input of GST on such expenses will be taken by consignee as shown in entry 4 of Accounting treatment in books of consignor).

3. Advance (if any) given by the Consignee to the Consignor

Consignor's Account Dr.

To Bills Payable Account or Bank Account

(Being advance given to the consignor against goods received from him)

4. For Sales by the Consignee

	Cash Account	Dr.	Sale amount (including GST)
or	Consignment Debtor's Account (If sold on credit)	Dr.	
	To Consignor's Account		(Sale Amount)
	To Output GST A/c		(GST Amount)

(Being goods sold on account of the consignor)

Consignor's Account has been credited because the amount of sales belongs to him.

5. For Commission on Sales

Consignor's Account	Dr.	(Total Amount)
To Commission Earned Account		(Commission)
To Output GST		(GST)

(Being commission earned on sale of goods received on consignment)

6. For Bad Debts

(*i*) If the consignee does not get del-credere commission :

Consignor's Account Dr.

To **Consignment** Debtor's Account

(Being bad debts on account of sales of goods received on consignment debited to Consignor's Account)

(*ii*) When the consignee gets *del-credere* commission :

Bad Debts Account Dr.

To **Consignment** Debtor's Account

(Being bad debts on account of sale of goods received on consignment treated as personal loss of the consignee because of getting *del credere* commission).

Bad Debts Account will ultimately be closed by transferring it to Profit and Loss Account. Some accountants prefer transfer of bad debts to Commission Earned Account and then net balance of commission **earned** is transferred to Profit and Loss Account.

7. For Remittance sent to the Consignor in Final Settlement of his Account.

Consignor's Account Dr.

To Bills Payable or Bank Account

(Being payment of the balance due to the consignor)

8. Payment of GST

Output GST A/c Dr.

To Input GST A/c

To Bank

(Being GST set off and balance paid to government)

Note : For set off rules of Input/Output GST, refer to chapter on GST in this book

ILLUSTRATION 1. ***(With GST when all goods sent to the consignee are sold by him).*** M/s Jaipuria & Co. of Delhi consigned on 15th March, 2025, 45 cases of glassware (cost price ₹ 41,235 and market value 48,000 ; GST rate is 12%) to Singh & Co. of Amritsar for sale on commission @ 5% on gross sale proceeds. The consignor paid freight and carriage amounting to ₹ 539. Rate of GST on commision is 18%.

The goods arrived at Amritsar on 20th March, 2025 and Singh & Co. paid clearing Charges ₹ 235; Sundry Charges ₹ 59, Carriage ₹ 102 and Godown Charges ₹ 90.

The goods were sold by Singh & Co. as under :

15 cases @ ₹ 1,003 per case, 22 cases @ ₹ 1,050 per case and the remainder for ₹ 10,000.

On June 21, 2025, Singh Co. sent a draft for ₹ 10,000 to M/s Jaipuria & Co. on account. On 1st July, 2025 Singh & Co. forwarded an Account Sales together with a Bill of Exchange for the balance.

Give Journal Entries and prepare Necessary Accounts to record the above transactions in the books of both the parties. Calculations are to be made to the nearest rupee. No GST is charged on expenses.

SOLUTION **In the Books of M/s Jaipuria & Co. (Consignor)**

JOURNAL ENTRIES

2025			₹	₹
Mar. 15	Consignment to Amritsar Account	Dr.	41,235	
	Singh & Co.	Dr.	5,760	
	To Goods sent on Consignment Account			41,235
	To Output IGST (48,000 × 12%)			5,760
	(Being goods sent on consignment to Singh & Co. of Amritsar)			
	Note. GST is charged on Market Value (not on cost price) of the goods sent on consignment as per GST Rules			
Mar. 15	Consignment to Amritsar Account	Dr.	539	
	To Cash Account			539
	(Being expenses incurred on goods sent on consignment)			
" 20	Consignment to Amritsar Account	Dr.	486	
	To Singh & Co.			486
	(Being expenses incurred by the consignee)			
April 20	Output IGST A/c	Dr.	5,760	
	To Bank A/c			5,760
	(Being Output IGST deposited with Government)			
June 21	Bank Account	Dr.	10,000	
	To Singh & Co.			10,000
	(Being a draft for ₹ 10,000 received from Singh & Co.)			
July 1	Singh & Co.	Dr.	48,145	
	To Consignment to Amritsar Account			48,145
	(Being gross proceeds of the consignment as per the Account Sales)			
" 1	Consignment to Amritsar Account	Dr.	2,407	
	Input IGST A/c	Dr.	433	
	To Singh & Co.			2,840
	(Being 5% commission on gross proceeds ₹ 48,145 payable to the consignee and 18% IGST as per GST rule)			
" 1	Bills Receivable Account	Dr.	40,579	
	To Singh & Co.			40,579
	(Being the amount due received)			

July 1	Consignment to Amritsar Account Dr.		3,478	
	To Profit and Loss Account			3,478
	(Being profit on consignment transferred)			
" 1	Goods sent on Consignment Account Dr.		41,235	
	To Trading Account			41,235
	(Being goods sent on consignment transferred to Trading Account)			

CONSIGNMENT TO AMRITSAR ACCOUNT

2025		₹	2025		₹
Mar. 15	To Goods sent on Consignment Account	41,235	July 1	By Singh & Co. (Sales)	48,145
" 15	To Cash Account (Expenses)	539			
" 20	To Singh & Co. (Expenses)	486			
July 1	To Singh & Co. (Commission)	2,407			
" 1	To Profit & Loss A/c (Profit transferred)	3,478			
		48,145			48,145

SINGH & CO.

2025		₹	2025		₹
Mar. 15	To Output IGST	5,760	March 20	By Consignment to Amritsar Account	486
July 1	To Consignment to Amritsar Account	48,145	June 21	By Bank Account	10,000
			July 1	By Consignment to Amritsar Account	2,407
				By Input IGST A/c	433
			" 1	By Bills Receivable Account	40,579
		53,905			53,905

GOODS SENT ON CONSIGNMENT ACCOUNT

2025		₹	2025		₹
July 1	To Trading Account	41,235	Mar. 15	By Consignment to Amritsar Account	41,235
		41,235			41,235

In the Books of Singh & Co. (Consignee)
JOURNAL ENTRIES

2025			₹	₹
Mar. 15	Input IGST A/c Dr.		5,760	
	To Jaipuria & Co.			5,760
	(Being goods received on consignment basis. IGST charged by Jaipuria)			
Mar. 20	M/s Jaipuria & Co. Dr.		486	
	To Cash Account			486
	(Being expenses paid on M/s. Jaipuria's consignment)			

June 21	M/s Jaipuria & Co.	Dr.	10,000	
	To Bank Account			10,000
	(Being amount sent by a draft of ₹ 10,000)			
?	Bank Account	Dr.	53,919	
	To M/s Jaipuria & Co.			48,145
	To Output IGST			5,774
	(Being goods sold on behalf of M/s Jaipuria & Co.)			
June 30	Output IGST A/c	Dr.	5,774	
	To Input IGST A/c			5,760
	To Bank A/c			14
	(Being GST set off and balance paid)			
July 1	M/s Jaipuria & Co.	Dr.	2,840	
	To Commission **Earned** Account			2,407
	To Output IGST A/c			433
	(Being 5% commission on sale proceeds on account of consignment and Output IGST @ 18%)			
July 1	M/s Jaipuria & Co.	Dr.	40,579	
	To Bills Payable Account			40,579
	(Being remittance of amount due to M/s Jaipuria & Co.			
July 30	Output IGST A/c	Dr.	433	
	To Bank Account			433
	(Being GST collected deposited)			

M/s JAIPURIA & CO.

2025		₹	2025		₹
Mar. 20	To Cash Account	486	March	By Bank A/c (Sales)	48,145
June 21	To Bank Account	10,000		By Output IGST	5,760
July 1	To Commission **Earned** A/c	2,407			
" 1	To Output IGST A/c	433			
" 1	To Bills Payable A/c	40,579			
		53,905			53,905

Note : The Output IGST collected in March is to paid by April 20th. The Input IGST for month of July shall be set off against Output IGST as and when it is credited in accounts. Till then it shall be shown as Current Assets in Balance Sheet.

Valuation of Unsold Stock

It is quite possible that all goods sent on consignment might not have been sold by the consignee up to the date when the final accounts of the consignor are prepared. It is, therefore, natural that stock on consignment should be properly valued and credited to the Consignment Account to ascertain correct profit or loss on consignment. Unsold stock is valued at cost or net realisable value, whichever is less principle emphasised in Ind. AS–2. While calculating the cost of stock, cost plus a proportionate share of non-recurring expenses is considered. It may be noted that **non-recurring expenses** are the expenses which are incurred to bring the goods to the godowns of the consignee such as packing and forwarding charges, freight, octroi duty, insurance in-transit, cartage of goods from railway station to the godowns of the consignee etc. But **recurring expenses** such as godown rent, storage, advertisement etc. incurred after the goods reach the godowns of the consignee are not taken into consideration for the valuation of stock on consignment. The stock on consignment will be shown as an asset in the Balance Sheet of the consignor. Following journal entry is passed to record the stock on consignment :

Consignment Stock Account	Dr.
To Consignment to........................Account	
(Being the value of stock on hand with the consignee)	

It may be noted carefully that no entry is passed for unsold goods in the books of the consignee as no entry is passed in the books of the consignee, when goods are received from the consignor. Moreover the consignor is the owner of the goods and not the consignee, so no entry is required for the unsold goods in the books of the consignee.

ILLUSTRATION 2. On 1st January, 2025 Rohit sends 150 sewing machines costing ₹ 30,000 to Anurag to be sold on behalf of the former at 5% commission on sales, Rohit paid ₹ 1,500 as freight and carriage for sending the machines. Anurag sent the account sales on 31st March, 2025 stating that:

(*i*) 120 sewing machines were sold for ₹ 27,000.

(*ii*) Expenses incurred on inward consignment were : Octroi ₹ 250 ; Carriage ₹ 50 ; Goodown Rent ₹ 2,100 and Advertisement and other Selling Expenses ₹ 1,500.

SOLUTION

Value of Consignment Stock on 31st March, 2025 will be calculated as under :

	Number of sewing machines consigned		150
Less :	Number of sewing machines sold		120
	Number of machines unsold (*i.e.*, consignment stock)		30
	Cost price of 150 swing machines :		30,000
			₹
	Cost price of 30 machines $\left(i.e.\ \frac{₹\ 30,000}{150} \times 30\right)$		6,000
Add :	Proportionate share of non-recurring expenses :	₹	
	Freight and carriage incurred by Rohit on 150 machines	1,500	
	Octroi on 150 machines paid by Anurag	250	
	Carriage on 150 machines paid by Anurag	50	
		1,800	
	Therefore, expenses on 30 machines $\left(\frac{₹\ 1,800}{150} \times 30\right)$		360
	Value of consignment stock on 31-3-2025		6,360

Value of Consignment Stock on 31-3-2025 if the net realisable value is ₹ 210.

In this case if net realisable value of one machine is ₹ 210, then ₹ 6,300 (*i.e.* ₹ 210 × 30) will be treated as value of stock and not ₹ 6,360 as calculated above. This is based on the principle that unsold goods will be valued at cost or net realisable value, whichever is less.

ILLUSTRATION 3. Himanshu sent out goods costing ₹ 80,000 to Navin so as to show 20% profit on invoice price. 40% goods were lost in transit. 60% of the goods received were sold half at invoice price and the balance at 25% above the invoice price. Rate of Commission is 10% on sales at invoice price *plus* 50% of gross sales *less* all commission exceeds sales at invoice price. Calculate the amount of commission.

SOLUTION **CALCULATION OF COMMISSION**

		₹
A.	Invoice Price of Goods Sent (₹ 80,000 + 25% on cost equivalent to 20% on invoice price)	1,00,000
B.	*Less* : Invoice Price of Goods Lost (₹ 1,00,000 × 40%)	40,000
C.	Invoice Price of Balance Goods (A – B)	60,000
	Invoice Price of Goods Sold (60% of ₹ 60,000)	36,000
	50% Sales at Invoice Price (50% of Rs,. 36,000)	18,000
	50% Sales at 25% above Invoice Price (50% of ₹ 36,000) × 125%	22,500
	Total Sales Proceeds	40,500
	10% Commission on Sales at Invoice Price (10% of 36,000)	3,600

Let Total Commission be = X

X – ₹ 3,600 = 50% (₹ 40,500 – ₹ X – ₹ 36,000) = ₹ 20,250 – 0.5 X – ₹ 18,000

X – ₹ 3,600 + 0.5*x* = ₹ 2,250

1.5*x* = ₹ 2,250 + ₹ 3,600

X = ₹ 5850/1.5 = ₹ 3,900

ILLUSTRATION 4. (*When unsold goods are with the consignee at the beginning and at the end of the period*). The Cochin Consignment Account in the books of Ranaji of Bombay showed a debit balance of ₹ 1,500 representing the cost of 10 bicycles on 1st January, 2025. On March 1, Ranaji sent a further consignment to Cochin of 40 bicycles costing ₹ 160 each. The freight and other charges amounted to ₹ 210. On 1st June, the Cochin Agent sent an Account Sales showing that 8 bicycles from the old stock realised ₹ 140 each and 25 bicycles from the second consignment realised ₹ 200 each and 15 bicycles remained in stock unsold. Two bicycles from the old stock being unsaleable at Cochin were returned to Bombay, for which the Cochin Agent sent a separate debit note for ₹ 30 being expenses incurred by him.

The Cochin agent is entitled to a selling commission of 5 per cent which covers all out-of-pocket expenses in respect of the consignment. Show the necessary accounts in the books of the consignor, supposing that he closes his accounts on 30th June and uses FIFO method for selling the goods.

SOLUTION **CONSIGNMENT TO COCHIN ACCOUNT**

2025		₹	2025			₹
Jan. 1	To Consignment Stock A/c (Opening Balance)	1,500	June 1	By Cochin Agent (Sales) :		
Mar. 1	To Goods Sent on Consignment A/c	6,400		8 bicycles @ ₹ 140 =	₹ 1,120	
" 1	To Bank A/c (Expenses)	210		25 bicycles @ ₹ 200 =	5,000	6,120
June 1	To Cochin Agent (5% commission on sales)	306		By Consignment Stock A/c :		
" 1	To Cochin Agent (Expenses on 2 bicycles returned)	30	" 3	Cost of 15 bicycles @ ₹ 160 =	₹ 2,400	
" 30	To Profit on Consignment transferred to Profit and Loss A/c	453		Proportionate Expenses: on 40 bicycles = ₹ 210 ∴ On 15 bicycles $= \frac{210}{40} \times 15 =$	79	2,479
			June 30	By Goods Sent on Consignment A/c (Returns : 2 bicycles @ ₹ 150)		300
		8,899				8,899

COCHIN AGENT ACCOUNT

2025		₹	2025		₹
June 1	To Consignment to Cochin A/c (Sales)	6,120	June 1	By Consignment to Cochin A/c (Commission)	306
			June 1	By Consignment to Cochin A/c (Expenses)	30
			" 30	By Balance c/d	5,784
		6,120			6,120
July 1	To Balance b/d	5,784			

GOODS SENT ON CONSIGNMENT ACCOUNT

2025		₹	2025		₹
June 30	To Consignment to Cochin A/c	300	Mar. 1	By Consignment to Cochin A/c	6,400
" 30	To Trading A/c (Transfer)	6,100			
		6,400			6,400

CONSIGNMENT STOCK ACCOUNT

2025		₹	2025		₹
Jan. 1	To Balance b/d	1,500	Jan. 1	By Consignment to Cochin A/c (transfer)	1,500
June 30	To Consignment to Cochin A/c	2,479	June 30	By Balance c/d	2,479
July 1	To Balance b/d	2,479			

Invoicing Goods Higher than Cost

Sometimes, the consignor is not interested to reveal actual cost of the goods consigned to the consignee so that the latter may not be in a position to know the actual profit made on the consignment. To achieve this objective the consignor sends to the consignee the proforma invoice charging goods not at cost but at higher price. Such invoice is prepared when goods are sent by the consignor to the consignee or head office to the branch. The effect of such a policy is that consignment account stands debited with a higher price of goods sent on consignment thereby reducing the profit on consignment. Similarly, unsold stock on consignment is valued at higher price thereby increasing the profit on consignment. Evidently, therefore, some adjustments should be made at the end of each balancing period if the correct profit or loss on consignment is to be ascertained. Following adjusting entries are made in the books of the consignor to nullify the effect of higher price.

(1) Goods sent on Consignment Account Dr.
 To Consignment Account
(Being the excess of invoice price of goods sent on consignment written back).

This entry is made with the amount of the difference between the higher price at which the consignment had been invoiced and actual cost of such consignment. The purpose of this entry is to write back the goods on cost to cancel the excess debit to consignment and excess credit to goods sent on consignment account given at the time of sending the goods to the consignee.

(2) Consignment Account Dr.
 To Consignment Stock Suspense or Reserve Account
(Being the excess of invoice value over cost price of unsold stock adjusted to write back the unsold stock at cost price)

Consignment stock will be shown in the balance sheet of the consignor as below :

BALANCE SHEET

Liabilities	₹	*Assets*	₹
		Consignment Stock *Less* : Consignment Stock Reserve or Suspense A/c	

There is no need of any adjustment in the books of the consignee because he is not in any way affected by the higher price of the goods. No entry is passed for the goods received from the consignor and unsold stock in the books of the consignee, so question of cancellation of the excess amount does not arise.

ILLUSTRATION 5. ***(When goods are sent to the Consignee at Invoice Price).*** Swastik Ltd. forwarded on 1st January, 2025, 100 bicycles to Narinder & Co. of Delhi to be sold on behalf of Swastik Ltd. The cost of one bicycle was ₹ 250, but the invoice price was ₹ 300 (Market Value for GST purpose assumed at ₹ 300 plus GST rate 12%). Swastic Ltd. incurred ₹ 1,000 on freight and insurance and received ₹ 10,000 as advance from Narinder & Co. Narinder & Co. paid ₹ 500 as carriage, ₹ 400 as rent and ₹ 300 as insurance and by 30th June, 2025 had disposed of 80 bicycles for ₹ 25,000. Narinder & Co. is entitled to commission on sale at 5 per cent on proforma invoice price and 25% of any surplus price realised. Narinder and Co. remitted the amount due from them by a bank draft. GST on commission is 18%.

You are required to give the Journal Entries to record the above transactions in the books of the consignor and the consignee and also write up the Ledger Accounts in the books of both the parties. Ignore GST on expenses.

SOLUTION

In the Books of Swastic Ltd. (Consignor)
JOURNAL ENTRIES

2025				₹	₹
Jan. 1	Consignment to Delhi Account	Dr.		30,000	
	Narinder & Co.	Dr.		3,600	
	To Goods sent on Consignment Account				30,000
	To Output CGST A/c				1,800
	To Output SGST A/c				1,800
	(Being 100 bicycles sent to Narinder & Co. of Delhi on consignment basis and invoiced @ ₹ 300)				
" 1	Consignment to Delhi Account	Dr.		1,000	
	To Bank Account				1,000
	(Being freight and insurance paid on account of goods sent on consignment)				
" 1	Bank Account	Dr.		10,000	
	To Narinder & Co.				10,000
	(Being advance payment received)				
Feb. 20	Output CGST A/c	Dr.		1,800	
	Output SGST A/c	Dr.		1,800	
	To Bank A/c				3,600
	(Being GST deposited to Government Account)				
June 30	Consignment to Delhi Account	Dr.		1,200	
	To Narinder & Co.				1,200
	(Being expenses incurred by Narinder & Co.)				

Date	Particulars		L.F.	Dr. ₹	Cr. ₹
June 30	Narinder & Co.	Dr.		25,000	
	To Consignment to Delhi Account				25,000
	(Being sale of 80 bicycles for ₹ 25,000 by the consignee)				
June 30	Consignment to Delhi Account	Dr.		1,450	
	Input CGST A/c	Dr.		130.5	
	Input SGST A/c	Dr.		130.5	
	To Narinder & Co.				1,711
	[Being commission payable to Narinder & Co. @ 5% on invoice price ₹ 24,000 (*i.e.*. 80 × ₹ 300) plus 25% on surplus ₹ 1,000 *i.e.* (₹ 25,000 – ₹ 24,000) ; (GST = 1,450 @ 18% as per GST Rule)]				
" 30	Bank Account	Dr.		15,689	
	To Narinder & Co.				15,689
	(Being amount due from Narinder & Co. received)				
" 30	Consignment Stock Account	Dr.		6,300	
	To Consignment to Delhi Account				6,300
	(Being the value of 20 bicycles left unsold @ ₹ 300 plus proportionate non-recurring expenses ₹ 300 *i.e.* $\frac{₹ 1,500}{100} \times 20$)				
" 30	Goods sent on Consignment Account	Dr.		5,000	
	To Consignment to Delhi Account				5,000
	(Being the excess of invoice price @ ₹ 50 per bicycle on 100 bicycles written back)				
June 30	Consignment to Delhi Account	Dr.		1,000	
	To Consignment Stock Suspense Account				1,000
	(Being the excess of invoice value over cost price @ ₹ 50 on 20 unsold bicycles written back)				
" 30	Consignment to Delhi Account	Dr.		1,650	
	To Profit and Loss Account				1,650
	(Being profit on consignment transferred)				
" 30	Goods sent on Consignment Account	Dr.		25,000	
	To Trading Account				25,000
	(Being transfer of balance of Goods sent on Consignment Account to Trading Account)				

CONSIGNMENT TO DELHI ACCOUNT

2025		₹	2025		₹
Jan. 1	To Goods sent on Consignment A/c	30,000	June 30	By Narinder & Co. (Sales)	25,000
" 1	To Bank (Expenses)	1,000	" 30	By Consignment Stock A/c	6,300
June 30	To Narinder & Co. (Expenses)	1,200	" 30	By Goods sent on Consignment A/c	5,000
" 30	To Narinder & Co. (Commission)	1,450			
" 30	To Consignment Stock Suspense A/c	1,000			
June 30	To Profit on Consignment transferred to Profit and Loss A/c	1,650			
		36,300			36,300

NARINDER & CO.

2025		₹	2025		₹
Jan. 1	To Output CGST	1,800	Jan. 1	By Bank Account	10,000
"	To Output SGST	1,800	June 30	By Consignment to Delhi A/c	1,200
June 30	To Consignment to Delhi A/c	25,000	" 30	By Consignment to Delhi A/c	1,450
			" 30	By Input CGST	130.5
			" 30	By Input SGST	130.5
			" 30	By Bank Account	15,689
		28,600			28,600

GOODS SENT ON CONSIGNMENT ACCOUNT

2025		₹	2025		₹
June 30	To Consignment to Delhi A/c	5,000	Jan. 1	By Consignment to Delhi A/c	30,000
" 30	To Trading Account	25,000			
		30,000			30,000

CONSIGNMENT STOCK ACCOUNT

2025		₹	2025		₹
June 30	To Consignment to Delhi A/c	6,300	Jan. 30	By Balance c/d	6,300
July 1	To Balance b/d	6,300			

CONSIGNMENT STOCK SUSPENSE ACCOUNT

2025		₹	2025		₹
June 30	To Balance c/d	1,000	June 30	By Consignment to Delhi	1,000
			July 1	By Balance b/d	1,000

In the Books of Narinder & Co.

JOURNAL ENTRIES

2025			₹	₹
Jan. 1	Input CGST	Dr.	1,800	
	Input SGST	Dr.	1,800	
	To Swastik Ltd.			3,600
	(Being Input of GST taken on goods received)			
Jan. 1	Swastik Ltd.	Dr.	10,000	
	To Bank Account			10,000
	(Being advance given on receipt of 100 bicycles to be sold on consignment basis)			
Jan. 1	Swastik Ltd.	Dr.	1,200	
	To Bank Account			1,200
	(Being expenses paid on goods on consignment)			
June 30	Bank Account	Dr.	28,000	
	To Swastik Ltd.			25,000
	To Output CGST A/c			1,500
	To Output SGST A/c			1,500
	(Being goods sold on the account of Swastik Ltd. CGST @ 6% and SGST @ 6% on ₹ 25,000)			

June 30	Swastik Ltd. Dr.			1,711	
	To Commission **Earned** Account				1,450
	To Output CGST A/c				130.5
	To Output SGST A/c				130.5
	(Being Commission due on sale proceeds with 18% GST as per GST Rule)				
" 30	Swastik Ltd. Dr.			15,689	
	To Bank Account				15,689
	(Being amount due on consignment remitted to Swastik Ltd.)				

SWASTIK LTD.

2025		₹	2025		₹
Jan. 1	To Bank Account (Advance)	10,000	June 30	By Bank Account (Sales)	25,000
Jan. 1	To Bank Account (Exp.)	1,200	Jan. 1	By Input CGST A/c	1,800
June 30	To Commission Earned with GST	1,450	"	By Input CGST A/c	1,800
" 30	To Output CGST A/c	130.5			
" 30	To Output SGST A/c	130.5			
" 30	To Bank Account	15,689			
		28,600			28,600

Accounting for Loss of Goods

The loss of goods sent on consignment is that of the consignor and not of the consignee, so the consignor alone is to make the entries for the loss of goods. The entries to adjust the loss of goods in the books of the consignor will depend upon the type of loss. Following are the two types of losses of goods :

(*a*) **Normal Loss.** It is that loss which is due to the nature of the goods consigned. Such loss may arise due to loading and unloading of the goods, cutting the bulk material into smaller parts, evaporation, drying, sublimation of goods etc. For example, some of the quantity of coal consigned is bound to be converted into dust because of loading and unloading. In other words, such loss is unavoidable because some of the goods are bound to be lost even after taking all precautions. Being normal such a loss is a part of the cost of the consignment, so no entry is passed in the books of the consignor. Anyhow, such type of loss is considered while calculating the cost of stock left unsold with the consignee. The value of unsold stock on consignment is increased because the value of stock is the proportion of the cost of the goods consigned and non-recurring expenses that the quantity of stock bears to the total quantity of goods consigned as diminished by the normal loss of goods. Suppose 100 tonnes of coal are consigned @ ₹ 150 per tonne, non-recurring expenses being ₹ 4,000. Further, if loss due to loading and unloading is 5 tonnes and if the quantity sold by the consignee is 85 tonnes, then the value of unsold stock of 10 tonnes will be as follows :

	₹
Cost of 100 tonnes of coal @ ₹ 150 per tonne	15,000
Add : Non-recurring expenses	4,000
Total cost of 100 tonnes	19,000

The cost of 100 tonnes becomes the cost of 95 tonnes because of a normal loss of 5 tonnes.

The cost of 95 tonnes of coal = ₹ 19,000

Therefore, value of 10 tonnes of stock = $\frac{₹\ 19,000}{95} \times 10 = ₹\ 2,000$

(*b*) **Abnormal Loss.** Such loss is an avoidable loss because it does not arise due to the nature of the goods. Such loss may arise due to bad luck (*i.e.*, destruction of goods by fire, mischief *i.e.*, theft of goods) and inefficiency (abnormal breakage due to careless handling). The value of such a loss is calculated at cost in the same way as the value of unsold stock on consignment and is credited to consignment account and debited to abnormal loss account or accidental loss account to ascertain the correct profit or loss of the consignment. If the stock is insured, the amount of claim admitted by insurance company should be debited to insurance company and credited to Abnormal Loss Account or Accidental Loss Account. Any amount realised on account of damaged goods should also be credited to Abnormal Loss Account. Commission paid on sale of damaged goods is also debited to Abnormal Loss Account. Balance of Abnormal Loss Account (if any) should be transferred ultimately to Profit and Loss Account.

ILLUSTRTION 6. **(*Calculation of Abnormal Loss and Value of Stock*)** A Consigned to B 1000 kgs. of certain goods at ₹ 200 per kg. incurring ₹ 5,000 as expenses. 100 kgs. were lost in transit. B spent ₹ 1,000 as non-recurring expenses and ₹ 3,000 as recurring expenses. B sold 600 kgs. of the goods 5 kgs. goods were lost due to breakage at B's godown which was considered to be normal. Calculate the amount of abnormal loss and the value of stock on consignment.

SOLUTION

Calculation of the Amount of Abnormal Loss

	₹
Cost of 100 kgs. lost in transit @ ₹ 200 per kg.	20,000
Add : Proportionate non-recurring expenses : $\frac{₹ 5,000}{1,000} \times 100$	500
Amount of Abnormal Loss	20,500

Calculation of the Value of Stock

	₹
Cost of goods consigned : 1,000 kgs. @ ₹ 200	2,00,000
Add : Expenses incurred by A	5,000
Cost before loss in transit	2,05,000
Less : Value of abnormal loss as calculated above	20,500
Value of remaining 900 kgs. (1000 – 100)	1,84,500
Add : Non-recurring expenses incurred by B	1,000
Cost of 895 kgs. (*i.e.* 900 kgs. – 5 kgs. normal loss)	1,85,500

Value of 295 kgs. Closing stock after sale $\frac{₹ 1,85,500}{895 \text{ kgs.}} \times 295$ kgs. = ₹ 61,142

Distinction Between Normal Loss and Abnormal Loss

Following are the main distinctions between normal loss and abnormal loss :

Basis of Distinction	*Normal Loss*	*Abnormal Loss*
1. Value of Loss	It is an unavoidable loss.	It is an avoidable loss.
2. Cause of Loss	It is caused due to inherent nature of goods, *e.g.,* evaporation, normal leakage or spoilage.	It is caused by abnormal reasons such as fire, theft, abnormal spoilage, etc.
3. Treatment in Cost	It is treated as a part of the cost.	It is not treated as a part of the cost.
4. Calculation of Value	Value of such loss is not calculated separately.	Value of such loss is calculated separately like the value of unsold stock.
5. Treatment in Accounts	No treatment in accounts except its value is adjusted by increasing the cost per unit.	Value of such loss is credited to Consignment Account in order to calculate the normal profit or loss on consignment.

6. Journal Entry	No journal entry is passed in accounts for such loss.	A separate journal entry is passed in accounts by debiting Abnormal Loss Account and crediting Consignment Account.
7. Realisation from Damaged Goods	Generally there is no realisation from damaged goods in case of this loss.	Amount realised from damaged goods is credited to Abnormal Loss Account. The balance in Abnormal Loss Account is transferred to Profit & Loss Account.

ILLUSTRATION 7. (*When there is abnormal loss of goods*). B whose accounting year ends on 31st May, 2025, consigned 200 bags of sugar, each bag costing ₹ 300 to A of Bombay on 1st April, 2025. He had paid ₹ 1,000 towards freight and insurance, 30 bags were damaged in transit and on 31st May, 2025 the consignor has received ₹ 2,000 on account of the damaged bags from the Insurance Company.

A took delivery of the goods on 10th April, 2025 and immediately accepted a bill drawn on him for ₹ 40,000 for 60 days. On 31st May, 2025, the consignee reported that:

(*i*) 140 bags were sold at ₹ 350 per bag ;

(*ii*) The damaged bags were sold at ₹ 110 per bag ; and

(*iii*) He had incurred the following expenses :

Godown rent ₹ 1,400 ; clearing charges ₹ 1,700 and carriage outwards ₹ 600.

He is entitled to a commission of 10% on the sale proceeds of all goods sold.

Assuming that A remits the balance by bank draft on 31st May, 2025, prepare Ledger Accounts ignoring GST in the books of B. Also assume that no portion of the expenses incurred by the consignee is attributable to the damaged bags.

SOLUTION

CONSIGNMENT TO BOMBAY ACCOUNT

2025		₹	2025		₹
April 1	To Goods sent on Consignment A/c	60,000	?	By Accidental Loss A/c (1)	9,150
				By A (Sales)	49,000
April 1	To Bank A/c (Expenses)	1,000	May 31	By Consignment Stock A/c (2)	9,450
May 31	To A (Expenses)	3,700	May 31	By Loss on Consignment transferred to Profit and Loss A/c	2,000
May 31	To A (10% commission on ₹ 49,000 sale of goods)	4,900			
		69,600			69,600

ACCIDENTAL LOSS ACCOUNT

2025		₹	2025		₹
?	To Consignment to Bombay A/c	9,150	May 31	By Bank A/c (Amount received from Insurance Co.)	2,000
May 31	To A (10% Commission on ₹ 3,300 sale)	330	May 31	By A (Sale of 30 bags @ ₹ 110 per bag)	3,300
			May 31	By Abnormal Loss transferred to Profit & Loss A/c	4,180
		9,480			9,480

A'S ACCOUNT

2025		₹	2025		₹
May 31	To Consignment to Bombay A/c	49,000	April 10	By Bills Receivable A/c	40,000

		₹			₹
May 31	To Accidental Loss A/c	3,300	May 31	By Consignment to Bombay A/c	3,700
			May 31	By Consignment to Bombay A/c	4,900
			May 31	By Accidental Loss A/c	330
			May 31	By Bank A/c	3,370
		52,300			52,300

GOODS SENT ON CONSIGNMENT ACCOUNT

2025		₹	2025		₹
May 31	To Trading A/c	60,000	April 1	By Consignment to Bombay A/c	60,000

BILLS RECEIVABLE ACCOUNT

2025		₹	2025		₹
April 10	To A	40,000	May 31	By Balance c/d	40,000
June 1	To Balance b/d	40,000			

CONSIGNMENT STOCK ACCOUNT

2025		₹	2025		₹
May 31	To Consignment to Bombay A/c	9,450	May 31	By Balance c/d	9,450
June 1	To Balance b/d	9,450			

Working Notes

(1) ***Valuation of Goods Destroyed by Fire***

		₹
Cost of 30 bags @ ₹ 300 per bag		9,000
Add : Proportionate freight and insurance charges $\left(\frac{₹\ 1,000 \times 30}{200}\right)$		150
		9,150

(2) ***Valuation of Consignment Stock***

		Nos.
No. of bags consigned		200
Less: No. of bags damaged	30	
No. of good bags sold	140	
		170
No. of bags remaining unsold		30
		₹
Cost of 30 bags @ 300 per bag		9,000
Add : Proportionate non-recurring expenses		
Freight and Insurance $\left(\frac{₹\ 1,000 \times 30}{200}\right)$		150
Clearing charges on 30 bags $\left(\frac{₹\ 1,700}{170} \times 30\right)$		300
		9,450

Where both Normal and Abnormal Losses Occur Simultaneously

In some cases it may be possible that both losses *i.e.*, normal and abnormal losses, are given in the question. While preparing consignment account normal loss is ignored. The valuation of abnormal loss is done on the same basis as has already been discussed. But while calculating the value of stock, the following procedure is to be followed :

(*i*) First of all deduct the quantity of normal loss from the total quantity without deducting anything from the total cost.

(*ii*) Then deduct the quantity as well as value of abnormal loss (without deducting anything received or receivable from the insurance company) from the rest of the quantity and cost as arrived at in (*i*) above.

(*iii*) Calculate average value of per unit by dividing the residual amount by the residual quantity.

(*iv*) Multiply with the units of unsold stock lying in the hands of the consignee by average cost of a unit as calculated in (*iii*) above. This will give the value of consignment stock which is to be shown on the credit side of the consignment account.

Valuation of Goods in Transit

Sometimes goods sent by the consignor do not reach to the consignee (*i.e.* in the way). Such goods are called Goods in Transit. These are in the nature of closing stock and need to be valued accordingly. Such goods are to be valued at cost *i.e.* basic cost of goods to the consignor plus all proportionate expenses of the consignor. It must be noted carefully that consignee's, expenses incurred will not be included in the cost and there will be no entry for goods in transit in the books of the consignee.

ILLUSTRATION 8. Shri Mehta of Bombay consigns 1,000 cases of goods costing ₹ 100 each to Sri Sundaram of Madras. Sri Mehta pays the following expenses in connection with the consignment.

Carriage ₹ 1,000; Freight ₹ 3,000; Loading charges ₹ 1,000.

Sri Sundaram sells 700 cases at ₹ 140 per case and incurs the following expenses :

Clearing charges ₹ 850; Warehousing and storage ₹ 1,700; Packing and selling expenses ₹ 600.

It is found that 50 cases have been lost in transit and 100 cases are still in transit.

Sri Sundaram is entitled to a commission of 10% on gross sales. Draw up the Consignment Account and Sundaram's Account in the books of Sri Mehta. Ignore GST.

CONSIGNMENT ACCOUNT

	₹		₹
To Goods sent on Consignment Account	1,00,000	By Sundaram (Sales)	
To Bank (Expenses)	5,000	700 cases @ ₹ 140 per case	98,000
To Sundaram (Expenses)	3,150	By Accidental Loss A/c (1)	5,250
To Sundaram (Commission)		By Goods in Transit A/c (2)	10,500
10% on ₹ 98,000 Sales	9,800	By Consignment Stock A/c (3)	15,900
To Profit on Consignment transferred to Profit and Loss Account	11,700		
	1,29,650		1,29,650

SUNDARAM'S ACCOUNT

	₹		₹
To Consignment A/c (Sales)	98,000	By Consignment A/c (Expenses)	3,150
		By Consignment A/c (Commission)	9,800
		By Balance c/d	85,050
	98,000		98,000

Working Notes :

(1) *Value of Accidental Loss*

	₹
Cost of 50 cases @ ₹ 100 per case	5,000
Add : Proportionate non-recurring expenses incurred by the Consignor *i.e.*, $\frac{50}{1,000}$ × ₹ 5,000	250
	5,250

(2) *Value of Goods in transit*

Cost of 100 cases @ ₹ 100 per case	10,000
Add : Proportioned non-recurring expenses incurred by the Consignor *i.e.* $\frac{100}{1,000}$ × ₹ 5,000	500
	10,500

(3) *Value of Closing Consignment Stock*

		₹
Cost of 150 cases @ ₹ 100 per case		15,000
Add : Proportionate non-recurring expenses incurred by the Consignor *i.e.* $\frac{150}{1,000} \times$ ₹ 5,000		750
Add : Proportionate non-recurring expenses incurred by the Consignee		
Clearing charges on 850 cases (1,000 cases consigned – 50 cases lost in transit—100 cases still in transit)	₹ 850	
Therefore, clearing charges on 150 cases $\left(\frac{₹ 850}{850} \times 150\right)$		150
		15,900

ILLUSTRATION 9. (*When both normal and abnormal losses occur simultaneously*). Oswal Mills, Ludhiana consigned 5,000 kgs. of Vanaspati Ghee to Vijay Dealers of Chandigarh. Each kg. ghee costs ₹ 8. Oswal Mills paid ₹ 50 as carriage, ₹ 250 as freight and ₹ 200 as insurance in transit. During transit 500 kgs. were accidentally destroyed for which the insurance company paid directly to the consignors ₹ 2,500 in full settlement of the claim.

After three months from the date of the consignment of the goods to Chandigarh, Vijay Dealers reported that 3,500 kgs. of ghee was sold @ ₹ 9.50 per kg. and expenses being : on godown rent, ₹ 500 and on salesman salary, ₹ 750. Vijay Dealers are entitled to a 5% commission on sales,. Vijay Dealers also reported a loss of 20 kgs. due to leakage. Prepare the necessary accounts, ignoring GST, in the books of both the parties.

SOLUTION

In the Books of Oswal Mills, Ludhiana

CONSIGNMENT TO CHANDIGARH ACCOUNT

	₹			₹
To Goods sent on Consignment A/c	40,000	By Bank (Insurance Claim)		2,500
To Cash A/c (Expenses)	500	By Profit & Loss A/c (Abnormal Loss)	(1)	1,550
To Vijay Dealers (Expenses)	1,250	By Vijay Dealers (Sales)		33,250
To Vijay Dealers (5% commission on sales ₹ 33,250)	1,663	By Consignment Stock A/c	(2)	7,973
To Profit on Consignment transferred to Profit and Loss A/c	1,860			
	45,273			45,273

VIJAY DEALERS

	₹		₹
To Consignment to Chandigarh A/c	33,250	By Consignment to Chandigarh A/c	1,250
		By Consignment to Chandigarh A/c	1,663
		By Balance c/d	30,337
	33,250		33,250
To Balance b/d	30,337		

GOODS SENT ON CONSIGNMENT ACCOUNT

	₹		₹
To Trading A/c	40,000	By Consignment to Chandigarh A/c	40,000

CONSIGNMENT STOCK ACCOUNT

	₹		₹
To Consignment to Chandigarh A/c	7,973	By Balance c/d	7,973
To Balance b/d	7,973		

In the Books of Vijay Dealers
OSWAL MILLS

	₹		₹
To Cash Account	1,250	By Cash A/c (Sales)	33,250
To Commission A/c	1,663		
To Balance c/d	30,337		
	33,250		33,250
		By Balance b/d	30,337

COMMISSION ACCOUNT

	₹		₹
To Profit & Loss A/c (Transfer)	1,663	By Oswal Mills	1,663

Working Notes :

(1) ***Value of Vanaspati Ghee Accidentally Destroyed***

	₹	₹
Cost of 5,000 kgs. @ ₹ 8 per kg.		40,000
Add : Expenses :		
Carriage	50	
Freight	250	
Insurance in Transit	200	
		500
Total cost of 5,000 kgs.		40,500
Therefore, cost of 500 kgs. accidentally destroyed $\left(\frac{₹\ 40,500 \times 500}{5,000}\right)$		4,050
Cost of remaining 4,500 kgs.		36,450
Value of goods accidentally destroyed		4,050
Less : Amount recovered from Insurance Company		2,500
Abnormal Loss		1,550

(2) ***Value of Stock on Consignment***

	Quantity	*Cost*
Total Cost of Goods Consigned	5,000 kgs.	₹ 40,500
Less : Abnormal Loss	500 kgs.	₹ 4,050
	4,500 kgs.	₹ 36,450
Less: Normal Loss	20 kgs.	–
Value of Remaining Stock	4,480 kgs.	36,450

$$\text{Value of Stock} = \frac{\text{Unsold Stock}}{\text{Remaining Stock}} \times \text{Value of Remaining Stock}$$

$$= \frac{980 \text{ kgs.}}{4{,}480 \text{ kgs.}} \times ₹\ 36{,}450 = ₹\ 7{,}973$$

QUESTIONS

OBJECTIVE TYPE

1. (*a*) When goods are sent on consignment, the account to be debited is :

   (*i*) Consignee's Personal Account. (*ii*) Consignment Account.

   (*b*) When goods consigned are sold by the consignee, the account to be debited in the books of consignee is :

   (*i*) Cash Account. (*ii*) Consignment Account. (*iii*) Consignor's Personal Account.

Ans. [(*a*) (*ii*), (*b*) (*i*).]

2. **Mention whether the following statements are Right or Wrong :**

   (*a*) No entry is to be passed by the consignee when he receives the goods from the consignor.

   (*b*) *Del Credere* commission is allowed to the consignee to cover abnormal loss.

   (*c*) The value of abnormal loss is credited to the Consignment Account.

   (*d*) Overriding commission is calculated on credit sales only.

   (*e*) The unsold consignment stock is valued at original cost of the goods.

   (*f*) When goods are invoiced at cost plus $33\frac{1}{3}\%$, the loading on invoice price is 25%.

   (*g*) Normal loss is unavoidable and arises due to the nature of the goods.

Ans. [(*a*) Right, (*b*) Wrong, (*c*) Right, (*d*) Wrong, (*e*) Wrong, (*f*) Right, (*g*) Right].

3. **Write the most appropriate answer from the given options in respect of the following :**

   (*a*) A consignee gets *del credere* commission for—

   (*i*) Selling of goods

   (*ii*) Bearing loss due to bad debts on consignment sales

   (*iii*) Selling goods on credit basis

   (*iv*) Selling goods beyond invoice price.

   (*b*) *Del credere* commission is payable on—

   (*i*) Total sales (*ii*) Net profit

   (*iii*) Credit sales (*iv*) Cash sales.

   (*c*) The Abnormal Loss on Consignment is credited to—

   (*i*) Profit and Loss Account (*ii*) Consignee's Account

   (*iii*) Consignment Account (*iv*) Insurance Company Account.

   (*d*) 2,000 kgs. of apples are consigned to a wholesaler, the cost being ₹ 3 per kg *plus* ₹ 400 of freight, it is known that a loss of 15% is unavoidable. The effective cost per kg will be :

   (*i*) ₹ 2.50 (*ii*) ₹ 3.76

   (*iii*) ₹ 1.70 (*iv*) ₹ 1.50.

   (*e*) Dinesh of Delhi consigns goods of the invoice price of ₹ 1,00,000 to Bharat of Ballabhgarh at cost *plus* 25%. The amount of loading is—

   (*i*) ₹ 25,000 (*ii*) ₹ 20,000

   (*iii*) ₹ 15,000 (*iv*) ₹ 32,500.

Ans. [(*a*) (*ii*); (*b*) (*iii*); (*c*) (*iii*); (*d*) (*ii*); (*e*) (*ii*)]

SHORT ANSWER TYPE

1. Explain in brief the following terms:

   (*i*) Consignor (*ii*) Consignee

   (*iii*) Del Credere Commission (*iv*) Overriding Commission

(*v*) Account Sales (*vi*) Normal Loss
(*vii*) Abnormal Loss (*viii*) Proforma Invoice.
(*ix*) Invoice (*x*) Loading.

2. Give four points of distinction between (*i*) Consignment and Sale (*ii*) Invoice and Account Sales.
3. What is Del Credere Commission ? Why is such commission paid ?
4. Describe the method of determining the value of unsold stock of goods sent on consignment. How do you close consignment stock account ? Illustrate.
5. Distinguish between 'overriding commission' and del credere commission.
6. Briefly explain abnormal loss in consignment.
7. What are recurring expenses in relation to consignment ? How is distinction between recurring and non-recurring expenses relevant in consignment accounts ?
8. How will you treat normal loss of goods in consignment accounts ?
9. How will you calculate the amount of abnormal loss after identifying the expenses to be included in cost ? Also give the accounting treatment of abnormal loss.
10. Give the justification for the consignor to draw a bill of exchange on the consignee before consignment is sold. Does the consignee run any risk in accepting such a bill ?
11. Give the accounting treatment of bad debts in the books of the consignor and consignee when :
    (*a*) del credere commission is allowed ?
    (*b*) del credere commission is not allowed ?
12. Explain, in brief, how you will calculate the value of unsold stock at the end, if normal and abnormal losses occur simultaneously in consignment accounts.
13. Distinguish between :
    (*a*) Consignment and Sales ; (*b*) Invoice and Proforma Invoice ; (*c*) Normal Loss and Abnormal Loss; (*d*) Recurring Expenses and Non-recurring Expenses.
14. Meeraj of Meerut consigned goods costing ₹ 20,000 to Giri of Hyderabad on consignment basis. Meeraj paid carriage and cartage ₹ 200 and insurance ₹ 300. On the way, 1/5th of the consignment was lost by fire and the insurance company admitted claim to the extent of ₹ 3,000. Ascertain the *amount of abnormal loss* and the actual loss incurred to him after the claim.

Ans. [Abnormal loss ₹ 4,100; Actual Loss ₹ 1,100]

15. Consignor consigned 200 litres of oil @ ₹ 10 per litre. Expenses for freight etc. came to ₹ 100. 140 litres of oil was sold by the consignee and he also reported a shortage of 20 litres due to leakage. Calculate *value of closing stock*. ***(B.Com. Panjab)***

Ans. [₹ 467]

16. On 15-6-25 A of Amritsar consigned to his agent B at Batala goods costing ₹ 20,000 paying carriage ₹ 150, freight ₹ 200 and insurance ₹ 100.

    B sold 3/4th of the consignment for ₹ 21,500 and had to bear the following expenses : Octroi Duty ₹ 120; Carriage ₹ 50; Godown Rent ₹ 250; Commission to Salesman ₹ 260. he was entitled to 10% commission. On 30-6-25 the closing date, the market price was 20% more than cost price. Find out the *value of closing stock*. ***(B.Com. Panjab)***

Ans. [₹ 5,155]

17. A consigned to B 200 cycles at proforma invoice price of ₹ 150, which was 25% above cost. B was entitled to commission at 5% on cost of goods sold plus 20% of excess price realised over cost price of goods sold. B sold 140 cycles at ₹ 180 each. Calculate the amount of *commission payable* to B. ***(B.Com. Panjab)***

Ans. [₹ 2,520]

LONG ANSWER TYPE

1. Define 'Consignment'. What is the difference between a consignment and a sale of goods ?
2. Why goods are sent to consignee at invoice price? What adjustment entries are recorded in the books of the consignor to find profit on consignment when goods are invoiced at proforma prices ?
3. Give journal entries in respect of consignment transactions in the books of consignor and consignee.
4. Write short notes on :
   (*a*) Del Credere Commission.
   (*b*) Treatment of Normal and Abnormal Losses in Consignment Account.
   (*c*) Valuation of Unsold Stock in Consignment.
   (*d*) Proforma Invoice.
   (*e*) Account Sale.
   (*f*) Non-recurring Expenses
   (*g*) Recurring Expenses.

PRACTICAL PROBLEMS

NO UNSOLD STOCK

1. **(With GST)** Ram & Co. of Kolkata consigned 50 cases of goods at ₹ 200 each (Market value ₹ 400 plus GST @ 12%) to Nathan of Mumbai. The consignor pays ₹ 200 for insurance and for freight ₹ 300. Nathan sent an account sales (all being intrastate) showing the gross proceeds at ₹ 24,000. The expenses paid by Nathan were dock dues ₹ 20, carriage ₹ 50, warehousing expenses ₹ 130. He sent the amount due to the consignor after deducting 4 per cent, GST rate 18% on commission. Give Journal Entries in the books of both the parties.

Ans. [Profit ₹ 12,340; Amount received from Nathan ₹ 22,840].

2. B. Ghosh of Bombay sent on consignment to C. Alok of Calcutta 300 cases @ ₹ 125 on 1st July, 2024 to be sold on his account and at his risk for 10% Commission. B. Ghosh incurred ₹ 3,000 expenses on despatching the goods to C. Alok. On July 10, 2024 B. Ghosh received a bill for ₹ 20,000 at 2 months from C. Alok. On September 30, 2024 C. Alok sent an account sales disclosing that 200 cases have been sold for ₹ 160 each and the remaining cases @ ₹ 150 each. The account sales also discloses that C. Alok has incurred unloading expenses ₹ 600 and selling expenses ₹ 900. He sends a draft for the net amount due. You are required to (*a*) prepare the Account Sales and (*b*) pass journal entries and prepare necessary accounts ignoring GST in the books of both the parties.

Ans. [(*a*) Balance Due ₹ 20,800 ; (*b*) Profit ₹ 300].

3. The Delhi Motors Ltd., Delhi consigned to their agent B in Bombay two motor cars (costing ₹ 80,000) for sale on the basis of 10% commission, B is to bear all landing charge in Bombay which amounted to ₹ 1,000. B sold one car for ₹ 50,000 and remitted ₹ 40,000 on account. The second car was sold for ₹ 48,000 but out of this sum ₹ 2,500 became bad debt.

   Pass Journal entries for bad debts only and open necessary ledger accounts ignoring GST in the books of both the parties.

   (*i*) If no *Del Credere* commission is given to the agent B.
   (*ii*) If B is to get 3% *Del Credere* commission in addition to ordinary commission.

Ans. (*i*) Profit ₹ 5,700 ; Balance due from B ₹ 45,700.
(*ii*) Profit ₹ 5,260 ; Balance due from B ₹ 45,260].

4. Auto Agencies have sold out the following goods on behalf of different parties for which they have incurred some expenses and are entitled to commission and reimbursement of expenses :

	X	Y	Z
	₹	₹	₹
Goods Received	10,000	15,000	18,000
Goods sold	12,000	13,000	22,000

Stock in hand	4,000	6,000	6,000
Remittance	10,000	11,000	20,000
Expenses	300	200	400
Commission	10%	6%	5%

Prepare the necessary accounts ignoring GST in the Books of Auto Agencies.

Ans. [Credit Balances : X– ₹ 500 ; Y ₹ 1,020, Z ₹ 500 ; Total Commission transferred to P/L A/c ₹ 3,080.]

Hint. [Prepare Consignor's A/c and Commission A/c in the books of Auto Agencies]

5. (With GST) Minerva Mills Ltd. of Bangalore sent 50 pieces of shirting to Fancy Stores, Delhi on consignment basis. The consignees are entitled to receive 5% commission (GST @ 18%) plus expenses. The cost of Minerva Mills Ltd. is ₹ 40 per piece (Market value is ₹ 50 for GST purpose ; GST rate is 12%). Fancy Stores, Delhi pay the following expenses :
Railway freight etc. ₹ 100 ; Godown rent & insurance ₹ 50.

Minerva Mills Ltd. draw on the consignees a draft for ₹ 1,000 which is duly accepted. It is discounted for ₹ 970. Later Fancy Stores, Delhi report that the entire consignment has been sold for ₹ 3,000. Show Journal Entries and important Ledger Accounts in the books of the consignor.

Ans. [Profit ₹ 670; Balance due from Fancy Stores ₹ 1,700].

VALUATION OF STOCK

6. On 1st July, 2024 Radio House of Delhi consigned 200 Radios to Banerjee Bros. of the Calcutta. The cost of each radio was ₹ 400. Radio House paid ₹ 5,000 for freight and insurance. On 7 July, 2024 Banerjee Bros. accepted a 3 months bill drawn upon them by Radio House for ₹ 50,000, Banerjee Bros. paid ₹ 2,200 as rent and ₹ 1,300 for advertisement and upto 31st December, 2024 (on which date Radio House close their books) they sold 180 radios at ₹ 500 each. Banerjee Bros. were entitled to a commission of 5% on sales.

Give Journal entries and prepare necessary accounts to record the above transactions in the books of the parties.

Ans. [Profit ₹ 5,500 ; Value of stock ₹ 8,500 ; Balance due from Banerjee Bros. ₹ 32,000].

7. Williams of Madras consigned 300 chests of tea at ₹ 2,000 per chest to Johnson of New Delhi paying freight ₹ 4,000 and other expenses ₹ 2,000. Johnson sold 250 chests at ₹ 2,500 per chest on credit and 25 chests at ₹ 2,200 per chest for cash. Johnson spent for freight and octroi ₹ 3,000 and other expenses ₹ 1,000. He remitted the amount due to Williams after deducting his commission at 5% (normal), $2\frac{1}{2}$% (overriding), and $\frac{1}{2}$% *del credere* (*Del Credere* commission to be given on total sales). Johnson found that one customer to whom credit of 40 days was allowed paid only ₹ 4,800 out of the total amount of ₹ 5,000 due from him in full settlement of account. Other customers paid the amount on due dates.

Pass journal entries ignoring GST in the books of both the parties.

Ans. [Profit ₹ 66,350 : Consignment Stock ₹ 50,750 ; Balance received ₹ 6,21,600].

INVOICE PRICE

8. Messrs Sudershan Lal & Co. of Delhi consigned 1,000 tins of pure ghee costing ₹ 60 per tin to their agents Chatterjee Ghee Stores at Calcutta. The tins were invoiced as proforma ₹ 80 per tin. The agents sold 400 tins at ₹ 80 per tin for cash and 400 tins at ₹ 82 per tin on credit. Messrs Sudershan Lal & Co. paid freight and carriage ₹ 500 and miscellaneous ₹ 200. They drew on Chatterjee Ghee Stores at 3 months for ₹ 45,000, which was duly accepted by the latter. The expenses incurred by the Chatterjee Ghee Stores were : carriage ₹ 250, octroi ₹ 50, storage ₹ 104, miscellaneous ₹ 200. They were entitled to 5 per cent commission and 2 per cent *del credere* commission on total gross sale proceeds. They sent their Account Sales to their principal showing as a deduction therefrom their commission and the various expenses incurred by them. A month later all the debtors except one who owed ₹ 200, paid cash and the Chatterjee Ghee Stores remitted the amount due on consignment.

Prepare necessary accounts ignoring GST in the books of both the parties.

Ans. [Profit ₹ 11,160 ; Value of Stock (at I.P.) ₹ 16,200 ; Balance received from Chatterjee Ghee Stores ₹ 14,660].

9. On 1st January, 2025 B of Bombay consigned 100 cases (cost price ₹ 7,500) at a proforma invoice of 25% profit on sale to his agent C of Chandigarh. On the same date B paid ₹ 600 as expenses. On 30th January, C took delivery and paid ₹ 1,200 for octroi and other duties and remitted ₹ 4,000 as an advance. On 31st January he sold 80 cases for ₹ 10,500 ; C is entitled to 5% commission on gross sales and 10% of the sales price in excess of invoice price.

Show Consignment A/c and C's Account in the books of B. C is required to maintain proportionate security with the consignor for unsold stock.

Ans. [Profit ₹ 2,285 ; Value of Stock at I.P. ₹ 2,360 ; Balance received from C ₹ 5,325, Commission ₹ 775].

10. Arun sends goods on consignment to Seemu. The terms are that Seemu will receive 10% commission on the price (which is cost plus 25%) and 20% of any price realised above the invoice price. Seemu will meet his expenses himself, goods to be sent freight paid.

Arun sent goods whose cost was ₹ 16,000 and spent ₹ 1,500 on freight, forwarding, etc. Seemu accepted a bill for ₹ 16,000 immediately on receiving the consignment. His expenses were ₹ 200 as rent and ₹ 100 as insurance. Seemu sold 3/4 of the goods for ₹ 19,500. Part of the sales were on credit and one customer failed to pay ₹ 400. Give Consignment Account and Seemu's Account in the books of Arun and Arun's Account in the books of Seemu ignoring GST.

Ans. [Profit ₹ 3,575 ; Value of Stock at I.P. ₹ 5,375 ; Commission ₹ 2,400 ; Balance due from Seemu ₹ 700].

LOSS OF GOODS

11. (*a*) The M. Coal Co. consigned to M. Sales Ltd. 200 tonnes of coal at a cost of ₹ 15,000 and paid ₹ 4,600 towards railway freight. M. Sales Company sold 100 tonnes and reported a shortage of 4 tonnes on the whole consignment. Calcutta the value of stock at the end.

(*b*) *X* consigned 100 packets of cosmetics, each costing ₹ 300 to his agent at Madras. He paid ₹ 400 towards freight and insurance, 15 packets were destroyed on the way. The consignee took delivery of the remaining packets and spent ₹ 700 as godown rent, ₹ 850 as clearing charges and ₹ 300 as carriage outwards. You are required to calculate the abnormal loss or cost of damage and the value of closing stock at the end, if the agent sells away 80 packets.

(*c*) 1,000 transistors each costing ₹ 80 were sent by A to B of Bombay on consignment basis. A paid freight amounting to ₹ 1,000 and cartage ₹ 100. B received only 900 sets as 100 sets were destroyed during transit. B incurred an expenditure of ₹ 1,000 on account of clearing charges and cartage. Calculate the abnormal loss on transistors destroyed during transit.

(*d*) Phillips Radio of Kanpur despatched 1,000 transistors at ₹ 70 each to Mohan Bros, Bombay. The consignors paid freight ₹ 750 ; cartage ₹ 50 and insurance ₹ 250. Mohan Bros. received only 900 sets and incurred ₹ 10,000 on octroi and other expenses, ₹ 500 for cartage and ₹ 600 on sales expenses. The consignee sold 600 sets only. You are required to calculate the value of closing stock.

Ans. [(*a*) ₹ 9,600 ; (*b*) ₹ 4,560 ; ₹ 1,570 ; (*c*) ₹ 8,110 ; (*d*) ₹ 24,815].

WHERE BOTH LOSSES OCCUR SIMULTANEOUSLY

12. R consigned 10,000 kgs. of Ghee at ₹ 20 per kg. He spent ₹ 5 per kg. as freight and insurance for sending the Ghee to his agent D at Delhi. On the way 100 kgs. of Ghee was lost due to the leakage (which are to be treated as normal loss) and 400 kgs. of Ghee was destroyed in transit. ₹ 8,500 was paid to the consignor directly by the Insurance Co. as insurance claim. D sold 7,500 kgs. at ₹ 40 per kg. He spent ₹ 32,000 on advertisement and recurring expenses. Calculate (*i*) the amount of abnormal loss, (*ii*) value of stock at the end, (*iii*) prepare Consignment A/c showing profit or loss on consignment, if D is entitled to 5% commission on sales.

Ans. [(*i*) ₹ 1,500 ; (*ii*) ₹ 50,526 ; (*iii*) Profit ₹ 63,526].

13. 1,000 bicycles were consigned by Premier Bicycle Co., Delhi to Superior Bros. Kanpur at ₹ 150 each Premier Co. paid freight ₹ 10,000 and insurance in transit ₹ 1,500. During transit 100 bicycles were totally damaged by fire. Superior Bros. took delivery of the remaining bicycles and paid ₹ 1,530 for octroi.

Superior Bros. sent a bank draft to Premier Co. for ₹ 50,000 as advance payment and later sent an Account Sales showing that 800 bicycles were sold at ₹ 220 each. Expenses incurred by Superior Bros. on godown rent and advertisement etc. amounted to ₹ 2,000. Superior Bros. is entitled to commission of 5%. Prepare the Consignment Account, Accidental Loss Account and Superior Bros. Account ignoring GST in the books of Premier Bicycle Co., Delhi, assuming that a claim from insurance company was settled for ₹ 14,000.

Ans. [Profit ₹ 34,640 ; Balance Due ₹ 1,13,670 ; Abnormal Loss ₹ 2,150 ; Value of Stock ₹ 16,320].

14. Pyare Lal & Sons of Delhi purchased 10,000 metres of cloth for ₹ 20,000, 5,000 metres sent on consignment to Ram Chand & Bros. of Ajmer at the selling price of ₹ 3 per metre. The consignors pay ₹ 500 for freight and ₹ 50 for packing etc. ₹ 10 for petty expenses.

Ram Chand & Bros. sell 4,000 metres at ₹ 4 per metre and incur ₹ 200 for sundry expenses. They are entitled to a commission of 5% on total sale proceeds plus a further 20% on any surplus price realised over ₹ 3 per metre.

3,000 metres are sold at Delhi directly at ₹ 3 a metre less ₹ 300 for expenses and commission. Owing to a fall in market the stock of cloth in hand is to be reduced by 10%.

Prepare the Consignment Account and Trading and Profit and Loss Account in the books of Pyare Lal & Sons and Pyare Lal & Sons' Account in the books of the Consignee.

Ans. [Profit on Consignment ₹ 5,552 ; Value of Stock ₹ 2,912 ; Gross Profit ₹ 2,600 ; Net Profit ₹ 7,852].

15. R of Ranchi consigned goods of the invoice price of ₹ 2,00,000 which is 25 per cent above cost to D of Delhi. The terms of the consignment were :

(*a*) Consignee to get a commission of 5 per cent on all sales.

(*b*) Any goods taken by the consignee himself or lost through consignee's negligence, shall be valued at cost plus $12\frac{1}{2}$ per cent and no commission will be allowed on them.

The expenses incurred by the consignor were : Carriage and freight ₹ 6,720 and ₹ 3,440. The consignor received ₹ 50,000 as advance against the consignment. Account sales together with a draft for the balance due was received by the consignor showing the following position.

Goods of the invoice price of ₹ 1,60,000 were sold for ₹ 2,48,000. Goods of the invoice price of ₹ 10,000 and ₹ 5,000 were taken by D and lost through his negligence respectively. Amounts of ₹ 1,720 on advertisement and ₹ 1,080 on selling expenses were incurred by D. Prepare Consignment Account and Consignee's Account in the books of consignor.

Ans. [Profit ₹ 97,410 ; Value of Stock at I.P. ₹ 26,270 ; Balance due from D ₹ 1,96,300].

16. The Bharat Cycles Ltd. of Delhi appointed B of Bombay as their selling agent on the following terms :

(*a*) Goods to be sold at invoice price or over :

(*b*) B to be entitled to a commission of $7\frac{1}{2}$% on the invoice price and 20% of any surplus price realised.

(*c*) The principals to draw on the agent a 30 days draft for 80% of the invoice price.

On 1st August, 2024, 1,000 bicycles were consigned to Naresh Kumar, each bicycle costing ₹ 64, including freight and invoiced at ₹ 80.

Before 31st December, 2024 (when the principal's books are closed), B met his acceptance on due date and sold off 820 bicycles at an average price of ₹ 93 per bicycle, the sale expenses being ₹ 1,250, and remitted the amount due by means of bank draft.

20 of the unsold bicycles were shop-spoiled and were to be valued at depreciation of 50%.

Prepare Consignment Account and B's A/c in the books of consignor.

Ans. [Profit ₹ 14,838 ; Value of Stock at I.P. ₹ 13,600 ; Amount received ₹ 3,958].

17. X of Calcutta sent, on 15th January, 2025, a consignment of 500 bicycles costing ₹ 100 each. Expenses of ₹ 700 were met by the consignor. Y of Bombay spent ₹ 1,500 for clearance and the selling expenses were ₹ 10 per bicycle.

Y sold on 4th April, 2025, 300 bicycles @ ₹ 160 per bicycle and again on 20th June, 2025, 150 bicycles @ ₹ 172.

Y was entitled to a commission of ₹ 25 per bicycle sold plus one fourth of the amount by which the gross sale proceeds less total commission thereon exceeded a sum calculated at the rate of ₹ 125 per bicycle sold. Y sent the amount due to X on 30th June, 2025.

You are required to show the Consignment Account and Y's Account in the books of X.

Ans. [Profit ₹ 9,810. Value of Stock ₹ 5,220 ; Commission ₹ 12,510].

18. Bhola consigned 40 machines to Ram on 1st January, 2024 on the following terms :

(*a*) All machines were to be sold 20% above the cost of each machine *i.e.* ₹ 10,000. Any deficit in selling price is to be borne by Ram while Ram is to retain 50% of any surplus price realised.

(*b*) Ram is to be paid 3% commission and 2% Del Credere commission on all sales.

Bhola incurred freight charges of ₹ 40,000 in consigning the machines. Ram sent Account Sales on 31st December, 2024 disclosing—

10 machines sold for ₹ 12,000 each. 5 machines sold for ₹ 10,000 each. 15 machines sold for ₹ 14,000 each.

Ram had incurred unloading charges of ₹ 4,000 and selling expenses of ₹ 6,000. He had collected the entire sale proceeds except ₹ 2,000 which had become a bad debt. Ram sent a bank draft for the net amount due to Bhola.

On 30th June, 2025 Ram sent a further Account Sales disclosing—

10 machines sold at ₹ 12,000 each. Selling expenses were ₹ 1,500. He also sent a draft for the net amount due. Bhola closes his books on 31st December each year.

Write up Consignment Account and Ram's Account for the year 2024 and upto 30th June, 2025.

Ans. [2024 : Profit ₹ 17,000 ; Value of Stock ₹ 1,11,000 : Draft received ₹ 3,46,000. 2025 : Profit ₹ 1,500 ; Draft received ₹ 1,12,500]

19. On October 1, 2024 Meena & Co. of Calcutta who sent 100 sewing machines on consignment to Nazma of Patna, spent ₹ 250 on packing. The cost of each machine was ₹ 112 but it was now invoiced at 25% above cost.

One case containing 5 machines was lost in transit. Nazma was asked to pay ₹ 475 as freight of the remaining machines. He had to spend ₹ 95 as cartage and octroi duty and ₹ 190 as godown rent. He sold 75 machines @ ₹ 190. He found 10 machines defective and therefore returned them to Calcutta at a cost of ₹ 50. Nazma is entitled to a commission of 5% on invoice price and 20% of any excess realised on the invoice price and 1% del credere commission. Nazma could not realise sale proceeds of 5 machines.

Prepare Consignment Account, Consignee's Account, Consignment Stock Account and Consignment Stock Reserve Account ignoring GST in the books of Meena & Co.

Ans. [Profit ₹ 3,470 ; Value of Stock at I.P. ₹ 1,485 ; Abnormal Loss ₹ 572.50 ; Balance due from Nazma ₹ 12,022.50].

20. On October 1, 2024 Mr. Achut of Bombay consigned 100 units of a commodity to Mr. Rao of Delhi. The goods were invoiced on October 1, 2024 at ₹ 150 so as to yield a profit of 50 per cent on cost. Mr. Achut incurred ₹ 1,000 on freight and insurance. Mr. Rao incurred ₹ 500 on freight and ₹ 800 on rent. Before 31st December, 2024, he sold 50 units for cash at ₹ 160 per unit, 20 units for ₹ 175 per unit on credit. He retained his commission 5 per cent and 1 per cent of the *del credere* arrangements on all sales and remitted the balance on 31st December, 2024. Mr. Rao noticed that 10 units were damaged on account of bad packing and he could sell them only for ₹ 80 per unit. A debtor for ₹ 1,000 to whom the goods were sold by Mr. Rao became insolvent and only 50 paise in a rupee was recovered. Mr. Rao sent an account sales on 31st December, 2024 detailing the transactions for the quarter ended on that date and he remitted the balance due.

Make necessary ledger entries in the books of Mr. Achut and Mr. Rao, assuming that Mr. Achut closes his books every 31st December. Ignore GST.

Ans. [Profit ₹ 1,960 ; Abnormal Loss ₹ 398 ; Value of Stock (I.P.) ₹ 4,052].

21. Mr. X of Bombay invoiced goods to his agent Y of Calcutta at selling price. The agent sends his report regarding sales and collection of book debts by him every month. He is entitled to a commission of 5% on cash collected and an allowance for expenses @ ₹ 2,000 per half-year. During the half-year ending 31st December, 2024, goods were invoiced to the agent X costing ₹ 5,00,000 plus freight and charges thereon, ₹ 75,000. During the same period, sales were made by the agent amounting to ₹ 6,84,000. Debts collected were ₹ 5,60,000 and discounts were allowed amounting to ₹ 5,975. The agent remitted to X ₹ 5,00,000.

Included in the consignments to the agent was a consignment of goods costing to X ₹ 12,500 partly damaged in transit. The consignment was insured and the claim was settled for ₹ 12,400.

At 31st December, 2024 the unsold stock in the hands of the agent represents cost to X of ₹ 75,000.

Prepare the Consignment Account and the Consignee's Account in the books of the Consignor ignoring GST.

Ans. [Profit ₹ 1,73,650 ; Value of Stock ₹ 86,250 ; Balance due from Y ₹ 1,48,025].

22. Dutt of Delhi makes sewing machines at a cost of ₹ 120. On 1st January, 2024 he consigned 200 of them, invoice price ₹ 150 to Khan at Madras to be sold on behalf of Dutt, Khan receiving a commission of 8% on sales plus 2% *del credere* and 10% of any profit that may remain on the basis of invoice price. Khan was to bear all expenses after the machines reach his godown. Dutt incurred ₹ 500 as forwarding expenses and Insurance.

10 machines were damaged during transit for which Dutt received ₹ 1,050 from insurers. Khan took delivery of remaining machines paying ₹ 1,140 as freight, octroi duty, cartage, etc. (Subsequently he also paid ₹ 500 as storage and other charges).

Khan sold 160 machines @ ₹ 180 ; 100 of them on credit out of which the proceeds of 5 machines could not be received because of the disappearance of the customer. Khan remitted the amount due to Dutt.

You are required to prepare the Consignment to Madras A/c and Khan's A/c in Dutt's Books.

Ans. [Profit ₹ 5,309 ; Abnormal Loss ₹ 175 ; Value of Stock (at Invoice Price) ₹ 4,755 ; Commission ₹ 2,931].

23. The Account sales received from an Agent disclosed that the total sales effected by him during 2024-25 amounted to ₹ 4,50,000. This included ₹ 3,12,500 for sales made at invoice price which is cost plus 25% and the balance at 10% above the invoice price. He incurred expenses to the tune of ₹ 5,000, out of which a sum of ₹ 1,800 is recurring in nature. Forwarding expenses of the Consignor totalled ₹ 2,400. The Agent had remitted the balance due from him through Bank Draft after deducting the expenses, 5% commission on gross sales, bad debts ₹ 850 and a bills payable accepted by him for ₹ 10,000.

The value of unsold stock at original cost lying with the Agent as on 31st March, 2025 amounted to ₹ 50,000.

You are required to prepare the Consignment Account and the Agents' Account in the books of the Consignor.

Ans. [Profit ₹ 69,950, Value of Unsold Stock ₹ 63,200 ; Goods sent on Consignment at I.P. ₹ 5,00,000 ; Draft received from Agent ₹ 4,11,650].

24. Given below is the relevant portion of a Trial Balance as on 31-3-2025. You are asked to give adjustment entries and open necessary Ledger Accounts after taking into consideration the information under the Trial Balance. Prepare also adjusted Trial Balance as on 31-3-2025 :

TRIAL BALANCE

as on 31-3-2025

	Dr.	*Cr.*
	₹	₹
Materials Consumed	3,75,000	
Stock as on 31-3-2025	50,000	
Suspense A/c of N.K. Sinha		20,000
Suspense A/c of S.K. Sinha	7,500	
Other Balance		4,12,500
	4,32,500	4,32,500

Information :

(*i*) Analysis of N.K. Sinha's account reveals that goods costing ₹ 30,000 were sent to him under consignment agreement. All the goods were sold except $\frac{1}{4}$(which was valued at cost) for ₹ 50,000 against which a cheque of ₹ 20,000 only was received. No entry was passed except that of cheque received. Commission @ 1% is payable to N.K. Sinha.

(*ii*) Similarly is joint venture agreement was entered into with S.K. Sinha for which an advance of ₹ 7,500 was made. It is now ascertained that the venture earned a Profit of ₹ 5,000 of which the proprietor's share is $\frac{3}{5}$ ths.

Ans. [(*i*) Profit on Consignment ₹ 27,000; Balance due from S.K. Sinha ₹ 10,500; Total of Adjusted Trial Balance ₹ 4,42,500; (*ii*) Debit S.K. Sinha with ₹ 3,000, Credit Profit and Loss A/c with ₹ 3,000]

CHAPTER

15

Accounting for Joint Ventures

Meaning of Joint Venture

A joint venture is usually a temporary partnership without the use of a firm name, limited to carrying out a particular business plan in which the persons concerned agree to contribute capital and to share profits or losses. The parties in a joint venture are known as co-venturers and their liability is limited to the adventure concerned for which they agree to contribute capital and share profits or losses. For example, *X* and *Y* decide to contribute ₹ 1,00,000 each and to invest the same in the purchase and sale of wheat. They purchased wheat costing ₹ 1,80,000 and incurred ₹ 20,000 as expenses. The entire wheat was sold by them for ₹ 3,00,000. Thus, they made a profit of ₹ 1,00,000 in this venture. Then *X* and *Y* share the profits in the agreed ratio say, equally. Each will get ₹ 50,000 share of profit.

Areas of Business where Joint Venture Form of Business can be adopted

(*i*) Joint Consignment of Goods, (*ii*) Underwriting of Shares or Debentures, (*iii*) Construction of a Building, (*iv*) Distribution of Goods, (*v*) Sale and Purchase of properties.

Characteristics of a Joint Venture

Following are the main characteristics of a joint venture :

(*a*) It is an agreement between two or more persons.

(*b*) It is a *temporary partnership* and comes to an end after the completion of a particular venture.

(*c*) The partnership is for a *specific venture,* so it is a particular partnership.

(*d*) The partnership is *without the use of a firm name.*

(*e*) The main *purpose* of a joint venture is to make profit and to distribute that profit among all co-venturers. Loss, if any, will also be borne by the co-venturers in the agreed ratio or equally if no agreement regarding ratio has been made.

(*f*) The venturers may do any type of business of their own during the course of the venture.

Benefits of Joint Venture

Following benefits will be available from Joint Venture business :

(*i*) **Sharing of Risk.** The risk in case of joint venture business will be borne by all co-adventurers as profit or loss on joint venture transactions are shared by all co-adventurers in a predetermined ratio.

(*ii*) **Financial Resources.** Adequate financial resources provided by two or more persons will be available to undertake relatively big projects requiring more capital.

(*iii*) **Sufficient Experience.** More people of different skills and experience can come together to undertake costly and profitable projects and execute them efficiently.

Difference Between Joint Venture and Consignment

Main differences between a joint venture and a consignment are :

Points of Distinction	*Joint Venture*	*Consignment*
1. Relation Between Parties	The relationship between the parties is that of owners.	The relationship between the parties is that of the principal and the agent.
2. Method(s) of Keeping Accounts	There are four methods of keeping accounts.	There is only one method of keeping accounts.
3. Continuity of Relationship Between Parties	The relationship is terminated as soon as the venture is over	The relationship will be there even after one transaction.
4. Ownership of Goods	Ownership is that of co-adventurers.	Ownership remains with the consignor though possession of goods passes from the consignor to the consignee.
5. Profit Earned	It belongs to the co-adventurers	It belongs to the consignor and not to the consignee.
6. Account Sales	It is not sent by one co-adven-turer to another.	It is sent by the consignee to the consignor.
7. Management	The co-venturers enjoy full powers to manage the business and contribute funds for the business.	The consignee being an agent has no powers except that he has simply to obey the instructions of his principal.
8. Finance	Money is contributed by all co-venturers in a certain proportion.	All money is invested by the consignor.
9. Risk	Risk is shared between venturers.	Sales are made at consignor's risk.
10. Scope	Its scope is wide as it covers many activities besides trade.	Its scope is limited only to trade.
11. Number of Parties	There are at least two co-adventurers but may be more than two.	There are usually two parties normally the principal and the agent.
12. Parties	The parties to a joint venture are called co-adventurers.	The parties to a consignment are called consignor and consignee.
13. Nature of Business	It may be undertaken for any legal business including sale and purchase of movable goods.	It is concerned only with sale of movable goods.

Distinction Between Joint Venture & Partnership

Important distinctions between joint venture and partnership are given below :

Basis of Distinction	*Joint Venture*	*Partnership*
1. Name of the Firm	It is carried on without a firm's name.	It is carried on with firm's name.
2. Co-venturers/ Partners	The parties are called co-venturers.	The parties are called partners.

3. Continuity	It is temporary partnership and comes to an end after the completion of a particular venture.	It is continuous and does not end after the completion of a particular venture.
4. Liability	The liability of co-venturers is limited to the adventure concerned for which they agree to contribute capital and share profits or losses.	The liability of partners is unlimited to the extent of their business and private estate.
5. Location of Business	It is generally local.	It may be located at different places.
6. Position of a Minor	In it, minor is generally not admitted.	A minor can be admitted only for benefits.
7. Application of the Act	No enactment is applicable.	Indian Partnership Act, 1932 is applicable.
8. No. of Partners/Members	There is no limit in it.	The numbers of partners is limited to 20 in ordinary trade and 10 in banking business.

Methods of Recording Joint Venture Transactions

It is necessary to maintain proper accounts of all transactions of joint venture so that correct profit or loss on joint venture may be ascertained. Following are the main methods of recording joint venture transactions.

(*a*) When one of the co-venturers is appointed to manage the joint venture.
(*b*) When separate set of books are not maintained for recording joint venture transactions.
(*c*) When separate set of books are kept for the joint venture.
(*d*) When joint venture transactions are recorded through the Memorandum Joint Venture Account.

These will be discussed in detail one by one.

(a) When one of the co-venturers is appointed to manage the joint venture

This method is followed when most of the buying and selling on account of joint venture is managed by one-conventurer. Other co-venturers are only to contribute their share of investment in the joint venture. All transactions relating to joint venture are recorded by the co-venturer so appointed in his books as follows :

(*i*) On receipt of cash from other co-venturers as their share of investment.
Cash Account Dr.
To Other Co-venturers' Accounts (with their respective contributions)

(*ii*) On purchase of goods
Joint Venture Account Dr.
To Cash Account (If purchased for cash)
or To Supplier's Account (If purchased on credit)

(*iii*) On supplying goods out of his stock
Joint Venture Account Dr.
To Purchases or Goods Account

(*iv*) On goods being supplied by other co-venturers
Joint Venture Account Dr.
To Other Co-venturers' Accounts

(*v*) On expenses incurred on account of joint venture
Joint Venture Account Dr.
To Cash Account

(*vi*) On sale of goods on account of joint venture
Cash Account Dr.
    To Joint Venture Account

(*vii*) If the working partner gets commission, the entry is :
Joint Venture Account Dr.
    To Commission Account

(*viii*) If unsold stock is taken by the working partner :
Goods Account Dr.
    To Joint Venture Account

If unsold stock is taken by other co-venturers :
Other Co-venturers' Accounts Dr.
    To Joint Venture Account

(*ix*) Joint Venture Account is closed by transferring the balance of the account, either profit or loss to Profit and Loss Account (working partner's share of profit) and Other Co-venturers' Accounts (their share of profit or loss).

(*a*) In case of a profit, the entry is :
Joint Venture Account Dr.
    To Profit and Loss Account
    To Other Co-venturers' Accounts

(*b*) In case of a loss on joint venture, the entry is :
Profit and Loss Account Dr.
Other Co-venturers' Accounts Dr.
    To Joint Venture Account

Thus, we have seen that Joint Venture is a nominal account. It is debited with the cost of goods purchased or supplied out of stock as well as with all expenses and is credited with sales and unsold stock.

(*x*) On completion of the joint venture, the amount due to the other co-venturers is ascertained and payment is made to them. The entry is

Other Co-venturers' Accounts Dr.
    To Cash or Bank Account

ILLUSTRATION 1. Ram, Mohan and Rahim were partners in a joint venture, each contributing ₹ 5,000. Ram purchased goods for ₹ 13,000 and also supplied goods worth ₹ 1,000 from his stock. Rahim also supplied goods to the value of ₹ 1,500 from stock and his expenses in connection with the supplying of goods on account of joint venture amounted to ₹ 50. Ram paid ₹ 250 for expenses in connection with the joint venture. Ram sold goods on behalf of the joint venture and realised ₹ 20,800. Ram was entitled to a commission of 5 per cent on sales. Unsold goods amounting to ₹ 500 were taken over by Mohan. Ram settled accounts of Mohan and Rahim by Bank draft.

Record these transactions in Ram's Journal and also prepare Joint Venture Account and Mohan and Rahim Accounts in Ram's Books.

SOLUTION

RAM'S JOURNAL

			₹	₹
	Bank Account	Dr.	10,000	
	To Mohan			5,000
	To Rahim			5,000
	(Being amount received from Mohan and Rahim for joint venture)			

	Joint Venture Account Dr. To Bank Account (Being goods purchased on account of joint venture)		13,000	13,000
	Joint Venture Account Dr. To Goods Account (Being goods supplied out of stock for joint venture)		1,000	1,000
	Joint Venture Account Dr. To Rahim (Being goods for ₹ 1,500 supplied for joint venture and expenses ₹ 50 incurred by Rahim)		1,550	1,550
	Joint Venture Account Dr. To Bank Account (Being expenses incurred in connection with joint venture)		250	250
	Bank Account Dr. To Joint Venture Account (Being goods sold on account of joint venture)		20,800	20,800
	Joint Venture Account Dr. To Commission Account (Being 5% commission on sale of ₹ 20,800 on account of joint venture)		1,040	1,040
	Mohan Dr. To Joint Venture Account (Being unsold goods taken by Mohan)		500	500
	Joint Venture Account Dr. To Profit and Loss Account To Mohan To Rahim (Being profit on joint venture transferred)		4,460	 1,486 1,487 1,487
	Mohan Dr. Rahim Dr. To Bank Account (Being amount remitted to Mohan and Rahim in settlement of their accounts)		5,987 8,037	 14,024

JOINT VENTURE ACCOUNT

	₹		₹
To Bank Account (Purchases)	13,000	By Bank Account (Sales)	20,800
To Goods Account (Goods supplied)	1,000	By Mohan (Unsold goods taken)	500
To Rahim (Goods and expenses)	1,550		
To Bank Account (Expenses)	250		
To Commission Account (5%)	1,040		
To Profit on Joint Venture transferred to: ₹			
Profit & Loss Account 1,486			
Mohan 1,487			
Rahim 1,487	4,460		
	21,300		21,300

CO-VENTURERS ACCOUNTS

	Mohan ₹	Rahim ₹		Mohan ₹	Rahim ₹
To Joint Venture A/c	500	—	By Bank A/c	5,000	5,000
To Bank A/c	5,987	8,037	By Joint Venture A/c	—	1,550
			By Joint Venture A/c (Profit)	1,487	1,487
	6,487	8,037		6,487	8,037

(b) When a separate set of books is not maintained for recording joint venture transactions

Under this method, each co-venturer opens a Joint Venture Account and the personal accounts of other co-venturers. The system of accounting is :

1. Each co-venturer debits Joint Venture Account with the cost of goods purchased and expenses incurred on account of joint venture. The credit is given to the Bank or to the Creditor's Account (if goods are purchased on credit and expenses not yet paid).

2. Each co-venturer also debits Joint Venture Account and credits the account of other co-venturer with the cost of goods purchased and expenses incurred by the other co-venturer on account of joint venture. It may be remembered that it is possible only if each co-venturer gives information regarding purchase of goods, sale of goods and expenses incurred by him to the other co-venturer.

3. When goods are sold on account of joint venture, Cash or Purchaser Account is debited and Joint Venture Account is credited with the amount of sale. If the goods are sold by the other co-venturer, personal account of the other co-venturer is debited and Joint Venture Account is credited with the amount of sale.

4. When any commission is receivable by the co-venturer, Joint Venture Account is debited and Commission Account is credited with the amount of the commission. If the commission is receivable by the other co-venturer, Joint Venture Account is debited and Personal Account of the other co-venturer is credited.

5. Sometimes, remittance is received by one co-venturer by getting the bill discounted accepted by the other co-venturer. This is done when one of the co-venturers makes the investment on account of joint venture. In such a case, loss on account of discounting the bill should be transferred to Joint Venture Account because loss on account of discount is to be borne by all the co-venturers. Entries in this connection are as follows :

In Drawer's Books		*In Acceptor's Books*	
(*i*) Bills Receivable Account	Dr.	(*i*) Other Co-venturer	Dr.
To Other Co-venturer		To Bills Payable Account	
(Being acceptance received)		(Being acceptance given)	
(*ii*) Bank Account	Dr.	(*ii*) No entry	
Discount Account	Dr.		
To Bills Receivable Account			
(Being bill discounted)			
(*iii*) Joint Venture Account	Dr.	(*iii*) Joint Venture Account	Dr.
To Discount Account		To Other Co-venturer	
(Being transfer of discount)		(Being transfer of discount)	

6. If unsold stock is taken by one-conventurer, Goods Account is debited and Joint Venture Account is credited in the books of co-venturer taking goods. If unsold goods are taken by the other co-venturer, Personal Account of the other co-venturer is debited and Joint Venture Account is credited.

7. Balance in Joint Venture Account will represent profit or loss and will be shared by all-coventurers in the agreed ratio or in the absence of any agreement equally. If there is a profit, each partner debits Joint

Venture Account and credits Profit and Loss Account with his own share and the other Co-Venturers' Accounts with their share of profit. In case of a loss, the entries will be reversed.

8. The balance in the personal account of any co-venturer will show the amount due from or due to him.

Under this method, each co-venturer will open the following accounts in his books :

(1) Joint Venture Account. It is a nominal account in nature and is prepared to ascertain the Profit or Loss.

(2) Co-venturers' Personal Accounts. Each venturer will keep personal accounts of other co-venturers to record transactions affected by them.

ILLUSTRATION 2. A of Ahmedabad and B of Mumbai enter into a joint venture to consign 100 bales to C at Kolkata to be sold on their joint account. They agree to share profits or losses equally.

A sent 50 bales valued at ₹ 60,000 and pays freight and expenses ₹ 1,200. B sent 50 bales valued at ₹ 55,000 and pays expenses for ₹ 900.

All the bales reached Kolkata in time. However, 5 bales were found to have been tampered with during the transit. A recovered ₹ 3,000 from the insurance company, C sold remaining bales for ₹ 1,35,000. He charged 3% as selling commission and deducted ₹ 1,500 towards expenses.

C remitted the balance amount to A by D/D on State Bank of India payable at Ahmedabad.

Record the above transactions in the books of A and B.

SOLUTION

A's Books

JOURNAL

			₹	₹
	Joint Venture Account	Dr.	60,000	
	To Bank Account			60,000
	(Being cost of goods purchased on account of joint venture)			
	Joint Venture Account	Dr.	1,200	
	To Bank Account			1,200
	(Being expenses incurred on account of joint venture)			
	Joint Venture Account	Dr.	55,000	
	To B			55,000
	(Being goods purchased by B on account of joint venture)			
	Joint Venture Account	Dr.	900	
	To B			900
	(Being expenses incurred by B on account of joint venture)			
	Bank Account	Dr.	3,000	
	To Joint Venture Account			3,000
	(Being amount received from insurance company on tampering with goods on account of joint venture)			
	C	Dr.	1,35,000	
	To Joint Venture			1,35,000
	(Being sales effected by C on account of joint venture)			
	Joint Venture Account	Dr.	4,050	
	To C			4,050
	(Being 3% commission on ₹ 1,35,000 payable to C)			
	Joint Venture Account	Dr.	1,500	
	To C			1,500
	(Being expenses incurred by C on account of joint venture)			

Bank Account	Dr.	1,29,450	
To C			1,29,450
(Being D/D received from C for the amount due from him)			
Joint Venture Account	Dr.	15,350	
To Profit and Loss Account			7,675
To B			7,675
(Being profit on joint venture transferred)			

JOINT VENTURE ACCOUNT

		₹		₹
To Bank Account (Goods)		60,000	By Bank Account (Insurance Claim)	3,000
" Bank Account (Expenses)		1,200	" C (Sales)	1,35,000
" B (Goods)		55,000		
" B (Expenses)		900		
" C (Selling Commission)		4,050		
" C (Expenses)		1,500		
To Profit on Joint Venture transferred to:				
Profit and Loss A/c	₹ 7,675			
B	₹ 7,675	15,350		
		1,38,000		1,38,000

B's ACCOUNT

	₹		₹
To Balance c/d	63,575	By Joint Venture A/c (Goods)	55,000
		By Joint Venture A/c (Expenses)	900
		By Joint Venture A/c (Profit)	7,675
	63,575		63,575
		By Balance b/d	63,575

C's ACCOUNT

	₹		₹
To Joint Venture A/c (Sales)	1,35,000	By Joint Venture A/c (Commission)	4,050
		By Joint Venture A/c (Expenses)	1,500
		By Bank A/c	1,29,450
	1,35,000		1,35,000

B's Books
JOURNAL

		₹	₹
Joint Venture Account	Dr.	60,000	
To A			60,000
(Being cost of goods purchased by A on account of joint venture)			

Particulars		Dr. (₹)	Cr. (₹)
Joint Venture Account	Dr.	1,200	
To A			1,200
(Being expenses incurred by A)			
Joint Venture Account	Dr.	55,000	
To Bank Account			55,000
(Being cost of goods purchased on account of joint venture)			
Joint Venture Account	Dr.	900	
To Bank			900
(Being expenses incurred on account of joint account)			
A	Dr.	3,000	
To Joint Venture Account			3,000
(Being amount received by A from insurance on account of joint venture)			
C	Dr.	1,35,000	
To Joint Venture Account			1,35,000
(Being sales effected by C on account of joint venture)			
Joint Venture Account	Dr.	4,050	
To C			4,050
(Being 3% commission on ₹ 1,35,000 payable to C)			
Joint Venture Account	Dr.	1,500	
To C`			1,500
(Being expenses incurred by C on account of joint venture)			
A	Dr.	1,29,450	
To C			1,29,450
(Being amount received by A from C)			
Joint Venture Account	Dr.	15,350	
To Profit and Loss Account			7,675
To A			7,675
(Being profit on joint venture transferred)			

JOINT VENTURE ACCOUNT

		₹		₹
To A (Goods)		60,000	By A (Insurance claim)	3,000
" A (Expenses)		1,200	" C (Sales)	1,35,000
" Bank (Goods)		55,000		
" Bank (Expenses)		900		
" C (Selling Commission)		4,050		
" C (Expenses)		1,500		
To Profit on Joint Venture transferred to:				
Profit and Loss A/c	₹ 7,675			
A	₹ 7,675	15,350		
		1,38,000		1,38,000

A's ACCOUNT

	₹		₹
To Joint Venture A/c :	3,000	By Joint Ventures A/c (Goods)	60,000
To C's A/c	1,29,450	By Joint Ventures A/c (Expenses)	1,200
		By Joint Ventures A/c (Profit)	7,675
		By Balance c/d	63,575
	1,32,450		1,32,450
To Balance b/d	63,575		

C's ACCOUNT

	₹		₹
To Joint Venture A/c (Sales)	1,35,000	By Joint Ventures A/c (Commission)	4,050
		By Joint Ventures A/c (Expenses)	1,500
		By A's A/c	1,29,450
	1,35,000		1,35,000

(c) When a separate set of books is kept for the joint venture

In this method, no individual co-venturer makes a record in his individual books but a complete set of double entry books is used for writing up joint venture transactions. The accounting treatment in this method is similiar to that of partnership transactions. This method is usually followed when the parties to a joint venture are at the same place and when the joint venture undertaken is sufficiently large. Under this method, a Joint Bank Account is opened, the co-venturers to a joint venture pay their share of investment into this account and the payments on account of joint venture are also recorded in this account. Accounts of the co-venturers are also opened. When the joint venture is completed, the amounts due to the co-venturers are ascertained and paid and books are thus closed.

The entries to be recorded in this method are as follows :

1. When the amount is contributed by the co-venturers :
   Joint Bank Account Dr.
   To Personal Account of each Co-venturer
2. When goods are purchased on account of joint venture :
   Joint Venture Account Dr.
   To Joint Bank Account (If purchased on cash)
   or To Supplier's Account (If purchased on credit)
3. For expenses incurred on account of joint venture :
   Joint Venture Account Dr.
   To Joint Bank Account
4. When goods are sold on account of joint venture :
   Joint Bank Account Dr. (if sold on cash)
   or Purchaser's Account Dr. (if sold on credit)
   To Joint Venture Account
5. Joint Venture Account is closed by transferring the balance (*i.e.*, profit or loss) of this account to all co-venturers in their profit or loss sharing ratio.
6. For payment of the amount due to co-venturers :
   Personal Accounts of the Co-venturers Dr.
   To Joint Bank Account

Under this method, following accounts are opened :

(1) Joint Venture Account. It is a nominal account in nature and used to calculate profit or loss on joint venture.

(2) Co-Venturers' Accounts. Each Co-venturer's Account is a personal account of each venturer and used to record transactions of venturer with joint business and to ascertain the amount due to/from them.

(3) Joint Bank Account. It is a personal account used to record cash and bank transactions.

It may be noted that there should be no balance in Joint Bank Account when all payments due on account of joint venture are made and the amounts due to the co-venturers are paid.

ILLUSTRATION 3. A and B enter into joint venture. A agrees to bring capital in cash. Accordingly a Joint Banking Account is opened by A for a sum of ₹ 80,000. B buys goods worth ₹ 50,000 as part of his share of capital. Further goods worth ₹ 1,18,000 were purchased from C paying ₹ 60,000 and balance by a promissory note signed by A and B.

The goods were sent to Calcutta for sale. Expenses totalling ₹ 5,000 were incurred in sending the goods. Part of goods were damaged and a sum of ₹ 25,000 were recovered from the insurance company. The balance goods were sold for ₹ 2,20,000.

Give journal entries to record the above transactions. Also prepare Joint Venture Account, Joint Bank Account and accounts of A and B assuming that the promissory note was duly honoured.

SOLUTION

JOURNAL ENTRIES

				₹	₹
	Joint Bank Account	Dr.		80,000	
	To A				80,000
	(Being amount contributed by A)				
	Joint Venture Account	Dr.		50,000	
	To B				50,000
	(Being goods purchased by B on account of joint venture)				
	Joint Venture Account	Dr.		1,18,000	
	To C				1,18,000
	(Being goods purchased from C on account of joint venture)				
	C	Dr.		1,18,000	
	To Joint Bank Account				60,000
	To Bills Payable Account				58,000
	(Being payment made to C)				
	Joint Venture Account	Dr.		5,000	
	To Joint Bank Account				5,000
	(Being expenses incurred on account of joint venture)				
	Joint Bank Account	Dr.		25,000	
	To Joint Venture Account				25,000
	(Being amount received from the insurance company for part of the goods damaged)				
	Joint Bank Account	Dr.		2,20,000	
	To Joint Venture Account				2,20,000
	(Being sales on account of joint venture)				

	Bills Payable Account Dr. To Joint Bank Account (Being payment of the promissory note on the due date)		58,000	58,000
	Joint Venture Account Dr. To A To B (Being profit on Joint venture transferred to A & B)		72,000	36,000 36,000
	A Dr. B Dr. To Joint Bank Account (Being payment made to co-venturers in final settlement of their accounts)		1,16,000 86,000	2,02,000

JOINT VENTURE ACCOUNT

	₹		₹
To B (Goods)	50,000	By Joint Bank Account (Insurance Claim)	25,000
" C (Goods)	1,18,000	By Joint Bank Account (Sales)	2,20,000
To Joint Bank Account (Expenses)	5,000		
To Profit on Joint Venture transferred to : A ₹ 36,000 B ₹ 36,000	72,000		
	2,45,000		2,45,000

A

	₹		₹
To Joint Bank Account	1,16,000	By Joint Bank Account	80,000
		" Joint Venture Account (Profit)	36,000
	1,16,000		1,16,000

B

	₹		₹
To Joint Bank Account	86,000	By Joint Venture Account (Goods)	50,000
		By Joint Venture Account (Profit)	36,000
	86,000		86,000

JOINT BANK ACCOUNT

	₹		₹
To A	80,000	By C	60,000
" Joint Venture Account	25,000	" Joint Venture Account	5,000
" Joint Venture Account	2,20,000	" Bills Payable Account	58,000

		By A	1,16,000
		" B	86,000
	3,25,000		3,25,000

Construction of Buildings, Bridges, Roads, etc.

Such work, being of a bigger nature, are usually undertaken by companies which become contractee. The consideration to be received by such companies is usually partly in cash and partly in the form of shares or debentures. Shares and Debentures are sold or taken over by co-venturers at agreed price in order to determine the overall profit/loss of the venture. The additional entries to be passed are given below :

	Debit	Credit
(*i*) For Contract price due	Contractee's A/c	Joint Venture A/c
(*ii*) For receipt of contract price	Joint Bank A/c (for cash), Shares/Debentures A/c (for shares/debentures)	Contractee
(*iii*) For sale of shares/debentures	Joint Bank A/c Co-adventurers A/c	Shares/Debentures A/c
(*iv*) Profit on sale of shares/debentures	Shares/Debentures A/c	Joint Venture A/c

Note : For loss on sale of shares/debentures—reverse entry.

ILLUSTRATION 4. Dilip and Raj are doing business separately as engineering contractors. They undertake jointly to build and instal new machinery for a company for a contract price of ₹ 1,34,000—₹ 84,000 payable in instalments in cash and the balance as fully paid shares in the new company. A bank account is opened in joint, Dilip paying ₹ 45,000 and Raj ₹ 20,000. They are to share profits and losses in the proportion of 3/5 and 2/5 respectively. Their transactions were as follows :

Amount advanced to suppliers for supply of materials ₹ 52,000 ; Value of materials supplied by suppliers ₹ 89,000 ; Balance amount paid to suppliers in full and final settlement ₹ 35,500 ; Paid Wages ₹ 36,000 ; Materials purchased in cash ₹ 2,500 ; Material supplied by Dilip from stock ₹ 9,250 ; Engineering consultant fees paid ₹ 3,250 ; Value of stock lost by fire and not covered by insurance ₹ 3,500.

The contract was completed and the price duly received.

Dilip took all the shares at the agreed value of ₹ 47,000 and Raj took the balance stock of materials worth ₹ 3,500 at an agreed value of ₹ 2,750.

Prepare Joint Venture Account, showing the resultant profit or loss and the accounts of Dilip and Raj and also Bank Account.

SOLUTION

JOINT BANK ACCOUNT

	₹		₹
To Dilip	45,000	By Suppliers A/c—(Materials)	52,000
" Raj	20,000	" Suppliers A/c—(Materials)	35,500
" Joint Venture A/c	84,000	" Joint Venture A/c—(Wages)	36,000
		" Joint Venture A/c—(Materials)	2,500
		" Joint Venture A/c (Consultant fees)	3,250
		" Dilip	4,400
		" Raj	15,350
	1,49,000		1,49,000

JOINT VENTURE ACCOUNT

	₹		₹
To Suppliers A/c—(Materials)	89,000	By Suppliers A/c—(Discount received)	1,500
" Joint Bank A/c—(Wages)	36,000	" Joint Bank A/c	84,000
" Joint Bank A/c—(Materials)	2,500	" Shares A/c	50,000
" Joint Bank A/c—		" Raj (Materials)	2,750
(Consultant's fees)	3,250	" Dilip—Loss	2,850
" Dilip—(Materials)	9,250	" Raj—(Loss)	1,900
" Shares A/c	3,000		
	1,43,000		1,43,000

DILIP

	₹		₹
To Shares A/c	47,000	By Joint Bank A/c	45,000
" Joint Venture A/c—(Loss)	2,850	" Joint Venture A/c	9,250
" Joint Bank A/c	4,400		
	54,250		54,250

RAJ

	₹		₹
To Joint Venture A/c	2,750	By Joint Bank A/c	20,000
" Joint Venture A/c—(Loss)	1,900		
" Joint Bank A/c	15,350		
	20,000		20,000

SHARES ACCOUNT

	₹		₹
To Joint Venture A/c	50,000	By Dilip	47,000
		" Joint Venture A/c	3,000
	50,000		50,000

Underwriting of Shares

Sometimes co-adventurers agree to underwrite the shares of a company for a consideration of underwriting commission which may be received partly in cash and partly in shares. If all the shares are not subscribed by the public, then underwriters will have to take up the shares not subscribed by the public and shares received as commission. The shares are ultimately sold or taken over by co-adventurers at an agreed price in order to calculate the overall profit or loss on joint venture. The additional entries to be passed are given below :

	Debit	**Credit**
(*i*) For receiving Commission	Joint Bank A/c Shares A/c	Joint Venture A/c
(*ii*) For taking up the shares not subscribed by public	Shares A/c	Joint Bank A/c Co-adventures' A/c
(*iii*) For sale of Shares	Joint Bank A/c Co-ventures' A/c	Shares A/c
(*iv*) For Profit on Shares	Shares A/c	Joint Venture A/c

Note : For loss on shares reverse entry.

ILLUSTRATION 5. (Underwriting of Shares) Gopal and Govind entered into a joint venture agreement to undertake the subscriptions of 50,000 Equity Shares of ₹ 10 each issued by a newly formed Limited Company at a premium of ₹ 2 per share. The underwriting commission is 4% as provided in the Articles.

Public subscriptions were received for 38,000 shares and the underwriters duly discharged their obligations by taking up the remaining shares. Gopal and Govind contributed ₹ 80,000 each and deposited the same in a Joint Bank Account. Sundry expenses incurred out of the Joint Bank amounted to ₹ 5,000. The underwriting commission was received by cheque.

Towards the end of the venture 10,000 shares were sold by them in the open market @ ₹ 14 per share and the rest of the shares were taken up by them equally @ ₹ 13 per share.

Profits of the venture were shared equally.

You are required to prepare the joint venture account, Joint Bank Account and the personal accounts of the co-venturers recording the above mentioned transactions.

SOLUTION

JOINT VENTURE ACCOUNT

		₹		₹
To Joint Bank A/c (Cost of 12,000 shares @ as 12 per share)		1,44,000	By Joint Bank A/c (Underwriting Commission : 4% on ₹ 6,00,000)	24,000
To Joint Bank A/c (Sundry expenses)		5,000	By Joint Bank A/c (Sale of 10,000 shares @ ₹ 14 per share)	1,40,000
" Profit to :	₹		" Gopal's A/c $\left(\frac{1}{2}\text{ Shares taken over}\right)$	13,000
" Gopal	20,500		By Gobind's A/c $\left(\frac{1}{2}\text{ Shares taken over}\right)$	13,000
Govind	20,500	41,000		
		1,90,000		1,90,000

JOINT BANK ACCOUNT

	₹		₹
To Gopal's A/c	80,000	By Joint Venture A/c (Sundry Expenses)	5,000
" Govind's A/c	80,000	" Joint Venture A/c (Cost of shares)	1,44,000
" Joint Venture A/c	1,40,000	" Gopal's A/c	87,500
" Joint Venture A/c (Underwriting Commission)	24,000	" Govind's A/c	87,500
	3,24,000		3,24,000

CO-VENTURERS' ACCOUNTS

	Gopal ₹	*Govind* ₹		*Gopal* ₹	*Govind* ₹
To Joint Venture A/c (Shares taken over)	13,000	13,000	By Joint Bank A/c	80,000	80,000
" Joint Bank A/c	87,500	87,500	" Joint Venture A/c (Profit)	20,500	20,500
	1,00,500	1,00,500		1,00,500	1,00,500

Sale of Plots through Developers

Sometimes co-adventurers act as developers in joint venture. They purchase land and incur certain expenses in order to develop the land. The land is divided into certain plots besides leaving some portion of land for providing various common facilities and for public roads. These plots are ultimately sold or are taken over by co-adventures at an agreed price. The profit or loss are shared by co-adventurers in proportion of the ratio in which they share profits and losses. This will be more clear from the following illustration.

ILLUSTRATION 6. Kailash and Gopal entered into a joint venture for the sale of plots of land. A Joint Bank Account was opened in which Kailash deposited ₹ 30 lakh and Gopal deposited ₹ 10 lakh. They agreed to share profits and losses in the ratio of their respective capitals.

A piece of land was purchased for ₹ 29 lakh. Legal and registration fees of ₹ 3 lakh were paid. A sum of ₹ 8 lakh was spent on development of the land. The land was divided into 40 plots. 30 plots were sold @ ₹ 1.5 lakh each and 6 plots were sold @ ₹ 1.2 lakh each. The brokerage of ₹ 2.2 lakh was paid for selling the plots. The remaining plots were taken over by Gopal and Kailash at the cost price in proportion of the ratio in which they shared profits and losses.

Prepare the Joint Venture Account, Joint Bank Account and the accounts of the two co-venturers.

SOLUTION

JOINT VENTURE ACCOUNT ₹ in lakhs

To Joint Bank A/c :			By Joint Bank A/c Plot sold	
Land Purchased		29.00	30 × 1.5 lakh	45.00
Legal Expenses		3.00	6 × 1.2 lakh	7.20
Development Expenses		8.00	By Kailash's A/c (3 plots)	3.00
Brokerage paid		2.20	By Gopal's A/c (one plot)	1.00
To Profit transferred to				
Co-Adventurer's A/cs :				
Kailash	10.5			
Gopal	3.5			
		14.00		
		56.20		56.20

CO-ADVENTURES ACCOUNT (₹ in lakhs)

	Kailash	Gopal		Kailash	Gopal
To Joint Venture A/c	3.00	1.00	By Joint Bank A/c	30.00	10.00
To Joint Bank A/c	37.50	12.50	By Joint Venture A/c (Profit)	10.50	3.50
	40.50	13.50		40.50	13.50

JOINT BANK ACCOUNT (₹ In Lakhs)

To Kailash's A/c	30.00	By Joint Venture A/c (Land Purchased + Legal Expenses + Development Expenses + Brokerage paid)	42.20
To Gopal's A/c	10.00	By Kailash's A/c	37.50
To Joint Venture A/c (Plot Sold)	52.20	By Gopal's A/c	12.50
	92.20		92.20

(d) Memorandum Joint Venture Account

This method is followed when each co-adventurer in a joint venture wants to make a record of joint venture transactions in his books. This method is an alternative of (B) method and operates as follows :

(*a*) Every co-adventurer will open a personal account called Joint Venture with—(name of the other co-adventurer) Account and the following entries will be recorded in this account.

(*i*) Joint Venture with________Account Dr.
To Cash or Creditors Account
(Being all payments or liabilities incurred on account of joint venture)

(*ii*) Cash or Debtors Account
To Joint Venture with________Account Dr.
(Being sales effected by him on account of Joint venture)

(*iii*) Joint Venture with________Account
To Goods Account
(Being goods supplied out of stock for joint venture)

(*iv*) Joint Venture with________Account
To Commission Account
(Being commission payable to us on sales on account of joint venture)

It may be noted that entries relating to joint venture effecting the co-adventurer regarding the joint venture transactions are to be recorded only in his books. Similarly, entries effecting other co-adventurers will be recorded by other co-adventurers in their books.

(*b*) In addition to the personal accounts as described above, a Memorandum Joint Venture Account is also opened with a view to ascertaining profit or loss on joint venture. To enable the preparation of Memorandum Joint Venture Account, each party sends to the other party a copy of the transactions effected by him. Memorandum Joint Venture Account can be compared with a Profit and Loss Account because all expenses and losses are debited to this account. It may be remembered by the students that the items appearing in the personal accounts of all co-adventurers are entered in the Memorandum Joint Venture Account on the same sides (debit or credit) as they appear in the personal accounts. The balance of Memorandum Joint Venture Account represents profit or loss on joint venture and each co-adventurer will make a record of profit or loss in his books as follows:

(*i*) Joint Venture with________Account Dr.
To Profit and Loss Account
(Being our share of profit on joint venture)

(*ii*) Profit and Loss Account
To Joint Venture with________Account
(Being our share of loss on joint venture)

It may be noted that Memorandum Joint Venture Account does not form part of the double entry system. It has been prepared to find out profit or loss on joint venture.

(*c*) The balance in Joint Venture with—Account will show the amount due to or due from the other co-adventurer.

ILLUSTRATION 7. Aswin of Chennai and Gupta of Delhi entered into a joint venture on 1-4-2024 for the purpose of buying second-hand cars, recondition and sell them as diesel-air-conditioned cars. Aswin has agreed to buy second-hand cars and recondition them and fit diesel engines. Gupta has agreed to fix air conditioners and sell them at Delhi. They have agreed to share the profits and losses equally and settle their accounts at the end of the each year.

Following are the details of purchase, sale and expenses incurred by Aswin and Gupta during the year 1-4-2024 to 31-3-2025.

	Aswin ₹	Gupta ₹
Cost of 10 cars purchased at average price	5,00,000	
Reconditioning expenditure	45,000	
Cost of 10 diesel engines	30,000	
Labour charges	18,000	32,000
8 Air conditioners purchased		4,00,000
Buying commission @ 5%	25,000	
Selling commission @ 5%		60,000
Sale value realised on sale of 8 cars		12,00,000
Expenses incurred		
Freight—Local	10,000	8,000
Delhi	30,000	—
Rent— Office	10,000	10,000
Garage	12,000	20,000
Insurance	16,000	20,000
Miscellaneous expenses	6,000	10,000

Gupta sent a cheque for ₹ 6,00,000 to Aswin on 1-3-2025. Of the balance of 2 cars, one car was met with accident on the way to garage before reconditioning and the insurance company settled the claim at ₹ 30,000 (received by Aswin) as a total loss. The old petrol engines were sold @ ₹ 500 per engine and one diesel engine was sold at ₹ 3,000 by Aswin. All of them were sold before 31-3-2025. Aswin retained the balance one car as a non-airconditioned diesel car for his personal use which was priced at average cost. Aswin/Gupta settled the balance due to/by them as on 31-3-2025 by sending a crossed cheque as the case may be.

Prepare : (1) Memorandum Joint Venture Account. (2) Joint Venture Account with Gupta in the Books of Aswin. (3) Joint Venture Account with Aswin in the Books of Gupta.

SOLUTION

MEMORANDUM JOINT VENTURE ACCOUNT

	₹			₹
To *Aswin* :		By *Aswin* :		
Cost of 10 Cars	5,00,000	Sale of Petrol Engines		
Reconditioning Expenses	45,000	(9 × ₹ 500)		4,500
Cost of 10 Diesel Engines	30,000	Sale of Diesel Engines		3,000
Labour Charges	18,000	Insurance Claim		30,000
Buying Commission	25,000	Cost of Car taken	(1)	68,389
Freight — Local	10,000	By *Gupta* :		
— Delhi	30,000	Sale Value of 8 Cars		12,00,000
Rent — Office	10,000			
— Garage	12,000			
Insurance	16,000			
Misc. Expenses	6,000			
To *Gupta* :				
Labour Charges	32,000			
Cost of 8 Air Conditioners	4,00,000			
Selling Commission	60,000			
Freight — Local	8,000			
Rent — Office	10,000			
— Garage	20,000			

		₹		₹
Insurance		20,000		
Misc. Expenses		10,000		
To Profit on Venture :				
Aswin	₹ 21,945			
Gupta	₹ 21,944			
		43,889		
		13,05,889		13,05,889

In the Books of Aswin

JOINT VENTURE WITH GUPTA ACCOUNT

	₹		₹
To Bank —Cost of Cars	5,00,000	By Bank (Advance from Gupta)	6,00,000
—Cost of Diesel Engines	30,000	—Sale of Petrol Engines	4,500
—Reconditioning Expenses	45,000	—Sale of Diesel Engines	3,000
—Labour Charges	18,000	—Insurance Claim	30,000
—Freight Local	10,000	—Motor Vehicle A/c	
—Freight Delhi	30,000	(Car taken over)	68,389
—Office Rent	10,000	By Bank (Balance received)	18,056
—Garage Rent	12,000		
—Buying Commission	25,000		
—Insurance	16,000		
—Misc. Expenses	6,000		
To P/L A/c (Share of Profit on Venture)	21,945		
	7,23,945		7,23,945

In the Books of Gupta

JOINT VENTURE WITH ASWIN ACCOUNT

	₹		₹
To Bank A/c :		By Bank (Sale of Cars)	12,00,000
—Advance given	6,00,000		
—Cost of Air Conditioners	4,00,000		
—Labour Charges	32,000		
—Freight Charges (local)	8,000		
—Office Rent	10,000		
—Garage Rent	20,000		
—Selling Commission	60,000		
—Insurance	20,000		
—Misc. Expenses	10,000		
To Profit & Loss A/c (Share of Profit)	21,944		
To Bank (Balance Paid)	18,056		
	12,00,000		12,00,000

Working Notes :

(1) ***Cost of non-airconditioner diesel car taken over by Aswin*** **:**

	₹
Cost of one car (1/10 of ₹ 5,00,000)	50,000
Reconditioning expenditure (1/9 of ₹ 45,000)	5,000
Cost of one diesel engine (1/10 of ₹ 30,000)	3,000
Labour charges incurred by Aswin (1/9 of ₹ 18,000)	2,000

Local freight charges incurred by Aswin (1/10 of ₹ 10,000)	1,000
Buying commission (1/10 of ₹ 25,000)	2,500
Office Rent incurred by Aswin (1/9 of ₹ 10,000)	1,111
Garage Rent incurred by Aswin (1/9 of ₹ 12,000)	1,333
Insurance charges paid by Aswin (1/9 of ₹ 16,000)	1,778
Misc. expenses incurred by Aswin (1/9 of ₹ 6,000)	667
	68,389

(2) If abnormal loss on joint venture is calculated separately by taking cost of car and proportionate local freight charges incurred by Aswin, then amount of abnormal loss will be ₹ 21,000 (*i.e.,* Cost ₹ 50,000 + ₹ 1,000 Share of Local Freight – 30,000 Claim Settled). In that case, profit on joint venture would be ₹ 64,889.

Interest

Sometimes the co-venturers to a joint venture agree to charge or allow interest on the debit and credit balances up to the date of the completion of the joint venture ; the Joint Venture Account in such a case should be treated similar to the Account Current. Interest allowed to the co-venturers being loss is debited to Joint Venture Account and interest charged to co-venturers being income is credited to Joint Venture Account to arrive at the amount of net profit divisible among them.

ILLUSTRATION 8. Vijay and Arun entered into a joint venture for purchase and sale of cotton. They agreed to share profits in the proportion of 2 : 1 and also to be entitled to an interest of 12% per annum (on monthly basis) on moneys invested as well as received. Following transactions took place in between themselves :

(*i*) On 1st January, 2025, Vijay purchased 1,000 bales of cotton @ ₹ 500 per bale, the brokerage being ₹ 10 per bale.

(*ii*) On 1st February, 2025, Arun purchased 500 bales of cotton @ ₹ 520 per bale, the brokerage being ₹ 10 per bale.

(*iii*) On 28th February, 2025, Vijay sold 800 bales of cotton @ ₹ 572 per bale, the brokerage being ₹ 12 per bale and took the proceeds to himself.

(*iv*) On 1st April, 2025, Arun sold 600 bales of cotton @ ₹ 580 per bale, the brokerage being ₹ 10 per bale and took the proceeds to himself.

It was also agreed that each co-venturer will at first sell from his own purchase and then, if need be, from the goods purchased by other co-venturer. The balance stock left unsold was taken by Vijay at cost on 30th April, 2025 when accounts were settled between the co-venturers.

You are required to show the accounts of co-venturers and Joint Venture Account as would appear when maintained in a separate set of books.

SOLUTION

JOINT VENTURE ACCOUNT

2025		₹	2025		₹
Jan. 1	To Vijay (Purchases – 1,000 bales @ ₹ 500 + ₹ 10 brokerage)	5,10,000	Feb. 28	By Vijay (Sales—800 bales @ ₹ 572—₹ 12 brokerage)	4,48,000
Feb. 1	To Arun (Purchases—500 bales@ ₹ 520 + ₹ 10 brokerage)	2,65,000	April 1	By Arun (Sales—600 bales @ ₹ 580—₹ 10 brokerage)	3,42,000
April 30	To Vijay (Interest @ 12% on ₹ 5,10,000 for 4 months from Jan. 1 to April 30 ₹ 20,400		" 30	By Vijay (100 unsold bales taken @ ₹ 510 *i.e.,* cost price of Vijay)	51,000

	Less : 12% on ₹ 4,48,000 sales made by him for 2 months from Feb. 28 to April 30 =	8,960	11,440			
April 30	To Arun (Interest @ 12% on ₹ 2,65,000 for 3 months from Feb. 1 to April 30 =	7,950				
	Less : 12% on ₹ 3,42,000 sales made by him for 1 month from April 1 to April 30 =	3,420	4,530			
April 30	To Profit on Joint Venture transferred to :					
	Vijay—2/3 share	33,353				
	Arun—1/3 share	16,677	50,030			
			8,41,000			8,41,000

VIJAY

2025		₹	2025		₹
Feb. 28	To Joint Venture Account (Sales)	4,48,000	Jan. 1	By Joint Venture A/c (Purchases)	5,10,000
April 30	To Joint Venture A/c (Unsold goods taken)	51,000	April 30	By Joint Venture A/c (Interest)	11,440
" 30	To Joint Bank A/c	55,793	" 30	By Joint Venture A/c (Profit)	33,353
		5,54,793			5,54,793

ARUN

2025		₹	2025		₹
April 1	To Joint Venture A/c (Sales)	3,42,000	Feb. 1	By Joint Venture A/c (Purchases)	2,65,000
			Apr. 30	By Joint Venture A/c (Interest)	4,530
			" 30	By Joint Venture A/c (Profit)	16,677
			" 30	By Joint Bank A/c	55,793
		3,42,000			3,42,000

JOINT BANK ACCOUNT

2025		₹	2025		₹
Apr. 30	To Arun	55,793	Apr. 30	By Vijay	55,793

Conversion of Consignment into Joint Venture

Whenever it is desired to convert consignment into joint venture, the following procedure is followed :

(*i*) The necessary accounts should be prepared relating to consignment in the books of consignor to calculate profit or loss on consignment and commission due to consignee.

(*ii*) On conversion of consignment into joint venture, the memorandum joint venture account is to be prepared without forming part of double entry to find out profit or loss on the joint venture as per new agreement. Accordingly value of goods at new rate, discount on bill and interest on capital are charged to this account to show profit distributable among co-venturers after charging commission on sales.

(*iii*) After comparing the amounts of above items in two accounts, an adjustment entry is to be passed in the books of consignor to bring change in the relationship between consignor and consignee (now co-venturer).

Co-venturer's (previously consignee) A/c Dr.
Profit & Loss Ac/ (to cancel excess profit)
To Trading A/c
To Interest A/c
To Discount A/c

This will be more clear from the following Illustration :

ILLUSTRATION 9. (*Conversion of consignment into joint venture*). On 1st April, 2025 Rakesh consigned 100 table fans to Mohan of Panipat, each table fan costing ₹ 200. The table fans were invoiced at ₹250 each. Freight and insurance charges paid by Rakesh amounted to ₹ 500. 5 table fans were damaged in transit and on 30th June, 2025 Rakesh received ₹ 500 on account of the damaged fans from the insurance company.

Mohan took delivery of the table fans and immediately accepted a bill drawn on him for ₹ 10,000 for 3 months. Rakesh got it discounted at 12% p.a. On 30th June, 2025, Mohan sent an Account Sales showing that :

(*i*) 85 tables fans at ₹ 260 each were sold.

(*ii*) The damaged fans were sold at ₹ 130 per fan.

(*iii*) He had incurred the following expenses:

Octroi and carriage inwards ₹ 200 ; Godown expenses ₹ 200 ; Selling expenses ₹ 500.

Mohan is entitled to a commission of ₹ 20 per table fan sold plus one-fifth of the amount by which the gross sale proceeds exceeds a sum calculated at the invoice price. The commission is not payable on the sale of damaged fans. Mohan remitted the balance due from him.

After the preparation of accounts on 30th June, 2025, it was decided that the relationship between Rakesh and Mohan should be one of joint venture, the cost of the table fans being taken at ₹ 220. Under the new agreement, Mohan is entitled to 5% commission on all sales and Rakesh is entitled to interest @ 12% p.a. on his capital outlay. Rakesh accounting year ends on 30th June, 2025.

SOLUTION **CONSIGNMENT TO PANIPAT ACCOUNT**

2025		₹	2025		₹
April 1	To Goods Sent on Consignment A/c	25,000	June 30	By Bank A/c (Insurance Claim)	500
" 1	To Cash A/c (Freight & Ins.)	500	" 30	By Mohan—Sales of 85 fans @ ₹ 260 each	22,100
	To Mohan (Ex.)	900	" 30	By Mohan—Sale of 5 damaged fans @ ₹ 130 each	650
June 30	To Mohan (Commission) : @ ₹ 20 on 85 fans ₹ 1,700 1/5 of the excess		June 30	By Consignment	

			₹				₹
		i.e. 1/5 (22,100 – 21,250) 170	1,870			Stock A/c : Invoice price of 10 fans @ ₹ 250 each ₹ 2,500	
" 30	To	Stock Reserve—on 10 fans @ ₹ 50 each	500			*Add* : Proportionate Freight & Insurance $\left(\frac{₹ 500}{100} \times 10\right)$ 50	
June 30	To	Profit on Consignment transferred to Profit & Loss A/c	2,050			Proportionate Octroi and Cartage $\left(\frac{₹ 200}{100} \times 10\right)$ 20	2,570
				June 30	By	Goods Sent on Consignment A/c —Loading on 100 table fans @ ₹ 50 each	5,000
			30,820				30,820

GOODS SENT ON CONSIGNMENT ACCOUNT

2025			₹	2025			₹
June 30	To	Consignment to Panipat A/c	5,000	April 1	By	Consignment to Panipat A/c	25,000
" 30	To	Trading A/c	20,000				
			25,000				25,000

MOHAN

2025			₹	2025			₹
June 30	To	Consignment to Panipat A/c (Sale proceeds of 85 fans)	22,100	April 1	By	Bills Receivable A/c	10,000
				June 30	By	Consignment to Panipat A/c (Expenses)	900
" 30	To	Consignment to Panipat A/c (Sale of damaged fans)	650	June 30	By	Consignment to Panipat A/c (Commission)	1,870
				" 30	By	Bank A/c	9,980
			22,750				22,750

MEMORANDUM JOINT VENTURE ACCOUNT

	₹			₹
To Goods—100 table fans @ ₹ 220	22,000	By Sales—85 fans @ ₹ 260		22,100
To Expenses (Rakesh)	500	By Sales—5 damaged fans @ ₹ 130		650
To Discount	300	By Insurance Claim		500
To Expenses (Mohan)	900	By Consignment Stock A/c	₹	
To Commission to Mohan—5% on (₹ 22,100 + ₹ 650)	1,138	Cost—10 fans @ ₹ 220 =	2,200	
To Interest to Rakesh (1)	384	Proportionate Freight and Insurance	50	

	₹	₹		₹	₹
To Stock Reserve on 10 fans @ ₹ 20 (*i.e.* ₹ 220 – ₹ 200)		200	Proportionate Octroi and Carriage	20	
To Profit on Joint Venture :	₹				2,270
Rakesh	49				
Mohan	49				
		98			
		25,520			25,520

(1) Interest is calculated as follows :

On ₹ 22,000 (goods) + ₹ 500 (expenses) – ₹ 9,700 proceeds of the bill *i.e.*, ₹ 12,800 for 3 months from April to June 30 @ 12%.

$$= ₹\ 12,800 \times \frac{12}{100} \times \frac{3}{12} = ₹\ 384$$

Under the new agreement of joint venture Mohan is to be credited with ₹ 1,187 (*i.e.*, ₹ 1,138 for commission plus ₹ 49 share of profit on joint venture). Previously under the consignment agreement he received ₹ 1,870 as commission. Therefore, he is to be debited with ₹ 683 (*i.e.* ₹ 1,870—₹ 1,187). Rakesh will now credit Trading A/c by ₹ 2,000 extra because fans are to be valued @ ₹ 220 per fan instead of ₹ 200. Rakesh will also give credit to Interest Account ₹ 384 and Discount Account ₹ 300. In case of consignment, Rakesh's profit was ₹ 2,050. Now, under the new agreement there is a profit of ₹ 49 only, so Rakesh's Profit and Loss Account should be debited with ₹ 2,001 (₹ 2,050—₹ 49) to cancel the excess profit. Following journal entry is needed to bring the change in the relationship, between Rakesh and Mohan—

		₹	₹
Mohan	Dr.	683	
Profit and Loss Account	Dr.	2,001	
To Trading Account			2,000
To Interest Account			384
To Discount Account			300
(Being adjustment of accounts on conversion of Consignment to Panipat to Joint Venture with Mohan)			

QUESTIONS

OBJECTIVE TYPE

1. Fill in the blanks :

(*a*) Joint Venture Account is a.........Account.

(*b*) Consignment Account is a.........Account.

(*c*) Joint Venture with Vishwanathan Account in the books of Swamy will disclose.........

(*d*) Under memorandum joint venture method, each co-venturer opens only one account which is in the nature of a.........

(*e*) When goods are taken away by the co-venturer maintaining accounts regarding joint venture, the account to be debited is.........

(*f*) The accounts to be credited for transferring profit on joint venture in the books of the co-venturer maintaining accounts regarding joint venture are.........

Ans. [(*a*) Nominal (*b*) Nominal (*c*) Personal Account of Vishwanathan (*d*) Personal Account (*e*) Goods Account (*f*) Profit and Loss Account and Other Party A/c (for his share)].

2. Tick the right answer :

(*a*) When goods are purchased for the joint venture, the account to be debited in separate set of books for keeping the accounts of joint venture is.........

(*i*) Purchases Account. (*ii*) Joint Venture Account.

(*b*) Memorandum Joint Venture Account is.........

(*i*) A personal account. (*ii*) A real account. (*iii*) A nominal account.

(*c*) When separate set of books are kept for maintaining the accounts of joint venture, then

(*i*) Memorandum Joint Venture Account is not opened.

(*ii*) Memorandum Joint Venture Account is opened.

(*d*) (*i*) Value of goods destroyed by fire is debited to Joint Venture Account.

(*ii*) Value of goods destroyed by fire is not debited to Joint Venture Account.

(*e*) Joint Venture Account is a :

(*i*) Nominal Account (*ii*) Real Account

(*iii*) Artificial Personal Account (*iv*) Representative Personal Account.

(*f*) If unsold goods costing ₹ 20,000 are taken over by a co-venturer for ₹ 15,000, the Joint Venture Account will be credited with—

(*i*) ₹ 20,000 (*ii*) ₹ 15,000

(*iii*) ₹ 5,000 (*iv*) ₹ 35,000.

Ans. [(*a*) (*ii*), (*b*) (*iii*), (*c*) (*i*), (*d*) (*ii*), (*e*) (*i*), (*f*) (*ii*)].

SHORT ANSWER TYPE

1. What is Joint Venture ?
2. Give three examples of business in which joint venture is used.
3. Give four characteristics of Joint Venture.
4. Distinguish between Joint Venture and Consignment.
5. Distinguish between Joint Venture and Partnership.
6. Name the methods of keeping Joint Venture accounts.
7. What is Memorandum Joint Venture Account ?
8. What is Joint Bank Account ? Why is it maintained in Joint Venture accounts ?
9. A and B were partners in a joint venture sharing profits and losses in the ratio of 4 : 1. A supplies goods to the value of ₹ 5,000 and incurs expenses amounting to ₹ 400. B supplies goods to the value of ₹ 4,000 and his expenses amount to ₹ 300. B sells goods on behalf of the joint venture and realises ₹ 12,000. B is entitled to a commission of 5% on sales. B settles his account by bank draft. Prepare the Joint Venture Account in A's books.

Ans. [Profit ₹ 1,700]

10. A purchased goods worth ₹ 50,000 for Joint Venture and spended ₹ 10,000 on packing, insurance, freight etc. He sends it to B, who received goods and spended ₹ 9,000. What Journal Entries will be passed, when Memorandum Joint Venture Methods is adopted ?
11. A and B enter into Joint Venture. A supplied goods of ₹ 80,000 and incurred expenses of ₹ 8,000. B supplied goods of ₹ 50,000 and incurred expenses of ₹ 3,000. B sold goods for ₹ 2,55,000. He gets 10% commission on sales. A gets ₹ 5,000 as salary. Profits are shared in 3 : 2 ratio.

Prepare *Joint Venture Account*.

Ans. [Profit ₹ 83,500; A's share : ₹ 50,100; B's Share : ₹ 33,400]

LONG ANSWER TYPE

1. Define a joint venture and give its various features. Name the different methods used to record joint venture transactions.
2. Distinguish joint venture from consignment and partnership.

3. Give the various journal entries to be passed in case where separate set of books are maintained for recording joint venture transactions.
4. What is a Memorandum Joint Venture Account ? Give the various journal entries when accounts are maintained under this method.
5. Give the various journal entries to be passed in case where no separate set of books are maintained for recording joint venture transactions.

PRACTICAL PROBLEMS

WHERE ONE COVENTURER MANAGES THE JOINT VENTURE

1. A and B entered into a joint speculation and purchase an old house with extensive grounds for ₹ 8,000, each contributing ₹ 4,000. For an agreed fee of ₹ 500 A is to manage the disposal of the property. Sales of internal fittings, windows, etc., amount to ₹ 1,700. A pays ₹ 300 for demolishing the house material of which realised ₹ 200. Sundry expenses paid by A were ₹ 100 and the whole of the land is eventually sold for ₹ 9,000. A and B share the net profits equally. A paying B his share by cheque.

   Record these transactions in A's Journal and show Joint Venture A/c and B's A/c in his ledger.

Ans. [Profit ₹ 2,000 ; Amount paid to B ₹ 5,000].

WHERE NO SEPARATE BOOKS ARE MAINTAINED

2. A and B were participants in a joint venture, sharing profits and losses in the proportion of 10 : 9 respectively. Each party maintains a complete record in his own books. A supplies goods to the value of ₹ 25,000 and incurs an expenditure of ₹ 500 on them ; and B supplies goods to the extent of ₹ 21,000 and his expenses thereon amounted to ₹ 1,000. A sells all the goods for ₹ 70,000 for which he is entitled to receive a commission at 5 per cent. Accounts are settled by bank draft. Give Journal Entries and prepare necessary accounts in the books of both the parties.

Ans. [Profit ₹ 19,000 ; Amount paid to B ₹ 31,000].

3. Mohan purchased 1,000 metres of Kashmir Silk @ ₹ 6 per metre and sent to Desai of Mumbai to be sold for mutual benefit. Mohan spent ₹ 200 on packing etc. Desai received the consignment and paid ₹ 500 as freight.

   Mohan drew upon Desai for ₹ 5,000. The draft was accepted and Mohan got it *discounted* for ₹ 4,850. Desai sold 900 metres @ ₹ 9 per metre and had to pay ₹ 252 as expenses.

   Mohan took over remaining quantity at *cost plus 10%*. Mohan is to be allowed commission on sales @ 5% and the profits are to be shared in the ratio of 3 (Mohan) : 2 (Desai).

   Prepare Ledger Accounts in the books of Mohan.

Ans. [Profit ₹ 1,330 ; Balance due from Desai ₹ 1,816 ; Value of goods taken over ₹ 737].

4. P and Q entered into a Joint Venture. Each party was to receive commission of 5% on the proceeds of goods sold by him, but any commission paid by him to Sales Agents was not to be allowed as a charge against the Joint Venture. Subject to this, the profit or loss was to be shared equally.

   They purchased goods at a cost of ₹ 30,000 which was paid by P, who drew a bill on Q at 3 months for ₹ 20,000. The bill was discounted by P at a cost of ₹ 240 chargeable against the venture and was met at maturity. All the goods were sold for cash. Other transactions relating to the venture were:

	By P ₹	By Q ₹
Payments for :		
Carriage	260	—
Travelling Expenses	120	240

Commission paid to Sales Agents	400	200
Sundry Expenses	120	80
Receipts for goods sold	17,200	18,800

The goods unsold cost ₹ 3,000 and P took them over at a price yielding a gross profit at half the average rate made on sales, and paid Q the amount due to him. Prepare Joint Venture Account in the books of P.

Ans. [Profit ₹ 6,640 ; Valuation of goods taken over by P ₹ 3,500].

5. A in Delhi enters into a Joint Venture with B in Mumbai to ship *cotton bales* to C in Japan. A sends cotton to the value of ₹ 15,000, pays railway freight etc. ₹ 750 and sundry expenses ₹ 800. B sends goods valued at ₹ 10,370 and pays freight and insurance ₹ 600 ; dock dues ₹ 100; custom charges ₹ 250 ; and other sundry expenses ₹ 250. A advances to B ₹ 3,000 on account of the Venture. B receives account sales and remittance of the net proceeds from C in Japan for the whole of the goods amounting to ₹ 40,000. Show how Joint Venture transactions will be recorded in the Ledgers of A and B.

Ans. [Profit ₹ 11,880 ; Amount received from B ₹ 25,490]

6. Ramesh and Suresh entered into a joint venture to purchase and sell *hosiery goods*. Profit and losses were to be shared equally. Ramesh financed the venture and Suresh undertook the sales on a commission of 5% on the sales proceeds. Ramesh purchased goods to the value of ₹ 50,000 less 5% trade discount, paid freight ₹ 1,500 and advanced ₹ 1,200 to Suresh to meet expenses. Suresh expended for carriage ₹ 300, rent ₹ 450, advertisement ₹ 200 and sundries ₹ 150. Sales made by Suresh amounted to ₹ 67,500. It was agreed that Ramesh should receive ₹ 2,500 as interest.

   Remaining unsold goods costing ₹ 2,500 were retained by Suresh and those were charged to him at a price to show the same rate of gross profit (without charging any expenditure) as that made on the total sales (excluding those goods taken).

   Give Journal Entries in the books of Ramesh and Suresh and also prepare the necessary Ledger Accounts in their books.

Ans. [Profit ₹ 15,275 ; Balance due from Suresh ₹ 60,337.50].

WHERE SEPARATE BOOKS ARE MAINTAINED

7. X and Y entered into a joint venture for purchase and sale of some *household items*. They agreed to share profit and losses in the ratio of their respective contributions. X contributed ₹ 10,000 in cash and Y ₹ 13,000. The whole amount was placed in a Joint Bank Account. Goods were purchased by X for ₹ 10,000 and expenses paid by Y amounted to ₹ 2,000. They also purchased goods for ₹ 15,000 through the Joint Bank Account. The expenses on purchase and sale of the articles amounted to ₹ 6,000, (including those met by Y). Goods costing ₹ 20,000 were sold for ₹ 45,000 and the balance was lost by fire.

   Prepare Joint Venture Account, Joint Bank Account and the Venturers' Accounts closing the venture.

Ans. [Profit ₹ 14,000 ; Amount paid to X and Y ₹ 28,000 and ₹ 21,000 respectively.

8. A and B doing business separately as *building contractors*, undertake jointly to construct a building for a newly started Joint Stock Company for a contract price of ₹ 1,00,000 payable as to ₹ 80,000 by instalments in cash and ₹ 20,000 in fully paid shares of the Company. A Banking Account is opened in their joint names, A paying in ₹ 25,000 and B ₹ 15,000. They are to share the profits and losses in the proportions of $\frac{2}{3}$ and $\frac{1}{3}$ respectively. Their transactions were as follows :

	₹		₹
Paid wages	30,000	Material supplied by B	4,000
Bought material	70,000	Architect's Fees paid by A	2,000
Material supplied by A	5,000		

The contract was completed and the price (cash and shares) duly received. The Joint Venture was closed by A taking up all the shares of the Company at an agreed valuation of ₹ 16,000 and B taking up the stock of materials at an agreed valuation of ₹ 3,000.

Show the necessary Ledger Accounts.

Ans. [Loss ₹ 12,000 ; Amount paid to A and B ₹ 8,000 and ₹ 12,000 respectively].

9. B and C of Kolkata undertake a joint venture in *Burma timber*. On 1st July, 2024, they opened a joint banking account with ₹ 25,000, towards which B contributed ₹ 15,000 and C ₹ 10,000. They agree to share profits and losses in proportion to their cash contributions. They remitted to their agent in Burma ₹ 22,100 to pay for timber purchased. Freight, insurance and other charges amounting to ₹ 3,900 were paid in Kolkata.

On 1st December, 2024, the sales amounted to ₹ 28,740, which enabled them to repay themselves the cash originally advanced, no account being taken of interest. They then decided to close the venture and C agreed to take over the balance of timber unsold for ₹ 1,260 which is to be deducted from his share of profit.

Prepare accounts, showing the amount of cash available for division by way of profit and how the same is divisible between B and C.

Ans. [Profit ₹ 4,000 divisible between B and C ₹ 2,400 and ₹ 1,600 respectively].

10. Arun, Ashok and Gopal entered into a joint venture agreement. According to the terms of agreement, Arun is to supervise the overall working of venture and a separate set of books is kept for record keeping. Arun is entitled to charge 5% commission on sales. Ashok and Gopal contributed ₹ 6,400 each. Goods are purchased from Om Swarup for ₹ 14,400 and from Arun's own stock for ₹ 4,800. An expenditure of ₹ 1,460 is incurred on account of joint venture.

All the goods are sold away for ₹ 24,400. The accounts of venture are settled and accounts closed.

Journalise the above transactions, and show Joint Venture A/c and other ledger accounts in the joint venture books.

Ans. [Profit ₹ 2,520 ; Amount paid to Arun, Ashok and Gopal ₹ 6,860, ₹ 7,240 and ₹ 7,240 respectively].

11. Rajeev and Ashok entered into a joint venture as *dealers in land* and opened a *Joint Banking Account* with ₹ 60,000 towards which Rajeev contributed ₹ 40,000. They agreed to share profits and losses in proportion to their cash contributions. They purchased a plot of land measuring 5,000 sq. meters for ₹ 50,000. It was decided to sell the land in smaller plots and a plan was got prepared at the cost of ₹ 1,200. In the said plan 1/5 of the total area of the land was left over for public roads and the remaining land was divided into 8 plots of equal size. Out of 8 plots 3 plots were sold @ ₹ 15 per square meter and the remaining 5 plots were sold @ ₹ 14 per square meter. Expenses incurred in connection with the plots were : registration expenses ₹ 4,000, stamp duty ₹ 400 and other expenses ₹ 1,000. Allow 2% on the sale proceeds as commission to Rajeev.

Journalise the above transactions and prepare necessary Ledger Accounts.

Ans. [Loss ₹ 250 ; Amount paid to Rajeev ₹ 40,983 and Ashok ₹ 19,917].

12. Chander and Sunder entered into a Joint Venture of one year agreeing to share profits and losses equally after allowing *interest on capital* at 5% per annum. Chander contributed ₹ 30,000 and Sunder ₹ 20,000 for which they opened a joint bank account. In addition, Chander invested ₹ 8,000 on goods.

They purchased from Inder goods for ₹ 71,500 and spent ₹ 3,800 by way of freight and insurance.

At the end of the year the bulk of the goods were sold for ₹ 98,740. The remaining goods were taken by Chander for ₹ 9,000. Selling expenses were ₹ 6,940.

Prepare Joint Venture Account, Joint Bank Account and also Joint Venture (Investment) Account in the books of Chander and Sunder.

Ans. [Profit ₹ 14,600 ; Amount paid to Chander and Sunder ₹ 38,200 and ₹ 28,300 respectively].

13. Ramesh and Suresh entered into a Joint venture sharing profits and losses as 3 : 2. They opened a Joint Bank Account and deposited ₹ 4,000 each. Ramesh purchased 8 tons of an item @ ₹ 600 per ton and his expenses were ₹ 1,300. Suresh purchased a second item of 100 tons @ ₹ 21 per ton and his expenses were ₹ 1,100. Expenses were met from private sources and purchases were paid from Joint Bank Account.

Suresh sold 6 tons of the first item @ ₹ 1,000 per ton and his selling expenses were ₹ 1,150. Ramesh sold 80 tons of the second item @ ₹ 50 per ton and his selling expenses were ₹ 1,200. All the sale proceeds were deposited in Joint Bank Account and expenses were met from private sources.

Prepare the following accounts in the books of Joint Venture of Ramesh and Suresh : (*a*) Joint Venture Account , (*b*) Joint Venturers' Accounts, (*c*) Joint Bank Account, (*d*) Working of closing stock valuation.

Ans. [Profit ₹ 515, Amount due to Ramesh ₹ 6,809 ; Amount due to Suresh ₹ 6,456 ; Value of Closing Stock ₹ 2,165].

14. Vikas and Vishal entered into a joint venture of *underwriting* 1,00,000 shares of ₹ 10 each at par issued by a joint stock company. The consideration for underwriting the shares was 2,500 other shares of ₹ 10 each fully paid to be issued to them.

The public took up 90,000 shares and the remaining 10,000 shares of the guaranteed issued were taken up by Vikas and Vishal who provide cash equally for the purchase of remaining shares. The entire share holding of the joint venture was then sold through other brokers : 50% at a price of ₹ 10 less brokerage 50 paise per share ; 20% at ₹ 9.50 less brokerage 50 paise per share and the balance were taken up by Vikas and Vishal equally at ₹ 9 per share. Expenses on account of joint venture were : advertisement ₹ 750 and other expenses ₹ 250. You are required to prepare ; (*a*) Joint Venture Account; (*b*) Joint Bank Account ; and (*c*) Accounts of Vikas and Vishal.

Ans. [Profit ₹ 14,625 ; Amount paid to Vikas and Vishal ₹ 40,437.50 each].

MEMORANDUM JOINT VENTURE

15. A and B entered into a joint venture for the purchase and sale of *materials auctioned by the Government*. A agreed to provide funds for the purchase of materials, and B to devote his time. The profit and loss was to be shared equally, subject to a credit of ₹ 500 to A by way of interest on his capital. A purchased materials worth ₹ 50,000 ; and drew a bill at two months for ₹ 20,000 on B which was duly accepted by the latter. The bill was discounted at a cost of ₹ 260. The various expenses relating to the venture were:

(*a*) A paid ₹ 250 for carriage, ₹ 100 for brokerage, and ₹ 50 for miscellaneous expenses.

(*b*) B paid ₹ 300 for commission, ₹ 200 for insurance, and ₹ 100 for miscellaneous expenses.

The total sales amounted to ₹ 72,000 (cash). There was, however, some stock of unsold goods which was taken over by both the parties, at ₹ 200 by A and at ₹ 300 by B. B paid the amount due to A. The expenses in connection with the discounting of the bill were to be treated as a charge against the venture.

Prepare Joint Venture Account in the books of A and B separately and a Memorandum Joint Venture Account.

Ans. [Profit ₹ 20,740 ; Amount received from B ₹ 41,330].

16. A and B decided to trade together in imported *watches*. Profits and losses were to be shared, A 2/3 and B 1/3.

On July 1, 2025 A purchased goods at a cost of ₹ 14,400 and half of the goods were handed over to B. On July 12, he bought another lot of watches of ₹ 4,800 and incurred expenses of ₹ 480.

On July 12, 2025 B purchased goods at a cost of ₹ 9,000 and on the same day sent to A a part of these goods costing ₹ 3,600 and paid ₹ 220 as carriage and freight. On July 15, A remitted sum of ₹ 4,000 to B.

All the goods were sold by both the parties at a uniform price of 33-1/3 per cent above cost, excluding expenses. Each of them collected cash proceeds on sales, except a sum of ₹ 800 owing to A which was ultimately treated as a business loss.

On September 30, the unsold goods valued at ₹ 3,000 at cost were in A's possession ; of these, goods costing ₹ 1,200 were taken by him and the remainder sold for ₹ 2,000. B disposed of all the goods except some damaged watches costing ₹ 600 which were written off as unsaleable.

On September 30, both the parties decided to close the business and to have a full settlement. You are required to prepare : (*a*) The Joint Venture Account as it wold appear in the books of A recording his transactions in regard thereto. (*b*) A Memorandum Account for the Joint Venture showing the net profit.

Ans. [Profit ₹ 6,300 ; Amount Received from B ₹ 8,680].

17. Red and Blue agree to enter into a joint venture to buy and sell *Television Sets*. Profits and losses were to be divided : Red two-thirds, Blue one-third.

On 3rd May, 2025 Red purchased three Television Sets for ₹ 2,800, ₹ 3,250 and ₹ 3,775 respectively. He bought a special cabinet costing ₹ 750 which he fixed for one of the sets, the old cabinet was not reusable. On 31st May, 2025 he sold two of the sets for ₹ 4,000 each paying the proceeds into his private bank account.

On 15th June, 2025 he sold the other set for ₹ 4,500, which amount he paid over to Blue, who paid it into his bank account.

On 4th May, 2025 Blue purchased a TV Set for ₹ 2,500 having incurred expenditure of ₹ 250 on repairing, sold it on 12th May, 2025 for ₹ 3,000, paying the proceeds into his own bank account. This set developed mechanical trouble and on 25th May 2025 Blue agreed to take the set back at a price of ₹ 2,850, which he paid out of his bank account. The set was still unsold at 30th June, 2025 and it was agreed that Blue should take it over for his personal use at a valuation of ₹ 2,650.

Other expenditure incurred was as follows :

	RED	*BLUE*
Travelling, Postage, etc.	80	64
Showroom charges	225	120

Red paid into his bank net receipts of ₹ 140 in respect of commission given by the Manufacturers.

On 1st July, 2025 the sum required in full settlement as between Red and Blue was paid by the party accountable.

You are required to prepare : (*a*) Account of the Joint Venture with Red as it would appear in the books of Blue ; and (*b*) Memorandum Joint Venture Account, showing the net profits.

Ans. [Profit ₹ 1,626 ; Amount paid to Red ₹ 3,824].

18. Desai of Delhi and Kapoor of Kanpur entered into a joint venture with the object of buying at sales any cheap *machinery* and re-selling the same. Desai to make purchases and Kapoor to effect sales and the profit or loss to be shared in the proportion of 2 : 3 ; ₹ 25,000 were remitted by Kapoor to Desai towards the joint venture.

Desai purchased machinery worth ₹ 20,000 and paid ₹ 9,500 for its repairs, $2\frac{1}{2}\%$ as buying commission and ₹ 900 other sundry expenses and then sent the machinery to Kanpur.

Kapoor took delivery of the machinery at his end incurring ₹ 1,500 for Railway freight and ₹ 700 for octroi. He sold part of the machinery for ₹ 35,000 and kept the remaining for himself at an agreed value of ₹ 7,500. His other expenses were—Godown Rent ₹ 450, Insurance ₹ 560, Brokerage ₹ 830 and other miscellaneous expenses ₹ 640.

Raise accounts for the joint venture to show how matters stand in each party's ledger and prepare a statement showing the results of the venture.

Ans. [Profit ₹ 6,920 ; Balance Due to Desai ₹ 8,668].

19. C of Kolkata and D of Delhi entered into a joint venture for the purpose of buying and selling second-hand motor cars, C to make purchases and D to effect sales. The profit or loss was to be shared as to C two-fifths and D three-fifths. A sum of ₹ 10,000 was remitted by D to C towards the venture.

C purchased 10 cars for ₹ 8,000, paid ₹ 4,350 for their reconditioning and sent them to Delhi. His other expenses were—Buying Commission $2\frac{1}{2}$ per cent and Sundry Expenses ₹ 350.

D took delivery of the cars by paying ₹ 750 for railway freight and ₹ 375 for octroi. He sold four cars at ₹ 1,600 each, two at ₹ 1,800 each and three at ₹ 2,250 each. He retained the remaining car for himself at an agreed value of ₹ 2,100. His expenses were—Insurance ₹ 150 ; Garage Rent ₹ 250; Brokerage ₹ 685 ; Sundries ₹ 450.

Each party's ledger contains a record of his own transactions on joint account. Prepare a statement showing the result of the venture and the account of the venture in each party's ledger as it will finally appear, assuming that the matter was finally settled between the parties.

Ans. [Profit ₹ 3,290 ; Amount received from D ₹ 4,216].

INTEREST

20. Ramlal and Shyamlal entered into a joint venture for purchase and sale of cotton. They agreed to share profits in the proportion of 2 : 1 and also to be entitled to an interest of 6% per annum (on monthly basis) on capital invested by each of them. Following transactions took place in between themselves :

(*i*) On 1st November, 2024, Ramlal purchased 700 bales of cotton @ ₹ 110 per bale, the brokerage being ₹ 4 per bale.

(*ii*) On 1st December, 2024, Shyamlal purchased 600 bales of cotton @ ₹ 124 per bale, the brokerage being ₹ 4 per bale.

(*iii*) On 1st January, 2025, Shyamlal sold 350 bales of cotton @ ₹ 138 per bale (the brokerage being ₹ 2 per bale) and took the proceeds to himself.

(*iv*) On 15th January, 2025, Ramlal sold 800 bales of cotton @ ₹ 132 per bale (the brokerage being ₹ 2 per bale) and took the sale proceeds to himself.

It was also agreed that each of the partners will at first sell from his own purchases and then, if required from the stock purchased by the other one. The balance of stock was to be divided between the partners in proportion of their profit sharing ratio, goods being valued at cost to the partner concerned.

On 31st January, 2025, the partners settled their accounts. Show the accounts of Ramlal, Shyamlal and the Joint Venture as would appear when maintained in a separate set of books.

Ans. [Profit ₹ 12,733 : Amount paid to Shyamlal ₹ 27,574 and received from Ramlal ₹ 27,574].

21. A and B entered into a joint venture of plucking and selling *apples*. They bought all the fruits in the 2024 season in the High Orchard at Kotgarh, paying ₹ 30,000 to the owner on August 1,2024. Labour was engaged to pluck and pack the fruit for which a sum of ₹ 5,000 was paid spread over a period of 2 months. A paid for the fruit as well as labour expenses.

The fruit was despatched to B in Delhi who sold it for ₹ 60,000. The sale proceeds were collected over the period of 2 months. At the end of the season some fruit was sold locally by A for ₹ 3,000. Settlement of accounts was made on October 31, 2024.

After (*a*) reckoning interest @ 12% p.a. for money invested as well as received, (*b*) allowing 5% commission to B on Sales made by him, and (*c*) salary of ₹ 1,000 p.m. to A for the season, the balance was to be divided equally.

Prepare Memorandum Joint Venture Account and Joint Venture Account with B in the books of A and Joint Venture Account with A in the books of B.

Ans. [Profit ₹ 23,230 ; Amount Received from B ₹ 46,585].

22. A and B enter into a joint venture sharing profits and losses equally. A purchased goods for ₹ 5,000 and B spent ₹ 1,000 for freight on 1st January, 2025. On the same day B bought goods worth ₹ 10,000 on credit. Further expenses were incurred as follows :

On 1-2-2025—₹ 1,500 by B.
On 1-3-2025—₹ 500 by A.

Creditors for goods were paid as follows :
1-2-2025—₹ 5,000 by A.
1-3-2025—₹ 5,000 by B.

Sales were made against cash as follows :
15-1-2025—₹ 3,000 by A.
31-1-2025—₹ 6,000 by B.
15-2-2025—₹ 3,000 by A.
1-3-2025—₹ 4,000 by B.

On 31st March, 2025 the balance stock was taken over by B at ₹ 9,000. The accounts between the venturers were settled by cash payment on this date. The venturers are entitled to *interest at 12%* per annum.

Prepare necessary Ledger Accounts in the books of the venturers.

Ans. [Profit ₹ 6,915 ; Amount received from B ₹ 8,092].

23. Wadekar and Pataudi enter into a joint venture to develop some building sites and sell them on the understanding that the result of the venture would be shared in the ratio of 4 : 5 between them. It is also agreed that any cash investment they make in the venture would be entitled to *interest at 10%* p.a.

They chose a five acre agricultural plot and purchased it for ₹ 60,000. They approached a nationalised bank which agreed to finance them to the extent of 80% of the cost at 16% interest per annum. The buying arrangements were finalised on 1st July 2024 and the vendors paid off on the same day. Balance of purchase consideration and also the registration expenses which came to 8% were met by Wadekar from out of his own resources.

Pataudi met the costs of preparation of the layout, advertisement etc. which were as under :

(*a*)	Levelling and engineering costs paid to architects and town planners on 1-8-2024	at ₹	250	per ground
(*b*)	Municipal fee on 1-9-2024	at ₹	400	per ground
(*c*)	Advertisement expenses met on 1-10-2024	₹	17,500	
(*d*)	Entertainment expenses on 31-12-2024	₹	1,120	

Plots were advertised for sale in newspapers on 15-9-2024 and on the basis of response ; the entire area was dealt with as under :

(*i*) 15% of the total area was to be left for roads, market place, police station and a park.

(*ii*) 10 plots each of 3, $2\frac{1}{2}$ and $1\frac{1}{2}$ grounds were made.

(*iii*) The balance area was taken equally by Wadekar and Pataudi at cost.

(*iv*) $1\frac{1}{2}$ ground plots carried a premium of 50%, $2\frac{1}{2}$ ground plots a premium of 40% and 3 ground plots a premium of 25% over cost.

(*v*) Pataudi to receive 8% of the sale proceeds as management fee for his efforts.

The entire transactions were put through by 31st December, 2024. Show Joint Venture Account and the statement of account settlement between the venturers.

(1 acre is equal to 18 grounds of 2,400 sq. feet each)

Ans. [Profit ₹ 10,455 ; Amount paid to : Wadekar ₹ 16,762 and Pataudi ₹ 92,898].

CONVERSION OF CONSIGNMENT INTO JOINT VENTURE

24. On 1st January, 2025, Singh of Amritsar, a manufacturer of *sports goods,* sent a consignment of 100 cricket bats to Bose of Kolkata to be sold on a consignment basis at a commission of 20%, such a commission to cover the consignee's expenses but not the freight charges of the goods to Kolkata. The cost of each bat is ₹ 100 but is invoiced to Bose at ₹ 150 each. A case containing 10 cricket bats was lost against which the consignor lodged a claim and collected from the insurance company ₹ 800. The consignee paid ₹ 540 as freight charges and spent a further sum of ₹ 400 as sales expenses. Consignor's expenses amounted to ₹ 500. The consignee accepted a bill of exchange drawn by Singh for 3 months (beginning with the date of despatch) for ₹ 10,000 which was discounted at 6% p.a. with the bankers. Bose sold 75 bats at ₹ 200 each and on 30th June 2025 remitted the balance due from him.

After making up the accounts on 30th June, 2025, the parties decide to convert their relationship to that of a joint venture on the terms that the cost of a bat would be taken of ₹ 150, Singh to get an interest of 8% p.a. on his investment and Bose to get a commission of 10% on sales. Venturers are to share profit and losses equally.

Prepare the necessary accounts in the books of Singh and indicate the adjustment Journal Entry required on conversion of the terms of despatch.

The working should form part of your answer.

Ans. [Profit on Consignment ₹ 3,675 ; Abnormal Loss ₹ 250 ; Value of Consignment Stock at I.P. ₹ 2,415 ; Balance received from Bose ₹ 1,460. *On Conversion* : Loss on Joint Venture ₹ 325 ; Net Amount due from Bose under Joint Venture ₹ 1,262].

CHAPTER 16

Account Current and Average Due Date

ACCOUNT CURRENT

When it is agreed that interest be charged on each transaction between the two parties, then an account current is prepared. Account current is a statement sent by one party to another with whom the party has dealings, showing in a chronological (date-wise) order, the various transactions that have been entered into between the two parties during the period covered by the statement along with the amount of interest that is due or payable together with details of calculation of interest. It is in the form of an account, having debit and credit sides and is a copy of the ledger account of the party to whom the statement is sent in the ledger of the party submitting the statement. **An account current may be defined as an account of the transactions between two parties during a particular period in which interest is calculated at an agreed rate on each debit and credit item and the net balance of interest is included on the debit or credit side of the account in the amount column.** It is a copy of the account appearing in the books of the sender with the additional column for interest on each item. In the heading of the account current, the name of the person to whom the account current is rendered, is shown first, then comes the phrase 'in Account Current with" and then the name of the person sending the account current is given. For example, if an Account Current is headed as "Dinesh in Account Current with Karan Singh" it means account of Dinesh in the ledger of Karan Singh. The statement itself is in the form of an account, having debit and credit sides and is a copy of the ledger account of the party to whom the statement is sent in the ledger of the party submitting the statement. However, additional columns are also provided on both sides to show how the amount of interest has been arrived at.

It is prepared when frequent transactions regularly take place between two parties. An account current is normally exchanged between the following parties :

(*i*) Merchants buying and selling goods on credit to each other. (*ii*) Supplier and customer when payments by customer are irregular. (*iii*) Principal and his agent. (*iv*) Lender and borrower. (*v*) Broker and his client. (*vi*) Head office and its branch. (*vii*) Consignor and consignee.

Methods of Calculation of Interest

Following are the various methods of calculation of interest :

1. By Interest Tables. Interest is calculated at an agreed rate on each item by ready made interest tables from the due date of the item to the date on which the account current is prepared. The interest columns on both sides of the account current are added and these totals are recorded into the principal account column on their respective sides.

2. By Product Method. In this method, the amount of each item is multiplied by the number of days or months for which interest is to be calculated, the product thus obtained is placed in the "product column" of the Account Current against the item. The product column are then balanced and the interest is calculated on the balance of the product for one day (if period calculated in days) or for one month (if period calculated in months) and is placed in the amount column of the side having bigger total of the products. The product method is based on the principle that interest on a certain amount for a number of days is the same as the interest on the product (amount × days) for one day. For example, interest on ₹ 730 for 10 days @ 10% p.a. is the same (*i.e.* ₹ 2) as interest on the product ₹ 7,300 (₹ 730 × 10 days) for one day.

For counting of days for which interest is to be charged, only one extreme date is counted and not both. Normally the day of the transaction is excluded and the last day of the period is included. But in case of previous balance brought forward, both extreme dates are counted *i.e.*, the first (opening) date will be counted because it would represent the balance that existed on the previous date. Further, it may be noted that days are to be calculated from the due date of the transaction and not the date of transaction because party becomes liable for interest from the due date of the transaction.

Red Ink Interest. If due date falls after the closing period of the account current, no interest should be allowed, rather interest should be deducted for the number of days by which the due date falls after the closing date of the account current. For example, the date of rendering of the account current is June 30, and on June 15, an acceptance for ₹ 500 is given by Ramesh to Suresh for 2 months. Due date of this bill will be August 18 including 3 days of grace. Therefore, interest on ₹ 500 for 49 days (from July 1 to August 18) will have to be deducted from the side of the account current on which the bill is entered. The product of this item (500 × 49) will be shown as a minus product and will be deducted from the totals of the products on the side on which the bills are recorded. In actual practice, the product of such an item the due date of which falls after the closing date of the account is written in red ink ; so it is known as red ink interest.

ILLUSTRATION 1. S.K. Surekha had the following transactions with T.L. Raisena :

2024			₹	2024			₹
Jan.	1	Balance due from Raisena	1,000	June	16	Purchased goods from him (Received on July 16)	15,000
Feb.	16	Purchased goods from him	6,000	Sept.	23	Paid him cash	3,000
"	28	Sold goods to him	10,000	Oct.	24	Accepted his bill for 3 months	5,000
Mar.	16	Received a cheque	3,000	Nov.	26	Received his acceptance for 2 months	8,000
Apr.	20	Sold him goods (Invoiced on May 3)	10,000				

You are asked to prepare an Account Current, with necessary columns of T.L. Raisena completed upto December 31, 2024 as will appear in the books of Surekha reckoning 5% interest on the balance due.

(*For Solution, please next page*)

3. By Interest Numbers. This method is slightly different from the product method. Under this method, each product (as obtained under the product method) is divided by 100 and the resulting figure is written against each item in the column headed Interest Numbers. The Interest number columns are then balanced and the interest on the balance of numbers is placed in the amount column of the side having bigger total of the numbers. In this method, the interest is ascertained by the following formula.

$$\text{Interest} = \frac{\text{Balance of Numbers} \times \text{Rate}}{365}$$

If the period of the account current is a leap year, the formula is :

$$\text{Interest} = \frac{\text{Balance of Numbers} \times \text{Rate}}{366}$$

If the period is calculated in number of months, the formula is :

$$\text{Interest} = \frac{\text{Balance of Numbers} \times \text{Rate}}{12}$$

It may be noted that balance of numbers has been multiplied by rate of interest alone and not divided by 100 because numbers have already been divided by 100.

SOLUTION (*ILLUSTRATION 1*)

T.L. RAISENA IN ACCOUNT WITH S.K. SUREKHA

as on 31-12-2024

Dr. Cr.

Due Date	Particulars	Days to Dec. 31	Product	Amount	Due Date	Particulars	Days to Dec. 31	Product	Amount
2024			₹	₹	2024			₹	₹
Jan, 1	To Balance b/d	365	3,65,000	1,000	Feb. 16	By Purchases	318	19,08,000	6,000
Feb. 28	To Sales	306	30,60,000	10,000	Mar. 16	By Bank	290	8,70,000	3,000
May 3	To Sales	242	24,20,000	10,000	July 16	By Purchases	168	25,20,000	15,000
Sep. 23	To Cash	99	2,97,000	3,000	2025 Jan. 29	By B/R (acceptance dated Nov. 26)	–29	(–)2,32,000	8,000
2025 Jan. 27	To Bills Payable (accepted on 24-10-2024)	–27	(–) 1,35,500	5,000	2024 Dec. 31	By Balance *contra*		9,41,000	
2024 Dec. 31	To Interest (on ₹ 9,41,000 @ 5% per annum for 1 day)			129					
Dec. 31	To Balance c/d			2,871					
			60,07,000	32,000				60,07,000	32,000
					2025 Jan. 1	By Balance b/d			2,871

Note. A bill of exchange or a promissory note other than payable on demand or at sight or on presentation falls due on the third day after the day on which it is stated to be payable.

4. Epoque Method. This method is the reverse of the product method. Interest is calculated from the commencement of the period of the account current to the date of each item. In calculating days for the purpose of interest both extreme dates, *i.e.*, opening day of the account current and the date of the item are taken as we did for the opening balance under the product method. Number of days thus ascertained are multiplied by the respective amounts to get the products. No interest will be charged or credited on the opening balance because of its showing zero as number of days but interest on the closing balance (before calculating interest) must be charged for the whole period of the account current. Interest is then calculated for one day at the agreed rate for the balance of the products and is *entered on the side showing shorter balance of products*.

ILLUSTRATION 2. Work out the problem given in illustration 1 by Epoque Method.

(*For* **SOLUTION**, *please see next page*)

5. Periodic Balance Method. This method of calculation of interest is followed by banks for calculating interest on overdrafts and saving bank accounts. The saving bank account of a customer shows deposit and withdrawals of a customer. After every deposit or withdrawal of amount balance of the account is taken. Every balance thus ascertained is multiplied by the number of days for which it remains unchanged and product for each balance is ascertained. The product can be debit or credit according to the nature of balance. Banks usually charge higher rate of interest for debit balance and allow lower rate for credit balance ; so debit products and credit products are totalled separately. If the interest on the credit products is more than the interest on the debit products, the balance of interest is credited to customer's account. Similarly, if the interest on the debit products is more than the interest on the credit products, the balance of interest is debited to customer's account.

It may be remembered that if on any one date more than one transaction takes place, minimum balance on that date will be considered for interest purposes because bank will allow interest on minimum balance.

ILLUSTRATION 3. Mr. Vastava opened a bank account on 1st March, 2025 with a deposit of ₹ 8,000. He pays in as follows :

20th March, ₹ 2,000 ; 10th April ₹ 5,000 ; 15th May ₹ 4,000 ; 10th June, ₹ 10,000 ; 27th June, ₹ 4,000. He draws out as below :

25th March, ₹ 11,000 ; 10th April ₹ 2,000 ; 25th April, ₹ 5,000.

A bill for ₹ 5,000 discounted with the bank on February 15, 2025 by Mr. Vastava is dishonoured on the due date on 17th May, 2025.

The bank debits Mr. Vastava with ₹ 25 as bank charges on 30th June, 2025.

Calculate the bank interest counting 10% on the customer's debit balances and 4% p.a. on credit balances and close the account on 30th June, 2025.

(*For* **SOLUTION** *please see page 15·6*)

AVERAGE DUE DATE

In business enterprises, a large number of receipts and payments by and from a single party may occur at different points of time. To simplify the calculation of interest involved for such transactions, the idea of average due date has been developed. **Average Due Date is a break-even date on which the net amount payable can be settled without causing loss of interest either to the borrower or the lender or average due date is an equated date of payment on which a single payment may be made in lieu of several payments due for payment on different dates,** so that neither the debtor nor the creditor is a loser from the point of view of interest. In the process of single payment on the average due date, certain payments become payable before their actual due dates whereas some other payments become payable after their due dates. In other words, average due date is the arithmetic average of various payments. The idea of average due date is important because interest is charged on the total amount due from the debtor for the number of days he makes payment after average due date.

SOLUTION (*ILLUSTRATION 2*)

T.L. RAISENA IN ACCOUNT WITH S. SUREKHA
as on 31-12-2024

Dr. Cr.

Date	Due Date	Particulars	Days to Jan. 1	Products	Amount	Date	Due Date	Particulars	Days to Jan. 1	Products	Amount
2024	2024			₹	₹	2024	2024			₹	₹
Jan. 1	Jan. 1	To Balance b/d	0	0	1,000	Feb. 16	Feb. 16	By Purchases	47	2,82,000	6,000
Feb. 28	Feb. 28	To Sales	59	5,90,000	10,000	Mar. 16	Mar. 16	By Bank	75	2,25,000	3,000
Apr. 20	May 3	To Sales	123	12,30,000	10,000	June 16	July 16	By Purchases	197	29,55,000	15,000
Sept. 23	Sep. 23	To Cash	266	7,98,000	3,000		2025				
	2025					Nov. 26	Jan. 29	By Bills Receivable	394	31,52,000	8,000
Oct. 24	Jan. 27	To Bills Payable	392	19,60,000	5,000						
	2024										
Dec. 31	Dec. 31	To Products for Bal. (₹ 3,000)	365	10,95,000							
Dec. 31	Dec. 31	To Balance of Products		9,41,000							
Dec. 31	Dec. 31	To Interest (on ₹ 9,41,000 – Balance of Products @ 5% p.a. for one day) : $\frac{₹\,9,41,000}{365} \times \frac{5}{100}$			129						
Dec. 31		To Balance c/d			2,871						
				66,14,000	32,000					66,14,000	32,000
						2025 Jan. 1		By Balance b/d			2,871

SOLUTION (*ILLUSTRATION 3*)

MR. VASTAVA IN ACCOUNT WITH....................BANK
as on 30th June, 2025

Date	Particulars	*With-drawals* ₹	*Deposits Cr.* ₹	*Dr. or Cr.*	*Balance* ₹	*Days*	*Products Debit* ₹	*Products Credit* ₹
2025								
March 1	By Cash		8,000	Cr.	8,000	19		1,52,000
" 20	By Cash		2,000	Cr.	10,000	5		50,000
" 25	To Self-Cheque	11,000		Dr.	1,000	16	16,000	
April 10	By Cash		5,000	Cr.	4,000	Nil		Nil
" 10	To Self-Cheque	2,000		Cr.	2,000	15		30,000
" 25	To Self-Cheque	5,000		Dr.	3,000	20	60,000	
May 15	By Cash		4,000	Cr.	1,000	2		2,000
" 17	To Bills Receivable Dishonoured	5,000		Dr.	4,000	24	96,000	
June 10	By Cash		10,000	Cr.	6,000	17		1,02,000
" 27	By Cash		4,000	Cr.	10,000	3		30,000
" 30	To Bank Charges	25		Cr.	9,975	0		
" 30	To Interest : On ₹ 1,72,000 (Total of debit products) @ 10% p.a. for one day ₹ 47 *Less* : Interest on ₹ 3,66,000 (Total of credit products) @ 4% p.a. for one day ₹ 40 ₹ 7	7		Cr.	9,968			
June 30	To Balance c/d	9,968						
		33,000	33,000				1,72,000	3,66,000

Instances Where Average Due Date is Used

Few instances where average due date can be used :

(*i*) Calculation of interest on drawings made by the proprietors or partners of a business firm at several points of time.

(*ii*) Settlement of accounts between a principal and an agent.

(*iii*) Settlement of contra accounts, that is, A and B sell goods to each other on different dates.

(*iv*) For making lump sum payment against various bills drawn on different dates with different due dates.

(*v*) This method is also helpful in the settlement of accounts in case of gradual realisation of assets on dissolution of the firm.

Types of Problems

Following are the two types of problems relating to the average due date :

1. Calculation of average due date when various payments are due on different dates and single payment is to be made by the debtor.

2. Calculation of average due date when amount is lent by the creditor in one instalment and repayment of the amount lent is to be made in various instalments.

Method of Ascertaining the Average Due Date in First Type of Problems

The average due date in such type of problems is calculated as follows :

1. Take any due date as the starting point. This should preferably be the earliest due date of the transactions. This is base date

2. Calculate the number of days from the starting point to the due date of each transaction. If the due date of a transaction is after the starting point, its number of days should be treated as 'plus' but if the due date of transaction is previous to the starting point, number of days should be marked 'minus'. In calculating the number of days, either of the dates is neglected.

3. Multiply the amount of each transaction to the nearest rupee by its respective number of days as calculated heretofore.

4. Add up the amounts and products.

5. Divide the total of the products by the total of the amounts and get the result approximately upto a whole number. This gives the number of days the average due date is away from the starting point.

6. Add the number of days calculated above to the starting point and the result will be the average due date.

The formula for calculating average due date is as follows :

$$\text{Average Due Date} = \text{Base Date} \pm \frac{\text{Total of Products}}{\text{Total of Amounts}}$$

Note : Whenever there is a sale of goods by two persons to each other on different dates, the formula for calculating average due date becomes :

$$\text{Base date} \pm \frac{\text{Difference in Products}}{\text{Difference in Amounts}}$$

ILLUSTRATION 4. Kaul and Nabhi are partners in a business and they have invested ₹ 40,000 and ₹ 30,000 respectively as capital on 1st January, 2024. Each partner has been withdrawing ₹ 500 at the end of each month (from January to December) for private expenses. According to the partnership deed interest is allowed on capital @ 8% p.a. and charged on drawings @ 6% p.a. Calculate the amount of interest to which each partner is entitled.

SOLUTION

CALCULATION OF AVERAGE DUE DATE

(January 31 is the starting point)

Due Date	*Amount*	*No. of Months from January 31*	*Product (Amount × No. of Months)*
2024	₹		₹
January 31	500	0	0
February 28	500	1	500
March 31	500	2	1,000
April 30	500	3	1,500
May 31	500	4	2,000
June 30	500	5	2,500
July 31	500	6	3,000
August 31	500	7	3,500
September 30	500	8	4,000
October 31	500	9	4,500
November 30	500	10	5,000
December 31	500	11	5,500
	6,000		33,000

Number of Months = $\frac{₹\ 33{,}000}{₹\ 6{,}000} = 5\frac{1}{2}$ months

Therefore, average due date is January 31 + $5\frac{1}{2}$ months = July 15

So interest on drawings will be charged from partners for $5\frac{1}{2}$ months from July 15, 2024 to December 31, 2024. Interest on drawings chargeable to each partner :

$$\frac{₹\ 6{,}000 \times 6 \times 11}{100 \times 2 \times 12} = ₹\ 165$$

The amount of interest to which partner is entitled = Interest on Capital – Interest on Drawings.

Therefore, Kaul is entitled to ₹ 3,200 $\left(\textit{i.e.,}\ ₹\ 40{,}000 \times \frac{8}{100}\right)$ – ₹ 165 = ₹ 3,035

Nabhi is entitled to ₹ 2,400 $\left(\textit{i.e.,}\ ₹\ 30{,}000 \times \frac{8}{100}\right)$ – ₹ 165 = ₹ 2,235

ILLUSTRATION 5. From the following details find out the average due date.

Date of Bill	*Amount (₹)*	*Usance of Bill*
29th January, 2025	5,000	1 month
20th March, 2025	4,000	2 months
12th July, 2025	7,000	1 month
10th August, 2025	6,000	2 months

SOLUTION

Calculation of Average Due Date

(Taking 3rd March, 2025 as Base Date)

Date of Bill 2025	*Term*	*Due Date 2025*	*Amount* (₹)	*No. of days from the base date i.e. 3rd March, 2025* (₹)	*Product* (₹)
29th January	1 month	3rd March (1)	5,000	0	0
20th March	2 months	23rd May	4,000	81	3,24,000
12th July	1 month	14th August (2)	7,000	164	11,48,000
10th August	2 months	13th October	6,000	224	13,44,000
			22,000		28,16,000

$$\text{Average Due Date} = \text{Base Date + Days equal to } \frac{\text{Sum of Products}}{\text{Sum of Amounts}}$$

$$= \text{3rd March, 2025} + \frac{28,16,000}{22,000}$$

$$= \text{3rd March, 2025 + 128 days = 9th July, 2025}$$

Working Notes :

1. Bill dated 29th January, 2025 has the maturity period of one month, but there is no corresponding date in February, 2025. Therefore, the last day of the month *i.e.* 28th February, 2025 shall be deemed maturity date and due date would be 3rd March, 2025 (after adding 3 days of grace).
2. Bills dated 12th July, 2025 has the maturity period of one month, due date (after adding 3 days of grace) falls on 15th August, 2025. 15th August being public holiday, due date would be preceding date *i.e.* 14th August, 2025.

ILLUSTRATION 6. Mr. B and Mr. G had the following mutual dealings and allow each other one month's credit. At the end of three months the accounts rendered are as follow:

Date	*Goods sold by Mr. B to Mr. G* (₹)	*Date*	*Goods sold by Mr. G to Mr. B* (₹)
July 20	35,000	July 25	24,000
August 17	30,000	August 16	22,000
September 13	32,000	September 5	25,000

You are required to calculate the date upon which the balance should be paid so that no interest is due either to Mr. B or Mr. G (consider 20 August as base date)

SOLUTION

Taking August 20 as the zero or base date (Aug. 20 + One month Credit = 20 Sept.)

For Mr. G's Payments :

Date of Transactions	*Due Date*	*Amount* (₹)	*No. of days from the base date*	*Products* (₹)
(1)	(2)	(3)	(4)	(5)
July 20	August 20	35,000	0	0
August 17	September 17	30,000	28	8,40,000
September 13	October 13	32,000	54	17,28,000
Amount due to G		97,000	Sum of Products	25,68,000

For Mr. B's Payments :

Taking August 20 as the zero or base date

Date of Transactions	*Due Date*	*Amount (₹)*	*No. of days from the base date*	*Products (₹)*
(1)	(2)	(3)	(4)	(5)
July 25	August 25	24,000	5	1,20,000
August 16	September 16	22,000	27	5,94,000
September 5	October 5	25,000	46	11,50,000
Amount due to B		71,000	Total Products	18,64,000

Excess of Mr. G's products over Mr. B's = ₹ 25,68,000 – ₹ 18,64,000
= ₹ 7,04,000

Excess amount due to Mr. B ₹ 97,000 – ₹ 71,000 = ₹ 26,000

Number of days from the base date to the date of settlement is

$\frac{₹\ 7,04,000}{₹\ 26,000}$ = 27.07 days (Hence it may be taken as 27 days or 28 days)

Hence the date of settlement of the balance is 27 days after Aug. 20th i.e., on Sept. 16. On Sept. 16, G has to pay B, ₹ 26,000 to clear the account.

Alternatively, the date of settlement of the balance is 28 days after August 20th, *i.e.,* On September 17, G has to pay B, ₹ 26,000 to clear the account.

ILLUSTRATION 7. A and B are partners in a firm and share profits and losses equally. A has withdrawn the following sums during the half year ending 30th June, 2025 :

Date	*Amount*
	₹
January 15	5,000
February 10	4,000
April 5	8,000
May 20	10,000
June 18	9,000

Interest on drawings is charged @ 10% per annum. Find out the average due date and calculate the interest on drawings to be charged on 30th June 2025. ***(IPCE May, 2014, Modified)***

SOLUTION

CALCULATION OF AVERAGE DUE DATE

(Base Date 15th January, 2025)

Date	*Amount (₹)*	*No. of days*	*Product*
January 15	5,000	0	0
February 10	4,000	26	1,04,000
April 5	8,000	80	6,40,000
May 20	10,000	125	12,50,000
June 18	9,000	154	13,86,000
	36,000		33,80,000

$$\text{Average due date} = \text{Base date} + \frac{\text{Total product}}{\text{Total amount}} \times \text{days}$$

$$= \text{15th Jan.} + \frac{33,80,000}{36,000} \text{ days}$$

= 15th Jan. + 94 days (approx.) = 19th April, 2025

Number of days from 19th April, 2025 to 30th June, 2025 = 72 days
Interest on drawings from 19th April to 30th June @ 10%.

$$= ₹\,36{,}000 \times \frac{72}{365} \times \frac{10}{100} = ₹\,710$$

Hence, interest on drawings ₹ 710 will be charged from A on 30th June, 2025.

ILLUSTRATION 8. Mehra owed ₹ 3,000 on 1st January, 2025 to Somesh. the following are the transactions that took place between them during 2025. It is agreed between the parties that interest @ 6% per annum is to be calculated on all transactions.

2025			₹	2025			₹
January	16	Somesh sold goods to Mehra	2,000	Feb.	10	Somesh pays cash	1,500
"	29	Somesh purchased goods from Mehra	1,500	March	7	Mehra accepts a bill drawn by Somesh for one month	2,000

They desire to settle their accounts by one single payment on 15th March, 2025. Ascertain the amount to be paid to the nearest rupee. Ignore days of grace.

(*For* **SOLUTION**, *please see next page*)

ILLUSTRATION 9. Rajeev owes Anil ₹ 2,000 on 1st July, 2025. He has accepted the following bills drawn upon him by Anil.

Bill for ₹ 800 drawn on 12th July payable one month after date.
Bill for ₹ 1,400 drawn on 1st August payable 2 months after date.
Rajeev has also received the following acceptances from Anil.
Bill for ₹ 500 drawn on 28th July payable three months after date.
Bill for ₹ 400 drawn on 29th July payable 2 months after date.
Bill for ₹ 600 drawn on 10th August payable after 2 months.
Bill for ₹ 1,000 drawn on 13th August payable after 3 months.

Rajeev wants to settle the account with Anil by one single payment on the equated date. Calculate the equated date and the amount to be paid on that date. Holidays during the period are:

Gazetted holidays : 15th August, 2nd October, and 31st October.
Emergency holiday : 16th November.

(*For* **SOLUTION**, *please see page 16·13*)

Method of Ascertaining Average Due Date in Second Type of Problems

Calculation of average due date is somewhat different in problems where the amount is lent in one instalment and repayment of the loan is made in various instalments. There average due date in such types of problems is calculated as follows :

1. Calculate number of days or months or years from the date of lending money to the date of each repayment of instalment.
2. Find out the total number of days or months or years of various repayments as calculated in step (1).
3. Divide the total as calculated in step (2) by number of instalments in which repayment of the loan is to be made.
4. The result obtained in step (3) is added to the date of commencement of loan to get the average due date.

SOLUTION (*ILLUSTRATION 8*)

MEHRA IN ACCOUNT WITH SURESH

(*January 1 is the starting point*)

Due Date	*Particulars*	*Amount*	*No. of Days*	*Products*	*Due Date*	*Particulars*	*Amount*	*No. of Days*	*Products*
2025		₹		₹	2025		₹		₹
Jan. 1	To Balance b/d	3,000	0	—	Jan. 29	By Purchases Account	1,500	28	42,000
Jan. 16	" Sales Account	2,000	15	30,000	April 10	" B/R Account	2,000	99	1,98,000
Feb. 10	" Cash Account	1,500	40	60,000		" Balance c/d	3,000		
	" Balance c/d			1,50,000					
		6,500		2,40,000			6,500		2,40,000

Number of Days $\frac{1,50,000}{3,000} = -50$ days. Days in minus because products are in favour of Mehra but the amount is against him.

∴ Average Due Date when single payment without any interest can be made is January 1—50 days = 12 November, 2024.

The payment is to made on 15th March, 2025. Therefore, interest from November 12,2024 to March 15 (for 123 days) will have to be paid along with ₹ 3,000.

∴ Interest on ₹ 3,000 for 123 days @ 6% p.a. is :

$$₹\ 3,000 \times \frac{6}{100} \times \frac{123}{365} = ₹\ 66.60 \text{ or } ₹\ 61 \text{ to the nearest rupee}$$

Hence, total payment to be made to settle the account is ₹ 3,000 + ₹ 61 = ₹ 3,061.

SOLUTION (*ILLUSTRATION 9*)

RAJEEV IN ACCOUNT WITH ANIL
(*July 1 is the starting point*)

Date	Due Date	Particulars	Amount	No. of Days	Products	Date	Due Date	Particulars	Amount	No. of Days	Products
2025	2025		₹		₹	2025	2025		₹		₹
July 1	July 1	To Balance b/d	2,000	0	0	July 12	Aug. 14	By Bills Receivable A/c	800	44	35,200
" 28	Oct. 30	To Bills Payable A/c	500	121	60,500	Aug. 1	Oct. 4	By Bills Receivable A/c	1,400	95	1,33,000
July 29	" 1	To Bills Payable A/c	400	92	36,800	Aug. 13		By Balance c/d	2,300		1,30,500
Aug. 10	" 13	To Bills Payable A/c	600	104	62,400						
Aug. 13	Nov. 17	To Bills Payable A/c	1,000	139	1,39,000						
			4,500		2,98,700						2,98,700

$$\text{Number of Days} = \frac{\text{Balance of products}}{\text{Balance of amounts}} = \frac{1,30,500}{2,300} = 57 \text{ days (to the nearest whole number)}$$

Therefore, equated date is July 1 + 57 days = August 27, 2025.

₹ 2,300 (amount due) should be paid on August 27, 2025, by Rajeev to settle his account with Anil.

Notes :

1. When the day (including 3 days of grace) on which a bill falls due is a gazetted holiday, the bill shall be deemed to be due on the next preceding business day. Hence, the due dates are August 14, October 1, October 30 and not August 15, October 2 and October 31.

2. When the day on which a bill is due is an emergency holiday, the bill shall be deemed to be due on the next following day. Hence, the due date is November 17 and not November 16.

Thus average due date is :

$$\text{Date of loan} + \frac{\text{Summation of number of days or months or years from the date of loan to the date of repayment of various instalments}}{\text{Number of instalments}}$$

ILLUSTRATION 10. ₹ 25,000 lent by Amrita to Pritma on 1st January, 2022 is repayable in 5 equal instalments commencing from 1st January, 2023. Calculate average due date and amount of each instalment at 10% p.a. interest.

SOLUTION

Calculation of summation of number of years from the date of loan to the date of repayment of each instalment is as follows :

1st instalment is paid after 1 year from the date of loan
2nd instalment is paid after 2 years from the date of loan
3rd instalment is paid after 3 years from the date of loan
4th instalment is paid after 4 years from the date of loan
5th instalment is paid after 5 years from the date of loan

Total 15 years

Number of instalments = 5

Average Due Date =

$$\text{Date of loan} + \frac{\text{Summation of number of years from the date of loan to the date of repayment of various instalments}}{\text{Number of instalments}}$$

$$= \text{January 1, 2022} + \frac{15}{5} \text{ years} = \text{January 1, 2022} + 3 \text{ years} = \text{January 1, 2025}$$

If loan was given on January 1, 2025, no interest would have been charged but the loan was given on January 1, 2022. Therefore, interest for 3 years from the date of loan to the average due date will be charged.

$\therefore$ Interest = ₹ $25,000 \times \frac{10}{100} \times 3 =$ ₹ 7,500

Amount of loan	₹	25,000
Add : Interest payable	₹	7,500
Total amount payable in 5 instalments	₹	32,500

$\therefore$ Amount payable per instalment = ₹ $\frac{32,500}{5}$ = ₹ 6,500

ILLUSTRATION 11. ₹ 40,000 lent by Sundaram to Chatterjee on 1st January, 2024 is repayable in four equal half yearly instalments commencing from 1st January, 2025. Calculate average due date and interest at 15% p.a.

SOLUTION

Calculation of summation of number of months from the date of loan to the date of repayment of each instalment is as follows :

1st instalment is paid after	12 months from the date of loan
2nd instalment is paid after	18 months from the date of loan
3rd instalment is paid after	24 months from the date of loan
4th instalment is paid after	30 months from the date of loan
Total	84 months

Number of instalments = 4

Average Due Date $= \text{January 1, 2024} + \frac{84}{4}$ months

$= \text{January 1, 2024} + 21 \text{ months} = \text{September 30, 2025}$

Interest will be charged for 21 months from the date of loan to the average due date.

$\therefore$ Interest $= ₹\ 40{,}000 \times \frac{21}{12} \times \frac{15}{100} = ₹\ 10{,}500.$

QUESTIONS

OBJECTIVE TYPE

1. Fill in the blanks :

(*a*) An account current is a copy of the account appearing in the books of the.........with the additional column for interest on each item.

(*b*) Epoque method of calculation of interest is the reverse of the.........

(*c*) An average due date is an.........date of payment on which a single payment may be made in lieu of.........due for payment on different dates.

(*d*) Red ink interest is the interest for the number of days by which the due date falls after the.........date of the account current.

Ans. [(*a*) Sender, (*b*) Product method, (*c*) Equated, Several Payments, and (*d*) Closing]

2. State with reasons whether the following statements are true or false :

(*a*) Average due date is the median average of several due dates for payments.

(*b*) If payment is made on the average due date it results in loss of interest to the creditor.

(*c*) In the calculation of average due date, only the due date of the first transaction must be taken as the base date.

Ans. [False (*a*; (*b*); (*c*)]

SHORT/LONG ANSWER TYPE

1. What is average due date ? How is it calculated ? What is the objective of calculating average due date? List out various instances where Average Due Date can be used.

2. Distinguish between Current Account and Account Current.

3. What do you mean by an Account Current ? Explain the different methods of calculating interest in Account Current.

4. Explain the following :

(*a*) Red ink Interest.

(*b*) Method of counting number of days for the calculation of interest.

5. Anand purchased goods from Amrita, the average due date for payment in cash is 10-8-2025 and the total amount due is ₹ 67,500. How much amount should be paid by Anand to Amrita, if total payment is made on following dates and interest is to be considered at the rate of 12% p.a.

(*i*) On average due date.

(*ii*) On 25th August, 2025.

(*iii*) On 30th July, 2025. ***(Inter IPC, Nov. 2015 Modified)***

Ans. [(*i*) ₹ 67,500 ; (*ii*) ₹ 67,833 ; (*iii*) ₹ 67,256]

PRACTICAL PROBLEMS

ACCOUNT CURRENT

1. From the following particulars prepare account current, as sent by Rose to Lily as on 31st March, 2025 by means of product method, charging interest @ 6% p.a.

Date	*Particulars*	*Amount*
1-1-2025	Balance due from Lily	8,500
10-1-2025	Sold Goods to Lily	14,700
15-1-2025	Purchased Goods from Lily	10,200
20-1-2025	Goods returned by Lily	2,500
25-2-2025	Lily paid by Cheque	9,500

Ans. [Interest ₹ 111.45; Dr. Balance ₹ 1111.45]

2. On January 1, 2025, X owed ₹ 5,000 to Y on account. During the three months ended March 31, 2025, the transactions were as follows in the books of Y :

	₹		₹
January 10—Received 2 bills for 2 months and 3 months respectively from X (₹ 2,000 each)	4,000	February 9—Paid cash to X	1,000
January 20—Met a bill for 2 months (due this day) drawn by X on November 17, 2024	1,000	February 19—Received from X	1,000
		March 1—Sold goods to X	1,000
		March 13—X's acceptance due this day dishonoured	

Prepare Account Current to be rendered to X on March 31, interest to be reckoned at 9% p.a.

Ans. [Interest ₹ 127.23 ; Dr. Balance ₹ 4,127.23].

3. From the following, prepare an Account Current as set by Arun to Bhola, on 30th June, 2025 charging interest on debits at the rate of 6% and on credits @ 4% per annum.

2025		₹	2025		₹
Jan. 1	Balance due from Bhola	600	Feb. 14	Bhola accepted Arun's drafts for one month	300
Jan. 10	Sold goods to Bhola	520	April 29	Goods sold to Bhola	615
Jan. 17	Bhola returned goods	125	May 15	Received cash from Bhola	700
Feb. 10	Bhola paid by cheque	400	June 5	Bhola accepted Arun's bill for 3 months	500

Ans. [Interest ₹ 27.21 ; Cr. Balance ₹ 262.79]

4. From the following transactions, draw up an Account Current by means of product up to 31st December, 2024 to be rendered by X to Y and give the amount of interest charging @ 8% per annum.

Date *2024*	*Particulars*	*Amount* *(₹ in thousands)*
July 1	Balance owing by Y	600
July 15	Goods sold to Y	900
August 21	Goods bought from Y	700
August 23	Cash received from Y	450
October 23	Y accepted X's bill at 3 months	300
November 1	Goods bought from Y	950
December 3	Accepted a bill drawn by Y at 3 months due date of bill is on Sunday)	400

On 31st December, 2024, X and Y settled their account after considering the interest factor. Show the cash amount received or paid by X on that date. **[*CA-PCE May, 2011, Modified*]**

Ans. [Interest ₹ 8,000; Paid to Y—₹ 4,92,000]

5. On 1st January, 2025 Om Prakash opened a Bank Current Account and deposited therein a sum of ₹ 15,000. He further paid in the following amounts : 15th January ₹ 6,000 ; 12th March ₹ 4,000 and 10th May ₹ 8,000. He withdrew ₹ 13,000 on 15th February ; ₹ 15,000 on 10th April and ₹ 7,000 on 15th June.

Show Om Prakash's Account in the Banker's Ledger reckoning interest at 5% per annum on the debit balances and 2 per cent per annum on the credit balances. Close the account on 30th June, 2025.

Ans. [Interest ₹ 70.63 ; Cr. Balance ₹ 1,929.37].

AVERAGE DUE DATE

6. Ajay owes Arun ₹ 2,050 on 1st January, 2025 and he purchases goods from Arun as follows :
12th January.........₹ 1,500 ; 13th February.........₹ 1,200
He also sells goods to Arun as follows :
20th January.........₹ 1,000 ; 18th March.........₹ 900.
He also accepts a bill for ₹ 2,000 drawn by Arun for one month on January 11. If Ajay wants to settle the account with Arun on 31st March, 2025 together with interest at 10% p.a., ascertain the amount he will have to pay to clear his account with Arun.

Ans. [₹ 900.07]
Hint. Average Due Date August 28, 2025.

7. R had the following bills receivable and bills payable against S. Calculate average due date when the payment can be made or received without any loss or gain of interest to either party.

Bills Receivable			*Bills Payable*		
Date of the Bill	*Amount (₹)*	*Tenure in months*	*Date of Bill*	*Amount (₹)*	*Tenure in months*
1-6-2025	9,000	3	29-5-2025	6,000	2
5-6-2025	7,500	3	3-6-2025	9,000	3
9-6-2025	10,000	1	10-6-2025	10,000	2
12-6-2025	8,000	2	13-6-2025	7,000	2
20-6-2025	12,000	3	27-6-2025	11,000	1

Holiday intervening in the period 15th August, 2025, 16th August, 2025, and 6th September, 2025.

Ans. [Average Due 27th January, 2026]

8. A.N. Kapoor had the following bills receivable and bills payable against J.N. Ramanathan.
Calculate the average due date when the payment can be made or received without any loss of interest to either party.
Note. Gazetted Holidays intervening in the period ; 15th August, 2025 and 2nd October, 2025, Emergency holiday, 18th September, 2025.

Bills Receivable			*Bills Payable*		
Date	*Amount ₹*	*Tenure*	*Date*	*Amount ₹*	*Tenure (Months)*
1-5-2025	2,000	4 months	10-5-2025	1,000	2
12-6-2025	1,500	2 months	29-5-2025	3,000	4
15-6-2025	3,000	3 months	6-6-2025	2,000	2
7-7-2025	1,000	2 months	17-6-2025	1,500	3
10-7-2025	2,500	1 month	30-6-2025	500	1

Ans. [August 26, 2025].

9. A trader allows his customers, credit for one week only beyond which he charges interest @ 12% per annum. Anil, a customer buys goods as follows :

Date of Sale / Purchase	*Amount* (₹)
January 2, 2025	6,000
January 28, 2025	5,500
February 17, 2025	7,000
March 3, 2025	4,700

Anil settles his account on 31st March, 2025. Calculate the amount of interest payable by Anil using average due date method. ***[CA IPCE May, 2010, Modified]***

Ans. [A.D.D. = 10th February, Interest ₹ 373.74]

10. T owes to K the following amounts :

₹ 7,000 due on 15th March, 2025; ₹ 12,000 due on 5th April, 2025; ₹ 30,000 due on 25th April, 2025; ₹ 20,000 due on 11th June, 2025.

He desires to make the full payment on 30th June, 2025 along with interest @ 10% per annum from the average due date. Find out the average due date and the amount of interest. Amount of interest may be rounded off to the nearest rupee. ***[IPCE, Nov. 2012 Modified]***

Ans. [ADD 1st May; Interest ₹ 1,131 (approx)]

11. A partner has been withdrawing ₹ 600 at the end of each month from January to December for private expenses. According to the partnership deed interest is charged on drawings @ 10% per annum. Calculate the amount of interest to be charged on drawings by the partner for the year.

Ans. [₹ 330].

12. ₹ 15,000 lent by Shiv Raj to Jain & Co. on 1st January, 2024 is repayable in 5 equal annual instalments commencing from 1st January, 2025. Calculate average due date and interest at 15% p.a.

Ans. [Jan. 1, 2023 ; ₹ 9,000].

13. Win owed ₹ 1,200 on 1st January, 2024 to Jim. the following transactions took place between the two parties :

2024			₹				₹
Jan.	16	Jim sold goods to Win	800	Feb.	10	Jim pays cash	600
Jan.	29	Jim purchased goods	600	Feb.	10	Win accepts a bill drawn by Jim for one month	700

It is desired to settle the account between the two parties by one single payment on 15th March together with interest @ 6% per annum. Ascertain the date and the amount paid.

Ans. [9th December, 2024 ; Total amount to be paid on 15th March including interest ₹ 1,320.52].

14. The following is the account of Anand in the ledger of Kamlesh :

2025			₹	2025			₹
January	1	To Balance b/d	15,000	March	25	By Returns	1,000
March	9	To Sales	30,000	April	10	By Cash	15,000
May	25	To Sales	7,000	June	3	By Cash	20,000
				June	30	By Balance c/d	16,000
			52,000				52,000

Calculate average due date and the amount of interest payable or receivable by Anand at 6% p.a. to 30th June, 2025.

Ans. [Sept. 22, 2025 ; ₹ 379].

CHAPTER

17

Partnership Accounts-I

The Indian Partnership Act of 1932 contains the main provisions which are applicable to partnership firms working in India. According to this Act "Partnership is the relation between persons who have agreed to share the profit of the business carried on by all or any of them acting for all". Individually the persons who work in the firm are called partners and the name with which all partners work collectively is called the firm's name. For example, A, B and C working in a firm will be called partners and 'ABC & Co.', the name with which these partners work collectively will be called firm's name.

Essential Features of a Partnership

Following are the essential features of a partnership firm :

(*i*) **Persons.** In order to constitute a partnership firm, there must be at least two persons. The maximum number in partnership is 20 in case the firm is doing ordinary business and 10 in case the firm is engaged in banking business.

(*ii*) **Agreement.** In order to have a partnership, it is necessary that there must be an agreement between partners.

(*iii*) **Sharing of profits.** It is one of the important terms to constitute a partnership firm. Generally sharing of profits (or losses) is one of the important elements to constitute a firm.

(*iv*) **Business.** It includes trade, vocation and profession. The firm must be engaged in a lawful business.

(*v*) **Management.** The management of the partnership firm will be done either by all the partners or any one of them on behalf of all other partners. There is mutual agency among the partners.

Partnership Deed

In the beginning all partners have mutual love and affection and they are ready to work in a team. Inspite of this, it is desirable that they must have their verbal or written agreement in order to avoid the future dispute among the partners. Usually written agreement is preferred so that it can be referred to by all the partners as and when need arises. The legal document signed by all partners and containing the terms and conditions regarding the conduct of partnership business, is called partnership deed. The terms and conditions are inserted in the form of clauses in the deed. Following are the *important clauses* in a partnership deed :

1. The name of the firm.
2. The nature of the business which the firm is supposed to do.
3. The amount of capital and how it is contributed by each partner.
4. The proportion in which the partners will share profits and losses.
5. The amount of drawings which a partner can draw from the firm.

6. Whether interest on capital will be allowed ? If so, then what will be the rate of interest charged on the drawings of the partners ?
7. What will be the authority of each partner ? Will some restrictions be imposed on the duties of the partners ?
8. What will be the duration of the firm ? Whether the firm will be dissolved at will or will continue for a fixed period or till the happening of a particular event or on the completion of a particular venture ?
9. How the amount of the goodwill of the firm will be ascertained at the time of change in profit sharing ratio, admission, retirement or death of a partner ?
10. Will some salary or remuneration or commission be allowed to any of the partners because of his working in the firm ?
11. How the annual accounts of the firm will be prepared ? Will the accounts be audited by an independent Chartered Accountant ? How the auditor will be appointed ?
12. In case of retirement or death of a partner, how the amount which is to be paid to the partner or his legal representatives is ascertained ? If the partners have taken a joint life policy or individual policies, the premium of which is being charged to the Profit and Loss Account and on the death of a partner, how the amount received from the insurance company and their surrender value will be distributed among the partners.
13. If a partner has given any amount of loan besides his capital, will interest be allowed to him ? If so, what will be the rate ?
14. In case a partner becomes insolvent, how the accounts of the firm will be settled ? Will the rule of *Garner* vs. *Murray* be applicable in this case ?
15. The circumstances in which the firm will be dissolved and the manner, in which the accounts will be settled in case of dissolution of a firm.
16. In case some dispute arises among the partners, how will it be settled ? Will it be referred to some arbitrator ?
17. Any other clause on which the partners may agree at the time of agreement.

Rules Applicable in Absence of an Agreement

Under the Partnership Act, 1932 the following rules will be applicable for proper accounting of the partnership firm in absence of an agreement among the partners :

1. Profits or losses of the firm will be shared equally by the partners. (Section 13)
2. Interest on capital will not be allowed to any partner. If agreed, the interest will be allowed only out of profits of the firm, *i.e.*, it would be an appropriation of profit payable only if profit warrants. It is chargeable only to the extent of the available profit. In case of losses no interest will be allowed. Similarly, no interest will be charged on drawings of the partners unless agreed upon. (Section 13)
3. If any partner has given a loan to the firm besides his share of capital, he will be allowed 6% interest on such loan. (Section 13)
4. No salary or remuneration will be allowed to any of the partners. In case salary is payable to the partner or partners, it would be an appropriation of profit *i.e.* it would be payable only if there is a profit (Section 13)
5. Every partner must take part in the management of the partnership business.
6. No person can be admitted without the consent of all existing partners.
7. The partnership books are to be kept at the place of business of the partnership and every partner may have access to and inspect and copy any of them.

Capital Accounts

Capital Accounts of the partners may be fixed or fluctuating.

(*i*) **Fixed Capital Accounts.** When the partners agree that the amount of capital contributed by them shall remain fixed and shall not be reduced or increased during the term of the partnership except by special agreement, the capital accounts are said to be fixed. Under such circumstances, it becomes necessary to have current accounts of the partners. The usual adjustments at the end of the period in regard to interest on capital, interest on drawings, salary or commission, profit or loss will be made in the current accounts. A credit balance in current account will be shown on the liabilities side and a debit balance on the assets side of the Balance Sheet. In case partners withdraw regularly a fixed amount, a separate Drawings Account can be opened to facilitate the calculation of interest on drawings so that balance of Drawings Account including interest on drawings may be transferred to Current Account by passing one entry.

(*ii*) **Fluctuating Capital Accounts.** When all the adjustments relating to interest on capital, interest on drawings, salary or commission, contribution of profit or loss will be made in the capital accounts, the balance of capital accounts will fluctuate from year to year and that is why these are known as fluctuating capital accounts.

Capital Ratio

Sometimes, partners agree to share their profits on the basis of effective capital employed. If capitals are fixed, profit will be distributed in that fixed capital ratio. But if capitals are fluctuating and partners introduce or withdraw capitals during the year, weighted average with reference to time has to be worked out to determine the ratio in which profit or loss will be shared.

ILLUSTRATION 1. A, B and C started a partnership firm on 1-1-2024. A introduced ₹ 10,000 on 1-1-2024 and further introduced ₹ 4,000 on 1-7-2024. B introduced ₹ 25,000 at first on 1-1-2024 but withdrew ₹ 5,000 from the business on 30-9-2024. C introduced ₹ 15,000 at the beginning on 1-1-2024, increased it by ₹ 5,000 on 1-4-2024 and reduced it to ₹ 10,000 on 1-11-2024.

During the year 2024 they made a net profit of ₹ 75,500. The partners decided to provide interest on their capitals at 10% p.a. and to divide the balance of profit in their effective capital contribution ratio.

Prepare the Profit and Loss Appropriation Account for the year ended 31-12-2024.

(CMA—Inter June, 2013 Modified)

SOLUTION

Calculation of Effective Capital Contribution :

			₹
A.	10,000 for 6 months	=	60,000
	14,000 for 6 months	=	84,000
			1,44,000
B.	25,000 for 9 months	=	2,25,000
	20,000 for 3 months	=	60,000
			2,85,000
C.	15,000 for 3 months	=	45,000
	20,000 for 7 months	=	1,40,000
	10,000 for 2 months	=	20,000
			2,05,000

Profit sharing ratio = Effective Capital Ratio = 144 : 285 : 205

Interest on Capital :

A. ₹ 1,44,000 × 10/100 × 1/12 = ₹ 1,200

B. ₹ 2,85,000 × 10/000 × 1/12 = ₹ 2,375

C. ₹ 2,05,000 × 10/100 × 1/12 = ₹ 1,708

PROFIT AND LOSS APPROPRIATION ACCOUNT

for the year ended 31-12-2024

Dr. Particulars		Amount (₹)	Particulars	*Cr.* Amount (₹)
To Interest on Capital	₹		By Profit & Loss A/c (Net Profit)	75,500
A	1,200			
B	2,375			
C	1,708	5,283		
To Share of Profits :	₹			
A 70,217 × 144/634 =	15,948			
B 70,217 × 285/634 =	31,565			
C 70,217 × 205/634 =	22,704	70,217		
		75,500		75,500

Usual Adjustments in Partnership Accounts

In case of sole trader's final accounts, the whole net profit is transferred to capital of the proprietor. But in case of partnership, adjustments relating to interest on capital, interest on drawings, partners' salary or commission are to be made in the Profit and Loss Appropriation Account after calculating the net profit of the firm. Then the remaining profit or loss will be divided among the partners in the profit sharing ratio. Following journal entries will be passed for distribution of profits among partners :

(*i*) *For Interest on Capital* (Interest on capitals is allowed to compensate the partners who have contributed more capitals in proportion to their profit sharing ratios).

Profit and Loss Appropriation Account Dr.
  To Partners' Capital (or Current) Accounts

(*ii*) *For Salary or Commission Payable to Partners*

Profit and Loss Appropriation A/c Dr.
  To Partners' Capital (or Current) Accounts

(*iii*) *For Interest on Drawings*

Partners' Capital (or Current) Accounts Dr.
  To Profit and Loss Appropriation A/c

(*iv*) *For Distribution of Profit*

Profit and Loss Appropriation A/c Dr.
  To Partners' Capital (or Current) Accounts

Note. If loss, reverse entry will be passed.

ILLUSTRATION 2. Good, Better and Best are in partnership sharing profits and losses in the ratio of 3 : 2 : 4. Their capital account balances as on 31st March, 2025 are as follows :

Good ₹ 1,70,000 (Cr.); Better ₹ 1,10,000 (Cr.); Best ₹ 1,22,000 (Cr.)

Following further information is provided :

1. ₹ 22,240 is to be transferred to General Reserve.
2. Good, Better and Best are paid monthly salary in cash amounting ₹ 2,400, ₹ 1,600 and ₹ 1,800 respectively.

3. Partners are allowed interest on their closing capital balances @ 6% p.a. and are charged interest on drawings @ 8% p.a.
4. Good and Best are entitled to commission @ 8% and 10% respectively of the net profit before making any appropriation.
5. Better is entitled to commission @ 15% of the net profit before charging Interest on Drawings but after making all other appropriations.
6. During the year Good withdrew ₹ 2,000 at the beginning of every month, Better ₹ 1,750 at the end of every month and Best ₹ 1,250 at the middle of every month.
7. Firm's Accountant is entitled to a salary of ₹ 2,000 per month and a commission of 12% of net profit after charging such commission.

The Net Profit of the firm for the year ended on 31st March, 2025 before providing for any of the above adjustments was ₹ 2,76,000.

You are required to prepare Profit and Loss Appropriation Account for the year ended on 31st March, 2025.

(CA—IPCE May, 2012 Modified)

SOLUTION

PROFIT AND LOSS APPROPRIATION ACCOUNT

for the year ended on 31st March, 2025

Particulars		₹	*Particulars*		₹
To General Reserve		22,240	By Net Profit (1)		2,25,000
To Salaries to Partners	₹		By Interest on Drawings (3)	₹	
Good	28,800		Good	1,040	
Better	19,200		Better	770	
Best	21,600		Best	600	
		69,600			2,410
To Interest on Capital :					
Good	10,200				
Better	6,600				
Best	7,320				
		24,120			
To Commission to Partners :					
Good (8% of ₹ 2,25,000)	18,000				
Better (4)	10,281				
Best (10% of ₹ 2,25,000)	22,500				
		50,781			
To Partners' Capital A/cs (Profit)					
Good	20,223				
Better	13,482				
Best	26,964				
		60,669			
		2,27,410			2,27,410

Working Notes :

(1) **PROFIT AND LOSS ACCOUNT**

Particulars	₹	*Particulars*	₹
To Salary (Firm's Accountant)	24,000	By Profit	2,76,000
To Commission (Firm's Accountant) (2)	27,000		
To Net Profit transferred to P & L Appropriation A/c	2,25,000		
	2,76,000		2,76,000

(2) **COMMISSION OF FIRM'S ACCOUNTANT**

$$= \frac{\text{Profit after salary of Firm's Accountant}}{(100 + 12)} \times 12 = \frac{(2,76,000 - 24,000)}{(100 + 12)} \times 12 = ₹\ 27,000$$

(3) **INTEREST ON DRAWINGS**

		₹
Good (at the beginning of every month)	$\left(₹\ 24,000 \times \frac{6.5}{12} \times 8\%\right)$	1,040
Better (at the end of every month)	$\left(₹\ 21,000 \times \frac{5.5}{12} \times 8\%\right)$	770
Best (at the middle of every month)	$\left(₹\ 15,000 \times \frac{6}{12} \times 8\%\right)$	600
		2,410

On the basis of average due date interest on drawings will be for the period as follows :

In case of Good for $6\frac{1}{2}$ months

In case of Better for $5\frac{1}{2}$ months

In case of Best for 6 months

(4) **COMMISSION OF BETTER**

Commission of Better = [Net profit for appropriation (excluding interest on drawings) – General reserve – Interest on capital – Salaries to partners – Commission to Good and Best] × 15%

Commission to Better = ₹ [2,25,000 – 22,240 – 24,120 – 69,600 – 18,000 – 22,500] × 15%

= ₹ 68,540 × 15% = ₹ 10,281.

Minor Partner

A partner who has not attained the age of majority is called a minor partner. As no agreement can be entered into with a minor, he can only be admitted to the benefits of an existing partnership with the consent of all the partners. A minor partner is not personally liable for the debts of the partnership firm but his share in the partnership property and profits of the firm will be liable for firm's debts and obligations. He will not be personally liable for any debt of the firm until he attains the age of majority. He is not liable to share the loss, if there is any. Within six months of his attaining majority or when he comes to know that he enjoys the benefits of partnership (whichever date is later), he has to elect whether or not he wants to continue as a partner. He must give public notice if he does not want to continue as a partner, otherwise he will be deemed to have elected to be a partner. He will become liable for the debts of the firm since he was admitted to the benefits of the partnership firm on his election as a partner.

ILLUSTRATION 3. Since 1st January, 2021 A, B and minor C are equal partners. Their Balance Sheet as on 31-12-2024 is as follows :

Liabilities		₹	*Assets*	₹
Sundry Creditors		40,000	Cash in hand	15,000
Accumulated Balance in			Cash at Bank	25,000
Profit & Loss A/c		60,000	Sundry Debtors	40,500
Capital Accounts :	₹		Stock in Trade	24,500
A	40,000		Plant & Machinery	35,000
B	40,000		Land & Building	60,000
C	20,000			
		1,00,000		
		2,00,000		2,00,000

(i) Accumulated balance in Profit and Loss Account as given in the Balance Sheet consists of the following :

Profit of 2022 ₹ 36,000, Loss of 2023 ₹ 18,000, and Profit of 2024 ₹ 42,000.

(ii) Analysis of the books of accounts disclosed the following errors :

(a) A machinery costing ₹ 12,000 purchased in 2023 was debited to Repairs Account. 10% depreciation on reducing balance method is provided on plant and machinery.

(b) ₹ 1,080 being the fixed deposit interest due to the firm used by A for his personal expenses in 2024.

(c) Goods costing ₹ 12,000 sent on sale or return basis have been recorded as credit sale. The firm's gross profit ratio is 20% on sales.

Prepare Partners' Capital Accounts and Balance Sheet of the firm as on 31-12-2024 giving effect to the above adjustments.

SOLUTION **CALCULATION OF CORRECT PROFIT FOR VARIOUS YEARS**

	2022	*2023*	*2024*
	₹	₹	₹
Profit (Loss) as given	36,000	(18,000)	42,000
Add : Machinery wrongly debited to Repairs Account		12,000	
Add : Fixed deposit interest of the firm used by A for personal expenses			1,080
	36,000	(6,000)	43,080
Less : 10% Depreciation on W.D.V. of Machinery	—	(1,200)	1,080
	36,000	(7,200)	42,000
Less : Gross Profit on ₹ 12,000 (Goods on sale or return basis wrongly treated as sale) not yet realised @ 25% on cost	—	—	3,000
Correct Profit (Loss)	36,000	(7,200)	39,000
Share of : A	12,000	(3,600)	13,000
B	12,000	(3,600)	13,000
C (Minor Partner)	12,000	—	13,000

C being minor partner will not share the loss of *2023* as a minor partner can be admitted to the benefits of the firm.

PARTNERS' CAPITAL ACCOUNTS

	A	*B*	*C*		*A*	*B*	*C*
	₹	₹	₹		₹	₹	₹
To Fixed Deposit Interest	1,080	—	—	By Balance b/d (Opening Capital)	40,000	40,000	20,000
To Balance c/d	60,320	61,400	45,000	By Profit/Loss (Transfer) (for 3 years)	21,400	21,400	25,000
	61,400	61,400	45,000		61,400	61,400	45,000

BALANCE SHEET OF A, B AND C

as at 31-12-2024

Liabilities	₹	*Assets*	₹
Sundry Creditors	40,000	Cash in hand	15,000

	₹			₹
Capital Accounts :		Cash at Bank		25,000
A	60,320	Sundry Debtors	(1)	25,500
B	61,400	Stock in Trade	(2)	36,500
C	45,000	Plant & Machinery (₹ 35,000 + ₹ 12,000 – ₹ 1,200 – ₹ 1,080)		44,720
		Land & Building		60,000
	2,06,720			2,06,720

	₹
(1) Sundry Debtors as given	40,500
Less : Goods on approval basis wrongly treated as credit sale (Cost ₹ 12,000 + ₹ 3,000 Profit = ₹ 15,000 Sale)	15,000
Debtors	25,500
(2) Stock as given	24,500
Add : Cost of goods sent on approval basis	12,000
Closing Stock	36,500

PAST ADJUSTMENTS

Sometimes, after closing the accounts of a partnership firm, it is discovered that there was some error or omission in those accounts. For example, interest on capitals or drawings may have been omitted at all, charged or allowed at high or too low a rate, profits and losses may have been distributed among the partners in a wrong proportion and so on. In order to correct these errors and omissions, adjustment entries are to be passed in the usual way.

ILLUSTRATION 4. A and B are partners sharing profits in the ratio of 5 : 3. Following is the Balance Sheet of the Firm on 31-3-2025 :

BALANCE SHEET
as at 31-3-2025

Liabilities	₹	*Assets*	₹
Capital :		Drawings	
A	80,000	A	5,000
B	20,000	B	3,000
		Other Assets	92,000
	1,00,000		1,00,000

Profit for the year 2024-25 was ₹ 16,000 and was divided between the Partners as per agreed ratio, but interest on capital @ 5% p.a. and on drawings @ 6% was inadvertently omitted. Interest on drawings may be calculated on an average basis for 6 months.

You are required to pass Journal Entry(ies)to make the adjustments in the Capital Accounts of A and B.

(ICWA Inter, Dec. 2014, Modified)

SOLUTION **CALCULATION OF CAPITAL ON 1-4-2024**

	Partner A	*Partner B*
Capital as at 31-3-2025	80,000	20,000
Less : Profit credited	10,000	6,000
Capital on 1-4-2024	70,000	14,000

(Figures in ₹)

Adjustments for :	Partner A		Partner B	
	Dr.	Cr.	Dr.	Cr.
	₹	₹	₹	₹
Interest on Capital @ 5%		3,500		700
Interest on Drawings @ 6% for 6 months	150		90	
Profit Written back	10,000		6,000	
Divisible Profit (₹ 16,000 + ₹ 240 – ₹ 4,200) = ₹ 12,040		7,525		4,515
Total	10,150	11,025	6,090	5,215
Net	(+) 875		(–) 875	

JOURNAL ENTRY

			₹	₹
	B's Capital A/c To A's Capital (Adjusting Entry for the adjustments omitted)	Dr.	875	875

ILLUSTRATION 5. A and B had been in partnership for many years as valuers, sharing profits equally, it had been their custom to ignore fee, earned on uncompleted matters, when preparing annual accounts. On 1st January, 2022 they entered into a new partnership agreement under which the profits earned in any year were to be distributed as follows :

Up to ₹ 8,000—equally.

Excess over ₹ 8,000—one-third to A and two-third to B.

Although they shared profits in accordance with new agreement, they continued to prepare their accounts upon the old basis, *i.e.*, ignoring fees earned on uncompleted work. At the end of 2024, it was pointed out to them that they were not following the terms of their agreement, and it was agreed that such correcting entries as might be necessary should be put through as on 31st December, 2024. The profits already dealt with were as follows :

2022—₹ 7,500, 2023—₹ 8,210 ; 2024—₹ 9,350.

The outstanding fees not brought into accounts were : On 31st December 2021 ₹ 960 ; On 31st December 2022 ₹ 1,280 ; On 31st December 2023 ₹ 1,550 ; On 31st December 2024 ₹ 920.

Assuming that the books were duly closed at the end of each year, give the entries necessary to correct the partners' accounts.

SOLUTION

As the fees outstanding had not been brought into accounts, the profit already dealt with are wrong. The correct profits after taking these fees into account would be as follows :

Year (1)	Profit as given (2)	Add Fees outstanding at the end of the year (3)	Less Fees outstanding at the beginning of the year (4)	Correct Profit (5) = (2) + (3) – (4)
	₹	₹	₹	₹
2021	—	960	—	960
2022	7,500	1,280	960	7,820
2023	8,210	1,550	1,280	8,480
2024	9,350	920	1,550	8,720

The profit already distributed and the profit as should have been distributed are given in the following table :

Year	*Profits as already distributed*			*Profit as should have been distributed*		
	Profit as given ₹	*A's share* ₹	*B's share* ₹	*Correct Profits* ₹	*A's share* ₹	*B's share* ₹
2021	—	—	—	960	480	480
2022	7,500	3,750	3,750	7,820	3,910	3,910
2023	8,210	4,070	4,140	8,480	4,160	4,320
2024	9,350	4,450	4,900	8,720	4,240	4,480
Total	25,060	12,270	12,790	25,980	12,790	13,190

A has been credited with ₹ 12,270 while he ought to have been credited with ₹ 12,790. Thus, he should be credited with ₹ 520 (₹ 12,790 – ₹ 12,270) more.

B has been credited with ₹ 12,790 while he ought to have been credited with ₹ 13,190. Thus, he should be credited with ₹ 400 (₹ 13,190 – ₹ 12,790) more.

Following entry is required to correct the Partners' Accounts :

		₹	₹
Outstanding Fees Account	Dr.	920	
To A's Capital Account			520
To B's Capital Account			400
(Being outstanding fees brought into account)			

ILLUSTRATION 6. A and B had been in partnership for many years sharing profits equally. After the profits for 2024 had been divided, it was agreed that with effect from January 1, 2024 they would share profits and losses in the ratio of 5 : 3. Profit for 2024 ₹ 1,04,000 as already taken in accounts was ascertained without taking into account the following facts :

	31-12-2023	*31-12-2024*
	₹	₹
Expenses paid in advance	2,000	1,500
Outstanding Expenses	3,000	4,000
Accrued Income	1,200	800

You are required to give the necessary adjusting entry/entries.

SOLUTION

		₹	₹
	Profit as already adjusted		1,04,000
Add :	Expenses paid in advance on 31-12-2024		1,500
	Outstanding Expenses on 31-12-2023		3,000
	Accrued Income on 31-12-2024		800
			1,09,300
Less :	Expenses paid in advance on 31-12-2023	2,000	
	Outstanding Expenses on 31-12-2024	4,000	
	Accrued Income on 31-12-2023	1,200	
			7,200
	Correct Profit for 2024		1,02,100
Adjustment of Profit for 2023			
	Expenses paid in advance		2,000
	Accrued Income		1,200
			3,200
Less :	Outstanding Expenses		3,000
	Increase in Profit for 2023		200

Statement Showing Adjustment

	A	B
	₹	₹
Adjusted Profit of ₹ 1,02,100 for 2024 in the ratio of 5 : 3	63,812.50	38,287.50
Add : Increase in Profit for 2023 ₹ 200 divided equally	100.00	100.00
	63,912.50	38,387.50
Less : Profit of ₹ 1,04,000 already credited equally	52,000.00	52,000.00
Amount to be debited or credited further	11,912.50	13,612.50
	(Cr.)	(Dr.)

Adjusting Entry

			₹	₹
2024 Dec. 31	Prepaid Expenses Account	Dr.	1,500	
	Accrued Income Account	Dr.	800	
	B's Capital Account	Dr.	13,612.50	
	To Outstanding Expenses Account			4,000
	To A's Capital Account			11,912.50
	(Being entry for adjustment as a result of bringing into account prepaid expenses, accrued income, outstanding expenses on 31-12-2024 and change in the profit sharing ratio from 1 : 1 to 5 : 3)			

ILLUSTRATION 7. Laurel and Hardy are partners of the firm LH & Co. from 1-4-2021. Initially both of them contributed ₹ 1,00,000 each as capital. They did not contribute any capital thereafter. They maintain accounts of the firm on mercantile basis. They were sharing profits and losses in the ratio of 5 : 4. After the accounts for the year ended 31-3-2025 were finalised, the partners decided to share profits and losses equally with effect from 1-4-2021. It was also discovered that in ascertaining the results in the earlier years certain adjustments, details of which are given below, had not been noted.

Year ended 31st March	*2022*	*2023*	*2024*	*2025*
	₹	₹	₹	₹
Profit as per accounts prepared and finalised	1,40,000	2,60,000	3,20,000	3,60,000
Expenses not provided for (as at 31st March)	30,000	20,000	36,000	24,000
Incomes not taken into account (as at 31st March)	18,000	15,000	12,000	21,000

Following is the Balance Sheet of the firm as on 31-3-2025 before adjustment of revised profits between Laurel and Hardy.

BALANCE SHEET LH & CO.

as at 31-3-2025

Liabilities	₹	*Assets*	₹
Capital Accounts :		Plant and Machinery	60,000
Laurel	2,11,500	Cash in hand	10,000
Hardy	1,51,500	Cash at Bank	5,000
Sundry Creditors	2,27,000	Stock in Trade	3,10,000
		Sundry Debtors	2,05,000
	5,90,000		5,90,000

You are required to Prepare : (*i*) Profit and Loss Adjustment Account; (*ii*) Capital Accounts of the partners; and (*iii*) Revised Balance Sheet of the firm. **(*CA—P.C.E.*)**

SOLUTION

(*i*) **PROFIT AND LOSS ADJUSTMENT ACCOUNT**

	₹		₹
To Outstanding Expenses A/c (Expenses for 4 years not provided in the past now considered)	1,10,000	By Laurel's Capital A/c (Share of Profit for four years credited in old ratio written back : $\frac{5}{9} \times ₹\ 10{,}80{,}000$)	6,00,000
To Net Profit for 4 years Credited to Capital Accounts in the new ratio of 1 : 1			
Laurel's Capital A/c $\left(\frac{1}{2} \times ₹\ 10{,}36{,}000\right)$	5,18,000	By Hardy's Capital A/c (Share of Profit for 4 years credited in old ratio written back : $\frac{4}{9} \times ₹\ 10{,}80{,}000$)	4,80,000
Hardy's Capital A/c $\left(\frac{1}{2} \times ₹\ 10{,}36{,}000\right)$	5,18,000	By Accrued Income A/c (Income for 4 years not taken into account previously now considered)	66,000
	11,46,000		11,46,000

(*ii*) **PARTNERS' CAPITAL ACCOUNTS**

	Laurel ₹	*Hardy* ₹		*Laurel* ₹	*Hardy* ₹
To Profit & Loss Adjustment A/c	6,00,000	4,80,000	By Balance b/d	2,11,500	1,51,500
To Balance c/d	1,29,500	1,89,500	By Profit & Loss Adjustment A/c	5,18,000	5,18,000
	7,29,500	6,69,500		7,29,500	6,69,500
			By Balance b/d	1,29,500	1,89,500

(*iii*) **BALANCE SHEET OF LH & CO.**
as on 1-4-2025

Liabilities	₹	*Assets*	₹
Capital Accounts :		Plant and Machinery	60,000
Laurel	1,29,500	Stock in Trade	3,10,000
Hardy	1,89,500	Sundry Debtors	2,05,000
Sundry Creditors	2,27,000	Accrued Income	66,000
Outstanding Expenses	1,10,000	Cash at Bank	5,000
		Cash in hand	10,000
	6,56,000		6,56,000

Note : It is assumed that expenses and incomes not taken into account in earlier years were totally ignored. These have been considered when decision of change in profit sharing ratio was made.

GUARANTEE

Sometimes, a partner is taken into the firm on the guarantee that he shall be given a minimum amount of the profits of the firm even if there are no profits or his share of profit falls short of the guaranteed amount. This guarantee to the new partner can be given by one of the existing partners or all the existing partners in order to encourage a senior partner or any sincere clerk of the business inducted to the benefits of partnership. For accounting purposes, the guaranteed amount due to the new partner should be deducted out of the total profits. Then profits of the remaining partners should be ascertained from the residue (*i.e.* total profit minus the guaranteed amount payable to the new partner) and divide the same in the new profit sharing ratio of the existing partners. Alternatively in case of guarantee given by the partner—

(*i*) The appropriation of profit should be made in the general course by applying the existing profit sharing ratio.

(*ii*) The minimum amount guaranteed is to be decided.

(*iii*) In case the guaranteed amount (*ii*) is more, the excess should be deducted from the share of profit of the partner giving guarantee and calculated under (*i*) above. The same amount should be added with the original share of profit of the partner to whom the guarantee has been given.

This will be more clear from the following illustrations :

ILLUSTRATION 8. M/s Neptune & Co.'s Balance Sheet as at 31st March, 2025 :

Liabilities		₹	*Assets*		₹
Bank Overdraft			Cash at Bank of India		800
(State Bank)		54,000	Sundry Debtors		2,80,000
Sundry Creditors		1,56,000	Stock		1,00,000
Capital Accounts :			Motor Cars :	₹	
Mr. *A* :	₹		Cost as per last B/S	1,60,000	
Balance as per last B/S	4,02,000		*Less*: Depreciation		
Add : Profit for the year	95,400		till date	54,000	
	4,97,400				1,06,000
Less : Drawings	40,000		Machinery :		
		4,57,400	Cost as per last B/S	3,00,000	
Mr. *B* :			*Less*: Depreciation		
Balance as per last B/S	2,00,000		till date	1,40,000	
Add : Profit for the year	95,400				1,60,000
	2,95,400		Land and Buildings		2,40,000
Less : Drawings	76,000				
		2,19,400			
		8,86,800			8,86,800

You have examined the foregoing Draft of the Balance Sheet and have ascertained that the following adjustments are required to be carried out :

(*i*) Land and Buildings are shown at cost less ₹ 60,000 being the proceeds of the sale during the year of premises costing ₹ 70,000.

(*ii*) Machinery having a net book value of ₹ 4,300 had been scrapped during the year. The original cost was ₹ 12,300.

(*iii*) ₹ 2,000 paid for the Licence fees for the year ending 30th September, 2025 had been written off.

(*iv*) Debts amounting to ₹ 10,420 were considered to be bad and further debts amounting to ₹ 5,400 were considered doubtful and required 100% provision. Provision for doubtful debts had previously been made for ₹ 10,000.

(*v*) An item in the inventory was valued at ₹ 37,400, but had a realisable value of ₹ 26,000 only. Scrap Material having a value of ₹ 6,600 had been omitted from the stock valuation.

(*vi*) The cashier had misappropriated ₹ 700.

(*vii*) The cash-book for the year ending 31st March, 2025 included payments amounting to ₹ 6,924, the cheques having been made out, but not despatched to suppliers until April, 2025.

(*viii*) Interest is to be allowed on the Partners' Opening Capital Account balances less drawings during the year at 9%.

You are required to prepare : (*a*) Profit & Loss Adjustment Account for the year. (*b*) Capital Accounts of the Partners.

SOLUTION

PROFIT AND LOSS ADJUSTMENT ACCOUNT

for the year ended 31st March, 2025

		₹			₹
To Land & Building Account (Loss on Sale)		10,000	By Partners' Capital Accounts :	₹	
To Machinery Account (Loss on Scrapping)		4,300	Mr. *A*	95,400	
To Provision for Doubtful Debts Account		5,820	Mr. *B*	95,400	1,90,800
To Stock Account (Fall in Market Value)		11,400	By Prepaid Licence Fee Account		1,000
To Cash (Misappropriated)		700	By Stock Account (Scrap material value)		6,600
To Interest on Capital :	₹				
Mr. *A*'s Capital A/c (9% on ₹ 3,62,000)	32,580				
Mr. *B*'s Capital A/c (9% on ₹ 1,24,000)	11,160	43,740			
To Profit transferred to Capital Accounts :	₹				
Mr. *A*	61,220				
Mr. *B*	61,220	1,22,440			
		1,98,400			1,98,400

PARTNERS' CAPITAL ACCOUNTS

	Mr. *A*	Mr. *B*		Mr. *A*	Mr. *B*
	₹	₹		₹	₹
31-3-2025			31-3-2025		
To Profit & Loss Adjustment A/c (Profit written back)	95,400	95,400	By Balance b/d	4,57,400	2,19,400
To Balance c/d	4,55,800	1,96,380	By Profit & Loss Adjustment A/c (Interest on Capital)	32,580	11,160
			By Profit & Loss Adjustment A/c (Net Profit)	61,220	61,220
	5,51,200	2,91,780		5,51,200	2,91,780
			1-4-2025		
			By Balance b/d	4,55,800	1,96,380

Note. Misappropriation of cash of ₹ 700 by cashier can also be debited to cashier. In that case, ₹ 700 will not be debited to Profit and Loss Adjustment Account and Profit transferred to partners will be ₹ 1,23,140.

ILLUSTRATION 9. Manu and Nilam are partners in a firm sharing profits and losses in the ratio of 3 : 1 respectively. On 1-10-2024 Olwin joins as a 1/6th partner for ₹ 56,000 capital and ₹ 12,000 premium for goodwill. From 1-10-2024 each partner is to get a salary @ ₹ 12,000 p.a. and existing partners guarantee a minimum of ₹ 20,000 p.a. (including profit share and salary) to Olwin.

The Trial Balance of the firm for the year ending on 31-3-2025 is given below :

	Dr.	*Cr.*
	₹	₹
Capital/Drawings :		
Manu	77,000	2,70,000
Nilam	43,000	90,000
Olwin	8,000	
Suspense (cash paid by Olwin)		68,000
Purchases	14,70,000	
Salaries (including partners' salary upto February, 2025)	1,65,000	
Furniture (cost on 1-4-2024)	64,000	
Motor vehicles (cost)		
Acquired on 1-4-2024	56,200	
Acquired on 31-1-2025	13,800	
Sales (to September ₹ 10,00,000)		15,00,000
General expenses	67,520	
Debtors/Creditors	1,73,800	2,44,520
Bank	34,200	
	21,72,520	21,72,520

Sales yielded a Gross Profit of 20% on sales until January, 2025.

On 31-3-2025 : Stock—₹ 2,67,500; Accrued expenses—₹ 7,080; Prepayments—₹ 1,600; To be withheld for income tax—₹ 12,600 (₹ 4,000 for Manu; ₹ 3,600 for Nilam and ₹ 5,000 for Olwin).

Depreciate vehicles @ 20% p.a. on cost and furniture @ 10% p.a. on cost.

Prepare Trading and Profit and Loss Account for the year ended 31-3-2025 and show the Capital Accounts of the partners.

SOLUTION

TRADING AND PROFIT AND LOSS ACCOUNT

for the year ending 31st March, 2025

	₹		₹
To Purchases	14,70,000	By Sales	15,00,000
To Gross Profit c/d	2,97,500	By Closing Stock	2,67,500
	17,67,500		17,67,500

	April to September	*October to March*		*April to September*	*October to March*
	₹	₹		₹	₹
To Salaries excluding Partners' Salaries for 5 months (₹ 1,65,000 – ₹ 3,000 × 5)	75,000	75,000	By Gross Profit b/d	2,00,000 (20% of ₹ 10,00,000 Sales)	97,500 (Balancing Figure (₹ 2,97,500 – ₹ 2,00,000)

Particulars				Particulars		
To General	₹			By Net Loss c/d		23,280
Expenses	67,520					
Add : Accrued						
Expenses	7,080					
	74,600					
Less : Pre-						
payments	1,600					
	73,000	36,500	36,500			
To Depreciation of :						
Furniture 10%		3,200	3,200			
Motor Vehicles 20%		5,620	6,080 (₹ 5,620 + ₹ 460 for 2 months on ₹ 13,800)			
To Net Profit c/d		79,680				
		2,00,000	1,20,780		2,00,000	1,20,780
To Net Loss b/d			23,280	By Net Profit b/d	79,680	
To Partners' Salaries				By Net Loss		
for 6 months	₹			transferred		
Manu	6,000			to Capital		
Nilam	6,000			Accounts:		
Olwin	6,000			Manu (3/4 share)		33,960
			18,000	Nilam (1/4 share)		11,320
To Net Profit transferred to Capital Accounts						
Manu (3/4 share)		59,760				
Nilam (1/4 share)		19,920				
Olwin			(1) 4,000			
		79,680	45,280		79,680	45,280

PARTNERS' CAPITAL ACCOUNTS

	Manu ₹	*Nilam* ₹	*Olwin* ₹		*Manu* ₹	*Nilam* ₹	*Olwin* ₹
To Drawings	77,000	43,000	8,000	By Balance b/d	2,70,000	90,000	
To Cash (Salaries drawn)	5,000	5,000	5,000	By Suspense (Capital)			56,000
To Income Tax Provision	4,000	3,600	5,000	By Suspense (Goodwill)	9,000	3,000	
To Profit & Loss A/c (Share of Loss for second half year)	33,960	11,320		By Salaries	6,000	6,000	6,000
				By Profit & Loss A/c (Share of Profit for first half year)	59,760	19,920	
To Balance b/d	2,24,800	56,000	48,000	By Profit & Loss A/c (Share of Profit for second half year)			4,000
	3,44,760	1,18,920	66,000		3,44,760	1,18,920	66,000

Working Note (1)

Olwin's minimum share guaranteed is ₹ 20,000 p.a. Therefore, for 6 months minimum amount payable to him is ₹ 10,000 out of which ₹ 6,000 is given as salary. The balance of ₹ 4,000 is his share of profit. The loss for second half year after giving ₹ 4,000 profit to Olwin is borne by Manu and Nilam in their profit/loss sharing ratio of 3 : 1.

Change in Constitution of the Firms

Subsequent to the formation of the partnership firm there may be a number of changes in the constitution of the firm without the firm coming to an end. Change in the constitution of the firm may be due to : admission of a new partner, retirement of a partner and death of a partner.

ADMISSION OF A PARTNER

Whenever a partner is admitted into the partnership firm, he acquires two rights *i.e.* (*i*) the right to share in the assets of the partnership, and (*ii*) the right to share in the profits of the business.

For the right to share in the assets of the partnership, the new partner usually brings in certain assets (mainly cash) equal to the amount of capital that he has agreed to contribute and these are credited to his capital account. In the event of termination of partnership, he would be entitled to receive back his capital.

The right to share in the profits of the business will reduce the profits of the existing partners as the same profits will now be divided among all the partners including a new partner. Old partners require the newcomer to make a payment for the benefit which he acquired from the old partners in the form of sharing future profits. In lieu of the right to share future profits, the new partner is required to pay some amount to the old partners which is known as premium. The term premium means payment that one has to make for the purpose of enjoying the fruits of another person's efforts. Following are the main points which usually require attention at the time of admission of a partner :

(*i*) Calculation of new profit sharing ratio. (*ii*) Revaluation of assets and liabilities. (*iii*) Treatment of goodwill. (*iv*) Adjustment of undistributed profits and losses. (*v*) Adjustment of capitals in order to bring these in proportion to profit sharing ratio.

These will be discussed in detail one by one.

Calculation of New Profit Sharing Ratio

The calculation of new profit sharing ratio will depend on the agreement between the old partners and the new partner but the following cases may arise while calculating the profit sharing ratio.

(*i*) If the new partners' share is given and nothing else is mentioned in the question, then it is presumed that the remaining partners will share the rest of the profits in the old ratio. For example, X and Y are partners sharing profits and losses in proportion of 2 : 1. They admit a new partner Z whom they give 1/6th share in profits. The new profit sharing ratio will be calculated as under :

Suppose the total share is 1.

The new partner Z takes 1/6 share out of 1.

$$\text{Rest of share } 1-\frac{1}{6}=\frac{5}{6}$$

$$\text{X's New share}=\frac{5}{6}\times\frac{2}{3}=\frac{5}{9}$$

$$\text{Y's New share}=\frac{5}{6}\times\frac{1}{3}=\frac{5}{18}$$

$$\therefore\ X:Y:Z=\frac{10}{18}:\frac{5}{18}:\frac{3}{18}=10:5:3$$

(*ii*) The new partner, in some cases, purchases his share of profit from the old partners in a particular ratio. New profit sharing ratio of the old partners will be calculated by deducting the proportion given to the new partner from the shares of old partner. For example, X and Y are partners sharing profits and losses in the proportion of 7 : 5. They agree to admit Z into partnership who is to get 1/6th share in profits. He acquires this share as 1/24th from X and 1/8 from Y. Now profit sharing ratio will be calculated as under:

The new partner Z acquires $\frac{1}{6}$th share in profits.

In which he takes $\frac{1}{24}$ from X and $\frac{1}{8}$ from Y

$\therefore$ X's new share $= \frac{7}{12} - \frac{1}{24} = \frac{14-1}{24} = \frac{13}{24}$

$\therefore$ Y's new share $= \frac{5}{12} - \frac{1}{8} = \frac{10-3}{24} = \frac{7}{24}$

Now X, Y, Z will share $= \frac{13}{24} : \frac{7}{24} : \frac{4}{24} = 13 : 7 : 4$

(*iii*) In some cases, old partner surrenders a particular proportion of his share in favour of a new partner. In this case, first of all surrendered proportion is to be calculated for each partner and then this will be deducted from his old profit sharing ratio in order to calculate his new profit sharing ratio. For example, A and B share profits in the ratio of 7 : 3. C was admitted as a partner. A surrendered 1/7th of his share and B 1/3rd of his share in favour of C. The new profit sharing ratio will be calculated as under :

A's old share $= \frac{7}{10}$

He surrenders $\frac{1}{7}$th of his share *i.e.* $\frac{1}{7}$ of $\frac{7}{10} = \frac{1}{10}$

$\therefore$ A's New share $= \frac{7}{10} - \frac{1}{10} = \frac{7-1}{10} = \frac{6}{10}$

B's old share $= \frac{3}{10}$

He surrenders $\frac{1}{3}$rd of his share *i.e.*, $\frac{1}{3}$ of $\frac{3}{10} = \frac{1}{10}$

$\therefore$ B's New share $= \frac{3}{10} - \frac{1}{10} = \frac{3-1}{10} = \frac{2}{10}$

C's share $= \frac{1}{10} + \frac{1}{10} = \frac{1+1}{10} = \frac{2}{10}$

$\therefore$ A : B : C $= \frac{6}{10} : \frac{2}{10} : \frac{2}{10} = 6 : 2 : 2 = 3 : 1 : 1.$

(*iv*) Sometimes, a new partner acquires his share from the old partners in a particular ratio. Then it becomes necessary to calculate the fraction of share which he got from each partner. This fraction should be deducted from the share of old partners in order to calculate the new profit sharing ratio. For example, Ram and Shyam are partners sharing profits and losses in the ratio of 3 : 1. They agreed to admit Mohan into the partnership firm. Mohan is given 1/4th share of future profits which he acquires in the ratio of 2 : 1 from Ram and Shyam. The new profit sharing ratio will be calculated as under :

Mohan gets from Ram $\frac{1}{4} \times \frac{2}{3} = \frac{2}{12}$

Mohan gets from Shyam $= \frac{1}{4} \times \frac{1}{3} = \frac{1}{12}$

Ram's share $= \frac{3}{4} - \frac{2}{12} = \frac{7}{12}$

Shyam's share $= \frac{1}{4} - \frac{1}{12} = \frac{2}{12}$

New profit sharing of Ram : Shyam : Mohan = 7 : 2 : 3.

Calculation of Sacrificing Ratio

Sacrificing ratio means the forgoing a fraction of share in favour of a new partner by the old ones. It is calculated at the time of admission of a partner by deducting new profit sharing ratio from the old profit sharing ratio of the partners. For example A and B are in partnership sharing profits in the ratio of 3 : 2 respectively. C is admitted into the partnership. The new profit sharing ratio will be A 5, B 3 and C 2. The sacrificing ratio will be calculated as under :

Sacrifice made by A $= \frac{3}{5} - \frac{5}{10} = \frac{1}{10}$

Sacrifice made by B $= \frac{2}{5} - \frac{3}{10} = \frac{1}{10}$

$\therefore$ Sacrificing ratio = **1 : 1**

ILLUSTRATION 10.

(i) Anil and Mukesh are partners sharing profits, and losses in the ratio of 3 : 2. Govind is admitted for 1/4th share of firm. Thereafter, Madan enters for 20 paisa in a rupee. Compute new profit sharing ratios under both the admission of partners.

(ii) Following Goodwill Account was opened by the partners R and S, on the admission of H as a new partner into firm Om and Sons. Calculate the share of profit agreed to be given to "H".

GOODWILL ACCOUNT

		₹			₹
1-4-2024	To R's Capital A/c	24,800	1-4-2024	By R's Capital A/c	12,400
1-4-2024	To S's Capital A/c	18,600	1-4-2024	By S's Capital A/c	12,400
			1-4-2024	By H's Capital A/c	18,600
		43,400			43,400

(iii) Ashok and Bala who where in partnership sharing 7/12 and 5/12 respectively admitted Chand as a partner giving him 1/5th share form 1-4-2024. The new profit sharing ratio is 7 : 5 : 3. Chand brought ₹ 96,000 towards goodwill to be shared by Ashok & Bala in their sacrificing ratio. The amount so brought was however credited to Chand's capital account by mistake.

The Trial Balance of the firm as on 31st March, 2025 is given below :

	Dr. (₹)	*Cr.* (₹)
Ashok's Capital		3,36,000
Bala's Capital		2,40,000
Chand's Capital		2,24,000
Sundry Creditors		48,000
Current year profit		2,20,000
Other Assets	7,70,000	
Ashok's drawings	1,45,600	
Bala's drawings	1,04,000	
Chand's drawings	20,400	
Chand in hand	28,000	
	10,68,000	10,68,000

Interest on drawings is to be ignored but interest on capital is to be charged at 5% per annum which was not made so far. Prepare new Balance Sheet as at 31-3-2025 giving effect to above adjustments/omissions. ***(CMA—Inter Dec., 2012 Modified)***

SOLUTION

(*i*) **(*a*) At the time of admission of Govind**

Let the total share of profit at the time of admission of Govind = 1

Share of New Partner: Govind $= \frac{1}{4}$

Remaining share of profit $= 1 - \frac{1}{4} = \frac{3}{4}$

Now, New share of Anil $= \frac{3}{4} \times \frac{3}{5} = \frac{9}{20}$

New share of Mukesh $= \frac{3}{4} \times \frac{2}{5} = \frac{6}{20}$

New ratio of Anil, Mukesh and Govind

$\frac{9}{20} : \frac{6}{20} : \frac{1}{4}$ *i.e.* $= 9 : 6 : 5$

(*b*) At the time of admission of Madan

Let total share at the time of admission of Madan = 1

Share of new partner : Madan $= \frac{1}{5}$ (*i.e.* 20 paise in a ₹)

Remaining share $= 1 - \frac{1}{5} = \frac{4}{5}$

Now, New share of Anil $= \frac{4}{5} \times \frac{9}{20} = \frac{9}{25}$

New share of Mukesh $= \frac{4}{5} \times \frac{6}{20} = \frac{6}{25}$

New share of Govind $= \frac{4}{5} \times \frac{5}{20} = \frac{5}{25}$

New ratio of Anil, Mukesh, Govind and Madan

$\frac{9}{25} : \frac{6}{25} : \frac{5}{25} : \frac{1}{5}$ *i.e.* $9 : 6 : 5 : 5$

(*ii*) **Share of H in profit sharing ratio may be calculated as follows :**

H's share $= \frac{\text{Share of H in Goodwill}}{\text{Total Goodwill}} = \frac{₹18,600}{₹43,400} = \frac{3}{7}$

(*iii*) **Working Note :**

(1) COMPUTATION OF CORRECT CAPITAL OF PARTNERS

	Ashok (₹)	*Bala (₹)*	*Chand (₹)*
Capital as per Trial Balance	3,36,000	2,40,000	2,24,000
Adjustment for Goodwill in sacrificing ratio (7 : 5)	56,000	40,000	(96,000)
	3,92,000	2,80,000	1,28,000
Interest on Capital @ 5%	19,600	14,000	6,400
	4,11,600	2,94,000	1,34,400
Share of Profit ₹ 2,20,000 minus interest on capital of ₹ 40,000 = ₹ 1,80,000 in 7 : 5 : 3 ratio	84,000	60,000	36,000
	4,95,600	3,54,000	1,70,400
Less : Drawings	1,45,600	1,04,000	20,400
Closing Capital	3,50,000	2,50,000	1,50,000

(2) CALCULATION OF SACRIFICING RATIO

Old Ratio	7/12	5/12	
New Ratio	7/15	5/15	3/15
Sacrificing Ratio = Old Ratio minus New Ratio	7/60	5/60	
i.e.	7 : 5 ratio		

BALANCE SHEET AS AT 31-3-2025 (after adjustments)

Particulars	₹	Particulars	₹
Capital Accounts :		Assets	7,70,000
Ashok	3,50,000	Cash on hand	28,000
Bala	2,50,000		
Chand	1,50,000		
Creditors	48,000		
	7,98,000		7,98,000

Revaluation of Assets and Liabilities

It is in the interest of all partners that revaluation of assets and liabilities is done at the time of admission of a partner. When a new partner is admitted into the business, it is natural that he should not be benefitted from any appreciation in the value of assets which has taken place nor he should suffer because of any depreciation in the value of assets. Same is the case with liabilities. Therefore, assets and liabilities are revalued at the time of admission of a new partner. The changes in the value of assets and liabilities are recorded in revaluation account (also known as profit and loss adjustment account) ; whatever profit or loss arises from such revaluation, should be credited or debited to the old partners' capital accounts in their old profit sharing ratio. Following journal entries will be passed in the books of the firm when values are to be altered in the books :

(*i*) *For any increase in the value of an asset*
Asset A/c Dr.
To Revaluation A/c

(*ii*) *For any decrease in the value of an asset*
Revaluation A/c Dr.
To Asset A/c

(*iii*) *For any increase in the value of liabilities*
Revaluation A/c Dr.
To Liabilities A/c

(*iv*) *For any decrease in the value of liabilities*
Liabilities A/c Dr.
To Revaluation A/c

(*v*) *For profit on revaluation*
Revaluation A/c Dr.
To Old Partners' Capital A/cs

(*vi*) *For any loss on revaluation*
Old Partners' Capital A/cs Dr.
To Revaluation A/c

Memorandum Revaluation Method

Sometimes the partners may agree that the value of assets and liabilities are not to be altered and in such a case increase or decrease in the amount of assets and liabilities is recorded in the Memorandum Revaluation Account but no corresponding entry is made in the assets and liabilities. The balance of Memorandum Revaluation Account is transferred to the Old Partners Capital Accounts in their old profit sharing ratio. In order to complete the double entry, entries made in the Memorandum Revaluation Account are reversed and the balance is transferred to Capital Accounts of all partners (including the new partner) in their new profit sharing ratio. Therefore, if Memorandum Revaluation Account reveals a loss on revaluation of assets and liabilities, the entries will be as given below :

(*i*) Old Partners' Capital A/cs Dr.
To Memorandum Revaluation A/c
(Being loss on revaluation transferred to old partners' capital accounts in old profit sharing ratio).

(*ii*) Memorandum Revaluation A/c Dr.
To All Partners' (including new) Capital A/cs
(Being reversal of the above in new profit sharing ratio)

In case revaluation of assets and liabilities shows a profit, reversal entries of the above two entries will be recorded.

It may be noted that value of assets and liabilities will not change and they will be recorded at old values in the Balance Sheet of the firm after the reconstitution. However, balances of Cash Account and Old Partners' Capital Accounts will change.

ILLUSTRATION 11. Mohan and Sohan are partners sharing profits in the proportions of two-third and one-third. Their Balance Sheet as at 31st March, 2025 stands as under :

	₹	₹		₹
Sundry Creditors		44,000	Cash	17,000
Capital Accounts :			Sundry Debtors	15,000
Mohan	30,000		Bills Receivable	4,000
Sohan	20,000		Stocks	25,000
		50,000	Furniture and Fixtures	3,000
			Land and Buildings	30,000
		94,000		94,000

Jag is admitted to partnership with effect from 1st April, 2025 on the following terms :

(*a*) That he brings in ₹ 15,000 as his capital for one-fourth share and pays ₹ 6,000 for goodwill half of which is to be withdrawn by Mohan and Sohan ; (*b*) That there is likely to be claim against the firm for damages for which provision to the extent of ₹ 1,500 is to be made ; (*c*) That a bill for ₹ 1,300 for electric charges has been omitted to be accounted is, therefore, to be provided for ; (*d*) That the stocks are to be reduced to ₹ 23,000 and Furniture and Fixture by ₹ 1,000 ; (*e*) That 5 per cent provision for Bad and Doubtful debts is to be created ; (*f*) That value of Land and Building is to be appreciated by 20 per cent ; (*g*) That included in the Sundry Creditors is an item of ₹ 1,200 which is not to be paid and therefore has to be written back ; (*h*) That the profit sharing ratio of the old partners will not change. (*i*) That ₹ 1,000 is to be received as commission by Mohan and Sohan has to be accounted for.

(*a*) Prepare Revaluation Account and a Balance Sheet after giving effect to the above.

(*b*) Prepare Memorandum Revaluation Account and the opening Balance Sheet of the firm as newly constituted assuming the value of liabilities and assets other than cash are not to be altered.

SOLUTION

(*a*) **REVALUATION ACCOUNT**

		₹		₹
To Provision for Damages		1,500	By Land and Buildings A/c	6,000
To Electricity Expenses Outstanding		1,300	By Sundry Creditors A/c	1,200
To Stock		2,000	By Commission Receivable A/c	1,000
To Furniture and Fittings		1,000		
To Provision for D/D		750		
To Profit to Capital A/cs :	₹			
Mohan	1,100			
Sohan	550			
		1,650		
		8,200		8,200

BALANCE SHEET OF M/s MOHAN, SOHAN AND JAG

as on April 1, 2025

Liabilities	₹	*Assets*		₹
Sundry Creditors	42,800	Cash	₹	35,000
Expenses Outstanding	1,300	Sundry Debtors	15,000	

Provision for Damages		1,500	*Less* : Provision for		
Capitals :			Doubtful Debts	750	
Mohan (₹ 30,000	₹				14,250
+ ₹ 2,000 + ₹ 1,100)	33,100		Bills Receivable		4,000
Sohan (₹ 20,000			Stocks		23,000
+ ₹ 1,000 + ₹ 550)	21,550		Furniture and Fixtures		2,000
Jag	15,000		Land and Buildings		36,000
		69,650	Commission Receivable		1,000
		1,15,250			1,15,250

(*b*) **MEMORANDUM REVALUATION ACCOUNT**

		₹			₹
To Provision for Damages A/c		1,500	By Land & Buildings A/c		6,000
To Electricity Charges Outstanding		1,300	By Sundry Creditors A/c		1,200
To Stock		2,000	By Commission Receivable		1,000
To Furniture and Fittings		1,000			
To Provision for D/D		750			
To Profit to Capital A/cs :	₹				
Mohan	1,100				
Sohan	550				
		1,650			
		8,200			8,200
To Reversal of entry for increase in value of assets and decrease in liabilities		8,200	By Reversal of entry for decrease in assets and increase in liabilities		6,550
			By Loss to Capital A/cs :	₹	
			Mohan (1/2)	825	
			Sohan (1/4)	412.50	
			Jag (1/4)	412.50	
					1,650
		8,200			8,200

BALANCE SHEET OF M/s MOHAN, SOHAN & JAG
as on April 1, 2025

Liabilities	₹	*Assets*	₹
Sundry Creditors	44,000.00	Cash	35,000.00
Capital A/cs :		Sundry Debtors	15,000.00
Mohan	32,275.00	Bills Receivable	4,000.00
Sohan	21,137.50	Stocks	25,000.00
Jag	14,587.50	Furniture & Fixtures	3,000.00
		Land & Buildings	30,000.00
	1,12,000.00		1,12,000.00

Treatment of Goodwill

Goodwill is the value of the reputation of a firm in respect of profits expected in future over and above the normal profits. It attaches itself to a business which has been yielding super profits in the past and where there is a reasonable likelihood of equally profitable conditions being maintained in the future. It is, thus, the present value of a firm's anticipated excess earning. It is the extra value attaching to a prosperous business beyond the intrinsic worth of the net assets. It is an intangible asset. It is not visible but it is subject to fluctuations. It does not become obsolete.

Factors Affecting the Value of Goodwill

Following are the main factors which affect the value of goodwill :

1. **Favourable Location of Site.** If the business is located in a prominent locality, its value will be more as compared to a locality which is not popular at all.
2. **Time Factor.** Time also increases the value of goodwill. The business or profession which is running for the last twenty years on profitable lines will have more value than a business or profession which has been established only two years back.
3. **Nature of the Business.** The nature of the business also affects its value of goodwill. If the business is dealing in necessary goods or it has a monopolistic type of business or the risk is less, in that case its value of goodwill will be more as compared to other business which has no such characteristics.
4. **Capital Requirements.** If the business requires more capital, the value of goodwill in such a business will be less as compared to a business where the capital required is less.
5. **Efficiency of Management.** If the management of a concern is more efficient and reputed, the value of goodwill in such a business will be more as compared to the business where the management is not efficient.
6. **Possibility of Competition.** The value of goodwill will be more in those businesses where there is no competition or competition is negligible.
7. **Miscellaneous Factors.** Sometimes money market conditions, peace in the country, government attitude and rising or declining tendency of profits also affect the valuation of goodwill.

Methods of Valuation of Goodwill

Method of valuation of goodwill is generally mentioned in the partnership deed. Following are the main methods of valuing the goodwill of a business :

1. **Average Profit Method.** Under this method, average of the profits of last three or four years is calculated. The average profit is multiplied by the number of years in which the anticipated profit will be available. For example, if the profits of 2023, 2024 and 2025 are ₹ 8,000,₹ 10,000 and ₹ 12,000 respectively and the goodwill is to be valued at twice of the average of the last three years' profits, the value of the goodwill will be calculated as under :

   Total Profit = ₹ 8,000 + ₹ 10,000 + ₹ 12,000 = ₹ 30,000

   Average Profit = ₹ 10,000 (*i.e.,* ₹ 30,000 ÷ 3)

   Value of Goodwill = ₹ 10,000 × 2 = ₹ 20,000
2. **Super Profit Method.** Under this method, it is assumed that a normal percentage of profit can be earned in the same type of business or industry on a certain amount of investment. For example, if the investment in the business is ₹ 50,000 and the normal rate of profit is 15%, then the normal profit will be ₹ 7,500 (*i.e.,* ₹ 50,000 × 15/100). This normal profit is compared with the actual profit earned. If the actual profit is more than the normal profit, there will be super profit. Suppose further that the actual profit is ₹ 10,000. Then ₹ 2,500 (*i.e.,* ₹ 10,000 – ₹ 7,500) will be super profit. The super profit is multiplied by the number of years in which the super profit will be available in future. For example, if the super profit will be available for three years, the value of goodwill will be ₹ 2,500 × 3 = ₹ 7,500.
3. **Capitalisation Method.** Under this method, the average profits are capitalised taking into consideration the general expectation in the same industry. Suppose the actual profits are ₹ 7,500 and the general expectation in the same type of industry is 10%, then the total value of the net assets (*i.e.* assets minus liabilities) will be ₹ 75,000 (*i.e.,* ₹ 7,500 × 100/10). If the actual net assets are ₹ 70,000, then the value of goodwill will be ₹ 5,000 (*i.e.,* ₹ 75,000 – ₹ 70,000).

Need for Valuing the Goodwill

Need for valuing the goodwill in case of partnership firm arises in the following circumstances :

(*i*) When the profit sharing ratio is changed. (*ii*) When a new partner is admitted. (*iii*) When a partner retires or dies. (*iv*) When two firms are amalgamated. (*v*) When a firm's business is dissolved or sold to a company.

When the Profit Sharing Ratio is Changed

If the partners of a firm decide to change the existing profit sharing ratio, then the partner who gains in this ratio will have to compensate the other partner. The compensation is the value of goodwill represented by the gain in the profit sharing ratio which one partner is purchasing from the other, previously belonging to the latter. Suppose A and B are partners sharing profits and losses in the ratio of 5 : 3. They decide that in future profit sharing ratio will be 3 : 1. The goodwill is valued at ₹ 80,000. A gains 1/8th share (*i.e.*, 3/4—5/8) and he must pay B ₹ 10,000 (*i.e.*, 1/8 of ₹ 80,000) for his share of profit which he gained from B.

ILLUSTRATION 12. A, B and C were partners sharing profits and losses 2 : 3 : 1. The position of the firm as on 1-4-2024 and 31-3-2025 was :

	1-4-2024	*31-3-2025*		*1-4-2024*	*31-3-2025*
	₹	₹		₹	₹
A's Capital	20,000	18,000	Fixed Assets	30,000	28,000
B's Capital	40,000	36,000	Debtors	40,000	37,000
C's Capital	10,000	9,000	Stock	20,000	65,000
General Reserve	30,000	72,000	Loans and Advances	32,000	22,000
Capital Reserve	12,000	12,000			
Bank Overdraft	10,000	5,000			
	1,22,000	1,52,000		1,22,000	1,52,000

On 1st April, 2024 the partners decided to change their profit and loss sharing ratio to 2 : 4 : 1. Goodwill was valued at ₹ 42,000. No entries were, however, passed to give effect to this change.

Pass journal entries in the books of the firm as on 31st March, 2025 and prepare Capital Accounts of the Partners.

SOLUTION

JOURNAL ENTRIES

Date	Particulars		Dr. ₹	Cr. ₹
2025			₹	₹
March 31	Capital Reserve Account	Dr.	12,000	
	To A's Capital Account			4,000
	To B's Capital Account			6,000
	To C's Capital Account			2,000
	(Capital Reserve transferred to Partners' Capital Accounts in the ratio of 2 : 3 : 1 on change in the profit sharing ratio)			
	General Reserve Account	Dr.	72,000	
	To A's Capital Account			22,000
	To B's Capital Account			39,000
	To C's Capital Account			11,000
	(General Reserve transferred to Partners' Capital Accounts : ₹ 30,000. *i.e.*, Reserve as on January 1 in the old profit sharing ratio and the balance ₹ 42,000 in the new profit sharing ratio)			

B's Capital A/c Dr.	3,000	
To A's Capital Account		2,000
To C's Capital Account		1,000
(Being B's Capital debited for goodwill for 3/42 share of gain and A's capital and C's Capital credited for 2/42 and 1/42 share of profit sacrificed respectively)		

CAPITAL ACCOUNTS

	A	B	C		A	B	C
	₹	₹	₹		₹	₹	₹
To Drawings	2,000	4,000	1,000	By Balance b/d	20,000	40,000	10,000
To A's Capital A/c	—	2,000	—	By General Reserve	22,000	39,000	11,000
To C's Capital A/c	—	1,000	—	By B's Capital A/c	2,000	—	1,000
To Balance c/d	46,000	78,000	23,000	By Capital Reserve	4,000	6,000	2,000
	48,000	85,000	24,000		48,000	85,000	24,000

Notes :

DISTRIBUTION OF GENERAL RESERVE

	As on April, 1 2024 (2 : 3 : 1)	*Addition during the year* (2 : 4 : 1)	*Total*
	₹	₹	₹
A	10,000	12,000	22,000
B	15,000	24,000	39,000
C	5,000	6,000	11,000
	30,000	42,000	72,000
Calculation of Drawings	A	B	C
	₹	₹	₹
Capital as on 1-4-2024	20,000	40,000	10,000
Less : Capital as on 31-3-2025	18,000	36,000	9,000
Drawings during the year	2,000	4,000	1,000

Accounting Standard Guidelines on Intangible Assets and Goodwill

According to Accounting Standards, an intangible asset should be recognised in the books of account only when three conditions are met: it must be clearly identifiable and have the characteristics of an asset; it must be expected to provide future economic benefits specifically to the enterprise and its cost must be measurable reliably. If any of these conditions is not satisfied, the intangible asset cannot be recognised.

Internally generated goodwill fails to meet these conditions. It is not a distinct, identifiable resource like a patent or trademark, it is difficult to assess future benefits derived from it, and there is no reliable method to measure its cost due to the absence of any monetary transaction. Hence, internally generated or inherent goodwill cannot be recognised as an asset in the books of account.

Only purchased goodwill, which arises when a firm pays an amount over and above the fair value of net assets acquired, qualifies for recognition. For example, if a business is purchased for ₹ 4,00,000 while its net assets are worth ₹ 3,50,000, the extra ₹ 50,000 is treated as purchased goodwill and can be recorded as an intangible asset.

In partnership firms, goodwill is often valued during events like admission, retirement, or change in profit-sharing ratio. However, if no consideration is paid, such goodwill is considered internally generated and should not be recorded in the books. Instead, adjustments for goodwill should be made through the partners' capital accounts. If any goodwill already exists in the books at the time of reconstitution, it should be written off immediately. Purchased goodwill should be amortised over the period during which benefits are expected to arise.

When a New Partner is Admitted

The various methods of treating goodwill in the books of the firm at the time of admission of a new partner are as under :

(*i*) **When the amount of goodwill is paid privately.** Occasionally the goodwill is not brought into the partnership books at all but is paid by separate cheque to the old partners by the newcomer and is treated as a matter outside the business. This method is most unscientific. Besides creating black money in the hands of old partners, it exposes the new partner to a serious disadvantage at least on two accounts. Firstly, if suppose the firm is dissolved soon after his admission, he can claim no compensation for the amount of goodwill paid by him on his admission and secondly had the entire amount of goodwill remained in business, it would have increased the firm's profits accordingly out of which new partner too would get a proportion of which he is thus totally deprived. In this case no entry is made in the books of accounts of the firm.

(*ii*) When the goodwill is received in cash and retained in the business. In this case, the amount of goodwill received is entered in the firm's books and is retained in the business as additional working capital after the old partners capital accounts have been duly credited with their legitimate shares *i.e.,* in the sacrificing ratio. Following journal entries will be passed in the books of the firm:

(*a*) Cash A/c Dr.
To Premium A/c
(Being cash brought in credited to premium account)

(*b*) Premium A/c Dr.
To Old Partners' Capital A/cs (in sacrificing ratio)

Alternatively only one entry may be passed as given below :

Cash A/c Dr.
To Old Partners' Capital Accounts (in sacrificing ratio)

(*iii*) **When the amount of goodwill is received in cash and withdrawn by old partners.** In this case, the goodwill is recorded as received in the books of the firm but is drawn immediately in cash by the old partners in the ratio of sacrifice made by them. Following entries are necessary to record the receipt and withdrawal of goodwill amount by old partners :

(*a*) *When the amount of goodwill is credited to old partners in the ratio of sacrifice made by them.*

(*i*) Cash A/c Dr.
To Premium A/c

(*ii*) Premium A/c Dr.
To Old Partners' Capital A/cs (in the sacrificing ratio)

Alternatively, the following entry may be passed :

Cash Account Dr.
To Old Partners' Capital Accounts

(*b*) *When the amount is withdrawn by old partners in cash.*

Old Partners' Capital Accounts Dr.
To Cash Account

(*iv*) **When the goodwill is not brought in cash.** Sometimes the amount of goodwill is not brought in cash by the newcomer then an adjustment of goodwill is made by debiting new partner's capital account and crediting the old partners' capital accounts in their sacrificing ratio. This entry will be for new partner's share of goodwill. The journal entry to be made in this case is as under:

New Partner's Capital A/c Dr.
To Old Partners' Capital Accounts (in sacrificing ratio)

(*v*) **When goodwill is already appearing in the books.** When the goodwill is already appearing in the firm's books, first of all goodwill is to be written off from the books by debiting old partners' capital accounts in their profit sharing ratio and crediting the goodwill account. Then the following entry is to be passed in the books of the firm for new partner's share of goodwill :

New Partner's Capital Account Dr.
To Old Partners' Capital Accounts (in their sacrificing ratio)

(*vi*) Sometimes new partner is unable to bring cash equal to his share of goodwill and goodwill is also appearing in the balance sheet. In this case, first of all write off the amount of goodwill shown in the books debiting the old partners' capital accounts. The cash brought by the new partner for goodwill and the difference in share of goodwill not brought in cash is to be debited to the capital account of new partner and corresponding credit is to be given to the old partners' capital accounts in their sacrificing ratio.

Journal entries to be passed are as under :

(*a*) Old Partners' Capital A/cs Dr.
To Goodwill A/c
(Being goodwill written off from the books)

(*b*) Cash A/c Dr. (Cash brought in by new partner)
New Partner's Capital A/c Dr. (Difference not brought in cash)
To Old Partners' Capital A/cs (in sacrificing Ratio)
(Being goodwill credited to old partners in sacrificing ratio)

(*vii*) **When goodwill is hidden (*i.e.*, not clearly given in the Balance Sheet or otherwise stated).**

In this case the goodwill is to be derived from the facts given in the question. For example A and B are equal partners with capitals of ₹ 8,000 and ₹ 7,000 respectively.

They admit C as a partner with 1/4th share in the profits of the firm. C brings ₹ 8,000 as his share of Capital. In this case the goodwill will be derived as under :

For 1/4 share the capital of C is ₹ 8,000

∴ Total capital of the firm is ₹ 32,000.

But the capital of A, B and C together is ₹ 8,000 + ₹ 7,000 + ₹ 8,000 = ₹ 23,000

∴ Value of Goodwill = Total Estimated Capital – Actual Capital = ₹ 32,000 – ₹ 23,000 = ₹ **9,000**

Further treatment will be the same as given in previous cases.

ILLUSTRATION 13. Hira and Meera are partners in a firm sharing profits and losses in the ratio of 3 : 2. Their capitals are ₹ 60,000 and ₹ 40,000 respectively. They admit Kamla as a new partner who will get 1/6 share in the profits of the firm. Kamla brings in ₹ 25,000 as her capital. Find out the amount of goodwill on the basis of the above information. Also show the calculations to find out their new profit sharing ratio.

SOLUTION

Calculation of New Profit Sharing Ratio

Total share = 1

The new partner, Kamla, gets $\frac{1}{6}$ share.

The remaining share $1-\frac{1}{6}=\frac{5}{6}$ will be divided between the old partners, Hira and Meera, in their old ratio of 3 : 2 as follows :

Hira's new share $=\frac{5}{6}\times\frac{3}{5}=\frac{1}{2}$.

Meera's new share $=\frac{5}{6}\times\frac{2}{5}=\frac{1}{3}$.

Kamla's share as given $=\frac{1}{6}$.

Therefore, new profit sharing ratio is $\frac{1}{2}:\frac{1}{3}:\frac{1}{6}$ or 3 : 2 : 1.

Calculation of the Amount of Goodwill

Kamla brings in ₹ 25,000 as capital for $\frac{1}{6}$ share.

Therefore, total capital of Hira & Meera for $\frac{5}{6}$ share should be = ₹ $25{,}000\times\frac{6}{1}\times\frac{5}{6}$ = ₹ 1,25,000.

Combined capital of Hira & Meera is ₹ 1,00,000 (*i.e.* ₹ 60,000 + ₹ 40,000)

Therefore, hidden goodwill is ₹ 1,25,000 – ₹ 1,00,000 = ₹ 25,000.

Goodwill of ₹ 25,000 will be credited to Capital Accounts of Hira and Meera in the ratio of 3 : 2.

Hira's share of goodwill = ₹ $25{,}000\times\frac{3}{5}$ = ₹ 15,000.

Meera's share of goodwill = ₹ $25{,}000\times\frac{2}{5}$ = ₹ 10,000.

ILLUSTRATION 14. W paid a premium to other partners of the firm at the time of his admission to the firm, with a condition that the firm will not be dissolved before expiry of five years. The firm is dissolved after three years. W claims refund of premium.

(*a*) List the criteria for the calculation of the amount of refund.

(*b*) Also list any two conditions when no claim in this respect will arise.

SOLUTION

If the firm is dissolved before the term expires, as is the case, W being a partner who has paid premium on admission will have to be repaid/refunded.

(a) *The criteria for calculation of refund* amount are :

(*i*) *Terms upon* which admission was made,

(*ii*) *The time period* for which it was agreed that the *firm will not be dissolved,*

(*iii*) The time period for which the firm has *already been in existence.*

(b) *No claim for refund will arise if* :

(*i*) The firm is dissolved *due to death* of a partner,

(*ii*) If the dissolution of the firm is basically because of misconduct of W,

(*iii*) If the dissolution is *through an agreement* and such agreement does not have a stipulation for refund of premium.

Adjustment of Undistributed Profits and Losses

If there appear some undistributed profits in the name of general reserve or profit and loss account (credit balance), that should be divided among the old partners in the old profit sharing ratio by passing the following journal entry :

General Reserve or Profit and Loss A/c	Dr.
To Old Partners' Capital A/cs	

The effect of this will be that in the new Balance Sheet no balance of General Reserve or Profit and Loss Cr. balance will appear. Similarly if profit and loss account (Dr. balance) is appearing on the assets side of the balance sheet, it should be closed by transfer to old partners' capital accounts in their old profit sharing ratio by passing the following entry :

Old Partners' Capital Accounts Dr.
  To Profit and Loss A/c

No loss will appear on the assets side in the new Balance Sheet.

Adjustment of Capitals of Partners to be Proportionate to Profit Sharing Ratio

It is often agreed among the partners that capital accounts of the partners should be adjusted on the admission of a partner, so that they may be in proportion to the new profit sharing ratio. This may be done either on the basis of new partner's capital or the newcomer may bring his share of capital on the basis of old partners' capital after adjustment.

(*i*) **When capitals are to be adjusted on the basis of new partner.** The total capital can be calculated on the basis of new partner's share and the amount of capital brought by him. Capital required for each partner can also be calculated on the basis of new profit sharing ratio. The required amount of capital will now be compared with the balance of amount in the capital account of each partner after all adjustments are made. If the balance is more than the required balance, the excess will be withdrawn by the partner from the firm or will be transferred to his Current Account. But if the balance is less than the required amount of capital, the deficiency will be brought by the partner in cash or will be transferred to his Current Account. Instructions in this respect must be noted carefully from the language of the question.

ILLUSTRATION 15. Following is the Balance Sheet of A, B and C sharing profits and losses in the proportion of 6 : 5 : 3 respectively :

	₹		₹
Creditors	18,900	Cash	1,890
Bills Payable	6,300	Debtors	26,460
General Reserve	10,500	Stock	29,400
A's Capital	35,400	Furniture	7,350
B's Capital	29,850	Land and Buildings	45,150
C's Capital	14,550	Goodwill	5,250
	1,15,500		1,15,500

They agreed to take D into partnership and give him 1/8 share on the following terms:

(*i*) That furniture be depreciated by ₹ 920 ;

(*ii*) That stock be depreciated by 10% ;

(*iii*) That a provision of ₹ 1,320 be made for outstanding repair bills ;

(*iv*) That the value of land and building having appreciated be brought upto ₹ 59,850 ;

(*v*) That the value of goodwill be ₹ 16,800 and D's share of goodwill is adjusted through capital accounts ;

(*vi*) That D should then bring in ₹ 16,100 as his capital ;

(*vii*) That after making the above adjustments the total capital of the firm should be ₹ 1,12,000 and be adjusted on the basis of the new profit sharing ratio in the business. Actual cash to be paid off or brought in by the partners as the case may be.

Pass the necessary journal entries and prepare Revaluation Account, Partners' Capital Accounts and Balance Sheet of the new firm.

SOLUTION

JOURNAL ENTRIES

Particulars		₹	₹
Revaluation A/c	Dr.	5,180	
To Furniture A/c			920
To Stock A/c			2,940
To Provision for Outstanding Repairs A/c			1,320
(Being the reduction in the value of assets and provision made for unpaid repair bill)			
Land & Building A/c	Dr.	14,700	
To Revaluation A/c			14,700
(Being appreciation in the value of land and building)			
Revaluation A/c	Dr.	9,520	
To A's Capital A/c			4,080
To B's Capital A/c			3,400
To C's Capital A/c			2,040
(Being the profit on revaluation transferred to Capital A/cs)			
General Reserve A/c	Dr.	10,500	
To A's Capital A/c			4,500
To B's Capital A/c			3,750
To C's Capital A/c			2,250
(Being general reserve distributed among the partners in the old profit sharing ratio)			
D's Capital A/c	Dr.	2,100	
To A's Capital A/c			900
To B's Capital A/c			750
To C's Capital A/c			450
(Being D's share of Goodwill distributed to old partners in their sacrificing ratio)			
Cash A/c	Dr.	16,100	
To D's Capital A/c			16,100
(Being the amount brought in by D as capital)			
A's Capital A/c	Dr.	2,250	
B's Capital A/c	Dr.	1,875	
C's Capital A/c	Dr.	1,125	
To Goodwill A/c			5,250
(Being existing amount of goodwill written off from the books)			
A's Capital A/c	Dr.	630	
B's Capital A/c	Dr.	875	
To Cash A/c			1505
(Being cash paid to A and B being excess of their share of proportionate capital)			
Cash A/c	Dr.	2,835	
To C's Capital A/c			2,835
(For cash brought in by C being short of his share of proportionate capital)			

REVALUATION ACCOUNT

	₹		₹
To Furniture A/c	920	By Land and Buildings	14,700
To Stock A/c	2,940		

To Provision for Outstanding Repairs A/c		1,320		
To Profit transferred to Capital A/cs :	₹			
A	4,080			
B	3,400			
C	2,040	9,520		
		14,700		14,700

CAPITAL ACCOUNTS

	A	B	C	D		A	B	C	D
	₹	₹	₹	₹		₹	₹	₹	₹
To Capital A/cs	—	—	—	2,100	By Balance b/d	35,400	29,850	14,550	—
To Goodwill	2,250	1,875	1,125	—	By Cash A/c	—	—	—	16,100
To Cash	630	875	—	—	By General Reserve	4,500	3,750	2,250	—
To Balance c/d (2)	42,000	35,000	21,000	14,000	By Revaluation A/c	4,080	3,400	2,040	—
					By D's Capital A/c	900	750	450	—
					By Cash	—	—	2,835	—
	44,880	37,750	22,125	16,100		44,880	37,750	22,125	16,100

BALANCE SHEET OF M/S A, B, C, D & CO.

Liabilities		₹	*Assets*	₹
Sundry Creditors		18,900	Cash (₹ 1,890+ ₹ 16,100 – ₹ 630 – ₹ 875 +₹ 2,835)	19,320
Bills Payable		6,300	Sundry Debtors	26,460
Provision for Outstanding Repairs		1,320	Stock	26,460
Capitals A/cs : (See note 2)	₹		Furniture	6,430
A	42,000		Land & Building	59,850
B	35,000			
C	21,000			
D	14,000	1,12,000		
		1,38,520		1,38,520

Working Note :

(1) ***Net Profit Sharing Ratio***

Profit of the whole firm = 1

D got 1/8th share

Remaining Share $1 - \frac{1}{8} = \frac{7}{8}$

A's new Share = $\frac{7}{8} \times \frac{6}{14} = \frac{6}{16}$

B's new share $= \frac{7}{8} \times \frac{5}{14} = \frac{5}{16}$

C's new share = $\frac{7}{8} \times \frac{3}{14} = \frac{3}{16}$

New shares are A : B : C : D = $\frac{6}{16} : \frac{5}{16} : \frac{3}{16} : \frac{2}{16}$

= 6 : 5 : 3 : 2

(2) ***Total Capital of the Firm*** **= ₹ 1,12,000**

A's Capital = ₹ 1,12,000 × $\frac{6}{16}$ = ₹ 42,000

B's Capital = ₹ 1,12,000 × $\frac{5}{16}$ = ₹ 35,000

C's Capital = ₹ 1,12,000 × $\frac{3}{16}$ = ₹ 21,000

D's Capital = ₹ 1,12,000 × $\frac{2}{16}$ = ₹ 14,000

***(ii)* When the new partner is required to bring in the amount of capital in proportion to his share in the firm.** Under such a case first of all, old partners' capital accounts balances (after making all adjustments) should be calculated. The total capital of the old partners will be for the remaining share *i.e.*, deducting new partner's share from the whole share. On this basis the total capital of the firm should be calculated and then new partner's share of the amount of capital can be easily calculated. For example, if after adjustments, the total capital of old partners' capital accounts comes to ₹ 33,000. The new partner's share is 1/4. The total will be ₹ 44,000 (*i.e.*, ₹ 33,000 × 4/3). The new partner will bring ₹ 11,000 *i.e.*, 1/4 of ₹ 44,000 as his share of capital in the firm.

ILLUSTRATION 16. Following was the Balance Sheet of 'A' and 'B', who were sharing profits and losses in the ratio of 2 : 1 on 31-12-2024 :

Liabilities	₹	*Assets*	₹
Capital Accounts		Plant and Machinery	12,00,000
A	10,00,000	Building	9,00,000
B	5,00,000	Sundry Debtors	3,00,000
Reserve Fund	9,00,000	Stock	4,00,000
Sundry Creditors	4,00,000	Cash	1,00,000
Bills Payable	1,00,000		
	29,00,000		29,00,000

They agreed to admit 'C' into the partnership on the following terms :

(*i*) The goodwill of the firm was fixed at ₹ 1,05,000.

(*ii*) That the value of stock and plant and machinery were to be reduced by 10%.

(*iii*) That a provision of 5% was to be created for doubtful debts.

(*iv*) That the building account was to be appreciated by 20%.

(*v*) There was an unrecorded liability of ₹ 10,000.

(*vi*) Investments worth ₹ 20,000 (Not mentioned in the Balance Sheet) were taken into account.

(*vii*) That the value of reserve fund, the values of liabilities and the values of assets other than cash are not to be altered.

(*viii*) 'C' was to be given one-fourth share in the profit and was to bring capital equal to his share of profit after all adjustments.

Prepare Memorandum Revaluation Account, Capital Accounts of the partners and Balance Sheet of the newly reconstituted firm.

SOLUTION

MEMORANDUM REVALUATION ACCOUNT

		₹		₹
To Stock		40,000	By Building	1,80,000
To Plant & Machinery		1,20,000	By Investments	20,000
To Provision for Doubtful Debts		15,000		
To Unrecorded Liability		10,000		
To Profit on Revaluation transferred to				
Old Partners in Old Ratio :	₹			
A's Capital A/c	10,000			
B's Capital A/c	5,000	15,000		
		2,00,000		2,00,000

	₹		₹
To Building	1,80,000	By Stock	40,000
To Investments	20,000	By Plant & Machinery	1,20,000
		By Provision for Doubtful Debts	15,000
		By Unrecorded Liability	10,000
		By Loss on Account of Reversal of Entries transferred to All Partners in their New Ratio of $\frac{1}{2}:\frac{1}{4}:\frac{1}{4}$	
		A's Capital A/c ₹ 7,500	
		B's Capital A/c ₹ 3,750	
		C's Capital A/c ₹ 3,750	15,000
	2,00,000		2,00,000

PARTNERS' CAPITAL ACCOUNTS

	A ₹	*B* ₹	*C* ₹		*A* ₹	*B* ₹	*C* ₹
To Goodwill (Written off in new profit ratio of $\frac{1}{2}:\frac{1}{4}:\frac{1}{4}$)	52,500	26,250	26,250	By Balance b/d	10,00,000	5,00,000	—
				By Goodwill	70,000	35,000	—
To Memorandum Revaluation A/c (Reversal Entry)	7,500	3,750	3,750	By Memorandum Revaluation A/c	10,000	5,000	—
To Reserve Fund (Reversal Entry)	4,50,000	2,25,000	2,25,000	By Reserve Fund	6,00,000	3,00,000	—
To Balance c/d	11,70,000	5,85,000	5,85,000(1)	By Cash (Bal. Fig.)			8,40,000
	16,80,000	8,40,000	8,40,000		16,80,000	8,40,000	8,40,000
				By Balance b/d	11,70,000	5,85,000	5,85,000

BALANCE SHEET OF THE NEWLY RECONSTITUTED FIRM OF A, B & C

as on 31-12-2024

Liabilities	₹	*Assets*	₹
Capital Accounts :		Building	9,00,000
A	11,70,000	Plant & Machinery	12,00,000
B	5,85,000	Stock	4,00,000
C	5,85,000	Sundry 'Debtors	3,00,000
Reserve Fund	9,00,000	Cash (₹ 1,00,000 + ₹ 8,40,000)	9,40,000
Sundry Creditors	4,00,000		
Bills Payable	1,00,000		
	37,40,000		37,40,000

Working Note :

(*i*) ***Calculation of Balance of Capital Account of C***

	₹
Closing Capitals of A & B after all adjustments are :	
A	11,70,000
B	5,85,000
Combined Capital of A & B	17,55,000

Combined profit share of A & B $\left(1 - \frac{1}{4} \text{ share of C}\right)$ $\frac{3}{4}$

Combined capital of A and B for $\frac{3}{4}$ share ₹ 17,55,000

Therefore, Balance of Capital A/c of C = ₹ 17,55,000 × $\frac{4}{3} \times \frac{1}{4}$ = ₹ 5,85,000.

ILLUSTRATION 17. R and S are partners in a business started in 2021 sharing profits and losses in the ratio of 5 : 4. After the accounts for the calendar year 2024 were made up and their proportionate shares taken note of in their individual accounts, they decided to share profits and losses equally from the year 2024. It was also discovered that in ascertaining the results in prior years certain adjustments, details of which are given below, had not been noted :

	2021	*2022*	*2023*	*2024*
Profits as per accounts prepared and finalised	₹ 24,000	26,000	30,000	36,000
Expenses not provided for (as at 31st December)	₹ 3,000	2,000	3,600	2,400
Incomes not taken into account	₹ 1,800	1,500	1,200	2,100

On 31st December, 2023, Reserves stood at ₹ 18,000. Capitals of R and S were ₹ 42,000 and ₹ 32,000 respectively as on 31st December, 2024.

On 1st January, 2025, N was decided to be admitted as a partner and was allotted 1/5th share. Goodwill was decided to be ascertained by capitalising at 20% the average profits of the immediately two preceding years before admission. N would bring in proportionate capital. Capitals of R and S are to be equal, the differences to be adjusted in their current accounts.

Profits for 2025 were ₹ 42,000. Drawings of R, S and N for the year were ₹ 18,000, ₹ 16,000 and ₹ 6,000 respectively.

Prepare Capital and Current Accounts of the Partners for 2025.

SOLUTION

(***For Partners' Capital and Current Accounts see next page***)

Working Notes :

(1) **PROFIT & LOSS ADJUSTMENT ACCOUNT (for 2024)**

		₹			₹
To Outstanding Expenses (2024) (Now adjusted not considered earlier in cash profit)		2,400	By Capital Accounts	₹	
			R	20,000	
			S	16,000	36,000
To Net Profit transferred to Capital Accounts (equally)	₹		(Cash profit of 2024 written back)		
R	19,050		By Capital Accounts		
S	19,050	38,100	R	1,333	
			S	1,067	2,400
			(Outstanding expenses ₹ 3,600 minus accrued income ₹ 1,200 of the year 2023 previously adjusted in 2024 written back)		
			By Accrued Income (2024) (Now Adjusted not taken earlier in cash profit)		2,100
		40,500			40,500

SOLUTION (*ILLUSTRATION 17*)

PARTNERS' CAPITAL ACCOUNTS

Date	Particulars	R	S	N	Date	Particulars	R	S	N
		₹	₹	₹			₹	₹	₹
2024 Dec. 31	To Profit & Loss Adjustment A/c (5 : 4) (Cash profit written back in old ratio)	20,000	16,000		2024 Dec. 31	By Balance b/d	42,000	32,000	
" 31	To Profit & Loss Adjustment A/c (5 : 4) (Outstanding expenses of ₹ 3,600 minus accrued income ₹ 1,200 pertaining to the year 2023 debited in old ratio of 5 : 4 being loss of 2023)	1,333	1,067		" 31	By Reserves (5 : 4)	10,000	8,000	
" 31	To Balance c/d	49,717	41,983		" 31	By Profit & Loss Adjustment A/c (1)	19,050	19,050	
		71,050	59,050				71,050	59,050	
2025 Jan. 1	To Current Accounts (Excess capital transferred)	20,417	12,683		2025 Jan. 1	By Balance b/d	49,717	41,983	
" 1	To Balance c/d	66,200	66,200	33,100	" 1	By Goodwill (2)	36,900	36,900	
					" 1	By Bank (3)			33,100
		86,617	78,883	33,100			86,617	78,883	33,100

PARTNERS' CURRENT ACCOUNTS

Date	Particulars	R	S	N	Date	Particulars	R	S	N
		₹	₹	₹			₹	₹	₹
2025 Dec. 31	To Drawings	18,000	16,000	6,000	2025 Jan. 1	By Capital A/cs	20,417	12,683	
" 31	To Balance c/d	19,217	13,483	2,400	Dec. 31	By Profit & Loss A/c	16,800	16,800	8,400
		37,217	29,483	8,400			37,217	29,483	8,400

(2) *Valuation of Goodwill*

For calculating the value of goodwill, adjusted profits for 2023 and 2024 are required. The same are calculated as follows :

	₹	2023 ₹	₹	2024 ₹
Cash Profits (as given)		30,000		36,000
Add : Outstanding expenses of previous year		2,000		3,600
Accrued income of current year		1,200		2,100
		33,200		41,700
Less: Outstanding expenses of current year	3,600		2,400	
Accrued income of previous year	1,500		1,200	
		5,100		3,600
Correct Profit		28,100		38,100
Total profits of 2023 and 2024 (₹ 28,100 + ₹ 38,100)				66,200
Average profits $\left(i.e. \frac{₹\ 66{,}200}{2}\right)$				33,100
Capitalised value of profits @ 20% $\left(₹\ 33{,}100 \times \frac{100}{20}\right)$				1,65,500
Less : Balance of Capital Accounts before N's admission as a partner				
R's Capital		49,717		
S's Capital		41,983		
				91,700
Value of Goodwill				73,800

(3) N brings in as capital = 1/5 of ₹ 1,65,500 = ₹ 33,100.

ILLUSTRATION 18. Anu and Manu are carrying on business in partnership and sharing profits and losses in the ratio of 5 : 3. The firm's Balance Sheet as on 31st March, 2025 was as follows :

Liabilities	*Amount* (₹)	*Assets*	*Amount* (₹)
Capital Accounts :		Building	3,80,000
Anu	2,80,000	Machinery	1,43,000
Manu	2,50,000	Furniture	85,000
Long-term Loan	2,00,000	Trade Receivables	1,64,000
Trade Payables	1,19,500	Inventories	48,400
Outstanding Liabilities	16,200	Investments	15,200
		Cash & Bank	30,100
	8,65,700		8,65,700

They decided to admit Ranu as a partner with effect from 1st April, 2025 on the following terms :

(*i*) Ranu will be paid 1/5 share in the future profits and new profit sharing ratio would be 5 : 3 : 2.

(*ii*) Ranu will bring ₹ 1,00,000 as his capital.

(*iii*) Goodwill of firms is to be valued at 2 years' purchase of average profit of past 3 years and Ranu will bring his share of goodwill in cash. The profits of past 3 years ending on 31st March were as under :

31st March, 2023	₹	87,000
31st March, 2024	₹	1,06,000
31st March 2025	₹	1,22,000

(*iv*) It was also agreed that the partners will not withdraw their share of goodwill nor will the gcodwill appear in the books of account.

(*v*) It was also decided to value the assets :

Building is to be appreciated by ₹ 50,000 and Machinery is to be depreciated by 10%. Furniture is revalued at ₹ 80,000. Investments at ₹ 16,000 and Inventories at ₹ 47,500.

Provision for doubtful debts is to be created on debtors @ 5%.

You are required to prepare Revaluation Account, Partners' Capital Accounts and Balance Sheet of the reconstituted firm as on 1st April, 2025.

SOLUTION

REVALUATION ACCOUNT

Particulars		₹	*Particulars*	₹
To Machinery A/c		14,300	By Building A/c	50,000
To Furniture A/c		5,000	By investments	800
To Provision for Doubtful Debts		8,200		
To Inventories		900		
To Partner's Capital A/c				
(Profit on revaluation)				
Anu (5/8)	14,000			
Manu (3/8)	8,400	22,400		
		50,800		50,800

PARTNER'S CAPITAL ACCOUNTS

Particulars	*Anu (₹)*	*Manu (₹)*	*Ranu (₹)*	*Particulars*	*Anu (₹)*	*Manu (₹)*	*Ranu (₹)*
To Balance c/d	3,20,250	2,74,150	1,00,000	By Balance b/d	2,80,000	2,50,000	
				By Profit on Revaluation	14,000	8,400	
				By Bank (Capital)	—	—	1,00,000
				By Bank (Goodwill)	26,250	15,750	—
	3,20,250	2,74,150	1,00,000		3,20,250	2,74,150	1,00,000

BALANCE SHEET (AFTER ADMISSION OF RANU)

as on 1st April, 2025

Liabilities		₹	*Assets*	₹
Capital Accounts :			Building	4,30,000
Anu	3,20,250		Machinery	1,28,700
Manu	2,74,150		Furniture	80,000
Ranu	1,00,000	6,94,400	Trade Receivable	1,55,800

Long-term Loan	2,00,000	Inventories	47,500
Trade Payable	1,19,500	Investments	16,000
Outstanding Liabilities	16,200	Cash and Bank	1,72,100
	10,30,100		10,30,100

Working Notes :

1. **Calculation of Goodwill:**

   $$\text{Average Profit} = \frac{87{,}000 + 1{,}06{,}000 + 1{,}22{,}000}{3} = ₹\ 1{,}05{,}000$$

   Two years' purchase of average profits = 1,05,000 × 2 = 2,10,000

   Goodwill to be brought in by Ranu = ₹ 2,10,000 × 2/10 = ₹ 42,000

2. **Calculation of Sacrificing Ratio = Old – New Ratio**

   Anu = 5/8 – 5/10 = 5/40

   Manu = 3/8 – 3/10 = 3/40

   Goodwill brought in by Ranu shared (at the profit sacrificing ratio) by :

	₹
Anu (₹ 42,000 × 5/8)	26,250
Manu (₹ 42,000 × 3/8)	15,750
	42,000

3. **Bank Balance after admission of Ranu:**

BANK ACCOUNT

Particulars	₹	*Particulars*	₹
To Balance b/d	30,100	By Balance c/d	1,72,100
To Anu's Capital A/c	26,250		
To Manu's Capital A/c	15,750		
To Ranu's Capital A/c	1,00,000		
	1,72,100		1,.72,100

Alternatively, goodwill can also be calculated the basis of weighted average profit, since the profit of the firm is on increasing trend.

ILLUSTRATION 19. Balance Sheet of Mr. Satyam, a practising Chartered Accountant as on 31st March, 2025 is as follows :

BALANCE SHEET

Liabilities	₹	*Assets*	₹
Capital	50,000	Building	40,000
General Reserve	10,000	Furniture	20,000
Profit and Loss Account for the year ended 31-3-2025	70,000	Car	30,000
		Bank Deposits (Client's Account)	20,000
Client's Accounts	30,000	Books and Library	40,000
Other Liabilities	5,000	Cash at Bank	10,000
		Cash in hand	5,000
	1,65,000		1,65,000

Further Information :

(I) His articled clerk, Mr. Anandan, who had qualified for the profession, was admitted as a partner from 1st August, 2024 on the following terms :

(*a*) Mr. Anandan was to be given 10% of the profits arising out of professional work only.

(*b*) Mr. Anandan was to have a guaranteed minimum of ₹ 15,000 per annum.

(*c*) Goodwill of the practice was valued at ₹ 50,000. It was agreed that Mr. Anandan would have no claim on the Goodwill, either present or future.

(*d*) Following incomes were outstanding as on 1st August, 2024 :

(*i*) Professional Fees ₹ 30,000 ; (*ii*) Rent Receivable ₹ 2,000 ; (*iii*) Liquidator's Remuneration ₹ 3,000.

(*e*) Building was to continue to be owned by Mr. Satyam and was partly used for the profession and partly let out. It was decided to charge the firm ₹ 500 per month as rent from 1st August, 2024. No adjustment has been made therefor in the accounts.

(II) Mr. Satyam was appointed as a liquidator of a company from 1st January, 2024. The remuneration received therefrom has also been included in the accounts.

(III) Profit and Loss Account balance was comprised as follows :

(*a*) Professional Income ₹ 60,000 ; (*b*) Liquidator's Remuneration ₹ 7,000 ; (*c*) Rent Receipts ₹ 2,500 ; (*d*) Interest on Client's Deposits ₹ 500.

(IV) The firm maintained books on cash basis.

Prepare Profit and Loss Appropriation Account, Capital Accounts and Balance Sheet of the firm after making necessary adjustments for the above.

SOLUTION

PROFIT & LOSS APPROPRIATION ACCOUNT

for the year ending 31st March, 2025

	Upto 31st July	From 1st Aug.		Upto 31st July	From 1st Aug.
	₹	₹		₹	₹
To Satyam's Capital Account (Rent)	—	4,000	By Profit and Loss A/c Professional Income	20,000	40,000
To Satyam's Capital Account (Balance)	20,000	26,000			
To Anandan's A/c (Minimum Guarantee)	—	10,000			
	20,000	40,000		20,000	40,000

CAPITAL ACCOUNTS

	Satyam	Anandan		Satyam	Anandan
	₹	₹		₹	₹
To Outstanding Fees written off	27,000	3,000	By Balance b/d	50,000	—
" Building A/c	40,000	—	" Outstanding Fees	30,000	—
To Balance c/d	82,500	7,000	By General Reserve	10,000	—
			" Liquidator's Remuneration	7,000	—
			" Rent Received	2,500	—
			" P. & L. App. A/c (Rent)	4,000	—
			" Profit (share)	46,000	10,000
	1,49,500	10,000		1,49,500	10,000

BALANCE SHEET OF M/s SATYAM & ANANDAN
as on 31st March, 2025

Liabilities	₹	₹	*Assets*	₹
Other Liabilities		5,000	Cash in hand	5,000
Client's A/c	30,000		Cash at Bank	10,000
Add : Interest received	500		Books & Library	40,000
		30,500	Bank Deposit (Client's A/c)	20,000
Capital A/cs :			Car	30,000
Satyam	82,500		Furniture	20,000
Anandan	7,000			
		89,500		
		1,25,000		1,25,000

Notes :

(1) Liquidators' remuneration has not been treated as professional income.

(2) Accrued professional income on 1-8-2024, ₹ 30,000, has been raised and written off to the partners' capital accounts.

(3) As the entire goodwill belongs to Satyam, as and when realised, so it has not been raised in the books.

(4) Building has been debited to Satyam's Capital Account as it is no longer property of the firm.

RETIREMENT OF A PARTNER

The only difference between admission and retirement of a partner is that in case of the former, the new partner joins the firm whereas in case of retirement, an old partner leaves the firm because of certain reasons as old age, ill health etc.

Important points which require attention in case of retirement of a partner are :

(*i*) Treatment of goodwill or premium. (*ii*) Revaluation of assets and liabilities. (*iii*) Calculation of new sharing or gaining ratio. (*iv*) Treatment of undistributed profits or losses. (*v*) Share of profit upto the date of retirement. (*vi*) Share in Life Policy. (*vii*) Calculation of total amount due to a retiring partner. (*viii*) Adjustment of capitals after retirement in order to be proportionate to the new profit sharing ratio. (*ix*) Settlement of total amount due to the retiring partner.

We shall now discuss these points one by one.

(*i*) Treatment of Goodwill. Goodwill is valued according to any of the methods (discussed previously) and as per provisions of the partnership deed. Following treatment may be given :

If any amount of goodwill is appearing in the balance sheet at the retirement of a partner, that should be written off by debiting all partners' capital accounts and crediting the goodwill account. Further, retiring partner's share of goodwill is to be calculated and credited to his capital account, the corresponding debit to be given to continuing partners' capital accounts in gaining ratio. In some cases, even the continuing partner may loose some share, in that case his account will also be credited with proportionate amount of premium (as compared to retiring partner's share) and corresponding debit given to other partner's capital account who has gained his share.

Continuing Partners' Capital A/cs. (in gaining ratio)
    To Retiring Partner's Capital A/c

(*ii*) Revaluation of Assets and Liabilities. Revaluation of assets and liabilities is to be done on the same basis as is done in case of admission of a partner. The only difference is that profit or loss on revaluation is to be divided among all the partners (including the retiring partner) in the profit sharing ratio in case of retirement of a partner. Assets and liabilities will then appear in the Balance Sheet at changed values.

Sometimes it may be desired not to alter the values of assets and liabilities in the books, a Memorandum Revaluation Account will be prepared. The first part of this account will be exactly the same as in case of Revaluation Account but in second part entries shall be reversed and the profit or loss of this part shall be divided among the continuing partners in their new profit sharing ratio.

***(iii)* Calculation of Gaining Ratio.** This ratio is calculated when a partner retires from a firm. If new ratio of the continuing partners is not given in the question, it is presumed that the remaining partners will continue to share in the old ratio existed between them prior to retirement of a partner *i.e.* they gain in the old ratio. If the new ratios of the partners are given in the question, the gaining ratio can be calculated by deducting the old ratios from the new ones. This ratio is very important as it helps to determine the amount of compensation to be paid by each of the remaining partners in the firm to the retiring partner.

***(iv)* Treatment of Undistributed Profits or Losses.** General reserve or credit balance of profit and loss account will be distributed by crediting to all the partners' capital accounts in their profit sharing ratio and will not be shown on the liabilities side of the Balance Sheet after distribution. Alternately, only retiring partner's share of these items may be credited to his account and residual amount of such accounts may be shown on the liabilities side of the Balance Sheet. Reverse treatment will be given if there is debit balance of profit and loss account on the assets side of the Balance Sheet.

***(v)* Share of Retiring Partner's Profit Upto the Date of Retirement.** If a partner retires in between the accounting year due to some reasons, his share of profit upto the date of retirement is to be calculated (on the basis of last year's profit or otherwise) and credited to his capital account, the corresponding debit to be given to profit and loss suspense account.

***(vi)* Share in the Life Policy.** If the partners have taken either joint life policy or individual life policies, and these have attained some surrender value, the share of retiring partner is calculated and credited to his capital account, the corresponding debit to be given to continuing partners in gaining ratio.

***(vii)* Calculation of Total Amount Due to a Retiring Partner.** The total amount due to a retiring partner may include *(i)* capital on the date of last Balance Sheet, *(ii)* interest or salary, if any, payable to him, *(iii)* share of profit or loss to the date of retirement, *(iv)* share in the goodwill of the firm, *(v)* share in the profit or loss on revaluation of assets and liabilities, *(vi)* share in the general reserve or profit and loss account appearing in the Balance Sheet. The total amount calculated will be transferred to the retiring partner's loan account. The entry will be :

Retiring Partner's Capital A/c
    To Retiring Partner's Loan A/c

***(viii)* Adjustment of Capital after Retirement in Order to be Proportionate to the Profit Sharing Ratio.** Sometimes after the retirement of a partner, the continuing partners decide to have a certain sum as to be the capital of the firm and that too should be in their new profit sharing ratio. From the total amount of the capital, the capital required by each partner is calculated with reference to his profit sharing ratio and compared with the existing balance in the capital account after making all adjustments. If surplus, the amount will be withdrawn by the partner concerned and if the balance is less than the required amount of his share of capital, he will have to bring the difference of amount in cash in firm's books.

***(ix)* Settlement of the Total Amount Due to the Retiring Partner.** Retiring partner will demand immediate payment of the balance due to him at the time of retirement but the financial resources of the firm may not permit the total amount due to a retiring partner to be paid in one instalment. Some amount may be paid immediately and the rest may be treated as retiring partner's loan to the firm at a certain rate of interest. Partner's loan account will be continuously shown on the liabilities side of the Balance Sheet till all the outstanding amount of the loan is paid by the firm to the retiring partner.

ILLUSTRATION 20. On 31st March, 2025 the Balance Sheet of M/s. A, B & C sharing profits and losses in proportion to their capitals, stood as follows :

Liabilities	₹	₹	*Assets*	₹
Capital Accounts :			Land and Buildings	2,00,000
A	2,00,000		Machinery	3,00,000

B	3,00,000		Closing Stock	1,00,000
C	2,00,000	7,00,000	Sundry Debtors	1,00,000
			Cash and Bank Balances	1,00,000
Sundry Creditors		1,00,000		
		8,00,000		8,00,000

On 31st March, 2025, A desired to retire from the firm and the remaining partners decided to carry on. It was agreed to revalue the assets and liabilities on that date on the following basis.

(1) Land and Buildings be appreciated by 30%. (2) Machinery be depreciated by 20%. (3) Closing stock to be valued at ₹ 75,000. (4) Provision for bad debts be made at 5%. (5) Old credit balances of Sundry Creditors ₹ 20,000 be written back. (6) Joint Life Policy of the partners surrendered and cash obtained ₹ 80,000. (7) Goodwill of the entire firm be valued at ₹ 1,40,000 and A's share of the Goodwill be adjusted in the accounts of B and C who share the future profits equally. No Goodwill Account being raised. (8) The total capital of the firm is to be the same as before retirement. Individual capitals be in their profit sharing ratio. (9) Amount due to A is to be settled 50% on retirement and the balance 50% within one year.

Prepare Revaluation Account, Capital Accounts of Partners, Cash Account and Balance Sheet as on 1-4-2025 of M/s B & C.

SOLUTION

REVALUATION ACCOUNT

		₹		₹
To Machinery		60,000	By Land & Buildings	60,000
To Closing Stock		25,000	By Sundry Creditors	20,000
To Provision for Bad Debts		5,000	By Cash & Bank A/c	
To Profit on Revaluation transferred			(Joint Life Policy surrendered)	80,000
to Capital A/cs :	₹			
A (2/7)	20,000			
B (3/7)	30,000			
C (2/7)	20,000			
		70,000		
		1,60,000		1,60,000

PARTNERS' CAPITAL ACCOUNTS

	A	B	C		A	B	C
	₹	₹	₹		₹	₹	₹
To A's Capital A/c				By Balance b/d	2,00,000	3,00,000	2,00,000
(Goodwill)		10,000	30,000	By Revaluation A/c	20,000	30,000	20,000
To Cash & Bank A/c				By B's Capital A/c	10,000		
(50% of amount due				By C's Capital A/c	30,000		
paid)	1,30,000			By Cash & Bank A/c	—	30,000	1,60,000
To A's Loan A/c	1,30,000						
(Balance transferred)							
To Balance c/d	—	3,50,000	3,50,000				
	2,60,000	3,60,000	3,80,000		2,60,000	3,60,000	3,80,000

CASH & BANK ACCOUNT

	₹		₹
To Balance b/d	1,00,000	By A's Capital A/c (Payment of 50% of the amount due to A)	1,30,000
To Revaluation A/c (Receipt of surrender value of joint life policy)	80,000	By Balance c/d	2,40,000
To B's Capital A/c	30,000		
To C's Capital A/c	1,60,000		
	3,70,000		3,70,000

BALANCE SHEET OF M/S. A, B & C

as at 1-4-2025

Liabilities		₹	*Assets*		₹
Partners' Capital Accounts :	₹		Land & Buildings		2,60,000
B	3,50,000		Machinery		2,40,000
C	3,50,000		Closing Stock	₹	75,000
		7,00,000	Sundry Debtors	1,00,000	
A's Loan		1,30,000	*Less* : Provision for Bad Debts	5,000	
Sundry Creditors		80,000			95,000
			Cash & Bank Balances		2,40,000
		9,10,000			9,10,000

Working Notes :

(2) *Calculation of Amount of Goodwill to be Credited to A and Debited to B and C.*

Goodwill of the firm ₹ 1,40,000

A's share of goodwill $\left(₹\ 1{,}40{,}000 \times \frac{2}{7}\right)$ ₹ 40,000

Goodwill of ₹ 40,000 should be debited to B and C in their gaining ratio of 1 : 3 calculated as follows :

B's Gaining Ratio = New Ratio – Old Ratio *i.e.* $\frac{1}{2} - \frac{3}{7} = \frac{1}{14}$

C's Gaining Ratio = $\frac{1}{2} - \frac{2}{7} = \frac{3}{14}$

Therefore, gaining ratio is 1/14 : 3/14 = 1 : 3

B should bear amount of goodwill = ₹ 40,000 × $\frac{1}{4}$ = ₹ 10,000

C should bear amount of goodwill = ₹ 40,000 × $\frac{3}{4}$ = ₹ 30,000.

ILLUSTRATION 21. (*Retirement of two partners and continuance of business by third partner*) Morning, Day and Night carry on business in partnership sharing the Profits and Losses in the proportion of 25%, 25% and 50% respectively. Their Balance Sheet as on 31-3-2025 was as under :

Liabilities		₹	*Assets*	₹
Sundry Creditors		1,20,000	Cash/Bank	1,00,000
General Reserves		80,000	Sundry Debtors	75,00,000
Capitals—	₹		Inventories	10,00,000
Morning	24,00,000		Fixed Assets W.D.V.	4,00,000
Day	24,00,000		Investment (At cost) (Market	
Night	50,00,000		Value ₹ 15,00,000)	10,00,000
		98,00,000		
		1,00,00,000		1,00,00,000

On 1st April, 2025, Morning and Day retired and Night continued the business. Night paid ₹ 36,00,000 to Morning and ₹ 36,00,000 to Day in full and final discharge of their claim in the partnership. This amount was brought in by Night for the purpose of payment to the retiring partners. None of the assets and liabilities are to be revalued.

You are asked to : (*i*) Pass accounting entries in relation to the above in the books of business unit. (*ii*) Prepare Balance Sheet of the business unit after the above transactions are recorded.

SOLUTION

In the Books of the Business Unit

JOURNAL ENTRIES

		₹	₹
Bank A/c	Dr.	72,00,000	
To Night's Capital A/c			72,00,000
(Being Capital brought by Night for payment to Morning and Day)			
Morning's Capital A/c	Dr.	36,00,000	
Day's Capital A/c	Dr.	36,00,000	
To Bank A/c			72,00,000
(Being Capitals paid on retirement)			
Night's Capital A/c	Dr.	24,00,000	
To Morning's Capital A/c			12,00,000
To Day's Capital A/c			12,00,000
(Being purchase of share of goodwill of Morning and Day by Night)			

BALANCE SHEET OF BUSINESS UNIT

(*After retirement of Morning and Day*)

Liabilities		₹	*Assets*	₹
Net Worth being Excess of Assets Over			Fixed Assets WDV	4,00,000
Liabilities Comprising of Night's	₹		Investment at cost	
Capital Contribution	98,00,000		(Market Value ₹ 15,00,000)	10,00,000
Add : Reserves	80,000		*Current Assets* :	
		98,80,000	Inventories	10,00,000
Current Liabilities			Sundry Debtors	75,00,000
Sundry Creditors		1,20,000	Cash/Bank	1,00,000
		1,00,00,000		1,00,00,000

ILLUSTRATION 22. A and B had started a firm of Chartered Accountants as equal partners under the style of "Y & Co" with effect from January 1, 2021. Each of the partners had contributed ₹ 1,000 towards the capital of the firm and was allowed to draw ₹ 200 per month. On January 1, 2022 they took in C as a third partner with equal share with the two original partners and he contributed ₹ 1,000 towards the capital of the firm. He too was entitled to draw ₹ 200 per month. A got a part-time job elsewhere from Jan. 1, 2023 and considering that he would be unable to devote his full time towards the business of the firm agreed to leave half of his share in the profits to be appropriated equally between B and C and his drawing was reduced to ₹ 100 per month since January, 2023, Later on, B got a full-time job from 1st January, 2024 and in consequence A had to leave his part-time job to devote his full-time in the firm. It was arranged that B would retain only a quarter of his earlier share in the firm and would be drawing nothing from January, 2024. A and C would be drawing at the rate of ₹ 300 per month instead. The interest surrendered by B would be appropriated equally by A and C. On 31st December, 2024 B decided to retire

altogether from the firm. You are required to ascertain the amount due to B by the firm from the following particulars :

(*a*) Assets and Liabilities position on relative dates :

Date	*Balance of Cash and at Bank*	*Outstanding Bills*	*Fixed Assets*	*Liabilities*
	₹	₹	₹	₹
31-12-2021	3,412	2,116	600	328
31-12-2022	5,219	3,417	1,000	736
31-12-2023	8,476	4,894	1,200	1,570
31-12-2024	9,787	6,158	1,600	1,345

(*b*) B's share of goodwill is to be taken at twice the amount of profits earned by him during the year 2024.

(*c*) The partners have drawn exactly what they could draw under the agreement and nothing else.

(*d*) No interest on capital or drawings is to be calculated.

SOLUTION

For the purpose of ascertaining the amount due to B on his retirement, his account should be credited in respect of his share of yearly profits and Goodwill and debited for the yearly drawings.

The yearly total profit will be arrived at by finding out the increase in net assets each year adding thereto the drawings made during the year and deducting therefrom further capital introduced during the year.

ASCERTAINMENT OF TOTAL YEARLY PROFIT

Particulars	*Years*			
	2021	*2022*	*2023*	*2024*
	₹	₹	₹	₹
Cash and Bank	3,412	5,219	8,476	9,787
Outstanding Bills	2,116	3,417	4,894	6,158
Fixed Assets	600	1,000	1,200	1,600
Total Closing Assets	6,128	9,636	14,570	17,545
Less : Closing Liabilities	328	736	1,570	1,345
Closing Net Assets	5,800	8,900	13,000	16,200
Less : Opening Net Assets		5,800	8,900	13,000
Increase in Net Assets	5,800	3,100	4,100	3,200
Add : Drawings during the year	4,800	7,200	6,000	7,200
	10,600	10,300	10,100	10,400
Less : Introduction of Capital	2,000	1,000		
Profits for the Years	8,600	9,300	10,100	10,400

CALCULATION OF PROFIT-SHARING RATIO AND DRAWINGS

Years	*A*	*B*	*C*	*Drawings*
				₹
2021	1/2	1/2	—	4,800
2022	1/3	1/3	1/3	7,200
2023	1/3 – 1/6 *i.e.* 1/6	1/3 + 1/12 *i.e.* 5/12	1/3 + 1/12 *i.e.* 5/12	6,000
2024	1/6 + 5/32 *i.e.* 31/96	5/12 – 5/16 *i.e.* 5/48	5/12 + 5/32 *i.e.* 55/96	7,200

B's CAPITAL ACCOUNT

		₹			₹
2021	To Cash —Drawings	2,400	2021	By Cash (Amount introduced)	1,000
2022	To Cash —Drawings	2,400		By P & L App. A/c— (1/2 share of ₹ 8,600)	4,300
2023	To Cash —Drawings	2,400	2022	By P & L App. A/c—(1/3 rd share of ₹ 9,300)	3,100
2024	Balance transferred to B's Loan A/c	8,657	2023	By P & L App. A/c— (5/12th share of ₹ 10,100)	4,208
			2024	By P & L App. A/c— (5/48th share of ₹ 10,400)	1,083
				By Goodwill	2,166
		15,857			15,857

Note. B's share of Goodwill has been taken at 2 times the amount of profits earned during the year 2024. Hence the required amount is 2 × ₹ 1,083 *i.e.* ₹ 2,166.

ILLUSTRATION 23. X and Y are partners sharing profits and losses in the ratio of 3 : 2. On 30th September, 2024 they admitted Z as a partner. The new profit sharing ratio agreed was 2 : 2 : 1.

At the time of admission Z brought in a fixture valued at ₹ 6,000 and a machinery worth ₹ 24,000. No accounting entry was passed for the fixture brought in by partner Z in the books of the firm.

Also at the time of admission the valuation of goodwill was made. The value of goodwill of X and Y was decided at ₹ 40,000 and value of goodwill of partner Z was fixed at ₹ 20,000. No effect was given to the goodwill value in the books of the firm.

On 31-3-2025, it was decided that partner X would retire and the other partners viz., Y and Z would continue the business of the firm by converting it into a company called YZ Ltd., with equal shareholding in the company.

The partners agreed as below :

(*i*) The goodwill of the firm shall be fixed at ₹ 80,000. Necessary effect for goodwill value not recorded earlier shall be given. The present goodwill value being ₹ 80,000 shall be reflected in the books of the company.

(*ii*) All the assets and liabilities of the firm shall be taken over by the company.

(*iii*) Partner X would take motor car of the firm at a value of ₹ 7,400.

(*iv*) A plant owned by the firm is sold for ₹ 6,000.

(*v*) The profit of the firm upto 30-9-2024 was ₹ 44,000.

(*vi*) Partner X agreed to leave ₹ 90,000 as loan with the firm in return for 12% interest per annum.

Following is the Trial Balance of the firm as on 31-3-2025 :

Particulars	*Dr.* ₹	*Cr.* ₹
Capital Account :		
X	—	80,000
Y	—	50,000
Z	—	24,000
Drawings Account :		
X	24,000	
Y	20,000	
Z	9,600	

Sundry Debtors	70,000	
Sundry Creditors	—	32,000
Plant (Book value of plant sold ₹ 8,000)	46,000	
Fixtures	14,000	
Stock	24,000	
Motor Car	5,400	
Cash at Bank	34,600	
Profit & Loss A/c (for the year)	—	59,600
	2,45,600	2,45,600

You are required to prepare : (*i*) Goodwill Adjustment Account. (*ii*) Profit & Loss Appropriation Account. (*iii*) Partners' Capital Accounts. (*iv*) Balance Sheet of YZ Ltd. after conversion.

SOLUTION

(*i*) **GOODWILL ADJUSTMENT ACCOUNT**

		₹			₹
2024 Sept. 30	To Partners' Capital A/cs :		2024 Sept. 30	By Partners' Capital A/cs :	
	X $\left(₹ 40,000 \times \frac{3}{5}\right)$	24,000		X $\left(\frac{2}{5} \times ₹ 60,000\right)$	24,000
	Y $\left(₹ 40,000 \times \frac{2}{5}\right)$	16,000		Y $\left(\frac{2}{5} \times ₹ 60,000\right)$	24,000
	Z	20,000		Z $\left(\frac{1}{5} \times ₹ 60,000\right)$	12,000
2025 March 31	To Partners' Capital A/cs :		2025 March 31	By Goodwill A/c (Goodwill raised)	80,000
	X	32,000			
	Y	32,000			
	Z	16,000			
		1,40,000			1,40,000

(*ii*) **CALCULATION OF PROFIT APPORTIONMENT**

	Total ₹	*X* ₹	*Y* ₹	*Z* ₹
Upto 30-9-2024 (In 3 : 2 Ratio)	44,000	26,400	17,600	—
From 1-10-2024 to 31-3-2025 (₹ 59,600 for the year—₹ 44,000 profit for first 6 months = ₹ 15,600 apportioned in the ratio 2 : 2 : 1)	15,600	6,240	6,240	3,120
Total Apportionment for the year	59,600	32,640	23,840	3,120

PROFIT AND LOSS APPORTIONMENT ACCOUNT

			₹		₹
To Plant (Loss on Sale of Plant)			2,000	By Motor Car (Profit) (₹ 7,400 – ₹ 5,400 Book Value)	2,000
To Profit transferred to Capital Accounts:		₹		By Profit & Loss A/c (Profit for the year)	59,600
	X	32,640			
	Y	23,840			
	Z	3,120			
			59,600		
			61,600		61,600

(*iii*) **PARTNERS' CAPITAL ACCOUNTS**

	Z	Y	Z		X	Y	Z
30-9-2024	₹	₹	₹	30-9-2024	₹	₹	₹
To Goodwill Adjustment A/c	24,000	24,000	12,000	By Balance b/d	80,000	50,000	
31-3-2025				By Plant & Machinery	—	—	24,000
To Motor Car	7,400	—	—	By Fixtures	—	—	6,000
To Drawings	22,000	20,000	9,600	By Goodwill Adjustment A/c	24,000	16,000	20,000
To 12% Loan	90,000	—	—	31-3-2025			
To Bank	25,240	—	—	By Profit & Loss Appropriation A/c	32,640	23,840	3,120
To Balance c/d	—	77,840	47,520	By Goodwill Adjustment	32,000	32,000	16,000
	1,68,640	1,21,840	69,120		1,68,640	1,21,840	69,120
To Bank (1)	—	15,160	—	By Balance c/d	—	77,840	47,520
To Shares of YZ Ltd.	—	62,680	62,680	By Bank (1)	—	—	15,160
	—	77,840	62,680		—	77,840	62,680

(*iv*) **BALANCE SHEET OF YZ LTD.**

as at 31-3-2025

	₹
I. Equity and Liabilities	
(1) *Shareholders' Funds*	
Share Capital :	
12,536 Equity Shares of ₹ 10 (assumed) each fully paid up	1,25,360
(All the above shares issued to A and B for conversion of firm into a limited company)	
(2) *Non-current Liabilities*	
12% Loan	90,000
(3) *Current Liabiities*	
Accounts Payable : Sundry Creditors	32,000
Total	2,47,360
II. Assets	
(1) *Non-current Assets*	
Plant (₹ 46,000 – ₹ 8,000)	38,000
Fixtures (₹ 14,000 + ₹ 6,000)	20,000
Goodwill	80,000
(2) *Current Assets*	
Stock	24,000
Trade Receivables : Sundry Debtors	70,000
Cash at Bank	15,360
Total	2,47,360

Working Notes

(1) Total capital of the firm before conversion

		₹
Y	₹ 77,840	
Z	₹ 47,520	
		1,25,360

Y and Z would continue the business of the firm by converting it into a company with equal shareholding in the company. Therefore, share capital of Y and Z would be ₹ 1,25,360 × $\frac{1}{2}$ = ₹ 62,680 each

Z should bring cash (₹ 62,680 – ₹ 47,520)	₹ 15,160
Y should withdraw cash to make his capital equal to Z (₹ 77,840 – ₹ 62,680)	₹ 15,160

(2) **BANK ACCOUNT**

	₹		₹
To Balance b/d	34,600	By X's Capital A/c	25,240
To Plant (Sale)	6,000	By Y's Capital A/c	15,160
To Z's Capital A/c (1)	15,160	By Balance c/d (2)	15,360
	55,760		55,760

ILLUSTRATION 24. A, B and C were in partnership sharing profits and losses in the ratio of 3 : 2 : 1. Balance Sheet of their business on 31st March, 2025 was as follows :

Liabilities		₹	*Assets*	₹
Capital Accounts :	₹		Machinery	80,000
A	60,000		Furniture	15,000
B	50,000		Motor Car	30,000
C	40,000		Stock	50,000
		1,50,000	Sundry Debtors	60,000
Sundry Creditors		72,000	Cash at Bank	37,000
Bank Loan		30,000		
Other Liabilities		20,000		
		2,72,000		2,72,000

A retired on 1st April, 2025 and the Partnership Deed provided *inter alia* that in the event of admission, death or retirement of a partner, the assets and liabilities are to be revalued and that the Goodwill of the firm is to be computed on the basis of 2 year's purchase of the correct profits of the last 4 years.

It is discovered that the accounts require adjustments owing to certain mistakes in the earlier years. On 1st October, 2022, repairs to machinery for ₹ 6,000 had been wrongly debited to Machinery Account ; and on 1st April, 2023, a piece of furniture whose book value was ₹ 2,000 was disposed off for ₹ 800 but the proceeds were wrongly credited to sales account. The partners have been charging depreciation on all fixed assets @ 10% p.a. on the reducing balance system on time basis. Profits for the last 4 years, without adjusting the above mentioned mistakes, were as follows:

2021-22 ₹ 20,000 ; 2022-23 ₹ 24,000 ; 2023-24 ₹ 32,000 ; 2024-25 ₹ 36,000.

Revaluation on the date of retirement was as under :

Machinery ₹ 90,000 ; Furniture ₹ 10,000 ; Motor Car ₹ 22,000.

B and C decided to share future profits after A's retirement, in the ratio of 3 : 2. It was further agreed that the retiring partner shall be credited with his due proportion of goodwill, without raising a goodwill account in the books.

A is to be paid 50% of the amount due to his retirement immediately and the balance is to be transferred to his Loan Account carrying interest @ 6% p.a. B and C are to bring necessary cash (in their new ratio) subject to the condition that a cash balance of ₹ 20,000 is to be maintained as working capital.

Show Capital Accounts of the partners and Balance Sheet of the firm after all the above mentioned transactions have been carried out. Ignore fractions. (All workings should form part of your answer.)

SOLUTION

CAPITAL ACCOUNTS

	A	B	C		A	B	C
	₹	₹	₹		₹	₹	₹
To Revaluation A/c (*i*)	1,500	1,000	500	By Balance b/d	60,000	50,000	40,000
To A's Capital A/c (*iii*) (Goodwill)	—	14,102	12,338	By B's Capital (Goodwill)	14,102	—	—
To Cash	42,470			By C's Capital (Goodwill)	12,338	—	—
To A's Loan A/c	42,470			By Cash (*iv*)		15,282	10,188
To Balance c/d		50,180	37,350				
	86,440	65,282	50,188		86,440	65,282	50,188

BALANCE SHEET OF M/s B & C
as on 1st April, 2025

Liabilities		₹	Assets	₹
Other Liabilities		20,000	Cash	20,000
A's Loan A/c		42,470	Sundry Debtors	60,000
Bank Loan		30,000	Stock	50,000
Sundry Creditors		72,000	Motor Car	22,000
Capital Accounts :	₹		Furniture	10,000
B	50,180		Machinery	90,000
C	37,350			
		87,530		
		2,52,000		2,52,000

Working Notes :

(*i*) **REVALUATION ACCOUNT**

		₹			₹	₹
To	Motor Car	8,000	By	Machinery		10,000
"	Furniture	5,000	"	Loss transferred to Capital A/cs :	₹	
				A	1,500	
				B	1,000	
				C	500	
						3,000
		13,000				13,000

(*ii*) **ADJUSTED PROFIT**

	2021-22	2022-23	2023-24	2024-25
	₹	₹	₹	₹
Reported Profit	20,000	24,000	32,000	36,000
Adjustments :				
Repairs wrongly capitalised	—	– 6,000	—	—
Depreciation on the above		+ 300	+ 570	+ 513
Sale of furniture shown as Sales on 1-4-2023	—	—	– 800	—
Loss on sale of furniture	—	—	– 1,200	—
Depreciation on Furniture Sold (Written off)			+ 200	+ 180
Adjusted Profit	20,000	18,300	30,770	36,693

	₹
Total profits for 4 years	1,05,763
Average	26,440
Goodwill (at 2 year's purchase)	52,880
A's Share of Goodwill (1/2)	26,440

(*iii*) *Gain by B and C on A's retirement*

B : $\frac{3}{5}-\frac{1}{3}=\frac{8}{30}$

C : $\frac{2}{5}-\frac{1}{6}=\frac{7}{30}$.

A's share of goodwill has been debited to B and C in the ratio of 8 : 7 *i.e.*, ₹ 14,102 to B and ₹ 12,338 to C.

(*iv*) *Cash brought in by B and C*

	₹
Amount due to A	84,940
Less : transferred to his Loan A/c	42,470
Amount payable	42,470
Surplus in existing cash balance (₹ 37,000 – ₹ 20,000 working capital)	17,000
Payable by B and C in the ratio of 3 : 2	25,470

Retirement and Admission

Sometimes in a firm a partner retires and a new partner is admitted at the same time so that working of the firm may not suffer because of funds and persons. In such a case first of all adjustments are to the made as are done at the time of retirement of a partner. Then the case of admission of a partner is taken for adjustment in the accounts. This will be clear from the working of the following Illustrations :

ILLUSTRATION 25 (*Retirement and Admission*). Ms. Naina, Ms. Radha and Ms. Khushi were partners in a firm sharing profits and losses in the ratio of 4 : 3 : 2. Balance Sheet of the firm as on 31-3-2024 was as follows :

Liabilities	*Amount (₹)*	*Assets*	*Amount (₹)*
Capital Accounts		Plant & Machinery	4,26,000
Naina	3,00,000	Stock	1,85,800
Radha	2,25,000	Debtors	1,30,500
Khushi	1,50,000	Bank Balance	92,700
Current Accounts :			
Naina	25,000		
Radha	12,500		
Khushi	18,750		
Creditors	1,03,750		
	8,35,000		8,35,000

On 1st April 2024, Ms. Naina retired. On her retirement goodwill is valued at ₹ 1,80,000. Ms. Radha and Ms. Khushi do not wish to rise Goodwill Account in the books.

Ms. Naina drew her balance of current account on 2nd April, 2024 and it is agreed to pay balance of her capital account over a period of two years by half yearly instalments with interest at 10% per annum.

On 1st Oct. 2024 Ms. Asmita (Daughter of Radha) admitted as a partner. Ms. Radha surrendered one third of her share of profit and loss in favour of Asmita and also transferred one third of her capital to Ms. Asmita. Ms. Asmita was manager in the firm with annual salary of ₹ 16,000, prior to admission as a partner.

The other bank transactions during the financial year 2024-25 were as follows : ₹

1. Payment to creditors 7,75,000
2. Received from debtors 11,25,000
3. Expenses paid 11,250
4. Asmita's salary paid 8,000
5. Partners' Drawings :
   - Ms. Radha 50,000
   - Ms. Khushi 41,250
   - Ms. Asmita 11,250
6. First instalment with interest paid to Ms. Naina on 1st Oct. 2024.
7. Plant and Machinery sold at ₹ 9,000 on 3rd April, 2024 (Cost ₹ 10,000 and Book value ₹ 7,000).
8. Balances as on 31st March, 2025 : Debtors ₹ 1,50,000, Creditors for purchases ₹ 1,25,000, Creditors for expenses ₹ 10,000 and Stock ₹ 1,71,250.
9. Depreciation is to be written off on Plant and Machinery ₹ 30,350.
10. Second instalment with interest paid to Ms. Naina on 1st April, 2025.

You are required to prepare : (*a*) Ms. Naina's Loan Account, (*b*) Partners' Capital Accounts, (*c*) Partners' Current Accounts, (*d*) Bank Account, and (*e*) Balance Sheet as on 31st March, 2025 in the books of the firm.
[*Adapted C.A. Inter (IPCE) Nov. 2015 Modified*]

SOLUTION

(*a*) **NAINA'S LOAN ACCOUNT**

		₹			₹
1-10-2024	To Bank $\left(\frac{₹\,3{,}80{,}000}{4} + ₹\,19{,}000\right)$	1,14,000	1-4-2024	By Capital A/c	3,80,000
			30-9-2024	By Interest—For 6 months @ 10% p.a. on 3,80,000	19,000
31-3-2025	To Balance c/d	2,99,250	31-3-2025	By Interest—For 6 months on ₹ 2,85,000 @ 10% p.a.	14,250
		4,13,250			4,13,250
				By Balance b/d	2,99,250

(*b*) **PARTNERS' CAPITAL ACCOUNTS**

	Naina	Radha	Khushi	Asmita		Naina	Radha	Khushi	Asmita
	₹	₹	₹	₹		₹	₹	₹	₹
To Naina's Capital A/c		48,000	32,000		By Balance b/d	3,00,000	2,25,000	1,50,000	–
To Asmita's Capital A/c		59,000			By Radha's Capital A/c	48,000	–		–
To Naina's Loan A/c	3,80,000	–	–	–	By Khushi's Capital A/c	32,000	–	–	–
To Balance c/d		1,18,000	1,18,000	59,000	By Radha's Capital A/c	–	–	–	59,000
	3,80,000	2,25,000	1,50,000	59,000		3,80,000	2,25,000	1,50,000	59,000

(*c*) **PARTNERS' CURRENT ACCOUNTS**

	Naina	Radha	Khushi	Asmita		Naina	Radha	Khushi	Asmita
	₹	₹	₹	₹		₹	₹	₹	₹
To Bank (Drawings)		50,000	41,250	11,250	By Balance b/d	25,000	12,500	18,750	
To Bank A/c	25,000				By P & L A/c upto :				
To Balance c/d		82,850	74,640	14,110	Sept. 30, 2024		69,630	46,420	
					March 31, 2025		50,720	50,720	25,360
	25,000	1,32,850	1,15,890	25,360		25,000	1,32,850	1,15,890	25,360

(*d*)

BANK ACCOUNT

	₹		₹
To Balance b/d	92,700	By Naina's Current Account	25,000
To Sundry Debtors	11,25,000	By Sundry Creditors	7,75,000
To Sale of Machine	9,000	By Sundry Expenses	11,250
		By Asmita's Salary	8,000
		By Naina's Loan Account	1,14,000
		By Current Account (Drawings) :	
		Naina	50,000
		Radha	41,250
		Khushi	11,250
		By Balance c/d	1,90,950
	12,26,700		12,26,700

(*e*)

BALANCE SHEET OF THE FIRM

as on March 31, 2025

		₹			₹
Creditors : Trade	1,25,000		Machinery	4,26,000	
Expenses	10,000	1,35,000	*Less* : Sold	(7,000)	
Naina's Loan Account		2,99,250	Depreciation	(30,350)	3,88,650
Partners' Capital Accounts :			Current Assets :		
Radha	1,18,000		Stock in Trade	1,71,250	
Khushi	1,18,000		Debtors	1,50,000	
Asmita	59,000	2,95,000	Bank Balance	1,90,950	5,12,200
Partners' Current Accounts :					
Radha	82,850				
Khushi	74,640				
Asmita	14,110	1,71,600			
		9,00,850			9,00,850

Working Notes :

(1) Calculation of Sales

DEBTORS ACCOUNT

	₹		₹
To Balance b/d	1,30,500	By Bank	11,25,000
To Sales (Bal. Fig.)	11,44,500	By Balance c/d	1,50,000
	12,75,000		12,75,000

Calculation of Purchases

CREDITORS ACCOUNT

	₹		₹
To Bank A/c	7,75,000	By Bal. b/d	1,03,750
To Balance c/d	1,25,000	By Purchase (Bal. fig.)	7,96,250
	9,00,000		9,00,000

*All Sales and purchases are considered to be on credit basis.

(2) Computation of Profits for the year ended March 31, 2025

TRADING AND PROFIT AND LOSS ACCOUNT

for the year ended March 31, 2025

		₹			₹
To Opening Stock		1,85,800	By Sales	(1)	11,44,500
To Purchases	(2)	7,96,250	By Closing Stock		1,71,250
To Gross Profit c/d		3,33,700			
		13,15,750			13,15,750

	Apr. 1 to Sept. 30 (₹)	Oct. 1 to Mar. 31 (₹)		Apr. 1 to Sept. 30 (₹)	Oct. 1 to Mar. 31 (₹)
To Sundry Expenses (11,250 + 10,000)	10,625	10,625	By Gross Profit b/d	1,66,850	1,66,850
			By Profit on Sale on Machine	2,000	—
To Depreciation on Machinery	15,175	15,175			
To Interest on Naina's Loan	19,000	14,250			
To Salary—Asmita	8,000				
To Profit Transferred to					
Radha's Capital A/c	69,630	50,720			
Khushi's Capital A/c	46,420	50,720			
Asmita's Capital A/c	—	25,360			
	1,68,850	1,66,850		1,68,850	1,66,850

(3) Adjustment of Goodwill at the Time of Retirement of Naina

		₹	₹
Radha's Capital A/c	Dr.	48,000	
Khushi's Capital A/c	Dr.	32,000	
To Naina's Capital A/c (₹ 1,80,000 × 4/9)			80,000
(Naina's share of goodwill adjusted among Radha and Khushi in their gaining ratio of 3 : 2)			

(4) New profit sharing ratio after admission of Asmita will be 2 : 2 : 1

Profits for the half year ended on 30-9-2024 will be distributed among Radha and Khushi in the ratio of 3 : 2 and profits for the half year ended on 31-3-2025 will be distributed among Radha, Khushi and Asmita in the ratio of 2 : 2 : 1.

ILLUSTRATION 26. (*Retirement & Admission*). Ram, Rahim and Robert are partners, sharing Profits and Losses in the ratio of 5 : 3 : 2. It was decided that Robert would retire on 31-3-2025 and in his place Richard would be admitted as a partner with new profit sharing ratio between Ram, Rahim and Richard at 3 : 2 : 1.

BALANCE SHEET OF RAM, RAHIM AND ROBERT

as on 31-3-2025

Liabilities	₹	*Assets*	₹
Capital Accounts :		Cash in Hand	20,000
Ram	1,00,000	Cash at Bank	1,00,000
Rahim	1,50,000	Sundry Debtors	5,00,000
Robert	2,00,000	Stock in Trade	2,00,000

General Reserve	2,00,000	Plant & Machinery	3,00,000
Sundry Creditors	8,00,000	Land & Building	5,30,000
Loan from Richard	2,00,000		
	16,50,000		16,50,000

Retirement of Robert and admission of Richard is on the following terms :

(*a*) Plant and Machinery to be depreciated by ₹ 30,000.

(*b*) Land and Building to be valued at ₹ 6,00,000.

(*c*) Stock to be valued at 95% of book value.

(*d*) Provision for doubtful debts @ 10% to be provided on debtors.

(*e*) General Reserve to be apportioned amongst Ram, Rahim and Robert.

(*f*) The firm's goodwill to be valued at 2 years' purchase of the average profits of the last 3 years. The relevant figures for the year ended 31st March are : 2022 — Profit ₹ 50,000 ; 2023— Profit ₹ 60,000 ; 2024 – Profit ₹ 55,000

(*g*) Out of the amount due to Robert ₹ 2,00,000 would be retained as loan by the firm and the balance will be settled immediately.

(*h*) Richard's capital should be equal to 50% of the combined capital of Ram and Rahim.

Prepare : (*i*) Capital Accounts of the partners; and (*ii*) Balance Sheet of the reconstituted firm.

(CA—PE-II, Nov. 2005 Modified)

SOLUTION

Dr. **PARTNERS' CAPITAL ACCOUNTS** Cr.

	Ram	Rahim	Robert	Richard		Ram	Rahim	Robert	Richard
	₹	₹	₹	₹		₹	₹	₹	₹
To Revaluation A/c (Loss) (W.N. 1)	10,000	6,000	4,000	—	By Balance b/d	1,00,000	1,50,000	2,00,000	—
To Loan from Robert A/c	—	—	2,00,000	—	By General Reserve	1,00,000	60,000	40,000	—
To Bank	—	—	58,000		By Goodwill (W.N. 2)	55,000	33,000	22,000	—
To Balance c/d	2,45,000	2,37,000	—	—					
	2,55,000	2,43,000	2,62,000	—		2,55,000	2,43,000	2,62,000	—
To Goodwill (4) (Written off in ratio of 3 : 2 : 1)	55,000	36,667	—	18,333	By Balance b/d	2,45,000	2,37,000	—	—
					By Richard's Loan A/c —transfer	—	—	—	2,00,000
To Balance c/d	1,90,000	2,00,333	—	1,95,167	By Bank	—	—	—	13,500
	2,45,000	2,37,000	—	2,13,500		2,45,000	2,37,000	—	2,13,500

BALANCE SHEET OF THE RECONSTITUTED FIRM

(after admission of Richard)

Liabilities	₹	*Assets*		₹
Sundry Creditors	8,00,000	Cash in hand		20,000
Loan from Robert	2,00,000	Cash at Bank (W.N. 3)	₹	55,500
Capital Accounts :		Debtors	5,00,000	

Ram	1,90,000	*Less* : Provision for Doubtful		
Rahim	2,00,333	Debts	50,000	
Richard	1,95,167			4,50,000
		Stock		1,90,000
		Plant & Machinery		2,70,000
		Land & Building		6,00,000
	15,85,500			15,85,500

Working Notes

(1) **REVALUATION ACCOUNT**

Liabilities	₹	*Assets*	₹
To Plant & Machinery	30,000	By Land & Building	70,000
To Stock	10,000	By Loss on Revaluation transferred to :	
To Provision for Doubtful Debts	50,000	Ram's Capital A/c	10,000
		Rahim's Capital A/c	6,000
		Robert's Capital A/c	4,000
	90,000		90,000

(2) ***Calculation of Goodwill***

	₹
Profit for the year ended 31-3-2022	50,000
Profit for the year ended 31-3-2023	60,000
Profit for the year ended 31-3-2024	55,000
	1,65,000

$$\text{Average Profit} = \frac{₹\ 1{,}65{,}000}{3} = ₹\ 55{,}000$$

Goodwill at 2 years' purchase = ₹ 55,000 × 2 = ₹ 1,10,000

(3) ***Calculation of Bank Balance***

BANK ACCOUNT

Liabilities	₹	*Assets*	₹
To Balance b/d	1,00,000	By Robert's Capital A/c	58,000
To Richard's Capital A/c	13,500	By Balance c/d	55,500
	1,13,500		1,13,500

(4) Goodwill should be recorded in the books only when some consideration in money or money's worth has been paid for it. Therefore, the goodwill raised at the time of retirement of Robert is to be written off in new ratio among remaining partners including new partner—Richard.

DEATH OF A PARTNER

The problems which arise in case of death of a partner are similar to those of a retiring partner except that the death of a partner may occur at any time whereas the retirement of a partner is planned *i.e.* he is allowed to retire on the last date of an accounting period. The deceased partner's capital account is credited with the balance of capital at the beginning of the year, interest on capital (if allowed), share of profit on revaluation of assets and liabilities, share of undistributed profits, share of profit to the date of death, his share of goodwill and the amount which is received from the Life Insurance Corporation of India (or surrender value in case of individual policies) and debited with drawings to the date of death, interest on drawings (if charged) and the balance is transferred to the executor's account of the deceased partner.

Moreover, under Section 37 of the Partnership Act, the executors of the deceased partner would be entitled to at their discretion either interest at 6% per annum on the amount due from the date of death to the date of payment or to that portion of the profit that is earned by the firm with the amount due to the deceased partner. Most of the points have already been discussed in the retirement of a partner but the following two points require special attention. (*i*) Calculation of deceased partner's share of profit. (*ii*) Treatment of life policy or policies.

These will be discussed one by one.

Calculation of Deceased Partner's Share of Profit

The deceased partner's share of profit is to be determined either on the basis of time or turnover :

(*a*) On the basis of time. In this case, it is assumed that the profit during the previous year has been earned uniformly in all months during the year, provided previous year is taken as the base for calculation of profit. Sometimes average profits of the past three or four years is taken as base rather than the previous year. Whatever base may be taken, it is to be multiplied by the period for which the deceased partner remained in the firm and also his profit sharing ratio at the time of his death. For example A, B, and C are partners in a firm sharing profits and losses in the ratio of 3 : 2 : 1. B dies on 14th March, 2025. The average of the last three years is ₹ 30,000. B's share of profit on the basis of time is calculated as under :

Average yearly profit = ₹ 30,000

Profit for 73 days *i.e.*, Jan. 1 to March 14, 2025 = $\frac{₹\ 30{,}000 \times 73}{365}$ = ₹ 6,000

B's share = 2/6 × ₹ 6,000 = ₹ 2,000.

(*b*) On the basis of turnover. In this method, average past profit is divided into two portions *i.e.*, before the death and after the death on the basis of ratio of turnover to the date of death to average turnover and then deceased partner's share is calculated and credited to his capital account. For example, A, B and C are partners in a firm sharing profits and losses in the ratio of 3 : 2 : 1. B dies on 14th March, 2025. Turnover from 1st January, to 14th March, 2025 is ₹ 42,000. Average turnover of the last three years is ₹ 60,000 and profit is ₹ 30,000. B's share of profit on this basis will be calculated as under :

Average turnover = ₹ 60,000

Sales to the date of death = ₹ 42,000.

∴ Profit to the date of death = ₹ 42,000 × $\frac{₹\ 30{,}000}{₹\ 60{,}000}$ = ₹ 21,000

∴ B's share of profit = $\frac{1}{3}$ × ₹ 21,000 = ₹ 7,000.

ILLUSTRATION 27. P, Q and R were carrying on a business in partnership, sharing profits and losses in the ratio of 5 : 3 : 2 respectively. The firm earned a profit of ₹ 3,60,000 for the accounting year ended 31st March, 2024 on which date the firm's Balance Sheet stood as follows :

BALANCE SHEET

as on 31st March, 2024

Liabilities	₹	*Assets*	₹
P's Capital	7,00,000	Freehold Land and Building	8,00,000
Q's Capital	5,70,000	Machinery	3,50,000
R's Capital	4,30,000	Furniture & Fixtures	1,02,000
Creditors	79,400	Stock	2,98,800

Outstanding Expenses	4,900	Debtors	1,60,000
		Cash at Bank	73,500
	17,84,300		17,84,300

P died on 31st August, 2024. According to firm's partnership deed, in case of death of a partner :

(*i*) Assets and Liabilities have to be revalued by an independent valuer.

(*ii*) Goodwill is to be calculated at two years' purchase of average profits for the last three completed accounting years and the deceased Partner's Capital Account is to be credited with his share of goodwill.

(*iii*) The share of the deceased partner in the profits for the period between end of the previous accounting year and the date of death is to be calculated on the basis of the previous accounting year's profits. Post death of P, Q and R will share profit in the ratio of 3 : 2.

Profits for the accounting years 2021-2022 and 2022-23 were as follows :

	₹
For the year ended 31st March, 2022	2,90,000
For the year ended 31st march, 2023	3,40,000

Drawings by P from 1st April 2024 to be date of his death totalled ₹ 46,000.

On revaluation, Freehold Land and Building was appreciated by ₹ 1,00,000; Machinery was depreciated by ₹ 10,000 and a Provision for Bad Debts was created @ 5% on Debtors as on 31st March 2024. P's sole heir was given ₹ 5,00,000 immediately and the balance along with interest @ 12% per annum was paid to him on 31st March, 2025.

Prepare Revaluation Account, P's Capital Account and P's Heir Account, giving important working notes. ***(C.A. Inter, May, 2013 Modified)***

SOLUTION

REVALUATION ACCOUNT

	₹	₹		₹
To Machinery		10,000	By Freehold Land & Building	1,00,000
To Provision for Doubtful Debts (5% of ₹ 1,60,000)		8,000		
To Capital Accounts :				
P (5/10 Share of Profit)	41,000			
Q (3/10 Share of Profit)	24,600			
R (2/5 Share of Profit)	16,400			
		82,000		
		1,00,000		1,00,000

P'S CAPITAL ACCOUNT

	₹		₹
To Drawings	46,000	By Balance b/d	7,00,000
To P's Heir Account (Balance transferred)	11,00,000	By Q's Capital A/c (2)	1,98,000
		By R's Capital A/c (2)	1,32,000
		By Profit and Loss Suspense A/c (3)	75,000
		By Revaluation A/c	41,000
	11,46,000		11,46,000

P'S HEIR ACCOUNT

		₹			₹
31-8-2024	To Bank A/c	5,00,000	31-8-2024	By P's Capital A/c	11,00,000
31-3-2025	To Bank A/c	6,42,000	31-3-2025	By Interest A/c	
				$\left(6,00,000 \times 12\% \times \frac{7}{12}\right)$	42,000
		11,42,000			11,42,000

Working Notes :

(1) Calculation of Gaining Ratio of Partners Q and R

	New share	Old share	Gaining share	Sacrificing share
P		5/10		5/10
Q	3/5	3/10	$\frac{3}{5}-\frac{3}{10}=\frac{6-3}{10}=\frac{3}{10}$	
R	2/5	2/10	$\frac{2}{5}-\frac{2}{10}=\frac{4-2}{10}=\frac{2}{10}$	

(2) Calculation of Goodwill

	₹
Profits for 3 years :	
2021-22	2,90,000
2022-23	3,40,000
2023-24	3,60,000
	9,90,000

Average Profit = 9,90,000/3 = ₹ 3,30,000

Goodwill = 3,30,000 × 2 = ₹ 6,60,000

Share of P in goodwill $=6,60,000 \times \frac{5}{10}$ = ₹ 3,30,000

Adjustment for P's share of goodwill through Q's and R's Capital Accounts (in their gaining ratio 3 : 2) :

Q's Capital A/c (3,30,000 × 3./5) ₹ 1,98,000

R's Capital A/c (3,30,000 × 2/5) ₹ 1,32,000

(2) Share of P in Profits for the period between 1-4-2024 to 31-8-2024 *i.e.* till the date of death

1st April, 2024 to 31st August, 2024 = 5 months

Profit for year 2023-24 = ₹ 3,60,000

Estimated profit for 5 months $= 3,60,000 \times \frac{5}{12}$ = ₹ 1,50,000

Share of P $= 1,50,000 \times \frac{5}{10}$ = ₹ 75,000

Treatment of Life Policy (or Policies)

When a partner dies, his legal representatives are required to be paid a large sum of money. If some arrangement is not made, it may affect the financial position as well as working of the partnership business. In order to provide funds to the legal representatives of the deceased partner, generally a joint life policy (or individual life policies for partners) is taken by the firm. The premium paid on such policy (policies) is charged to the Profit and Loss Account. Joint Life Policy will be an asset of the firm and deceased partner has a right to share any profit or loss on such a policy. So, any claim which is received by the firm on the death of a partner is divided among the partners and credited to their capital accounts in their profit sharing ratio.

If the partners have taken individual life policies and the premiums of such individual policies are charged to profit and loss account of the firm, the deceased partner has a right to share the amount not only received from Life Insurance Corporation of India but also the surrender value which the other partners' policies acquired at the time of death. Surrender value is the value which is payable immediately to the insured on surrendering all rights of the policy (or policies) to the corporation. This will be more clear from the following illustration.

Treatment of Joint Life Policy

There are three methods of dealing with the Joint Life Policy :

(*a*) When the premiums are written off to Profit and Loss Account. Under this method, the premium paid on the joint life policy is debited to the Profit and Loss Account and whatever amount is received from the corporation on the date of death of a partner is divided among the partners in their profit sharing ratio. Following journal entries will be passed.

(*i*) *When insurance premium is paid*

Insurance Premium A/c Dr.
 To Bank

(*ii*) *When charged to Profit and Loss Account*

Profit and Loss A/c Dr.
 To Insurance Premium A/c

(*iii*) *When the amount is received on the death of a partner*

Bank A/c Dr.
 To Joint Life Policy A/c

(*iv*) *When the amount received is distributed among the partners in their profit sharing ratio*

Joint Life Policy A/c Dr.
 To Partners' Capital A/cs

(*b*) When premiums are to be written off through Joint Life Policy Reserve Account. Under this method, the following entries are passed :

(*i*) *When premium is paid*

Joint Life Policy A/c Dr.
 To Bank A/c

(*ii*) **When a reserve equal to premium paid is created out of profit and loss**

Profit and Loss A/c Dr.
 To Joint Life Policy Reserve A/c

(*iii*) **When excess of Joint Life Policy over surrender value is written off to Joint Life Policy Reserve Account**

Joint Life Policy Reserve A/c Dr.
 To Joint Life Policy A/c

(*iv*) **When the amount of joint policy is received**

Bank A/c Dr.
 To Joint Life Policy A/c

(*v*) **When the balance of Joint Life Policy Reserve Account is transferred to Joint Life Policy Account**

Joint Life Policy Reserve A/c Dr.
 To Joint Life Policy A/c

(*vi*) **When balance of joint life policy is distributed among the partners**

Joint Life Policy A/c Dr.
 To Partners' Capital A/cs

(c) When surrender value is to be treated as an asset. Under this case, the amount of premium paid is debited to Joint Life Policy Account which is reduced to its surrender value by appropriate debit to the Profit and Loss Account. The balance in joint life policy will be shown as an asset in the Balance Sheet. The amount received on the death of a partner on account of joint life policy from the insurance company is credited to Joint Life Policy Account and the balance standing in Joint Life Policy Account after the receipt of the amount of the policy is closed by transferring it to all partners in their profit sharing ratio. The journal entry for closing the balance of Joint Life Policy Account is :

Joint Life Policy Account Dr.
  To Partners' Capital Accounts

ILLUSTRATION 28. Ramu, Shamu and Raju were partners sharing profits and losses in the ratio of 3 : 2 : 2. Their Balance Sheet as on 1-1-2024 was as follows :

Liabilities		₹	*Assets*	₹
Capital Accounts			Fixed Assets	80,000
Ramu	30,000		Stock	15,000
Shamu	20,000		Debtors	12,000
Raju	20,000		Cash & Bank	1,951
		70,000		
Reserves		14,000		
Creditors		24,951		
		1,08,951		1,08,951

On 1st October, 2024, Ramu died. His heirs agreed that :

(i) Goodwill of the firm be valued at 2 years' purchase of average profit of past three years. Profits for the years 2021, 2022 and 2023 were ₹ 30,000, ₹ 40,000 and ₹ 47,600 respectively giving these profits weights of 1, 2 and 3 respectively.

(ii) Fixed assets be revalued at ₹ 1,01,000.

(iii) Profit to be shared, earned in subsequent period after death of Ramu till settlement of his executors' claim.

Ramu's heirs account was settled on 31-12-2024 by bringing in required cash by remaining partners in equal proportion leaving cash balance of ₹ 1,234. Each partner had drawn @ ₹ 1,000 per month for personal use.

Profit for the current year after charging depreciation of ₹ 9,000 (₹ 6,000 for first three quarters and ₹ 3,000 for last quarter) was ₹ 46,600 earned evenly through-out the year.

You are requested to prepare Profit & Loss Appropriation A/c, Cash & Bank A/c, Ramu's Executor's A/c and Partners' Capital Accounts for the year ended on 31-12-2024 assuming remaining partners decided not to retain goodwill in the books. ***(CA—PCE 11/2010 Modified)***

SOLUTION

(i) **PROFIT & LOSS ACCOUNT**

	₹ (for nine months)	₹ (for three months)		₹ (for nine months)	₹ (for three months)
To Depreciation	6,000	3,000	By Profit (1)		
To Net Profit	35,700	10,900	₹ 55,600 in 9 : 3 Ratio	41,700	13,900
	41,700	13,900		41,700	13,900

PROFIT & LOSS APPROPRIATION ACCOUNT

	₹ (for nine months)	₹ (for three months)		₹ (for nine months)	₹ (for three months)
To Partners' Capital A/cs			By Net Profit	35,700	10,900
Ramu	15,300	–			
Shamu	10,200	3,043			
Raju	10,200	3,044			
To Ramu's Executor A/c (2)	—	4,813			
	35,700	10,900		35,700	10,900

(ii) PARTNERS' CAPITAL ACCOUNTS AS ON 31ST OCTOBER, 2024

	Ramu (₹)	Shamu (₹)	Raju (₹)		Ramu (₹)	Shamu (₹)	Raju (₹)
To Drawings A/c	9,000	9,000	9,000	By Balance b/d	30,000	20,000	20,000
To Ramu's Executors A/c	87,414	—	—	By Reserves A/c	6,000	4,000	4,000
To Balance c/d	—	55,276	55,276	By Goodwill* (3)	36,114	24,076	24,076
				By Fixed Assets	9,000	6,000	6,000
				By Profit & Loss Appropriation A/c	15,300	10,200	10,200
	96,414	64,276	64,276		96,414	64,276	64,276

(iii) PARTNERS' CAPITAL ACCOUNTS

as on 31-12-2024

	Shamu (₹)	Raju (₹)		Shamu (₹)	Raju (₹)
To Drawings A/c	3,000	3,000	By Balance b/d	55,276	55,276
To Goodwill A/c	42,133	42,133	By Cash	62,255	62,255
To Balance c/d	75,441	75,442	By Profit & Loss Appropriation A/c	3,043	3,044
	1,20,574	1,20,575		1,20,574	1,20,575

(iv) RAMU'S EXECUTORS' ACCOUNT

as on 31-12-2024

	₹		₹
To Bank	92,227	By Balance b/d	87,414
		By P & L Appropriation A/c	4,813
	92,227		92,227

* Goodwill should be recorded in the books only when some consideration in money or money's worth has been paid for it. However, in the above solution, goodwill has been raised in the books at the time of death of a partner and written off by the remaining partners, as per the information given in the question.

(v) **CASH & BANK ACCOUNT**

	₹		₹
To Balance b/d	1,951	By Ramu's Executors A/c	92,227
To Shamu's Capital A/c	62,255	By Partners' Capital A/cs (Drawings) :	
To Raju's Capital A/c	62,255	Ramu	9,000
		Shamu	12,000
		Raju	12,000
		By Balance c/d	1,234
	1,26,461		1,26,461

Working Notes :

1. Profit for the year before depreciation :

	₹
Profit after depreciation	46,600
Add : Depreciation	9,000
Profit before depreciation	55,600

2. As per Section 37 of the Partnership Act, in case of settlement of deceased partner's account on the date other then the date of death, the executor of deceased partner has a choice to take

Either—

(A) Profit Earned on Un-settled Capital $= \text{Profit} \times \dfrac{\text{Unsettled Capital as on 1-10-24}}{\text{Total Capital as on 1-10-24}}$

$$= ₹10{,}900 \times \frac{₹\,87{,}414}{₹\,(87{,}414 + 55{,}276 + 55{,}276)}$$

$$= ₹10{,}900 \times \frac{87{,}414}{1{,}97{,}966} = ₹\,4{,}813$$

Or

(B) Interest on Capital @ 6% *i.e.* ₹ 87,414 × 6% × 3/12 = ₹ 1,311

Option A is beneficial, therefore heirs of Ramu will opt for proportionate share of profit *i.e.* ₹ 4,813.

3. Valuation of Goodwill :

	₹	*Weight*	*Product* ₹
Profit for 2021	30,000	1	30,000
2022	40,000	2	80,000
2023	47,600	3	1,42,800
	1,17,600	6	2,52,800

Weighted Average Profit $= \dfrac{2{,}52{,}800}{6} = ₹\,42{,}133$

Goodwill = 2 years' purchase of average profit = ₹ 42,133 × 2 = ₹ 84,266.

ILLUSTRATION 29. A, B and C were trading in Partnership sharing profits and losses in the proportion of 4 : 3 : 3. The balances in the books of the firm as on 31st December, 2024, subject to final adjustment, were as follows :

	Debit ₹	*Credit* ₹
Capital and Drawing Accounts		
A	24,000	1,50,000
B	36,000	75,000
C	36,000	90,000

Land and Buildings	1,20,000	
Furniture and Fixtures	22,500	
Stock	1,87,500	
Debtors	30,000	
Bank Account	60,000	
Creditors		45,000
Profit for the year before charging interest		1,56,000
Total	5,16,000	5,16,000

C died on 30th June, 2024. The Partnership Deed provided that : (1) Interest was to be credited on Capital Accounts of partners at 10% per annum on the balance at the beginning of the year. (2) On the death of a partner—(*i*) Goodwill was to be valued at three year's purchase of average annual profits of three years upto the date of death, after deducting interest on capital employed at 8% p.a. and a fair remuneration for each of the partners ; (*ii*) Fixed Assets were to be valued by an independent valuer and all other assets and liabilities to be taken at book value; and (3) Whenever necessary, profit or loss should be apportioned on a time basis.

You ascertain that :—(*a*) Profits for three years before charging partners' interest were : 2021 ₹ 1,68,000 ; 2022 ₹ 1,89,000 ; 2023 ₹ 1,80,000 ; (*b*) The independent valuation at the date of death revealed : Land and Buildings ₹ 1,50,000 ; Furniture and Fixtures ₹ 15,000 (*c*) A fair remuneration for each of the partners would be ₹ 37,500 per annum and that the Capital Employed in the business to be taken as ₹ 3,90,000 throughout. It was agreed between the partners that—(*i*) Goodwill was not to be shown as an asset of the firm as on 31st December, 2024. Therefore, adjustment for goodwill was to be made in Capital Accounts ; (*ii*) The amount due to C's estate was to remain as loan with the firm carrying interest at 12% per annum ; (*iii*) A and B would share profits equally from the date of death of C ; (*iv*) Depreciation on revised value of assets would be ignored.

You are required to prepare (1) Partners' Capital Accounts and Current Accounts ; and (2) Balance Sheet of the firm as on 31st December, 2024. Working should be done correct to the nearest rupee.

SOLUTION

CAPITAL ACCOUNTS

	A	B	C		A	B	C
	₹	₹	₹		₹	₹	₹
To C's Current A/c (3)	—	—	12,825	By Balance b/d	1,50,000	75,000	90,000
To C's Capital A/c	9,990	19,980	—	By Revaluation A/c (3)	9,000	6,750	6,750
To C's Executors A/c	—	—	1,13,895	By A's Capital (4)	—	—	9,990
To Balance c/d	1,49,010	61,770	—	By B's Capital (4)	—	—	19,980
	1,59,000	81,750	1,26,720		1,59,000	81,750	1,26,720

CURRENT ACCOUNTS

	A	B	C		A	B	C
	₹	₹	₹		₹	₹	₹
To Balance b/d	24,000	36,000	36,000	By Interest on Capital	15,000	7,500	4,500
To Balance c/d	45,858	20,133	—	By Profit upto 30th June (2)	24,900	18,675	18,675
				By Profit upto 31st Dec. (2)	29,958	29,958	—
				By C's Capital	—	—	12,825
	69,858	56,133	36,000		69,858	56,133	36,000

BALANCE SHEET

as on 31-12-2024

Liabilities		₹	*Assets*	₹
Creditors		45,000	Bank	60,000
C's Executor's A/c (1)	₹	1,20,729	Debtors	30,000
Capital A/cs : A	1,49,010		Stock	1,87,500
B	61,770		Furniture & Fittings	15,000
		2,10,780	Land & Buildings	1,50,000
Current A/cs : A	45,858			
B	20,133			
		65,991		
		4,42,500		4,42,500

Working Notes :

(1) **C's EXECUTORS ACCOUNT**

	₹		₹
To Balance c/d	1,20,729	By C's Capital A/c	1,13,895
		By Interest	6,834
	1,20,729		1,20,729

(2) **PROFIT & LOSS ACCOUNT**

	Upto 30th June 2024 ₹	*Upto 31st Dec. 2024* ₹		*Upto 30th June 2024* ₹	*Upto 31st Dec. 2024* ₹
To Interest on Capital					
A	7,500	7,500	By Profit	78,000	78,000
B	3,750	3,750			
C	4,500	—			
To Interest on C's Loan		6,834			
To Profit transferred to Current A/cs :					
A	24,900	29,958			
B	18,675	29,958			
C	18,675	—			
	78,000	78,000		78,000	78,000

(3) **REVALUATION ACCOUNT**

		₹		₹
To Furniture & Fixtures		7,500	By Building	30,000
To Capital A/cs :	₹			
A	9,000			
B	6,750			
C	6,750			
		22,500		
		30,000		30,000

(4) ***Calculation of Goodwill***

			₹	₹
Profits upto	30th June, 2022	1/2 of 2021	84,000	
		1/2 of 2022	94,500	
				1,78,500
"	30th June, 2023	1/2 of 2022	94,500	
		1/2 of 2023	90,000	
				1,84,500
Profits upto	30th June, 2024	1/2 of 2023	90,000	
		1/2 of 2024	78,000	
				1,68,000
	Total Profit for three years			5,31,000
	Average Profit			1,77,000
Less : Interest on capital employed 8% on ₹ 3,90,000			31,200	
Fair remuneration to partners ₹ 37,500 × 3			1,12,500	
				1,43,700
				33,300

	A	*B*	*C*
Three years' purchase—₹ 99,900 (*i.e.*, ₹ 33,300 × 3)			
₹ 99,900 allocated among partners	39,960	29,970	29,970
Goodwill to be debited 1 : 1	49,950	49,950	–
Goodwill to be debited or credited	9,990 (Dr.)	19,980 (Dr.)	29,970 (Cr.)

ILLUSTRATION 30. A, B and C are partners in a firm sharing profits and losses in the proportion of 4 : 3 : 2 respectively. Balance Sheet as at 30th June, 2022, at which date A died, is as under :

BALANCE SHEET

Liabilities	₹	*Assets*	₹
Sundry Creditors	2,000	Cash	1,000
Bank Overdraft	5,000	Debtors	10,000
Reserve Fund	9,000	Stock	16,000
Partners' Current Accounts :		Motor Car	2,000
A	7,000	Furniture	1,000
B	4,000	Machinery	20,000
C	3,000	Building	30,000
Capital Accounts :			
A	20,000		
B	20,000		
C	10,000		
	80,000		80,000

The Partnership Agreement provided that on the death of a partner :

(*i*) The firm shall be continued by the other partners ;

(*ii*) Goodwill to be valued on the basis of two years' profits on the average of the three preceding years ;

(*iii*) Fixed and floating assets to be revalued ; and

(*iv*) The amount ascertained to be due to the deceased partner's legal representatives to be treated as loan to the firm. One-third of the amount plus interest at 6 per cent per annum on the balance outstanding being paid on 30th June each year until fully repaid.

The profits of the three preceding years were ₹ 30,000, ₹ 45,000 and ₹ 60,000 respectively. On revaluation as at 30th June, 2022 the amount for Building, Machinery, Furniture, Motor Car and Stock came to ₹ 60,000 ; ₹ 80,000 ; ₹ 3,000 ; ₹ 5,000 and ₹ 21,000 respectively whilst the Debtors were considered good at the book figure less 10 per cent provision for doubtful debts.

You are asked to prepare by giving effect to the above adjustments in the books of the firm : (*a*) Revaluation Account ; (*b*) Deceased Partner's Capital Account ; (*c*) The Legal Representatives' Loan Account for the three years ended 30th June, 2025. (Calculations to be made to the nearest rupee).

SOLUTION

REVALUATION ACCOUNT

		₹		₹
To Provision for Doubtful Debts		1,000	By Building	30,000
To Profit transferred to			By Machinery	60,000
Capital A/cs :	₹		By Furniture	2,000
A	44,000		By Motor Car	3,000
B	33,000		By Stock	5,000
C	22,000	99,000		
		1,00,000		1,00,000

A'S CAPITAL ACCOUNT

	₹		₹
To A's Executors Loan A/c	1,15,000	By Balance b/d	20,000
		By Revaluation A/c	44,000
		By Current A/c	7,000
		By Goodwill A/c $\left(\frac{4}{9} \times ₹\ 90,000\right)$	40,000
		By Reserve Fund	4,000
	1,15,000		1,15,000

A'S EXECUTORS' LOAN ACCOUNT

		₹			₹
2023			2022		
June 30	To Bank A/c $\left(\frac{₹\ 1,15,000}{3} + ₹\ 6,900\right)$	45,233	July 1	By A's Capital A/c	1,15,000
			2023		
			June 30	By Interest A/c	6,900
June 30	To Balance c/d	76,667			
		1,21,900			1,21,900
2024			2023		
June 30	To Bank A/c $\left(\frac{₹\ 1,15,000}{3} + ₹\ 4,600\right)$	42,933	July 1	By Balance b/d	76,667
			2024		
			June 30	By Interest A/c	4,600
June 30	To Balance c/d	38,334			
		81,267			81,267

2025 June 30	To Bank A/c	40,634	2024 July 1	By Balance b/d	38,334
			2025 June 30	By Interest A/c	2,300
		40,634			40,634

Application of Section 37 of the Partnership Act

In the absence of any agreement, the retired partner or the executors of the decreased partner would be entitled at their discretion either interest at 6% per annum on the amount due from the date of retirement/death to the date of payment or that portion of the profit that is earned by the firm with the amount due to the retired partner or the decreased partner.

	₹
A's Capital A/c as on the date of *C*'s death	66,714
B's Capital A/c as on the date of *C*'s death	83,286
Amount due to *C*'s executors as on 30-9-2024	52,000
Total amount with which profit is earned	2,02,000

Interest on ₹ 52,000 @ 6% p.a. for 6 months for 1-10-2024 to 31-3-2025	₹ 1,560
Portion of profit earned by the firm with the amount due to the legal heirs of *C*	
$\frac{\text{₹ 25,000 (Profit for second half year)} \times \text{₹ 52,000}}{\text{₹ 2,02,000}} =$	₹ 6,436

Legal heirs would opt for the higher amount of ₹ 6,436.

Amount Due to Legal Heirs of C as on 31-3-2025	₹
Balance in *C*'s Executor's A/c	52,000
Portion of Profit	6,436
Total Amount Due to Legal Heirs of *C*	58,436

ILLUSTRATION 31. A, B and C were partners, sharing Profits and Losses in the ratio of 5 : 3 : 2 respectively. On 31st March, 2024 their Balance Sheet stood as follows :

Liabilities	₹	*Assets*	₹
A's Capital	7,79,000	Plant and Machinery	13,62,000
B's Capital	7,07,800	Furniture and Fittings	2,36,000
C's Capital	6,86,200	Stock	7,02,000
Creditors	4,91,000	Debtors	1,91,000
		Cash at Bank	1,73,000
	26,64,000		26,64,000

On 31st July, 2024 A died. According to partnership deed, on the death of a partner, the capital account of the deceased partner was to be credited with :

(*i*) his share of profit for the relevant part of the year of death calculated on the basis of profit earned during the immediately preceding accounting year, and

(*ii*) his share of goodwill.

Goodwill was to be valued at two years' purchase of the average profits of immediately preceding three accounting years. The profits, as per books of account, were as follows :

	₹
For accounting year ended 31st March, 2022	3,29,000
For accounting year ended 31st March, 2023	3,46,000
For accounting year ended 31st March, 2024	3,78,000

However, while going through the books of account on A's death, it came to light that ₹ 30,000 worth of wages were spent on installation of a new machinery, but the sum was not capitalised; the machinery was put into operation on 1st October, 2023. Depreciation was provided on the machinery @ 20% per annum.

On 1st October, 2024 A's son D was admitted into partnership with immediate effect on the following terms :

(*a*) D would get one-fourth share in the profits of the firm, while the relative profit sharing ratio between B and C would remain unchanged.

(*b*) The final balance of A's capital Account would be credited to D's Capital Account.

(*c*) An adjustment would be made in the Capital Accounts for D's share of goodwill. The basis of valuation of firm's goodwill would be the same as was adopted at the time of the death of his father.

On 31st March, 2025 Profit and Loss Account of the firm showed that the firm had earned a profit of ₹ 4,16,000 for the year. The respective drawings accounts showed that while B and C had withdrawn ₹ 60,000 each during the year, D's drawings totalled ₹ 30,000. Drawings Accounts are closed at the end of the year by transfer to respective capital accounts.

You are required to :

(*i*) Prepare a statement showing distribution of profits for the accounting year ended 31st March, 2025; and

(*ii*) Pass Journal Entries for all the transactions relating to death of the partner, D's admission into partnership, and at the end of the year relating to transfer of Drawings Accounts and distribution of profit for the year.

SOLUTION

(*i*) Statement Showing Distribution of Profits for the Accounting Year Ended 31st March, 2025

	₹	₹
Net profit for the year ended 31-3-2025		4,16,000
A's Share of Profit :		
(*a*) Deceased partner A's share for 4 months from 1-4-2024 to 31-7-2024 (1)	67,500	
(*b*) A's executor share of profit for 2 months from 1-8-2024 to 30-9-2024 (5)	28,021	
		95,521
B's Share of Profit :		
(*a*) B's share of profit for 4 months from 1-4-2024 to 31-7-2024 (3)	42,700	
(*b*) B's share of profit for 2 months from 1-8-2024 to 30-9-2024 (6)	24,787	
(*c*) B's share of profit for 6 months from 1-10-2024 to 31-3-2025 (10)	93,600	
		1,61,087
C's share of Profit :		
(*a*) C's share of profit for 4 months from 1-4-2024 to 31-7-2024 (3)	28,467	
(*b*) C's share of profit for 2 months from 1-8-2024 to 30-9-2024 (6)	16,525	
(*c*) C's share of profit for 6 months from 1-10-2024 to 31-3-2025 (10)	62,400	
		1,07,392
D's share of profit for 6 months from 1-10-2024 to 31-3-2025 (10)		52,000
		4,16,000

(ii) **JOURNAL ENTRIES**

Date	Particulars		Dr. ₹	Cr. ₹
2024 July 31	Machinery A/c	Dr.	27,000	
	To A's Capital A/c			13,500
	To B's Capital A/c			8,100
	To C's Capital A/c			5,400
	[Being wages spent on installation of new machinery capitalised (after providing ₹ 3,000 depreciation @ 20% p.a. for 6 months from 1-10-2023 to 31-3-2024 on ₹ 30,000) and credited to Partners' Capital Accounts in the ratio of 5 : 3 : 2]			
2024 July 31	Profit and Loss Suspense A/c	Dr.	67,500	
	To A's Capital A/c			67,500
	[Being A's share of profit for 4 months from 1-4-2024 to 31-7-2024 (1)]			
"	Goodwill A/c	Dr.	7,20,000	
	To A's Capital A/c			3,60,000
	To B's Capital A/c			2,16,000
	To C's Capital A/c			1,44,000
	[Being Goodwill raised on A's death (2)]			
"	A's Capital A/c	Dr.	12,20,000	
	To A's Executor A/c			12,20,000
	[Being balance due to A on his death transferred to his executor's account (4)]			
October 1	Profit and Loss Suspense A/c	Dr.	28,021	
	To A's Executor's A/c			28,021
	[Being profit earned out of the unsettled capital for 2 months from 1-8-2024 to 30-9-2024 credited to A's Executor A/c (5)]			
"	A's Executor's A/c	Dr.	12,48,021	
	To D's Capital A/c			12,48,021
	[Being amount due to A's executor transferred to D's Capital A/c as per working note no. (7)]			
October 1	B's Capital A/c	Dr.	3,24,000	
	C's Capital A/c	Dr.	2,16,000	
	D's Capital A/c	Dr.	1,80,000	
	To Goodwill A/c			7,20,000
	(Being goodwill written off and debited to partners in the new profit sharing ratio of 9 : 6 : 5)			
2025 March 31	B's Capital A/c	Dr.	60,000	
	C's Capital A/c	Dr.	60,000	
	D's Capital A/c	Dr.	30,000	
	To B's Drawings A/c			60,000
	To C's Drawings A/c			60,000
	To D's Drawings A/c			30,000
	(Being drawings transferred to Capital Accounts)			

March 31	Profit and Loss Appropriation A/c	Dr.	4,16,000	
	To Profit and Loss Suspense A/c			95,521
	To B's Capital A/c			1,61,087
	To C's Capital A/c			1,07,392
	To D's Capital A/c			52,000
	(Being distribution of profits as shown in statements of distribution of profits as per working notes (3), (6) and (10) and balance of Profit and Loss Suspense Account transferred to Profit and Loss Appropriation Account)			

Working Notes :

(1) Computation of A's Share in Profit for 4 months from 1-4-2024 to 31-7-2024

A's share in profits for the period of 1-4-2024 to 31-7-2024 is to be calculated on the basis of profit earned during the immediately previous accounting year ended on 31st March, 2024.

	₹
Profit for the year ended 31st March, 2024	3,78,000
Add : Capital expenditure of wages spent on installation of new machinery wrongly treated as revenue expenditure, now capitalised	30,000
	4,08,000
Less : Depreciation on ₹ 30,000 @ 20% p.a. for 6 months from 1-10-2023 to 31-3-2024	3,000
Correct Profit for the year ending 31st March, 2024	4,05,000

Profit for 4 months on the basis of last year's profit = ₹ 4,05,000 × $\frac{4}{12}$ = ₹ 1,35,000

A's share in profit = ₹ 1,35,000 × $\frac{5}{10}$ = ₹ 67,500

(2) Valuation of Goodwill

	₹
Profit for the year ended 31st March, 2022	3,29,000
Profit for the year ended 31st March, 2023	3,46,000
Profit for the year ended 31st March, 2024	(1) 4,05,000
Total Profit	10,80,000

Average Profit = ₹ $\frac{10,80,000}{3}$ = ₹ 3,60,000

Goodwill at two years' purchase = ₹ 3,60,000 × 2 = ₹ 7,20,000

(3) Distribution of Profits for 4 months ended 31st July, 2024

	₹
Net Profit for the year ending 31st March, 2025	4,16,000
Net Profit for 4 months from 1-4-2024 to 31-7-2024 $\left(₹ 4,16,000 \times \frac{4}{12}\right)$	1,38,667
A's share [See working note no. (1)]	67,500
B's share 3/5 of (₹ 1,38,667 – ₹ 67,500)	42,700
C's share 2/5 of (₹ 1,38,667 – ₹ 67,500)	28,467
	1,38,667

(4) **PARTNERS' CAPITAL ACCOUNTS**

as on 31st July, 2024

	A	B	C		A	B	C
	₹	₹	₹		₹	₹	₹
To Drawings (for 4 months)		20,000	20,000	By Balance b/d	7,79,000	7,07,800	6,86,200
To A's Executor's A/c	12,20,000			By Plant & Machinery	13,500	8,100	5,400
To Balance c/d		9,54,600	8,44,067	By Goodwill	3,60,000	2,16,000	1,44,000
				By Profit for 4 months (W.N. 3)	67,500	42,700	28,467
	12,20,000	9,74,600	8,64,067		12,20,000	9,74,600	8,64,067

(5) **Application of Section 37 of the Partnership Act**

Either

(*i*) Interest on ₹ 12,20,000 @ 6% p.a. for 2 months = ₹ 12,200

or

(*ii*) Profit earned out of unsettled capital of ₹ 12,20,000 of A

$$₹\ 4,16,000 \times \frac{2}{12} \times \frac{₹\ 12,20,000}{₹\ (12,20,000 + 9,54,600 + 8,44,067)} = ₹\ 28,021 \text{ (approx.)}$$

In the absence of specific agreement amongst partners on the above subject matter, the representatives of the deceased partner can receive at their option, interest at the rate of 6% p.a. or share of profit earned from the amount due to the deceased partner.

In the above case, it would be rational to assume that A's executor would opt for ₹ 28,021.

(6) **Distribution of Profit for 2 Months ended 30th September, 2024**

		₹
Net Profit	$\left(₹\ 4,16,000 \times \frac{2}{12}\right)$	69,333
A's executor's share [See working note (5)]		28,021
B's share	$\left(₹\ 41,312 \times \frac{3}{5}\right)$	24,787
C's share	$\left(₹\ 41,312 \times \frac{2}{5}\right)$	16,525
		69,333

(7) **A'S EXECUTOR'S ACCOUNT**

(31-7-2024 to 1-10-2024)

	₹		₹
1-10-2024 To D's Capital A/c	12,48,021	31-7-2024 By A's Capital A/c	12,20,000
		1-10-2024 By Profit & Loss Suspense A/c (5)	28,021
	12,48,021		12,48,021

(8) **PARTNERS' CAPITAL ACCOUNTS**

(1st August, 2024 to 30th Sept., 2024)

	B	C		B	C
30-9-2024	₹	₹	1-8-2024	₹	₹
To Drawings			By Balance b/d	9,54,600	8,44,067
(for 2 months)	10,000	10,000	30-9-2024		
To Balance c/d	9,69,387	8,50,592	By P & L A/c(6)	24,787	16,525
	9,79,387	8,60,592		9,79,387	8,60,592

(9) ***Calculation of New Profit Sharing Ratio***

D's share $= \frac{1}{4}$

B's new share = 3/4 × 3/5 = 9/20

C's new ratio = 3/4 × 2/5 = 6/20

D's new share $= \frac{1}{4}$ or 5/20

New profit sharing ratio of B, C and D is 9 : 6 : 5.

(10) ***Distribution of Profits for 6 months from 1-10-2024 to 31-3-2025***

	₹
Net Profit for the year ending 31-3-2025	4,16,000
Net Profit for 6 months (assuming profit was earned uniformly throughout the year : ₹ 4,16,000 × $\frac{6}{12}$)	2,08,000
B's share $\left(₹\ 2,08,000 \times \frac{9}{20}\right)$	93,600
C's share $\left(₹\ 2,08,000 \times \frac{6}{20}\right)$	62,400
D's share $\left(₹\ 2,08,000 \times \frac{5}{20}\right)$	52,000
	2,08,000

AMALGAMATION OF FIRMS

Amalgamation of firms takes place when two or more firms working independently amalgamate themselves and in their place a new firm is formed to take over their businesses. This is done to avoid competition, to reduce unnecessary advertisement expenditure, to gain monopoly in the market, to have more capital and skill and to have internal and external economies of large scale production. As a result of the amalgamation, the partners of the old firms (*i.e.,* the firms which are amalgamated) become the partners of the new firm formed. Amalgamation of firms may be made possible by the following ways:

(*i*) When two or more sole traders decide to amalgamate to form a new partnership.

(*ii*) When one existing partnership firm absorbs a sole proprietorship.

(*iii*) When one existing partnership firm absorbs another partnership firm.

(*iv*) When two or more existing partnership firms amalgamate and form a new firm.

Objectives of Amalgamation of Firms

The objectives of amalgamation of firms are as follows :

1. **Economics of Large Scale Production.** Amalgamation of firms will provide more resources to use than individual firms. It will help in increasing the scale of operations and as a result advantages of a large scale firm can be availed.
2. **Avoiding Cut Throat Competition.** Amalgamation of two or more firms will be helpful in avoiding disastrous results of cut throat competition.
3. **Growth.** Growth or expansion is essential for the survival of a firm. A firm may not grow rapidly through internal expansion or growth. Merger of two or more firms enable satisfactory and balanced growth because of availability of large funds and superior management emerging from the amalgamation of firms.
4. **Better Financial Planning.** Amalgamated firms will be able to use their financial resources in a better way and overall profit may increase.
5. **Monopoly.** Two or more firms carrying on similar lines of business may amalgamate to have monopoly in a particular trade.
6. **Diversification.** Two or more firms operating in different lines can diversify their activities by amalgamating themselves. Amalgamation is a good method of bringing diversification because it will bring together the experiences of different firms specialising in different lines of activities.
7. **Economic Necessity.** Sometimes, Government may force two or more sick firms to merge themselves to improve their financial position and overall working.
8. **Liberalisation of the Indian Economy.** One of the reason of amalgamation of firms may be the liberalisation of the Indian economy. Liberalisation is forcing firms to merge themselves to increase the scale of operations so that they may face global competition successfully.
9. **Reduction in Expenses.** Amalgamation of firms will be helpful in reducing management and marketing expenses and there will be no duplication of fixed expenses.
10. **Utilisation of Tax Shields.** Amalgamation will be helpful in set off the accumulated losses of one firm against the future profit of the other firm and will enable the amalgamated firm to avail tax benefits.

Problems Connected with the Amalgamation of Firms

Following problems may arise when existing firms are amalgamated to form a new company:

(*a*) The new firm may take over some assets and liabilities at book value and some assets and liabilities at revised values.

(*b*) The new firm may not take over some assets and liabilities of the existing firms.

(*c*) The new firm may agree to pay some amount for the goodwill which may be more or less than the amount of goodwill, if any, already appearing in the books of the existing firms.

Accounting Treatment in the Books of the Amalgamating Firms

Following steps may be taken to close the books of the old firms :

(*i*) All assets and liabilities should be revalued in order to ascertain the true capital brought by each partner into the new firm. For this purpose each firm will prepare a Revaluation Account relating to its own assets and liabilities and profit or loss on revaluation will be transferred to the Partners' Capital Accounts in the profit sharing ratio. This revaluation is done in the same way as was done at the time of admission or retirement of a partner.

(*ii*) All reserves, profits and losses appearing in the Balance Sheets of old firms are transferred to the Partners' Capital Accounts in their profit sharing ratio.

(*iii*) If some assets and liabilities are not taken over by the new firm, these are closed by transfer to capital accounts of the partners in the ratio of their capitals and not in the profit sharing ratio. Division of assets and liabilities taken over by the partners is done in the ratio of capitals because it amounts to return or addition of Capital.

(*iv*) Goodwill, if valued, should be raised in the firm's books by passing necessary entries.

(*v*) New Firm's Account is debited with the difference of assets and liabilities taken over by passing the following entry :

New Firm's A/c Dr.
Liabilities A/c Dr.
To Assets A/c

Assets and liabilities are taken at revised values for the purpose of the above entry.

(*vi*) Partners' Capital Accounts (*i.e.* final amount due) are closed by transfer to the new firm's account by passing the following entry :

Partners' Capital A/cs Dr.
To New Firm's A/c

Books of the New Firm

Books of the new firm are opened by passing the following entries :

(*i*) Assets (taken over) Dr.
To Liabilities (taken over)
To Capital A/cs of the Partners
as calculated in step (*vi*) above.

(*ii*) Adjust capital accounts of the partners in the light of the requirements of the new firm such as a partner brings in capital or withdraws it ; entry for that is passed.

Where two or more existing proprietorship firms are amalgamated and form a new firm

ILLUSTRATION 32. Following were the Balance Sheets as at 31st March, 2025 of two firms M/s A and B and M/s C & D.

	A & B	*C & D*		*A & B*	*C & D*
	₹	₹		₹	₹
Creditors	3,000	25,000	Stock	50,000	75,000
Bills Payable	6,000	—	Debtors	30,000	45,000
Bank Overdraft	—	10,300	Premises	20,000	—
Capitals :			Plant & Machinery	5,000	20,000
A	50,000		Bank	1,500	—
B	50,000		Furniture	500	300
C		52,500	Defence Bonds	2,000	
D		52,500			
	1,09,000	1,40,300		1,09,000	1,40,300

The two firms decided to amalgamate their businesses as from 1st April, 2025. For this purpose it was agreed that the Premises and Plant and Machinery belonging to A and B should be taken over by the new firm M/s ABC & D at ₹ 25,000 and ₹ 10,000 respectively. C & D were to be credited with ₹ 5,000 for the value of certain patent rights they possessed, which became the property of the partnership and which were not included in their Balance Sheet. All the other assets were taken over at the values stated in the respective Balance Sheets, except the Defence Bonds belonging to A & B, which were not taken over. Both firms undertook to discharge their own liabilities, and it was agreed that A & B should introduce cash to make their capitals equal to that of C & D.

Pass the necessary Journal Entries in the books of the old firms and the Opening Entries in the books of M/s ABC & D. Prepare also Balance Sheet of the new firm.

SOLUTION

Books of M/s A and B

JOURNAL ENTRIES

			₹	₹
2025 April, 1	Plant and Machinery Account	Dr.	5,000	
	Premises Account	Dr.	5,000	
	To Revaluation Account			10,000
	(Being appreciation in the value of Plant and Machinery and Premises)			
April, 1	Revaluation Account	Dr.	10,000	
	To A's Capital Account			5,000
	To B's Capital Account			5,000
	(Being distribution of profit on revaluation between A and B)			
"	Creditors Account	Dr.	3,000	
	Bills Payable Account	Dr.	6,000	
	To A's Capital Account			4,500
	To B' Capital Account			4,500
	(Being transfer of liabilities not taken over by the new firm to the Capital Accounts of A and B)			
"	A's Capital Account	Dr.	1,000	
	B' Capital Account	Dr.	1,000	
	To Defence Bonds A/c			2,000
	(Being transfer of asset not taken over by the new firm to the Capital Accounts of A and B)			
April, 1	M/s A B C & D	Dr.	1,17,000	
	To Bank			1,500
	To Stock			50,000
	To Debtors			30,000
	To Premises			25,000
	To Plant and Machinery			10,000
	To Furniture			500
	(Being taking over of various assets by the firm)			
"	A's Capital Account	Dr.	58,500	
	B's Capital Account	Dr.	58,500	
	To M/s ABC & D			1,17,000
	(Being transfer of capital to new firm)			

Books of M/s C and D

JOURNAL ENTRIES

			₹	₹
2025 April, 1	Patent Rights Account	Dr.	5,000	
	To Revaluation Account			5,000
	(Being patent rights brought into accounts)			

Date	Particulars		Dr. ₹	Cr. ₹
April, 1	Revaluation Account	Dr.	5,000	
	To C's Capital Account			2,500
	To D's Capital Account			2,500
	(Being distribution of balance of revaluation between C and D)			
2025 April, 1	Creditors Account	Dr.	25,000	
	Bank Overdraft Account	Dr.	10,300	
	To C's Capital			17,650
	To D's Capital			17,650
	(Being transfer of liabilities not taken over to the Capital Accounts of C and D)			
April, 1	M/s A B C & D	Dr.	1,45,300	
	To Stock			75,000
	To Debtors			45,000
	To Plant and Machinery			20,000
	To Patents			5,000
	To Furniture			300
	(Being taking over of various assets by the new firm of M/s A B C & D)			
April, 1	C's Capital Account	Dr.	72,650	
	D's Capital Account	Dr.	72,650	
	To M/s A B C & D			1,45,300
	(Being transfer of Capital Accounts to new firm)			

Books of M/s A B C & D
JOURNAL ENTRIES

Date	Particulars		₹	₹
2025 April, 1	Bank Account	Dr.	1,500	
	Stock Account	Dr.	50,000	
	Debtors Account	Dr.	30,000	
	Premises Account	Dr.	25,000	
	Plant and Machinery Account	Dr.	10,000	
	Furniture Account	Dr.	500	
	To A's Capital Account			58,500
	To B's Capital Account			58,500
	(Being taking over of Assets of A and B)			
2025 April, 1	Stock Account	Dr.	75,000	
	Debtors Account	Dr.	45,000	
	Plant and Machinery Account	Dr.	20,000	
	Patents Account	Dr.	5,000	
	Furniture Account	Dr.	300	
	To C's Capital Account			72,650
	To D's Capital Account			72,650
	(Being taking over of Assets of C and D)			
"	Bank Account	Dr.	28,300	
	To A's Capital Account			14,150
	To B's Capital Account			14,150
	(Being introduction of cash by A and B to make their capitals equal to C and D)			

BALANCE SHEET OF M/s A B C & D

as at 1st April, 2025

Liabilities		₹	Assets	₹
Capital Accounts :	₹		Cash at Bank	29,800
A	72,650		Sundry Debtors	75,000
B	72,650		Stock	1,25,000
C	72,650		Patents Rights	5,000
D	72,650		Furniture and Fixtures	800
		2,90,600	Plant and Machinery	30,000
			Premises	25,000
		2,90,600		2,90,600

ILLUSTRATION 33. X and Y are partners of X & Co. sharing profits and losses in the ratio of 3 : 1 and Y and Z are partners of Y & Co. sharing profits and losses in the ratio of 2 : 1.

On 31st March, 2025, they decide to amalgamate and form a new firm M/s X Y Z & Co. wherein X, Y and Z would be partners sharing profits and losses in the ratio of 3 : 2 : 1.

Balance Sheets of the two firms on the above date were as under :

Liabilities	*X & Co.*	*Y & Co.*	*Assets*	*X & Co.*	*Y & Co.*
	₹	₹		₹	₹
Capitals :			*Fixed Assets* :		
X	4,80,000	—	Building	1,00,000	—
Y	3,20,000	4,00,000	Machinery	3,00,000	3,20,000
Z	—	2,00,000	Furniture	40,000	12,000
Reserves	1,00,000	3,00,000	Current Assets :		
Creditors	2,40,000	2,32,000	Stock	2,40,000	2,80,000
Due to X & Co.	—	2,00,000	Debtors	3,20,000	4,00,000
Bank Loan	1,60,000	—	Cash at Bank	60,000	1,80,000
			Cash in hand	40,000	20,000
			Due from Y & Co.	2,00,000	—
			Advances	—	1,20,000
	13,00,000	13,32,000		13,00,000	13,32,000

The amalgamated firm took over the business on the following terms :

(*a*) Building of X & Co. was valued at ₹ 2,00,000.

(*b*) Machinery of X & Co. was valued at ₹ 4,50,000 and that of Y & Co. at ₹ 4,00,000.

(*c*) Goodwill valued X & Co. ₹ 1,00,000 and Y & Co. ₹ 82,000 but the same will not appear in the books of XYZ & Co.

(*d*) Partners of the new firm will bring necessary cash to pay other partners to adjust their capitals according to the profit sharing ratio.

Show Journal Entries in the books of M/s XYZ & Co. and prepare Balance Sheet as on 31-3-2025.

SOLUTION

In the Books of M/s XYZ & Co.
JOURNAL ENTRIES

2025			₹	₹
March 31	Goodwill A/c Dr.		1,00,000	
	Building A/c Dr.		2,00,000	
	Machinery A/c Dr.		4,50,000	
	Furniture A/c Dr.		40,000	
	Stock A/c Dr.		2,40,000	
	Debtors A/c Dr.		3,20,000	
	Bank A/c Dr.		60,000	
	Cash A/c Dr.		40,000	
	Due from Y & Co. A/c Dr.		2,00,000	
	To Creditors A/c			2,40,000
	To Bank Loan A/c			1,60,000
	To X's Capital A/c (1)			8,17,500
	To Y's Capital A/c (1)			4,32,500
	(Being assets and liabilities of X & Co. taken over)			
March 31	Goodwill A/c Dr.		82,000	
	Machinery A/c Dr.		4,00,000	
	Furniture A/c Dr.		12,000	
	Stock A/c Dr.		2,80,000	
	Debtors A/c Dr.		4,00,000	
	Bank A/c Dr.		1,80,000	
	Cash A/c Dr.		20,000	
	Advances A/c Dr.		1,20,000	
	To Creditors A/c			2,32,000
	To Due to X & Co. A/c			2,00,000
	To Y's Capital Account (2)			7,08,000
	To Z' Capital A/c (2)			3,54,000
	(Being assets and liabilities of Y & Co. taken over)			
March 31	X's Capital A/c Dr.		91,000	
	Y's Capital A/c Dr.		60,667	
	Z's Capital A/c Dr.		30,333	
	To Goodwill A/c			1,82,000
	(Being goodwill written off in the ratio of 3 : 2 : 1)			
March 31	Bank A/c Dr.		3,69,833	
	To X's Capital A/c (3)			3,38,500
	To Z's Capital A/c (3)			31,333
	(Being cash brought in by X and Z to make capital proportionate)			
March 31	Y's Capital A/c (3) Dr.		3,69,833	
	To Bank A/c			3,69,833
	(Being excess capital withdrawn)			
" 31	Due to X & Co. Dr.		2,00,000	
	To Due from Y & Co.			2,00,000
	(Being elimination of mutual items of the merged firms X & Co. and Y & Co.)			

BALANCE SHEET OF M/S X Y Z CO.
as at March 31, 2025

Liabilities	₹	*Assets*	₹
Capital Accounts :		Building	2,00,000
X	10,65,000	Machinery	8,50,000
Y	7,10,000	Furniture	52,000
Z	3,55,000	Stock	5,20,000
Creditors	4,72,000	Debtors	7,20,000
Bank Loan	1,60,000	Advances	1,20,000
		Cash at Bank	2,40,000
		Cash in hand	60,000
	27,62,000		27,62,000

Working Notes :

(1) **CAPITAL ACCOUNTS (In the Books of X & Co.)**

	X	Y		X	Y
	₹	₹		₹	₹
To Capital A/c—M/s XYZ & Co. (Transfer)	8,17,500	4,32,500	By Balance b/d	4,80,000	3,20,000
			By Reserves	75,000	25,000
			By Goodwill	75,000	25,000
			By Revaluation A/c (Profit on Revaluation of Building & Machinery)	1,87,500	62,500
	8,17,500	4,32,500		8,17,500	4,32,500

(2) **CAPITAL ACCOUNTS (In the Books of Y & Co.)**

	Y	Z		Y	Z
	₹	₹		₹	₹
To Capital A/c—M/s XYZ & Co. (Transfer)	7,08,000	3,54,000	By Balance b/d	4,00,000	2,00,000
			By Reserves	2,00,000	1,00,000
			By Goodwill	54,667	27,333
			By Revaluation A/c (Profit on Revaluation of Machinery)	53,333	26,667
	7,08,000	3,54,000		7,08,000	3,54,000

(3) ***Calculation of Capital Adjustments***

	X	Y	Z	*Total Capital of All Partners*
	₹	₹	₹	₹
Capital transferred from X & Co.	8,17,500	4,32,500	—	
Capital transferred from Y & Co.	—	7,08,000	3,54,000	
	8,17,500	11,40,500	3,54,000	
Less : Goodwill written off in new ratio of 3 : 2 : 1	91,000	60,667	30,333	
(*a*)	7,26,500	10,79,833	3,23,667	21,30,000

Proportionate Capital according to ratio of 3 : 2 : 1. (b)	10,65,000	7,10,000	3,55,000	21,30,000
Amount to be brought in to make proportionate capital (b) – (a)	3,38,500	—	31,333	
Amount to be withdrawn to make proportionate capital (a) – (b)	—	3,69,833	—	

ILLUSTRATION 34. A and B are partners of AB & Co. sharing profits and losses in the ratio of 2 : 1 and C and D are partners of CD & Co. sharing profits and losses in the ratio of 3 : 2. On 1st April 2025, they decided to *amalgamate and form a new firm* M/s AD & Co. wherein all the partners of both the firms would be partners sharing profits and losses in he ratio of 2 : 1 : 3 : 2 respectively to A, B, C and D.

Their Balance Sheets on that date were as under :

Liabilties	*AB & Co.* (₹)	*CD & Co.* (₹)	*Assets*	*AB & Co.* (₹)	*CD & Co.* (₹)
Capitals :			Building	75,000	90,000
A	1,50,000		Machinery	1,20,000	1,00,000
B	1,00,000		Furniture	15,000	12,000
C		1,20,000	Stock	24,000	36,000
D		80,000	Debtors	65,000	78,000
Reserves	66,000	54,000	Due from CD & Co.	47,000	
Coeditors	52,000	35,000	Cash at Bank	18,000	15,000
Due to AB & Co.		47,000	Cash in hand	4,000	5,000
	3,68,000	3,36,000		3,68,000	3,36,000

The amalgamated firm took over the business on the following terms :

(*a*) Building was taken over at ₹ 1,00,000 and ₹ 1,25,000 of AB & Co. and CD & Co. respectively and machinery was taken over at ₹ 1,25,000 and ₹ 1,10,000 of AB & Co. and CD & Co. respectively.

(*b*) Goodwill of AB & Co. was worth ₹ 75,000 and that of CD & Co. was worth ₹ 50,000. Goodwill Account was not to be opened in the books of the new firm, the adjustments being recorded through Capital Accounts of the partners.

(*c*) Provision of doubtful debts has to be carried forward at ₹ 5,000 in respect of debtors of AB & Co. and ₹ 8,000 in respect of CD & Co.

You are required :

(*i*) Compute the adjustments necessary for goodwill.

(*ii*) Pass the Journal Entries in the books of AD & Co. assuming that excess/deficit capital (taking D's capital as base) with reference to share in profits are to be transferred to Current Accounts.

(CA, IPCE May, 2010 Modified)

SOLUTION

(*i*) **ADJUSTMENT FOR RAISING & WRITING OFF OF GOODWILL**

	Goodwill raised in old profit sharing ratio			*Goodwill written off in new ratio*	*Difference*
	AB & Co. ₹	*CD & Co.* ₹	*Total* ₹	*AD & Co.* ₹	₹
A	50,000		50,000 Cr.	31,250 Dr.	18,750 Cr.
B	25,000		25,000 Cr.	15,625 Dr.	9,375 Cr.
C		30,000	30,000 Cr.	46,875 Dr.	16,875 Dr.
D		20,000	20,000 Cr.	31,250 Dr.	11,250 Dr.
	75,000	50,000	1,25,000	1,25,000	

(*ii*) **In the Books of AD & Co.**

JOURNAL ENTRIES

Date	Particulars		Debit	Credit
2025			₹	₹
April 1	Building A/c	Dr.	1,00,000	
	Machinery A/c	Dr.	1,25,000	
	Furniture A/c	Dr.	15,000	
	Stock A/c	Dr.	24,000	
	Debtors A/c	Dr.	65,000	
	CD & Co. A/c	Dr.	47,000	
	Cash at Bank A/c	Dr.	18,000	
	Cash in Hand A/c	Dr.	4,000	
	To Provision for Doubtful Debts A/c			5,000
	To Creditors A/c			52,000
	To A's Capital A/c (2a)			2,10,667
	To B's Capital A/c (2a)			1,30,333
	(Being the sundry assets and liabilities of AB & Co. taken over at the values stated as per the agreement)			
	Building A/c	Dr.	1,25,000	
	Machinery A/c	Dr.	1,10,000	
	Furniture A/c	Dr.	12,000	
	Stock A/c	Dr.	36,000	
	Debtors A/c	Dr.	78,000	
	Cash at Bank A/c	Dr.	15,000	
	Cash in Hand A/c	Dr.	5,000	
	To Provision for Doubtful Debts A/c			8,000
	To Creditors A/c			35,000
	To AB & Co. A/c			47,000
	To C's Capital A/c (2b)			1,74,600
	To D's Capital A/c (2b)			1,16,400
	(Being the sundry assets and liabilities of CD & Co. taken over at the values stated as per the agreement)			
	C's Capital A/c	Dr.	16,875	
	D's Capital A/c	Dr.	11,250	
	To A's Capital A/c			18,750
	To B's Capital A/c			9,375
	(Being adjustment in Capital Accounts of the partners on account of goodwill)			
	AB & Co. A/c	Dr.	47,000	
	To CD & Co. A/c			47,000
	(Being mutual indebtedness of AB & Co. and CD & Co. cancelled)			
	A's Capital A/c	(4) Dr.	1,24,267	
	To A's Current A/c			1,24,267
	(Being excess amount in A's Capital A/c transferred to A's Current A/c)			
	B's Capital A/c	(4) Dr.	87,133	
	To B's Current A/c			87,133
	(Being excess amount in B's Capital A/c transferred to B's Current A/c) (3)			

Working Notes :

(1) PROFIT ON REVALUATION

		AB & Co. ₹	CD & Co. ₹
Building	(₹ 1,00,000 – ₹ 75,000)	25,000	
	(₹ 1,25,000 – ₹ 90,000)		35,000
Machinery	(₹ 1,25,000 – ₹ 1,20,000)	5,000	
	(₹ 1,10,000 – ₹ 1,00,000)		10,000
		30,000	45,000
Less : Provision for Doubtful Debts		(5,000)	(8,000)
		25,000	37,000

(2) BALANCE OF CAPITAL ACCOUNTS OF PARTNERS ON TRANSFER OF BUSINESS TO AD & CO.

(*a*) AB & Co.

	A's Capital ₹	B's Capital ₹
Balance as per the Balance Sheet	1,50,000	1,00,000
Reserves in the Profit and Loss Sharing Ratio	44,000	22,000
Profit on Revaluation in the Profit and Loss Sharing Ratio (1)	16,667	8,333
	2,10,667	1,30,333

(*b*) CD & Co.

	C's Capital ₹	D's Capital ₹
Balance as per the Balance Sheet	1,20,000	80,000
Reserves in the Profit and Loss Sharing Ratio	32,400	21,600
Profit on Revaluation in the Profits and Loss sharing Ratio (1)	22,200	14,800
	1,74,600	1,16,400

(3) CALCULATION OF ADJUSTMENT FOR GOODWILL

	A's Capital ₹	B's Capital ₹	C's Capital ₹	D's Capital ₹
Adjustment for Goodwill in the Old Ratio of 2 : 1 & 3 :2	50,000 Cr.	25,000 Cr.	30,000 Cr.	20,000 Cr.
Adjustment for Total Goodwill of 1,25,000 for writing off in the New Ratio of 2 : 1 : 3 : 2	31,250 Dr.	15,625 Dr.	46,875 Dr.	31,250 Dr.
Net Adjustment	18,750 Cr.	9,375 Cr.	16,875 Dr.	11,250 Dr.

(4) CALCULATION OF CAPITAL OF EACH PARTNER IN THE NEW FIRM

Particulars		A ₹	B ₹	C ₹	D ₹
Balance as per (2)		2,10,667	1,30,333	1,74,600	1,16,400
Adjustment for Goodwill	(3)	18,750	9,375	(16,875)	(11,250)
		2,29,417	1,39,708	1,57,725	1,05,150
Total Capital ₹ 4,20,600 (*i.e.* 1,05,150 × 8/2 (*i.e.* ₹ 4,20,600) in the New Ratio of 2 : 1 : 3 : 2		(1,05,150)	(52,575)	(1,57,725)	(1,05,150)
Transfer to Current Account		1,24,267 Cr.	87,133 Cr.	—	—

ILLUSTRATION 35. Firm X & Co. consists of partners A and B sharing Profits and Losses in the ratio of 3 : 2. Firm Y & Co. consists of partners B and C sharing Profits and Losses in the ratio of 5 : 3.

On 31st March, 2025 it was decided to amalgamate both the firms and form a new firm XY & Co., wherein A, B and C would be partners sharing Profits and Losses in the ratio of 4 : 5 : 1.

BALANCE SHEETS
as at 31-3-2025

Liabilities	*X & Co.*	*Y & Co.*	*Assets*	*X & Co.*	*Y & Co.*
Capitals :			Cash in Hand/Bank	40,000	30,000
A	1,50,000	—	Debtors	60,000	80,000
B	1,00,000	75,000	Stock	50,000	20,000
C	—	50,000	Vehicles	—	90,000
Reserve	50,000	40,000	Machinery	1,20,000	—
Creditors	1,20,000	55,000	Building	1,50,000	—
	4,20,000	2,20,000		4,20,000	2,20,000

Following were the terms of amalgamation :

(*i*) Goodwill of X & Co. was valued at ₹ 75,000. Goodwill of Y & Co. was valued at ₹ 40,000. Goodwill account not to be opened in the books of the new firm but adjusted through the Capital accounts of the partners.

(*ii*) Building, Machinery and Vehicles are to be taken over at ₹ 2,00,000. ₹ 1,00,000 and ₹ 74,000 respectively.

(*iii*) Provision for doubtful debts at ₹ 5,000 in respect of X & Co. and ₹ 4,000 in respect Y & Co. are to be provided.

You are required to :

(*i*) Show, how the Goodwill value is adjusted amongst the partners.

(*ii*) Prepare Balance Sheet of XY & Co. as at 31-3-2025 by keeping partners Capitals in their profit sharing ratio by taking capital of 'B' as the basis. The excess or deficiency to be kept in the respective Partners' Current accounts.

SOLUTION

(*i*) ADJUSTMENT FOR RAISING AND WRITING OFF OF GOODWILL

	Raised in old profit sharing ratio		*Total*	*Written off in new ratio*	*Difference*
	X & Co. (3 : 2)	*Y & Co. (5 : 3)*			
	₹	₹	₹	₹	₹
A	45,000	—	45,000 Cr.	46,000 Dr.	1,000 Dr.
B	30,000	25,000	55,000 Cr.	57,500 Dr.	2,500 Dr.
C	—	15,000	15,000 Cr.	11,500 Dr.	3,500 Cr.
	75,000	40,000	1,15,000	1,15,000	Nil

(*ii*) BALANCE SHEET OF XY & CO. (NEW FIRM)
as on 31-3-2025

Liabilities		₹	*Assets*	₹
Capital A/cs :			Vehicles	74,000
A	(2)	1,72,000	Machinery	1,00,000
B	(2)	2,15,000	Building	2,00,000
C	(2)	43,000	Stock	70,000

		₹		₹
Current A/cs :			Debtors	1,31,000
A	(2)	22,000	Cash & Bank	70,000
C	(2)	18,000		
Creditors		1,75,000		
		6,45,000		6,45,000

Working Notes :

(1) ***Balance of Capital Accounts at the Time of Amalgamation of Firms***

X & Co. (Profit & Loss Sharing Ratio 3 : 2)	*A's Capital*	*B's Capital*
	₹	₹
Balance as per Balance Sheet	1,50,000	1,00,000
Add : Reserves	30,000	20,000
Revaluation Profit (Building)	30,000	20,000
Less : Revaluation Loss (Machinery)	(12,000)	(8,000)
Provision for Doubtful Debts	(3,000)	(2,000)
	1,95,000	1,30,000

Y & Co. (Profit & Loss Sharing Ratio 5 : 3)	*B's Capital*	*C's Capital*
	₹	₹
Balance as per Balance Sheet	75,000	50,000
Add : Reserves	25,000	15,000
Less : Revaluation Loss (Vehicle)	(10,000)	(6,000)
Provision for Doubtful Debts	(2,500)	(1,500)
	87,500	57,500

(2) ***Balance of Capital Accounts in the Balance Sheet of the New Firm as on 31-3-2025***

	A	*B*	*C*
	₹	₹	₹
Balance b/d : X & Co.	1,95,000	1,30,000	—
Y & Co.	—	87,500	57,500
	1,95,000	2,17,500	57,500
Adjustment for Goodwill	(1,000)	(2,500)	3,500
	1,94,000	2,15,000	61,000
Total Capital ₹ 4,30,000 (B's Capital *i.e.* ₹ 2,15,000 × 2) to be Contributed in 4 : 5 : 1 Ratio	1,72,000	2,15,000	43,000
Transfer to Current Account	22,000	—	18,000

QUESTIONS

OBJECTIVE TYPE

1. **In each of the following cases indicate the *alternative* which you consider to be correct.**

(*a*) On the admission of a partner if the goodwill is raised at full value, it should be debited to—(*i*) cash account ; (*ii*) old partners' capital accounts ; (*iii*) goodwill account.

(*b*) If assets and liabilities are adjusted at the time of admission of a partner and profit is resulted, it should be credited to the capital accounts of—(*i*) all partners in their new profit sharing ratio ; (*ii*) the old partners in their new profit sharing ratio ; (*iii*) the old partners in their old profit sharing ratio.

(*c*) A and B are partners sharing profits in the ratio of 3 : 2. C is admitted paying a premium of ₹ 2,000 for 1/4th share of profit. B will get—(*i*) ₹ 800 ; (*ii*) ₹ 500 ; (*iii*) ₹ 1,200.

(*d*) Any amount to be written off after the admission of a partner is transferred to the capital accounts of all partners in—(*i*) their capital ratio ; (*ii*) new profit sharing ratio ; (*iii*) old profit sharing ratio.

(*e*) In the case of retirement of a partner, goodwill at its full value is credited to the account/accounts of—(*i*) only retiring partner, (*ii*) all partners, (*iii*) only remaining partners.

(*f*) In the case of retirement of a partner, profit on revaluation is credited to the capital accounts of the partners—(*i*) equally, (*ii*) in their profit sharing ratio, (*iii*) in proportion to their capitals.

(*g*) When any partner retires or dies and the remaining partners carry on the business with the firm's property without any final settlement of accounts, the outgoing partner or executors of the deceased partner are entitled to :

(*i*) Interest at 6% p.a. of the amount due to the retiring partners or executors of the deceased partner; (*ii*) such share of the profits as may be attributable to the use of the amount due ; (*iii*) either of the above two at the option of the outgoing partner or executors of the deceased partner.

(*h*) Revaluation Account is a—

(*i*) Nominal Account (*ii*) Real Account
(*iii*) Personal Account (*iv*) None of the above.

(*i*) At the time of admission of new partner, reserves and undistributed profits are credited to Old Partners' Capital Accounts in—

(*i*) Old profit-sharing ratio (*ii*) New profit-sharing ratio
(*iii*) The ratio of sacrifice (*iv*) The ratio of gain.

(*j*) Goodwill brought in by an incoming partner in cash to join a partnership firm is shared by the old partners in their—

(*i*) Ratio of capitals (*ii*) New profit sharing ratio
(*iii*) Ratio of sacrifice (*iv*) Old profit sharing ratio.

(*k*) If partnership deed is silent on the point, interest allowed on Partners' Capital Accounts will be —

(*i*) @ 6% per annum (*ii*) @ 5% per annum
(*iii*) @ 8% per annum (*iv*) Nil.

(*l*) The maximum number of partners in a non-banking partnership firm can be—

(*i*) Ten (*ii*) Twenty
(*iii*) Fifty (*iv*) Seven.

(*m*) To provide funds to pay to the deceased partner's heirs in case of death of a partner, the partners generally—

(*i*) Create a sinking fund (*ii*) Take a joint life policy
(*iii*) Create a reserve fund (*iv*) Open a separate bank account.

(*n*) Incoming partner does not pay for goodwill but the Goodwill A/c is raised and credited in

(*i*) Old profit sharing ratio (*ii*) New profit sharing ratio

(*iii*) Sacrifice ratio (*iv*) Gaining ratio.

(*o*) In the absence of an agreement amongst the partners, loan given by a partner to the firm will be at an interest at the rate of

(*i*) 5% (*ii*) 6%

(*iii*) 8% (*iv*) 10%.

Ans. [(*a*) (*iii*) ; (*b*) (*iii*) ; (*c*) (*i*) ; (*d*) (*ii*) ; (*e*) (*ii*) ; (*f*) (*ii*) ; (*g*) (*iii*) ; (*h*) (*i*); (*i*) (*i*); (*j*) (*iii*); (*k*) (*iv*); (*l*) (*ii*); (*m*) (*ii*); (*n*) (*i*); (*o*) (*ii*)].

2. Indicate whether the following statements are True or False :

(*a*) Revaluation account is opened in each firm's books for revaluation of assets and liabilities when amalgamation of firms takes place.

(*b*) If some assets and liabilities are not taken over by the new firm, these should be transferred to the capital accounts of the partners in their profit sharing ratio.

(*c*) Final amount due to partners is closed by transfer to the new firm's account which is formed by amalgamation of firms.

(*d*) A joint stock company converts itself into a partnership firm to get the advantages of limited liability.

(*e*) Shares and debentures received from the purchasing company are distributed amongst partners in the ratio of their final amount due in the absence of an agreement.

(*f*) In the case of sale of a firm to a company the profit or loss on sale is ascertained through a revaluation account.

(*g*) Realisation accounts are prepared to close the books of the amalgamated firms.

(*h*) Partnership deed is different from partnership agreement.

Ans. [True : (*a*), (*c*), (*e*), (*h*) False (*b*), (*d*), (*f*), (*g*)].

3. Fill in the blanks :

(*a*) Current accounts of the partners should be opened when the capitals are........

(*b*) In the absence of a partnership deed, profits and losses are divided by partners......

(*c*) In the absence of an agreement, interest on partner's loan shall be paid @......

(*d*) In the absence of an agreement, partners shall......salaries.

(*e*) A, B and C share profits and losses in the ratio of 1/2, 1/3 and 1/6 respectively. D, a new partner, is given 1/8 share. Then the new profit sharing ratio will be......

(*f*) A and B are equal partners. They admit C and D as partners with $\frac{1}{5}$ and $\frac{1}{6}$ share respectively. Then the new ratio will be...................

(*g*) A partner admitted into the partnership firm acquires two rights *i.e.* (*i*) the right to share in the assets of the partnership and (*ii*) the right to share......

(*h*) Revaluation account is a......account.

(*i*) Th balance of revaluation account is transferred to the old partners' capital accounts in their......

(*j*) Goodwill is an......asset.

(*k*) The amount of goodwill received in cash from a new partner is transferred to the old partners capital accounts......

(*l*) At the time of admission of a new partner, if the value of goodwill is overstated in the books, it is written back by......

(*m*) A...........partner does not have liability to share the loss incurred by a firm.

Ans. [(*a*) fixed ; (*b*) equally ; (*c*) 6% p.a. ; (*d*) not be paid ; (*e*) 7/16, 7/24, 7/48, 1 /8, (*f*) 19 : 19 : 12 : 10 ; (*g*) in the profits of the business ; (*h*) nominal account; (*i*) old profit sharing ratio; (*j*) intangible; (*k*) in their sacrificing ratio; (*l*) debiting the excess amount to the old partners' capital accounts in their old profit sharing ratio and crediting goodwill account accordingly ; (*m*) minor].

SHORT ANSWER TYPE

1. Give the meaning and definition of partnership.
2. Explain the essential features of partnership.
3. Define partnership deed.
4. Give the provisions of Partnership Act applicable to accounts in the absence of agreement.
5. How will you deal with the following terms while preparing partnership accounts?
   (*i*) Interest on Capital. (*ii*) Interest or Drawings. (*iii*) Salary/Commission to a partner. (*iv*) Interest on loan advanced to a partner.
6. Distinguish between fixed capital accounts and fluctuating capital accounts.
7. Explain the necessity of partners' current accounts.
8. Why are adjustments necessary after closing the partnership accounts ?
9. Give the meaning of the term "Minimum Guaranteed Profit".
10. Enumerate the main points which usually require attention at the time of admission of a partner.
11. Enumerate the cases that may arise while calculating the new profit sharing ratio.
12. What is Memorandum Revaluation Account ? What purpose does it serve ?
13. Distinguish between Revaluation Account and Memorandum Revaluation Account.
14. Define Goodwill.
15. Enumerate the factors that affect the Valuation of Goodwill.
16. State the circumstances under which goodwill of a partnership firm may have to be valued.
17. Enumerate the different methods used for valuation of goodwill.
18. Explain the super profit method of valuation of goodwill of a partnership firm.
19. Give the meaning of sacrificing ratio at the time of admission of a partner.
20. Distinguish between sacrificing and gaining ratios.
21. Enumerate the various methods of recording goodwill in partnership book on the admission of a partner.
22. How will you adjust the undistributed profits and losses appearing in the Balance Sheet of the firm at the time of admission of a partner ?
23. How will you adjust the capital accounts of the partners at the time of admission of a partner on the basis of a new partner ?
24. How capital accounts of partners are adjusted when the new partner is required to bring in the amount of capital in proportion to his share in the firm ?
25. Distinguish between admission and retirement of a partner.
26. Enumerate the main points which require attention in case of retirement of a partner.
27. Name three methods of dealing with the Joint Life Policy.
28. A, B and C are partners in a firm sharing profits and losses in the ratio of 4 : 3 : 2. B decides to retire from the firm. Calculate the new profit sharing ratio of A and C in the following circumstances:
   (*i*) If B gives his share to A and C in the original ratios of A and C. (*ii*) If B gives his share to A and C in equal proportion. (*iii*) If B gives his share to A and C in the ratio of 3 : 1. (*iv*) If B gives his share to A only.

Ans. [(*i*) 2 : 1 ; (*ii*) 11 : 7 ; (*iii*) 25 : 11 ; (*iv*) 7 : 2]

LONG ANSWER TYPE

1. Write short notes on : (*a*) Essential features of a partnership. (*b*) Partnership deed. (*c*) Fixed and fluctuating capitals.
2. What clauses should be inserted in a partnership deed to avoid any future dispute among the partners ? Give illustrations.
3. Explain the rules applicable, in absence of an agreement among the partners, for proper accounting of the partnership firm.
4. Explain : (*a*) Revaluation Account and (*b*) Memorandum Revaluation Account.
5. Define goodwill and state the factors upon which it depends and the methods which may be adopted to evaluate it. How it is treated on the admission of a partner ?
6. How will you treat the following items ?
   (*a*) When goodwill appears in the books at partial amount and the new partner brings his share of goodwill in cash.
   (*b*) When goodwill appears in the books at partial amount and the new partner does not bring his share of goodwill in cash.
   (*c*) When goodwill appears in the books at partial amount and the new partner brings in cash only a part of the total amount of his share of goodwill.
7. Define goodwill and explain its treatment in the books of account on admission of a new partner,
   (*a*) when no goodwill account appears in the books and the new partner brings cash for his share of goodwill and
   (*b*) when goodwill account appears in the books at its full value and the new partner brings cash for his share of goodwill.
8. Why is it necessary to make adjustments in the book value of assets and liabilities at the time of admission of a partner ? Give journal entries that have to be passed regarding this aspect.
9. (*a*) Explain briefly various methods of valuation of Goodwill.
   (*b*) Give the treatment of goodwill at the time of admission of a partner when: (*i*) Goodwill raised. (*ii*) Goodwill raised and written-off. Give a practical example to explain the above mentioned circumstances.
10. How is goodwill treated in the books of accounts on the retirement of a partner ?
11. What are the objectives of taking a joint life policy by the partnership firm ? Describe the various methods of treatment of joint life policy in the books of account.
12. What clauses should be inserted in a partnership deed in order to avoid any dispute on retirement or death of a partner ? Give illustrations.
13. What do you mean by amalgamation of firms ? What entries are passed to close the books of the firms which are amalgamated ?
14. How will you treat assets and liabilities not taken over by the new firms in the books of the amalgamated firms?

PRACTICAL PROBLEMS

APPROPRIATION OF PROFIT

1. A, B and C are in partnership and during the year 2025 earn ₹ 83,000, A and B are entitled to 5% per annum interest on their capitals of ₹ 60,000 and ₹ 1,00,000 respectively ; while C, who has no capital in the firm is entitled to a salary of ₹ 12,000 per annum. C is also entitled to a commission of 5% on the profits after charging interest, salary and commission.

   It is further agreed that the residue of profits should be appropriated as to 20% for a charity fund and the balance shared equally by A and B.

Prepare Profit and Loss Appropriation Account and Partners' Capital and Current Accounts for the year 2025, if the drawings of the partners during the year were : A ₹ 10,000 ; B ₹ 9,000 ; C ₹ 13,000.

Ans. [Profit ₹ 48,000 : Current A/cs Balances : A—₹ 17,000 ; B—₹ 20,000 ; C—₹ 2,000].

2. A, B and C are in partnership with respective fixed capitals of ₹ 40,000, ₹ 30,000 and ₹ 20,000. B and C are entitled to annual salaries of ₹ 2,000 and ₹ 1,500 respectively payable before division of profits. Interest on capital is allowed at 5 per cent per annum, but interest is not charged on drawings. Of the first ₹ 12,000 divisible as profit in any year, A is entitled to 50 per cent, B to 30 per cent and C to 20 per cent. Annual profits in excess of ₹ 12,000 are divisible equally. The profit for the year ended 31st December, 2024 was ₹ 20,100 after debiting partners salaries but before charging interest on capitals. The partners drawings for the year were : A ₹ 8,000, B ₹ 7,500 and C ₹ 4,000. The balance on the partners' current accounts on 1st January 2024 were—A ₹ 3,000 credit; B ₹ 500 credit ; C ₹ 1,000 debit.

Prepare Profit and Loss Appropriation Account and the Partners' Current Accounts for the year 2024.

Ans. [Profit ₹ 15,600 ; Current Accounts Balances : A—₹ 4,200 ; B—₹ 1,300 ; C—₹ 1,100].

3. On 1st July, 2024, L, M and N commence a business in partnership. L puts in ₹ 60,000 at first but withdraws ₹ 20,000 at the end of six months. M introduces ₹ 50,000 at first and increases it to ₹ 60,000 at the end of four months but withdraws ₹ 20,000 at the end of eight months. N brings in ₹ 50,000 at first but increases it by ₹ 40,000 at the end of seven months.

During the year ended 30th June, 2025 they make a net profit of ₹ 45,000. Show how the partners should divide the amount on the basis of the effective capital employed by each partner.

Ans. [Profit : ₹ 45,000 ; Profit sharing ratio of L, M and N = 3 : 3 : 4].

4. A and B were equal partners but owing to the special ability of A it was agreed that B should, out of his share pay A a salary of ₹ 6,000 p.a. The accounts at 31st December, 2023 showed the following results:

Capital A (1-1-2023) ₹ 40,000 ; Capital B (1-1-2023) ₹ 50,000 ; Net Profit before charging interest on capital ₹ 31,000 ; Drawings A ₹ 7,000 ; Drawings B ₹ 8,000 ; Paid by B to A in cash on account of salary ₹ 4,000.

For the year ending 31st December, 2024 upon similar lines, the figures are as follows:

Net Profit ₹ 34,600 ; Drawings A ₹ 7,500 ; Drawings B ₹ 8,000 ; Paid by B to A in cash on account of salary ₹ 3,000 ;

After charging 10% p.a. interest on capital (disregarding interest on drawings and salary), write up the Capital Account of each partner for two years 2023 and 2024.

Ans. [Balances in Capital Accounts : A ₹ 62,500 ; B ₹ 62,600]

PAST ADJUSTMENTS AND GUARANTEES

5. XYZ & Co. is a partnership concern, having three partners X, Y, Z. Their fixed Capital Accounts stood at ₹ 30,000, ₹ 15,000 and ₹ 15,000 respectively on 1st January, 2024.

Deed of partnership provided that :

(*a*) Z should be allowed a remuneration of ₹ 3,000 per annum.

(*b*) Interest @ 5 per cent per annum has to be allowed on Capital.

(*c*) Balance Profit/Loss is to be divided in the proportion of 2 : 2 : 1.

Ignoring the above terms, the profit of ₹ 18,000 for the year ended 31st December, 2024 is divided equally.

You are now required to pass the Journal Entry to rectify the error.

Ans. [Debit Y's Current A/c with ₹ 450 and Credit X's and Z's Current Accounts with ₹ 300 and ₹ 150 respectively].

6. Weak, Able and Lazy are in partnership sharing profits and losses in the ratio of 2 : 1 : 1. It is agreed that interest on capital will be allowed @ 5 per cent per annum and interest on drawings will be charged @ 4 per cent per annum. (No interest will be charged or allowed on current accounts).

Following are the particulars of the Capital, Current and Drawings Accounts of the partners :

	Weak	*Able*	*Lazy*
	₹	₹	₹
Capital (1-1-2024)	75,000	40,000	30,000
Current Account (1-1-2024)	10,000	5,000	5,000 (Dr.)
Drawings	15,000	10,000	10,000
Interest on Drawings (2024)	500	250	350

The draft accounts for 2024 showed a net profit of ₹ 60,000 before taking into account interest on capital and drawings and subject to following rectifications of errors :

(*a*) Life insurance premium of Weak amounting to ₹ 750 paid by the firm on 31st December, 2024 has been charged to Miscellaneous Expenditure A/c.

(*b*) Repairs of machinery amounting to ₹ 10,000 has been debited to Plant Account and depreciation thereon charged @ 20 per cent.

(*c*) Travelling expenses of ₹ 3,000 of Able for a pleasure trip to U.K. paid by the firm on 30th June, 2024 has been debited to Travelling Expenses A/c.

You are required to prepare the Profit and Loss Appropriation Account for the year ended 31st December, 2024 and the Partners' Current Accounts for the year.

Ans. [Profit ₹ 49,600 ; Balances in Current Accounts : Weak ₹ 22,300 (Cr.) ; Able ₹ 6,150 (Cr.) ; Lazy ₹ 1,450 (Dr.)]

7. Ram and Rahim are in partnership sharing profits and losses in the ratio of 3 : 2. As Ram on account of his advancing year's feels that he cannot work as hard as before, the chief clerk of the firm, Ratan, is admitted as a partner with effect from January 1, 2024 and becomes entitled to one tenth of the net profits and nothing else, the mutual ratio between Ram and Rahim remained unaltered.

Before becoming a partner, Ratan was getting a salary of ₹ 500 per month together with a commission of 4% of the net profits after deducting his salary and commission.

It is provided in the Partnership Deed that the share of Ratan's profit as partner in excess of the amount to which he would have been entitled if he had continued as the chief clerk, should be taken out of Ram's share of profit.

The net profit for the year ended December 31, 2024 amounted to ₹ 1,10,000.

You are required to prepare Profit and Loss Appropriation Account of the year ended 31st December, 2024.

Ans. [Ram ₹ 59,000 ; Rahim ₹ 40,000 and Ratan ₹ 11,000].

8. P, Q. and R were in partnership sharing profits and losses in the ratio of 6 : 3 : 1. They decided to take S into partnership with effect from 1st April, 2024 on the following terms and conditions :

(*i*) S is to bring in his proportionate share of goodwill in cash. Goodwill is not to be brought into the books but necessary adjustments are to be made in the old partners' capital accounts. (*ii*) Goodwill to be valued at 60% of the average annual profits of the previous three or four years whichever is the higher. (*iii*) The average profits for the purpose of goodwill for the past years, ending 31st March 2024, 2023, 2022 and 2021 were ₹ 48,300, ₹ 30,000, ₹ 31,200 and ₹ 42,200 respectively. (*iv*) The new profit sharing ratio between P, Q, R and S will be 3 : 3 : 3 : 1. (*v*) S should bring in ₹ 20,000 as capital. (*vi*) The new partner is to receive an annual salary of ₹ 12,000 in addition to his share of profit. R personally guaranteed that the aggregate of salary and share of profit of the new partner shall not be less than ₹ 25,000 per annum.

The draft accounts for the year ended 31st March, 2025 showed a profit of ₹ 1,32,800 before taking into account Salary of S.

Show the Journal Entries (including cash entries) passed at the time of admission of the partner and also the distribution of the net profit for the year ended 31st March, 2025, between the partners.

Ans. [Profit : P—₹ 36,240 ; Q—₹ 36,240 ; R—₹ 35,320 ; S—₹ 13,000].

9. Anju and Manju are in partnership sharing profits and losses in 7 : 3. As a mark of appreciation of the services of their Senior Officer Sreenjoy, they took him into partnership on January 1, 2024 giving him one-tenth share of the profits only. The mutual ratio between Anju and Manju remains unaltered.

Before becoming a partner, Sreenjoy was getting a salary of ₹ 4,000 per mensem and a commission of 5% on the net profits after charging his salary and commission.

It was also agreed that any excess over his former remuneration to which Sreenjoy as a partner becomes entitled is to be provided out of Anju's share of profit.

The net profits for the year ended December 31, 2024 amounted to ₹ 19,80,000. Prepare Profit and Loss Appropriation Account for the year ended December 31, 2024 showing the distribution of the net profits amongst the partners.

Ans. [Anju ₹ 12,30,000 ; Manju ₹ 5,52,000 ; Sreenjoy ₹ 1,98,000].

ADMISSION OF A PARTNER

10. Messrs A, B and C is a firm sharing profits and losses in the ratio of 2 : 2 : 1. Their Balance Sheet as on 31st March, 2025 is as below :

Liabilities		₹	*Assets*	₹
Sundry Creditors		12,850	Land and Buildings	25,000
Outstanding Liabilities		1,500	Furniture	6,500
General Reserve		6,500	Stock of Goods	11,750
Capital Accounts :			Sundry Debtors	5,500
	₹		Cash in hand	140
A	12,000		Cash at Bank	960
B	12,000			
C	5,000			
		29,000		
		49,850		49,850

The partners have agreed to take D as a partner with effect from 1st April, 2025 on the following terms :

(1) D shall bring ₹ 5,000 towards his capital. (2) The value of stock should be increased by ₹ 2,500. (3) Provision for bad and doubtful debts should be provided at 10% of the debtors. (4) The furniture depreciated by 10%. (5) The value of land and buildings should be enhanced by 20%. (6) The value of the goodwill is ₹ 15,000 and is to be adjusted through capital accounts. (7) General Reserve will be transferred to the Partners' Capital Accounts. (8) The new profit sharing ratio shall be—A 5/15 ; B 5/15 ; C 3/15 and D 2/15.

The outstanding liabilities include ₹ 1,000 due to E which has been paid by A. Necessary entries were not made in the books.

Prepare (*i*) Revaluation Account, (*ii*) Capital Accounts of the partners, and (*iii*) Balance Sheet of the firm as newly constituted (Journal entries are not required).

Ans. [Profit on Revaluation ₹ 6,300 ; Capital A/cs Balances ; A—₹ 19,120 ; B—₹ 18,120 ; C—₹ 7,560 and D ₹ 3,000 ; B/S Total ₹ 61,150].

11. Raju, Shastri and Tanka are partners in a firm, sharing profits and losses in the ratio of 5 : 3 : 2. Their Balance Sheet as on 31st March, 2024, stood as follows :

Liabilities	₹	*Assets*	₹
Sundry Creditors	25,000	Cash at Bank	10,000

		₹		₹	₹
General Reserve		20,000			
Shastri's Loan Account		15,000	Sundry Debtors	22,000	
Capital Accounts :	₹		*Less* : Provision for		
Raju	25,000		Bad Debts	2,000	
Shastri	10,000				20,000
Tanka	5,000		Furniture		10,000
		40,000	Plant and Machinery		35,000
			Stock		25,000
		1,00,000			1,00,000

From 1st April, 2024, the partners decided to change their profit sharing ratio as 2 : 1 : 2 instead of their former ratio of 5 : 3 : 2 and for that purpose the following adjustments were agreed upon :

(*i*) The Provision for Bad Debts was to be raised to 10%.

(*ii*) Furniture was to be appreciated by ₹ 5,200.

They did not, however, want to alter the book values of the assets and reserves but record the change by passing one single Journal entry.

Profit and Loss Account of the firm for the year ended 31st March, 2025, showed a net profit of ₹ 22,900.

You are required :

(*a*) to show the Journal entry adjusting the partners' capitals as on 1st April, 2024, and

(*b*) to prepare the Profit and Loss Appropriation Account for the year ended 31st March, 2025, after taking into consideration the following adjustments :

(*i*) Interest on Capital at 5% p.a. (*ii*) Interest on Shastri's Loan, and (*iii*) Transfer 25% of the divisible profit to the Reserve Fund after charging such Reserve.

Ans. [Debit Tanka's Capital A/c with ₹ 5,000 and Credit each Raju's Capital and Shastri's Capital Accounts with ₹ 2,500 ; Profit ₹ 16,000].

12. A, B and C were partners sharing profits and losses in the ratio of 3 : 2 : 1. On 1st January, 2025, they admitted D into partnership on the following terms :

D is to have one-sixth share which he purchased entirely from A, paying A ₹ 40,000 for the share of goodwill (through the books of the firm). Of this amount A was to withdraw ₹ 30,000 and D to bring in proportionate capital. It was further agreed that investments should be reduced to their market value, *viz.* ₹ 18,000 and that plant should be reduced to ₹ 29,000. A sum of ₹ 3,000 included in creditors was to be written back as there was no liability to pay the amount.

The Balance Sheet on 31st December, 2024 was as follows :

Liabilities	₹	*Assets*	₹
Creditors	1,05,000	Cash at Bank	40,000
Capital A/cs :		Debtors	60,000
A	60,000	Stock	50,000
B	40,000	Investments at cost	30,000
C	20,000	Furniture and Fitting	10,000
		Plant	35,000
	2,25,000		2,25,000

The profits for 2025 were ₹ 60,000 and the drawings were ₹ 15,000 for A and B each and ₹ 7,500 for C and D each.

Pass the necessary Journal Entries on D's admission. Also, prepare Partners' Capital Accounts and Balance Sheet of the new firm as on 31st December, 2025 assuming that profits during the year 2025 were wholly in cash.

Ans. [Balance in Capital Accounts : A ₹ 67,500 ; B ₹ 40,000 ; C ₹ 20,000 ; D ₹ 25.500 ; B/S Total ₹ 2,55,000].

13. Following is the Balance Sheet of A, B and C sharing Profits and Losses in the proportion of 6/14, 5/14 and 3/14 respectively :

	₹		₹
Creditors	37,800	Cash	3,780
Bills Payable	12,600	Debtors	52,920
General Reserve	21,000	Stock	58,800
Capital Accounts :		Furniture	14,700
A	70,800	Land and Building	90,300
B	59,700	Goodwill	10,500
C	29,100		
	2,31,000		2,31,000

They agreed to take D into partnership and give him 1/8th share on the following terms : (*i*) That furniture be depreciated by ₹ 1,840. (*ii*) That stock be depreciated by 10%. (*iii*) That a provision of ₹ 2,640 be made for outstanding repair bills. (*iv*) That the value of land and building, having appreciated, be brought upto ₹ 1,19,700. (*v*) That the present value of goodwill is ₹ 28,140. Existing goodwill shown in the Balance Sheet is to be written off. The new partner's share in increase in the value of goodwill may be adjusted through capital accounts. (*vi*) That D should bring in ₹ 29,400 as his capital. (*vii*) That the total capital of the firm, should be ₹ 2,35,200 and the Capital accounts of old partners be adjusted on the basis of new profit-sharing ratio in the business. Actual cash is to be paid off or brought in by the old partners, as the case maybe.

Prepare a Revaluation Account, Partners' Capital Accounts and the Balance Sheet of the new firm. ***(CA—PE-I, May 2006 Modified)***

Ans. [Profit on Revaluation ₹ 19,040; New Profit Sharing Ratio A : B : C : D = 6 : 5 : 3 : 2 ; Balance Sheet Total ₹ 2,88,240 ; Cash brought by A, B, and C ₹ 3,795, ₹ 2,463 and ₹ 8,197 respectively]

14. Mr. Srinivas and Mr. Raja are partners, who share Profits of the firm in the ratio of 1 : 2. The firm's Balance Sheet as on 31st December, 2024 was as under :

Liabilities		*Amount* (₹)	*Assets*	*Amount* (₹)
Capital Accounts :	₹		Furniture & Fixtures	16,000
Mr. Srinivas	1,20,000		Premises	2,10,000
Mr. Raja	2,40,000		Stock	84,000
		3,60,000	Sundry Debtors	68,500
Sundry Creditors		35,000	Cash & Bank Balance	16,500
		3,95,000		3,95,000

They agree to admit Mr. Anil into partnership on the following terms and conditions :

(*a*) Premises have to be valued higher by 15%.

(*b*) Depreciate furniture and fixture by 6%

(*c*) Provision for Doubtful Debts @ 5% to be created on Sundry debtors.

(*d*) The value of firm's goodwill be fixed at ₹ 50,000. Goodwill account shall be written back to the Partner's accounts in accordance with the new profit sharing ratio.

(*e*) Mr. Anil shall bring ₹ 1,00,000 for his 1/4th share of profits.

(*f*) Share capital of partners to be maintained according to the profit sharing based on capital brought in by incoming partner.

Prepare Revaluation A/c, Capital A/cs of partners and Balance Sheet after admission of new partner Mr. Anil.

Ans. [Profit on Revaluation ₹ 77,115 Cash brought by Mr. Anil ₹ 12,500; Cash paid to Srinivas and Raja ₹ 33,205 and ₹ 66,410 respectively. Balance Sheet Total ₹ 4,35,000]

15. Following is the Balance Sheet of Messrs. A and B as on 31st March, 2024 :

Liabilities	₹	₹	*Assets*	₹
A's Capital	40,000		Land and Buildings	50,000
B's Capital	50,000		Stock	30,000
		90,000	Debtors	20,000
A's Loan		10,000	Investments :	
General Reserve		10,000	6% Debentures in X Ltd.	20,000
Liabilities		20,000	Cash	10,000
		1,30,000		1,30,000

It was agreed that Mr. C is to be admitted for a fifth share in the future profits from 1st April, 2024. He is required to contribute cash towards goodwill and ₹ 10,000 towards capital.

Following further information is furnished :

(*i*) The partners A and B shared the profits in ratio of 3 :2.

(*ii*) Mr. A was receiving a salary of ₹ 500 p.m. from the very inception of the firm in 1998 in addition to share of profit.

(*iii*) The future profit ratio between A, B and C will be 3 : 1 : 1. Mr. A will not get any salary after the admission of Mr. C.

(*iv*) (*a*) The goodwill of the firm shall be determined on the basis of 2 years' purchase of the average profits from business of the last 5 years. The particulars of the profits for the year ended 31st March are as under :

2020 Profit ₹ 20,000 ; 2021 Loss ₹ 10,000 ; 2022 Profit ₹ 20,000 ; 2023 Profit ₹ 25,000 ; 2024 Profit ₹ 30,000.

The above profits and losses are after charging the salary of Mr. A. The profits of the year ended 31st March, 2020 included an extraneous profit of ₹ 30,000 and the loss of the year ended 31st March, 2021 was on account of loss by strike to the extent of ₹ 20,000.

(*b*) It was agreed that the value of the goodwill of the firm shall appear in the books of the firm.

(*v*) The trading profit before depreciation for the year ended 31st March, 2025 was ₹ 40,000.

(*vi*) The liabilities as on 31st March, 2024 included a sum of ₹ 10,000 due to contractors in respect of the construction of the Building. This bill was settled in full on 31st December, 2024 on a payment of ₹ 8,000.

(*vii*) The partners had drawn each ₹ 1,000 p.m. as drawings.

(*viii*) The value of other Assets and Liabilities as on 31st March, 2025 was as under :

Building (before Depreciation) ₹ 60,000 ; Stock ₹ 40,000 ; Debtors—Nil ; Investments ₹ 20,000 ; Liabilities—Nil.

(*ix*) Provide Depreciation at 5% on Land and Building on the closing balance and interest at 6% on A's loan.

Prepare Profit and Loss Account for the year ended 31st March, 2025, Capital Accounts and Balance Sheet as on that date.

Ans. [Net Profit ₹ 37,600; Balance Sheet Total ₹ 1,69,720; Building Purchase ₹ 12,000 ; Cash at the end of the year ₹ 13,120]

16. Following was the Balance Sheet of 'A' and 'B', who were sharing profits and losses in the ratio of 2 : 1 on 31-12-2024 :

Liabilities	₹	*Assets*	₹
Capital Accounts		Plant and Machinery	12,00,000
A	10,00,000	Building	9,00,000
B	5,00,000	Sundry Debtors	3,00,000
Reserve Fund	9,00,000	Stock	4,00,000
Sundry Creditors	4,00,000	Cash	1,00,000
Bills Payable	1,00,000		
	29,00,000		29,00,000

They agreed to admit 'C' into the partnership on the following terms :

(*i*) The goodwill of the firm was fixed at ₹ 1,05,000.

(*ii*) That the value of stock and plant and machinery were to be reduced by 10%.

(*iii*) That a provision of 5% was to be created for doubtful debts.

(*iv*) That the building account was to be appreciated by 20%.

(*v*) There was an unrecorded liability of ₹ 10,000.

(*vi*) Investments worth ₹ 20,000 (Not mentioned in the Balance Sheet) were taken into account.

(*vii*) That the value of reserve fund, the values of liabilities and the values of assets other than cash are not to be altered.

(*viii*) 'C' was to be given one-fourth share in the profit and was to bring capital equal to his share of profit after all adjustments.

Prepare Memorandum Revaluation Account. Capital Accounts of the partners and Balance Sheet of the newly reconstituted firm.

Ans. [Profit on Revaluation ₹ 15,000; Cash brought by C ₹ 8,40,000; Balance Sheet Total ₹ 37,40,000]

[**Hint :** (*i*) New Profit Sharing Ratio A : B : C = 2 : 1 : 1. (*ii*) Closing Capital of C ₹ 5,85,000; (*iii*) Adjustment of Goodwill—Debit C's Capital A/c with ₹ 26,250 and credit A and B's Capital Accounts with ₹ 17,500 and ₹ 8,750 respectively.]

17. Deepal and Sheetal are partners in a firm sharing profits in the ratio of 2 : 1. Their Balance Sheet on 31st December, 2024 was as under :

Liabilities	₹	*Assets*		₹
Creditors	1,400	Bank		1,004
Investment Provision	400	Bills Receivable	₹	2,500
Workmen Compensation Fund	1,200	Debtors	4,000	
General Reserve	2,100	*Less* : Provision	500	
Capital A/cs :				3,500
Deepal	6,000	Stock		3,000
Sheetal	4,900	Investments		5,000
		Goodwill		996
Total	16,000			16,000

On the above date, Chetal is admitted for 2/5th share in the profits of the firm.

Following revaluations were made at the time of admission ;

(1) Accrued incomes not appearing in the books ₹ 100. (2) Market value of investments is ₹ 4,500. (3) Claim on account of workmen's compensation is estimated at ₹ 150. (4) Provision for Doubtful Debts is required at ₹ 600. (5) X, an old customer, whose account was written off as bad, has promised to pay ₹ 350 in settlement of his full claim. (6) The firm had purchased machinery on

hire-purchase system for ₹ 3,000 of which only ₹ 100 are to be paid. Both machinery and unpaid liability did not appear in the Balance Sheet. (7) There was a joint life policy on the lives of Deepal and Sheetal for ₹ 15,000. Surrender value of the policy on the date of admission amounted to ₹ 2,400. It was decided to record this as an asset of the new firm. (8) Chetal is required to bring in cash ₹ 10,000 as capital and ₹ 2,400 as her share of goodwill.

You are required to prepare—Revaluation A/c, Partners' Capital Accounts, Balance Sheet of the new firm after the admission of Chetal.

Ans. [Profit ₹ 6,600 ; Capital A/cs Balances ; Deepal ₹ 12,736 ; Sheetal ₹ 8,268 ; Chetal ₹ 10,000 ; B/S Total ₹ 33,154].

18. B was in practice as a Chartered Accountant, and on 31st March, 2024 his position was as follows :

Cash at Bank ₹ 1,500 ; Due by clients ₹ 18,600 ; Furniture and Office Equipments ₹ 3,800 ; Estimated value of incompleted work ₹ 4,000 ; Sundry Creditors ₹ 900.

During the past four years C was his articled clerk, and as from 1st April, 2024 B agreed to admit him as a partner on the following terms :

C is to introduce capital equal to one-third of the amount as being B's capital on 31st March, 2024, and to pay a premium equal to two year's purchase of a third share of the net profit based on the average for the last three years. The net profits for the three years ended on 31st March, 2022, 2023 and 2024 were ₹ 13,000 ; ₹ 15,000 and ₹ 17,000 respectively.

50 per cent of the premium money is to be withdrawn by B.

The partners are to receive 5 per cent interest on capitals before distributing profits, *viz.* B—three-fourths and C—one-fourth. The profit for the year ended 31-3-2025, before charging interest on capital amounts to ₹ 20,050.

You are required to show the opening Balance Sheet of the new firm and Profit and Loss Appropriation Account for the year ended 31st March, 2025.

Ans. [Profit ₹ 18,000 ; B/S Total ₹ 41,900].

19. Laurel and Hardy are partners of the firm LH & Co., from 1-4-2021. Initially both of them contributed ₹ 1,00,000 each as capital. They did not contribute any capital thereafter. They maintain accounts of the firm on mercantile basis. They were sharing profits and losses in the ratio of 5 : 4. After the accounts for the year ended 31-3-2025 were finalized, the partners decided to share profits and losses equally with effect from 1-4-2021.

It was also discovered that in ascertaining the results in the earlier years certain adjustments, details of which are given below, had not been noted.

Year ended 31st March	*2022*	*2023*	*2024*	*2025*
	₹	₹	₹	₹
Profit as per Accounts Prepared and Finalized	1,40,000	2,60,000	3,20,000	3,60,000
Expenses not Provided for (as at 31st March)	30,000	20,000	36,000	24,000
Incomes not taken into Account (as at 31st March)	18,000	15,000	12,000	21,000

The partners decided to admit Chaplin as a partner with effect from 1-4-2025. It was decided that Chaplin would be allotted 20% share in the firm and he must bring 20% of the combined capital of Laurel and Hardy.

Following is the Balance Sheet of the firm as on 31-3-2025 before admission of Chaplin and before adjustment of revised profits between Laurel and Hardy.

BALANCE SHEET OF LH & CO.

as on 31-3-2025

Liabilities	₹	*Assets*	₹
Capital Accounts :		Plant and Machinery	60,000
Laurel	2,11,500	Cash on hand	10,000

Hardy	1,51,500	Cash at Bank	5,000
Sundry Creditors	2,27,000	Stock in Trade	3,10,000
		Sundry Debtors	2,05,000
	5,90,000		5,90,000

You are required to prepare : (*i*) Profit and Loss Adjustment Account; (*ii*) Capital Accounts of the partners; and (*iii*) Balance Sheet of the firm after the admission of Chaplin.

(PCE—May 2014 Modified)

Ans. [(*i*) Loss ₹ 44,000; (*ii*) Capital brought by Chaplin ₹ 63,800; Balances in Capital A/cs : Laurel ₹ 1,29,500; Hardy ₹ 1,89,500; Balance Sheet Total ₹ 7,19,800]

20. Ajay, Vijay and Sanjay are partners sharing Profit & Loss in the ratio of 2 : 3 : 1. The Balance Sheet of the firm as on 31-3-2025 is as follows :

Liabilities	₹	*Assets*	₹
Capital A/c :		Furniture & Fixture	30,000
Vijay's Capital	85,000	Office Equipment	20,000
Sanjay's Capital	68,000	Motor Car	60,000
General Reserve A/c	30,000	Stock	40,000
Sundry Creditors	25,000	Sundry Debtors	20,000
		Cash at Bank	18,000
		Ajay's Capital	20,000
	2,08,000		2,08,000

Kamal is admitted as a new partner with effect from 1st April, 2025 by receiving 1/4 share in the Profit & Loss of the firm. The profit or loss sharing ratios between other partners remain same as before. It was agreed that Kamal would bring some private furniture worth ₹ 3,000 and private stock worth ₹ 5,000 and balance in cash towards his capital.

The following adjustments are to be made prior to Kamal's admission :

1. Goodwill of the firm is to be valued at 2 years purchase of the average profit of last 3 years. The profits for the last 3 years were ₹ 35,900, ₹ 38,200 and ₹ 31,500. However on checking of the past records it was noticed that on 1-4-2021 a new furniture costing, ₹ 8,000 was purchased but wrongly debited to revenue and also in years 2022-23, a purchase invoice for ₹ 4,000 has been omitted in the book. The firm charged depreciation on furniture @ 10% on original cost. You calculation of goodwill is to be made on the basis of correct profits. It is agreed among existing partners that Sanjay's interest in the goodwill of the firm is only up to value of ₹ 42,000.
2. Motor Car is taken over by Vijay at ₹ 70,000.
3. Office equipment is revalued at ₹ 25,000.
4. Expenses incurred but not paid of ₹ 6,500 are provided for.
5. Value of the stock is to be reduced by 5%.
6. Kamal is to bring proportionate capital. Capital of Vijay, Ajay and Sanjay are also to be adjusted in profit sharing ratio.

Assuming the above adjustments are duly carried out, show Revaluation Account, Partners' Capital Accounts and Balance Sheet of the firm after Kamal's admission.

(CA Inter, IPCE May 2016 Modified)

Ans. [Profit on Revaluation ₹ 2,500; Capital Accounts : Ajay ₹ 39,232; Vijay ₹ 58,847; Sanjay ₹ 19,616; Kamal ₹ 39,232; B/S Total ₹ 1,92,427]

RETIREMENT OF A PARTNER

21. On 31st December, 2024, Balance Sheet of A, B and C who were sharing profits and losses in proportion of their capitals stood as follows :

Liabilities		₹	*Assets*		₹
Creditors		10,800	Cash at Bank	₹	8,000
Capital Accounts :	₹		Debtors	10,000	
A	45,000		*Less* : Provision	200	
B	30,000				9,800
C	15,000		Stock		9,000
		90,000	Machinery		24,000
			Land & Building		50,000
		1,00,800			1,00,800

B retires and the following re-adjustment of assets and liabilities have been agreed upon before ascertainment of the amount payable to B:

(*i*) That out of the amount of insurance which was debited entirely to Profit and Loss Account, ₹ 1,000 be carried forward for unexpired insurance ; (*ii*) That the Land and Building be appreciated by 10% ; (*iii*) That the Provision of Doubtful Debts be brought upto 5% on Debtors ; (*iv*) That Machinery be depreciated by 5% ; (*v*) That a provision of ₹ 1,500 be made in respect of an outstanding bill for repairs; (*vi*) That the goodwill of the entire firm be fixed at ₹ 18,000 and B's share of the same be adjusted into the accounts of A and C who are going to share future profits in the proportion of 3/4 and 1/4 respectively (no goodwill account being raised) ; (*vii*) That the entire capital of the firm as newly constituted be fixed at ₹ 60,000 between A and C in the proportion of 3/4 and 1/4 after passing entries in their accounts for adjustments, *i.e.* actual cash to be paid off or to be brought in by the continuing partners as the case may be ; (*viii*) That B be paid ₹ 5,000 in cash and the balance be transferred to his Loan Account.

Prepare Revaluation Account, Capital Accounts of the partners and Balance Sheet of the firm of A and C.

Ans. [Profit on Revaluation ₹ 3,000 ; B/S Total ₹ 1,04,300 ; B's Loan ₹ 32,000 ; A and C brought ₹ 3,000 and ₹ 1,000 respectively].

22. On 31st March, 2025, Balance Sheet of P, Q, and R sharing profits and losses in proportion to their capitals stood as follows :

Liabilities	₹	*Assets*	₹
Capital Accounts :		Land and Building	30,000
Mr. P	20,000	Plant and Machinery	20,000
Mr. Q	30,000	Stock of Goods	12,000
Mr. R	20,000	Sundry Debtors	11,000
Sundry Creditors	10,000	Cash and Bank Balances	7,000
	80,000		80,000

On 1st April, 2025, P desired to retire from the firm and remaining partners decided to carry on the business. It was greed to revalue the assets and liabilities on that date on the following basis :

(*i*) Land and Building be appreciated by 20%.

(*ii*) Plant and Machinery be depreciated by 20%.

(*iii*) Stock of goods to be valued at ₹ 10,000.

(*iv*) Old credit balances of sundry creditors, ₹ 2,000 be written back.

(*v*) Provisions for bad debts should be provided at 5%.

(vi) Joint Life Policy of the partners surrendered and cash obtained ₹ 7,550.

(vii) Goodwill of the entire firm is valued at ₹ 14,000 and P's share of the goodwill is adjusted in the A/cs of Q and R, who would share the future profits equally. No goodwill account being raised.

(viii) The total capital of the firm is to be the same as before retirement. Individual capitals are in their profit sharing ratio.

(ix) Amount due to Mr. P is to be settled on the following basis :

50% on retirement and the balance 50% within one year.

Prepare (a) Revaluation Account, (b) Capital Accounts of the partners, (c) Cash Account and (d) Balance Sheet of the new firm M/s Q & R as on 1-4-2025. ***(PE-I, Nov. 2013 Modified)***

Ans. [(a) Profit on Revaluation ₹ 7,000; (b) Amount transferred to P's Loan ₹ 13,000; Balance in each Capital A/cs of Q and R ₹ 35,000; (c) Cash Balance ₹ 20,550; (d) Balance Sheet Total ₹ 91,000]

[**Hint :** Amount brought by Q and R ₹ 3,000 and ₹ 16,000 respectively.]

23. Balance Sheet of X, Y and Z who were sharing profits in the ratio of 4 : 3 : 2 respectively stood as follows on 31st December, 2024 :

Liabilities		₹	*Assets*	₹	₹
Sundry Creditors		4,140	Cash at Bank		3,300
Capital Accounts :	₹		Sundry Debtors	3,045	
X	12,000		*Less* : Provision	105	
Y	9,000				2,940
Z	6,000		Stock		4,800
		27,000	Plant & Machinery		5,100
			Land and Building		15,000
		31,140			31,140

Y having given notice to retire from the firm, the following adjustments in the books of the firm were agreed upon :

(a) That Land and Building be appreciated by 10 per cent ; (b) The provision for bad debts is no longer necessary ; (c) That the Stock be appreciated by 20 per cent ; (d) The adjustment be made in the accounts to rectify a mistake previously made whereby Y was credited in excess by ₹ 810 while X and Z were debited in excess by ₹ 420 and ₹ 390 respectively ; (e) That the goodwill of the firm be valued at ₹ 5,400 and Y's share of the same be adjusted to that of X and Z who are going to share in future profits in the ratio of 2 : 1 ; (f) That the entire capital of the firm, as newly constituted, will be readjusted by bringing in or paying of cash so that the future capital of X and Z be in the ratio of 2 : 1.

Pass Journal Entires and prepare Balance Sheet of the new firm, showing Y's balance as loan.

Ans. [Profit on Revaluation ₹ 2,565 ; B/S Total ₹ 33,705 ; X brings ₹ 120 and Z is paid ₹ 120].

24. A, B and C are partners, sharing profit and losses equally. Their assets and liabilities as at 30-6-2025 were as follows :

Liabilities		₹	*Assets*	₹
Partners' Capitals :	₹		Land & Freehold Property	1,00,000
A	1,00,000		Plant & Machinery	2,00,000
B	1,00,000		Furniture & Equipment	50,000
C	2,00,000		Stock in Trade	1,00,000
		4,00,000	Sundry Debtors	1,00,000

Partners' Current A/cs			Balance with Bankers	1,50,000
A	50,000			
B	75,000			
C	25,000			
		1,50,000		
Sundry Creditors		1,50,000		
		7,00,000		7,00,000

On 1-7-2025, A retires and it is agreed that he should be paid in full on that date all his dues. For this purpose, Goodwill is to be calculated on the basis of 3 years' purchase of past 3 years' profits which amounted to ₹ 1,00,000, ₹ 1,20,000, and ₹ 1,40,000 respectively.

In order to meet this obligation, a bank loan was arranged as at 1-7-2025 for ₹ 2,00,000 by pledging the fixed assets as security.

Further, to compensate a loyal manager D, it is agreed between B and C that D should be admitted as a partner, who should bring in over and above a capital of ₹ 1,00,000, his share of Goodwill in cash to serve as working capital. B and C agreed to forego 1/3 of their individual share of profits to D.

You are required to give effect to the above transactions on 1-7-2025 by passing necessary Journal Entries in the partnership books and to prepare an opening Balance Sheet of the firm as on that date.

Ans. [B/S Total ₹ 8,50,000].

25. A, B and C were carrying on business in partnership, sharing profits and losses in the ratio of 2 : 1 : 1. On 31st December, 2024, B decided to retire from the firm and the following terms and conditions were agreed upon.

(*a*) A typewriter purchased on 1st January, 2023, for ₹ 1,200 and charged to office expenses account in 2023 has to be brought into account after allowing 15% per annum depreciation on reducing instalment basis ; (*b*) Furniture and fittings are to be written down by Rs 603 and Stock by ₹ 5,000 ; (*c*) The provisions for Bad and Doubtful Debts standing in the books at ₹ 4,000 are to be reduced by 25% ; (*d*) A liability in respect of workmen's compensation for ₹ 2,100, not acknowledged by the partnership as a valid claim is, however, to be provided for ; (*e*) Goodwill of the firm is valued at ₹ 24,000 ; (*f*) The Capital Accounts of the partners on 31st December, 2024, stood at ; A ₹ 20,001, B ₹ 15,001 and C ₹ 10,001.

A and C agree that Goodwill Account shall not continue in the books and the amount payable to B shall be brought in by them in their new profit sharing ratio.

You are required to pass Journal entries to record the above transactions.

Ans. [Amount paid to B ₹ 19,542].

26. A, B and C are in partnership sharing profits and losses in proportion of 2 : 2 : 1 respectively. It was agreed that, in case of retirement of a partner, the value of goodwill shall be determined at $1\frac{1}{2}$ year's purchase of the average profit of the last four years. C retired from the business with effect from 1st July, 2025, and the following matters came up for consideration in connection therewith :

(*i*) Capital expenditure of ₹ 3,000 incurred on 15th November, 2021, wrongly debited to purchases account is to be written back and depreciation at 10% is to be charged annually on the closing balances on reducing balance method ; (*ii*) No adjustment was made for goods worth ₹ 1,000 taken over by A on 28th March, 2025 ; (*iii*) The profits for four years ended on 30th June, 2022, 2023, 2024 and 2025 were ₹ 12,000, ₹ 15,000, ₹ 14,000 and ₹ 16,000 respectively, (*iv*) C's Capital Account stood at ₹ 55,000 as on 30th June, 2025.

You are required to draw up C's Capital Account and to find out the amount finally due to him.

Ans. [Amount of C's Loan ₹ 60,092].

RETIREMENT & ADMISSION

27. Gold, Silver and Diamond are partners in a firm sharing Profits and Losses in the ratio of 5 : 3 : 2. Gold retires on 1st April, 2025 on which date Balance Sheet of the firm stood as under :

BALANCE SHEET

as at 1st April, 2025

Liabilities		₹	*Assets*	₹
Capital Accounts :	₹		Goodwill	10,000
Gold	80,000		Furniture	30,000
Silver	50,000		Office Equipments	25,000
Diamond	40,000		Building	60,000
		1,70,000	Stock	77,000
General Reserve		20,000	Sundry Debtors	75,000
Sundry Creditors		90,000	Cash	18,000
Bills Payable		15,000		
		2,95,000		2,95,000

It is provided in the Deed of Partnership that in the event of death or retirement of a partner, goodwill is to be valued at 2 years' purchase of the average profits of the last 4 years. The profits for the last 4 years were :

2024-25 ₹ 30,000 ; 2023-24 ₹ 24,000 ; 2022-23 ₹ 20,000 ; 2021-22 ₹ 18,000.

Furniture and Building are revalued at ₹ 25,000 and ₹ 75,000 respectively. Stock is overvalued by 10%.

It was decided that Gold should be paid ₹ 50,000 immediately on retirement and the balance on his Capital Account is to be treated as a loan to the firm. Silver and Diamond contributed necessary sums in equal proportion for payments to Gold and to leave ₹ 20,000 Cash as working capital. Assuming the above mentioned arrangements are given effect to, you are required to show Revaluation Account, Cash Account and Capital Accounts of the partners.

Ans. [Profit on Revaluation ₹ 3,000 ; Cash Balance ₹ 20,000 ; Capital : Silver ₹ 93,700 & Diamond ₹ 77,800 ; Gold's Loan ₹ 59,500].

28. A, B and C were partners, sharing profits and losses in the proportions of 3 : 2 : 2 respectively. Balance Sheet of the firm as on 1st January, 2024 was as follows :

Liabilities		₹	*Assets*	₹
Capital Accounts :	₹		Plant and Machinery	36,000
A	50,000		Furniture	14,000
B	40,000		Stock in hand	56,000
C	35,000		Sundry Debtors	48,000
		1,25,000	Cash at Bank	9,000
Overdraft from Bank		10,000		
Sundry Creditors		28,000		
		1,63,000		1,63,000

A retired on 1st January, 2024, on which date D was admitted as a new partner. For the purpose of adjusting the rights as between the old partners, Goodwill was to be valued at ₹ 42,000 and Sundry Debtors and Stock in hand were to be reduced by ₹ 8,000 and ₹ 6,000 respectively. A was to receive ₹ 22,000 in cash on the date of retirement and the balance due to him was to remain on loan at 8% per annum, interest payable on 31st December each year on which date firm closed its accounts.

D was to bring in ₹ 50,000 in cash as his capital on the date of admission.

The new partners were to share profits and losses equally after allowing interest on loan from A.

The net profit for the year ended 31st December, 2024 was ₹ 33,200 before taking into account interest on loan from A.

Show the Ledger Accounts, giving effect to the above facts :

(*a*) Capital Accounts of the new partners as on 31st December, 2024, (*b*) A's Loan Account as on 31st December, 2024 and Profit and Loss Appropriation Account for the year ended 31st December, 2024.

Ans. [(*a*) Capital Balances—B—₹ 58,000 ; C—₹ 53,000 ; and D—₹ 60,000, (*b*) A's Loan Balance ₹ 43,200, Share of Profits B, C and D ₹ 10,000 each].

29. P and Q were working in partnership sharing profits and losses equally. On 31-12-2024 P decided to retire and in his place, his son R was admitted as a partner from 1st January, 2025 with 1/3rd share in profit.

The Balance sheet of the firm as on 31-12-2024 was as follows :

Liabilities		₹	*Assets*	₹
Sundry Creditors		14,700	Goodwill	15,000
Capitals :	₹		Land & Buildings	40,050
P	54,000		Motor Car	12,000
Q	48,300		Furniture	9,300
		1,02,300	Sundry Debtors	24,150
			Cash at Bank	16,500
		1,17,000		1,17,000

It was decided as follows :

(*a*) The Goodwill should be raised to ₹ 20,000. (*b*) The motor car would be taken over by P at its book value. (*c*) The value of Land and Buildings would be increased by ₹ 8,280. (*d*) Q and R would introduce sufficient capital to pay off P and to leave thereafter a sum of ₹ 7,350 as Bank Balance, in a manner to make their capitals in proportion to their share of profits. (*e*) The capital payable by R was to be gifted to him by his father. (*f*) The new partners decided not to show goodwill as an asset.

The above arrangements were duly complied with. Show Partners' Capital Accounts and Bank A/c.

Ans. [Capital A/cs Balances : Q ₹ 49,620, R ₹ 24,810].

30. A, B and C are partners of the firm ABC & Co., sharing profits and losses in the ratio of 5 : 3 : 2. Following is the Balance Sheet of the firm as at 31-3-2025 :

BALANCE SHEET

as on 31-3-2025

Liabilities	₹	*Assets*	₹
Partners' Capital Accounts :		Goodwill	1,00,000
A	4,50,000	Building	10,50,000
B	1,30,000	Machinery	6,50,000
C	1,70,000	Furniture	2,15,000
Investment Fluctuation Reserve	1,00,000	Investments (Market Value ₹ 75,000)	60,000
Contingency Reserve	75,000	Stock	6,50,000
Long-term Loan	15,00,000	Sundry Debtors	6,95,000
Bank Overdraft	2,20,000	Advertisement Suspense	25,000
Sundry Creditors	8,00,000		
	34,45,000		34,45,000

It was decided that B would retire from the partnership on 1-4-2025 and D would be admitted as a partner on the same date. Following adjustments are agreed amongst the partners for the retirement/admission :

(*i*) Goodwill is to be valued at ₹ 5,00,000, but the same will not appear as an asset in the books of the firm.

(*ii*) Building and machinery are to be revalued at ₹ 10,00,000 and ₹ 5,20,000 respectively.

(*iii*) Investments are to be taken over by B at the market value.

(*iv*) Provision for doubtful debts to be maintained at 20% on sundry debtors.

(*v*) The capital of the reconstituted firm will be ₹ 10,00,000 to be contributed by the partners A, C and D in their new profit sharing ratio of 2 : 2 : 1.

(*vi*) Surplus funds, if any, will be used to pay the bank overdraft.

(*vii*) Amount due to retiring partner B will be transferred to his loan account.

Prepare : (*i*) Revaluation Account; (*ii*) Capital Accounts of the partners; and (*iii*) Balance Sheet of the firm after reconstitution.

Ans. [Loss on Revaluation ₹ 3,04,000; Amount transferred to B's Loan ₹ 1,28,800; Balance Sheet Total ₹ 34,28,800]

[**Hint :** Cash Balance ₹ 4,87,800; Sacrificing Ratio A and B = 1 : 3; Gaining Ratio of C and D = 1 : 1]

31. Ram, Rahim and Robert are partners, sharing Profits and Losses in the ratio of 5 : 3 : 2. It was decided that Robert would retire on 31-3-2025 and in his place Richard would be admitted as a partner with new profit sharing ratio between Ram, Rahim and Richard at 3 : 2 : 1.

BALANCE SHEET OF RAM, RAHIM AND ROBERT

as on 31-3-2025

Liabilities	₹	*Assets*	₹
Capital Accounts :		Cash in Hand	20,000
Ram	1,00,000	Cash at Bank	1,00,000
Rahim	1,50,000	Sundry Debtors	5,00,000
Robert	2,00,000	Stock in Trade	2,00,000
General Reserve	2,00,000	Plant & Machinery	3,00,000
Sundry Creditors	8,00,000	Land & Building	5,30,000
Loan from Richard	2,00,000		
	16,50,000		16,50,000

Retirement of Robert and admission of Richard is on the following terms :

(*a*) Plant and Machinery to be depreciated by ₹ 30,000.

(*b*) Land and Building to be valued at ₹ 6,00,000.

(*c*) Stock to be valued at 95% of book value.

(*d*) Provision for doubtful debts @ 10% to be provided on debtors.

(*e*) General Reserve to be apportioned amongst Ram, Rahim and Robert.

(*f*) The firm's goodwill to be valued at 2 years purchase of the average profits of the last 3 years.

The relevant figures are :

Year ended 31-3-2022 — Profit ₹ 50,000
Year ended 31-3-2023 — Profit ₹ 60,000
Year ended 31-3-2024 — Profit ₹ 55,000

(*g*) Out of the amount due to Robert ₹ 2,00,000 would be retained as loan by the firm and the balance will be settled immediately.

(*h*) Richard's capital should be equal to 50% of the combined capital of Ram and Rahim.

Prepare : (*i*) Capital Accounts of the partners; and (*ii*) Balance Sheet of the reconstituted firm.

Ans. [Loss on Revaluation ₹ 20,000 ; Capital Balances of Ram and Rahim (after Robert's retirement) ₹ 2,45,000 and ₹ 2,37,000 respectively. Capital Balances (after admission of Richard Ram ₹ 1,90,000 ; Rahim ₹ 2,00,333 and Richard ₹ 1,95,167 respectively. Balance Sheet Total ₹ 15,85,500]

DEATH OF A PARTNER

32. X, Y and Z were trading in partnership sharing profits and losses as 4 : 3 : 3 respectively. The accounts of the firm are made up to 31st December every year.

The deed provided that, on the death of a partner, goodwill to be valued at 3 years' average profits of 3 years ending up to the date of death, after deducting interest @ 8% on capital employed and a fair remuneration to each partner. The profits are assumed to be earned evenly through the year.

On 30th June, 2025, X died and it was agreed to adjust goodwill in the capital accounts without showing any amount of goodwill in the balance sheet. It was agreed that for the purpose of valuation of goodwill, fair remuneration to each partner would be ₹ 15,000 p.a. and the capital employed would be ₹ 1,56,000 and Y and Z were to continue the partnership sharing profits and losses equally after the death of X.

Following were the amounts of profits of various years before charging interest on capital employed and remuneration to partners.

2022 ₹ 67,200 ; 2023 ₹ 75,600 ; 2024 ₹ 72,000 ; 2025 ₹ 62,400.

Compute the value of goodwill and show the entry in the books of the firm.

Ans. [Value of Goodwill ₹ 39,960; The entry to be passed is:

Y's Capital A/c	**Dr.**	**₹ 7,992**	
Z's Capital A/c	**Dr.**	**₹ 7,992**	
To X's Capital A/c			**₹ 15,984].**

33. A, B and C carried on business in partnership sharing profits and losses in proportion of 1/2, 1/3, and 1/6 respectively.

The partnership deed provided that on the death of a partner his executors be paid as under :

(*a*) The amount lying to the credit of his capital account on the date of death, less drawings made during the period, (*b*) His share of profit till the date of death be taken at the sum calculated on the average of the last three completed years' profit. (*c*) A Goodwill Account be raised on the basis of the two years' purchase of the average of profits of the last three years :

The firm had insured the partners' lives severally. A for ₹ 10,000, B for ₹ 7,500 and C for ₹ 5,000. The premiums were charged to Profit and Loss Account.

The Capital Accounts to carry interest at 6% per annum.

A died on 31st March, 2025.

The Balance Sheet on 1st January, 2025 showed their capitals as under :

A ₹ 20,000 ; B ₹ 15,000 and C ₹ 10,000.

A had drawn ₹ 3,500 during the period 1st January, 2025 to 31st March, 2025.

The surrender value on 31st March, 2025 amounted in each case to one-half of the sum assured.

The annual profits for the last three completed years were ₹ 7,480, ₹ 8,000 and ₹ 9,000.

Prepare A's Executor's Account.

Ans. [₹ 34,105].

34. Firm ABC consisted of 3 partners, A, B and C, sharing profits and losses in the ratio of 5 : 3 : 2 respectively. The partner A died on February 20, 2025. Profit and Loss Account for the period upto date of death and Balance Sheet as on that date were prepared. The Balance Sheet as on that date was as below :

Liabilities		₹	*Assets*	₹
Capitals :	₹		Goodwill	6,000
	A—12,000		Machinery	35,000
	B—16,000		Furniture	6,000
	C—12,000		Stock	9,000
		40,000	Debtors	15,000
Loan from A		5,000	Bank	3,000
General Reserve		7,000		
Creditors		22,000		
		74,000		74,000

In addition to the assets shown above the Firm had 3 life policies in the name of each partner, for insured value of ₹ 20,000 each, the premiums of which were charged to Profit and Loss Account.

According to the Partnership Deed, on death of a partner, the assets and liabilities are to be revalued by a valuer. The revalued figures were :

(1) Machinery ₹ 45,000, Debtors are subject to a Provision for Doubtful Debts at 10% and Furniture at ₹ 7,000. The value of goodwill of the firm is ₹ 21,000 and is to be adjusted through capital accounts. (2) Provision for Taxation to be created for ₹ 1,500. (3) Death-claim for policy in the name of A will be realised in full and the surrender values of the other 2 policies were ₹ 7,500, each.

The business will be continued by B and C, henceforth sharing profits and losses equally. The net balance due to A is transferred to A's Executors Account, which will be paid off later. Life Policy Account is not to be shown in the books of the new firm.

Show Capital Accounts, Revaluation Account and the new Balance Sheet of the firm.

Ans. [Profit on Revaluation ₹ 9,500 ; A's Executors A/c ₹ 44,500 ; Capital A/cs ; B—₹ 21,450 ; C—₹ 8,050 ; B/S Total ₹ 97,500].

35. Brown and Smith are partners. The Partnership Deed provides *inter alia* :

(*i*) That the accounts be balanced on 31st December each year ; (*ii*) That the profits be divided as follows : Brown one half, Smith one-third and carried to a Reserve Account one-sixth ; (*iii*) That in the event of death of a partner, his Executors will be entitled to be paid out ; (*a*) The capital to his credit at date of death. (*b*) His proportion of Reserve at date of the last Balance Sheet, (*c*) His proportion of profits to date based on the average profits of the last three completed years, (*d*) By way of Goodwill his proportion of total profits for the preceding three years.

On 31 December, 2024, the Ledger Balances were :

	₹	₹
Brown 's Capital		90,000
Smith's Capital		60,000
Reserve		30,000
Bills Receivable	20,000	
Investments	50,000	
Cash	1,40,000	
Creditors		30,000
	2,10,000	2,10,000

The Profits for the three years were 2022, ₹ 42,000 ; 2023, ₹ 39,000 and 2024 ₹ 45,000.

Smith died on 1st May, 2025. Show the workings of Smith's *(i)* Share of Reserve, *(ii)* Share of Profits, and *(iii)* Share of Goodwill and draw up Smith's Executor's Account as would appear in the firm's Ledger transferring the amount to his Loan Account.

Ans. [Amount due to Smith's Executors, ₹ 1,28,000].

36. A, B and C were partners, sharing profits and losses in the ratio of 3: 2 : 1. In order to meet the financial requirements in case of death of a partner, the firm took a joint life policy for ₹ 12,000 on 1st January, 2021 paying an annual premium of ₹ 1,000. The firm closes its books on 31st December, each year and the policy was shown at its surrender value each year. Such values as at 31st December each year were as follows : 2021 : Nil ; 2022 : ₹ 240 ; 2023 : ₹ 540 ; 2024 : ₹ 800. B died on 30th September, 2025 and the policy money was received on 18th November, 2025 :

Show the accounts relating to joint life policy under various cases.

37. Amir and Bamir entered into partnership on 1st January, 2022, the former introducing a capital of ₹ 90,000 and the latter ₹ 30,000. They effect a policy of insurance for ₹ 45,000 upon their joint lives in order to enable the survivor, in case of death of one, to pay out in cash part of the other's interest. The net profits before charging interest on capital as at the beginning of each year, at 6 per cent per annum and on drawings (averaged at 4 per cent per annum), were as follows :

Year	Net Profits	Amir's drawings	Bamir's drawings
	₹	₹	₹
2022	34,800	10,000	5,000
2023	37,628	12,000	7,000
2024	38,100	14,000	7,500

Profits and losses were divided between Amir and Bamir in the ratio of two and one respectively.

The annual insurance premium which is ₹ 3,000 is charged to Profit and Loss Account as a business expense.

On 31st March, 2025, Amir died. According to the terms of the partnership deed the deceased partner's executors are entitled to receive his share of the capital as it stood on 31st December, 2024 plus his three months' share of the profit calculated upon the previous year's rate of profit and share of goodwill which is reckoned at two-thirds of the two year purchase of the previous three years' profits after adjusting for interest on capital and drawings but without deducting the premium paid on the joint life insurance policy.

Make up Amir's Executors Account. The goodwill is not be shown in the books of continuing partner.

Workings of adjusted net profits and computation of Amir's share of goodwill will be considered as part of the answer. Calculations are to be made to the nearest rupee ignoring fractions, wherever arising.

Ans. [Amount due to Amir's Executors ₹ 2,09,488].

38. You are given the Balance Sheet of M/s X & Co. as on 31-12-2024 consisting of three partners—Mr. J, Mr. W and Mr. N, who were sharing profits and losses equally.

BALANCE SHEET OF M/S X AND CO.

as on 31-12-2024.

Liabilities	₹	*Assets*	₹
Capital Accounts		Plant and Machinery	23,650
Mr. J	10,000	Furniture	4,500
Mr. W	16,000	Stock	20,000
Mr. N	14,000	Debtors	20,540
Creditors	10,000	Cash	11,310
6% Loan	30,000		
	80,000		80,000

Mr. N died on 1-1-2025. Following information is available :

(*a*) ₹ 2,260 received from Mr. Y as rent was credited to Y's account. He has already a debit balance for other transactions.

(*b*) Machine purchased on 26-12-2024 for ₹ 6,000 was debited to purchases account. Erection charges of ₹ 1,000 were charged to repairs account.

(*c*) Interest of ₹ 2,408 was paid in advance. But the entire amount was charged to Profit and Loss Account in 2024.

(*d*) Machinery is valued at 20% below the book value after adjustment of (*b*) above.

(*e*) Debtors are estimated to be worth 95% of book value.

(*f*) Goodwill account is to be raised to the extent of deceased partner's share. Goodwill is to be valued at three year's purchase of the average profit of the year 2022, 2023 and 2024 and goodwill not to be shown in the books of the new firm.

Profit for the years 2022 and 2023 were ₹ 18,000 and ₹ 20,000 respectively. Profit for the year 2024 subject to the adjustments (*a*), (*b*) and (*c*) above was ₹ 13,842.

One half of the dues to the deceased are to be met immediately by cash to be brought in by continuing partners in their profit sharing ratio. Balance will coninue as loan with 12% interest p.a. in the name of the executor of the deceased partner.

Show necessary accounts and Balance Sheet of the firm after one half of the dues are paid off.

(C.A. *Inter*)

Ans. [N's Executor's Loan A/c ₹ 18,318 (Cr.) ; Capital Accounts : J ₹ 20,625 (Cr.) and W ₹ 26,625 (Cr.) ; B/S Total ₹ 1,05,568].

AMALGAMATION

39. A and B are partners sharing profits and losses equally in a business similar to that carried on by C. In order to avoid competition they decided to amalgamate the two businesses by taking over the assets and liabilities of C and admitting him into partnership with them as from 1st April, 2025. Their Balance Sheets as on 31st March, 2025 were as follows :

Liabilities		*A & B*	*C*	*Assets*		*A & B*	*C*
		₹	₹			₹	₹
Sundry Creditors		15,000	37,500	Cash	₹	300	700
Bank Overdraft		5,000	32,000	Debtors	35,000		
Bills Payable		—	3,000	*Less* : Provision for			
Loan		—	10,500	Bad Debts	1,500		
Capital A/cs :	₹					33,500	25,000
A	20,000			Stock		21,200	26,300
B	15,000			Investment		—	27,000
		35,000	—	C's Capital Overdrawn		—	4,000
		55,000	83,000			55,000	83,000

The new partnership is to be carried on as A, B and C and it was agreed among all the partners that the Book Debts of both the businesses should be provided with Bad Debts provisions at 10% and the stock to be reduced by 5% for the purpose of amalgamation and that the investments of C should be valued at ₹ 35,000 and that C was to be credited with a sum of ₹ 5,100 for Goodwill. It was further agreed that in order to raise the total capital of the firm to ₹ 60,000 each partner shall introduce such sum as would make his capital in the new business equal to one third of the capital. Goodwill is not to be shown in the books of the new firm.

Give Journal Entries in the books of the new firm and show amalgamated Balance Sheet as at 1st April, 2025.

Ans. [Balance Sheet Total ₹ 1,57,900].

40. Two firms 'P & Q' and 'R & S' agreed to amalgamate their businesses. Their positions as on March 31, 2025 were as follows :

BALANCE SHEETS
as on 31 March, 2025

Liabilities	*P & Q*	*R & S*	*Assets*	*P & Q*	*R & S*
Creditors	1,04,000	52,000	Cash at Bank	1,56,000	65,000
Capitals :			Debtors	1,30,000	1,04,000
P	1,82,000		Stock in Trade	42,000	26,000
Q	1,30,000		Furniture	10,000	13,000
R		91,000	Office Building	78,000	
S		65,000			
	4,16,000	2,08,000		4,16,000	2,08,000

Creditors and debtors were not taken over by the new firm PQRS. Office building was retained by P and Q but the new firm agreed to pay a monthly rent of ₹ 400. The cash required for working of the new firm was estimated at ₹ 1,30,000 to be provided by the partners in their new profit sharing proportion as under:

P = 3/10 ; Q = 3/10 ; R = 2/10 ; S = 2/10.

(1) Give Journal entries in the books of P & Q and R & S.

(2) Give the opening balance sheet of PQRS. State your assumptions, if any, clearly.

Ans. [Balance Sheet Total of the firm PQRS = ₹ 2,21,000 ; Capitals of the partners : P = ₹ 69,334 ; Q = ₹ 60,666 ; R = ₹ 48,750 and S = ₹ 42,250].

Hint. [It is assumed that cash is also not taken over by the new firm because cash required in the new firm is contributed by the partners in the ratio of P = 3/10 ; Q = 3/10 ; R = 2/10 ; and S = 2/10].

CHAPTER 18

Partnership Accounts-II

DISSOLUTION

The Indian Partnership Act, 1932 recognises the difference between the 'dissolution of partnership' and 'dissolution of firm'. The dissolution of *partnership* between all the partners of a firm is called the dissolution of the firm. Thus, it is the complete breakdown of a partnership and partners do not continue the firm. On the other hand, dissolution of the partnership means a reconstitution of the firm due to the retirement of a partner or the insolvency of a partner or the death of a partner and the remaining partners provide for the continuance of the firm in pursuance of an express or implied agreement to that effect. On dissolution of a firm the firm's assets are realised and the liabilities are discharged because the firm is to be closed, whereas on dissolution of a partnership, the share of the outgoing partner is ascertained and the firm is not closed.

Distinction Between Dissolution of Partnership and Dissolution of a Firm

Following are the main distinctions between dissolution of partnership and dissolution of a firm :

Point of Distinction	*Dissolution of Partnership*	*Dissolution of a Firm*
1. Meaning	It means discontinuance of relationship between partners but the business is not terminated and a firm continues its business.	It means dissolution of partnership of all partners of the firm along with winding up of the business of the entire firm. The business of the firm is closed.
2. Books of Accounts	In this case, books of accounts may not be closed.	In this case, books of accounts are closed.
3. Dissolution	It does not mean dissolution of firm.	It means dissolution of partnership also.
4. Nature	It is voluntary and is dissolved by mutual agreement and through the process of reconstitution without the intervention of court.	It may be both voluntary and compulsory. A firm can also be dissolved by Court's orders.
5. Settlement of Assets and Liabilities	In this case, assets and liabilities are revalued and new Balance Sheet is drawn.	In this case, assets are sold and realised and liabilities are paid off.
6. Economic Relationship	Such relationship may remain or change as the case may be.	Such relationship between the partners comes to an end.

Modes of Dissolution of Firm

The various ways in which a firm may be dissolved are given as under :

1. **Dissolution by agreement.** A firm is dissolved when all the partners agree that it should be dissolved. A partnership firm is the creation of an agreement ; similarly a firm can be dissolved by an agreement.
2. **Dissolution on the happening of contingencies.** A firm is dissolved in any of the following ways unless there is a contract between the partners to the contrary. These are: (*i*) by the expiry of the term of duration of the firm, (*ii*) by the completion of the adventure for which the firm was constituted, (*iii*) by the death of a partner, and (*iv*) by the adjudication of a partner as insolvent.
3. **Dissolution by notice of partnership at will.** When the partnership is at will, the firm may be dissolved at any time by any partner giving notice in writing to all the other partners of his intention to dissolve the firm.
4. **Compulsory dissolution or dissolution by the operation of law.** A firm is compulsorily dissolved in different ways as : (*i*) When all the partners except one become insolvent. (*ii*) When all the partners become insolvent. (*iii*) When the business becomes illegal. (*iv*) Where the number of partners exceed twenty in case of ordinary business or ten in case of banking business.
5. **Dissolution by the court.** At the suit of a partner, a court may order the dissolution of the firm in different ways as : (*i*) when a partner becomes of *unsound mind*, (*ii*) when a partner suffers from *permanent incapacity* and becomes incapable of performing his duties as a partner, (*iii*) when a partner is *guilty of misconduct* affecting the business of the firm, (*iv*) when a partner *commits wilful or persistent breaches* of agreement, (*v*) when a partner has *transferred the whole of his interest* in the firm to a third party or when his share has been attached under a decree or sold under process of law, (*vi*) when the *business of the firm cannot be carried on except at a loss*, and (*vii*) when the court is satisfied as to grounds which render it *just and equitable to* dissolve the firm.

Settlement of Accounts on Dissolution

The mode of settlement of accounts on a dissolution of the firm is as follows as given in Section 48 of the Indian Partnership Act, 1932.

In settling the accounts of a firm after dissolution, the following rules shall, subject to agreement by the partners, be observed—

(*a*) **Losses, including deficiencies of capital,** shall be paid first out of profits, next out of capital, and lastly, if necessary, by the partners individually in the proportions in which they are entitled to share profits.

(*b*) **The assets of the firm,** including any sums contributed by the partners to make up deficiencies of capital, shall be applied in the following manner and order :

(*i*) in paying the debts of the firm to third parties ;

(*ii*) in paying to each partner rateably what is due to him from the firm for advances as distinguished from capital ;

(*iii*) in paying to each partner rateably what is due to him on account of capital ; and

(*iv*) the residue, if any, shall be divided among the partners in the proportions in which they are entitled to share profits.

Dissolution Before Expiry of a Fixed Term (Section 50)

If a partner on his admission in the firm has paid a premium (*i.e.* goodwill) to the other partners with a stipulation that the firm will not be dissolved before the expiry of a certain period, he will be entitled to a suitable refund of the premium if the firm is dissolved before the term has expired. However, no claim in this respect will arise if :

(*i*) The firm is dissolved due to the death of a partner.

(*ii*) The dissolution is mainly due to the partner's (claiming refund) own misconduct.

(*iii*) The dissolution is as a result of an agreement containing no provision for the return of the premium or any part of it.

The refund of the premium will be such as is reasonable having regard to the terms upon which the admission was made and to the length of the period agreed and the period expired upto the dissolution date. Any refund of premium that becomes due on the dissolution will be debited to other partners' capital accounts in their profit sharing ratio and credited to the refund claiming partner's capital account.

Firm Debts and Private Debts

Where there are partnership debts and private debts of the partners in their individual capacity, the *assets of the firm* shall be applied in the first instance in payment of the debts of the firm and surplus of assets, if any, would be paid to the partners in the proportion in which they were entitled to share profits. Similarly, the *private property of each partner* shall be applied first in the payment of his private debts, and the surplus of private assets, if any, would be handed over to the firm if the firm needs it for the payment of its debts.

Example 1. Ramesh and Suresh are two equal partners in a firm and the following is the position of that firm at the time of dissolution :

	Firm's Debts	*Firm's Assets*
	₹ 80,000	₹ 1,00,000 Realisable Value
	Private Debts	Private Estate
Ramesh	₹ 25,000	₹ 10,000
Suresh	Nil	₹ 20,000

In this case, firm's assets amounting to ₹ 1,00,000 would be utilised to pay firm's debts of ₹ 80,000 and the surplus of ₹ 20,000 (*i.e.,* ₹ 1,00,000 – ₹ 80,000) would be shared by Ramesh and Suresh equally. In other words, Ramesh can use his share of surplus of ₹ 10,000 in firm's assets for paying his private debts and Suresh can retain his share of surplus with him.

Example 2. Suppose the position of the partners Ramesh and Suresh at the time of dissolution is as follows :

	Private Liabilities	*Private Estate*
	₹	₹
Ramesh	30,000	25,000
Suresh	20,000	35,000

In this case, private estate of Ramesh of ₹ 25,000 would be used in the first instance to pay his private liabilities of ₹ 30,000 and as there is no surplus left, nothing is available for paying the debts of the firm. Suresh's private estate of ₹ 35,000 would be utilised in the first instance to pay his private liabilities of ₹ 20,000 and the surplus of ₹ 15,000 (*i.e.,* ₹ 35,000 – ₹ 20,000) can be used for meeting the debts of the firm, if need arises.

Distinction Between Firm's Debts and Private Debts

Following are the main distinctions between Firm's Debts and Private Debts.

Basis of Distinction	*Firm's Debts*	*Private Debts*
1. Incurrence of Debts	These are incurred by the firm.	These are incurred by a partner in his individual capacity.
2. Liability of Partner(s)	All partners are jointly and severally liable.	Only concerned partner is liable.

3. **Use of Firm's Property**	Firm's property will be utilised first for firm's debts.	For these debts, only share of concerned partner in excess of firm's property over firm's debts can be used.
4. **Use of Private Property**	For these debts, only the excess of partner's private property over his private debts can be used.	For these debts, private property shall be used first.

Realisation Account

Realisation Account is prepared in order to realise the assets of the firm and the amount so realised is utilized for the payment of liabilities of firm according to the provisions of the Act. If there are any expenses incurred by the firm in realising the assets of the firm (known as realisation expenses) they are debited to this account. The difference between the two sides of this account discloses either the profit or loss on realisation and will be transferred to Partners' Capital Accounts in their profit sharing ratio.

Difference Between Realisation Account and Revaluation Account

Following are the main distinctions between Realisation Account and Revaluation Account.

Basis of Distinction	*Realisation Account*	*Revaluation Account*
1. **Time Factor**	It is prepared at the time of dissolution of the firm.	It is prepared at the time of admission, retirement, death of the partner etc.
2. **Recording of Assets and Liabilities**	It records the book value and the realised value of assets and liabilities.	It records increase or decrease in the value of assets and liabilities.
3. **Purpose**	Its main purpose is to realize the assets of the firm and to utilize this amount in payment of liabilities of the firm.	Its main purpose is to revalue the assets and liabilities of the firm on admission, retirement or death of the partner in order to ensure that no partner benefits or suffers due to change in partnership.
4. **Profit**	Profit or loss due to this effect is distributed among all the partners.	The profit or loss, thus, revealed is distributed among the old partners entitled for it.
5. **Expenses**	It contains an entry for the expenses of dissolution.	It does not contain any entry for the expenses incurred on revaluation of assets and liabilities.
6. **Effect**	It records the effect of realisation of various assets and payment of various liabilities. After opening this account, all the accounts in the ledger are closed *i.e.* there is winding up.	It records the effect of revaluation of assets and liabilities. The firm continues after opening this account.

Entries on Dissolution

A firm is closed on the dissolution, so books of account should also be closed. Books of account can be closed only if all the assets are realised in cash or otherwise, disposed of and all outside liabilities are paid off as also the partners' loans and capitals. The Balance Sheet of the firm is prepared on the date, the dissolution of the firm takes place to know the book value of assets and liabilities of the firm on that date. Following steps are taken to close the books of account.

1. For Closing Assets' Accounts. A Realisation Account is opened and all the assets at their book values (except cash and bank balances and debit balance of Profit and Loss Account) are transferred to the debit side of Realisation Account. The entry is :

Realisation Account Dr.
To Assets Account (individually)
(Being transfer of various assets at book values to Realisation Account)

Cash and Bank Accounts are not ordinarily closed by transfer to Realisation Account, but these accounts are automatically closed when the balances of Capital Accounts are finally paid. But if all the assets are taken over by any one in case of *sale of the firm*, then Cash and Bank Account (like other assets) will also be closed by transfer to Realisation Account.

The various assets against which *provisions* (*i.e.*, provision for doubtful debts, provision for depreciation, joint life policy reserve etc.) exist should be closed by transfer to Realisation Account at gross figures. The provisions should be transferred separately to Realisation Account because these are separate accounts in the books. The entry for closing the provisions is :

Provision for Doubtful Debts Dr.
Provision for Discounts Dr.
Provision for Depreciation Dr.
Joint Life Policy Reserve Dr.
Contingency Reserve Dr.
Investment Fluctuation Fund Dr.
To Realisation Account
(Being transfer of various provisions to Realisation Account)

The entry for closing the *debit balance of* Profit and Loss Account representing accumulated losses is :

Partners' Current Accounts (If the capitals are fixed) Dr.
or Partners' Capital Accounts (If the capitals are fluctuating) Dr.
To Profit and Loss Account
(Being transfer of accumulated losses)

2. For Closing Outside Liabilities' Accounts. All the liabilities to third parties are closed by transfer to Realisation Account. The entry is :

Employees Provident Fund Account Dr.
Sundry Creditors Account Dr.
Bills Payable Account Dr.
Outsider's Loan Account (other than partner) Dr.
Bank Overdraft Account Dr.
Outstanding Expenses Account Dr.
To Realisation Account
(Being transfer of liabilities to third parties)

Liabilities to third parties do not include loan accounts, current accounts and capital accounts of the partners, reserve fund and credit balance of Profit and Loss Account. Loan accounts, current accounts and capital accounts of the partners are not closed by transfer to Realisation Account but these accounts are closed when final payment is made to the partners after all the outsiders have been paid. Entry for the close of reserve fund and credit balance of Profit and Loss Account is :

Reserve Fund Dr.
Profit and Loss Account Dr.
To Partners' Capital Accounts
(Being transfer of Reserve Fund and Profit and Loss Account to Partners' Capital Accounts in their profit sharing ratio).

3. For Realising Assets. Assets may either be sold for cash, or may be taken over by any of partners, or may be taken over by any creditor in full or part payment of the amount due to him. If the assets are sold for cash, the entry is :

Cash Account Dr.
To Realisation Account
(Being assets sold for cash)

If the assets are taken over by any partner, the entry is :

Partner's Capital Account Dr.
To Realisation Account
(Being assets taken over by the partner)

If any asset is taken over by any creditor in part or full payment of the amount due to him, the value placed on the asset taken over is deducted from the amount due to the creditor and the balance of the amount due will be paid to him. Entry for the asset taken over by the creditor is not made but entry for the net payment to the creditor is made.

4. For Payment of Liabilities. First of all, payment of liabilities to third parties will be made and the entry is :

Realisation Account Dr.
To Cash or Bank Account
(Being payment of liabilities to third parties)

It may be noted that Realisation Account has been debited in place of liabilities accounts because liabilities accounts have already been closed by transfer to Realisation Account.

If some partner agrees to pay liabilities to third parties, the entry is :

Realisation Account
To Partner's Capital Account
(Being liabilities agreed to be paid by the partner)

5. For Expenses of Realisation :

Realisation Account
To Cash or Bank Account
(Being expenses incurred in connection with the dissolution of the firm)

If a partner agrees to bear all expenses of realisation in consideration of an agreed amount to be paid to him, the entry is made for the agreed amount as follows :

Realisation Account Dr.
To Partner's Capital Account
(Being expenses of realisation payable to the partner)

No entry is passed in the firm's books for the actual expenses of realisation because these expenses become the personal loss of the partner. In such a case, if actual expenses of realisation are paid by the firm, the entry is :

Partner's Capital Account Dr.
To Cash/Bank Account
(Being actual expenses of realisation agreed to be paid by the partner and paid by the firm)

6. For Closing Realisation Account. Realisation Account is a nominal account ; it is closed to find out profit or loss made or suffered on the realisation of assets and payment of outside liabilities. If the credit side of Realisation Account is more than the debit side, a profit has been made and should be transferred to Partners' Capital Accounts. The entry is :

Realisation Account
To Partners' Capital Accounts Dr.
(Being profit on realisation transferred to Capital Accounts of the partners in their profit sharing ratio).

If the debit side of Realisation Account is more than the credit side, a loss has been incurred and the entry is :

Partners' Capital Accounts Dr.
To Realisation Account

(Being loss on realisation transferred to Capital Accounts of the partners in their profit and loss sharing ratio).

7. Payment of Partner's Loan. After making the payment to third parties, the loan due to a partner is paid and the entry is :

Partner's Loan Account Dr.
To Cash/Bank Account
(Being the payment of partner's loan)

Note. Partners' loans or advances should be paid off after setting off against them any debit balance in the Capital Account of the concerned partner.

8. Closing of Current Accounts. Balances of Current Accounts of the partners (if any) should be closed by transfer to the Capital Accounts of the partners. The entry is :

(*a*) If Current Accounts show credit balances :

Partners' Current Accounts Dr.
To Partners' Capital Accounts
(Being transfer of credit balances of current accounts)

(*b*) If Current Accounts show debit balances :

Partners' Capital Accounts Dr.
To Partners' Current Accounts
(Being transfer of debit balances of current accounts)

9. For Closing Capital Accounts. If the Capital Account of any partner shows a debit balance, he should bring in cash to settle his account with the firm. The entry is :

Cash/Bank Account Dr.
To Partner's Capital Account
(Being amount due from the partner received)

Last of all, the amount due to the partners is paid and the entry is :

Partners' Capital Accounts
To Cash/Bank Account
(Being amount due to the partners paid).

Treatment of Goodwill on Dissolution

No special treatment is given to goodwill, it is treated like other assets. If it appears in the books on the dissolution date, it is closed by transferring it to the debit side of Realisation Account. If it *does not appear in the books* on the dissolution date and some amount is realised for goodwill, the entry is :

Cash/Bank Account Dr.
To Realisation Account
(Being amount realised for goodwill)

Treatment of Unrecorded Assets and Liabilities

It is possible that on the dissolution date there may be some assets and liabilities which may not be appearing in the books. Such assets and liabilities have not been recorded in the books, so question of their transfer to Realisation Account does not arise. But entries are recorded when such assets or liabilities are realised or paid.

When an *unrecorded asset is realised or taken over by a partner*, the entry is :

Cash/Bank Account Dr.
Partner's Capital Account Dr.
To Realisation Account

(Realisation of unrecorded asset being income credited to Realisation Account).

When an *unrecorded liability is paid or assumed by a partner* :

Realisation Account Dr.
To Cash/Bank Account
To Partner's Capital Account

(Payment of unrecorded liability being loss debited to Realisation Account).

ILLUSTRATION 1. P, Q and R were partners sharing Profit & Loss in the ratio of 3 : 2 : 1. They decided to dissolve the business as on 31st March, 2025 when their Balance Sheet was as follows :

Liabilities		*Amount* (₹)	*Assets*	*Amount* (₹)
Capital A/cs :			Land & Building	4,85,000
P	3,55,000		Machinery	1,88,000
Q	2,20,000		Furniture	1,05,000
R	1,25,000	7,00,000	Stock	55,800
General Reserve		1,50,000	Trade Debtors	1,56,000
Employees Provident Fund		60,000	Cash & Bank	44,200
Trade Creditors		1,24,000		
		10,34,000		10,34,000

The following information is given to your :

(*i*) There was an unrecorded investment which was sold for ₹ 30,000.

(*ii*) One of the creditors agreed to take over some items of furniture of Bank value ₹ 25,000 at 24,000. The rest of the creditors were paid at a discount of 5%.

(*iii*) Out of the trade debtors ₹ 9,000 proved bad, remaining were fully realised.

(*iv*) The other assets were realised as under :

Land & Building	₹ 5,25,000
Machinery	₹ 1,70,000
Furniture	Remaining taken over by P at ₹ 75,000
Stock	₹ 60,000

(*v*) Expenses of dissolution amounted to ₹ 18,700.

(*vi*) There was an outstanding bill for repairs which had to be paid for ₹ 3,500.

You are required to prepare :

(1) Realisation A/c

(2) Cash & Bank A/c

(3) Partners' Capital A/c in the books of partnership firm.

SOLUTION

REALISATION ACCOUNT

Particulars	(₹)	Amount (₹)	Particulars	(₹)	Amount (₹)
To Sundry Assets :			By Creditors		1,24,000
Debtors	1,56,000		By Employee's Provident Fund		60,000

Stock	55,800		By Bank A/c :		
Furniture	1,05,000		Land and Building	5,25,000	
Plant & Machinery	1,88,000		Debtors	1,47,000	
Land and Building	4,85,000	9,89,800	Stock	60,000	
To Bank-Creditors :			Machinery	1,70,000	
(W. No. 1)		95,000	Unrecorded Investment	30,000	9,32,000
To Bank A/c Ourstanding Bill			By P's Capital A/c		
for Repairs		3,500	(Furniture taken over)		75,000
To Bank A/c (Expenses)		18,700			
To Bank (Employee Provident					
Fund)		60,000			
To Profit transferred to :					
P's Capital A/c	12,000				
Q's Capital A/c	8,000				
R's Capital A/c	4,000	24,000			
		11,91,000			11,91,000

PARTNERS' CAPITAL ACCOUNTS

Particulars	*P* (₹)	*Q* (₹)	*R* (₹)	*Particulars*	*P* (₹)	*Q* (₹)	*R* (₹)
To Realisation A/c	75,000			By Balance b/d	3,55,000	2,20,000	1,25,000
To Bank	3,67,000	2,78,000	1,54,000	By General Reserve	75,000	50,000	25,000
				By Realisation Profit	12,000	8,000	4,000
	4,42,000	2,78,000	1,54,000		4,42,000	2,78,000	1,54,000

BANK ACCOUNT

Particulars	₹	*Particulars*	₹
To Balance b/d	44,200	By Realisation A/c (Liabilities Paid)	1,77,200
To Realisation A/c (Assets realised)	9,32,000	By P's Capital A/c	3,67,000
		By Q's Capital A/c	2,78,000
		By R's Capital A/c	1,54,000
	9,76,200		9,76,200

Working Note 1:

PAYMENT TO TRADE CREDITORS

Particulars	*Amount* (₹)
Trade Creditors as per Balance Sheet	1,24,000
Less : Furniture (Book Value ₹ 25,000 accepted at ₹ 24,000)	24,000
	1,00,000
Less : Discount @ 5%	5,000
Amount paid to Creditors	95,000

ILLUSTRATION 2. A, B, and C are partners of a firm of Chartered Accountants having office at Bombay, Hyderabad and Bhopal, sharing profits and losses in the ratio of 5 : 3 : 2 respectively. The Statement of Affairs of the firm as at 31st March, 2025 is shown below :

	₹	₹
Capital Accounts :		
A		15,000
B		12,000
C		6,000
Current Accounts :		
A		7,550
B	2,575	
C	1,115	
Accounts Payable		4,915
Accounts Receivable :		
Bombay	12,000	
Hyderabad	8,625	
Bhopal	9,875	
Goodwill	5,000	
Cash in hand	575	
Cash with Banks	5,700	

On that date, due to old age A desires to retire from the firm and other two partners agree and it is decided that B would take over the Bombay and Hyderabad offices and C would take over the Bhopal office with the respective assets and liabilities . You are given the following additional information :

(*a*) A's share of goodwill is valued at Rs 15,000 and this would be bought by B and C in their profit sharing ratios.

(*b*) Accounts payable include rent of the Bhopal office for the months of February and March, 2025 at the monthly rate of ₹ 250 and the balance represents outstanding expenses of Bombay and Hyderabad office.

(*c*) Cash in hand is to be utilised to pay A and other settlements *inter-se* to take place before 1st May, 2025.

(*d*) Accounts receivable to be discounted at 2%.

Draw up accounts necessary to give effect to the above and to close the books of the firm. **(*C.A. Inter*)**

SOLUTION

REALISATION ACCOUNT

	₹	₹		₹	₹
To Accounts Receivable :			By Accounts Payable		4,915
Bombay	12,000		By B (Value of net assets taken over)	(1)	15,797
Hyderabad	8,625		By C (Value of net assets taken over)	(2)	9,178
Bhopal	9,875	30,500	By Loss on Realisation transferred to Capital Accounts :	₹	
To Goodwill		5,000	A—5/10 share	2,805	
			B—3/10 share	1,683	
			C—2/10 share	1,122	5,610
		35,500			35,500

BANK ACCOUNT

	₹		₹
To Balance b/d	5,700	By A's Capital A/c	34,745
" Cash in hand	575		
" B's Capital A/c	17,055		
" C's Capital A/c	11,415		
	34,745		34,745

PARTNERS' CURRENT ACCOUNTS

	A	*B*	*C*		*A*	*B*	*C*
	₹	₹	₹		₹	₹	₹
To Balance b/d		2,575	1,115	By Balance b/d	7,550		
" Capital A/c (Transfer)	7,550			" Capital A/c (Transfer)		2,575	1,115
	7,550	2,575	1,115		7,550	2,575	1,115

CAPITAL ACCOUNTS

	A	*B*	*C*		*A*	*B*	*C*
	₹	₹	₹		₹	₹	₹
To Current A/cs		2,575	1,115	By Balance b/d	15,000	12,000	6,000
To Realisation A/c (Net assets taken over)		15,797	9,178	By Current A/c	7,550		
				" B's Capital (Goodwill)	9,000		
To Realisation A/c (Loss)	2,805	1,683	1,122	By C's Capital (Goodwill)	6,000		
" A's Capital A/c (Goodwill)		9,000	6,000	" Bank (Cash introduced)		17,055	11,415
" To Bank	34,745						
	37,550	29,055	17,415		37,550	29,055	17,415

Working Notes :

Value of net assets taken over is calculated as follows :

	(1) B (Bombay and Hyderabad Offices)		(2) C (Bhopal Office)
	₹		₹
Accounts Receivable	20,625		9,875
Less : 2% Discount	413		197
	20,212		9,678
Less : Accounts Payable	4,415	(₹ 4,915 – ₹ 500)	500 (Rent for 2 months)
Net Assets	15,797		9,178

ILLUSTRATION 3. A, B and C were partners in a business, sharing profits and losses in the ratio of 2 : 1 : 1. Their Balance Sheet as at 31-3-2025 is as follows :

BALANCE SHEET
as at 31-3-2025

(Figures in ₹ '000)

Liabilities			*Assets*		
Fixed Capital :			Fixed Assets		300
A	200		Investments		50
B	100		Current Assets :		
C	100		Stock	100	
		400	Debtors	60	
Current Accounts :			Cash & Bank	150	
A	40				310
B	20				
		60			
Unsecured Loans		200			
		660			660

On 1-4-2025, it is agreed among the partners that BC (P) Ltd., a newly formed company with B and C having each taken up 100 shares of ₹ 10 each will take over the firm as a going concern including goodwill but excluding cash & bank balances. Following points are also agreed upon :

(*a*) The Goodwill will be valued at 3 years purchase of super profit.

(*b*) The actual profit for the purpose of goodwill valuation will be ₹ 1,00,000.

(*c*) Normal rate of return will be 15% on fixed capital.

(*d*) All other assets and liabilities will be taken over at book values.

(*e*) The purchase consideration will be payable partly in shares of ₹ 10 each and partly in cash. Payment in cash being to meet the requirement to discharge A, who has agreed to retire.

(*f*) B and C are to acquire equal interest in the new company.

(*g*) Expenses of liquidation ₹ 40,000.

You are required to prepare the necessary Ledger Accounts.

SOLUTION

Calculation of Goodwill

	₹
Actual profit for the purpose of goodwill valuation	1,00,000
Less : Normal profit @ 15% on fixed capital of ₹ 4,00,000	60,000
(Fixed capital : A ₹ 2,00,000	
B ₹ 1,00,000	
C ₹ 1,00,000 ₹ 4,00,000)	
Super Profit	40,000
Goodwill at 3 Years' Purchase : ₹ 40,000 × 3	1,20,000

Calculation of Purchase Consideration

	₹
Fixed Assets	3,00,000
Investments	50,000
Stock	1,00,000
Debtors	60,000
Goodwill	1,20,000
Value of Assets taken over	6,30,000
Less : Unsecured Loans	2,00,000
Purchase Consideration	4,30,000

Necessary Ledger Accounts

REALISATION ACCOUNT

	₹		₹	₹
To Fixed Assets	3,00,000	By Unsecured Loans		2,00,000
To Investments	50,000	By BC (P) Ltd.		4,30,000
To Stock	1,00,000	By Loss on Realisation		
To Debtors	60,000	transferred to :	₹	
To Goodwill	1,20,000	A's Capital A/c	20,000	
To Bank (Expenses)	40,000	B's Capital A/c	10,000	
		C's Capital A/c	10,000	
				40,000
	6,70,000			6,70,000

PARTNERS' CAPITAL ACCOUNTS

	A ₹	B ₹	C ₹		A ₹	B ₹	C ₹
To Realisation A/c (Loss)	20,000	10,000	10,000	By Balance b/d	2,00,000	1,00,000	1,00,000
To Shares in BC (P) Ltd.		1,30,000	1,30,000	By Current A/cs (Transfer)	40,000	20,000	
To C's Capital A/c (Capital Adjustment)		10,000		By Goodwill	60,000	30,000	30,000
				By B's Capital A/c (Capital Adjustment)			10,000
To Bank	2,80,000						
	3,00,000	1,50,000	1,40,000		3,00,000	1,50,000	1,40,000

BC (P) LTD.

	₹		₹
To Realisation A/c (Purchase Consideration)	4,30,000	By Bank	1,70,000
		By Shares in BC (P) Ltd.	2,60,000
	4,30,000		4,30,000

BANK ACCOUNT

	₹		₹
To Balance b/d	1,50,000	By Realisation A/c (Expenses)	40,000
To BC (P) Ltd. (Bal. figure)	1,70,000	By A's Capital A/c	2,80,000
	3,20,000		3,20,000

SHARES IN BC (P) LTD.

	₹		₹
To BC (P) Ltd.	2,60,000	By B's Capital A/c	1,30,000
		By C's Capital A/c	1,30,000
	2,60,000		2,60,000

ILLUSTRATION 4. A, B and C have been carrying on business as wholesale grocers and they share profits 7/15, 5/15 and 3/15 respectively. On 31st December, 2024 they dissolve partnership. The Balance Sheet of the firm on that date was as follows :

Liabilities		₹	*Assets*	₹
Sundry Creditors		2,500	Land and Building	7,500
Loan		6,000	Plant and Fittings	2,250
Capitals :	₹		Stock-in-Trade	10,650
A	9,000		Horse, Cart & Harness	1,000
B	6,000		Sundry Debtors	3,000
C	2,500		Cash	1,600
		17,500		
		26,000		26,000

A and B wanted C to join them in floating the concern as a private company but C refused and A and B arranged to pay C out and then to form the company.

The agreements between A, B and C were as follows :

A and B took over the liabilities at the book figures plus ₹ 500 allowed for realisation expenses ; they also took over the cash ; and the Horse, Cart and Harness were sold for cash realising ₹ 740.

The other assets A and B agree to take over as follows :

Land and Building ₹ 10,000 ; Plant and Fittings less 10 per cent ; Stock less 20 per cent ; Debtors at ₹ 2,115.

A and B having paid the realisation expenses ₹ 500 and having paid out C by providing the required cash in the same proportion as they share profits and losses (*inter-se*) proceed to sell the assets as they stand to Punjab Trading Co. Ltd., for ₹ 12,000 cash and ₹ 12,000 in fully paid shares. A and B take shares in the *same proportion as they share profits and losses.*

A and B then pay off the liabilities themselves and close the partnership books.

You are required to show only (*a*) Cash Account, (*b*) Capital Accounts, (*c*) Realisation Account, (*d*) Punjab Trading Co. Ltd. Account. Assume that all the above transactions are put through and completed on 31st December, 2024.

SOLUTION

Books of M/s A, B and C

REALISATION ACCOUNT

			₹				₹
To	Land & Building		7,500	By	Sundry Creditors		2,500
"	Plant and Fittings		2,250	"	Loan		6,000
"	Stock-in-Trade		10,650	"	Cash (Realisation of Horse, Cart and Harness)		740
"	Horse, Cart and Harness		1,000	"	A & B Joint A/c :	₹	
"	Sundry Debtors		3,000		Land & Buildings	10,000	
"	Cash		1,600		Plant and Fittings	2,025	
"	A & B Joint A/c :	₹			Stock	8,520	
	Creditors	2,500			Debtors	2,115	
	Loan	6,000			Cash	1,600	
	Realisation Expenses	500					24,260
			9,000	By	Loss on Realisation :		
					A	700	
					B	500	
					C	300	
							1,500
			35,000				35,000

CASH ACCOUNT

	₹		₹
To Balance b/d	1,600	By Realisation A/c (Transfer)	1,600
" Realisation Account (Horse, Cart and Harness)	740	" C's Capital A/c	2,200
" A's Capital A/c	852		
" B's Capital A/c	608		
	3,800		3,800

CAPITAL ACCOUNTS

	A ₹	B ₹	C ₹		A ₹	B ₹	C ₹
To Realisation A/c (Loss)	700	500	300	By Balance b/d	9,000	6,000	2,500
To A & B Joint A/c	9,152	6,108	—	By Cash A/c (Amount brought to pay C in 7 : 5 ratio)	852	608	
To Cash A/c	—	—	2,200				
	9,852	6,608	2,500		9,852	6,608	2,500

A AND B JOINT ACCOUNT

	₹		₹
To Realisation Account (Assets taken over)	24,260	By Realisation Account (Liabilities taken over)	9,000
		" A's Capital Account	9,152
		" B's Capital Account	6,108
	24,260		24,260

Books of M/s A and B
REALISATION ACCOUNT

	₹	₹		₹
To Land & Building		10,000	By Liability for Realisation Expenses	500
" Plant & Fittings		2,025	" Sundry Creditors	2,500
" Stock		8,520	" Loan	6,000
" Debtors		2,115	" Punjab Trading Co. Ltd. (Assets sold)	24,000
" Cash (Sundry Creditors)		2,500		
" Cash (Realisation Expenses)		500		
To Cash (Loan)		6,000		
" Profit on Realisation transferred to Capitals :				
A	782			
B	558	1,340		
		33,000		33,000

PUNJAB TRADING CO. LTD.'s ACCOUNT

	₹		₹
To Realisation A/c	24,000	By Cash Account	12,000
		" Shares Account	12,000
	24,000		24,000

CASH ACCOUNT

	₹		₹
To Sundries (Cash from old firm)	1,600	By Realisation A/c (Expenses)	500
" Punjab Trading Co. Ltd.	12,000	" Realisation A/c (Loan)	6,000
		" Realisation A/c (Creditors)	2,500
		" A's Capital A/c	2,934
		" B's Capital A/c	1,666
	13,600		13,600

CAPITAL ACCOUNTS

	A	B		A	B
	₹	₹		₹	₹
To Shares A/c	7,000	5,000	By Sundry Assets	9,152	6,108
" To Cash A/c	2,934	1,666	" Realisation A/c (Profit)	782	558
	9,934	6,666		9,934	6,666

Working Note (1) :

Cash brought in by A and B has been calculated as follows :

	₹
Amount due to C	2,200
Less : Cash realisation on sale of horse, cart & harness	740
Balance to be brought by A and B in the ratio of 7 : 5	1,460

Therefore, A brings $\left(₹\,1{,}460 \times \frac{7}{12}\right)$ ₹ 852

B brings $\left(₹\,1{,}460 \times \frac{5}{12}\right)$ ₹ 608

ILLUSTRATION 5. A and B, who make up their accounts annually to 31st December were in partnership sharing profits and losses in the ratio of 2 : 1. No interest was charged on drawings or credited to capital.

Following was the summary of the balances as on 31st December, 2024.

	₹		₹
Fixture and Fittings	22,000	Partners' Capital A/cs :	
Leasehold Premises	50,000	A	31,000
Stock (Opening)	7,600	B	10,000
Debtors	1,800	Loan from A at 8% p.a.	20,000
Purchases	48,000	Creditors	6,400
General Expenses	16,000	Sales	1,04,000
Partners' Drawings :		Depreciation on Motor Vehicle	
A	6,000	as on 1-1-2024	3,600

B	4,800	Bank Overdraft	26,200
Motor Vehicle (at Cost)	9,000		
Wages	36,000		
	2,01,200		2,01,200

For the purpose of closing of accounts on 31-12-2024, closing stock was valued at ₹ 6,200 and furniture and fittings at ₹ 18,000. Provision for depreciation on motor vehicle is to be made at 20% p.a. calculated on cost and for accrued general expenses ₹ 1,200. In addition one year's interest is to be provided on A's loan.

The partnership was dissolved on 1-1-2025, it being agreed that :

(*i*) A should take over stock for ₹ 4,000.

(*ii*) B should take over motor vehicle at ₹ 2,700 and part of the fittings and fixtures for ₹ 7,500.

(*iii*) Interest on A's loan should cease with effect from 1-1-2025.

During January, 2025 the following transactions took place :

(*a*) Leasehold Premises were sold, realising a net amount of ₹ 60,000.

(*b*) ₹ 1,600 was collected from debtors and the balance was taken over by A.

(*c*) A portion of the fittings and fixtures were auctioned and realised ₹ 10,000. It was also agreed that the balance of fixtures and fittings should be taken over by B for ₹ 500.

(*d*) Creditors and accrued general expenses were paid in full.

(*e*) Realisation expenses amounted to ₹ 1,400.

(*f*) All amounts receivable and payable by A and B were settled.

Prepare : (1) Profit and Loss Account for the year ended 31st December, 2024 excluding profit or loss arising on dissolution. (2) Realisation Account. (3) Cash Account for January, 2025. (4) Partners' Accounts showing the final settlement of dissolution.

SOLUTION

PROFIT AND LOSS ACCOUNT OF M/s A AND B

for the year ended 31st December, 2024

		₹			₹
To Opening Stock		7,600	By Sales		1,04,000
" Purchases		48,000	" Closing Stock		6,200
" Wages		36,000			
" Gross Profit c/d		18,600			
	₹	1,10,200			1,10,200
To General Expenses	16,000		By Gross Profit b/d		18,600
Add : Accrued	1,200	17,200	" Net Loss transferred to Capital Accounts :	₹	
" Depreciation on Motor Vehicle @ 20% on ₹ 9,000		1,800	A—2/3 share	4,000	
			B—1/3 share	2,000	6,000
To Loss on Fixtures and Fittings (₹ 22,000 – ₹ 18,000)		4,000			
" Interest on Loan from A @ 8% on ₹ 20,000		1,600			
		24,600			24,600

REALISATION ACCOUNT

		₹			₹
To Stock (Closing)		6,200	By A's Capital Account (Stock taken over)		6,000
" Fixtures and Fittings (Revalued Amount)		18,000	" B's Capital Account :	₹	
" Leasehold Premises		50,000	Motor Vehicles taken over	2,700	
" Debtors		1,800	Fixtures taken over	7,500	10,200
" Motor Vehicles (₹ 9,000 – ₹ 3,600 – ₹ 1,800) (Depreciated Value)		3,600	" Cash Account (Debtors)		1,600
" Cash Account (Realisation Expenses)		1,400	" A's Capital Account (Balance of debtors taken)		200
To Profit on Realisation transferred Capital A/cs :	₹		" Cash Account (Fixtures)		10,000
A—2/3 share	5,000		By B's Capital Account (Balance of fixtures taken)		500
B—1/3 share	2,500	7,500	" Cash Account (Premises)		60,000
		88,500			88,500

CASH ACCOUNT

	₹		₹
To Realisation Account (Debtors)	1,600	By Bank Overdraft	26,200
" Realisation Account (Fixtures)	10,000	" A's Loan Account	20,000
" Realisation Account (Premises)	60,000	" Interest on A's Loan	1,600
" B's Capital Account	5,000	" Creditors	6,400
		" Realisation Account (Expenses)	1,400
		" Accrued Expenses Account	1,200
		" A's Capital Account	19,800
	76,600		76,600

PARTNERS' CAPITAL ACCOUNTS

	A	*B*		*A*	*B*
	₹	₹		₹	₹
To Drawings Account	6,000	4,800	By Balance b/d	31,000	10,000
" Profit & Loss A/c (Loss)	4,000	2,000	" Realisation A/c (Profit on Realisation Account)	5,000	2,500
" Realisation A/c :			" Cash Account	—	5,000
Stock taken over	6,000	—			
Motor Vehicles taken over	—	2,700			
Fixtures taken over (₹ 7,500 + ₹ 500)	—	8,000			
Debtors taken over	200	—			
" Cash Account	19,800				
	36,000	17,500		36,000	17,500

Note. Alternatively, Sundry Creditors, Loan from A, Interest on Loan from A, Accrued Expenses and Bank Overdraft can be transferred to Realisation Account on the credit side and their payment is shown on the debit side of Realisation Account.

ILLUSTRATION 6. A, B and C have been in partnership since 1st July, 2006. C received a fixed and guaranteed share of ₹ 2,500 per annum and the balance of profits and losses divisible between A and B in the proportion of three-fifths and two-fifths respectively.

On 1st July, 2024, A and B mutually agreed with C that he should be entitled to a one-tenth share in the partnership and C paid the sum of ₹ 500 into the partnership funds on that date for his share of goodwill.

The firm was dissolved on 30th June, 2025 as B had disclosed prior to that date that he had been responsible for the following irregularities :

(1) The value of stock on hand on 30th June, 2024 had been inflated by B by ₹ 2,500 to cover goods (at their cost price) removed and sold by him personally for ₹ 2,500. The partners agreed that the stock should have realised ₹ 3,000. The stock on 30th June, 2025 was correctly valued at ₹ 17,875.

(2) Cheques received from old debtors in June, 2025, amounting to ₹ 1,500 (and in respect of which no discount was allowable) had been omitted from the books of account and appropriated by B for his own use.

(3) In March, 2025 B had got some private work done by the firm's printers : bills amounting to ₹ 200 had been passed through firm's books and debited to Printing and Stationery Account.

The Balance Sheet as on 30th June, 2025 (before making adjustments on account of B's disclosure) was as follows :

	₹	₹		₹	₹
Trade Creditors	20,000		Sundry Fixed Assets		2,500
Less : Reserve for Discount	500		Stock		17,875
		19,500	Trade Debtors	39,000	
Bank Overdraft		1,000	*Less* : Provision for Discount	1,950	
Partners' Capitals :					37,050
A	35,100		Cash		775
B	2,250				
C	350				
		37,700			
		58,200			58,200

The goodwill and other assets except cash were taken over by A for ₹ 60,000. Final settlement was made on July 31, 2025, B having agreed to make good the amount due by him to the partnership. The creditors were also paid on that date, discount being allowed as per provision. B is not to be penalised for his irregularities.

Pass Journal Entries in respect of B's irregularities and prepare Ledger Accounts to close the books of the firm.

SOLUTION

Adjustment entry regarding stock is to be made as follows :

	A ₹	B ₹	C ₹
Profit was inflated by ₹ 2,500 because of inflation in stock on 30-6-2024 ; so excess credit was given to partners A and B in proportion to 3 : 2.	1,500	1,000	—
Profit was understated because of inflation in opening stock on 1-7-2024 (Closing stock becoming opening stock) ; so excess debit given to partners A, B & C in proportion to 27 : 18 : 5 (new ratio).	1,350	900	250
Excess credit or debit given previously	150 Cr.	100 Cr.	250 Dr.

	A	B	C
Debit for goods removed by B	–	3,000	–
Credit for goods removed by B to be given to A and B in their old ratio of 3 : 2 ; C is not to share because goods were removed before C's admission.	1,800	1,200	–
Adjustments Required	1,650 Cr.	1,900 Dr.	250 Cr.

Note. Excess credit or debit given previously is reversed so that it is cancelled.

JOURNAL ENTRIES

			₹	₹
	B's Capital Account	Dr.	1,900	
	To A's Capital Account			1,650
	To C's Capital Account			250
	[Being adjustment (as explained above) for stock taken by B]			
	B's Capital A/c	Dr.	1,500	
	To Sundry Debtors			1,500
	(Being money realised from debtors and appropriated by B)			
	Provision for Discount Account	Dr.	75	
	To A's Capital A/c			45
	To B's Capital A/c			30
	(Being amount of provision for discount not allowable written back to old partners A and B in their old profit sharing ratio of 3 : 2. C is not to share because provision is in respect of debtors of the old firm)			
	B's Capital A/c	Dr.	200	
	To Profit and Loss Adjustment A/c			200
	(Being private work of B done by firm's printers charged to printing and stationery instead of to B)			
	Profit and Loss Adjustment A/c	Dr.	200	
	To A's Capital A/c			108
	To B's Capital A/c			72
	To C' Capital A/c			20
	(Being profit transferred to A, B and C in their new profit sharing ratio of 27 : 18 : 5)			

REALISATION ACCOUNT

		₹		₹
To Sundry Fixed Assets		2,500	By Provision for Discount (₹ 1,950 – ₹ 75)	1,875
" Stock		17,875	" Trade Creditors	20,000
" Trade Debtors (₹ 39,000 – ₹ 1,500)		37,500	" Bank Overdraft	1,000
" Reserve for Discount on Creditors		500	" A's Capital A/c—Sundry Assets	60,000
" Bank—Sundry Creditors		19,500		
" Bank—Bank Overdraft		1,000		
" Profit transferred to Capital Accounts:	₹			
A	2,160			
B	1,440			
C	400	4,000		
		82,875		82,875

BANK ACCOUNT

	₹		₹
To Balance b/d	775	By Realisation A/c—Sundry Creditors	19,500
" A's Capital A/c	20,937	" Realisation A/c—Bank Overdraft	1,000
		" B's Capital A/c	192
		" C's Capital A/c	1,020
	21,712		21,712

CAPITAL ACCOUNTS

	A	B	C		A	B	C
	₹	₹	₹		₹	₹	₹
To A's Capital A/c (for stock)		1,650		By Balance b/d	35,100	2,250	350
" C's Capital A/c (for stock)		250		" B's Capital A/c (for stock)	1,650	—	250
" Sundry Debtors		1,500		" Provision for Discount A/c	45	30	—
" Profit and Loss Adjustment A/c		200		" Profit and Loss Adjustment A/c	108	72	20
" Realisation A/c —Sundry Assets	60,000			" Realisation A/c (Profit)	2,160	1,440	400
" Bank	—	192	1,020	" Bank	20,937	—	—
	60,000	3,792	1,020		60,000	3,792	1,020

ILLUSTRATION 7. On 31st March, 2024, Sri Raman acquires on payment of ₹ 80,000 the business of M/s Gupta and Singh taking over at book value the following assets and liabilities :

Debtors ₹ 35,000 ; Furniture ₹ 3,000 ; Stock ₹ 46,000 ; Creditors ₹ 10,000.

There was no change between 1st January, 2024 and 31st March, 2024 in the book value of the assets and liabilities not taken over.

The same set of books has been continued after the acquisition and no entries for the acquisition have been passed except for the payment of ₹ 80,000 made by Sri Raman.

From the following balance sheet and trial balance prepare Business Purchase Account, Profit and Loss Account for the year ended 31st December 2024, and Balance Sheet as at that date.

BALANCE SHEET

as at 31st December, 2023

Liabilities		₹	*Assets*	₹
Capital Account :			Furniture	3,000
	₹		Investments	5,000
Sri Gupta	30,000		Insurance Policy	2,000
Sri Singh	20,000		Stock	40,000
		50,000	Debtors	30,000
Bank Loan		18,000		
Creditors		12,000		
		80,000		80,000

On 31st December, 2024, the Trial Balance is :

	₹	₹
Stock	40,000	
Furniture	3,000	
Investments	5,000	
Insurance Policy	2,000	
Business Purchase Account	80,000	
Bank Loan		18,000
Capital :		
Gupta		30,000
Singh		20,000
Raman		30,000
Bank	3,000	
Debtors	48,000	
Creditors		15,000
Purchases	3,20,000	
Expenses	12,000	
Sales		4,00,000
	5,13,000	5,13,000

Closing Stock ₹ 50,000

SOLUTION

BUSINESS PURCHASE ACCOUNT

	₹		₹
To Balance b/d	80,000	By Bank Loan (Not taken)	18,000
To Investments (Not taken)	5,000	By Gupta's Capital A/c	30,000
To Insurance Policy (Note taken)	2,000	By Singh's Capital A/c	20,000
		By Goodwill (1)	6,000
		By Profit & Loss A/c (2) (Balancing figure, profit for 3 months from January 1, 2024 to March 31, 2024)	13,000
	87,000		87,000

PROFIT AND LOSS ACCOUNT OF MR. RAMAN

for the year ended 31st December, 2024

	₹		₹
To Opening Stock	40,000	By Sales	4,00,000
" Purchases	3,20,000	By Closing Stock	50,000
" Expenses	12,000		
" Gupta & Singh (Profit upto 31st March)	13,000		
" Net Profit transferred to Raman's Capital A/c	65,000		
	4,50,000		4,50,000

BALANCE SHEET OF MR. RAMAN
as on 31st December, 2024

Liabilities		₹	*Assets*	₹
Sundry Creditors	₹	15,000	Cash at Bank	3,000
Raman's Capital	30,000		Sundry Debtors	48,000
Add : Profit	65,000		Stock in Trade	50,000
		95,000	Furniture	3,000
			Goodwill	6,000
		1,10,000		1,10,000

Working Notes :

(1) *Calculation of Goodwill*

	₹
Value of Assets taken over :	
Stock	46,000
Debtors	35,000
Furniture	3,000
	84,000
Less : Creditors	10,000
Value of Net Assets taken over	74,000
Goodwill (Balancing figure)	6,000
Purchase Consideration	80,000

(2) *Calculation of Profit for three months ending 31st March belonging to Gupta and Singh*

It can be calculated by seeing increase in net assets for 3 months from January 1, 2024 to March 31, 2024 shown as below :

	as on 1st January	*as on 31st March*
	₹	₹
Furniture	3,000	3,000
Stock	40,000	46,000
Debtors	30,000	35,000
	73,000	84,000
Less : Creditors	12,000	10,000
Net Assets	61,000	74,000
Profit equal to increase in value of net assets	13,000	—
	74,000	74,000

Insolvency of a Partner—Garner *vs.* Murray Rule

If a partner' Capital Account shows a debit balance on the dissolution of the firm, he is to pay the debit balance to the firm to settle his account. But if such a partner is insolvent *i.e.*, unable to satisfy his debt to the firm, then his deficiency which he is not able to bring will be borne by the other solvent partners in accordance with the decision in *Garner* vs. *Murray*. In this case it was ruled that, in the absence of any agreement to the contrary, the deficiency on the insolvent partner's Capital Account must be borne by other solvent partners in proportion to their capitals which stood before the dissolution of the firm. The effect of this ruling is to make a distinction between an ordinary loss due to trading or realisation of assets and loss on account of insolvency of a partner. The loss on account of the insolvency of a partner is a capital loss and as such should be borne by the other solvent partners in proportion to their capitals. The practice before this decision was to share the deficiency of the insolvent partner by the solvent partners in their profit and loss sharing ratios. No distinction was observed between trading loss and capital loss.

Another ruling in *Garner* vs. *Murray* case is that the solvent partners should bring in cash equal to their share of loss on realisation. This ruling has been given to bring the capital accounts of the solvent partners to the figures they stood before transferring the loss on realisation. A large majority of the accountants are of the view that the second ruling given in the *Garner* vs. *Marray* case is a useless ruling. The argument advanced by them against this ruling is that it is unreasonable to ask a solvent partner to bring in cash his share of loss on realisation when he already has a credit balance in his Capital Account. The only point to be kept in mind is that the deficiency of the insolvency partner should be borne by the solvent partners in proportion to their capitals which stood before debiting the loss on realisation.

Fixed and Fluctuating Capitals

While determining the capital ratio of the solvent partners, distinction should be observed between fixed and fluctuating capital. If the capitals of the partners have been agreed to be fixed, then no adjustment is required for accumulated profits or losses, interest on capitals, drawings etc. and deficiency of the insolvent partner is borne by the solvent partners in proportion to their agreed fixed capitals. All adjustments relating to accumulated profits or losses, reserves, interest on capitals and drawings will be recorded in the current accounts of the partners. The deficiency of the insolvent partner will be ascertained after transferring the balance of the insolvent partner's Current Account to his Capital Account. The deficiency of the insolvent partner should be transferred to the Current Accounts of the solvent partners in proportion to their agreed fixed capitals. The entry is :

Solvent Partners' Current Accounts Dr.

To Insolvent Partner's Capital Account

(Being transfer of the deficiency of the insolvent partner to the solvent partners' current accounts in proportion to their agreed fixed capitals)

But if the capital accounts are maintained on fluctuating basis, then Capital Accounts should be adjusted for reserves, profits or losses, interest on capitals and drawings and the capitals thus arrived at should be the basis of ratio according to which the deficiency of the insolvent partner is to be borne by the solvent partners. It may be remembered that the loss on realisation is not to be taken into consideration while ascertaining the capital ratio of the solvent partners because deficiency of the insolvent partner is to be met by the solvent partners in proportion to their capitals which stood before the dissolution of the firm. The entry for meeting the deficiency is :

Solvent Partners' Capital Accounts Dr.

To Insolvent Partner's Capital Account

(Being transfer of the deficiency of the insolvent partner to the solvent partner's capital accounts).

The criticism of the decision in *Garner* vs. *Murray* is that it violates the principles of natural justice and equity. If some solvent partner is having a debit balance in his Capital Account on the dissolution date, he will not have to bear the loss on account of the deficiency of the insolvent partner because capital ratios of the solvent partners are based on their respective credit balances. Thus, solvent partner having a debit balance in his Capital Account is not to meet any share of the deficiency even though he may be financially more sound as compared to other solvent partners.

Applicability of Garner Vs. Murray in India

Some people are of the view that in India the decision in Garner vs. Murray does not apply. But there is nothing in the Indian Partnership Act, 1932 which goes against the rule laid down in Garner vs. Murray case. Therefore, it would be safe to follow it till an Indian Court definitely gives decision contrary to the decision given in Garner vs. Murray. Loss on realisation brought in cash by the solvent partners as given in Garner vs. Murray decision may not be followed taking it as an undesirable ruling.

If an examination problem states that the rule in Garner vs. Murray is to be followed, the solvent partners should bring in cash their respective shares of loss on realisation. If no mention is made of Garner vs. Murray decision in the problem to be solved, the solvent partners may not be required to bring their shares of loss on realisation in cash. But the other ruling given in the case is to be followed. That is, in the absence of any agreement to the contrary, the solvent partners should bear the loss arising due to the insolvency of a partner in proportion to their capitals which stood before the dissolution of the firm.

Non-Applicability of Garner Vs. Murray Rule

1. When the solvent partner has a debit balance in the Capital Account.
   Only solvent partners will bear the loss of capital deficiency of the insolvent partner in their capital ratio. If incidentally a solvent partner has a debit balance in his Capital Account, he will escape the liability to bear the loss due to insolvency of another partner.
2. When the firm has only two partners.
3. When there is an agreement between the partners to share the deficiency in Capital Account of insolvent partner.
4. When all the partners of the firm are insolvent.

ILLUSTRATION 8. G, S & J were partners sharing profits and losses in the ratio of 4 : 3 : 2, no partnership salary or interest on capital being allowed. Their Balance Sheet as on 31-3-2025 is as follows :

Liabilities	*Amount* (₹)	*Amount* (₹)	*Assets*	*Amount* (₹)	*Amount* (₹)
Partners' Fixed Capital A/cs :			Fixed Assets :		
G	24,000		Goodwill	48,000	
S	24,000		Land	9,600	
J	12,000	60,000	Plant and Machinery	15,360	
Partners' Current A/c :			Motor Car	840	73,800
G	600		Current Assets :		
S	10,800		Stock		4,680
J	(480)	10,920	Trade Debtors	2,400	
Loan from G		9,600	*Less* : Provision	120	2,280
Trade Creditors		14,880	Cash at Bank		240
			Miscellaneous Losses :		
			Profit & Loss Sale		14,400
		95,400			95,400

On 1st April, 2025, the partnership was dissolved. Moto car was taken over by G at a value of ₹ 600, but no cash was given specifically in respect of this transaction. Sale of other assets realised the following amounts.

Particulars	₹
Goodwill	Nil
Land	8,400
Plant & Machinery	6,000
Stock	3,600
Trade Debtors	1,920

Trade creditors were paid ₹ 14,040 in full settlement of their debts. The cost of dissolution amounted to ₹ 1,800. The loan from G was repaid; G and S both were fully solvent and able to bring in any cash required but J was forced into bankruptcy and was only able to bring 1/2 of the amount due.

You are required to prepare :

(*i*) Cash and Bank account

(*ii*) Realisation account, and

(*iii*) Partners' Fixed Capital Accounts (after transferring current accounts balances)

Apply Garner *Vs*. Murray rule.

SOLUTION

CASH & BANK ACCOUNT

		₹		₹
To Balance b/d		240	By Realisation A/c : Creditors	14,040
To Realisation A/c :			By Realisation A/c : Expenses	1,800
Land		8,400	By G's Loan A/c	9,600
Plant and Machinery		6,000	By G's Capital A/c	16,280
Stock		3,600	By S's Capital A/c	28,680
Trade Debtors		1,920		
To Capital Accounts :				
G	27,200			
S	20,400			
J	2,640	50,240		
		70,400		70,400

REALISATION ACCOUNT

	₹			₹
To Goodwill	48,000	By Trade Creditors		14,880
To Land	9,600	By Provision for Bad Debts		120
To Plant and Machinery	15,360	By Bank :		
To Motor Car	840	Land	8,400	
To Stock	4,680	Plant and Machinery	6,000	
To Sundry Debtors	2,400	Stock	3,600	
To Bank (Creditors)	14,040	Debtors	1,920	19,920
To Bank (Expenses)	1,800	By G (Car)		600
		By Capital Accounts : (Loss)		
		G	27,200	
		S	20,400	
		J	13,600	61,200
	96,720			96,720

PARTNERS' FIXED CAPITAL ACCOUNTS

	G	S	J		G	S	J
	₹	₹	₹		₹	₹	₹
To Current A/c (Transfer)	5,800	—	3,680	By Balance b/d	24,000	24,000	12,000
To Realisation A/c (Loss)	27,200	20,400	13,600	By Current A/c (Transfer)	—	6,000	—
To Realisation A/c (Car)	600	—	—	By Bank	—	—	2,640

To J's Capital A/c (Deficiency)	1,320	1,320	—	By Bank * (Realisation Loss)	27,200	20,400	—
To Bank*	16,280	28,680	—	By G & S (Deficiency)	—	—	2,640
	51,200	50,400	17,280		51,200	50,400	17,280

Note :

1. G, S and J will bring cash to make good their share of the loss on realisation.
2. As per Garner *Vs.* Murray rule, solvent partners—G and S have to bear the loss due to insolvency of a partner J in their fixed capital ratio.

*Alternatively, posting may be done for the net amount being received from/paid to G and S respectively.

Working Note :

Current account balances of partners have been arrived after adjusting profit and loss account debit balance as follows :

	Current account balance	Profit & Loss		
G	600	(6,400)	5,800	Dr.
S	10,800	(4,800)	6,000	Cr.
J	(480)	(3,200)	3,680	Dr.

ILLUSTRATION 9. Ram, Rahim and Auntony were in partnership sharing profits and losses in the ratio of 1/2, 1/3 and 1/6 respectively. They decided to dissolve the partnership firm on 31-3-2025 when the Balance Sheet of the firm appeared as under :

BALANCE SHEET OF THE FIRM

as on 31-3-2025

Liabilities		₹	*Assets*	₹
Sundry Creditors		5,67,000	Goodwill A/c	4,56,300
Bank Overdraft		6,06,450	Plant and Machinery	6,07,500
Joint Life Policy Reserve		2,65,500	Furniture	64,650
Loan from Mrs. Ram		1,50,000	Stock	2,36,700
Capital Accounts :	₹		Sundry Debtors	5,34,000
Ram	4,20,000		Joint Life Policy	2,65,500
Rahim	2,25,000		Commission Receivable	1,40,550
Auntony	1,20,000	7,65,000	Cash on Hand	48,750
		23,53,950		23,53,950

Following details are relevant for dissolution :

(*i*) The joint life policy was surrendered for ₹ 2,32,500.

(*ii*) Ram took over goodwill and plant and machinery for ₹ 9,00,000.

(*iii*) Ram also agreed to discharge bank overdraft and loan from Mrs. Ram.

(*iv*) Furniture and stocks were divided equally between Ram and Rahim at an agreed valuation of ₹ 3,60,000.

(*v*) Sundry debtors were assigned to firm's creditors in full satisfaction of their claims.

(*vi*) Commission receivable was received in toto in time.

(*vii*) A bill discounted was subsequently returned dishonoured and proved valueless ₹ 30,750 (including ₹ 500 noting charges).

(*viii*) Ram paid the expenses of dissolution amounting to ₹ 18,000.

(*ix*) Auntony agreed to receive ₹ 1,50,000 in full satisfaction of his rights, title and interest in the firm.

You are required to show accounts relating to closing of books on dissolution of the firm.

SOLUTION

REALISATION ACCOUNT

		₹			₹
To Goodwill A/c		4,56,300	By Sundry Creditors A/c		5,67,000
To Plant & Machinery A/c		6,07,500	By Joint Life Policy Reserve A/c		2,65,500
To Furniture A/c		64,650	By Cash A/c : (Joint Life Policy)		2,32,500
To Stock A/c		2,36,700	By Ram's Capital A/c :		
To Sundry Debtors A/c		5,34,000	Goodwill, Plant &	₹	
To Joint Life Policy A/c		2,65,500	Machinery	9,00,000	
To Ram's Capital A/c :			Furniture, Stocks	1,80,000	
(Dissolution Expenses)		18,000			10,80,000
To Cash A/c :			By Rahim's Capital A/c :		
Bill Dishonoured		30,750	(Furniture, Stocks)		1,80,000
To Partners' Capital Accounts :					
(Profit on realisation)	₹				
Ram	55,800				
Rahim	37,200				
Auntony	18,600				
		1,11,600			
		23,25,000			23,25,000

CAPITAL ACCOUNTS

	Ram	Rahim	Auntony		Ram	Rahim	Auntony
	₹	₹	₹		₹	₹	₹
To Realisation A/c :				By Balance b/d	4,20,000	2,25,000	1,20,000
Goodwill and Plant and Machinery	9,00,000	—	—	By Bank Overdraft A/c	6,06,450	—	—
Furniture and Stocks	1,80,000	1,80,000	—	By Loan from Mrs. Ram A/c	1,50,000	—	—
To Auntony's Capital A/c	6,840	4,560	—	By Realisation A/c : (Dissolution Exp.)	18,000	—	—
To Cash A/c	—	—	1,50,000	By Realisation A/c : (Profit on Realisation)	55,800	37,200	18,600
To Cash A/c (Balancing figure)	1,63,410	77,640	—	By Partners' Capital A/cs :	—	—	—
				Ram (3/5 of ₹ 11,400)	—	—	6,840
				Rahim (2/5 of ₹ 11,400)	—	—	4,560
	12,50,250	2,62,200	1,50,000		12,50,250	2,62,200	1,50,000

CASH ACCOUNT

	₹		₹
To Balance b/d	48,750	By Realisation A/c :	
To Realisation A/c : (Joint Life Policy)	2,32,500	(Bill dishonoured)	30,750
To Commission Receivable A/c	1,40,550	By Partners' Capital Accounts :	
		Ram	1,63,410
		Rahim	77,640
		Auntony	1,50,000
	4,21,800		4,21,800

Note : No entry is required regarding the assignment of sundry debtors to sundry creditors in full satisfaction of their claims.

ILLUSTRATION 10. A, B, C and D are sharing profits and losses sin the ratio 5 : 5 : 4 : 2. Frauds committed by C during the year were found out and it was decided to dissolve the partnership on 31st March, 2025 when their Balance Sheet was as under :

Liabilities	*Amount*	*Assets*	*Amount*
	₹		₹
Capitals		Building	1,20,000
A	90,000	Stock	85,500
B	90,000	Investments	29,000
C	—	Debtors	42,000
D	35,000	Cash	14,500
General Reserve	24,000	C	15,000
Trade Creditors	47,000		
Bills Payable	20,000		
	3,06,000		3,06,000

Following information is given to you :

(*i*) A cheque for ₹ 4,300 received from debtor was not recorded in the books and was misappropriated by C.

(*ii*) Investments costing ₹ 5,400 were sold by C at ₹ 7,900 and the funds transferred to his personal account. This sale was omitted from the firm's books.

(*iii*) A creditor agreed to take over investments of the book value of ₹ 5,400 at ₹ 8,400. The rest of the creditors were paid off at a discount of 2%.

(*iv*) The other assets realised as follows :

Building 105% of book value ; Stock ₹ 78,000 ; Investments The rest of investments were sold at a profit of ₹ 4,800 ; Debtors The rest of the debtors were realised at a discount of 12%

(*v*) The bills payable were settled at a discount of ₹ 400.

(*vi*) The expenses of dissolution amounted to ₹ 4,900

(*vii*) It was found out that realisation from C's private assets would only be ₹ 4,000.

Prepare the necessary Ledger Accounts.

SOLUTION

REALISATION ACCOUNT

	₹		₹
To Building	1,20,000	By Trade Creditors	47,000
To Stock	85,500	By Bills Payable	20,000

		₹		₹	₹
To Investments		29,000	By Cash :		
To Debtors		42,000	Building	1,26,000	
To Cash—Creditors paid (1)		37,828	Stock	78,000	
To Cash—Expenses		4,900	Investments (2)	23,000	
To Cash—Bills Payable (₹ 20,000 – ₹ 400)		19,600	Debtors (3)	33,176	
To Profit on Realisation transferred to					2,60,176
Partners' Capital A/cs :	₹		By Debtors—Unrecorded		4,300
A	171		By Investments—Unrecorded		7,900
B	171				
C	137				
D	69				
		548			
		3,39,376			3,39,376

CASH ACCOUNT

		₹		₹
To Balance b/d		14,500	By Realisation—Creditors paid	37,828
To Realisation—Assets realised	₹		By Realisation—Bills Payable	19,600
Building	1,26,000		By Realisation—Expenses	4,900
Stock	78,000		By Capital Accounts :	
Investments	23,000		A	90,531
Debtors	33,176		B	90,531
		2,60,176	D	35,286
To C's Capital A/c		4,000		
		2,78,676		2,78,676

PARTNERS' CAPITAL ACCOUNTS

	A	B	C	D		A	B	C	D
	₹	₹	₹	₹		₹	₹	₹	₹
To Balance b/d			15,000		By Balance b/d	90,000	90,000	—	35,000
To Debtors —Misappropriation			4,300		By General Reserve	7,500	7,500	6,000	3,000
To Investments —Misappropriation			7,900		By Realisation Profit	171	171	137	69
					By Cash A/c			4,000	
					By A's Capital A/c			7,140	
To C's Capital A/c (4)	7,140	7,140		2,783	By B's Capital A/c			7,140	
To Cash A/c	90,531	90,531		35,286	By D's Capital A/c			2,783	
	97,671	97,671	27,200	38,069		97,671	97,671	27,200	38,069

Working Notes :

(1) Amount paid to creditors

	₹
Book value	47,000
Less : Creditors taking over investments	8,400
	38,600
Less : Discount @ 2%	772
	37,828

(2) Amount received from sale of investments

	₹
Book Value	29,000
Less : Misappropriated by C	5,400
	23,600
Less : Taken over by a creditor	5,400
	18,200
Add : Profit on sale of investments	4,800
	23,000

(3) Amount received from debtors

	₹
Book Value	42,000
Less : Unrecorded receipt	4,300
	37,700
Less : Discount @ 12%	4,524
	33,176

(4) Deficiency of C

	₹
Balance of Capital as on 31-3-2025 (Dr.)	15,000
Debtors—Misappropriation	4,300
Investment—Misappropriation	7,900
	27,200
Less : Realisation Profit	(137)
General Reserve	(6,000)
Contribution from Private Assets	(4,000)
Net Deficiency of Capital	17,063

This deficiency of ₹ 17,063 in C's Capital Account will be shared by other partners A, B and D in their capital ratio of 97,500 : 97,500 : 38,000 which is after transferring the share of General Reserve.

Accordingly,

A's share of deficiency $= \left[17{,}063 \times \frac{97{,}500}{2{,}33{,}000}\right] =$ ₹ 7,140

B's share of deficiency $= \left[17{,}063 \times \frac{97{,}500}{2{,}33{,}000}\right] =$ ₹ 7,140

D's share of deficiency $= \left[17{,}063 \times \frac{38{,}000}{2{,}33{,}000}\right] =$ ₹ 2,783

ILLUSTRATION 11. The firm of A and B has four partners and as on 31st March, 2025, its Balance Sheet stood as follows :

	₹		₹
Capital A/cs :		Land	50,000
A	2,00,000	Building	2,50,000
B	2,00,000	Office Equipment	1,25,000
C	1,00,000	Computers	70,000
Current A/cs :		Debtors	4,00,000
A	50,000	Stocks	3,00,000
B	1,50,000	Cash at Bank	75,000
C	1,10,000	Other Current Assets	22,600
Loan from NBFC	5,00,000	Current A/c :	
Current Liabilities	70,000	D	87,400
	13,80,000		13,80,000

The partners have been sharing profit and losses in the ratio of 4 : 4 : 1 : 1. It has been agreed to dissolve the firm on 1-4-2025 on the basis of the following understanding :

(*a*) Following assets are to be realised to the extent indicated with respect to the book values :

Land 200% ; Building 120% ; Computers 70% ; Debtors 95% ; Stocks 90% ;

(*b*) In the case of the loan, the lenders are to be paid at their insistence at a prepayment premium of 1%.

(*c*) D is insolvent and no amount is recoverable from him. His father, C, however, agrees to bear 50% of his deficiency. The balance of the deficiency is agreed to be apportioned according to law.

Assuming that the realisation of the assets and discharge of liabilities is carried out immediately, show Realisation A/c, Partners' Capital Accounts and Cash Account.

SOLUTION

REALISATION ACCOUNT

		₹			₹
To Land		50,000	By Loan from NBFC		5,00,000
To Building		2,50,000	By Current Liabilities		70,000
To Office Equipment		1,25,000	By Cash A/c (Assets Realised) :	₹	
To Computers		70,000	Land $\left(₹ 50,000 \times \frac{200}{100}\right)$	1,00,000	
To Debtors		4,00,000			
To Stocks		3,00,000			
To Other Current Assets		22,600	Building $\left(₹ 2,50,000 \times \frac{120}{100}\right)$	3,00,000	
To Cash A/c (Loan from NBFC ₹ 5,00,000 + 1% of ₹ 5,00,000)		5,05,000			
To Cash A/c (Current Liabilities)		70,000	Office Equipment	1,25,000	
To Profit on Realisation transferred to :	₹		Computers $\left(₹ 70,000 \times \frac{70}{100}\right)$	49,000	
Current A/cs A(4/10)	9,600				
B (4/10)	9,600		Debtors $\left(₹ 4,00,000 \times \frac{95}{100}\right)$	3,80,000	
C (1/10)	2,400				
D (1/10)	2,400	24,000	Stocks $\left(₹ 3,00,000 \times \frac{90}{100}\right)$	2,70,000	
			Other Current Assets	22,600	12,46,600
		18,16,600			18,16,600

PARTNERS' CURRENT ACCOUNTS

	A	B	C	D		A	B	C	D
	₹	₹	₹	₹		₹	₹	₹	₹
To Balance b/d	—	—	—	87,400	By Balance b/d	50,000	1,50,000	1,10,000	—
To Partners' Capital A/cs (Transfer)	59,600	1,59,600	1,12,400	—	By Realisation A/c (Profit)	9,600	9,600	2,400	2,400
					By D's Capital A/c (Transfer)				85,000
	59,600	1,59,600	1,12,400	87,400		59,600	1,59,600	1,12,400	87,400

PARTNERS' CAPITAL ACCOUNTS

	A	B	C	D		A	B	C	D
	₹	₹	₹	₹		₹	₹	₹	₹
To D's Current A/c				85,000	By Balance b/d	2,00,000	2,00,000	1,00,000	—
To D's Capital A/c (50% of D's deficiency)			42,500		By Partners' Current A/cs	59,600	1,59,600	1,12,400	
To D's Capital A/c (Balance of deficiency borne in capital ratio of 2 : 2 : 1)	17,000	17,000	8,500	—	By C's Capital A/c (50% of D's Deficiency)				42,500
To Cash A/c (final settlement)	2,42,600	3,42,600	1,61,400	—	By A's Capital A/c				17,000
					By B's Capital A/c				17,000
					By C's Capital A/c (as per contra)				8,500
	2,59,600	3,59,600	2,12,400	85,000		2,59,600	3,59,600	2,12,400	85,000

CASH ACCOUNT

	₹		₹
To Balance b/d	75,000	By Realisation A/c (Loan from NBFC)	5,05,000
To Realisation A/c (Assets Realised)	12,46,600	By Realisation A/c (Current Liabilities)	70,000
		By Capital A/cs : A	2,42,600
		B	3,42,600
		C	1,61,400
	13,21,600		13,21,600

When All Partners are Insolvent

When all partners are insolvent and are not able to bring the amount due from them then the creditors of the firm cannot be paid in full. Then there are two methods for closing the books of accounts of the firm.

(a) Where outside liabilities are not transferred to Realisation Account

Following procedure is followed.

(*i*) Sundry assets (except cash in hand or at bank) are transferred to the debit side of Realisation Account as usual.

(*ii*) On realisation of assets, Realisation Account is credited.

(*iii*) For realisation expenses, Realisation Account is debited and Cash Account is credited.

(*iv*) If any liability is secured, then the liability will be paid on priority basis to the extent of realisation of that asset.

(*v*) Amount brought by any partner from his private estate is credited to his Capital Account and debited to Cash Account.

(*vi*) Cash Account is prepared in order to calculate the amount available for payment to unsecured outside liabilities. The balance in unsecured outside liabilities account represents amount not paid to these creditors and is closed by transfer to Deficiency Account.

(*vii*) Capital Accounts (after all entries) are closed by transferring their balances to Deficiency Account.

(*viii*) Deficiency account, if prepared, will tally.

This will be more clear from the following illustrations.

ILLUSTRATION 12. Balance Sheet of A, B and C, who are sharing profits and losses in the ratio of 2 : 2 : 1, was as follows on 31st March, 2025, the date of dissolution :

BALANCE SHEET OF A, B AND C
as on March 31, 2025

Liabilities	₹	*Assets*	₹
Sundry Creditors	1,20,000	Cash	1,000
Bank Loan (with a charge on Stock)	50,000	Stock	60,000
Capitals :		Other Assets	1,09,000
A	30,000	Goodwill	30,000
B	20,000	Capital :	
		C	20,000
	2,20,000		2,20,000

Stock realised ₹ 52,000 and other assets were sold for ₹ 90,000.

Expenses on realisation amounted to ₹ 3,000.

Assuming that all the partners are insolvent, prepare necessary ledger accounts to close the books of the firm.

SOLUTION

REALISATION ACCOUNT

	₹	₹		₹	₹
To Sundry Assets :			By Cash (Other Assets)		90,000
Stock	60,000		By Cash (Stock)		52,000
Other assets	1,09,000		By Loss to Capital A/c		
Goodwill	30,000		A	24,000	
		1,99,000	B	24,000	
To Cash (Realisation Expenses)		3,000	C	12,000	
					60,000
		2,02,000			2,02,000

CASH ACCOUNT

	₹		₹
To Balance b/d	1,000	By Realisation A/c (Expenses)	3,000
" Realisation A/c (Other Assets)	90,000	" Bank Loan A/c	50,000
" Realisation A/c (Stock)	52,000	" Sundry Creditors A/c	90,000
	1,43,000		1,43,000

SUNDRY CREDITORS ACCOUNT

	₹		₹
To Cash A/c	90,000	By Balance b/d	1,20,000
" Deficiency A/c	30,000		
	1,20,000		1,20,000

CAPITAL ACCOUNTS

	A	B	C		A	B	C
	₹	₹	₹		₹	₹	₹
To Balance b/d			20,000	By Balance b/d	30,000	20,000	
" Realisation A/c	24,000	24,000	12,000	" Deficiency A/c		4,000	32,000
" Deficiency A/c	6,000						
	30,000	24,000	32,000		30,000	24,000	32,000

DEFICIENCY ACCOUNT

	₹		₹
To B's Capital A/c	4,000	By Sundry Creditors A/c	30,000
" C's Capital A/c	32,000	" A's Capital A/c	6,000
	36,000		36,000

(*b*) ***If the effect of realisation of all assets and liabilities is to be passed through Realisation Account.*** Sometimes it is specifically required in the question that all matters relating to realisation of assets and payments of liabilities are to be passed through Realisation Account, then creditors are also transferred to the credit side of Realisation Account. Secured creditors (to the extent of realisation of security) are always paid on priority basis. Unsecured creditors will be paid (by debiting Realisation Account) the balance of cash available together with whatever can be received from the private estates of the partners after expenses of realisation are met. Capital Accounts' balances will be transferred to Deficiency Account which shall be automatically closed. It is to be noted carefully that Partners' Capital Accounts will not be closed according to Garner *vs*. Murray.

ILLUSTRATION 13. A, B and C are three partners sharing profits and losses in the ratio of 2 : 2 : 1. Below is the Balance Sheet when the firm was dissolved.

Liabilities	₹	*Assets*	₹
Sundry Creditors	1,50,000	Plant and Machinery	48,000
A's Loan	20,000	Land and Buildings	40,000
A's Capital A/c	40,000	Furniture	2,000
B's Capital A/c	20,000	Sundry Debtors	20,000
		Stock	56,000
		Cash	4,000
		Profit and Loss Account	50,000
		C's Capital Account	10,000
	2,30,000		2,30,000

The assets realised as follows : Plant and Machinery ₹ 20,000 ; Land and Buildings ₹ 35,000 ; Furniture ₹ 500 ; Sundry Debtors ₹ 9,500 and Stock ₹ 31,000. The position of the partners was as follows :

	Private Estate	*Private Liabilities*
	₹	₹
A	16,000	12,000
C	10,000	13,000

B was able to pay 25 paise in the rupee of what was payable on his account to the firm. The expenses of realisation amounted to ₹ 1,000.

Prepare ledger accounts passing all matters relating to realisation of assets and payment of liabilities through realisation account.

SOLUTION

REALISATION ACCOUNT

	₹			₹
To Plant and Machinery	48,000	By Sundry Creditors		1,50,000
" Land and Buildings	40,000	" Cash (Assets realised)		96,000
To Furniture	2,000	By Loss on Realisation transferred		
" Sundry Debtors	20,000	to Capital A/cs :	₹	
" Stock	56,000	A—2/5 share	10,667	
" Cash (Realisation Expenses)	1,000	B—2/5 share	10,667	
" Cash (Payment of Creditors)	1,05,667	C—1/5 share	5,333	
				26,667
	2,72,667			2,72,667

CASH ACCOUNT

	₹		₹
To Balance b/d	4,000	By Realisation A/c (Expenses)	1,000
" Realisation Account (Assets Realised)	96,000	By Realisation A/c (Creditors)	1,05,667
" A's Capital Account	4,000		
" B's Capital Account (1)	2,667		
	1,06,667		1,06,667

A's LOAN ACCOUNT

	₹		₹
To A's Capital Account (Transfer)	20,000	By Balance b/d	20,000

CAPITAL ACCOUNT

	A	B	C		A	B	C
	₹	₹	₹		₹	₹	₹
To Balance b/d			10,000	By Balance b/d	40,000	20,000	
" P & L A/c	20,000	20,000	10,000	" A's Loan A/c	20,000		
" Realisation A/c	10,667	10,667	5,333	" Cash (1) A/c	4,000	2,667	
" Deficiency	33,333			" Deficiency A/c		8,000	25,333
	64,000	30,667	25,333		64,000	30,667	25,333

DEFICIENCY ACCOUNT

	₹		₹
To B's Capital A/c	8,000	By A's Capital A/c	33,333
" C's Capital A/c	25,333		
	33,333		33,333

Working Note :

(1) Amount brought in by B has ben determined as follows :

Suppose the amount brought in by B is *x. i.e.* 1/4 of the amount due from him.

Amount of cash available to creditors after the realisation of assets is :

	₹
Cash in hand on the dissolution date	4,000
Add : Assets realised	96,000
	1,00,000
Less : Realisation expenses	1,000
	99,000
Add : Cash realised from A's private estate	4,000
	1,03,000
Add : Cash brought in by B (as assumed above)	x
Cash available for payment to creditors	1,03,000 + x

After making the payment of cash available to the creditors, Realisation Account will appear as follows :

	₹		₹
To Plant and Machinery	48,000	By Sundry Creditors	1,50,000
" Land and Buildings	40,000	" Cash (Assets realised)	96,000
" Furniture	2,000		
" Sundry Debtors	20,000		
To Stock	56,000		
" Cash (Realisation Expenses)	1,000		
" Cash (Creditors)	1,03,000 + x		

Loss on Realisation = Total of Debit Side – Total of Credit Side

$$= 2{,}70{,}000 + x - 2{,}46{,}000 = 24{,}000 + x$$

B's Share of loss on realisation is $\frac{2}{5}$ *i.e.* $\frac{2}{5}(24{,}000 + x)$

$$= 9{,}600 + \frac{2}{5}x$$

B's Capital Account after transferring loss on realisation will appear as follows :

	₹		₹
To Profit and Loss Account	20,000	By Balance b/d	20,000
" Realisation Account (Loss)	$9{,}600 + \frac{2}{5}x$		

Amount due from B = ₹ 29,600 + $\frac{2}{5}x$ – ₹ 20,000 = ₹ 9,600 + $\frac{2}{5}x$

We have assumed 1/4 amount to be brought in by B as x, so total amount due from B will be equivalent to $4x$.

$$\therefore\ 4x = ₹\ 9{,}600 + \frac{2}{5}x$$

$$20x = ₹\ 48{,}000 + 2x$$

$$18x = ₹\ 48{,}000$$

$$x = \frac{₹\ 48{,}000}{18} = ₹\ 2{,}667.$$

Hence amount brought in by B is ₹ 2,667.

Gradual Realisation of Assets and Piecemeal Distribution

In all the problems on dissolution so far attempted by us, we have assumed that all assets are realised immediately on the date of the dissolution and the accounts of all the creditors and partners are settled on the same date. But this assumption is unrealistic because normally the process of realising the assets takes a long time and cash is distributed as and when it is realised as the partners in such a case may not wish to wait till all the assets are realized. It is universally accepted practice that an interim distribution is made to the partners for their claim (after paying off all creditors) as and when cash is available. Under such a case when there is a gradual realisation of assets, it is necessary to avoid the unpleasant consequences of a partner's account being overdrawn distributing cash of various realisations of assets in such a way that the final unpaid balance of the capital of each partner is left in his profit sharing ratio. In other words, the various realisations of assets should be distributed in such a way that even if the remaining assets do not realise anything, no partner should receive more than the amount to which he is ultimately entitled after being debited with the share of total loss on realisation.

Priority of Distribution

On a gradual realisation of assets, the cash realised is distributed in the following order to avoid the excess payment to any partner :

(1) Expenses of realisation are to be paid in the first instance as these get preference over unsecured creditors.

(2) Then the debts of the firm to **third parties** (if more than one creditor, then in proportion of the amounts due) must be paid out in full prior to any partner being paid any amount in respect of his loan and capital.

(3) **Secured creditors** should get preference over unsecured creditors. But their preference is subject to the realisation of asset kept with them as security, otherwise they are to be treated like unsecured creditors.

(4) After the creditors have been paid off, the amount due to a partner as loan should be paid. When the loans are due to more than one partner, the cash available should be paid rateably.

(5) After the payment of outside liabilities and loans due to the partners, the capitals of the partners are paid. Partners' capitals consist of balance in capital and current accounts and share in the undistributed profits or loss and reserves.

Methods of Distribution of Cash Among Partners

1. The debts of the firm to third parties must be paid out in full prior to any partner being paid any amount in respect of his loan and capital ; secured creditors should get preference over unsecured creditors. But their preference is subject to the realisation of asset kept with them as security otherwise they are to be treated like unsecured creditors. **Expenses of realisation are to get preference over unsecured creditors.**
2. After the creditors have been paid off, the amount due to a partner as loan should be paid. When the loans are due to more than one partner, the cash available should be rateably distributed.
3. After the payment of outside liabilities and loans due to the partners, the capitals of the partners are paid.

Following are the two methods of cash distribution among partners as and when realised :

1. Proportionate (or Higher Relative) Capital Method

If the capitals of the partners are in the ratio of their profit sharing arrangement, then each of them is paid out according to his capital ratio at each distribution. If the capitals of the partners are not in the profit sharing ratio, then the first cash available (after making the payment of outside liabilities and loans due to the partners) for distribution amongst the partners should be paid to those partners whose capitals are more than their profit sharing ratios to bring their capitals to their profit sharing levels. After this the cash available is distributed amongst all the partners according to the profit sharing ratio. The unpaid balances of capital accounts will represent loss on realisation and this loss will be exactly in the profit and loss sharing ratio of the partners.

The cash available for distribution amongst the partners cannot be distributed according to the profit and loss sharing ratio unless the capitals of the partners are in the profit and loss sharing ratio because that will not leave the unpaid balances of the capital accounts in the profit and loss sharing ratio of the partners. Following example will make this point clear :

For example, X and Y are partners with capitals of ₹ 40,000 and ₹ 20,000 and share the profits and losses in the ratio of 5 : 2. If after paying off the creditors, two more instalments of ₹ 28,000 and ₹ 11,000 are collected and all the distribution is made according to the profit sharing ratio, the result will be as follows :

	X	*Y*
	₹	₹
Amount Due	40,000	20,000
1st instalment of ₹ 28,000 distributed in the profit sharing ratio of 5 : 2	20,000	8,000
Balance due	20,000	12,000
2nd instalment of ₹ 11,000 distributed in the ratio of 5 : 2.	7,857	3,143
Balance left unpaid or loss on realisation	12,143	8,857

The balance remaining unpaid is not in the profit sharing ratio of 5 : 2, so the distribution of cash in the profit sharing ratio is wrong.

Similarly, the cash available for distribution amongst partners cannot be distributed in the ratio of capitals of the partners, because then the partners will have to bear the loss on realisation according to the ratio of capitals. If cash is distributed in the ratio of capitals, the following would be the position in the above case :

	X	*Y*
	₹	₹
Amount Due	40,000	20,000
1st instalment of ₹ 28,000 distributed in the ratio of capitals 40,000 : 20,000 *i.e.* 2 : 1	18,667	9,333
Balance Due	21,333	10,667
2nd instalment of ₹ 11,000 distributed in the ratio of 2 : 1	7,333	3,667
Balance left unpaid or loss on realisation	14,000	7,000

The distribution according to the ratio of capitals is also wrong, the loss on realisation is not according to the profit and loss sharing ratio of 5 : 2.

If cash available is distributed first to those partners whose capitals are more than their profit sharing ratios, the position in the above example will be as follows :

	X	*Y*
	₹	₹
Amount Due	40,000	20,000
First instalment of ₹ 28,000 ; ₹ 4,000 paid to Y to bring his capital to the profit sharing ratio	–	4,000
	40,000	16,000
₹ 24,000 distributed in the profit sharing ratio of 5 : 2	17,143	6,857
Balance Due	22,857	9,143
Second instalment of ₹ 11,000 distributed in the ratio of 5 : 2	7,857	3,143
Balance left unpaid or loss on realisation	15,000	6,000

This method of distribution of cash amongst the partners is correct because balance left unpaid on account of capitals or loss on realisation is according to the profit and loss sharing ratio.

ILLUSTRATION 14. Ajay Enterprises, a partnership firm in which A, B and C are three partners sharing profits and losses in the ratio of 4 : 3 : 3. Balance Sheet of the firm as on 31st December, 2024 is as below :

Liabilities	₹	*Assets*	₹
A's Capital	15,000	Factory Building	24,160
B's Capital	7,500	Plant & Machinery	16,275
C's Capital	15,000	Debtors	5,400
B's Loan A/c	4,500	Stock	12,390
Sundry Creditors	16,500	Cash at Bank	275
	58,500		58,500

On Balance Sheet date all the three partners have decided to dissolve their partnership. Since the realisation of assets was protracted, they decided to distribute amounts as and when feasible and for this purpose they appoint C who was to get as his remuneration 1% of the value of the assets realised other than cash at bank and 10% of the amount distributed to the partners.

Assets were realised piece-meal as under :

First instalment ₹ 18,650; Second intalment ₹ 17,320; Third instalment ₹ 10,000; Last intalment ₹ 7,000; Dissolution expenses were provided for estimated amount of ₹ 3,000; The creditors were settled finally for ₹ 15,900.

Prepare a statement showing *distribution of cash* amongst the partners by *'Highest Relative Capital Method'*. ***(CA-IPCE, May, 2015 Modified)***

SOLUTION

STATEMENT SHOWING DISTRIBUTION OF CASH AMONGST THE PARTNERS BY HIGHEST RELATIVE CAPITAL METHOD (HRCM)

		Creditors	*B's Loan*	*Capitals*		
	₹	₹	₹	*A (₹)*	*B (₹)*	*C (₹)*
Balance due		16,500	4,500	15,000	7,500	15,000
On receipt of 1st instalment amount	18,650					
Add : Cash at Bank	275					
	18,925					
Less : Dissolution Expenses provided for	(3,000)					
	15,925					
Less : C's Remuneration of 1% on Assets realised 18,650 × 1%)	(187)					
	15,738					
Less : Payment made to Creditors	(15,738)	(15,738)				
Balance due	Nil	762				
On realisation of 2nd instalment	17,320					
Less : C's Remuneration of 1% on assets realised (17,320 × 1%)	(173)					
	17,147					
Less : Payment made to creditors (settled for the total ₹ 15,900 – ₹ 15,738)	(162)	(162)				
	16,985	600				

Particulars				A	B	C
Transferred to P & L A/c		Nil				
Less : Payment for B's Loan A/c	(4,500)		(4,500)			
Amount available for Distribution to Partners	12,485		Nil			
Less : C's Remuneration of 10% of the amount distributed to partners (12,485 × 10/110)	(1,135)					
Balance Distributed to Partners on the basis of HRCM	11,350					
Less : Paid to C (1)	(3,750)					(3,750)
	7,600					11,250
Less : Paid to A and C in 4 : 3 (1)	(7,600)			(4,343)	—	(3,257)
Balance due	—			10,657	7,500	7,993
On realisation of 3rd instalment	10,000					
Less : C's remuneration of 1% on assets realised (10,000 × 1%)	(100)					
	(9,900					
Less : C's remuneration of 10% of the amount distributed to partners (9,900 × 10/110)	(900)					
	9,000					
Less : Paid to A and C in 4 : 3 ratio excess amount remaining in their Capital Accounts as compared to B's Capial A/c	(1,150)			(657)		(493)
	7,850			10,000	7,500	7,500
Less : Now, paid to A, B and C in 4 : 3 : 3	(7,850)			(3,140)	(2,355)	(2,355)
Balance due	—			6,860	5,145	5,145
On Realisation of 4th and last instalment	7,000					
Less : C's remuneration of 1% on assets realised (7,000 × 1%)	(70)					
	6,930					
Less : C's Remuneration of 10% of the amount distributed to partners (6,930 × 10/110)	(630)					
	6,300					
Less : Paid to A, B and C in 4 : 3 : 3	(6,300)			(2,520)	(1,890)	(1,890)
Loss suffered by partners				4,340	3,255	3,255

Working Note :

(1) **Calculation of amount paid to partners on the basis of Highest Relative Capital Method**

HIGHER RELATIVE CAPITAL METHOD (HRCM)

		A	B	C
		₹	₹	₹
Balance of Capital Accounts	(A)	15,000	7,500	15,000
Profit Sharing Ratio		4	3	3
Capital—Profit Sharing Ratio [(A) ÷ (Profit Ratio)]		3,750	2,500	5,000
Capital in Profit Sharing Ratio taking B's Capital as base	(B)	10,000	7,500	7,500
Excess of A's Capital and C's Capital [(A) – (B) = (C)]	(C)	5,000	nil	7,500

Again repeating the process for A and C				
Profit Sharing Ratio		4		3
Capital—Profit Sharing Ratio [(C) ÷ (Ratio)]		1,250		2,500
Capital in Profit Sharing Ratio taking A's Capital as base	(D)	5,000		3,750
Excess Capital to be paid first	(C – D) = (E)	Nil		3,750

Therefore, first ₹ 3,750 will be paid to C. Then A and C will receive in proportion of 4 : 3 upto ₹ 8,750 to bring the capital of all partners A, B and C in proportion to their profit sharing ratio. Thereafter, balance available will be paid to all partners *viz.* A, B and C in their profit sharing ratio of 4 : 3 : 3.

ILLUSTRATION 15. Ananth Associates is a reputed firm. On account of certain misunderstanding between the partners, it was decided to dissolve the firm as on 31st December, 2024. Their Balance Sheet as on 31st December, 2024 was as follows :

Liabilities	₹	₹	*Assets*	₹
Capitals :			Land and Buildings	7,00,000
Ananth	3,00,000		Other Fixed Assets	3,00,000
Kishore	2,00,000		Stock in Trade	2,00,000
Kumar (Minor)	1,00,000		Debtors	4,00,000
		6,00,000	Bills	1,50,000
Mortgage Loans		3,00,000	Goodwill	30,000
Bank O.D.		3,00,000	Cash	20,000
Other Loans		2,00,000		
Creditors		2,00,000		
Kumar's Loan		2,00,000		
		18,00,000		18,00,000

It was decided that Mr. Ananth shall be in-charge of Realisations. He shall set apart ₹ 10,000 towards expenses. He shall be paid a remuneration of 5 per cent on the amounts distributed to the partners towards their contributions other than loans. Assets realised are as under :

		₹
1-1-2025	Debtors	3,50,000
15-1-2025	Fixed Assets	4,00,000
1-2-2025	Debtors	50,000
15-2-2025	Bills	1,40,000
1-3-2025	Fixed Assets	50,000
15-3-2025	Land and Buildings	8,00,000

Prepare a statement showing how the money received on various dates will be distributed according to *proportionate capital method* assuming :

(*a*) The actual expenses of realisation amounted to ₹ 20,005.

(*b*) The firm is solvent.

(*c*) The profit sharing ratio was as under :

	Profit	*Loss*
Ananth	2	1
Kishore	2	1
Kumar	1	Nil
	5	2

(*d*) The final dissolution is made on 15th March, 2025.

SOLUTION

While solving the illustration, it has been assumed that mortgage loans are on the security of fixed assets and bank overdraft is on the security of stock-in-trade. Further, secured creditors are treated as unsecured except when the security concerned is realised.

(For Statement of Distribution of Cash see next two pages)

STATEMENT SHOWING DISTRIBUTION OF CASH

Particulars		Mortgage Loans	Bank O.D.	Other Loans	Creditors	Kumar's Loan	Ananth's Capital	Kishore's Capital	Kumar's Capital
	₹	₹	₹	₹	₹	₹	₹	₹	₹
Amount due		3,00,000	3,00,000	2,00,000	2,00,000	2,00,000	3,00,000	2,00,000	1,00,000
Cash in hand	20,000								
Less : Amount kept for realisation expenses	10,000								
Distributed among outsiders (3 : 3 : 2 : 2)	10,000	3,000	3,000	2,000	2,000	—	—	—	—
Balance Due		2,97,000	2,97,000	1,98,000	1,98,000	2,00,000	3,00,000	2,00,000	1,00,000
First Realisation on 1-1-2025	3,50,000								
Less : Distributed among outsiders (3 : 3 : 2 : 2)	3,50,000	1,05,000	1,05,000	70,000	70,000	—	—	—	—
Balance Due		1,92,000	1,92,000	1,28,000	1,28,000	2,00,000	3,00,000	2,00,000	1,00,000
Second Realisation of Fixed Assets on 15-1-2025	4,00,000								
Less : Balance of Mortgage Loans being secured paid first	1,92,000	1,92,000							
Distributed among outsiders (3 : 2 : 2)	2,08,000		89,143	59,429	59,428	—	—	—	—
Balance Due		—	1,02,857	68,571	68,572	2,00,000	3,00,000	2,00,000	1,00,000
Third Realisation of Debtors on 1-2-2025	50,000								
Less : Distributed among outsiders (3 : 2 : 2)	50,000		21,429	14,285	14,286	—	—	—	—
Balance Due			81,428	54,286	54,286	2,00,000	3,00,000	2,00,000	1,00,000
Fourth Realisation of Bills on 15-2-2025	1,40,000								
Less : Distributed among outsiders (3 : 2 : 2)	1,40,000		60,000	40,000	40,000	—	—	—	—
Balance Due			21,428	14,286	14,286	2,00,000	3,00,000	2,00,000	1,00,000
Fifth Realisation of Fixed Assets on 1-3-2025	50,000								
Less : Distributed among outsiders (3 : 2 : 2)	50,000		21,428	14,286	14,286	—	—	—	—
Balance Due			—	—	—	2,00,000	3,00,000	2,00,000	1,00,000

Sixth Realisation of Land and Buildings on 15-3-2025	8,00,000								
Less : Additional payment of realisation expenses (₹ 20,005 – ₹ 10,000)	10,005								
	7,89,995								
Less : Payment of Kumar's Loan	2,00,000					2,00,000			
Amount available for partners' Capitals	5,89,995					—	3,00,000	2,00,000	1,00,000
Less : Ananths' Commission @ $\frac{5}{105}\left(i.e. ₹\ 5,89,995 \times \frac{5}{105}\right)$	28,095								
	5,61,900								
Less : Kumar's Capital paid first because he suffers no share in loss on account of being minor partner	1,00,000								1,00,000
	4,61,900						3,00,000	2,00,000	—
Less : Paid to Ananth to make his capital equal to that of Kishore	1,00,000						1,00,000		
	3,61,900						2,00,000	2,00,000	—
Less : Distributed equally between Ananth and Kishore	3,61,900						1,80,950	1,80,950	
Balance Due							19,050	19,050	Nil*

* Kumar will get 1/5 share (*i.e.,* share of profit) of what remains after paying ₹ 19,050 to each Ananth and Kishore out of the proceeds of stock-in-trade. If stock does not realise any amount, amount unpaid to Ananth and Kishore will become loss on realisation. Kumar has been paid first because he is not to share any loss on realisation.

2. Maximum Loss Method

An alternative method of piecemeal distribution of cash amongst partners is to calculate the maximum possible loss on every realisation after the outside liabilities and the partners' loans have been paid. The amount available for distribution amongst partners is compared with the total amount of capitals payable to partners and the maximum possible loss is ascertained on the assumption that in future assets will not realise any amount. The maximum possible loss so ascertained is deducted from the capitals of the partners in the profit and loss sharing ratio and the balance left in the capital accounts after deducting the maximum possible loss will be the amount payable to the partners. But if a partner's share of maximum possible loss is more than the amount standing to the credit of his capital account, he should be treated as insolvent and his deficiency (only that portion of his share of maximum possible loss which is more than his capital) should be debited to the capital accounts of the other partners in the proportion of their capitals which stood on the dissolution date as stated in the case of Garner *vs.* Murray. The amount standing to the credit of the partners after debiting share of maximum loss and share of the insolvent partner's deficiency will be equal to the cash available for distribution amongst the partners. At the time of next realisation the opening balances of their original capitals less the amounts already paid to them will be the basis for calculating the maximum possible loss. This process of maximum possible loss is repeated on each realisation till all the assets are disposed off.

ILLUSTRATION 16. Pinku, Rinku and Tinku were in partnership sharing profits and losses in the ratio of 3 : 2 : 1. Their Balance Sheet on 31st December, 2024 was as follows :

Liabilities	₹	*Assets*	₹
Sundry Creditors	30,000	Cash	3,000
Tinku's Loan Account	5,000	Stock	25,000
Capital Accounts :		Sundry Debtors	35,000
Pinku	15,000	Bills Receivable	3,000
Rinku	15,000	Furniture and Fittings	9,000
Tinku	10,000		
	75,000		75,000

Bills receivable were accepted on 1st November, 2024 payable after three months.

On 1st January, 2025, the firm was dissolved. The assets realised and the expenses were as follows :

	Stock	*Debtors*	*Furniture and Fittings*	*Expenses*
	₹	₹	₹	₹
January 31	5,000	7,000	2,000	600
February 28	9,000	10,000	3,500	1,000
March 31	6,000	11,000	—	3,000
April 30	2,500	4,500	2,000	900

Bills receivable were duly honoured.

Prepare a statement showing the distribution of Cash by Maximum Loss Method. Assume payments were made on the last day of the months. Also write up the Cash Account and Partners' Capital Accounts.

SOLUTION

The cash available for distribution each month is as follows :

	Stock +	Debtors +	Bills Receivable +	Furniture & Fittings	– Expenses	= Cash Available
	₹	₹	₹	₹	₹	₹
January 31	5,000	7,000	—	2,000	600	13,400
February 28	9,000	10,000	3,000	3,500	1,000	24,500

March	31	6,000	11,000	—	—	3,000	14,000
April	30	2,500	4,500	—	2,000	900	8,100

STATEMENT SHOWING DISTRIBUTION OF CASH

		Creditors	*Tinku's Loan*	*Pinku's Capital*	*Rinku's Capital*	*Tinku's Capital*
		₹	₹	₹	₹	₹
Amount Due		30,000	5,000	15,000	15,000	10,000
Cash in hand paid to Creditors		3,000	—	—	—	—
Balance Due		27,000	5,000	15,000	15,000	10,000
1st Realisation of ₹ 13,400 on January 31 paid to Creditors		13,400	—	—	—	—
Balance Due	₹	13,600	5,000	15,000	15,000	10,000
2nd Realisation on February 28	24,500					
Less : Paid to Creditors	13,600	13,600	—	—	—	—
	10,900					
Less : Payment of Tinku's Loan	5,000	—	5,000	—	—	—
		—	—	15,000	15,000	10,000
Cash available for distribution among partners	5,900					
Maximum possible loss is Capitals—Cash available *i.e.* ₹ 15,000 + ₹ 15,000 + ₹ 10,000 – ₹ 5,900 = ₹ 34,100. This loss is divided among partners in the ratio of 3 : 2 : 1.				– 17,050	– 11,367	– 5,683
				– 2,050	3,633	4,317
Pinku's deficiency allocated to Rinku and Tinku in their capital ratios *i.e.* 15,000 : 10,000				+ 2,050	– 1,230	– 820
Amount paid to Rinku and Tinku					2,403	3,497
Balance Due				15,000	12,597	6,503
3rd Realisation on March 31 is ₹ 14,000. Maximum possible loss is ₹ 20,100 (*i.e.* ₹ 15,000 + ₹ 12,597 + ₹ 6,503 – ₹ 14,000 cash available). This loss is divided in the profit sharing ratio of 3 : 2 : 1				10,050	6,700	3,350
Amount paid to the partners				4,950	5,897	3,153
Balance Due (Balance after 2nd realisation—Amount paid on 3rd realisation) 4th Realisation on April 30	8,100			10,050	6,700	3,350
Maximum loss is ₹ 12,000 (10,050 + 6,700 + 3,350 – 8,100)				6,000	4,000	2,000
Amount paid to the partners				4,050	2,700	1,350

CASH ACCOUNT

2025		₹	2025		₹
Jan. 1	To Balance b/d	3,000	Jan. 1	By Realisation A/c (Creditors)	3,000
" 31	" Realisation Account (Assets Realised)	14,000	" 31	" Realisation A/c (Expenses)	600
			" 31	" Realisation A/c (Creditors)	13,400
Feb. 28	" Realisation Account (Assets Realised)	25,500	Feb. 28	" Realisation A/c (Expenses)	1,000
			" 28	" Realisation A/c (Creditors)	13,600
Mar. 31	" Realisation Account (Assets Realised)	17,000	" 28	" Tinku's Loan A/c	5,000
			" 28	" Rinku's Capital A/c	2,403
Apr. 30	" Realisation Account (Assets Realised)	9,000	" 28	" Tinku's Capital A/c	3,497
			Mar. 31	" Realisation A/c (Expenses)	3,000
			" 31	" Pinku's Capital A/c	4,950
			" 31	" Rinku's Capital A/c	5,897
			" 31	" Tinku's Capital A/c	3,153
			Apr. 30	" Realisation A/c (Expenses)	900
			" 30	" Pinku's Capital A/c	4,050
			" 30	" Rinku's Capital A/c	2,700
			" 30	" Tinku's Capital A/c	1,350
		68,500			68,500

CAPITAL ACCOUNTS

		Pinku	Rinku	Tinku			Pinku	Rinku	Tinku
		₹	₹	₹			₹	₹	₹
2025					2025				
Feb. 28	To Cash A/c	—	2,403	3,497	Jan. 1	By Balance b/d	15,000	15,000	10,000
Mar. 31	To Cash A/c	4,950	5,897	3,153					
Apr. 30	To Realisation A/c (Loss)	6,000	4,000	2,000					
" 30	To Cash A/c	4,050	2,700	1,350					
		15,000	15,000	10,000			15,000	15,000	10,000

ILLUSTRATION 17. Monika, Sonika and Ronika share profit and losses in the preportion of 2 : 1 : 1. Their Balance Sheet is as follows :

Liabilities	₹	*Assets*	₹
Sundry Creditors	10,000	Plant and Machinery	25,500
Sonika's Loan	6,000	Stock	15,500
Ronika's Loan	4,000	Furniture	5,000
Reserve Fund	8,000	Sundry Debtors	17,000
Contingency Reserve	6,000	Cash in hand	6,000
Monika's Capital	40,000	Loan to Monika	20,000
Sonika's Capital	10,000		
Ronika's Capital	5,000		
	89,000		89,000

The firm is dissolved, and the assets are realised as follows :

1st Realisation ₹ 12,000 ; 2nd Realisation ₹ 25,000 ; 3rd and Final Realisation ₹ 19,000.

On the dissolution date, there was a contingent liability of ₹ 2,000 against the firm which was settled at ₹ 1,500 at the time of 2nd realisation. Realisation expenses were estimated at ₹ 2,000 but these actually amounted to ₹ 1,200. The firm was found to pay ₹ 600 out of third realisation for which no provision was made. Sonika took over stock valued at ₹ 1,000 at the time of 3rd realisation.

Prepare a statement showing the distribution of cash by Maximum Loss Method.

SOLUTION

STATEMENT SHOWING DISTRIBUTION OF CASH

Particulars		*Creditors*	*Sonika's Loan*	*Ronika's Loan*	*Monika's Capital*	*Sonika's Capital*	*Ronika's Capital*
Amount Due	₹	10,000	6,000	4,000	20,000 (40,000 – 20,000 Loan)	10,000	5,000
Add: Reserve fund credited to the Capitals in the profit sharing ratio of 2 : 1 : 1.					4,000	2,000	2,000
Add : Contingency Reserve	₹ 6,000						
Less : Liability	₹ 2,000						
Credited to the Capitals in the ratio of 2 : 1 : 1	₹ 4,000				2,000	1,000	1,000
Amount due on the dissolution date		10,000	6,000	4,000	26,000	13,000	8,000
Cash in hand	₹ 6,000						
Less : Amount kept for realisation expenses	₹ 2,000						
	4,000						
Less : Amount kept for Contingent Liability	2,000						
Amount paid to the creditors	2,000	2,000	—	—	—	—	—
Balance Due		8,000	6,000	4,000	26,000	13,000	8,000
1st Realisation	₹ 12,000						
Less : Paid to Creditors	8,000	8,000					
Partners' loan paid in the ratio of their loans	4,000		2,400	1,600			
Balance Due		—	3,600	2,400	26,000	13,000	8,000
Add : Profit on contingent liability in the ratio of 2 : 1 : 1					250	125	125
2nd Realisation	₹ 25,000						
Less : Partners' loans paid	6,000	—	3,600	2,400	—	—	—
	19,000	—	—	—	26,250	13,125	8,125
Add : Cash saved on payment of contingent liability (₹ 2,000 – ₹ 1,500)	500						
Total cash available for distribution among partners	19,500						

Maximum loss is ₹ 28,000 (*i.e.* ₹ 26,250 + ₹ 13,125 + ₹ 8,125 – ₹ 19,500) which is debited to the capitals in the profit sharing ratio of 2 : 1 : 1.		—	—	—	14,000	7,000	7,000
Amount paid to partners					12,250	6,125	1,125
Balance Due					14,000	7,000	7,000
3rd Realisation	₹ 19,000						
Add : Cash available due to saving in realisation expenses (₹ 2,000 – ₹ 1,200)	800						
	19,800						
Add : Stock taken by Sonika	1,000						
	20,800						
Less : A new liability paid for which no provision was made	600						
Cash available for distribution among partners	20,200						
Maximum loss is ₹ 7,800 (₹ 14,000 + ₹ 7,000 + ₹ 7,000 – ₹ 20,200) which is distributed in the ratio of 2 : 1 : 1					3,900	1,950	1,950
Amount paid to partners					10,100	*5,050	5,050

*₹ 4,050 cash and ₹ 1,000 stock.

ILLUSTRATION 18. Ramesh, Rajesh and Rakesh are three partners in a firm and share profits and losses in the proportion of 3/10, 5/10 and 2/10 respectively. Their Balance Sheet on 31st December, 2024 is as follows :

Liabilities		₹	*Assets*	₹
Sundry Creditors		17,000	Cash in hand	4,000
Capitals :	₹		Other Assets	70,000
Ramesh	38,000		Profit and Loss Account	10,000
Rajesh	26,000			
Rakesh	3,000			
		67,000		
		84,000		84,000

The partnership is dissolved and the assets are realised as follows :

	Book value of assets realised	*Amount realised*
2025	₹	₹
January 31	30,000	25,000
February 28	25,000	15,000
March 31	15,000	10,000

Rakesh is insolvent and a sum of ₹ 1,400 is recovered from his estate in full settlement. Prepare a statement showing how the distribution should be made by following the maximum possible loss method. Also prepare the necessary accounts to close the books of the firm.

SOLUTION **STATEMENT SHOWING DISTRIBUTION OF CASH**

Particulars		Creditors	Ramesh's Capital	Rajesh's Capital	Rakesh's Capital
		₹	₹	₹	₹
Amount Due		17,000	38,000	26,000	3,000
Less : Loss shown in the Balance Sheet debited to the Capital Accounts in the profit sharing ratio of 3 : 5 : 2.		—	3,000	5,000	2,000
		17,000	35,000	21,000	1,000
Cash in hand paid to Creditors		4,000	—	—	—
Balance Due		13,000	35,000	21,000	1,000
Less : Loss on 1st Realisation on January 31, ₹ 5,000 (Book value of assets ₹ 30,000 – Realisable Value ₹ 25,000) debited to Capital Accounts in the profit sharing ratio of 3/10 : 5/10 : 2/10			1,500	2,500	1,000
		13,000	33,500	18,500	—
	₹				
1st Realisation on January 31, 2025	25,000				
Less : Paid to creditors	13,000	13,000	—	—	—
Cash available for partners	12,000	—	33,500	18,500	—
Less : Maximum Loss (₹ 33,500 + ₹ 18,500 – ₹ 12,000)	40,000		12,000	20,000	8,000
			21,500	– 1,500	– 8,000
Deficiency of Rajesh and Rakesh debited to Ramesh			– 9,500	+ 1,500	+ 8,000
Cash paid to Ramesh			12,000	—	—
Capital after 1st realisation (after loss on 1st realisation and payment of ₹ 12,000 to Ramesh)			21,500	18,500	—
Less : Loss on 2nd realisation of Feb. 28, ₹ 10,000 debited to Capital Accounts in the profit sharing ratio of 3/10 : 5/10 : 2/10			3,000	5,000	2,000
			18,500	13,500	– 2,000
2nd Realisation on February 28, 2025	15,000				
Less : Maximum Loss (₹ 18,500 + ₹ 13,500 – ₹ 2,000 – ₹ 15,000)	15,000		– 4,500	– 7,500	– 3,000
			14,000	6,000	– 5,000
Rakesh's deficiency allocated to Ramesh and Rajesh in the ratio of their Capitals on the dissolution date *i.e.* ₹ 35,000 : ₹ 21,000			– 3,125	– 1,875	+ 5,000
Cash paid to Ramesh and Rajesh			10,875	4,125	—

Capitals after Feb. 28, 2025 (after loss on 2nd realisation and payment of 2nd instalment to partners)			7,625	9,375	–2,000
3rd Realisation on March 31, 2025	10,000				
Maximum Loss (₹ 7,625 + ₹ 9,375 – ₹ 2,000 – ₹ 10,000)	5,000		– 1,500	– 2,500	– 1,000
			6,125	6,875	– 3,000
Less : Amount paid by Rakesh			—	—	1,400
			6,125	6,875	– 1,600
Rakesh's deficiency allocated to Ramesh and Rajesh in the ratio of their Capitals on the dissolution date *i.e.* ₹ 35,000 : ₹ 21,000.			– 1,000	– 600	+ 1,600
Cash paid to Ramesh and Rajesh			5,125	6,275	—

REALISATION ACCOUNT

2025		₹	2025		₹
Jan. 1	To Sundry Assets	70,000	Jan. 1	By Sundry Creditors	17,000
" 1	" Cash Account (Cash in hand paid to Creditors)	4,000	" 31	" Cash Account (Assets realised)	25,000
" 31	" Cash A/c (Payment to Creditors)	13,000	Feb. 28	" Cash Account (Assets realised)	15,000
			Mar. 31	" Cash Account (Assets realised)	10,000
			Mar. 31	By Loss on Realisation transferred to Capital Accounts : ₹ Ramesh—3/10 share 6,000 Rajesh—5/10 share 10,000 Rakesh—2/10 share 4,000	20,000
		87,000			87,000

CASH ACCOUNT

2025		₹	2025		₹
Jan. 1	To Balance b/d	4,000	Jan. 1	By Realisation A/c (Creditors)	4,000
" 31	" Realisation A/c (Assets realised)	25,000	" 31	" Realisation A/c (Creditors)	13,000
			" 31	" Ramesh's Capital A/c	12,000
Feb. 28	" Realisation A/c (Assets realised)	15,000	Feb. 28	" Ramesh's Capital A/c	10,875
			" 28	" Rajesh's Capital A/c	4,125
Mar. 31	" Realisation A/c (Assets realised)	10,000	Mar. 31	" Ramesh's Capital A/c	5,125
			" 31	" Rajesh's Capital A/c	6,275
" 31	" Rakesh's Capital A/c	1,400			
		55,400			55,400

CAPITAL ACCOUNTS

		Ramesh	*Rajesh*	*Rakesh*			*Ramesh*	*Rajesh*	*Rakesh*
		₹	₹	₹			₹	₹	₹
2025					2025				
Jan. 1	To Profit & Loss A/c	3,000	5,000	2,000	Jan. 1	By Balance b/d	38,000	26,000	3,000
					Mar.31	By Cash A/c			1,400

Date	Particulars				Date	Particulars			
Jan. 31	To Cash A/c	12,000			Mar.31	By Ramesh's Capital A/c (5/8 share of deficiency)			1,000
Feb. 28	To Cash A/c	10,875	4,125		" 31	By Rajesh's Capital A/c (3/8 share of deficiency)			600
Mar. 31	To Realisation A/c (Loss)	6,000	10,000	4,000					
" 31	To Rakesh's Capital A/c	1,000	600						
" 31	To Cash A/c	5,125	6,275						
		38,000	26,000	6,000			38,000	26,000	6,000

CONVERSION OF A PARTNERSHIP INTO A LIMITED COMPANY OR SALE TO A COMPANY

Conversion of partnership means changing the status of the partnership firm into a joint stock company. A new company is formed to take over the business of the firm. Conversion is just like a sale of partnership business to a new company. This process will result in the dissolution of the firm. The partners of the firm will become shareholders of the company as they have been allotted shares by the company for taking over the business.

The object of such conversion is to take some advantages of joint stock company over partnership firm. Such advantages are :

(*i*) Liability of the shareholders will become limited.

(*ii*) The company can collect more fund for expansion of its business.

(*iii*) The entity of the company will be separate from its members. The admission, death, and insolvency of the members will not affect the continuity of the company.

(*iv*) To take advantages of less rate of income-tax, etc.

(*v*) To enjoy the benefits of large scale production.

(*vi*) To have continuous existence of the business unit.

Purchase Consideration

Purchase consideration is the amount paid by the purchasing company to the vendor firm for taking over its assets and liabilities. The company may take over all assets or liabilities or any of them. The value of such assets taken over and liabilities assumed may be book value or current value depends upon agreement between them. The amount of purchase consideration may be paid in any form as shares, debentures of the company and cash. Purchase consideration ascertainment is very important as it affects accounting entries in the books.

Methods of Calculation of Purchase Consideration

There are different methods of calculating purchase consideration but here only the following three methods are discussed.

1. Lumpsum Method. When a fixed amount or lumpsum is given by the purchasing company to the vendor firm, it is called lumpsum method of purchase consideration. For example, R Ltd. paid ₹ 2,00,000 to M/s AB & Co. for purchase of business, it is a case of lump sum method of purchase consideration.

2. Net Payment Method. Under this method, the purchase consideration is the total of all the payments made by company to the vendor firm in the form of shares, debentures and cash. For example, X Co. Ltd. is formed to take over all the assets and liabilities of the firm of M/s X, Y & Z for ₹ 2,00,000 which is to be paid by the allotment of 12,000 shares of ₹ 10 each fully paid and balance in cash. It is not necessary that the company may take all assets and assume all liabilities. If any asset is not takenover by the company, the same may be sold by the firm in the market or may be taken over by one of the partners at an agreed value. Similarly if liabilities are not assumed by the company, then they should be paid by the firm itself.

3. Net Assets Method. Under this method the total of all assets taken over by the company at agreed value is calculated and the agreed value of liabilities assumed is deducted. The balance is the purchase consideration, *i.e.*,

Purchase Consideration = Agreed value of assets taken over – Agreed value of liabilities assumed.

For example, X Co. Ltd. took over the following assets at the value mentioned against them :

	₹		₹
Building	6,00,000	Debtors	4,00,000
Stock	3,00,000	Goodwill	2,00,000

The company agreed to pay to the creditors ₹ 5,00,000. The purchase consideration will be calculated as under :

	₹
Agreed value of assets taken over	
Building	6,00,000
Stock	3,00,000
Debtors	4,00,000
Goodwill	2,00,000
	15,00,000
Less : Agreed value of creditors assumed	5,00,000
Purchase Consideration	10,00,000

Accounting Procedure

The partnership firm's accounts are closed in the same way as we have discussed earlier. Realisation Account is opened and assets and liabilities taken over by the company are transferred to Realisation Account at their book values. The Company formed will be debited with the amount agreed to be paid by it for the purchase of the firm and Realisation Account credited. Besides this treatment, the following points may be noted :

1. Treatment of assets not taken over. If some assets are not taken over by the purchasing company, then such assets are not transferred to Realisation Account and will be disposed of by the partnership firm. In such a case, the entry is :

Cash/Bank Account Dr.
  To Relevant Asset Account
(Being asset not taken over by the purchasing company disposed of by the firm)

Any balance left in the Asset Account (so sold) being profit or loss is transferred to Realisation A/c.

2. Treatment of liabilities not taken over. The liabilities not taken over by the purchasing company are not transferred to Realisation Account but should be paid off separately. The entry is :

Liability (not taken over) Account Dr.
  To Cash/Bank Account
(Being payment of the liability not taken over by purchasing company)

The balance (if any) left in the liability account being profit or loss is transferred to Realisation Account and liability account is closed.

3. Treatment of purchase consideration. Following journal entry is passed in the books of the firm.

Purchasing Company's Account Dr.
  To Realisation Account
(Being the purchase consideration debited to the Purchasing Company)

4. Treatment of purchase price from the purchasing company. Usually the purchasing company will pay the purchase price in cash, shares and debentures. The entry for this is :

Cash Account	Dr.
Shares in Purchasing Company	Dr.
Debentures in Purchasing Company	Dr.
To Purchasing Company's Account	

(Being receipt of the purchase consideration from the purchasing company)

5. Distribution of shares and debentures amongst partners. Shares and debentures received from the purchasing company are distributed amongst partners in the proportions agreed upon. In the absence of such agreement, shares and debentures can be distributed by following the two bases given below as advocated by two groups of accountants :

(*i*) According to one group of accountants, shares and debentures received should be distributed among partners in the same ratio in which they distribute profits or losses. The logic behind this basis is that profit or loss due to appreciation or depreciation in the value of shares or debentures should be divided like other profits or losses and no distinction should be made between trading profits and losses and profits and losses due to shares and debentures. Keeping in view this logic, shares and debentures should be divided amongst partners in proportion to their profit sharing ratio.

(*ii*) According to another group of accountants, shares and debentures should be distributed amongst partners in the ratio of their final claims after realisation. In support of this basis of distribution their contention is that under Section 48 (*b*) (*iii*) of the Partnership Act, 1932 assets of the firm must be used in paying to each partner rateably what is due to him on account of capital.

The two points of views given above can be resolved by following the procedure given below :

(*i*) Shares and debentures received from the purchasing company should be valued according to their present worth (*i.e.*, market rate). Any profit or loss as a result of such revaluation should be transferred to Partners' Capital Accounts in their profit sharing ratio.

(*ii*) Shares and debentures so revalued as per (*i*) should be distributed among partners in the ratio of their final claims *i.e* amount finally due to them.

(*iii*) In the absence of any information of the present worth of shares and debentures it may be presumed that shares and debentures are worth their book values and there is no profit or loss on shares and debentures. In such a case, shares and debentures should be divided among partners in proportion to their final claims.

It may be noted that *shares and debentures will be distributed to the nearest whole number because fraction of a share or debenture cannot be issued.*

Assets and liabilities not taken over by the purchasing company can also be closed by transferring them to Realisation Account. If assets and liabilities are closed in this way, then the amount realised on sale of assets is debited to Cash/Bank Account and credited to Realisation Account and amount paid on discharging such liabilities, is debited to Realisation Account and credited to Cash/Bank Account.

Apportionment of Shares Amongst the Partners—Maintenance of Mutual Relationship

Sometimes students may be required to suggest equitable basis for distribution of shares amongst partners (specifically when a partnership is converted into a company), so as to maintain their mutual relationship as previously existed among them when they cease to be partners and become members of the joint stock company. Maintenance of mutual relationship among partners relates to mutually agreed upon profit sharing ratio and partners may also receive salaries and interest on capital. So far as salaries are concerned, these can be paid in a company only to the employees or whole-time directors and partners can be compensated for the salaries they were getting as partners by giving them whole-time directorship or some important posts as employees. Interest on capital to partners is given to compensate them if their capitals are more than their profit sharing ratio. In a company, profits belong to equity shareholders after the payment of fixed rate of preference dividend. Therefore, for maintenance of mutual relationship among partners as previously existed among them, equity shares in the new company (formed by converting partnership firm into a company) should be given to the erstwhile partners in the ratio in which they shared profit of the partnership firm and for the excess capital (*i.e.* more than the profit sharing ratio), the partners should get preference shares carrying dividend at the rate at which interest was paid on capitals taking interest as an appropriation of profit.

Suppose A, B and C share profits and losses in the ratio of 5 : 3 : 2 after allowing interest on capital @ 10% p.a. and have capitals of ₹ 1,00,000, ₹ 80,000 and ₹ 50,000 respectively on 31st December, 2024. On 1st January, 2025, the business of the partnership firm was converted into a private limited company and was valued at ₹ 2,70,000. A scheme of capitalisation whereby the mutual interest of erstwhile partners may remain intact will be as follows :

	A	*B*	*C*
	₹	₹	₹
Capitals on 31-12-2024	1,00,000	80,000	50,000
Add : Goodwill [₹ 2,70,000 value of business – Capitals (₹ 1,00,000 + ₹ 80,000 + ₹ 50,000)]	20,000	12,000	8,000
	$\left(40,000 \times \frac{5}{10}\right)$	$\left(40,000 \times \frac{3}{10}\right)$	$\left(40,000 \times \frac{2}{10}\right)$
	1,20,000	92,000	58,000
Less : Taking A's Capital as base, Capitals in the profit sharing ratio of 5 : 3 : 2	1,20,000	72,000	48,000
Excess Capital	—	20,000	10,000
Equity Shares to be given	1,20,000	72,000	48,000
10% Preference Shares (For Excess Capital)	—	20,000	10,000

ILLUSTRATION 19. (***Net Assets Method***) Anivash, Rohit and Madwesh were carrying on business in partnership sharing Profits and Losses in the ratio of 5 : 4 : 3 respectively. The Trial Balance of the firm as on 31st March, 2025 was the following :

Particulars	*Dr.* (₹)	*Cr.* (₹)
Plant and Machinery at Cost	1,05,000	—
Stock	60,200	—
Sundry Debtors	85,000	—
Sundry Creditors	—	1,05,200
Capital A/cs :		
Avinash	—	70,000
Rohit	—	50,000
Madwesh	—	30,000
Drawings A/cs :		
Avinash	30,000	—
Rohit	25,000	—
Madwesh	20,000	—
Depreciation on Plant and Machinery	—	35,000
Trading Profit for the year	—	1,29,800
Cash at Bank	94,800	—
	4,20,000	4,20,000

Additional information :

(*a*) Interest on Capital Accounts at 10% on the amount standing to the credit of partners' Capital Accounts at the beginning of the year was not provided before preparing the above Trial Balance.

(*b*) On 31st March, 2025 they formed a Private Ltd. Company Anagha (P) Ltd. to take over the partnership business.

(*c*) You are further informed as under :

(*i*) Plant and Machinery is to be transferred at ₹ 80,000.

(*ii*) Equity Shares of ₹ 10 each of the company are to be issued to the partners at par in such numbers to ensure that by reason of their share holdings alone they will have the same rights of sharing Profits and Losses as they had in the partnership. Balance, if any, in their Capital Accounts will be settled by giving $7\frac{1}{2}$% Preference Share at par.

(*iii*) Before transferring the business, the partners withdrew by cash from partnership the following amounts over and above the drawings as shown in the Trial Balance :
(*a*) Avinash ₹ 20,000 ; (*b*) Rohit ₹ 10,600 ; (*c*) Madwesh ₹ 14,200.

(*iv*) All Assets and Liabilities except Plant and Machinery and the Bank Balance are to be transferred at their value in the books of the partnership as at 31st March, 2025.

(*v*) You are required to prepare :

(*a*) Profit and Loss Adjustment Account for the year ending 31st March, 2025.

(*b*) Capital Accounts showing all the adjustments required to dissolve the partnership.

(*c*) A statement showing the number of shares of each class to be issued by the company to each of the partners to settle their accounts.

(*d*) Prepare Balance Sheet of the company Anagha (P) Ltd. as on 31-3-2025 after take over of the business.

SOLUTION

In the Books of Avinash, Rohit & Madwesh

(*a*) PROFIT & LOSS ADJUSTMENT ACCOUNT

for the year ended 31st March, 2025

		₹		₹
To Interest on Capital :	₹		By Profit	1,29,800
Avinash	7,000		By Plant and Machinery	10,000
Rohit	5,000			
Madwesh	3,000			
		15,000		
To Capital A/cs (Profit)				
Avinash	52,000			
Rohit	41,600			
Madwesh	31,200			
		1,24,800		
		1,39,800		1,39,800

(*b*) PARTNERS' CAPITAL ACCOUNTS

	Avinash	Rohit	Madwesh		Avinash	Rohit	Madwesh
	₹	₹	₹		₹	₹	₹
To Drawings as per Trial Balance	30,000	25,000	20,000	By Balance b/d	70,000	50,000	30,000
To Additional Drawings	20,000	10,600	14,200	By Profit & Loss Adjustment A/c	52,000	41,600	31,200
To Balance c/d	79,000	61,000	30,000	By Interest on Capital	7,000	5,000	3,000
	1,29,000	96,600	64,200		1,29,000	96,600	64,200

To Equity Shares	50,000	40,000	30,000	By Balance b/d	79,000	61,000	30,000
To Preference Shares	29,000	21,000					
	79,000	61,000	30,000		79,000	61,000	30,000

(c) STATEMENT SHOWING THE NUMBER AND CLASSES OF SHARES ISSUED TO PARTNERS

	Avinash ₹	*Rohit* ₹	*Madwesh* ₹
Closing Capital Balance (after adjustments)	79,000	61,000	30,000
Taking Madwesh's Capital as base for ensuring same rights of shareholding—Equity shares of ₹ 10 each to be issued	50,000	40,000	30,000
Balance to be settled by issue of $7\frac{1}{2}$% Preference Shares	29,000	21,000	–

(d) BALANCE SHEET OF ANAGHA (P) LTD.

as on 31st March, 2025

(after takeover of the business)

Liabilities	₹	*Assets*	₹
Share Capital :		*Fixed Assets :*	
12,000 Equity Shares of ₹ 10 each at par (issued for consideration other than cash)	1,20,000	Plant and Machinery	80,000
		Current Assets :	
		Stock	60,200
$7\frac{1}{2}$% Preference Shares (Issued for consideration other than cash)	50,000	Debtors	85,000
		Cash at Bank	50,000
Current Liabilities & Provisions :			
Sundry Creditors	1,05,200		
	2,75,200		2,75,200

Working Note :

***Calculation of Purchase Consideration* :**

	₹
Plant and Machinery	80,000
Stock	60,200
Debtors	85,000
Cash at Bank (₹ 94,800 – ₹ 44,800)	50,000
	2,75,200
Less : Sundry Creditors	1,05,200
	1,70,000

ILLUSTRATION 20. Ali and Beta were carrying on business, sharing profits and losses equally. The firm's Balance Sheet as at 31-12-2024 was :

Liabilities		₹	*Assets*	₹
Sundry Creditors		1,44,000	Stock	1,44,000
Bank Overdraft		84,000	Machinery	3,60,000
Capital A/cs :	₹		Debtors	1,68,000
Ali	3,36,000		Joint Life Policy	21,600
Beta	3,12,000	6,48,000	Leasehold Premises	81,600
			Profit & Loss A/c	62,400

	₹		₹	₹
		Drawings A/c :	₹	
		Ali	24,000	
		Beta	14,400	38,400
	8,76,000			8,76,000

The business was carried on till 30-6-2025. The partners withdrew the amounts equal to half the amount of profit made during the period of six months ended on 30-6-2025, in equal proportion. The profit was calculated after charging depreciation at 10% p.a. on machinery and after writing off 5% on leasehold premises. In the half year, sundry creditors were reduced by ₹ 24,000 and bank overdraft by ₹ 36,000.

On 30-6-2025, stock was valued at ₹ 1,80,000 and debtors at ₹ 1,44,000; the Joint Life Policy had been surrendered for ₹ 21,600 before 30-6-2025 and other items remained the same as at 31-12-2024.

On 30-6-2025, the firm sold the business to a limited company. The value of goodwill was fixed at ₹ 2,40,000 and the rest of the assets were valued on the basis of the Balance Sheet as at 30-6-2025. The company paid the purchase consideration in equity shares of ₹ 10 each.

You are required to prepare :

(*a*) Balance Sheet of the firm as at 30-6-2025;

(*b*) Realisation Account; and

(*c*) Partners' Capital Accounts showing the final settlement between them.

SOLUTION

BALANCE SHEET OF THE FIRM

as on June 30, 2025

Liabilities	₹	*Assets*		₹
Sundry Creditors (1,44,000 – 24,000)	1,20,000	Leasehold Premises	81,600	
Bank Overdraft (84,000 – 36,000)	48,000	*Less* : Written off 5%	4,080	77,520
Total Capital of Ali and Beta on		Machinery	3,60,000	
30-6-2025 (Bal. Fig.)	5,75,520	*Less* : Depreciation for $\frac{1}{2}$ year		
		@ 10% p.a.	18,000	3,42,000
		Stock		1,80,000
		Debtors		1,44,000
	7,43,520			7,43,520

STATEMENT OF PROFIT AND LOSS OF THE FIRM

for the half year ending June 30, 2025

			₹
Total Capital of the Firm as on 30-6-2025 as per Balance Sheet			5,75,520
Less : Capital on 31-12-2024 :	*Ali*	*Beta*	
	₹	₹	
Capital as given in Balance Sheet as at 31-12-2024	3,36,000	3,12,000	
Less : Drawings	24,000	14,400	
	3,12,000	2,97,600	
Less : $\frac{1}{2}$ Share of ₹ 62,400 loss	31,200	31,200	
	2,80,800	2,66,400	
Total Capital as on 31-12-2024 (₹ 2,80,800 + ₹ 2,66,400)			5,47,200
Net Increase in Capital (after Drawings)			28,320

Since drawings are half of the profits, actual profit earned by the firm for 6 months is ₹ 28,320 × 2 = ₹ 56,640.

(1) Calculation of Purchase Consideration

	₹	₹
Total Assets as per Balance Sheet as on 30-6-2025		7,43,520
Add : Goodwill agreed to be paid		2,40,000
		9,83,520
Less : External Liabilities on 30-6-2025 :	₹	
Sundry Creditors	1,20,000	
Bank Overdraft	48,000	
		1,68,000
Net Assets taken over *i.e.* Purchase Consideration		8,15,520

(2) REALISATION ACCOUNT

	₹		₹
To Machinery	3,42,000	By Creditors	1,20,000
To Leasehold Premises	77,520	By Bank Overdraft	48,000
To Stock	1,80,000	By Shares in Company	
To Debtors	1,44,000	(Equal to Purchase Consideration)	8,15,520
To Profit on Realisation transferred to :			
Ali : 1/2 share	1,20,000		
Beta : 1/2 share	1,20,000		
	9,83,520		9,83,520

(3) PARTNERS' CAPITAL ACCOUNT

2025		*Ali*	*Beta*			*Ali*	*Beta*
June 30	To Drawings	14,160	14,160	Jan. 1	By Balance b/d	2,80,800	2,66,400
June 30	To Shares in Co. (Bal. Figure) (Distribution of shares equal to the amount Due)	4,14,960	4,00,560	June 30	By Profit (for 6 months)	28,320	28,320
					By Realisation A/c (Share of Profit)	1,20,000	1,20,000
		4,29,120	4,14,720			4,29,120	4,14,720

ILLUSTRATION 21. (Net Assets Method) Mr. M and Mr. D were carrying on business as equal partners. The firm's Balance Sheet as on 31st December, 2024 was as follows :

Liabilities	₹	*Assets*	₹
Sundry Creditors	65,500	Stock	54,000
Bank Overdraft	30,000	Plant and Machinery	1,82,000
Bills Payable	12,500	Office Furniture	15,000
Capital Accounts :		Book Debts	73,000
M	1,50,000	Joint Life Policy	9,500
D	1,48,000	Leasehold Premises	34,500
		Profit and Loss A/c (Debit Balance)	26,000
		Drawings Account :	
		M	9,000
		D	3,000
	4,06,000		4,06,000

The business was carried on till 30th June, 2025. The partners withdrew in equal amounts half the amount of profits made during the period of six months (from January-June 2025) after 10% p.a. had been written off leasehold premises, 10% p.a. off plant and machinery and 5% p.a. off office furniture. Meanwhile sundry creditors were reduced by ₹ 10,000. On 30th June, 2025 stock was valued at ₹ 63,400. Bills payable were reduced by ₹ 2,300 and bank overdraft by ₹ 15,000. Book debts were valued at ₹ 65,000, the joint life policy was realised for ₹ 9,500 and the amount was utilised to reduce the bank overdraft and other items remained the same as on 31st December, 2024.

On 30th June, 2025 the firm sold the business to a Limited Company. The value of the goodwill was estimated at ₹ 1,08,000 and the rest of the assets were valued on the basis of the Balance Sheet as on 30th June 2025. The Company paid the purchase consideration in fully paid equity shares of ₹ 10 each, at par.

You are required to prepare a Realisation Account and Capital Accounts of the partners as on 30th June, 2025.

SOLUTION

REALISATION ACCOUNT

2025			₹	2025			₹
June 30	To Leasehold Premises		32,775	June 30	By Sundry Creditors		55,500
	To Plant & Machinery		1,72,900		By Bank Overdraft (₹ 30,000 – ₹ 15,000 – ₹ 9,500 Proceeds of Joint Life Policy)		5,500
	To Office Furniture		14,625		By Bills Payable		10,200
	To Stock		63,400		By Limited Company	(3)	3,85,500
	To Book Debts		65,000				
	To Profit on Realisation transferred to :	₹					
	M's Capital A/c	54,000					
	D's Capital A/c	54,000	1,08,000				
			4,56,700				4,56,700

PARTNERS' CAPITAL ACCOUNTS

2025		M ₹	D ₹	2025		M ₹	D ₹
Jan. 1	To Profit & Loss A/c (Debit Balance)	13,000	13,000	Jan. 1	By Balance b/d	1,50,000	1,48,000
" 1	To Drawings	9,000	3,000	June 30	By Profit & Loss A/c (2)	17,500	17,500
June 30	To Drawings (Half of Profit upto June 30, 2025 withdrawn)	8,750	8,750	" 30	By Realisation A/c (Profit)	54,000	54,000
June 30	To Shares in Limited Company	1,90,750	1,94,750				
		2,21,500	2,19,500			2,21,500	2,19,500

Working Notes :

(1) ***Statement Showing Value of Net Assets as at 30th June, 2025.***

	₹	₹
Leasehold Premises	34,500	
Less : Depreciation @ 10% p.a. for 6 months	1,725	
		32,775

	₹	₹
Plant and Machinery	1,82,000	
Less : Depreciation @ 10% p.a. for 6 months	9,100	
		1,72,900
Furniture	15,000	
Less : Depreciation @ 5% p.a. for 6 months	375	
		14,625
Stock		63,400
Book Debts		65,000
		3,48,700
Less : Sundry Creditors	55,500	
Bank Overdraft (₹ 15,000 – ₹ 9,500 Proceeds of Joint Life Policy. It has been assumed that bank overdraft of ₹ 15,000 is before crediting proceeds of Joint Life Policy)	5,500	
Bills Payable	10,200	
		71,200
Value of Net Assets as on June 30, 2025		2,77,500

(2) *Calculation of Profit Earned from Jan. 1, 2025 to June 30, 2025.*

	₹	₹	₹
Net Assets as on 30th June, 2025			2,77,500
Less : Net Assets as on 1st January, 2025 :			
Stock		54,000	
Plant and Machinery		1,82,000	
Office Furniture		15,000	
Book Debts		73,000	
Joint Life Policy		9,500	
Leasehold Premises		34,500	
		3,68,000	
Less : Sundry Creditors	65,500		
Bank Overdraft	30,000		
Bills Payable	12,500		
		1,08,000	
			2,60,000
Increase in Net Assets after Drawings			17,500
Add : Profit withdrawn by partners			17,500
Net Profit for 6 months from 1-1-2025 to 30-6-2025			35,000

(3) *Calculation of Purchase Consideration* :

	₹
Value of Net Assets as on 30th June, 2025 as per Working Note (1)	2,77,500
Add : Goodwill	1,08,000
Purchase Consideration	3,85,500

ILLUSTRATION 22. (Net Assets Method) Shri A, Shri B and Shri C are equal partners of M/s ABC & Co. Balance Sheet of the firm as on 31st December, 2024 was as follows :

Liabilities	₹	*Assets*	₹
Shri A's Account	5,00,000	Land	5,00,000

Shri B's Account	10,00,000	Plant and Machinery	20,00,000
Loans from Banks	50,00,000	Buildings	7,00,000
Creditors	10,00,000	Stocks	30,00,000
		Debtors	10,00,000
		Shri C's Account	3,00,000
	75,00,000		75,00,000

On that date, it is decided to convert the partnership into a limited company on the following terms :

(*a*) Land to be valued at ₹ 15,00,000.

(*b*) Plant and Machinery to be valued at ₹ 25,00,000.

(*c*) Depreciation amounting to ₹ 2,00,000 to be written off buildings.

(*d*) A provision of 10 per cent of book value to be made for obsolete stocks.

(*e*) A provision for doubtful debts to be made at 10 per cent of the debtors.

(*f*) A discount of 6 per cent would be earned on creditors when paid out.

(*g*) The new company will issue 12,000 equity shares of ₹ 100 each credited as fully paid up, such share capital being valued at ₹ 15,00,000 and the balance payable is to be discharged by issue of 8 per cent debenture certificates of ₹ 1,000 each.

Show the necessary ledger accounts to close the books of ABC & Co. and show the opening balance sheet of the new company. You may assume that (*i*) all partners are solvent and have sufficient cash resources as may be necessary for purposes of settling accounts, and (*ii*) shares and cash are divided equally among the partners.

SOLUTION

M/s A B C & Co's Books

REALISATION ACCOUNT

	₹		₹
To Land	5,00,000	By Creditors	10,00,000
" Plant	20,00,000	" Loan from Banks	50,00,000
" Buildings	7,00,000	" Limited Co. (Purchasing Co.) (1)	21,60,000
" Stocks	30,00,000		
" Debtors	10,00,000		
To Profit on Realisation transferred to Capital A/cs : ₹ A 3,20,000; B 3,20,000; C 3,20,000	9,60,000		
	81,60,000		81,60,000

LIMITED CO. (*i.e.*, Purchasing Co.)

	₹		₹
To Realisation Account	21,60,000	By Shares in Limited Co.	15,00,000
		" 8% Debentures in Limited Co.	6,60,000
	21,60,000		21,60,000

SHARES IN LIMITED CO's ACCOUNT

	₹		₹
To Limited Co.	15,00,000	By A's Capital Account	5,00,000
		" B's Capital Account	5,00,000
		" C's Capital Account	5,00,000
	15,00,000		15,00,000

8% DEBENTURES IN LIMITED CO's ACCOUNT

	₹		₹
To Limited Co.	6,60,000	By A's Capital Account	80,000
		" B's Capital Account	5,80,000
	6,60,000		6,60,000

CASH ACCOUNT

	₹		₹
To C's Capital Account	7,20,000	By A's Capital Account	2,40,000
		" B's Capital Account	2,40,000
		" C's Capital Account	2,40,000
	7,20,000		7,20,000

PARTNERS' CAPITAL ACCOUNTS

	A	B	C		A	B	C
	₹	₹	₹		₹	₹	₹
To Balance b/d			3,00,000	By Balance b/d	5,00,000	10,00,000	
To Shares in Limited Co.	5,00,000	5,00,000	5,00,000	By Realisation A/c (Profit)	3,20,000	3,20,000	3,20,000
" Cash (2)	2,40,000	2,40,000	2,40,000	" Cash (3)			7,20,000
" 8% Debentures in Limited Co. (Balancing figure)	80,000	5,80,000					
	8,20,000	13,20,000	10,40,000		8,20,000	13,20,000	10,40,000

BALANCE SHEET OF PURCHASING CO.
as on 1st January 2025

		₹
I. Equity and Liabilities		
(1) *Shareholders' Funds*		
(a) Share Capital :		
12,000 Equity Shares of ₹ 100 each		
(All the above shares are issued for purchase of business)		12,00,000
(b) Reserves and Surplus :		
Securities Premium A/c (on 12,000 shares @ ₹ 25 per share)		3,00,000
(2) *Non-current Liabilities*		
Secured Loans : 8% Debentures		6,60,000
Unsecured Loans : Bank Loans		50,00,000
(3) *Current Liabilities*	₹	
Creditors	10,00,000	
Less : Reserves for Discount	60,000	
		9,40,000
Total		81,00,000

		₹
II. Assets		
(1) *Non-current Assets*		
Land		15,00,000
Buildings		5,00,000
Plant and Machinery		25,00,000
(2) *Current Assets*		
Stocks	₹	27,00,000
Debtors	10,00,000	
Less : Provision for Doubtful Debts	1,00,000	9,00,000
Total		81,00,000

Working Notes :

(1) *Calculation of Purchase Consideration*

	₹	₹
Value of Assets taken over :		
Land		15,00,000
Plant and Machinery		25,00,000
Buildings	7,00,000	
Less : Depreciation	2,00,000	5,00,000
Stock	30,00,000	
Less : 10% Provision for Obsolete Stock	3,00,000	27,00,000
Debtors	10,00,000	
Less : 10% Provision for Doubtful Debts	1,00,000	9,00,000
		81,00,000
Less : Liabilities taken over :		
Creditors	10,00,000	
Less : 6% Reserve for Discount	60,000	
	9,40,000	
Bank Loan	50,00,000	59,40,000
Purchase Consideration Payable by the Purchasing Co.		21,60,000

Purchase consideration is to be settled by :

	₹
(*i*) Issue of 12,000 Equity Shares of ₹ 100 each @ ₹ 125 per share	15,00,000
(*ii*) Issue of 660 Debentures of ₹ 1,000 each (*i.e.* balancing amount)	6,60,000
	21,60,000

(2) *Calculation of the amount of cash to be distributed equally* *among all partners* :

	₹	₹
A's Claim : A's credit balance after profit on realisation	8,20,000	
Less : Shares taken over	5,00,000	3,20,000
B's Claim : B's credit balance after profit on realisation	13,20,000	
Less : Shares taken over	5,00,000	8,20,000
		11,40,000
Less : Debentures to be distributed only between A and B because their accounts show credit balances		6,60,000
Amount to be received in cash equally by A and B		4,80,000

(3) ***Calculation of the amount of cash to be brought by C.***

	₹	₹
Amount due from C : C's credit balance (*i.e.*, profit on realisation)		3,20,000
Less : Debit balance	3,00,000	
Shares taken over	5,00,000	
		8,00,000
		4,80,000

Therefore, C is to bring in ₹ 4,80,000 which can be distributed equally between A and B, *i.e.*, ₹ 2,40,000 each. But as per question, each partner is to get equal cash, so C should bring in ₹ 7,20,000 to distribute ₹ 4,80,000 between A and B equally and pay himself (*i.e.*, C) ₹ 2,40,000.

ILLUSTRATION 23. Mr. B and Mr. E are partners sharing Profits and Losses in the ratio of 3 : 2. On 30th September, 2024 they admit Mr. C as a partner, and the new profit ratio is 2 : 2 : 1. C brought in Fixture ₹ 3,000 and cash ₹ 10,000, the goodwill being (*i*) B and E ₹ 20,000 and (*ii*) C ₹ 10,000 but neither figure is to be brought into the books.

On 31st March, 2025, the partnership is dissolved, B retiring and the other two partners forming a company called BC Limited with equal capitals, taking over all remaining assets and liabilities, goodwill being agreed at ₹ 40,000 and brought into books of the company. B agrees to take over the business car at ₹ 3,700 : Plant was sold for ₹ 3,000 being in excess of requirements. The profits of the two preceding years were ₹ 17,200 and ₹ 19,000 respectively and it was agreed that for the half year ended 30th September, 2024, the net profit was to be taken as equal to the average of the two preceding years and the current year.

No entries had been made when C entered, except cash. No new book being opened by BC Company Ltd., B agreed to leave ₹ 50,000 as loan to the company, secured by 12% Debentures. Following is the Trial Balance as on 31st March, 2025 :

	Debit	*Credit*
	₹	₹
Capital Accounts :		
B	—	35,000
E	—	20,000
C	—	10,000
Drawings Accounts :		
B	6,000	—
E	5,000	—
C	2,800	—
Debtors & Creditors	31,000	12,000
Plant (Book value of plant sold ₹ 4,000)	23,000	—
Fixtures	7,000	—
Motor Car	2,700	—
Stock on 31st March, 2025	13,000	—
Bank	16,300	—
Profit & Loss A/c for the year	—	29,800
	1,06,800	1,06,800

Prepare : (1) Goodwill Adjustment Account ; (2) Capital Accounts of Partners ; (3) Profit and Loss Appropriation Account .

SOLUTION

(1) GOODWILL ADJUSTMENT ACCOUNT

Date	Particulars	₹	₹	Date	Particulars	₹	₹
2024 Sept. 30	To Partners' Capital A/cs : (Goodwill raised)	₹		2024 Sept. 30	By Partners' Capital A/cs : (Goodwill written off)	₹	
	B	12,000			B	12,000	
	E	8,000			E	12,000	
	C	10,000	30,000		C	6,000	30,000
2025 March 31	To Partners' Capital A/cs : (Goodwill raised)			2025 March 31	By Goodwill A/c (Goodwill raised transferred from Goodwill Adjustment A/c to Goodwill A/c)		40,000
	B	16,000					
	E	16,000					
	C	8,000	40,000				
			70,000				70,000

(2) PARTNERS' CAPITAL ACCOUNTS

Particulars	*B*	*E*	*C*	Particulars	*B*	*E*	*C*
2025 March 31	₹	₹	₹	2025 31st March	₹	₹	₹
To Goodwill adjustment A/c (not recorded earlier)	12,000	12,000	6,000	By Balance b/d	35,000	20,000	10,000
To Drawings	6,000	5,000	2,800	By Fixtures (not recorded earlier)			3,000
To Motor Car	3,700			By Profit & Loss Appropriation A/c (1)	16,320	11,920	1,560
To B's Loan (secured by 12% Debentures)	50,000			By Goodwill adjustment A/c (not recorded earlier)	12,000	8,000	10,000
To Bank A/c	7,620			By Goodwill Adjustment A/c	16,000	16,000	8,000
To Bank A/c		7,580		By Bank A/c			7,580
To Share Capital A/c		31,340	31,340				
	79,320	55,920	40,140		79,320	55,920	40,140

(3) PROFIT AND LOSS APPROPRIATION ACCOUNT

for the year ended 31st March, 2025

Particulars		₹	₹	Particulars	₹
To Partners' Capital Accounts :		₹		By Profit & Loss A/c	29,800
B	(1)	16,320			
E	(1)	11,920			
C	(1)	1,560	29,800		
			29,800		29,800

Working Notes :

(1) ***Calculation of Profit transferred to Capital Accounts :***

	₹
Calculation of half yearly profit to 30th September, 2024 :	
Profit of the preceding 2 years (₹ 17,200 + ₹ 19,000)	36,200
Add : Current year's profit	29,800
	66,000
Profit for 6 months ending 30th September $\left(₹\ 66{,}000 \times \frac{1}{3}\right)$	22,000
∴ Profit for next 6 months ending 31st March, 2025 (Current year's profit ₹ 29,800 – Profit for 6 months ₹ 22,000)	7,800
Current year's profit	29,800

	B	E	C
	₹	₹	₹
Division of Profit for first 6 months (3 : 2)	13,200	8,800	–
Division of Profit for 6 months ending 31st March, 2025 in the ratio of 2 : 2 : 1	3,120	3,120	1,560
	16,320	11,920	1,560

(2) ***Calculation of Share Capital of B C Ltd.***

Total Capital of the firm E and C before converting the firm into a Company.

		₹
E's Capital A/c	See Capital	38,920
C's Capital A/c	Accounts	23,760
Share Capital of the Company		62,680

E and C should have equal share in B C Ltd. *i.e.* ₹ 31,340

E should withdraw cash equal to excess capital (₹ 38,920 – ₹ 31,340) = ₹ 7,580

C should bring in cash to make his contribution equal (₹ 31,340 – ₹ 23,760) = ₹ 7,580

(3) ***Calculation of Balance of Cash at Bank***

BANK ACCOUNT

	₹		₹
To Balance b/d	16,300	By B's Capital A/c	7,620
To Plant A/c (Sale of Plant)	3,000	By E's Capital A/c	7,580
To C's Capital A/c (Amount brought in)	7,580	By Balance c/d	11,680
	26,880		26,880

(4) ***Calculation of Profit and Loss on Sale and Take Over of Assets***

	₹
Profit on motor car taken over (₹ 3,700 – ₹ 2,700)	1,000
Less : Loss on sale of plant (₹ 4,000 – ₹ 3,000)	1,000
Net profit or loss	Nil

QUESTIONS

OBJECTIVE TYPE

1. **Fill in the blanks :**

(*a*) Unrecorded liability paid at the time of dissolution is to be debited to.........account.

(*b*) When an unrecorded asset is realised at the time of dissolution of the firm, cash account is debited and.........account is credited.

(*c*) Goodwill account appearing in the books on the dissolution date is closed by transferring it to.........side of the ....account.

(*d*) Entry for the asset taken over by a creditor is.........but entry for the net payment to the creditor is passed.

(*e*) When the firm is dissolved, reserve fund is transferred to.........in their profit sharing ratio.

(*f*) After making the payment to third parties, the.........due to a partner is paid.

(*g*) The practice before Garner *vs.* Murray decision was to share the deficiency of the insolvent partner by the solvent partners in their.........ratio.

(*h*) According to the decision in Garner *vs.* Murray, in the absence of any agreement to the contrary, the deficiency of the insolvent partner must be borne by other solvent partners in proportion to.........

(*i*) X, Y and Z are partners. X became insolvent on 20-6-2025. The Capital Account balance of partner Y is on the debit side. Partner Y is solvent. Partner Y should .... the loss arising on account of the insolvency of partner X.

Ans. [(*a*) realisation ; (*b*) realisation ; (*c*) debit, realisation ; (*d*) not passed ; (*e*) partners' capital/current accounts ; (*f*) loan ; (*g*) profit and loss sharing ratio ; (*h*) capitals which stood before dissolution of the firm ; (*i*) not bear].

2. **Indicate whether the following statements are true or false.**

(*a*) Realisation account is a real account.

(*b*) On the dissolution of a firm the firm is closed, whereas on a dissolution of the partnership, the share of the outgoing partner is determined and the firm is not closed.

(*c*) While determining the capital ratio of the solvent partners in which deficiency of the insolvent partner is to be borne by the solvent partners, distinction should not be made between fixed and fluctuating capitals.

(*d*) Before Garner *vs.* Murray decision, no distinction was made between trading loss and capital loss.

(*e*) If some solvent partner is having a debit balance in his capital account on the dissolution date, he will not have to bear the loss on account of the deficiency of the insolvent partner.

(*f*) When there is gradual realisation of assets on the dissolution of a firm, the various realisation of assets should be distributed in such a way that even if the remaining assets do not realise anything, no partner should receive more than the amount to which he is ultimately entitled after having debited with the share of total loss on realisation.

(*g*) A partnership is dissolved on the death of a partner.

Ans. [True (*b*), (*d*), (*e*) & (*f*) ; false (*a*) ; (*c*) & (*g*)].

3. **Choose the correct answer for the following Multiple Choice Questions :**

(A) On dissolution of a firm cash in hand is transferred to—

(*i*) Realisation Account, (*ii*) Capital Accounts of the partners in profit sharing ratio, (*iii*) Cash Account, (*iv*) Creditors Account.

(B) On dissolution of a partnership, the Realisation Account is debited with :

(*i*) All the liabilities of the firm, (*ii*) Cash received from the sale of the assets, (*iii*) Any asset taken over by one of the partners, (*iv*) All assets to be realised.

Ans. [(A) (*iii*); (B) (*iv*)]

SHORT ANSWER TYPE

1. What do you mean by Realisation Account ?
2. What is the difference between dissolution of the firm and partnership dissolution ?
3. What is meant by an unrecorded asset ? How do you deal with it at the time of dissolution of a firm?
4. How would you treat an unrecorded asset taken by one of the partners at the time of dissolution of a firm?
5. Mention any four circumstances under which a partnership firm is dissolved.
6. What Journal entry do you pass when excess capital is to be transferred to Partners Current Accounts ?
7. What do you mean by Realisation Account ? How do you close this account ?
8. Bring out two important decisions of Garner *Vs.* Murray.
9. When all the partners are insolvent how the deficiency is treated ?
10. Write the rule laid down (or decision) in Garner *Vs.* Murray. Is it applicable in India or not?
11. How do you close the creditors account when all the partners are insolvent ?
12. What is piecemeal distribution of cash ?
13. Total capital of partners P, Q, R and S was ₹ 81,000 on the date of dissolution. Their profit sharing ratio was 3 : 2 : 4 : 1 and capital ratio was 30 : 14 : 16 : 21. Prepare a statement of surplus capital.
14. Write down the order of payments under piecemeal distribution of cash.
15. What are the assumptions under Maximum Loss Method of piecemeal distribution of cash?

LONG ANSWER TYPE

1. Bring out clearly the difference between dissolution of partnership and dissolution of firm. State how and under what circumstances a firm may be dissolved.
2. State the legal provisions for adjusting losses and distributing assets on the dissolution of a partnership where no agreement to the contrary exists.
3. What do you mean by dissolution of a firm ? Give the entries needed to close the books of the firm upon its dissolution.
4. What is a Realisation Account ? How does it differ from Revaluation Account ?
5. How is the debit balance of a partner's capital account to be treated in the event of dissolution of a firm ?
6. Examine the underlying principles of Garner *vs.* Murray decision in the dissolution of partnership with suitable illustrations. State when is this rule not applicable.
7. How should accounts be finally adjusted when all the partners are insolvent ?
8. Write short notes on the following : (*i*) Garner *vs.* Murray Decision. (*ii*) Piecemeal Distribution.

PRACTICAL PROBLEMS

DISSOLUTION

1. X, Y and Z were sharing profits in the ratio of 3 : 1 : 1 respectively. They decided to dissolve their firm on 31st March, 2025 when their position was as follows :

Liabilities		₹	*Assets*		₹
Capitals :	₹		Machinery		51,000
X	82,500		Furniture		3,000
Y	30,000		Stock	₹	23,400
Z	21,000		Debtors	72,600	
		1,33,500	*Less* : Provision for Bad Debts	3,600	
Loan		4,500			69,000
Sundry Creditors		18,000	Cash in Hand		9,600
		1,56,000			1,56,000

(*i*) X agreed to takeover furniture at ₹ 2,400, debtors amounting to ₹ 60,000 at ₹ 51,600 and also the creditors at their book value.

(*ii*) Y agreed to takeover stock at ₹ 21,000 and a part of the machinery at ₹ 21,600 (being book value *less* 10%).

(*iii*) Z agreed to takeover the remaining machinery at 90% of the book value *less* ₹ 300 as allowance. He also assumed the responsibility for the payment of loan together with accrued interest ₹ 90 (not recorded in the books).

(*iv*) Dissolution expenses amounted to ₹ 810.

(*v*) The remaining debtors were sold to a debt-collecting agency at 50% of book value.

Prepare important Ledger Accounts to close the books of account.

Ans. [Loss on Realisation ₹ 20,400 ; Final Payment to X—₹ 34,260 ; Amount brought by Y and Z ₹ 16,680 and ₹ 2,490 respectively]

2. X, Y, and Z sharing profits in the ratio of 2 : 2 : 1 agreed upon dissolution of their partnership on 30th June, 2024 on which date their Balance Sheet was as under :

Liabilities		₹	*Assets*		₹
Capital—X		80,000	Fixed Assets		1,00,000
Capital—Y		60,000	Life Policy		
Reserve Fund		20,000	(at surrender value)		20,000
Joint Life Policy Fund	₹	20,000	Debtors	20,000	
Creditors	38,000		*Less* : Provision	1,000	
Less : Reserve for Discount	1,000				19,000
		37,000	Stock at invoice price	20,000	
Salary Outstanding		4,000	*Less* : Price unloading	4,000	
					16,000
			Investments	16,000	
			Less : Fluctuation Fund	1,000	
					15,000
			Capital Account—Z		4,000
			Bank		47,000
		2,21,000			2,21,000

Investments were taken over by X at ₹ 12,000 ; creditors of ₹ 20,000 were taken over by Y who has agreed to settle account with them at ₹ 19,800. Remaining creditors were paid at ₹ 15,000. Joint life policy was surrendered and fixed assets realised ₹ 1,40,000. Stock and debtors realised ₹ 14,000 and 18,000 respectively. One customer, whose account was written off as bad, now paid ₹ 1,600 which is not included in ₹ 18,000 above. There was one unrecorded asset estimated at ₹ 6,000, half of which was handed over to an unrecorded liability of ₹ 10,000 in settlement of claim of ₹ 5,000 and remaining half was sold in the market which realised ₹ 2,600.

Y took over the responsibility of completing dissolution and he is granted salary of ₹ 800 p.m. Actual realisation expenses amounting to ₹ 2,200 were paid by the firm, but were to be borne by Y. Dissolution was completed and final payments were made on 31st October, 2024.

You are required to prepare Ledger Accounts in the books of the firm.

Ans. [Profit ₹ 52,200; Payment made to X ₹ 96,880; Y ₹ 1,09,680; Z ₹ 10,440]

3. Aman Bhuvan, Chaman and Dron shared profits and losses in the ratio of 2 : 3 : 3 : 2 respectively. On 31st March, 2025, their Balance Sheet stood as follows :

Liabilities		₹	*Assets*		₹
Creditors		2,00,000	Sundry Assets		3,10,000
Bhuvan's Loan		50,000	Cash at Bank		10,000
Capitals :	₹		Drawings :	₹	
Aman	90,000		Aman	10,000	
Bhuvan	60,000		Chaman	20,000	
Chaman	60,000				30,000
Dron	40,000		Accumulated Loss		1,50,000
		2,50,000			
		5,00,000			5,00,000

The position of the partners was as follows :

	Private Estates (₹)	*Private Liabilities* (₹)
Aman	1,00,000	1,50,000
Bhuvan	2,00,000	60,000
Chaman	50,000	30,000
Dron	80,000	90,000

The assets (excluding cash at bank) realised at ₹ 2,70,000. Expenses on dissolution came to ₹ 10,000. Prepare Ledger Accounts closing the books on dissolution of the firm.

Ans. [Loss on Realisation ₹ 50,000; Final Payment to Aman ₹ 40,000; Total of Bank Account ₹ 3,00,000]

4. A, B and C are partners in a firm sharing profits and losses in the ratio of 5 : 3 : 2. They agreed to dissolve the firm on 31st March, 2025 on which date their Balance Sheet was as follows :

Liabilities		₹	*Assets*	₹
Capital A/cs :			Goodwill	3,000
A	₹ 10,000		Furniture	10,000
C	₹ 70,000		Joint Life Policy	
		80,000	(At Surrender Value)	20,000
Reserve Fund		10,000	Sundry Debtors	40,000
Joint Life Policy Fund		20,000	Stock	22,000
Sundry Creditors		18,000	Cash at Bank	30,000
Outstanding Rent		2,000	Current A/c—B	5,000
		1,30,000		1,30,000

Furniture and stock were taken over by A at an agreed valuation of ₹ 12,000 and ₹ 15,000 respectively. Joint Life Policy was surrendered and Sundry Debtors were realised in full after allowing a discount of 20%. Sundry Creditors were taken over by B who agreed to settle account with them at ₹ 17,000. The Realisation expenses amounted to ₹ 1,000.

You are required to prepare Ledger Accounts in the books of the firm.

Ans. [Profit on Realisation ₹ 4,000 ; Payment to : B ₹ 16,200 and C ₹ 72,800 ; Amount received from A ₹ 10,000].

5. Naveen and Vishal have been in business together for the last three years ending 31st December, 2024 at which date they agree to dissolve. The capitals at the commencement of the business were ₹ 30,000 and ₹ 20,000. Profit and losses were shared in the ratio of 3 : 2. The result of three years before allowing 10% interest on capitals were :

		₹
2022	Profit	30,000
2023	Profit	22,200
2024	Loss	5,380

Drawings of each partner were ₹ 4,000 per year. Creditors on the date of dissolution were ₹ 16,400. The assets realised ₹ 75,000. Expenses of dissolution amount to ₹ 550. Give the necessary accounts to close the books of the firm.

Ans. [Loss on Realisation ₹ 14,770. Final Payment to Naveen and Vishal ₹ 37,478 and ₹ 20,572 respectively].

6. A, B and C are partners sharing profits and losses in the ratio of 5 : 3 : 2 respectively. On 31st December, 2024 they decided to dissolve the partnership firm and on that date their Balance Sheet was as follows :

BALANCE SHEET

as on 31-12-2024

Liabilities		₹	*Assets*		₹
Capital :	₹		Cash	₹	10,000
A	80,000		Debtors	42,000	
C	70,000		*Less*: Provision	2,000	
		1,50,000			40,000
General Reserve		20,000	B's Capital		10,000
Creditors		60,000	Land & Building		80,000
Bills Payable		20,000	Stock		45,000
Mrs. C's Loan		10,000	Furniture		30,000
Investment Fluctuation Fund		5,000	Bills Receivable		25,000
			Investments		25,000
		2,65,000			2,65,000

The terms of dissolution are as follows :

(*a*) ₹ 19,000 were paid to a creditor as against only ₹ 13,000 provided for in the books of accounts.

(*b*) There were bad debts of ₹ 7,000 and discount of 10% was allowed to debtors.

(*c*) Bills Payable due on an average after 3 months were paid immediately at a discount of 12% p.a.

(*d*) Investment realised ₹ 22,000 ; land and building was sold for ₹ 1,00,000, stock realised 20% less.

(*e*) C agreed to pay Mrs. C's loan and took over furniture at ₹ 28,000.

(*f*) A rebate of ₹ 1,000 was given to bills receivable and expenses of dissolution were ₹ 3,000 which were paid by B.

Prepare necessary Ledger Accounts.

Ans. [Loss on Realisation ₹ 6,900; Paid to A and C ₹ 86,550 and ₹ 54,620 respectively. B brings ₹ 3,070. Total Cash A/c ₹ 2,26,570].

7. P, Q and R carrying on business as merchants and sharing profits and losses in the ratio of 2 : 2 : 1, dissolved their firm as on December 31, 2024 on which date their Balance Sheet was as follows :

Liabilities		₹	*Assets*		₹
Sundry Creditors		20,300	Cash at Bank		4,500
Reserve Fund		10,000	Stock	₹	16,000
Joint Life Policy Reserve		8,000	Debtors	10,000	
Capital A/cs :	₹		*Less* : Provision	500	
P	15,000				9,500
Q	15,000		Joint Life Policy		11,000
R	3,000		Premises		30,300
		33,000			
		71,300			71,300

Note. There is a bill for ₹ 1,000 under discount. The bill was received from Z.

The assets except cash at bank and joint life policy were sold to a company which paid ₹ 65,000 in cash. The life policy was surrendered and ₹ 11,300 were received. Z proved insolvent and a dividend of 50% was received from his estate. Sundry creditors were paid ₹ 19,500 in full settlement. Expenses amounted to ₹ 3,000.

Prepare Realisation Account, Cash Account and the Partners' Capital Accounts.

Ans. [Profit on Realisation ₹ 6,500 ; Final Payment to P ₹ 24,920 ; Q ₹ 24,920 and R ₹ 7,960].

8. A, B and C were partners sharing profits and losses in the ratio of 3 : 2 : 1 respectively. On account of differences amongst them, they agree to dissolve the partnership on 31st December, 2024, on which date a Balance Sheet was prepared and it stood as under :

Liabilities	₹	*Assets*	₹
Capital Accounts :		Goodwill	30,420
A	28,000	Plant and Machinery	40,500
B	15,000	Furniture	4,310
C	8,000	Stock	15,780
Loan from A's wife	10,000	Book Debts	35,600
Sundry Creditors	37,800	Joint Life Policy	17,700
Bank Overdraft	40,430	Accrued Agency Commission	9,370
Life Policy Fund	17,700	Cash at Bank	3,250
	1,56,930		1,56,930

The life policy was surrendered for ₹ 15,500. Interest on drawings to date of dissolution was A ₹ 600, B ₹ 400, C ₹ 200. A took over Goodwill and Plant and Machinery for ₹ 60,000 and agreed to discharge his wife's loan and Bank Overdraft. Furniture and Stock were divided equally between A and B at an agreed valuation of ₹ 24,000. The Book Debts were assigned to the creditors of the firm in full satisfaction of their claim. The agency commission was recovered in time. A bill of ₹ 2,000 under discount was returned dishonoured with noting charges ₹ 50 and subsequently it proved valueless. The expenses of dissolution, *viz*. ₹ 1,200 were agreed to be paid by A. C agreed to the above arrangement on payment to him of ₹ 10,000 in full satisfaction of his right, title and interest in the firm.

You are required to state Realisation, Cash and Final Accounts of the Partners on completion of the dissolution proceedings. (Journal entries are not required).

Ans. [Loss on Realisation ₹ 6,860 : Final Repayment to A and B ₹ 10,894 and ₹ 5,176 respectively].

Hints. (1) Expenses borne by A have been taken as expenses not met by A.
(2) Joint Life Policy and Life Policy Fund have not been transferred to Realisation Account.

9. Following is the Balance Sheet at 31st March, 2025 of Antony, Birdy and Costello carrying on business in partnership sharing profits and losses as 2 : 2 : 1.

Liabilities		₹	*Assets*	₹
Capital Accounts :	₹		Fixed Assets	70,000
Antony	40,000		Sundry Debtors	30,000
Birdy	25,000		Stock	10,000
		65,000	Cash	5,000
Mortgage Loan		40,000	Capital Account (Dr. Balance) :	
Reserve		6,000	Costello	6,000
Sundry Creditors		10,000		
		1,21,000		1,21,000

They decided to dissolve the partnership and the following arrangements were agreed upon :

(1) Fixed assets included :

(*i*) Motor Car—₹ 5,500 taken over by Birdy at an agreed value of ₹ 9,000 after necessary repairing costs amounting to ₹ 2,000 to be borne by the firm.

(*ii*) Land and Building—₹ 50,000 subject to mortgage loan, taken over by Antony at an agreed value of ₹ 60,000 subject to mortgage loan to be taken over at ₹ 40,000.

(2) Other assets excluding cash and creditors are taken over by Eureka Limited in consideration of issue of 5,000 equity shares of ₹ 10 each fully paid. These shares are taken over at a total agreed value of ₹ 48,000 equally by Antony and Birdy.

(3) A creditor for ₹ 2,500 not provided for in the books had to be paid.

Prepare the following accounts assuming that the final settlement was made by the partners bringing in the amounts due from them :

(1) Realisation Account, (2) Partners' Capital Accounts, (3) Cash Account.

Ans. [Profit on Realisation ₹ 12,500 ; Costello and Birdy Bring Cash ₹ 2,300 and ₹ 600 respectively. Final Payment to Antony, ₹ 3,400].

10. Lion and Tiger were in partnership sharing profits and losses in the ratio of 3 : 1. Following is the Balance Sheet of the partnership as at 31st March, 2025 :

Liabilities		₹	*Assets*	₹
Capital Accounts	₹		Fixed Assets	21,000
Lion	24,000		Stock	11,200
Tiger	8,000		Debtors	19,600
		32,000	Cash at Bank	3,720
Current Accounts :				
Lion	4,200			
Tiger	2,000			
		6,200		
Loan—Tiger		3,000		
Creditors		14,320		
		55,520		55,520

Elephant Ltd. agreed to take over stock and fixed assets, excluding the value of motor car ₹ 4,100 for a consideration of ₹ 48,000 which is to be satisfied by payment of cash ₹ 16,000, allotment of 160 Preference Shares of ₹ 100 each, valued at ₹ 75 per share, and the balance by allotment of 1,600 Equity Shares of the face value of ₹ 10 each.

The debtors realised ₹ 19,200 and the creditors were settled for ₹ 14,000.

Following were agreed between the partners :

(1) The Equity Shares should be allotted in the ratio of the partners' capital accounts as per Balance Sheet.

(2) Lion to take over the motor car at an agreed value of ₹ 4,200.

(3) The Preference Shares to be allotted to Tiger to the value of his loan and the remaining to be allotted equally between the partners.

(4) Balance remaining to be settled in cash.

You are required to show : Realisation Account, Partners' Capital A/cs, Bank Account, and Statement showing distribution of shares.

Ans. [Profit on Realisation ₹ 19,920 : Final Repayment to Lion and Tiger by Cash ₹ 19,440 and ₹ 5,480 respectively].

11. P, Q and R carrying on business sharing profits and losses equally agreed to dissolve the partnership on 31-3-2025. Balance Sheet of the partnership as on that date is as follows :

Capital and Liabilities		₹	*Property and Assets*	₹
Capital Accounts :	₹		Land and Building	20,000
P	25,000		Plant and Machinery	25,000
Q	20,000		Furniture and Fixture	5,000
R	18,000		Stock	15,000
		63,000	Sundry Debtors	18,000
Loan from S		10,000	Cash and Bank Balances	7,000
Creditors		17,000		
		90,000		90,000

It was decided that P and Q would take over the following assets at figures shown against each of them :

	₹
Land and Building	25,000
Plant and Machinery	15,000
Furniture	7,000

S agreed to take the entire stock in full settlement of his loan. Sundry debtors were realised at ₹ 15,000 and creditors were settled at ₹ 18,000.

P and Q decided to form a partnership sharing profits and losses in the ratio of 2 : 1 and it was agreed that the firm will require a total capital of ₹ 60,000 and P and Q should bring sufficient capital for the purpose in such proportion that their capitals should be in the profit sharing ratios.

Draw up relevant accounts to close the books of P, Q and R and prepare the opening Balance Sheet of P and Q.

Ans. [Loss on Realisation ₹ 12,000 ; Balance Sheet Total of the New Firm ₹ 70,000].

Hint. The above answer of ₹ 70,000 is on the assumption that R is paid all the cash available with the old firm and the remaining balance of ₹ 10,000 in R's Capital Account has been treated as a loan to the new firm.

12. A, B and C decided to dissolve their partnership on 30th June, 2025. Their Balance Sheet is as follows:

Liabilities	₹	*Assets*	₹
Creditors	3,400	Cash at Bank	2,500
Capitals :		Debtors	6,200
A	12,000	Stock	3,700
B	9,000	Loose Tools	800
C	6,000	Motor Vehicles	1,200
		Plant and Machinery	6,000
		Freehold Premises	10,000
	30,400		30,400

B and C agreed to form a new partnership to carry on the business and it is agreed that they shall acquire from the old firm the following assets at figures shown below :

Stock ₹ 4,000 ; Loose Tools ₹ 500 ; Motor Vehicles ₹ 2,500 ; Plant and Machinery ₹ 7,800 ; Freehold Premises ₹ 8,400 ; Goodwill ₹ 6,000.

The partnership agreement of A, B and C provides that trading profits or loss shall be divided in the ratio of 3 : 2 : 1 and that capital profits or losses shall be divided in proportion of their respective capitals.

Debtors realised ₹ 5,900 and discounts amounting to ₹ 72 are secured on payments due to creditors.

Prepare the necessary accounts of A, B and C giving effect to these transactions and draw up the opening Balance Sheet of B and C who bring the necessary cash to pay in the ratio of 3 : 2.

Ans. [Profit on Realisation ₹ 7,272 ; B/S Total ₹ 29,200 ; B's Capital ₹ 17,522 ; C's Capital ₹ 11,678].

INSOLVENCY OF A PARTNER

When all Partners are not Insolvent

13. Following was the Balance Sheet of a firm as at 31st March, 2025 :

Liabilities	₹	*Assets*	₹
Creditors	2,04,800	Bank Balance	11,000
P's Loan A/c	60,000	Debtors	1,92,120
Q's Loan A/c	24,000	Stock	1,28,000
P's Current A/c	42,400	Machinery	57,200
Q's Current A/c	5,000	Land	1,68,000
Current Accounts :		R's Current A/c	19,880
P	1,20,000		
Q	80,000		
R	40,000		
	5,76,200		5,76,200

It was decided to dissolve the firm on that date. The assets (with the exception of bank balance) realised ₹ 4,53,600. The firm had to pay ₹ 3,000 for an outstanding bill not recorded in the books. R became insolvent and ₹ 2,000 were realised from his estate. Prepare necessary Ledger Accounts in the books of the firm when—

(*i*) Partners' capitals were fixed; and

(*ii*) Garner *vs.* Murray rule was followed.

Ans. [Loss on Realisation ₹ 94,720 ; R's Deficiency of ₹ 9,453 to be borne by P and Q in the ratio of 3 : 2 ; Final Payment to P—₹ 1,56,728 and ₹ 81,219 respectively]

14. Following was the Balance Sheet of P, Q and R on 31st March, 2025.

Liabilities	₹	*Assets*	₹
P's Capital	25,000	Freehold Property	10,000
R's Capital	15,000	Furniture	5,000
P's Current Account	1,000	Stock-in-trade	23,100
R's Current Account	500	Debtors	30,000
Sundry Creditors	30,000	Cash	2,500
Loan on Mortgage of Freehold Property	4,000	Q's Current Account	4,900
	75,500		75,500

The partners shared profits and losses in the proportion of 6 : 3 : 5. It was decided to dissolve the partnership as on the date of the balance sheet.

The asset realise as under :

Freehold Property ₹ 6,000 ; Furniture ₹ 2,000 ; Stock-in-trade ₹ 15,000 ; Debtors ₹ 20,000.

The expenses of realisation amounted to ₹ 2,000. The sundry creditors agreed to take 75 paise in the rupee in full satisfaction. It was ascertained that Q has become insolvent. A dividend of 50 paise in the rupee was received from the Court Receiver.

Write up Realisation Account, Bank Account, Capital and Current Accounts of the partners. Indicate the basis adopted for distributing the deficiency in the Capital Account.

Ans. [Loss on Realisation ₹ 19,600 ; Final Repayment to P and R—₹ 23,156 and ₹ 13,794 respectively].

15. A, B and C are partners in a firm sharing profits and losses in the ratio of 2 : 2 : 1. They decided to dissolve and appoint B to realise the assets and distribute the proceeds for which he is to receive as his remuneration 5% of the amounts ultimately paid to A and C but in lieu of this he is to bear all expenses of realisation.

Balance Sheet of the firm on the date of dissolution is as under :

Liabilities	₹	*Assets*	₹	₹
Creditors	1,317	Debtors	4,229	
A's Capital	3,960	*Less* : Provision	211	
B's Capital	2,970			4,018
		Stock		1,872
		Cash		290
		Other Assets		1,710
		C – (Overdrawn)		357
	8,247			8,247

B informs of the following realisations :

Debtors ₹ 3,462 ; Stock ₹ 1,444 ; Goodwill ₹ 50 ; Other Assets ₹ 914.

Creditors which were not recorded in books are now paid ₹ 100.

Expenses of realisation amount to ₹ 310. C is able to contribute only ₹ 100 beyond which he expresses his insolvency.

Close books of the firm.

Ans. **[Loss on Realisation ₹ 1,970 ; Commission paid to B—₹ 140 and Final Repayment to A —₹ 2,800 and B— ₹ 2,043 respectively].**

16. Lean, Stout and Thin were partners sharing profits and losses in the ratio of 3 : 2 : 1. On 31st December, 2024 their Balance Sheet was as follows :

Liabilities	₹	*Assets*		₹
Sundry Creditors	30,000	Cash at Bank		9,500
Bills Payable	5,000	Stock		15,500
Lean's Loan Account	6,000	Sundry Debtors		32,000
Reserve Fund	12,000	Furniture		5,000
Profit and Loss Account	6,000	Plant and Machinery		21,000
Capital Accounts :		Drawings :	₹	
Lean	20,000	Lean	4,000	
Stout	15,000	Stout	1,000	
				5,000
		Thin's Capital Account		6,000
	94,000			94,000

The assets realised as follows :

Stock ₹ 12,200 ; Sundry Debtors ₹ 30,100 ; Furniture ₹ 4,200.

Plant and Machinery is taken over by Lean at ₹ 18,000. A contingent liability for Bill Receivable discounted materialised to the extent of ₹ 600. Realisation expenses amounted to ₹ 600. Thin is insolvent but his estate pays ₹ 1,900. Prepare necessary accounts to close the books of the firm, if the capitals are fluctuating.

Ans. **[Loss on Realisation ₹ 10,200 ; Final Repayment to Lean and Stout ₹ 5,444 and ₹ 18,756 respectively].**

17. Menon, Mitra, Mehra and Morarka were partners in a firm sharing profits and losses in the ratio of 4 : 3 : 2 : 1. Their Balance Sheet as on 31st December, 2024 stood as follows :

Liabilities	₹	*Assets*	₹
Accounts Payable	10,000	Machinery	40,000
Capital A/cs :		Goodwill	10,000
Menon	30,000	Book Debts	8,000
Mitra	20,000	Stock	4,000
Mehra	3,000	Capital A/c : Morarka	1,000
	63,000		63,000

Morarka did not have any private assets or liabilities. The firm was dissolved by the partners. Prepare Ledger Accounts to close the books of the firm under each of the following two circumstances :

(*a*) The partners agreed to sell the fixed assets to Selecta Limited which allotted 2,250 fully paid equity shares of ₹ 10 each (at the market value of ₹ 13) and paid cash ₹ 10,000. Stock and Book Debts were realised at book value, and the cost of realisation amounted to ₹ 450. Mehra had sufficient private assets.

(*b*) Mehra could contribute ₹ 500 only from his personal resources.

The partners disposed of the assets through an auctioneer ; the machiney realised ₹ 30,000 and Stock and Book Debts ₹ 10,000. The cost of realisation amounted to ₹ 3,000.

Ans. [Loss on Realisation ₹ 11,200 (1st case) ; Distribution of Shares : Menon ₹ 16,562 ; Mitra ₹ 11,037 ; Mehra ₹ 1,651 ; Loss on Realisation ₹ 25,000 (2nd case)].

18. A, B, C and D were equal partners. Their Balance Sheet on the date of the dissolution was as follows :

Liabilities		₹	*Assets*		₹
Creditors		45,000	Sundra Assets		63,000
Bills Payable		5,000	Cash at Bank		2,000
B's Loan Account		3,000	Profit and Loss Account		16,000
Capital Accounts :			Drawings :	₹	
	₹		B	3,000	
A	23,000		C	3,000	
B	6,000		D	3,000	
C	4,000				9,000
D	4,000				
		37,000			
		90,000			90,000

The assets realised ₹ 56,000. The expenses of realisation amounted to ₹ 1,000. The position of the partners on the date of the dissolution was as follows :

	Private Estate	*Private Liabilities*
	₹	₹
A	20,000	23,000
B	16,000	10,000
C	14,000	12,000
D	8,000	9,000

Prepare the Ledger Accounts to close the books of the firm.

Ans. [Loss on Realisation ₹ 8,000].

19. A, B and C were in partnership sharing profits and losses in the ratio of 1/5, 3/10 and 1/2. Following is their Balance Sheet as on June, 30, 2025, when they decided to dissolve :

Liabilities	₹	*Assets*	₹
Capital of A	3,000	Cash	1,000
Capital of B	4,000	Plant and Machinery	5,000
Capital of C	3,000	Sundry Debtors	20,000
Trade Creditors	12,000	Advance to A	2,000
Loan from Bank on Book Debts, Plant etc.	14,000	Loss to date	8,000
	36,000		36,000

The assets realised ₹ 20,000. A has private estate which is valued at ₹ 4,000. B is insolvent. From C's estate a dividend of 50 paise in a rupee is received.

Show the Realisation Account and the accounts of the partners assuming that all entries relating to dissolution are passed through Realisation Account.

Ans. [Loss on Realisation ₹ 5,000 ; Final Payment to A—₹ 15,238 ; B and C bring ₹ 6,098 and ₹ 4,066 respectively].

20. P, Q and R are partners, sharing profits and losses in the proportion of one-half, one-third and one-sixth respectively. The partnership was dissolved on 31st March, 2025 on which date the Balance Sheet of the firm was as follows :

Liabilities	₹	*Assets*	₹
P's Capital	16,830	Sundry Assets	13,500
Q's Capital	11,832	Sundry Debtors	6,830
Reserve	7,200	Bills Receivable	5,036
Sundry Creditors	29,964	Stock	9,032
		R's Account	25,000
		Cash in hand	6,428
	65,826		65,826

The lives of the Partners were insured severally for P, ₹ 20,000 ; Q ₹ 10,000 ; and R ₹ 12,000. The premiums were charged to Profit and Loss Account. On the date of dissolution the surrender value of each of the policies was 30% of the sum assured. P took over his policy but the policies of Q and R were surrendered. In the course of realisation it was found :

(1) that a liability of ₹ 3,000 for purchase of goods in 2023-24 had been omitted from the Balance Sheet and that the goods had been included in the value of stock :

(2) that bills receivable amounting to ₹ 7,000 which were discounted by the firm were dishonoured and proved to be valueless.

P agreed to take over the goodwill of the firm at ₹ 5,000. The bills receivable were retired by the acceptors for ₹ 4,800. The remaining assets realised ₹ 20,798. The expenses of realisation amounted to ₹ 1,200. R is insolvent but his estate pays ₹ 4,200.

Preapre the final accounts of the partners, closing the books of the firm and show the result of the dissolution.

Ans. [Loss on Realisation ₹ 12,000 ; R's Deficiency of ₹ 20,000 divided between P and Q in the ratio of 25,230 : 17,432].

21. A, B and C are partners in a firm dealing in fancy goods, and sharing profits and losses in the ratio of 2 : 2 : 1 respectively, decided to dissolve and appoint B to realise the assets and distribute the proceeds. B is to receive 5% of the amounts coming to A and C as his remuneration, and is to bear all the expenses of realisation.

Following is the Balance Sheet prepared by the firm as on the date of dissolution :

Liabilities		₹	*Assets*		₹
Creditors		1,247		₹	
Capitals :			Debtors	4,229	
	₹		*Less* : Povision for Bad Debts	211	
A	4,106				4,018
B	3,080		Stock-in-Trade		1,872
		7,186	Cash		476
			Other Assets		1,710
			C— Overdrawn		357
		8,433			8,433

B reports the result of realisation as follows :

Debtors realise ₹ 3,462 ; Stock-in-Trade realises ₹ 1,444 ; Goodwill is sold for ₹ 50 ; The other assets realise ₹ 909.

Creditors were omitted from the Balance Sheet to the amount of ₹ 100. The expenses of realisation amounted to ₹ 100.

C informs his partners that he is possessed of ₹ 100 only, and they agree that, if as a result of the realisation, he is still indebted to more than this amount, they will accept it in full settlement. Prepare Dissolution Accounts.

Ans. [Loss on Realisation ₹ 1,982 ; B's Commission ₹ 147].

WHEN ALL PARTNERS ARE INSOLVENT

22. A, B and C were equal partners in a firm. Their Balance Sheet as on 31st March, 2025 was as follows :

Liabilities	₹	*Assets*	₹
A's Capital	1,60,000	Building	4,00,000
C's Capital	1,00,000	Machinery	4,00,000
A's Loan	2,00,000	Furniture and Fixtures	1,60,000
Creditors	10,00,000	Stock	1,60,000
		Book Debts	2,00,000
		Cash at Bank	10,000
		B's Capital (Overdrawn)	1,30,000
	14,60,000		14,60,000

The firm was dissolved as all the partners were declared insolvent. The assets realised as under : Book debts : 45% less; Building: ₹ 1,60,000; Stock : ₹ 1,00,000; Machinery : ₹ 2,00,000; and Furniture's and fixtures : ₹ 40,000. Realisation expenses were ₹ 10,000.

The private assets and private liabilities of the partners were as follows :

Partner	*Private Assets*	*Private Liabilities*
	(₹)	(₹)
A	2,50,000	2,50,000
B	2,00,000	1,80,000
C	2,30,000	2,50,000

Prepare Realisation Account, Bank Account, Creditors Account, Deficiency Account and Partners' Capital Accounts.

Ans. [Loss on Realisation ₹ 7,20,000, Cash Paid to Creditors ₹ 6,30,000; Total of Deficiency A/c ₹ 4,90,000]

23. X, Y and Z are partners sharing profits and losses in the ratio of 3 : 2 : 1. Below is their Balance Sheet as on 30th June, 2025 when they decided to dissolve the firm :

Liabilities	₹	*Assets*	₹
Sundry Creditors	51,000	Fixed Assets	50,000
Depreciation Fund	7,000	Current Assets	19,100
X's Loan	10,000	(including cash ₹ 1,600)	
X's Capital Account	15,000	Z's Capital Account	3,900
Y's Capital Account	8,000	Profit and Loss Account	18,000
	91,000		91,000

The assets realised ₹ 35,000. The position of the partners on the date of the dissolution was as follows :

	Private Estate	*Private Liabilities*
	₹	₹
X	9,000	7,500
Z	4,000	5,000

Y was able to pay 20 paise in the rupee of what was payable on his account to the partnership. The expenses of realisation amounted to ₹ 500. Prepare Ledger Accounts, passing all matters relating to realisation of assets and payment of liabilities through Realisation Account. Clearly show your calculation regarding cash brought in by Y.

Ans. [Loss on Realisation ₹ 13,071 ; Cash paid to Creditors ₹ 38,071 ; Y brings ₹ 471].

PIECEMEAL DISTRIBUTION

Proportionate (or Higher Relative) Capital Method

24. Orange, Apple and Banana were in partnership sharing profits and losses in the ratio of 3 : 2 : 1. They decided to dissolve the partnership and to distribute the sale proceeds as and when realised.

The partners' capitals were : Orange ₹ 10,000, Apple ₹ 9,000 and Banana ₹ 5,000. Apple's loan (Cr.) amounted to ₹ 3,000.

Sundry creditors amounted to ₹ 6,000.

The assets were realised as under.

	Stock	*Furniture*	*Debtors*	*Expenses*
	₹	₹	₹	₹
July	3,000	300	2,000	500
August	2,000	100	1,500	200
September	2,500	—	2,000	300
October	3,000	—	1,500	200

You are required to draw up a statement showing the distribution of Cash and the Journal Entry for closing finally the Capital Accounts of the partners by following the proportionate capital method.

Ans.

	Orange	**Apple**	**Banana**
	₹	₹	₹
Sept.	**—**	**1,933**	**1,467**
Oct.	**1,850**	**1,633**	**817**

25. P, Q and R are partners sharing profits and losses in the ratio of 1/4 : 1/4 : 1/2. They decided to dissolve their business on 31-3-2025, when their Balance Sheet was as follows :

BALANCE SHEET

Liabilities	₹	*Assets*	₹
Capital Accounts :			
P	10,000	Fixed Assets	82,000
Q	15,000	Stock	15,000
R	25,000	Debtors	18,000
Trade Creditors	20,000	Cash	5,000
Secured Loan (Secured on the fixed assets of the firm)	10,000		
Unsecured Loan	20,000		
Bank Overdraft (Secured against stock and book debts)	20,000		
	1,20,000		1,20,000

P is insolvent. Realisations are to be distributed monthly to creditors and partners in the order of priority. Realisations monthwise were :

2025		₹	2025		₹
April	Fixed Assets	17,000	June	Fixed Assets	12,000
	Stock and Debtors	4,000		Stock and Debtors	4,000

May	Fixed Assets	15,000	July	Fixed Assets	8,800
	Stock and Debtors	2,000		Stock and Debtors	Nil

Prepare a statement showing distribution of cash by Proportionate Capital Method and the Capital Accounts of the partners.

Ans. [Loss on Realisation ₹ 52,200 ; Final Payment to Q out of ₹ 3,006 Contributed by R = ₹ 806].

26. The firm of LMS was dissolved on 31-3-2025, on which date its Balance Sheet stood as follows :

Liabilities	₹	*Assets*	₹
Creditors	2,00,000	Fixed Assets	45,00,000
Bank Loan	5,00,000	Cash and Bank	2,00,000
L's Loan	10,00,000		
Capital :			
L	15,00,000		
M	10,00,000		
S	5,00,000		
	47,00,000		47,00,000

Partners share profits equally. A firm of Chartered Accountants is employed to realise the assets and distribute the cash after discharge of liabilities. Their fees which are to include all expenses is fixed at ₹ 1,00,000. No loss is expected on realisation since fixed assets include valuable land and buildings.

Realisations are :

S. No.	*Amount in ₹*
1 (including balance of Cash & Bank)	5,00,000
2	15,00,000
3	15,00,000
4	30,00,000
5	30,00,000

The Chartered Accountant firm decided to pay off the partners in '*Higher Relative Capital Method*'. You are required to prepare a statement showing distribution of cash with necessary workings. (*C.A. Inter*)

Ans.

	L	***M***	***S***
	₹	₹	₹
3rd Instalment	**8,66,667 (*i.e.* ₹ 3,00,000 + ₹ 5,00,000 + ₹ 66,667)**	**5,66,667 (*i.e.* ₹ 5,00,000 + ₹ 66,667)**	**66,666**
4th Instalment	**10,00,000**	**10,00,000**	**10,00,000**
5th Instalment	**10,00,000**	**10,00,000**	**10,00,000**

27. The partners P, Q and R have called you to assist them in winding up the affairs of their partnership on 31-12-2024. Their Balance Sheet as on that date is given below :

Liabilities	*Amount* (₹)	*Assets*	*Amount* (₹)
Capital Accounts :		Land & Building	50,000
P	65,000	Plant and Machinery	46,000
Q	50,500	Furniture & Fixture	10,000
R	32,000	Stock	14,500
Sundry Creditors	16,000	Debtors	14,000

		Cash at Bank	9,000
		Loan P	13,000
		Loan Q	7,000
	1,63,500		1,63,500

(*a*) The partners share profit and losses in the ratio of 4 : 3 : 2.

(*b*) Cash in distributed to the partners at the end of each month.

(*c*) A summary of liquidation transactions are as follows :

January 2025 :

₹ 9,000—Collected from debtors balance is uncollectable; ₹ 8,000—Received from the sale of entire furniture; ₹ 1,000—Liquidation expenses paid; and ₹ 6,000—Cash retained in the business at the end of month.

February 2025 :

₹ 1,000—Liquidation expenses paid; As part payment of his capital, R accepted a machinery for ₹ 9,000 (book value ₹ 3,500); and ₹ 2,000—Cash retained in the business at the end of month.

March 2025 :

₹ 38,000—Received on the sale of remaining plant and machinery; ₹ 10,000—Received from the sale of entire stock; ₹ 1,700—Liquidation expenses paid; ₹ 41,000—Received on sale of land and building; and No Cash is retained in the business.

You are required to prepare a schedule of cash payments amongst the partners by "Higher Relative Capital Method." ***(CA-IPCE May, 2014 Modified)***

Ans. [

	P	***Q***	***R***
January (₹)	**–**	**–**	**3,000**
February (₹)	**–**	**3,000**	**9,000**
			(Machinery given)
March (₹)	**41,689**	**32,767**	**14,844**
Loss	**10,311**	**7,733**	**5,156**]

MAXIMUM LOSS METHOD

28. A, B and C share profits and losses in the proportion of 1/2, 1,3 and 1/6. Their Balane Sheet is as follows :

Li abilities	₹	*Assets*	₹
A's Capital	3,000	Assets *less* Liabilities	8,000
B's Capital	3,000		
C's Capital	2,000		
	8,000		8,000

The partnership is dissolved, and the assets are realised as follows :

1st Realisation ₹ 1,000 ; 2nd Realisation ₹ 1,500 ; 3rd and Final Realisation ₹ 2,500.

The partners desire to withdraw immeditely such cash as is available for division among them rather than wait until all the assets have been sold.

Prepare a Statement showing how the distribution should be made and prepare Partners' Capital Accounts by following the *Maximum Possible Loss Method.*

Ans.

Realisation	***A***	***B***	***C***
	₹	₹	₹
I	**–**	**367**	**633**
II	**250**	**800**	**450**
III	**1,250**	**833**	**417**

29. A, B and C share profits and losses in the proportion of 4/10, 5/10 and 1/10. Their Balance Sheet is as follows :

Liabilities	₹	*Assets*	₹
Sundry Creditors	10,000	Cash in hand	3,000
A's Loan	6,000	Other Assets	56,000
B's Loan	3,000		
Reserve Fund	6,000		
Contingency Reserve	4,000		
A's Capital Account	15,000		
B's Capital Account	12,000		
C's Capital Account	3,000		
	59,000		59,000

The partnership is dissolved, and the assets are realised as follows :

First Realisation ₹ 10,000 ; Second Realisation ₹ 20,000 ; Third Realisation ₹ 17,000.

On the date of the dissolution, there was a contingent liability of ₹ 1,000 against the firm which was settled at ₹ 700 at the time of second realisation. Realisation expenses were estimated at ₹ 2,000 but those actually amounted to ₹ 1,500. C took stock worth ₹ 500 at the time of third realisation. The firm was forced to pay ₹ 600 out of third realisation for which no provision was made in the books.

Prepare a statement showing how the distribution should be made by following the *Maximum Loss Method.*

Ans.

Realisation	***A***	***B***	***C***
	₹	₹	₹
II	**7,520**	**2,650**	**1,130**
III	**6,960**	**8,700**	**1,740**

30. Balance Sheet of X, Y and Z as at December 31, 2024 (on which date they decided to dissolve their firm) was as under :

BALANCE SHEET

Liabilities		₹	*Assets*	₹
Capitals :			Cash in hand	5,000
	₹		Other Assets	65,000
X	20,000			
Y	30,000			
Z	10,000			
		60,000		
Sundry Creditors		10,000		
		70,000		70,000

The partnership deed provided that the loss arising on account of un-recovered deficiency of any partner in the event of dissolution should be borne by the remaining partners in the ratio in which such remaining partners' capitals stood on the eve of dissolution. Subject thereto, the profits and losses were to be shared in the ratio of 1 : 2 : 1.

Upon dissolution, the realisations of other assets were as under :

Date	*Book value of assets realised*	*Amount realised*
2025	₹	₹
January, 31	21,000	9,000
February, 28	36,000	4,000
March, 31	8,000	4,000

The patners decided to distribute the available cash amongst themselves in a manner which is most conservative.

Show, with the aid of necessary workings, the accounts of the partners, Realisation A/c and Cash/Bank A/c. Show, with the aid of necessary workings, the accounts of the partners, Realisation A/c and Cash/Bank A/c by following the *Maximum Possible Loss Method*. Z was insolvent and was unable to contribute anything towards his deficiency.

Ans.

Realisation	**X**	**Y**	**Z**
	₹	₹	₹
January 31	**4,000**	—	—
February 28	**1,800**	**2,200**	—
March 31	**1,400**	**2,600**	

Loss on Realisation ₹ 48,000.

SALE OF FIRM TO A COMPANY

31. Amit and Asit were in partnership sharing profits and losses : Amit two thirds ; Asit one third. The summarised partnership Balance Sheet as on March 31, 2025, was as follows :

Liabilities		₹	*Assets*		₹
Fixed Capital Accounts :			Fixed Assets		70,000
Amit	50,000		Current Assets :	₹	
Asit	40,000		Stock	35,000	
		90,000	Debtors	65,000	
Current Accounts :			Balance at Bank	15,000	
Amit	20,000				1,15,000
Less : Asit	10,000				
		10,000			
Loan—Asit		30,000			
Creditors		55,000			
		1,85,000			1,85,000

The fixed assets included two motor cars having book values of ₹ 8,000 and ₹ 6,000 respectively.

The partners desiring to retire from business accepted the offer of Western India Limited to acquire the stock and fixed assets, other than the motor cars, at an agreed purchase price of ₹ 1,60,000.

The purchase consideration was to be satisfied by a cash payment of ₹ 56,000, the allotment by the company to the partners of 400, 5% preference shares of ₹ 100 each and the balance by the allotment by the company to the partners of 900 equity shares of ₹ 100 each.

The debtors realised ₹ 61,000 and the creditors were settled for ₹ 51,000.

The partners agreed that the following should be the basis of distribution on dissolution of the partnership.

(1) Amit to take over one car at a valuation of ₹ 12,000 and Asit the other at ₹ 8,000.

(2) Asit to be allotted preference shares to the value of his loan, the remainder to be allotted to Amit.

(3) The equity shares to be allotted in proportion of fixed capitals.

(4) Both the preference and equity shares to be valued at ₹ 80 per share.

(5) The balances to be settled in cash. You are required to prepare :

(*a*) Realisation Account ; (*b*) the Bank Account ; and (*c*) the Partners' Capital Accounts showing the final settlement between them.

Ans. [Profit on Realisation ₹ 75,000 ; Cash Payment to Amit and Asit ₹ 66,000 and ₹ 15,000 respectively].

Hints Purchase consideration comes to ₹ 1,60,000 valuing shares @ ₹ 80 per share as shown below :

	₹
Cash	56,000
400 preference shares @ ₹ 80 per share	32,000
900 equity shares @ ₹ 80 per share	72,000
	1,60,000

32. 'S' and 'T' were carrying on business as equal partners. Their Balance Sheet as on 31st March, 2025 stood as follows :

Liabilities		₹	*Assets*	₹
Capital Accounts :			Stock	2,70,000
S	6,40,000		Debtors	3,65,000
T	6,60,000		Furniture	75,000
		13,00,000	Joint Life Policy	47,500
Creditors		3,27,500	Plant	1,72,500
Bank Overdraft		1,50,000	Building	9,10,000
Bills Payable		62,500		
		18,40,000		18,40,000

The operations of the business were carried on till 30th September, 2025, S and T both withdrew in equal amounts, half the amount of profits made during the current period of 6 months after 10% per annum had been written off on building and plant and 5% per annum written off on furniture. During the current period of 6 months, creditors were reduced by ₹ 50,000, Bills payable by ₹ 11,500 and Bank overdraft by ₹ 75,000 (after surrender of joint life policy). The Joint Life policy was surrendered for ₹ 47,500 on 30th September, 2025. Stock was valued at ₹ 3,17,000 and debtors at ₹ 3,25,000 on 30th September, 2025. The other items remained the same as on 31st March, 2025.

On 30th September, 2025 the firm sold its business to ST Ltd. The value of goodwill was estimated at ₹ 5,40,000 and the remaining assets were valued on the basis of the Balance Sheet as on 30th September, 2025. The ST Ltd. paid the purchase consideration in equity shares of ₹ 10 each. You are required to prepare a Realisation Account and Capital Accounts of the partners.

Ans. [Profit on Realisation ₹ 5,40,000; Shares divided among S and T ₹ 9,30,000 and ₹ 9,50,000]

Hint : Capital on 30-9-2025 ₹ 13,40,000; Net Profit (after drawings) ₹ 40,000; Purchase Consideration ₹ 18,80,000.

33. A, B and C carrying on business in partnership (profit and loss sharing ratio being 1/2, 1/3 and 1/6 respectively) decide to form a private limited company ABC Co. (Private) Ltd., with an authorised capital of ₹ 1,20,000 divided into 90,000 equity shares of ₹ 1 each and 30,000, 6% preference shares of ₹ 1 each. The company is incorporated on 31-3-2025 and takes over the business goodwill and some of the assets of the firm as on 31-3-2025, on which date the Balance Sheet of the firm is as given hereunder :

Liabilites		₹	*Assets*	₹
Creditors		5,600	Cash at Bank	17,200
A's Loan		8,000	Debtors	10,400
Current Accounts :			Current Account :	
	A	5,850	B	4,200
	C	4,150	Stock in Trade	36,000
Capital Accounts :			Furniture and Fixtures	1,200
	A	30,000	Scooters	3,600
	B	20,000	Machinery	13,000
	C	12,000		
		85,600		85,600

A who retires, is presented with a scooter, book value being ₹ 1,200. The company takes over the remaining scooter for ₹ 2,000. A takes over all the debtors and agrees to pay off creditors. He also received certain furniture for which he is charged ₹ 300. The company agrees to discharge A's loan by issuing to him 6,000 preference shares of ₹ 1 each fully paid and the balance in cash. C is the owner of the premises from where the business of the firm is carried on. C agrees to sell the above premises to the company for ₹ 20,000 in consideration whereof he agrees to receive 20,000 preference shares of ₹ 1 each fully paid.

The company takes over the remaining furniture at ₹ 600 ; stock at ₹ 33,200 ; Cash at Bank and macinery at book value. The goodwill is valued at ₹ 8,000 for the purpose of taking over.

The purchase consideration is to be discharged by the issue to the partners at par ₹ 60,000 equity shares of ₹ 1 each in proportion to final balance of their combined Capital and Current Accounts and the balance is to be paid in cash.

Preliminary expenses amounting to ₹ 800 are paid by the company.

Prepare—(*i*) Realisation Account, (*ii*) Combined Capital and Current Accounts of Partners, (*iii*) Opening Balance Sheet of the Limited Company.

Ans. [Profit on Realisation ₹ 4,500 ; B/S Total ₹ 86,000].

34. A, B and C were in partnership. Following was their Balance Sheet as on 30-9-2024.

Liabilities	₹	*Assets*	₹
Capital of A	6,000	Cash at Bank	6,000
Capital of B	9,000	Goodwill	3,000
Capital of C	5,000	Debtors	24,000
Creditors	25,000	Plant and Machinery	15,000
Loan from B	5,000	Loss to Date	2,000
	50,000		50,000

They shared profits 1/4 : 1/2 : 1/4. On differences having arisen B wished to retire. It was agreed that A and C should pay him his capital without adjusting the losses and the loan was to continue. A and C paid B from their own funds.

They immediately admitted D as 2/5 partner on his bringing in proportionate share of capital and also ₹ 2,000 for goodwill. Hereafter A and C agreed to share in the ratio of 1 : 2.

On 31-12-2024 they sold the business to X and Z Ltd. who paid a total of ₹ 34,000 inclusive of ₹ 2,000 for profits upto 31-12-2024. This was paid as to ₹ 20,000 in 1 Rupee shares and the balance in cash.

Show partners' Capital Accounts assuming that they decided to distribute the shares so as to maintain their rights in the company in the way as in the firm.

Ans. [Profit on Realisation ₹ 3,667 ; B/S Total on Dissolution ₹ 60,333 ; Final Repayment to A, B and C ₹ 6,633 ; ₹ 1,767 and ₹ 5,600 respectively].

35. Kapoor and Jain were carrying business sharing profits and losses equally. The firm's Balance Sheet as at 31st December, 2024 was as follows :

Liabilities	₹	*Assets*	₹
Sundry Creditors	60,000	Stock	60,000
Bank Overdraft	35,000	Machinery	1,50,000
Capital Accounts :		Debtors	70,000
Kapoor	1,40,000	Joint Life Policy	9,000
Jain	1,30,000	Leasehold Premises	34,000
		Profit and Loss Account	26,000
		Drawings Accounts :	
		Kapoor	10,000
		Jain	6,000
	3,65,000		3,65,000

The business was carried on till 30th June, 2025. The partners withdrew in equal amounts half the amount of profits made during the period of six months after charging depreciation at 10% p.a. on Machinery and after writing off 5% on Leasehold Premises. In the half year, Sundry Creditors were reduced by ₹ 10,000 and Bank Overdraft by ₹ 15,000.

On 30th June, 2025, Stock was valued at ₹ 75,000 and Debtors at ₹ 60,000; the Joint Life Policy had been surrendered for ₹ 9,000 before 30th June, 2025 and other items remained the same as at 31st December, 2024.

On 30th June, 2025, the firm sold the business to a Limited Company. The value of goodwill was fixed at ₹ 1,00,000 and the rest of the assets were valued on the basis of the Balance Sheet as at 30th June, 2025.

The company paid the purchase consideration in Equity shares of ₹ 10 each.

You are required to prepare : (*a*) Balance Sheet of the firm as at 30-6-2025 (*b*) Realisation Account. (*c*) Partners' Capital Accounts showing the final settlement between them.

Ans. [(*a*) B/S Total ₹ 3,09,800; (*b*) Profit on Realisation ₹ 1,00,000; Final Payment to : Kapoor ₹ 1,69,000 Shares and ₹ 3,000 Cash and Jain ₹ 1,69,000 Shares].

Hints : (1) Profit for 6 months from 1-1-2025 to 30-6-2025 ₹ 23,600.

(2) It has been assumed that shares have been divided between partners in their profit sharing ratio.

36. Suchandra, Ashmita and Kasturi were running partnership business sharing Profit and Losses in 2 : 2 : 1 ratio. Their Balance Sheet as on 31-3-2025 stood as follows : (₹ in 000's)

Liabilities	₹	₹	*Assets*	₹	₹
Fixed Capital :			Fixed Assets		920.00
Suchandra	690.00		Investment		115.00
Ashmita	460.00		Current Assets :		
Kasturi	230.00		Stock	230.00	
		1,380.00	Debtors	632.50	
Current Account :			Cash at Bank	287.50	
Suchandra	138.00				1,150.00
Kasturi	92.00				
		230.00			

Unsecured Loan		230.00			
Current Liabilities		345.00			
		2,185.00			2,185.00

On 1-4-2025, they agreed to form new company Tata (P) Ltd. with Ashmita and Kasturi each taking up 460 equity shares of ₹ 10 each, which shall take over the firm as going concern including Goodwill, but excluding cash and bank balance.

Followings are also agreed upon :

(*a*) Goodwill will be valued at 3 years purchase of super profit.

(*b*) The actual profit for the purpose of Goodwill valuation will be ₹ 4,60,000.

(*c*) The normal rate of return will be 18% p.a. on Fixed Capital.

(*d*) All other assets and liabilities will be taken at Book value.

(*e*) Ashmita and Kasturi are to acquire interest in the new company at the ratio of 3 : 2.

(*f*) The purchase consideration will be payable partly in shares of ₹ 10 each and partly in cash. Payment in cash given to meet the requirement to discharge Suchandra, who has agreed to retire.

(*g*) Realisation expenses amounted to ₹ 1,17,300.

You are required to close the books of the firm by passing necessary Journal Entries.

Ans. [Purchase Consideration ₹ 19,57,300 Value of Goodwill ₹ 6,34,800 ; Amount payable by Ashmita to Kasturi ₹ 11,500; Cash paid to ₹ 10,35,000; Shares distributed among Ashmita and Kasturi ₹ 6,.55,500 and ₹ 4,37,000]

37. R, K and C have carried on business as drapers for 20 years and on 31st March, 2025 their Balance Sheet was as under :

Liabilities		₹	*Assets*	₹
Bank Overdraft		20,000	Plant and Machinery	32,000
Creditors for Suppliers		30,000	Premises	50,000
Creditors for Expenses		18,000	Sundry Debtors	48,000
Capital Accounts (Fixed)	₹		Stock in Trade	40,000
R	30,000		Cash and Bank Balances	8,000
K	20,000			
C	20,000			
		70,000		
Current Accounts :				
R	16,000			
C	24,000			
		40,000		
		1,78,000		1,78,000

The Profit and Losses were shared in the ratio of fixed capital on 31st March, 2025. The partners agreed that due to old age R would retire from the firm when its goodwill be valued and proportionate share credited to R. It was also decided that premises appearing in the books at cost would be valued at their market value of ₹ 80,000 and allotted to R in satisfaction of his dues. Any excess or deficit would be settled in cash. It was also agreed that Stock in Trade and debtors would be taken at 90% of the book value and an unrecorded liability of bonus of ₹ 10,000 to staff brought into books. Goodwill of the firm was to be taken at ₹ 70,000.

After R's retirement, the business was carried on by K and C sharing profits and losses equally and till 30th June, 2025, the firm had made a net profit of ₹ 30,000 after crediting each partner's Capital Account with ₹ 500 p.m. as salary. No drawings were made by the partners in the quarter.

K and C now find that they cannot continue the business and decide to sell it to a private limited company as and from 1st July, 2025. The company is to take over the entire business for a consideration of ₹ 90,000 which the vendors agree to take 40% in 14% secured debentures and the balance in cash. To enable the company to pay the vendors and also leave it with a working capital of ₹ 20,000, the Company makes issue of equity shares of ₹ 10 each at par.

Show the Balance sheet of the Company after the take over the business of K and C.

All workings should form part of your answer.

Ans. [Profit on Adjustment ₹ 11,200; Cash paid to R ₹ 800; Total of Revised Balance Sheet (after R's retirement) ₹ 1,18,400; Balance Sheet Total of K & C as on 3th June, 2025 ₹ 73,400; Balance Sheet Total of Pvt. Ltd. as on 1st July, 2025 ₹ 1,10,000]

38. On 31st March, 2024 Sri Raman acquires on payment of ₹ 80,000 the business of M/s Gupta and Singh taking over at book value the following assets and liabilities :

Debtors ₹ 35,000 ; Furniture ₹ 3,000 ; Stock ₹ 46,000 ; Creditors ₹ 10,000.

There was no change between 1st January, 2024 and 31st March, 2024 in the book value of the assets and liabilities not taken over.

The same set of books has been continued after the acquisition and no entries for the acquisition have been passed except for the payment of ₹ 80,000 made by Sri Raman.

From the following Balance Sheet and Trial Balance prepare Business Purchase. Account, Profit and Loss Account for the year ended 31st December, 2024 and Balance Sheet as at that date.

BALANCE SHEET

as on 31st December, 2023

Liabilities		₹	*Assets*	₹
Capital Accounts :	₹		Furniture	3,000
			Investments	5,000
Sri Gupta	30,000		Insurance Policy	2,000
Sri Singh	20,000		Stock	40,000
		50,000	Debtors	30,000
Bank Loan		18,000		
Creditors		12,000		
		80,000		80,000

On 31st December, 2024 the trial balance is :

	Dr. ₹	*Cr.* ₹
Stock	40,000	
Furniture	3,000	
Investments	5,000	
Insurance policy	2,000	
Business Purchase Account	80,000	
Bank Loan		18,000
Capitals :		
Gupta		30,000
Singh		20,000
Raman		30,000
Bank	3,000	
Debtors		48,000
Creditors		15,000

Purchases	3,20,000	
Expenses	12,000	
Sales		4,00,000
	5,13,000	5,13,000

Closing Stock ₹ 50,000.

Ans. [Profit for 3 months from 1-1-2024 to 31-3-2024 ₹ 13,000 ; Profit for 9 months from 1-4-2024 to 31-12-2024 ₹ 65,000 ; Balance Sheet Total ₹ 1,10,000].

Hint. Amount of goodwill paid by Mr. Raman for acquiring the business of M/s Gupta and Singh ₹ 6,000.

39. P, Q and R are partners sharing profits and losses in the ratio 3 : 2 : 1 after allowing interest on capital @ 9% p.a. Their Balance Sheet as at 31st March, 2025 is as follows :

Liabilities		₹	*Assets*	₹
Capital Accounts :	₹		Plant & Machinery	1,08,000
P	50,000		Fixtures	20,000
Q	30,000		Stock	50,000
R	20,000		Sundry Debtors	30,000
		1,00,000		
Reserve Fund		60,000		
Creditors		48,000		
		2,08,000		2,08,000

They applied for *conversion of the firm* into a Private Limited "Company named PQR Pvt. Ltd. and the certificate was received on 1-4-2025. They decided to maintain same profit sharing ratio and to preserve the priority in regard to repayment of capital as far as possible. For that purpose, they decided to insert a clause of issuance of Preference shares in Memorandum of Association in addition to issuance of Equity shares of ₹ 10 each.

On 1-4-2025, the value of goodwill is to be determined on the basis of 2 years' purchase of the average profit from the business of the last 5 years. The particulars of profits are as under :

		₹
Year ended 31-3-2021	Profit	10,000
Year ended 31-3-2022	Loss	5,000
Year ended 31-3-2023	Profit	18,000
Year ended 31-3-2024	Profit	27,000
Year ended 31-3-2025	Profit	30.000

The loss for the year ended 31-3-2022 was on account of loss by strike to the extent of ₹ 10,000.

It was agreed that rest of the assets are valued on the basis of the Balance Sheet as at 31-3-2025 except Plant and Machinery which is valued at ₹ 1,02,000.

You are required to prepare (*a*) the Balance Sheet of the Company as at 1-4-2025, (*b*) Partners' Capital Accounts and (*c*) Statement showing the final settlement between the partners taking "Q's capital as basis. ***(CA IPCE Nov. 2015 Modified)***

Ans. [(*a*) B/S Total ₹ 2,38,000; Profit on sale of business ₹ 36,000; (*c*) Equity Shares—P—90,000; Q—60,000 and R—30,000. 10,000 preference shares (5,000 shares to each P and R).

Hint : Value of Goodwill ₹ 36,000. Purchase consideration ₹ 1,90,000.

ADMISSION /RETIREMENT/CONVERSION

40. The following is the Balance Sheet of M/s P and Q as on 31st March, 2024 :

Liabilities	₹	*Assets*	₹
Capital Accounts :		Machinery	54,000
P	50,000	Furniture	5,000
Q	30,000	Investment	50,000
Reserves	20,000	Stock	20,000
Loan Account of Q	15,000	Debtors	21,000
Creditors	40,000	Cash	5,000
	1,55,000		1,55,000

It was agreed that Mr. R is to be admitted for a fourth share in the future profits from 1st April, 2024. He is required to contribute cash towards goodwill and ₹ 15,000 towards capital.

The following further information is furnished :

(*a*) P & Q share the profits in the ratio 3 : 2.

(*b*) P was receiving salary of Rs; 750 p.m. from the very inception of the firm in 2010 in addition to share of profit.

(*c*) The future profit ratio between P, Q & R will be 2 : 1 : 1. P will not get any salary after the admission of R.

(*d*) It was agreed that the value of goodwill of the firm shall appear in the books of the firm. The goodwill of the firm shall be determined on the basis of 3 years' purchase of the average profits from business of the last 5 years. The particulars of the profits for the year ended 31st March are as under :

Year	2020	2021	2022	2023	2024
Profit / Loss	25,000	12,500	(2,500)	35,000	30,000

The above Profits and Losses are after charging the Salary of P. The Profit of the year ended 31st March, 2020 included an extraneous profit of ₹ 40,000 and the loss for the year ended 31st March, 2022 was on account of loss by strike to the extent of ₹ 20,000.

(*e*) The cash trading profit for the year ended 31st March, 2025 was ₹ 50,000 before depreciation.

(*f*) The partners had drawn each ₹ 1,000 p.m. as drawings.

(*g*) The values of other assets and liabilities as on 31st March, 2025 were as under :
Machinery (before depreciation) ₹ 60,000; Furniture (before depreciation) ₹ 10,000; Investment ₹ 50,000; Stock ₹ 15,000; Debtors ₹ 30,000; Creditors ₹ 20,000.

(*h*) Provide depreciation @ 10% on Machinery and @ 5% on Furniture on the Closing Balance and interest is accumulated @ 6% on Q's loan. The loan along with interest would be repaid within next 12 months.

(*i*) Investments are held from inception of the firm and interest is received @ 10% p.a.

(*j*) The partners applied for *conversion of the firm into a Private Limited Company*. Certificate was received on 1st April, 2025. They decided to convert Capital A/cs of the partners into share capital in the ratio of 2 : 1 : 1 on the basis of a total Capital as on 31st March, 2025. If necessary, partners have to subscribe to fresh capital or withdraw.

Prepare Profit and Loss Account of the firm for the year ended 31st March, 2025 and Balance Sheet of the Company on 1st April, 2025.

Ans. [Profit ₹ 47,600; Balance Sheet Total ₹ 1,77,500; Value of Goodwill ₹ 60,000; R gained 1/4 (sacrificed by P 1/10 and Q 3/20); R's share of goodwill ₹ 15,000 credited to P—₹ 6,000 and Q—₹ 9,000; Partners' Capital Accounts Balances : P—₹ 79,800; Q—₹ 46,900; R—₹ 14,900. Total of Balance Sheet of firm ₹ 1,77,500; Cash Balance ₹ 19,000. Distribution of Shares : P—70,800; Q and R each 35,400. P and Q should withdraw ₹ 9,000 and ₹ 11,500 and R should subscribe shares of ₹ 20,500]

41. X and Y are partners sharing profits and losses in the ratio of 3 : 2. On 30th September, 2024 they admitted Z as a partner. The new profit sharing ratio agreed was 2 : 2 : 1.

At the time of admission Z brought in a fixture valued at ₹ 6,000 and a machinery worth ₹ 24,000. No accounting entry was passed for the fixture brought in by partner Z in the books of the firm.

Also at the time of admission the valuation of goodwill was made. The value of goodwill of X and Y was decided at ₹ 40,000 and value of goodwill of partner Z was fixed at ₹ 20,000. No effect was given to the goodwill value in the books of the firm.

On 31-3-2025, it was decided that partner X would retire and the other partners *viz.,* Y and Z would continue the business of the firm by converting in into a company called YZ Ltd., with equal share holding in the company.

The partners agreed as below :

(*i*) The goodwill of the firm shall be fixed at ₹ 80,000. Necessary effect for goodwill value not recorded earlier shall be given. The present goodwill value being ₹ 80,000 shall be reflected in the books of the company.

(*ii*) All the assets and liabilities of the firm shall be taken over by the company.

(*iii*) Partner X would take motor car of the firm at a value of ₹ 7,400.

(*iv*) A plant owned by the firm is sold for ₹ 6,000.

(*v*) The profit of the firm upto 30-9-2024 was ₹ 44,000.

(*vi*) Partner X agreed to leave ₹ 90,000 as loan with the firm in return for 12% interest per annum.

Following is the Trial Balance of the firm as on 31-3-2025 :

Particulars	*Dr.* ₹	*Cr.* ₹	
Capital Accounts :			
X	—	80,000	
Y	—	50,000	
Z	—	24,000	
Drawings Account :			
X	22,000	–	
Y	20,000	—	
Z	9,600	—	
Sundry Debtors	70,000	—	
Sundry Creditors	–	32,000	
Plant (Book value of plant sold ₹ 8,000)	46,000	—	
Fixtures	14,000	–	
Stock		24,000	—
Motor Car		5,400	–
Cash at Bank	34,600	—	
Profit and Loss A/c (for the year)	—	59,600	
	2,45,600	2,45,600	

You are required to prepare :

(*i*) Goodwill Adjustment Account ; (*ii*) Profit and Loss Appropriation Account ; (*iii*) Partners' Capital Accounts ; (*iv*) Balance Sheet of YZ Ltd. after conversion.

Ans. [(*ii*) Profit ₹ 59,600 (X : ₹ 32,640; Y : ₹ 23,840 and Z ₹ 3,120]

(*iii*) Cash ₹ 15,160 paid to Y and brought by Z; Total Capital ₹ 1,25,360 (Y—₹ 62,680 and Z—₹ 62,680]

(*iv*) Balance Sheet Total ₹ 2,47,360]

CHAPTER 19

Financial Statements of Not-for-Profit Organisations

Meaning of Profitable Organisations and Not-for-Profit Organisations

Profitable organisations are those organisations which are engaged in trading and manufacturing activities. The main motive of such organisation is to earn profit. Funds in such organisations are contributed by the proprietors in the form of capital and accumulated reserves. In order to ascertain the cost of goods manufactured, gross profit and net profit (or loss), such organisations prepare, Manufacturing, Trading and Profit and Loss Account for a specified period and Balance Sheet on a particular date.

On the other hand, ***Not-for-profit organisations* are those organisations whose main object is not to earn profit but to render valuable services to its members and to the society.** Clubs, associations, hospitals, educational institutions, trade unions, charitable institutions, etc., are the examples of such organisations. People join such organisations for mutual entertainment, for protection, for professional reasons or for the promotion of art and culture. Such organisations are not required to prepare Profit and Loss Account as their main function is not trading or making profit. Such organisations prepare Receipts and Payments Account, Income and Expenditure Account and a Balance Sheet in order to ascertain Cash in hand or at Bank, Surplus or deficit and various assets, liabilities and capital or general fund respectively. Funds in such organisations are represented by capital fund which comprises of donations, subscriptions, surplus, etc.

Distinction Between Profitable and Not-for-Profit Organisations

Basis of Distinction	*Profitable Organisations*	*Not-for-Profit Organisations*
1. Motive	The main motive is to earn profit.	The main motive is to render service to members and society.
2. Funds	Funds are represented by capital contributed by proprietors and accumulated reserves.	Funds are represented by capital fund comprising in the form of donations subscriptions and surplus.
3. Financial Statements	These include Manufacturing A/c, Trading A/c, Profit & Loss A/c and Balance Sheet.	There include Receipts and Payments A/c, Income and Expenditure A/c and Balance Sheet.
4. Surplus/Profit	The balance of the Profit & Loss A/c is either net profit or net loss.	The balance of the Income and Expenditure A/c is either surplus or deficit.

Books and Accounts to be Maintained in Not-for-Profit Organisations

In order to avoid the chances of misappropriation of goods, and embezzlement of members money, it is essential to maintain proper books such as Register of Members', Minute Books to record the proceedings of meetings, Cash Receipt Journal, Cash Payment Journal and Journal Proper. Proper accounts in such organisations must be able to disclose as to what is the total amount of receipts and payments of cash, whether income is more than the expenditure or *vice versa* and what is the financial position of the organisation at the end of the accounting year. In order to achieve this, the Secretary or Treasurer is required to prepare the following and submit these to the members in annual meeting : (*i*) Receipts and Payments Account ; (*ii*) Income and Expenditure Account ; (*iii*) Balance Sheet.

Now each of these will be discussed in detail.

I. Receipts and Payments Account

Receipts and Payments Account is a real account. Debit what comes in and credit what goes out (or Increase in an asset is debited and decrease in an asset is credited) is the basic rule of double entry which is followed while preparing this account. It is a summary of cash book and is different from the cash book as an item of expense is written in the Cash book as many times as it is paid (say rent, if paid monthly will be written twelve times) but in the Receipts and Payments Account, it is written only once *i.e.,* in summary form. It is maintained on cash basis of accountancy and is prepared in not-for-profit organisations in lieu of cash book. Like cash book, receipts of cash are written on the debit side and payments on the credit side. All receipts and payments, whether these are relating to the current, preceding or succeeding period or are of capital or revenue nature, are written in this account. Opening balance of this account shows cash in hand or at bank at the beginning of the accounting period and closing balance shows cash in hand or at bank at the end of accounting period. No distinction is made whether the payment has been made in cash or cheque except opening and closing balances of cash and bank transactions are merged. As all types of accounts, *i.e.,* personal, real and nominal are written in this account, so it is not necessary to prepare a Balance Sheet along with this account. No adjustments for outstanding expenses, prepaid expenses, provision for doubtful debts or depreciation are made in this account as it is prepared on cash basis of accounting. It is prepared only for a specific period say for a month or a year. But this account does not show expenses and income on accrual basis. Moreover, it does not show whether the concern is able to meet its day to day expenses out of its income. Following is the specimen of a Receipts and Payments Account.

.... (Name of the entity)

RECEIPTS AND PAYMENTS ACCOUNT

for the year ending on ....

Receipts	₹	*Payments*	₹
To Balance b/d :		By Balance b/d (Overdraft)	
Cash		By Annual Sports Expenses	
Bank		By Salaries & Wages	
To Subscriptions :		By Rent, Rates & Taxes	
for previous year		By Insurance	
for current year		By Purchase of Fixed Assets	
for next year		*e.g.,* Furniture, Invest-	
To Entrance Fees		ments, Sports Equipments	
To Donations for Capital Asset		etc.	
e.g., Building		By Books & Periodicals	
To Donations :		By Audit Fees	
General		By Printing & Stationery	
Specific		By Honorarium	
To Life Membership Fees		By Bank Charges	

To Legacies		By Postage & Telegrams	
To Grant from Government		By Water & Electricity	
To Contribution for Annual Dinner		By Conveyance and Travelling	
To Dividend & Interest		By Repairs & Maintenance	
To Rent		By Sundry Expenses	
To Receipt on Annual Sports		By Annual Dinner Expenses	
To Sale of Old Magazines and Newspapers		By Balance c/d	
		Cash —	
To Sale of Old Sports Materials		Bank —	
To Sundry Receipts			
To Balance c/d (Overdraft)			

ILLUSTRATION 1. A Golf Club has kept its accounts on cash basis and the figures for 2025 are given below. You are required to prepare Receipts and Payments Account for the year.

	₹		₹
Entrance fees received	2,500	Secretary's Honorarium	1,500
Subscriptions received	19,800	Cash in Hand (at 1-1-2025)	2,350
Green fees received	600	Locker rent received	500
Expenses paid	27,250	Cost of investment bought during the year	1,100
Surplus on Bar Account	7,500		

SOLUTION

Golf Club
RECEIPTS AND PAYMENTS ACCOUNT FOR 2025

Receipts	₹	*Payments*	₹
To Balance b/d	2,350	By Expenses	27,250
" Entrance Fees	2,500	" Secretary's Honorarium	1,500
" Subscriptions	19,800	" Investment	1,100
" Green Fees	600	" Balance c/d (Bal. Fig.)	3,400
" Locker Rent	500		
" Surplus on Bar Account	7,500		
	33,250		33,250

Distinction Between Receipts and Payments Account and Cash Book

Basis of Distinction	*Receipts & Payments A/c*	*Cash Book*
1. Period	It is a summary of cash book and prepared at the end of accounting year.	It is written daily.
2. Recording of Transactions	Transactions are not written date-wise.	Transactions are written date-wise.
3. Institutions	Institutions working on no profit and no loss basis prepare this account.	All commercial institutions prepare this book.

4. Sides	There are two sides in this account, *i.e.,* left hand side is receipts side and right-hand side is payments side.	There are two sides of this book, *i.e.,* left-hand side is debit side and right-hand side is credit side.
5. Ledger Folio	There is no column of ledger folio.	There is a separate column for ledger folio on both sides of this book.

II. Income and Expenditure Account

Income and Expenditure Account is a nominal account. Debit all losses or expenses and credit all incomes and gains (or expenses decrease the equity and incomes increase the equity) will be followed while preparing this account. It is prepared in not-for-profit organisations in lieu of Profit and Loss Account. Incomes are shown on the credit side and expenses on the debit side. There is no opening balance but closing balance will show either surplus *i.e.,* excess of income over expenditure or deficit *i.e.,* excess of expenditure over income. Only revenue items are taken into consideration *i.e.,* capital items are totally excluded and income and expenditure of the current year are taken into consideration and income and expenditure relating to the preceding or succeeding periods are excluded while preparing this account. This account is prepared on accrual basis of accountancy and thus all adjustments relating to prepaid or outstanding expenses and incomes, provision for depreciation or doubtful debts will be made. Only nominal accounts are taken into consideration for the preparation of this account and for personal and real accounts a Balance Sheet must be prepared alongwith this account. Following is the specimen of an Income and Expenditure Account.

INCOME AND EXPENDITURE ACCOUNT

for the year ending ....20..

Expenditure	₹	*Income*	₹
To Salaries		By Subscriptions	
To Rent, Rates and Taxes		By Entrance Fees	
To Printing and Stationery		(If not capitalised)	
To General Expenses		By General Donations	
To Charities		(Small amount)	
To Wages of Groundsmen		By Rent of Hall	
To Honorarium		By Sale of Newspapers	
To Postage and Telegrams		By Sale of Grass	
To Bank Charges		By Grants from Government or	
To Telephone Expenses		Local Authorities	
To Upkeep of Ground		By Interest received	
To Newspapers and Periodicals		By Advertisements in Year Book	
To Entertainment Expenses		By Profit on Sale of Assets	
To Repairs		By Proceeds of Concerts	
To Conveyance		By Fees from Non-members	
To Electricity Charges		By Dividend received	
To Car Expenses		By Annual Dinner Contributions	
To Audit Fees		By Lockers Rent	
To Refreshment Expenses		By Income from Refreshments	
To Insurance		By Sports Fees	
To Miscellaneous Expenses		By Miscellaneous Receipts or	

To Interest To Sports Expenses To Loss on Sale of Assets To Depreciation on Assets To Surplus *i.e.,* Excess of Income Over Expenditure*		Sundry Income By Deficit *i.e.,* Excess of Expenditure Over Income*	

* The balancing figure is either Surplus or Deficit.

Distinction Between Receipts & Payments Account and Income & Expenditure Account

Following are the main points of distinction between the two accounts :

Basis of Distinction	*Receipts and Payments Account*	*Income and Expenditure Account*
1. Type of Account	It is a real account.	It is a nominal account.
2. In Lieu Of	It is prepared in not-for-profit organisations in lieu of cash book.	It is prepared in not-for-profit organisations in lieu of Profit and Loss Account.
3. Sides	Receipts are shown on the debit side and payments on the credit side.	Incomes (receipts) are shown on the credit side and expenditure (payments) on the debit side.
4. Opening Balance	There can be opening balance which represents cash in hand or at bank.	There is no opening balance.
5. Closing Balance	This shows cash in hand or at bank at the end of the accounting year.	There is no closing balance but the difference between the two sides shows either surplus or deficit.
6. Capital and Revenue Items	All items whether of capital or revenue nature are shown in this account.	Only revenue items are taken into consideration while preparing this account *i.e.,* capital items are totally excluded.
7. Period	All receipts and payments whether relating to the current period, succeeding or preceding periods are taken into consideration.	Only current period's incomes and expenditures are taken into consideration while preparing this account *i.e.,* incomes and expenditures relating to succeeding or preceding periods are excluded.
8. Balance Sheet	It is not necessary to prepare balance sheet along with this account.	The balance sheet must be pre-pared in order to accommodate real and personal accounts along with this account.
9. Adjustments	No adjustments are required to be made at the end of the year.	In order to find out the true income or expenditure of the current year, all adjustments are made at the end of the year.
10. Non Cash Items	It does not record non-cash items *e.g.* depreciation.	It records non-cash items.
11. Basis of Accountancy	It is prepared on cash basis of accountancy.	It is prepared on accrual basis of accountancy.

Conversion of Receipts & Payments Account into an Income & Expenditure Account

When it is desired to convert a Receipts and Payments Account into an Income and Expenditure Account, following steps are to be taken :

1. Leave the opening and closing balance of cash and bank given in the receipts and payments account.
2. Take only revenue items of income and expenditure and leave all those items which are of capital nature.
3. Make all adjustments for outstanding and prepaid incomes and expenses, provision for depreciation or bad debts etc.
4. Take items only for the current period *i.e.,* items relating to the preceding and succeeding periods are to be ignored. For calculating the figures for the current year, the following proforma will be helpful :

	₹	₹
Amount of Income/Expenditure as per Receipts & Payment Account	xxx	
Add :		
1. Creditors for Expenses or Subscription in arrear or due at the end of the period	xxx	
2. Stock/Prepaid Expenses or Subscription paid in Advance at the beginning of the period.	xxx	xxx
		xxx
Less :		
1. Creditors for Expenses or Subscription in arrear or due at the beginning of the period	xxx	
2. Stock/Prepaid Expenses or Subscription paid in Advance at the end of the period.	xxx	xxx
Amount to be shown as Income or Expenditure in Income & Expenditure A/c		xxx

ILLUSTRATION 2. From the following particulars, prepare Income and Expenditure Account of the Calcutta Golf Club for the year ended 31st December, 2024.

	₹		₹
Subscriptions received for 2024	10,500	Expenses for 2024 paid	8,000
Entrance Fees received for 2024	750	Expenses unpaid	230
Subscriptions and Entrance Fees for 2023		Liabilities for 2024 paid (estimated ₹ 700)	600
(estimated ₹ 150) realised	280	Audit Fees for 2024 not paid	200
Subscriptions and Entrance Fees for 2025	1,550	Profit on Service Account net	2,300
Subscriptions for 2024 to be taken at		Interest on Loans paid	320
(due ₹ 2,000)	1,000	Capital Expenditure written off	1,200
Miscellaneous Fees	2,100	Surplus from 2023 A/c	4,000
Provide for depreciation ₹ 680 for this year.		Capital Expenditure in 2024	2,120

SOLUTION

Calcutta Golf Club
INCOME AND EXPENDITURE ACCOUNT
for the year ended 31st December, 2024

Expenditure	₹	Income	₹
To Expenses (₹ 8,000 + ₹ 230)	8,230	By Subscription and Entrance	
" Audit Fees	200	Fees [₹ 10,500 + ₹ 750	12,380
" Interest on Loans	320	+ ₹ 1,000 + ₹ 130]	

	₹		₹
To Capital Expenditure (Written off)	1,200	By Miscellaneous Fees	2,100
" Depreciation	680	" Liabilities provided in excess last year (₹ 700 – ₹ 600)	100
" Surplus (Bal. Fig.)	6,250	" Profit on Service Account	2,300
	16,880		16,880

III. Balance Sheet

Balance Sheet in not-for-profit organisations is prepared in the usual way and contains particulars of assets and liabilities on the date on which it is prepared. Excess of assets over liabilities is called as Capital (or General) Fund and is made up of surplus of income over expenditure and certain items which are capitalised. Separate accounts are to be maintained for funds raised for specific purposes. If beginning capital fund is not given in the question, then Balance Sheet at the beginning of the period is to be made in order to calculate this fund. Following is the specimen of a Balance Sheet of such organisations :

BALANCE SHEET

as on.................,20..

Liabilities	₹	*Assets*	₹
Income Received in Advance		Cash in hand	
Outstanding Expenses		Cash at Bank	
Bank Overdraft		Fixed Deposits	
General Donations (Huge amount)		Outstanding Subscriptions	
Specific Donations (*e.g.*, Donations for Building)		Interest Outstanding	
		Prepaid Expenses	
Special Funds (such as Tournament Fund, etc.)		Rent Receivable	
		Investments	
Less Expenses (if any)		Government Securities	
Legacies		Typewriters	
Life Membership Fees		Stock of Stamps	
Capital Fund		Stock of Sports Materials	
Add: Excess of Income over Expenditure		Stock of Medicines	
		Stock of Stationery	
(or)		Books	
Less: Excess of Expenditure over Income		Furniture	
		Land and Buildings	
		Grounds	
		Medical Equipment and Instruments	
		Less: Depreciation (if any)	
		Electric Installations	
		Crockery	
		Deficiency	

Treatment of Some Important Items

There are certain items which are peculiar to not-for-profit organisations and require special treatment while preparing the final accounts of such organisations.

1. Legacy. It is the amount which a not-for-profit organisations will receive as per will of a deceased person. It will be given on the debit side of the receipts and payments account. It should be capitalised being an item of non-recurring nature and should be shown on the liabilities side of the Balance Sheet.

2. Donations. Donations are the amounts which are given to the not-for-profit organisations as gifts by members of a society. It is also given on the receipts side of the receipts and payments account. Donations may be (*i*) general donations and (*ii*) specific donations. Their treatment is given as under :

(*i*) ***General Donation.*** When the donor does not lay down any specific condition for using the amount of donation, then it is called as general donation. It can be treated either as an item of income (if the amount is small) or can be capitalised (if the amount is big one). If nothing is clear whether the amount is small or big, it can be treated in any manner, but a note should be appended regarding the treatment of such amount.

(*ii*) ***Specific Donation.*** If the donation is for a specific purpose, say for the construction of a room or pavillion, then it is called specific donation. It should be capitalised and will be shown on the liabilities side of Balance Sheet.

3. Sale of an Asset. If an asset is sold, the amount realised should be compared with its book value in order to find out profit or loss on the sale of an asset. If profit, it will be shown on the credit side and if loss on the debit side of Income and Expenditure Account. The amount realised from the sale will appear on the debit side of Receipts and Payments Account.

4. Entrance Fees. This fee is paid by the members to cover additional expenses incurred when a member joins. Accountants differ on the treatment of entrance fees. Some prefer to treat it as capital expenditure as it is heavy and received once from the members. But others say that it should be treated as income as it is a regular source of income of such concerns because of regular entry of members in each period and credited to Income and Expenditure Account. However, instructions in the question must be noted carefully. In absence of any specific instructions it should be treated as routine income.

5. Life Membership Fees. It is paid only once in lieu of annual subscriptions, so it should be capitalised and should be shown on the liabilities side of Balance Sheet.

6. Sale of Old Newspapers or Obsolete Items. Any amount realised from the sale of such items will be given on the debit side of Receipts and Payments Account and should be treated as item of income. It should be shown on the credit side of Income and Expenditure Account.

7. Fund Based Accounting and Non-Fund Based Accounting. Generally not-for-profit concerns establish funds for some specific purpose say Prize Distribution Fund or Building Fund. The payments or expenses incurred for the purpose of the fund are debited to it. Similarly, incomes earned on the investment of the fund are credited to it. *The accounting of incomes and expenses for which specific fund exists is termed as Fund Based Accounting.* Fund Based Accounting is an exception to the general rule that all items of revenue or income and expenses are transferred to Income and Expenditure Account. However, there are certain items of income or expenses for which no specific fund exists. The accounting for such incomes or expenses is termed as *Non-Fund Based Accounting.* These items are credited or debited to Income and Expenditure Account.

If there is a specific fund as Prize Distribution Fund or Building Fund and there are certain items of incomes and expenditure relating to such fund, then income or expenditure should not be shown in Income and Expenditure Account but income will be added to the fund and expenses deducted from such fund on the liabilities side of Balance Sheet. Suppose the following figures are given :

	Dr.	*Cr.*
	₹	₹
Prize Distribution Fund	—	10,000
Prize Distribution Fund Investment	10,000	—
Interest received on such investment	—	500
Prizes distributed	400	—

The interest and prizes distributed will not be treated as items of income or expenditure and will not be shown in the Income and Expenditure Account. Instead these will be shown on the liabilities side as under :

		₹	₹
	Prize Distribution Fund	10,000	
Add :	Interest	500	
		10,500	
Less :	Prizes distributed	400	
			10,100

EXAMPLE. How would you treat the following items in case of a not-for-profit organisations ?

(*i*) Tournament Fund ₹ 35,000. Tournament Expenses ₹ 10,000. Receipts from Tournament ₹ 15,000.

(*ii*) Billiard Match Expenses ₹ 5,500.

(*iii*) Prize Fund ₹ 15,000. Interest on Prize Fund Investment ₹ 1,500. Prizes paid ₹ 2,500. Prize Fund Investments ₹ 12,000.

(*iv*) Receipts from cinema show tickets ₹ 10,000. Expenses on cinema show ₹ 2,500.

SOLUTION

(*i*) There is a specific Tournament Fund. The treatment is done as under :

Liabilities Side :

	₹
Tournament Fund	35,000
Add : Receipts from Tournament	15,000
	50,000
Less : Tournament Expenses	10,000
Balance to remain on the Liabilities side as Tornament Fund	40,000

(*ii*) There is no specific fund. Hence ₹ 5,500 incurred on Billiard Match Expenses would be shown on the debit side of Income and Expenditure Account. It is the case of expenses independent of any fund.

(*iii*) There is a specific fund. The treatment will be as under :

Liabilities Side :

	₹
Prize Fund	15,000
Add : Interest	1,500
	16,500
Less : Prizes paid	2,500
	14,000

Note : Interest on Fund Investment is not added to Fund Investment Account as the amount upon receipt is debited to either Cash or Bank Account. The Assets side of Balance Sheet stands increased because of its impact on the receipts side of Receipts and Payments Account. However, if the amount of interest is also invested then investment could increase. Prize Fund Investments are to be shown as an asset in the Balance Sheet.

(*iv*) There is no specific fund. Receipts from cinema show tickets would be shown on the credit side of Income and Expenditure A/c and expenses on cinema show would be shown on the debit side of Income and Expenditure Account.

It is to be noted carefully that if the fund is less than the expenses, then the balance of expenses not covered by fund is shown in the Income and Expenditure Account.

8. Endowment Fund. A fund which provides permanent means of support for any person or institution or a donation which is meant to cover expenditure on a particular purpose in the future is called endowment fund. It is a capital receipt and recorded on the debit side of Receipts and Payments Account in the year of receipt. It is capitalised and shown on the liabilities side of the Balance Sheet.

9. Honorarium. Any amount paid to a person (who is not an employee of the organisation) for rendering services to the organisation is called honorarium. For example, if a payment is made to a doctor (who is not an employee of the hospital) for treating the patient and providing services of a specialised nature is honorarium and will be shown on the credit (payment) side of Receipts and Payments Account. From there it is posted to the debit (Expenditure) side of Income and Expenditure Account.

10. Sale of Sports Materials. Sports material is an asset but it is a consumable asset. When the asset say bats, balls, nets etc. are totally consumed and its utility is over, then any amount realised from the sale of such old items will be treated as income and will be credited to Income and Expenditure Account. This is found in the receipt side of Receipts and Payments Account.

11. Other Capital Payments. Such expenditure as purchase of books, furniture, investments, building etc. treated as capital expenditure is shown on the assets side of Balance Sheet.

12. Other Revenue Receipts. Such receipts as rents proceeds from entertainment concerts shows, lectures and interest on investments are treated as revenue receipts and shown on the credit side of Income and Expenditure Account.

13. Subscriptions Subscriptions are major recurring source of income of non-profit entities and are paid by members periodically. Subscriptions received during the year appear on the debit side of Receipts & Payments Account and subscriptions relating to the current period are shown on the income side of Income & Expenditure Account. To ascertain the amount of subscription to be shown in Income and Expenditure A/c, it can be computed in any of the following ways:

(*a*) In Statement Form, (*b*) In Account Form and (*c*) In Equation Form.

(a) In Statement Form

STATEMENT SHOWING THE COMPUTATION OF SUBSCRIPTION INCOME FOR THE YEAR

	₹	₹
Subscriptions Received during the year		xx
Add : (*i*) Outstanding Subscriptions at the end of the current year	xx	
(*ii*) Subscription received in advance at the beginning of the current year	xx	
		xx
Less : (*i*) Outstanding Subscription at the beginning of the year	xx	
(*ii*) Subscriptions received in advance at the end of the current year	xx	
		xx
Subscription Income to be Credited to Income & Expenditure A/c		xx

(b) In Account Form

SUBSCRIPTION ACCOUNT

	₹		₹
To Outstanding Subscription b/d (Balance in the beginning)	—	By Subscription Received in Advance (Balance in the beginning)	—
To Income & Expenditure A/c (Balancing figure)		By Cash (given on the debit side of Receipts and Payments A/c)	
To Subscription Received in Advance c/d (At the end)		By Subscription Outstanding c/d (Balance at the end)	

(c) In Equation Form. Following equation may be adopted for computation of subscription income for the current year :

$$SI = SR + OS_2 + AS_1 - OS_1 - AS_2$$

where SI = Subscription Income for the current accounting year

SR = Subscription Received during the current accounting year

OS_2 = Outstanding Subscription at the end of the current year
AS_1 = Advance Subscription in the beginning of the current year
OS_1 = Outstanding Subscription in the beginning of the current year
AS_2 = Advance Subscription at the end of the current year.

ILLUSTRATION 3. From the following extract of Receipts and Payments Account and the additional information, you are required to calculate the Income from Subscription for the year ending March 31, 2025 and show them in the Income & Expenditure Account, and the balance Sheet of a Club.

AN EXTRACT OF RECEIPTS AND PAYMENTS ACCOUNT

for the year ending 31st March, 2025

Receipts		₹	*Payments*	₹
To Subscription				
2023-24	4,000			
2024-25	20,000			
2025-26	5,000	29,000		

Information :

(*i*)	Subscription outstanding on 31-3-2024	₹ 5,000
(*ii*)	Subscription outstanding on 31-3-2025	₹ 4,000
(*iii*)	Subscription received in advance on 31-3-2024 for 2024-25	₹ 5,000

(CA IPCE May, 2014 Modified)

SOLUTION

INCOME AND EXPENDITURE ACCOUNT

for the year ending 31st March, 2025

	₹	₹
By Subscription : Received	20,000	
Add : Outstanding 31-3-2025 (4,000 – 1,000) (See Note)	3,000	
Add : Received in advance last year for 2024-25	5,000	28,000

BALANCE SHEET

As on 31st March, 2025 (Extract)

Liabilities	₹	*Assets*	₹	₹
Subscription received in Advance for year 2025-26	5,000	Subscription Outstanding		
		2023-24	1,000	
		2024-25	3,000	4,000

Note : Subscription outstanding on 31-3-2025 as given in the question is ₹ 4,000. It has been considered that last year outstanding ₹ 1,000 has also been included in this amount.

14. Grant from Government and Government Agencies. Some not-for-profit entities may receive grants from government and/or government agencies or from local or national or international agencies. The treatment depends on the nature of grant. If the grant is for a specific purpose as purchase or acquisition or construction of a fixed asset, being of capital nature, is shown on the liabilities side of Balance Sheet. But if the grant is for general purpose (*i.e.*, not for a specific purpose), it is treated as revenue receipt and is shown on the credit side of Income and Expenditure Account.

15. Bank Balance as per Pass Book. If bank balance as per pass book is given, it is desirable to calculate the bank balance as per cash book by preparing bank reconciliation statement to be shown in the Balance Sheet.

16. Expenses Involving Stocks. Sometimes opening and closing stock balances of certain items *e.g.*, sports materials, printing and stationery, tinned provision, crockery etc. are given besides purchase of such items. In order to calculate the actual expenditure to the shown on the debit side of Income and Expenditure, the following procedure is adopted:

	₹	₹
Purchase/Payments as per Receipts & Payments A/c	xx	
Add: Opening Stock of such items	xx	
Creditors at the end of the year for such items	xx	
Advance payment at the beginning of the year		xx
Less: Closing Stock of such items	xx	
Creditors at the beginning of the year for such items	xx	
Advance payment at the end of the year		xx
Actual Expenditure during the current year		xx

ILLUSTRATION 4. From the following particulars, calculate the amounts to be shown in the Income and Expenditure Account during the year 2024 :

(*i*) Amount paid for stationery during the year as per Receipts and Payments Account ₹ 1,080

	on 1-1-2024	*on 31-12-2024*
	₹	₹
Stock of Stationery	300	50
Creditors for Stationery	200	130
Advance payment for Stationery	20	30

(*ii*) Subscription received during the year as per Receipts & Payments Account ₹ 28,680

	on 1-1-2024	*on 31-12-2024*
	₹	₹
Subscription outstanding	2,400	3,000
Subscription received in advance	1,800	1,080

(*iii*) Subscription received in 2024 as :
2023 ₹ 10,000 ; 2024 ₹ 90,000 ; 2025 ₹ 8,000.

		₹	₹
Subscription outstanding in 2023		15,000	
Subscription outstanding for 2024		20,000	
Subscription received in advance in 2023	for 2024		13,000
	for 2025		4,000
Life Membership subscription received in 2024			2,000

(*iv*) During the year ended 31st March, 2025, Sachin Cricket Club received subscriptions for the year ending 31st March, as follows :
2024—₹ 12,000; 2025—₹ 6,15,000; 2026—₹ 18,000.
There are 500 members and annual subscriptions is ₹ 1,500 per member.
On 31st March, 2025, a sum of ₹ 15,000 was still in arrears for subscriptions for the year ended 31st March, 2024.
Ascertain the amount of subscriptions that will appear on the credit side of Income and Expenditure Account for the year ended 31st March, 2025. Also show how the items would appear in the Balance Sheet as on 31st March, 2024 and the Balance Sheet as on 31st March, 2025. ***(IPCE Nov. 2015 Modified)***

SOLUTION

		₹	₹
(*i*)	Amount paid for Stationery during the year		1,080
	Add : Stock of Stationery on 1-1-2024	300	
	" Advance payment for Stationery on 1-1-2024	20	
	" Creditors for Stationery on 31-12-2024	130	
			450
			1,530
	Less : Creditors for Stationery on 1-1-2024	200	
	" Stock of Stationery on 31-12-2024	50	
	" Advance payment for Stationery on 31-12-2024	30	
			280
	Expenditure on Stationery to be shown in Income and Expenditure Account		1,250

		₹	₹
(*ii*)	Subscriptions received during the year		28,680
	Add : Subscriptions outstanding on 31-12-2024	3,000	
	" Subscriptions received in advance on 1-1-2024	1,800	
			4,800
			33,480
	Less : Subscriptions outstanding on 1-1-2024	2,400	
	" Subscription received in advance on 31-12-2024	1,080	
			3,480
	Subscription received to be shown in the Income and Expenditure Account		30,000

		₹
(*iii*)	Subscription received in 2024	90,000
	Add : Subscription outstanding in 2024	20,000
	" Subscription received in Advance in 2023 for 2024	13,000
	Amount of subscription to be shown in Income and Expenditure A/c	1,23,000

(*iv*) Amount of subscription for the year 2024-25 ₹

INCOME AND EXPENDITURE ACCOUNT (AN EXTRACT)
OF SACHIIN CRICKET CLUB
for the year ended 31st March, 2025

	₹		₹
		By Subscription (500 members × ₹ 1,500 per member)	7,50,000

BALANCE SHEET OF SACHIN CRICKET CLUB
as on 31st March 2024 (An Extract)

Liabilities	₹	*Assets*	₹
		Subscription Receivable (15,000 + 12,000)	27,000

BALANCE SHEET OF SACHIN CRICKET CLUB

as on 31st March 2025 (An Extract)

Liabilities	₹	*Assets*		₹
Unearned Subscription	18,000	Outstanding Subscription of	₹	
		2023-24	15,000	
		2024-25 (₹ 7,50,000 – ₹ 6,15,000)	1,35,000	
				1,50,000

Distinction Between Income and Expenditure Account and Profit & Loss Account

Basis of Distinction	*Income and Expenditure Account*	*Profit and Loss Account*
1. Object	The object of this account is to ascertain Surplus (Excess of Income over Expenditure) or Deficit (Excess of Expenditure over Income).	The object of this account is to ascertain net profit or net loss.
2. Concerns	This account is prepared in not-for-profit organisations.	This account is prepared in profitable organisations.
3. Basis of Preparation	This account is prepared on the basis of Receipts and Payments Account and additional information.	This account is prepared on the basis of trial balance and additional information.
4. Balance	The balance of this account is termed as surplus or deficit.	The balance of this account is called net profit or net loss.

Types of Problems

Following are the main types of problems a reader is required to face :

Type I. *Where Income and Expenditure and Balance Sheet is to be prepared from a given Receipts & Payments A/c with additional information.*

ILLUSTRATION 5. From the following Receipts and Payments Account of a Club and from the information supplied prepare Income and Expenditure Account for the year ended 31st March, 2025 and the Balance Sheet as on that date :

RECEIPTS AND PAYMENTS ACCOUNT

		₹		₹
To Balance b/d		7,000	By Tournament Expenses	1,100
" Donation for Building		8,000	" Furniture	2,000
" General Donations		200	" Curtains	800
" Legacies (to be capitalised)		6,000	" Crockery purchased	1,000
To Sale of Old Furniture (cost ₹80)		75	By Sports Material	1,200
" Endowment Fund Receipts		10,000	" Salaries	1,300
" Sale of Newspapers		400	" Honorarium	2,600
" Sale of Sports Material		80	" Charities	8,000
" Rent received from use of Hall		1,500	" Advertisements	250
" Advertisement in the year book		400	" Rent and Taxes	1,400
" Proceeds of Concerts		1,200	" Advance against construction of Building	5,000
" Subscriptions :	₹		" Cost of Entertainment	1,450
2023-24	600			
2024-25	14,000		" Payment to Creditors of last year	400

2025-26	800		By Electric Installation Expenses		3,000
		15,400	" Library Books		800
To Tournament Fund		1,500	" Newspapers		1,300
			" Postage		700
			" Bar Expenses including Purchases		1,600
			" 7% Investments purchased on 1st October, 2024		10,000
			" Balance		7,855
		51,755			51,755

***Information* :**

(*a*) Balance on 31st March, 2025
Sports Material ₹ 100 ; Bar Stock ₹ 120 ; Postage ₹ 20 ; Crockery ₹ 2,000.

(*b*) Subscription outstanding on 31st March, 2025 was ₹ 700.

(*c*) Salary outstanding on 31st March, 2025 was ₹ 50.

(*d*) Salary paid included ₹ 80 paid for 2023-24 and ₹ 10 for 2025-26.

(*e*) Investments included investments out of Building Donations ₹ 8,000.

(*f*) Depreciate crockery on the following basis :

1/5 of their value is to be written off in the year of purchase and 2/5th in each of the next two years. Of the stock of crockery as on 1-4-2024 (₹ 2,000) one-half was one year old and the other half two years old.

SOLUTION **INCOME AND EXPENDITURE ACCOUNT OF A CLUB**

for the year ended 31st March, 2025

Expenditure	₹	₹	*Income*	₹	₹
To Salaries	1,300		By General Donations		200
Add : Outstanding	50		" Sale of Newspapers		400
	1,350		" Sale of Sports Material		80
Less : for 2023-24 & 2025-26	90		" Rent for Use of Halls		1,500
		1,260	" Advertisement		400
" Honorarium		2,600	" Proceeds of Concerts		1,200
" Charities		8,000	" Subscription	14,000	
" Advertisement		250	*Add* : Outstanding	700	
" Rent and Taxes		1,400			14,700
" Cost of Entertainment		1,450	" Interest Accrued		
" Newspapers		1,300	$\left(₹\,2{,}000 \times \frac{7}{100} \times \frac{6}{12}\right)$		
" Postage	700				70
" *Less*: Stock in hand on 31-3-2025	20		" Deficit—Excess of Expenditure		
		680	over Income		2,675
To Bar Purchases	1,600				
Less: Stock in hand	120				
		1,480			
" Loss on Sale of Furniture		5			
" Sports Material	1,200				
Less: Stock on 31-3-2025	100				
		1,100			
" Depreciation on Crockery (1)		1,700			
		21,225			21,225

BALANCE SHEET
as on 31st March, 2025

Liabilities	₹	₹	*Assets*	₹
Salary outstanding		50	Cash in hand	7,855
Subscription in advance		800	Accrued Interest (₹ 280 + ₹ 70)	350
Tournament Fund	1,500		Salary paid in advance	10
Less: Expenses	1,100		Subscription outstanding	700
		400	Stock of : Sports Materials	100
Donation for Building	8,000		Bar	120
Add : Interest on Investment	280		Postage	20
		8,280	Advance for construction of Building	5,000
Capital Fund (2)	9,120		Investment	10,000
Add: Legacies	6,000		Electric Installation	3,000
	15,120		Crockery	
Less: Deficit	2,675		(₹ 2,000 + ₹ 1,000 – ₹ 1,700)	1,300
		12,445	Curtains	800
Endowment Fund		10,000	Library Books	800
			Furniture less sold (₹ 2,000 – ₹ 80)	1,920
		31,975		31,975

Working Notes :

(1) *Calculation of Depreciation on Crockery* : ₹

(*a*) Stock of crockery one year old ₹ 1,000. This is to be used for two years. Therefore half of this is to be depreciated this year. 500

(*b*) Stock of crockery two years old ₹ 1,000. Since this crockery has already been used for two years, this is the last year of its life. The whole amount shall be written off. 1,000

(*c*) Crockery purchased during the year ₹ 1,000. This is the first year, thus 1/5th of this amount shall be written off. 200

Total Depreciation 1,700

(2) *Calculation of Beginning Capital Fund* :

BALANCE SHEET
as on 1-4-2024

	₹		₹
Creditors	400	Cash in hand	7,000
Salary outstanding	80	Subscription outstanding	600
Capital Fund (Balancing figure)	9,120	Crockery	2,000
	9,600		9,600

ILLUSTRATION 6. The Receipts and Payments Account of Vandana Sports Club for the year ended 31st March, 2025 are as follows :

RECEIPTS AND PAYMENTS ACCOUNT

Receipts		*Amount* (₹)	*Payment*	*Amount* (₹)
To Balance b/d			By Salaries	1,55,000
Cash in Hand	5,200		By Rent & Electricity	69,750
Cash at Bank	35,500	40,700	By Library Books	10,500

To Subscriptions	2,95,000	By Newspaper and Magazines		16,600
To Entrance Fees	50,000	By Sports Equipment		28,500
To Miscellaneous Income	19,850	By Sundry Expenses		71,050
To Interest on Investments	8,000	By Balance c/d		
		Cash in hand	8,750	
		Cash at Bank	53,400	62,150
	4,13,550			4,13,550

Details of other assets and liabilities are furnished as follows :

Particulars	*31st March 2024*	*31st March 2025*
Salaries Outstanding	10,200	12,400
Outstanding Rent and Electricity	6,500	7,600
Investment (8% Govt. Bonds)	1,00,000	1,00,000
Interest Accrued on Bonds	2,000	2,000
Subscription Receivable	18,700	20,600
Subscription received in Advance	7,000	8,400
Furniture	65,500	
Sports Equipment	41,500	
Library Books	22,000	

The closing values of furniture and sports equipment are to be determined after charging depreciation at 10% and 15% respectively inclusive of additions, if any during the year. The Club's library books are revalued at the end of every year and the value at the end of 31st March, 2025 was ₹ 30,000. 60% of the Entrance fee is to be capitalised,.

You are required to prepare :

(*i*) Income and Expenditure Account for the year ended 31st March, 2025

(*ii*) Balance Sheet as on 31st March, 2025.

SOLUTION

In the Books of Vandana Sports Club
INCOME AND EXPENDITURE ACCOUNT
for the year ending 31st March, 2025

Expenditure		*Amount (₹)*	*Income*	*Amount (₹)*
To Salaries (W.N. 2)		1,57,200	By Subscription (WN 2)	2,95,500
To Rent & Electricity (W.N. 2)		70,850	By Interest on Investments	8,000
To Magazines & Newspapers		16,600	By Misc. Income	19,850
To Sundry Expenses		71,050	By Entrance Fees	20,000
To Depreciation :				
Furniture	6,550			
Sports Equipment	10,500			
Library Books	2,500	19,550		
To Excess of Income Over Expenditure		8,100		
		3,43,350		3,43,350

BALANCE SHEET
on 31st March, 2025

Liabilities	(₹)	*Amount* (₹)	*Assets*	(₹)	*Amount* (₹)
Capital Fund:			Furniture Cost	65,500	
Opening Balance (W.N. 1)	2,66,700		*Less* : Depreciation	(6,550)	58,950
Add : Excess of Income over			Sports Equipment:		
Expenditure	8,100		Opening Balance	41,500	
Entrance Fees (60%)	30,000	3,04,800	Addition	28,500	
Subscription received in				70,000	
Advance		8,400	*Less* : Depreciation	(10,500)	59,500
Outstanding Expenses :			Library Books:		
Salaries	12,400		Opening Balance	22,000	
Rent & Electricity	7,600	20,000	Addition	10,500	
				32,500	
			Less : Depreciation	(2,500)	30,000
			Investments (8% Bonds)		1,00,000
			Cash in hand		8,750
			Cash at Bank		53,400
			Subscription Receivable		20,600
			Interest accrued on Bonds		2,000
		3,33,200			3,33,200

Alternatively, the capitalised portion of entrance fee of ₹ 30,000 may be shown separately in the liability side.

Working Notes:

1.

BALANCE SHEET
as on 31st March, 2024

Liabilities		₹	*Assets*	₹
Outstanding Expenses :			Furniture	65,500
Salaries	10,200		Library Books	22,000
Rent & Electricity	6,500	16,700	Sports Equipment	41,500
Subscription Received in Advance		7,000	Investments	1,00,000
Capital Fund (Balancing figure)		2,66,700	Cash in hand	5,200
			Cash at Bank	35,500
			Subscription Receivable	18,700
			Interest Accrued	2,000
		2,90,400		2,90,400

2.

		Salaries (₹)	Rent & Electricity (₹)
(*i*)	**Expenses**		
	Paid during the year	1,55,000	69,750
	Add : Outstanding on 31-3-2025	12,400	7,600
		1,67,400	77,350
	Less : Outstanding on 31-3-2024	(10,200)	(6,500)
	Expenditure for the year	1,57,200	70,850

(*ii*)	**Depreciation :**		
	(*a*) Furniture @ 10% on ₹ 65,500		6,550
	(*b*) Sports Equipment @ 15% on ₹ 70,000		10,500
	(*c*) Library Books	32,500	
	Revalued at	(30,000)	2,500
			19,550
(*iii*)	**Subscription :**		
	Received as per Receipt and Payment A/c		2,95,000
	Add : Receivable on 31-3-2025		20,600
	Add : Prepaid as on 31-3-2024		7,000
			3,22,600
	Less : Receivable on 31-3-2024		(18,700)
	Less : Prepaid as on 31-3-2025		(8,400)
			2,95,500
(*iv*)	**Entrance Fees :**		
	Received as per Receipt and Payment A/c		50,000
	Less : Capitalised		(30,000)
	Charged to Income & Expenditure		20,000

ILLUSTRATION 7. Following is the Receipts and Payments Account of the "Three Hundred Club" for the year ending 31st March, 2025 :

Receipts	₹	₹	*Payments*	₹
Opening Balance			Honoraria to Secretary and Treasurer	4,800
Cash in hand	150		Rates and Taxes etc.	1,260
Balance as per Bank			Printing and Stationery	470
Pass Book	8,230		Other Miscellaneous Expenses	1,530
		8,380	Groundman's Wages	840
Subscriptions		10,710	Expenditure on Fetes	2,390
Receipts from Fetes		2,400	Payments for Bar Purchases	5,770
Net Proceeds of Variety Entertainment		4,270	Repairs etc.	320
Bank Interest		230	New Car (*Less* Sale Proceeds of Old Car	
Bar Takings		7,450	₹ 3,000)	12,600
Cash Over-spent		20	Closing Balance as per Bank Pass Book	3,480
		33,460		33,460

You are given the following additional information :

		1-4-2024 ₹	*31-3-2025* ₹
(1)	Subscription due	1,200	980
(2)	Unpresented cheques being payment on printing	90	30
(3)	Club Premises at cost	29,000	—
(4)	Depreciation on Club Premises	18,800	—
(5)	Car at cost	12,190	—

(6)	Depreciation on Car	10,290	–
(7)	Value of Bar Stock	710	870
(8)	Amount due for Bar Purchases	590	430

(9) Cash overspent represents amount of honorarium to the treasurer not drawn due to shortage of funds. But the total salary payable to him for the year was already included in ₹ 4,800.

(10) Depreciation is to be provided @ 5% p.a. on the written down value of the Club premises and at 15 per cent p.a. on car for the whole year.

You are required to adjust bank balance according to Cash Book and prepare :

(*i*) An income and expenditure account of the club for the year ending 31st March, 2025 and

(*ii*) A Balance Sheet as at 31st March, 2025.

SOLUTION

Three Hundred Club

INCOME AND EXPENDITURE ACCOUNT

for the year ended 31st March, 2025

	₹	₹		₹	₹
To Honorarium to Secretary		4,800	By Subscriptions	10,710	
" Rates and Taxes		1,260	*Add*: Outstanding		
" Printing and Stationery	470		on 31-3-2025	980	
Add : Outstanding at the end	30			11,690	
			Less : Outstanding	1,200	
	500		on 1-4-2024		10,490
Less: Outstanding on 1-4-2024	90		" Receipts from Fetes		2,400
		410	" Net Proceeds of Variety		
" Miscellaneous Expenses		1,530	Entertainments		4,270
" Groundman's Wages		840	" Bank Interest		230
			" Bar Takings		7,450
To Bar Expenses : Purchases	5,770		By Profit on Sale of Motor Car		
Add: Beginning Bar Stock	710		[(₹ 3,000 – ₹ 1,900 *i.e.*		
" Outstanding	430		₹ 12,190 – ₹ 10,290]		1,100
₹	6,910				
Less: Bar Closing Stock 870					
Outstanding on					
1-4-2024 590					
	1,460				
		5,450			
" Repairs		320			
" Fetes Expenses		2,390			
" Depreciation :					
Premises	510				
Motor Car	2,340				
		2,850			
" Surplus—Excess of Income over Expenditure		6,090			
		25,940			25,940

BALANCE SHEET
as on 31st March, 2025

		₹			₹
Outstanding Liabilities for Purchases		430	Cash and Bank Balances on hand		
Outstanding Liabilities for Expenses	₹	20	and at Bank (₹ 3,480 – ₹ 30)		3,450
Capital Fund on 1-4-2024	(1) 21,710		Outstanding Subscriptions		980
Add: Surplus	6,090		Bar Stock		870
		27,800	Motor Car	15,600	
			Less: Depreciation	2,340	
					13,260
			Club Premises	29,000	
			Less: Depreciation to date		
			(₹ 18,800 + ₹ 510)	19,310	
					9,690
		28,250			28,250

Working Note :

(1) *Calculation of Beginning Capital Fund as at 1-4-2024*

BEGINNING BALANCE SHEET
as at 1-4-2024

	₹		₹
Outstanding Liabilities for Purchases	590	Cash in hand	150
Capital Fund (Balancing figure)	21,710	Cash at Bank (₹ 8,230 – ₹ 90)	8,140
		Bar Stock	710
		Subscription Due	1,200
		Club Premises (₹ 29,000 – ₹ 18,800)	10,200
		Car (₹ 12,190 – ₹ 10,290)	1,900
	22,300		22,300

ILLUSTRATION 8. Following is the Receipts and Payments Account of Sydney Club for the year ended 31st March, 2025:

Receipts	₹	*Payments*	₹
Opening Balance		Salaries	1,20,000
Cash	10,000	Creditors	15,20,000
Bank	3,850	Printing and Stationery	70,000
Subscription Received	2,02,750	Postage	40,000
Entrance Donation	1,00,000	Telephones and Telex	52,000
Interest Received	58,000	Repairs and Maintenance	48,000
Sale of Assets	8,000	Glass and Table Linen	12,000
Miscellaneous Income	9,000	Crockery and Cutlery	14,000
Receipts at		Garden Upkeep	8,000
Coffee Room	10,70,000	Membership Fees	4,000
Wines and Spirits	5,10,000	Insurance	5,000
Swimming Pool	80,000	Electricity	28,000
Tennis Court	1,02,000	*Closing Balance*	
		Cash	8,000
		Bank	2,24,600
	21,53,600		21,53,600

The Assets and Liabilities as on 1-7-2024 were as follows :

Fixed Assets (net) ₹ 5,00,000 ; Stock ₹ 3,80,000 ; Investment in 12% Government Securities ₹ 5,00,000 ; Outstanding Subscription ₹ 12,000 ; Prepaid Insurance ₹ 1,000 ; Sundry Creditors ₹ 1,12,000 ; Subscription received in advance ₹ 15,000 ; Entrance Donation Received pending membership ₹ 1,00,000 ; Gratuity Fund ₹ 1,50,000.

Following adjustments are to be made while drawing up the Accounts :

(*i*) Subscription received in advance as on 31st March, 2025 was ₹ 18,000.

(*ii*) Outstanding Subscription as on 31st March, 2025 was ₹ 7,000.

(*iii*) Outstanding Expenses are Salaries ₹ 8,000 and Electricity ₹ 15,000.

(*iv*) 50% of the Entrance Donation was to be capitalised. There was no pending membership as on 31st March, 2025.

(*v*) The cost of assets sold net as on 01-7-2024 was ₹ 10,000.

(*vi*) Depreciation is to be provided at the rate of 10% on assets.

(*vii*) A sum of ₹ 20,000 received in October 2024 as Entrance Donation from an applicant was to be refunded as he has not fulfilled the requisite membership qualifications. The refund was made on 3-6-2025.

(*viii*) Purchases made during the year amounted to ₹ 15,00,000.

(*ix*) The value of closing stock was ₹ 2,10,000.

(*x*) The club as a matter of policy charges off to Income and Expenditure Account all purchases made on account of crockery, cutlery, glass and linen in the year of purchase.

You are required to prepare an Income and Expenditure Account for the year ended 31st March, 2025, and the Balance Sheet as on 31st March, 2025 alongwith necessary workings.

(CA—PCE—June, 2009 Modified)

SOLUTION

Sydney Club
INCOME AND EXPENDITURE ACCOUNT
for the year ended 31-3-2025

Expenditure	₹	*Income*	₹
To Salaries		By Subscription	
(₹ 1,20,000 + ₹ 8,000)	1,28,000	(₹ 2,02,750 + ₹ 7,000 +	
To Printing & Stationery	70,000	₹ 15,000 – ₹ 12,000 –	
To Postage	40,000	₹ 18,000)	1,94,750
To Telephone & Telex	52,000	By Entrance Donation	
To Repairs & Maintenance	48,000	(₹ 1,00,000 + ₹ 1,00,000 –	
To Glass & Table Linen	12,000	₹ 20,000 – ₹ 90,000)	90,000
To Crockery & Cutlery	14,000	By Interest (₹ 58,000 + ₹ 2,000)	60,000
To Garden Upkeep	8,000	By Misc. Income	9,000
To Membership Fees	4,000	By Profits from Operations	92,000
To Insurance (₹ 5,000 + ₹ 1,000)	6,000	(₹ 10,70,000 + ₹ 5,10,000 +	
To Electricity		₹ 80,000 + ₹ 1,02,000 –	
(₹ 28,000 + ₹ 15,000)	43,000	₹ 16,70,000 (*i.e.* ₹ 3,80,000	
To Loss on Sale of Assets		opening stock + ₹ 15,00,000	
(₹ 10,000 – ₹ 8,000)	2,000	purchases – ₹ 2,10,000 closing stock)	
To Depreciation		By Deficit – Excess of Expenditure	
(10% on ₹ 4,90,000)	49,000	over Income	30,250
	4,76,000		4,76,000

BALANCE SHEET
as on 31st March, 2025

Liabilities		₹	*Assets*	₹
Outstanding Expenses (₹ 8,000 + ₹ 15,000)		23,000	Fixed Assets (₹ 5,00,000 – ₹ 10,000 – ₹ 49,000)	4,41,000
Entrance Donations Refundable		20,000	Stock	2,10,000
Subscription received in advance		18,000	Investments	5,00,000
Sundry Creditors (₹ 1,12,000 + ₹ 15,00,000 –₹ 15,20,000)		92,000	Subscription Outstanding	7,000
Gratuity Fund		1,50,000	Interest Accrued	2,000
Capital Fund	₹ (1) 10,29,850		Bank	2,24,600
Add : Entrance Fees Capitalised	90,000		Cash	8,000
	11,19,850			
Less : Deficit	30,250	10,89,600		
		13,92,600		13,92,600

Working Note :

(1) ***Calculation of Beginning Capital Fund***

BALANCE SHEET
as on 1-4-2024

Liabilities	₹	*Assets*	₹
Sundry Creditors	1,12,000	Fixed Assets	5,00,000
Subscription Received in Advance	15,000	Stock	3,80,000
Entrance Donation Received in Advance	1,00,000	Investments	5,00,000
Gratuity Fund	1,50,000	Subscription Outstanding	12,000
Capital Fund (Balancing figure)	10,29,850	Prepaid Expenses	1,000
		Cash	10,000
		Bank	3,850
	14,06,850		14,06,850

ILLUSTRATION 9. New Delhi Recreation Club consists of a badminton section and a football section. The Balance Sheet of the Club as on 1-1-2024 is as under :

Liabilities	₹	*Assets*	₹
Accumulated Fund	36,450	Club House	21,200
		Badminton Court (Cost ₹ 20,000)	12,000
		Equipments	2,500
		Cash and Bank	750
	36,450		36,450

Following is the Receipts and Payments Account for the year ended 31-12-2024 :

Receipts	₹	*Payments*	₹
To Balance b/d	750	By New Badminton Court	8,000
To Ten-year Badminton Membership	6,000	By Prizes for Tournament :	
To Subscriptions : Badminton	3,200	Badminton	1,000
Football	650	Football	12,000

	₹		₹
To Tournament Entry Fees :		By Football Kit	1,200
Badminton	1,000	By Rates of Club House	500
Football	4,000	By General Expenses	4,650
To Collection at Football Matches	17,300	By Balance c/d	5,550
	32,900		32,900

In order to help pay for the new badminton court, ten-year badminton membership were offered for sale, at the beginning of 2024 at ₹ 200 each. It is the club's policy to write off the cost of the badminton court over a ten-year period. Equipments are to be depreciated at 10%. The football kit can be considered to possess a nil value.

Prepare :

(*a*) An Income and Expenditure Account for the year ended 31-12-2024, showing the net surplus/deficit arising separately from the badminton section and football section.

(*b*) The Balance Sheet as on 31-12-2024.

SOLUTION

(3)

New Delhi Recreation Club
INCOME AND EXPENDITURE ACCOUNT
for the year ended 31-12-2024

	Badminton	*Football*		*Badminton*	*Football*
	₹	₹		₹	₹
To Depreciation on Badminton Court (10% on ₹ 20,000 + ₹ 8,000)	2,800	—	By Ten Year Badminton Membership (1/10th of ₹ 6,000)	600	—
To Prizes for Tournament	1,000	12,000	By Subscriptions	3,200	650
To Football Kit	—	1,200	By Tournament Entry Fees	1,000	4,000
To Surplus c/d	1,000	8,750	By Collection at Football Matches	—	17,300
	4,800	21,950		4,800	21,950
To Depreciation on Equipments (10% on ₹ 2,500)		250	By Net Surplus b/d (₹ 1,000 + ₹ 8,750)		9,750
To Rates of Club House		500			
To General Expenses		4,650			
To Surplus		4,350			
		9,750			9,750

BALANCE SHEET
as on 31-12-2024

Liabilities	₹	₹	*Assets*	₹	₹
Accumulated Fund :	36,450		Club House		21,200
Add : Surplus	4,350	40,800	Badminton Court (₹ 12,000 + ₹ 8,000)	20,000	
Ten Year Badminton Memberships (₹ 6,000 – ₹ 600)		5,400	*Less* : Depreciation	2,800	17,200
			Equipments	2,500	
			Less : Depreciation	250	2,250
			Cash at Bank		5,550
		46,200			46,200

Type III. ***When Balance Sheets at the beginning and at the end are to be prepared from a given Receipts and Payments Account and Income and Expenditure Account.***

Sometimes Income and Expenditure and Receipts and Payments Accounts are given in the question and it is required to prepare the Balance Sheet both at the beginning as well as at the end of the period. In such a case the following procedure may be adopted :

1. From the particulars given in the question prepare the Balance Sheet at the beginning of the year.
2. Compare the *'Receipts side'* of the Receipts and Payments Account to 'Income side' of Income and Expenditure Account to ascertain (*i*) subscription in arrears of the previous and current years, (*ii*) income received in advance, and (*iii*) sale of an asset during the year.
3. Similarly, compare the *'payments side'* of the Receipts and Payments Account to 'expenditure side' of the Income and Expenditure Account in order to ascertain (*i*) outstanding expenses during the year, (*ii*) prepaid expenses during the year, (*iii*) stock of stationery in hand, (*iv*) depreciation on assets, and (*v*) purchase of an asset during the year.

ILLUSTRATION 10. From the following accounts taken from the books of the S.S. Hospital for the year ending 31st March, 2025, you are required to prepare its opening (1-4-2024) and its closing (31-3-2025) Balance Sheets.

RECEIPTS AND PAYMENTS ACCOUNT

	₹		₹
To Balance :		By Payments :	
Cash	600	Furniture Purchased	1,000
Bank	7,000	Instruments Purchased	2,000
Govt. Securities	1,80,000	Surgery and Dispensary	1,500
To Receipts :		Diet Expenses	2,500
Subscriptions	30,000	Rent and Taxes	2,400
Donations	6,000	Insurance	500
Interest	10,000	Office Expenses	1,200
Miscellaneous	500	Salaries	24,000
		Miscellaneous Expenses	200
		By Closing Balances :	
		Cash	1,800
		Bank	17,000
		Govt. Securities	1,80,000
	2,34,100		2,34,100

INCOME AND EXPENDITURE ACCOUNT

	₹	₹		₹	₹
To Salaries :			By Subscriptions :		
Paid	24,000		Receipts	30,000	
Less : For 2023-24	1,500		*Less* : for 2023-24	10,000	
	22,500			20,000	
Add : Outstanding	1,000		*Add* : Outstanding	8,000	
		23,500			28,000
To Diet Expenses		2,500	By Donations		6,000
" Surgery and Dispensary Expenses		1,500	" Interest :		
			Received	10,000	
" Rent and Taxes :			*Less* : for 2023-24	2,500	
Paid	2,400			7,500	
Less : for 2023-24	200		*Add* : Outstanding	2,500	
	2,200				10,000

Add : Outstanding	250		By Miscellaneous Receipts	500
		2,450		
" Insurance	500			
Less : Prepaid	100			
		400		
" Office Expenses		1,200		
" Miscellaneous Expenses		200		
" Depreciation :				
Building @ $2\frac{1}{2}\%$		5,000		
Furniture @ 10%		400		
Instruments @ 20%		1,200		
" Surplus		6,150		
		44,500		44,500

Depreciation on all assets has been worked for the full year. Value of building is exclusive of the cost of land of the hospital amounting to ₹ 50,000. Govt. Securities of the face value of ₹ 2,00,000 (cost ₹ 1,80,000) represent investment of the Endowment Fund of the Hospital.

SOLUTION

S.S. Hospital

BALANCE SHEET

as at 1-4-2024

		₹			₹
Capital Fund (Balancing figure)		2,75,400	Land		50,000
Endowment Fund		1,80,000	Instruments	(1)	4,000
Outstanding Expenses :	₹		Furniture	(1)	3,000
Salaries	1,500		Buildings	(1)	2,00,000
Rent and Taxes	200		Interest outstanding		2,500
		1,700	Subscription outstanding		10,000
			Government Securities		1,80,000
			Bank		7,000
			Cash in hand		600
		4,57,100			4,57,100

BALANCE SHEET

as on 31st March, 2025

	₹	₹		₹	₹
Capital Fund on			Land		50,000
1-4-2024	2,75,400		Instruments	4,000	
Add : Surplus	6,150		*Add* : Purchased in		
		2,81,550	2024-25	2,000	
Endowment Fund		1,80,000		6,000	
Outstanding Expenses			*Less* : Depreciation	1,200	
Salaries	1,000				4,800
Rent & Taxes	250		Furniture	3,000	
		1,250	*Add* : Purchased	1,000	
				4,000	
			Less : Depreciation	400	
					3,600

		Building	2,00,000	
		Less : Depreciation	5,000	
				1,95,000
		Prepaid Insurance		100
		Outstanding Interest		2,500
		Outstanding Subscription		8,000
		Government Securities		1,80,000
		Bank		17,000
		Cash in hand		1,800
	4,62,800			4,62,800

Working Note. (1) Assets values have been calculated as under :

Assets	*Depreciation*	*Amount of Depreciation*	*Full Value of Asset*	*Less Purchased during 2024-25*	*Value on 1-4-2024*
		₹	₹	₹	₹
Building	$2\frac{1}{2}$%	5,000	2,00,000 (5,000 × 100/2.5)	—	2,00,000
Furniture	10%	400	4,000 (400 × 100/10)	1,000	3,000
Instruments	20%	1,200	6,000 (1,200 × 100/20)	2,000	4,000

Type IV. *When a Receipts and Payments Account is to be prepared from a given Income and Expenditure Account and the accompanying notes.*

Sometimes Income and Expenditure Account is given alongwith its accompanying notes and it is required to prepare the Receipts and Payments Account. In such a case the following procedure may be adopted :

(1) All expenditure whether capital or revenue or relating to the current, succeeding and preceding period incurred during the year must be shown on the credit side of this account.

(2) All receipts of cash whether captial or revenue or relating to the current, succeeding and preceding period should go to the debit side of this account.

(3) Opening and Closing Balances of Receipts and Payments Account are to be taken into consideration.

(4) Eliminate all adjustments relating to provisions for doubtful debts or depreciation which were made for preparing income and expenditure account.

(5) Purchase or sale of assets can be calculated by comparing the net value of the assets on two dates *i.e.* at the beginning and the end of the year.

ILLUSTRATION 11. Income and Expenditure Account of City Sports Club for the year ended 31st March, 2025 was as follows :

Expenditure	*Amount*	*Income*	*Amount*
	₹		₹
To Salaries	1,20,000	By Subscriptions	1,60,000
To Printing and Stationery	6,000	By Entrance Fees	10,000
To Rent	12,000	By Contribution for Annual dinner	20,000
To Repairs	10,000	By Profit on Annual Sports meet	
To Sundry Expenses	8,000	(realised in cash)	20,000

To Annual Dinner Expenses	30,000		
To Interest to Bank	6,000		
To Depreciation on Sports Equipment	6,000		
To Excess of Income over Expenditure	12,000		
	2,10,000		2,10,000

The above account had been prepared after the following adjustments :

	₹
Subscription Outstanding on 31-3-2024	12,000
Subscriptions received in Advance on 31-3-2024	9,000
Subscriptions received in Advanced on 31-3-2025	5,400
Subscriptions Outstanding on 31-3-2025	15,000

Salaries outstanding at the beginning and at the end of the financial year were ₹ 8,000 and ₹ 10,000 respectively. Sundry expenses included prepaid insurance expenses of ₹ 1,200.

The Club owned a freehold ground valued ₹ 2,00,000. The Club has sports equipment on 1-4-2024 valued at ₹ 52,000. At the end of the year, after depreciation, the sports equipment amounted to ₹ 54,000. The Club raised a loan of ₹ 40,000 from a bank on 1-1-2024, which was unpaid till 31-3-2025. On 31-3-2025, cash in hand was ₹ 32,000.

Prepare Receipts and Payments Account of the Club for the year ended 31st March, 2025 and Balance Sheet as on that date. ***(CA—IPCE—Nov. 2009 Modified)***

SOLUTION

City Sports Club
RECEIPTS AND PAYMENTS ACCOUNT
for the year ended 31st March, 2025

Receipts	*Amount*	*Payments*	*Amount*
	₹		₹
To Balance b/d (Bal. Fig.)	27,800	By Salaries :	
To Subscription :		for 2023-2024	8,000
for 2023-2024	12,000	for 2024-2025	1,10,000
for 2024-2025 (3)	1,36,000	By Printing and Stationery	6,000
for 2025-2026	5,400	By Rent	12,000
To Entrance Fees	10,000	By Repairs	10,000
To Contribution for Annual Dinner	20,000	By Sundry Expenses (₹ 8,000 + ₹ 1,200)	9,200
To Profit on Annual Sports Meet	20,000	By Annual Dinner Expenses	30,000
		By Interest to Bank	6,000
		By Sports Equipment (2)	8,000
		By Balance c/d	32,000
	2,31,200		2,31,200

BALANCE SHEET
as at 31st March, 2025

Liabilities	(₹)	(₹)	*Assets*	(₹)	(₹)
Capital Fund (1)	2,34,800		Freehold Ground		2,00,000

Add : Excess of Income over Expenditure	12,000		Sports Equipment	52,000	
			Add : Additions during the year (Bal. Fig.)	8,000	
				60,000	
		2,46,800	*Less* : Depreciation	6,000	
Bank Loan		40,000			54,000
Outstanding Salaries		10,000	Subscription in Arrear		15,000
Subscription in Advance		5,400	Prepaid Insurance		1,200
			Cash in hand		32,000
		3,02,200			3,02,200

Working Notes :

(1) Calculation of Opening Balance of Capital Fund :

BALANCE SHEET

as at 31st March, 2024

	₹		₹
Capital Fund (Bal. Fig.)	2,34,800	Freehold Ground	2,00,000
Bank Loan	40,000	Sports Equipment	52,000
Outstanding Salaries	8,000	Subscription in Arrear	12,000
Subscription in Advance	9,000	Cash in hand	27,800
	2,91,800		2,91,800

(2) Sports Equipment Account

	₹		₹
To Balance b/d	52,000	By Depreciation Account	6,000
To Bank Account (Addition)	8,000	By Balance c/d	54,000
	60,000		60,000

(3) Subscription received during 2024-25

Particular	₹	₹
Subscription for 2024-25 as per Income and Expenditure A/c		1,60,000
Less : Subscription outstanding as on 31-3-2025	15,000	
Less : Subscription received in advance as on 31-3-2024	9,000	
		24,000
Subscription received during 2024-25		1,36,000

ILLUSTRATION 12. Following is the Income and Expenditure Account of Victoria Club for the year ending 31st March, 2025 :

Expenditure	*Amount* ₹	*Income*	₹	*Amount* ₹
To Salaries & Wages	19,000	By Subscription		30,000
To Misc. Expenses (Including Insurance)	2,000	By Entrance Fees received		1,000
To Audit Fees	1,000	By Annual Sports Income		
To Chief Executives' Honorarium	4,000	Receipts	6,000	
		Less : Expenses	3,000	
To Printing & Stationery	1,800			3,000

Expenditure	₹	₹	Income	₹
To Annual Day Celebration	₹			
Expenses	6,000			
Less : Donation	4,000			
		2,000		
To Interest on Bank Loan		600		
To Depreciation on Sports Equipment		1,200		
To Excess of Income Over Expenditure		2,400		
		34,000		34,000

Additional Information :

		31-3-2024 (₹)	*31-3-2025* (₹)
(*i*)	Subscription outstanding	2,400	3,000
(*ii*)	Subscription received in advance	1,800	1,080
(*iii*)	Salaries outstanding	1,600	1,800
(*iv*)	Sports equipment (after deducting depreciation)	10,400	10,800
(*v*)	Prepaid Insurance	—	240
(*vi*)	Cash in Hand	?	6,400

(*vii*) The Club owned a Sports' ground of ₹ 40,000

(*viii*) The Club took a loan of ₹ 8,000 from a Bank during the year 2023-24, which was not paid in 2024-25.

(*ix*) Audit fee of 2024-25 was outstanding, but audit fees of ₹ 800 for 2023-24 was paid in 2024-25.

Prepare Receipts and Payments Account for the year ending 31st March, 2025 and a Balance Sheet o that date.

SOLUTION

Victoria Club
RECEIPTS AND PAYMENTS ACCOUNT
for the year ended 31-3-2025

Receipts	₹	₹	*Payments*	₹	₹
To Balance b/d (Bal. Fig.)		5,560	By Salaries & Wages	19,000	
To Subscription	30,000		*Add* : Outstanding at the beginning of the year	1,600	
Add : Outstanding at the beginning of the year	2,400			20,600	
Advance received at the end of the year	1,080		*Less* : Outstanding at the end of the year	1,800	
	33,480				18,800
Less : Outstanding at the end of the year ₹ 3,000			By Audit Fees (for last year)		800
			By Purchase of Sports Equipments (2)		1,600
Advance received at the beginning of the year 1,800			By Misc. Expenses	2,000	
			Add : Prepaid Insurance	240	
					2,240
	4,800		By Chief Executive's Honorarium		4,000
		28,680	By Printing & Stationery		1,800
To Donation		4,000	By Expenses on Annual Sports		3,000
To Entrance Fees		1,000	By Annual Day Celebration Expenses		6,000
To Receipts for Annual Sports		6,000	By Interest on Bank Loan		600
			By Balance c/d		6,400
		45,240			45,240

BALANCE SHEET
as on 31-3-2025

Receipts	₹	₹	*Payments*	₹
Salaries Outstanding		1,800	Cash	6,400
Audit Fees Outstanding		1,000	Subscription Outstanding	3,000
Bank Loan		8,000	Sports Equipment	
Subscription Received in Advance		1,080	(₹ 10,400 + ₹ 1,600(2) – ₹ 1,200)	10,800
	₹		Sports Ground	40,000
Capital Fund	(1) 46,160		Prepaid Insurance	240
Add : Surplus	2,400			
		48,560		
		60,440		60,440

Working Notes

(1) ***Calculation of Beginning Capital Fund***

BALANCE SHEET
as on 31-3-2024

Liabilities	₹	*Assets*	₹
Salaries Outstanding	1,600	Cash	5,560
Audit Fees Outstanding	800	Subscription Outstanding	2,400
Subscription Received in Advance	1,800	Sports Ground	40,000
Bank Loan	8,000	Sports Equipment less Depreciation	10,400
Capital Fund (Bal. Fig.)	46,160		
	58,360		58,360

(2) ***Calculation of Purchase of Sports Equipments***

SPORTS EQUIPMENT ACCOUNT

	₹		₹
To Balance b/d	10,400	By Depreciation	1,200
To Bank (Purchase : Bal. Fig.)	1,600	By Balance c/d	10,800
	12,000		12,000

ILLUSTRATION 13. From the following Income & Expenditure Account of Premium Sports Club for the year ended 31st Mach, 2025, you are required to prepare Receipts & Payments Account for the year ended 31st March, 2025 and Balance Sheet as on that date :

Expenditure	*Amount* ₹	*Income*	*Amount* ₹
To Salaries	1,18,800	By Subscriptions	4,20,000
To Rent	2,16,000	By Entrance Fee	1,20,000
To Printing & Stationery	28,000	By Profit on sale of Sports Material	5,500
To Postage & Telephone	41,600	By Interest on 8% Govt. Bonds	12,000
To Membership Fee	3,200	By Sale of Old Newspaper	11,600
To Electricity Charges	38,500		

To Garden Upkeep	19,300		
To Sports Material Utilised	62,800		
To Repairs & Maintenance	18,700		
To Depreciation	13,000		
To Miscellaneous Expenses	5,700		
To Surplus carried to Capital Fund	3,500		
	5,69,100		5,69,100

The following additional information is provided to you :

(*a*)

	Balances as on 1-4-2024	*Balances as on 31-3-2025*
Fixed Assets	2,40,000	?
Bank Balance	8,300	?
Stock of Sports Material	43,450	35,670
Outstanding Subscription	10,200	5,700
Subscription received in advance	2,400	4,900
8% Government Bonds	1,50,000	1,50,000
Outstanding Salaries	16,000	14,300
Outstanding Rent	21,000	15,000
Advance for Stationery	1,350	1,550
Outstanding Repairs & Maintenance	1,200	Nil
Creditors for purchase of Sports Material	3,400	4,200

(*b*) Some of Fixed Assets were purchased on 1-10-2024 and depreciation is to be charged @ 5% p.a.

(*c*) Sports Material worth ₹ 72,000 was purchased on credit during the year.

(*d*) The Club became member of State Table Tennis Association on 1-1-2025 when it paid fee up to 31-12-2025.

(*e*) 50% of Entrance Fees is to be capitalised.

(*f*) Interest on 8% Government Bonds was received for two quarters only.

(*g*) A Fixed Deposit of ₹ 80,000 was made on 31st March, 2025. ***(CA May, 2012 Modified)***

SOLUTION

RECEIPTS AND PAYMENTS ACCOUNT OF PREMIUM SPORTS CLUB

for the year ended 31st March, 2025.

Receipts	₹	*Income*	₹
To Cash at Bank (Opening)	8,300	By Salaries (6)	1,20,500
To Subscription (1)	4,27,000	By Rent (7)	2,22,000
To Entrance Fees (2)	2,40,000	By Printing and Stationery (8)	28,200
To Interest on 8% Govt. Bond (3)	6,000	By Postage and Telephone	41,600
To Sale of Old Newspaper	11,600	By Membership Fee (9)	12,800
To Sale of Sports Material (4)	22,480	By Electricity Charges	38,500
		By Garden upkeep	19,300
		By Payment to Creditors for Sports Material (5)	71,200
		By Purchase of Fixed Assets (10)	40,000
		By Repairs and Maintenance (11)	19,900

		By Misc. Expenses	5,700
		By Fixed Deposit made	80,000
		By Cash at Bank (Closing) (bal. fig.)	15,680
	7,15,380		7,15,380

BALANCE SHEET OF PREMIUM SPORTS CLUB
as on 31st March, 2025

Liabilities		₹	*Assets*		₹
	₹			₹	
Capital Fund :			Fixed Assets	2,40,000	
Opening Balance (12)	4,09,300		*Add* : Additions (10)	40,000	
Add : Surplus	3,500			2,80,000	
		4,12,800	*Less* : Depreciation	13,000	
Entrance Fees		1,20,000			2,67,000
Subscription Received in Advance		4,900	Fixed Deposit		80,000
Outstanding Expenses			Investments in 8% Govt. Bonds		1,50,000
Salary	14,300		Stock of Sports Material		35,670
Rent	15,000		Subscription Receivable		5,700
		29,300	Membership Fee paid in Advance		9,600
Creditors for Purchase of			Prepaid Printing and Stationery Charges		1,550
Sports Material		4,200	Outstanding Interest on 8% Govt. Bonds		6,000
			Cash at Bank		15,680
		5,71,200			5,71,200

Working Notes :

1. ***Subscription received during the year***

	₹	₹
Subscription for the year ended 31st March, 2025		4,20,000
Less : Subscription receivable on 31-3-2025	5,700	
Less : Subscription received in advance on 1-4-2024	2,400	
		(8,100)
		4,11,900
Add : Subscription receivable on 1-4-2024	10,200	
Add : Subscription received in advance on 31-3-2025	4,900	
		15,100
		4,27,000

2. ***Entrance Fees received during the year***

Entrance Fees as per Income and Expenditure Account	₹ 1,20,000
Add : Capitalised Entrance Fees (50%)	₹ 1,20,000
	₹ 2,40,000

3. ***Interest on 8% Government Bond***

	₹
Interest as per Income and Expenditure Account	12,000
Less : Outstanding Interest for 2 quarters [12,l000 × 6/12)]	(6,000)
	6,000

4. ***Sales Price of Sports Material Sold***

	₹
Stock of Sports Material on 1-4-2024	43,450
Add : Purchase of Sports Material during the year	72,000
	1,15,450
Less : Stock of Sports Material on 31-3-2025	(35,670)
Cost of Sports Material consumed in the club and for sale	79,780
Less : Sports material consumed in the club	(62,800)
Cost of Sports Material sold	16,980

Sales Price of sports material sold = ₹ 16,980 Cost + ₹ 5,500 Profit = ₹ 22,480

5. ***Payment to Creditors for Sports Material***

	₹
Purchase of Sports Material	72,000
Less : Closing Creditors for Purchase of Sports Material on 31-3-2025	(4,200)
	67,800
Add : Opening Creditors for Purchase of Sports Material on 1-4-2024	3,400
	71,200

6. ***Salaries paid during the year***

	₹
Salaries as per Income and Expenditure Account	1,18,800
Less : Outstanding Balance as on 31-3-2025	(14,300)
	1,04,500
Add : Outstanding Balance as on 1-4-2024	16,000
	1,20,500

7. ***Rent paid during the year***

	₹
Rent as per Income and Expenditure Account	2,16,000
Less : Outstanding Balance as on 31-3-2025	(15,000)
	2,01,000
Add : Outstanding Balance as on 1-4-2024	21,000
	2,22,000

8. *Printing and Stationery paid during the year*

	₹
Printing and Stationery as per Income and Expenditure Account	28,000
Less : Prepaid Balance as on 1-4-2024	(1,350)
	26,650
Add : Prepaid Balance as on 31-3-2025	1,550
	28,200

9. *Membership Fee paid during the year*

	₹
Membership Fee as per Income and Expenditure Account	3,200
Add : Prepaid Balance as on 31-3-2025 [(3,200/3 × 9]	9,600
	12,800

10. *Fixed Asset purchased during the year*

	₹
Depreciation during the year	13,000
Less : Depreciation on Opening Balance of Fixed Asset	(12,000)
Depreciation on New Purchase of Fixed Asset during the year	1,000
Cost of Asset purchased during the year $\left(₹ 1,000 \times \frac{12}{6} \times \frac{100}{5}\right)$	40,000

11. *Repairs and Maintenance paid during the year*

	₹
Repairs and Maintenance as per Income and Expenditure Account	18,700
Add : Outstanding Balance as on 1-4-2024	1,200
	19,900

12. BALANCE SHEET OF PREMIUM SPORTS CLUB

as on 1st April, 2024

Liabilities	₹	*Assets*	₹
Capital Fund (Bal. Fig.)	4,09,300	Fixed Assets	2,40,000
Subscription Received in Advance	2,400	Investments in 8% Government Bonds	1,50,000
Outstanding Expenses :		Stock of Sports Material	43,450
Salary	16,000	Subscription receivable	10,200
Rent	21,000	Prepaid Printing and Stationery Charges	1,350
Repairs and Maintenance	1,200	Bank	8,300
Creditors for Purchase of Sports Material	3,400		
	4,53,300		4,53,300

Note : It is assumed that Premium "Sports Club has purchased all the sports equipment on credit basis only.

Type V. *Where Bar Trading Account alongwith Income and Expenditure and Balance Sheet is to be prepared.*

ILLUSTRATION 14. ABC sports and Social Club's financial year ends on 31st March. The assets and liabilities of the club at dates stated were as follows :

	At 31-3-2024	*At 31-3-2025*
	₹	₹
Equipment	25,000	28,000
Subscriptions in arrears	2,000	1,800
Subscription in advance	1,300	1,100
Creditors for Bar Stocks	3,500	4,300
Bar stocks	8,000	6,000
Electricity owing	1,050	1,400
Raffle (Lottery) Fund	500	?
Bank Balance	7,230	?

For the year ending 31 March 2025, cash receipts and payments made were :

	₹		₹
Subscriptions (including ₹ 600 of arrears from previous year)	21,000	Affiliation fees (for *four years*)	1,000
		Purchases of Equipment	8,000
Bar takings	41,000	Bar Stocks	20,500
Annual dinner/dance sale of tickets	24,000	Barman's Wages	7,500
Sale of raffle tickets	1,800	Catering (dinner/dance)	14,400
		Hire of Band (dinner/dance)	3,000
		Raffle Prizes	600
		Rent of Hall	15,000
		Printing and Postage	2,000
		Electricity	5,810
		Honorary Secretary's Expenses	1,220
		Repairs to Equipment	3,000

Note. Subscription arrears of previous year written off ₹ 400. Prepare (*i*) A Bar Trading Account; (*ii*) Income and Expenditure Account for the year ending 31st March 2025; and (*iii*) A Balance Sheet as on that date.

SOLUTION

BAR TRADING ACCOUNT
for the year ended 31-3-2025

	₹		₹
To Opening Stock	8,000	By Bar Takings	41,000
To Purchases (₹ 20,500 + ₹ 800)	21,300	By Closing Stock	6,000
To Wages	7,500		
To Profit transferred to Income & Expenditure A/c	10,200		
	47,000		47,000

INCOME AND EXPENDITURE ACCOUNT
for the year ended 31-3-2025

Expenditure	₹	₹	*Income*	₹
To Bad Debts written off		400	By Subscription	21,400
To Affiliation Fees	1,000		By Bar Trading A/c (Profit)	10,200
Less : Prepaid	750	250	By Annual Dinner/Dance Sale of Tickets	24,000

To Depreciation on Equipment				
(₹ 8,000 + ₹ 25,000 – ₹ 28,000)		5,000		
To Catering (Dinner/Dances)		14,400		
To Hire of Band		3,000		
To Rent of Hall		15,000		
To Printing & Postage	₹	2,000		
To Electricity	5,810			
Add : Outstanding	350			
		6,160		
To Honorary Secretary's Expenses		1,220		
To Repairs to Equipment		3,000		
To Surplus		5,170		
		55,600		55,600

BALANCE SHEET

as on 31-3-2025

Liabilities		₹	*Assets*	₹
Subscription in Advance		1,100	Bank Balance	
Creditors for Bar Stock		4,300	(₹ 87,800 + ₹ 7,230 – ₹ 82,030)	13,000
Electricity Charges Due		1,400	Bar Stock	6,000
Raffle Fund			Subscription in Arrear	1,800
(₹ 500 + ₹ 1,800 – ₹ 600)	₹	1,700	Prepaid Affliation Fees	750
Capital Fund (1)	35,880		Equipments	28,000
Add : Surplus	5,170			
		41,050		
		49,550		49,550

Working Notes :

Calculation of Beginning Capital Fund

BALANCE SHEET

as on 1-4-2024

Liabilities	₹	*Assets*	₹
Subscription in Advance	1,300	Equipments	25,000
Creditors for Bar Stock	3,500	Subscription in Arrear	2,000
Electricity Due	1,050	Bar Stock	8,000
Raffle Fund	500	Bank	7,230
Capital Fund (Bal. fig.)	35,880		
	42,230		42,230

Type VI. ***Where Receipts & Payments A/c, Income and Expenditure Account and Balance Sheet are to be Prepared.***

ILLUSTRATION 15. Following informations were obtained from the books of Dignity Foundation Recreation Club as on 31-3-2025. At the end of the first year of the club you are asked to prepare Receipts and Payments Account, Income and Expenditure Account for the year ended 31-3-2025 and a Balance Sheet as at 31-3-2025 on mercantile basis :

(*i*) Donations received for building and library ₹ 1,00,000

(*ii*) Other revenue income and actual receipts :

	Revenue Income	*Actual Receipts*
	₹	₹
Entrance Fees	20,000	20,000
Subscription	17,000	16,000
Locker Rent	800	800
Sundry Income	1,400	860
Refreshment Account		20,000

(*iii*) Other revenue expenditure and actual payments :

	Revenue Expenditure	*Actual Payments*
	₹	₹
Land (Cost ₹ 10,000)	—	10,000
Furniture (Cost ₹ 1,46,000)	—	1,30,000
Salaries	6,000	5,800
Maintenance of Club	3,000	2,000
Rent	6,000	6,000
Refreshment Account	—	12,000

Donations to the extent of ₹ 12,500 were utilised for the purchase of library books, balance was still unutilised. In order to keep it safe, 9% Government bonds of ₹ 80,000 were purchased on 31-3-2025. Remaining amount was put in the bank on 31-3-2025 under the term deposit. Depreciation at 10% p.a. was to be provided for the whole year on Furniture and Library Books.

SOLUTION

Dignity Foundation Recreation Club

RECEIPTS AND PAYMENTS ACCOUNT

for the year ending 31st March, 2025

Receipts	₹	*Payments*	₹
To Donations for Building and Library	1,00,000	By Land	10,000
To Entrance Fees	20,000	By Furniture	1,30,000
To Subscription	16,000	By Salaries	5,800
To Locker Rent	800	By Maintenance of Club	2,000
To Sundry Income	860	By Rent	6,000
To Refreshment A/c	20,000	By Refreshment A/c	12,000
To Balance c/d (Overdraft) (Balancing Fig.)	1,08,140	By Library Books	12,500
		By 9% Govt. Bonds	80,000
		By Term Deposit (₹ 1,00,000 – ₹ 12,500 – ₹ 80,000)	7,500
	2,65,800		2,65,800
		By Balance b/d	1,08,140

INCOME AND EXPENDITURE ACCOUNT

for the year ending 31st March, 2025

Expenditure	₹	₹	*Income*	₹	₹
To Salaries	5,800		By Entrance Fees		20,000
Add : Outstanding	200		By Subscription	16,000	
		6,000	*Add* : Outstanding	1,000	
To Maintenance of Club	2,000				17,000

Add : Outstanding	1,000		By Locker Rent		800
		3,000	By Sundry Income	860	
To Rent		6,000	*Add* : Outstanding		
To Depreciation @ 10%			(₹ 1,400 – ₹ 860)	540	
Furniture	14,600				1,400
Library Books	1,250		By Refreshment Receipts	20,000	
		15,850	*Less* : Expenditure on		
To Capital Fund (Excess of			Refreshment	12,000	
Income Over Expenditure)		16,350			8,000
		47,200			47,200

BALANCE SHEET

as at 31-3-2025

Liabilities		₹	*Assets*	₹	₹
Capital Fund (Surplus)		16,350	Land		10,000
Building and Library Fund		1,00,000	Furniture	1,46,000	
Creditors for Expenses :	₹		*Less* : Depreciation	14,600	
Salaries Due	200				1,31,400
Maintenance of Club	1,000		Library Books	12,500	
		1,200	*Less* : Depreciation	1,250	
Bank Overdraft		1,08,140			11,250
Creditors for Furniture			9% Govt. Bonds		80,000
(₹ 1,46,000 – ₹ 1,30,000)		16,000	Bank Term Deposit		7,500
			Subscription Receivable		1,000
			Sundry Income Receivable		540
		2,41,690			2,41,690

Accounting for Educational Institutions

Educational institutions in India are mostly registered as societies under the Indian Societies Registration Act of 1860. The Societies are autonomous bodies with office bearers consisting of President, Secretary, Treasurer and Executive Committee Members. The General Body consists of all the members of the society. In case of a society which runs many colleges and schools, there is a governing body also including Principal of each college or Headmaster of each school as members for managing the affairs of each individual college or school.

The basic aim of an educational institution is not to earn profit but it is to spread education at a cheaper rate. There are four main sources through which amounts are collected by the educational institutions for running their activities. These sources are :

1. Fees collected from students in the form of admission fees, tuition fees, science fees, examination fees, fines etc.
2. Security deposits from students such as library security.
3. Donations from public.
4. Grants received from the Government such as maintenance grant, equipment grant, building grant, etc.

Separate registers should be kept for the sources of collection given above. A Collection Register should be maintained for collection of tuition fees, admission fees, laboratory fees, fines, building fund etc. from students. A Students' Ledger must be maintained and an account of each student should be opened in this ledger to keep a record of the various types of fees due from him and amounts realised from him from time to time. Fees due from a student should be debited to his account and fees collected should be credited to his account. Fee concessions and irrecoverable fees should be sanctioned by the higher authority or Managing Committee and these should be noted in the accounts of the students who have been given fee concessions or whose irrecoverable fees have been written off. Periodical reconciliation should be made for the fees which should have been collected from the students and fees which have been actually collected and fees outstanding should be ascertained.

As regards payments, the following may be the various items on which payments are made by an educational institution :

1. Pay and allowances to teaching staff, office staff and menial staff.
2. Provident fund contribution.
3. Books for library.
4. Newspapers and magazines.
5. Medical Inspection.
6. Examination expenses, *i.e.* printing of question papers and supply of answer books and other examination material.
7. Functions and festivals.
8. Sports and games.
9. Extra-curricular excursions and visits.
10. Prizes for co-curricular activities.
11. Laboratory equipment.
12. Audio-visual education.
13. Furniture—Purchase and its repair.
14. Building repairs.
15. Distribution of scholarships and stipends.
16. Electric and telephone charges.
17. Purchase of stationery for office use.
18. Audit fees.

All the educational institutions usually follow financial year (*i.e.* 1st April to 31st March) as their accounting year and they are required to prepare an Income and Expenditure Account and Balance sheet for each financial year to know surplus or deficiency of each accounting year and financial position of their institutions at the end of each accounting year. The preparation of Income and Expenditure Account and Balance Sheet has already been discussed in detail.

Consolidation of Accounts

For a society running many educational institutions, the problem of Consolidation of accounts of various institutions under its control will arise. This problem can be simplified if the consolidation of accounts is done step by step. A separate register should be kept by the society for consolidation of the summarised figures of all the institutions under its control. For example, if tuition fees are to be consolidated, it is to be done as given below :

		₹
	Institute-wise opening balance of tuition fees outstanding	…………
Add :	Institute-wise tuition fees due during the year	…………
		…………
Less :	Institute-wise tuition fees received during the year	…………
	Tution fees outstanding at the end of the year	…………

Similarly, all other items can be consolidated and with consolidated figures Consolidated Income and Expenditure Account and Consolidated Balance Sheet are prepared to have a consolidated view of all institutions.

ILLUSTRATION 16. Novel **Education Society** supplied the following information :

INCOME AND EXPENDITURE ACCOUNT

for the year ending 31st March, 2025

Expenditure	₹ (in '000)	*Income*	₹ (in '000)
To Salaries	830	By Subscriptions	4,780
To Scholarships	4,130	By Government Grant	530

To Rent	280	By Proceeds of Tickets for Entertainment	830
To General Expenses	310	By Advertisements in Souvenir	510
To Audit Fees	60	By Interest on Bank Fixed Deposit (for full year @ 6% per annum)	150
To Printing Tickets and Souvenir	150		
To Cost of Entertainment	350		
To Loss on Sale of Furniture (Book Value, ₹ 80,000)	30		
To Depreciation on Furniture	60		
To Surplus, *i.e.,* Excess of Income over Expenditure	600		
	6,800		6,800

RECEIPTS AND PAYMENTS ACCOUNT

for the year ended 31st March, 2025

Receipts	₹ (in '000)	*Payments*	₹ (in '000)
To Balance b/f	380	By Salaries	940
To Subscriptions	4,600	By Scholarships	4,010
To Government Grant	530	By Rent	260
To Sale of Tickets	830	By General Expenses	310
To Advertisements in Souvenir	460	By Printing of Tickets and Souvenir	120
to Interest on Bank Fixed Deposits	100	By Cost of Entertainment	350
To Sale of Furniture	50	By Furniture	200
		By Balance c/f	760
	6,950		6,950

On 31st March, 2024, subscriptions due were ₹ 1,50,000, furniture on that date was ₹ 6,00,000. Prepare Balance Sheets as at 31st March, 2024 and 31st March, 2025.

SOLUTION

BALANCE SHEET OF NOVEL EDUCATION SOCIETY

as on 31st March, 2024

Liabilities	₹ '000	*Assets*	₹ '000
Salaries Outstanding	110	Cash at Bank/in Hand	380
Capital Fund—Balancing Figure	3,520	Subscription due	150
		6% Bank Fixed Deposit (1)	2,500
		Furniture	600
	3,630		3,630

BALANCE SHEET OF NOVEL EDUCATION SOCIETY

as on 31st March 2025

Liabilities	₹ '000	*Assets*		₹ '000
Scholarships Outstanding (4,130 – 4,010)	120	Cash at Bank/in hand		760
Rent Outstanding (280 – 260)	20	Subscription due (2)		330
Audit Fees Outstanding (not yet paid)	60	Due for Advertisements in Souvenir :	₹ '000	
Printing Expenses Outstanding (150 – 120)	30	Income	510	

	₹ '000				
Capital Fund :			Less : Receipts	460	
Opening Balance	3,520				50
Add : Surplus for the year	600		Interest Accrued on Investments		50
		4,120	(150 Interest – 100 Received)		
			6% Bank Fixed Deposits		2,500
			Furniture :		
			Opening Balance	600	
			Add : Addition	200	
				800	
			Less : Sale	80	
				720	
			Less : Depreciation	60	
					660
		4,350			4,350

Working Notes

(1) *Calculation of 6% Bank Fixed Deposits*

	₹ '000
Interest on Bank Fixed Deposit for full year @ 6% per annum	150
Therefore, Investment in Fixed Deposit $\left(150 \times \frac{100}{6}\right)$	2,500

(2) *Calculation of Subscriptions Due on 31st March, 2025*

	₹ '000	₹ '000
Subscription Income for the year as per Income & Expenditure A/c		4,780
Total Receipts of Subscriptions as per Receipts & Payments A/c	4,600	
Less : Subscriptions received on account of previous year (*i.e.* Subscription due last year)	150	
		4,450
Subscriptions due on 31st March, 2025		330

ILLUSTRATION 17. Modern **City School** is a privately run educational institution. Its Balance Sheet as on 31st March, 2024 was as follows :

Liabilities	₹	*Assets*	₹
Capital Fund	20,00,000	Land	8,00,000
Development Fund	10,00,000	School Buildings	15,00,000
Special Donation Fund	6,00,000	School Bus	8,00,000
General Fund	6,50,000	Furniture	2,00,000
Employee Super Annuation Fund	5,00,000	Laboratory Equipment	
Outstanding Salaries (March, 2025)		Science Lab	50,000
Teaching Staff	1,50,000	Computer Lab	2,00,000
Non-teaching Staff	80,000	Library Books	2,50,000
Outstanding Electricity Bill	20,000	Investment in Govt. Securities	8,00,000
		Tuition Fee Outstanding	60,000
		Cash and Bank	3,40,000
	50,00,000		50,00,000

RECEIPTS AND PAYMENTS ACCOUNT
for the year ended 31st March, 2025

	₹		₹
Opening Balance	3,40,000	Salaries	
Admission Fee	9,00,000	Teaching Staff	58,00,000
Tuition Fee	80,00,000	Non-teaching Staff	10,00,000
Contribution to Special Donation		Purchase of Library Books	1,00,000
Funds (from Ex-students)	3,00,000	Purchase of Science Lab Equipment	50,000
Interest on Investments	75,000	Purchase of Computers	60,000
		Construction of New School Buildings	4,00,000
		Purchase of School Bus	6,00,000
		Purchase of Govt. Securities	5,00,000
		Education Tour Expenses	1,50,000
		Annual Function	1,00,000
		Building Maintenance Expenses	1,50,000
		Purchase of New Furniture	60,000
		Electricity	80,000
		Printing, Postage, Stationery and Other Expenses	1,40,000
		Closing Balance	4,25,000
	96,15,000		96,15,000

Following further information is available :

(1) Interest accrued but not received ₹ 10,000

(2) The school has decided to charge depreciation as follows :

School buildings (excluding new construction)	5%
School furniture (excluding new additions)	10%
Lab equipment	
Science Lab (old & new)	8%
Computer Lab (old & new)	20%
School Bus (excluding the one newly acquired during the year)	15%
Library Books (old & new)	10%

(3) Amount to be contributed to employee superannuation fund during the year ₹ 1,50,000

(4) Outstanding expenses at the end of the year :

Staff Salaries	
Teaching Staff	₹ 80,000
Non-teaching Staff	₹ 20,000
Telephone Bill	₹ 2,000

(5) Building Contractor's Bills outstanding as on 31st March, 2025 ₹ 70,000

(6) Tuition Fee receivable as on 31st March, 2025 ₹ 50,000

(7) Admission Fee includes ₹ 2,50,000 representing collection towards development fund.

You are required to prepare an Income and Expenditure Account for the year ended 31st March, 2025 and a Balance Sheet as on that date. *(ICWA State II, December, 2006 Modified)*

SOLUTION

Modern City School
INCOME AND EXPENDITURE ACCOUNT
for the year ended 31st March, 2025

	₹		₹
To Salaries :		By Tuition Fees	
Teaching Staff (₹ 58,00,000 + ₹ 80,000 – ₹ 1,50,000)	57,30,000	(₹ 80,00,000 – ₹ 60,000 + ₹ 50,000)	79,90,000
Non-teaching Staff (₹ 10,00,000 + ₹ 20,000 – ₹ 80,000)	9,40,000	By Admission Fees (₹ 9,00,000 – ₹ 2,50,0000	6,50,000
To Contribution to Super Annuation Fund	1,50,000	By Interest on Investments	
To Educational Tours	1,50,000	(₹ 75,000 + ₹ 10,000)	85,000
To Annual Function	1,00,000		
To Electricity (₹ 80,000 – ₹ 20,000)	60,000		
To Printing and Stationery, etc. (₹ 1,40,000 + ₹ 2,000)	1,42,000		
To Building Maintenance	1,50,000		
To Depreciation :			
School Building $\left(₹ 15,00,000 \times \frac{5}{100}\right)$	75,000		
Furniture $\left(₹ 2,00,000 \times \frac{10}{100}\right)$	20,000		
Science Laboratory Equipment (₹ 50,000 + ₹ 50,000) × $\frac{8}{100}$	8,000		
Computer Laboratory Equipments (₹ 2,00,000 + ₹ 60,000) × $\frac{20}{100}$	52,000		
School Bus (₹ 8,00,000 × .15)	1,20,000		
Library Books $\left(₹ 2,50,000 + ₹ 1,00,000\right) \times \frac{10}{100}$	35,000		
Surplus—Excess of Income over Expenditure	9,93,000		
	87,25,000		87,25,000

BALANCE SHEET
as on 31st March, 2025

Liabilities	₹	*Assets*	₹
Capital Fund	20,00,000	Land	8,00,000
Development Fund (₹ 10,00,000 + ₹ 2,50,000)	12,50,000	School Building (₹ 15,00,000 + ₹ 4,00,000 + ₹ 70,000 – ₹ 75,000)	18,95,000
Special Donation Fund (₹ 6,00,000 + ₹ 3,00,000)	9,00,000	Furniture	
General Fund		(₹ 2,00,000 + ₹ 60,000 – ₹ 20,000)	2,40,000
(₹ 6,50,000 + ₹ 9,93,000)	16,43,000	Laboratory Equipments :	
Employee Superannuation Fund		Science (₹ 50,000 + ₹ 50,000	
(₹ 5,00,000 + ₹ 1,50,000)	6,50,000	– ₹ 8,000)	92,000

Outstanding Expenses :		Computer :	
Salaries : Teaching	80,000	(₹ 2,00,000 + ₹ 60,000 – ₹ 52,000)	2,08,000
Non-teaching	20,000	Library Books (₹ 2,50,000 + ₹ 1,00,000	
Telephone	2,000	– ₹ 35,000	3,15,000
Payable to Building Contractor	70,000	School Bus (₹ 8,00,000 + ₹ 6,00,000	
		– ₹ 1,20,000)	12,80,000
		Investments	13,00,000
		Receivables :	
		Tuition Fees	50,000
		Accrued Interest	10,000
		Cash and Bank	4,25,000
	66,15,000		66,15,000

Accounting for Students' Hostels

Many educational institutions run students' hostels to provide boarding facilities to students who belong to far off places. Government gives grants to hostels in abundance so that students living in villages and remote areas may have boarding facilities at a cheaper rate at places where educational institutions are located. A hostel is run at no profit no loss basis, so it prepares like other organisations without profit-motive the following :

(*a*) Receipts and Payment Account. (*b*) Income and Expenditure Account. (*c*) Balance Sheet.

Following may be the various types of incomes for a hostel :

1. Room rent.
2. Rent of furniture and appliances like fans, heaters, geysers, etc.
3. Electric and water charges.
4. Reading room fee.
5. Common room fee.
6. Medical fee.
7. Room service charges.
8. Admission fee.
9. Establishment charges.
10. Mess charges.
11. Grants.

Expenses for a hostel may be of the following types :

1. Establishment expenses.
2. Repairs and maintenance.
3. Electricity expenses.
4. Water charges.
5. Newspapers and magazines.
6. Indoor games material.
7. Depreciation.
8. Rent of accommodation if hired.
9. Medical expenses.
10. Provision for mess.

A security register should be separately maintained for keeping a record of the securities deposited by the students when they take admission in the hostel. Such securities are to be refunded to the students when they leave the hostel.

ILLUSTRATION 18. From the following Trial Balance and additional information, prepare Income and Expenditure Account for the year ending 31st December, 2024 and a Balance Sheet as on that date.

SARASWATI HOSTEL

	₹	₹
Land	5,00,000	
Building	42,00,000	
Furniture and Fixtures	1,50,000	
Fans	50,000	
Heaters	5,000	

		₹	₹
Room Rent			2,35,000
Rent for Fans, Heaters, etc.			11,000
Electricity and Water Charges			19,000
Mess Fees			11,80,000
Mess Charges extra for Guests			20,000
Room Service Charges			6,000
Annual Day Collection			7,000
Opening Stock :	Food	21,000	
	Fuel	3,000	
	Drinks	2,000	
	Sundries	4,000	
Purchases :	Food	7,10,000	
	Fuel	60,000	
	Drinks	90,000	
	Sundries	10,000	
Wages :	Mess	2,25,000	
	Others	65,000	
Electricity and Water Charges		28,000	
Repairs and Maintenance		22,000	
Indoor Games Material		15,000	
Common Room Expenses		16,000	
Medical Expenses		13,000	
Grants—Youth Welfare Department			2,00,000
Investments—Govt. Securities		5,00,000	
Income from Investments			55,000
Security Deposit			2,67,000
Capital Fund			47,00,000
General Fund			3,00,000
Cash at Bank		3,11,000	
		70,00,000	70,00,000

Additional Information :

(1) Closing Stock : Food ₹ 15,000 ; Fuel ₹ 5,000 ; Drinks ₹ 3,000 ; and Sundries ₹ 2,000.

(2) Provide Depreciation : Building 5% ; Furniture and Fixtures 15% ; Fans 20% and Heaters 20%.

SOLUTION **INCOME AND EXPENDITURE ACCOUNT OF SARASWATI HOSTEL**

for the year ending 31st December, 2024

Expenditure	₹	₹	*Income*	₹
To Mess Expenses :			By Room Rent	2,35,000
Food : Opening Stock	21,000		By Rent for Fans, Heaters etc.	11,000
Add : Purchases	7,10,000		By Electricity and Water Charges	19,000
	7,31,000		By Mess Fees	11,80,000
Less : Closing Stock	15,000		By Mess Charges for Guests	20,000
		7,16,000	By Room Service Charges	6,000
Drinks : Opening Stock	2,000		By Annual Day Collection	7,000
Add : Purchases	90,000		By Income from Investments	55,000
	92,000		By Grants	2,00,000
Less : Closing Stock	3,000			
		89,000		

Fuel : Opening Stock	3,000			
Add : Purchases	60,000			
	63,000			
Less : Closing Stock	5,000			
		58,000		
Sundries : Opening Stock	4,000			
Add : Purchases	10,000			
	14,000			
Less : Closing Stock	2,000			
		12,000		
To Wages : Mess	2,25,000			
Others	65,000			
		2,90,000		
To Electricity & Water Charges		28,000		
To Repairs & Maintenance		22,000		
To Indoor Games Material		15,000		
To Common Room Expenses		16,000		
To Medical Expenses		13,000		
To Depreciation :				
Building	2,10,000			
Furniture	22,500			
Fans	10,000			
Heaters	1,000			
		2,43,500		
To Excess of Income Over Expenditure		2,30,500		
		17,33,000		17,33,000

BALANCE SHEET OF SARASWATI HOSTEL

as on 31st December, 2024

Liabilities		₹	*Assets*		₹
Capital Fund		47,00,000	Land	₹	5,00,000
General Fund :	₹		Building	42,00,000	
Opening Balance	3,00,000		*Less* : Depreciation	2,10,000	
Add : Excess of Income					39,90,000
over Expenditure	2,30,500		Furniture & Fixtures	1,50,000	
		5,30,500	*Less* : Depreciation	22,500	
Security Deposit		2,67,000			1,27,500
			Fans	50,000	
			Less : Depreciation	10,000	
					40,000
			Heaters	5,000	
			Less : Depreciation	1,000	
					4,000
			Investments :		
			Govt. Securities		5,00,000

		Closing Stock :		
		Food	15,000	
		Fuel	5,000	
		Drinks	3,000	
		Sundries	2,000	
				25,000
		Cash at Bank		3,11,000
	54,97,500			54,97,500

Accounts of Hospitals

As hospitals are non-profit institutions, they prepare Receipts and Payment Account, Income and Expenditure Account and Balance Sheet as other organisations without profit motive prepare.

Various items of income in case of a hospital may be the following :

1. Room and bed rents.
2. Food charges.
3. Medical care.
4. Operating room charges.
5. Delivery room charges.
6. Anaesthesia charges.
7. X-ray charges.
8. Laboratory charges.
9. Pharmacy charges.
10. Physical therapy.
11. Dentistry income.
12. Collections on patient's accounts written off.
13. Contributed services of personnel. Under this item, value of donated service of full time or part time personnel who do not receive full salaries or other monetary compensation is taken. Entry for this is :

    Salaries Account Dr.

    To Contributed Services Account.
14. Grants—Sponsors and Government for operating needs of the hospital. Grants received for providing fixed assets like building, furniture and fixed equipment are capitalised.
15. Subscriptions
16. Donations—Cash and value free supplies.
17. Fees from nurses getting training in nurses training school.
18. Interest on investments.
19. Miscellaneous income.

Various types of expenses in case of a hospital may be the following :

1. Salaries and wages.
2. Diet expenses.
3. Surgery and dispensary expenses.
4. Office expenses.
5. Depreciation.
6. Repairs and maintenance.
7. Laundry and linen expenses.
8. Operation plant and X-ray plant expenses.
9. Laboratory and pharmacy expenses.
10. Motor service expenses.
11. Other expenses.

To get total income or expenses under each head, columnar Charges Book, Purchases Book and Cash Book should be prepared. A Patient Account should be opened for each patient in the Patients' Accounts Receivable Ledger to keep a record of daily charges charged to the patient and amount deposited by him/her and finally amount due to or from him/her when he/she is discharged. The ruling of the Patient's Accounts Receivable Ledger is shown on the **next page**.

PATIENTS' ACCOUNTS RECEIVABLE LEDGER

Name.. Indoor/Outdoor...................... Ward.................... Room/Bed No.................

Address....................................... Admitted on....................... Discharged on........................

Salary/Wages per month..................

Date	Room/Bed Charges ₹	Food Charges ₹	Medical Care ₹	Operation Charges ₹	Delivery Charges ₹	Anaesthesia Charges ₹	X-ray Charges ₹	Pharmacy Charges ₹	Lab. Charges ₹	Other Charges ₹	Total ₹	Conce-ssion ₹	Amount Deposited ₹	Balance	
														Dr.	Cr.

ILLUSTRATION 19. Surya Trust runs a **charitable hospital and a dispensary** and for the year ended 31st March, 2025, the following balances were extracted from its books :

		Dr. ₹	*Cr.* ₹
Capital Fund			18,00,000
Donation received in the year			12,00,000
Fees received from patients			6,00,000
Recovery for amenities—rent etc.			5,50,000
Recovery for food supplies			2,80,000
Surgical Equipments		9,10,000	
Buildings, Theatres etc.		6,40,000	
Consumption of			
Medicines	2,40,000		
Foodstuffs	1,80,000		
Chemicals etc.	60,000		
		4,80,000	
Closing Stock of :			
Medicines etc.	40,000		
Foodstuffs	8,000		
Chemicals etc.	2,000		
		50,000	
Sales of Medicines (dispensary)			6,20,000
Opening Stock of Medicines (dispensary)		1,10,000	
Purchases of Medicines (dispensary)		6,00,000	
Salaries :			
Administrative staff	60,000		
Doctors, nurses, etc.	3,00,000		
Assistants at dispensary	30,000		
		3,90,000	
Electricity and power charges etc.			
Hospital	2,10,000		
Dispensary	4,000		
		2,14,000	
Furniture, fittings and equipments		1,60,000	
Ambulance		60,000	
Postage, telephone charges etc. *less* recovery		52,000	
Subscription to medical journals		42,000	
Ambulance maintenance charges less recoveries			1,600
Consumption of linen, bedsheets, etc.		1,80,000	
Fixed Deposit (made on 10-8-2023 for three years at interest of 11% p.a.)		10,00,000	
Cash in hand		12,100	
Cash at Bank		70,500	
Sundry Debtors (dispensary)		1,21,000	
Sundry Creditors (dispensary)			82,000
Remuneration to trustees, trust office expenses etc.		42,000	
		51,33,600	51,33,600

Additional information :

(*i*) The dispensary supplies medicines to Hospital on requisitions and delivery notes; for which no adjustment has been made in the books. Cost of such supplies in the year was ₹ 1,20,000.

(*ii*) Stock of medicines at close at dispensary was ₹ 80,000;

(*iii*) Donations were received towards the corpus of the trust;

(*iv*) Stock of medicines on 31st March, 2025 at the Hospital included ₹ 8,000 worth of medicines belonging to patients; this has not been considered in arriving the figure of consumption of medicines;

(*v*) One of the well-wishers donated Surgery Equipment, whose market value was ₹ 80,000 on 15th August, 2024;

(*vi*) The Hospital is to receive a grant of 25% of the amount spent on treatment of poor patients from the local branch of the Red Cross Society. Such expenditure in the year was ₹ 1 lakhs.

(*vii*) Out of the fees recovered from the patients, 10% is to given to specialists as retained.

(*viii*) Depreciations on assets, on closing balances, is to be provided on :

Surgical Equipments	20%
Buildings	5%
Furniture and Fittings	10%
Ambulance	30%

Prepare Income and Expenditure of the Dispensary, Trust and Hospital for the year ended 31st March, 2025 and Statement of Affairs of the Trust as on that date.

(*CA—IPCE Nov. 2009 Modified & I.C.W.A. Inter*)

SOLUTION

Surya Trust

INCOME AND EXPENDITURE OF THE DISPENSARY

for the year ending 31st March, 2025

Expenditure	₹	*Income*	₹
To Opening Stock of Medicines	1,10,000	By Sales of Medicines	6,20,000
To Purchases of Medicines	6,00,000	By Supplies of Medicines to Hospital	1,20,000
To Salaries of Assistants	30,000	By Closing Stock of Medicines etc.	80,000
To Electric Charges	4,000		
To Surplus carried to the General Trust Income and Expenditure A/c	76,000		
	8,20,000		8,20,000

INCOME AND EXPENDITURE ACCOUNT OF THE HOSPITAL

for the year ending 31st March, 2025

Expenditure	₹	₹	*Income*	₹
To Consumption of			By Fees recovered from Patients	6,00,000
Medicines	2,40,000		By Recovery for Amenities—	
Add : Supplies of			Rent etc.	5,50,000
Medicines			By Recovery for Food Supplies	2,80,000
from Dispensary	1,20,000		By Ambulance Receipts less	
Medicines belonging			Maintenance Charges	1,600
to Patients	8,000		By Grants receivable from Red Cross	
		3,68,000	(25% of ₹ 1,00,000)	25,000

To Consumption of Food Stuffs		1,80,000	By Excess of Expenditure over	
To Consumption of Chemicals		60,000	Income *i.e.* Deficit	2,67,400
To Salaries to :				
Doctors, Nurses, etc.	3,00,000			
Administrative Staff	60,000			
		3,60,000		
To Returns due to Specialists —10% of ₹ 6,00,000 Fees from Patients		60,000		
To Electricity and Power Charges		2,10,000		
To Subscription to Journals		42,000		
To Consumption of Linen, Bed sheets, etc.		1,80,000		
To Depreciation of :				
Surgical Equipments @ 20% on ₹ 9,90,000	1,98,000			
Building @ 5% on ₹ 6,40,000	32,000			
Furniture & Fittings @ 10% on ₹ 1,60,000	16,000			
Ambulance @ 30% on ₹ 60,000	18,000			
		2,64,000		
		17,24,000		17,24,000

INCOME AND EXPENDITURE ACCOUNT OF THE TRUST

for the year ending 31st March, 2025

	₹		₹
To Deficit in Hospital A/c	2,67,400	By Surplus from Dispensary	76,000
To Postage, Telephone Charges etc. less Recoveries	52,000	By Interest due on Fixed Deposit @ 11% on ₹ 10,00,000	1,10,000
To Remuneration to Trustees, Truste Office Expenses etc.	42,000	By Net Deficit of the Trust for the year	1,75,400
	3,61,400		3,61,400

STATEMENT OF AFFAIRS OF SURYA TRUST

as on 31-3-2025

Liabilities	₹	₹	*Assets*	₹	₹
Sundry Creditors (Dispensary)		82,000	Cash in hand		12,100
Returns due to Specialists		60,000	Cash at Bank		70,500
Capital Fund as on 1-4-2024	18,00,000		Fixed Deposit	10,00,000	
Add : Donations	12,00,000		*Add* : Interest Due	1,10,000	
Market Value of Gift of Equipment	80,000				11,10,000
			Sundry Debtors		1,21,000
			Grant Receivable from Red Cross		25,000
	30,80,000		Stock of Medicines		80,000
Less : Deficit for the year	1,75,400		Stock in the Hospital :		
		29,04,600	Medicines (40,000 – 8,000)	32,000	
			Food Stuffs	8,000	
			Chemicals etc.	2,000	
					42,000

		Surgical Equipments	9,10,000	
		Add : Gift Received	80,000	
			9,90,000	
		Less: Depreciation	1,98,000	
				7,92,000
		Ambulance	60,000	
		Less : Depreciation	18,000	
				42,000
		Furniture & Fittings	1,60,000	
		Less : Depreciation	16,000	
				1,44,000
		Building, Theatre, etc.	6,40,000	
		Less : Depreciation	32,000	
				6,08,000
	30,46,600			30,46,600

QUESTIONS

OBJECTIVE TYPE

1. Fill in the Blanks :

(*i*) ...... Account is a summary of cash transactions.

(*ii*) All ...... and revenue items are recorded in Receipts and Payments Account.

(*iii*) Receipts and Payments Account records transactions relating to ...... periods.

(*iv*) Income and Expenditure Account is prepared from transactions relating to ...... items only.

(*v*) The difference between Income and Expenditure or *vice versa* is called ....

(*vi*) Difference between assets and liabilities is called ...... Fund.

(*vii*) When there is specific fund, income and expenditure relating to that are adjusted on the ...... side of Balance Sheet.

(*viii*) Four main sources through which amounts are collected by the educational institutions are (*i*) fees collected from students, (*ii*) security deposits from students, (*iii*) donations from public, and (*iv*)...........

(*ix*) Account of each student is opened in ....

(*x*) All the educational institutions should maintain...........for various types of collections.

(*xi*) All the educational institutions usually follow...........as their accounting year.

(*xii*) A...........should be separately maintained for keeping a record of the securities.

(*xiii*) Under contributed services of personnel, value of ....of full time or part time personnel who do not receive full salaries or other monetary compensation is taken.

(*xiv*) A patient account should be opened for each patient in the ....

Ans. [(*i*) Receipts and Payment; (*ii*) Capital; (*iii*) All; (*iv*) revenue; (*v*) Surplus or deficit; (*vi*) Capital or General; (*vii*) liabilities; (*viii*) grants received from the Government; (*ix*) students' ledger; (*x*) a Collection Register; (*xi*) financial year; (*xii*) Security Register; (*xiii*) donated service; (*xiv*) Patients' Accounts Receivable Ledger]

2. State with reasons whether the following statements re 'True' or False' :

(*i*) Receipts and Payments Account is merely summary of cash transactions.

(*ii*) The receipts and payments account records receipts and payments of revenue nature only.

(*iii*) If there appears sports fund, the expenses incurred on sports activities will be taken into income and expenditure account.

(*iv*) Receipts and Payments Account highlights total income and expenditure.
(*v*) Only revenue items are disclosed in Income and Expenditure Account.
(*vi*) Subscriptions in advance in the current year are treated as assets of the Not For Profit Organisation.
(*vii*) In case there is a Prize Fund, any income received or accrued from this fund would be added to Prize Fund Account.
(*viii*) Receipts from the sale of an old furniture is considered as on ordinary income.

Ans. [True : (*i*), (*v*), (*vii*); False : (*ii*), (*iii*), (*iv*), (*vi*), (*vii*)]

3. In each of the following cases, indicate which you consider to be correct :

(*a*) Not-for-profit organisations institutions prepare :
(*i*) Profit and loss account (*ii*) manufacturing account (*iii*) Income and expenditure account.

(*b*) Receipt and Payments Account is :
(*i*) A nominal account (*ii*) A real account (*ii*) A personal account.

(*c*) Receipts and Payment Account shows :
(*i*) Income and expenditure (*ii*) Cash receipts and payments (*iii*) Assets and liabilities.

(*d*) Income and expenditure account reveals :
(*i*) Cash in hand (*ii*) Surplus or deficiency (*iii*) Capital account.

(*e*) Income and expenditure account records transactions of :
(*i*) Revenue nature only, (*iii*) Capital nature only, (*iii*) Both capital and revenue nature.

(*f*) Subscription received in advance is :
(*i*) an income (*ii*) an Asset (*iii*) liability.

(*g*) Subscription in arrears (given in adjustment) are shown on the :
(*i*) Credit side of income and expenditure account and assets side of the balance sheet, (*ii*) Debit side of income and expenditure and liabilities side of the balance sheet, (*iii*) only on the assets side of balance sheet.

(*h*) Donation received for a specific purpose :
(*i*) should be credited to a separate account and shown on the liabilities side of the Balance Sheet (*ii*) should be credited to income and expenditure account (*iii*) should not be recorded at all.

(*i*) If there is a prize fund then prizes awarded, expenses and income are transformed to :
(*i*) Income and expenditure account, (*ii*) Assets side of the Balance Sheet, (*iii*) The liability side of the balance sheet, (*iv*) Both income and expenditure account and to balance sheet.

(*j*) Admission fee income should be :
(*i*) capitalised (*ii*) treated as a revenue (*iii*) treated as revenue unless the amount is pretty large (*iv*) treated as a liability.

(*k*) Income and Expenditure Account is a
(*i*) Real account (*ii*) Personal account (*iii*) Nominal account (*iv*) None of these.

Ans. [(*a*) : (*iii*) ; (*b*) : (*ii*) ; (*c*) : (*ii*) ; (*d*) : (*ii*) ; (*e*) : (*i*) ; (*f*) : (*iii*) ; (*g*) : (*i*) ; (*h*) : (*i*) ; (*i*) : (*iii*) ; (*j*) : (*iii*); (*k*) : (*iii*)].

SHORT ANSWER TYPE

1. "Receipts and Payments Account is a real account". Explain this in about 100 words.
2. Give four points of distinction between Receipts and Payments Account and Income and Expenditure Account.
3. Give four points for conversion of Receipts and Payments Account into Income and Expenditure Account.

4. How will you convert Income and Expenditure Account into Receipts and Payments Account ?

5. How are donations treated in Income and Expenditure Account and Balance Sheet ?

6. How will you treat the following items while preparing final accounts of not-for-profit organisations:

(*a*) Specific Donations
(*b*) Entrance fees
(*c*) Subscription
(*d*) Life Membership Fees.
(*e*) Legacy
(*f*) Honorarium
(*g*) Specific Fund and related expenses and items of income.

7. Ascertain the missing information :

	(*i*) ₹	(*ii*) ₹
Outstanding Expenses :		
This year	2,000	1,200
Last year	3,000	1,800
Accrued Income :		
This year	1,000	1,600
Last year	1,500	1,000
Prepaid Expenses :		
This year	850	980
Last year	600	560
Income received in advance :		
This year	1,400	1,180
Last year	890	490
Income on Cash Basis (This year)	42,850	?
Income on Accrual Basis (This year)	?	38,970

Ans. [(*i*) ₹ 43,090 ; (*ii*) ₹ 38,040].

8. How will you deal with the following case while preparing the final accounts as on 31st March, 2025 :

BALANCE SHEET
as on 1st April, 2024

Liabilities	₹	*Assets*	₹
Creditors for sports Materials	150	Sports Material	200

RECEIPTS AND PAYMENTS ACCOUNT
for the year ended 31st March, 2025

Liabilities	₹	*Assets*	₹
Sports Material	90	Sports Material	3,500

Additional Information : Sports Material in Hand on 31st March, 2025 ₹ 550.

Ans. [Amount to be shown as expenditure in the Income and Expenditure Account ₹ 3,000. Sports Material to be shown as an asset in the Balance Sheet as at 31-3-2025 ₹ 550].

9. How will you deal with the following items while preparing for the Delhi Cricket Club, its Income and Expenditure Account for the year ended 31st March, 2025 and its Balance Sheet as on that date.

(*i*) Donations received during the year for the construction of Pavilion ₹ 7,54,000 ; Expenditure incurred upto 31-3-2025 on its construction ₹ 5,92,000 ; (The construction work is continuing, the total estimated ; expenditure of construction of Pavilion being ₹ 20,00,000) ; (*ii*) Tournament Fund; Balance as on 1st April, 2024 ₹ 3,760 ; Subscriptions received during the year ₹ 18,400 ;

Expenditure incurred during the year on conducting tournaments ₹ 20,200 ; (*iii*) Life-membership fees received during the year ₹ 16,000. Give reasons for your answer.

Ans. **[(*i*) ₹ 1,62,000 (*i.e.* ₹ 7,54,000 – ₹ 5,92,000) shown on the liabilities side of the Balance Sheet.**

(*ii*) ₹ 1,960 (*i.e.* ₹ 3,760 + ₹ 18,400 –₹ 20,200) is shown on the liabilities side in the Balance Sheet.

(*iii*) ₹ 16,000 is capitalised and shown on the liabilities side of the Balance Sheet.

10. How will you deal with the following in the Income and Expenditure Account and Balance Sheet of a club as on 31st March, 2025 ?

	₹		₹
Subscription received during 2024-25	25,000	Subscription received in advance as on 1-4-2024	7,500
Subscription Outstanding on 1-4-2024	5,000		
Subscription Outstanding on 31-3-2025	10,000	Subscription received in advance as on 31-3-2025	5,000

Ans. **[₹ 32,500].**

11. Prepare "Subscription Account' from the following items for the year ending on 31st March 2025 : (*i*) Subscriptions in arrear on 31st March, 2024 ₹ 500 ; (*ii*) Subscriptions received in advance at 31st March, 2024 for 2024-25 ₹ 1,100 ; (*iii*) Total Subscriptions received during 2024-25 (including ₹ 400 for 2023-24, ₹ 1,200 for 2025-26) ₹ 35,400 ; (*iv*) Subscriptions outstanding for 2024-25 ₹ 400.

Ans. **[₹ 35,300 to be taken as Income in Income & Expenditure A/c].**

12. Calculate what amount will be posted to Income and Expenditure Account for the year ending 31st March, 2025 : Stock of Stationery on 1st April, 2024 ₹ 600 ; Creditors for Stationery on 1st April, 2024 ₹ 400 ; Advances paid for Stationery Carried Forward from 2023-24 ₹ 40 ; Amount paid for Stationery during the year 2024-25 ₹ 2,160 ; Stock of Stationary on 31st March 2025 ₹ 100 ; Creditors for Stationery on 31st March, 2025 ₹ 260 ; Advances paid for Stationery on 31st March, 2025 ₹ 60.

Ans. **[Stationery actually used during the year ₹ 2,500]**

13. Rangakarmi, an amateur theatre organisation, charges its members an annual subscription of ₹ 200 per member. It accrues for subscription owing at the end of each year and also adjusts for subscriptions received in advance. The organisation closes its accounts every year at 31st December. Following particulars are available :

(1) On 1st January, 2024, 20 members owed ₹ 4,000 for the year 2023.

(2) In December 2023, 5 members paid ₹ 1,000 for the year 2024.

(3) During the year 2024, the organisation received cash subscriptions of ₹ 85,000. The details are:

For 2023	₹	4,000
For 2024	₹	79,000
For 2025	₹	2,000
Total	₹	85,000

(4) At close of 31st December 2024, 15 members had not paid their 2024 subscriptions. Prepare the subscriptions account. ***(ICWA—Stage II, June 2006 Modified)***

Ans. **[Subscription of ₹ 83,000 will be transferred and shown on credit side of Income and Expenditure Account]**

14. The following information of M/s. TT Club is related for the year ended 31st March, 2025 :

1. *Balances*	*As on 1-4-2024*	*As on 31-3-2025*
	₹	₹
Stock of Sports Material	75,000	1,12,500
Amount due for Sports Material	67,500	97,500

Subscription due	11,250		16,500
Subscription received in advance	9,000		5,250
2. Subscription received during the year		₹ 3,75,000	
3. Payments for Sports Material during the year		₹ 2,25,000	

You are required to :

(A) Ascertain the amount of Subscription and Sports Material that will appear in Income and Expenditure Account for the year ended 31-3-2025 and

(B) Also show how these items would appear in the Balance Sheet as on 31-3-2025.

(Inter IPC, Nov. 2015 Modified)

Ans. [Amounts to appear in Income and Expenditure A/c : Subscription ₹ 3,84,000 as Income and Sports Material ₹ 2,17,500 as Expenditure ; Amounts to Appear in Balance Sheet : Subscription Received in Advance ₹ 5,250 as a Liability; Subscription Receivable ₹ 16,500 as an Asset; Amount Due for Sports Material ₹ 97,500 as a Liability; Stock of Sports Material ₹ 1,12,500 as an Asset.]

LONG ANSWER TYPE

1. Distinguish between profitable and not-for-profit organisations. Why is it necessary to keep the books of accounts in case of such concerns ?
2. Discuss the main characteristics of Receipts and Payments Account and Income and Expenditure Account. In what concerns these are prepared ?
3. Distinguish between a Receipts and Payments Account and an Income and Expenditure Account. How will you convert a Receipts and Payment Account into an Income and Expenditure Account ?
4. How will you treat the following while preparing final accounts of not-for-profit organisations ?
   (*i*) Legacy ; (*ii*) Donations ; (*iii*) Entrance Fees ; (*iv*) Sale of an asset ; (*v*) Life Membership fees ; (*vi*) Sale of old newspapers or obsolete items ; (*vii*) Treatment of specific funds.
5. How will you prepare the Balance Sheet both at the beginning and at the end of the accounting period from a given Receipts and Payments Account and an Income and Expenditure Account ?
6. What procedure will you follow to prepare Receipts and Payments Account from a given Income and Expenditure Account with accompanying notes ?
7. How would you deal with (*i*) Donations—general and specific and (*ii*) Legacy, in the final accounts of a not-for-profit organisations ?
8. What types of persons prepare receipts and expenditure account. What are the special features of the type of account ?
9. Distinguish between Profit & Loss Account and Income and Expenditure Account.
10. Write a note on Receipts & Expenditure Account.
11. Distinguish between Receipts & Payments A/c and Cash Book.
12. Write short notes on the following : (*a*) Accounting for educational institutions. (*b*) Accounting for hostels. (*c*) Accounting for hospitals.

PRACTICAL PROBLEMS

PREPARATION OF INCOME & EXPENDITURE ACCOUNT AND BALANCE SHEET FROM TRIAL BALANCE

1. From the following Trial Balance, prepare an Income and Expenditure Account of the *Delhi Club* for the year ended 31st March, 2025 and a Balance Sheet as on that date. Depreciate Furniture by

10%, Billiards Tables and Accessories by 20% and China Glass, Cutlery, etc. by $33\frac{1}{3}$%. Of the subscriptions ₹ 400 is paid in advance and ₹ 250 is in arrears. ₹ 300 is owing for salaries to staff.

Dr. Balances :	₹	*Dr. Balances* :	₹
Furniture	2,500	Cost of Annual Dinner	760
Billiards Table & Accessories (bought in 2023)	1,250	Sundry Debtors	1,170
		Cash at Bank	4,800
China, Glass, Cutlery, etc.	333	Cash in Hand	174
Repairs	734	*Cr. Balances* :	₹
Salaries and Wages	2,262	Members' Subscription	10,560
Rent and Telephone	3,194	Sundry Receipts from Billiards, etc.	1,743
Fuel and Light	1,618	Sale of Tickets for Entertainment	3,234
Cost of Entertainment	2,190	Sundry Creditors	2,600
Sundry Expenses	1,600	Entrance Fees	448
		Capital Fund	4,000

Ans. [Surplus ₹ 2,566 ; B/S Total ₹ 9,866].

2. Mary Sports Club provides the following Receipts & Payments for the year ending 31st March, 2025 :

RECEIPTS AND PAYMENTS ACCOUNT

Receipts	*Amount* ₹	*Payments*	*Amount* ₹
To Cash & Bank Balances b/d	36,900	By Municipal Taxes	6,800
To Subscription	57,300	By Salaries	36,000
To Donations (received for meeting capital expenditure)	25,000	By Electricity Charges	2,300
		By Sports Material	4,000
To Interest on Investments	5,000	By Books for Library	17,000
To Other Income	1,200	By Newspapers	1,425
		By Miscellaneous Expenses	1,235
		By Cash & Bank Balances c/d	56,640
	1,25,400		1,25,400

Assets	*As on 31-3-2024*
(1) Books at Library	22,000
(2) Furniture & Fixtures	20,000
(3) Subscription Receivable	7,500
(4) Investment	75,000
(5) Accrued Interest on Investment	1,750
(6) Sports Material	12,000

Assets as on 31-3-25 are as follows :

(1) Subscription receivable—₹ 17,500; (2) Accrued Interest on Investments—₹ 1,750

Outstanding Expenses	*31-3-2024*	*31-3-2025*
(*a*) Salaries	4,000	6,000
(*b*) Newspapers	350	450
(*c*) Municipal Taxes	850	950
(*d*) Electricity Charges	1,350	1,500

Depreciation to be provided at the following rates :

Furniture and Fixtures @ 10% p.a.; Sports Material @ 25% p.a.; Books at Library @ 10% p.a.

You are required to prepare Mary Sports Club's Opening Balance Sheet as on 1-4-2024, Income and Expenditure Account for the year ended on 31st March, 2025 and Balance Sheet as on that date. Assume that additions in Sports Materials and Library Books are made at the beginning of the year.

Ans. [Beginning Capital Fund ₹ 1,68,600; Surplus ₹ 13,540; Balance Sheet Total ₹ 2,15,990]

PREPARATION OF INCOME & EXPENDITURE ACCOUNT AND BALANCE SHEET FROM GIVEN RECEIPTS & PAYMENTS A/C AND ADDITIONAL INFORMATION

3. Following is the statement of Receipts and Payments of *Krishna Charitable Institution* for the year 2024-25.

Receipts		₹	*Payments*	₹
To Balance :	₹		By Charities	14,500
Cash on Deposit	5,000		By Salaries	2,600
Cash on Current A/c	2,400		By Rent and Taxes	1,200
Cash in hand	300		By Printing	300
		7,700	By Postage	100
To Donations		8,000	By Advertisement	250
" Subscriptions		7,000	By Furniture	750
" Endowment Fund Receipts		15,000	By Insurance	750
" Legacies		3,000	By Investments	14,000
" Interest on Investment		9,500	By Advance Building	5,000
" Interest on Deposit		150	By Balance—Cash on Deposit	8,000
" Sales of old Newspaper		75	Cash on Current Account	2,250
			Cash in hand	725
		50,425		50,425

Prepare the Income and Expenditure Account for the year ended 31st March, 2025 after considering the following :

(*a*) It was decided to treat one-half of the amounts received on account of Donations as income.

(*b*)

	1-4-2024	*31-3-2025*
	₹	₹
Rent Due	250	300
Prepaid Rent	350	200
Salaries Due	150	450
Advertisement Due	100	150
Subscription Due	200	400
Subscription paid in Advance	400	500

(*c*) Interest on Investments ₹ 400, though accrued, was not actually received.

Ans. [Surplus ₹ 975]

4. From the following particulars, which relate to a Musical Society, prepare an Income and Expenditure Account and a Balance Sheet as at 31st March, 2025.

BALANCE SHEET

as on 31st March, 2024

Liabilities	₹	*Assets*	₹
Outstanding Rent	425	Cash at Bank	3,000

Capital Fund	15,575	Government Securities	10,000
		Accrued Interest	125
		Outstanding Subscription	400
		Library Books	1,000
		Furniture and Fittings	1,475
	16,000		16,000

The transactions for the year were :

Receipts : Subscription ₹ 2,500; Proceeds received from Entertainment and Lectures ₹ 1,000; Interest on Securities ₹ 475; Entrance fees received ₹ 500; Sale proceeds of old chairs ₹ 75 (Book Value ₹ 100).

Payments : Rent ₹ 600; Printing ₹ 150; Advertising ₹ 200; Sundries ₹ 55; Government Securities ₹ 2,500; Furniture ₹ 400; Library Books ₹ 300; Cost of Entertainment ₹ 750.

Following were outstanding as on 31st March, 2025; Printing ₹ 75; Rent ₹ 100; Interest on securities ₹ 150 and Subscription ₹ 325.

Ans. **[Surplus ₹ 2,895; Balance Sheet Total ₹ 18,645].**

Hint. Prepare Receipts and Payments Account to find cash balance on 31st March, 2025, which is ₹ 2,595.

5. Balance Sheet of a *Public Library* stood as follows on the 31st March, 2024 :

Liabilities	₹	*Assets*	₹	₹
Outstanding Creditors for Expenses	700	Cash at Bank		4,000
Creditors on Accounts	4,300	Sundry Debtors :		
Capital Fund :		For Subscriptions outstanding	1,000	
Accumulated Excess of Income over Expenditure	70,000	For Lecture Hall	400	1,400
		Investment in 5% Government Loans		6,000
		Library Books		20,000
		Furniture		3,500
		Buildings		40,000
		Prepaid Insurance		100
	75,000			75,000

Cash transactions for the year ending 31st March, 2025 were as follows :

Receipts	₹	*Payments*	₹
To Bank Balance	4,000	By Payment to Creditors on Open Accounts	4,300
" Entrance Fees	1,200	" Additions to Library Books	1,400
" Subscriptions	12,500	" Electric Light	300
" Proceeds from Lectures and Entertainments	4,500	" Municipal Taxes	1,100
" Rent Received from Use of Hall	1,500	" Repairs	800
" Interest on Investments	200	" Insurance	350
To Sale of Old Newspapers	450	By Electric Installation Expenses	2,000
" Sale of Old Furniture	100	" Payment to Creditors for Expenses (last year)	700

		To Printing and Stationery	500
		" Sundry Expenses	250
		" Postage	420
		" Subscription to Periodicals	1,400
		" Cost of Investments Bought	3,000
		" Salaries	3,600
		" Balance at Bank	4,330
	24,450		24,450

Insurance was prepaid to the extent of ₹ 75 and subscription outstanding amounted to ₹ 1,800, ₹ 250 were owing for use of Lecture Hall and ₹ 300 for interest on investments had accrued due. There were creditors outstanding for new steel shelves acquired during the year amounting to ₹ 1,750. There were also owing for salaries ₹ 500 and stationery ₹ 75. Entrance Fees are to be capitalised. Depreciate Buildings by 2%, Electric Installation and Furniture by 5% each and Library Books by 10%; such depreciation to be calculated on the opening balance of the assets in question.

You are required to prepare an Income and Expenditure Account and a Balance Sheet for the year ended 31st March, 2025.

Ans. [Surplus ₹ 7,805 ; B/S Total ₹ 81,330].

6. Receipts and Payments of *Bombay Gymkhana* for the year ending 31st March, 2025 are as under:

	₹		₹
To Balance on 1st April, 2024	1,375	By Salaries	4,760
" Donations	10,430	" Taxes	390
" Subscription	7,445	" Wages	1,440
" Entrance Fees	1,200	" Printing and Stationery	630
" Interest etc.	1,330	" Postage	120
" Surplus from Matches	2,700	" Repairs	950
		" Subscription of Newspapers	1,230
		" Balance on 31-3-2025	14,960
	24,480		24,480

You are required to prepare the Income and Expenditure Account for the year 2024-25 and Balance Sheet as at 31st March, 2025 on the basis of the following additional information :

(*a*) The subscription to newspapers included ₹ 20 paid for the year 2023-24 and ₹ 30 for the year 2025-26.

(*b*) Half the amount of entrance fees and 10% of the surplus income from matches should be credited to Building Fund Account. The credit balance in this account as on 1st April, 2024 was ₹ 3,000.

(*c*) All the donations are to be credited to the Capital Fund.

(*d*) Following bills were outstanding on 31st March, 2025.
Wages ₹ 150 ; Stationery ₹ 72 ; Furniture Purchased ₹ 250.

(*e*) Depreciate Building and Motor Car by 10% and Furniture by ₹ 70.

(*f*) Subscription received ₹ 40 for the year 2025-26.

(*g*) Other assets on 1st April, 2024 were :

Buildings ₹ 11,000 ; Furniture ₹ 3,200 ; Investment ₹ 3,000 ; Motor Car ₹ 3,200.

Ans. [Surplus ₹ 583 : B/S Total ₹ 34,150 ; Beginning Capital Fund ₹ 18,755].

7. Following is the Receipts and Payments Account of the Delhi Literary Society for the year ended 31st March, 2025 :

	₹		₹
To Cash at Bank	12,500	By Salaries	2,500
To Subscriptions	52,500	By Printing and Stationery	1,250
To Annual Day Receipts	26,800	By Annual Day Expenses	1,500
To Mushaira Receipts	22,500	By Mushaira Expenses	10,000
To Dividends on Shares	2,500	By Telephone Charges	2,500
		By Sundry Expenses	2,000
		By Shares Purchased	75,000
		By Postage and Telegrams	2,200
		By Building Maintenance	6,340
		By Cash at Bank	13,510
	1,16,800		1,16,800

Following further information is furnished :

1. The value of the Building owned by the Society stood at ₹ 50,000 as at 1st April, 2024. Depreciation at 5 per cent has to be provided.
2. There were 200 members paying subscriptions at the rate of ₹ 250 per annum each.
3. As on 1st April 2024 no subscriptions had been received in advance but subscriptions were outstanding to the extent of ₹ 1,000 as at 31st March, 2024 and on 31st March, 2025 subscriptions outstanding were ₹ 1,500.
4. Postage Stamps worth ₹ 250 were with the Secretary at the beginning of the year and the stamps at the end of the value of ₹ 150.
5. The investment in shares at the beginning of the year was to the extent of ₹ 5,000
6. An amount of ₹ 250 in respect of the Annual Day Receipts was yet to be received.
7. The rent of the theatre (amounting ₹ 2,500) where the Mushaira (poetic symposium) was held is still to be paid.
8. Hire of telephone to the extent of ₹ 300 is paid in advance.

You are required to prepare the Income and Expenditure Account for the year ended 31st March, 2025 and the Balance Sheet as at that date.

Ans. [Surplus ₹ 68,960 ; B/S Total ₹ 1,43,210 ; Beginning Capital Fund ₹ 68,750].

8. Following is the Receipts and Payments Account of *Saraswati Club* for the year ended 31st March, 2025 :

		₹			₹
Cash in hand (1-4-2024)		1,500	Bank Overdraft (1-4-2024)		3,100
Subscriptions :	₹		Investment in Securities		3,000
2023-24	300		Furniture (old)		1,450
2024-25	16,200		Salaries		6,200
2025-26	150		Stationery & Printing		890
		16,650	Misc. Expenses		1,420
Income from Entertainments		310	Balance on 31-3-2025 :	₹	
Entrance Fees		670	Cash in Hand	550	
Interest on Securities		480	Cash at Bank	3,100	
Sale proceeds of old chairs (Book value ₹ 120)		100			3,650
		19,710			19,710

Prepare Income and Expenditure Account of the club for the year ended 31st March, 2025 and a Balance Sheet as at that date having due regard to the following additional information :

(i) The Club has 1,800 members, each paying an annual subscription of ₹ 10. Subscription amounting to ₹ 90 are still in arrears in respect of the year 2023-24.

(ii) Stock of stationery on 31st March, 2024 was ₹ 125 and at 31st March, 2025 ₹ 87.

(iii) Entrance fees are to be capitalised.

(iv) Salary of ₹ 550 for March, 2025 is outstanding. Expenses accruing at 31st March, 2024 amounted to ₹ 132. The club has paid ₹ 500 in the year 2023-24 towards telephone charges of which ₹ 125 relate to 2024-25.

(v) As on 31st March, 2024 Premises stand in books at ₹ 24,500 and Investments at ₹ 6,500. Depreciate Premises and Furniture by 5 per cent.

Ans. [Surplus ₹ 8,387 ; B/S Total ₹ 39,665 ; Beginning Capital Fund ₹ 29,908].

9. Following is the Receipts and Payments Account of M/s *Tiptop Club* for the year ended 31st March, 2025 :

Receipts	₹	*Payments*	₹
To Cash in hand on 1st April, 2024	9,000	By Payments for Cosmetics	15,000
To Subscription	45,000	By Honorarium to Beautician	8,000
To Donation	4,500	By Salaries	18,000
To Interest on Investments at 6% for the year	3,000	By Sundry Expenses	1,000
		By Rent for Building	12,000
To Fashion Show Proceeds	50,500	By Equipments Purchased	13,000
		By Fashion Show Expenses	34,000
		By Cash in hand on 31st March, 2025	11,000
	1,12,000		1,12,000

***Additional Information* :**

	On 1st April, 2024	*On 31st March, 2025*
(i) Subscription due	500	2,000
(ii) Subscription received in advance	1,500	1,000
(iii) Stock of cosmetics	10,000	7,000
(iv) Amount due to cosmetics suppliers	8,000	11,000
(v) Rent paid in advance	1,000	1,500
(vi) Salary outstanding	1,500	2,000
(vii) Value of Equipments	21,500	29,000
(viii) Value of Furniture and Fixtures	40,000	36,000

You are required to prepare Income and Expenditure Account for the year ended 31st March, 2025 and Balance Sheet as on that date of M/s Tiptop Club. Show all workings.

Ans. [Surplus ₹ 1,500 ; Balance Sheet Total ₹ 1,36,500 ; Beginning Capital Fund ₹ 1,21,000]

10. Following is the Receipts and Payments Account of Mayur Club for the year ended 31st March, 2025 :

Receipts	₹	*Payments*	₹
Opening Balance (1-4-2024)		Payments :	
Cash on hand	39,100	Sports Materials	3,04,500
Cash at Bank	50,000	Salaries	3,15,000

Receipts :		Equipment Purchased on 1-10-24	60,000
Subscriptions :		Bank Fixed Deposits on 31-3-25	1,50,000
For the year 2023-24	18,000	Rent	1,48,500
For the year 2024-25	9,63,000	Ground Maintenance	22,120
For the year 2025-26	4,500	Insurance	38,400
Interest on Bank		Stationery	3,450
Fixed Deposits @ 10%	45,000	Sundry Expenses	5,880
		Closing Balance as on 31-3-2025	
		Cash on hand	31,750
		Cash at Bank	40,000
	11,19,600		11,19,600

Following additional information is provided to you :

(*i*) The club has 220 members. The annual subscription is ₹ 4,500 per member.

(*ii*) Depreciation to be provided on furniture at 10% p.a. and on sports equipment at 15% p.a.

(*iii*) On 31st March, 2025, stock of sports material in hand (after members use during the year) is valued at ₹ 78,000 and stock of stationery at ₹ 3,150. Rent for 1 month is outstanding. Unexpired insurance amounts to ₹ 9,600.

(*iv*) On 31st March, 2024 the club had the following assets :

Furniture ₹ 2,70,000 ; Sports Equipment ₹ 1,80,000 ; Bank Fixed Deposit ₹ 4,50,000 ; Stock of Stationery ₹ 1,500 ; Stock of Sports Material ₹ 73,500 ; Unexpired Insurance ₹ 8,400 ; Subscription in Arrear ₹ 22,500.

Note : There was no liability on 31-3-2024.

You are required to prepare :

(*i*) Income and Expenditure Account; and

(*ii*) Balance Sheet as at 31st March, 2025.

Ans. [Surplus ₹ 1,32,500; Balance Sheet Total ₹ 12,45,500; Beginning Capital Fund ₹ 10,95,000]

11. Following is the Receipts and Payments A/c of a club for the year ending 31st March, 2025 :

Receipts			₹	*Payments*			₹
To Balance			4,200	By Rent			14,000
" Donation			14,000	" Salary :			
" Subscriptions :				2023-24	₹	2,800	
2023-24	₹	2,100		2024-25	₹	8,400	
2024-25	₹	39,900					11,200
2025-26	₹	2,800		" Sports Material			12,600
			44,800	" Interest (6% Loan)			1,050
" Interest on Investments			2,800	" Match Expenses			5,600
" Entrance Fees			9,800	" Newspapers			1,400
				" Balance			29,750
			75,600				75,600

Outstanding subscription for 2024-25 was ₹ 2,800. Entrance fees for 2024-25 ₹ 1,400 was outstanding. Donation amount includes special donation for Match Fund ₹ 7,000. Outstanding expenses for 2024-25 were : Rent ₹ 1,400 ; Salary ₹ 2,800 and Repairs ₹ 700.

On 1st April 2024 the club had : Building ₹ 28,000 ; Sports Materials ₹ 14,000 ; Furniture ₹ 14,000 ; Match Fund Investments ₹ 21,000 (Interest accrued on that ₹ 700 was outstanding for the year 2024-25) ; Match Fund ₹ 21,000. Income for the year 2023-24 was ₹ 8,400. Sports Materials were valued at ₹ 17,500 on 31-3-2025.

Prepare Income and Expenditure A/c and Balance Sheet as on 31-3-2025

Ans. [Surplus ₹ 22,050 ; Capital Fund on 1-4-2024 ₹ 42,000 ; B/S Total ₹ 1,15,150].

12. Following is the Receipts and Payments Account of the *Delhi Club* for the year ended 31st March, 2025.

RECEIPTS AND PAYMENTS ACCOUNT

for the year ended 31st March, 2025

		₹			₹
To Balance b/f	₹		By Secretary's Remuneration		6,000
Cash	2,000		" Salary to Staff		5,000
Bank	10,000		" Canteen Expenses		12,000
		12,000	" Construction of Building		15,000
" Subscription—			" Balance c/d	₹	
For 2024-25	5,000		Cash	800	
For 2023-24	200		Bank	2,000	
For 2025-26	100				2,800
		5,300			
" Interest from 5% Govt. Security (purchased in the past at discount of 1%)		2,000			
" Sale of Old Furniture		1,000			
" Sale of Newspapers		500			
" Canteen Collection		10,000			
" Donation received for Building Fund		10,000			
		40,800			40,800

With the additional information given below, prepare Income and Expenditure Account for the year ended 31st March, 2025 and Balance Sheet as on that date :

	As on 31st March, 2024	*As on 31st March, 2025*
	₹	₹
(*a*) Subscription receivable	1,000	?
(*b*) Subscription received in advance	200	100
(*c*) Salaries to Staff outstanding	2,000	1,000
(*d*) Canteen Expenses prepaid	1,000	500
(*e*) Furniture etc.	10,000	?
(*f*) Construction expenses outstanding		2,000

(*g*) Subscription due for the year 2024-25 was ₹ 5,500

(*h*) The book value of furniture sold was ₹ 3,000.

(*i*) Charge Depreciation on furniture at 10% on the closing net balance.

Ans. [Deficit ₹ 7,200 ; B/S Total ₹ 67,300 ; Beginning Capital Fund ₹ 61,400].

13. From the following information available from the records of the *Indian Sports Association*, prepare an Income and Expenditure Account for the year ended 31st March, 2025.

	₹		₹
Subscription received	25,000	Tournament prizes awarded	7,000
Upkeep of playground	3,000	Donation received	11,000

Entrance fees received	8,000	Stock of Refreshment on 1-4-2024	540
Rent paid	1,200	Purchase of Canteen Stores and Refreshments	8,460
Salaries and wages	3,200	Cash and Bank Balances	47,000
Travelling expenses	900	Tournament Fund	10,000
Stock of equipment (1-4-2024)	9,000	General Fund	30,000
Tournament expenses	14,000	Subscription in arrears (1-4-2024) (For 2022-23 ₹ 2,000 ; For 2023-24 ₹ 12,000)	14,000
Printing and Stationery	3,000		
General charges	6,000		
Tournament fees received	25,000		
		Creditors for expenses	3,300

(*a*) Equipment is to be valued on the basis of revaluation at the end of the year. The Committee of Management has decided to have the equipment valued at 85% of its book value on 1st April 2024.

(*b*) Subscription in arrears as on 31st March, 2025 were as follows :
For 2022-23 ₹ 2,000 ; For 2023-24 ₹ 3,000 ; For 2024-25 ₹ 13,000

During the year, arrear subscription totalling ₹ 9,000 relating to the year 2023-24 had been collected.

(*c*) Donation of ₹ 11,000 include ₹ 4,000 received on tournament account.

(*d*) 25% of the entrance fees has to be capitalised.

(*e*) Stock of refreshments as on 31st March, 2025 was as under :

Value of provisions, stores, etc. ₹ 2,000 ; Value of eatables and perishables ₹ 500 ; Value of aerated water bottles, cigarettes, etc. ₹ 300

The Committee of Management decides to adhere to the scheme of valuation of these items as hitherto followed *viz* :

(*i*) to value provisions and stores at cost ;

(*ii*) the stock of perishables and eatables on the basis of realised sale proceeds on the subsequent day to the closing of accounts ; and

(*iii*) aerated water bottles and cigarettes at 80% of their purchase price.

Sales of eatables on 1st April, 2025 amounted to ₹ 275.

(*f*) The Association had printed its annual report for 2024-25 and the bill due from the printers is for ₹ 500. Another bill for the brochure brought out for the tournament is also pending settlement and is for ₹ 1,200.

Ans. [Surplus ₹ 16,365].

14. Following was the Balance Sheet of the *Delhi Manufacturers Association* as at 31st March, 2025 :

Liabilities	₹	*Assets*	₹	₹
Capital Fund	78,000	Furniture & Fixtures		4,000
Amount Payable (Souvenir)	5,000	Office Equipment		20,000
Staff Provident Fund	11,000	Staff Provident Fund Investments		8,600
Advertisements received in advance (Souvenir)	2,000	Loans out of Provident Fund		1,500
Prize Fund	10,000	Prize Fund Investments		10,000
		Stock of Stationery & Printing		600
		Cash in Hand		250
		Cash at Bank :		
		Other	60,150	
		Provident Fund	900	61,050
	1,06,000			1,06,000

Staff Provident Fund Investments are 4% Government Loan, purchased at 86. Transactions during the year 2024-25 are as follows :

	₹		₹
Subscriptions from members	75,000	Establishments	20,000
Donation for building	50,000	Loan to employees against the Provident Fund	1,000
Staff Provident Fund			
—Contribution by employees	3,000	Accounts payable (Souvenir)	9,500
—Repayment of Loan	500	Provident Fund (Repayment)	5,000
Interest on Prize Fund Investments	500	Rent, Rates, Expenses	5,000
Advertisement in Souvenir	8,000	Printing & Stationery	1,200
Disbursements :		Purchase of land for building	45,000
Propaganda expenses	62,300	Prizes	400

Expenses still payable in respect of souvenir are ₹ 1,500 ; Stationery stock is valued at ₹ 400. Furniture and fixtures and office equipment are to be depreciated @ 10%.

Prepare Income and Expenditure Account of the Association for the year ended March, 31, 2025 and Balance Sheet as on that date. The Association's contribution to the Provident Fund is the same as that of the employees.

Ans. [Deficit ₹ 15,100 ; B/S Total ₹ 1,36,500 ; Closing Cash and Bank Balance ₹ 47,500].

15. Following is the Receipts and Payments Account of a *Sports Club* for the year ended 31st December, 2024 :

Receipts	₹	*Payments*	₹
To Balance b/d	7,500	By Salaries	14,000
To Subscriptions (including ₹ 2,000 for the year 2023)	40,000	By Match Expenses	28,000
To Donations	15,000	By 12% Investments on 1-1-2024	40,000
To Life Membership Fees	35,000	By Sports Materials	15,000
To Sale of Furniture at Book Value	5,000	By Printing & Stationery	12,000
To Entrance Fees	10,000	By Honorarium	5,000
To Interest on 10% Investments for full year	20,000	By Furniture	15,000
To Match Fund	40,000	By Magazines and Journals	10,000
To Donations for Building Fund	45,000	By Books	35,000
To Sale of Newspapers	2,500	By Municipal Taxes	6,000
		By Balance c/d	40,000
	2,20,000		2,20,000

Additional Information :

(*i*) Position of the Club on January 1, 2024 was as follows :

Subscriptions due ₹ 3,000 ; Furniture ₹ 10,000 ; Books ₹ 20,000 ; Building ₹ 1,25,000 ; Stock of Sports Materials ₹ 4,500 ; Creditors for Printing ₹ 2,500.

(*ii*) The Club has 1,000 members each paying an annual subscription of ₹ 50. 20 members paid their subscription in advance in 2023. In the year 2024, subscription was received in advance from 15 members.

(*iii*) Municipal Taxes are paid every year on 1st April.

(*iv*) One member donated a Billiard Table worth ₹ 50,000.

(*v*) Books worth ₹ 46,000 on 31st December, 2024 and stock of sports materials on that date amounted to ₹ 4,000.

(*vi*) 12% investments include ₹ 30,000 invested from donations received for building fund.

Prepare Income and Expenditure Account for the year ended 31st December, 2024 and a Balance Sheet as on that date.

Ans. [Surplus ₹ 19,700; Balance Sheet Total ₹ 5,44,050; Beginning Capital Fund ₹ 3,68,000]

16. Following is the Receipts and Payment Account of *Sodepore Recreation Club* for the year ended 31-12-2024 :

		₹		₹
To Cash in hand		1,000	By Rent of Club House	2,600
Cash at Bank		12,000	By Painting of Club House	1,400
To Members' Subscription	₹		By Wages of Ground Maintenance	3,000
2023	200		By General Expenses	2,600
2024	3,600		By Electricity Charges	3,600
2025	400		By Investment	20,000
		4,200	By Secretary's Honorarium	1,200
To Life Membership Subscription		4,000	By Annual Meeting Expenses	800
To Sale of Ticket of Annual Exhibition		20,000	By Sports Equipment	3,600
To Sale of Refreshment		24,000	By Purchase of Refreshment	11,000
To Interest on Investment		2,600	By Printing & Stationery	1,000
To Sale of Furniture (Original Cost			By Insurance	600
1-1-2019, ₹ 1,000)		200	By Cash in hand	4,000
			By Cash at Bank	12,600
		68,000		68,000

Following information is available to you :

(*a*) On 31-12-2023 outstanding subscription for 2023 was ₹ 300.

(*b*) On 31-12-2023 advance subscription for 2024 received was ₹ 100.

(*c*) On 31-12-2024 outstanding subscription for 2024 was ₹ 600.

(*d*) A life membership scheme was introduced in 2023. Under this scheme, life membership premium is ₹ 1,000 and it was to be apportioned to income 1/10th every year over a period of 10 years. Life membership subscription totalling ₹ 5,000 was collected during 2023.

(*e*) On 1-1-2024 Investment was ₹ 40,000 and accrued interest on such date was ₹ 2,400.

(*f*) On 1-1-2023 furniture costing ₹ 16,000 were purchased and it was decided to write off depreciation on furniture and sports equipment @ 10% on cost.

(*g*) In 2023 a plot of land was purchased for ₹ 20,000 to construct Club House.

(*h*) Other assets and liabilities of the club were (all figures in rupees) as follows :

	Stock of Refreshment	*Prepaid Insurance*	*Accrued Rent*	*Creditors for Refreshment*
31-12-2023	₹ 3,800	₹ 140	₹ 400	₹ 800
31-12-2024	₹ 4,200	₹ 100	₹ 200	₹ 1,000

Prepare (*i*) an Income and Expenditure Account for the year ending 31-12-2024 and (*ii*) Balance Sheet as at 31-12-2024 of Sodepur Recreation Club.

Ans. [Surplus ₹ 19,300; Balance Sheet Total ₹ 1,17,640; Beginning Capital Fund ₹ 89,140]

PREPARATION OF BALANCE SHEET BOTH AT THE BEGINNING AND AT THE END OF THE YEAR

17. From the following information given in the books of a *sports club,* prepare Balance Sheet as on 31st March, 2025.

RECEIPTS & PAYMENTS ACCOUNT

For the year ending 31-3-2025

Receipts	₹	*Payments*	₹
To Balance b/d	8,400	By Salaries	16,000
" Entrance Fees	4,000	" Investments	40,000
" Subscriptions :		" Advertising	1,000
2023-24	1,200	" Printing and Stationery	3,600
2024-25	50,000	By Insurance Premium	2,400
2025-26	800	" Balance c/d	5,400
To Interest Received	4,000		
	68,400		68,400

INCOME AND EXPENDITURE ACCOUNT

for the year ending on 31-3-2025

Expenditure	₹	*Income*	₹
To Salaries	16,800	By Subscription	51,000
" Advertising	1,000	" Entrance Fees	4,000
" Printing and Stationery	3,000	" Interest Received	4,000
To Audit Fees	2,000		
" Insurance Premium	2,000		
" Depreciation :			
on Sports Equipments	15,000		
on Furniture	800		
" Excess of Income over Expenditure	18,400		
	59,000		59,000

Assets & Liabilities of the club on 1-4-2024 included Sports Equipment ₹ 50,000 ; Ground and Pavilion ₹ 80,000 ; and Furniture ₹ 8,000. Subscription in arrears on that date were ₹ 1,600 subscription received in advance were ₹ 500 and Creditors for Stationery ₹ 600.

Ans. [B/S Total ₹ 1,68,900 ; Capital Fund on 1-4-2024 ₹ 1,46,900].

18. Given below are Receipts and Payments Account and Income and Expenditure Account of a Club for the year ending 31st March 2025. Prepare Balance Sheets both in the beginning and at the end.

RECEIPTS AND PAYMENTS ACCOUNT

for the year ending 31st March, 2025

Receipts	₹	*Payments*	₹
To Balance b/d	4,000	By Salaries	6,000
To Endowment Fund	2,000	By Advertisement	1,200
" Subscription	10,200	" Provisions	6,800
" Entrance Fees	800	" Printing & Stationery	700
" Donation for Books	1,300	" Deposit in Bank	1,000
" Entertainment	4,000	" Sports Material	2,800
" Sale of Furniture (cost		" Creditors (2023-24)	1,300
price ₹ 800)	700	" Investment at 96	1,920

		By Purchased on 30-9-2024	
		Interest 4%	
		" Balance c/d	1,280
	23,000		23,000

INCOME AND EXPENDITURE ACCOUNT
for the year ended 31st March, 2025

Expenditure	₹	*Income*	₹
To Sale of Furniture (Loss)	100	By Subscription	10,000
" Salaries	6,700	" Entrance Fees	400
" Advertisement	1,000	" Interest on Investments	
" Audit Fees	300	at 4% on ₹ 2,000	80
" Provisions	6,000	" Entertainment	4,000
To Printing and Stationery	750	By Excess of Expenditure	
" Sports Material	2,000	over Income	2,370
	16,850		16,850

Ans. [Beginning Capital Fund ₹ 3,500 ; Total of B/S (1-4-2024) ₹ 6,720 ; B/S Total (31-3-2025) ₹ 6,080].

Hints.

(1) Difference between the two figures of subscription has been treated as subscription received in advance at the end of the year. Alternatively such difference can be treated as subscription outstanding at the beginning of the year.

(2) Difference between the two figures of advertisement has been treated as prepaid advertisement at the end of the year. Alternatively it can be treated as advertisement outstanding at the beginning of the year.

PREPARATION OF RECEIPTS AND PAYMENTS ACCOUNT

19. Income and Expenditure Account for the year ended 31st March, 2025 of *South Asia Club* is given below :

Expenditure	₹	*Income*	₹
To Salaries & Wages	47,500	By Subscription	75,000
To Miscellaneous Expenses	5,000	By Entrance Fee	2,500
To Audit Fee	2,500	By Contribution for Annual Day	
To Executive's Honorarium	10,000	(After deducting expenses	
To Sports Day Expenses	5,000	₹ 7,500)	7,500
To Printing & Stationery	4,500		
To Interest on Bank Loan	1,500		
To Depreciation on Sports Equipment	3,000		
To Excess of Income over Expenditure	6,000		
	85,000		85,000

Following additional information is also available :

		31-3-2024	*31-3-2025*
		₹	₹
(1)	Subscription Received in Advance	4,500	2,700
(2)	Subscription Outstanding	6,000	7,500

(3)	Salaries Outstanding	4,000	4,500
(4)	Sports Equipment (After deducting depreciation)	26,000	27,000
(5)	Cash in hand on 31-3-2025 was ₹ 16,000.		
(6)	The club took a 5% loan of ₹ 30,000 from a bank during 2023-24 for which interest was not paid in the financial year 2024-25.		

Prepare Receipts and Payments Account of South Asia Club for the year ending 31st March, 2025.

Ans. [Cash in Hand on 1-4-2024 ₹ 12,300]

Hint. Subscription received during the year ₹ 71,700; Salaries and wages paid during the year ₹ 47,000 ; Sports Equipment purchased during the year ₹ 4,000.

20. Income and Expenditure Account of *Bombay Club* for the year ended 31st March, 2025 is as follows :

	₹		₹
To Salaries	48,000	By Subscriptions	1,30,000
To Rent	12,000	By Entrance Fees	20,000
To Printing & Stationery	3,000	By Contribution for Annual	
To Travelling Expenses	6,000	Dinner	16,000
To Annual Dinner Expenses	14,000	By Profit on Annual Sports	2,000
To Secretary's Honorarium	12,000		
To General Expenses	6,000		
To Interest and Bank Charges	1,800		
To Audit Fees	2,000		
To Books & Periodicals	3,000		
To Depreciation in Sports Equipment	2,500		
To Excess of Income over Expenditure	57,700		
	1,68,000		1,68,000

Income and Expenditure Account has been prepared after the following adjustments :

	31-3-2024	*31-3-2025*
	₹	₹
Subscription outstanding	12,000	8,000
Subscription received in advance	9,000	14,000
Salaries outstanding	4,000	3,000

Audit fees for the year has not been paid. Previous year's audit fees ₹ 1,500 was paid during the year.

The club's Assets on 31st March, 2024 were as follows :

Freehold Land ₹ 1,00,000 ; Sports Equipments ₹ 26,000.

At the end of the year, after depreciation the equipments amounted to ₹ 27,000. Bank loan of ₹ 10,000 as on 31st March, 2024 was still due at the end of the current year. On 31st March, 2025 Cash at Bank amounted to ₹ 69,700.

Prepare Receipts and Payments Account for the year ended 31st March, 2025 and Balance Sheet as on that date.

Ans. [Cash at Bank on 1-4-2024 ₹ 4,500 ; B/S Total ₹ 2,04,700 ; Beginning Capital Fund ₹ 1,18,000].

21. Following is the Income and Expenditure Account of *Kanpur Youth Club* for the year ended 31st March, 2025.

INCOME AND EXPENDITURE ACCOUNT

for the year ended 31st March, 2025

	₹		₹
To Salaries	19,500	By Subscription	68,000
" Rent	4,500	" Donation	5,000
" Printing	750		
" Insurance	500		
" Audit Fees	750		
" Games & Sports	3,500		
" Subscription written off	350		
" Miscellaneous expenses	14,500		
" Loss on sale of furniture	2,500		
" Depreciation :			
Sports Equipments	6,000		
Furniture	3,100		
" Excess of Income over Expenditure	17,050		
	73,000		73,000

Additional Information :

	31-3-2024	*31-3-2025*
	₹	₹
Subscriptions in arrear	2,600	3,700
Advance Subscription	1,000	1,500
Outstanding expenses :		
Rent	500	800
Salaries	1,200	350
Audit Fees	500	750
Sports Equipments less depn.	25,000	24,000
Furniture less depn.	30,000	27,900
Prepaid Insurance	—	150

Book value of Furniture sold is ₹ 7,000. Entrance fees capitalised ₹ 4,000. On 1st April, 2024 there was no cash in hand but a Bank Overdraft for ₹ 15,000. On 31st March 2025, Cash in hand amounted to ₹ 850 and the rest was Bank balance.

Prepare Receipts and Payments Account of the club for the year ended 31st March, 2025.

Ans. [Cash at Bank ₹ 7,250].

Hint. Subscription received ₹ 67,050 ; Purchase of Sports Equipments ₹ 5,000 ; Purchase of Furniture ₹ 8,000 ; Sale of Furniture ₹ 4,500.

22. From the following particulars relating to *Ramakrishna Mission Charitable Hospital* prepare (*i*) Receipts and Payments Account for the year ended 31st March, 2025, and (*ii*) Balance Sheet as on 31st March, 2025.

INCOME AND EXPENDITURE ACCOUNT

for the year ended 31st March,2025

Expenditure	₹	*Income*	₹
To Medicines used	29,980	By Subscriptions	56,000
To Honorarium to Visiting Doctors	12,000	By Donations	9,500
To Salaries	27,500	By Interest on Investments	
To Printing and Stationery	1,100	@ 11% p.a.	11,000

	₹		₹	₹
To Electricity and Water	475	By Income from Film	₹	
To Rent	6,000	Show Proceeds	11,450	
To Depreciation on Furniture and Fixtures	2,100	*Less* : Expenses	780	10,670
To Depreciation on Equipment	3,250			
To Surplus, *i.e.*, Excess of Income over Expenditure	4,765			
	87,170			87,170

Additional information :

		On 1-4-2024	31-3-2025
		₹	₹
(*i*)	Subscriptions Due	120	160
(*ii*)	Subscriptions Received in Advance	64	100
(*iii*)	Electricity and Water Bills Unpaid	92	115
(*iv*)	Stock of Medicines	7,820	9,750
(*v*)	Estimated Value of Equipment	11,600	13,900
(*vi*)	Furniture and Fixture (cost less depreciation)	21,000	18,900
(*vii*)	Land	—	10,000
(*viii*)	Interest Accrued on Investments in 11% Debentures costing ₹ 1,02,500 (face value ₹ 1,00,000)	3,750	3,750
(*ix*)	Cash in Hand	340	160
(*x*)	Cash at Bank	9,000	?

Ans. [Cash at Bank ₹ 1,834 ; Capital Fund on 1-4-2024 ₹ 1,55,974 ; B/S Total ₹ 1,60,954].
Hints. Subscription Received ₹ 55,996, Medicines Consumed ₹ 31,910 ; Purchase of Equipment ₹ 5,550.

23. The *Lok Kalyan Dispensary* had the following Income and Expenditure Account for 2024-25 :

Expenditure		₹	*Income*	₹
To Salaries		23,500	By Subscriptions	25,000
To Surgery and Dispensary		3,000	By Interest	9,000
To Rent and Taxes		500	By Donations	4,000
To Insurance		200	By Miscellaneous Receipts	300
To Office Expenses		800		
To Depreciation :	₹			
Buildings	3,750			
Furniture	120			
Instruments	100	3,970		
To Surplus of Income over Expenditure		6,330		
		38,300		38,300

Other information is as follows :	31-3-2024	31-3-2025
	₹	₹
Cash in hand and at Bank	?	18,700
Government Securities (face value ₹ 2,00,000)	1,80,000	1,80,000
Subscription outstanding	7,000	10,000

Subscription Received in advance	500	600
Salaries unpaid	1,000	1,500
Furniture	2,000	1,980
Land and Building	2,00,000	1,96,250
Instruments	3,500	3,900
Surgery expenses due	200	300
Stock of medicines	300	100

You are required to prepare Receipts and Payments Account for 2024-25 and also Balance Sheet as on 31-3-2025.

Ans. [Beginning Cash in hand and at Bank ₹ 11,100 ; B/S Total ₹ 4,10,930 ; Beginning Capital Fund ₹ 4,02,200].

24. "Citizens Club" was registered in a city and the Accountant prepared the following Receipts and Payment Account for the year ended March 31, 2025 and showed a deficit of ₹ 14,520.

Receipts	₹	*Payments*	₹
To Subscription	62,130	By Premises Purchased on 1-4-2024	30,000
To Fair Receipts	7,200	By Honorarium to Secretary	12,000
To Variety Show Receipts (net)	12,810	By Rent	2,400
To Interest	690	By Rates and Taxes	3,780
To Bar Collection	22,350	By Printing and Stationery	1,410
To Cash Spent More	1,000	By Sundry Expenses	5,350
To Deficit	14,520	By Wages	2,520
		By Fair Expenses	7,170
		By Bar Purchases— Payments	17,310
		By Repairs	960
		By New Car (Less Proceeds of Old Car ₹ 9,000)	37,800
	1,20,700		1,20,700

Following additional information could be obtained.

	1-4-2024 ₹	*31-3-2025* ₹
Cash in Hand	450	
Bank Balance as per Pass Book	24,690	10,440
Cheques issued not presented for Sundry Expenses	270	90
Subscription due	3,600	2,940
Premises at cost	87,000	1,17,000
Accumulated Depreciation on Premises	56,400	
Car at cost	36,570	46,800
Accumulated Depreciation on Car	30,870	
Bar Stock	2,130	2,610
Creditors for Bar Purchases	1,770	1,290

Cash overspent represents honorarium to Secretary not withdrawn due to cash deficit. His annual honorarium is ₹ 12,000. Depreciation on premises and car is to be provided at 5 per cent and 20 per cent on written down value.

You are required to prepare correct Receipts and Payments Account, Income and Expenditure Account and Balance Sheet as at March 31, 2025.

Ans. [Cash Balance ₹ 10,350 ; Surplus 43,490 ; B/S Total ₹ 1,10,910 ; Capital Fund (Beginning ₹ 65,130].

PREPARATION OF TRADING ACCOUNTS OF RESTUARANT AND BAR AND INCOME AND EXPENDITURE A/C AND BALANCE SHEET

25. The balances from the books of Neo Club on 31-3-2025 were extracted as follows :

	₹		₹
Furniture on 31-3-2024	840	Purchases for Bar	8,224
Furniture additions from 1-4-2024 to 31-3-2025	542	Rent and Rates	3,490
Furniture & Fittings on 31-3-2024	292	Wages	6,234
Billiard Table and Accessories on 31-3-2024	890	Postage and Telegrams Expenses	1,799
China Glass, Cutlery and Linen on on 31-3-2024	200	Electricity Charges	1,758
Stock in Restaurant on 31-3-2024	357	Sundry Expenses	1,349
Stock in Bar on 31-3-2024	30	Cash on Hand on 31-3-2025	136
Restaurant Takings	16,168	Cash at Bank on 31-3-2025	920
Bar Takings	13,050	Bank Deposits	2,833
Billiards and Sundry Receipts	2,566	Sundry Debtors	749
Subscription from Members	3,150	Sundry Creditors	1,785
Interest on Deposits	87	Capital Fund on 31-3-2024	4,624
Purchases for Restaurant	10,787		

You are requested to prepare separate Trading Accounts for Restaurant and Bar and the Income and Expenditure Account for the year ended 31-3-2025 together with the Balance Sheet as on that date, after making adjustments for the following :

(*a*) Cost of food etc. to staff is estimated at ₹ 5,500 of which ₹ 5,000 is to be credited to Restaurant and ₹ 500 to Bar. (*b*) Stocks on 31-3-2025 were ₹ 23 and ₹ 295 for Restaurant and Bar respectively. (*c*) Depreciation shall be provided at 10% for Furniture, Fixture and Fittings, Billiards Table and Accessories to the nearest multiple of a rupee. (*d*) Subscriptions due on 31-3-2025 were ₹ 500 and Sundry Expenses of ₹ 500 were outstanding on the same date. (*e*) One half of china glass, cultery and lien on 31-3-2024 shall be written off during the year ending on 31-3-2025.

Ans. [Gross Profit—Restaurant ₹ 10,047 ; Bar ₹ 5,591 ; Surplus ₹ 955 ; Balance Sheet Total ₹ 7,864].

PREPARATION OF RECEIPTS AND PAYMENTS ACCOUNT, INCOME AND EXPENDITURE ACCOUNT AND BALANCE SHEET

26. The *Association of Veterinary Physicians* had the following Balance Sheet as at 31st March, 2025.

BALANCE SHEET

as at 31st March, 2025

Liabilities	₹	*Assets*	₹
Sundry Creditors (for Purchase of Stationery)	700	Cash in Hand	100
Salaries Outstanding	600	Bank Balance	9,200
Capital Fund	18,900	Fixed Deposit with Bank	10,000
		Miscellaneous Advances	250
		Interest Receivable on F.D.	250
		Subscriptions Receivable	400
	20,200		20,200

The Association consists of 200 members and the annual subscription is ₹ 100 per member. All payments are through cheques except petty cash payments. Following is the summary of the Petty Cash Book for the year 2024-25.

PETTY CASH SUMMARY

	₹		₹
To Balance (1-4-2024)	100	By Miscellaneous Expenses	5,900
To Receipts from Bank	6,000	By Balance (31-3-2025)	200
	6,100		6,100

Analysis of the bank statements for 2024-25 shows the following payments :

	₹		₹
Sundry creditors (for purchase of stationery)	1,800	Miscellaneous expenses	600
Salaries	7,700	Towards additional Fixed Deposits	
Subscriptions to periodicals	1,200	1-10-2024	5,000
Withdrawals for petty cash	6,000		

With reference to the above, you are required to prepare : (*a*) Receipts and Payments Account for the year 2024-25 ; (*b*) Income and expenditure account for the year ended 31st March, 2025 ; (*c*) Balance Sheet as at 31st March, 2025,

After taking into Account the following additional information :

(*i*) Fixed deposits are for long-term and carry interest at 10% per annum. During the year interest received totalled ₹ 1,000.

(*ii*) On 31st March, 2025 the following were outstanding :

Salaries ₹ 700 ; For purchase of stationery : ₹ 200.

(*iii*) Subscription Receivable as at 31st March, 2025 : ₹ 500.

Ans. [Closing Bank Balance ₹ 7,800 ; Surplus ₹ 4,200 ; B/S Total ₹ 24,000].

27. From the following information relating to *Mukesh Social Club,* you are required to prepare :

(*a*) an Income and Expenditure Account (including profit or loss on bar) for the year ended 31st March, 2025,

(*b*) a Balance Sheet at that date :

(*i*) A summary of cash book for the year 2024-25 is as follows :

	₹		₹
Bar balance as on 1st April, 2024	836	Bar Supplies	13,461
Annual Subscriptions	3,668	Bar Wages	1,099
Bar Takings	15,392	Salaries and Wages	1,365
Hire of Rooms	146	Office Expenses	424
Income from Investments	315	Lighting and Heating	372
Sale of Investments	328	Rates and Insurance	287
		Miscellaneous Expenses	303
		Investments	1,400
		Furniture (Purchased on 30th Sept. 2024)	900
		Bank Balance as on 31st March, 2025	1,074
	20,685		20,685

(*ii*) The balance at bank on 1st April, 2024 represented ₹ 336 on current account and ₹ 500 on deposit account. All the receipts shown in the above summary were paid into the Current Account except for ₹ 51 deposit account interest (included in income from investments) and all payments were made from the Current Account. During 2024-25, ₹ 300 were transferred from the Current Account to the Deposit Account.

(*iii*) Following items were outstanding at 31st March.

	2024	*2025*
	₹	₹
Subscriptions in arrears	79	98
Salaries and wages accrued	33	41
Creditors for bar supplies	1,217	1,325
Stock of stationery	56	65
Subscriptions in advance	14	26
Telephone bill outstanding	29	37
Electricity charges unpaid	31	44
Debtors for bar sales	12	49
Repairs account outstanding	9	53
Bar wages accrued	21	23
Stock of coke	40	57
Rates and insurance prepaid	62	73
Stock of Bar supplies	1,422	1,989

(*iv*) At 31st March, 2024, the club owned the following assets which are shown at cost. At 31st March, 2024 they had been in the ownership of the club for the number of years indicated :

	₹	
Freehold Premium	6,000	12 years
Furniture	1,000	12 years
Furniture	800	5 years
Investments	3,000	4 years

(*v*) The club is providing for the depreciation of Freehold Premises of $2\frac{1}{2}\%$ per annum and of Furniture at 10% per annum both rates being calculated on original cost.

Ans. [Surplus ₹ 2,400 ; Bar Profit ₹ 1,326 ; B/S Total ₹ 12,702 ; Capital Fund ₹ 8,753].

28. The *United Club* closes its accounts on calendar year basis. It runs a pantry and general services. On 1st April, 2024 on the persuasion of some members, it laid a tennis court on the understanding that half of laying the court would be met by the said members individually and that the maintenance of the court would be subsidised fully by them.

Following figures are furnished to you by the accountant of the Club for the year ended 31st March, 2025.

	₹		₹
General Fund	1,25,000	Rent outstanding on 1-4-2024	1,500
Admission Fees from Members	10,000	Pantry Purchases	40,000
Membership Subscriptions (includes the amount to be contributed by members towards the Capital Cost of Tennis Court)	57,000	Salaries and Wages	30,000
		Tennis Court Laying Expenses	4,000
		Marker's Wages	1,800
Audit Fees	250	Salaries of Stewards, Bearers and Cooks	24,080
Subscriptions outstanding on 1-4-2024	3,000	Sundry Creditors for Pantry Purchases	2,630
Pantry Stock on 1-4-2024	300	Subscriptions to Books and Periodicals	17,060

Bank Balance	1,275	Sports Equipments	19,800
Cash in hand	95	Furniture and Fittings (Pantry)	24,770
Pantry Sales	70,000	Fixed Deposits with Banks	70,000
Tennis Court Maintenance		Library	8,000
Collections	5,000	Rent	21,000
		Printing and Stationery	5,700

1. 2024-25 subscriptions in arrears are ₹ 1,400 and 2025-26 subscriptions received this year are ₹ 480.
2. The monthly rent is ₹ 1,500.
3. Fixed deposits in Banks were made : ₹ 15,000 on 1st June, 2024 : ₹ 30,000 on 1st January 2025 and the balance on 1st February, 2025. Interest on these deposits for the current year has not been received and is at 8% per annum.
4. Depreciation at the rate of 15% on Library, 10% on furniture and fittings and 30% on sports equipments is to be provided.
5. In connection with the inauguration of the tennis court, the club on its own brought out a souvenir. Printing expenses on this came to ₹ 1,000 and these remain unpaid on 31st March. Amounts due from the advertisers ₹ 1,500. These figures have not been taken into account by the accountant.
6. Salaries and wages of ₹ 30,000 include salary of ₹ 9,000 to the Manager of the club. Manager's salary is to be distributed between Pantry, General and Tennis court in the ratio of 3 : 2 : 1 and the rest among the departments in the ratio of 5 : 4 : 1.
7. Bills for supplies of provisions to the Pantry in March, 2025 amounting to ₹ 1,750 have not been paid and taken into account.
8. Pantry stock on hand on 31st March, 2025 is valued at cost of ₹ 250.
9. Subscriptions to periodicals to the extent of ₹ 3,950 have been paid in advance.

You are required to prepare the Income and Expenditure Account in columnar form for the year ended 31st March, 2025 and the Balance Sheet on that date.

Ans. [Surplus (General) ₹ 1,620 ; Deficit (Pantry) ₹ 13,357 ; Deficit Recoverable from Tennis Players ₹ 400 ; B/S Total ₹ 1,29,123].

29. From the following details and information pertaining to Agarwal Nursing Home, you are required to prepare an Income and Expenditure Account and the Balance Sheet as at 31st March, 2025.

(*a*) The Nursing Home was started on 1st April, 2022 with ₹ 1,50,000 as Capital. For the years ended 31st March, 2023 and 31st March, 2024, a loss of ₹ 14,000 and a profit of ₹ 32,000 were made.

(*b*) The equipments and machinery installed in the Nursing Home were financed fully by the State Bank of India to the extent of ₹ 3,50,000. The loan taken on 1st April, 2022 from the Bank carries an interest of 16% p.a. on diminishing balances and the principal is to be repaid in ten equal half-yearly installments due on 30th September and the 31st March along with interest. The commitments upto 1st April, 2024 have been discharged by the business.

(*c*) From the Nursing Home's daily patient register, you notice the following :

(*i*) Bills are raised on a weekly basis for payment by patients

(*ii*) Bills raised upto 24th March, 2025 are ₹ 11,45,500.

(*iii*) Bills yet to be raised for the last week are ₹ 23,500.

(*d*) All receipts are banked with the State Bank of India in a Current Account and all expenses, except ₹ 500 every week for petty cash expenses, are met by cheques. Following is the summary of bank transactions :

	₹		₹
Deposits received from patients	11,30,000	Purchase of detergents	20,000
Discounts received from drug		Power and lighting bills	70,100
manufacturers and agents	12,000	Machinery, Maintenance and	

Withdrawals :		Repairs	30,000
Salaries and wages to Doctors		Withdrawals by partners	48,000
and other staff	4,50,000	Rent for premises	30,000
Payments to creditors for drugs etc.	3,75,000		

The Bank has debited the current account with the loan instalments and interest due on the specified dates. A sum of ₹ 2,700 has also been debited by the Bank towards insurance premium on the fire risks against machinery cover on behalf of the insured.

(*e*) Balances as on 1st April, 2024 :

	₹		₹
1. Sundry Creditors for drugs and medicines	25,000	6. Stock of medicines	23,000
2. Salary due to staff	30,000	7. Cash imprest	500
3. Rent due for March, 2024	2,500	8. Interest-free Loan taken from the Disabled Warriors Society, Delhi	1,38,000
4. Accounts receivable	30,000		
5. Furniture and Fixtures	1,80,000		

(*f*) Amounts due on 31st March, 2025 :

1. Salary to Staff	15,000	3. Rent due for March, 2025	2,500
2. Amounts due for purchases made	18,000	4. Stock of medicines	12,000

The Nursing Home is run by a partnership consisting of Mrs. and Mr. Agarwal (both being doctors) who are entitled to a salary of ₹ 2,000 and ₹ 1,000 per month respectively. Husband and wife share capital and profits and losses in the same ratio as their salary entitlements.

Drawings over and above the salary entitlements to be transferred to capital accounts of the partners in the same ratio as capital.

Depreciation on equipments and machinery to be charged at 10% on the straightline method and on furniture and fixtures at 15% of their book value.

Ans. **[Profit ₹ 59,400 ; B/S Total ₹ 5,28,900].**

PREPARATION OF RECEIPTS AND PAYMENTS ACCOUNT, INCOME AND EXPENDITURE ACCOUNT AND BALANCE SHEET OF EDUCATIONAL INSTITUTIONS, STUDENTS' HOSTELS AND HOSPITALS

30. Prepare Income and Expenditure Account and Balance Sheet from the following Receipts and Payments Account and Balance Sheet of a Public School.

RECEIPTS AND PAYMENTS ACCOUNT

for the year ending 31st March, 2025

Receipts	₹	*Payments*		₹
To Opening Balance (1-4-2024)	1,00,000	By Pay and Allowances :		
" Tuition Fees	1,45,000		₹	
" Fines	5,000	Teaching staff	2,70,000	
" Grants-in-Aid	2,90,000	Office staff	60,000	
" Interest on Securities	2,000	Menial staff	22,000	
" Rent from use of Hall	4,700			3,52,000
" Examination Fees	6,000	" Provident Fund Contribution :		
		Teaching staff	22,500	
		Office staff	5,000	
		Menial staff	1,500	
				29,000
		" Books for Library		25,000

	₹		₹
		By Newspapers and Magazines	2,000
		" Science Equipment	2,500
		" Science Contingencies	2,000
		" Postage and Telegrams	2,300
		" Repairs to Buildings	2,700
		" General Charges	2,400
		" Audit Fee	1,000
		" Municipal Tax	500
		" Outstanding Creditors	3,000
		" Closing Balance (31-3-2025)	1,28,300
	5,52,700		5,52,700

BALANCE SHEET

as on 31-3-2024

Liabilities	₹	*Assets*	₹
Outstanding for Expenses	3,000	Cash	1,00,000
Building Fund	5,05,000	Furniture	1,75,000
General Reserve	4,50,000	Investments	50,000
Income and Expenditure Account	2,13,500	Library Books	1,25,000
		Land and Buildings	7,10,000
		Outstanding Tuition Fee	11,500
	11,71,500		11,71,500

On 31-3-2025 tuition fee outstanding was ₹ 16,500 and salaries outstanding for teaching staff were ₹ 15,000. Provide depreciation on Land and Buildings 2%, Furniture 10% and Library Books 10%. Science equipment is to be completely written off.

Ans. **[Excess of Expenditure over Income ₹ 400 ; B/S Total 11,83,100].**

31. The cashier of a Charitable Trust furnishes you with the following information to enable you to prepare the final accounts of the trust :

	Dr. ₹	*Cr.* ₹
Interest		30,000
Rent		12,000
Donation of Clinic Fund		6,000
Sundry collections from parties		3,000
Salaries	6,000	
Medicines and Surgical Expenses	14,000	
Clinical Equipments purchased	5,000	
Educational Scholarships	10,000	
Printing, Stationery and Postage	800	
Travelling Expenses of Trustees	1,000	
Conveyance Allowance to staff	200	
Furniture purchased	4,000	
Investments (purchased on the last day of the year)	10,000	
Cash and Bank Balances :		
Cash	1,600	1,000
Bank	13,400	14,000
	66,000	66,000

Trust fund originally consisted of Buildings valued at ₹ 1,50,000. 9% Government securities of the face value of ₹ 3,50,000 (Cost of ₹ 3,20,000) and the Bank Balance of ₹ 10,000.

Bank interest collectable at the end of the year was ₹ 2,500. Interest accrued on investments at the beginning of the year was ₹ 3,500, and at the end of the year ₹ 5000. The Trust owed suppliers of medicines ₹ 1,200 and ₹ 800 respectively at the beginning and at the end of the year. Furniture at the beginning of the year was valued at ₹ 3,000.

You have to provide depreciation on the book values of buildings at $2\frac{1}{2}$%and on other assets at 20%. ***(I.C.W.A. Final)***

Ans. [Excess of Income over Expenditure ₹ 11,250 ; B/S Total ₹ 5,08,350 ; Trust Fund at the beginning of the year ₹ 4,80,000 ; Capital Fund at the beginning of the year ₹ 10,300].

Hints. (1) Cash ₹ 1,000 and Bank Balance ₹14,000 given as credit balance in the information are to be taken as balances of Cash and Bank at the beginning of the year. These are taken wrongly as credit balances by the cashier because cash in hand can never be a credit balance. Receipts and Payments Account will tally only if we take these figures as opening balances of cash and bank. To make this point clear, Receipts and Payments Account is given below :

(1) **RECEIPTS AND PAYMENTS ACCOUNT**

	₹		₹
To Balance b/d		By Capital Payments :	
Cash	1,000	Investments	10,000
Bank	14,000	Clinical Equipments	5,000
To Capital Fund :		Furniture	4,000
Donation for Clinic Fund	6,000	By Revenue Payments :	
To Revenue Receipts :		Salaries	6,000
Interest	30,000	Medicines and Surgical Expenses	14,000
Rent	12,000	Educational Scholarships	10,000
Sundry Collections	3,000	Printing etc.	800
		Travelling Expenses	1,000
		Conveyance Allowance	200
		By Balance c/d	
		Cash	1,600
		Bank	13,400
	66,000		66,000

(2) **OPENING BALANCE SHEET**

	₹	₹		₹
Trust Fund consisted of :			Building	1,50,000
Buildings	1,50,000		Furniture	3,000
Govt. Securities	3,20,000		Investments	3,20,000
Bank Balance	10,000		Accrued Interest	3,500
		4,80,000	Bank	14,000
Creditors for Supplies		1,200	Cash	1,000
Capital Fund (Balancing figure)		10,300		
		4,91,500		4,91,500

CHAPTER

20

Self-Balancing Ledger and Sectional Balancing

When all the accounts are kept in one ledger, a trial balance can be extracted as a test of the arithmetical accuracy of the accounts though certain errors may not be revealed by such trial balance. If the trial balance total disagrees, the number of entries for a small business being relatively few, the books can be easily and quickly checked so as to locate the errors. However, when the firm has grown and the accounting work has been so sub-divided that there are several or many ledgers, a trial balance, the total of which does not agree, can result in a great deal of unnecessary checking before the errors are found. What is required, in fact, is a type of trial balance for each ledger or a section of the groups of ledgers and this requirement is met by self balancing ledgers or sectional balancing.

Meaning of Self-balancing System

A self balancing ledger is one whose balances when extracted, forms a complete trial balance. For self balancing purposes, the ledger is divided into three sections :

1. General Ledger. It contains all the real and nominal accounts as well as such personal accounts except trade debtors and trade creditors.

2. Purchases (or Bought or Creditors) Ledger. It contains the accounts of persons from whom goods are bought on credit.

3. Sales (or Sold or Debtors) Ledger. It contains the accounts of persons to whom goods are sold on credit.

General ledger is usually in the charge of an accountant whereas purchases and sales ledger (known as trade or subsidiary ledgers) are placed in the charge of accounts clerk. When there are a large number of customers and suppliers, purchases and sales ledgers may further be subdivided into sections—***(a)* alphabetically** as A—G, H—L, M—R, S—Z ; ***(b)* departmentally** as A Department, B Department, Hosiery Department, Drapery Department ; or ***(c)* geographically,** as local, provincial, national, international.

PROCEDURE OF SELF-BALANCING

It is quite evident from the divisions of the ledger that none of the ledgers contains all the information required for the preparation of a trial balance. For example, from the sales book the items are posted to the debit of the customer's concerned account in the sales ledger. The total of the sales book is posted to the credit of the sales account and being a nominal account is opened in the General ledger. Thus, sales ledger will be having all debit entries with the result neither of them is complete in itself for the preparation of a trial balance. Similarly, from the purchases book, the items are posted to the credit of suppliers' accounts in the purchase ledger and total of purchases is posted to the debit of purchases account and being a nominal account, it will be opened in the general ledger. Thus, purchase ledger contains credit entry while the general ledger contains the debit entry. These examples clearly show that none of the three ledgers contains in itself all the data for the preparation of a trial balance independently.

In order to make each ledger self balancing it is necessary that the ledger which contains debit entry should be provided with a credit entry and the one which contains debit entry should be provided with the credit entry. This is achieved by opening an extra account called General Ledger Adjustment Account in each of the sales and purchases ledger and two accounts *i.e.,* sales ledger adjustment account and purchase ledger adjustment account in the general ledger. Contra entries of that already recorded in one ledger will be posted to the adjustment accounts in each ledger. Such contra entries are made in monthly or periodical totals in order to save the clerical labour. As every entry in the ledger has its contra posting (in total) in the Adjustment Account which is opened at the end of each ledger, the double entry of every transaction is recorded in the same ledger. A separate trial balance can be prepared from each ledger in which balance on adjustment account opened at the end of the ledger is included and such trial balance must agree provided all the transactions are recorded correctly.

In order to make the ledgers self balancing, relevant changes will have to be made in the subsidiary books. **Analysis columns** will be added to the cash book, journal and to all other books of original entry. Specimens of cash book and journal proper are given on the next page.

The information required for the preparation of accounts under self-balancing system is obtained from the following subsidiary books :

1. **Cash Book.** Cash received from sundry debtors, cash paid to sundry creditors, discount received from creditors and discount allowed to debtors.
2. **Purchases Book.** Amount of credit purchases during a specified period.
3. **Sales Book.** Amount of credit sales made during a specified period.
4. **Purchases Returns Book.** Amount of purchases returns during a specified period.
5. **Sales Returns Book.** Amount of sales returns during a specified period.
6. **Bills Receivable Book.** Total amount of bills received from sundry debtors during a specified period.
7. **Bills Payable Book.** Total amount of bills accepted and given to creditors during a specified period.
8. **Journal.** Opening balances, bad and doubtful debts, interest, dishonour of bills etc.

Journal Entries for Self-Balancing Sales Ledger

All debtors accounts are opened in the Sales ledger and entries are made on the debit side of these accounts from the sales book. In order to make this ledger self balancing, a General Ledger Adjustment Account is opened in sales ledger and all entries in totals appearing on the debit side of various debtors accounts will be shown on the credit side of this account and all credit entries of various debtors accounts on the debit side of this account.

In order to make the general ledger self-balancing a Sales Ledger Adjustment Account is opened in the general ledger. It will contain all entries of General Ledger Adjustment Account (in sales ledger) but on reverse sides *i.e.* all entries appearing on the debit side of various debtors accounts are debited to Sales Ledger Adjustment Account (in general ledger) and all credit entries in the various debtors accounts are credited to Sales Ledger Adjustment Account (in general ledger).

Following Journal Entries are passed to make the sales ledger self-balancing :

(i) For credit sales, bills receivable dishonoured, interest and expenses charged to debtors during the period.

Sales Ledger Adjustment A/c Dr.
(in General Ledger)
To General Ledger Adjustment A/c
(in Sales Ledger)

(Contd. on page 20.4)

CASH BOOK

Dr. (Receipts) **Cr. (Payments)**

Date	Particulars	V.N.	L.F.	Discount	Cash	Bank	Bought Ledger	Sold Ledger	Date	Particulars	V.N.	L.F.	Discount	Cash	Bank	Bought Ledger	Sold Ledger

JOURNAL PROPER

Date	Particulars	L.F.	Amount	Amount	Bought Ledger		Sold Ledger	
			Dr.	Cr.	Dr.	Cr.	Dr.	Cr.

(ii) For total of cash received from debtors, discount allowed to them, bills received, sales returns and bad debts written off.

General Ledger Adjustment A/c
(in Sales Ledger)
To Sales Ledger Adjustment A/c
(in General Ledger)

ILLUSTRATION 1. From the following particulars you are required to write up the individual Debtors Accounts and the General Ledger Adjustment Account (in Sales Ledger) and Sales Ledger Adjustment Account (in General Ledger) of Raj Kumar (who keeps his Ledger on self-balancing system) during the month of July, 2025 :

Individual Debtors' Balances on 1st July, 2025 :

A ₹ 510 ; B ₹ 540 ; C ₹ 630 ; D ₹ 390.

Transactions during the month of July, 2025 :

July

2 Sold goods to A, ₹ 570
9 Received from B on Account, ₹ 100.
11 Received from A, ₹ 500 in full settlement of his balance on 1st July, 2025.
13 Sold goods to B, ₹ 200.
14 B returned goods, which were damaged in transit ₹ 60.
18 Received from C ₹ 600 and allowed him discount, ₹ 30.
19 Received from A, a bills of exchange for ₹ 400 accepted by R payable on 25th July.
22 Received from B, ₹ 300.
25 A's acceptance returned dishonoured.
27 *D became insolvent* and 30 paise in the rupee was received from his estate in full and final settlement.
30 Sold goods to C ₹ 340.

SOLUTION

In Sales Ledger

A

2025		₹	2025		₹
July 1	To Balance b/d	510	July 11	By Cash	500
July 2	" Sales	570	July 11	" Discount	10
" 25	" B/R (dishonoured)	400	" 19	" B/R	400
			" 31	" Balance c/d	570
		1,480			1,480

B

2025		₹	2025		₹
July 1	To Balance b/d	540	July 9	By Cash	100
" 13	" Sales	200	" 14	" Returns Inwards	60
			" 22	" Cash	300
			" 31	" Balance c/d	280
		740			740

C

2025		₹	2025		₹
July 1	To Balance b/d	630	July 18	By Cash	600
" 30	" Sales	340	" 31	" Discount	30
			" 31	" Balance c/d	340
		970			970

D

2025		₹	2025		₹
July 1	To Balance b/d	390	July 27	By Cash	117
				" Bad Debts	273
		390			390

GENERAL LEDGER ADJUSTMENT ACCOUNT IN SALES LEDGER

	₹		₹
To Sales Ledger Adjustment A/c (in General Ledger) :		By Balance b/d	2,070
		" Sales Ledger Adjustment A/c (in General Ledger) :	
Cash	1,617		
Discount	40	Sales	1,110
Returns Inwards	60	B/R (dishonoured)	400
B/R	400		
Bad Debts	273		
Balance c/d	1,190		
	3,580		3,580
		By Balance b/d	1,190

SALES LEDGER ADJUSTMENT ACCOUNT

(in General Ledger)

	₹		₹
To Balance b/d	2,070	By General Ledger Adjustment A/c (in Sales Ledger) :	
" General Ledger Adjustment A/c (in Sales Ledger)		Cash	1,617
Sales	1,110	Discount	40
B/R (dishonoured)	400	Returns Inwards	60
		B/R	400
		Bad Debts	273
		" Balance c/d	1,190
	3,580		3,580
To Balance b/d	1,190		

Journal Entries for Self-Balancing Purchases Ledger

All creditors accounts are opened in the purchases ledger and entries are made on the credit side of these accounts from the purchases book. In order to make this ledger self balancing, a General Ledger

Adjustment Account is opened in the purchases ledger and all entries in total appearing on the credit side of the various creditors will be shown on the debit side of this account and all debit entries of various creditors accounts are shown on the credit side of this account.

In order to make the general ledger self balancing, a Purchase Ledger Adjustment Account is opened in the general ledger. It will contain all entries of General Ledger Adjustment Account (in purchases ledger) but on the reverse side *i.e.* all entries appearing on the credit side of various creditors accounts are credited to Purchases Ledger Adjustment Account (in general ledger) and all debit entries in the various creditors accounts are debited to Purchases Ledger Adjustment Account (in general ledger).

Following Journal Entries are passed to make the Purchases Ledger Self Balancing :

(i) For credit purchases, bills payable dishonoured, interest and expenses charged by creditors.

General Ledger Adjustment A/c Dr.
(in Purchases Ledger)
To Purchases Ledger Adjustment A/c
(in General Ledger)

(ii) For total cash paid to creditors, discount received, bills accepted and purchases returns.

Purchases Ledger Adjustment A/c Dr.
(in General Ledger)
To General Ledger Adjustment A/c
(in Purchases Ledger)

ILLUSTRATION 2. On 1st June the creditors balances in a Trader's Ledger were as follows :

A ₹ 1,700 ; B ₹ 1,800 ; C ₹ 1,650 ; D₹ 2,100 ; E ₹ 1,300 and F ₹ 1,900. Following transactions occurred during the month :

June		₹	June		₹
2	Bought goods from A	1,850	22	Bought goods from D	1,600
8	Paid to F on account	900	25	Returned goods to G	230
9	Trader accepted A's draft		27	Paid to B (discount ₹ 60)	1,740
	(discount ₹ 50)	950	28	Bought goods from E	2,200
11	Returned goods to E	300		Paid to G (discount ₹ 70)	1,700
12	Bought goods from G	2,000	29	Trader accepted F's draft	
14	Paid to E (discount ₹ 10)	990		(discount ₹ 40)	1,000
19	Bought goods from B	1,500	30	Bought goods from F	1,600
21	Paid to D (discount ₹ 100)	2,000		Paid to A on account	700

You are required to write up individual Creditors' A/cs, General Ledger Adjustment A/c (in Bought Ledger) and Bought Ledger Adjustment Account (in General Ledger).

SOLUTION

In Purchase Ledger

A

		₹			₹
June 9	To Bills Payable A/c	950	June 1	By Balance b/d	1,700
	" Discount A/c	50	" 2	" Purchases	1,850
June 30	" Bank A/c	700			
" 30	" Balance c/d	1,850			
		3,550			3,550
			July 1	By Balance b/d	1,850

B

		₹			₹
June 27	To Bank	1,740	June 1	By Balance b/d	1,800
	" Discount	60	" 19	" Purchases	1,500
" 30	" Balance c/d	1,500			
		3,300			3,300
			July 1	By Balance b/d	1,500

C

		₹			₹
June 30	To Balance c/d	1,650	June 1	By Balance b/d	1,650
			July 1	By Balance b/d	1,650

D

		₹			₹
June 21	To Bank	2,000	June 1	By Balance b/d	2,100
" 30	" Discount	100	" 22	" Purchases	1,600
" 30	" Balance c/d	1,600			
		3,700			3,700
			July 1	By Balance b/d	1,600

E

		₹			₹
June 11	To Returns Outwards	300	June 1	By Balance b/d	1,300
" 14	" Bank	990	" 28	" Purchases	2,200
	" Discount	10			
" 30	" Balance c/d	2,200			
		3,500			3,500
			July 1	By Balance b/d	2,200

F

		₹			₹
June 8	To Bank	900	June 1	By Balance b/d	1,900
" 29	" B/P	1,000	" 30	" Purchases	1,600
	" Discount	40			
" 30	" Balance c/d	1,560			
		3,500			3,500
			July 1	By Balance b/d	1,560

G

		₹			₹
June 25	To Returns Outward	230	June 12	By Purchases	2,000
" 28	" Bank	1,700			
" 28	" Discount	70			
		2,000			2,000

GENERAL LEDGER ADJUSTMENT ACCOUNT
(in Bought Ledger)

		₹			₹
June 1	To Balance b/d	10,450	June 30	By Bought Ledger Adjustment A/c (in General Ledger) :	
" 30	" Bought Ledger Adjustment A/c (in General Ledger) :			Bank	8,030
	Purchases	10,750		Discount	330
				Bills Payable	1,950
				Returns Outward	530
			" 30	" Balance c/d	10,360
		21,200			21,200
July 1	To Balance b/d	10,360			

BOUGHT LEDGER ADJUSTMENT ACCOUNT
(in General Ledger)

		₹			₹
June 30	To General Ledger Adjustment A/c (in Bought Ledger) :		June 1	By Balance b/d	10,450
	Bank	8,030	" 30	General Ledger Adjustment A/c (in Bought Ledger) :	
	Discount	330		Purchases	10,750
	Bills Payable	1,950			
	Returns Outward	530			
" 30	" Balance c/d	10,360			
		21,200			21,200
			July 1	By Balance b/d	10,360

ILLUSTRATION 3. Prepare the General Ledger Adjustment Account in creditors ledger for the year ending 31st March, 2025 from the following information :

Sundry creditors as on 1-4-2024 ₹ 2,30,000.

Total purchases amounted to ₹ 8,25,000 including purchase of trade investment for ₹ 45,000 (face value ₹ 50,000). The total cash purchases were 60% more than the credit purchases.

Cash paid to creditors during the year was 50% of the aggregate of the opening creditors and credit purchases for the period. Creditors allowed a cash discount of ₹ 8,000.

A cheque paid to creditors ₹ 7,000 was dishonoured.

Goods returned to suppliers ₹ 11,000.

Bills receivables amounting to ₹ 30,000 endorsed in favour of a creditor in the month of February, 2025.

(Inter ITC Nov. 2015 Modified)

SOLUTION

CREDITORS' LEDGER
GENERAL LEDGER ADJUSTMENT ACCOUNT
for the year ended 31-3-2025

		₹	₹			₹	₹
1-4-2024	To Balance b/d		2,30,000	31-3-2025	By Creditors Ledger Adjustment A/c :		
31-3-2025	To Creditors Ledger						

	Adjustment A/c :				Bank (1)	2,65,000	
	Purchases (1)	3,00,000			Discount Received	8,000	
	Cheque paid				Returns	11,000	
	dishonoured	7,000	3,07,000		Bills Receivable		
					Endorsed	30,000	3,14,000
					By Balance c/d		2,23,000
			5,37,000				5,37,000

Working Note (1) :

Calculation of Credit Purchases and Cash Paid to Creditors

If credit purchases are 100%, then cash purchases will be 60% higher *i.e.* 100% + 60% = 160%

Thus, credit purchases and cash purchases are in ratio of 100 : 160 *i.e.* 5 : 8. Hence credit purchases are 5/13 of ₹ (8,25,000 – 45,000) = ₹ 3,00,0000

Cash paid to creditors is 50% of (2,30,000 + 3,00,000) = ₹ 2,65,000.

Transfer from One Ledger to Another

Sometimes goods are purchased from and sold to the same person but his personal account will be kept both in purchases and sales ledger. Settlement of such person's account will be made by deducting one account from the other and paying or being paid the balance. The same person cannot be a debtor and creditor of the firm, so his smaller account must be transferred to the greater, either from the purchases ledger to sales ledger or from sales ledger to the purchases ledger, as the case may be. Transfer entries must be made through the journal in order to avoid omission of such cases from the accounts. Suppose Hitesh's Account in purchases ledger shows a balance of ₹ 3,000 and in sales ledger a balance of ₹ 5,000. The former will, therefore, be transferred to the latter. Following entries are passed for this purpose :

Hitesh (in Purchases Ledger)	Dr.	3,000	
To Hitesh (in Sales Ledger)			3,000
(For transfer of balance from Hitesh's Account in purchases ledger to his account in sales ledger)			

Following adjustment entries will also be made :

(*i*)	Purchases Ledger Adjustment A/c (in General Ledger)	Dr.	3,000	
	To General Ledger Adjustment A/c (in Purchases Ledger)			3,000
	(For amount transferred from purchases ledger to sales ledger)			
(*ii*)	General Ledger Adjustment A/c (in Sales Ledger)	Dr.	3,000	
	To Sales Ledger Adjustment A/c (in General Ledger)			3,000
	(For amount transferred from sales ledger to purchases ledger)			

ILLUSTRATION 4. Make the transfer and self-balancing entries for the following :

1. Sold goods to Ram ₹ 8,000, purchased goods from Ram ₹ 500.
2. Purchased goods from Mehta Bros. ₹ 700, sold goods to them 600.
3. Sold goods for ₹ 100 to Ramji Dass, the clerk, in the firm in payment of the outstanding salary due to him.

SOLUTION

JOURNAL

				₹	₹
1.	(*a*) Ram (in the Bought Ledger) Dr. To Ram (in the Sales Ledger) (For the transfer of the smaller amount)			500	500
	(*b*) Purchases Ledger Adjustment Account Dr. (in General Ledger) To General Ledger Adjustment Account (in Purchases Ledger)			500	500
	(*c*) General Ledger Adjustment Account Dr. (in Sales Ledger) To Sales Ledger Adjustment Account (in General Ledger)			500	500
2.	(*a*) Mehta Bros. (in Purchases Ledger) Dr. To Methta Bros. (in Sales Ledger) (For the transfer of smaller amount)			600	600
	(*b*) Purchases Ledger Adjustment Account Dr. (in General Ledger) To General Ledger Adjustment Account (in Purchases Ledger)			600	600
	(*c*) General Ledger Adjustment Account Dr. (in Sales Ledger) To Sales Ledger Adjustment Account (in General Ledger)			600	600
3.	(*a*) Salary Outstanding Account (G.L.) Dr. To Sales Account (For transfer)			100	100
	(*b*) General Ledger Adjustment Account Dr. (in Sales ledger) To Sales Ledger Adjustment Account (in General Ledger) (For self balancing the Sales Ledger and General Ledger) (Second entry will not be needed as only two ledgers are affected)			100	100

Contra Balances

We know that the purchases ledger should contain all credit balances and the sales ledger all debit balances. But in practice it sometimes happens that in some of the purchases ledger accounts there are sundry small debit balances and also that in the sales ledger accounts there are sundry small credit balances. When goods are sold a charge for packages is included in sales. When the account is settled in cash and subsequently when packages are empty and returned, they have to be credited. At balancing time, there may not be any debit balance in the account to offset this credit. Sometimes mistakes are found in accounts after these are settled and their rectification may require crediting of such accounts with a certain amount. Both debit and credit balances are brought forward in adjustment accounts. For example, suppose the purchases ledger balances amount to ₹ 24,540 after deducting ₹ 460, the total of sundry debit balances therein, balances in the sales ledger amount to ₹ 54,750 after deducting ₹ 250, the total of sundry credit balances therein ; the adjustment account in general ledger will appear as follows :

General Ledger

PURCHASES LEDGER ADJUSTMENT ACCOUNT

		₹			₹
Jan. 1	To Balance b/d	460	Jan. 1	By Balance b/d	25,000

SALES LEDGER ADJUSTMENT ACCOUNT

		₹			₹
Jan. 1	To Balance b/d	55,000	Jan. 1	By Balance b/d	250

ILLUSTRATION 5. From the following details write General Ledger Adjustment Accounts (in Bought and Sold Ledgers) and the Bought and Sold Ledger Adjustment Accounts (in General Ledger) as on 31 March, 2025 :

			₹		₹
Debtors (1-4-2024)		Dr.	17,425	Bills accepted for creditors	7,400
Debtors	-do-	Cr.	320	Provision for Bad Debts	900
Creditors	-do-	Cr.	27,408	Discount allowed to debtors but later on disallowed	100
Creditors	-do-	Dr.	210		
Purchases			25,200	Cash received from debtors	8,700
Sales			28,209	Discount allowed to creditors	1,020
Sales Returns			208	Cash paid to debtors	25
Purchases Returns			714	Cash Purchases	4,320
Cash paid to creditors			12,700	Cash Sales	7,400
Bills received from debtors			9,300	Bad debts written off	215
Bill dishonoured			200	Discount allowed to debtors	215
Credit Balance in Sales Ledger (on 31-3-2025)			4,241	Transfer from creditors to debtors ledger	1,242
Debit Balance in Bought Ledger (on 31-3-2025)			2,678	Bad.Debts received	250

SOLUTION

General Ledger

PURCHASE LEDGER ADJUSTMENT ACCOUNT

	₹		₹
To Balance b/d	210	By Balance b/d	27,408
To General Ledger Adjustment A/c (in Purchases Ledger)		By General Ledger Adjustment A/c (in Purchases Ledger) :	
Purchases Returns	714	Purchases	25,200
Cash	12,700	By Balance c/d	2,678
B/P	7,400		
Discount	1,020		
Transfer	1,242		
To Balance c/d	32,000		
	55,286		55,286

SOLD LEDGER ADJUSTMENT ACCOUNT

	₹		₹
To Balance b/d	17,425	By Balance b/d	320
To General Ledger Adjustment A/c		By General Ledger Adjustment A/c	
(in Sales Ledger)		(in Sales Ledger)	
Sales	28,209	Sales Returns	208
Cash	25	Discount	215
Bills dishonoured	200	B/R	9,300
Discount disallowed	100	Cash	8,700
To Balance c/d	4,241	Transfer	1,242
		Bad debts	215
		By Balance c/d	30,000
	50,200		50,200

GENERAL LEDGER ADJUSTMENT ACCOUNT

(in Purchases Ledger)

	₹		₹
To Balance b/d	27,408	By Balance b/d	210
To Purchases Ledger Adjustment A/c		By Purchases Ledger Adjustment A/c	
(in General Ledger) :		(in General Ledger A/c) :	
Purchases	25,200	Purchases Returns	714
To Balance c/d	2,678	Cash	12,700
		B/P	7,400
		Discount	1,020
		Transfer	1,242
		By Balance c/d	32,000
	55,286		55,286

GENERAL LEDGER ADJUSTMENT ACCOUNT

(in Sales Ledger)

	₹		₹
To Balance b/d	320	By Balance b/d	17,425
To Sales Ledger Adjustment A/c		By Sales Ledger Adjustment A/c	
(in General Ledger) :		(in General Ledger)	
Sales Returns	208	Sales	28,209
Discount	215	Cash	25
B/R	9,300	Bills dishonoured	200
Cash	8,700	Discount disallowed	100
Transfer	1,242	By Balance c/d	4,241
Bad Debts	215		
To Balance c/d	30,000		
	50,200		50,200

Note. Cash Purchases, Cash Sales, Provision for Bad Debts and Bad Debts Recovered do not affect the preparation of all adjustment accounts.

SECTIONAL BALANCING SYSTEM

Under sectional balancing system only a section of the group of ledgers is self-balanced. Usually the main ledger (*i.e.,* general ledger) is made self-balancing and for this purpose a control account is maintained in the general ledger for each of the sales and purchases ledger. In other words, two personal accounts (*i.e.,* total accounts), namely, Total Debtors Account and Total Creditors Account are opened in the general ledger to make it self-balancing. Correctness of the posting of the sales and bought ledger can be checked by preparing Total Debtors and Total Creditors Accounts in the general ledger. Thus, under sectional balancing system, a trial balance is prepared only for the general ledger.

Difference Between Self-Balancing & Sectional Balancing System

Following are the main distinctions between the two systems :

(*i*) Under self-balancing system, *all* the ledgers are *self-balanced* and a total balance of each ledger can be prepared in order to check the arithmetical accuracy of each ledger whereas under sectional balancing only a section of the group of ledgers is self-balancing.

(*ii*) Under sectional balancing usually the main ledger is made self-balancing and for this purpose a *control account* is maintained in the general ledger for each of the sales and purchase ledger but in self-balancing system control or adjustments accounts are opened in each ledger.

(*iii*) Under sectional balancing, a *trial balance* is prepared only in the general ledger whereas in self-balancing system, a trial balance is prepared in each of the ledgers independently.

(*iv*) Under self-balancing ledger, in each ledger *double entry is completed* whereas in sectional ledgers double entry is completed only in general ledger. Personal accounts in debtors and creditors ledgers are maintained on single entry basis.

Total Debtors Account

This account is debited with the sum of all the items which have been debited in detail to individual personal accounts in the sales ledgers and credited with the sum of all the items which have been credited to such accounts. The balance of this account should, therefore, be equal to the sum of all balances appearing in the sales ledgers.

The total of the various items of debit and credit which are extracted from the various books appear in the Total Debtors' Account and are given in the following specimen :

Dr. **TOTAL DEBTORS ACCOUNT** Cr.

Dr.	Cr.
1. Opening Debit Balance (from Opening Entry)	1. Opening Credit Balance (from Opening Entry)
2. Credit Sales (from Sales Book)	2. Cash received from Debtors (from Cash Book)
3. B/R Dishonoured (from Journal)	3. Discount allowed to Debtors (from Cash Book)
4. Total Creditors A/c (B/R endorsed dishonoured)—(from Journal)	4. Sales Return (from Returns Inwards Book)
5. Interest & Expenses Charged (from Journal)	5. Bills Receivable (from B/R Book)
6. Refund to Debtors (from Cash Book)	6. Bad Debts Allowances (from Journal)
7. Transfers (from Journal)	7. Transfers (from Journal)
8. Closing Balance, if any	8. Closing Balance of Debtors

Total Creditors Account

This account operates as a control account of the bought ledger and should disclose a balance equal to the total of all the individual balances in this ledger. This account is raised in a similar manner to that of

Total Debtors Account. The various debit and credit items along with their source books which appear in Total Creditors Account are given as follows :

Dr. **TOTAL CREDITORS ACCOUNT** Cr.

Dr.	Cr.
1. Opening Debit Balance of Creditors (From Opening Entry)	1. Opening Balance of Creditors (from Opening Entry)
2. Cash Paid to Creditors (from Cash Book)	2. Purchases (from Purchases Book)
3. Discount received (from Cash Book)	3. Bills Payable Dishonoured (from Journal)
4. Returns Outwards (from Purchase Returns Book)	4. Interest and Expenses (from Journal)
5. Bills Payable (from B/P Book)	5. Total Debtors A/c (B/R endorsed dishonoured)—(from Journal)
6. B/R (Endorsed) (from Journal)	6. Refund from Creditors (from Cash Book)
7. Transfers (from Journal)	7. Closing Debit Balance of Creditors
8. Closing Balance of Creditors	

ILLUSTRATION 6. Following particulars are obtained from books of a Company for the year ended 31st March, 2025 :

	₹		₹
Cash Sales	25,000	Bills Receivable dishonoured	2,500
Credit Purchases	2,80,000	Return Inward	8,500
Collection from Debtors	4,25,000	Payments to Creditors	1,62,000
Bills Receivable received	20,000	Discount allowed	3,000
Discount Received	2,500	Debtors' cheque returned dishonoured	7,500
Cash Purchases	12,000	Credit Sales	4,90,000
Bills Payable paid	6,500	Bills Receivables collected	10,000
Recovery of Bad Debts	1,500	Return Outward	3,700
Bills Receivable discounted with Bank	8,000	Bills Receivable endorsed to creditors	7,900
Interest charged on overdue Customer's Accounts	1,200	Overpayments refunded by suppliers	600
Endorsed Bills Receivable dishonoured (noting charges ₹ 75)	5,500	Bad Debts	1,000
Bills Payable accepted	16,000	**Opening Balances**	
		Sundry Debtors	78,000
		Sundry Creditors	85,000

You are required to prepare Total Debtors Account and Total Creditors Account.

SOLUTION

TOTAL DEBTORS ACCOUNT

	₹		₹
To Balance b/d	78,000	By Cash	4,25,000
To Bank (Cheque Dishonoured)	7,500	By Discount Allowed	3,000
To B/R (Dishonoured)	2,500	By B/R	20,000
To Interest	1,200	By Returns Inward	8,500
To Sales	4,90,000	By Bad Debts	1,000
To Sundry Creditors (Endorsed Bill Dishonoured with Noting Charges)	5,575	By Balance c/d	1,27,275
	5,84,775		5,84,775

TOTAL CREDITORS ACCOUNT

	₹		₹
To Cash	1,62,000	By Balance b/d	85,000
To B/R (Endorsed)	7,900	By Purchases	2,80,000
To Discount Received	2,500	By Sundry Debtors A/c	
To Bills Payable	16,000	(Endorsed B/R Dishonoured	
To Return Outward	3,700	with Noting Charges)	5,575
To Balance c/d	1,79,075	By Cash (Over Payments Refunded)	600
	3,71,175		3,71,175

Advantages of Self-Balancing Ledgers

Following are the main advantages of self-balancing ledgers :

1. It is easy to locate the errors under self-balancing system. Delay in balancing is minimised thereby saving time, money and labour.
2. It is easy to compile trial balance before individual personal ledger balances are absorbed. It also facilitates the preparation of both interim accounts and draft final accounts.
3. It enables accounting system that would otherwise be unwieldy, to be divided into self contained sections.
4. The control accounts provide a quick means of ascertaining the upto-date amounts owing to and by the business. This information can be very useful to the management.
5. It acts as a check on the honesty of clerks in charge of personal ledgers.
6. The information regarding proprietor's capital, profit and loss etc. contained in the general ledger can be kept confidential from the office staff, if general ledger is kept in the charge of the Partner or a trustworthy assistant.
7. It provides a good method of office control by distinguishing the efficient clerks from the inefficient clerks.

Thus this system can be used with profit in those cases where either a large number of customers and suppliers require alphabetical or regional classification or when it is desired to prepare final accounts periodically.

Errors Affecting Self-Balancing Ledgers

We have already discussed the various types of errors and how to rectify them in a previous chapter. The same technique with a little deviation can be applied to the correction of errors affecting self-balancing errors. We must judge whether the error in question :

(*i*) affects the total of a Subsidiary Book ; or

(*ii*) It relates to a transfer of amount from one ledger to another ledger.

If the error affects the total of a subsidiary book (*i.e.* sales book, purchases book, sales and purchases returns book, bills receivable and bills payable books and cash column for receipt from sundry debtors and payments to sundry creditors), the error is rectified by making a self-balancing entry in addition to the usual entry for rectifying the error. For example, if the total of the sales book is less by ₹ 200 it will affect sales account, sales ledger adjustment account (in general ledger) and general ledger adjustment account (in sales ledger). The error will be corrected as under :

		Dr.	Cr.
(*i*)	Suspense A/c Dr.	₹ 200	
	To Sales		₹ 200
	(For entry made for correcting sales account)		
(*ii*)	Sales Ledger Adjustment A/c Dr.	₹ 200	
	(in General Ledger)		

To General Ledger Adjustment A/c ₹ 200
(in Sales Ledger)
(For additional self-balancing entry passed for correcting adjustment accounts)

If the error relates to a transfer of account from one ledger to another ledger and does not affect the total of some subsidiary book with respect of purchases and sales, then no entry is required to be passed for correcting adjustment accounts. Only one usual entry will be passed to correct the error. For example, if goods purchased from Ram Prakash for ₹ 500 are posted to Ram Parshad's A/c as ₹ 50 the error will be corrected by passing the following entry :

Suspense A/c	Dr.	450	
Ram Parshad's A/c		50	
To Ram Parkash			500
(For entry made for correcting the two personal accounts)			

ILLUSTRATION 7. A firm has adopted the self-balancing system with their purchase and sale ledgers, the adjustment accounts for these being kept in the general ledger. Since the date on which accounts were last made up the following errors have been discovered :

(*a*) an overcast of ₹ 100 in the sales book ;
(*b*) an item of ₹ 420 in the returns outwards book has been posted to the personal account as ₹ 240;
(*c*) a credit of ₹ 2,140 for goods returned has been entered in the account of a customer in the Sales Ledger, no other entry whatever being made ;
(*d*) discount amounting to ₹ 150 received during a certain month have not been posted to discount account in the General Ledger (The posting to the other accounts concerned has been correctly made);
(*e*) a trade discount of ₹ 100 has been debited to a supplier's account in the bought ledger and posted direct to the credit of purchases account in the general ledger, no further entry being made ;
(*f*) the posting to the sales ledger adjustment account of a bill for ₹ 300 received from a customer has been omitted ;
(*g*) Goods returned for ₹ 150 by Rajesh were not entered in the books ;
(*h*) a cheque for ₹ 500 received from Umesh was wrongly posted to the account of Suresh.

Rectify the above errors.

SOLUTION

				₹	₹
(*a*)	(*i*) Sales A/c To Suspense A/c (For correction of overcasting)	Dr.		100	100
	(*ii*) General Ledger Adjustment A/c (in Sales Ledger) To Sales Ledger Adjustment A/c (in General Ledger) (For additional entry for correcting adjustment A/cs)	Dr.		100	100
(*b*)	(*i*) Creditors To Suspense A/c (For correction of wrong posting)	Dr.		180	180
	(*ii*) No additional entry needed as the total accounts were already correct)				
(*c*)	(*i*) Sales Returns A/c To Suspense A/c (Goods returned omitted to be debited to Sales Returns A/c now recorded)	Dr.		2,140	2,140

	Particulars		Dr.	Cr.
	(*ii*) General Ledger Adjustment A/c (in Sales Ledger) To Sales Ledger Adjustment A/c (in General Ledger) (For additional entry for correcting adjustment account)	Dr.	2,140	2,140
(*d*)	(*i*) Suspense A/c To Discount A/c (For correction of Discount account)	Dr.	150	150
	(*ii*) No additional entry is required			
(*e*)	(*i*) Bought Ledger Adjustment A/c (In General Ledger) To General Ledger Adjustment A/c (in Bought Ledger) (For self-balancing entry for trade discount not done as yet)	Dr.	100	100
(*f*)	Suspense A/c To Sales Ledger Adjustment A/c (For correction of an omission)	Dr.	300	300
(*g*)	(*i*) Return Inwards A/c To Rajesh A/c (Entry for omission of Sales Returns)	Dr.	150	150
	(*ii*) General Ledger Adjustment A/c (in Sales Ledger) To Sales Ledger Adjustment A/c (in General Ledger) (Entry in the adjustment account arising out of the omission of entry regarding sales returns)	Dr.	150	150
(*h*)	(*i*) Suresh A/c To Umesh A/c (Amount wrongly credited to the former A/c instead of to latter A/c, now rectified)	Dr.	500	500
	(*ii*) General Ledger Adjustment A/c (in Sales Ledger) To Sales Ledger Adjustment A/c (in General Ledger) (Correcting entry in total account relating to Sales Ledger)	Dr.	500	500
	(*iii*) Sales Ledger Adjustment A/c (in General Ledger) To General Ledger Adjustment A/c (in Sales Ledger) (Correction of the entry in total relating to Sales Ledger)	Dr.	500	500

QUESTIONS

OBJECTIVE TYPE

1. In each of the following cases indicate the alternative which you consider to be correct.

(*a*) Sold Ledger Adjustment Account is opened in :
(*i*) sold ledger, (*ii*) bought ledger, (*iii*) general ledger, (*iv*) sold ledger as well as in bought ledger.
(*b*) Goodwill Account is opened in :
(*i*) debtors ledger, (*ii*) creditors ledger, (*iii*) general ledger.
(*c*) Bought Ledger Adjustment Account is opened in :
(*i*) bought ledger, (*ii*) sold ledger, (*iii*) general ledger, (*iv*) sold ledger as well as in bought ledger.
(*d*) Provision for doubtful debts is opened in :
(*i*) debtors ledger, (*ii*) creditors ledger, (*iii*) general ledger.
(*e*) General Ledger Adjustment Account is opened in :
(*i*) bought ledger, (*ii*) sold ledger, (*iii*) general ledger, (*iv*) both sold ledger and bought ledger.
(*f*) Bills receivable from X will be taken to :
(*i*) general ledger, (*ii*) debtors ledger, (*iii*) creditors ledger.
(*g*) The adjustment of cash sales will appear in :
(*i*) Sales Ledger Adjustment Account, (*ii*) Bought Ledger Adjustment Account, (*iii*) none of the above two accounts.
(*h*) Bad Debts previously written off now recovered affects :
(*i*) General Ledger Adjustment in sales ledger, (*ii*) General Ledger Adjustment in bought ledger, (*iii*) none of these.
(*i*) The adjustment for bills receivable dishonoured will appear in :
(*i*) Sales Ledger Adjustment Account, (*ii*) Bought Ledger Adjustment Account, (*iii*) None of these.

Ans. [(*a*) : (*iii*), (*b*) : (*iii*), (*c*) : (*iii*), (*d*) : (*iii*), (*e*) : (*iv*), (*f*) : (*i*), (*g*) : (*iii*), (*h*) : (*iii*), (*i*) : (*i*)].

2. Fills in the blanks :

(1) Creditors ledger is called.........
(2) Debtors Ledger Adjustment Account is opened in............ledger and is equivalent to.........Account.
(3) In case of old machinery sold to X, the account of old machinery is taken to............and that of X to............
(4) The term 'Trade Creditors' means a person from whom such goods in which he deals are purchased on.........
(5) The disagreement of total balance in the creditors ledger gives a hint that the mistake is committed in any of the accounts relating to.........
(6) At the time of transfer from one ledger to another the personal account in.........ledger is debited and the same personal account in............ledger is credited.
(7) In sectional balancing system only......ledger is made self-balancing and.........account and.........account are used.
(8) Sectional balancing system is the self-balancing of a.........of the group of ledgers.

Ans. [(1) Bought or Purchases Ledger ; (2) General, Total Debtors ; (3) General Ledger, General Ledger ; (4) Credit basis ; (5) Creditors ; (6) Creditors, Debtors, (7) General, Sales Ledger Adjustment, Purchase Ledger Adjustment ; (8) Section].

3. State which of the following statements are True or False :

(*a*) Sales Ledger Adjustment Account in the General Ledger is just reverse of General Ledger Adjustment Account in the Sales Ledger.

(*b*) General Ledger contains all accounts except the personal accounts of trade debtors and trade creditors.

(*c*) Self-balancing system can be introduced even in small concerns where only one ledger is maintained.

(*d*) With the introduction of self-balancing system there will be no errors in the ledgers.

(*e*) Self-balancing and sectional balancing are synonymous terms.

(*f*) In sectional balancing system, a trial balance is prepared only for the General Ledger.

(*g*) No entry for self-balancing is required when a transaction affects only one ledger.

Ans. [True : (*a*) ; (*b*) ; (*f*) ; (*g*) ; False : (*c*) ; (*d*) ; (*e*)].

SHORT ANSWER TYPE

1. What is self-balancing system of ledgers ?
2. How are Ledgers made self-balancing ?
3. Give two advantages of self-balancing ledgers system.
4. Write a note on (*i*) Contra balances, (*ii*) Transfers from one ledger to another ledger.
5. What is sectional balancing ?
6. Distinguish between self-balancing and sectional balancing.
7. What are the main advantages of sectional balancing ?
8. What is general ledger kept under self-balancing ledgers system ?
9. What are the self-balancing entries required to adjust transfer of debtors balance to Creditors Account?
10. Give two objects of self-balancing ledgers system.
11. What are the other names for debtors ledger ?
12. The summarised analysis of the accounts of the outstanding debtors of Ganapathi Ltd. at the date of 13-3-2025 (Annual Closing) of amount as under :

Debtors	*Goods Sold during the year (₹)*	*Goods returned during the year (₹)*	*Cash and Cheques received during the year (₹)*	*Discount allowed during the year (₹)*	*Bills of Exchange received during the year (₹)*
A	6,000	—	4,000	1,000	—
B	4,000	1,000	2,000	—	—
C	10,000	—	6,000	—	—
D	20,000	2,000	12,000	1,000	2,000
F	24,000	3,000	16,000	2,000	2,000

Debtors' balance at the beginning of the year was ₹ 9,000. Out the above receipts of a bill for ₹ 1,400 given by D was dishonoured, noting charges amounting to ₹ 40.

Required :

Prepare General Ledger Adjustment Account in Debtors Ledger.

Ans. [Credit Balance of General Ledger Adjustment A/c ₹ 20,440]

LONG ANSWER TYPE

1. What do you understand by "Self-Balancing System of Ledger" ? How are the ledgers made self-balancing ? State the advantages of this system.
2. What is Sectional Balancing ? Distinguish it from Self-Balancing Ledgers.

3. In a business where the system of self-balancing of ledgers is adopted there are two Bought Ledgers, *viz.* (*i*) Inland, and (*ii*) Foreign ; three Sold Ledgers *viz.* (*i*) Local, (*ii*) Provincial, and (*iii*) Foreign and one General Ledger. Give Proforma rulings of the Cash Book, Sales Book, Purchases Book, Bills Receivable Book, Bills Payable Book and the Journal suitable for that business.
4. Write a note on : (*i*) Contra balances, (*ii*) Transfer from one ledger to another ledger.
5. It is said that in a system of sectional balancing, errors are easily and quickly located. Is it correct ? If so, how is it made possible ?
6. What is sectional ledger ? Briefly explain the system of sectional balancing. State the advantages of sectional balancing.
7. A company keeps its Ledger upon self-balancing principle. You are required to describe the operation of this system and its advantages, illustrating your answer with proforma examples and explaining the sources of the entries made by you.

PRACTICAL PROBLEMS

1. In a business three Ledgers are kept in use, *viz.* (*i*) a Creditors' Ledger, (*ii*) a Debtors' Ledger, and (*iii*) a General Ledger which are kept on the self-balancing system. Following is a summary of the transactions with the Debtors and Creditors of the business for the month of March, 2025. Open the *necessary Adjustment Accounts in the respective Ledgers :*

	₹		₹
Debtors' Balance 1-3-2025	40,000	Received Bills Receivable	7,500
Creditors' Balance 1-3-2025	46,250	Bills Payable Accepted	3,750
Credit Sales	24,500	Returns Outwards	1,500
Credit Purchases	11,250	Returns Inwards	2,195
Received Cash from Debtors	19,500	Allowances to Debtors	680
Discount allowed to them	500	Allowances from Creditors	375
Paid Cash to Creditors	24,690	Bad Debts written off	1,125
Discount allowed by them	810	Bills Receivable Dishonoured	940

Ans. [SL Adj. A/c (Dr.) ₹ 33,940 ; PL Adj. A/c (Cr.) 26,375].

2. ESS BEE Ltd. have three ledgers in use *viz.*, a Debtors' Ledger, a Creditors' Ledger and a Nominal Ledger which are all kept on the system of Self-Balancing. From the following particulars, prepare (*i*) *Debtors' Ledger Adjustment Account and (ii) Creditors' Ledger Adjustment Account in the Nominal Ledger.*

1-10-2024	₹		₹
Balance of Sundry Debtors	32,000	Bills Payable accepted	3,000
Balance of Sundry Creditors	37,000	Bills Receivable received	6,000
31-3-2025		Returns Inwards	1,750
Credit Purchases	9,000	Returns Outwards	1,200
Credit Sales	19,600	Rebate allowed to Debtors	550
Cash Sales	1,500	Rebate allowed by Creditors	300
Paid to Creditors	19,750	Provision for Doubtful Debts	320
Discount allowed by them	650	Bad Debts	900
Cash received from Debtors	15,600	Bills Receivable Dishonoured	750
Discount allowed to Debtors	400		

Ans. [DL Adj. A/c (Dr.) ₹ 27,150 ; CL Adj. A/c (Cr.) ₹ 21,100].

3. From the following information prepare Sales Ledger Adjustment Accounts in General Ledger under self-balancing system :

	₹		₹
Sundry Debtors Opening Balances :		Bills Receivable dishonoured	10,000
Debit	2,00,000	Bills Receivable discounted	40,000
Credit	10,000	Provision for Bad Debts	10,000
Cash and Cheque Receipts	8,00,000	Bad Debts recovered	5,000
Credit Sales	10,00,000	Transfer from Debtors' Ledger to Creditors' Ledger	5,000
Discount allowed	30,000		
Returns Inward	20,000	Transfer from Creditors' Ledger to Debtors' Ledger	6,000
Bad Debts	15,000		
Bills Receivable received	1,00,000	Closing Credit Balance in Sundry Debtors	20,000

Ans. [S.L. Adjustment A/c (Dr.) ₹ 2,44,000].

4. Following details were extracted from the books of X Limited for the six months ended 31st March, 2025.

	₹		₹
Sundry debtors' balances total,		Purchases returns	180
October 1, 2024	1,920	Interest charged to debtors	10
Supplier's balance total		Debtors cheques dishonoured	70
October 1, 2024	1,210	Discount allowed	350
Cash paid to suppliers	7,610	Bills payable accepted	
Cash received from debtors	12,990	(including renewals)	890
Credit purchases	8,840	Bills payable withdrawn	
Cash purchases	4,500	upon renewed	200
Discount received	280	Interest on bills payable renewed	20
Bad debts written off	50	Cash sales	8,200
Sales returns	90	Credit sales	13,300

Prepare *Sold Ledger Adjustment Account and Bought Ledger Adjustment Account in General Ledger.*

Ans. [S.L. Adj. A/c (Dr.) ₹ 1,820 ; B.L. Adj. A/c (Cr.) ₹ 1,310].

5. From the following particulars write up necessary Adjustment A/cs as they would appear in General Ledger :

	₹
Debtors' balance in General Ledger Adj. A/c	(Cr.) 49,850
Creditors' balance in General Ledger Adj. A/c	(Dr.) 28,010

	₹		₹
Credit Sales	40,400	Returns outward	2,240
Cash Sales	18,080	Bills Payable accepted	5,300
Cash Purchases	15,930	Bills Receivable received	3,500
Credit Purchases	27,600	B/R dishonoured	325
Creditors paid off	26,500	Interest charged for dishonoured bill	20
Received from Debtors	44,100	Allowances	1,605
Discount allowed to the business	1,450	Bad debts	1,495
Discount allowed by the business	1,540	Transfer from Debtors	
Returns Inward	1,795	Ledger to Creditors Ledger	400

Ans. [DL Adj. A/c (Dr.) Balance ₹ 36,160 ; CL Adj. A/c (Cr.) Balance ₹ 19,720].

6. Prepare Bought Ledger Adjustment and Sales Ledger Adjustment Account as would appear in the General Ledger of M/s Hindustan Traders for the year ended 31st March, 2025 from the following information :

Opening Balances (1-4-2024)

	Dr. ₹	*Cr.* ₹
Bought Ledger	2,610	35,820
Sales Ledger	43,860	720

Transactions during the year :

	₹		₹
Purchases	1,98,540	Discount received	4,980
Purchases Returns	7,680	Cash refunded to the debtors	520
Sales	2,62,470	Bills Receivable received	12,360
Sales Returns	3,510	Bills Payable issued	6,750
Cash received from debtors	2,28,630	Bills Receivable dishonoured	750
Discount allowed	8,460	Transfer from Bought to Sales Ledger	100
Cash paid to the creditors	1,75,290	Transfer from Sales to Bought Ledger	40

Closing Balance (31-3-2025) :

Bought Ledger	(Dr.)	2,310
Sales Ledger	(Dr.)	1,360

Ans. [P.L. Adj. A/c (Cr.) Balance ₹ 39,220 ; S.L. Adjustment A/c (Dr.) Balance ₹ 55,140].

7. From the following particulars which have been extracted from the books of Gulzar & Co. for the year ended 31st March, 2025 prepare *General Ledger Adjustment Account in Creditors Ledger* and *Debtors Ledger Adjustment Account in the General Ledger* :

	Dr. ₹	*Cr.* ₹
Debtors Balance 1-4-2024	20,000	300
Creditors balance 1-4-2024	200	15,000

Transactions during the year :

	₹		₹
Purchases (including cash ₹ 4,000)	12,000	Bills receivable endorsed	800
Sales (including cash ₹ 6,000)	25,000	Bills receivable as endorsed dishonoured	300
Cash paid to suppliers in full settlement of claim of ₹ 9,000	8,500	Bills receivable discounted	1,400
Cash received from customers in full settlement of claim of ₹ 15,000	14,100	Bills receivable dishonoured	400
		Interest charged on dishonoured bill	30
Bills payable accepted (including renewals)	2,000	Transfer from one ledger to another ledger	600
Bills payable withdrawn upon renewals	500	Returns (Cr.)	700
Interest on bills payable renewed	20	Debtors Balance 31-3-2025 (Cr.)	450
Bills receivable received	3,000	Creditors Balance 31-3-2025 (Cr.)	10,870

Ans. [DL Adj. A/c (in General Ledger) ₹ 21,280 (Dr.); GL Adj. A/c (in Creditors Ledger) ₹ 350 (Cr.)].

8. Mr. Bee, the proprietor of Make Honey Company, keeps his accounts under the self-balancing system. You are required to prepare *Total Debtors A/c and Total Creditors A/c* from the following particulars in the respective ledgers :

Opening Balances :

	Dr.	Cr.
	₹	₹
Debtors' balances	21,420	1,070
Creditors' balances	740	25,350

Transactions during the month :

	₹		₹
Purchases	65,290	Interest charged to debtors	570
Sales	88,580	Cheques from debtors dishonoured	1,500
Purchase returns	2,320	Interest charged by creditors	90
Sales returns	1,370	Bills receivable dishonoured	700
Cash and cheques received from debtors	70,510	Bad debts written off	1,575
Bills receivable	5,300	Bills receivable discounted (discount ₹ 100)	4,800
Cash paid to creditors	59,365	Reserve for bad and doubtful debts	1,520
Bills payable accepted	5,400	Bills payable honoured	6,300
Cash discount received	1,820	Debtors' balances (Cr.)	570
Cash discount allowed	2,370	Creditors' balances (Dr.)	1,850

Included in the debtors was an amount of ₹ 1,650 due from Mr. G. from whom goods worth ₹ 750 had been purchased. Mr. G. agreed to set off his claim against the amount due from him.

Ans. [Debtors Adjustment A/c ₹ 30,395 ; Creditors Adjustment A/c ₹ 22,185].

9. Write up (*a*) *Total Debtors' Account* and (*b*) *Total Creditors'* Account recording the following transactions for the year ended 31-3-2025 bringing down the balance on that date :

	₹		₹
Sales	2,04,000	Bad Debts written off	1,100
Purchases	1,40,000	Cash received in respect of debit balance in creditors account	1,100
Cash received from debtors	1,55,000	Returns inward	9,900
Cash paid to creditors	1,37,000	Bills received	40,000
Allowances to customers on goods damaged	2,000	Returns outward	1,500
Amount due to suppliers as shown by creditors ledger offset against amount due from the same concern as shown by debtors ledger	1,400	Bills receivable dishonoured	2,500
		Discounts received	3,000
		Discount allowed	2,500
Cash received in respect of debts previously written off	1,300	Cash refunded to the debtor	500

On 1-4-2024 the debtors ledger balances were ₹ 18,300 debit and ₹ 190 credit while the creditors ledger balances on the same date were ₹ 16,500 credit and ₹ 1,100 debit. On 31-3-2025 there were no credit balances in debtors ledger except those outstanding on 1-4-2024 and no debit balances in the creditors ledger.

Ans. [(*a*) ₹ 13,400 ; (*b*) ₹ 13,600].

10. From the following particulars prepare "General Ledger Adjustment Account" in Sales Ledger :

Due by : A.B. ₹ 170 ; B.C. ₹ 180 ; C.D. ₹ 195 ; E.F. ₹ 300.

Credit balance : B.G. ₹ 130 ; F.D. ₹ 30.

June 2	Sold goods to A.B. ₹ 185. Received from B.C. on account ₹ 100.	June 21	Received from E.F. ₹ 295 in full settlement.
" 9	Drew a bill on A.B. ₹ 250 which he accepted payable after 3 months.	" 22	Sold goods to E.F. for ₹ 250
		" 23	M.N. returned goods ₹ 50

June 11 Returned goods to B.G. ₹ 30.
" 12 Sold goods to M.N. ₹ 200.
" 14 Received from C.D. ₹ 189 in full settlement of dues.
" 19 Sold goods to F.D. ₹ 150.
June 27 Received from A.B. ₹ 100 allowing him discount ₹ 5
" 28 Sold goods to R.G. ₹ 200
Received from E.F. ₹ 200, discount ₹ 3.
" 28 Received as advance from S.M. ₹ 300.

Ans. [Cr. Balance ₹ 597].

11. From the following particulars prepare the relevant adjustment account as would appear in the General Ledger of Mr. Vasu for the month of March, 2025.

Date	*Particulars*
1	Purchases from Mr. X ₹ 2,000.
2	Paid ₹ 1,600 after adjusting the initial advance in full to Mr. X.
11	Paid ₹ 1,000 to Mr. R towards the purchases made in February in full.
13	Paid advance to Mr. Y. ₹ 3,000.
14	Purchased goods from Mr. A ₹ 4,000.
25	Returned goods worth ₹ 500 to Mr. A.
26	Settled the balance due to A at a discount of 10 per cent.
27	Goods Purchased from Mr. Y. ₹ 2,500 against the advance paid on 13th.
28	Received back the advance from Mr. P paid on 28th February, 2025, ₹ 2,000.
30	Purchases from B ₹ 2,000.
31	Goods returned to Q ₹ 750. The goods were originally purchased for cash in February.

Ans. [Balance (Cr.) ₹ 2,000 ; (Dr.) ₹ 1,250].

12. Following information is available from the books of a trader from January 1 to March 31, 2025 :

(1) Total Sales amounted to ₹ 60,000 including the sale of old furniture for ₹ 1,200 (Book Value ₹ 3,500). The total Cash Sales were 80% less than the total Credit Sales.

(2) Cash collection from debtors amounted to 60% of the aggregate of the opening debtors and the Credit Sales for the period. Debtors were allowed Cash discounts for ₹ 2,600.

(3) Bills Receivable drawn during the three months totalled ₹ 6,000, of which bills amounting to ₹ 3,000 were endorsed in favour of suppliers. Out of these endorsed B/R, a B/R for ₹ 600 was dishonoured for non-payment, as the party became insolvent, his estate realising nothing.

(4) Cheques received from Sundry Customers for ₹ 6,000 were dishonoured ; a sum of ₹ 500 is irrecoverable ; Bad Debts written off in the earlier years realised ₹ 2,500.

(5) Sundry Debtors, as on 1st January 2025, stood at ₹ 40,000.

You are required to show the *Debtors Ledger Adjustment Account in the Ledger.*

Ans. [Dr. Balance ₹ 32,500].

13. Mr. Patel maintains his ledgers on self-balancing system. The transactions from January 1 to April 30, 2025 are given below. You are required to prepare General Ledger Adjustment Account as will appear in the Debtors' Ledger :

(1) *Opening Balance* (1-1-2025) :
Debtors Ledger ₹ 78,000.

(2) Cash Sales – ₹ 12,000 (being 10% of total Sales).

(3) Collection from customers (other than collections on Bills Receivable) amounted to ₹ 1,10,000 which included the following :

(*a*) A sum of ₹ 3,000 realised from the estate of an insolvent customer (at 0.60 paise per Rupee).

(*b*) ₹ 6,500 received from a customer as advance for sale.

(*c*) ₹ 4,000 received from a debtor after adjustments of an advance of ₹ 2,000 made in December, 2024.

(*d*) ₹ 1,250 received from a party whose account was written off in earlier years.

(4) Interest charged to customers on overdue accounts ₹ 2,600.

(5) Bills Receivable drawn during the period ₹ 18,500.

(6) Bills Receivable collected during the period ₹ 10,600 (including ₹ 5,900 collected on Bills Receivable drawn during November and December, 2024)

(7) Bills Receivable dishonoured on maturity ₹ 1,700.

(8) Bills Receivable endorsed to Suppliers – ₹ 6,000, out of which Bill Receivable for ₹ 2,000 was discounted by Creditors at 5% duly met at maturity. Bills Receivable for ₹ 3,000 were dishonoured on maturity (noting charges being ₹ 20) and Bills Receivable amounting to ₹ 1,000 will mature in May 2025.

(9) Returns Inward – ₹ 11,600.

(10) Transfer from creditors ledger to debtors ledger – ₹ 6,900.

Ans. [Cr. Balance ₹ 50,070].

14. Messrs Pioneer & Co., are maintaining accounts on self-balancing system. On 31-3-2025 the General Ledger discloses the following balances :

Sales Ledger Adjustment Account	Dr.	₹	35,235
Bought Ledger Adjustment Account	Cr.	₹	15,530

On scrutinising the ledger, the following mistakes were noticed :

(*a*) A credit purchase of ₹ 4,350 has been credited to the Sales Ledger Adjustment Account though the payment has been debited to the Bought ledger Adjustment Account. However, in the subsidiary books, these two entries have been entered only in the Bought Ledger.

(*b*) ₹ 1,000 paid to B for goods purchased have been debited to the Sales Ledger Adjustment Account. In the subsidiary books, party's account shows a debit balance in the Sales Ledger and a credit balance in the Bought Ledger.

(*c*) ₹ 4,750 were due from A in the Sales Ledger as against ₹ 7,740 due to him for purchases made and entered in the Bought Ledger.

(*d*) The Sales Ledger Balances disclose that sums aggregating ₹ 740 have to be written off as Bad Debts and Discounts.

Prepare the necessary Journal Entries in the General Ledger and other subsidiary books.

15. From the following information available from the books of a trader from 1-1-2025 to 31-3-2025, you are required to draw up the Debtors Ledger Adjustment Account in the General Ledger :

(*i*) Total sales amounted to ₹ 2,00,000 including the sale of machine for ₹ 6,800 (book value ₹ 12,000). The total cash sales were 85% less than the total credit sales.

(*ii*) Cash collections from debtors amounted to 70% of the aggregate of the opening debtors and credit sales for the period. Debtors were allowed a cash discount of ₹ 20,000.

(*iii*) Bills receivable drawn during the three months totalled ₹ 45,000 of which bills amounting to ₹ 20,000 were endorsed in favour of suppliers. Out of the endorsed bills, one bill for ₹ 6,000 was dishonoured for non-payment as the party became insolvent, his estate realised nothing.

(*iv*) Cheque received from debtors ₹ 15,000 were dishonoured, a sum of ₹ 3,500 was irrecoverable, Bad debts written off in the earlier year's realised ₹ 15,000.

(*v*) Sundry debtors as on 1-1-2025 stood at ₹ 1,50,000. ***(C.A. Inter, IPCE, May, 2016 Modified)***

Ans. [Debtors Ledger Adjustment Account Balance on 31-3-2025 ₹ 41,900 Dr.]

Hints : Credit Sales ₹ 1,68,000 $\left(i.e.\ \frac{100}{115} \times ₹\ 1,93,200\right)$; Bad Debts ₹ 9,500.

CHAPTER

21

Single Entry or Accounts from Incomplete Records

The term 'Single Entry' is vaguely used to define the method of maintaining accounts which does not exactly follow the principles of double entry system. It does not mean (as the name goes) that there is one entry for each transaction *i.e.* only one account is given debit or credit for each transaction. But it simply means that principles of the double entry system are not being followed for all transactions. Under this method, usually the personal accounts of the debtors and creditors are kept and impersonal accounts—real and nominal accounts, may not be maintained in the books. There are two types of single entry :

1. Pure Single Entry. Under this type of single entry, the dual-aspect of each transaction is ignored. Only the personal accounts of the debtors and creditors are kept, all real and nominal accounts are not maintained altogether in the books.

2. Single Entry in the Popular Sense. This method of single entry goes beyond the maintaining of the personal accounts, yet falls short of a complete system of double entry. Under this, some subsidiary books are also written up but the postings are made therefrom of such entries as relate to personal accounts.

Kohler has defined single entry system as follows :

"A system of book-keeping in which as a rule only records of cash and personal accounts are maintained, it is always incomplete double entry varying with the circumstances."

Single entry in the popular sense may consist of (*i*) double entry for certain transactions such as cash received from debtors or cash paid to creditors, (*ii*) single entry in respect of some transactions such as purchase of fixed assets, payment of expenses etc., and (*iii*) no entry in respect of some transactions such as bad debts, depreciation, loss of stock by fire etc.

From the above description it becomes clear that single entry is not any particular system of accounting but rather it is the double entry system in an incomplete and disjointed form.

Difference Between Single Entry and Double Entry

Following are the main differences :

(*i*) The single entry method of maintaining accounts is an incomplete record of the financial transactions whereas the double entry method of maintaining accounts is a complete record of the financial transactions.

(*ii*) All accounts, personal as well as impersonal, are maintained in the double entry method whereas in the single entry only personal accounts may be maintained.

(*iii*) Books maintained by the single entry system are not as reliable as they are in case of the double entry system because a complete record of transactions is not maintained.

(*iv*) Trial Balance cannot be prepared as it can be prepared in the double entry system, so arithmetical accuracy cannot be checked. In the double entry system, Trial Balance can be prepared because a complete record of transactions is maintained, so arithmetical accuracy of the books can be checked.

(*v*) In the single entry method, Trading and Profit and Loss Account and Balance Sheet cannot be prepared because a complete record of real and nominal accounts is not available in the books. On the other hand, both these statements can be prepared in the double entry system because a complete record of all accounts is available in the books.

Defects of Single Entry

Single entry suffers from the following defects :

1. It is not a scientific method of accounting because it does not record the two-fold aspect of each transaction.

2. No trial balance can be prepared as it does not record the dual aspect of each transaction. Therefore, so the arithmetical accuracy of the books cannot be checked.

3. In the absence of nominal accounts, trading and profit and loss account cannot be prepared.

4. In the absence of real accounts, it is not possible to know the exact financial position of the business on any particular day by preparing a Balance Sheet.

5. Internal check is not possible, so the possibility of fraud or misappropriation is greater in case of single entry than in the case of double entry system.

6. Accounts prepared on the basis of the single entry do not inspire confidence in the outsiders owing to the lack of any test for their arithmetical accuracy. Therefore, information obtained from accounts maintained on the basis of the single entry will be taken with doubt.

7. It is difficult to ascertain the value of the business, specially of goodwill if the proprietor wishes to sell his business.

8. Joint stock companies cannot follow this method of accounting on account of legal requirements of full disclosure, so this system is suitable in case of small proprietary or partnership concerns.

Inspite of the above defects, the single entry method of maintaining accounts is quite popular with small firms which cannot afford to spend money on an elaborate system of double entry of maintaining accounts.

Preparation of Statement of Affairs

In the absence of real accounts in the books maintained on the single entry, it is not possible to prepare the Balance Sheet of the business. Therefore, to judge the financial position of the business, a statement known as Statement of Affairs showing various assets and liabilities on a particular date is prepared from such information as may be available. Following points should be considered while preparing a Statement of Affairs :

1. The cash book should be balanced and cash in hand should be verified with the balance as shown by the Cash Book.
2. The bank balance as shown by the Cash Book should be reconciled with the balance as per Pass Book.
3. The list of debtors and creditors should be prepared from the personal accounts maintained in the ledger.
4. Stock-in-trade should be taken and valued at cost or market price, whichever is lower.
5. Values of fixed assets should be ascertained from vouchers or any other source of information as may be available. Depreciation, if any, on fixed assets should be provided.
6. All outstanding expenses and incomes should be considered and shown in the Statement of Affairs.

7. Similarly, expenses paid in advance and incomes received in advance should also be provided and shown in the Statement of Affairs.
8. Excess of assets over liabilities should be taken as capital of the proprietor on the date when the Statement of Affairs is prepared.

Differences Between Statement of Affairs and Balance Sheet

Following are the main distinctions between Statement of Affairs and Balance Sheet:

Points of Distinction	*Statement of Affairs*	*Balance Sheet*
1. Purpose	It shows the financial position as well as to find out the capital in ascertaining the trading profit or loss for a particular period.	It shows the financial position of the business as on a particular date.
2. Source	It is prepared from ledger balances and partly from other particulars and estimates, etc.	It is prepared from balances only.
3. Accounting Method	It is prepared when accounts are maintained under single entry system.	It is prepared when accounts are maintained under double entry system.
4. Reliability	It is not regarded as reliable as it is based partly on accounts and partly on other information.	It is reliable as it is based on actual figures.
5. Capital Account	Capital is the excess of assets over liabilities.	Capital Account is taken from the ledger.
6. Trial Balance	Trial Balance is not prepared.	Trial Balance is prepared before balance sheet.
7. Omission	In this statement omission of assets or liabilities cannot be traced.	In it omission of any asset or liability can be easily be traced as the totals will not tally.

Ascertainment of Profit under the Single Entry System

Profit under this system can be ascertained by two methods *i.e.* (1) Statement of Affairs or Net Worth Method, (2) Conversion Method.

1. Statement of Affairs or Net Worth Method

Trading and Profit and Loss cannot be prepared from books maintained on single entry basis because nominal accounts are not maintained in the ledger. Then, how to find out the profit or loss for the year ? Following procedure is followed for the ascertainment of the profit or loss from the single entry books.

1. First of all, a Statement of Affairs at the beginning of the year *i.e.* of last year is prepared to determine the amount of capital of the proprietor at the beginning of the year.

2. Similarly, a Statement of Affairs at the close of the year is prepared to determine the amount of capital at the end of the year.

3. Drawings made by the proprietor during the year should be added to the amount of capital at the end of the year as ascertained in step (2) on the plea that the capital would have been more to that extent had there been no such drawings.

4. Similarly, capital introduced during the year should be deducted from the capital at the end, for the reason that the capital at the end would have been less by that amount had there been no such additions to the capital during the year.

5. Capital at the beginning of the year as ascertained in step (1) should be deducted from the capital at the end of the year as adjusted in steps (3) and (4) and the difference will be either a trading profit or loss.

If the adjusted capital at the end exceeds the capital at the beginning, the excess will be profit for the year. If the adjusted capital at the end of the year is less than the capital at the beginning of the year, the difference will be loss for the year because adjusted capital at the end can be reduced by loss.

6. Interest on capital and interest on drawings (if any) are adjusted in profit or loss as derived in step (5) to arrive at net profit or loss for the year.

ILLUSTRATION 1. On 1-7-2024, Nikita Mittal commenced her business with ₹ 5,00,000. On 1-10-2024 she sold her private investments (Cost ₹ 50,000, Face value ₹ 40,000) at 125% of face value and brought the proceeds into her business. Her drawings were ₹ 1,000 p.m. Goods costing ₹ 11,000 were taken by her for personal use. On 31-3-2025, Capital before the following adjustments is ₹ 7,00,000, Outstanding Expenses ₹ 21,000 and Prepaid Expenses ₹ 4,000. Provide Interest on Capital @ 12% p.a. and for group incentive to staff @ 5% on Net Profit after charging such incentive and interest on capital. Calculate the Profit/Loss for the year ended 31st March, 2025. ***(CWA(F) Dec., 2010 Modified)***

SOLUTION **STATEMENT OF PROFIT**

				₹
A.	Capital at the end			7,00,000
B.	*Add* : Drawings during the year (₹ 9,000 Cash Drawings for 9 months + ₹ 11,000 Goods)			20,000
C.	*Less* : Additional capital introduced during the year [₹ 40,000 Face Value of Investments + 25% of ₹ 40,000]			(50,000)
D.	"Adjusted Capital at the end (A + B – C)			6,70,000
E.	*Less* : Capital in the beginning			5,00,000
F.	Profit subject to Adjustments (D – E)			1,70,000
G.	*Less* : Adjustments :		₹	
	+ Outstanding Expenses		21,000	
	– Prepaid Expenses		4,000	
			17,000	
	+ Interest on Capital	₹		
	(12% × 5,00,000 × 9/12)	45,000		
	(12% × 50,000 × 6/12)	3,000		
			48,000	
				65,000
H.	Net Profit before Group Incentive for the year [F – G]			1,05,000
I.	*Less* : Group Incentive to Staff [₹ 1,05,000 × 5/105]			5,000
J.	Net Profit [H – I]			1,00,000

ILLUSTRATION 2. A, B and C run a business sharing profits and losses in proportion of 2 : 2 : 1. On 1st January, 2025 their respective capitals were ₹ 96,000, ₹ 90,000 and ₹ 84,000. On 30th June, 2025 the following was the position :

	₹
Creditors	30,000
Furniture	9,000
Book Debts	1,80,000
Stock	90,000
Cash in hand and at Bank	36,000

The drawings of the partners respectively were ₹ 12,000, ₹ 9,000 and ₹ 6,000 during the half-year. Each partner is entitled to an interest at the rate of 5% p.a. on capital. Interest on drawings was calculated as ₹ 600 for A, ₹ 450 in case of B and ₹ 300 in case of C.

You are required to prepare :

(*i*) A Statement of Affairs as on 30th June, 2025.

(*ii*) Calculate the profits for the half-year ending on 30th June, 2025 and allocate the same amongst the partners. Also calculate capital of each partner as on 30th June, 2025.

SOLUTION

(*i*) **STATEMENT OF AFFAIRS OF A, B & C**

as on 30th June, 2025

Liabilities	₹	*Assets*	₹
Capital (Bal. Fig.)	2,85,000	Furniture	9,000
Creditors	30,000	Stock	90,000
		Book Debts	1,80,000
		Cash in Hand and at Bank	36,000
	3,15,000		3,15,000

(*ii*) **STATEMENT SHOWING PROFIT AND LOSS OF PARTNERS A, B AND C**

for six months ending on 30th June, 2025

Particulars	₹
Capital as on 30th June, 2025	2,85,000
Add : Drawings of A, B and C (₹ 12,000 + ₹ 9,000 + ₹ 6,000)	27,000
Add : Interest on Drawings of A, B and C (₹ 600 + ₹ 450 + ₹ 300)	1,350
	3,13,350
Less : Interest on Capital of A, B and C for $\frac{1}{2}$ year @ 5% p.a. (₹ 2,400 + ₹ 2,250 + ₹ 2,100)	6,750
	3,06,600
Less : Capital as on 1st January, 2025 of A, B and C (₹ 96,000 + ₹ 90,000 + ₹ 84,000)	2,70,000
Net Profit	36,600

STATEMENT SHOWING ALLOCATION OF PROFITS AND OTHER ADJUSTMENTS IN THE CAPITAL ACCOUNTS OF A, B AND C

Particulars	*A* (₹)	*B* (₹)	*C* (₹)
Capital as on 1st January, 2025	96,000	90,000	84,000
Add : Net Profit in the ratio of 2 : 2 : 1	14,640	14,640	7,320
Add : Interest on Capital @ 5% p.a. for 6 months	2,400	2,250	2,100
	1,13,040	1,06,890	93,420
Less : Drawings	(12,000)	(9,000)	(6,000)
Less : Interest on Drawings	(600)	(450)	(300)
Capital as on 30th June, 2025	1,00,440	97,440	87,120

ILLUSTRATION 3. A, B and C were in partnership and towards the end of 2024 most of their books and records were destroyed in a fire. Balance Sheet as on 31st December, 2023 was as follows :

	₹	₹		₹
Creditors		5,500	Cash	2,400
Capitals :			Debtors	3,600

A	4,500		Stock	6,500
B	3,000		Machinery	1,440
C	1,500		Fixtures and Fittings	600
		9,000	Advance Payments	35
Current Accounts :			Current Account :	
A	145		C	170
B	100			
		245		
		14,745		14,745

The partners' drawings during 2024 have been proved at A—₹ 1,400, B—₹ 1,000 and C—₹ 650, On 31st December 2024 Cash was ₹ 3,200, Debtors ₹ 4,025, Stock ₹ 5,900, Advance Payment ₹ 25, and Creditors ₹ 6,040. Machinery is to be depreciated by 10% per annum and Fixtures and Fittings at $7\frac{1}{2}$%. 5% interest is to be allowed on capitals. The partners share profits in the proportions of 1/2, 1/3 and 1/6.

You are required to prepare a statement showing the net trading profit for the year 2024 and the division of the same between the partners, together with the Balance Sheet as on 31st December, 2024.

SOLUTION

STATEMENT OF AFFAIRS OF M/s A, B & C

as at 31st December, 2024

Liabilities		₹	*Assets*		₹
Creditors		6,040	Cash		3,200
Capitals :	₹		Debtors		4,025
A	4,500		Stock		5,900
B	3,000		Advance Payment		25
C	1,500			₹	
		9,000	Machinery	1,440	
			Less : 10% Depreciation	144	
					1,296
			Fixtures and Fittings	600	
			Less : $7\frac{1}{2}$% Depreciation	45	
					555
			Combined Current Accounts of A, B and C (Excess of liabilities over assets)		39
		15,040			15,040

STATEMENT OF PROFIT AND LOSS

for the year ending 31st December, 2024

		₹
Combined Current Accounts of A, B and C on 31-12-2024		– 39
Add : Drawings during the year :	₹	
A	1,400	
B	1,000	
C	650	
		3,050
		3,011

Less : Combined Current Accounts of A, B and C on 1-1-2024 :		
A	145	
B	100	
C	– 170	
		75
Profit before Allowing Interest on Capital		2,936
Less : Interest on Capital @ 5% p.a.		
A : On ₹ 4,500 for one year	225	
B : On ₹ 3,000 for one year	150	
C : On ₹ 1,500 for one year	75	
		450
Net Profit made during the year		2,486
Divided among A, B and C as follows :		₹
A—1/2 of ₹ 2,486		1,243
B—1/3 of ₹ 2,486		829
C—1/6 of ₹ 2,486		414

BALANCE SHEET OF M/s A, B & C

as at 31st December, 2024

Liabilities		₹	*Assets*		₹
Creditors		6,040	Cash		3,200
Capitals :	₹		Debtors		4,025
A	4,500		Stock		5,900
B	3,000		Advance Payment		25
C	1,500			₹	
		9,000	Machinery	1,440	
A's Current Account :			*Less* : 10% Depreciation	144	
Balance on 1-1-2024	145				1,296
Add : Interest	225		Fixtures and Fittings	600	
Profit	1,243				
	1,613		*Less* : $7\frac{1}{2}$% Depreciation	45	
Less : Drawings	1,400				555
		213	C's Current Account :		
B's Current Account :			Balance on 1-1-2024 170		
Balance on 1-1-2024	100		*Add* : Drawings 650		
Add : Interest	150			820	
Profit	829		*Less* : Interest 75		
	1,079		Profit 414		
Less : Drawings	1,000			489	
		79			331
		15,332			15,332

ILLUSTRATION 4. A took B in partnership on 1st January, 2022 on the basis of the following statement as on the same date prepared from A's books kept by Single Entry :

Liabilities	₹	*Assets*	₹
Creditors	48,000	Furniture and Fittings	15,000
A's Capital	78,000	Debtors	75,000
		Stock	30,000
		Cash at Bank	6,000
	1,26,000		1,26,000

B is to pay a premium of ₹ 12,000 out of his share of profits exceeding ₹ 7,500 per annum over which sum he is not to draw on any account. The new firm takes over the assets and discharges the liabilities and A's Capital is as agreed as per the above statement. B is to bring in ₹ 15,000 as Capital which he did on 1st January, 2022. The profits are to be divided as A 2/3rd and B 1/3rd and 5% interest is to be allowed on the opening balance of capital each year. A's drawings were ₹ 18,000, ₹ 16,200 and ₹ 17,400 for years 2022, 2023 and 2024 respectively and B drew ₹ 7,500 each year. The firm's assets and liabilities exclusive of the capitals on 31st December, 2022, 2023 and 2024 were as follows :

	2022	*2023*	*2024*
	₹	₹	₹
Assets	1,50,000	1,48,500	1,71,000
Liabilities	52,500	45,000	48,000

Amounts due from B to A in respect of premium were to be transferred from his capital to A's capital.

Make out a statement showing profit or loss each year and write up Partners' Capital Accounts.

SOLUTION

STATEMENT OF PROFIT AND LOSS

for the year ending 31st December, 2022

		₹
Excess of assets over liabilities *i.e.*, Capital on 31-12-2022		
(₹ 1,50,000 – 52,500)		97,500
Add : Drawings during the year (A : ₹ 18,000 + B : ₹ 7,500)		25,500
		1,23,000
Less : Capitals of A and B on 1-1-2022 (₹ 78,000 + ₹ 15,000)		93,000
Profit before allowing interest on capitals		30,000
Less : Interest on capitals	₹	
A—5% on ₹ 78,000	3,900	
B—5% on ₹ 15,000	750	
		4,650
Net Profit for the year 2022		25,350
A—2/3rd share (₹ 25,350 × 2/3) =	₹ 16,900	
B—1/3rd share (₹ 25,350 × 1/3) =	₹ 8,450	
	25,350	

STATEMENT OF PROFIT AND LOSS

for the year ending 31st December, 2023

		₹
Excess of assets over liabilities *i.e.* Capital on 31-12-2023 (₹ 1,48,500 – ₹ 45,000)		1,03,500
Add : Drawings during the year (A : ₹ 16,200 + B : ₹ 7,500)		23,700
		1,27,200
Less : Capitals of A and B as on 1-1-2023		97,500
Profit before allowing interest on capitals		29,700
Less : Interest on Capitals :	₹	
A—5 per cent on ₹ 81,750 (1)	4,088	
B—5 per cent on ₹ 15,750 (2)	787	
		4,875
Net Profit for the year 2023		24,825
A's Share of Profit—2/3 share	16,550	
B's Share of Profit—1/3rd share	8,275	
	24,825	

STATEMENT OF PROFIT AND LOSS

for the year ending 31st December, 2024

	₹	₹
Excess of assets over liabilities *i.e.* Capital on 31-12-2024 (₹ 1,71,000 – ₹ 48,000)		1,23,000
Add : Drawings during the year (A : ₹ 17,400 + B : ₹ 7,500)		24,900
		1,47,900
Less : Capitals of A and B as at 1-1-2024		1,03,500
Profit before allowing interest on capitals		44,400
Less : Interest on Capitals :		
A—5 per cent on ₹ 86,963 (3)	4,348	
B—5 per cent on ₹ 16,537 (4)	827	
		5,175
Net Profit for the year 2024		39,225
	₹	
A's Share of Profit—2/3rd share $\left(₹ 39,225 \times \frac{2}{3}\right) =$	26,150	
B's Share of Profit—1/3rd share $\left(₹ 39,225 \times \frac{1}{3}\right) =$	13,075	
	39,225	

A'S CAPITAL ACCOUNT

2022		₹	2022		₹
Dec. 31	To Drawings	18,000	Jan. 1	By Balance b/d	78,000
Dec. 31	To Balance c/d	81,750	Dec. 31	By Interest on Capital	3,900
			Dec. 31	By Profit—2/3rd share	16,900
			Dec. 31	By B's Capital—Transfer	950
		99,750			99,750

Date	Particulars	₹	Date	Particulars	₹
2023			2023		
Dec.31	To Drawings	16,200	Jan. 1	By Balance b/d (1)	81,750
Dec.31	To Balance c/d	86,963	Dec. 31	By Interest on Capital	4,088
			Dec. 31	By Profit—2/3rd share	16,550
			Dec. 31	B's Capital—Transfer	775
		1,03,163			1,03,163
2024			2024		
Dec.31	To Drawings	17,400	Jan. 1	By Balance b/d (3)	86,963
Dec.31	To Balance c/d	1,05,636	Dec. 31	By Interest on Capital	4,348
			Dec. 31	By Profit—2/3rd share	26,150
			Dec. 31	By B's Capital—Transfer	5,575
		1,23,036			1,23,036
			2025		
			Jan 1	By Balance b/d	1,05,636

B's CAPITAL ACCOUNT

Date	Particulars	₹	Date	Particulars	₹
2022			2022		
Dec.31	To Drawings	7,500	Jan. 1	By Bank	15,000
Dec.31	To A's Capital—Transfer	950	Dec. 31	By Interest on Capital	750
Dec.31	To Balance c/d	15,750	Dec. 31	By Profit—1/3rd share	8,450
		24,200			24,200
2023			2023		
Dec.31	To Drawings	7,500	Jan. 1	By Balance b/d (2)	15,750
Dec.31	To A's Capital—Transfer	775	Dec. 31	By Interest on Capital	787
Dec.31	To Balance c/d	16,537	Dec. 31	By Profit—1/3rd share	8,275
		24,812			24,812
2024			2024		
Dec 31	To Drawings	7,500	Jan. 1	By Balance b/d (4)	16,537
Dec.31	To A's Capital—Transfer	5,575	Dec. 31	By Interest on Capital	827
Dec.31	To Balance c/d	17,364	Dec. 31	By Profit—1/3rd share	13,075
		30,439			30,439
			2025		
			Jan 1	By Balance b/d	17,364

ILLUSTRATION 5. Lokesh, who keeps books by single entry, had submitted his Income-tax returns to Income-tax authorities showing his incomes to be as follows :

		₹			₹
Year ending March 31, 2020	=	33,075	Year ending March 31, 2023	=	61,875
Year ending March 31, 2021	=	33,300	Year ending March 31, 2024	=	54,630
Year ending March 31, 2022	=	35,415	Year ending March 31, 2025	=	41,670

The Income-tax Officer is not satisfied as to the accuracy of the incomes returned. You are appointed as a consultant to assist in establishing correctness of the incomes returned and for that purpose you are given the following information :

(*a*) Business liabilities and assets at March 31, 2019 were :

Creditors : ₹ 32,940, Furniture & Fittings : ₹ 22,500, Stock : ₹ 24,390 (at selling price which is 25% above cost), Debtors : ₹ 11,025, Cash at Bank and in hand ₹ 15,615.

(*b*) Lokesh owed his brother ₹ 18,000 on March 31, 2019. On February 15, 2022 he repaid this amount and on April 1, 2024, he lent his brother ₹ 13,500.

(*c*) Lokesh owns a house which he purchased in 2003 for ₹ 90,000 and a car which he purchased on October 2020 for ₹ 33,750. In January, 2024, he bought debentures in X Ltd. having face value of ₹ 40,000 for ₹ 33,750.

(*d*) In May, 2024 a sum of ₹ 13,500 was stolen from his house.

(*e*) Lokesh estimates that his living expenses have been 2019-20—₹ 13,500; 2020-21—₹ 18,000; 2021-22—₹ 27,000; 2022-23, 2023-24 and 2024-2025—₹ 31,500 p.a. exclusive of the amount stolen.

(*f*) On March 31, 2025 business liabilities and assets were : Creditors ₹ 37,800, Furniture, Fixtures and Fittings ₹ 40,500, Stock ₹ 54,330 (at selling price with a gross profit of 25%), Debtors ₹ 26,640, Cash-in-hand and at Bank ₹ 29,025.

From the information submitted, prepare statements showing whether or not the incomes declared by Lokesh are correct.

SOLUTION

STATEMENT OF AFFAIRS OF LOKESH

as on ......

Liabilities	*31-3-2019*	*31-3-2025*	*Assets*	*31-3-2019*	*31-3-25*
	₹	₹		₹	₹
Creditors	32,940	37,800	Furnitures, Fixtures and Fittings	22,500	40,500
Loan from Brother	18,000	—	Stock		
Capital (Bal. Fig.)	1,07,712	2,70,112	$\left(₹\,24{,}390 \times \frac{100}{125} = ₹\,19{,}512\right)$	19,512	40,747 (54,330 × 75%)
			Debtors	11,025	26,640
			Cash in Hand and at Bank	15,615	29,025
			Loan to Brother	—	13,500
			Building (House)	90,000	90,000
			Car	—	33,750
			Debentures in X Ltd.	—	33,750
	1,58,652	3,07,912		1,58,652	3,07,912

STATEMENT OF PROFIT

	₹	₹
Capital as on 31-3-2025		2,70,112
Add : Drawings from 2019-20 to 2024-25 [₹ 13,500 + ₹ 18,000 + ₹ 27,000 + ₹ 31,500 + ₹ 31,500 + ₹ 31,500]	1,53,000	
Add : Amount stolen in May, 2024	13,500	
		1,66,500
Adjusted Capital at the end		4,36,612
Less : Opening Capital on 31-3-2019		1,07,712
Net Profit during the year		3,28,900

Less : Profits as shown by Income-tax return from 31-3-2020 to 31-3-2025 (₹ 33,075 + ₹ 33,300 + ₹ 35,415 + ₹ 61,875 + ₹ 54,630 + ₹ 41,670]		2,59,965
Understatement of Income		68,935

ILLUSTRATION 6. Suresh does not maintain his books of accounts under the double entry system but keeps slips of papers from which he makes up his annual accounts. He has borrowed moneys from a bank to whom he has to render figures of profits every year. He has given to the bank the following profit figures :

Year ending 31st December	*Profits* ₹	*Year ending 31st December*	*Profits* ₹
2020	20,000	2023	48,000
2021	32,000	2024	55,000
2022	35,000		

The bank appoints you to audit the statements and verify whether the figures of profits reported are correct or not ; for this purpose, the following figures are made available to you :

(*a*) Position as on 31st December, 2019 : Sundry Debtors ₹ 20,000 ; Stock on trade (at 95% of the cost) ₹ 47,500 ; Cash in hand and at bank ₹ 12,600 ; Trade Creditors ₹ 6,000 ; Expenses due ₹ 1,600.

(*b*) In December, 2020, he had advanced ₹ 8,000 to A for purchase of a vacant land. The property was registered in March, 2022 after payment of balance consideration of ₹ 32,000. Costs of registration incurred for this were ₹ 7,500.

(*c*) Suresh purchased jewellery for ₹ 15,000 for his daughter in October, 2022, Marriage expenses incurred in January, 2023 were ₹ 24,000.

(*d*) A new V C R was purchased by him in March 2024 for ₹ 18,000 and presented by him to his friend in November 2024.

(*e*) His annual household expenses amounted to a minimum of ₹ 24,000.

(*f*) The position of assets and liabilities as on 31st December 2024 was found to be : Overdraft with bank (secured against property) ₹ 12,000 ; Trade creditors ₹ 10,000 ; Expenses payable ₹ 600 ; Sundry debtors (including ₹ 600 due from a peon declared insolvent by the court) ₹ 28,800 ; Stock in trade (at 125% of cost to reflect market value) ₹ 60,000 and Cash in hand ₹ 250.

It is found that the rate of profit has been uniform throughout the period and the proportion of sales during the years to total sales for the period was in the ratio of 3 : 4 : 4 : 6 : 8.

Ascertain the annual profits and indicate differences, if any, with those reported by Suresh to the bank earlier.

All workings are to form part of your answer.

SOLUTION

STATEMENT OF AFFAIRS

as on 31-12-2019

Liabilities	₹	*Assets*	₹
Trade Creditors	6,000	Cash in hand and at Bank	12,600
Outstanding Expenses	1,600	Sundry Debtors	20,000
Capital (Balancing figure)	75,000	Stock on Trade (At cost) $\left(₹\,47{,}500 \times \frac{100}{95}\right)$	50,000
	82,600		82,600

STATEMENT OF AFFAIRS
as on 31-12-2024

Liabilities	₹	Assets		₹
Bank Overdraft (Secured against property)	12,000	Cash in hand		250
Trade Creditors	10,000	Sundry Debtors	28,800	
Outstanding Expenses	600	*Less* : Bad Debts	600	28,200
Capital (Balancing figure)	53,850	Stock in Trade (At cost) $\left(₹ 60,000 \times \frac{100}{125}\right)$		48,000
	76,450			76,450

STATEMENT SHOWING PROFIT
for the period 1-1-2020 to 31-12-2024

		₹
	Capital as on 31-12-2024 as per Statement of Affairs	53,850
Add :	Drawings for 5 years @ ₹ 24,000 per annum	1,20,000
	Purchase of Property	47,500
	Purchase of Jewellery and Marriage Expenses	39,000
	Purchase of VCR for friend	18,000
		2,78,350
Less :	Capital as at 1-1-2020 as per Statement of Affairs	75,000
	Net Profit for 5 years	2,03,350

STATEMENT SHOWING ANNUAL PROFIT AND THEIR DIFFERENCES WITH REPORTED PROFIT
for the period 2020 to 2024

Year	*Apportionment Ratio of Sales*	*Annual Profit in the Ratio of Sales*	*Profit Reported to Bank*	*Difference*
		₹	₹	₹
2020	3	24,402	20,000	+ 4,402
2021	4	32,536	32,000	+ 536
2022	4	32,536	35,000	– 2,464
2023	6	48,804	48,000	+ 804
2024	8	65,072	55,000	+ 10,072
	25	2,03,350	1,90,000	+ 13,350

Total profits for 5 years have been apportioned in the ratio of 3 : 4 : 4 : 6 : 8 to get annual profits.

ILLUSTRATION 7. A and B started business on January 1, 2023 with ₹ 50,000 as capital contributed equally but the profit sharing ratio was 3 : 2. Their drawings were ₹ 300 and ₹ 200 per month respectively. They had kept no account except the following information :

	31-12-2023	*31-12-2024*
	₹	₹
Machinery at cost	20,000	25,000
Stock in Trade	30,000	30,000
Debtors	50,000	60,000
Cash	2,000	500

Creditors	30,000	20,000
Outstanding Expenses	4,000	3,000
Bank Balance (as per Pass Book)	6,000	8,000

Provision is to be made for depreciation at 10 per cent on the cost of machinery as at end of each year. Debtors on 31-12-2023 include ₹ 5,000 for goods sent on consignment at 25 per cent above cost, and the goods were not sold until 2023. A cheque for ₹ 1,000 had been deposited on 31-12-2023 but was credited on 2-1-2024.

Cheque for ₹ 2,000 issued on 26-12-2024 was presented on 3-1-2025. A cheque for ₹ 1,000 was deposited by a customer on 27-12-2024. A cheque for ₹ 500 directly deposited in December, 2024 was dishonoured but no adjustment for these were made.

Determine profits for 2023 and 2024 and draw up a Balance Sheet as at 31st December, 2024.

SOLUTION **STATEMENT OF AFFAIRS OF M/S A & B**

as on 31-12-2023

Liabilities	₹	*Assets*		₹
Creditors	30,000	Cash in hand		2,000
Outstanding Expenses	4,000	Cash at Bank (1)		7,000
Capital—Excess of Assets over		Debtors (2)		45,000
Liabilities	72,000	Stock-in-trade		30,000
		Stock on Consignment (2)	₹	4,000
		Machinery	20,000	
		Less : 10% Depreciation	2,000	
				18,000
	1,06,000			1,06,000

Notes : (1) Bank Balance, ₹ 6,000 as per Pass Book has been increased by ₹ 1,000 to arrive at the bank balance as per Cash Book because a cheque of ₹ 1,000 deposited must have been entered in the Cash Book. There is no need of adjustment in the balance of debtors because it must have already been posted to the customer's account from whom cheque was received.

(2) An amount of ₹ 5,000 has been deducted from debtors for goods sent on consignment because goods included in debtors have not been sold upto 31st December, 2023. Goods sent on consignment treated as sales must be treated as stock. Hence, the cost of goods sent on consignment treated as sales must be treated as stock. Hence, the cost of goods sent on consignment ₹ 4,000 (*i.e.* 5,000 × 100/125) has been taken as stock on consignment not sold.

STATEMENT OF PROFIT AND LOSS OF M/s A & B

for the year ended December 31, 2023

			₹
	Capital of A and B as at 31st December, 2023		72,000
Add :	Drawings during the year	₹	
	A	3,600	
	B	2,400	
			6,000
			78,000
Less :	Capital of A and B as at 1st January, 2023		50,000
	Profit made during the year 2023		28,000
	A's Share of Profit (3/5)		16,800
	B's Share of Profit (2/5)		11,200

STATEMENT OF AFFAIRS OF M/S A AND B

as on 31-12-2024

Liabilities	₹	*Assets*		₹
Creditors	20,000	Cash in hand		500
Outstanding Expenses	3,000	Cash at Bank (1)		6,000
Capital—Excess of assets over		Debtors (2)		59,500
liabilities	93,500	Stock-in-trade		30,000
			₹	
		Machinery at Cost	25,000	
		Less : Depreciation for		
		2023 @ 10% on ₹		
		₹ 20,000 = 2,000		
		for 2024@ 10% on		
		₹ 25,000 = 2,500		
			4,500	
				20,500
	1,16,500			1,16,500

STATEMENT OF PROFIT AND LOSS

for the year ending 31st December, 2024

		₹	₹
	Capital of A and B as at 31-12-2024		93,500
Add :	Drawings during the year	₹	
	A	3,600	
	B	2,400	
			6,000
			99,500
Less :	Capital of A and B as at 1-1-2024		72,000
	Profit made during the year 2024		27,500
	A's share of profit (3/5)		16,500
	B's share of profit (2/5)		11,000

Working Notes :

(1) Balance at Bank as per Pass Book has been reduced by ₹ 2,000 to arrive at the balance as per Cash Book which was reduced when cheque was issued. No adjustment in balance at bank as per Pass Book is needed for a cheque for ₹ 1,000 deposited by a customer and a cheque for ₹ 500 dishonoured to arrive at balance as per Cash Book because the bank balance as per Pass Book is already adjusted.

(2) **DEBTORS' ACCOUNT**

	₹		₹
To Balance b/d (as given)	60,000	By Bank (Cheque deposted by a customer)	1,000
To Bank (cheque dishonoured)	500	By Balance c/d	59,500
	60,500		60,500
To Balance b/d	59,500		

BALANCE SHEET OF M/S A & B
as on 31-12-2024

Liabilities		₹	*Assets*		₹
Creditors		20,000	Cash in hand		500
Outstanding Expenses		3,000	Cash at Bank		6,000
Capital Accounts			Debtors		59,500
A :			Stock	₹	30,000
Amount contributed on	₹		Machinery at Cost	25,000	
1-1-2023	25,000		*Less* : Depreciation written off		
Profit for 2 years			2023 ₹ 2,000		
(2023 & 2024)	33,300		2024 ₹ 2,500		
				4,500	
	58,300				20,500
Less : Drawings for 2 years	7,200				
B :		51,100			
Amount contributed on 1-1-2023	25,000				
Profit for 2 years (2023 & 2024)	22,200				
	47,200				
Less : Drawings for 2 years	4,800				
		42,400			
		1,16,500			1,16,500

2. Conversion Method

According to conversion method if it is desired to change the system of accounting from single entry to double entry on a given date, the following procedure should be adopted :

1. A Statement of Affairs should be prepared on the date on which the change is to be made. It should be seen that cash and bank balances as shown in the Statement of Affairs must agree with the Cash Balance as shown by the Cash Book and the Bank Balance as shown by the Bank column of the Cash Book respectively. Similarly, the amounts of debtors and creditors shown in the Statement of Affairs should agree with the totals of debit and credit balances extracted from the individual accounts of debtors and creditors. For bringing into books the various assets and liabilities appearing in the Statement of Affairs, an opening journal entry should be made as follows :

Various Assets Account Dr.

To Various Liabilities Account

To Capital Account

(Being balances brought forward from the Statement of Affairs)

The books will thus be opened under the double entry. In future all transactions should be recorded according to the double entry system *i.e.* first through proper subsidiary books and then posted to the ledger.

Conversion of Books of Last Year from Single Entry into Double Entry

If a businessman wants to convert the books of 2024 maintained on single entry system into double entry system in 2025, he should follow the following procedure, which is based on the assumption that proper subsidiary books have been maintained under the single entry system :

1. A Statement of Affairs at the beginning of the year 2024 should be prepared and posted from it all those accounts which have not been maintained already.

2. Cash Book should be gone through and entries relating to impersonal accounts should be posted to their respective accounts as these items were not posted to impersonal accounts under the single entry system. This should complete the double entry of the Cash Book.

3. Similarly, totals of other subsidiary books as were not posted to the impersonal accounts should be posted to their respective accounts. For example, the total of the Purchases Book will be debited to Purchases Account and that of the Returns Inwards Book should be debited to Returns Inwards Account.

4. Now, the personal accounts, which have already been kept under the single entry system, should be scrutinised in order to find out the items which have been made direct therein without passing through one of the subsidiary books *e.g.*, bad debts, discounts, allowances, etc., might have been credited direct to the personal accounts. Such items should be posted to their respective impersonal accounts so that the two-fold effect of such transactions may be completed.

5. If a Petty Cash Book is maintained, the monthly analysis should be posted to the debit of the various accounts for expeneses and the total credited to Petty Cash Account.

6. After completing the double entry of all the transactions of the previous year, a trial balance should then be prepared to test the arithmetical accuracy of the books. After taking into consideration the necessary adjustments like outstanding expenses and incomes, depreciation, provision for bad debts and discounts, Trading and Profit and Loss Account and Balance Sheet should be prepared in the usual manner.

If only the Cash Book is maintained and the transactions other than cash affecting personal accounts are recorded directly to the personal accounts in the Ledger, a different procedure of conversion should be followed as given below :

(*i*) A Statement of Affairs, as described earlier, at the beginning of the year should be prepared.

(*ii*) Cash Book should be investigated into and all such items as were not posted previously to the real and nominal accounts should be posted to their respective accounts.

(*iii*) A careful analysis of all the items shown on both the sides of the personal accounts should be made. **The analysis of the debit side of the Debtors' Accounts will disclose the following :**

(*a*) Opening balances as shown in Statement of Affairs at the beginning of the year,
(*b*) Credit Sales,
(*c*) Dishonoured Bills Receivable,
(*d*) Transfers.

The analysis of the credit side of Debtors' Accounts will reveal the following facts :

(*a*) Cash received from debtors,
(*b*) Discount allowed to debtors,
(*c*) Bills Receivable received from debtors,
(*d*) Returns inwards,
(*e*) Bad debts,
(*f*) Allowances made to customers,
(*g*) Transfers.

The totals of these analysis columns as were not previously posted to the impersonal accounts will be debited or credited to their respective impersonal accounts (*e.g.* Sales Account, Bills Receivable Account, Returns Inwards Account, Bad Debts Account etc.), the corresponding credit or debit being given to a Total Debtors Account.

Similarly, the analysis of the credit side of the Creditors' Account will show :

(*a*) Opening balances as shown in the Statement of Affairs at the beginning of the year,
(*b*) Credit purchases,
(*c*) Bills payable dishonoured or renewed,
(*d*) Transfers.

The analysis of the debit side of the Creditors' Account will disclose :

(*a*) Cash paid to creditors,
(*b*) Discounts allowed by creditors,
(*e*) Returns outwards,
(*f*) Allowances and rebates allowed by creditors.

(*c*) Bills Payable given to creditors,
(*d*) Bills Receivable endorsed in favour of creditors,
(*g*) Transfers.

The totals of these analysis columns will be journalised by debiting or crediting the respective impersonal accounts, the corresponding credit or debit being given to Total Creditors Account.

The double entry of all the transactions would thus be completed and the trial balance should be prepared to test the arithmetical accuracy of the work. After the preparation of the trial balance, final accounts can be prepared in the usual way.

Some Practical Hints

The solution of practical problems relating to conversion of single entry into double entry is beset with a number of difficult points; so some practical hints are given below for the convenience of the students :

1. Ascertainment of credit sales and credit purchases. Usually a question on single entry does not give the figures of credit sales and credit purchases so to find them out a Total Debtors Account and a Total Creditors Account is prepared as follows :

Dr. **PROFORMA OF A TOTAL DEBTORS ACCOUNT** Cr.

	₹		₹
To Balance b/d (Opening Balance)		By Cash	
" Bills Receivable (Dishonoured)		" Bank	
To Freight (Charged)		" Bills Receivable	
" Interest on Overdue Accounts		By Discounts	
" Transfers		" Returns Inwards	
" Cash (Refund for returns)		" Allowances	
" Credit Sales (Balancing figure)		" Transfers	
		" Bad Debts	
		" Balance c/d (Closing Balance)	

Dr. **PROFORMA OF A TOTAL CREDITORS ACCOUNT** Cr.

	₹		₹
To Cash		By Balance b/d (Opening Balance)	
" Bank		" Cash (Refund for returns, etc.)	
" Bills Payable		" Bills Payable (dishonoured)	
" Returns Outwards		" Transfers	
" Discounts		" Credit Purchases (Balancing figure)	
" Allowances and Rebates			
" Transfers			
" Balance c/d (Closing Balance)			

2. Ascertainment of Opening and Closing Debtors and Creditors when Credit Sales and Purchases are given. In such a case, the opening or closing balances of debtors and creditors can easily be ascertained by preparing the Total Debtors Account and Total Creditors Account as shown in (1) above. The balancing figures in the Total Debtors Account and Total Creditors Account will be opening or closing balances of debtors and creditors.

3. Ascertainment of Bills Receivable and Bills Payable. Sometimes the question may not give the opening or closing balances of Bills Receivable and Bills Payable. Such figures can be found out by preparing the Bills Recivable Account and Bills Payable Account as shown below :

Dr. **BILLS RECEIVABLE ACCOUNT** Cr.

	₹		₹
To Balance b/d (Opening Balance)		By Cash (Bills receivable matured during the year)	
" Sundry Debtors (B/R received during the year)		" Sundry Debtors (B/R dishonoured)	
		" Sundry Creditors (B/R endorsed)	
		" Balance c/d (Closing Balance)	

Dr. **BILLS PAYABLE ACCOUNT** Cr.

	₹		₹
To Cash		By Balance b/d (Opening Balance)	
" Sundry Creditors (B/P dishonoured)		" Sundry Creditors (Acceptances given during the year)	
" Balance c/d (Closing Balance)			

In either case the missing figure would be the balancing one.

4. Ascertainment of Opening and Closing Stock when Rate of Gross Profit is given. These figures will be calculated as follows :

Opening Stock = Cost of Goods Sold (*i.e.* Sales – Gross Profit) + Closing Stock – Purchases

Closing Stock = Opening Stock + Purchases – Cost of Goods Sold.

5. Ascertainment of Opening Balance of Capital, an Asset or a Liability. Such a missing figure can be ascertained by preparing the opening Statement of Affairs. The missing item would be the balancing figure in the Statement of Affairs.

6. Ascertainment of Cash and Bank Balances. Sometimes opening and closing balances of cash in hand or cash at bank are not given, such figures can be ascertained by preparing the columnar Cash Book. When all the known items are writen up in the Cash Book, the balancing figure would be the missing item and such missing item can be any one of the following items :

(*i*) Opening balance of cash in hand and cash at bank
(*ii*) Closing balance of cash in hand and cash at bank
(*iii*) Cash sales
(*iv*) Cash purchases
(*v*) Payments to creditors
(*vi*) Receipts from debtors
(*vii*) Expenses
(*viii*) Drawings
(*ix*) Cash missing etc.

If a combined figure of cash and bank balance is given in the question, either cash or bank balance (depending upon the information given in the question) should be ascertained first and then the other figure is ascertained by taking the difference between the combined figure and the balance calculated first.

7. Accounts relating to different expenses, incomes, fixed assets, long term liabilities, outstanding expenses and outstanding incomes are also prepared with the help of Receipts and Payments Account and additional information available.

8. Identification of Drawings/Personal Expenses. It is normal in case of single entry system, that no distinction is made between business expenses and personal expenses. While making accounts from incomplete records, it is important to identify the transactions related to personal expenses met from business cash or drawings made. Few examples of such expenses are household expenses met from business cash, life insurance premiums of proprietor/partners/family members paid from business cash.

9. Additions made by proprietors/partners. In single entry, any fresh investments made in business by proprietors/partners may not be easily traceable. So it becomes important to trace such transactions and account them properly in the books of accounts, so that true profits may be calculated and accurate financial position is depicted. Few examples of such transactions are interest and dividends of personal investments are reflected in business or rent from non business property is collected and added to business cash.

ILLUSTRATION 8. From the following information, calculate closing stock on 31st March, 2025 and total sales and total purchases for the year ended 31st March, 2025 :

	On 31st March, 2024 (₹)	*On 31st March, 2025* (₹)
Debtors	6,77,000	5,60,000
Creditors	5,00,000	3,60,000
Bills Payable	4,00,000	5,20,000
Bills Receivable	1,80,000	1,50,000
Stock	2,50,000	?

Transactions during the year ended 31st March, 2025 :

	₹		₹
Discount allowed to Customers	22,000	Bad Debts	60,000
Discount allowed by Suppliers	15,000	Bills Receivable Dishonoured	32,000
Bills Payable Discharged	7,20,000	Cash paid to Creditors	26,00,000
Bills Receivable Collected	4,40,000	Cash received from Debtors	45,00,000
Returns Inwards	1,82,000	Cash Sales	8,25,000
Returns Outwards	94,000	Cash Purchases	21,00,000

Uniform sale price of goods was cost plus 25%.

SOLUTION

BILLS RECEIVABLE ACCOUNT

	₹		₹
To Balance b/d	1,80,000	By Cash A/c (Collection)	4,40,000
To Debtors (Bal. Figure)	4,42,000	By Debtors (BR Dishonoured)	32,000
(Bills Receivable Drawn)		By Balance c/d	1,50,000
	6,22,000		6,22,000

SUNDRY DEBTORS ACCOUNT

	₹		₹
To Balance b/d	6,77,000	By Cash A/c (Received)	45,00,000
To Bills Receivable (Dishonoured)	32,000	By Discount	22,000
To Credit Sales (Balancing Figure)	50,57,000	By Bad Debts	60,000
		By Bills Receivable A/c	4,42,000
		By Returns Inwards	1,82,000
		By Balance c/d	5,60,000
	57,66,000		57,66,000

BILLS PAYABLE ACCOUNT

	₹		₹
To Cash	7,20,000	By Balance b/d	4,00,000
To Balance c/d	5,20,000	By Creditors (Bal. Figure)	8,40,000
		(Acceptances Given)	
	12,40,000		12,40,000

CREDITORS ACCOUNT

	₹		₹
To Cash A/c	26,00,000	By Balance b/d	5,00,000
To Discount	15,000	By Purchases (Balancing Figure)	34,09,000
To Returns Outwards	94,000		
To Bills Payable (Issued)	8,40,000		
To Balance c/d	3,60,000		
	39,09,000		39,09,000

Net Sales = Cash Sales + Credit Sales
= ₹ 8,25,000 + ₹ 50,57,000 = ₹ **58,82,000**

Net Purchases = Cash Purchases + Credit Purchases
= ₹ 21,00,000 + ₹ 34,09,000 = ₹ **55,09,000**

Value of Closing Stock = Opening Stock + Purchases – Cost of Goods sold

Cost of Goods sold = Sales – 20% of Sales *i.e.* 25% of Cost
= ₹ 58,82,000 – (20% × ₹ 58,82,000)
= ₹ 58,82,000 – ₹ 11,76,400 = ₹ **47,05,600**

Closing Stock :		₹
Opening Stock	=	2,50,000
Purchases	=	55,09,000
		57,59,000
Less : Cost of Goods Sold	=	47,05,600
Closing Stock	=	10,53,400

ILLUSTRATION 9. Mr. X runs a retail business. Suddenly he finds on 31-3-2025 that his Cash and Bank balances have reduced considerably. He provides you the following information :

(*i*) *Balances*	*31-3-2024*	*31-3-2025*
	₹	₹
Sundry Debtors	35,400	58,800
Sundry Creditors	84,400	22,400
Cash at Bank	1,08,400	2,500
Cash in Hand	10,400	500
Rent (Outstanding for one month)	2,400	3,000
Stock	11,400	20,000
Electricity and Telephone Bills—Outstanding		6,400

(*ii*) Bank Pass-book reveals the following :

Total Deposits ₹ 10,34,000

Withdrawals :

Creditors ₹ 8,90,000 ; Professional Charges ₹ 34,000 ; Furnitures and Fixtures (acquired on 1-10-24) ₹ 54,000 ; Proprietor's Drawings ₹ 1,61,900. (*iii*) Rent has been increased from January, 2025.

(*iv*) Mr. X deposited all cash sales and collections from debtors after meeting wages, shop expenses, rent, electricity and telephone charges.

(*v*) Mr. X made all purchases on credit.

(*vi*) His credit sales during the year amounted to ₹ 9,00,000.

(*vii*) He incurred ₹ 6,500 per month towards wages.

(*viii*) He incurred following expenses :
(*a*) Electricity and telephone charges ₹ 24,000 (paid)
(*b*) Shop expenses ₹ 18,000 (paid).

(*ix*) Charge depreciation on furniture and fixtures @ 10% p.a.
Finalise the accounts of Mr. X and compute his profit for the year ended 31-3-2025. Prepare his Statement of Affairs and reconcile the profit and capital balance.

SOLUTION

TRADING AND PROFIT & LOSS ACCOUNT OF MR. X

for the year ending 31st March, 2025

	₹			₹
To Opening Stock	11,400	By Sales :	₹	
To Purchases (2)	8,28,000	Cash (4)	2,97,500	
To Wages (₹ 6,500 × 12)	78,000	Credit	9,00,000	
To Gross Profit c/d	3,00,100			11,97,500
		By Closing Stock		20,000
	12,17,500			12,17,500
To Professional Charges	34,000	By Gross Profit b/d		3,00,100
To Rent (3)	30,600			
To Electricity & Telephone (₹ 24,000 + ₹ 6,400)	30,400			
To Shop Expenses	18,000			
To Depreciation on Furniture $\left(₹\,54{,}000 \times \frac{10}{100} \times \frac{1}{2}\right)$	2,700			
To Net Profit transferred to Capital A/c	1,84,400			
	3,00,100			3,00,100

STATEMENT OF AFFAIRS OF MR. X

as on 31-3-2024 and 31-3-2025

Liabilities	*31-3-24*	*31-3-25*	*Assets*		*31-3-24*	*31-3-25*
	₹	₹			₹	₹
Outstanding Expenses :			Cash		10,400	500
Rent	2,400	3,000	Bank		1,08,400	2,500
Electricity & Telephone		6,400	Sundry Debtors		35,400	58,800
Sundry Creditors	84,400	22,400	Stock	₹	11,400	20,000
Capital Account (Balancing Fig.)	78,800	1,01,300	Furniture	54,000		
			Less : Depreciation	2,700		
						51,300
	1,65,600	1,33,100			1,65,600	1,33,100

RECONCILIATION OF PROFIT AND CAPITAL BALANCE

	₹
Capital on 31-3-2025 as per Statement of Affairs	1,01,300
Add : Drawings during the year	1,61,900
	2,63,200

Less : Capital on 1-4-2024	78,800
Profit for the year ending 31st March, 2025	1,84,400
Profit as Profit & Loss A/c	1,84,400
Thus Profit is Reconciled	

Working Notes

(1) ***Calculation of Cash Received from Debtors***

TOTAL DEBTORS ACCOUNT

	₹		₹
To Balance b/d	35,400	By Cash (Balancing Figure)	8,76,600
To Credit Sales	9,00,000	By Balance c/d	58,800
	9,35,400		9,35,400

(2) ***Calculation of Credit Purchases***

TOTAL CREDITORS ACCOUNT

	₹		₹
To Bank	8,90,000	By Balance b/d	84,400
To Balance c/d	22,400	By Credit Purchases (Bal. Fig.)	8,28,000
	9,12,400		9,12,400

(3) ***Calculation of Amount of Rent Paid and Rent for the year***

	₹
Payment of rent outstanding as on 31-3-2024 during the year	2,400
Payment of rent for 9 months from 1-4-2024 to 31-12-2024 @ ₹ 2,400 per month	21,600
Payment of rent for 2 months from 1-1-2025 to 28-2-2025 @ ₹ 3,000 per month	6,000
Rent paid in cash during the year	30,000
Add : Rent outstanding on 31-3-2025	3,000
	33,000
Less : Rent outstanding on 31-3-2024	2,400
Rent payable for the year ending 31-3-2025	30,600

(4) ***Calculation of Cash Sales***

CASH BOOK

	Cash	*Bank*		*Cash*	*Bank*
	₹	₹		₹	₹
To Balance b/d	10,400	1,08,400	By Bank (Deposits) (C)	10,34,000	
To Sundry Debtors (1)	8,76,600		By Wages	78,000	
To Cash Sales (Bal. Figure)	2,97,500		By Rent (3)	30,000	
To Cash (Total Deposits) (C)		10,34,000	By Electricity & Telephone	24,000	
			By Shop Expenses	18,000	
			By Professional Charges		34,000

			By Sundry Creditors		8,90,000
			By Furniture		54,000
			By Drawings		1,61,900
			By Balance c/d	500	2,500
	11,84,500	11,42,400		11,84,500	11,42,400

ILLUSTRATION 10. Harshit Traders are carrying on the retail business of electrical goods. They keep their books of account under single entry system. The Balance Sheet as on 31st March, 2024 was as follows :

Liabilities	*Amount* (₹)	*Assets*	*Amount* (₹)
Capital A/c	6,05,000	Motor Vehicle	1,10,000
Trade Creditors	75,200	Furniture	73,500
Salary Payable	9,000	Stock in Trade	1,70,800
		Trade Debtors	1,45,400
		6% Investments	60,000
		Cash in Hand and at Bank	1,29,500
	6,89,200		6,89,200

The summary of Cash and Bank Book for the year ended 31st March, 2025 was given as below :

Receipts	*Amount* (₹)	*Payments*	*Amount* (₹)
Cash in Hand & at Bank on 1st April, 2024	1,29,500	Cash Purchases	9,48,400
		Payment to Trade Creditors	75,45,000
Cash Sales	10,22,400	Salaries	4,12,800
Receipts form Trade Debtors	85,52,000	Rent & Taxes	2,51,600
Interest on Investments	3,600	Sundry Expenses	1,38,400
		Drawings	2,40,000
		Cash in Hand & at Bank on 31st March, 2025	1,71,300
	97,07,500		97,07,500

Additional information:

(*i*) Gross Profit ratio of 12.5% on Sales is maintained throughout the year.

(*ii*) During the year, discount allowed to Trade debtors was for ₹ 62,500 and discount received from Trade Creditors amounted to ₹ 35,000.

(*iii*) As on 31st March, 2025. The closing balances to Trade Debtors and Trade Creditors were ₹ 2,20,500 and ₹ 1,05,600 respectively.

(*iv*) On 31st March, 2025 an amount of ₹ 14,800 was outstanding towards Salary.

(*v*) Depreciation @ 10% p.a. to be charged on Motor Vehicle and Furniture.

You are required to prepare Trading and Profit & Loss account for the year ended 31st March, 2025 and Balance Sheet as on that date.

SOLUTION

In the Book of Harshit Traders
TRADING AND PROFIT AND LOSS ACCOUNT
for the year ended 31st March, 2025

Particulars	(₹)	*Amount* (₹)	*Particulars*	(₹)	*Amount* (₹)
To Opening Stock		1,70,800	By Sales		
To Purchases			Cash	10,22,400	
Cash	9,48,400		Credit (W.N. 1)	86,89,600	97,12,000
Credit (W.N. 2)	76,10,400	85,58,800	By Closing Stock (Bal. Fig.)		2,31,600
To Gross Profit c/d					
(12.5% of 97,12,000)		12,14,000			
		99,43,600			99,43,600
To Rent & Taxes		2,51,600	By Gross Profit b/d		12,14,000
To Salaries (W.N. 3)		4,18,600	By Discount received		35,000
To Sundry Expenses		1,38,400	By Interest on Investment		3,600
To Discount Allowed		62,500			
To Depreciation	11,000				
(10% on					
(1,10,000 & 73,500))	7,350	18,350			
To Net Profit (b/f)		3,63,150			
		12,52,600			12,52,600

BALANCE SHEET
as at 31st March, 2025

Liabilities	(₹)	*Amount* (₹)	*Assets*	(₹)	*Amount* (₹)
Capital			Motor Vehicle	1,10,000	
Opening Balance	6,05,000		*Less* : Depreciation	(11,000)	99,000
Less : Drawing	(2,40,000)		Furniture & Fittings	73,500	
	3,65,000		*Less* : Depreciation	(7,350)	66,150
Add : Net Profit for the years	3,63,150	7,28,150	Closing Stock		2,31,600
Trade Creditors		1,05,600	Trade Receivable		2,20,500
Outstanding Salary		14,800	6% Investment		60,000
			Cash in Hand & at Bank		1,71,300
		8,48,550			8,48,550

Working Notes:

1. **TRADE DEBTORS ACCOUNT**

	₹		₹
To Balance b/d	1,45,400	By Cash/Bank	85,52,000
To Credit Sales (Bal. fig.)	86,89,600	By Discount Allowed	62,500
		By Balance c/d	2,20,500
	88,35,000		88,35,000

2. **TRADE CREDITORS ACCOUNT**

	₹		₹
To Cash/Bank	75,45,000	By Balance b/d	75,200
To Discount Received	35,000	By Purchases Credit	76,10,400
To Balance c/d	1,05,600		
	76,85,600		76,85,600

2. **COMPUTATION OF SALARY TO BE CHARGED TO PROFIT & LOSS ACCOUNT**

	₹
Salary Expenses paid (as per Cash Book)	4,12,800
Less : Outstanding Expenses as on 31-3-2024	(9,000)
	4,03,800
Add : Outstanding Expenses as on 31-3-2025	14,800
	4,18,600

ILLUSTRATION 11. Sri Sandipan, a trader, keeps the following records for his transactions:

(*i*) A Purchase Book in which he enters all his purchases invoices and cancels them as and when payment is made.

(*ii*) A Sales Book in which he enters all his sales bills and marks them off as and when each is received.

(*iii*) All the collections were deposited into the Bank and payments were made through cheques only except for petty payments which he met from his personal drawings.

(*iv*) At the end of each year, he prepares a Profit and Loss A/c on cash basis.

(*v*) As Sri Sandipan likes to admit Sri Rana Pratap as a partner of his business, he requests you to prepare his Trading and Profit & Loss Account for the year ended 31st December, 2024 and the Balance Sheet on that date.

You are furnished the following information for the said purpose :

Bank Pass Book shows the following payments :

(*a*)	Paid for purchases including ₹ 2,660 in respect of the previous period for which a sum of ₹ 377 is still outstanding	₹ 25,880
(*b*)	Salaries and Wages	₹ 6,822
(*c*)	Rent, Rates, Stationery and Insurance	₹ 5,166
(*d*)	Additions to Furniture	₹ 1,220
(*e*)	Advertising including ₹ 250 for the quarter ending 31st March, 2025	₹ 1,440
(*f*)	Repairs to Premises	₹ 644
(*g*)	Personal drawings of Sri Sandipan, out of which he has paid ₹ 577 for coolie and cartage, postage, entertainment and miscellaneous expenses in connection with business.	₹ 4,400

Sri Sandipan had stock of ₹ 10,660 on hand at the beginning of the year. This included some old defective items, which he disposed off for ₹ 755 but he had forgotten to deposit the sale proceeds in his Bank account. The stock at the end amounted to ₹ 8,220.

Cash received for sales amounted to ₹ 47,880 of which ₹ 7,110 were collections in respect of the previous year. Outstanding debtors at the end of the year were ₹ 9,655. His Purchase Book for the year discloses that invoices of the total value of ₹ 2,177 have not been cancelled. He had a Bank balance of ₹ 1,255 as on 31st December, 2024. The list of Furniture & Fittings at the end of the period was ₹ 6,255. Expenses outstanding amount ₹ 644. No other information is available with the trader, Sri Sandipan.

SOLUTION

Working Notes :

(1) ***Calculation of Balance at Bank as at 1-1-2024***

BANK ACCOUNT

		₹			₹
31-12-24	To Total Debtors	47,880	1-1-24	By Balance b/d—O/D (Bal. Fig.)	1,053
			31-12-24	By Creditors	25,880
				By Salaries & Wages	6,822
				By Rent, Rates, Stationery & Insurance	5,166
				By Furniture	1,220
				By Advertising	1,440
				By Repairs to Premises	644
				By Drawings	4,400
				By Balance c/d	1,255
		47,880			47,880

(2) ***Calculation of Capital as at 1-1-2024***

BALANCE SHEET
as on 1-1-2024

Liabilities	₹	*Assets*	₹
Bank Overdraft (1)	1,053	Trade Debtors	7,110
Trade Creditors (₹ 2,660 + ₹ 377)	3,037	Stock	10,660
Capital (Opening) [Balancing Fig.]	18,715	Furniture (₹ 6,255 – ₹ 1,220 Purchase during the year)	5,035
	22,805		22,805

(3) ***Calculation of Sales during 2024***

TRADE DEBTORS ACCOUNT

		₹			₹
1-1-24	To Balance b/d	7,110	31-12-24	By Bank A/c	47,880
	To Sales (Balancing Fig.)	50,425	"	By Balance c/d	9,655
		57,535			57,535

(4) ***Calculation of Purchases for the year 2024***

TRADE CREDITORS ACCOUNT

		₹			₹
	To Bank A/c	25,880	1-1-24	By Balance b/d	3,037
31-12-24	To Balance c/d (₹ 2,177 + ₹ 377 outstanding for 2023)	2,554		By Purchases (Balancing Fig.)	25,397
		28,434			28,434

(5) *Calculation of Drawings during the year 2024*

DRAWINGS ACCOUNT

		₹		₹
	To Bank A/c	4,400	By Petty Expenses	577
	To Sales (Collection Retained)	755	By Capital A/c—Transfer	4,578
		5,155		5,155

TRADING AND PROFIT & LOSS ACCOUNT

for the year ended 31-12-2024

Particulars		₹	*Particulars*		₹
To Opening Stock		10,660	By Sales	(3)	50,425
To Purchases	(4)	25,397	By Closing Stock		8,220
To Gross Profit c/d		23,343	By Disposal of Defective—Items		755
		59,400			59,400
To Salaries & Wages		6,822	By Gross Profit b/d		23,343
To Rent, Rates, Stationery		5,166			
To Repairs to Premises		644			
To Advertising (₹ 1440 – ₹ 250 Prepaid)	₹	1,190			
To Petty Expenses	577				
Add : Outstanding	644				
		1,221			
To Net Profit		8,300			
		23,343			23,343

BALANCE SHEET

as at 31-12-2024

Liabilities		₹	*Assets*	₹
Capital (Opening)	(1) 18,715		Furniture & Fittings	6,255
Add : Profit	8,300		Stock	8,220
	27,015		Trade Debtors	9,655
Less : Drawings	(5) 4,578		Prepaid Advertising	250
		22,437	Cash at Bank	1,255
Trade Creditors		2,554		
Outstanding Expenses		644		
		25,635		25,635

ILLUSTRATION 12. Following information relates to the business of Mr. Shiv Kumar, who requested you to prepare a Trading and Profit & Loss Account for the year ended 31st March, 2025 and a Balance Sheet as on that date :

(*a*)	*Balance as on 31st March, 2024* ₹	*Balance as on 31st March, 2025* ₹
Building	3,20,000	3,60,000
Furniture	60,000	68,000
Motor Car	80,000	80,000

Stocks	—	40,000
Bills Payable	28,000	16,000
Cash and Bank Balances	1,80,000	1,04,000
Sundry Debtors	1,60,000	—
Bills Receivable	32,000	28,000
Sundry Creditors	1,20,000	—

(*b*) Cash transactions during the year included the following besides certain other items :

	₹		₹
Sale of Old Papers and Miscellaneous Income	20,000	Cash Purchase	48,000
Miscellaneous Trade Expenses (including salaries etc.)	80,000	Payment to Creditors	1,84,000
Collection from Debtors	2,00,000	Cash Sales	80,000

(*c*) Other information :

(*i*) Bills receivable drawn during the year amount to ₹ 20,000 and Bills payable accepted ₹ 16,000.

(*ii*) Some items of old furniture, whose written down value on 31st March, 2024 was ₹ 20,000 was sold on 30th September, 2024 for ₹ 8,000. Depreciation is to be provided on Building and Furniture @ 10% p.a. and on Motorcar @ 20% p.a. Depreciation on sale of furniture to be provided for 6 months and for additions to Building for whole year.

(*iii*) Of the Debtors, a sum of ₹ 8,000 should be written off as Bad Debt and a provision for doubtful debts is to be provided @ 2%.

(*iv*) Mr. Shiv Kumar has been maintaining a steady gross profit rate of 30% on turnover.

(*v*) Outstanding salary on 31st March, 2024 was ₹ 8,000 and on 31st March, 2025 was ₹ 10,000. On 31st March, 2024 Profit and Loss Account had a credit balance of ₹ 40,000.

(*vi*) 20% of total sales and total purchase are to be treated as for cash.

(*vii*) Additions in Furniture Account took place in the beginning of the year and there was no opening provision for doubtful debts.

SOLUTION

TRADING AND PROFIT AND LOSS ACCOUNT OF MR. SHIV KUMAR

for the year ending 31st March, 2025

	₹	₹		₹	₹
To Opening Stock (Balancing Figure)		80,000	By Sales :		
To Purchases :			Cash	80,000	
Cash	48,000		Credit $\left(\frac{80}{20} \times ₹\ 80{,}000\right)$	3,20,000	4,00,000
Credit $\left(\frac{80}{20} \times ₹\ 48{,}000\right)$	1,92,000	2,40,000			
To Gross Profit (30% of ₹ 4,00,000 Sales)		1,20,000	By Closing Stock		40,000
		4,40,000			4,40,000
To Miscellaneous Expenses	80,000		By Gross Profit b/d		1,20,000
Less : Outstanding Salary last year	8,000		By Sale of Old Papers and Miscellaneous Income		20,000
	72,000		By Net Loss transferred to Capital A/c		25,840
Add : Outstanding Salary this year	10,000	82,000			

To Depreciation on :				
Building 10%	36,000			
Furniture : 10% on ₹ 20,000				
furniture sold for $\frac{1}{2}$ year	1,000			
10% on ₹ 68,000	6,800			
Motor Car 20%	16,000			
		59,800		
To Loss on Sale of Furniture (₹ 20,000 – ₹ 1,000 Dep.— ₹ 8,000 Value Realised)		11,000		
To Bad Debts		8,000		
To Provision for Doubtful Debts (2% of ₹ 2,52,000 Closing Debtors)		5,040		
		1,65,840		1,65,840

BALANCE SHEET OF SHIV KUMAR

as on 31st March, 2025

Liabilities		₹	*Assets*		₹
Outstanding Salary		10,000	Cash in hand and at Bank		1,04,000
Bills Payable		16,000	Bills Receivable	₹	28,000
Sundry Creditors (3)	₹	1,12,000	Sundry Debtors (1)	2,52,000	
Capital as on 1-4-2024 (6)	7,16,000		*Less* : Provision for Doubtful Debts @ 2%	5,040	
Add : Profit & Loss A/c's Balance as at 1-4-2024	40,000				2,46,960
	7,56,000		Closing Stock		40,000
Less : Net Loss for the year	25,840		Motor Car	80,000	
		7,30,160	*Less* : 20% Depreciation	16,000	
					64,000
			Furniture	60,000	
			Less : Written down value of Furniture sold	20,000	
				40,000	
			Add : Purchase of Furniture during the year (5)	28,000	
				68,000	
			Less : 10% Depreciation	6,800	
					61,200
			Building	3,20,000	
			Add : Addition during the year	40,000	
				3,60,000	
			Less : 10% Depreciation	36,000	
					3,24,000
		8,68,160			8,68,160

Working Notes :

(1) ***Calculation of Debtors as at 31-3-2025***

SUNDRY DEBTORS ACCOUNT

	₹		₹
To Balance b/d	1,60,000	By Cash/Bank A/c	2,00,000
To Sales (Credit)	3,20,000	By Bills Receivable A/c	20,000
		By Bad Debts	8,000
		By Balance c/d (Bal. Figure)	2,52,000
	4,80,000		4,80,000
To Balance b/d	2,52,000		

(2) ***Calculation of Amount Received on Account of Bills Receivable during the Year 2024-25***

BILLS RECEIVABLE ACCOUNT

	₹		₹
To Balance b/d	32,000	By Cash/Bank A/c (Balancing figure)	24,000
To Sundry Debtors (Bills drawn during the year)	20,000	By Balance c/d	28,000
	52,000		52,000
To Balance b/d	28,000		

(3) ***Calculation of Balance of Creditors as at 31-3-2025***

SUNDRY CREDITORS ACCOUNT

	₹		₹
To Cash/Bank A/c	1,84,000	By Balance b/d	1,20,000
To Bills Payable A/c (Bills accepted)	16,000	By Purchases A/c (Credit)	1,92,000
To Balance c/d (Bal. Figure)	1,12,000		
	3,12,000		3,12,000
		By Balance b/d	1,12,000

(4) ***Calculation of Amount Paid on Account of Bills Payable***

BILLS PAYABLE ACCOUNT

	₹		₹
To Cash/Bank A/c (Bal. Fig.)	28,000	By Balance b/d	28,000
To Balance c/d	16,000	By Sundry Creditors A/c	16,000
	44,000		44,000
		By Balance b/d	16,000

(5) ***Calculation of Furniture Purchased for Cash during the Year 2024-25***

CASH/BANK ACCOUNT

	₹		₹
To Balance b/d	1,80,000	By Miscellaneous Trade Expenses	80,000
To Miscellaneous Income	20,000	By Cash Purchases	48,000
To Sundry Debtors A/c	2,00,000	By Sundry Creditors A/c	1,84,000

To Cash Sales	80,000	By Bills Payable A/c (4)	28,000
To Sale of Furniture	8,000	By Addition to Building	40,000
To Bills Receivable A/c (2)	24,000	By Addition to Furniture (Balancing Figure)	28,000
		By Balance c/d	1,04,000
	5,12,000		5,12,000

(6) ***Calculation of Capital as at 1-4-2024***

BALANCE SHEET

as at 1-4-2024

Liabilities	₹	*Assets*	₹
Outstanding Salary	8,000	Cash in hand and at Bank	1,80,000
Bills Payable	28,000	Bills Receivable	32,000
Sundry Creditors	1,20,000	Sundry Debtors	1,60,000
Profit & Loss A/c	40,000	Stock	80,000
Capital (Balancing Figure)	7,16,000	Motor Car	80,000
		Furniture	60,000
		Building	3,20,000
	9,12,000		9,12,000

ILLUSTRATION 13. Shri Rashid furnishes you with the following information relating to his business :

(*a*) ***Assets and liabilities as on***

	1-1-2024	*31-12-2024*
	₹	₹
Furniture (w.d.v.)	6,000	6,350
Stock at cost	8,000	7,000
Sundry debtors	16,000	?
Sundry creditors	11,000	15,000
Prepaid expenses	600	700
Unpaid expenses	2,000	1,800
Cash in hand and at bank	1,200	625

(*b*) Receipts and payments during 2024 :

Collections from debtors, after allowing discount of ₹ 1,500 amounted to ₹ 58,500.

Collections on discounting of bills of exchange, after deduction of discount of ₹ 125 by the bank, totalled to ₹ 6,125.

Creditors of ₹ 40,000 were paid ₹ 39,200 in full settlement of their dues.

Payment for freight inwards ₹ 3,000.

Amounts withdrawn for personal use ₹ 7,000.

Payment for office furniture ₹ 1,000.

Investment carrying annual interest of 4% were purchased at ₹ 96 (Face Value ₹ 100) on 1st July, 2024 and payment made therefor.

Expenses including salaries paid ₹ 14,500.

Miscellaneous receipts ₹ 500.

(*c*) Bills of exchange drawn on and accepted by customers during the year amounted to ₹ 10,000. Of these, bills of exchange of ₹ 2,000 were endorsed in favour of creditors. An endorsed bill of exchange of ₹ 400 was dishonoured.

(*d*) Goods costing ₹ 900 were used as advertising materials.
(*e*) Goods are invariably sold to show a gross profit of 33 and 1/3% on sales.
(*f*) Difference in cash book, if any, is to be treated as further drawings or introduction by Shri Rashid.
(*g*) Provide at 2.5% for doubtful debts on closing debtors.

Rashid asks you to prepare Trading and Profit and Loss Account for the year ended 31st December, 2024 and Balance Sheet as on that date.

SOLUTION

TRADING AND PROFIT & LOSS ACCOUNT

for the year ending 31st December, 2024

	₹	₹		₹
To Opening Stock		8,000	By Sales (3)	73,050
To Purchases (2)	45,600		By Closing Stock	7,000
Less : For Advertising	900			
		44,700		
To Freight Inwards		3,000		
To Gross Profit c/d (3)		24,350		
		80,050		80,050
To Sundry Expenses (6)		14,200	By Gross Profit b/d	24,350
To Advertisement		900	By Interest on Investment	
To Discount allowed—	₹		$\left(₹\,100 \times \frac{4}{100} \times \frac{1}{2}\right)$	
Debtors	1,500			2
Bills Receivable	125			
		1,625	By Discount received	800
To Depreciation on Furniture		650	By Miscellaneous Income	500
To Provision for Doubtful Debts		486		
To Net Profit		7,791		
		25,652		25,652

BALANCE SHEET

as on 31st December, 2024

Liabilities	₹	₹	*Assets*	₹	₹
Capital as on 1st			Furniture (w.d.v.)	6,000	
January, 2024 (1)	18,800		Additions during the year	1,000	
Less : Drawings (5)	7,904			7,000	
	10,896		*Less* : Depreciation	650	
Add : Net Profit	7,791				6,350
		18,687	Investment		96
Sundry Creditors		15,000	Interest Accrued		2
Outstanding Expenses		1,800	Closing Stock		7,000
			Sundry Debtors (4)	19,450	
			Less : Provision for Doubtful Debts	486	
					18,964
			Bills Receivable (7)		1,750
			Cash in Hand and at Bank		625
			Prepaid Expenses		700
		35,487			35,487

Working Notes :

(1) ***Calculation of Capital on 1st January, 2024***

BALANCE SHEET

as on 1st January, 2024

Liabilities	₹	*Assets*	₹
Capital (Balancing figure)	18,800	Furniture (w.d.v.)	6,000
Creditors	11,000	Stock at Cost	8,000
Outstanding Expenses	2,000	Sundry Debtors	16,000
		Cash in Hand and at Bank	1,200
		Prepaid Expenses	600
	31,800		31,800

(2) ***Calculation of Purchases made during the year***

SUNDRY CREDITORS ACCOUNT

	₹		₹
To Cash and Bank A/c	39,200	By Balance b/d	11,000
To Discount Received A/c	800	By Sundry Debtors A/c	400
To Bills Receivable A/c	2,000	By Purchases A/c (Balancing figure)	45,600
To Balance c/d	15,000		
	57,000		57,000

(3) ***Calculation of Sales made during the year***

	₹	₹
Opening Stock		8,000
Purchases	45,600	
Less : For Advertising	900	
		44,700
Freight Inwards		3,000
		55,700
Less : Closing Stock		7,000
Cost of Goods Sold		48,700
Add : Gross Profit (@ 50% on Cost equivalent to $33\frac{1}{3}$% on Sales)		24,350
Sales		73,050

(4) ***Calculation of Debtors on 31-12-2024***

SUNDRY DEBTORS ACCOUNT

	₹		₹
To Balance b/d	16,000	By Cash and Bank A/c	58,500
To Sales A/c	73,050	By Discount Allowed A/c	1,500
To Sundry Creditors A/c		By Bills Receivable A/c	10,000
(Bill dishonoured)	400	By Balance c/d (Balancing figure)	19,450
	89,450		89,450

(5) *Calculation of Additional Drawings by Mr. Rashid*

CASH AND BANK ACCOUNT

	₹		₹
To Balance b/d	1,200	By Freight Inwards A/c	3,000
To Sundry Debtors A/c	58,500	By Furniture A/c	1,000
To Bills Receivable A/c	6,125	By Investment A/c	96
To Miscellaneous Income A/c	500	By Expenses A/c	14,500
		By Creditors A/c	39,200
		By Drawings A/c [₹ 7,000 + ₹ 904 Bal. Fig. (Additional Drawings)]	7,904
		By Balance c/d	625
	66,325		66,325

(6) *Calculation of Amount of Expenses Debited to Profit and Loss A/c*

EXPENSES ACCOUNT

	₹		₹
To Prepaid Expenses A/c (on 1-1-2024)	600	By Outstanding Expenses A/c (on 1-1-2024)	2,000
To Bank A/c	14,500	By Profit and Loss A/c (Balancing figure)	14,200
To Outstanding Expenses A/c (on 31-12-2024)	1,800	By Prepaid Expanses A/c (on 31-12-2024)	700
	16,900		16,900

(7) *Calculation of Bills Receivable on 31-12-2024*

BILLS RECEIVABLE ACCOUNT

	₹		₹
To Debtors A/c	10,000	By Creditors A/c	2,000
		By Bank A/c	6,125
		By Discount on Bills Receivable A/c	125
		By Balance c/d (Balancing figure)	1,750
	10,000		10,000

ILLUSTRATION 14. Following is the Balance Sheet of Sanjay, a small trader as on 31-3-2024.

Liabilities	*(₹'000)*	*Assets*	*(₹'000)*
Capital	200	Fixed Assets	145
Creditors	50	Stock	40
		Debtors	50
		Cash in Hand	5
		Cash at Bank	10
	250		250

A fire destroyed the accounting records as well as the closing cash of the trader on 31-3-2025. However, the following information was available :

(*a*) Debtors and creditors on 31-3-2025 showed an increase of 20% as compared to 31-3-2024.

(*b*) Credit Period :

Debtors—1 month Creditors—2 months

(*c*) Stock was maintained at the same level throughout the year.

(*d*) Cash sales constituted 20% of total sales.

(*e*) All purchases were for credit only.

(*f*) Current ratio as on 31-3-2025 was exactly 2.

(*g*) Total expenses excluding depreciation for the year amounted to ₹ 2,50,000.

(*h*) Depreciation was provided at 10% on the closing value of fixed assets.

(*i*) Bank and cash transactions :

(1) Payments to creditors included ₹ 50,000 by cash. (2) Receipts from debtors included ₹ 5,90,000 by way of cheques. (3) Cash deposited into the bank ₹ 1,20,000. (4) Personal drawings from bank ₹ 50,000. (5) Fixed assets purchased and paid by cheques ₹ 2,25,000.

You are required to prepare : (*a*) Trading and Profit & Loss Account of Sanjay for the year ended 31-3-2025 and (*b*) Balance Sheet on that date. For your exercise, assume cash destroyed by fire is written off in the Profit and Loss Account. ***(C.A.—PCE)***

SOLUTION

Books of Sanjay

TRADING AND PROFIT & LOSS ACCOUNT

for the year ending 31-3-2025 *(Figures in ₹ '000)*

To Opening Stock		40	By Sales : (1)		
" Purchases		360	Cash	180	
" Gross Profit c/d		540	Credit	720	
					900
			" Closing Stock		40
		940			940
To Expenses		250	By Gross Profit b/d		540
" Depreciation		37			
" Cash Destroyed	(5)	10			
" Net Profit transferred to Capital A/c		243			
		540			540

BALANCE SHEET

as on 31-3-2025

Liabilities	(₹ '000)	(₹ '000)	*Assets*	(₹ '000)	(₹ '000)
Capital	200		Fixed Assets (₹ 145 + ₹ 225)	370	
Add : Net Profit	243		*Less* : Depreciation	37	
	443				333
Less : Drawings	50				
		393	Stock		40
Creditors		60	Debtors		60
			Cash at Bank		20
		453			453

Working Notes :

Other Computations :

(1) ***Calculation of cash received from debtors***

Debtors Opening Balance		= ₹ 50,000
Closing Balance	= ₹ 50,000 + 20%	= ₹ 60,000
Credit Sales	= ₹ 60,000 × 12	= ₹ 7,20,000
Total Sales	$= 7,20,000 \times \frac{100}{80}$	= ₹ 9,00,000
Cash Sales	= ₹ 9,00,000 × 20%	= ₹ 1,80,000
Receipt of Cash from Debtors (₹ 50,000 + ₹ 7,20,000 – ₹ 60,000 – ₹ 5,90,000 by cheques)		= ₹ 1,20,000

(2) ***Payment made to creditors by cheques***

Creditors Opening Balance	= ₹ 50,000	
Closing Balance	= ₹ 50,000 + 20%	= ₹ 60,000
Credit Purchases	= ₹ 60,000 × 6	= ₹ 3,60,000
Payment by cheques (₹ 50,000 + ₹ 3,60,000 – ₹ 60,000 – ₹ 50,000 by cash)		= ₹ 3,00,000

(3) ***Calculation of Closing Bank Balance*** **:**

Creditors *i.e.* current liability : = ₹ 60,000

Current Assets 2 times ; current ratio being 2) = ₹ 60,000 × 2 = ₹ 1,20,000

Bank Balance = Current Assets – Stock – Debtors
= (₹ 1,20,000 – ₹ 40,000 – ₹ 60,000) = ₹ 20,000

(4) ***Calculation of Expenses by Cheques*** **: (Balancing fig. in Bank A/c)**

Fig. (₹ '000) (10 + 590 + 120 – 300 – 50 – 225 – 20) = (₹ '000) 125

Expenses by Cash = 250 – 125 = (₹ '000) 125

(5) ***Calculation of Cash destroyed = (Balancing figure in Cash A/c)***

Calculation of Cash destroyed by fire

CASH & BANK ACCOUNT (₹ '000)

	Cash	Bank		Cash	Bank
To Balance b/d	5	10	By Creditors (2)	50	300
To Debtors (1)	120	590	By Drawings		50
To Cash Sales	180		By Bank (Cash Deposited)	120	
To Cash			By Expenses (4)	125	125
(Deposited into bank)		120	By Assets		225
			By Cash Destroyed (Balancing figure)	(*a*) 10	
			By Balance c/d (3)		20
	305	720		305	720

(*a*) Fig. (₹ '000) (5 + 120 + 180 – 50 – 120 – 125) = 10

ILLUSTRATION 15. Following is the Balance Sheet of Sri Agni Dev as on 31st March, 2024 :

Liabilities	₹	*Assets*	₹
Capital Account	2,52,500	Machinery	1,20,000
Sundry Creditors for Purchases	45,000	Furniture	20,000

		Stock	33,000
		Debtors	1,00,000
		Cash in hand	8,000
		Cash at Bank	16,500
	2,97,500		2,97,500

Riots occurred and fire broke out on the evening of 31st March, 2025, destroying the books of account and Furniture. The cashier was grievously hurt and the cash available in the cash box was stolen.

The trader gives you the following information :

(*i*) Sales are effected as 25% for cash and the balance on credit. His total sales for the year ended 31st March, 2025 were 20% higher than the previous year. All the sales and purchases of goods were evenly spread throughout the year (as also in the last year).

(*ii*) Terms of credit

Debtors 2 Months ; Creditors 1 Month.

(*iii*) Stock level was maintained at ₹ 33,000 all throughout the year.

(*iv*) A steady Gross Profit rate of 25% on the turnover was maintained throughout. Creditors are paid by cheques only, except for cash purchases of ₹ 50,000.

(*v*) His private records and the Bank Pass-book disclosed the following transactions for the year.

(*a*)	Miscellaneous Business Expenses	₹ 1,57,500 (including ₹ 5,000 paid by cheque and ₹ 7,500 was outstanding as on 31st March, 2025)
(*b*)	Repairs	₹ 3,500 (paid by cash)
(*c*)	Addition to Machinery	₹ 60,000 (paid by cheque)
(*d*)	Private Drawings	₹ 30,000 (paid by cash)
(*e*)	Travelling Expenses	₹ 18,000 (paid by cash)
(*f*)	Introduction of Additional Capital by depositing in to the Bank.	₹ 5,000

(*vi*) Collection from debtors were all through cheques.

(*vii*) Depreciation on Machinery is to be provided @ 15% on the Closing Book Value.

(*viii*) The cash stolen is to be charged to the Profit and Loss Account.

(*ix*) Loss of furniture is to be adjusted from the Capital Account.

Prepare Trading, Profit and Loss Account for the year ended 31st March, 2025 and a Balance Sheet as on that date. Make appropriate assumptions wherever necessary. All workings should form part of your answer. ***(CA—PE-II)***

SOLUTION

TRADING AND PROFIT & LOSS ACCOUNT OF SHRI AGNI DEV

for the year ended 31st March, 2025

		₹			₹
To Opening Stock		33,000	By Sales	(1)	9,60,000
To Purchases	(3)	7,20,000	By Closing Stock		33,000
To Gross Profit c/d		2,40,000			
		9,93,000			9,93,000
To Business Expenses		1,57,500	By Gross Profit b/d		2,40,000
To Repairs		3,500			
To Depreciation		27,000			

		₹		₹
To Travelling Expenses		18,000		
To Loss by theft	(7)	1,500		
To Net Profit transferred to Capital A/c		32,500		
		2,40,000		2,40,000

BALANCE SHEET OF SHRI AGNI DEV

as on 31st March, 2025

Liabilities			₹	*Assets*		₹
Sundry Creditors		(4)	55,833	Stock in Trade		33,000
Bank Overdraft			2,667	Sundry Debtors (2)	₹	1,20,000
Outstanding Expenses			7,500	Machinery	1,80,000	
		₹		*Less* : Depreciation	27,000	
Capital		2,52,500				1,53,000
Add : Fresh Capital		5,000				
Net Profit		32,500				
₹		2,90,000				
Less : Drawings	30,000					
Loss of Furniture	20,000					
		50,000				
			2,40,000			
			3,06,000			3,06,000

Working Notes :

(1) ***Calculation of Sales during 2024-25***

	₹
Debtors as on 31st March, 2024 (Being equal to 2 months credit sales)	1,00,000
Total Credit Sales in 2023-24 ₹ 1,00,000 × 6	6,00,000
Cash Sales, being equal to 1/3 of credit sales or 1/4 of the total	2,00,000
Total Sales in 2023-24	8,00,000
Increase in sales (20%)	1,60,000
Total Sales during 2024-25	9,60,000

	₹
Cash Sales (1/4 of total sales)	2,40,000
Credit Sales (3/4 of total sales)	7,20,000

(2) Debtors equal to 2 months credit sales $\left(₹\,7{,}20{,}000 \times \frac{2}{12}\right)$ 1,20,000

(3) ***Purchases***

Sales in 2024-25	9,60,000
Gross Profit @ 25%	2,40,000
Cost of goods sold being purchases (as there is no change in stock levels)	7,20,000

(4) Sundry Creditors for goods ₹ (₹ 7,20,000 – ₹ 50,000 Cash Purchases) ÷ 12 $= \frac{₹\,6{,}70{,}000}{12} =$ ₹ 55,833

(5) ***Collection from Debtors***

	₹
Opening Balance	1,00,000
Add : Credit Sales	7,20,000
	8,20,000
Less : Closing Balance	1,20,000
Collection from Debtors by Cheques	7,00,000

(6) ***Payment to Creditors***

	₹
Opening Balance	45,000
Add : Credit purchases (₹ 7,20,000 – ₹ 50,000)	6,70,000
	7,15,000
Less : Closing Balance	55,833
Payment to Creditors by Cheques	6,59,167

(7) ***Calculation of Cash Loss by Theft***

CASH BOOK

	₹	₹		₹	₹
To Balance b/d	8,000	16,500	By Payment to Creditors (6)	50,000	6,59,167
To Collection from Debtors (5)	—	7,00,000	By Misc. Expenses	1,45,000	5,000
To Sales	2,40,000	—	By Repairs	3,500	—
To Additional Capital	—	5,000	By Addition to Machinery	—	60,000
To Balance c/d (overdraft)		2,667	By Travelling Expenses	18,000	—
			By Private Drawings	30,000	—
			By Balance c/d (loss by theft)	1,500	—
	2,48,000	7,24,167		2,48,000	7,24,167

ILLUSTRATION 16. Mr. Dinesh, a trader, does not keep his books on a double entry basis. The following information is available from his books and other records for the year ended 31st March, 2025. On the basis of the following information, compile a Trading Account, Profit and Loss Account for the year ended 31st March, 2025 and Balance Sheet as at that date.

	31-3-2024	*31-3-2025*
	₹	₹
(1) Liabilities and Assets :		
Bank Balance	20,000	9,400
Cash Balance	3,000	2,000
Prepaid Expenses	5,000	7,000
Stock	70,000	60,000
Debtors for Sales	2,30,000	—
Bills Receivable	—	—
Furniture at written down value	70,000	82,000
Creditors for purchases	2,20,000	2,60,000
Outstanding Liabilities for expenses	30,000	15,000
(2) Receipts and payments during 2024-25 :		
Collection from Debtors (after allowing $2\frac{1}{2}$% discount)		5,85,000
Proprietor's Drawings		50,000

Capital introduced by Proprietor	95,150
Purchase of Furniture in the middle of the year	20,000
14% Government Securities purchased at 96% on 1-4-2024	96,000
Expenses	2,00,000
Sale of Scrap	5,000
Payment to Creditors (after receiving 2% discount)	3,92,000
Proceeds of Bills Receivable discounted at 2%	61,250

(3) Sales are made so as to realise a profit of $33\frac{1}{3}\%$ on sale proceeds.

(4) Goods worth ₹ 5,000 were taken by the Proprietor.

(5) During the year bills receivable worth ₹ 1,50,000 were drawn on debtors. Of these, bill amounting to ₹ 30,000 were endorsed in favour of the creditors. Of this later amount, a bill for ₹ 5,000 was dishonoured by the debtor.

(6) Sales and purchases are made only on credit. *(ICWA—Final)*

SOLUTION

TRADING AND PROFIT & LOSS ACCOUNT
for the year ending 31st March, 2025

	₹	₹		₹
To Opening stock		70,000	By Sales (3)	7,05,000
To Purchases (2)	4,65,000		By Closing Stock	60,000
Less : Drawings by proprietor	5,000			
		4,60,000		
To Gross Profit c/d		2,35,000		
		7,65,000		7,65,000
To Expenses (8)		1,83,000	By Gross Profit b/d	2,35,000
To Depreciation (6)		8,000	By Interest on Securities	14,000
To Discount on Debtors		15,000	By Discount	8,000
To Discount on Bills Receivable		1,250	By Sale of Scrap	5,000
To Net Profit		54,750		
		2,62,000		2,62,000

BALANCE SHEET
as on 31st March, 2025

Liabilities		₹	*Assets*	₹
Outstanding Expenses	₹	15,000	Cash in Bank	9,400
Sundry Creditors		2,60,000	Cash in Hand	2,000
Capital Opening (1)	1,48,000		Prepaid Expenses	7,000
Add : Introduced during the			Interest accrued on Investment	14,000
year (7)	95,150		Bills Receivable (5)	57,500
Add : Profit for the year	54,750		Sundry Debtors (4)	1,90,000
	2,97,900		Stock-in-trade	60,000
Less : Drawings	55,000		Investments 14% Govt. Securities	
		2,42,900	(Nominal value 1,00,000)	96,000

			₹	
		Fixed Assets		
		Furniture	90,000	
		Less : Depreciation	8,000	
				82,000
	5,17,900			5,17,900

Working Notes :

(1) *Calculation of Opening Capital Balance*

BALANCE SHEET

as on 31st March, 2024

Liabilities	₹	*Assets*	₹
Sundry Creditors	2,20,000	Furniture	70,000
Outstanding Expenses	30,000	Stock-in-trade	70,000
Capital (Balancing figure)	1,48,000	Sundry Debtors	2,30,000
		Prepaid Expenses	5,000
		Cash at Bank	20,000
		Cash in Hand	3,000
	3,98,000		3,98,000

(2) *Calculation of Credit Purchases :*

TOTAL CREDITORS ACCOUNT

	₹		₹
To Cash at Bank	3,92,000	By Balance b/d	2,20,000
To Discount	8,000	By Sundry Debtors (bills dishonoured)	5,000
To Bills Receivable	30,000	By Purchases (Balancing figure)	4,65,000
To Balance c/d	2,60,000		
	6,90,000		6,90,000

(3) *Calculation of Sales during the year*

		₹
Stock on 1st April, 2024		70,000
Purchases		4,65,000
	₹	5,35,000
Less : Closing Stock	60,000	
Less : Drawn by Proprietor	5,000	
		65,000
Cost of Goods Sold		4,70,000
Add : Profit 50% on Cost or $33\frac{1}{3}$% on Selling Price		2,35,000
		7,05,000

(4) *Calculation of Debtors at the end*

TOTAL DEBTORS ACCOUNT

	₹		₹
To Balance b/d	2,30,000	By Cash/Bank	5,85,000
To Sales	7,05,000	By Discount	15,000

To Sundry Creditors (bill dishonoured after endorsement)	5,000	By Bills Receivable	1,50,000
		By Balance c/d (Balancing figure)	1,90,000
	9,40,000		9,40,000

(5) ***Calculation of Bills Receivable at the end***

BILLS RECEIVABLE ACCOUNT

	₹		₹
To Sundry Debtors	1,50,000	By Sundry Creditors	30,000
		By Cash/Bank	61,250
		By Discount	1,250
		By Balance c/d (Balancing figure)	57,500
	1,50,000		1,50,000

(6) ***Calculation of Depreciation on Furniture***

FURNITURE ACCOUNT

	₹		₹
To Balance b/d	70,000	By Depreciation (Balancing figure)	8,000
To Cash/Bank (Purchase)	20,000	By Balance c/d	82,000
	90,000		90,000

(7) ***Calculation of Capital Introduced***

CASH/BANK ACCOUNT

	₹		₹
To Balance b/d	23,000	By Sundry Creditors	3,92,000
To Sundry Debtors	5,85,000	By Furniture A/c	20,000
To Bills Receivable	61,250	By 14% Govt. Securities	96,000
To Sale of Scrap	5,000	By Expenses	2,00,000
To Capital A/c		By Drawings	50,000
(Fresh Capital Introduced)	95,150	By Balance c/d	11,400
	7,69,400		7,69,400

(8) ***Calculation of Expenses Charged to Profit and Loss A/c***

	₹	₹
Paid		2,00,000
Add : Outstanding on 31-3-2025		15,000
Add : Prepaid on 31-3-2024		5,000
		2,20,000
Less : Outstanding on 31-3-2024	30,000	
Less : Prepaid on 31-3-2025	7,000	37,000
		1,83,000

ILLUSTRATION 17. Following is the Balance Sheet of the retail business of Shri Srinivas as at 31st December, 2024 :

Liabilities	₹	*Assets*	₹
Sri Srinivas's Capital	1,00,000	Furniture	10,000
Liabilities for Goods	20,500	Stock	70,000
Rent	1,000	Debtors	25,000
		Cash at bank	14,500
		Cash in hand	2,000
	1,21,500		1,21,500

You are furnished with the following information :

(1) Sri Srinivas sells his goods at a profit of 20% on sales.

(2) Goods are sold for cash and credit. Credit customers pay by cheques only.

(3) Payments for purchases (all credit basis) are always made by cheques.

(4) It is the practice of Sri Srinivas to send to the bank every weekend the collections of the week after paying every week, salary of ₹ 300 to the clerk, Sundry expenses of ₹ 50 and personal expenses ₹ 100.

Analysis of the Bank Pass-book for the 13 weeks period ending 31st March, 2025 disclosed the following :

	₹		₹
Payments to creditors	75,000	Following are the balances on	
Payments of rent upto 31-3-2025	4,000	31st March, 2025 :	
Amounts deposited into the bank	1,25,000	Stock	40,000
(include ₹ 30,000 received from		Debtors	30,000
debtors by cheques)		Creditors for goods	36,500

On the evening of 31st March, 2025 the Cashier absconded with the available cash in the cash box. There was no cash deposit on the week ended on that date.

You are required to prepare a statement showing the amount of cash defalcated by the cashier and also a Profit and Loss Account for the period ended 31st March, 2025 and a Balance Sheet as on that date.

SOLUTION

STATEMENT SHOWING THE AMOUNT OF CASH DEFALCATED BY THE CASHIER

	₹	₹
Cash balance as on 1-1-2025		2,000
Add : Cash sales		1,16,250
		1,18,250
Less : Salary to clerk (₹ 300 × 13)	3,900	
Sundry expenses (₹ 50 × ₹ 13)	650	
Drawings of Sri Srinivas (₹ 100 × 13)	1,300	
Deposit into bank (₹ 1,25,000 – ₹ 30,000)	95,000	1,00,850
Cash balance as on 31-3-2025 (defalcated by cashier)		17,400

TRADING AND PROFIT AND LOSS ACCOUNT OF SRI SRINIVAS

for the 13 week period ended 31st March, 2025

		₹		₹	₹
To Opening Stock		70,000	By Sales :		
To Purchases	(1)	91,000	Cash (4)	1,16,250	
To Gross Profit c/d		30,250	Credit (3)	35,000	
					1,51,250
			By Closing Stock		40,000
		1,91,250			1,91,250
To Salaries		3,900	By Gross Profit b/d		30,250
To Rent (₹ 4,000 – ₹ 1,000)		3,000			
To Sundry Expenses		650			
To Loss of cash by theft		17,400			
To Net Profit transferred to Capital Account		5,300			
		30,250			30,250

BALANCE SHEET OF SRI SRINIVAS

as on 31st March, 2025

Liabilities		₹	*Assets*		₹
Liabilities for Goods	₹	36,500	Cash at Bank	(5)	60,500
Capital as on 1-1-2025	1,00,000		Debtors		30,000
Add : Profit	5,300		Stock		40,000
	1,05,300		Furniture		10,000
Less : Drawings	1,300				
		1,04,000			
		1,40,500			1,40,500

Working Notes :

(1) *Calculation of Credit Purchases*

CREDITORS ACCOUNT

	₹		₹
To Bank A/c	75,000	By Balance b/d	20,500
To Balance c/d	36,500	By Purchases A/c (Balancing figure)	91,000
	1,11,500		1,11,500

(2) *Calculation of Total Sales*

	₹
Opening Stock	70,000
Add : Purchases	91,000
	1,61,000
Less : Closing Stock	40,000
Cost of Goods Sold	1,21,000
Add : Gross Profit (25% on cost)	30,250
Total Sales	1,51,250

(3) *Calculation of Credit Sales*

DEBTORS ACCOUNT

	₹		₹
To Balance b/d	25,000	By Bank A/c	30,000
To Credit Sales (Bal. fig.)	35,000	By Balance c/d	30,000
	60,000		60,000

(4) *Calculation of Cash Sales*

	₹
Total Sales (2)	1,51,250
Less : Credit Sales	35,000
Cash Sales	1,16,250

(5) *Calculation of Bank Balance as on 31-3-2025*

BANK ACCOUNT

	₹		₹
To Balance b/d	14,500	By Creditors A/c	75,000
To Debtors A/c	30,000	By Rent A/c	4,000
To Cash A/c	95,000	By Balance c/d	60,500
	1,39,500		1,39,500

Note : The amount defalcated by the cashier may be treated as recoverable, then ₹ 17,400 may be shown as sundry advances on assets side in the Balance Sheet and net profit for the 13 week period ending 31st March, 2025 would amount to ₹ 22,700.

ILLUSTRATION 18. A is importer of fancy goods, operating from rented premises, which is on lease of ₹ 1,000 per month. He prepares his accounts as on 31st December, each year. On the night of December 31st, 2024 all his books and records were destroyed in a fire.

Following was his summarised financial position as on 31st December, 2023 :

Fixed Assets : Motor Car ₹ 20,000 ; Furniture ₹ 10,000.

Current Assets : Stock-in-trade (at cost) ₹ 2,00,500 ; Debtors ₹ 24,000 ; Balance at Bank ₹ 27,060 ; Cash in Hand ₹ 590 ; Prepaid Rates ₹ 500.

Current Liabilities : Creditors for purchases ₹ 1,10,200 ; Accrued rent ₹ 2,000 ; Due for Hire Purchase Instalments ₹ 2,790.

Following further information is also available :

(*a*) A buys goods for resale only from one manufacturer in Japan, who allows a rebate of 3% of the goods purchased by him in excess of ₹ 5,00,000 in a calendar year. The rebate due for the year ended 31st December, 2024 was ₹ 12,480.

(*b*) All goods are sold at a standard gross profit margin of 40% on selling price. Any rebate due is to be ignored for the purpose.

(*c*) Stock at cost on 31st December, 2024 amounted to ₹ 90,200.

(*d*) Weekly cash expenses out of cash sales (before depositing the same into the bank) has been:

Drawings ₹ 300 ; Carriage Outward ₹ 500 ; Petrol ₹ 100 ; General Expenses ₹ 50.

Cash in hand on 31st December, 2024 amounted to ₹ 1,670.

(e) His bank statements for the year reveal the following information :

	₹		₹
Paid for purchases of goods	10,10,500	Printing and Stationery	6,400
Car Expenses	6,680	Advertisement	12,280
Rent	13,000	Insurance (for business)	3,000
Rates for the year ended 31st March, 2025	3,200	Lorry Hire Charges	48,700
		General Expenses	36,230
Hire Purchase Instalments (Final Payments)	3,040	Drawings	37,000
Salaries	1,12,460	Balance as on 31st December, 2024	2,31,800
Travelling Expenses	36,800		

(f) Depreciation on motor car and furniture is to be provided @ 30% and 15% respectively.

Prepare Trading and Profit and Loss Account for the year ended on 31st December, 2024 and Balance Sheet as on that date. ***(C.A. Inter)***

SOLUTION

TRADING AND PROFIT AND LOSS ACCOUNT OF A

for the year ending 31st December, 2024

		₹		₹
To Opening Stock		2,00,500	By Sales (2)	17,10,500
To Purchases (1)		9,16,000	By Closing Stock	90,200
To Gross Profit c/d		6,84,200		
		18,00,700		18,00,700
To Salaries		1,12,460	By Gross Profit b/d	6,84,200
To Rent @ ₹ 1,000 p.m.		12,000	By Rebate on Purchases	12,480
To Rates (3,200 – 800 + 500)		2,900		
To Car Expenses including Petrol ₹ 5,200		11,880		
To Travelling Expenses		36,800		
To Printing & Stationery		6,400		
To Advertisement		12,280		
To Insurance		3,000		
To Carriage Outward		26,000		
To General Expenses :	₹			
Cash Payment	2,600			
By Bank	36,230	38,830		
To Lorry Hire Charges		48,700		
To Hire Purchase Interest :				
Instalment Payment (Final)	3,040			
Less : Due as on 31-12-2024	2,790	250		
To Depreciation :				
On Motor Car @ 30%	6,000			
On Furniture @ 15%	1,500	7,500		
To Net Profit transferred to Capital A/c		3,77,680		
		6,96,680		6,96,680

BALANCE SHEET OF A
as at 31st December, 2024

Liabilities		₹	*Assets*	₹	₹
A's Capital on 1-1-2024	(8)	1,67,660	Fixed Assets :		
Add : Profit for the year		3,77,680	Motor Car	20,000	
		5,45,340	*Less* : Depreciation	6,000	
Less : Drawings		52,600			14,000
		4,92,740	Furniture	10,000	
Sundry Creditors	(7)	3,220	*Less* : Depreciation	1,500	
Accrued Rent :	₹				8,500
Rent paid during 2024	13,000		Current Assets :		
Less : Accrued Rent 2023	2,000		Stock-in-trade at cost		90,200
Payment for 2024	11,000		Sundry Debtors	(6)	1,49,990
Due for 2024 @			Prepaid Rates		800
₹ 1,000 p.m.	12,000		Balance at Bank		2,31,800
		1,000	Cash in hand		1,670
		4,96,960			4,96,960

Working Notes :

(1) ***Calculation of Purchases***

	₹
Purchases for which rebate not allowed	5,00,000
Purchases in excess of ₹ 5,00,000 for which 3% rebate is allowed. Rebate allowed is ₹ 12,480 ; therefore, purchases for which rebate is allowed ₹ 12,480 × $\frac{100}{3}$	4,16,000
Total Purchases	9,16,000

(2) ***Calculation of Sales***

	₹
Opening Stock	2,00,500
Add : Purchases	9,16,000
	11,16,500
Less : Closing Stock	90,200
Cost of Goods Sold	10,26,300

Rate of Gross Profit 40% on Sales

Therefore, Sales $= \frac{100}{60}$ of Cost of Sales $= \frac{100}{60} \times$ ₹ 10,26,300

= ₹ 17,10,500

(3) ***Calculation of Cash Sales***

CASH ACCOUNT
(*For 52 weeks*)

	₹		₹
To Balance b/d	590	By Drawings (₹ 300 × 52)	15,600
To Cash Sales (Bal. figure)	50,480	By Carriage Outward (₹ 500 × 52)	26,000
		By Petrol (₹ 100 × 52)	5,200
		By General Expenses (₹ 50 × 52)	2,600
		By Balance c/d	1,670
	51,070		51,070

(4) *Calculation of Credit Sales*

		₹
Total Sales		17,10,500
Less : Cash Sales	(3)	50,480
Credit Sales		16,60,020

(5) *Calculation of Amount Received from Debtors*

BANK ACCOUNT

	₹		₹
To Balance b/d	27,060	By Total Creditors A/c	10,10,500
To Total Debtors A/c (Balancing figure)	15,34,030	By Car Expenses	6,680
		By Rent	13,000
		By Rates	3,200
		By H.P. Instalments	3,040
		By Salaries	1,12,460
		By Travelling Expenses	36,800
		By Printing & Stationery	6,400
		By Advertisement	12,280
		By Insurance	3,000
		By Lorry Hire Charges	48,700
		By General Expenses	36,230
		By Drawings	37,000
		By Balance c/d	2,31,800
	15,61,090		15,61,090

(6) *Calculation of Debtors as at 31-12-2024*

TOTAL DEBTORS ACCOUNT

	₹		₹
To Balance b/d	24,000	By Bank (5)	15,34,030
" Credit Sales (4)	16,60,020	" Balance c/d (Balancing figure)	1,49,990
	16,84,020		16,84,020

(7) *Calculation of Creditors as at 31-12-2024*

TOTAL CREDITORS ACCOUNT

	₹		₹
To Bank	10,10,500	By Balance b/d	1,10,200
" Rabate	12,480	" Purchases (1)	9,16,000
" Balance c/d (Balancing figure)	3,220		
	10,26,200		10,26,200

(8) *Calculation of Capital as at 1-1-2024*

STATEMENT OF AFFAIRS

as at 1-1-2024

Liabilities	₹	*Assets*	₹
Creditors	1,10,200	Motor Car	20,000
Accrued Rent	2,000	Furniture	10,000

Due for Hire Purchase Instalments	2,790	Stock-in-trade	2,00,500
Capital as at 1-1-2024		Debtors	24,000
(Balancing figure)	1,67,660	Prepaid Rates	500
		Balance at bank	27,060
		Cash in hand	590
	2,82,650		2,82,650

ILLUSTRATION 19. Shri Kakubhai is operating a small maufacturing business. He did not keep adequate records to determine his income or prepare a proper Balance Sheet. Following particulars are furnished to you :

STATEMENT OF AFFAIRS

	31-12-2023	*31-12-2024*		*31-12-2023*	*31-12-2024*
	₹	₹		₹	₹
Sundry Creditors	50,000	65,000	Cash in hand	1,400	1,800
Loan from Babubhai	—	18,000	Cash at Bank	12,000	8,200
Kakubhai's Capital	3,63,400	3,34,000	Sundry Debtors	55,600	41,200
			Stock of Raw Materials	15,000	24,000
			Stock of Finished Goods	66,000	72,000
			Fixed Assets	1,90,000	2,20,000
			Investments	73,400	49,800
	4,13,400	4,17,000		4,13,400	4,17,000

Your examination of the available records reveals the following additional information :

(*i*) Sundry Debtors as at the end of the year do not include the sum of ₹ 9,200 due from a customer as full collection from him was considered doubtful. However, prior to the time you start your work, you find that the above account was settled for ₹ 7,000.

(*ii*) The stocks of finished goods have been valued at sale price. The average margin of profit on sales was 30% at 31st December, 2023 and 40% at 31st December, 2024. Raw materials were valued at cost.

(*iii*) Sundry Debtors include the sum of ₹ 2,000 in respect of goods sent on consignment on 30th December, 2024. The same has been billed at sale price.

(*iv*) The details of investments are as under :

Name of the Company	*Shares*	*Face Value* ₹	*31-12-2023* ₹	*31-12-2024* ₹
A Ltd.	400	100	40,000	40,000
B Ltd.	334	100	33,400	—
C Ltd.	196	50	—	9,800
			73,400	49,800

(*a*) The shares of A Ltd. were acquired in 2021 for ₹ 54,000.

(*b*) The shares of B Ltd. were purchased in June, 2019 for ₹ 34,000 and sold in April, 2024 for ₹ 44,000.

(*c*) The shares of C Ltd. were purchased in June, 2024 for ₹ 14,000.

(*v*) The loan from Babubhai was utilised for making a gift to the proprietor's newly born daughter.

(*vi*) The figures of Cash and Bank are amounts appearing as the balances on his bank statements as on 31st December, 2023 and 31st December, 2024 respectively. By reviewing subsequent Bank statements, you find the following :

(*a*) A deposit of ₹ 4,000 made on 31st December, 2023 was not recorded by the bank until 4th January, 2024. A cheque for ₹ 1,800 issued prior to 31st December, 2023 was not presented to Bank until January, 2024.

(*b*) A deposit of ₹ 8,000 from a customer was entered by the Bank on 30th December, 2024. Shri Kakubhai did not receive notice of this collection until 6th January, 2025.

(*vii*) Following expenditures were made during the year 2024 :

(*a*) Advance payment of tax ₹ 12,000 ; (*b*) Household and personal expenses ₹ 51,200.

You are required to prepare (*i*) a Statement of Shri Kakubhai's Income for the year ended 31st December, 2024, (*ii*) his Balance Sheet as on that date, and (*iii*) supporting schedules.

SOLUTION

STATEMENT OF AFFAIRS OF KAKUBHAI

as at 31-12-2023

Liabilities	₹	*Assets*		₹
Sundry Creditors	50,000	Cash in hand		1,400
Capital (Bal. figure)	3,60,400	Cash at Bank	(1)	14,200
		Sundry Debtors		55,600
		Stock of Raw Material at Cost		15,000
		Stock of Finished Goods at Cost	(2)	46,200
		Investments	(3)	88,000
		Fixed Assets		1,90,000
	4,10,400			4,10,400

STATEMENT OF AFFAIRS OF KAKUBHAI

as at 31-12-2024

Liabilities	₹	*Assets*		₹
Sundry Creditors	65,000	Cash in hand		1,800
Loan from Babubhai	18,000	Cash at Bank	(4)	200
Capital—Excess of assets		Sundry Debtors	(5)	46,200
over liabilities	3,33,600	Stock of Raw Materials at Cost		24,000
		Stock of Finished Goods at Cost	(6)	44,400
		Investments	(7)	68,000
		Fixed Assets		2,20,000
		Advance Payment of Tax		12,000
	4,16,600			4,16,600

STATEMENT OF INCOME OF KUKUBHAI

for the year ending December 31, 2024

	₹	₹
Capital as at 31-12-2024 as per Statement of Affairs		3,33,600
Add : Drawings during the year :		
Household and Personal Expenses	51,200	
Gift to the proprietor's daughter	18,000	
		69,200
		4,02,800
Less : Capital as at 1-1-2024 as per Statement of Affairs		3,60,400
Profit for the year 2024		42,400

BALANCE SHEET OF KAKUBHAI

at at 31-12-2024

		₹		₹
Sundry Creditors		65,000	Cash in hand	1,800
Loan from Babubhai		18,000	Cash at Bank	200
Capital Account :	₹		Sundry Debtors	46,200
Balance on 1-1-2024	3,60,400		Stock of Raw Materials at Cost	24,000
Add : Profit for the year	42,400		Stock of Finished Goods at Cost	44,400
	4,02,800		Investments	68,000
Less : Drawings	69,200		Fixed Assets	2,20,000
		3,33,600	Advance Payment of Tax	12,000
		4,16,600		4,16,600

Working Notes :

(1) *Bank Balance as on 31-12-2023*

	₹
Balance as per Bank Statement as on 31-12-2023	12,000
Add : Deposit not recorded by the Bank	4,000
	16,000
Less : Cheques not presented for payment upto 31-12-2023	1,800
Balance at bank as per Cash Book as on 31-12-2023	14,200

(2) *Stock of Finished Goods as on 31-12-2023*

	₹
Value of stock of finished goods at price (given)	66,000
Less : 30% profit included $\left(₹\ 66,000 \times \frac{30}{100}\right)$	19,800
Value of Stock at cost	46,200

(3) *Investments as on 31-12-2023*

	₹
Shares in A Ltd. at Cost	54,000
Shares in B Ltd. at Cost	34,000
Value of Investments at cost	88,000

Investments have been valued at cost because they have been held as a fixed asset.

(4) *Cash at Bank as on 31-12-2024*

	₹
Balance as per Bank Statement	8,200
Less : Deposit from customer into the bank not entered in the Cash Book	8,000
Bank Balance as per Cash Book	200

(5) *Sundry Debtors on 31-12-2024*

	₹
Balance as given	41,200
Less : Sale proceeds of goods consigned on 30-12-2024 included in debtors	2,000
	39,200
Add : Debtors of ₹ 9,200 settled for ₹ 7,000 not included in debtors*	7,000
	46,200

*Even though the item occurs after 31-12-2024 but it takes place before the preparation of the Balance Sheet, so it has been taken.

(6) *Stock of Finished Goods as on 31-12-2024*

	₹
Value of stock at sale price (given)	72,000
Add : Stock with the consignee at sale price	2,000
	74,000
Less : 40% profit included $\left(₹\,74{,}000 \times \frac{40}{100}\right)$	29,600
Value of stock at cost	44,400

(7) *Investments as on 31-12-2024*

	₹
Shares in A Ltd. at cost	54,000
Shares in C Ltd. at cost	14,000
	68,000

Note. The profit on the sale of shares in B Ltd. during 2024, ₹ 10,000 gets automatically adjusted in the profit of ₹ 42,400 for the year 2024 because the sale price of ₹ 44,000 must have increased the bank balance as on 31-12-2024. Increased bank balance increased capital, so profit for 2024 was increased. Thus, profit on sale of shares does not require any adjustment.

ILLUSTRATION 20. Sunrise Traders is a retail trading company having its head office in Calcutta and a branch at Bombay. The selling price is determined at a fixed percentage on cost price. The records maintained at the head office and the branch were incomplete. The summarised trial balance of the books of Sunrise Traders on 31-12-2024 was as follows :

	₹	₹
Stock as at 31-12-2023 (H.O.)	35,000	
Furniture (H.O.) at cost	13,000	
Depreciation to 31-12-2023		4,300
Furniture (Branch) at cost	4,200	
Profit & Loss A/c on 31-12-2023		5,000
Capital		20,000
General Reserve		6,000
Balance at Bank	29,000	
Drawings	2,000	
Cash received from branch		60,000
Imprest at branch	200	
Debtors and Creditors	20,000	30,500
Administrative expenses (H.O.)	35,400	
Administrative expenses (Branch)	4,500	
Purchases (H.O.)	3,50,000	
Sales (H.O.)		3,67,500
	4,93,300	4,93,300

(1) All the goods were received by the branch from head office for resale with the exception of goods purchased by the branch at ₹ 4,800 paid from branch takings before banking.

(2) Goods amounting to ₹ 70,000 at selling price were sent by H.O. to branch during the year but these transactions were not entered in head office books.

(3) Furniture is to be depreciated at 10% of the cost.

(4) A commission of 10% on the net profit of the branch is payable to the Branch Manager. The net profit of the branch is to be determined after charging such commission, depreciation on branch furniture, and ₹ 600 payable to head office as supervision charges.

(5) The closing stock at H.O. at cost was ₹ 35,000 and at branch at selling price was ₹ 10,200.

(6) Sundry expenses for ₹ 300 were incurred by branch which were paid before sending the remittance to head office.

(7) On 31-12-2024 the cash in hand was ₹ 400 and debtors were ₹ 500 at the branch. You are required to prepare :

(*a*) Trading and Profit & Loss A/c for the year ended 2024.

(*b*) Balance Sheet as at 31-12-2024.

SOLUTION

TRADING AND PROFIT AND LOSS ACCOUNTS OF SUNRISE TRADERS

for the year ending 31st December, 2024

	H.O.	*Branch*		*H.O.*	*Branch*
	₹	₹		₹	₹
To Opening Stock	35,000		By Sales	3,67,500	(1) 65,800
" Purchases	3,50,000	4,800	" Goods Sent to Branch (2)	56,000	
" Goods from H.O.		(2) 56,000	" Closing Stock	35,000	8,160
" Gross Profit c/d	73,500	13,160			
	4,58,500	73,960		4,58,500	73,960
To Administrative Expenses	35,400	(3) 4,800	By Gross Profit b/d	73,500	13,160
" Depreciation	1,300	420	" Supervision Charges	600	
" Supervision Charges		600			
" Branch Manager's Commission $\left(\frac{10}{110} \times ₹\ 7{,}340\right)$		667			
" Net Profit	37,400	6,673			
	74,100	13,160		74,100	13,160

BALANCE SHEET OF SUNRISE TRADERS

as on 13-12-2024

Liabilities		₹	*Assets*		₹
	₹			₹	
Capital	20,000		Furniture at H.O.	13,000	
Less : Drawings	2,000		*Less* : Depreciation to date		
		18,000	(₹ 4,300 + ₹ 1,300)	5,600	
General Reserve		6,000			7,400
Profit & Loss Account :			Furniture at Branch	4,200	
Opening Balance	5,000		*Less* : Depreciation	420	
Profit for the year :					3,780
H.O.	37,400		Stock: H.O.	35,000	
Branch	6,673		Branch	8,160	
		49,073			43,160
Sundry Creditors		30,500	Debtors: H.O.	20,000	
Manager's Commission Payable		667	Branch	500	
					20,500
			Cash at Bank : H.O.	29,000	
			Branch	400	
					29,400
		1,04,240			1,04,240

Working Notes :

(1) ***Calculation of Sales at Branch***

Sales are made at a fixed percentage of profit on cost. So to calculate sales at branch, first rate of gross profit should be ascertained.

	₹	₹
Sales at H.O.		3,67,500
Add : Goods invoiced to branch at selling price		70,000
		4,37,500
Less : Cost of Sales		
Opening stock at H.O.	35,000	
Add : Purchases by H.O.	3,50,000	
	3,85,000	
Less : Closing Stock at H.O.	35,000	3,50,000
Gross Profit		87,500

Gross Profit included in Sales

$$\text{Rate of Gross Profit} = \frac{\text{Gross Profit}}{\text{Sales}} \times 100$$

$$= \frac{₹\ 87,500}{₹\ 4,37,500} \times 100 = 20\%$$

Sales at Branch **:**

	₹	₹
Goods invoiced by H.O. at selling price :		70,000
Add : Retail price of goods purchased by branch :		
Cost	4,800	
Add : Profit @ 20% on sales or $\frac{20}{80}$ of cost $\left(i.e.\ \frac{20}{80} \times ₹\ 4,800\right)$	1,200	6,000
		76,000
Less : Closing Stock at branch at selling price		10,200
Sales at Branch		65,800

(2) ***Calculation of Cost of Goods sent to Branch*** **:**

	₹
Selling price of goods sent to Branch	70,000
Less : 20% profit included therein	14,000
Cost of goods sent to Branch	56,000

(3) ***Calculation of Administration Expenses of Branch***

	₹
As given in the trial balance	4,500
Add : Sundry expenses incurred by the branch	300
	4,800

ILLUSTRATION 21. On 31st December, 2024, John's books and records were destroyed by fire. Following information was available :

(*a*) Balance Sheet of John as on 31st December, 2023 was as follows :

Capital and Liabilities		₹	*Property and Assets*	₹
Capital		4,20,000	Fixtures	1,00,000
Creditors :	₹		Stock	1,50,000
Goods	94,000		Debtors	1,20,000
Electricity Charges	2,000		Rates in advance	4,500
Accounting Charges	5,000		Cash in hand	15,000
		1,01,000	Cash at Bank	1,31,500
		5,21,000		5,21,000

(*b*) The insurance company agreed to pay ₹ 95,000 per fixtures and ₹ 1,05,000 for stock without production of accounts; the stock, however, was ₹ 1,15,000.

(*c*) From bank statements and cheque books which were in his house, the following information on payments was available :

	₹		₹
Personal Expenses	80,000	Rates	13,500
Sundry Expenses	6,500	Rent	51,700
Accountancy Charges	8,000	Goods for Resale	21,58,000
Electricity	7,500	Fixtures	20,000

(*d*) Total bankings for the year amounted to ₹ 24,50,200.

(*e*) All cash takings were banked with the exception of the following payments during the year:

(*i*) An assistant's salary of ₹ 18,000 per annum.

(*ii*) Goods for resale averaging ₹ 10,500 per month.

(*iii*) Drawings varied between ₹ 20,000 and ₹ 30,000 per month.

(*f*) ₹ 2,500 per month for 9 months was received in cash for subletting a portion of the shop and this was not banked.

(*g*) During the year sale proceeds for waste paper amounting to ₹ 30,500 were paid into the Bank.

(*h*) On 31-12-2024 (*a*) Debtors were ₹ 2,05,000. (*b*) Creditors for goods were ₹ 90,000, for electricity ₹ 800, for accounting charges ₹ 750 and for rent ₹ 4,700. (*c*) Rates in advance ₹ 6,500. (*d*) Cash in hand ₹ 17,000. (*e*) During the year a bad debt of ₹ 6,000 was incurred. (*f*) The rate of gross profit as a percentage of sale was 20%.

You are required to compile a Trading and Profit and Loss Account for the year ended 31st December, 2024 and Balance Sheet as on that date.

SOLUTION **TRADING AND PROFIT AND LOSS ACCOUNT OF JOHN**

for the year ending 31st December, 2024

		₹		₹	₹
To Opening Stock		1,50,000	By Sales	(2)	28,93,750
To Purchases	(1)	22,80,000	By Insurance Claim		1,05,000
To Gross Profit c/d		5,78,750	By Profit & Loss A/c (Fire claim not admitted) :		
			Value of stock destroyed	1,15,000	
			Less : Claim admitted	1,05,000	
					10,000
₹		30,08,750			30,08,750

To Rent	51,700		By Gross Profit b/d	5,78,750
Add : Outstanding (31-12-2024)	4,700		By Sale Proceeds for Waste Paper	30,500
		56,400	By Rent Received	22,500
To Rates	13,500			
Add : Paid in Advance on 1-1-2024	4,500			
	18,000			
Less : Paid in Advance on 31-12-2024	6,500			
		11,500		
To Salary of the Assistant		18,000		
To Sundry Expenses		6,500		
To Electricity	7,500			
Add : Outstanding (31-12-2024)	800			
	8,300			
Less : Outstanding (1-1-2024)	2,000			
		6,300		
To Accountancy Charges	8,000			
Add : Outstanding (31-12-2024)	750			
	8,750			
Less : Outstanding (31-12-2023)	5,000			
		3,750		
To Trading A/c (Loss of Stock)		10,000		
To Value of Fixtures Destroyed by Fire (₹ 1,00,000 + ₹ 20,000)	1,20,000			
Less : Claim Admitted	95,000			
		25,000		
To Bad Debts		6,000		
To Net Profit transferred to Capital Account		4,88,300		
		6,31,750		6,31,750

BALANCE SHEET OF JOHN

as on 31-12-2024

Liabilities		₹	*Assets*		₹
Creditors for Goods		90,000	Cash in hand		17,000
Expenses Outstanding :	₹		Cash at Bank	(4)	2,36,500
Electricity	800		Sundry Debtors		2,05,000
Accountancy Charges	750		Insurance Claim Due (₹ 95,000 + ₹ 1,05,000)		2,00,000
Rent	4,700				
		6,250	Rates Prepaid		6,500
Capital as on 1-1-2024	4,20,000				
Add : Net Profit	4,88,300				
	9,08,300				

Less : Drawings (4)	3,39,550	5,68,750		
		6,65,000		6,65,000

Working Notes :

(1) ***Calculation of Purchases***

CREDITORS ACCOUNT

	₹		₹
To Cash (₹ 10,500 × 12)	1,26,000	By Balance b/d	94,000
To Bank	21,58,000	By Purchases (Balancing figure)	22,80,000
To Balance c/d	90,000		
	23,74,000		23,74,000

(2) ***Calculation of Sales***

	₹
Opening Stock (1-1-2024)	1,50,000
Add : Purchases	22,80,000
	24,30,000
Less : Closing Stock on 31-12-2024 *i.e.* stock destroyed by fire	1,15,000
Cost of goods sold	23,15,000
Add : Gross profit @ 20% on sale or 25% of cost	5,78,750
Sales	28,93,750

(3) ***Calculation of Amount Received from Debtors***

DEBTORS ACCOUNT

		₹		₹
To Balance b/d		1,20,000	By Bad Debts	6,000
To Sales	(2)	28,93,750	By Cash (Balancing figure)	28,02,750
			By Balance c/d	2,05,000
		30,13,750		30,13,750

(4) ***Calculation of Cash Drawings and Bank Balance as on 31-12-2024***

CASH BOOK

		Cash	*Bank*		*Cash*	*Bank*
		₹	₹		₹	₹
To Balance b/d		15,000	1,31,500	By Sundry Expenses		6,500
To Proceeds for Waste				By Accountancy Charges		8,000
Paper			30,500	By Electricity		7,500
To Cash (₹ 24,50,200				By Rates		13,500
– ₹ 30,500)			24,19,700	By Rent		51,700
To Rent (₹ 2,500 × 9)		22,500		By Creditors (Goods for		
To Debtors	(3)	28,02,750		Resale)	1,26,000	21,58,000
				By Fixtures		20,000
				By Assistant's Salary	18,000	
				By Bank	24,19,700	

			By Drawings	2,59,550 (Bal. fig.)	80,000
			By Balance c/d	17,000	2,36,500 (Bal. fig.)
	28,40,250	25,81,700		28,40,250	25,81,700

ILLUSTRATION 22. Mr. Slipshod started business as a provision merchant on 1st January, 2023. He opened a Bank Account for the business with ₹ 25,000 and immediately spent ₹ 12,500 on Fixtures and Fittings. The only records kept were of cash sales which amounted in 2023 to ₹ 37,500 and in 2024 to ₹ 45,000. There were no credit sales. Following facts were ascertained :

(*a*) All expenses of the business had been met by cheques, and an analysis of the Bank Book showed the following payments in the two years :

Purchases (of which ₹ 37,000 related to 2023) ₹ 63,750 ; Rent and Rates ₹ 5,100 ; Salaries ₹ 11,000 ; Advertising ₹ 1,400 ; Other Expenses ₹ 2,880.

(*b*) Value of the stock on 31st December, 2024 was ₹ 15,000. No stock was taken on 31st December, 2023, but a uniform rate of gross profit was assumed.

(*c*) Liabilities outstanding at 31st December, 2024 were :

Purchases ₹ 7,500 ; Advertising ₹ 500 ; Other Expenses (Light, Heat, Telephone, etc.) ₹ 170.

(*d*) Amounts paid in advance at 31st December, 2024 were :

Rates ₹ 100 ; Other Expenses (insurance) ₹ 50.

(*e*) All business expenses arose equally in two periods.

(*f*) Goods were taken from stock for private consumption, the estimated cost being ₹ 500 in 2023 and ₹ 750 in 2024.

(*g*) Private drawings amounting to ₹ 6,620 were met out of cash receipts and the balance was banked.

(*h*) Private income of ₹ 2,250 had been paid into the Bank. The fixtures and fittings are to be written off over 10 years in equal instalments. On the basis of foregoing information, you are required to prepare :

(1) Trading and Profit and Loss Accounts for each of the years 2023 and 2024.

(2) Balance Sheet at 31st December, 2024.

SOLUTION

To find out the stock on 31st December, 2023, a figure necessary for the preparation of the Trading and Profit and Loss Account for the year 2023, we prepare a combined Trading Account for the two years 2023 and 2024 to ascertain the rate of gross profit in two years because rate of gross profit will help us in ascertaining the balancing figure of closing stock in the Trading Account for the year 2023.

COMBINED TRADING ACCOUNT FOR 2023 & 2024

	₹	₹		₹	₹
To Purchases	63,750		By Sales : 2023	37,500	
Add : Outstanding	7,500		2024	45,000	
	71,250				82,500
Less : Goods taken for private consumption (₹ 500 + ₹ 750)	1;250		" Closing Stock		15,000
		70,000			
To Gross Profit		27,500			
		97,500			97,500

$$\text{Rate of Gross Profit} = \frac{\text{Gross Profit}}{\text{Sales}} \times 100 = \frac{₹\ 27,500}{₹\ 82,500} \times 100 = 33\frac{1}{3}\%$$

Another figure which is missing is the balance at bank, so we prepare Bank Account to find out the balance at bank.

BANK ACCOUNT FOR 2023 & 2024

		₹		₹
To Capital Account	₹	25,000	By Fixtures & Fittings	12,500
" Cash Sales	82,500		" Purchases	63,750
Less : Drawings	6,620		" Rent and Rates	5,100
		75,880	" Salaries	11,000
To Capital Account			" Advertising	1,400
(private income banked)		2,250	" Other Expenses	2,880
			" Balance c/d (Bal. fig.)	6,500
		1,03,130		1,03,130
To Balance b/d		6,500		

TRADING AND PROFIT AND LOSS ACCOUNT OF MR. SLIPSHOD

		2023	2024		2023	2024
		₹	₹		₹	₹
To Opening Stock		—	11,500	By Sales	37,500	45,000
" Purchases ₹	₹			" Closing Stock		
37,000	34,250			(Balancing figure for 2023)	11,500	15,000
Less : Goods taken for personal use 500	750					
		36,500	33,500			
To Gross Profit						
($33\frac{1}{3}\%$ of sales)		12,500	15,000			
		49,000	60,000		49,000	60,000
To Salaries		5,500	5,500	By Gross Profit b/d	12,500	15,000
" Rent and Rates	5,100					
Less : Prepaid	100					
		2,500	2,500			
" Advertising	1,400					
Add : Outstanding	500					
		950	950			
To Other Expenses	2,880					
Add : Outstanding	170					
	3,050					
Less : Prepaid	50					
		1,500	1,500			

	2023	2024		2023	2024
To Depreciation on Fixtures and Fittings (10% on ₹ 12,500)	1,250	1,250			
" Net Profit transferred to Capital A/c	800	3,300			
	12,500	15,000		12,500	15,000

BALANCE SHEET OF SLIPSHOD

as on 31st December, 2024

Liabilities			₹	*Assets*		₹
Sundry Creditors for Purchases			7,500	Cash at Bank		6,500
Advertising Expenses Outstanding			500	Stock		15,000
Other Expenses Outstanding			170	Prepaid Rates		100
Capital Account :		₹		Prepaid Insurance		50
Introduced on 1-1-2023		25,000			₹	
Private Income paid in	₹	2,250		Fixtures & Fittings :	12,500	
Profits : 2023—₹	800			*Less* : Depreciation @ 10%		
2024—₹	3,300			p.a. for 2 years	2,500	
		4,100				10,000
		31,350				
Less : Drawings	₹					
Cash	6,620					
Goods	1,250					
		7,870				
			23,480			
			31,650			31,650

ILLUSTRATION 23. On April 1, 2024, Shri Lall bought all the shares of Royal Stores Private Ltd. of which he became the Managing Director. The company carried on its operations in a rented shop from which it sold cosmetics and confectionery. The company did not keep double-entry accounts, but you are provided with the following information :

(*i*) Balance Sheet of the Company as on 31st March, 2024 :

	₹		₹
Paid up share capital : 5,000		Fixed Assets :	
shares of ₹ 10 each	50,000	Fixtures and Fittings at cost	30,000
Profit and Loss Account	10,500	Current Assets :	
Creditors :		Stock at Cost :	
Cosmetics	2,500	Cosmetics	5,000
Confectionery	2,000	Confectionery	3,000
Outstanding Rent	500	Unpaid Accounts :	
		Confectionery	500
		Prepaid :	
		Rates and Insurance	2,500
		Balance with Bank	23,500
		Cash on hand	1,000
	65,500		65,500

(*ii*) Analysis of the Bank statements for the year ended March 31, 2025 :

	₹
Paid in :	
Assumed to be takings	2,45,000

Withdrawn :

Purchase of Cosmetics ₹ 1,00,000 ; Purchase of Confectionery ₹ 1,10,000 ; Repairs ₹ 4,000 ; Rent ₹ 6,000 ; Rates and Insurance ₹ 10,000 ; Electricity ₹ 4,000 ; Sri Lall ₹ 15,000.

(*iii*) Following were paid out of takings

Salaries ₹ 15,000 ; Confectionery Purchased ₹ 1,500 ; Trade Expenses ₹ 1,250 ; Cosmetics Purchased ₹ 5,000.

(*iv*) Shri Lall had taken from the shop cosmetics for his own consumption and paid into the till the cost price of ₹ 4,550.

(*v*) Following are the gross profit percentages with reference to sales :

Cosmetics	9%
Confectionery	30%

(*vi*) On 31st March, 2025, there were :

	Stocks at cost	*Debtors Prepayments and Float*	*Liabilities*
	₹	₹	₹
Cosmetics	4,850		2,000
Confectionery	3,500	1,000	3,000
Rent			500
Rates and Insurance		2,750	
Cash in till		250	
Accountancy/Audit			2,000

(*vii*) Shri Lall has instructed you to regard any shortage in cash as being due to amounts withdrawn by him and requested that his aggregate withdrawals be treated as being in part-payment of his agreed director' remuneration of ₹ 25,000 for the year.

You are required to prepare :

(*a*) Trading and Profit and Loss Account for the year ended March 31, 2025 showing separately the gross profit from (*i*) Cosmetics and (*ii*) Confectionery (Ignore depreciation and taxation),

(*b*) Balance Sheet as on March 31, 2025,

(*c*) Total Debtors and Total Creditors Accounts, and

(*d*) An account in columnar form for cash and bank transactions.

SOLUTION

(*a*)

Royal Stores Private Limited
TRADING AND PROFIT AND LOSS ACCOUNT
for the year ending 31st March, 2025

	Cos-metics	*Confec-tionery*	*Total*		*Cos-metics*	*Confec-tionery*	*Total*
	₹	₹	₹		₹	₹	₹
To Opening Stock	5,000	3,000	8,000	By Sales (2)	1,10,000	1,60,000	2,70,000
" Purchases	1,04,500	1,12,500	2,17,000	" Goods for personal use	4,550		4,550
" Gross Profit c/d	9,900	48,000	57,900	" Closing Stock	4,850	3,500	8,350
	1,19,400	1,63,500	2,82,900		1,19,400	1,63,500	2,82,900
To Salaries		₹	15,000	By Gross Profit b/d			
" Rates and Insurance		10,000		Cosmetics			9,900

	Add : Prepaid last year	2,500		Confectionery	48,000
		12,500		By Net Loss Carried to Balance Sheet	9,100
	Less : Prepaid this year	2,750			
			9,750		
To	Rent	6,000			
	Less : Outstanding last year	500			
		5,500			
	Add : Outstanding this year	500			
			6,000		
To	Repairs		4,000		
"	Electricity		4,000		
"	Trade Expenses		1,250		
"	Accountancy/Audit		2,000		
"	Director's Remuneration		25,000		
			67,000		67,000

(*b*) **BALANCE SHEET OF ROYAL STORES PRIVATE LIMITED**

as at 31st March, 2025

		₹
I. Equity and Liabilities		
(1) *Shareholders' Funds*		
(*a*) Share Capital :		
5,000 Shares of ₹ 10 each fully paid		50,000
(*b*) Reserves and Surplus :		
Surplus Account (*i.e.* Profit & Loss A/c)	₹	
As at 1-4-2024	10,500	
Less : Net Loss for 2024-25	9,100	
		1,400
(2) *Current Liabilities*		
Trade Creditors (₹ 2,000 + ₹ 3,000)		5,000
Accountancy/Audit Outstanding		2,000
Rent Outstanding		500
Director's Remuneration Outstanding		2,950
Total		61,850
II. Assets		
(1) *Non-current Assets*		
Fixed Assets : Fixtures & Fittings at Cost		30,000
(2) *Current Assets*		
Stock (₹ 4,850 Cosmetics + ₹ 3,500 Confectionery)		8,350
Sundry Debtors (Confectionery)		1,000
Cash in hand		250
Cash at Bank		19,500
Prepaid Expenses		2,750
Total		61,850

(*c*) **TOTAL DEBTORS ACCOUNT**

	Cosmetics	*Confectionery*		*Cosmetics*	*Confectionery*
	₹	₹		₹	₹
To Balance b/d	—	500	By Cash (Balancing fig.)	1,10,000	1,59,500
" Sales (2)	1,10,000	1,60,000	" Balance c/d		1,000
	1,10,000	1,60,500		1,10,000	1,60,500

TOTAL CREDITORS ACCOUNT

	Cosmetics	*Confectionery*		*Cosmetics*	*Confectionery*
	₹	₹		₹	₹
To Bank Account	1,00,000	1,10,000	By Balance b/d	2,500	2,000
To Cash Account	5,000	1,500	By Purchases (Balancing figure)	1,04,500	1,12,500
" Balance c/d	2,000	3,000			
	1,07,000	1,14,500		1,07,000	1,14,500

(*d*) **CASH BOOK**

		Cash	*Bank*			*Cash*	*Bank*
		₹	₹		₹	₹	₹
To Balance b/d		1,000	23,500	By Creditors :			
" Cash			2,45,000	Cosmetics	1,00,000		
" Shri Lall (Sales at cost)		4,550		Confectionery	1,10,000		2,10,000
" Debtors :	₹			" Bank		2,45,000	
Cosmetics	1,10,000			" Repairs			4,000
Confectionery	1,59,500	2,69,500		" Rent			6,000
				" Rates & Insurance			10,000
				" Electricity			4,000
				" Sri Lall			15,000
				" Salaries		15,000	
				" Purchases : Confectionery		1,500	
				Cosmetics		5,000	
				" Trade Expenses		1,250	
				" Sri Lall (Balancing fig.)		7,050	
				" Balance c/d		250	19,500
		2,75,050	2,68,500			2,75,050	2,68,500

Working Notes :

(1) **SRI LALL'S CURRENT ACCOUNT**

	₹		₹
To Bank (Drawings)	15,000	By Director's Remuneration	25,000
" Cash (Drawings)	7,050		
" Balance c/d	2,950		
	25,000		25,000

(2) *Calculation of Amount of Sales*	*Cosmetics*	*Confectionery*
	₹	₹
Opening Stock	5,000	3,000
Purchases as per Creditors Account	1,04,500	1,12,500
	1,09,500	1,15,500
Less : Closing Stock	4,850	3,500
	1,04,650	1,12,000
Less : Goods taken by Sri Lall at cost	4,550	—
Cost of Goods sold	1,00,100	1,12,000
Gross Profit, 9/91 and 30/70	9,900	48,000
Sales	1,10,000	1,60,000

QUESTIONS

OBJECTIVE TYPE

1. Find out the missing figure :

(*a*)

	Opening stock	*Closing stock*	*Sales*	*Carriage inward*	*Purchases*	*Gross profit ratio*
		₹	₹	₹	₹	₹
(*i*)	50,000	70,000	5,60,000	10,000	?	25% on Turnover
(*ii*)	60,000	75,000	?	15,000	5,00,000	20% on Turnover

(*b*)

Net Profit	₹ 50,000
Fixed Expenses (including depreciation)	₹ 80,000
Gross profit ratio	25% on Turnover
Cost of sale	?

Ans. [(*a*) (*i*) ₹ 4,30,000. (*ii*) ₹ 6,25,000; (*b*) ₹ 3,90,000].

2. **State whether the following statements are true or false :**

(*a*) Trial Balance can be prepared in case the books are maintained according to single entry system.

(*b*) Real and nominal accounts are maintained if books are kept according to single entry system.

(*c*) Capital at the beginning of the accounting year is ascertained by preparing Cash Account.

(*d*) The figure of credit sale is ascertained by preparing Total Debtors' Account.

(*e*) For ascertaining net profit according to net worth method of single entry, Profit and Loss Account is prepared.

(*f*) If rate of gross profit is 25% on cost, it will be 20% on sales.

(*g*) Under net worth method of single entry, profit is ascertained by calculating the increase in net worth after adjusting for drawings and additions to capital.

(*h*) Cash sales are ascertained by preparing Total Debtors' A/c.

Ans. [Correct : (*d*) ; (*f*) ; (*g*) ; False : (*a*) ; (*b*) ; (*c*) ; (*e*) ; (*h*)].

3. Choose the most appropriate answer :

(*a*) The capital at the beginning of the accounting year in case of single entry system is determined by preparing :

(*i*) Opening Statement of Affairs ; (*ii*) Cash Account ; (*iii*) Bank Account.

(*b*) Single entry can be adopted by :

(*i*) Small firms ; (*ii*) Joint stock companies ; (*iii*) Registered co-operative societies.

(*c*) In case of net worth method of single entry, profit is ascertained by :

(*i*) Comparing the capital at the beginning of the accounting period and the capital at the end of the accounting period ; (*ii*) Preparing a Profit and Loss Account ; (*iii*) Preparing a Balance Sheet.

(*d*) The amount of credit sale is ascertained by :

(*i*) Preparing Total Debtors' Account ; (*ii*) Preparing Trading Account ; (*iii*) Preparing Statement of Affairs.

(*e*) Opening Capital ₹ 30,000, Closing Capital ₹ 15,000, Loss during the year ₹ 8,000. Drawings ₹ 7,000, Additional Capital introduced will be :

(*i*) Nil (*ii*) 8,000

(*iii*) 16,000 (*iv*) 23,000

Ans. [(*a*) (*i*) ; (*b*) (*i*) ; (*c*) (*i*) ; (*d*) (*i*) ; (*e*) (*i*)].

SHORT ANSWER TYPE

1. What is single entry book keeping ?
2. State the two merits and two demerits of Single Entry.
3. Give two differences between Statement of Affairs and Balance Sheet.
4. **From the information given below, calculate the required items :**

(*a*) Capital at the beginning of the year :

Capital at the end of the year ₹ 70,000 ; drawings during the year ₹ 10,000 ; capital introduced during the year ₹ 5,000 ; profit during the year ₹ 20,000.

(*b*) Sales :

Cost of goods sold ₹ 5,40,000 ; rate of profit 25% on sales.

(*c*) Purchases :

Creditors at the beginning of the year ₹ 40,000 ; Closing creditors ₹ 45,000; Cash paid to creditors ₹ 1,50,000 ; discount allowed by creditors ₹ 5,000 ; returns outwards ₹ 8,000 ; acceptances given to creditors during the year Rs. 50,000.

(*d*) Purchases :

Cost of goods sold ₹ 8,00,000 ; opening stock ₹ 1,00,000 ; closing stock ₹ 1,20,000.

(*e*) Cost of goods sold :

Sales ₹ 8,40,000 ; rate of gross profit on cost 20%.

(*f*) Stock at the end of the year :

Sales Rs, 6,00,000 ; opening stock ₹ 50,000 ; purchases ₹ 5,00,000 ; wages (productive) ₹ 10,000; carriage inward ₹ 7,000 ; rate of gross profit on cost 20%.

(*g*) Bills received from customers :

Opening balance of B/R Rs. 15,000 ; B/R endorsed in favour of creditors ₹ 2,000 ; B/R collected (*i.e.* honoured) ₹ 8,000 ; B\R dishonoured ₹ 1,000 ; closing balance of B/R ₹ 20,000.

(*h*) From the following information calculate the total purchases :

	₹		₹
Bills payable 1.1.2024	12,000	Cash paid to creditors	60,400
Creditors 1.1.2024	10,000	Returns outwards	2,400
Bills payable 31.12.2024	16,000	Cash purchases	41,600
Creditors 31.12.2024	12,000	Discount allowed by creditors	200
Bills payable paid during the year	17,800		

Ans. [(*a*) ₹ 55,000 ; (*b*) ₹ 7,20,000 ; (*c*) ₹ 2,18,000 ; (*d*) ₹ 8,20,000 ; (*e*) ₹ 7,00,000 ; (*f*) ₹ 67,000 ; (*g*) ₹ 16,000 (*h*) ₹ 1,28,400].

5. Find out the value of opening stock with the help of the following particulars :

	₹		₹
Purchases made during the year	1,40,000	Wages and freight	3,500
Sales made during the year	2,10,000	Rate of gross profit on cost	50%
Closing stock	14,000		

Ans. [₹ 10,500].

6. Find out the profit of Mr. A from the following information :

Capital at the beginning of the year	₹ 20,00,000
Drawings made by Mr. A	₹ 2,00,000
Capital at the end of the year	₹ 25,00,000
Additional capital introduced during the year	₹ 1,00,000

Ans. [Profit ₹ 6,00,000] ***(CA—PCE Nov. 2009 Modified)***

7. On 1st April, 2024, Chhotu started business with an initial Capital of ₹ 70,000. On 1st October, 2024, he introduced additional capital of ₹ 40,000. On 7th of every month, he withdraws ₹ 5,000 for household expenses. On 31st March, 2025 his Assets and Liabilities were ₹ 2,00,000 and ₹ 70,000 respectively.

Ascertain the profit by Chhotu during the year ended 31st March, 2025.

(CA—*IPCE Nov. 2009 Modified*)

Ans. [Profit ₹ 80,000]

8. If the percentage of discount on marked price is $33\frac{1}{3}$ and the discount is ₹ 1,200. Find the selling price and marked price.

Ans. [Marked Price ₹ 3,600 ; Selling Price ₹ 2,400].

9. Calculate the missing figure :

	₹		₹
Capital in the beginning ?			
Capital at the end	36,000	Drawings	5,600
Capital introduced	9,400	Loss	2,800

Ans. [₹ 35,000].

10. Calculate the missing figure :

	₹		₹
Capital introduced	70,800	Loss	5,600
Further capital introduced	18,800	Closing capital	?
Drawings	11,200		

Ans. [₹ 72,800].

11. Find out the value of opening stock with the following particulars :

	₹		₹
Opening Stock	?	Cash sales	1,70,000
Purchases made during the year	2,80,000	Wages and freight	7,000
Sales during the year :		Closing stock	28,000
Credit sales	2,50,000	Rate of Gross Profit on Sales	20%

Ans. [77,000].

12. From the following information furnished by X & Co., prepare Total Debtors Account.

Sales (includes Cash Sales of ₹ 7,000)	68,000	Return Inward	700
Collections from Debtors (Cash)	57,000	Bad Debts Written off	
Discount allowed	2,000	—Now Recovered	500
Bad Debts Written off	1,500	Provision for Doubtful Debts	1,200
Cheques Received	10,000	Balance Outstanding on 1-3-2025	
Cheques Dishonoured	2,000	(Receivable)	20,000

Ans. [Balance Outstanding at the end of March, 2025 ₹ 11,800]

13. Attempt the following :

A company sold 20% of the goods on cash basis and the balance on credit basis. Debtors are allowed $1\frac{1}{2}$ month's credit and their balance as on 31-3-2025 is ₹ 1,25,000. Assume that the sale is uniform throughout the year. Calculate the credit sales and total sales of the company for the year ended 31-3-2025. ***(C.A. Inter, Nov. 2015 Modified)***

Ans. [Credit Sales ₹ 10,00,000; Total Sales ₹ 12,50,000]

14. Answer the question :

Prepare Total Creditors Account for the year ended 31-3-2025 from the date given below :

	₹
Creditors Balance on 1-4-2024	38,000
Credit Purchases during the year	2,67,000
Bills Payable Accepted	62,000
Cash paid to Creditors	1,37,000
B/R Endorsed to Creditors	16,000
Endorsed B/R Dishonoured	3,000
B/P Dishonoured	2,000
Purchase Returns	11,000
Discount Received	6,000
Transfer from Debtors Ledger	7,000

(C.A. Inter, Dec. 2014 Modified)

Ans. [Creditors Balance as on 31-3-2025 ₹ 71,000]

LONG ANSWER TYPE

1. What do you understand by Single Entry ? What are its disadvantages ? How does it differ from the Double Entry System ?
2. How will you calculate profit under the Single Entry Method of maintaining accounts ?
3. State briefly how you would convert a set of books, which had been kept on the Single Entry into the Double Entry with a prospective effect and retrospective effect.
4. Distinguish between Statement of Affairs and Balance Sheet.
5. "Single entry system of book-keeping is an unscientific, incomplete and defective system." Explain this statement.

PRACTICAL PROBLEMS

1. R had ₹ 3,00,000 in Bank on 1st January, 2024 when he started his business. He closed his accounts on 31st of March, 2025. His single-entry books (in which he did not maintain any accounts for the bank) showed his position as follows :

	On 31-3-2024 ₹	*On 31-3-2025* ₹
Cash-in-hand	2,000	3,000
Stock-in-Trade	19,000	29,000
Debtors	1,000	2,000
Creditors	5,000	3,000

On 1st February, 2024 he began drawing ₹ 800 per month for his personal expenses from the cash box of the business.

His accounts in the Bank had the following entries :

	Deposits ₹	Withdrawals ₹
1-1-2024	3,00,000	—
1-1-2024 to 31-3-2024	—	2,23,000
1-4-2024 to 31-3-2025	2,30,000	2,70,000

The above withdrawals included payments by cheques of ₹ 2,00,000 and ₹ 60,000 respectively during the periods from 1st January to 31st March, 2024 and from 1st April, 2024 to 31st March, 2025 for the purchase of machinery for the business ; and the deposits after 1st January, 2024 consisted wholly of sale price received from customers by cheques.

Draw up R's statement of affairs as at 31st March, 2024 and 31st March, 2025 respectively and work out his profit or loss for the year ended 31st March, 2025. Also work out his profit or loss for the three months from 1-1-2024 to 31-3-2024.

Ans. [Capital as at 31-3-2024 ₹ 2,94,000 ; Capital as at 31-3-2025 ₹ 3,28,000 ; Profit ₹ 43,600 for the year ended 31-3-2025. Loss ₹ 4,400 for the three months ended 31-3-2024].

2. From the following information, prepare a statement showing the profit of the firm for the year ending 31st March, 2025 as well as the Balance Sheet as on that date :

X and Y carrying on business in partnership and sharing profits and losses in proportion of 2 : 1, has the following balances to the credit of their accounts shown in the firm as at 1st April, 2024 :

X ₹ 34,500 ; Y ₹ 18,000.

On 31st March, 2025, the position of the business was as follows :

Cash in hand ₹ 6,750 ; Cash at Bank ₹ 5,000 ; Sundry Debtors ₹ 25,000 ; Stock ₹ 33,000 ; Furniture ₹ 4,200 ; Sundry Creditors for goods ₹ 19,500 and Sundry Creditors for expenses ₹ 3,900.

During the year, X had drawn ₹ 9,900 from the firm. He had also taken some goods worth ₹ 1,200 for his personal use. He had sold some goods of the business for ₹ 2,700 and retained the proceeds himself. He had personally paid to some of the employees of the firm ₹ 4,950 towards their salaries, which he was entitled to be reimbursed. Y had withdrawn ₹ 3,750 in cash and also taken some goods worth ₹ 750 for his personal use. He had personally paid towards some expenses of the firm ₹ 2,400, which he was entitled to be reimbursed.

Ans. [Profit ₹ 9,000 : Balance Sheet Total ₹ 73,950].

3. Ajay, Sanjay and Naval are in partnership and keep their books by Single Entry. The State of Affairs of the firm as on 30th September, 2023 was as under :

		₹		₹
Bills Payable		700	Cash in Hand	1,250
Expenses Outstanding		650	Cash at Bank	3,450
Creditors		7,700	Bills Receivable	3,000
Capital Accounts :	₹		Debtors	10,200
Ajay	5,000		Stock	8,400
Sanjay	5,000		Sanjay's Current Account	930
Naval	5,000			
		15,000		
Ajay's Current Account		2,150		
Naval's Current Account		1,030		
		27,230		27,230

The position of the firm on 30th September, 2024 was :

Cash in hand ₹ 1,400; Cash at Bank ₹ 3,570; Debtors ₹ 12,300; Stock ₹ 9,360; Bills Payable ₹ 500. Creditors ₹ 6,200 and 4% G.P. Notes of the face value of ₹ 2,000 purchased at 97%.

Each partner had drawn ₹ 250 per month in the middle of every month during the year. 8% interest on capital and drawings drawn during the year is to be charged. On 1st April, 2024 each partner had introduced ₹ 1,500 as further capital in the firm.

Ascertain the profit or loss made by the firm during the year ending September 30, 2024 and show the Balance Sheet as on that date.

Ans. [Combined Current Accounts at the end ₹ 2,370 ; Net Profit ₹ 8,100 ; B/S Total ₹ 29,460].

CONVERSION METHOD

4. Rulia Ram does not maintain regular books but keeps only a memoranda of his transactions. He furnishes the following information for the year ending 30th September, 2024 :

(*i*) Total collections from debtors in cash—₹ 16,500.

(*ii*) Payments received against Bills Receivable in cash—₹ 1,750

(*iii*) Cash sales (as gathered from cash sales invoices)—₹ 8,200.

(*iv*) The abstract of the Bank Account for the year ending 30th September, 2024 is as follows :

	₹		₹
To Cash Deposited Out of Collections	23,870	By Overdraft as on 1-10-2023	2,500
		By Personal Drawings	1,500
		By Salaries to Staff	4,800
		By Interest and Bank Charges	50
		By General Expenses	4,560
		By Payment to Creditors	8,400
		By Payment against Bills Payable	900
		By Balance on 30-9-2024	1,160
	23,870		23,870

(*v*) Other Balances on 1st October, 2023 are as follows :

Stock ₹ 5,300 ; Debtors ₹ 14,000 ; Provision for Doubtful Debts ₹ 700 ; Furniture ₹ 1,000; Bills Receivable ₹ 1,200 ; Buildings ₹ 8,000 ; Cash in hand ₹ 100 ; General Expenses Outstanding ₹ 200 ; Creditors ₹ 4,100 ; Bills Payable ₹ 700.

(*vi*) He purchased one cycle for ₹ 320 on 1st January, 2024.

(*vii*) Besides the cash balance with the cashier, the following are the other balances as on 30th September, 2024 :

Stock ₹ 5,900 ; Bills Receivable ₹ 1,140 ; Debtors ₹ 17,000 ; Creditors ₹ 4,500 ; Bills Payable ₹ 650 ; General Expenses Outstanding ₹ 500.

Prepare Trading and Profit and Loss Account for the year ending 30th September, 2024 and the Balance Sheet as on that date after providing for depreciation at 10% p.a. on all fixed assets, 5% provision for doubtful debts and 2% provision for discount.

Ans. [G.P. ₹ 20,340 ; N.P. ₹ 9,233 ; B/S Total ₹ 34,783].

Hints. Acceptances received during the year ₹ 1,690 ; Credit Sales ₹ 21,190 ; Acceptances given during the year ₹ 850 ; Credit Purchases ₹ 9,650 ; Cash Balance at the end ₹ 2,360.

5. X is a small trader. He maintains no books but only an account with a bank in which all takings are lodged after meeting business expenses and his personal drawings and in which payments for business purchases are passed through.

You are required to ascertain his trading results for the year ended March 31, 2025, and the financial position of the business as on that date from the following information supplied by X :

(*i*) The bank statement shows deposits of ₹ 12,030 and withdrawals of ₹ 11,850.

(ii) ₹ 1,000 had been placed in fixed deposit account on December 31, 2023 at 8 per cent per annum and withdrawn with interest on June 30, 2024.

(iii) The assets and liabilities on March 31st, 2025 were : Stock ₹ 2,100 ; Book Debts ₹ 1,150 ; Bank Balance ₹ 320 ; Furniture ₹ 2,000 ; and Trade Creditors ₹ 400.

(iv) In the absence of reliable information, estimates are supplied on the following matters :

(a) The stock and book debts have each increased by ₹ 100 during the year.

(b) The trade creditors were ₹ 200 on April 1, 2024.

(c) During the year the personal expenses amounted to ₹ 1,000 and business expenses ₹ 1,700.

Ans. [G.P. ₹ 1,840 ; N.P. ₹ 160 ; B/S Total ₹ 5,570].

Hints : Capital Beginning ₹ 6,010 ; Bank (Beginning Balance) ₹ 140 ; Sales ₹ 13,790; Purchases ₹ 12,050.

6. Following information is supplied from which you are required to prepare Profit and Loss Account for the year ended 31st December, 2024 and Balance Sheet at that date :

Assets and Liabilities	*1-1-2024*	*31-12-2024*
	₹	₹
Sundry Assets	18,000	20,000
Stock	14,000	19,000
Cash in Hand	8,200	4,800
Cash at Bank	2,200	8,000
Debtors	?	26,000
Creditors	12,000	9,800
Miscellaneous Expenses outstanding	1,000	600

Details relative to the year's transactions are :

	₹		₹
Receipts in the year and discount credited to Debtors' Accounts	2,45,000	Cash purchases	10,000
		Salary and wages paid out of Bank	18,000
Returns from Debtors	6,000	Miscellaneous expenses paid by cash	5,000
Bad Debts	1,000	Drawings by cash	9,400
Sales—Cash and Credit	3,00,000	Purchase of Sundry Assets by cheque	2,000
Returns to Creditors	3,000	Cash withdrawn from Bank	21,000
Payments to Creditors by cheques	2,36,200	Cash sales deposited in Bank	?
Receipts from Debtors deposited into Bank	2,43,000	Discount allowed by creditors	4,000

Ans. [Cash Sales ₹ 40,000 ; Debtors on 1-1-2024 ₹ 18,000 ; Credit Purchases ₹ 2,41,000 ; Capital on 1-1-2024 ₹ 47,400 ; Gross Profit ₹ 51,000 ; Net Profit ₹ 29,400 ; B/S Total ₹ 77,800].

7. Mr. PQ has a small trading business for which the following procedures are followed :

(1) All collections are deposited with the bank each day.

(2) All payments except petty expenses are made by cheques.

(3) To meet petty expenses a cheque of ₹ 500 is withdrawn from the bank on the 1st day of each month.

(4) Mr. PQ makes personal drawings from the bank.

Following figures are available from Mr. PQ's records.

	1-1-2024	*31-12-2024*
	₹	₹
Cash in Hand	320	200
Balance in Bank	2,500	5,000 (Overdraft)
Debtors	20,000	30,000

Creditors	20,000	30,000
Stock of goods	10,000	30,000
Payments made to creditors during the year		20,000
Sales made during the year		30,000

Mr. PQ spent during the year ₹ 200 from the office cash for his personal expenses.

Prepare Profit and Loss Account for the year ended on 31st December, 2024 and Balance Sheet as on that date from the above information.

Ans. [G.P. ₹ 20,000 ; N.P. ₹ 14,080 ; B/S Total ₹ 60,200].

Hints : Amount received from customers ₹ 20,000 ; Credit Purchases ₹ 30,000 ; Cash paid for sundry expenses ₹ 5,920 ; Drawings ₹ 1,700 ; Capital Beginning ₹ 12,820.

8. Mr. Reddy does not maintain complete records of his business but gives you the following information:

	31st March, 2025	*31st March, 2024*
	₹	₹
Machineries	2,00,000	1,50,000
Sundry Creditors	86,000	?
Sundry Debtors	?	93,000
Stock in Trade	70,000	50,000
Cash in Hand	2,600	1,500
Furniture	27,000	30,000
Cash at Bank	15,600	18,700

His cash transactions for the year ended 31st March, 2025 included the following (besides certain other items) :

	₹		₹
Payments to Creditors	4,10,000	Cash Purchases	1,30,000
Cash Sales (25% of total Sales)	1,70,000	Collection from Debtors	5,27,000
Business Expenses	82,000	Withdrawn for Household Expenses	30,000

He maintains a uniform rate of gross profit of 25% on turnover. Outstanding business expenses on 31st March, 2025 amounted to ₹ 5,000. Addition of new machinery was made on October 1, 2024. Some old furniture (book value ₹ 6,000) was sold during the year and the proceeds stands credited to Furniture Account.

Provide depreciation on Machineries @ 15% p.a. and on Furniture @ 10% p.a. (excluding sold item).

Mr. Reddy requests you to prepare a Trading and Profit and Loss Account for the year ended 31st March, 2025 and a Balance Sheet as on that date.

Ans. [Gross Profit ₹ 1,70,000 ; Net Profit ₹ 51,350 ; B/S Total ₹ 3,59,550].

Hints : Debtors at the end ₹ 76,000 ; Opening balance of creditors ₹ 96,000 ; Depreciation (10% of ₹ 24,000) ₹ 2,400.

9. Following information relates to the business of Shri Bhagwan Singh who has asked you to prepare a Trading and Profit and Loss Account for the year ended 31st March, 2025 and a Balance Sheet as on that date :

	Balances as on 31-3-2024	*Balances as on 31-3-2025*
	₹	₹
A. Building	80,000	90,000
Furniture	15,000	20,000
Motor Car	20,000	20,000
Stock	?	10,000

Debtors	40,000	?
Creditors	30,000	?
Cash and Bank Balances	45,000	26,000
Bills Receivable	8,000	7,000
Bills Payable	7,000	4,000

B. Cash transactions during the year included the following besides certain other items—

	₹		₹
Sale of old papers	5,000	Cash Purchases	12,000
Miscellaneous Trade Expenses		Payment to Creditors	46,000
(including salaries etc)	20,000	Cash Sales	20,000
Collection from Debtors	50,000		

C. Other information :

(*a*) Bills Receivable drawn during the year amount to ₹ 5,000 and bills payable accepted ₹ 4,000.

(*b*) An item of old furniture whose written down value on 31-3-2024 was ₹ 5,000 was sold on 30-9-2024 for ₹ 2,000. Depreciation is to be provided on Building and Furniture @ 10% p.a. and on Motor Car @ 20% p.a.

(*c*) Of the debtors a sum of ₹ 2,000 should be written off as bad debt and a provision for doubtful debts is to be provided @ 2%.

(*d*) Shri Bhagwan Singh has been maintaining a steady gross profit rate of 30% on turnover.

(*e*) Outstanding salary on 31-3-2024 was ₹ 2,000 and on 31-3-2025 was ₹ 2,500.

(*f*) Profit and Loss Account had a credit balance of ₹ 10,000 on 31-3-2024.

(*g*) 20% of total sales and total purchases are to be treated as for cash.

Ans. [Gross Profit ₹ 30,000 ; Net Loss ₹ 6,760 ; B/S Total ₹ 2,19,740].

10. Archana Enterprises maintain their books of accounts under single entry system. The Balance Sheet as on 31st March, 2024 was as follows :

Liabilities	*Amount* (₹)	*Assets*	*Amount* (₹)
Capital A/c	6,75,000	Furniture & Fixtures	1,50,000
Trade Creditors	7,57,500	Stock	9,15,000
Outstanding Expenses	67,500	Trade Debtors	3,12,000
		Prepaid Insurance	3,000
		Cash in Hand and at Bank	1,20,000
	15,00,000		15,00,000

The following was the summary of cash and bank book for the year ended 31st March, 2025 :

Receipts	*Amount* (₹)	*Payments*	*Amount* (₹)
Cash in hand and at Bank on		Payment to Trade Creditors	1,24,83,000
1st April, 2024	1,20,000	Sundry Expenses paid	9,31,050
Cash Sales	1,10,70,000	Drawings	3,60,000
Receipts from Trade Debtors	27,75,000	Cash in Hand and at Bank	
		on 31st March, 2025	1,90,950
	1,39,65,000		1,39,65,000

Additional Information :

(*i*) Discount allowed to trade debtors and received from trade creditors amounted to ₹ 54,000 and ₹ 42,500 respectively (for the year ended 31st March, 2025).

(*ii*) Annual fire insurance premium of ₹ 9,000 was paid every year on 1st August for the renewal of the policy.

(*iii*) Furniture and fixtures were subject to depreciation @ 15% p.a. on diminishing balance method.

(*iv*) The following are the balances as on 31st March, 2025 :

Stock	₹ 9,75,000
Trade debtors	₹ 3,43,000
Outstanding expenses	₹ 55,200

(*v*) Gross profit ratio of 10% on sales is maintained throughout the year.

You are required to prepare Trading and Profit & Loss Account for the year ended 31st March, 2025, and Balance Sheet as on that date. ***(CAIPCC Nov., 2019 Modified)***

Ans. [Gross Profit ₹ 13,93,000 ; Net Profit ₹ 4,40,250 ; B/S Total ₹ 16,39,450; Credit Sales ₹ 28,60,000; Sundry Expenses charged to Profit & Loss A/c ₹ 9,18,750].

11. Alok does not maintain proper books of accounts. From the following information, prepare Trading and Profit and Loss Account for the year ending 30th September, 2024 and a Balance Sheet as on that date :

	As on 30-9-2023	*As on 30-9-2024*
	₹	₹
Stock	5,200	5,800
Debtors	10,300	11,400
Cash	1,500	1,270
Furniture	1,200	1,500
Creditors	4,100	3,750
Bills Receivable	600	800
Bills Payable	1,500	1,000
Bank Overdraft	3,000	—

Analysis of other transactions is as follows :

	₹		₹
Cash paid to Creditors	21,500	Discount received	800
Cash received from Debtors	27,800	Bad Debts	200
Salaries	7,200	Returns Inwards	500
Office Expenses	1,200	Returns Outwards	300
Rent	2,400	Payments made against Bills Payable	1,800
Cash Sales	13,500	Cash received against Bills Receivable	1,300
Cash Purchases	4,200	Bills Receivable dishonoured during the year	400
Discount allowed	600	Drawings	1,100

Provide 5% interest on capital

Ans. [G.P. ₹ 17,850 ; N.P. ₹ 6,410 ; B/S Total ₹ 20,770].

Hints : Credit sales ₹ 31,700 ; Bills accepted by customers ₹ 1,900 ; Credit purchases ₹ 23,550 ; Acceptances given ₹ 1,300 ; Loss of cash ₹ 130 ; Capital beginning ₹ 10,200.

12. Ram carried on business as retail merchant. He has not maintained regular account books. However, he always maintained ₹ 10,000 in cash and deposited the balance into the Bank Account. He informs you that he has sold goods at a profit of 25% on sales.

Following information is given to you :

Assets and Liabilities	*As on 1-4-2024*	*As on 31-3-2025*
Cash in Hand	10,000	10,000
Sundry Creditors	40,000	90,000
Cash at Bank	50,000 (Cr.)	80,000 (Dr.)
Sundry Debtors	1,00,000	3,50,000
Stock in Trade	2,80,000	?

Analysis of his bank pass book reveals the following information :

(*a*) Payment to creditors ₹ 7,00,000 ; (*b*) Payment for business expenses ₹ 1,20,000 ; (*c*) Receipts from debtors ₹ 7,50,000 ; (*d*) Loan from Laxman ₹ 1,00,000 taken on 1-10-2024 at 10% per annum ; (*e*) Cash deposited in the bank ₹ 1,00,000.

He informs you that he paid creditors for goods ₹ 20,000 in cash and salaries ₹ 40,000 in cash. He has drawn ₹ 80,000 in cash for personal expenses. During the year Ram had not introduced any additional capital. Surplus cash if any, to be taken as cash sales.

Prepare :

(*i*) Trading and Profit and Loss Account for the year ended 31-3-2025.

(*ii*) Balance Sheet as at 31st March, 2025.

Ans. [Gross Profit ₹ 3,10,000 ; Net Profit ₹ 1,45,000 ; B/S Total ₹ 5,60,000].

13. K Azad, who is in business as a wholesaler in sunflower oil, is a client of your accounting firm. You are required to draw up his final accounts for the year ended 31-3-2025 :

From the files, you pick up his Balance Sheet as at 31-3-2024 reading as below :

BALANCE SHEET
as at 31-3-2024

Liabilities	₹	*Assets*		₹
K. Azad's Capital	1,50,000	Cash and Bank Balances	₹	75,000
Creditors for Oil Purchases	2,00,000	Debtors		1,60,000
12% Security Deposit from Customers	50,000	Stock of Oil (125 tins)		1,25,000
Creditors for Expenses :		Furniture	30,000	
Rent	6,000	*Less* : Depreciation	3,000	
Salaries	4,000			27,000
Commission	20,000	Rent Advance		12,000
		Electricity Deposit		1,000
		Three-Wheeler Tempo Van	40,000	
		Less : Depreciation	10,000	
				30,000
	4,30,000			4,30,000

A summary of the rough Cash Book of K. Azad for the year ended 31-3-2025 is as below :

CASH AND BANK SUMMARY

Receipts	₹		₹
Cash Sales	5,26,500	*Payments*	
Collections from Debtors	26,73,500	Landlord	79,000
		Salaries	48,000
		Miscellaneous Office Expenses	12,000

Commission	20,000
Personal Income-tax	50,000
Transfer on 1-10-2024 to 12% p.a. on Fixed Deposit	6,00,000
Creditors for Oil Suppliers	24,00,000

A scrutiny of the other records gives you the following information :

(i) During the year oil was purchased at 250 tins per month basis at a unit cost of ₹ 1,000. 5 tins were damaged in transit in respect of which insurance claim has been preferred. The surveyors have since approved the claim at 80%. The damaged ones were sold for ₹ 1,500 which is included in the cash sales. One tin has been used up for personal consumption. Total number of tins sold during the year was 3,000 at a unit price of ₹ 1,750.

(ii) Rent until 30-9-2024 was ₹ 6,000 per month and was increased thereafter by ₹ 1,000 per month. Additional advance rent of ₹ 2,000 was paid and this is included in the figure of payments to landlord.

(iii) Provide depreciation at 10% and 25% of WDV on furniture and tempo van respectively.

(iv) It is further noticed that a customer has paid ₹ 10,000 on 31-3-2025 as security deposit by cash. One of the staff has defalcated (Apply conservatism principle). The claim against the Insurance Company is pending.

You are requested to prepare final accounts for the year ended 31-3-2025.

Ans. [Gross Profit ₹ 22,50,000; Net Profit ₹ 21,26,300; Balance Sheet Total ₹ 30,98,300.]

Hints : Closing Stock (119 tons) ₹ 1,19,000; Loss of damaged stock transferred to P/L A/c ₹ 500; Debtors at the end ₹ 22,11,500; Creditors at the end ₹ 8,00,000; Cash and Bank Balance at the end ₹ 66,000.

14. A and B who had conducted separate business of merchants as sole traders agreed on 28th February, 2025 to enter into partnership as from 1st April, 2025. B had not kept proper records and in order to establish the interests of the partners on 1st April, 2025 it was arranged that B should carry on business for the month of March, 2025 and upon the results of that month, their respective interests in the partnership would be determined.

Following is a summary of B's transactions for the month of March, 2025 :

	₹		₹
Cash at Bank on 28th February, 2025 as per Bank statement	5,200	Sundry creditors—28th February, 2025	18,900
Unpresented cheques at that date	6,150	Cash at Bank on 31st March, 2025 as per Bank statement	11,840
Furniture as per valuation	22,000	Unpresented cheques—31st March, 2025	2,080
Sundry debtors—28th February, 2025	19,000		

Credit sales during the month, the cost of which was ₹ 4,520, amounted to ₹ 7,100. Included in these sales was a sale at ₹ 3,200, the cost of which was ₹ 1,800 and these goods were not delivered until 3rd April, 2025.

	₹		₹
Credit purchases including goods received on 2nd April, 2025 and costing ₹ 2,500	11,420	Cash disbursements were :	
Stock in hand, taken on 31st March, 2025 and priced at cost, amounted to	30,000	Commission	1,800
A credit note was issued on 9th March, 2025 for an overcharge in an invoice dated 26th February, 2025	800	Salaries and Expenses	1,600
Cash receipts were :		Rent	400
Debtors	13,000	Creditors (after deducting ₹ 100 discount)	9,900
Cash sales (cost of goods sold ₹ 9,600)	13,450	Drawings	2,000
		Bank charges and interest	40

You are required to prepare B's statement of Assets and Liabilities and Capital as at 31st March, 2025 and Revenue Statement for the month then ended. Depreciation may be disregarded. Assume that sales and purchases are effected only on delivery of goods. ***(ICWA—Final)***

Ans. [Net Profit ₹ 1,290; Balance Sheet Total ₹ 70,860]

Hints : Stock in hand as on 28-2-2025 ₹ 33,400; Bank balance as on 28-2-2025 ₹ 950; Bank balance as on 31-3-2025 ₹ 9,760; Sundry debtors as on 28-2-2025 ₹ 18,200; Capital as on 28-2-2025 ₹ 53,750; Debtors as on 31-3-2025 ₹ 9,100; Creditors as on 31-3-2025 ₹ 17,820.

15. Sri Gangadhar was appointed on Saturday, 29th December, at 2 p.m. to join as a Cashier on Monday, 31st December. Balance Sheet as on Saturday, 29th December was as under :

Liabilities	₹	*Assets*	₹
Capital	60,000	Fixed Assets	38,000
Creditors	16,000	Stock	16,000
Outstanding Liabilities	1,000	Debtors	12,000
		Bank	8,000
		Cash	3,000
	77,000		77,000

He worked for 13 weeks (*i.e.,* up to Saturday, 30th March), on a salary of ₹ 60 per week. Every week end, the proprietor withdrew ₹ 200 for himself and paid the weekly salaries of the Cashier. After meeting all the weekly disbursements, the entire Cash Balance was deposited in the Bank in the first hour of each Monday. Other expenses per week paid in cash were ₹ 40 on an average.

No cash purchase was made and creditors were paid only by cheque. But sales were usually for cash and all sales were at fixed prices fetching 25% profit on selling price. Credit sales were all noted in a diary. All unpaid bills to be paid to creditors were kept in a separate file.

On 30th March, debtors as per diary amounted to ₹ 16,000 and creditors ₹ 14,000. All the outstanding liabilities for expenses were cleared in the meantime. Credit sales during the period amounted to ₹ 12,000. Stock on 31st March was taken and valued at cost of ₹ 10,000.

Transactions with Bank over the thirteen weeks are given below :

	₹		₹
Balance 29-12-XX	8,000	Creditors	22,000
Deposits—Debtors' cheque	2,000	Expenses and rent (including	
Cash	18,000	opening outstanding)	2,600
		Balance on 30-3-......	3,400
	28,000		28,000

The Cashier did not report on 1st April, Monday for work and the balance in the till was missing. Debtors and creditors were then circularised and debtors actually amounted to ₹ 14,000. Creditors amounted to ₹ 14,000. But it was discovered that goods returned ₹ 800 to creditors against cash payment by them was not at all recorded in the books.

There was a fidelity guarantee insurance policy for ₹ 10,000. Ascertain the amount of defalcation for claim to be made on the Insurance Company.

All working notes are to form part of your answer.

Ans. [Purchases ₹ 20,000; Cash collected from debtors ₹ 6,000; Cash Sales ₹ 21,600; Cash deposited into the bank ₹ 18,000; Total defalcation ₹ 11,500 (*i.e.* ₹ 800 from sundry creditors, ₹ 2,000 from sundry debtors and ₹ 8,700 cash from till. Defalcation Loss transferred to P/L A/c ₹ 1,500]

16. Green trades as Fair Travel Agency, effecting sales of tickets for Tour Operators Ltd., Air Lines and Railways. The commissions earned thereon are at the rates of 10%, $7\frac{1}{2}$% and 7% respectively. The accounts are made up to October 31 in each year.

The balances as on October 31, 2024 were as follows :

	₹	₹
Capital		51,000
Deposits from customers for Tour Operators Ltd.		20,000
P.A.Y.E.		2,500
Accountancy		1,500
Advertising		1,000
Rates		1,000
Fixtures and fittings	10,000	
Motor car	9,000	
Debtors for rail tickets	5,000	
Debtors for air tickets	1,000	
Rent in advance	1,250	
Bank balance	50,750	
	77,000	77,000

You obtained the following information :

(1) From bank statements, returned cheques and the paying-in-slips for the year ended October 31, 2025 :
Banking (cheques and cash) ₹ 8,20,000 ; Payments for tickets—Tour Operators Ltd. ₹ 6,20,000 ; Air Lines ₹ 65,000 ; Railways ₹ 70,000 ; Rent (4 quarters) ₹ 5,000 ; Electricity ₹ 900 ; Accountancy ₹ 1,500 ; Rates ₹ 3,000 ; P.A.Y.E. ₹ 9,100 ; Advertising ₹ 6,250 ; Balance at bank on October 31, 2025 ₹ 90,000 ;

(2) Weekly expenditure (52 weeks) defrayed from cash takings before banking :
Petty expenses ₹ 10 ; Staff wages ₹ 400 (net) ; Drawings ₹ 200.

(3) From audit statements the following liabilities on October 31, 2025 were disclosed :
Rates ₹ 1,100 ; Advertising ₹ 500 ; Railway ₹ 13,700 ; Tour Operators Ltd. ₹ 5,500 ; Airlines ₹ 1,600 ; Accountancy ₹ 1,500.

(4) Customers' deposits on October 31, 2025 all for Tour Operators Ltd., were ₹ 10,000 and debtors for tour rail tickets were ₹ 1,000.

(5) Depreciation of car and fixtures is calculated at 25% p.a. and 10% p.a. on the reducing balances respectively, and

(6) Green agrees that any cash difference should be transferred to his Drawings Account.

You are required to prepare :

(*a*) Profit and Loss account for the year ended on October 31, 2025 showing separately the commission from each class of tickets sold ; and

(*b*) Balance Sheet as on October 31, 2025.

Ignore taxation.

Ans. [N.P. ₹ 33,780 ; B/S Total ₹ 1,08,000].

Hints : Debtors for Tours ₹ 6,95,000 ; Cash amount received from tours ₹ 6,85,000 ; Drs. for sale of tickets ₹ 72,000 ; Amount received from air customers ₹ 73,000 ; Commission on rail travel ₹ 6,300; Amount received from railway customers ₹ 94,000 ; Amount of Drawings ₹ 280.

17. Doll and Dolly are in partnership sharing profits and losses equally. They keep their books by Single Entry System. No ready figures are available for total sales but they maintain a steady gross profit rate of 25% on sales.

An abstract of their cash transactions for the year ended 30th June, 2025 is given below :

Receipts	₹	*Payments*	₹
Cash in hand	10,800	Salaries	22,000
Receipts from Customers	2,70,000	Rent	4,400
Cash Sales	32,000	Advertising	1,800
		Printing	1,600
		General Expenses	19,100
		Payment to Trade Creditors	2,24,000
		Doll's Drawings	4,000
		Cash in hand	35,900
	3,12,800		3,12,800

Following balances are available from their books as on 30th June, 2024 and 30th June, 2025.

	as on 30-6-2024	*as on 30-6-2025*
	₹	₹
Stock-in-trade	44,000	50,000
Sundry Debtors	?	70,000
Sundry Creditors	46,800	37,000
Furniture	6,000	?

Other information :

(*a*) Discount allowed, ₹ 2,800.

(*b*) Discount earned, ₹ 2,400.

(*c*) Outstanding printing, ₹ 500.

(*d*) Capital of Doll as on 30th June, 2024 was ₹ 4,000 more than Capital of Dolly.

(*e*) Provide depreciation on Furniture @ 10% p.a.

From the above you are required to prepare :

(*i*) Trading and Profit and Loss Account for the year ended 30th June, 2025 and

(*ii*) Balance Sheet as on that date, in the books of Doll and Dolly.

Ans. [G.P. ₹ 70,200 ; N.P. ₹ 19,800 ; B/S Total ₹ 1,61,300].

Hints : Total Sales ₹ 2,80,800 ; Credit Purchases ₹ 2,16,600 ; Debtors on 30-6-2024 ₹ 94,000 ; Capital on 30-6-2024 Doll ₹ 56,000 and Dolly ₹ 52,000].

18. Suresh runs a Circulating Library and his accounts are in a mess. One Bank Account has been used for both the business as well as his personal transactions. After looking into his record and questioning him you gather the following informations :

	₹
(1) Payment for magazines for the year ended 31st March, 2025	19,400
(2) Payment of other expenses for the year ended 31st March, 2025	6,160
(3) Payment of delivery peon's wages for the year ended 31st March, 2025	4,400
(4) Subscriptions Collected	43,390

(5) He has taken ₹ 1,000 per month in cash from the subscriptions to pay his wife for their personal expenses depositing the balance of collection into the Bank.

(6) During the year he bought a second hand car (not for the business) from a friend for ₹ 8,000. However, as the friend owed him ₹ 500 for subscriptions, the matter was settled by a cheque for the difference.

(7) An assurance policy on his life matured during the year and realised ₹ 14,000.

(8) Suresh cashed cheque for ₹ 2,400 for a friend and this cheque was dishonoured. The friend is repaying by instalments and owes ₹ 1,000 on 31st March, 2025.

(9) Other personal payments by cheque total ₹ 4,700.

(10) Magazine subscription for the year amounting to ₹ 800 had to be written off by Suresh as irrecoverable.

(11) The cash collected included ₹ 1,200 in respect of magazine subscriptions written off irrecoverable in a previous year.

(12) Suresh runs the business from his flat for which a rent of ₹ 180 per month is included in the payments for other expenses ₹ 6,160. The living accommodation may be regarded as two-thirds of the whole.

Following balances may be accepted as correct :

	31st March, 2024	*31st March, 2025*
	₹	₹
Cash in Hand	230	140
Bank Balance	9,440	11,760
Subscriptions Receivable considered good	3,660	4,210
Creditors for Purchase of Magazines	1,800	1,680
Stock of Magazines at cost	4,900	1,660

You are required to prepare : (1) A Cash and Bank Summary Account for the year ; (2) Suresh (Proprietor's) Account for the year ; (3) An Income and Expenditure Account for the Circulating Library for the year ended 31st March, 2025 ; and (4) A Balance Sheet as at 31st March, 2025.

Ans. [Proprietor's A/c Balance on 31-3-2025 ₹ 16,090 ; Excess of Income over Expenditure ₹ 12,800 ; B/S Total ₹ 17,770 ; Capital as at 1-4-2024 ₹ 16,430].

19. Following is the Balance Sheet of Manish and Suresh as on 1st April, 2024 :

Liabilities	₹	*Assets*	₹
Capital :		Building	1,00,000
Manish	1,50,000	Machinery	65,000
Suresh	75,000	Stock	40,000
Creditors for Goods	30,000	Debtors	50,000
Creditors for Expenses	25,000	Bank	25,000
	2,80,000		2,80,000

They give you the following additional information :

(*i*) Creditors' velocity 1.5 months and Debtors' velocity 2 months.

(*ii*) Stock level is maintained uniformly in value throughout all over the year.

(*iii*) Depreciation on machinery is charged @ 10%. Depreciation on building @ 5% in the current year.

(*iv*) Cost price will go up by 15% as compared to last year and also sales in the current year will increase by 25% in volume.

(*v*) Rate of gross profit remains the same.

(*vi*) Business expenses are ₹ 50,000 for the year. All expense are paid off in cash.

(*vii*) Closing stock is be valued on LIFO Basis.

Prepare Trading and Profit and Loss Account; Trade Debtors A/c and Trade Creditors A/c for the year ending 31-3-2025. ***(Inter IPCE May, 2016 Modified)***

Ans. [Gross Profit ₹ 86,250; Net Profit ₹ 24,750]

Hints : Sales for the current year ₹ 4,31,250; Cost of Goods sold ₹ 3,45,000; Rate of Gross Profit 20% on Sales; Debtors ₹ 71,875; Creditors ₹ 43,125.

CHAPTER

22

Royalty Accounts

Introduction

There are some special rights over something which are possessed by some persons. For example, a landlord possesses an exclusive right over some property say mine or quarry in his land. A patentee who has invented something new has an exclusive right over his patent rights. An author has an exclusive copyright over the work or his writing in the form of a book. These rights either can be used by these persons themselves or can be given to some other person on lease basis for some consideration. If the second option is adopted, there comes into existence a royalty agreement. A *royalty agreement* is an agreement between two parties, *i.e.,* the person who gives out his special rights and the person who takes out the special right on lease for a consideration. The person who gives out some special right over something to another person for a consideration is called *lessor or landlord* or *patentee or an author.* The person who takes out some special right from its owner on lease for a consideration is called *lessee or tenet or patentor or publisher.*

Terms Used in Royalty Agreements

There are some special terms which generally are used in royalty agreements. The meaning of such terms must be clear to the reader. The special terms are :

(*i*) **Landlord.** The person who gives out his some special rights over something say mining rights or patent rights or copy rights, on lease to another person for a consideration is called the landlord, or lessor or patentee or an author.

(*ii*) **Lessee.** The person who takes out the special rights from its owner on lease for a consideration is called lessee or patentor or publisher.

(*iii*) **Royalty.** Royalty is a periodical payment based on output or sale for the use of a certain asset or right like mine, copyright or patent to its owner. Thus, royalty is paid by the lessee of a mine to the owner of the mine, by the manufacturer to the patentee or by the publisher to the author of the book. Royalty is also paid by concerns dealing in raising of earth, clay stone or by concerns engaged in collection of forest products as lac, honey, etc. to the landlord or the Government from whom lease has been taken to continue their activities.

Types of Royalties. There are three types of royalties (*i*) Mining royalty, (*ii*) Patent royalty, and (*iii*) Copyright royalty.

Mining Royalty is the periodical payment generally based on output, made by the lessee of a mine or quarry to the lessor or the landlord (*i.e.,* owner of the mine or quarry).

Patent Royalty is the periodical payment based on output, made by the lessee of a patent or patent right to be lessor or the patentee (*i.e.,* the holder of the patent right).

Copyright Royalty is also the periodical payment based on sales, made by the lessee of a copyright (*i.e.,* the publisher) to the lessor (*i.e.,* the author).

The bases on which royalty is calculated in various cases are given below :

(*a*) Author of a book—No. of books sold.

(*b*) Owner of a mine—Quantity of coal produced.

(*c*) Scientist holding a patent—Output.

(*d*) An owner of an oil well—Quantity of oil extracted.

The lessee making the payment of royalty treats it as ordinary business expenditure and debits Royalty Account. Thus, Royalty Account is a nominal account and is closed at the end of every accounting year by transferring it to Profit and Loss Account. Strictly speaking, royalty based on output is a part of cost of production and as such should be transferred to Trading or Manufacturing or Production Account ; royalty based on sales is a selling expenditure and as such should be transferred to Profit and Loss Account.

It may be remembered that a lump-sum payment for the outright purchase of a patent, mine or book is not treated as royalty but is a capital expenditure and recorded as a fixed asset.

(*iv*) Minimum (or Dead or Certain or Fixed) Rent. Royalty agreements are usually associated with a clause that the lessor or landlord must receive a minimum amount whatever be the production or sales in a particular period. Such minimum amount is known as minimum rent or dead rent or fixed rent. The fixation of such rent is in the interest of the landlord because it guarantees him the receipt of the minimum amount in case of low output or sales. Further, it gives incentive to the lessee to increase the production or sales. Since the guarantee is for the payment of a minimum amount, it has the effect of paying actual royalty based on output or sales or minimum rent, whichever is higher. In the absence of minimum rent, the lessee may acquire rights from different landlords to obviate competition and deliberately may under-utilise such rights. For example, M/s. Kalyani Publishers printed a book on Advanced Accountancy at a minimum rent of ₹ 2,00,000 per annum royalty being payable @ ₹ 75 per copy sold and the number of copies sold in the first year is 2,000 and in the second year is 4,000. In this case, M/s. Kalyani Publishers will have to pay ₹ 2,00,000 (*i.e.,* minimum rent) to the authors in the first year even though the royalty works out to be ₹ 1,50,000 for 2,000 copies @ ₹ 75 per copy sold. In the second year ₹ 3,00,000 as royalty for 4,000 copies @ ₹ 75 per copy sold will be paid to the authors even though the minimum rent is ₹ 2,00,000.

(*v*) Shortworkings (or Redeemable Dead Rent). The excess of minimum rent over actual royalty calculated on the basis of output or sales is termed as shortworking. In the example cited above, there is a shortworking of ₹ 50,000, *i.e.,* ₹ 2,00,000 minimum rent—₹ 1,50,000 actual royalty for 2,000 copies @ ₹ 75 per copy in the first year. There is no shortworking in the second year because actual royalty of ₹ 3,00,000 is more than the minimum rent of ₹ 2,00,000. Normally shortworkings are during gestation period or due to abnormal working conditions during the early periods of lease as the activity level is low in that period.

(*vi*) Ground (or Surface) Rent. It is the fixed yearly or half yearly rent payable by the lessee to the landlord in addition to the minimum rent.

(*vii*) Right of Recouping Shortworkings. Usually in the first few years of the royalty agreement, the work does not gather the required momentum because of the time taken in the preparation for starting the production or pushing up the sales, so shortworkings arising in the first few years may not be due to inefficiency of the lessee. Keeping this in view, royalty agreement may contain a clause that shortworkings (*i.e.,* excess amount paid in earlier years) are recoverable by the lessee in subsequent years when royalties are in excess of the minimum rent. The right of getting back the excess payment made by the lessee in earlier years is called the right of recoupment of shortworkings. The right of recoupment of shortworkings can be :

(*a*) Restricted (*i.e.,* fixed) to a certain period, or

(*b*) Unrestricted (*i.e.,* floating).

When the lessee gets the right of recoupment of shortworkings for a certain period (say four or five years) commencing from the date of the royalty agreement, the right is said to be restricted or fixed. Any shortworking arising beyond this period cannot be reimbursed. But when the lessor allows the lessee to recoup any shortworking within two or three subsequent or following years, then the right is said to be unrestricted or floating because this can be availed of in any year when shortworking arises.

Shortworkings should be carried forward and shown on the assets side in the Balance Sheet so long as they are recoverable and shortworkings which could not be recouped during the allowed period of recoupment should be closed by transferring to the Profit and Loss Account. **If there is no provision in the royalty agreement for recoupment of shortworkings, the same should be transferred to the Profit and Loss Account in the very year of the shortworkings.**

The problem of shortworkings or its recoupment does not arise if the royalty agreement does not contain a clause of minimum rent. In such a case, the payment of royalty is simply based on output or sales.

***(vii)* Recoupment of Shortworkings.** It means the recovery of shortworkings of the previous years out of surplus royalty of subsequent years. Following conditions can be there for recoupment of shortworkings :

(*a*) The shortworkings are recouped when there is surplus *i.e.*, excess of royalty over minimum rent.

(*b*) The recoupment of shortworkings is to be done within the agreed period as given in the agreement.

(*c*) If shortworkings could not be recouped within the agreed period, it will be transferred to Profit & Loss Account in the year in which the right of recoupment is lost. By this process, shortworkings account gets closed and will not appear as an asset in the balance sheet.

The journal entries to be passed in the books of lessee and lessor are given alongwith other journal entries in case the royalties are recouped and not recouped within stipulated time.

***(viii)* Surplus.** It indicates the excess of actual amount of royalty over minimum rent.

Surplus = Actual Royalty – Minimum Rent.

Shortworkings can be recouped only when the lessee has a right to recoup and there is a surplus.

Distinction Between Rent and Royalty

Following are the main distinctions between rent and royalty :

	Rent	*Royalty*
1. Nature of Assets	It is the consideration payable for the use of only tangible assets as building, machinery etc.	It is the consideration payable for the use of special right for both tangible and intangible assets. (*i.e.*, patents, copy-rights etc.)
2. Basis of Payment	It is mostly payable on the basis of time as weekly, monthly or yearly.	It is paid on the basis of production, yield or sale.
3. Fixed or Variable	The amount of rent is generally fixed with regard to time.	The amount of royalty is variable and is calculated in accordance with production or sales.
4. Minimum Rent	There is no concept of minimum rent.	It generally contains a clause in the agreement to pay minimum rent.
5. Parties	The parties are known as tenant and landlord.	The parties are known as lessee/ patentee/publisher and lessor/ patent holder/author etc.

Accounting Entries in the Books of the Lessee

(I) When there are no royalties in a year

(*a*) *If Minimum Rent is not opened*

Shortworkings A/c Dr.

To Landlord's A/c

(*b*) *If Minimum Rent is opened*

(*a*) Minimum Rent A/c
To Landlord A/c

(*b*) Shortworkings A/c Dr.
To Minimum Rent A/c

(*c*) Landlord Dr. (with the amount of minimum rent paid)
To Bank

(*d*) Profit and Loss or Production Account Dr. (with the actual amount of royalties transferred)
To Royalties Account

(II) When royalties are less than the minimum rent and shortworkings are recoverable in subsequent years :

If Minimum Rent or Dead Rent Account is not Opened

(*a*) Royalties Account Dr. (with the actual amount of royalties earned)
Shortworkings Account Dr. (with the difference between the minimum rent and the actual royalties earned)
To Landlord (with the minimum rent)

Entries for the payment to landlord and for transfer of royalties to Profit and Loss Account will be the same as in (*i*) discussed afterwards.

The debit balance of the Shortworking Account will be carried forward and shown as an asset in the Balance Sheet till it is recoupable.

If Minimum Rent or Dead Rent Account is Opened in the Books

(*a*) Minimum Rent Account Dr.
To Landlord
(Being minimum rent payable to the landlord)

(*b*) Royalties Account Dr.
Shortwokings Account Dr.
To Minimum Rent Account
(Being actual amount of royalties earned and excess amount payable to the landlord debited to Shortworkings Account to make up the amount of minimum rent).

(*c*) Landlord Dr.
To Bank
(Being the amount of minimum rent paid)

(*d*) Profit and Loss Account or Production Account Dr.
To Royalties Account
(Being actual amount of royalties transferred)

The only difference in two methods is that entry (*a*) in the first method requires two entries (*a*) and (*b*) in the second method, other entries being same.

(III) When royalties are equal to minimum rent in a year

As there will be no shortworkings, no minimum rent account is opened. So, the entry for the amount payable to the landlord will be

Royalties A/c
To Landlord A/c

Other entries will be the same as in case of (*ii*) above.

(IV) When royalties exceed the minimum rent and shortworkings are recouped :

(*a*) Royalties Account Dr.
To Landlord
(Being the amount of royalties earned by the landlord)

(*b*) Landlord Dr. (with actual royalties earned)
To Shortworkings (with the amount which can be recouped)
To Bank Account (with the amount paid)

(*c*) Profit and Loss or
Production Account Dr.
To Royalties Account
(Being actual royalties earned transferred to the Profit and Loss Account)

Entries (*a*) and (*b*) can also be shown as follows :

(*a*) Royalties Account Dr. (with actual royalties earned)
To Shortworkings Account (with the amount which can be recouped)
To Landlord (with the difference)

(*b*) Landlord Dr.
To Bank Account
(Being amount paid to the landlord)

The debit balance (if any) in the Shortworkings Account which is no longer recoupable should be written off to Profit and Loss Account as follows :

Profit and Loss Account Dr.
To Shortworkings Account
(Being transfer of irrecoverable shortworkings)

ILLUSTRATION 1. ***(When royalty is to be recouped within fixed period).*** Bengal Coal Limited leased a colliery on 1st January, 2021 at a minimum rent of ₹ 15,000 merging into a royalty of ₹ 1 per ton with a stipulation to recoup shortworkings over the *first three years of the lease*. The output for the first four years of the lease was 8,000 ; 13,000 ; 21,000 and 18,000 tons respectively. Draft the necessary journal entries in the books of the company giving effect to the above.

SOLUTION

ANALYTICAL TABLE

Year	*Output (Tons)*	*Royalties @ ₹ 1 per ton*	*Short-workings*	*Surplus*	*Recoup-ment*	*Shortworkings not recoupable*	*Paid to Landlord*
		₹	₹	₹	₹	₹	₹
2021	8,000	8,000	7,000(15,000 – 8,000)	—	—	—	15,000
2022	13,000	13,000	2,000(15,000 – 13,000)	—	—	—	15,000
2023	21,000	21,000	—	6,000(21,000 – 15,000)	6,000	3,000(9,000 – 6,000)	15,000
2024	18,000	18,000	—	3,000(18,000 – 15,000)			18,000

JOURNAL ENTRIES IN THE BOOKS OF BENGAL COAL LTD.

Date	Particulars		L.F.	₹	₹
2021 Dec. 31	Royalties Account	Dr.		8,000	
	Shortworkings Account	Dr.		7,000	
	To Landlord				15,000
	(Being royalties @ ₹ 1 per ton on 8,000 tons and shortworkings ₹ 7,000 due to make up the minimum amount of ₹ 15,000)				
" 31	Landlord	Dr.		15,000	
	To Bank Account				15,000
	(Being the payment of minimum rent)				
Dec. 31	Production Account	Dr.		8,000	
	To Royalties Account				8,000
	(Being transfer of actual royalties to Production Account)				
2022 Dec. 31	Royalties Account	Dr.		13,000	
	Shortworkings Account	Dr.		2,000	
	To Landlord				15,000
	(Being royalties @ ₹ 1 per ton on 13,000 tons subject to a minimum rent of ₹ 15,000)				
Dec. 31	Landlord	Dr.		15,000	
	To Bank Account				15,000
	(Being the payment of minimum rent)				
" 31	Production Account	Dr.		13,000	
	To Royalties Account				13,000
	(Being transfer of royalties)				
2023 Dec. 31	Royalties Account	Dr.		21,000	
	To Landlord				21,000
	(Being royalties @ ₹ 1 per ton on 21,000 tons)				
" 31	Landlord	Dr.		21,000	
	To Shortworkings Account			6,000	
	To Bank Account				27,000
	(Being minimum rent of ₹ 15,000 paid to the landlord and ₹ 6,000 shortworkings recouped)				
" 31	Production Account	Dr.		21,000	
	To Royalties Account				21,000
	(Being transfer of royalties for the year)				
" 31	Profit and Loss Account	Dr.		3,000	
	To Shortworkings Account				3,000
	(Being transfer of irrecoverable shortworkings)				
2024 Dec. 31	Royalties Account	Dr.		18,000	
	To Landlord				18,000
	(Being royalties due @ ₹ 1 per ton on 18,000 tons)				
Dec. 31	Landlord	Dr.		18,000	
	To Bank Account				18,000
	(Being payment of royalties)				
" 31	Production Account	Dr.		18,000	
	To Royalties Account				18,000
	(Being transfer of royalties to Profit and Loss A/c)				

ILLUSTRATION 2. (*When there is special condition for recoupment of shortworkings*). Mohan took a mine on lease for 20 years. Rate of royalty is ₹ 1 per ton. Minimum rent is ₹ 8,000 per year. Next year shortworkings of that year will not be recouped in which yield will be less than 4,000 tons and the year in which royalty will be more than minimum rent, only 50% of excess will be used for recoupment of shortworkings.

Prepare the Necessary Accounts in the books of lessee when the yield for first four years respectively is 3,500 tons, 7,000 tons, 7,500 tons and 9,000 tons.

SOLUTION

ANALYTICAL TABLE

Year	Output (tons)	Royalties @ ₹ 1 for ton	Minimum Rent	Shortworkings	Surplus	Shortworkings recouped	Shortworkings not recouped	Paid to Landlord
		₹	₹	₹	₹	₹	₹	₹
I	3,500	3,500	8,000	4,500	—	—	(1) 4,500	8,000
II	7,000	7,000	8,000	1,000	—	—	—	8,000
III	7,500	7,500	8,000	500	—	—	1,000	8,000
IV	9,000	9,000	8,000		1,000	500	—	8,500

(1) Shortworking of year I cannot be recouped next year because output of this year is less than 4,000 tons. Hence, this shortworking has become non-recoupable in year I.

In the Books of Lessee (Mohan)

ROYALTIES ACCOUNT

Year		₹	Year		₹
I	To Landlord A/c	3,500	I	By Profit & Loss A/c	3,500
II	To Landlord A/c	7,000	II	By Profit & Loss A/c	7,000
III	To Landlord A/c	7,500	III	By Profit & Loss A/c	7,500
IV	To Landlord A/c	9,000	IV	By Profit & Loss A/c	9,000

SHORTWORKINGS ACCOUNT

Year		₹	Year		₹
I	To Landlord A/c	4,500	I	ByProfit & Loss A/c	4,500
II	To Landlord A/c	1,000	II	By Balance c/d	1,000
III	To Balance b/d	1,000	III	By Profit & Loss A/c	1,000
	To Landlord A/c	500		By Balance c/d	500
		1,500			1,500
IV	To Balance b/d	500	IV	By Landlord A/c	500

LANDLORD ACCOUNT

Year		₹	Year		₹
I	To Bank A/c	8,000	I	By Royalties A/c	3,500
				By Shortworkings A/c	4,500
		8,000			8,000
II	To Bank A/c	8,000	II	By Royalties A/c	7,000
				By Shortworkings A/c	1,000
		8,000			8,000

		₹			₹
III	To Bank A/c	8,000	III	By Royalties A/c	7,500
				By Shortworkings A/c	500
		8,000			8,000
IV	To Shortworkings A/c	500	IV	By Royalties A/c	9,000
	To Bank A/c	8,500			
		9,000			9,000

PROFIT & LOSS ACCOUNT

Year		₹	*Year*		₹
I	To Royalties A/c	3,500			
	To Shortworkings A/c	4,500			
II	To Royalties A/c	7,000			
III	To Royalties A/c	7,500			
	To Shortworkings A/c	1,000			
IV	To Royalties A/c	9,000			

ILLUSTRATION 3. (***When amount of shortworkings or surplus or royalty is given***)**.** The Bharat Mining Company holds a lease of a coal mine for a period of 20 years, commencing from 1st April, 2019. The lease provided for the payment on 15th April, 2020 and (annually thereafter) a royalty of ₹ 2 per ton on coal produced in the previous year subject to a minimum rent of ₹ 8,000 per year. Shortworkings can be recouped out of royalty in excess of the minimum rent for the next two years only. In the year of strike the minimum rent was to be regarded as having been reduced proportionately having regard to the length of stoppage. The first year in respect of which minimum rent was payable expired on 31st March, 2020. The excess paid for the first year was ₹ 3,750, of the second year ₹ 3,000. In the third year the surplus was ₹ 3,200 and of the fourth year ₹ 4,000. In the fifth year actual royalties amounted to ₹ 14,000 and in the sixth year ₹ 7,500 only. During the sixth year there was a stoppage due to strike lasting three months.

Write up the Necessary Accounts in the books of Bharat Mining Company.

SOLUTION

ANALYTICAL TABLE

Year	*Royalty*	*Minimum Rent*	*Short-workings*	*Surplus*	*Recoup-able*	*Unrecoup-able*	*Paid to landlord*
	₹	₹	₹	₹	₹	₹	₹
2020	4,250	8,000	3,750	—	—	—	8,000
2021	5,000	8,000	3,000	—	—	—	8,000
2022	11,200	8,000	—	3,200	3,200	550	8,000
2023	12,000	8,000	—	4,000	3,000	—	9,000
2024	14,000	8,000	—	6,000	—	—	14,000
2025	7,500	6,000	—	1,500	—	—	7,500

ROYALTIES ACCOUNT

		₹			₹
2020 Mar. 31	To Landlord	4,250	2020 Mar. 31	By Production A/c	4,250
2021 Mar. 31	" Landlord	5,000	2021 Mar. 31	" Production A/c	5,000
2022 Mar. 31	" Landlord	11,200	2022 Mar. 31	" Production A/c	11,200

2023 Mar. 31	"	Landlord	12,000	2023 Mar. 31	"	Production A/c	12,000
2024 Mar. 31	"	Landlord	14,000	2024 Mar. 31	"	Production A/c	14,000
2025 Mar. 31	"	Landlord	7,500	2025 Mar. 31	"	Production A/c	7,500

SHORTWORKINGS ACCOUNT

			₹				₹
2020 Mar. 31	To	Landlord	3,750	2020 Mar. 31	By	Balance c/d	3,750
2020 Apr. 1	"	Balance b/d	3,750				
2021 Mar. 31	"	Landlord	3,000	2021 Mar. 31	"	Balance c/d	6,750
			6,750				6,750
2021 April 1	"	Balance b/d	6,750	2022 Mar. 31	"	Landlord	3,200
				Mar. 31	"	Profit and Loss A/c	550
				Mar. 31	"	Balance c/d	3,000
			6,750				6,750
2022 Apr. 1	"	Balance b/d	3,000	2023 Mar. 31	"	Landlord	3,000

LANDLORD

			₹				₹
2020 Mar. 31	To	Balance c/d	8,000	2020 Mar. 31	By	Royalty Account	4,250
				" 31	"	Shortworkings A/c	3,750
			8,000				8,000
Apr. 15	"	Bank Account	8,000	Apr. 1	"	Balance b/d	8,000
2021 Mar. 31	"	Balance c/d	8,000	2021 Mar. 31	"	Royalties Account	5,000
					"	Shortworkings A/c	3,000
			16,000				16,000
Apr. 15	To	Bank Account	8,000	Apr. 1	By	Balance b/d	8,000
2022 Mar. 31	"	Shortworkings A/c	3,200	2022 Mar. 31	"	Royalties Account	11,200
" 31	"	Balance c/d	8,000				
			19,200				19,200
Apr. 15	"	Bank Account	8,000	Apr. 1	"	Balance b/d	8,000
2023 Mar. 31	"	Shortworkings A/c	3,000	2023 Mar. 31	"	Royalties Account	12,000
" 31	"	Balance c/d	9,000				
			20,000				20,000

Apr. 15	"	Bank Account	9,000	Apr. 1	"	Balance b/d	9,000
2024				2024			
Mar. 31	"	Balance c/d	14,000	Mar. 31	"	Royalties Account	14,000
			23,000				23,000
Apr. 15	"	Bank Account	14,000	Apr. 1	"	Balance b/d	14,000
2025				2025			
Mar. 31	"	Balance c/d	7,500	Mar. 31	"	Royalties Account	7,500
			21,500				21,500
Apr. 15	"	Bank Account	7,500	Apr. 1	"	Balance b/d	7,500

Payment of Nazrana or Lease Premium in Addition to Royalty

In some cases, the lessee may agree to pay lumsum amount to the lessor in addition to royalty. This extra payment in addition to royalty is known as nazrana or lease premium or goodwill. Under such a situation a Nazrana Account is opened in the books of the lessee and lessor. *In the books of the lessee,* the whole amount of nazrana is debited to 'Nazrana Account'. This account being a capital expenditure for the lessee, can be written off every year during the period of the lease by debiting Profit and Loss Account and crediting Nazrana Account. *In the books of the lessor* the amount received as nazrana is credited to Nazrana Account and equal amount is credited to Profit and Loss Account each year during the life of lease. The balance in Nazrana Account is shown as an asset (in lessee's books) and as liability (in the books of the lessor).

ILLUSTRATION 4. *(Payment of Nazrana).* On January 1, 2022, a Brick Co. acquired a lease of 15 years from Mr. X on lease for getting earth. Terms of lease are :

(*a*) annual rate of royalty is ₹ 1 per 100 cubic feet of earth taken out.
(*b*) minimum rent is ₹ 12,000 per annum.
(*c*) on 1st January, 2022, company gave ₹ 1,50,000 to X for nazrana.
(*d*) short workings can be recouped during first 4 years only.
(*e*) annual royalty is paid on 31st December, each year.

Brick making company extracted earth in the following manner :

Years	*2022*	*2023*	*2024*	*2025*
Earth in cubic feet	10,00,000	15,00,000	9,00,000	14,00,000

Open Nazrana Account, Royalty Account and Shortworkings Account in the books of Brick Co.

SOLUTION

ANALYTICAL TABLE

Year	*Earth (Cu. feet)*	*Royalties*	*Short-workings*	*Short workings recouped*	*Short-workings unrecouped*	*Amount paid to landlord*
	₹	₹	₹	₹	₹	₹
2022	10,00,000	10,000	2,000	—	—	12,000
2023	15,00,000	15,000	—	2,000	—	13,000
2024	9,00,000	9,000	3,000	—	—	12,000
2025	14,00,000	14,000	—	2,000	1,000	12,000

NAZRANA ACCOUNT

Dr.		₹		Cr.	₹
2022			2022		
Jan. 1	To Bank A/c	1,50,000	Dec. 31	By Profit & Loss A/c	
				$\left(\frac{1}{15} \times 1,50,000\right)$	10,000
			"	By Balance c/d	1,40,000
		1,50,000			1,50,000
2023			2023		
Jan. 1	To Balance b/d	1,40,000	Dec. 31	By Profit & Loss A/c	10,000
			"	By Balance c/d	1,30,000
		1,40,000			1,40,000
2024			2024		
Jan. 1	To Balance b/d	1,30,000	Dec. 31	By Profit & Loss A/c	10,000
			"	By Balance c/d	1,20,000
		1,30,000			1,30,000
2025			2025		
Jan. 1	To Balance b/d	1,20,000	Dec. 31	By Profit & Loss A/c	10,000
			"	By balance c/d	1,10,000
		1,20,000			1,20,000

ROYALTY ACCOUNT

Dr.		₹		Cr.	₹
2022	To Landlord	10,000	2022	By Production A/c	10,000
2023	To Landlord	15,000	2023	By Production A/c	15,000
2024	To Landlord	9,000	2024	By Production A/c	9,000
2025	To Landlord	14,000	2025	By Production A/c	14,000

SHORTWORKINGS ACCOUNT

Dr.		₹		Cr.	₹
2022	To Landlord	2,000	2022	By Balance c/d	2,000
2023	To Balance b/d	2,000	2023	By Landlord	2,000
2024	To Landlord	3,000	2024	By Balance c/d	3,000
2025	To Balance b/d	3,000	2025	By Landlord	2,000
				By Profit & Loss A/c	1,000
		3,000			3,000

Stoppage of Work due to Strike/Lockout/Accident etc.

Generally minimum rent is fixed taking into consideration the minimum expected output under normal conditions. Whenever there is stoppage of work due to abnormal reasons as strike, lockout, accident or for any other reason, the minimum rent is required to be adjusted as provided for in the agreement. Such agreement may have the following arrangements :

(*i*) **Non-application of the condition of minimum rent.** In such a case the clause of minimum rent is not applied. Actual royalties will discharge all rental obligations. There will not be any shortworkings or surplus.

(*ii*) **Reduction in the amount of minimum rent.** If there is any clause in the agreement, regarding reduction in the amount of minimum rent, it can take the following form :

(*a*) Minimum rent is reduced *proportionately* to the length of the stoppage of work during the relevant year.

(*b*) Minimum rent can be reduced by a *fixed percentage* or by a fixed amount in the year of stoppage.

ILLUSTRATION 5. (***When minimum rent is reduced proportionately in case of strike***) Mr. Sharma took a lease of Mines from Mr. Singhania with effect from 1st January 2003 for a period of 20 years. The terms of agreement provided for the payment of royalty @ ₹ 0.60 per ton raised, subject to a minimum rent of ₹ 12,000 per annum, with a right to recoup shortworkings, within a period of 3 years immediately succeeding the year in which the short-working arises. It was further agreed that the minimum rent should be reduced *proportionately*, in case of strikes or lock-outs in any year.

You are furnished with the following details :

Year	2019	2020	2021	2022	2023	2024
Tons raised	23000	18700	15400 (there was a strike period of 3 months)	19000	20600	22600

The balance in Shortworkings Account as on January 1, 2019 was ₹ 4,900 of which ₹ 2,200 arose in 2017 and the balance in 2018.

You are required to show Royalty Account, Shortworkings A/c and Mr. Singhania's A/c in the Books of Mr. Sharma for all the above 6 years. ***(ICWA Final)***

SOLUTION

ANALYTICAL TABLE

Year	*Tons raised*	*Royalty @ 60 p.*	*Minimum Rent*	*Short-workings*	*Surplus*	*Recouped*	*Not Recouped*	*Paid to Landlord*
		₹	₹	₹	₹	₹	₹	₹
2019	23,000	13,800	12,000	—	1,800	1,800	400	12,000
2020	18,700	11,220	12,000	780	—	—	2,700	12,000
2021	15,400	9,240	9,000	—	240	240	—	9,000
2022	19,000	11,400	12,000	600	—	—	—	12,000
2023	20,600	12,360	12,000	—	360	360	180	12,000
2024	22,600	13,560	12,000	—	1,560	600	—	12,960

ROYALTY ACCOUNT

		₹			₹
31-12-2019	To Singhania's A/c	13,800	31-12-2019	By Production A/c	13,800
31-12-2020	To Singhania's A/c	11,220	31-12-2020	By Production A/c	11,220
31-12-2021	To Singhania's A/c	9,240	31-12-2021	By Production A/c	9,240
31-12-2022	To Singhania's A/c	11,400	31-12-2022	By Production A/c	11,400
31-12-2023	To Singhania's A/c	12,360	31-12-2023	By Production A/c	12,360
31-12-2024	To Singhania's A/c	13,560	31-12-2024	By Production A/c	13,560

SHORT WORKINGS ACCOUNT

		₹			₹
1-1-2019	To Balance b/d	4,900	31-12-2019	By Singhania's A/c	1,800
			"	By Profit & Loss A/c	400
			"	By Balance c/d	2,700
		4,900			4,900
1-1-2020	To Balance b/d	2,700	31-12-2020	By Profit & Loss A/c	2,700
31-12-2020	To Singhania's A/c	780	"	By Balance c/d	780
		3,480			3,480
1-1-2021	To Balance b/d	780	31-12-2021	By Singhania's A/c	240
			"	By Balance c/d	540
		780			780
1-1-2022	To Balance b/d	540	31-12-2022	By Balance c/d	1,140
31-12-2022	To Singhania's A/c	600			
		1,140			1,140
1-1-2023	To Balance b/d	1,140	31-12-2023	By Singhania's A/c	360
			"	By Profit & Loss A/c	180
			"	By Balance c/d	600
		1,140			1,140
1-1-2024	To Balance b/d	600	31-12-2024	By Singhania's A/c	600

SINGHANIA'S ACCOUNT

		₹			₹
31-12-2019	To Shortworkings A/c	1,800	31-12-2019	By Royalty A/c	13,800
"	To Bank A/c	12,000			
		13,800			13,800
31-12-2020	To Bank A/c	12,000	31-12-2020	By Royalty A/c	11,220
			31-12-2020	By Shortworkings A/c	780
		12,000			12,000
31-12-2021	To Shortworkings A/c	240	31-12-2021	By Royalty A/c	9,240
"	To Bank A/c	9,000			
		9,240			9,240
31-12-2022	To Bank A/c	12,000	31-12-2020	By Royalty A/c	11,400
			31-12-2020	By Shortworkings A/c	600
		12,000			12,000
31-12-2023	To Shortworkings A/c	360	31-12-2023	By Royalty A/c	12,360
	To Bank A/c	12,000			
		12,360			12,360
31-12-2024	To Shortworkings A/c	600	31-12-2024	By Royalty A/c	13,560
	To Bank A/c	12,960			
		13,560			13,560

Creation of Provision Against Shortworkings

Sometimes, it may not be possible to recoup the shortworkings out of future payments of royalty due to some factors physical or economical even though the period to recover the same still has not lapsed. In such cases, provision against shortworkings should be created in the year in which shortworkings arise with the amount of shortworkings of that year by passing the following entry:

Profit and Loss Account Dr.
To Provision Against Shortworkings Account
(Being provision against shortworkings created)

When shortworkings are actually recovered, the balance in the Provision Against Shortworkings Account should be reduced by transfer to the Profit and Loss Account by passing the following entry :

Provision Against Shortworkings Account Dr.
To Profit and Loss Account
(Being recoupment of shortworkings)

In case it is clear that shortworkings are no longer recoupable, the following entry is to be passed :

Provision Against Shortworkings Account Dr.
To Shortworkings Account
(Being provision against shortworkings eliminated on account of irrecoverable shortworkings)

After shortworkings are recouped, the excess provision against shortworkings is credited to Profit and Loss Account as a prior period adjustment because Profit & Loss Account was debited when provision against shortworkings was created. Entry for excess provision is :

Provision Against Shortworkings Account Dr.
To Profit & Loss Account
(Being transfer of excess provision after shortworkings are recouped)

The above method of creation of provision against shortworkings is adopted when the amount of shortworkings is substantial and chances of recovery of shortworkings are uncertain.

ILLUSTRATION 6. (*When provision against shortworkings is to be maintained*) Mining Corporation Ltd. obtained a lease of coal field for 99 years from Mr. Landlord on following terms from 1st January, 2022.

(*a*) Mining Corporation will develop the land and will bear the cost of development.

(*b*) Royalties will be ₹ 2 per tonne of coal raised during the period.

(*c*) Minimum rent will be ₹ 10,000 for the first year with an annual increase of ₹ 1,000 till it reaches ₹ 15,000.

(*d*) Shortworkings, if any, are recoverable within first three years only. Mining Corporation Ltd. developed the land at the cost of ₹ 2 crores and estimated coal deposit of 20 lakhs of tonnes. It was decided to depreciate this expenditure on Depletion Method of depreciation.

The coal raised by Mining Corporation is as under :

Year	2022	2023	2024	2025
Production in tonnes	1,000	2,000	10,000	15,000

You are required to prepare : Royalties Account, Shortworkings Account, Landlord Account and Provision Against Shortworkings Account.

SOLUTION

ANALYTICAL TABLE

Year	Production	Rate of Royalty per tonne	Royalty	Minimum Rent	Shortworkings	Surplus	Recoupment	Shortworkings not recoupable	Payment to Landlord
	Tonnes	₹	₹	₹	₹	₹	₹	₹	₹
2022	1,000	2	2,000	10,000	8,000	—	—	—	10,000
2023	2,000	2	4,000	11,000	7,000	—	—	—	11,000
2024	10,000	2	20,000	12,000	—	8,000	8,000	7,000	12,000
2025	15,000	2	30,000	13,000	—	17,000	—	—	30,000

In the Books of Mining Corporation Ltd.

ROYALTIES ACCOUNT

		₹			₹
2022	To Landlord A/c	2,000	2022	By Production A/c	2,000
2023	To Landlord a/c	4,000	2023	By Production A/c	4,000
2024	To Shortworkings A/c	8,000	2024	By Production A/c	20,000
	To Landlord A/c	12,000			
		20,000			20,000
2025	To Landlord A/c	30,000	2025	By Production A/c	30,000

SHORTWORKINGS ACCOUNT

		₹			₹
2022	To Landlord A/c	8,000	2022	By Balance c/d	8,000
2023	To Balance b/d	8,000	2023	By Balance c/d	15,000
	To Landlord A/c	7,000			
		15,000			15,000
2024	To Balance b/d	15,000	2024	By Royalties A/c	8,000
				By Provision Against Shortworkings	7,000
		15,000			15,000

LANDLORD ACCOUNT

		₹			₹
2022	To Bank A/c	10,000	2022	By Royalties A/c	2,000
				By Shortworkings A/c	8,000
		10,000			10,000
2023	To Bank A/c	11,000	2023	By Royalties A/c	4,000
				By Shortworkings A/c	7,000
		11,000			11,000
2024	To Bank A/c	12,000	2024	By Royalties A/c	12,000
2025	To Bank A/c	30,000	2025	By Royalties A/c	30,000

PROVISION AGAINST SHORTWORKINGS ACCOUNT

		₹			₹
2022	To Balance c/d	8,000	2022	By Profit & Loss A/c	8,000
2023	To Balance c/d	15,000	2023	By Balance b/d	8,000
				By Profit & Loss A/c	7,000
		15,000			15,000
2024	To Profit & Loss A/c	8,000	2024	By Balance b/d	15,000
	To Shortworkings A/c	7,000			
		15,000			15,000

Note. Cost of the development of land ₹ 2 crores is not to be considered as its is a capital expenditure. It has nothing to do with royalty accounts. Cost of ₹ 2 crores will be recovered from production by way of depreciation by following depletion method of depreciation as given below :

$$\text{Depreciation per tonne} = \frac{\text{Cost of the Development of the Land}}{\text{Quantity of Estimated Coal Deposit}} = \frac{₹\ 2 \text{ crores}}{20 \text{ lakhs tonnes}} = ₹\ 10$$

Every year Production Account will be charged depreciation @ ₹ 10 per tonne of output produced.

ILLUSTRATION 7. ***(When minimum rent is reduced (i) on proportionate basis in case of strike and (ii) certain percentage of the period of lockout)*** New Steel Ltd. obtained a lease from Old Coal Ltd., for a coal mine on 1st January, 2019 on the following terms and conditions :

(1) Royalty at ₹ 1 per tonne raised.

(2) Minimum rent ₹ 24,000 per annum.

(3) Recoupment of shortworking of each year during three years following subject to a maximum of ₹ 5,000 p.a.

(4) In the event of strike the minimum rent would be taken *pro rata* on the basis of actual working days but in the event of lockout, the lessee would enjoy a concession in respect of minimum rent for 50% of the period of lockout.

Besides the above, New Steel Ltd. have been granted a cash subsidy equal to 25% of the unrecoupable shortworkings by the Central Government up to the first five years of the lease.

Working up to first six years is as follows :

Year	2019	2020	2021	2022	2023	2024
Actual Royalty (₹)	14,000	20,400	32,200	27,200	21,600	19,400
					(Strike 2 months)	(Lockout for 4 months)

Show the ledger accounts in the books of New Steel Ltd.

SOLUTION

ROYALTY ACCOUNT

		₹			₹
2019			2019		
Dec. 31	To Old Coal Ltd.	14,000	Dec. 31	By Production A/c	14,000
2020			2020		
Dec. 31	To Old Coal Ltd.	20,400	Dec. 31	By Production A/c	20,400
2021			2021		
Dec. 31	To Old Coal Ltd.	32,200	Dec. 31	By Production A/c	32,200
2022			2022		
Dec. 31	To Old Coal Ltd.	27,200	Dec. 31	By Production A/c	27,200

Date	Particulars	₹	Date	Particulars	₹
2023			2023		
Dec. 31	To Old Coal Ltd.	21,600	Dec. 31	By Production A/c	21,600
2024			2024		
Dec. 31	To Old Coal Ltd.	19,400	Dec. 31	By Production A/c	19,400

SHORTWORKINGS ACCOUNT

Date	Particulars	₹	Date	Particulars	₹
2019			2019		
Dec. 31	To Old Coal Ltd.	10,000	Dec. 31	By Balance c/d	10,000
2020			2020		
Jan. 1	To Balance b/d	10,000	Dec. 31	By Balance c/d	13,600
Dec. 31	To Old Coal Ltd.	3,600			
		13,600			13,600
2021			2021		
Jan. 1	To Balance b/d	13,600	Dec. 31	By Old Coal Ltd.	5,000
			Dec. 31	By Balance c/d	8,600
		13,600			13,600
2022			2022		
Jan. 1	To Balance b/d	8,600	Dec. 31	By Old Coal Ltd.	3,200
			Dec. 31	By Cash (Subsidy)	450
			Dec. 31	(25% of ₹ 1,800)	
			Dec. 31	By Profit & Loss A/c	1,350
			Dec. 31	By Balance c/d	3,600
		8,600			8,600
2023			2023		
Jan. 1	To Balance b/d	3,600	Dec. 31	By Old Coal Ltd.	1,600
			Dec. 31	By Cash (Subsidy), (25% of ₹ 2,000)	500
			Dec. 31	By Profit & Loss A/c	1,500
		3,600			3,600
2024			2024		
Dec. 31	To Old Coal Ltd.	600	Dec. 31	By Balance c/d	600
2025					
Jan. 1	To Balance b/d	600			

OLD COAL LTD.

Date	Particulars	₹	Date	Particulars	₹
2019			2019		
Dec. 31	To Bank A/c	24,000	Dec. 31	By Royalty A/c	14,000
			Dec. 31	By Shortworkings A/c	10,000
		24,000			24,000
2020			2020		
Dec. 31	To Bank A/c	24,000	Dec. 31	By Royalty A/c	20,400
				By Shortworkings A/c	3,600
		24,000			24,000

2021			2021		
Dec. 31	To Shortworkings A/c	5,000	Dec. 31	By Royalty A/c	32,200
Dec. 31	To Bank A/c	27,200			
		32,200			32,200
2022			2022		
Dec. 31	To Shortworkings A/c	3,200	Dec. 31	By Royalty A/c	27,200
Dec. 31	To Bank A/c	24,000			
		27,200			27,200
2023			2023		
Dec. 31	To Shortworkings A/c	1,600	Dec. 31	By Royalty A/c	21,600
Dec. 31	To Bank A/c	20,000			
		21,600			21,600
2024			2024		
Dec. 31	To Bank A/c	20,000	Dec. 31	By Royalty A/c	19,400
			Dec. 31	By Shortworkings A/c	600
		20,000			20,000

Income Tax

If there is a provision in the income tax law that the payer of royalty should deduct tax at source at the prescribed rate and tax so deducted shall be deposited to the credit of the Central Government within a specified time. The landlord will get the amount of royalty or minimum rent after adjustment of tax. The total amount of royalty (including tax) will be charged to Profit & Loss (or Production) A/c.

ILLUSTRATION 8. ***(When deduction of Income Tax is to be made at Source)*** Agro (India) Ltd. Madras, entered into a collaboration agreement with Agro (U.K.) Ltd., Birmingham, under which the former were to pay the latter, commencing with the date on which they started production, a royalty @ 5% of sales during each quarter of the calendar year, subject to deduction of tax in India (which may be assumed @ 50%) so however that the remittance in any such quarter should not be less than £ 500, the 'shortworking' being recoupable from out of royalty payable in subsequent quarters during the same calendar year but not beyond.

Following are the sales figures of Agro (India) Ltd. :

Quarter	30-9-2023	31-12-2023	31-3-2024	30-6-2024	30-9-2024	31-12-2024
Sales (₹)	1,00,000	2,00,000	5,00,000	3,36,000	6,00,000	12,00,000

The production had begun on 1-7-2023, the rate of exchange may be taken at £ 1 = ₹ 13-1/3 for remittances upto 6-6-2024 and thereafter at £ = ₹ 21. The remittance has been made in each case within one month from the end of the relevant quarters.

Show Royalty Account, Agro (U.K.) Account and Shortworkings Account.

SOLUTION

ROYALTY ACCOUNT

		₹			₹
2023			2023		
Sep. 30	To Agro (U.K.) Ltd.	5,000	Dec. 31	By Profit and Loss Account	15,000
Dec. 31	To Agro (U.K.) Ltd.	10,000			
		15,000			15,000

2024			2024		
Mar. 31	To Agro (U.K.) Ltd.	25,000	Dec. 31	By Profit and Loss Account	1,31,800
June 30	To Agro (U.K.) Ltd.	16,800			
Sep. 30	To Agro (U.K.) Ltd.	30,000			
Dec. 31	To Agro (U.K.) Ltd.	60,000			
		1,31,800			1,31,800

SHORTWORKINGS ACCOUNT

		₹			₹
2023			2023		
Sep. 30	To Agro (U.K.) Ltd.	8,333	Dec. 31	By Profit & Loss A/c	11,666
Dec. 31	To Agro (U.K.) Ltd.	3,333			
		11,666			11,666
2024			2024		
June 30	To Agro (U.K.) Ltd.	4,200	Sep. 30	By Agro (U.K.) Ltd.	4,200

AGRO (U.K.) LTD.

		₹			₹
2023			2023		
Oct. 31	To Tax Payable A/c	6,667	Sep. 30	By Royalty A/c	5,000
" 31	" Bank A/c	6,666	" 30	" Shortworkings A/c	8,333
Dec. 31	" Balance c/d	13,333	Dec. 31	" Royalty A/c	10,000
			" 31	" Shortworkings A/c	3,333
		26,666			26,666
2024			2024		
Jan. 31	To Tax Payable A/c	6,667	Jan. 1	By Balance b/d	13,333
" 31	" Bank A/c	6,666	Mar. 31	" Royalty A/c	25,000
April 30	" Tax Payable A/c	12,500	June 30	" Royalty A/c	16,800
" 30	" Bank A/c	12,500	" 30	" Shortworkings A/c	4,200
July 31	" Tax Payable A/c	10,500	Sep. 30	" Royalty A/c	30,000
" 31	" Bank A/c	10,500	Dec. 31	" Royalty A/c	60,000
Oct. 31	" Shortworkings A/c	4,200			
" 31	" Tax Payable A/c	12,900			
Oct. 31	" Bank A/c	12,900			
Dec. 31	" Balance c/d	60,000			
		1,49,333			1,49,333
2025			2025		
Jan. 31	To Tax Payable A/c	30,000	Jan. 31	By Balance b/d	60,000
" 31	To Bank A/c	30,000			
		60,000			60,000

Note. The minimum payment after tax up to 30-4-2024 is ₹ 6,666 (*i.e.* £ 500 @ ₹ 13.33 per £). To this an equal amount is added for tax, therefore, minimum rent is ₹ 13,333 (*i.e.* £ 1,000 @ ₹ 13.33 per £).

The minimum payment after tax after 6-6-2024 is ₹ 10,500 (*i.e.* £ 500 @ ₹ 21 per £). To this an equal amount for tax is added to arrive at the amount of minimum rent. Thus, minimum rent after 6-6-2024 is ₹ 21,000 (*i.e.* ₹ 10,500 + ₹ 10,500].

Copyright Royalties

Copyright means the sole right granted by law to an author to publish and sell his book in the market. The author generally gives this right to a firm of publishers, who will undertake to do the production and sales of the book for a consideration. This consideration may be a lumpsum payment or a fixed percentage as agreed between the author and the publishers on the number of books sold multiplied by the printed price of the books sold. The number of copies sold can be calculated in the following manner :

			No.
Opening Stock of Books			× ×
Add : Number of Books Printed			× ×
	Books available		× ×
Less :	Specimen Books	× ×	
	Waste Books	× ×	
	Closing Stock of Books	× ×	
			× ×
No. of Books Sold during the year			

OR

No. of Copies Sold = Copies Printed + Opening Stock – Closing Stock

Generally copyright agreements do not contain any clause for the payment of minimum amount of royalty. Hence, the problem of shortworkings, recoupment of shortworkings or writing off shortworkings to Profit and Loss Account does not arise in such cases. But if there is any clause for the payment of minimum rent, then treatment of shortworkings will be same as discussed earlier.

ILLUSTRATION 9. ***(Where no. of copies sold are to be calculated besides recoupment of shortworkings within a fixed period)*** Mr. Jain wrote a book on Advanced Accountancy and got it published with M/s Kalyani Publishers on the terms that royalties will be paid @ ₹ 50 per copy sold subject to a minimum rent of ₹ 1,50,000 with a right of recoupment of shortworkings over the first three years of the royalty agreement. From the following details write up (*i*) Minimum Rent Account, (*ii*) Royalties Account, (*iii*) Shortworkings Account, and (*iv*) Mr. Jain's Account.

Year	2021	2022	2023	2024
Number of Copies Printed	2,000	3,000	4,000	5,000
Closing Stock	100	200	400	500

SOLUTION

In this problem, it is necessary to find out the number of copies sold because royalty is to be paid on the basis of number of copies sold. Number of copies sold is found out as follows :

Number of copies sold = Copies printed + Opening stock – Closing stock

Number of Copies sold in					Royalty @ ₹ 50
2021	=	2,000 + Nil – 100	=	1,900 Copies	₹ 95,000
2022	=	3,000 + 100 – 200	=	2,900 Copies	₹ 1,45,000
2023	=	4,000 + 200 – 400	=	3,800 Copies	₹ 1,90,000
2024	=	5,000 + 400 – 500	=	4,900 Copies	₹ 2,45,000

MINIMUM RENT ACCOUNT

		₹			₹
2021			2021		
Dec. 31	To Mr. Jain	1,50,000	Dec. 31	By Royalties Account	95,000
				By Shortworkings A/c	55,000
		1,50,000			1,50,000

2022			2022		
Dec. 31	To Mr. Jain	1,50,000	Dec. 31	By Royalties Account	1,45,000
			" 31	By Shortworkings A/c	5,000
		1,50,000			1,50,000

ROYALTIES ACCOUNT

		₹			₹
2021			2021		
Dec. 31	To Minimum Rent A/c	95,000	Dec. 31	By Profit & Loss A/c	95,000
2022			2022		
Dec. 31	To Minimum Rent A/c	1,45,000	Dec. 31	By Profit & Loss A/c	1,45,000
2023			2023		
Dec. 31	To Mr. Jain	1,50,000	Dec. 31	By Profit & Loss A/c	1,90,000
" 31	To Shortworkings A/c	40,000			
		1,90,000			1,90,000
2024			2024		
Dec. 31	To Mr. Jain	2,45,000	Dec. 31	By Profit & Loss A/c	2,45,000

SHORTWORKINGS ACCOUNT

		₹			₹
2021			2021		
Dec. 31	To Minimum Rent A/c	55,000	Dec. 31	By Balance c/d	55,000
2022			2022		
Jan. 1	To Balance b/d	55,000	Dec. 31	By Balance c/d	60,000
Dec. 31	" Minimum Rent A/c	5,000			
		60,000			60,000
2023			2023		
Jan. 1	To Balance b/d	60,000	Dec. 31	By Royalties Account	40,000
			" 31	" Profit & Loss A/c	20,000
		60,000			60,000

MR. JAIN

		₹			₹
2021			2021		
Dec. 31	To Bank Account	1,50,000	Dec. 31	By Minimum Rent A/c	1,50,000
2022			2022		
Dec. 31	To Bank Account	1,50,000	Dec. 31	By Minimum Rent A/c	1,50,000
2023			2023		
Dec. 31	To Bank Account	1,50,000	Dec. 31	By Royalties Account	1,50,000
2024			2024		
Dec. 31	To Bank Account	2,45,000	Dec. 31	By Royalties Account	2,45,000

Damage Payable by the Lessor (Author) to the Lessee (Publisher)

In case of lease of copyrights, the royalty agreement may contain a clause that the author should revise the book and give the revised manuscript to the publishers for publication within a stipulated period failing which the author should pay some compensation of damage to the publisher. If there is such a clause in the agreement and there is default on the part of the author he becomes liable to pay damages or compensation to the publishers. Following journal entries will be passed :

In the Books of the Publishers

Author's A/c Dr.
To Damages Receivable A/c

Damages receivable by the publisher from the author are not actually received in cash. These are generally set off against the royalty payable to the author. The entry for the payment of the net amount to the author will be passed. Damages receivable account will be closed by transfer its balance to the credit side of Profit & Loss Account.

In the Books of the Author

Such damages payable by the author to the publishers is a loss to him. The journal entry will be

Damages Payable A/c Dr.
To Publishers A/c

The damages payable by the author to the publishers are not actually paid in cash. These are generally set off against the royalty receivable from the publishers. The entry for the net receipt of the amount of royalty will be passed in the books of the author. Damages Payable A/c will be closed by transfer to the debit side of Profit & Loss Account.

ILLUSTRATION 10. ***(Where damages are deducted from the amount of royalty)*** Professor Lal wrote a book and gave Kalyani Publishers the publishing rights on the following terms with effect from 1-1-2021 :

(*i*) Royalties @ 10% on published price of the copies sold.
(*ii*) Minimum payment of ₹ 60,000 in the first year and ₹ 1,00,000 per annum thereafter.
(*iii*) Right to deduct in following two years any excess of minimum rent paid over actual royalties in any year.
(*iv*) Revision of book by the author on request and to pay ₹ 6,000 per month to Kalyani Publishers for every month of delay after six months of request made by the Publishers.
(*v*) In the event of delay the condition of minimum amount payable was not to be applied. On 1-1-2024 request for revision was made and the revised manuscript was supplied by the author on 1-11-2024.

Prepare Ledger Accounts in the books of the publisher based on the following information—

Year	*2021*	*2022*	*2023*	*2024*	*2025*
Copies sold (number)	1,500	4,900	5,000	4,000	5,000
Printed price per copy (₹)	200	200	250	250	250

SOLUTION

ANALYTICAL TABLE

Year	*Sales*	*Royalties*	*Min. Rent*	*Short-Workings*	*Surplus*	*Reco-uped*	*Written off*	*Carried*	*Payment*
	₹	₹	₹	₹	₹	₹	₹	₹	₹
2021	3,00,000	30,000	60,000	30,000	—	—	—	30,000	60,000
2022	9,80,000	98,000	1,00,000	2,000	—	—	—	32,000	1,00,000
2023	12,50,000	1,25,000	1,00,000	—	25,000	25,000	5,000	2,000	1,00,000
2024	10,00,000	1,00,000	—	—	—	—	2,000	—	76,000
2025	12,50,000	1,25,000	1,00,000	—	25,000	—	—	—	1,25,000

Notes : In the year 2024 as per agreement—

(1) Condition of minimum rent is not applicable.

(2) Royalty payable works out to be ₹ 1,00,000.

(3) But because of delay of four months in the submission of manuscript by the author, the publisher shall deduct. ₹ 24,000 (*i.e.,* ₹ 6,000 × 4), Hence, the net royalty payable is ₹ 76,000.

ROYALTIES ACCOUNT

		₹			₹
2021	To Kundan Lal	30,000	2021	By Profit & Loss A/c	30,000
2022	To Kundan Lal	98,000	2022	By Profit & Loss A/c	98,000
2023	To Kundan Lal	1,25,000	2023	By Profit & Loss A/c	1,25,000
2024	To Kundan Lal	1,00,000	2024	By Profit & Loss A/c	1,00,000
2025	To Kundan Lal	1,25,000	2025	By Profit & Loss A/c	1,25,000

SHORTWORKINGS ACCOUNT

		₹			₹
2021	To Kundan Lal	30,000	2021	By Balance c/d	30,000
2022	To Balance b/d	30,000	2022	By Balance c/d	32,000
	To Kundan Lal	2,000			
		32,000			32,000
2023	To Balance b/d	32,000	2023	By Kundan Lal	25,000
				By Profit & Loss A/c	5,000
				By Balance c/d	2,000
		32,000			32,000
2024	To Balance b/d	2,000	2024	By Profit & Loss A/c	2,000

DAMAGES RECEIVABLE ACCOUNT

		₹			₹
2024	To Profit & Loss A/c	24,000	2024	By Kundan Lal	24,000

KUNDAN LAL

		₹			₹
2021	To Bank A/c	60,000	2021	By Royalties A/c	30,000
				By Shortworkings A/c	30,000
		60,000			60,000
2022	To Bank A/c	1,00,000	2022	By Royalties A/c	98,000
				By Shortworkings A/c	2,000
		1,00,000			1,00,000
2023	To Bank A/c	1,00,000	2023	By Royalties A/c	1,25,000
	To Shortworkings A/c	25,000			
		1,25,000			1,25,000

2024	To Bank A/c	76,000	2024	By Royalties A/c	1,00,000
	To Damages Receivable A/c	24,000			
		1,00,000			1,00,000
2025	To Bank A/c	1,25,000	2025	By Royalties A/c	1,25,000

Accounting Entries in the Books of the Lessor (or Landlord)

In the books of the lessor (or landlord) receiving the royalties, the treatment will be the reverse of what we have done so far. Following entries will be recorded :

(1) **When the royalties received are less than the minimum rent and shortworkings are recoverable out of future years,** the following entries are made :

(*a*)	Lessee's Account	Dr.	(with minimum rent)
	To Royalties Receivable Account		(with actual royalties)
	To Shortworkings (or Royalty) Suspense Account		(with the difference)
(*b*)	Bank Account	Dr.	(with the amount received)
	To Lessee's Account		
(*c*)	Royalties Receivable Account	Dr.	(with the amount of royalties earned transferred)
	To Profit & Loss Account		

The credit balance of Shortworkings Suspense Account will be carried forward and shown as a liability in the Balance Sheet till it is recoupable.

It is called "Shortworkings or Royalty Suspense Account" because the extra payment over the actual royalty that the landlord receives, can be recovered by the lessee from the excess working when the royalty is more than the minimum rent. The matter of recovery is uncertain which depends on future working which is uncertain. That is why it is called Royalty or Shortworkings Suspense.

(2) **When the royalties earned exceed the minimum rent and shortworkings are recovered,** the entries are as follows :

(*a*)	Lessee's Account	Dr.	(with the amount of royalties earned)
	To Royalties Receivable Account		
(*b*)	Shortworkings Suspense Account	Dr.	(with the amount of shortworkings recovered)
	To Lessee's Account		
(*c*)	Bank Account	Dr.	(with the amount due received)
	To Lessee's Account		
(*d*)	Royalties Receivable Account	Dr.	(with the amount of actual royalties earned)
	To Profit and Loss Account		

If any balance of Shortworkings Suspense Account is no longer recoverable, it should be transferred to Profit and Loss Account as follows :

Shortworkings Suspense Account	Dr.
To Profit and Loss Account	

ILLUSTRATION 11. ***(Where entries are to be made in the books of landlord)*** Bihar Coal Ltd. leased a colliery from Himalaya Coal Ltd. on 1st January, 2020 at a minimum rent of ₹ 30,000 merging into a royalty of ₹ 1.50 per ton with power to recoup shortworkings during the first three years of the lease. The output of the colliery for the five years of the lease was 9,000, 15,000, 27,000, 17,000 and 28,000 tons respectively.

Pass the journal entries for five years for the above transactions in the books of Himalaya Coal Ltd.

SOLUTION

ANALYTICAL TABLE

Year	Output (tons)	Royalty Receivable	Short-workings	Surplus	S.W. Recouped	S.W. not Recouped	Paid to Landlord
		₹	₹	₹	₹	₹	₹
2020	9,000	13,500	16,500	—	—	—	30,000
2021	15,000	22,500	7,500	—	—	—	30,000
2022	27,000	40,500	—	10,500	10,500	13,500	30,000
2023	17,000	25,500	4,500	—	—	4,500	30,000
2024	28,000	42,000	—	12,000	—	—	42,000

JOURNAL ENTRIES IN THE BOOKS OF HIMALAYA COAL LTD.

Date	Particulars		L.F.	₹	₹
2020 Dec. 31	Bihar Coal Ltd.	Dr.		30,000	
	To Royalties Receivable Account				13,500
	To Shortworkings Suspense Account				16,500
	(Being the minimum amount due from Bihar Coal Ltd.—royalties @ ₹ 1.50 per ton on 9,000 tons and ₹ 16,500 treated as shortworkings to make up the minimum amount of ₹ 30,000)				
Dec. 31	Bank Account	Dr.		30,000	
	To Bihar Coal Ltd.				30,000
	(Being the amount of royalties received)				
Dec. 31	Royalties Receivable Account	Dr.		13,500	
	To Profit and Loss Account				13,500
	(Being amount of royalties receivable transferred to Profit and Loss account)				
2021 Dec. 31	Bihar Coal Ltd.	Dr.		30,000	
	To Royalties Receivable Account				22,500
	To Shortworkings Suspense Account				7,500
	(Being minimum amount due from Bihar Coal Ltd.—royalties @ ₹ 1.50 per ton on 15,000 tons and ₹ 7,500 taken as shortworkings to make up the minimum amount of ₹ 30,000)				
Dec. 31	Bank Account	Dr.		30,000	
	To Bihar Coal Ltd.				30,000
	(Being amount due received from Bihar Coal Ltd.)				
Dec. 31	Royalties Receivable Account	Dr.		22,500	
	To Profit and Loss Account				22,500
	(Being transfer of Royalties Receivable Account to Profit and Loss Account)				
2022 Dec. 31	Bihar Coal Ltd.			40,500	
	To Royalties Receivable Account				40,500
	(Being royalties earned @ ₹ 1.50 per ton on 27,000 tons)				

Dec. 31	Shortworkings Suspense Account Dr. To Bihar Coal Ltd. (Being Shortworkings suspense recouped by Bihar Coal Ltd. in excess of minimum rent)		10,500	10,500
Dec. 31	Bank Account To Bihar Coal ltd. (Being minimum rent received from Bihar Coal Ltd.)		30,000	30,000
Dec. 31	Royalties Receivable Account Dr. Shortworkings Suspense Account Dr. To Profit and Loss Account (Being transfer of royalties receivable and irrecoverable balance in Shortworkings Suspense Account to Profit and Loss Account)		40,500 13,500	54,000
2023 Dec. 31	Bihar Coal Ltd. Dr. To Royalties Receivable Account To Shortworkings Suspense Account (Being minimum rent due from Bihar Coal Ltd.—royalties @ ₹ 1.50 per ton on 17,000 tons and shortworkings ₹ 4,500 to make up the minimum rent of ₹ 30,000)		30,000	25,500 4,500
Dec. 31	Bank Account Dr. To Bihar Coal Ltd. (Being receipt of minimum rent from Bihar Coal Ltd.)		30,000	30,000
Dec. 31	Royalties Receivable Account Dr. Shortworkings Suspense Account Dr. To Profit and Loss Account (Being transfer of royalties receivable and shortworkings to Profit and Loss Account ; shortworkings cannot be carried forward because it is recoverable during the first three years of the lease).		25,500 4,500	30,000
2024 Dec. 31	Bihar Coal Ltd. Dr. To Royalties Receivable Account (Being royalties earned @ ₹ 1.50 per ton on 28,000 tons)		42,000	42,000
Dec. 31	Bank Account Dr. To Bihar Coal Ltd. (Being amount due from Bihar Coal Ltd. received)		42,000	42,000
Dec. 31	Royalties Receivable Account Dr. To Profit and Loss Account (Being transfer of royalties receivable to Profit and Loss Account)		42,000	42,000

Sub-lease (Or Sub-royalty)

Sometimes, the terms of the original lease may empower the lessee to sublet a part of the land to another person as a sub-lessee. In such a case, the status of the original lessee will be two fold : as lessee paying royalties to the landlord and as sub-lessor receiving royalties from the sub-lessee. As lessee he maintains Royalties Payable Account, Shortworkings Recoupable Account and Landlord's Account and as sub-lessor he maintains Royalties Receivable Account, Shortworkings Allowable Account and Sub-lessee's Account.

The entries in the books of sub-lessee and landlord will be in the lines of those of lessee and landlord as discussed earlier.

A point of importance in case of sub-lease is that production or sales by the sub-lessee under sub-lease will be considered to be production or sales under the original lease and royalties payable to the original landlord will be calculated on the basis of total production or sales of both the lessee and the sub-lessee.

ILLUSTRATION 12. Cochin Coals Ltd. holds a lease of coal mine for 20 years. It sub-leased a part of the coal mine to Dhanbad Coals Ltd. The details of output in tons are given below :

Year	*Cochin Coals (Tons)*	*Dhanbad Coals (Tons)*
2022-23	10,000	4,000
2023-24	12,000	7,000
2024-25	14,000	8,000

As per lease, Cochin Coals has to pay ₹ 100 per ton and a minimum rent being ₹ 15,00,000. Dhanbad Coals had to pay ₹ 120 per ton to Cochin Coals by way of royalty.

Show Royalty Account in the books of Cochin Coals Ltd. for the said 3 years reflecting both Royalty receivable from Dhanbad Coals and Royalty payable to the Landlord. ***(ICAI-I, Dec., 2018 Modified)***

SOLUTION

In the Books of Cochin Coals Ltd.

ROYALTY PAYABLE ACCOUNT

		₹		₹
31-3-2023	To Landlord A/c		By Royalty Receivable A/c (4,000 × 120)	4,80,000
	₹ 100 (10,000 + 4,000)	14,00,000	By Profit & Loss A/c	9,20,000
		14,00,000		14,00,000
31-3-2024	To Landlord A/c		By Royalty Receivable A/c (7,000 × 120)	8,40,000
	₹ 100 (12,000 + 7,000)	19,00,000	By Profit & Loss A/c	10,60,000
		19,00,000		19,00,000
31-3-2025	To Landlord A/c		By Royalty Receivable A/c (8,000 × 120)	9,60,000
	₹ 100 (14,000 + 8,000)	22,00,000	By Profit & Loss A/c	12,40,000
		22,00,000		22,00,000

Note. There will be shortworkings of ₹ 1,00,000 (*i.e.* ₹ 15,00,000 Minimum Rent – ₹ 14,00,000 Royalty Payable) for the year 2022-23 and it will be debited to Profit and Loss A/c of the same year as there is no clause of recoupment of shortworkings in the agreement.

ILLUSTRATION 13. (***Sub-lease***) On 1st January, 2021 Hari obtained a mining lease on a term that on every ton of output a royalty of 50 paise is payable subject to a minimum rent of ₹ 12,000 per annum. On 1st July, 2022, Hari granted a sub-lease of part of this mine to Ram on the basis that a royalty of 75 paise per ton of output merging into a minimum of ₹ 5,000 per annum.

The recoupment of shortworkings was limited under the principal lease to a period of first three years of lease and under the sub-lease to a period upto 31st December, 2023.

From the following information you are required to show ledger accounts in the book of Hari :

Year	*Output in tons*	
	Own	*Sub-lease*
2021	18,000	—
2022	16,000	3,000
2023	18,000	9,000
2024	15,000	10,000

SOLUTION (*For Analytical Table, please see the next page*)

SOLUTION (*ILLUSTRATION 13*)

ANALYTICAL TABLE

Year	*Output*			*Royalty Pavable @50 paise*	*Recoupable*	*Royalty Receivable @ 75 paise*	*Shortworkings Allowable*	*Shortworkings not recoupable*
	Own	*Sub-lease*	*Total*					
	Tons	Tons	Tons	₹	₹	₹	₹	₹
2021	18,000	—	18,000	9,000 (18,000 × 50 P.)	3,000 (12,000 – 9,000)	—	—	—
2022	16,000	3,000	19,000	9,500 (19,000 × 50 P.)	2,500 (12,000 – 9,500)	2,250 (3,000 × 75 P)	250 (2,500 – 2,250) (See Note)	—
2023	18,000	9,000	27,000	13,500 (27,000 × 50 P.)	–1,500 (12,000 – 13,500)	6,750 (9,000 × 75 P.)	–250	4,000
2024	15,000	10,000	25,000	12,500 (25,000 × 50 P.)		7,500 (10,000 × 75 P.)		

Note. Royalty payable by Hari has been calculated on the total output.

In the Books of Hari

ROYALTY PAYABLE ACCOUNT

		₹			₹
31-12-2021	To Landlord	9,000	31-12-2021	By Profit & Loss A/c	9,000
31-12-2022	To Landlord	9,500	31-12-2022	By Royalty Receivable A/c (on 3,000 tons @ 50 paise)	1,500
			31-12-2022	By Profit & Loss A/c	8,000
		9,500			9,500
31-12-2023	To Landlord	13,500	31-12-2023	By Royalty Receivable A/c (on 9,000 tons @ 50 paise)	4,500
			31-12-2023	By Profit & Loss A/c	9,000
		13,500			13,500
31-12-2024	To Landlord	12,500	31-12-2024	By Royalty Receivable A/c (on 10,000 tons @ 50 paise)	5,000
			31-12-2024	By Profit & Loss A/c	7,500
		12,500			12,500

Note. Alternatively royalty payable may be transferred to Production Account.

SHORTWORKINGS RECOUPABLE ACCOUNT

		₹			₹
31-12-2021	To Landlord	3,000	31-12-2021	By Balance c/d	3,000
1-1-2022	To Balance b/d	3,000	31-12-2022	By Balance c/d	5,500
31-12-2022	To Landlord	2,500			
		5,500			5,500
1-1-2023	To Balance b/d	5,500	31-12-2023	By Landlord	1,500
			31-12-2023	By Profit & Loss A/c	4,000
		5,500			5,500

LANDLORD'S ACCOUNT

		₹			₹
31-12-2021	To Bank A/c	12,000	31-12-2021	By Royalty Payable A/c	9,000
			31-12-2021	By Shortworkings Recoupable A/c	3,000
		12,000			12,000
31-12-2022	To Bank A/c	12,000	31-12-2022	By Royalty Payable A/c	9,500
			31-12-2022	By Shortworkings Recoupable A/c	2,500
		12,000			12,000

		₹			₹
31-12-2023	To Shortworkings Recoupable A/c	1,500	31-12-2023	By Royalty Payable A/c	13,500
31-12-2023	To Bank A/c	12,000			
		13,500			13,500
31-12-2024	To Bank A/c	12,500	31-12-2024	By Royalty Payable A/c	12,500

ROYALTY RECEIVABLE ACCOUNT

		₹			₹
31-12-2022	To Royalty Payable A/c	1,500	31-12-2022	By Ram	2,250
31-12-2022	To Profit & Loss A/c	750			
		2,250			2,250
31-12-2023	To Royalty Payable A/c	4,500	31-12-2023	By Ram	6,750
31-12-2023	To Profit & Loss A/c	2,250			
		6,750			6,750
31-12-2024	To Royalty Payable A/c	5,000	31-12-2024	By Ram	7,500
31-12-2024	To Profit & Loss A/c	2,500			
		7,500			7,500

SHORTWORKINGS ALLOWABLE ACCOUNT

		₹			₹
31-12-2022	To Balance c/d	250	31-12-2022	By Ram	250
31-12-2023	To Ram	250	1-1-2023	By Balance b/d	250

RAM'S ACCOUNT

		₹			₹
31-12-2022	To Royalty Receivable A/c	2,250	31-12-2022	By Bank A/c	2,500
31-12-2022	To Shortworkings Allowable A/c	250			
		2,500			2,500
31-12-2023	To Royalty Receivable A/c	6,750	31-12-2023	By Shortworkings Allowable A/c	250
			31-12-2023	By Bank A/c	6,500
		6,750			6,750
31-12-2024	To Royalty Receivable A/c	7,500	31-12-2023	By Bank A/c	7,500

Note. In case of sub-lease minimum rent for the year 2022 will be for half year from July 1, 2022 to December 31, 2022 because sub-lease was granted on July 1, 2022. Therefore, minimum rent for 2022 is ₹ 2,500 $\left(i.e.\frac{1}{2} \times ₹\ 5{,}000\right)$.

Note. It may be clearly noted that in those cases where royalty payable and royalty receivable are calculated on different bases such as royalty payable is calculated on production and the calculation of royalty receivable is done on sales, it will be desirable not to transfer royalties receivable to Royalties Payable Account. They will be transferred independently to Production Account if calculation is based on production and Profit and Loss Account if the basis of calculation is on sales as has been done in the illustration given below :

ILLUSTRATION 14. (*Sub-lease*) Dobsons Ltd. took a licence for production of a foreign medicine from Johnson Ltd. at royalty of ₹ 1 per bottle produced.

Dobsons Ltd. issued a sub-licence to Medico Ltd. on the basis of a royalty payment of ₹ 1.25 per bottle sold. Minimum royalty payable by Medico Ltd. was fixed at ₹ 15,000 per annum with a right to recoup shortworkings in the following year.

From the given details prepare Royalty Receivable Account, Royalty Payable Account and Shortworkings Account in the books of Dobsons Ltd.

	Dobsons Ltd.		*Medico Ltd.*	
	Sales	*Closing Stock*	*Production*	*Closing Stock*
1st year	50,000	5,000	10,000	2,000
2nd year	70,000	8,000	18,000	4,000
3rd year	1,00,000	10,000	25,000	5,000

SOLUTION

Royalty receivable is to be calculated on the basis of number of bottles sold, so first number of bottles sold by Medico Ltd. is calculated to find out the amount of royalty receivable.

Number of bottles sold = Bottles produced + Opening stock – Closing stock

Number of bottles sold in 1st year = 10,000 + Nil – 2,000 = 8,000

Number of bottles sold in 2nd year = 18,000 + 2,000 – 4,000 = 16,000

Number of bottles sold in 3rd year = 25,000 + 4,000 – 5,000 = 24,000

Royalty receivable in 1st year on 8,000 bottles @ ₹ 1.25 per bottle = ₹ 10,000

Royalty receivable in 2nd year on 16,000 bottles @ ₹ 1.25 per bottle = ₹ 20,000

Royalty receivable in 3rd year on 24,000 bottles @ ₹ 1.25 per bottle = ₹ 30,000

ROYALTY RECEIVABLE ACCOUNT

		₹			₹
1st Year	To Profit & Loss A/c	10,000	1st year	By Medico Ltd.	10,000
2nd Year	To Profit & Loss A/c	20,000	2nd year	By Medico Ltd.	20,000
3rd Year	To Profit & Loss A/c	30,000	3rd year	By Medico Ltd.	30,000

Royalty payable in case of sub-lease is calculated on the basis of total output ; so first total output is calculated by adding the production of Dobsons Ltd. and Medico Ltd.

	Production of Dobsons Ltd. (Sale + Closing Stock – Opening Stock)	Production of Medico Ltd.	Total Production
1st year	50,000 + 5,000 – Nil = 55,000	10,000	65,000
2nd year	70,000 + 8,000 – 5,000 = 73,000	18,000	91,000
3rd year	1,00,000 + 10,000 – 8,000 = 1,02,000	25,000	1,27,000

Royalty payable in 1st year on 65,000 bottles @ ₹ 1 = ₹ 65,000

Royalty payable in 2nd year on 91,000 bottles @ ₹ 1 = ₹ 91,000

Royalty payable in 3rd year on 1,27,000 bottles @ ₹ 1 = ₹ 1,27,000

ROYALTY PAYABLE ACCOUNT

		₹			₹
1st Year	To Johnson Ltd.	65,000	1st year	By Production A/c	65,000
2nd year	To Johnson Ltd.	91,000	2nd year	By Production A/c	91,000
3rd year	To Johnson Ltd.	1,27,000	3rd year	By Production A/c	1,27,000

SHORTWORKING ALLOWABLE ACCOUNT

		₹			₹
1st Year	To Balance c/d	5,000	1st year	By Medico Ltd. (15,000 – 10,000)	5,000
2nd year	To Medico Ltd.	5,000	2nd year	By Balance b/d	5,000

Shortworking Account can be prepared only in case of a sub-licence given to Medico Ltd. because a condition of minimum rent of ₹ 15,000 has been agreed upon. It cannot be prepared in case of original licence given to Dobsons Ltd. because of no condition of the minimum rent.

ILLUSTRATION 15. (*Sub-lease*) On 1st April, 2021 Global Limited, patentees of a new type of electric razor issued a license to Arthar Limited for the manufacture and sale of razors., On the same date, Arthar Limited issued to Allied Limited a sub-license for the same purpose. The license issued by Global Limited provided for a royalty of ₹ 10 per razor produced, subject to a minimum sum of ₹ 75,000 per annum, and sub-license issued by Arthar Limited provided for a royalty of ₹ 15 per razor sold, subject to a minimum sum of ₹ 30,000 per annum. Both the license and sub-license provided that, should the royalties for any year be less than the specified minimum, the shortworkings could be recouped, out of royalties, in excess of the minimum amount falling due for payment in the immediately following two years.

From the following information, prepare Royalties Payable A/c, Royalties Receivable Account, Royalties Adjustment Account, Shortworkings Recoupable Account and Shortworkings Allowable Account in the books of Arthar Limited for the years ended 31st March, 2022, 2023 and 2024 :

Arthar Limited

	Sales	*Stock*
31-3-2022	3,000 razors	500 razors
31-3-2023	5,000 razors	1,500 razors
31-3-2024	4,900 razors	2,000 razors

Allied Limited

	Production	*Stock*
31-3-2022	2,000 razors	440 razors
31-3-2023	3,000 razors	500 razors
31-3-2024	2,400 razors	100 razors

(*Adapted C.A. Inter*)

SOLUTION

ANALYTICAL TABLE OF ROYALTIES PAYABLE

Year ended	*Total Production by Arthar Ltd. and Allied Ltd. (Units)*	*Actual Royalties @ ₹ 10 per unit*	*Shortworkings (Actual Royalties – Minimum Rent)*	*Shortworkings Recouped (Royalties – Minimum Rent)*	*Shortworkings not Recoverable*	*Payment to Global Ltd.*
		₹	₹	₹	₹	₹
31-3-2022	5,500	55,000	20,000	—		75,000
31-3-2023	9,000	90,000		15,000		75,000
31-3-2024	7,800	78,000		3,000	2,000	75,000

Note. Production = Sales + Closing Stock – Opening Stock.

ANALYTICAL TABLE OF ROYALTIES RECEIVABLE

Year ended	Sales by Allied Ltd.	Royalties Receivable @ ₹ 15 per unit	Minimum Rent	Short-workings	Short-workings Allowed	Short workings lapsed	Amount Received from Allied Ltd.
	Units	₹	₹	₹	₹	₹	₹
31-3-2022	1,560	23,400	30,000	6,600	—	—	30,000
31-3-2023	2,940	44,100	30,000	—	6,600	—	37,500
31-3-2024	2,800	42,000	30,000	—	—	—	42,000

Note. Sales = Opening Stock + Production – Closing Stock.

In the Books of Arthar Ltd.

ROYALTIES PAYABLE ACCOUNT

Date	Particulars	₹	Date	Particulars	₹
31-3-2022	To Global Ltd. A/c	55,000	31-3-2022	By Production A/c (3,500 × ₹ 10)	35,000
			31-3-2022	By Royalties Adjustment A/c (2,000 × ₹ 10)	20,000
		55,000			55,000
31-3-2023	To Global Ltd. A/c	90,000	31-3-2023	By Production A/c (6,000 × ₹ 10)	60,000
			31-3-2023	By Royalties Adjustment A/c (3,000 × ₹ 10)	30,000
		90,000			90,000
31-3-2024	To Global Ltd. A/c	78,000	31-3-2024	By Production A/c (5,400 × ₹ 10)	54,000
			31-3-2024	By Royalties Adjustment A/c (2,400 × ₹ 10)	24,000
		78,000			78,000

ROYALTIES RECEIVABLE ACCOUNT

Date	Particulars	₹	Date	Particulars	₹
31-3-2022	To Royalties Adjustment A/c (1,560 × ₹ 10)	15,600	31-3-2022	By Allied Ltd. A/c	23,400
31-3-2022	To Profit & Loss A/c	7,800			
		23,400			23,400
31-3-2023	To Royalties Adjustment A/c (2,940 × ₹ 10)	29,400	31-3-2022	By Allied Ltd. A/c	44,100
31-3-2023	To Profit & Loss A/c	14,700			
		44,100			44,100
31-3-2024	To Royalties Adjustment A/c (2,800 × ₹ 10)	28,000	31-3-2024	By Allied Ltd. A/c	42,000
31-3-2024	To Profit & Loss A/c	14,000			
		42,000			42,000

ROYALTIES ADJUSTMENT ACCOUNT

Date	Particulars	₹	Date	Particulars	₹
31-3-2022	To Royalties Payable A/c	20,000	31-3-2022	By Royalties Receivable A/c	15,600
			31-3-2023	By Balance c/d	4,400
		20,000			20,000
1-4-2022	To Balance b/d	4,400	31-3-2023	By Royalties Receivable A/c	29,400
31-3-2023	To Royalties Payable A/c	30,000	31-3-2023	By Balance c/d	5,000
		34,400			34,400
1-4-2023	To Balance b/d	5,000	31-3-2024	By Royalties Receivable A/c	28,000
31-3-2024	To Royalties Payable A/c	24,000	31-3-2024	By Balance c/d	1,000
		29,000			29,000
1-4-2024	To Balance b/d	1,000			

Note. The balance in Royalties Adjustment A/c represents the royalties paid to Global Ltd. but not yet recovered from Allied Ltd.

SHORTWORKINGS RECOUPABLE ACCOUNT

Date	Particulars	₹	Date	Particulars	₹
31-3-2022	To Global Ltd. A/c	20,000	31-3-2022	By Balance c/d	20,000
1-4-2022	To Balance b/d	20,000	31-3-2023	By Global Ltd. A/c	15,000
			31-3-2023	By Balance c/d	5,000
		20,000			20,000
1-4-2023	To Balance b/d	5,000	31-3-2024	By Global Ltd. A/c	3,000
			31-3-2024	By Profit & Loss A/c	2,000
		5,000			5,000

SHORTWORKINGS ALLOWABLE ACCOUNT

Date	Particulars	₹	Date	Particulars	₹
31-3-2022	To Balance c/d	6,600	31-3-2022	By Allied Ltd. A/c	6,600
31-3-2023	To Allied Ltd. A/c	6,600	1-4-2023	By Balance b/d	6,600

QUESTIONS

OBJECTIVE TYPE

1. **Fill in the blanks :**

(*a*) Shortworking is the excess of minimum rent over........ for the year.

(*b*) Shortworkings recoverable in future are shown in the Balance Sheet on the..........

(*c*) Royalty is calculated either on the basis of ....

(*d*) When shortworkings are recovered, debit is given to............

(*e*) Irrecoverable shortworkings are transferred to .... Account.

(*f*) Royalty account is a................account.

(*g*) The right of recoupment of shortworkings can be............

Ans. [(*a*) royalty payable ; (*b*) assets side ; (*c*) output or sales ; (*d*) Landlord's Account ; (*e*) Profit and Loss ; (*f*) nominal ; (*g*) restricted or unrestricted].

2. State whether the following statements are true or false :

(*a*) Royalty Account is a real account.

(*b*) When the shortworkings become irrecoverable, the same are debited to the Trading Account.

(*c*) Royalty paid on sales is debited to the Profit and Loss Account.

(*d*) The fixation of minimum rent guarantees the landlord the receipt of the minimum amount in case of low output or sales.

(*e*) Royalty Account is closed by transferring it to the Landlord's Account.

(*f*) Shortworkings should be carried forward and shown in the Balance Sheet so long as they are recoverable.

Ans. [True : (*c*), (*d*) and (*f*) ; False : (*b*) and (*e*)].

3. Choose the correct answer :

(*a*) Royalty Account is :
(*i*) Nominal A/c, (*ii*) Personal Account, (*iii*) Real Account.

(*b*) Shortworkings can be recouped out of
(*i*) Minimum rent (*ii*) Excess of actual Royalty over minimum rent
(*iii*) Excess of minimum rent over actual royalty
(*iv*) Profit and Loss Account.

(*c*) The lessee's right to recoup shortworking's related to :
(*i*) first four years (*ii*) terms of the agreement (*iii*) Subsequent three years.

(*d*) Royalty payable is debited by lessee to :
(*i*) Royalty A/c (*ii*) Landlord A/c (*iii*) Profit & Loss A/c.

(*e*) Royalty earned by the lessor is credited to :
(*i*) Sub-lease A/c (*ii*) Profit & Loss A/c (*iii*) Royalty Receivable A/c

(*f*) In case of right to recoupe shortworkings has expired, the balance of shortworkings is transferred to :
(*i*) Landlord A/c (*ii*) Profit & Loss A/c (*iii*) Royalty A/c.

Ans. [(*a*) (*i*); (*b*) (*ii*); (*c*) (*ii*); (*d*) (*i*); (*e*) (*iii*); (*f*) (*ii*)]

SHORT ANSWER TYPE

1. What is royalty ?
2. What is minimum (or dead) rent ?
3. What is the purpose of fixing minimum rent ?
4. Why and how is minimum rent fixed in royalties ?
5. Define shortworking.
6. What do you mean by recoupment of shortworkings ? How is shortworking recouped.
7. What is meant by surface rent ?
8. What do you understand by fixed and floating recoupment of shortworkings.
9. Write a note on sub-lease.

LONG ANSWER TYPE

1. What do you mean by 'royalty' ? Point out the importance of minimum rent in the royalty agreement.
2. What is the purpose of fixing minimum rent in royalty agreements ? Why and how is minimum rent fixed in royalties ?
3. Define shortworkings and explain how Shortworkings Account is maintained in the books of the lessee.

4. What do you mean by recoupment of shortworkings ? How is shortworking recouped ?
5. Explain the following terms in reference to royalty accounts :
   (*i*) Surface Rent
   (*ii*) Fixed and Floating recoupment of shortworkings.
6. Give the entires in the books of the lessee and the landlord when the royalty is more than the minimum rent and shortworkings of the previous years are to be recouped.
7. Write short notes on the following : (*a*) Minimum (or Dead) Rent. (*b*) Royalties Receivable. (*c*) Sub-lease. (*d*) Shortworkings Suspense Account.

PRACTICAL' PROBLEMS

1. (***Where shortworkings are to be recouped within fixed period***). The Bihar Coal Company Ltd. are lessee of a mine on a royalty of 50 paise per ton of coal raised, with a dead rent of ₹ 30,000 per annum, and power to recoup shortworkings during the first five years of the lease. The output for the first three years was as follows :

   1st year 15,000 tons ; 2nd year 50,000 tons ; 3rd year 75,000 tons.

   Draft the necessary journal entries in the books of the company giving effect to the above. You are also required to write up the Minimum Rent Account, Royalties Account, Shortworkings Account, Landlord's Account and Profit and Loss Account.

Ans. [Debit Balance in Shortworkings Account at the end of 3rd year ₹ 20,000].

2. Maniram Singh, who had patented a circular TV antenna, granted Sky Enterprise a licence for ten years to manufacture and sell the product on the following terms :
   (1) Sky Enterprise was to pay Maniram a royalty of ₹ 10 for each antenna sold.
   (2) The minimum royalty for each of the first three years covered by the licence was to be ₹ 50,000. After these years royalties were to be payable on the actual numbers of antennas sold.
   (3) If royalties on antennas sold amounted to less than ₹ 50,000. Sky Enterprise was entitled to deduct the deficiencies from royalties in excess of the sum payable in respect of each of the first *three years of* the agreement.

   The numbers of antennas sold in the first four years ending 31st March were as follows :

2022	2023	2024	2025
4,300	4,900	5,450	5,250

   You are required to present the following Ledger Accounts recording the above transactions in respect of royalties in the books of Sky Enterprise :

   (*a*) Royalties Account; (*b*) Short-workings Account; (*c*) The Account of Maniram Singh.

Ans. [Irrecoverable Shortworkings Debited to Profit & Loss Account : 2024 ₹ 3,500].

3. (***Where actual royalties earned are paid in case of strike***). Mineral Ltd. Leased a property from Sarkar at a royalty of ₹ 1.50 per ton with a minimum rent of ₹ 10,000 per annum. Each year's excess of minimum rent over royalties is recoverable out of royalties of next five years. In the event of a strike and the minimum rental not being reached, the lease provided that the actual royalties earned for the year discharged all rental obligation for the year.

   The results of working of the property are given below :

Year	2018	2019	2020	2021	2022	2023	2024 (Strike year)	2025
Actual Royalty (₹)	Nil	3,300	9,000	11,100	14,000	15,000	8,000	15,200

   Write up Minimum Rent Account and Royalties Account showing the amount charged to Profit and Loss Account each year.

Ans. [Amount Charged to Profit and Loss Account : 2018 Nil; 2019 ₹ 3,300 ; 2020 ₹ 9,000; 2021 ₹ 11,100; 2022 ₹ 14,000; 2023 ₹ 15,000; 2024 ₹ 14,600; 2025 ₹ 15,200; Irrecoverable Shortworking in 2024 ₹ 6,600].

4. ***(Where entries are to be made in the books of landlord).*** A company leased a colliery from the Swatantra Coal Ltd. on 1st January 2022 at a minimum rent of ₹ 40,000 merging into a royalty of ₹ 1 per ton with power to recoup shortworkings over the first three years of the lease. The output of the colliery for first four years was 18,000 tons, 32,000 tons 48,000 tons and 38,000 tons respectively.

   Pass the necessary Journal Entries for each of the four years in the books of Swatantra Coal Ltd.

Ans. [Irrecoverable Shortworking Suspense Credited to Profit and Loss Account ; 2024 ₹ 22,000; 2025 ₹ 2,000].

5. ***(Where actual royalties and minimum rent are given to calculate shortworkings and surplus and actual royalties earned are paid in case of strike).*** M owned certain patent rights. He granted a licence to N to use such rights on royalty basis. Following are the relevant particulars :

Year	1st	2nd	3rd	4th (Strike)	5th
Actual Royalties (₹)	5,000	10,000	8,000	8,000	14,000
Minimum Rent (₹	8,000	9,000	10,000	12,000	13,000

   The deficiency of any year is to be set off against royalty payable in excess of the minimum rent in two following years. In the event of strike and the minimum rent not being realised, it was provided that the actual royalties earned for the year would be the full royalty obligation for the year.

   You are required to show the Royalties Account, M's Account and Shortworkings Account in the books of N. ***(I.C.W.A Inter)***

Ans. [Irrecoverable Shortworking Debited to Profit and Loss Account : 3rd year ₹ 2,000 ; 5th year ₹ 1,000].

6. ***(Where shortworkings are to be recouped within floating period).*** On 1st January, 2020, Hiren, patentee of a new type of article required in engineering concern, issued a licence to Subir for 5 years for the manufacture and sale of the article on the following terms and conditions :

   (*a*) Royalty of ₹ 15 per article manufactured.

   (*b*) Minimum rent of ₹ 15,000 per annum.

   (*c*) Recoupment of shortworkings out of royalties in excess of minimum rent during the two years immediately following subject to a maximum of ₹ 6,000 per annum.

   (*d*) Accounts were to be settled annually on 31st December.

   The number of articles manufactured for the five years was as follows :

Year	2021	2022	2023	2024	2025
Nos.	100	1,100	2,600	400	2,200

   You are required to show the (*a*) Royalties Account, (*b*) Shortworkings Account, and (*c*) Hiren's Account in the books of Subir. ***(Adopted I.C.W.A, Inter)***

Ans. [Irrecoverable Shortworkings Debited to Profit and Loss A/c : 2023 ₹ 6,000 ; 2025 ₹ 3,000].

7. ***(Where production is to be calculated and shortworkings are to be recouped in next year only).*** On 1st January, 2021, Bright Limited, patentees of a new type of gas-burner, issued a licence to Popular Limited for the manufacture and sale of burners for five years on the following terms :

   (*a*) Popular Ltd. to pay a royalty of ₹ 100 for every burner *manufactured* subject to a minimum rent of ₹ 50,000 per annum.

   (*b*) If, for any year, the royalties calculated on burners manufactured amount to less than the minimum rent, Popular Ltd. may recoup the shortworkings against royalties payable in excess of the minimum rent in the *next year only, but not afterwards*.

   (*c*) Payment to be made on 31st December.

Sales and closing stock of burners for five years were :

Year	2021	2022	2023	2024	2025
Sales (Units)	200	400	600	550	230
Stock on 31st Dec. (Units)	50	100	70	150	20

You are required to show the (*i*) Royalties, (*ii*) Shortworkings, and (*iii*) Bright Ltd.'s Accounts in the books of Popular Ltd. who close their accounts on 31st December in each year. **(*I.C.W.A. Inter*)**

Ans. [Irrecoverable Shortworkings Debited to Profit and Loss Account : 2022 ₹ 25,000 ; 2025 ₹ 40,000]

Note. Shortworkings of 2025 cannot be carried forward to the next year as the license for the manufacture and sale of burners for five years expires on 31-12-2025.

8. (***Sub-lease***) Madurai Bottles Ltd. obtain on 1st July, 2022, the selling franchise for the southern districts of Tamil Nadu from the Madras Bottles Ltd., for the sale of their products in that area on payment of 50 paise *per bottle sold for a period of five years.*

Simultaneously, Madurai Bottles Ltd., enter into an arrangement with Tirunelveli Bottles Ltd., under which the latter organisation has been licensed by the former to manufacture and sell aerated water for the same period of five years of the same brand on payment of 90 paise per bottle manufactured every year.

Madras Bottles Ltd. are to be paid a minimum royalty of ₹ 50,000 per annum, any shortworkings being recouped within a year after the shortfall.

From the following details, prepare Royalty Payable, Royalty Receivable and Shortworkings Accounts in the ledger of Madurai Bottles Ltd.

Tirunelveli Bottles Ltd :		*(No. of Bottles)*	
	Opening Stock	*Sales*	*Closing Stock*
	₹	₹	₹
Year ended 30th June, 2023		12,500	2,500
Year ended 30th June, 2024	2,500	60,000	10,000
Year ended 30th June, 2025	10,000	80,000	5,000
Madurai Bottles Ltd. :			
(Out of own production)			
Year ended 30th June, 2023		40,000	
Year ended 30th June, 2024		60,000	
Year ended 30th June, 2025		1,20,000	

Ans. [Irrecoverable Shortworking Debited to Profit and Loss Account ; 30th June, 2024 ₹ 13,750].

9. (***Where royalties are to be paid subject to deduction of income tax***). Menthol India Ltd., entered into a collaboration agreement with Menthol U.K. Ltd. under which the Indian company is to pay the London Company, commencing with the date of start of production in the Indian factory, a royalty at 1% of sales during each quarter, subject to deduction of income-tax at 30%, so that the remittance in any quarter should not be less than £ 400. Shortworkings are recoupable from out of royalty payable in subsequent quarters within the same calendar year and not beyond.

Following figures of sales are made available to you :

Quarters ended	30-9-2023	31-12-2023	31-5-2024	30-8-2024	30-9-2024	31-12-2024
Sales (₹)	4,00,000	6,00,000	10,00,000	16,00,000	10,00,000	14,00,000

Production commenced on 1st July, 2023. Rate of exchange to be adopted for remittances will be £ 1= ₹ 20 for 2023 payments and £ 1 = ₹ 22 for 2024 payments. Remittance of each quarter's royalty was made within 30 days of the end of the quarter.

Draw Royalty Account, Menthol U.K. Ltd.'s Account and Shortworkings Account in the books of Menthol India Ltd. for the year ended 31st Dec. 2024. **(*CA Inter*)**

Ans. [Irrecoverable Shortworking transferred to Profit and Loss Account : 2023 ₹ 12,858; 2024 ₹ 1,142].

10. (*Sub-lease*) M/s Coal Extractors Ltd. took lease of a coal mine from M/s Coal Mines Ltd. at an annual Dead Rent of ₹ 10,000 subject to a royalty payable @ ₹ 2 per ton extracted. Shortworkings are recoupable one year after shortworkings arise.

Coal Extractors Ltd., sub-leased a part of the mine to Miner's Co-operative at an annual Dead Rent of ₹ 5,000 subject to a royalty payable @ ₹ 1 per ton extracted. The right to recoup shortworkings arise one year after shortworkings take place. However, such right lapses at the end of the year in which shortworkings become recoupable.

Details of extraction are as follows :

Year	2022	2023	2024	2025
Coal Extractors Ltd. (Tons)	2,000	3,000	4,000	5,000
Miner's Co-operative (Tons)	2,000	3,000	4,000	5,000

In 2025 the whole mine was closed for 6 months due to a mine collapse.

Show Royalty Payable Account, Shortworkings Repayable Account, Coal Mines Ltd. Account and Miners Co-operative Account in the books of Coal Extractors Ltd.

Ans. [Shortworkings Repayable A/c transferred to Profit and Loss Account : 2023 ₹ 3,000 ; 2024 ₹ 2,000].

Hint. In 2025 dead rent will be 50% as the mine was closed for 6 months due to a mine collapse.

11. (*Typical—where amount of royalty is to be calculated*) Following balances appeared in the books of a lessee as on January 1, 2022.

Landlord's Account (Cr.) ₹ 28,000.

Shortworkings Account (Dr.) ₹ 6,000 (out of which ₹ 3,000 arose in 2021, Rs 2,000 in 2020 and the rest in 2019)

The Agreement of Royalty provided the following :

(*a*) Minimum Rent ₹ 56,000 p.a.

(*b*) The power to recoup shortworkings within 3 years immediately following the year in which it arises.

(*c*) Payments to the landlord to be made as under :

50% of the amount is payable in the year in which it becomes due and the balance of 50% in the next year.

You are given the following particulars from 2022 to 2025 :

Year	*Payments to Landlord*	*Shortworkings*	*Shortworkings recouped*
	₹	₹	₹
2022	56,000	—	800
2023	58,000	—	5,000
2024	58,000	2,000	—
2025	60,000	—	2,000

You are required to show the Royalty Account and Shortworking Account from 2022 to 2025.

Ans. [Irrecoverable Shortworking transferred to Profit & Loss Account in 2022 = ₹ 200].

12. (*Sub-lease*) Jalal Ltd. took lease of a colliery from Halal Ltd. on 1 April, 2020 with a right to sub-lease the property. Under the terms of the lease, a royalty of ₹ 20 per tonne is payable, rent being ₹ 3,00,000 a year payable annually on 31 March. Jalal Ltd. is entitled to recoup shortworkings out of the excess workings throughout the terms of the lease.

Jalal Ltd. granted a sub-lease of a part of the property to Belal Ltd. from 1 Apri,l 2021 for a royalty of ₹ 25 per tonne merging into a minimum rent of ₹ 2,00,000 per annum payable annually on 31st March. Belal Ltd. is entitled to recoup shortworkings of any year out of the excess workings of the subsequent year.

The output was as follows :

	Jalal Ltd.	*Belal Ltd.*
	Tonnes	*Tonnes*
Year ended 31 March, 2021	8,000	—
Year ended 31 March, 2022	9,000	6,000
Year ended 31 March, 2023	12,000	7,000
Year ended 31 March, 2024	13,000	8,000
Year ended 31 March, 2025	14,000	8,000

Show in the books of Jalal Ltd. :

Royalty Payable Account ; Royalty Receivable Account ; Halal Ltd. (Landlord) Account ; Belal Ltd. Account

13. ***(Sub-lease)*** Nabipur Ltd. owns certain patent rights. It has granted a license to Asoke Ltd. to use such rights on royalty basis. The royalty is payable at Rs 50 per unit produced. Asoke Ltd. has issued a sub-licence to Kaniska Ltd. on the basis of a royalty of ₹ 60 per unit sold. The minimum royalty payable by Kaniska Ltd. is fixed at ₹ 75,000 per annum. Shortworkings can be recouped within one year from the last date of the year in which they occur.

Following particulars are available for the first three years of working :

	Asoke Ltd.		*Kaniska Ltd.*	
Year	*Sales (Units)*	*Closing Stock (Units)*	*Production (Units)*	*Closing Stock (Units)*
1	6,000	1,500	600	300
2	7,500	3,000	3,000	600
3	13,500	4,500	4,500	1,350

You are required to :

(*a*) Prepare in the books of Asoke Ltd. a statement showing analysis of royalties receivable and royalties payable, and

(*b*) show Royalty Receivable Account and Royalty Payable Account in the books of Asoke Ltd.

[**Hint :** Own Production = Sales + Closing Stock – Opening Stock
Sales = Production + Opening Stock – Closing Stock]

CHAPTER 23

Accounting for Leasing

Introduction

In the world of business, acquiring assets like buildings, machinery, vehicles, or equipment is often essential for running day-to-day operations or expanding capacity. But buying these fixed assets outright can be costly and may not always be the smartest financial decision—especially for startups, growing businesses, or companies facing a cash crunch. This is where **leasing** offers a smart and flexible alternative.

Leasing allows a business to use an asset without owning it. Instead of paying a large sum upfront, the business (called the **lessee**) pays periodic rentals to the owner (called the **lessor**) for using the asset over an agreed period. This simple arrangement makes it possible for companies to access expensive assets, conserve cash, and maintain financial flexibility.

Leasing has become a popular financing method around the world—especially for assets that lose value over time, like vehicles or machinery. It helps businesses keep pace with changing technology and market demands without being tied down by long-term ownership or heavy capital investments.

From an accounting perspective, leasing also affects how a company presents its financial position. Earlier, lease obligations were often not shown in the balance sheet (a practice known as **off-balance sheet financing**), but modern accounting standards now require greater transparency. Understanding how leases are classified and recorded is therefore vital for accurate financial reporting.

CONCEPT OF LEASE

Meaning of Lease

A lease is a contractual agreement in which one party (**lessor**) grants the other party (**lessee**) the right to use an asset for a specific period in exchange for periodic payments called **lease rentals**. The ownership of the asset remains with the lessor, but the lessee is entitled to use the asset as per the terms and conditions specified in the lease agreement. A lease allows the lessee to **control and use** the asset without the need to invest large sums of money upfront to purchase it. For the lessor, leasing becomes a way to earn income from assets they own but do not use directly. Leasing is a form of **asset-based financing** where the use of the asset is separated from its ownership.

LEGAL AND ACCOUNTING PERSPECTIVES

Legal Perspective

In India, lease agreements are primarily governed by the following laws:

1. **The Indian Contract Act, 1872** – Governs the formation, validity, and enforceability of lease agreements as contracts between parties.

2. **The Transfer of Property Act, 1882** – Specifically deals with leases of immovable property, defining lease, lessor, lessee, duration, rights, and obligations.
3. **The Indian Stamp Act & Registration Act** – Mandates proper stamping and registration of lease deeds, especially for long-term leases, to ensure legal enforceability.

The **lease deed** or agreement forms the basis of the relationship between the lessor and the lessee and must clearly mention terms such as lease period, rent, renewal options, responsibilities for maintenance, taxes, penalties, and termination conditions.

Accounting Perspective

From an accounting standpoint, lease transactions must be reported in a manner that reflects the *substance over form* – that is, the economic reality rather than merely the legal form. To achieve this, lease accounting in India is governed by specific accounting standards.

1. Indian Accounting Standard (Ind AS) 17 – "Leases" (Applicable for periods before adoption of Ind AS 116)

- **Classification**: Leases are classified into (*a*) **Finance Lease** – where risks and rewards of ownership transfer to the lessee (*b*) **Operating Lease** – where ownership remains with the lessor.
- **Lessee Accounting**: In finance lease- Recognises leased asset and corresponding liability and in operating lease- Recognises lease rentals as an expense on a straight-line basis.
- **Lessor Accounting**: In finance lease- Recognises receivable at the net investment in lease and in operating lease- Keeps the asset in books and recognise rental income.

2. Indian Accounting Standard (Ind AS) 116 – "Leases"(*Replaces Ind AS 17 for periods beginning on or after April 1, 2019*)

- **Lessee Accounting**: Requires lessees to recognise most leases on the **balance sheet**. It recognises a **Right-of-Use (ROU) Asset** and a **Lease Liability** at the present value of future lease payments. Expense is split into **depreciation of ROU asset** and **interest on lease liability**.
- **Lessor Accounting**: Lessor accounting remains largely similar to Ind AS 17. It continues to classify leases as **finance or operating leases**, with recognition and income treatment accordingly.
- **Exemptions**: Lessees may choose not to apply Ind AS 116 for **short-term leases** (less than 12 months) and **low-value leases** (such as small office equipment)

Key Terms in Leasing

Understanding leasing requires familiarity with some technical terms commonly used in lease agreements and accounting. The following definitions, drawn from Indian Accounting Standards and practical applications, will help build a strong conceptual base.

1. **Lessor:** The lessor is the legal owner of the asset who grants the right to use the asset to another party (the lessee) for a specified period in exchange for lease payments.
2. **Lessee:** The lessee is the party who obtains the right to use the asset from the lessor for an agreed period by paying lease rentals.
3. **Non-Cancellable Lease:** A lease is non-cancellable if it can be cancelled only under limited conditions, such as occurrence of a rare event, with the lessor's permission, renewal with the same or similar lease terms, payment of a significant penalty by the lessee. This ensures a strong binding commitment between the parties.
4. **Inception of the Lease:** This is the date when both parties agree to the key terms and conditions of the lease in writing. It marks the beginning of the lease arrangement, even if the actual use of the asset starts later.

5. **Lease Term :** The lease term includes (*a*) The non-cancellable period of the lease, and (*b*) any optional extension periods that are reasonably certain to be exercised by the lessee. It represents the total expected duration for which lease payments are to be made.
6. **Minimum Lease Payments (MLP):** These are the total payments that the lessee is required to make during the lease term, excluding (*a*) Contingent rent (*b*) Taxes, and (*c*) Maintenance and insurance costs (if borne by the lessee). It may also include (*a*) Any guaranteed residual value (by the lessee or a third party) in case of lessee accounting, and (*b*) The residual value guaranteed to the lessor in case of lessor accounting.
7. **Fair Value:** Fair value is the price at which an asset can be exchanged, or a liability settled in an open, unbiased transaction between well-informed parties.
8. **Useful Life:** This is either (*a*) The period during which the asset is expected to be used by the lessee, or (*b*) The total units of output (like machine hours or production units) expected to be derived from the asset.
9. **Residual Value:** This is the expected fair value of the leased asset at the end of the lease term.
10. **Interest Rate Implicit in the Lease:** This is the discount rate at which the present value of minimum lease payments and the unguaranteed residual value equals the fair value of the leased asset at the lease's inception. It is crucial in calculating the asset and liability values in finance leases.
11. **Gross Investment in the Lease:** This refers to the total of (*a*) Minimum lease payments from the lessee, and (*b*) Any unguaranteed residual value expected to accrue to the lessor.
12. **Unearned Finance Income:** This is the difference between the gross investment and its present value. It represents the total interest income the lessor will earn over the lease period.
13. **Net Investment in the Lease :** It is calculated as: **Net Investment** = Gross Investment – Unearned Finance Income This is the actual value of the lease receivable on the lessor's books.
14. **Bargain Option:** An option that allows the lessee to renew the lease or purchase the asset at a price significantly lower than the expected fair market value, making it almost certain the lessee will exercise it.
15. **Estimated Economic Life of the Asset:** This refers to the total time span during which the leased asset is expected to be economically usable, considering the intended purpose of the asset.
16. **Unguaranteed Residual Value:** This is the portion of the residual value of the asset at the end of the lease that is not guaranteed by the lessee or any third party. It represents the lessor's risk.
17. **Contingent Rent:** These are lease payments that vary based on factors such as lessee's sales revenue, asset usage levels, changes in market interest or price indices. Such rents are not fixed and are accounted for separately from minimum lease payments.
18. **Right-of-Use Asset (ROU Asset):** An asset that represents the lessee's right to use a leased asset over the lease term. Recognised along with a lease liability at lease commencement.
19. **Initial Direct Costs:** These are incremental costs directly attributable to negotiating and arranging a lease, such as legal fees or commission. Under **lessor accounting**, these are often capitalised. Under **lessee accounting**, treatment may differ under Ind AS 17 and 116.

Nature and Purpose of Leasing

Leasing is often preferred over outright purchase because it:

(*i*) Reduces the need for **initial capital investment**.

(*ii*) Provides access to **updated technology or equipment**.

(*iii*) Helps businesses maintain **financial flexibility** and liquidity.

(*iv*) Offers **tax advantages** in certain jurisdictions.

(*v*) May improve **debt-equity ratios** and other financial indicators.

Advantages of Leasing

1. **No Ownership Risk.** The lessee is not exposed to the risks of ownership such as asset obsolescence or decline in market value.
2. **Low Initial Investment.** Leasing allows the use of expensive assets without large upfront payments, helping preserve cash.
3. **Flexibility.** Lease agreements can be customised in terms of duration, payment structure, and renewal options.
4. **Tax Benefits.** Lease rentals are often fully deductible as business expenses, reducing taxable income.
5. **Improved Liquidity.** Since the lessee doesn't have to pay the full cost of the asset, more funds remain available for other operations.
6. **Off-Balance Sheet Financing** (under earlier standards like AS 19). Operating leases do not appear as liabilities on the balance sheet, improving the financial ratios of the lessee.
7. **Access to Latest Technology.** Leasing enables periodic replacement of old or obsolete assets, ensuring up-to-date equipment is always in use.
8. **Easy Availability of Assets.** Leasing is often easier to arrange than loans, especially for startups or companies with limited credit history.

Disadvantages of Leasing

1. **No Ownership Rights.** The lessee never becomes the owner and cannot benefit from appreciation in asset value.
2. **Higher Overall Cost.** Total lease payments over time may exceed the cost of buying the asset outright.
3. **Fixed Financial Obligation.** The lessee is required to pay lease rentals throughout the lease period, even if the asset becomes obsolete or is underutilised.
4. **No Capital Gain.** The lessee cannot sell the asset and therefore does not earn any gain from its resale.
5. **Usage Restrictions.** Lease agreements may impose restrictions on asset use, customisation, or subleasing.
6. **Penalties for Early Termination.** Exiting the lease before the agreed term can attract penalties and create legal complications.
7. **Not Suitable for All Assets.** Some specialised or customised assets may not be available on lease.
8. **Impact on Credit Position** (under newer standards like Ind AS 116). Lease liabilities are shown on the balance sheet, which can affect debt ratios and borrowing capacity.

Classification of Leases

A lease is a contractual arrangement where the lessor (owner) permits the lessee (user) to use an asset in return for periodic lease payments over an agreed period. As per Indian Accounting Standards, leases are classified into two broad categories:

1. Operating Lease
2. Finance Lease

1. Operating Lease (*Cancellable Lease*)

An operating lease is a lease that ***does not transfer substantially all the risks and rewards*** associated with ownership of the asset to the lessee. In other words, the lessor continues to retain ownership benefits, including the risks of obsolescence, idle time, and residual value.

Key Characteristics:

(*i*) The lease term is significantly shorter than the useful life of the asset (typically less than 75%).

(*ii*) The lease generally includes a cancellation clause, allowing the lessee to terminate the lease with notice.

(*iii*) The asset remains the property of the lessor, and the lessee does not get the option to own the asset.
(*iv*) Maintenance, insurance, and repairs are usually the responsibility of the lessor.
(*v*) The lease rentals may not fully recover the cost of the asset during the primary lease period.
(*vi*) Risk of obsolescence or damage is borne by the lessor.

2. Finance Lease (Non-Cancellable Lease)

A *finance lease* is a lease that **transfers substantially all the risks and rewards** associated with ownership of the asset to the lessee, even if the legal title may or may not be eventually transferred. In substance, the lessee enjoys the benefits of ownership and bears related risks, such as obsolescence and wear and tear.

Key Characteristics:

(*i*) The lease term covers a *major portion of the useful life* of the asset (typically *75% or more* of the economic life).
(*ii*) The lease is *non-cancellable* by either party, except under rare circumstances.
(*iii*) The lessee generally has the *option to purchase* the asset at the end of the lease period, often at a *bargain price.*
(*iv*) *Risks and rewards* of ownership, including maintenance, insurance, and obsolescence, are borne by the *lessee.*
(*v*) The *present value of minimum lease payments* is substantially equal to or more than the fair value of the leased asset at the inception of the lease.
(*vi*) The lease agreement may include a *bargain renewal* or *purchase option*, indicating intention to retain long-term control over the asset.

Distinction between Operating Lease and Finance Lease

Following are the main distinctions between the two types of leases :

Basis of Difference	Finance Lease	Operating Lease
Ownership	Risks and rewards of ownership are substantially transferred to the lessee.	Risks and rewards remain with the lessor.
Lease Term	Covers a major part of the asset's economic life (typically ≥ 75%).	Lease term is significantly shorter than the economic life of the asset.
Cancellation Clause	Usually, non-cancellable.	Generally cancellable with prior notice.
Option to Purchase	Usually includes a bargain purchase option.	Generally, no option to purchase at the end of the lease term.
Depreciation	Charged by the lessee, as the asset is capitalised in their books.	Charged by the lessor, since the asset remains their property.
Accounting Treatment (Lessee)	Recognises leased asset and liability. Lease payments split into interest & principal.	Treats lease rental as revenue expense in P&L on a straight-line basis.
Accounting Treatment (Lessor)	Derecognises asset and recognises receivable; records interest income.	Retains asset and records lease rental as income; depreciates the asset.
Capitalisation in Books	Asset and liability both are capitalised in the lessee's books.	Neither asset nor liability is capitalised in lessee's books.
Maintenance & Repairs	Usually borne by the lessee.	Usually borne by the lessor.
Residual Risk	Borne by the lessee.	Borne by the lessor.
Examples	Lease of machinery with option to purchase at nominal price.	Short-term vehicle or equipment rental without ownership rights.

ACCOUNTING TREATMENT

Accounting for Finance Lease

(*a*) In the Books of the Lessee

(*i*) At the inception of a finance lease, the lessee shall recognise both a leased asset and a lease liability in the books of account. The amount to be recorded will be the fair value of the leased asset, or, if lower, the present value of the minimum lease payments (MLPs) from the lessee's perspective. To determine the present value of MLPs, the discount rate to be used is the interest rate implicit in the lease, if this can be readily determined. If not, the lessee's incremental borrowing rate should be applied.

(*ii*) It is not appropriate to offset the lease liability against the leased asset in the financial statements. The lease liability should be disclosed separately on the balance sheet—classified as either a current liability or long-term liability, depending on the timing of the payment obligations.

(*iii*) Any initial direct costs incurred by the lessee—such as legal charges, commissions, and documentation fees—related to the acquisition of the finance lease should be capitalised as part of the cost of the leased asset.

(*iv*) Each lease payment made by the lessee must be apportioned between two components (*a*) Finance charge (interest expense), and (*b*) Reduction of the outstanding lease liability. The finance charge is to be recognised in such a way that it results in a constant periodic rate of interest on the remaining balance of the lease liability throughout the lease term.

(*v*) A finance lease results in two types of expenses for the lessee in each accounting period (*a*) Depreciation expense on the leased asset, and (*b*) Finance (interest) expense on the lease liability. The depreciation policy for leased assets should follow the same principles as that applied to similar owned assets. If there is no reasonable certainty that the lessee will gain ownership of the asset by the end of the lease term, the asset should be depreciated over the shorter of the lease term or its useful life.

JOURNAL ENTRIES IN THE BOOKS OF THE LESSEE

Date		*L.F.*	*Dr. (₹)*	*Cr. (₹)*
(*i*)	**For asset taken on Finance Lease at the time of inception of Lease :**			
	Asset under Lease A/c		×××	
	To Lease Liability A/c/Lessor A/c			×××
	(The entry will be passed with an amount equal to fair value of the leased asset or present value of the minimum lease payment, whichever is less)			
(*ii*)	**On Capitalisation of Initial Direct Cost (if any) :**			
	Asset under Lease A/c		×××	
	To Bank A/c			×××
(*iii*)	**On Payment of lease Rental :**			
	Lease Liability A/c/Lessor A/c		×××	
	To Bank A/c			×××
(*iv*)	**For Finance Charge due for the year :**			
	Finance Charge A/c		×××	
	To Lessor A/c			×××

(v)	**On Charging Depreciation on Asset taken on Finance Lease :**			
	Depreciation A/c		×××	
	To Asset under Lease A/c			×××
(vi)	**At the end of the year for Finance Charge and Depreciation :**			
	Profit & Loss/Statement of Profit & Loss A/c		×××	
	To Finance Charge A/c			×××
	To Depreciation on Asset under Lease A/c			×××
(vii)	**For Purchase of the Asset on the Termination of the Lease :**			
	Asset A/c		×××	
	To Bank A/c			×××

(b) In the Books of the Lessor

(i) At the inception of a finance lease, the lessor should record a lease receivable equal to the net investment in the lease. The net investment is the gross investment in the lease (i.e., the total of minimum lease payments from the lessee and any unguaranteed residual value) discounted at the interest rate implicit in the lease.

(ii) The asset given on lease is derecognised from the books of the lessor, and replaced by a lease receivable, reflecting the lessor's right to receive lease payments over time.

(iii) The finance income (i.e., interest income) is recognised over the lease term based on a pattern that reflects a constant periodic rate of return on the net investment in the lease. This ensures that income recognition aligns with the financial reality of the lease arrangement.

(iv) Initial direct costs incurred by the lessor in connection with negotiating and arranging the lease should be either (a) Recognised immediately as an expense, or (b) Allocated over the lease term as part of the net investment in the lease, depending on the accounting policy followed.

(v) The lease receivable should be presented in the balance sheet under financial assets. It should be appropriately classified as current or non-current based on the timing of expected cash flows.

(vi) As the risks and rewards associated with ownership are transferred to the lessee, the lessor does not charge depreciation on the leased asset after the commencement of the lease. The asset is treated as sold under a financing arrangement.

JOURNAL ENTRIES IN THE BOOKS OF LESSOR

Date		*L.F.*	*Cr. (₹)*
(i)	**For Asset given on Finance Lease :**		
	Lease Receivable A/c/Lessee A/c		[With Net Investment]
	To Asset A/c		
(ii)	**For Receipt of Lease Rental :**		
	Bank A/c		[With Actual Lease Rental]
	To Lease Receivable A/c		[With Principal Amount]
	To Finance Income A/c		[With Finance Income]
(iii)	**For Transfer to Profit & Loss A/c**		
	Finance Income/Interest Income A/c		×××
	To Profit & Loss A/c		×××

Notes :

1. **Gross Investment (GI) =** Minimum Lease Payment (MLP) from Lessor's Point of view + Unearned Residual Value.
2. **Net Investment (NI)** = PV of Gross Investment

Or

Gross Investment – Unearned Finance Income

3. **Unearned Finance Income (UFI)** = Gross Investment – Net Investment
4. The discounting rate for calculations is the implicit rate of interest in the Lease.

   Fair Value (PV of MLP + PV of UGRV)

Accounting for Operating Lease

(*a*) In the Books of the Lessee

(*i*) In the case of an operating lease, the lessee does not recognise any leased asset or liability in the balance sheet, as the risks and rewards incidental to ownership remain with the lessor.

(*ii*) Lease rentals paid by the lessee are treated as a revenue expenditure, charged to the Profit and Loss Account on an accrual basis over the lease term. Unless another basis better reflects the pattern of benefit received, the straight-line method is generally used to allocate the lease expense evenly across the lease term.

(*iii*) If lease rentals paid during a period exceed the expense accrued, the excess is shown as Prepaid Lease Rental (an asset). Conversely, if the rentals paid are less than the accrued lease expense, the shortfall is treated as Outstanding Lease Rental (a liability).

(*iv*) The lessee is not responsible for depreciation, as the asset is not capitalised in its books. Likewise, the lessee does not account for any residual value or finance cost under this arrangement.

OPERATING LEASE

JOURNAL ENTRIES IN THE BOOKS OF LESSEE

(*i*)	**On recording of Rent Expenses** Rent Expense A/c To Lessor A/c (To be recorded on uniform basis or straight line basis over the lease term)	}	Amount of Rent Expenses $= \dfrac{\text{Total Expenses}}{\text{Period of Lease}}$	
(*ii*)	**On making payment of Lease Rent** Lessor A/c To Bank A/c		×××	×××
(*iii*)	**On transferring lease rental the end of the year** Profit & Loss/Statement of Profit & Loss A/c To Rent Expenses A/c		×××	×××

(*b*) In the Books of the Lessor

(*i*) The leased asset remains a fixed asset in the books of the lessor. Ownership, along with the associated risks such as obsolescence or idle time, continues to rest with the lessor.

(*ii*) The lessor charges depreciation on the leased asset as per its normal depreciation policy, in accordance with the provisions of applicable accounting standards and company law.

(*iii*) Lease income (i.e., rentals received) is recognised as revenue in the Profit and Loss Account on a systematic and rational basis. If the pattern of earning income is not significantly variable, the straight-line basis is generally considered appropriate for recognising lease income.

(*iv*) Any initial direct costs incurred by the lessor in negotiating and arranging the lease (such as legal fees, broker commissions, etc.) should be expensed in the year in which they are incurred, unless another method is more appropriate under the accounting policy of the entity.

(*v*) The leased asset should be presented as part of Property, Plant, and Equipment (PPE) in the lessor's balance sheet, and lease rental income should be disclosed separately in the income statement.

JOURNAL ENTRIES IN THE BOOKS OF LESSOR

	Particulars		L.F.	Dr. (₹)	Cr. (₹)
(*i*)	**For Recording Lease Rental Income (Due)**				
	Operating Lease Receivable A/c	Dr.		×××	
	To Lease Rental Income A/c				×××
(*ii*)	**For Receipt of Lease Rental Income**				
	Bank A/c	Dr.		×××	
	To Operating Lease Receivable A/c				×××
(*iii*)	**For Charging Depreciation on Leased Asset**				
	Depreciation A/c	Dr.		×××	
	To Leased Asset A/c				×××
(*iv*)	**At the end of Year transfer to Profit & Loss A/c**				
	(*a*) For Rental Income				
	Lease Equalisation A/c*	Dr.		×××	
	Lease Rental Income A/c	Dr.		×××	
	To Profit & Loss A/c				×××
	To Statement of Profit & Loss A/c				×××
	To Lease Equalisation A/c*				×××
	(*b*) For Depreciation				
	Profit & Loss A/c	Dr.		×××	
	Statement of Profit & Loss A/c	Dr.		×××	
	To Depreciation A/c				×××

***Note:** Either of the two will appear in particular year regarding a Leased asset.

ILLUSTRATION 1. Mr. A has taken a car on lease from XYZ Ltd. for a period of 5 years. As per the terms of the agreement, Mr. A has the option to purchase the car at the end of the lease term for ₹ 20,000. It is estimated that the fair market value of the car at the end of 5 years will be ₹ 2,00,000.

Based on the above information:

(*a*) Identify the type of lease in the hands of Mr. A along with justification of the classification. (*b*) State the accounting treatment in the books of the lessee at the inception of the lease. (*c*) Pass the journal entry at the inception assuming the present value of minimum lease payments is ₹ 4,80,000 and the fair value of the car is ₹ 5,00,000.

SOLUTION

(*a*) The lease is classified as a **Finance Lease**. As per AS 19 – *Leases* (*and also **Ind AS 116***), a lease is classified as a finance lease if it transfers substantially all the risks and rewards incidental to ownership of the asset. In this case, Mr. A has the option to purchase the car at a bargain price of ₹ 20,000, while the expected market value at that time is ₹ 2,00,000. Since the option price is significantly lower than the fair market value, it is reasonably certain that Mr. A will exercise the option. Hence, the lease meets the criteria for a finance lease.

(*b*) **Accounting Treatment in the Books of Lessee:** At the inception of the lease, the lessee (Mr. A) should recognise:

- The leased asset and a corresponding lease liability in the books.
- The amount to be recognised is the present value of minimum lease payments, or fair value, whichever is lower.
  Here: Fair value = ₹ 5,00,000 & Present value of MLP = ₹ 4,80,000
  Hence, both asset and liability will be recorded at ₹ 4,80,000.

(*c*) **Journal Entry in the Books of Lessee:**

Leased Car A/c	Dr.	₹ 4,80,000	
To Lease Liability A/c			₹ 4,80,000
(Being leased car recognised as asset and corresponding lease obligation created)			

ILLUSTRATION 2. XYZ Ltd. has taken a property on lease from ABC Ltd. for a period of 32 years. The expected economic life of the property is 40 years. a) Identify the type of leasealong with jusification b) State the appropriate accounting treatment as per AS 19 in the books of the lessee at the inception of the lease.

SOLUTION:

(*a*) The lease should be classified as a **Finance Lease**. According to AS 19 – Leases, a lease is classified as a finance lease if it transfers substantially all the risks and rewards incidental to ownership of the asset to the lessee. One of the indicators of a finance lease is when the lease term covers a major part of the economic life of the asset — typically taken as 75% or more.

Here: Lease Term = 32 years; Economic Life = 40 years; Percentage of lease term to economic life = (32 ÷ 40) ₹ 100 = **80%**

Since the lease term covers **80%** of the economic life of the property, which is greater than the 75% threshold, the lease is classified as a **finance lease**.

(*b*) **Accounting Treatment in the Books of Lessee:** At the inception of a finance lease, the lessee should:

- Recognise the **ieased asset** and a corresponding **lease liability** in the balance sheet.
- The value to be recognised is the **lower of the fair value of the asset** and the **present value of minimum lease payments (MLP).**

Additionally:

- Depreciation on the leased asset should be charged over the **lease term** or **useful life**, whichever is shorter, if ownership is not transferred.
- Lease payments should be apportioned between **finance charge** and **reduction of lease liability** using the effective interest rate method.

ILLUSTRATION 3: On 1st April 2024, **ABC Ltd. (Lessee)** acquired machinery on a finance lease from **XYZ Ltd. (Lessor)** under the following terms:

Fair value of the machinery: ₹ 10,00,000; Lease term: 4 years

Annual lease rental: ₹ 2,89,000, payable at the end of each year; Estimated useful life of the asset: 5 years

Guaranteed residual value by lessee: ₹ 1,00,000

Interest rate implicit in the lease (IRR): 10% p.a.

Present value of minimum lease payments: ₹ 10,00,000

Ownership is transferred to lessee at the end of lease term. Depreciation is charged on straight line basis over useful life

(*a*) Pass necessary journal entries in the books of ABC Ltd. (Lessee) for the first year ended 31st March 2025.

(*b*) Pass journal entries in the books of XYZ Ltd. (Lessor) for the same period.

SOLUTION

In the Books of the Lessee – ABC Ltd.

1. As per AS 19, the lessee should record the leased asset and lease liability at the present value of minimum lease payments, i.e., ₹ 10,00,000.
2. Depreciation on leased asset (for the year ending 31st March 2025). Since ownership is transferred, depreciation is charged over useful life of 5 years:
   Depreciation=₹ 10,00,000 ÷ 5 = ₹ 2,00,000 per annum
3. We must break up the lease rental of ₹ 2,89,000 into interest and principal. Interest for Year 1 = 10% of ₹ 10,00,000 = ₹ 1,00,000 Principal repayment = ₹ 2,89,000 – ₹ 1,00,000 = ₹ 1,89,000

JOURNAL ENTRIES IN ABC LTD.'S BOOKS (LESSEE)

Date	Particulars			Debit (₹)	Credit (₹)
01-04-2024	Machinery A/c	Dr.		10,00,000	
	To Lease Liability A/c				10,00,000
	(Being machinery acquired on finance lease, capitalised at PV of lease payments)				
31-03-2025	Depreciation A/c	Dr.		2,00,000	
	To Machinery A/c				2,00,000
	(Being depreciation charged on machinery for the year				
31-03-2025	Finance Charges A/c	Dr.		1,00,000	
	Lease Liability A/c	Dr.		1,89,000	
	To Bank A/c				2,89,000
	(Being lease rental paid including interest and principal repayment)				
31-03-2025	P&L A/c	Dr.		2,00,000	
	To Depreciation A/c				2,00,000
	(Being depreciation transferred to P&L)				
31-03-2025	P&L A/c	Dr.		1,00,000	
	To Finance Charges A/c				1,00,000
	(Being finance charges transferred to P&L)				

In the Books of the Lessor – XYZ Ltd.

1. Derecognise asset and recognise lease receivable- Since it is a finance lease, the lessor treats it as a sale-type transaction.
2. Interest income and lease receipt for Year 1

Interest income = 10% of ₹ 10,00,000 = ₹ 1,00,000 Principal received = ₹ 1,89,000

JOURNAL ENTRIES IN XYZ LTD.'S BOOKS (LESSOR)

Date	Particulars			Debit (₹)	Credit (₹)
1-04-2024	Lease Receivable A/c	Dr.		10,00,000	
	To Machinery A/c				10,00,000
	(Being machinery derecognised and lease receivable recognised)				
31-03-2025	Bank A/c	Dr.		2,89,000	
	To Lease Receivable A/c				1,89,000
	To Interest Income A/c				1,00,000
	(Being lease rental received and apportioned between interest and principal)				
31-03-2025	Interest Income A/c	Dr.		1,00,000	
	To P&L A/c				1,00,000
	(Being interest income transferred to P&L)				

ILLUSTRATION 4. Annual lease rent = ₹ 40,000 at the end of each year

Lease period = 5 years

Guaranteed residual value = ₹ 14,000.

Fair value at the inception (beginning) of lease = ₹ 1,50,000

Interest rate implicit on lease is 12.6%. The present value factors at 12.6% are 0.89, 0.79, 0.7, 0.622, 0.552 at the end of first, second, third, fourth and fifth year respectively.

Show the Journal entry to record the asset taken on finance lease in the books of the lessee.

(CA IPCE, Nov. 2015)

SOLUTION

In the Books of Lessee

JOURNAL ENTRY

		₹	₹
	Asset A/c Dr. To Lessor (Being recognition of finance lease as an asset and a liability)	1,49,888	1,49,888

Working Note : (1)

Year (1)	*Lease Payments (₹) (2)*	*Discounting Factor (12.6%) (3)*	*Present Value of Lease Payment (₹) (4) = 2 × 3*
1	40,000	0.89	35,600
2	40,000	0.79	31,600
3	40,000	0.70	28,000
4	40,000	0.622	24,880
5	40,000	0.552	22,080
5	14,000 (GRV)	0.552	7,728
			1,49,888

ILLUSTRATION 5. Following particulars are available about the lease :

Lessor's cost of leased computer	₹ 59,000
Fair value of the leased computer at the inception of the lease (1-1-2021)	₹ 60,000

The lease term is four years. The rental is ₹ 35,000; ₹ 16,000; ₹ 8,000 and ₹ 4,500 respectively in these four years, payable in advance every year. The estimated residual value of the computer at the end of the leased term is 5% of the cost of the asset to the lessor. The lessee has the right to continue the lease at the end of the aforesaid lease term at a nominal rent. The relevant statutory WDV depreciation rate is 40%.

(*a*) State whether the lease should be classified as finance lease or an operating lease.

(*b*) Give journal entries for the finance lease in the books of lessee when financing cost transacted was 14%.

(CA—Nov. 2012 Modified)

SOLUTION

(*a*) **CALCULATION OF THE STATUS OF THE LEASE**

Year	*Lease Payment*	*Discount Factor @ 14% p.a.*	*Present Value of Lease Payment (Lease Payment X Discount Factor)*
	₹		₹
0	35,000	1.000	35,000
1	16,000	0.8772 (1.000 ÷ 1.14)	14,035

2	8,000	0.7695 (0.8772 ÷ 1.14)	6,156
3	4,500	0.6750 (0.7695 ÷ 1.14)	3,038
4	3,000 (Residual value to be paid)	0.5921 (0.6750 ÷ 1.14)	1,776
	66,500		60,005

Note : Amount paid in the beginning of year 1 can be taken as zero year. Similarly, amount paid in the beginning of 2nd year can be considered as paid at the end of 1st year and so on.

Since the present value of the lease payments is approximately equal to the fair value (₹ 60,000) of the leased asset, the lease should be classified as finance lease.

Total Finance Charges = Total Lease Payments – Fair Value of Lease

₹ 66,500 – ₹ 60,000 = ₹ 6,500

CALCULATION OF FINANCE CHARGES INCLUDED IN EVERY INSTALMENT

Year	*Fair Value of the lease*	*Finance Charges @ 14% of Outstanding Liability in the Beginning of the year*	*Lease Payment*	*Reduction in Outstanding Liability*	*Outstanding Liability*
	₹	₹	₹	₹	₹
1-1-2021	60,000	—	35,000	35,000	25,000 (60,000 – 35,000)
31-12-2021		3,500 $\left(25,000 \times \frac{14}{100}\right)$	16,000	12,500 (16,000 – 3,500)	12,500 (25,000 – 12,500)
31-12-2022	—	1,750 $\left(12,500 \times \frac{14}{100}\right)$	8,000	6,250 (8,000 – 1,750)	6,250 (12,500 – 6,250)
31-12-2023		875 $\left(6,250 \times \frac{14}{100}\right)$	4,500	3,625 (4,500 – 875)	2,625 (6,250 – 3,625)
31-12-2024		375 (Bal. Figure)	3,000	2,625 (3,000 – 325)	— (2,625 – 2,625)
		6,500			

In the Books of the Lessee
JOURNAL ENTRIES

Date		*L.F.*	*Dr.*	*Cr.*
			₹	₹
1-1-2021	Leased Computer A/c Dr. To Lessor's A/c (Being fair value of the computer purchased on lease recorded)		60,000	60,000
1-1-2021	Lessor's A/c Dr. To Bank A/c (Being payment of first instalment)		35,000	35,000

Date	Particulars		Dr. (₹)	Cr. (₹)
31-12-2021	Finance Charges A/c	Dr.	3,500	
	To Lessor's A/c			3,500
	(Being finance charges due)			
31-12-2021	Depreciation A/c	Dr.	24,000	
	To Leased Computer A/c			24,000
	(Being 40% depreciation on the fair value of the computer : $\frac{40}{100} \times$ ₹ 60,000)			
31-12-2021	Profit & Loss A/c	Dr.	27,500	
	To Finance Charges A/c			3,500
	To Depreciation A/c			24,000
	(Being transfer of finance charges and depreciation to Profit & Loss A/c			
1-1-2022	Lessor's A/c	Dr.	16,000	
	To Bank A/c			16,000
	(Being payment of second instalment in advance)			
31-12-2022	Finance Charges A/c	Dr.	1,750	
	To Lessor's A/c			1,750
	(Being finance charges due)			
	Depreciation A/c	Dr.	14,400	
	To Leased Computer A/c			14,400
	(Being depreciation @ 40% on written down value of ₹ 36,000)			
	Profit & Loss A/c	Dr.	16,150	
	To Depreciation A/c			14,400
	To Finance Charges A/c			1,750
	(Being depreciation and finance charges transferred to Profit & Loss A/c)			
1-1-2023	Lessor's A/c	Dr.	8,000	
	To Bank A/c			8,000
	(Being payment of third instalment in advance)			
31-12-2023	Finance Charges A/c	Dr.	875	
	To Lessor's A/c			875
	(Being finance charges due)			
31-12-2023	Depreciation A/c	Dr.	8,640	
	To Leased Computer A/c			8,640
	(Being depreciation @ 40% on written down value of ₹ 21,600)			
31-12-2023	Profit & Loss A/c	Dr.	9,515	
	To Depreciation A/c			8,640
	To Finance Charges			875
	(Being finance charges and depreciation transferred to Profit & Loss A/c)			
1-1-2024	Lessor's A/c	Dr.	4,500	
	To Bank A/c			4,500
	(Being payment of fourth instalment in advance)			

31-12-2024	Finance Charges A/c	Dr.	375	
	To Lessor's A/c			375
	(Being finance charges due)			
31-12-2024	Lessor's A/c	Dr.	3,000	
	To Bank A/c			3,000
	(Being residual value of the leased computer paid)			
31-12-2024	Depreciation A/c	Dr.	5,184	
	To Lease Computer A/c			5,184
	(Being depreciation @ 40% on written down value of ₹ 12,960)			
31-12-2024	Profit & Loss A/c	Dr.	5,559	
	To Depreciation A/c			5,184
	To Finance Charges A/c			375
	(Being transfer of depreciation and finance charges to Profit & Loss A/c)			

ILLUSTRATION 6. A & Co. acquired machinery on lease from B and Co. on April 1, 2025 on the following terms :

Lease Term—5 years; Fair value of machinery—₹ 45,00,000; Useful life—15 years.

Annual lease rental payable at ₹ 4,00,000, ₹ 3,00,000, ₹ 2,00,000, ₹ 60,000 and ₹ 40,000.

Present value are 0.8696, 0.7561, 0.6575, 0.5718, and 0.4972 for the first, second, third, fourth and firth year respectively at 15% IRR.

Depreciation: 10% p.a. on straight line basis.

(*i*) Whether the lease an Operating lease or Finance lease giving reasons.

(*ii*) How would this lease be accounted for in the books of the lessor and lessee ?

Pass journal entries for this purpose for first year in the books of both lessor and the lessee, assuming that accounts are closed on 31st March every year.

SOLUTION

(*i*) The given lease is operating lease due to the following reasons :

Present Value of minimum lease payments is substantially lower than the fair value of the asset as shown below :

Present Value of MLP:

= (₹ 4,00,000 × 0.8696) + (₹ 3,00,000 × 0.7561) + (₹ 2,00,000 × 0.6575) + (₹ 60,000 × 0.5718) + (₹ 40,000 × 0.4972)

= ₹ 3,47,840 + 2,26,830 + 1,31,500 + 34,308 + 19,900 = ₹ 7,60,378

Fair value of Machinery = ₹ 45,00,000

ILLUSTRATION 7. R Limited (the Lessee) acquired a machinery on lease from S Limited (the Lessor) on January 1, 2022. The lease term covers the entire economic life of the machinery, *i.e.,* 3 years. The fair value of the machinery on January 1, 2022 is ₹ 3,50,000. The lease agreement requires the lessee to pay an amount of ₹ 1,50,000 per year beginning December 31, 2022. The lessee has guaranteed a residual value of ₹ 11,400 on December 31, 2024 to the lessor. The lessor, however, estimates that the machinery will have a salvage value of only ₹ 10,000 on December 31, 2024. The implicit rate of interest is 15% p.a. Compute the value of machinery to be recognised by the lessee and also the finance charges every year on the basis of Ind. AS–17. P.V. Factor of 15% in three years is 2.283.

SOLUTION

The value of machinery to be recognised by the lessee would be the fair value of machinery ₹ 3,50,000.

CALCULATION OF FINANCE CHARGES

Year		Finance Charge	Lease Payment	Reduction in Outstanding Liability	Outstanding Liability
		₹	₹	₹	₹
Year 1	Jan. 1	—	—	—	3,50,000
	Dec. 31	52,500	1,50,000	97,500	2,52,500
		(15% of 3,50,000)		(1,50,000 – 52,500)	(3,50,000 – 97,500)
Year 2	Dec. 31	37,875	1,50,000	1,12,125	1,40,375
		(15% of 2,52,500)		(1,50,000 – 37,875)	(2,52,500 – 1,12,125)
Year 3	Dec. 31	21,056	1,50,000	1,28,944	11,431 (1)
		(15% of 1,40,375)		(1,50,000 – 21,056)	(1,40,375 – 1,28,944)

(1) The difference between this figure (₹ 11,431) and guaranteed residual value of ₹ 11,400 is due to approximation in calculating the interest rate implicit in the lease.

ILLUSTRATION 8. An equipment is leased for 3 years and its useful life is 5 years. Both the cost and the fair value of the equipment are ₹ 3,00,000. The amount will be paid in 3 instalments and at the termination of lease lessor will get back the equipment. The unguaranteed residual value at the end of 3 years is ₹ 40,000. The (internal rate of return) IRR of the investment is 10%. The present value of annuity factor of ₹ 1 due at the end of 3rd year at 10% IRR is 2.4868. The present value of ₹ 1 due at end of third year at 10% rate of interest is 0.7513.

(*i*) State with reason whether the lease constitutes finance lease.

(*ii*) Calculate unearned finance income.

SOLUTION

(*i*) Residual value at the end of 3rd year = ₹ 40,000 and P/V factor for ₹ 1 at the end of 3rd year = 0.7513

Therefore, present value of residual value (₹ 40,000 × 0.7513) = ₹ 30,052.

Present Value of minimum lease payments = ₹ 30,00,000 – ₹ 30,052 = ₹ 2,69,948

Proportion of minimum lease payments to fair value is 89.58% $\left(i.e.\ \frac{₹\ 2,69,948}{₹\ 3,00,000}\right)$.

It is substantial portion of fair value of ₹ 3,00,000, therefore, lease constitutes a finance lease. Moreover, lease period of three years covers major part of the lease of the asset (5 years). Hence it is a finance lease.

(*ii*) Calculation of Unearned Finance Income

	₹
Annual lease payment to the lessor $\left(\frac{₹\ 2,69,948}{2.4868}\right)$	1,08,552
Gross investment in lease for 3 years (₹ 1,08,552 × 3)	3,25,656
Add : Unguaranteed residual value	40,000
Gross investment in lease	3,65,656
Less : Cost of the investment	3,00,000
Unearned Finance Income	65,656

Note : Annual lease payment has been calculated on the basis that the present value of lease payments plus residual value is equal to the fair value *i.e.* cost of the asset.

ILLUSTRATION 9. R Ltd. (the lessee) acquired machinery on lease from S Ltd. (the lessor) on January 1, 2022. The lease term covers the entire economic life of the machinery, *i.e.* 3 years. The fair value of the machinery on January 1, 2022 is ₹ 3,50,000. The lease agreement requires the lessee to pay an amount of ₹ 1,50,000 per year beginning December 31, 2022. The lessee has guaranteed a residual value of ₹ 11,400 on December 31, 2024 to the lessor. The lessor, however, estimates that the machinery will have a salvage value of only ₹ 10,000 on December 31, 2024. The implicit rate of interest is 15% p.a. Compute the value of machinery to be recognised by the lessee and also the finance charges every year on the basis of AS–19. Present value factors at 15% for 3 years are :

1st year—0.8695 ; 2nd year—0.7561 ; Third year—0.6575.

SOLUTION

At the inception of a finance lease, the lessee should recognise the lease as an asset and a liability. Such recognition should be at an amount equal to the fair value of the leased asset at the inception of the lease. However, if the fair value of the leased asset exceeds the present value of the minimum lease payments from the standpoint of the lessee, the amount recorded as an asset and a liability should be the present value of the minimum lease payments from the standpoint of the lessee.

In the present case fair value of the machinery is ₹ 3,50,000 and the net present value of minimum lease payments from the standpoint of the lessee is ₹ 3,49,961 as calculated below :

	Lease Payment	*P/V Factor*	*Present Value*
	₹	₹	₹
Year 1	1,50,000	0.8695	1,30,425
Year 2	1,50,000	0.7561	1,13,415
Year 3	1,50,000	0.6575	98,625
Year 3	11,400	0.6575	7,496
	(Guaranteed Residual Value)		3,49,961

As the present value of minimum lease payments is less than the fair value of the leased asset, the machinery should be recognised by the lessee at ₹ 3,49,961.

ILLUSTRATION 10. B&P Ltd. availed a lease from N&L Ltd. the conditions of the lease terms are as under :

(*i*) Lease period is 3 years, in the beginning of the year 2022, for equipment costing ₹ 10,00,000 and has an expected useful life of 5 years.

(*ii*) The Fair market value is also ₹ 10,00,000.

(*iii*) The property reverts back to the lessor on termination of the lease.

(*iv*) The unguaranteed residual value is estimated at ₹ 1,00,000 at the end of the year 2024.

(*v*) 3 equal annual payments are made at the end of each year.

Consider IRR = 10%.

The present value of ₹ 1 due at the end of 3rd year at 10% rate of interest is ₹ 0.7513.

The present value of annuity of ₹ 1 due at the end of 3rd year at 10% IRR is ₹ 2.4868.

(*a*) State whether the lease constitute finance lease and (*b*) also calculate unearned Finance income.

(*CA IPCE*)

SOLUTION

(*a*) **COMPUTATION OF ANNUAL LEASE PAYMENT TO THE LESSOR**

	₹
Cost of Equipment	10,00,000
Unguaranteed Residual Value	1,00,000

Present Value of Residual Value after third year @ 10% (₹ 1,00,000 × 0.7513)	75,130
Fair Value to be recovered from lease payments (₹ 10,00,000 – ₹ 75,130)	9,24,870
Present Value of Annuity for three years is 2.4868	
Annual Lease Payment = ₹ 9,24,870/2.4868	3,71,911.70

The present value of lease payment *i.e.*, ₹ 9,24,870 equal 92.48% of the fair market value *i.e.*, 10,00,000. As the present value of minimum lease payments substantially covers the initial fair value of the leased asset and lease term (*i.e.* 3 years) covers the major part of the life of asset (*i.e.* 5 years). Therefore, it constitutes a *finance lease*.

(*b*) **COMPUTATION OF UNEARNED FINANCE INCOME**

	₹
Total Lease Payments (₹ 3,71,911.70 × 3)	11,15,735
Add : Unguaranteed Residual Value	1,00,000
Gross Investment in the Lease	1,215,735
Less : Present Value of Investment (Lease Payments and Residual Value) (₹ 75,130 + ₹ 9,24,870)	(10,00,000)
Unearned Finance Income	2,15,735

ILLUSTRATION 11. A Ltd. leased a machinery to B Ltd. on the following terms :

	(*₹ in lakhs*)
Fair value of the machinery	20
Lease term	5 years
Lease Rental per annum	5
Guaranteed residual value	1
Expected residual value	2
Internal Rate of Return	15%

Depreciation is provided on straight line method @ 10% per annum. Ascertain unearned financial income and necessary entries may be passed in the books of the lessee in the first year.

SOLUTION

CALCULATION OF MINIMUM LEASE PAYMENTS AND UNGUARANTEED RESIDUAL VALUE

Year	Minimum Lease Payments	Discount Factor at 15% (Noted from P/V Tables)	Present Value
	₹		₹
1	5,00,000	0.8696	4,34,800
2	5,00,000	0.7561	3,78,050
3	5,00,000	0.6575	3,28,750
4	5,00,000	0.5718	2,85,900
5	5,00,000	0.4972	2,48,600
5	1,00,000 (Guaranteed Residual Value)	0.4972	49,720
	Present Value of Lease Payments for Lessee		17,25,820
5	1,00,000 Unguaranteed Residual Value)	0.4972	49,720
	Present Value of Lease Payments for Lessor		17,75,540

CALCULATION OF UNEARNED FINANCE INCOME

	₹
Minimum lease payments for 5 years @ ₹ 5,00,000 per annum	25,00,000
Guaranteed residual value	1,00,000
Unguaranteed residual value	1,00,000
Gross Investment	27,00,000
Less : Present value of lease payments for lessor as calculated above	17,75,540
Unearned Finance Income	9,24,460

JOURNAL ENTRIES IN THE BOOKS OF B LTD.

			₹	₹
At the inception of lease				
Machinery Account	Dr.		17,25,820	
To A Ltd.'s Account				17,25,820
(Being lease of machinery recorded at present value)				
At the end of the first year of lease				
Finance Charges Account	Dr.		2,58,873	
To A Ltd.'s Account				2,58,873
(Being 15% finance charges on ₹ 17,25,820 for first year due)				
A Ltd.'s Account	Dr.		5,00,000	
To Bank Account				5,00,000
(Being lease rent paid to the lessor for first year)				
Depreciation Account	Dr.		1,72,582	
To Machinery Account				1,72,582
(Being depreciation provided @ 10% on ₹ 17,25,820)				
Profit & Loss Account	Dr.		4,31,455	
To Finance Charges Account				2,58,873
To Depreciation Account				1,72,582
(Being depreciation and finance charges transferred to Profit & Loss Account)				

ILLUSTRATION. 12. On 1st April 2024, **Lessor Ltd.** leased out machinery to **Lessee Ltd.** under an operating lease agreement for a period of **3 years**. The annual lease rent is ₹ 1,50,000, payable at the end of each financial year. The expected useful life of the machinery is 10 years. The ownership of the asset remains with Lessor Ltd., and the lease is cancellable. Assume the depreciation is charged @10% per annum on the cost of machinery of ₹ 10,00,000.

Pass journal entries in the books of (*a*) Lessee Ltd. (*b*) Lessor Ltd. for the **first year ending 31st March 2025**.

SOLUTION

(*a*) In the Books of Lessee Ltd. Since it is an operating lease, the lease rent is treated as a revenue expense and recorded on an accrual basis.

JOURNAL ENTRY

Date	*Particulars*		*L.F.*	*Debit (₹)*	*Credit (₹)*
31-Mar-2025	Lease Rent A/c	Dr.		1,50,000	
	To Bank A/c				1,50,000
	(Being lease rent paid for the year)				

(*b*) In the Books of Lessor Ltd. Lessor continues to treat the machinery as a **fixed asset** and charges **depreciation** as per its normal policy. Lease rent received is recognised as **revenue income**.

JOURNAL ENTRIES

Date	*Particulars*		*L.F.*	*Debit (₹)*	*Credit (₹)*
31-Mar-2025	Bank A/c	Dr.		1,50,000	
	To Lease Rent Income A/c				1,50,000
	(Being lease rent received for the year)				
31-Mar-2025	Depreciation A/c	Dr.		1,00,000	
	To Machinery A/c				1,00,000
	(Being depreciation charged @10% on ₹ 10,00,000)				
31-Mar-2025	Profit and Loss A/c	Dr.		1,00,000	
	To Depreciation A/c				1,00,000
	(Being depreciation transferred to P&L)				
31-Mar-2025	Lease Rent Income A/c	Dr.		1,50,000	
	To Profit and Loss A/c				1,50,000
	(Being lease rent income transferred to P&L)				

DISCLOSURE

Disclosures in the Financial Statements

Disclosure should be made of the amount of assets that are the subject of finance leases at each Balance Sheet date. Liabilities, differentiating between the current and long-term portions, should also be disclosed.

Commitments for minimum lease payments under finance leases and under non-cancellable operating leases with a term of more than one year should be disclosed in summary form giving the amounts and periods in which the payments will become due.

Disclosure should be made of significant financing restrictions, renewal or purchase options, contingent rentals and other contingencies arising from leases.

Disclosure should be made of the basis used for allocating income so as to produce a constant periodic rate of return, indicating whether the return relates to the net investment outstanding or the net cash investment outstanding in the lease. If more than one basis is used, the bases should be disclosed.

When a significant part of the lessor's business comprises operating leases, the lessor should disclose the amount of assets by each major class of asset together with the related accumulated depreciation at each balance sheet date.

Apart from the disclosures recommended in the above paragraphs, the lessor should disclose the accounting policies followed with regard to accounting for income under finance lease, valuation of assets given on lease and charge for depreciation.

Sale and Lease Back Transactions

A sale and lease back transaction includes the sale of an asset by the vendor and leasing of the same asset back to the vendor. The seller gets the right to use the same asset as also increasing its liquidity position. It is like eating the cake and having it too. The benefit of depreciation is available to the buyer.

Accounting Treatment :

1. **If lease back is financial lease**—Any profit or loss of sale proceeds over the carrying amount should not be immediately recognized as profit or loss in the financial statement of seller lessee.

It should be deferred and amortised over lease term in proportion to the depreciation of leased assets.

2. **If lease back is operating lease**—Any profit or loss is recognized immediately when sale price is equal to fair value.

If sale price 'below'" fair value :

Profit—recognize profit immediately.

Loss—recognize loss immediately if not compensated by future lease payments.

Loss—defer and amortise loss if loss is compensated by future lease payments.

ILLUSTRATION 13. Global Ltd. has initiated a lease for three years in respect of an equipment costing ₹ 1,50,000 with expected useful life of 4 years. The asset would revert to Global Limited under the lease agreement. The other information available in respect of lease agreement is :

(*i*) The unguaranted residual value of the equipment after the expiry of the lease term is estimated at ₹ 20,000.

(*ii*) The implicit rate of interest is 10%.

(*iii*) The annual payments (to be made at the end of each accounting year) have been determined in such a way that the present value of the lease payment plus the residual value is equal to the cost of asset.

Ascertain in the hands of Global Ltd. (*i*) The annual lease payment. (*ii*) The unearned finance income (*iii*) The segregation of finance income, and also (*iv*) Show how necessary items will appear in its Profit and Loss Account and Balance Sheet for the various years. **(*CA Final*)**

SOLUTION

(*i*) *Calculation of Annual Lease Payment**	₹
Cost of Equipment	1,50,000
Unguaranteed Residual Value	20,000
P.V. of residual value for 3 years @ 10% (₹ 20,000 × 0.751)	15,020
Fair value to be recovered from Lease Payment (₹ 1,50,000 – ₹ 15,020)	1,34,980
P.V. Factor for 3 years @ 10%	2.487
Annual Lease Payment (₹ 1,34,980 ÷ PV Factor for 3 years @ 10%, *i.e.,* 2.487)	54,275

(*ii*) *Unearned Financial Income*	₹
Total Lease Payments (₹ 54,275 × 3)	1,62,825
Add : Residual Value	20,000
Gross Investments	1,82,825
Less : Present Value of Investments (₹ 1,34,980 + ₹ 15,020)	1,50,000
Unearned Financial Income	32,825

(*iii*) Segregation of Finance Income

Year	*Lease Rental*	*Finance Charges @ 10% on Outstanding amount of the year*	*Repayment*	*Outstanding Amount*
	₹	₹	₹	₹
0	—	—	—	1,50,000
I	54,275	15,000	39,275	1,10,725
II	54,275	11,073	43,202	67,523
III	74,275**	6,752	67,523	—
	1,82,825	32,825	1,50,000	

**₹ 74,275 includes unguaranted residual value of equipment amounting ₹ 20,000.

(*iv*) *Profit & Loss Amount (Relevant Extracts)*

Credit Side		₹
I Year	By Finance Income	15,000
II Year	By Finance Income	11,073
III Year	By Finance Income	6,752

BALANCE SHEET (Relevant Extracts)

Assets Side		₹	₹
I Year	Lease Amouunt Receivable	1,50,000	
	Less : Amount Received	39,275	
			110,725
II Year	Lease Amouunt Receivable	1,10,725	
	Less : Received	43,202	
			67,523
III Year	Lease Amount Receivable	67,523	
	Less : Amount received	47,523	
		20,000	
	Residual Value	20,000	
			Nil

Notes to Balance Sheet

		₹
Year I	Minimum Lease Payments (₹ 54,275 + ₹ 54,275)	1,08,550
	Residual Value	20,000
	Unearned Finance Income	1,28,550
	Less : Unearned Finance Income (₹ 11,073 + ₹ 6,752)	17,825
	Receivable	1,10,725
Classification :		₹
	Not later than 1 Year	43,202
	Later than 1 year but not more than 5 years	67,523
	Total	1,10,725
Year II	Minimum Lease Payments	54,275
	Add : Residual Value (Estimated)	20,000
		74275
	Unearned Finance Income	6,752
	Lease Receivable (not later than one year)	67,523
Year III	Lease Receivables (including residual value)	67,523
	Less : Amount received	67,523
		Nil

QUESTIONS

SHORT/LONG ANSWER TYPE

1. Why leasing is becoming more popular these days as a method of finance?
2. Define leasing. Explain the different types of leases.
3. State concisely the difference between the operating and financing lease giving an example of each.

OR

Distinguish between operating and financial lease. What are the situations when each type of such leasing arrangement is suitable for the lessee ?

OR

Explain operating lease or financial lease. ***(B.Com. Hons. Delhi)***

Distinguish between operating and financial lease. What are the situations when each type of such leasing arrangement is suitable for the lessee ?

4. Discuss the advantages and disadvantages of leasing.
5. "Leasing transaction accelerates industrial growth." Comment.
6. Write notes on :

   (*i*) Lease term (*ii*) Bargain option (*iii*) Minimum lease payment (*iv*) Interest rate implicit in the lease (*v*) Leasing or Buying decisions.
7. Mention the guidelines to treat a lease in the financial statements of the lessor and the lessee.
8. What is Leasing ? What is its need ? Explain the accounting practices relating to lease in the context of Indian Companies.
9. Bring out the nature of leasing. How would you evaluate it in relation to other sources of finance ?
10. What is Leasing ? What are its types ? Give the situations in which each is suitable.
11. What is lease financing ? Distinguish between financial lease and operating lease. Evaluate leasing decisions in relation to buying decisions.
12. Define the term Finance Lease. State any three situations when a lease would be classified as finance lease. ***(CA IPCE Nov. 2012)***
13. Explain the procedure for accounting for leases. Is it same for all types of leases ?
14. Suraj Ltd. wishes to obtain a machine costing ₹ 30 lakhs by way of lease. The effective life of the machine is 14 years, but the company requires it only for the first 5 years. It enters into an agreement with Ashok Ltd. for a lease rental for ₹ 3 lakhs p.a. payable in arrears and the implicit rate of interest is 15%. The chief accountant of Suraj Ltd. is not sure about the treatment of these lease rentals and seeks your advice.

Ans. [Present value of minimum lease payments for 5 years at 15% P/V factor is ₹ 10.08 lakhs which is much less than the fair value of ₹ 30 lakhs. Therefore, it is a case of operating lease and lease rental paid every year is taken as an expense in the statement of profit and loss]

15. Compute the Minimum Lease Payment in the following independent situations where A and B are the lessor and lessee respectively :
   (*i*) Monthly Lease Rent = ₹ 25,000, Lease term 32 months, C, a third party, provides a guarantee on behalf of B to A, that ₹ 55,000 will be paid as residual value.
   (*ii*) Monthly Lease Rent = ₹ 15,000 for 48 months, together with 2.5% of the sales revenue per annum. B guarantees to pay A ₹ 10,000 as residual value of the asset.

Ans. [(*i*) ₹ 8,55,000; (*ii*) ₹ 7,30,000]

16. Classify the following into either operating lease or financial lease based on the information provided. Give suitable explanation for your answer :

(*i*) Economic life of the asset is 10 years, lease term is 9 years, but the asset is not acquired at the end of lease term.

(*ii*) Lease payments to be recognised as an expense in the statement of Profit and Loss A/c of a lessee.

(*iii*) Economic life of the asset is 5 years, lease term is 2 years, but the asset is of special nature and has been procured only for the use of the lessee.

Depreciation on the leased asset is charged by the lessor in his books.

Ans. [Finance Lease (*i*) & (*iii*) ; Operating Lease (*ii*)]

PRACTICAL PROBLEMS

1. The following particulars are available about Lease.

Lessor's cost of the leased Asset ₹ 1,18,000

Fair Value of the lease asset at the inception of the lease (1-1-25) ₹1,20,000

The lease term is four years. The rental value is ₹ 70,000, ₹ 32,000, ₹ 16,000, ₹ 9,000.

Respectively in these four years payable in advance every year .The estimated residual value the asset at the end of the leased period is 55 of the cost of the Asset to the lessor. The lessee has the right to continue to lease at the end of the aforesaid lease term at A nominal rent. The relevant statutory written down value depreciation rate of 40%.

1. Prepare the status of lease and calculate the Finance charges included in every instalment.
2. Show the Journal Entries in the books of and lessor when financing cost was 14%.

Ans. [(*i*) Finance lease, Finance Charges ₹ 13,000]

2. LTK Ltd (Lesse) acquired a generator on lease from PK Electronics Ltd(Lessor) on January1, 2022.The lease term covers 3 years(estimated Useful life of Generator) The fair value of the Generator on January 1, 2021 is ₹ 1,75,000. According to the lease agreement, lessee has to pay an amount of Rs 75,000 per year in the beginning December, 2021. The lessee has guaranteed a residual value of ₹ 5,700 on December 31, 2024 to the lessor The lessor ,however estimates that the salvage value of the Generator will be only 5,000on December 2024. The implicit rate of interest is 15% p.a. Compute the value of generator to be recognized by the lesee and also the finance charges every year on the basis of AS19 P.V.Factor of 15% in three years is 2.283

Ans. [Fair Value of generator ₹ 1,75,000. Finance charges ₹ 5,716]

3. From the information given below, determine whether the lease is Financial or operating. Lessor's cost of the based asset ₹ 1,60,000 fair value of the based Asset on 1.1.2025. ₹ 1,60,000 (Inceaption of the lease) The lease is for 4 years and the rentals, which have to be paid in the advance at the beginning of each year, are ₹ 80,000, ₹ 50,000, ₹ 30,000 and ₹ 20,000 respectively. The estimated residual value of the based asset at the end of the lease term is 5% of the cost of the leaser. The lesser expects a return of 18 % on Investment.

Ans. [Finance Lease]

4. Lessee Ltd. took a machine on lease from Lessor Ltd., the fair value being ₹ 7,00,000. The economic life of the machine as well as the lease term is 3 years. At the end of each year Lessee Ltd., pays ₹ 3,00,000. Guaranteed Residual Value (GRV) is ₹ 22,000 on expiry of the lease. Implicit Rate of Return (IRR) is 15% p.a., and present value factors at 15% are 0.869, 0.756 and 0.657 at the end of first, second and third years respectively.

Calculate the value of machine to be considered by Lessee Ltd. and the interest (Finance charges) in each year. ***(CA—Final, Nov. 2010 Modified)***

Ans. [Value of Machine ₹ 6,99,054; Interest : 1st year ₹ 1,04,858, 2nd year ₹ 75,587 and 3rd year ₹ 41,925.]

5. R Ltd. has taken the assets on lease from S Ltd. Following information is given below :

Lease term	= 4 years
Fair value at inception of lease	= ₹ 32,00,000
Lease Rent	= ₹ 10,00,000 p.a. at the end of year
Guaranteed Residual Value	= ₹ 2,00,000
Expected Residual Value	= ₹ 6,00,000
Implicit Interest Rate	= 14.97%

Do the accounting in the books of Lessee and the Lessor if the lease rent is ₹ 10,00,000 p.a. at the end of year.

6. S. Square Private Limited has taken machinery on lease from S.K. Ltd. The information is as under :

Lease term = 4 years

Fair value at inception of lease = ₹ 20,00,000

Lease Rent = ₹ 6,25,000 p.a. at the end of year

Guaranteed residual value = ₹ 1,25,000

Expected residual value = ₹ 3,75,000

Implicit interest rate = 15%

Discounted rates for 1st year, 2nd year, 3rd year and 4th year are 0.8696, 0.7561, 0.6575 and 0.5718 respectively.

Calculate the value of the lease liability. ***(Adapted CA Final Nov. 2010)***

Ans. [Present value of minimum lease payments ₹ 18,55,850 is less than fair value at the inception of lease *i.e.* ₹ 20,00,000, therefore the lease liability should be recognised at ₹ 18,55,850].

CHAPTER

24

Hire Purchase System and Instalment Purchase System

Hire Purchase System

There are different ways by which goods can be sold *i.e.* possession as well as ownership of goods will be passed from the seller to the purchaser. Goods can be sold **for cash,** *i.e.,* where ownership and possession is immediately passed from the seller to the purchaser and purchaser also makes the payment in cash at the time of taking the delivery of goods. Goods can be sold **on credit** also where ownership and possession of goods passes immediately from the seller to the buyer but the payment is deferred, *i.e.,* made after sometimes. Another way of selling goods is either on hire purchase or instalment purchase system system.

Under **hire purchase system**, the buyer acquires the possession of the goods immediately and agrees to pay the total hire purchase price in instalments, each instalment is treated as a hire charge until the payment of the last instalment when ownership of goods passes from the seller to the buyer. In case the buyer makes any default in the payment of any instalment, the seller will have a right to repossess these goods from the buyer and forfeit the amount already received treating it as a hire charge. But if the buyer is paying all the instalments on the due dates, the seller has no right to repossess these goods from the buyer. Thus, this system is advantageous both to the buyer and the seller. The buyer gets the facility of paying the total amount in instalments and the seller is able to sell more goods under this system receiving the price in instalments with the added security to repossess the goods in case the buyer makes any default in the payment of any instalment.

Features of Hire Purchase System

Following are the main features of the hire purchase system :

***(i)* Agreement.** There is an agreement between the seller and the purchaser.

***(ii)* Possession.** The possession of goods immediately passes from the seller to the buyer on signing the agreement.

***(iii)* Down Payment.** The hire purchaser generally pays an amount on signing the agreement or at the time of delivery of goods.

***(iv)* Instalments.** The buyer will make payment in instalments over a period of time.

***(v)* Ownership.** The ownership of the goods will remain with the seller and passes to the buyer on payment of the last instalment.

***(vi)* Constituents of Hire Purchase Instalment.** Each instalment consists partly of a financial charge (interest) and partly of capital payment (cash price) and is treated as hire charge till the last instalment is paid.

(*vii*) Option to Return the Goods. The buyer has an option to return the goods to the seller and can terminate the agreement if he does not want to pay the rest of the instalments.

(*viii*) Repossession. If there is any default in payment of any instalment, the seller has a right to repossess the goods sold on hire purchase and forfeit the amount already received either as down payment or in instalments.

We know from our common experience that if the goods are purchased for cash, the price will be less than if the goods are purchased under hire purchase system. This is because of the fact that hire purchase price includes some element of interest (*i.e.,* financing charges) besides the cash price (*i.e.,* H.P. Price = Cash Price + Interest). It is essential to split the total hire purchase price into two parts, *i.e.,* (*i*) payment towards cash price to be treated as capital expenditure for the purchase of an asset, and (*ii*) interest to be charged to profit and loss account treating it as a revenue expense.

HIRE PURCHASE AGREEMENT

Hire Purchase agreement means an agreement under which goods are let on hire and under which the hirer has an option to buy the goods as per terms of the agreement and includes the following stipulations :

(*i*) Possession of goods is delivered by the owner thereof to a person on condition that such person pays the agreed amount in periodical instalments ;

(*ii*) The property in the goods is to be transferred to the hirer on payment of the last instalments ; and

(*iii*) Such a person has a right to terminate the agreement at any time before the property is so transferred.

Contents of the Hire Purchase Agreement [Sec. 3 and 4]

The Hire Purchase Agreement must be in writing and signed by the both Hire Vendor & Hire Purchaser. A surety, if any, must sign the agreement. The contents of the hire purchase agreement must include the following :

(*i*) The *hire purchase price* of the goods to which it relates.

(*ii*) The *cash price* of the goods.

(*iii*) The date of commencement of the agreement.

(*iv*) The number of instalments by which the hire purchase price is to be paid, the amount of each of those instalments and the date, or the mode of determining the date, upon which it is payable, and the person to whom and the place where it is payable.

(*v*) The goods to which the agreement relates in a manner sufficient to identify them.

(*vi*) Where any part of the hire purchase price is to be paid otherwise than by cash or by cheque, the hire purchase agreement shall contain a description of that part of the hire purchase price, and

(*vii*) Where any of the above requirement has not been complied with, the hirer may institute a suit for getting the hire purchase agreement rescinded, and the court may, if it is satisfied that the failure to comply with any such requirements has prejudiced the hirer, rescind the agreement on such terms as it thinks fit in the circumstances of the case.

Terms Used in Hire Purchase Agreement Transactions

Following are the main terms which are frequently used in hire purchase transactions and their understanding is necessary.

(*i*) **Hire Purchaser or Hirer.** He is the buyer of goods.

(*ii*) **Hire Vendor**. He is the seller of the goods.

(*iii*) **Cash Price**. It is the price on which purchaser can buy the goods for cash. It is the value of goods to be recorded in the books of account.

(*iv*) **Hire Purchase Price**. It is total amount which the hire purchaser is required to pay to the hire vendor. Hire purchase price is the aggregate of cash price and interest on outstanding amount.

(*v*) **Down Payment.** It is the price which is paid by the hire purchaser to the vendor at the time of agreement and taking the possession of the goods.

(*vi*) **Goods Repossessed.** It means goods taken back by the hire vendor from the hire purchaser in case he makes any default in the payment of any instalment.

(*vii*) **Interest**. It is the cost of borrowed funds to buy the asset. It is the excess of hire purchase price over cash price.

(*viii*) **Instalments**. These are convenient amounts in which hire purchase price is split.

(*ix*) **Stock with Customers (or H.P. Stock).** It is the value of goods with the hire purchasers for which instalments will become due in the subsequent accounting periods.

(*x*) **Instalments Due (or H.P. Debtors)**. These are instalments which are due in the accounting period but not paid by the hire purchaser.

Accounting For Hire Purchase Transactions

There are two parties in the hire purchase agreement *i.e.*, buyer and seller. The method of recording hire purchase transactions in the account books depends upon the nature of goods, *i.e.*, whether they are of considerable value or of comparatively small value.

(I) In Case of Goods of Considerable Value

In the books of Hire Purchaser

There are three methods of recording hire purchase transactions in the books of the buyer.

1. Cash Price Method (*i.e.* **Treating the goods as outright property of the hirer).** Some accountants are of the opinion that goods purchased on hire purchase system should be treated as property of the business by the buyer on the assumption that asset has been purchased with the intention of paying all the instalments on the due dates to acquire the asset for the business. Under this method, following Journal Entries are to be passed in the books of the buyer.

(*i*) *When an asset is purchased on hire purchase system*

Asset Account Dr. (With cash price)
  To Hire Vendor Account

(*ii*) *For cash down payment on delivery*

Hire Vendor Account Dr.
  To Cash/Bank Account

(*iii*) *For interest due at the end of the year*

Interest Account Dr.
  To Hire Vendor Account

(*iv*) *For the payment of the first instalment*

Hire Vendor Account Dr.
  To Bank Account

(*v*) *For depreciation charge*

Depreciation Account Dr.
  To Asset Account

Alternatively a firm may maintain Provision for Depreciation A/c instead of charging to hire purchase Asset Account. In such a case the Journal Entry is :

Profit & Loss Account Dr.
  To Provision for Depriciation for Asset
    on Hire Purchase and Asset on Hire Purchase is shown at its historical cost.

(*vi*) *For transfer of interest and depreciation to Profit and Loss Account*

Profit & Loss Account Dr.

To Interest Account

To Depreciation Account

Note. *Entries (iii), (iv), (v) and (vi) will be repeated in subsequent years.*

Asset in this case will be shown in the Balance Sheet after deducting depreciation and balance due to the vendor from the asset's beginning balance.

2. Treating the goods as not becoming the property of the hirer. Under this method, goods purchased under hire purchase system will not become the property of the buyer until all the instalments are paid. Following Journal Entries are made in the books of the buyer :

(*i*) *When an asset is purchased on hire purchase*

No entry

(*ii*) *For cash down payment on delivery of the asset*

Asset Account Dr.

To Bank Account

(*iii*) *When the first instalment becomes due* :

Asset Account Dr. (Payment towards cash price)

Interest Account Dr. (For Interest)

To Hire Vendor Account (Amount of instalment)

(*iv*) *When the first instalment is paid*

Hire Vendor Account Dr.

To Bank Account

(*v*) *When depreciation is charged*

Depreciation Account Dr.

To Asset Account

(*vi*) *When interest and depreciation accounts are closed by transfer to Profit and Loss Account.*

Profit and Loss Account Dr.

To Interest Account

To Depreciation Account

Notes. *Entries (iii) to (vi) will be repeated in subsequent years.*

Asset will be shown in the Balance Sheet at purchase cost minus the depreciation.

3. Interest Suspense Method. Under this method asset is debited with cash price, difference between hire purchase price and cash price is also debited to Interest Suspense Account and corresponding total credit is given to the vendor. Interest included in each instalment is credited to Interest Suspense Account by giving debit to Interest Account. Following Journal Entries are passed in the books of the buyer.

(*i*) *When an asset is purchased on hire purchase system*

Asset Account Dr. (With cash price)

Interest Suspense Account Dr. (Difference between hire purchase price and cash price)

To Hire Vendor Account (With total hire purchase price)

(*ii*) *For cash down payment on delivery*

Hire Vendor Account Dr.

To Cash/Bank Account

(*iii*) *For interest due at the end of the year*

Interest Account Dr.

To Interest Suspense Account

(*iv*) *For the payment of the first instalment*
Hire Vendor Account Dr.
To Bank Account

(*v*) *For depreciation charge*
Depreciation Account Dr.
To Asset Account

(*vi*) *For transfer of interest and depreciation to Profit and Loss Account.*
Profit & Loss Account Dr.
To Interest Account
" Depreciation Account

Note. *Entries (iii) to (vi) will be repeated in subsequent years.*

Under this method asset will be shown in the Balance Sheet at cash price less depreciation charged and balance due less Suspense Account balance.

Note. Generally the first method is adopted for the purpose of examination and has been followed in solving illustrations and problems.

In the Books of Hire Vendor

1. First method. Under this method, the following entries are passed in the books of the vendor :

(*i*) *When goods are sold on hire purchase*
Hire Purchaser's Account Dr.
To Hire Sales Account
Hire Sales Account is ultimately closed by transfer to Trading Account.

(*ii*) *For cash received on delivery*
Cash/Bank Account Dr.
To Hire Purchaser's Account

(*iii*) *For interest due on instalment at the end of the year*
Hire Purchaser's Account
To Interest Account

(*iv*) *For receipt of the amount of instalment*
Cash/Bank Account Dr.
To Hire Purchaser's Account

(*v*) *For transferring the balance of interest to Profit and Loss Account*
Interest Account Dr.
To Profit and Loss Account

Note. *Entries (iii) to (v) will be repeated in subsequent years.*

2. **Second Method.** Under this method, the difference between the hire purchase price and the cash price is credited to the Interest Suspense Account and Hire Sale Account is also credited with cash price corresponding debit being given to Hire Purchaser's Account. As and when the interest becomes due on each instalment, it is credited to Interest Account corresponding debit given to Interest Suspense Account. Following Journal Entries are passed in the books of the vendor.

(*i*) *When goods are sold on hire purchase*
Hire Purchaser's Account Dr. (With total H.P. Price)
To Hire Sales Account (With Cash Price)
To Interest Suspense Account (With difference between H.P. Price and Cash Price)

(ii) *For cash received on delivery*
Cash/Bank Account Dr.
To Hire Purchaser's Account

(iii) *For interest due on instalment at the end of the year.*
Interest Suspense Account Dr.
To Interest Account

(iv) *For receipt of the amount of instalment*
Cash/Bank Account Dr.
To Hire Purchaser's Account

(v) *For transfer of interest to Profit and Loss Account*
Interest Account Dr.
To Profit and Loss Account

Note. *Entries from (iii) to (v) will be repeated in subsequent years.*

Note. Generally the first method is followed in examination. Hence this method has been followed in solving illustrations and problems.

Calculation of Interest/Cash Price

Hire purchase price consist of cash price (down payment and instalments to be paid over the particular period. Instalments consist of two elements (1) amount due towards the principal amount of Hire purchase price, (2) Interest due on payments outstanding. It is important to calculate the amount of interest and segregate it from principal amount for proper accounting. At times in the problems, the interest rate may not given, so the students will have calculate the interest first and then proceed further. In some cases, the cash price is not given, so calculations are to be made accordingly. Following illustration will help in understanding various situations and calculations.

ILLUSTRATION 1. (*Where all the particulars are given*) Following are the particulars relating to hire purchase :

Purchaser—Ram & Co. Seller—Shyam & Co.

Date of purchase—Jan. 1, 2022 Goods purchased—Machine

Cash Price—₹ 12,894.

Payments—₹ 2,000 on signing of the agreement and the balance in the three equal annual instalments of ₹ 4,000 due on 31st December each year.

Rate of Interest—5% per annum.

Depreciation—20% on the written down value each year.

Make Journal entries and prepare necessary Ledger Accounts in the books of both the parties and show the Machinery in the Balance Sheet as on 31st December, 2023. Calculations are to be made to the nearest rupee.

SOLUTION

Working Notes

(1) ***Calculation of principal and interest included in each instalment***

	Cash Price	Interest	Instalments: Payment towards Cash Price	Instalments: Interest
	₹	5%	₹	₹
	12,894			—
Less : Paid on 1-1-2022	2,000		2,000	
	10,894			545

Less : Paid on 31-12-2022	3,455		3,455	
	7,439			372
Less : Paid on 31-12-2023	3,628		3,628	
	3,811			189
Less : Paid on 31-12-2024	3,811		3,811	
	—	Total	12,894	1,106

(2) ***Calculation of Depreciation***

		₹
	Cash Price on 1-1-2022	12,894
Less :	Depreciation @ 20% for 2022	2,579
	Balance on 1-1-2023	10,315
Less :	Depreciation @ 20% for 2023	2,063
	Balance on 1-1-2024	8,252
Less :	Depreciation @ 20% for 2024	1,650
	Balance on 1-1-2025	6,602

JOURNAL ENTRIES

			2022		*2023*		*2024*	
			Dr.	*Cr.*	*Dr.*	*Cr.*	*Dr.*	*Cr.*
			₹	₹	₹	₹	₹	₹
Jan. 1	Machinery A/c	Dr.	12,894		—		—	
	To Shyam & Co.			12,894		—	—	
	(Purchase of machinery on H.P.)							
"	Shyam & Co.	Dr.	2,000		—		—	
	To Cash			2,000		—	—	
	(Cash down payment)							
Dec. 31	Interest A/c	Dr.	545		372		189	
	To Shyam & Co.	Dr.		545		372		189
	(Interest credited to vendor)							
"	Shyam & Co.	Dr.	4,000		4,000		4,000	
	To Cash			4,000		4,000		4,000
	(Payment of instalment)							
Dec. 31	Depreciation A/c	Dr.	2,579		2,063		1,650	
	To Machinery A/c			2,579		2,063		1,650
	(Depreciation charged to asset A/c)							
Dec. 31	Profit & Loss A/c	Dr.	3,124		2,435		1,839	
	To Interest A/c			545		372		189
	" Depreciation A/c			2,579		2,063		1,650
	(For balance of Interest & Depreciation transferred to Profit & Loss A/c)							

Ledger

MACHINERY ACCOUNT

Date	Particulars	₹	Date	Particulars	₹
2022 Jan. 1	To Shyam & Co.	12,894	2022 Dec. 31	By Depreciation A/c	2,579
			"	" Balance c/d	10,315
		12,894			12,894
2023 Jan. 1	" Balance b/d	10,315	2023 Dec. 31	" Depreciation A/c	2,063
			"	" Balance c/d	8,252
		10,315			10,315
2024 Jan. 1	" Balance b/d	8,252	2024 Dec. 31	" Depreciation A/c	1,650
			"	" Balance c/d	6,602
		8,252			8,252
2025 Jan. 1	" Balance b/d	6,602			

SHYAM & CO. ACCOUNT

Date	Particulars	₹	Date	Particulars	₹
2022 Jan. 1	To Cash	2,000	2022 Jan. 1	By Machinery A/c	12,894
Dec. 31	" Cash	4,000	Dec. 31	" Interest A/c	545
	" Balance c/d	7,439			
		13,439			13,439
2023 Dec. 31	" Cash	4,000	2023 Jan. 1	" Balance b/d	7,439
	" Balance c/d	3,811	Dec. 31	" Interest A/c	372
		7,811			7,811
2024 Dec. 31	" Cash	4,000	2024 Jan. 1	" Balance b/d	3,811
			Dec. 31	" Interest A/c (Bal. fig.)	189
		4,000			4,000

INTEREST ACCOUNT

Date	Particulars	₹	Date	Particulars	₹
31-12-2022	To Shyam & Co. A/c	545	31-12-2022	By Profit & Loss A/c	545
31-12-2023	" Shyam & Co. A/c	372	31-12-2023	" Profit & Loss A/c	372
31-12-2024	" Shyam & Co. A/c	189	31-12-2024	" Profit & Loss A/c	189

DEPRECIATION ACCOUNT

Date	Particulars	₹	Date	Particulars	₹
31-12-2022	To Machinery A/c	2,579	31-12-2022	By Profit & Loss A/c	2,579

31-12-2023	-do-	2,063	31-12-2023	"	Profit & Loss A/c	2,063
31-12-2024	-do-	1,650	31-12-2024	"	Profit & Loss A/c	1,650

BALANCE SHEET

as on 31st December, 2023

	Assets	₹	₹
	Machinery on H.P.	10,315	
	Less : Depreciation	2,063	
		8,252	
	Less : Due to Shyam & Co.	3,811	4,441

In the Books of Shyam & Co.

JOURNAL ENTRIES

			2022		*2023*		*2024*	
			Dr.	*Cr.*	*Dr.*	*Cr.*	*Dr.*	*Cr.*
			₹	₹	₹	₹	₹	₹
Jan. 1	Ram & Co. To Hire Sales A/c (Machinery sold on H.P.)		12,894	12,894	—	—	—	—
"	Cash A/c To Ram & Co. (Cash received on delivery)	Dr.	2,000	2,000	—	—	—	—
Dec. 31	Ram & Co. To Interest A/c (Interest charged to Ram & Co.)	Dr.	545	545	372	372	189	189
Dec.31	Cash A/c To Ram & Co. A/c (Instalment received)	Dr.	4,000	4,000	4,000	4,000	4,000	4,000
"	Interest A/c To Profit & Loss A/c (For balance on Interest A/c transferred to Profit & Loss A/c)	Dr.	545	545	372	372	189	189
"	Hire Sales A/c To Trading A/c (For transfer of Sale to Trading A/c)	Dr.	12,894	12,894				

Ledger

RAM & CO's ACCOUNT

2022		₹	2022		₹
Jan. 1	To Hire Sales A/c	12,894	Jan. 1	By Cash	2,000
Dec. 31	" Interest A/c	545	Dec. 31	" Cash	4,000
			"	" Balance c/d	7,439
		13,439			13,439

2023			2023		
Jan. 1	To Balance b/d	7,439	Dec. 31	By Cash	4,000
Dec. 31	" Interest A/c	372	"	" Balance c/d	3,811
		7,811			7,811
2024			2024		
Jan. 1	To Balance b/d	3,811	Dec. 31	By Cash	4,000
Dec. 31	" Interest A/c	189			
		4,000			4,000

HIRE SALES ACCOUNT

		₹			₹
2022			2022		
Dec. 31	To Trading A/c	12,894	Jan. 1	By Ram & Co.'s A/c	12,894

INTEREST ACCOUNT

		₹			₹
31-12-2022	To Profit & Loss A/c	545	31-12-2022	By Ram & Co.'s A/c	545
31-12-2023	To Profit & Loss A/c	372	31-12-2023	By Ram & Co. A/c	372
31-12-2024	To Profit & Loss A/c	189	31-12-2024	By Ram & Co.' A/c	189

ILLUSTRATION 2. (*Where all particulars are given and instalments are inclusive of interest*) Samir Dunga, the owner of a printing press, prepares final accounts annually to 31st December. On 31st December, 2021 he purchased a printing machine on hire purchase from Sreeram Enterprise. The cash price of the machine was ₹ 4,00,000. Dunga made a down payment of ₹ 1,00,000 on the date of purchase. He paid three instalments of ₹ 1,20,634 each on 31st December, 2022, 31st December 2023 and 31st December, 2024. The vendor charged interest at 10 per cent per annum on the outstanding balance on 1st January each year. Machine Account was maintained at cost and a separate Depreciation Provision Account was created to record accumulated depreciation. Dunga charged depreciation at 25 per cent on a reducing balances basis.

Required :

(*a*) Prepare the following accounts in the books of Dunga for the period of the contract : Machinery on Hire Purchase Account. Sreeram Enterprise Account. Hire Purchase Interest Payable Account and Provision for Depreciation on Machinery Account.

(*b*) Show how the above matters would be reflected on the Balance Sheet of Dunga on 31st December 2022.

Sreeram Enterprise prepares final accounts to 31st December, on which date it charges Dunga with the interest due.

SOLUTION

(*a*) **MACHINERY (ON H.P.) ACCOUNT**

		₹			₹
31-12-2021	To Sreeram Enterprises A/c	4,00,000	31-12-2021	By Balance c/d	4,00,000
1-1-2022	To Balance b/d	4,00,000	31-12-2022	By Balance c/d	4,00,000
1-1-2023	To Balance b/d	4,00,000	31-12-2023	By Balance c/d	4,00,000
1-1-2024	To Balance b/d	4,00,000	31-12-2024	B Balance c/d	4,00,000

SREERAM ENTERPRISE (VENDOR) ACCOUNT

		₹			₹
31-12-2021	To Bank A/c	1,00,000	31-12-2021	By Machinery A/c	4,00,000
"	To Balance c/d	3,00,000			
		4,00,000			4,00,000
31-12-2022	To Bank A/c	1,20,634	1-1-2022	By Balance b/d	3,00,000
"	To Balance c/d	2,09,366	31-12-2022	By H.P. Interest Payable A/c	30,000
		3,30,000			3,30,000
31-12-2023	To Bank A/c	1,20,634	1-1-2023	By Balance b/d	2,09,366
"	To Balance c/d	1,09,668	31-12-2023	By H.P. Interest Payable A/c	20,936
		2,30,302			2,30,302
31-12-2024	To Bank A/c	1,20,634	1-1-2024	By Balance b/d	1,09,668
			31-12-2024	By H.P. Interest Payable A/c (Bal. fig.)	10,966
		1,20,634			1,20,634

H.P. INTEREST PAYABLE ACCOUNT

		₹			₹
31-12-2022	To Sreeram Enterprise A/c	30,000	31-12-2022	By Profit & Loss A/c	30,000
31-12-2023	To Sreeram Enterprise A/c	20,936	31-12-2023	By Profit & Loss A/c	20,936
31-12-2024	To Sreeram Enterprise A/c	10,966	31-12-2024	By Profit & Loss A/c	10,966

PROVISION FOR DEPRECIATION ON MACHINERY ACCOUNT

		₹			₹
31-12-2022	To Balance c/d	1,00,000	31-12-2022	By Profit & Loss A/c	1,00,000
31-12-2023	To Balance c/d	1,75,000	1-1-2023	By Balance b/d	1,00,000
			31-12-2023	By Profit & Loss A/c	75,000
		1,75,000			1,75,000
31-12-2024	To Balance c/d	2,31,250	1-1-2024	By Balance b/d	1,75,000
			31-12-2024	By Profit & Loss A/c	56,250
		2,31,250			2,31,250

(*b*) **BALANCE SHEET**

as on 3-12-2022 (relevant portion only)

Liabilities	₹	*Assets*	₹	₹
Sreeram Enterprise A/c (Liability for Machine on H.P.)	2,09,366	Machinery on H.P. at Cost	4,00,000	
		Less : Accumulated Depreciation	1,00,000	3,00,000

Calculation of Interest by Product Method. When cash price, hire purchase price and the amounts of various instalments are given but rate of interest is not given, the following procedure is adopted :

Hire Purchase Price – Cash Price = Total Interest

Hire Purchase Price – First Payment = First Balance

First Balance – Second Payment = Second Balance

Second Balance – Third Payment = Third Balance

These balances are multiplied by the period for which the amounts remain outstanding in order to calculate the product. The total interest is apportioned in the ratio of individual product to the total product. Interest in each period will be deducted from the payment made for each period in order to calculate the amount of instalment. This will be more clear from the following Example.

EXAMPLE. (*Calculation of Interest by Product Method*). X purchased from Y a machine on Hire-Purchase System on 1st January 2025. Its hire-purchase price was ₹ 95,000 and cash price was ₹ 86,800. ₹ 5,000 was paid on delivery, ₹ 10,000 was paid after 4 months, ₹ 15,000 was paid after 6 months, ₹ 30,000 was paid after 9 months and ₹ 35,000 was paid after 12 months. The date of payment of each instalment is counted from the date of purchase of machinery.

Calculate interest in each instalment and cash price portion included in each instalment.

SOLUTION

Total Interest = H.P. Price – Cash Price
= ₹ 95,000 – ₹ 86,800
= ₹ 8,200

Instal-ment No.	Period	Amount	Product	Interest $\frac{₹\,8{,}200}{₹\,8{,}20{,}000} = \frac{1}{100}$	Cash Price Portion of Instalment
		₹	₹	₹	
1.	4 months	₹ 90,000	₹ 90,000 × 4 = 3,60,000	3,600	₹ 10,000 – ₹ 3,600 = ₹ 6,400
2.	6 – 4 = 2 months	₹ 90,000 – 10,000 = ₹ 80,000	₹ 80,000 × 2 = 1,60,000	1,600	₹ 15,000 – ₹ 1,600 = ₹ 13,400
3.	9 – 6 = 3 months	₹ 80,000 – 15,000 = ₹ 65,000	₹ 65,000 × 3 = 1,95,000	1,950	₹ 30,000 – ₹ 1,950 = ₹ 28,050
4.	12 – 9 = 3 months	₹ 65,000 – ₹ 30,000 = ₹ 35,000	₹ 35,000 × 3 = 1,05,000	1,050	₹ 35,000 – ₹ 1,050 = ₹ 33,950
			8,20,000	8,200	₹ 81,800

Calculation of interest when rate is not given. If cash price and each instalment amount together with down payment is given but rate of interest is not given, then total interest will be calculated by deducting cash price from the total hire purchase price. Total interest should be divided in the ratio of amount outstanding for each year.

Example. On 1st January, 2021 Messrs XYZ & Co. took delivery from ABC Co. Ltd., of a machine on hire-purchase system, ₹ 1,500 being paid on delivery and the balance in five instalments of ₹ 3,000 each, payable annually on 31st December. The cash price of the machine was ₹ 15,000. Calculate the amount of interest for each year.

SOLUTION

	₹
2021 Amount outstanding for interest after down payment	15,000
2022 Amount outstanding for interest after 1st instalment	12,000
2023 Amount outstanding for interest after 2nd instalment	9,000
2024 Amount outstanding for interest after 3rd instalment	6,000
2025 Amount outstanding for interest after 4th instalment	3,000

Total interest for all the five years is ₹ 1,500 (*i.e.* ₹ 16,500hire purchase price – ₹ 15,000 cash price) which should be divided in the ratio of 5 : 4 : 3 : 2 : 1 for all these years.

Hence the interest comes to

	₹		₹
2021	₹ 1,500 × $\frac{5}{15}$ = 500	2024	₹ 1,500 × $\frac{2}{15}$ = 200
2022	₹ 1,500 × $\frac{4}{15}$ = 400	2025	₹ 1,500 × $\frac{1}{15}$ = 100
2023	₹ 1,500 × $\frac{3}{15}$ = 300		

Calculation of Cash Price, when it is not given (or Work Back Method). Sometimes in the question the cash price is not given. The asset account cannot be debited with more than the cash price of the asset, so it becomes essential to find out the cash price first before solving such type of questions. The procedure to calculate cash price is to take up the final instalment first and to deduct the interest from it. Interest can be calculated for one year by multiplying the sum due at the end of the year by the formula : $\frac{\text{Rate of Interest}}{100 + \text{Rate of Interest}}$. Suppose *x* owes *y* ₹ 100, interest being 10% p.a. At the end of one year *x* will have to pay ₹ 110 out of which ₹ 10 is for interest. Hence 10/110 of the sum due at the end of the year will be interest. If this interest is deducted from the sum due at the end of the year, the residual will be the sum due at the beginning of the year. This will also be the amount due at the end of the last but one year after paying the annual instalment. The total of these two (amount due + annual instalment) will give the sum due at the end of the last but one year. That year's interest will be calculated by multiplying the sum due by 10/110 and so on the process continues for other previous years also. If the instalments are half yearly and rate of interest is given per annum then it should be reduced to half for the purpose of calculating interest out of the total amount.

ILLUSTRATION 3. X Ltd. had purchased a machinery on hire purchase system from Y Ltd. The terms are that X Ltd. would pay ₹ 20,000 down on signing the agreement and 4 annual instalments of ₹ 11,000 each commencing from the beginning of the next year. X Ltd. charged depreciation at the rate of 10 per cent per annum on cost under diminishing balance-system. Y Ltd. charged interest at the rate of 10 per cent per annum in their hire purchase contract. Prepare Machinery Account and Y Ltd. Account for 5 years in the books of X Ltd.

SOLUTION

In the Books of X Ltd.
MACHINERY ACCOUNT

Year		₹	Year		₹
I	To Y Ltd. (1)	54,869	I	By Depreciation A/c	5,487
			I	" Balance c/d	49,382
		54,869			54,869

		₹			₹
II	To Balance b/d	49,382	II	By Depreciation A/c	4,938
				" Balance c/d	44,444
		49,382			49,382
III	To Balance b/d	44,444	III	By Depreciation A/c	4,444
				" Balance c/d	40,000
		44,444			44,444
IV	To Balance b/d	40,000	IV	By Depreciation A/c	4,000
				" Balance c/d	36,000
		40,000			40,000
V	To Balance b/d	36,000	V	By Depreciation A/c	3,600
				" Balance c/d	32,400
		36,000			36,000
VI	To Balance b/d	32,400			

Y Ltd.

Year		₹	Year		₹
I	To Bank A/c	20,000	I	By Machinery A/c	54,869
	" Balance c/d	38,356		" Interest A/c	3,487
		58,356			58,356
II	To Bank A/c	11,000	II	By Balance b/d	38,356
	" Balance c/d	30,091		" Interest A/c	2,735
		41,091			41,091
III	To Bank A/c	11,000	III	By Balance b/d	30,091
	" Balance c/d	21,000		" Interest A/c	1,909
		32,000			32,000
IV	To Bank A/c	11,000	IV	By Balance b/d	21,000
	" Balance c/d	11,000		" Interest A/c	1,000
		22,000			22,000
V	To Bank A/c	11,000	V	By Balance b/d	11,000

Working Note :

(1) ***Calculation of Cash Price & Interest***

No. of Instalment	*Closing Balance*	*Amount of Instalment*	*Total*	*Interest @ 1/11*	*Opening Balance*
	₹	₹	₹	₹	₹
IV	—	11,000	11,000	1,000	10,000
III	10,000	11,000	21,000	1,909	19,091
II	19,091	11,000	30,091	2,735	27,356
I	27,356	11,000	38,356	3,487	34,869

Cash Price = Down Payment + ₹ 34,869

= ₹ 20,000 + ₹ 34,869 = ₹ 54,869

Calculation of Cash Price when references to annuity table, rate of interest and instalments are given:

Sometimes in the question a reference to annuity table where in present value of the annuity for a number of years at a certain rate of interest is given, the cash price is calculated by multiplying the amount of instalment and the value of annuity and adding in the product the down payment. This will be more clear from the following illustration.

Calculation of interest when rate and cash price is not given :

When cash price and rate of interest is not given and it is desired to calculate the amount of interest included in each instalment, then the question will be solved through forming equation for each instalment and solving them. This will be clear from the following illustration.

Example. M/s India Motors Ltd. sells scooters on the hire purchase system. The terms of payment for the sale of a scooter are ₹ 1,000 on delivery, ₹ 1,040 at the end of the first year, ₹ 960 at the end of the second year and ₹ 880 at the end of the third year, inclusive of finance charges or interest. Calculate amount of interest included in each instalment.

SOLUTION

Suppose the Cash price paid in each instalment is 'P' and interest (i)

Then First instalment $P + 3i$ = ₹ 1040 ...(*i*)

Second instalment $P + 2i$ = ₹ 960 ...(*ii*)

Third instalment $P + i$ = ₹ 880 ...(*iii*)

(Interest in first instalment will be three times as compared to the third instalment because amount due will be for 3 instalments).

Adding (*ii*) and (*iii*) $2P + 3i$ = ₹ 1,840 ...(*iv*)

Deducting (*i*) from (*iv*) *i.e.* P = ₹ 800

∴ Cash price paid each time is ₹ 800.

∴ Interest in each instalment is as under :

No. of Instalment	*Instalment paid*	*Cash price paid*	*Interest paid*
	₹	₹	₹
1	1,040	800	240
2	960	800	160
3	880	800	80

Note. Assume (*i*) the difference in various instalments (leaving down payment) is due to the difference of interest *i.e.* all payments towards cash price are equal. (*ii*) Rate of interest is uniform all through.

Purchase Through Financial Institution

When an asset is purchased on hire purchase, the purchaser sometimes gets it finance through some financial institution. In such a case, the instalments are paid to financial institution instead of vendor and right on the property will be that of financial institution. Such method is applied in case of more valuable assets as Motor, Truck, Tractor, etc. which are purchased with the help of some financial institution. In such a case an account of financial institution (instead of vendor) will be opened in the books of purchaser but other accounts will be the same.

ILLUSTRATION 4. On 1st January, 2022 X Ltd. acquired a tractor of the cash price of ₹ 1,76,000. The purchase of the tractor was financed by Delhi Finance Corporation to whom X Ltd. paid ₹ 56,000 on 1st January, 2022 and instalments (exclusive of interest) of ₹ 40,000 at the end of each year are to be paid. The rate of interest was 15% per annum.

X Ltd. writes off depreciation at 20% per annum on diminishing balance method. Tractor met with an accident on 1st April, 2024 and X Ltd. received from the insurance company ₹ 84,000 as claim. The debt of Delhi Finance Corporation was discharged on that date.

SOLUTION

In the Books of X Ltd.

TRACTOR ACCOUNT

		₹			₹
1-1-22	To Delhi Finance Corpn.	1,76,000	31-12-22	By Depreciation A/c	35,200
			"	By Balance c/d	1,40,800
		1,76,000			1,76,000
1-1-23	To Balance b/d	1,40,800	31-12-23	By Depreciation A/c	28,160
				By Balance c/d	1,12,640
		1,40,800			1,40,800
1-1-24	To Balance b/d	1,12,640	1-4-24	By Depreciation A/c (for 3 months)	5,632
			"	By Bank A/c (Insurance Claim)	84,000
			31-12-24	By Profit & Loss A/c	23,008
		1,12,640			1,12,640

DELHI FINANCE CORPORATION ACCOUNT

		₹			₹
1-1-22	To Bank A/c	56,000	1-1-22	By Tractor A/c	1,76,000
31-12-22	To Bank A/c (₹ 40,000 + ₹ 18,000)	58,000	31-12-22	By Interest A/c (15% of ₹ 1,20,000)	18,000
"	To Balance c/d	80,000			
		1,94,000			1,94,000
31-12-23	To Bank A/c (₹ 40,000 + ₹ 12,000)	52,000	1-1-23	By Balance b/d	80,000
"	To Balance c/d	40,000	31-12-23	By Interest A/c (15% on ₹ 80,000)	12,000
		92,000			92,000
1-4-24	To Bank A/c (Final Payment)	41,500	1-1-24	By Balance b/d	40,000
			1-4-24	By Interest A/c $\left(₹ 40,000 \times \frac{15}{100} \times \frac{3}{12}\right)$	1,500
		41,500			41,500

When the Vendor Charges Insurance Premium from the Purchaser

The vendor remains the owner of the property or goods till the last instalment is paid by the hire purchaser. In order to avoid any risk to the property, the vendor gets the insurance policy and the premium paid is charged to the hire purchaser. The hire purchaser will pass the journal entry for insurance premium as is passed for interest at the end of the year. Insurance Premium Account is closed by transfer to the Profit & Loss A/c at the end of the year and is paid to the vendor alongwith the instalment. Following Journal Entries are passed :

In the Books of Purchaser

(*i*) *When the amount of insurance premium is due*

Insurance Premium A/c Dr.
  To Vendor A/c

(*ii*) *When insurance premium is paid*

Vendor A/c Dr.
  To Bank A/c

In the Books of Vendor

(*i*) *When the insurance premium is paid*

Hire Purchaser A/c Dr.
  To Bank A/c

(*ii*) *When the amount of insurance premium is received*

Bank A/c Dr.
  To Hire Purchaser A/c

ILLUSTRATION 5. Delhi Engineering Works purchase a machinery on hire purchase system. The cash price of the machinery is ₹ 64,000, the deposit is ₹ 6,400 and four annual instalments of ₹ 14,400 are to be paid, commencing a year after delivery. In addition, interest is to be paid at 7% on yearly balances and the purchaser is to pay to the seller an insurance premium of 25 paise per annum on the outstanding balances.

Show the Vendor's Account and Insurance Premium Account in the books of the purchaser for the agreement period.

SOLUTION

In the Books of Delhi Engineering Works

VENDOR'S ACCOUNT

Year		₹	Year		₹
1st	To Bank A/c	6,400	1st	By Machinery A/c	64,000
	To Bank A/c (₹ 14,400 + ₹ 4,032 + ₹ 144)	18,576		By Interest A/c (7% on ₹ 57,600)	4,032
	To Balance c/d	43,200		By Insurance Premium $\left(₹\,57,600 \times \frac{25}{100} \times \frac{1}{100}\right)$	144
		68,176			68,176
2nd	To Bank A/c (₹ 14,400 + ₹ 3,024 + ₹ 108)	17,532	2nd	By Balance b/d	43,200
	To Balance c/d	28,800		By Interest A/c (7% on ₹ 43,200)	3,024
				By Insurance Premium $\left(₹\,43,200 \times \frac{25}{100} \times \frac{1}{100}\right)$	108
		46,332			46,332
3rd	To Bank A/c (₹ 14,400 + ₹ 2,016 + ₹ 72)	16,488	3rd	By Balance b/d	28,800
				By Interest A/c (7% on ₹ 28,800)	2,016

	To Balance c/d	14,400		By Insurance Premium $\left(₹\,28,800 \times \frac{25}{100} \times \frac{1}{100}\right)$	72
		30,888			30,888
4th	To Bank A/c (₹ 14,400 + ₹ 1,008 + ₹ 36)	15,444	4th	By Balance b/d	14,400
				By Interest A/c (7% on ₹ 14,400)	1,008
				By Insurance Premium $\left(₹\,14,400 \times \frac{25}{100} \times \frac{1}{100}\right)$	36
		15,444			15,444

INSURANCE PREMIUM ACCOUNT

Year		₹	Year		₹
1st	To Vendor's A/c	144	1st	By Profit & Loss A/c	144
2nd	To Vendor's A/c	108	2nd	By Profit & Loss A/c	108
3rd	To Vendor's A/c	72	3rd	By Profit & Loss A/c	72
4th	To Vendor's A/c	36	4th	By Profit & Loss A/c	36

Transfer of Asset by the Hire Purchaser

Sometimes the hire purchaser, with the consent of the vendor, transfers the asset to some other person after paying some instalments during the period of hire purchase agreement. In such a case the hire purchaser receives some amount in lieu of the instalments paid by him and gives the responsibility of payment of future instalments due on such asset to the person to whom the asset is transferred. Following entries will be passed in the books of the transferee.

Asset A/c	Dr.	
To Transferor's A/c		[For the amount agreed to be paid to the hire purchaser]
To Vendor's A/c		[For cash price of remaining instalments]

Transferee will calculate depreciation on the total amount debited to the asset account and will pass all entries as might have been passed in the books of the transferor.

ILLUSTRATION 6. A Ltd. entered into a hire purchase agreement with B Ltd. for the purchase of 100 wagons over a period of three years from January 1, 2024 by half-yearly instalments of ₹ 7,385 payable on June 30 and December 31 each year, the cash price being ₹ 400 per wagon and the rate of interest 6% p.a. with half-yearly rest.

On January 1, 2025 after paying two instalments A Ltd. transferred their rights in the agreement to C Ltd. for a consideration of ₹ 10,000. C Ltd. paid sum to A Ltd. on 1st January, 2025 and the next instalments to B Ltd. on due dates.

Show in the form of Journal Entries how the transactions should appear in the books of C Ltd. upto 30th June, 2025 when its financial year ended writing off depreciation @ 10% p.a. Calculations may be done to the nearest rupee.

SOLUTION

JOURNAL (*of C Ltd.*)

				₹	₹
2025					
Jan. 1	Wagons Account	Dr.		37,444	
	To A Ltd.				10,000
	To B Ltd.				27,444 (1)
	(Being 100 wagons taken over on hire purchase system as per agreement)				
Jan. 1	A Ltd.	Dr.		10,000	
	To Bank				10,000
	(Being payment made to A Ltd.)				
June 30	Interest Account	Dr.		823	
	To B Ltd. (2)				823
	(Being interest on ₹ 27,444 at 6% p.a. for 6 months)				
June 30	B Ltd.	Dr.		7,385	
	To Bank				7,385
	(Being payment of instalment)				
June 30	Depreciation Account	Dr.		1,872	
	To Wagons Account				1,872
	(Being depreciation at 10% p.a. on ₹ 37,444 for 6 months)				
"	Profit and Loss Account	Dr.		2,695	
	To Interest Account				823
	To Depreciation Account				1,872
	(Interest and depreciation transferred to Profit and Loss Account)				

Working Notes :

(1) ***Calculation of Amount Due to B. Ltd.***

B. LTD.'s ACCOUNT (*in the books of A Ltd.*)

2024		₹	2024		₹
June 30	To Bank A/c	7,385	Jan. 1	By Wagons A/c	40,000
Dec. 31	" Bank A/c	7,385	June 30	" Interest A/c $\left(\frac{6}{100} \times ₹\ 40{,}000 \times \frac{1}{2}\right)$	1,200
"	" Balance c/d	27,444	Dec. 31	By Interest A/c $\left(\frac{6}{100} \times ₹\ 33{,}815 \times \frac{1}{2}\right)$	1,014
		42,214			42,214

The amount of ₹ 27,444 is due to B Ltd. from A Ltd. will now have to be paid by C Ltd. to B Ltd.

(2) ***Calculation of interest***

$$\frac{6}{100} \times \frac{6}{12} \times ₹\ 27{,}444 = ₹\ 823 \textit{ approx.}$$

Default and Repossession

When the buyer makes default in the payment of any instalment the vendor has a right to repossess the goods sold on hire purchase and forfeit whatever amount he has already received treating it as a hire charge. There are two possibilities in repossession of goods *i.e.*, (*i*) when the vendor takes back the complete repossession of asset and (*ii*) when the vendor takes repossession of only a part of the total asset sold to the hire purchaser.

I. *When the vendor takes back the complete repossession of asset*

Entries for interest and depreciation will be passed in the books of buyer and vendor except the entry for payment upto the date of default.

Buyer will close the account of the vendor by transferring its balance to Asset Account by debiting Vendor's Account and crediting Asset Account. Any balance left in Asset Account will represent loss and will be closed by transfer to the Profit and Loss Account.

Vendor will close the account of the hire purchaser by transferring its balance to Goods Repossessed Account. This account will further be debited with expenses incurred in repairing or overhauling goods and credited with sale price. The balance will represent profit or loss on repossessed goods and will be closed by transfer to Profit and Loss Account.

Journal Entries in the Books of Hire Purchaser

(1) Entry for interest due in the year of default

Interest A/c Dr.
    To Vendor's A/c

(2) For transferring credit balance (including interest) in Vendor's A/c to Asset A/c in case of possession of entire goods

Vendor's A/c Dr.
    To Asset A/c

(3) For providing depreciation for current year in current period

Depreciation A/c Dr.
    To Asset A/c

(4) The balance in Asset A/c being loss on default or surrender is closed by transferring to Profit & Loss A/c

Profit & Loss A/c Dr.
    To Asset A/c

Journal Entries in the Books of Vendor

(1) Entry for interest due in the year of default

Hire Purchaser A/c Dr.
    To Interest A/c

(2) On Repossession of Goods

Goods Repossessed A/c Dr.
    To Hire Purchaser A/c

(3) For expenses incurred on goods repossessed to make them fit for sale

Goods Repossessed A/c
    To Cash/Bank A/c

(4) For cash received from sale of repossessed goods

Cash/Bank A/c Dr.
    To Goods Repossessed A/c

(5) Any balance left in Goods Repossessed A/c is profit or loss on repossession and is transferred to Profit & Loss A/c

***(i)* If Profit**

Goods Repossessed A/c Dr.
To Profit & Loss A/c

***(ii)* If Loss**

Profit & Loss A/c Dr.
To Goods Repossessed A/c

ILLUSTRATION 7. P purchased a machine on hire-purchase system for ₹ 56,000 payment to be made, ₹ 15,000 down and 3 instalments of ₹ 15,000 each at the end of each year. Rate of interest is charged at 5% per annum. Buyer is depreciating the asset at 10% p.a. on written down value method.

Because of financial difficulties, P after having paid down payment and first instalment at the end of the 1st year, could not pay second instalment and seller took possession of the machine. Seller after expending ₹ 357 on repairs of the asset sold it away for ₹ 30,110.

Open Ledger accounts in the books of both the parties to record the transactions.

SOLUTION

In the Books of P

MACHINERY ACCOUNT

Year		₹	Year		₹
I			I		
Jan. 1	To Hire Vendor	56,000	Dec. 31	By Depreciation @ 10%	5,600
			"	" Balance c/d	50,400
		56,000			56,000
II			II		
Jan. 1	To Balance b/d	50,400	Dec. 31	By Depreciation	5,040
			"	" Hire Vendor	29,453
			"	" P. & L. A/c (Loss on Default) (Balancing Figure)	15,907
		50,400			50,400

HIRE VENDOR ACCOUNT

Year		₹	Year		₹
I			I		
Jan. 1	To Bank A/c	15,000	Jan. 1	By Machinery A/c	56,000
Dec. 31	" Bank A/c	15,000	Dec. 31	" Interest A/c	2,050
"	" Balance c/d	28,050			
		58,050			58,050
II			II		
Dec. 31	To Machinery A/c	29,453	Jan. 1	By Balance b/d	28,050
			Dec. 31	" Interest A/c	1,403
		29,453			29,453

In the Books of Hire Vendor

P's ACCOUNT

Year		₹	Year		₹
I			I		
Jan. 1	To Hire Sales A/c	56,000	Jan. 1	By Bank A/c	15,000
Dec. 31	" Interest A/c	2,050	Dec. 31	" Bank A/c	15,000
			"	" Balance c/d	28,050
		58,050			58,050
II			II		
Jan. 1	To Balance b/d	28,050	Dec. 31	By Goods Repossessed A/c	29,453
Dec. 31	" Interest A/c	1,403			
		29,453			29,453

GOODS REPOSSESSED ACCOUNT

Year		₹	Year		₹
II			II		
Dec. 31	To P	29,453	Dec. 31	By Sales	30,110
"	To Cash (Expenses)	357			
	" Profit & Loss A/c (Profit on Repossession)	300			
		30,110			30,110

PROFIT & LOSS ACCOUNT

			₹
		By Goods Repossessed A/c	300

II. *When the vendor takes repossession of only a part of the total asset sold to the hire purchaser*

In this case also entries for interest and depreciation will be passed in the books of the purchaser and vendor except the entry for payment upto the date of default.

Both the hire purchaser and vendor will not close Vendor's Account and Hire Purchaser's Account in their respective books but an entry will be passed with the agreed value of that asset which has been taken back by the vendor. The vendor will generally agree to take back a part of asset only at enhanced rate of depreciation.

The hire purchaser will calculate the value of the asset left with him by the vendor by providing normal rate of depreciation and will keep this amount as asset in the Asset Account. The asset account balance will show profit or loss on default and will be transferred to the profit and loss account. Repossessed Goods Account in the books of the vendor will be prepared on the same lines as it was prepared in (I) above.

ILLUSTRATION 8. Monica purchased on 1st January, 2022 two Maruti vans from Neeru on hire purchase system. The cash price was payable as ₹ 24,000 down for each van and the balance in 3 equal instalments together with interest @ 10 per cent per annum. The amount of last instalment including interest was ₹ 70,400. Depreciation was to be provided at 20 per cent per annum on reducing balances. Monica paid the two instalments on 31-12-2022 and 31-12-2023 but could not pay the instalment due on 31-12-2024.

Neeru repossessed one Maruti van adjusting its value against the amount due. The repossession was done on the basis of 25% depreciation on original cost method. Neeru spent ₹ 10,000 on van repossessed and sold it for ₹ 62,000.

Show the necessary accounts in the books of both the parties.

SOLUTION

Working Note :

(1) ***Calculation of Cash Price of 2 Vans***

H.P. Instalment ₹ 70,400

Rate of Interest 10%

Cash Price of Instalment = ₹ 70,400 $\times \frac{100}{110}$ = ₹ 64,000

Total Cash Price of 2 Vans = ₹ 64,000 × 3 + Down Payment ₹ 24,000 × 2

= ₹ 1,92,000 + ₹ 48,000 = ₹ 2,40,000

(2) ***W.D. Value of One Van Repossessed***

		₹
	Cost of one Van	1,20,000
Less :	Depreciation @ 25% for three years	90,000
	W.D.V. on 31-12-2024	30,000

(3) ***W.D. Value of One Van Retained***

	₹
Cost	1,20,000
Less : Dep. @ 20%	24,000
	96,000
Less : Dep. 20%	19,200
	76,800
Less : Dep. 20%	15,360
	61,440

In the Books of Monica

VAN ACCOUNT

		₹			₹
2022			2022		
Jan. 1	To Neeru's A/c	2,40,000	Dec. 31	By Depreciation A/c	48,000
			"	Balance c/d	1,92,000
		2,40,000			2,40,000
2023			2023		
Jan. 1	To Balance b/d	1,92,000	Dec. 31	By Depreciation A/c	38,400
			"	Balance c/d	1,53,600
		1,92,000			1,92,000
2024			2024		
Jan. 1	To Balance b/d	1,53,600	Dec. 31	By Depreciation A/c	30,720
			"	By Neeru's A/c	30,000
			"	By P/L A/c (Bal. fig.) (Loss on default)	31,440
			"	" Balance c/d	61,440
		1,53,600			1,53,600

NEERU'S ACCOUNT

		₹			₹
2022			2022		
Jan. 1	To Bank A/c	48,000	Jan. 1	By Van A/c	2,40,000
Dec. 31	To Bank A/c		Dec. 31	By Interest A/c	19,200
	(₹ 64,000 + ₹ 19,200)	83,200			
	To Balance c/d	1,28,000			
		2,59,200			2,59,200
2023			2023		
Dec. 31	To Bank A/c		Jan. 1	By Balance b/d	1,28,000
	(₹ 64,000 + ₹ 12,800)	76,800	Dec. 31	By Interest	12,800
" 31	" Balance c/d	64,000			
		1,40,800			1,40,800
2024			2024		
Dec. 31	To Van A/c	30,000	Jan. 1	By Balance b/d	64,000
" 31	To Balance c/d	40,400	Dec. 31	By Interest	6,400
		70,400			70,400

In the Books of Neeru

MONICA'S ACCOUNT

		₹			₹
2022			2022		
Jan. 1	To Hire Sale	2,40,000	Jan. 1	By Bank A/c	48,000
Dec. 31	To Interest A/c	19,200	Dec. 31	By Bank A/c	83,200
			"	By Balance c/d	1,28,000
		2,59,200			2,59,200
2023			2023		
Jan. 1	To Balance b/d	1,28,000	Dec. 31	By Bank A/c	76,800
Dec. 31	To Interest	12,800	"	By Balance c/d	64,000
		1,40,800			1,40,800
2024			2024		
Jan. 1	To Balance b/d	64,000	Dec. 31	By Goods Repossessed	30,000
Dec. 31	To Interest A/c	6,400	"	By Balance c/d	40,400
		70,400			70,400

GOODS REPOSSESSED ACCOUNT

	₹		₹
To Monica's A/c	30,000	By Bank (Sale)	62,000
To Bank	10,000		
To P/L A/c (Profit on Repossession)	22,000		
	62,000		62,000

ILLUSTRATION 9. Roman Co. purchased five machines from Ramos Ltd., on 1st January, 2022 on hire purchase system. The cash price of each machine is ₹ 1,20,000. The mode of payments was as follows :

(*i*) 15% of cash price down ; (*ii*) 25% of cash price at the end of each year for 4 years.

Roman Co. writes off 15% depreciation annually on diminishing balance. The payment due to 31st December, 2023 could not be made. Ramos Lt d. agreed to leave three machines with the buyer on the condition that the value of the other two machines would be adjusted against the amount due, the machines being valued at cost less 25% depreciation on diminishing balance.

Show the necessary accounts in the books of Roman Co.

SOLUTION

In the Books of Roman Co.

MACHINERY ACCOUNT

Date	Particulars	₹	Date	Particulars	₹
2022			2022		
Jan. 1	To Ramos Ltd.	6,00,000	Dec. 31	By Depreciation A/c	90,000
			"	By Balance c/d	5,10,000
		6,00,000			6,00,000
2023			2023		
Jan. 1	To Balance b/d	5,10,000	Dec. 31	By Depreciation A/c	76,500
			"	By Ramos Ltd. (2)	1,35,000
			Dec. 31	By Profit & Loss A/c (Loss on default) (Bal. fig.)	38,400
			"	By Balance c/d (3)	2,60,100
		5,10,000			5,10,000
2024					
Jan. 1	To Balance b/d	2,60,100			

RAMOS LTD. ACCOUNT

Date	Particulars	₹	Date	Particulars	₹
2022			2022		
Jan. 1	To Bank (15% of 6,00,000)	90,000	Jan. 1	By Machinery A/c	6,00,000
Dec. 31	To Bank	1,50,000	Dec. 31	By Interest A/c (1)	36,000
"	To Balance c/d	3,96,000			
		6,36,000			6,36,000
2023			2023		
Dec. 31	To Machinery A/c (2)	1,35,000	Jan. 1	By Balance b/d	3,96,000
"	To Balance c/d	2,88,000	Dec. 31	By Interest A/c (1)	27,000
		4,23,000			4,23,000
			2024		
			Jan. 1	By Balance b/d	2,88,000

Working Notes :

(1) ***Calculation of Interest***

Year	*Amount Outstanding* ₹	*Ratio*	*Interest* ₹
Jan. 1, 2022	6,00,000	4	36,000 $\left(i.e., 90,000 \times \frac{4}{10}\right)$
Jan. 1, 2023	4,50,000	3	27,000 $\left(i.e., 90,000 \times \frac{3}{10}\right)$
Jan. 1, 2024	3,00,000	2	18,000 $\left(i.e., 90,000 \times \frac{2}{10}\right)$
Jan. 1, 2025	1,50,000	1	9,000 $\left(i.e., 90,000 \times \frac{1}{10}\right)$

(2) *Calculation of Value of 2 Machines taken up by Ramos Ltd.*

	₹
Cost of 2 Machines	2,40,000
Less : Depreciation @ 25% for 2022	60,000
	1,80,000
Less : Depreciation @ 25% for 2023	45,000
Value on 31-12-2023	1,35,000

(3) *Calculation of Value of 3 Machines retained by Roman Co.*

	₹
Cost of 3 Machines	3,60,000
Less : Depreciation @ 15% for 2022	54,000
	3,06,000
Less : Depreciation @ 15% for 2023	45,900
Value on 31-12-2023	2,60,100

Provision against Free Maintenance

When goods are sold with the guarantee for free maintenance or service for a stipulated period, a provision should be created for free maintenance and servicing out of the sales as sales include a charge for free maintenance. This amount may be credited to a separate account called Maintenance Suspense Account. Actual maintenance expenses are debited to this account and the difference between the actual and estimated expenses should be treated as profit or loss. But one point which requires attention is that if the guarantee is for one year, it will involve two years, *i.e.,* half of current year and half of next year. Similarly if the guarantee is for two years, it will involve half of current year, the whole of the next year and half of the third year assuming that sales in the first year are made in the middle of the year. Generally in the initial period actual maintenance expenses will be less as compared to the estimated expenses, but if in a certain period actual expenses are more than the estimated expenses, the difference must be charged to Profit and Loss Account and corresponding credit given to Maintenance Suspense Account. The balance of Maintenance Suspense Account after the guarantee period is over, is transferred to Profit and Loss Account.

Following entries may be passed in the books of the Vendor :

(*i*) *For sales including maintenance charges made*

Hire Purchase A/c Dr.
  To Hire Sales A/c

(*ii*) *For transfer of maintenance charges to Maintenance Suspense A/c*

Hire Sales A/c Dr.
  To Maintenance Suspense A/c

(*iii*) *For interest due on assets sold*

Hire Purchaser A/c Dr.
  To Interest A/c

(*iv*) *For receipt of Instalment*

Bank A/c Dr.
  To Hire Purchaser A/c

(*v*) *For payment of actual cost of maintenance*

Maintenance Suspense A/c Dr.
  To Cash A/c

(vi) *For transfer of excess of actual cost of maintenance to Profit & Loss A/c*
Profit & Loss A/c Dr.
To Maintenance Suspense A/c

(vii) *For transfer of excess of Maintenance Suspense to Profit & Loss A/c*
Maintenance Suspense A/c Dr.
To Profit & Loss A/c

(viii) *For transfer of interest to P/L A/c*
Interest A/c Dr.
To Profit & Loss A/c

Note : Interest will be calculated on cost price including the amount of repairs.

ILLUSTRATION 10. Cash price of a machine is ₹ 3,000 and Hire-Purchase price is ₹ 4,000. This machine is sold on Hire-Purchase System on 1st January, 2023 and payment is made in four six-monthly instalment of ₹ 1,000 each. It was agreed that the machine will be maintained free of charge for a period of two years. The actual expenses of maintenance were ₹ 100 and ₹ 250 for the first and second years respectively, though past experience showed that they are ₹ 500 of which ₹ 70 are for the first year. Pass the necessary Journal entries in the books of the Hire Vendor and open the Hire Maintenance Suspense Account.

SOLUTION

2023				Dr. ₹	Cr. ₹
Jan. 1	Hire-Purchaser To Hire Sales A/c (Being sales made)	Dr.		3,000	3,000
	Hire Sales A/c To Maintenance Suspense A/c (Being transfer made)	Dr.		500	500
June 30	Hire-Purchaser To Interest A/c (Being interest for half year due)	Dr.		400	400
	Bank A/c To Hire-Purchaser (Being receipt of instalment)	Dr.		1,000	1,000
Dec. 31	Hire-Purchaser To Interest A/c (Being interest for half year due)	Dr.		300	300
	Bank A/c To Hire-Purchaser (Being receipt of second instalment)	Dr.		1,000	1,000
	Maintenance Suspense A/c To Cash A/c (Being actual expenses made)	Dr.		100	100

	Profit and Loss A/c Dr. To Maintenance Suspense A/c (Being excess of actual maintenance expenses over estimated)		30	30
	Interest A/c Dr. To Profit and Loss A/c (Being transfer of interest of Profit and Loss A/c)		700	700
2024 June 30	Hire-Purchaser Dr. To Interest A/c (Being interest for half year due)		200	200
	Bank A/c Dr. To Hire-Purchaser (Being receipt of instalment)		1,000	1,000
Dec. 31	Hire-Purchaser Dr. To Interest A/c (Being interest for half year due)		100	100
	Bank A/c Dr. To Hire-Purchaser (Being receipt of third instalment)		1,000	1,000
	Maintenance Suspense A/c Dr. To Cash A/c (Being payment of actual expenses of maintenance)		250	250
Dec. 31	Maintenance Suspense A/c Dr. To Profit and Loss A/c (Being transfer balance of Maintenance Suspense A/c to Profit and Loss A/c)		180	180
	Interest A/c Dr. To Profit and Loss A/c (Being transfer of interest to Profit and Loss A/c)		300	300

MAINTENANCE SUSPENSE ACCOUNT

		₹			₹
2023			2023		
Dec. 31	To Cash A/c	100	Jan. 1	By Hire Sales	500
"	To Balance c/d	430	Dec. 31	By P. & L. A/c (₹ 100 – ₹ 70)	30
		530			530
2024			2024		
Dec. 31	To Cash A/c	250	Jan. 1	By Balance b/d	430
"	To P. & L. A/c	180			
		430			430

Working Note :

(*i*) ***Calculation of Interest***

Sales Price ₹ 4,000 – Cash Price ₹ 3,000 = ₹ 1,000 Interest.

Instalment	Outstanding Instalment	Ratio	Interest
			₹
I	4	4/10	$\frac{1,000 \times 4}{10} = 400$
II	3	3/10	$\frac{1,000 \times 3}{10} = 300$
III	2	2/10	$\frac{1,000 \times 2}{10} = 200$
IV	1	1/10	$\frac{1,000 \times 1}{10} = 100$
	10		1,000

Goods of Comparatively Small Value

When numerous goods of small value are being sold by a firm under hire purchase system on different dates, then it becomes inconvenient and impracticable to maintain separate account for each customer and to calculate interest in respect of sale of each type of goods. Following method can be adopted under these circumstances :

(*a*) A subsidiary book under the name of Hire Purchase Register may be maintained to record name of the article, cost price, selling price, number of instalments, down payment and many small columns for recording the receipt of instalments as and when received. The specimen ruling of this register is as under :

HIRE PURCHASE REGISTER

Date of Contract	Name of Customer	Name of Article	Cost Price	Selling Price	Number of Instalment	Down Payment	Date of Payments							
							1st	2nd	3rd	4th	5th	6th	7th	8th

(*b*) From this register, the following information will be collected at the end of the financial year :

(*i*) Cost price of the goods sold on hire purchase to various customers ;

(*ii*) Total cash received from customers ;

(*iii*) Total instalments due but not paid by customers. This may be due to the delay on the part of the customers.

(*iv*) Cost price of the goods lying in the hands of customers on which instalments have not become due. The total amount of unpaid and not due instalments gives the cost price of the goods in the hands of customers and is known at 'Stock out on Hire at cost price'. The value of such items can be ascertained in the following ways provided the gross profit margin is uniform :

(*i*) $\frac{\text{Amount of unpaid instalments}}{\text{Amount of hire purchase amount}} \times \text{Cost}$

or (*ii*) Unpaid instalments – Gross profit margin

or (*iii*) $\frac{\text{No. of unpaid instalments}}{\text{No. of instalments including down payment}} \times \text{Cost}$

Note. In case *(iii)*, the amount of down payment must be the same as that of instalment.

The cost price of unpaid and not due instalments (or stock at the end) will be calculated and will be shown on the credit side of trading account.

Accounting Procedure for Preparing Hire Purchase Trading Account

After obtaining the necessary information from the hire purchase register, a hire purchase trading account can be prepared.

Following Journal Entries will be passed in the books of the vendor.

(i) When goods are sold on hire purchase

Hire Purchase Trading A/c
  To Goods Sold on Hire Purchase A/c] with H.P. Price

(ii) On receipts of instalments

Cash A/c Dr.
  To Hire Purchase Trading A/c

(iii) For instalments due at the end of the year but not received

Instalments Due or H.P. Debtors A/c Dr.
  To Hire Purchase Trading A/c

Note. For opening balance of instalment due, a reverse entry will be passed.

(iv) For goods repossessed due to non-payment of instalments

Repossessed Goods A/c Dr.
  To Hire Purchase Trading A/c] with the estimated value of goods received

(v) For goods lying with customers in respect of which instalments are not due :

Hire Purchase Stock A/c Dr.
  To Hire Purchase Trading A/c] at H.P. Price

Note. For opening stock of such goods reverse entry will be passed.

(vi) To remove the loading in hire purchase sales

Goods Sold on Hire Purchase A/c Dr.
  To Hire Purchase Trading A/c] For loading only

(vii) To remove the loading in closing stock

Hire Purchase Trading A/c
  To Stock Reserve A/c] For loading only

Note. For removing the loading in opening stock, reverse entry will be passed.

(viii) Hire Purchase Trading Account is now complete and will show profit or loss which will be closed by transfer to Profit and Loss Account.

(a) If Profit

Hire Purchase Trading A/c Dr.
  To P. & L. A/c

(b) If Loss

P. & L. A/c Dr.
  To H.P. Trading A/c

At the beginning of the next year Instalment Due Account, Hire Purchase Stock Account and Stock Reserve Account will be closed by transfer to the Hire Purchase Trading Account.

ILLUSTRATION 11. Sonam Corporation sells goods on hire purchase basis. The hire purchase price is cost plus 50%. From the following particulars (all figures are at invoice price) prepare Hire Purchase Trading Account for the year ended 31st March, 2025 :

	₹
Instalments not yet due on 1-4-24	3,00,000
Instalments due on 1-4-24	1,50,000
Goods sold on hire purchase during the year	9,00,000
Instalments collected from HP debtors	6,80,000
Stock with customers at hire purchase price	4,50,000
Goods re-possessed during the year	60,000
On 31-3-2025 Goods repossessed were valued at Cost less 40%	

(CA—Inter Modified)

SOLUTION

HIRE PURCHASE TRADING ACCOUNT

for the year ended 31-3-2025

	₹		₹
To Opening Balance :		By Hire Purchase Stock Reserve (Opening)	1,00,000
Hire Purchase Stock	3,00,000	By Bank (Instalments Collected)	6,80,000
Hire Purchase Debtors	1,50,000	By Goods Repossessed (3)	24,000
To Goods sold on Hire Purchase	9,00,000	By Goods Sold on Hire Purchase (Loading)	3,00,000
To Hire Purchase Stock Reserve (Closing)	1,50,000	By Closing Balances:	
To Profit & Loss A/c	2,14,000	Hire Purchase Stock	4,50,000
		Hire Purchase Debtors (2)	1,60,000
	17,14,000		17,14,000

Working Notes :

(1) MEMORANDUM HIRE PURCHASE STOCK ACCOUNT

	₹		₹
To Balance b/d	3,00,000	By Hire Purchase Debtors a/c (Bal. Fig.)	7,50,000
To Goods sold on Hire Purchase	9,00,000	By Balance c/d	4,50,000
	12,00,000		12,00,000

(2) MEMORANDUM HIRE PURCHASE DEBTORS ACCOUNT

	₹		₹
To Balance b/d	1,50,000	By Bank/Cash	6,80,000
To Hire Purchase Stock A/c (1)	7,50,000	By Goods Repossessed	60,000
		By Balance c/d (Bal. Fig.)	1,60,000
	9,00,000		9,00,000

(3) Value of goods re-possessed : $\left(₹\,60{,}000 \times \frac{100}{150} \times \frac{60}{100}\right) = ₹\,24{,}000$

ILLUSTRATION 12. M/s Deep Electronic sells TVs on hire purchase basis. Cost price per set ₹ 28,000. Cash sale price ₹ 30,100 and hire purchase price is 33,600 for 12 monthly instalments payable by 10th of every month. However, the buyer has to make cash down payment ₹ 3,600 at the time of purchase. Hire purchase transactions (No. of sets) are 150 : January—10; February—12; March—10; April—12; May—10; June—10; July—10; August—15; September—11; October—20; November—20; and December—10. All instalments are duly collected. Show the necessary Journal Entries (without narration) and prepare Hire Purchase Trading Account.

SOLUTION

JOURNAL ENTRIES

			₹	₹
(*i*) For cash down payment at the time of hire transaction.	Cash/Bank A/c	Dr.	5,40,000	
	To Hire Purchase Sale			5,40,000
(*ii*) When instalmens falls due	Instalments Due A/c	Dr.	18,72,500	
	To Hire Purchase Sale			18,72,500
(*iii*) On collection of instalments	Cash/Bank A/c	Dr.	18,72,500	
	To Instalments Due			18,72,500
(*iv*) For instalments not yet due at the end of the year	Hire Purchase Stock A/c	Dr.	26,27,500	
	To Trading A/c			26,27,500
(*v*) For Stock Reserve	Stock Reserve A/c	Dr.	4,37,916	
	To Hire Purchase Stock A/c			4,37,916

HIRE PURCHASE TRADING ACCOUNT

	₹		₹
To Shop Stock A/c (₹ 28,000 × 150)	42,00,000	By Hire Purchase Sale A/c	24,12,500
To Stock Reserve A/c	4,37,916	By Stock with Customers A/c	
To Profit & Loss A/c (Profit)	4,02,084	(at hire purchase price)	26,27,500
	50,40,000		50,40,000

Working Notes :

Total No. of Transactions 150

Cash down ₹ 3,600 × 150 = ₹ 5,40,000

Instalments Collected/Due

Transactions	***No. of Instalments Collected***			***No. of Instalmens Due***		
January	10 × 11 (1)	=	110	10 × 1	=	10
February	12 × 10	=	120	12 × 2	=	24
March	10 × 9	=	90	10 × 3	=	30
April	12 × 8	=	96	12 × 4	=	48
May	10 × 7	=	70	10 × 5	=	50
June	10 × 6	=	60	10 × 6	=	60
July	10 × 5	=	50	10 × 7	=	70
August	15 × 4	=	60	15 × 8	=	120
September	11 × 3	=	33	11 × 9	=	99
October	20 × 2	=	40	20 × 10	=	200
November	20 × 1	=	20	20 × 11	=	220
December	10 × 0	=	0	10 × 12	=	120
			749			1051

Total Instalments 1800 (*i.e.* 150 × 12) or 749 Collected + 1051 Due = 1800.

Amount collected for 749 instalments

$$= \frac{₹\ 33{,}600 - ₹\ 3{,}600}{12} \times 749 = ₹\ \mathbf{18{,}72{,}500}$$

Amount not yet due

$$= \frac{₹\ 33{,}600 - ₹\ 3{,}600}{12} \times 1051 = ₹\ \mathbf{26{,}27{,}500}$$

Cash Down = ₹ 3,600 × 150 = ₹ **5,40,000**

Total Hire Purchase Amount (₹ 33,600 × 150) = ₹ **50,40,000**

Hire Vendor should recognise the amount of instalmens collected and cash down value (*i.e. ₹ 5,40,000 + ₹ 18,72,500) ₹* ***24,12,500 as sale.*** *Balance of ₹ 26,27,500 is value of goods lying with customers at hire purchase price.* Stock Reserve should be computed and deducted from such amount to show Hire Purchase

$$\text{Stock at cost} = \text{Goods lying with Hire Purchase at Hire Purchase Price} \times \frac{\text{Cost Price}}{\text{Hire Purchase Price}}$$

$$\text{Stock at Cost} = ₹\ 26{,}27{,}500 \times \frac{₹\ 28{,}000}{₹\ 33{,}600} = ₹\ 21{,}89{,}584$$

Stock Reserve = ₹ 26,27,500 – 21,89,584 = ₹ **4,37,916**

Ist instalment of January's transaction will be collected by 10th February, therefore, instalment of January's transaction collected in the year will be 11

ILLUSTRATION 13. From the following information of M/s Chennai Traders, you are required to prepare Hire Purchase Trading Account to ascertain the profit made during the financial year 2024-25.

Chennai Traders sell goods on hire purchase basis at cost plus 25%. Following details are available : (All figure are at invoice price)

	₹
(1) Instalments not due on 31st March, 2024	4,50,000
(2) Instalments due and collected during the financial year 2024-25	12,00,000
(3) Instalments due but not collected during the financial year 2024-25 which includes ₹ 15,000 for which goods were repossessed	75,000
(4) Instalments not due on 31st March, 2025 including ₹ 30,000 for which goods were repossessed	5,55,000
(5) Instalments collected on repossessed stock	22,500
(6) M/s Chennai Traders valued repossessed stock at 60% of original cost.	

(CA—Inter Modified)

SOLUTION

In the Books of M/s Chennai Traders

HIRE PURCHASE TRADING ACCOUNT (at Invoice Value)

	₹		₹
To Goods with Customers (31st March, 2024)	4,50,000	By Stock Reserve (Opening)	90,000
To Goods Sold on Hire Purchase (3)	13,50,000	By Hire Purchase Sales (1)	12,75,000
To Bad Debts (4)	3,000	By Goods Sold on Hire Purchase (Loading) (3)	2,70,000
To Loss on Repossession (W.N. 2)	3,600	By Goods with Customers (31st March, 2025)	5,25,000
To Stock Reserve (Closing)	1,05,000		
To Profit & Loss A/c (Transfer of H.P. Profit)	2,48,400		
	21,60,000		21,60,000

Working Notes :

(1) Hire Purchase Sales

	₹
Instalments due and Collected	12,00,000
Add : Instalments due but not Collected	75,000
	12,75,000

(2) Loss on Repossessed Goods

	₹
Hire Purchase Price of Repossessed Goods :	
Instalments collected	22,500
Instalments due	15,000
Instalments not due	30,000
	67,500
Cost of repossessed goods (₹ 67,500 × 100/125)	54,000
Valuation of repossessed goods (₹ 54,000 × 60/100)	32,400
Less : Cost of instalments due + Instalments not yet due (₹ 15,000 + 30,000) × 100/125	(36,000)
Loss on repossession	3,600

(3) Goods taken from Shop Stock :

	₹
Hire Purchase Sales (12,00,000 + 75,000)	12,75,000
Add : Stock with customers as on 31st March 2025 (₹ 5,55,000 – ₹ 30,000)	5,25,000
Less : Stock with Customers as on 31st March, 2024	(4,50,000)
	13,50,000

Loading on goods taken from shop stock = ₹ 13,50,000 × (25/125) = ₹ 2,70,000.

(4) Bad Debts

	₹
Instalments due but not collected on repossessed goods	15,000
Add : Insalments not yet due on repossessed goods at cost $\left(₹ 30,000 \times \frac{100}{125}\right)$	24,000
	39,000
Less : Cost of instalments due and not yet due	(36,000)
	3,000

In other words ₹ 15,000 × (25/125) = ₹ 3,000

ILLUSTRATION 14. Sameera Corporation sells Computers on Hire-purchase basis at cost plus 25%. Terms of sales are ₹ 5,000 as down payment and 10 monthly instalments of ₹ 2,500 for each computer. From the following particulars, prepare Hire-purchase Trading A/c for the year 2024-25 :

As on 1st April, 2024 last instalment on 20 computers was outstanding as this was not due upto the end of the previous year. During 2024-25, the firm sold 120 computers. As on 31st March, 2025 the position of instalments outstanding was as under :

Instalments due but not collected	4 Instalments on 4 computers and Last Instalment on 9 Computers
Instalments not yet due	6 Instalments on 50 Computers, 4 Instalments on 20 Computers and Last Instalment on 40 Computers.

Two Computers on which 8 instalments were due and one instalment not yet due on 31-3-2025, had to be repossessed. Repossessed stock is valued at 50% of cost. All other instalments have been received.

SOLUTION

Hire Purchase Price = ₹ 5,000 Down Payment + ₹ 25,000 on 10 Instalments = ₹ 30,000

Cost of Computer = ₹ 30,000 $- \frac{25}{125} \times$ ₹ 30,000 = ₹ 24,000

HIRE PURCHASE TRADING ACCOUNT

for the year ending 31st March, 2025

	₹		₹
To Hire Purchase Stock (1-4-2024) (Last Instalment on 20 Computers @ ₹ 2,500)	50,000	By Bank Account (1)	24,92,500
To Goods Sold on Hire Purchase (120 × ₹ 30,000)	36,00,000	By Goods Repossessed A/c $\left(2 \times ₹\ 24{,}000 \times \frac{50}{100}\right)$	24,000
To Stock Reserve $\left(\frac{25}{125} \times ₹\ 10{,}50{,}000\right)$	2,10,000	By Instalments Due (4 × 4 + 1 × 9 = 25 Instalments of ₹ 2,500 each)	62,500
To Profit & Loss A/c (Transfer of Profit)	4,99,000	By Hire Purchase Stock [(6 × 50 + 4 × 20 + 1 × 40) × ₹ 2,500]	10,50,000
		By Stock Reserve $\left(\frac{25}{125} \times ₹\ 50{,}000\right)$	10,000
		By Goods Sold on Hire Purchase $\left(\frac{25}{125} \times ₹\ 36{,}00{,}000\right)$	7,20,000
	43,59,000		43,59,000

Working Note

(1) ***Calculation of Amount Collected during the Year 2024-25***

	₹	₹	₹
Down payment on 120 computers @ ₹ 5,000			6,00,000
Add : Instalments collected			
(*a*) Last instalment on 20 computers outstanding as on 1-4-2024 (20 × ₹ 2,500)			50,000
(*b*) Instalments due and collected on 120 computers sold during the year :			
Total instalments on 120 computers (10 × 120 × ₹ 2,500)		30,00,000	
Less : Instalments due but not collected :			
4 instalments on 4 computers @ ₹ 2,500 (*i.e.* 4 × 4 × ₹ 2,500)	40,000		
Last Instalment on 9 computers (9 × ₹ 2,500)	22,500		
8 instalments on 2 repossessed computers (8 × 2 × ₹ 2,500)	40,000		
		1,02,500	
		28,97,500	
Less : Instalments not due as on 31-3-2025 :			
6 instalments on 50 computers (6 × 50 × ₹ 2,500)	7,50,000		
4 instalments on 20 computers (4 × 20 × ₹ 2,500)	2,00,000		
Last instalment on 40 computers (40 × ₹ 2,500)	1,00,000		
One instalment on 2 repossessed computers (1 × 2 × ₹ 2,500)	5,000		
		10,55,000	
			18,42,500
Amount collected during the year 2024-25			24,92,500

Stock and Debtors Method

This is an alternative method of calculating profit or loss of those traders who sell a number of goods of comparatively small value daily on the hire purchase system. Instead of preparing one H.P. Trading Account to calculate the profit, Hire Purchase Stock Account, Hire Purchase Debtors Account, Shop Stock Account and Hire Purchase Adjustment Account are prepared. Following entries are passed relating to hire purchase transactions :

(*i*) *When goods are purchased for shop stock*

Shop Stock A/c	Dr.	(Cost price)
To Purchases A/c		

(*ii*) *When goods are sold on hire purchase*

Hire Purchase Stock A/c	Dr.	(At sale price)
To Goods Sold on H.P A/c		

(*iii*) *For total instalments which become due*

Hire Purchase Debtors A/c	Dr.	(H.P. Price)
To Hire Purchase Stock A/c		

(*iv*) *When cash is received from debtors*

Cash A/c	Dr.	
To Hire Purchase Debtors A/c		

(*v*) *When goods are repossessed on default and loss is transferred to Hire Purchase Adjustment A/c*

Goods Repossessed A/c	Dr.	[For realisable value]
H.P. Adjustment A/c	Dr.	[Loss]
To Hire Purchase Debtors A/c		[Instalments due and not received in cash]
To Hire Purchase Stock A/c		[For instalments not yet due]
To H.P. Adjustment A/c		[Profit on Repossession]

(*vi*) *For transfer of goods sold on H.P.*

Goods Sold on H.P. A/c	Dr.	
To H.P. Adjustment A/c		[Loading]
To Trading A/c		[Cost price]

(*vii*) *For reserve on closing stock*

Hire Purchase Adjustment A/c	Dr.	[For Loading]
To Stock Reserve A/c		

(*viii*) *For reserve on opening stock*

Stock Reserve A/c	Dr.	[For Loading]
To Hire Purchase Adjustment A/c		

(*ix*) *For profit or loss on hire purchase*

(*a*) *If Profit*		(*b*) *If Loss*	
H.P. Adjustment A/c	Dr.	Profit & Loss A/c	Dr.
To Profit & Loss A/c		To H.P Adjustment A/c	

ILLUSTRATION 15. Harish sells goods on hire purchase at cost plus 50%. From the following particulars relating to the hire-purchase department for the year ending 31st March, 2025, prepare H.P. Debtors A/c ; Shop Stock A/c ; H.P. Stock A/c ; H.P. Adjustment A/c ; Goods Sold on H.P. A/c and Stock Reserve A/c.

		₹
April 1 2024	Stock with hire-purchase customers at selling price	4,500
	Stock at shop at cost	9,000
	Instalments due	2,500

April 1 2024 to 31st March, 2025	Cash received from customers	30,000
	Hire Expenses	1,250
	Goods purchased during the year	30,000
March 31, 2025	Instalments due customers paying	4,500
	Goods repossessed (instalments due ₹ 1,000) valued at	250
	Stock at shop at cost (excluding repossessed goods)	10,000

Verify your result by preparing H.P. Trading Account.

SOLUTION

HIRE PURCHASE STOCK ACCOUNT

		₹		₹
To Balance b/d		4,500	By H.P. Debtors A/c (1)	33,000
To Goods Sold on H.P. A/c	₹		By Balance c/d (Bal. figure) (3)	15,000
Cost (2)	29,000			
Profit	14,500			
		43,500		
		48,000		48,000

HIRE PURCHASE DEBTORS ACCOUNT

	₹		₹
To Balance b/d	2,500	By Cash	30,000
To Hire Purchase Stock A/c (1)		By Goods Repossessed A/c	250
(Instalment due)		By H.P. Adjustment A/c	750
(Balancing figure)	33,000	By Balance c/d	4,500
	35,500		35,500

SHOP STOCK ACCOUNT

	₹		₹
To Balance b/d	9,000	By Cost of Goods Sold on H.P.	
To Purchases A/c	30,000	(Bal. figure) (2)	29,000
		By Balance c/d	10,000
	39,000		39,000

H.P. ADJUSTMENT ACCOUNT

	₹		₹
To Stock Reserve A/c	5,000	By Stock Reserve	1,500
To H.P. Drs. A/c (Loss)	750	By Goods Sold on H.P. A/c	14,500
To Hire Expenses	1,250		
To Profit & Loss A/c (Profit)	9,000		
	16,000		16,000

GOODS SOLD ON H.P. ACCOUNT

	₹		₹
To H.P. Adjustment A/c	14,500	By H.P. Stock A/c	43,500
To Trading A/c	29,000		
	43,500		43,500

STOCK RESERVE ACCOUNT

	₹		₹
To H.P Adjustment A/c	1,500	By Balance b/d	1,500
To Balance c/d	5,000	By H.P. Adjustment A/c	5,000

Note. Numbers in Brackets are given successive steps.

H.P. TRADING ACCOUNT

	₹		₹
To Stock with Customers	4,500	By Cash A/c	30,000
To Instalment Due	2,500	By Goods Repossessed A/c (₹ 1,000)	250
To Goods Sold on H.P. A/c	43,500	By H.P. Stock A/c	15,000
To Stock Reserve A/c	5,000	By Instalment Due A/c	4,500
To Hire Expenses	1,250	By Stock Reserve A/c	1,500
To Net Profit	9,000	By Goods Sold on H.P. A/c	14,500
	65,750		65,750

ILLUSTRATION 16. (*Partial Repossession & H.P. Trading*). Shri Nikhil commenced business on 1st April, 2024. During the year ended 31st March, 2025 purchases amounted to ₹ 54,000 and ordinary sales ₹ 62,000. In addition the following sales were made under Hire Purchase arrangements :

Article	*Cost*	*Sales Price*	*Initial amount paid*	*Monthly Instalment*	*No. of Instalments paid during the year*
	₹	₹	₹		
Radio	600	900	100	20 of ₹ 40	8
Washing Machine	800	1,200	120	12 of ₹ 90	2
Record Player	700	1,000	100	18 of ₹ 50	4

After 4 instalments had been paid on Record Player it was returned on 29th March, 2025.

Stock in trade on 31st March, 2025 excluding Record Player returned amounted to ₹ 7,000.

Prepare : (*i*) Hire Purchase Trading Account, (*ii*) General Trading A/c ; (*iii*) Goods Repossessed Account and (*iv*) Memorandum Hire-Purchase Debtors Account for the year ended 31st March, 2025.

Note. The value of goods returned may be taken at cost equivalent.

SOLUTION

Sh. Nikhil

HIRE PURCHASE TRADING ACCOUNT

	₹			₹
To Purchases	2,100	By Cash received :	₹	
To Gross Profit	330	Radio	420	
		Washing Machine	300	
		Record Player	300	
				1,020
		By Goods Repossessed A/c $\left(\frac{₹\,700}{₹\,1{,}000} \times ₹\,700\right)$ (Cost of Record Player)		490

		By Stock in hands of customers at cost equivalent (₹ 320 + ₹ 600)	920
	2,430		2,430

GENERAL TRADING ACCOUNT

	₹	₹		₹
To Purchases	54,000		By Sales	62,000
Less : Cost of goods sold on H.P.	2,100		By Closing Stock	7,000
		51,900		
To Gross Profit		17,100		
		69,000		69,000

GOODS REPOSSESSED ACCOUNT

	₹		₹
To Hire Purchase Trading A/c (Cost of Record Player)	490	By Balance c/d	490

MEMORANDUM H.P. DEBTORS ACCOUNT

	₹		₹
To Sale Price of Goods delivered on Hire Purchase (₹ 900 + ₹ 1,200 + ₹ 1,000)	3,100	By Cash received	1,020
		" Goods repossessed (at H.P. Price)	700
		" Balance c/d	1,380
	3,100		3,100
To Balance b/d	1,380		

Working Note :

Calculation of the Value of Stock at Cost Equivalent

$$\text{Cost Equivalent} = \frac{\text{Instalments Outstanding}}{\text{Sale Price}} \times \text{Cost Price}$$

	Cost	*H.P. Sale Price*	*Initial Payment*	*Instalments Paid*	*Instalments Outstanding*	*Cost Equivalent*
	₹	₹	₹	₹	₹	₹
Radio	600	900	100	8 × 40 = 320	12 × 40 = 480	320 $\left(i.e.\ 480 \times \frac{600}{900}\right)$
Washing Machine	800	1,200	120	2 × 90 = 180	10 × 90 = 900	600 $\left(i.e.\ 900 \times \frac{800}{1,200}\right)$
Record Player	700	1,000	100	4 × 50 = 200	14 × 50 = 700	490 $\left(i.e.\ 700 \times \frac{700}{1,000}\right)$
Total			320	700		

ILLUSTRATION 17. Delhi Traders commenced business in 2023 selling goods on hire purchase basis on the following terms :

Cost	*Selling price*	*Deposit payable*	*Instalments payable*
₹ 2,000	₹ 3,000	20%	12 Monthly

Monthly instalments are payable on the last date of the month in which the sale takes place. Other details are :

	2023	*2024*
Sales	300 Nos.	600 Nos.
Instalments Received	₹ 3,75,000	₹ 10,70,000

Sales take place evenly throughout the year. In 2024, 40 items sold in 2023 on which a total of 300 instalments had been received were repossessed.

Show ledger accounts for both the years in the books of Delhi Traders.

SOLUTION

HIRE PURCHASE TRADING ACCOUNT

for the year ending 31st December, 2023

	₹		₹
To Goods sold on H.P. (300 × ₹ 3,000)	9,00,000	By Hire Purchase Debtors A/c [Cash & Instalments Due *i.e.,* ₹ 1,80,000 + ₹ 3,90,000]	5,70,000
" Stock Reserve (1/3 of ₹ 3,30,000)	1,10,000	" H.P. Stock A/c (1)	3,30,000
" Net Profit transferred to P. & L. A/c	1,90,000	" Goods sold on H.P. (1/3 of ₹ 9,00,000)	3,00,000
	12,00,000		12,00,000

HIRE PURCHASE TRADING ACCOUNT

for the year ending 31st December, 2024

	₹		₹
To H.P. Stock (Opening Balance)	3,30,000	By Stock Reserve (opening)	1,10,000
" Goods sold on H.P. A/c (600 × ₹ 3,000)	18,00,000	" Hire Purchase Debtors A/c [Cash and Instalments Due ₹ 14,70,000 – ₹ 36,000] (3)	14,34,000
" Stock Reserve (1/3 of ₹ 6,60,000)	2,20,000	" Repossessed Goods A/c (2/3 of ₹ 36,000)	24,000
" Net Profit transferred to Profit and Loss A/c	4,78,000	" H.P. Stock A/c (2)	6,60,000
		" Goods sold on H.P. (Loading)	6,00,000
	28,28,000		28,28,000

HIRE PURCHASE DEBTORS ACCOUNT

		₹			₹
2023	To H.P. Trading A/c	5,70,000	2023	By Cash — Down payment	1,80,000
				— Instalments	3,75,000
				" Balance c/d	15,000
		5,70,000			5,70,000

2024			2024		
	To Balance b/d	15,000		By Cash — Down Payment	3,60,000
	" H.P. Trading A/c	14,34,000		— Instalments	10,70,000
				" Balance c/d	19,000
		14,49,000			14,49,000

Working Notes :

(1) ***Calculation of instalments due in 2023 and 2024 from sales of 2023***

	Units Sold	*Per Unit in 2023*	*Total in 2023*	*Per unit in 2024*	*Total in 2024*
January	25	12	300	—	—
February	25	11	275	1	25
March	25	10	250	2	50
April	25	9	225	3	75
May	25	8	200	4	100
June	25	7	175	5	125
July	25	6	150	6	150
August	25	5	125	7	175
September	25	4	100	8	200
October	25	3	75	9	225
November	25	2	50	10	250
December	25	1	25	11	275
			1,950		1,650
Amount of each instalment (₹)			200		200
Total amount (₹)			3,90,000		3,30,000

(2) On the basis of 2023 instalments due in 2024 will be ₹ 7,80,000 (*i.e.,* ₹ 3,90,000 × 2) and value of stock lying with customers will be ₹ 6,60,000 (*i.e.,* ₹ 3,30,000 × 2) (amount of instalments due in 2025). Sales in 2024 being double as compared to 2024, so figures have been multiplied by 2.

(3) *Amount due from customers*

	₹
Ex-2023 Sales	3,30,000
Ex-2024 Sales :	
Down payment (600 × ₹ 600)	3,60,000
Hire Purchase instalments	7,80,000
	14,70,000
Less : Instalments due on repossessed sales 180 (*i.e.,* 480 – 300) × ₹ 200 =	36,000
	14,34,000

ILLUSTRATION 18. (*Where goods are sold both for cash and hire purchase*). Venus Enterprises sells goods for cash and hire purchase. The rate of gross profit for hire purchase sales is 32 per cent on cost, and cash sales are made at the hire purchase price as reduced by 1/11th.

The Trading Account is constructed on the basis that full credit is taken on hire purchase deliveries as well as on the cash basis.

The hire purchase trading did not commence till 1st February, 2024.

The Trading Account of the concern for the year ended 31st December, 2024 was as follows :

	₹		₹
To Opening Stock	2,10,000	By H.P. Sales	13,39,800
To Purchases	10,75,000	*Less* : Returns	14,850
			13,24,950
To Gross Profit	3,54,950	By Cash Sales	1,80,000
		" Closing Stock	1,35,000
	16,39,950		16,39,950

Instalments received during the year amounted to ₹ 7,96,950. Returns of ₹ 14,850 represents unpaid instalments on repossessed goods ; which have been included in closing stock at a valuation of ₹ 10,000. The original cost of repossessed goods is ₹ 15,000.

Ascertain the correct profit of the concern on hire purchase and general trading by preparing Hire Purchase Trading Account, General Trading Account and Goods Repossessed Account.

SOLUTION

HIRE PURCHASE TRADING ACCOUNT

	₹		₹	₹
To Shop Stock A/c (Cost of goods sold on hire purchase : ₹ 13,39,800 $\times \frac{100}{132}$)	10,15,000	By H.P. Sales A/c (Instalments Collected)		7,96,950
		By Repossessed Goods at cost		15,000
To Repossessed Goods A/c— Transfer of Instalments Collected. [₹ 15,000 + ₹ 4,800 *i.e.* 32% of ₹ 15,000) – ₹ 14,850]	4,950	By H.P. Stock A/c (at hire purchase price) (₹ 13,39,800 – ₹ 7,96,950 – ₹ 14,850)	5,28,000	
		Less : Stock Reserve (₹ 5,28,000 $\times \frac{32}{132}$)	1,28,000	4,00,000
To Profit & Loss A/c (Profit)	1,92,000			
	12,11,950			12,11,950

GENERAL TRADING ACCOUNT

	₹		₹
To Shop Stock A/c (Cost of Goods Sold on H.P. : ₹ 1,80,000 $\times \frac{100}{120}$)	1,50,000	By Sales	1,80,000
To Gross Profit	30,000		
	1,80,000		1,80,000

REPOSSESSED GOODS ACCOUNT

	₹		₹
To Hire Purchase Trading A/c	15,000	By Hire Purchase Trading A/c	4,950
		" Shop Stock A/c	10,000
		" Profit & Loss A/c (Loss)	50
	15,000		15,000

Working Note :

SHOP STOCK ACCOUNT

	₹		₹
To Balance b/d	2,10,000	By H.P. Trading A/c	10,15,000
To Purchases	10,75,000	By General Trading A/c	1,50,000
To Repossessed Goods A/c	10,000	By Balance c/d [Value of unsold goods at cost price ₹ 1,20,000 plus ₹ 10,000 repossessed goods at current price which is less than the cost)	1,30,000
	12,95,000		12,95,000

ILLUSTRATION 19. Krishna Agencies started business on 1st April, 2024. During the year ended 31st March, 2025, they sold undermentioned durables under two schemes - Cash Price Scheme (CPS) and Hire Purchase Scheme (HPS).

Under the CPS they priced the goods at cost plus 25% and collected it on delivery.

Under the HPS the buyers were required to sign a Hire-purchase Agreement undertaking to pay for the value of the goods including finance charges in 30 instalments, the value being calculated at Cash Price plus 50%.

Following are the details available at the end of 31st March, 2025 with regard to the products :

Product	*Nos. purchased*	*Nos. sold under CPS*	*Nos. sold under HPS*	*Cost per unit*	*No. of instalments due during the year*	*No. of instalments received during the year*
				₹		
TV Set	90	20	60	16,000	1,080	1,000
Washing Machines	70	20	40	12,000	840	800

Following were the expenses during the year :

Rent ₹ 1,20,000 ; Salaries ₹ 1,44,000 ; Commission to Salesmen ₹ 12,000 ; Office Expenses ₹ 1,20,000.

From the above information, you are required to prepare :

(*a*) Hire-purchase Trading Account, and

(*b*) Trading and Profit & Loss Account.

SOLUTION

(*a*) **In the Books of Krishna Agencies**

HIRE PURCHASE TRADING ACCOUNT

for the year ended 31st March, 2025

		₹			₹
To Goods sold on H.P. A/c :			By Bank A/c- cash received		
TVs			TVs (1,000 × ₹ 1,000)		
(60 × ₹ 30,000)	₹ 18,00,000			₹ 10,00,000	
Washing Machines			Washing Machines		
(40 × ₹ 22,500)	₹ 9,00,000	27,00,000	(800 × ₹ 750)	₹ 6,00,000	16,00,000

To H.P. Stock Reserve $\left[₹ 9,90,000 \times \frac{87.5}{187.5}\right]$	4,62,000	Instalment Due A/c : TVs (80 × ₹ 1,000)	₹ 80,000	
		Washing Machines (40 × ₹ 750)	₹ 30,000	
To Profit & Loss A/c	7,98,000			1,10,000
		By Goods sold on H.P. A/c : (Cancellation of loading) $\left[₹ 27,00,000 \times \frac{87.5}{187.5}\right]$		12,60,000
		" H.P. Stock (2)		9,90,000
	39,60,000			39,60,000

(*b*) **TRADING AND PROFIT & LOSS ACCOUNT**

for the year ended 31st March, 2025

		₹			₹
To Purchases :			By Sales :		
TVs (90 × ₹ 16,000)	₹ 14,40,000		TVs (20 × ₹ 20,000)	₹ 4,00,000	
Washing Machines (70 × ₹ 12,000)	₹ 8,40,000		Washing Machines (20 × ₹ 15,000)	₹ 3,00,000	
		22,80,000			7,00,000
" Gross Profit c/d		1,40,000	" Goods sold on H.P. A/c (₹ 27,00,000 – ₹ 12,60,000)		14,40,000
			" Shop Stock (3)		2,80,000
		24,20,000			24,20,000
To Salaries		1,44,000	By Gross Profit b/d		1,40,000
" Rent		1,20,000	" H.P. Trading A/c (H.P. Profit)		7,98,000
" Commission		12,000			
" Office Expenses		1,20,000			
" Net Profit		5,42,000			
		9,38,000			9,38,000

Working Notes :

(1) ***Calculation of per Unit Cash Price, H.P. Price and Instalment Amount***

Product	*Cost*	*Cash Price (Cost × 1.25)*	*H.P. Price (Cost Price × 1.5)*	*Instalments Amount (H.P. Price/No. of Instalments)*
	₹	₹	₹	₹
T.V. Sets	16,000	20,000	30,000	1,000 (*i.e.* ₹ 30,000 ÷ 30)
Washing Machines	12,000	15,000	22,500	750 (*i.e.* ₹ 22,500 ÷ 30)

(2) *Calculation of H.P. Stock as on 31-3-2025*

Product	Total No. of Instalments (Nos)	Instalments due in 2024-25	Instalments not due in 2024-25	H.P. Stock
				₹
T.V. Set	1,800	1,080	720	7,20,000 (*i.e.* 720 × 1,000)
Washing Machine	1,200	840	360	2,70,000 (*i.e.* 360 × 750)
				9,90,000

(3) *Calculation of Shop Stock as on 31-3-2025*

Product	Nos. Purchased	Nos. Sold	Balance	Amount
	₹	₹	₹	₹
T.V. Sets	90	80	10	1,60,000 (*i.e.* 10 × 16,000)
Washing Machine	70	60	10	1,20,000 (*i.e.* 10 × 12,000)
				2,80,000

ILLUSTRATION 20. A Company started business on 1st April, 2024. The business is to sell radio sets and refrigerators both for cash and on hire-purchase basis. Information about the terms is given below:

	Radio Sets	*Refrigerators*
Sale Price (₹)	600	2,800
Cost (₹)	400	2,000
Cash down for hire-purchase (₹)	100	400
Monthly instalment (₹)	25	200
Number of instalments	20	12

The company purchased goods costing ₹ 96,000 and sales excluding hire-purchase transactions amounted to ₹ 63,900. Stock on 31st March, 2025 was valued at ₹ 7,210. Hire-purchase transactions were as follows :

	Number sold	*Instalments collected*	*Instalments due (customers paying)*
Radio Sets	40	520	30
Refrigerators	20	110	10

3 radio sets and 2 refrigerators on which only eight instalments were collected were repossessed and were valued at ₹ 2,433 ; after reconditioning at a cost of ₹ 400 these were sold for ₹ 3,633. This is not included in the figure of stock mentioned above.

Prepare (*i*) Hire Purchase Trading Account and Profit & Loss Account.

(*ii*) H.P. Stock Account, Hire Purchase Debtors Account, Goods Repossessed Account and H.P. Adjustment Account under Stock and Debtors System.

SOLUTION

(*i*) **HIRE PURCHASE TRADING ACCOUNT**

		₹			₹
2025			2025		
March 31	To Goods Sold on Hire Purchase A/c (1)	80,000	March 31	By Cash (2)	50,800
				" Goods Repossessed A/c	2,433
March 31	To H.P. Stock Reserve (on instalments not yet due) (4)	7,069		By Instalments Due	2,750
"	To P. & L. A/c	16,864		" Goods Sold on Hire Purchase A/c (Loading) (₹ 80,000 – ₹ 56,000)	24,000
				" Balance c/d (3)	23,950
		1,03,933			1,03,933

PROFIT AND LOSS ACCOUNT

	₹	₹		₹
To Purchases	96,000		By Sales	63,900
Less : Goods sold on H.P.	56,000	40,000	" Stock	7,210
			" Profit on H.P.	16,864
" Profit		48,774	" Profit on Goods Repossessed	800
		88,774		88,774

(*ii*) **H.P. STOCK ACCOUNT**

		₹			₹
To Goods sold on H.P. A/c	(1)	80,000	By H.P. Debtors A/c (Instalments falling due)	(6)	53,550
			By Goods Repossessed A/c (Instalments not yet due on repossessed goods)	(5)	2,500
			By Balance c/d (Instalments not yet due)	(3)	23,950
		80,000			80,000

HIRE PURCHASE DEBTORS ACCOUNT

		₹			₹
To H.P. Stock A/c	(6)	53,550	By Cash Collected	(2)	50,800
			By Balance c/d (30 × ₹ 25 + 10 × ₹ 200)		2,750
		53,550			53,550

GOODS REPOSSESSED ACCOUNT

		₹		₹
To H.P. Stock A/c (Instalments to be written off)	(6)	2,500	By H.P. Adjustment A/c	67
			" Balance c/d	2,433
		2,500		2,500

	₹		₹
To Balance b/d	2,433	By Cash (Sale)	3,633
" Cash	400		
" Profit & Loss A/c (Profit on Goods Repossessed)	800		
	3,633		3,633

H. P. ADJUSTMENT ACCOUNT

		₹		₹
To Goods Repossessed A/c (Loss on repossession of goods)		67	By Goods sold on H.P. A/c —Loading	24,000
" Stock Reserve A/c	(4)	7,069	" Gross Repossessed A/c (Profit on sale of repossessed goods)	800
" Profit & Loss A/c		17,664		
		24,800		24,800

Working Notes :

(1) ***Amount of Hire Purchase Cost and Price are worked out as follows :***

	Cost	*Hire Purchase Price*
	₹	₹
Radio Sets	40 × ₹ 400 = 16,000	40 × ₹ 600 = 24,000
Refrigerators	20 × ₹ 2,000 = 40,000	20 × ₹ 2,800 = 56,000
	56,000	80,000

(2) ***Cash Collected***

	Radio Sets	*Refrigerators*
	₹	₹
Down Payment	100 × 40 = 4,000	20 × 400 = 8,000
Instalments Collected	520 × 25 = 13,000	110 × 200 = 22,000
Amount Collected on Goods Repossessed	3 × 8 × 25 = 600	2 × 8 × 200 = 3,200
	17,600	33,200

Total Cash Collected = ₹ 17,600 + ₹ 33,200 = ₹ 50,800

(3) ***Instalments not yet due :***

Radio Sets

Total Instalments on 37 radio sets (37 × 20)	740
Less : Instalments collected and due	550
Instalments not yet due	190
Amount of instalments not yet due 190 × ₹ 25 =	₹ 4,750

Refrigerators :

Total instalments on 18 refrigerators (18 × 12)	216
Less : Instalments collected & due	120
Instalments not yet due	96

Amount of instalments not yet due = 96 × ₹ 200 = ₹ 19,200

Total amount of instalments not yet due = ₹ 4,750 + ₹ 19,200 = ₹ 23,950

(4) ***Stock Reserve :***

	Radio sets	*Refrigerators*
	₹	₹
H.P. Price	600	2,800
Cost	400	2,000
Profit	200	800

Reserve required $= \frac{200}{600} \times 4{,}750$ $= ₹\ 1{,}583$; $\frac{800}{2{,}800} \times 19{,}200$ $= ₹\ 5{,}486$

∴ Total Reserve required = ₹ 1,583 + ₹ 5,486 = ₹ 7,069

(5) ***Instalments not due on repossessed goods***

	₹
Radio Sets 12 × ₹ 25 × 3 =	900
Refrigerators 4 × ₹ 200 × 2 =	1,600
	2,500

(6) ***Hire Purchase Total Amount Receivable Radio Sets***

		₹	₹
Cash Down (40 × ₹ 100)	=	4,000	
Instalments received and due 550 × ₹ 25	=	13,750	
Instalments received on repossessed goods (3 × 8 × ₹ 25)	=	600	
			18,350
Refrigerators			
Cash Down (20 × ₹ 400)	=	8,000	
Instalments received and due (120 × ₹ 200)	=	24,000	
Instalments received on repossessed goods (2 × 8 × ₹ 200)	=	3,200	
			35,200
			53,550

ILLUSTRATION 21. Majestice & Co. commenced business on 1st April, 2024 dealing in the radio sets and record players. They sell goods both directly as well as on hire purchase. You are furnished with the following information for the year ended 31st March, 2025 :

		Radio Sets	*Record Players*
Purchases	No.	1000	100
Sales : Direct for Cash	No.	800	50
On hire-purchase	No.	40	20
To employees as explained below	No.	3	2
Purchase cost per unit		₹ 400	₹ 1,200
Direct sales price per unit		₹ 500	₹ 1,500
Terms of hire purchase sale :			
Cash down at the time of delivery		₹ 100	₹ 300
Monthly instalments		₹ 50	₹ 150
Number of instalments		10	12
Instalments collected		260	110
Instalments due but not collected		15	10

During the year firm repossessed 3 radio sets and 2 record players for failure to pay instalments. The hire purchase customers had paid only 4 instalments each in respect of these radio sets and record players. At the time of repossession, the radio sets were valued at ₹ 200 each and the record players were valued at ₹ 500 each. The firm spent ₹ 30 per radio set and ₹ 70 per record player on reconditioning. These sets were sold to employees at a concessional rate of ₹ 300 per radio set and ₹ 700 per record player and the amounts were recovered from their salaries before the close of the year.

Prepare columnar accounts to show the "earnings" during the year.

SOLUTION

Majestic & Co.

HIRE PURCHASE TRADING ACCOUNT

for the year ended 31st March, 2025

	Radio Set	*Record Player*	*Total*		*Radio Set*	*Record Player*	*Total*
	₹	₹	₹		₹	₹	₹
To Goods sold on H.P. (4)	24,000	42,000	66,000	By Cash/Bank A/c (5)	17,000	22,500	39,500
To Stock Reserve (on instalments not yet due) (9)	2,140	7,800	9,940	By Goods Repossessed A/c	600	1,000	1,600
To Profit & Loss A/c	5,560	8,800	14,360	By Instalments Due (7)	750	1,500	2,250
				By Stock out on Hire Purchase (8)	5,350	15,600	20,950
				By Goods Sold on H.P. (Loading)	8,000	18,000	26,000
	31,700	58,600	90,300		31,700	58,600	90,300

GOODS SOLD ON HIRE PURCHASE ACCOUNT

	₹	₹	₹		₹	₹	₹
To H.P. Trading A/c	8,000	18,000	26,000	By H.P. Trading A/c	24,000	42,000	66,000
To Purchases A/c	16,000	24,000	40,000				
	24,000	42,000	66,000		24,000	42,000	66,000

PURCHASES ACCOUNT

	₹	₹	₹		₹	₹	₹
To Suppliers (1)	4,00,000	1,20,000	5,20,000	By Goods Sold on H.P. (2)	16,000	24,000	40,000
				By Trading A/c (3)	3,84,000	96,000	4,80,000
	4,00,000	1,20,000	5,20,000		4,00,000	1,20,000	5,20,000

TRADING AND PROFIT & LOSS ACCOUNT

for the year ended 31st March, 2025

	₹	₹	₹		₹	₹	₹
To Purchases (3)	3,84,000	96,000	4,80,000	By Sales	4,00,000	75,000	4,75,000
To Gross Profit c/d	80,000	15,000	95,000	By Closing Stock	64,000	36,000	1,00,000
	4,64,000	1,11,000	5,75,000		4,64,000	1,11,000	5,75,000
To Profit subject to Sundry Expenses	85,770	24,060	1,09,830	By Gross Profit b/d	80,000	15,000	95,000
				" H.P. Trading A/c	5,560	8,800	14,360
				" Goods Repossessed A/c	210	260	470
	85,770	24,060	1,09,830		85,770	24,060	1,09,830

Working Notes :

	Radio Sets	Record Players	Total
	₹	₹	₹
(1) Purchases : 1,000 × ₹ 400	4,00,000		
100 × ₹ 1,200		1,20,000	5,20,000
(2) Cost of goods sold on H.P.			
40 × ₹ 400	16,000		
20 × ₹ 1,200		24,000	40,000
(3) Cost of goods transferred to Trading Account [(1) – (2)]	3,84,000	96,000	4,80,000
(4) H.P. selling price of goods sold on H.P.			
40 × ₹ 600	24,000		
20 × ₹ 2,100		42,000	66,000
(5) Cash collected			
Down payment			
40 × ₹ 100	4,000		
20 × ₹ 300		6,000	10,000
Instalments collected			
260 × ₹ 50	13,000		
110 × ₹ 150		16,500	29,500
	17,000	22,500	39,500
(6) Instalments due on repossessed sets			
3 × 6 × ₹ 50	900		
2 × 8 × ₹ 150		2,400	3,300
(7) Instalments Due			
15 × ₹ 50	750		
10 × ₹ 150		1,500	2,250
(8) Instalments not yet due			
[400 – (260 + 18 + 15)] × ₹ 50	5,350		
[240 – (110 + 16 + 10)] × ₹ 150		15,600	20,950
(9) Stock Reserve	₹	₹	
(*a*) Cost	400	1,200	
Less : Payment Cash Down	100	300	
Balance	300	900	
(*b*) Amount of instalments to be collected	500	1,800	
(*c*) Difference (*b*) – (*a*)	200	900	
Instalments not yet due	5,350	15,600	
Reserve required ₹ 5,350 × $\frac{200}{500}$	2,140		
₹ 15,600 × $\frac{900}{1,800}$		7,800	

ILLUSTRATION 22. A company sells goods on Hire Purchase on the basis 25% down, the balance with 20% interest thereon being payable in 8 equal quarterly instalments on 30th June, 30th September, 31st December and 31st March each year. The first instalment is payable at the end of the quarter in which the sale is made. The company transfers 50%, 30% and 20% of the interest to Profit and Loss Account in the first, second and third years respectively.

Balance on 1-4-2024 : Hire Purchase Debtors ₹ 75,375, Hire Purchase Interest Suspense ₹ 9,900.

Hire purchase sales (exclusive of interest) which have evenly occurred over each of the three calendar years are :

2022-2023 ₹ 80,000, 2023-24 ₹ 1,00,000, 2024-25 ₹ 76,000. All dues were promptly paid in each year.

Make out for the year 2024-25—(1) Hire Purchase Debtors Account, (2) Hire Purchase Suspense Account.

SOLUTION

HIRE PURCHASE DEBTORS ACCOUNT

Date	Particulars		₹	Date	Particulars	₹
2024		₹		2025		
April 1	To Balance b/d		75,375	Mar. 31	By Bank (1) (25% of ₹ 76,000)	19,000
to Mar. 31	" Hire Purchase Sales :			" 31	By Bank (3)	79,875
	Sale price	76,000		" 31	By Balance c/d (3)	63,900
	Interest (1)	11,400	87,400			
			1,62,775			1,62,775
2025 April 1	To Balance b/d		63,900			

HIRE PURCHASE INTEREST SUSPENSE ACCOUNT

Date	Particulars		₹	Date	Particulars	₹
2025 March 31	To Profit & Loss A/c	(1)	12,600	2024 April 1	By Balance b/d	9,900
March 31	" Balance c/d		8,700	2025 March 31	" H.P. Debtors A/c	11,400
			21,300			21,300

Working Notes :

(1) ***Calculation of Total Amount of Instalment & Interest***

Year	*Sale Price (excluding interest)*	*Down Payment (25%)*	*Balance due (75%)*	*Interest @ 20% on the balance due*	*Total amount of instalment*
	₹	₹	₹	₹	₹
2022-23	80,000	20,000	60,000	12,000	72,000
2023-24	1,00,000	25,000	75,000	15,000	90,000
2024-25	76,000	19,000	57,000	11,400	68,400

Transfer of Interest to Profit and Loss A/c on 31-3-2025

20% of ₹ 12,000 + 30% of ₹ 15,000 + 50% of ₹ 11,400 = ₹ 12,600

(2) ***Instalments falling due in three years***

	Total Instalments	*First Year*	*Second Year*	*Third Year*
Sale in 1st Quarter	8	4	4	—
Sale in 2nd Quarter	8	3	4	1
Sale in 3rd Quarter	8	2	4	2
Sale in 4th Quarter	8	1	4	3
	32	10	16	6

For each year's sale 10/32, 16/32, 6/32, is receivable in the first, second and the third year of sales respectively.

(3) ***Calculation of instalments received in 2024-25 and outstanding debtors of 1st April, 2024 and 31st March, 2025.***

	Total instalments received in 2024-25	*Outstanding on 1-4-2024*	*Outstanding on 31-3-2025*
	₹	₹	₹
2022-23 Sales	72,000 × 6/32 = 13,500	72,000 × 6/32 = 13,500	—
2023-24 Sales	90,000 × 16/32 = 45,000	90,000 × 22/32 = 61,875	90,000 × 6/32 = 16,875
2024-25 Sales	68,400 × 10/32 = 21,375	—	68,400 × 22/32 = 47,025
	79,875	75,375	63,900

ILLUSTRATION 23. A manufacturing company purchased machinery on Hire Purchase basis on 1st June, 2024. Soon after installation the machine was giving troubles and finally broke down on 14th August, 2024. The suppliers agreed to replace the machine. A new agreement was signed for that purpose and a sum of ₹ 500 was paid for cancelling the first agreement by the manufacturing company. Following are the necessary particulars :

		1st Machine	*2nd Machine*
(1)	Date of Purchase	1-6-2024	31-8-2024
(2)	Cash Price	₹ 35,000	₹ 42,860
(3)	Initial Payment	₹ 6,920	—
(4)	Allowance for Payments made under cancelled agreement		₹ 9,500
(5)	Hire charges	₹ 3,240	₹ 3,840
(6)	Hire Purchase Price	₹ 38,240	₹ 46,700
(7)	Number of instalments	18	24
(8)	Instalments payable every month commencing	1st July 2024	1st October 2024

(9) All payments were made on due dates.

(10) Ignore Depreciation on Machinery.

You have to prepare Machinery on H.P. A/c, Hire Purchase Company's Account, Hire Purchase (Machine) Disposal Account and Hire Purchase Interest Suspense Account, in the books of the manufacturing company for the year ending 31st March, 2025.

SOLUTION

MACHINERY ON H.P. ACCOUNT

		₹			₹
2024 June 1	To Hire Purchase Company's A/c	35,000	2024 Aug. 14	By H.P. (Machine) Disposal A/c	35,000
Aug. 31	To Hire Purchase Company's A/c	42,860	2025 Mar. 31	By Balance c/d	42,860
2025 April 1	To Balance b/d	42,860			

H.P. INTEREST SUSPENSE ACCOUNT

		₹			₹
2024			2024		
June 1	To Hire Purchase Company's A/c	3,240	Aug. 14	By Hire Purchase Company's A/c	2,577
Aug. 31	" Hire Purchase Company's A/c	3,840	"	Interest A/c (on 1st machine)	663
			2025		
			Mar. 31	" Interest A/c (on 2nd machine)	1,881
			"	" Balance c/d	1,959
		7,080			7,080
2025					
April 1	To Balance b/d	1,959			

HIRE PURCHASE COMPANY ACCOUNT

		₹			₹
2024			2024		
June 1	To Bank	6,920	June 1	By Machinery on Hire Purchase A/c	35,000
July 1	To Bank	1,740	"	By H.P. Interest Suspense A/c	3,240
Aug. 1	To Bank	1,740	Aug. 31	By Machinery on H.P. A/c	42,860
Aug. 14	To H.P. Interest Suspense A/c (amount written back)	2,577	"	By H.P. Interest Suspense A/c	3,840
"	To H.P. (Machine) Disposal A/c (allowance for payments)	9,500			
"	To H.P. (Machine) Disposal A/c	25,263			
Oct. 1	To Bank	1,550			
Nov. 1	To Bank	1,550			
Dec. 1	To Bank	1,550			
2025					
Jan. 1	To Bank	1,550			
Feb. 1	To Bank	1,550			
Mar. 1	To Bank	1,550			
Mar. 31	To Balance c/d	27,900			
		84,940			84,940
			2025		
			April 1	By Balance b/d	27,900

H.P. (MACHINE) DISPOSAL ACCOUNT

		₹			₹
2024			2024		
Aug. 14	To Machinery on Hire Purchase A/c	35,000	Aug. 14	By Hire Purchase Co. A/c	25,263
	To Bank (cancellation charges)	500	Aug. 31	" (allowance)	9,500
			"	" Profit & Loss A/c	737
		35,500			35,500

Working Notes :

(1) *Calculation of Monthly Instalments*

	1st Machine	*2nd Machine*
	₹	₹
Hire Purchase Price	38,240	46,700
Less : Initial payment	6,920	—
Initial Allowance	—	9,500
	31,320	37,200
Total Instalments	18	24
Monthly Instalment	1,740	1,550

(2) *Total payment made in respect of the first machine*

	₹
Down payment	6,920
Two monthly instalments @ ₹ 1,740 each	3,480
	10,400
Less : Allowance given by H.P. company	9,500
Total Loss	900
Less : Interest included in the two instalments	663
Loss to be written off to which is to be added the cancellation charge	237

(3) *Calculation of Interest*

	1st Machine	*2nd Machine*
	₹	₹
Total H.P. charges	3,240	3,840
Sums of Digits		
[18 + 17 + ... + 1]	171	—
[24 + 23 + ... + 1]	—	300
Sums of the digits		
for first two months	35	—
for the seven months	—	147
Interest for the months		
$\left(₹\,3{,}240 \times \frac{35}{171}\right)$	663	—
$\left(₹\,3{,}840 \times \frac{147}{300}\right)$	—	1,881

ILLUSTRATION 24. (H.P./Lease Basis) B and S commenced trading on 1st April, 2024 as traders in electronic machines. The profits were shared by them in the ratio of 2 : 1 after charging agreed equal salaries.

As on 31st March, 2023, the following draft Profit and Loss Account has been prepared:

	₹		₹
To Purchases	6,36,000	By Sales	7,92,000
To Wages & Salaries	1,03,500	By Hire Purchase Interest	33,600
To Salary to Partners	54,000	By Lease Rent	3,600
To General Expenses	42,440	By Stock (at Cost)	1,08,000
To Net Profit for the year	1,01,260		
	9,37,200		9,37,200

You are also informed that :

(*a*) The firm deals in only one type of machine which costs ₹ 1,200 and is sold at a uniform gross profit of $33\frac{1}{3}\%$ on selling price.

(*b*) Due to a decline in sale in the latter part of the year, the partners had sold some machines on hire purchase for initial payment of ₹ 360 and 24 monthly payments of ₹ 80 each, the interest being equally allocated among 24 instalments.

Some other machines were also given on lease for ₹ 50 p.m.

The first monthly instalment and the first lease rent is due in the month of delivery.

At the end of the five-year period of lease, the machines are not likely to have any scrap value.

(*c*) The number of machines sent out other than on account of Cash Sales were :

	Hire Purchase	*Lease*
October	20	10
November	24	12
December	26	18
	70	40

(*d*) Machines on lease have been included in stock in hand as on 31st March, 2025.

You are required to redraft Trading and Profit & Loss Account in accordance with correct accounting principles. Give your workings and reasons for the alterations suggested.

SOLUTION

TRADING & PROFIT & LOSS ACCOUNT OF M/s. B & S

for the year ended 31st March, 2025

		₹		₹
To Purchases (530 machines)		6,36,000	By Sales (370 × ₹ 1,800)	6,66,000
" Gross Profit c/d		2,22,000	" Goods Sold on H.P. (70 × ₹ 1,200)	84,000
			" Goods given on Lease	48,000
			" Closing Stock (50 × ₹ 1,200) (1)	60,000
		8,58,000		8,58,000
To Wages & Salaries		1,03,500	By Gross Profit b/d	2,22,000
" General Expenses		42,440	" Gross Profit on H.P. Sales (3)	11,080
" Depreciation on leased machines (4)		1,440	" H.P. Interest (2)	2,680
" Salary to Partners :	₹		" Lease Rent (72 × ₹ 50)	3,600
B	27,000			
S	27,000	54,000		
To Net Profit to :				
B	25,320			
S	12,660	37,980		
		2,39,360		2,39,360

Reasons for Alteration of Profit & Loss A/c

(*i*) Sales should be credited with only the proceeds of 370 machines *i.e.*, excluding hire purchase sales.

(*ii*) The whole price of ₹ 480 should not be treated as profit as interest must be spread over three financial years. The profit on hire purchase sales has also to be treated similarly.

(*iii*) Depreciation must be provided on machines given on lease basis.

Working Notes :

(1) *Closing Stock at Shop*

	₹
Cost of Closing Stock	1,08,000
Cost per machine	1,200
No. of machines = $\frac{₹\ 1,08,000}{₹\ 1,200}$	90
Less : given on lease	40
∴ No. of machines in closing stock	50

(2) *Calculation of Interest Collected*

		₹	₹
H.P. Sales Price : Down payment			360
	Instalments 24 × ₹ 80		1,920
			2,280
Normal Sale Price : Cost		1,200	
Add :	$33\frac{1}{3}$% on Sale or $\frac{1}{2}$ of Cost	600	
			1,800
Total Interest recoverable in 24 instalments			480

Interest recoverable per month = $\frac{₹\ 480}{24}$ = ₹ 20

H.P. Interest Collected			No. of Instalments
Oct.	20 × 3	=	60
Nov.	24 × 2	=	48
Dec.	26 × 1	=	26
			134

Interest collected for the current year = 134 × ₹ 20 = ₹ 2,680.

(3) *Gross Profit Collected on H.P. Sales*

Amount collected against normal selling price	₹
Down Payment (70 × ₹ 360)	= 25,200
Instalments excluding interest @ ₹ 60 each (134 × ₹ 60)	= 8,040
	33,240
Profit realised @ $33\frac{1}{3}$% of the amount collected ₹ 33,240	11,080

(4) *Depreciation on leased machines*

		Months
Oct.	10 × 3	= 30
Nov.	12 × 2	= 24
Dec.	18 × 1	= 18
		72

Monthly Depreciation = $\frac{₹\ 1200}{60}$ = ₹ 20 [As the life is only 5 years]

Total Depreciation 72 × ₹ 20 = ₹ 1,440

ILLUSTRATION 25. Mr. Glostar commenced business on 1st April, 2024. He sells washing machines of a standard type and size on hire purchase terms. The total amount, including interest payable for each washing machine is ₹ 4,500. Customers are required to pay an initial deposit of ₹ 900, followed by eight quarterly instalments of ₹ 450 each. Following trial balance is extracted from Mr. Glostar's books as on 31-3-2025 :

TRIAL BALANCE

Particulars	*Debit*	*Credit*
	₹	₹
Capital	—	15,00,000
Furniture	1,50,000	—
Purchases	27,00,000	—
Cash Collected from Customers	—	11,47,500
Salaries and Wages	1,92,000	—
Office Expenses	82,500	—
Creditors	—	2,49,000
Bank Overdraft	—	2,94,000
Bank Interest	6,000	—
Drawings	60,000	
	31,90,500	31,90,500

850 machines were sold during the year on hire purchase terms. Mr. Glostar has decided to take credit of profits and interest in proportion to cash collections. He purchases at a cost of ₹ 3,000 each. Provide 8% depreciation on furniture.

You are required to prepare the Hire Purchase Trading A/c, Profit & Loss A/c and Balance Sheet as on that date. All workings are to be shown.

SOLUTION

HIRE PURCHASE TRADING ACCOUNT, PROFIT AND LOSS ACCOUNT

for the year ending 31s March, 2025

	₹		₹
To Purchases (900 washing machines @ ₹ 3,000 each)	27,00,000	By Sales (850 × ₹ 4,500)	38,25,000
To Provision for Unrealised Profit (2)	8,92,500	By Closing Stock (50 washing machines @ ₹ 3,000 each)	1,50,000
To Gross Profit c/d	3,82,500		
	39,75,000		39,75,000
To Salaries and Wages	1,92,000	By Gross Profit b/d	3,82,500
To Office Expenses	82,500		
To Interest	6,000		
To Depreciation on Furniture (8% on ₹ 1,50,000)	12,000		
To Net Profit transferred to Capital A/c	90,000		
	3,82,500		3,82,500

BALANCE SHEET
as on 31-3-2025

Liabilities		₹	*Assets*	₹	₹
Creditors		2,49,000	Hire Purchase Debtors (2)	26,77,500	
Bank Overdraft		2,94,000	*Less* : Provision for Unrealised		
	₹		Profit	8,92,500	
Capital as on 1-4-2024	15,00,000				17,85,000
Add : Net Profit	90,000		Closing Stock		1,50,000
	15,90,000		Furniture	1,50,000	
Less : Drawings	60,000		*Less* : Depreciation	12,000	
		15,30,000			1,38,000
		20,73,000			20,73,000

Working Notes

(1) ***Calculation of Hire Purchase Debtors***

	₹
Total hire sale value of 850 washing machines @ ₹ 4,500 each	38,25,000
Less : Cash collected from hire purchase customers	11,47,500
Hire Purchase Debtors on 31-3-2025	26,77,500

(2) ***Calculation of Unrealised Profit***

	₹
Hire purchase price of each machine	4,500
Less : Cost of each machine	3,000
Profit on each machine	1,500

Total Profit on 850 machines sold @ ₹ 1,500, *i.e.,* total profit on ₹ 38,25,000 hire sale value 12,75,000

Therefore, unrealised profit on ₹ 26,77,500 (as calculated above) hire purchase debtors (*i.e.* amount not yet realised) :

$$\frac{₹\ 12,75,000}{₹\ 38,25,000} \times ₹\ 26,77,500 \qquad 8,92,500$$

INSTALMENT PURCHASE SYSTEM

Under instalment purchase system, the possession as well as ownership passes from the seller to the buyer immediately on entering the agreement but the buyer agrees to pay the total price in instalments. If the buyer makes any default in the payment of any instalment, the seller has no right to repossess the goods. The seller can file a suit in the court of law for recovery of the price.

Distinction Between Hire Purchase System and Instalment Purchase System

Following are the main points of distinction between the two systems :

***(i)* Nature of contract.** Hire purchase is an agreement of hiring whereas instalment purchase system is an agreement of sale.

***(ii)* Ownership.** Under hire purchase system, ownership remains with the seller until the payment of last instalment but under instalment purchase system the ownership passes from seller to the buyer immediately on entering the agreement.

***(iii)* Return of goods**. Under hire purchase agreement, goods can be returned if the buyer does not want to pay rest of the instalments, but under instalment purchase system, the goods cannot be returned by the buyer to the seller unless there is some default on the part of the seller.

***(iv)* Rights of disposal.** Under hire purchase system, the buyer cannot sell, destroy, transfer, damage or pledge the goods but under instalment purchase system, the buyer can do all these things.

(v) Rights of seller. Under hire purchase system, the seller can repossess the goods if the buyer makes any default in the payment of any instalment but under instalment purchase system, the seller can sue in the court of law for price if the buyer makes default in payment of any instalment.

(vi) Right of forfeiture of instalments received under hire purchase system. In case of default in the payment of instalments, hire vendor has a right to forfeit the instalments already received treating it as hire charge but in case of instalment purchase system, the seller cannot forfeit the instalments already received, he can sue only for the unpaid balance.

(vii) Risk under hire purchase system. Under hire purchase system, loss occurring to goods has to be borne by the hire vendor as the risk lies with the ownership but in case of instalment purchase system, any such loss will have to be borne by the buyer.

(viii) Responsibility of normal repairs. Under hire purchase system, the responsibility of normal repairs lies with hire vendor being owner of goods but in case of instalment purchase system, the seller is not at all responsible for the normal repairs as the purchaser is the owner of goods from the very beginning.

Accounting Entries

In Buyer's Books

Following entries are passed in the books of the buyer under instalment system :

(i) *When an asset is purchased on instalment purchase system*

Asset Account	Dr.	(With cash price)
Interest Suspense Account	Dr.	(Difference between total price and cash price)
To Vendor's Account (with total instalment purchase price)		

(ii) *For cash down payment on delivery*

Vendor's Account Dr.
To Cash/Bank Account

(iii) *For interest due at the end of the year*

Interest Account Dr.
To Interest Suspense Account

(iv) *For the payment of the first instalment*

Vendor's Account Dr.
To Bank Account

(v) *For depreciation charge*

Depreciation Account Dr.
To Asset Account

(vi) *For transfer of interest and depreciation to profit and loss account*

Profit & Loss Account Dr.
To Interest Account
To Depreciation Account

Note. *Entries (iii) to (vi) will be repeated in subsequent years.*

In Vendor's Books

Following entries are to be passed in the books of the vendor :

(i) *When goods are sold on instalment purchase system*

Purchaser's Account	Dr.	(with total price)
To Sales Account		(with cash price)
To Interest Suspense Account		(with difference between total price and cash price)

(ii) *For cash received on delivery*
Cash/Bank Account Dr.
To Purchaser's Account

(iii) *For interest due on instalment at the end of the year*
Interest Suspense Account Dr.
To Interest Account

(iv) *For receipt of the amount of instalment*
Cash/Bank Account Dr.
To Purchaser's Account

(v) *For transfer of Interest to Profit and Loss Account*
Interest Account Dr.
To Profit and Loss Account

Note. *Entries from (iii) to (v) will be repeated in subsequent years.*

ILLUSTRATION 26. On 1st January, 2022, Om Oil Company purchased an oil machine on the instalment system. The cash price of the machine was ₹ 11,175 and payment was to be made as follows :

₹ 3,000 was to be paid on the signing of the agreement and the balance in three instalments of ₹ 3,000 each at the end of each year, 5% interest is charged by the Delhi Manufacturing Company per annum. Om Oil Company has decided to write off 10 per cent annually on the diminishing balance of the cash price.

Prepare necessary Accounts in the books of purchaser and vendor. Calculations are to be made to the nearest rupee.

SOLUTION

In the Books of Om Oil Co.

MACHINERY ACCOUNT

		₹			₹
2022 Jan. 1	To Delhi Manufacturing Co.	11,175	2022 Dec. 31	By Depreciation A/c	1,118
			"	" Balance c/d	10,057
		11,175			11,175
2023 Jan. 1	To Balance b/d	10,057	2023 Dec. 31	By Depreciation A/c	1,006
			"	" Balance c/d	9,051
		10,057			10,057
2024 Jan. 1	To Balance b/d	9,051	2024 Dec. 31	By Depreciation A/c	905
				" Balance c/d	8,146
		9,051			9,051

INTEREST SUSPENSE ACCOUNT

		₹			₹
2022 Jan. 1	To Delhi Manufacturing Co.	825	2022 Dec. 31	By Interest A/c	409
			"	" Balance c/d	416
		825			825
2023 Jan. 1	To Balance b/d	416	2023 Dec. 31	By Interest A/c	279
			"	" Balance c/d	137
		416			416
2024 Jan. 1	To Balance b/d	137	2024 Dec. 31	By Interest A/c	137

DELHI MANUFACTURING COMPANY ACCOUNT

		₹			₹
2022			2022		
Jan. 1	To Bank	3,000	Jan. 1	By Machinery A/c	11,175
Dec. 31	To Bank	3,000	"	" Interest Suspense A/c	825
"	To Balance c/d	6,000			
		12,000			12,000
2023			2023		
Dec. 31	To Bank	3,000	Jan. 1	By Balance b/d	6,000
"	To Balance c/d	3,000			
		6,000			6,000
2024			2024		
Dec. 31	To Bank	3,000	Jan. 1	By Balance b/d	3,000

INTEREST ACCOUNT

		₹			₹
31-12-2022	To Interest Suspense A/c	409	31-12-2022	By P. & L. A/c	409
31-12-2023	To Interest Suspense A/c	279	31-12-2023	By P. & L. A/c	279
31-12-2024	To Interest Suspense A/c	137	31-12-2024	By P. & L. A/c	137

In the Books of Delhi Manufacturing Co.

OM OIL COMPANY ACCOUNT

		₹			₹
2022			2022		
Jan. 1	To Sales	11,175	Jan. 1	By Bank A/c	3,000
"	To Interest Suspense A/c	825	Dec. 31	By Bank A/c	3,000
			"	By Balance c/d	6,000
		12,000			12,000
2023			2023		
Jan. 1	To Balance b/d	6,000	Dec. 31	By Bank	3,000
			"	By Balance c/d	3,000
		6,000			6,000
2024			2024		
Jan. 1	To Balance b/d	3,000	Dec. 31	By Bank	3,000

INTEREST SUSPENSE ACCOUNT

		₹			₹
2022			2022		
Dec. 31	To Interest A/c	409	Jan. 1	By Om Oil Co.	825
"	To Balance c/d	416			
		825			825

2023 Dec. 31 "	To Interest A/c To Balance c/d	279 137	2023 Jan. 1	By Balance b/d	416
		416			416
2024 Dec. 31	To Interest A/c	137	2024 Jan. 1	By Balance b/d	137

INTEREST ACCOUNT

		₹			₹
31-12-2022	To P. & L. A/c	409	31-12-2022	By Interest Suspense A/c	409
31-12-2023	To P. & L. A/c	279	31-12-2023	By Interest Suspense A/c	279
31-12-2024	To P. & L. A/c	137	31-12-2024	By Interest Suspense A/c	137

When the asset is given on hire purchase to the person from whom it is purchased on instalment system

There may be a case when asset is given on hire purchase to the same person from whom it is purchased on instalment system. The hire charges are adjusted, at the end of each period against the amount due to the vendor on account of principal and interest, any difference being settled in cash. The working under such a case will be more clear from the following illustration :

ILLUSTRATION 27. On 1st January, 2022 A sells a truck to B, on the instalment payment system, on the following conditions :

(1) The purchase price of the truck is ₹ 1,00,000.

(2) This amount is payable to A in four equal annual instalments along with 12% interest per annum on the outstanding balance, the first instalment being payable on the date of sale.

B in turn, hires out the truck to A for a monthly hire of ₹ 3,000 per month from 1st January, 2022. The hire charges are to be adjusted, at the end of each year, against the amount due to A on account of principal and interest, any difference being settled in cash.

B, charges 20% depreciation (on the written-down-value method) on the truck.

All payments are made as per the agreement. On 1st January 2025, the truck is sold by B to A for ₹ 15,000 in cash.

Show in B's books, Truck Account, Interest Suspense Account, Hire Charges Account, Interest Account and A's Account.

SOLUTION **In the Books of B**

TRUCK ACCOUNT

		₹			₹
2022 Jan. 1	To A	1,00,000	2022 Dec. 31 "	By Depreciation A/c By Balance c/d	20,000 80,000
		1,00,000			1,00,000
2023 Jan. 1	To Balance b/d	80,000	2023 Dec. 31 "	By Depreciation A/c " Balance c/d	16,000 64,000
		80,000			80,000

2024			2024		
Jan. 1	To Balance b/d	64,000	Dec. 31	By Depreciation A/c	12,800
			"	" Balance c/d	51,200
		64,000			64,000
2025			2025		
Jan. 1	To Balance b/d	51,200	Jan. 1	By B	15,000
			"	" Profit & Loss A/c (Loss on Sale)	36,200
		51,200			51,200

INTEREST SUSPENSE ACCOUNT

		₹			₹
2022			2022		
Jan. 1	To A's Account (Total interest)	18,000	Dec. 31	By Interest (12% on ₹ 75,000)	9,000
			"	" Balance c/d	9,000
		18,000			18,000
2023			2023		
Jan. 1	To Balance b/d	9,000	Dec. 31	By Interest A/c	6,000
			"	" Balance c/d	3,000
		9,000			9,000
2024			2024		
Jan. 1	To Balance b/d	3,000	Dec. 31	By Interest A/c	3,000

HIRE CHARGES ACCOUNT

		₹			₹
31-12-2022	To Profit & Loss A/c	36,000	31-12-2022	By A	36,000
31-12-2023	To Profit & Loss A/c	36,000	31-12-2023	By A	36,000
31-12-2024	To Profit & Loss A/c	36,000	31-12-2024	By A	36,000

INTEREST ACCOUNT

		₹			₹
31-12-2022	To Interest Suspense A/c	9,000	31-12-2022	By Profit & Loss A/c	9,000
31-12-2023	To Interest Suspense A/c	6,000	31-12-2023	By Profit & Loss A/c	6,000
31-12-2024	To Interest Suspense A/c	3,000	31-12-2024	By Profit & Loss A/c	3,000

A'S ACCOUNT

		₹			₹
2022			2022		
Jan. 1	To Bank	25,000	Jan. 1	By Truck A/c	1,00,000
Dec. 31	" Hire Charges A/c	36,000	"	" Interest Suspense A/c	18,000
"	" Balance c/d	57,000			
		1,18,000			1,18,000

2023			2023		
Dec. 31	To Hire Charges A/c	36,000	Jan. 1	By Balance b/d	57,000
"	" Balance c/d	23,000	"	By Cash	2,000
		59,000			59,000
2024			2024		
Dec. 31	To Hire Charges	36,000	Jan. 1	By Balance b/d	23,000
			"	" Cash	5,000
			Dec. 31	" Balance c/d	8,000
		36,000			36,000
2025			2025		
Jan. 1	To Balance b/d	8,000	Jan. 1	By Cash	23,000
"	" Truck A/c	15,000			
		23,000			23,000

Note. (1) Calculation of Cash Settlement.

	Principal + Interest	*High Charges + Sale Proceeds*	*Amount Received*
	₹	₹	₹
On 1-1-2023	₹ 25,000 + 9,000 = 34,000	36,000	2,000
On 1-1-2024	₹ 25,000 + 6,000 = 31,000	36,000	5,000
On 1-1-2025	₹ 25,000 + 3,000 = 28,000	36,000 + 15,000 = 51,000	23,000

ILLUSTRATION 28. ABC Associates entered into a financial agreement on 1-4-2024 with Flexible Leasing Ltd. for lease of a car. The price of the car was ₹ 2,00,000 and the quarterly lease rentals wee agreed at ₹ 90 per thousand payable at the beginning of every quarter. ABC Associates kept up their payments but by 25-3-2025 they approached and obtained the consent of the leasing company for treating the arrangement as one of Hire-purchase from the beginning on the following terms :

Period : 3 years

Quarterly hire : ₹ 30,000 payable at the beginning of the quarter.

It was agreed that the loan rentals paid will be treated as hire monies and that the balance due upto 31-3-2025 will be settled by ABC Associates on that date with interest @ 18% p.a. on various instalments during the year. The rate of depreciation on the car is 25%.

Show Flexible Leasing Ltd.'s A/c and Interest Suspense A/c in the books of ABC Associates for the year 2024-25. Calculations are to be rounded off to the nearest rupee. ***(C.A. Inter)***

SOLUTION

In the Books of ABC Associates

FLEXIBLE LEASING LIMITED ACCOUNT

2025		₹	2025		₹
Mar. 25	To Lease Rental A/c	72,000	Mar. 25	By Car on H.P. A/c	2,00,000
" 31	To Bank A/c (1)	53,400	" 31	By Interest Suspense A/c (2)	1,60,000
" 31	To Balance c/d	2,40,000	" 31	By Interest A/c	5,400
		3,65,400			3,65,400

INTEREST SUSPENSE ACCOUNT

2025		₹	2025		₹
Mar. 25	To Flexible Leasing Ltd. A/c (2)	1,60,000	Mar. 31	By Interest on Hire Purchase A/c (2)	72,727
			"	By Balance c/d	87,273
		1,60,000			1,60,000

Working Notes :

1. ***Calculation of Balance Payable on 31st March, 2025 and the Amount of Interest***

CALCULATION OF DIFFERENCE PAYABLE ON 31-3-2025 AND INTEREST

Date	*Quarterly Hire Charges*	*Quarterly Lease Rentals Paid*	*Difference Payable*	*Interest (18% p.a.) From*	*To*	*Amount Interest*
	₹	₹	₹			₹
1-4-2024	30,000	18,000	12,000	1-4-2024	31-3-2025	2,160
1-7-2024	30,000	18,000	12,000	1-7-2024	31-3-2025	1,620
1-10-2024	30,000	18,000	12,000	1-10-2024	31-3-2025	1,080
1-1-2025	30,000	18,000	12,000	1-1-2025	31-3-2025	540
		72,000	48,000			5,400

Amount Payable on 31st March, 2025 :	₹
Balance due	48,000
Interest due	5,400
	53,400

(2) ***Ascertainment of Total Amount of Interest on Hire Purchase***

	₹
Hire Purchase Price of the Car (₹ 30,000 × 12 instalments)	3,60,000
Less : Cash Price	2,00,000
Total Amount of Interest	1,60,000

(3) ***Calculation of Interest on Hire Purchase Attributable to the Year 2024-25***

Date	*Interest Calculation*	*Interest*
		₹
1-4-2024	—	—
1-7-2024	₹ 1,60,000 × $\frac{11}{66}$	26,667
1-10-2024	₹ 1,60,000 × $\frac{10}{66}$	24,242
1-1-2025	₹ 1,60,000 × $\frac{9}{66}$	21,818
		72,727

QUESTIONS

OBJECTIVE TYPE

1. **State whether the following statements are TRUE or FALSE :**

(*i*) There is no difference between Hire Purchase and Instalment system.

(*ii*) In Hire Purchase system, the ownership immediately passes to the Vendor on down payment.

(*iii*) There is a difference between instalment purchase and credit sale.

(*iv*) Each instalment includes payment towards cash price and interest.

(*v*) Depreciation on fixed assets purchased on hire purchase system is charged in the books of purchaser.

(*vi*) Total interest is apportioned to the different instalments on the basis of amount due at different instalments.

(*vii*) If there is a default in the payment of any instalment (in case of hire purchase system), the vendor has a right to repossess the goods.

(*viii*) The vendor has a right to reposses the goods sold on hire purchase even if all instalments are paid by purchaser in time.

(*ix*) Under hire purchase system, the purchaser becomes owner immediately on payment of signing amount.

(*x*) Under hire purchase system, down payment has to be made compulsarily,

(*xi*) Cash price instalment does not include interest.

(*xii*) In the event of default in the payment of any instalment, the hire vendor can only sue for recovery of money under hire purchase system.

(*xiii*) Hire Purchase Trading Account is prepared to find out profit or loss under stock and debtors system.

(*xiv*) Hire purchase debtors and Instalment Not Due means the same.

(*xv*) Hire Purchase Stock Account is debited with the total amount which has become due (including down payment) during the accounting period under Stock and Debtors System.

(*xvi*) Stock at Shop Account is credited with the cost price of goods sold on hire purchase under Stock and Debtors System.

(*xvii*) Hire purchase Stock Account is credited with instalments not due on goods repossessed under Stock and Debtors System.

(*xviii*) Hire Purchase Debtors Account is credited with the instalments not due on goods repossessed under Stock and Debtors System.

(*xix*) Goods Repossessed Account is credited with the loss on repossession of goods under Stock and Debtors System.

Ans. **[TRUE : (*iii*), (*iv*), (*v*), (*vi*), (*vii*),** (*xi*), (*xvi*), (*xix*); **FALSE : (*i*), (*ii*), (*viii*),** (*ix*), (*x*), (*xii*), (*xiii*), (*xiv*), (*xv*), (*xvii*), (*xviii*)**]**

2. Choose the Correct Answer from the given options :

(*a*) The amount paid at the time of hire purchase agreement is known as :

(*i*) Cash price (*ii*) Down payment
(*iii*) First Instalments (*iv*) Hire purchase price

(*b*) In Hire Purchase system cash price plus interest is known as :

(*i*) Capital value of asset (*ii*) Book value of asset
(*iii*) Hire purchase price of asset (*iv*) Hire purchase charges.

(*c*) Total interest on hire purchase goods is the difference between—

(*i*) Hire purchase price and cash price
(*ii*) Hire purchase price and down payment
(*iii*) Cash price and first instalment
(*iv*) None of the above.

(*d*) Depreciation on hire purchase asset is claimed by

(*i*) Hire Vendor (*ii*) Hire Purchaser
(*iii*) Hire Vendor or hire purchaser as per agreement
(*iv*) No depreciation is claimed till the last instalment is paid/received.

(*e*) Under instalment payment system ownership of goods

(*i*) is transferred at the time of last instalment (*ii*) is not transferred

(*iii*) is transferred at the time of agreement (*iv*) none of the above.

Ans. [(*a*) (*ii*); (*b*) (*iii*); (*c*) (*i*); (*d*) (*ii*); (*e*) (*iii*)]

SHORT ANSWER TYPE

1. What is Hire Purchase System ?
2. Distinguish between Hire Sale and Credit Sale.
3. Give two merits of Hire Purchase System.
4. State two disadvantages of Hire Purchase System to the Hire Vendor and Vendee.
5. Give two points of distinctions between Hire Purchase System and Instalment Purchase System.
6. Explain in brief (*i*) Down Payment ; (*ii*) Cash Price ; (*iii*) Goods Repossessed ; (*iv*) Hire Purchaser.
7. Should depreciation be charged on fixed assets purchased on Hire Purchase in the books of Hire Purchaser ?
8. Why each instalment is broken into two parts—payment towards cash price and interest ?
9. Give journal entries to be passed in the books of Hire Purchaser and Vendor when there is : (*i*) Complete repossession or (*ii*) Partial repossession on default in the payment of any instalment.

OR

Discuss the accounting treatment of repossessed goods on default made by hire purchaser.

10. Give a specimen of Hire Purchase Trading Account.
11. What is Stock and Debtors System in case of Hire Purchase System ?
12. P Purchased a T.V. on hire purchase system. The cash price of the T.V. was ₹ 7,200. He agrees to pay four quarterly instalments of ₹ 2,000 each. Calculate *interest* for each quarter.

Ans. [Interest ₹ 320, ₹ 240, ₹ 160, ₹ 80].

13. One machine whose cash price is ₹ 81,800 is purchased for ₹ 90,000 on hire purchase system. Payment of hire purchase price is made after the date of purchase in the following manner :

At the end of 4 months ₹ 10,000; at the end of 6 months ₹ 15,000; at the end of 9 months ₹ 30,000; at the end of 12 months ₹ 35,000.

Machine is purchased on 1-1-2025 and the date of payment of each instalment is counted from this date. Open the *Hire Vendor Account* in the books of the Hire Purchaser.

Ans. [Interest included in : Instalment I ₹ 3,600; Instalment II ₹ 1,600; Instalment III ₹ 1,950; Instalment IV ₹ 1,050].

14. On 1-1-2023, Bajaj Autos Ltd. sold a scooter on hire purchase system to Vikram Enterprises. ₹ 2,000 was to be paid on signing the agreement and the balance in three instalments of ₹ 2,000 each at the end of the year, commencing from the year 2023. The seller charged interest at 5% p.a. Calculate the amount of interest in each *instalment* and also the amount of *cash price.*

Ans. [Cash Price ₹ 7,447; Interest : 2023 ₹ 272; 2024 ₹ 186; 2025 ₹ 95]

15. Rajesh acquired on 1-1-2024 a machine under a hire purchase agreement which provides for 5 half yearly instalments of ₹ 6,000 each, the first being due on 1st July, 2024. Assuming that the applicable rate of interest is 10% per cent per annum. Calculated the cash price of the machine.

Ans. [₹ 25,977]

16. Hitesh purchased a truck on hire purchase system. As per terms he is required to pay ₹ 1,40,000 down, ₹ 1,06,000 at the end of the first year, ₹ 98,000 at the end of second year and ₹ 1,10,000 at the end of the third year. Interest is charged @ 10% p.a. Calculate cash price of the truck and interest paid with each instalment.

Ans. [Cash Price ₹ 4,00,000; Interest paid in instalments : I—₹ 26,000; II—₹ 18,000; III—₹ 10,000]

17. A purchased a machine on Hire-purchase system. The cash price of the machine was ₹ 1,86,250. He paid ₹ 50,000 on signing of the agreement and rest in three annual instalments of ₹ 50,000 each. Calculate **interest for each year.**

Ans. [Interest ₹ 6,875, ₹ 4,583, ₹ 2,292].

18. Mr. X purchased a machine on hire purchase system. He made cash payment of ₹ 30,000 and the balance was payable in 5 annual instalments of ₹ 60,000 each. The cash price of the machine is ₹ 3,00,000. Assume that the purchase was made on 1st April and the annual instalments are payable on 31st March of every year. Calculate the **amount of interest for each year.**

(CA—*PCE Nov. 2009*)

Ans. [Interest ₹ 10,000, ₹ 8,000, ₹ 6,000, ₹ 4,000 and ₹ 2,000 for I to Vth year respectively]

19. On 1st April, 2023, Fasttrack Motors Co. sells a truck on *hire purchase basis* to Teja Transport Co. for a total hire purchase price of ₹ 9,00,000 payable as to ₹ 2,40,000 as down payment and the balance in three equal annual instalments of ₹ 2,20,000 each payable on 31st March 2024, 2025 and 2026.

The hire vendor charges interest @10% per annum.

You are required to ascertain the **cash price** of the truck for Teja Transport Co. Calculations may be made to the nearest rupee. ***(CA—Inter Nov. 2012 Modified)***

Ans. [₹ 7,87,107]

20. M/s RG & Co. sells goods on hire purchase adding 50% to cost. From the following figures prepare Hire Purchase Trading Account.

Goods with Customers on 1-1-2025,		Cash received from customers during the year
Instalments not yield due	₹ 27,000	₹ 1,00,500
Goods sold on Hire Purchase		Instalments due that not received at the end
during 2025	₹ 1,27,500	of the year, customer paying ₹ 9,000.

All figures are on the basis of hire purchase.

Ans. [Profit ₹ 36,500; Stock with Customers on 31-12-2025 ₹ 45,000]

LONG ANSWER TYPE

1. What do you understand by Hire-Purchase System ? In what respects does it differ from Instalment System ?
2. What are the various journal entries to be passed in the books of hire-purchaser and vendor in case the goods are sold under hire-purchase system ?
3. Discuss the accounting treatment of repossessed goods on default made by hire purchaser.
4. Write a note on Hire Purchase Trading Account.
5. Messrs Rama and Krishna sell daily a number of small articles of very small value on the hire-purchase system and request you to recommend to them a simple but satisfactory system of keeping accounts. What will be your advice to them ?
6. Discuss briefly the main provisions of the Hire Purchase Act, 1972 which are relevant for accounting purposes.
7. What is instalment purchase system ? Discuss the Journal Entries to be passed in the books of purchaser and vendor.
8. Please indicate the distinction between hire purchase, instalment purchase and financial lease.

(ICWA—Final)

PRACTICAL PROBLEMS

HIRE PURCHASE SYSTEM

1. The Chennai Company purchased a machine from the Mumbai Machine Company on Hire Purchase agreement on 1st January, 2023 paying cash ₹ 10,000 and agreeing to pay three further instalments of ₹ 10,000 each on 31st December of every year. The cash price of the machine is ₹ 37,250 and the Chennai Company charges interest at 5% per annum. The Chennai Company writes off ten per cent every year of cash value of the machine on the reducing instalment system.

   (*a*) Journalise the entries and open the necessary accounts in the books of both the companies.

   (*b*) How will the Machinery Account appear in the Balance Sheet of Chennai Company as on 31st December 2024 ?

   Note. Calculations are to be made to the nearest rupee.

Ans. [(*a*) Interest 2023 ₹ 1,363 ; 2024 ₹ 931 & 2025 ₹ 456 ; Balance in Machinery A/c ₹ 27,155 ; (*b*) ₹ 20,628].

2. Dobsons Ltd. had purchased a machinery on hire-purchase system from Hind Machinery Ltd. The terms are that they would pay ₹ 20,000 down on 1-1-2023 and 5 annual instalments of ₹ 11,000 each commencing from 1-1-2024. They charged depreciation on machinery at the rate of 15 per cent under diminishing balance system.

   Hind Machinery Ltd. had charged interest at the rate of 10 per cent per annum.

   Show the "Machinery Account" and "Hind Machinery Ltd. Account" to record the above transactions in the books of Dobsons Ltd. till the instalments are paid off. Dobsons' accounting year ended on 31st December in each year.

Ans. [Interest ₹ 4,170, ₹ 3,487, ₹ 2,736, ₹ 1,909 and ₹ 1,000 ; Cash Price ₹ 61,698].

3. Happy Valley Florists Ltd. acquired a delivery van on hire purchase on 1-4-2021 from Ganesh Enterprises. The terms were as follows :

Particulars	*Amount* (₹)
Hire Purchase Price	1,80,000
Down Payment	30,000
1st instalment payable after 1 year	50,000
2nd instalment after 2 years	50,000
3rd instalment after 3 years	30,000
4th instalment after 4 years	20,000

   Cash price van ₹ 1,50,000 and depreciation is charged at 10% WDV.

   You are required to :

   (*i*) Calculate Total Interest and Interest included in each instalment.

   (*ii*) Prepare Van A/c, Ganesh Enterprises A/c in the books of Happy Valley Florists Ltd. up to 31-3-2025. ***(CA IPCE, May, 2014 Modified)***

Ans. [Total Interest ₹ 30,000. Interest : 1st year—₹ 14,062; 2nd year—₹ 9,375; 3rd year—₹ 4,688; 4th year—₹ 1,875]

4. On 1st January, 2022 X Ltd. purchased a motor-car from Y Ltd. on the hire-purchase system, the cash price of which was payable as ₹ 12,000 down and the balance in 3 equal annual instalments together with interest @ 10% p.a. The amount of the last instalment including interest was ₹ 17,600. Depreciation was to be provided at 20% p.a. on the reducing balances.

   At the end of 3 years of service the Motor Car was sold for ₹ 30,000 cash.

Show (*a*) Motor-Car Account and (*b*) Vendor's Account in the books of the buyer for 3 years to 31st December, 2024.

Ans. [Cash Price ₹ 60,000 ; Interest 2022 ₹ 4,800 ; 2023 ₹ 3,200 and 2024 ₹ 1,600 ; Loss on Sale ₹ 720].

5. Coconut Growers purchase a machinery on instalment basis from Y Machinery Co. Ltd. on the following terms :
   (*a*) Cash down payment at the time of signing the agreement ₹ 12,000.
   (*b*) Five annual instalments of ₹ 7,700, the first to commence at the end of twelve months from the date of cash down payment.
   (*c*) Interest at 10% p.a. is charged by the seller.
   (*d*) Depreciation at 20% p.a. WDV basis is written off from the machinery.
   (*e*) Machinery is sold for ₹ 15,000 on completion of payments of instalments.
   Show the Machinery Account and Y Machinery Co. Ltd. A/c for the entire period.

Ans. [Cash Price ₹ 41,189, Interest I—₹ 2,919, II—₹ 2,441, III—₹ 1,915, IV—₹ 1,336 & V year ₹ 700, Profit on Sale ₹ 1,503].

6. On July 1, 2024, Eastern Printers purchased a printing machine on a hire purchase basis, payments to be made ₹ 10,000 on the said date and the balance in three half yearly instalments of ₹ 8,200, ₹ 7,440 and ₹ 6,300 commencing from December 31, 2024. The vendor charged interest at 10 per cent per annum calculated on half yearly rests.
   Eastern Printers close their books annually on December 31, and provide depreciation at 10 per cent per annum on diminishing balance in each year.
   Determine the cash price of the machine and show the necessary ledger accounts in the books of Eastern Printers.

Ans. [Cash Price ₹ 30,000 ; Interest ₹ 1,000 ; ₹ 640 and ₹ 300].

7. On 1st January, 2024, X & Co. entered into an agreement to purchase 200 Sewing Machines on hire-purchase system from Y & Co. Price was to be paid in equal half yearly instalments of ₹ 14,770 on 30th June and 31st December each year for three years. Cash price was ₹ 400 per sewing machine and rate of interest was 6% per annum payable on half yearly balances.
   On 1st January, 2025 after paying two instalments X & Co. transferred the machines to Z & Co. after receiving ₹ 20,000. Z & Co. paid this amount to X & Co. immediately and remaining instalments to Y & Co. on due dates.
   Record the above transactions in the books of Z & Co. by way of Journal Entries for the financial year ended 30th June, 2025. Charge depreciation on sewing machines @ 10% p.a.

Ans. [Balance due to Y & Co. on 31-12-2024 ₹ 54,889; Z will pay to Y interest of ₹ 1,647 on 30th June, 2025].

DEFAULT AND COMPLETE REPOSSESSION

8. Delhi Ltd. purchased from Mumbai Co. three machines costing ₹ 40,000 each on the Hire-Purchase System. Payment was to be made ₹ 30,000 down and the remainder in three equal instalments together with interest at 5%. Delhi Ltd. writes off depreciation @ 20% on the diminishing balance. It paid the instalment due at the end of the first year but could not pay the next.
   Give the necessary Ledger Accounts in the books of both the parties for two years if the hire vendor took possession of all the three machines. The hire vendor spent ₹ 5,800 on getting the machines thoroughly overhauled and sold them for ₹ 70,000.

Ans. [Loss on Default ₹ 13,800 ; Profit to Vendors ₹ 1,200].

9. On 1 April 2022 Bharat Travel Agency acquired a luxury car on hire purchase terms making a down payment of ₹ 50,000 from Sullab Auto Ltd. According to the hire purchase terms, Bharat Travel Agency would have to pay the remaining amount in four equal annual instalments of ₹ 1,26,188 each, commencing from 31 March, 2023. The agreed rate of interest was 10% per annum and the interest was included in the instalment amount of ₹ 1,26,188.

On 31 March 2025 when the third instalment became due, Bharat Travel Agency expressed its inability to make any further payment and, consequent upon which, Sulabh Auto Ltd. re-possessed the car. The car was depreciated by Bharat Travel Agency at 10% per annum based on the diminishing balance method.

Show the car account and Sulabh Auto Ltd. account in the books of Bharat Travel Agency to give effect to the above. Bharat Travel Agency prepares its annual accounts on 31st March every year.

Ans. [Loss on Default ₹ 87,146; Cash Price ₹ 4,50,000; Interest ₹ 40,000; ₹ 31,380 and ₹ 21,900].

10. A machinery is sold on hire purchase. The term of payment is four annual instalments of ₹ 6,000 at the end of each year commencing from the date of agreement. Interest is charged @ 20% and is included in the annual payment of ₹ 6,000.

Show Machinery Account and Hire Vendor Account in the books of the purchaser who defaulted in the payment of the third yearly payment whereupon the vendor repossessed the machinery. The purchaser provides depreciation on the machinery @ 10% per annum on written down value basis.

All workings should form part of your answer. ***(ICWA—Stage II, Dec. 2011)***

Ans. [Loss on Default ₹ 324; Interest : 1st year ₹ 3,106, 2nd year ₹ 2,528, 3rd year ₹ 1,833; Cash Price ₹ 15,533]

DEFAULT AND PARTIAL REPOSSESSION

11. Mumbai Ltd. purchased three machines costing ₹ 1,00,000 each from Hindustan Machines Ltd. as on 1st January, 2022 on hire-purchase system. The terms were :

Payment on delivery ₹ 25,000 for each machine and balance of the principal amount by 3 equal instalments plus interest at 15% per annum to be paid at the end of each year.

Mumbai Ltd. writes off 25% depreciation each year on diminishing balance method.

Mumbai Ltd. paid the instalment due on 31st December, 2022 and 31st December, 2023 but could not pay the final instalment.

Hindustan Ltd. repossessed two machines adjusting values against the amount due. The repossession was done on 1st January, 2025 on the basis of 40% depreciation on the diminishing balance method.

You are required to :

(*a*) Write up the Ledger Accounts in the books of Mumbai Ltd. showing the above transactions upto 1-1-2025, and

(*b*) Show the disclosure of the balances arising from the above in the Balance Sheet of Mumbai Ltd. as on 31st December, 2024.

Ans. [Loss on Repossession ₹ 41,175].

12. On 1st April, 2023, Turant Transport Ltd. acquired 3 trucks at the cash sale price of ₹ 9,00,000 each on hire purchase from Hind Motors Ltd. The terms include cash down of ₹ 5,40,000 and payment of the residue in two equal annual instalments together with interest at 9% per annum at the end of the year. First year dues were paid, but Turant Transport Ltd. could not pay the next instalment. Turant Transport Ltd. wrote off depreciation @ 20% annually on diminishing balance. Hind Motors Ltd., however, agreed to leave one truck with the hire purchaser and adjust the value of two other trucks against the outstanding amount due. The trucks were valued on the basis of 30% annual depreciation on their written down value.

Show important Ledger Accounts in the books of both the parties assuming that the acquired trucks were sold on 30th April, 2025 for ₹ 9,75,000 after incurring repair expenses of ₹ 68,000. Both the companies close their books of account on 31st March every year.

Ans. [Loss on Repossession ₹ 2,70,000 ; Profit on Sale ₹ 25,000].

13. Srikumar bought 2 cars from 'Fair Value Motors Pvt. Ltd. on 1-4-2022 on the following terms :

Down Payment	6,00,000
1st Instalment at the end of first year	4,20,000

2nd Instalment at the end of 2nd year 4,90,000
3rd Instalment at the end of 3rd year 5,50,000
Interest is charged at 10% p.a.

Srikumar provides depreciation @ 25% on the diminishing balances :

On 31-3-2025 Srikumar failed to pay the 3rd instalment upon which 'Fair Value Motors Pvt. Ltd.' repossessed 1 car. Srikumar agreed to leave one car with Fair Value Motors Pvt. Ltd. and adjusted the value of the car against the amount due. The car taken over was valued on the basis of 40% depreciation annually on written down basis. The balance amount remaining in the vendor's account after the above adjustment was paid by Srikumar after 3 months with interest @ 20% p.a.

You are required to :

(*i*) Calculate the cash price of the cars and the interest paid with each instalment.

(*ii*) Prepare Car Account and Fair Value Motors Pvt. Ltd. Account in the books of Srikumar assuming books are closed on March 31, every year. Figures may be rounded off to the nearest rupee. ***(CA-Inter November, 2016 Modified)***

Ans. [Loss on default ₹ 1,85,288; Value on car repossessed ₹ 1,94,400; Balance on Car A/c ₹ 3,79,687]

14. On 1st April, 2024, Bombay Transport Ltd. purchased from Delhi Motors five trucks costing ₹ 3,00,000 each on the hire-purchase system. The payment was to be made as follows :

- 10% of cash price down; and
- 25% of cash price at the end of the four subsequent half years.

The payment due on 31st March, 2025 could not be made and hence the trucks were seized by the vendor. But after negotiation, the hire-purchaser was allowed to keep three trucks on the condition that the value of other two trucks would be adjusted against the amount due, the trucks being valued at cost less 25% depreciation. Bombay Transport Ltd. closes its books on 31st March each year and the depreciation is charged at 15% per annum on the original cost of trucks.

The vendor spent ₹ 60,000 on getting the trucks repaired and sold them for ₹ 5,00,000.

Prepare necessary Ledger Accounts in the books of both the parties.

Ans. [Loss on Default ₹ 60,000; Loss on Repossession ₹ 10,000; Balance in Trucks (on H.P.) A/c ₹ 7,65,000; Balance due from Hire Purchaser ₹ 6,30,000]

15. X purchased seven machines on Hire Purchase on 1st July, 2024. The cash purchase price of each machine was ₹ 50,000. He was to pay 20% of the cash purchase price at the time of delivery and the balance in five half-yearly instalments starting from 31st December, 2024 with interest @ 5% per annum.

On X's failure to pay the instalment due on 30th June, 2025 it was agreed that X could return 3 machines to the vendor and remaining 4 would be retained by him. The vendor agreed to allow him a credit for the amount paid towards cash price against these 3 machines less 25%.

Show the relevant accounts in the books of X assuming that the books are closed in June every year and depreciation @ 20% is charged on Machinery.

Ans. [Loss on Default ₹ 79,500 ; Amount Credited in respect of three machines returned ₹ 40,500; Balance in Machinery Account ₹ 1,60,000].

16. On 1st January, 2024, Ashok acquired furniture on the hire-purchase system from Real Aids Ltd., agreeing to pay four semi-annual instalments of ₹ 800 each, commencing on 30th June, 2024. The cash price of the items was ₹ 3,010 and an interest of 5% per annum was chargeable.

On 30th September, 2024, Ashok expresses his inability to continue and Real Aids seized the property. It was agreed that Ashok would pay the due proportion of the instalment upto the date of seizure and also a further sum of ₹ 200 towards depreciation. At the time of repossession, Real Aids valued the furniture at ₹ 1,500.

The company after incurring ₹ 200 towards repairs of the furniture sold the items for ₹ 1,800 on 15th October, 2024.

Show the Ledger Accounts as they would appear in the books of Real Aids Ltd. working out the profit or loss on the transactions assuming that the company passes hire-purchase transactions through its books as sales.

Ans. [Loss on Valuation of Repossessed Goods ₹ 213.82 ; Profit on Repossessed Goods ₹ 100 ; Net Loss ₹ 10.00].

17. In a sale transaction under hire-purchase sale, the amount payable over two years was ₹ 4,800 inclusive of hire charges of ₹ 800. During the first year, buyer paid a total sum of ₹ 2,600 and requested the seller to repossess the article. The estimated value of the repossessed stock was assessed at ₹ 2,000 and cost of repossession amounted to ₹ 100. The hire-purchase agreement provided for a refund on the basis of revaluation of repossessed stock. The repossessed stock was subsequently sold for ₹ 3,000 after effecting repairs of ₹ 250. Show Hire Purchase Debtor's, Repossessed Stock and Hire-purchase Charges Accounts in the books of the seller.

Ans. [Cash Refund ₹ 100 ; Profit on Repossession ₹ 750].

PROVISION AGAINST FREE MAINTENANCE

18. During 2024 ten television sets were sold with free maintenance warranty for two years. It is estimated that the cost of free maintenance for each television will be ₹ 300, ₹ 120 for the first year and ₹ 180 for the second year. Actual costs incurred were ₹ 700 in 2024 and ₹ 1,400 in 2025. Show *Maintenance Suspense Account* for two years. Books are closed on 31st December each year.

19. M/s Tolly Electro manufactures T.V. sets and sells them both for cash and on hire purchase. The cash price is ₹ 8000 and hire purchase price is ₹ 10,000, payable ₹ 2,000 down and the balance in four equal half-yearly instalments. The warranty period for each set is 2 years from the date of sale and the estimated amount of after sales maintenance is ₹ 800 for each set of which ₹ 300 will be for the first year.

During the year 2025 Tolly Electro sold 100 sets on cash basis and 200 sets on hire purchase basis and incurred an amount of ₹ 40,000 on the after sales service.

Pass the necessary Journal Entries and show *Maintenance Suspense Account* for the year 2025.

HIRE PURCHASE TRADING ACCOUNT/STOCK DEBTORS SYSTEM

20. A Trader sold out goods on *hire purchase* at a profit of 25% on cost price.

Prepare (*i*) Hire Purchase Stock A/c (*ii*) Shop Stock A/c (*iii*) Hire Purchase Debtors' Account and (*iv*) Hire Purchase Adjustment Account in the books of the trader from the following details :

		₹
Stock in Godown on 1-4-2024		6,00,000
	on 31-3-2025	5,00,000
Overdue Instalments :		
	on 1-4-2024	40,000
	on 31-3-2025	60,000
Goods with Customers on Hire Purchase on 1-4-2024		7,20,000
Purchases		12,92,000
Instalments received		12,00,000

Ans. [Profit ₹ 2,44,000]

Hint : Cost of Goods Sold on H.P. ₹ 13,92,000; Closing Balance of H.P. Stock ₹ 12,40,000; Instalments due during the year ₹ 12,20,000]

21. X Ltd. which sells a patent product on hire-purchase terms, has the following transactions for the year to 31st March, 2025. The gross profit is 25 per cent on selling price :

2024		₹
April 1	Stock out on hire at hire-purchase price	40,000
	Stock on hand (at shop)	5,000
	Instalments due (customers still paying)	3,000

April 1, 2024 to 31st March , 2025	Cash received in instalments during the year	80,000
31st March 2025	Stock out on hire at Hire-purchase price	46,000
	Stock on hand (at shop)	7,000
	Instalments due (customers still paying)	5,000

Prepare the necessary accounts to find out Gross Profit of X Ltd. for the year ending 31st March, 2025.

Ans. [Profit ₹ 20,500].

Hints. Purchases ₹ 68,000 ; Instalments due during the year ₹ 82,000 ; Goods sold on H.P. ₹ 88,000.

22. Deepak sells goods on hire purchase at cost plus 60%. From the following particulars for the year ending on 31-3-2025, prepare all accounts under stock and debtors system. Calculate the profit earned:

1-4-2024	Stock with hire purchase customers at selling price	12,000
	Stock at the shop at cost	5,000
	Instalments overdue	8,000
31-3-2025	Total instalments that fell due during the year	1,89,440
	Cash received from customers (including down payment of ₹ 15,440)	1,75,440
	Goods repossessed (Instalments due ₹ 500)	400
	Stock at the shop at cost (including goods repossessed ₹ 400)	2,000
	Purchases	1,20,000
	Hire expenses	3,400

Also prepare H.P. Trading Account to verify your results.

Ans. [₹ 67,540].

Hint. Cost of Goods Sold on H.P. ₹ 1,23,400 ; H.P. Stock Balance at the end ₹ 20,000.

23. Wye sells goods on Hire-purchase at cost plus 50%. Prepare Hire Purchase Trading Account from the information given below :

	₹		₹
Stock with Customers on Hire-purchase Price (Opening)	1,62,000	Goods Repossessed (instalments not due ₹ 36,000)	9,000
Stock in hand at Shop (Opening)	3,24,000	Stock at Shop excluding Repossessed Goods (Closing)	3,60,000
Instalments Overdue (Opening)	1,35,000	Cash Received during the year	10,35,000
Purchases during the year	10,80,000	Instalments Overdue (Closing)	1,62,000

The vendor spent ₹ 2,000 on goods repossessed and then sold it for ₹ 15,000.

Ans. [Profit ₹ 3,43,000]

Hint. Goods Sold on H.P ₹ 15,66,000; Instalments Due at the end ₹ 6,30,000, Instalments due during the year ₹ 5,04,000.

24. Sound Co. records transactions relating to its *hire-purchase business* on Stock Debtors system. It sold to Rasheed a tape recorder for which Rasheed was required to pay in all ₹ 1,200 in the form of 12 monthly instalments of ₹ 100 each. Rasheed paid four instalments in time but thereafter stopped paying instalments. Sound Co., after the seventh instalment had also become due (but before the eighth instalment had fallen due) repossessed the tape-recorder. The company valued the repossessed tape recorder at ₹ 850.

In the books of the company, pass a Journal Entry to record the effect of repossession of tape-recorder from Rasheed.

Hint.	Debit Repossessed Stock A/c	850
	Credit Instalments Due A/c	300
	Credit Hire-Purchase Stock A/c	500
	Credit Profit & Loss or H.P. Adjustment A/c	50

25. A trader has delivered goods to his customers on *hire-purchase system* at hire-purchase price amounting to ₹ 27,500. He normally sells goods in the open market at retail price showing a gross profit of 20% on that price. In order to sell goods at hire purchase price he adds 10% to retail price to cover enhanced risk.

During the year, goods costing ₹ 2,400 were returned by a hire-purchaser, who had paid nothing. These goods are valued at cost on March 31, 2025. Instalments received during the year were ₹ 7,700.

You are required to prepare Hire-purchase Trading Account for the year ending March 31, 2025, so that profit to be taken into account in such proportion of the profit as instalment received bear to the total goods out on hire-purchase.

Ans. [Profit ₹ 2,100 ; Total Stock in the hands of Customers at H.P. Price ₹ 16,500].

26. Mr. Bhalla commenced business on 1st April, 2024. He effected cash sales as well as on 'hire-purchase' basis. During the year 2024-25, his purchases amounted to ₹ 14,500. The cash sales were for ₹ 12,000. Following items were sold on hire-purchase basis as per the following particulars :

	Cost	*Sales Price*	*Initial Payment*	*Instalments paid during the year*
	₹	₹	₹	₹
Radio	200	350	50	125
Cycle	210	350	75	125
Encyclopaedia	400	600	100	150

The instalments on Encyclopaedia could not be kept up and the same was repossessed on 30th November, 2024. The closing stock including the Encyclopaedia amounted to ₹ 5,000.

Prepare Hire-purchase Trading Account, Memorandum Hire-purchase Debtors Account, Goods Repossessed A/c, and General Trading Account for the year ended 31st March, 2025.

Ans. [H.P. Profit ₹ 238 ; Gross Profit ₹ 3,077].

27. Sunshine Company sells goods for cash and on *hire purchase*, the latter being the cash retail price plus 12.5% thereon. Following are the particulars for the year ended 31st December, 2024 :

			₹
Stock at Hire Purchase Price customers on 1-1-2024			29,700
Purchase during the year			1,58,400
Stock at Shop :	On 1-1-2024	22,000	
	On 31-12-2024	26,400	
			48,400
Cash Sales during the year			
79,200			
Cash received during the year (Hire purchase instalments)			1,01,750
Instalments due but not received :			
	On 1-1-2024		4,400
	On 31-12-2024		6,600
Hire purchase sales during the year			1,18,800

Prepare : (*a*) General Trading Account, (*b*) Hire Purchase Trading Account, (*c*) Hire Purchase Sales Account.

for the year ended 31st December, 2024.

Ans. [General Profit ₹ 66,000; Profit on H.P. ₹ 26,950]

Hint. H.P Price of Closing Stock with Customers ₹ 44,500; Cost of Retail Sales ₹ 66,000.

28. On January 1, 2024, Raman commences business to sell transistor sets on hire-purchase at 50% above the cost. The hire-sale price of a set is ₹ 150 and the hire-purchaser is required to pay 20% cash down and the residue in 12 monthly instalments. The first instalment is payable on the last day of the month in which the set is sold on hire-purchase. During 2024, 60 sets are so sold and the instalment receipts amount to ₹ 3,800.

All the instalments are duly received except for six sets on which a total of 12 instalments is received. These sets are, therefore, repossessed in 2025.

Prepare Hire-purchase Trading Accounts for 2024 and 2025. Assume that hire- purchases were evenly made throughout the year. Also the arrears (if any) of 2024 are considered good in that year.

Ans. [Profit 2024—₹ 1,900 ; 2025—₹ 900].

29. ABC Ltd. sells goods on Hire-purchase by adding 50% above cost from the following particulars, prepare Hire-purchase Trading Account to reveal the profit for the year ended 31-3-2025 :

		₹
1-4-2024	Instalments due but not collected	10,000
1-4-2024	Stock at shop (at cost)	36,000
1-4-2024	Instalments not yet due	18,000
31-3-2025	Stock at shop	40,000
31-3-2025	Instalments due but not collected	18,000

Others details :

Total instalments became due	1,32,000
Goods purchased	1,20,000
Cash received from customers	1,21,000

Goods on which due instalments could not be collected were repossessed and valued at 30% below original cost. The vendor spent ₹ 500 on getting goods overhauled and then sold for ₹ 2,800.

Ans. [Profit ₹ 43,300].

Hints: Goods Sold on H.P. ₹ 1,74,000 ; Loss on Repossession of Goods ₹ 1,600 ; Profit on Sale of Repossessed Goods ₹ 900]

30. Kamala Agencies started business on 1st April, 2024. During the year ended 31st March, 2025 they sold under mentioned durables under *two schemes*—Cash Price Scheme (C.P.S.) and Hire Purchase Scheme (H.P.S.)

Under the C.P.S. they priced the goods at cost plus 25% and collected it on delivery.

Under the H.P.S. the buyers were required to sign a Hire Purchase Agreement undertaking to pay for the value of the goods including finance charges in 30 instalments, the value being calculated at cash price plus 50%.

Following are the details available at the end of 31st March, 2025 with regard to the products :

Product	*Nos. purchased*	*Nos. sold under C.P.S.*	*Nos. sold under H.P.S.*	*Cost per unit ₹*	*No. of instalments due during the year*	*No. of instalments received during the year*
T.V. Sets	90	20	60	16,000	1,080	1,000
Washing Machines	70	20	40	12,000	840	800

Following were the expenses during the year :

Rent ₹ 1,08,000 ; Salaries ₹ 1,50,000 ; Commission to Salesmen ₹ 12,000 ; Office Expenses ₹ 1,26,000.

From the above information, you are required to prepare : (*a*) Hire Purchase Trading Account, and (*b*) Trading and Profit & Loss Account.

Ans. [Hire Purchase Profit ₹ 7,98,000 ; Gross Profit ₹ 1,40,000 ; Net Profit ₹ 5,42,000]

31. Computer Point sells computers on Hire-purchase basis at cost plus 25%. Terms of sale are ₹ 5,000 down payment and eight monthly instalments of ₹ 2,500 for each computer.

Following transactions took place during the financial year 2024-25 :

Number of instalments not yet due as on 1-4-2024	=	25
Number of instalments due but not collected as on 1-4-2024	=	5

During the financial year 240 computers were sold. Out of the above sold computers during the year the outstanding positions were as follows as on 31-3-2025 :

Instalments not yet due :

(*i*) Eight instalments on 50 computers. (*ii*) Six instalments on 30 computers. (*iii*) Two instalments on 10 computers.

Instalments due but not collected :

Two instalments on 5 computers during the year. Two computers on which five instalments were due and two instalments not yet due were repossessed out of sales effected during current year. Repossessed stock is valued at 50% of cost. All instalments have been received. You are asked to prepare Hire-Purchase Trading Account for the year ending on 31-3-2025.

Ans. [Profit ₹ 8,97,500]

[**Hint :** Cash collected during the year ₹ 45,15,000; Value of Repossessed Computers ₹ 20,000; Hire Purchase Sales ₹ 45,65,000]

32. M/s Multistore Limited sells goods both on cash and *hire purchase basis* and record hire purchase transactions on *"Stock and Debtors System"*. It closes its books of accounts on 31st March every year. On 1st May, 2024, it sold to Manas a Scooter and a LCD TV.

The other information is as follows :

Particulars	*Scooter*	*LCD TV*
Cost Price (₹)	30,000	40,000
Down Payment (₹)	5,000	6,000
Number of Instalments payable	12	6
Amount of each Instalment (₹)	2,800	7,600
Mode of payment	Monthly	Quarterly
1st Instalment due on	1st June, 2024	1st July, 2024

Manas paid all the instalmens due except for those due on 1st January, 2025. It was decided that M/s Multistore Limited will take back Scooter at an agreed price of ₹ 22,000 and excess amount, if any, will be adjusted against the instalmens due of LCD TV.

Scooter repossessed was sold for ₹ 24,500 after incurring repair charges of ₹ 1,000.

Prepare necessary Ledger Accounts to record the above transactions and find out the profit.

(IPCE May, 2012 Modified)

Ans. [Profit ₹ 21,700]

Hint. H.P. Price : Scooter ₹ 38,600; LCDTV = ₹ 51,600; Profit on H.P. Sale ₹ 20,200.

33. Rosemary Enterprises sells its merchandise under instalment schemes. Legal title to the goods is not relinquished until the customer fully pays the instalments. A summary of the transactions of the firm for the first four years of its existence is given below :

	2022	*2023*	*2024*	*2025*
	₹	₹	₹	₹
Sales on instalment basis	6,66,000	9,50,000	10,20,000	11,04,000
Opening Stock	—	1,20,000	1,60,000	2,40,000
Stock at Close	1,20,000	1,60,000	2,40,000	3,20,000
Purchases	6,75,000	8,00,000	8,55,200	9,20,000
Amounts realised from customers :				
2022 Sales	2,20,000	2,80,000	1,00,000	55,000
2023 Sales	—	4,00,000	2,80,000	2,00,000
2024 Sales	—	—	4,80,000	4,00,000
2025 Sales	—	—	—	3,50,000

Indicate the realised profit for each of these years.

Ans. [	*2022*	*2023*	*2024*	*2025*
Amount of Gross Profit Realised	36,667	1,26,667	1,87,867	2,28,852].
Hints. (*i*) Rate of Gross Profit (%)	16.67	20	24	23.91

(*ii*) Amount of realised profit = Amount realised from customers in a particular year × Gross profit rate for that year.

34. Fancy Ltd. sells Tape Recorders and T.V. sets both on hire purchase and on cash basis. The terms are as follows :

	Tape Recorders	*T.V. Sets*
	₹	₹
Cash Price	1,000	4,000
Cost	800	3,200
Cash down for hire purchase	200	1,000
Monthly instalment	100	275
No. of instalments	10	12

Fancy Ltd. purchased goods costing ₹ 10,00,000 in all and made cash sales totalling ₹ 8,50,000. Closing Stock in hand on 31-3-2025 was valued at ₹ 1,00,000. Hire purchase transactions were as follows :

	No. Sold	*Instalments Collected*	*Instalment due (Customers paying)*
T.V. Sets	20	110	10
Tape Recorders	40	260	15

2 T.V. sets and 3 Tape recorders on which only 4 instalments were collected were repossessed and were valued at ₹ 3,000. These are not included in the figure of stock mentioned above.

Prepare Accounts to show the Profit and Loss on hire purchase transactions and the overall profit or loss made by the Company.

Ans. [Profit on H.P. Transactions ₹ 23,917, Net Profit ₹ 69,917].

35. Neeta Limited commenced business on April 1, 2024. The business is to sell VCPs and VCRs both for cash and on hire-purchase basis. Information about terms is given below :

	VCPs	*VCRs*
	₹	₹
Cash Price	10,000	30,000
Cost	8,000	24,000
Cash down for hire-purchase	2,000	6,000
Monthly Instalment	1,000	3,000
Number of Instalments	10	12

The company purchased goods costing ₹ 1,00,00,000 in all and made cash sales totalling ₹ 86,00,000. Stock in hand on 31st March, 2025 was valued at ₹ 12,00,000. Hire-purchase transactions were as follows :

	Number Sold	*Instalments collected*	*Instalments Due (customers paying)*
VCPs	20	110	10
VCRs	40	260	15

3 VCPs and 2 VCRs on which only 4 instalments were collected were repossessed and were valued at ₹ 32,000. This is not included in the figure of stock mentioned above. Prepare accounts showing the profit or loss made by the company by adopting Stock and Debtors system.

Ans. [H.P. Profit ₹ 5,02,333 ; Net Profit ₹ 14,22,333].

Hints. Goods Sold on H.P. ₹ 19,20,000 ; H.P. Stock at the end ₹ 6,29,000 ; Cash received from H.P. Debtors ₹ 11,70,000 ; Loss on Revaluation of Goods Repossessed ₹ 34,000 ; Stock Reserve required at the end ₹ 2,63,667.

36. The hire purchase department of New Appliances Ltd. sells television sets and room coolers. This department was started in 2024-25. The relevant information for the year ended 31st March, 2025 is as follows :

	Television	Room Cooler
	₹	₹
Cost	5,400	2,000
Cash Price	6,300	2,400
Cash down Payment	900	400
Monthly Instalment	600	200
Number of instalments	10	12

During the year 200 television sets and 240 room coolers were sold on hire purchase basis. Four television sets on which 3 instalments only could be collected and 8 room coolers on which 5 instalments had been collected were repossessed. They were valued at ₹ 20,000 ; after reconditioning at a cost of ₹ 2,000, they were sold outright for ₹ 28,000. Other instalments collected and those due (customers still paying) were respectively as follows :

Television sets	540 and 40
Room Coolers	800 and 60

Prepare accounts on stock and debtors system to reveal the profit of the department.

Ans. [Profit ₹ 2,00,057].

37. Shockers Ltd. commenced business on 1st April, 2024 selling electric generators. They deal in one type only which costs ₹ 6,000 and is sold at a uniform gross profit margin of one-third of selling price. At 31st March, 2025 the company produces the following draft accounts :

REVENUE ACCOUNT

	₹		₹
Purchases	7,20,000	Cash Sales	6,39,000
Salaries : Staff	70,000	Hire Purchase Sales	1,00,000
Director	40,000	Stock at Cost	2,34,000
Overhead Expenses	65,000		
Net Profit for the year	78,000		
	9,73,000		9,73,000

BALANCE SHEET

	₹		₹
Equity Shares of ₹ 10, each	4,00,000	Stock at Cost	2,34,000
Net Profit for the year	78,000	Hire Purchase Debtors	67,200
Creditors	46,000	Bank	2,22,800
	5,24,000		5,24,000

Following information is relevant :

(*i*) Because of a decline in sales towards the end of the year, the directors decided to sell some of the generators on *hire purchase terms* for a deposit of ₹ 2,000 and 10 monthly instalments of ₹ 800 each. Both the deposit and the first monthly instalments are to be paid in the month of delivery.

(*ii*) The number of generators sent out on hire purchase was :
January, 2025—2 ; February, 2025—2 ; March, 2025—6

The directors agree that the gross profit on hire purchase sales is to be taken on the basis that gross profit is earned in proportion to the total cash received in the accounting period and that hire purchase interest is earned in proportion to the instalments received in the accounting period.

Required :

(*a*) General Trading Account, Hire Purchase Trading Account and Profit and Loss A/c for the year ended 31st March, 2025 showing clearly the gross profit on cash sales and the profit taken on hire purchase sales ;

(*b*) Balance Sheet as at 31st March, 2025.

Ans. [(*a*) Gross Profit on General Trading ₹ 2,13,000, H.P. Trading A/c Profit ₹ 9,840 ; Net Profit ₹ 49,440 ;

(*b*) B/S Total ₹ 4,95,440].

Hints. Proportion of Gross Profit taken to Trading A/c ₹ 9,840, Stock on H.P. at Cost of ₹ 38,640.

INSTALMENT PURCHASE SYSTEM

38. On 1st Jan. 2025 a company purchased wagons on the instalment system. The cash price of the wagons was ₹ 59,600 and the payment was to be made as follows :

₹ 16,000 was to be paid on agreement and the balance in 3 instalments of ₹ 16,000 each at the end of each year. 5% interest per annum is charged by the Wagon company. The buyers have decided to write off 10% annually on the diminishing cash value. Prepare necessary Ledger Accounts in the books of the buyer.

Ans. [Interest—₹ 2,180; ₹ 1,489 and ₹ 731]

39. Vijay purchased a motor car from Mysore Motors on 1st January, 2024 on *Instalment system*. The payment is to be made as follows :

₹ 40,000 on delivery, ₹ 76,000 at the end of the first year, ₹ 60,000 at the end of the second year, and ₹ 55,000 at the end of the third year.

Interest at 10% p.a. is included in these instalments. Vijay charged depreciation on the Motor Car at 20% p.a. on the diminishing balance.

You are required to prepare necessary Accounts in the books of Vijay and show the interest calculation.

Ans. [Cash Price ₹ 2,00,000; Interest : 2024—₹ 16,000; 2025—₹ 10,000 and ₹ 2026—₹ 5,000; Balance in Motor Car Account ₹ 1,02,400]

40. On January 1, 2021, A acquires a machine from B on *instalment* buying @ 10% p.a. interest which is yearly chargeable. The buyer agrees to pay to the seller ₹ 2,00,000 on January 1, 2021, ₹ 1,21,000 on December 31, 2022, ₹ 1,33,100 on December 31, 2023 and finally ₹ 1,46,410 on December 31, 2024. A duly discharges all these sums.

Prepare Machinery Account, Seller's Account, and Interest Suspense Account for the first two years in A's books. Assume that A provides for depreciation @ 20% p.a. on diminishing balance method at the accounting date 31st December each year.

Ans. [Cash Price ₹ 5,00,000 ; Interest — 2021 ₹ 30,000 ; 2022 ₹ 33,000 ; 2023 ₹ 24,200 ; 2024 ₹ 13,310].

CHAPTER

25

Branch Accounting

Introduction

In order to increase the sales, business houses are required to make available their products over a larger territory and may generally split their business into certain divisions or parts. If the various parts or divisions are located in different parts of the same city as Chandni Chowk, Karol Bagh, Connaught Place, Nehru Place (in Delhi) or in different cities of the same country as Kolkata, Chennai, Mumbai, Kanpur, Begaluru and Delhi (in India) or in different countries of the world as Canada, U.S.A., England, Japan, U.S.S.R., China, France and Germany, these are known as branches. Head office controls the activities of various branches.

Objects (or Purposes) of Branch Accounting

Main object of keeping branch accounts is dependent on the nature of the business and specific need of a particular branch. The objects of keeping the branch accounts acceptable to all businesses are :

(*i*) To know the profit or loss of each branch separately. (*ii*) To ascertain the financial position of each branch on a particular date. (*iii*) To know the cash and goods requirements of various branches. (*iv*) To evaluate the progress and performance of each branch. (*v*) To calculate commission for payment to the managers, if based on profits of branch. (*vi*) To know the profitability of each branch and type of business for expansion of the business. (*vii*) To give concrete suggestions for the improvement in the working of the various branches. (*viii*) To meet the requirements of specific enactments as all branches of a company must keep the accounts for audit purposes.

Types of Branches

From accounting point of view, the following are the main types of branches :

(*a*) Dependent Branches (Branches not keeping full system of accounting ;

(*b*) Independent Branches (Branches keeping full system of accounting) ; and

(*c*) Foreign branches.

(*a*) Dependent Branch (Branches Not Keeping Full System of Accounting)

Following are the main features of such branches :

(*i*) Such branches *sell only those goods which are received from the head office* and are not usually allowed to make purchases in the open market except with the express permission of the head office.

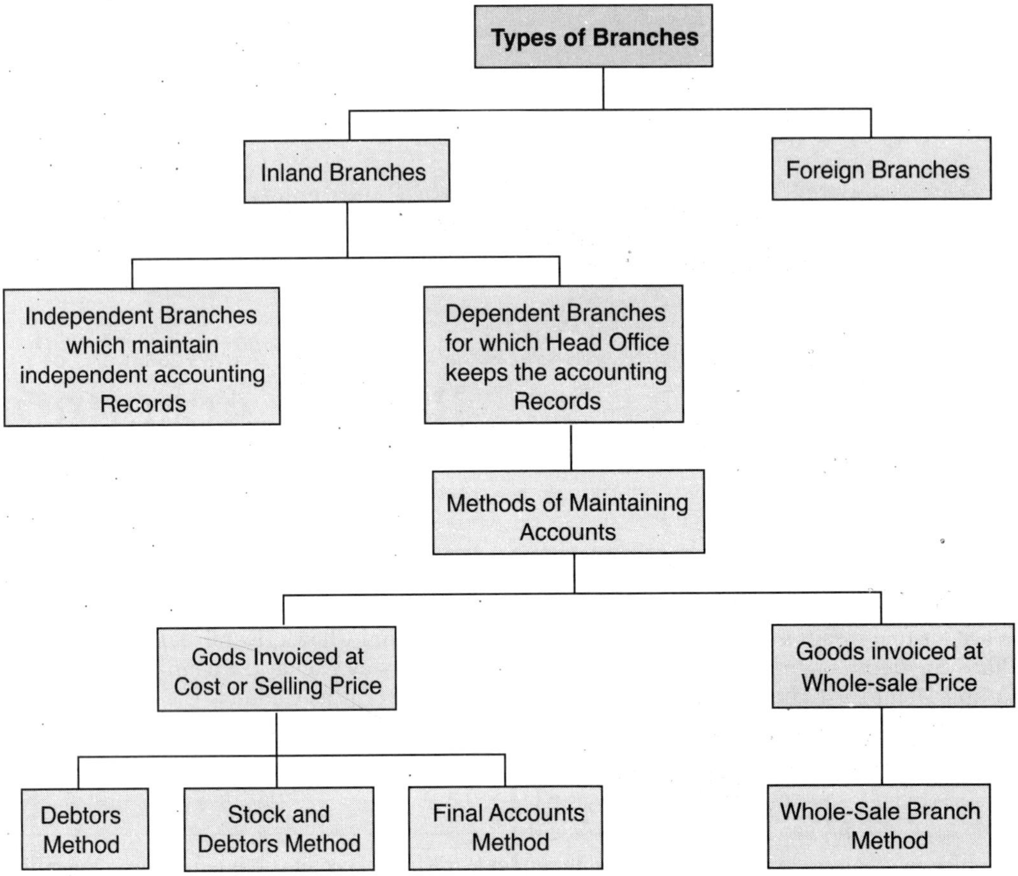

(ii) Goods are supplied by the Head Office to such branches *either at cost price or at invoice price.*

(iii) All *expenses* of the branch such as rent, salary of staff, advertisement etc., are paid by the head office.

(iv) *Petty expenses* such as cartage, entertainments, freights etc. are paid by the branch manager out of petty cash book balance. Such book is maintained at the branch either as simple petty cash book or on imprest system.

(v) The *amount received from cash sales or cash received from the debtors* is either remitted to the head office daily or deposited in the account of the head office at some local bank.

(vi) The branch manager is normally expected to sell the *goods for cash only* but he may be authorised to sell goods on credit in certain cases.

(vii) Such branches do not maintain their own books of account. All records are maintained by head office.

Accounting Records For Branch

The branches with the above features, do not keep proper set of books of accounts. In order to supply the requisite accounting information to the head office at regular interval, each branch keeps some *memorandum records,* such as the Stock Register, the Cash Book and the Petty Cash Book. The *Stock Register* is maintained with a view to keep a record of all goods received from the head office, or returns made to head office during that period, sales made at the branch during the period, breakages and losses of goods and balance of stock available in hand at the close of the accounting period. The *cash book* is maintained to keep record of cash transactions such as cash sales, receipts from branch debtors and cash remitted to head office from time to time. The purpose of maintaining the *Petty Cash Book* is to record small payment of expenses such as carriage, postage, conveyance and entertainment etc. If, however, the branch is authorised to make *credit sales,* a Sales Day Book and a Debtors Ledgers will also be required to be maintained.

Accounting Records For Head Office (*or* System of Accounting for Branch)

Branches not keeping full system of accounting do not keep proper accounts but accounts are maintained in the head office books only. Thus, the system of accounting for branch to be adopted by the head office *depends on* the size of the branch, the degree of control sought to be exercised, the nature and volume of business transactions and the special circumstances under which the branch is operating etc. Following are the *main ways* in which the head office may keep the branch accounts in its books :

(1) Debtors System (2) Final Account System. (3) Stock and Debtors System (4) Wholesale Branch System.

1. Debtors System

This system also called synthetic method is *adopted generally in those branches which are fairly small in size.* Under this system, the head office opens a *separate account for each branch* in order to record all transactions relating to the branch. This account is a nominal account in nature and is prepared to calculate profit and loss for each branch. The goods supplied by the head office to the branch may be either at cost price or at cost plus profit. Following are the *journal entries* which are passed in the books of the head office to record branch transactions.

Transactions	Debit	Credit
(*i*) When goods are sent to branch	Branch A/c	Goods sent to Branch A/c
(*ii*) For return of goods to H.O.	Goods sent to Branch A/c	Branch A/c
(*iii*) For transferring the balance of Goods Sent to Branch A/c	Goods sent to Branch A/c	Purchases A/c (in trading concerns) or Trading A/c (in mfg. concerns)
(*iv*) When cheque or draft is sent for branch expenses	Branch A/c	Bank A/c
(*v*) When cheque or draft is received for remittance	Bank A/c	Branch A/c
(*vi*) When goods are supplied by the branch to another branch under instructions of head office.	Goods sent to Branch A/c	Branch A/c
(*vii*) When goods are supplied by head office but not received by the branch.	Goods in Transit A/c	Branch A/c
(*viii*) When remittances are sent by the branch but not received by the head office.	Cash-in-transit A/c	Branch A/c
(*ix*) For closing balances of assets	Branch Assets A/c	Branch A/c
(*x*) For beginning balances of assets (next year)	Branch A/c	Branch Assets A/c
(*xi*) For closing balances of liabilities	Branch A/c	Branch Liabilities A/c
(*xii*) For opening balances of liabilities (next year)	Branch Liabilities A/c	Branch A/c
(*xiii*) For branch profit	Branch A/c	General Profit & Loss A/c
(*xiv*) For branch loss	General Profit & Loss A/c	Branch A/c

In short, Branch Account is debited with the opening balance of branch assets, goods sent to branch account less returns, cheques sent for expenses of the branch and branch liabilities at the end and credited by branch liabilities at the beginning, cheques received for remittances and closing balances of branch assets. The difference between the two sides will be profit or loss of the branch.

Branch Account (in the books of head office) will appear as under after posting of the entries :

Branch Account
(IN H.O. BOOKS)

To Branch Cash in hand	Opening Balances of Branch Assets	XXX	By Branch Liabilities A/c (Opening Creditors and Outstanding Expenses)	XXX
To Branch Stock		XXX	By Bank (Remittances by the branch *i.e.,* cash sales + cash received from debtors either through branch debtors or direct from branch debtors—any amount spent by branch manager)	XXX
To Branch Debtors		XXX		
To Branch Furniture		XXX		
To Branch Prepaid Insurance ......etc.		XXX		
To Goods sent to Branch A/c *Less* Goods Returned to Head Office		XXX	By Branch Cash in hand (Closing Balances of Branch Assets)	XXX
To Goods sent by other Branches		XXX	By Branch Stock	XXX
To Bank (expenses paid by H.O.)		XXX	By Branch Debtors	XXX
To Branch Liabilities A/c (Closing Creditors and Outstanding Expenses)		XXX	By Branch Furniture	XXX
			By Branch Prepaid Rent /Insurance......etc.	XXX
*To General Profit & Loss A/c (Profit)		XXX	*By General Profit & Loss A/c (Loss)	XXX
Total		XXX	Total	XXX

Treatment of Certain Branch Transactions

(1) Branch expenses paid by the branch out of petty cash. If the petty cash book is *not maintained on Imprest System* then such expenses will be deducted from the branch cash and at the close reduced balance of cash will be shown on the credit side of the branch account. Such expenses need not be shown in the branch account. If such expenses are re-imbursed by the head office to the branch (*if the petty cash is maintained on imprest system*), then these must be debited to the branch account. However, same opening and closing balances of petty cash will be shown on the debit and credit side respectively of the branch account.

(2) Depreciation of fixed assets. This is not shown in the branch account. But closing balance of the fixed assets will be shown on the credit side of the branch account after deduction of the amount of depreciation.

(3) Credit sales, bad debts, sales returns, allowances, and discount allowed pertaining to branch. These items are pertaining to the debtors account and **will not be shown in the branch account.** However, these items will be taken into consideration while ascertaining the amount of opening or closing balance of debtors or amount received from debtors which are shown in the branch account. If the branch has received a bill of exchange it will be sent to head office. The entry will then be debit bills of exchange and credit branch account.

(4) Goods in transit. Goods in transit is the difference between goods sent by head office and received by the branch. Such goods will be shown either on the both sides of the branch account or will be ignored totally while preparing the branch account.

(5) Purchase of fixed assets by the branch. If the branch has purchased any fixed assets, then on one hand Branch Account will be **credited** by the head office and on the other the remittance from the branch will be reduced by the amount. If branch has purchased the asset on **credit basis** and liability arising from such purchase will be shown on the debit side of branch account.

(6) Sale of fixed asset. If the **sale is for cash,** cash remittances will increase from the branch but asset will reduce in value to be shown on the credit side of the branch account. **Loss or profit arising from such sale of fixed asset** will not be shown in the branch account as this is automatically adjusted through the above adjustments.

(7) Losses. Losses due to pilferage, wastage and other losses of stock due to normal or abnormal reasons are also completely ignored while preparing branch account under this method.

(8) Amount received from Insurance Company. When the branch has received any compensation from the insurance company for loss of stock or for any other asset damaged at the branch, such amount will be remitted to the head office. As a result, the amount so received will be added to the amount to be remitted to the head office. If the amount is not yet received from the insurance company till the end of accounting period, the claim due from the insurance company will be taken as an asset and shown on the credit side of branch account.

(9) Preparation of Debtors Account. If cash received from debtors or opening or closing balance of debtors is missing, Branch Debtors Account should be prepared to find out the missing figure.

(10) Bills Receivable received from branch debtors. If a bill is received from debtors at branch, then bills receivable account is debited and debtors account is credited. Further, if the bill is discounted by the branch, the branch cash account is debited and bills receivable account is credited with the net amount. Discount on bills receivable discounted is automatically adjusted in the amount remitted to head office and is never debited to branch account.

The main defect of this method is that it does not provide full information for analysis of Branch Profit and Loss. To overcome this problem, a separate Branch Trading & Profit and Loss Account has to be prepared, which is, of course, a Memorandum Account not forming part of the full system of accounting.

ILLUSTRATION 1. A firm is having its Head Office at Delhi and Branch at Chandigarh. Following are the transactions of the Head Office with Branch for the year ended 31st December, 2024.

	₹		₹
Petty Cash at Branch 1-1-2024	12,500	Cheque sent to branch for :	
Stock at Branch on 1-1-2024	7,50,000	Establishment Expenses	2,50,000
Furniture at Branch on 1-1-2024	4,50,000	Petty Cash	75,000
Goods supplied to Branch during		Salary Outstanding on 31-12-2024	25,000
the year	37,75,000	Petty Expenses incurred by Branch	67,500
Goods returned by branch	25,000	Stock at Branch on 31-12-2024	10,00,000
Cash Sales at Branch	52,50,000		
Depreciate Furniture @ 10% per annum			

Prepare Branch Account after passing necessary Journal Entries and also show the relevant items of the Branch in the Balance Sheet in the books of the Head Office.

SOLUTION

In the Books of the Head Office

JOURNAL ENTRIES

			Dr. ₹	Cr. ₹
2024				
Jan. 1	Chandigarh Branch A/c	Dr.	12,12,500	
	To Branch Stock A/c			7,50,000
	To Branch Petty Cash A/c			12,500
	To Branch Furniture A/c			4,50,000
	(Being branch opening assets transferred to Branch A/c)			

Jan. 1 to Dec. 31	Chandigarh Branch A/c To Goods Sent to Branch A/c (Being goods sent to Branch)	Dr.	37,75,000	37,75,000
"	Chandigarh Branch A/c To Bank A/c (Being cheque sent to branch for establishment expenses and petty expenses)	Dr.	3,25,000	3,25,000
"	Goods sent to Branch A/c to Chandigarh Branch A/c (Being goods returned by Branch)	Dr.	25,000	25,000
"	Bank A/c To Chandigarh Branch A/c (Being sale proceeds received from Branch)	Dr.	52,50,000	52,50,000
Dec. 31	Chandigarh Branch A/c To Branch Outstanding Salary A/c (Being adjustment entry for Branch closing liability)	Dr.	25,000	25,000
"	Branch Stock A/c Branch Petty Cash A/c Branch Furniture A/c To Chandigarh Branch A/c (Being adjustment entry for Branch Closing assets)	Dr. Dr. Dr.	10,00,000 20,000 4,05,000	14,25,000
"	Chandigarh Branch A/c To General Profit & Loss A/c (Being profit at Branch transferred to Profit and Loss A/c)	Dr.	13,62,500	13,62,500

CHANDIGARH BRANCH ACCOUNT

2024		₹	2024		₹
Jan. 1	To Branch Stock A/c	7,50,000	Jan. 1 to Dec. 31	By Bank A/c (Cash Sales)	52,50,000
"	To Branch Petty Cash A/c	12,500	Dec. 31	By Branch Stock A/c	10,00,000
"	To Branch Furniture A/c	4,50,000	"	By Branch Petty Cash A/c (₹ 12,500 + ₹ 75,000 – ₹ 67,500)	20,000
Jan. 1 to Dec. 31	To Goods Sent to Branch A/c ₹ 37,75,000 *Less* : Goods Sent to Branch A/c (Returns) 25,000	37,50,000	"	By Branch Furniture A/c (₹ 4,50,000 – ₹ 45,000 Depreciation)	4,05,000
"	To Bank A/c Establishment Exp. Petty Cash	 2,50,000 75,000			
Dec. 31	To Branch Outstanding Salary A/c	25,000			
"	To General Profit & Loss A/c (Branch Profit transferred)	13,62,500			
		66,75,000			66,75,000

BALANCE SHEET OF ...
as at 31st December, 2024

Liabilities	₹	*Assets*		₹
Chandigarh Branch Outstanding Salary	25,000	Chandigarh Branch Stock		10,00,000
Profit & Loss A/c	13,62,500	Chandigarh Branch Petty Cash	₹	20,000
(Chandigarh Branch Profit)		Chandgarh Branch Furniture	4,50,000	
		Less : Depreciation	45,000	
				4,05,000

ILLUSTRATION 2. Manju Traders, Delhi, have a branch at Mumbai. From the following particulars relating to the branch for the year ending 31-3-2025, prepare Branch Account in the head office books :

	₹		₹
Balances on 1-4-2024 :		Discount allowed to debtors	100
Stock at Branch	10,000	Cash sent to Branch for	
Branch Debtors	4,000	Rent	2,100
Petty Cash	500	Salaries (₹ 200 p.m.)	2,400
Furniture	2,000	Petty Cash	1,000
Prepaid Insurance	150	Insurance (Annual upto 30-6-2025)	600
Salaries Outstanding	200	Goods returned by branch	1,000
Goods sent to branch during the year	80,000	Goods returned by debtors	2,000
Cash sales during the year	1,30,000	Stock on 31-3-2025	5,000
Credit sales during the year	40,000	Petty expenses paid by branch	690
Cash received from debtors	35,000	Sale of furniture on 1-10-2024 (book	
Cash paid by debtors direct to		value of furniture on 1-10-2024	
head office	2,000	was ₹ 475)	400

Provide depreciation on furniture @ 10% p.a. Goods costing ₹ 2,500 were damaged in transit and a sum of ₹ 2,000 was recoverable from the insurance company in full settlement of the claim. The branch manager is entitled to a commission of 10% of profit of branch after charging such commission.

SOLUTION

In the Books of Manju Traders
MUMBAI BRANCH ACCOUNT

	₹	₹		₹	₹
To Branch Stock A/c		10,000	By Branch Outstanding Salaries A/c		200
" Branch Debtors A/c		4,000	" Cash (Remittances) :		
" Branch Petty Cash A/c		500	Cash Sales	1,30,000	
" Branch Furniture A/c		2,000	Cash received from		
" Branch Prepaid Insurance A/c		150	Debtors	35,000	
" Goods sent to Branch A/c	80,000		Cash paid by Branch		
Less : Returns from Branch	1,000		Debtors direct to H.O.	2,000	
		79,000	Sale of Furniture	400	
					1,67,400
" Bank A/c :			" Branch Stock A/c		5,000
Rent	2,100		" Branch Petty Cash A/c		
Salaries	2,400		" (₹ 500 + ₹ 1,000 – ₹ 690)		810
Petty Cash	1,000		" Branch Debtors A/c (1)		4,900
Insurance	600		" Branch Furniture A/c (2)		1,350
		6,100			

	₹		₹
To Salaries Outstanding A/c	200	By Branch Prepaid Insurance A/c (1/4 of ₹ 600)	150
" Manager's Outstanding Commission $\left(\frac{10}{110} \text{ of } ₹\, 79{,}860\right)$	7,260	" Insurance Company Claim A/c	2,000
" General Profit & Loss A/c (Profit)	72,600		
	1,81,810		1,81,810

Working Notes : (1) ***Calculation of Debtors at the end***

DEBTORS ACCOUNT

	₹		₹
To Balance b/d	4,000	By Cash A/c (received from debtors)	35,000
" Sales (credit) A/c	40,000	" Cash A/c (cash paid by debtors direct to H.O.)	2,000
		" Sales Returns A/c	2,000
		" Discount A/c	100
		" Balance c/d (Bal. fig.)	4,900
	44,000		44,000

(2) Value of Furniture (sold on 1-10-2024) on 1-4-2024 is ₹ 475 × $\frac{100}{95}$ = ₹ 500. The remaining value of furniture on 1-4-2024 is ₹ 1,500 (*i.e.,* ₹ 2,000 – ₹ 500) and used for the whole year. So after charging depreciation @ 10% p.a., its value after depreciation on 31-3-2025 is ₹ 1,350. Loss on sale of furniture ₹ 100 (*i.e.* ₹ 500 – ₹ 400) will not be taken into account. While preparing Branch Account ₹ 400 received from sale of furniture will be added to cash received from branch.

Invoice Price Method

When the goods are sent by the head office to the branch at invoice price, *i.e.,* cost plus some percentage of profit, the **branch manager is required to sell the goods at invoice price only.** Goods are marked on invoice price to achieve the following objectives :

(*i*) In order to **keep secret from the branch manager the cost price of the goods and profit made,** so that the branch manager may not start a rival and competitive business with the concern; and

(*ii*) In order to **have effective control on stock *i.e.,* stock** at any time must be equal to opening stock plus goods received from head office minus sales made at the branch.

Accounting Adjustments Required in Head Office Books

The branch records are not in any way affected due to invoicing of goods at cost plus profit. But, in order to calculate the profit or loss made by the branch, some accounting adjustments, as stated below, are required to be passed in the Books of the H.O. for eliminating the profit element included in branch opening stock, goods sent to branch less returns made by branch to head office and branch closing stock.

(*i*) *For adjustment of excess price of the opening stock (or in transit) at branch*

Stock Reserve A/c Dr.
  To Branch A/c

(*ii*) *For adjustment of excess price of the closing stock of unsold goods at branch*

Branch A/c Dr.
  To Stock Reserve A/c

(*iii*) *For adjustment of excess price of goods sent to branch less returns to head office*

Goods sent to Branch A/c Dr.
  To Branch A/c

Closing stock should always be valued at cost or net realisable value, whichever is lower. This is based on the principle of conservatism, *i.e,* no profit should be anticipated and all losses should be provided. Moreover, the unsold stock lying in the branch will not earn any profit unless sold. Therefore, it is necessary to make provision for the profit element included in the unsold stock.

Calculation of Mark-up or Load

For calculating loading or excess price, the following **procedure** is adopted :

Suppose goods are invoiced at **cost plus 25%.** If the cost is ₹ 100, profit is ₹ 25, selling price therefore, is ₹ 125. The ratio of profit to selling price is 25/125 or 1/5. Adjustments for the difference or excess price in value between the invoice price and the cost price, therefore, will be made on the basis of 1/5 of the invoice price. **If the percentage is given on sale** price as 25% on sale price, then suppose the sale price is ₹ 100, the profit will be ₹ 25. Therefore, cost will be ₹ 75. So the percentage on cost will be $\frac{25}{75} \times 100 = 33\frac{1}{3}\%$ or ($\frac{1}{3}$ of cost).

ILLUSTRATION 3. Bata Ltd. has a head office and many retail branches which are supplied goods from the head office at 20% profit on sales price. Accounts are kept at head office from where all expenses (except petty expenses) are paid. Such petty expenses are paid by the branches which are allowed to maintain petty cash balances of ₹ 2,300 on *Imprest system.* From the following balances as shown by the books, prepare Branch Account.

Balances on 1-4-2024 :			
Petty cash in hand at branch	2,300	Cash purchases by the branch (on permission from head office)	40,500
Stock in hand at branch at sales price	50,000	Credit purchases	99,800
Sundry debtors at branch	24,000	*Payments made by the head office* :	
Sundry creditors at branch	11,200	Rent for one year (paid on 1st July, 2024)	2,800
Furniture and fixture at branch	28,000	Salaries	12,000
Rent prepaid (upto 30th June, 2024)	1,300	Insurance paid for the year ending 30-6-2025	960
Transactions for the year ended 31-3-2025 were as follows :		*Payment made by the branch* :	
Goods sent to branch (*Less* : Returns)	4,04,000	Petty expenses	480
		Balances on 31-3-2025 :	
Cash sales at branch	5,80,000	Stock at Sales Price	37,500
Credit sales at branch	95,000	Creditors at the end	23,000
Allowances to debtors	1,500	Write off 10% depreciation on furniture	
Cash received from customers	80,000		
Bad debts to be written off	1,200		

SOLUTION

In the Books of Bata Ltd.
BRANCH ACCOUNT

		₹		₹
To Branch Petty Cash A/c		2,300	By Branch Creditors A/c	11,200
" Branch Stock A/c		50,000	" Cash A/c (remittance) (3)	5,31,500
" Branch Debtors A/c		24,000	" Branch Stock A/c	37,500
" Branch Furniture & Fixture A/c		28,000	" Branch Debtors A/c (1)	36,300
" Branch Rent Prepaid A/c		1,300	" Branch Petty Cash A/c (4)	2,300
" Goods sent to Branch A/c		4,04,000	" Branch Furniture A/c	25,200
" Bank A/c :	₹		" Branch Rent Prepaid A/c	700
Rent	2,800		" Branch Insurance Prepaid A/c	240

Salaries	12,000		By Stock Reserve A/c		10,000
Insurance	960		" Goods Sent to Branch A/c		80,800
		15,760			
" Bank A/c (Petty Expenses)		480			
" Branch Creditors A/c		23,000			
" Stock Reserve A/c		7,500			
" General Profit & Loss A/c (Profit)		1,79,400			
		7,35,740			7,35,740

Working Notes :

(1) **DEBTORS ACCOUNT**

	₹		₹
To Balance b/d	24,000	By Allowances	1,500
" Sales (Credit)	95,000	" Bad Debts	1,200
		" Cash	80,000
		" Balance c/d (Bal. fig.)	36,300
	1,19,000		1,19,000

(2) **CREDITORS ACCOUNT**

	₹		₹
To Cash (Bal. fig.)	88,000	By Balance b/d	11,200
" Balance c/d	23,000	" Purchases (Credit)	99,800
	1,11,000		1,11,000

(3) **CASH ACCOUNT**

	₹		₹
To Cash Sales	5,80,000	By Purchases	40,500
" Debtors	80,000	" Creditors (2)	88,000
		" Cash Remitted (Bal. fig.)	5,31,500
	6,60,000		6,60,000

(4) **PETTY CASH ACCOUNT**

	₹		₹
To Balance b/d	2,300	By Cash (Petty Expenses)	480
" Cash (Reimbursement of Expenses)	480	" Balance c/d	2,300
	2,780		2,780

2. Final Account System

According to this system, the profit or loss made by the branch is determined by preparing Branch Trading and Profit & Loss Account at cost price. It should be carefully noted that all expenses (direct and indirect) whether paid by the head office or by the branch are debited to the Trading and Profit & Loss Account prepared for the branch. The profit and loss as disclosed by this account is exactly same as that of the branch account prepared according to Debtors/Synthetic system. It should be further noted that the branch Trading and Profit & Loss Account is only a memorandum account not forming part of the full accounting system. If the branch account is also prepared, in addition to the branch Trading & Profit and Loss Account, then such a branch account will be treated as a personal account and not considered in the nature of a nominal account under the Debtors system. Then branch account under such circumstances, will show a debit balance which will be equal to net worth or net assets available at branch at the end of the accounting period. The working of this system will be clear from the following illustration.

ILLUSTRATION 4. A Delhi merchant has a Branch at Chennai to which he charges out the goods at cost plus 25%. The Chennai Branch keeps its own Sales Ledger and transmits all cash received to the Head Office every day. All expenses are paid from the Head office. The transactions for the Branch were as follows :

	₹		₹
Stock (1-4-2024) at I.P.	11,000	Returns Inwards	500
Debtors (1-4-2024)	100	Cheques sent to Branch :	
Petty Cash	100	Rent	600
Cash Sales	2,650	Wages	200
Credit Sales	23,950	Salaries and other expenses	900
Goods sent to Branch at I.P.	20,000	Stock (31-3-2025)	13,000
Collection on ledger accounts	21,000	Debtors	2,000
Goods returned to H.O. at I.P.	300	Petty Cash (31-3-2025) including	
Bad Debts	300	miscellaneous income ₹ 25,	
Allowances to Customers	250	not remitted	125

Prepare the Branch Trading and Profit & Loss Account and Branch Account for the year 31-3-2025.

SOLUTION

BRANCH TRADING AND PROFIT & LOSS ACCOUNT

for the year ending 31-3-2025

		₹		₹	₹
To Opening Stock			By Sales :		
(₹ 11000 – ₹ 2,200)		8,800	Cash	2,650	
To Goods Sent to Branch A/c	₹		Credit	23,950	
(₹ 20,000 – ₹ 4,000)	16,000			26,600	
Less : Returns to H.O.			*Less* : Returns	500	
(₹ 300 – ₹ 60)	240	15.760			26,100
" Wages		200	By Closing Stock		
" Gross Profit c/d		11,740	(₹ 13,000 – ₹ 2,600)		10,400
		36,500			36,500
		₹			₹
" Bad Debts		300	" Gross Profit b/d		11,740
" Allowances		250	" Accrued Income		25
" Rent		600			
" Salaries & Other Expenses		900			
" Net Profit		9,715			
		11,765			11,765

BRANCH ACCOUNT (PERSONAL) ACCOUNT

	₹	₹		₹
To Opening Balances :			By Cash (Remittances)	
Stock		8,800	(₹ 2,650 + ₹ 21,000)	23,650

Debtors		100	By Balance c/d	
Petty Cash		100	(₹ 10,400 + ₹ 2,000 + ₹ 125)	12,525
To Goods Sent to Branch A/c	16,000			
Less : Returns to H.O.	240			
		15,760		
" Bank A/c (Expenses)		1,700		
" Profit		9,715		
		36,175		36,175

3. Stock and Debtors System

There is yet another method of calculating profit and loss of a branch which is popularly known as 'Stock & Debtors' System or 'Analytical Method'. It is an elaborate method of keeping branch accounts and is considered very useful where the branch turnover is sufficiently large and where a greater degree of control is sought to be exercised by the head office over the branch. According to this system, instead of opening one Branch Account, as is done in case of Debtors system, separate accounts are opened for various transactions at branch. According to this system, a separate ledger for each branch will have to be maintained at head office for keeping accounts, such as Branch Stock, Branch Debtors, Goods sent to Branch,Branch Expenses, and Branch Asset etc. Branch Cash or Petty Cash Account may sometime be required to be maintained if the branch is permitted to use the available cash for making certain payments. Preparation of Branch Stock Account will, however, vary from branch to branch depending upon the method of charging out the goods sent to branch. Goods may be charged to Branch at cost or selling price.

(a) Goods Charged to Branch at Cost Price

In this case the following accounts are prepared in the books of head office :

1. Branch Stock Account. This account is similar to that of the Branch Trading Account where items like goods received from head office, goods returned to head office, goods sold by branch and goods returned by customers to the branch etc. are dealt with. This account is debited with opening stock at branch, goods sent to branch and goods returned to the branch by customers. This account is credited with cash sales, credit sales made by the branch, the goods returned by branch to the head office and closing stock at branch. The balance of this account represents gross profit or gross loss and the same is transferred to Branch Profit & Loss Account.

2. Goods Sent to Branch Account. This account maintained in the books of the head office is credited with goods sent to branch and is debited with goods returned by branch. At the end of the accounting period, the balance of this account is transferred to Purchases Account in case of trading concern and to Trading Account in case of a manufacturing concerns.

3. Branch Debtors Account. This account is prepared when the branch sells goods on credit. It is necessary for recording all transactions concerning branch debtors and for ascertaining the balance of debtors at branch.

4. Branch Petty Cash Account. This account is maintained where the branch makes some petty cash payments. This account is debited with the balance of petty cash available in hand at the beginning of the accounting year and with cash sent to the branch by the head office for petty cash and is credited with all petty cash expenses incurred by the branch. The balance of this petty cash account represents petty cash available in hand at the end of the accounting period.

5. Branch Profit & Loss Account. This account is prepared to ascertain the profit or loss made by the branch during the accounting period. Gross profit or loss at the branch, as determined from the Branch Stock Account, is transferred to this account. The various branch expenses or losses are debited and if there is any income, the same should be credited to this Branch Profit & Loss Account. The balance of this account represents net profit or net loss for the year.

6. Branch Cash Account. This account is maintained for recording all cash transactions relating to the branch. This account is considered quite essential where the branch is permitted to purchase goods locally and to incur expenses at branch out of cash available with the branch.

Following journal entries will be required for preparation of branch accounts according to 'Stock & Debtors' system in the books of H.O.

Transactions	*Debit*	*Credit*
1. Goods sent to branch	Branch Stock A/c	Goods sent to Branch A/c
2. Goods returned by branch	Goods sent to Branch A/c	Branch Stock A/c
3. Cash sales at branch remitted to H.O.	Branch Cash A/c	Branch Stock A/c
4. Credit Sales at branch	Branch Debtors A/c	Branch Stock A/c
5. Returns from customers	Branch Stock A/c	Branch Debtors A/c
6. Bad Debts & Discount etc. allowed	Branch Expenses A/c	Branch Debtors A/c
7. Cash received from branch debtors remitted to H.O.	Branch Cash A/c	Branch Debtors A/c
8. Shortage of goods in branch stock	Branch P/L A/C	Branch Stock A/c
9. Surplus of goods in branch stock	Branch Stock A/c	Branch P/L A/c
10. Expenses paid by head office	Branch Expenses A/c	Cash A/c
11. Transfer of branch expenses to branch P/L A/c	Branch P/L A/c	Branch Expenses A/c
12. Goods in transit	Good in Transit A/c	Branch Stock A/c
13. Good lost in transit being abnormal loss	Branch P/L A/c Insurance Claim Receivable A/c (if any claim is admitted)	Branch Stock A/c
14. Cash in Transit	Cash in Transit A/c	Branch Cash A/c
15. Transfer of branch gross profit	Branch Stock A/c	Branch P/L A/c
16. Transfer of branch net profit	Branch P/L A/c	General P/L A/c

ILLUSTRATION 5. M/s Bharat Enterprise Ltd. invoices goods to their various branches at cost, and the branches sell on credit as well as for cash. From the following details relating to Bengaluru Branch, prepare necessary accounts in the books of head office :

	₹		₹
Stock on 1st January, 2024	15,000	Allowances to customers	300
Stock on 31st December, 2024	14,000	Returns from customers	600
Debtors on 1st January, 2024	25,000	Bad Debts written off	500
Debtors on 31st December, 2024	35,000	Discount allowed to customers	2,000
Cash at branch on 1st Jan. 2024	500	Remittance from branch	70,000
Cash sent to branch	1,500	Rent & Taxes	1,500
Goods sent to branch	50,000	Salaries	5,000
Goods returned by branch	500	General Trade Charges	1,500
Cash sales	32,000	Normal Loss of goods due to wastage	1,000
Credit sales	58,000	Abnormal Loss of goods due to pilferage	2,000

SOLUTION

In the Books of Head Office

BRANCH STOCK ACCOUNT

2024		₹	₹	2024		₹
Jan. 1	To Balance b/d		15,000	Dec. 31	By Cash A/c (Sales)	32,000
Dec. 31	" Goods sent to Branch A/c	50,000		" "	" Branch Debtors A/c (Credit Sales)	58,000

Dec. 31	*Less* : Returns to H.O. 500	49,500	Dec. 31	By Branch P/L A/c (Pilferage of goods)	2,000
	To Branch Debtors A/c (Sales Returns)	600	"	" Balance c/d	14,000
	" Branch P/L A/c (Gross Profit)	40,900			
		1,06,000			1,06,000

BRANCH DEBTORS ACCOUNT

2024		₹	2024		₹
Jan. 1	To Balance b/d	25,000	Dec. 31	By Branch Cash A/c (Bal. Fig.)	44,600
Dec 31	" Branch Stock A/c	58,000	" "	" Branch Expenses : ₹	
			" "	Allowance 300	
			" "	Discount 2,000	
			" "	Bad Debts 500	2,800
			" "	" Branch Stock A/c (Sales Returns)	600
			" "	" Balance c/d	35,000
		83,000			83,000

BRANCH CASH ACCOUNT

2024		₹	2024	₹	₹
Jan. 1	To Balance b/d	500	Dec. 31	By Branch Expenses :	
Dec. 31	" General Cash A/c	1,500		Rent & Taxes 1,500	
	" Branch Stock A/c	32,000		Salaries 5,000	
	" Branch Debtors A/c	44,600		General Trade Charges 1,500	8,000
			" "	" General Cash A/c	70,000
			" "	" Balance c/d	600
		78,600			78,600

GOODS SENT TO BRANCH ACCOUNT

2024		₹	2024		₹
Dec. 31	To Purchases A/c (Transfer)	49,500	Dec. 31	By Branch Stock A/c	49,500

BRANCH EXPENSES ACCOUNT

2024		₹	2024		₹
Dec. 31	To Branch Cash A/c ₹		Dec. 31	By Branch P/L A/c	10,800
	Rent & Taxes 1,500				
	Salaries 5,000				
	General Trade charges 1,500	8,000			
	" Branch Debtors A/c	2,800			
		10,800			10,800

BRANCH PROFIT & LOSS ACCOUNT

2024		₹	2024		₹
Dec. 1	To Branch Expenses :		Dec. 31	By Branch Stock A/c (Gross Profit)	40,900
	Allowances	300			
	Discount	2,000			
	Bad Debts	500			
	Rent & Taxes	1,500			
	Wages & Salaries	5,000			
	General Trade Charges	1,500			
	" Branch Stock: (Cost of goods pilfered)	2,000			
	" Net profit transferred to General P/L A/c	28,100			
		40,900			40,900

(b) Goods Charged to Branch at Selling Price

The Stock and Debtors system, as discussed above is particularly considered very useful and appropriate where goods are invoiced to the branch at Selling Price. A brief description of various accounts opened in the books of head office is given below :

1. Branch Stock Account. This account is prepared in the same way as that when goods are invoiced at cost, except that all entries are made at invoice price. This method of accounting helps the head office to exercise a better control over the branch stock. This account clearly brings into focus the shortage or surplus in stock at branch. The balance of this account, after posting all the relevant entries should be equal to the stock in hand available at branch, unless there is any surplus or shortage. The profit or the 'load' included in such surplus or shortage should be transferred to Branch Adjustment Account while the cost of such surplus or shortage should be adjusted to Branch Profit & Loss Account.

2. Branch Adjustment Account. This account is prepared for ascertaining the amount of gross profit earned by the branch. This is done by eliminating the profit element or the 'loading' included in the value of opening and closing stock at branch, goods sent to branch, less returns made by branch to head office and in surplus or shortage in branch stock etc. The balance of the account represents the gross trading profit or loss which is then transferred to Branch Profit & Loss Account.

3. Goods Sent to Branch Account. The purpose of preparing this account is to ascertain the exact value of the goods sent to the branch during the accounting period. This account is credited with the value of goods sent to branch at selling price and is debited with the value of goods returned by the branch at the same invoice value. After adjusting the 'Loading' *i.e.,* the profit included in such goods, the balance of this account is transferred to Purchases Account.

4. Branch Profit & Loss Account. This account is prepared to ascertain the net profit or loss at the branch. The branch gross profit or loss as shown by Branch Adjustment account is transferred to Branch Profit & Loss Account. The branch expenses, shortage of stock at cost value and losses of stock etc. are debited to this account. This account is further credited with incomes and gains, if any at branch and cost value of surplus in branch stock etc. The balance of the account represents net profit or loss made at the branch during the accounting period, which is finally transferred to General Profit & Loss Account.

5. Stock Reserve/Suspense Account. This account is prepared to adjust the loading included in the value of opening and closing stock at branch. This account is credited with the loading included in the closing stock at branch and its balance is carried forward to the next accounting period.

Apart from the above, other accounts which are required to be prepared according to 'Stock & Debtors' system under method (B) referred to above, are **Branch Expenses Account, Branch Debtors Account, Branch Cash Account and Branch Assets Account** etc. These accounts are prepared in the same way as those when goods sent to branch are charged at cost, as already stated in method (A) above.

Following Journal Entries are made relating to various types of transactions under this method :

(*i*) *When goods are sent to branch*

Branch Stock A/c Dr.

To Goods Sent to Branch A/c

Note. Reverse entry will be passed for goods returned by branch to Head Office.

(*ii*) *When sales are made by the branch*

(*a*) *For Cash Sales*

Cash A/c Dr.

To Branch Stock A/c

(*b*) *For Credit Sales*

Branch Debtors A/c Dr.

To Branch Stock A/c

(*iii*) (*a*) *When cash or bill is received from Debtors*

Cash or Bills Receivable A/c Dr.

To Branch Debtors A/c

(*b*) *When bill of exchange is discounted from the bank by head office*

Bank A/c Dr.

Branch Expenses (Discount on Bill) A/c Dr.

To Bills Receivable A/c

(*iv*) *For discount allowed, allowances and bad debts*

Branch Expenses A/c Dr.

To Branch Debtors A/c

(*v*) *For agreed allowances to customers off selling price already taken into account while invoicing*

Branch Adjustment A/c Dr.

To Branch Stock A/c

(*vi*) *When goods are returned by branch debtors*

Branch Stock A/c Dr.

To Branch Debtors A/c

(*vii*) *When goods are returned by branch debtors direct to head office*

Goods sent to Branch A/c (Cost)

Branch Adjustment A/c (Loading)

To Branch Debtors A/c

(*viii*) *For normal loss of stock*

Branch Adjustment A/c Dr. [with full value]

To Branch Stock A/c

(*ix*) *For abnormal loss, waste or leakage or shortage of stock*

Branch Adjustment A/c Dr. [with loading only]

Branch Profit & Loss A/c Dr. [with cost]

To Branch Stock A/c

Note. Reverse entry for Surplus in Stock.

Due to loss of goods in transit or theft and pilferages at branch, abnormal losses may arise. In such cases the Branch Stock Account must be credited with such abnormal losses. This is necessary to find out stock discrepancies for other reasons. The loading on abnormal losses is to be debited to Branch Adjustment Account and the cost of goods to Branch Profit and Loss Account.

(*x*) *For transfer of goods from one branch to another branch*

Transferor Branch		*Transferee Branch*	
Goods sent to Branch A/c	Dr.	Branch Stock A/c	Dr.
Branch Adjustment A/c	Dr.	To Goods sent to Branch A/c	
To Branch Stock A/c		To Branch Adjustment A/c	

(*xi*) *For apparent profit over the invoice price*

Branch Stock A/c Dr.
To Branch Adjustment A/c

(*xii*) *For Branch expenses paid in cash*

Branch Expenses A/c Dr.
To Cash

(*xiii*) *For closing branch expenses account (excluding cash in hand at the end) to Branch P. & L. Account*

Branch Adjustment A/c Dr. (for non-recurring expenses)
Branch Profit & Loss A/c Dr. (for recurring expenses)
To Branch Expenses A/c

(*xiv*) *For adjustment of excess price of the opening stock*

Stock Reserve A/c Dr.
To Branch Adjustment A/c

(*xv*) *For adjustment of excess price of the closing stock*

Branch Adjustment A/c Dr.
To Stock Reserve A/c

(*xvi*) *For adjustment of excess price of goods sent to branch*

Goods sent to Branch A/c Dr.
To Branch Adjustment A/c

(*xvii*) *For insurance claim received or recoverable*

Bank / Insurance Claim Dr.
To Branch P. & L. A/c

(*xviii*) *For transfer of balance of Branch Adjustment A / c (i.e., gross profit)*

Branch Adjustment A/c Dr.
To Branch P. & L. A/c

(*xix*) *For transfer of profit or loss to general profit and loss account*

(*a*) *If profit*		(*b*) *If loss*	
Branch P. & L. A/c	Dr.	General P. & L. A/c	Dr.
To General P. & L. A/c		To Branch P. & L. A/c	

(*xx*) *For closing the goods sent to branch account*

Goods sent to Branch A/c Dr.
To Purchases or Trading A/c

ILLUSTRATION 6. A company with its head office at Kolkata has branches at Mumbai and Delhi. Goods are invoiced to the branch at cost plus $33\frac{1}{3}\%$ which is the selling price. Following information is given in respect of Delhi branch for the year ended 31st March, 2025 :

	₹		₹
Goods sent to Branch (invoice price)	4,80,000	Branch Debtors' balance (1-4-2024)	30,000
Stock at Branch (1-4-2024) at invoice price	24,000	Discounts allowed	1,000
		Bad debts	1,500
Cash Sales	1,76,000	Stock at Branch (31-3-2025) at Invoice price	48,000
Returns from Customers	6,000		
Branch Adjustment A/c (Cr.)	6,000	Branch Debtors' balance (31-3-2025)	36,500
Branch Expenses (of which non-recurring ₹ 1,000) paid by the H.O.	54,500	Collections from Debtors	2,66,000
Normal Loss at I.P.	700	Branch Debtors' cheques returned dishonoured	5,000
Goods lost in transit at I.P.	10,000	Transfer from Delhi Branch to Mumbai Branch	4,000
Claim recoverable from the Insurance Co. for loss in transit	9,000	Allowances to customers off selling price (already adjusted while invoicing)	300
Goods returned by branch debtors direct to H.O.	4,000		

You are required to prepare the necessary Accounts under Stock and Debtors system to reveal the profit of the branch for the year 2024-25.

SOLUTION

BRANCH STOCK ACCOUNT

	₹		₹
To Balance b/d	24,000	By Cash (Sales)	1,76,000
" Goods Sent to Branch A/c	4,80,000	" Branch Debtors A/c (credit)	2,80,000
" Branch Debtors A/c (Sales Returns)	6,000	" Branch Adj. A/c (I.P. of Normal Loss)	700
" Branch Adjustment A/c (Apparent Profit) (Bal. fig.)	9,000	" Branch Adj. A/c (Agreed Allowances)	300
		" Branch Adj. A/c (Loading of Ab. Loss)	2,500
		" Branch P & L A/c (Cost of Ab. Loss)	7,500
		" Branch Adjustment A/c (Loading of Goods Transferred)	1,000
		" Goods sent to Branch A/c (Cost)	3,000
		" Balance c/d	48,000
	5,19,000		5,19,000

BRANCH DEBTORS ACCOUNT

	₹		₹	₹
To Balance b/d	30,000	By Goods Sent to Branch (Cost of goods returned direct to H.O.)		3,000
" Bank (Cheques dishonoured)	5,000	By Branch Adjustment A/c (Loading of goods returned direct to H.O.)		1,000
To Branch Stock A/c (Credit sales) (Bal. fig.)	2,80,000	" Branch Stock (Sales Returns)		6,000
		" Branch Expenses A/c :		
		Discount	1,000	
		Bad Debts	1,500	2,500
		" Cash		2,66,000
		" Balance c/d		36,500
	3,15,000			3,15,000

BRANCH EXPENSES ACCOUNT

	₹		₹
To Cash	54,500	By Branch Adj. A/c (Non-recurring)	1,000
" Branch Debtors A/c	2,500	By Branch P. & L. A/c (Recurring)	56,000
	57,000		57,000

BRANCH ADJUSTMENT ACCOUNT

	₹		₹
To Stock Reserve	12,000	By Stock Reserve	6,000
" Branch Stock (Normal Loss)	700	" Goods Sent to Branch	1,20,000
" Branch Stock A/c	300	" Branch Stock A/c (Apparent Profit)	9,000
" Branch Stock A/c (Loading of Abnormal Loss)	2,500		
" Branch Debtors A/c	1,000		
" Branch Expenses A/c	1,000		
" Branch Stock A/c (Transfer)	1,000		
" Branch P & L A/c (Gross Profit)	1,16,500		
	1,35,000		1,35,000

BRANCH PROFIT & LOSS ACCOUNT

	₹		₹
To Branch Expenses	56,000	By Branch Adjustment A/c	1,16,500
" Branch Stock A/c (Cost of Ab. Loss) 9,000	7,500	" Insurance Co. (Insurance Claim recoverable)	
" General P. & L. A./c (Net Profit)	62,000		
	1,25,500		1,25,500

GOODS SENT TO BRANCH ACCOUNT

	₹		₹
To Branch Adjustment A/c (Loading)	1,20,000	By Branch Stock A/c	4,80,000
" Branch Debtors A/c (Cost of goods returned direct to H.O.)	3,000		
" Branch Stock A/c (Transfer)	3,000		
" Trading A/c	3,54,000		
	4,80,000		4,80,000

ILLUSTRATION 7. Sellwell Ltd. has two branches, in Cochin and Bengaluru. During the year ended 31st March, 2024 goods have been invoiced to the Cochin branch at 20% above cost and to the Bengaluru branch at 25% above cost. The branches do not maintain complete books of accounts but the following figures are available for the year ended 31st March, 2025 :

	Cochin	*Bengaluru*
	₹	₹
Opening Stock at invoice price	10,000	10,000
Goods sent to Branch at cost	50,000	40,000
Amount remitted by Branch	80,000	80,000

Amount remitted by Head Office	15,000	15,000
Goods returned by branch at invoice price	3,000	—
Cash as on 1-4-2024	2,000	1,000
Cash as on 31-3-2025	1,000	500
Goods returned by customers at Branch at selling price	5,000	4,000
Expenses at Branch in Cash	5,000	3,000

All sales at the Branches are for cash. During the year Cochin Branch purchased fixed assets worth ₹ 4,000 and this amount is included in the figure of branch expenses. Cochin branch transferred to the Bengaluru Branch stock costing ₹ 5,000 during the year. The Bengaluru Branch remitted ₹ 2,000 to the Cochin Branch also during the year. There was a closing stock of ₹ 24,000 valued at invoice price at the Cochin Branch. There was no closing stock at the Bengaluru Branch. The Branch Stock Adjustment Account in the Head Office books showed the following position as on 1st April, 2024 :

For Cochin—₹ 2,500 (Cr.); For Bengaluru—₹ 2,000 (Cr.).

Prepare Branch Stock Account, Branch Adjustment Account, Goods sent to Branch Account, Branch Cash Account and Branch Profit and Loss Account in the Head Office books ignoring depreciation.

SOLUTION

Sellwell Ltd.

BRANCH STOCK ACCOUNT

	Bangalore	Cochin		Bangalore	Cochin
	₹	₹		₹	₹
To Opening Stock	10,000	10,000	By Branch Cash A/c (See Branch Cash A/c)	76,000	73,500
To Goods sent to Branch A/c (Invoice Bill)	60,000	50,000	By Goods sent to Branch —Returns	3,000	—
To Branch Cash A/c (Goods returned)	5,000	4,000	By Goods sent to Branch —transfer (₹ 5,000 + 20% of ₹ 5,000)	6,000	
To Goods sent to Branch (transfer, ₹ 5,000 + 25% of ₹ 5,000)	—	6,250	By Closing Stock	24,000	
To Branch Adjustment A/c (Apparent Profit over invoice price : Bal. fig.)	34,000	3,250			
	1,09,000	73,500		1,09,000	73,500

BRANCH ADJUSTMENT ACCOUNT

	₹	₹		₹	₹
To Goods Sent to Branch A/c (Loading on Returns) (₹ 1,000 on transfer + ₹ 500 on returns to H.O.)	1,500	—	By Balance b/d (Reserve against opening stock)	2,500	2,000
To Branch Profit & Loss A/c (Profit)	41,000	16,500	By Goods Sent to Branch A/c (Loading) (1/6 of ₹ 60,000)	10,000	—
To Balance c/d (1/6 of ₹ 24,000)	4,000	—	(1/5 of ₹ 50,000) + ₹ 1,250 on transfer)	—	11,250
			By Branch Stock A/c	34,000	3,250
	46,500	16,500		46,500	16,500

GOODS SENT TO BRANCH ACCOUNT

	₹	₹		₹	₹
To Branch Stock A/c (Returns)	3,000	—	By Branch Stock A/c	60,000	50,000
To Branch Stock A/c (Transfer)	6,000	—	By Branch Stock A/c (transfer)	—	6,250
To Branch Stock Adjustment A/c	10,000	11,250	By Branch Stock Adjustment A/c	1,500	
To Purchases (Balancing Figure)	42,500	45,000			
	61,500	56,250		61,500	56,250

BRANCH PROFIT & LOSS ACCOUNT

	Bangalore	*Cochin*		*Bangalore*	*Cochin*
	₹	₹		₹	₹
To Branch Expenses	5,000	3,000	To Branch Adjustment A/c		
To Net Profit to			(G. Profit)	41,000	16,500
General Profit & Loss A/c	36,000	13,500			
	41,000	16,500		41,000	16,500

BRANCH CASH ACCOUNT

	₹	₹		₹	₹
To Balance b/d	2,000	1,000	By Bank (Remittance to H.O.)	80,000	80,000
To Bank (Remittance from H.O.)	15,000	15,000	By Branch Stock A/c (Returns)	5,000	4,000
To H.O. A/c (from			By Branch Expenses A/c	5,000	3,000
Bengaluru Branch)	2,000	—	By Fixed Assets	4,000	—
To Branch Stock A/c (Sales)	76,000	73,500	By H.O. A/c (to Cochin Branch)	—	2,000
(Balancing Figure)			By Balance c/d	1,000	500
	95,000	89,500		95,000	89,500

ILLUSTRATION 8. A Head Office sends goods to its branch at cost plus 10%. On other sales the Head Office makes a uniform profit of $33\frac{1}{3}\%$.

The Branch sells goods at a uniform profit of 25%.

Following transactions took place during the year ended 31st March, 2025 :

(*i*) Head Office purchases amounted to ₹ 7,32,000 and purchase returns were ₹ 30,825 and discounts allowed by suppliers amounted to ₹ 15,045.

(*ii*) Sales by Head Office amounted to ₹ 5,40,000. Goods sent by Head Office to Branch at invoice price amounted to ₹ 2,72,250. Discounts allowed to customers were ₹ 4,950.

(*iii*) Goods sent to Branch on 31st March, 2025 amounting to ₹ 33,000 were in transit.

(*iv*) Goods purchased by the Branch locally were of ₹ 91,312.

(*v*) Establishment and other expenses at Head Office were of ₹ 1,40,130 and at the Branch of ₹ 40,238.

(*vi*) Sales by the Branch amounted to ₹ 3,60,000; discount allowed to customers was ₹ 2,820 and cost of goods lost in transit was ₹ 4,005.

(*vii*) Stock of goods at the Branch as on 31st March, 2025 included goods received from Head Office for ₹ 57,750.

Prepare a columnar Trading and Profit & Loss Account for Head Office and the Branch for the year ended 31st March, 2025.

SOLUTION

TRADING AND PROFIT & LOSS ACCOUNT

for the year ended 31st March, 2025

	H.O. ₹	Branch ₹	Total ₹		H.O. ₹	Branch ₹	Total ₹
To Purchases less Returns (₹ 7,32,000 – ₹ 30,825)	7,01,175	91,312	7,92,487	By Sales	5,40,000	3,60,000	9,00,000
To Goods from H.O.	—	2,39,250	2,39,250	" Goods sent to Branch less in transit (₹ 2,72,250 – ₹ 33,000)	2,39,250	—	2,39,250
" Gross Profit c/d	2,01,750	90,000	2,91,750	By Branch P.& L A/c (Goods lost in transit)	—	4,005	4,005
				" Closing Stock (*i*) & (*ii*)	1,23,675	56,557	1,80,232
	9,02,925	4,20,562	13,23,487		9,02,925	4,20,562	13,23,487
To Expenses	1,40,130	40,238	1,80,368	By Gross Profit b/d	2,01,750	90,000	2,91,750
" Discount allowed	4,950	2,820	7,770	" Discount received	15,045	—	15,045
" Br. Trading A/c (Goods lost in transit)	—	4,005	4,005				
" Stock Reserve (1/11 of ₹ 57,750)	5,250	—	5,250				
" Net Profit	66,465	42,937	1,09,402				
	2,16,795	90,000	3,06,795		2,16,795	90,000	3,06,795

Working Notes :

(*i*) ***Calculation of Closing Stock at H.O. (including in transit)***

	₹	₹
Purchases	7,32,000	
Less : Returns	30,825	
		7,01,175
Cost of Sales of :		
H.O. $\left(₹\ 5{,}40{,}000 \times \frac{2}{3}\right)$	3,60,000	
Branch $\left(₹\ 2{,}39{,}250 \times \frac{10}{11}\right)$	2,17,500	
		5,77,500
Value of Closing Stock at H.O.		1,23,675

(*ii*) ***Calculation of Closing Stock at Branch***

	₹	₹
Branch Purchases		91,312
Goods received from H.O.		2,39,250
		3,30,562
Cost of sales of Branch Sales (₹ 3,60,000 – ₹ 90,000)	2,70,000	
Goods lost in transit	4,005	2,74,005
		56,557

(*iii*) Goods in transit can be included in Branch Stock also and the adjustments should be made accordingly.

4. Distinction Between Wholesale and Retail Profit at Branch

Sometimes head office also sells goods at retail or list price besides sending the goods to branches at wholesale prices. The difference between the retail price and wholesale price will be the profit made by the branch. Suppose if an article costs to head office ₹ 100 and it is supplied to the branches at ₹ 160 at wholesale price but both head office and branches sell goods at ₹ 200, then, profit made by the branch will be ₹ 40 (*i.e.,* ₹ 200 – ₹ 160) and not ₹ 100 (₹ 200 – ₹ 100).

The goods are sent by the head office to the branches at wholesale prices and if all the goods are sold there is no problem but if some goods remain unsold at the end of the accounting year, these unsold goods at the branches must be reduced to cost price by making a stock reserve for unrealised profit for the difference between the wholesale and cost price and will be debited to the head office profit and loss account, as previously the head office must have earned profit while sending goods to the branches. This will be more clear from the following illustration.

EXAMPLE. Following is the information of the Jammu branch of Best Ltd., New Delhi for the year ending 31st March, 2025 from the following :

(1) Goods are invoiced to the branch at cost plus 20%. (2) The sale price is cost plus 50%. (3) Other informations :

	₹		₹
Stock as on 1-4-2024 at I.P.	2,20,000	Sales during the year	12,00,000
Goods sent during the year at I.P.	11,00,000	Expenses incurred at the branch	45,000

Ascertain : (*i*) the profit earned by the branch during the year. (*ii*) branch stock reserve in respect of unrealized profit.

SOLUTION

(*i*) Calculation of profit earned by the branch

In the Books of Jammu Branch
TRADING ACCOUNT

Particulars	Amount	*Particulars*	Amount
	₹		₹
To Opening Stock	2,20,000	By Sales	12,00,000
To Goods received from Head Office	11,00,000	By Closing Stock (1)	3,60,000
To Expenses	45,000		
To Gross Profit	1,95,000		
	15,60,000		15,60,000

(*ii*) Stock reserve in respect of unrealised profit

= ₹ 3,60,000 × (20/120) = ₹ 60,000

Working Note :

	₹
Cost Price	100
Invoice Price	120
Sale Price	150

(1) Calculation of closing stock at invoice price

	₹	
Opening Stock at Invoice Price	2,20,000	
Goods received during the year at Invoice Price	11,00,000	
	13,20,000	
Less : Cost of Goods sold at Invoice Price	(9,60,000)	[₹12,00,000 × (120/150)]
Closing Stock	3,60,000	

Note : It is assumed that all figures given in the question are at invoice price.

ILLUSTRATION 9. (***Where penalty is charged from manager for shortage of goods***): Premier company has two branch retail shops X and Y, with a separate Manager. The ratio of Gross Profit to selling price is constant at each shop at 25% throughout the year to 31st March, 2025.

Each branch manager is entitled to a commission of 10% of the net profit earned by his branch, calculated before charging his commission but subject to a deduction from such commission equal to 15% of any ascertained deficiency of the Branch Stock. All goods are supplied by the head office to these branches. From information given below, calculate the commission due to each Manager for the year 2024-25.

	Branch X	*Branch Y*
	₹	₹
Stock at 1-4-2024 at cost	18,684	12,484
Goods to Branches at cost	72,420	43,480
Sales	90,320	58,560
Drawing of Commission A/c by Manager	500	300
Miscellaneous expenses	12,280	9,020
Stock at 31-3-2025 at cost	20,832	10,952

SOLUTION

In the Books of Premier Co.

BRANCH TRADING ACCOUNT

	Branch X	Branch Y		Branch X	Branch Y
	₹	₹		₹	₹
To Opening Stock	18,684	12,484	By Sales	90,320	58,560
To Goods Sent to Branches A/c	72,420	43,480	By Closing Stock	20,832	10,952
To Gross Profit c/d (25% on Sales)	22,580	14,640	By Branch P. & L. A/c (Shortage of Stock) (Balancing figures)	2,532	1,092
	1,13,684	70,604		1,13,684	70,604

BRANCH PROFIT & LOSS ACCOUNT

for the year ended 31st March, 2025

	Branch X	Branch Y		Branch X	Branch Y
	₹	₹		₹	₹
To Misc. Expenses	12,280	9,020	By Gross Profit b/d	22,580	14,640
To Trading A/c (Shortage of Stock)	2,532	1,092			
To Net Profit c/d	7,768	4,528			
	22,580	14,640		22,580	14,640

COMPUTATION OF MANAGER'S COMMISSION DUE

	Branch X	Branch Y
	₹	₹
Commission @ 10% of Net Profit	777	453
Less : Penalty 15% for Shortage of Stock	380	164
	397	289
Less : Drawings	500	300
Commission Overdrawn	103	11

ILLUSTRATION 10. Following is the Trial Balance of Woodwine & Co. Ltd. as on 31st March, 2025 :

	Head Office		*Branch Office*	
	Dr.	Cr.	Dr.	Cr.
	₹	₹	₹	₹
Share Capital :				
Authorised & Issued 50,000 shares of ₹ 10 each		5,00,000		
Branch Fittings	6,000			
H.O. Remittances			2,12,660	
Purchases	4,92,180			
Goods sent to Branch		2,50,920		
Head Office Stock 1-4-2024	98,460			
Branch Office Stock 1-4-2024 (at wholesale price)	58,440			
Fixed Assets H.O.	4,92,660			
Sundry Debtors	1,72,800		14,250	
Head Office A/c				11,900
Sales		7,45,620		2,40,420
Branch Purchases	2,50,920			
Sundry Creditors		60,800		
Branch Remittances		2,12,660		
Cash at Bank	1,82,100		2,000	
Cash in Hand	500		100	
Profit & Loss A/c		2,54,000		
Branch A/c	11,900			
Expenses—H.O.	2,65,840			
—Branch	11,680		23,310	
Branch Stock Adjustment A/c		19,480		
	20,43,480	20,43,480	2,52,320	2,52,320

Head Office supplies the Branch with all the goods required, and these are charged out at retail selling price, which is cost plus 100%. At the end of the year an adjustment is made to reduce the price charged to the wholesale price, which is cost plus 50%.

Books are kept at the Branch to record sales and certain cash transactions. All cash received by the branch is paid to the bank to the credit of head office, but to Branches a local bank account, worked on imprest for the payment of sundry expenses, the remittances being made monthly by the H.O.

The values of stock on hand on 31st March, 2025 were—H.O. ₹ 94,600 and Branch (at retail selling price) ₹ 92,000.

From the above, prepare a columnar Trading and Profit & Loss A/c for the year ended 31st March, 2025 and a Balance Sheet on that date. Ignore taxation, Journal Entries are not required.

SOLUTION **TRADING AND PROFIT & LOSS ACCOUNT**

for the year ended 31st March, 2025

	H.O.	Branch		H.O.	Branch
	₹	₹		₹	₹
To Opening Stock	98,460	58,440	By Sales	7,45,620	2,40,420
" Purchases	4,92,180	—	" Transfer to Branch		
" Transfer from H.O.			(at wholesale price)	1,88,190	—
(₹ 2,50,920 × 3/4)	—	1,88,190	" Closing Stock	94,600	69,000
" Gross Profit c/d	4,37,770	62,790	(₹ 92,000 × 3/4)		
	10,28,410	3,09,420		10,28,410	3,09,420

To Sundry Expenses	2,65,840	34,990	By Gross Profit b/d	4,37,770	62,790
" Stock Reserve (1/3 of ₹ 69,000)	23,000		" Stock Reserve (1/3 of ₹ 58,440)	19,480	
" Net Profit c/d	1,68,410	27,800			
	4,57,250	62,790		4,57,250	62,790

BALANCE SHEET
as at 31st March, 2025

	₹	₹		₹	₹
Share Capital			H.O. Fixed Assets		4,92,660
Authorised, Issued and Paid-up			Branch Fittings		6,000
50,000 shares of ₹ 10 each		5,00,000	Br. Stock in Trade	69,000	
Profit & Loss Account			*Less* : Reserve	23,000	
Last year	2,54,000				46,000
This year : H.O.	1,68,410		H.O. Stock in Trade		94,600
Branch	27,800		Sundry Debtors : H.O.		1,72,800
		4,50,210	Branch		14,250
Sundry Creditors		60,800	Cash at Bank : H.O.		1,82,100
			Branch		2,000
			Cash in Hand		600
		10,11,010			10,11,010

(*b*) Independent Branch (Branch Keeping Full System of Accounting)

Branch keeping full system of accounting or independent branches are those branches which also purchase goods from the market besides getting the goods from the head office. They can also supply goods to the head office, pay expenses from the cash realised and deposit cash in their own account. In other words, these branches operate as an independent units for all practical purposes but their only link with the head office is that they are owned by the head office and whatever their profit or loss will be, that belongs to the head office.

Such branches keep complete set of double entry books and prepare their own trial balance, trading and profit and loss account and balance sheet. Such branches open head office account in their books. This account is debited by cash sent to the head office, goods supplied to head office, payment made by the branch for purchase of assets and loss to be borne by the head office and credited by cash received from the head office, goods received from the head office, depreciation of branch fixed assets, charge made by head office for rendering services and profit earned by the branch. Similarly, the head office will also maintain a branch account for each branch. This account will have the same entries but on the reverse sides.

Now we deal with certain transactions which require special attention.

(*i*) **Purchase of Branch Fixed Assets**. Generally the branch fixed assets are maintained in the books of head office. When an asset is purchased, the following entries are passed.

	Head Office Books		*Branch Books*	
(*a*) If the payment is made by the branch	Branch Fixed Assets A/c To Branch A/c	Dr.	Head Office A/c To Cash	Dr.
(*b*) If the payment is made by the head office	Branch Fixed Assets A/c To Bank	Dr.	No Entry	

(*ii*) Depreciation of Fixed Assets. As branch fixed assets are maintained in the books of head office so entries relating to depreciation will also be passed through head office account. Following entry will be passed :

H.O. Books		*Branch Books*	
Branch A/c	Dr.	P. & L. A/c	Dr.
To Branch Fixed Assets A/c		To Head Office A/c	

(*iii*) **Head Office Expenses**. If some services such as administration or technical are rendered by the head office to the branch then a proportionate charge for such expenses will be made to each branch by the head office and entry for that will be as follows :

H.O. Books		*Branch Books*	
Branch A/c	Dr.	P. & L. A/c	Dr.
To P. & L. A/c		To Head Office A/c	

(*iv*) **Reconciliation of Transit Items.** The balance of head office account (in branch books) and branch account (in head office books) should normally be the same and one will make debit and other will credit for all transactions affecting these accounts. But these accounts may differ in balances because of the following reasons :

(*a*) **Cash in Transit.** Sometimes the branch is remitting the cash to the head office before the close of the accounting year, say on 28th March, when the accounts are closed on 31st March. While remitting the cash to the head office the branch will debit the head office account but if the remittance is received by the head office after the closing date of the accounting year, say on 4th April, then head office will not give a credit for the same amount of remittance on 31st March, so the two balances, *i.e.,* H.O. A/c (in Branch books) and Branch Account (in H.O. books) will differ. In order to reconcile these balances, an adjusting entry will be passed in the books of branch or head office (if the intimation of such remittance is received by the head office).

Branch Books			*Head Office Books*	
Cash in Transit A/c	Dr.	OR	Cash in Transit A/c	Dr.
To Head Office A/c			To Branch A/c	

(*b*) *Goods in Transit.* Similarly the two balances may differ because of goods in transit. Suppose the head office sent goods to the branch on 28th March but those goods were received by the branch on 4th April (next year). Head office must have debited the account of branch in its books but there will be no corresponding credit to head office account in the books of branch; so on the last day of accounting year, *i.e.,* 31st March the head office will pass the following adjusting entry :

Goods in Transit A/c	Dr.
To Branch A/c	

Cash in transit or goods in transit will be shown as an asset in the balance sheet.

(*v*) **Inter-branch Transactions**. If the head office has many branches and there is a possibility that some branch may supply goods or send cash to the other branch, such transactions among the branches are called inter-branch transactions. Such transactions may be recorded either by maintaining a current account of a branch in another branch's books or such transactions may be recorded by all branches by passing entries through head office account. For example, if goods are supplied by Kolkata branch to Delhi branch and the head office is at Mumbai, then the following journal entries will be passed in the books of head office and the branches :

Mumbai Books		*Kolkata Books*		*Delhi Books*	
Delhi Branch A/c	Dr.	Head Office A/c	Dr.	Goods Received from Other Branches A/c	Dr.
To Kolkata Branchs A/c		To Goods Supplied to Other Branches A/c		To Head Office A/c	

(*vi*) **Cash Paid by Branch on Behalf of H.O**. If the branch has paid some cash (say for purchases made by H.O.) on behalf of H.O., then the following entries will be passed in the books of H.O and the branch :

H.O. Books		*Branch Books*	
Purchases A/c	Dr.	H.O. A/c	Dr.
To Branch A/c		To Cash A/c	

(*vii*) **Cash Collected by Branch on Behalf of H.O.** If the branch has collected some cash on behalf of H.O. (say for calls in arrears from the shareholders of H.O.,) then the following journal entries will be passed in the books of H.O. and the branch :

H.O. Books		*Branch Books*	
Branch A/c	Dr.	Cash A/c	Dr.
To Calls in Arrears A/c		To H.O. A/c	

(*viii*) **If a Bill is Drawn by one Branch on another Branch.** If a bill is drawn by Agra Branch on Mumbai Branch and the H.O. is at Delhi, then the following entries will be passed in the books of H.O. and branches :

H.O. Books		*Agra Branch*		*Mumbai Branch*	
Agra Branch A/c	Dr.	B/R A/c	Dr.	H.O. A/c	Dr.
To Bills Payable		To H.O. A/c		To B/P A/c	
B/R A/c	Dr.				
To Mumbai Branch					

ILLUSTRATION 11. A and Co. Limited having its Head Office at Delhi with Branches at Lucknow and Allahabad closes its annual accounts on 31st December, when the following transactions have taken place :

(*a*) Remittances of ₹ 4,500 made by Lucknow Branch to its Head Office on 30th December, received by Head Office on 5th January (next year).

(*b*) Goods valuing ₹ 2,200 despatched by Allahabad Branch on 27th December, under instructions from the Head Office and received by the Lucknow Branch on 30th December.

(*c*) Depreciation amounting to ₹ 1,100 on Lucknow Branch Fixed Assets when accounts of such assets are maintained at the Head Office.

(*d*) Goods worth ₹ 9,000 despatched by Head Office to Allahabad Branch on 30th December, received by that branch on 7th January (next year).

(*e*) Lucknow Branch paid ₹ 400 dividend to a local shareholder on behalf of the Head Office.

(*f*) A sum of ₹ 600 being arrears of call money was received by the Allahabad branch from a shareholder in November but was not communicated to the Head Office till 3rd January (next year).

(*g*) Lucknow branch draws a bill receivable for ₹ 5,000 on Allahabad branch which sends its acceptance.

Pass adjusting Journal Entries in the books of Head Office and Branches.

SOLUTION **In the Books of H.O.**

JOURNAL ENTRIES

			₹	₹
(*a*)	No entry or alternatively the following entry will be passed if intimation has been received by H.O. : Cash in Transit A/c Dr. To Lucknow Branch (Cash remitted by Lucknow branch still in transit)		4,500	4,500
(*b*)	Lucknow Branch A/c Dr. To Allahabad Branch A/c (Being goods transferred from Allahabad to Lucknow branch under our instructions)		2,200	2,200

(c)	Lucknow Branch A/c Dr. To Lucknow Fixed Assets A/c (Depreciation charged on Lucknow branch fixed assets)		1,100	1,100
(d)	Goods in Transit A/c Dr. To Allahabad Branch A/c (Goods sent by us still in transit)		9,000	9,000
(e)	Dividend A/c Dr. To Lucknow Branch A/c (Dividend paid by Lucknow branch on our behalf)		400	400
(f)	Allahabad Branch A/c Dr. To Calls in Arrears A/c (Calls in arrear received by Allahabad branch on our behalf)		600	600
(g)	(i) Lucknow Branch A/c Dr. To Bills Payable A/c (Being bill drawn by Lucknow branch on Allahabad branch)		5,000	5,000
	(ii) Bills Receivable A/c Dr. To Allahabad Branch (Being bills accepted by Allahabad branch)		5,000	5,000

II IN THE BOOKS OF LUCKNOW BRANCH

(a)	No Entry or if the intimation is received, then Head Office A/c Dr. To Bank A/c (Being remittance made to head office)	4,500	4,500
(b)	Good Received from Other Branches A/c Dr. To Head Office A/c (Being goods received from Allahabad branch through H.O.)	2,200	2,200
(c)	Profit & Loss A/c Dr. To Head Office A/c (Depreciation charged on Fixed Assets)	1,100	1,100
(d)	No Entry		
(e)	Head Office A/c Dr. To Cash A/c (Dividend paid on behalf of H.O.)	400	400
(f)	×		

III. IN THE BOOKS OF ALLAHABAD BRANCH

(a)	×		
(b)	Head Office A/c Dr. To Goods Supplied to Other Branches A/c (Goods despatched to Lucknow branch through H.O.)	2,200	2,200
(c)	×		
(d)	×		
(e)	×		
(f)	Cash A/c Dr. To Head Office A/c (Calls in arrears collected on behalf of head office.)	600	600

(g)	Bills Receivable A/c Dr. To Head Office A/c (Acceptance from Allahabad branch received)	5,000	5,000	(g)	Head Office A/c Dr. To Bills Payable A/c (Acceptance given to Lucknow branch)	5,000	5,000

ILLUSTRATION 12. Show Adjustment Journal Entry along with working notes in the books of head office at the end of April, 2025 for incorporation of inter branch transactions assuming that only head office maintains different branch account in its books :

(A) Delhi Branch :

(i) Received goods from Mumbai ₹ 1,40,000 and ₹ 60,000 from Kolkata.

(ii) Sent goods to Chennai ₹ 1,00,000, Kolkata ₹ 80,000

(iii) Bill receivable received ₹ 80,000 from Chennai

(iv) Acceptances sent to Mumbai ₹ 1,00,000, Kolkata ₹ 40,000

(B) Mumbai Branch (Apart from the above):

(i) Received goods from Kolkata ₹ 60,000, Delhi ₹ 80,000

(ii) Cash sent to Delhi ₹ 60,000, Kolkata ₹ 28,000

(C) Chennai Branch (Apart from the above):

(i) Received goods from Kolkata ₹ 1,20,000

(ii) Acceptances and cash sent to Kolkata ₹ 80,000, Kolkata ₹ 40,000 respectively.

(D) Kolkata Branch (Apart from the above):

(i) Sent goods to Chennai ₹ 1,40,000

(ii) Paid cash to Chennai ₹ 60,000

(iii) Acceptance sent to Chennai ₹ 60,000. ***(CA – Inter May, 2017 Modified)***

SOLUTION

INTER-BRANCH TRANSACTIONS

		Delhi	Mumbai	Chennai	Kolkata
		₹	₹	₹	₹
A.	**Delhi Branch**				
(1)	Received goods	2,00,000 (Dr.)	1,40,000 (Cr.)		60,000 (Cr.)
(2)	Sent goods	1,80,000 (Cr.)		1,00,000 (Dr.)	80,000 (Dr.)
(3)	Received Bills Receivable	80,000 (Dr.)		80,000 (Cr.)	
(4)	Sent Acceptance	1,40,000 (Cr.)	1,00,000 (Dr.)		40,000 (Dr.)
B.	**Mumbai Branch**				
(5)	Received goods	80,000 (Cr.)	1,40,000 (Dr.)		60,000 (Cr.)
(6)	Sent cash	60,000 (Dr.)	88,000 (Cr.)		28,000 (Dr.)
C.	**Chennai Branch**				
(7)	Received goods			1,20,000 (Dr.)	1,20,000 (Cr.)
(8)	Sent cash and acceptances			1,20,000 (Cr.)	1,20,000 (Dr.)
D.	**Kolkata Branch**				
(9)	Sent goods			1,40,000 (Dr.)	1,40,000 (Cr.)
(10)	Sent cash			60,000 (Dr.)	60,000 (Cr.)
(11)	Sent acceptances			60,000 (Dr.)	60,000 (Cr.)
		60,000 (Cr.)	12,000 (Dr.)	2,80,000 (Dr.)	2,32,000 (Cr.)

ILLUSTRATION 13. Head Office of a business and its branch keep their own books and each prepares its own Profit and Loss Account. Following are the balances appearing in the two sets of books as on 31st March, 2025, after the ascertainment of profit and after making all adjustments except those referred to below :

	Head Office		*Branch Office*	
	Dr.	*Cr.*	*Dr.*	*Cr.*
	₹	₹	₹	₹
Capital		1,00,000		
Fixed Assets	36,000		16,000	
Stock	34,200		10,740	
Debtors & Creditors	7,820	3,960	4,840	1,920
Cash	10,740		1,420	
Profit & Loss		14,660		3,060
Branch Office Account	29,860			
Head Office Account				28,020
	1,18,620	1,18,620	33,000	33,000

Pass Journal Entries necessary (in both sets of books) to record the adjustment dealing with the following and prepare a Balance Sheet as on 31st March, 2025.

(*a*) On 31st March, the branch had sent a cheque for ₹ 1,000 to the head office, neither received by them nor credited to the branch till next month.

(*b*) Goods valued at ₹ 440 had been forwarded by the head office to the branch and invoiced on 30th March, but were neither received by the branch nor dealt with in their books till next month.

(*c*) It was agreed that the branch should be charged with ₹ 300 for administration services rendered by the head office during the year.

(*d*) Stock stolen in transit from the head office to the branch and charged to the branch by the head office but not credited to the head office in the branch books as the branch manager declined to admit any liability, ₹ 400 (not covered by insurance).

(*e*) Depreciation of branch assets, of which accounts are maintained by the head office not provided for ₹ 250.

(*f*) The balance of profit shown by the branch is to be transferred to the head office books.

SOLUTION

HEAD OFFICE JOURNAL

				₹	₹
(*a*)	Goods in Transit A/c	Dr.		440	
	To Branch Account				440
	(Being goods invoiced on 30th March not yet received by the branch)				
(*b*)	Branch Account	Dr.		300	
	P. & L. A/c				300
	(Being charge for services rendered by H.O. to Branch)				
(*c*)	Profit and Loss A/c	Dr.		400	
	To Branch A/c				400
	(Being the amount of uninsured stock stolen on way to branch)				
(*d*)	Branch Account	Dr.		250	
	To Branch Assets A/c				250
	(Being depreciation on branch assets maintained by H.O.)				
(*e*)	Branch A/c	Dr.		2,510	
	To General Profit and Loss A/c				2,510
	(Being Branch profit transferred to General P. & L. A/c)				

BRANCH OFFICE JOURNAL

				₹	₹
(*a*)	Cash in Transit A/c	Dr.		1,000	
	To Head Office A/c				1,000
	(Being cash sent on 31st March, not received by H.O.)				
(*b*)	P. & L. A/c	Dr.		300	
	To Head Office A/c				300
	(Being charge for administrative services rendered by H.O.)				
(*c*)	P. & L. A/c	Dr.		250	
	To Head Office A/c				250
	(Being charge of Depreciation on assets maintained by H.O.)				
(*d*)	Profit & Loss A/c	Dr.		2,510	
	To Head Office A/c				2,510
	(Being profit at Branch transferred to Head Office A/c)				

BALANCE SHEET

as on 31st March, 2025

Liabilities		₹	*Assets*	₹	₹
Capital		1,00,000	Fixed Assets :		
Creditors :	₹		Head Office	36,000	
Head Office	3,960		Branch (₹ 16,000 – ₹ 250)	15,750	51,750
Branch	1,920	5,880	Stock :		
Profit & Loss A/c :			Head Office	34,200	
Head Office (14,660 + 300 – 400)	14,560		Branch	10,740	
Branch	2,510	17,070	In transit	440	45,380
			Debtors :		
			Head Office	7,820	
			Branch	4,840	12,660
			Cash :		
			Head Office	10,740	
			Branch	1,420	
			In Transit	1,000	13,160
		1,22,950			1,22,950

ILLUSTRATION 14. From the following information, prepare—

(*a*) Reconciliation of Head Office Account in Branch Books and of the Branch Account in the Head Office Books; and

(*b*) The Trading and Profit & Loss Account of the Head Office—for the year ended 31st December, 2024.

	Head Office	Branch
	₹	₹
Opening Stock	10,000	4,500
Purchases	1,15,000	—
Sales	2,05,000	1,55,000
Other Expenses	15,200	6,200
Closing Stock	5,200	3,100

The Branch books show the Head Office Account at ₹ 9,000 (Cr.) and the Head Office books show the Branch Account at ₹ 24,000 (Dr.) The Branch receives all its supplies from the Head Office, which are invoiced at 25% over cost. During the year, the Head Office sent invoices to the Branch to the tune of ₹ 1,04,500. The Head Office credits its Sales Account with the invoice price of the goods sent to the Branch.

The Head Office billed the Branch for ₹ 12,000 on 31st December, 2024 representing the Branch's share of the expenses incurred by the Head Office. The said expenses had not been recorded in the books of the Branch.

The expenses of the Branch are met by the Head Office from time to time for which amounts are sent in advance to the Branch. A sum of ₹ 3,000 sent to the Branch by the Head Office on 29th December, 2024 in this connection, was received by the Branch on 3rd January, 2025.

(I.C.W.A. Inter)

SOLUTION

RECONCILIATION ACCOUNT OF HEAD OFFICE ACCOUNT

(In Branch Books)

	₹		₹
To Balance (as per H.O. Books)	24,000	By Balance b/d	9,000
		By Head Office Expenses (Share of Expenses Billed by H.O.)	12,000
		By H.O. Cash in Transit	3,000
	24,000		24,000

RECONCILIATION ACCOUNT OF BRANCH ACCOUNT

(In H.O. Books)

	₹		₹
To Balance b/d	24,000	By Remittance in Transit (Cash sent by H.O. yet in transit)	3,000
		By H.O. Expenses (Expenses billed for branch's share of expenses but not yet recorded in Branch's Books)	12,000
		By Balance (as per Branch's Books)	9,000
	24,000		24,000

TRADING AND PROFIT AND LOSS ACCOUNT

for the year ending 31st December, 2024

	H.O.	Branch	Total		H.O.	Branch	Total
	₹	₹	₹		₹	₹	₹
To Opening Stock	10,000	4,500	14,500	By Sales	1,00,500	1,55,000	2,55,500
To Purchases	1,15,000	—	1,15,000	By Goods sent to Branch	1,04,500	—	1,04,500
To Goods from H.O.	—	1,04,500	1,04,500	By Closing Stock	5,200	3,100	8,300
To Gross Profit c/d	85,200	49,100	1,34,300				
	2,10,200	1,58,100	3,68,300		2,10,200	1,58,100	3,68,300
To Other Expenses	15,200	6,200	21,400	By Gross Profit b/d	85,200	49,100	1,34,300
To H.O. Expenses	—	12,000	12,000	By Stock Reserve $\left(₹\,4{,}500 \times \frac{25}{125}\right)$	900	—	900
To Stock Reserve $\left(₹\,3{,}100 \times \frac{25}{15}\right)$	620	—	620				
To Net Profit	70,280	30,900	1,01,180				
	86,100	49,100	1,35,200		86,100	49,100	1,35,200

Incorporation of Branch Trial Balance in Head Office Books

Head office and its various branches are under one organisation and it is, therefore, necessary that head office should prepare only one combined balance sheet (if not the trading and profit and loss account) for the benefit of the shareholders and the outsiders. For this purpose, the head office is required to incorporate the branch trial balance in its books. The process by which consolidated balance sheet of the whole business is prepared is known as incorporation of the branch trial balance. Following are the two methods for doing this :

First Method. Under this method branch trading and profit & loss account is prepared to incorporate all revenue items. Assets, liabilities and profit are also incorporated through branch account in order to prepare the consolidated balance sheet. Following journal entries are passed in this connection :

(*i*) *For debit side items of trading account as opening stock, net purchases and direct expenses*

Branch Trading A/c Dr.

To Branch A/c

(*ii*) *For credit side items of trading account such as net sales and closing stock*

Branch A/c Dr.

To Branch Trading A/c

(*iii*) *For transfer of gross profit or gross loss*

(*a*) *If gross profit*

Branch Trading A/c Dr.

To Branch P. & L. A/c

(*b*) *If gross loss*

Branch P. & L. A/c Dr.

To Branch Trading A/c

(*iv*) *For total of various expenses and losses which appear on the debit side of profit and loss account*

Branch Profit & Loss A/c Dr.

To Branch A/c

(*v*) *For total of incomes and gains which appear on the credit side of profit and loss account*

Branch A/c Dr.

To Branch Profit & Loss A/c

(*vi*) *For transfer of net profit (or loss) to general profit and loss account*

(*a*) *If Profit*

Branch P. & L. A/c Dr.
To General P. & L. A/c

(*b*) *If loss*

General P. & L. A/c Dr.
To Branch P. & L. A/c

(*vii*) *For total of various branch assets*

Branch Assets (individually) A/c Dr.
To Branch A/c

(*viii*) *For total of various branch liabilities*

Branch A/c Dr.
To Branch Liabilities A/c (individually)

ILLUSTRATION 15. Give Journal entries for incorporation of Delhi Branch accounts in the Head Office books and show the Branch Account in Head Office books after incorporating therein the assets and liabilities.

The Trial Balance as on 31st March, 2025 is as under :

	Dr.	*Cr.*
	₹	₹
Manufacturing Expenses	10,000	
Salaries	10,000	
Wages	40,000	
Cash in hand	2,000	
Purchases	80,000	
Goods received from H.O.	15,000	
Rent	4,000	
General Expenses	5,000	
Sales		1,50,000
Purchases Returns		1,000
Opening Stock	30,000	
Discount earned		1,000
Debtors	15,000	
Creditors		5,000
H.O. Account		54,000
	2,11,000	2,11,000

Closing stock at Branch ₹ 30,000. Depreciation is to be provided on Branch Machinery of ₹ 50,000 @ 20 per cent and Branch Furniture of ₹ 3,000 @ 15 per cent. Rent outstanding is ₹ 500.

SOLUTION

Head Office Books

JOURNAL

			₹	₹
2025 Mar. 31	Delhi Branch Account Dr.		10,450	
	To Branch Machinery Account			10,000
	To Branch Furniture Account			450
	(Being the depreciation on Branch Fixed Assets charged to Branch)			

Date	Particulars		Dr. (₹)	Cr. (₹)
Mar. 31	Delhi Trading Account	Dr.	1,74,000	
	To Delhi Branch Account			1,74,000
	(Being the total of the following items in Branch Trial Balance debited to Branch Trading Account :			
		₹		
	Stock	30,000		
	Purchases *less* Returns	79,000		
	Wages	40,000		
	Manufacturing Expenses	10,000		
	Goods received from Head Office	15,000		
		1,74,000		
Mar. 31	Delhi Branch Account	Dr.	1,80,000	
	To Delhi Trading Account			1,80,000
	(Being the total of the following items at Branch credited to Branch Trading Account)			
		₹		
	Sales	1,50,000		
	Branch Stock	30,000		
		1,80,000		
Mar. 31	Delhi Trading Account	Dr.	6,000	
	To Delhi Profit and Loss Account			6,000
	(Being the transfer of gross profit)			
Mar. 31	Delhi Profit and Loss Account	Dr.	29,950	
	To Delhi Branch Account			29,950
	(The total of the following expenses at Branch debited to Branch Profit and Loss Account)			
		₹		
	Rent (including outstanding)	4,500		
	Salaries	10,000		
	General Expenses	5,000		
	Depreciation	10,450		
		29,950		
Mar. 31	Delhi Branch Account	Dr.	1,000	
	To Delhi Profit and Loss Account			1,000
	(Being the discount earned at Delhi credited to Branch Profit and Loss Account)			
Mar. 31	General Profit and Loss A/c	Dr.	22,950	
	To Branch Profit and Loss Account			22,950
	(Being the loss transferred to Profit and Loss Account of the Head Office)			
Mar. 31	Delhi Debtors Account	Dr.	15,000	
	Delhi Cash Account	Dr.	2,000	
	Delhi Stock Account	Dr.	30,000	
	To Delhi Branch Account			47,000
	(Being the transfer of various assets at Branch to Head Office books)			

Mar. 31	Delhi Branch Account Dr.		5,500	
	To Branch Creditors Account			5,000
	To Branch Expenses Outstanding Account			500
	(Being the transfer of liabilities at Branch to Head Office books)			

DELHI BRANCH ACCOUNT (IN H. O. BOOKS)

2025		₹	2025		₹
Mar. 31	To Balance b/d	54,000	Mar. 31	By Delhi Trading Account—(Opening Stock, Purchases, etc.)	1,74,000
"	" Branch Machinery A/c (Dep.)	10,000	"	" Delhi Profit and Loss Account— (Expenses)	29,950
"	" Branch Furniture A/c (Dep.)	450	"	" Branch Assets	47,000
"	" Delhi Trading Account—(Sales and Stock)	1,80,000			
"	" Delhi Profit and Loss Account— (Discount)	1,000			
"	" Branch Liabilities	5,500			
		2,50,950			2,50,950

Second Method. Under this method Branch Trading and Profit & Loss Account is prepared as a Memorandum Account and entry for transferring the net profit (or loss) is passed in the books of head office. No entries are passed for incorporating branch assets and liabilities in the books of the head office with the result that Branch Account in the books of head office will show balance equal to net worth (*i.e.,* total assets—total liabilities).

ILLUSTRATION 16. A Mumbai merchant opens a new branch in Delhi which trades independently of the Head Office. The transactions of the Branch for the year ended 31-3-2025 are as under :

			₹		₹
Goods supplied by Head Office			20,000	Cash received from Customers	30,400
Purchases from Outsiders—		₹		Cash paid to Creditors	14,200
	Credit	15,500		Expenses paid by Branch	8,950
	Cash	3,000	18,500	Furniture purchased by Branch on Credit	3,500
Sales :	Credit	25,000		Cash received from Head Office initially	4,000
	Cash	4,600	29,600	Remitted to Head Office	11,000

Prepare Branch Trading and Profit & Loss Account and Branch Account in the Head Office Books after incorporation of the Branch Trial Balance taking the following into consideration:

(*a*) Accounts of the Branch Fixed Assets are maintained in H.O. Books :
(*b*) Write off Depreciation on furniture at 5 per cent per annum.
(*c*) A remittance of ₹ 2,000 from the Branch to the Head Office is in transit.
(*d*) Branch Closing Stock is valued at ₹ 12,000.

SOLUTION

In the Books of H.O.
DELHI BRANCH TRADING AND PROFIT & LOSS ACCOUNT
for the year ending 31-3-2025

	₹		₹	₹
To Goods supplied by Head Office	20,000	By Sales : Cash	4,600	

		₹				
To Purchases :					Credit	25,000	
Cash	15,500					29,600
Credit	3,000	18,500	" Closing Stock		12,000
" Gross Profit c/d		3,100			
		41,600			41,600
" Expenses		8,950	" Gross Profit b/d		3,100
" Depreciation on Furniture		175	" Net Loss transferred to General P. & L. A/c		6,025
		9,125			9,125

DELHI BRANCH ACCOUNT

	₹			₹
To Cash	4,000	By Furniture	₹	3,500
" Goods Sent to Branch	20,000	" Remittance	11,000	
" Branch Furniture	175	*Less* : In Transit	2,000	
				9,000
		By General P. & L. A/c		6,025
		" Balance c/d (₹ 15,850 – ₹ 10,200) (See Note)		5,650
	24,175			24,175

Note. *S. Assets* : Closing Stock ₹ 12,000 + Cash in transit ₹ 2,000 + Cash in hand ₹ 1,850 [*i.e.,* ₹ 4,000 + ₹ 4,600 + ₹ 30,400 – ₹ 14,200 – ₹ 8,950 – ₹ 3,000 – ₹ 11,000] = ₹ 15,850.

Liabilities = S. Crs. ₹ 1,300 (*i.e.,* ₹ 15,500 – ₹ 14,200) + Creditors for Furniture ₹ 3,500 + Advance from Debtors ₹ 5,400 (*i.e.,* ₹ 30,400 – ₹ 25,000) = ₹ 10,200.

Sometimes it becomes difficult for the branch to pass entries in its books because of non-availability of full information from the head office of value of goods sent and value of anything done by the head office on behalf of branch. In such a case, all the revenue items are closed by transferring them to the head office as final accounts cannot be prepared by the branch because of inadequate information.

ILLUSTRATION 17. Good Luck Ltd. of Kolkata has a branch at Chennai, to which the goods sold are supplied from Kolkata, but the cost thereof is not recorded in the Head Office Books. On 31st March, 2024, the Branch Balance Sheet was as follows :

Liabilities	₹	*Assets*	₹
Creditors Balance	80,000	Debtors Balance	2,50,000
Head Office	1,79,000	Building Extension A/c —Closed by transfer to H.O. A/c	—
		Cash at Bank	9,000
	2,59,000		2,59,000

During the six months ending 30th September, 2024, the following transactions took place at Chennai :

	₹		₹
Sales (all on Credit)	3,10,000	Salaries (inclusive of advance of ₹ 3,000)	8,900
General Expenses	2,200		
Wages paid	28,700	Manager's Salary	6,000
Fire Insurance (Paid for one year)	3,600	Collection from Debtors	1,90,000

Remittance to H.O.	62,800	Discount allowed	9,000
Cash paid to Creditors	70,000	Discount earned	1,500
Building Account (further payment)	6,000	Purchases (all on credit)	66,000

As on 30th September, 2024, Cash in hand was ₹ 1,900 and at Bank ₹ 8,900.

Set out the Head Office Account at Chennai Books and the Branch Balance Sheet as on 30th September, 2024 (on the same lines as on 31st March, 2024). Also give Total Debtors Account and Total Creditors Account.

SOLUTION

In the Books of Chennai Branch
HEAD OFFICE ACCOUNT

2024		₹	2024		₹
April 1	To Cash	62,800	April 1	By Balance b/d	1,79,000
Sept. 30	" Sundries (Revenue items (Dr.) Less pre-payment)	1,19,600	Sept. 3	" Sundries [Revenue items (Cr.)]	3,11,500
	" Building A/c	6,000			
	" Balance c/d	3,02,100			
		4,90,500			4,90,500

BALANCE SHEET OF CHENNAI BRANCH
as on 30th September, 2024

Liabilities	₹	*Assets*	₹
Sundry Creditors (2)	74,500	Sundry Debtors (1)	3,61,000
Head Office A/c	3,02,100	Advance Salary	3,000
		Prepaid Insurance	1,800
		Building Extension A/c (transferred to H.O. A/c)	—
		Cash in Hand	1,900
		Cash at Bank	8,900
	3,76,600		3,76,600

(1) **TOTAL DEBTORS ACCOUNT**

	₹		₹
To Balance b/d	2,50,000	By Cash	1,90,000
" Sales	3,10,000	" Discount	9,000
		" Balance c/d (Balancing figure)	3,61,000
	5,60,000		5,60,000

(2) **TOTAL CREDITORS ACCOUNT**

	₹		₹
To Bank	70,000	By Balance b/d	80,000
" Discount	1,500	" Purchases	66,000
" Balance c/d (Balancing figure)	74,500		
	1,46,000		1,46,000

ILLUSTRATION 18. Mr. Chena Swami of Chennai trades in Refined Oil and Ghee. It has a branch at Salem. He despatches 30 tins of Refined Oil @ ₹ 1,500 per tin and 20 tins of Ghee ₹ 5,000 per tin on 1st of every month. The Branch has incurred expenditure of ₹ 45,890 which is met out of its collections; this is in addition to expenditure directly paid by Head Office.

Following are the other details :

	Chennai H.O. Amount (₹)	*Salem B.O.* Amount (₹)
Purchases :		
Refined Oil	27,50,000	
Ghee	48,28,000	
Direct Expenses	6,35,000	
Expenses paid by H.O.		76,800
Sales :		
Refined Oil	24,10,000	5,95,000
Ghee	38,40,500	14,50,000
Collection during the year (including Cash Sales)		20,15,000
Remittance by Branch to Head Office		19,50,000

Balance as on	*Chennai H.O.*	
	1-4-2024 Amount (₹)	31-3-2025 Amount (₹)
Stock :		
Refined Oil	44,000	8,90,000
Ghee	10,65,000	15,70,000
Building	5,10,000	7,14,780
Furniture & Fixtures	88,600	79,740

Balance as on	*Salem Branch Office*	
	1-4-2024 Amount (₹)	31-3-2025 Amount (₹)
Stock :		
Refined Oil	22,500	19,500
Ghee	40,000	90,000
Sundry Debtors	1,80,000	?
Cash in hand	25.690	?
Furniture & Fixtures	23,800	21,420

Additional information :

(*i*) Addition to Building on 1-4-2024 ₹ 2,41,600 by H.O.

(*ii*) Rate of depreciation: Furniture & Fixtures @ 10% and Building @ 5% (already adjusted in the above figure) (*iii*) The Branch Manager is entitled to 10% commission on overall organisational profits after charging such commission.

(*iv*) The General Manager is entitled to a salary of ₹ 20,000 per month.

(*v*) General expenses incurred by Head Office is ₹ 1,86,000.

You are requested to prepare Branch Account in the Head Office books and also prepare Chena Swami's Trading and Profit & Loss Account (excluding branch transactions) for the year ended 31st March, 2025.

(CA -Inter Nov. 2016 Modified)

SOLUTION

In the books of Mr. Chena Swami

SALEM BRANCH ACCOUNT

	₹		₹
To Balance b/d		By Bank (Remittance to H.O.)	19,50,000
Opening stock :		By Balance c/d	
Ghee	40,000	Closing stock:	
Oil	22,500	Refined oil	19,500
Debtors	1,80,000	Ghee	90,000
Cash on hand	25,690	Debtors	2,10,000
Furniture & Fittings	23,800	Cash on hand	44,800
To Goods sent to Branch A/c		Furniture & Fitting	21,420
Refined Oil (30 × 1500 × 12)	5,40,000		
Ghee (20 × 5000 × 12)	12,00,000		
To Bank (Expenses paid by H.O.)	76,800		
To Net Profit transferred to General P & L A/c	2,26,930		
	23,35,720		23,35,720

Mr. Chena Swami

TRADING AND PROFIT AND LOSS ACCOUNT

for the Year ended 31st March, 2025

(Excluding Branch Transaction)

		₹		₹
To Opening Stock :			By Sales :	
Refined Oil		44,000		24,10,000
Ghee		10,65,000		38,40,500
To Purchases :	₹		By Closing Stock :	
Refined Oil	27,50,000			8,90,000
Less : Goods Sent to				15,70,000
Branch	5,40,000	22,10,000		
Ghee	48,28,000			
Less : Goods Sent to				
Branch	12,00,000	36,28,000		
To Direct Expenses		6,35,800		
To Gross Profit		11,27,700		
		87,10,500		87,10,500

	₹		₹
To Manager's Salary	2,40,000	By Gross Profit	11,27,700
To General Expenses	1,86,000	By Branch Profit transferred	2,26,930
To Depreciation :			
Furniture (₹ 88,600 – ₹ 79,740)	8,860		
Building (₹ 5,10,800 + ₹ 2,41,600 – ₹ 7,14,780)	37,620		
To Manager's Commission @ 10% (₹ 8,82,150 (*i.e.,* ₹ 13,54,630 – ₹ 4,72,480) × 10/110)	80,195		
To Net Profit	8,01,955		
	13,54,630		13,54,630

Working Notes :

(1) **DEBTORS ACCOUNT**

	₹		₹
To Balance b/d	1,80,000	By Cash Collections	20,15,000
To Sales made during the year :		By Balance c/d (Bal. Figure)	2,10,000
Refined oil	5,95,000		
Ghee	14,50,000		
	22,25,000		22,25,000

(2) **BRANCH CASH ACCOUNT**

	₹		₹
To Balance b/d	25,690	By Remittance	19,50,000
To Collections	20,15,000	By Expenses	45,890
		By Balance c/d (Bal. Figure)	44,800
	20,40,690		20,40,690

(3) Branch managers generally get commission based on the Branch profits and not on overall organisational profits. The commission of branch manager is computed as 10% on overall organisational profits after charging such commission.

(4) Since the amount of cash sales was not given specifically in the question, total amount of cash collections during the year amounting ₹ 20,15,000 has been considered as collection from Debtors.

ILLUSTRATION 19. M/s Shah & Co. commenced business on 1-4-2024 with Head Office at Mumbai and a Branch at Chennai. Purchases were made exclusively by the Head Office, where the goods were processed before sale. There was no loss or wastage in processing.

Only the processed goods received from Head Office were handled by the Branch. The goods were sent to branch at processed cost plus 10%.

All sales, whether by head office or by the Branch, were at uniform gross profit of 25% on their respective cost.

Following is the Trial Balance as on 31-3-2025.

	Head Office		*Branch*	
	Dr. ₹	Cr. ₹	Dr. ₹	Cr. ₹
Capital		3,10,000		
Drawings	55,000			
Purchases	19,69,500			

Cost of processing	50,500			
Sales		12,80,000		8,20,000
Goods sent to Branch		9,24,000		
Administrative Expenses	1,39,000		15,000	
Selling Expenses	50,000		6,200	
Debtors	3,09,600		1,13,600	
Branch Current A/c	3,89,800			
Creditors		6,01,400		10,800
Bank Balance	1,52,000		77,500	
Head Office Current Account				2,61,500
Goods received from H.O.			8,80,000	
	31,15,400	31,15,400	10,92,300	10,92,300

Following further information is provided :

(*i*) Goods sent by Head Office to the Branch in March, 2025 of ₹ 44,000 were not received by the Branch till 2-4-2025.

(*ii*) A remittance of ₹ 84,300 sent by the Branch to Head Office was also similarly not received upto 31-3-2025.

(*iii*) Stock taking at the Branch disclosed a shortage of ₹ 20,000 (at selling price to the branch).

(*iv*) Cost of unprocessed goods at head Office on 31-3-2025 was ₹ 1,00,000.

Prepare Trading and Profit and Loss Account in columnar form and Balance Sheet of the business as a whole as at 31-3-2025.

SOLUTION

In the Books of Shah & Co.
TRADING AND PROFIT & LOSS ACCOUNT
for the year ended 31-3-25

	H.O.	*Branch*	*Total*		*H.O.*	*Branch*	*Total*
	₹	₹	₹		₹	₹	₹
To Purchases	19,69,500	—	19,69,500	By Sales	12,80,000	8,20,000	21,00,000
To Cost of Processing	50,500	—	50,500	By Goods sent to Branch A/c	9,24,000	—	—
To Goods received from H.O. A/c	—	8,80,000	—	By Stock Shortage	—	16,000	16,000
To Gross Profit c/d	3,40,000	1,64,000	5,04,000	By Goods in Transit	—	—	44,000
				By Closing Stock Processed Goods (1)	56,000	2,08,000	2,64,000
				Unprocessed Goods	1,00,000	—	1,00,000
	23,60,000	10,44,000	25,24,000		23,60,000	10,44,000	25,24,000
To Admn. Expenses	1,39,000	15,000	1,54,000	By Goods Profit b/d	3,40,000	1,64,000	5,04,000
To Selling Expenses	50,000	6,200	56,200				
To Stock Shortage	—	16,000	16,000				
To Stock Reserve (2)	22,909	—	22,909				
To Net Profit	1,28,091	1,26,800	2,54,891				
	3,40,000	1,64,000	5,04,000		3,40,000	1,64,000	5,04,000

BALANCE SHEET
as at 31st March, 2025

Liabilities	₹	₹	*Assets*		₹	₹
Creditors : H.O.	6,01,400		Debtors :	H.O.	3,09,600	
Branch	10,800			Branch	1,13,600	
		6,12,200				4,23,200
Capital	3,10,000		Closing Stock :			
Add : Net Profit	2,54,891		Processed Goods :			
	5,64,891			H.O.	56,000	
Less : Drawings	55,000			Branch	2,08,000	
		5,09,891			2,64,000	
			Less : Stock Reserve (2)		18,909	
						2,45,091
			Unprocessed Goods			1,00,000
			Bank Balance :	H.O.	1,52,000	
				Branch	77,500	
						2,29,500
			Goods in Transit [₹ 44,000 – ₹ 4,000)(2)]			40,000
			Cash in Transit			84,300
		11,22,091				11,22,091

Working Notes :

(1) *Calculation of Closing Stock*

		₹	₹
Stock at Head Office :			
Cost of goods processed (₹ 19,69,500 + ₹ 50,500 – ₹ 1,00,000)			19,20,000
Less : Cost of goods sold to Branch	₹ 9,24,000 × $\frac{100}{110}$	8,40,000	
Cost of goods sold	₹ 12,80,000 × $\frac{100}{125}$	10,24,000	
			18,64,000
Stock of Processed Goods with H.O.			56,000
Stock at Branch :			₹
Goods received from H.O. (at invoice price)		₹	8,80,000
Less : Invoice value of goods sold	$\left(₹ 8,20,000 \times \frac{100}{125}\right)$	6,56,000	
Invoice value of shortage of stock	$\left(₹ 20,000 \times \frac{100}{125}\right)$	16,000	
			6,72,000
Stock at Branch at Invoice Price			2,08,000
Less : Stock Reserve	$\left(₹ 2,08,000 \times \frac{10}{110}\right)$		18,909
Stock of Processed Goods with Branch (at cost)			1,89,091

(2) Stock Reserve

		₹
Unrealised Profit on Branch Stock	$\left(₹ 2,08,000 \times \frac{10}{110}\right)$	18,909
Unrealised Profit on Goods in Transit	$\left(₹ 44,000 \times \frac{10}{110}\right)$	4,000
		22,909

Difference Between Independent Branch and Dependent Branch

Following are the main differences between independent branch and dependent branch:

Basis	Independent Branch	Dependent Branch
1. System of Accounting	It keeps full system of accounting at its place.	Its accounts are maintained at head office level. Only Cash Register, Debtors Register are maintained at branch.
2. Type of Goods Sold	Such branch sells goods both received from head office and that of purchased made by it.	Such branches sells only those goods which are received from head office. It is not allowed to make own purchases in the ordinary course of business.
3. Payment of Expenses	Such branches keep amount of cash required to meet regular nature of expenses themselves.	Expenses of regular nature like salary, rent etc are normally paid by head office. Branch managers normally are allowed to incur petty expenses only.
4. Remittance of Cash	Such branches are not required to remit all daily collections of cash to head office.	All daily collections from sales and debtors will be deposited in Head Office Account in some local bank or remitted to head office.
5. Trial Balance	Such branches extract trial balance from the ledger maintained at branch level.	No trial balance is required to be extracted as accounts are maintained at head office.
6. Reconciliation	Reconciliation between the accounts maintained at branch and head office is to be made before finalising the accounts.	No need of any reconciliation as accounts are maintained at head office level.
7. Preparation of Final Accounts	Trading and Profit and Loss Account is prepared in normal way as the accounts are kept following double entry system.	Different methods as Debtors System, Final Account System, Stock and Debtors System etc. are followed for preparation of accounts under dependent branches.

(*c*) Foreign Branches

When a branch is located in a foreign country it is called a foreign branch. Such branch will keep its books of accounts in foreign currency. The main problem which the head office is to face under this type of branch is to convert the branch trial balance from the foreign currency to the currency of that country where a head office is working in order to incorporate the branch trial balance in the books of head office. Otherwise for all purposes, this branch is treated as an independent branch.

Accounting for Foreign Branches

For the purpose of accounting, AS 11 (revised 2003) classifies the foreign branches into two types :

(*i*) Integral Foreign Operations (IFO)

(*ii*) Non-integral Foreign Operation (NFO)

Both types of Foreign Branches are discussed below :

(1) Integral Foreign Branches (IFO)

It is a foreign operation, the activities of which are an integral part of those of the reporting enterprise. This foreign operation branch does its business outside India as if it is an extension to the Indian business. For example—if the foreign branch imports goods from India, sells the goods in foreign country and then remits the foreign currency collected from customers to the head office in India.

As there are frequent cash flows, changes in forex rates directly affects the operating cash flows of the reporting entity.

Consider some more examples of IFO—

- If a foreign branch is responsible for sourcing the raw material from that country and forwarding the same to its head office India.
- A foreign branch is responsible for marketing and finding customers, getting the orders and forwarding the same to head office in India.

Technique for Foreign Currency Translation in Financial Statements

Following are the standard recommendations for foreign currency translation for Integral Foreign Operations.

Item	*Rate*
Revenue items	Average Rate for the year
Opening Stock	Opening Rate, *i.e.,* Rates prevalent at the beginning of the accounting period.
Closing Stock	Closing Rate, *i.e.,* Rates prevalent at the close of the accounting period.
Fixed Assets	Translated at the original rate. If there is change in the value of foreign currency liabilities, adjustment should be made to cost of Fixed Assets in rupees.
Depreciation	Rate used for translation of value of Fixed Assets on which depreciation is calculated.
Current Assets	Closing Rate
Current Liabilities	Closing Rate
Long-term Liabilities	Closing Rate
Head Office Account	Balance in 'Head Office Account' in Branch Books is taken at the Indian Rupees for which 'Branch Account' in the head office stands. It must be ensured that all transactions are accounted for in both the books.

On translation of branch trial balance as above, a difference would arise due to application of different exchange rates. Such difference is accounted in a separate account called Exchange Difference Account. The exchange difference may be either a gain or a loss and is to be recognised in branch Profit and Loss Account.

(2) Non-Integral Foreign Operations (NFO)

It is a foreign operation that is not an integral Foreign operation. This foreign operation/branch does business independently and accumulates cash and other monetary items and remits foreign currency occasionally. As there are no frequent cash flows, changes in forex rates will have little or no direct effect on the operating cash flows of the reporting entity. Consider the example wherein a foreign branch procures the raw material and pays it in the local currency, manufactures or provides services, uses surplus for future plans, if requires funds, it borrows in its local currency and occasionally sends money to head office in India. Normally, the reporting entity looks at the non-integral operations as an investment.

Translation Technique of Financial Statements of Non Integral Foreign Operations (NFO)

Item	*Rate*
Revenue Items	Average Rate for the year
All Assets and Liabilities	Closing Rate

The exchange difference on translation is carried in the balance sheet in separate reserve called "foreign currency translation reserve". This difference represents unrealised exchange difference and is recognised in Profit and Loss A/c in the year of disposal of non-integral foreign operations.

ILLUSTRATION 20. Karan Enterprises having its Head Office in Mangalore, Karnataka has a branch in Greenville, USA. Following is the trial balance of Branch as at 31-3-2025 :

Particulars	*Amount ($) Dr.*	*Amount ($) Cr.*
Fixed Assets	8,000	
Opening Inventory	800	
Cash	700	
Goods Received from head office	2,800	
Sales		24,050
Purchases	11,800	
Expenses	1,800	
Remittance to Head Office	2,450	
Head Office Account		4,300
	28,350	28,350

(*i*) Fixed assets were purchased on 1st April, 2021.

(*ii*) Depreciation at 10% p.a. is to be charged on fixed assets on straight line method.

(*iii*) Closing inventory at branch in $ 700 as on 31-3-2025.

(*iv*) Goods received from Head Office (H) were recorded at ₹ 1,85,500 in HO books.

(*v*) Remittances to HO were recorded at ₹ 1,62,000 in HO books.

(*vi*) HO account is recorded in HO books at ₹ 2,84,500.

(*vii*) Exchange rates of US Dollar at different dates can be taken as :

1-4-2021 ₹ 63

1-4-2024 ₹ 65 and

31-3-2025 ₹ 67

Prepare the trial balance after been converted into Indian rupees in accordance with AS-11.

(*CA IPCC Nov. 2019 Modified*)

SOLUTION

TRIAL BALANCE OF FOREIGN BRANCH (CONVERTED INTO INDIAN RUPEES)

as on March 31, 2025

Particulars	*$ (Dr.)*	*$ (Cr.)*	*Conversion Basis*	*Rate*	*₹ (Dr.)*	*₹ (Cr.)*
Fixed Assets	8,000		Transaction Date Rate	63	5,04,000	
Opening Inventory	800		Opening Rate	65	52,000	
Goods Received from H.O.	2,800		Actual		1,85,500	
Sales		24,050	Average Rate	66		15,87,300
Purchases	11,800		Average Rate	66	7,78,800	
Expenses	1,800		Average Rate	66	1,18,800	
Cash	700		Closing Rate	67	46,900	
Remittance to H.O.	2,450		Actuals		1,62,000	
H.O. Account		4,300	Actuals			2,84,500
Exchange Rate Difference			Balancing Figure		23,800	
	28,350	28,350			18,71,800	18,71,800
Closing Stock	700		Closing Rate	67	46,900	
Depreciation	800		Fixed Asset Rate	63	50,400	

ILLUSTRATION 21. DM Ltd., Delhi has a branch in London. London branch is an integral foreign operation of DM Ltd. At the end of the year 31st March, 2025, the branch furnishes the following trial balance in U.K. Pound :

Particulars	£ Dr.	£ Dr.
Fixed Assets (Acquired on 1st April, 2021)	24,000	
Stock as on 1st April, 2024	11,200	
Goods from Head Office	64,000	
Expenses	4,800	
Debtors	4,800	
Creditors		3,200
Cash at Bank	1,200	
Head Office Account		22,800
Purchases	12,000	
Sales		96,000
	1,22,000	1,22,000

In Head Office books, Branch Account stood as shown below :

LONDON BRANCH ACCOUNT

Particulars	₹	*Particulars*	₹
To Balance b/d	20,10,000	By Bank A/c	52,16,000
To Goods sent to Branch	49,26,000	By Balance c/d	17,20,000
	69,36,000		69,36,000

Following further information is given :

(*a*) Fixed assets are to be depreciated @ 10% p.a. on straight line basis.

(*b*) On 31st March, 2025 : Expenses Outstanding = £ 400 ; Prepaid Expenses = £ 200 ; Closing Stock = £ 8,000

(*c*) Rate of Exchange : 1st April, 2021 : ₹ 70 to £ 1 ; 1st April, 2024 : ₹ 76 to £ 1 ; 31st March, 2025 : ₹ 77 to £ 1; Average : ₹ 75 to £ 1

You are required to prepare :

(*i*) Trial balance, incorporating adjustments of outstanding and prepaid expenses, converting U.K. pound into Indian rupees.

(*ii*) Trading and Profit and Loss Account for the year ended 31st March, 2025 and Balance Sheet as on that date of London branch as would appear in the books of Delhi head office of DM Ltd.

SOLUTION

(*i*) **TRIAL BALANCE OF LONDON BRANCH**
as on 31st March, 2025

Particulars	U.K. Pound	Rate per U.K. Pound	Dr.(₹)	Cr. (₹)
Fixed Assets	24,000	70	16,80,000	
Stock (as on 1st April, 2024)	11,200	76	8,51,200	
Goods from Head Office	64,000	(as given in Branch A/c)	49,26,000	
Sales	96,000	75		72,00,000

Purchases	12,000	75	9,00,000	
Expenses (4,800 + 400 – 200)	5,000	75	3,75,000	
Debtors	4,800	77	3,69,600	
Creditors	3,200	77		2,46,400
Outstanding Expenses	400	77		30,800
Prepaid Expenses	200	77	15,400	
Cash at Bank	1,200	77	92,400	
Head Office Account		—		17,20,000
Difference in Foreign Exchange Translation				12,400
			92,09,600	92,09,600

Closing Stock will be (£ 8,000 × ₹ 77) = ₹ 6,16,000

(ii) **TRADING AND PROFIT AND LOSS ACCOUNT**

for the year ended 31st March, 2025

Particulars	Amount	*Particulars*	Amount
	₹		₹
To Opening Stock	8,51,200	By Sales	72,00,000
To Purchases	9,00,000	By Closing Stock	6,16,000
To Goods from Head Office	49,26,000		
To Gross Profit	11,38,800		
	78,16,000		78,16,000
To Expenses	3,75,000	By Gross Profit	11,38,800
To Depreciation	1,68,000	By Profit due to Foreign Exchange	
To Net Profit	6,08,200	Difference	12,400
	11,51,200		11,51,200

(iii) **BALANCE SHEET**

as on 31st March, 2024

Liabilities		₹	*Assets*	₹	₹
Head Office :	₹		Fixed Assets	16,80,000	
Balance	17,20,000		*Less* : Depreciation	1,68,000	
Add : Net Profit	6,08,200				15,12,000
		23,28,200	Debtors		3,69,600
Outstanding Expenses		30,800	Prepaid Expenses		15,400
Creditors		2,46,400	Closing Stock		6,16,000
			Cash at Bank		92,400
		26,05,400			26,05,400

ILLUSTRATION 22. Goodluck Ltd. carried on a manufacturing business. It exported some of its products through an overseas branch which is an integral foreign operations and whose currency is "Dhabus". The branch carries out the final assembly operations before selling the goods. The Trial Balance of the Head Office and the Branch as on 31-3-2025 was as under :

	Head Office		*Branch*	
	Dr. ₹	*Cr.* ₹	*Dr.* *Dhabus*	*Cr.* *Dhabus*
Freehold Building at cost	14,000		63,000	
Debtors/Creditors	8,900	9,500	36,000	1,560

Sales		1,04,000		4,32,000
Issued Share Capital		40,000		
Components sent to Branch		35,000		
Head Office/Branch	60,100			5,04,260
Branch-Cost of sales			3,60,000	
Provision for depreciation of machinery		1,500		56,700
H.O. cost of sales (including goods sent to branch)	59,000			
Administrative cost	15,200		18,000	
Stock on 31-3-2025	28,900		11,520	
Profit and Loss Account		2,000		
Machinery at cost	6,000		1,26,000	
Remittances		28,000	2,72,000	
Cash at bank	4,600		79,200	
Selling and distribution costs	23,300		28,800	
	2,20,000	2,20,000	9,94,520	9,94,520

Following adjustments are to be made :

1. The cost of sales figure includes a depreciation charge of 10 per cent per annum on the cost of machinery.

2. A provision of ₹ 300 for unrealised profit in the Branch stock is to be made

3. On 26th March, 2025 the Branch remitted 16,000 Dhabus. This amount was received by the H.O. on 4th April, 2025 and realised ₹ 1,990.

4. During February, 2025 a customer of the Branch by mistake paid the H.O. for goods supplied by the Branch. The amount due from him was Dhabus 320 which realised ₹ 36. It has been correctly dealt with by H.O. but not yet entered in the Branch account.

5. Provide commission at 5 per cent of the net profits of the Branch after charging such commission which is payable to the Branch Manager.

6. The exchange rates were (*a*) on 1st April, 2024 : 10 Dhabus = 1 Rupee ; (*b*) On 31-3-2025 : 8 Dhabus = 1 Rupee ; (*c*) Average Rate for the year : 9 Dhabus = 1 Rupee ; (*d*) On date of purchase of building and machinery : 7 Dhabus = 1 Rupee

You are required to prepare for internal use :

(A) Branch Trial Balance (after above adjustments) in H.O. currency.

(B) Detailed Trading and Profit and Loss Accounts of H.O. and the Branch for the year ending 31st March, 2025.

(C) Balance Sheet as at 31st March, 2025 (combined figures of the H.O. and the Branch). Ignore Taxation.

SOLUTION

Trial Balance of Goodluck Ltd.

(A) CONVERSION OF THE BRANCH

	Dhabus Dr.	Dhabus Cr.	Rate per ₹	Dr. ₹	Cr. ₹
Freehold Buildings	63,000		7	9,000	—
Debtors (36,000 – 320)	35,680		8	4,460	
Creditors		1,560	8		195
Sales		4,32,000	9		48,000
Head Office		5,03,940	—		60,100
Cost of Sales (3,60,000 – 12,600)	3,47,400		9	38,600	

Depreciation	12,600		7	1,800	
Provision for Depreciation on Machinery		56,700	7		8,100
Administrative Cost	18,000		9	2,000	
Stock on 31-3-2025	11,520		8	1,440	
Machinery at Cost	1,26,000		7	18,000	
Remittances (28,000 + 1,990)	2,72,000		—	29,990	
Cash at Bank	79,200		8	9,900	
Selling & Distribution Cost	28,800		9	3,200	
Difference in Exchange					1,995
	9,94,200	9,94,200		1,18,390	1,18,390

TRADING AND PROFIT & LOSS ACCOUNT

for the year ending 31-3-2025

	Branch	*H.O.*	*Total*		*Branch*	*H.O.*	*Total*
	₹	₹	₹		₹	₹	₹
To Cost of Sales (excluding depreciation)	38,600	58,400	97,000	By Sales	48,000	1,04,000	1,52,000
" Gross Profit c/d	9,400	80,600	90,000	" Goods sent to Branch Account	—	35,000	35,000
	48,000	1,39,000	1,87,000		48,000	1,39,000	1,87,000
To Administrative Cost	2,000	15,200	17,200	By Gross Profit b/d	9,400	80,600	90,000
" Selling and Distribution Expenses	3,200	23,300	26,500				
" Depreciation	1,800	600	2,400				
" Commission to Branch Manager	150		150				
" Stock Reserve		300	300				
" Net Profit c/d	2,250	41,200	43,450				
	9,400	80,600	90,000		9,400	80,600	90,000

PROFIT AND LOSS APPROPRIATION ACCOUNT

	₹		₹	₹
To Balance c/d	45,450	By Balance b/d		2,000
		" Net Profit for the year		
		H.O.	41,200	
		Branch	2,250	
				43,450
	45,450			45,450

BALANCE SHEET OF GOOD LUCK LTD.

as on 31-3-2025

Liabilities	₹	*Assets*		₹
Share Capital :		Fixed Assets :		
Authorised	?	Freehold Building at Cost	₹	23,000
Issued and Subscribed	40,000	Machinery at Cost	24,000	
Shares of ₹......each		*Less* : Depreciation	9,600	
Reserves and Surplus :				14,400
Profit and Loss A/c	45,450	Investments		Nil

Exchange Reserve	1,995	Current Assets, Loans and Advances :	
Secured Loans	nil	Current Assets	
Unsecured Loans	nil	Stock-in-trade (at cost)	30,040
Current Liabilities and Provisions :		Sundry Debtors	13,360
Sundry Creditors	9,695	Cash at Bank	14,500
Commission due to Branch Manager	150	Cash in Transit	1,990
		Loans and Advances	Nil
	97,290		97,290

Working Note :

The Branch Manager will be entitled to commission on profit according to the Branch Books. The profit before such commission is 25,200 Dhabus, as shown below :

	Dhabus	*Dhabus*
Sales		4,32,000
Less : Cost of Sales	3,60,000	
Administration Cost	18,000	
Selling & Distribution Cost	28,800	4,06,800
Profit		25,200

Commission 5/105 of Dhabus 25,200 = 1,200 Dhabus

Converted at the rate of 8 Dhabus a rupee = $\frac{1,200}{8}$ = ₹ 150.

ILLUSTRATION 23. An Indian company Moon Star Limited has a branch at Verginia (USA). The Branch is a non-integral foreign operation of the Indian Company. The Trial Balance of the Branch as at 31st March, 2025 is as follows :

Particulars	*US $*	
	Dr.	*Cr.*
Office Equipments	48,000	
Furniture and Fixtures	3,200	
Stock (April 1, 2024)	22,400	
Purchases	96,000	
Sales	—	1,66,400
Goods Sent from HO	32,000	
Salaries	3,200	
Carriage Inward	400	
Rent, Rates & Taxes	800	
Insurance	400	
Trade Expenses	400	
Head Office Account	—	45,600
Sundry Debtors	9,600	
Sundry Creditors	—	6,800
Cash at Bank	2,000	
Cash in Hand	400	
	2,18,800	2,18,800

The following further informations are given :

(1) Salaries Outstanding $ 400.

(2) Depreciate Office Equipment and Furniture & Fixtures @ 10% p.a. at written down value.

(3) The Head Office sent goods to Branch for ₹ 15,80,000.

(4) The Head Office shown an amount of ₹ 20,50,000 due from Branch.

(5) Stock on 31st March, 2025—$ 21,500.

(6) There were no transit items either at the start or at the end of the year.

(7) On April 1, 2023 when the fixed assets were purchased the rate of exchange was ₹ 43 to one $. On Aril 1, 2024, the rate was ₹ 47 per $. On March 31, 2025 the rate was ₹ 50 per $. Average Rate during the year was ₹ 45 to one $.

Prepare :

(*a*) Trial balance incorporating adjustments given converting dollars into rupees.

(*b*) Trading, Profit and Loss Account for the year ended 31st March, 2025 and Balance Sheet as on date depicting the profitability and net position of the Branch as would appear in the books of Indian company for the purpose of incorporating in the main Balance Sheet.

(CA IPCE May, 2015 Modified)

SOLUTION

In the Books of Moon Star Ltd.—An Indian Company

TRIAL BALANCE AFTER ADJUSTMENT (IN RUPEES) OF VERGINIA (USA) BRANCH

as on 31st March, 2025

Particulars	Dr. US $	Cr. US $	Conversion Rate	Dr. ₹	Cr. ₹
Office Equipment (48,000 – 4,800 Dep.)	43,200		50	21,60,000	
Depreciation on Office Equipment	4,800		50	2,40,000	
Furniture and Fixtures (3,200 – 320 Dep.)	2,880		50	1,44,000	
Depreciation on Furniture and Fixtures	320		50	16,000	
Stock (1st April, 2024)	22,400		47	10,52,800	
Purchases	96,000		45	43,20,000	
Sales		1,66,400	45		74,88,000
Goods sent from H.O.	32,000		as given in H.O.	15,80,000	
Carriage Inward	400		45	18,000	
Salaries (3,200 + 400 Outstanding)	3,600		45	1,62,000	
Outstanding Salaries		400	50		20,000
Rent, Rates and Taxes	800		45	36,000	
Insurance	400		45	18,000	
Trade Expenses	400		45	18,000	
Head Office A/c		45,600	as given in H.O.		20,50,000
Trade Debtors	9,600		50	4,80,000	
Trade Creditors		6,800	50		3,40,000
Cash at Bank	2,000		50	1,00,000	
Cash in hand	400		50	20,000	
Exchange Gain (Bal. Fig.)					4,66,800
	2,19,200	2,19,200		1,03,64,800	1,03,64,800

(b) TRADING AND PROFIT AND LOSS ACCOUNT OF VERGINIA BRANCH

for the year ended 31st March, 2025

	₹		₹
To Opening Stock	10,52,800	By Sales	74,88,000
To Purchases	43,20,000	By Closing Stock (21,500 US $ × 50)	10,75,000
To Goods from Head Office	15,80,000		
To Carriage Inward	18,000		
To Gross Profit c/d	15,92,200		
	85,63,000		85,63,000
To Salaries	1,62,000	By Gross Profit b/d	15,92,200
To Rent, Rates and Taxes	36,000		
To Insurance	18,000		
To Trade Expenses	18,000		
To Depreciation on Office Equipment	2,40,000		
To Depreciation on Furniture and Fixtures	16,000		
To Net Profit c/d	11,02,200		
	15,92,200		15,92,200

BALANCE SHEET OF VERGINIA BRANCH

as on 31st March, 2025

Liabilities		₹	*Assets*		₹
	₹			₹	
Head Office A/c	20,50,000		Office Equipment	24,00,000	
Add : Net Profit	11,02,200		*Less* : Depreciation	2,40,000	
		31,52,200			21,60,000
Foreign Currency Translation Reserve		4,66,800	Furniture and Fixtures	1,60,000	
Trade Creditors		3,40,000	*Less* : Depreciation	16,000	
Outstanding Salaries		20,000			1,44,000
			Closing Stock		10,75,000
			Trade Debtors		4,80,000
			Cash in hand		20,000
			Cash at Bank		1,00,000
		39,79,000			39,79,000

QUESTIONS

OBJECTIVE TYPE

1. State whether the following statements are true or false :

(i) A dependent branch is one which does not maintain its own set of accounting books to ascertain financial results.

(ii) Under debtors system Branch Account discloses profit or loss of the branch.

(iii) Under debtors system, Branch Account is credited with opening balances of branch assets.

(*iv*) Under debtors system no entry in required in Branch Account for branch expenses paid by the branch out of petty cash.

(*v*) Depreciation less furniture appears on the debit side of branch account.

(*vi*) The system of calculating profit by preparing one Branch Account for each branch, called Branch Account, is termed as Debtors System.

(*vii*) Bad Debts and discount allowed to debtors are not shown in Branch Account.

(*viii*) Under debtors system the Branch Account is real account.

(*ix*) The books of a dependent branch are maintained by head office under debtors system.

(*x*) If a bill has been discounted by the branch, the amount of discount is debited to Branch Account under debtors system as it is a loss at the branch.

(*xi*) Under the stock and debtors system Branch Stock Account is a nominal account.

(*xii*) Under the stock and debtors system branch profit is ascertained by opening Branch Adjustment Account.

(*xiii*) Branch Stock Account is always prepared at cost price.

(*xiv*) The invoice price is the price at which goods are sold to customers by the branch.

(*xv*) Branch Adjustment Account is prepared to determine gross profit or gross loss of the branch.

(*xvi*) When goods are supplied to the branch at cost price, the difference in two sides of Branch Stock Account is known as surplus or shortage.

(*xvii*) There is no relationship between closing balance of Branch Adjustment Account and the opening balance of Branch Profit and Loss Account.

(*xviii*) Under final account system of branch accounting; Branch Trading and Profit and Loss Account is a memorandum account.

(*xix*) An independent branch is one which is situated within the territories of country of head office.

(*xx*) In the case of branch keeping full system of accounting, entry for depreciation of fixed assets (when these are maintained in head office books) in the books of branch is as follows :

Profit and Loss Account Dr.

To Head Office Account

(*xxi*) The balances shown by Head Office Account (in branch books) and Branch Account (in head office books) are always equal although the nature of balances differ.

(*xxii*) Cash-in-transit is the amount which is sent by head office to branch or remitted by branch to head office, but not received by branch in former case and by head office in later case.

(*xxiii*) Abnormal loss is directly debited to Branch Adjustment Account.

(*xxiv*) Goods returned by customers direct to branch are shown in the debit as well as credit side of the Branch Account under Debtors System.

(*xxv*) At profit-margin of 20% on sale price is equivalent to 25% profit on cost.

(*xxvi*) Under stock and debtors system no entry is required for normal loss of stock.

Ans. [True : (*i*), (*ii*), (*iv*), (*vi*), (*vii*), (*xii*), (*xv*), (*xviii*), (*xx*), (*xxii*), (*xxv*); False : (*iii*), (*v*), (*viii*), (*ix*), (*x*), (*xi*), (*xiii*), (*xiv*), (*xvi*), (*xvii*), (*xix*), (*xxi*), (*xxiii*), (*xxiv*), (*xxvi*)]

SHORT ANSWER TYPE

1. How do we ascertain closing debtors of a branch ?
2. What are the main types of branches from accounting point of view ?
3. Give any three objectives of branch accounting.
4. How will you ascertain remittance from a branch ?
5. What adjustment entries are made by the head office when goods are sent to branch at invoice price.

6. How will you ascertain closing stock of a branch in stock and debtors system of maintaining branch accounts ?
7. Journalise the following transactions in the head office books when branches are keeping full system of accounting.
   (*a*) Depreciation on branch fixed assets when their accounts are maintained in head office books.
   (*b*) Goods in transit.
8. How will you incorporate branch asset and liabilities in the head office books in case of an independent branch.
9. What is the journal entry for incorporating branch profit in the head office books when branch trading and profit and loss account is prepared as a memorandum account?
10. How will you convert foreign branch floating assets and floating liabilities in head office books ?
11. How will you convert revenue items of a foreign branch in the books of head office ?
12. Goods are sent from head office to a branch at a price so as to include a 25% profit on transfer price. What will be the amount of reserve on a closing stock of ₹ 15,000 at the branch.

Ans. [₹ 3,750]

13. Explain 'goods in transit' and 'cash in transit'.
14. Explain the accounting procedure for branch on the basis of Debtor System and Final Account System.
15. Briefly explain foreign branch types.

LONG ANSWER TYPE

1. What are the main classes of Branch Accounts ? Give the ruling and column headings of goods supplied to branches (Branch Books maintained at the Head Office) with five imaginary entries.
2. In respect of dependent branch, the Head Office (under Branch accounting method) follows certain methods of accounting. List them out clearly.
3. What are the objects of keeping Branch Accounts ? Contrast and compare the methods of charging goods sent to branches at (*i*) Cost price, (*ii*) Fixed percentage over cost, (*iii*) Retail selling price.
4. What is the purpose behind creating a reserve for the unsold stock in the branch, where stocks are sent by the head office at invoice price ?
5. What do you understand by the term 'Branch Adjustment Account' ? Explain clearly.
6. What do you understand by an Independent Branch? What books are maintained by such a branch and how are its accounts incorporated in the books of the main office so as to prepare the consolidated accounts ?
7. What do you understand by inter-branch transactions ? Which is the best method of dealing with these ?
8. With respect to Branch Accounts, how will you deal with the following matters (*a*) Goods supplied by Branch to Head Office; (*b*) Remittance-in-transit; (*c*) Depreciation of Branch Fixed Assets; and (*d*) Goods-in-Transit.
9. Give Journal Entries for incorporating the branch trial balance in the books of head office.
10. Distinguish between Branch Account and Departmental Accounts.
11. Write a note on Stock and Debtors System.
12. Write a note on Dependent and Independent Branches.
13. State the reasons for the difference between the balances of Branch Account in the Head Office books and the Head Office Account in the books of the Branch. How would you reconcile the balances of the two accounts ?

14. Explain the technique of translation of Financial Statements of foreign branch which is integral foreign operation.

15. At what rate will you convert the following items appearing in the T.B. of a foreign branch in case of IFO ? (*i*) Head Office balance; (*ii*) Depreciation on fixed assets; (*iii*) Remittance by the branch; and (*iv*) Provision for bad & doubtful debts.

16. A firm sells goods at cost plus 25 per cent. How would you record the return of goods of ₹ 4,500 (at selling price) from the branch stock to the head office under the stock debtors integrated system of accounting ?

			₹	₹
Hint.	Goods sent to Branch A/c	Dr.	3,600	
	Branch Adjustment A/c	Dr.	900	
	To Branch Stock A/c			4,500

PRACTICAL PROBLEMS

DEBTORS SYSTEM AT COST PRICE

1. From the following details relating to Delhi branch for the year ending March 31, 2025, prepare Branch Account in the books of Head office. Show your workings clearly.

	₹		₹	₹
Balances as on 1-4-2024 :		Goods returned by Branch		2,000
Stock	25,000	Goods returned by Debtors		1,000
Debtors	10,000	Cash sent to Branch for Expenses :		₹
Furniture	6,000	Rent (₹ 800 p.m.)	9,600	
Petty Cash	1,000	Salary (₹ 4,000 p.m.)	48,000	
Insurance Pre-paid	300	Petty Cash	2,000	
Salaries Outstanding	4,000	Insurance		
Goods sent to Branch during the year	2,00,000	(upto June 2025)	1,200	60,800
Cash Sales during the year	2,70,000	Petty Cash Expenses		2,200
Total Sales	3,50,000	Discount Allowed to Debtors		500
Cash received from Debtors	65,000	Stock on 31-3-2025		15,000
Cash paid by Debtors direct to H.O.	5,000	Depreciation on Furniture at 10% p.a.		

Goods costing ₹ 2,500 were damaged in transit and a sum of ₹ 2,000 was recovered from the insurance company in full settlement of the claim. The manager is entitled to a commission of 5% of profit at branch after charging such commission.

Ans. [Profit ₹ 77,048; Debtors at the end ₹ 18,500; Petty Cash Balance ₹ 800; Manager's Commission ₹ 3,852].

2. A Company with its Head Office at Mumbai has a Branch at Kolkata. The Branch receives all goods from Head Office who also remits cash for all expenses. Sales are made by the branch on credit as well as for cash.

Total sales by the Branch for the year ended 31st March, 2025 amounted to ₹ 5,60,000 out of which 20% is cash sales. Following further information is relevant.

	1-4-2024	*31-3-2025*
	₹	₹
Stock in trade	25,000	36,000
Debtors	60,000	48,000
Petty Cash	120	180

Expenses actually incurred by the Branch during the year were :
Salaries ₹ 36,000 ; Rent ₹ 12,000 ; Petty expenses ₹ 5,600.

All sales are made by the Branch at cost plus 25%.

You are required to prepare Kolkata Branch Account in the Books of Head Office for the year ended 31st March, 2025.

Ans. **[Profit ₹ 58,400].**

Hints. Goods sent to branch = Total Sales – Loading + Closing Stock – Opening Stock = ₹4,59,000; Collection from Debtors ₹ 4,60,000; Cash remitted for branch petty expenses ₹ 5,660.

3. Jain Bros. operate a retail branch at Delhi. All purchases are made by the head office at Chennai; goods being charged out to the branch at cost price. All cash received by the branch is remitted to Chennai. Branch petty expenses are paid out of an *imprest* which is reimbursed by the head office from time to time. From the following particulars relating to Delhi Branch, you are required to prepare Branch Account (for calculating profit) in the books of head office.

	₹		₹
1-4-2024		Petty expenses paid by the branch out of imprest	700
Stock at cost	8,000		
Petty cash	800	Cash sales during the year	70,000
Plant	10,000	Sale of the plant on October 1, 2024 (book value of the plant on the date of sale ₹ 900)	800
31-3-2025			
Stock at cost	7,000		
Goods sent to branch	50,000	Expenses paid by the head office	5,000

It is required to write off the plant at 20% p.a.

Ans. **[Profit ₹ 11,300; Value of Plant at the end ₹ 7,200].**

4. T of Kolkata has a branch at Dibrugarh. The branch does not maintain separate books of accounts. The branch has the following assets and liabilities on 31st August, 2024 and 30th September, 2024:

	31st August, 2024 ₹	*30th September, 2024* ₹
Stock of ten	1,80,000	1,50,000
Advance to Suppliers	5,00,000	4,50,000
Bank Balance	75,000	1,00,000
Prepaid Expenses	10,000	12,000
Outstanding Expenses	13,000	11,000
Creditors for Purchases	3,00,000	to be ascertained

During the month, Dibrugarh branch :

(*a*) received by electronic mail transfer ₹ 10,00,000 from Kolkata head office;

(*b*) purchased tea worth ₹ 12,00,000;

(*c*) sent tea costing ₹ 12,30,000 to Kolkata, freight of ₹ 80,000 being payable at the destination by the receiver;

(*d*) spent ₹ 25,000 on office expenses;

(*e*) paid ₹ 3,00,000 as advance to suppliers;

(*f*) paid ₹ 6,50,000 to suppliers in settlement of outstanding dues.

In addition, T informs you that the Kolkata office had directly paid ₹ 3,50,000 to Dibrugarh suppliers by cheques drawn on bank accounts in Kolkata during the month.

T informs you that for the purpose of accounting, Dibrugarh branch is not treated as an outsider. He wants you to write the following accounts relating to the transactions of the Dibrugarh branch as would appear in the books of Kolkata head office.

(*i*) Dibrugarh Tea Stock Account ; (*ii*) Advance to Dibrugarh Suppliers' Account ; (*iii*) Dibrugarh Suppliers' Account ; (*iv*) Dibrugarh Bank Account ; (*v*) Dibrugarh Branch Expenses Account.

DEBTORS SYSTEM AT INVOICE PRICE

5. Bauxite Industries, Mumbai has a branch in Cochin to which office goods are invoiced at cost plus 25%. The branch sells both for cash and on credit. Branch Expenses are paid direct from Head Office and the Branch has to remit all cash received into the Head Office Bank Account at Cochin.

From the following details, relating to year 2024-25 prepare Branch Account in the Head Office Ledger and ascertain the Branch Profit. Branch does not maintain any books of account but sends weekly returns to the Head Office.

	₹		₹
Goods received from Head Office at invoice price	6,00,000	Discount allowed to Debtors	6,000
Returns to Head Office at invoice price	12,000	Bad Debts in the year	4,000
Stock at Cochin as on 1-4-2024	60,000	Sales Returns at Cochin Branch	8,000
Sales in the year (Cash)	2,00,000	Rent, Rates, Taxes at Branch	18,000
—do— (Credit)	3,60,000	Salaries, Wages, Bonus at Branch	60,000
Sundry Debtors at Cochin as on 1-4-2024	72,000	Office Expenses	6,000
Cash received from Debtors	3,20,000	Stock at Branch on 31st March, 2025 at invoice price	1,20,000

Ans. [Profit ₹ 35,600; Debtors at the end ₹ 94,000].

6. Pawan & Co. of Delhi has a branch at Jaipur. Goods are invoiced to the branch at cost plus 25%. The branch is instructed to deposit the receipts everyday in the Head Office Account with the bank. All the expenses are paid through cheque by the head office except petty cash expenses which are paid by the Branch.

From the following information, you are required to prepare Branch Account in the books of Head Office :

	₹		₹
Stock at Invoice Price on 1-4-24	1,64,000	Goods Invoiced to Branch by Head Office	12,56,000
Stock at Invoice Price on 31-3-25	1,92,000	Expenses paid by Head Office	2,64,000
Debtors as on 1-4-24	63,400	Petty Expenses paid by the Branch	20,900
Debtors as on 31-3-25	84,300	Furniture acquired by the branch on 1-10-24 (Payment was made by the branch from cash sales and collection from debtors)	5,000
Furniture & Fixtures as on 1-4-24	46,800		
Cash Sales	8,02,600		
Credit Sales	7,44,200		

Depreciation to be provided on branch furniture and fixtures @ 10% p.a. on WDV basis.

Ans. [Profit ₹ 2,74,570; Cash received from Debtors ₹ 7,23,300; Cash remitted by Branch to H.O. ₹ 15,00,000]

7. X Ltd., Mumbai, started on 1st April, 2024, has two branches at Kanpur and Lucknow. All goods sold at the Branches are received from the Head Office invoiced at cost plus 25%. All expenses relating to Branches are paid by the Head Office. Each Branch has its own Sales Ledger and sends weekly statements. All cash collections are remitted daily to Head Office by the Branches. Following particulars relating to the year ended 31st March, 2025 have been extracted from the weekly statements sent by the Branches :

	Kanpur ₹	Lucknow ₹
Credit Sales	1,25,200	1,10,000
Cash Sales	78,600	85,200
Sales Returns	2,300	1,200
Sundry Debtors	34,500	23,600
Rent and Rates	3,200	4,500
Bad Debts	6,000	—

Salaries	16,000	18,000
General Expenses	2,600	1,500
Goods received from H.O.	1,50,000	1,25,000
Advertisement	7,500	5,200
Stock on 31st March, 2025	45,000	35,000

You are required to prepare Branch Accounts as they would appear in the books of the Head Office, showing the Profit or Loss for the period. ***(C.A. Inter)***

Ans. [Profit : Kanpur ₹ 82,200; Lucknow ₹ 92,800].

Hint. Cash received from Debtors : Kanpur ₹ 82,400 : Lucknow ₹ 85,200.

8. S.P. who carried on a retail business opened a branch X on 1-1-2025 where all sales were on credit basis. All goods required by the branch were supplied from the Head Office and were invoiced to the branch at 10% above cost. Following were the transactions during 1-1-2025 to 31-3-2025.

	Jan.	*Feb.*	*March*
	₹	₹	₹
Goods sent to Branch (Purchase price)	40,000	50,000	60,000
Sales as shown by the branch monthly reports	38,000	42,000	55,000
Cash received from Debtors and remitted to H.O.	20,000	51,000	35,000
Returns to H.O. (Invoice Price to Branch)	1,200	800	2,400

The stock of goods held by the branch on March 31, 2025 amounted to ₹ 53,900 at invoice price to branch. Record these transactions in the Head Office books, showing balances as on 31st March, 2025 and the branch gross profit for the three months ended on that date.

All workings should form part of your answer. ***(C.A. Inter)***

Ans. [Profit ₹ 38,000; Debtors at the end ₹ 29,000].

9. A business has three branches at Coimbatore, Trivandrum and Bengaluru. The Head Office at Chennai purchases goods and sends them to branches, to be sold at a uniform percentage of profit on cost. Following particulars are made available to you to enable you to prepare a Combined Trading Account for the year ended 31st March, 2025 :

	Chennai	*Coimbatore*	*Trivandrum*	*Bengaluru*
	₹	₹	₹	₹
Stock on 1st April, 2024	54,000	16,000	12,500	10,000
Purchases during the year	2,74,000			
Sales	—	1,80,000	1,20,000	1,00,000
Stock on 31st March, 2025	28,000	6,000	5,000	2,500
Branch Accounts :				
Coimbatore	15,000			
Trivandrum	32,000			
Bengaluru	4,000			
Remittances from branches	3,20,000	1,50,000	1,00,000	70,000

Chennai Office invoices goods to the branches at fixed sales prices but maintains branch accounts in its ledgers at cost price.

Show Branch Accounts in Chennai Head Office Books. ***(C.A. Inter)***

Ans. [Gross Profit : Coimbatore ₹ 36,000; Trivandrum ₹ 24,000; Bengaluru ₹ 20,000; Total ₹ 80,000].

Balances in Branch A/cs : Coimbatore ₹ 37,000; Trivandrum ₹ 46,000; Bengaluru ₹ 28,000].

Hint. Rate of Profit on Invoice Price = **20%.**

10. Jaico Limited invoices goods to its Kanpur Branch at cost plus 25% thereon. Both Cash and Credit Sales are effected by the branch. The branch expenses are paid direct from the H.O. The details of transactions available for the year ending 31st March, 2025 are :

	₹		₹
Goods received at Kanpur from Head Office at invoice price	40,000	Cash received from Debtors	29,500
Returns to Head Office at invoice price	800	Discounts allowed to customers	300
Stock at Kanpur on 1st April, 2024 at invoice price	8,000	Returns from customers at selling price	700
Credit Sales for the year	30,000	Rent, Rates etc.	60
Cash Sales	18,700	Salaries and Wages	1,200
Debtors as on 1st April, 2024	5,200	Sundry Expenses	300
Bad Debts	500	Stock as on 31st March, 2025 at invoice price	6,000

Record the above transactions in the Branch Account in the Head Office Ledger and close the accounts as on 31st March, 2025 and show how the relevant items will appear in the Head Office's Balance Sheet on that date.

Ans. [Profit ₹ 12,680; Debtors at the end ₹ 4,200].

11. The Head Office of a company invoices goods to its Delhi Branch at cost plus 20%. The Delhi Branch also purchases independently from local parties goods for which payments are made by the Head Office. All the cash collected by the Branch is banked on the same day to the credit of the Head Office and all expenses are directly paid by the Head Office except for a petty cash account maintained by the branch for which periodical transfers are made from the Head Office.

From the following particulars show the Branch Account as maintained in the Head Office books, reflecting the branch profit for the year ended 31-3-2025 :

	₹	₹		₹	₹
Petty Cash Balance :			Sundry Debtors on 31-3-2025		24,000
1-4-2024		2,000	Goods sent to Branch from H.O. at invoice price		60,000
31-3-2025		1,850	Transfer from H.O. for petty cash expenses		2,500
Cash received from Debtors		1,25,000	Bad Debts		1,000
Stock on 1-4-2024 :			Discounts to customers		2,000
Transferred from H.O. at invoice price	24,000		Branch expenses		30,000
Directly purchased by Branch	16,000	40,000	Stock on 31-3-2025:		
Cash Sales		45,000	Transferred from H.O. at invoice value	18,000	
Credit Sales		1,30,000	Directly purchased by Branch	12,000	30,000
Direct Purchases		45,000			
Returns from Customers		3,000			

Ans. [Profit ₹ 32,350; Debtors on 1-4-2024 ₹ 25,000].

12. ABC Ltd. Delhi invoices goods to its Mumbai and Kolkata offices at 20% less than the list price which is cost *plus* 50% with instructions that cash sales are to be made at invoice price and credit sales at list price. Following information is available of the transactions of Delhi Branch for the year ended on 31st March, 2023.

Particulars	*Amt. (₹)*
Opening Stock at Cost to Branch	1,80,000
Opening Balance of Debtors	20,000
Goods sent to Mumbai (at cost to H.O.)	2,20,000

Goods received by Mumbai Branch till close of the year	2,52,000
Cash Sales	60% of Net Credit Sales
Goods returned by Credit Customers to Mumbai Branch	75,000
Goods returned by Mumbai Branch to H.O.	84,000
Loss of Goods by Fire at Mumbai (at Invoice Price)	6,000
Insurance claim recovered by Mumbai Office from the Insurance Company	80% of the Cost of loss
Loss of Goods at Mumbai through Normal Pilferage (at list price)	6,000
Discount allowed to Mumbai Branch Credit Customers	27,000
Mumbai Branch Expenses paid by Delhi H.O. (including Insurance Premium of ₹ 4,000 paid for the year ending on 30th June, 2025)	19,000
Outstanding Mumbai Branch Expenses	3,625
Provision is to be made for Discount on Debtors	6,075
Cash collected from Credit Customers	1,73,000
Closing Debtors at Mumbai Branch	45,000

Mumbai Branch Manager is entitled to a commission @ 5% of per profits after charging such commission. Round off Commission to the nearest rupee.

Answer the following :

(*a*) Calculate the Closing Stock of the Branch.

(*b*) Calculate Net Sales of the Branch.

(*c*) Calculate net Profits of the Branch.

(*d*) Prepare Mumbai Branch Account under Debtors Method for the year ended 31st March, 2025.

Ans. [(*a*) ₹ 22,200; (*b*) ₹ 3,00,000; (*c*) Net Profit ₹ 36,000].

FINAL ACCOUNTS SYSTEM

13. Shree Nanak of Mumbai has a branch at Delhi. Goods are invoiced to the Branch at cost *plus* 20%. The expenses of the Branch are paid from Mumbai and the Branch keeps a Sales Journal and the Debtors' Ledger only. From the information supplied by the Branch, prepare Trading and Profit & Loss Account of the Branch for the year ending 31st March, 2025 and show the Account of the Branch as it would appear in the books of the Head Office.

	₹		₹
Opening Stock (at invoice price)	12,000	Goods received from Head Office	15,000
Closing Stock (at invoice price)	9,000	Goods in Transit from Head Office on 31st March, 2025	1,800
Credit Sales	20,500		
Cash Sales	8,750	Expenses paid by Head Office for the branch	5,200
Receipts from debtors	18,950		
Sundry Debtors on 31st March, 2025	4,580		

Ans. [G.P. ₹ 14,250; N.P. ₹ 9,050; Branch A/c's Balance ₹ 12,080; Beginning Debtors ₹ 3,030].

Hint. Goods sent to Branch = Goods received from H.O. + Goods in Transit

STOCK AND DEBTORS SYSTEM

14. On October 1, 2024 the goods invoiced by Kolkata Head Office of a trader to its Chennai Branch were ₹ 48,000 at selling price, being $33\frac{1}{3}\%$ on cost price. For six months ended 31-3-2025, the branch return showed that the sales were ₹ 29,000. The goods invoiced at ₹ 2,000 were returned by the Branch to the Head Office. The closing stock at Chennai Branch on 31-3-2025 was ₹ 16,800 at selling price.

Record the above transactions showing Chennai Branch Stock Account, Chennai Branch Adjustment Account, Chennai P. & L. A/c, and Goods Sent to Branches Account in Kolkata Head Office Books and balance them at 31-3-2025.

Ans. [Gross Profit ₹ 7,250; Net Profit ₹ 7,100 ; Shortage ₹ 200].

15. Delhi head office supplies goods to its branch at Kanpur at invoice price which is cost plus 50%. All cash received by the branch is remitted to Delhi and all Branch expenses are paid by the head office. From the following particulars related to Kanpur branch for the year 2024-25, prepare :

(*i*) Branch Account, and

(*ii*) Branch Stock Account, Branch Debtors Account, Branch Expenses Account and Branch Adjustment Account in the books of the head office so as to find out the gross profit and net profit made by the branch.

	₹			₹
Stock with Branch on 1-4-2024		Discount allowed to Debtors		2,400
(at Invoice Price)	60,000	Expenses (Cash paid by		
Branch Debtors on 1-4-2024	12,000	Head Office) :	₹	
Petty Cash Balance on 1-4-2024	100	Rent	2,400	
Goods received from Head Office		Salaries	24,000	
(at Invoice Price)	1,86,000	Petty Cash	1,000	
Goods Returned to Head Office	3,000			27,400
Credit Sales less Returns	84,000	Cash Sales		1,04,000
Allowance to Customer off		Stock with Branch on 31-3-2025		
Selling Price (already adjusted		(at Invoice Price)		54,000
while invoicing)	2,000	Petty Cash Balance on 31-3-2025		100
Cash received from Debtors	90,000			

Ans. [Gross Profit ₹ 62,000; Net Profit ₹ 32,200; Apparent Profit ₹ 1,000].

16. Sehwag & Co., with headquarters at Chennai, maintains a branch at Kochi. Goods are invoiced to the Kochi branch at cost plus 25%. In respect of the Kochi branch, the following information pertaining to the year ended 31-3-2025 are made available to you :

	₹		₹
Goods sent to Branch at Invoice Price	6,25,000	Amounts Received from Branch Debtors	
	3,40,000		
Cash Sales effected by Branch	1,76,000	Cheques of Customers which	
Goods Returned by Customers to Branch	10,000	got Dishonoured	8,000
Bad Debts	5,000	Branch Expenses met in Cash	72,900
Discounts Allowed to Customers	2,000		

	As on 31-3-2024	*As on 31-3-2025*
	₹	₹
Stock at Branch (at Invoice Price)	1,25,000	1,75,000
Branch Debtors	40,000	95,000

Adopting the Stock and Debtors System, you are required to prepare the following Ledger Accounts, as appearing in the Books of Head Office : (*a*) Kochi Branch Debtors Account; (*b*) Kochi Branch Stock Account; (*c*) Kochi Branch Adjustment Account and (*d*) Kochi Profit & Loss Account.

Ans. [Gross Profit ₹ 1,13,750; Net Profit ₹ 30,100]

[**Hint :** Shortage of Stock ₹ 5,000]

17. Neo Ltd. with headquarters at Mumbai, maintains a branch at Goa. Goods are invoiced cost plus 25%. In respect of Goa branch, the following information pertaining to the year ended 31st March, 2025 are made available to you :

	₹		₹
Goods sent to Branch (at Invoice Price)	6,75,000	Amount received from Branch Debtors	3,25,000
Goods returned by Branch during the year (at Invoice Price)	24,000	Cheques of Customers which got Dishonoured	8,000
Cash Sales effected by Branch	1,85,000	Branch Expenses met in Cash	72,500
		Sales Return at Goa Branch	10,000
Discount allowed to Customers	2,500	Bad Debts	5,500

	On 31st March, 2025	*On 31st March, 2024*
Branch Debtors	1,05,000	50,000
Stock at Branch (at Invoice Price)	2,36,000	1,50,000

Adopting the Stock and debtors system, you are required to prepare the following Ledger Accounts, as appearing in the books of the Head Office : (*i*) Goa Stock Account; (*ii*) Goa Branch Debtors Account; (*iii*) Goa Branch Adjustment Account; (*iv*) Goa Branch Profit and Loss Account.

Ans. [Gross Profit ₹ 1,13,000, Net Profit ₹ 32,500]

18. ABC Ltd. has two branches at Delhi and at Mumbai. Goods are invoiced to Branches at cost plus 50%. All expenses of branch are paid by Head Office. Following information is available of the transactions of Delhi Branch for the year ended on 31st March, 2025.

Particulars	*Amt. (₹)*
Opening Stock at Cost to Branch	2,67,000
Opening Balance of Debtors	65,000
Goods sent to Branch (including goods invoiced at ₹ 15,000 to Branch on 31st March but not received by Branch before close of the financial year	7,83,000
Goods received from Mumbai Branch	6,000
Goods transferred to Mumbai branch	51,000
Goods returned by Delhi branch to HO	11,700
Goods returned by Credit Customers to Delhi Branch	5,700
Goods returned by credit customers directly to HO	1,200
Agreed allowances to customers off the selling price (already taken into account while invoicing)	1,000
Normal Loss due to wastage and deterioration of stock (at cost to Branch)	1,000
Loss in Transit (at invoice price)	6,600
Insurance Claim received by Branch (Cost of Loss less 8%)	
Cash Sales	32,000
Credit Sales	7,29,400
Branch Expenses (including Insurance charges ₹ 5000 and Branch Manager's Commission ₹ 12,000)	50,000
Bad Debts	1,000
Discount Allowed	500

The Branch Manager is entitled to a commission of 10% of profit of Branch after charging such commission.

Required: Prepare Branch Stock Account, Branch Adjustment Account and Branch Profit and Loss Account assuming the closing stock at Branch at its cost as per physical verification amounted to ₹ 2,10,000 and closing balance of Debtors is 70,000.

Ans. [Gross Profit ₹ 2,49,833; Net Profit ₹ 1,88,771].

Hint. [Cost of Shortage ₹ 2,333]

19. Red and Co. of Mumbai started a branch at Bengaluru on 1-4-2024 to which goods were sent at 20% above cost. The branch makes both cash sales and credit sales. Branch expenses are met from branch cash and balance money remitted to H.O. The branch does not maintain double entry books of account and necessary accounts relating to branch are maintained in H.O. Following further details are given for the year ending on 31-3-2025 :

	₹		₹
Cost of Goods sent to Branch	1,00,000	Closing Cash on hand at Branch on 31-3-2025	4,000
Goods received by Branch till 31-3-2025 at Invoice Price	1,08,000	Cash Remitted by H.O. to Branch during the year	6,000
Credit Sales for the year	1,16,000	Closing Stock in hand at Branch at Invoice Price	12,000
Closing Debtors on 31-3-2025	41,600	Expenses Incurred at Branch	24,000
Bad Debts Written Off during the year	400		
Cash Remitted to H.O.	86,000		

Draw up the necessary Ledger Accounts like Branch Debtors Account, Branch Stock Account, Goods sent to Branch Account, Branch Cash Account, Branch Expenses Account and Branch Adjustment A/c for ascertaining gross profit and Branch Profit and Loss A/c for ascertaining Branch Profit.

Ans. [Gross Profit ₹ 70,000; Net Profit ₹ 45,600]

20. A Head Office at Mumbai has a branch at Chennai in charge of a manager. The ratio of gross profit on turnover at the Branch was 25 per cent constant throughout the year.

The branch manager is entitled to a commission of 10 per cent of the profit earned by the Branch calculated before charging his commission, but subject to a deduction from such commission a sum equal to 50 per cent of any ascertained deficiency of branch stock. All goods were supplied to the Branch by Head Office.

From the following figures extracted from the branch books, calculate the commission due to the manager for the year ended 31st March, 2025 :

	₹		₹
Stock on 1-4-2024 at cost	31,210	Establishment Expenses	22,550
Goods received from Head Office at cost	1,08,700	Drawings by manager against commission	1,000
Sales	1,46,400	Stock on 31-3-2025 at selling price	39,880

Ans. [Net Profit ₹ 13,850; Commission due ₹ 285; Deficiency ₹ 200].

21. PQ Ltd., Kolkata, started a branch in Mumbai on 1st April, 2024 to which goods were sent at 20% above cost. The branch makes both credit and cash sales. Branch expenses are met from branch cash and balance money remitted to H.O. The branch does not maintain double entry books of account and necessary accounts relating to branch are maintained in H.O.

Following further details are given for year ended on 31st March, 2025 :

	₹		₹
Cost of goods sent to Branch	50,000	Cash remitted to H.O.	43,000
Goods received by Branch till 31st March, 2025 at invoice price	54,000	Cash in hand at Branch on 31st March, 2025	2,000
Credit sales for the year	48,000	Cash remitted by H.O. to Branch during the year	3,000
Debtors as on 31st March, 2025	20,800	Closing stock at Branch at invoice price	6,000
Bad Debts and Discount written off	200	Expenses incurred at Branch	12,000

Show the necessary Ledger A/cs in the books of the Head Office (Under Stock and Debtors System) and determine Profit and Loss of the Branch for the year ended on 31st March, 2025.

Ans. [Gross Profit ₹ 35,000; Net Profit ₹ 22,800; Cash received from Debtors ₹ 27,000 and from Sales ₹ 27,000].

22. A Head Office in Patna has two branches at Chennai and at Delhi. Goods are consigned to them at loaded figures of 10 per cent and 20 per cent on cost respectively. During the year, the invoices to the branches are ₹ 44,000 and ₹ 60,000 respectively.

Included in the item ₹ 44,000 are invoices for goods costing ₹ 12,000 invoiced to Chennai Branch at ₹ 13,200 which should have been invoiced to Delhi Branch. Sales are all for cash, being Chennai Branch ₹ 22,000 and Delhi Branch ₹ 50,400. It may be assumed that the closing stocks are correct.

Prepare (*i*) Branch Stock Account; (*iii*) Goods sent to Branches Account; and (*iii*) Branch Adjustment Account in the books of Head Office.

Ans. [Profit : Chennai ₹ 2,000; Delhi ₹ 8,400].

23. Chennai Ltd. invoices goods to its branch at cost plus $33\frac{1}{3}$%. From the following particulars prepare Branch Stock Account, Branch Stock Adjustment Account and Branch Profit & Loss Account as they would appear in the books of Head Office :

	₹
Stock at Commencement at Branch at invoice price	1,50,000
Stock at Close at Branch at invoice price	1,20,000
Goods sent to branch during the year at invoice price (including goods invoiced at ₹ 20,000 to branch on 31-3-2025 but not received by branch before close of the year)	10,00,000
Return of goods to Head Office (invoice price)	50,000
Cash Sales at Branch	9,00,000
Credit Sales at Branch	50,000
Invoice value of goods pilfered	10,000
Normal loss at Branch due to shortage and deterioration of stock (at invoice price)	15,000

Chennai Ltd. closes its books on 31st March, 2025.

Ans. [Gross Profit ₹ 2,37,500; Net Profit ₹ 2,30,000; Excess of Sale Price Over Invoice Price ₹ 15,000].

24. Omni Corporation Ltd. has two branches—one at Jaipur and another at Lucknow. Good are invoiced to branches at cost plus 50%. Branches remit all cash received to head office and all expenses are paid by the head office. From the following particulars, prepare the necessary accounts on the '*stock and debtors system*' to show the profit earned at Jaipur branch during the year ended 31st March, 2025 :

	₹		₹
Stock on 1st April, 2024	93,000	Goods returned by branch to head office	12,000
Debtors on 1st April, 2024	68,000	Goods transferred from Lucknow branch to Jaipur branch	15,000
Goods sent to branch at cost	3,40,000	Shortage of stock at the branch	4,500
Sales at Branch :		Discount allowed to customers	2,000
Cash	2,50,100	Cash expenses at branch	54,000
Credit	3,10,000		
Cash collected from debtors	3,04,000		

Ans. [Gross Profit ₹ 1,86,700 ; Net Profit ₹ 1,27,700].

25. Concept & Co., with its Head Office at Mumbai has a branch at Nagpur. Goods are invoiced to the Branch at cost plus $33\frac{1}{3}$%. Following information is given in respect of the branch for the year ended 31st March, 2025 :

	₹		₹
Goods sent to Branch (Invoice Price)	4,80,000	Discount allowed	1,000
Stock at Branch on 1-4-2024 (Invoice Price)	24,000	Bad debts	1,500
		Collection from Debtors	2,70,000

Cash Sales	1,80,000	Branch debtors cheques returned dishonoured	5,000
Return of goods by customers to be Branch	6,000	Stock at Branch on 31-3-2025 (Invoice price)	48,000
Branch expenses (paid in cash)	53,500		
Branch debtors balance on 1-4-2024	30,000	Branch debtors balance on 31-3-2025	36,500

Prepare, under the *Stock and Debtors System,* the following Ledger Accounts in the books of the Head Office : (*i*) Nagpur Branch Stock Account (*ii*) Nagpur Branch Debtors Account (*iii*) Nagpur Branch Adjustment Account.

Also compute shortage of stock at branch, if any.

Ans. [Gross Profit ₹ 1,13,500 ; Net Profit ₹ 56,000 ; Shortage of Stock at Branch ₹ 2,000].

26. Shyam Traders of Delhi, a firm of traders, has a branch at Hyderabad. In order to maintain strict control over stock, it invoices goods to the branch at the selling price including profit of 25% on selling price. From the following particulars, prepare Branch Stock Account, Branch Debtors Account, Branch Adjustment Account and Branch Profit & Loss Account :

	₹		₹
Branch Stock on 1st April, 2024 (*at invoice price*)	3,00,000	Cash Received from Debtors	8,00,000
		Bad debts written off	5,000
Branch Debtors on 1st April, 2024	2,28,000	Discount allowed to Branch Customers	6,000
Goods Invoiced to Branch at Invoice Price during the year 2024-25	13,40,000	Cash Expenses at the Branch	1,34,000
		Branch Stock on 31st March, 2025 (*at invoice price*)	2,68,000
Sales at branch during the year :			
Cash	6,20,000		
Credit	7,48,000		

Ans. [Gross Profit ₹ 3,42,000 ; Net Profit ₹ 1,94,000; Shortage of Stock at Branch ₹ 4,000].

27. Multi Chained Stores Ltd. Delhi has its branches at Lucknow and Chennai. It charges goods to its branches at cost plus 25%. Following information is available of the transactions of the Lucknow Branch for the year ended 31st March, 2025 :

			₹
Stock at Branch on 1-4-2024 at I.P.			30,000
Debtors on 1-4-2024			10,000
Transactions during the year :			
Goods sent to Lucknow Branch at I.P.			3,25,000
Goods returned to H.O. at I.P.			10,000
Good returned by Lucknow debtors direct to H.O.			5,000
Cash sales			1,09,000
Cash received from Lucknow debtors			1,70,000
Allowances to Lucknow customers off selling price (already adjusted while invoicing)			2,000
Normal Loss at I.P.			1,000
Goods Lost in fire at I.P.			5,000
Insurance Co. paid to H.O. for loss by fire at Lucknow		₹	3,000
Cash sent for Expenses :	Recurring	32,820	
	Non-recurring	1,000	33,820
Bad Debts at Branch			500
Goods transferred to Chennai Branch under H.O. advice			15,000
Goods returned by Debtors			500

	₹
Branch Debtors cheques dishonoured	2,000
Stock at Branch on 31-3-2025 at I.P.	48,500
Debtors on 31-3-2025	14,000

Prepare all accounts under Stock and Debtors System.

Ans. **[Gross Profit ₹ 63,300; Net Profit ₹ 28,980].**

Hint. Credit Sales ₹ 1,78,000; Apparent Profit ₹ 13,000.

28. Mumbai Traders Ltd. sends goods to its Chennai Branch at cost plus 25 per cent. Following particulars are available in respect of the Branch for the year ended 31st March, 2025 :

	₹		₹
Opening Stock at Branch at cost to Branch	80,000	Sales	12,19,000
Goods sent to Branch at invoice price	12,00,000	Expenses	60,000
Loss-in-transit at invoice price	15,000	Closing stock at Branch at cost to Branch	40,000
Pilferage at invoice price	6,000	Recovered from Insurance Company against loss-in-transit	10,000
Normal Loss at Invoice Price	3,000		

Show Ledger Accounts in the head office books for : (*a*) Branch Stock Account, (*b*) Goods sent to Branch Account, (*c*) Branch Adjustment Account, (*d*) Branch Profit and Loss Account.

Ans. **[Gross Profit ₹ 2,40,800; Net Profit ₹ 1,74,000].**

29. B.S. Ltd. operates a retail branch at Ranchi. All purchases are made by the Head Office at Kolkata. Goods for the branch being delivered to it direct and charged out at selling price, which is cost price plus 50 per cent. All cash received by the branch is remitted to Kolkata. Branch expenses are paid by the branch out of an impress account which is reimbursed by Kolkata every month.

The branch keeps a Sales Ledger and certain essential subsidiary books; otherwise all branch transactions are recorded in the books of the Kolkata office.

On April 1, 2024, Stock-in-Trade at the Branch, at selling price amounted to ₹ 48,660 and Debtors ₹ 6,440.

During the year ended 31st March, 2025, the following transactions took place at the branch :

	₹		₹
Goods received by the branch at selling price	1,21,800	Agreed allowances to customers off selling price (already taken into account while invoicing)	970
Cash Sales	64,150	Cash received from Debtors	42,600
Credit Sales	51,280	Debtors written off irrecoverable	650
Goods returned to Kolkata at selling price	1,560	Cash discount allowed	1,120
Expenses	17,290		

A consignment of goods despatched to the branch in March, 2025 at a selling price of ₹ 1,200 was not received by the branch until 6th April, 2025 and had not been included in its stock figure. On 31-3-2025, physical stock at the branch, at selling price amounted to ₹ 52,200.

You are required to write up Branch Stock Account, Branch Adjustment Account and Branch Profit and Loss Account (in the books of Kolkata) for the year ended 31st March, 2025.

Ans. **[G.P. ₹ 37,830; N.P. ₹ 18,570].**

30. A & Co. has two retail branches, X and Y, selling goods supplied to them by the company's central warehouse. All such supply of goods are charged at fixed selling price of cost plus 50 per cent. Sales are mainly for cash but branch managers are authorised to give limited credit in appropriate cases. Statement of accounts are sent by the Head Office to credit customers at monthly intervals with the request that they remit direct to Head Office where entire accounting is centralised.

On 31st March, 2025, summarised branch statements show the following particulars in respect of the transactions of the branch X :

	₹		₹
Stock at selling price on 1st April, 2024	2,67,000	Goods returned by customers to branch	5,700
Debtors on 1st April, 2024	14,000	Goods returned by credit customers to H.O.	1,200
Cash Sales	7,29,400	Goods transferred by branch to branch	45,000
Cash remitted to H.O. by credit customers	28,000	Goods sent to branch by H.O. (at selling price)	7,83,000
Goods returned by branch to H.O.	11,700	Bad Debts written off	1,500

The amount due by credit customers as on 31st March, 2025 was ₹ 9,600 and apart from goods (of the sales value of ₹ 6,600) lost in transit from H.O. to branch the actual stock on that date was in agreement with the book figures. A claim was made against the carrier in respect of lost stock and the sum of ₹ 5,000 was accepted in full settlement.

You are required to record whole of the foregoing in Ledger Accounts in the H.O. books.

Ans. **[Gross Profit ₹ 2,51,500; Net Profit ₹ 2,50,600].**

31. Mumbai Soap Mills Ltd. has two branches, at Kolkata and at Chennai. Goods are invoiced to branches at cost plus 50%. Branches remit all cash received to the Head Office and all expenses are met by the Head Office. From the following particulars prepare the necessary accounts on Stock and Debtors system, to show the profit earned at the branches during the year ending 31-3-2025.

	Kolkata	*Chennai*
	₹	₹
Stock on 1-4-2024 (invoice price)	9,300	15,600
Debtors on 1-4-2024	6,800	8,700
Goods invoiced to Branches (Cost Price)	34,000	36,000
Sales at Branches :		
Cash	25,010	35,000
Credit	31,000	30,100
Cash Collected from Debtors	30,400	29,800
Goods returned by Debtors	1,200	1,500
Good returned by Branch to Head office	1,500	—
Goods transferred from Chennai to Kolkata	2,100	2,100
Surplus in Stock	—	300
Shortage in Stock	450	—
Discount allowed to Customers	200	350
Expenses at Branches	5,400	6,700

Ans. **[Gross Profit : Kolkata ₹ 18,270; Chennai ₹ 21,200; Net Profit : Kolkata ₹ 12,370; Chennai ₹ 14,350].**

32. Gulshan Stores Ltd. with its head office in Kolkata invoiced goods to its branch at Patna at 20% less than the list price which is cost plus 100% with instructions that cash sales were to be made at the invoice price and credit sales at the catalogue price (*i.e.*, list price).

From the following particulars available from the branch, prepare Branch Stock Account, Branch Adjustment Account, Branch Profit and Loss Account and Branch Debtors Account for the year ending 31st December, 2024.

	₹		₹
Stock on 1-1-2024 (invoice price)	6,000	Cash from debtors	42,817
Debtors on 1-1-2024	5,000	Expenses at branch	8,683
Goods received from head office (invoice price)	66,000	Remittances to head office	60,000
		Debtors on 31-12-2024	12,183
Sales : Cash	23,000	Stock on 31-12-2024 (invoice price)	8,800
Credit	50,000		

(ICWA—Final)

Ans. **[Gross Profit ₹ 33,625; Net Profit ₹ 24,817]**

Hint : Stock Shortage ₹ 200, Apparent Profit ₹ 10,000.

33. Novelties Ltd. with its Head Office in Delhi, invoiced goods to its branch at Mumbai at 20% less than the catalogue price which is cost plus 50%, with instructions that cash sales were to be made at invoice price and credit sales at catalogue price less discount at 15% on prompt payment.
From the following particulars available from the Branch, prepare Branch Trading and Profit & Loss Account for the year ended 31st March, 2025 (showing adjustments) in the Head Office books so as to show the actual profit or loss on the Branch for the year :

	₹		₹
Stock on 1st April, 2024 (invoice price)	12,000	Discount allowed to Debtors	13,365
Debtors on 1st April, 2024	10,000	Expenses at the Branch	6,000
Goods received from Head Office (invoice price)	1,32,000	Remittance to Head Office	1,20,000
Sales (Cash)	46,000	Debtors on 31st March, 2025	11,000
Sales (Credit)	1,00,000	Cash in hand on 31st March, 2025	5,635
Cash realised from Debtors	85,635	Stock on 31st March, 2025 (invoice price)	15,000

It was further reported that a part of stock at the Branch was lost by fire (not covered by insurance) during the year whose value is to be ascertained; and a provision should be made for discount to be allowed to debtors as on 31st March, 2025 on the basis of the year's trend of prompt payment.

Ans. **[G.P. ₹ 41,000; Net Profit ₹ 17,798 ; Invoice Value of Stock Destroyed ₹ 3,000; Provision for Discount ₹ 1,337.]**

WHOLESALE AND RETAIL PROFIT AT BRANCH

34. Beta Ltd. having head office at Mumbai has a branch at Nagpur. The head office does wholesale trade only at cost plus 80%. The goods are sent to branch at the wholesale price *viz.,* cost plus 80%. The branch at Nagpur is wholly engaged in retail trade and the goods are sold at cost to H.O. plus 100%.
Following details are furnished for the year ended 31st March, 2025 :

	Head Office (₹)	*Branch* (₹)
Opening Stock (as on 1-4-2024)	2,25,000	—
Purchases	25,50,000	—
Goods sent to Branch (Cost to H.O. plus 80%)	9,54,000	—
Sales	27,81,000	9,50,000
Office Expenses	90,000	8,500
Selling Expenses	72,000	6,300
Staff Salary	65,000	12,000

You are required to prepare Trading and Profit and Loss Account of the Head Office and Branch for the year ended 31st March, 2025.

Ans.

	H.O. ₹	***Branch*** ₹
Gross Profit	**16,60,000**	**95,000**
Net Profit	**13,89,000**	**68,200**
Closing Stock	**7,00,000**	**99,000**
Stock Reserve ₹ 44,000		

35. A head office sends goods to branch and dealers at 20% less than the list price. Goods are sold to customer at cost plus 10%. From the following particulars, ascertain the Profit made at Head Office and Branch on the whole sale basis :

	Head Office	Branch
	₹	₹
Opening Stock at Cost (in case of branch at wholesale price)	10,000	8,000
Purchases	1,00,000	
Goods sent to Branch (at I.P.)	48,000	
Goods sold to Dealers	40,000	
Sales	85,000	40,000
Expenses	11,000	6,000

Ans. [G.P.—H.O. : ₹ 75,500 ; Branch : ₹ 8,000; N.P.—H.O. : ₹ 58,500; Branch : ₹ 2,000; Closing Stock—H.O. ₹ 12,500 ; Branch ₹ 24,000]

36. Rahul Ltd. operates a number of retail outlets to which goods are invoiced at wholesale price which is cost plus 25%. These outlets sell goods at the retail price which is wholesale price plus 20%. Following is the information regarding one of the outlets for the year ended 31st March, 2025 :

	₹		₹
Stock at the outlet 1-4-2024	30,000	Goods lost by fire	?
Goods invoiced to the outlet during the year	3,24,000	Expenses of the outlet for the year	20,000
		Stock at the outlet 31-3-2025	36,000
Gross profit made by the outlet	60,000		

You are required to prepare the following in the books of Rahul limited for the year ended 31-3-2025 : (*a*) Outlet Stock Account ; (*b*) Outlet Profit & Loss Account ; (*c*) Stock Reserve Account.

Ans. [Net Profit ₹ 22,000].

Hint : Retail Sale Price ₹ 3,60,000; Goods lost by fire ₹ 18,000.

INDEPENDENT BRANCHES

37. Give Journal Entries for the following transactions in the books of Delhi Head Office and Kanpur Branch Office :

(*i*) Goods sent by the head office on 28th March worth ₹ 150 to its Kanpur branch not received by the branch upto 31st March.

(*ii*) Goods sent by Mumbai branch to Kanpur branch for ₹ 300 are yet to be recorded.

(*iii*) Kanpur branch paid ₹ 3,000 for a machine purchased by the head office in Kanpur.

(*iv*) Provide depreciation at 10% on furniture (₹ 20,000) when Kanpur branch furniture account is maintained in the Head Office books.

(*v*) A remittance of ₹ 8,500 made by Kanpur Branch to the Head Office on 28th March was received by the latter on 4th April.

(*vi*) Mumbai branch paid ₹ 100 dividend to a local shareholder on behalf of the Head Office.

(*vii*) Kanpur Branch collected ₹ 2,000 from a Kanpur customer of the Head Office.

38. A Kolkata firm whose accounting year ends on 31st March, has two branches one at Agra and the other at Varanasi. The branches keep a complete set of books. On 31st March, 2025, the Agra and Varanasi Branch Accounts in the Kolkata books showed debit balances of ₹ 30,450 and ₹ 45,000 respectively before taking the following information into account :

(*a*) Goods valued ₹ 2,000 were transferred from Agra to Varanasi under instructions from Head Office.

(*b*) The Agra Branch collected ₹ 2,500 from an Agra customer of the Head Office.

(*c*) The Varanasi Branch paid ₹ 5,000 for certain goods purchased by the Head Office.

(*d*) ₹ 5,000 remitted by the Agra Branch to Kolkata on 29th March, 2025 received in Kolkata on 3rd April.

(*e*) The Varanasi Branch received on behalf of the Head Office ₹ 1,500 as dividend from a Varanasi Company.

(*f*) For the year 2024-25, the Agra Branch showed a net loss of ₹ 1,250 and the Varanasi Branch a net profit of ₹ 5,400.

Pass Journal entries to record these matters in the Head Office books, and write up the two Branch Accounts therein.

Ans. [Debit Balances : Agra ₹ 24,700 and Varanasi ₹ 48,900].

39. Pass necessary Journal entries in the books of an independent Branch of a Company, wherever required, to rectify or adjust the following :

(*i*) Income of ₹ 2,800 allocated to the Branch by Head Office but not recorded in the Branch books.

(*ii*) Provision for doubtful debts, whose accounts are kept by the Head Office, not provided earlier for ₹ 1,000.

(*iii*) Branch paid ₹ 3,000 as salary to a Head Office Manager, but the amount paid has been debited by the Branch to Salaries Account.

(*iv*) Branch incurred traveling expenses of ₹ 5,000 on behalf of other Branches, but not recorded in the books of Branch.

(*v*) A remittance of ₹ 1,50,000 sent by the Branch has not been received by Head Office on the date of reconciliation of Accounts.

(*vi*) Head Office allocates ₹ 75,000 to the Branch as Head Office expenses, which has not yet been recorded by the Branch.

(*vii*) Head Office collected ₹ 30,000 directly from a Branch Customer. The intimation of the fact has been received by the Branch only now.

(*viii*) Goods dispatched by the Head office amounting to ₹ 10,000, but not received by the Branch till date of reconciliation. The Goods have been received subsequently. **(*CA IPCE, May, 2014*)**

40. A Kolkata Head Office passes one entry at the end of each month to adjust the position arising out of inter-branch transactions during the month. From the following inter-branch transactions in April, 2024 make journal entries in the books of Kolkata Head Office.

(*a*) Delhi Branch

(*i*) Received goods from Nagpur Branch ₹ 9,000 and Ahmedabad Branch ₹ 6,000.

(*ii*) Sent goods to Ahmedabad Branch Rs. 15,000 and Nagpur Branch Rs. 12,000.

(*iii*) Received B/R from Ahmedabad Branch ₹ 9,000.

(*iv*) Sent acceptances to Nagpur Branch ₹ 6,000 and Ahmedabad Branch ₹ 3,000.

(*b*) Kanpur Branch [apart from (*a*) above]

(*i*) Received goods from Nagpur Branch ₹ 15,000 and Delhi Branch Rs. 6,000.

(*ii*) Cash sent to Nagpur Branch ₹ 3,000 and Delhi Branch ₹ 9,000.

(*c*) Nagpur Branch [apart from (*a*) and (*b*) above].

(*i*) Sent goods to Ahmedabad Branch ₹ 9,000.

(*ii*) Received B/R from Ahmedabad Branch ₹ 6,000.

(*iii*) Received cash from Ahmedabad Branch ₹ 5,000.

Ans. [Ahmedabad ₹ 1,000 Dr.; Kanpur ₹ 9,000 Dr. ; Delhi ₹ 9,000 Cr.; and Nagpur ₹ 1,000 Cr.].

41. Following balances are extracted from the books of the branch :

	₹		₹
Stock on 1-4-2024	39,000	Wages	8,000
Head Office (Credit)	42,000	Salaries	2,500
Sundry Debtors	15,000	Carriage & Freight	1,200
Purchases	34,500	Rent, Rates, etc.	1,200
Goods received from H.O.	42,500	Office Expenses	300
Returns to H.O.	2,000	Cash in Hand	350
Sales	96,000	Cash at Bank	1,450
Sundry Creditors	6,000	Stock on 31-3-2025	42,600

The Head Office sent goods worth ₹ 7,500 to the Branch on 30th March, 2025, but the Branch received the same on 7th April, 2025. The Branch remitted to Head Office ₹ 4,500 on 27th March, 2025, but the money was received by Head Office on 2nd April, 2025. The Branch Account in the Head Office books showed a debit balance of ₹ 54,000 on 31st March 2025. Branch Plant and Machinery Account appeared in the Head Office books at ₹ 24,000 on 31st March, 2025 which was to be depreciated by 5 per cent.

Make the necessary Journal Entries in the books of the Head Office and the Branch for reconciling their accounts. Give also the Journal Entries to incorporate the Branch Trial Balance in the Head Office books.

Ans. [G.P. ₹ 15,400; N.P. ₹ 10,200].

42. The head office of a business and its branch keep their own books and each prepares its own profit and loss account. Following are the balances appearing in the two sets of books as on 31st March, 2025 after the ascertainment of profit and after making all adjustments except those referred below :

	Head Office		*Branch*	
	Dr.	Cr.	Dr.	Cr.
	₹	₹	₹	₹
Capital		1,00,000		
Fixed Assets	26,000	—	16,000	—
Stock	34,000	—	10,700	—
Debtors & Creditors	7,800	1,200	4,800	1,900
Cash	10,700	—	1,400	—
Profit & Loss	—	7,160	—	3,000
Branch Account	29,860	—	—	28,000
	1,08,360	1,08,360	32,900	32,900

Set out the Balance Sheet of the business as on 31-3-2025 and the Journal entries necessary to record the following adjustments in the books of H.O. :

(*a*) On 29th March, the branch had sent a cheque for ₹ 1,200 to the Head Office, not received by H.O. till next month.

(*b*) It was agreed that the branch should be charged with ₹ 250 for the services rendered by the H.O. to the branch.

(*c*) Depreciation on branch assets, the accounts of which are maintained by the H.O. not provided for ₹ 325.

(*d*) The profit of the branch is to be transferred to the H.O.

Ans. [Branch Profit ₹ 2,425; B/S Total ₹ 1,12,935].

43. Puskar Enterprise has its head office in Ranchi and a branch in Imphal. Following Trial Balance has been extracted from the books of account as at 31st March, 2025 :

	Head Office		*Branch*	
	Dr.	*Cr.*	*Dr.*	*Cr.*
	₹	₹	₹	₹
Capital		16,50,000		
Debtors	3,00,000		1,80,000	
Creditors		1,50,000		
Purchases	27,42,000			
Sales		25,50,000		13,11,000
Goods sent to branch at invoice price		11,40,000	11,25,000	

Fixed Assets (Net)	10,50,000		2,00,000	
Stock (1 April, 2024)	24,000		60,000	
Stock Adjustment (unrealised profit)		12,000		
Head Office/Branch Current A/c	5,25,000			3,60,000
Administrative and Selling Expenses	8,41,500		74,500	
Cash and Bank	46,500		39,000	
Provision for Bad Debts		27,000		7,500
	55,29,000	55,29,000	16,78,500	16,78,500

Other relevant information :

(1) All goods are purchased by the head office. Goods are sent to branch at cost plus 25 per cent

(2) Stocks at 31 March, 2025 were valued at :

H.O. ₹ 36,000

Branch ₹ 45,000 (invoice price)

(3) Depreciation is to be provided on fixed assets at 10% on book value.

(4) Bad debt provision is to be maintained at 5% on debtors as at the end of the year.

(5) Cash in transit from branch to head office at 31 March, 2025 was ₹ 1,50,000.

(6) Goods in transit from head office to branch at 31st March, 2025 at invoice price was ₹ 15,000.

Prepare, in columnar form, Branch and Head Office Trading and Profit & Loss Accounts for the year ended 31st March, 2025 and a Combined Balance Sheet for Pushkar Enterprise as on the date.

Ans.

	H.O.	***Branch***
	₹	₹
Gross Profit	**9,60,000**	**1,71,000**
Net Profit	**25,500**	**75,000**
Balance Sheet Total ₹ 19,00,500		

44. Messrs. Dhyanchand & Co., Kanpur, have a branch in Delhi. The Delhi branch deals not only in the goods from the head office but also buys some auxiliary goods and deals in them. They, however, do not prepare any profit & loss account but close all the accounts to the head office at the end of the year and open them afresh on the basis of advice from their head office. The fixed assets accounts are also maintained at the head office. The goods from the head office are invoiced at selling prices to give a profit of 20% on the sale price. The goods sent from the branch to the head office are at cost. From the following, prepare Branch Account, Branch Trading and Profit & Loss Account and Branch Assets Account in the head office books :

TRIAL BALANCE OF DELHI BRANCH AS ON 31-3-2025

	Dr.	*Cr.*
	₹	₹
Head office opening balance, 1-4-2024	15,000	
Goods from head office	50,000	
Purchases	20,000	
Sales		1,00,000
Opening stock (H.O. goods at invoice price)	4,000	
Opening stock of other goods	500	
Goods to head office		3,000
Salaries	7,000	
Rent	3,000	
Office expenditure	2,000	
Cash in hand	500	

Cash at bank	4,000	
Head office current account		15,000
Sundry debtors	15,000	
Sundry creditors		3,000
	1,21,000	1,21,000

The branch balances on 1 April, 2024 were as under :

Furniture ₹ 5,000; Sundry debtors ₹ 9,500; Cash ₹ 1,000; Creditors ₹ 30,000; Stock (H.O. goods at invoice price) ₹ 4,000; Other goods ₹ 500. The closing stock at branch of the head office goods at invoice price is ₹ 3,000 and that of purchased goods at cost is ₹ 1,000. Depreciation is to be provided at 10% on branch assets.

Ans. [Gross Profit ₹ 42,700; Net Profit ₹ 30,200; Balance in Delhi Branch Account ₹ 20,500; Remittance to H.O. ₹ 32,000].

45. Following is the Trial Balance of Meerut Branch as on 31st March, 2025 :

	Dr. ₹	*Cr.* ₹
Delhi Head Office	3,240	
Stock, 1st April, 2024	6,000	
Purchases	97,800	
Goods Received from Head Office	19,000	
Sales		1,38,000
Goods Supplied to Head Office		6,000
Salaries	4,500	
Debtors	3,700	
Creditors		1,850
Rent	1,960	
Sundry Office Expenses	1,470	
Cash at Bank	1,780	
Furniture	6,000	
Depreciation on Furniture	400	
	1,45,850	1,45,850

Stock at branch on 31st March, 2025 was valued at ₹ 7,700.

Meerut Branch Account in the head office books on 31st March, 2025 stood at ₹ 460 (debit balance). On 28th March, 2025, the head office forwarded goods of the value of ₹ 3,700 to the branch where they were received on 3rd April, 2025.

(*i*) Prepare Trading and Profit & Loss Account of Meerut Branch for the year ended 31st March, 2025 and its Balance Sheet as on that date.

(*ii*) Pass Journal Entries in the books of the head office to incorporate the above-mentioned trial balance, and

(*iii*) Show Meerut Branch Account as it would be closed in head office's ledger.

Ans. [(*i*) Gross Profit ₹ 28,900; Net Profit ₹ 20,570; B/S Total ₹ 19,180. (*ii*) Total of Meerut Branch ₹ 1,54,010].

46. B and C are partners sharing profits and losses in the proportions of 2/3 and 1/3 respectively. B managed the Mumbai Office and C managed the Kanpur Office. On 31st March, 2025, the Trial Balance stood as follows :

Mumbai Office		*Kanpur Office*	
Stock, 1st April	1,08,000	Stock, 1st April	78,000
Kanpur Office (Dr.)	45,000	Mumbai Office (Cr.)	36,000
B's Capital	2,04,000	C's Capital	48,000
Purchases	1,92,000	Book Debts	30,000
Sales	3,12,000	Purchases	1,02,000
Plant at Mumbai	72,000	Sales	1,44,000
Plant at Kanpur	48,000	Creditors	12,000
Book Debts	45,000	Wages	24,000
Creditors	42,000	Carriage and Cartage	2,400
Wages	36,000	Cash in hand	3,600
Carriage and Cartage	5,400	Stock on 31st March	85,200
Cash in hand	6,600		
Stock on 31st March	1,00,800		

Interest on Capitals is to be allowed at 5% and Depreciation @ 5% is to be charged on Plant.

Pass the necessary Journal Entries in the books of both offices (except those relating to Trading and Profit and Loss Account) and prepare separately the Final Accounts and the Balance Sheets of the Mumbai and Kanpur offices.

Ans. [Mumbai—G.P. ₹ 71,400; N.P. ₹ 57,600; B/S Total ₹ 3,06,600; Kanpur—G.P. ₹ 22,800; N.P. ₹ 18,000; B/S Total ₹ 1,27,800].

47. A Mumbai firm has a branch at Kanpur where a complete set of double entry books is kept. All purchases are made in Mumbai and stock required by the Kanpur branch is invoiced to it by the Head Office at selling price less 20 per cent, the branch manager is entitled to a commission equal to one-half of the net profit earned by the branch on the basis of such invoice price.

Following are the balances extracted from the Mumbai and Kanpur books on 31st March, 2025 :

	Mumbai		*Kanpur*	
	₹	₹	₹	₹
Capital		20,000		
Sundry Creditors		931		27
Goodwill	1,000			
Cash	1,793		49	
Sundry Debtors	3,973		1,438	
Stock at Mumbai on 1-4-2024 at cost	11,482			
Stock at Kanpur on 1-4-2024 as invoiced (cost being ₹ 1,431)			1,792	
Purchases	28,724			
Goods invoiced to Branch		6,305	7,715	
Salaries and Wages	2,280		846	
Sundry Expenses	1,399		369	
Kanpur Branch Account	1,176			
Head Office Account				2,847
Sales		25,331		9,575
Furniture	740		240	
	52,567	52,567	12,449	12,449

Depreciate Furniture at 5 per cent. The stock in hand on 31st March, 2025 at Mumbai was valued at ₹ 15,427 and at Kanpur at ₹ 1,542 at cost and ₹ 1,847 at invoice price.

A remittance of ₹ 100 sent by the Branch was in transit on 31st March, 2025.

Prepare the firm's Profit and Loss Account for the year ended 31st March, 2025 (showing the profit made in each town separately) and the Balance Sheet as on that date.

Ans. [Profit—Mumbai ₹ 3,141; Kanpur ₹ 1,810; B/S Total ₹ 26,253].

48. M/s Triplex, Mumbai has a Branch at Poona to which goods are invoiced at cost plus 25 per cent. The Branch also purchases goods locally.

Trial Balance of the Head Office for the year ended 31st March, 2025 was as follows :

	Dr. ₹	*Cr.* ₹
Capital		2,50,000
Sundry Fixed Assets	1,50,000	
Stock	60,000	
Sundry Debtors	58,000	
Sundry Creditors		43,000
Cash at Bank	17,500	
Goods sent to Branch (at invoice price)		1,50,000
Goods returned from Branch (invoice price)	5,000	
Poona Branch Account	2,96,000	
Purchases	10,50,000	
Sales		12,50,000
Sundry Expenses	56,500	
	16,93,000	16,93,000

Closing Stock : Head Office ₹ 50,000.
Branch ₹ 1,00,000 at cost (exclusive of stock of ₹ 10,000 at Invoice Value in transit from H.O. to branch).

Following are the balances in the books of the Poona Branch for the year ended 31st March, 2025 :

	₹
Purchases (other than goods received from the H.O.)	5,80,000
Sales	6,50,000
Sundry Debtors	35,000
Sundry Creditors	21,000
Sundry Fixed Assets	1,00,000
General Expenses	41,000
Cash at Bank (Not taking into account the cash in transit of ₹ 10,000 from H.O. to branch)	2,500
Opening Stocks (all stocks from Purchases outside)	53,500

Provide depreciation at 10 per cent on Fixed Assets.

From the foregoing information, prepare a Consolidated Trading and Profit and Loss Account (showing separately the figures of Profit/Loss for the Head Office and Branch) and Balance Sheet.

Ans. [Gross Profit—H.O. : ₹ 3,06,000; Branch : ₹ 8,500; Net profit—H.O. : ₹ 2,34,500; Net Loss : Branch—₹ 42,500; B/S Total ₹ 5,06,000].

49. The branches of a multiple shop company are supplied from the Head Office with goods at cost. The branches pay wages and minor items of petty cash, but otherwise all expenses are paid by the Head Office.

From the weekly returns of the branches, the following summaries are prepared :

CASH ACCOUNT

(Branches), *Year 2024-25*

		₹			₹
2024 April 1	To Balance b/d	1,200	2025 March 31	By Cash Purchases	4,360
2025 March 31	To Cash Sales	4,13,680		Wages	1,12,500
	To Cash on Ledger A/cs	12,350		Expenses	2,320
				Amount banked	3,06,550
				By Balance c/d	1,500
		4,27,230			4,27,230
	To Balance b/d	1,500			

DEBTORS' ACCOUNT

(Branches), *Year 2024-25*

		₹			₹
2024 April 1	To Balance b/d	890	2025 March 31	By Cash	12,350
2025 March 31	To Sales	14,350		By Allowances	480
				By Balance c/d	2,410
		15,240			15,240
	To Balance b/d	2,410			

Branches Current Account (in Head Office books) appears in summarized form as follows :

		₹	₹			₹
2024 April 1	To Balance			2024 April 1	By Balance :	
	Cash	1,200		2025	Rent & Rates	4,340
	Debtors	890		March 31	" Bank	3,06,550
	Stocks	16,380		March 31	" Balance c/d	60
	Fitting	10,000				
			28,470			
2025 March 31	To Goods		2,26,500			
	To Cash					
	Rent & Rates		20,200			
	Salaries		32,300			
	Sundry Expenses		2,480			
	Fittings		1,000			
			3,10,950			3,10,950
	To Balance b/d		60			

On 31st March, 2025 stock at the branches was ₹ 20,400; liabilities were for rent and rates ₹ 6,320; and for salaries, ₹ 1,000.

Prepare statements of Branches Trading Account for the year ended 31st March, 2025 and Branches Balance Sheet as on that date (depreciation written off 10 per cent on fittings) and complete the Current Account in the Head Office books.

Ans. [G.P. ₹ 88,690; N.P. ₹ 26,830; B/S Total ₹ 34,210].

50. XY Company of Kolkata has a Branch at Delhi. Goods sold at Delhi are supplied from Kolkata but no charge is made in the books as between the Branch and the Head Office. On 31st March, 2025 the Branch Balance Sheet after closing the books was as follows :

Liabilities	₹	*Assets*	₹
Creditors' Balances	40,000	Debtors' Balances	2,00,000
Head office	1,68,000	Building Extension Account closed by Head Office A/c	—
		Cash at Bank	8,000
	2,08,000		2,08,000

For the six months ending on September 30, 2025, the following transactions took place at Branch :

	₹		₹
Sales	2,40,000	Cash collections from Debtors	1,60,000
Purchases	48,000	Discounts allowed	8,000
Wages paid	20,000	Discounts earned	1,200
Salaries (inclusive of advance of ₹ 2,000)	4,000	Cash paid to Creditors	60,000
		Cash sent to Bank	80,000
General Expenses	1,600	Building Account (further payment to contractors)	4,000
Fire Insurance Premium paid for one year	3,200	Cash in Hand	1,600
Manager's Salary for 9 months	7,200	Cash at Bank	28,000

Set out the Head Office Account in the Delhi books as on 30th September, 2025 to show the entries after the books are closed and also the Branch Balance Sheet on the same date assuming to be made upon the same lines as on 31st March, 2025.

Ans. [H.O. A/c Balance ₹ 2,80,800; B/S Total ₹ 3,07,600].

51. A trader commenced business on 1st April, 2024 establishing a head office and one branch. Purchases were made exclusively by the head office where the goods were processed before sales. There was no loss or wastage in processing. Only processed goods received from head office were handled by the branch and these were charged to the branch, at processed cost plus 10%.

All sales, whether by H.O. or the branch, were at uniform gross profit of 25% on the cost after processing. From the following information prepare Profit and Loss Account for the year and Balance Sheet as on 31st March, 2025.

Capital ₹ 2,20,000; Drawings ₹ 25,000; Purchases ₹ 19,93,350; Cost of processing ₹ 34,650; Sales—H.O. ₹ 14,20,000. Sales—Branch ₹ 6,40,000; Goods sent to Branch ₹ 6,51,200; Selling and General Expenses ₹ 2,41,000; Debtors ₹ 3,22,000; Creditors ₹ 5,85,750; Branch Current A/c ₹ 2,05,550; Balance at Bank ₹ 1,96,000.

Following information is relevant : (*i*) Stock taking at Branch disclosed a shortage of ₹ 5,000 (at selling price). (*ii*) Goods charged by head office to branch during the year include ₹ 11,000 not received by branch during the year. A remittance of ₹ 43,750 from Branch to head Office was not received before April, 2025. The necessary adjustments in respect of these items are to be made in head office books, (*iii*) Cost of unprocessed goods at head office on 31st March, 2025 was ₹ 1,80,000.

Ans. [Net Profit ₹ 1,67,000; B/S Total ₹ 9,47,750].

52. Following Trial Balance is extracted from the books of the Nagpur Branch of XYZ Ltd., as on 31st March, 2025 :

	₹		₹
Debit Balances :		Branch Expenses	9,000
Stock Opening at Invoice Price	25,000	Current Account with H. Office	58,500

Branch Debtors	10,000	*Credit Balances* :	
Cash in hand	500	Branch Creditors	3,000
Goods received from Head Office	80,000	Branch Sales	1,80,000

As on that date, closing stocks with branch at invoice price were valued at ₹ 30,000. There was an amount of ₹ 18,500 remitted by the branch on 31st March, which had not been received by the Head Office on that date. The head office had sent goods, costing ₹ 20,000 to the Branch on 29th March. These had not been received by the Branch till the closing date.

The Head Office enters in its books all goods sent to the branch at cost. The branch enters these in its books at invoice price but sells them at an even high one. At the end of each year the difference is adjusted by being debited to the Branch and credited to the Profit and Loss Account in the books of the Head Office. The proportionate difference between cost and invoice price, was the same at all relevant times.

The credit balance as on 31st March, 2024 of the Branch Account in the Head Office books, was ₹60,000 before making any of the above adjustments (though the above mentioned despatch of goods of ₹ 20,000 on 29th March, had of course, been duly debited to the Branch Account).

Prepare Branch Profit and Loss Account and Head Office Profit and Loss Account (relevant portion only) for the year ended 31st March, 2025.

Ans. [Balance in Branch A/c ₹ 58,500; Branch Net Profit ₹ 96,000; H.O. Net Profit ₹ 1,33,500].

53. Anil and Sunil are partners of a business having Head Office in Delhi and branch at Kolkata. Anil looks after the Delhi Office and Sunil looks after the Kolkata branch. Anil is entitled to 40% of the profits made at Delhi while Sunil is entitled to 30% of the profits at Kolkata. The balance profits/losses are shared equally.

Following trial balances as on 31st March, 2025 are furnished to you :

	Delhi		*Kolkata*	
	Dr.	Cr.	Dr.	Cr.
	₹	₹	₹	₹
Opening Stock at cost	30,000	—	40,000	—
Purchases & Returns	1,80,000	10,000	2,75,000	15,000
Goods sent to :				
Kolkata	—	50,000	—	—
Delhi	—	—	—	70,000
Goods received from :				
Kolkata	65,000	—	—	—
Delhi	—	—	48,000	—
Sales & Returns	15,000	3,15,000	20,000	3,70,000
Expenses	28,000	—	39,000	—
Customers Accounts	64,000	4,000	71,000	3,000
Suppliers Accounts	2,000	32,000	1,000	51,000
Bank Account	70,000	—	—	6,000
Fixed assets-opening (WDV)	50,000	—	80,000	—
Kolkata Branch Account	—	5,000	—	—
Delhi Head Office Account	—	—	17,000	—
Capital & Drawing Accounts :				
Anil	30,000	83,000	4,000	35,000
Sunil	5,000	40,000	25,000	70,000
	5,39,000	5,39,000	6,20,000	6,20,000

You are informed that :

(*a*) On 30th March, 2025 Delhi head office remitted ₹ 5,000 by bank draft to Kolkata Branch. The envelope was received by the branch on 2nd April, 2025.

(*b*) Stock at cost on 31st March, 2025 was worth :
(*i*) ₹ 46,000 at Delhi; and (*ii*) ₹ 54,000 at Kolkata.

(*c*) Depreciation is to be provided at 10%.

(*d*) 10% of the cash expenses relating to the Head Office are to be treated as overheads incurred on behalf of the branch.

You are asked by the partners to prepare :

(1) Trading and Profit & Loss Account for the year ended 31st March, 2025 for Delhi Head Office and Kolkata Branch in columnar form :

(2) Consolidated Balance Sheet of the firm as on 31st March, 2025; and

(3) Branch and Head Office Accounts in respective books.

Ans. [G.P. : Delhi ₹ 1,31,000, Kolkata ₹ 1,26,000; Net Profit : Delhi ₹ 1,00,800, Kolkata ₹ 76,200; (2) B/S Total, ₹ 4,37,000; (3) Cr. Balance in Kolkata Branch A/c (in H.O. books) ₹ 9,200, Dr. Balance in Delhi H.O. A/c (in Kolkata books) ₹ 9,200].

54. XY & Co., commenced business on 1-4-2024 with head Office at Calicut and a Branch at Tiruchur.

All goods were purchased by Head Office and normally packed immediately but on 31-3-2025, goods costing ₹ 5,000 remained unpacked.

Only packed goods were sent to the Branch charged at selling price less 10%.

Following information is furnished to you as on 31st March, 2025 from the Head Office and Branch Office books :

	Head Office	*Branch*
	₹	₹
Capital account	40,000	—
Drawings by Proprietor	10,000	—
Purchases	4,00,000	—
Packing materials bought	6,000	—
Sales	3,20,000	1,00,000
Despatch of goods to Branch	1,13,400	—
Selling expenses	16,000	800
Clerks' salary, wages, etc.	20,000	3,000
Sundry Debtors	28,000	4,200
Sundry Creditors	26,600	5,000
Current Accounts :		
Head Office (Credit balance)		12,000
Branch Office (Debit balance)	19,000	—
Bank Balances	1,000	1,000
Goods Received from Head Office	—	1,08,000

You are further informed that :

(*a*) Sales by Head Office were at a uniform gross profit, after charging packing materials, of 20% on the fixed selling price;

(*b*) Sales at branch were at fixed selling price;

(*c*) Goods invoiced and despatched by head Office to Branch in March, 2025 for ₹ 5,400 were received in the Branch only on 10th April, 2025;

(*d*) Stock of packing materials on hand as on 31st March, 2025 was valued at ₹1,000;

(*e*) Remittance of ₹ 1,600 from the Branch to the Head office was in transit on 31-3-2025;

(f) ₹ 2,000 worth of stock at selling price was damaged at the Branch. For valuing stock, this was reduced by ₹ 1,090 below the invoice cost of the Branch. It was decided that the Head Office and the Branch would share equaliy the loss occasioned by this and also the deficit in stock, ascertained on actual stock taking at the Branch of goods at selling price of ₹ 500.

Prepare Profit and Loss Accounts of the Tiruchur and Calicut Offices and also a Balance Sheet as at 31-3-2025 of the business.

Ans. [Gross Profit : H.O. ₹ 76,600; Branch ₹ 10,000; Net Profit : H.O. ₹ 37,480, Branch ₹ 5,430; B/S Total ₹ 1,04,510].

Hint. Closing Stock : Head Office ₹ 43,200, Branch ₹ 16,460.

55. A trader commenced business on 1st April, 2024 at a head office and one branch. Purchases were made exclusively by the head office where the goods were processed before sale. There was no loss or wastage in processing.

Only processed goods received from head office were handled by the branch and these were charged to the branch at processed cost plus 10 per cent.

All sales whether by head office or the branch, were at uniform gross profit of 25 per cent on the processed cost.

Following Trial Balances as on 31st March, 2025 were extracted from the books :

	Head Office		*Branch*	
	Dr.	*Cr.*	*Dr.*	*Cr.*
	₹	₹	₹	₹
Capital		2,20,000		
Drawings	25,000			
Purchases	19,93,350			
Cost of Processing	34,650			
Sales		14,20,000		6,40,000
Goods sent to Branch/received by Branch		6,51,200	6,40,200	
Selling and General Expenses	2,24,000		27,000	
Debtors/Creditors	2,30,000	5,83,350	92,000	2,400
Branch/Head Office Current Accounts	2,05,550			1,50,800
Balance at Bank	1,62,000		34,000	
	28,74,550	28,74,550	7,93,200	7,93,200

Following information is relevant :

(i) Goods charged by head office to branch in March 2025, at ₹ 11,000 were not received by the branch until April 1, 2025. A remittance of ₹ 43,750 from the branch to head office, in March 2025 was not received at head office until April 2025. The necessary adjustments, in respect of these items, are to be made in head office books.

(ii) Stock-taking at branch disclosed shortage of ₹ 5,000 (at selling price).

(iii) Cost of unprocessed goods at head office as on 31st March, 2025 was ₹ 1,80,000.

You are required to prepare, in columnar form, Trading and Profit and Loss Account and Balance Sheet of the head office, branch and the business as a whole.

Ans. [

	Branch	***H.O.***	***Total***
	₹	₹	₹
Gross Profit	**76,800**	**3,43,200**	**4,20,000**
Net Profit (Before unrealised profit)	**45,800**	**1,18,800**	**1,64,600**

Balance Sheet Total ₹ 9,37,750]

56. A limited company has its Head Office in Delhi and a Branch in Mumbai where a separate set of books is used. Following are the trial balances extracted on 31st March, 2025 :

Head Office

TRIAL BALANCE

	₹	₹
Share Capital		
(Authorised :		
10,000 Equity shares of ₹ 100 each) :		
Issued; 8,000 Equity shares		8,00,000
Profit & Loss Account 1-4-2024		25,310
Interim Dividend paid—December, 2024	30,000	
General Reserve		1,00,000
Fixed Assets	5,30,000	
Stock	2,22,470	
Debtors and Creditors	50,500	21,900
Profit for 2024-25		82,200
Cash Balance	62,730	
Branch Current Account	1,33,710	
	10,29,410	10,29,410

BRANCH TRIAL BALANCE

	₹	₹
Fixed Assets	95,000	
Profit for 2024-25		31,700
Stock	50,460	
Debtors and Creditors	19,100	10,400
Cash Balance	6,550	
Head Office Current Account		1,29,010
	1,71,110	1,71,110

The difference between the balances of Current Accounts in the two sets of books is accounted for as follows :

(*a*) Cash remitted by the Branch on 31st March, 2025, but received by the Head office on 1st April, 2025—₹ 3,000.

(*b*) Stock stolen in transit from Head Office and charged to the Branch by the Head Office, but not credited to Head Office in the Branch books as the Branch Manager declined to admit any liability (not covered by insurance)—₹ 1,700.

Give Branch Current Account in the Head Office books after incorporating Branch Trial Balance through Journal. Also prepare the Company's Balance Sheet as on 31st March, 2025. ***(C.A. Inter)***

Ans. [B/S Total ₹ 10,39,810; Profit and Loss A/c Balance (of H.O.) to be shown in B/S ₹ 1,07,510].

Foreign Branches

57. On 31st December, 2024 the following balances appeared in the books of Kolkata Branch of an English firm having its head office in New York :

	Amount in ₹	*Amount in ₹*
Stock on 1st January, 2024	93,600	
Purchases and Sales	6,25,000	9,37,500
Debtors and Creditors	3,06,000	2,04,000

Bills Receivable and Payable	81,600	71,400
Salaries and Wages	40,000	—
Rent, Rates sand Taxes	42,500	—
Furniture	36,400	—
Bank Account	2,27,460	—
New York Account	—	2,39,660
	14,52,560	14,52,560

Stock on 31st December, 2024 was ₹ 2,55,000.

Branch Account in New York books showed a debit balance of $ 5,360 on 31st December, 2024 and Furniture appeared i the Head Office books at $ 700.

The rate of exchange on 31st December 2023 was ₹ 52 and on 31t December, 2024 was ₹ 51. The average rate for the year was ₹ 50.

Prepare in the Head Office books the Profit and Loss Account and the Balance Sheet of the branch.

(CA PCE November, 2012 Modified)

Ans. [Gross Profit $ 9,450, Net Profit $ 7,000; Balance Sheet Total $ 17,760]

Hint : Exchange transaction loss $ 800.

58. Carlin & Co. has head office at New York (U.S.A.) and branch at Mumbai (India). Mumbai branch furnishes you with its trial balance as on 31st March, 2025 and the additional information given thereafter :

	Dr.	*Cr.*
		Rupees in thousands
Stock on 1st April, 2024	300	—
Purchases and Sales	800	1,200
Sundry Debtors and Creditors	400	300
Bills of Exchange	120	240
Wages and Salaries	560	—
Rent, Rates and Taxes	360	—
Sundry Charges	160	—
Computers	240	—
Bank balance	420	—
New York office a/c	—	1,620
	3,360	3,360

Additional information :

(*a*) Computers were acquired from a remittance of US $ 6,000 received from New York head office and paid to the suppliers. Depreciate computers at 60% for the year.

(*b*) Unsold stock of Mumbai branch was worth ₹ 4,20,000, on 31st March, 2025.

(*c*) The rates of exchange may be taken as follows :

(*i*) on 1-4-2024 @ ₹ 40 per US $. (*ii*) on 31-3-2025 @ ₹ 42 per US $. (*iii*) average exchange rate for the year @ ₹ 41 per US $. (*iv*) conversion in $ shall be made up to two decimal accuracy.

You are asked to prepare in US dollars the Revenue Statement for the year ended 31st March, 2025 and the Balance Sheet as on that date of Mumbai branch as would appear in the books of New York head office of Carlin & Co. You are informed that Mumbai Branch Account showed a debit balance of US $ 39609.18 on 31-3-2025 in New York books and there were no items pending reconciliation.

Ans. [Gross Loss US $ 1402.45; Net Loss US $ 17685.38; Balance Sheet Total US $ 34780.95]

59. An Indian company has a branch at Washington. Its Trial Balance as at 30th September, 2024 is as follows :

	Dr. *US $*	*Cr.* *US $*
Plant and Machinery	1,20,000	—
Furniture and Fixtures	8,000	—
Stock, Oct. 1, 2023	56,000	—
Purchases	2,40,000	—
Sales	—	4,16,000
Goods from Indian Co. (H.O.)	80,000	—
Wages	2,000	—
Carriage inward	1,000	—
Salaries	6,000	—
Rent, Rates and Taxes	2,000	—
Insurance	1,000	—
Trade Expenses	1,000	—
Head Office A/c	—	1,14,000
Trade Debtors	24,000	—
Trade Creditors	—	17,000
Cash at Bank	5,000	—
Cash in hand	1,000	—
	5,47,000	5,47,000

Following further information is given : 1. Wages outstanding—$ 1,000. 2. Depreciate Plant and Machinery and Furniture and Fixtures @ 10 per cent p.a. on W.D.V. method. 3. The Head Office sent goods to Branch for ₹ 39,40,000. 4. The Head Office shows an amount of ₹ 43,00,000 due from Branch. 5. Stock on 30th September, 2024—$ 52,000. 6. There were no in transit items either at the start or at the end of the year. 7. On September 1, 2022, when the fixed assets were purchased, the rate of exchange was ₹ 38 to one $. On October 1, 2023, the rate was ₹ 39 to one $. On September 30, 2024, the rate was ₹ 41 to one $. Average rate during the year was ₹ 40 to one $.

You are asked to prepare :

(*a*) Trial Balance incorporating adjustments given under 1 to 4 above, converting dollars into rupees;

(*b*) Trading and Profit and Loss Account for the year ended 30th September, 2024 and Balance Sheet as on that date depicting the profitability and net position of the branch as would appear in India for the purpose of incorporating in the main Balance Sheet.

Ans. **[(*a*) Exchange Gain ₹ 7,00,000 ; Total of the Converted Trial Balance ₹ 2,23,78,000 ; (*b*) Net Profit ₹ 27,01,600 ; B/S Total ₹ 77,39,600]**

60. S & M Ltd., Mumbai, have a branch in Sydney, Australia. At the end of 31st March, 2025, the following ledger balances have been extracted from the books of the Mumbai Office and the Sydney office :

	Mumbai (₹ thousands)		*Sydney (Austr. dollars thousands)*	
	Debit	*Credit*	*Debit*	*Credit*
Share Capital	—	2,000	—	—
Reserves & Surplus	—	1,000	—	—
Land	500	—	—	—
Buildings (Cost)	1,000	—	—	—

Buildings Dep./Reserve	—	200	—	—
Plant & Machinery (Cost)	2,500	—	200	—
Plant & Machinery Dep. Reserve	—	600	—	130
Debtors/Creditors	280	200	60	30
Stock (1-4-2024)	100	—	20	—
Branch Stock Reserve	—	4	—	—
Cash & Bank Balances	10	—	10	—
Purchases/Sales	240	520	20	123
Goods sent to Branch	—	100	5	—
Managing Director's Salary	30	—	—	—
Wages & Salaries	75	—	45	—
Rent	—	—	12	—
Office Expenses	25	—	18	—
Commission Receipts	—	256	—	100
Branch/H.O. Current A/c	120	—	—	7
	4,880	4,880	390	390

Following information is also available

(i) Stock as at 31-3-2025 : Mumbai ₹ 1,50,000 ; Sydney A$ 3,125

(ii) Head Office always sent goods to the Branch at cost plus 25%.

(iii) Provision is to be made for doubtful debts at 5%.

(iv) Depreciation is to be provided on buildings at 10% and on plant and machinery at 20% on written down value.

(v) The Managing Director is entitled to 2% commission on net profits.

(vi) Income tax is to be provided at 47.5%.

You are required :

(a) To convert the Branch Trial Balance into rupees; using the following rates of exchange : Opening rate A$ = ₹ 20 ; Closing rate A$ = ₹ 24 ; Average rate A$ = ₹ 22 ; For Fixed Assets A$ = ₹ 18.

(b) To prepare the Trading and Profit and Loss for the year ended 31st March, 2025 showing to the extent possible H.O. results and Branch results separately. (Balance Sheet not required). Assume this as IFO. ***(C.A. Inter)***

Ans. [Gross Profit (Total) ₹ 2,271 ; Net Profit ₹ 988 ; Exchange Loss ₹ 216 ; Depreciation : H.O. ₹ 460, Branch ₹ 252 ; M.D. Commission ₹ 41 (all figures in ₹ '000)]

61. The Washington Branch of XYZ Limited, Mumbai sent the following trial balance as on 31st December, 2024 :

	$	*$*
Head Office A/c	—	22,800
Sales	—	84,000
Debtors and Creditors	4,800	3,400
Machinery	24,000	—
Cash at Bank	1,200	—
Stock, 1 January, 2024	11,200	—
Goods from H.O.	64,000	—
Expenses	5,000	—
	1,10,200	1,10,200

In the books of head office, Branch A/c stood as follows :

WASHINGTON BRANCH ACCOUNT

	₹		₹
To Branch b/d	8,10,000	By Cash	28,76,000
To Goods sent to Branch	29,26,000	By Balance c/d	8,60,000
	37,36,000		37,36,000

Goods are sent to the branch at cost plus 10% and the branch sells goods at invoice price plus 25%. Machinery was acquired on 31st January, 2020, when $ 1.00 = ₹ 40.

Rates of exchange were : 1st January, 2024 $ 1.00 = ₹ 46 ; 31st December, 2024 $ 1.00 = ₹ 48 ; Average $ 1.00 = ₹ 47.

Machinery is depreciated @ 10% and the branch manager is entitled to a commission of 5% on the profits of the branch.

You are required to : (*i*) Prepare Branch Trading & Profit & Loss A/c in dollars. (*ii*) Convert the Trial Balance of branch into Indian currency and prepare Branch Trading & Profit and Loss A/c and Branch A/c in the books of head office.

Ans. [(*i*) Gross Profit $ 16,800; Net Profit $ 8,930; Total of Trial Balance ₹ 49,71,200; Gross Profit ₹ 8,90,800; Net Profit ₹ 4,90,240]

[**Hint :** Manager's Commission ₹ 22,560; Closing Stock ₹ 3,84,000]

CHAPTER 26

Departmental Accounts

When a business sells different types of goods or carries on several activities under one roof, it is generally split up into a number of departments. This is generally done to have smooth and efficient running of a business. A department is generally a physical part of the rest of the business. It is not separated geographically from the other departments, though treated a separate profit centre. When a business is divided into several departments, internal information about operating results of each department is required. This enables the management to take decisions relating to pricing, closure etc. after taking into consideration the different rates of growth, profitability and degree of risk of different departments.

Objectives of Departmental Accounts

When all the divisions of a business are located under one roof and it is desired to ascertain the profit or loss of each department or class of goods separately, then departmental accounts are prepared. The main objects of preparing such accounts are :

(*i*) To have comparison of the results of a particular department with previous year and also with the other departments of the same concern ;

(*ii*) To know the **comparative results** of different departments in the same year;

(*iii*) To assess the **position of stock** in each department;

(*iv*) To identify **areas of weakness** for cost control and improvement of efficiency;

(*v*) To help the proprietor in formulating policy to expand the business on proper lines so as to optimise the profits of the concern ;

(*vi*) To allow departmental managers' commission on the basis of the profits of their departments ; and

(*vii*) To generate information which may be helpful for planning, control, evaluation of performance of each department and for taking various managerial decisions.

Advantages of Departmental Accounts

Following are the main advantages of departmental accounts :

1. Performance Evaluation. The trading results of each department may help to evaluate the performance of each department. The sales of that department which gives maximum profit may be pushed up by special efforts. The profitability of each department may help the management for taking decision whether to drop a department or add a new one. The overall profits of the organisation can be increased by having friendly rivalries among different departments. The departmental managers and staff can be suitably rewarded on the basis of the departmental results.

2. Growth Potential. The growth potentials of a department can be evaluated by having comparison with the other departments.

3. **Proper Allocation of Expenses.** Expenses that relate to particular department are estimated on actual basis. Therefore, costs and profits of each department is estimated more accurately. It helps to have comparison of various expenses of each department with the previous period or with other departments of the same concern.

4. **Justification of Capital Outlay.** It helps the management to determine the justification of proper use of capital invested in each department. The users of accounting information like the shareholders, investors, creditors etc. can be provided more detailed information.

5. **Measurement of Efficiency.** It helps to know the efficiency of each department by calculating stock turnover ratio of each department to reveal the fast or slow movement of various items of stock.

6. **Planning and Control.** The information provided by departmental accounts may be helpful to management for future intelligent planning and control.

Methods of Departmental Accounts

The accounting system which is adopted for a departmental organisation depends upon the need to identify the different expenses and revenues of each department so that profit of each may be ascertained accurately. It must be designed in such a manner so that it may provide maximum information and is simple to understand and operate.

Following are the two methods of keeping Departmental Accounts :

(*i*) Where separate set of books are maintained for each department, and

(*ii*) Where accounts of all departments are maintained together in columnar books.

(i) Where separate set of books are maintained for each department

This method of accounting is followed in very large organisations or where the maintenance of separate books for each department is compulsory as per some law of the land. For example, general insurance companies in India are required to have separate books of accounts for each type of business, *i.e.,* Fire, Marine, Accident, etc. Under this method, each department is treated as a separate unit and accounts are kept independently. Trading results of each department are combined at the end of the year to get trading results of the organisation as a whole. This method is costly in operation and rarely used. This is generally employed in large businesses such as large general stores, insurance companies, etc. such departments are also known as independent departments.

(ii) Where accounts of all departments are maintained together in Columnar Books

Under this method the entire book keeping records are maintained by a central accounts department. This method is generally used in small concerns. A department generally does not maintain a full double entry book keeping system but records are kept in analytical or columnar books relating to purchases, sales, stock, returns inwards, return outwards, and direct expenses such departments are also known as dependent departments.

Departments in a particular concern may be classified according to functions, *e.g.,* purchasing, selling, finance, production, subsidiary services (*e.g.,* transport, packing, repairs, etc.). In order to ascertain the gross profit earned by different departments, departmental trading account is prepared in columnar form. There is no difficulty in ascertaining the figures of opening stock, closing stock, purchases (net), sales (net) and direct expenses if columnar form of books are maintained.

Departmental Expenses

Expenses of a business can be broadly divided into following two categories :

1. **Direct Expenses.** Expenses relating to a particular department are called direct expenses. They are charged to respective department. For example wages, staff salaries, packing, material etc.

2. Indirect Expenses. Expenses relating to more than one department are called indirect expenses. They are further divided into—

(*a*) Expenses which can be allocated. (*b*) Expenses which cannot be allocated.

These are discussed as under :

Allocation of Departmental Expenses

1. There are certain expenses which can be specially incurred for a particular department : for example, salary paid to salesman in sales department, may be charged directly to the sales department.

2. There are certain expenses which can be precisely charged to specific departments as these departments are benefited by these expenses such as lighting will be charged to the departments according to separate meters or on the basis of number of **light** points.

Apportionment of Departmental Expenses

Problems arise only in indirect expenses which are common for the concern as a whole and may be relating to sales, distribution, administration, finance and till these are distributed among the departments on some suitable basis, the net profits of different departments cannot be ascertained. Such expenses which cannot be directly related to a particular department or cannot have precise allocation, may be divided among the different departments as follows :

(*i*) **Selling Expenses.** These expenses include discount allowed, bad debts, selling commission, carriage on sales and should be divided among the different departments on the basis of sales. **It must be noted carefully that sales for this purpose also include transfers to other departments.**

(*ii*) **Building Expenses**. Rent and rates, insurance on building, repairs, etc. are expenses which are relating to building or premises and should be distributed among the different departments according to the space occupied by each department. If any department is enjoying any special benefit, then charge for these expenses must be adjusted according to the special benefit enjoyed by a particular department. **Departments having front location must bear more charges as compared to departments in rear part of the building.**

(*iii*) **Heating and Lighting**. If there are no separate meters, these may be apportioned among the different departments on the basis of points, lamps used, area or inversely to the number of windows.

(*iv*) **Power.** It should be apportioned on the basis of probable usage as determined by numbers and types of machines adjusted where necessary according to running hours in absence of separate meters for each department.

(*v*) **Advertising**. It should be apportioned on the basis of advertising space used by the different departments or on the basis of advertisement for the benefit of all departments must be apportioned equally among the departments.

(*vi*) **Insurance Premium.** It must be seen whether the insurance premium has been paid for stock, premises or loss of profit or workmen's compensation and should be apportioned on the basis of stock carried, proportion of premises occupied, profits earned in the preceding years and wages respectively but if there exists any abnormal feature relating to any department, that may be considered while apportioning such expenses. For example, if a department is dealing in oil or its employee's job is more risky as compared to other departments, then some more amount must be charged to such departments.

(*vii*) **Depreciation.** It should be allocated among the different departments on the basis of assets employed in each department.

(*viii*) **Labour Welfare Expenses**. These should be apportioned among the different departments on the basis of number of employees working in each department.

Following table (in summary form) will help to know the proper basis for apportionment of some important expenses among various departments.

Expenses	*Basis*
1. Sales Expenses as travelling salesman's salary and commission, selling expenses, after sales service, discount allowed, bad debts, freight outwards, provision for discount on debtors, sales manager's salary and other benefits etc.	Sales of each department
2. All expenses relating to building as rent, rates, taxes, air conditioning expenses, heating, insurance of building etc.	Area or value of floor space.
3. Lighting and Heating (*e.g.* energy expenses)	Consumption of energy each department.
4. Insurance on Stock	Average stock carried
5. Insurance on Plant & Machinery	Value of Plant of Machinery
6. Group Insurance Premium	Direct wages
7. Power	H.P. or H.P. × Hours worked
8. Depreciation, Renewals & Repairs	Value of assets in each department otherwise on time basis.
9. Canteen Expenses and Labour Welfare Expenses	No. of employees
10. Works Manager's Salary	Time spent in each department
11. Carriage Inward	Purchases of each department
12. Interest on Loan	Utilisation of loan amount in each department (if can be identified), otherwise in combined P & L A/c
13. Profit & Loss on Sale of Investment	Value of investments sold in each department (if value can be identified), otherwise in combined P & L A/c.
14. Wages/Salaries	Time devoted to each department.

4. There are certain expenses which cannot be allocated on some equitable basis such as debenture interest, share transfer office expenses, general manager's salary etc. should not be apportioned. Profits of all departments should be brought down in Combined Income Account and such expenses should be debited and non-departmental profits credited to this account without making any effort for its apportionment among different departments.

Distinction Between Departmental Accounts and Branch Accounts

Important distinctions between Departmental Accounts and Branch Accounts are given below :

Basis of Differences	*Departmental Accounts*	*Branch Accounts*
1. Location	Departments are always in Inland	It is either Inland or Foreign
2. Establishment of Departments	All departments of a Business remain generally under one roof.	Branch of a concern is established at different place in the same town or at different town.
3. Motive	Departments are made to increase the efficiency of the Business.	Branch is opened to increase the Sale.
4. Maintenance of Accounts	All accounts are maintained at one place and Departmental Trading and Profit and Loss Account is prepared accordingly.	In case of branch, all branch accounts are kept at Head Office except cash, customers and stock registers are maintained at branch. But in case of

		independent branch all accounts are kept at branch and a branch prepares its own Trading and Profit & Loss Account.
5. Allocation of Common Expenses	Departments are not geographically separated from each other, so problem of allocation of common expenses among different departments arises.	As branches are geographically separated from each other so the problem of allocation of common expenses among different branches does not arise.
6. Adjustments and Reconciliation of Accounts	The question of adjustments and reconciliation of accounts does not arise in departmental accounts.	In case of independent branch some adjustments and reconciliation of head office and the branch accounts are required to be done at the end of the year.
7. Problem of foreign currency	The problem of conversion of foreign currency into home currency does not arise.	The problem of conversion of foreign branch figures may arise at the time of finalisation of accounts of head office.
8. Growth	Departments are confined to local business and can grow vertically within the same roof.	Branches cater to a wider market and can expand and grow geographically.
9. Operations of Organisation	Departments are confined to a single place unless similar organisations are opened elsewhere.	Branches can be started anywhere in the world. So there can be local and foreign branches.

ILLUSTRATION 1. Following balances for the year ended 31st March, 2025 were extracted from the books of Shri Bikram Singh :

	₹		₹
Stock on 1-4-2024		Salaries	12,600
Radios	45,000	Publicity Expenses	8,900
Watches	21,000	Rent, Rates and Taxes	3,200
Sales :		Commission	10,600
Radios	2,94,000	Miscellaneous Expenses	5,000
Watches	1,46,000	Interest Received	400
Purchases :		Provision for Bad and Doubtful Debts	800
Radios	2,25,000		
Watches	1,15,000		

Prepare Departmental Trading and Profit and Loss Account for the year ended 31st March, 2025 after taking into account the following :

(*i*) Stock as on 31st March, 2025 was :

Radios ₹ 30,000 ; Watches ₹ 24,000

(*ii*) An amount of ₹ 1,200 out of Sundry Debtors of ₹ 16,800 has to be written off as bad and the provision for doubtful debts has to be increased thereafter to 10 per cent of the debts outstanding.

(*iii*) Following expenses are outstanding a on 31st March, 2025 :

Publicity ₹ 1,300 ; Salaries ₹ 1,200 ; Commission ₹ 1,700.

(*iv*) Provide 10 per cent depreciation on Furniture and Fixtures of ₹ 12,400.

(*v*) Revenue items to be allocated in the ratio of 2 : 1 as between Radios and Watches.

Ignore fractions of a Rupee in calculations.

SOLUTION

DEPARTMENTAL PROFIT AND LOSS ACCOUNT

for the year ending 31st March, 2025

	Radios	Watches	Total		Radios	Watches	Total
	₹	₹	₹		₹	₹	₹
To Opening Stock	45,000	21,000	66,000	By Sales	2,94,000	1,46,000	4,40,000
To Purchases	2,25,000	1,15,000	3,40,000	By Closing Stock	30,000	24,000	54,000
To Gross Profit c/d	54,000	34,000	88,000				
	3,24,000	1,70,000	4,94,000		3,24,000	1,70,000	4,94,000
To Salaries	9,200	4,600	13,800	By Gross Profit b/d	54,000	34,000	88,000
To Publicity	6,800	3,400	10,200	By Interest (2 : 1)	267	133	400
To Rent, Rates & Taxes	2,133	1,067	3,200				
To Commission	8,200	4,100	12,300				
To Miscellaneous Expenses	3,333	1,667	5,000				
To Depreciation on Furniture	827	413	1,240				
To Bad Debts	800	400	1,200				
To Provision for Bad & Doubtful Debts (₹ 1,560 – ₹ 800)	507	253	760				
To Net Profit	22,467	18,233	40,700				
	54,267	34,133	88,400		54,267	34,133	88,400

Inter-department Transfers

Sometimes goods or employment of staff or performance of services are transferred from one department to another department. As each department is treated as a separate profit centre, so it is necessary to have separate records for such inter-departmental transfers. Generally a weekly or monthly Departmental Transfer Analysis Sheet is prepared to record all inter-departmental transfers. The proforma of this sheet may be as under :

DEPARTMENTAL TRANSFER ANALYSIS SHEET

		Supplying Departments			*Receiving Departments*		
		Dept. A	*Dept. B*	*Dept. C*	*Dept. A*	*Dept. B*	*Dept. C*
2025		₹					
April	5	4,000	—	—	—	4,000	—
"	10	—	5,000	—	5,000	—	—
"	25	—	—	3,000	—	3,000	—
"	30	2,000	—	—	—	—	2,000
Total		6,000	5,000	3,000	5,000	7,000	2,000

At the end of the week/month the following entry is passed for transfer :

Receiving Department A/c Dr. (Transfer Price)

To Supplying Department A/c

Transfer price can be (1) cost based or (2) market price based. Sometimes dual pricing is also used. These are discussed below :

ILLUSTRATION 2. Deepa Ltd. had 3 departments D1, D2, D3. Informations relating to the *departments* are as follows :

	Departments		
	D1 (₹)	*D2 (₹)*	*D3 (₹)*
Opening Stock	30,000	40,000	60,000
Direct Materials Consumed	80,000	1,20,000	—
Wages	50,000	1,00,000	—
Closing Stock	40,000	1,40,000	80,000
Sales	—	—	3,40,000

Stocks of each departments are valued at cost of the department concerned. Stocks of D1 are transferred to D2 at a margin of 50% above departmental cost. Stocks of D2 are transferred to D3 department at a margin of 10% above departmental cost.

Other relevant expenses were :

Salaries ₹ 20,000; Printing and Stationery ₹ 10,000; Rent ₹ 60,000; Interest paid ₹ 40,000; and Depreciation ₹ 30,000.

Allocate expenses in the ratio of departmental gross profits. Opening figures of reserves for unrealised profits on departmental stocks were :

D2—₹ 10,000 and D3—₹ 20,000.

Prepare Departmental Trading and Profit & Loss Account.

SOLUTION (For Departmental Trading and Profit & Loss Account please see next page)

Working Notes :

(1) Cost of Transfer :

$$D1-(30{,}000 + 80{,}000 + 50{,}000 - 40{,}000)\frac{150}{100} = ₹\ 1{,}80{,}000$$

$$D2-(40{,}000 + 1{,}20{,}000 + 1{,}00{,}000 + 1{,}80{,}000 - 1{,}40{,}000)\frac{110}{100} = ₹\ 3{,}30{,}000$$

(2) Calculation of Unrealised Profit on Stock :

$$\text{Closing Stock of D2 includes cost of D1} = ₹\ 1{,}40{,}000 \times \frac{₹\ 1{,}80{,}000}{4{,}00{,}000} = ₹\ 63{,}000$$

$$\text{Unrealised Profit} = ₹\ 63{,}000\ \frac{50}{150} = ₹\ 21{,}000$$

Closing Stock (wholly transferred from D2) ₹ 80,000

$$\text{Profit}\left(\frac{10}{110} \times 80{,}000\right) = ₹\ 7{,}273$$

Cost as per D2 (₹ 80,000 – ₹ 7,273) = ₹ 72,727

$$\text{Proportionate transfer from A} = ₹\ 72{,}727 \times \frac{₹\ 1{,}80{,}000}{4{,}00{,}000} = ₹\ 32{,}727$$

$$\text{Unrealised Profit} = ₹\ 32{,}727 \times \frac{50}{150} = ₹\ 10{,}909$$

Total Unrealised Profit of D3 = ₹ 7,273 + ₹ 10,909 = ₹ 18,182

SOLUTION (*Illustration 2*)

DEPARTMENTAL TRADING AND PROFIT & LOSS ACCOUNT

Particulars	*D1*	*D2*	*D3*	*Total (₹)*	*Particulars*	*D1*	*D2*	*D3*	*Total (₹)*
To Opening Stock	30,000	40,000	60,000	1,30,000	By Sales	—	—	3,40,000	3,40,000
To Direct Material	80,000	1,20,000	—	2,00,000	By Transfer	1,80,000	3,30,000	—	5,10,000
To Wages	50,000	1,00,000	—	1,50,000	By Closing Stock	40,000	1,40,000	80,000	2,60,000
To Transfer	—	1,80,000	3,30,000	5,10,000	Stock				
To Gross Profit c/d	60,000	30,000	30,000	1,20,000					
	2,20,000	4,70,000	4,20,000	11,10,000		2,20,000	4,70,000	4,20,000	11,10,000
To Salaries	10,000	5,000	5,000	20,000	By Gross Profit b/d	60,000	30,000	30,000	1,20,000
To Printing &					By Loss c/d	20,000	10,000	10,000	40,000
Stationery	5,000	2,500	2,500	10,000					
To Rent	30,000	15,000	15,000	60,000					
To Interest	20,000	10,000	10,000	40,000					
To Depreciation	15,000	7,500	7,500	30,000					
	80,000	40,000	40,000	1,60,000		80,000	40,000	40,000	1,60,000
To Loss b/d				40,000	By Stock Reserve b/d :				
To Stock Reserve					D2				10,000
D2				21,000	D3				20,000
D3				18,182	By Net Loss				49,182
				79,182					79,182

ILLUSTRATION 3. Department R sells goods to Department S at a profit of 25% on cost and Department T at 10% profit on cost. Department S sells goods to R and T at a profit of 15% and 20% on sales respectively. Department T charges 20% and 25% profit on cost to Department R and S respectively.

Department manages are entitled to 10% commission on net profit subject to unrealized profit on departmental sales being eliminated. Departmental profits after charging manager's commission, but before adjustment of unrealized profit, are as under :

Department R ₹ 54,000 ; Department S ₹ 40,500 ; Department T ₹ 27,000.

Stocks lying at different departments at the end of the year are as under :

	Deptt. R ₹	*Deptt. S* ₹	*Deptt. T* ₹
Transfer from Department R	—	22,500	16,500
Transfer from Department S	21,000	—	18,000
Transfer from Department T	9,000	7,500	—

Find out the correct departmental profits after charging manager's commission.

SOLUTION

STATEMENT SHOWING CORRECT DEPARTMENTAL PROFITS

	Departments		
	R	*S*	*T*
	₹	₹	₹
Profit	54,000	40,500	27,000
Add : Managerial Commission (1/9)	6,000	4,500	3,000
	60,000	45,000	30,000
Less : Unrealised Profit on Stock (Refer W.N.)	(6,000)	(6,750)	(3,000)
	54,000	38,250	27,000
Less : Managers' Commission @ 10%	(5,400)	(3,825)	(2,700)
	48,600	34,425	24,300

Working Note (1) :

CALCULATION OF UNREALISED PROFIT

	Department R (₹)	*Department S* (₹)	*Department T* (₹)	*Total* (₹)
Transfer by :				
R Department to	—	₹22,500 × $\frac{25}{125}$ = ₹4,500	16,500 × $\frac{10}{110}$ = ₹1,500	6,000
S Department to	₹21,000 × $\frac{15}{100}$ = ₹3,150	—	₹18,000 × $\frac{20}{100}$ = ₹3,600	6,750
T Department to	₹9,000 × $\frac{20}{120}$ = ₹1,500	₹7,500 × $\frac{25}{125}$ = ₹1,500	—	3,000

Cost Based Transfer Price

Under this method of pricing the prices may be based on actual cost or total cost or standard cost or marginal cost. Standard cost is preferred to actual cost as the inefficiency of one department is not allowed to pass to another department. When goods are transferred at full cost, the fixed cost of supplying department becomes the variable cost of the receiving department.

Market Based Transfer Price

Sometimes goods or services are transferred from one department to another department at selling price and there are also unsold goods at the end of the period. A department cannot earn anything by selling the goods to another department. That is why this method does not give any advantage to either the selling or buying department, compared with trading with outsiders. So unrealised profit in the unsold goods must be debited to the department who supplied the goods to another department in the form of stock reserve. Such reserves are to be made both for opening and closing stocks by passing following entries :

(*i*) *For closing stock*

General Profit & Loss A/c

To Provision for Unrealised Profit on Stock or Stock Reserve A/c

(*ii*) *At the beginning of the next year*

Provision for Unrealised Profit on Stock or Stock Reserve A/c Dr.

To General Profit & Loss A/c

Dual Pricing

In order to motivate both the departments the buying and selling departments may be debited and credited respectively with two different prices. For example, the buying department may be debited with cost price and the selling department with the market price.

ILLUSTRATION 4. Green & Co. has two Departments P and Q. Department P sells goods to Department Q at normal selling prices. From the following particulars prepare Departmental Trading and Profit and Loss Account for the year ended 31-3-2025 and also ascertain the Net Profit to be transferred to Balance Sheet :

Particulars	*Department P* ₹	*Department Q* ₹
Opening Stock	1,00,000	NIL
Purchases	23,00,000	2,00,000
Goods from Department P	—	7,00,000
Wages	1,00,000	1,60,000
Travelling Expenses	10,000	1,40,000
Closing Stock at cost to the Department	5,00,000	1,80,000
Sales	23,00,000	15,00,000
Printing and Stationery	20,000	16,000

Following expenses incurred for both the departments were not apportioned between the Departments :

(*a*) Salaries ₹ 2,70,000 ; (*b*) Advertisement expenses ₹ 90,000 ; (*c*) General expenses ₹ 8,00,000 ; (*d*) Depreciation @ 25% on the machinery value of ₹ 48,000, Advertisement expenses are to be apportioned in the turnover ratio. Salaries in 2 : 1 ratio and Depreciation in 1 : 3 ratio between the Departments P and Q. General expenses are to be apportioned in 3 : 1 ratio.

SOLUTION

Green & Co.

DEPARTMENTAL TRADING AND PROFIT & LOSS ACCOUNT

for the year ended 31st March, 2025

	Deptt. P ₹	Deptt. Q ₹		Deptt. P ₹	Deptt Q ₹
To Opening Stock	1,00,000	—	By Sales	23,00,000	15,00,000
To Purchases	23,00,000	2,00,000	By Transfer to Deptt. Q	7,00,000	
To Transfer from Deptt. P	—	7,00,000	By Closing Stock	5,00,000	1,80,000
To Wages	1,00,000	1,60,000			

	P	Q		P	Q
To Gross Profit c/d	10,00,000	6,20,000			
	35,00,000	16,80,000		35,00,000	16,80,000
To Salaries (2 : 1)	1,80,000	90,000	By Gross Profit b/d	10,00,000	6,20,000
To Travelling Expenses	10,000	1,40,000			
To Printing & Stationery	20,000	16,000			
To Advertisement Expenses (23 : 15) (1)	54,474	35,526			
To General Expenses (3 : 1)	6,00,000	2,00,000			
To Depreciation on Machinery (1 : 3)	3,000	9,000			
To General P & L A/c (Profit)	1,32,526	1,29,474			
	10,00,000	6,20,000		10,00,000	6,20,000

GENERAL PROFIT AND LOSS ACCOUNT

for the Year ended 31-3-2025

	₹		₹	₹
To Provision for Unrealised Profit on Stock of Deptt. Q (2)	46,667	By Departmental Trading & P/L A/c		
		Deptt. P	1,32,526	
To Net Profit transferred to B/S.	2,15,333	Deptt. Q	1,29,474	2,62,000
	2,62,000			2,62,000

Working Notes :

(1) ***Apportionment of advertisement expenses***

These are apportioned on the basis of outside sales made by two departments as no advertising effort is required for inter departmental transfers.

(2) ***Calculation of Unrealised Profit on Stock of Deptt. Q.***

Gross Profit % on Sales of Deptt P

$$\frac{₹\ 10,00,000}{₹\ 30,00,000} \times 100 = 33\frac{1}{3}\%$$

Proportion of stock transferred by P included in closing stock of Q

$$\frac{₹\ 7,00,000}{₹\ 9,00,000} \times ₹\ 1,80,000 = ₹\ 1,40,000$$

∴ Provision for unrealised profit is :

$$= 33\frac{1}{3}\% \text{ of } ₹\ 1,40,000 = ₹\ \mathbf{46,667.}$$

ILLUSTRATION 5. M/s Bright and Co. had four departments A, B, C and D. Each department being managed by a departmental manager whose commission was 10% of the respective departmental profit, subject to a minimum of ₹ 6,000 in each case. Inter departmental transfers took place at a loaded price as follows :

From Department		A to Department	B	10% above cost	
"	"	A to "	D	20%	" "
"	"	C to "	D	20%	" "
"	"	C to "	B	20%	" "

For the year ended 31st March, 2025 the firm had already prepared and closed the departmental Trading and Profit & Loss Account. Subsequently it was discovered that the closing stocks of departments had included interdepartmentally transferred goods at loaded price of cost price. From the following information prepare a statement recomputing the departmental profit or loss :

	Deptt. A	Deptt. B	Deptt. C	Deptt. D
	₹	₹	₹	₹
Final Profit/Loss	38,000 (Loss)	50,400 (Profit)	72,000 (Profit)	1,08,000 (Profit)
Interdepartmental transfers included at loaded price in the departmental Stock		(₹ 22,000 from Deptt. A and ₹ 48,000 from Deptt. C)	—	(₹ 3,600 from Deptt. C and ₹ 1,200 from Deptt. A)

SOLUTION

STATEMENT SHOWING RECOMPUTATION OF DEPARTMENTAL PROFIT & LOSS

Departments	A	B	C	D
	₹	₹	₹	₹
Final Profit/Loss (already computed)	– 38,000	50,400	72,000	1,08,000
Add : Departmental manager commission @ 10% of Deptt. profit subject to a minimum of ₹ 6,000 (1)	+ 6,000	6,000	8,000	12,000
Profit before Deptt. Manager's Commission	–32,000	56,400	80,000	1,20,000
Less : Profit earned through transfer of goods at loaded price remaining in stock at transfer price (2)	– 2,200	—	– 8,600	—
Corrected departmental profit (before manager's commission)	– 34,200	56,400	71,400	1,20,000
Less : Manager's Commission @ 10% of profit subject to a minimum of ₹ 6,000	– 6,000	6,000	7,140	12,000
Departmental profit after manager's commission	– 40,200	50,400	64,260	1,08,000

Working Note :

(1) ***Calculation of Manager's Commission***

If Department profit is ₹ 100 then commission is ₹ 10 and final profit is ₹ 90. On final profit of ₹ 90, commission is ₹ 10 *i.e.,* commission is 1/9 of final profit.

Deptt.	Profit/Loss	Commission
	₹	
A	– 38,000	6,000
B	50,400	6,000 (*i.e.* ₹ 50,400 × 1/9 = ₹ 5,600) less than ₹ 6,000.
C	72,000	8,000 (*i.e.* ₹ 72,000 × 1/9 = ₹ 8,000)
D	1,08,000	12,000 (*i.e.* ₹ 10,800 × 1/9 = ₹ 12,000)

(2) ***Calculation of unrealised profit on stock transfer*** ₹

Deptt A : ₹ 22,000 to Deptt. B @ 110% ; profit thereon ₹ 22,000 × $\frac{10}{110}$ = 2,000

₹ 1,200 to Deptt. D @ 120% ; Profit thereon ₹ 1,200 × $\frac{20}{120}$ = 200

2,200

Deptt. C :	₹ 48,000 to Deptt. B @ 120%; profit thereon ₹ 48,000 × $\frac{20}{120}$ =	8,000
	₹ 3,600 to Deptt. D @ 120% ; profit thereon ₹ 3,600 × $\frac{20}{120}$ =	600
		8,600

ILLUSTRATION 6. The firm, M/s K Creations has two Departments, Dyed fabric and Readymade garments. Readymade garments are made by the firm itself. Both dyed fabric and readymade garments have independent market. Some of readymade garment department's requirement is supplied by Dyed Fabric Department at its usual Selling Price.

From the following figures, prepare departmental Trading and Profit & Loss Account for the year ended 31st March, 2025

Particulars	*Dyed Fabric Department*	*Readymade garments department*
Opening Stock as on April 1, 2024	5,40,000	15,20,000
Purchases (excluding Inter Department transfers)	20,12,080	1,50,00,000
Sales (excluding Inter Department transfers)	31,06,000	3,12,50,000
Transfer to Readymade Garment	5,00,000	—
Direct Wages	3,00,000	67,30,000
Direct Expenses	1,00,000	19,50,000
Plant and Equipment for Dyeing/Stitching Readymade Garments (WDV as on April 1, 2024)	5,00,000	15,00,000
Rent and Warehousing	4,50,000	12,00,000
Stock as on March 31st 2025	6,00,000	22,50,000

The following further information are available for necessary consideration :

(*i*) The Stock in Readymade garments department may be considered as consisting of 60% of dyed fabric and 40% of Other Expenses.

(*ii*) the Dyed Fabric Department earned a Gross Profit @ 30% in 2023-2024.

(*iii*) On the plant and equipment, depreciation @ 20% p.a. to be provided.

(*iv*) The following expenses incurred for both the departments were not apportioned between the departments :

	₹
(*a*) Salaries	2,70,000
(*b*) Advertisement expenses	90,000
(*c*) General expenses	8,00,000

(*v*) Salaries in 1 : 2 ratio, Advertisement expenses in the turnover ratio and General expenses in 1 : 3 ratio are to be apportioned between the Dyed Fabric Department and Readymade Department respectively.

(Intermediate (New) Examination, July, 2021 Modified)

SOLUTION ***(For Departmental Trading and Profit & Loss Account see next page)***

SOLUTION ((*Illustration 6*)

M/s K Creations
DEPARTMENTAL TRADING AND PROFIT & LOSS ACCOUNT
for the year ended 31st March 2025

Particulars	*Dyed Fabric Department*	*Readymade Garments Department*	*Total*	*Particulars*	*Dyes Fabric Department*	*Readymade Garments Department*	*Total*
	(₹)	(₹)	(₹)		(₹)	(₹)	(₹)
To Opening Stock	5,40,000	15,20,000	20,60,000	By Sales	31,06,000	3,12,50,000	3,43,56,000
To Purchases	20,12,080	1,5,00,000	1,70,12,080	By Transfer to			
To Transfer from				Readymade			
Dyed Fabric Deptt.		5,00,000	5,00,000	Garments	5,00,000		5,00,000
To Direct Wages	3,00,000	67,30,000	70,30,000	By Closing Stock	6,00,000	22,50,000	28,50,000
To Direct Expenses	1,00,000	19,50,000	20,50,000				
To Depreciation*	1,00,000	3,00,000	4,00,000				
To Gross Profit	11,53,920	75,00,000	86,53,920				
To	42,06,000	3,35,00,000	3,77,06,000	Total	42,06,000	3,35,00,000	3,77,06,000
To Rent and Warehousing	4,50,000	12,00,000	16,50,000	By Gross Profit	11,53,920	75,00,000	86,53,920
To Salaries	90,000	1,80,000	2,70,000				
To Advertisement Exp.	8,137	81,863	90,000				
To General Expenses	2,00,000	6,00,000	8,00,000				
To Net Profit	4,05,783	54,38,137	58,43,920				
	11,53,920	75,00,000	86,53,920		11,53,920	75,00,000	86,53,920

PROFIT AND LOSS ACCOUNT (COMBINED)

Particulars	Amt. (₹)	Particulars	Amt. (₹)
To Unrealised Profit (WN)	1,58,400	By Net Profit	58,43,920
To General Net Profit	56,85,520		
	58,43,920		58,43,920

Calculation of Stock Reserve

Rate of Gross Profit of Dyed Fabric Department for the year 2024-25

= 11,53,920/(31,06,000 + 5,00,000) × 100 = 32%

Closing stock of Dyed Fabric in Readymade Garments Department

= 22,50,000 × 60% = ₹ 13,50,000

Stock reserve required for unrealised profit @ 32% on closing stock

= 13,50,000 × 32% = ₹ 4,32,000

Stock reserve for unrealised profit included in opening stock of Readymade Garments Department = ₹ 15,20,000 × 60% × 30% = ₹ 2,73,600

Additional stock reserve required = ₹ 4,32,000 – ₹ 2,73,600 = ₹ 1,58,400

Multiple Market Transfer Pricing on Reciprocal Basis

Where inter departmental transfers are made on reciprocal basis, then how to calculate the unrealised profit on unsold stock of different departments is shown in the following illustration :

ILLUSTRATION 7. Terad & Co. has two departments A and B. From the following particulars, prepare Departmental Trading Account and Consolidated Trading Account for the year ended 31st March, 2025.

	Departments	
	A	***B***
	₹	₹
Opening Stock (at cost)	1,00,000	60,000
Purchases	4,60,000	3,40,000
Carriage	10,000	10,000
Wages	60,000	40,000
Sales (excluding inter-transfer)	7,00,000	5,60,000
Purchased goods transferred :		
by B to A	50,000	—
by A to B	—	40,000
Finished Goods transferred :		
by B to A	1,75,000	—
by A to B	—	2,00,000
Return of Finished Goods :		
by B to A	50,000	—
by A to B	—	35,000
Closing Stock :		
Purchased goods	22,500	30,000
Finished goods	**1,20,000**	**70,000**

Purchased goods have been transferred at their respective departmental purchase cost and finished goods at departmental market price. 20% of finished closing stock at each department represented finished goods received from other department.

SOLUTION

DEPARTMENTAL TRADING ACCOUNT
for the year ended 31-3-2025

	Deptt. A ₹	Deptt. B ₹		Deptt. A ₹	Deptt. B ₹
To Opening Stock	1,00,000	60,000	By Sales	7,00,000	5,60,000
To Purchases	4,60,000	3,40,000	By Transfer of Purchased Goods	40,000	50,000
To Carriage	10,000	10,000	By Transfer of Finished Goods	2,00,000	1,75,000
To Wages	60,000	40,000	By Return of Finished Goods	35,000	50,000
To Transfer of Purchased Goods	50,000	40,000	By Closing Stock :		
To Transfer of Finished Goods	1,75,000	2,00,000	Purchased Goods	22,500	30,000
To Return of Finished Goods	50,000	35,000	Finished Goods	1,20,000	70,000
To Gross Profit c/d	2,12,500	2,10,000			
	11,17,500	9,35,000		11,17,500	9,35,000

PROFIT & LOSS ACCOUNT

	₹		₹
To Stock Reserve		By Gross Profit	
A	7,200	A Deptt.	2,12,500
B	3,500	B Deptt.	2,10,000
To Net Profit	4,11,800		
	4,22,500		4,22,500

Working Notes :

(1) ***Stock Reserve for A Deptt.***

$$\frac{\text{Gross Profit}}{\text{Sales + Transfer of Finished Goods to B – Return of Finished Goods by B}} \times 20\% \text{ of Finished Stock of B}$$

$$= \frac{₹\ 2,12,500}{₹\ 7,00,000 + 2,00,000 - 50,000} \times 20\% \text{ of } ₹\ 70,000 = \frac{₹\ 2,12,500}{₹\ 8,50,000} \times ₹\ 14,000 = ₹\ \mathbf{3,500}$$

(2) ***Stock Reserve of B Department***

$$\frac{₹\ 2,10,000}{₹\ 5,60,000 + ₹\ 1,75,000 - ₹\ 35,000} \times 20\% \text{ of } ₹\ 1,20,000 = \frac{₹\ 2,10,000}{₹\ 7,00,000} \times ₹\ 24,000 = ₹\ \mathbf{7,200}$$

ILLUSTRATION 8. A Ltd. has a factory which has two manufacturing departments X and Y. Part of the output of X Department is transferred to Y Department for further processing and the balance is directly transferred to the Selling Department. The entire production of Y Department is transferred to the Selling Department. Inter-departmental stock transfers are made as follows :

X Department to Y Department at $33\frac{1}{3}\%$ over departmental cost.

X Department to Selling Department at 50% over departmental cost.

Y Department to Selling Department at 25% over departmental cost.

Following information is given for the year ended 31st March, 2025 :

	Department X		Department Y		Selling Department	
	M.T.	₹	M.T.	₹	M.T.	₹
Opening Stocks	60	60,000	20	40,000	50	1,45,000
Raw Material Consumption	90	1,00,000	20	20,000	—	—
Labour charges	—	50,000	—	80,000	—	—
Sales	—	—	—	—		5,00,000
Closing Stock	30	—	50	—	60	—

Out of the total production in X Department 30 M.T. were for transfer to the Selling Department. Apart from these stocks which were transferred during the year the balance output and the entire Opening and Closing Stocks of X Department were for transfer to Y Department. The per tonne material and labour consumption in X department on production to be transferred directly to the selling department is 300 per cent of the labour, and material consumption on production meant for Y Department.

Prepare Departmental Profit and Loss Account ignoring material wastages.

SOLUTION. (***For Departmental Profit and Loss Account see next page***)

Working Notes :

(1) *Department X*

	Qty. M.T.	Amount ₹	₹
Total Production	150	2,10,000	
Transfer from X Dept. @ 1,000 M.T.	120	1,20,000	
Closing Stock (out of production of X Dept.)	30	30,000	
Cost of Transfer to Y Dept.	90	90,000	
Add : Loading $33\frac{1}{3}\%$		30,000	
		1,20,000	
			1,20,000
Cost of Transfer to Selling Dept. (30 M.T. equal to 90 M.T. @ ₹ 1,000 per M.T.)	30	90,000	
Add : Loading 50%		45,000	
			1,35,000
Total Transfer Value from X to Y and Selling Dept.	120		2,55,000
Department Y			
Total Production	130	2,60,000	
Less : Closing Stock $\left(\frac{₹\ 2,60,000}{130} \times 50\right)$	50	1,00,000	
	80	1,60,000	
Add : Loading 25%		40,000	
			2,00,000

(2) *Value of Closing Stock of Selling Dept.*

Total Stock	160	4,80,000
Value of Closing Stock $\left(\frac{60}{160} \times ₹\ 4,80,000\right)$	60	1,80,000

SOLUTION (*Illustration 8*)

DEPARTMENTAL PROFIT AND LOSS ACCOUNT
for the year ending 31st March, 2025

	X Dept.		Y Dept.		Selling Dept.			X Dept.		Y Dept		Selling Dept.	
	Qty. M.T.	*Amount*	*Qty. M.T.*	*Amount*	*Qty. M.T.*	*Amount*		*Qty. M.T.*	*Amount*	*Qty. M.T.*	*Amount*	*Qty. M.T.*	*Amount*
		₹		₹		₹			₹		₹		₹
To Opening Stock	60	60,000	20	40,000	50	1,45,000	By Stock Transferred	120	2,55,000	80	2,00,000		
" Raw Materials Consumption	90	1,00,000	20	20,000			" Sales					100	5,00,000
" Labour Charges		50,000		80,000			" Closing Stock	30	30,000	50	1,00,000	60	1,80,000
" Stock Transferred from X Dept.			90	1,20,000	30	1,35,000							
" Stock Transferred from Y Dept.					80	2,00,000							
" Gross Profit		75,000		40,000		2,00,000							
	150	2,85,000	130	3,00,000	160	6,80,000		150	2,85,000	130	3,00,000	160	6,80,000

ILLUSTRATION 9. ABC Ltd. has several departments. Goods supplied to each department are debited to a Memorandum Departmental Stock Account at cost plus a fixed percentage (mark-up) to give the normal selling price. The amount of mark-up is credited to a Memorandum Departmental Markup account. If the selling price of goods is reduced below its normal selling prices, the reduction (mark-down) will require adjustment both in the stock account and the mark-up account. The mark-up for department X for the last three years has been 20%. Figures relevant to department X for the year ended 31st March, 2025 were as follows :

Stock as on 1st April, 2024, at cost	₹ 1,50,000
Purchases at cost	₹ 4,30,000
Sales	₹ 6,50,000

It is further ascertained that :

(1) Shortage of stock found in the year ending 31-3-2025, costing ₹ 4,000 were written off.

(2) Opening stock on 1-4-2024 including goods costing ₹ 12,000 had been sold during the year and had been marked-down in the selling price by ₹ 1,600. The remaining stock had been sold during the year.

(3) Goods purchased during the year were marked down by ₹ 3,600 from a cost of ₹ 30,000. Marked-down stock costing ₹ 10,000 remained unsold on 31-3-2025,.

(4) The departmental closing stock is to be valued at cost subject to adjustment for mark-up and mark-down.

You are required to prepare for the year ended 31st March, 2025 :

(*i*) Departmental Trading Account for department X for the year ended 31st March, 2025 in the books of head office.

(*ii*) Memorandum Stock Account for the year ended 31st March, 2025.

(*iii*) Memorandum Mark-up account for the year ended 31st March, 2025.

(*CA IPCC, Nov. 2019 Modified*)

SOLUTION

(*i*) **In the Books of Head Office**

DEPARTMENT TRADING ACCOUNT FOR DEPARTMENT X

for the year ending on 31-3-2025

Particulars	₹	*Particulars*	₹
To Opening Stock	1,50,000	By Sales	6,50,000
To Purchases	4,30,000	By Shortage	4,000
To Gross Profit c/d	1,05,000	By Closing Stock	31,000
	6,85,000		6,85,000

(*ii*) **MEMORANDUM STOCK ACCOUNT (for Department X) (at selling price)**

Particulars	₹	*Particulars*	₹
To Balance b/d		By Profit & Loss A/c (Cost of Shortage)	4,000
(₹ 1,50,000 + 20% of ₹ 1,50,000)	1,80,000	By Memorandum Departmental Mark-up A/c	
To Purchases		(Load on Shortage) (₹ 4,000 × 20%)	800
(₹ 4,30,000 + 20% of ₹ 4,30,000)	5,16,000	By Memorandum Departmental Mark-up A/c	
		(Mark-down on Current Purchases)	3,600
		By Debtors A/c (Sales)	6,50,000
		By Memorandum Departmental Mark-up A/c	
		(Mark Down on Opening Stock)	1,600
		By Balance c/d	36,000
	6,96,000		6,96,000

(*iii*) **MEMORANDUM DEPARTMENTAL MARK-UP ACCOUNT**

Particulars	₹	*Particulars*	₹
To Memorandum Departmental Stock A/c (₹ 4,000 × 20/100)	800	By Balance b/d (₹ 1,80,000 × 20/120)	30,000
To Memorandum Departmental Stock A/c	3,600	By Memorandum Departmental Stock A/c (₹ 5,16,000 × 20/120)	86,000
To Memorandum Departmental Stock A/c	1,600		
To Gross Profit transferred to Profit & Loss A/c	1,05,000		
To Balance c/d [(₹ 36,000 + 1,200*) × 20/120 – ₹ 1,200]	5,000		
	1,16,000		1,16,000

*[₹ 3,600 × 10,000/30,000] = ₹ 1,200. Alternatively, this adjustment of ₹ 1,200 may be routed through Memorandum Stock Account.

Working Notes :

(*i*) Calculation of Cost of Sales

		₹
A	Sales as per Book	6,50,000
B	*Add* : Mark-down in Opening Stock (given)	1,600
C	*Add* : Mark-down in Sales Out of Current Purchases (₹ 3,600 × 20,000/30,000)	2,400
D	Value of Sales if there was no Mark-down (A + B + C)	6,54,000
E	*Less* : Gross Profit (20/120 of ₹ 6,54,000) subject to Mark Down	(1,09,000)
F	Cost of Sales (D – E)	5,45,000

(*ii*) Calculation of Closing Stock

		₹
A	Opening Stock	1,50,000
B	*Add* : Purchases	4,30,000
C	*Less* : Cost of Sales	(5,45,000)
D	*Less* : Shortage	(4,000)
E	Closing Stock (A + B – C – D)	31,000

ILLUSTRATION 10. Southern Store Ltd. is a retail store operating two departments. The company maintains a memorandum stock account and memorandum mark up account for each of the departments. Supplies issued to the departments are debited to the memorandum stock account of the department at cost plus the mark up and departmental sales are credited to this account. The mark up on supplies issued to the departments is credited to the mark up account for the department. When it is necessary to reduce the selling price below the normal selling price *i.e.* cost plus mark up, the reduction (mark down) is entered in the memorandum stock account and in the mark up account. Department Y has a mark up of $33\frac{1}{3}\%$ on cost and Department Z 50% on cost.

Following information has been extracted from the records of Southern Stores Ltd. for the year ended 31st March, 2025.

	Department Y	*Department Z*
	₹	₹
Stock on 1-4-2024 at cost	24,000	36,000
Purchases	1,62,000	1,90,000
Sales	2,10,000	2,85,000

(1) The stock of Department Y at 1st April, 2024 includes goods on which the selling price has been marked down by ₹ 510. These goods were sold in April, 2024 at the reduced price.

(2) Certain goods purchased in 2024-25 for ₹ 2,700 for department Y, were transferred during the year to department Z, and sold for ₹ 4,050. Purchase and sale are recorded in the purchases of department Y and the sales of department Z respectively, but no entries in respect of the transfer have been made.

(3) Goods purchased in 2024-25 were marked down as follows :

	Department Y	*Department Z*
	₹	₹
Cost	8,000	21,000
Mark down	800	4,100

At the end of the year there were some items in the stock of the department Z, which had been marked down to ₹ 2,300. With this exception all goods were marked down in 2024-25 were sold during the year at the reduced prices.

(4) During stock taking at 31st March, 2025 goods which had cost ₹ 240 were found to be missing in department Y. It was determined that the loss should be regarded as irrecoverable.

(5) The closing stock in both departments are to be valued at cost for the purpose of the annual accounts.

You are required to prepare for each department for the year ended 31st March, 2025: (*a*) Trading Account (*b*) Memorandum Stock Account, and (*c*) Memorandum Mark up Account.

SOLUTION

Southern Stores Ltd.
TRADING ACCOUNT
for the year ended 31st March, 2025

	Deptt. Y	Deptt. Z		Deptt. Y	Deptt. Z
	₹	₹		₹	₹
To Opening Stock at Cost	24,000	36,000	By Sales	2,10,000	2,85,000
To Purchases	1,62,000	1,90,000	By Transfer to Deptt. Z	2,700	
To Transfer from Y Deptt.		2,700	By Goods Lost	240	
To Gross Profit	51,518	92,496	By Closing Stock at cost (1)	24,578	36,196
	2,37,518	3,21,196		2,37,518	3,21,196

MEMORANDUM STOCK ACCOUNT

	₹	₹		₹	₹
To Balance b/d	32,000	54,000	By Balance b/d	510	
To Purchases A/c	1,62,000	1,90,000	By Sales	2,10,000	2,85,000
To Memorandum Mark up A/c	54,000	95,000	By Transfer	2,700	
To Transfer		2,700	By Memorandum Mark up A/c (on transfer)	900	
To Memorandum Mark up A/c		1,350	By Memorandum Mark down A/c (marked down)	800	4,100

To Memorandum Mark up A/c (on marked down goods still in stock) (2)		344	By Loss of Stock	240	
			By Memorandum Mark up A/c (on lost stock)	80	
			By Balance c/d (closing stock)	32,770	54,294
	2,48,000	3,43,394		2,48,000	3,43,394

MEMORANDUM MARK UP ACCOUNT

	Y Deptt.	Z Deptt.		Y Deptt.	Z Deptt.
	₹	₹		₹	₹
To Balance b/d	510		By Balance b/d	8,000	18,000
To Memorandum Stock A/c (on transfer)	900		By Memorandum Stock A/c (Mark up on Purchases)	54,000	95,000
To Memorandum Stock A/c (Mark down)	800	4,100	By Memorandum Stock A/c (Mark up on transfer)		1,350
To Memorandum Stock A/c (Mark down on goods destroyed)	80		By Memorandum Stock A/c (Mark down on goods still in stock)		344
To Gross Profit (Balancing figure)	51,518	92,496			
To Balance c/d	8,192	18,098			
	62,000	1,14,694		62,000	1,14,694

Working Notes :

(1) *Calculation of Stock at Cost*

	Y Deptt.	Z. Deptt.
	₹	₹
Closing Stock at Invoice Price	32,770	54,294
At Cost	(3/4) 24,578	(2/3) 36,196

(2) *Marked down in unsold stock of Z Deptt.*

$$\frac{\text{Mark down} \times \text{Value of Stock}}{\text{Value after mark down}} = \frac{₹\,4100 \times ₹\,2300}{₹\,27400} = ₹\,344.$$

(3) *Verification of Gross Profit*

	Y Deptt.	Z Deptt.
	₹	₹
Sales	2,10,000	2,85,000
Add : Reduction	510	–
Add : Reduction mark down	800	3,756 (4,100 – 344)
	2,11,310	2,88,756
Gross Profit	(1/4) 52,828	(1/3) 96,252
Less : Marked down	1,310	3,756
Gross Profit as per Memorandum Mark up A/c	51,518	92,496

QUESTIONS

OBJECTIVE TYPE

1. **Fill in the blanks :**

   (*a*) When inter-departmental transfer is based on market price and there are unsold goods out of the transferred goods at the end of the accounting period, provision must be made for the .... on unsold goods included in the stock lying with the transferee department.

   (*b*) Department accounts are prepared to know separately the .... of each department.

   (*c*) Selling expenses should be divided among the different departments on the basis of ....

   (*d*) Building expenses should be divided among the different departments according to the .... by each department.

Ans. [(*a*) unrealised profit ; (*b*) profit ; (*c*) sales ; (*d*) space occupied].

2. **State how the following expenses are allocated among the different departments :**

   (*i*) Rent & Taxes [On the basis of floor space]
   (*ii*) Repairs to Machines [On the basis of value of machineries]
   (*iii*) Labour Welfare Exp. [On the basis of No. of workers or wages of each deptt.]
   (*iv*) Bad Debts [On the basis of sale ratio]
   (*v*) Carriage Inward [On the basis of purchase ratio]
   (*vi*) Depreciation of Assets [On the basis of ratio of assets values of each department]
   (*vii*) Discount Allowed [On the basis of departmental turnover ratio]

3. **Choose the Correct Answer**

   Goods are transferred from Department X to Department Y at a price so as to include a profit of 33.33% on cost. If the value of closing stock of Department Y is ₹ 18,000, then the amount of stock reserve on closing stock will be –

   (*a*) ₹ 6,000; (*b*) ₹ 4,500; (*c*) ₹ 9,000; (*d*) None of the above.

Ans. [(*b*)]

SHORT ANSWER TYPE

1. What is meant by a department ?
2. Give three objectives of preparing departmental accounts.
3. List atleast five advantages of departmental accounts.
4. Give three disinctions between departmental accounts and branch accounts.
5. What are inter-departmental transfers ?
6. What adjustment entries are to be passed when goods are transferred from one department to another department at market price ?
7. What is Dual Pricing ?
8. List the various bases for apportionment of common expenses.
9. Mixed goods were purchased for ₹ 1,00,000 and later they were sorted into three categories *X*, *Y*, *Z* as follows :

   X 1,000 – Selling Price ₹ 20 each. *Y* 2,000 – Selling Price ₹ 22.50 each. *Z* 2,400 – Selling Price ₹ 25 each.

   All categories yield the same rate of profit. Calculate the purchase price of each category.

Ans. [*X*–₹ 16,000 ; *Y*–₹ 36,000 and *Z*–₹ 48,000]

LONG ANSWER TYPE

1. What are departmental accounts & Give the objects and advantages of preparing departmental accounts ?
2. List the differences between Branch and Departmental System of Accounting.
3. Ddescribe the method of the allocation of expenses in the preparation of departmental accounts.
4. What are departmental accounts ? Explain the basis of allocation of expenses over various departments.
5. How would the following expenses be distributed among various departments :

   (*i*) Rent, (*ii*) Managing Director's salary and commission, (*iii*) Advertisement charges, (*iv*) Insurance premium, (*v*) Income-tax, (*vi*) Interest on borrowed capital, (*vii*) Depreciation, (*viii*) Establishment expenses, (*x*) Lighting.
6. How are the inter departmental transactions are recorded in Departmental Accounts ?

PRACTICAL PROBLEMS

1. From the following Trial Balance, prepare Departmental Trading and Profit and Loss Account for the year ended 31st March, 2025 and Balance Sheet as at that date.

TRIAL BALANCE

		Debit	*Credit*
		₹	₹
Stock 1.4.2024	Department A	17,000	
	Department B	14,500	
Purchases	Department A	35,400	
	Department B	30,200	
Sales	Department A	—	60,800
	Department B	—	51,250
Wages	Department A	8,200	
	Department B	2,700	
Rent, rates, taxes and insurance		9,390	
Sundry expenses		3,600	
Salaries		3,000	
Lighting and heating		2,100	
Discount allowed		2,220	
Discounts received		—	650
Advertising		3,680	
Carriage inwards		2,340	
Furniture and fittings		3,000	
Plant and machinery		21,000	
Sundry debtors		6,060	
Sundry creditors		—	18,600
A's Capital Account		—	47,660
A's Drawings		4,500	
Cash in hand		170	
Cash at Bank		9,900	
		1,78,960	1,78,960

Following information is also provided :

(a) Internal transfer of goods from Dept. A to Department B ₹ 420.

(b) The items, rent, taxes and insurance, sundry expenses, lighting and heating, salaries and carriage inwards, to be apportioned 2/3 to Department A and 1/3 to Department B.

(c) Advertising to be apportioned equally.

(d) Discount allowed and received are apportioned on the basis of departmental sales and purchases (excluding transfers) correct to nearest ₹ 10.

(e) Depreciation at 10 per cent per annum on furniture and fitting and on plant and machinery. This is to be charged 3/4 to Department A and 1/4 to Department B.

(f) Services rendered by Department B to Department A included in wages ₹ 500.

(g) Stock as at 31.3.2025—A Dept. ₹ 16,740 and B Dept. ₹ 12,050.

(h) Fixed assets remain unchanged during the year.

Ans. [Gross Profit A ₹ 15,300 : B ₹ 15,200 ; Net Profit B ₹ 6,010 ; Net Loss—A ₹ 1,250].

2. From the following data, prepare Departmental Trading and Profit and Loss Account and thereafter the Combined Income Account revealing the concern's true results for the year ended 31st March, 2025.

	Departments	
	A	*B*
	₹	₹
Stock (1st April)	40,000	—
Purchases from outside	2,00,000	20,000
Wages	10,000	1,000
Transfer of goods from Department A	—	50,000
Stock (31st March) at cost to the Department	30,000	10,000
Sales to outsiders	2,00,000	71,000

B's entire stock represents goods from Department A which transfers them at 25% above its cost. Administrative and selling expenses amount to ₹ 15,000 which are to be allocated between departments A and B in the ratio of 4 : 1 respectively.

Ans. [Gross Profit—A ₹ 30,000 ; B ₹ 10,000 ; Profit—A ₹ 18,000 ; B ₹ 7,000; Combined Net Profit ₹ 23,000].

3. A Ltd. has three departments X, Y and Z. From the following particulars given by M/s A Ltd., compute

(a) the value of stock as on 31 March, 2025, and

(b) the departmental results.

(i)

	X	*Y*	*Z*
	₹	₹	₹
Stock (1-4-2024)	12,000	18,000	6,000
Purchases	73,000	62,000	24,000
Actual Sales	86,250	79,700	37,300
Gross profit on normal selling price	20%	25%	$33\frac{1}{3}$%

(ii) During the year certain items were sold at a discount given below and these discounts were reflected in the values of sale stated above :

	Departments		
	X	*Y*	*Z*
	₹	₹	₹
Sales at normal price	5,000	1,500	500
Sales at actual price	3,750	1,200	300

Ans. [

	X	Y	Z
(a) Value of Stock (₹)	**15,000**	**20,000**	**5,000**
(b) Gross Profit (₹)	**16,250**	**19,700**	**12,300]**

4. M/s Highway Garage consists of three departments, Spares, Service and Repairs, each department being managed by a departmental manager whose commission was respectively 5%, 10% and 10% of the respective departmental profits, subject, however, to a minimum of ₹ 3,000 in each case. Inter-departmental transfers take place at a "loaded" price as follows :

From Spares to Service	5% above cost
From Spares to Repairs	10% above cost
From Repairs to Service	10% above cost

In respect of the year ended March 31, 2025, the firm had already prepared and closed the departmental trading and profit and loss account. Subsequently it was discovered that the closing stocks of various departments had included inter-departmentally transferred goods at "loaded" price instead of the correct cost price. From the following information prepare a Statement Recomputing the Departmental Profit or Loss :

	Spares	*Services*	*Repairs*
	₹	₹	₹
Final Net Profit/Loss	19,000 (Loss)	25,200 (Profit)	36,000 (Profit)
Inter-departmental transfer included at "loaded" price in the departmental Stocks		32,500 (10,500 from Spares and 22,000 from Repairs)	2,100 (from Spares)

Ans. [Real Net Profit : Service ₹ 25,200 ; Repairs ₹ 34,200 ; and Spares Loss ₹ 19,691].

5. From the undermentioned information and instructions, prepare Departmental Trading and Profit and Loss Account in columnar form of the three departments of the Outfitters Ltd. :

	Tailoring	*Ladies' Wear*	*Outfitting*
	₹	₹	₹
Stock, January 1-4-2024	41,280	33,975	93,721
Stock, 31-3-2025	32,840	43,828	81,626
Purchases for the year	2,10,342	75,296	1,39,109
Returns (purchases)	14,382	5,629	1,823
Sales for the year	4,00,173	1,54,085	3,62,189
Returns (sales)	Nil	3,259	11,217
Wages	72,823	30,084	24,613

Goods were transferred as follows (all at cost) :

Tailoring to ladies' wear, ₹ 389 and to outfitting ₹ 6,679 ; Ladies' wear to tailoring ₹ 5,315 ; Outfitting to tailoring ₹ 4,271 and to ladies' wear ₹ 5,801.

Apportion equally : stationery ₹ 921 ; postage ₹ 663 ; general charges ₹ 30,627 ; insurance ₹ 1,785 and depreciation, ₹ 5,460.

Allocate the following further expenditure as you think best and append notes stating the basis selected for each item.

Establishment ₹ 63,395 ; bad debts, ₹ 19,823; advertising, ₹ 7,293 and income tax, ₹ 11,028.

Rent and taxes, ₹ 45,437 is to be spilt up in proportion to space occupied, *i.e.,* tailoring 4, ladies wear 2, outfitting 3, others 2.

Approximate apportionment is all that is necessary ; charge any odd balance to outfitting department.

Ans. [

	Tailoring	*Ladies'Wear*	*Outfitting*
G.P. (₹)	**1,20,432**	**60,053**	**1,80,371**
N.P. (₹)	**44,776**	**17,802**	**1,13,874**
N.P. after I.T. (₹)	**41,972**	**16,680**	**1,06,772**

]

6. The following balances as at 31-12-2025 have been extracted from the books of David, the proprietor of a departmental store having two departments X and Y :
Salaries and Wages ₹ 1,42,500; Maintenance ₹ 12,360; Rent ₹ 27,050; Advertising ₹ 15,000; Sundry Debtors ₹ 41,900; Sundry Creditors ₹ 16,800; Provision for doubtful debts ₹ 5,000; Investments ₹ 50,000; Furniture ₹ 46,500; Cash ₹ 21,550; Capital Account ₹ 2,00,880; Drawings ₹ 75,120.
The records relating to the stocks are : (all figure in ₹)

	Stock on 1-1-2025	*Purchases*	*Purchase Returns*	*Stock on 31-12-2025*
Department X	10,700	94,600	900	21,000
Department Y	68,000	2,20,980	2,200	61,600

Additional Information :

(*a*) Department X sells articles for ₹ 40 each which is equivalent to 80% above cost price, while Department Y sells articles of ₹ 60 each which is equivalent to double the cost price.

(*b*) Write off bad debts ₹ 3,300 and maintain the provision for doubtful debts at 10% of the remaining outstanding debtors. These amounts should be apportioned equally between Department X and Department Y.

(*c*) Provide ₹ 4,000 investment income due to be received.

(*d*) Provide ₹ 1,150 rent due to be paid.

(*e*) Depreciate furniture by 10%.

(*f*) All general expenses (including depreciation) should be apportioned between department X and department Y on the basis of the number of articles sold by these departments during the year.

You are required to prepare Departmental Trading and Profit and Loss Account for the year ended 31-12-2025 and a Balance Sheet as on that date.

7. FGH Ltd. has three departments I.J.K. Following information is provided for the year ended 31-3-2025 :

	I	*J*	*K*
	₹	₹	₹
Opening Stock	5,000	8,000	19,000
Opening reserve for unrealised profit	—	2,000	3,000
Materials consumed	16,000	20,000	—
Direct Labour	9,000	10,000	—
Closing Stock	5,000	20,000	5,000
Sales	—	—	80,000
Area occupied (sq. mtr.,)	2,500	1,500	1,000
No. of employees	30	20	10

Stocks of each department are valued at costs to the department concerned. Stocks of I are transferred to J at cost plus 20% and stocks of J are transferred to K at a gross profit of 20% on sales. Other common expenses are salaries and staff welfare ₹ 18,000, rent ₹ 6,000.

Prepare Departmental Trading, Profit and Loss Account for the year ending 31-3-2025.

Ans. [

	I	*J*	*K*
Gross Profit (₹)	5,000	12,000	6,000
Net Profit (₹)	(7,000)	4,200	1,800

]

8. Brahma Limited has three departments and submits the following information for the year ending on 31st March, 2025 :

	A	*B*	*C*	*Total (₹)*
Purchases (units)	5,000	10,000	15,000	
Purchases (Amount)				8,40,000
Sales (units)	5,200	9,800	15,300	
Selling Price (₹ per unit)	40	45	50	
Closing Stock (units)	400	600	700	

You are required to prepare Departmental Trading Account of Brahma Limited assuming that the rate of profit on sales is uniform in each case.

Ans. [

	A	*B*	*C*
Gross Profit (₹)	83,200	1,76,400	3,06,000
Purchases (₹)	1,20,000	2,70,000	4,50,000
Opening Stock (units)	600	400	1,000
Closing Stock (₹)	9,.600	16,200	21,000]

[**Hint.** Profit Margin Ratio = 40%

9. A departmental stores carries on its business through five departments A, B, C, D and E.

(*i*) Following information for 2024-25 is now made available to you :

Salaries and Commission ₹ 11,020 ; Rent and Rates ₹ 2,900 ; Insurance ₹ 1,160 ; Miscellaneous Expenses ₹ 2,610.

All these expenses are chargeable to each department in proportion to the cost of the articles sold in the respective departments.

(*ii*) Following balances as at 31-3-2025 were ascertained :

	A	*B*	*C*	*D*	*E*
	₹	₹	₹	₹	₹
Opening Stock at cost	10,000	6,000	15,000	8,000	9,000
Purchases	1,00,000	60,000	20,000	52,000	60,000
Sales	96,000	62,000	19,000	46,000	60,000
Closing Stock at cost	23,000	8,000	6,000	2,000	11,000

Prepare the profits and loss accounts to show the final result of each department and also the combined results with respective percentages on sales.

Ans. [Profit ; Dept–A ₹ 3,693 ; B ₹ 462 ; Loss : Dept—C ₹ 11,769 ; D ₹ 15,538 & E ₹ 1,538].

10. Following purchases were made by a business house having three departments :

Department A 1,000 units
Department B 2,000 units } at a total of ₹ 1,00,000
Department C 2,400 units

Stocks on 1st January were :

Department A 120 units
Department B 80 units, and
Department C 152 units.

The sales were :

Department A 1,020 units @ ₹ 20.00 each.
Department B 1,920 units @ Rs 22.50 each.
Department C 2,496 units @ ₹ 25.00 each.
The rate of gross profit is the same in each case.

Prepare Departmental Trading Accounts.

Ans. [G.P. : A ₹ 4,080 ; B ₹ 8,640 and C ₹ 12,480].

11. The directors of Departmental Stores Ltd. wish to ascertain, approximately, the net profits of the "A", "B" and "C" departments separately for the quarter ended March 31, 2025. It is found impracticable actually to take stock on that date but an adequate system of departmental accounts is in use and the normal rates of gross profit for the departments concerned are 40%, 30% and 20% on turnover, respectively. Indirect expenses are charged in proportion to departmental turnover.

Following are the figures for each department :

	A	B	C
	₹	₹	₹
Stock as on 1.1.2025	30,000	35,000	15,000
Purchases to 31-3-2025	35,000	37,500	23,500
Sales to 31-3-2025	60,000	50,000	30,000
Direct Expenses	10,100	7,250	3,550

Total indirect expenses for the period (including those relating to other departments) were ₹ 21,000 on total sales of Rs 4,20,000.

Prepare a statement showing gross profit, net profit after making reserve for stock at 10% in respect of each department.

Ans. [Gross Profit : A ₹ 24,000 ; B ₹ 15,000 ; C ₹ 6,000 ; Net Profit : A ₹ 17,090, B ₹ 8,025 and C ₹ 2,695].

12. Department A sells goods to Department B at a profit of 20% on cost and Department C at 15% profit on cost. Department B sells goods to A and C at a profit of 10% and 20% on sales respectively. Department C sells goods to A and B at 15% and 10% profit on cost respectively.

Departmental managers are entitled to 10% commission on net profit subject to unrealised profit on departmental sales being eliminated. Departmental profits after charging manager's commission, but before adjustment of unrealised profit are as under :

Department A ₹ 36,000; Department B ₹ 27,000; Department C ₹ 18,000.

Stocks lying at different departments at the end of the year are as below :

	Departments		
	A (₹)	*B (₹)*	*C (₹)*
Transfer from Department A	—	7,200	5,750
Transfer from Department B	19,000	—	15,000
Transfer from Department C	4,600	3,300	—

Find out correct *departmental profits* after charging manager's commission.

Ans. [Correct Profit—Departments : A—₹ 34,245; B—₹ 22,590; C—₹ 17,190]

13. A concern has two departments, X and Y. From the following particulars, prepare a Consolidated Trading Account for the year ending 31st March, 2025 :

	X	Y
	₹	₹
Opening stock at cost	20,000	12,000
Purchases	92,000	68,000
Carriage	2,000	2,000
Wages	12,000	8,000
Sales	1,40,000	1,12,000
Purchased goods transferred :		
by 'Y' to 'X'	10,000	
by 'X' to 'Y'		8,000
Finished goods transferred :		
by 'Y' to 'X'	35,000	
by 'X' to 'Y'		40,000
Returns of finished goods :		
by 'Y' to 'X'	10,000	
by 'X' to 'Y'		7,000

Closing stock :		
(*i*) Purchased goods	4,500	6,000
(*ii*) Finished goods	24,000	14,000

You are informed that purchased goods have been transferred mutually at their respective departmental purchase cost and finished goods at departmental market price and that 25% of the finished stock (closing) at each department represented finished goods received from the other department.

Ans. [Gross Profit : X ₹ 42,500 ; Y ₹ 42,000 ; Net Profit : X ₹ 41,625 ; Y ₹ 40,200].

14. X Ltd. has a factory which has two Manufacturing Departments A and B. Part of the output of 'A' Department is transferred to 'B' Department for further processing and balance is directly transferred to the Selling Department. The entire production of 'B' Department is transferred to the Selling Department. Inter-Department Stock transfers are made as follows :

'A' Department to 'B' Department at 20% over departmental cost. 'A' Department to Selling Department at 30% over departmental cost. 'B' Department to Selling Department at 25% over departmental cost.

Following information is given for the year ending 31st March, 2025 :

	Department A		*Department B*		*Selling*	
	M.T.	₹	M.T.	₹	M.T.	₹
Opening Stock	60	60,000	20	40,000	50	1,60,000
Raw Material consumption	100	1,10,000	30	30,000		
Labour charges		60,000		80,000		
Sales						6,00,000
Closing Stock	40		60		60	

Out of total production in 'A' Department 30 M.T. were for transfer to the Selling Department and the Balance to 'B' Department. The per tonne material and labour consumption in 'A' Department on production to be transferred directly to the Selling Department is 200 per cent of the labour and material consumption on production meant for 'B' Department. Prepare Departmental Profit and Loss Account.

Ans. [Profit : Dept. A—₹ 44,640 ; Dept. B—₹ 50,490 ; Selling Department—₹ 2,81,286].

CHAPTER 27

Voyage Accounts

Shipping companies are required to ascertain the profit or loss of a particular voyage and for this purpose they are to adopt some system of accounting, known as Voyage Accounting. If the shipping companies are plying a number of ships in the sea, the overall profit or loss for all ships is ascertained by preparing General Profit and Loss account. But if the profit or loss of a particular route or voyage is to be calculated, then a Voyage Account is prepared. Voyage Account is similar to an ordinary Profit and Loss Account. Each voyage covers outward and return journey of the vessel.

At the top of the Voyage Account, details regarding name of the ship, place of departure and destination, time of starting voyage, date of completion of voyage, time taken by the voyage etc. are given. Voyage Account is a nominal account. All expenses relating to the voyage including wages and salaries of the crew, captain and other staff, stores consumed, insurance, depreciation, commission, brokerage etc. are debited to this account whilst all earnings, freight, primage and passage money are credited. Voyage Account is prepared in the following proforma :

NAME OF THE SHIP

Voyage No. ....   Date of Commencement ....
From .... to ....   Date of Arrival ....

VOYAGE ACCOUNT

Particulars	₹	*Particulars*	₹
To Brokerage & Address Commission		By Freight :	
To Insurance on Freight		Outward	
To Consumable Stores		Inward	
To Depreciation on Ship/Hull		By Primage	
To Port Charges		By Passage Money	
To Stevedoring Expenses		By Voyage in Progress A/c (Expenses relating to unfinished voyage on the date of closing of books of account)	
To Bunker Cost			
To Lighterage			
To Salaries & Wages			
To Light House Charges		By Profit & Loss A/c (Loss on Voyage) (Balancing Figure)	
To Repairs & Renewals			
To Overheads			

To Provision for Freight on Incomplete Voyage (freight and primage received in advance relating to voyage in progress) To Profit & Loss A/c (Profit on voyage) (Balancing Figure)			

Treatment of Special Items

It is customary for shipping companies to keep separate Voyage Account for each vessel in order to ascertain the profit or loss which results from each voyage. In form a Voyage Account is similar to an ordinary Profit and Loss Account. Each voyage covers both outward and return journey of the vessel. All expenses relating to the voyage, including wages and salaries of the crew, captain and other staff, stores consumed, insurance, depreciation, commission, brokerage etc. are debited to this account whilst all earnings, freight, primage and passage money are credited.

Debit Side Items

Following points merit special attention in connection with Voyage Accounts :

1. Brokerage and commission. Apart from port charges, duties, harbour wages and other expenses on the voyage, a brokerage to the charterer's agent is usually paid and an address commission is payable to the charters themselves—both being computed on the freights earned. Sometimes, the managers are also entitled to a commission on freights earned. Address commission may also become payable to brokers for procurement of freights from different parties. Address commission is calculated as a percentage of freight (including primage, if any) earned by the shipping company.

2. Insurance. The charges against the voyage must be exactly applicable to the particular voyage *e.g.* a ship may be insured for a whole year but the amount chargeable against the voyage must be such portion as is applicable to the duration thereof as if the voyage is for one month; one-twelfth of the annual premium payable should be charged against the voyage.

3. Stores. If any stock of stores is bought for use during the voyage, then on ship's return the stores in hand must be valued and brought into account. Stores consumed (opening stock + purchases – closing stock) is to be debited.

4. Depreciation. In order to ascertain the true results of each voyage, Voyage Account must be charged with such item as depreciation on ship and tackle, repairs, renewals and replacements thereof.

5. Bunker Cost. It refers to the amount spent on fuel, coal, diesel and fresh water used for the purpose of voyage.

6. Port charges. These charges are paid to the port authorities for allowing the ship to use port for loading and unloading of cargo.

7. Stevedoring charges. These charges are paid for loading and unloading of cargo on and from the ship.

9. Salaries and Wages. Salaries and wages paid to the crew are charged to Voyage Account.

10. Light House Charges. Light house is a tower in the midst of navigable waters equipped with optical or radio-electrical instruments to show path to the ships. The charges paid to the port authorities for various facilities like radio signal, becon light etc. provided by such light houses are known as light house charges.

Credit Side Items

1. Freight. The amount charged by the shipping company from the cargo owners for the cargo loaded on the ship is known as freight. It includes both freight on outward and inward journey.

2. Passage Money. The fare collected by the company from the passengers who are carried on the ship alongwith merchandise by the captain is called passage money.

3. Primage. It is additional freight just like surcharge on freight originally collected for the captain of the ship now-a-days is treated as income of the shipping company.

Note : Provision for freight on incomplete voyage and voyage in progress are discussed afterwards in this chapter.

ILLUSTRATION 1. Following details are furnished by a Shipping Company in connection with voyage No. 45 which was commenced from port A on 1st February, 2025. The ship arrived at port D on 31st March, 2025 when the voyage was completed.

2,000 tons and 500 tons were loaded at port A for port D and C respectively. Another 300 tons were loaded at C for D. The freight charges were :

A to D ₹ 100 per ton ; A to C ₹ 80 per ton ; C to D ₹ 50 per ton.

The freight is subject to 10% primage, 5% address commission and 3% brokerage. The freight was insured at $\frac{1}{2}$%. The Hull was insured for the voyage @ 1%. Depreciation is provided @ 5% p.a.

Cost of the ship is ₹ 12 lakhs. The expenses at different ports were as under :

	A	*B*	*C*	*D*
	₹	₹	₹	₹
Port charges	5,000	1,000	3,000	3,000
Coal	18,000	—	4,000	
Captains' expenses	1,200	800	600	900
Harbour wages	4,000	—	3,000	2,500

Stores purchased at commencement amounted to ₹ 8,000. Opening Stock of stores was ₹ 5,000 and Closing Stock is estimated at ₹ 2,000. Stock of coal at close is estimated at ₹ 4,500 as against stock of ₹ 1,500 at the beginning.

Salaries and wages of sailors etc. amount to ₹ 12,000 per month. Prepare Voyage Account for the period ending 31st March, 2025.

SOLUTION

VOYAGE ACCOUNT

for the period ending 31st March, 2025

		₹			₹
To Port Charges (₹ 5,000 + ₹ 1,000 + ₹ 3,000 + ₹ 3,000)		12,000	By Freight		
To Coal :	₹		A to D 2,000 Tons @ ₹ 100 per ton	2,00,000	
Opening Stock	1,500		A to C 500 Tons @ ₹ 80 per ton	40,000	
Add : Purchases	22,000		C to D 300 Tons @ ₹ 50 per ton	15,000	2,55,000
	23,500				
Less : Closing Stock	4,500	19,000			
To Captains Expenses (₹ 1,200 + ₹ 800 + ₹ 600 + ₹ 900)		3,500	By Primage (10% on ₹ 2,55,000)		25,500
To Harbour Wages (₹ 4,000 + ₹ 3,000 + ₹ 2,500)		9,500			
To Address Commission (5% of 2,80,500)		14,025			
To Brokerage (3% of ₹ 2,80,500)		8,415			
To Insurance Premium					
Freight $\frac{1}{2}$% of ₹ 2,80,500		1,403			
Hull 1% of ₹ 12 lakh		12,000			

To Stores (₹ 5,000 + ₹ 8,000 – ₹ 2,000)	11,000		
To Depreciation $\left(₹ 12,00,000 \times \frac{5}{100} \times \frac{2}{12}\right)$	10,000		
To Salaries & Wages (₹ 12,000 × 2)	24,000		
To Net Profit	1,55,657		
	2,80,500		2,80,500

ILLUSTRATION 2. Packard Steamship Ltd. owns a tramp steamer by name, M.V. Vaikunt, which was chartered on a voyage on 1st March, 2025, on the following terms :

(*i*) Mumbai to Basra with general cargo at ₹ 500 per tonne. The charter stipulates for an address commission to the charterers at 2% of the freight payable on raising the bill of lading together with a brokerage of 5% to the charterer's agent, one-third of which is repayable to the ship.

(*ii*) Basra to Dubai with fertilisers at ₹ 240 per tonne. Address commission of 2% on freight is payable to charterers and a brokerage of 1% is payable to agents on signing the charter.

The vessel is insured with Lloyds on an annual premium of ₹ 6,60,000. The master of the vessel is entitled to 1% of the net profits of each voyage after charging such commission.

Further details are :

Repairs and Renewals : at Mumbai ₹ 40,000, and at Basra ₹ 18,000.

Stores Supplies and Provisions : at Mumbai ₹ 1,40,000, at Basra ₹ 1,60,000 and at Dubai ₹ 90,000 out of which ₹ 40,000 was in stock at the conclusion of voyage.

Consumption of Bunkers : Fuel oil 6 tonnes a day, diesel 2 tonnes a day, and fresh water 25 tonnes a day while the vessel is in port and fuel oil 15 tonnes a day, diesel 2 tonnes a day and fresh water 25 tonnes a day while sailing. Fuel oil, diesel and fresh water cost ₹ 1,200, ₹ 2,500 and ₹ 50 per tonne respectively.

Stevedoring charges : at Mumbai ₹ 20 per tonne; at Basra ₹ 15 per tonne for loading and ₹ 20 per tonne for discharging; and at Dubai ₹ 12 per tonne for load/discharge.

Captain's expenses : at Basra ₹ 16,000 and at Dubai ₹ 20,000.

Port charges : at Mumbai ₹ 60,000; at Basra ₹ 70,000 and at Dubai ₹ 54,000.

The vessel loaded the following cargo :

at Mumbai—general cargo—8,000 tonnes, out of which 6,000 tonnes were to be discharged at Basra and the rest at Dubai. The freight from Mumbai to Dubai was fixed at ₹ 600 per tonne net.

at Basra—fertiliser—for discharge at Dubai—6,000 tonnes.

The vessel completed the voyage on 30th April 2025. Number of sailing days as per ship's log came to 16.

Prepare a Voyage Account bearing in mind that the company has to provide towards special survey repairs of the vessel ₹ 24 lakhs every year.

SOLUTION

Packard Steamship Ltd.

VOYAGE ACCOUNT OF M.V. VAIKUNT

from 1st March to 30th April, 2025

		₹			₹
To Port Charges		1,84,000	By Freight :		
" Stevedoring Charges :			Mumbai to Basra		
Loading at Mumbai—			6,000 tonnes	₹	
8,000 tonnes	₹		@ ₹ 500/tonne	30,00,000	
@ ₹ 20/tonne	1,60,000		Mumbai to Dubai		
Unloading at Basra—			2,000 tonnes		
6,000 tonnes @ ₹ 20	1,20,000		@ ₹ 600/tonne		12,00,000

	₹	₹		₹	₹
Loading at Basra			Basra to Dubai		
6,000 tonnes @ ₹ 15	90,000		6,000 tonnes @		
Unloading at Dubai			₹ 240/tonnes	14,40,000	56.40.000
8,000 tonnes @ ₹ 12	96,000		" Refund of Brokerage		
	50,000		(1/3 of ₹ 1,50,000)		
		4,66,000	By Stock of Stores, Supplies		
To Captain's Expenses		36,000	and Provisions		40,000
" Stores, Supplies and Provisions		3,90,000			
" Repairs & Renewals :					
At Mumbai	40,000				
At Basra	18,000				
Provision for Special Survey Repairs $\left(\frac{2}{12} \times ₹\ 24,00,000\right)$	4,00,000	4.58.000			
To Consumption of Bunkers :					
For 16 Sailing Days @ ₹ 24,250 (1)	3,88,000				
For 45 days stay at port @ ₹ 13,450 (2)					
	6,05,250	9.93.250			
" Insurance $\left(\frac{2}{12} \times ₹\ 6,60,000\right)$		1,10,000			
" Address Commission :					
2% on ₹ 30,00,000	60,000				
2% on ₹ 14,40,000	28,800	88.800			
" Brokerage :					
5% on ₹ 30,00,000	1,50,000				
1% on ₹ 14,40,000	14,400	1.64.400			
" Commission to Master $\left(\frac{1}{101} \text{ of } ₹\ 28,39,550\right)$		28,114			
" Net Profit on Voyage		28,11,436			
		57,30,000			57,30,000

Working Notes :

(1) ***Cost of Consumption of Bunkers per day on Sailing Days* :**

	₹
Fuel Oil : 15 tonnes @ ₹ 1,200 per tonne	18,000
Diesel : 2 tonnes @ ₹ 2,500 per tonne	5,000
Fresh Water : 25 tonnes @ ₹ 50 per tonne	1,250
	24,250

(2) ***Consumption of Bunkers per day during Stay at Port***

	₹
Fuel oil : 6 tonnes @ ₹ 1,200 per tonne	7,200
Diesel : 2 tonnes @ ₹ 2,500 per tonne	5,000
Fresh Water : 25 tonnes @ ₹ 50 per tonne	1,250
	13,450

Voyage-in-Progress (Incomplete Voyage). At the time of closing the books of accounts at the end of the year, it is possible that voyage may not be complete and it may still be in progress. In such a case, special treatment is required for the following items :

1. Freight received on incomplete journey.
2. Expenses related to incomplete journey.

1. Freight Received on Incomplete Journey. Though the entire freight (including primage) being income, is credited to Voyage Account yet it is unearned income as the journey of the ship is incomplete and is required to be carried forward. Instead of deducting from freight on credit side, a provision for freight (including primage) is made and shown on the debit side of Voyage Account under the heading *"Provision for Incomplete Voyage"* (*i.e.* voyage in progress).

2. Expenses Related to Incomplete Journey. If the income of the incomplete journey is carried forward, it is desirable that expenses relating to incomplete voyage are also carried forward so that matching concept may not be violated. Unexpired expenses are credited to Voyage Account as *"Voyage in Progress"* in order to ascertain the correct profit of the period.

Unexpired expenses are to be carried forward on the basis of their nature as :

(*i*) Expenses related to freight.

(*ii*) Expenses not related to freight (*i.e.* Standing Expenses).

(*iii*) Actual identifiable expenses.

***(i)* Expenses Related to Freight**. Expenses (as address commission, agent's commission and freight insurance) related to return journey are carried forward in proportion to freight of return journey to that of total freight of journey. For example, if the total freight is ₹ 5,00,000 including return freight of ₹ 2,00,000 and the total expenses are ₹ 1,00,000. Then such expenses related to return journey are calculated as follows :

$$\frac{\text{Return Freight}}{\text{Total Freight}} \times \text{Expenses related to freight} = \frac{₹\ 2{,}00{,}000}{₹\ 5{,}00{,}000} \times ₹\ 1{,}00{,}000 = ₹\ \mathbf{40{,}000}$$

Note : If the insurance premium on freight is paid on the policy on the basis of time, then freight insurance will be treated as part of Standing Expenses.

***(ii)* Expenses Not Related to Freight**. The proportion of non-freight (standing) expenses to be carried forward depends upon the position of the ship and the amount of expenses incurred. Some of the possibilities are discussed as under :

(*a*) ***When return journey is incomplete.*** In such a case 1/2 of the standing expenses are carried forward.

(*b*) ***When return journey is half way back.*** The treatment of expenses depends upon whether the expenses incurred are for the entire voyage or till date :

(*i*) *Total expenses of voyage given.* If the freight of return journey is not recognised as revenue then expenses of return journey (1/2 of total) should be carried forward.

(*ii*) *Expenses till date given.* Total expenses are incurred for $1\frac{1}{2}$ journey. Out of these ($1\frac{1}{2}$) expenses 1/2 are related to return journey. The proportion of expenses to be carried forward to total expenses are calculated as under :

$$\frac{\text{Expenses on Incomplete Journey}}{\text{Total Expenses}} = \frac{\frac{1}{2}}{1\frac{1}{2}} = \frac{1}{3}$$

***(iii)* One round trip and single way.** Where the ship has completed one round trip and she is on her half way back for single way and

(*a*) *Expenses of total voyage are given.* In this case 1/3 of the expenses should be carried forward. The proportion of expenses of incomplete journey to be carried forward is calculated as under :

$$\frac{\text{Expenses on Incomplete Journey}}{\text{Total Expenses}} = \frac{1}{1+1+1} = \frac{1}{3}$$

(*b*) *Expenses are given till date.* In this case 1/5 of the expenses should be carried forward. The proportion of incomplete journey to be carried forward is calculated as under :

$$\frac{\text{Expenses on Incomplete Journey}}{\text{Total Expenses}} = \frac{\frac{1}{2}}{2\frac{1}{2}} = \frac{1}{5}$$

ILLUSTRATION 3. Great India Shipping Co. Ltd. of Mumbai acquired a new ship M.V. Sumudra at a cost of ₹ 37,50,000. The ship was ready for service on 1st April, 2025. An insurance policy was taken out at 2% p.a. on the ship, freight was insured at ₹ 10,000 per annum. During 3 months ended 30th June, 2025, the ship completed one round trip to Kolkata and was half through the second trip (single way) to Kolkata.

The ship carried the following Cargo : To Kolkata 9,000 tons @ ₹ 300 per ton ; From Kolkata 10,000 tons @ ₹ 270 per ton ; To Kolkata 12,000 tons @ ₹ 250 per ton.

5% commission was paid to agents in addition to 1% address commission. The expenses were as follows:

	₹		₹
Salaries and wages of the crew	8,00,000	Stevedoring at ₹ 20 per ton	6,20,000
Fuel	4,00,000	Share of overheads for the ship for the period	2,50,000
Sundry stores	80,000		
Port dues (Mumbai ₹ 70,000, Kolkata ₹ 50,000)	1,20,000		

Provide depreciation for the period at 5% per annum.

Prepare Voyage Account for the period of three months ending 30th June, 2025.

SOLUTION

Great India Shipping Co. Ltd.
VOYAGE ACCOUNT
from 1-4-2025 to 30th June, 2025

	₹		₹	₹
To Salaries & Wages	8,00,000	By Freight		
" Fuel	4,00,000	9000 tons	₹	
" Sundry Stores	80,000	@ ₹ 300 per ton	27,00,000	
" Port Dues	1,20,000	10,000 tons		
" Stevedoring	6,20,000	@ ₹ 270 per ton	27,00,000	
" Overheads	2,50,000	12,000 tons		
" Commission (5% on ₹ 84,00,000)	4,20,000	@ ₹ 250 per ton	30,00,000	
" Address Commission (1% of ₹ 84,00,000)	84,000			84,00,000
		By Voyage in Progress (1)		7,62,958
" Insurance on Freight $\left(\frac{1}{4}\text{ of ₹ } 10,000\right)$	2,500			
" Insurance $\left(\frac{1}{4}\text{ of } 2\% \text{ on ₹ } 37,50,000\right)$	18,750			
" Depreciation (5% on ₹ 37,50,000 for 3 months)	46,875			
" Provision for Incomplete Voyage (Freight)	30,00,000			
" Net Profit transferred to Profit & Loss A/c	33,20,833			
	91,62,958			91,62,958

Working Notes :

(1) *Calculation of Voyage in Progress.*

	₹
5% Commission on ₹ 30,00,000	1,50,000
1% Address Commission on ₹ 30,00,000	30,000
Stevedoring @ ₹ 20 per ton for 12,000 tons	2,40,000
Salaries and wages (1/5th)	1,60,000
Fuel (1/5th)	80,000
Sundry Stores (1/5th)	16,000
Overheads (1/5th)	50,000
Insurance on Freight (1/5th)	500
Insurance on Ship (1/5th)	3,750
Depreciation (1/5th)	9,375
Port Dues (1/3rd of ₹ 70,000 Port Dues at Mumbai) (2)	23,333
	7,62,958

(2) The ship started from Mumbai to Kolkata and reached Mumbai in the 1st round trip.

In the second round trip it again started from Mumbai.

When the ship first started from Mumbai, it did only loading. On returning back it did unloading and loading. Since the question is silent about the time spread, a reasonable approximation may be made of port dues taking 1/3 for incomplete voyage.

ILLUSTRATION 4. M.V. Indian Glory owned by the Hindustan Shipping Company Ltd. is on the Mumbai—London lines trade. Her daily standing charges (fixed costs) are ₹ 45,000. In the period between 1st July and 31st December, 2024, the ship had finished one round voyage to London and on the date when the books of accounts of the company were closed at the end of the year, the vessel was on her way to London, having sailed out of Mumbai after midnight of 21st December. Loading for London commenced on 1-12-2024.

From the following details prepare a Voyage Account.

***Freight earned* :**

(*a*) *Complete voyage—Mumbai to London*

(*i*) 20,000 tonnes textiles at ₹ 280 per tonne.

(*ii*) 10,000 tonnes copra at ₹ 340 per tonne.

On textiles, a surcharge of 10% was also recovered.

London to Mumbai

32,000 tonnes of urea at ₹ 300 per tonne.

(*b*) Unfinished voyage :

30,000 tonnes of general cargo at ₹ 240 per tonne plus a surcharge of 15%.

***Expenses* :**

(*a*) Stevedoring expenses :

(*i*) at ₹ 20 per tonne at Mumbai for general cargo and ₹ 25 per tonne for textiles and copra.

(*ii*) at London a uniform rate of £ 1 per tonne.

(*b*) Fuel consumption

(*i*) on sailing days : 30 tonnes of fuel oil per day.
5 tonnes of diesel per day.

(*ii*) on days in port : 10 tonnes of fuel oil per day.
5 tonnes of diesel per day.

(*iii*) cost per tonne : Fuel oil ₹ 1,400 per tonne
Diesel ₹ 2,500 per tonne

(*c*) Port dues : At London—£ 2,000
at Mumbai—₹ 2,40,000 (inclusive of ₹ 60,000 for the incomplete voyage).

(*d*) Sundry Stores : ₹ 60,000.

(*e*) During the period, the vessel was in Mumbai port for 70 days and in London port for 40 days.

(*f*) Conversion rate per £ 1 could be assumed at ₹ 20.

SOLUTION

M.V. Indian Glory
VOYAGE ACCOUNT
from 1st July to 31st December, 2024

		₹			₹
To Standing Charges (184 days @ ₹ 45,000 per day)		82,80,000	By Freight 20,000 tonnes @ ₹ 308 (*i.e.* ₹ 280 plus 10% of ₹ 280)	₹ 61,60,000	
To Stevedoring Expenses : 30,000 tonnes textile & copra @ ₹ 25 per tonne at Mumbai	₹ 7,50,000		10,000 tonnes copra @ ₹ 340 per tonne	34,00,000	
30,000 tonnes textile & copra @ ₹ 20 per tonne at London	6,00,000		32,000 tonnes urea @ ₹ 300 per tonne	96,00,000	
32,000 tonnes of urea @ ₹ 20 per tonne at London	6,40,000		30,000 tonnes of general cargo @ ₹ 276 (*i.e.* ₹ 240 plus 15% of ₹ 240)	82,80,000	
32,000 tonne of urea @ ₹ 20 per tonne at Mumbai	6,40,000				2,74,40,000
30,000 tonnes of general cargo @ ₹ 20 per tonne at Mumbai	6,00,000		By Voyage in Progress (2)		31,66,500
		32,30,000			
To Fuel Consumed (1)		69,48,000			
To Port Dues at Mumbai	2,40,000				
at London (2,000 × ₹ 20)	40,000				
		2,80,000			
To Sundry Stores		60,000			
To Voyage in Progress (30,000 tonnes @ ₹ 276)		82,80,000			
To Net Profit		35,28,500			
		3,06,06,500			3,06,06,500

Working Notes :

(1) *Calculation of Fuel Consumed* :

	Tonnes	Fuel Oil ₹	Tonnes	Diesel ₹
Stay at port 110 days	1,100 tonnes (10 tonnes per day) @ ₹ 1,400 per tonne	15,40,000	550 tonnes (5 tonnes per day) @ ₹ 2,500 per tonne	13,75,000
During journey 74 days	30 tonnes per day *i.e.,* 2,220 @ ₹ 1,400 per tonne	31,08,000	370 tonnes (5 tonnes per day) @ ₹ 2,500 per tonne	9,25,000
		46,48,000		23,00,000

Total amount of Fuel Consumed = ₹ 69,48,000.

(2) *Calculation of Voyage in Progress* :

	Fuel Oil Tonnes	Diesel Tonnes	₹
Fuel consumption :			
At port 21 days	210	105	
Sailing days—10	300	50	
	510	155	
Rate per tonne	₹ 1,400	₹ 2,500	
	₹ 7,14,000	₹ 3,87,500	11,01,500
Stevedoring charges (30,000 tonnes @ ₹ 20 per tonne)			6,00,000
Port charges (given)			60,000
Standing charges for 31 days @ ₹ 45,000 per day			13,95,000
Sundry stores (1/6 on time basis)			10,000
			31,66,500

ILLUSTRATION 5. S.S. Jalaksha voyaged from Visakhapattanam for Kolkata on 1st February, 2025. On 31st March, 2025, when the accounts of the company are closed, S. S. Jalaksha was on her way back to Visakhapattanam from Kolkata on Voyage No. 707, having covered half of the return voyage. Following details of expenses and income for the entire voyage to and from Kolkata are furnished :

		₹			₹
Freight charges		8,00,000	Insurance of :	Ship for the voyage	1,00,000
Port charges		30,000		Freight	40,000
Salary of crew		80,000	Depreciation of the ship for the two		
Consumption of :	Coal	1,40,000	months of the voyage		80,000
	Stores	60,000			

Primage is at 10% on freight charges. Address commission is at 5% on freight charges and primage. Only ₹ 3,00,000 freight was available on return journey to Visakhapattanam. Three-fourths of the total voyage including return journey is complete on 31st March, 2025. Of the total expenses, expenses unconnected with freight shall be carried forward as "in process" for the balance of the journey. As freight is actually earned only on completion of a voyage, you have to carry forward the freight in respect of the return journey as well as all incidental incomes.

Prepare Voyage Account for the period 1st February, 2025 to 31st March, 2025.

SOLUTION

In the Books of S.S. Jalaksha
VOYAGE NO. 707 ACCOUNT
from 1st February, 2025 to 31st March, 2025

	₹		₹	₹
To Port Charges	30,000	By Freight Outward	5,00,000	
To Salary of Crew	80,000	*Add:* Primage 10%	50,000	
To Consumption of Coal	1,40,000			5,50,000
To Consumption of Stores	60,000	By Freight Inward	3,00,000	
To Insurance of Ship	1,00,000	*Add:* Primage 10%	30,000	
Total Expenses Unconnected with Freight for the Entire Voyage	4,10,000			3,30,000
To Depreciation of the Ship	80,000	By Voyage in Progress :		
To Insurance Charges on Freight	40,000	$\frac{1}{2}$ of Total Expenses for the Entire Voyage Unconnected with Freight		
To Address Commission @ 5% on :		$\left(\frac{1}{2}\times ₹\ 4,10,000\right)$	2,05,000	
Freight Outward @ 5% on ₹ 5,50,000	27,500	$\frac{1}{3}$ of Depreciation		
Freight Inward @ 5% on ₹ 3,30,000	16,500	$\left(i.e., \frac{80,000}{1}\times\frac{1}{3}\right)$	(1) 26,667	
To Provision for Incomplete Voyage :				
Freight and Primage on Inward Journey	3,30,000	Address Commission on on Freight Inward	16,500	
To Profit on Voyage	2,39,167	Insurance Charges on Freight $\left(₹\ 40,000\times\frac{3,00,000}{8.00.000}\right)$	15,000	
				2,63,167
	11,43,167			11,43,167

(1) Note : One outward journey and $\frac{1}{2}$ of return journey is complete. Therefore, $\frac{1}{3}$rd $\left(i.e., \frac{\frac{1}{2}}{1\frac{1}{2}}\right)$ of depreciation has been carried forward.

QUESTIONS

OBJECTIVE TYPE

1. **Fill in the blanks :**
   (*a*) Voyage Account is a............account.
   (*b*) Voyage Account is prepared to ascertain............from each voyage.

Ans. [(*a*) Nominal; (*b*) Profit or loss].

2. **State whether the following statements are true or false :**
   (*a*) Passage money is treated as income in Voyage Account.
   (*b*) Profit/Loss is ascertained only for completed voyage while preparing Voyage Account.
   (*c*) Address Commission is calculated as a percentage on freight only.
   (*d*) Voyage Account is a nominal account.
   (*e*) Voyage account is prepared to ascertain profit from all ships owned by shipping company.

Ans. [True : (*a*), (*b*), (*d*). False : (*c*), (*e*)].

SHORT/LONG ANSWER TYPE

1. Explain the meaning of the following terms :
(*a*) Primage ; (*b*) Address Commission; (*c*) Passage Money.
2. What is a Voyage Account.
3. What is voyage in progress ? How is it calculated ?
4. Discuss the nature, necessity and method of preparing Voyage Account. What will be the position if voyage is in progress ?
5. How will you calculate profit in case of incomplete voyage ? Explain by taking a practical example.

Or

What will be the position of voyage in progress ?

PRACTICAL PROBLEMS

1. The S.S. Obyssey undertook a voyage from Athens to Kolkata starting on 1st January, 2025 and reaching on 31st March, 2025. The cargo consisted of 900 tons of food grains and 100 tons of engineering goods. The freight charges were ₹ 150 per ton for foodgrains and ₹ 100 per ton for engineering goods. In addition primage was 10%. Brokerage was payable at 5%. The expenses were :

	Athens	*Kolkata*
	₹	₹
Coal and Diesel	20,000	—
Port Charges	9,000	2,000
Harbour wages	3,000	1,000
Loading charges	2,000	—
Other expenses were :		
Stores	10,000	
Discharging expenses	2,000	
Postage	1,000	
Salaries of crew	10,000	

The ship was insured for ₹ 10,00,000 at 1% for Voyage Policy of Hull. The freight was insured @ $\frac{1}{2}$%. Depreciation is charged on the written down value of the ship at 5% per annum. The value as on 1st January, 2025 was ₹ 8,00,000. Prepare Voyage Account.

Ans. [Profit ₹ 70,727].

2. M.V. Indian Empress is regularly employed on cargo trade between India and East Africa. She set on her voyage on 1st July, 2025 and arrived at her destination on 14th August, 2025. You are required to prepare a Voyage Account bearing in mind the following particulars:
   (*i*) The vessel was purchased in 2003 for ₹ 100 lakhs and at the time of purchase had 16 years of working life left (Depreciation on ships is charged on straight line basis).
   (*ii*) Standing cost per day excluding recovery of depreciation is ₹ 22,000.
   (*iii*) The vessel consumes daily 14 tonnes of fuel oil, 2 tonnes of diesel and 15 tonnes of fresh water. The costs of these are ₹ 1,000, ₹ 1,350 and ₹ 20 per tonne respectively.
   (*iv*) The vessel loaded the under-mentioned cargo :
   4,000 tonnes on which freight of ₹ 375 per tonne was charged and 3,500 tonnes on which the rate of freight was ₹ 190 per tonne;

Both the rates are to be enhanced by a surcharge of 20% over the basic rates.

(*v*) Freight brokers were to be paid a brokerage of $2\frac{1}{2}$ %.

(*vi*) Port charges at the loading and discharging ports were ₹ 40,000 and ₹ 85,000 respectively.

Ans. [Net Profit ₹ 5,75,995].

3. S.S. Kanishka sailed from Kolkata on 1-2-2025 and arrived at Chennai port on 31-3-2025 via Vishakhapatnam port on Voyage No. 403. Following goods were loaded :

1,000 M.T. and 200 M.T. at Kolkata port for Chennai port and Vishakhapatnam port respectively. Another 500 M.T. were loaded at Vishakhapatnam for Chennai. The freight charges were :

Kolkata port to Chennai port ₹ 600 per M.T. ; Kolkata port to Vishakhapatnam port ₹ 500 per M.T. ; Vishakhapatnam port to Chennai port ₹ 400 per M.T.

The freight is subject to 10% primage, 5% address commission and 2.5% brokerage. The freight was insured at 1/2%. The hull was insured for the Voyage at 1%. Depreciation was provided at 3% p.a. The cost of the ship is ₹ 1 crore. Following were the expenses incurred at different ports :

	Kolkata	*Vishakhapatnam*	*Chennai*
	₹	₹	₹
Port charges	36,000	20,000	20,000
Coal	1,00,000	30,000	—
Captain's contingencies	7,000	2,000	10,000
Harbour wages	10,000	20,000	15,000

Stores purchased for the Voyage amounted to ₹ 50,000. Opening Stock of stores was ₹ 40,000 and closing stock was estimated at ₹ 30,000. Stock of coal at close was estimated at ₹ 30,000 as against stock of ₹ 10,000 at the beginning. The ship will not come back to Kolkata port in the near future as part of the voyage programme. Salaries and wages amounted to ₹ 80,000 p.m.

Prepare Voyage No. 403 Account.

Ans. [Profit ₹ 2,90,800].

4. S.S. Jalasakti sailed from Mumbai on 1st February, 2025 and arrived at Kolkata on 31st March, 2025 via Marmagoa, Cochin and Vishakhapatnam. She was loaded with 800 tons of cotton at Mumbai for Vishakhapatnam. At Cochin a further load of 600 tons of coconut oil was booked for Kolkata. Besides, 100 tons of textiles were also loaded at Mumbai for Marmagoa. The freight charges were as follows :

Mumbai to Vishakhapatnam ₹ 80 per ton. Mumbai to Marmagoa ₹ 25 per ton. Cochin to Kolkata ₹ 60 per ton.

Plus Primage 10% and subject to commission at 4% and Brokerage at 2%.

Following were the expenses at different ports :

	Mumbai	*Marmagoa*	*Cochin*	*Vishakhapatnam*	*Kolkata*
	₹	₹	₹	₹	₹
Coal	14,000			2,000	
Port charges	4,000	600	1,000	1,000	3,000
Captain's Expenses	800	500	300	600	700
Harbour Wages	1,200	700	1,100	1,200	2,000
Loading charges	1,600		1,200		

Following were the other expenses :

Stores supplied ₹ 8,400 ; Discharging Expenses ₹ 5,200 ; Despatching of Funds ₹ 400 ; Interest on Advances ₹ 500 ; Postage bills ₹ 600.

The ship was insured for ₹ 5,00,000 at 1.5% premium for the Voyage and the total freight was insured at $\frac{1}{2}$% premium. Depreciation is to be charged on the book value of the ship at ₹ 4,50,000 at 4% p.a. The wages of the sailors are ₹ 8,400 per month.

Prepare Voyage Account.

Ans. **[Net Profit ₹ 25,521].**

5. M.V. Indian Glory is employed on conference trade and is on a regular run between India and the United Kingdom. The Conference freight rate is ₹ 200 per freight tonne to be enhanced by a surcharge of 20% for port congestion and an adjustment of + $7\frac{1}{2}$% for currency factor.

The vessel arrived in Kolkata on 20th February, 2025 and started loading cargo. Loading was over on 1st March (morning) when she set sail for London where she arrived on the night of the 20th of March, 2025. Unloading of the cargo was over and the vessel commenced her next employment on 1st April, 2025 (evening). The total voyage time was calculated at 40 days.

At Kolkata, the ship took in 8,500 freight tonnes. Following direct expenses were incurred :

		₹
(*i*)	Entry fee, tug hire, berth hire at Kolkata	72,000
(*ii*)	Port charges at London	85,000
(*iii*)	Hooghly river dues and lighthouse dues	7,600

(*iv*) Insurance premia on cargo at 0.25% of the basic freight rate.

(*v*) Stevedoring charges are ₹ 18 and ₹ 25 per freight tonne at Kolkata and London respectively.

(*a*) During port stay—4 tonnes of fuel oil and 25 tonnes of fresh water per day.

(*b*) On sailing days—12 tonnes of fuel oil and 10 tonnes of fresh water per day.

Cost of fuel oil—₹ 1,350 per tonne and cost of fresh water—₹ 25 per tonne.

(*vi*) Annual costs of maintenance of ship (you can adopt 360 days as normal working days in a year) :

(*a*) Salaries to officers and crew ₹ 30,00,000 ; (*b*) Insurance premia ₹ 12,15,000 ; (*c*) Repairs and maintenance ₹ 25,00,000 ; (*d*) Interest on loan and capital ₹ 11,25,000 ; (*e*) Working life of vessel bought for ₹75 lakhs is to be taken as six years.

(*vii*) Freight brokerage at $1\frac{1}{2}$% is payable.

Kindly draw a Voyage Account and ascertain the result of the voyage.

Ans. **[Profit on voyage ₹ 1,66,255].**

VOYAGE IN PROGRESS

6. J.J. Jaltranga commenced a voyage on 1st October, 2024 from Mumbai to Chennai. The details of complete voyage, *i.e.* Mumbai to Chennai and back to Mumbai, were as follows :

	₹		₹
Coal Consumption	70,000	Freight	4,00,000
Port Charges	14,000	Stores Consumed	30,000
Depreciation	40,000	Salaries	48,000
Sundry Expenses	4,000	Insurance—Ship	40,000
Wages	8,000	Insurance—Freight	16,000

Primage and address commission are 10% and 5% respectively. Freight relating to the return journey amounted to ₹ 1,20,000 only. The accounts are closed on 31st December The ship was on her half way back to Mumbai on the date of closing the accounts. Prepare Voyage Account upto 31st December, 2024.

Ans. **[Net Profit ₹ 1,54,400; Voyage in Progress ₹ 1,38,400].**

7. Bharat Shipping Ltd. of Mumbai acquired a new ship, M.V. Jalabahi at a cost of ₹ 25,00,000. The ship was ready for service on January 1, 2025. Upto 31st March, 2025, the ship had made 2 complete voyages one to London and back and was half way through the next to London. The ship carried the following freight :

To London 7,500 tonnes @ ₹ 30 per tonne.

From London 9,000 tonnes @ ₹ 25 per tonne.
Unfinished Voyage 9,500 tonnes @ ₹ 25 per tonne.
Following expenses were incurred :

		₹		₹
Salaries & Wages of Crew		80,000	Stevedoring @ ₹ 2 per tonne	52,000
Fuel		40,000	Share of overhead for the ship for the period	30,000
Sundry Stores		8,000		
Port Dues:	₹			
Mumbai	8,400			
London	6,000	14,400		

You are further informed that 5% commission was paid to agents in addition to 1% Address Commission. An insurance policy was taken out @ 2% p.a. on the ship and freight was insured at a premium of ₹ 1,200 p.a.

You are required to prepare Voyage Account for the period of 3 months ending on 31st March, 2025.

Ans. [Profit ₹ 2,41,760; Voyage in Progress ₹ 70,210].

8. S.S. Himalaya set on voyage from Kolkata to Mumbai. On 31st Dec. on which date the accounts are to be closed, the return voyage has not been completed. The details for the entire voyage to Mumbai and back to Kolkata completed after 31st December were :

Freight ₹ 4,00,000; Coal consumption ₹ 70,000; Stores consumed ₹ 30,000; Port charges ₹ 15,000; Salaries of crew ₹ 40,000; Depreciation ₹ 40,000; Insurance—ship ₹ 20,000; Insurance—freight ₹ 8,000; Primage 10%; Address Commission 5%; Only ₹ 1,50,000 freight was available on return journey. Prepare Voyage Account upto 31st December.

Ans. [Net Profit ₹ 1,48,750, Voyage in Progress ₹ 1,18,750 (*i.e.* $\frac{1}{2}$ of total expenses excluding address commission and freight insurance ₹ 1,07,500 + 3/8 of address commission and freight insurance ₹ 30,000 or ₹ 11,250].

CHAPTER 28

Accounting for Packages and Containers

Packages or containers may be of two types, *viz.*, primary and secondary. The former relates to those packages which form part of the products. The cost of such containers is included in the cost of the products. The other type relates to those containers which are required for distribution of goods to the customers.

Accounting Treatment

Accounting for packages or containers is done to achieve the following objectives :

(*a*) To exercise control on movement of containers to ensure that containers are properly returned by customers and due credit is given to them if these are charged separately.

(*b*) To see that there is no misappropriation of containers.

(*c*) To find out profit or loss on containers separately from the main product when a separate charge is made for containers.

The treatment of containers in the accounts will depend upon the policy of the individual concern. This may be :

1. Containers Non-returnable. When containers are not returnable, there are two alternatives, *i.e.*, whether a separate charge is made or not made for these containers.

(*a*) ***When a separate charge is not made***. The charge for the containers in this case will be included in the sale price of the goods. A containers stock account should be kept which will be debited with opening stock of containers and purchases and credited with closing stock, the balance being the expense of containers during the period of the accounts being written off as distribution expense to Profit and Loss Account or if desired, can be charged to Trading or Manufacturing Account as a part of the cost of putting the goods in a saleable condition.

(*b*) ***When a separate charge is made.*** Sometimes when containers are non-returnable, a separate charge is made for them. These charges should be entered in a separate column in the Sales Day Book or Journal. In this case a containers account is opened which will be debited with opening stock of containers and purchases and credited with amount charged to customers and closing stock of containers. As the charge made to the customer is generally higher than cost price, the balance of this account will represent the profit or loss on container. for the period and will be transferred to profit and loss account.

2. Containers Returnable. When containers are returnable, there can be two cases, *i.e.*, when no separate charge is made and when a separate charge is made.

(*a*) ***When no separate charge is made***. The double entry book-keeping will be similar to that in 1 (*a*) except that opening and closing stock will be divided between containers in the warehouse and those in the hands of the customers. Stock must be brought into the accounts at cost less adequate depreciation. Further entries will be necessary in the books, however, in order to keep a check on containers. Each container should have an identification number and columns should be provided in the Sales Day Book or Journals and in customer's account for these numbers. When goods are sent to a customer, the containers' number will be entered in the special column in the Day Book or Journal and posted to the column on the debit side of the customer's account. When containers are returned the number will be entered in a book kept for this purpose at the gate, from which it will be posted to the column of the credit side of the customer's account. Periodical cancellation of numbers appearing on both the sides of the account will reveal the numbers of the containers still in the hands of the customers. Following Journal entries are passed in this case:

(*i*) *For purchases of containers by the firm*
Containers Stock A/c Dr.
To Cash/Bank/Creditors A/c

(*ii*) *When goods are sold in containers*
Customer's A/c Dr.
To Sales A/c

Selling price is so adjusted that it covers the cost of the container. In case customer does not return the container, no further entry is required. It is assumed that the container too has been purchased by the customer along with the goods in the container.

(*iii*) *When containers are returned*
Sales Return A/c Dr. (with depreciated value of containers)
To Customers A/c

(*iv*) *When containers are repaid*
Containers Stock A/c Dr.
To Cash/Bank A/c

(*v*) *When containers are destroyed or lost*
Profit & Loss A/c Dr.
To Containers Stock A/c

(*vi*) *For depreciation on containers*
Profit & Loss A/c Dr.
To Containers Stock A/c

Containers Stock both with the customers and in hand at the end of the period will be shown on the credit side of the containers stock account.

(b) When a separate charge is made. Containers are sometimes charged separately at cost but more usually at a price in excess of cost in order to cover depreciation charges, repairs and bad debts. Similarly credit given for returns is often less than the price at which the containers are charged out. A time limit is often imposed after which containers are not returnable. There are various alternative methods of dealing with these transactions in the books.

Method (I)

Following journal entries will be passed under this case :

(*i*) *For purchase of containers*
Containers Trading A/c Dr. (with purchase price)
To Purchases A/c

(*ii*) *For containers sent to customers*
Customers A/c Dr. (with chargeable price)
To Containers Trading A/c

(*iii*) *For provision required in respect of containers sent*
Containers Trading A/c Dr. (with return price)
To Containers Provision or Reserve or Deposit A/c

(*iv*) *For containers returned by customers*
Containers Provision A/c Dr. (with return price)
To Customers A/c

(*v*) *For Containers retained by customers*
Containers Provision A/c Dr. (with return price)
To Containers Trading A/c

(*vi*) *For Containers destroyed by Fire*
Profit & Loss A/c Dr.
To Containers Trading A/c

(*vii*) *For Containers sold as scrap*
Cash/Bank A/c Dr.
To Containers Trading A/c

(*viii*) *For amount spent on repairs / maintenance*
Containers Trading A/c Dr.
To Cash/Bank A/c

(*ix*) *For containers stock at end*
Containers Stock A/c
To Containers Trading A/c

Note. Reverse entry for opening stock of containers.

(*x*) *For profit on Containers Trading Account*
Containers Trading A/c Dr.
To Profit & Loss A/c

After passing these entries, the following two accounts can be prepared :

Containers Trading Account. This account is a nominal account and shows profit or loss. The *debit side* of this account shows—(*i*) Containers in stock and with customers at cost price ; (*ii*) Purchases at purchase price ; (*iii*) Return price of containers sent to customers (without mentioning the number). The *credit side* shows—(*i*) Containers sent to customers at chargeable price (without mentioning the number); (*ii*) Containers destroyed by fire or other reasons ; (*iii*) Cash realised from sale of scrap ; (*iv*) Containers retained by the customers at return price ; and (*v*) balance of containers in hand and with customers dividing into new and old containers.

Containers Provision or Reserve or Deposit Account. This account does not disclose any profit or loss and is *debited* by (*i*) containers returned by customers at return price ; (*ii*) containers retained by customers at return price ; (*iii*) provision necessary at return price for those containers which are in the hands of customers. This account is *credited* by (*i*) the balance of containers in the hands of customers at return price as beginning provision ; (*ii*) containers sent to customers at return price. The two sides of this account must tally.

ILLUSTRATION 1. A manufacturer sells his products in containers charging them out at ₹ 22 each. Customers are credited by ₹ 18 each if the containers are returned within six weeks. For accounting purposes at closing all stocks with customers and in factory are valued at ₹ 14 each except those representing new ones which are valued at their purchase price, *i.e.,* ₹ 15. Following particulars are available for the year ended 31st March, 2025 :

	Nos.		Nos.
Containers with customers (1-4-2024)	6,800	Containers sold as scrap (for ₹ 300)	50
Containers sent out to customers	10,500	Containers in hand (1-4-2024)	5,000
Containers returned by customers	3,400	Containers with customers (31-3-2025)	4,600
Containers destroyed by fire	200		

Purchases during the year totalled to ₹ 1,65,000.

You are required to prepare Containers Trading Account and Containers Provision Account.

SOLUTION

CONTAINERS TRADING ACCOUNT

	Rate	No.	Amount		Rate	No.	Amount
	₹		₹		₹		₹
To Balance b/d	14	5,000	70,000	By Customers A/c			
In hand with customers	14	6,800	95,200	10,500	22		2,31,000
To Purchases	15	11,000	1,65,000	By Profit & Loss A/c			
" Containers Provision A/c 10,500	18		1,89,000	(Destroyed by fire)	14	200	2,800
To Profit & Loss A/c			78,800	By Cash (Sale as Scrap)		50	300
				By Containers Provision A/c (retained)	18	(1) 9,300	1,67,400
				By Balance c/d : In hand	15	(2) 8,650	1,29,750
				Customers Old	14	2,250	31,500
				New	15	2,350	35,250
		22,800	5,98,000			22,800	5,98,000

CONTAINERS PROVISION ACCOUNT

	₹	No.	₹		₹	No.	₹
To Customers (Returns)	18	3,400	61,200	By Balance b/d	18	6,800	1,22,400
" Containers Trading A/c (Retained)	18	9,300	1,67,400	" Containers Trading A/c	18	10,500	1,89,000
To Balance c/d	18	4,600	82,800				
		17,300	3,11,400			17,300	3,11,400

Working Notes :

(1) ***Containers retained by customers***

	No.	No.
Opening Stock with customers		6,800
Containers sent		10,500
		17,300
Less : Returned	3,400	
" Returnable	4,600	
		8,000
		9,300

(2) ***Containers in hand***

Opening Stock	5,000
Purchases	11,000
Received from customers	3,400
	19,400

Less :	Sent to customers	10,500	
	Destroyed by fire	200	
	Sold as Scrap	50	
			10,750
			8,650

(3) ***Containers with customers***

New (11,000 – 8,650 Containers in hand)	2,350
Old (Balancing figure)	2,250
	4,600

Method (II)

(*a*) Containers Stock Account. This is a real account prepared at cost price and will not disclose any profit or loss. This account is *debited* by (*i*) Balance of containers stock in hand and with customers ; (*ii*) Purchase of containers at purchase price and *credited by* (*i*) containers retained by customers ; (*ii*) loss of containers destroyed, lost or scrapped; (*iii*) stock of containers in hand and with customers dividing into new and old containers.

(*b*) Containers Trading Account. This is a nominal account and will show profit or loss on the issue of containers. This account is *debited by* (*i*) containers retained by the customers (at cost) ; (*ii*) cost of containers sold as scrap ; (*iii*) maintenance cost of packages, and *credited by* (*i*) rental of containers sent to customers ; (*ii*) sale of retained containers at return price ; (*iii*) Cash realised from sale of scrapped containers. The difference between the two sides will be profit or loss on containers.

Following accounts are prepared by solving the illustration 1 under this method :

CONTAINERS STOCK ACCOUNT

	Rate	No.	Amount		Rate	No.	Amount
	₹		₹		₹		₹
To Balance b/d				By Containers			
In hand	14	5,000	70,000	Trading A/c			
With Customers	14	6,800	95,200	(Containers retained			
" Purchases	15	11,000	1,65,000	by customers)	14	9,300	1,30,200
				" P. & L. A/c (Cost of			
				containers destroyed)	14	200	2,800
				" Containers Trading A/c			
				(Cost of containers sold			
				as scrap)	14	50	700
				" Balance c/d			
				With customers			
				Old	14	2,250	31,500
				New	15	2,350	35,250
				In hand	15	8,650	1,29,750
		22,860	3,30,200			22,800	3,30,200

CONTAINERS TRADING ACCOUNT

	Rate	No.	Amount		Rate	No.	Amount
	₹		₹		₹		₹
To Containers Stock				By Customers A/c			
A/c (retained)	14	9,300	1,30,200	(Rental of 10,500			

To Containers Stock A/c (Cost of containers sold as scrap)	14	50	700	containers)	4		42,000
" Profit & Loss A/c (Profit)			78,800	" Customers A/c Sale of 9,300 drums	18	9,300	1,67,400
				" Cash—realised from the sale of containers as scrap		50	300
		9,350	2,09,700			9,350	2,09,700

PROFIT & LOSS ACCOUNT

	₹		₹
To Containers Stock A/c (Cost of Containers destroyed by Fire)	2,800	By Containers Trading A/c	78,800

MEMORANDUM CUSTOMERS ACCOUNT

	Rate	No.	Amount		Rate	No.	Amount
	₹		₹		₹		₹
To Balance b/d	18	6,800	1,22,400	By Containers Returned	18	3,400	61,200
To Containers sent out	18	10,500	1,89,000	By Containers Sold (Retained)	18	9,300	1,67,400
				" Balance c/d	18	4,600	82,800
		17,300	3,11,400			17,300	3,11,400

Method (III)

Journal entries to be recorded in the third method are as follows :

1. For purchase of containers

Containers Stock A/c	Dr.	(with purchase price of containers)
To Bank A/c		

2. When containers are sent out to customers :

(*a*) Customers A/c	Dr.	(with chargeable price)
To Containers Trading A/c		
(*b*) Containers Trading A/c	Dr.	(with return price)
To Containers Provision A/c		

3. For containers returned by the customers :

Containers Provision A/c		(with return price)
To Customers A/c		

4. For Containers retained by customers :

(*a*) Containers Provision A/c	Dr.	(with return price)
To Containers Trading A/c		
(*b*) Containers Trading A/c	Dr.	(with cost of containers retained)
To Containers Stock A/c		

5. When Containers are sold as scrap :

(*a*) Bank A/c	Dr.	(with amount realised)
To Containers Trading A/c		

(*b*) Containers Trading A/c Dr. (with cost of containers sold as scrap)
To Containers Stock A/c

6. If Containers are destroyed in an accident or by fire :
Profit and Loss A/c Dr. (with cost of containers lost by fire or accident)
To Containers Stock A/c

7. For transfer of profit on trading in containers :
Containers Trading A/c Dr. (with profit disclosed by Containers Trading A/c)
To Profit & Loss A/c

8. For depreciation provided on containers :
Containers Trading A/c Dr. (with depreciation *i.e.,* reduction in value of containers)
To Containers Stock A/c

Note. In the above mentioned entries, book value of containers instead of cost of containers will be credited if depreciation has been provided earlier on containers.

Containers Stock Account will be the same as in method (*ii*). But Containers Trading Account and Containers Reserve Account are prepared as given below :

CONTAINERS TRADING ACCOUNT

	Rate	Amount		Rate	Amount
	₹	₹		₹	₹
To Containers Reserve A/c (10,500 containers)	18	1,89,000	By Customers A/c (10,500 Containers)	22	2,31,000
To Containers Stock A/c (Cost of drums retained 9,300)	14	1,30,200	By Containers Reserve A/c (Provision of 9,300 drums not required)	18	1,67,400
" Containers Stock A/c —Cost of Drums Sold as Scrap	14	700	" Cash—Sale proceeds of containers sold as scrap		300
" Profit & Loss A/c		78,800			
		3,98,700			3,98,700

CONTAINERS RESERVE ACCOUNT

	Rate	No.	Amount		Rate	No.	Amount
	₹		₹		₹		₹
To Customers A/c	18	3,400	61,200	By Balance b/d	18	6,800	1,22,400
" Containers Trading A/c	18	9,300	1,67,400	" Containers Trading A/c	18	10,500	1,89,000
" Balance c/d	18	4,600	82,800				
		17,300	3,11,400			17,300	3,11,400

MISCELLANEOUS ILLUSTRATIONS

ILLUSTRATION 2. Packers Ltd. sells its products charging them out at ₹ 50 each. Customers are credited by ₹ 45 each if the containers are returned within 2 months. All stocks with the customers and in the factory on the date of closing are valued at ₹ 40 each, except those representing new ones which are valued at their purchase price. The opening stock with customers and in factory has been valued at ₹ 50 each. Following particulars with regard to the containers are available for the year ended 31st March, 2025:

	No. of Containers		*No. of Containers*
Stock with customers (1-4-2024)	6,800	Returnable stock with customers (31-3-2025)	4,000
Stock in factory (1-4-2024)	8,200	Stock in factory (31-3-2025)	10,700
Sent out to customers	60,000	Purchased during the year	₹ 1,20,000
Returned by customers	60,600		
Sold as scrap (for ₹ 30 each)	100		

Prepare Containers Stock Account and Containers Reserve Account. ***(C.A. Inter)***

(For Solution see next page)

Working Notes :

(1) **Containers Retained by Customers :**

MEMORANDUM CUSTOMERS ACCOUNT (QUANTITY COLUMN)

	Qty. Nos.		*Qty. Nos.*
To Balance b/d	6,800	By Containers returned	60,600
" Containers sent out	60,000	" Containers retained	2,200
		" Balance c/d	4,000
	66,800		66,800

(2) **Containers Purchased :**

		Nos.	*Nos.*
Opening Stock :			
In factory		8,200	
With customers		6,800	
			15,000
Less : Containers retained by customers		2,200	
Containers scrapped		100	
			2,300
	(A)		12,700
Closing Stock :			
In factory		10,700	
With customers		4,000	
	(B)		14,700
Purchased (B – A)			2,000

SOLUTION

Packers Ltd.

CONTAINERS STOCK ACCOUNT

Particulars	Qty.	Rate	Amount	Particulars	Qty.	Rate	Amount
	Nos.	₹	₹		Nos.	₹	₹
To Balance b/d				By Containers Trading A/c	2,200	50	1,10,000
In factory	8,200	50	4,10,000	" Contaners Trading A/c			
With customers	6,800	50	3,40,000	(Loss on valuation of stock)			1,27,000
To Purchases	2,000	60	1,20,000	" Containers Trading A/c	100	50	5,000
				" Balance c/d			
				In Factory			
				—Old	8,700	40	3,48,000
				—New	2,000	60	1,20,000
				With customers	4,000	40	1,60,000
	17,000		8,70,000		17,000		8,70,000

CONTAINERS RESERVE ACCOUNT

	Qty.	Rate	Amount		Qty.	Rate	Amount
	Nos.	₹	₹		Nos.	₹	₹
To Containers Debtors A/c				By Balance b/d	6,800	45	3,06,000
(Containers returned)	60,600	45	27,27,000	" Containers Trading A/c			
" Containers Trading A/c				—Containers sent out	60,000	45	27,00,000
(Containers retained) (1)	2,200	45	99,000				
" Balance c/d	4,000	45	1,80,000				
	66,800		30,06,000		66,800		30,06,000

ILLUSTRATION 3. A manufacturer sells his goods to customers in containers. Following information is given in respect of the year 2024-25 :

	Number		*Number*
Purchases during the year	60,000	With customers on 31-3-2025 (Returnable)	10,000
Sent out to customers	50,000	Returns from customers	4,000
Fully destroyed	200	With customers on 1-4-2024 (Returnable)	6,000
Sold as scrap (₹ 1,000)	400		
At godown 1-4-2024	12,000		

Purchases during the year amounted to ₹ 6,00,000. Hire charge is ₹ 4 per container. Chargeable price is 80% above cost. Cost price of container is constant over the last 3 years.

Prepare Containers Stock Account and Containers Suspense Account. ***(C.A. Inter)***

SOLUTION

CONTAINERS STOCK ACCOUNT

	Qty.	Rate	Amount		Qty.	Rate	Amount
	Nos.	₹	₹		Nos.	₹	₹
To Opening Stock				By Containers Trading A/c (Retained)	42,000	10	4,20,000
At Godown	12,000	10	1,20,000				
With Customers	6,000	10	60,000	By Profit & Loss A/c (Destroyed)	200	10	2,000
To Purchases	60,000	10	6,00,000				
				By Containers Trading A/c (Cost of containers sold as scrap)	400	10	4,000
				By Closing Stock			
				At Godown	25,400	10	2,54,000
				With customers	10,000	10	1,00,000
	78,000		7,80,000		78,000		7,80,000

CONTAINERS SUSPENSE ACCOUNT

	Qty.	Rate	Amount		Qty.	Rate	Amount
	Nos.	₹	₹		Nos.	₹	₹
To Containers Trading A/c (Retained)	42,000	14	5,88,000	By Balance b/d (with Customers)	6,000	14	84,000
To Return from Customers	4,000	14	56,000	By Containers Trading A/c	50,000	14	7,00,000
To Balance c/d (with customers)	10,000	14	1,40,000				
	56,000		7,84,000		56,000		7,84,000

Working Notes :

(1) *No. of Containers Retained by Customers :*

	Nos.
Nos. with Customers on 1-4-2024	6,000
Add : Sent out	50,000
	56,000

	Nos.	
Less : Returns	4,000	
Closing Balance with Customers on 31-3-2025	10,000	
		14,000
		42,000

(2) *Closing Stock of Containers at Godown 31-3-2025*

	Nos.	Nos.
At Godown on 1-4-2024		12,000
With Customers on 1-4-2024		6,000
		18,000
Add : Purchases		60,000
		78,000
Less : Fully Destroyed	200	
Sold as Scrap	400	
Retained	42,000	
With Customers 31-3-2025	10,000	
		52,600
		25,400

ILLUSTRATION 4. Hard Luck Chemicals Ltd. deliver goods to customers in drums (which are valued in books at ₹ 30 each) charging them out at ₹ 60 each. Customers are credited with ₹ 40 each, if the drums are returned within six weeks. Following information is supplied to you :

	Drums		*Drums*
Stock in hand on 1st April, 2024	2,000	Drums returned by customers	4,600
Drums with customers on 1st April, 2024 (Still returnable)	4,200	Drums destroyed in an accident	60
Purchases at ₹ 50 each	3,000	Drums sold as scrap for ₹ 1,000	100
Drums sent out to customers	6,400	Repairs carried out to drums ₹ 3,500	—

On 31st March, 2025, 3,800 drums were with customers and could be returned within the following week.

You are required to show Drums Stock Account, Drums Trading Account and Memorandum Customers Account in the books of the Company.

SOLUTION

DRUMS STOCK ACCOUNT

	Nos.	₹		Nos.	₹
To Balance b/d			By Drums Trading A/c		
In hand	2,000	60,000	(See Memorandum		
With Customers	4,200	1,26,000	Customers A/c)		
To Purchases A/c	3,000	1,50,000	(Drums retained)	2,200	66,000
			By Profit & Loss A/c		
			(Destroyed)	60	1,800
			By Drums Trading A/c		
			(Sold as Scrap)	100	3,000
			By Balance c/d		
			With Customers	3,800	1,14,000
			In Hand : Old	40	1,200
			New	3,000	1,50,000
	9,200	3,36,000		9,200	3,36,000

DRUMS TRADING ACCOUNT

	Nos.	₹		Nos.	₹
To Drums Stock A/c (retained)	2,200	66,000	By Customers A/c (Rental of 6,400 drums @ ₹ 20 each)		1,28,000
To Drums Stock A/c (Sold as scrap)	100	3,000	By Customers A/c (Sale of 2,200 drums @ ₹ 40 each)	2,200	88,000
To Cash—Repairs		3,500	By Cash—realised by Sale of drums as Scrap	100	1,000
To Profit & LossA/c		1,44,500			
	2,300	2,17,000		2,300	2,17,000

MEMORANDUM CUSTOMERS ACCOUNT

	Nos.	₹		Nos.	₹
To Balance b/d	4,200	1,68,000	By Drums returned	4,600	1,84,000
To Drums sent out	6,400	2,56,000	By Drums sold being not returnable (Bal. fig.)	2,200	88,000
			Balance c/d	3,800	1,52,000
	10,600	4,24,000		10,600	4,24,000

ILLUSTRATION 5. Chennai Chemical Ltd. supply their products in returnable drums which are charged at ₹ 20 each. Customers returning the drums with in a month are credited with ₹ 18. The company's procedure is to retain ₹ 18 in deposit account till the date of expiry of the option period for return of the drums. Following particulars are available from the books :

	₹		₹
Returnable drums as on 1-4-2024	8,000	Drums returned by customers in 2024-25	2,88,000
Drums in stock as on 1-4-2024	16,000	Drums returnable on 31-3-2025	15,000
Drums purchased during 2024-25 at ₹ 15 per drum	20,000	Drums scrapped in 2024-25—sold for ₹ 10,000	2,000
Drums sent to customers during 2024-25	3,00,000		

All drums as on 31-3-2024 and 31-3-2025 are to be valued at ₹ 10 each. All the amount due in respect of drums have been collected from the customers.

You are asked to show the Ledger Accounts for the year 2024-25 : (*a*) Drums Stock A/c (*b*) Drums Debtors A/c (*c*) Drums Deposits A/c and (*d*) Drums Trading A/c.

SOLUTION

Chennai Chemicals Ltd.
DRUMS STOCK ACCOUNT

	Nos.	₹		Nos.	₹
To Balance c/d			By Drums Trading A/c (Scrapped)	2,000	20,000
With customers	8,000	80,000			
In hand	16,000	1,60,000	By Drums Trading A/c (retained) (*i*)	5,000	50,000
To Purchases	20,000	3,00,000			

	Nos.	₹			Nos.	₹
			By Drums Trading A/c (Depreciation on 20,000 drums @ ₹ 5 per drum)			1,00,000
			By Balance c/d			
			With customers		15,000	1,50,000
			In hand	(*ii*)	22,000	2,20,000
	44,000	5,40,000			44,000	5,40,000

DRUMS TRADING ACCOUNT

	₹		₹
To Drums Stock A/c (cost of drums scrapped)	20,000	By Bank (Sale of scrap)	10,000
To Drums Stock A/c (cost of drums retained)	50,000	By Drums Deposit A/c (5,000 @ ₹ 18)	90,000
To Drums Stock A/c (Depreciation)	1,00,000	By Drums Debtors A/c (Hire charge 3,00,000 × ₹ 2)	6,00,000
To Profit & Loss A/c (Profit)	5,30,000		
	7,00,000		7,00,000

DRUMS DEBTORS ACCOUNT

	Nos.	₹		Nos.	₹
To Balance b/d	8,000	1,60,000	By Drums Deposit A/c (Returns)	2,88,000	51,84,000
To Drums Trading A/c (3,00,000 × ₹ 2)		6,00,000	By Drums retained	5,000	—
To Drums Deposit A/c (3,00,000 × ₹ 18)	3,00,000	54,00,000	By Bank (Bal. fig.)		6,76,000
			By Balance c/d : @ ₹ 20	15,000	3,00,000
	3,08,000	61,60,000		3,08,000	61,60,000

DRUMS DEPOSIT ACCOUNT

	Nos.	₹		Nos.	₹
To Drum Debtors (Returns)	2,88,000	51,84,000	By Balance b/d	8,000	1,44,000
To Drums Trading A/c (Retained)	5,000	90,000	By Drums Debtors (Sent out)	3,00,000	54,00,000
To Balance c/d	15,000	2,70,000			
	3,08,000	55,44,000		3,08,000	55,44,000

Working Notes :

(*i*) ***Calculation of drums retained***

	Nos.
Opening stock of drums with customers	8,000
Add : Sent out during the year	3,00,000
	3,08,000
Less : Returned by Customers	2,88,000
	20,000
Less : Returnable	15,000
Retained by customers	5,000

(ii) Calculation of closing balance of drums in hand

	Nos.
Opening stock of drums	16,000
Add : Purchases	20,000
Add : Returned by customers	2,88,000
	3,24,000
Less : Sent out to customers	3,00,000
	24,000
Less : Scrapped during the year	2,000
Closing Balance	22,000

ILLUSTRATION 6. Lubricants Ltd. sells oil in drums which are charged at ₹ 10 each. Customers returning drums within a month are credited with ₹ 8.

Following information is available from the books :

		Nos.
(a)	Returnable drums as on 1-1-2024	4,000
(b)	Drums physically in stock as on 1-1-2024	8,000
(c)	Drums purchased in 2024 at ₹ 5 each	30,000
(d)	Drums sent out in 2024	5,00,000
(e)	Drums scrapped in 2024 (sold for ₹ 5,000)	2,000
(f)	Drums returned by the customers	4,80,000
(g)	Drums sent out in December, 2024 lying with customers	10,000

(h) All drums as on 1st January, 2024 were valued at ₹ 2 each

(j) All drums as on 31st December, 2024 are to be valued at 50 per cent below cost price.

(k) Amount due from (Drums) Debtors as on 1st January, 2024 ₹ 10,000.

(l) Amount received from (Drums) Debtors during the year — ₹ 11,00,000.

Prepare Ledger Accounts in the books of Lubricants Ltd.

SOLUTION

DRUMS TRADING ACCOUNT

	Rate	Nos.	Amount		Rate	Nos.	Amount
	₹		₹		₹		₹
To Balance b/d				By Drums Drs. A/c		—	50,00,000
With Customers	2	4,000	8,000	" Cash	2.5	2,000	5,000
In Stock	2	8,000	16,000	" Drums Provision A/c			
" Purchases	5	30,000	1,50,000	(Retained)	8	(1)14,000	1,12,000
" Drums Provision A/c	8		40,00,000	" Balance c/d			
" Net Profit			10,08,000	With Customers	2.5	10,000	25,000
				In Stock	2.5	(2)16,000	40,000
		42,000	51,82,000			42,000	51,82,000

DRUMS PROVISION ACCOUNT

	Rate	Nos.	Amount		Rate	Nos.	Amount
	₹		₹		₹		₹
To Drums Debtors A/c				By Balance b/d	8	4,000	32,000
(Returns)	8	4,80,000	38,40,000	" Drums Trading A/c	8	5,00,000	40,00,000

To Drums Trading A/c (Retained)	8	14,000	1,12,000				
" Balance c/d	8	10,000	80,000				
		5,04,000	40,32,000			5,04,000	40,32,000

DRUMS DEBTORS ACCOUNT

	₹		₹
To Balance b/d	10,000	By Drums Provision A/c (Returns)	38,40,000
To Drums Trading A/c (Sent out)	50,00,000	By Bank	11,00,000
		By Balance c/d	70,000
	50,10,000		50,10,000
To Balance b/d	70,000		

Working Notes :

(1) *Drums retained by Customers*

		Nos.
Opening Stock with Customers		4,000
Drums sent		5,00,000
	Nos.	5,04,000
Less : Returned	4,80,000	
Returnable	10,000	
		4,90,000
Drums retained by Customers		14,000

(2) *Containers in hand*

		Nos.
Opening Stock		8,000
Purchases		30,000
Received from Customers		4,80,000
	Nos.	5,18,000
Less : Sent to Customers	5,00,000	
Sold as Scrap	2,000	
		5,02,000
Containers in hand on 31-12-2024		16,000

ILLUSTRATION 7. ABC Ltd. supplies their products in returnable drums. A drum is invoiced @ ₹ 80, but if it is returned within a month, a credit of ₹ 70 is given to the customs. A drum costs ₹ 70 to the company and its life is estimated at 12 years at the end of which the scrap value in likely to be ₹ 10. Following particulars are supplied to you :

Stock in hand as on 1-4-2024	28,000	Purchases	2,000
Stock with customers as on 1-4-2024	20,000	Sent out to customers	1,20,000
Stock in hand as on 31-3-2025	?	Returned by customers	1,26,000
Stock with customers as on 31-3-2025	12,000	Scrapped (sold for ₹ 16,000) (useful life being over)	3,000

Method of charging depreciation-straight line

Prepare Drums Trading Account and Profit and Loss Account and Drums Reserve Account.

SOLUTION

DRUMS TRADING AND PROFIT AND LOSS ACCOUNT

for the year ending 31st March, 2025

	Rate	Nos.	Amount		Rate	Nos.	Amount
	₹		₹		₹		₹
To Balance b/d				By Customers A/c	80		96,00,000
In hand	70	28,000	19,60,000	(1,20,000 × ₹ 80)			
With Customers	70	20,000	14,00,000	By Bank A/c			
To Bank (Purchases)	70	2,000	1,40,000	(Sale of drums			
To Drum Reserve A/c	70		84,00,000	scrapped)		3,000	16,000
(1,20,000 × ₹ 70)				By Drum Reserve A/c			
To Gross Profit c/d			11,86,000	(Reserve on drums			
				retained not required)	70	(1) 2,000	1,40,000
				By Provision for Depreciation A/c (Accumulated depreciation @ ₹ 60 on 3,000 drums scrapped after useful life of 12 years being over)			1,80,000
				By Balance c/d			
				In hand	70	(2) 33,000	23,10,000
				With Customers	70	12,000	8,40,000
		50,000	1,30,86,000			50,000	1,30,86,000
To Provision for Depreciation A/c (Depreciation on 45,000 drums @ ₹ 5 for the year)			2,25,000	By Gross Profit b/d			11,86,000
To Net Profit			9,61,000				
			11,86,000				11,86,000

DRUMS RESERVE ACCOUNT

for the year ending 31st March, 2025

	Rate	Nos.	Amount		Rate	Nos.	Amount
	₹		₹		₹		₹
To Customers A/c				By Balance b/d	70	20,000	14,00,000
(Reserve on drums				By Drums Trading A/c			
returned not required)	70	1,26,000	88,20,000	(Reserve on drums			
To Drum Trading A/c				sent out)	70	1,20,000	84,00,000
(Reserve on drums							
retained)	70	2,000	1,40,000				

To Balance c/d	70	12,000	8,40,000				
		1,40,000	98,00,000			1,40,000	98,00,000
				By Balance b/d	70	12,000	8,40,000

Working Notes :

1. ***Calculation of Number of Drums Retained by Customers***

		Nos.
No. of drums with customers as on 1-4-2024		20,000
Add : Sent out during the year 2024-25		1,20,000
	Nos.	1,40,000
Less : No. of drums returned by customers	1,26,000	
Stock with customers as on 31-3-2025	12,000	
		1,38,000
Number of drums retained by customers		2,000

2. ***Calculation of Number of Drums in Hand as on 31-3-2025***

		Nos.
Stock as on 1-4-2024		28,000
Add : Purchases		2,000
No. of drums returned by customers		1,26,000
	Nos.	1,56,000
Less : No. of drums sent out to customers	1,20,000	
No. of drums scrapped	3,000	
		1,23,000
No. of drums in hand as on 31-3-2025		33,000

QUESTIONS

SHORT/LONG ANSWER TYPE

1. How are containers not returnable treated in accounts ?
2. What are the items recorded as the debit and credit sides of a Containers Stock Account ?
3. Discuss the method of Accounting for Package and Containers ?
4. Discuss the accounting treatment of containers when these are returnable.
5. Discuss the accounting treatment of containers when these are (*i*) returnable and (*ii*) non-returnable.
6. Write short notes on : (*i*) Containers Stock A/c, (*ii*) Containers Suspense A/c, (*iii*) Customers Control A/c and (*iv*) Containers Trading Account.
7. Explain the difference between retained containers and returnable containers.
8. In case of returnable containers, the three accounts usually opened are : (*a*) Containers Stock Account, (*b*) Containers Suspense Account, (*c*) Containers Trading Account. Give the items debited and credited in these accounts by giving the specimens of these accounts.

PRACTICAL PROBLEMS

1. Messrs Internal Trading Company despatch their returnable packages to the customers. Following policy has been adopted by the management in regard to pricing and valuation of stock in their books and Balance Sheet :

   (1) The packages in hand are valued at cost and those with the customers at cost price less 25%.

(2) The packages are invoiced to the customers at cost price plus 25%.

(3) Full credit is given to the customers for the packages returned by them.

Following information is furnished to you :

(*i*) Value of packages as per Balance Sheet as on 31st March, 2024 :

(*a*) In hand ₹ 600 ; (*b*) With the customers ₹ 400.

(*ii*) Packages purchased during the year — ₹ 2,000.

(*iii*) Packages sent to the customers at invoice rate — ₹ 5,600.

(*iv*) Packages returned by the customers at invoice rate — ₹ 4,400.

Calculate the value of the packages in hand and those with the customers as on 31st March, 2025 to be shown in the Balance Sheet.

Ans. [Value of Packages in hand, ₹ 1,640 ; Value of packages with customers, ₹ 1,120; Value to be shown in B/S ₹ 2,760].

2. X Ltd. supplies goods to customers in packages, which are priced at 20 p. each in the accounts books. The company charges them at 40 p. each but credits the customers at 35 p. each when the packages are returned within a specified period. On 1st January, 2024, there were 2,000 packages in stock and 4,000 packages in the hands of customers. The company made fresh purchases at 25 p. each of 5,000 packages during the year upto 31st December, 2024 and sent out to customers, 7,000 packages. 7,400 packages were returned to the company and 250 packages were sold as scrap for ₹ 25. At the end of the year 2,600 packages were in the hands of the customers to be returned. Show the Ledger Accounts to record the above transactions.

Ans. [Profit ₹ 475].

Hints [:Packages retained by customers 1,000 ; Containers in Hand (New 5,000 + Old 2,150) 7,150].

3. On 1-4-2024 stock of packages in hand was ₹ 8,000 (valued in the books at cost less 25%) and ₹ 1,200 in the hands of customers at invoice price, which is cost plus 50%.

For the year ended 31st March, 2025, packages were charged out at cost plus 50% and full credit was given in respect of those returned in good condition. Packages sent out during the year were ₹ 16,000 (invoice price) and returns (all in good condition) ₹ 10,000. Customers retained packages at an invoice price of ₹ 300 and closing stock of packages in hand at cost ₹ 6,666.67.

Write up necessary Accounts.

Ans. [Profit ₹ 150].

Hint : [Purchases—Nil, Packages with customers at cost price ₹ 3,450.]

4. G.B. sold a product which required expensive containers. These cost ₹ 10 each and were invoiced to customers at ₹ 15 each on the basis of sale or return within two months.

In his impersonal ledger G.B. maintained a Customers Control Account, a Containers Stock Account and to record the unrealised profit on containers in the hands of customers, a "Containers' Suspense Account".

On April 1, 2024 there were 70 containers in stock and in addition 60 in the hands of customers which had been delivered to them within the previous two months.

During the six months ended September 30, 2024, 380 containers had been despatched to customers and 320 had been returned within two months ; 40, which had not been returned had been duly paid for by the customers ; 100 containers had been purchased, 20 had been scrapped after return and sold for cash in September, 2024 for ₹ 5 each. Repairs to other containers returned cost ₹ 100, paid in cash.

You are required to write up the three accounts in G.B's Impersonal Ledger recording these transactions, bringing down the balances as on September 30, 2024.

Ans. [Profit—Nil ; Stock with customers ₹ 1,200 (80 containers) ; Stock in hand ₹ 900 (90 containers)].

5. P. Co. Ltd. sells its products in returnable packages. Customers are charged at ₹ 5 for each package at the time of sale and credited with ₹ 4 if the packages are returned in two months. In case the packages are returned in a damaged condition credit is given for ₹ 2.

Following figures are available for the year ended on 31-3-2025 :

	Nos.	₹
Returnable package with customers as on 1-4-2024	20,000	40,000
Stock in hand as on 1-4-2024	5,000	10,000
Packages purchased during the year	15,000	45,000
Returnable packages with customers as on 31-3-2025	10,000	
Packages sent during the year	50,000	
Packages returned in damaged condition during the year	5,000	
Packages not returned within the scheduled time during the year	20,000	

All stock is to be valued at cost, assuming that FIFO method was followed for the purpose of despatch to customers. Damaged packages are to be valued at 50% of cost.

Write up the necessary Ledger Accounts.

Ans. [Profit ₹ 95,000].

Hints : Packages returned 40,000 ; Stock in Hand 10,000. In both cases 5,000 damaged are included.

6. Mumbai Chemical Ltd. supply their products in returnable containers. A container is invoiced to the customer at ₹ 40 but if it is returned within two months, a credit of ₹ 35 is given to the customer. A container costs ₹ 35 to the company and its life is estimated at 6 years at the end of which scrap value is likely to be ₹ 5. Following particulars are supplied to you :

	Nos.		*Nos.*
Containers with customers (1-4-2024)	10,000	Containers purchased during the year	1,000
Containers in stock (1-4-2024)	14,000	Containers condemned during the year, useful life being over	1,500
Containers sent to customers during the year 2024-25	60,000	Amount realised by sale of condemned containers	₹ 8,000
Containers returned by customers	63,000		
Containers returnable	6,000		

Depreciation is to be provided on straight line basis.

Prepare Containers Trading Account for the year and ascertain the profit or loss earned or incurred in the year.

Ans. [Net Profit ₹ 1,88,000].

Hints : Containers retained 1,000 ; Closing stock at shop 16,500 containers.

7. A firm sells its goods in containers bought at ₹ 20 each. Customers are charged at ₹ 24 per container and are allowed ₹ 16 for each container returned within a given period. For stock taking purposes, all containers in the factory and in the hands of customers are valued at ₹ 14 each.

From the following information, draw up the necessary Accounts in the books of the firm for the year ended 31st March, 2025 :

	Number of Containers		*Number of Containers*
In the factory at 1st April 1, 2024	9,000	Purchased during the year 2024-25	12,000
With customers at 1st April 1, 2024 (Returnable)	7,200	Sent to customers during the year 2024-25	20,000
With customers at 31st March, 2025 (Returnable)	5,800	Returned by customers during the year 2024-25	13,600

Ans. [Profit ₹ 1,03,600].

Hints : Containers retained by customers 7,800 ; Containers in factory 14,600.

8. A Manufacturer sells his products in containers charging them out at ₹ 12 each. Customers are credited by ₹ 10 each if the containers are returned within 3 months. For accounting purposes at closing, all stocks with customers and in factory are valued at ₹ 8 each except representing new ones which are valued at their purchase price. Following particulars are available for the year ended 30th June, 2025 :

	No. of Containers		*No. of Containers*
Stock with Customers on 1-7-2024 (all returnable)	1,200	Purchases during the year (at a uniform rate) totalled to ₹ 5,040	?
Stock in hand on 1-7-2024	900	Sent to Customers	6,500
Stock with Customers on 30-6-2025 (all returnable)	1,000	Returned by Customers	6,000
Stock in hand on 30-6-2025	800	Destroyed by fire	100
		Sold as scrap for ₹ 300	60

You are required to prepare (*a*) Containers Trading Account and (*b*) Containers Suspense Account in the books of the Manufacturer for the year ended 30th June, 2025.

Ans. **[Profit ₹ 14,220].**

Hints : Containers Retained 700 ; No. of Containers Purchased 560.

9. A manufacturer sends its products in Drums costing ₹ 30 each, charges its customers at ₹ 40 each, allows credit to customers at ₹ 35 each if returned in due time and values the stock of drums for Balance Sheet purpose at ₹ 20 each on the average at depreciated value.

From the following particulars, prepare the Drums Trading Account, Deposit (Reserve) for Drums Account for the year ending 31st March, 2025 and show how the relevant items will appear in the Profit and Loss Account and Balance Sheet as on 31st March, 2025 :

			Number of Drums
Stock in hand, 1-4-2024	5,000	Stock in hand, 31-3-2025	?
Stock with customers, 1-4-2024 (Returnable)	6,000	Sold for cash ₹ 4,500, as old/defective	450
Purchases in 2024-25	9,000	Scrapped (of no value)/Rejected	50
Set out to customers in 2024-25	25,000	Retained by and treated as sold to customers	?
Returned by customers in 2024-25	16,000	Repaired old drums for ₹ 1,000	600
Stock with customers, 31-3-2025 (Returnable)	12,000		

Ans. **[Profit ₹ 74,500].**

Hints : Closing Stock in Hand 4,500 ; Retained by customers 3,000.

10. M sells his goods in special packages costing ₹ 25 each. Packages are charged out at ₹ 40 each to customers and credited at ₹ 30 each if returned in good condition within 3 months. For stock-taking purpose, all packages in factory and in the hands of customers are valued at ₹ 20 each.

On April 1, 2024 there were 4,500 packages in the factory and 7,800 in the hands of the customers for less than three months.

During the year ended March 31, 2025 13,000 packages were purchased by M, some packages were charged out to customers and they had retained 5,500 packages. The customers had been given credit for ₹ 2,37,000 on account of returns within the stipulated period. 200 packages, sound but no longer suitable for M's goods, were sold for ₹ 2,000. 300 packages were destroyed as they had been damaged beyond repairs and some were required at a cost of ₹ 1,000.

On March 31, 2025 there were 12,700 packages in the factory, out of which 3,400 were new.

For the year ended March 31, 2025 prepare : (*i*) Packages Trading Account and (*ii*) Packages Suspense Account.

Ans. **[Profit ₹ 1,09,000].**

Hints : Packages issued during the year 12,200 ; Packages returned by customers 7,900 ; Stock with customers at the end 6,600.

11. X sells his goods in boxes which he charged out to customers at ₹ 6 each. Customers are allowed a credit of ₹ 4 per box returned within 60 days of sale.

While closing his accounts for the year ended 30th September, 2023, X valued the stock of boxes in his factory and returnable boxes in the hands of customers invoiced within 60 days of the close of accounting year, at ₹ 2 per box. The number of such boxes was 10,000 and 25,000 respectively.

For the year ended 30th September, 2024, the following transactions took place :

50,000 boxes were purchased at ₹ 2.50 per box.

80,000 were charged to customers.

75,000 were returned by customers.

2,500 boxes out of those returned were scrapped and sold for ₹ 1,500.

1,000 boxes were damaged by rain and discarded.

At close of the year, 15,000 boxes were with customers. Cash received on account of rentals and sales from customers was ₹ 2,50,000.

Record the above transactions in the books of X and draw Memorandum Debtors Account, Boxes Stock Account, Boxes Trading Account and Boxes Debtors Account.

Ans. [Value of boxes with customers, 15,000 @ ₹ 2 = ₹ 30,000 ; Value of boxes at shop, 1,500 @ ₹ 2 + 50,000 @ ₹ 2.50 = ₹ 1,28,000 ; Gross Profit ₹ 1,86,500 ; Net Profit ₹ 1,84,500].

CHAPTER

29

Accounting for Goods Sent on Sale or Return Basis

We very often find that a firm in order to promote its sales sends goods to the customers with an option either to retain or to return the goods within a stipulated time. Such delivery of goods to customers, subject to such an option, is known as 'goods on sale or return' or 'goods on approval' basis. According to section 24 of the Sale of Goods Act, 1893, in respect of such goods, the sale will take place on the property in the goods pass to the buyer :

(i) when he signifies his approval or acceptance to the seller ;

(ii) when he does some act adopting the transaction ;

(iii) if he does not signify his approval or acceptance to the seller but retains the goods without giving notice of rejection, on the expiry of the specified time (if a time has been fixed) or on the expiry of a reasonable time (if no time has been fixed).

Delivery of goods on approval basis, simply indicates a mere change of 'possession' and not a transfer of 'ownership' untill and unless the customer signified his approval or the stipulated time has expired. So pending receipt of approval, or expiry of stipulated time the goods sent by a firm on sale or return basis can not be legally deemed to be a 'sale' in the true sense of the term. No profit, therefore, arises or accrues to the seller from out of such transactions until the transaction turns into an actual sale. In other words, if the goods sent on sale or return basis is regarded as sale, profit will be anticipated thereon which may never be actually realised and the Balance sheet will not exhibit a true and fair view of financial position of the firm. Hence, a special accounting method to record this type of sale or return transactions becomes necessary.

Accounting records for sale or return transactions : The method of recording goods sent on sale or return basis depends upon the circumstances and the number of transactions involved. This sort of transactions may be divided into the following three distinct categories :

(A) When the number of transactions are few.

(B) When the transactions are moderately large in number.

(C) When the transactions are numerous.

(A) When the number of transactions are few

In case, where the transactions are very few in number, there is no need to keep a separate set of record. We should adopt the following procedure for recording such transactions :

IN THE BOOKS OF THE SELLER

Date	Particulars		L.F.	Dr.	Cr.
?	(*i*) **When goods are sent on approval :** Sundry Debtors a/c	Dr.		(at SP)	
	To Sales a/c				(at SP)
	(Being the goods sent on approval but treated as actual sales)				
?	(*ii*) **When the goods are returned :** Sales a/c/Returns Inward a/c	Dr.		(at SP)	
	To Sundry Debtors a/c				(at SP)
	(Being the goods returned by customers on approval A/c)				
	(*iii*) **When the goods are approved :** No journal entry is required.				
?	(*iv*) **When the goods are sold at a higher price than the selling price :** Sundry Debtors A/c	Dr.			
	To Sales A/c				
	(Being the difference for extra price adjusted)				
?	(*v*) **If the goods are sold at a lower price than the selling price :** Sales A/c	Dr.			
	To Sundry Debtors A/c				
	(Being the difference in price reduction adjusted)				
	(*vi*) **If any goods are lying with the customers on approval at the close of the accounting period, which are neither approved nor returned.**				
?	(*a*) Sales A/c	Dr.		(at SP)	
	To Debtors Suspense A/c				(at SP)
	(Being the adjustment for goods still lying with customers on approval but neither approved nor returned)				
	(*b*) Stock on Sale or Return A/c	Dr.			at cost/ market price, whichever is lower.
	To Trading A/c				
	(Being the value of unsold stock on sale or return a/c brought into account)				

N.B. (*i*) Journal Entry No (*vi*) should be reversed at the beginning of the subsequent accounting period.

(*ii*) Credit balance in 'Debtors Suspense a/c' should be shown by way of deduction from Sundry Debtors on the asset side of the Balance Sheet.

(*iii*) Stock with customers should be brought into account either at cost or at the net realisable value, whichever is less.

ILLUSTRATION 1. Mr. A, a trader, despatched goods costing ₹ 16,000 to his customer Mr. B on sale or return basis after charging a gross profit of 25% on cost. Mr. A had treated the transaction as credit sale at the time of despatch of the goods.

Pass Journal entries in the books of Mr. A, if : (*i*) the customer had approved the goods; (*ii*) the customer had rejected all the goods; (*iii*) the customer had retained half of the goods while rejecting the other half.

SOLUTION

In the Boos of A
JOURNAL

		₹	₹
(1) *When goods are sent on approval*			
B's A/c	Dr.	20,000	
To Sales A/c			20,000
(Being goods sent on approval treated as credit sale)			
(2) (*i*) *When goods are approved by customer, no entry is to be passed*			
(*ii*) *When customer rejects all the goods*			
Sales A/c	Dr.	20,000	
To B's A/c			20,000
(Being entry for credit sale reversed on rejection of the goods by the customer)			
(*iii*) *When the customer retains half the goods while rejecting the other half :*			
Sales A/c	Dr.	10,000	
To B's A/c			10,000
(Being entry for credit sale reversed for the rejected portion, *i.e.,* half of the goods.)			

Working Note :	₹
Cost of goods sent on approval	16,000
Add : Gross Profit @ 25% of the Cost	4,000
Sale Price	20,000

ILLUSTRATION 2. Rajesh Brothers sell their goods to their approved customers on 'sale or return' basis treating all such transactions as actual sales at the time of despatch. They sent on 15th December goods costing ₹ 1,000 to Rama Stores at 20% profit on sale and passed the goods through Sales Day Book. How would you adjust the transaction on 31st December, if Rama Stores consent is pending ?

SOLUTION

JOURNAL ENTRIES IN THE BOOKS OF THE TRADER

			₹	₹
Dec. 15	Sundry Debtors (M/s Rama Stores) A/c	Dr.	1,250	
	To Sales A/c			1,250
	(Being the goods sent to M/s Rama Stores on approval but treated as actual sales)			
Dec. 31	Sales A/c	Dr.	1,250	
	To Debtors Suspense A/c			1,250
	(Being the adjustment for goods still lying with customers on approval but neither approved nor returned)			
Dec. 31	Stock on Sale or Return A/c	Dr.	1,000	
	To Trading A/c			1,000
	(Being the value of unsold stock on sale or return a/c brought into account)			

N.B. (*i*) Journal Entry No. (2) should be reversed at the commencement of the subsequent accounting period.
(*ii*) Credit balance in 'Debtors Suspense a/c' should be shown by way of deduction from Sundry Debtors on the assets side of the Balance Sheet.

(B) When the transactions are moderately large in number

When the transactions are moderately large in number *i.e.,* neither more nor less, these are recorded in a different manner: under this method, a separate day book called 'Sale or Return Day Book' is maintained from which necessary ledger postings are made.

SALE OR RETURN DAY BOOK

Goods Sent				Goods Returned				Goods Sold				Balance
Date	Particulars	F	Amount	Date	Particulars	F	Amount	Date	Particulars	F	Amount	₹

(*i*) When the goods are sent on approval, the record is made in the 'goods sent' column of the above day book. This is just an aid to memory. From this column, no ledger posting is made as the customers are not treated as debtors and the transactions are not regarded as sales.

(*ii*) When the goods are returned, an entry is made in the 'goods returned' column of the day book and no ledger posting is made therefrom.

(*iii*) When the goods are approved and sold, an entry is made in the goods sold column. The personal accounts of the individual customers are debited in the ledger and the Sales a/c is credited in the ledger with the monthly total of the goods sold column. This is a simple process.

(*iv*) At the end of the accounting period, balance of goods left with the customers is shown in last 'balance' column of the day book and this is brought into account as closing stock of goods lying unsold with customers on approval. But it must be valued either at cost price or at net realisable value whichever is less. This is done by means of a journal entry debiting Stock on Sale or Return A/c and crediting Trading A/c.

(C) When there are numerous transactions

This method is particularly suitable when transactions relating to Sale or Return are numerous. Under this method, a separate day book called 'Sale or Return Day Book' is maintained along with a seperate ledger called 'Sale or Return Ledger' also known as 'Kacha Ledger'. When such a book is maintained (a specimen of which is given below), the following procedure should be adopted for recording the transactions in the ledger on the basis of the entries in the Sale or Return Day Book.

SALE OR RETURN DAY BOOK

Goods Sent				Returns				Sales				Balance
Date	Particulars	F	Amount	Date	Particulars	F	Amount	Date	Particulars	F	Amount	₹

(*i*) When the goods are sent on approval, the entries are shown in the 'goods sent' column. The individual personal accounts of the customers are debited and the 'Sale or Return A/c' is credited with the monthly total in the Sale or Return Ledger. Nothing is posted in the main ledger.

(*ii*) When the goods are returned, it is shown in the 'Return Column'. The individual customers accounts are credited and the Sale or Return A/c is debited in the Sale or Return Ledger. Here too, nothing is posted to the main ledger.

(*iii*) When the goods are retained by customers or otherwise treated as approved, the entries are shown in the 'Sales' column. The individual customers accounts are debited in the Sales/Main Ledger and the monthly total of the sales column is credited to Sales a/c in the General/Main Ledger. Moreover, the individual customers accounts are credited in the Sale or Return Ledger and the monthly total of the sales column is debited to Sale or Return Account in the Sale or Return Ledger. This will cancel the customers accounts in the Sale or Return Ledger.

(*iv*) The value of goods sent but not yet approved at the end of the accounting period as shown in the 'balance' column of the Sale or Return Day Book represents the unsold stock with customers on approval which should be brought into account either at cost price or at market price whichever is less by debiting stock on Sale or Return Account and crediting Trading Account.

ILLUSTRATION 3. M/s Tinkoo Ram and Sons sent out goods on approval as follows :

Jan. 15	X ₹ 1,300 ; Jan. 28	Returned ₹ 1,100. Retained rest.
Jan. 20	Y ₹ 1,200 ; Jan. 28	Retained all.
Jan. 30	Z ₹ 2,500 ; Jan. 30	No intimation.

Record the above transactions maintaining books on Double Entry Principles.
Give Journal and Ledger Entries. Cost of goods sold on Jan. 30 is ₹ 2,000.

SOLUTION **JOURNAL ENTRIES**

	In the Sale or Return Ledger		₹	₹		*In the Main Ledger*			
?	X's A/c	Dr.	1,300						
	Y's A/c	Dr.	1,200						
	Z's A/c	Dr.	2,500						
	To Sale or Return A/c			5,000					
	(Being the goods sent to customers on approval but treated as actual sales)					No Entry			
?	Sale or Return a/c	Dr.	1,100						
	To X's a/c			1,100					
	(Being the goods returned by customers on approval a/c)					No Entry			
?	Sale or Return A/c	Dr.	1,400						
	To X's A/c			200					
	To Y's A/c			1,200					
	(Being cancellation of Sales in the Sale or Return Ledger on approval by customers)					No Entry			
					?	X's A/c	Dr.	200	
						Y's A/c	Dr.	1,200	
						To Sales A/c			1,400
						(Being the actual sales brought into account on approval by customers)			
					?	Stock on Sale or Return A/c	Dr.	2,000	
						To Trading A/c			2,000
						(Being the unsold stock on sale or return basis brought into account)			

IF PASSED THROUGH THE SALE OR RETURN DAY BOOK

Goods Sent				Returns				Goods Approved				Balance
Date	Particulars	F	₹	Date	Particulars	F	₹	Date	Particulars	F	₹	₹
Jun.15	X		1,300	?	X		1,100	?	X		200	
" 20	Y		1,200					?	Y		1,200	
" 30	Z		2,500									2,500
			5,000				1,100				1,400	2,500

In the Sale or Return Ledger

SALE OR RETURN ACCOUNT

		₹			₹
?	To X	1,100	Jan. 31	By Sundries	5,000
	" X	200			
	" Y	1,200			
	" Balance c/d	2,500			
		5,000			5,000

X's ACCOUNT

		₹			₹
Jan. 15	To Sale or Return A/c	1,300	?	By Sale or Return A/c	1,100
			?	" Sale or Return A/c	200
		1,300			1,300

Y's ACCOUNT

		₹			₹
Jan. 20	To Sale or Return A/c	1,200	?	By Sale or Return A/c	1,200
		1,200			1,200

Z's ACCOUNT

		₹			₹
Jan. 30	To Sale or Return A/c	2,500	?	By Balance c/d	2,500
		2,500			2,500

In the Main/General Ledger

X's ACCOUNT

		₹			₹
?	To Sales	200			

Y's ACCOUNT

		₹			₹
?	To Sales	1,200			

SALES ACCOUNT

		₹			₹
			?	By Sundries	1,400

ILLUSTRATION 4. Ramkrishna Bhandar sends out goods on approval to a few customers and includes the same in the Sales Account. On 31st March, 2025 the sundry debtors balance stood at ₹ 1,00,000 which included ₹ 7,000 goods sent on approval against which no intimation was received during the year. These goods were sent out at 25 per cent over and above cost price to Amit ₹ 4,000 and Birdy ₹ 3,000.

Amit sent intimation of acceptance on 30th April and Birdy returned the goods on 10th April, 2025.

Make adjustment entries and show how these items will appear in the Balance Sheet on 31st March, 2025. Show also the Journal Entries to be made during April 2025.

SOLUTION

JOURNAL ENTRIES IN THE BOOKS OF THE TRADER

				₹	₹
2025 March 31	Sales A/c	Dr.		7,000	
	To Debtors Suspense A/c				7,000
	(Being the adjustment for goods still lying with customers on approval but not yet approved)				
	Stock on Sale or Return A/c	Dr.		5,600	
	To Trading A/c				5,600
	(Being the unsold stock on Sale or Return A/c brought into account)				
April 1	Debtors Suspense A/c	Dr.		7,000	
	To Sales				7,000
	(Bring the cancellation of the adjusting entry of previous accounting period).				
April 10	Return Inward A/c	Dr.		3,000	
	To Sundry Debtors A/c				3,000
	(Being the goods returned sent on approval a/c)				

N.B.

(*i*) Credit balance in 'Debtors Suspense A/c' should be shown by way of deduction from Sundry Debtors on the assets side of the Balance Sheet.

(*ii*) Stock has been valued as : $\frac{₹\,7000 \times 100}{125} = ₹\,5{,}600$.

ILLUSTRATION 5. ABC Limited supplied goods on sale or return basis to customers.

Goods are to be returned within 15 days from the date of dispatch, failing which it is treated as sales. The books of BC Limited are closed on 31st March, 2025. The particulars of the same are as under :

Date of Dispatch	*Partly Name*	*Amount*	*Remarks*
10-3-2025	PQR	25,000	No information till 31-3-2025
12-3-2025	DEF	15,000	Returned on 16-3-2025
15-3-2025	GHI	40,000	Goods worth ₹ 8,000 Returned on 20-3-2025
20-3-2025	DEF	10,000	Goods Retained on 24-3-2025
25-3-2025	PQR	22,000	Goods Retained on 28-3-2025
30-3-2025	XYZ	35,000	No information till 31-3-2025

SOLUTION

In the Books of 'ABC'

GOODS ON SALES OR RETURN, SOLD AND RETURNED DAY BOOK

Date 2025	Party to whom goods sent	L.F.	Amount (₹)	Date 2025	Sold (₹)	Returned (₹)
March 10	M/s PQR		25,000	March 25	25,000	—
March 12	M/s DEF		15,000	March. 16	—	15,000
March 15	M/s GHI		40,000	March 20	32,000	8,000
March 20	M/s DEF		10,000	March 24	10,000	—
March 25	M/s PQR		22,000	March 28	22,000	—
March 30	M/s GHI		35,000	—		
			1,47,000		89,000	23,000

GOODS ON SALES OR RETURN TOTAL ACCOUNT

Date	Particulars	Amount (₹)	Date	Particulars	Amount (₹)
2025			2025		
Mar. 31	To Returns	23,000	Mar. 31	By Goods Sent on Sales or	
	To Sales	89,000		Return	1,47,000
	To Balance c/d	35,000			
		1,47,000			1,47,000

ILLUSTRATION 6. A firm sends goods on sale or return basis ; customers' having the choice of returning the goods within a month. During April, 2025, the following are the details of the goods sent :

2025	*Customer*	*Value* ₹	*Proforma Invoice No.*
April 2	A	10,000	004
4	B	18,000	007
16	C	25,000	023
20	D	8,000	032
24	E	21,000	041
28	F	30,000	049

Within the stipulated time, A and C returned the goods while B, D and E informed that they have accepted the goods. Prepare Sale or Return Day Book. Show the following accounts in the books of the firm:

Sale on Approval Account and Customers for Sale on Approval Account as on 15th May, 2025. Also prepare accounts in the main ledger.

SOLUTION

SALE OR RETURN DAY BOOK

Goods Sent				Goods Returned				Goods Approved				Balance
Date	Particulars	F	Amount	Date	Particulars	F	Amount	Date	Particulars	F	Amount	Amount
2025			₹	2025			₹	2025			₹	₹
Apr. 2	A		10,000	May 2	A		10,000	May 4	B		18,000	
" 4	B		18,000	" 15	C		25,000	" 15	D		8,000	

Apr 16	C		25,000				May 15	E		21,000	
" 20	D		8,000								
" 24	E		21,000							30,000	
" 28	F		30,000								
			1,12,000			35,000				47,000	30,000

N.B. Ledger postings have been shown upto 15th May 2025.

In the Sale or Return Ledger
IN THE BOOKS OF THE FIRM
SALE ON APPROVAL A/C

		₹			₹
2025			2025		
May 15	To Sundries	35,000	April 30	By Sundries	1,12,000
" 15	" Sundries	47,000			
" 15	" Balance c/d	30,000			
		1,12,000			1,12,000
			2025		
			May 16	By Balance b/d	30,000

A's ACCOUNT

			₹			₹
2025				2025		
April 2	To Sale on Approval A/c		10,000	May 2	By Sale on Approval A/c	10,000

B's ACCOUNT

			₹			₹
2025				2025		
April 4	To Sale on Approval A/c		18,000	May 4	By Sale on Approval A/c	18,000

C's ACCOUNT

			₹			₹
2025				2025		
April 16	To Sale on Approval A/c		25,000	May 15	By Sale on Approval A/c	25,000

D's ACCOUNT

			₹			₹
2025				2025		
April 20	To Sale on Approval A/c		8,000	May 15	By Sale on Approval A/c	8,000

E's ACCOUNT

			₹			₹
2025				2025		
April 24	To Sale on Approval A/c		21,000	May 15	By Sale on Approval A/c	21,000

F's ACCOUNT

			₹			₹
2025				2025		
April 28	To Sale on Approval A/c		30,000	May 15	By Balance c/d	30,000
May 15	To Balance b/d		30,000			

In the Main Ledger

B's ACCOUNT

		₹			₹
2025 May 4	To Sales	18,000			

D's ACCOUNT

		₹			₹
2025 May 15	To Sales	8,000			

E's ACCOUNT

		₹			₹
2025 May 15	To Sales	21,000			

SALES ACCOUNT

		₹			₹
			2025 May 15	By Sundries	47,000

QUESTIONS

OBJECTIVE TYPE

1. **State whether the following statements are True or False :**
   (*a*) There is difference between 'Sales or Return Day Book' and 'Sales and Return Day Book'.
   (*b*) At the end of the year goods sent on approval basis shall not be taken as closing stock for preparing final accounts.
   (*c*) Double Entry System is followed for recording where a large number of transactions are made on Sales or Return Basis.
   (*d*) Sales or Return Account is not a part of the main ledger.
   (*e*) It is necessary to make adjustment entry on return of goods, when such goods are sent on sale or return basis.
   (*f*) Goods sold on approval or return basis are not recorded as credit sales initially when they are sent-out.

Ans. [True (*a*), (*c*), (*d*), (*e*). False : (*b*), (*f*)].

SHORT/LONG ANSWER TYPE

1. How will you account for goods sent on 'sale or return' basis when such transactions are numerous ?
2. Discuss the accounting treatment for goods sent on sale or return when (*i*) the number of transactions are few, (*ii*) there are many transactions, and (*iii*) there are too many transactions.
3. Write a note on "goods sent on sale or return basis".

PRACTICAL PROBLEMS

1. A Gas Company sends out its gas stoves to dealers on 'Sale or Return'. All such transactions are, however, treated like actual sales and are passed through the Day Book. Just before the end of the

financial year, 100 stoves, which had cost them ₹ 150 each, have been sent to a dealer on 'Sale or Return' and have been debited to his account at ₹ 200 each, out of which only 20 stoves are sold at ₹ 220 each.

Show the entries in the Journal of the Company to adjust these transactions for the purpose of preparing the final accounts for the year ended March 31, 2025.

2. A trader has credited certain items of sales "on approval" aggregating ₹ 10,000 to sales account. Of these goods to the value of ₹ 3,000 have been returned and taken into stock at cost of ₹ 1,500 though the record of return was omitted in the accounts ; and in respect of another parcel of ₹ 1,000 (cost being ₹ 500), the period of approval did not expire on closing date.

Show adjustment and correcting entries in the books of the trader.

3. A trader sends goods to his customers on Sale or Return basis. All such transactions are, however, treated like actual sales and are passed through the Day Book. Following transactions took place during the year 2025 :

			₹
June	8	Sent goods to customers on Sale or Return basis at cost plus 20%	80,000
"	29	Goods returned by customers	30,000
October	12	Received sales intimation from customers for goods valued at	35,000

Assuming that the date of final accounts was 31st December, give Journal Entries for the above transactions.

4. B.S. sends out goods on approval to a few customers and include the same in Sale Account. On 31-3-2025 the stock in hand amounted to ₹ 80,000 and the Sundry Debtors balance stood at ₹ 1,50,000 which include ₹ 10,000 for goods sent on approval against which no intimation was received during the year. These goods were sent out at 25% above cost and were sent to R ₹ 4,000 and B ₹ 6,000.

On 20th April B returned the goods and on 25th April R intimated of his intention to retain the goods.

Make adjustment entries and show how these items will appear in the Balance Sheet on 31-3-2025 and show what Journal Entries would be made in April, 2025.

5. A. Mehta who keeps a special set of books for his business sends out goods on sale or return as follows :

		₹		
Jan. 1	B	500	Jan. 4	All retained
Jan. 9	C	250	Jan. 10	Returned ₹ 150 Retained ₹ 100
Jan. 16	D	700	Jan. 19	All retained
Jan. 23	C	250	Jan. 25	All returned
Jan. 30	B	400	Jan. 31	No intimation as to sale and goods not yet returned
Jan. 31	E	500		—Do—

Show Day Books, Goods on Sale or Return Total Account and Ledger Account.

6. Automobiles Ltd., sent out motor cars on "Sale or Return'. They maintained a separate set of books for this type of business. During the month of April, 2025, they sent out motor cars on 'Sale or Return' as follows :

2025			₹	2025		
April	2	Y & Co. Ltd.	10,000	April	7	Returned
"	16	X & Co. Ltd.	15,000	"	20	Retained
"	20	Y & Co. Ltd.	16,000	"	25	Returned
"	28	Y & Co. Ltd.	20,000			No intimation received as to approval and car not yet returned.

Show the Day Book.

7. Messrs Awaaz Electronics supplied goods on Sale or Return basis, the particulars of which are as under :

Date of Despatch	*Party's Name*	*Amount*	*Other Particulars*
		₹	
10-3-2025	ABC Co.	2,600	14-3-2025 — Returned
15-3-2025	XYZ Co.	3,400	17-3-2025 — Sold
20-3-2025	PQR Co.	1,900	25-3-2025 — Goods worth ₹ 800 returned
27-3-2025	XYZ Co.	2,200	— No intimation 31-3-2025
28-3-2025	PQR Co.	1,700	-do-

The books of Awaaz Electronics are closed on 31st day of March each year.

Exhibit the entries as they would appear in the books of Awaaz Electronics *viz.* the "Goods sent on Sale or Return Day Book", "Goods on Sale or Return & Sold Returned Day Book" and show how the "Goods on Sale or Return Total Account" would appear.

Ans. [Balance of Goods on Sale or Return ₹ 3,900]

8. Messrs Condensed Book Publishers sent consignment of their publications to the following customers on sale or return basis in the first week of April 2025:

	₹		₹
Menon, Madras	500	Govind, Bombay	1,000
Narain, Madras	200	Ghosh, Calcutta	450
Ramesh, Bombay	300	Poddar, Calcutta	250

The letter to the customers mentioned that if the books were not approved by them, they should be returned within one month, failing which they would be treated as sold. By the end of that month, the customers from Madras had retained the books, while those from Calcutta had returned them in time. Mr. Govind of Bombay had accepted one of the consignments of ₹ 700 but returned the others and the time of approval had not yet expired for Mr. Ramesh. Show the entries in the sale or return day book.

9. A Torch Company sends out its torches to dealers on sale or return basis. All such transactions are treated as actual sales and are passed through the Day Book. Just before the end of the financial year, 100 torches, which cost them ₹ 300 each, have been sent to a dealer on Sale or Return basis and have been debited to his account at ₹ 350 each; out of which only 30 torches are sold.

How would you adjust these transactions for the purpose of the company's Profit and Loss Account and Balance Sheet ?

10. M/s Barua and Co. sends out their goods to dealers on 'Sale or Return' basis. All such transactions are, however, treated like actual sales and are passed through the Day Book. Just before the end of the financial years, goods of the sales value of ₹ 25,000 have been sent on 'Sale or Return' basis and have been debited to their account. These goods have neither been approved nor returned. The sale price was arrived at after adding 25% on cost.

How would you adjust these transactions for the purpose of the M/s Barua & Co's Profit & Loss Account and Balance Sheet ?

CHAPTER

30

Investment Accounts

An enterprise holds investments for a variety of reasons. Such investments form a significant aspect of the operations of an enterprise in certain cases. Therefore, the evaluation of the performance of such an enterprise depends upon the return earned through such investments.

Investments are assets held by an enterprise for earning income by way of dividends, interest, and rentals, for capital appreciation, or for other benefits to the investing enterprise. Assets held as stock-in-trade are not 'investments'.

Forms of Investment

Now, these investments can be in the form of certificates or documents such as shares of an enterprise or they can be in a physical form like building.

Furthermore, the investment may be a debt other than short or long term loan or trade debt. Such an investment represents the monetary amount owed to the holder of such an investment who earns an interest for lending such an amount.

On the other hand, an enterprise may invest in the net assets of another company by acquiring equity shares of such a company.

Now, the investments for which there exists an active market, the value of such investments shall be taken as the market value. This is because the market value provides the closest estimate for fair value of such investments.

The market value is nothing but the amount that is received from the sale of an investment in the open market. Such an amount is also adjusted for expenses incurred before the disposal of such an investment.

But, where an active market for investments does not exist, other means are adopted to determine the fair value of such investments. The fair value refers to the amount for which an asset is exchanged between a buyer and seller in an arm's length transaction.

Classification of Investments

The financial statement of an enterprise presents fixed assets, investments and current assets into different categories. As far as investments are concerned, these are classified into long term investments and current investments. As per AS 13 also, investments are classified as:

A. Current Investments. Current Investments are investments which by their nature are readily realisable and are intended to be held for less than a year from the date when such investment is done.

Carrying Amount of Current Investments

Current investments must be carried in financial statements at lower of cost and fair value which is determined either by category of investment or on an individual investment basis, however, not on the overall basis.

If there is any decline in the fair value or any reversal of such a decline, then they are to be included in the P&L of the enterprise.

B. **Long-Term Investments.** Long-term investments are investments other than the current investments, even though they might be freely marketable.

Carrying Amount of Long-Term Investments

Long-term investments must always be carried in financial statements at their cost. The carrying amount of the long term investment is typically the cost of such an investment. However, if there is a permanent reduction in the value of the long term investment, the carrying amount of such an investment is also reduced.Such a reduction is charged to P&L statement. However, such a reduction in the carrying amount is reversed when there is an increase in the value of such an investment or the reasons that lead to a reduction in its carrying amount do not exist anymore.

The carrying amount of a long term investment is determined by considering the cost of every individual investment made.

Cost of Investments

- The cost of investments include charges related to acquisition of brokerage, duties, and fees
- **Non-cash consideration** – In case investments are acquired, or partly acquired, by

  (*i*) issuing shares

  (*ii*) issuing other securities

  (*iii*) any other asset,

  The cost of acquisition is the fair value of securities which are issued or the assets which are given up. The fair value might not essentially be same as the par or nominal value of securities which are issued. It might be prudent to consider fair value of such investment acquired in case it's more evident
- **Interest, dividend or other receivables** – Dividends, interest and other receivables that are in connection with the investments are usually considered as income, is the ROI (return on the investment).However, in certain conditions, such inflows signify a recovery of the cost and doesn't form part of the income. For instance, an enterprise is yet to acquire an interest bearing investment for which the interest becomes due. Such an interest is not regarded as an income. Rather it is included in the price paid for the investment. Thus, when such an enterprise receives interest subsequently, it is allocated between pre-acquisition and post-acquisition periods. The pre-acquisition portion of the interest received is deducted from the cost of such an investment. Likewise, an enterprise may treat the dividends on equity shares declared from pre-acquisition profits in a similar way.

  However, where it is difficult to allocate such an income between pre and post-acquisition periods, the enterprise may reduce the cost of its investment by the amount of dividends receivable. This can only happen in cases where the dividends to be received clearly represent the recovery of a portion of cost of investment.
- **Right Shares** – In case right shares offered are subsequently subscribed for, cost of such right shares is then added to carrying the amount of original holding.

In case the rights aren't subscribed for, however, are sold, sale proceeds from the sale of such rights are transferred to P/L statement. But, where an investment is acquired on a cum-right basis and market value of the investment immediately after becoming ex-right is less than the cost for which such investment was acquired, it might be prudent to apply the proceeds from the sale of rights to reduce carrying the amount of the investment to the market value.

ILLUSTRATION 1. MY Ltd. had acquired 200 equity shares of YZ Ltd. at ₹ 105 per share on 1-1-2025 and paid ₹ 200 towards brokerage, stamp duty and STT. On 31st March, 2025 Shares of YZ Ltd. were traded at ₹ 110 per share. At what value investment is to be shown in the Balance Sheet of MY Ltd. as at 31st March, 2025.

SOLUTION **CALCULATION OF COST OF INVESTMENT**

Particulars	₹
Purchase Price of Equity Shares of YZ Ltd. (200 shares × ₹ 105 per share)	21,000
Add : Brokerage, Stamp duty and STT	200
Cost of Investment	21,200

If the investment is long then it will be shown at cost. Therefore value of investment will be ₹ 21,200. However, if the investment is a current investment, then it will be shown at lower of cost (*i.e.* ₹ 21,200) or net realisable value (*i.e.* ₹ 200 × 110 = 22,000). Therefore, value of investment will be ₹ 21,200.

Investment Property

Investment property is investments that are made in land or buildings which aren't envisioned to be used significantly for use, or in business operations of, the investing company.

Disposal of Investments

When an asset is disposed of, the difference between proceeds received from disposal and the carrying amount of investment is recognized in the P&L statement. Such a difference is also adjusted for any expenses incurred with respect to disposal of such investments.

However, there are cases where only a part of an individual investment is disposed of. In such a case, the carrying amount of a portion of such investment is determined on the basis of the average carrying amount of the total investment.

Reclassification of Investments

Following are the ways in which investments can be reclassified.

The first one relates to the case where long term investments are reclassified as current investments. In such a case, investments are transferred at an amount that is lower of cost and its carrying amount at the date of transfer.

The second one relates to the case where current investments are reclassified as long term investments. In such a case, investments are transferred at an amount that is lower of cost and fair value at the date of transfer.

Disclosures in the Financial Statements

An enterprise needs to make the following disclosures pertaining to investments made in its P&L statement.

- Accounting policies followed to determine the carrying amount of investments
- Amounts represented in P&L statement for:
  - (*i*) Interest, dividends and rentals on current investments and long term investments separately. Further, an enterprise must state the gross income and the amount of TDS must be shown under advance taxes paid.
  - (*ii*) Profit and losses arising on disposing current investments and changes arising in the carrying amount of such investments
  - (*iii*) Profit and losses arising on disposing long term investments and changes arising in the carrying amount of such investments

- Major restrictions on ownership right, realisation of investments or the remittance of income and disposal proceeds
- Total amount of quoted and unquoted investments. This would help in determining the total market value of quoted investments.
- Other disclosures as demanded by the statutory authority

Accounting for investments is done according to AS–16, **Accounting for Investments,** which specifies how accounting for investments is done in financial statements and related disclosure requirements. AS 13 does not deal with following :

(1) Bases for recognisation of interest, dividends and rentals earned on investments.

(2) Operating or financial leases.

(3) Investment of retirement benefit plans and life Insurance enterprises.

(4) Institutions which are formed under Central or State Government Act or declared under Companies Act, 2013 like mutual funds, Banks, Venture Capital Funds, etc.

EXAMPLE. How will you deal with following in the financial statement of the Paridhi Electronics Ltd. as on 31-3-2025 ?

(*i*) Paridhi Electronics Ltd. invested in the shares of another unlised company on 1st May 2021 at a cost of ₹ 3,00,000 with the intention of holding more than a year. The published accounts of unlisted company received in January, 2025 reveals that the company has incurred cash losses with decline market share and investment of Paridhi Electronics Ltd. may not fetch more than ₹ 45,000.

(*ii*) Also Paridhi Electronics Ltd. has current investment (X Ltd.'s shares) purchased for ₹ 5 lakhs, which the company want to reclassify as long term investment. The market value of these investments as on date of Balance Sheet was ₹ 2.5 lakhs. ***(CA. Inter Nov. 2020 Modified)***

SOLUTION

(*i*) Investments are classified as long term investments should be carried in the financial statements at cost. However, provision for diminution shall be made to recognise a decline, other than temporary, in the value of the investments, such reduction being determined and made for each investment individually. It is further stated that indicators of the value of an investment are obtained by reference to its market value, the investee's assets and results and the expected cash flows from the investment.

On this basis, the facts of the given case clearly suggest that the provision for diminution should be made to reduce the carrying amount of shares to ₹ 45,000 in the financial statements for the year ended 31st March, 2025 and charge the difference of loss of ₹ 2,55,000 to Profit and Loss account.

(*ii*) Where investments are reclassified from current to long-term, transfers are made at the lower of cost of fair value at the date of transfer.

In the given case, the market value of the investment (X Ltd. shares) is ₹ 2.50 lakhs, which is lower than its cost *i.e.,* ₹ 5 lakhs. Therefore, the transfer to long term investments should be made at cost *i.e.,* ₹ 2.50 lakhs. The loss of ₹ 2.50 lakhs should be charged to profit and loss account.

Investment Accounts

The accounts of investments are kept in the same way as the accounts of any other asset. A separate investment account should be opened for each kind of security and on the head of the account particulars regarding the nature of the security, dates when interest or dividend is due, the date of redemption etc. should be stated. When the number of investments carried is large, a separate Investment Ledger is employed for recording all investment accounts.

Purposes of maintaining an investment ledger are as follows :

1. It helps in keeping a record of each security separately.
2. It helps to ascertain the value of securities at the end of the accounting period.

3. It is helpful in collection of interest and dividend as and when they become due.
4. It is helpful in ascertaining the amount of accrued income at the end of the accounting period.
5. It facilitates the determination of the profit or loss on sale of any security.

On the purchase of an investment, Investment Account will be debited and Cash Account credited with the cost thereof *i.e.,* the purchase price plus the bank's or broker's commission and on the sale of investment, Cash Account will be debited and Investment Account credited with the net proceeds realised.

Interest or Dividend Account. In addition to the accounts of investments it will be necessary to maintain an Interest or Dividend Account for recording the income derived from various investments. It means that there will be as many investment accounts as the different kinds of securities held ; but there will be only one Interest or Dividend Account for recording the income derived from all of them.

Investment Transactions

In writing up investment accounts special attention should be given to the purchase and sale of securities-cum-dividend or ex-dividend.

Cum-Dividend (or Cum-Interest) Quotations

On fixed investments interest goes on accruing day by day but it is paid periodically on fixed dates. The transactions of investments do not necessarily take place on those dates and so at the time of the sale of investment, it has to be settled as to who will get the next instalment which in the absence of an agreement goes to the purchaser. A company pays dividend on a share to the person whose name appears on the date of the payment of dividend in the books of the company as its holder. Even if a person has held a share for as long a period of eleven months but has sold it to another shortly before the payment of dividend, the company would pay dividend to the new purchaser and not to the former holder. Naturally, therefore, the seller charges the purchaser a price which, in his opinion, includes dividend accrued on the share upto the date of sale. The share is then said to have been sold "cum-dividend" or together with dividend, the right of receiving dividend being passed on to the purchaser. It should, therefore, be noted that **when an investment is purchased cum-dividend or cum-interest the purchaser pays for it a higher price than the normal price, the difference representing the dividend or interest accrued on the investment upto the date of purchase. Therefore, while debiting Investment Account with the purchase price, the same should be split up into the normal price and the dividend/interest accrued, the normal price being debited to Investment Account and the dividend or interest accrued debited to the Dividend or the Interest Account.**

Similarly, when an investment is sold cum-dividend or cum-interest, the price received includes dividend or interest accrued on the investment upto the date of sale. Therefore, it should be split into the normal price and the dividend or interest accrued, the normal price being credited to the particular Investment Account and the dividend or interest accrued credited to the Dividend or the Interest Account. In respect of *Government securities price quoted is ex-interest* unless otherwise stated whereas in respect of Non-Government securities, it is cum-interest unless otherwise stated.

Accounting Entries

In the Books of the Buyer

(*i*) *On an investment being purchased as cum-dividend (or cum interest)*

Shares in—Co. Ltd. or Investment A/c	Dr.	(Capital cost)
Dividend or Interest A/c	Dr.	(Dividend or Interest)
(on Investment A/c)		
To Bank		(Capital Cost & Dividend or Interest)

Actual Purchase Price or Capital Cost of Investment = (Purchase Price + Purchase Expenses – Interest for the period from the last interest payable to the date of transaction)

(*ii*) *On receipt of dividend or interest*

Bank A/c	Dr.	With the amount of Dividend or Interest
To Dividend or Interest (on Investment A/c)		

(*iii*) *For Accrued Interest*

Accrued Interest A/c	Dr.
To Interest A/c	

Note. At the close of the accounting period, the balance of Interest or Dividend Account will be transferred to P & L. A/c.

In the Books of the Seller

(1) *On an investment being sold cum-dividend (or cum-interest)*

Bank A/c	Dr.	(Amount received)
To Shares in — Co. Ltd. or Investment A/c		(Actual sale price)
To Dividend or Interest (on Investment A/c)		(Dividend or Interest)

Actual Sale Price of Investment = Sale Price – Sale Expenses – Accrued Interest for the period from the last interest payable date to the date of sale.

(2) *On receipt of dividend or interest*

Bank A/c	Dr.	For amount of Dividend or Interest
To Dividend or Interest A/c		

ILLUSTRATION 2. On 31st January, 2025, X purchased for cash from Y four 6% ₹ 100 Debentures of the Mehta Ltd. at ₹ 110 $\frac{1}{2}$% cum-interest ; interest being payable on 1st June and 1st December each year.

How will you record the transaction in the books of X and Y if each party had to pay bank commission of 25 paise per cent on face value?

SOLUTION **IN THE BOOKS OF X**

	₹
Purchase Price of 4 Debentures @ ₹ 110.50 each cum-interest	442
Add : Bank Commission @ 25 paise per cent on ₹ 400 face value	1
Total Cost	443
Less : Accrued interest for the past 2 months from Dec. 1, 2024 to Jan. 31, 2025 @ 6% p.a. on ₹ 400	4
Value of Investment	439

JOURNAL

				₹	₹
2025 Jan. 31	Investment A/c	Dr.		439	
	Interest A/c	Dr.		4	
	To Cash A/c				443
	(Being purchase of investment at ₹ 110 $\frac{1}{2}$% cum-interest plus commission paid)				

Note. On June 1, total interest for 6 months shall be credited in the books. Commission paid on purchase is capitalised.

IN THE BOOKS OF Y

	₹
Cum-interest price of security	442
Less : Bank commission paid	1
Total Cost	441
Less : Accrued interest	4
Capitalised Cost of Investment	437

JOURNAL

			₹	₹
2025 Jan. 31	Cash A/c Dr.		441	
	To Investment A/c			437
	To Interest A/c			4
	(Being the sale of investment at ₹ $110\frac{1}{2}$% cum-interest less commission paid)			

Ex-Dividend or Ex-Interest Quotations

When an investment is purchased "Ex-Dividend or Ex-Interest" the price paid is below the normal price, *i.e.*, it is arrived at after deducting from the normal price dividend or interest receivable on the investment from the date of interest or dividend payment to the date of purchase. Therefore, when an investment is purchased Ex-Dividend or Ex-Interest, the purchaser has to pay to the seller the accrued interest upto the date of purchase in addition to the price paid for the investment. Unless otherwise stated, the price quotation will be cum-interest quotation.

ILLUSTRATION 3. Work out the problem given in Illustration 2 if the quotation is ex-interest.

SOLUTION

IN THE BOOKS OF X

	₹
Purchase price of 4 debentures @ ₹ 110.50 ex-interest	442
Add : Bank Commission @ 25 paise per cent on ₹ 400, the face value of 4 debentures @ ₹ 100	1
Total Cost of Investment	443

JOURNAL ENTRIES

			₹	₹
2025 Jan. 31	Investment Account Dr.		443	
	Interest Account Dr.		4	
	To Cash Account			447
	(Being purchase of 4 debentures @ ₹ 110.50 ex-interest plus commission ₹ 1 and interest paid for 2 months from Dec. 1 to Jan. 31 @ 6% p.a. on ₹ 400 face value of debentures)			

IN THE BOOKS OF Y

	₹
Selling price of 4 debentures @ 110.50 ex-interest	442
Less : Bank Commission paid @ 25 paise per cent on ₹ 400	1
Net amount realised on account of sale of investment	441

JOURNAL ENTRIES

			₹	₹
2025 Jan. 31	Cash Account Dr. To Investment Account To Interest Account (Being purchase of 4 debentures @ ₹ 110.50 ex-interest minus commission ₹ 1 and interest received for 2 months @ 6% p.a. on ₹ 400, the face value of 4 debentures)		445	 441 4

Difference Between Cum-Interest and Ex-Interest

Following are the main differences between Cum-Interest and Ex-Interest :

(1) In case of cum-interest **purchase price** includes the interest accrued upto the date of purchase whereas this is not included in case of ex-interest.

(2) In case of cum-interest nothing is payable for **interest accrued** whereas it is payable in case of ex-interest.

(3) In case of cum-interest, **purchase price is more than the real price** of the security but purchase price is the real price in case of ex-interest.

Balancing the Investment Account

When the whole of an investment has been sold, the difference between the two sides of an Investment Account will be profit or loss on the sale.

Where only part of an investment has been sold during the year, the cost of the remaining investment will be brought down as a balance in the Investment Account and the difference between its two sides will be profit or loss on the investments sold.

When the investment is a fixed asset, any profit or loss made on the sale thereof will be of a capital nature and should be treated accordingly.

ILLUSTRATION 4. On 1st June, 2024 Mr. Arthur purchased ₹ 9,000 5% debentures of ₹ 100 each in the Patel Engineering Works Ltd. at ₹ 105 cum-interest, interest being payable on 31st March and 30th September each year. Expenses on Stamps amounted to ₹ 80. On 1st November, 2024 he sold ₹ 3,000 debentures at ₹ 107 cum-interest.

Brokerage is payable on each transaction @$\frac{1}{8}$% on nominal value. Make entries in Arthur's books and show Investment Account and Interest Account as on 31st December, 2024.

SOLUTION

JOURNAL ENTRIES

			Dr. ₹	Cr. ₹
2024 June 1	Investment A/c (1) Dr. Interest A/c Dr. To Bank A/c (Being investment made in ₹ 9,000 5% debentures of ₹ 100 each at ₹ 105 cum-interest; 5% p.a. interest for 2 months of April and May included in the purchase price deducted from the purchase price and debited to Interest A/c; brokerage @ $\frac{1}{8}$ % on ₹ 9,000 nominal value and stamp fee ₹ 80 added to the purchase price of the investment)		(1)9,466.25 75.00	 9,541.25

Sept. 30	Bank A/c Dr. To Interest A/c (Being interest received on ₹ 9,000 nominal value of debentures @ 5% p.a. for 6 months)		225.00	225.00
Nov. 1	Bank A/c Dr. To Investment A/c To Interest A/c (Being investment of nominal value of ₹ 3,000 sold at ₹ 107 cum-interest; interest for October month @ 5% p.a. deducted from sale value and brokerage ₹ 3.75 paid @ $\frac{1}{8}$% on ₹ 3,000 nominal value also deducted from the selling price of the investment)		3,206.25	(2) 3,193.75 12.50
Nov. 1	Investment A/c Dr. To Profit & Loss A/c (Profit on sale of investment transferred to Profit & Loss A/c)		(3) 38.33	38.33
Dec. 31	Accrued Interest A/c Dr. To Interest A/c (Being accrued interest on ₹ 6,000 nominal value @ 5% p.a. for 3 months from October 1 to Dec. 31)		75	75
Dec. 31	Interest A/c Dr. To Profit and Loss A/c (Being interest on investment earned during the year transferred to Profit & Loss A/c)		237.50	237.50

INVESTMENT ACCOUNT

(5% Debentures of Patel Engineering Works Ltd.)

(Interest Payable on 31st March and 30th September)

		Nominal Value	Amount			Nominal	Amount Value
2024		₹	₹	2024		₹	₹
June 1	To Bank A/c	9,000	9,466.25	Nov. 1	By Bank A/c	3,000	3,193.75
Nov. 1	To Profit & Loss A/c		38.33	Dec. 31	By Balance c/d	6,000	6,310.83
		9,000	9,504.58			9,000	9,504.58
2025							
Jan. 1	To Balance b/d	6,000	6,310.83				

INTEREST ACCOUNT

2024		₹	2024		₹
June. 1	To Bank A/c	75.00	Sept. 30	By Bank A/c	225.00
Dec. 31	To Profit & Loss A/c	237.50	Nov. 1	By Bank A/c	12.50
			Dec. 31	By Accrued Interest A/c	75.00
		312.50			312.50

Working Notes :

(1) ***Purchase Price of ₹ 9,000 Debentures on June 1, 2024***

		₹
Amount paid ₹ 9,000 × $\frac{105}{100}$		9,450.00
Add: Brokerage $\frac{1}{8} \times \frac{1}{100}$ × ₹ 9,000		11.25
Stamp fee		80.00
Total amount paid		9,541.25
Less :Interest for 2 months (April & May) ₹ 9,000 × $\frac{2}{12} \times \frac{5}{100}$		75.00
Amount to be Debited to Investment A/c		9,466.25

(2) ***Sale Value of Investment on November 1, 2024***

		₹
Gross sale proceed : ₹ 3,000 × $\frac{107}{100}$		3,210.00
Less : Amount paid for brokerage $\frac{1}{8} \times \frac{1}{100}$ × ₹ 3,000	₹ 3.75	
Interest included in gross sale proceed for month of October ₹ 3,000 × $\frac{5}{100} \times \frac{1}{12}$	₹ 12.50	
		16.25
Amount to be credited to Investment A/c		3,193.75

(3) ***Profit on Sale of Investment***

	₹
Purchase Price of ₹ 9,000 Debentures	9,466.25
	₹
Therefore, Purchase Price of ₹ 3,000 Debentures $\left(\frac{₹\ 9,466.25}{₹\ 9,000} \times ₹\ 3,000\right)$	3,155.42
	₹
Selling Price of Investment	3,193.75
Less: Purchase Price of Investment	3,155.42
Profit on Sale of Investment	38.33

ILLUSTRATION 5. Mr. Harsh provides the following details relating to his holding in 10% debentures (face value of ₹ 100 each) of Exe Ltd. held as current assets :

1-4-2024	Opening Balance—12,500 debentures, Cost ₹ 12,25,000
1-6-2024	Purchased 9,000 debentures @ ₹ 98 each ex-interest
1-11-2024	Purchased 12,000 debentures @ ₹ 115 each cum interest
31-1-2025	Sold 13,500 debentures @ ₹ 110 each cum-interest
31-3-2025	Market value of debentures @ ₹ 115 each

Due dates of interest are 30th June and 31st December.

Brokerage at 1% is to be paid for each transaction. Mr. Harsh closes his books on 31-3-2025. Show investment account as it would appear in his books assuming FIFO method is followed.

(CA IPCC Nov., 2019 Modified)

SOLUTION

INVESTMENT ACCOUNT OF MR. HARSH

for the year ending on 31-3-2025

(Scrip : 10% Debentures of Exe Limited)

(Interest Payable on 30th June and 31st December)

Date	Particulars	Nominal Value ₹	Interest ₹	Cost ₹	Date	Particulars	Nominal Value ₹	Interest ₹	Cost ₹
1-4-24	To Balance b/d	12,50,000	31,250	12,25,000	30-6-24	By Bank 21,500 × 100 × 10% × 1/2	–	1,07,500	–
1-6-24	To Bank (ex-interest) (W.N. 1)	9,00,000	37,500	8,90,820	31-12-25	By Bank 33,500 × 100 × 10% × 1/2		1,67,500	
1-11-24	To Bank (cum-interest) (W.N. 2)	12,00,000	40,000	13,53,800	31-1-25	By Bank (W.N. 3)	13,50,000	11,250	14,58,900
31-1-25	To Profit & Loss A/c (W.N. 3)			1,34,920	31-1-25	By Balance c/d (W.N. 4)	20,00,000	50,000	21,45,640
31-3-25	To Profit & Loss A/c (Bal. fig.)		2,27,500						
		33,50,000	3,36,250	36,04,540			33,50,000	3,36,250	36,04,540

Working Notes :

1. **Purchase of debentures on 1-6-2024**

   Interest element = 9,000 × 100 × 10% × 5/12 = ₹ 37,500

   Investment element = (9,000 × 98) + [1% (9,000 × 98)] = ₹ 8,90,820

2. **Purchase of debentures on 1-11-2024**

   Interest element = 12,000 × 100 × 10% × 4/12 = ₹ 40,000

   Investment element = 12,000 × 115 × 101% less 40,000 = ₹ 13,53,800

3. **Profit on sale of debentures as on 31-1-2025**

Particulars	₹
Sales Price of Debentures (13,500 × ₹ 110)	14,85,000
Less : Brokerage @ 1%	(14,850)
	14,70,150
Less : Interest (1,35,000/12)	(11,250)
	14,58,900
Less : Cost of Debentures [(12,25,000 + (8,90,820 × 1,00,000/9,00,000)]	(13,23,980)
Profit on Sale	1,34,920

4. **Valuation of closing balance as on 31-3-2025 :**

   Market value of 20,000 Debentures at ₹ 115 = ₹ 23,00,000

Cost of	8,000 Debentures	=	8,90,820/9,000 × 8,000	=	7,91,840
	12,000 Debentures	=			13,53,800
	Total				21,45,640

   Value at the end is ₹ 21,45,640, *i.e.,* which is less than market value of ₹ 23,00,000.

ILLUSTRATION 6. Mr. Shape dealt on the stock exchange and had purchased and sold leading scripts but did not maintain his accounts in a proper manner. He furnished the following data :

Investments in hand as at July 1, 2024

300 3% Conversion Loan 2024-25 of ₹ 100 each purchased at ₹ 60.

250 Equity Shares of ₹ 10 each of Everlite Limited at ₹ 18 per share.

1000 9% Preference Shares of ₹ 100 each of Prosperous Limited at ₹ 95.

Transactions during the year

Purchases :750 Equity Shares of ₹ 10 each of Everlite Limited at ₹ 23.

250 Equity Shares of ₹ 10 each of Small Limited at ₹ 9.

125 Equity Shares of ₹ 10 each of Bright Shipping Limited at ₹ 12.

Sold : 100 3% Conversion Loan 2024-25 at ₹ 65.

100 6% Preference Shares of Prosperous Limited at ₹ 99.

Interest / Dividends Received

3% Conversion Loan—Interest received ₹ 900.

9% Preference Shares of Prosperous Limited at ₹ 9,000.

Everlite Limited—Dividend at 20 per cent on 1,000 Shares—₹ 2,000.

Everlite Limited issued Bonus Shares and Mr. Shape received 1,000 Equity Shares of the Company as Bonus Shares.

You are required to show Investment Account in the Books of Mr. Shape.

SOLUTION

IN THE BOOKS OF MR. SHAPE

INVESTMENT ACCOUNT

	₹		₹
To Balance b/d		By Bank :	
300—3% Conversion Loan of ₹ 100 each (purchased at ₹ 60 each)	18,000	Sale of 100—3% Conversion Loan @ ₹ 65 per share	6,500
250—Equity Shares of ₹ 10 each of Everlite Ltd. (Purchased at ₹ 18 per share)	4,500	Sale of 100, 9% Pref. Shares of Prosperous Co. Ltd. @ ₹ 99 per share	9,900
1,000—9% Pref. Shares of ₹ 100 each (purchased at ₹ 95 each) of Prosperous Ltd.	95,000	By Balance c/d :	
To Bank : Purchase 750 Equity Shares of ₹ 10 of Everlite Ltd. at ₹ 23 each	17,250	200—3% Conversion Loan of ₹ 100 each	12,000
250 Equity Shares of ₹ 10 each of Small Ltd. at ₹ 9 each	2,250	1000 Equity Shares of Everlite Ltd. of ₹ 10 each	21,750
125 Equity Shares of ₹ 10 each of Bright Shipping Ltd. at ₹ 12 each	1,500	900—9% Pref. Shares of ₹ 100 each of Prosperous Ltd.	85,500
To Profit and Loss A/c (Profit on sale)		250—Equity Shares of ₹ 10 each of Small Ltd.	2,250
100—3% Conversion Loan	500	125—Equity Shares of ₹ 10 each at ₹ 12 each	1,500
9% Pref. Shares of Prosperous Ltd.	400		
	1,39,400		1,39,400

Columnar Investment Accounts

Concerns holding a large number of investments may find it more convenient to employ a separate ledger called an Investment Ledger, for keeping the accounts of all their investments. Such a ledger is kept on the columnar system and is ruled differently from an ordinary ledger. As the issuing authority of a security pays interest to the holder at a certain rate calculated on its face value, it is desirable that the face value (also known as the nominal value) as well as the interest or dividend received should appear side by side with the capital invested in it. Therefore, the Investment Ledger is provided with three columns on either side headed 'Nominal value', Interest or Dividend and Capital or Principal Investment. The name of each investment is written at the top of the account followed by the rate of interest or dividend, if the same is fixed on the dates when it is payable ; when an investment is purchased "cum-dividend", "ex-dividend" its cost is analysed into the normal price and the dividend or interest accrued and an entry is made on the credit side of the Cash Book, from where it is posted to the respective columns on the debit side of the particular Investment Account in the Investment Ledger. When the whole or part of the investment is sold, the price received, similarly split up into the normal price and the dividend or interest accrued, is entered on the debit side of the Cash Book, from where it is posted to the respective columns on the credit side of the particular Investment Account in the Investment Ledger. Expenses by way of brokerage, stamps etc., will be debited to the capital account. When dividend or interest accrued on an investment is received, it is first entered on the debit side of the Cash Book and then posted to the credit side of the particular Investment Account in the 'Dividend or Interest' column in the Investment Ledger. At the close of the financial year, the dividend or interest accrued on different investments, but not received, is brought into account by crediting the 'Dividend or Interest' columns of the different investment accounts in the Investment Ledger and bringing down such balances as an asset after the accounts have been balanced.

The first column is of Nominal value and in it on the credit is entered the nominal value of investments on hand and the totals on both sides will then agree.

The second column is of Interest or Dividend and it will always show a credit balance representing interest or dividend on investments for the period and it will be carried to the Profit and Loss Account.

The third column is for Capital or Principal. In this column against the closing balance will be entered the **value of securities** is hand and the difference of the two sides will show profit or loss on the sale of investments during the period. Value of securities in hand is the lower of cost and fair value.

ILLUSTRATION 7. Bonanzaa Limited held on 1st April, 2024 ₹ 2,00,000 of 9% **Government Loan** (2029) at ₹ 1,90,000. (Face Value of Loan ₹ 100 each). Three months' interest had accrued on the above date. On 31st May, 2024 the company purchased the same Government Loan of the face value of ₹ 80,000 at ₹ 95 (net) cum-interest. On 1st June, 2024, ₹ 60,000 face value of the loan was sold at ₹ 94 (net) ex-interest. Interest on the loan was paid each year on 30th June and 31st December and was credited by the bank on the same date. On 30th November, 2024 ₹ 40,000 face value of Loan was sold at ₹ 97 (net) cum-interest. On 1st December, 2024 the company purchased the same loan ₹ 10,000 at par ex-interest. On 1st March, 2025 the company sold ₹ 10,000 face value of the loan at ₹ 95 ex-interest. The market price of the loan on 31st March, 2025 was ₹ 96. Draw up 9% Government Loan (2029) Account in the books of Bonanzaa Limited. First in first out method shall be followed and the balance of the loan held by the company shall be valued at total average cost or market price whichever is lower. Calculations shall be made to the nearest rupee or multiple thereof. ***(C.A. Inter)***

SOLUTION. ***(For 9% Government Loan (2029) Account see next page)***

SOLUTION (*ILLUSTRATION 7*)

In the Books of Bonanzaa Ltd.

9% GOVERNMENT LOAN (2029) ACCOUNT

(*Interest payable on 30th June and 31st December*)

Dr. *Cr.*

Date	Particulars	Nominal Value	Income	Capital	Date	Particulars	Nominal Value	Income	Capital
2024		₹	₹	₹	2024		₹	₹	₹
April 1	To Balance b/d (1)	2,00,000	4,500	1,90,000	June 1	By Bank A/c	60,000	2,250	56,400
May 31	" Bank A/c	80,000	3,000	73,000	" 30	" Bank A/c	—	9,900	—
Dec. 1	" Bank A/c	10,000	375	10,000		(Interest for 6 months)			
					Nov. 30	" Bank A/c	40,000	1,500	37,300
					Dec. 31	" Bank A/c	—	8,550	—
						(Interest for 6 months)			
2025					2025				
Mar. 31	" Profit & Loss A/c	—	18,525		March 1	" Bank A/c	10,000	150	9,500
					" 31	" Profit & Loss A/c	—	—	1,300
						(Loss on sale) (2)			
					" "	" Balance c/d (3)	1,80,000	4,050	1,68,500
		2,90,000	26,400	2,73,000			2,90,000	26,400	2,73,000

Working Notes :

(1) Interest accrued on balance of Govt. Loan as on 1-4-2024 :

Interest on ₹ 2,00,000 @ 9% for 3 months = ₹ 2,00,000 × 9/100 × 1/4 = ₹ 4,500.

(2) Loss on sale of 9% Govt. Loan: Since FIFO basis is to be followed, the sales have been made out of the balance of 9% Govt. Loan in hand as on 1-4-2024.

(A) Cost of ₹ 1,10,000 9% Govt. Loan sold during 2024-25
= ₹ 1,90,000 × 1,10,000/2,00,000 = ₹ 1,04,500

(B) Sale proceeds of ₹ 1,10,000 9% Govt. Loan = ₹ 1,03,200
Loss on sale of 9% Govt. Loan (A-B) ₹ 1,300

(3) Cost of closing balance of 9% Govt. Loan on FIFO basis : The face value of balance of 9% Govt. Loan as on 31-3-2025 is ₹ 1,80,000. The cost of 9% Govt. Loan as on 31-3-2025 is arrived at as per FIFO basis as below :

	Nominal Value	*Actual Cost*
	₹	₹
Balance out of opening stock of 9% Govt. Loan	90,000	85,500
Balance out of May, 2024 purchase	80,000	73,000
Balance out of December, 2024 purchase	10,000	10,000
	1,80,000	1,68,500

Average cost of 9% Govt. Loan per unit = ₹ 1,68,500/1,800 = ₹ 93.61

Market price of 9% Govt. Loan per unit = ₹ 96.00

Average cost being lower, the closing balance of 9% Govt. Loan is valued at average cost.

Interest accrued on ₹ 1,80,000 @ 9% for 3 months = ₹ 1,80,000 × 9/100 × 1/4 = ₹ 4,050.

ILLUSTRATION 8. During the year ended 31st December 2024, Ivory Investments Ltd. purchased and sold investments as per details below :

31st March—Purchased 10,000, 5 per cent **Debentures** of ₹ 100 each of Asbestos Ltd. at ₹ 97, brokerage and stamp duty amounting to ₹ 25,600. Interest is payable on the debentures on 1st July and 1st January.

1st May—Purchased 10,000, 6 per cent Cumulative Preference Shares of ₹ 100 each of Andhra Cements Ltd. at ₹ 95, brokerage and stamp duty being ₹ 24,200. Dividends are payable on 30th June and 31st December.

1st July—Sold ₹ 6,00,000 Debentures of Asbestos Ltd. at ₹ 99 per hundred, less brokerage, etc. ₹ 3,600.

1st October—Purchased a further 4,000, 6 per cent, Cumulative Preference Shares of ₹ 100 of Andhra Cements Ltd. at ₹ 90, brokerage and stamp duty being ₹ 8,600.

Write up the Ledger Accounts of the two investments for the year 2024.

*(For **SOLUTION** see pages 30·16 & 30·17)*

ILLUSTRATION 9. On July 1, 2024, Madurai Investment Ltd. held ₹ 2,00,000 6% **debentures** of Chartered Gerald Ltd. which appeared in the books at ₹ 1,93,000. Interest is payable on July 31 and January 31. On October 1, 2024, a further ₹ 1,00,000 debentures in Chartered Gerald Ltd. were bought at ₹ 98 cum interest and on January 1, 2025, a further ₹ 60,000 debentures were bought at ₹ 97 ex-interest.

On March 31, 2025, ₹ 1,60,000 debentures were sold at ₹ 101 cum-interest and on June 1, 2025, ₹ 1,20,000 debentures were sold at ₹ 102 ex-interest.

Show Investment Account for the period ending on June 30, 2025.

*(For **SOLUTION** see page 30·18)*

SOLUTION (*ILLUSTRATION 8*)

INVESTMENT ACCOUNT

(5% Debentures of Asbestos Limited)

Dr. Cr.

Date	Particulars	Face Value ₹	Interest ₹	Investment ₹	Date	Particulars	Face Value ₹	Interest ₹	Investment ₹
31-3-2024	To Cash 9,70,000 *Add* : Brokerage 25,600 9,95,600	10,00,000	12,500 (For 3 months on 10,00,000)	9,83,100	1-7-2024	By Cash (Interest)	—	25,000	—
					"	" Cash Sold @ 99%— 5,94,000 *Less* : Expenses 3,600 5,90,400	6,00,000	—	5,90,400
31-12-2024	To Profit & Loss Account (1)	—	—	540	31-12-2024	By Accrued Interest $\left(4,00,000 \times \frac{5}{100} \times \frac{6}{12}\right)$	—	10,000	—
31-12-2024	To Profit & Loss Account	—	22,500		"	" Balance c/d (at Cost)	4,00,000	—	3,93,240
		10,00,000	35,000	9,83,640			10,00,000	35,000	9,83,640

(1) *Calculation of Profit on Sale of Debentures on 1-7-2024*

Amount realised on sale of debentures (nominal value ₹ 6,00,000)	₹	5,90,400
Less : Purchase of ₹ 6,00,000 Debentures $\left(\frac{9,83,100}{10,00,000} \times 6,00,000\right)$	₹	5,89,860
Profit on Sale of Debentures	₹	540

INVESTMENT ACCOUNT
(6% Cum. Pref. Shares in Andhra Cements Limited)

Dr. *Cr.*

Date	Particulars	Face value ₹	Dividend ₹	Investment ₹	Date	Particulars	Face value ₹	Dividend ₹	Investment ₹
1-5-2024	To Cash 9,50,000 *Add* : Brokerage and Stamp Duty 24,200 9,74,200	10,00,000	20,000 (For 4 months on 10,00,000)	9,54,200	30-6-2024	By Cash (Dividend) $\left(10,00,000 \times \frac{6}{100} \times \frac{6}{12}\right)$	—	30,000	—
1-10-2024	To Cash 3,60,000 *Add* : Brokerage 8,600 3,68,600	4,00,000	6,000	3,62,600	31-12-2024	" Cash (Dividend) $\left(14,00,000 \times \frac{6}{100} \times \frac{6}{12}\right)$	—	42,000	—
31-12-2024	To Profit & Loss Account	—	46,000	—	" "	" Balance (at Cost) c/d	14,00,000	—	13,16,800
		14,00,000	72,000	13,16,800			14,00,000	72,000	13,16,800

SOLUTION (*ILLUSTRATION 9*)

INVESTMENT ACCOUNT

(6% Debentures of Chartered Gerald Ltd.)

Interest payable on July 31 and January 31

Date	Particulars	Nominal Value	Interest	Investment	Date	Particulars	Nominal Value	Interest	Investment
2024		₹	₹	₹	2024		₹	₹	₹
July 1	To Balance b/d	2,00,000	(1) 5,000	1,93,000	July 31	By Bank $\left(2,00,000 \times \frac{6}{100} \times \frac{1}{2}\right)$		6,000	
Oct. 1	To bank A/c	1,00,000	(2) 1,000	(2) 97,000					
2025					2025				
Jan. 1	To Bank A/c	60,000	(3) 1,500	(3) 58,200	Mar. 31	By Bank $\left(3,60,000 \times \frac{6}{100} \times \frac{1}{2}\right)$		10,800	
Mar. 31	To Profit & Loss A/c			(5) 5,600	Mar. 31	By Bank	1,60,000	(4) 1,600	(4) 1,60,000
June 1	To Profit & Loss A/c			(6) 6,200	June 1	By Bank	1,20,000	2,400 (For 4 months)	1,22,400
June 30	To Profit & Loss A/c		15,300		June 30	By Balance c/d	80,000	2,000 (For 5 months	77,600
		3,60,000	22,800	3,60,000			3,60,000	22,800	3,60,000
July 1	To Balance b/d (Interest accrued for 5 months)	80,000	2,000	77,600					

Working Notes

(1) Interest accrued on 1-7-2024 from the last date of payment of interest *i.e.* March 31, 2024

Interest Accrued for 5 months = ₹ 2,00,000 × $\frac{5}{12} \times \frac{6}{100}$ = ₹ 5,000

(2) *Purchase of Debentures on 1-10-2024*

₹ 1,00,000 @ ₹ 98 cum-interest $\left(₹ 1,00,000 \times \frac{98}{100}\right)$	₹	98,000
Less : Interest included therein for 2 months from August 1 to Oct. 1 $\left(₹ 1,00,000 \times \frac{2}{12} \times \frac{6}{100}\right)$	₹	1,000
Amount paid for Debentures	₹	97,000

(3) *Purchase of Debentures on 1-1-2025*

₹ 60,000 debentures @ ₹ 97 ex-interest $\left(₹ 60,000 \times \frac{97}{100}\right)$	₹	58,200
Separate payment for interest (being ex-interest) for 5 months from August 1 to Dec. 31 $\left(₹ 60,000 \times \frac{5}{12} \times \frac{6}{100}\right)$	₹	1,500

(4) *Sale of Debentures on 31-3-2025*

₹ 1,60,000 debentures @ ₹ 101 cum-interest $\left(₹ 1,60,000 \times \frac{101}{100}\right)$	₹	1,61,600
Less : Interest for 2 months from Feb. 1, 2025 to March 31, 2025 included in the sale price $\left(₹ 1,60,000 \times \frac{2}{12} \times \frac{6}{100}\right)$	₹	1,600
Amount realised on account of Debentures	₹	1,60,000

(5) *Profit on Sale of Debentures on 31-3-2025*

	₹
Amount realised on sale of ₹ 1,60,000 debentures (4)	1,60,000
Less : Purchase price of ₹ 2,00,000 debentures appearing in book on 1-7-240₹ 1,93,000	
Therefore, purchase price of ₹ 1,60,000 debentures $\left(\frac{₹ 1,93,000}{₹ 2,00,000} \times ₹ 1,60,000\right)$	1,54,400
Profit on sale of ₹ 1,60,000 debentures	5,600

(6) *Profit on Sale of Debentures on June 1, 2025*

		₹
Amount realised on sale of ₹ 1,20,000 debentures @ ₹ 102 ex-interest $\left(₹ 1,20,000 \times \frac{102}{100}\right)$		1,22,400
Less : Purchase price : (Following First in First Out Method)		
Sale ₹ 40,000 out of balance of 1-7-2024 $\left(\frac{₹ 1,93,000}{₹ 2,00,000} \times ₹ 40,000\right)$	= ₹ 38,600	
Sale ₹ 80,000 out of debentures purchased on 1-10-2024 $\left(\frac{₹ 97,000}{₹ 1,00,000} \times ₹ 80,000\right)$	₹ 77,600	
		1,16,200
Profit on sale of ₹ 1,20,000 debentures		6,200

ILLUSTRATION 10. Unique Investment Corporation has done the following transactions in 6% State **Government Stock** between 1st September, 2023 and 31st July, 2025 and all these transactions are Cum-interest excepting those marked Ex-interest. Interest is payable half-yearly on 1st February and 1st August. The accounting period ends on 30th June every year.

1st September 2023—Purchased ₹ 10,000 stock @ 101.50.

1st October 2023—Purchased ₹ 25,000 stock @ 101.

1st November 2023—Sold ₹ 15,000 stock @ 103.25.

1st November 2023—Purchased ₹ 5,000 stock @ 103.

15th January 2024—Sold ₹ 10,000 stock @ 105 Ex-interest.

1st March 2024—Sold ₹ 4,000 stock @ 102.50.

15th July 2024—Purchased ₹ 5,000 stock @ 101.25 Ex-interest.

1st November 2024—Purchased ₹ 5,000 stock @ 102.

15th January 2025—Sold ₹ 15,000 stock @ 103.

1st July 2025—Purchased ₹ 2,000 stock @ 102.

Write up Investment Account in the books of the Corporation, showing the profits and losses on the transactions using the **average cost method** and also showing the amount of interest for each accounting period duly realised.

SOLUTION *(For 6% State Government Stock A/c see next page)*

SCHEDULE OF PROFIT OR LOSS ON SALES

(Average cost method)

		Nominal	*Cost*	*Realised*	*Profit*	*Loss*
2023		₹	₹	₹	₹	₹
Sept. 1	Purchase	10,000	10,100			
Oct. 1	Purchase	25,000	25,000			
		35,000	35,100			
Nov. 1	Sale	15,000	15,043[1]	15,262.50	219.50	
		20,000	20,057			
Nov. 1	Purchase	5,000	5,075			
		25,000	25,132			
2024						
Jan. 15	Sale	10,000	10,053[2]	10,525	472.00	
		15,000	15,079			
Mar. 1	Sale	4,000	4,021[3]	4,080	59.00	
		11,000	11,058		750.50	
July 15	Purchase	5,000	5,063			
		16,000	16,121			
Nov. 1	Purchase	5,000	5,025			
		21,000	21,146			
2025						
Jan. 1	Sale	15,000	15,104[4]	15,037.50		66.50
		6,000	6,042			

Notes. (1) $\frac{15}{35} \times$ ₹ 35,100 = ₹ 15,043 (approx) ; (2) $\frac{10}{25} \times$ ₹ 25,132 = ₹ 10,053 (approx) ;

(3) $\frac{4}{15} \times$ ₹ 15,079 = ₹ 4,021 (approx) ; (4) $\frac{15}{21} \times$ ₹ 21,146 = ₹ 15,104 (approx).

SOLUTION (*ILLUSTRATION 10*)

6% STATE GOVERNMENT STOCK
(*Interest payable half-yearly on 1st February & 1st August*)

Date	*Particulars*	*Nominal*	*Income*	*Capital*	*Date*	*Particulars*	*Nominal*	*Income*	*Capital*
2023		₹	₹	₹	2023		₹	₹	₹
Sept. 1	To Cash : Purchase at ₹ 101.50	10,000	50	10,100	Nov. 1	By Cash : Sale at ₹ 103.25	15,000	225	15,262.50
Oct. 1	" Cash : Purchase at ₹ 101	25,000	250	25,000	2024 Jan. 15	" Cash : Sale at ₹ 105 ex-interest	10,000	275	10,525.00
Nov. 1	" Cash : Purchase at ₹ 103	5,000	75	5,075	Feb. 1	" Interest on ₹ 15,000 at 6% p.a. for half year		450	
2024 June 30	" Income & Exp. A/c Profit on transaction			750.50	Mar. 1	" Cash : Sale at ₹ 102.50	4,000	20	4,080.00
	Interest for period		870		June 30	" Balance c/d Stock at average cost (Accruing interest thereon (for 5 months)	11,000	275	11,058.00
		40,000	1,245	40,925.50			40,000	1,245	40,925.50
2024 July 1	To Balance b/d	11,000	275	11,058	2024 Aug. 1	By Interest on ₹ 16,000 at 6% p.a. for half year		480.00	
July 15	" Cash : Purchase at 101.25 ex-interest	5,000	137.50	5,062.50	2025 Jan. 15	" Cash : Sale at ₹ 103	15,000	412.50	15,037.50
Nov. 1	" Cash : Purchases at ₹ 102	5,000	75	5,025.00	Feb. 1	" Bank (Int. on ₹ 6,000 for $\frac{1}{2}$ year)		180.00	
2025 June 30	" Income & Exp. A/c Interest for the period		710		June 30	" Income & Exp. A/c (Loss on transaction)			66.00
					"	" Balance c/d Stock at average cost Accruing interest for 5 months	6,000	125.00	6,042.00
		21,000	1,197.50	21,145.50			21,000	1,197.50	21,145.50
July 1	" Balance b/d	6,000	125	6,042					
"	" Cash : Purchase at ₹ 102.	2,000	50	1,990					

Equity Shares Accounts

Equity shares are known as variable income bearing securities because income on investment in shares depends on the rate of dividend declared by a company. Following are the peculiar features in case the investment accounts are prepared regarding equity shares :

***(i)* Purchase of Equity Shares.** If shares are purchased with the intention to hold for short-term period, then these will be shown at the realisable value. However, if equity shares are acquired with an intention to hold for long-term then these will be shown at cost in the Balance Sheet of the Company. However, provision for diminution shall be made to recognise a decline, if other than temporary, in the value of shares. Investment in shares, gold and silver acquired for long-term period should be shown at cost though their realisable value have been increased.

EXAMPLE. M/s Innovative Garments Manufacturing Company Limited invested in the shares of another company on 1st October, 2024 at a cost of ₹ 2,50,000. It also earlier purchased Gold of ₹ 4,00,000 and Silver of ₹ 2,00,000 on 1st March, 2023. Market value as on 31st March, 2025 of above investments are as follows :

Shares ₹ 2,25,000; Gold ₹ 6,00,000; Silver ₹ 3,50,000.

How above investments will be shown in the books of accounts of M/s Innovative Garments Manufacturing Company Limited for the year ending 31st March, 2025.

SOLUTION

If shares are purchased with an intention to hold for short-term period, then these will be shown at the realisable value of ₹ 2,25,000 as on 31st March, 2025.

However, if *equity shares are acquired with an intention to hold for long-term period, then these will be shown at cost* of ₹ 2,50,000 in the Balance Sheet of the company. However, provision for diminution shall be made to recognize a decline, if other than temporary, in the value of shares.

Investment acquired for long-term period shall be shown at cost. Gold and silver are generally purchased with an intention to hold it for long-term period until and unless given otherwise. Hence, the investment in Gold and Silver (purchased on 1st March, 2023) shall continue to be shown at cost as on 31st Mach, 2025 *i.e.,* ₹ 4,00,000 and ₹ 200,000 respectively, though their realizable values have been increased.

***(ii)* Bonus Shares.** When successful companies issue bonus shares to capitalise their reserves, the shareholders are not required to pay any amount for such shares. The number of shares will be entered in the number column and nothing will be added in the amount of principal or capital column. When bonus shares are sold, the profit on such shares is calculated by deducting average cost of shares sold from sale price of bonus shares. Valuation of investment in shares should be made at market value or average cost price of shares, whichever is lower.

ILLUSTRATION 11. H purchased 500 **equity shares** of ₹ 100 each in the ABC Company Limited for ₹ 62,500 inclusive of brokerage and stamp duty. Some years later the company decided to capitalise its profit and to issue to the holders of equity shares one equity share as Bonus for every equity share held by them. Prior to capitalization, the shares of ABC Company Limited were quoted at ₹ 175 per share. After the capitalization, the shares were quoted at ₹ 92.50 per share. H sold the Bonus shares and received ₹ 90 per share. Show Investment A/c in H's books on average cost basis. ***(Adapted CA—Inter)***

SOLUTION

In the Books of H

INVESTMENT ACCOUNT (EQUITY SHARES OF ABC CO. LTD.)

Particulars	*Face Value* ₹	*Cost* ₹	*Particulars*	*Face Value* ₹	*Cost* ₹
To Balance b/d	50,000	62,500	By Bank A/c	50,000	45,000
To Bonus Shares A/c	50,000	—	By Balance c/d (2)	50,000	31,250

To Profit & Loss A/c (Profit on Sale) (1)		13,750				
	1,00,000	76,250			1,00,000	76,250

Working Notes :

(1) Calculation of Profit on Sale of Bonus Shares : ₹

Sale Price of Bonus Shares	45,000
Less : Average Cost of shares sold $\left(\frac{₹ 62,500}{1,00,000} \times 50,000\right)$ =	31,250
Profit	13,750

(2) Value of Closing Investment :

Market Value of Shares $\left(\frac{₹ 50,000}{100} \times 92.50\right)$ = 46,250

Cost Price of Shares (1) = 31,250

Value of investment will be lower of market value or average cost price, *i.e.* ₹ 31,250

ILLUSTRATION 12. On 1-4-2024, Mr. T. Shekharan purchased 5,000 equity shares of ₹ 100 each in V Ltd. @ ₹ 120 each from a broker, who charged 2% brokerage. He incurred 50 paise per ₹ 100 as cost of shares transfer stamps. On 31-1-2025 bonus was declared in the ratio of 1 : 2. Before and after the record date of bonus shares, the shares ere quoted at ₹ 175 per share and ₹ 90 per share respectively. On 31-3-2025, Mr. T. Shekharan sold bonus shares to a broker, who charged 2% brokerage.

Show the Investment Account in the books of T. Shekharan, who held the shares as Current Assets and closing value of investments shall be made at cost or market value, whichever is lower. ***(CA—Inter)***

SOLUTION

In the Books of T. Shekharan
INVESTMENT ACCOUNT IN EQUITY SHARES OF V LTD.
for the year ended 31st March, 2025

Date	Particulars	Nominal Value (₹	Cost (₹)	Date	Particulars	Nominal Value (₹)	Cost (₹)
1-4-2024	To Bank A/c (1)	5,00,000	6,15,000	31-3-2025	By Bank A/c	2,50,000	2,20,500
31-3-2025	To Bonus Shares	2,50,000	—	31-3-2025	By Balance c/d	5,00,000	(4) 4,10,000
31-3-2025	To Profit & Loss A/c		(3) 15,500				
		7,50,000	6,30,500			7,50,000	6,30,500

Working Notes :

(1) *Cost of equity shares purchased on 1st April, 2024*
= Cost + Brokerage + Cost of transfer stamps
= 5,000 × ₹ 120 + 2% of ₹ 6,00,000 + 1/2% of ₹ 6,00,000 = ₹ 6,15,000

(2) *Sale proceeds of equity shares sold on 31st March, 2025*
= Sale Price – Brokerage
= 2,500 × ₹ 90 – 2% of ₹ 2,25,000 = ₹ 2,20,500

(3) *Profit on sale of bonus shares on 31st March, 2025*
= Sales Proceeds – Average Cost
Sales Proceeds = ₹ 2,20,500

Average Cost = ₹ [6,15,000 × 2,50,000/7,50,000]
= ₹ 2,05,000
Profit = ₹ 2,20,500 – ₹ 2,05,000 = ₹ 15,500.

(4) *Valuation of equity shares on 31st March, 2025*

Cost = ₹ [6,15,000 × 5,00,000/7,50,000] = ₹ 4,10,000 *i.e.* ₹ 82 per share

Market Value = 5,000 shares × ₹ 90 = ₹ 4,50,000

Closing stock of equity shares has been valued at ₹ 4,10,000 *i.e.* cost being lower than the market value.

(*iii*) **Rights Shares.** If shares are first offered to the existing shareholders as a matter of their right, such shares are called right shares. Such shares may be purchased by the shareholder or the right may be renunciated in favour of a third party for a consideration. If the shares are purchased, the number of shares and amount paid will be entered in the number and principal columns respectively. If the rights are not subscribed for but are sold in the market, the amount received will be entered only in the Profit & Loss Account. It is further stated that when right shares offered are subscribed for, the cost of the right shares is added to the carrying amount of the original holding. If rights are not subscribed for but are sold in the market, the sale proceeds are taken to the profit and loss statement. However, where the investments are acquired on cum-right basis and the market value of investments immediately after their becoming ex-right is lower than the cost for which they were acquired, it may be appropriate to apply the sale proceeds of rights to reduce the carrying amount of such investments to the market value."

(*iii*) If shares are purchased as cum-dividend, it is not possible to calculate the amount of dividend until it is declared. Then the total price paid is entered in the principal column and as and when dividend is received, it is entered in the capital column on the credit side.

Following Illustrations will clear these points.

ILLUSTRATION 13. Tandon carried out the following transactions in the **shares** of Bright Ltd.:

(*a*) On 1st April, 2024 he purchased 20,000 **equity shares** of ₹ 1 each fully paid for ₹ 30,000 on cum-right basis.

(*b*) On 15th May, 2024, Tandon sold 4,000 shares for ₹ 7,600.

(*c*) At a meeting on 15th June, 2024, the company decided :

(*i*) to make a bonus issue of one fully paid share for every four shares held on 1st June 2024, and

(*ii*) to give its members the right to apply for one share for every five shares held on 1st June, 2024 at a price of ₹ 1.50 per share of which 75 paise is payable on or before 15th July, 2024, and the balance, 75 paise per share, on or before 15th September, 2024.

The shares issued under (*i*) and (*ii*) were not to rank for dividend for the year ending 31st December, 2024.

(*d*) Tandon received his bonus shares and took up 2,000 shares under the rights issue, paying the sums thereon when due and selling the rights to the remaining shares at 40 paise per share ; the proceeds were received on 30th September, 2024.

(*e*) On 15th March, 2025, he received a dividend from Bright Ltd. of 15 per cent in respect of the year ended 31st December, 2024.

(*f*) On 30th March, he received ₹ 14,000 for the sale of 10,000 shares.

You are required to record these transactions in Investments Account in Tandon's books for the year ended 31st March 2025, transferring any profits or losses on these transactions. Apply Average basis. Expenses and tax to be ignored.

(*For* **SOLUTION** *see page next page*)

SOLUTION (*ILLUSTRATION 13*)

In the Books of Mr. Tandon

INVESTMENT ACCOUNT (SHARES IN BRIGHT LIMITED)

Dr. Cr.

Date	Particulars	No. of Shares	Income	Principal Amount	Date	Particulars	No. of Shares	Income	Principal Amount
2024			₹	₹	2024			₹	₹
April 1	To Bank (Purchases)	20,000	—	30,000	May 15	By Bank (Sales)	4,000	—	7,600
May 15	" Profit & Loss A/c (1)	—	—	1,600	Sept. 30	" Bank (Sale of Right) (1,200 @ 40 paise)	—	—	480
June 15	" Bonus Issue	4,000	—	—	2025				
July 15	" Bank @ 75 p. paid on 2,000 shares)	2,000	—	1,500	Mar. 15	" Bank (Dividend) (15% on ₹ 16,000)		2,400	—
Sept. 15	" Bank @ 75 p. paid on 2,000 shares)	—	—	1,500	" 30	" Bank (Sale)	10,000	—	14,000
2025					" 31	" Balance c/d $\left(\frac{12,000}{22,000} \times 26,520\right)$	12,000	—	14,465
Mar. 30	" Profit & Loss A/c (2)			1,945					
" 31	" Profit & Loss A/c transferred	—	2,400	—					
		26,000	2,400	36,545			26,000	2,400	36,545

Working Notes :

(1) Sale on 15-5-2024 : Cost of 4,000 shares @ ₹ 1.50 — ₹ 6,000

Sale Price — ₹ 7,600

Profit — ₹ 1,600

(2) Cost of 10,000 shares sold : ₹

Cost of 22,000 shares (₹ 24,000 + ₹ 3,000) — 27,000

Less : Amount received from rights — 480

Cost of 22,000 shares — ₹ 26,520

∴ Cost of 10,000 shares $\left(\frac{₹ 26,520}{22,000} \times 10,000\right)$ — ₹ 12,055

Profit on 10,000 shares (₹ 14,000 – ₹ 12,055) — ₹ 1,945

ILLUSTRATION 14. On 1st January, 2024 X Ltd. had 10,000 **equity shares** of ₹ 10 each in Alpha Ltd. purchased ₹ 1,25,000. The company unlike investment companies does not make any apportionment of dividends (received or receivable) in between capital and revenue.

On 15th May, 2024, Alpha Ltd. made a **bonus issue** of one fully paid share for every two held. In addition, on the same day **right shares** were issued at 3 for every 5 held on that date at a premium of ₹ 3, ₹ 7 to be paid on application and balance in call after a month. These shares are not to rank for dividend for the year ending 30th June, 2024. 1/3 right shares were taken up by X Ltd. and balance rights being sold at ₹ 2 each on 25th May, 2024.

On 15th October, 2024, the company declared a dividend of 20% for the year ending 30th June, 2024.

Make out Investment Account in the books of X Ltd. Ignore income tax.

[*Adapted B.Com. (Hons.) Calcutta*]

(*For* **SOLUTION** *see next page*)

ILLUSTRATION 15. On 1-4-2024. Mr. S had 25,000 equity shares of X Ltd. at a book value of ₹ 15 per share (face value ₹ 10).

On 20-6-2024, he purchases further 5,000 shares of X Ltd. at ₹ 16 per share. Directors of X Ltd. announced a bonus and rights issue. No dividend was payable on these issues. The terms of issue were as follows :

Bonus — basis 1 : 6 (16-8-2024);

Rights — basis 3 : 7 (31-8-2024) price ₹ 15 per share :

Due date for payment—30-9-2024 :

Rights are transferable in full or in part.

Accordingly Mr. S sold 1/3rd of his entitlement to Mr. T for a consideration of ₹ 2 per share.

Dividend at 20% for the year ending 31-3-2024 was declared by X Ltd. and Mr. S received the same on 31-10-2024.

Dividend for the shares acquired by him on 20-6-2024 are to be adjusted against the cost of purchase.

On 25-11-2024 Mr. S sold 25,000 equity shares at a premium of ₹ 5 per share.

Prepare Investment Account and Profit and Loss Account in the books of Mr. S assuming that he closes his books on 31-12-2024 and shares are valued at average cost.

SOLUTION

Books of S

INVESTMENT ACCOUNT (*Equity Shares in X Ltd.*)

Date	Particulars	No. of Shares	₹	Date	Particulars	No. of Shares	₹
1-4-2024	To Balance b/f	25,000	3,75,000	30-9-2024	By Bank		
20-6-2024	To Bank	5,000	80,000		(Sale of Rights)	—	10,000
16-8-2024	To Bonus Shares (1)	5,000	—	31-10-2024	By Bank (Dividend)	—	10,000
30-9-2024	To Bank (Rights)	10,000	1,50,000	25-11-2024	By Bank		
25-11-2024	To Profit on Sale (6)	—	50,000		(Sale of Shares)	25,000	3,75,000
				31-12-2024	By Balance c/d (5)	20,000	2,60,000
		45,000	6,55,000			45,000	6,55,000

(*Contd. on page 30.28*)

SOLUTION (*ILLUSTRATION 14*)

INVESTMENT ACCOUNT
(Equity Shares in Alpha Ltd.)

Date	Particulars	No. of Shares	Nominal Value	Amount	Date	Particulars	No. of Shares	Nominal Value	Amount
2024			₹	₹	2024			₹	₹
Jan. 1	To Balance b/d	10,000	1,00,000	1,25,000	May 25	By Bank (Sale of right on 4,000 shares @ ₹ 2 per share)			8,000
May 15	To Bonus Issue	5,000	50,000	—					
" 15	To Bank (@ ₹ 7 as application money on 2,000 right shares)	2,000	20,000	14,000	Dec. 31	By Balance c/d	17,000	1,70,000	1,43,000
June 15	To Bank (@ ₹ 6 balance of issued price of 2,000 right shares)			12,000					
		17,000	1,70,000	1,51,000			17,000	17,000	1,51,000
2025									
Jan. 1	To Balance b/d	17,000	1,70,000	1,43,000					

Notes : (1) Dividend income of ₹ 20,000 (*i.e.* 20% dividend on ₹ 1,00,000 nominal value shares) will be transferred to Profit and Loss Account.

(2) Number of bonus shares @ 1 for every 2 shares held = $10,000 \times \frac{1}{2} = 5,000$.

(3) Number of right shares @ 3 for every 5 held = $10,000 \times \frac{3}{5} = 6,000$.

Dr. **PROFIT & LOSS ACCOUNT** Cr.

		₹			₹
31-12-2024	To Balance c/f	1,00,000	31-10-2024	By Dividend (4)	50,000
			25-11-2024	By Profit on Sale of Shares (6)	50,000
		1,00,000			1,00,000

Working Notes :

(1) Bonus shares = 30,000 × 1/6 = 5,000 shares

(2) Right shares = $\frac{25{,}000 + 5{,}000 + 5{,}000}{7} \times 3$ = 15,000 shares

(3) Sale of Rights = 15,000 × 1/3 = 5,000 shares @ ₹ 2 = ₹ 10,000

(4) Dividend received on 25,000 shares at ₹ 2 per share = ₹ 50,000

(5) Cost of 20,000 shares on 31-12-2024

$= \frac{₹\ 3{,}75{,}000 + ₹\ 80{,}000 + ₹\ 1{,}50{,}000 - ₹\ 10{,}000 - ₹\ 10{,}000}{45{,}000 \text{ shares}} \times 20{,}000 \text{ shares} = ₹\ 2{,}60{,}000$

(6) Profit on Sale

Cost of 20,000 shares is ₹ 2,60,000

So, cost of 25,000 shares = $\frac{₹\ 2{,}60{,}000}{20{,}000} \times 25{,}000 = ₹\ 3{,}25{,}000$

Profit on sale = ₹ 3,75,000 – ₹ 3,25,000 = ₹ 50,000

ILLUSTRATION 16. On 1st April, 2024, XY Ltd. has 15,000 equity shares of ABC Ltd. at a book value of ₹ 15 per share (face value ₹ 10 per share). On 1st June, 2024, XY Ltd. acquired 5,000 equity shares of ABC Ltd. for ₹ 1,00,000 on cum right basis. ABC Ltd. announced a bonus and right issue.

(1) Bonus was declared, at the rate of one equity share for every five shares held, on 1st July 2024.

(2) Right shares are to be issued to the existing shareholders on 1st September 2024. The company will issue one right share for every 6 shares at 20% premium. No dividend was payable on these shares.

(3) Dividend for the year ended 31-3-2024 was declared by ABC Ltd. @ 20%, which was received by XY Ltd. on 31st October, 2024.

XY Ltd.

(*i*) Took up half the right issue.

(*ii*) Sold the remaining rights for ₹ 8 per share.

(*iii*) Sold half of its share holding on 1st January, 2025 at ₹ 16.50 per share. Brokerage being 1%.

You are required to prepare Investment Account of XY Ltd,. for the year ended 31st March 2025 assuming the shares are being valued at average cost. ***(CA—Inter)***

SOLUTION

In the Books of XY Ltd.
INVESTMENT IN EQUITY SHARES OF ABC LTD.
for the year ended 31st March, 2025

		No. of Shares	Income ₹	Capital ₹			No. of Shares	Income ₹	Capital ₹
2024					2024				
April 1	To Balance b/d	15,000	—	2,25,000	Sept. 1	By Bank A/c (3)	—	—	16,000
June 1	To Bank A/c	5,000	—	1,00,000	2024				
July 1	To Bonus				Oct. 31	By Bank A/c (5)	—	30,000	10,000
	Issue (1)	4,000			2025				

Sept. 1 2025	To Bank A/c (2)	2,000	—	24,000	Jan. 1	By Bank A/c (4)	13,000	—	2,12,355
Mar. 31	To P & L A/c (4)	—	—	50,855	Mar. 31	By Balance c/d (6)	13,000	—	1,61,500
"	To P & L A/c	—	30,000	—					
		26,000	30,000	3,99,855			26,000	30,000	3,99,855

Working Notes :

(1) Calculation of No. of Bonus Shares Issued

$$\text{Bonus Shares} = \frac{15{,}000 \text{ shares} + 5{,}000 \text{ shares}}{5} \times 1 = 4{,}000 \text{ shares}$$

(2) Calculation of Right Shares Subscribed

$$\text{Right Shares} = \frac{15{,}000 \text{ shares} + 5{,}000 \text{ shares} + 4{,}000 \text{ shares}}{6} = 4{,}000 \text{ shares}$$

$$\text{Shares subscribed by XY Ltd.} = \frac{4{,}000}{2} = 2{,}000 \text{ shares}$$

Value of right shares subscribed = 2,000 shares @ ₹ 12 per share = ₹ 24,000

(3) Calculation of Sale of Right Entitlement

2,000 shares × ₹ 8 per share = ₹ 16,000

(Since shares are purchased cum right basis, therefore, amount received from sale of rights will be credited to Investment A/c)

(4) Calculation of Profit on Sale of Shares

Total holding = 15,000 shares original
5,000 shares purchased
4,000 shares bonus
2,000 shares right shares
26,000 shares

50% of the holding were sold

13,000 shares (*i.e.* 26,000 × 1/2) were sold.

Cost of total holdings of 26,000 shares (on average basis)
= ₹ 2,25,000 + ₹ 1,00,000 + ₹ 24,000 − ₹ 16,000 − ₹10,000 = ₹ 3,23,000

Average Cost of 13,000 shares would be

$$= \frac{₹\ 3{,}23{,}000}{26{,}000} \times 13{,}000 = ₹\ 1{,}61{,}500$$

	₹
Sale proceeds of 13,000 shares (13,000 × ₹ 16.50)	2,14,500
Less : 1% Brokerage	2,145
	2,12,355
Less : Cost of 13,000 shares	1,61,500
Profit on Sale	50,855

(5) Dividend received on investment held as on 1st April, 2024

= 15,000 shares × ₹ 10 × 20% = ₹ 30,000 will be transferred to Profit and Loss A/c

Dividend received on shares purchased on 1st June, 2024

= 5,000 shares × ₹ 10 × 20% = ₹ 10,000 will be adjusted to Investment A/c

Note : It is presumed that no dividend is received on bonus shares as bonus shares are declared on 1st July, 2024 and dividend pertains to the year ended 31-3-2024.

(6) Calculation of closing value of shares (on average basis) as on 31st March, 2025

$13{,}000 \times \frac{₹\ 3{,}23{,}000}{26{,}000}$ = ₹ 1,61,500. Closing value of shares would be ₹ 1,61,500.

ILLUSTRATION 17. Mr. Brown has made following transactions during the financial year 2024-25 :

Date	*Particulars*
1-5-2024	Purchased 24,000 12% **Bonds** of ₹ 100 each at ₹ 84 cum-interest. Interest is payable on 30th September and 31st March every year.
15-6-2024	Purchased ₹ 1,50,000 **equity shares** of ₹ 10 each in Alpha Limited for ₹ 25 each through a broker, who charged brokerage @ 2%.
10-7-2024	Purchased 60,000 equity shares of ₹ 10 each in Beeta Limited for ₹ 44 each through a broker, who charged brokerage @ 2%.
14-10-2024	Alpha Limited made a **bonus issue** of two shares for every three shares held.
31-10-2024	Sold 80000 shares in Alpha Limited for ₹ 22 each.
1-1-2025	Received 15% interim dividend on equity shares of Alpha Limited.
15-1-2025	Beeta Limited made a **right issue** of one equity share for every four shares held at ₹ 5 per share. Mr. Brown exercised his option for 40% of his entitlements and sold the balance rights in the market at ₹ 2.25 per share.
1-3-2025	Sold 15,000 12% Bonds at ₹ 90 ex-interest.
15-3-2025	Received 18% interim dividend on equity shares of Beeta Limited. Interest on 12% Bonds was duly received on due dates.

Prepare separate **Investment Account** for 12% Bonds, Equity Shares of Alpha Limited and Equity Shares of Beeta Limited in the books of Mr. Brown for the year ended on 31st March, 2025. ***(CA—Inter)***

SOLUTION

In the Books of Mr. Brown

12% BONDS

for the year ended 31st March, 2025

		No.	Interest Income ₹	Amount ₹			No.	Interest Income ₹	Amount ₹
2024					2024				
May 1	To Bank A/c	24,000	24,000	19,92,000	Sept. 30	By Bank (Interest)	—	1,44,000	
2025					2025				
March	To P & L A/c (1)	—	—	1,05,000	Mar. 1	By Bank A/c	15,000	75,000	13,50,000
31	To P & L A/c		2,49,000		2025				
					Mar. 31	By Bank (Interest)		54,000	
						By Balance c/d	9,000	—	7,47,000
		24,000	2,73,000	20,97,000			24,000	2,73,000	20,97,000

INVESTMENT IN EQUITY SHARES OF ALPHA LTD.

for the year ended 31st March, 2025

		No.	Dividend Income ₹	Amount ₹			No.	Dividend Income ₹	Amount ₹
2024					2024				
June 15	To Bank A/c	1,50,000	—	38,25,000	Oct. 31	By Bank A/c	80,000	—	17,60,000
Oct. 14	To Bonus Issue (1,50,000/3 × 2)	1,00,000	—	—	2025	By Bank A/c			
					Jan. 1	—Dividend		2,55,000	

2025 Mar. 31	To P & L A/c (3)			5,36,000	Mar. 31	By Balance c/d	1,70,000	—	26,01,000
	To P & L A/c		2,55,000						
		2,50,000	2,55,000	43,61,000			2,50,000	2,55,000	43,61,000

INVESTMENT IN EQUITY SHARES OF BEETA LTD.

for the year ended 31st March, 2025

		No.	*Dividend Income* ₹	*Amount* ₹			*No.*	*Dividend Income* ₹	*Amount* ₹
2025 June 10	To Bank A/c	60,000	—	26,92,800	2025 Jan. 15	By Bank A/c (6)	—	—	20,250
2025 Jan. 15	To Bank A/c (5)	6,000	—	30,000	Mar. 15	By Bank—Dividend	—	1,18,800	
Mar. 31	To P & L A/c	—	1,18,800	—	2025 Mar. 31	By Balance c/d (Bal. fig.)	66,000	—	27,02,550
		66,000	1,18,800	27,22,800			66,000	1,18,800	27,22,800

Working Notes :

(1) Profit on sale of 12% Bonds

Sale Price	₹ 13,50,000
Less : Cost of Bonds Sold $= \frac{19,92,000}{24,000} \times 15,000$	₹ 12,45,000
Profit on Sale	₹ 1,05,000

QUESTIONS

OBJECTIVE TYPE

1. **State whether the following statements are TRUE or FALSE :**
   (*a*) Cum-dividend price is not the real price of investment.
   (*b*) Closing balance of investment is valued at cost or market price whichever is less.
   (*c*) Bonus shares are recorded at nominal value in the investment account.
   (*d*) Brokerage is added in the purchase value of investment in the books of purchaser.
   (*e*) Brokerage is not deducted from the sale value of investment in the books of seller.
   (*f*) Ex-interest price is more than the Cum-interest price.
   (*g*) Only FIFO method is used to calculate cost of closing balance of investment.

Ans. [True (*a*), (*b*), (*d*). False : (*c*), (*e*), (*f*), (*g*)].

2. **Fill in the blanks :**
   (*a*) Investment Account is.................Account.
   (*b*) Sale of right is a..............receipt in case of right issue.
   (*c*) Brokerage is...........in the cost of investment in the books of purchaser of investment.
   (*d*) Interest accrued upto the date of sale of investment added ....price.

Ans. [(*a*) Real, (*b*) Capital, (*c*) added, (*d*) Ex-interest].

SHORT ANSWER TYPE

1. **Discuss the** nature and purpose of investment account.
2. What do you mean by Investment Ledger ?
3. Distinguish between Cum-Interest and Ex-Interest.
4. How are investment accounts prepared when there is issue of bonus shares and right shares by the company ?
5. How will you account for sale of rights in the preparation of Investment Accounts ?
6. What is Ex-dividend and cum-dividend quotation ?
7. What is cum-interest-quotation of securities ?

LONG ANSWER TYPE

1. What are the special features of Investment Accounts ? How are stock exchange transactions (sale & purchase of securities) recorded in books ?
2. What do you understand by Investment Account ? How is it prepared ? Explain the terms 'cum-interest' and 'ex-interest' in relation to such account with the help of suitable examples.
3. What benefits an investor gets by preparing an Investment Account ? Is there any difference in preparation of Investment Account for Shares and Debentures ? Explain giving examples.

PRACTICAL PROBLEMS

1. On 1-1-2024 6% 200 **Debentures** of ₹ 100 each in **Y Ltd.** were held as investments by X Ltd. at a cost of ₹ 18,200. Interest is payable on 31st December.

   On 1-4-2024 ₹ 4,000 of such debentures were purchased by X Ltd. @ ₹ 98 and on 1-9-2024 ₹ 6,000 Debentures were sold at ₹ 96 ex-interest. On 1-12-2024 ₹ 8,000 Debentures were sold @ ₹ 99 cum-interest. On 31-12-2024 X Ltd. sold ₹ 10,000 Debentures @ ₹ 95 ex-interest.

   Prepare Investment Account for 6% Debentures of Y Ltd. in the Books of X Ltd. Ignore Income Tax.

Ans. [Interest transferred to P. & L. A/c ₹ 1,220 ; Profit on All Sales ₹ 680 (*i.e.* 300 + 200 + 180)].

2. Mr. A held on 1st January, 2024, ₹ 1,00,000 of $3\frac{1}{2}$% **Government Loan** at ₹ 95,000. Three months interest had accrued. On 31st May he purchased a further ₹ 40,000 of the Loan @ ₹ 96 (net) cum-interest. On 31st July, ₹ 30,000 of the Loan was sold at ₹ 94 (net) ex-interest. On 30th November ₹ 20,000 of the Loan was sold at ₹ 96 (net) cum-interest. Interest on the Loan was paid each year on 31st March and 30th September and was collected on 4th April and 5th October. The price of the Loan on 31st December, 2024 was ₹ 96. Draw up the Loan Account. Ignore income-tax and paise.

Ans. [Interest transferred to Profit & Loss A/c ₹ 3,822 ; Loss on Sale ₹ 217 *i.e.*, ₹ 300 – ₹ 83].

3. On 1st April, 2024, **X, Y and Co.** held 9% **debentures** in Banbury Ltd. of the face value of ₹ 10,000 at cost of ₹ 8,000. Market value on that date was ₹ 9,000. Interest is payable on 31st December every year. On 1st December, 2024 debentures of nominal value of ₹ 6,000 were purchased for ₹ 5,000 ex-interest and on 31st December, 2024 debentures of nominal value of ₹ 2,000 were sold cum-interest for ₹ 1,900. On 1st January, 2025 debentures of nominal value of ₹ 6,000 were bought at ₹ 5,800. The market value of the debentures on 31st March, 2025 was at ₹ 90.

   Make out Investment Account in the books of X, Y and Co., showing profit or loss on sale of investment. Stocks on 31st March each year are valued at lower of cost (apply FIFO method) and market price.

Ans. [Interest transferred to P. & L. A/c ₹ 1,170 ; Value of Holding ₹ 17,200 ; Capital Profit on Sale ₹ 120].

4. **Mr. Investor** furnishes the following details relating to his holding in 6% **Government Bonds :**

Opening Balance : Face value ₹ 60,000 – Cost ₹ 59,000

1-3-2024 100 units purchased Ex-interest at ₹ 98.

1-7-2024 Sold 200 Ex-interest out of the original holding at ₹ 100.

1-10-2024 Purchased 50 units at ₹ 98 Cum-interest.

1-11-2024 Sold 200 units Ex-interest at ₹ 99 out of the original holdings.

Interest dates are 30th September and 31st March. Mr. Investor closes his books every 31st December. Show the Investment Account as it would appear in his books.

Ans. [Interest transferred to P. & L. A/c ₹ 3,375, Value of Holding ₹ 34,367, Profit on 1st Sale ₹ 333, 2nd Sale ₹ 134].

5. **Jaipur Investment Ltd.** hold 1,000 15% **Debentures** of ₹ 100 each in Udaipur Industries Ltd. as on 1st April, 2024, at a cost of ₹ 1,05,000. Interest is payable on 30th June and 31st December each year. On 1st May, 2024, 500 Debentures are purchased-cum-interest at ₹ 53,500. On 1st November, 2024, 600 Debentures are sold ex-interest at ₹ 57,300. On 30th November, 2024, 400 Debentures are purchased ex-interest at ₹ 38,400. On 31st December, 2024, 400 debentures are sold cum-interest for ₹ 55,000.

Prepare investment account valuing holding on 31st March, 2025 at cost (applying FIFO method).

(C.A. Inter)

Ans. [Interest transferred to P. & L. A/c ₹ 18,625 ; Value of Holding on 31st March ₹ 89,400; Total Profit on Sale of Debentures ₹ 4,300].

6. Rose Ltd. had made an investment of ₹ 500 lakhs in the equity shares of Nose Ltd. on 10-1-2025. The realisable value of such investment on 31-3-2025 became ₹ 200 lakhs as Nose Ltd. lost a case of patent rights. Rose Ltd. follows financial year as accounting year. How will you recognise this reduction in Financial statements for the year 2024-25.

BONUS SHARES

7. On 1-4-2024, Mr. Krishna Murty purchased 1,000 equity shares of ₹ 100 each in TELCO Ltd. @ ₹ 120 each from a Broker, who charged 2% brokerage. He incurred 50 paise per ₹ 100 as cost of shares transfer stamps. On 31-1-2025 Bonus was declared in the ratio of 1 : 2. Before and after the record date of bonus shares, the shares were quoted at ₹ 175 per share and ₹ 90 per share respectively. On 31-3-2025 Mr. Krishna Murty sold bonus shares to a Broker, who charged 2% brokerage.

Show the Investment Account in the books of Mr. Krishna Murty, who held the shares as current asset and closing value of investments shall be made at Cost or Market value, whichever is lower.

(CA—Inter)

Ans. [Profit on Sale of Bonus shares ₹ 3,100 ; Value of Equity shares on 31-3-2025 ₹ 82,000]

8. On 1-4-2024, Mr. Sharma purchased 2,000 equity shares of ₹ 100 each in Reliance Ltd. @ ₹ 130 each from a Broker, who charged 1% brokerage. He incurred 50 paise per ₹ 100 as cost of shares transfer stamps. On 31-1-2025 Bonus was declared in the ratio of 1 : 2. Before and after the record date of bonus shares, the shares were quoted at ₹ 135 per share and ₹ 82 per share respectively. On 31-3-2025, Mr. Sharma sold bonus shares to a broker at market price who charged 1% brokerage.

Show the Investment Account for the year ended 31st March, 2025 in the books of Mr. Sharma, who held the shares, as current assets and closing value of investments shall be made at Cost or Market value whichever is lower. ***(CA—PCE, Nov. 2015 Modified)***

Ans. [Value of Holding (₹ 2,00,000 shares) ₹ 1,64,000]

[**Hint :** Cost of Equity Shares Purchased on 1-4-2024 ₹ 2,63,900; Sale Proceed of Bonus Shares Sold on 31-3-2025 ₹ 81,180; Loss on Sale of Bonus Shares on 31-3-2025 ₹ 6,787]

9. A Limited purchased 5000 equity shares (face value 100 each) of Allianz Limited for ₹ 105 each on 1st April, 2024. The shares were quoted cum Dividend. On 5th May, 2024, Allianz Limited

declared and paid dividend of 2% for year ended 31st March 8, 2024. On 30th June, 2024 Allianz Limited issued Bonus shares in ratio of 1 : 5. On 1st October, 2024 Allianz Limited issued rights share in the ratio of 1 : 12 @ 45 per share. A limited subscribed to half of the rights issue and the balance was sold at ₹ 5 per right entitlement. The company declared interim dividend of 1% on 30th November, 2024. Right shares were not entitled to dividend. The company sold 3,000 shares on 31st December, 2024 at 95 per share. The company A Ltd. incurred 2% as brokerage while buying and selling shares. You are required to prepare investment Accounting books of A Ltd.

Ans. [Profit on Sale of Shares ₹ 21,660 ; Value of Holding on 31st March, 2025 ₹ 2,79,110]

10. On 1-5-2024, Mr. Mishra purchased 800 equity shares of ₹ 10 each in Fillco Ltd. @ ₹ 50 each from a broker who charged 5%. He incurred 20 paisa per ₹ 100 as cost of shares transfer stamps. On 31-10-2024, bonus was declared in the ratio 1 : 4. The shares were quoted at ₹ 110 and ₹ 60 per share before and after the record date of bonus shares respectively. On 30-11-2024, Mr. Mishra sold the bonus shares to a broker who charged 5%. You are required to prepare Investment Account in the books of Mr. Mishra for the year ending 31-12-2024 and closing value of investment shall be made at cost or market value whichever is lower.

Ans. [Profit on Sale of Shares ₹ 2,984 ; Value of Holding on 31st Dec., 2024 ₹ 33,664]

11. In 2023, M/s. Wye Ltd. issued 12% fully paid debentures of ₹ 100 each, interest being payable half yearly on 30th September and 31st March of every accounting year.

On 1st December, 2024, M/s, Bull & Bear purchased 10,000 of these debentures at ₹ 101 cum-interest price, also paying brokerage @ 1% of cum-interest amount of the purchase. On 1st March, 2025 the film sold all of these debentures at ₹ 106 cum-interest price, again paying brokerage @ 1% of cum-interest amount.

Prepare Investment Account in the books of M/s Bull & Bear for the period 1st December, 2024 to 1st March, 2025.

Ans. [Profit : ₹ – 700 (*i.e. loss*)]

BONUS SHARES AND RIGHT SHARES

12. On 1st April, 2024, Singh had 20,000 **equity shares** in X Ltd. Face value of the shares was ₹ 10 each but their book value was ₹ 16 per share.

On 1st June, 2024, Singh purchased 5,000 more equity shares in the company at a premium of ₹ 4 per share.

On 30th June, 2024, the Directors of X Ltd. announced a bonus and rights issue. Bonus was declared at the rate of one equity share for every five shares held and these shares were received on 2 August, 2024.

The terms of the rights issue were :

(*a*) Rights shares to be issued to the existing holders on 10th August, 2024.

(*b*) Rights issue would entitle the holders to subscribe to additional equity shares in the company at the rate of one share per every three held at ₹ 15 per share—the whole sum being payable by 30th September, 2024.

(*c*) Existing shareholders may, to the extent of their entitlement, either wholly or in part, transfer their rights to outsiders.

(*d*) Singh exercised his option under the rights issue of 50% of his entitlements and the balance of rights, he sold to Ananth for a consideration of ₹ 1.50 per share.

(*e*) Dividends for the year ended 31st March, 2024, at a rate of 15% were declared by the company and received by Singh on 20th October, 2024.

(*f*) On 1st November, 2024 Singh sold 20,000 equity shares at a premium of ₹ 3 per share.

Show the Investment Account as it would appear in Singh's book as on 31-3-2025 and the value of shares held (Average Basis) on that date assuming the accounting year is April 1 to March 31.

Ans. [Loss on Sale of 20,000 Shares ₹ 1,429; Value of Holding on 31st March, 2025 ₹ 1,96,071]

13. Smart Investments made the following investments in the year 2024-25 :

12% State Government Bonds having face value ₹ 100

Date	*Particulars*
1-4-2024	Opening Balance (1,200 bonds) book value of ₹ 1,26,000
2-5-2024	Purchased 2,000 bonds @ ₹ 100 cum interest
30-9-2024	Sold 1,500 bonds at ₹ 105 ex interest.

Interest on the bonds is received on 30th June and 31st December, each year.

Equity Shares of X Ltd.

15-4-2024	Purchased 5,000 equity shares @ ₹ 200 on cum right basis Brokerage of 1% was paid in addition (Face Value of shares ₹ 10)
3-6-2024	The company announced a **bonus** issue of 2 shares for every 5 shares held.
16-8-2024	The company made a **rights** issue of 1 share for every 7 shares held at ₹ 250 per share. The entire money was payable by 31-8-2024.
22-8-2024	Rights to the extent of 20% was sold @ ₹ 60. The remaining rights were subscribed.
2-9-2024	Dividend @ 15% for the year ended 31-3-2024 was received on 16-9-2024.
15-12-2024	Sold 3,000 shares @ ₹ 300. Brokerage of 1% was incurred extra.
15-1-2025	Received interim dividend @ 10% for the year 2024-25
31-3-2025	The shares were quoted in the stock exchange @ ₹ 220.

Prepare Investment Accounts in the books of Smart Investments. Assume that the average cost method is followed. ***(CA—Inter Modified)***

Ans. [Investment in 12% Govt. Bonds A/c—Value on 31-3-2025 ₹ 1,68,937.50; Equity Shares—Balance (4,800 Shares) Valued at ₹ 7,32,615]

Hint : Profit on Sale of Bonds on 30-9-2024 ₹ 8,437.50; Cost of Equity Shares ₹ 10,10,000; Sale Proceeds of Equity Shares on 15-12-2024 ₹ 8,91,000; Profit on Sale of Shares on 15-12-2024 ₹ 4,33,115.

14. Akash Ltd. had 4,000 equity share of X Limited, at a book value of ₹15 per share (face value of ₹10 each) on 1st April 2024. On 1st September 2024. Akash Ltd. acquired 1,000 equity shares of Limited at a premium of ₹ 4 per share. X limited announced a *bonus and right issue* for existing shareholders

The terms of bonus and right issue were :

(1) Bonus was declared, at the rate of two equity shares for every five equity shares held on 30th September, 2024.

(2) Right shares are to be issued to the exisrting shareholders on 1st December, 2024. The company issued two right shares for every seven shares held at 25% premium. No dividend was payable on these shares. The whole sum being payable by 31st December, 2024.

(3) Existing shareholders were entitled to transfer their right to outsiders, either wholly or in part.

(4) Akash Ltd. exercised its option under the issue for 50% of its entitlements and sold the remaining rights for ₹ 8 per share.

(5) Dividend for the year ended 31st March 2024, at the rate of 20% was declared by the company and received by Akash Ltd., on 20th January 2025.

(6) On 1st February 2025, Akash Ltd. sold half of its share holdings at a premium of ₹ 4 per share.

(7) The market price of share on 31-3-2025 was ₹13 per share.

You are required to prepare the investment Account of Akash Ltd. for the year ended 31st March, 2025 and determine the value of share held on that date assuming the investment as current investment. ***(CA – Inter May, 2017 Modified)***

Ans. [Value of Investment at the end ₹ 42,250 ; Cost of shares sold ₹ 13,750; Sale of right entitlement ₹ 8,000; Dividend received on Investment ₹ 2,000]

15. Mr. Z has made following transactions during the financial year 2024-25 :

Investment 1 : 8% Corporate Bonds having face value ₹ 100.

Date	*Particulars*
1-6-2024	Purchased 36,000 Bonds at ₹ 86 cum-interest. Interest is payable on 30th September and 31st Mach, every year.
15-2-2025	Sold 24,000 Bonds at ₹ 92 ex-interest

Interest on the bonds is received on 30th September and 31st March.

Investment 2 : Equity Shares of G Ltd. having face value ₹ 10.

Date	*Particulars*
1-4-2024	Opening Balance 8,000 equity shares at a book value of ₹ 190 per share
1-5-2024	Purchased 7,000 equity shares @ ₹ 230 on cum right basis; Brokerage of 1% was paid in addition.
15-6-2024	The company announced a bonus issue of 2 shares for every 5 shares held
1-8-2024	The company made a rights issue of 1 share for every 7 shares held at ₹ 230 per share. The entire money was payable by 31-8-2024.
25-8-2024	Rights to the extent of 30% of his entitlements was sold @ ₹ 75 per share. The remaining rights were subscribed.
16-9-2024	Dividend @ ₹ 6 per share for the year ended 31-3-2024 was received on 16-9-2024. No dividend payable on right issue and Bonus issue.
1-12-2024	Sold 7,000 shares @ 260 per share. Brokerage of 1% was incurred extra.
25-1-2025	Received interim dividend @ ₹ 3 per share for the year 2024-25.
31-3-2025	The shares were quoted in the stock exchange @ ₹ 260.

Both investments have been classified as Current investment in the books of Mr. Z on 15th May 2025, Mr. Z decides to reclassify investment in equity shares of G Ltd. as long-term investment. On 15th May 2025, the shares were quoted in the stock exchange @ ₹ 180.

You are required to :

(*i*) Prepare Investment Accounts in the books of Mr. Z for the year 2024-25, assuming that the average cost method is followed.

(*ii*) Profit and Loss Account for the year 2024-25, based on the above information.

(*iii*) Suggest values at which investment in equity shares should be reclassified in accordance with AS-13. ***(CA – Inter May, 2021 Modified)***

Ans. [Valuation of Bond at the end of year—₹ 10,16,000; Profit on Sale of Bonds—₹ 1,76,000; Valuation of equity shares at year end—₹ 25,00,100 (16,100 shares); Amount of right shares subscribed—₹ 4,83,000; Dividend received—₹ 42,000 (to be treated as Capital receipt; Profit on sale of shares—₹ 7,14,800]

CHAPTER

31

Insolvency Accounts

Meaning of Insolvent

According to popular usage, an insolvent is one who is not able to pay his liabilities as and when claimed. But in legal sense the term insolvent can be applied to a person whose liabilities exceed his assets and against whom an order of adjudication has been passed by the competent court. The proceedings taken by the court in case of insolvent person are known as insolvency proceedings.

Insolvency Laws in India

There are two acts dealing with insolvency affairs in India :

1. The Presidency Towns Insolvency Act, 1909 which applies to the persons residing in the Presidency Towns of Mumbai, Kolkata and Chennai.

2. The Provincial Insolvency Act, 1920 which applies to the persons residing in the rest of India.

The Insolvency Acts mentioned above are applicable to individuals, partnership firms or Hindu undivided families. In case of joint stock companies, the term liquidation (and not insolvency) is used and the Companies Act, 2013 is applicable. There is a significant difference between insolvency and liquidation. Insolvency takes place only when an individual or a partnership firm or a Hindu undivided family is unable to pay its liabilities whereas liquidation may take place even when a company has sufficient amount to pay its debts.

The two insolvency acts referred to above are similar except in some points. Both the acts are based on the English Bankruptcy Act. These acts will be considered only insofar as they are relevant to the Accounting aspect.

When can a Person be Declared Insolvent ?

Two conditions must be fulfilled before a person can be declared insolvent by a competent court. The first condition is that he must be a debtor and he must have inadequate assets for repayment in full of his liabilities. The second condition is that he must have committed an act of insolvency. An act of insolvency can be defined as some act of the debtor which shows that he is not in a position to make the full payment of his liabilities. An act of insolvency may take place in any of the following circumstances :

1. When the debtor makes a transfer of all or substantially all of his property to a third person for the benefit of his creditors.

2. When the debtor transfers his property or any part thereof with the intent to defeat or delay his creditors.

3. When the debtor transfers his property for fraudulent preference. Fraudulent preference takes place when the debtor prefers one creditor to another and pays the preferred creditor more than what he would

have received had the assets been proportionately distributed among creditors of the debtor. Upon an order of adjudication the preferred creditor will have to return the money received by him.

4. When any of the property of the debtor is sold or attached for a period of not less than 21 days in execution of the decree of any court. Under the Provincial Insolvency Act, only a sale in execution is an act of insolvency.

5. When the debtor notifies any of his creditors that he has suspended, or that he is about to suspend, payment of his debts.

6. When the debtor petitions the court to be adjudged an insolvent.

7. When the debtor is imprisoned in execution of a court decree for payment of money.

8. If with intent to defraud or delay his creditors ;

(*a*) the debtor departs from or remains out of India ;

(*b*) the debtor departs from his dwelling house or usual place of business or otherwise absents himself ;

(*c*) the debtor secludes himself so as to deprive his creditors of the means of communicating with him.

Legally a person can be called insolvent only if an order of adjudication is passed against him by a competent court. Before the court can pass an order of adjudication, there must be a petition presented to it either by a creditor or by the debtor himself. Petition by a creditor or creditors can be made only if (1) the debt, singly or jointly, is at least ₹ 500; and (2) the debtor commits an act of insolvency within three months of the petition. After presentation of the petition, the court fixes a date for hearing and then it either rejects the petition or makes an order of adjudication.

Under the Presidency Towns Insolvency Act, the order of adjudication relates back to the first available act of insolvency and under the Provincial Insolvency Act, its relates back to the date of the presentation of the petition. This doctrine is known as *Doctrine of Relation Back*. Therefore, the insolvency of a person commences, not from the date when the order of adjudication is passed, but from an earlier date.

The official who is appointed to conduct the insolvency proceedings after the order of adjudication is passed is known as Official Assignee in Presidency Towns and Official Receiver in other places. After the order of adjudication is passed, the property of the insolvent vests in the Official Assignee or Receiver who proceeds to realise the assets and distribute the sale proceeds of the assets in the following order :

(*a*) Fully secured creditors to be paid in full. (*b*) Partly secured creditors to the extent they are secured. (*c*) Realisation expenses and remuneration of the Official Receiver or Assignee. (*d*) Preferential creditors. (*e*) Unsecured creditors including the uncovered balance of partly secured creditors.

The Order of Discharge. After the order of adjudication, the insolvent debtor may apply to the court for an order of discharge. After hearing the insolvent debtor and examining the conduct of the insolvent as reported by the Official Assignee or Receiver, the court may issue an order of discharge which frees the insolvent from his previous debts except to Government, debt incurred by fraud and liability of maintenance.

Interest. Creditors can claim interest on their debts upto the date of the order of adjudication. If the property of the debtor is sufficient to make the payment of creditors in full and a surplus exists, interest will be paid to the creditors for the period after the order of adjudication at the rate of 6% per annum.

Voluntary Transfers. If a person transfers his property to another without consideration, it is called a voluntary transfer. Under the Presidency Towns Insolvency Act, all voluntary transfers of property made by the insolvent without consideration during two years preceding the order of adjudication shall be void and inoperative and in case of Provincial Insolvency Act, such transfers are voidable and not void as against the Receiver and may be annulled by the court. In Provincial Insolvency Act, voluntary transfers become inoperative if made within 2 years of the petition of insolvency. But voluntary transfers made by the insolvent will not be void in the following cases :

(*a*) when the transfer is made before and in consideration of marriage ; and (*b*) when the transfer is made in favour of a purchase or encumbrance in good faith and for valuable consideration.

Doctrine of Reputed Ownership. According to this doctrine, goods in the possession, order or disposition of a trading insolvent in his business with the consent of their true owner and under the circumstances the trader insolvent appears to be their true owner, will be treated as assets of the insolvent for distribution to his creditors. The doctrine does not apply in the following cases :

1. Immovable properties. 2. Goods which were in the possession of the insolvent as repairer or carrier. 3. Goods in the possession of the insolvent as trustee or administrator.

Insolvency Accounts

Upon being adjudicated the insolvent has to submit (1) A Statement of Affairs as on the date of order ; and (2) A Deficiency Account.

The form of the Statement of Affairs prescribed by rules made under the Presidency Towns Insolvency Act is given below. Under the Provincial Insolvency Act, there is no provision for the submission of a Statement of Affairs to be submitted under the Presidency Towns Insolvency Act.

STATEMENT OF AFFAIRS

(*As required by the Indian Insolvency Act*)

In the Court of Justice
IN INSOLVENCY

To the insolvent, — You are required to fill up carefully and accurately, this sheet and the several sheets, A, B, C, D, E, F, G and H, showing the state of your affairs on the day on which the order of adjudication was made against you *viz.,* the .... day of .... 20 ....

Such sheets, when filled up will constitute your Schedule and must be verified by Oath or Declaration.

Gross Liabilities	*Liabilities (as stated and estimated by the Debtor)*	*Expected to Rank*	*Assets (as stated and estimated by the Debtor)*	*Estimated to Produce*
₹				₹
	Unsecured Creditors as per List A		Property as per List E, *viz.,*	
	Fully Secured Creditors as per List B		(*a*) Cash at Bankers	
	Less : Estimated value of securities		(*b*) Cash in Hand	
	Less : Amount thereof carried to List C		(*c*) Cash deposited with solicitor for cost of petition	
	Balance thereof *contra*		(*d*) Stock-in-Trade	
	Partly Secured Creditors as per List C		(*e*) Machinery	
	Less : Estimated value of securities		(*f*) Trade Fixtures, Fittings, Utensils, etc.	
	Preferential Creditors as per List D (Creditors for rent, taxes, salaries and wages, etc.) payable in full as per *contra*		(*g*) Furniture	
			(*h*) Life Policies	
			(*i*) Other property	
			Book Debts as per list F, *viz.,* :	
			Good	
			Doubtful	
			Bad	
			Estimated to produce	

			Bills of Exchange or other similar securities on hand as per List G Estimated to produce Surplus from securities in the hands of creditors fully secured (per *contra*) *Deduct :* Creditors for preferential rent, rates, taxes, wages, etc. (per *contra*) Deficiency as explained in List H	

I/We................make oath, solemnly affirm, and say, that the above statement and the several lists hereunto annexed marked A, B, C, D, E, F, G and H are to the best of my/our knowledge and belief, a full and complete of my/our affairs on the date of the above-mentioned order of adjudication made against me/us.

Affirmed / Sworn at,......... this .... day of

before Commissioner (Signature).................

Statement of Affairs like Balance Sheet is divided into two parts, namely, liabilities and assets. Liabilities of the insolvent debtor are classified into four lists as follows :

Unsecured Creditors as per List A. This list will include all creditors who have no security to fall back upon in case of non-payment of their dues, *e.g.,* trade creditors, bills payable, bank overdraft, Mrs. loan out of her *stridhan*, amount payable on account of contingent liabilities (*i.e.* bills discounted likely to be dishonoured, partly paid shares held, uncompleted contracts guarantees given for others etc. any other loan which is not secured and non-preferential amount due for wages, salaries, rent etc.

Loan from Wife. A loan from wife is usually assumed to be given from her personal property, *i.e., stridhan*. Such type of loan is treated like other loans taken and makes wife a creditor of the insolvent. If it is proved that loan has been given by wife out of the money given to her by her husband, then her position is not like other creditors and loan will not be included in the list of creditors. *In such a case, loan is taken as the capital of the insolvent.*

Interest. Interest is not allowed to a creditor after the date of insolvency. But if all claims have been paid in full, then interest at 6% p.a. is allowed upto the date of payment.

Fully Secured Creditors as per List B. This list will include all those creditors who have sufficient securities of the insolvent debtor to meet their claims. Any surplus of securities in the hands of fully secured creditors after meeting their claims, if not otherwise charged, will be shown on the assets side of the Statement of Affairs and will be available for distribution among the unsecured creditors.

Partly Secured Creditors as per List C. These creditors are not fully secured and have insufficient securities to meet their claims. The unsatisfied amount of these creditors is written in the expected to rank column like unsecured creditors because they are to rank for dividend for the unsatisfied amount.

Preferential Creditors for Rent, Rates, Taxes and Wages as per List D. Such creditors get preference over other unsecured creditors, so they are known as preferential creditors. By law, the following are the preferential creditors :

(*a*) All debts due to Government or any local authority, *e.g.,* taxes

(*b*) The salary of any clerk or wages of any servant or labourer in respect of the services rendered to the insolvent during four months preceding the date of the presentation of the insolvency petition, subject to the following limits :

(*i*) Under the Presidency Towns Insolvency Act — ₹ 300 for such clerk and ₹ 100 for each such servant or labourer.

(*ii*) Under the Provincial Insolvency Act — ₹ 20 for each such clerk, servant or labourer.

(*c*) One month's rent due to the landlord is preferential in the Presidency Towns Insolvency Act. **Rent is not at all preferential in the Provincial Insolvency Act.**

Assets of the insolvent debtor shown in the Statement of Affairs have also been grouped into four lists as follows :

Property as per List E. All assets except book debts, bills of exchange in hand and assets kept as securities with the fully secured or partly secured creditors are included in this list.

Book Debts as per List F. The book debts are divided into three parts as follows :

(*i*) Good ; (*ii*) Doubtful ; (*iii*) Bad

Bills of Exchange or Other Similar Securities in hand as per List G.

Deficiency Account as per list H. This list shows the amount of deficiency which the insolvent debtor is not able to pay to his creditors.

Points to be Noted while Preparing Statement of Affairs

1. While preparing the Statement of Affairs of an individual, no distinction should be observed between business assets and liabilities and private assets and liabilities. In other words, private assets and liabilities of the insolvent debtor are treated in the same way as assets and liabilities of the business are treated. But a distinction is observed between assets and liabilities of the partnership firm and private assets and liabilities of the partners. Private assets of the partners are first utilised for making the payment of private liabilities, and if there is a surplus after meeting private liabilities, it can be utilised to pay the firm's liabilities and is included in property as per List E.

2. All the property of the insolvent debtor [excluding the tools of his trade, the necessary wearing apparel, bedding, cooking utensils (the total value of all these things exceeding ₹ 300 will be included in case of the Presidency Towns Insolvency Act), Properties held by him in trust for others and all *stridhan*] is shown on the assets side of the Statement of Affairs. Assets mortgaged with fully or partly secured creditors are not shown on the assets side. Only surplus left in the hands of fully secured creditors after meeting their claims is shown on the assets side after List G unless the surplus is to be used for paying partly secured creditors.

3. The amount of fully secured creditors is not shown in the 'expected to rank column' on the liabilities side because such creditors are not to rank for dividend.

4. The amount of partly secured creditors is shown in the inner column from which the estimated value of securities is deducted and the unsecured balance of such creditors is shown in expected to rank column on the liabilities side.

5. The amount of the preferential creditors is deducted from the assets side after taking the total of lists E, F and G because such creditors are paid before the unsecured creditors.

6. Contingent liabilities expected to rank *e.g.,* bills discounted to be dishonoured are included in unsecured creditors as per List A.

Difference Between Balance Sheet and Statement of Affairs

Following are various points of differences between Balance Sheet and Statement of Affairs:

1. A Balance Sheet shows assets at book values, while a Statement of Affairs shows assets at book values, as well as realisable value.

2. A Balance Sheet shows intangible assets such as goodwill and prepaid expenses while a Statement of Affairs does not show such items.

3. A Balance Sheet gives information about capital, profit or loss, drawings and interest on capital whereas a Statement of Affairs excludes all such items.

4. A Statement of Affairs shows the amount (*i.e.,* deficiency) which the insolvent debtor is not able to pay to his creditors while a Balance Sheet does not show such a figure.

5. A Statement of Affairs is prepared on the date on which order of adjudication is passed against the debtor whereas a Balance Sheet is prepared usually at the end of each accounting period.

6. A Balance Sheet of an individual or a partnership firm is not prepared according to any act whereas a Statement of Affairs is prepared according to the rules given in the Insolvency Act.

7. A Balance Sheet separates personal assets and liabilities from trade assets and liabilities whereas a Statement of Affairs integrates personal and business assets and liabilities in case of individual insolvents.

8. A Balance Sheet shows contingent liabilities (if at all shown) as a footnote but they do not form part of the total of the liabilities side but a Statement of Affairs includes contingent liabilities to the extent expected to rank.

Difference Between Presidency Towns Insolvency Act and Provincial Insolvency Act

Basis of Distinction	*Presidency Town Insolvency Act.*	*Provincial Insolvency Act*
1. Act	This Act was enacted in 1909	This Act was enacted in 1920
2. Where applies	This Act applies to the persons residing in the towns of Mumbai, Kolkata and Chennai	This Act applies to the persons residing in the rest of India
3. Maximum limit of preferential amount	Under this Act, Maximum limit of preferential amount of a clerk is ₹ 300 and of a servant or labourer ₹ 100.	Under this act the maximum limit of preferential amount per clerk per servant and per labourer is ₹ 20.
4. Rent	One month's rent due to the landlord is preferential under this Act.	Rent is not at all preferential under this Act.
5. Goods or Assets left with insolvent	Under this Act domestic goods upto the value of ₹ 300 are left with the insolvent.	Under this Act, only those assets are left with the insolvent which have been exempted under the Code of Civil Procedure, 1908

EXAMPLE 1. Calculate the amount of preferential and unsecured creditors from the following figures pertaining to an insolvent debtor according to Presidency Towns Insolvency Act and Provincial Insolvency Act.

	₹		₹
Sales Tax	**25,000**	**Wages of 2 servants for 4 months**	**800**
Income Tax	**15,000**	**Wages of 5 labourers for 3 months**	**3,000**
Municipal Tax	**5,000**	**Salary of the Manager**	**5,000**
4 Months' Rent due to landlord	**20,000**	**Salary of 2 clerks for 4 months**	**2,400**

SOLUTION

Statement Showing the Calculation of Preferential Creditors and Unsecured Creditors

Amount Due	*Particulars*	*Under Presidency Insolvency Act*		*Under Provincial Insolvency Act*	
		Preferential Creditors	*Unsecured Creditors*	*Preferential Creditors*	*Unsecured Creditors*
₹		₹	₹	₹	₹
25,000	Sales Tax	25,000	—	25,000	—
15,000	Income Tax	15,000	—	15,000	—

5,000	Municipal Tax	5,000	—	5,000	—
20,000	4 months' rent due to landlord	5,000	15,000	—	20,000
800	Wages of 2 servants for 4 months	200	600	40	760
3,000	Wages of 5 labourers for 3 months	500	2,500	100	2,900
5,000	Salary of the manager	—	5,000	—	5,000
2,400	Salary of 2 clerks for 4 months	600	1,800	40	2,360
76,200	Total	51,300	24,900	45,180	31,020

EXAMPLE 2. From the following ascertain the creditors to be shown under list A and D :

	₹		₹
Creditors on open account	**55,000**	**B/R discounted (expected to Rank ₹ 3,000)**	**9,000**
Bills payable	**10,500**	**Income tax payable**	**550**
Creditor having lien on stock	**8,000**	**Creditors for salaries & wages (preferential ₹ 600)**	**2,200**
Bills of Exchange	**4,000**		
Stock (estimated to produce)	**6,000**		

SOLUTION

	₹	₹
Unsecured creditors as per list 'A'		
1. Creditors on open account	55,000	
2. B/P	10,500	
3. Creditors for salaries and wages over and above preferential limits (₹ 2,200 – ₹ 600)	1,600	
4. Liability on bills discounted	3,000	
		70,100
Creditors for rent, taxes, wages etc. payable in full as per list 'D'		
1. Creditors for salaries and wages	600	
2. Income tax payable	550	
		1,150

ILLUSTRATION 1. Mr. Shankar of Mumbai finding himself unable to meet his creditors, has to prepare a Statement of Affairs, for which the following particulars are available on the date of his adjudication as insolvent as on 31-3-2025 :

Leasehold property ₹ 2,00,000, estimated to realise, ₹ 1,90,000.

Plant & Machinery ₹ 80,000, estimated to realise ₹ 60,000.

Stock in Trade ₹ 40,000, estimated to realise ₹ 28,000.

Book debts : Good ₹ 1,20,000, Doubtful ₹ 10,000, estimated to realise 50%, Bad ₹ 28,000, Bills in Hand ₹ 7,500.

Life Policy for ₹ 50,000, whose Surrender Value is ₹ 10,000 held by the insurance company against a loan of ₹ 4,000.

Household Furniture ₹ 7,200, Household Debts ₹ 5,800.

Bills Discounted ₹ 12,000, ₹ 4,000 likely to be dishonoured.

Loan on Mortgage of Leasehold ₹ 1,00,000, Cash in Hand ₹ 200.

Bank Overdraft secured by Personal Guarantee of Shankar's Brother, and Second Mortgage on Leasehold ₹ 1,00,000.

Unsecured Creditors ₹ 3,00,000, Loan from Naresh ₹ 5,000 secured by a second charge on Life Policy. Ground Rent on Household for three months accrued ₹ 750.

He could not pay his office clerks (two persons) salaries for six months ₹ 3,000 and also Rates & Taxes amounting to ₹ 3,000 due to Government.

Prepare Statement of Affairs of Mr. Shankar as on 31-3-2025.

SOLUTION

STATEMENT OF AFFAIRS OF MR. SHANKAR

as on 31-3-2025

Gross Liabilities	*Liabilities (as stated and estimated by Debtor)*		*Expected to Rank*	*Assets (as stated and estimated by Debtor)*	*Book Value*	*Estimated to Produce*
₹		₹	₹		₹	₹
	Unsecured Creditors			Property as per List E		
3,20,700	as per List A	(1)	3,12,700	*viz.,*		
	Creditors Fully			(*a*) Cash	200	200
1,09,000	Secured as per			(*b*) Stock in Trade	40,000	28,000
	List B (2)	1,09,000		(*c*) Plant & Machinery	80,000	60,000
	Estimated Value of			(*d*) Furniture	7,200	7,200
	Securities	2,00,000		Book Debts as per List F		
	Surplus	91,000		Good	1,20,000	1,20,000
	Less : Amount thereof			Doubtful	10,000	5,000
	carried to List C	90,000		Bad	28,000	—
	Balance as per			Bills of Exchange as per		
	Contra	1,000		List G	7,500	
	Creditors Partly			Estimated to Realize		7,500
1,00,000	Secured as per List C	1,00,000		Surplus from Securities in		
	Less : Estimated Value			the hands of Creditors		
	of Securities	90,000	10,000	Fully Secured (as per		
	Preferential Creditors			Contra)		1,000
	(Creditors for				2,92,900	2,28,900
	Salaries, Wages,			Deduct Preferential		
	Rent etc.) payable in			Creditors (as per Contra)		3,850
3,850	full as per List D	3,850				2,25,050
	Deducted as per			Deficiency as Explained		
	Contra	3,850		in List H		97,650
5,33,550			3,22,700			3,22,700

Working Notes :

(1) ***Unsecured Creditors as per List A***

	₹
Household Debtors	5,800
Bills Discounted likely to be dishonoured	4,000
Unsecured Creditors	3,00,000
Two months rent (one month rent is preferential)	500
Clerk's Salary (in excess of ₹ 300 per clerk) (₹ 3,000 – ₹ 600)	2,400
	3,12,700

The gross liabilities of unsecured creditors includes full amount ₹ 12,000 of discounted bills.

(2) ***Fully Secured Creditors as per List B***

	Amount	Security
	₹	₹
Loan from Insurance Company	4,000	10,000
Naresh	5,000	
Loan on Mortgage of Leasehold	1,00,000	1,90,000
	1,09,000	2,00,000

Note : Since the Surrender Value is ₹ 10,000, both the Insurance Company and Naresh can be fully covered leaving a surplus of ₹ 1,000.

(3) ***Partly Secured Creditors as per List C***

Bank Overdraft of ₹ 1,00,000 will be partly secured because after meeting the first charge on Leasehold, ₹ 90,000 will be left which is insufficient to meet Bank Overdraft fully. The personal Guarantee of Shankar's brother cannot be considered for preparing Shankar's Statement of Affairs.

(4) ***Preferential Creditors as per List D***

	₹
One month's rent	250
Salaries of two clerks (₹ 300 × 2)	600
Rates and Taxes	3,000
Preferential Creditors	3,850

As Shankar is a resident of Mumbai, the Presidency Towns Insolvency Act, 1909 will apply to him, and accordingly Preferential Creditors will be calculated.

Deficiency Account (List H)

The purpose of preparing the Deficiency Account is to explain how the deficiency, as shown in the Statement of Affairs, has been arrived at. This account shows how the capital introduced by the insolvent debtor has been lost along with unpaid amount of the creditors. This account is prepared in the same way as the Capital Account is prepared with the difference that the sides of the Deficiency Account are opposite to those of a Capital Account. The specimen form of the Deficiency Account is as follows :

DEFICIENCY ACCOUNT (LIST H)

	₹		₹
Excess of assets over liabilities, *i.e.*, capital on		Excess of liabilities over assets	
Net profit arising from carrying on of business after deducting usual trade expenses		Net loss arising from carrying on of business after deduction from profits, usual trade expenses	
Income or profit from other sources *e.g.*,		Bad Debts as per List F	
(*i*) Interest on capital		Expenses incurred since ....other than usual trade expenses, *viz.*,	
(*ii*) Excess of private assets over private liabilities		Household Expenses (Drawings)	
(*iii*) Profit on realisation of any asset		Other Losses :	
Deficiency as per Statement of Affairs		Loss on realisation of assets	
		Loss through dishonour of discounted bills	
		Speculation losses	
		Loss through betting	
		Excess of private liabilities over private assets, etc.	

From the above specimen it is clear that on the debit side the capital and all other items (*i.e.*, profits) that increase capital are shown and on credit side all losses and drawings are written. The difference between the two sides is deficiency as shown in the Statement of Affairs. The deficiency arises because losses and drawings outweigh capital and profits.

ILLUSTRATION 2. Satta Ram filed a petition in bankruptcy on 31st December, 2024. His books showed the following balances :

		₹	₹	₹
Fixtures and Fittings (estimated to produce ₹ 400)			1,030	
Stock-in-trade (estimated to produce ₹ 5,000)			7,210	
Trade Creditors				7,940
Bills Payable				8,700
Sundry Debtors	– Good	3,800		
	– Doubtful (estimated at 50%)	8,000		
	– Bad	8,000		
			19,800	
Bank Overdraft				6,900
Capital				4,500
			28,040	28,040

Liability on bills discounted ₹ 2,500, expected to rank ₹ 600. His life policy (surrender value ₹ 2,000) given as security for a loan of ₹ 1,500 at 10% interest paid up to the preceding 30th June. Mrs. Satta Ram gave up jewellery valued at ₹ 1,200 to the Official Receiver. Official Receiver completed certain pending transactions which resulted in a profit of ₹ 200. There is a creditor of ₹ 100 (included in trade creditors) who is not to rank for dividend. Income-tax due amounted to ₹ 1,540.

Prepare Statement of Affairs and Deficiency Account.

SOLUTION

Unsecured Creditors as per List A

	₹
Trade Creditors	7,940
Less : Creditors not to rank for dividend	100
	7,840
Bills Payable	8,700
Bank Overdraft	6,900
Bills likely to be dishonoured	600
	24,040

Fully Secured Creditors as per List B

	Amount	*Value of Security*
	₹	₹
Private loan on the security of life policy	1,500	2,000
Interest @ 10% p.a. on ₹ 1,500 for 6 months (from July 1, 2024 to December 31, 2024) not paid	75	
	1,575	

Preferential Creditors as per List D

	₹
Income-tax due	1,540

STATEMENT OF AFFAIRS OF MR. SATTA RAM
as at 31st December, 2024

Gross Liabilities	*Liabilities*		*Expected to Rank*	*Assets*	*Book Value*	*Expected to Produce*
₹		₹	₹		₹	₹
	Unsecured Creditors as per			Property as per List E :		
25,940	List A		24,040	Stock-in-trade	7,210	5,000
	Fully Secured Creditors			Fixtures & Fittings	1,030	400
1,575	as per List B	1,575		Mrs. Jewellery		1,200
	Less : Estimated			Profit from completing		
	Value of Securities	2,000		pending transactions		200
				Book Debts as per		
	Surplus as per contra	425		List F :		
	Preferential Creditors			Good	3,800	3,800
1,540	as per List D	1,540		Doubtful	8,000	
	Deducted as per contra	1,540		Bad	8,000	
				Estimated to produce		4,000
				Surplus from securities in the hands of fully secured creditors		425
					28,040	15,025
				Preferential creditors deducted as per contra		1,540
						13,485
				Deficiency as explained in List H		10,555
29,055			24,040			24,040

Notes (1) The gross liability for unsecured creditors is ₹ 25,940. ₹ 2,500 (and not ₹ 600) in respect of liability for discounted bills should be added for calculation of gross liability.

(2) No distinction has been made between business assets and business liabilities and private assets and private liabilities because the insolvent debtor is an individual.

DEFICIENCY ACCOUNT (LIST H)

		₹			₹
Excess of assets over liabilities *i.e.*, capital on 31-12-2024		4,500	Loss on book debts as per List F :		12,000
Income or profit from other sources :			Other losses :		
Profit from completing	₹		Loss on realisation of fixtures	₹	
pending transactions	200		and fittings	630	
Excess of private assets			Loss on realisation of stock	2,210	
over private liabilities (1)	85		Bills likely to be dishonoured	600	3,440
Creditors not to rank for dividend	100	385			
Deficiency as per Statement of Affairs		10,555			
		15,440			15,440

Working Notes :

(1) *Excess of private assets over private liabilities has been arrived at as follows :*

	₹	₹
Mrs. Jewellery		1,200
Life Policy		2,000
Total of private assets		3,200
Less : Private Loan on security of life policy	1,500	
Interest on loan @ 10% p.a. for 6 months	75	
Income Tax due	1,540	
		3,115
Excess of private assets over private liabilities		85

ILLUSTRATION 3. Following is the Balance Sheet of Mr. Brown as at 31st March, 2025. He has filed a petition in the court for being declared as insolvent :

Liabilities	₹	*Assets*		₹
Capital	18,000	Goodwill		5,000
Bank Loan (Secured)		Machinery		20,000
by First Charge on Building)	80,000	Building		1,15,000
Loan from Finance Co.,	30,000	Investment in Shares		5,000
(Secured by Second Charge		Furniture		7,000
on Building)		Stock		9,000
Sundry Creditors	59,000	*Debtors* :	₹	
Sales Tax Payable	8,000	Goods	14,000	
Loan from Wife	5,000	Doubtful	8,000	
		Bad	2,000	
				24,000
		Cash and Bank		15,000
	2,00,000			2,00,000

Mr. Brown estimated that except the following, all tangible assets are realisable :

(*i*) A machinery ₹ 5,000 included in the Balance Sheet has no value.

(*ii*) Debtors (unrealisable) ₹ 7,600.

(*iii*) Non-moving stock ₹ 3,000.

(*iv*) Useless furniture ₹ 4,000.

(*v*) Investment has no value.

Further Information :

(*i*) Building expected to realise ₹ 1,20,000.

(*ii*) Loan was given by his wife from her personal sources.

(*iii*) A bill discounted for ₹ 10,000 is likely to be dishonoured

(*iv*) One creditor forgoes his claim for ₹ 4,000.

(*v*) Mr. Brown started his business on 1-4-2021. His household expenses upto 31-3-2025 are ₹ 48,000. His private Life Insurance Policy matured for ₹ 30,000 on 31-3-2025.

He made profit of ₹ 40,000 upto 31-3-2023.

He incurred loss of ₹ 50,000 from 1-4-2023 to 31-3-2025.

Also, he suffered speculation loss of ₹ 10,000 in the year ended 31-3-2025.

Based on the above information, prepare Statement of Affairs of Mr. Brown as on 31-3-2025 and Deficiency Account.

SOLUTION

STATEMENT OF AFFAIRS

as on 31st March, 2025

Gross Liabilities	*Liabilities (as stated and estimated by debtor)*	*Expected to Bank*	*Assets (as stated and estimated by debtor*	*Book Value*	*Estimated to Produce*
₹		₹		₹	₹
70,000	Unsecured Credited as per List A	70,000	Property as per List E :		
80,000	Creditor Fully Secured as ₹		Cash at Bank	15,000	15,000
	per List B 80,000		Stock	9,000	6,000
	Less : Estimated Value of		Machinery	20,000	15,000
	Securities 1,20,000		Furniture	7,000	3,000
	Surplus 40,000		Goodwill	5,000	—
	Less : Amount Carried		Investment in Shares	5,000	—
	to List C 30,000		Book Debts as per List F :		
	Balance thereof to Contra 10,000		Good	14,000	14,000
	Creditor Partly Secured		Doubtful	8,000	2,400
30,000	as per List C 30,000		Bad	2,000	—
	Less : Surplus carried			85,000	55,400
	from List B 30,000		Surplus from Securities		
	—		in the hands of Fully		
		—	Secured Creditors		
	Preferential Creditors		(as per Contra)		10,000
8,000	Payable in Full as per List D				65,400
	Sale Tax Payable 8,000		*Less* : Preferential		
	Less : Deducted as per		Creditors as per		
	Contra 8,000		Contra		8,000
	—				57,400
		—	Deficiency as Explained		
			in List H		12,600
1,88,000		70,000			70,000

DEFICIENCY ACCOUNT (LIST H)

	₹		₹	₹
Excess of Assets over Liabilities as on 1-4-2021 (Bal. Fig.)	56,000	Net Loss arising from Business since 1-4-2023		50,000
Net Profit Arising from Business upto 31-3-2023	40,000	Bad Debts as per List F		7,600
Profit on Realisation of :		Drawings for Household Expenses		48,000
Building	5,000	Loss on Realisation of :		
Life Policy Matured	30,000	Furniture	4,000	
Creditors Forgone Claims	4,000	Machinery	5,000	
Deficiency as per Statement of Affairs	12,600	Stock	3,000	
		Goodwill	5,000	
		Investments	5,000	
				22,000
		Loss on Dishonour of Bill		10,000
		Speculation Loss		10,000
	1,47,600			1,47,600

ILLUSTRATION 4. Din Dayal of Delhi commenced business on 1st January, 2020 with a capital of ₹ 65,000. His profits for three years were ₹ 35,400 ; he did not prepare proper accounts for the next two years. His drawings averaged ₹ 4,800 per annum.

On 31st December, 2024 an order of adjudication was made against him when his affairs were as follows :

	₹
Building : Cost ₹ 60,000 estimated to realise	20,000
Plant and Machinery : Cost ₹ 28,000 estimated to realise	10,000
Book Debts : Good ₹ 12,000 ; Doubtful ₹ 4,000 estimated to realise ₹ 1,000 and Bad ₹ 10,000	
Bills Receivable discounted and expected to rank	5,000
Preferential Creditors	1,000
Creditors partly secured (security : life policy estimated to be worth ₹ 8,000)	23,000
Mortgage on Buildings	10,000
Unsecured Creditors	40,000
Household Furniture	3,000
Household Debts	2,000
Furniture : Cost ₹ 2,000 estimated to realise	800
Stock : Cost ₹ 16,000 estimated to realise	11,000
Cash in hand	200

Mrs. Din Dayal gave up jewellery valued at ₹ 2,500 to the Official Receiver. You are required to prepare a Statement of Affairs and a Deficiency Account from the above particulars.

SOLUTION

Profit or loss for the two years, 2023 and 2024, is not given in the problem ; so Trial Balance is prepared to find it out.

TRIAL BALANCE
as on 31-12-2024

		₹			₹
Building		60,000	Capital on 1-1-2020	65,000	
Plant and Machinery	₹	28,000	*Add* : Profit for 3 years	35,400	
Book Debts — Good	12,000			1,00,400	
Doubtful	4,000		*Less* : Drawings for 5 years	24,000	
Bad	10,000	26,000			76,400
Furniture		2,000	Preferential Creditors		1,000
Stock		16,000	Creditors Partly Secured		23,000
Cash in hand		200	Mortgage on Buildings		10,000
Loss for the two years, 2023 and 2024 (balancing figure)		18,200	Unsecured Creditors		40,000
		1,50,400			1,50,400

STATEMENT OF AFFAIRS OF DIN DAYAL
as on 31st December, 2024

Gross Liabilities	Liabilities (as stated and estimated by the debtor)		Expected to Rank	Assets (as stated and estimated by the debtor)	Book Value	Expected to Produce
₹		₹			₹	₹
47,000	Unsecured Creditors as per List A :	(1)	47,000	Property as per List E : Cash in hand	200	200

	Creditors fully			Stock	16,000	11,000
	secured as per	₹		Machinery	28,000	10,000
10,000	List B	10,000		Furniture	2,000	800
	Estimated value			Household Furniture		3,000
	of security	20,000		Jewellery of Wife		2,500
	Surplus as per *contra*	10,000		Book Debts as per		
	Creditors partly secured			List F :		
23,000	as per List C	23,000		Good	12,000	12,000
	Less : Estimated value			Doubtful	4,000	1,000
	of security	8,000		Bad	10,000	—
			15,000		72,200	40,500
	Preferential Creditors			Surplus as per *contra*		10,000
1,000	as per List D	1,000				50,500
	Deducted as per contra	1,000		Preferential Creditors		
				deducted as per *contra*		1,000
						49,500
				Deficiency as		
				explained in List H		12,500
81,000			62,000			62,000

DEFICIENCY ACCOUNT

	₹			₹
Excess of assets over liabilities *i.e.*, Capital on 1-1-2020	65,000	Net loss arising from carrying on business from 1-1-2020 to the date of adjudication		18,200
Net Profit arising from carrying on business from 1-1-2020 to adjudication date after deducting usual trade expenses	35,400	Bad Debts as per List F		13,000
Income or profit from other sources :		Expenses incurred since 1-1-2020 other than usual trade expenses *viz.*, Household Expenses		24,000
Excess of private assets over private liabilities (2)	11,500	Other Losses :		
Deficiency as per Statement of Affairs	12,500	Loss on realisation of	₹	
		Stock	5,000	
		Machinery	18,000	
		Furniture	1,200	
		Building	40,000	
		Loss on Bills Discounted	5,000	
				69,200
	1,24,400			1,24,400

Working Notes :

(1) ***Calculation of Amount of Unsecured Creditors***

	₹
Unsecured Creditors	40,000
Bills likely to be dishonoured	5,000
Household debts	2,000
	47,000

(2) ***Calculation of Excess of Private Assets over Private Liabilities :***

	₹
Life Policy	8,000
Household furniture	3,000
Jewellery of wife	2,500
	13,500
Less : Household debts	2,000
	11,500

ILLUSTRATION 5. The assets of a merchant on 30th June, 2025 as shown by his books were ₹ 45,000 and his liabilities ₹ 31,000. He filed his insolvency petition and estimated his deficiency to be ₹ 22,000. After making the above estimate, he found that the following items were not recorded in his books :

(*a*) Interest @ 10% on his capital from 1st January, 2025.
(*b*) Amount due as wages ₹ 200 ; as salaries ₹ 500 ; as rates and taxes ₹ 300 ; as rent ₹ 500.
(*c*) A contingent liability for ₹ 3,000 on bills discounted by him for ₹ 8,000.
(*d*) A loan of ₹ 5,000 taken from a friend for the marriage of his daughter.

SOLUTION

STATEMENT OF AFFAIRS OF MERCHANT
as at 30th June, 2025

Gross Liabilities	*Liabilities*		*Expected to Rank*	*Assets*	*Book Value*	*Expected to Produce*
₹			₹		₹	₹
	Unsecured Creditors			Property as per List E		
44,500	as per List A	(1)	39,500	Book Debts as per List F	45,000	(3) 9,000
—	Creditors Fully Secured			Bills of Exchange as per List G		
	as per List B	—		Surplus from securities		
	Less : Estimated			in the hands of fully secured		
	value of securities	—		creditors as per *contra*		—
	Surplus to *contra*				45,000	9,000
—	Creditors Partly			*Deduct :* Preferential		
	Secured as			Creditors as per *contra*		1,000
	per List C	—			8,000	
	Less : Estimated			Deficiency as explained in List H		31,500
	value of securities	—				
	Creditors for Rent,					
	Rates, Taxes, Wages, etc.,					
	payable in full as per	₹				
1,000	List D (2)	1,000				
	Deducted as per *contra*	1,000				
45,500			39,500			39,500

DEFICIENCY ACCOUNT (LIST H)

	₹		₹
Excess of assets over liabilities on		Other Losses :	
30th June, 2025, *i.e.*, Capital	14,000	Loss on realisation of assets	36,000

Deficiency as per Statement of Affairs	31,500	Loss due to expenses : ₹	
		Wages 200	
		Salaries 500	
		Rates and Taxes 300	
		Rent 500	1,500
		Bills discounted likely to be dishonoured	3,000
		Private liability of loan taken from the friend for the marriage of the daughter	5,000
	45,500		45,500

Working Notes :

(1) ***The amount of unsecured creditors has been calculated as follows :***

	₹
Liabilities	31,000
Rent	500
Bills discounted likely to be dishonoured	3,000
Friend's loan	5,000
	39,500

The gross liability of unsecured creditors is ₹ 44,500 ; ₹ 5,000 in respect of bills discounted not likely to be dishonoured have also been added.

(2) ***The amount of preferential creditors is*** **:**

	₹
Wages	200
Salaries	500
Rates and Taxes	300
	1,000

(3) While filing his petition, the merchant stated his deficiency as ₹ 22,000 and liabilities as ₹ 31,000. This shows that the assets must have realisable value of ₹ 9,000 (₹ 31,000 – ₹ 22,000) because only at this value he can estimate his deficiency of ₹ 22,000.

(4) Interest on capital for 6 months has not been considered as the proprietor cannot get anything on becoming insolvent unless all the creditors are paid in full.

ILLUSTRATION 6. Mr. X files a petition in insolvency as at December 31, 2024, on which date his position was :

Liabilities		*Assets*	₹
Trade Creditors	30,000	Plant and Machinery (realisable value, ₹ 55,000)	80,000
Bills Payable	20,000	Sundry Trade Debtors (Bad ₹ 15,500 and Doubtful ₹ 6,000 with 50% realisation)	36,500
Creditors with lien on stocks	25,000	Patents (realisable value Nil)	20,000
Creditors having a charge on Plant & Machinery	20,000	Furniture (realisable value ₹ 500)	1,000
Payable for Salaries & Taxes	800	Stock (realisable value ₹ 17,500)	28,500
		Cash	1,500

The insolvent commenced business on 1st Jan., 2020. After depreciation of plant and machinery at ₹ 5,000 p.a. and allowing interest on capital at ₹ 4,000 p.a. and a salary to proprietor at ₹ 1,500 p.a. the trading resulted in profits of ₹ 6,000 in 2020, ₹ 5,000 in 2021, and losses of ₹ 7,000 each in 2022 and 2023 and ₹ 10,400 in 2024. The drawings during the period amounted to ₹ 26,000.

From the foregoing prepare Statement of Affairs and Deficiency Account as on 31st December 2024.

SOLUTION

In the given problem the capital of X is not given. Hence Trial Balance is prepared to know the capital. The difference between credit side total and debit side total of trial balance is assumed as capital. The trial balance is given below :

TRIAL BALANCE OF MR. X

As on Dec. 31st, 2024

Particulars	*Debit Amount* (₹)	*Credit Amount* (₹)
Plant and Machinery	80,000	
Sundry Trade Debtors	36,500	
Patents	20,000	
Furniture	1,000	
Stock	28,500	
Cash	1,500	
Trade Creditors		30,000
Bill Payable		20,000
Creditors with lien on Stocks		25,000
Creditors having a charge on Plant & Machinery		20,000
Payable for Salaries and Taxes		800
Interest on Capital (₹ 4,000 × 5 yrs.)		20,000
Salary to Proprietor (₹ 1,500 × 5 yrs.)		7,500
Profits for 2 years (₹ 6,000 + ₹ 5,000)		11,000
Loss for 3 years (₹ 7,000 + ₹ 7,000 + ₹ 10,400)	24,400	
Drawings	26,000	
Difference in Trial Balance : Capital introduced (Balancing fig.)		83,600
	2,17,900	2,17,900

STATEMENT OF AFFAIRS OF X

As on 31st Dec., 2024

Gross Liabilities	*Liabilities*		*Expected to Rank*	*Assets*	*Book Value*	*Expected to Produce*
₹			₹		₹	₹
	Unsecured Creditors			Assets as per list 'E'		
50,000	as per list 'A'		50,000	Patents	20,000	
	Fully Secured Creditors			Furniture	1,000	500
	as per list	₹		Cash	1,500	1,500
20,000	'B'	20,000		Book Debts as per list		
	Less : Estimated			'F'		
	value of security	55,000		Good	15,000	15,000
	Surplus carried			Doubtful	6,000	3,000
	as per *contra*	35,000		Bad	15,500	—
	Partly Secured			B/E as per list G		
	Creditors as per				59,000	20,000

25,000	List 'C'	25,000		Surplus as per *contra*		35,000
	Less : Estimated value of securities	17,500				55,000
			7,500	*Less* : Preferential Creditors as per *contra*		800
						54,200
800	Preferential Creditors as per list 'D'	800		Deficiency as explained in list 'H'		3,300
	Deducted as per *contra*	800				
95,800			57,500			57,500

DEFICIENCY ACCOUNT (LIST H)

	₹			₹
Capital (Excess of assets over liabilities as on 1-1-2020)	83,600	Net Loss for 3 years (₹ 7,000 + ₹ 7,000 + ₹ 10,400)		24,400
Interest on Capital for 5 yrs. (₹ 4,000 × 5)	20,000	Drawings		26,000
		Bad Debts (₹ 15,500 + ₹ 3,000)		18,500
Salary to proprietor for 5 yrs. (₹ 1,500 × 5)	7,500	Loss on realisation of assets :	₹	
		Patents	20,000	
Net Profit for 2 yrs. (₹ 6,000 + ₹ 5,000)	11,000	Plant & Machinery	25,000	
		Furniture	500	
Deficiency as per Statement of Affairs	3,300	Stock	11,000	
				56,500
	1,25,400			1,25,400

Insolvency of Partnership Firms

While attempting the problems relating to insolvency of individuals the students must have noticed that no distinction was observed between business assets and liabilities and private assets and liabilities. Both were treated alike for the preparation of the Statement of Affairs. But this is not in the case of insolvency of partnership firms and a distinction is observed between the assets and liabilities of the partnership firm and private assets and liabilities of the partners. The assets of the firm are used first for paying liabilities of the firm and if a surplus remains after paying the firm's liabilities, a partner can use his share of the surplus for the payment of his private liabilities. In the same way, private assets of the individual partners are first utilised for the payment of their individual private liabilities and if there is a surplus in any partner's private estate, it shall be treated as part of the partnership property and can be utilised for the payment of firm's liabilities.

Separate Statement of Affairs and Deficiency Accounts are prepared for the partnership firm and for each of the partners. Surplus from the private estates of the partners is transferred to the firm's Statement of Affairs and is shown in "Property as per List E". It is also shown in the Deficiency Account as "Income from other Sources". But the private deficiency of a partner is not transferred to the firm's Statement of Affairs and Deficiency Account because firm's assets are used first for the payment of firm's liabilities.

Another point of importance in case of insolvency of partnership is that if a creditor of the partnership firm has taken some private property of the partner as security, then such a private asset will not be considered as security for ascertaining the nature of the creditor, whether fully secured or partly secured. The reason for doing so is that such creditor should try to get first whatever he can from the firm and for the remaining unpaid balance (not paid by the firm), he should sell the private property of the partner held by him. Suppose, there is a bank overdraft of ₹ 50,000 against the firm secured by the mortgage of A's house worth ₹ 30,000. The total creditors including bank overdraft who are to rank for dividend are ₹ 4,50,000 and the total amount available from the realisation of assets is ₹ 2,70,000. The bank will get from the firm $\frac{₹\ 2,70,000}{₹\ 4,50,000} \times ₹\ 50,000 = ₹\ 30,000$ and for the remaining unpaid amount of ₹ 20,000 (*i.e.* ₹ 50,000 – ₹ 30,000), the bank will sell the house of A and realise ₹ 30,000. The bank will keep ₹ 20,000 for the recovery of its unpaid amount by the firm and give the balance of house to the Official Assignee or Receiver for the payment of A's private liabilities.

ILLUSTRATION 7. Following are the particulars of the joint and separate estates of the firm and partners A and B :

	Firm	*A*	*B*		*Firm*	*A*	*B*
Liabilities :	₹	₹	₹	*Assets :*	₹	₹	₹
Capitals : A	16,000			Debtors	12,000	—	—
B	12,000			Stock	40,000	—	—
Creditors	60,000	4,000	16,000	Furniture	4,000	4,000	4,000
Preferential Creditors	4,000	—	—	Building	28,000	—	—
Mortgage on Building	16,000	—	—	Investments	—	8,000	8,000
B/P	20,000	—	—	Plant	40,000	—	—
Excess of Assets over				Capital A and B	—	16,000	12,000
Liabilities	—	24,000	8,000	Cash	4,000	—	—
	1,28,000	28,000	24,000		1,28,000	28,000	24,000

B/P was secured by second charge on Building and B's personal guarantee and B's investment as collateral security. Estimated realisable values are :

Firm's Assets : Building ₹ 22,000 ; Plant ₹ 8,000 ; Furniture ₹ 2,000 ; Stock ₹ 16,000 ; Debtors : Good ₹ 4,000 ; Doubtful ₹ 4,000 (realisable value ₹ 2,000); Bad ₹ 4,000.

A's Assets : Furniture ₹ 2,000 ; Investments ₹ 6,000.

B's Assets : Furniture ₹ 2,000 ; Investments ₹ 4,000.

From the particulars given above, prepare Statement of Affairs and Deficiency Accounts of the joint estate as also the private estate of the partners.

SOLUTION

The first point to note before preparing firm's Statement of Affairs is :

Is there any surplus in any partner's private estate ? There is no surplus in B's estate because B's private property is not sufficient even to pay B's private liabilities. But there is a surplus of ₹ 4,000 in A's estate calculated as below :

Realisable value of A's private assets :		₹
	Furniture	2,000
	Investments	6,000
		8,000
Less :	Private Liabilities (A's Creditors)	4,000
	Surplus in A's Estate	4,000

Surplus of ₹ 4,000 in A's estate can be utilised for paying creditors of the firm ; so it will be shown as a property in the firm's Statement of Affairs.

STATEMENT OF AFFAIRS A AND B

as at ....

Gross Liabilities	Liabilities		Expected to Rank	Assets	Book Value	Expected to Produce
₹			₹		₹	₹
	Unsecured Creditors			Property as per List E		
60,000	as per List A		60,000	Cash	4,000	4,000
	Fully Secured Creditors	₹		Stock	40,000	16,000
16,000	as per List B	16,000		Plant	40,000	8,000
	Less : Estimated			Furniture	4,000	2,000
	value of securities	22,000		Surplus from A's Estate		4,000
	Carried to List C :	6,000		Books Debts as per List F :		
20,000	Partly Secured Creditors			Good	4,000	4,000
	as per List C	20,000		Doubtful	4,000	
	Less : Estimated value			Bad	4,000	
	of security	6,000		Estimated to produce		2,000
			14,000		1,00,000	40,000
	Creditors for Rent,			Creditors for rent,		
	Rates, Taxes, Wages,			rates, taxes, wages,		
4,000	etc., payable in full					
	as per List D	4,000		etc. deducted as per *contra*		4,000
	Deducted as per *contra*	4,000				36,000
				Deficiency as explained in List H		38,000
1,00,000			74,000			74,000

The amount of B/P is ₹ 20,000. The holder of B/P realises ₹ 6,000 by having a second charge on building and for the balance of the amount, the holder will be considered as unsecured creditor of the firm. The holder of B/P realises ₹ 6,811 as follows :

The partnership firm pays for ₹ 74,000 = ₹ 36,000

Therefore, the firm pays for ₹ 14,000 (*i.e.* ₹ 20,000 – ₹ 6,000) $= \frac{₹\ 36,000}{₹\ 74,000} \times ₹\ 14000 = ₹\ 6,811.$

For the balance of the amount of B/P, *i.e.,* ₹ 14,000 – ₹ 6,811 = ₹ 7,189, the holder of B/P has B's personal guarantee and investments ; so this amount will be realised from B. Since the unsatisfied amount of B/P is ₹ 7,189 and the realisable value of investments is ₹ 4,000, the holder of B/P should be treated as partly secured creditor of B.

DEFICIENCY ACCOUNT OF A AND B (LIST H)

	₹			₹
Excess of assets over liabilities		Bad debts as per List F		6,000
i.e., Capital as on	28,000	Other Losses :		
Income or profit from other sources :		Loss on realisation of :	₹	
Surplus from A's estate	4,000	Plant	32,000	
Deficiency as per Statement of Affairs	38,000	Furniture	2,000	
		Stock	24,000	
		Building	6,000	
				64,000
	70,000			70,000

STATEMENT OF AFFAIRS OF A

₹		₹		₹	₹
4,000	Unsecured Creditors as per List A	4,000	Property as per List E Furniture	4,000	2,000
	Surplus carried to the firm of A and B as explained in List H	4,000	Investments	8,000	6,000
4,000		8,000		12,000	8,000

SURPLUS ACCOUNT OF A

	₹		₹	₹
Excess of Assets over Liabilities *i.e.,* Capital	24,000	Loss on realisation of :		
		Investments	2,000	
		Furniture	2,000	
				4,000
		Loss of Capital in the firm		16,000
		Surplus as per Statement of Affairs		4,000
	24,000			24,000

STATEMENT OF AFFAIRS OF B

₹		₹	₹		₹	₹
16,000	Unsecured Creditors as per List A		16,000	Property as per List E : Furniture	4,000	2,000
7,189	Partly Secured Creditors as per List C	7,189		Deficiency as explained in List H		17,189
	Less : Estimated value of security	4,000				
			3,189			
23,189			19,189		4,000	19,189

DEFICIENCY ACCOUNT OF B

	₹		₹	₹
Excess of Assets over Liabilities	8,000	Loss on realisation of :		
Deficiency as per Statement of Affairs	17,189	Investments	4,000	
		Furniture	2,000	
				6,000
		Loss on payment due to guarantee		7,189
		Loss of Capital in the firm		12,000
	25,189			25,189

ILLUSTRATION 8. Ploughman and Carter are equal partners. Insolvency petition is filed on 30-6-2025. The Balance Sheet as on 30-6-2025 is as follows (realisable value indicated in brackets) :

	₹		₹
Mortgage Loan (on Freehold)	40,000	Freehold (1,20,000)	1,60,000
Bank Overdraft (secured by second mortgage on Freehold)	1,60,000	Plant and Machinery (72,000)	1,20,000
		Fixtures (4,000)	12,000

Preferential Creditors	6,000	Stock (40,000)	80,000
Unsecured Creditors	2,00,000	Debtors (60,000)	1,00,000
Capital—Ploughman	88,000	Cash	2,000
		Carter—Capital Overdrawn	20,000
	4,94,000		4,94,000

The overdraft is secured, in addition to second mortgage, by Ploughman's personal guarantee against which his investments have been deposited. Ploughman's investments are estimated to realise ₹ 64,000 and after meeting his guarantee his private estate was insolvent. Carter was solvent and ₹ 38,000 was available from his estate for firm's creditors.

Prepare :

(*a*) Statement of Affairs (including rate of dividend for unsecured creditors).

(*b*) Deficiency Account.

(*c*) Capital Accounts in the Ledger (assuming realisations are as per estimates).

SOLUTION

STATEMENT OF AFFAIRS OF PLOUGHMAN AND CARTER

as on 30th June, 2025

Gross Liabilities	*Liabilities (as stated and estimated by the debtor)*		*Expected to Rank*	*Assets (as stated and estimated by the debtor)*	*Book Value*	*Expected to Produce*
₹			₹		₹	₹
	Unsecured Creditors			Property as per List E :		
2,00,000	as per List A		2,00,000	Cash	2,000	2,000
	Fully Secured Creditors	₹		Stock	80,000	40,000
40,000	as per List B	40,000		Plant and Machinery	1,20,000	72,000
	Less : Estimated Value			Fixtures	12,000	4,000
	of Securities	1,20,000		Surplus from Carter's		
		80,000		Estate		38,000
	Less : Transfer to					1,56,000
	List C	80,000		Book Debts as per List F	1,00,000	60,000
	Partly Secured				3,14,000	2,16,000
	Creditors as			Preferential Creditors		
1,60,000	per List C	1,60,000		deducted as per *contra*		6,000
	Less : Estimated					2,10,000
	Value of Securities	80,000		Deficiency as explained		
			80,000	in List H		70,000
	Preferential Creditors					
6,000	as per List D	6,000				
	Deducted as per					
	contra	6,000				
4,06,000			2,80,000			2,80,000

Rate of dividend per rupee of unsecured creditors is :

$$\frac{\text{Available assets for unsecured creditors}}{\text{Amount of unsecured creditors}} = \frac{₹\ 2,10,000}{₹\ 2,80,000} = 75 \text{ paise}$$

DEFICIENCY ACCOUNT (LIST H)

	₹		₹	₹
Excess of Assets over Liabilities,		Bad Debts as per List F		40,000
i.e., Capital on 30-6-2025	68,000	Loss on Realisation of Other		
Income from Other Sources :		Assets :		
Surplus from Carter's Estate	38,000	Stock	40,000	
Deficiency as per Statement of Affairs	70,000	Plant & Machinery	48,000	
		Fixtures	8,000	
		Freehold	40,000	
				1,36,000
	1,76,000			1,76,000

CAPITAL ACCOUNTS

	Ploughman	Carter		Ploughman	Carter
	₹	₹		₹	₹
To Balance b/d		20,000	By Balance b/d	88,000	
" Realisation A/c (Loss on Realisation of Assets ₹ 1,76,000 divided equally)	88,000	88,000	" Cash (Surplus from Carter's Estate)		38,000
			" Creditors (Deficiency)		70,000
	88,000	1,08,000		88,000	1,08,000

Insolvency and Bankruptcy Code, 2016 (IBC)

There were multiple laws in India dealing with insolvency and bankruptcy which were not aiding lenders in effective and timely recovery of stressed assets, causing undue strain on the Indian credit system. Thus, the Government of India has come out with a consolidated legislation i.e. Insolvency and Bankruptcy Code, 2016 ("Code") effective May, 2016 for speedy resolution of insolvency and bankruptcy of Companies, LLPs, Individuals and Partnership Firms.

Key Objectives of the Code

The Insolvency and Bankruptcy Code, 2016 is intended to strike the right balance of interest of all stakeholders of the business enterprise so that the corporates and other business entities enjoy availability of credit and at the same time the creditor do not have to bear the losses on account of default. The purpose of enactment of the Insolvency and Bankruptcy Code, 2016 is as follows :

(*a*) To consolidate and amend the laws relating to re-organisation and insolvency resolution of corporate persons, partnership firms and individuals.

(*b*) To fix time periods for execution of the laws in a time bound manner.

(*c*) To maximise the value of assets of interested persons.

(*d*) To promote entrepreneurship.

(*e*) To increase availability of credit.

(*f*) To balance the interests of all the stakeholders including alternation in the order of priority of payment of Government dues.

(*g*) To establish an Insolvency and Bankruptcy Board of India as a regulatory body for insolvency and bankruptcy law.

Regulatory Mechanism

The Insolvency and Bankruptcy Code, 2016 provides a new regulatory mechanism with an institutional set-up comprising of five pillars :

- Insolvency and Bankruptcy Board of India (IBBI)
- Insolvency Professional Agencies (IPAs)
- Insolvency Professionals (IPs)
- Information Utilities (IUs)
- Adjudicating Authority (AA)

Insolvency and Bankruptcy Code paves a new path for individual insolvency. The Code was brought into revolutionise insolvency processes in the country and establish consolidated procedures for corporate and individual insolvency.

As of new, the entire gamut of authorities in relation to Insolvency and Bankruptcy Code, 2016 are in place. The provisions relating to corporate insolvency resolutions, including fast track resolution, corporate liquidation and voluntary liquidation have been operationalised successfully. The provisions related to individual solvency are discussed below :

Individual Solvency

Individual insolvency framework pursues the objectives enshrined in the Code. It prevents creditors from harming the debtor by racing to be the first to recover their dues, and thereby facilitates resolution of insolvency. It facilitates an individual to get in and get out of business, undeterred by honest business failure, and thereby promotes entrepreneurship. It increases creditor's expected returns and thereby promotes availability of credit. It does not take away future income of the debtor after fresh/earned start and thereby does not undermine incentive to work. It relieves the debtor of the burden of debt and isolates minimum assets for his subsistence, while improving the prospects of realisation for creditors, thereby ensuring fairness and equity. These objectives are extremely important in the Indian context, where proprietorship and partnership firms have significant contribution to income and employment, and informal financial creditors (FCs) account for a significant share of credit.

Framework

In case of default by an individual, a creditor typically had two remedies - against the person of the debtor and / or against his property. Historically, the remedy was directed against the person. In ancient times, the creditor had the liberty to take the debtor, and often his family, into debt slavery. Reportedly, Genghis Khan used to hang the debtor who became bankrupt for the third time. The 19th century insolvency enactments provided considerable relief to debtors from harassment, while allowing creditors relief against the property of the debtor. A recent research ('Bombay's People 1860-98, Insolvents in the City' by Asiya Siddiqui) evidences that 85% of the 20,980-odd petitioners, who filed for bankruptcy in Mumbai between 1860 and 1898, got protection from arrest or detention.

Two subsequent enactments, namely, the Presidency Towns Insolvency Act, 1909 and the Provincial Insolvency Act, 1920, are in force today. The Code makes several improvements over these two enactments. With its' focus on rehabilitation of the debtor as opposed to adjudging him as insolvent, the Code: (*a*) provides an objective trigger for initiation of insolvency resolution process instead of relying on the commission of an 'act of insolvency'; (*b*) mandates a moratorium which provides a breathing space for the debtor and creditors to negotiate a repayment plan; (*c*) uses independent and qualified professionals to assist the stakeholders and the AA in conduct of processes; (*d*) prescribes a linear process, in which bankruptcy typically follows the failure of the insolvency resolution process; (*e*) enables automatic discharge instead of requiring that discharge be granted by the AA on the satisfaction that the insolvent has conducted himself well in the run up to and during insolvency; (*f*) provides a more comprehensive regime, including a debt relief in the form of 'fresh start', and keeps certain assets of the debtor beyond the reach of creditors for the subsistence of the debtor.

Part III

Part III of the Code provides for three processes for individual insolvency resolution, on default of a threshold amount:

(*a*) Fresh Start Process: This is available only to those debtors who have an annual income ≤ Rs. 60,000, assets < Rs. 20,000, debts ≤ Rs. 35,000 and do not have a dwelling unit. Only the debtor can file an application for fresh start for discharge of his debt. A resolution professional (RP) examines the application and submits a report to the AA, recommending acceptance or rejection of the application. On consideration of the report of the RP the AA passes an order, either admitting or rejecting the application. If the application is admitted, the creditors have an opportunity to object to the process on limited grounds. On conclusion of the process, the AA passes an order for the discharge of the debtor or revokes the admission of the application. The discharge order writes off the unsecured debts, allowing the debtor to start afresh, subject to an entry in the credit history.

(*b*) Insolvency Resolution Process: This provides a framework for the debtor and creditors to collectively renegotiate a repayment plan under the supervision of an RR The debtor or a creditor may make an application for initiation of the process. If the application is admitted by the AA, a public notice is issued inviting claims from all creditors. The debtor then prepares a repayment plan, in consultation with the RP If the plan is approved by 75% of the voting share of the creditors, and thereafter by the AA, the RP supervises its implementation. On execution of the repayment plan, the AA issues a discharge order releasing the debtor from its liability in terms of the plan, and the debtor gets an 'earned start'.

(*c*) Bankruptcy Process: If resolution process fails or repayment plan is not implemented, the debtor or creditor may make an application for the initiation of bankruptcy process. If the application is admitted, the AA passes a bankruptcy order and appoints a bankruptcy trustee, followed by an invitation of claims from creditors. The bankruptcy trustee investigates the affairs of the bankrupt, realises the estate of the bankrupt and distributes the proceeds in accordance with the priority provided in the Code. He submits a report of administration of the estate of the bankrupt to the committee of creditors for approval. On expiry of one year from the bankruptcy commencement date or within seven days of the approval by the committee of creditors, the bankruptcy trustee applies for a discharge order and the AA passes a discharge order. This discharge order releases the debtor from the bankruptcy debt. The bankrupt, however, suffers certain disabilities during the period of bankruptcy process.

Difference between Vis-a-vis Corporate Insolvency and Individual Insolvency

Individual insolvency framework differs from that of corporate insolvency on many aspects:

(*a*) Corporates are artificial persons with a broadly uniform structure. The Code provides a uniform process for resolution of their insolvency. It, however, categorises individuals into three categories and expects customised processes for resolution of each of the categories.

(*b*) There is no automatic debt relief in case of corporate entities. Individual insolvency, however, offers a fresh start process which grants automatic debt relief for a set of debtors where chance of recovery is low as compared to the efforts involved. While a corporate resolution process may yield into liquidation process, fresh start process never yields into bankruptcy process.

(*c*) A corporate entity and its business can be re-organised or liquidated and sold in bits and pieces. The business, if any, of an individual can be re-organised. The individual cannot, however, be liquidated or sold.

(*d*) Commencement of liquidation is automatic on failure of corporate resolution process. However, it is not so in the case of individual insolvency. A fresh application needs to be made either by the debtor or a creditor for commencement of the bankruptcy process, after failure of resolution process.

(*e*) Only on completion of liquidation, a corporate is dissolved. The bankruptcy process does not affect or is not affected by the existence of the debtor. It is not closed even on the death of the debtor.

(*f*) The Code does not envisage an RP to supervise the implementation of resolution plan for corporates. However, he supervises implementation of repayment plan under the individual insolvency.

(*g*) The National Company Law Tribunal is the AA for insolvency of corporate entities and personal guarantors to corporate entities undergoing corporate processes. The Debt Recovery Tribunal is the AA for insolvency of individuals.

Phasing

The Code envisages insolvency resolution of three categories of individuals, namely, personal guarantors to corporate debtors (CDs), partnership firms and proprietorship firms, and other individuals. Each category is unique and needs a separate dispensation for resolution of its insolvency. A category may have several sub-categories, each of which may require customised process. Further, the stakeholders need guidance on how to use the insolvency processes to their advantage. Given the scale of the country with 1.3 billion citizens, the road to implementing the insolvency regime for individuals is an uphill one and the learning curve is very steep. An appropriate phasing and sequencing of implementation of individual insolvency is essential, in sync with the legislative intention.

In the first phase, the provisions of the Code dealing with insolvency and bankruptcy of personal guarantors to corporates may be implemented.* This would complement the corporate insolvency regime and put personal guarantors and corporate guarantors on a level playing field. The provisions of the Code dealing with insolvency of partnership and proprietorship firms may be implemented in the second phase. In the third phase, the provisions of the Code dealing with insolvency of other individuals may be implemented. This would enable learnings from earlier phases for design of the dispensation for subsequent phases and to have all stakeholders on board for the efficient implementation of Part III of the Code.

QUESTIONS

OBJECTIVE TYPE

1. **Fill in the blanks :**
   (*a*) Loss on bills discounted and likely to be dishonoured is included in List...... and shown on the .... side of the Deficiency Account.
   (*b*) Excess of private assets over private liabilities is shown on the.......side of the Deficiency Account.
   (*c*) The unsecured creditors having a prior claim over the others are called .... creditors.
   (*d*) If the realisable value of an asset is more than its book value, the difference will appear on the..........side of the Deficiency Account.
   (*e*) Statement of Affairs is prepared to record the amount of..........and Deficiency Account is prepared to explain the.........of the deficiency.

Ans. [(*a*) A : right hand ; (*b*) left hand ; (*c*) preferential ; (*d*) left hand ; (*e*) deficiency, causes].

2. **Indicate the correct answers :**
   (*a*) Preferential creditors are shown under
   (*i*) List A (*ii*) List D (*iii*) List E.
   (*b*) Under the Presidency Towns Insolvency Act, rent due to the landlord is preferential for a period of
   (*i*) one month (*ii*) two months (*iii*) three months
   (*c*) Amount due to Government or local authority is a
   (*i*) secured claim (*ii*) unsecured claim (*iii*) preferential claim.
   (*d*) Book debts are shown under
   (*i*) List A (*ii*) List E (*iii*) List F.
   (*e*) Under the Provincial Insolvency Act, rent due to the landlord is preferential for a period of
   (*i*) one month (*ii*) three months (*iii*) Rent is not preferential.

Ans. [(*a*) (*ii*), (*b*) (*i*), (*c*) (*iii*), (*d*) (*iii*), (*e*) (*iii*)].

* The phase was implemented with effect from 1st December, 2019. It applies to personal guarantors of corporate debtors.

3. State the effect of the following in the Statement of Affairs and Deficiency Account with reasons :

(*i*) 24 months before the declaration of insolvency, a private house of ₹ 40,000 was transferred to his wife without consideration and a private bungalow of ₹ 60,000 to his daughter in consideration of her marriage.

(*ii*) The insolvent has private assets worth ₹ 80,000 including '*Stridhan*' of ₹ 25,000 of his spouse and private liabilities worth ₹ 35,000.

(*iii*) Out of the unsecured creditors of ₹ 80,000 a loan taken from wife of ₹ 28,000 has been included. Wife has paid this sum out of her '*Stridhan*'.

(*iv*) Bills Received of ₹ 20,500 were discounted out of which bills worth ₹ 12,000 are not expected to be dishonoured.

4. How will you treat the following items while preparing statement of affairs and deficiency account ?

(*a*) The insolvent has transferred a small private house of ₹ 6,00,000 to his daughter in consideration of her marriage.

(*b*) ₹ 40,000 loan from wife has been included in unsecured creditors of ₹ 1,60,000. Wife has paid this loan out of her Stridhan.

(*c*) 18 months before the declaration of insolvency a private house of ₹ 4,00,000 was transferred to his wife without consideration.

(*d*) The insolvent has private assets worth ₹ 1,50,000 including Stridhan of ₹ 25,000 of his spouse and private liabilities worth ₹ 50,000.

(*e*) Bills received of ₹ 20,000 were discounted out of which bills worth ₹ 12,000 are not expected to be dishonoured.

SHORT ANSWER TYPE

1. How do you treat loan from wife under Insolvency Act ?

2. What is Deficiency Account ?

3. What is to be given in Property as per List E ?

4. How will you treat bills likely to be dishonoured in case of Insolvency Accounts ?

5. What do you mean by fraudulent preference ?

6. What do you mean by doctrine of reputed ownership ?

7. How will you deal with voluntary transfer in case of Insolvency Accounts ?

8. How do you treat wife's jewellery of ₹ 20,000 surrendered by her to the court in insolvency statements ?

9. What do you mean by preferential creditors ?

10. From the following ascertain the **creditors** to be shown under Lists A and D :

	₹		₹
Creditors on Open Account	55,000	B/R discounted (expected to Rank ₹ 3,000)	9,000
B/P	10,500	Income-tax payable	550
Creditors having lien on Stock	8,000	Creditors for Salaries and Wages	
Bills of exchange	4,000	(Preferential ₹ 600)	2,200
Stock (estimated to produce)	6,000		

Ans. [List 'A' ₹ 70,100 ; List 'D' ₹ 1,150]

11. From the following figures of an insolvent, prepare the **Statement of Affairs** as at 31st Dec., 2024. Cash ₹ 320 ; Stock-in-trade ₹ 1,000 ; Debtors-Good ₹ 7,000. Debtors-doubtful ₹ 1,800 ; Debtors-bad ₹ 1,500. Fixtures & Fittings ₹ 564. Investment in Shares ₹ 50 ; Unsecured Creditors (including ₹ 1,000 of his wife, given from stridhan) ₹ 13,000 ; Secured Creditors ₹ 2,500 ; Value of Securities held by secured Creditors ₹ 3,500. Preferential claims for Rent, Rates & Taxes ₹ 190.

Stock realises ₹ 666, Fixtures & Fittings ₹ 282, Investments in shares, the book value, and the bad and doubtful debts together ₹ 600.

Ans. [Deficiency ₹ 3,272]

12. Prepare **Deficiency Account** from the following details :—

	₹		₹
Excess of assets over liabilities	20,000	Loss from betting	8,000
Net loss from business	6,500	Net Profit from Business	10,000
Income from other sources	4,000	Bad debts	12,000
Household expenses	32,000	Loss on realisation of assets	9,640

Ans. [Deficiency ₹ 34,140]

13. From the following particulars prepare **Deficiency Account :**

	₹		₹
Net Loss from 2023 to 2025	18,000	Loss on Bills Discounted	2,000
Gift declared void	1,000	Net Profit in 2021 and 2022	5,000
Excess of Assets over Liabilities (1-1-2021)	20,000	Loss on Sale of Assets	5,000
Bad Debts	10,000	Interest on Capital	1,000
Profit on Sale of Assets	2,000	Loss through Speculation	2,000
Household Expenses	3,000	Surplus from Private Property	4,000

Ans. [Deficiency ₹ 7,000]

14. The assets of a Merchant on 30th June, 2025 as shown by his books were ₹ 56,000 and liabilities ₹ 44,000. He filed his insolvency petition in the court and estimated his deficiency to be ₹ 30,000. After making the above estimate, he found that the following items were not included.

Interest at 6% on his capital from 1st January, 2025. A contingent liability for ₹ 2,500 on bills discounted by him for ₹ 10,000.

Amounts due as wages ₹ 300, as Salaries ₹ 700, as rent ₹ 300 and rates and taxes ₹ 200.

Prepare his **Statement of Affairs.**

Ans. [Deficiency ₹ 34,000]

15. From the following ascertain the **creditors** to be shown under Lists A and D

	₹		₹
Creditors on open accounts	55,000	Bills Receivable discounted	
Creditors having lien on stock	8,000	(expected to rank 3,000)	9,000
Bills of Exchange	4,000	Income tax payable	550
Stock & (estimated to produce)	6,000	Creditors for salaries and wages	
		(preferential ₹ 60)	2,200

Ans. [List A ₹ 60,140 ; List D ₹ 610]

16. Ascertain the amount of **creditors** to be shown under Lists B and C.

	₹		₹
Plant (estimated to produce ₹ 25,000)	35,000	Creditors having lein on shares	10,000
First mortgage on Plant	22,000	Trade creditors	30,000
Second mortage on Plant	15,000	Creditors for salaries and wages	1,500
Shares (estimated to produce ₹ 6,000)	8,000	Bills payable	5,000

Ans. [List B—₹ 22,000 ; List C ₹ 25,000].

17. The assets of Gopal as on 30-6-2024 as shown by his books were ₹ 70,000 and his liabilities ₹ 60,000. He filed his petition for insolvency and estimated his deficiency to be ₹ 40,000. He found subsequently that the following were not passed through his account books :

(*a*) Interest @ 6% p.a. on his capital from 1st Jan., 2024.

(*b*) A contingent liability of ₹ 3,000 on bills discounted by him for ₹ 12,000.

(*c*) Preferential payments ₹ 1,600. Prepare only **Deficiency Account.**

Ans. [Deficiency ₹ 44,600]

18. Garib is insolvent. From the following data prepare **appropriate lists of Creditors :**

	₹		₹
Total Creditors	90,000	Book value of Building	40,000
Creditors (Secured with 1st charge on Buildings)	20,000	Realisable value of Building	35,000
Creditors (Secured with 2nd charge on Buildings)	25,000		

Ans. [List B ₹ 20,000 ; List C Gross ₹ 25,000 expected value of security ₹ 15,000 ; List A ₹ 45,000].

19. Prepare **Deficiency Account** from the following information :

	₹		₹
Capital on 1-1-2024 (opening)	800	Loss on sale of assets	500
Bad debts	1,000	Interest on capital	100
Profit on sale of assets	200	Loss through speculation	200
Household expenses	300	Surplus from private property	400
Loss on bills discounted	200	Gift declared void	100
Profit in first two years	500	Loss in next three years	1,800

Ans. [Deficiency ₹ 1,900].

20. Mohd. Zaved had on 31st March, 2025 assets of ₹ 66,000 including a machinery valued in the books at ₹ 6,000 (estimated to realise 70% of the book value) and furniture valued ₹ 2,000 (estimated to produce 40%). He also had liabilities ₹ 40,000 of which ₹ 3,000 were fully secured against the machinery and liabilities of ₹ 1,000 were secured against furniture. He filed his petition in insolvency and estimated his deficiency to be ₹ 20,000 before taking into account the following items :

(*i*) Interest on his capital @ 6% from 30th June, 2025.

(*ii*) Bills discounted ₹ 1,000 expected to rank ₹ 500.

(*iii*) Wages ₹ 700; Rent ₹ 800; Salaries ₹ 2,000; Income-tax ₹ 100; Sales-tax ₹ 50; House-tax ₹ 50.

(*iv*) Mohd. Zaved is a reputed owner of a property worth ₹ 8,000.

Prepare his revised **Statement of Affairs and Deficiency Account.**

Ans. [Deficiency ₹ 24,000; Deficiency A/c Total ₹ 50,000]

LONG ANSWER TYPE

1. Mention the various lists that have to be prepared in support of the Statement of Affairs prepared under the Indian Insolvency Law, giving short particulars as to the contents of each of them.
2. Explain the difference between a Statement of Affairs and a Balance Sheet.
3. What is Deficiency Account ? How is it prepared ?
4. What do you mean by Preferential Creditors ? How are they shown in the Statement of Affairs ?
5. Is there any difference between insolvency of an individual and insolvency of a partnership firm ? If so, explain it.
6. What do you mean by fraudulent preference ? Has it any effect on the Statement of Affairs and the Deficiency Account ?
7. How will you deal with joint and separate estates of partners in insolvency ?
8. Explain the insolvency procedure laid down by the legislation in India.

PRACTICAL PROBLEMS

INSOLVENCY OF INDIVIDUALS

1. Mr. A is insolvent. He supplies to you the following information as on 31-3-2025 :

	₹		₹
Cash in hand	10,000	Book Debts (Doubtful) Expected to realize 40%	5,50,000
Creditors for Goods	10,00,000		
Taxes due to Government	35,000	Bills Discounted (₹ 40,000 bad)	1,40,000
Bank Loan Secured by Lieu on Stock	1,50,000	Loan from Nathan secured by second charge on stock	2,00,000
Furniture (Expected to Realize ₹ 50,000)	75,000		
Stock (expected to realize 50%)	6,00,000	Bills receivable (₹ 40,000 bad)	1,00,000
Book Debts (Good)	4,50,000		

Mr. A started business four years ago with a capital of ₹ 4,50,000. He drew ₹ 75,000 each year for private purposes, but did not maintain proper books of accounts. Mrs. A gave up her jewellery valued ₹ 1,00,000 to the receiver.

Prepare **Statement of Affairs** of Mr. A as on 31-3-2025 and Deficiency Account as on that date.

Ans. [Deficiency ₹ 2,35,000; Total of Deficiency A/c ₹ 10,35,000]

[**Hints :** Unsecured Creditors Gross ₹ 11,40,000 (expected to rank ₹ 10,40,000). Accumulated Profit (₹ 2,50,000) can be ascertained by preparing Trial Balance.]

2. Mr. Seth of Mumbai finds himself insolvent on 31st December, 2024. His position was as follows :

	₹		₹
Cash in hand	300	Bills Payable	28,000
Bills of Exchange	4,800	Bank Overdraft	12,000
Debtors : Good	8,000	Liability on bills discounted (estimated to rank ₹ 6,000)	10,000
Doubtful (Estimated to realise 80%)	2,400		
Bad	1,000	Creditors secured by life policy (worth ₹ 8,000)	13,000
Furniture (estimated to realise ₹ 5,000)	7,000		
Machinery (estimated to realise ₹ 41,000)	50,000	Household utensils	300
Stock-in-trade (estimated to realise ₹ 32,000)	40,000	Life policy not charged	6,000
		Mortgages (holding the security worth ₹ 70,000)	50,000
Household Debts	1,000		
Rent due to Landlord for 2 months	1,200	Creditors holding a second charge on the assets held by fully secured creditors (to the extent of ₹ 14,000)	18,000
Wages due to servant for five months	100		
Clerk's salaries for 4 months in arrears	1,700		
Rates and taxes due	1,000		
Mrs. Loan	11,000	Works Manager's salary due for last 2 months	2,000
Trade Creditors	45,000		

Prepare **Statement of Affairs.** Estimating the cost of winding up at ₹ 1,200, state the rate of dividend which could be expected to be paid to the creditors.

Ans. [Deficiency ₹ 12,980 ; Dividend @ 88 paise per rupee].

3. Ganpat files his petition for insolvency on 31st December, 2024 with the following particulars :

	₹
Sundry Debtors : Good ₹ 5,000, Doubtful ₹ 15,250 (estimated to produce ₹ 10,000) ; Bad ₹ 5,000	
100 shares in Textiles Ltd. (estimated to produce ₹ 7,500)	12,500
Mining shares (estimated to produce ₹ 38,000)	42,500
Loss through speculation	7,500
Creditors on open accounts	45,000

Creditors holding a second charge on mining shares to the extent of ₹ 15,000	17,500
Creditors holding a first charge on mining shares	20,000
Bills Payable	2,500
Bills Receivable discounted (of which ₹ 1,750 is likely to be dishonoured)	3,500
Creditors for rates, taxes, wages etc. (of which ₹ 1,250 is preferential)	1,500
Furniture (estimated to produce ₹ 1,500)	2,000
Cash in hand	60
Stock-in-trade (estimated to realise ₹ 15,000)	19,440
Bills Receivable (estimated to produce ₹ 3,500)	5,000

He started with a capital of ₹ 30,000 on 1st January, 2023 and business resulted in a profit of ₹ 5,000 and ₹ 3,750 for the first two years respectively and loss of ₹ 2,500 for the third year after allowing ₹ 1,500 as interest on capital each year. Withdrawals for the entire period amounted to ₹ 13,000.

Prepare **Statement of Affairs and Deficiency Account.**

Ans. [Deficiency ₹ 7,690 ; Total of Deficiency A/c ₹ 50,940].

4. Shyam Mohan filed a petition in bankruptcy on 30th June. His books showed the following balances :

	₹	₹
Cash in hand	10	
Fixtures and Fittings (estimated to produce ₹ 80)	250	
Stock-in-trade (estimated to produce ₹ 1,200)	1,800	
Sundry Creditors :		
Trade Creditors		2,000
Bills Payable		2,200
Sundry Debtors :		
Good	1,000	
Doubtful (Expected to realise 50%)	2,000	
Bad	2,000	
Bank Overdraft		1,200
Capital		1,660
	7,060	7,060

Liability on bills discounted ₹ 500, expected to rank ₹ 100. His household furniture was valued at ₹ 250. He owned a house valued at ₹ 750, having a mortgage on it of ₹ 600 at 4%. Interest paid up to the preceding 31st December.

Preferential Creditors amounted to ₹ 35 (included in sundry creditors) and ₹ 15 for rates on the house.

Prepare **Statement of Affairs and Deficiency Account.**

Ans. [Deficiency ₹ 1,837 ; Total of Deficiency A/c ₹ 3,870].

5. A filed his petition in Bankruptcy on 30th June, 2025. Prepare his Statement of Affairs and Deficiency Account from the following information.

The stock-in-trade cost ₹ 72,000 of which ₹ 6,000 worth is in the hands of a creditor for ₹ 10,000 who is entitled to exercise a lien : Book Debts : Good Rs 97,500. Doubtful ₹ 1,200 worth ₹ 400, Bad ₹ 1,500; Fixtures and Fittings (after depreciation) ₹ 2,300 ; Cash in hand ₹ 100.

Bills Receivable ₹ 11,000 (held by bankers) against overdraft of ₹ 40,000—balance of which is secured by a second mortgage on debtor's freehold property and by the guarantee of his brother. Customers' bills under discount ₹ 15,000 of which ₹ 2,000 is ascertained to be bad and ₹ 1,000 is doubtful. Freehold property ₹ 30,000 subject to a first mortgage of ₹ 20,000. The unsecured creditors amount to ₹ 2,98,000 in addition to the claims for rates, taxes and wages amounting to ₹ 2,400. The Stock-in-trade and the Book Debts (outside the bills) are estimated to be realised at 75% of their face value, and the freehold property which cost ₹ 28,000 is valued at ₹ 22,000. Subject to the modifications stated above, the assets are worth their book values.

You learn that the debtor had a surplus of assets of ₹ 50,000 on 1st January, 2023 since when he has withdrawn ₹ 30,000 per annum in equal monthly instalments. His profits for the year ended 31st December, 2023, were ₹ 21,000 and for 2024 ₹ 4,200 since which time he has not made up his books.

From these details, you are required to prepare as nearly as may be in statutory form (*a*) **Statement of Affairs,** and (*b*) **Deficiency Account.**

Ans. [Deficiency ₹ 2,10,475 ; Total of Deficiency A/c ₹ 2,85,675 ; Loss for 2025 ₹ 1,55,000].

6. The capital in the business of X on 31st December, 2023 was ₹ 7,000. During the year ended 31st December, 2024, he sustained a trading loss of ₹ 7,800 and his drawings out of the business were ₹ 7,000. Owing to his unsatisfactory financial position, he was compelled to file his petition, and a receiving order was made against him on 31st December, 2024. His assets consisted of :

(*a*) Book debts ₹ 10,000 of which ₹ 8,000 were considered good and the remaining estimated to produce ₹ 1,000.

(*b*) Stock (cost ₹ 15,000) estimated to produce ₹ 10,000.

(*c*) Machinery (cost ₹ 16,000) estimated to produce ₹ 11,000.

(*d*) Freehold house valued at ₹ 12,000, the deeds of which were lodged with the bank as security for an overdraft on business account of ₹ 8,000.

(*e*) His life policy (surrender value of ₹ 2,000) given as part security for a private loan of ₹ 3,000.

(*f*) His trade creditors amounted to ₹ 40,400 and he owed ₹ 400 to his clerk, being salaries for the two months ended 30th June, 2024.

(*g*) Bills had been discounted amounting to ₹ 3,000 in respect of which it was estimated that X would be liable for ₹ 1,000.

Prepare his **Statement of Affairs and Deficiency Account.** Estimating the cost of winding up at ₹ 800, state the amount of dividend which could be expected to be paid.

Ans. [Deficiency ₹ 8,800 ; Expected Dividend per rupee 0.775 ; Deficiency A/c Total ₹ 26,800].

7. On 31st December, 2024 Shri Y files his petition in bankruptcy on which date the Receiving Order was made. You are instructed by the Official Receiver in Bankruptcy to assist the debtor in the preparation of a **Deficiency Account and Statement of Affairs.** Your investigation discloses the following :

Assets	*Book Value*	*Estimated to produce*
	₹	₹
Freehold property to a first mortgage thereon having been given to fully secured creditors and a second charge limited to ₹ 10,000 to partly secured creditors.	1,20,000	1,00,000
Stock-in-trade	56,000	39,000
Trade Fixtures and Fittings	8,000	3,000
Book Debts :		
Good	61,000	61,000
Doubtful	27,000	20,000
Bad	17,000	Nil
Bills Receivable	3,000	Nil
Cash in hand	1,000	1,000

Liabilities

His liabilities amounted to ₹ 3,50,000 of which ₹ 74,000 was fully secured, ₹ 38,000 partly secured, liabilities for rent, wages etc. were ₹ 4,500 claimed to be preferential. There was also contingent liability on bills under discount of ₹ 27,400 of which ₹ 2,000 was expected to rank. He has household furniture of the estimated value of ₹ 2,500 and life policies of the surrender value of ₹ 5,000. The two latter items were not in his books of accounts. Out of liabilities for rent, etc. ₹ 2,000 was admitted as preferential.

On 1st January, 2022 Y's capital was ₹ 1,30,000. During the three intervening years, trading results, interest on capitals, and drawings were as follows :

	Trading Results		*Drawings*	*Interest on Capital*
	₹		₹	₹
To 31st December, 2022	4,000	Profit	8,000	6,000
To 31st December, 2023	75,000	Loss	10,000	6,500
To 31st December, 2024			15,000	1,500

Out of drawings, Mrs. Y purchased ornaments for ₹ 5,000 which she offers to Mr. Y for paying loans. These are estimated to fetch ₹ 6,000, ₹ 30,000 loss in 2023 (included in ₹ 75,000 above) was due to speculation.

Ans. [Deficiency ₹ 1,14,500 ; Deficiency A/c Total ₹ 2,76,000 ; Loss for 2024 ₹ 97,000].

8. A merchant became insolvent on 1-1-2025 on which date his total assets were ₹ 75,000 and liabilities ₹ 65,000 and he estimated a deficiency of ₹ 20,000 before taking the following items into consideration which were not passed through his account books :

(1) Interest on his capital of ₹ 25,000 @ 6% for one year.

(2) A contingent liability for ₹ 3,000 on bills discounted by him for ₹ 8,000.

(3) Amount due as wages ₹ 300 ; as salaries ₹ 600 ; as rent ₹ 500 ; as rates and taxes ₹ 1,000.

(4) A loan of ₹ 5,000 taken from a friend for the marriage of his daughter, and ₹ 2,000 from his wife.

Prepare a **Statement of Affairs and a Deficiency Account.**

Ans. [Deficiency ₹ 32,400 ; Total of Deficiency A/c ₹ 57,400].

INSOLVENCY OF PARTNERSHIP FIRMS

9. A and B are in partnership and file their petitions in bankruptcy. From the following particulars prepare **Statement of Affairs and Deficiency Accounts** of the joint estate as also the private estates of the partners:

BALANCE SHEET

	A and B	A	B		A and B	A	B
	₹	₹	₹		₹	₹	₹
Mortgage on Freehold	12,000	—	—	Freehold	24,000	—	—
Bank Overdraft	12,000	—	—	Plant	26,000	—	—
Sundry Creditors	49,600	6,000	11,600	Furniture	1,600	4,000	4,800
Preferential Creditors	400	—	—	Stock	22,000	—	—
Capital A	12,000	—	—	Debtors	20,000	—	—
Capital B	8,000	—	—	Investments	—	10,000	3,200
Surplus	—	20,000	4,400	Cash	400	—	—
				Capital in A and B	—	12,000	8,000
	94,000	26,000	16,000		94,000	26,000	16,000

The bank overdraft was secured by a second mortgage on freehold, and B's personal guarantee, supported by the deposit of B's investment as collateral security.

Freehold ₹ 18,000 ; Plant ₹ 12,000 ; Furniture ₹ 600 ; Stock ₹ 12,400 ; Debtors : good ₹ 10,300 ; doubtful ₹ 4,000 (estimated to realise 50 paise in a rupee) ; bad ₹ 5,700 ; A's assets ; Furniture ₹ 2,400; Investments ₹ 8,000 ; B's assets ; Furniture ₹ 3,200 and investments ₹ 1,200.

Ans.

		Firm	*A*	*B*
Deficiency	**(Surplus)**	**₹ 13,900**	**(4,400)**	**8,700**
Deficiency A/c	**(Surplus) Total**	**₹ 38,300**	**(20,000)**	**13,100**

10. A firm of Kane and Rane file their petition in bankruptcy and you are asked to draw up **Statement of Affairs and Deficiency Account** as on December 31, 2024 from the following information :

Sundry assets on December 31, 2024 amounted to ₹ 1,22,184 (estimated to realise ₹ 94,600) as against ₹ 1,20,000 on January 1, 2020. The sundry creditors on December 31, 2024 amounted to ₹ 1,07,270 as against ₹ 92,686 on January 1, 2020.

The capital accounts (excluding the current accounts) on December 31, 2024 showed a credit of ₹ 20,000.

The partners' drawings amounted to ₹ 2,800 p.a. (₹ 1,600 for Kane and ₹ 1,200 for Rane).

Trading results after charging ₹ 1,000 p.a. interest on capitals and ₹ 400 p.a. Rane's salary, were : 2020 profit ₹ 2,600 ; 2021 profit ₹ 800 ; 2022 loss ₹ 3,200 ; 2023 profit ₹ 400 ; 2024 loss ₹ 6,000.

On January 1, 2020 Rane had introduced further cash of ₹ 4,000 duly credited to his capital account.

Ans. [Deficiency (firm) ₹ 12,670 ; Total of Deficiency A/c ₹ 50,784 ; Current A/cs on 1-1-2024 ₹ 7,314].

11. Following particulars of M/s Unfortunate, a firm consisting of two partners, Abdul and Rahim are given :

(*a*) The firm was formed two years ago. The firm made a profit of ₹ 15,000 in the first year. Then it incurred substantial losses.

(*b*) Mohamed, a minor, was admitted to the benefits of partnership from the beginning.

(*c*) The firm is insolvent.

(*d*) The financial position, of the firm and the partners, is given as follows :

Liabilities

	Firm	*Abdul*	*Rahim*	*Mohamed*
	₹	₹	₹	₹
Mortgage Loan	22,000	—	—	—
Unsecured Creditors	10,000	2,000	5,000	—
Preferential Creditors	10,000	—	—	—

Assets

	Book Value	*Realisable Value*			
Building	20,000	25,000			
Other Assets	20,000	5,000	—	1,000	10,000
	40,000	30,000		1,000	10,000

(*e*) Other assets of Mr. Mohamed included ₹ 5,000 deposited in a bank. This represented the share of profit drawn from the firm.

(*f*) The partners Abdul and Rahim each had contributed ₹ 10,000, and the minor has contributed ₹ 5,000, when the business commenced. The partners shared profits equally.

Prepare **Statements of Affairs** of the firm and its two partners and also the firm's **Deficiency Account.**

Ans. [Firm's Deficiency ₹ 12,000 ; Total of Statement of Affairs ₹ 10,000 ; Total of Firm's Deficiency Account ₹ 57,000 ; Abdul's Deficiency ₹ 2,000 ; Rahim's Deficiency ₹ 4,000].

Hints : (1) It is assumed that since Mohamed has drawn his share of profit in the first year, the other partners also have drawn profits.

(2) There can be no recovery from Mohamed's estate as he is a minor partner. A minor can only be admitted to the benefits of the firm, he cannot be held responsible for firm's losses.

(3) Net loss for the second year is ₹ 27,000 on the assumption that first year's profit ₹ 15,000 is withdrawn by all partners.

12. A and B are carrying on business in a partnership sharing profits and losses in the proportion of two-third and one-third. They filed their petition in Bankruptcy on 30th September, 2024, when their Balance Sheet showed the following position :

BALANCE SHEET

as on 30th September, 2024

	₹		₹
Bank Overdraft secured by a charge on Machinery	30,000	Machinery	18,000
Sundry Creditors	64,500	Furniture	2,500
Bills Payable	5,000	Stock	14,200
A's Capital	12,400	Debtors (including ₹ 3,000 for dishonoured bills and ₹ 2,000 doubtful of recovery)	29,500
B's Capital	4,200	Investments	12,800
		A's Drawings	6,200
		B' Drawings	3,000
		Speculation Losses carried forward	20,300
		Cash	1,400
		Profit and Loss Account	8,200
	1,16,100		1,16,100

The assets of the firm are estimated to realise as under :

Machinery ₹ 12,000 ; Furniture ₹ 2,000 ; Investments ₹ 16,500 and Stock ₹ 2,000.

The Bank Overdraft was further secured by a charge on B's cottage. Creditors include ₹ 1,200 due to preferential creditors and ₹ 5,400 in respect of claim against the firm, which is not excepted to rank.

It is expected that A's private estate would show a deficit of ₹ 4,100. B had no personal property other than the cottage, which is expected to realise ₹ 8,000.

Prepare the **Statement of Affairs and the Deficiency Account** of the firm.

Ans. [Deficiency ₹ 22,700 ; Total of Deficiency A/c ₹ 51,400].

CHAPTER 32

Insurance Claims

Insurance means a contract of indemnity (guarantee) whereby one party, called the insurer, undertakes to indemnify (compensate) the loss suffered by other party, called the insured, on the happening of some unforeseen event in consideration of a fixed sum of money, called the premium.

Business enterprises get insured against the *loss of stocks* on the happening of certain events such as fire, flood, theft, earthquake etc. Sometimes, an enterprise also take insurance against consequential *loss of profit* due to decrease in turnover, increase in expenses etc. Such policy is known as loss of profit or consequential loss policy.

In this chapter, we will study Insurance claims for these two aspects.

1. Claim for loss of stock
2. Claim for loss of profit.

Stock Insurance

Every business unit has to keep a sufficient quantity of stock in the business premises for meeting the requirements of sales or manufacturing the goods. The stock kept in the business premises is subject to risk of loss by fire. For protecting itself against such loss, a business unit takes a fire insurance policy covering the loss of stock by fire. A fire insurance policy which covers loss of stock by fire is known as loss of stock policy in which the insurance company undertakes to compensate the business unit for loss of stock by fire in consideration of a payment called premium.

A fire in a business place destroys a number of assets such as building, machinery, furniture, stock, etc., so it is in the interest of a business unit to take a fire insurance policy to indemnify itself against the loss of stock and other assets resulting from fire. A fire insurance claim is lodged with the insurance company for the loss of stock and other assets by fire. It is easy to lodge claim for the loss of all assets except stock-in-trade because books of account maintain accounts of such assets except (usually) stock-in-trade.

Calculation of the Amount of Claim to be Lodged for the Loss of Stock by Fire

To lodge claim for the loss of stock by fire, value of stock-in-trade on the date of fire has to be estimated. Various points which are considered for the estimation of stock in hand on the date of fire are given below :

1. Gross Profit Ratio. Most important point is the percentage of gross profit on sales so that cost of goods sold during the year of fire may be ascertained. In the absence of any special circumstances, the percentage of gross profit on sales earned last year is applied to the current year (*i.e.,* the year of fire). So, Trading Account of last year may be referred to determine the gross profit ratio of last year. Where stocks records are maintained and not destroyed by fire, gross profit ratio is not necessary.

2. Determination of value of stock on the date of fire. Next step is to prepare Memorandum Trading Account of the current year upto the date of fire on the basis of opening stock, purchase and sales from the beginning of the year upto the date of fire and estimated gross profit on the basis of last year's gross profit ratio. The balancing figure in the Memorandum Trading Account will be the estimated value of stock in hand on the date of fire.

3. Determination of value of salvage stock. Third step is to deduct the value of stock salvaged, if any, from the value of stock as ascertained in step 2 ; the resultant figure is the amount of claim for the loss of stock to be lodged with the insurance company.

Salvage refers to goods saved from fire. The insurer has the right to take away the goods salvage. But, usually, goods are retained by the insured himself.

The treatment of salvage depends upon the fact of each case. If such salvaged goods are retained by the insured, then the value of salvaged stock should be deducted from the value of stock as on the date of fire to determine amount of claim for loss of stock.

4. Determination of Loss of Stock

Value of stock on the date of fire	×××
Less Salvaged Value	×××
Loss of Stock	×××

For calculating the claim, in addition to three points above, the following aspects should also be considered :

(*i*) **If stock in trade of last year was not valued at cost, it should be adjusted to cost to ascertain the correct percentage of gross profit on sales to be applied to the current year.** For example, if closing stock of last year was valued at ₹ 90,000 being 10% below cost, it should be adjusted to ₹ 1,00,000 $\left(i.e., \quad ₹\ 90{,}000 \times \frac{100}{90}\right)$ for the purpose of preparing Trading Account of the last year and the Memorandum Trading Account of the current year. **Goods distributed as free samples and goods taken by the proprietor or partners, if any, should also be adjusted** in Trading Account of the last year and Memorandum Trading of the current year.

(*ii*) **If there is a poor selling line stock in opening and/or closing stock, such stock should be eliminated from the Trading Account of the last year to get the gross profit ratio of the current year.** Any sale of poor selling line should also be deducted from the total sales to find out normal sales because gross profit ratio is to be applied to the normal sales. The same procedure is to be followed for poor selling line stock and sales in case of Memorandum Trading Account.

(*iii*) **When gross profit ratios for a number of years are given, an average of these ratios may be ascertained for finding out the gross profit ratio to be applied to the current year.** But it is not advisable to take the average gross profit ratio in case of a continuous and persistent fall in the rate of gross profit from year to year, rather a reasonably declining rate of gross profit as compared to the previous year or weighted average of previous years should be applied in the current year. Similarly, in case gross profit ratios for a number of years shown, an upward trend, weighted average can be calculated or a reasonably increasing rate of gross profit as compared to the previous year can be applied in the current year.

(*iv*) **Expenses of Salvage Operations.** Fire fighting expenses incurred on the date of fire for the purpose of salvaging the goods from fire are to be added (if allowed) before calculating the total loss or gross claim and applying the average clause.

ILLUSTRATION 1. ***(Determination of loss of stock).*** On 20th July, 2025 the godown and the business premises of a merchant were affected by fire. From the accounting records salvaged, the following information is made available to you :

	(₹)
Stock of Goods on 1st April, 2024	1,00,000
Stock of Goods at 10% lower than cost on 31st March, 2025	1,08,000
Purchases of Goods for the year 1st April, 2024 to 31st March, 2025	4,20,000
Sales for the same period	6,00,000
Purchases less returns from 1st April, 2025 to 20th July, 2025	1,40,000
Sales Returns for the above period	3,10,000

Sales up to 20th July, 2025 included ₹ 40,000 for which goods had not been despatched. Purchases up to 20th July, 2025 did not include ₹ 20,000 for which purchase invoices had not been received from suppliers, though goods had been received at the godown.

Goods salvaged from the accident were worth ₹ 12,000 and these were handed over to the insured. Ascertain the value of the claim for the loss of goods/stock which could be preferred to the insurer.

(CMA Inter June, 2024 Modified)

SOLUTION

Dr. **TRADING ACCOUNT** Cr.

for the year ended 31-3-2025

Particulars	*Amount (₹)*	*Amount (₹)*	*Particulars*	*Amount (₹)*	*Amount (₹)*
To Opening Stock		1,00,000	By Sales		6,00,000
To Purchases		4,20,000	By Closing Stock	1,08,000	
To Gross Profit		2,00,000	*Add* : Under Valuation $\left[\frac{10}{90}\text{ of } 1,08,000\right]$	12,000	
					1,20,000
		7,20,000			7,20,000

Rate of Gross Profit in 2024-25 = $\frac{₹\ 2,00,000}{₹\ 6,00,000} \times 100 = 33\frac{1}{3}\%$ on sales.

The net purchases in current year should be ₹ 1,40,000 + ₹ 20,000

Similarly, Sales = ₹ 3,10,000 – ₹ 40,000 = ₹ 2,70,000

Dr. **MEMORANDUM TRADING ACCOUNT** Cr.

for the period of 1-4-2025 to 20-7-2025

Particulars	*Amount (₹)*	*Particulars*	*Amount (₹)*
To Opening Stock	1,20,000	By Sales	2,70,000
To Purchases	1,60,000	By Closing Stock (Balancing Fig.)	1,00,000
To Gross Profit $\left[\frac{1}{3}\text{ of ₹ } 2,70,000\right]$	90,000		
	3,70,000		3,70,000

STATEMENT OF CLAIM FOR LOSS OF STOCK

	(₹)
Estimated Value of Stock on 20-7-2025	1,00,000
Less : Value of Salvaged Stock	12,000
Stock Lost by Fire	88,000

5. Determination of Insurance Claim. The insurer may be fully/over insured or underinsured. How insurance claim will be determined is depicted by way of diagram below :

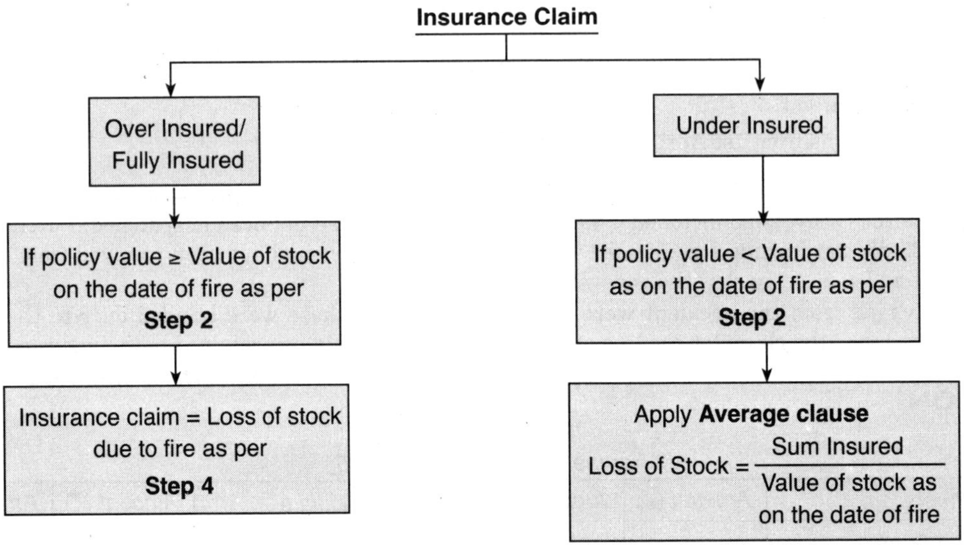

Following terms are explained below :

(*i*) Under insurance

(*ii*) Average clause

(*i*) **Under Insurance.** When an Insurance Policy is taken to cover loss of profit, under insurance occurs if the sum assured falls short of the amount for which the cover should have been taken. For loss of profit in the event of fire, the insurable amount is calculated by applying the rate of gross profit to the turnover of 12 months preceding the date of fire.

The insurer applies "Average Clause" to determine the amount of valid claim in the event of under insurance. The insured has to bear a portion of the loss himself.

Suppose standard sales are ₹ 1,25,000 but owing to dislocation caused by fire, sales amount to ₹ 1,00,000. If the applicable gross profit is 20% of the sales. The amount for which cover should have been taken would be 20% of ₹ 1,25,000, *i.e.,* ₹ 25,000. When cover is less than ₹ 25,000, the insurer will settle claim with a proportionately lesser amount.

(*ii*) **Average Clause.** A fire insurance policy usually includes an average clause to discourage the under insurance of stock or any asset. The effect of this clause is that if the value of stock or any asset insured on the date of fire is more than the amount of policy taken, the full value of stock or any asset destroyed does not become payable to the insured but the insurance company pays the proportion of the loss which the amount of policy taken bears to the total value of stock or any asset in hand on the date of fire. For example, if the value of insurance policy for the loss of stock is ₹ 1,00,000 and stock in hand on the date of fire is ₹ 1,40,000 out of which stock destroyed is estimated to be ₹ 70,000. The claim admitted by the insurance company will be as follows :

$$\text{Value of stock destroyed} \times \frac{\text{Value of Insurance Policy}}{\text{Value of stock on the date of fire}}$$

$$₹\,70{,}000 \times \frac{₹\,1{,}00{,}000}{₹\,1{,}40{,}000} = ₹\,50{,}000.$$

Therefore, insurance claim admitted will be proportionately reduced to ₹ 50,000 and the total value of stock destroyed by fire (*i.e.,* ₹ 70,000) will not be admissible to the insured.

It may also be noted that Fire Insurance being the contract of indemnity, a claim can be put across only for the actual amount of the loss, not exceeding the insured value. Following points should be kept in mind while determining the amount of claim.

(*i*) **Total loss.** Amount of claim is equal to actual loss. That is, if goods are fully insured, the amount of claim is restricted to policy amount only.

(*ii*) Partial Loss

(*a*) **Without average clause.** Claim is equal to the lower of actual loss or the sum insured.

(*b*) **With average clause.** Amount of claim is proportionately reduced, considering the ratio of the policy amount to the value of stock as on the date of fire.

ILLUSTRATION 2. (***Where average clause is not applicable***) On 29th August, 2025, the godown of a trader caught fire and a large part of the stock of goods was destroyed. However, goods costing ₹ 1,08,000 could be salvaged incurring fire fighting expenses amounting to ₹ 4,700.

Trader provides you the following additional information :

	₹
Cost of stock on 1st April, 2024	7,10,500
Cost of stock on 31st March, 2025	7,90,100
Purchases during the year ended 31st March, 2025	56,79,600
Purchases from 1st April, 2025 to the date of fire	33,10,700
Cost of goods distributed as samples for advertising from 1st April, 2025 to the date of fire	41,000
Cost of goods withdrawn by trader for personal use from 1st April, 2025 to the date of fire	2,000
Sales for the year ended 31st March, 2025	80,00,000
Sales from 1st April, 2025 to the date of fire	45,36,000

The insurance company also admitted fire fighting expenses. Trader had taken the fire insurance policy for ₹ 9,00,000 with an average clause.

Calculate the **amount of the claim** that will be admitted by the insurance company.

(CA—IPCE, Nov. 2012 Modified)

SOLUTION

MEMORANDUM TRADING ACCOUNT

for the period 1st April, 2025 to 29th August 2025

			₹		₹
To Opening Stock		₹	7,90,100	By Sales	45,36,000
To Purchases		33,10,700		By Closing Stock (Bal. Fig.)	8,82,600
Less : Advertisement	41,000				
Drawings	2,000	43,000	32,67,700		
To Gross Profit [30% of Sales (1)]			13,60,800		
			54,18,600		54,18,600

STATEMENT OF INSURANCE CLAIM

	₹
Value of Stock Destroyed by Fire	8,82,600
Less : Salvaged Stock	(1,08,000)
Add : Fire Fighting Expenses	4,700
Insurance Claim	7,79,300

Note : Since policy amount is more than claim amount, **average clause will not apply.** Therefore, claim amount of ₹ 7,79,300 will be admitted by the Insurance Company.

Working Notes :

(1) *Calculation of Gross Profit Ratio for 2024-25*

TRADING ACCOUNT

for the year ended 31st March, 2025

	₹		₹
To Opening Stock	7,10,500	By Sales	80,00,000
To Purchases	56,79,600	By Closing Stock	7,90,100
To Gross Profit (Bal. Fig.)	24,00,000		
	87,90,100		87,90,100

Rate of Gross Profit in 2024-25 $= \frac{\text{Gross Profit}}{\text{Sales}} \times 100 = \frac{24,00,000}{80,00,000} \times 100 = 30\%$

ILLUSTRATION 3. (*Where average clause is to be applied*). Fire occurred in the premises of Gharib Dass on 1st April, 2025 and a considerable part of the stock was destroyed. The stock salvaged was ₹ 56,000. A fire insurance policy for ₹ 3,42,000 was taken to cover loss of stock by fire. You are required to ascertain the insurance claim which the company should claim from the insurance company for the loss of stock by the fire from the following particulars :

	₹		₹
Purchases for the year 2024	18,76,000	Stock on 1st January, 2024	2,88,000
Sales for the year 2024	23,20,000	Stock on 31st December, 2024	4,84,000
Purchases from 1st January, 2025 to 1st April, 2025	3,64,000	Wages paid during the year 2024	2,00,000
Sales from 1st January, 2025 to 1st April, 2025	4,80,000	Wages paid during 1st January, 2025 to 1st April, 2025	36,000

Fire also broke out on 21st December, 2024 and destroyed stock of the estimated cost of ₹ 1,00,000.

There was a practice in the concern to value stock at cost less 10%, but all of a sudden this practice was changed and stock on 31st December, 2024 was valued at cost plus 10%.

SOLUTION

TRADING ACCOUNT OF GHARIB DASS

for the year ending 31st December, 2024

	₹		₹
To Stock on 1-1-2024 $\left(₹\,2,88,000 \times \frac{100}{90}\right)$	3,20,000	By Sales	23,20,000
		By Closing Stock $\left(₹\,4,84,000 \times \frac{100}{110}\right)$	4,40,000
To Purchases	18,76,000		
To Wages	2,00,000	By Stock destroyed by fire	1,00,000
To Gross Profit	4,64,000		
	28,60,000		28,60,000

Percentage of Gross Profit to sales $= \frac{\text{Gross Profit}}{\text{Sales}} \times 100 = \frac{₹\,4,64,000}{₹\,23,20,000} \times 100 = 20\%.$

Stock destroyed on 21st December, 2024 has been shown on the credit side of the Trading Account for the year 2024 to ascertain correct percentage of gross profit.

MEMORANDUM TRADING ACCOUNT OF GHARIB DASS

upto 1st April, 2025

	₹		₹
To Stock on 1-1-2025	4,40,000	By Sales	4,80,000
To Purchases	3,64,000	By Closing Stock	4,56,000
To Wages	36,000	(Balancing figure)	
To Gross Profit (20% of ₹ 4,80,000)	96,000		
	9,36,000		9,36,000

		₹
	Value of stock on 1st April, 2025	4,56,000
Less :	Stock salvaged	56,000
	Stock destroyed by fire	4,00,000

The average clause will apply as the value of stock on the date of fire, ₹ 4,56,000, is more than the sum assured of ₹ 3,42,000. Therefore, the insurance claim to be lodged will be :

$$\frac{\text{Value of Policy}}{\text{Value of stock on the date of fire}} \times \text{Value of stock destroyed}$$

$$= \frac{₹\ 3{,}42{,}000}{₹\ 4{,}56{,}000} \times ₹\ 4{,}00{,}000 = ₹\ 3{,}00{,}000.$$

ILLUSTRATION 4. ***(Where goods on approval had been sent).*** A fire occurred in the premises of M/s Preet Enterprises on the right of 28th September, 2025. The firm has taken an Insurance Policy for ₹ 5,00,000 which is subject to average clause. The value of goods salvaged was estimated at ₹ 62,500. The firm continues to maintain the same rate of Gross Profit as during the preceding year.

The following information were available :

	Particulars	₹
(*i*)	Stock at Cost on 1st April, 2024	5,25,000
(*ii*)	Stock at Cost on 31st March, 2025	4,20,000
(*iii*)	Purchases for the year ended 31st March, 2025	37,35,000
(*iv*)	Sales for the year ended 31st March, 2025	48,00,000
(*v*)	Purchases from 1st April, 2025 to 28th September, 2025	27,22,000
(*vi*)	Sales from 1st April, 2025 to 28th September, 2025	33,30,000

Additional Information :

(*i*) Purchase upto 28th September, 2025 did not include ₹ 1,20,000 for which purchase invoice had not been received from suppliers through the goods had been received in the warehouse.

(*ii*) Sale value of goods distributed for advertisement from 1st April, 2025 to 28th September, 2025 is ₹ 90,000.

(*iii*) Sales upto 28th September, 2025 include ₹ 90,000 for which the goods had not been dispatched.

(*v*) On 1st July, 2025, goods worth ₹ 1,50,000 was sold to Ram and Co. on approval basis which was included in the sales but not approval had been received for 2/3rd of the goods sold to them till 28th September, 2025.

You are required to ascertain the amount of claim to be lodged with the Insurance Company for Loss of Stock. ***(Intermediate Examination, November, 2022 Modified)***

SOLUTION

(a) Computation of claim for loss of stock

	₹
Stock on the date of Fire (*i.e.* on 28-9-2025)	5,98,000
Less : Stock Salvaged	(62,500)
Stock Destroyed by Fire (Loss of Stock)	5,35,500

Amount of claim :

$$= \frac{\text{Insured value}}{\text{Total cost of stock on the date of fire}} \times \text{Loss of stock}$$

(Average clause is applicable as insurance policy amount (₹ 5,00,000) is less than the value of closing stock *i.e.* ₹ 5,98,000)

5,00,000/5,98,000 × 5,35,500 = ₹ 4,47,742 (rounded off)

TRADING ACCOUNT

for the year ended 31-3-2425

Particulars	₹	*Particulars*	₹
To Opening Stock	5,25,000	By Sales	48,00,000
To Purchases	37,35,000	By Closing Stock at Cost	4,20,000
To Gross Profit	9,60,000		
	52,20,000		52,20,000

Rate of Gross Profit $= \frac{9,60,000}{48,00,000} = 20\%$

MEMORANDUM TRADING ACCOUNT

(1-4-25 to 28-9-25)

Particulars		₹	*Particulars*	₹
To Opening Stock		4,20,000	By Sales (W.N.. 2)	31,40,000
To Purchases	₹ 27,22,000		By Goods with Customers*	
Add : Purchases for			(for approval) (W.N. 1)	80,000
which invoice			By Cost of Goods distributed**	72,000
not received	₹ 1,20,000	28,42,000	By Closing Stock (Bal. Fig.)	5,98,000
To Gross Profit (₹ 3,40,000 × 20%)		6,28,000		
		38,90,000		38,90,000

* For financial statement purposes, this would form part of closing stock (since there is no sale). However, this has been shown separately for computation of claim for loss of stock since the goods were physically not with the entity and, hence, there was no loss of such stock.

** This may alternatively be shown as deduction from purchases on the debit side of the Memorandum Trading Account.

Working Notes :

1. **Calculation of Goods with Customers**

   Since no approval for sale has been received for the goods of ₹ 1,00,000 (*i.e.* 2/3 of ₹ 1,50,000) hence, these should be valued at cost *i.e.* ₹ 1,00,000 – 20% of ₹ 1,00,000 = ₹ 80,000.

2. **Calculation of Actual Sales**

   Total Sales – Goods not Dispatched – Sale of Goods on Approval (2/3rd)
   = Sales (₹ 33,30,000 – ₹ 90,000 – ₹ 1,00,000) = ₹ 31,40,000

ILLUSTRATION 5. (*Where effect of price rise is to taken*). From the following figures, calculate the amount of claim to be lodged with the insurance company for loss of stock :

	₹		₹
Stock at cost on 1st January, 2023	90,000	Sales during 2023	6,00,000
Stock at cost on 1st January, 2024	70,000	Sales from 1st January, 2024	
Purchases during 2023	4,00,000	to 30th September, 2024	8,80,000
Purchases from 1st January, 2024			
to 30th September, 2024	6,00,000		

You are informed that :

(*a*) In 2024 the cost of purchases have risen by 20% above the level prevailing in 2023;
(*b*) In 2024 the selling prices have gone up by 10% over the levels prevailing in 2023 ;
(*c*) Salvage value is ₹ 5,000.

SOLUTION

TRADING ACCOUNT
for the year ending 31st December, 2023

	₹		₹
To Opening Stock	90,000	By Sales	6,00,000
To Purchases	4,00,000	By Closing Stock	70,000
To Gross Profit (30% on sales)	1,80,000		
	6,70,000		6,70,000

$$\text{Percentage of Gross Profit on Sales in 2023} = \frac{₹\ 1,80,000}{₹\ 6,00,000} \times 100 = 30\%$$

MEMORANDUM TRADING ACCOUNT
for 9 months ending 30th Sept., 2024

		₹			₹
To Opening Stock		70,000	By Sales	₹	
" Purchases		6,00,000	Out of Opening Stock (1)	1,10,000	
" Gross Profit :			Out of Current		
On sales of opening	₹		Purchases (3)	7,70,000	
stock (2)	40,000		By Closing Stock		8,80,000
On sales out of			(Balancing figure)		12,000
Current Purchases (3)	1,82,000				
		2,22,000			
		8,92,000			8,92,000

Working Notes

(1) *Sales out of Opening Stock* :

		₹
	Selling Price in 2023 (say)	100
Less :	Gross Profit in 2023 derived from Trading A/c (2023)	30
	Cost of Sales in 2023	70
	Selling Price in 2024 (*i.e.,* 100 + 10%)	110
Less :	Cost of Opening Stock for ₹ 110 Sales	70
	Gross Profit on ₹ 110 Sales	40

Therefore, Selling Price of Opening Stock = $\frac{110}{70}$ × ₹ 70,000 = ₹ 1,10,000

		₹
(2) *Gross Profit on Sales of Opening Stock* :		
Selling Price		1,10,000
Less : Cost of Opening Stock		70,000
Gross Profit		40,000
(3) *Sales out of Current Purchases and Profit thereon*		₹
Sales at 2023 rate (say)		100
Add : 10% Increase in Price		10
Sales at 2024 rate		110
Less : Cost of Sales	₹	
Cost of Sales at 2023 rate	70	
Add : 20% increase $\left(i.e. \frac{20}{100} \times ₹\ 70\right)$	14	
		84
Profit on Sales of ₹ 110		26
Total Sales in 2024		8,80,000
Less : Sales of Opening Stock		1,10,000
Sales out of Current Purchases		7,70,000

Therefore, Gross Profit on Sales out of Current Purchases

$$= \frac{26}{110} \times ₹\ 7,70,000 = ₹\ 1,82,000.$$

ILLUSTRATION 6. ***(Where figures are missing for preparation of Memorandum Trading A/c)***
A fire occurred in the premises of M/s Durga & Co. on 15 May, 2025. The entire stock as well as books and records were destroyed. From the Balance Sheet of the previous accounting year ended on 31-3-2025, you find the following items :

	₹		₹
Cash at Bank	60,000	Creditors	1,80,000
Cash in hand	300	Stock in trade	50,000
Debtors	2,00,000		

Following further information is available to you :

(1) To meet daily wages, a cheque of ₹ 12,000 is drawn from the bank on the first working day of each month and a maximum of ₹ 300 is kept in the till on any day;

(2) There was no cash purchase or cash sales;

(3) All collections are deposited into bank each day;

(4) Sundry expenses, other than wages, paid by cheque amount to ₹ 6,000 per month, drawn on the second day of each month;

(5) Debtors confirm their dues of ₹ 2,50,000 ;

(6) The only creditor of the business which supplies goods to it, confirms that the business owes ₹ 2,00,000 after it had paid ₹ 2,40,000 by cheque during the period from 1-4-2025 to 15-5-2025;

(7) Balance at bank on 15-5-2025 was ₹ 42,000 ;

(8) The business usually makes a gross profit of 25% on sales which it is expected to maintain in 2025-26 also.

Prepare a statement showing the insurance claim recoverable. ***(I.C.W.A. Final)***

SOLUTION

MEMORANDUM TRADING ACCOUNT

for the period from 1-4-2025 to 15-5-2025 (the date of fire)

	₹		₹
To Stock (on 1-4-2025)	50,000	By Sales (3)	3,08,000
To Purchases (4)	2,60,000	By Closing Stock (Balancing Figure)	1,03,000
To Wages (1)	24,000		
To Gross Profit (25% on ₹ 3,08,000 Sales)	77,000		
	4,11,000		4,11,000

STATEMENT SHOWING THE INSURANCE CLAIM RECOVERABLE

	₹
Estimated value of stock on the date of fire	1,03,000
Less : Salvage of stock	Nil
Insurance Claim Recoverable for Loss of Stock	1,03,000

Working Notes

(1) *Calculation of Wages*

CASH ACCOUNT

	₹		₹
To Balance b/d	300	By Wages (Balancing Figure)	24,000
To Bank (Amount withdrawn from bank for April and May @ 12,000 per month)	24,000	By Balance c/d (Maximum balance kept on any day)	300
	24,300		24,300

(2) *Calculation of Amount Received from Debtors*

BANK ACCOUNT

	₹		₹
To Balance b/d	60,000	By Creditors	2,40,000
To Debtors (Amount received from Debtors) (Balancing Figure)	2,58,000	By Cash	24,000
		By Sundry Expenses (for April & May)	
		By Balance c/d	42,000
	3,18,000		3,18,000

(3) *Calculation of Sales*

DEBTORS ACCOUNT

	₹		₹
To Balance b/d	2,00,000	By Bank (2)	2,58,000
To Sales (Balancing Figure)	3,08,000	By Balance c/d	2,50,000
	5,08,000		5,08,000

(4) *Computation of Purchases*

CREDITORS ACCOUNT

	₹		₹
To Bank	2,40,000	By Balance b/d	1,80,000
To Balance c/d	2,00,000	By Purchases (Balancing Figure)	2,60,000
	4,40,000		4,40,000

ILLUSTRATION 7. ***(Where two fires occur besides calculating average Gross Profit Ratio & Salvage operation expenses)*** A fire occurred in the premises of M/s Low Luck Traders twice during the accounting year 2024-25, that is on 31st July, 2024 and again on 30th November, 2024. From the following particulars, calculate the claim to be lodged in respect of the goods lost by fire on the aforementioned dates :

(1) The stock as at 31st March, 2024 was valued at ₹ 9,90,000.

(2) The purchases from 1st April, 2024 to 31st July, 2024 amounted to ₹ 35,60,000 and included furniture purchased for ₹ 10,000.

(3) Sales for the period from 1st April, 2024 to 31st July, 2024 amounted to ₹ 50,00,000.

(4) The purchases from 1st August, 2024 to 30th November, 2024 amounted to ₹ 49,50,000 of which goods costing ₹ 1,05,000 were received on 10th December, 2024.

(5) The sales for the period from 1st August, 2024 to 30th November, 2024 amounted to ₹ 60,60,000 out of which sales on "sales or return' basis amounted to ₹ 1,00,000. No intimation was received from the customers in respect of 60% of the goods sold on approval basis.

(6) Information regarding sales and gross profit of the last three years was as follows:

Year	*Sales*	*Gross Profit*
	₹	₹
2021-22	1,00,00,000	12,00,000
2022-23	1,20,00,000	9,60,000
2023-24	1,35,00,000	13,40,000

(7) In the beginning of the year 2024-25, the selling price was raised by 20%.

(8) The closing stock of 2023-24 was undervalued by ₹ 10,000.

(9) The value of the goods salvaged on 31st July, 2024 was ₹ 3,00,000.

(10) The value of the goods salvaged on 30th November, 2024 was also ₹ 3,00,000.

(11) The expenses of the salvage operations were ₹ 20,000 on 31st July, 2024 and ₹ 10,000 on 30th November, 2024.

(12) The firm had taken out a fire insurance policy of ₹ 6,00,000 on 1st April, 2024. At the time of receiving the insurance claim on 31st July, 2024, no additional premium was paid for restoration of the insurance policy to its original amount. The policy was subject to the average clause.

SOLUTION

Calculation of Rate of Gross Profit for 2024-25

$$\text{Gross Profit Ratio} = \frac{\text{Gross Profit}}{\text{Sales}} \times 100$$

$$\text{2021-22} = \frac{₹\ 12{,}00{,}000}{₹\ 1{,}00{,}00{,}000} \times 100 = 12\%$$

$$\text{2022-23} = \frac{₹\ 9{,}60{,}000}{₹\ 1{,}20{,}00{,}000} \times 100 = 8\%$$

$$\text{2023-24} = \frac{₹\ 13{,}50{,}000}{₹\ 1{,}35{,}00{,}000} \times 100 = 10\%$$

(Gross Profit = ₹ 13,40,000 as given + ₹ 10,000 for undervaluation of Closing Stock)

Average Gross Profit Ratio = $\frac{12\% + 8\% + 10\%}{3}$ = 10%

	Past	*2024-25*
Sales	100	120 (100 + 20% Increase)
Gross Profit	10	30 (120 – 90)
Cost	90 (100 – 10)	90 (Cost remaining same as in the past)

Therefore, Rate of Gross Profit for 2024-25 $= \frac{\text{Gross Profit}}{\text{Sales}} \times 100 = \frac{30}{120} \times 100 = 25\%$

MEMORANDUM TRADING ACCOUNT

for the period commencing 1-4-2024 to 31-7-2024 the date of first fire

		₹		₹
To Opening Stock (1-4-2024) (₹ 9,90,000 + ₹ 10,000)	₹	10,00,000	By Sales	50,00,000
To Purchases	35,60,000		By Stock on the date of fire (Balancing figure)	8,00,000
Less : Furniture Purchased	10,000			
		35,50,000		
To Gross Profit (25% of Sales)		12,50,000		
		58,00,000		58,00,000

		₹
	Stock on the date of fire on 31-7-2024	8,00,000
Less :	Goods salvaged	3,00,000
		5,00,000
Add :	Expenses of salvage operations	20,000
	Loss by fire	5,20,000

Value of Claim on 31-7-2024 $= \frac{\text{Value of Policy}}{\text{Stock on the date of fire}} \times \text{Loss by fire}$

$= \frac{₹\ 6,00,000}{₹ 8,00,000} \times ₹\ 5,20,000 = ₹\ 3,90,000.$

MEMORANDUM TRADING ACCOUNT

for the period from 1-8-2024 to 30-11-2024 the second date of fire

	₹	₹		₹	₹
To Opening Stock (*i.e.* Value of goods salvaged on 1-8-2024)		3,00,000	By Sales	60,60,000	
			Less : Sales on Approval	60,000	
To Purchases	49,50,000				60,00,000
Less : Goods not yet received	1,05,000		By Stock lying with customers (Cost of goods on approval basis)		
		48,45,000	*i.e.* ₹ 60,000 × $\frac{75}{100}$)		45,000
To Gross Profit (25% of Sales)		15,00,000	By Stock on the date of fire (Balancing figure)		6,00,000
		66,45,000			66,45,000

		₹
	Stock on the date of fire	6,00,000
Less :	Value of goods salvaged	3,00,000
		3,00,000
Add :	Expenses of salvage operations	10,000
	Loss by second fire in the same financial year	3,10,000

$$\text{Value of claim on 30-11-2024} = \frac{\text{Value of Policy remaining after meeting first claim during the year 2024-25}}{\text{Stock on the date of fire}} \times \text{Loss by fire}$$

$$= \frac{₹\,6{,}00{,}000 - ₹\,3{,}90{,}000}{₹\,6{,}00{,}000} \times ₹\,3{,}10{,}000 = ₹\,1{,}08{,}500.$$

Ascertainment of Claim when Abnormal Items of Goods are available (or Poor Selling Goods)

Abnormal items of goods are those which cannot be sold at the normal price or has a slow rate of turnover. Such goods may include some poor selling of stock of goods and are generally valued at below cost and thus reduce the gross profit. In order to determine the normal rate of gross profit the stock and sale proceeds of these goods are to be eliminated from the total sales and stock. Trading Account in such a case is prepared in columnar form to show separately the normal and abnormal items. Following are the main steps involved in calculating the claim in the presence of abnormal lines of goods :

Step 1 : Preparation of Last Year Trading Account

While preparing Last Year Trading Account stock, purchases and sales of normal goods must be considered in arriving the gross profit. In other words, value of abnormal goods included in opening stock, purchases, sales and closing stock must be deducted from the respective items.

Step 2 : Calculation of Rate of Gross Profit on Sales

Rate of gross profit on sales must be calculated with reference to gross profit on sale of normal goods and sales of normal goods only by the following formula :

$$\text{Rate of Gross Profit (on normal sales)} = \frac{\text{Gross Profit on Sale of Normal Goods}}{\text{Sales of Normal Goods}} \times 100$$

Step 3 : Preparation of Memorandum Trading Account

While preparing this account, value of abnormal goods included in opening stock, purchases and sales must be deducted from the respective items and is to be shown in a separate column for abnormal items. Gross profit must be calculated on the sales value of normal goods by applying rate of gross profit on normal sales as calculated in step (2). The balancing figure will be closing stock of normal goods on the date of fire.

Step 4 : Calculation of Actual Amount of Loss

Actual amount of loss can be calculated by using the following format :

	₹
Stock of Normal Goods on the date of Fire (from Memorandum Trading A/c)	×××
Stock of Abnormal Goods on the date of Fire	×××
	×××
Less : Stock Salvaged	×××
	×××
Add : Expenses for Extinguishment of Fire	×××
Actual Loss of Stock	×××

Step 5 : Calculation of Amount of Claim

There would not be any difference in calculation of amount of claim on account of existence of abnormal goods. Calculation of claim is also based on the extent of insurance. If the amount of policy is less than the total stock (both normal and abnormal), then average clause is applied as there is under insurance.

ILLUSTRATION 8. (*Where poor selling goods are in stock*). On 25th June, 2025 a fire broke out in the premises of Unlucky Co. All the stocks were destroyed except some which were partly damaged and sold subsequently for ₹ 7,900.

From the following particulars ascertain the claim to be submitted to the Insurance Company assuming that the policy was for ₹ 20,000.

	₹		₹
Stock as on 1st January, 2025	24,400	Purchases during the year 2024	1,53,500
Purchases upto the date of the fire	73,000	Sales during the year 2024	1,96,500
Sales upto the date of the fire	97,000	Stock as on 1st January, 2024	18,500

The stock as on 1st January, 2024 included a special item valued ₹ 5,600 which was sold at a profit of 20% on sales. A part of this item was sold in 2024 while the balance was sold on 3rd May, 2025 for ₹ 2,500. Except for this item, the gross profit on all other items was at a uniform rate throughout the period.

SOLUTION

TRADING ACCOUNT OF UNLUCKY CO.

for the year ending 31st December, 2024

	Normal Items	*Abnormal Items*		*Normal Items*	*Abnormal Items*
	₹	₹		₹	₹
To Opening Stock	12,900	5,600	By Sales	1,92,000	(1)4,500
To Purchases	1,53,500	—	By Closing Stock	22,400	(2)2,000
To Gross Profit	48,000	900			
	2,14,400	6,500		2,14,400	6,500

(1) ***Sales value of special item is calculated as follows*** :

		₹
	Cost of special item	5,600
Add :	25% profit on cost which is equivalent to 20% on sales	1,400
		7,000
	Total sales value of the special item	7,000
Less :	Sale of special item in 2025	2,500
	Sale of special item in 2024	4,500

(2) ***Cost of the sale of special item in 2025*** :

	₹
Sale value	2,500
Less : 20% Profit included therein $\left(₹\,2{,}500 \times \frac{20}{100}\right)$	500
Cost	2,000

$$\text{Gross Profit on Normal Sales} = \frac{\text{Gross Profit on Normal Sales}}{\text{Normal Sales}} \times 100$$

$$= \frac{₹\,48{,}000}{₹\,1{,}92{,}000} \times 100 = 25\%$$

MEMORANDUM TRADING ACCOUNT OF UNLUCKY CO.

upto 25th June, 2025

	Normal Items	Abnormal Items		Normal Items	Abnormal Items
	₹	₹		₹	₹
To Stock on 1-1-2025	22,400	2,000	By Sales	94,500	2,500
To Purchases	73,000	—	By Stock on 25-6-2025	24,525	
To Gross Profit (25% on Normal Sales and balancing figure in case of abnormal items)	23,625	500			
	1,19,025	2,500		1,19,025	2,500

	₹
Value of stock on the date of fire	24,525
Less : Sale of partly damaged stock	7,900
Value of stock destroyed by fire	16,625

$$\text{Claim to be lodged} = \text{Value of stock destroyed} \times \frac{\text{Insurance Policy}}{\text{Value of stock on the date of fire}}$$

$$= ₹\ 16,625 \times \frac{₹\ 20,000}{₹\ 24,525} = ₹\ 13,558$$

ILLUSTRATION 9. ***(Where poor selling goods are in stock)*** On 15th December, 2024 the premises of NAGAR LTD. were destroyed by fire, but sufficient records were saved from which the following particulars were ascertained :

	₹
Stock at cost on 1st April, 2023	2,20,500
Stock at cost on 31st March, 2024	2,38,800
Purchases *less* returns, year ended 31st March, 2024	11,94,000
Sales *less* returns, year ended 31st March, 2024	14,61,000
Purchases *less* returns, 1st April, 2024 to 15th December, 2024	10,15,000
Sales *less* returns, 1st April, 2024 to 15th December, 2024	11,62,000

In valuing stock for Balance Sheet as at 31st March, 2024 ₹ 6,900 had been written off for certain stock which was a poor selling line, having cost of ₹ 20,700. A portion of these goods were sold in June, 2024 at a loss of ₹ 750 on the original cost of ₹ 10,350. The remainder of this stock was now estimated to be worth the original cost. Subject to the above exception gross profit had remained at a uniform rate throughout. The stock salvaged was ₹ 17,500. The stock was insured for ₹ 2,50,000.

Required : Calculate the amount of claim to be lodged with the insurance company for loss of sotck.

(ICMA – Inter June, 2015 Modified)

SOLUTION

TRADING ACCOUNT

for the year ended 31.3.2024

	Normal item (₹)	Abnormal item (₹)	Total (₹)		Normal item (₹)	Abnormal item (₹)	Total (₹)
To Opening Stock A/c	2,20,500	—	2,20,500	By Sales *less* Returns A/c	14,61,000	—	14,61,000
To Purchases *less* Returns	11,73,300	20,700	11,94,400	By Closing Stock (2,38,800 + 6,900)	2,25,000	20,700	2,45,700
To Gross Profit	2,92,200	–	2,92,200				
	16,86,000	20,700	17,06,700		16,86,000	20,700	17,06,700

$$\text{Rate of Gross Profit} = \frac{(2{,}92{,}000 \times 100)}{14{,}61{,}000} = 20\%$$

MEMORANDUM TRADING ACCOUNT

For the period of 1st April, 2024 to 15th December, 2024

	Normal item (₹)	Abnormal item (₹)	Total (₹)		Normal item (₹)	Abnormal item (₹)	Total (₹)
To Opening Stock A/c	2,25,000	20,700	2,45,700	By Sales	11,52,400	9,600	11,62,000
To Purchases	10,15,000	—	10,15,000	By Loss	—	750	750
To Gross Profit (20% of ₹ 11,52,400)	2,30,480	—	2,30,480	By Closing Stock (B/f)	3,18,080	10,350	3,28,430
	14,70,480	20,700	14,91,180		14,70,480	20,700	14,91,180

Account of Loss of Stock :

Value of Stock on date of fire	3,28,430
Less : Stock Salvaged	17,500
Loss of Stock by fire	3,10,930

Since the value of the stock is more than the Insurance policy. Average Clause should be applied.

Application of Average Clause :

$$\text{Amount of Claim} = \text{Loss of Stock by Fire} \times \frac{\text{Insured Amount}}{\text{Value of Stock on Date of Fire}}$$

$$= 3{,}10{,}930 \times \frac{2{,}50{,}000}{3{,}28{,}430} = \text{₹ } \mathbf{2{,}36{,}679}$$

ILLUSTRATION 10. (*Where claim for stock of damaged goods is to be calculated*). The premises of Sulav Enterprise, a proprietary concern, were damaged by fire on 12th February, 2025. As a result, some trading stock was totally destroyed, and in addition, stock costing ₹ 96,000 was partly damaged. The insurance company agreed to reduce the value of the damaged stock to ₹ 52,800. On 31st December, 2024, the stock-in-trade of the concern was valued at ₹ 4,12,000. Subsequently the following purchases were made:

	₹		₹
8th January, 2025	1,09,920	14th February, 2025	42,400
21st January, 2025	72,000	20th February, 2025	2,24,000
27th January, 2025	5,360	8th March, 2025	1,37,600

Additional information for the three months ended 31st March, 2025 is given below :

(*a*) 50% of the damaged goods were sold before 31st March, 2025 at a profit of 15%.

(*b*) With the exception of the damaged goods, the firm has earned a gross profit of 30% of the cost of goods sold.

(*c*) The sales during the three months ended 31st March, 2025 were ₹ 5,64,360.

(*d*) The undamaged stock at 31st March, 2025 was valued at ₹ 2,03,280.

(*e*) The firm has an insurance cover for loss and damage to stock by fire.

Prepare a statement of insurance claim.

SOLUTION

	₹
Total sales during 3 months	6,65,360
Less: Sales of partly damaged goods $\left(\frac{1}{2} \times \text{₹ } 52{,}800 \times \frac{115}{100}\right)$	30,360
Sales of undamaged stock	6,24,000

Computation of Cost of Damaged Stock

	₹	₹
Stock as at 31-12-2024		4,12,000
Add: Purchases during 1-1-2025 to 31-3-2025		5,91,280
		10,03,280
Less : Cost of partly damaged stock		96,000
		9,07,280
Less : Cost of undamaged stock sold :		
Sales of undamaged stock	6,24,000	
Less: Gross profit included therein $\left(₹\,6{,}24{,}000 \times \frac{30}{130}\right)$	1,44,000	4,80,000
Expected balance of undamaged stock		4,27,280
Less: Actual cost of undamaged stock valued on 31-3-2025		2,03,280
Stock completely destroyed		2,24,000

Statement of Insurance Claim

	₹
Cost of stock completely destroyed	2,24,000
Add : Agreed value of partly damaged stock	52,800
Total claim for Stock Damaged	2,76,800

ILLUSTRATION 11. ***(Where slow item of goods is there besides calculating average G.P. Ratio)*** The premises of P were destroyed by fire on 30-6-2025. Following figures, however, were collected from various sources. Prepare a statement of claim in respect of the loss of stock for submission to the Fire Insurance Company. The firm closes its books on 31st December every year.

Details	*2022*	*2023*	*2024*	*30-6-2025*
	₹	₹	₹	₹
Opening Stock	20,000	22,000	11,800	34,020
Purchases less returns	1,60,000	1,45,000	1,70,000	35,000
Sales less returns	2,00,000	1,98,500	1,87,500	26,000
Freight (Inwards)	5,000	3,000	5,000	1,000
Freight (Outwards)	6,000	7,000	3,000	250

In 2022, while valuing closing stock, a slow moving item costing ₹ 5,000 was valued at ₹ 4,000. This was sold for ₹ 4,500 in 2023. In 2023, an item costing ₹ 6,000 was wrongly valued at ₹ 7,000. This was sold for ₹ 5,500 in 2024. In 2024, a slow moving item, costing ₹ 12,000 was valued at ₹ 10,000 ; 50% of which was sold before 30-6-2025 for ₹ 6,000. The value of salvage was ₹ 8,000.

SOLUTION

TRADING ACCOUNT OF P

	2022	2023	2024		2022	2023	2024
	₹	₹	₹		₹	₹	₹
To Opening Stock	20,000	22,000	11,800	By Sales	2,00,000	1,98,500	1,87,500
Less : Abnormal Item		4,000	7,000	*Less* : Sales of Abnormal Item		4,500	5,500
		18,000	4,800			1,94,000	1,82,000

To Purchases	1,60,000	1,45,000	1,70,000	By Closing Stock (at Cost)	23,000	10,800	36,020
To Freight (Inwards)	5,000	3,000	5,000				
To Gross Profit	38,000	38,800	38,220				
	2,23,000	2,04,800	2,18,020		2,23,000	2,04,800	2,18,020

Note. The item of freight (outwards) has not been considered in the Trading Account because this item is debited to the Profit and Loss Account :

Percentage of Gross Profit on Sales

$$2022 = \frac{₹\ 38,000}{₹\ 2,00,000} \times 100 = 19\% \qquad 2023 = \frac{₹\ 38,800}{1,94,000} \times 100 = 20\%$$

$$2024 = \frac{₹\ 38,220}{₹\ 1,82,000} \times 100 = 21\%$$

From the above it is evident that ratio of gross profit to sales is increasing by 1% every year, so ratio of gross profit for 2025 can be taken as 22% (*i.e.* 1% more than of 2024). Alternatively, weighted average of gross profits of 2022, 2023 and 2024 can be calculated by assigning weights, 1, 2 and 3 respectively as follows :

Year	*% of Gross Profit*	*Assumed Weights*	*Product of G.P. & Weights*
2022	19	1	19
2023	20	2	40
2024	21	3	63
		6	122

$$\text{Average \% of Gross Profit on Sales} = \frac{122}{6} = 20.33\%$$

MEMORANDUM TRADING ACCOUNT OF P

for the 6 months ending June 30, 2025

	₹		₹
To Opening Stock (at Cost)	36,020	By Sales	26,000
Less : Cost of Slow Moving Item	12,000	*Less* : Sale of Slow Moving Item	6,000
	24,020		20,000
To Purchases	35,000	By Closing Stock (Balancing figure)	44,420
To Freight (Inwards)	1,000		
To Gross Profit (22% on ₹ 20,000)	4,400		
	64,420		64,420

Amount of Claim

	₹
Value of Stock as per Memorandum Trading A/c	44,420
Add : 50% of the cost of slow moving item not yet sold $\left(\frac{50}{100} \times ₹\ 12,000\right)$	6,000
	50,420
Less : Stock salvaged	8,000
Claim to be lodged	42,420

ILLUSTRATION 12. ***(Where value of stock and rate of G.P. is to be calculated).*** On 2nd June, 2025, the stock of Shri Daga was destroyed by fire but sufficient records were saved from which the following particulars were ascertained :

	₹		₹
Stock at cost—1st April, 2024	90,000	Sales—year ended 31st March, 2025	6,00,000
Stock at cost—31st March, 2025		Purchases—1-4-25 to 2-6-25	1,50,000
(at 10% lower than cost)	1,08,000	Sales—1-4-25 to 2-6-25	3,20,000
Purchases—year ended 31st March, 2025	4,30,000		

Sales up to 2nd June, 2025 included ₹ 50,000 for which goods had not been despatched.

Purchases up to 2nd June, 2025 included machinery purchased for ₹ 10,000 and did not included ₹ 20,000 for which purchase invoices had not been received from suppliers though goods have been received at the godown.

The value of stock salvaged from the accident was worth ₹ 15,000 and this was handed over to the insured. Ascertain the amount of claim for loss of stock.

SOLUTION

Working Notes :

(1) ***Ascertainment of the Rate of Gross Profit for the Previous Year*** **:**

	₹	₹
Stock as on 1-4-2024		90,000
Add : Purchases		4,30,000
		5,20,000
Less : Stock as on 31-3-2025	1,08,000	
Adjustment for under valuation $\left(₹\ 1{,}08{,}000 \times \frac{10}{90}\right)$	12,000	
		1,20,000
		4,00,000
Gross Profit (Bal. Fig.)		2,00,000
Sales		6,00,000

Rate of Gross Profit on Sales = $\frac{₹\ 2{,}00{,}000}{₹\ 6{,}00{,}000} \times 100 = \mathbf{33\frac{1}{3}\%}$

(2) ***Ascertainment of Stock on 2nd June, 2025***

	₹	₹
Opening Stock at Cost		1,20,000
Purchases	1,50,000	
Less : Machinery purchased	10,000	
	1,40,000	
Add : Adjustment of Goods received (Invoices not received)	20,000	
		1,60,000
		2,80,000
Less : *Cost of Goods Sold* :		
Sales	3,20,000	
Less : Goods not yet delivered	50,000	
	2,70,000	
Less : Gross Profit $33\frac{1}{3}\%$ on Sales	90,000	
		1,80,000
Value of Stock on 2nd June, 2025		1,00,000

STATEMENT OF INSURANCE CLAIM

	₹
Value of Stock on 2nd June, 2025	1,00,000
Less : Salvage Value	15,000
Insurance Claim	85,000

Consequential Loss or Loss of Profit Insurance

Consequential loss insurance indemnifies the insured any loss of profit suffered by him consequent on the destruction of business properties by fire. An ordinary fire insurance policy covers the loss on account of stock or properties destroyed by fire, but it does not cover loss of profit due to inability to produce or sell on account of fire. Therefore, a separate policy known as consequential loss policy is taken to cover the following losses due to fire :

(*a*) Loss of profit due to inability to produce and sell.

(*b*) Loss of standing (or fixed) charges due to their non-recovery or less recovery because of no production or less production as a result of fire.

(*c*) Increased cost of working as a result of fire such as renting a new business place temporarily for conducting the business operations.

Explanation of Certain Terms

It is desirable to know the meaning of following terms in connection with making claim on loss of profit policies.

(*a*) Gross Profit. It is calculated by adding the amount of insured standing charges to the net profit. In case of net loss, gross profit is the amount of insured standing charges such a proportion of any net trading loss as the amount of the insured standing charges bear to all standing charges (*i.e.* Insured + uninsured) of the business.

(*b*) Net Profit. In order to calculate net profit of the business, due provision should be made for all standing and other charges including depreciation but before any deduction of any taxation chargeable on profits from the net trading profits resulting from business of the insured at the premises.

(*c*) Insured Standing Charges. These charges are specified in the policy. Which the insured desires to recover in case of an accident. Such charges include :

> (*i*) Rent, rates and taxes not related with profits of the business, (*ii*) Interest on debentures and loans, (*iii*) salaries of permanent staff, (*iv*) Wages of skilled workers, (*v*) Directors' fees, (*vi*) Auditor's fees, (*vii*) Advertising, (*viii*) Travelling, and (*ix*) Unspecified standing charges (not exceeding 5% of the amount of specified standing charges).

(*d*) Turnover. The money paid or payable to the insured for goods sold and delivered and for services rendered.

(*e*) Annual Turnover. The turnover during the twelve months immediately preceding the date of the damage.

(*f*) Standard Turnover. The turnover during that period in the twelve months immediately before the date of damage which corresponds with the indemnity period.

(*g*) Rate of Gross Profit. The rate of gross profit earned on the turnover during the financial year immediately before the date of the damage.

(*h*) Indemnity Period. The period beginning with the occurrence of the damage and ending not later than 12 months thereafter during which the results of the business shall be affected in consequence of the damage.

Difference Between Fire Insurance Policy and Loss of Profit Policy

Basis of Distinction	*Fire Insurance Policy*	*Loss of Profit Policy*
1. Coverage	This policy covers loss of or damage to insured property such as building, stock, etc.	This policy covers loss of gross profit sustained in consequent of a business interruption.
2. Subject Matter	The subject matter of this insurance policy is tangible and covers material property.	In this case of insurance policy, it is intangible and covers the earning capacity of the business.

Computation of Claim for Loss of Profit. Following procedure is followed for the calculation of claim for loss of profit :

(1) Calculate short sales by comparing the sales made during the abnormal period in the year of fire with the sales of the same period of the year preceding the year of fire. In this connection, it may be remembered that calculation of short sales is to be made for the period of dislocation due to fire or the period of indemnity for which policy is taken, whichever is less. For example, if the indemnity period is 4 months whereas dislocation of the business takes place for 3 months, the amount of short sales is to be calculated for 3 months. But if dislocation continues for 6 months, the amount of short sales is to be calculated for 4 months because loss on account of short sales beyond the indemnity period will not be allowed by the insurance company.

(2) Calculate rate of gross profit of the financial year preceding the year of fire. Calculation of rate of gross profit for loss of profit policy is different from the normal rate of gross profit as described earlier in this chapter. It is calculated as follows :

$$\text{Rate of Gross Profit} = \frac{\text{Net Profit + Insured Standing Charges}}{\text{Sales of the financial year preceding the year of fire}} \times 100$$

(3) Calculate loss of profit on short sales by applying the rate of gross profit as calculated in step (2).

(4) Add increased cost of working incurred to mitigate the effect of the loss on account of short sales to the loss of profit as calculated in step (3). The claim for increased cost of working is restricted to the lowest of the following amounts :

(*a*) Actual increased working expenses

(*b*) $$\frac{\text{Gross Profit on annual (adjusted) turnover}}{\text{Gross Profit as mentioned above + Standing Charges not insured}} \times \text{Additional Expenses}$$

Some author apply the insured formula.

Or $$\frac{\text{Net Profit (for the last completed year) + Insured Constant Expenses}}{\text{Net Profit + All Constant Expenses}} \times \text{Increased Working Cost}$$

(*c*) Gross profit on sales resulting from the increased working expenses.

(5) Deduct the amount of expenses saved as a result of fire from the total claim as calculated in step (4) and the resultant figure will be the amount of gross claim for loss of profit.

(6) The gross claim as calculated in step (5) is subject to the average clause as follows :

$$\text{Gross Claim} \times \frac{\text{Amount of Policy}}{\text{Gross Profit on 12 months' sales (adjusted) immediately preceding the date of fire}}$$

The figure so calculated will be the amount of claim for loss of profit to be lodged with the insurance company. It may be remembered that the average clause is to be applied only if the amount of the policy is less than the gross profit on the adjusted turnover of 12 months preceding the date of fire. For the calculation of the adjusted turnover, adjustments are made to the turnover of 12 months immediately preceding the date of fire as may be necessary to provide for the trend of the business. For example, if 20% increase in sales is expected in the year of fire, turnover of 12 months immediately preceding the date of fire will be increased by 20% to get the figure of adjusted turnover. Similarly, the amount of short sales will be adjusted if any increase or decrease is to be expected in the year of fire.

EXAMPLE. A trader intends to take a loss of profit policy with indemnity period of 6 months, however, he could not decide the policy amount. From the following details, suggest the policy amount :

	₹
Turnover in last financial year	4,50,000
Standing Charges in last financial year	90,000

Net profit earned in last year was 10% of turnover and the same trend expected in subsequent year.
Increase in turnover expected 25%.
To achieve additional sales, trader has to incur additional expenditure of ₹ 31,250.

SOLUTION

(*a*) **Calculation of Gross Profit**

$$\text{Gross Profit} = \frac{\text{Net Profit + Standing Charges}}{\text{Turnover}} \times 100 = \frac{₹\,45{,}000 + ₹\,90{,}000}{₹\,4{,}50{,}000} \times 100 = 30\%$$

(*b*) **Calculation of policy amount to cover loss of profit**

	₹
Turnover in the last financial year	4,50,000
Add : 25% increase in turnover	1,12,500
	5,62,500
Gross Profit on increased Turnover (5,62,500 × 30%)	1,68,750
Add : Additional Standing Charges	31,250
	2,00,000

Therefore, the trader should go in for a loss of profit policy of ₹ 2,00,000.

ILLUSTRATION 13. (***Claim for Loss of Profit***). On 1st November, 2024 a severe fire broke out in the premises of Ill Luck Co. Ltd. The indemnity period lasted for 4 months during which the sales of the company were reduced to ₹ 2,00,000 only. The company closes its account on 30th June every year. Profit and Loss Account for the year ended 30th June, 2024 is given below :

PROFIT AND LOSS ACCOUNT

for the year ended 30th June, 2024

	₹		₹
Opening Stock	5,00,000	By Sales	47,50,000
Purchases	30,00,000	" Closing Stock	2,50,000
Variable Expenses	7,87,500		
Standing Charges	3,62,500		
Net Profit	3,50,000		
	50,00,000		50,00,000

The company took a loss of profit policy for a sum of ₹ 6,00,000. The sales of the company for the 12 months ending the date of fire were ₹ 50,00,000 and for the 4 months from 1st November, 2020 to 28th February, 2024 were ₹ 15,00,000.

It was noted that the sales for the first four months of the year under indemnity were 20% higher than previous year. Compute the claim for loss of profit.

SOLUTION

Calculation of Amount of Short Sales :	₹
Sales from 1-11-2023 to 28-2-2024	15,00,000
Add : 20% increase expected in the current year	3,00,000
	18,00,000
Less : Sales from 1-11-2024 to 28-2-2025	2,00,000
Short Sales	16,00,000

Calculation of Gross Profit :

$$\frac{\text{Net Profit + Standing Charges}}{\text{Sales}} \times 100$$

$$\frac{₹\,3,50,000 + ₹\,3,62,500}{₹\,47,50,000} \times 100 = \frac{₹\,7,12,500}{₹\,47,50,000} \times 100 = 15\%$$

Gross Profit on sales for the 12 months ending the date of fire :

15% on ₹ 50,00,000 = ₹ 7,50,000

Loss of Profit :

$$15\% \text{ on short sales } \left(i.e., \frac{15}{100} \times ₹\,16,00,000 \right) = ₹\,2,40,000$$

Claim of Loss :

$$\text{Loss of Profit} \times \frac{\text{Amount of Policy}}{\text{Gross Profit on preceding 12 month's adjusted sales}}$$

$$= ₹\,2,40,000 \times \frac{₹\,6,00,000}{15\% \text{ of } ₹\,50,00,000 \times \frac{120}{100}} = ₹\,1,60,000.$$

ILLUSTRATION 14. (*Claim for Loss of Profit*). From the following information, you are required to work out claim under the Loss of Profits insurance policy.

1. Cover—Gross Profit—₹ 1,00,000.
2. Indemnity period—Six months.
3. Damage—due to a fire accident on 28th December—accounting year ends on 31st December.
4. Net Profit plus all standing charges in the prior accounting year—₹ 1,50,000.
5. Standing charges uninsured—₹ 25,000.
6. Turnover of the last accounting year was ₹ 5,00,000, the rate of gross profit being 25%.
7. The annual turnover, namely, the turnover for 12 months immediately preceding the fire—₹ 5,20,000.
8. As a consequence of fire, there was a reduction in certain insured standing charge at the rate of ₹ 25,000 per annum.
9. The standard turnover ₹ 2,60,000.
10. Increased cost of working during the period of indemnity was ₹ 20,000.
11. Turnover during the period of indemnity was ₹ 1,00,000 and out of this turnover of ₹ 80,000 was maintained due to increased cost of working.

SOLUTION

Calculation of Short Sales :

	₹
Standard turnover	2,60,000
Turnover during the indemnity period	1,00,000
Short Sales	1,60,000

Calculation of Rate of Gross Profit

$$\frac{\text{Net profit plus all standing charges − Uninsured standing charges}}{\text{Sales of the last accounting year}} \times 100$$

$$= \frac{₹\,1,50,000 - ₹\,25,000}{₹\,5,00,000} \times 100 = 25\%$$

Amount of Claim

	₹	₹
Loss of profit on short sales of ₹ 1,60,000 @ 25%		40,000
Add : Increased cost of working :		
Actual amount of increased cost	20,000	
Gross profit @ 25% on turnover for 12 months		

immediately preceding the date of fire $\left(₹\,5{,}20{,}000 \times \frac{25}{100}\right)$	1,30,000	
Gross profit as above plus uninsured standing charges (1,30,000 + 25,000)	1,55,000	
Claim for increased cost of working $\left(₹\,20{,}000 \times \frac{1{,}30{,}000}{1{,}55{,}000}\right)$		16,774
[Gross profit @ 25% on additional sales of ₹ 80,000 due to increased cost $\left(\frac{25}{100} \times ₹\,80{,}000\right) = ₹\,20{,}000$ is more than ₹ 16,774, so claim admissible is ₹ 16,774]		
	56.774	56,774
Less : Saving in standing charges for $\frac{1}{2}$ year $\left(₹\,25{,}000 \times \frac{1}{2}\right)$		12,500
		44,274

Application of Average Clause

$$\frac{\text{Sum Insured}}{\text{Gross Profit on preceding 12 month's sales}} \times \text{Amount of Claim}$$

$$= \frac{₹\,1{,}00{,}000}{25\%\text{ of }₹\,5{,}20{,}000} \times ₹\,44{,}274 = \frac{₹\,1{,}00{,}000}{₹\,1{,}30{,}000} \times ₹\,44{,}274 = ₹\,34{,}057.$$

Therefore, claim for loss of profit to be lodged is ₹ 34,057.

ILLUSTRATION 15. (***Claim for Loss of Profit***). A fire occurred on 1st July, 2024, in the premises of Arolite Ltd. and business was practically disorganised upto 30th November, 2024. From the books of account, the following information was extracted :

	₹		₹
Actual turnover from 1st July, 2024 to 30th November, 2024	60,000	Insured standing charges for the last financial year	60,000
Turnover from 1st July, 2023 to 30th November, 2023	2,00,000	Turnover for the last financial year	5,00,000
Net Profit for the last financial year	90,000	Turnover for the year ending 30th June, 2024	5,50,000
Total standing charges for the year	72,000		

The company incurred additional expenses amounting to ₹ 9,000 which reduced the loss in turnover. There was also a saving during the indemnity period of ₹ 2,486.

The company holds a 'loss of profit' policy for ₹ 1,65,000 having an indemnity period for 6 months. There had been a considerable increase in trade and it had been agreed that an adjustment of 20% be made in respect of upward trend in turnover.

Compute claim under "loss of profit insurance" assuming that all sales during the indemnity period are because of additional cost.

SOLUTION

Calculation of Short Sales

	₹
Standard turnover : Sales from 1-7-2023 to 30-11-2023	2,00,000
Add : 20% increase in sales due to upward trend in turnover	40,000
	2,40,000
Less : Sales during the indemnity period, 1st July, 2024 to 30th November, 2024	60,000
Short Sales	1,80,000

Calculation of Rate of Gross Profit

$$\frac{\text{Net profit + Insured standing charges}}{\text{Turnover for the last financial year}} \times 100 = \frac{₹\,90{,}000 + ₹\,60{,}000}{₹\,5{,}00{,}000} \times 100 = 30\%$$

Calculation of Amount of Claim

		₹
Loss of profit on short sales of ₹ 1,80,000 @ 30%		54,000
Add: Additional expenses—Lowest of the following amounts		
	₹	
(*i*) Actual amount of additional expenses	9,000	
(*ii*) Gross profit on additional sales of ₹ 60,000 during the indemnity period @ 30%	18,000	
(*iii*) Gross profit @ 30% on turnover for 12 months immediately preceding the date of fire ₹ 6,60,000 *i.e.,* 30% of (₹ 5,50,000 + 20% increase of ₹ 5,50,000)	1,98,000	
Gross profit as above plus uninsured expenses (₹ 1,98,000 + ₹ 12,000)	2,10,000	

$$\text{Additional expenses} \times \frac{\text{Gross profit}}{\text{Gross profit + Uninsured expenses}}$$

$$₹\,9{,}000 \times \frac{₹\,1{,}98{,}000}{₹\,1{,}98{,}000 + ₹\,12{,}000} = ₹\,8{,}486$$

Therefore, claim for additional expenses is the third figure of ₹ 8,486 because it is the lowest	8,486
	62,486
Less: Saving in expenses	2,486
Amount of claim	60,000

Application of Average Clause

$$\text{Net Claim} = \text{Amount of claim} \times \frac{\text{Sum insured}}{\text{Gross profit on preceding 12 months sales (adjusted)}}$$

$$₹\,60{,}000 \times \frac{₹\,1{,}65{,}000}{₹\,1{,}98{,}000} = ₹\,50{,}000$$

ILLUSTRATION 16. A fire occurred in the premises of M/s Kirti & Co. on 15th December, 2024. The working remained disturbed upto 15th March, 2025 as a result of which sales got adversely affected. The firm had taken out an insurance policy with an average clause against consequential losses for ₹ 2,50,000.

Following details are available from the quarterly sales tax return filed/GST return filed :

Sales	*2021-22* (₹)	*2022-23* (₹)	*2023-24* (₹)	*2024-25* (₹)
From 1st April to 30th June	3,80,000	3,15,000	4,11,900	3,24,000
From 1st July to 30th September	1,86,000	3,92,000	3,86,000	4,42,000
From 1st October to 31st December	3,86,000	4,00,000	4,62,000	3,50,000
From 1st January to 31st March	2,88,000	3,19,000	3,80,000	2,96,000
Total	12,40,000	14,26,000	16,39,900	14,12,000

A period of 3 months (*i.e.* from 16-12-2024 to 15-3-2025) has been agreed upon as indemnity period.

Sales from 16-12-2023 to 31-12-2023	68,000
Sales from 16-12-2024 to 31-12-2-24	Nil
Sales from 16-3-2024 to 31-3-2024	1,20,000
Sales from 16-3-2025 to 31-3-2025	40,000

Net profit was ₹ 2,50,000 and standing charges (all insured) amounted to ₹ 77,980 for the year ending 31st March, 2024.

You are required to calculate the loss of profit claim amount. ***(CA-IPCC Nov., 2022 Modified)***

SOLUTION

Gross Profit Ratio	₹
Net Profit for the year 2023-24	2,50,000
Add : Insured Standing Charges	77,980
Ratio of Gross Profit = $\frac{3,27,980}{16,39,900}$ = 20%	3,27,980

Calculation of Short Sales

Indemnity period : 16-12-2024 to 15-3-2025

Standard sales to be calculated on basis of corresponding period of year 2023-24.

	₹
Sales for period 16-12-2023 to 31-12-2023	68,000
Sales for period 1-1-2024 to 15-3-2024 (Note 1)	2,60,000
Sales for period 16-12-2023 to 15-3-2024	3,28,000
Add : Upward Trend in Sales (15%) (Note 2)	49,200
Standard Sales (adjusted)	3,77,200
Actual Sales of Disorganised period	
Calculation of Sales from 16-12-2024 to 15-3-2025	
Sales for period 16-12-2024 to 31-12-2024	Nil
Sales for 1-1-2025 to 15-3-2025 (₹ 2,96,000 – ₹ 40,000)	2,56,000
Actual Sales	2,56,000
Short Sales (₹ 3,77,200 – ₹ 2,56,000)	1,21,200

Loss of Gross Profit

Short Sales × Gross Profit Ratio = 1,21,200 × 20%	24,240

Application of Average Clause

$$\text{Net Claim} = \text{Gross Claim} \times \frac{\text{Policy Value}}{\text{Gross Profit on Annual Turnover}}$$

$$= 24,240 \times \frac{2,50,000}{3,26,240 \text{ (W.N. 3)}}$$

Amount of Loss of Profit Claim = ₹ 18,575

Working Notes :

1. **Sales for period 1-1-2024 to 15-3-2024**

	₹
Sales for 1 Jan. to 31 March (2023-24) (given)	3,80,000
Less : Sales for 16-3-2024 to 31-3-2024 (given)	(1,20,000)
Sales for Period 1-1-2024 to 15-3-2024	2,60,000

2. **Calculation of Upward Trend in Sales**

	₹
Total Sales in year 2021-22	12,40,000
Increase in Sales in year 2022-23 as compared to 2021-22	1,86,000

$$\% \text{ increase} = \frac{1,86,000\ (14,26,000 - 12,40,000)}{12,40,000} = 15\%$$

Increase in sales in year 2023-24 as compared to year 2022-23

$$\% \text{ increase} = \frac{2,13,900\ (16,39,900 - 14,26,000)}{14,26,000} = 15\%$$

Thus annual percentage increase trend is of 15%

3. **Gross Profit on Annual Turnover**	₹
Sales from 16-12-2023 to 30-12-2024 (adjusted) (68,000 × 1.15)	78,200
1-1-2024 to 31-3-2024 (adjusted (3,80,000 × 1.15)	4,37,000
1-4-2024 to 30-6-2024	3,24,000
1-7-2024 to 30-9-2024	4,42,000
1-10-2024 to 15-12-2024 (3,50,000 – Nil)	3,50,000
Sales for 12 months just before date of fire*	16,31,200
Gross Profit on Adjusted Annual Sales @ 20%	3,26,240

Note : Alternatively, the annual adjusted turnover may be computed as ₹ 17,98,000 (₹ 15,64,000 × 1.15) considering the annual % increase trend for the entire period of last 12 months preceding to the date of fire. In that case, the gross profit on adjusted annual sales @ 20% will be computed as ₹ 3,59,720 and net claim will be computed accordingly.

ILLUSTRATION 17. (*Claim for Loss of Profit/Stock*). The cost structure of All-in-one Ltd. is as under:

Materials 30% ; Labour 20% ; Variable Overheads 20% ; Fixed Overheads 15% ; Net Profit 15%; Sales for 2024 amounted to ₹ 30,00,000.

Future sales are expected to increase by 60% in 2025 and on that basis loss of profit policy was taken on 1-1-2025. All expenses were incurred.

In 2025, opening stock was ₹ 4,00,000. There was fire on 1st September and dislocation continued up to 30th November. During which period sales amounted to ₹ 3,00,000. Sales for the corresponding period in the previous year were ₹ 8,00,000. Though 60% increase was budgeted, actual sales were only 25% higher. Sales in 2025 upto 31st August amounted to ₹ 7,50,000. Purchases during the period were ₹ 5,00,000. There was no opening stock or closing stock of finished goods, cost structure remained same as before. Calculate the insurance claim for (*a*) loss of profit and (*b*) loss of stock.

SOLUTION

(*a*) ***Calculation of Insurance Claim for Loss of Profit***

Net Profit Percentage	15% of Sales	
Fixed Overheads	15% of Sales	
Therefore, Rate of Gross Profit = 15% + 15% = 30%		
		₹
Sales during dislocation period of previous year, *i.e.,* Sales from 1-9-2024 to 30-11-2024		8,00,000
Add : 25% upward trend		2,00,000
		10,00,000
Less : Actual sales during dislocation period of 1-9-2025 to 30-11-2025		3,00,000
Short Sales		7,00,000
Loss of Profit @ 30% on ₹ 7,00,000 Short Sales		2,10,000
Therefore, Claim for Loss of Profit		2,10,000

Average clause need not be applied because loss of profit is fully insured. Loss of profit policy was taken on the basis of 60% expected increase in sales whereas actual sales were higher by 25%.

(*b*) *Calculation of Insurance Claim for Loss of Stock*

	₹
Opening Stock of Materials on 1-1-2025	4,00,000
Add : Purchases during 1-1-2025 to 30-8-2025	5,00,000
	9,00,000
Less : Material consumed @ 30% of sales made during 1-1-2025 to 30-8-2025 (30% of 7,50,000 Sales)	2,25,000
Loss of Stock by Fire	6,75,000
Therefore, Insurance Claim for Loss of Stock	6,75,000

ILLUSTRATION 18. (*Calculation of Amount of Policy*) CCL wants to take up a Loss of profit policy. Turnover during the current year is expected to increase by 20%. The company will avail overdraft facilities from its bank @ 15% interest to boost up the sales. The average daily overdraft balance will be around ₹ 3 lakh. All other fixed expenses will remain same. Following further details are also available from the previous year's account :

Total Variable Expenses ₹ 24,00,000 ; Fixed Expenses : Salaries ₹ 3,30,000 ; Rent, Rates and Taxes ₹ 30,000 ; Travelling Expenses ₹ 50,000 ; Postage, Telegram, Telephone ₹ 60,000 ; Directors' Fees ₹ 10,000 ; Audit Fees ₹ 20,000 ; Miscellaneous Income ₹ 70,000 ; Net Profit ₹ 4,20,000

Determine the amount of policy to be taken for the current year.

SOLUTION

CALCULATION OF GROSS PROFIT OF THE PREVIOUS YEAR

		₹
Net Profit		4,20,000
Less : Miscellaneous Income		70,000
Operating Profit		3,50,000
Add : Fixed Expenses :	₹	
Salaries	3,30,000	
Rent, Rates & Taxes	30,000	
Travelling Expenses	50,000	
Postage, Telegram & Telephone	60,000	
Directors' Fees	10,000	
Audit Fees	20,000	
		5,00,000
Gross Profit		8,50,000

DETERMINATION OF THE AMOUNT OF THE POLICY

	₹
Gross Profit on the basis of last year's sales	8,50,000
Add : Increase in Gross Profit because of 20% Expected Increase in Sales	1,70,000
Expected Gross Profit in the current year	10,20,000
Add : Increased standing charges to be covered : 15% of ₹ 3,00,000 overdraft facilities	45,000
Policy to be taken for the Current year	10,65,000

ILLUSTRATION 19. (*Claim for Loss of Profit*). A loss of profit policy was taken for ₹ 80,000. Fire occurred on 15th March, 2025. Indemnity period was for three months. Net profit for 2024 year ending on 31st December was ₹ 56,000 and standing charges (all insured) amounted to ₹ 49,600. Determine insurance claims from the following details available from quarterly sales tax returns :

Sales	*2022*	*2023*	*2024*	*2025*
	₹	₹	₹	₹
From Ist January to 31st March	1,20,000	1,30,000	1,42,000	1,30,000
From 1st April to 30th June	80,000	90,000	1,00,000	40,000
From 1st July to 30th September	1,00,000	1,10,000	1,20,000	1,00,000
From 1st October to 31st December	1,36,000	1,50,000	1,66,000	1,60,000
Total Sales	4,36,000	4,80,000	5,28,000	4,30,000

Sales from 16-3-2024 to 31-3-2024 were ₹ 28,000.
Sales from 16-3-2025 to 31-3-2025 were ₹ Nil.
Sales from 16-6-2024 to 30-6-2024 were ₹ 24,000, and
Sales from 16-6-2025 to 30-6-2025 were ₹ 6,000.

SOLUTION

Calculation of Short Sales.

Short sales are to be calculated for indemnity period of 3 months from the date of fire *i.e.* from 16-3-2025 to 15-6-2025.

				₹
	Sales for the period from 16-3-2024 to 31-3-2024			28,000
			₹	
Add :	Sales for the period from 1-4-2024 to 30-6-2024		1,00,000	
Less :	Sales from 16-6-2024 to 30-6-2024		24,000	
				76,000
				1,04,000
Add :	Increase in % of sales noticed *i.e.* 10% (Calculation shown below)			10,400
	Expected Sales from 16-3-2024 to 15-6-2024			1,14,400
Less :	Sales from 16-3-2025 to 15-6-2025 :			
	Sales from 16-3-2025 to 31-3-2025		Nil	
	Sales from 1-4-2025 to 30-6-2025	₹ 40,000		
Less :	Sales from 16-6-2025 to 30-6-2025	₹ 6,000		
			34,000	
				34,000
	Short Sales for the Indemnity Period			80,400

		₹
	10% increase in sales has been noticed as calculated below :	
	Sales for the year 2023	4,80,000
Less :	Sales for the year 2022	4,36,000
	Increase in sales in 2023 as compared to 2022	44,000

$$\% \text{ Increase} = \frac{₹\ 44{,}000}{₹\ 4{,}36{,}000} \times 100 = 10\% \text{ Approx.}$$

		₹
	Sales for the year 2024	5,28,000
Less :	Sales for the year 2023	4,80,000
	Increase in sales 2024 as compared to 2023	48,000

$$\% \text{ Increase} = \frac{₹\ 48{,}000}{₹\ 4{,}80{,}000} \times 100 = 10\%$$

$$\text{Average \% Increase} = \frac{10\% + 10\%}{2} = 10\%$$

Calculation of Gross Profit Ratio for the year 2024

$$= \frac{\text{Net Profit + Standing Charges}}{\text{Sales for 2024}} \times 100 = \frac{₹\ 56{,}000 + ₹\ 49{,}600}{₹\ 5{,}28{,}000} \times 100 = 20\%$$

Loss of Profit on Short Sales = Short Sales × Gross Profit Ratio
= ₹ 80,400 × 20% = ₹ 16,080

Calculation of Adjusted Sales for the period of 12 months ending on 15-3-2025 i.e. the date of fire.

		₹
	Sales from 16-3-2024 to 31-3-2024	28,000
Add :	Sales from 1-4-2024 to 30-6-2024	1,00,000

	Sales from 1-7-2024 to 30-9-2024		1,20,000
	Sales from 1-10-2024 to 31-12-2024		1,66,000
	Sales from 1-1-2025 to 31-3-2025	₹ 1,30,000	
Less :	Sales from 16-3-2025 to 31-3-2025	Nil	
			1,30,000
	Sales for 12 months from 16-3-2024 to 15-3-2025		5,44,000
Add :	10% increase expected		54,400
	Adjusted sales for 12 months preceding the date of fire		5,98,400

Gross Profit on Adjusted Sales @ 20% = $₹\ 5,98,400 \times \frac{20}{100} = ₹\ 1,19,680$

Calculation of Amount of Claim by Application of Average Clause

$$\text{Claim} = \text{Loss of Profit on Short Sales} \times \frac{\text{Amount of Policy}}{\text{Gross Profit on Adjusted Sales of 12 months preceding the date of fire}}$$

$$= ₹\ 16,080 \times \frac{₹\ 80,000}{₹\ 1,19,680} = ₹\ 10,749$$

ILLUSTRATION 20. ***(Claim for Loss of Stock/Profit).*** S & M Ltd. give the following Trading and Profit and Loss Account for the year ended 31st December, 2024 :

TRADING AND PROFIT AND LOSS ACCOUNT

for the year ended 31st December, 2024

	₹		₹
To Opening Stock	50,000	By Sales	8,00,000
" Purchases	3,00,000	" Closing Stock	70,000
" Wages (₹ 20,000 for skilled labour)	1,60,000		
" Manufacturing Expenses	1,20,000		
" Gross Profit	2,40,000		
	8,70,000		8,70,000
" Office Administrative Expenses	60,000	" Gross Profit	2,40,000
" Advertising	20,000		
To Selling Expenses (fixed)	40,000		
" Commission on Sales	48,000		
" Carriage Outward	16,000		
" Net Profit	56,000		
	2,40,000		2,40,000

The company had taken out policies both against loss of stock and against loss of profit, the amounts being ₹ 80,000 and ₹ 1,72,000. Fire occurred on 1st May, 2025 and as a result of which sales were seriously affected for the period of 4 months. You are given the following further information :

(*a*) Purchases, wages and other manufacturing expenses for the first 4 months of 2025 were ₹ 1,00,000, ₹ 50,000 and ₹ 36,000 respectively.

(*b*) Sales for the same period were ₹ 2,40,000.

(*c*) Other sales figures were as follows :

From 1st January 2024 to 30th April 2024 ₹ 3,00,000 ; From 1st May 2024 to 31st August 2024 ₹ 3,60,000 ; From 1st May 2025 to 31st August 2025 ₹ 60,000.

(*d*) Due to rise in wages, net profit during 2025 was expected to decline by 2% on sales.

(*e*) Additional expenses incurred during the period after fire amounted to ₹ 1,40,000. The amount of the policy included ₹ 1,20,000 for expenses leaving ₹ 20,000 uncovered. Ascertain the claim for stock and for loss of profit.

All workings should form part of your answer.

SOLUTION

Calculation of Amount of claim for Loss of Stock

$$\text{Rate of Gross Profit in 2024} = \frac{\text{Gross Profit for 2024}}{\text{Sales for 2024}} \times 100 = \frac{₹\,2,40,000}{₹\,8,00,000} \times 100 = 30\%$$

In 2025, gross profit and net profit is expected to decline by 2% because of rise in wages, hence the rate of gross profit in 2025 will be 28% (*i.e.,* 30% – 2%).

MEMORANDUM TRADING ACCOUNT

for 4 months ending 1st May, 2025

	₹		₹
To Opening Stock on 1-1-2025	70,000	By Sales	2,40,000
" Purchases	1,00,000	By Closing Stock (Balancing	
" Wages	50,000	figure)	83,200
" Manufacturing Expenses	36,000	(*i.e.,* Stock destroyed by fire)	
" Gross Profit (28% on Sales)	67,200		
	3,23,200		3,23,200

Value of stock destroyed by fire is ₹ 83,200 but claim for loss of stock will be limited to ₹ 80,000 which is the amount of insurance policy.

Calculation of Loss of Profit

	₹
(*i*) *Short Sales*	
Sales from May 1, 2024 to August 31, 2024	3,60,000
Less : 20% decline observed in 2025 over 2024 (Jan. 1, 2025 to April 30, 2025 ₹ 2,40,000 instead of ₹ 3,00,000 for the same period in 2024 : % decline in sales in 2025 = $\frac{₹\,60,000}{₹\,3,00,000} \times 100 = 20\%$)	72,000 (20% 3,60,000)
Turnover expected during dislocation period	2,88,000
Less : Actual sales from May 1, 2025 to August 31, 2025	60,000
Short Sales	2,28,000

(*ii*) *Gross Profit Ratio*

$$\frac{\text{Net Profit (2024) + Insured Standing Charges}}{\text{Sales (2024)}}$$

$$= \frac{₹\,56,000 + ₹\,1,20,000}{₹\,8,00,000} \times 100 \qquad = 22\%$$

Less : Expected decrease due to increase in wages = 2%

Gross Profit Ratio 20%

(*iii*) *Loss of Gross Profit on Short Sales*

20% of ₹ 2,28,000 Short Sales ₹ 45,600

(*iv*) ***Calculation of Preceding 12 months' Adjusted Sales***

	₹
Sales for the year 2024 (Jan. 1 to Dec. 31)	8,00,000
Less : Sales from 1-1-2024 to 30-4-2024	3,00,000
Sales from May 1, 2024 to Dec. 31, 2024	5,00,000
Add : Sales from Jan. 1, 2025 to April 30, 2025	2,40,000
Sales from 1-5-2024 to 30-4-2025	7,40,000
Less : 20% Reduction	1,48,000
Adjusted sales for 12 months' preceding the date of fire	5,92,000

(*v*) ***Calculation of Amount Allowable for Additional Expenses***

Lowest of the following amounts :

(*a*) Actual expenses ₹ 1,40,000

(*b*) Gross profit @ 20% on actual sales of ₹ 60,000 during the indemnity period ₹ 12,000

(*c*) Additional expenses $\times \frac{\text{Gross profit on adjusted sales}}{\text{Gross profit + Uninsured expenses as above}}$

$$₹\ 1,40,000 \times \frac{20\% \text{ of } ₹\ 5,92,000}{20\% \text{ of } ₹\ 5,92,000 + ₹\ 20,000}$$

$$₹\ 1,40,000 \times \frac{₹\ 1,18,400}{₹\ 1,38,400} = \qquad ₹\ 1,19,769$$

Lowest of the above three figures is ₹ 12,000, so claim allowable for additional expenses is for ₹ 12,000.

(*vi*) *Calculation of Amount of Claim for Loss of Profit*

	₹
Gross profit on short sales as calculated in (*iii*)	45,600
Add : Additional expenses allowable	12,000
Amount of claim	57,600

Note. Average clause will not apply on the amount of claim because the amount of the policy ₹ 1,72,000 against loss of profit is higher than the gross profit of ₹ 1,18,400 on adjusted annual sales of ₹ 5,92,000.

ILLUSTRATION 21. (*Claim for Loss of Profit*). Stores Ltd. which runs a shop makes up its accounts annually to 31st January. For the year ended 31st January, 2023, the Profit and Loss Account was summarised as under :

	₹	₹
Sales		21,60,000
Less : Cost of Sales (not after discount received)	9,38,400	
Wages	4,80,000	
		14,18,400
Gross Profit		7,41,600
Less : Fixed Charges (including shop assistants salary)		5,41,600
Net Profit		2,00,000

On 1st October, 2023, a fire occurred as a result of which no trading was possible till February 1, 2024. On that date half the shop was reopened for business, the other half reopened on 1st April, 2024. The Consequential Loss Policy covered gross profit and workroom wages and accountancy charges at ₹ 5,000 or 2% of the amount of the claim before such charges whichever is greater. The insurers agreed that :

(1) Turnover increased by 15% p.a. (2) Workroom wages increased by 10% p.a. (3) The period 1st Oct. to 31st Dec. accounts for one half of the annual turnover. (4) Fixed charges and wages occur evenly throughout the year. (5) Discounts received equal 1% of turnover.

You are required to compute the consequential loss claim.

SOLUTION

Calculation of Rate of Gross Profit

		₹	₹	₹
	Sales			21,60,000
Less :	Cost of Sales	9,38,400		
Add :	Discount @ 1% on Sales	21,600		
			9,60,000	
	Wages		4,80,000	
				14,40,000
	Gross Profit			7,20,000

Rate of Gross Profit on Sales = $\frac{₹\,7,20,000}{₹\,21,60,000} \times 100 = 33\frac{1}{3}\%$

Calculation of Short Sales

		₹
Sales (last financial year)		21,60,000
Add : 15% increase expected		3,24,000
Expected Annual Sales for 2023-24		24,84,000
		₹
Sales from 1-10-2023 to 31-12-2023 $\left(\frac{1}{2}\text{ of annual sales}\right)$		12,42,000
Sales for the month of January 2024 $\left(\frac{1}{9}\text{ of remaining 9 months' sales } \textit{i.e.} \frac{1}{9}\text{ of ₹ 12,42,000}\right)$		1,38,000
Add : Sales for 2 months of Feb. 2024 and March 2024 :		
Annual sales for the year ending on 31st January, 2024	₹	
as calculated above	24,84,000	
Add : 15% increase expected $\left(\frac{15}{100} \times ₹\,24,84,000\right)$	3,72,600	
Expected turnover for 2024-25	28,56,600	
Turnover for 3 months of October 2024 to Dec. 2024 $\left(\frac{1}{2} \times ₹\,28,56,600\right)$	14,28,300	
Turnover for remaining 9 months	14,28,300	
Therefore, expected sales for 2 months of Feb. 2024 and March 2024 for half the shop opened $\left(\frac{1}{2} \times \frac{₹\,14,28,300}{9} \times 2\right)$		1,58,700
Loss of sales or short sales for the dislocation period of October 1, 2023 to March 31, 2024		15,38,700

Calculation of Loss of Profit

		₹
Gross Profit @ $33\frac{1}{3}\%$ on short sales $\left(33\frac{1}{3}\%\text{ of } 15,38,700\right)$		5,12,900
Add : Discount @ 1% on ₹ 15,38,700		15,387
Add : Workroom wages from 1st October 2023 to 31st January 2024 :	₹	
Annual wages for 2022-23	4,80,000	
Add : 10% increase expected	48,000	
Annual wages for 2023-24	5,28,000	

Therefore, wages for 4 months from 1st October, 2023 to 31st January, 2024 $\left(₹\,5,28,000 \times \frac{4}{12}\right)$		1,76,000
Add : Workroom wages for 2 months from Feb. 1, 2024 to March 31, 2024 falling in the next financial year ending 31st January, 2025	₹	
Wages for the financial year 2023-24 as calculated above	5,28,000	
Add : Expected increase @ 10%	52,800	
Expected wages for 2024-25	5,80,800	
Therefore, wages for 2 months of Feb. 1, 2024 to March 31, 2024 belonging to the financial year of 2024-25 for half shop not reopened $\left(₹\,5,80,800 \times \frac{2}{12} \times \frac{1}{2}\right)$		48,400
		7,52,687
Add : Accounting charges ₹ 5,000 or 2% of above, whichever is greater *i.e.* 2% of ₹ 7,52,687		15,054
Amount of Consequential Loss Claim		7,67,741

ILLUSTRATION 22. (*Claim for Loss of Stock/Profit*). Bherumal has a small plastic goods factory. His sales mark up uniformly, is :

	% of selling price
Ex-factory cost	$33\frac{1}{3}$
Administration, etc. (all insured)	$16\frac{2}{3}$
Advertising and sales promotion	$33\frac{1}{3}$
Net profit	$16\frac{2}{3}$
	100

His selling expenditure is strictly incurred on the basis of sales and no part of it is fixed. He closes his accounts on March 31 each year.

A fire took place in his premises on June 30, 2025 which destroyed the stock of finished goods completely and also dislocated his business for the next three months. Earlier he had insured against fire, both in respect of stock of goods as well as in respect of loss of profits, the latter providing for indemnity as per usual method of calculation. All his records were also destroyed by fire ; but he could ascertain from the office file of his income tax and sales tax adviser that his stock of finished goods on March 31, 2025 was ₹ 25,000, and that his turnover figures were as below :

Period		*Sales*	*Purchases*
		₹	₹
April-June	30, 2024	12,000	
July-Sept.	30, 2024	15,000	
Oct.-Dec.	31, 2024	9,000	
Jan.-March	31, 2025	18,000	
April	30, 2025	11,000	7,000
May	31, 2025	8,000	4,000

He estimates that his turnover of sale and purchases for the month of June, 2025 would be the same as the figure for the preceding month.

His turnover of sales for the quarter ended September 30, 2025 was nil and his normal operations could be commenced from October 1, 2025. He estimated that the item of factory cost during the three months ended June 30, 2025 excluding consumption of raw materials would be ₹ 2,000. The loss of profit was in the sum of ₹ 30,000.

Show a statement showing the claim to be submitted in respect of **loss of stock and loss of profits** including in detail the basis for calculations.

SOLUTION

Statement Showing Loss of Stock

	₹	₹
Opening stock on April 1, 2025 (*i.e.*, stock on 31st March, 2025)		25,000
Add : Purchases from April 1, 2025 to June 30, 2025 :		
April 30, 2025	7,000	
May 31, 2025	4,000	
June 30, 2025 (same as in May 2025)	4,000	
		15,000
		40,000
Less : Cost of goods sold :		
Sales during April 1, 2025 to June 30, 2025		
April 30, 2025	11,000	
May 31, 2025	8,000	
June 30, 2025 (same as in May 2025)	8,000	
	27,000	
Less : Gross Profit @ $66\frac{2}{3}\%$	18,000	
		9,000
Claim to be submitted in respect of loss of stock		31,000

Calculation of Claim for Loss of Profit

(1) ***Calculation of trend of sales***

	₹	
Sales of the immediately preceding 3 months from the date of fire		
April 2025	11,000	
May 2025	8,000	
June 2025	8,000	
		27,000
Less : Sales of the corresponding period in 2024, *i.e.*, sales for the quarter June 30, 2024		12,000
Increase in sales during 2025		15,000
Rate of increase in sales $\left(\frac{₹\,15{,}000}{₹\,12{,}000} \times 100\right)$		125%

(2) ***Calculation of short sales***

	₹
Sales during the dislocation period of the previous year, *i.e.*, June 30, 2024 to September 30, 2024	15,000
Add : Increase in sales at 125% as calculated in (1) above	18,750
Expected sales during the dislocation period	33,750
Less : Actual sales during the dislocation period	Nil
Short Sales	33,750

(3) ***Calculation of rate of gross profit***

Net profit + Insured Administration expenses

$16\frac{2}{3}\% + 16\frac{2}{3}\% = 33\frac{1}{3}\%$

(4) Calculation of loss of profit on short sales

$33\frac{1}{3}$% of short sales (*i.e.*, $33\frac{1}{3}$% of ₹ 33,750) ₹ 11,250

(5) Calculation of preceding 12 month's adjusted sales

	₹
Sales of 3 months ending September 30, 2024	15,000
Sales of 3 months ending December 31, 2024	9,000
Sales of 3 months ending March 31, 2025	18,000
Total Sales of 9 months	42,000
Add : Expected increase @ 125% in sales $\left(₹ 42,000 \times \frac{125}{100}\right)$	52,500
	94,500
Add : Sales of the next 3 months (April 1, 2025 to June 30, 2025)	27,000
Total sales of 12 months immediately preceding the date of fire	1,21,500

(5) Calculation of amount of claim for loss of profit

$$\frac{\text{Amount of Policy}}{\text{Loss of profit on preceding 12 months' adjusted sales}} \times \text{Loss of profit on short sales}$$

$$= \frac{₹ 30,000}{33\frac{1}{3}\% \text{ of } ₹ 1,21,500} \times ₹ 11,250 = ₹ 8,333.$$

ILLUSTRATION 23. A furniture firm maintained books of account on cash basis. Fire occurred on 30th June, 2025 in the premises of the firm destroying portion of stock and records. However, the following data are available :

	Rupees in lakhs	
Year	*2023*	*2024*
Sales	20	40
Purchases	16	24
Stock at Start at Cost	—	4
Stock at Close at Cost	4	5
Bills Payable not recorded at year end	2	3
Bills Receivables not recorded at year end	5	4

Transactions of the firm for the period from 1-1-2025 to 30-6-2025 were as follows :

Sales 25 lakhs. Purchases ₹ 14 lakhs. Bills payable not recorded as at 30th June, 2025—₹ 3 lakhs. Bills receivables not recorded as at 30th June, 2025—₹ 5 lakhs.

You are informed that the firm used to include collection charges of repairs and cost of repairs (rate of markup is cost plus 50%) in the sales and purchases respectively. Collection of repairs charges were as follows :

Year, 2023	₹ 3 lakhs
Year, 2024	₹ 6 lakhs
For the period from 1-1-2025 to 30-6-2025	₹ 6 lakhs

It is agreed with the insurer that the results of the operations for the period from 1-1-2025 to 30-6-2025 should be based on the average of the gross profit ratio of the calendar year 2023 and 2024. Firm's stock was insured for ₹ 2 lakhs and the policy contains 60% co-insurance clause. Stock salvaged is agreed at ₹ 48,000.

From the data given, calculate : (*a*) Correct amount of sales for the years 2023 and 2024 respectively; (*b*) Correct amount of purchases for the year 2023 and 2024 respectively; (*c*) Gross profit for the above two years respectively; (*d*) Average of the gross profit ratios; (*e*) Correct amount of sale and purchases for the period from 1-1-2025 to 30-6-2025; (*f*) Working to show the value of stock lost in fire; (*g*) The amount of claim for loss of stock. ***(ICWA—Stage II)***

SOLUTION

(*a*) *Correct Amount of sales* (₹ *in lakhs*)

	2023	2024
Sales as given	20	40
Add : Bills Receivable not Recorded at year end	5	4
	25	44
Less : B/R Not Recorded at the beginning of the year	—	5
	25	39
Less : Repair Collections	3	6
	22	33

(*b*) *Correct Amount of Purchases*

	2023	2024
Purchases as given	16	24
Add : Bills Payable not Recorded at year end	2	3
	18	27
Less : B/P not Recorded at beginning of the year	—	2
	18	25
Less : Cost of Repairs included in Purchases	*2	*4
	16	21

$* 3 \times \frac{2}{3} = 2; 6 \times \frac{2}{3} = 4$

(*c*) ***Gross Profit Earned***

		2023	2024
Sales	(A)	22	33
Less : Cost of Sales :			
Opening Stock		–	4
Purchases		16	21
		16	25
Less : Closing Stock		4	5
	(B)	12	20
Gross Profit (A) – (B)		**10**	**13**
Gross Profit Ratio		45.45%	39.39%

(*d*) **Average Gross Profit** $\frac{45.45\% + 39.39\%}{2} = 42.42\%$

(*e*) (*i*) ***Correct Amount of Sales for the Current Period***

	₹ *in lakhs*
Sales as given	25
Add : B/R as on 30-6-2025 Unrecorded	5
	30
Less : BRS on 1-1-2025 Unrecorded	4
	26
Less : Repair Collections	6
	20

(ii) Correct Amount of Purchases for the Current Period

	₹ in lakhs
Purchases as given	14
Add : B/P on 30-6-2025 Unrecorded	3
	17
Less : B/P on 1-1-2025	3
	14
Less : Cost of Repairs $6 \times \frac{2}{3} =$	4
	10

(f) ***TRADING ACCOUNT** **(₹ in lakhs)**

	₹		₹
To Opening Stock	5	By Sales	20
Add : Purchases	10	Closing Stock (Balancing Fig.)	3.48
	15		
To Gross Profit at 42.42%	8.48		
	23.48		23.48

*This can be given in statement form if the student prefers.

	₹ in lakhs
Closing Stock as at 30-6-2025	3.48
Less : Value of Stock Salvaged	0.48
Loss of Stock	3.00

(g) Amount of Claim

60% of ₹ 3.48 lakhs = 2.09 (Rounded off)

Claim ₹ 3 lakhs × $\frac{2}{2.09}$ = ₹ 2.87 lakhs.

Accounting Entries for Fire Claims

1. On admission of the fire claim :

(a) If the claim relates to loss of stock :

Stock losses can be of two types, namely, (1) loss on account of stock destroyed—where goods are totally lost ; and (2) loss on account of stock damaged—when goods are not totally lost but may be damaged to some extent by fire. The entry for the claim admitted in case of stock is :

(i) Insurance Company Dr.

To Stock Destroyed Account

To Stock Damaged Account

(Being entry for the claim admitted for stock destroyed and stock damaged)

(ii) Entry for the actual cost of stock lost is :

Stock Destroyed Account Dr.

Stock Damaged Account Dr.

To Trading Account

(Being cost of stock destroyed and damaged transferred to Trading Account)

(*iii*) Entry for the sale of damaged goods :
Bank Account Dr.
To Stock Damaged Account
(Being amount realised on sale of damaged stock)

(*iv*) Difference of Stock Destroyed Account and Stock Damaged Account being loss or profit is transferred to Profit and Loss Account.

2. On admission of claim for loss of profit :
Insurance Company Account Dr.
To Profit and Loss Account (Amount of loss of profit relating to current year)
To Profit and Loss Suspense Account
(Amount of loss of profit pertaining to next year)

On receipt of money relating to loss of profit claim :
Bank Account Dr.
To Insurance Company

3. On admission of claim relating to fixed assets :
Insurance Company Account
To Fixed Assets
(Being claim admitted by the insurance company for fixed assets destroyed by fire)

Difference in book value of fixed assets, claim admitted in relation thereto being loss or profit transferred to Profit & Loss Account.

ILLUSTRATION 24. A fire occurred on 21st May, 2024 in the factory of Messrs Bombay Steel Traders. Following particulars are obtained as regards the costs and book values of various assets affected by fire, the amounts claimed and admitted by the Yoga Kshema Insurance Company Limited.

	Book value	*Claimed*	*Admitted*
	₹	₹	₹
Buildings	50,000	60,000	45,000
Plant and machinery	70,000	75,000	60,000
Fittings	12,000	15,000	13,500
Stock damaged	28,000	30,000	17,000
Stock destroyed	45,000	50,000	40,000
Loss of profit	—	55,000	37,000
Fire expenses	—	1,200	1,200

The buildings, plant and machinery and fittings were completely destroyed by fire and most of the stock lying in a godown adjacent to the factory was also destroyed. The damaged goods saved were sold for ₹ 13,000. The claim admitted for loss of profit was ₹ 9,000 in respect of the profit for the remaining portion of the year ended 30th September, 2024 and ₹ 28,000 for six months thereafter when a new factory was built. The actual fire expenses incurred were ₹ 1,200. The insurance company paid the amount for all claims on 27th September, 2024.

Make journal entries in the books of Messrs. Bombay Steel Traders to record the above particulars including the cash book entries.

SOLUTION

BOOKS OF MESSRS BOMBAY STEEL TRADERS
JOURNAL ENTRIES

				₹	₹
	Yoga Kshema Insurance Company	Dr.		2,13,700	
	To Buildings A/c				45,000
	" Plant and Machinery A/c				60,000
	" Fittings A/c				13,500
	" Stock Damaged A/c				17,000

To Stock Destroyed A/c " Profit and Loss A/c " Profit and Loss Suspense A/c " Fire Expenses A/c (Being various claims admitted by the insurance company)			40,000 9,000 28,000 1,200
Stock Damaged A/c Dr. Stock Destroyed A/c Dr. To Trading A/c [Being book value of stock damaged and stock destroyed credited to Trading A/c]		28,000 45,000	73,000
Bank A/c Dr. To Stock Damaged Account (Being sale of damaged goods)		13,000	13,000
Stock damaged A/c Dr. To Profit and Loss A/c (Being balance of damaged goods transferred to Profit and Loss A/c)		2,000	2,000
Profit and Loss A/c Dr. To Stock Destroyed A/c [Being balance of stock destroyed (*i.e.*, less claim admitted) transferred to Profit and Loss A/c]		5,000	5,000
Profit and Loss A/c Dr. To Building A/c " Plant and Machinery A/c (Being difference between book value and claim admitted transferred to Profit and Loss A/c)		15,000	5,000 10,000
Fittings A/c Dr. To Profit and Loss A/c (Being difference between book value and claim admitted being profit credited to Profit and Loss A/c)		1,500	1,500
Fire Expenses A/c Dr. To Bank (Being payment of fire expenses)		1,200	1,200
Bank A/c Dr. To Yoga Kshema Insurance Company A/c (Being receipt of various claims admitted by the insurance company on account of loss by fire)		2,13,700	2,13,700

Profit and Loss Suspense Account relating to claim for loss of profit for the next year will be credited to Profit and Loss Account in the next year.

ILLUSTRATION 25. Bijlee Ltd. is a manufacturing company. The Balance Sheet of the company as on 31st March, 2024, included the following assets :

	₹	₹
Fixed Assets :		
Freehold Factory at cost		2,50,000
Plant at Cost	1,40,000	
Less : Accumulated Depreciation	40,000	
		1,00,000

Current Assets :

Stock	1,85,000

These assets were insured for the following sums :

Factory Buildings	3,00,000
Plant	1,60,000
Stock	1,60,000

On 30th June, 2024, the factory and its contents, which included the above items, were totally destroyed by fire, apart from the stock salvaged. Following bases were agreed with the insurance company :

	₹
Factory Building	2,80,000
Plant	1,50,000
Stock (subject to average)	2,40,000

The total stock at the date of the fire was valued at ₹ 3,00,000 of which ₹ 60,000 was salvaged. The claim was paid on 30th September, 2024.

The freehold land was estimated by the Directors to have cost ₹ 40,000 out of the total cost of land and buildings of ₹ 2,50,000.

Record the foregoing in the books of the company and show how these would be disclosed in the accounts of the company for the year ended 31st March, 2025.

SOLUTION

(1) ***Amount transferred to Capital Reserve***

As the amount of insurance claim admitted in connection with factory building and plant is more than their purchase price, the excess amount is credited to capital reserve being capital profit. It is calculated as follows :

	₹	₹
Insurance claims for factory building		2,80,000
Less : Cost value of factory building :		
Freehold factory at cost	2,50,000	
Less : Value of land included in cost of freehold factory as estimated by the Directors	40,000	
		2,10,000
		70,000
Capital profit on factory building		
Add : Capital profit on plant :		
Insurance claim admitted for plant	1,50,000	
Less : Plant at cost	1,40,000	
		10,000
Total Capital Reserve		80,000

(2) *Amount transferred to General Reserve*

As insurance claim admitted for plant is more than the purchase price of the plant, provision for depreciation on plant, ₹ 40,000, is no longer required and is transferred to general reserve.

(3) ***Loss on Stock destroyed by fire and not covered by insurance***

	₹
Value of stock on the date of the fire	3,00,000
Less : Stock salvaged	60,000
Loss of stock by fire	2,40,000

Loss of stock by fire is subjected to the average clause because stock is under insured :

$$\text{Insurance claim} = \text{Loss of stock} \times \frac{\text{Value of policy of stock}}{\text{Value of stock on the date of fire}}$$

$$= ₹\ 2,40,000 \times \frac{₹\ 1,60,000}{₹\ 3,00,000} = ₹\ 1,28,000$$

	₹
Loss of stock by fire	2,40,000
Less : Insurance claim	1,28,000
Loss of stock not covered by insurance	1,12,000

JOURNAL ENTRIES

Date	Particulars		L.F.	₹	₹
2024 Sept. 30	Insurance Company Account	Dr.		5,58,000	
	To insurance Claim Account				5,58,000
	(Being claim admitted by the insurance company for loss arising from destruction by fire : Factory Buildings ₹ 2,80,000 ; Plant ₹ 1,50,000 and Stock ₹ 1,28,000)				
Sept. 30	Bank Account	Dr.		5,58,000	
	To Insurance Company Account				5,58,000
	(Being receipt of insurance claim)				
2025 Mar. 31	Freehold Land Account	Dr.		40,000	
	Insurance Claim Account	Dr.		2,80,000	
	To Freehold Factory Account				2,50,000
	To Capital Reserve Account				70,000
	(Being transfer of cost of land to Land Account and excess of insurance claim admitted over purchase price of factory building to Capital Reserve)				
Mar. 31	Insurance Claim Account	Dr.		1,50,000	
	Provision for Depreciation on Plant Account	Dr.		40,000	
	To Plant Account				1,40,000
	To Capital Reserve Account				10,000
	To General Reserve Account				40,000
	(Being excess of insurance claim admitted over original cost of plant transferred to Capital Reserve and provision for Depreciation no longer required transferred to General Reserve)				
Mar. 31	Insurance Claim Account	Dr.		1,28,000	
	Profit and Loss Account	Dr.		1,12,000	
	To Trading Account				2,40,000
	(Being total value of stock destroyed by fire transferred to Trading Account and loss of stock not covered by insurance transferred to Profit & Loss Account)				

Workmen's Compensation Insurance

An employer can get an insurance policy to cover his liability to his workmen who suffer injuries when they work in the organisation. In case of such a policy, insurance premiums are based on total wages paid. But premiums are paid in advance before actual wages become payable. Therefore, premiums paid in advance are calculated on the previous year's wages subject to adjustment when actual figures for current year's wages are available. When premium is paid, it is debited to Workmen's Compensation Insurance Suspense Account. At the end of the year, the insured will calculate the exact premium due on the basis of actual wages for the period and will debit Workmen's Compensation Insurance Account and credit Workmen's Compensation Insurance Suspense Account. The balance in Workmen's Suspense Account will be carried forward for adjustment in cash. All this has been made clear in the illustration given below :

ILLUSTRATION 26. Fairdeal Ltd. has taken a Workmen's Compensation Policy on 1st October, 2023 at a premium of 2% on wages. Give the necessary journal entries on the basis of following particulars :

(1)	Wages from 1st October, 2022 to 30th September, 2023	48,00,000
(2)	Wages from 1st October, 2023 to 31st March, 2024 (year end)	28,00,000
(3)	Wages from 1st April, 2024 to 30th September, 2024	25,00,000
(4)	Claims received and settled during March, 2024	50,000
(5)	Insurance Company reimbursed the claims in April, 2024	

SOLUTION

FAIR DEAL LTD.
JOURNAL ENTRIES

Date	Particulars		L.F.	₹	₹
2023 Oct. 1	Workmen's Compensation Insurance Suspense A/c	Dr.		96,000	
	To Bank A/c				96,000
	(Being provisional premium paid @ 2% on ₹ 48,00,000 wages of immediately preceding 12 months)				
2024 Mar. 31	Workmen's Compensation Insurance A/c	Dr.		56,000	
	To Workmen's Compensation Insurance Suspense A/c				56,000
	(Being premium @ 2% on ₹ 28,00,000 actual wages till year end 31st March, 2024 transferred to Workmen's Compensation Insurance A/c as expense)				
" 31	Insurance Company A/c	Dr.		50,000	
	To Bank A/c				50,000
	(Being claims paid to Workers recoverable from the insurance company)				
April ?	Bank A/c	Dr.		50,000	
	To Insurance Company A/c				50,000
	(Being amount of claims recovered from insurance company)				
Oct. 1	Workmen's Compensation Insurance A/c	Dr.		50,000	
	To Workmen's Compensation Insurance Suspense A/c				40,000
	To Bank				10,000
	(Being premium amount @ 2% on ₹ 25,00,000 wages paid from 1-4-2024 to 30-9-2024 debited to Workmen's Compensation Insurance A/c as expense of the period ; ₹ 40,000 provided out of balance lying in Workmen's Compensation Insurance A/c and payment of shortfall of ₹ 10,000 in premium paid earlier)				

QUESTIONS

OBJECTIVE TYPE

1. **Fill in the blanks :**

   (*i*) The average clause in a loss of stock policy discourages......

   (*ii*) The difference between standard turnover and actual turnover during the indemnity period is......

   (*iii*) The average clause in case of a loss of stock policy is applied when the value of stock on the date of fire is more than the......

   (*iv*) Rate of gross profit in case of a loss of profit insurance is determined by applying the formula ......

   (*v*) Loss of profit insurance is also known as......

Ans. **[(*i*) under insurance of stock ; (*ii*) short sales ; (*iii*) amount of policy taken ;**

(*iv*) $$\frac{\textbf{Net profit + Insured standing charges}}{\textbf{Sales of the financial year preceding the year of fire}} \times 100$$

(*v*) consequential loss insurance]

2. Select the correct answer :

(*a*) The loss of profit policy covers loss of profit due to :

(*i*) Loss of sales

(*ii*) Non-recovery of standing charges

(*iii*) Loss of sales as well as loss of insured standing charges.

(*b*) The objective of inserting average clause in loss of stock policy is to :

(*i*) Encourage under-insurance

(*ii*) Discourage full insurance of stock

(*iii*) Encourage full insurance of stock.

(*c*) A building worth ₹ 10,00,000 is insured for ₹ 6,00,000. It is completely destroyed by fire. The loss to be admitted by the insurance company will be :

(*i*) ₹ 10,00,000 ; (*ii*) ₹ 6,00,000 ; (*iii*) ₹ 5,00,000 ; (*iv*) None of these.

(*d*) A firm took an insurance policy against fire for ₹ 50,000. The policy contained an average clause. A fire occurred. On the date of fire, goods costing ₹ 75,000 were available in the stores. Goods salvaged totalled ₹ 15,000. The insurance company will admit a claim for—

(*i*) ₹ 75,000; (*ii*) ₹ 60,000; (*iii*) ₹ 50,000; (*iv*) ₹ 40,000.

Ans. **[(*a*) (*iii*) ; (*b*) (*i*) ; (*c*) (*ii*) ; (*d*) (*iv*)].**

SHORT ANSWER TYPE

1. What do you mean by Gross Profit Ratio ?
2. What do you mean by under insurance ?
3. Why is an average clause included in Fire Insurance Policy ?
4. What is an Average clause in fire insurance claim ?

OR

Describe the significance of average clause in a fire insurance policy with an example.

(*PCE Nov. 2018*)

5. What is the formula for determining the amount of claim for loss of profits, when average clause is applicable ?
6. How do you ascertain the amount of claim under a fire insurance claim ?
7. What is a consequential loss policy ?

LOSS OF STOCK BY FIRE

8. A fire occurred in the premises of Mr. Y on June 15, 2025 and a considerable part of the stock was destroyed.

The value of the stock saved was ₹ 4,000.

The books disclosed that on 1st April, 2025 the stock was valued at ₹ 45,000 ; the purchases up to the date of fire amounted to ₹ 1,25,000 and the sales to ₹ 1,80,000. On investigation, it was found that during the past five years, the average gross profit on sales was 30%.

You are required to prepare a statement showing the amount Mr. Y should claim from the insurance company in respect of stock destroyed by fire.

Ans. **[₹ 40,000].**

9. Loss of stock by fire ₹ 2,00,000. Amount of Policy ₹ 1,71,000, Total Value of Stock ₹ 2,28,000. Calculate the amount of fire claim by applying average clause.

Ans. **[₹ 1,50,000]**

10. A fire occurred in the godown of a company on 20-3-2025. All stocks were destroyed except to the extent of ₹ 13,000. From the following figures ascertain the claim amount in respect of loss of stock by fire.

	₹		₹
Stock on 1-1-2024	40,000	Stock on 31-12-2024	24,000
Purchases during 2024	1,40,000	Purchases during 2025 upto date of fire	1,46,000
Sales during 2024	2,00,000	Sales during 2025 upto the date of fire	1,60,000

Stock was always valued at 80% of the cost.

Ans. **[Gross Profit Ratio 20% ; Claim Amount ₹ 48,000]**

11. In January, 2025 a firm took an insurance policy for ₹ 60 lakhs to insure goods in its godown against fire subject to average clause. On 7th March, 2025 a fire broke out destroying goods costing ₹ 44 lakhs. Stock in the godown was estimated at ₹ 80 lakhs. Compute the amount of insurance claim.

Ans. **[₹ 33 lakhs]**

12. For the year ending 31st December, 2024, the Sales, Purchases, Opening Stock and Closing Stock of a Trader was ₹ 5,00,000, ₹ 3,80,000, ₹ 65,000 and ₹ 52,000 respectively. Some goods were destroyed by fire (without realization of any value) during the year. If the Trader earned Gross Profit @ 25% on Sales for the year, calculate the value of goods destroyed by fire.

Ans. **[₹ 18,000]**

LOSS OF PROFIT POLICY

13. Comet Limited has loss of profit insurance policy of ₹ 21,00,000. The period of indemnity is three months. A fire occurred on 31st March, 2025. Following information is available :

	₹		₹
Sales for the year ended 31st December 2024	70,00,000	Standing charges for 2024	16,00,000
		Profit for 2024	5,00,000
Sales for the period from 1-4-2024 to 31-3-2025	80,00,000	Saving in standing charges because of fire	50,000
Sales for the period from 1-4-2024 to 30-6-2024	18,00,000	Additional expenses to reduce loss of turn over	1,00,000
Sales for the period from 1st April 2025 to 30th June 2025	1,20,000		

Compute the claim to be made on the insurance company.

Ans. **[Short Sales ₹ 16,80,000; Gross Profit Ratio 30%; Admissible Increased Working Cost ₹ 36,000; Gross Claim ₹ 4,90,000; Net Claim ₹ 4,28,750]**

14. Due to flood, business of Mr. Singh was dislocated from 1-4-2024 to 31-8-2024 (5 months). From the following details, calculate the amount of claim to be lodged in respect of loss of profit policy.

Particulars	₹
Policy Amount	1,25,000
Turnover from 1-4-2024 to 31-8-2024	2,40,000
Standing charges from 1-4-2024 to 31-8-2024	60,000
Turnover during 1-4-2023 to 31-3-2024	12,00,000
Gross Profit Ratio	10% on Sales
Standard charges for the year 2023-24	84,000

The turnover for the year 2024-2025 was anticipated to increase by 10% over the turnover of the preceding year.

Ans. **[Amount of Claim ₹ 56,000]**

[**Hint :** Short Sales ₹ 3,10,000; Increase cost of working ₹ 25,000]

LONG ANSWER TYPE

1. Explain in short, the following principles and term of **insurance business** :
(*i*) Principle of Indemnity; (*ii*) Insurable interest; (*iii*) Principle of "UBERRIMAE FIDEI"; (*iv*) Catastrophic Loss.
2. How loss due to short sales is calculated in connection with loss of profits policy ? ***(I.C.W.A. Inter)***
3. Explain the procedure of determining the amount of claim for the loss of stock to be lodged with the insurance company.
4. How will you ascertain the claim for loss of profit as a result of fire ?
5. What do you mean by "Loss of Profit Insurance" ? What items would normally be covered by such an insurance ?
6. Write short notes on :
(*a*) Gross Profit Ratio ; (*b*) Memorandum Trading Account ; (*c*) Average Clause ; (*d*) Indemnity Period ; (*e*) Short Sales.
7. Explain any two of the following terms :
(*a*) Standing charges ; (*b*) Average clause ; (*c*) Increased cost for workings.

PRACTICAL PROBLEMS

LOSS OF STOCK INSURANCE

1. A fire occurred in the premises of a merchant on 18th September, 2024 and a considerable part of the stock was destroyed. The value of the stock saved was ₹ 8,200.
The books disclosed that on 1st April, 2024 the stock was valued at ₹ 66,850, the purchases to the date of fire amounted to ₹ 1,85,000 and the sales to ₹ 2,82,500. Goods costing ₹ 500 were taken for personal use and goods sold for ₹ 2,500 were returned to the merchant. On investigation it is found that during the past five years the average gross profit on the cost was 25%.
You are required to prepare a statement showing the amount the merchant should **claim from the insurance company** in respect of stock destroyed by fire.

Ans. **[₹ 19,150].**

2. On 28th February, 2024, in Volatile Ltd., the entire stock except stock costing ₹ 62,000 was destroyed due to fire. Determine the **amount of loss** on the basis of following information :

	₹		₹
Stock on 1st April, 2023	1,80,000	Stock on 31st March, 2024	1,12,500
Purchases during the year ended 31st March, 2024	7,00,000	Purchases during 2024-25 (till the date of fire)	7,30,000
Sales during the year ended 31st March, 2024	10,00,000	Sales during 2024-25 (till the date of fire)	8,00,000

In the company, the stock is valued at 10% below the cost.

Ans. **[Amount of Claim ₹ 1,73,000]**

3. On 10th January, 2025, a fire occurred in the godown of Bright Electricals. All the stock was burnt. Each year, Bright Electricals values the stock at cost less 10%. From the following additional information, ascertain the **value of stock on the date of fire :**

	₹		₹
Stock on 1st April, 2023	7,20,000	Stock on 31st March, 2024	4,50,000
Purchases during the year ended 31st March, 2024	28,00,000	Purchases from 1st April, 2024 to date of fire	29,20,000
Sales during the year ended 31st March, 2024	40,00,000	Sales from 1st April, 2024 to date of fire	32,00,000

Ans. **[₹ 9,40,000]**

4. A fire occurred in the premises of Ranjan on 25th November, 2024 when a large part of the stock was destroyed. The value of salvaged stock was ₹ 1,50,000. Ranjan gives you the following information for the period 1st April, 2024 to 25th November, 2024 :

(*i*) Purchases : ₹ 8,05,000. (*ii*) Sales : ₹ 9,00,000. (*iii*) Goods costing ₹ 5,000 were taken away by Ranjan for his personal use. (*iv*) Cost price of the stock on 1st April, 2024 : ₹ 4,00,000.

Over the last few years, Ranjan has been selling goods at a consistent rate of gross margin of $33\frac{1}{3}\%$ on sales.

The insurance policy is for ₹ 5,00,000. It includes an average clause.

Ranjan asks you to prepare a **statement of claim** to be made on the insurance company.

Ans. **[₹ 3,75,000]**

5. A fire occurred in the workshop of Mr. A on 31st March, 2025, where a large part of the stock was destroyed. Scrap realised ₹ 7,500. Mr. A gives you the following information for the period of 1st January to 31st March, 2025 :

		₹
(*i*)	Purchases	42,500
(*ii*)	Sales	45,000

(*iii*) Goods costing ₹ 1,000 were taken by Mr. A for personal use.

(*iv*) Cost price of stock on 1st January, 2025 was ₹ 20,000.

(*v*) Over the past few years, Mr. A has been selling goods at a consistent gross profit margin of 30%.

(*vi*) The Insurance Policy was for ₹ 25,000. It included an average clause. Prepare a **statement of claim** to be made on the Insurance Company by Mr. A.

Ans. **[Amount of Claim ₹ 18,750]**

6. On 2-6-2025 the stock of Mr. Black was destroyed by fire. However, following particulars were furnished from the records saved :

	₹		₹
Stock at cost on 1-4-2024	1,35,000	Sales for the year ended 31-3-2025	9,00,000
Stock at 90% of cost on 31-3-2025	1,62,000	Purchases from 1-4-2025 to 2-6-2025	2,25,000
Purchases for the year ended 31-3-2025	6,45,000	Sales from 1-4-2025 to 2-6-2025	4,80,000

Sales upto 2-6-2025 includes ₹ 75,000 being the goods not dispatched to the customers. The sales invoice price is ₹ 75,000.

Purchases upto 2-6-2025 includes a machinery acquired for ₹ 15,000.

Purchases upto 2-6-2025 does not include goods worth ₹ 30,000 received from suppliers, as invoice not received upto the date of fire. These goods have remained in the godown at the time of fire.

Value of stock salvaged from fire ₹ 22,500 and this has been handed over to the insurance company.

The insurance policy is for ₹ 1,20,000 and it is subject to average clause. Ascertain the **amount of claim** for loss of stock.

Ans. **[₹ 1,20,000]**

[**Hint :** G.P. Ratio = $33\frac{1}{3}\%$]

7. On 1st April, 2025, a trader took out a Fire Insurance Policy containing an average clause covering his stock for ₹ 7,50,000. His practice was to place his selling price at cost plus $33\frac{1}{3}\%$. He closes his book on 31st March, every year.

On 31st December, 2025, a fire broke out at premises and destroyed much of his stock. The salvaged stock was valued at ₹ 3,00,000. During the period of nine months preceding the fire, his purchases amounted to ₹ 30,50,000 and sales to ₹ 42,00,000. On 1st April, 2025, the stock was valued at ₹ 10,00,000.

Prepare a statement showing the **amount of claim.**

Ans. [Amount of Claim ₹ 5,00,000]

8. Fire occurred in the premises of Bad Luck Ltd. on 20th February, 2025. The company has taken out a fire insurance policy of ₹ 1,00,000 covering its stock in trade and the policy was subject to average clause. From the following particulars ascertain the **claim to be lodged.**

	₹		₹
Stock on 1st January, 2024	90,000	Sales Returns during the year 2024	10,000
Purchases during the year 2024	3,65,000	Purchases from 1-1-2025 to date of fire	84,000
Purchases Returns during the year 2024	5,000	Sales from 1-1-2025 to date of fire	1,03,000
Stock on 31st December, 2024	1,26,000	Sales Returns from 1-1-2025 to date of fire	4,000
Sales for the year 2024	4,10,000	Value of stock saved	19,800

It was the practice of the concern to value stocks at cost less 10%.

Ans. [₹ 86,326].

ASCERTAINMENT OF CLAIM WHEN ABNORMAL ITEMS ARE AVAILABLE

9. On 30th September, 2024, the stock of Fred Perry was lost in a fire accident. From the available records, the following information is made available to you to enable you to prepare a **statement of claim** on the insurers :

	₹		₹
Stock at cost on 1-4-2023	37,500	Sales less returns for the year	
Stock at cost on 31-3-2024	52,000	ended 31-3-2024	3,15,000
Purchases less returns for the		Purchases less returns upto 30-9-2024	1,45,000
year ended 31-3-2024	2,53,750	Sales less returns up to 30-9-2024	1,84,050

In valuing stock on 31-3-2024, due to obsolescence 50% of the value of the stock which originally cost ₹ 6,000 had been written off. In May 2024, three-fourths of this stock had been sold at 90% of the original cost and it is now expected that the balance of the obsolete stock would also realise the same price. Subject to the above, gross profit had remained uniform throughout.

Stock to the value of ₹ 7,200 was salvaged.

Ans. [Amount of Claim to be Lodged = ₹ 53,150].

10. On 11-11-2024 the premises of Rocky Ltd. was destroyed by fire. Following information is made available :

	₹		₹
Stock as on 1-4-2023	3,75,000	Purchases from 1-4-2024	
Purchases from 1-4-2023 to 31-3-2024	5,20,000	to 11-11-2024	3,41,000
Sales from 1-4-2023 to 31-3-2024	8,55,000	Sales from 1-4-2024 to	
Stock as on 31-3-2024	2,00,000	11-11-2024	4,35,500

In valuing the stock on 31-3-2024, due to damage 50% of the value of the stock which originally cost ₹ 22,000 was written off.

In June, 2024 about 50% of this stock was sold for ₹ 5,500 and the balance of obsolete stock is expected to realize the same price (*i.e.,* 50% of the original cost).

The gross profit ratio is to be assumed as uniform in respect of other sales. Stock salvaged from fire amounts to ₹ 11,500.

Compute the **value of stock lost in fire.**

Ans. [₹ 1,80,000]

11. Malcom owns a retail stationery shop which was partly destroyed by fire on 27th June, 2025. The stock was insured for ₹ 13,000.

The Balance Sheet drawn on 31st December, 2024 included, *inter alia,* the following items:

	₹
Stock	12,500
Creditors	3,500

On examination of the books of account for the subsequent period up to the date of the fire, the following particulars were obtained :

	₹
Sales	88,800
Payments to creditors for goods	75,000
Creditors as on 27-6-2025	1,800

A physical check of stock after the fire showed that items undamaged were ₹ 7,000.

The normal rate of gross profit is 25 per cent on cost but the stock on 31st December, 2024 included items of discontinued line totalling ₹ 3,800 which were all sold during the next two months at cost.

You are required to compute the **amount of claim** to be made to the insurer.

Ans. [₹ 6,500].

12. On 1st April, 2025 the stock of Mr. Hariprasad was destroyed by fire but sufficient records were saved from which following particulars were ascertained :

Stock at cost 1 Jan, 2024	1,47,000	Sales Year ended 31st Dec. 2024	9,74,000
Stock at cost 31 Dec, 2024	1,59,200	Purchases 1-1-2025 to 31-3-2025	3,24,000
Purchases year ended 31 Dec. 2024	7,96,000	Sales 1-1-2025 to 31-3-2025	4,62,400

In valuing the stock for the Balance Sheet at 31st Dec. 2024 ₹ 4,600 had been written off on certain stock which was a poor selling line having cost ₹ 13,800. A portion of these goods were sold in March, 2025 at a loss of ₹ 500 on original cost of ₹ 6,900. The remainder of this stock was now estimated to be worth its original cost. Subject to the above exception gross profit had reminded at a uniform rate throughout the year.

The value of stock salvaged was ₹ 11,600. The policy was for ₹ 1,00,000 and was subject to average clause.

Work out the amount of the claim of loss by fire. ***(CA – Inter Nov. 2016 Modified)***

Ans. [₹ 90,009]

13. On 1st April, 2025, the godown of Hindustan Limited was destroyed by fire. From the books of account, the following particulars are gathered :

Stock at cost on 1st January, 2024 ₹ 27,570 ; Stock as per Balance Sheet on 31st December, 2024 ₹ 51,120 ; Purchases during 2024 ₹ 2,71,350 ; Purchases from 1st January, 2025 to 31st March, 2025 ₹ 75,000 ; Sales during 2024 ₹ 3,51,000 ; Sales from 1st January, 2025 to 31st March, 2025 ₹ 91,500 ; Value of goods salvaged ₹ 6,300.

Goods of which original cost was ₹ 3,600 had been valued at ₹ 1,500 on 31st December, 2024. These were sold in March 2025 for ₹ 2,700. Except this transaction, the rate of gross profit had remained constant.

On 31st March, 2025 goods worth ₹ 15,000 had been received by the godown-keeper but had not been entered in the purchases account.

Calculate the **value of goods destroyed by fire.**

Ans. [₹ 71,160].

14. ***(Where slow item of goods is there besides calculating average G.P. Ratio)*** The premises of P were destroyed by fire on 30-6-2025. Following figures, however, were collected from various sources. Prepare a **statement of claim** in respect of the loss of stock for submission to the Fire Insurance Company. The firm closes its books on 31st December every year.

Details	*2022*	*2023*	*2024*	*30-6-2025*
	₹	₹	₹	₹
Opening Stock	20,000	22,000	11,800	34,020
Purchases less returns	1,60,000	1,45,000	1,70,000	35,000
Sales less returns	2,00,000	1,98,500	1,87,500	26,000
Freight (Inwards)	5,000	3,000	5,000	1,000
Freight (Outwards)	6,000	7,000	3,000	250

In 2022, while valuing closing stock, a slow moving item costing ₹ 5,000 was valued at ₹ 4,000. This was sold for ₹ 4,500 in 2023. In 2023, an item costing ₹ 6,000 was wrongly valued at ₹ 7,000. This was sold for ₹ 5,500 in 2024. In 2024, a slow moving item, costing ₹ 12,000 was valued at ₹ 10,000 ; 50% of which was sold before 30-6-2025 for ₹ 6,000. The value of salvage was ₹ 8,000.

Ans. **[Amount of Claim ₹ 42,420].**

Hint. [G.P. Ratio : 2022—19% ; 2023—20% and 2024—21% Weighted Average G.P. Ratio = 20.33% ; Value of Stock on the date of loss ₹ 44,420]

15. A fire occurred in the premises of Shri Romesh on 1st April, 2025 and a considerable part of the stock was destroyed. The stock salvaged was ₹ 1,12,000. Shri Romesh had taken a fire insurance policy for ₹ 6,84,000 to cover the loss of stock by fire.

You are required to **ascertain the insurance claim** due from the insurance company for the loss of stock by fire. Following particulars are available :

Purchases for the year 2024 ₹ 37,52,000 ; Sales for the year 2024 ₹ 46,40,000 ; Purchases from 1st January, 2025 to 1st April, 2025 ₹ 7,28,000 ; Sales from 1st January, 2025 to 1st April, 2025 ₹ 9,60,000 ; Stock on 1st January, 2024 ₹ 5,76,000 ; Stock on 31st December, 2024 ₹ 9,68,000 ; Wages paid during the year 2024 ₹ 4,00,000 ; Wages paid during 1st January, 2025 to 1st April, 2025 ₹ 72,000

Shri Romesh had in June 2024 consigned goods worth ₹ 2,00,000 which were lost in an accident. As there was no insurance the loss was borne by him in full.

Stock at the end of each year and till the end of Calendar Year 2023 had been valued at cost less 10%. From 2024, however, there was a change in the valuation of closing stock which was ascertained by adding 10% to its cost.

Ans. **[₹ 6,00,000]**

16. A fire occurred on 1st October, 2025 in the premises of Sure Success Ltd.

From the following figures, calculate the **amount of claim to be lodged** with the Insurance Company for loss of stock :

	₹		₹
Stock at cost on 1-1-2024	1,35,000	Purchases from 1-1-2025 to 30-9-2025	9,00,000
Stock at cost on 1-1-2025	1,05,000	Sales during 2024	9,00,000
Purchases during 2024	6,00,000	Sales from 1-1-2025 to 30-9-2025	13,20,000

You are informed that :

(*i*) In 2025 the cost of purchases have risen by 20% above the level prevailing in 2024.

(*ii*) In 2025 the selling prices have gone up by 10% over the levels prevailing in 2024.

(*iii*) Salvage value is ₹ 6,000.

Ans. **[₹ 12,000].**

17. The factory premises of Toy Company were engulfed in fire on 31st March, 2025 as a result of which a major part of stock was burnt to ashes. The stock was covered by policy for ₹ 1,00,000 subject to average clause.

The records at the Office revealed following information :

1. (*a*) The Company sold goods to Dealers on one month credit at Dealers' price which is catalogue price less 15%. A cash discount is allowed @ 5% for immediate payment.

   (*b*) The goods are also sold to Agents at Catalogue Price less 10% against cash payment.

   (*c*) Goods are sent to branches at Catalogue Price.

   (*d*) Catalogue Price is cost + 100%.

2. The Sales/Despatch during period upto date of fire is—

   (*a*) Sale to Dealer ... ₹ 3,40,000 (Without cash discount)

   (*b*) Sale to Dealer ... ₹ 3,23,000 (Net of Cash Discount)

(c) Sale to Agents ... ₹ 90,000
(d) Despatch to Branches ... ₹ 3,00,000

3. Stock on 1st January, 2025 was ₹ 2,50,000 at Catalogue Price. Purchases at Cost from 1st January, 2025 to 31st March, 2025. ... ₹ 6,25,000
4. Salvaged Stock valued at ... ₹ 45,000

Compute the **amount of claim to be lodged.**

Ans. [₹ 70,000].

18. A fire occurred on the premises of a businessman on 30th June, 2025, destroying the greater part of his stock. No stock records have been maintained. Following information was ascertained from his books which were not involved in the fire.

	₹		₹
Value of stock on 1st January, 2025	12,500	Sales in 2022	2,50,000
Purchases from 1st January, 2025		Sales in 2023	1,60,000
to 30th June, 2025	45,500	Sales in 2024	1,90,000
Sales for the above period	56,600	Gross Profit in 2022	75,000
Purchases in 2022	2,20,000	Gross Profit in 2023	32,000
Purchases in 2023	1,75,000	Gross Profit in 2024	19,000
Purchases in 2024	1,50,000	Value of stock saved from fire	2,500

Prepare a statement showing the **amount to be claimed** from the Insurance Company, mentioning any further factors which you consider should be taken into consideration when preparing the claim.

Ans. [₹ 1,730 ; Rate of Gross Profit 5% (assumed) because of decreasing trend].

LOSS OF PROFIT INSURANCE

19. A firm has decided to arrange for a **loss of profits insurance** and you are required to finalise **the sum to be insured on a full insurance basis** from the following figures for the last financial year ; it is anticipated that for the current financial year, turnover will increase by 10% and that all standing (fixed) expenses will remain unchanged.

	₹	₹
Total Variable Expenses		21,00,000
Fixed Expenses :		
Wages and salaries to skilled employees and salaries to administration staff	3,00,000	
Depreciation of all fixed assets	1,00,000	
Insurance premium	10,000	
Audit Fees	4,000	
Directors' Fees	4,000	
Travellers' Expenses (including Motor Car Expenses)	40,000	
Postage, Cables and Telephones	3,000	
Trade subscriptions	1,000	
Rent, Rates and Taxes	30,000	
		4,92,000
Non-operating Income		50,000
Net Profit		4,08,000

Ans. [₹ 9,35,000].

20. From the following details find out the **claim under a loss of profit policy :**

Indemnity periods	6 months	Standing Charges for 2023	
Policy value	₹ 30,000	accounting year (all insured)	₹ 17,000

Date of Fire 1-4-2024		Sales from 1-4-2023 to 31-3-2024	₹ 1,60,000
Dislocation upto 1-8-2024		Sales from 1-4-2024 to 1-8-2024	₹ 15,000
Sales for 2023 accounting year	₹1,20,000	Sales from 1-4-2023 to 1-8-2023	₹ 50,000
Net Profit for 2023 accounting year	₹ 13,000		

There is a clear 10% upward trend in business. ***(ICWA—Stage II, Dec. 2007 Modified)***

Ans. [Short Sales ₹ 40,000; Claim ₹ 6,818]

21. On December 31, 2024 a fire damaged the premises of Behl Bros. Ltd. and the business of the company was disorganised until March 31, 2025. The company was insured under a loss of profit policy for ₹ 26,000 with a six months period of indemnity.

The company's accounts for the year ended October 31, 2024 showed a turnover of ₹ 70,000 with a net profit of ₹ 8,000. The amount of standing charges covered by the insurance and debited in that year was ₹ 20,000. The turnover for the 12 months ended December 31, 2024 was ₹ 78,000. The turnover during the period the business was dislocated amounted to ₹ 8,000 while during the corresponding period in the preceding year it was ₹ 17,000. A sum of ₹ 2,000 was spent as additional expenses to mitigate the effect of the loss, there being however, no saving in standing charges as a result of the fire.

Prepare a **claim to be submitted** in respect of the **consequential loss policy.**

Ans. [₹ 4,667].

22. From the following particulars ascertain the claim to be lodged in respect of the **consequential loss policy :**

(*a*) Fire occurred on July 1, 2025 and affected sales for 3 months.

(*b*) Sales for 3 months ending 30th September in 2024 and 2025 were ₹ 1,50,000 and ₹ 50,000 respectively.

(*c*) The policy was for ₹ 4,50,000 with a six months period of indemnity.

(*d*) Sales for 12 months ended June 30, 2025 were ₹ 19,00,000.

(*e*) Accounts are prepared on 31st December. The net profit for 2024 amounted to ₹ 2,50,000 after debiting standing charges totalling ₹ 1,10,000. Sales for 2024 were ₹ 18,00,000.

(*f*) A sum of ₹ 3,500 was spent as additional expenses to mitigate the effect of the loss.

Ans. [₹ 23,500].

23. Madhu & Co. effected a policy of insurance covering loss of profits and standing charges to the extent of ₹ 5 lakhs (based upon previous year's profits) plus an allowance of ₹ 1,00,000 for profit and standing charges expected to accrue from increased turnover, the period of indemnity being 3 months. The turnover for the previous year ended 31st March was ₹ 15 lakhs and the ensuing year was estimated at ₹ 18 lakhs.

A fire occurred on 1st November. Following relative figures have been ascertained :

Month	*Sales Previous year*	*Sales Budget Current year*	*Actual Sales*
	₹	₹	₹
November	80,000	96,000	Nil
December	1,10,000	1,32,000	Nil
January	1,20,000	1,44,000	32,000

Upon investigation, you find that the increased sales for the past seven months were over-estimated by 50% and the ratio of expenses was consistent with such reduction. The additional expenses of carrying on the business during partial disablement amounted to ₹ 7,000.

Prepare **statement of claim** against insurance company and show workings.

Ans. [₹ 1,10,000].

Hint . Short sales ₹ 3,09,000. Short sales are to be calculated increasing sales of November, December and January of previous year by 10%.

24. A fire occurred on 1st February, 2025, in premises of Pioneer Ltd., a retail store and business was partially disorganised upto 30th June, 2025. The company was insured under a **loss of profits** for ₹ 1,25,000 with a six months period of indemnity. From the following information, compute **the amount of claim under the loss of profit policy.**

Actual turnover from 1st February, 2025 to 30th June, 2025 ₹ 80,000 ; Turnover from 1st February, 2024 to 30th June, 2024 ₹ 2,00,000 ; Turnover from 1st February, 2024 to 31st January, 2025 ₹ 4,50,000 ; Net Profit for last financial year ₹ 70,000 ; Insured standing charges for last financial year ₹ 56,000 ; Total standing charges for last financial year ₹ 64,000 ; Turnover for the last financial year ₹ 4,20,000.

The company incurred additional expenses amounting to ₹ 6,700 which reduced the loss in turnover. There was also a saving during the indemnity period of ₹ 2,450 in the insured standing charges as a result of the fire.

There had been a considerable increase in trade since the date of the last annual accounts and it has been agreed that an adjustment of 15% be made in respect of the upward trend in turnover.

Ans. **[₹ 39,390].**

25. On 1st May, 2024 a fire occurred in the factory of ABC Manufacturing Co. Ltd. and claims against the General Insurance Co. Ltd. were admitted on 5th August as follows :

	Original Cost	*Book Value*	*Claimed*	*Admitted*
	₹	₹	₹	₹
Repairs to factory	—	—	1,35,000	90,000
Plant destroyed	3,60,000	2,25,000	3,15,000	2,70,000
Repairs to Plant	—	—	27,000	22,500
Stock destroyed	4,50,000	3,15,000	4,50,000	3,87,000
Stock damaged	—	—	45,000	36,000
Loss of Profit	—	—	90,000	45,000
Charges for fire brigade	—	—	7,200	6,300

The amounts claimed for repairs to factory and plant and the fire brigade charges were paid by the Company.

Give the **Journal Entries** in the Company's books and state how the final differences if any, should be treated in Company's Accounts including the profit or loss on account of insurance.

Ans. **[Treatment of Final Differences :**

(1) Profit and Loss A/c will be debited with—Repairs to Factory A/c ₹ 45,000 ; Repairs to Plant A/c ₹ 4,500 ; Fire Brigade Charges A/c ₹ 900

(2) Profit and Loss A/c will be credited with Claims received on Loss of Profits & Stocks ₹ 4,68,000

(3) ₹ 45,000 profit on plant destroyed account will be credited to Capital Reserve A/c and shown on the liabilities side of the Balance Sheet.]

26. On 1st April, 2024, Hindustan Aeromania Co. Ltd., whose financial year ends on 30th June, took out an insurance policy with the Bogus Insurance Co. Ltd. to cover against Workmen's Compensation Risk for the year ending 31st March, 2025.

The premium was payable at the rate of 1 per cent of wages paid during the year. On taking out of the policy there was payable an amount calculated at that rate on the wages paid for the year to 31st March, 2024, and subsequently, on 7th April, 2025 an adjustment was effected for the actual premium payable.

On 1st April, 2025, the insurance was renewed for a further year. In the mean time the claims arising under the first policy amounted to ₹ 35,000 due to certain mishaps in test flights of the planes assembled by the company. Consequently, for the year ending 31st December, 2025, the premium rates were raised to 1.50 per cent of wages paid for the year ending 31st March, 2025, the amount payable on the taking out of the policy being calculated on the wages for the year ended 31st March, 2025. Adjustment is made on 7th April as before.

The actual wages were as follows :

	₹		₹
Year ended 31st March, 2024	1,00,000	Nine months ended 31st March, 2025	70,000
Three months ended 30th June, 2024	20,000	Three months ended 30th June, 2025	30,000

How will you pass Journal Entries entries for these transactions in the books of Hindustan Aeromania Co. Ltd.? Give also the appropriate closing Journal Entries in the books of the same company.

27. There was a serious fire in the premises of M/s Fortunate on 1st September, 2024. Their business activities were interrupted until 31st December, 2024, when normal trading conditions were re-established. M/s Fortunate are insured under the loss of profit policy for ₹ 42,000 the period of indemnity being six months.

You are able to ascertain the following information :

(1) The net profit for the year ended 31st December, 2023 was ₹ 20,000.

(2) The annual insurable standing charges amounted to ₹ 30,000 of which ₹ 2,000 were not included in the definition of insured standing charges under the policy.

(3) The additional cost of working in order to mitigate the damage caused by the fire amounted to ₹ 600, and but for this expenditure, the business would have had to shut down.

(4) The saving in insured charges in consequence of the fire amounted to ₹ 1,500.

(5) The turnover for the period of four months ended April 30, August 31 and December 31, for each of the years 2023 and 2024 was as under :

	₹	₹	₹
2023	65,000	80,000	95,000
2024	70,000	80,000	15,000

You are required to **compute the relevant claim** under the terms of the **loss of profits policy.**

Ans. [₹ 12,922].

28. A fire occurred in the premises of a timber merchant on the night of 31st December, 2024. Goods worth ₹ 25,000 only could be salvaged. Following further information is available :

(1) The accounting year ends on 31st March every year.

(2) The closing stock on 31st March, 2024 was valued at ₹ 1,10,000. This was 10% above the cost.

(3) The purchases during the period from 1st April, 2024 to 31st December, 2024 amounted to ₹ 5,50,000 as per the Purchases Register. However goods worth ₹ 30,000 were received on 3rd January 2025.

(4) The sales during the period from 1st April, 2024 to 31st December, 2024 amounted to ₹ 6,45,000 and included goods sold on approval basis for which the period of approval was not yet over on 31st December, 2024. The goods so sold on approval basis had been invoiced at ₹ 30,000, which was 50% above cost.

(5) On 30th December, 2024 goods worth ₹ 60,000 had been sent to a Commission Agent on consignment basis.

(6) The wages paid during the period from 1st April, 2024 to 31st December, 2024 amounted to ₹ 40,000 and included ₹ 10,000 paid to workers engaged in construction work.

(7) The amount spent on carriage inwards during the period from 1st April, 2024 to 31st December, 2024 was ₹ 25,000.

(8) It was agreed to take the gross profit ratio as the weighted average of the gross profit ratios of the preceding four years.

For this purpose, greater weightage was to be given to later years. Also, an item purchased in July, 2024 for ₹ 20,000 and sold in August, 2024 at a loss of ₹ 5,000 was to be considered separately.

(9) The gross profit and sales of the preceding four years were as follows :

Year	*Gross Profit*	*Sales*
	₹	₹
2020-21	1,04,000	4,00,000
2021-22	90,000	4,50,000
2022-23	1,15,200	4,80,000
2023-24	1,52,800	5,10,000

(10) The merchant had obtained a policy of ₹ 1,00,000 to cover the loss of stock by fire and the policy contained the average clause.

You are required to determine the **amount of claim to be lodged** with the insurance company for the **stock destroyed by fire.**

Ans. **[₹ 80,000].**

29. Ramda & Sons had taken out policies (without Average Clause) both against loss of stock and loss of profit, for ₹ 2,10,000 and ₹ 3,20,000 respectively. A fire occurred on 1st July, 2024 and as a result of which sales were seriously affected for a period of 3 months.

Trading and Profit & Loss A/c of Ramda & Sons for the year ended on 31st March, 2024 is given below:

	₹		₹
To Opening Stock	96,000	By Sales	12,00,000
To Purchases	7,56,000	By Closing Stock	1,85,000
To Wages	1,58,000		
To Manufacturing Expenses	75,000		
To Gross Profit *c/d*	3,00,000		
	13,85,000		13,85,000
To Administrative Expenses	83,600	By Gross Profit *b/d*	3,00,000
To Selling Expenses (Fixed)	72,400		
To Commission on Sales	34,200		
To Carriage Outward	49,800		
To Net Profit	60,000		
	3,00,000		3,00,000

Further detail provided is as below :

(*a*) Sales, Purchases, Wages and Manufacturing Expenses for the period 1-4-2024 to 30-6-2024 were ₹ 3,36,000, ₹ 2,14,000, ₹ 51,000 and ₹ 12,000 respectively.

(*b*) Other Sales figure were as follows :
From 1-4-2023 to 30-6-2023 ₹ 3,00,000; From 1-7-2023 to 30-9-2023 ₹ 3,20,000; From 1-7-2024 to 30-9-24 ₹ 48,000.

(*c*) Due to decrease in the material cost, Gross Profit during 2024-25 was expected to increase by 5% on sales.

(*d*) ₹ 1,98,000 were additionally incurred during the period after fire. The amount of policy included ₹ 1,56,000 for expenses leaving ₹ 42,000 uncovered. **Compute the claim for stock, loss of profit and additional expenses.** ***(CA—IPCE, May, 2012 Modified)***

Ans. **[Claim for Loss of Stock ₹ 2,10,000; Loss of Profit ₹ 82,432; ₹ 11,040 Admissible Additional Expenses]**

CHAPTER 33

Accounting Standards

The Institute of Chartered Accountants of India being the premier accounting body in India has tried to improve its accounting standards continuously in the country. However, the most important step in developing accounting standards in the country has been setting up of an Accounting Standards Board in 1977. Important function of this Board is to formulate accounting standards so that such standards will be established by the Council of the Institute of Chartered Accountants. It has been made clear by the Institute that while formulating the accounting standards, the Accounting Standards Board (ASB) will keep in view customs, usages, applicable laws and the business environments in India and the Institute of Cost Accountants of India and the International Accounting Standards issued by the International Accounting Standards Committee. It is gratifying to note that the Institute of Chartered Accountants of India and the Institute of Cost Accountants of India are both members of International Accounting Standards Committee. This development will go a long way in the uniform adoption of International Accounting Standards in the country. The standards formulated by Accounting Standards Board are initially recommendatory in nature, but many organisations in the corporate sector have adopted these standards voluntarily. In the formulation and finalisation of accounting standards, the Accounting Standards Board seeks the views and guidance of industrial concerns, governments and other interested parties. The establishment of the Accounting Standards Board (ASB) itself marked a commendable effort by the Institute of the Chartered Accountants in its endeavour to formulate and harmonise accounting practices, and has played a significant role in improving corporate practices.

PREFACE TO THE STATEMENTS OF ACCOUNTING STANDARDS

1. Formation of the Accounting Standards Board

1.1. The Institute of Chartered Accountants of India (ICAI), recognising the need to harmonise the diverse accounting policies and practices in use in India, constituted the Accounting Standards Board (ASB) on 21st April, 1977.

1.2. The composition of the ASB is fairly broad-based and ensures participation of all interest-groups in the standard-setting process. Apart from the elected members of the Council of the ICAI nominated on the ASB, the following are represented on the ASB:

- *(i)* Nominee of the Central Government representing the Department of Company Affairs on the Council of the ICAI.
- *(ii)* Nominee of the Central Government representing the Office of the Comptroller and Auditor General of India on the Council of the ICAI.
- *(iii)* Nominee of the Central Government representing the Central Board of Direct Taxes in the Council of the ICAI.

(*iv*) Representative of the Institute of Cost and Works Accountants of India.

(*v*) Representative of the Institute of Company Secretaries of India.

(*vi*) Representatives of Industry Associations (1 from Associated Chambers of Commerce and Industry (ASSOCHAM), 1 from Confederation of Indian Industry (CII) and 1 from Federation of Indian Chambers of Commerce and Industry (FICCI).

(*vii*) Representative of Reserve Bank of India.

(*viii*) Representative of Securities and Exchange Board of India.

(*ix*) Representative of Controller General of Accounts.

(*x*) Representative of Central Board of Excise and Customs.

(*xi*) Representatives of Academic Institutions (1 from Universities and 1 from Indian Institutes of Management).

(*xii*) Representative of Financial Institutions.

(*xiii*) Eminent professionals co–opted by the ICAI (they may be in practice or in industry, government, education, etc.).

(*xiv*) Chairman of the Research Committee and the Chairman of the Expert Advisory Committee of the ICAI, if they are not otherwise members of the Accounting Standards Board.

(*xv*) Representative(s) of any other body, as considered appropriate by the ICAI.

2. Objectives and Functions of the Accounting Standards Board

2.1. Following are the objectives of the Accounting Standards Board:

(*i*) To conceive of and suggest areas in which accounting standards need to be developed.

(*ii*) To formulate Accounting Standards with a view to assisting the Council of the ICAI in evolving and establishing Accounting Standards in India.

(*iii*) To examine how far the relevant International Accounting Standard/ International Financial Reporting Standard (see paragraph 2.3 below) can be adapted while formulating the Accounting Standard and to adapt the same.

(*iv*) To review, at regular intervals, the Accounting Standards from the point of view of acceptance or changed conditions, and, if necessary, revise the same.

(*v*) To provide, from time to time, interpretations and guidance on Accounting Standards.

(*vi*) To carry out such other functions relating to Accounting Standards.

2.2. Important function of the ASB is to formulate Accounting Standards so that such standards may be established by the ICAI in India. While formulating the Accounting Standards, the ASB will take into consideration the applicable laws, customs, usages and business environment prevailing in India.

2.3. The ICAI, being a full-fledged member of the International Federation of Accountants (IFAC), is expected, *inter alia,* to actively promote the International Accounting Standards Board's (IASB) pronouncements in the country with a view to facilitate global harmonisation of accounting standards. Accordingly, while formulating the Accounting Standards, the ASB will give due to consideration to International Accounting Standards (IASs) issued by the International Accounting Standards Committee (Predecessor body to IASB) or International Financial Reporting Standards (IFRSs) issued by the IASB, as the case may be, and try to integrate them, to the extent possible, in the light of the conditions and practices prevailing in India.

2.4. The Accounting Standards are issued under the authority of the Council of the ICAI. The ASB has also been entrusted with the responsibility of propagating the Accounting Standards and of persuading the concerned parties to adopt them in the preparation and presentation of financial statements. The ASB will provide interpretations and guidance on issues arising from Accounting Standards. The ASB will also review the Accounting Standards at periodical intervals and, if necessary, revise the same.

3. General Purpose Financial Statements

3.1. For discharging its functions, the ASB will keep in view the purposes and limitations of financial statements and the attest function of the auditors. The ASB will enumerate and describe the basic concept to which accounting principles should be oriented and state the accounting principles to which the practices and procedures should conform.

3.2. The ASB will clarify the terms commonly used in financial statements and suggest improvements in the terminology wherever necessary. The ASB will examine the various current alternative practices in vogue and endeavour to eliminate or reduce alternatives within the bounds of rationality.

3.3. Accounting Standards are designed to apply to the general purpose financial statements and other financial reporting, which are subject to the attest function of the members of the ICAI. Accounting Standards apply in respect of any enterprise (whether organised in corporate, co-operative or other forms) engaged in commercial, industrial or business activities, irrespective of whether it is profit oriented or it is established for charitable or religious purposes. Accounting Standards will not, however, apply to enterprises only carrying on the activities which are not of commercial, industrial or business nature. (*e.g.*, an activity of collecting donations and giving them to flood affected people). Exclusion of an enterprise from the applicability of the Accounting Standards would be permissible only if no part of the activity of such enterprise is commercial, industrial or business in nature. Even if a very small proportion of the activities of an enterprise is considered to be commercial, industrial or business in nature, the Accounting Standards would apply to all its activities including those which are not commercial, industrial or business in nature.

3.4. The term 'General Purpose Financial Statements' includes balance sheet, statement of profit and loss, a cash flow statement (wherever applicable) and statements and explanatory notes which form part thereof, issued for the use of various stakeholders, Governments and their agencies and the public. References to financial statements in this Preface and in the standards issued from time to time will be construed to refer to General Purpose Financial Statements.

3.5. Responsibility for the preparation of financial statements and for adequate disclosure is that of the management of the enterprise. The auditor's responsibility is to form his opinion and report on such financial statements.

4. Scope of Accounting Standards

4.1. Efforts will be made to issue Accounting Standards which are in conformity with the provisions of the applicable laws, customs, usages and business environment in India. However, if a particular Accounting Standard is found to be not in conformity with law, the provisions of the said law will prevail and the financial statements should be prepared in conformity with such law.

4.2. The Accounting Standards by their very nature cannot and do not override the local regulations which govern the preparation and presentation of financial statements in the country. However, the ICAI will determine the extent of disclosure to be made in financial statements and the auditor's report thereon. Such disclosure may be by way of appropriate notes explaining the treatment of particular items. Such explanatory notes will be only in the nature of clarification and therefore need not be treated as adverse comments on the related financial statements.

4.3. The Accounting Standards are intended to apply only to items which are material. Any limitations with regard to the applicability of a specific Accounting Standard will be made clear by the ICAI from time to time. The date from which a particular Standard will come into effect, as well as the class of enterprises to which it will apply, will also be specified by the ICAI. However, no standard will have retroactive application, unless otherwise stated.

4.4. The Institute will use its best endeavours to persuade the Government, appropriate authorities, industrial and business community to adopt the Accounting Standards in order to achieve uniformity in preparation and presentation of financial statements.

4.5. In formulation of Accounting Standards, the emphasis would be on laying down accounting principles and not detailed rules for application and implementation thereof.

4.6. The Standards formulated by the ASB include paragraphs in bold italic type and plain type, which have equal authority. Paragraphs in bold italic type indicate the main principles. An individual standard should be read in the context of the objective stated in that standard and this Preface.

4.7. The ASB may consider any issue requiring interpretation on any Accounting Standard. Interpretations will be issued under the authority of the Council. The authority of Interpretation is the same as that of Accounting Standard to which it relates.

5. Procedure for Issuing an Accounting Standard

Broadly, the following procedure is adopted from formulating Accounting Standards:

5.1. The ASB determines the broad areas in which Accounting Standards need to be formulated and the priority in regard to the selection thereof.

5.2. In the preparation of Accounting Standards, the ASB will be assisted by Study Groups constituted to consider specific subjects. In the formation of Study Groups, provision will be made for wide participation by the members of the Institute and others.

5.3. The draft of the proposed standard will normally include the following :

- (*a*) Objective of the Standard,
- (*b*) Scope of the Standard,
- (*c*) Definitions of the terms used in the Standards,
- (*d*) Recognition and measurement principles, wherever applicable,
- (*e*) Presentation and disclosure requirements.

5.4. The ASB will consider the preliminary draft prepared by the Study Group and if any revision of the draft is required on the basis of deliberations, the ASB will make the same or refer the same to the Study Group.

5.5. The ASB will circulate the draft of the Accounting Standard to the Council members of the ICAI and the following specified bodies for their comments:

- (*i*) Department of Company Affairs (DCA)
- (*ii*) Comptroller and Auditor General of India (C&AG)
- (*iii*) Central Board of Direct Taxes (CBDT)
- (*iv*) The Institute of Cost and Works Accountants of India (ICWAI)
- (*v*) The Institute of Company Secretaries of India (ICSI)
- (*vi*) Associated Chambers of Commerce and Industry (ASSOCHAM), Confederation of Indian Industry (CII) and Federation of Indian Chambers of Commerce and Industry (FICCI)
- (*vii*) Reserve Bank of India (RBI)
- (*viii*) Securities and Exchange Board of India (SEBI)
- (*ix*) Standing Conference of Public Enterprises (SCOPE)
- (*x*) Indian Bank's Association (IBA)
- (*xi*) Any other body considered relevant by the ASB keeping in view the nature of the Accounting Standard

5.6. The ASB will hold a meeting with the representatives of specified bodies to ascertain their view on the draft of the proposed Accounting Standard. On the basis of comments received and discussion with the representatives of specified bodies, the ASB will finalise the Exposure Draft of the proposed Accounting Standard.

5.7. The Exposure Draft of the proposed standard will be issued for comments by the members of the Institute and the public. The Exposure Draft will specifically be sent to specified bodies (as listed above), stock exchanges, and other interest groups, as appropriate.

5.8. After taking into consideration the comments received, the draft of the proposed standard will be finalised by the ASB and submitted to the Council of the ICAI.

5.9. The Council of the ICAI will consider the final draft of the proposed Standard, and if found necessary, modify the same in consultation with the ASB. The Accounting standard on the relevant subject will then be issued by the ICAI.

5.10. For a substantive revision of an Accounting Standard, the procedure followed for formulation of a new Accounting Standard, as detailed above, will be followed.

5.11. Subsequent to issuance of an Accounting Standard, some aspect(s) may require revision which are not substantive in nature. For this purpose, the ICAI may make limited revision to an Accounting Standard. The procedure followed for the limited revision will substantially be the same as that to be followed for formulation of an Accounting Standard, ensuring that sufficient opportunity is given to various interest groups and general public to react to the proposal for limited revision.

6. Compliance with the Accounting Standards

6.1. The Accounting Standards will be mandatory from the respective date(s) mentioned in the Accounting Standard(s). The mandatory status of an Accounting Standard implies that while discharging their attest functions, it will be the duty of the members of the Institute to examine whether the Accounting Standard is complied with in the presentation of financial statements covered by their audit. In the event of any deviation from the Accounting Standard, it will be their duty to make adequate disclosures in their audit reports so that the users of financial statements may be aware of such deviation.

6.2. Ensuring compliance with the Accounting Standards while preparing the financial statements is the responsibility of the management of the enterprise. Statutes governing certain enterprises require of the enterprises that the financial statements should be prepared in compliance with the Accounting Standards, e.g., the Companies Act, 1956 (section 211), and the Insurance Regulatory and Development Authority (Preparation of Financial Statements and Auditor's Report of Insurance Companies Regulations, 2000.

6.3. Financial Statements cannot be described as complying with the Accounting Standards unless they comply with all the requirements of each applicable Standard.

Meaning and Definition of Accounting Standards

Accounting standards are written/policy documents issued by the government or professional institutes or other regulatory body covering various aspects of recognition, measurement, treatment, presentation and disclosure of accounting transactions in the financial statements. According to **T.P. Ghosh** "Accounting Standards are the policy documents issued by the recognised expert accountancy body relating to various aspects of measurement, treatment and disclosure of accounting transactions and events." **Kohler** has also defined accounting standard as "a mode of conduct imposed on accountants by custom, law or professional body."

Significance of Accounting Standards

Accounting Standards play an important role to facilitate uniform preparation and reporting of general purpose financial statements published annually for the benefit of various users of such statements. They are very useful for investors and other external groups in assessing the progress and prospects of alternative investments in different entities in different countries. Standards will help all users of reading financial statements on a true and fair view on uniform basis. They become reliable, uniform and consistent. Accounting standards will raise the standards of audit itself in its tasks of reporting in the financial statements. The standard accounting reports published shall be easily aggregated and used particularly if they are concerned with the meaning-fulness of the number for the purposes of economic planning, market analysis and the like. All of these factors have been important determinants of the establishment of accounting standards.

Advantages and Disadvantages of Setting Accounting Standards

The Accounting Standards seek to describe the accounting principles, the valuation techniques and methods of applying the accounting principles in the preparation and presentation of financial statements so that they may give a true and fair view. The ostensible purpose of the standard setting bodies is to promote the dissemination of timely and useful financial information to investors and certain other parties having an interest in entities' economic performance. The setting of accounting standards has the following advantages :

(*i*) Standards *reduce* to a reasonable extent *or eliminate altogether confusing variations in the accounting treatment* used to prepare financial statements.

(*ii*) There are certain areas where important information are not statutorily required to be disclosed. *Standards may call for disclosure beyond that required by law.*

(*iii*) The application of accounting standards would, to a limited extent, *facilitate comparison of financial statements of enterprises* situated in different parts of the world and also of different enterprises situated in the same country. However, it should be noted in this respect that differences in the institutions, traditions and legal systems from one country to another give rise to differences in accounting standards practiced in different countries.

(*iv*) *Accounting standards are the tools to remove the financial conflict between different groups of society.* It is true that the interest of each stake holder is different so there will be conflict between their interests. The Accounting standards will provide uniformity in the accounting treatment. Hence each party will have the knowledge of the affairs ; it will reduce the financial conflicts between different groups of society.

However, there are some *disadvantages* of setting of accounting standards :

(*i*) Alternative solutions to certain accounting problems may have arguments to recommend them. Therefore, the *choice between different alternative accounting treatments may become difficult.*

(*ii*) There may be *trend towards rigidity and away from flexibility* in applying the accounting standards.

(*iii*) Accounting standards *cannot override the statute.* The standards are required to be framed within the ambit of prevailing statutes.

INDIAN ACCOUNTING STANDARDS

A brief summary of the recognition, measurement, presentation and disclosure requirements under the Indian Accounting Standards (referred to as Ind AS or Standards in the guide) prescribed under section 133 of the Companies Act, 2013, as notified under the Companies (Indian Accounting Standard) Rules, 2015, in a simple and concise manner is discussed in this section.

It aims to present the fundamental concepts and principles of Ind AS in brief. It provides a high-level understanding of Ind AS rather than a set of detailed definitive interpretations of standards. The application of Ind AS to a specific company or a transaction is a matter of judgement given its particular facts and circumstances.

The arrangement of this section is as follows:

A. Applicability and Accounting Principles of Indian Accounting Standards (Ind AS)

B. Standards related to financial reporting and disclosures

(*i*) First-time adoption of Ind AS: Ind AS 101

(*ii*) Presentation of financial statements: Ind AS 1

(*iii*) Statement of cash flows: Ind AS 7

(*iv*) Accounting policies, changes in accounting estimates and errors: Ind AS 8

(*v*) Events after the reporting period: Ind AS 10

(*vi*) Non-current assets held for sale and discontinued operations: Ind AS 105

(*vii*) Fair value measurement: Ind AS 113

(*viii*) Operating segments: Ind AS 108

(*ix*) Related-party disclosures: Ind AS 24

(*x*) Separate financial statements: Ind AS 27
(*xi*) Earnings per share: Ind AS 33
(*xii*) Interim financial reporting: Ind AS 34
(*xiii*) Investment property: Ind AS 40

C. Standards providing guidance on financial statement line items

(*i*) Revenue from contracts with customers: Ind AS 115
(*ii*) Inventories: Ind AS 2
(*iii*) Income taxes: Ind AS 12
(*iv*) Property, plant and equipment: Ind AS 16
(*v*) Leases: Ind AS 17
(*vi*) Employee benefits: Ind AS 19
(*vii*) Share-based payment: Ind AS 102
(*viii*) Accounting for government grants and disclosure of government assistance: Ind AS 20
(*ix*) Effects of changes in foreign exchange rates and financial reporting in hyper inflationary economies: Ind AS 21 and Ind AS 29
(*x*) Borrowing costs: Ind AS 23
(*xi*) Impairment of assets: Ind AS 36
(*xii*) Provisions, contingent liabilities and contingent assets: Ind AS 37
(*xiii*) Intangible assets: Ind AS 38

D. Business acquisition and consolidation

(*i*) Business combinations: Ind AS 103
(*ii*) Consolidated financial statements: Ind AS 110
(*iii*) Joint arrangements: Ind AS 111
(*iv*) Disclosure of interest in other entities: Ind AS 112
(*v*) Investment in associates and joint ventures: Ind AS 28

E. Financial instruments

(*i*) Financial instruments: Ind AS 109
(*ii*) Financial instruments (presentation and disclosures): Ind AS 32,Ind AS 107, Ind AS 113 and Ind AS 109

F. Industry specific standards

(*i*) Insurance contracts: Ind AS 104
(*ii*) Exploration for and evaluation of mineral resources: Ind AS 106
(*iii*) Regulatory deferral accounts: Ind AS 114
(*iv*) Agriculture: Ind AS 41

G. Ind AS and IFRS: A comparison

H. List of standards: IAS/IFRS vs Ind AS

1. APPLICABILITY & ACCOUNTING PRINCIPLES OF INDIAN ACCOUNTING STANDARDS (IND AS)

Presently, the Institute of Chartered Accountants of India (ICAI) has issued 39 Indian Accounting Standards (Ind AS) which have been notified under the Companies (Indian Accounting Standards) Rules, 2015 ("Ind AS Rules"), of the Companies Act, 2013.

Applicability of Ind AS

As per the notification released by the Ministry of Corporate Affairs (MCA) on 16 February 2015, the roadmap for Ind AS implementation is as follows:

Financial Year	Mandatorily Applicable To:
2016-17	Companies (listed and unlisted) whose net worth is equal to or greater than 500 crore INR
2017-18	Unlisted companies whose net worth is equal to or greater than 250 crore INR and all listed companies
2018-19 onwards	When a company's net worth becomes greater than 250 crore INR
2015-16 or later	Entities, not under the mandatory road- map, may later voluntarily adopt Ind AS

Whenever a company gets covered under the roadmap, Ind AS becomes mandatory, its holding, subsidiary, associate and joint venture companies will also have to adopt Ind AS (irrespective of their net worth). For the purpose of computing the net worth, reference should be made to the definition under the Companies Act, 2013. In accordance with section 2 (57) of the Companies Act, 2013, net worth is computed as follows:

Net worth *means the aggregate value of the paid-up share capital and all reserves created out of the profits and securities premium account, after deducting the aggregate value of the accumulated losses, deferred expenditure and miscellaneous expenditure not written off, as per the audited balance sheet, but does not include reserves created out of revaluation of assets, write-back of depreciation and amalgamation.*

Ind AS will apply to both consolidated as well as standalone financial statements of a company. While overseas subsidiary, associate or joint venture companies are not required to prepare standalone financial statements under Ind AS, they will need to prepare Ind AS adjusted financial information to enable consolidation by the Indian parent.

Presently, insurance companies, banking companies and non- banking finance companies (NBFCs) are not required to apply Ind AS. The Ind AS rules are silent when these companies are subsidiaries, associates or joint ventures of a parent covered under the roadmap. It appears that these companies will need to report Ind AS adjusted financial information to enable consolidation by the parent.

In case of conflict between Ind AS and the law, the provisions of law will prevail and financial statements are to be prepared in compliance with the law.

Principles of Ind AS

The entities' general purpose financial statements give information about performance, position and cash flow that is useful to a different users in making financial decisions. These users include shareholders, creditors, employees and the general public.

A complete set of financial statements under Ind AS includes the following:

- Balance sheet at the end of the period
- Statement of profit and loss for the period
- Statement of changes in equity for the period
- Statement of cash flows for the period; notes, comprising a summary of significant accounting policies and other explanatory information
- Comparative financial information in respect of the preceding period as specified
- Balance sheet as at the beginning of the preceding period when an entity applies an accounting policy retrospectively or makes a retrospective restatement of items in its financial statements, or when it reclassifies items in its financial statements having an impact on the balance sheet as at the beginning of the preceding period.

India has chosen a path of International Financial Reporting Standards (IFRS) convergence rather than adoption. Hence, Ind AS are primarily based on the IFRS issued by the International Accounting Standards Board (IASB). However, there are certain carve-outs from the IFRS. There are also certain general differences between Ind AS and IFRS. These differences are stated here under:

- The transitional provisions given in each of the standards under IFRS have not been given in Ind AS, since all transitional provisions related to Ind AS, wherever considered appropriate, have been included in Ind AS 101, First-Time Adoption of Indian Accounting Standards, corresponding to IFRS 1, First-Time Adoption of International Financial Reporting Standards.
- Different terminology is used in Ind AS when compared to IFRS, e.g. the term 'balance sheet' is used instead of 'statement of financial position' and 'statement of profit and loss' is used instead of 'statement of comprehensive income'.

2. STANDARDS RELATED TO FINANCIAL REPORTING AND DISCLOSURES

First-Time Adoption Of IND AS: IND AS 101

An entity moving from Indian GAAP to Ind AS needs to apply the requirements of Ind AS 101. It applies to an entity's first Ind AS financial statements and the interim reports presented under Ind AS 34, 'Interim financial reporting', which are part of that period.

The basic requirement is for full retrospective application of all Ind AS, effective at the reporting date. However, there are a number of optional exemptions and mandatory exceptions to the requirement of retrospective application.

The exemptions cover standards for which it is considered that retrospective application could prove too difficult or could result in a cost likely to exceed related benefits to users. The exemptions are optional. Any, all or none of the exemptions may be applied.

The **optional exemptions** relate to the following:

- Share-based payment transactions
- Insurance contracts
- Deemed cost
- Leases
- Cumulative translation differences
- Investment in subsidiaries, joint ventures and associates
- Assets and liabilities of subsidiaries, joint ventures and associates
- Compound financial instruments
- Designation of previously recognised financial instruments
- Fair value measurement of financial assets or financial liabilities at initial recognition
- Decommissioning liabilities included in the cost of property, plant and equipment
- Financial assets or intangible assets accounted for in accordance with service concession arrangements
- Borrowing costs
- Extinguishing financial liabilities with equity instruments
- Severe hyperinflation
- Joint arrangements
- Stripping costs in the production phase of a surface mine
- Designation of contracts to buy or sell a non-financial item
- Revenue from contracts with customers
- Non-current assets held for sale and discontinued operations

Further, there are **mandatory exceptions** in applying the Ind AS requirements as summarised below:

- Derecognition of financial assets and liabilities
- Hedge accounting

- Non-controlling interests
- Classification and measurement of financial assets
- Impairment of financial assets
- Embedded derivatives
- Government loans
- Estimates

Comparative information is prepared and presented on the basis of Ind AS. Almost all adjustments arising from the first-time application of Ind AS are adjusted against opening retained earnings (or, if appropriate, another category of equity) of the first period that is presented on an Ind AS basis. Disclosures of certain reconciliations from Indian GAAP to Ind AS are required.

Presentation of Financial Statements: Ind AS 1

The objective of financial statements is to provide information that is useful in making economic decisions. This standard prescribes the basis for the presentation of general purpose financial statements in order to ensure comparability both with the entity's financial statements of previous periods and with those of other entities. It sets out overall requirements for the presentation of financial statements, guidelines for their structure and minimum requirements for their content.

Financial statements are prepared on a going concern basis unless management intends either to liquidate the entity or to cease trading, or has no realistic alternative but to do so. Management prepares its financial statements, except for cash flow information, under the accrual basis of accounting. There are minimum disclosures to be made in the financial statements and in the notes under Ind AS.

An entity shall present a single statement of profit and loss, with profit and loss and other comprehensive income presented in separate sections within the same statement. The sections shall be presented together with the profit and loss section presented first, followed directly by the other comprehensive section. An entity shall present, with equal prominence, all of the financial statements in a complete set of financial statements. Financial statements disclose corresponding information for the preceding period, unless a standard or interpretation permits or requires otherwise.

1. Material Items

The nature and amount of items of income and expense are disclosed separately where they are material. Disclosure may be in the statement or in the notes. Such income and expenses might include restructuring costs; write-downs of inventories or property, plant and equipment; litigation settlements; and gains or losses on disposals of property, plant and equipment.

2. Presentation Of True And Fair View

Financial statements shall present a true and fair view of the financial position, financial performance and cash flows of an entity. The application of Ind AS, with additional disclosures when necessary, is resumed to result in financial statements that present a true and fair view.

3. Going Concern And Accrual Basis Of Accounting

An entity shall prepare financial statements on a going concern basis unless management intends to either liquidate the entity or cease trading, or has no realistic alternative but to do so.

An entity shall prepare its financial statements, except for cash flow information, using the accrual basis of accounting.

4. Offsetting

An entity shall not offset assets and liabilities or income and expenses, unless required to or permitted by Ind AS.

5. Balance Sheet

The balance sheet presents an entity's financial position at a specific point in time. Subject to meeting certain minimum presentation and disclosure requirements, management may use its judgement regarding the form of presentation, such as which sub-classifications to present and what information to disclose on the face of the statement or in the notes.

Ind AS 1 specifies that the following items, as a minimum, are presented on the face of the balance sheet:

- **Assets**: Property, plant and equipment; investment property; intangible assets; financial assets; investments accounted for using the equity method; biological assets; deferred tax assets; current tax assets; inventories; trade and other receivables; and cash and cash equivalents
- **Equity**: Issued capital and reserves attributable to the parent's owners; and non-controlling interest
- **Liabilities**: Deferred tax liabilities; current tax liabilities; financial liabilities; provisions; and trade and other payables
- **Assets and liabilities held for sale**: The total of assets classified as held for sale and assets included in disposal groups classified as held for sale; and liabilities included in disposal groups classified as held for sale in accordance with Ind AS 105, 'non-current assets held for sale and discontinued operations'.

Current and non-current assets and liabilities are presented as separate classifications in the statement, unless the presentation based on liquidity provides reliable and more relevant information.

6. Statement Of Profit And Loss

The statement of profit and loss presents an entity's performance over a specific period. The statement of profit and loss includes all items of income and expense and includes each component of other comprehensive income classified by nature.

Items to be presented in statement of profit and loss

Ind AS 1 specifies certain items presented in the statement of profit and loss.

Additional line items or sub-headings are presented in this statement when relevant to an understanding of the entity's financial performance. Any item of income or expense is not presented as extraordinary item in the statement of profit and loss or in the notes. The expenses are classified in the statement of profit and loss based on the nature of expense.

7. Other Comprehensive Income

An entity shall present items of other comprehensive income grouped into those that will be reclassified subsequently to profit or loss and those that will not be reclassified. An entity shall disclose reclassification adjustments relating to the components of other comprehensive income. An entity presents each component of other comprehensive income in the statement either as:

(*i*) Net of its related tax effects, or

(*ii*) Before its related tax effects, with the aggregate tax effect of these components shown separately.

An entity needs to also disclose reclassification adjustments relating to components of other comprehensive income.

8. Statement Of Changes in Equity

The following items are presented in the statement of changes in equity:

- Total comprehensive income for the period, showing separately the total amounts attributable to the parent's owners and to non-controlling interest
- For each component of equity, the effects of retrospective application or retrospective restatement recognised in accordance with Ind AS 8, 'Accounting policies, changes in accounting estimates, and errors'.

- For each component of equity, reconciliation between the carrying amount at the beginning and the end of the period, separately disclosing changes resulting from the following:
  - → Profit or loss
  - → Other comprehensive income
  - → Transactions with owners in their capacity as owners, showing separately contributions by and distributions to owners and changes in ownership interests in subsidiaries that do not result in a loss of control
  - → Any item recognised directly in equity such as capital reserve on bargain purchase in a business combination transaction

The amounts of dividends recognised as distributions to owners during the period, and the related amount of dividends per share, shall be disclosed.

9. Statement Of Cash Flows

Cash flow statements are addressed in a separate summary dealing with the requirements of Ind AS 7.

10. Notes To The Financial Statements

The notes are an integral part of the financial statements. Notes provide information additional to the amounts disclosed in the 'primary' statements. They also include accounting policies, critical accounting estimates and judgements, disclosures on capital and puttable financial instruments classified as equity. Ind AS-1requires disclosures regarding reconciliation between the carrying amount at the beginning and the end of the period for each component of equity including disclosure regarding recognition of bargain purchase gain arising on business combination in line with the treatment prescribed in this regard in Ind AS 103.

Statement of Cash Flows: Ind AS 7

The statement of cash flows (cash flow statement) is one of the primary statements in financial reporting (along with the statement of profit and loss, the balance sheet and the statement of changes in equity). It presents the generation and use of 'cash and cash equivalents' by category (operating, investing and finance) over a specific period of time. It provides users with a basis to assess the entity's ability to generate and utilise its cash.

Operating activities are the entity's revenue-producing activities.

Investing activities are the acquisition and disposal of long-term assets (including business combinations) and investments that are not cash equivalents.

Financing activities are the changes in equity and borrowings.

Management may present operating cash flows by using either the direct method (gross cash receipts/payments) or the indirect method (adjusting net profit or loss for non-operating and non- cash transactions, and for changes in working capital).

Cash flows from investing and financing activities are reported gross separately (that is, gross cash receipts and gross cash payments) unless they meet certain specified criteria.

Interest paid and interest and dividends received are classified as financing cash flows and investing cash flows respectively. This is because they are costs of obtaining financial resources or returns on investments. Dividends paid should be classified as cash flows from financing activities because they are costs of obtaining financial resources. Cash flows relating to taxation on income are classified and separately disclosed under operating activities unless they can be specifically attributed to investing or financing activities. The total that summarises the effect of the operating, investing and financing cash flows is the movement in the balance of cash and cash equivalents for the period. Bank borrowings are generally considered as financing activities. However, bank overdrafts, which are repayable on demand form an integral part of an entity's cash management, are included as a component of cash and cash equivalents.

Separate disclosure is made of significant non-cash transactions (such as the issue of equity for the acquisition of a subsidiary or the acquisition of an asset through a finance lease).

Non-cash transactions include impairment losses/reversals, depreciation, amortisation, fair value gains/losses and income statement charges for provisions.

Accounting Policies, Changes in Accounting Estimates and Errors: Ind AS 8

An entity follows the accounting policies required by Ind AS relevant to the circumstances of the entity. However, for some situations, standards offer a choice. There are other situations where no guidance is given by Ind AS. In these situations, management needs to select appropriate accounting policies.

Management uses its judgement in developing and applying an accounting policy that results in relevant and reliable information. Reliable information demonstrates faithful representation, substance over form, neutrality, prudence and completeness. If there is no Ind AS or interpretation that is specifically applicable, management needs to consider the applicability of the requirements in Ind AS on similar and related issues, and then the definitions, recognition criteria and measurement concepts for assets, liabilities, income and expenses in the framework. In making the judgement on the selection of accounting policies, management may also first consider the most recent pronouncements of IASB and in absence thereof, those of the other standard-setting bodies that use a similar conceptual framework to develop accounting standards, other accounting literature and accepted industry practices, to the extent that these do not conflict with Ind AS.

Accounting policies need to be applied consistently to similar transactions and events (unless a standard permits or requires otherwise).

Changes in Accounting Policies

Changes in accounting policies made on adoption of a new standard are accounted for in accordance with the transition provisions (if any) within that standard. If specific transition provisions do not exist, a change in policy (whether required or voluntary) is accounted for retrospectively (that is, by restating all comparative figures presented) unless this is impracticable.

Issue of New or Revised Standards not yet Effective

Standards are normally published in advance of the required implementation date. In the intervening period, where a new or revised standard relevant to an entity has been issued but is not yet effective, management discloses this fact. It also provides the known or reasonably estimable information relevant to assessing the impact the application of the standard might have on the entity's financial statements in the period of initial recognition.

Changes in Accounting Estimates

An entity prospectively recognises changes in accounting estimates by including the effects in profit or loss in the period affected (the period of the change and future periods), except if the change in estimate gives rise to changes in assets, liabilities or equity. In this case, it is recognised by adjusting the carrying amount of the related asset, liability, or equity in the period of the change.

Errors

Errors may arise from mistakes and oversights or misinterpretation of information.

Errors discovered in a subsequent period are prior-period errors.

Material prior-period errors are adjusted retrospectively (that is, by restating comparative figures) unless this is impracticable (that is, it cannot be done, after 'making every reasonable effort to do so').

Events After the Reporting Period: Ind AS 10

It is not generally practicable for preparers to finalise financial statements without a period of time elapsing between the balance sheet date and the date on which the financial statements are approved for issue. The question therefore arises whether events occurring between the balance sheet date and the date of approval (that is, events after the reporting period) should be reflected in the financial statements.

Events after the reporting period are either adjusting events or non-adjusting events. Adjusting events provide further evidence of conditions that existed at the balance sheet date, for example, determining after the year end the consideration for assets sold before the year end. Non-adjusting events relate to conditions that arose after the balance sheet date–for example, announcing a plan to discontinue an operation after the year end.The carrying amounts of assets and liabilities at the balance sheet date are adjusted only for adjusting events or events that indicate that the going-concern assumption in relation to the whole entity is not appropriate. Significant non-adjusting post-balance-sheet events, such as the issue of shares or major business combinations, are disclosed.

Dividends proposed or declared after the balance sheet date but before the financial statements have been approved for issue are not recognised as a liability at the balance sheet date. Details of these dividends are, however, disclosed.

An entity discloses the date on which the financial statements were approved for issue and the persons approving the issue and, where necessary, the fact that the owners or other persons have the ability to amend the financial statements after issue.

Non-Current Assets held for Sale And Discontinued Operations : Ind AS 105

Ind AS 105, 'Non-current assets held for sale and discontinued operations', is relevant when any disposal occurs or is planned including distribution of non-current assets to shareholders. The held-for-sale criteria in Ind AS 105 apply to non-current assets (or disposal groups) whose value will be recovered principally through sale rather than through continuing use. The criteria do not apply to assets that are being scrapped, wound down or abandoned. Ind AS 105 defines a disposal group as a group of assets to be disposed of, by sale or otherwise, together as a group in a single transaction, and liabilities directly associated with those assets that will be transferred in the transaction.

The non-current asset (or disposal group) is classified as 'held for sale' if it is available for immediate sale in its present condition and its sale is highly probable. A sale is 'highly probable' where:

- There is evidence of management commitment
- There is an active programme to locate a buyer and complete the plan
- The asset is actively marketed for sale at a reasonable price compared to its fair value
- The sale is expected to be completed within 12 months of the date of classification
- Actions required to complete the plan indicate that it is unlikely that there will be significant changes to the plan or that it will be withdrawn. A non-current asset (or disposal group) is classified as 'held for distribution to owners' when the entity is committed to such distribution (that is, the assets must be available for immediate distribution in their present condition and the distribution must be highly probable). For a distribution to be highly probable, actions to complete the distribution need to have been initiated and should be expected to be completed within one year from the date of classification. Actions required to complete the distribution need to indicate that it is unlikely that significant changes to the distribution will be made or that the distribution will be withdrawn. The probability of shareholders' approval (if required in the jurisdiction) should be considered in the assessment of 'highly probable'.

Non-current assets (or disposal groups) classified as held for sale or as held for distribution are:

- Measured at the lower of the carrying amount and fair value less costs to sell
- Not depreciated or amortised
- Presented separately in the balance sheet (assets and liabilities should not be offset)
- A discontinued operation is a component of an entity that can be distinguished operationally and financially for financial reporting purposes from the rest of the entity and:
- Represents a separate major line of business or geographical area of operation
- Is part of a single coordinated plan to dispose of a separate major line of business or major geographical area of operation
- Is a subsidiary acquired exclusively with a view for resale

An operation is classified as discontinued only at the date on which the operation meets the criteria to be classified as held for sale or when the entity has disposed of the operation. Although balance sheet information is neither restated nor re-measured for discontinued operations, the statement of profit and loss information does have to be restated for the comparative period. Discontinued operations are presented separately in the statement of profit and loss and the cash flow statement. There are additional disclosure requirements in relation to discontinued operations. The date of disposal of a subsidiary or disposal group is the date on which the control passes. The consolidated income statement includes the results of a subsidiary or disposal group up to the date of disposal and the gain or loss on disposal.

Fair Value Measurement: Ind AS 113

Ind AS 113 defines fair value as 'The price that would be received to sell an asset or paid to transfer a liability in an orderly transaction between market participants at the measurement date' The key principle is that fair value is the exit price from the perspective of market participants who hold the asset or owe the liability at the measurement date. It is based on the perspective of market participants rather than the entity itself, so fair value is not affected by an entity's intentions towards the asset, liability or equity item that is being fair valued.

A fair value measurement requires management to determine four things:

- The particular asset or liability that is the subject of the measurement (consistent with its unit of account)
- The highest and best use for a non-financial asset
- The principal (or most advantageous) market
- The valuation technique (Ind AS 113 para B2)

Ind AS 113 addresses how to measure fair value but does not stipulate when fair value can or should be used.

Operating Segments: Ind AS 108

Segment guidance requires an entity to disclose information that enables users of the financial statements to evaluate the nature and financial effects of the business activities and the economic environments through the eyes of management ('management approach'). The identification of an entity's operating segments is the core determinant for the level of information included in the segment disclosures. Operating segments are components of an entity, identified based on the breakout of information contained in the internal reports that are regularly used by the entity's chief operating decision-maker (CODM) to allocate resources and to assess performance.

Reportable segments are individual operating segments or a group of operating segments for which segment information must be separately reported (that is, disclosed). Aggregation of one or more operating segments into a single reportable segment is permitted (but not required) where certain conditions are met, the principal condition being that the operating segments should have similar economic characteristics. Whether multiple operating segments can be aggregated into a single reportable segment is a matter of significant judgement.

For each segment disclosed, entities are required to provide a measure of profit or loss in the format viewed by the CODM, as well as a measure of assets and liabilities if such amounts are regularly provided to the CODM. Other segment disclosures include revenue from customers for each group of similar products and services, revenue by geography and dependence on major customers. Additional detailed disclosures of performance and resources are required if the CODM reviews these amounts. A reconciliation of the total amount disclosed for all segments to the primary financial statements is required for revenue, profit and loss, and other material items reviewed by the CODM.

Related-Party Disclosures: Ind AS 24

Under Ind AS 24, disclosures are required in respect of an entity's transactions with related parties. Related parties include the following:

- Parents
- Subsidiaries

- Fellow subsidiaries
- Associates of the entity and other members of the group
- Joint ventures of the entity and other members of the group
- Members of key management personnel of the entity or of a parent of the entity (and close members of their families)
- Persons with control, joint control or significant influence over the entity (and close members of their families)
- Post-employment benefit plans
- Entities (or any of their group members) providing key management personnel services to the entity or its parent

Finance providers are not related parties simply because of their normal dealings with the entity. Management discloses the name of the entity's parent and, if different, the ultimate controlling party. Relationships between a parent and its subsidiaries are disclosed irrespective of whether there have been transactions with them.

Where there have been related party transactions during the period, management discloses the nature of the relationship, as well as information about the transactions and outstanding balances, including commitments, necessary for users to understand the potential impact of the relationship on the financial statements. Disclosure is made by category of related party and by major type of transaction. Items of a similar nature may be disclosed in aggregate, except when separate disclosure is necessary for an understanding of the effects of related party transactions on the entity's financial statements.

Management only discloses that related party transactions which were made on terms equivalent to those that prevail in arm's length transactions if such terms can be substantiated. An entity is exempt from the disclosure of transactions (and outstanding balances) with a related party that is either a government that has control, joint control or significant influence over the entity or is another entity that is under the control, joint control or significant influence of the same government as the entity. Where the entity applies the exemption, it discloses the name of the government and the nature of its relationship with the entity. It also discloses the nature and amount of each individually significant transaction and the qualitative or quantitative extent of any collectively significant transactions.

Separate Financial Statements: Ind AS 27

This standard shall be applied in accounting for investments in subsidiaries, joint ventures and associates when an entity elects, or is required by law, to present separate financial statements.

Separate financial statements are those presented by a parent (that is, an investor with control of a subsidiary) or an investor with joint control of, or significant influence over, an investee, in which the investments are accounted for at cost or in accordance with Ind AS 109, 'Financial instruments'. Financial statements in which the equity method is applied are not separate financial statements. These may be termed as 'consolidated financial statements'. Similarly, the financial statements of an entity that does not have a subsidiary, associate or joint venturer's interest in a joint venture are not separate financial statements. Separate financial statements shall be prepared in accordance with all applicable Ind AS, except as follows:

When an entity prepares separate financial statements, it shall account for investments in subsidiaries, joint ventures and associates either at cost, or in accordance with Ind AS 109.

The entity shall apply the same accounting for each category of investments. Investments accounted for at cost shall be accounted for in accordance with Ind AS 105, 'Non-current assets held for sale and discontinued operations', when they are classified as held for sale (or included in a disposal group that is classified as held for sale). The measurement of investments accounted for in accordance with Ind AS 109 is not changed in such circumstances.

An entity shall recognise a dividend from a subsidiary, a joint venture or an associate in profit or loss in its separate financial statements when its right to receive the dividend is established.

Earnings Per Share: Ind AS 33

Earnings per share (EPS) is a ratio widely used by financial analysts, investors and others to gauge an entity's profitability and to value its shares. EPS is normally calculated in the context of ordinary shares of the entity. Earnings attributable to ordinary shareholders are therefore determined by deducting from net income the earnings attributable to holders of more senior equity instruments.

Basic EPS is calculated by dividing the profit or loss for the period attributable to the equity holders of the parent by the weighted average number of ordinary shares outstanding (including adjustments for bonus and rights issues).

Diluted EPS is calculated by adjusting the profit or loss and the weighted average number of ordinary shares by taking into account the conversion of any dilutive potential ordinary shares. Potential ordinary shares are those financial instruments and contracts that may result in issuing ordinary shares such as convertible bonds and options (including employee share options).

Basic and diluted EPS for both continuing and total operations are presented with equal prominence in the statement of profit and loss for each class of ordinary shares. Separate EPS figures for discontinued operations are disclosed in the same statement or in the notes.

Interim Financial Reporting: Ind AS 34

No Ind AS require an entity to publish interim financial statements. However, the publication of interim financial statements is required for listed entities under requirements of the listing agreement. For interim financial information, the entity needs to follow measurement and recognition principles laid down in this standard or the relevant Ind AS as applicable. For the purpose of disclosure, listed entities use the format as per the listing agreement.

In case of entities not preparing interim financial statements pursuant to the listing agreement but required to report interim financial information for any other purposes, they may either prepare full Ind AS financial statements (conforming to the requirements of Ind AS 1, 'Presentation of financial statements') or condensed financial statements. Condensed reporting is the more common approach. Condensed financial statements include a condensed balance sheet, a condensed statement of profit and loss, a condensed statement of cash flows, a condensed statement of changes in equity and selected explanatory notes.

An entity generally uses the same accounting policies for recognising and measuring assets, liabilities, revenues, expenses and gains and losses at interim dates as those to be used in the current year annual financial statements. There are special measurement requirements for certain costs that can only be determined on an annual basis (for example, items such as tax that is calculated based on an estimated full-year effective rate) and the use of estimates in the interim financial statements. An impairment loss recognised in a previous interim period in respect of goodwill is not reversed.

As a minimum requirement, current period and comparative figures (condensed or complete) are disclosed as follows:

- **Balance Sheet** as of the current interim period end with comparatives for the immediately preceding year end
- **Statement Of Profit Or Loss**-current interim period, financial year to date and comparatives for the same preceding periods (interim and year to date)
- **Cash Flow Statement** and **Statement of Changes in Equity** – financial year to date with comparatives for the same year to date period of the preceding year
- **Explanatory Notes** - Ind AS 34 sets out criteria to determine what information should be disclosed in the interim financial statements. These include the following:
- Materiality on the overall interim financial statements
- Unusual or irregular items
- Changes since previous reporting periods that have had a significant effect on the interim financial statements (of the current or previous reporting financial year)
- Relevance to the understanding of estimates used in the interim financial statements.

The overriding objective is to ensure that an interim financial report includes all information relevant to understanding an entity's financial position and performance during the interim period.

Investment Property: Ind AS 40

Certain properties are classified as investment properties for financial reporting purposes in accordance with Ind AS 40, 'Investment property', as the characteristics of these properties differ significantly from owner-occupied properties. It is the current value of such properties and changes to those values that are relevant to users of financial statements.

Investment property is property (land or a building, or part of a building or both) held by an entity to earn rentals and/or for capital appreciation. This category includes such property in the course of construction or development. Any other properties are accounted for as property, plant and equipment (PPE) or inventory in accordance with the following:

- Ind AS 16, 'Property, plant and equipment', if they are held for use in the production or supply of goods or services
- Ind AS 2, 'Inventories', as inventory, if they are held for sale in the ordinary course of business.

Initial measurement of an investment property will be at cost. Subsequent measurement of investment properties to be carried at cost less accumulated depreciation and any accumulated impairment losses. However, the fair value of the investment property is disclosed in the notes.

3. STANDARDS PROVIDING GUIDANCE ON FINANCIAL STATEMENT LINE ITEMS

Revenue From Contracts With Customers: Ind AS 115

In May 2014, the Financial Accounting Standards Board (FASB) and IASB issued the converged standard on revenue recognition ASC 606 and IFRS 15, 'Revenue from contracts with customers'. The MCA, while notifying the Ind AS, has chosen the IFRS 15 path, ensuring convergence with IFRS.

The standard contains principles that an entity will apply to determine the measurement of revenue and timing of when it is recognised. The underlying principle is that an entity will recognise revenue to depict the transfer of goods or services to customers at an amount it expects to be entitled to in exchange for those goods or services. The standard can significantly change how entities recognise revenue, especially those that currently apply industry-specific guidance. The standard will also result in a significant increase in the volume of disclosures related to revenue. While applying the new standard, entities will have to follow the following five-step process:

Identify the contract with a customer

Contracts can be oral or written. Following are the important criteria to consider before accounting for each contract:

- The parties have approved the contract and intend to perform their respective obligations.
- Each party's rights regarding the goods or services to be transferred can be identified.
- The payment terms can be identified.
- The risk, timing or amount of the entity's future cash flows are expected to change (that is, the contract has commercial substance).
- It is probable that the entity will collect the consideration to which it will be entitled in exchange for goods or services transferred.

Identify the separate performance obligations in the contract

A performance obligation is a promise to transfer a distinct good or service (or a series of distinct goods or services that are substantially the same and have the same pattern of transfer) to a customer. The promise can be explicit, implicit or implied by an entity's customary business practice. The objective of identifying distinct performance obligations is to depict the transfer of goods or services to the customer. Identifying performance obligations is more challenging when there are multiple explicit or implicit promises in a contract.

Determine the transaction price

The transaction price is the amount of consideration that an entity expects to be entitled to in exchange for transferring promised goods or services to a customer, excluding amounts collected on behalf of a third party (for example, some sales taxes). Determining the transaction price is more complex if the arrangement involves variable consideration, a significant financing component, non-cash consideration or consideration payable to a customer.

Allocate the Transaction Price to the Separate Performance Obligations

The transaction price is allocated to the separate performance obligations in a contract based on the relative stand-alone selling prices of the goods or services promised. This allocation is made at contract inception and not adjusted to reflect subsequent changes in the standalone selling prices of those goods or services. The best evidence of standalone selling price is the observable price of a good or service when the entity sells that good or service separately. Management will need to estimate the selling price of goods or services that do not have an observable standalone selling price, and maximise the use of observable inputs while making that estimate. Possible estimation methods include, but are not limited to the following:

- Expected cost plus and appropriate margin
- Assessment of market prices for similar goods or services adjusted for entity-specific costs and margins
- Residual approach, in limited circumstances
- Discounts and variable consideration will typically be allocated proportionately to all of the performance obligations in the contract. A discount or variable consideration can be allocated to one or more separate performance obligations, rather than to all performance obligations in the arrangement if the following conditions are met:
- The entity regularly sells each distinct good or service (or each bundle of distinct goods or services) on a standalone basis.
- The entity regularly sells, on a standalone basis, a bundle of some of the goods or services at a discount to the standalone selling prices of the goods or services in that bundle.
- The discount attributable to the bundle of goods or services is substantially the same as the discount in the contract.

For example, when a product is sold with a subsequent service, basis above, revenue is allocated initially to the product component and the service component; it is recognised separately thereafter when the criteria for revenue recognition are met for each component.

Recognise Revenue When (or as) Each Performance Obligation is Satisfied

The final step in the model is recognising revenue. An entity will recognise revenue when (or as) a good or service is transferred to the customer and the customer obtains control of that good or service. Control of an asset refers to an entity's ability to direct the use of and obtain substantially all of the remaining benefits (that is, the potential cash inflows or savings in outflows) from the asset. Directing the use of an asset refers to a customer's right to deploy that asset, to allow another entity to deploy that asset in its activities or to restrict another entity from deploying that asset.

The standard requires management to determine when the control of a good or service has been transferred to the customer. The timing of revenue recognition can change for some transactions when compared to current guidance, which is more focussed on the transfer of risks and rewards. Though the transfer of risks and rewards is an indicator of whether control has been transferred, additional indicators also need to be considered. For example, an entity that transfers control of a good to a customer but retains some economic risks might need to record revenue when the control over good transfers, while under existing guidance revenue recognition might be delayed until all of the economic risks have also transferred.

An entity needs to determine during contract inception whether the control of a good or service will be transferred over time or at a point in time. This determination needs to depict the transfer of benefits to the customer and should be evaluated from the customer's perspective. An entity should first assess whether the performance obligation is satisfied over time. If not, the good or service transfers at a point in time.

Recognition of Revenue Over Time

An entity will recognise revenue over time if any of the following criteria are met:

- The customer concurrently receives and consumes the benefits provided by the entity's performance as the entity performs.
- The entity's performance creates or enhances a customer- controlled asset.
- The entity's performance does not create an asset with an alternative use and the entity has a right to payment for performance completed to date.

Recognition of Revenue at a Point in time

An entity will recognise revenue at a point in time (when control transfers) for performance obligations that do not meet the criteria for recognition of revenue over time. To determine when a customer obtains control and an entity satisfies a performance obligation, the entity should consider the concept of control and the following indicators:

- The entity has a present right to payment for the asset.
- The entity transferred legal title to the asset.
- The entity transferred physical possession of the asset.
- The entity transferred significant risk and rewards of ownership to the customer.
- The customer accepted the asset.

Additional Considerations

Certain additional concepts in Ind AS 115, dealt with in greater detail than in today's GAAP guidance, have been summarised below:

Multiple element arrangements. Understanding what a customer expects to receive as a final product is necessary to assess whether goods or services need to be combined and accounted as a single performance obligation or multiple elements. Some contracts contain a promise to deliver multiple goods or services, but the customer is not purchasing the individual items. The customer, instead, is purchasing the final good or service which is the aggregate of those individual items. Judgement, based on proper application of the principles envisaged in Ind AS 115, will determine whether a contract involves a single or multiple separate performance obligations. The guidance provided in Ind AS 115 is more detailed and explicit for such situations compared to the current accounting practices.

Variable consideration. Entities may agree to provide goods or services for consideration that varies upon certain future events which may or may not occur. Examples include refund rights, performance bonuses and penalties. This can sometimes be driven by the past practice of an entity or industry, for example, if there is a history of providing discounts or concessions after the goods are sold.

Under current practice (pre Ind AS 115), it is not uncommon to defer revenue until the contingency is resolved. However, upon adoption of Ind AS 115, an estimate of variable consideration needs to be made at contract inception and a reassessment may be required at each reporting date. Even if the entire amount of variable consideration fails to meet this threshold, management will need to consider whether a portion does meet the criterion. This amount is recognised as revenue when goods or services are transferred to the customer and can affect entities in industries where variable consideration is currently not recorded until all contingencies are resolved. Management will need to reassess estimates at each reporting period, and adjust revenue accordingly. This can result in early revenue recognition in comparison with current practice.

Time value of money. Some contracts provide the customer or the entity with a significant financing benefit (explicitly or implicitly). This is because performance by an entity and payment by its customer might occur at significantly different times. Under the new standard, an entity needs to adjust the transaction price for the time value of money if the contract includes a significant financing component. The standard provides certain exceptions to applying this guidance and a practical expedient which allows entities to ignore time value of money if the time between transfer of goods or services and payment is less than one year. Presently, such financing benefit is not identified and separated under the current Indian GAAP. This aspect will impact entities which have significant advance or deferred payment arrangements.

Contract costs. Entities sometimes incur costs (such as sales commissions or mobilisation activities) to obtain or fulfil a contract. Contract costs that meet certain criteria will be capitalised as assets and amortised as revenue under the new standard. Such capitalised costs will require a periodic review for recoverability and impairment, if applicable.

Disclosures. Further, the disclosures required in Ind AS 115 are far more elaborate than the prevalent practice. For instance, quantitative and qualitative information will have to be provided about significant judgements and changes in those judgements that management makes to determine revenue.

Service concession arrangements: Appendix C to Ind AS 115. Appendix C to Ind AS 115 'Service concession arrangements' sets out the accounting requirements for service concession arrangements while Appendix D to Ind AS 115 'Services concession arrangements: Disclosures' contains disclosure requirements. Appendix C and D of Ind AS 115 apply to public-to-private service concession arrangements in which the public sector body (the grantor) controls and/or regulates the services provided with the infrastructure by the private sector entity (the operator). The concession arrangement also addresses to whom the operator needs to provide the services and at what price. The grantor controls any significant residual interest in the infrastructure. As the infrastructure is controlled by the grantor, the operator does not recognise the infrastructure as its property, plant and equipment; nor does the operator recognise a finance lease receivable for leasing the public service infrastructure to the grantor, regardless of the extent to which the operator bears the risk and rewards incidental to ownership of the assets.

The operator recognises a financial asset to the extent that it has an unconditional contractual right to receive cash irrespective of the usage of the infrastructure or an intangible asset to the extent that it receives a right (a license) to charge users of the public service. Under both the financial asset and the intangible asset models, the operator accounts for revenue and costs relating to construction or upgrade services in accordance with Ind AS 115, 'Revenue from contracts with customers'. The operator recognises revenue and costs relating to operation services in accordance with Ind AS 115. Any contractual obligation to maintain or restore infrastructure, except for upgrade services, is recognised in accordance with Ind AS 37, 'Provisions, contingent liabilities and contingent assets'.

Inventories: Ind AS 2

Inventories are initially recognised at the lower of cost and net realisable value (NRV). Cost of inventories includes import duties, non-refundable taxes, transport and handling costs and any other directly attributable costs, less trade discounts, rebates and similar items. Costs such as abnormal amount of wasted materials, storage costs, administrative costs and selling costs are excluded from the cost of inventories. NRV is the estimated selling price in the ordinary course of business, less the estimated costs of completion and estimated selling expenses.

Techniques for the measurement of the cost of inventories, such as the standard cost method or the retail method, may be used for convenience if the results approximate cost. Ind AS 2, 'Inventories', requires the cost for items that are not interchangeable or that have been segregated for specific contracts to be determined on an individual-item basis. The cost of other inventory items used is assigned by using either the first- in, first-out (FIFO) or weighted average cost formula. Last-in, first-out (LIFO) is not permitted. An entity uses the same cost formula for all inventories of similar nature and use to the entity. A different cost formula may be justified where inventories have a different nature or use. The cost formula used is applied on a consistent basis from period to period.

An entity may purchase inventories on deferred payment terms. When the arrangement effectively contains a financing element, that element, for example a difference between the purchase price for normal credit terms and the amount paid, is recognised as interest expense over the period of the financing.

Income Taxes: Ind AS 12

Ind AS 12 deals only with taxes on income, comprising current tax and deferred tax.

Current tax expense for a period is based on the taxable and deductible amounts to be used for the computation of the taxable income for the current year. An entity recognises a liability in the balance sheet in respect of current tax expense for the current and prior periods to the extent unpaid. It recognises an asset if current tax has been overpaid.

Current tax assets and liabilities for the current and prior periods are measured at the amount expected to be paid to (recovered from) the taxation authorities, using the tax rates and tax laws that have been enacted or substantively enacted by the balance sheet date.

Tax payable based on taxable profit seldom matches the tax expense that might be expected based on pre-tax accounting profit. The mismatch can occur because Ind AS recognition criteria for items of income and expense are different from the treatment of items under tax law.

Deferred tax accounting seeks to deal with this mismatch. It is based on the temporary differences between the tax base of an asset or liability and its carrying amount in the financial statements. For example, if an asset is revalued upwards but not sold, the revaluation creates a temporary difference (if the carrying amount of the asset in the financial statements is greater than the tax base of the asset), and the tax consequence is a deferred tax liability.

Deferred tax is provided in full for all temporary differences arising between the tax bases of assets and liabilities and their carrying amounts in the financial statements, except when the temporary difference arises from the following:

- Initial recognition of goodwill (for deferred tax liabilities only)
- Initial recognition of an asset or liability in a transaction which is not a business combination and which affects neither accounting profit nor taxable profit
- Investments in subsidiaries, branches, associates and joint ventures, but only when certain criteria apply.

Deferred tax assets and liabilities are measured at the tax rates that are expected to apply to the period when the asset is realised or the liability is settled based on tax rates (and tax laws) that have been enacted or substantively enacted by the balance sheet date. The discounting of deferred tax assets and liabilities is not permitted.

Generally, the measurement of deferred tax liabilities and deferred tax assets reflects the tax consequences that would follow based on what the entity expects, at the balance sheet date, to recover or settle the carrying amount of its assets and liabilities. The expected manner of recovery of land with an unlimited life is always through sale. For other assets, the manner in which management expects to recover the asset (that is, through use or through sale or through a combination of both) is considered at each balance sheet date. Management only recognises a deferred tax asset for deductible temporary differences to the extent that it is probable that taxable profit will be available against which the deductible temporary difference can be utilised. This also applies to deferred tax assets for unused tax losses carried forward. Current and deferred tax is recognised in profit or loss for the period, unless the tax arises from a business combination or a transaction or event that is recognised outside profit or loss, either in other comprehensive income or directly in equity in the same or different period. The accompanying tax consequences, for example, a change in tax rates or tax laws, a reassessment of the recoverability of deferred tax assets or a change in the expected manner of recovery of an asset are recognised in profit or loss, except to the extent that they relate to the items previously charged or credited outside of profit or loss.

Property, Plant and Equipment: Ind AS 16

Property, plant and equipment (PPE) is recognised when the cost of an asset can be reliably measured and it is probable that the entity will obtain future economic benefits from the asset.

PPE is measured initially at cost. Cost includes the fair value of the consideration given to acquire the asset (net of discounts and rebates) and any directly attributable cost of bringing the asset to working condition for its intended use (inclusive of import duties and non-refundable purchase taxes). Directly attributable costs include the cost of site preparation, delivery, installation costs, relevant professional fees and the estimated cost of dismantling and removing the asset and restoring the site (to the extent that such a cost is recognised as a provision). Classes of PPE are carried at historical cost less accumulated depreciation and any accumulated impairment losses (the cost model), or at a revalued amount less any accumulated depreciation and subsequent accumulated impairment losses (the revaluation model). The depreciable amount of PPE (being the gross carrying value less the estimated residual value) is depreciated on a systematic basis over its useful life.

Subsequent expenditure relating to an item of PPE is capitalised if it meets the recognition criteria. PPE may comprise parts with different useful lives. Depreciation is calculated based on each individual part's life. In case of replacement of one part, the new part is capitalised to the extent that it meets the recognition criteria of an asset, and the carrying amount of the parts replaced is derecognised.

The cost of a major inspection or overhaul of an item occurring at regular intervals over the useful life of the item is capitalised to the extent that it meets the recognition criteria of an asset. The carrying amounts of the parts replaced are derecognised.

Leases: Ind AS 17

A lease gives one party (the lessee) the right to use an asset over an agreed period of time in return for payment to the lessor. Leasing is an important source of medium and long- term financing; and accounting for leases can have a significant impact on lessees' and lessors' financial statements.

Leases are classified as finance or operating leases at inception, depending on whether substantially all the risks and rewards of ownership transfers to the lessee. Under a finance lease, the lessee has substantially all of the risks and rewards of ownership. All other leases are operating leases. Leases of land and buildings are considered separately under Ind AS.

Under a finance lease, the lessee recognises an asset held under a finance lease and a corresponding obligation to pay rentals. The lessee depreciates the asset.

The lessor recognises the leased asset as a receivable. The receivable is measured at the 'net investment' in the lease–the minimum lease payments receivable, discounted at the internal rate of return of the lease, plus the unguaranteed residual that accrues to the lessor.

Under an operating lease, the lessee does not recognise an asset and lease obligation. The lessor continues to recognise the leased asset and depreciates it. The rentals paid are normally charged to the income statement of the lessee and credited to that of the lessor on a straight-line basis unless another systematic basis is more representative of the time pattern of the user's benefit or if the payments to the lessor are agreed to increase in line with expected general inflation to compensate for the lessor's expected inflationary cost increases. Linked transactions with the legal form of a lease are accounted for on the basis of their substance–for example, a sale and leaseback where the seller is committed to repurchase the asset may not be a lease in substance if the 'seller' retains the risks and rewards of ownership and substantially the same rights of use as before the transaction.

Equally, some transactions that do not have the legal form of a lease are in substance leases if they are dependent on a particular asset that the purchaser can control physically or economically.

Employee Benefits: Ind AS 19

The accounting for employee benefits, for pensions in particular, is complex. The liabilities in defined benefit pension plans are frequently material. They are long-term and difficult to measure, and this gives rise to difficulty in measuring the cost attributable to each year.

Employee benefits are all forms of consideration given or promised by an entity in exchange for services rendered by its employees. These benefits include salary-related benefits (such as wages, profit-sharing, bonuses and compensated absences, such as paid holiday and long-service leave), termination benefits (such as severance and redundancy pay) and post- employment benefits (such as retirement benefit plans). Ind AS

19 is relevant for all employee benefits except for those to which Ind AS 102, share-based payments, applies. Post-employment benefits include pensions, post-employment life insurance and medical care. Pensions are provided to employees either through defined contribution plans or defined benefit plans. Recognition and measurement for short-term benefits are relatively straightforward, because actuarial assumptions are not required and the obligations are not discounted. However, long- term benefits, particularly post-employment benefits, give rise to more complicated measurement issues.

Defined Contribution Plans

Accounting for defined contribution plans is straightforward. The cost of defined contribution plans is the contribution payable by the employer for that accounting period.

Defined Benefit Plans

Accounting for defined benefit plans is complex because actuarial assumptions and valuation methods are required to measure the balance sheet obligation and the expense. The expense recognised generally differs from the contributions made in the period.

Subject to certain conditions, the net amount recognised on the balance sheet is the difference between the defined benefit obligation and the plan assets.

To calculate the defined benefit obligation, estimates (actuarial assumptions) regarding demographic variables (such as employee turnover and mortality) and financial variables (such as future increases in salaries and medical costs) are made and included in a valuation model. The resulting benefit obligation is then discounted to a present value. This normally requires the expertise of an actuary. Where defined benefit plans are funded, the plan assets are measured at fair value.

Where no market price is available, the fair value of plan assets is estimated, for example, by discounting expected future cash flows using a discount rate that reflects both the risk associated with the plan assets and the maturity of those assets. Plan assets are tightly defined, and only assets that meet a strict definition may be offset against the plan's defined benefit obligations, resulting in a net surplus or net deficit that is shown on the balance sheet.

At each balance sheet date, the plan assets and the defined benefit obligations are re-measured. The income statement reflects the change in the surplus or deficit, except for contributions made to the plan and benefits paid by the plan, along with business combinations and re-measurement gains and losses. Re-measurement gains and losses comprise actuarial gains and losses, return on plan assets (comprise amounts included in net interest on the net defined benefit liability or asset) and any change in the effect of the asset ceiling (excluding amounts included in net interest on the net defined benefit liability or asset). Remeasurements are recognised in other comprehensive income.

The amount of pension expense (income) to be recognised in profit or loss is comprised of the following individual components, unless they are required or permitted to be included in the costs of an asset:

- **Service costs** (present value of the benefits earned by active employees)
- **Net interest costs** (unwinding of the discount on the defined benefit obligations and a theoretical return on plan assets)

Service costs comprise the 'current service costs', which are the increase in the present value of the defined benefit are resulting from employee services in the current period, 'past-service costs' (as defined below and including any gain or loss on curtailment) and any gain or loss on settlement.

Net interest on the net defined benefit liability (asset) is defined as, 'the change during the period in the net defined benefit liability (asset) that arises from the passage of time' (Ind AS 19 para 8). The net interest cost can be viewed as comprising theoretical interest income on plan assets, interest cost on the defined benefit obligation (that is, representing the unwinding of the discount on the plan obligation) and interest on the effect of the asset ceiling (Ind AS 19 para 124).

Net interest on the net defined benefit liability (asset) is calculated by multiplying the net defined benefit liability (asset) by the discount rate, both as determined at the start of the annual reporting period, taking account of any changes in the net defined benefit liability (asset) during the period as a result of contribution and benefit payments (Ind AS 19 para 123). The discount rate applicable to any financial year is an appropriate government bond rate. However, subsidiaries, associates, joint ventures and branches domiciled outside India shall discount post-employment benefit obligations arising on account of post-employment benefit plans using the rate determined by reference to market yields at the end of the reporting period on high quality corporate bonds. In case such subsidiaries, associates, joint ventures and branches are domiciled in countries where there is no deep market in such bonds, the market yield (at the end of the reporting period) on government bonds of that country shall be used. Net interest on the net defined benefit liability (asset) can be viewed as effectively including theoretical interest income on plan assets.

Past-service costs are defined as a change in the present value of the defined benefit obligation for employee services in prior periods, resulting from a plan amendment (the introduction or withdrawal of, or changes to, a defined benefit plan) or a curtailment (a significant reduction by the entity in the number of employees covered by a plan). Past-service costs need to be recognised as an expense generally when a plan amendment or curtailment occurs. Settlement gains or losses are recognised in the income statement when the settlement occurs.

Appendix B, 'Ind AS 19–The limit on a defined benefit asset, minimum funding requirements and their interaction', provides guidance on assessing the amount that can be recognised as an asset when plan assets exceed the defined benefit obligation, creating a net surplus. It also explains how the pension asset or liability may be affected by a statutory or contractual minimum funding requirement.

Share-Based Payment: Ind AS 102

Ind AS 102 applies to all share-based payment arrangements. A share-based payment arrangement is defined as: An agreement between the entity (or another group entity or any shareholder of any group entity) and another party (including an employee) that entitles the other party to receive:

- Cash or other assets of the entity for amounts that are based on the price (or value) of equity instruments (including shares or share options) of the entity or another group entity, or
- Equity instruments (including shares or share options) of the entity or another group entity.

The most common application is employee share schemes such as share option schemes. However, entities sometimes also pay for other expenses such as professional fees, and for the purchase of assets by means of share-based payment.

The accounting treatment under Ind AS 102 is based on the fair value of the instruments. Both the valuation of and the accounting for awards sometimes can be difficult due to the complex models that may need to be used to calculate the fair value of options, and also due to the variety and complexity of schemes. In addition, the standard requires extensive disclosures.

The result generally is reduced reported profits, especially in entities that use share-based payment extensively as part of their remuneration strategy.

All transactions involving share-based payment are recognised as expenses or assets over underlying vesting period. Equity-settled share-based payment transactions are measured at the grant date fair value for employee services; and, for non-employee transactions, at the fair value of the goods or services received at the date on which the entity recognises the goods or services. If the fair value of the goods or services cannot be estimated reliably—such as employee services and circumstances in which the goods or services cannot be specifically identified—the entity uses the fair value of the equity instruments granted.

Equity-settled share-based payment transactions are not re-measured once the grant date fair value has been determined. The treatment is different for cash-settled share-based payment transactions—cash-settled awards are measured at the fair value of the liability. The liability is re-measured at each balance sheet date through the date of settlement, with changes in fair value recognised in the income statement.

Accounting for Government Grants and Disclosure of Government Assistance: Ind AS 20

Government grants are recognised when there is reasonable assurance that the entity will comply with the conditions related to them and that the grants will be received.

Grants related to income are recognised in profit or loss on a systematic basis over the periods necessary to match them with the related costs that they are intended to compensate. They are either offset against the related expense or presented as separate income. The timing of such recognition in profit or loss will depend on the fulfilment of any conditions or obligations attached to the grant.

Grants related to assets are presented as deferred income in the balance sheet. Profit or loss will be affected by deferred income being recognised as income systematically over the useful life of the related asset.

Cash movements related to purchase of assets and receipt of related grants are disclosed as separate items in the statement of cash flows. Non-monetary grants are required to be accounted at fair value.

Effects of Changes in Foreign Exchange Rates and Financial Reporting in Hyperinflationary Economies: Ind AS 21 and Ind AS 29

Many entities do business with overseas suppliers or customers, or have overseas operations. This gives rise to two main accounting issues:

- Some transactions (for example, those with overseas suppliers or customers) may be denominated in foreign currencies. These transactions are expressed in the entity's own currency (functional currency) for financial reporting purposes.
- A parent entity may have foreign operations such as overseas subsidiaries, branches or associates. The functional currency of these foreign operations may be different to the parent entity's functional currency and therefore the accounting records may be maintained in different currencies. Because it is not possible to combine transactions measured in different currencies, the foreign operation's results and financial position are translated into a single currency, namely that in which the group's consolidated financial statements are reported (presentation currency). The methods required for each of the above circumstances have been summarised below.

Expressing Foreign Currency Transactions in the Entity's Functional Currency

A foreign currency transaction is expressed in an entity's functional currency using the exchange rate at the transaction date. Foreign currency balances representing cash or amounts to be received or paid in cash (monetary items) are retranslated at the end of the reporting period using the exchange rate on that date. Exchange differences on such monetary items are recognised as income or expense for the period, except where an entity has opted for the exemption given in Ind AS 101, allowing it to continue the policy adopted for accounting for exchange differences arising from translation of long-term foreign currency monetary items recognised in the financial statements for the period ending immediately before beginning of the first Ind AS financial reporting period as per the previous GAAP.

Such an entity may continue to apply the accounting policy so opted for such long-term foreign currency monetary items under previous GAAP. Non-monetary balances that are not re-measured at fair value and are denominated in a foreign currency are expressed in the functional currency using the exchange rate at the transaction date. Where a non-monetary item is re-measured at fair value in the financial statements, the exchange rate at the date when fair value was determined is used.

Translating Functional Currency Financial Statements into A Presentation Currency

Assets and liabilities are translated from the functional currency to the presentation currency at the closing rate at the end of the reporting period. The income statement is translated at exchange rates at the dates of the transactions or at the average rate if that approximates the actual rates. All resulting exchange differences are recognised in other comprehensive income.

Change in Functional Currency

When there is a change in functional currency of either the reporting entity or a significant foreign operation, Ind AS 21 requires disclosure of that fact and the reason for the change in functional currency along with disclosure of the date of change in functional currency. The effect of a change in functional currency is accounted for prospectively.

The financial statements of a foreign operation that has the currency of a hyperinflationary economy as its functional currency are first restated in accordance with Ind AS 29, 'Financial reporting in hyperinflationary economies'. All components are then translated to the presentation currency at the closing rate at the end of the reporting period. Disclosure regarding the duration of the hyperinflationary situation existing in the economy needs to be provided.

Financial Reporting In Hyperinflationary Economies

In a hyperinflationary economy, reporting of operating results and financial position in the local currency without restatement is not useful. Money loses purchasing power at such a rate that comparison of amounts from transactions and other events that have occurred at different times, even within the same accounting period, is misleading.

Ind AS 29 applies to the financial statements of entities reporting in the currency of a hyperinflationary economy. Presentation of the information required by this standard as a supplement to unrestated financial statements is not permitted. Furthermore, separate presentation of the financial statements before restatement is discouraged.

The financial statements of an entity whose functional currency is the currency of a hyperinflationary economy, whether they are based on a historical cost approach or a current cost approach, shall be stated in terms of the measuring unit current at the end of the reporting period.

The corresponding figures for the previous period required by Ind AS 1, 'Presentation of financial statements', and any information in respect of earlier periods shall also be stated in terms of the measuring unit current at the end of the reporting period. For the purpose of presenting comparative amounts in a different presentation currency, paragraphs 42(b) and 43 of Ind AS 21, 'The effects of changes in foreign exchange rates', apply. The gain or loss on the net monetary position shall be included in profit or loss and separately disclosed.

The restatement of financial statements in accordance with this standard requires the application of certain procedures as well as judgement. The consistent application of these procedures and judgements from period to period is more important than the precise accuracy of the resulting amounts included in the restated financial statements.

The restatement of financial statements in accordance with this standard requires the use of a general price index that reflects changes in general purchasing power. It is preferable that all entities that report in the currency of the same economy use the same index. When an economy ceases to be hyperinflationary and an entity discontinues the preparation and presentation of financial statements prepared in accordance with this standard, it shall treat the amounts expressed in the measuring unit current at the end of the previous reporting period as the basis for the carrying amounts in its subsequent financial statements.

Borrowing Costs: Ind AS 23

Under Ind AS 23, 'Borrowing costs', borrowing costs directly attributable to the acquisition, construction or production of a qualifying asset are to be capitalised. An entity shall recognise other borrowing costs as an expense in the period in which it incurs them.

Borrowing costs are interest and other costs that an entity incurs in connection with the borrowing of funds.

A qualifying asset is an asset that necessarily takes a substantial period of time to get ready for its intended use or sale.

An entity shall begin capitalising borrowing costs as part of the cost of a qualifying asset on the commencement date. The commencement date for capitalisation is the date when the entity first meets all of the following conditions:

- Incurs expenditures for the asset
- Incurs borrowing costs
- Undertakes activities that are necessary to prepare the asset for its intended use or sale.

An entity shall suspend capitalisation of borrowing costs during extended periods in which it suspends active development of a qualifying asset.

An entity shall cease capitalising borrowing costs when substantially all the activities necessary to prepare the qualifying asset for its intended use or sale are complete.

Impairment of Assets: Ind AS 36

Nearly all assets "current and non-current" are subject to an impairment test to ensure that they are not overstated on the balance sheet.

The basic principle of impairment is that an asset may not be carried on the balance sheet above its recoverable amount. Recoverable amount is defined as the higher of the asset's fair value less costs of disposal and its value in use. Fair value less costs of disposal is the price that would be received to sell upon disposal of an asset in an orderly transaction between market participants at the measurement date, less costs of disposal. Guidance on fair valuing is given in Ind AS 113, 'Fair value measurement'. Value in use requires management to estimate the future pre-tax cash flows to be derived from the asset and discount them using a pre-tax market rate that reflects current assessments of the time value of money and the risks specific to the asset.

All assets, subject to the impairment guidance, are tested for impairment where there is an indication that the asset may be impaired. Certain assets (goodwill, indefinite lived intangible assets and intangible assets that are not yet available for use) are also tested for impairment annually even if there is no impairment indicator. This impairment test may be performed any time during the annual period, provided it is performed at the same time every year. When considering whether an asset is impaired, both external indicators (for example, significant adverse changes in the technological, market, economic or legal environment or increases in market interest rates) and internal indicators (for example, evidence of obsolescence or physical damage of an asset or evidence from internal reporting that the economic performance of an asset is, or will be, worse than expected) are considered.

Recoverable amount is calculated at the individual asset level. However, an asset seldom generates cash flows independently of other assets, and most assets are tested for impairment in groups of assets described as cash-generating units (CGUs). A CGU is the smallest identifiable group of assets that generates inflows that are largely independent from the cash flows from other CGUs.

The carrying value of an asset is compared to the recoverable amount (being the higher of value in use or fair value less costs of disposal). It is not always necessary to determine both an asset's fair value less cost of disposal and its value in use. If either of these amounts exceeds the carrying amount, the asset is not impaired and it is not necessary to estimate the other amount. An asset or CGU is impaired when its carrying amount exceeds its recoverable amount. Any impairment is allocated to the asset or assets of the CGU, with the impairment loss recognised in profit or loss. Goodwill acquired in a business combination is allocated to the acquirer's CGUs or groups of CGUs that are expected to benefit from the synergies of the business combination. However, the largest group of CGUs permitted for goodwill impairment testing is an operating segment before aggregation. An impairment loss recognised in prior periods for an asset other than goodwill shall be reversed if, and only if, there has been a change in the estimates used to determine the asset's recoverable amount since the last impairment loss was recognised. An impairment loss recognised for goodwill is not reversed in a subsequent period.

Provisions, Contingent Liabilities And Contingent Assets: Ind AS 37

A liability is a 'present obligation of the entity arising from past events, the settlement of which is expected to result in an outflow from the entity of resources embodying economic benefits'. A provision falls within the category of liabilities and is defined as 'a liability of uncertain timing or amount'.

Recognition and Initial Measurement

A provision is recognised when: the entity has a present obligation to transfer economic benefits as a result of past events; it is probable (more likely than not) that such a transfer will be required to settle the obligation; and a reliable estimate of the amount of the obligation can be made.

The amount recognised as a provision is the best estimate of the expenditure required to settle the obligation at the balance sheet date, measured at the expected cash flows discounted for the time value of money. Provisions are not recognised for future operating losses.

A present obligation arises from an obligating event and may take the form of either a legal obligation or a constructive obligation. An obligating event leaves the entity with no realistic alternative to settle the obligation. If the entity can avoid future expenditure by its future actions, it has no present obligation, and no provision is required. For example, an entity cannot recognise a provision based solely on the intent to incur expenditure at some future date or the expectation of future operating losses. An obligation does not generally have to take the form of a 'legal' obligation before a provision is recognised. An entity may have an established pattern of past practice that indicates to other parties that it will accept certain responsibilities and as a result has created a valid expectation on the part of those other parties that it will discharge those responsibilities (that is, the entity is under a constructive obligation). If an entity has an onerous contract (the unavoidable costs of meeting the obligations under the contract exceed the economic benefits expected to be received under it), the present obligation under the contract is recognised as a provision. Impairments of any assets dedicated to the contract are recognised before making a provision.

Restructuring Provisions

There are specific requirements for restructuring provisions. A provision is recognised when the following points are met: (a) a detailed formal plan identifying the main features of the restructuring; and (b) a valid expectation in those affected that the entity will carry out the restructuring by starting to implement the plan or by announcing its main features to those affected.

A restructuring plan does not create a present obligation at the balance sheet date if it is announced after that date, even if it is announced before the financial statements are approved. A sale or termination of a business might fall under the definition of restructuring. No obligation arises in respect of restructuring costs associated with the sale of an operation until the entity is committed to the sale (that is, there is a binding sale agreement). The provision includes only incremental costs necessarily resulting from the restructuring and not those associated with the entity's ongoing activities. Any expected gains on the sale of assets are not considered in measuring a restructuring provision.

Reimbursements

An obligation and any anticipated recovery are presented separately as a liability and an asset respectively; however, an asset can only be recognised if it is virtually certain that settlement of the obligation will result in a reimbursement, and the amount recognised for the reimbursement should not exceed the amount of the provision. The amount of any expected reimbursement is disclosed. Net presentation is permitted only in the income statement.

Subsequent Measurement

Management performs an exercise at each balance sheet date to identify the best estimate of the expenditure required to settle the present obligation at the balance sheet date, discounted at an appropriate rate. The increase in provision due to the passage of time (that is a consequence of the discount rate) is recognised as borrowing cost.

Contingent Liabilities

Contingent liabilities are possible obligations whose existence will be confirmed only on the occurrence or non-occurrence of uncertain future events outside the entity's control, or present obligations that are not recognised because of the following: (a) It is not probable that an outflow of economic benefits will be required to settle the obligation; or (b) the amount cannot be measured reliably.

Contingent liabilities are not recognised but are disclosed and described in the notes to the financial statements, including an estimate of their potential financial effect and uncertainties relating to the amount or timing of any outflow, unless the possibility of settlement is remote.

Contingent Assets

Contingent assets are possible assets whose existence will be confirmed only on the occurrence or non-occurrence of uncertain future events outside the entity's control. Contingent assets are not recognised. When the realisation of income is virtually certain, the related asset is not a contingent asset; it is recognised as an asset.

Contingent assets are disclosed and described in the notes to the financial statements, including an estimate of their potential financial effect if the inflow of economic benefits is probable.

Levies

Appendix C, 'Levies', is an interpretation of Ind AS 37, 'Provisions, contingent liabilities and contingent assets'. Ind AS 37 sets out criteria for the recognition of a liability, one of which is the requirement for the entity to have a present obligation as a result of a past event (known as an obligating event). The interpretation clarifies that the obligating event that gives rise to a liability to pay a levy is the activity described in the relevant legislation that triggers the payment of the levy.

Intangible Assets: Ind AS 38

An intangible asset is an identifiable non-monetary asset without physical substance. The identifiable criterion is met when the intangible asset is separable (that is, when it can be sold, transferred or licensed), or where it arises from contractual or other legal rights.

Separately Acquired Intangible Assets

Separately acquired intangible assets are recognised initially at cost. Cost comprises the purchase price, including import duties and non-refundable purchase taxes and any directly attributable costs of preparing the asset for its intended use. The purchase price of a separately acquired intangible asset incorporates assumptions about the probable economic future benefits that may be generated by the asset.

Internally Generated Intangible Assets

The process of generating an intangible asset is divided into a research phase and a development phase. No intangible assets arising from the research phase may be recognised. Intangible assets arising from the development phase are recognised when the entity can demonstrate the following:

- Its technical feasibility
- Its intention to complete the developments
- Its ability to use or sell the intangible asset
- How the intangible asset will generate probable future economic benefits (for example, the existence of a market for the output of the intangible asset or for the intangible asset itself)
- The availability of resources to complete the development
- Its ability to measure the attributable expenditure reliably

Any expenditure written off during the research or development phase cannot subsequently be capitalised, if the project meets the criteria for recognition at a later date.

The costs relating to many internally generated intangible items cannot be capitalised and are expensed as incurred. This includes research, start-up and advertising costs. Expenditure on internally generated brands, mastheads, customer lists, publishing titles and goodwill are not recognised as intangible assets.

Intangible Assets Acquired in a Business Combination

If an intangible asset is acquired in a business combination, both the probability and measurement criterion are always considered to be met. An intangible asset will therefore always be recognised, regardless of whether it has been previously recognised in the acquiree's financial statements.

Subsequent Measurement

Intangible assets are amortised unless they have an indefinite useful life. Amortisation is carried out on a systematic basis over the useful life of the intangible asset.

An intangible asset has an indefinite useful life when, based on an analysis of all the relevant factors, there is no foreseeable limit to the period over which the asset is expected to generate net cash inflows for the entity. Intangible assets with finite useful lives are considered for impairment when there is an indication that the asset has been impaired. Intangible assets with indefinite useful lives and intangible assets not yet in use are tested annually for impairment and whenever there is an indication of impairment.

4. BUSINESS ACQUISITION AND CONSOLIDATION

Business Combinations: Ind AS 103

A business combination is a transaction or event in which an entity–('acquirer') obtains control of one or more businesses ('acquire(s)'). Under Ind AS 110, an investor controls an investee when the investor is exposed, or has rights, to variable returns from its involvement with the investee and has the ability to affect those returns through its power over the investee. A number of factors such as equity shareholding, control of the board and contractual agreements may influence which entity has control. There is a presumption of control if an entity owns more than 50% of the equity shareholding in another entity, though this may not always be the case.

Business combinations occur in a variety of structures. Ind AS 103, 'Business combinations', focusses on the substance of the transaction, rather than the legal form. The overall result of a series of transactions is considered if there are a number of transactions among the parties involved. For example, any transaction contingent on the completion of another transaction may be considered linked. Judgement is required to determine when transactions should be linked.

All business combinations within Ind AS 103's scope are accounted for using the acquisition method. The acquisition method views a business combination from the perspective of the acquirer and can be summarised in the following steps:

- Identify the acquirer
- Determine the acquisition date
- Recognise and measure the identifiable assets acquired, liabilities assumed and any non-controlling interest in the acquiree
- Recognise and measure the consideration transferred for the acquiree
- Recognise and measure goodwill or a gain from a bargain purchase (as capital reserve)

The acquiree's identifiable assets (including intangible assets not previously recognised), liabilities and contingent liabilities are generally recognised at their fair value. Fair value is measured in accordance with Ind AS 113. If the acquisition is for less than 100% of the acquiree, there is a non-controlling interest. The non-controlling interest represents the equity in a subsidiary that is not attributable directly or indirectly to the parent. The acquirer can elect to measure the non-controlling interest at its fair value or at its proportionate share of the identifiable net assets.

The consideration for the combination includes cash and cash equivalents and the fair value of any non-cash consideration given. Any equity instruments issued as part of the consideration are fair valued. If any of the consideration is deferred, it is discounted to reflect its present value at the acquisition date, if the effect of discounting is material.

Consideration includes only those amounts paid to the seller in exchange for control of the entity. Consideration excludes amounts paid to settle pre-existing relationships, payments that are contingent on future employee services and acquisition- related costs.

A portion of the consideration may be contingent on the outcome of future events or the acquired entity's performance ('contingent consideration'). Contingent consideration is also recognised at its fair value at the date of acquisition. The accounting for contingent consideration after the date of acquisition depends on whether it is classified as a liability (re-measured to fair value each reporting period through profit and loss) or as equity (no subsequent re-measurement). The classification as either a liability or equity is determined with reference to the guidance in Ind AS 32, 'Financial instruments: Presentation'.

Goodwill is recognised for the future economic benefits arising from assets acquired that are not individually identified and separately recognised. Goodwill is the difference between the consideration transferred, the amount of any non-controlling interest in the acquiree and the acquisition-date fair value of any previous equity interest in the acquiree over the fair value of the identifiable net assets acquired. If the non-controlling interest is measured at its fair value, goodwill includes amounts attributable to the non-controlling interest. If the non-controlling interest is measured at its proportionate share of identifiable net assets, goodwill includes only amounts attributable to the controlling interest–that is, the parent. Goodwill is recognised as an asset and tested annually for impairment or more frequently if there is an indication of impairment.

In rare situations, for example, a bargain purchase as a result of a distressed sale, it is possible that no goodwill will result from the transaction. Rather, a bargain gain arises. Ind AS 103 requires the same to be recognised in other comprehensive income and accumulated in equity as capital reserve, unless there is no clear evidence for the underlying reason for classification of the business combination as a bargain purchase, in which case, it shall be recognised directly in equity as capital reserve.

For business combinations between entities that are under common control, there is specific guidance included in Ind AS 103. Such business combinations are accounted for using the pooling of interests method. Under the pooling of interests method:

- All assets and liabilities of the acquiree are reflected at their previous carrying values in the books of the acquirer.
- No adjustments are made to reflect any fair values, nor are any new assets recognised.
- The only adjustment permitted is the adjustment towards uniform accounting policies.

Consolidated Financial Statements: Ind AS 110

The principles concerning consolidated financial statements under Ind AS 110 are set out in Ind AS 110, 'Consolidated financial statements'. Ind AS 110 has a single definition of control.

Ind AS 110's objective is to establish principles for presenting and preparing consolidated financial statements when an entity controls one or more entities. Ind AS 110 sets out the requirements for when an entity needs to prepare consolidated financial statements, defines the principles of control, explains how to apply the principles of control and explains the accounting requirements for preparing consolidated financial statements (Ind AS 110 para 2).

The key principle in the standard is that control exists, and consolidation is required, only if the investor possesses power over the investee, has exposure to variable returns from its involvement with the investee and has the ability to use its power over the investee to affect its returns. The core principle is that a consolidated entity presents a parent and its subsidiaries as if they are a single economic entity. Ind AS 110 provides guidance on the following issues when determining who has control:

- Assessment of the purpose and design of an investee
- Relevant activities and power to direct those
- Nature of rights—whether substantive or merely protective in nature
- Assessment of voting rights and potential voting rights
- Whether an investor is a principal or an agent while exercising its controlling power
- Relationships between investors and how they affect control
- Existence of power over specified assets only

Ind AS 110 will affect some entities more than others.

The consolidation conclusion is not expected to change for most straightforward entities. However, changes can result where there are complex group structures or where structured entities are involved in a transaction. Those most likely to be affected potentially include investors in the following entities:

- Entities with a dominant investor that does not possess a majority voting interest, where the remaining votes are held by widely-dispersed shareholders (de facto control)
- Structured entities, also known as special purpose entities
- Entities that issue or hold significant potential voting rights
- Asset management entities

In difficult situations, the precise facts and circumstances will affect the analysis under Ind AS 110. Ind AS 110 does not provide 'bright lines' and requires consideration of many factors, such as the existence of contractual arrangements and rights held by other parties, in order to assess control.

Ind AS 110 does not contain any disclosure requirements; these are included within Ind AS 112 which has greatly increased the amount of required disclosures. Reporting entities should plan for, and implement, the processes and controls that will be required to gather the additional information.

When the proportion of the equity held by non-controlling interests changes, an entity shall adjust the carrying amounts of the controlling and non-controlling interests to reflect the changes in their relative interests in the subsidiary. The entity shall recognise directly in equity any difference between the amount by which the non-controlling interests are adjusted and the fair value of the consideration paid or received, and attribute it to the owners of the parent. This is a significant change from the current Indian GAAP practice of how increase or decrease in a subsidiary's equity interest is accounted. When a parent loses control of a subsidiary, it shall:

- **Derecognise:**
  - The assets (including any goodwill) and liabilities of the subsidiary at their carrying amounts at the date when control is lost; and
  - The carrying amount of any non-controlling interests in the former subsidiary at the date when control is lost (including any components of other comprehensive income attributable to them).
- **Recognise:**
  - The fair value of the consideration received, if any, from the transaction, event or circumstances that resulted in the loss of control;
  - If the transaction, event or circumstances that resulted in the loss of control involves a distribution of shares of the subsidiary to owners in their capacity as owners, that distribution; and
  - Any investment retained in the former subsidiary at its fair value at the date when control is lost.
- Reclassify to profit or loss, or transfer directly to retained earnings if required by other Ind AS, the amounts recognised in other comprehensive income in relation to the subsidiary
- Recognise any resulting difference as a gain or loss in profit or loss attributable to the parent

Again, this is a significant change from the current Indian GAAP practice of how decrease of equity interest in a subsidiary is accounted, especially the concept of fair valuing the remaining interest in the investment.

Entities that meet the definition of an investment entity are exempt from consolidating underlying investees that they control. Instead, they are required to account for these subsidiaries at fair value through profit or loss under Ind AS 109.

Joint Arrangements: Ind AS 111

A joint arrangement is a contractual arrangement where at least two parties agree to share control over the activities of the arrangement. Unanimous consent towards decisions about relevant activities between the parties sharing control is a requirement in order to meet the definition of joint control.

Joint arrangements can be joint operations or joint ventures. The classification is principle based and depends on the parties' exposure in relation to the arrangement. When the parties' exposure to the arrangement only extends to the net assets of the arrangement, the arrangement is a joint venture.

Joint operators have rights to assets and obligations for liabilities. Joint operations are often not structured through separate vehicles. When a joint arrangement is separated from the parties and included in a separate vehicle, it can be either a joint operation or a joint venture. In such cases, further analysis is required on the legal form of the separate vehicle, the terms and conditions included in the contractual agreement and sometimes, other facts and circumstances. This is because in practice, the latter two can override the principles derived from the legal form of the separate vehicle.

Joint operators account for their rights to assets and obligations for liabilities. Joint ventures account for their interest by using the equity method of accounting.

Disclosure of Interest In Other Entities: Ind AS 112

Ind AS 112 provides for extensive disclosures on consolidated financial statements. The key disclosures required are outlined below:

- Significant judgements and assumptions in determining control, joint control or significant influence, the type of joint arrangement when the arrangement is through separate vehicles to be disclosed,
- Disclosure by the investment entity about significant judgements and assumptions it made in determining that it is an investment entity,
- To understand the composition of the group, interest that non-controlling interests have in the group's activities and cash flows in the interest in subsidiaries,
- For each unconsolidated subsidiary, an investment entity shall disclose the subsidiary's name, the principal place of business (and country of incorporation if different from the principal place of business) of the subsidiary, and the proportion of ownership interest held by the investment entity and, if different, the proportion of voting rights held,
- An entity having interest in joint arrangement and associates shall disclose information that enables users of its financial statements to evaluate the following:
    - The nature, extent and financial effects of its interests in joint arrangements and associates, including the nature and effects of its contractual relationship with the other investors with joint control of, or significant influence over, joint arrangements and associates
    - The nature of, and changes in, the risks associated with its interests in joint ventures and associates
- An entity having interest in unconsolidated structured entities shall disclose information that enables users of its financial statements:
    - To understand the nature and extent of its interests in unconsolidated structured entities
    - To evaluate the nature of, and changes in, the risks associated with its interests in unconsolidated structured entities

Investment in Associates and Joint Ventures: Ind AS 28

Ind AS 28, 'Investments in associates and joint ventures', requires that interests in such entities are accounted for using the equity method of accounting. An associate is an entity in which the investor has significant influence, but which is neither a subsidiary nor a joint venture of the investor. Significant influence is the power to participate in the financial and operating policy decisions of the investee, but not to control those policies. It is presumed to exist when the investor holds at least 20% of the investee's voting power. It is presumed not to exist when less than 20% is held. These presumptions may be rebutted. A joint venture is a joint arrangement where the parties have joint control and have rights to the arrangement's net assets.

Associates and joint ventures are accounted for using the equity method unless they meet the criteria to be classified as 'held for sale' under Ind AS 105, 'Non-current assets held for sale and discontinued operations'. Under the equity method, the investment in the associate or joint venture is initially carried at cost. It is increased or decreased to recognise the investor's share of the profit or loss of the associate or joint venture after the date of acquisition.

Investments in associates or joint ventures are classified as non-current assets and presented as one line item in the balance sheet (inclusive of goodwill arising on acquisition). Investments in associates or joint ventures are tested for impairment in accordance with Ind AS 36, 'Impairment of assets', as single assets if there are impairment indicators.

If an investor's share of its associate's or joint venture's losses exceeds the carrying amount of the investment, the carrying amount of the investment is reduced to nil. Recognition of further losses is discontinued, unless the investor has an obligation to fund the associate or joint venture or the investor has guaranteed to support the associate or joint venture. In the separate (non-consolidated) financial statements of the investor, the investments in associates or joint ventures are carried at cost or as financial assets in accordance with Ind AS 109.

5. FINANCIAL INSTRUMENTS

Financial Instruments: Ind AS 109

Classification, recognition and measurement principles and certain disclosure requirements for financial instruments are addressed in three standards:

- Ind AS 107, 'Financial Instruments: Disclosure', which deals with disclosures
- Ind AS 32, 'Financial Instruments: Presentation', which deals with distinguishing debt from equity and with guidance on netting of financial instruments
- Ind AS 109, 'Financial Instruments', which contains requirements for recognition and measurement

The objective of the three standards is to establish requirements for all aspects of accounting for financial instruments, including distinguishing debt from equity, netting, recognition, derecognition, measurement, hedge accounting, and disclosures.

The standards' scope is broad. The standards cover all types of financial instruments, including receivables, payables, investments in bonds and shares, borrowings and derivatives. They also apply to certain contracts to buy or sell non-financial assets (such as commodities) that can be net-settled in cash or another financial instrument.

For guidance on fair value measurement and related disclosures, refer to Ind AS 113, 'Fair value measurement'.

The key concepts of classification, measurement and recognition for financial instruments are discussed in this section.

Nature and Characteristics of Financial Instruments

Financial instruments include a wide range of assets and liabilities, such as trade debtors, trade creditors, loans, finance lease receivables and derivatives. They are recognised and measured according to Ind AS 109's requirements and are disclosed in accordance with Ind AS 107, and for fair value disclosures under Ind AS 113.

Financial instruments represent contractual rights or obligations to receive or pay cash or other financial assets. Non-financial items have a more indirect, non-contractual relationship to future cash flows. A financial asset is cash; a contractual right to receive cash or another financial asset; a contractual right to exchange financial assets or liabilities with another entity under potentially favourable conditions; or an equity instrument of another entity. A financial liability is a contractual obligation to deliver cash or another financial asset; or to exchange financial instruments with another entity under potentially unfavourable conditions.

An equity instrument is any contract that evidences a residual interest in the entity's assets after deducting all of its liabilities.

A derivative is a financial instrument that derives its value from an underlying price or index; requires little or no initial net investment; and is settled at a future date.

Embedded Derivatives in Host Contracts

Some financial instruments and other contracts combine a derivative and a non-derivative in a single contract. The derivative part of the contract is referred to as an 'embedded derivative'. Its effect is that some of the contract's cash flows vary in a way similar to a standalone derivative. For example, the principal amount of a bond may vary with changes in a stock market index. In this case, the embedded derivative is an equity derivative on the relevant stock market index.

Ind AS 109 specifically prohibits bifurcation of embedded derivatives for financial assets. Embedded derivatives in relation to financial liabilities, that are not 'closely related' to the rest of the contract, are separated and accounted for as stand-alone derivatives (that is, measured at fair value). An embedded derivative is not 'closely related' if its economic characteristics and risks are different from those of the rest of the contract. Ind AS 109 sets out many examples to help determine when this test is (and is not) met. Analysing contracts for potential embedded derivatives is one of the more challenging aspects of Ind AS 109.

Classification and Measurement of Financial Instruments

All financial assets and liabilities are measured initially at fair value under Ind AS 109. The fair value of a financial instrument is normally the transaction price, that is, the fair value of the consideration given or received. However, in some circumstances, the transaction price may not be indicative of fair value. Ind AS permits departure from the transaction price only if fair value is evidenced by a quoted price in an active market for an identical asset or liability (that is, a Level 1 input) or based on a valuation technique that uses only data from observable markets. The way financial instruments are classified under Ind AS 109 drives how they are subsequently measured and where measurement changes are accounted for.

Financial Assets: Debt Instruments

Business Model Assessment

Ind AS 109 requires that all financial assets are subsequently measured at amortised cost, fair value through other comprehensive income (FVOCI) or fair value through profit or loss (FVPL) based on the business model for managing financial assets and their contractual cash flow characteristics. The business model is determined by the entity's key management personnel in the way that assets are managed and their performance is reported. The business model is determined at a level that reflects how groups of financial assets are managed together to achieve a particular business objective. It is not an instrument-by-instrument analysis. Rather it can be performed at a higher level of aggregation.

- An entity's business model for managing financial assets is a matter of fact and not merely an assertion. It is typically observable through the activities that the entity undertakes to achieve the objective of the business model. The business model for managing financial assets is not determined by a single factor or activity. Instead, management has to consider all relevant evidence available at the date of the assessment. Such relevant evidence includes, but is not limited to the following:

-- How the performance of the business model (and the financial assets held within) is evaluated and reported to the entity's key management personnel

-- The risks that affect the performance of the business model (and the financial assets held within) and, in particular, the way those risks are managed

-- How managers of the business are compensated (for example, whether the compensation is based on the fair value of the assets managed or the contractual cash flows collected)

Contractual Cash Flow Analysis

Once the business model assessment has been performed, management needs to assess whether the asset's contractual cash flows solely represent payments of principal and interest (the SPPI condition). This condition is necessary for the financial asset or the group of financial assets to be classified at the amortised cost or FVOCI.

Ind AS 109 provides definitions of principal and interest, which will help management to make a preliminary assessment of whether contractual cash flows solely represent payments of principal and interest:

Principal is the fair value of the financial asset at initial recognition. However, that principal amount might change over the life of the financial asset (for example, if there are repayments of principal).

Interest is typically the compensation for the time value of money and credit risk. However, interest can also include consideration for other basic lending risks (for example, liquidity risk) and costs (for example, servicing or administrative costs) associated with holding the financial asset for a period of time, as well as a profit margin.

Ind AS 109 establishes that instruments with contractual cash flows that are SPPI on the principal amount outstanding are consistent with a basic lending arrangement. Management has to assess whether contractual cash flows are SPPI in the currency in which the financial asset is denominated.

Contractual features that introduce exposure to risks or volatility in the contractual cash flows unrelated to a basic lending arrangement, such as exposure to changes in equity or commodity prices, do not give rise to contractual cash flows that are SPPI. For example, convertible bonds and profit participating loans will not meet the SPPI condition.

A financial asset is measured at the amortised cost if both of the following criteria are met:

- The asset is held to collect its contractual cash flows
- The asset's contractual cash flows represent SPPI

Financial assets included within this category are initially recognised at fair value and subsequently measured at the amortised cost.

A financial asset is measured at FVOCI, if both of the following criteria are met:

- The objective of the business model is achieved both by collecting contractual cash flows and selling financial assets
- The asset's contractual cash flows represent SPPI

Financial assets included within the FVOCI category are initially recognised and subsequently measured at fair value. Movements in the carrying amount are recorded through OCI, except for the recognition of impairment gains or losses, interest revenue as well as foreign exchange gains and losses which are recognised in profit and loss. Where the financial asset is derecognised, the cumulative gain or loss previously recognised in OCI is reclassified from equity to profit or loss.

FVPL is the residual category. Financial assets need to be classified as FVPL if they do not meet the criteria of FVOCI or amortised cost. Financial assets included within the FVPL category need to be measured at fair value with all changes recorded through profit or loss.

Regardless of the business model assessment, an entity can elect to classify a financial asset at FVPL, if doing so reduces or eliminates a measurement or recognition inconsistency (accounting mismatch). Reclassifications between the categories are permitted, although they are expected to be rare.

Financial Assets: Equity Instruments

Investments in equity instruments are always measured at fair value. Equity instruments are those that meet the definition of equity from the perspective of the issuer as defined in Ind AS 32. Equity instruments that are held for trading are required to be classified as FVPL. For all other equities, management has the ability to make an irrevocable election on initial recognition, on an instrument-by-instrument basis, to present changes in fair value in OCI rather than profit or loss. If this election is made, all fair value changes, excluding dividends that are a return on investment, will be included in OCI. There is no recycling of amounts from OCI to profit and loss (for example, on sale of an equity investment), nor are there any impairment requirements. However, the entity might transfer the cumulative gain or loss within equity.

Financial Liabilities

Financial liabilities are measured at the amortised cost using effective interest rate method unless they are classified as FVPL. Financial liabilities are classified as FVPL if they are designated at initial recognition as such (subject to various conditions), if they are held for trading or are derivatives (except for a derivative, that is, a financial guarantee contract or a designated and effective hedging instrument). For liabilities designated at FVPL, changes in fair value related to changes in own credit risk are presented separately in OCI. Amounts in OCI relating to own credit are not recycled to profit or loss even when the liability is derecognised and the amounts are realised. However, the standard does allow transfers within equity.

Derivatives

Derivatives (including separated embedded derivatives) are measured at fair value. All fair value gains and losses are recognised in profit or loss except where the derivatives qualify as hedging instruments in cash flow hedges or net investment hedges.

Financial Liabilities and Equity

The classification of a financial instrument by the issuer as either a liability (debt) or equity can have a significant impact on an entity's gearing (debt-to-equity ratio) and reported earnings. It can also affect the entity's debt covenants.

The critical feature of a liability is that under the terms of the instrument, the issuer is or can be required to deliver either cash or another financial asset to the holder; it cannot avoid this obligation. For example, a debenture under which the issuer is required to make interest payments and redeem the debenture for cash is a financial liability.

An instrument is classified as equity when it represents a residual interest in the issuer's assets after deducting all its liabilities; or, put another way, when the issuer has no obligation under the terms of the instrument to deliver cash or other financial assets to another entity. Ordinary shares or common stock where all the payments are at the discretion of the issuer are examples of equity of the issuer.

In addition, the following types of financial instrument are accounted for as equity, provided they have particular features and meet specific conditions:

- Puttable financial instruments (for example, some shares issued by co-operative entities and some partnership interests)
- Instruments or components of instruments that impose on the entity an obligation to deliver to another party a pro rata share of the net assets of the entity only on liquidation (for example, some shares issued by limited life entities)

The classification of the financial instrument as either debt or equity is based on the substance of the contractual arrangement of the instrument rather than its legal form. This means, for example, that a redeemable preference share, which is economically the same as a bond, is accounted for in the same way as a bond. The redeemable preference share is therefore treated as a liability rather than equity, even though legally it is a share of the issuer.

Other instruments may not be as straightforward. An analysis of the terms of each instrument in light of the detailed classification requirements is necessary, particularly as some financial instruments contain both liability and equity features. Such instruments, for example, bonds that are convertible into a fixed number of equity shares, are accounted for as separate liability and equity (being the option to convert if all the criteria for equity are met) components.

The treatment of interest, dividends, losses and gains in the income statement follows the classification of the related instrument. If a preference share is classified as a liability, its coupon (preference dividend) is shown as interest cost.

However, the discretionary coupon on an instrument that is treated as equity is shown as a distribution within equity.

Recognition and Derecognition

Recognition

Recognition for financial assets and financial liabilities tends to be straightforward. An entity recognises a financial asset or a financial liability at the time it becomes a party to a contract.

Derecognition

Derecognition is the term used for ceasing to recognise a financial asset or financial liability on an entity's balance sheet. These rules are more complex.

Assets

An entity that holds a financial asset may raise finance using the asset as security for the finance or as the primary source of cash flow to repay the finance. Derecognition requirements of Ind AS

109 determine whether the transaction is a sale of the financial assets (and therefore the entity ceases to recognise the assets) or whether finance has been secured on the assets (and the entity recognises a liability for any proceeds received). This evaluation can be straightforward. For example, it is clear with little or no analysis that a financial asset is derecognised in an unconditional transfer of it to an unconsolidated third party, with no risks and rewards of the asset being retained.

Conversely, derecognition is not allowed where an asset has been transferred, but substantially all the risks and rewards of the asset have been retained through the terms of the agreement. However, the analysis may be more complex in other cases. Securitisation and debt factoring are examples of more complex transactions where derecognition will need careful consideration.

Liabilities

An entity may only cease to recognise (derecognise) a financial liability when it is extinguished–that is, when the obligation is discharged, cancelled or expires, or when the debtor is legally released from the liability by law or by the creditor agreeing to such a release.

Impairment

Ind AS 109 outlines a three-stage model (general model) for impairment based on changes in credit quality since initial recognition.

Stage 1 includes financial instruments that have not had a significant increase in credit risk since the initial recognition or have low credit risk at the reporting date. For these assets, 12-month expected credit losses (ECL) are recognised and interest revenue is calculated on the gross carrying amount of the asset (that is, without deduction for credit allowance). 12-month ECL result from default events that are possible within 12 months after the reporting date. It is not the expected cash shortfalls over the 12-month period but the entire credit loss on an asset weighted by the probability that the loss will occur in the next 12 months.

Stage 2 includes financial instruments that have had a significant increase in credit risk since the initial recognition (unless they have low credit risk at the reporting date) but that do not have objective evidence of impairment. For these assets, lifetime ECL are recognised, but interest revenue is still calculated on the gross carrying amount of the asset. Lifetime ECL are the expected credit losses that result from all possible default events over the expected life of the financial instrument. EPL are the weighted average credit losses with the probability of default (PD) as the weight.

Stage 3 includes financial assets that have objective evidence of impairment at the reporting date. For these assets, lifetime ECL are recognised and interest revenue is calculated on the net carrying amount (that is, net of credit allowance).

ECL are a probability-weighted estimate of credit losses. A credit loss is the difference between the cash flows that are due to an entity in accordance with the contract and the cash flows that the entity expects to receive discounted at the original effective interest rate. Since ECL consider the amount and timing of payments, a credit loss arises even if the entity expects to be paid in full, but later than when contractually due.

The model includes some operational simplifications for trade receivables, contract assets and lease receivables as they are often held by entities that do not have sophisticated credit risk management systems. These simplifications eliminate the need to calculate 12-month ECL and to assess when a significant increase in credit risk has occurred. For trade receivables or contract assets that do not contain a significant financing component, the loss allowance needs to be measured at the initial recognition as well as throughout the life of the receivable at an amount equal to lifetime ECL. As a practical expedient, a provision matrix may be used to estimate ECL for these financial instruments.

For trade receivables or contract assets which contain a significant financing component in accordance with Ind AS 115 and lease receivables, an entity has an accounting policy choice. It can either apply the simplified approach (measuring the loss allowance at an amount equal to lifetime ECL at initial recognition and throughout its life), or apply the general model.

As an exception to the general model, if the credit risk of a financial instrument is low at the reporting date, management can measure impairment using 12-month ECL, and so it does not have to assess whether a significant increase in credit risk has occurred.

Hedge Accounting

Hedging is the process of using a financial instrument (usually a derivative) to mitigate all or some of the risk of a hedged item. Hedge accounting changes the timing of recognition of gains and losses on either the hedged item or the hedging instrument so that both are recognised in profit or loss within the same accounting period, in order to record the economic substance of the combination of the hedged item and instrument.

To qualify for hedge accounting, an entity must (a) formally designate and document a hedge relationship between a qualifying hedging instrument and a qualifying hedged item at the inception of the hedge, and (b) both at inception and on an ongoing basis, demonstrate that the hedge is effective.

There are three types of hedge relationships:

- Fair value hedge: A hedge of the exposure to changes in the fair value of a recognised asset or liability, or a firm commitment
- Cash flow hedge: A hedge of the exposure to variability in cash flows of a recognised asset or liability, a firm commitment or a highly probable forecast transaction
- Net investment hedge: A hedge of the foreign currency risk on a net investment in a foreign operation

For a fair value hedge, the hedged item is adjusted for the gain or loss attributable to the hedged risk. That element is included in the income statement where it will offset the gain or loss on the hedging instrument.

For an effective cash flow hedge, gains and losses on the hedging instrument are initially included in other comprehensive income. The amount included in other comprehensive income is the lesser of the fair value of the hedging instrument and hedge item. Where the hedging instrument has a fair value greater than the hedged item, the excess is recorded within the profit or loss as ineffectiveness. Gains or losses deferred in other comprehensive income are reclassified to profit or loss when the hedged item affects the income statement. If the hedged item is the forecast acquisition of a non-financial asset or liability, the entity may choose an accounting policy of adjusting the carrying amount of the non-financial asset or liability for the hedging gain or loss at acquisition, or leaving the hedging gains or losses deferred in equity and reclassifying them to profit and loss when the hedged item affects profit or loss.

Hedges of a net investment in a foreign operation are accounted for similarly to cash flow hedges. A retrospective effectiveness testing is not required under Ind AS 109. Ind AS 109 requires ensuring that the hedge ratio is appropriate. Companies need to verify that the hedge ratio is aligned with the requirement of their economic hedging strategy (risk management strategy). Deliberate imbalances must be avoided. A mismatch of weightings between the hedged item and the hedging instrument should not be used to achieve an accounting outcome that is inconsistent with the purpose of hedge accounting. This doesn't imply that the hedge relationship must be perfect, but the weightings of the hedging instruments and hedged item actually used cannot be selected in order to introduce ineffectiveness. Companies need to carefully document their hedging strategy and financial instrument classification at inception. Ind AS 109 prohibits voluntary de-designation of hedges if risk management strategy of the company has not changed.

Financial Instruments (Presentation and Disclosures): Ind AS 32, Ind AS 107, Ind AS 113 and Ind AS 109

There have been significant developments in risk management concepts and practices in recent years. New techniques have evolved for measuring and managing exposures to risks arising from financial instruments. This, coupled with the significant volatility experienced in the financial markets, has increased the need for more relevant information and greater transparency about an entity's exposures arising from financial instruments and how those risks are managed. Financial statement users and other investors need such information to make more informed judgements about risks that entities run from the use of financial instruments and their associated returns.

Ind AS 107 sets out disclosure requirements that are intended to enable users to evaluate the significance of financial instruments for an entity's financial position and performance, and to understand the nature and extent of risks arising from those financial instruments to which the entity is exposed.

All entities that have financial instruments are affected–even simple instruments such as borrowings, accounts payable and receivable, cash and investments.

Disclosures are required to be made for the risks including credit risk, liquidity risk and market risk. Further, Ind AS 107 and Ind AS 113 require disclosure of a three-level hierarchy for fair value measurement as well as some specific quantitative disclosures for financial instruments at the lowest level in the hierarchy. The disclosure requirements apply to all entities and not just to banks and financial institutions.

Ind AS 109 requires detailed qualitative and quantitative disclosures in relation to impairment. Ind AS 32 includes presentation requirements and rules for liability, equity, compound financial instruments and offsetting financial asset and financial liability.

6. INDUSTRY SPECIFIC STANDARDS

Insurance Contracts: Ind AS 104

Insurance contracts are contracts where an entity accepts significant insurance risk from another party (the policyholder) by agreeing to compensate the policyholder if the insured event adversely affects the policyholder. The risk transferred in the contract must be insurance risk, which is any risk except for financial risk.

Ind AS 104, 'Insurance contracts', applies to all issuers of insurance contracts whether or not the entity is legally an insurance company. It does not apply to accounting for insurance contracts by policyholders.

This Ind AS prescribes a liability adequacy test. An insurer shall assess at the end of each reporting period whether its recognised insurance liabilities are adequate, using current estimates of future cash flows under its insurance contracts. If that assessment shows that the carrying amount of its insurance liabilities is inadequate in the light of the estimated future cash flows, the entire deficiency shall be recognised in profit or loss. Disclosure is particularly important for information relating to insurance contracts. Ind AS 104 has two main principles for disclosure. Entities need to disclose the following:

- Information that identifies and explains the amounts in its financial statements arising from insurance contracts
- Information that enables users of its financial statements to evaluate the nature and extent of risks arising from insurance contracts

Exploration for and Evaluation of Mineral Resources: Ind AS 106

Ind AS 106, 'Exploration for and evaluation of mineral resources', addresses the financial reporting for the exploration for and evaluation of mineral resources. It does not address other aspects of accounting by entities engaged in the exploration for and evaluation of mineral reserves (such as activities before an entity has acquired the legal right to explore or after the technical feasibility and commercial viability to extract resources have been demonstrated).

Activities outside the scope of Ind AS 106 are accounted for as per the applicable standards (such as Ind AS 16, 'Property, plant and equipment', Ind AS 37, 'Provisions, contingent liabilities and contingent assets', and Ind AS 38, 'Intangible assets').

The accounting policy adopted for the recognition of exploration and evaluation assets should result in relevant and reliable information. Ind AS 106 permits companies in this sector to continue applying policies for the recognition of exploration and evaluation assets that were followed under the previous GAAP. The accounting policy may be changed only if the change makes the financial statements more relevant and no less reliable, or more reliable and no less relevant.

Exploration and evaluation assets are initially measured at cost. They are classified as tangible or intangible assets, according to the nature of the assets acquired. Management applies that classification consistently. After recognition, management applies either the cost model or the revaluation model to the exploration and evaluation assets, based on Ind AS 16, 'Property, plant and equipment', or Ind AS 38, 'Intangible assets', according to the nature of the assets. As soon as technical feasibility and commercial viability are determined, the assets are no longer classified as exploration and evaluation assets.

The exploration and evaluation assets are tested for impairment when facts and circumstances suggest that the carrying amounts may not be recovered. The assets are also tested for impairment before reclassification out of exploration and evaluation. The impairment is measured, presented and disclosed according to Ind AS 36, 'Impairment of assets', except that exploration and evaluation assets are allocated to cash-generating units or groups of cash-generating units no larger than a segment.

Management discloses the accounting policy adopted, as well as the amount of assets, liabilities, income and expense and investing cash flows arising from the exploration and evaluation of mineral resources. Appendix B, 'Stripping costs in the production phase of a surface mine', contained in Ind AS 16, 'Property, plant and equipment', applies to waste removal costs incurred in surface mining activity during the production phase.

Regulatory Deferral Accounts: Ind AS 114

Regulatory deferral account balances arise when an entity provides goods or services to customers at a price or rate that is subject to rate regulation.

The standard permits the rate regulated entity to account for 'regulatory deferral account balances' in accordance with the previous GAAP in its initial adoption and the subsequent financial periods. An entity subject to rate regulation coming into existence after the Ind AS comes into force or an entity whose activities become subject to rate regulation subsequent to preparation and presentation of its first Ind AS financial statements shall be entitled to apply the requirements of the previous GAAP in respect of such rate regulated activities.

This standard, therefore, provides an exemption from para 11 of Ind AS 8, 'Accounting policies, changes in accounting estimates and errors', which requires an entity to consider the requirement of Ind AS dealing with similar matters and the requirement of conceptual framework when setting its accounting policies.

The entities are permitted to continue to apply the previous GAAP accounting policies for the recognition, measurement, impairment and derecognition of regulatory deferral account balances except if the change makes the financial statements more relevant to the economic decision-making needs of users and no less reliable, or more reliable and no less relevant to those needs.

However, the presentation of such amounts shall comply with the presentation requirements of this standard, which may require changes in the entity's previous GAAP presentation policies.

Agriculture: Ind AS 41

Agricultural activity is defined as the managed biological transformation and harvest of biological assets (living animals and plants) for sale or for conversion into agricultural produce (harvested product of biological assets) or into additional biological assets.

The biological assets are categorised into consumable biological assets and bearer biological assets. Consumable biological assets are those that are to be harvested as agriculture produce or sold as biological assets. Bearer biological assets are those other than consumable biological assets. Bearer biological assets are not agricultural produce but, rather, are held to bear produce.

All biological assets other than bearer plants are usually measured at fair value less costs to sell, with the change in the carrying amount reported as part of profit or loss from operating activities.Costs to sell are the incremental costs directly attributable to the disposal of an asset, excluding finance costs and income taxes Bearer plants are measured in accordance with Ind AS 16, 'Property, plant, and equipment'.

The table below provides examples of biological assets, agricultural produce, and products that are the result of processing after harvest:

Biological assets	Agricultural produce	Products that are the result of processing after harvest
Sheep	wool	Yarn, carpet
Dairy Cattle	Milk	Cheese
Sugarcane	Harvested cane	Sugar
Cotton plants	Harvested cotton	Thread, clothing

Some plants, for example, tea bushes, grape vines, oil palms and rubber trees, usually meet the definition of a bearer plant and are within the scope of Ind AS 16, Property, plant & Equipment. However, the produce growing on bearer plants, for example, tea leaves, grapes, oil palm fruit and latex, is within the scope of Ind AS 41.

7. IND AS AND IFRS: A COMPARISON

India has chosen the path of IFRS convergence and not adoption. Though Ind AS has come a long way and is now quite close to IFRS, certain differences between the IFRS and Ind AS still remain. We call them carve-outs or carve-ins. The carve outs/ins in some key areas are summarised below:

Presentation

- Under Ind AS, the breach of a material provision of a long- term loan will be classified as current except where before the approval of the financial statements for issue, the lender had agreed not to demand payment as a consequence of the breach. A similar exemption is unavailable in IFRS. Consequently, adjusting events under Ind AS 10 has been modified to include events where the lender had agreed to not demand payment as a consequence of the breach of material provision of a long-term loan, before the approval of the financial statement for issue.

- The option to present other comprehensive income in a separate statement is not available under Ind AS. Accordingly, only one statement comprising both profit or loss and other comprehensive income will be presented. The single statement approach requires all items of income and expense to be recognised in the statement of comprehensive income, while the two-statement approach requires two statements to be prepared, one displaying components of profit or loss (separate income statement) and the other beginning with profit or loss and displaying components of other comprehensive income. IFRS provides an option either to follow the single-statement approach or to follow the two- statement approach.
  - Ind AS also does not allow the presentation of expenses by function; only the classification of expense by 'nature' is permitted. Under IFRS, this is a policy election.
  - IFRS allows the option to present inflows and outflows of interest and dividends in the operating activities section of the cash flow statement. Ind AS does not have this option for non-financial entities. Interest and divided inflows and outflows are required to be reported in the investing and financing sections of the cash flow statement respectively.
  - Under IFRS, EPS is not required in separate financial statements if both consolidated and separate financial statements are presented. Under Ind AS, the disclosure of EPS is required in both consolidated as well as separate financial statements.
  - Under Ind AS, where any item of income and expense, which is otherwise required to be recognised in profit or loss in accordance with Ind AS, is debited or credited to the securities premium account or other reserves, the amount in respect thereof shall be deducted from profit or loss from continuing operations for the purpose of calculating EPS. There is no such provision in IFRS.

Acquisitions

- Under IFRS, the bargain purchase gain or negative goodwill arising on business combinations is recognised in profit or loss. Under Ind AS, the bargain purchase gain can be recognised either in other comprehensive income or capital reserve but not in profit or loss. Similar to business combination, bargain purchase gain on the acquisition of an associate is also not recognised in profit or loss.
- Under Ind AS, common control transactions are to be accounted based only on the book values of assets and liabilities. IFRS also allows a fair value option.

Leases

- Under Ind AS, where the escalation of operating lease rentals is in line with the expected general inflation so as to compensate the lessor for expected inflationary cost, rentals are not required to be recognised as an expense on a straight- line basis. Under IFRS, this is considered contingent rent if linked to the index.

Derivatives

- Ind AS introduces an exception to the IFRS definition of a 'financial liability'. Ind AS classifies a conversion option embedded in a convertible bond denominated in a foreign currency as an equity instrument if it entitles the holder to acquire a fixed number of the entity's own equity instruments for a fixed amount of cash, and the exercise price is fixed in any currency. This is not provided in IFRS. Therefore, it will not be required to be fair valued at each balance sheet date under Ind AS. Under IFRS, this conversion option is treated as a derivative liability. This is one of the most significant differences between Ind AS and IFRS.

Property, Plant And Equipment

- Under Ind AS, investment property is to be accounted using only the cost model, with the disclosure of fair value. Under IFRS, both cost and fair value options of accounting are available.
- IFRS permits the treatment of property interest held in an operating lease to be classified as investment property, if the definition of investment property is otherwise met and a fair value model is applied. In such cases, the operating lease will be accounted as if it were a finance lease. However, there is no such option under Ind AS.

Government Grants

- IFRS gives an option to measure non-monetary government grants related to assets (tangible and intangible) either at their fair value or at nominal value. Ind AS requires the measurement of such grants only at their fair value.
- IFRS gives an option to present the grants related to assets either by setting up the grant as deferred income or by deducting the grant in arriving at the carrying amount of the asset. Ind AS requires the presentation of such grants in the balance sheet as deferred income.

Related Parties

- Under IFRS, certain relationships are specifically mentioned and considered to meet the definition of close members of the family of a person. These relationships are expanded in Ind AS to include brother, sister, father and mother of a person.
- Under Ind AS, the related-party disclosures do not apply where providing such disclosures will conflict with the entity's duties of confidentiality provided under a statute or by a regulator or similar competent authority. IFRS does not provide such an exemption.

Associates

- When it is impracticable, Ind AS 28 allows the exemption from use of uniform accounting policies to perform equity method accounting of associates. IFRS does not allow this option.

Others

- Under IFRS, standards on segment information and EPS are applicable to only those companies which are listed or are in the process of being listed. Ind AS does not provide any such exemption for the applicability of standards. In the absence of any exemption under the Companies Act, 2013, and the rules made thereunder, all companies applying Ind AS will have to apply standards on segment information and EPS.

Companies will need to carefully evaluate the Ind AS transition provisions and accounting policy elections, in case they wish to bring their Ind AS financial information closer to IFRS. This may be more important for those entities planning international fund raising or listing, as they may require IFRS compliant financial statements for that purpose.

Sr. No.	IAS/IFRS Reference	IAS/IFRS Name	Ind AS Reference	Ind AS Name
1	IAS 1	Presentations of financial Statements	Ind AS 1	Presentations of financial Statements
2	IAS 2	Inventories	Ind AS 2	Inventories
3	IAS 7	Statement of cash flows	Ind AS 7	Statement of cash flows
4	IAS 8	Accounting Policies, changes In accounting estimate And errors	Ind AS 8	Accounting Policies, changes In accounting estimate And errors

5	IAS 10	Events after the reporting Period	Ind AS 10	Events after the reporting Period
6	IAS 11	Construction Contracts		
7	IAS 12	Income taxes	Ind AS 12	Income taxes
8	IAS 16	Property, plant & Equipment	Ind AS 16	Property, plant & Equipment
9	IAS 17	Leases	Ind AS 17	Leases
10	IAS 18	Revenue		
11	IAS 19	Employee Benefits	Ind AS 19	Employee Benefits
12	IAS 20	Accounting for govt. grants & disclosure of govt. Assistance	Ind AS 20	Accounting for govt. grants & disclosure of govt. Assistance
13	IAS 21	The effects of changes in foreign Exchange rates	Ind AS 21	The effects of changes in foreign Exchange rates
14	IAS 23	Borrowing costs	Ind AS 23	Borrowing costs
15	IAS 24	Related-party disclosures disclosures	Ind AS 24	Related-party disclosures disclosures
16	IAS 26	Accounting & reporting by Retirement benefit plans		
17	IAS 27	Separate financial statements	Ind AS 27	Separate financial statements
18	IAS 28	Investment in associates and Joint ventures	Ind AS 28	Investment in associates and Joint ventures
19	IAS 29	Financial reporting in hyper-Inflationary economies	Ind AS 29	Financial reporting in hyper-Inflationary economies
20	IAS 31	Interest In joint ventures		
21	IAS 32	Financial Instruments: Presentations	Ind AS 32	Financial Instruments: Presentations
22	IAS 33	Earnings per Share	Ind AS 33	Earnings per Share
23	IAS 34	Interim financial Reporting	Ind AS 34	Interim financial Reporting
24	IAS 36	Impairment of assets	Ind AS 36	Impairment of assets
25	IAS 37	Provisions, contingent liabilities and contingent assets	Ind AS 37	Provisions, contingent liabilities and contingent assets
26	IAS 38	Intangible Assets	Ind AS 38	Intangible Assets
27	IAS 39	Financial Instrument Recognition	Ind AS 39	Financial Instrument Recognition
28	IAS 40	Investment property	Ind AS 40	Investment property
29	IAS 41	Agriculture	Ind AS 41	Agriculture
30	IFRS 1	First time adoption of International Financial Reporting Standards	Ind AS 101	First time adoption of Indian Accounting Standards
31	IFRS 2	Share based payment	Ind AS 102	Share based payment
32	IFRS 3	Business combinations	Ind AS 103	Business combinations
33	IFRS 4	Insurance contracts	Ind AS 104	Insurance contracts

34	IFRS 5	Non-current assets held for sale and discontinued operations	Ind AS 105	Non-current assets held for sale and discontinued operations
35	IFRS 6	Exploration for and evaluation of mineral resources	Ind AS 106	Exploration for and valuation of mineral resources
36	IFRS 7	Financial instruments: Disclosures	Ind AS 107	Financial instruments: Disclosures
37	IFRS 8	Operating segments	Ind AS 108	Operating segments
38	IFRS 9	Financial instruments	Ind AS 109	Financial instruments
39	IFRS 10	Consolidated financial statements	Ind AS 110	Consolidated financial statements
40	IFRS 11	Joint arrangements	Ind AS 111	Joint arrangements
41	IFRS 12	Disclosure of interest in other entities	Ind AS 112	Disclosure of interest in other entities
42	IFRS 13	Fair value measurement	Ind AS 113	Fair value measurement
43	IFRS 14	Regulatory deferral accounts	Ind AS 114	Regulatory deferral accounts
44	IFRS 15	Revenue from contracts with customer	Ind AS 115	Revenue from contracts with customer

Sr. No.	IAS/IFRS Reference	IAS/IFRS Name	Ind AS Reference	Ind AS Name
1	IFRIC 1	Changes in existing decommissioning, restoration and similar liabilities	Appendix A To Ind AS 16	Changes in existing decommissioning, restoration and similar liabilities
2	IFRIC 2	Members' shares in co-operative entities and similar instruments		
3	IFRIC 4	Determining whether an arrangement contains a lease	Appendix C to Ind AS 17	Determining whether an arrangement contains a lease
4	IFRIC 5	Rights to interests arising from decommissioning, restoration and environmental rehabilitation funds	Appendix A to Ind AS 37	Rights to interests arising from decommissioning, restoration and environmental rehabilitation funds
5	IFRIC 6	Liabilities arising from participating in a specific market—waste electrical and electronic equipment	Appendix B to Ind AS 37	Liabilities arising from participating in a specific market—waste electrical and electronic equipment
6	IFRIC 7	Applying the restatement approach under IAS 29-Financial reporting in hyperinflationary economies	Appendix A to Ind AS 29	Applying the restatement approach under IAS 29-Financial reporting in hyperinflationary economies
7	IFRIC 10	Interim financial reporting and impairment	Appendix A to Ind AS 34	Interim financial reporting and Impairment
8	IFRIC 12	Service concession arrangements	Appendix C to Ind AS 115	Service concession arrangements
9	IFRIC 13	Customer loyalty programmes	Not applicable	Not applicable. Superseded by Ind AS 115

10	IFRIC 14	The limit on a defined benefit asset, minimum funding requirements and their interaction	Appendix B to Ind AS 19	The limit on a defined benefit asset, minimum funding requirements and their interaction
11	IFRIC 15	Agreements for the construction of real estate	Not applicable	Not applicable. Superseded by Ind AS 115
12	IFRIC 16	Hedges of a net investment in a foreign operation	Appendix C to Ind AS 109	Hedges of a net investment in a foreign operation
13	IFRIC 17	Distributions of non-cash assets to owners	Appendix A to Ind AS 10	Distributions of non-cash assets to owners
14	IFRIC 18	Transfers of assets from customers	Not applicable	Not applicable. Superseded by Ind AS 115
15	IFRIC 19	Extinguishing financial liabilities with equity Instruments	Appendix D to Ind AS 109	Extinguishing financial liabilities with equity instruments
16	IFRIC 20	Stripping costs in the production phase of a surface mine	Appendix B to Ind AS 16	Stripping costs in the production phase of a surface mine
17	IFRIC 21	Levies	Appendix C to Ind AS 37	Levies
18	SIC 7	Introduction of the Euro		
19	SIC 10	Government assistance–No specific relation to operating activities	Appendix A to Ind AS 20	Government assistance–No specific relation to operating activities
20	SIC 12	Consolidation– Special Purpose Entities	Not applicable	Not applicable. Superseded by Ind AS 110
21	SIC 13	Jointly controlled entities–Non-monetary contributions by venturers	Not applicable	Not applicable. Superseded by Ind AS 111
22	SIC 15	Operating leases– Incentives	Appendix A to Ind AS 17	Operating leases– Incentives
23	SIC 25	Income taxes– Changes in the tax status of an enterprise or its shareholders	Appendix A to Ind AS 12	Income taxes– Changes in the tax status of an enterprise or its shareholders
24	SIC 27	Evaluating the substance of transactions in the legal form of a lease	Appendix B to Ind AS 17	Evaluating the substance of transactions in the legal form of a lease
25	SIC 29	Service concession arrangements disclosures	Appendix D to Ind AS 115	Service concession arrangements disclosures
26	SIC 31	Revenue–Barter transactions involving advertising services	Not applicable	Not applicable. Superseded by Ind AS 115
27	SIC 32	Intangible assets– website costs	Appendix A to Ind AS 38	Intangible assets– Website costs

Need for Convergence with IFRSs

The globalisation of the business world and the regulations, which support it, as well as the development of e-commerce make it imperative to have a single globally accepted financial reporting system. A number of multi-national companies are establishing their businesses in various countries with emerging economies and vice versa. The entities in emerging economies are increasingly accessing the global markets to fulfill their capital needs by getting their securities listed on the stock exchanges outside their country. Capital markets are, thus, becoming integrated consistent with this World-wide trend. More and more Indian companies are also being listed on overseas stock exchanges. Sound financial reporting structure is imperative for economic well-being and effective functioning of capital markets.

The use of different accounting frameworks in different countries, which require inconsistent treatment and presentation of the same underlying economic transactions, creates confusion for users of financial statements. This confusion leads to inefficiency in capital markets across the world. Therefore, increasing complexity of business transactions and globalisation of capital markets call for a single set of high quality accounting standards. High standards of financial reporting strengthen the trust investors place in financial and non-financial information. Thus, it has become the need of the day to have a single set of globally accepted accounting standards has prompted many countries to pursue convergence of national accounting standards with IFRSs.

Benefits of achieving convergence with IFRSs

The economy, investors, industry and accounting professionals all stand to gain from the convergence.

(i) **The Economy :** The convergence benefits the economy by increasing growth of its international business. It assists the maintenance of orderly and efficient capital markets and also helps to increase the capital formation and thereby economic growth. It encourages international investors to invest and thereby leads to more foreign capital flows to the country.

(ii) **Investors :** The investors who wish to invest outside their own country want the information that is more relevant, reliable, timely and comparable across the jurisdictions. Financial statements prepared using a common set of accounting standards help investors better understand investment opportunities as opposed to financial statements prepared using a different set of national accounting standards. To understanding the financial statements better, global investors have to incur more cost in terms of the time and efforts to convert the financial statements so that they can confidently compare opportunities. Investors' confidence would be strong if accounting standards used are globally accepted. Convergence with IFRSs add to investors' understanding and confidence in high quality financial statements.

(iii) **The industry :** The industry is able to raise capital from foreign markets at lower cost if it can create confidence in the minds of foreign investors that their financial statements comply with globally accepted accounting standards. With the diversity in accounting standards from country to country, enterprises which operate in different countries face a multitude of accounting requirements prevailing in the countries. The burden of financial reporting reduces with convergence of accounting standards because it simplifies the process of preparing the individual, group financial statements, and thereby reduces the costs of preparing the financial statements using different sets of accounting standards.

(iv) **The accounting professionals :** It offers accounting professionals more opportunities in any part of the world if same accounting practices prevail throughout the world. They are able to advise the clients on financial reporting to fulfil the compliance of any regulatory body of any country of the world.

Problems And Challenges

Despite several benefits as may be looked out by the different people, there will be several challenges that will be faced on the way of IFRS convergence.

1. Difference in GAAP and IFRS : Adoption of IFRS means that the entire set of financial statements will be required to undergo a drastic change. The differences are wide and very deep routed.It would be a challenge to bring about awareness of IFRS and its impact among the users of financial statements.

2. Training and Education : Lack of training facilities and academic courses on IFRS will also pose challenge in India. There is a need to be educated on IFRS and its application. Charles Noski, former chief financial officer and Vice Chairman of the Board ofAT&T Corporation and a former Deloitte &Touche partner noted that"Educating 100,000 employees on how they must do their business is not a trivial activity,"

3. Legal and Regulatory considerations : Currently, the reporting requirements are governed by various regulators in India and their provisions override other laws. IFRS does not recognise such overriding laws. The regulatory and legal requirements in India will pose a challenge unless the same is been addressed by respective regulatory.

4. Taxation : IFRS convergence would affect most of the items in the financial statements and consequently the tax liabilities would also undergo a change. Thus the taxation laws should address the treatment of tax liabilities arising on convergence from Indian GAAP to IFRS.

5. Fair value Measurement : IFRS uses fair value as a measurement base for valuing most of the items of financial statements. The use of fair value accounting can bring a lot of volatility and subjectivity to the financial statements. It also involves a lot of hard work in arriving at the fair value and valuation experts have to be used.

6. Re-negotiation of Contract : The contracts would have to be re-negotiated which is also a big challenge. This is because the financial results under IFRS are likely to be very different from those under the Indian GAAP

7. Reporting systems : Companies would have to ensure that the existing business reporting model is amended to suit the reporting requirements of IFRS. The information systems should be designed to capture new requirements related to fixed assets, segment disclosures, related party transactions, etc.

Conversion is much more than a technical accounting issue. IFRS or Ind AS may significantly affect any number of a company's day-to-day operations and may even impact the reported profitability of the business itself. Since the timeline in the roadmap is no longer valid , the new implementation date for Ind AS is awaited from the MCA. It is unclear if the MCA will release a fresh roadmap or just amend the implementation date. Understanding IFRS or Ind AS and its implications is a business imperative for Indian companies.

QUESTIONS

OBJECTIVE TYPE

1. Objective of Financial Accounting Standards is to

(*i*) (*a*) Improve the reliability of the financial statements

(*b*) Hormonise accounting policies

(*c*) Make the reliability of the financial data

(*d*) All of the above.

(*ii*) Which Ind AS relates to Statement of Cash Flows ?
 (*a*) Ind AS 3
 (*b*) Ind AS 7
 (*c*) Ind AS 12
 (*c*) Ind AS 20

(*iii*) Which Ind AS relates to leases ?
 (*a*) Ind AS 23
 (*b*) Ind AS 24
 (*c*) Ind AS 17
 (*d*) Ind AS 12

(*iv*) Ind AS in India are issued by
 (*a*) Reserve Bank of India
 (*b*) Central Government
 (*c*) Institute of Chartered Accountants of India.

(*v*) Which Ind AS relates to Events after the Reporting Period ?
 (*a*) Ind AS 10
 (*b*) Ind AS 16
 (*c*) Ind AS 19
 (*d*) Ind AS 24

Ans. [(*i*) (*d*); (*ii*) (*b*); (*iii*) (*c*); (*iv*) (*c*); (*v*) (*a*)]

2. Which of the following statements are correct ?
 (*i*) Ind AS 1 relates to Presentation of Financial Statements
 (*ii*) Ind AS 16 relates to Property, Plant and Equipment.
 (*iii*) Ind AS 12 relates to Employee Benefits.
 (*iv*) Ind AS 23 relates to Borrowing Costs.
 (*v*) Ind AS 38 relates to Intangible Assets.

Ans. [Correct : (*i*); (*ii*); (*iv*); (*v*)]

3. Fill in the blanks :
 (*i*) Ind AS 10 relates to ....
 (*ii*) Ind AS 12 relates to ....
 (*iii*) Ind AS 27 relates to ....
 (*iv*) Ind AS 2 relates to ....
 (*v*) Ind AS 21 relates to ....

Ans. [*i*) Events after the Reporting Period; (*ii*) Income Taxes; (*iii*) Separate Financial Statements; (*iv*) Inventories; (*v*) The Effects of Changes in Foreign Exchange Rates]

SHORT/LONG ANSWER TYPE

1. What are Accounting Standards ? Discuss the main objectives of such standards.

OR

Define the term 'accounting standard'. How does a standard differ from a concept ?

OR

What is the legal status of accounting standards in India ?

OR

What is meant by accounting standards ? State briefly the merits of issuing accounting standards.

2. Write a note on Formation of the Accounting Standards Board set up in India.
3. State the objectives and functions of the Accounting Standards Board.

4. Write a note on Scope of Accounting Standards.
5. Describe briefly the procedure for issuing an Accounting Standard. Write a note on compliance with the Accounting Standards.
6. Explain briefly the advantages and disadvantages of setting Accounting Standards.
7. Write a note on the significance of Accounting Standards.

   OR

   Write a note on the significance of accounting standards. Are all Indian Accounting Standards mandatory from the very beginning ?
8. Give a list of Ind-ASs.
9. Compare the Ind AS with International Financial Reporting System. (IFRS)

CHAPTER **34**

International Financial Reporting Standards (IFRS)

What is IFRS ?

It means a principle based Accounting Standard (AS) drafted in comparatively simple and clear language than most of Indian **ASs.** Indian ASs are rule based. The term IFRS has both, a narrow and a broad meaning. Narrowly, IFRS refers to the new numbered series of pronouncements that the IASB is issuing, as distinct from the IAS series issued by its predecessor IASC.

- More broadly, IFRS refers to the entire body of IASB pronouncements, including Standards and Interpretation approved by the IASB, IASC, and SIC.
- IFRS is principle based Standards, drafted lucidly and easy to understand and apply. However, the application of IFRS requires an increased use of fair values for measurement of assets and liabilities.
- The focus in IFRS is more towards getting the balance sheet right and hence brings significant volatility in the income statement.

International Financial Reporting Standards (IFRS)

International Financial Reporting Standards (IFRS) are the globally accepted accounting standards issued by International Accounting Standards Board (IASB). They explain how different types of business transactions and events should be reported in financial statements. They also include guidelines and interpretations approved by IASB. The main objective of IFRS is to make international comparisons as easy as possible.

The IFRS Foundation and the IASB

The International regulatory framework consists of :

1. The International Financial Reporting Standards Foundation (IFRS Foundation)
2. The International Accounting Standards Board (IASB)
3. The International Financial Reporting Standards Advisory Council (IFRSAC)
4. The International Financial Reporting Standards Interpretations Committee (IFRSIC).

The IFRS Foundation is an independent, not-for-profit private sector organisation working in the public interest. It was founded in March 2001 as the IASC Foundation as a not-for-profit corporation incorporated in the United States and is the parent entity of the IASB. In March 2010, the IASC

Foundation changed its name to the IFRS Foundation to reflect more clearly what the Foundation does which is the publication and promotion of IFRS.

The governance and oversight of the IFRS Foundation and its standard-setting bodies rests with the Trustees. The Trustees are appointed for a renewable term of three years and must have an understanding of the issues relevant to the setting and development of IFRS but are not involved in a technical capacity. Six of the Trustees must be selected from the Asia/Oceania region, six from Europe, six from North America, one from Africa, one from South America and two from the rest of the world. The Trustees are publicly accountable to a Monitoring Board of public authorities.

The International Accounting Standards Board is an independent, privately-funded accounting standard setter based in London. It is a part of the International regulatory framework, reporting to the IFRS Foundation. From April 2001 the IASB assumed accounting standard setting responsibilities from its predecessor body, the International Accounting Standards Committee (IASC). The IASB has an important role to play in the regulation of financial information as it is responsible for issuing IFRS, which are then adopted for use in many different jurisdictions. Since 2001, almost 120 countries have required or permitted the use of IFRS in preparing financial information which makes the IASB the most important accounting body worldwide. The remaining major economies have timelines in place for changing over from national accounting standards to convergence with IFRS in the near future.

In India, convergence with IFRS is being done in the form of Ind AS. The Ministry of Corporate Affairs (MCA) is designated as the nodal Ministry for converging Indian GAAP' with IFRS/Ind AS and has notified 39 Ind AS till date. The roadmap for phase wise implementation of Ind AS was notified by MCA in 2015.

The industry has started Ind-AS implementation (from April 1, 2016) and there is a remarkable development. Example of few of the Companies following Ind AS in India: 1. Infosys. Ltd. 2. Wipro Ltd. 3. Dr. Reddys Lab Ltd. 4. Bharti Airtel Ltd. 5. Sterlite Industries Ltd. 6. Tata Motors Ltd. 7. Seimens Ltd. 8. Tata Consultancy Ltd. 9. Great Eastern Energy Corporation Ltd. 10. Noida Toll Bridge.

Features of IFRS

The main features of IFRS are as follows :

1. IFRS are principle-based accounting standards as compared to rule-based accounting standards as is the case with Indian Accounting standards.
2. IFRS are drafted in a clear and simple language and are easy to understand and apply.
3. IFRS emphasise that various transactions should be treated on the basis of their economic substance rather than their legal form.
4. Under the IFRS, the fixed assets are recorded at current cost.
5. Under IFRS, the assets, liabilities, revenues and expenses are reported in its functional currency which means the currency of the place where the entity operates.
6. Under IFRS the useful lie of the assets has to be computed again and again until the asset is actually removed from the books of accounts.
7. IFRS make it compulsory to adopt Component Accounting. Under component accounting, depreciation is not calculated simply on the total value of an asset but on the cost of important parts of the equipment or asset.

Need for IFRS

1. **Uniformity.** IFRS provides single set of accounting standards that would enable internationally standardize and assure better quality on a global screen.
2. **International capital.** IFRS would also permit international capital to flow more freely, enabling companies to develop consistent global practices on accounting problems.
3. **Regulators.** IFRS would be beneficial to regulators too, as a complexity associated with needing understand various reporting regimes would be reduced.
4. **Investors.** IFRS gives a better understanding to the financial statements and assess the

investment opportunities other than Home Country. Financial Statements follow IFRS give better and cohesive information to the investors.

5. **Accounting professionals.** IFRS also benefits the Accounting Professionals in a way that they will able to sell their services in the different part of world. Accounting Professionals can provide their services, those countries which follow IFRS.

Assumptions in IFRS

1. **Going Concern Assumption :** The first assumption is that the life of the business is infinite, *i.e.,* the entity would continue to exist for an indefinite period of time in the future.
2. **Accrual Assumption :** According to this assumption, transactions are recorded on accrual basis, *i.e.,* as and when the transactions occur, the date of settlement being immaterial.
3. **Measuring Unit Assumption :** Under this assumption assets are shown in the Balance Sheet at current or fair value. Similarly, liabilities are shown at that amount which would be required to settle them.
4. **Assumption of Constant Purchasing Power :** It is assumed that the value of capital would be adjusted to price index at the end of each financial year.

Scope of IFRS

- IASB Standards are known as International Financial Reporting Standards (IFRSs).
- All International Accounting Standards (IAS's) and Interpretations issued by the former IASC" and SI continue to be applicable unless and until they are amended or withdrawn.
- IFRS's apply to the general-purpose financial statements and other financial reporting by profit-oriented entities—those engaged in commercial, industrial, financial and similar activities regardless of their legal form.
- Entities other than profit-oriented business entities may also find IFRSs appropriate.
- General purpose financial statements are intended to meet the common needs of shareholders, creditors, employees, and the public at large for information about an entity's financial position, performance, and cash flows.
- Other financial reporting includes information provided outside financial statements that assists in the interpretation of a complete set of financial statements or improves users ability to make efficient economic decisions.
- IFRS apply to individual company and consolidated financial statements.
- A complete set of financial statements includes a balance sheet, an income statement, a cash flow statement, a statement showing either all changes in equity or changes in equity other than those arising from investments by a distributions to owners, a summary of accounting policies, and explanatory notes.
- If an IFRS allow both a 'benchmark' and an 'allowed alternative' treatment, financial statements may be described as conforming to IFRS whichever treatment is followed.
- In developing Standards, IASB intends not to permit choices in accounting treatment. Further, IASB intends to reconsider the choices in existing IASs with a view to reducing the number of those choices.
- The provision of IAS 1 that conformity with IAS requires compliance with every applicable IAS an Interpretation requires compliance with all IFRSs as well.

Difference between IFRS and Indian GAAP or Accounting Standards

(*i*) IFRS are based on **Principles** contrary to the Indian Accounting Standards which are based on **Rules.** For example, under schedule VI of the Companies Act, Redeemable Preference Shares are shown under the head 'Share Capital' but IFRS require that it should be shown under the head 'Loans.'

(*ii*) IFRS are based on the concept of 'Fair Value' but Indian Accounting Standards are based on the concept of 'Historical Cost' concept.

Difficulties or Challenges in Adopting IFRS

Following are the difficulties or challenges in adopting IFRS by India :

(*i*) **Concept :** IFRS are more principle-based on there is a scope of subjective judgement. The information in the financial statements is presented on the basis of **substance rather than rule.**

On the other hand **Indian Accounting Standards** are rigid being rules-based. Subjective judgement is not permitted in Indian Accounting Standards.

(*ii*) **Legal compliance :** Application of IFRS is totally based on the investors' needs. Their interests are given priority over law.

On the other hand, in **Indian Accounting Standards** the legal compliance gets priority over investor's needs.

(*iii*) **Framework provided :** IFRS provide a wide framework for financial reporting.

No such framework is present for **Indian Accounting Standards.**

(*iv*) **True and fair view :** In IFRS true and fair concept has no relevance.

In Indian Accounting Standards, there is an emphasis on the concept of true and fair view.

(*v*) **Presentation of financial statements :** IFRS clearly provide guidelines and overall requirement in presenting financial statements of companies.

Indian Accounting standards do not define clear requirements for disclosure in the financial statements.

Objectives of IFRSs

1. To develop a single set of high quality, understandable and enforceable global accounting standards that will form the stable platform for international accounting.
2. The correct adoption of IFRSs will bring more transparency and a higher degree of comparability, both of which promise many benefits for the organisations as well as economies.
3. To promote the use and rigorous application of those standards.
4. To take account of as appropriate, the special needs of small and medium-sized entities and emerging economies.
5. To bring about convergence of national accounting standards and International Accounting Standards and International Financial Reporting Standards (IFRS) to high quality solutions.
6. To make the information included in financial statements reliable so that users can take correct decisions.
7. To report the information on time *i.e.* undue delays should be avoided.
8. To identify the trends in the financial position and performance so that users must be able to compare the financial statements of different enterprises.

Structure of IFRS vis-a-vis Indian GAAP

Indian Pronouncements	*IFRS Pronouncements*
1. 28 (29) Accounting Standards mandatory (minus AS-8)	1. 29 (41)-IASs issued by IASC
2. 3 Standards on Financial Instruments; AS 30, AS 31 and AS 32 still not mandatory	2. 9-IFRSs issued by IASB
3. Accounting Standards Interpretations	3. 18 (19)-Interpretations originated by the International Financial Reporting Interpretations Committee (IFRIC).
4. Guidance Notes	4. 11 (34)-Interpretations issued by the former Standing Interpretations Committee (SIC).
5. Expert Advisory Options	

Note : Figures inside brackets are numbers of pronouncements made so far and figures outside the brackets are the number of pronouncements which are in force at present.

Since 2001 the Accounting Standards issued by the International Accounting Standard Board are designated as International Financial Reporting Standards (IFRSs). IASB achieves its objectives primarily by developing and publishing International Financial Reporting Standards (IFRSs) for general purpose financial statements and other financial reporting. The objective of International Financial Reporting Standards is to meet the common information needs of wide range of users such as shareholders, creditors, employees and public at large relating to financial statements. So far IASB has issued seventeen Financial Reporting Standards given as follows :

IFRS-1. First-time Adoption of International Financial Reporting Standards
IFRS-2. Share-based Payment
IFRS-3. Business Combinations
IFRS-4. Insurance Contracts
IFRS-5. Non-current Assets Held for Sale and Discontinued Operations
IFRS-6. Exploration for and Evaluation of Mineral Resources
IFRS-7. Financial Instruments : Disclosures
IFRS-8. Operating Segments
IFRS-9. Financial Instruments
IFRS 10. Consolidated Financial Statements
IFRS 11. Joint Arrangements
IFRS 12. Disclosure of Interests in Other Entities
IFRS 13. Fair Value Measurement
IFRS 14. Regulatory Deferral Accounts
IFRS 15. Revenue from Contracts with Customers
IFRS 16. Leases
IFRS 17. Insurance Contract

A brief explanation of these International Financial Reporting Standards is given below :

IFRS-1—First Time Adoption of International Financial Reporting Standards

When an organisation that reports under an accounting framework other than the International Financial Reporting Standards such as Indian Accounting Standards decides to adopt IFRS, it has to comply with certain requirements prescribed by IFRS on conversion to IFRS. IASB makes it incumbent upon all new entrants to IFRS to compulsorily pass the International Financial Reporting Standard 1 (IFRS-1) test on conversion of their accounting framework to IFRS. This standard is gaining importance day by day as more and more countries of the world are adopting IFRS as their national accounting standards.

The objective of this IFRS is to make sure that an entity's first IFRS financial statements and its interim financial reports for part of the period covered by those financial statements contain high quality information that (*a*) is transparent for users and comparable over all periods presented; (*b*) provides a suitable starting point for accounting in accordance with International Financial Reporting Standards; and (*c*) can be generated at a cost that does not exceed the benefits to users.

An entity shall prepare and present an opening IFRS statement of financial position at the date of transition to IFRSs. This is the starting point in accordance with IFRSs.

An entity shall use the same accounting policies in its opening IFRS statement of financial position and throughout all periods presented in its first IFRS financial statements. In general, those accounting policies shall comply with each IFRS effective at the end of its first IFRS reporting period.

In general, IFRS requires an entity to do the following in the opening IFRS statement of financial position that it prepares as a starting point for its accounting under IFRSs.

(*a*) recognise all assets and liabilities whose recognition is required by IFRSs;
(*b*) not recognise items as assets or liabilities if IFRSs do not permit such recognition;

(*c*) reclassify items that it recognised in accordance with previous GAAP as one type of asset, liability or component of equity in accordance with IFRSs; and

(*d*) apply IFRSs in measuring all recognised assets and liabilities.

An entity makes estimates in accordance with IFRSs for the opening statement to financial position and all other periods covered by the financial statements. An entity shall explain how the transition from previous GAAP to IFRSs affected its reported financial position, financial performance and cash flows.

IFRS-2—Share-based Payment

Entities often grant shares or share option to employees, directors and other parties as remuneration packages or in exchange for goods and services acquired. The objective of IFRS-2 is to specify the financial reporting of share-based payment transactions and to show the effects of such transactions (including associated expenses) on profit or loss and financial position.

IFRS-2 identifies three types of share based transactions as follows :

1. Equity-settled share-based payment transactions.
2. Cash-settled share-based payment transactions.
3. Share-based payment transactions with cash alternative.

This standard also applies to transfers of equity instruments of the entity's parent or equity instruments of another entity in the same group as the entity, to parties that have supplied goods or services to the entity.

Equity-settled share-based payment transactions are those in which the entity receives goods or services as consideration for equity instruments of the entity. This standard requires an entity to measure the goods or services received and the corresponding increase in equity at the fair value of goods are services received, unless that fair value cannot be estimated reliably. If the fair value of the goods or services cannot be estimated reliably by the entity, then the entity is required to measure the value of the goods or services received and the corresponding increase in equity indirectly by reference to the fair value of the equity instruments granted.

Cash-settled share-based payment transactions are those in which the entity acquires goods or services by incurring liabilities to the supplier of those goods or services for amounts that are based on the price or value of the entity's shares or other equity instruments of the entity. For such type of transactions the entity shall measure the goods or services acquired and the liability incurred at the fair value of the liability. Until the liability is settled, the entity is required to remeasure the fair value of the liability at each reporting date and at the date of settlement, with any changes in fair value recognised in profit or loss for the period.

Share-based payment transactions with cash alternative are those transactions in which the entity receives or acquires goods or services and the terms of the arrangement provide either the entity or the supplier of those goods or services with a choice of whether the entity settles the transaction in cash or by issuing equity instruments. For share-based payment transactions in which the terms of the arrangement provide either the entity or the supplier of goods or services with a choice whether the entity settles the transaction in cash or by issuing equity instruments, the entity is required to account for that transaction, or component of that transaction as a cash settled share-based payment transaction if, and to the extent that, the entity has incurred a liability to settle in cash, or as an equity-settled share-based payment transaction if, and to the extent that, no such liability has been incurred.

As per this standard, an entity shall disclose information that enables users of the financial statements to understand the nature and extent of share-based payment arrangements that existed during the period and the effect of share-based payment transactions on the entity's profit or loss for the period and on its financial position. The entity is also required to disclose how the fair value of the goods or services acquired, or the fair value of the equity instruments granted, during the period was determined.

IFRS-3—Business Combination

The objective of IFRS-3 is to specify the financial reporting to be provided by an entity when it undertakes a business combination. IFRS-3 establishes principles and requirements for how an acquirer recognises and measure in its financial statements the identifiable assets acquired, the liabilities assumed and any non-controlling interest in the acquire. It also establishes principles and requirements for recognising and measuring the goodwill acquired in the business combination or a gain from a bargain purchase and for determining what information to disclose to enable users of the financial statements to evaluate the nature and financial effects of the business combination.

As per this IFRS, a business combination must be accounted for by applying the acquisition method, unless it is a combination involving entities or businesses under common control. One of the parties to a business combination is identified as the acquirer, being the entity that obtains control of the other business (the acquire). It may be noted that formations of a joint venture or the acquisition of an asset or a group of assets that does not constitute a business are not business combinations.

Core principle of IFRS-3 is that an acquirer of a business recognises the assets acquired and liabilities assumed at their acquisition date fair values and discloses information that enables users to evaluate the nature and financial effects of the acquisition.

As per IFRS-3, the acquirer shall measure the cost of a business combination as the aggregate of the fair values, at the date of exchange, of assets given, liabilities assumed, and equity instruments issued by the acquirer, in exchange for control of the business of the acquire plus any costs directly attributable to the business combination. The acquirer shall at the acquisition date recognise goodwill acquired in a business combination as an asset and initially measure that goodwill at its cost, being the excess of the cost of the business combination over the acquirer's interest in the net fair value of the identifiable assets, liabilities and contingent liabilities.

When a business combination provides for an adjustment to the cost of the combination contingent on future events, the acquirer should include the amount of that adjustment in the cost of combination at the acquisition date if the adjustment can be measured reliably. After a business combination, the acquirer should disclose any adjustments recognised in the current reporting period that relate to business combinations that occurred in the current or previous reporting periods.

IFRS-4—Insurance Contracts

The objective of IFRS-4 is to specify the financial reporting for insurance contracts by any entity that issues such contracts until the Board completes the second phase of its project on insurance contracts. In particular, this IFRS requires limited improvements to accounting by insurers for insurance contracts and disclosure that identifies and explains the amounts in an insurer's financial statements arising from insurance contracts and helps users of those financial statements understand the amount, timing and uncertainty of future cash flows from insurance contracts.

IFRS-4 applies to all insurance contracts (including reinsurance contracts) that an entity issues and to reinsurance contracts that it holds, except for specified contracts covered by other IFRSs. It does not apply to other assets and liabilities of an insurer, such as financial assets and financial liabilities. This IFRS does not cover accounting by policyholders.

As per this IFRS, an insurer is required to assess at each reporting date whether its recognised insurance liabilities are adequate using current estimates of future cash flows under its insurance contracts. If the assessment shows that the carrying amount of its insurance liabilities is inadequate in the light of the estimated future cash flows, the entire deficiency should be recognised in profit and loss statement.

IFRS-4 permits an insurer to change its accounting policies for insurance contracts if, and only if, the change makes the financial statements more relevant to the economic decision-making needs of users and no less reliable, or more reliable and no less relevant. This IFRS requires an insurer to disclose information that identifies and explains the amounts in its financial statements arising from insurance contracts. An insurer should also disclose information that enables users of the financial statements to understand the amount, timing and uncertainty of future cash flows arising from insurance contracts.

IFRS-5—Non-Current Assets Held for Sale and Discontinued Operations

The objective of IFRS-5 is to specify the accounting for assets held for sale, and the presentation and disclosure of discontinued operations. In particular, this IFRS requires.

Held for Sale—assets that meet the criteria to be classified as held for sale to be measured at the lower of carrying amount and fair value less costs to sell, and depreciation on such assets to cease;

Disposal Group—an asset classified as held for sale and the assets and liabilities included within a disposal group classified as held for sale to be presented separately in the statement of financial position; and

Discontinued Operation—the results of discontinued operations to be presented separately in the statement of comprehensive income.

As per IFRS-5, an entity shall classify a non-current asset or disposal group as held for sale if its carrying amount will be recovered principally through a sale transaction rather than through continuing use. For this the asset or disposal group must be available for immediate sale in its present condition subject only to terms that are usual and customary for sale of such asset or disposal group and its sale must be highly probable. For the sale to be highly probable, the appropriate level of management must be committed to a plan to sell the asset or disposal group, and an active programme to locate a buyer and complete the plan must have been initiated. An entity shall not classify as held for sale a non-current asset (or disposal group) that is to be abandoned. This is because its carrying amount will be recovered principally through continued use. Further, an entity shall present and disclose information that enables users of the financial statements to evaluate the financial effects of discontinued operations and disposal of non-current assets or disposal groups.

IFRS-6—Exploration for and Evaluation of Mineral Resources

The objective of IFRS-6 is to specify the financial reporting for the exploration and evaluation of mineral resources. As per this IFRS, exploration and mineral expenditures are expenditures incurred by an entity in connection with the exploration for and evaluation of mineral resources before the technical feasibility and commercial viability of extracting a mineral resource are demonstrable. Exploration for and evaluation of mineral resources has been defined as the search for mineral resources including minerals, oil, natural gas and similar non-regenerative resources after the entity has obtained legal rights to explore in a specific area, as well as the determination of the technical feasibility and commercial viability of extracting the mineral resource.

As per this IFRS, exploration and evaluation assets shall be measured at cost. Exploration and evaluation assets are exploration and evaluation expenditures recognised as assets in accordance with the entity's accounting policy. An entity adopting IFRS-6 may continue to use the accounting policies applied immediately before adopting the IFRS.

Exploration and evaluation assets shall be assessed for impairment when facts and circumstances suggest that the carrying amount of an exploration and evaluation asset may exceed its recoverable amount. In such a case, the entity shall measure, present and disclose any resulting impairment loss.

As per this IFRS, an entity shall determine an accounting policy for allocating exploration and evaluation assets to cash-generating units or groups of cash-generating units for the purpose of assessing such assets for impairment. Each cash-generating unit or group of units to which an exploration and evaluation asset is allocated shall not be larger than an operating segment determined in accordance with IFRS-8, Operating Segments. Further, an entity shall disclose information that identifies and explains the amounts recognised in its financial statements arising from the exploration for and evaluation of mineral resources.

IFRS-7—Financial Instruments : Disclosures

IFRS-7 deals with the disclosure requirements in relation to all risks arising from financial instruments and applies to an entity that holds financial instruments. The objective of this IFRs is to require entities to provide disclosures in their financial statements that enable users to understand the significance of financial instruments for the entity's financial position and performance and the nature and extent of risk arising from the financial instruments to which the entity is exposed during the period at the reporting dates.

This IFRS prescribes specific disclosure of certain policies relating to financial instruments such as criteria for designating financial assets and financial liabilities at fair value through profit or loss and accounting policy for financial assets that are subject to re-negotiation terms. Disclosure for fair value determination should be made, whether the fair value is based on quoted prices or valuation techniques.

Risk information disclosure requirement is of relevance where user of the financial statements uses these for predicting future financial position and performance. There are three types of risks (*i.e.* credit risk, liquidity risk and market risk) which arise from financial instruments. Credit risk is that risk that one party to a financial instrument will incur a financial loss for the other party by failing to discharge an obligation. Liquidity risk arises when the entity will encounter difficulty in meeting obligation associated with financial liabilities. It may not have required cash or cash equivalent to meet its financial obligation resulting in default. Market risk arises when the fair value or future cash flows of a financial instrument will fluctuate because of changes in market prices. For each type of risk, the entity should disclose the exposure to the risk and how they arise and the entity's objective, policies and processes for managing the risks and methods used to measure the risk. Any changes to these disclosures from the previous accounting period should also be reported.

Note : There is no difference between IFRS-7 and AS-32. Please refer to AS-32.

IFRS-8—Operating Segments

IFRS-8 requires publicly held entities to report certain information about the following :

- their products and services
- the geographic areas in which they operate
- their major customers.

This IFRS specifies how an entity should report about its operating segments in annual financial statements and also requires an entity to report selected information about its operating segments in interim financial reports. It also sets out requirements for related disclosures about products and services, geographical areas and major customers.

IFRS-8 applies to the separate or individual financial statements of an entity and to the consolidated financial statements of group with a parent :

- whose debt or equity instruments are traded in a public market; or
- that files or in the process of filing its (consolidated) financial statements with a securities commission or other regulatory organisation for the purpose of issuing any class of instruments in a public market.

However, when both separate and consolidated financial statements for the parent are presented in a single financial report, segment information need be presented only on the basis of the consolidated financial statements.

An operating segment is a component of an entity :

- that engages in business activities from which it may earn revenues and incur expenses (including revenues and expenses relating to transactions with other components of the same entity);
- whose operating results are reviewed regularly by the entity's chief operating decision maker to make decisions about resources to be allocated to the segment and assess its performance; and
- for which discrete financial information is available.

IFRS-8 requires an entity to report financial and descriptive information about its reportable segments. Reportable segments are operating segments or aggregations of operating segments that meet specified criteria as given below :

- its reported revenue, from both external customers and intersegment salers or transfers, is 10% or more of the combined revenue, internal and external, or all operating segments.
- profit or loss is 10% or more, in absolute amount, of the greater of (*a*) the combined profit of all operating segments that did not report a loss; and (*b*) the combined loss of all operating segments that reported a loss; or
- its assets are 10% or more of the combined assets of all operating segments.

Further, if the total external revenue reported by operating segments constitutes less than 75% of the entity's revenue, additional operating segments must be identified as reportable segments until at least 75% of the entity's revenue is included in reportable segments.

When an operating segment is first identified as a reportable segment according to the quantitative thresholds, comparative data should be presented, unless the necessary information is not available and the cost to develop it would be excessive.

IFRS-8 requires an entity to give description information about the way the operating segments were identified and the types of products and services from which each operating segments derives its revenues. It also requires an entity to give information about the reported segment profit or loss, segment assets and segment liabilities and the basis of measurement. This IFRS requires reconciliations of total reportable segment revenues, total profit or loss, total assets and liabilities and other amounts disclosed for reportable segments to corresponding amounts in the entity's financial statements.

IFRS-9—Financial Instruments

IFRS 9 *Financial Instruments* includes requirements for recognition and measurement, derecognition and hedge accounting. The IASB is adding to the standard as it completes the various phases of its comprehensive project on financial instruments, and so it will eventually form a complete replacement for AS 39 *Financial Instruments: Recognition and Measurement.*

Objective

The objective of this IFRS is to establish principles for the financial reporting of *financial assets* and *financial liabilities* that will present relevant and useful information to users of financial statements for their assessment of the amounts, timing and uncertainty of an entity's future cash.

Scope

An entity shall apply this IFRS to all items within the scope of IAS 39 *Financial Instruments: Recognition and Measurement.*

Initial measurement of financial instruments

All financial instruments are initially measured at fair value plus or minus, in the case of a financial asset or financial liability not at fair value through profit or loss, transaction costs.

Subsequent Measurement of Financial Assets

IFRS 9 divides all financial assets that are currently in the scope of IAS 39 into two classifications - those measured at amortised cost and those measured at fair value. Classification is made at the time the financial asset is initially recognised, namely when the entity becomes a party to the contractual provisions of the instrument.

Debt Instruments

A debt instrument that meets the following two conditions can be measured at amortised cost (net of any write down for impairment)

- **Business model test:** The objective of the entity's business model is to hold the financial asset to collect the contractual cash flows (rather than to sell the instrument prior to its contractual maturity to realise its fair value changes).
- **Cash flow characteristics test:** The contractual terms of the financial asset give rise on specified dates to cash flows that are solely payments of principal and interest on the principal outstanding.

All other debt instruments must be measured at fair value through profit or loss (FVTPL).

Fair Value Option

Even if an instrument meets the two amortised cost tests, IFRS 9 contains an option to designate a financial asset as measured at FVTPL if doing so eliminates or significantly reduces a measurement or recognition inconsistency (sometimes referred to as an 'accounting mismatch') that would otherwise arise from measuring assets or liabilities or recognising the gains and losses on them on different bases.

Equity Instruments

All equity investments in scope of IFRS 9 are to be measured at fair value in the statement of financial position, with value changes recognised in profit or loss, except for those equity investments for which the entity has elected to report value changes in 'other comprehensive income'. There is no 'cost exception' for unquoted equities.

Other comprehensive income' option

If an equity investment is not held for trading, an entity can make an irrevocable election at initial recognition to measure it at fair value through other comprehensive income (FVTOCI) with only dividend income recognised in profit or loss.

Measurement Guidance

Despite the fair value requirement for all equity investments, IFRS 9 contains guidance on when cost may be the best estimate of fair value and also when it might not be representative of fair value.

Subsequent Measurement of Financial Liabilities

IFRS 9 doesn't change the basic accounting model for financial liabilities under IAS 39. Two measurement categories continue to exist: fair value through profit or loss (FVTPL) and amortised cost. Financial liabilities held for trading are measured at FVTPL, and all other financial liabilities are measured at amortised cost unless the fair value option is applied.

Fair Value Option

IFRS 9 contains an option to designate a financial liability as measured at FVTPL if

- doing so eliminates or significantly reduces a measurement or recognition inconsistency (sometimes referred to as an 'accounting mismatch') that would otherwise arise from measuring assets or liabilities or recognising the gains and losses on them on different bases, or
- the liability is part or a group of financial liabilities or financial assets and financial liabilities that is managed and its performance is evaluated on a fair value basis, in accordance with a documented risk management or investment strategy, and information about the group is provided internally on that basis to the entity's key management personnel.

A financial liability which does not meet any of these criteria may still be designated as measured at FVTPL when it contains one or more embedded derivatives that would require separation.

IFRS 9 requires gains and losses on financial liabilities designated as at fair value through profit or loss to be split into the amount of change in the fair value that is attributable to changes in the credit risk of the liability, which shall be presented in other comprehensive income, and the remaining amount of change in the fair value of the liability which shall be presented in profit or loss. The new guidance allows the recognition of the full amount of change in the fair value in the profit or loss only if the recognition of changes in the liability's credit risk in other comprehensive income would create or enlarge an accounting mismatch in profit or loss. That determination is made at initial recognition and is not reassessed.

Amounts presented in other comprehensive income shall not be subsequently transferred to profit or loss, the entity may only transfer the cumulative gain or loss within equity.

Derecognition of Financial Assets

The basic premise for the derecognition model in IFRS 9 (carried over from IAS 39) is to determine whether the asset under consideration for derecognition is:

- an asset in its entirety or
- specifically identified cash flows from an asset (or a group of similar financial assets) or
- a fully proportionate (pro rata) share of the cash flows from an asset (or a group of similar financial assets). or
- a fully proportionate (pro rata) share of specifically identified cash flows from a financial asset (or a group of similar financial assets)

Once the asset under consideration for derecognition has been determined, an assessment is made as to whether the asset has been transferred, and if so, whether the transfer of that asset is subsequently eligible for derecognition.

An asset is transferred if either the entity has transferred the contractual rights to receive the cash flows, or the entity has retained the contractual rights to receive the cash flows from the asset, but has assumed a contractual obligation to pass those cash flows on under an arrangement that meets the following three conditions:

- the entity has no obligation to pay amounts to the eventual recipient unless it collects equivalent amounts on the original asset
- the entity is prohibited from selling or pledging the original asset (other than as security to the eventual recipient),
- the entity has an obligation to remit those cash flows without material delay

Once an entity has determined that the asset has been transferred, it then determines whether or not it has transferred substantially all of the risks and rewards of ownership of the asset. If substantially all the risks and rewards have been transferred, the asset is derecognised. If substantially all the risks and rewards have been retained, derecognition of the asset is precluded.

If the entity has neither retained nor transferred substantially all of the risks and rewards of the asset, then the entity must assess whether it has relinquished control of the asset or not. If the entity does not control the asset then derecognition is appropriate; however if the entity has retained control of the asset, then the entity continues to recognise the asset to the extent to which it has a continuing involvement in the asset.

Derecognition of Financial Liabilities

A financial liability should be removed from the balance sheet when, and only when, it is extinguished, that is, when the obligation specified in the contract is either discharged or cancelled or expires.] Where there has been an exchange between an existing borrower and lender of debt instruments with substantially different terms, or there has been a substantial modification of the terms of an existing financial liability, this transaction is accounted for as an extinguishment of the original financial liability and the recognition of a new financial liability. A gain or loss from extinguishment of the original financial liability is recognised in profit or loss.

Derivatives

All derivatives, including those linked to unquoted equity investments, are measured at fair value. Value changes are recognised in profit or loss unless the entity has elected to treat the derivative as a hedging instrument in accordance with IAS 39, in which case the requirements of IAS 39 apply.

Embedded Derivatives

An embedded derivative is a component of a hybrid contract that also includes a non-derivative host, with the effect that some of the cash flows of the combined instrument vary in a way similar to a stand-alone derivative. A derivative that is attached to a financial instrument but is contractually transferable independently of that instrument, or has a different counterparty, is not an embedded derivative, but a separate financial instrument.

The embedded derivative concept of IAS 39 has been included in IFRS 9 to apply only to hosts that are not assets within the scope of the standard, Consequently, embedded derivatives that under IAS 39 would have been separately accounted for at FVTPL because they were not closely related to the financial host asset will no longer be separated. Instead, the contractual cash flows of the financial asset are assessed in their entirety, and the asset as a whole is measured at FVTPL if any of its cash flows do not represent payments of principal and interest. The embedded derivative concept of IAS 39 is now included in IFRS 9 and continues to apply to financial liabilities and hosts not within the scope of the standard (e.g. leasing contracts, insurance contracts, contracts for the purchase or sale of a non-financial items).

Reclassification

For financial assets, reclassification is required between FVTPL and amortised cost, or vice versa, if and only if the entity's business model objective for its financial assets changes so its previous model assessment would no longer apply.

If reclassification is appropriate, it must be done prospectively from the reclassification date. An entity does not restate any previously recognised gains, losses, or interest.

IFRS 9 does not allow reclassification where:

- the 'other comprehensive income' option has been exercised for a financial asset, or
- the fair value option has been exercised in any circumstance for a financial assets or financial liability.

Hedge Accounting

The hedge accounting requirements in IFRS 9 are optional. If certain eligibility and qualification criteria are met, hedge accounting allows an entity to reflect risk management activities in the financial statements by matching gains or losses on financial hedging instruments with losses or gains on the risk exposures they hedge.

The hedge accounting model in IFRS 9 is not designed to accommodate hedging of open, dynamic portfolios. As a result for a fair value hedge of interest rate risk of a portfolio of financial assets or liabilities an entity can apply the hedge accounting requirements in IAS 39 instead of those in IFRS 9.

Qualifying Criteria for Hedge Accounting

A hedging relationship qualifies for hedge accounting only if all of the following criteria are met:

1. the hedging relationship consists only of eligible hedging instruments and eligible hedged items.
2. at the inception of the hedging relationship there is formal designation and documentation of the hedging relationship and the entity's risk management objective and strategy for undertaking the hedge.
3. the hedging relationship meets all of the hedge effectiveness requirements (see below)

Hedging Instruments

Only contracts with a party external to the reporting entity may be designated as hedging instruments.

A hedging instrument may be a derivative (except for some written options) or non-derivative financial instrument measured at FVTPL unless it is a financial liability designated as at FVTPL for which changes due to credit risk are presented in OCI. For a hedge of foreign currency risk, the foreign currency risk component of a non-derivative financial instrument, except equity investments designated as FVTOCI, may be designated as the hedging instrument.

IFRS 9 allows a proportion (e.g. 60%) but not a time portion (eg the first 6 years of cash flows of a 10 year instrument) of a hedging instrument to be designated as the hedging instrument. IFRS 9 also allows only the intrinsic value of an option, or the spot element of a forward to be designated as the hedging instrument. An entity may also exclude the foreign currency basis spread from a designated hedging instrument.

IFRS 9 allows combinations of derivatives and non-derivatives to be designated as the hedging instrument.

Combinations of purchased and written options do not qualify if they amount to a net written option at the date of designation.

Hedged Items

A hedged item can be a recognised asset or liability, an unrecognised firm commitment, a highly probable forecast transaction or a net investment in a foreign operation and must be reliably measurable.

An aggregated exposure that is a combination of an eligible hedged item as described above and a derivative may be designated as a hedged item.

The hedged item must generally be with a party external to the reporting entity however as an exception the foreign currency risk of an intragroup monetary item may qualify as a hedged item in the consolidated financial statements if it results in an exposure to foreign exchange rate gains or losses that are not fully eliminated on consolidation. In addition, the foreign currency risk of a highly probable forecast intragroup transaction may qualify as a hedged item in consolidated financial statements provided that the transaction is denominated in a currency other than the functional currency of the entity entering into that transaction and the foreign currency risk will affect consolidated profit or loss.

An entity may designate an item in its entirety or a component of an item as the hedged item. The component may be a risk component that is separately identifiable and reliably measurable; one or more selected contractual cash flows; or components of a nominal amount.

A group of items (including net positions is an eligible hedged item only if:

1. it consists of items individually, eligible hedged items;
2. the items in the group are managed together on a group basis for risk management purposes; and
3. in the case of a cash flow hedge of a group of items whose variabilities in cash flows are not expected to be approximately proportional to the overall variability in cash flows of the group:
   (*a*) it is a hedge of foreign currency risk; and
   (*b*) the designation of that net position specifies the reporting period in which the forecast transactions are expected to affect profit or loss, as well as their nature and volume

For a hedge of a net position whose hedged risk affects different line items in the statement of profit or loss and other comprehensive income, any hedging gains or losses in that statement are presented in a separate line from those affected by the hedged items.

Accounting for Qualifying Hedging Relationships

There are three types of hedging relationships:

Fair value hedge: a hedge of the exposure to changes in fair value of a recognised asset or liability or an unrecognised firm commitment, or a component of any such item, that is attributable to a particular risk and could affect profit or loss (or OCI in the case of an equity instrument designated as at FVTOCI).

For a fair value hedge, the gain or loss on the hedging instrument is recognised in profit or loss (or OCI, if hedging an equity instrument at FVTOCI and the hedging gain or loss on the hedged item adjusts the carrying amount of the hedged item and is recognised in profit or loss. However, if the hedged item is an equity instrument at FVTOCI, those amounts remain in OCI. When a hedged item is an unrecognised firm commitment the cumulative hedging gain or loss is recognised as an asset or a liability with a corresponding gain or loss recognised in profit or loss.

If the hedged item is a financial instrument measured at amortised cost any hedge adjustment is amortised to profit or loss based on a recalculated effective interest rate. Amortisation may begin as soon as an adjustment exists and shall begin no later than when the hedged item ceases to be adjusted for hedging gains and losses.

Cash flow hedge: a hedge of the exposure to variability in cash flows that is attributable to a particular risk associated with all, or a component of, a recognised asset or liability (such as all or some future interest payments on variable-rate debt) or a highly probable forecast transaction, and could affect profit or loss.

For a cash flow hedge the cash flow hedge reserve in equity is adjusted to the lower of the following (in absolute amounts):

- the cumulative gain or loss on the hedging instrument from inception of the hedge; and
- the cumulative change in fair value of the hedged item from inception of the hedge.

The portion of the gain or loss on the hedging instrument that is determined to be an effective hedge is recognised in OCI and any remaining gain or loss is hedge ineffectiveness that is recognised in profit or loss.

If a hedged forecast transaction subsequently results in the recognition of a non-financial item or becomes a firm commitment for which fair value hedge accounting is applied, The amount that has been accumulated in the cash flow hedge reserve is removed and included directly in the initial cost or other carrying amount of the asset or the liability. In other cases The amount that has been accumulated in the cash flow hedge reserve is reclassified to profit or loss in the same period(s) as the hedged cash flows.

When an entity discontinues hedge accounting for a cash flow hedge, if the hedged future cash flows are still expected to occur, the amount that has been accumulated in the cash flow hedge reserve remains there until the future cash flows occur; if the hedged future cash flows are no longer expected to occur, that amount is immediately reclassified to profit or loss.

A hedge of the foreign currency risk of a firm commitment may be accounted for as a fair value hedge or a cash flow hedge.

Hedge of a net investment in a foreign operation (as defined in IAS 21), including a hedge of a monetary item that is accounted for as part of the net investment, is accounted for similarly to cash flow hedges:

- the portion of the gain or loss on the hedging instrument that is determined to be an effective hedge is recognised in OCI; and
- the ineffective portion is recognised in profit or loss.

The cumulative gain or loss on the hedging instrument relating to the effective portion of the hedge is reclassified to profit or loss on the disposal or partial disposal of the foreign operation.

Hedge Effectiveness Requirements

In order to qualify for hedge accounting, the hedge relationship must meet the following effectiveness criteria at the beginning of each hedged period:

- there is an economic relationship between the hedged item and the hedging instrument;
- the effect of credit risk does not dominate the value changes that result from that economic relationship; and
- the hedge ratio of the hedging relationship is the same as that actually used in the economic hedge

Rebalancing and Discontinuation

If a hedging relationship ceases to meet the hedge effectiveness requirement relating to the hedge ratio but the risk management objective for that designated hedging relationship remains the same, an entity adjusts the hedge ratio of the hedging relationship (i.e. rebalances the hedge) so that it meets the qualifying criteria again.

An entity discontinues hedge accounting prospectively only when the hedging relationship (or a part of a hedging relationship) ceases to meet the qualifying criteria (after any rebalancing). This includes instances when the hedging instrument expires or is sold, terminated or exercised. Discontinuing hedge accounting can either affect a hedging relationship in its entirety or only a part of it (in which case hedge accounting continues for the remainder of the hedging relationship).

Time Value of Options

When an entity separates the intrinsic value and time value of an option contract and designates as the hedging instrument only the change in intrinsic value of the option, it recognises some or all of the change in the time value in OCI which is later removed or reclassified from equity as a single amount or on an amortised basis (depending on the nature of the hedged item) and ultimately recognised in profit or loss.

This reduces profit or loss volatility compared to recognising the change in value of time value directly in profit or loss.

Forward Points and Foreign Currency Basis Spreads

When an entity separates the forward points and the spot element of a forward contract and designates as the hedging instrument only the change in the value of the spot element, or when an entity excludes the foreign currency basis spread from a hedge the entity may recognise the change in value of the excluded portion in OCI to be later removed or reclassified from equity as a single amount or on an amortised basis (depending on the nature of the hedged item) and ultimately recognised in profit or loss.This reduces profit or loss volatility compared to recognising the change in value of forward points or currency basis spreads directly in profit or loss.

Credit Exposures Designated at FVTPL

If an entity uses a credit derivative measured at FVTPL to manage the credit risk of a financial instrument (credit exposure) it may designate all or a proportion of that financial instrument as measured at FVTPL if:

- the name of the credit exposure matches the reference entity of the credit derivative ('name matching'); and
- the seniority of the financial instrument matches that of the instruments that can be delivered in accordance with the credit derivative.

An entity may make this designation irrespective of whether the financial instrument that is managed for credit risk is within the scope of IFRS 9 (for example, it can apply to loan commitments that are outside the scope of IFRS 9). The entity may designate that financial instrument at, or subsequent to, initial recognition, or while it is unrecognised and shall document the designation concurrently.

If designated after initial recognition, any difference in the previous carrying amount and fair value is recognised immediately in profit or loss .

An entity discontinues measuring the financial instrument that gave rise to the credit risk at FVTPL if the qualifying criteria are no longer met and the instrument is not otherwise required to measure the instrument at FVTPL. The fair value at discontinuation becomes its new carrying amount.

Disclosures

IFRS 9 amends some of the requirements of IFRS 7 *Financial Instruments: Disclosures* including added disclosures about investments in equity instruments designated as at FVTOCI.

IFRS-10—Consolidated Financial Statements

IFRS 10 *Consolidated Financial Statements* outlines the requirements for the preparation and presentation of consolidated financial statements, requiring entities to consolidate entities it controls. Control requires exposure or rights to variable returns and the ability to affect those returns through power over an investee.

IFRS 10 was issued in May 2011 and applies to annual periods beginning on or after 1 January 2013.

Objective

The objective of IFRS 10 is to establish principles for the presentation and preparation of consolidated financial statements when an entity controls one or more other entities.

The Standard:

- requires a parent entity (an entity that controls one or more other entities) to present consolidated financial statements
- defines the principle of control, and establishes control as the basis for consolidation

- set out how to apply the principle of control to identify whether an investor controls an investee and therefore must consolidate the investee
- sets out the accounting requirements for the preparation of consolidated financial statements
- defines an investment entity and sets out an exception to consolidating particular subsidiaries of an investment entity.

Key Definitions

Consolidated financial statements	The financial statements of a group in which the assets, liabilities, equity, income, expenses and cash flows of the parent and its subsidiaries are presented as those of a single economic entity
Control of an investee	An investor controls an investee when the investor is exposed, or has rights, to variable returns from its involvement with the investee and has the ability to affect those returns through its power over the investee
Investment entity	An entity that:
	(*a*) obtains funds from one or more investors for the purpose of providing those investor(s) with investment management services
	(*b*) commits to its investor(s) that its business purpose is to invest funds solely for returns from capital appreciation, investment income, or both, and
	(*c*) measures and evaluates the performance of substantially all of its investments on a fair value basis.
Parent	An entity that controls one or more entities
Power	Existing rights that give the current ability to direct the relevant activities
Protective rights	Rights designed to protect the interest of the party holding those rights without giving that party power over the entity to which those rights relate
Relevant activities	Activities of the investee that significantly affect the investee's returns

Control

An investor determines whether it is a parent by assessing whether it controls one or more investees. An investor considers all relevant facts and circumstances when assessing whether it controls an investee. An investor controls an investee when it is exposed, or has rights, to variable returns from its involvement with the investee and has the ability to affect those returns through its power over the investee.

An investor controls an investee if and only if the investor has all of the following elements:

- power over the investee, i.e. the investor has existing rights that give it the ability to direct the relevant activities (the activities that significantly affect the investee's returns)
- exposure, or rights, to variable returns from its involvement with the investee
- the ability to use its power over the investee to affect the amount of the investor's returns.

Power arises from rights. Such rights can be straightforward (e.g. through voting rights) or be complex (e.g. embedded in contractual arrangements). An investor that holds only protective rights cannot have power over an investee and so cannot control an investee

An investor must be exposed, or have rights, to variable returns from its involvement with an investee to control the investee. Such returns must have the potential to vary as a result of the investee's performance and can be positive, negative, or both.

A parent must not only have power over an investee and exposure or rights to variable returns from its involvement with the investee, a parent must also have the ability to use its power over the investee to affect its returns from its involvement with the investee.

When assessing whether an investor controls an investee an investor with decision-making rights determines whether it acts as principal or as an agent of other parties. A number of factors are considered in making this assessment. For instance, the remuneration of the decision-maker is considered in determining whether it is an agent.

Accounting Requirements

Preparation of Consolidated Financial Statements

A parent prepares consolidated financial statements using uniform accounting policies for like transactions and other events in similar circumstances.

However, a parent need not present consolidated financial statements if it meets all of the following conditions:

- it is a wholly-owned subsidiary or is a partially-owned subsidiary of another entity and its other owners, including those not otherwise entitled to vote, have been informed about, and do not object to, the parent not presenting consolidated financial statements
- its debt or equity instruments are not traded in a public market (a domestic or foreign stock exchange or an over-the-counter market, including local and regional markets)
- it did not file, nor is it in the process of filing, its financial statements with a securities commission or other regulatory organisation for the purpose of issuing any class of instruments in a public market, and
- its ultimate or any intermediate parent of the parent produces consolidated financial statements available for public use that comply with IFRSs.

Investment entities are prohibited from consolidating particular subsidiaries

Furthermore, post-employment benefit plans or other long-term employee benefit plans to whichIAS 19 *Employee Benefits* applies are not required to apply the requirements of IFRS 10.

Consolidation Procedures

Consolidated financial statements:

- combine like items of assets, liabilities, equity, income, expenses and cash flows of the parent with those of its subsidiaries
- offset (eliminate) the carrying amount of the parent's investment in each subsidiary and the parent's portion of equity of each subsidiary
- eliminate in full intragroup assets and liabilities, equity, income, expenses and cash flows relating to transactions between entities of the group (profits or losses resulting from intragroup transactions that are recognised in assets, such as inventory and fixed assets, are eliminated in full).

A reporting entity includes the income and expenses of a subsidiary in the consolidated financial statements from the date it gains control until the date when the reporting entity ceases to control the subsidiary. Income and expenses of the subsidiary are based on the amounts of the assets and liabilities recognised in the consolidated financial statements at the acquisition date.

The parent and subsidiaries are required to have the same reporting dates, or consolidation based on additional financial information prepared by subsidiary, unless impracticable. Where impracticable, the most recent financial statements of the subsidiary are used, adjusted for the effects of significant transactions or events between the reporting dates of the subsidiary and consolidated financial statements. The difference between the date of the subsidiary's financial statements and that of the consolidated financial statements shall be no more than three months

Non-controlling Interests (NCIs)

A parent presents non-controlling interests in its consolidated statement of financial position within equity, separately from the equity of the owners of the parent.

A reporting entity attributes the profit or loss and each component of other comprehensive income to the owners of the parent and to the non-controlling interests. The proportion allocated to the parent and non-controlling interests are determined on the basis of present ownership interests.

The reporting entity also attributes total comprehensive income to the owners of the parent and to the non-controlling interests even if this results in the non-controlling interests having a deficit balance.

Changes in Ownership Interests

Changes in a parent's ownership interest in a subsidiary that do not result in the parent losing control of the subsidiary are equity transactions (i.e. transactions with owners in their capacity as owners). When the proportion of the equity held by non-controlling interests changes, the carrying amounts of the controlling and non-controlling interests area adjusted to reflect the changes in their relative interests in the subsidiary. Any difference between the amount by which the non-controlling interests are adjusted and the fair value of the consideration paid or received is recognised directly in equity and attributed to the owners of the parent.

If a parent loses control of a subsidiary, the parent

- derecognises the assets and liabilities of the former subsidiary from the consolidated statement of financial position
- recognises any investment retained in the former subsidiary at its fair value when control is lost and subsequently accounts for it and for any amounts owed by or to the former subsidiary in accordance with relevant IFRSs. That fair value is regarded as the fair value on initial recognition of a financial asset in accordance with IFRS 9 *Financial Instruments* or, when appropriate, the cost on initial recognition of an investment in an associate or joint venture
- recognises the gain or loss associated with the loss of control attributable to the former controlling interest.

Investment entities Consolidation Exemption

[**Note**: The investment entity consolidation exemption was introduced by *Investment Entities*, issued on 31 October 2012 and effective for annual periods beginning on or after 1 January 2014.]

IFRS 10 contains special accounting requirements for investment entities. Where an entity meets the definition of an 'investment entity' , it does not consolidate its subsidiaries, or apply IFRS 3 *Business Combinations* when it obtains control of another entity.

An entity is required to consider all facts and circumstances when assessing whether it is an investment entity, including its purpose and design. IFRS 10 provides that an investment entity should have the following typical characteristics

- it has more than one investment
- it has more than one investor
- it has investors that are not related parties of the entity
- it has ownership interests in the form of equity or similar interests.

The absence of any of these typical characteristics does not necessarily disqualify an entity from being classified as an investment entity.

An investment entity is required to measure an investment in a subsidiary at fair value through profit or loss in accordance with IFRS 9 *Financial Instruments* or IAS 39 *Financial Instruments: Recognition and Measurement*. However, an investment entity is still required to consolidate a subsidiary where that subsidiary provides services that relate to the investment entity's investment activities.

Because an investment entity is not required to consolidate its subsidiaries, intragroup related party transactions and outstanding balances are not eliminated

Special requirements apply where an entity becomes, or ceases to be, an investment entity.

The exemption from consolidation only applies to the investment entity itself. Accordingly, a parent of an investment entity is required to consolidate all entities that it controls, including those controlled through an investment entity subsidiary, unless the parent itself is an investment entity.

Disclosure

There are no disclosures specified in IFRS 10. Instead, IFRS 12 *Disclosure of Interests in Other Entities* outlines the disclosures required.

IFRS-11—Joint Arrangements

IFRS 11 *Joint Arrangements* outlines the accounting by entities that jointly control an arrangement. Joint control involves the contractually agreed sharing of control and arrangements subject to joint control are classified as either a joint venture (representing a share of net assets and equity accounted) or a joint operation (representing rights to assets and obligations for liabilities, accounted for accordingly).

IFRS 11 was issued in May 2011 and applies to annual reporting periods beginning on or after 1 January 2013.

Objective

The main objective of IFRS 11 is that a party to a joint arrangement determines the type of joint arrangement in which it is involved by assessing its rights and obligations and accounts for those rights and obligations in accordance with that type of joint arrangement.

Key definitions

Joint arrangement	An arrangement of which two or more parties have joint control
Joint control	The contractually agreed sharing of control of an arrangement, which exists only when decisions about the relevant activities require the unanimous consent of the parties sharing control
Joint operation	A joint arrangement whereby the parties that have joint control of the arrangement have rights to the assets, and obligations for the liabilities, relating to the arrangement
Joint venture	A joint arrangement whereby the parties that have joint control of the arrangement have rights to the net assets of the arrangement
Joint venturer	A party to a joint venture that has joint control of that joint venture
Party to a joint arrangement	An entity that participates in a joint arrangement, regardless of whether that entity has joint control of the arrangement
Separate vehicle	A separately identifiable financial structure, including separate legal entities or entities recognised by statute, regardless of whether those entities have a legal personality

Joint Arrangements

A joint arrangement is an arrangement of which two or more parties have joint control.

A joint arrangement has the following characteristics:

- the parties are bound by a contractual arrangement, and
- the contractual arrangement gives two or more of those parties joint control of the arrangement.

A joint arrangement is either a joint operation or a joint venture.

Joint Control

Joint control is the contractually agreed sharing of control of an arrangement, which exists only when decisions about the relevant activities require the unanimous consent of the parties sharing control.

Before assessing whether an entity has joint control over an arrangement, an entity first assesses whether the parties, or a group of the parties, control the arrangement (in accordance with the definition of control in IFRS 10 *Consolidated Financial Statements*).

After concluding that all the parties, or a group of the parties, control the arrangement collectively, an entity shall assess whether it has joint control of the arrangement. Joint control exists only when decisions about the relevant activities require the unanimous consent of the parties that collectively control the arrangement.

The requirement for unanimous consent means that any party with joint control of the arrangement can prevent any of the other parties, or a group of the parties, from making unilateral decisions (about the relevant activities) without its consent.

Types of Joint Arrangements

Joint arrangements are either joint operations or joint ventures:

- A **joint operation** is a joint arrangement whereby the parties that have joint control of the arrangement have rights to the assets, and obligations for the liabilities, relating to the arrangement. Those parties are called joint operators.
- A **joint venture** is a joint arrangement whereby the parties that have joint control of the arrangement have rights to the net assets of the arrangement. Those parties are called joint venturers.

Classifying Joint Arrangements

The classification of a joint arrangement as a joint operation or a joint venture depends upon the rights and obligations of the parties to the arrangement. An entity determines the type of joint arrangement in which it is involved by considering the structure and form of the arrangement, the terms agreed by the parties in the contractual arrangement and other facts and circumstances.

Regardless of the purpose, structure or form of the arrangement, the classification of joint arrangements depends upon the parties' rights and obligations arising from the arrangement.

A joint arrangement in which the assets and liabilities relating to the arrangement are held in a separate vehicle can be either a joint venture or a joint operation.

A joint arrangement that is not structured through a separate vehicle is a joint operation. In such cases, the contractual arrangement establishes the parties' rights to the assets, and obligations for the liabilities, relating to the arrangement, and the parties' rights to the corresponding revenues and obligations for the corresponding expenses.

Financial Statements of Parties to a Joint Arrangement

Joint operations

A joint operator recognises in relation to its interest in a joint operation:

- its assets, including its share of any assets held jointly;
- its liabilities, including its share of any liabilities incurred jointly;
- its revenue from the sale of its share of the output of the joint operation;
- its share of the revenue from the sale of the output by the joint operation; and
- its expenses, including its share of any expenses incurred jointly.

A joint operator accounts for the assets, liabilities, revenues and expenses relating to its involvement in a joint operation in accordance with the relevant IFRSs.

The acquirer of an interest in a joint operation in which the activity constitutes a business, as defined in IFRS 3 *Business Combinations*, is required to apply all of the principles on business combinations accounting in IFRS 3 and other IFRSs with the exception of those principles that conflict with the guidance in IFRS 11

These requirements apply both to the initial acquisition of an interest in a joint operation, and the acquisition of an additional interest in a joint operation (in the latter case, previously held interests are not remeasured).

A party that participates in, but does not have joint control of, a joint operation shall also account for its interest in the arrangement in accordance with the above if that party has rights to the assets, and obligations for the liabilities, relating to the joint operation.

Joint ventures

A joint venturer recognises its interest in a joint venture as an investment and shall account for that investment using the equity method in accordance with IAS 28 *Investments in Associates and Joint Ventures* unless the entity is exempted from applying the equity method as specified in that standard.

A party that participates in, but does not have joint control of, a joint venture accounts for its interest in the arrangement in accordance with IFRS 9 *Financial Instruments* unless it has significant influence over the joint venture, in which case it accounts for it in accordance with IAS 28 (as amended in 2011).

Separate Financial Statements

The accounting for joint arrangements in an entity's separate financial statements depends on the involvement of the entity in that joint arrangement and the type of the joint arrangement:

Disclosure

There are no disclosures specified in IFRS 11. Instead, IFRS 12 *Disclosure of Interests in Other Entities* outlines the disclosures required.

IFRS-12—Disclosure of Interests in Other Entities

IFRS 12 *Disclosure of Interests in Other Entities* is a consolidated disclosure standard requiring a wide range of disclosures about an entity's interests in subsidiaries, joint arrangements, associates and unconsolidated 'structured entities'. Disclosures are presented as a series of objectives, with detailed guidance on satisfying those objectives.

IFRS 12 was issued in May 2011 and applies to annual periods beginning on or after 1 January 2013.

Objective and Scope

The objective of IFRS 12 is to require the disclosure of information that enables users of financial statements to evaluate:

- the nature of, and risks associated with, its interests in other entities
- the effects of those interests on its financial position, financial performance and cash flows.

Where the disclosures required by IFRS 12, together with the disclosures required by other IFRSs, do not meet the above objective, an entity is required to disclose whatever additional information is necessary to meet the objective.

IFRS 12 is required to be applied by an entity that has an interest in any of the following:

- subsidiaries
- joint arrangements (joint operations or joint ventures)
- associates
- unconsolidated structured entities

IFRS 12 does not apply to certain employee benefit plans, separate financial statements to whichIAS 27 *Separate Financial Statements* applies (except in relation to unconsolidated structured entities and investment entities in some cases), certain interests in joint ventures held by an entity that does not share in joint control, and the majority of interests in another entity accounted for in accordance with IFRS 9 *Financial Instruments*.

Key Definitions

Interest in Another Entity	Refers to contractual and non-contractual involvement that exposes an entity to variability of returns from the performance of the other entity. An interest in another entity can be evidenced by, but is not limited to, the holding of equity or debt instruments as well as other forms of involvement such as the provision of funding, liquidity support, credit enhancement and guarantees. It includes the means by which an entity has control or joint control of, or significant influence over, another entity. An entity does not necessarily have an interest in another entity solely because of a typical customer supplier relationship.
Structured Entity	An entity that has been designed so that voting or similar rights are not the dominant factor in deciding who controls the entity, such as when any voting rights relate to administrative tasks only and the relevant activities are directed by means of contractual arrangements.

Significant Judgements and Assumptions

An entity discloses information about significant judgements and assumptions it has made (and changes in those judgements and assumptions) in determining:

- that it controls another entity
- that it has joint control of an arrangement or significant influence over another entity
- the type of joint arrangement (i.e. joint operation or joint venture) when the arrangement has been structured through a separate vehicle.

Interests in Subsidiaries

An entity shall disclose information that enables users of its consolidated financial statements to:

- understand the composition of the group
- understand the interest that non-controlling interests have in the group's activities and cash flows
- evaluate the nature and extent of significant restrictions on its ability to access or use assets, and settle liabilities, of the group
- evaluate the nature of, and changes in, the risks associated with its interests in consolidated structured entities
- evaluate the consequences of changes in its ownership interest in a subsidiary that do not result in a loss of control
- evaluate the consequences of losing control of a subsidiary during the reporting period.

Interests in Unconsolidated Subsidiaries

In accordance with IFRS 10 *Consolidated Financial Statements*, an investment entity is required to apply the exception to consolidation and instead account for its investment in a subsidiary at fair value through profit or loss.

Where an entity is an investment entity, IFRS 12 requires additional disclosure, including:

- the fact the entity is an investment entity information about significant judgements and assumptions it has made in determining that it is an investment entity, and specifically where the entity does not have one or more of the 'typical characteristics' of an investment entity
- details of subsidiaries that have not been consolidated (name, place of business, ownership interests held)
- details of the relationship and certain transactions between the investment entity and the subsidiary (e.g. restrictions on transfer of funds, commitments, support arrangements, contractual arrangements)
- information where an entity becomes, or ceases to be, an investment entity

An entity making these disclosures are not required to provide various other disclosures required by IFRS 12

Interests in Joint Arrangements and Associates

An entity shall disclose information that enables users of its financial statements to evaluate:

- the nature, extent and financial effects of its interests in joint arrangements and associates, including the nature and effects of its contractual relationship with the other investors with joint control of, or significant influence over, joint arrangements and associates
- the nature of, and changes in, the risks associated with its interests in joint ventures and associates.

Interests in Unconsolidated Structured Entities

An entity shall disclose information that enables users of its financial statements to:

- understand the nature and extent of its interests in unconsolidated structured entities
- evaluate the nature of, and changes in, the risks associated with its interests in unconsolidated structured entities.

IFRS-13—Fair Value Measurement

IFRS 13 *Fair Value Measurement* applies to IFRSs that require or permit fair value measurements or disclosures and provides a single IFRS framework for measuring fair value and requires disclosures about fair value measurement. The Standard defines fair value on the basis of an 'exit price' notion and uses a 'fair value hierarchy', which results in a market-based, rather than entity-specific, measurement.

Objective

- defines fair value
- sets out in a single IFRS a framework for measuring fair value
- requires disclosures about fair value measurements.

IFRS 13 applies when another IFRS requires or permits fair value measurements or disclosures about fair value measurements (and measurements, such as fair value less costs to sell, based on fair value or disclosures about those measurements), except for:

- share-based payment transactions within the scope of IFRS 2 *Share-based Payment*
- leasing transactions within the scope of IAS 17 *Leases*
- measurements that have some similarities to fair value but that are not fair value, such as net realisable value in IAS 2 *Inventories* or value in use in IAS 36 *Impairment of Assets*.

Additional exemptions apply to the disclosures required by IFRS 13.

Key Definitions

Fair Value	The price that would be received to sell an asset or paid to transfer a liability in an orderly transaction between market participants at the measurement date
Active Market	A market in which transactions for the asset or liability take place with sufficient frequency and volume to provide pricing information on an ongoing basis
Exit price	The price that would be received to sell an asset or paid to transfer a liability
Highest and Best Use	The use of a non-financial asset by market participants that would maximise the value of the asset or the group of assets and liabilities (e.g. a business) within which the asset would be used

Most Advantageous Market	The market that maximises the amount that would be received to sell the asset or minimises the amount that would be paid to transfer the liability, after taking into account transaction costs and transport costs
Principal Market	The market with the greatest volume and level of activity for the asset or liability

Fair Value Hierarchy

Overview

IFRS 13 seeks to increase consistency and comparability in fair value measurements and related disclosures through a 'fair value hierarchy'. The hierarchy categorises the inputs used in valuation techniques into three levels. The hierarchy gives the highest priority to (unadjusted) quoted prices in active markets for identical assets or liabilities and the lowest priority to unobservable inputs.

If the inputs used to measure fair value are categorised into different levels of the fair value hierarchy, the fair value measurement is categorised in its entirety in the level of the lowest level input that is significant to the entire measurement (based on the application of judgement).

Level 1—Inputs

Level 1 inputs are quoted prices in active markets for identical assets or liabilities that the entity can access at the measurement date.

A quoted market price in an active market provides the most reliable evidence of fair value and is used without adjustment to measure fair value whenever available, with limited exceptions.

If an entity holds a position in a single asset or liability and the asset or liability is traded in an active market, the fair value of the asset or liability is measured within Level 1 as the product of the quoted price for the individual asset or liability and the quantity held by the entity, even if the market's normal daily trading volume is not sufficient to absorb the quantity held and placing orders to sell the position in a single transaction might affect the quoted price.

Level 2—Inputs

Level 2 inputs are inputs other than quoted market prices included within Level 1 that are observable for the asset or liability, either directly or indirectly.

Level 2 inputs include:

- quoted prices for similar assets or liabilities in active markets
- quoted prices for identical or similar assets or liabilities in markets that are not active
- inputs other than quoted prices that are observable for the asset or liability, for example
  - interest rates and yield curves observable at commonly quoted intervals
  - implied volatilities
  - credit spreads
- inputs that are derived principally from or corroborated by observable market data by correlation or other means ('market-corroborated inputs').

Level 3—Inputs

Level 3 inputs inputs are unobservable inputs for the asset or liability.

Unobservable inputs are used to measure fair value to the extent that relevant observable inputs are not available, thereby allowing for situations in which there is little, if any, market activity for the asset or liability at the measurement date. An entity develops unobservable inputs using the best information available in the circumstances, which might include the entity's own data, taking into account all information about market participant assumptions that is reasonably available.

Measurement of fair value

Overview of fair value measurement approach

The objective of a fair value measurement is to estimate the price at which an orderly transaction to sell the asset or to transfer the liability would take place between market participants at the measurement date under current market conditions. A fair value measurement requires an entity to determine all of the following:

- the particular asset or liability that is the subject of the measurement (consistently with its unit of account)
- for a non-financial asset, the valuation premise that is appropriate for the measurement (consistently with its highest and best use)
- the principal (or most advantageous) market for the asset or liability
- the valuation technique(s) appropriate for the measurement, considering the availability of data with which to develop inputs that represent the assumptions that market participants would use when pricing the asset or liability and the level of the fair value hierarchy within which the inputs are categorised.

Guidance on Measurement

IFRS 13 provides the guidance on the measurement of fair value, including the following:

- An entity takes into account the characteristics of the asset or liability being measured that a market participant would take into account when pricing the asset or liability at measurement date (e.g. the condition and location of the asset and any restrictions on the sale and use of the asset)
- Fair value measurement assumes an orderly transaction between market participants at the measurement date under current market conditions
- Fair value measurement assumes a transaction taking place in the principal market for the asset or liability, or in the absence of a principal market, the most advantageous market for the asset or liability
- A fair value measurement of a non-financial asset takes into account its highest and best use
- A fair value measurement of a financial or non-financial liability or an entity's own equity instruments assumes it is transferred to a market participant at the measurement date, without settlement, extinguishment, or cancellation at the measurement date
- The fair value of a liability reflects non-performance risk (the risk the entity will not fulfil an obligation), including an entity's own credit risk and assuming the same non-performance risk before and after the transfer of the liability
- An optional exception applies for certain financial assets and financial liabilities with offsetting positions in market risks or counterparty credit risk, provided conditions are met (additional disclosure is required).

Valuation Techniques

An entity uses valuation techniques appropriate in the circumstances and for which sufficient data are available to measure fair value, maximising the use of relevant observable inputs and minimising the use of unobservable inputs.

The objective of using a valuation technique is to estimate the price at which an orderly transaction to sell the asset or to transfer the liability would take place between market participants and the measurement date under current market conditions. Three widely used valuation techniques are:

- **market approach** – uses prices and other relevant information generated by market transactions involving identical or comparable (similar) assets, liabilities, or a group of assets and liabilities (e.g. a business)
- **cost approach** – reflects the amount that would be required currently to replace the service capacity of an asset (current replacement cost)

- **income approach** – converts future amounts (cash flows or income and expenses) to a single current (discounted) amount, reflecting current market expectations about those future amounts.

In some cases, a single valuation technique will be appropriate, whereas in others multiple valuation techniques will be appropriate.

Disclosure

Disclosure Objective

IFRS 13 requires an entity to disclose information that helps users of its financial statements assess both of the following:

- for assets and liabilities that are measured at fair value on a recurring or non-recurring basis in the statement of financial position after initial recognition, the valuation techniques and inputs used to develop those measurements
- for fair value measurements using significant unobservable inputs (Level 3), the effect of the measurements on profit or loss or other comprehensive income for the period.

Disclosure Exemptions

The disclosure requirements are not required for:

- plan assets measured at fair value in accordance with IAS 19 *Employee Benefits*
- retirement benefit plan investments measured at fair value in accordance with IAS 26*Accounting and Reporting by Retirement Benefit Plans*
- assets for which recoverable amount is fair value less costs of disposal in accordance withIAS 36 *Impairment of Assets*.

Identification of Classes

Where disclosures are required to be provided for each class of asset or liability, an entity determines appropriate classes on the basis of the nature, characteristics and risks of the asset or liability, and the level of the fair value hierarchy within which the fair value measurement is categorised.

Determining appropriate classes of assets and liabilities for which disclosures about fair value measurements should be provided requires judgement. A class of assets and liabilities will often require greater disaggregation than the line items presented in the statement of financial position. The number of classes may need to be greater for fair value measurements categorised within Level 3.

Some disclosures are differentiated on whether the measurements are:

- Recurring fair value measurements – fair value measurements required or permitted by other IFRSs to be recognised in the statement of financial position at the end of each reporting period
- Non-recurring fair value measurements are fair value measurements that are required or permitted by other IFRSs to be measured in the statement of financial position in particular circumstances.

Specific Disclosures Required

To meet the disclosure objective, the following minimum disclosures are required for each class of assets and liabilities measured at fair value (including measurements based on fair value within the scope of this IFRS) in the statement of financial position after initial recognition (note these are requirements have been summarised and additional disclosure is required where necessary):

- the fair value measurement at the end of the reporting period*
- for non-recurring fair value measurements, the reasons for the measurement*
- the level of the fair value hierarchy within which the fair value measurements are categorised in their entirety (Level 1, 2 or 3)*
- for assets and liabilities held at the reporting date that are measured at fair value on a recurring basis, the amounts of any transfers between Level 1 and Level 2 of the fair value hierarchy, the

reasons for those transfers and the entity's policy for determining when transfers between levels are deemed to have occurred, separately disclosing and discussing transfers into and out of each level

- for fair value measurements categorised within Level 2 and Level 3 of the fair value hierarchy, a description of the valuation technique(s) and the inputs used in the fair value measurement, any change in the valuation techniques and the reason(s) for making such change (with some exceptions)*
- for fair value measurements categorised within Level 3 of the fair value hierarchy, quantitative information about the significant unobservable inputs used in the fair value measurement (with some exceptions)
- for recurring fair value measurements categorised within Level 3 of the fair value hierarchy, a reconciliation from the opening balances to the closing balances, disclosing separately changes during the period attributable to the following:
  - total gains or losses for the period recognised in profit or loss, and the line item(s) in profit or loss in which those gains or losses are recognised – separately disclosing the amount included in profit or loss that is attributable to the change in unrealised gains or losses relating to those assets and liabilities held at the end of the reporting period, and the line item(s) in profit or loss in which those unrealised gains or losses are recognised
  - total gains or losses for the period recognised in other comprehensive income, and the line item(s) in other comprehensive income in which those gains or losses are recognised
  - purchases, sales, issues and settlements (each of those types of changes disclosed separately)
  - the amounts of any transfers into or out of Level 3 of the fair value hierarchy, the reasons for those transfers and the entity's policy for determining when transfers between levels are deemed to have occurred. Transfers into Level 3 shall be disclosed and discussed separately from transfers out of Level 3
- for fair value measurements categorised within Level 3 of the fair value hierarchy, a description of the valuation processes used by the entity
- for recurring fair value measurements categorised within Level 3of the fair value hierarchy:
  - a narrative description of the sensitivity of the fair value measurement to changes in unobservable inputs if a change in those inputs to a different amount might result in a significantly higher or lower fair value measurement. If there are interrelationships between those inputs and other unobservable inputs used in the fair value measurement, the entity also provides a description of those interrelationships and of how they might magnify or mitigate the effect of changes in the unobservable inputs on the fair value measurement
  - for financial assets and financial liabilities, if changing one or more of the unobservable inputs to reflect reasonably possible alternative assumptions would change fair value significantly, an entity shall state that fact and disclose the effect of those changes. The entity shall disclose how the effect of a change to reflect a reasonably possible alternative assumption was calculated
- if the highest and best use of a non-financial asset differs from its current use, an entity shall disclose that fact and why the non-financial asset is being used in a manner that differs from its highest and best use*.

'' in the list above indicates that the disclosure is also applicable to a class of assets or liabilities which is not measured at fair value in the statement of financial position but for which the fair value is disclosed.*

Quantitative disclosures are required to be presented in a tabular format unless another format is more appropriate.

IFRS-14—Regulatory Deferral Accounts

Overview

IFRS 14 *Regulatory Deferral Accounts* permits an entity which is a first-time adopter of International Financial Reporting Standards to continue to account, with some limited changes, for 'regulatory deferral account balances' in accordance with its previous GAAP, both on initial adoption of IFRS and in subsequent financial statements. Regulatory deferral account balances, and movements in them, are presented separately in the statement of financial position and statement of profit or loss and other comprehensive income, and specific disclosures are required.

IFRS 14 was originally issued in January 2014 and applies to an entity's first annual IFRS financial statements for a period beginning on or after 1 January 2016.

Scope

IFRS 14 is permitted, but not required, to be applied where an entity conducts rate-regulated activities and has recognised amounts in its previous GAAP financial statements that meet the definition of 'regulatory deferral account balances' (sometimes referred to 'regulatory assets' and 'regulatory liabilities')

Key definitions

Rate regulation	A framework for establishing the prices that can be charged to customers for goods and services and that framework is subject to oversight and/or approval by a rate-regulator
Rate regulator	An authorised body that is empowered by statute or regulation to establish the rate or range of rates that bind an entity. The rate regulator may be a third-party body or a related party of the entity, including the entity's own governing board, if that body is required by statute or regulation to set rates both in the interest of customers and to ensure the overall financial viability of the entity
Regulatory deferral account balance	The balance of any expense (or income) account that would not be recognised as an asset or a liability in accordance with other Standards, but that qualifies for deferral because it is included, or is expected to be included, by the rate regulator in establishing the rate(s) that can be charged to customers

Accounting Policies for Regulatory Deferral Account Balances

IFRS 14 provides an exemption from paragraph 11 of IAS 8 *Accounting Policies, Changes in Accounting Estimates and Errors* when an entity determines its accounting policies for regulatory deferral account balances. Paragraph 11 of IAS 8 requires an entity to consider the requirements of IFRSs dealing with similar matters and the requirements of the *Conceptual Framework* when setting its accounting policies.

The effect of the exemption is that eligible entities can continue to apply the accounting policies used for regulatory deferral account balances under the basis of accounting used immediately before adopting IFRS ('previous GAAP') when applying IFRSs, subject to the presentation requirements of IFRS 14 .

Entities are permitted to change their accounting policies for regulatory deferral account balances in accordance with IAS 8, but only if the change makes the financial statements more relevant and no less reliable, or more reliable and not less relevant, to the economic decision-making needs of users of the entity's financial statements. However, an entity is not permitted to change accounting policies to start to recognise regulatory deferral account balances.

Presentation in financial statements

The impact of regulatory deferral account balances are separately presented in an entity's financial statements. This requirements applies regardless of the entity's previous presentation policies in respect of regulatory deferral balance accounts under its previous GAAP. Accordingly:

- Separate line items are presented in the statement of financial position for the total of all regulatory deferral account debit balances, and all regulatory deferral account credit balances
- Regulatory deferral account balances are not classified between current and non-current, but are separately disclosed using subtotals
- The net movement in regulatory deferral account balances are separately presented in the statement of profit or loss and other comprehensive income using subtotals

The Illustrative examples accompanying IFRS 14 set out an illustrative presentation of financial statements by an entity applying the Standard.

Disclosures

IFRS 14 sets out disclosure objectives to allow users to assess:

- the nature of, and risks associated with, the rate regulation that establishes the price(s) the entity can charge customers for the goods or services it provides - including information about the entity's rate-regulated activities and the rate-setting process, the identity of the rate regulator(s), and the impacts of risks and uncertainties on the recovery or reversal of regulatory deferral balance accounts
- the effects of rate regulation on the entity's financial statements - including the basis on which regulatory deferral account balances are recognised, how they are assessed for recovery, a reconciliation of the carrying amount at the beginning and end of the reporting period, discount rates applicable, income tax impacts and details of balances that are no longer considered recoverable or reversible.

Effective date

Where an entity elects to apply it, IFRS 14 is effective for an entity's first annual IFRS financial statements that are for a period beginning on or after 1 January 2016. The standard can be applied earlier, but the entity must disclose when it has done so.

IFRS-15—Revenue from Contracts with Customers

Objective

The objective of IFRS 15 is to establish the principles that an entity shall apply to report useful information to users of financial statements about the nature, amount, timing, and uncertainty of revenue and cash flows arising from a contract with a customer. Application of the standard is mandatory for annual reporting periods starting from 1 January 2017 onwards. Earlier application is permitted.

Scope

IFRS 15 *Revenue from Contracts with Customers* applies to all contracts with customers except for: leases within the scope of IAS 17 *Leases*; financial instruments and other contractual rights or obligations within the scope of IFRS 9 *Financial Instruments,* IFRS 10 *Consolidated Financial Statements*, IFRS 11 *Joint Arrangements*, IAS 27 *Separate Financial Statements* and IAS 28 *Investments in Associates and Joint Ventures*; insurance contracts within the scope of IFRS 4*Insurance Contracts*; and non-monetary exchanges between entities in the same line of business to facilitate sales to customers or potential customers.

A contract with a customer may be partially within the scope of IFRS 15 and partially within the scope of another standard. In that scenario:

- if other standards specify how to separate and/or initially measure one or more parts of the contract, then those separation and measurement requirements are applied first. The transaction price is then reduced by the amounts that are initially measured under other standards;
- if no other standard provides guidance on how to separate and/or initially measure one or more parts of the contract, then IFRS 15 will be applied.

Key definitions

Contract	An agreement between two or more parties that creates enforceable rights and obligations.
Customer	A party that has contracted with an entity to obtain goods or services that are an output of the entity's ordinary activities in exchange for consideration.
Income	Increases in economic benefits during the accounting period in the form of inflows or enhancements of assets or decreases of liabilities that result in an increase in equity, other than those relating to contributions from equity participants.
Performance obligation	A promise in a contract with a customer to transfer to the customer either: • a good or service (or a bundle of goods or services) that is distinct; or • a series of distinct goods or services that are substantially the same and that have the same pattern of transfer to the customer.
Revenue	Income arising in the course of an entity's ordinary activities.
Transaction price	The amount of consideration to which an entity expects to be entitled in exchange for transferring promised goods or services to a customer, excluding amounts collected on behalf of third parties.

Accounting Requirements for Revenue

The five-step model framework

The core principle of IFRS 15 is that an entity will recognise revenue to depict the transfer of promised goods or services to customers in an amount that reflects the consideration to which the entity expects to be entitled in exchange for those goods or services. This core principle is delivered in a five-step model framework:

- Identify the contract(s) with a customer
- Identify the performance obligations in the contract
- Determine the transaction price
- Allocate the transaction price to the performance obligations in the contract
- Recognise revenue when (or as) the entity satisfies a performance obligation.

Application of this guidance will depend on the facts and circumstances present in a contract with a customer and will require the exercise of judgment.

Step 1: Identify the Contract with the Customer

A contract with a customer will be within the scope of IFRS 15 if all the following conditions are met:

- the contract has been approved by the parties to the contract;
- each party's rights in relation to the goods or services to be transferred can be identified;
- the payment terms for the goods or services to be transferred can be identified;

- the contract has commercial substance; and
- it is probable that the consideration to which the entity is entitled to in exchange for the goods or services will be collected.

If a contract with a customer does not yet meet all of the above criteria, the entity will continue to re-assess the contract going forward to determine whether it subsequently meets the above criteria. From that point, the entity will apply IFRS 15 to the contract.

The standard provides detailed guidance on how to account for approved contract modifications. If certain conditions are met, a contract modification will be accounted for as a separate contract with the customer. If not, it will be accounted for by modifying the accounting for the current contract with the customer. Whether the latter type of modification is accounted for prospectively or retrospectively depends on whether the remaining goods or services to be delivered after the modification are distinct from those delivered prior to the modification. Further details on accounting for contract modifications can be found in the Standard.

Step 2: Identify the Performance Obligations in the Contract

At the inception of the contract, the entity should assess the goods or services that have been promised to the customer, and identify as a performance obligation:

- a good or service (or bundle of goods or services) that is distinct; or
- a series of distinct goods or services that are substantially the same and that have the same pattern of transfer to the customer.

A series of distinct goods or services is transferred to the customer in the same pattern if both of the following criteria are met:

- each distinct good or service in the series that the entity promises to transfer consecutively to the customer would be a performance obligation that is satisfied over time (see below); and
- a single method of measuring progress would be used to measure the entity's progress towards complete satisfaction of the performance obligation to transfer each distinct good or service in the series to the customer.

A good or service is distinct if both of the following criteria are met:

- the customer can benefit from the good or services on its own or in conjunction with other readily available resources; and
- the entity's promise to transfer the good or service to the customer is separately idenitifable from other promises in the contract.

Factors for consideration as to whether a promise to transfer the good or service to the customer is separately identifiable include, but are not limited to:

- the entity does not provide a significant service of integrating the good or service with other goods or services promised in the contract.
- the good or service does not significantly modify or customise another good or service promised in the contract.
- the good or service is not highly interrelated with or highly dependent on other goods or services promised in the contract.

Step 3: Determine the Transaction Price

The transaction price is the amount to which an entity expects to be entitled in exchange for the transfer of goods and services. When making this determination, an entity will consider past customary business practices.

Where a contract contains elements of variable consideration, the entity will estimate the amount of variable consideration to which it will be entitled under the contract. [IFRS 15:50] Variable consideration can arise, for example, as a result of discounts, rebates, refunds, credits, price concessions, incentives, performance bonuses, penalties or other similar items. Variable consideration is also present if an entity's right to consideration is contingent on the occurrence of a future event.

The standard deals with the uncertainty relating to variable consideration by limiting the amount of variable consideration that can be recognised. Specifically, variable consideration is only included in the transaction price if, and to the extent that, it is highly probable that its inclusion will not result in a significant revenue reversal in the future when the uncertainty has been subsequently resolved.

However, a different, more restrictive approach is applied in respect of sales or usage-based royalty revenue arising from licences of intellectual property. Such revenue is recognised only when the underlying sales or usage occur.

Step 4: Allocate the Transaction Price to the Performance Obligations in the Contracts

Where a contract has multiple performance obligations, an entity will allocate the transaction price to the performance obligations in the contract by reference to their relative standalone selling prices. If a standalone selling price is not directly observable, the entity will need to estimate it.

IFRS 15 suggests various methods that might be used, including:

- Adjusted market assessment approach
- Expected cost plus a margin approach
- Residual approach (only permissible in limited circumstances).

Any overall discount compared to the aggregate of standalone selling prices is allocated between performance obligations on a relative standalone selling price basis. In certain circumstances, it may be appropriate to allocate such a discount to some but not all of the performance obligations.

Where consideration is paid in advance or in arrears, the entity will need to consider whether the contract includes a significant financing arrangement and, if so, adjust for the time value of money. A practical expedient is available where the interval between transfer of the promised goods or services and payment by the customer is expected to be less than 12 months.

Step 5: Recognise Revenue when (or as) the Entity Satisfies a Performance Obligation

Revenue is recognised as control is passed, either over time or at a point in time.

Control of an asset is defined as the ability to direct the use of and obtain substantially all of the remaining benefits from the asset. This includes the ability to prevent others from directing the use of and obtaining the benefits from the asset. The benefits related to the asset are the potential cash flows that may be obtained directly or indirectly. These include, but are not limited to:

- using the asset to produce goods or provide services;
- using the asset to enhance the value of other assets;
- using the asset to settle liabilities or to reduce expenses;
- selling or exchanging the asset;
- pledging the asset to secure a loan; and
- holding the asset.

An entity recognises revenue over time if one of the following criteria is met:

- the customer simultaneously receives and consumes all of the benefits provided by the entity as the entity performs;
- the entity's performance creates or enhances an asset that the customer controls as the asset is created; or
- the entity's performance does not create an asset with an alternative use to the entity and the entity has an enforceable right to payment for performance completed to date.

If an entity does not satisfy its performance obligation over time, it satisfies it at a point in time. Revenue will therefore be recognised when control is passed at a certain point in time. Factors that may indicate the point in time at which control passes include, but are not limited to:

- the entity has a present right to payment for the asset;
- the customer has legal title to the asset;
- the entity has transferred physical possession of the asset;
- the customer has the significant risks and rewards related to the ownership of the asset; and
- the customer has accepted the asset.

Contract Costs

The incremental costs of obtaining a contract must be recognised as an asset if the entity expects to recover those costs. However, those incremental costs are limited to the costs that the entity would not have incurred if the contract had not been successfully obtained (e.g. 'success fees' paid to agents). A practical expedient is available, allowing the incremental costs of obtaining a contract to be expensed if the associated amortisation period would be 12 months or less.

Costs incurred to fulfil a contract are recognised as an asset if and only if all of the following criteria are met:

- the costs relate directly to a contract (or a specific anticipated contract);
- the costs generate or enhance resources of the entity that will be used in satisfying performance obligations in the future; and
- the costs are expected to be recovered.

These include costs such as direct labour, direct materials, and the allocation of overheads that relate directly to the contract.

The asset recognised in respect of the costs to obtain or fulfil a contract is amortised on a systematic basis that is consistent with the pattern of transfer of the goods or services to which the asset relates.

Further Useful Implementation Guidance in Relation to Applying IFRS 15

These topics include:

- Performance obligations satisfied over time
- Methods for measuring progress towards complete satisfaction of a performance obligation
- Sale with a right of return
- Warranties
- Principal versus agent considerations
- Customer options for additional goods or services
- Customers' unexercised rights
- Non-refundable upfront fees
- Licensing
- Repurchase arrangements
- Consignment arrangements
- Bill-and-hold arrangements
- Customer acceptance
- Disclosures of disaggregation of revenue

These topics should be considered carefully when applying IFRS 15.

Presentation in Financial Statements

Contracts with customers will be presented in an entity's statement of financial position as a contract liability, a contract asset, or a receivable, depending on the relationship between the entity's performance and the customer's payment.

A contract liability is presented in the statement of financial position where a customer has paid an amount of consideration prior to the entity performing by transferring the related good or service to the customer.

Where the entity has performed by transferring a good or service to the customer and the customer has not yet paid the related consideration, a contract asset or a receivable is presented in the statement of financial position, depending on the nature of the entity's right to consideration. A contract asset is recognised when the entity's right to consideration is conditional on something other than the passage of time, for example future performance of the entity. A receivable is recognised when the entity's right to consideration is unconditional except for the passage of time.

Contract assets and receivables shall be accounted for in accordance with IFRS 9. Any impairment relating to contracts with customers should be measured, presented and disclosed in accordance with IFRS 9. Any difference between the initial recognition of a receivable and the corresponding amount of revenue recognised should also be presented as an expense, for example, an impairment loss.

Disclosures

The disclosure objective stated in IFRS 15 is for an entity to disclose sufficient information to enable users of financial statements to understand the nature, amount, timing and uncertainty of revenue and cash flows arising from contracts with customers. Therefore, an entity should disclose qualitative and quantitative information about all of the following:

- its contracts with customers;
- the significant judgments, and changes in the judgments, made in applying the guidance to those contracts; and
- any assets recognised from the costs to obtain or fulfil a contract with a customer.

Entities will need to consider the level of detail necessary to satisfy the disclosure objective and how much emphasis to place on each of the requirements. An entity should aggregate or disaggregate disclosures to ensure that useful information is not obscured.

In order to achieve the disclosure objective stated above, the Standard introduces a number of new disclosure requirements.

QUESTIONS

OBJECTIVE TYPE

1. State giving reasons, whether the following statements are 'TRUE' or 'FALSE' :

(*i*) International Financial Reporting Standards are issued by International Accounting Standards Board.

(*ii*) IFRS are rule-based.

(*iii*) Under IFRS, the fixed assets are valued at historical cost.

(*iv*) IFRS create common or uniform provision for the valuation of assets and liabilities.

(*v*) Under IFRS, it would be difficult to commit fraud.

Hints :

(*i*) True. International Financial Reporting Standards are issued by International Accounting Standards Board.

(*ii*) False. IFRS are principle-based.

(*iii*) False. Under IFRS, the fixed assets are valued at current cost.

(*iv*) True. IFRS create common or uniform provision for the valuation of assets and liabilities.

(*v*) True. IFRS require the companies to report the essence of each minute transaction which has to be finally audited and approved. Thus, it would be difficult to commit fraud.

SHORT/LONG ANSWER TYPE

1. What is IFRS ? Give objectives behind IFRSs.
2. Explain salient features of each International Financial Reporting Standard.
3. Give the need for IFRS
4. What re various assumptions of IFRS.
5. Explain th scope of IFRS.
6. Give differences between IFRS and Indian GAPP or Accounting Standards.
7. Explain in brief the various International Financial Reporting Standards formulated by International Accounting Standard Board.
8. Give the latest of IFRS.

CHAPTER 35

Accounts of Co-operative Societies

Introduction

From time to time, the Government has been encouraging the establishment of co-operative societies in order to help the weaker sections of the society. Various co-operative societies operative in various areas like consumer co-operative societies, producer co-operative societies, service co-operative societies, marketing co-operative societies, industrial co-operative societies etc. have come into existence in India for the benefit of members who form them.

Co-operative societies are institutions dealing in all kinds of business transactions. It becomes necessary for them to maintain accounts in proper and systematic manner. Persons of limited means and weaker sections of the community joined together to meet their common economic needs in the initial stages of organisation of co-operative societies. The persons who controlled their administration and accounts were totally ignorant about the principles of double entry book-keeping. They, however, evolved an indigenous form of account keeping to suit their convenience and understanding. The dual aspects of any transaction are denoted by the symbols 'Dr.' and 'Cr.' according to the principles of double entry book-keeping. The words 'Dr.' and 'Cr.' do not convey any specific meaning but they can be understood by their operational significance. The words 'Dr.' and 'Cr.' create confusion for a layman and thus two alternative words 'Receipts' and 'Payments' are used to convey the two-fold aspect of a transaction. The Accounts of Co-operative Societies follow the principles of Double Entry Book-keeping but with certain modifications in the procedures. These modifications are made for the convenience of those persons who are entrusted with responsibility of maintaining the accounts of co-operative societies.

Co-operative societies are established under the Co-operative Societies Act, 1912. Some of the states have adopted this Act without any change, while some other states have introduced some changes in it.

As per **Section 6 of the Co-operative Societies Act, 1912,** any ten persons who are competent to enter into contract and who wish to form a co-operative society may make an application to the Registrar of Co-operative Societies of the state, wherein they propose to establish the co-operative society. The society is managed by the managing committee, the members of which are elected annually at the general meeting of the society. Each registered society is required to frame its own by-laws which have got to be registered with the Registrar of co-operative societies. Any change in the by-laws will be effective only if it has been approved by the Registrar of the Co-operative Societies.

From the liability point of view, the co-operative societies may be of two types, namely, limited liability societies and unlimited liability societies. The liability of the members of a limited liability society is limited. In the event of loss the members cannot be made liable to pay more than the nominal value of shares held by them. No member other than a registered society can own more than 20% of the shares of the society or the value of the shares should not increase more than ₹ 1,000. The liability of the members will be unlimited if the object of the society is to raise funds in order to lend money to its members or where the majority of the members are creditors of the society.

ACCOUNTS

Day Book—A Journal

The two-fold aspect of a transaction has to be recorded according to the principles of double entry. Separate journal entries are not passed according to the practice followed in the maintenance of accounts of co-operative societies. All transactions are directly entered in the Day Book which is the book of original entry in the co-operative account keeping. All cash and non-cash transactions are recorded in it.

Day Book has two sides *i.e.* Receipts and Payments. Generally, two columns are kept, one for cash and the other for adjustment both on the receipt and payment sides. A cash transaction is either a receipt or payment of money. If it is a receipt of money, it is recorded in the cash column on the Receipts side of the Day Book. If it is a payment of cash, it is recorded in the cash column of the Payments side. If it is a non-cash transaction (for example, a credit transaction and adjustment) the two items of accounts of a transaction are entered in the Adjustment column both on the Receipts and Payments side of the Day Book. This book serves the purpose of the journal in double entry book-keeping as it records all cash and non-cash transactions of a co-operative institution.

Day Book—A Ledger for Cash Account

As all cash transactions are recorded straight way in the Day Book, it may be considered as the ledger for the Cash Account. Once the cash transactions are posted in this book, these are not posted further. The other accounts involving cash transactions are only further posted to the concerned ledgers. Thus, Day book serves the purpose of a ledger for the Cash Account in a co-operative institution.

Day Book with Cash and Adjustment Columns

Following is specimen ruling of a Day Book with Cash and Adjustment Columns generally maintained in a co-operative institution :

DAY BOOK WITH CASH AND ADJUSTMENT COLUMNS

Date	Particulars	R. No.	L.F.	Cash	Adjustment	Date	Particulars	R. No.	L.F.	Cash	Adjustment

ILLUSTRATION 1. Record the following transactions in the Day Book with Cash and Adjustment Columns of a service Co-operative Society which started functioning from May 1, 2025.

2025 May		₹	2025 May		₹
1	Share Capital Received	7,500	15	Board Meeting Expenses	25
	Invested in the Shares in DCCB		16	Purchased Consumer Goods	4,500
	(Distt. Central Coop. Bank)	3,000	17	Share Suspense received	1,575
	Share Fee received	375	18	Deposited into the DCC Bank	1,500
2	Purchased Consumer Goods	3,750	19	Transport charges paid	450

3	Sold Consumer Goods	3,150	20	Stationery	75
4	Stationery	150	21	Withdrawn from DCC Bank	1,050
5	Crop Loan (ST) from DCCB	30,000	22	Sold Fertilizer on credit to J	750
6	Loan issued to members : A ₹ 7,500 ; B ₹ 9,000 ; C ₹ 6,000 : D ₹ 3,000 ; E ₹ 4,500.		23	Received from H	225
			24	Share Suspense received on May 17, adjusted as follows : (*a*) Share Capital ₹ 900, (*b*) Share Fee ₹ 45	
7	Purchased Furniture	450			
8	Purchase of Fertilizer from Zila Marketing Society on credit	3,000	25	Recovered from F	600
9	Deposited in the DCC Bank	1,500	26	Invested in the shares of State Consumers Federation	750
10	Purchased Consumer Goods from Janta Bazar on credit	3,750	27	Recovery of Loan from B : Principal ₹ 1,500 ; Interest ₹ 75	
11	Paid for Postage	15			
12	Sold Fertilizer on credit to : F ₹ 2,400 ; G ₹ 1,500		28	Paid Rent Advance	300
			29	Withdrawn from Bank	1,500
13	Sold Consumer Goods on credit to : H ₹ 300 ; I ₹ 150		30	Paid Electricity Charges	10
			31	Paid Salary	300
14	Received Cash Sales of Consumer Goods	7,800			

SOLUTION (*Please see next page*)

Ledger Postings

Posting of all accounts is done in their respective ledgers except Cash Account. In case of double entry system one aspect of the transaction is debited in one ledger and the other of it is credited in another ledger. This is not applicable in case of Co-operative Accounting System. The accounts that are kept in the Day Book on the Receipts side are posted to the debit side of the respective ledgers. Similarly, the accounts kept in the Day Book on the payments side are posted on the credit side of the respective ledgers.

ILLUSTRATION 2. Post all the transactions that are entered in the Day Book in Illustration 1.

SOLUTION

SHARE CAPITAL ACCOUNT

Date	Receipts	DBF	Amount ₹	Date	Payment	DBF	Amount ₹
2025							
May 1	Cash		7,500				
24	Share Suspense		900				
			8,400				

SHARE FEE ACCOUNT

			₹				
2025							
May 1	Cash		375				
24	Share Suspense		45				
			420				

(*Contd. on page 35·5*)

SOLUTION (*ILLUSTRATION 1*)

DAY BOOK WITH CASH AND ADJUSTMENT COLUMNS OF A SERVICE CO-OPERATIVE SOCIETY

Transactions from 1-5-2025 to 31-5-2025

Date	Particulars (Receipts)	L.F.	Cash ₹	Adjustments ₹	Date	Particulars (Payments)	L.F.	Cash ₹	Adjustments ₹
2025					2025				
May 1	Share Capital		7,500		May 1	Shares in DCC Bank		3,000	
1	Share Fee		375		2	Purchase of Consumer Goods		3,750	
3	Sale of Consumer Goods		3,150		4	Stationery		150	
5	Crop Loan from DCCB		30,000		6	Loan to : A———		7,500	
8	Zila Marketing Society (1)			3,000		B———		9,000	
10	Janata Bazar			3,750		C———		6,000	
12	Sale of Fertilizers (2)			3,900		D———		3,000	
13	Sale of Consumer Goods			450		E———		4,500	
14	Cash Sales of Consumer Goods		7,800		7	Furniture		450	
17	Share Suspense		1,575		8	Purchase of Fertilizer (1)			3,000
21	DCC Bank		1,050		9	DCC Bank		1,500	
22	Sale of Fertilizer			750	10	Purchase of Consumer Goods			3,750
23	H's A/c		225		11	Postage		15	
24	Share Capital			900	12	F's A/c (2)			2,400
24	Share Fee			45		G's A/c			1,500
25	F's A/c		600		13	H's A/c			300
27	B's A/c					I's A/c			150
	Principal		1,500		15	Board's Meeting Expenses		25	
	Interest		75		16	Purchase of Consumer Goods		4,500	
29	DCC Bank		1,500		18	DCC Bank		1,500	
					19	Transport Charges		450	
					20	Stationery		75	
					22	J's A/c			750
					24	Share Suspense			945
					26	Shares of State Consumers Federation		750	
					28	Rent Advance		300	
					30	Electricity Charges		10	
					31	Salary		300	
						Cash Balance		8,575	
			55,350	12,795				55,350	12,795

(1) Purchase of Fertilizer from Zila Marketing Society on credit should be shown under adjustment column on the Payments side and Zila Marketing Society should be kept under Adjustment Column of the Receipts side.

(2) Sale of Fertilizer to F on credit should be shown under Adjustment Column of the Receipts side of Day Book and personal account of F should be shown under adjustment column on the Payment side.

SHARES IN DCC BANK ACCOUNT

				2025			₹
				May 1	Cash		3,000
							3,000

PURCHASE OF CONSUMER GOODS ACCOUNT

				2025			₹
				May 2	Cash		3,750
				10	Janta Bazar		3,750
				16	Cash		4,500
							12,000

ZILA MARKETING SOCIETY ACCOUNT

			₹				
2025 May 8	Purchase of Fertilizer		3,000				
			3,000				

JANTA BAZAR's ACCOUNT

2025			₹				
May 10	Purchase of Consumer Goods		3,750				
			3,750				

DCC BANK CURRENT ACCOUNT

2025			₹	2025			₹
May 21	Cash		1,050	May 9	Cash		1,500
29	Cash		1,500	18	Cash		1,500
			2,550				3,000

INTEREST ON MEMBERS' LOAN ACCOUNT

2025			₹				
May 27	Cash		75				
			75				

STATIONERY ACCOUNT

				2025			₹
				May 4	Cash		150
				20	Cash		75
							225

SALE OF CONSUMER GOODS ACCOUNT

			₹				₹
2025							
May 3	Cash		3,150				
13	H's A/c		300				
13	I's A/c		150				
14	Cash		7,800				
			11,400				

DCC BANK CROP LOAN ACCOUNT

			₹				₹
2025							
May 5	Cash		30,000				
			30,000				

LOAN ACCOUNT OF 'A'

			₹				₹
				2025			
				May 6	Cash		7,500
							7,500

LOAN ACCOUNT OF 'B'

			₹				₹
2025				2025			
May 27	Cash		1,500	May 6	Cash		9,000
			1,500				9,000

LOAN ACCOUNT OF 'C'

			₹				₹
				2025			
				May 6	Cash		6,000
							6,000

LOAN ACCOUNT OF 'D'

			₹				₹
				2025			
				May 6	Cash		3,000
							3,000

LOAN ACCOUNT OF 'E'

			₹				₹
				2025			
				May 6	Cash		4,500
							4,500

FURNITURE ACCOUNT

							₹
				2025			
				May 7	Cash		450
							450

PURCHASE OF FERTILIZER ACCOUNT

							₹
				2025			
				May 8	Zila Marketing Society		3,000
							3,000

POSTAGE ACCOUNT

							₹
				2025			
				May 11	Cash		15
							15

G's ACCOUNT

							₹
				2025			
				May 12	Fertilizer Sales		1,500
							1,500

SALE OF FERTILIZER ACCOUNT

			₹				
2025							
May 12	F's A/c		2,400				
" 12	G's A/c		1,500				
" 22	J's A/c		750				
			4,650				

LOAN ACCOUNT OF 'F'

			₹				₹
2025				2025			
May 25	Cash		600	May 12	Sale of Fertilizer		2,400
			600				2,400

LOAN ACCOUNT OF 'H'

			₹				₹
2025				2025			
May 23	Cash		225	May 13	Sale of Consumer Goods		300
			225				300

LOAN ACCOUNT OF 'I'

				2025			₹
				May 13	Sale of Consumer Goods		150
							150

BOARD'S MEETING EXPENSES ACCOUNT

				2025			₹
				May 15	Cash		25
							25

SHARE SUSPENSE ACCOUNT

2025			₹	2025			₹
May 17	Cash		1,575	May 24	Share Capital		900
					Share Fee		45
			1,575				945

TRANSPORT CHARGES ACCOUNT

				2025			₹
				May 19	Cash		450
							450

LOAN ACCOUNT OF 'J'

				2025			₹
				May 22	Sale of Fertilizer		750
							750

SHARES OF STATE CONSUMERS' FEDERATION ACCOUNT

				2025			₹
				May 26	Cash		750
							750

RENT ADVANCE ACCOUNT

				2025			₹
				May 28	Cash		300
							300

ELECTRICITY CHARGES ACCOUNT

				2025			₹
				May 30	Cash		10
							10

SALARY ACCOUNT

				2025			₹
				May 31	Cash		300
							300

Closing of Ledgers

All accounts except nominal accounts are balanced under double entry system of book-keeping. Only totals are kept in case of nominal accounts and balance is struck in the Trading and Profit and Loss Account. No attempt is made to close the balance for all accounts in case of co-operative accounting. The Receipts as well as Payments side in all the accounts are totalled and kept as they are. But personal ledgers are balanced as and when members clear their dues or when fresh advances are made.

Receipts & Payments Statement

Receipts and Payments Statement is prepared for a specified period from the totals found in all the ledgers. Thus it is a summary of the Day Book. As it is prepared from the totals of Receipts and Payments sides of the ledgers, so there are no opening and closing balances.

ILLUSTRATION 3. Prepare Receipts and Payments Statement for the month of May, 2025 on the basis of posting made in different ledgers in Illustration 2.

SOLUTION

RECEIPTS AND PAYMENTS STATEMENT OF A SERVICE SOCIETY

for the month of May, 2025

Receipts		₹	*Payments*		₹
Share Capital		8,400	Shares in DCC Bank		3,000
Share Fee A/c		420	Purchase of Consumer Goods		12,000
Zila Marketing Society		3,000	DCC Bank Current A/c		3,000
Janata Bazar		3,750	Stationery		225
DCC Bank Current A/c		2,550	Loans to members :	₹	
Interest on Members Loan		75	A	7,500	
Sale of Consumers Goods		11,400	B	9,000	
DCC Bank Crop. Loan A/c		30,000	C	6,000	
Sale of Fertilizer		4,650	D	3,000	
Loans Recovered :	₹		E	4,500	
B	1,500		F	2,400	
F	600		G	1,500	
H	225		H	300	
		2,325	I	150	
Share Suspense		1,575	J	750	
					35,100
			Furniture		450

		Purchase of Fertilizer	3,000
		Postage	15
		Board's Meeting Expenses	25
		Share Suspense	945
		Transport Charges450	
		Shares of State Consumers Federation	750
		Rent Advance	300
		Electric Charges	10
		Salary	300
		Cash Balance	8,575
	68,145		68,145

Distinction between Receipts and Payments Statement and Trial Balance

Receipts and Payments Statement	*Trial Balance*
1. It is prepared out of the totals of Receipts and Payments from the respective ledgers for a particular period only.	1. It is prepared from all the accounts *i.e.* balances of personal and real accounts and totals of the nominal accounts.
2. It confines itself only to transactions relating to a particular period for which it is prepared and thus does not take cognizance of the balances remaining in the ledgers of the previous period.	2. It also takes into account the Debit and Credit balances outstanding of all accounts in the previous period.
3. It shows only the total of the transactions of a particular period.	3. It is not possible to know the transactions carried on within a particular period either of receipts or payments from trial balance.
4. It gives a clear picture of all transactions effected during the year for a co-operative institution and helps for further management decisions.	4. It provides the basic data for preparation of final accounts and helps to check the arithmetical accuracy of accounts.
5. As it contains only the totals of the different transactions, it is not possible to prepare final accounts exclusively with the help of this statement. Previous year's Balance Sheet is required for final accounts.	5. As it contains all balances standing in the different ledgers, it is not necessary to refer to the previous Balance Sheet of the business concern.

FINAL ACCOUNTS

Final accounts of a co-operative society will include Trading and Profit & Loss Account and Balance Sheet. These are prepared from the Receipts and Payments statement of a particular period. Adjustment items should be taken into consideration in Receipts and Payments statement for the preparation of Final Accounts. Nominal items are taken to the Trading and Profit & Loss Account. Such accounts under the Receipts side represent incomes and those under the payments side expenditures. As regards real and personal accounts are concerned, the items kept under the Receipts side represent the Liabilities and those under the Payments side represent Assets. If a particular item appears on both the Receipts and Payments side, a balance should be struck between the two and resulting figure could either be a receipt balance or a payment balance. A receipt balance is a liability and a payment balance is an asset. The Balance Sheet is prepared on the basis of the balances struck for various items of accounts under the Receipts and Payments side.

Profit of a co-operative society can be appropriated in the following order :

(*a*) As per Section 33 of the Co-operative Societies Act, 1912, the first 25% of the net profit earned during any year should be transferred to a Reserve Fund.

(*b*) The balance of profits and the past profits available for distribution can be distributed to the members to such an extent and under such conditions as may be laid down by the rules or by-laws, but as per Section 35 dividend to members should not be more than 6.25%.

(*c*) A registered co-operative society may, with the sanction of the Registrar, contribute an amount not exceeding 10% of the net profit remaining after the compulsory transfer to Reserve Fund, for any charitable purpose as defined in Section 2 of the Charitable Endowment Act, 1890.

(*d*) A co-operative society with unlimited liability can distribute profits only with the general or special order of the State Government.

ILLUSTRATION 4. From the following Balance Sheet as on 31-12-2023 and Receipts and Payments Statement from 1-1-2024 to 31-12-2024 of a **Marketing** Co-operative Society, prepare a **Trading and Profit and Loss Account** for the year 2024 and a **Balance Sheet** as on 31-12-2024 taking into account the adjustments given below :

BALANCE SHEET

as at 31-12-2023

Liabilities	₹	*Assets*	₹
Share Capital :		Cash in hand	26,300
Members	1,58,000	Cash at DCC Bank	2,50,000
Government	1,30,000	Shares in Marketing Federation	45,000
Reserve Fund	86,000	Fixed Deposit in DCC Bank	47,700
Building Fund	63,000	Cement Security Deposit	1,55,700
Agriculture Stabilisation Fund	12,000	Building	6,30,000
Staff Security Deposit	20,000	Furniture	54,000
Staff Provident Fund Deposit	70,000	Members' Produce Loan	22,68,000
DCC Bank Cash Credit Loan	25,00,000	Consignment as per Contra	9,00,000
Consignment Account	10,00,000	Closing Stock	8,00,000
Value of Consignment as per Contra	9,00,000	Arbitration Fee from Members	10,000
Share Suspense	5,000	Stock Shortage Recoverable	20,200
General Suspense	25,000		
Establishment Charges Outstanding	16,000		
Profit for 2023	2,21,900		
	52,06,900		52,06,900

RECEIPTS AND PAYMENTS STATEMENT

for the year 2024

	₹		₹
Opening Balance	26,300	Purchase of Fertilizers	26,00,000
Sale of Fertilizers	30,00,000	Purchase of Foodgrains	8,65,000
Sale of Foodgrains	11,40,000	Share Suspense	2,700
Staff Security Deposit	9,000	General Suspense	68,000
Staff Provident Fund Deposit	27,000	Scooter Advance	11,000

Reserve Fund	27,000	Electricity Charges	2,700
Building Fund	20,000	Interest on Bank Cash	
Agriculture Stabilisation Fund	25,000	Credit Loan	20,000
Members' Produce Loan	9,00,000	Establishment Charges	2,05,000
DCC Bank Cash Credit Loan	18,00,000	Meeting Expenses	9,000
Share Suspense	8,000	Members' Produce Loan	13,50,000
General Suspense	35,000	Consignment Account	18,10,000
Consignment Account	18,00,000	Staff Security Deposit	5,000
Interest on Members' Produce Loan	1,00,000	Staff Provident Fund Deposit	9,000
Stock Shortages	10,000	DCC Bank Current Account	3,50,000
DCC Bank Current Account	5,00,000	DCC Bank Cash Credit Loan	18,50,000
Commission on Consignment	60,000	Profit for the previous year	2,21,900
Miscellaneous Receipts	18,000	Closing Balance	1,26,000
	95,05,300		95,05,300

Adjustments :

(*a*) Establishment Charges due ₹ 10,000.
(*b*) Depreciate furniture by 10% and building by 5%.
(*c*) Closing Stock ₹ 9,60,000.
(*d*) Consignment Stock ₹ 18,00,000.

SOLUTION

TRADING AND PROFIT AND LOSS ACCOUNT OF A MARKETING CO-OPERATIVE SOCIETY

for the year ending December 31, 2024

		₹		₹
Opening Stock		8,00,000	Sale of Fertilizers	30,00,000
Purchase of Fertilizers		26,00,000	Sale of Foodgrains	11,40,000
Purchase of Foodgrains		8,65,000	Closing Stock	9,60,000
Gross Profit c/d		8,35,000		
	₹	51,00,000		51,00,000
Establishment Charges	2,05,000		Gross Profit b/d	8,35,000
Less : Outstanding			Interest on Members' Produce Loan	1,00,000
Previous Year	16,000		Commission on Consignment	60,000
	1,89,000		Miscellaneous Receipts	18,000
Add : Outstanding 2024	10,000			
		1,99,000		
Interest on Bank Cash Credit Loan		20,000		
Meeting Expenses		9,000		
Electricity Charges		2,700		
Depreciation on :	₹			
Furniture	5,400			
Building	31,500			
Net Profit		36,900		
		7,45,400		
		10,13,000		10,13,000

BALANCE SHEET OF A MARKETING CO-OPERATIVE SOCIETY

as at December 31, 2024

Liabilities	₹	₹	*Assets*	₹
Share Capital :			Cash in hand	1,26,000
Members	1,58,000		Cash at DCC Bank	1,00,000
Government	1,30,000		Shares in Marketing Federation	45,000
		2,88,000	Fixed Deposit in DCC Bank	47,700
Reserve Fund		1,13,000	Cement Security Deposit	1,55,700
Building Fund		83,000	Building less Depreciation	5,98,500
Agriculture Stabilisation Fund		37,000	Furniture less Depreciation	48,600
Staff Security Deposit		24,000	Members' Produce Loan	27,18,000
Staff Provident Fund Deposit		88,000	Consignment Stock as per Contra	18,00,000
DCC Bank Cash Credit Loan		24,50,000	Closing Stock	9,60,000
Consignment Account		9,90,000	Stock Shortage Recoverable	10,200
Value of Consignment as per Contra		18,00,000	Arbitration Fee from Members	10,000
Share Suspense		10,300	General Suspense	8,000
Establishment Charges Due		10,000	Scooter Advance	11,000
Net Profit for 2024		7,45,400		
		66,38,700		66,38,700

Note : Profit for year 2023 was distributed during the year 2024 because it has been shown as a payment in the Receipts and Payment Account for the year 2024.

ILLUSTRATION 5. From the following Balance Sheet as on 31-12-2023 and Receipts and Payments Statement from 1-1-2024 to 31-12-2024 of a **Milk Supply** Co-operative Society, prepare a **Trading, Profit and Loss Account** for the year 2024 and a **Balance Sheet** as on 31-12-2024 taking into consideration the adjustments given below :

BALANCE SHEET

as on 31-12-2023

	₹		₹
Share Capital :		Cash in Hand	12,800
(*a*) Members	43,700	Cash at Bank	2,00,000
(*b*) Government	20,000	Fixed Deposit in Bank	28,000
Reserve Fund	53,200	Shares in Dairy Union	42,000
Building Fund	70,000	Loans to Members	1,92,500
Staff Security Deposit	16,100	Office Rent Advance	2,100
Milk Coupon Account	2,800	Transport Advance	11,200
Bonus to Members	30,800	Furniture	21,000
Dividend to Members	4,200	Cattle Shed	42,000
Milk Suppliers' Account :		Closing Stock of Bran	65,800
(*a*) Members	2,00,000		
(*b*) Non-members	59,000		
Members' Thrift Deposit	42,000		
Yard Rent Due	11,200		
Audit Fee Outstanding	11,200		
Sales Tax Provision	7,700		

Depreciation Reserve :			
(*a*) Furniture	1,500		
(*b*) Cattle Shed	2,000		
Share Suspense	1,400		
Net Profit for 2023	40,600		
	6,17,400		6,17,400

RECEIPTS AND PAYMENTS STATEMENT

for the year ending 31st December, 2024

Receipts	₹	*Payments*	₹
Opening Balance	12,800	Loans to Members	2,16,300
Share Capital (Members)	5,600	Share Capital (Members)	1,400
Sale of Bran	4,13,000	Purchases of Bran	3,45,800
Milk Order Deposits	59,500	Establishment Charges	1,38,600
Milk Handling Commission	1,24,500	Printing and Stationery	20,300
Interest on Loans (Members)	12,000	Milk Purchase Account :	
Loans to Members	2,55,500	(*a*) Members	36,20,000
Manure Sales	4,900	(*b*) Non-members	4,47,000
Bank Withdrawals	19,60,000	Bank Remittance	21,28,700
Milk Suppliers' Account :		Sales Tax	7,700
(*a*) Members	36,20,000	Milk Transportation Charges	17,500
(*b*) Non-members	4,61,000	Members' Thrift Deposit	18,900
Sale of Milk (Coupons)	35,84,000	Postage	2,100
Sale of Milk (Cash)	4,85,800	Office Rent	14,000
Milk Coupon Account	35,92,400	Electricity Charges	2,800
Interest on Fixed Deposit	4,200	Contingencies	9,100
Staff Security Deposit	5,600	Furniture	5,600
Cattle Shed Rent	4,800	Yard Rent	21,000
Members Thrift Deposit	19,600	Milk Suppliers' Account :	
Miscellaneous Receipts	18,800	(*a*) Members	35,05,000
		(*b*) Non-members	4,85,000
		Milk Coupon Account	35,84,000
		Purchases Advance	14,000
		General Body Expenses	4,200
		Closing Balance	35,000
	1,46,44,000		1,46,44,000

Adjustments :

(1) Closing Stock of Bran ₹ 48,500.

(2) Provide for the following items for 2024 :

(*a*) Yard Rent ₹ 5,000 ; (*b*) Printing and Stationery ₹ 800 ; Establishment Charges ₹ 3,000 ; Sales Tax ₹ 6,000 ; Audit Fee ₹ 6,000.

(3) Depreciate Furniture and Cattle Shed by 10% on cost. Milk order deposits should be treated as sales.

SOLUTION

TRADING AND PROFIT AND LOSS ACCOUNT OF A MILK SUPPLY CO-OPERATIVE SOCIETY

for the year ending 31st December, 2024

Particulars		₹	Particulars	₹
Opening Stock of Bran		65,800	Sale of Milk (Coupons)	35,84,000
Purchases of Bran		3,45,800	Sale of Milk (Cash)	4,85,800
Milk Purchases :			Sale of Bran	4,13,000
(*a*) Members		36,20,000	Milk Order Deposits	59,500
(*b*) Non-members		4,47,000	Manure Sales	4,900
Milk Transportation Charges		17,500	Closing Stock of Bran	48,500
Gross Profit c/d		99,600		
		45,95,700		45,95,700
	₹		Gross Profit b/d	99,600
Establishment Charges	1,38,600		Milk Handling Commission	1,24,500
Add : Outstanding	3,000		Interest on Loans (Members)	12,000
		1,41,600	Interest on Fixed Deposit	4,200
Yard Rent	21,000		Cattle Shed Rent	4,800
Less : Previous Year's			Miscellaneous Receipts	18,800
Outstanding	11,200			
	9,800			
Add : Outstanding for 2024	5,000			
		14,800		
Printing & Stationery	20,300			
Add : Outstanding	800			
		21,100		
Audit Fee for 2024 Outstanding		6,000		
Postage		2,100		
Office Rent		14,000		
Electricity Charges		2,800		
Contingencies		9,100		
General Body Expenses		4,200		
Sales Tax Provision		6,000		
Depreciation on :	₹			
Furniture	2,660			
Cattle Shed	4,200			
		6,860		
Net Profit		35,340		
		2,63,900		2,63,900

BALANCE SHEET OF A MILK SUPPLY CO-OPERATIVE SOCIETY

as on 31-12-2024

Liabilities	₹	*Assets*	₹
Share Capital :		Cash in Hand	35,000
(*a*) Members	47,900	Cash at Bank (₹ 2,00,000	3,68,700
(*b*) Government	20,000	+₹ 21,28,700 – ₹ 19,60,000)	
Reserve Fund	53,200	Fixed Deposit in Bank	28,000
Building Fund	70,000	Shares in Dairy Union	42,000

		₹			₹	₹
Staff Security Deposit		21,700	Loans to Members			1,53,300
Milk Coupon Account		11,200	Office Rent Advance			2,100
Milk Suppliers' Account :			Transport Advance			11,200
(*a*) Members		3,15,000	Purchases Advance			14,000
(*b*) Non-members		35,000	Closing Stock of Bran		₹	48,500
Share Suspense		1,400	Cattle Shed		42,000	
Bonus to Members		30,800	*Less* : Depreciation			
Dividend to Members		4,200	(₹ 2,000 + ₹ 4,200)		6,200	
Member's Thrift Deposit		42,700				35,800
Yard Rent due		5,000	Furniture on 1-1-2024		21,000	
Audit Fee Outstanding		17,200	*Add* : Purchases		5,600	
Sales Tax Provision		6,000			26,600	
Printing & Stationery			*Less* : Depreciation		4,160	
Outstanding		800	(₹ 1,500 + ₹ 2,660)			22,440
Establishment Charges						
Outstanding	₹	3,000				
Accumulated Profit	40,600					
Add : Profit for 2024	35,340					
		75,940				
		7,61,040				7,61,040

ILLUSTRATION 6. U, N, I, T and Y have come together and formed "UNITY' **Milk** Producers' Society. UNITY collects the milk from each one of its members and usually sells it to a few hotels on a regular basis. The monthly quota of each member is fixed at 3000 litres. If a member fails to supply that quantity, his share of profit will be in proportion to milk actually delivered by him ; there being no penalty. If a member were to exceed his quota, every extra litre supplied by him will qualify to share in profits at 50% weightage. A settlement is made at the end of every month.

For the month of May 2025, the relevant details were :

(A) Milk supplied by the members

U	3000	litres
N	2800	litres
I	3400	litres
T	4000	litres
Y	4000	litres
	17,200	litres

(B) Other Details

	Amount (₹)
Milk purchased from members	1,20,400
Sales	1,89,200
Administrative expenses	10,400
Credit given to customers for curdled milk	2,400

(C) Members' Accounts—dues to members for purchases

U	₹ 7,000
T	₹ 17,500

There was no opening or closing stock for the month of May 2025.

Prepare the Society's **Profit and Loss A/c** and **Members' Statement of Account.**

SOLUTION

In the Books of 'Unity' Milk Producers' Society
PROFIT & LOSS ACCOUNT
for the Month of May 2025

	₹		₹	₹
To Purchases	1,20,400	By Sales	1,89,200	
To Administrative Expenses	10,400	*Less* : Spoilage	2,400	
To Net Profit for the month	56,000			1,86,800
	1,86,800			1,86,800
To Members' A/cs (1) ₹		By Net Profit b/d		56,000
U $\left(\frac{3}{16} \times ₹\ 56,000\right)$ 10,500				
N $\left(\frac{7}{40} \times ₹\ 56,000\right)$ 9,800				
I $\left(\frac{1}{5} \times ₹\ 56,000\right)$ 11,200				
T $\left(\frac{7}{32} \times ₹\ 56,000\right)$ 12,250				
Y $\left(\frac{7}{32} \times ₹\ 56,000\right)$ 12,250				
	56,000			
	56,000			56,000

MEMBERS' STATEMENT OF ACCOUNT

	U	*N*	*I*	*T*	*Y*	*Total*
Due for Purchases (₹)	7,000	—	—	17,500	—	24,500
Share of Profit (₹)	10,500	9,800	11,200	12,250	12,250	56,000
Dues to Members (₹)	17,500	9,800	11,200	29,750	12,250	80,500

Working Notes

Members who have supplied in excess of 3,000 litres will qualify for extra profit equivalent to 1 litre for every two litres sold. Thus equivalent units for I will be 3,200 litres and for T and Y they will be 3,500 litres each ; making a total of 16,000 equivalent litres. Therefore, proportions of each in profit are as follows :

$$U = \frac{3,000}{16,000} = \frac{3}{16} \quad I = \frac{3,200}{16,000} = \frac{1}{5}$$

$$N = \frac{2,800}{16,000} = \frac{7}{40} \quad T \text{ and } Y = \frac{3,500}{16,000} = \frac{7}{32}$$

QUESTIONS

OBJECTIVE TYPE

1. **Which of the following statements are correct :**

(*a*) Two alternative words 'Receipts' and 'Payments' for 'Dr.' and 'Cr.' are used to convey the two fold aspect of transactions in case of Co-operative accounting.

(*b*) Only cash transactions are recorded in the Day Book in the co-operative account keeping.

(c) In case of a co-operative society, Day Book serves the purpose of journal in double entry book-keeping as it makes a record of all cash and non-cash transactions.

(d) Day Book does not serve the purpose of a ledger for the Cash Account in a Co-operative institution.

(e) In case of co-operative accounting, the accounts that are kept in the Day Book on the payments side are posted to the debit side of the respective ledgers.

(f) Receipts and Payments Statement is a summary of the Day Book.

Ans. [(*a*) ; (*c*) ; (*f*)].

SHORT/LONG ANSWER TYPE

1. What do you mean by Co-operative Accounts ? In what way are they different from other types of accounts ?
2. What is a Day Book ? Discuss how it is maintained. What do you understand by Adjustment column in the Day Book ?
3. Bring out clearly the similarities and differences between the Co-operative Accounting and the Double Entry System of Accounting.
4. Give the procedure adopted for the preparation of the Receipts and Payments Statement.
5. Distinguish between Receipts and Payments Statement and a Trial Balance.
6. Explain how posting is made from the Day Book to the different ledgers.
7. Describe, in detail, the procedure for the preparation of Final Accounts in co-operative institutions.

PRACTICAL PROBLEMS

1. Following are the transactions of a **service** co-operative society for the month of June, 2025 :

2025 June		₹
1	Opening Cash Balance	8,575
	Cash Purchase of Consumers Goods	1,500
2	Sale of Consumer Goods on Credit to B	750
3	Purchased Fertilizer from Zila Marketing Society on Credit	7,500
4	Distributed Loans in the form of Fertilizer to (₹): K 750; L 900; M 1,200; N 600; O 750	4,200
5	Sale of Fertilizer in Cash	2,700
6	Loans Recovered from	
	C : Principal	3,000
	Interest	60
	D : Principal	750
	Interest	15

2025 June		₹
11	Sale of Consumer Goods	600
12	Paid Purchase Advance by Cheque to Secretary	1,500
13	Secretary purchased consumers goods worth ₹ 1,200 and refunded the balance amount	
14	Recovered Loan from :	
	F : Principal	1,500
	Interest	18
	G : Principal	1,500
	Interest	15
15	Sale of Consumer Goods	900
16	DCC Bank Loan Remitted	7,500
17	Disbursed loan to P by cheque drawn on Bank Loan (ST) A/c	3,000
18	Purchased Stationery	150
19	Spent for Postage	35
20	Loan recovered from A	1,500
21	The Board Meeting resolved to adjust	

Date	Particulars	₹
7	Remitted into Bank (Current A/c)	3,000
	Remitted into Bank Co-op. Loan A/c :	
	Principal	6,000
	Interest	150
8	Cash remitted into Janta Bazar on Account	1,500
9	Loan Recovered from :	
	A :	
	Principal	4,500
	Interest	75
	B :	
	Principal	4,500
	Interest	60
	C :	
	Principal	1,500
	Interest	15
10	Share Suspense Received	160

Date	Particulars	₹
	Share Suspense A/c ₹ 315—towards Shares ₹ 300 and ₹ 15 towards Share Fee	
22	Board Meeting Expenses	30
23	₹ 1,500 paid towards DCC Bank Crop Loan A/c	
24	Purchased Furniture for ₹ 600	
25	Paid ₹ 1,500 to Zila Marketing Society by Cheque	
26	Conveyance charges paid to Secretary for attending court work ₹ 10	
27	Transport charges paid ₹ 225	
28	Postage Expenses ₹ 15	
29	Sale of Empties ₹75	
30	Paid salary by cash ₹ 300, Rent ₹ 300 by cheque	

Post the above transactions in the Day Book for the month of June, 2025.

Ans. [Cash Closing Balance ₹ 9,803].

2. Post all the transactions that are entered in the Day Book (in Problem 1).

3. Prepare Receipts and Payments Statement for the month of June, 2025 on the basis of posting made in different ledgers (in Problem 2).

4. From the following Balance Sheet as on 31-12-2023 and Receipts and Payments Statement for the year 2024 of **a Service** Co-operative Society, prepare **final accounts** for the year 2024 considering the adjustments given below :

BALANCE SHEET

as on 31-12-2023

Liabilities	₹	*Assets*	₹
Share Capital :		Cash in hand	3,000
Members	2,00,000	Cash at Bank	1,60,000
Government	1,00,000	National Saving Certificates	1,80,000
Reserve Fund	6,00,000	Loans to Members	15,00,000
Government Subsidy	1,60,000	Furniture	10,000
Bank Borrowings	12,00,000	Building	1,70,000
Rent Outstanding	3,000	Shortage Recoverable	2,000
General Suspense	4,000	Closing Stock	3,00,000
Net Profit for 2023	58,000		
	23,25,000		23,25,000

RECEIPTS AND PAYMENTS STATEMENT

for the year ending 31st December, 2024

Receipts	₹	*Payments*	₹
Opening Balance	3,000	Loans to Members	8,00,000
Loans to Members Recovered	11,50,000	Bank Borrowings	12,00,000
Bank Borrowings	10,00,000	Interest on Bank Borrowings	1,50,000
Interest	2,20,000	Purchases	5,00,000

Shortage Recovered	1,000	Establishment Charges	50,000
Admission and Share Fee	2,000	Rent	43,000
Share Capital (Members)	25,000	Sales Tax paid	2,000
Sales	7,00,000	Refund of Share Capital (Members)	10,000
Bank Current Account	20,000	Bank Current Account	3,00,000
		Closing Balance	66,000
	31,21,000		31,21,000

Adjustments **:**

1. Stock on 31-12-2024 ₹ 1,50,000 ; 2. Appropriation of Net Profit for the year 2023 is to be made as: (*a*) Reserve Fund ₹ 14,500 ; (*b*) Dividend ₹ 18,000 ; (*c*) Bonus to Staff ₹ 25,500 ; 3. Admission and Share Fee to be added to Reserve Fund. 4. Depreciate Furniture by 10% and Building by 5%.

Ans. [Gross Profit ₹ 48,000 ; Net Profit ₹ 18,500 ; Balance Sheet Total ₹ 21,57,500].

5. From the following Balance Sheet as on June 30, 2024 and Receipts and Payments Statement from 1-7-2024 to 30-6-2025 of an **Industrial** Co-operative Society, prepare a **Trading, Profit and Loss Account** for the year ending 30th June, 2025 and a **Balance Sheet** as on 30-6-2025 taking into account the adjustments given below :

BALANCE SHEET

as on 30-6-2024

Liabilities	₹	*Assets*	₹
Share Capital :		Cash in hand	4,000
Members	5,00,000	Cash at Bank	95,000
Government	2,00,000	Shares in Co-operative Woollen Mill	50,000
Reserve Fund	50,000	Shares in Industrial Co-operative Bank	40,000
Wages Equalisation Fund	10,000	Members' Advance	8,20,000
Price Equalisation Fund	8,000	Wages Advance to Members	55,000
Loan from Government	10,00,000	Trade Debtors	45,000
Bank Cash Credit Loan	3,00,000	Share Capital Loan to Members	1,50,000
Trade Creditors	70,000	Closing Stock	2,30,000
Thrift Deposit	20,000	Furniture	35,000
Audit Fee Outstanding	3,000	Plant and Machinery	4,50,000
Cash Difference	2,000	Building	2,50,000
Profit	71,000	Arbitration Fee Recoverable	4,000
		Amount Recoverable from Ex-Secretary	6,000
	22,34,000		22,34,000

RECEIPTS AND PAYMENTS STATEMENT

for the period from July 1, 2024 to June 30, 2025

Receipts	₹	*Payments*	₹
Sales	33,00,000	Purchases	25,00,000
Members' Advance	6,00,000	Shares in Industrial Co-operative Bank	5,00,000
Wages Advance to Members	6,50,000	Bank Current Account	3,00,000
Members' Share Capital	20,000	Wages	8,00,000
Thrift Deposit	80,000		

Bank Current Account	2,00,000	Wages Advance to Members	7,00,000
Bank Cash Credit Loan	12,00,000	Establishment Charges	2,00,000
Share Capital Loan to Members	30,000	Octroi	2,000
Arbitration Fee Recovery	3,000	Carriage	8,000
Trade Debtors	35,000	Bonus to Members	10,000
Miscellaneous Income	5,000	Bonus to Staff	8,000
Opening Balance	4,000	Dividend	35,000
		Selling Expenses	6,000
		Repayment of Govt. Loan	5,00,000
		Audit Fee	5,000
		Interest on Loans	30,000
		Bank Cash Credit Loan	5,00,000
		Closing Balance	23,000
	61,27,000		61,27,000

Adjustments :

(1) Closing Stock ₹ 3,00,000. (2) Depreciate fixed assets by 10%. (3) Provide ₹ 2,000 for audit fee. (4) Profit distribution is as follows : Bonus to Members ₹ 10,000 ; Bonus to Staff ₹ 11,250 ; Dividend ₹ 35,000 ; Reserve Fund ₹ 7,750 ; Wages Equalisation Fund ₹ 4,000 ; Price Equalisation Fund ₹ 3,000.

Ans. [Gross Profit ₹ 60,000 ; Net Loss ₹ 2,48,500 ; B/S Total ₹ 24,80,000].

CHAPTER 36

Contract Accounts

Contract accounts are prepared where the work is undertaken to customers' requirements and each order is of long duration as compared to small job. The work is generally of constructional nature. A construction contract is a contract for the construction of an asset or of a combination of assets which together constitute a single substantial project. This covers various activities as construction of plants (including site preparation), bridges, roads, dams, ships, buildings, complex parts of equipments, production of motion pictures etc. That is why this method is used by builders, civil engineering contractors, constructional and mechanical engineering firms etc. These contracts are negotiated in a number of ways.

Distinguishing Features of Contract Accounts

Following are the main distinguishing features of contract accounts :

***(i)* Higher Proportion of Direct Costs**. As most of the items of expenses can be directly identified with a contract, though indirect, are treated as direct expenses. Expenses on telephone installed at site, site power usage, site vehicles, transportation are treated as direct expenses.

***(ii)* Low Indirect Costs**. The only item of indirect cost may be Head office expenses. Such cost represents only a small proportion of the contract cost and is absorbed usually on some overall basis such as percentage of total contract cost.

***(iii)* Problem of Cost Control**. The large scale of some contracts and the size of the site may create some major problems of cost control consuming material usage and losses, pilferage, labour supervision and utilisation, damage to and loss of plant and tools etc.

***(iv)* Surplus Materials**. Surplus material, if any, will be either credited to the contract account with the cost of material at the end of the contract or will be debited to the new contract account, if directly transferred to another contract. If the material is not required immediately, it will be stored and the cost debited to a stock account.

Types of Contracts

Generally there are three types of contracts :

***(i)* Fixed Price Contracts**. Under these both parties agree to a fixed contract price.

***(ii)* Fixed Price Contracts** but in some cases subject to Escalation Clause (discussed afterwards).

***(iii)* Cost Plus Contracts**. Under these contracts no fixed price could be settled. The contractor is reimbursed for allowable or otherwise defined costs plus a percentage of these costs or a fixed fee towards profit.

Each contract is considered as a separate unit of cost and is allotted a distinguishing number. A separate account is kept for each individual contract ; usually a greater part of the work is carried out at the contract site itself, so the whole expenditure can be charged direct to the contract. However, the overheads relating to the office and central stores require apportionment among the various contracts on some arbitrary basis such as percentage of wages, materials or prime cost or percentage of total contract cost.

Recording of Costs of Contract

A Contract Ledger is maintained in which a separate account is opened for each contract undertaken by a contractor. A Contract Ledger is so ruled out as to give maximum information. A specimen ruling of the same is given below :

CONTRACT LEDGER

Form No. ....
Contract No. ....
Site ....
Completion Date ....
Remarks ....

Contract Price ....
Terms of Payment ....
Retention Money ....
Work Certified ....
Date .... ₹
Date .... ₹

Dr. *Cr.*

Date	*Particulars*	*Folio*	*Materials*	*Wages*	*Direct Expenses*	*Plant*	*Sub-contract Costs*	*Establishment Charges*	*Total*	*Date*	*Particulars*	*Folio*	*Materials*	*Wages*	*Direct Expenses*	*Plant*	*Sub-contract Costs*	*Establishment Charges*	*Total*

Each contract is considered as a separate unit of cost and is allotted a distinguishing number. A separate account is kept for each individual contract ; usually a greater part of the work is carried out at the contract site itself, so the whole of the expenditure can be charged direct to the contract. However, the overhead relating to the office, central stores etc. require apportionment among the various contracts on some arbitrary basis such as percentage of wages, materials or prime cost.

The recording procedure of the following items may be noted carefully :

1. Materials. Materials purchased directly or supplied from the store or transferred from other contracts will appear on the debit side. Materials returned to store will appear on the credit side. Amount received from the sale of surplus materials will appear on the credit side, any profit or loss arising from the sale will be transferred to the Profit and Loss Account. Materials stolen or destroyed by fire will be transferred to the Profit and Loss Account. In case any compensation is receivable from the insurance company for loss of materials, the amount due from insurance company is shown in the Balance Sheet. The loss which is not compensated is debited to Profit & Loss Account. Materials in hand at the end of the year will appear on the credit side. Sometimes materials are transferred from one contract to another contract. Contract receiving the materials is debited and the contract giving up the materials is credited. Normal wastage incurred in stores and materials should be charged to contracts by inflating the rates at which materials are priced out. Stores used in the manufacture of tools should be charged to Works Expenses A/c. Sometimes, it happens that the contractee under the terms of the contract, supplies some materials which do not affect the contract price. The value of such material should not be debited to Contract Account but a note will have to be kept to account for the quantity received and issued on a separate memorandum record.

Treatment of material in contract costing is as follows :

CONTRACT ACCOUNT

	₹		₹
To Stock of Materials	××	By Material transferred to Another Contract	××
To Material Issued from Stores	××	By Material Returned to Store	××
To Material Purchases at Site	××	By Material Loss	××
To Transfer of Material from Another Contract	××	By Material Sold	××
		By Stock of Material at Site	××

2. Labour or Wages. All labour employed at the contract site should be regarded as direct labour and charged direct to the contract concerned. Where possible, separate wages sheets should be prepared for each contract. If this is not possible, a Wages Analysis Sheet should be prepared wherein should be entered the particulars of the daily or weekly time sheets. The total of each column should be posted to be debit of the appropriate contract. Wages accrued or outstanding at the end of the period should appear on the debit side of the contract account.

3. Site (or Direct) Expenses. All site expenses (other than materials and wages) are charged to individual contract as and when they are incurred.

4. Indirect Expenses (or Overheads). There are certain expenses (such as salaries of engineers, surveyors, supervisors etc. engaged on various contracts, stores expenses, administrative and office expenses) which cannot be directly charged to contracts. Such expenses may be distributed on several contracts on some suitable basis as a percentage of materials or labour.

5. Plant and Machinery. Careful records of plant and machinery must be maintained to ensure that none is lost or improperly disposed of and that the contract is duly charged for the use of plant. There are **two methods** in use for charging contracts for the use made of plant and machinery :

(i) Contract Account debited with full value of the plant and credited with depreciated value at the end. The cost price of the plant or book value of the plant, if the plant is old, is debited to the contract, the corresponding credit being given to the plant account. When the plant is returned, the depreciated value is credited to the contract, the corresponding debit being given to the plant account. This method is used when the plant is required for daily *use at* the site for a long period or when the *plant is likely to work out before the contract is completed*.

This method requires the revaluation of the plant at the close of each financial year, so that the depreciated value may be credited to the contract account. Further, the method does not provide information to check the economic development of the plant. If the plant is charged to a contract, there is a possibility of the plant being retained after the work is completed so that it cannot be used elsewhere.

(ii) Contract account debited with an hourly rate of depreciation. A charge for the use of the plant may be made to the contract on the basis of the time for which the plant is made use of by the contract. To determine the charge to be made an "*Upkeep Account*" should be maintained for each plant to which should be debited the cost of maintenance, depreciation, fuel, oil etc. A *hire rate* is fixed with the help of this account and the contract is charged at this rate. This method is more scientific as compared to the first. This can be easily applied where a machine *is used for a short time*. For costly plants like *cranes* this method is useful as the cranes may be used for some hours only.

When calculating plant at site or in hand, plant returned to store, plant sold, plant destroyed etc. should be taken into consideration as shown below.

VALUE OF PLANT AT SITE

		₹
Cost of plant sent to Site		××
Less : Cost of plant returned to Store	××	
Cost of plant Sold	××	
Cost of Plant destroyed	××	
Cost of plant at site	××	
		××
		××
Less : Depreciation		××
Value of plant at site		××

6. Sub-contracts. Generally work of a specialised character *e.g.,* the installation of lifts, electrical fittings, Door setting and special flooring, is passed out to any other contractor by the main contractor. In such cases the work performed by the sub-contractors forms a direct charge to the contracts concerned. Sub-contract cost will be shown on the debit side of the Contract Account.

7. Extra Work. In most of the contracts additional work or variations of the work originally contracted for, are required by the contractee. The additional work, being outside the original contract, will be subject to a separate charge. If the additional work is quite substantial, it should be treated as a separate contract and a separate account should be opened for it. If it is not very substantial, expenses incurred upon extra work should appear on the debit side of the contract account as 'cost of extra work' and the extra amount which the contractee has agreed to pay should be added to the contract price.

8. Defective Work. If the work done by the contractor is defective, it will not be paid by the contractee. Cost of rectification of such defective work is debited to contract account.

9. Penalties. The contractee may impose penalties on the contract when there is a delay in completion of the contract or there are defects in its execution. In some contracts such penalties are normally anticipated. Normal penalties are debited to Contract Account but abnormal penalties are debited to Costing Profit & Loss Account.

Recording of Value and Profit on Contracts

1. Certificate of Work Done. When a contractor is engaged on a contract for a considerable time, his financial resources could become severely strained. A large amount of working capital would be required if he did not receive payment until the completion of the contract. It is a normal practice particularly in the case of large contracts for the contractee to pay the contractor sums of money on account during the period of the contract. These sums will be paid against certificates by surveyors or architects acting for the contractee certifying the value of work so far performed. Work certification is desired both by contractor and contractee as it helps to monitor the progress of work done, is a basis of payment by the contractee, facilitates estimation of profit and helps to get loan against work certified. In many cases, the terms of the contract provide that the whole of the amount shown by the certificate shall not be paid immediately but a percentage thereof shall be retained by the contractee until some time after the contract is completed. The sum retained is called *retention money*. The object of this retention is to place the contractee in a favourable position, should faulty work arise or penalties become payable by reason of late completion of the contract. If the work has not been certified, the contractee would not make any advance on it. Such work which has been done but not certified is called *work uncertified i.e.,* work done since certification. Work certified and work uncertified will appear on the credit side of the contract account under the heading 'work-in-progress'. If the work certified is not given, cash received from the contractee and retention money are given, the amount of work certified should be calculated first. For example, if ₹ 20,000 is received from the contractee after deducting 20% retention money, work certified will be : ₹ (20,000 × 100) ÷ 80 = ₹ 25,000.

EXAMPLE

I. *Calculate Work Certified* if (*a*) contract price ₹ 4,00,000 work certified 80%. (*b*) Cash received ₹ 8,00,000 being 80% of work certified.

II. *Calculate work uncertified if* : (*a*) Total cost incurred to date ₹ 5,00,000, cost of work certified ₹ 4,00,000. (*b*) Total cost incurred to date ₹ 6,00,000 to complete 60% of the contract work. The architect gave certificate for 50% of the contract price.

III. *Calculate cash received if* : (*a*) Work certified ₹ 8,00,000, Payment received from the Contractee 80%. (*b*) Contract price ₹ 12,00,000, Work certified 80% , Payment received from the Contractee 90%.

SOLUTION

I. (*a*) Work Certified = Contract Price × Work Certified as a percentage of Contract Price.

= ₹ 4,00,000 × 80% = ₹ 3,20,000

(*b*) Work Certified $= \dfrac{\text{Cash Received}}{\text{Cash as percentage of Work Certified}} = \dfrac{₹\,8{,}00{,}000}{80\%}$

= ₹ **10,00,000**

II. (*a*) Cost of Work Uncertified = ₹ 5,00,000 – ₹ 4,00,000 = ₹ **1,00,000**

(*b*) Cost of Work Uncertified $= ₹\,6{,}00{,}000 \times \dfrac{10\%}{60\%}$ = ₹ **1,00,000**

III. (*a*) Cash Received = ₹ 8,00,000 × 80% = ₹ **6,40,000**

(*b*) Cash Received = ₹ 12,00,000 × 80% × 90% = ₹ **8,64,000**

On receipt of certificate, one of the following accounting methods may be adopted :

(*a*) Credit the appropriate contract account with the value mentioned in the certificate and debit personal account of the contractee. Cash received is credited to the contractee's account and the balance is shown as a debtor representing retention money, or

(*b*) The contract account is credited with the value of the certificate and the contractee's account is debited with the amount payable immediately and a special Retention Money Account is debited with amount so retained, or

(*c*) The contract account is credited with the value of the certified work and work-in-progress account is debited. Whenever any amount is received from the contractee, cash account is debited and contractee's account is credited. Until contract is completed, amount received from contractee shows advance payments and is deducted from work-in-progress in the Balance Sheet. When contract is completed, contractee's account is debited with the contract price and the contract account is credited. This method has been adopted in the worked illustrations of this chapter.

Notional Profit

Notional Profit is also treated as estimated profit which can be calculated by subtracting the "Value of Work Certified" and "Cost of Work Certified". A contract may take several years in completion therefore notional profit is calculated every year based on the certified work. Even the cost of work un-certified is also treated as the part of "Value of Contract" for the purpose of calculating the Notional Profit because the organisation will surely collect the cost of work uncertified from customers.

EXAMPLE : A contract is proposed with contract price of ₹ 30 lakhs. ABC Pvt. Ltd. is ready to accept the project with all the prescribed terms and conditions of the contract. At the end of first year cost of work performed by ABC is ₹ 5 lakh and the value of certified work at the end of first year is ₹ 10 lakh. ABC has also incurred cost of ₹ 2 lakh which is not yet certified till the end of first year.

You are required to calculate the Notional Profit of ABC Pvt. Ltd. at the end of first year.

SOLUTION

Particulars	*Amount (₹)*
Value of Work Certified at the end of 1st year	10,00,000.00
Add : Cost of Work not yet Certified at the end of 1st year	2,00,000.00
Total Value of Contract	12,00,000.00

Less : Cost of Work up-to-date	5,00,000.00
Notional Profit at the end of 1st year	7,00,000.00

Estimated Profit

Estimated profit is used to evaluate the overall profitability of the contract based on Contract Price, Cost incurred till date, and estimated additional cost to be incurred to complete the contract. Estimated Profit is likely to arise on the completion of contract and it is the excess of contract price over the estimated total estimated cost of contract (either cost incurred till date or estimated additional cost or any cost for contingency).

EXAMPLE : ABC Pvt. Ltd. is engaged in a construction contract of ₹ 15 lakh and cost of ₹ 8 lakh is already incurred till date. Additional cost of ₹ 3 lakh is expected to complete the contract.

You are required to compute the Estimated Profit of the contract.

SOLUTION

Particulars	*Amount (₹)*
Contract Price	15,00,000.00
Less : Total Cost incurred till date	8,00,000.00
Profit till date	7,00,000.00
Less : Estimated Additional Cost	3,00,000.00
Estimated Profit	4,00,000.00

2. Profit or Loss on Incomplete Contract. Large contracts take a number of years to complete. So their cost can be ascertained only when they are completed. Even after the contract is completed, a proportion of contract price (the retention money) may be still outstanding from the contractee. The retention money is payable in full only when there is no faulty work and the contract is executed in time. So it is not possible to ascertain the profit or loss till the contract is completed and the period fixed for the payment of retention money has expired. Theoretically, therefore, profit or loss on contracts should be brought into account only when the contracts are completed. However, this procedure leads to considerable fluctuations in annual profits of the contractor. The year in which the contract is completed may show unusually large profits and other years may even show losses. Such serious fluctuations *in profits may affect the remuneration or dividend payable to owners*. So, it is desirable to calculate the **notional profit in contract costing** which represents the difference between the value of work certified and cost of work certified.

Notional Profit = Value of work certified – (Cost of work to date – Cost of work not yet certified)

Because of the above considerations, it is felt desirable to take into account a reasonable proportion of the notional profit on incomplete contracts depending upon the completion stage (*i.e.*, the ratio of work certified to total contract price) subject to the following principles :

Principles to be followed While taking Credit for Profit on Complete Contracts

The portion of profit to be credited to costing profit and loss account depends on the stage of completion of a contract. The stage of completion of the contract refers to certified work only and uncertified work is not considered.

The transfer of profit to the costing profit and loss account is done as under :

(*i*) **Contract less than 25% complete :** If the contract has just started or it is less than 25% complete, no profit is taken into account.

(*ii*) **Contract is 25% or more but less than 50% complete :** In this case one third of the notional profit, reduced in the ratio of cash received to work certified, may be transferred to the profit and loss account. The amount of profit to be transferred to the profit and loss account may be determined by using the following formula :

$$\frac{1}{3} \times \text{Notional Profit} \times \frac{\text{Cash Received}}{\text{Work Certified}} \text{ or \% of Cash Received}$$

(*iii*) **Contract is 50% or more but less than 90% complete :** In this case, two third of the notional profit, reduced by the portion of cash received to work certified may be transferred to the profit and loss account. In this case the formula to be used is as under :

$$\frac{2}{3} \times \text{Notional Profit} \times \frac{\text{Cash Received}}{\text{Work Certified}} \text{ or \% of Cash Received}$$

(*iv*) **Contracts nearing completion, say between 90% and 100% complete :** When a contract is nearing completion or 90% or more work has been done on a contract. The amount of profit to be credited to costing profit and loss account may be determined by ***using any one of the following formula.***

(*a*) $\text{Estimated Profit} \times \frac{\text{Work Certified}}{\text{Contract Price}}$

(*b*) $\text{Estimated Profit} \times \frac{\text{Work Certified}}{\text{Contract Price}} \times \frac{\text{Cash Received}}{\text{Work Certified}}$

or $\text{Estimated Profit} \times \frac{\text{Cash Received}}{\text{Contract Price}}$

(*c*) $\text{Estimated Profit} \times \frac{\text{Cost of Work to Date}}{\text{Estimated Total Cost}}$

(*v*) **Loss on Incompleted Contracts.** In the event of a loss on uncompleted contracts, this should be transferred in full to the Profit and Loss Account, whatever be the stage of completion of the contract.

EXAMPLE. A contract expected to be completed in year 4, exhibits the following information:

End of Year	*Value of work certified*	*Cost of work to date*	*Cost of work not yet certified*	*Cash received*
	(₹)	(₹)	(₹)	(₹)
1.	0	50,000	50,000	0
2.	3,00,000	2,30,000	10,000	2,75,000
3.	8,00,000	6,60,000	20,000	7,50,000

The contract price is ₹ 10,00,000 and the estimated profit is 20%.

You are required to calculate, how much profit should have been credited to the Profit and Loss A/c by the end of years 1, 2 and 3.

SOLUTION

End. of year	*Value of Work Certified (₹)*	*Cost of Work Certified**	*National Profit***	*Amount that should have been credited to Profit and Loss A/c by the end of year*
		(₹)	(₹)	(₹)
1	0	0	0	0
2	3,00,000	2,20,000	80,000	$\frac{1}{3} \times 80{,}000 \times \frac{2{,}75{,}000}{3{,}00{,}000} = 24{,}444$
3	8,00,000	6,40,000	1,60,000	$\frac{2}{3} \times 1{,}60{,}000 \times \frac{7{,}50{,}000}{8{,}00{,}000} = 1{,}00{,}000$

Workings :

End of Year	*Completion of Contract*	*Profit Credited to P & L Account*
Year 1	Less than 25 per cent	No Profit Credited
Year 2	25 per cent or more than 25 per cent but less than 50 per cent.	$\text{Cumulative Profit} = \frac{1}{3} \times \text{Notional Profit} \times \frac{\text{Cash Received}}{\text{Value of Work Certified}}$

Year 3	50 per cent or more than 50 per cent but less than 90 per cent.	Cumulative Profit = $\frac{2}{3}$ × Notional Profit × $\frac{\text{Cash Received}}{\text{Value of Work Certified}}$

* Cost of Work Certified = Cost of work to date – Cost of work not yet certified

** Notional Profit = Value of work certified – Cost of work certified)

Valuation of Work-in-Progress

Contracts in progress mean contracts which have not yet been completed. Such uncompleted contracts are also referred to as work-in-progress. All expenditure incurred on the uncompleted contract should be shown on the assets side of the Balance Sheet under the heading 'work-in-progress'. When profit is taken in respect of uncompleted contracts, the work-in-progress stated in the Balance Sheet should also include the profit, *i.e.,* valuation of work-in-progress is done by adding the profit and loss to the cost of the contracts. Suppose, the following is the expenditure on a contract commenced on 1-1-2025.

Materials ₹ 1,20,000, Wages ₹ 1,64,400, Plant ₹ 20,000, Business Charges ₹ 8,600. The work certified and value of materials at the end of the year are ₹ 3,00,000 and ₹ 10,000 respectively. Plant is to be depreciated at 10%. The profit transferred to Profit & Loss Account is ₹ 8,000 out of ₹ 15,000 notional profit. The cost of work done is ₹ 2,85,000 *i.e.,* [₹ 1,20,000 + ₹ 1,64,400 + ₹ 20,000 + ₹ 8,600 – ₹ 18,000 – ₹ 10,000] and the profit transferred to Profit and Loss Account is ₹ 8,000. Therefore, work in progress is ₹ 2,93,000.

Alternately the contractor should prepare Work-in-progress Account. On the debit side of this account work certified and uncertified is shown and on the credit side profit in reserve *i.e.,* the portion of the profit not transferred to Profit and Loss Account is shown, the difference of debit and credit side is work-in-progress. Work-in-Progress Account prepared from example given above will be as under :

WORK IN PROGRESS ACCOUNT

	₹		₹
To Contract A/c	3,00,000	By Contract A/c (Reserve)	7,000
		" Balance c/d	2,93,000
	3,00,000		3,00,000

All cash received on account of such uncompleted contracts should be shown in the Balance Sheet as a deduction from the work-in-progress. The contractee should never be shown as a debtor for the contract price until the contract has been completed. At the same time, he should not be shown as a creditor for the cash received.

If the expenditure on uncompleted contracts includes the value of plant at site and materials at site these items may be shown separately in the Balance Sheet. Thus instead of showing the total expenditure under the heading of work-in-progress, expenditure may be split up and shown, under the headings of 'plant at sites', 'materials at sites' and 'work-in-progress'.

ILLUSTRATION 1. A firm of building contractors began to trade on 1st April, 2024. Following was the expenditure on the contract for ₹ 3,00,000.

Materials issued to contract ₹ 51,000 ; Plant used for contract ₹ 15,000 ; Cost of moving plant, material etc. to the site ₹ 1,000 ; Wages incurred ₹ 80,000 ; Other Expenses incurred ₹ 5,000.

Cash received on account by 31st March, 2025, amounted to ₹ 1,28,000 being 80% of the work certified. Of the plant and materials charged to the contract, plant which cost ₹ 3,000 and materials which cost ₹ 2,500 were lost. On 31st March, 2025 plant which cost ₹ 2,000 was returned to stores, the cost of work done but uncertified was ₹ 1,000 and materials costing ₹ 2,300 were in hand on site.

Charge 15% depreciation on plant, and take to the Profit and Loss Account 2/3 of the profit received. Prepare a Contract Account, Contractee's Account and Extracts from Balance Sheet from the above particulars.

SOLUTION

CONTRACT ACCOUNT

	₹		₹	₹
To Materials	51,000	By Profit & Loss A/c		
" Wages	80,000	Plant Lost	3,000	
" Plant	15,000	Materials Lost	2,500	
" Cost of Moving Plant, Material etc.	1,000			5,500
" Other Expenses	5,000	By Plant Returned to store	2,000	
" Notional Profit c/d	27,000	*Less* : Depreciation	300	
				1,700
		By Plant at site	10,000	
		Less : Depreciation	1,500	
				8,500
		" Materials at site		2,300
		" Work-in-Progress A/c :		
		Work certified	1,60,000	
		Work uncertified	1,000	
				1,61,000
	1,79,000			1,79,000
To Profit & Loss Account : $\left(₹ 27,000 \times \frac{2}{3} \times 80\%\right)$	14,400	By Notional Profit b/d		27,000
" Work-in-progress A/c (Reserve)	12,600			
	27,000			27,000

CONTRACTEE'S ACCOUNT

	₹		₹
To Balance c/d	1,28,000	By Cash	1,28,000

BALANCE SHEET

as on 31st March, 2025

	₹	₹		₹	₹
Profit & Loss A/c	14,400		*Work-in-Progress :*		
Less : Loss of Plant & Materials	5,500		Work Certified	1,60,000	
		8,900	Work Uncertified	1,000	
				1,61,000	
			Less : Reserve	12,600	
				1,48,400	
			Less : Cash received	1,28,000	
					20,400
			Plant *less* Depreciation		10,200
			Materials at site		2,300

Profit on Uncompleted Contracts (Modern Approach)

According to this approach, two methods of calculating the profits on uncompleted contracts are used by contractors. These are :

***(i)* Percentage of Completion Method.** Under this method the profit is determined at the end of each accounting period before the completion of the entire contract.

***(ii)* Completion Contract Method.** Under this method, the profit is recognised only when the contract is completed or substantially completed.

Method *(i)* may be adopted only if the following conditions are satisfied :

(a) The cost attributable to the different stages of completion of the contract activity can be clearly identified. For this purpose each stage of contract should be distinguished as separate cost centre or profit centre. This is necessary to match the cost with the revenue till the stage of completion and to find out the resultant profit attributable to the proportion of work completed.

(b) There must exist adequate estimating process so that both costs to complete the contract and the percentage of contract performance completed at the end of the accounting period can be reliably estimated. The stage of completion can be determined by calculating the proportion that costs incurred to date bear to the estimated total costs of the contract activity.

(c) The costs attributable to the contract generally start with the signing of the contract and end when the contract is nearing completion. Cost incurred before signing a contract is applicable if such cost can be directly associated with a specific contract and there is every probability that the contract will be obtained. The costs may be divided into three classes :

(i) **Costs directly related to a specific contract** as cost of moving equipment to site, site labour costs and supervision, material used for construction, expenses incurred at the site, depreciation of plant and equipment used etc.

(ii) **Costs allocable to contracts** as design, technical assistance, insurance, fabrication of materials elsewhere including overheads etc.

(iii) **Costs apportioned to contracts** as general administration and finance costs, research and development cost, depreciation of idle plant and equipment etc.

(iv) Credit is to be given for the materials and other revenue sources, surplus to requirements transferred to other contracts etc.

(d) Progress payments and advance received from customers cannot generally be treated as equivalent to revenue earned. The revenue is to be based on the percentage of completion of work.

(e) The amount of loss, if any, estimated on the revised estimate of the uncompleted work, is to be deducted from the present revenue.

EXAMPLE 1. M/s Excellent Construction Company Limited under took a contract to construct a building for ₹ 3 crore on 1st September, 2024. On 31st March, 2025 the company found that it had already spent ₹ 1 crore 80 lakhs on the construction. Prudent estimate of additional cost for completion was ₹ 1 crore 40 lakhs. What amount should be charged, to revenue in the final accounts for the year ended on 31st March, 2025 ?

SOLUTION

CALCULATION OF ESTIMATED COST OF CONSTRUCTION

	₹ in crores
Cost of Construction incurred till date	1.80
Add : Estimated Future Cost	1.40
Total Estimated Cost of Construction	3.20

Percentage of Completion of Contract till date to total estimated cost of construction

= ₹ (1./80/3.20) × 100 = 56.25%

Proportion of Total Contract Value Recognised as Revenue

= Contract Price × Percentage of Completion

= ₹ 3 crores × 56.25% = ₹ 1.6875 crores

EXAMPLE 2. Ms Highway. Constructions undertook the construction of a highway on 1-4-2024. The contract was to be completed in 2 years. The contract price was estimated at ₹ 150 crores. Up to 31-3-2025 the company incurred ₹ 120 crores on the construction. The engineering involved in the project estimated that a further ₹ 45 crores would be incurred for completing the work.

What amount should be charged to revenue for the year 2024-25 ? Show the extract of the Profit & Loss A/c in the books of M/s High way Constructions. ***(CA IPCE May, 2014 Modified)***

SOLUTION

STATEMENT SHOWING THE AMOUNT TO BE CHARGED TO REVENUE

	₹ in crores
Cost of Construction incurred upto 31-3-2025	120
Add : Estimated Future Cost	45
Total Estimated Cost of Construction	165
Degree of Completion (120/165 × 100)	72.73%
Revenue Recognised (72.73% of 150)	109 (approx.)
Total Foreseeable Loss (165 – 150)	15
Less : Loss for the Current year (120 – 109)	11
Loss to be provided for	4

PROFIT AND LOSS ACCOUNT (EXTRACT)

	₹ in crores		*₹ in crores*
To Construction Costs	120	By Contact Price	109
To Provision for Loss	4	By Net Loss	15
	124		124

Work-in-Progress

The total expenditure cumulative to the year end is treated as work-in-progress, if no profit is taken in the accounts. The amount of profit is to be added to the progress cost, if profit is included for the adoption of the percentage of completion method. For Balance Sheet purposes, payments received from the contractee from time to time is normally taken separately as advance and shown on the Liabilities side of the Balance Sheet. Alternatively, the advance may be deducted from the Cost (and profit) and only one figure kept on the assets side.

ILLUSTRATION 2. A large contract is to be completed in five stages. The completion stage at the end of an accounting period shows the present position. It is a fixed price contract without any escalation clause.

Phases	*Estimate*		*Actual Cost*	*Contract Price*
	Original	*Revised up-to-date*		
	₹	₹	₹	₹
1. Certified	60,000	64,000	62,000	80,000
2. Completed but not certified	20,000	22,000	21,000	30,000

3. Completed 75%	20,000	22,000	16,600	26,000
4. Completed 25%	40,000	48,000	12,400	60,000
5. Incomplete	24,000	30,000	—	28,000
	1,64,000	1,86,000	1,12,000	2,24,000

Evaluate the profit to be taken in the accounts of the period if the contractor adopts (*a*) The percentage of completion method (*b*) The completed contract method. Also show the work-in-progress in the Balance Sheet, if ₹ 80,000 is received as final payment for completion of first phase.

SOLUTION

(*a*)

Phase	*Actual cost* ₹	*% of completion*	*Balance estimate* ₹	*Total* ₹	*Contract Price* ₹	*Profit (Loss)* ₹
1	62,000		—	62,000	80,000	18,000
2	21,000		—	21,000	30,000	9,000
3	16,600	25%	5,500	22,100	26,000	
4	12,400	75%	36,000	48,400	60,000	
5	—	100%	30,000	30,000	28,000	(2,000)
						25,000

(*b*) No profit can be taken into account till all phases are complete.

BALANCE SHEET

Liabilities	*Under (a)* ₹	*Under (b)* ₹	*Assets*	*Under (a)* ₹	*Under (b)* ₹
Advance*	80,000	80,000	Work-in-progress (1,12,000 + 25,000 Profit)	1,37,000	1,12,000

Note. *Advance can also be deducted from the work-in-progress on the assets side of the Balance Sheet.

ILLUSTRATION 3. Nirman Ltd. follows the 'percentage of completion' method for recognising revenue on construction contracts. From the following particulars made available to you, you are required to determine the results of contracts X, Y and Z to be included in the Profit and Loss Account of the Company for the year ended 31st March, 2025.

₹ in crores

Contract	*X*	*Y*	*Z*
Date of commencement	15.4.2024	1.10.2024	5.8.2023
Expected date of completion	15.5.2025	1.7.2025	30.4.2025
Contract value	₹ 313.00	1,247.00	80.00
Advance received and outstanding	20.60	120.00	3.00
Value of work certified	250.00	47.00	75.00
Value of work done but not certified	16.50	20.00	1.00
Progress of payments received (net of advance recovery)	168.00	42.30	52.00
Costs incurred till 31-3-2025	239.00	75.00	72.00
Estimate of costs to complete	27.00	—	9.00
Profits recognised till 31-3-2024	—	—	1.50

SOLUTION

	Contract X ₹	Contract Y ₹	Contract Z ₹
(A) Cost incurred till 31.3.2025	2,39,00,00,000	75,00,00,000	72,00,00,000
(B) Estimated cost till completion	27,00,00,000	Unascertainable	9,00,00,000
(C) Total Estimated cost	2,66,00,00,000	Unascertainable	81,00,00,000
(D) Total Contract Value	3,13,00,00,000	12,47,00,00,000	80,00,00,000
(E) Expected Profit/Loss on Contract (D – C)	47,00,00,000	Unascertainable	(1,00,00,000)
(F) Proportionate revenue to be recognised till 31-3-2025 $\left[E \times \frac{(A)}{(C)}\right]$	42,22,93,333	Unascertainable	(1,00,00,000)
(G) Revenue recognised till previous year end	Nil	Nil	1,50,00,000
(H) To be recognised for 2024-25 (F – G)	42,22,93,333	Unascertainable	(2,50,00,000)

Notes :

(1) As the *Contract X* is to be completed soon after close of the accounting year, 100% of the estimated profit can be recognised.

(2) *Contract Y* is in very initial stage. As such it will be carried in books at cost. It will be imprudent to take into account any profit.

(3) *Contract Z* anticipates a loss of ₹ 1 crore on completion. A loss estimate needs to be recognised in full and not just in proportion to cost done. Further till 31.3.2024 a profit of ₹ 1.5 crore was already recognised. Hence 2024-25 accounts will show a loss of ₹ 2.5 crores to set right the cumulative position.

Cost Plus Contract

Cost plus contract is a contract in which the value of the contract is ascertained by adding a certain percentage of profit over the total cost of the work. It is generally adopted in those cases where the probable cost of the contract cannot be computed in advance with a reasonable degree of accuracy. Such contracts are undertaken for production of special articles not usually manufactured, *e.g.*, production of newly designed aircraft component or in case of urgent repairs of ships, vehicles, power house, etc. or in case of construction during war time. Government prefers to give contract on cost plus basis.

Such contracts are advantageous both to the contractor and the contractee. From the *contractor's point of view*, this method protects him from the risks of fluctuations in market prices of material, labour and other services. He knows in advance, the profit he can expect on the order when completed. Moreover, there is no risk of incurring loss on the contracts as all agreed costs are recovered. If the contractor is unscrupulous, he may deliberately inflate cost in order to obtain higher profits. In order to avoid disputes in future, he must settle the admissible costs such as supervision, fixed overhead and losses such as allowances for wastage, scrap, normal loss etc. When bills are tendered, the burden of proving each item charged, falls on the shoulders of the manufacturer. However, this system may put a premium on inefficiency in so far as the contractor whose costs are highest, obtains highest profit. There is no incentive to find more efficient methods of production or to reduce costs, as the contractor can obtain no benefit from any saving thereby effected.

From *contractee's point of view*, this method ensures that the price paid will depend on cost rather than on arbitrary commitment to a specific price. Thus in uncertain market the contractee is suitably fortified and he pays only reasonable price. This method is suitable when he provides raw materials, tools, etc., to contractor. In general, it is observed that the cost to the buyer tends to be higher than the cost which could be obtained by other forms of contract.

ILLUSTRATION 4. A Car Manufacturing Company undertook on cost plus basis an order from a transport company for the overhaul of 100 engines. Spare parts of engines were to be supplied by the transport company. It was agreed that the basic cost would be negotiated on the basis of the actual cost of overhaul of the first ten engines.

The manufacturing company submitted the following actual cost after overhauling the first ten engines :

Cost per Engine : (1) Direct labour cost ₹ 150 ; (2) Variable overhead @ 100% on direct labour ₹ 150 ; (3) Miscellaneous supplies ₹ 10 ; (4) Stores overhead ₹ 50 ; (5) Fixed overhead @ 100 per cent on direct labour ₹ 150

The variable, fixed and stores overhead rates are those normally applied by the company. In reviewing the items of expenses included in the various classes of overhead it was noticed.

(*a*) Variable overhead included advertisement expenses of ₹ 3 lakhs and share of tooling expenses of ₹ 1 lakh for its own make of cars.

(*b*) Fixed overhead included depreciation amounting to ₹ 5 lakh for a special purpose plant solely used for the manufacture of bodies of its own make of car.

(*c*) Stores overhead included expenses of purchases department and stores organisation.

As the Accountant of the transport company, what advice would you give to your Managing Director about the resonableness or otherwise of the cost claimed by the manufacturing company ?

SOLUTION

The Car Manufacturing Company has undertaken the work of overhauling of the engines on cost plus basis. Since the spare parts are to be supplied by the customer, it is finally a maintenance job and no store-keeping or purchasing is involved for spare parts. As such the stores overheads should not be allowed to be charged except for a normal sum for miscellaneous supplies.

Variable overheads include advertisement expenses of ₹ 3 lakhs. The advertisement expense has nothing to do with overhauling of engines and it appears that the advertisement cost is purely for promoting the sales of the car of the company. So the expense is to be disallowed. Similarly the tooling expenses of ₹ 1 lakh for its own make of cars has no concern with overhauling and must be disallowed.

Fixed expenses include depreciation of ₹ 5 lakhs for a special purpose plant. This plant is for the car making and not one intended for overhauling. As such, it cannot be included in the cost of overhauling estimate.

As we have no information of total variable overheads and total fixed overheads, let us assume ₹ 10 lakhs each. In this case the variable expenses after disallowing advertisement and tooling expenses are reduced to ₹ 6,00,000 *i.e.*, 60%. Similarly, after disallowing ₹ 5 lakhs for plant depreciation, the fixed overheads come down ₹ 5 lakhs, *i.e.*, 50%. Now we can work out an estimated cost per engine as follows :

	Cost per engine
	₹
1. Direct labour cost	150
2. Variable overhead @ 60% on direct labour	90
3. Miscellaneous supplies	10
4. Stores overhead say 50% of misc. supplies	5
5. Fixed overhead @ 50% of direct labour after eluminating depreciation of special purpose plant	75
Total	330

Escalation Clause

This is a clause which is provided in the contract to cover up any changes in the price of the contract due to changes in the price of raw materials and labour or change in utilisation of factor of production. The object of this clause is to safeguard the interest on both sides against unfavourable change in the prices. Thus, in a contract with the transport undertaking, it may be provided that the price per ton-mile will increase or decrease for each rise or fall of price of petrol by 10% of the prevailing price. Here the contractor has to produce sufficient proof of excess costs before the customer agrees to reimburse such cost. Moreover, the basis on which the factor prices are based, is laid down in the contract.

ILLUSTRATION 5. The escalation clause of a Construction Contract runs as under :

You will be allowed escalation on this contract at the net consumption of 50 kgs. of Steel, 1,000 kgs. of cement and 80 C.M. of aggregate per 100 C.M. of R.C.C. with a margin of 5 per cent in steel, 5 per cent in cement and 12·5% in aggregate. The variation in price will be based on those ruling on the base date *viz.*

₹ 650 per tonne of steel ; and ₹ 120 per tonne of cement ; and ₹ 50 per 100 C.M. of aggregate.

The contract is for 4 lakhs C.M. of R.C.C. and the average price per unit quantity of materials consumed indicated an increase of 15 per cent in steel, 20 per cent in cement and a decrease of 5 per cent in aggregate, while the consumption of materials showed an excess of 12·5 per cent of the quantity admissible for each material (exclusive of margin), and 20% increase in aggregate.

Find the material cost variation contributed by (*a*) price and (*b*) consumption. Workout the claim to be preferred against the purchaser.

SOLUTION

	Consumption				*Price*	*Cost*
	Net	*Margin*		*Gross*		
					₹	₹
Steel (tonne)	200	5%	10	210	650	1,36,500
Cement (tonne)	4,000	5%	200	4,200	120	5,04,000
Aggregate (100 cm.)	3,200	12·5%	400	3,600	50	1,80,000
Total						8,20,500

MATERIAL COST VARIANCE

	Estimate			*Actual*			*Variance* (1)	
	Qty.	*Price*	*Cost*	*Qty.*	*Price*	*Cost*	*Price*	*Consumption*
	1	2	3	4	5	6	7	8
		₹	₹		₹	₹	₹	₹
Steel (Tonne)	210	650	1,36,500	225	747.50	1,68,187.50	21,937.50	9,750
Cement (Tonne)	4,200	120	5,04,000	4,500	144.00	6,48,000.00	1,08,000.00	36,000
Aggregate (100 cm.)	3,600	50	1,80,000	3,840	47.50	1,82,400.00	–9,600.00	12,000
			8,20,500			9,98,587.50	1,20,337.50	57,750

Claim to be preferred :

			₹
Steel	210 @ ₹ 97.50	= ₹ 20,475	
Cement	4,200 @ ₹ 24.00	= ₹ 1,00,800	
			1,21,275
Less : Aggregate 3,600 @ ₹ 2.50 =			9,000
			₹ 1,12,275

(1) Price Variance = Actual Qty. × Difference in Price
Consumption Variance = Estimated Price × Difference in Qty.

Target Costing

Under this method the targets of volume of production and targets of various expenditures of production are fixed before hand and constant efforts are made not to exceed the expenditure targets unless there is a corresponding increase in the volume of production over the target fixed. *Thus, the contractor receives an agreed sum of profit over his predetermined costs.* If actual costs are below the target fixed, the contractor is entitled to a bonus which is a proportion of saving thus made.

EXAMPLE. Sky Limited are Heavy Engineering Contractors specialising in construction of Flyovers. The company just entered into a contract with a local municipal corporation for building a flyover. No activity has started on this contract.

As per the terms of the contract, Dee Limited will receive an additional ₹ 50 lakhs if the construction of the flyover were to be finished within a period of two years from the commencement of the contract. The Accountant of Dee Limited wants to recognise this revenue since in the past the company has been able to meet similar targets very easily.

With reference to relevant Accounting Standard, discuss whether the accountant's proposal to recognise incentive receipt as contract revenue is correct or not.

SOLUTION

'Construction Contracts', incentive payments are additional amounts payable to the contractor if specified performance standards are met or exceeded. For example, a contract may allow for an incentive payment to the contractor for early completion of the contract. Incentive payments are included in contract revenue when both the conditions are met :

(*i*) the contract is sufficiently advanced that it is portable that the specified performance standards will be met or exceeded; and

(*ii*) the amount of the incentive payment can be measured reliably.

In the given problem, the contract has not even begun and hence the contract (Sky Limited) should not recognise any revenue of this contract. Therefore, the accountant's contention for recognising ₹ 50 lakhs as revenue is not correct.

MISCELLANEOUS ILLUSTRATIONS

ILLUSTRATION 6. A contractor secured a contract to supply and erect machinery for the sum of ₹ 7,50,000. He was to receive payments on account from time to time equal to 90% of the certified value of the work done.

He commenced work on 1st January, 2024 and incurred the following expenditure during the year : Plant and Tools ₹ 70,000 ; Machinery & Stores ₹ 2,00,000 ; Wages ₹ 1,50,000 ; Sundry Expenses ₹ 30,000 and Establishment Charges ₹ 40,000.

A part of machinery costing ₹ 20,000 was unsuitable to the contract and immediately sold at a profit of ₹ 5,000.

The value of Plant and Tools on 31st December, 2024 was ₹ 40,000 and the value of Machinery & Stores in hand ₹ 30,000.

By 31st January, 2025 he had received payments on account amounting to ₹ 4,38,750 being 90% of the certified value of work done upto 31st Dec., 2024.

In order to calculate the profit made on the contract upto 31st Dec., 2024 the contractor estimated the further expenditure that would be incurred in completing the contract and took to the credit of Profit and Loss A/c for the year that proportion of the estimated net profit to be realised on contract which the certified value of the work done bore to the contract price. He estimated :

(*a*) That contract would be completed in a further period of six months.

(*b*) That Plant and Tools would have a residual value of ₹ 10,000 upon the completion of the contract.

(*c*) That the cost of Machinery and Stores required in addition to those in stock on 31st December, 2024 would be ₹ 1,00,000 and that further Sundry Expenses of ₹ 20,000 would be incurred.

(*d*) That the wages on the contract for the 6 months to 30th June, 2025 would amount to ₹ 80,000.

(*e*) That the Establishment would cost the same sum per month as in the previous year.

(*f*) That $2\frac{1}{2}\%$ of the total cost of the contract (excluding this percentage) should be provided for contingencies.

Prepare Contract Account for the year ended 31st December, 2024 and show your calculations of the Profit & Loss A/c for the year.

SOLUTION

CONTRACT ACCOUNT

for the year ended 31st December, 2024

	₹		₹
To Plant & Tools	70,000	By Sale of Plant	25,000
To Machinery & Stores	2,00,000	By Work-in-progress :	
" Wages	1,50,000	Work Certified $\left(₹ 4,38,750 \times \frac{100}{90}\right)$	4,87,500
" Sundry Expenses	30,000		
" Establishment Charges	40,000		
" Profit & Loss A/c		" Plant & Tools in hand	40,000
(Profit on sale of plant)	5,000	" Machinery and Stores in hand	30,000
" Notional Profit c/d	87,500		
	5,82,500		5,82,500
To Profit & Loss A/c*	34,450	By Notional Profit b/d	87,500
" Work-in-progress A/c (Reserve)	53,050		
	87,500		87,500

* Profit to be credited to Profit and Loss Account has been calculated as under :

	₹	₹
Cost to date		4,90,000
Less : Cost of plant sold		20,000
		4,70,000
Estimated further expenditure :		
Machinery & Stores	1,00,000	
Sundry Expenses	20,000	
Wages	80,000	
Establishment Charges	20,000	
		2,20,000
		6,90,000
Less : Residual value of plant		10,000
		6,80,000
Provision for contingencies ($2\frac{1}{2}\%$ on ₹ 6,80,000)		17,000
Estimated Total Cost		6,97,000
Profit (Estimated)		53,000
Contract Price		7,50,000

∴ Profit to be credited to Profit & Loss Account

$$= \text{Estimated Profit} \times \frac{\text{Work Certified}}{\text{Total Contract Price}} = ₹\ 53{,}000 \times \frac{₹\ 4{,}87{,}500}{₹\ 7{,}50{,}000} = ₹\ 34{,}450.$$

ILLUSTRATION 7. Modern Construction Ltd. commenced a contract on 1st Jan, 2024. The total contract was for ₹ 10,00,000 (estimated by the contractor) and was accepted by Modern Construction Ltd. at 10% less. It was decided to estimate the total profit and to take to the credit of Profit & Loss A/c the proportion of estimated profit on cash basis which the work completed bore to the total contract. Actual expenditure in 2024 and estimated expenditure in 2025 are given below :

	2024 *(Actual)* ₹	*2025* *(Estimated)* ₹
Materials	1,50,000	2,60,000
Labour : Paid	1,00,000	1,20,000
Accrued	10,000	—
Plant purchased	80,000	—
Expenses	40,000	71,000
Plant returned to store on 31st Dec. (cost)	20,000	50,000 (on 30/9/2025)
Materials at site	10,000	—
Work certified	4,00,000	Full
Work uncertified	15,000	—
Cash received	3,00,000	Full

The plant is subject to annual depreciation @ 20% of cost. The contract is likely to be completed on 30 Sept., 2025. Prepare the Contract Account. Assume that the plant costing ₹ 10,000 has been exhausted on the contract site during the course of second year and may be treated as a normal loss.

SOLUTION

CONTRACT ACCOUNT

		₹			₹
To Materials	₹	1,50,000	By Plant returned to store		
To Labour : Paid	1,00,000		(₹ 20,000 – Dep. ₹ 4,000)		16,000
Accrued	10,000		By Plant at site		
		1,10,000	(₹ 60,000 – Dep. ₹ 12,000)		48,000
To Plant		80,000	By Materials at site		10,000
To Expenses		40,000	By Work-in-Progress :	₹	
To Notional Profit c/d		1,09,000	Work certified	4,00,000	
			Work uncertified	15,000	
					4,15,000
		4,89,000			4,89,000
To Profit and Loss A/c $\left(\frac{₹\ 1{,}27{,}500^{*}}{₹\ 9{,}00{,}000} \times ₹\ 4{,}00{,}000 \times 75\%\right)$		42,500	By Notional Profit b/d		1,09,000
To Work-in-Progress (Reserve)		66,500			
		1,09,000			1,09,000

*The figure has been arrived at after preparing an Estimated Contract Account.

ESTIMATED CONTRACT ACCOUNT

(2024-25)

	₹		₹	₹
To Materials (₹ 1,50,000 + ₹ 2,60,000)	4,10,000	By Plant returned to store :		
To Labour (₹ 1,10,000 + ₹ 1,10,000)	2,20,000	on 31-12-2024	16,000	
To Plant	80,000	on 30-9-2025	32,500	

	₹		₹
To Expenses	1,11,000	(₹ 50,000 – ₹ 17,500 Dep.	
To Profit made to date	1,27,500	for 21 months)	48,500
		By Contractee's Account	9,00,000
	9,48,500		9,48,500

ILLUSTRATION 8. Construction Ltd. commenced work on a contract worth ₹ 40 crores on 1st April, 2023. During 2023-24, they purchased construction materials worth ₹ 9.2 crores. During the same period, wages to the tune of ₹ 6 crores were paid. Site overheads for the period amounted to ₹ 1.50 crores.

The company hired plant from an associated concern. The plant was valued at the commencement of contract and at periodic intervals. Plant valued at ₹ 2.5 crores was introduced on 1st April, 2023. The valuation on 31st March, 2024 stood at ₹ 60 lakhs. This was after the plant-scrap was sold for ₹ 15 lakhs which Construction Ltd. was allowed to remain. Certain materials worth ₹ 30 lakhs were found to be unsuitable for the contract and had to be sold at a loss of 20%. On 31st March, 2024, the value of materials on hand stood at ₹ 55 lakhs. Work certified for the year was ₹ 20 crores against which 75% payment had been received from the contractee. Work done but not certified as on 31st March, 2024 was ₹ 3 crores (at cost). The same was subsequently certified for ₹ 3.5 crores.

The expected date of completion of the contract is 31st December, 2024. The estimated expenditure on wages during 2024-25, till completion of the contract, is ₹ 5 crores. Site overheads are expected to incur at 10% extra per month costs over 2023-24 figures. Besides the materials in stock on 31st March, 2024, a further ₹ 8.5 crores worth of materials would be necessary to complete the contract. Fresh plant valued at ₹ 1.5 crores is expected to be introduced during 2024-25 and the residual value of this, at the completion of work, will be ₹ 40 lakhs. It is the policy of the company to provide for 2% of the contract value as contingencies and closing down expenses.

Prepare, from the details given, Construction Materials Account, Plant Account and Contract Account for 2023-24. Profits are to be based in proportion to costs incurred in line with the relevant international accounting standard.

SOLUTION

CONSTRUCTION MATERIALS ACCOUNT

2023-24	₹	2023-24	₹
To Purchases	9,20,00,000	By Bank $\left(₹\,30,00,000 \times \frac{80}{100}\right)$	24,00,000
		By Loss on Sale of Materials transferred to Profit & Loss A/c	6,00,000
		By Contract A/c (Bal. Figure)	8,35,00,000
		By Balance c/d (Closing Stock)	55,00,000
	9,20,00,000		9,20,00,000

PLANT ACCOUNT

2023-24	₹	2023-24	₹
To Associated Company	2,50,00,000	By Contract A/c (Bal. Figure)	1,90,00,000
		By Balance c/d	60,00,000
	2,50,00,000		2,50,00,000

CONTRACT ACCOUNT

2023-24	₹	2023-24	₹
To Construction Materials	8,35,00,000	By Bank (Sale of Plant—Scrap)	15,00,000

	₹		₹
To Plant (used)	1,90,00,000	By Work-in-Progress A/c : ₹	
To Wages	6,00,00,000	Work Certified 20,00,00,000	
To Site Overheads	1,50,00,000	Work Uncertified 3,00,00,000	
Cost to date	17,75,00,000		23,00,00,000
To Notional Profit c/d	5,40,00,000		
	23,15,00,000		23,15,00,000
To Profit & Loss A/c (See Working Note)	2,29,40,300	By Notional Profit b/d	5,40,00,000
To Work-in-Progress A/c (Reserve)	3,10,59,700		
	5,40,00,000		5,40,00,000

Working Note :

CALCULATION OF ESTIMATED PROFIT ON TOTAL CONTRACT

	₹	₹
Contract Price		40,00,00,000
Less : Cost to date upto 31-3-2024	17,75,00,000	
Less : Sale of Plant—scrap	15,00,000	
Net cost to date upto 31-3-2024	17,60,00,000	
Add : Further cost to be incurred from 1-4-2024 to 31-12-2024 for the completion of the contract :		
Material in hand on 31-3-2024 to be used	55,00,000	
Plant in hand on 31-3-2024 to be used	60,00,000	
Further material required	8,50,00,000	
Wages estimated	5,00,00,000	
Fresh plant required	1,50,00,000	
Site Overheads for 9 months $\left(\frac{₹\ 1,50,00,000}{12} \times 9 \times \frac{110}{100}\right)$	1,23,75,000	
	34,98,75,000	
Less : Residual value of plant	40,00,000	
	34,58,75,000	
Add : Provision for contingencies and closing down expenses : 2% on ₹ 40 crores the contract price	80,00,000	
Total Estimated Cost	35,38,75,000	35,38,75,000
Total Estimated Profit on Total Contract		4,61,25,000

Calculation of Profit to be transferred to Profit and Loss A/c for the year 2023-24

$$\frac{\text{Cost to date}}{\text{Total Estimated Cost}} \times \text{Estimated Profit}$$

$$\frac{₹\ 17,60,00,000}{₹\ 35,38,75,000} \times ₹\ 4,61,25,000 = ₹\ 2,29,40,300.$$

ILLUSTRATION 9. A contractor, who prepares his account on 31st December each year, commenced a contract on 1st April, 2024. The costing records concerning the said contract reveal the following information on 31st December, 2024 :

Materials charged to site ₹ 2,58,100 ; Labour engaged ₹ 5,60,500 ; Foremen's salary ₹ 79,300.

Plants costing ₹ 2,60,000 had been on site for 146 days. Their working life is estimated at 7 years and their final scrap value at ₹ 15,000. A supervisor, who is paid ₹ 4,000 p.m., has devoted approximately three-fourths of his time to this contract. The administrative and other expenses amount to ₹ 1,40,000. Materials in hand at site on 31st December, 2024 cost ₹ 25,400. Some of the material costing ₹ 4,500 was found unsuitable and was sold for ₹ 4,000 and a part of the plant costing ₹ 5,500 (on 31-12-2024) unsuited to the contract was sold at a profit of ₹ 1,000.

The contract price was ₹ 22,00,000 but it was accepted by the contractor for ₹ 20,00,000. On 31st December, 2024, two-thirds of the contract price agreed to be paid was completed. Architect's certificate had been issued covering 50% of the cost of contract and ₹7,50,000 had so far been paid on account. Prepare Contract Account and state how much profit or loss according to conventional approach should be included in the financial accounts to 31st December, 2024. Workings should be clearly given. Depreciation is charged on time basis.

Also prepare Contractee's Account and show how these accounts would appear in the Balance Sheet as on 31st December, 2024.

SOLUTION

CONTRACT ACCOUNT

(for the period between 1st April & 31st Dec. 2024)

	₹			₹
To Materials	2,58,100	By Materials at Site		25,400
To Labour	5,60,500	By Bank (Material sold)		4,000
To Foremen's Salary	79,300	By Profit & Loss A/c (Loss on material sold)		500
To Supervisor's Salary $\left(\frac{3}{4} \times ₹\ 4{,}000 \times 9 \text{ months}\right)$	27,000	By Cost of Work Done c/d		10,49,000
To Depreciation of Plant $\left(\frac{₹\ 2{,}60{,}000 - ₹\ 15{,}000}{7} \times \frac{146}{365}\right)$	14,000			
To Administration & Other Expenses	1,40,000			
	10,78,900			10,78,900
To Cost of Work Done b/d	10,49,000	By Work-in-Progress :	₹	
To Notional Profit c/d	2,13,250	Work Certified	10,00,000	
		Work Uncertified	(1) 2,62,250	12,62,250
	12,62,250			12,62,250
To Profit & Loss A/c $\left(\frac{2}{3} \times ₹\ 2{,}13{,}250 \times \frac{₹\ 7{,}50{,}000}{₹\ 10{,}00{,}000}\right)$	1,06,625	By Notional Profit b/d		2,13,250
To Work in Progress (Reserve)	1,06,625			
	2,13,250			2,13,250

CONTRACTEE'S ACCOUNT

	₹		₹
To Balance c/d	7,50,000	By Cash	7,50,000

BALANCE SHEET AS ON 31ST DECEMBER, 2024

(Extracts only)

Liabilities	₹	*Assets*		₹
Profit & Loss A/c		*Work-in-Progress* :	₹	
(₹ 1,06,625 + ₹ 1,000		Work Certified	10,00,000	
Profit on Sale of Plant		Work Uncertified	2,62,250	
– ₹ 500 Loss on			12,62,250	
Sale of Material)	1,07,125	*Less* : Reserve	1,06,625	
			11,55,625	
		Less : Cash received	7,50,000	4,05,625
		Materials at Site		25,400
		Plant at Site		
		(₹ 2,60,000 + ₹ 1,000 Profit – ₹ 14,000		
		Depreciation – ₹ 6,500 Cash Sale)		2,40,500

Working Note :

(1) *Cost of Work Uncertified*

Cost of 2/3rd of the Contract ₹ 10,49,000

Hence Total Cost of the Contract = ₹ 10,49,000 $\times \frac{3}{2}$ = ₹ 15,73,500

The cost of 50% of the contract which has been completed and certified by the architect is ₹ 7,86,750 (₹ 15,73,500 ÷ 2)

The cost of the contract, which has been completed but not certified by the architect is ₹ 2,62,250 (*i.e.* ₹ 10,49,000 – ₹ 7,86,750)

Indian Accounting Standard–(Ind. As–115)—Revenue from Contracts with Customers. The main provisions of this standard have been given in separate chapter.

EXAMPLE

GTI Ltd. negotiates with Bharat Oil Corporation Ltd. (BOCL), for construction of "Retail Petrol & Diesel Outlet Stations". Based on proposals submitted to different Regional Offices of BOCL, the final approval for one outlet each in Region X, Region Y, Region Z is awarded to GTI Ltd. A single agreement is entered into between two. The agreement lays down values for each of the three outlets *i.e.*, ₹ 102 lacs, ₹ 150 lacs, ₹ 130 lacs for Region X, Region Y, Region Z respectively. Agreement also lays down completion time for each Region.

Comment whether GTI Ltd. will treat it as single contract or three separate contracts.

(CA – Inter Nov. 2016)

SOLUTION

When a contract covers number of assets, the construction of each asset should be treated as a separate construction contract when :

(*a*) separate proposals have been submitted for each asset ;

(*b*) each asset has been subject to separate negotiation and the contractor and customer have been able to accept or reject that part of the contract relating to each asset ; and

(*c*) the costs and revenues of each asset can be identified.

In the given case, each outlet is submitted as a separate proposal to different Zonal Offices, which can be separately negotiated, and costs and revenues thereof can be separately identified. Hence, each asset will be treated as a "single contract" even if there is one single agreement for contracts.

Therefore, three separate contract accounts must be recorded and maintained in the books of GTI Ltd. For each contract, principles of revenue and cost recognition must be applied separately and net income will be determined for each asset.

ILLUSTRATION 10. A firm of contractors obtained a contract for construction of bridges across river Revathi. Following details are available in the records kept for the year ended 31st March, 2025 :

	₹ (in lakhs)		₹ (in lakhs)
Total Contract Price	1,000	Estimated further cost to completion	495
Work Certified	500	Progress Payment Received	400
Work not certified	105	To be Received	140

The firm seeks your advice and assistance in the presentation of accounts keeping in view the requirements of "Accounting for Construction Contracts" issued by the Institute of the Chartered Accountants of India.

SOLUTION

(a) Amount of Foreseeable Loss

	(₹ in lakhs)
Work Certified	500
Work Uncertified	105
Estimated Further Cost to Completion	495
Total Cost of Construction	1,100
Less : Total Contract Price	1,000
Total Forseeable Loss	100

Note : A forseeable loss on the entire contract should be provided for in the financial statements irrespective of the amount of work done and the method of accounting followed. (Para 35 of AS-7).

(b) Construction Work-in-Progress i.e. Costs Incurred to Date

	₹ (in lakhs)
Work Certified	500
Work Uncertified	105
Construction Work-in-Progress	605
Total Cost of Construction as per (*a*)	1,100
% of Construction Work-in-Progress $\left(\frac{605}{1,100} \times 100\right)$	55%

(c) Proportion of Total Contract Value Recognised as Revenue as per Para 10(b) (ii) of AS-7

55% of ₹ 1,000 lakhs = ₹ 550 lakhs

	₹ in lakhs
Revenue Recognised	550
Less : Cost of Construction Work-in-Progress	605
Loss to be shown in the Profit and Loss for 2024-25	55

(d) Disclosure Requirements as per AS-7

	₹ in lakhs
(*i*) Cost incurred to date on Work-in-Progress	605
Less : Transferred to Profit & Loss A/c as Cost of Sales	605
	Nil

(*ii*) Profit & Loss A/c (Extract)

Revenue	550
Less : Cost of Sales	605
Loss	55
Add : Provision for loss on contract (Bal. Fig.)	45
Net loss including forseeable loss	100

(*iii*) Balance Sheet (Extract)

Debtors (*i.e.* revenue recognised)	550
Less : Progress payment received and receivable (400 + 140)	540
	10

ILLUSTRATION 11. On 1st December, 2024, Vishwakarma Construction Co. Ltd. undertook a contract to construct a building for ₹ 85 lakhs. On 31st March, 2025 the company found that it had already spent ₹ 64,99,000 on the construction. Prudent estimate of additional cost for completion was ₹ 32,01,000. What is the additional provision for foreseeable loss, which must be made in the final accounts for the year ended 31st March, 2025 ? ***(CA Final)***

SOLUTION

	₹
Cost incurred till 31st March, 2025	64,99,000
Add : Prudent estimate of additional cost for completion	32,01,000
Total Cost of Construction	97,00,000
Less : Contract Price	85,00,000
Total Foreseeable Loss	12,00,000

Contract Work in Progress = $\frac{₹\ 64{,}99{,}000}{₹\ 97{,}00{,}000} \times 100 =$ **67%**

Proportion of total contract value recognised as turnover = 67% of ₹ 85,00,000 = ₹ 56,95,000

Loss to be recognised in one year ended 31st march, 2025 = ₹ 64,99,000 – ₹ 56,95,000 = ₹ **8,04,000**

Since the total foreseeable loss is ₹ 12,00,000, an additional provision of ₹ 3,96,000 is required to be made.

ILLUSTRATION 12. An amount of ₹ 9,90,000 was incurred on a contract work upto 31-3-2025. Certificates have been received to date to the value of ₹ 12,00,000 against which ₹ 10,80,000 has been received in cash. The cost of work done but not certified amounted to ₹ 22,500. It is estimated that by spending an additional amount of ₹ 60,000 (including provision for contingencies) the work can be completed in all respects in another two months. The agreed contract price of work is ₹ 12,50,000. Compute a conservative estimate of the profit to be taken to the Profit and Loss Account.

SOLUTION

COMPUTATION OF ESTIMATE OF PROFIT

Particulars	₹
Expenditure incurred upto 31-3-2025	9,90,000
Estimated Additional Expenses (including Provision for Contingencies)	60,000
Estimated Cost (A)	10,50,000
Contract Price (B)	12,50,000
Total Estimated Profit [(B – A)]	2,00,000
Percentage of Completion (9,90,000/10,50,000) × 100	94.29

Computation of estimate of the profit to be taken to Profit and Loss Account :

$$\text{Total Estimated Profit} \times \frac{\text{Expenses incurred till 31-3-2025}}{\text{Total Estimated Cost}}$$

$$₹\,2,00,000 \times \frac{₹\,9,90,000}{₹\,10,50,000} = ₹\,1,88,571$$

When the outcome of a construction contract can be estimated reliably, contract revenue and contract costs associated with the construction contract should be recognised as revenue and expenses respectively by reference to the stage of completion of the contract activity at the reporting date. Thus estimated profit amounting ₹ 1,88,571 should be recognised as revenue in the Statement of Profit and Loss.

ILLUSTRATION 13. ABC Ltd. is a construction company, which has undertaken three contracts. Information for the pervious year along with other details is provided to you below :

	Contract A (₹ 000)	*Contract B* (₹ 000)	*Contract C* (₹ 000)
Contract Price	1,760	1,485	2,420
Balances brought forward at the beginning of the year			
Material on site		20	30
Written down value of Pant and Machinery		77	374
Wages accrued		5	10
Transactions during previous year :			
Profit previously transferred to Profit and Loss A/c			35
Cost of Work Certified (Cost of Sales)		418	814
Transactions during current year :			
Material delivered to site	88	220	396
Wages Paid	45	100	220
Salaries and other cost	15	40	50
Written down value of plant issued to site	190	35	
Head Office expenses apportioned during the year	10	20	50
Balances carried forward at the end of the year :			
Material on site	20		
Written down value of Plant and Machinery	150	20	230
Wages accrued	5	10	15
Value of work certified at the end of the year	200	860	2,100
Cost of work not certified at the end of the year			55

The agreed retention rate is 10% of the value of work certified by the contractee's architect. Contract C is scheduled to be handed over to the contractee in the near future. It is estimated that ₹ 3,05,000 shall be needed to be spent in addition to what has been tabulated above to complete this particular contract. This amount includes an allowance for plant depreciation, construction services and for contingencies.

You are required to prepare Contract Accounts for each of the three contracts and recommend how much profit or loss should be taken up for the year.

SOLUTION

CONTRACT ACCOUNTS (*₹ in '000*)

	A	B	C		A	B	C
To Material on Site b/d	—	20	30	By Wages Accrued b/d		5	10
To Plant on Site b/d	—	77	374	By Material on Site c/d	20		
To Material Control A/c	88	220	396	By Plant on Site c/d	150	20	230
To Wages Control A/c	45	100	220	By Cost of Work not			
To Salaries & Other Cost	15	40	50	Certified c/d			55

To Plant Control A/c	190	35		By Cost of Sales—Current Period (Balance) c/d	183	497	840
To Wages Accrued c/d	5	10	15				
To Apportionment of HO Expenses	10	20	50				
	353	522	1,135		353	522	1,135
To Cost of Sales b/d	183	497	840	By Attributable Sales Revenue (Current Period)*	183	442	1,153
To Profit taken this period			313	By Loss taken		55	
	183	497	1,153		183	497	1,153
To Cost of Work not Certified b/d			55	By Wages Accrued b/d	5	10	15
To Material on Site b/d	20						
To Plant on Site b/d	150	20	230				

*Profit taken plus cost of sales for the current period or cost of sales less loss to date

Notes :

(1) Profit/loss on the three contracts are calculated by deducting the cost of sales (both previous years and current year) from the value of work certified

		(₹ 000)
Contract A	17	(₹ 200 – ₹ 183)
Contract B	(55)	(₹ 860 – ₹ 915 (*i.e.* 497 + 418)
Contract C	446	(₹ 2,100 – ₹ 1,654)

Recommendation

Computation of profit taken for Contract C is as follows :	(₹ 000)
Cost of work certified (cost of sales to date = 814 + 840)	1,654
Cost of work not certified	55
Estimated costs to complete	305
Estimated cost of contract	2,014
Contract price	2,420
Anticipated profit	406

$$\text{Profit taken} = \frac{(0.90 \times ₹\ 2{,}100)}{₹\ 2{,}420} \times ₹\ 446 \text{ less profit previously transferred}$$

$$= ₹\ 3{,}48{,}000 - ₹\ 35{,}000 = ₹\ 3{,}13{,}000$$

(2) No profit has been taken for Contract A as it is in very early stage of completion

(3) Prudence concept has been utilised for Contract B. All loss has been taken.

QUESTIONS

OBJECTIVE TYPE

1. Indicate whether the following statements are true or false :

(*i*) Contract account is a method applied in constructive industry.

(*ii*) Most of the items of costs are direct in contract accounts.

(*iii*) In cost plus contract the contractor runs a risk of incurring loss.

(*iv*) Final contract price to be paid is certain in cost plus contracts.

(*v*) Escalation clause in a contract provides that the contract price is fixed.

(*vi*) In contract accounts, credit is taken only for a part of the profit on incomplete contracts.
(*vii*) Work certified includes profit element also.

Ans. [True : (*i*), (*ii*), (*vi*), (*vii*) ; False (*iii*), (*iv*), (*v*)].

2. Fill in the blanks :

(*i*) In contract accounts, the unit is a.........
(*ii*) ....in a contract, provides that the contract price would be suitably enhanced on the happening of a specified contingency.
(*iii*) The loss incurred on an incomplete contract is transferred to......... Account.
(*iv*) When the completion stage of the contract is more than half, the profit to be credited to Profit and Loss Account will be equal to.........
(*v*) In.........contracts, the contractor will get cost plus a stipulated profit.
(*vi*) When a contract is debited with the original cost of the plant, it should be credited with......at the end of the year.
(*vii*) When the completion stage of a contract is less than 1/4, the total expenditure on the contract is transferred to.........Account.
(*viii*) If the contract is almost complete, the amount of profit generally transferred to profit and loss account is equal to......

Ans. **[(*i*) contract, (*ii*) Escalation clause, (*iii*) Profit and Loss, (*iv*)** $\frac{2}{3} \times$ **Notional Profit** $\times \frac{\textbf{Cash Received}}{\textbf{Work Certified}}$, **(*v*) Cost plus, (*vi*) depreciated value of plant, (*vii*) Work-in-Progress, (*viii*) Estimated Profit** $\times \frac{\textbf{Work Certified}}{\textbf{Contract Price}}$**]**

SHORT ANSWER TYPE

1. Enumerate four advantages of cost plus contract to the contractor and the contractee.
2. What is Escalation clause ?
3. Give the four formulae which are used for transferring profit to profit and loss account when the contract is almost complete ?
4. What is Work-in-Progress ? How is it shown in the Contractor's Balance Sheet ?
5. What is Retention Money ? Why is it kept by he contractee ?
6. Explain briefly the distinguishing features of contract accounts.

LONG ANSWER TYPE

1. Suggest a system of accounts in detail suitable for a public contractor using heavy plant and carrying out contracts at long distances from his head office.
2. There are two methods of charging a contract cost account for use of Plant. Describe the two methods and state which method is preferable and why ?
3. Theoretically it may not be correct to bring into account any profit or loss on uncompleted contracts, but in practice strict adherence to this principle may have important consequences. Discuss the *pros and cons* of the question. How would such profit be ordinarily computed ?
4. What are the different methods of calculating profit on an incomplete contract ? Give illustrations.
5. Explain the basic principles to be followed in determining the amount for profit on uncompleted contracts.
6. What is a 'cost plus' contract ? Discuss the advantages of cost plus contracts to the manufacturer and the buyer.

7. Write short notes on : (*a*) Retention money, (*b*) Escalation clause, (*c*) Work-in-progress (*d*) Target Costing, and (*e*) cost-plus contracts.
8. Discuss the procedure followed in accounting for costs under contract costing.
9. In Contract Costing how will you treat cost of acquiring large heavy duty cranes and other material moving equipment purchased specifically for the construction of a bridge across a river ?"
10. Explain percentage of completion method is respect of Construction Contracts as per Accounting Standard 7. **(CA—*P.E.-II*)**

PRACTICAL PROBLEMS

1. (*a*) Compute a **conservative estimate of profit** on a contract (which has been 80% complete) from the following particulars. Illustrate at least 4 methods of computing the profit :

	₹		₹
Total Expenditure to date	85,000	Contract Price	1,53,000
Estimated further expenditure to		Work Certified	1,00,000
complete the contract		Work not Certified	8,500
(including contingencies)	17,000	Cash Received	81,600

Ans. [Estimated Profit ₹ 51,000 ; Profit transferred to Profit & Loss A/c under different methods can be ₹ 33,333 ; 27,200 ; ₹ 42,500 ; ₹ 34, 680].

(*b*) Following information is supplied regarding a contract in progress :

	₹	*Stage of Completion* %
Erection Cost to date	7,500	25
Fabrication Cost to date :		
Materials	60,000	60
Wages & Other Expenses	47,500	50
	1,15,000	
Contract value	2,00,000	

Calculate (*i*) the estimated profit or loss at the completion of the contract and (*ii*) the estimated profit or loss to date.

Ans. [(*i*) Loss ₹ 25,000 ; (*ii*) Loss ₹ 12,778].

(*c*) On 1st December 2024, BC Co. Ltd. undertook a contract to construct a building of ₹ 21.25 lakhs. On 31st March, 2025 the company found that it had already spent ₹ 16,24,750 on the construction. Prudent estimate of additional cost for completion was ₹ 8,00,250. What amount should be charged to revenue in the final accounts for the year ended 31st March, 2025 ? **(*CA PCE*)**

Ans. [₹ 14,23,750]

2. A firm of building contractors began to trade on 1-1-2024. Following was the expenditure on a contract for ₹ 6,00,000 :

	₹		₹
Material issued from stores	1,50,000	Direct expenses paid	22,000
Material purchased for the contract	40,000	Establishment expenses	10,000
Plant installed at cost	70,000	Direct expenses accrued due on 31-12-2024	3,000
Wages paid	2,40,000	Wages accrued due on 31-12-2024	4,000

Of the plant and materials charged to the contract, plant which cost ₹ 5,000 and materials costing ₹ 4,000 were lost. Some part of the materials costing ₹ 2,500 were sold at a profit of ₹ 500. On 31st December, 2024 plant which cost ₹ 2,000 was returned to stores and plant which cost ₹ 3,000 was transferred to some other contract.

The work certified was ₹ 4,80,000 and 80% of the same was received in cash. The cost of work done but uncertified was ₹ 3,000. Charge depreciation on plant at 10% p.a. You are required to prepare the **Contract Account** for the year ended 31st December, 2024 by transferring to the Profit or Loss Account the portion of profit, if any which you consider reasonable.

Also prepare **Contractee's Account, Work-in-progress Account** and **Balance Sheet** in the books of the contractor.

Ans. [Notional Profit ₹ 14,000 ; Profit transferred to Profit & Loss A/c ₹ 7,467 ; Work-in-Progress ₹ 4,76,467].

3. Y Ltd. undertook a contract No. 80 for ₹ 7,50,000. Contract Account showed the following particulars :

2023 :

Material ₹ 30,000, Wages ₹ 25,000, Overheads ₹ 10,000, Plant ₹ 1,00,000 and Materials at site at close ₹ 3,000.

2024 :

Materials ₹ 1,00,000, Wages ₹ 60,000, Overheads ₹ 15,000, Materials returned ₹ 8,000. The Plant at its depreciated value was transferred to contract No. 88. Uncertified work ₹ 15,000.

2025 :

Materials ₹ 1,60,000, Wages ₹ 1,00,000, Overheads ₹ 28,000 and Materials Sold ₹ 4,000.

The amount of work certified at the end of the first year was ₹ 1,00,000. The work certified upto the end of the second year was ₹ 4,00,000 and the work certified in the third year was ₹ 3,50,000. 80 per cent of the certified work was received in cash.

Profits to be taken credit for are one-third and one-half on cash basis in each of the two years respectively. Depreciate plant by 10 per cent on balance at the beginning of each year.

Prepare Accounts in Respect of the Contract at the end of each year.

(ICWA, Stage 2, Dec. 2006 Modified)

Ans. [Profit transferred to Profit & Loss A/c : 2023 ₹ 7,467; 2024 ₹ 62,613; 2025 ₹ 1,44,920]

4. Following is the Trial Balance of Premier Construction Company, engaged on the execution of Contract No. 747, for the year ended 31st December, 2024 :

	₹	₹
Contractee's Account : Amount received		
Creditors		3,00,000
Buildings		72,000
Creditors	1,60,000	
Bank Balance	35,000	
Capital Account		5,00,000
Materials	2,00,000	
Wages	1,80,000	
Expenses	47,000	
Plant	2,50,000	
	8,72,000	8,72,000

The work on Contract No. 747 was commenced on 1st January, 2024. Materials costing ₹ 1,70,000 were sent to the site of the contract but those of ₹ 6,000 were destroyed in an accident. Wages of ₹ 1,80,000 were paid during the year. Plant costing ₹ 50,000 was used on the contract all through the year. Plant with a cost of ₹ 2 lakhs was used from 1st January to 30th September and was then returned to the stores. Materials of cost of ₹ 4,000 were at site on 31st December, 2024.

The contract was for ₹ 6,00,000 and the contractee pays 75% of the work certified. Work certified was 80% of the total contract work at the end of 2024. Uncertified work was estimated at ₹ 15,000 on 31st December, 2024.

Expenses are charged to the contract at 25% of Wages. Plant is to be depreciated at 10% for the entire year.

Prepare **Contract No. 747 Account** for the year 2024 and make out **Balance Sheet** as on 31st December, 2024 in the books of Premier Construction Co.

Ans. [Notional Profit ₹ 90,000 ; Profit taken to Profit & Loss A/c ₹ 37,500 ; B/S Total ₹ 5,96,500].

5. AB contractors obtained a contract to build houses, the contract price being ₹ 4,00,000. Work commenced on 1st January, 2024 and the expenditure incurred during the year was—Plant and tools : ₹ 20,000 ; Stores and materials : ₹ 72,000 ; Wages : ₹ 65,000 ; Sundry expenses : ₹ 5,300 ; and Establishment charge : ₹ 11,700.

Certain materials costing ₹ 12,000 were unsuited to the contract and were sold for ₹ 14,500. A portion of the plant was scrapped and sold for ₹ 2,300.

The value of the plant and tools one sites on 31st December, 2024 was ₹ 6,200 and the value of stores and materials in hand ₹ 3,400. Cash received on account was ₹ 1,40,000 representing 80% of the work certified. The cost of the work done but not certified was ₹ 21,900, and this was certified later for ₹ 25,000.

AB decided (*i*) to estimate what further expenditure would be incurred in completing the contract ; (*ii*) to compute from this estimate and the expenditure already incurred, the total profit that would be made on the contract ; and (*iii*) to take to the credit of profit and loss account for the year 2024 that proportion of the total profit which correspond to the work certified by 31st December bore to the total contract price. The estimate was as follows :

(*a*) That the contract would be completed by 30th September, 2025.

(*b*) That the wages on the contract in 2025 would amount to ₹ 71,500.

(*c*) That the cost of stores and materials required in addition to those in stock on 31st December, 2024 would be 68,600 and that further expenses relating to contract would amount to ₹ 6,000.

(*d*) That a further Rs 25,000 would have to be laid out on plant and tools and that residual value of the plant and tools on 30th September, 2025 would be ₹ 3,000.

(*e*) That the establishment charges would cost the same per month as in 2024.

(*f*) That $2\frac{1}{2}$% of the total cost of the contract (excluding this percentage) would be due to defects, temporary maintenance and contingencies. Prepare **Contract Account** for the year ended 31st December, 2024 and show your calculation of the amount credited to the Profit and Loss Account for the year.

Ans. [Notional Profit—₹ 46,800 ; Profit transferred to Profit & Los A/c ₹ 24,067 ; Estimated Profit ₹ 55,011].

6. Khelaram commenced a contract on 1-7-2023. The price agreed for the contract was ₹ 8,00,000. At the end of the year on 30-6-2024, the contract was in advance stage of completion and it as decided to arrive at the notional profit on the basis of the total contract. The contract is expected to be completed by the end of December, 2024. Actual expenditure for the years 2023-24 and 2024-25 till December, 12 are as under :

Expenditure	*Actual till 30-6-2024* (₹)	*Estimated for 2024-25 (upto Dec., 2024)* (₹)
Materials	2,00,000	70,000
Labour	90,000	25,000
Plant Purchased (at Original Cost)	60,000	
Miscellaneous Expenses	30,000	6,000
Plant Returned to Store on 30-6-2024 (Original Cost)	12,000	—
Plant Returned to Store on 31-12-2024 (Original Cost)	—	24,000
Materials at Site	8,000	Nil
Work Certified	6,00,000	8,00,000
Work Uncertified	20,000	Nil
Cash Received	5,80,000	8,00,000

Charge Depreciation at 20% p.a. on Plant on Straight Line Basis.

You are asked to prepare the **Contract Account** for the year ended 30-6-2024.

Ans. [Notional Profit ₹ 2,96,000. Estimated Profit ₹ 3,62,200; Profit transferred to Profit & Loss Account ₹ 2,62,595]

7. Kapur Engineering Company undertakes long term contract which involves the fabrication of prestressed concrete blocs and the erection of the same on consumer's site.

Following information is supplied regarding the contract which is incomplete on 31st March, 2025.

Cost incurred :

		₹
Fabrication cost to date —		
Direct Materials		2,80,000
Direct Labour		90,000
Overheads		75,000
		4,45,000
Erection cost to date		15,000
	Total	4,60,000
Contract price		8,19,000
Cash received on account		6,00,000

Technical estimate of work completed to date —

Fabrication : Direct Materials 80% ; Direct Labour and overheads 75% ; Erection 25%.

You are required to prepare a statement for submission to the management indicating :

(*a*) the estimated profit on the completion of the contract.

(*b*) the estimated profit to date on the contract.

Ans. [(*a*) ₹ 1,89,000 ; (*b*) ₹ 1,38,000 or ₹ 1,38,462].

8. A contractor, who prepares his account on 31st December each year, commenced a contract on 1st April, 2024. The costing records concerning the said contract reveal the following information on 31st December, 2024 :

	₹
Materials charged to site	2,58,100
Labour engaged	5,60,500
Foremen's salary	79,300

Plants costing ₹ 2,60,000 had been on site for 146 days. Their working life is estimated at 7 years and their final scrap value are ₹ 15,000. A supervisor, who is paid ₹ 4,000 p.m., has devoted approximately three-fourths of his time to this contract. The administrative and other expenses amount to ₹ 1,40,000. Materials in hand at site on 31st December, 2024 cost ₹ 25,400. Some of the material costing ₹ 4,500 was found unsuitable and was sold for ₹ 4,000 and a part of the plant costing ₹ 5,500 (on 31.12.2024) unsuited to the contract was sold at a profit of ₹ 1,000.

The contract price was ₹ 22,00,000 but it was accepted by the contractor, for ₹ 20,00,000. On 31st December, 2024, two-thirds of the contract price agreed to be paid of work done was completed. Architect's certificate had been issued covering 50% of the cost of contract and ₹ 7,50,000 had so far been paid on account. Prepare **Contract Account** and state how much profit or loss should be included in the financial accounts to 31st December, 2024. Workings should be clearly given. Depreciation is charged on the time basis.

Also prepare **Contractee's Account** and show how these accounts would appear in the **Balance Sheet** as on 31st December, 2024.

Ans. [Notional Profit ₹ 2,13,250 ; Profit transferred to Profit & Loss A/c ₹ 1,06,625 ; WIP ₹ 11,55,625; Cost of uncertified work ₹ 2,62,250 (*i.e.*, cost of work done 10,49,000 – ₹ 7,86,750 *i.e.*, 50% of cost of contract].

9. M/s Tom Dick obtained a contract to build quarters, the price being ₹ 1,00,000. Work was started on 1st April, 2024 and the following expenses were incurred :

Plant ₹ 5,000 ; Stores ₹ 18,000 ; Wages ₹ 16,250 ; Sundry Expenses ₹ 1,325 ; Establishment Charges ₹ 2,925.

A part of the material was unsuitable and was sold for ₹ 3,625 (cost being ₹ 3,000). A portion of plant was scrapped and disposed of for ₹ 575.

The value of plant on 31st March, 2025 was ₹ 1,550 and of stores ₹ 850. Cash received on account was ₹ 35,000, representing 80% of the work certified. The work uncertified was valued at ₹ 5,475 and this was certified later for ₹ 6,250.

M/s. Tom and Dick decided to estimate what further expenditure would be incurred in completing the contract, compute form this estimate and the expenditure already incurred, the total profit that would be made on the contract and to take to credit of Profit & Loss A/c for the year 2024-25, that portion of the total which corresponded to the work certified on 31-3-2025.

Their estimate reveals that contract would be completed after 9 months, till then wages likely to be incurred ₹ 17,875. The cost of stores etc. required in addition to those in stocks on 31-3-2025 would be ₹ 17,150, and that further contract expenses would amount to ₹ 1,500. A further investment of ₹ 6,250 would be required on Plant which would be valued on 31-12-2025 at ₹ 750. The establishment charges would be same on monthly basis, as in the preceding year. Lastly 2% of the total cost of the contract should be kept as reserve for contingencies.

Prepare **Contract, Stores and Plant Accounts** for the year ended 31-3-2025, and also show your calculation of the amount, credited to Profit & Loss A/c for the year.

Ans. [Notional Profit ₹ 11,700 ; Profit transferred to Profit & Loss A/c ₹ 6,185.83].

10. Delux Limited undertake a contract for ₹ 5,00,000 on 1st July, 2024. On 30th June, 2025 when the accounts are closed, the following details about the contract were gathered :

Materials Purchased ₹ 1,00,000 ; Wages paid ₹ 45,000 ; General expenses ₹ 10,000 ; Plant purchased ₹ 50,000 ; Materials on hand 30-6-2025 ₹ 25,000 ; Wages Accrued 30-6-2025 ₹ 5,000 ; Work certified ₹ 2,00,000 ; Cash received ₹ 1,50,000 ; Work uncertified ₹ 15,000 ; Depreciation of Plant ₹ 5,000.

The above contract contained an escalation clause which reads as follows :

"In the event of prices of materials and rates of wages increase by more than 5%, the contract price would be increased accordingly by 25% of the rise in the cost of material and wages beyond 5% in each case."

It was found that since the date of signing the agreement the prices of material and wage rates increased by 25%. The value of the work certified does not take into account the effect of the above clause.

Prepare **Contract Account.** Workings should form part of the answer.

Ans. [Notional Profit ₹ 80,000 ; Profit transferred to Profit & Loss A/c ₹ 20,000].

Hint. Credit ₹ 5,000 for Contract Escalation.

11. The escalation of a long term contract stipulates the following quantities and rate of materials of A, B and C and following number of labour hours of X, Y and Z and their rates of pay. The actuals are shown below :

Materials	*Qty.*	*Rate*	*Actual*	
	(Tons.)	*₹*	*Qty.* (Tons)	*Rate*
A	500	50	750	45
B	1,000	30	900	35
C	20	1,000	21	1,010

Labour	*Hours*	*Hourly Rate*	*Hours*	*Hourly Rate*
X	4,800	2.00	4,500	2.25
Y	2,400	1.00	3,000	1.50
Z	9,600	1.50	10,000	1.50

Compute the amount of final claim so far as rate is concerned.

Ans. [Material Claim ₹ 77,700 ; Labour Claim ₹ 28,800].

12. A contractor has entered into a long term contract at an agreed price of ₹ 1,75,000 subject to an escalation clause for materials and wages as spelt out in the contract and corresponding actuals are as follows :

	Standard ₹	*Actual* ₹
Materials :		
A	5,000 Kgs. @ 5/-	5,050 Kgs. @ 4.80
B	3,500 Kgs. @ 8/-	3,450 Kgs. @ 7.90
C	2,500 Ltrs. @ 6/-	2,600 Ltrs. @ 6.60
Wages :	₹	₹
P	2,000 Hrs. @ 7/-	2,100 Hrs. @ 7.20
Q	2,500 Hrs. @ 7.50	2,450 Hrs. @ 7.50
R	3,000 Hrs. @ 6.50	3,100 Hrs. @ 6.60

Reckoning the full actual consumption of materials and wages the Company has claimed a final price of ₹ 1,77,360. Give your analysis of the admissible escalation claim and indicate the **final price payable.**

Ans. [Final Price Payable ₹ 1,75,850].

13. Following trial balance was extracted from the books of Jubilee Contractors as on 31st March, 2025 :

	Dr. ₹	*Cr.* ₹
Capital account		15,00,000
Buildings	5,00,000	
Equipment	12,50,000	
Contractees' accounts		15,00,000
Wages	3,50,000	
Expenses	1,80,000	
Bank	1,80,000	
Creditors		3,10,000
Materials	5,00,000	
Work-in-progress		
Contract No. 25 (1-4-2024)	5,00,000	
Contract No. 25 (1-4-2024)		1,50,000
	34,60,000	34,60,000

When the accounting year started on 1-4-2024. Contract No. 25 was in progress. This was completed on 30-6-2024. A new contract, Contract No. 26 was started on 1-4-2024. Following further particulars concerning these two contracts are available :

	Contract No. 25 ₹	*Contract No. 26* ₹
Materials sent to site	1,00,000	3,00,000
Wages paid	50,000	3,00,000
Materials lost at site by accident	—	15,000
Materials at site at the end of the year	—	20,000

Contract value	7,50,000	20,00,000
Work certified upto 31-3-2024	5,00,000	—
Work certified during the year	Full extent	?
Payment on certification	80%	90%
Uncertified work at the end of the year (estimated)	—	75,000

Expenses are charged at 50% of wages. Depreciation is provided at 10% on equipment and 2% on buildings. Equipment depreciation is to be allocated as 30% to Contract No. 25 and 70% to Contract No. 26.

Prepare : (*a*) **Contract No. 25 and Contract No. 26 Accounts; (*b*) Contractees' Accounts; (*c*) Profit and Loss Account** for the year ended 31-3-2025; and (*d*) Balance Sheet as on 31st March, 2025. ***(I.C.W.A. Final)***

Ans. [Profit transferred to Profit & Loss A/c : Contract No. 25 ₹ 1,87,500 and Contract No. 26 ₹ 1,63,500; B/S Total ₹ 21,31,000].

Hint : *Calculation of the Value of Work Certified in Case of Contract No. 26.*

	₹
Total cash received from contractees	15,00,000
Less : Cash received on account of Contract No. 25 (80% of ₹ 7,50,000; it is assumed that 20% is still pending even though the contract is completed. It is given in the problem that payment on certification is 80%)	6,00,000
Cash received on account of Contract No. 26	9,00,000
Payment on Certification in Case of Contract No. 26	90%
Work Certified in Case of Contract No. 26 $\left(\frac{100}{90} \times ₹ 9,00,000\right)$	10,00,000

CHAPTER

37

Computerised Accounting System

Before discussing Computer Accounting System, it is desirable to have some idea relating to various aspects of computer and its related terms.

The word 'computer' comes from the word 'compute' which means to calculate. The initial objective for inventing the computer was to create a fast calculating machine. However, now-a-days more than 80% of the work done by computers is of non-mathematical nature. In real sense computer may be defined as a device that processes information or data.

Data can be like biodata of various applicants when computer is used for recruiting personnel, or the marks obtained by various students in various subjects when the computer is used to prepare results or numbers of different types in case of application of computers for scientific research problems, etc.

Data may come in various shapes and sizes depending upon the type of computer application. A computer can store, process, and retrieve data as and when desired. For this reason computers are also known as *data processor*. Data processor can gather data from various incoming sources, merge (process of mixing) them all, sort (arranging in some sequence—ascending or descending) them in a desired order and print them in the desired format.

Role of the Computer in Accounting

Computers play a very important role in the field of accounting. They can be used as accounting machines and perform all the functions which accounting machines perform as described earlier. Some of the important accounting functions which they perform are given below :

(*a*) Transaction Recording. One of the basic functions of accounting is recording of the financial transactions that take place in a business unit. Transactions must be recorded accurately and regularly for making available up-to-date accounting information to the management. Manual accounting may not be able to keep pace with the increase in the size of the business. In manual accounting transactions may be recorded accurately but it is possible that errors may be committed in posting and there may be delay in posting. In computers, the operations of recording and posting are done with one entry at a great speed, the result is that all records become automatically correct if original entry is correct. With the use of computers, up-to-date information relating to recording of transactions is available to the management in time for taking timely decisions. Ledgers contain up-to-date information and balance of any account at any time is available without any loss of time. Printed bills and printed cheques can also be made available by the use of computers. By using computers, space and paper required for the storage of accounting records is reduced. Time required for the maintenance of accounts is considerably reduced because computers can do the accounting work at a very high speed.

(*b*) Payroll Accounting. Computers are very helpful in payroll accounting. Every business enterprise is required to calculate the wages and salaries due to each worker and employee. For this payroll for each department and a permanent payroll record for each employee is required, so that there may be timely distribution of wages and salaries. Manual handling of payroll accounting of a business enterprise employing hundreds and thousands of employees may take a long time and errors may be committed in the calculations of wages and salaries due to employees resulting into incorrect and delayed payment of wages and resentment among employees. Computerised payroll accounting can solve all these problems and can ensure prompt and accurate distribution of wages and salaries. It will help in keeping employees of the business enterprise satisfied.

(c) Inventory Control. The objective of inventory control is to provide material for production at economical prices, at right time, in right quantity and quality. Computers help in controlling the inventories by generating the reports at speed and with accuracy. These reports are like stock ledger, value stock statement, statement of stock out, rejections, purchase etc. Moreover accounting through computer increases the accessibility of all departments to the information required as soon as the information is fed into the software. Through the use of ERP systems, the information as to when the inventory is required can be extracted by the suppliers. This will reduce the time lags and thereby reduce cost.

COMPUTERISED ACCOUNTING SYSTEM

One must remember that the basic fundamentals of accounting remain same whether the books of accounts are maintained manually or are computerised. The basic principles of debit and credit remain same while recording the transactions of income, expenditure, purchase or sales. However, since the medium of recording is different in case of computerised accounting, the dependence on software being used is high. Selection of software and its use require certain precautions as well.

One of earliest computerised systems catering to the requirement of large business enterprises is Transaction Processing Systems (TPS). The main purpose of any TPS is to record, process, validate and store transactions that occur in various functional areas of the business for subsequent retrieval and usage.

Computerised Accounting system is one of the TPS. This system is concerned with the processing of the financial transactions only. Only those transactions which can be expressed in terms of money can be processed. (Money Measurement Principle).

Comparison Between Manual and Computerised Accounting

Accounting is the process of identifying, recording, classifying and summarising financial transactions to make financial statements and to interpret these for final analysis.

- **Identification.** The identification of transactions using accounting principles is same and common in both manual and computerised accounting system.
- **Recording.** Recording in manual accounting is through books of original entry (Journal and then to Ledgers) while the data is stored in well designed accounting database in Computerised System.
- **Classification.** In manual system, transactions recorded in books of original entry (Journal) are then classified by posting to Ledger accounts. This results in recording the entries once again. This means there is duplicacy of work. In computerised accounting system there is no such duplicacy. The stored transactions are processed and classified in the form of Ledger accounts by the inbuilt functions of the software. The basic data can be processed in different kinds of reports.
- **Summarising.** In manual system, the transactions are summarised by ascertaining the balances of all accounts to make Trial Balance. Preparation of Ledger accounts become prerequisite for preparing the Trial Balance. However, in computerised system, the original data is processed and gives the output in the form of Trial Balance. The preparation of various accounts in the Ledger is not a necessary step in case of computerised accounting system.
- **Financial Statements.** In manual system, in order to prepare financial statements, Trial Balance is a must. However, in case of computerised accounting, the generation of financial statements is independent of Trial Balance and such statements can be prepared by direct processing from the data originally stored in accounting database. Conceptually the accounting process is same irrespective of technology being used.

Need for Computerised Accounting

Every business has numerous processes. Some are simple and others complex. In addition to this when the volumes of the business increase, the company will need to maintain highly accurate and up-to-date accounting records.

The need of the Computerised Accounting System arises because of the advantages offered by it in terms of speed, accuracy and lower costs. Computerised accounting system helps to simplify, integrate and streamline all the business processes cost effectively.

Salient Features of Computerised Accounting

- **Fast, Powerful, Simple and Integrated.** Computerised accounting is designed to automate and integrate all the business operations, such as sales, finance, purchase, inventory and manufacturing. With computerised accounting, accurate data business information is literally at the fingertips. The computerised accounting combined with enhanced MIS, Multi-lingual and Data organization capabilities help the company simplify all the business processes easily and cost-effectively.
- **Complete Visibility.** Computerised accounting gives the company sufficient time to plan, increase the customer base and enhance customer satisfaction. With Computerised accounting the company will have greater visibility into the day-to-day business operations and access to vital information.
- **Enhanced User Experience.** Computerised accounting allows the company to enter data in a variety of ways which makes work pleasure. Adapting to the specific business needs is possible.
- **Accuracy and Speed.** Computerised accounting has user-definable templates which provide fast, accurate data entry transactions; thereafter all documents and reports can be generated automatically, at the press button.
- **Scalability.** Computerised accounting adapts to the current and future needs of the business. The scope of reporting is flexible as compared to manual system. In addition to this scope of reporting can be easily expanded without much of additional efforts.
- **Power.** Computerised accounting has the ability to handle huge volumes of transactions without compromising on speed or efficiency.
- **For Improved Business Performance.** Computerised accounting is a highly integrated application that transforms the business processing performance enhancing features which encompass accounting, inventory, reporting and statutory processes. This helps the company access information faster, and takes quicker decisions. Computerised accounting also guarantees real-time optimization of operations and enhanced communication.
- **Quick Decision Making.** Generates real-time comprehensive MIS reports and ensures access to complete and critical information instantly. The quickness with which decision can be taken is largely dependent on how fast the required information is available.
- **Reliability.** The information processed into reports in computerised accounting system are accurate and, therefore, reliable.

Fundamentals of Computerised Accounting System

Computerised Accounting System (CAS) has two basic requirements as mentioned :

- **Accounting Framework.** It constitutes the application environment in terms of accounting principles, groupings and codification structure. These are the pre-requisites of any computerised accounting systems.
- **Operating Procedure.** A well designed operating procedure blended with the operating environment of the organisation is required to work with the computerised accounting system.

  The computerised accounting system is one of the data base-oriented applications wherein the transactions data is stored in well organised database. The user operates on such database using the required interface and also takes the desired reports by suitable transformation of stored data into information.

The use of computers in Computerised Accounting System (or any other database-oriented application) has four basic requirements.

- **Front end Interface.** It is an interactive link or dialog between the user and database-oriented software through which the user communicates to back-end database. The users in the organisation could be Administrator, Accountant, Operators, and such others.
- **Back-end Database.** It is the data storage system that is hidden from the users and responds to the requirements of the user to the extent the user is authorised to access.
- **Data Processing.** It is the sequence of actions that are taken to transform the data into decision useful information.
- **Reporting System.** It is an integrated set of objects that constitute the report. A good reporting system should be well designed, flexible and displays the reports on monitor.

In brief, the CAS should be well designed and organised in such a manner so as to ensure that the system can be operated smoothly without any problems and hindrances.

ACCOUNTING SOFTWARES

Earlier when accounting softwares were not in use, businesses had to spend resources and time to maintain huge data of accounts department. Transfer of data from one department to other took long time. Maintenance of data manually also lead to more chances of errors. In order to overcome these limitations, the business organisations have started depending on computers for accounting.

For this purpose, various accounting tools are available for recording the business transactions like Spread Sheet, Pre-Packaged Accounting Software, and Customised Software etc. Larger organisations are also using ERP (Enterprises Resource Planning) Package to manage the business process across the all branches and departments.

Spread Sheet: Accounting can also be maintained on spread sheet package by using the knowledge and skills of spread sheet software to record and control the business transactions.

Spread sheet provides the facility of physical control of data by protected shared drive, with restricted access and read/write access, and provides password protection on cells and formulas.

Apart from above, spread sheet also allows grouping of accounts, replication of cell contents, formulas & macros, pivot tables, calculations and functions to maintain the accounting records in computer.

Pre-Packaged Software: Along with so many advantages, spread sheet has its own limitations as well like double entry & reports are not processed automatically in spread sheet without any formula. Therefore, spread sheet is not useful for large organisation where large volume of data is involved in business transactions.

Pre-packaged softwares are available in market and specially designed for some small and medium size organisation to maintain computerised records. These softwares are available in compact disk (CD) which is very easy to install and use to records the accounting transaction in personal computer with the help of these softwares. A network version of these softwares is also available in market that can perform from various workstation and client system attached with network. This software is required to install in the server to administrate all the client system and records all transaction electronically with the help of network.

These softwares are generally maintain all the basic records of business along with other business transactions like Organisation's Names, Address, Contact Numbers, and Other Details like tax registration numbers like GSTIN, PAN, TAN etc. After feeding basic details in software, accounting records can be maintain on software with the help of accounts along with their codes into master file of software. Once these basic parameters are set in software and master file are updated, pre-packaged software is ready for computerised accounting.

Customised Accounting Software: Pre-packaged softwares are really useful to fulfil the business needs to maintain computerised records. However, pre-packaged softwares are standard accounting package which are based on predefined rules and principles. Businesses are growing and becoming more complex in which standard package may not be able handled these complexities.

Customised softwares are specially designed for the requirement of any specific organisation. This is needed due to different and typical nature of business or any additional functional requirement that is not fulfilled in pre-packaged softwares. It is an integrated software package that covers all the accounting functions of organisation. This software is designed by analyst based on requirement and specification of user of software.

Implementation of customised software is merely depends upon the requirement of organisation so proper research is needed regarding every functional area and its requirement before deciding to develop a customised software.

Enterprises Resources Planning (ERP): Accounting softwares are designed to fulfil and integrate the requirement of all accounting functions of organisation. However, ERP is designed to integrate all business process across the entire enterprises. This is automatically updated software as per the latest changes and requirement of organisation that is the main limitation of customised software and other accounting softwares. However, other accounting softwares are not compatible to adapt the changes of law and function of organisation.

ERP is a latest accounting software package that integrates all functional process of business for optimum use of all resources. ERP package ensures one database, one application, and one user interface for entire organisation.

For this purpose, accounting softwares are used for recording the business transactions related to receipts, payments, purchase sales, inventory etc. There are different standard financial accounting softwares available in the market like EX, WINCA, DacEary and Tally.

Accounting software is computer software that records and processes accounting transactions within financial modules. Each functional module deals with a particular area of accounting. For example accounts receivable module covers accounting transactions of receipts from customers who owe money to organisation for goods and services provided to them and payroll module covers the details of employees and salaries to be paid to them. It shall generate reports of salaries due, paid, leaves taken, taxes deducted, allowances paid etc.

Benefits of Accounting software are it requires less effort, offers speed, human errors are eliminated, lower expenses on data collection and data transfer, generate reports fast, and also assists other business areas like inventory management, budget preparation, asset management, taxation and payroll. These softwares can also be customised in accordance to the company's need.

TALLY—INTRODUCTION

Tally is the most popular and widely accepted software because of it simplicity, flexibility and speed. Over a period of time, tally as a software for financial accounting has evolved into powerful tool for providing business solutions. Different versions of Tally available in market are Tally 5, Tally 7.2, Tally 9, Tally.ERP 9, Tally Prime 6.1.

Tally has moved from single user environment to multi-user environment. The latest version Tally Prime 6.1 has been improved a lot from the previous versions as it permits integration of data at various geographical locations. This software provides complete business solutions and it integrates the functionalities of various departments such as inventory, payroll accounts etc. It provides fast reports. Tally comes with simple user friendly interface and it is easy to install.

Single user Tally can be operated only at one computer and the multiuser software can be installed to many computers connected through LAN. Retail chains can use the multi-user software to run at its retail units, which can be controlled from one place. It allows business to collaborate and work at multiple locations. The features of this software simplify the business processes. It also helps small business units to give easy and fast service to customers.

WORKING WITH TALLY

The computer must be installed with Tally software in order to start working through Tally. To start double click on the Tally icon on the desktop or else find it from Start → My Programs → Tally. The screen which appears when Tally is started is the Gateway of Tally Screen. This Gateway of Tally is the centre of control of this software. The screen will appear as follows :

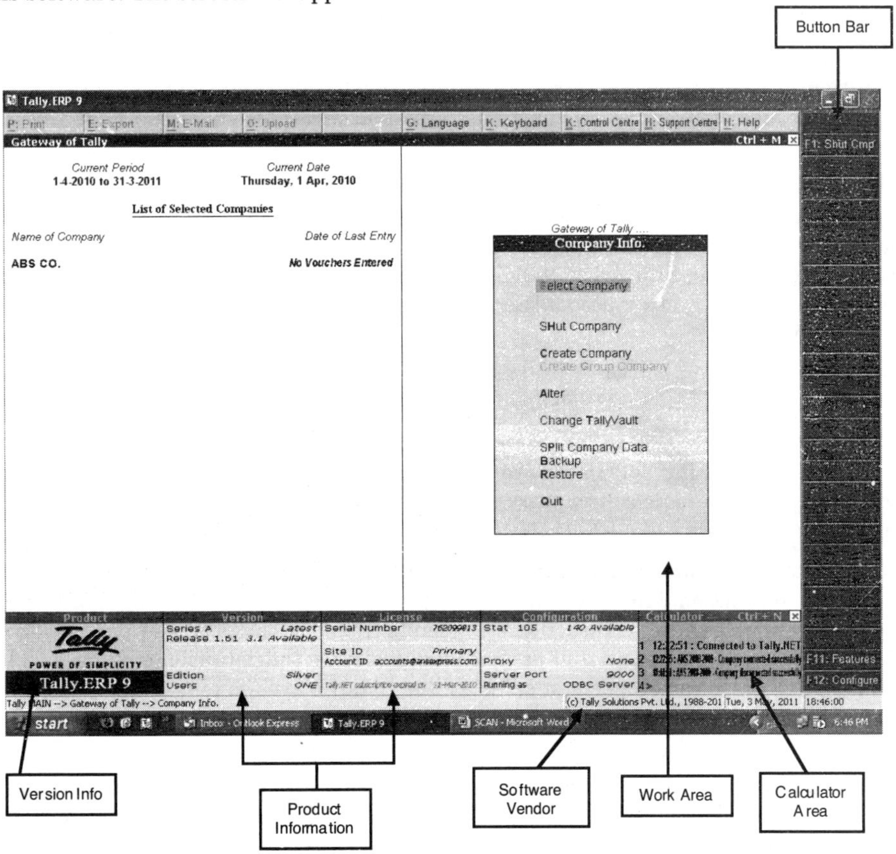

Fig. 1 : Gateway of Tally

The Gateway of Tally has four sections

1. Product Information
2. Work Area
3. Calculator Area
4. Button Bar

1. Product Information

This section displays the Tally version, Edition, License details, and Configuration. In the above printed screen version is Tally.ERP 9, Series A, Silver, limited (ore) user, Licenced to anspress.com Serial Number.

2. Work Area

Work Area is divided into two parts :

1. Left-hand side part
2. Right-hand side part

The left-hand side part in Work Area provides information of **Current Period, Current Date** and **List of Selected Companies** whose records are maintained in Tally.

The right-hand side part in the Work Area screen displays the **Company Information** menu. It consists of the following :

1. Masters (for defining ledger, group, sub-group, inventory)
2. Transactions/Vouchers entry (for recording transactions)
3. Reports (for viewing the balance sheet, profit and loss account, and other reports)

HOT KEYS. Hot keys are the text that are capitalized and are red in colour on all the menu screens. Typing any of the Hot Keys in the **Company Info Screen** will either take you to that particular screen or it may display the sub-menus within that Option.

For example from screen shown in Fig. 1 typing **A** would open *Accounts Info screen* and typing **V** would open *Accounting Vouchers.*

3. Calculator Area

Press [**Ctrl + N**] to activate the calculator functionality. Calculator Area is used for calculator functions. Any type of independent calculation can be done using calculator to get quick answers.

4. Button Bar

The buttons are designed to make working in Tally easier and in an efficient way. These buttons vary from one screen to another based on the screen functionality. The buttons appear on the right hand side of the Tally screen. Only buttons relevant to the current screen will be active and the inactive buttons are greyed. These buttons are enabled with the short cut keys (like **F1, F2** and so on). You can either click on these buttons or you can press the short cut keys to access.

On this screen, Tally displays the following buttons (keys).

Buttons Displayed at Tally Screen

Button	*Purpose*	*Remarks*
(Alt + H)	Help	To access Tally's online context-sensitive help.
(Alt + W)	Web Browser	To access the Web Browser directly from Tally.
F1	Select Cmp	To access data from other data directories either on the local system or through the network.
F1 (underlined)	Shut Cmp	Close the activated company.
F2	Date	Change date
F2 (underlined)	Period	Change the financial period
F3 (underlined)	Cmp Info	Enter the company related information
F11	Features	To select or modify different features of a company
F12	Configure	To access the configuration settings to manage the information put into Tally. Here, access the General Configuration to set country specific defaults. Use if before creating a company.

The use of function keys along with SHIFT and CTRL key is explained below :

1. Buttons with a character or function key underlined means you have to press underlined character or the function key along with SHIFT key.
2. Buttons with a character or function key double underlined means you have to press character or the function key along with CTRL key.
   For example,
   F1 : Press this shortcut function key to select a company
   F1 (underlined) : Press SHIFT+F1 to shut a company
   F8 (double underlined) : Press CTRL+F8 to select the Credit Note voucher
3. To toggle between Work area and Calculator :
   Ctrl+M : Press Ctrl + M to access the Gateway of Tally.
   Ctrl+N : Press Ctrl + N to access the Calculator/ODBC Server frame.
4. To exit from Tally. In order to exit from Tally, select Quit (or Press Esc Key, at Tally Main Menu. A confirmation is sought. Press Y or click at Yes button to exit from Tally.

ACCOUNTING PROCESS IN TALLY

The process of preparing final accounts in Tally can broadly be classified into four steps :

	Company Creation →	Group Formation →	Ledger Creation →	Voucher Creation
STEPS	1 →	2 →	3 →	4

Company Creation

Company means any entity for which set of accounts is to be prepared. It may be a company, partnership firm, sole proprietorship firm, etc.

To create a company in Tally, the following steps are taken :

Step I. Click F3 : Comp Info (Fig. 2) menu displays *Create Company* option (Fig. 3). In order to create company double click this option (Alternatively press C from Keyboard), the company creation screen will appear as follows : (Fig. 3)

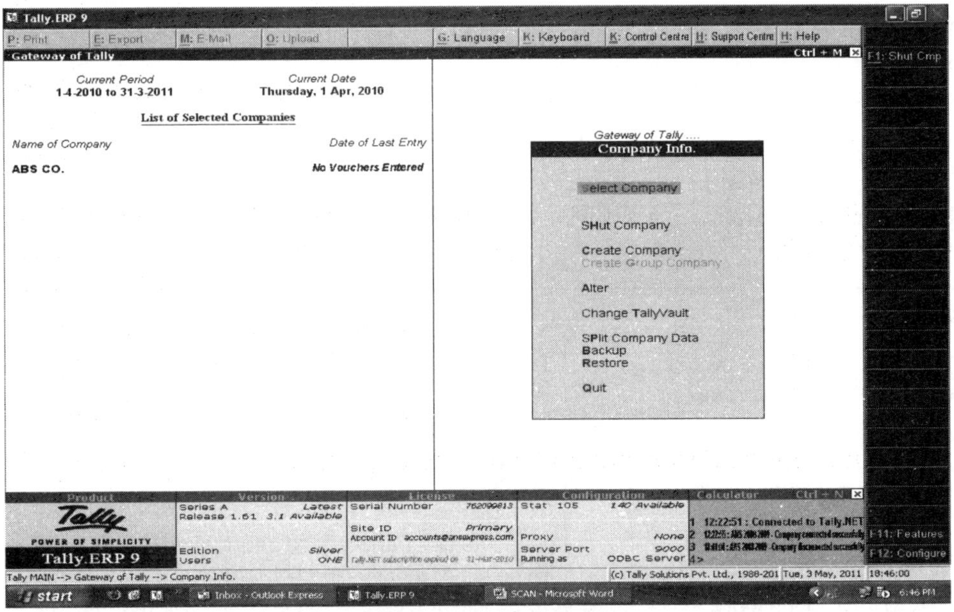

Fig. 2 : Company Info Menu Screen

Company Creation **Ctrl + M**

Directory :
Name :
Mailing Name :
Address :
E-mail Address :
Income Tax Number :
Local Sales Tax Number :
Inter State Sales Tax Number :
Currency Symbol :
Maintain :
Financial Year From :
Books Beginning From :
Tally Vault Password :
(WARNING : Forgetting your TallyVault password will render your data unusable)

Use Security Control :

Base Currency Information

Base Currency Symbol :
Formal Name :
Number of Decimal Places : Show Amounts in Millions ?
Is Symbol suffixed to Amounts ? : Put a space between Amounts and Symbols ?

Fig. 3 : Company Creation Screen

Step 2. The company creation screen shows various fields. This fields are required to be filled up. Some of the fields are compulsory and others are optional.

The fields in Company Creation screen are :

Field Name	***Particulars***
Directory	The default data Drive and Path is displayed and cursor skips this field on the presumption that you wish to keep data for the Company at same Directory. To alter the data *Directory,* press **Backspace** to move cursor on this field, enter the Drive and Path where you wish to keep data files for the Company.
Name	Enter *Name* for the Company. Tally accepts long Names. Tally reduces the font width according to available space in the display because of 'Auto-fit' technology application in the program. Name entered here would appear in *List of Companies* for selection of a Company and in all internal reports (*e.g.,* Display of Balance Sheet). Information in this field is mandatory.
Mailing Name	By default the *Name* entered in previous field is carried as *Mailing Name.* Mailing Name is printed in External Reports (*e.g.,* Confirmation stmt, Invoice etc.)
Address	Enter Address for the Company. On pressing **Enter** at a line, Tally would prompt another line, you can enter as many lines as you need. To terminate further entry, press **Enter** on blank line to move cursor to next field.
E-Mail Address	Enter Company's E-Mail address that would by default be carried at *From E-Mail* when you select to E-Mail a report. Information in this field is optional.
Income Tax Number	Enter your Company's Income Tax Permanent Account Number (PAN). If PAN is not allotted as yet, you may enter the General Index Register (GIR) Number.
Local Sales tax Number	Enter Local Sales Tax Registration Certification No. & Date (if the company is registered under Sales Tax Act), which you can print in Inventory Documents (*e.g.,* Invoice, Delivery Note). Information in this field is optional, not printed in Accounts report, you may leave blank for a company maintaining *Accounts Only.*
Inter-state Sales Tax Number	Enter here the Central Sales Tax Number & Date, if applicable for the Company to print in Inventory Documents. It's an optional field.
Current Symbol	Enter *Symbol* for the Currency in which *Books of Accounts* for the company is to be maintained (*e.g.,* ₹). This becomes the *Base Currency* symbol for the Company. Information in this field is mandatory.
Maintain	With Tally you can maintain (1) *Accounts only,* (2) *Inventory Only,* (3) *Accts-with-inv* for a Company. To maintain Financial Accounts only, select *Accounts only.* To maintain Inventory but no financial accounts (*e.g.,* Warehouse), select *Inventory only.* To maintain both Accounts and Inventory, select *Accts-with-Inv.*
Financial Year From	Enter beginning date of *Financial Year.* If you follow April-March financial year, enter 1st April of the beginning year (*e.g.* 1-4-2001).
Books Beginning From	In this field you enter the *Date* from which your books actually *begins from.* Normally *Books Beginning From* and *Financial Year From* would be same. Tally carries the date you enter in pervious field, press **Enter** to accept it or enter the Date from which you actually wish to maintain books in Tally.

TallyVault Password	To store data in encrypted form, opt to *TallyVault* the company data. You would be prompted to enter TallyVault Password and repeat the same at next prompt. If do not wish to opt TallyVault, just press **Enter** at this prompt.
Use Security Control	To restrict access to Company's data only to Authorised Users, say *Yes* to create Administrator. Enter Name of Administrator, Password and confirm the same at next field. If you do not wish any Security Control, respond *No.*

In bottom part you enter details of base Currency entered at the *Currency Symbol* field in the top section.

Base Currency Symbol	The Currency Symbol entered at *Currency Symbol* field (at top section) is displayed here for information—however you cannot alter it here.
Formal Name	Enter *Formal Name* for the *Base Currency.* Example : Indian Rupees, US Dollar, Australian Dollar, Hongkong Dollar, etc. Must be different from Currency Symbol.
Number of Decimal Places	Enter here number of decimal places for the Currency (for Dollar, Pound, Rupees—it is 2, for Dinars—3) to express in decimals.
Show Amount in Millions	For visual clarity, large Amounts are formatted by separators. To format in *Millions,* say *Yes,* respond *No* to format in *Lacs.*
Is Symbol	To put Currency Symbol before amount, say *No* (*e.g.,* US $ 1000, ₹ 1000)
Suffixed to Amounts ?	To print after amount, say *Yes.*
Put a Space Between Amount and Symbol	If you want a blank space between the amount and symbol, say *Yes.* If no space is required between amount and symbol, say *No.*

Step 3. On completing the total information, you will be asked Accept ? Yes or No. Click Yes to save the whole information. Now the company has been created and would be displayed under 'List of Selected Companies'.

PROCESS OF SELECTION OF A COMPANY

To select a company or shut a company or alter any information in the company already created, you need to have company Info. Menu. For invoking *'Company Info.'* menu, press *Alt* and *F3* keys simultaneously. This gives you the Company Information Screen as shown in Fig. 2.

The **Company Information menu** comprises of :

- **Select Company.** To select or load a company. A company can be selected only if it exists. It can be selected in the following way :

  (*a*) Select the option *Select Company* in this menu by pressing **S.**

  (*b*) Highlight the company to be selected with the help of arrow keys from the displayed List of Companies and press *Enter.*

- **Shut Company.** To shut a company. Shutting a company means unloading it. You can shut a company in the following way :

  (*a*) Select the option *Shut Company* in this menu by Pressing **H.**

  (*b*) Highlight the Company you wish to shut down from the List of Companies and press *Enter.*

  This Company can be loaded again as and when desired.

- **Create Company.** To Create a company. The steps for creating a company have been discussed.

- **Alter.** To Alter or modify the information relating to a company. You can make alterations to a company in the following way :

  (*a*) Press **A** key to select the *Alter* option from the *Company Info.* menu.

  (*b*) Highlight the Company you wish to alter from the List of Companies and press *Enter.* You have Company Alteration Screen.

GROUP FORMATION

The next step in preparation of final account after creating/selecting a company is *Group information* grouping of accounts and the resulting hierarchy of Ledger accounts from the part of accounting frame work of Computerised Accounting System.

To develop well-structured, flexible and informative set of data it is very important to classify the accounts. The way of classification of accounts will affect the accounting system's ability to store and retrieve the transaction data. Classifying means grouping or categorising accounts according to some common basis. The grouping should result in meaningful categories of accounts.

A set of accounts, which has some common characteristic(s), constitute an accounting group. The concept of grouping is used to create a hierarchy of Ledger accounts so that a logical accounting framework is put to place to design, develop and use a computerised accounting system. A group created by such categorisation of accounts must be a named group so as to represent the category. For example, Ledger of Trade Debtors consists of accounts of customers and Ledger of Trade Creditors contains account of suppliers. Both the Ledgers are Subsidiary Ledgers and the remaining accounts are bunched together to constitute the main Ledger. The Main Ledger is a default Ledger, which contains all other accounts that are not specifically classified in a system of accounting. The objective of system of control accounts is to exercise control over Subsidiary Ledgers and to provide quick information and expedite reporting. Therefore, under this system, two types of Ledgers : General and Specialised are maintained. The proxy account for of the subsidiary ledgers, also called control account is maintained in the general ledger. The main ledger with these control accounts is called as general ledger. Subsidiary ledger with the corresponding control account is called Specialised Ledger.

Under this system, every control account in the general ledger is posted with aggregates of different classes of transactions pertaining to their respective specialised ledgers. As a result, the final balance in the control accounts is exactly equal to aggregate of balances in each of the accounts of specialised ledger represented by such a control account.

GROUP FORMATION IN TALLY

Tally follows the 'Single Ledger' concept of accounting, which is the modern way of managing accounts. This is in direct contrast to Subsidiary Ledger Accounting. Thus, all financial entries are performed using ledgers or account heads. Ledger account head are created to identify transactions.

To single ledger concept does eliminate the need for sub-ledgers and corresponding control accounts in General Ledger. To comply with requirements of financial accounts, in Tally ledger accounts are identified and classified according to their nature in particular groups. This group ledger information is useful for presentation of summarized accounting data in the form of reports.

At the highest level of grouping, accounts are classified into capital or revenue—more specifically into assets, liabilities, income and expenditure. Based on mercantile accounting principles, Tally provides a set of **reserved groups** and allows you to modify their names or crate sub-groups.

Groups have a hierarchical organization. At the top of the hierarchy are Primary Groups. These are the main asset, liability, income or expenditure groups of accounts that determine the entire accounting and their presentation, i.e., whether a ledger affects Profit & Loss Account (as a revenue item) or goes into the Balance Sheet (as a capital item).

Primary Groups of Capital Nature

1. Capital Account
   (*a*) Reserves and Surplus [Retained Earnings]
2. Loans (Liability)
   Bank OD Accounts [Bank OCC Accounts]
   (*a*) Secured Loans
   (*b*) Unsecured Loans
3. Current Liabilities
   (*a*) Duties and Taxes
   (*b*) Provisions
   (*c*) Sundry Creditors

4. Fixed Assets
5. Investments
6. Current Assets
   (a) Bank Accounts
   (b) Cash-in-hand
   (c) Deposits
   (d) Loans & Advances
   (e) Stock-in-hand
   (f) Sundry Debtors
7. Suspense Account
8. Miscellaneous Expenses
9. Branch/Divisions

Primary Groups of Revenue Nature

10. Sales Account
11. Purchase Account
12. Direct Income
13. Indirect Income
14. Direct Expenses
15. Indirect Expenses

For forming more groups in the selected company, highlight *Accounts Info.* in Tally Main Screen and press *Enter* or press hot key **A.**

Gateway of Tally → *Accounts Info* → *Groups* : Double click on Groups/Press **G** on keyboard/ select Group from arrow keys and then press *Enter*.

Following screen is displayed—

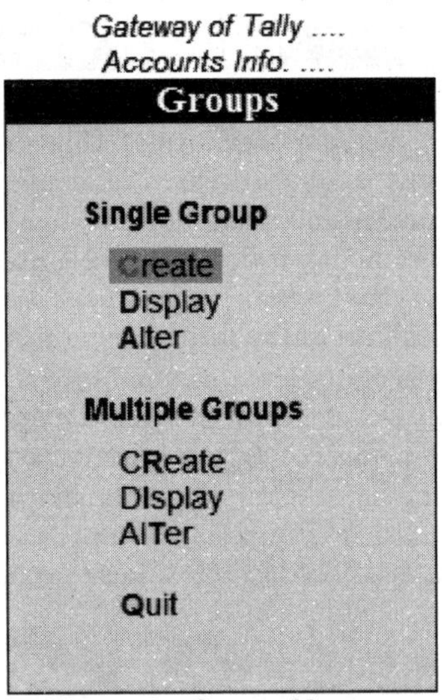

Figure 4 : Group Menu

You may create, alter, or display a single Group or multiple Groups.

Single group option is useful when you wish to work on one group at a time. Multiple groups option is used when work is to done on many sub-groups at a time. It is a time and labour saving option in a list format.

SINGLE GROUP

Gateway of Tally → Accounts info → Groups → Single Create

Buttons in single group screen

F3 : Company. to work with a different company. In the creation mode, you can create groups in the other company. In alter mode, you can copy the information by accepting the screen (<enter> or <Ctrl>+<A>). The old company's information remains.

F3 : Cmp Info. To work on the same report of another company. Available only in display mode.

To enable you to switch some advanced areas on/off without having to quit from the current screen.

F11 : Features. To change company features.

F12 : Configure. To change configuration of master information.

For the scope of our illustration we would set all the options to **NO.**

Note

1. Configuration changes affect all companies whereas Features changes affect only the company for whom features are changed.
2. Advanced mode allows entry of additional information as follows :
   - Creation of Primary Group
   - Control behaviour like sub-ledger
   - Used for calculation of taxes and discounts in invoices.

If you have not opted for advanced entries in masters, you will need to enter only the following information to create a group :

Name of Group. Enter the name of the desired group or sub-group. (*e.g.,* Misc. Expenses)

Alias. Give an alias to allow access the group using the Alias in addition to its name; or leave it blank (*e.g.,* for Misc. expenses, you can give 'Other Expenses' or even an alphanumeric code, say 'Exp123', as an alias).

Under. Specify under which existing (Parent) group the sub-classification is needed. Here if required, you can create a new Parent Group by using **<Alt>+<C>.**

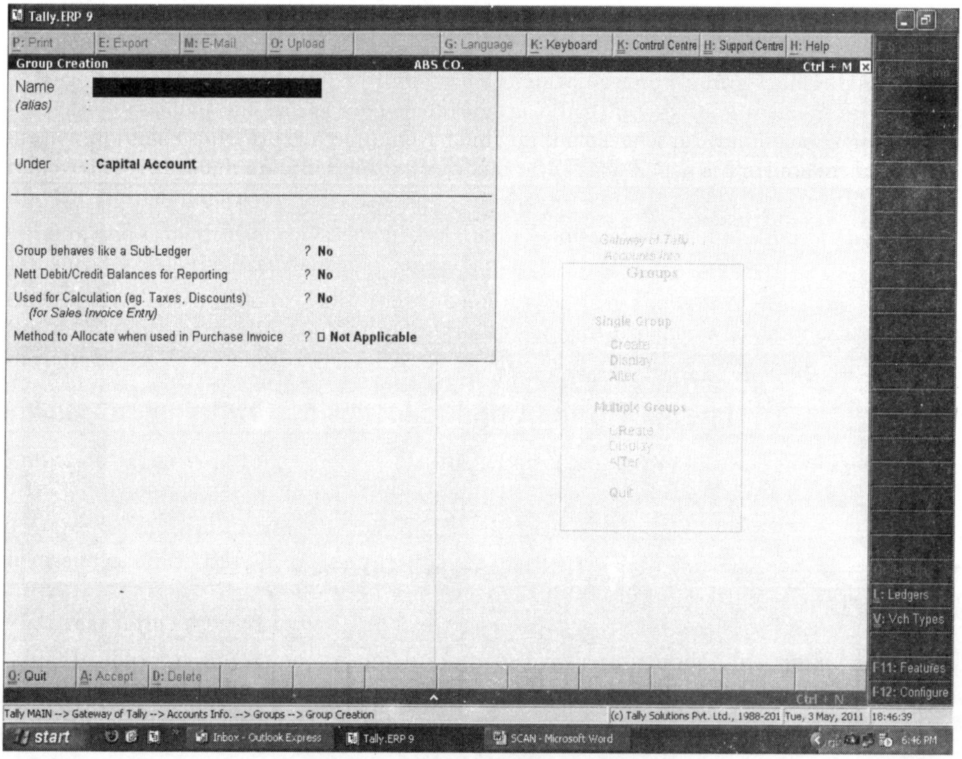

Fig. 5 : Group Creation Screen

Following are applicable only when advanced mode is activated :

Under. If it is a new primary group, select **Primary** (requirement of a new primary group would be extremely rare but the option exists). Creation of new Primary Group is not allowed if Advanced entries are not permitted (set to **No**).

If a new Primary Group is created, you must specify whether it is an asset, liability, income or expenditure by selecting the appropriate option. If you specify an income or expenditure you may also determine whether it affects gross profits by suitably answering the question—

Does it affect Gross Profits ? **Yes/No.**

Group behaves like sub-ledger?

To display **Sundry Debtors** without Ledger break-up in statements. Normally Sundry Debtors would have a large number of ledger accounts under it and it can be exploded during display to show ledger balances. To avoid this detailed display, choose **Yes.**

Used for Calculation (*e.g.* taxes, discounts) ?

Used if ledgers under this group would have percentages for discounts/taxes to be used for invoice entry.

Display Groups

To find out the list of groups existing the system follow the path: Gateway of Tally → Accounts Info → Groups → Single Group → Display and get the following Display Group Screen:

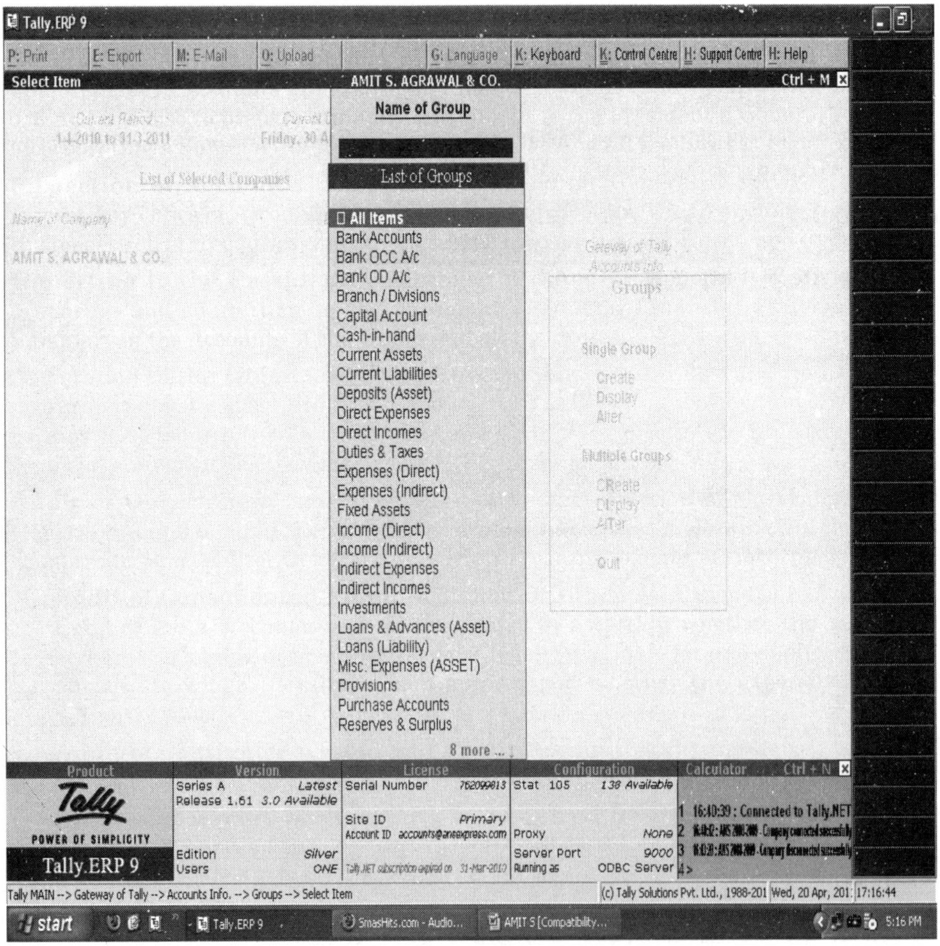

Fig. 6 : Display Group Screen

For Altering or modifying a group :

Gateway of Tally → Accounts Info → Groups → Single Alter

Group Alteration

Name **Capital Account**
(*alias*)
Under ☐ Primary
Nature of Group ? Liabilities
Group behaves like a Sub-Ledger ? No
Used for Calculation (e.g. Taxes, Discount) ? No
(*for Sales invoice Entry*)
Method to Allocate when used in Purchase Invoice ? ☐ Not Applicable
Net Debit/Credit Balances for Reporting ? No

Fig. 7 : Group Alteration Screen

For permanently deleting a group : First remove all ledgers specified under this group and then press the key combination Alt + D.

MULTIPLE GROUPS

This menu option is used to crate multiple groups with in the same screen simultaneously.

Gateway of Tally → Accounts Info → Groups → Multiple Create

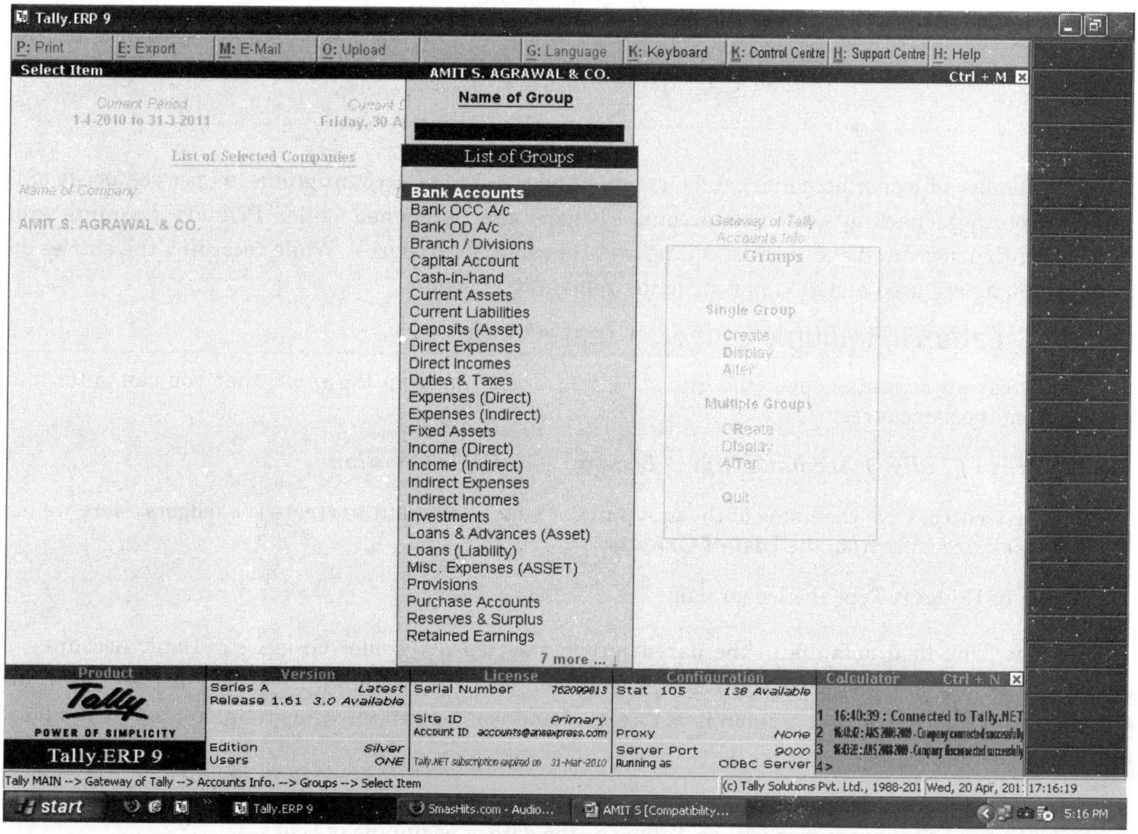

Fig. 8 : Multiple Group Creation Screen

LEDGER CREATION IN TALLY

At the time of creation of a company, Tally automatically creates two ledgers. Cash and Profit and Loss Account. Rest of the ledgers have to be created.

To create a ledger account Gateway of Tally → Account Info. → Ledgers → Single Create.

If all features and configure options are set to No, the following ledger screen will appear with four prompts namely name, alias, under and opening balance.

Ledger Creation		Ctrl + M
Name :		Total Op. Bal.
(alias) :		
Under :		
Inventory values are affected ?		No
Opening Balance :		
Name :	Mailing and Related Details	
	Income Tax No. :	
Address :	Sales Tax No. :	

Any number of ledger accounts can be created under different account groups as per the needs of the organisation. *E.g.,* packing expenses account (ledger) can be opened under Primary accounts group 'Marketing Expenses' and sub-groups 'Selling and Distribution expenses'. While recording the entries only ledger accounts are used and grouping structure remains transparent.

Ledger Creation in Multiple Ledgers Create Mode

This gives an advantage over the *Single Ledger Create* mode in the sense that you can enter many ledgers from the same screen.

Gateway of Tally → Accounts Info → Ledger → Multiple Creation

Under Group. Give the name of the group under which you want to create the ledgers. Here we have selected Bank Accounts from the **List of Groups.**

Name of Ledger. Type the ledger name.

Under. This field defaults to the parent group selected for 'Under Group' *e.g.* Bank Accounts. All entries in this column would be the same. You cursor skips this column. However, in case the **'Under Group'** field is 'all Items', this column is not skipped and you may specify the group. You are then allowed to even create a new group.

Opening Balance. Type the opening balance of the ledger account. This is the opening balance of the account when you first put your books on Tally, *i.e.,* the date of beginning of books.

Following screen shows creation of ledger accounts in Multiple Ledger Creation Mode Under Group : All items :

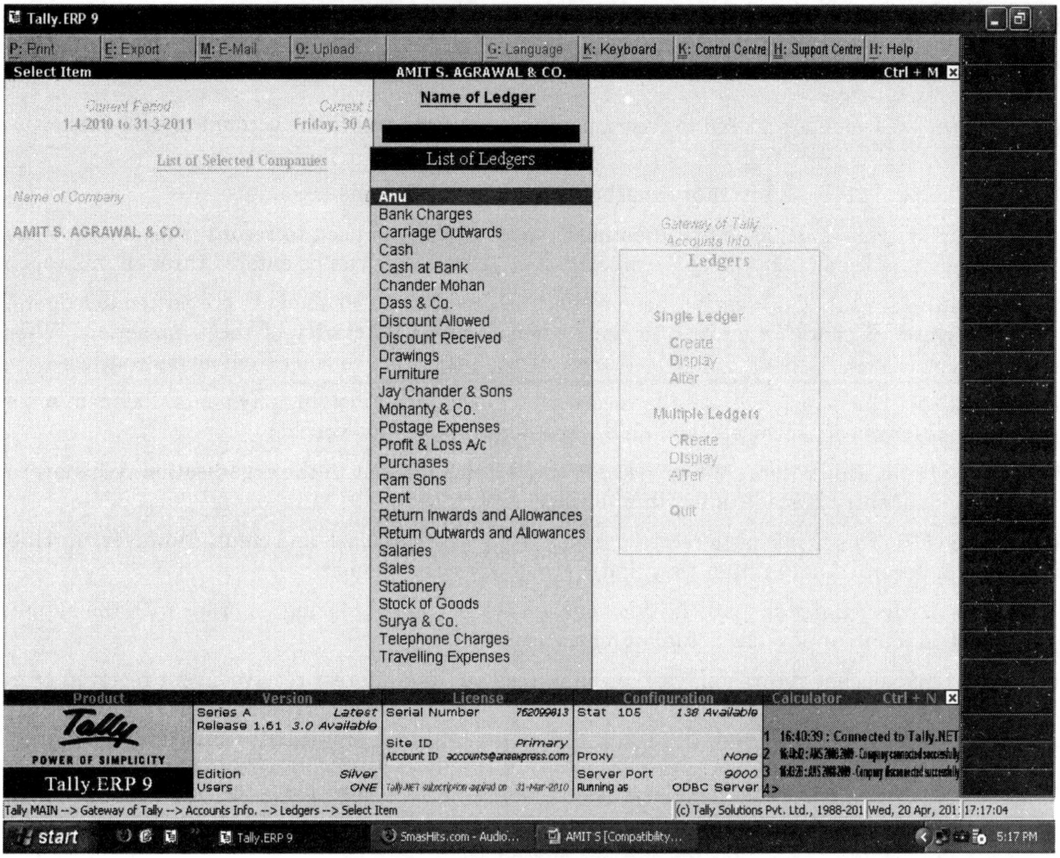

Fig. 9 : Ledger Creation Screen

VOUCHER CREATION

Process of Making a Voucher Entry

A voucher is a basic document used for recording transactions. It is a key to all business information. All the business transactions are entered through vouchers in Tally. While entering the transaction, the double entry system of accounting is to be followed and for each debit, there must be a corresponding credit. Accounts for the purpose of recording are classified into : Personal, Real and Nominal A/cs. All of you are aware of the basic rules of debit and credit which are given below :

1. Personal A/cs
   - Debit the Receiver
   - Credit the giver
2. Real A/cs
   - Debit what comes in
   - Credit what goes out
3. Nominal A/cs
   - Debit all expenses and losses
   - Credit all incomes and gains

Tally provides 16 pre-defined voucher types which fulfill normal transaction needs. If there is a need to create more voucher types, Tally allows the user to do so. The voucher types available in Tally are :

Contra (F4). To record the transactions where debit and credit accounts are cash and bank a/c only.

Credit Note. To record transactions like sales returns by customer where the account of the party is to be credited.

Debit Note. This voucher is used to record purchases returns where the account of the supplier is to be debited.

Delivery Note. This is an inventory voucher and will not affect the accounts.

Journal (F7). This voucher is an adjustment voucher. This is used to record transactions where no physical movement of funds takes place. Depreciation on fixed assets can be entered through this voucher.

Memorandum (F10). This voucher has no effect on accounts as no amounts are posted to ledgers from this voucher. Entry is made in such a voucher when there is no clarity of the transaction. When the transaction becomes clear later on, it can be transferred to respective voucher from memo voucher.

Payment(F5). This voucher is used to record all transactions involving payments. Payment of salary, electricity bill, purchase of assets, etc. will all be recorded through this voucher.

Physical Stock. This records the physical stock of items present in the organisation. Whenever stock taking is conducted, entry is made under this voucher.

Purchase (F9). This is meant to record purchases of goods both cash and credit. However, purchases of assets are not be recorded here rather they find place in payment voucher.

Purchase Order. Entry is made in this voucher at the time of placing an order with the supplier. It has no effect on accounts unless the actual purchases are made.

Receipt. This voucher records all cash or bank receipts like interest received, rent received or money received from sale of fixed assts.

Receipt Note. This is an inventory voucher and will not affect accounts.

Rejections In. This is to record the inventory items which have been rejected by customers. The accounting aspect is dealt with credit note.

Rejections Out. It records rejection of goods purchased.

Reversing Journal. This is a memo-voucher and has no effect on accounts.

Sales (F8). This voucher records all sales whether on cash or credit. Sales of fixed assets do not find any place here.

Sales Order. This is used to record any order for sale of goods received by customers.

Stock Journal. This voucher has no effect on accounts. It is used to transfer stocks from one location to another.

While making a voucher entry, *the following steps are to be taken* :

1. Check the date of voucher to be entered. To change the date, press F2 function key. Type the required date and press Enter.
2. Identify the voucher type of transaction like purchase, sale, receipt, payment etc. Select the type of voucher by pressing appropriate function key.
3. Identify ledger accounts in the transaction.
4. Identify the debit and credit accounts according to the rules of accounting.
5. Identify the amount of debit and credit.
6. Enter the voucher by selection debit and credit accounts and then type respective amounts and narration.
7. Select Accept Yes.

After making entries through vouchers, ledger accounts will possess some balances. The closing balances of ledger accounts are shown in a statement known as Trial Balance. The format of Trial Balance is as follows :

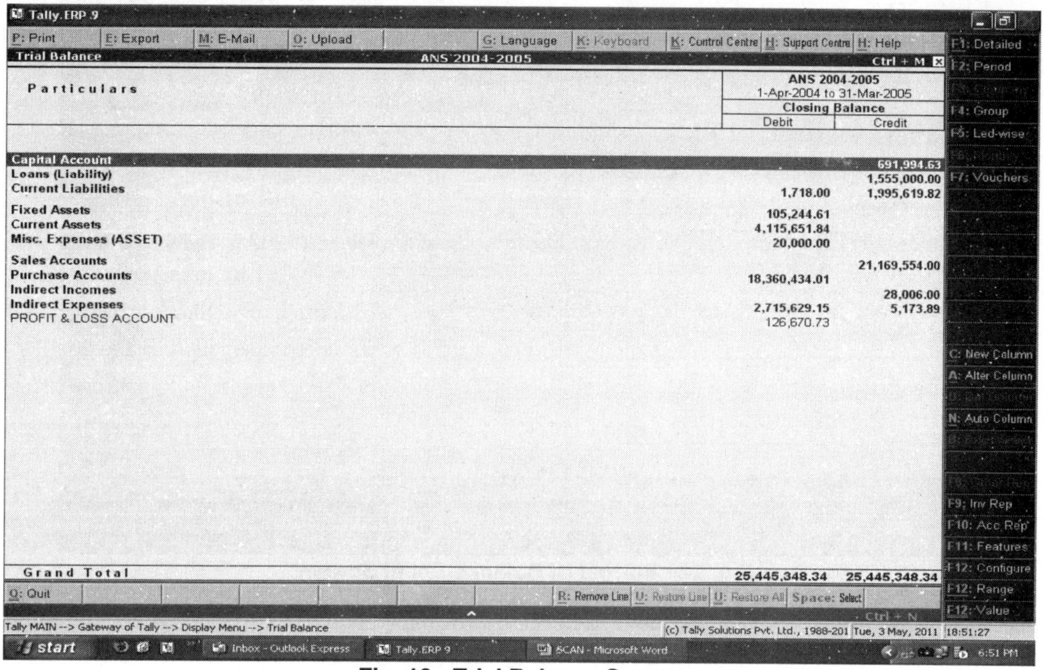

Fig. 10 : Trial Balance Screen

Tally transfers amounts from the trial balance automatically to the Profit and Loss A/c and Balance Sheet. The format of P/L A/c is :

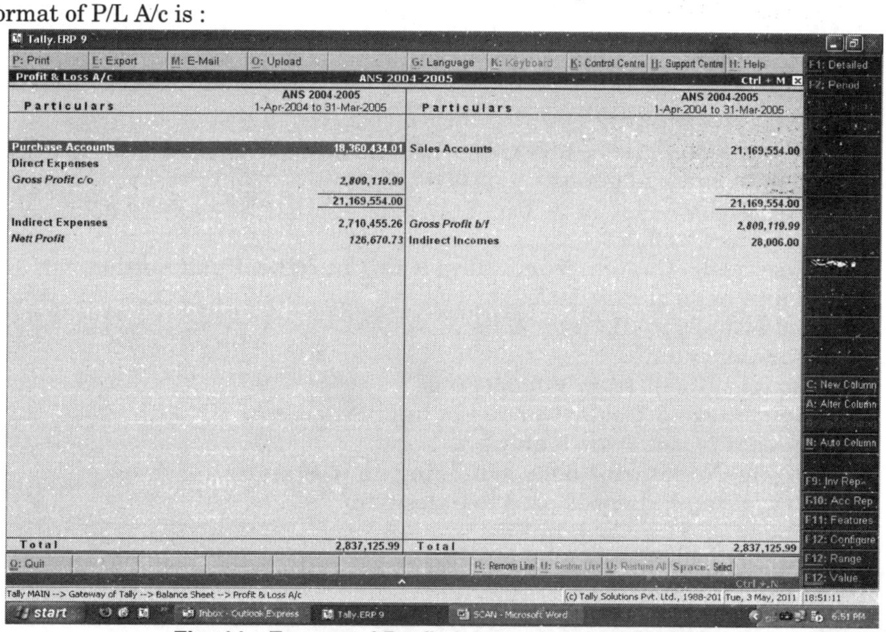

Fig. 11 : Format of Profit & Loss Account Screen

Profit and Loss will show the net profit of the business automatically.

Balance Sheet displays the financial position of the business for which information is automatically gathered from Trial Balance. The prime source of information is, however, vouchers.

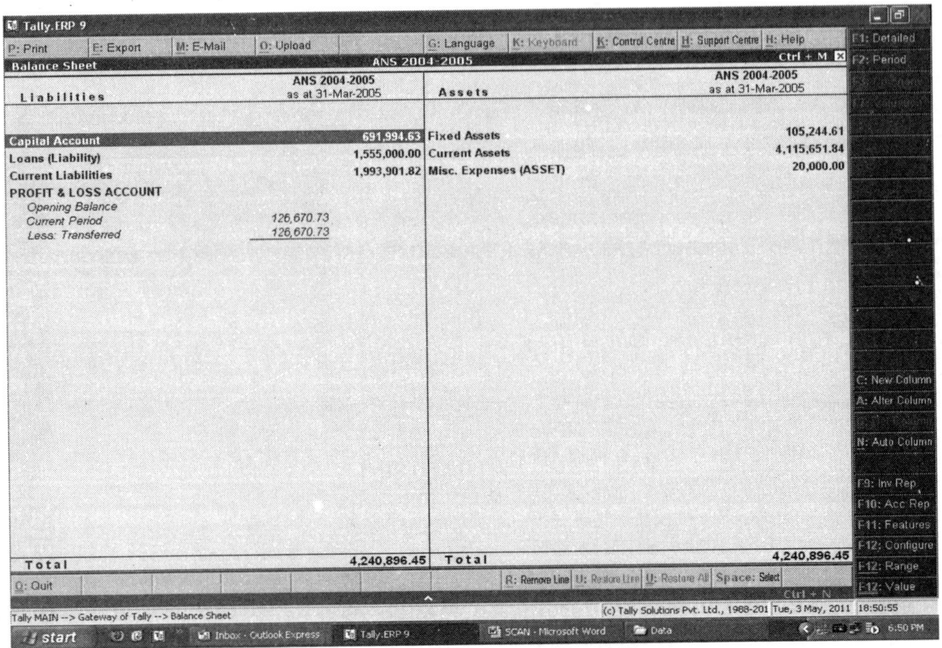

Fig. 12 : Format of Balance Sheet Screen

Once Tally is loaded, it makes the job of an accountant easy. The accountant has to supply only the basic information or he has to make only voucher entries and rest is taken care by Tally. Tally user can easily get reports like Trial Balance, Profit and Loss A/c and Balance Sheet without much effort and botheration.

ILLUSTRATION 1. Enter the following transactions in the Journal of Amit S. Agrawal & Co., post them to the Ledger, Prepare Trial Balance, P & L A/c and Balance Sheet using Tally,.ERP 9 software.

			₹
2005 Apr.	**1**	**Assets in hand: Cash ₹ 2,520; Cash at Bank ₹ 92,400 Rahul & Co. ₹ 27,000; Stock of goods ₹ 1,05,600.**	
		Liabilities : Surya & Co. ₹ 15,520; Vikash Sons ₹ 12,000; Amit Capital ₹ 2,00,000	
	2	**Received a Cheque from Rahul & Co., in full & Final Settlement**	**26,600**
	3	**Sold Goods to Roy & Co.**	**5,600**
	4	**Sold Goods to Chander & Sons**	**5,760**
		Carriage paid	**140**
	5	**Bought Goods from Vikash Sons**	**12,480**
		Paid Surya & Co. by Cheque in full Settlement	**15,200**
	6	**Bought Goods from Mohit**	**25,200**
	7	**Roy & Co. return Goods, not being up to Standard**	**400**
		Travelling Expenses paid to Salesman	**588**
		Goods sold for Cash to Vijay	**3,200**
	10	**Paid for Stationery**	**264**
		Postage Stamps	**60**
	13	**Returned Goods to Mohit (not being up to mark)**	**1,200**
		Mohit also admit claim for Breakage of Goods	**400**
	15	**Paid for Furniture by Cheque**	**2,800**
	16	**Goods used Personally by Proprietor**	**200**
	17	**Sold Goods to Rahul & Co.**	**20,000**

19	**Roy & Co. pay by Cheque**	**5,200**
20	**Cheque received from Chander & Sons**	**5,760**
22	**Bank returned Chander & Sons Cheque being Dishonoured**	
23	**Sold Goods to Ajay for Cash**	**9,200**
24	**Cash Deposited with Bank**	**8,000**
27	**Cheque sent to Mohit (Discount allowed ₹ 200)**	**23,400**
29	**Paid Telephone Charges**	**92**
30	**Paid Salaries**	**2,400**
	Paid Rent	**1,200**
	Bank Charges	**40**
	Drew for personal use out of Bank	**2,000**
	Received claim from Rahul & Co., for defects on Goods supplied to them; Claim admitted	**600**

Additional Information : Closing stock is valued at ₹ 1,20,000.

STEP-I Company Creation

For creating a company you first click on :

F3 : *Cmp Info* button on the Button Panel to have the *Company Info.* Menu. You get the Company Info screen. Now select *Create Company* option from Company Info menu either by double clicking on '*Create Company*' or by pressing **C** from keyboard. You will get the Company creation screen. The particulars of Amit S. Agrawal & Co. are filled up by imaginary information as required information relating to the company is not given in the illustration. After filling the particulars, you will find the screen in the following format :

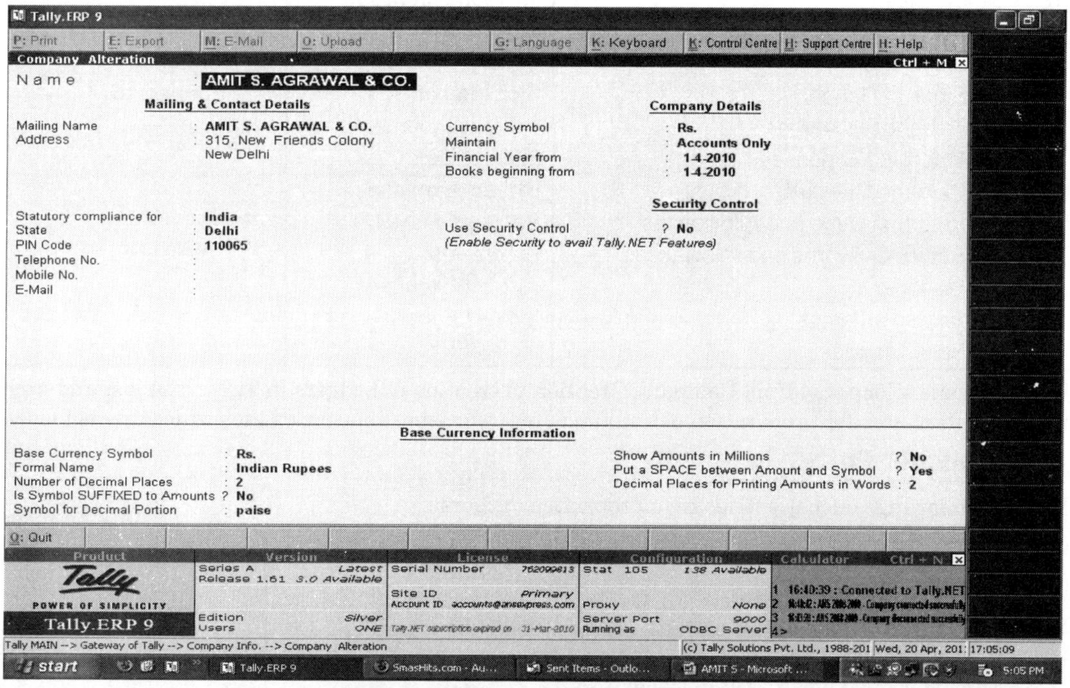

Fig. 13 : Company Creation Screen

Finally, confirm company creation by pressing the *Enter* key or 'Y' key to accept all declaration for the company.

Now the next step is to form Groups.

STEP-II Group formation

In our illustration, we need not create any group as its scope is limited to use of default groups predefined in Tally.

STEP-III Ledger Creation

Following ledgers need to be created for our illustration :

S. No.	Ledger Account	Under Group	Opening Balance (₹)
1.	Capital Account	Capital Account	2,00,000 (Cr.)
2.	Cash	Cash in hand	2,520 (Dr.)
3.	Cash at Bank	Bank Accounts	92,400 (Dr.)
4.	Mohit	Sundry Creditors	—
5.	Roy & Co.	Sundry Debtors	—
6.	Discount Allowed	Indirect Expenses	—
7.	Discount Received	Indirect Income	—
8.	Drawings	Capital Account	—
9.	Furniture	Fixed Assets	—
10.	Chander & Sons	Sundry Debtors	—
11.	Rahul & Co.	Sundry Debtors	27,000 (Dr.)
12.	Purchases	Purchases	—
13.	Vikash Sons	Sundry Creditors	12,000 (Dr.)
14.	Roy & Co.	Sundry Debtors	—
15.	Rent	Indirect Expenses	—
16.	Salaries	Indirect Expenses	—
17.	Sales	Sales Account	—
18.	Surya & Co.	Sundry Creditors	15,520 (Cr.)
19.	Stock of Goods	Stock-in-hand	1,05,600 (Dr.)
20.	Telephone Charges	Indirect Expenses	—
21.	Travelling Expenses	Indirect Expenses	—
22.	Carriage Outward	Indirect Expenses	—
23.	Return Inwards and Allowances	Sales	—
24.	Return Outwards and Allowances	Purchases	—
25.	Stationery	Indirect Expenses	—
26.	Postage Stamps	Indirect Expenses	—
27.	Bank Charges	Indirect Expenses	—

We have come a long way from Company Creation to creation of Ledgers in Tally. The last and probably the most important step for preparation of final accounts is passing voucher entries which are as follows.

STEP-IV Voucher Entry

Pass the following voucher entries in appropriate vouchers :

Date			₹	₹
April 2	**Receipt Voucher**			
	By Cash at Bank	Dr.	26,600	
	To Rahul & Co. (Sundry Debtors)			26,600
	(Being cheque received from Rahul & Co.)			
	Journal Voucher			
	By Discount Allowed	Dr.	400	
	To Rahul & Co. (Sundry Debtors)			400
	(Being discount allowed to Mohanty & Co. for prompt payment)			

Date	Particulars		Dr.	Cr.
April 3	**Sales Voucher**			
	By Roy & Co. (Sundry Debtors)	Dr.	5,600	
	To Sales			5,600
	(Being goods sold on credit to Roy & Co.)			
April 4	**Sales Voucher**			
	By Chander & Sons (Sundry Debtors)	Dr.	5,960	
	To Sales			5,960
	(Being goods sold on credit to Chander & Sons)			
	Payment Voucher			
	By Carriage Outwards	Dr.	140	
	To Cash			140
	(Being carriage paid)			
April 5	**Purchase Voucher**			
	By Purchases	Dr.	12,480	
	To Vikash Sons (Sundry Creditors)			12,480
	(Being goods purchased on credit)			
	Payment Voucher			
	By Surya & Co. (Sundry Creditors)	Dr.	15,200	
	To Cash at Bank			15,200
	(Being payment made to Surya & Co. in full settlement)			
	Journal Voucher			
	By Surya & Co.	Dr.	320	
	To Discount Received			320
	(Being discount received from Surya & Co.)			
April 6	**Purchase Voucher**			
	By Purchases	Dr.	25,200	
	To Mohit (Sundry Creditors)			25,200
	(Being goods purchased on credit)			
April 7	**Credit Note**			
	By Return Inwards and Allowances	Dr.	400	
	To Roy & Co. (Sundry Debtor)			400
	(Being goods returned by Roy & Co.)			
	Payment Voucher			
	By Travelling Expenses	Dr.	588	
	To Cash			588
	(Being travelling expenses paid)			
	Receipt Voucher			
	By Cash	Dr.	3,200	
	To Sales			3,200
	(Being goods sold for cash to Vijay)			
April 10	**Payment Voucher**			
	By Stationery	Dr.	264	
	To Cash			264
	(Being stationery purchased)			

Date	Particulars		Dr. Amount	Cr. Amount
	Payment Voucher By Postage Expense To Cash (Being postage purchased)	Dr.	60	60
April 13	**Debit Note** By Mohit (Sundry Creditors) To Returns Outwards and Allowances (Being goods returned to Mohit)	Dr.	1,200	1,200
	Debit Note By Mohit To Return Outwards & Allowances (Being claim admitted by Mohit for breakage of goods)	Dr.	400	400
April 15	**Payment Voucher** By Furniture To Cash at Bank (Being furniture purchased)	Dr.	2,800	2,800
April 16	**Journal Voucher** By Drawings To Purchases (Being goods withdrawn for personal use)	Dr.	200	200
April 17	**Sales Voucher** By Rahul & Co. (Sundry Debtors) By Sales (Being goods sold on credit)	Dr.	20,000	20,000
April 19	**Receipt Voucher** By Cash at Bank To Roy & Co. (Being a cheque received from Roy & Co.)	Dr.	5,200	5,200
April 20	**Receipt Voucher** By Cash at Bank To Chander & Sons (Being a cheque received from Chander & Sons)	Dr.	5,760	5,760
April 22	**Payment Voucher** By Chander & Sons To Cash at Bank (Being cheque of Chander & Sons dishonoured)	Dr.	5,760	5,760
April 23	**Receipt Voucher** By Cash To Sales (Being goods sold for cash to Ajay)	Dr.	9,200	9,200
April 24	**Contra** By Cash at Bank To Cash (Being cash deposited into bank)	Dr.	8,000	8,000

April 27	**Payment Voucher**			
	By Mohit	Dr.	23,400	
	To Cash at Bank			23,400
	(Being payment made to Mohit)			
April 27	**Journal Voucher**			
	By Mohit	Dr.	200	
	To Discount Received			200
	(Being discount received from Mohit)			
April 29	**Payment Voucher**			
	By Telephone Charges	Dr.	92	
	To Cash			92
	(Being telephone charges paid)			
April 30	**Payment Voucher**			
	By Salaries	Dr.	2,400	
	To Cash			2,400
	(Being salaries paid)			
April 30	**Payment Voucher**			
	By Rent	Dr.	1,200	
	To Cash			1,200
	(Being Rent paid)			
April 30	**Payment Voucher**			
	By Bank Charges	Dr.	40	
	To Cash at Bank			40
	(Being charges debited by bank)			
April 30	**Payment Voucher**			
	By Drawings	Dr.	2,000	
	To Cash at Bank			2,000
	(Being cash withdrawn from bank for personal use)			
April 30	**Journal Voucher**			
	By Return Inwards and Allowances	Dr.	600	
	To Mohanty & Co.			600
	(Being claim for defects on goods supplied admitted)			

Now that we have followed the four-step procedure of computerized accounting, *i.e.,*

1. Company Creation
2. Group Formation
3. Ledger Creation
4. Voucher Creation

We can proceed to see the further required reports like Trial Balance, Profit and Loss Account, Balance Sheet and Ratio Analysis Report.

STEP-IV Trial Balance

Tally automatically prepares Trial Balance, Profit and Loss Account, and Balance Sheet from the information entered.

Gateway of Tally → Reports → Display → Trial Balance

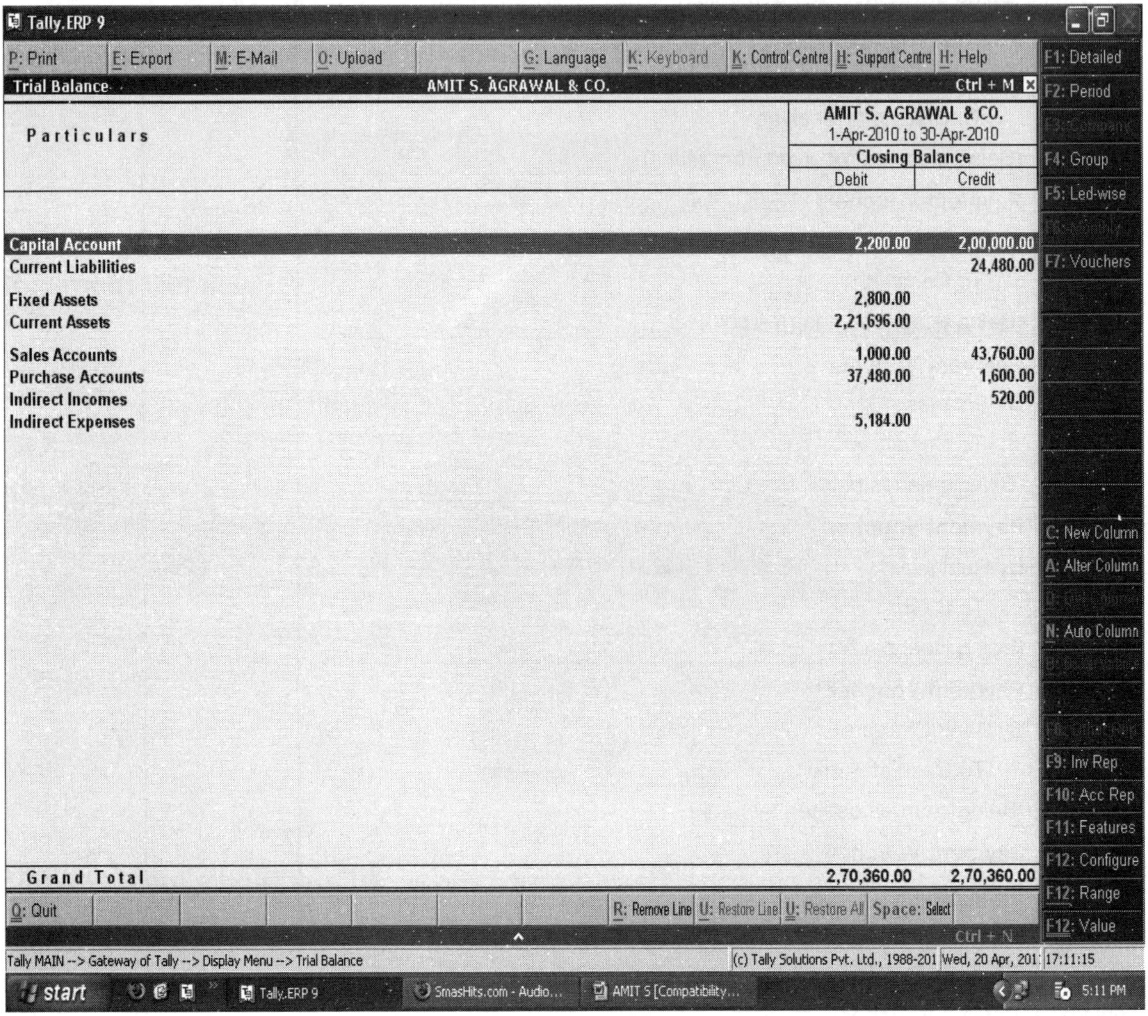

Trial Balance — AMIT S. AGRAWAL & CO.

Particulars	AMIT S. AGRAWAL & CO. 1-Apr-2010 to 30-Apr-2010 Closing Balance	
	Debit	Credit
Capital Account	2,200.00	2,00,000.00
Current Liabilities		24,480.00
Fixed Assets	2,800.00	
Current Assets	2,21,696.00	
Sales Accounts	1,000.00	43,760.00
Purchase Accounts	37,480.00	1,600.00
Indirect Incomes		520.00
Indirect Expenses	5,184.00	
Grand Total	2,70,360.00	2,70,360.00

Fig. 14 : Trial Balance

Entering Closing Stock. Enter closing stock value ₹ 60,000 under stock-in-hand group through Alteration mode that allows you to specify date and closing balance for that date. You can enter closing stock value either through

(*i*) Accounts Info → Ledger → Alter mode; or

(*ii*) In Balance Sheet by drilling down Current Assets → Stock in Hand → Ledger; or

(*iii*) From Profit and Loss Account by drilling down Opening or Closing Stock.

STEP-V Profit and Loss Account

Gateway of Tally → Report → Profit & Loss A/c

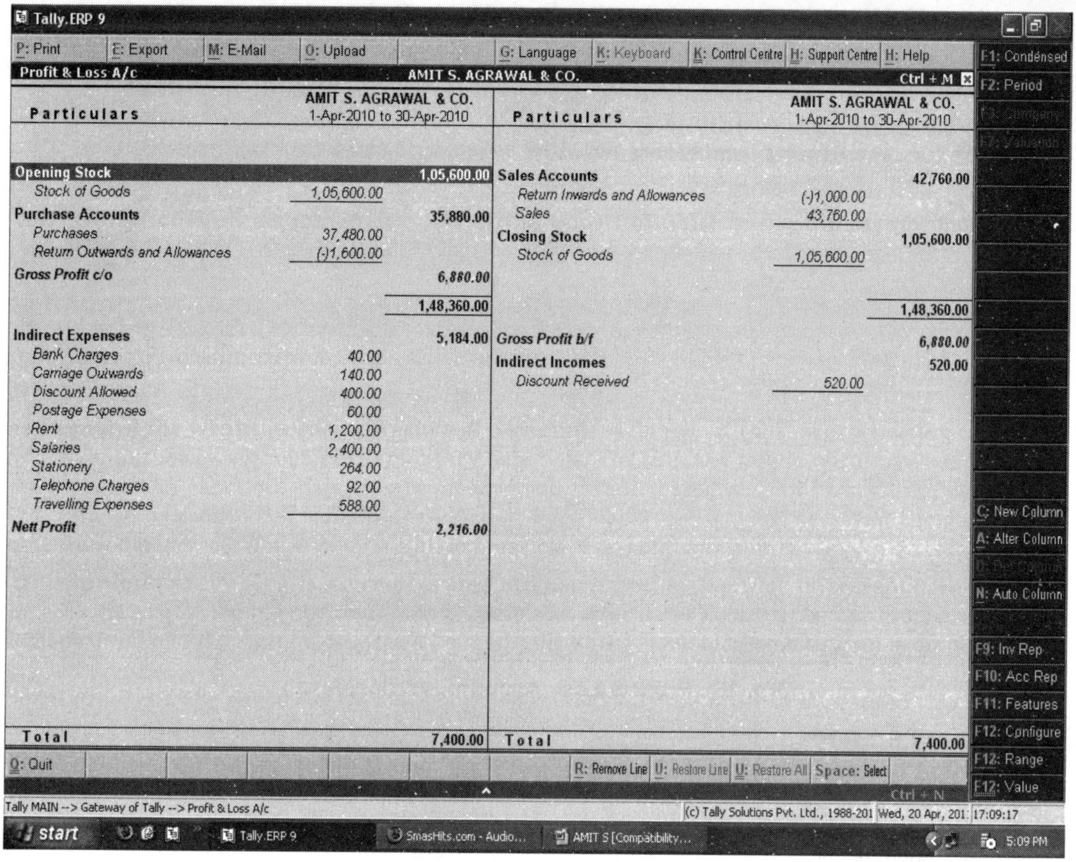

Tally.ERP 9

Profit & Loss A/c — AMIT S. AGRAWAL & CO.

Particulars	AMIT S. AGRAWAL & CO. 1-Apr-2010 to 30-Apr-2010		Particulars	AMIT S. AGRAWAL & CO. 1-Apr-2010 to 30-Apr-2010	
Opening Stock		1,05,600.00	**Sales Accounts**		42,760.00
Stock of Goods	1,05,600.00		*Return Inwards and Allowances*	(-)1,000.00	
Purchase Accounts		35,880.00	*Sales*	43,760.00	
Purchases	37,480.00		**Closing Stock**		1,05,600.00
Return Outwards and Allowances	(-)1,600.00		*Stock of Goods*	1,05,600.00	
Gross Profit c/o		6,880.00			
		1,48,360.00			1,48,360.00
Indirect Expenses		5,184.00	**Gross Profit b/f**		6,880.00
Bank Charges	40.00		**Indirect Incomes**		520.00
Carriage Outwards	140.00		*Discount Received*	520.00	
Discount Allowed	400.00				
Postage Expenses	60.00				
Rent	1,200.00				
Salaries	2,400.00				
Stationery	264.00				
Telephone Charges	92.00				
Travelling Expenses	588.00				
Nett Profit		2,216.00			
Total		7,400.00	**Total**		7,400.00

Fig. 15 : Profit & Loss Account Screen

One can also invoke Profit & Loss Configuration screen by pressing F12 from keyboard.

Configuration

Show Vertical Profit & Loss	?	Yes
Show Percentages	?	No
Show with Gross Profit	?	Yes
Appearance of Names	:	Name Only
Scale Factor for Values	:	Default

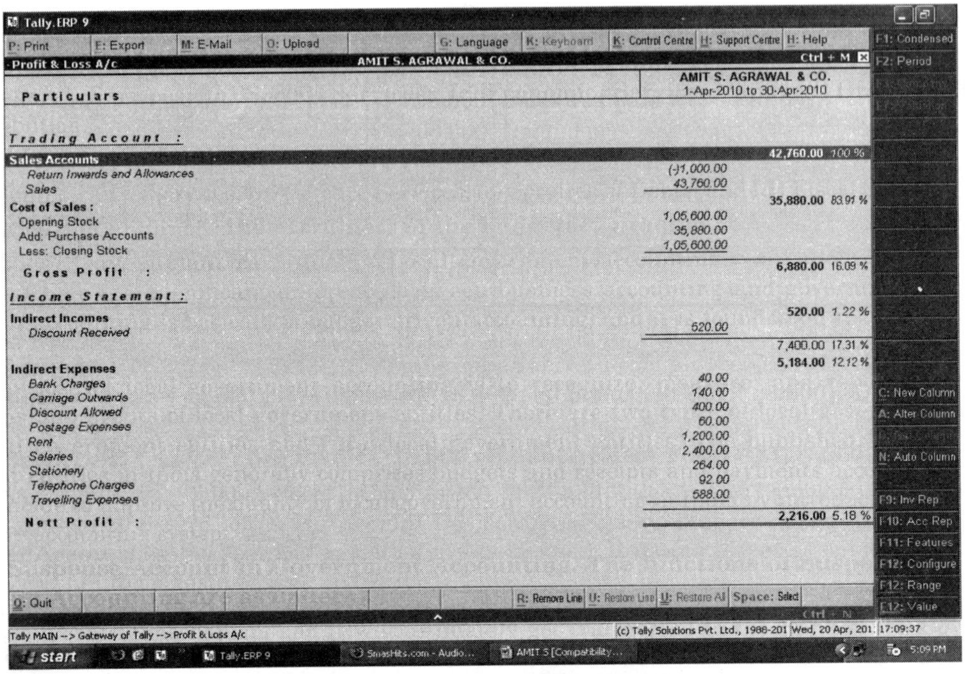

Fig. 16 : Profit & Loss Account (Vertical form)

STEP-VI Balance Sheet

Gateway of Tally → Reports → Balance Sheet

For a detailed view of balance sheet, click *__F1__* : *Detailed* in Button Bar, you get the detailed balance sheet screen as shown below :

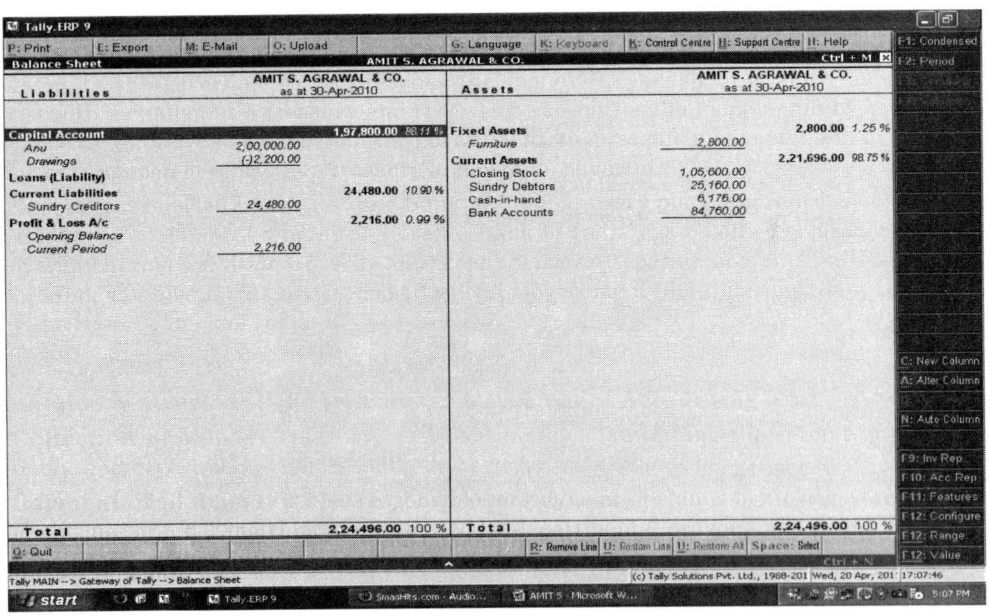

Fig. 17 : Balance Sheet Screen

For presenting balance sheet in vertical form, one can also invoke Balance Sheet configuration screen by pressing *F12* from keyboard or by clicking *F12* : *Configure* in Button Bar. You get the following screen :

Configuration

Show Vertical Balance Sheet	?	**Yes**
Show Percentages	?	No
Show Working Capital figures	?	Yes
Method of showing Balance Sheet	?	Liabilities/Assets
Appearance of Names	:	Name Only
Scale Factor for Values	:	Default

Write 'Yes' against 'Show Vertical Balance Sheet' and then press *enter* again and again till you get the Vertical Balance Sheet. It will be as follows :

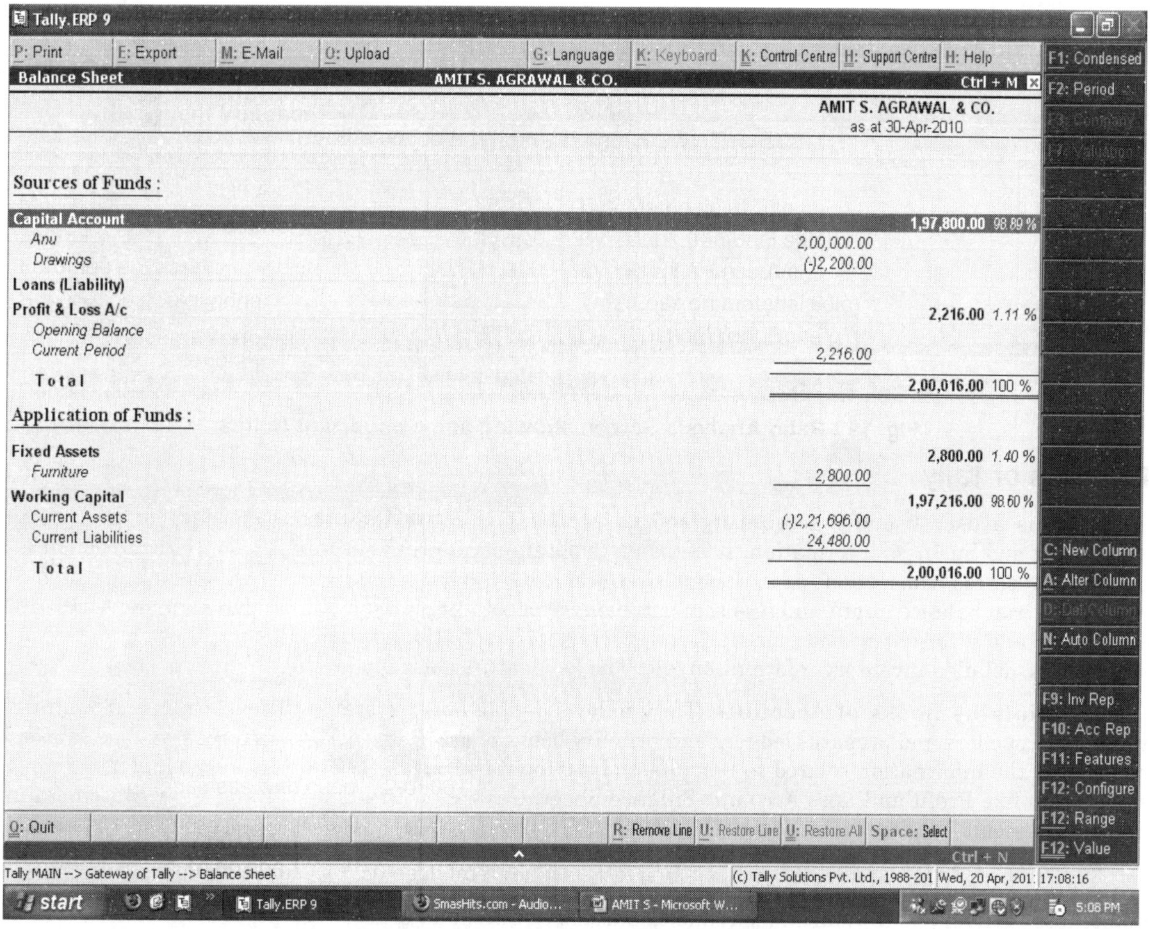

Fig. 18 : Vertical View of Balance Sheet

For detailed view of Vertical Balance Sheet, press **Alt + F1** keys or click on **F1 :** ***Detailed*** in Button Bar, you will get Detailed view of Vertical Balance Sheet.

We can also explore some other reports like Ratio analysis, Cash flow, Funds flow and other books like Sales register, purchase etc. can be also be generated.

STEP-VII Ratio Analysis Screen

Highlight ratio analysis and press *Enter* key or simply press hot key **R**, principal groups and principal ratios displayed on screen.

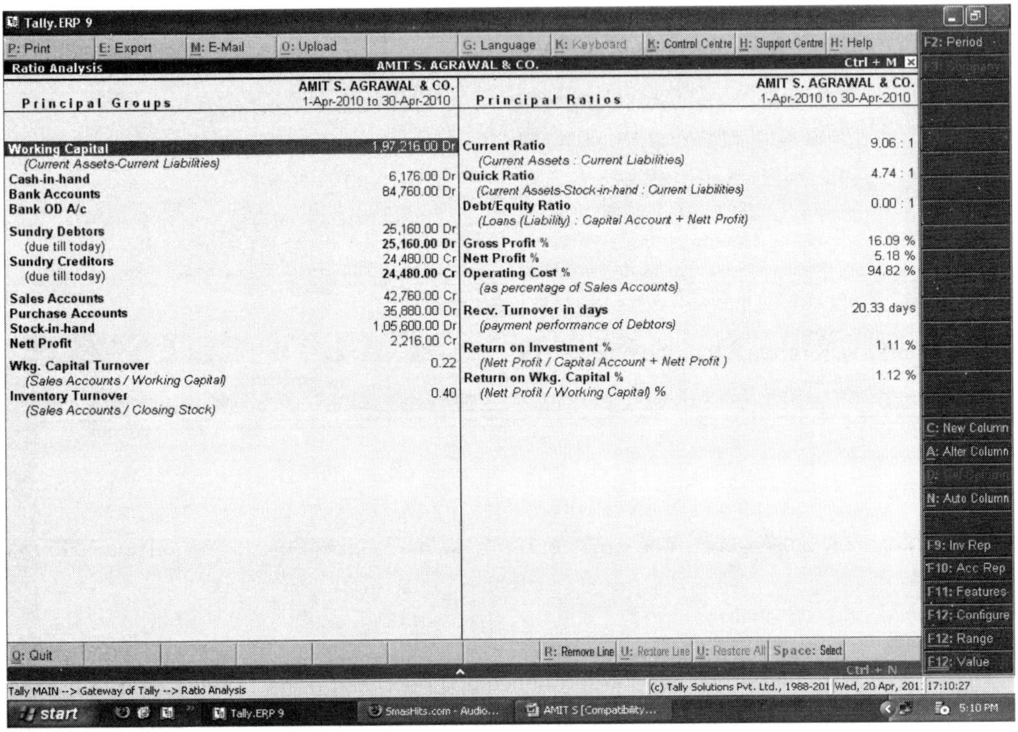

Fig. 19 : Ratio Analysis Screen showing some important Ratios

Features of Tally

Tally is a user friendly accounting software package. It provides the user with all the possible accounting and business information. It helps us to obtain accounting outputs. The only requirement is to enter the business transactions as and when they occur. Rest is left to Tally which will ensure maintenance of ledgers, trial balance, profit and loss account, balance sheet, comparison of financial statement with other companies and different periods, preparation of bank reconciliation statement, fund flows and cash flow statements, detailed inventory information, etc. The key features of Tally are highlighted below :

1. Maintains Books of Accounts. Tally follows double entry system of book keeping. It maintains records of vouchers and prepares ledgers and primary books of accounts such as cash book and bank book. It records all the information related to receipts and payments of business. Tally maintains all the financial statements like Profit and Loss Account, Balance Sheet, Cash Flow Statement, Fund Flow Statement and Stock Statement.

2. Voucher Types. Vouchers is the main document to record business transactions. Tally provides 16 pre-defined types of vouchers to record various transactions. The list of voucher types include credit note, debit note, delivery note, journal, payment, purchase, purchase order, receipt, receipt note, reversing journal, sales, sales order, physical stock and stock journal. Tally also gives a scope to the user to define different types of vouchers according to his requirements. The user can also have voucher numbering as per his needs. In other words, Tally provides flexibility in defining voucher types and voucher numbering.

3. Classification of Account-heads. Tally follows the 'Single Ledger' concept of accounting which includes both Personal and Nominal accounts. All accounting entries are made using ledgers or account heads. These ledgers have no meaning without proper classification. Tally allows the user to define ledgers according to requirements and also to group ledger accounts right at the time of creating them. This grouping and classification will be reflected in reports and statements at all times which proves to be meaningful. Everything is readily available as per needs and hence does not cause delay in reporting and decision-making.

4. Drill Down Display. It is possible to drill down to grass root level in Tally. One can view any group, ledger or voucher at a particular point of time. *E.g.* while viewing Profit and Loss A/c, the user can select any item of income or expenditure and can drill down till the vouchers. Similarly when Balance Sheet is studied, any item of asset or liability may be chosen and relevant information checked from the vouchers.

5. Printing of Vouchers, Cheques, etc. Tally facilitates the printing of vouchers which are entered by the user. The voucher can be printed as soon as it is entered. Printing could also be done for vouchers entered at previous dates and in previous periods. Tally also provides the facility of printing cheques, formal receipts and letters. For printing cheques, say yes to 'Enable Cheque Printing' option and enter the name of the company as signatory and name of the Bank for which account, cheque is to be printed.

6. Accounting Year of Choice. When the business is started in the middle of the financial year, the date of financial year does not coincide with the date of initiating business. *E.g.*, a business is started on 1st September 2009 and we don't want to have our accounting year as 1st June 2009 to 31st May 2010 rather we want to follow financial year say from 1st April 2010 to 31st March 2011. This can very easily be followed in Tally as when a company is created, Tally displays two heads—Financial Year From and Books Beginning From. Here two different dates *viz.* 1st April, 2010 and 1st June, 2010 can be entered under two heads respectively.

7. Split Financial Years. Tally's flexible period-less accounting permits entry of data for any number of years. Splitting financial years enables the user to retain most benefits. *E.g.,* four years data of a company from 1-1-08 to 31-12-11 are available which is to be split. Tally permits any date as the split point, however the beginning of the latest accounting year is recommended as the split point. In the above example, two new companies will be created—one with data from 1-1-08 to 31-12-2010, *i.e.,* three years, and the other for 1-1-2011 to 31-12-2011. This way, the historical data for three years will be preserved as one company and current financial year, as another.

8. Multiple Financial Years. The user is required to mention the beginning of financial year at the time of creation of a company. After that, he can maintain accounts for any number of periods by shifting from one period to another. He can also compare the information of one period with another period easily.

9. Quick Selection of Another Company. Tally provides the user to create and maintain any number of companies. If the user is working on one particular company and immediately wants to shift to another company, it can easily be done in Tally. To activate another company, click on the 'Name of Company' at Gateway under the 'List of Selected Companies'. Now the user can work on newly activated company. Hence two or more than two companies can be worked upon simultaneously without much botheration.

10. Multi Currency. When a company is created in Tally, currency symbol in which books of accounts are to be maintained is to be specified. This currency symbol is known as base currency. Besides base currency, Tally allows to record transactions in foreign currency, raise invoices in foreign currency and maintain bank accounts in foreign exchange. The user can print and view all reports in any currencies. However, in order to have meaningful reporting and analysis, a common currency, *i.e.,* base currency has to be used.

At the time of mentioning the currency in Tally, symbol along with formal name of the currency is to be given. *e.g.,* ₹ mentioned alone will not serve the purpose because it is the base currency in India and Nepal. So formal name *i.e.,* Indian Rupees has to be mentioned if it is company in India. Similarly for dollars, US dollars, Canadian dollars or Australian dollars has to be specified. By doing so, Tally would not be giving wrong picture by consolidating the accounts of two companies recorded in US dollars and Australian dollars and hence accuracy can be ensured.

11. Chronological Reporting. Tally produces all reports on the basis of the date of transactions and not on the basis of date of actual entry. This enables the books of accounts to represent accurate information.

12. Multi-Columnar Reporting. Tally displays columnar reports in ledgers, Cash Book, Bank Book, Purchase and Sales Registers. The information related to all reports is available for different periods and different companies. The user can compare and analyse the relevant information for multiple periods and different companies. This saves lot of time and energy as the required information is available on the same screen. Such kind of reporting helps the management in taking accurate and prompt decisions.

13. Filtering Report. Reports can be filtered through query. The user can give multiple query parameters and ask Tally to filter report suitable for 'All' or 'Any'. This is done as per the needs of the user.

14. Reconciliation of Bank Accounts. Reconciliation of bank accounts manually is known to all of you. Tally provides this facility of reconciliation and makes the things simpler for the user. The transactions which have not been cleared by the bank are highlighted. The data from which the user wants to reconcile his bank accounts, *i.e.,* 'Effective date of reconciliation' has to be mentioned along with the other basic information. Press F5 for reconciliation.

15. Post Dated Vouchers and Cheques. Another feature present in Tally is to include post dated vouchers and cheques. In case you have received a post dated cheque, it can be entered without affecting the books of accounts. Such post dated cheque will be considered as receipt only on the date specified in the cheque. Any post dated payment issued to the creditor will be treated as payment only on the date specified in the voucher. In this way there are no chances of forgetting and skipping the transactions.

16. Memorandum Vouchers. Such vouchers are not posted to ledgers and thus do not affect the books of accounts. These are prepared when the user has incomplete information or when he wants to make suspense payments. Memorandum vouchers are used in scenario management. Scenario management is a management tool used for forecasting by entering provisional figures in memorandum vouchers without affecting the main books. This is useful in reporting and decision making.

17. Creation and Copying of Masters. When a new company is created, many ledgers are to be created which if created in multiple screen in Tally a lot of time can be saved. Also when a similar company is created, the same account heads for expenses and incomes, assets and liabilities can be copied from the existing company to the new company in order to save time and effort.

18. Reporting on Day to Day Basis. Tally provides cash books, bank books and other ledgers on daily basis. The user can have information on average daily cash and bank balances.

19. Reporting on Percentage Basis. Tally provides the facility of presenting all financial statements on a percentage basis. Balance Sheet, Profit and Loss A/c, Cash Flow Statement, etc. are shown in percentages. This option to show percentages can be activated by pressing F12 (configuration). *E.g.,* if Profit and Loss is to be depicted in percentages, then all the account heads will be shown as percentage of sales.

20. Fund Flow and Cash Flow. Tally readily provides Funds Flow Statement by consolidating the information required for it and saves the botheration of the user. Tally also tracks the movement in cash inflow and outflow by preparing Cash Flow Statement.

21. Interest Calculations. Tally helps the user in calculating the interest automatically based on the instructions given by the user. Interest is to be calculated on outstanding balance amounts and outstanding bills, invoices, transactions (Receivables and Payables). F11 (features) contains the option to activate interest calculations for the company. After activating it, activate the interest calculation option for each ledger for which interest is to be calculated. The rate of interest along with the interest style has to be specified. Tally calculates interest but does not record it in the books. The user himself enters the interest into books by passing debit notes and credit notes as per his requirements. Interest is calculated on simple and compound basis.

22. Group Company. Different companies under the same management are required to consolidate their accounts to present the financial position of the group of companies as a whole. This is an outstanding feature of Tally that one can consolidate the accounts of any number of companies at any time, as well as keep them separate. The user can bring the companies together and also separate them as per his will. Consolidation of accounts of branch companies or sister concerns help management in viewing the performance of the group as a whole and also view the efficiency of the individual company separately. This exercise helps in effective decision-making.

23. Cost Centres. A cost centre can be said to be any unit of an organisation for which costs are collected. By providing cost centres, Tally allocates all the items of expenses to cost centres. When income is also attached with the cost, the cost centre can be formed as profit centre. *e.g.,* you could have a department, a machine or a worker as a cost centre. If a salesman is treated as a cost centre, then all the ledgers showing expenses related to salesman like salary, commission, travelling allowance, daily allowance etc. will be allocated to the salesman (cost centre). The performance of the salesman can be evaluated by keeping a note of cost incurred on him and revenue generated by him in terms of sales.

24. Budgets. Tally allows the user to create budgets for each and every possible function like finance, marketing, bank, sales, purchases, etc. There could be creation of optimistic budget, realistic budget, pessimistic budget, etc. The budgets act as a control tool as actuals are compared with budget figures to bring out the deviations and variances. The budget figures can be set for each account head or ledger.

25. Variance Analysis. Tally makes variance analysis possible with the help of budgets. Variance analysis reports depict the variance of actual figures from the budget figures and help the management in critical decision-making.

26. Ratio Analysis. Ratio analysis helps in finding out the actual position of the company. It highlights the short term as well as long term financial position, liquidity and profitability of the company. Tally helps the user in analysing the performance of the company with the use of ratios rather than depending on absolute figures. Tally provides with all the major ratios like current ratio, debt-equity ratio, gross profit ratio, return on working capital, receivables turnover, etc. In order to have ratio analysis, select Ratio Analysis from 'Gateway of Tally' is depicted as follows :

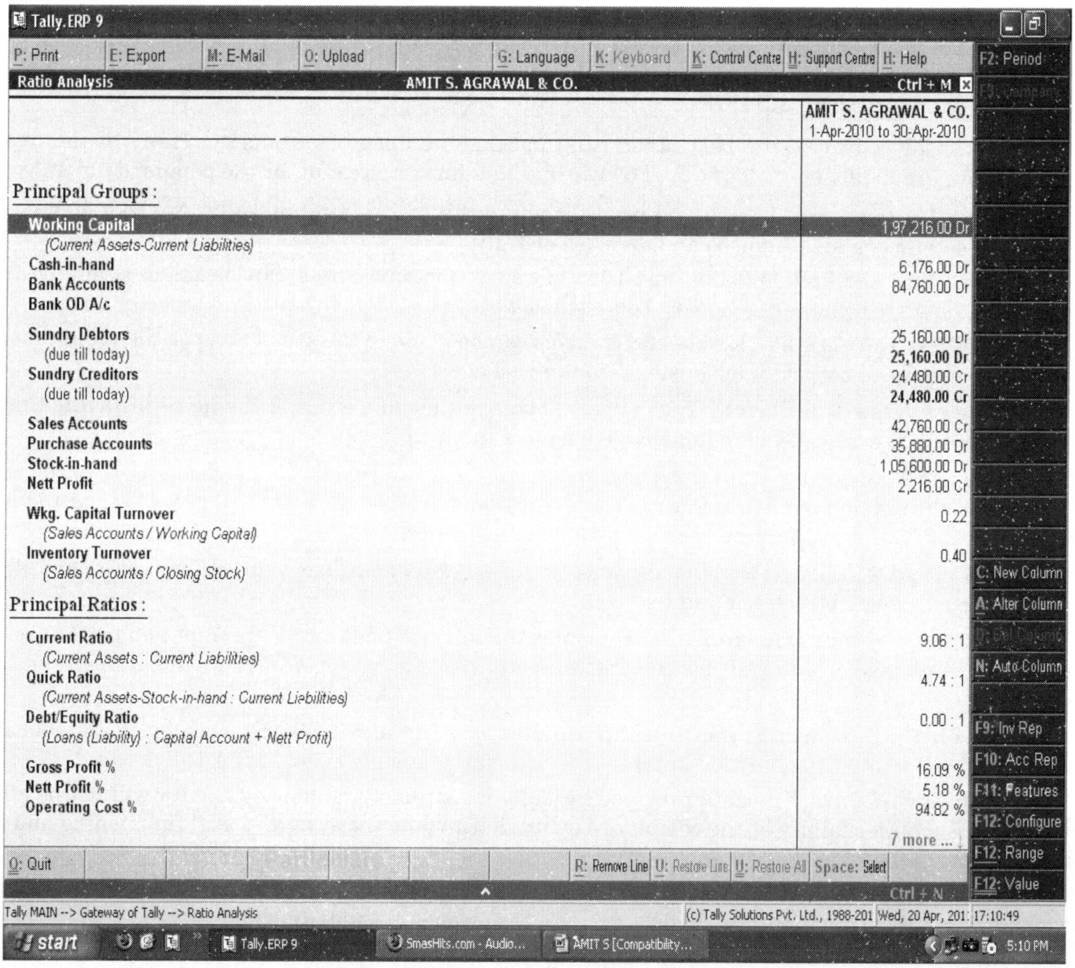

Fig. 20 : Ratio Analysis Statement

27. Import/Export of Data. Data can easily be imported and exported in Tally. We can get the data from any other software to Tally. Data can easily be exported from Tally to other softwares.

28. ODBC Compliance. Tally is ODBC compliant which means that any programme like MS Excel, Oracle etc. that is ODBC compliant can use data from Tally. With this facility, the user can extract data out of Tally and design his own report formats in other ODBC compliant software's.

29. E-Capabilities. Tally has extensive internet capabilities. E-mail, Web-publishing and data interchange over the Internet are easily achieved from within Tally. Reports in Tally can be E-mailed directly from Tally. Even invoices, purchase orders etc. can be e-mailed instead of sending printed ones. Tally allows the user to upload reports, price lists, range of products etc. on the website directly from Tally.

30. Graphical Analysis of Data. Tally provides graphical (Bar graph) analysis of data. One can have deeper analysis with the help of pictures. Graphical analysis of various reports like sales register, purchase register, Fund Flow, Cash Flow etc. can be made for different periods. In this way management is able to locate the boom and depression periods and is able to take better decisions.

31. Simplifies Income Tax for both Employees and Employers. The Income tax computations sheet and IT Returns can be generated as per the latest Income Tax Rules. It also provides quarterly and yearly returns which are required to be filed by the Employer.

32. Image/Logo Printing. The print capability is enhanced to print logo in the reports generated from Tally.ERP 9. The Comp[any Logo can be printed for any reports like Sales Invoice, Pay Slips, Debit/Credit Note, Receipt/Payment Vouchers, etc.

Tally as an Accounting Software

Tally is considered to be the best accounting package because of its merits. Many of the features discussed above are in fact merits of Tally. Following points further account for the popularity of Tally.

1. Easy to Understand. There is no need for any technical training in Tally. Anybody having basic knowledge of accounting and English can make use of Tally.

2. Speed. With the help of Tally, any type of report for any period can be made available in few seconds. Manual accounting can in no way be matched with Tally.

3. Flexibility. Tally is quite flexible and changes can be made in the system as per the requirements of the user. The user need not adapt his business to the package.

4. Saving of Time and Effort. There is no wastage of time and effort. Tally helps in saving time and effort which could be used elsewhere to manage business in a better way.

5. Codes not Mandatory. Tally does not require any codes to be followed in the system. Accounts and stock items can be entered by their names as such. Tally was the first package in the world to introduce the No codes concept. Tally supports the user if he wants to use codes.

6. User Friendly. Tally is user friendly and provides online help. The user can make use of Tally just by reading what appears on the computer screen.

7. Quick and Prompt Decisions. Tally enables the management to take prompt and better decisions. Management does not have to wait for reports, they are readily available in the manner required by the management.

8. Control. Business can be controlled in a better way through Tally. Everything is systematic and there is no scope for any irregularities. Internal check is automatically exercised in Tally.

9. Reliability of Data. The data provided by Tally is extremely reliable. The data will not be affected even if there is a power failure or the computer is shut down while the system is still functioning and hence there will be no data loss.

10. Security. Tally provides great security. The user can have individual passwords and define multiple levels of security as per his needs.

11. Easy Installation. Tally has simple and rapid installation. It has a simple menu driven installation procedure. It does not take more than one minute to install Tally on the local hard disk.

FUNDS FLOW STATEMENT

The funds flow report in Tally reflects the movement of the entire working capital. It includes operational funds, rise and fall in inventories, creditors and debtors apart from cash and bank and acquisition and sale of fixed assets. The statement reveals the sources of the Funds and their application. Tally automatically tracks all transactions entered and readily provides a Funds flow statement.

To view Funds Flow

- △ Go to Gateway Tally > Display ? Cash/Funds flow > Funds Flow
- △ Press ALT F2, change period - From 1-10-2006 to 31-3-2007
- △ Select a month

Step No. 1 Enter into Tally Accounting Software
Double Click on Tally Icon.

Step No. 2 Creation of Company
Company Info menu → Create ↵ (Give Name, Address, Financial Year etc.)

Step No. 3 Creation of Accounts
Path : Gateway of Tally → Accounts Info → Ledger Accounts → Create ↵

Create the following accounts :

Ledger	**Under**
Equity Capital	Capital
Debentures	Secured Loans
Tax Payable	Current Liabilities
Accounts Payable	Current Liabilities
Interest Payable	Current Liabilities
Dividend Payable	Current Liabilities
Fixed Asset	Fixed Asset
Long-term Investment	Investment
Work-in-Progress	Stock-in-hand
Stock-in-Trade	Stock-in-hand
Accounts Receivable	Current Asset
Cash in hand	

To Save the ledgers Press Control + A

Step No. 4 Creation of Units of measurement
Path : Gateway of Tally → Inventory Info → Units of measurement → Create ↵

Step No. 5 Creation of Stock Item
Path : Gateway of Tally → Inventory Info → Stock item → Create ↵

Step No. 6 Posting of transaction through appropriate accounting vouchers
Path : Gateway of Tally → Voucher Entry

Step No. 7 After completion the voucher entries Reports Generation
Path : Gate of Tally → Display → Cash/Funds flow → Funds flow

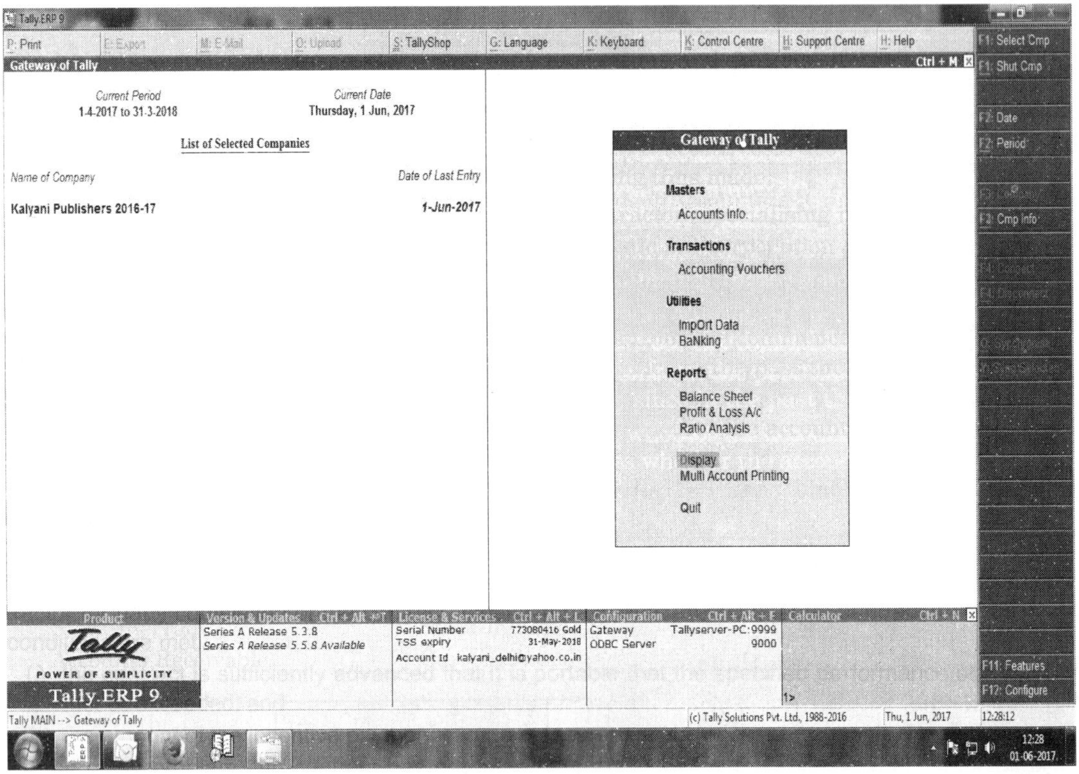
Gateway of Tally
Current Period
1-4-2017 to 31-3-2018
Current Date
Thursday, 1 Jun, 2017
List of Selected Companies
Name of Company
Date of Last Entry
Kalyani Publishers 2016-17
1-Jun-2017
Gateway of Tally
Masters
Accounts Info.
Transactions
Accounting Vouchers
Utilities
ImpOrt Data
BaNking
Reports
Balance Sheet
Profit & Loss A/c
Ratio Analysis
Display
Multi Account Printing
Quit

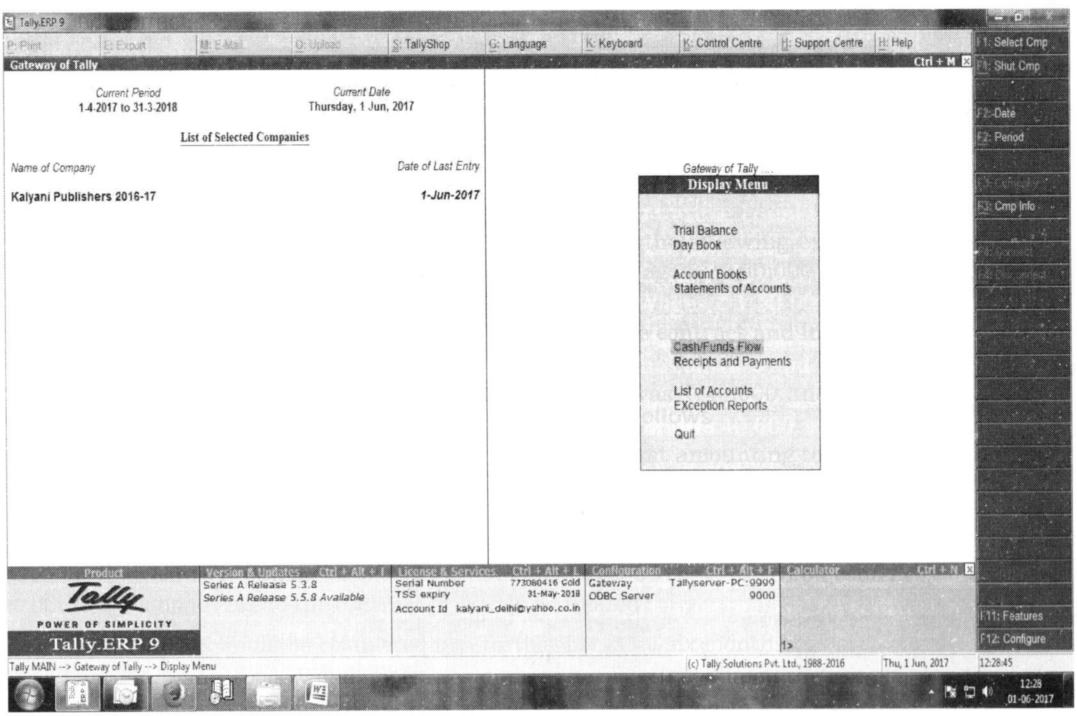
Gateway of Tally
Current Period
1-4-2017 to 31-3-2018
Current Date
Thursday, 1 Jun, 2017
List of Selected Companies
Name of Company
Date of Last Entry
Kalyani Publishers 2016-17
1-Jun-2017
Gateway of Tally ...
Display Menu
Trial Balance
Day Book
Account Books
Statements of Accounts
Cash/Funds Flow
Receipts and Payments
List of Accounts
EXception Reports
Quit

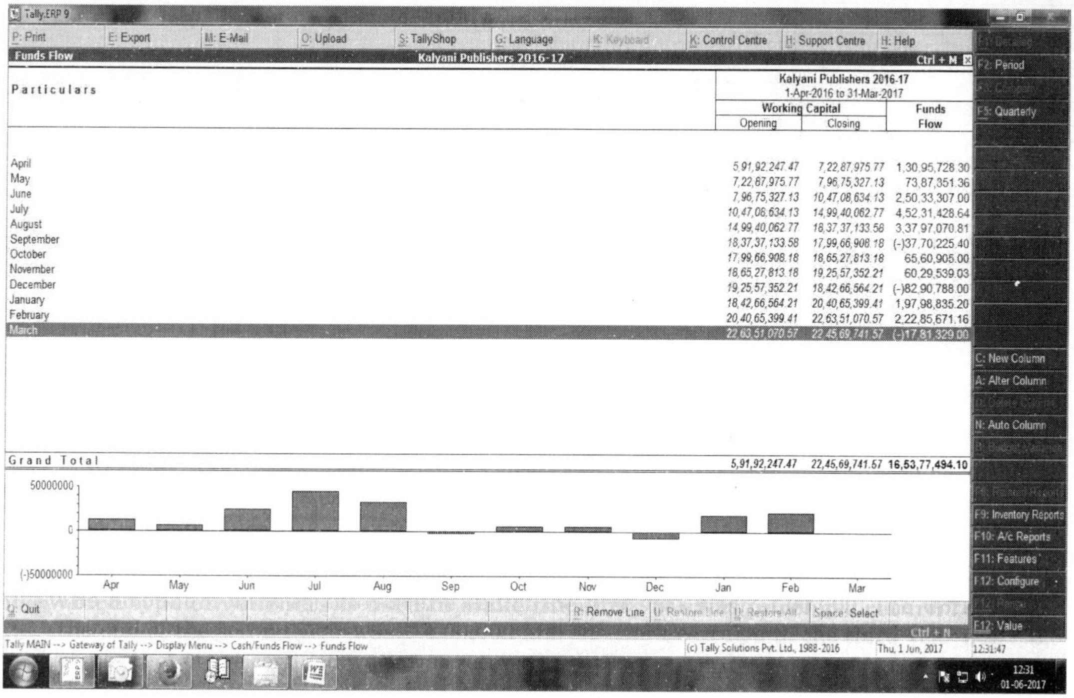

ILLUSTRATION 2

Show the Funds flow statement of XYZ Company. With the following accounts.

8 Fixed assets (a) Land (b) Building (c) Machinery (d) Furniture (e) Goodwill (f) Patents (g) Plant (h) Trade marks

5 Current assets (a) Trade Debtors (b) Stock c) Bills Receivable (d) Bank (e) Cash 3 Loan accounts (a) Loan from Andhra Bank (b) Loan from Raman (c) Mortgage Loan 1 Capital account

Under relevant groups with imaginary figures.

SOLUTION

Step 1:

Give a Double click on Tally icon

Step 2:

Create a Company by pressing Alt+F3 Button to select Company Information

Select Create Company or Hot Key character C from the key board. Fill All the Details and select type of a company as **Accounts only** and save it by pressing **Ctrl + A.**

Step 3 :

Gate Way of Tally → Accounts info –> Ledgers → Single/ Multiple Ledgers → Create

S. No.	Ledger	Group	Opening Balance
1	Land	Fixed assets	100000
2	Building	Fixed assets	200000
3	Machinery	Fixed assets	15000

4	Furniture	Fixed assets	8000
5	Goodwill	Fixed assets	2000
6	Patents	Fixed assets	100000
7	Plant	Fixed assets	500000
8	Trade Marks	Fixed assets	700000
9	Trade Debtors	Sundry Debtors	50000
10	Stock	Stock in hand	10000
11	Bills Receivable	Current assets	6000
12	Bank	Bank Accounts	10000
13	Cash	Cash in hand	100000
14	Loan from Andhra Bank	Loan accounts	50000
15	Loan from Raman	Loan accounts	5000
16	Mortgage Loan	Secured Loan	1000000
17	Capital	Capital	200000

Step 4 :

Gate way of Tally - Display → funds/cashflow → fund flow

ILLUSTRATION 3

Prepare funds flow from the information given below :

Name of the Account	Dr. ₹	Cr. ₹
Furniture	20,000	—
Machinery	1,00,000	—
Buildings	2,00,000	—
Capital	—	3,00,000
Cash	10,000	
Bills Payable	—	60,000
Trade Debtors	1,60,000	
Trade Creditors	—	1,30,000

SOLUTION

Step 1 :

Give a Double click on Tally icon

Step 2 :

Create a Company by pressing Alt+F3 Button to select Company Information

Select Create Company or Hot Key character C from the key board Fill All the Demi's and select type of a company as Accounts only and save it by pressing Ctrl + A.

Step 3 :

Gate Way of Tally → Accounts Info → Ledgers Single/Multiple Ledgers → Create

S. No.	Ledger	Group	Opening Balance
1	Furniture	Fixed Assets	20,000 Dr
2	Machinery	Fixed Assets	1,00,000 Dr
3	Buildings	Fixed Assets	2,00,000 Dr

4	Capital	Capital Accounts	3,00,000 Cr
5	Bills Payable	Current Liabilities	60,000 Cr
6	Trade Debtors	Sundry Debtor	1,60,000 Dr
7	Trade Creditors	Sundry Creditor	1,30,000 Cr

Step 4 :

Gate Way of Tally → Accounts Info → Ledger Single Ledger → Alter → Select Cash enter the opening balance 10,000 ₹ & save

Step 5 :

Gate way of Tally → Display → Funds / Cash flow → Funds flow

ILLUSTRATION 4

Prepare funds flow statement from the given transactions:

	₹
Started business with capital	3,00,000
Cash deposited into the SBI	40,000
Cash purchases	20,000
Cash Sales	24,000
Paid Rent	2,400

SOLUTION

Step 1 :

Give a Double click on Tally icon

Step 2 :

Create a Company by pressing Alt + F3 Button to select Company Information

Select Create Company or Hot Key character C from the key board. Fill All the Details and select type of a company as **Accounts only** and save it by pressing **Ctrl** + **A.**

Step 3 :

Gate Way of Tally → Accounts Info → Ledgers Single/ Multiple Ledgers → Create

S. No.	Ledger	Group
1	Capital	Capital Accounts
2	SBI	Bank Account
3	Cash Purchase	Purchase Account
4	Cash Sales	Sales Account
5	Rent	Indirect Expenses

Step 4 :

Gate way of Tally → Accounting Voucher

Date	Particulars	Function Key	Debit	Credit
	Receipt Voucher	F6		
	Cash A/c Dr		3,00,000	
	To Capital A/c			3,00,000

	Contra Voucher	F4		
	Bank A/c Dr		40,000	
	To Cash A/c			40,000
	Payment Voucher	F5		
	Purchase A/c Dr		20,000	
	To Cash A/c			20,000
	Receipt Voucher	F6		
	Cash A/c Dr		24,000	
	To Sales			24,000
	Payment Voucher	F5		
	Rent A/c Dr		2,400	
	To Cash A/c			2,400

Step 5 :

Gate Way of fally → Display funds/cashflow fundsflow

ILLUSTRATION 5

Prepare Fundsflow statement.

Madhan started business with cash ₹ 5,00,000

Purchased 15 colour TVs @ 15,000 each for cash

Paid carriage on purchase ₹ 2000

Sold 10 CTVs @ 20,000 each for cash

Sold 3 CTVs @ 20,000 each to Mr. Ramana on credit paid salaries ₹ 1,000

Closing stock valued at ₹ 30,000.

SOLUTION

Step 1 :

Give a Double click on Tally icon

Step 2 :

Create a Company by pressing Alt+F3 Button to select Company Information

Select Create Company or Hot Key character C from the key board. Fill All the Details and select type of a company as **Accounts with Inventory** and save it by pressing **Ctrl + A.**

Step 3 :

Gate Way of Tally → Accounts Info Ledgers → Single/ Multiple Ledgers → Create

Dadhan Capital	Capital
Purchases	Purchases
Carriage	Direct Expenses
Sales	Sales
Ramana	Sundry Debtors
Salaries	indirect Expenses
Closing Stock	Stock in hand

Step 4 :

Gateway of Tally → Accounting Vouchers

Date	Particulars		Function Key	Debit	Credit
	Receipt Voucher		F6		
	Cash A/c	Dr		5,00,000	
	To Capital A/c				5,00,000
	Payment Voucher		F5		
	Purchases A/c	Dr		2,25,000	
	To Cash A/c				2,25,000
	Payment Voucher		F5		
	Carriage A/c	Dr		2,000	
	To Cash A/c				2,000
	Receipt Voucher		F6		
	Cash A/c	Dr		2,00,000	
	To Sales A/c				2,00,000
	Sales Voucher		F8		
	Ramana A/c	Dr		60,000	
	To Sales A/c				60,000
	Payment Voucher		F5		
	Salaries A/c	Dr		1,000	
	To Cash A/c				1,000

Step 5 :

Gateway of Tally → Display → Funds/Cash Flow → Funds Flow

ILLUSTRATION 6

Mr. Rahul started business with ₹ 3,00,000

Purchased 10 colour TVs @ 15,000 each for cash

Purchased 10 colour TVs @ 15,000 each from Manoj

Sold 18 CTVs @ 18,000 each for cash

Paid salaries ₹ 1,000 and rent ₹ 1,000

Unsold stock ₹ 27,000.

Prepare fundsflow statement.

SOLUTION

Step 1 :

Give a Double click on Tally icon

Step 2 :

Create a Company by pressing Alt+F3 Button to select Company Information

Select Create Company or Hot Key character C from the key board. Fill All the Details and select type of a company as **Accounts with Inventory** and save it by pressing **Ctrl + A.**

Step 3 :

Gate Way of Tally → Accounts Info → Ledgers → Single/Multiple Ledgers → Create

Rahul Capital	Capital
Purchases	Purchases
Manoj	Sundry Creditor
Sales	Sales
Salaries	Indirect Expenses
Rent	Indirect Expenses
Closing Stock	Stock in Hand

Step 4 :

Gateway of Tally → Accounting Vouchers

Date	Particulars		Function Key	Debit	Credit
	Receipt Voucher		F6		
	Cash A/c	Dr		3,00,000	
	To Rahul Capital A/c				3,00,000
	Payment Voucher		F5		
	Purchases A/c	Dr		1,50,000	
	To Cash A/c				1,50,000
	Purchase Voucher		F9		
	Purchase A/c	Dr		1,50,000	
	To Manoj A/c				1,50,000
	Receipt Voucher		F6		
	Cash A/c	Dr		3,24,000	
	To Sales A/c				3,24,000
	Payment Voucher		F5		
	Salaries A/c	Dr		1,000	
	To Cash A/c				1,000
	Payment Voucher		F5		
	Rent A/c	Dr		1,000	
	To Cash A/c				1,000

Step 5 :

Gateway of Tally → Display → Cash/Funds Flow → Funds Flow

ILLUSTRATION 7

Show the fundsflow given below.

Name of the Account	Dr. (₹)	Cr. (₹)
Capital		10,00,000
S.Creditors		1,00,000

Bank Loan		1,00,000
Buildings	8,00,000	
S. Debtors	2,00,000	
Motorcar	2,00,000	

SOLUTION

Step 1 :

Give a Double click on Tally icon

Step 2 :

Create a Company by pressing Alt+F3 Button to select Company Information

Select Create Company or Hot Key character C from the key board. Fill All the Details and select type of a company as **Accounts only** and save it by pressing **Ctrl + A.**

Step 3 :

Gate Way of Tally → Accounts Info Ledgers → Single/ Multiple Ledgers → Create

S. No.	Ledger	Group	Opening Balance
1	Capital	Capital Account	5,00,000 Cr
2	S. Creditors	Sundry Creditors	50,000 Cr
3	Bank Loan	Loan accounts	50,000 Cr
4	Buildings	Fixed Assets	4,00,000 Dr
5	S. Debtors	Sundry Debtors	1,00,000 Dr
6	Motor car	Fixed Assets	1,00,000 Dr

Step 4 :

Gate way of Tally → Display → Funds/cashflow → fundsflow

Cash Flow Statement

The cash flow statement in Tally helps in tracking the movement of cash in a business i.e., Cash Inflow and Outflow (for both cash & bank).

The report also displays the net flow for any period. We can obtain a daily cash flow statement or activate Average Cash inflow/outflow Details for any period.

To View Cash Flow

△ Go to Gateway of Tally > Display > Cash/Funds flow > Cash flow

△ Press ALT + F2 change period - from 1-10-2006 to 31-3-2007

△ Select a month and press enter

△ At the cash flow summary, Click F4 : Daily flow to view the daily cash flow

Note : We can also set periodicity to use to daily in F12 : Configure of the cash flow summary screen.

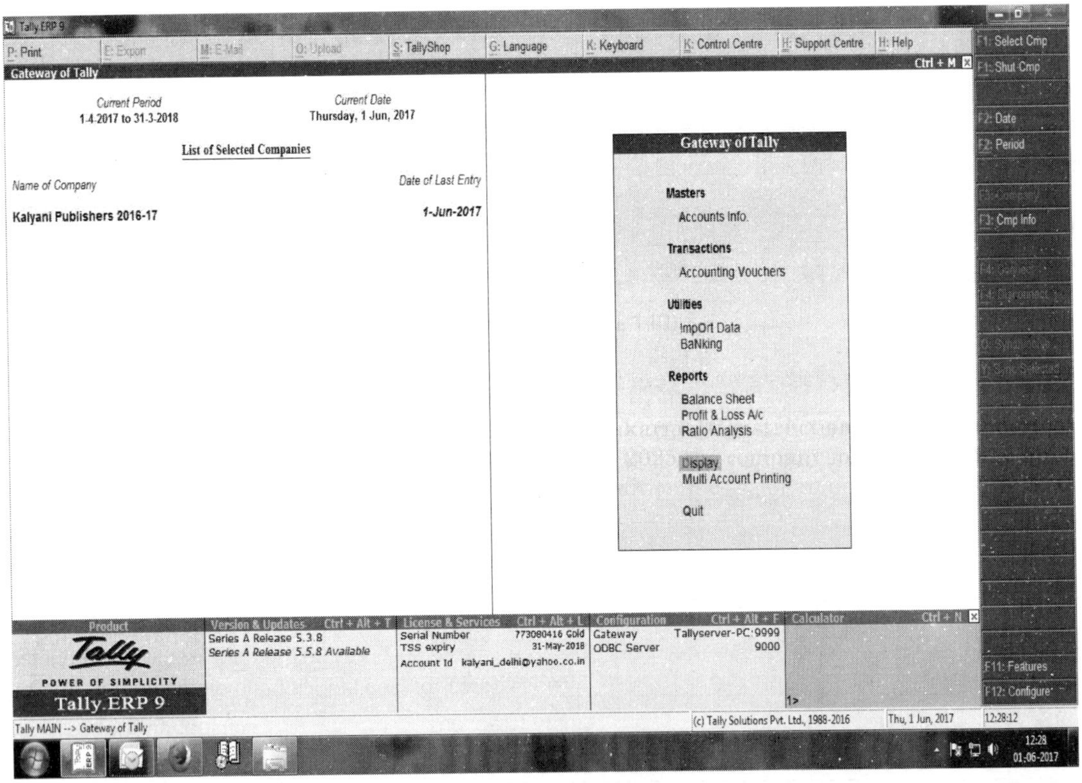
Tally.ERP 9
P: Print
E: Export
M: E-Mail
O: Upload
S: TallyShop
G: Language
K: Keyboard
K: Control Centre
H: Support Centre
H: Help
Gateway of Tally
Ctrl + M
F1: Select Cmp
F1: Shut Cmp
F2: Date
F2: Period
F3: Cmp Info
F11: Features
F12: Configure
Current Period
1-4-2017 to 31-3-2018
Current Date
Thursday, 1 Jun, 2017
List of Selected Companies
Name of Company
Date of Last Entry
Kalyani Publishers 2016-17
1-Jun-2017
Gateway of Tally
Masters
Accounts Info.
Transactions
Accounting Vouchers
Utilities
ImpOrt Data
BaNking
Reports
Balance Sheet
Profit & Loss A/c
Ratio Analysis
Display
Multi Account Printing
Quit
Product
Version & Updates Ctrl + Alt + T
Series A Release 5.3.8
Series A Release 5.5.8 Available
License & Services Ctrl + Alt + L
Serial Number 773080416 Gold
TSS expiry 31-May-2018
Account Id kalyani_delhi@yahoo.co.in
Configuration Ctrl + Alt + F
Gateway Tallyserver-PC:9999
ODBC Server 9000
Calculator Ctrl + N
POWER OF SIMPLICITY
Tally.ERP 9
Tally MAIN --> Gateway of Tally
(c) Tally Solutions Pvt. Ltd., 1988-2016
Thu, 1 Jun, 2017
12:28:12

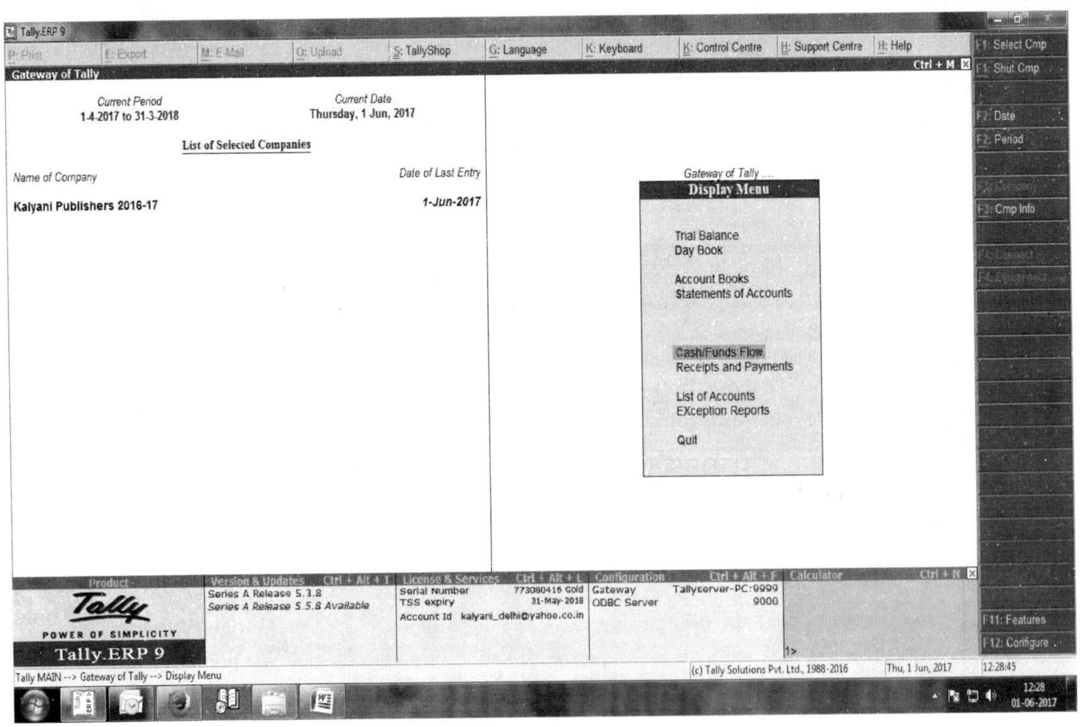
Tally.ERP 9
P: Print
E: Export
M: E-Mail
O: Upload
S: TallyShop
G: Language
K: Keyboard
K: Control Centre
H: Support Centre
H: Help
Gateway of Tally
Ctrl + M
F1: Select Cmp
F1: Shut Cmp
F2: Date
F2: Period
F3: Cmp Info
F11: Features
F12: Configure
Current Period
1-4-2017 to 31-3-2018
Current Date
Thursday, 1 Jun, 2017
List of Selected Companies
Name of Company
Date of Last Entry
Kalyani Publishers 2016-17
1-Jun-2017
Gateway of Tally ....
Display Menu
Trial Balance
Day Book
Account Books
Statements of Accounts
Cash/Funds Flow
Receipts and Payments
List of Accounts
EXception Reports
Quit
Product
Version & Updates Ctrl + Alt + T
Series A Release 5.3.8
Series A Release 5.5.8 Available
License & Services Ctrl + Alt + L
Serial Number 773080416 Gold
TSS expiry 31-May-2018
Account Id kalyani_delhi@yahoo.co.in
Configuration Ctrl + Alt + F
Gateway Tallyserver-PC:9999
ODBC Server 9000
Calculator Ctrl + N
POWER OF SIMPLICITY
Tally.ERP 9
Tally MAIN --> Gateway of Tally --> Display Menu
(c) Tally Solutions Pvt. Ltd., 1988-2016
Thu, 1 Jun, 2017
12:28:45

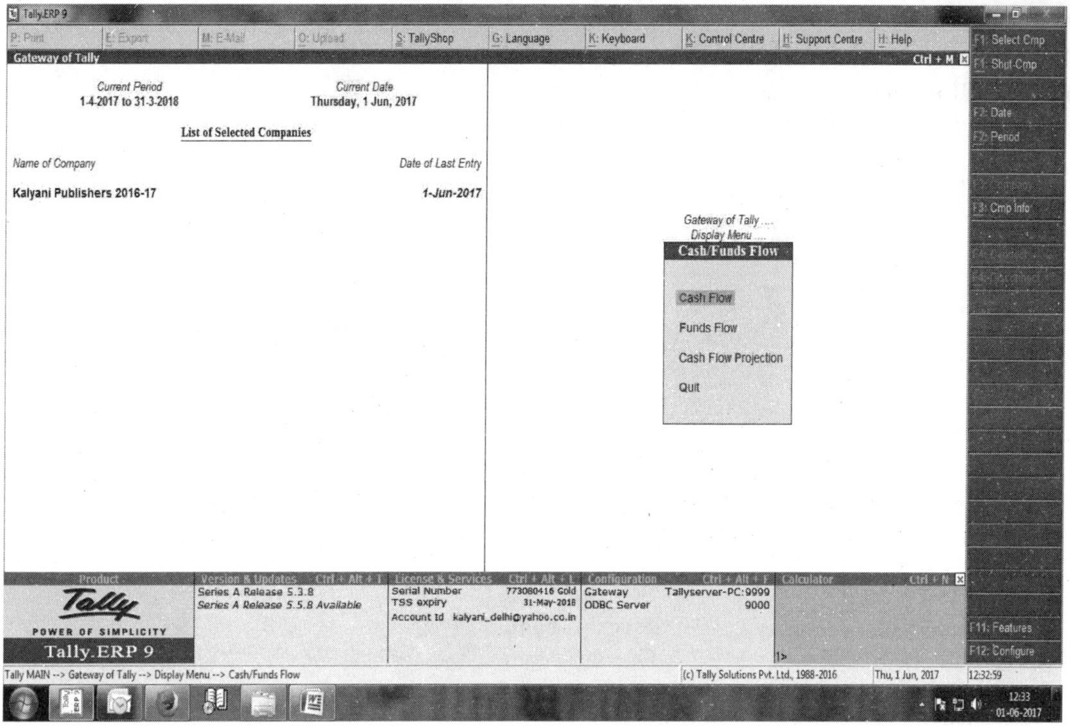

Tally.ERP 9
P: Print
E: Export
M: E-Mail
O: Upload
S: TallyShop
G: Language
K: Keyboard
K: Control Centre
H: Support Centre
H: Help
Gateway of Tally
Ctrl + M
F1: Select Cmp
F1: Shut Cmp
F2: Date
F2: Period
F3: Cmp Info
Current Period
1-4-2017 to 31-3-2018
Current Date
Thursday, 1 Jun, 2017
List of Selected Companies
Name of Company
Date of Last Entry
Kalyani Publishers 2016-17
1-Jun-2017
Gateway of Tally ....
Display Menu ....
Cash/Funds Flow
Cash Flow
Funds Flow
Cash Flow Projection
Quit
Product
Version & Updates Ctrl + Alt + T
Series A Release 5.3.8
Series A Release 5.5.8 Available
License & Services Ctrl + Alt + L
Serial Number 773080416 Gold
TSS expiry 31-May-2018
Account Id kalyani_delhi@yahoo.co.in
Configuration Ctrl + Alt + F
Gateway Tallyserver-PC:9999
ODBC Server 9000
Calculator Ctrl + N
Tally
POWER OF SIMPLICITY
Tally.ERP 9
F11: Features
F12: Configure
Tally MAIN --> Gateway of Tally --> Display Menu --> Cash/Funds Flow
(c) Tally Solutions Pvt. Ltd., 1988-2016
Thu, 1 Jun, 2017
12:32:59
12:33
01-06-2017

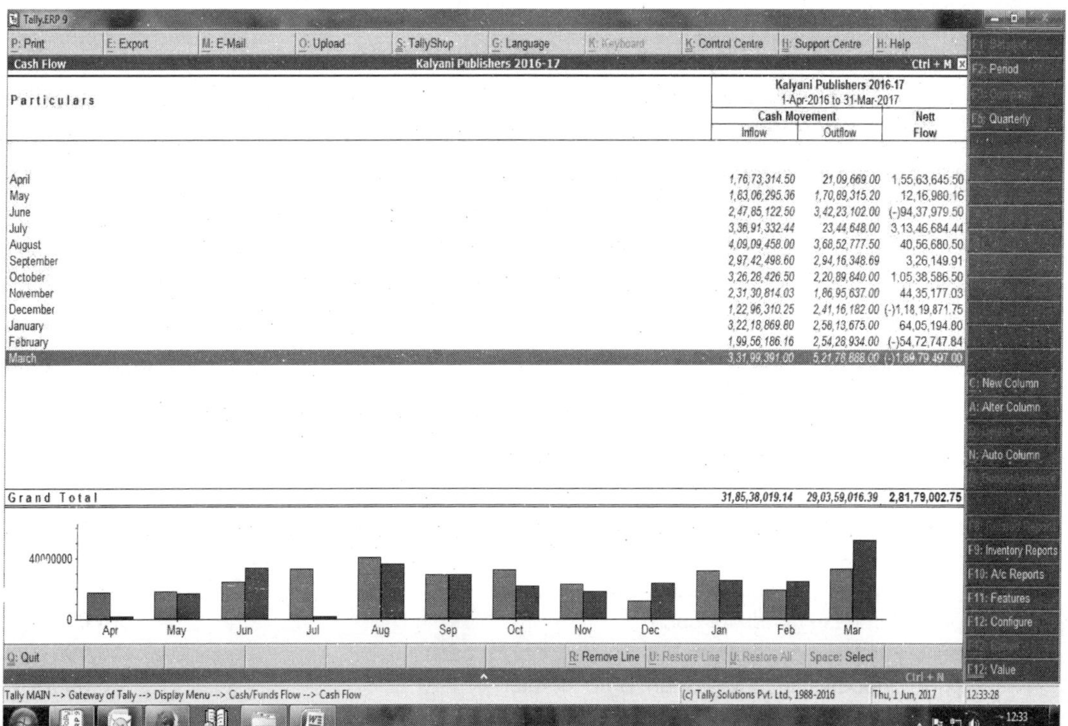

Tally.ERP 9
P: Print
E: Export
M: E-Mail
O: Upload
S: TallyShop
G: Language
K: Keyboard
K: Control Centre
H: Support Centre
H: Help
Cash Flow
Kalyani Publishers 2016-17
Ctrl + M
F2: Period
F5: Quarterly
Particulars
Kalyani Publishers 2016-17
1-Apr-2016 to 31-Mar-2017
Cash Movement
Inflow
Outflow
Nett Flow
April 1,76,73,314.50 21,09,669.00 1,55,63,645.50
May 1,83,06,295.36 1,70,89,315.20 12,16,980.16
June 2,47,85,122.50 3,42,23,102.00 (-)94,37,979.50
July 3,36,91,332.44 23,44,648.00 3,13,46,684.44
August 4,09,09,458.00 3,68,52,777.50 40,56,680.50
September 2,97,42,498.60 2,94,16,348.69 3,26,149.91
October 3,26,28,426.50 2,20,89,840.00 1,05,38,586.50
November 2,31,30,814.03 1,86,95,637.00 44,35,177.03
December 1,22,96,310.25 2,41,16,182.00 (-)1,18,19,871.75
January 3,22,18,869.80 2,58,13,675.00 64,05,194.80
February 1,99,56,186.16 2,54,28,934.00 (-)54,72,747.84
March 3,31,99,391.00 5,21,78,888.00 (-)1,89,79,497.00
Grand Total 31,85,38,019.14 29,03,59,016.39 2,81,79,002.75
C: New Column
A: Alter Column
N: Auto Column
40000000
0
Apr May Jun Jul Aug Sep Oct Nov Dec Jan Feb Mar
F9: Inventory Reports
F10: A/c Reports
F11: Features
F12: Configure
F12: Value
Q: Quit
R: Remove Line
U: Restore Line
U: Restore All
Space: Select
Ctrl + N
Tally MAIN --> Gateway of Tally --> Display Menu --> Cash/Funds Flow --> Cash Flow
(c) Tally Solutions Pvt. Ltd., 1988-2016
Thu, 1 Jun, 2017
12:33:28
12:33
01-06-2017

Step No : 1 Enter into Tally Accounting Software
Double Click on Tally Icon.

Step No : 2 Creation of Company
Company Info menu → Create ↲ (Give Name, Address, Financial Year etc.)

Step No : 3 Creation of Accounts
Path : Gateway of Tally → Accounts info → Ledger Accounts → Create ↲

Create the following accounts

Ledger	**Under**
Equity Capital	Capita
Debentures	Secured Loans
Tax Payable	Current Liabilities
Accounts Payable	Current Liabilities
Interest Payable	Current Liabilities
Dividend Payable	Current Liabilities
Fixed Asset	Fixed Assets
Long-term Investment	Investment
Work-in-Progress	Stock-in-hand
Stock-in-Trade	Stock-in-hand
Accounts Receivable	Current Asset
Cash in hand	

To save the Ledgers Press Control + A

Step No : 4 Creation of Units of measurement
Path : Gateway of Tally → Inventory Info → Units of measurement → Create ↲

Step No : 5 Creation of Stock Item
Path : Gateway of Tally → Inventory Info Stock item → Create ↲

Step No : 6 Posting of transaction through appropriate accounting vouchers
Path : Gateway of Tally → Voucher Entry

Step No : 7 After completion the voucher entries Reports Generation
Path : Gate of Tally Display → Cash / Fundsflow → fund flow

ILLUSTRATION 8

Enter 10 cash and 5 bank transactions with imaginary figures and prepare a Cashflow Statement.

SOLUTION

Assume some of the 10 cash and 5 Bank transactions as follows

1.	Bank Balance	20,000
2.	April 1 Rarnu stated business with cash	50,000
3.	April 2 Deposit in the bank	5,000
4.	April 3 Furniture purchased for cash	2,000
5.	April 5 Purchase goods for cash	4,000
6.	April 8 Purchase goods from M/s Sham & co. for cash	10,000
7.	April 16 Goods sold to M/s Sham & co for cash	6,000
8.	April 18 Goods sol on credit to Ramesh	3,000
9.	April 19 Received cash from Ramesh	3,000
10.	April 21 Paid Daily wages	1,000

11. April 22 Paid Rent 30,000
12. April 22 Paid salary 20,000
13. April 23 Paid Postage Exp. 1,000
14. April 24 Paid to Rajesh ₹ 10,000 by cheque
15. April 24 Paid to Mahesh Babu ₹ 25,000 by cheque
16. April 25 Received a cheque from Ragini ₹ 38,000
17. April 30 Received from Sneha ₹ 50,000 by cheque

Step 1 :

Give a Double click on Tally icon

Step 2 :

Create a Company by pressing Alt+F3 Button to select Company Information

Select Create Company or Hot Key character C from the key board. Fill All the Details and select type of a company as Accounts only and save it by pressing Ctrl + A.

Step 3 :

Gate Way of Tally → Accounts Info → Ledgers → Single/Multiple Ledgers → Create

S. No.	Ledger	Group
1	Ramu Capital	Capital A/c
2	Bank	Bank A/c
3	Furniture	Fixed Assets
4	Purchase	Purchase A/c
5	M/s Sham & co	Sundry Creditor
6	Ramesh	Sundry Debtor
7	Wages	Direct Expenses
8	Rent	Indirect Expenses
9	Salary	Indirect Expenses
10	Postage Expenses	Indirect Expenses
11	Rajesh	Sundry Debtor
12	Mahesh Babu	Sundry Debtor
13	Ragini	Sundry Creditor
14	Sneha	Sundry Creditor

Step 4:

Gate way of Tally → Accounting Voucher

Date	Particulars	Function Key	Debit	Credit
1	Receipt Voucher	F6		
	Cash A/c Dr		50000	
	To Ramu Capital A/c			50000

2	Contra Voucher		F4		
	Bank A/c	Dr		5000	
	To Cash A/c				5000
	Payment Voucher		F5		
	Furniture A/c	Dr		2000	
	To Cash A/c				2000
4	Payment Voucher		F5		
	Purchase A/c	Dr		4000	
	To Cash A/c				4000
5	Payment Voucher		F5		
	Purchase A/c	Dr		10000	
	To Cash A/c				10000
6	Receipt Voucher		F6		
	Cash A/c	Dr		6000	
	To Sales				6000
7	Sales Voucher		F8		
	Ramesh A/c	Dr		3000	
	To Sales A/c				3000
8	Payment Voucher		F5		
	Ramesh A/c	Dr		3000	
	To Cash A/c				3000
9	Payment Voucher		F5		
	Wages A/c	Dr		1000	
	To Cash A/c				1000
10	Payment Voucher		F5		
	Rent A/c	Dr		30000	
	To Cash A/c				30000
11	Payment Voucher		F5		
	Salaries A/c	Dr		20000	
	To Cash A/c				20000
12	Payment Voucher		F5		
	Postage A/c	Dr		1000	
	To Cash				1000
13	Payment Voucher		F5		
	Rajesh A/c	Dr		10000	
	To Bank A/c				10000

14	Payment Voucher	F5		
	Mahesh Babu A/c Dr		25000	
	To Bank			25000
15	Receipt Voucher	F6		
	Bank A/c Dr		38000	
	To Ragini			38000
16	Receipt Voucher	F6		
	Bank A/c Dr		50000	
	To Sneha A/c			50000

Step 5:

Gate way of Tally > Display → Funds flow / Cash flow → Cashflow

ILLUSTRATION 9

Prepare a cashflow statement for the following cash transactions.

(a) Srinu brought in cash towards Capital ₹ 75,000.
(b) Deposited into bank ₹ 60,000
(c) Purchased goods ₹ 9,000
(d) Sale of goods worth ₹ 21,000
(e) Paid to Raju (a supplier) ₹ 15,000
(f) Received from Ramu (a customer) ₹ 18,000.

SOLUTION :

Step 1 :

Give a Double click on Tally icon

Step 2 :

Create a Company by pressing Alt + F3 Button to select Company Information

Select Create Company or Hot Key character C from the key board. Fill All the Details and select type of a company as Accounts only and save it by pressing Ctrl + A.

Step 3 :

Gate Way of Tally → Accounts Info → Legers → Single/Multiple Ledgers → Create

S. No.	Ledger	Group
1	Srinu Capital	Capita! A/c
2	Bank	Bank A/c
3	Purchase	Purchase A/c
4	Sales	Sales A/c
5	Raju	Sundry Creditor
6	Ramu	Sundry Debtor

Step 4 :

Gate way of Tally → Accounting Voucher

Date	Particulars		Function Key	Debit	Credit
	Receipt Voucher		F6	75,000	
	Cash A/c	Dr			75,000
	To Srinu Capital A/c				
	Contra Voucher		F4	60,000	
	Bank A/c	Dr			60,000
	To Cash A/c				
	Payment Voucher		F5	9,000	
	Purchase A/c	Dr			9,000
	To Cash A/c				
	Receipt Voucher		F6	2,000	
	Cash A/c	Dr			2,000
	To Sales				
	Payment Voucher		F5	15,000	
	Raju A/C	Dr			15,000
	To Cash A/c				
	Receipt Voucher		F6	18,000	
	Cash A/c	Dr			18,000
	To Ramu A/c				

Step 5 :

Gate way of Tally → Display Cash/fundflow Cashflow Select Cash Book Press Enter Key twice to see cash transactions.

ILLUSTRATION 10

Prepare cashflow for the following bank transactions in Andhra Bank and ascertain Bank balance.

Balance at Bank ₹ 4,00,000

Paid to Srikanth ₹ 20,000 by cheque

Paid to Balu ₹ 50,000 by cheque

Received a cheque from Radha ₹ 76,000

Received from Sneha ₹ 1,00,000 by cheque.

SOLUTION

Step 1:

Give a Double click on Tally icon

Step 2 :

Create a Company by pressing Alt + F3 Button to select Company Information

Select Create Company or Hot Key character C from the key board. Fill All the Details and select type of a company as **Accounts only** and save it by pressing **Ctrl + A.**

Step 3 :

Gate Way of Tally → Accounts Info → Legers → Single/ Multiple Ledgers → Create

S. No.	Ledger	Group	Opening Balance
1	Bank	Bank A/c	2,00000
2	Srikanth	Sundry Creditor	
3	Balu	Sundry Creditor	
4	Sales	Sales A/c	
5	Radha	Sundry Debtor	
6	Sneha	Sundry Debtor	

Date	Particulars		Function Key	Debit	Credit
	Payment Voucher		F5		
	Srikanth A/c	Dr		10,000	
	To Bank A/c				10,000
	Payment Voucher		F5		
	Balu A/c	Dr		25,000	
	To Cash A/c				25,000
	Receipt Voucher		F6		
	Bank A/c	Dr		38,000	
	To Radha				38,000
	Receipt Voucher		F6		
	Bank A/c	Dr		50,000	
	To Sneha				50,000

Step 5 :

Gate way of Tally → Display → Cash / Funds flow- -? Cashflow

ILLUSTRATION 11

Create a company of your own and generate a cash book with 10 transactions each,with imaginary figures and show cashflow statement.

SOLUTION

The following are the transactions of Andhra Co. Ltd.

1. Started business with cash ₹ 2,0000
2. purchase 100 litres of coconut oil @ ₹ 100 per litres from Kerala Co.Ltd.
3. Purchased 500 soaps @ ₹ 50 each from Hindustan Lever Ltd.
4. Purchased 1000 @ ₹ 20 each detergent soaps form Nirma washing Co.Ltd,
5. Purchase 1000 Kgs of rice ₹ @ 15 per kg on cash basis from konaseema Rice Ltd.
6. Purchased 500 Kgs of rice ₹ 20 per Kg from Punjab rice Ltd.
7. Sold 400 soaps @ ₹ 60 each to X Ltd
8. Sold 1000 Kgs of rice @ 20 each to Y lid

9. Sold 800 liters of coconut oil on cash basis @ ₹ 125 each
10. Purchase Furniture ₹ 5000
11. Sold 1000 detergent soaps on cash basis @ ₹ 25
12. Purchase weighting machine for @ ₹ 2000
13. charge depreciation on furniture and weighing machine @ 10% each
14. Returned 10 liters of coconut oil to kejala Co.Ltd due to expiry date
15. Paid rent ₹ 2000 by cheque.
16. Paid sales promotion expenses ₹ 5,000
17. Cheque recaved from 'X' Ltd ₹ 20,000
18. Cash received form 'Y' Ltd ₹ 15,000
19. Cheque sent to Kerala Co. Ltd. For ₹ 8000
20. Cash given to Hindustan Ltd ₹ 25,000
21. Cheque send to Nrma Washing Co.Ltd ₹ 20,000

SOLUTION :

Step 1 :

Give a Double click on Tally icon

Step 2 :

Create a Company by pressing Alt+F3 Button to select Company Information

Select Create Company or Hot Key character C from the key board. Fill All the Details and select type of a company as **Accounts with Inventory** and save it by pressing **Ctrl + A.**

Step 3 :

Gate Way of Tally → Accounts Info → Legers → Single/ Multiple Ledgers → Create

S. No.	Ledger	Group
1	Capital	Capital Account
2	Credit purchases	Purchase
3	Kerala co & Ltd	Sundry creditors A/c
4	Hindustan lever Ltd	Sundry creditors A/c
5	Nirma washing co & L.td	Sundry creditors A/c
6	Konaseema Rice Ltd	Sundry creditors A/c
7	Punjab Rice Ltd.	Sundry creditors A/c
8	Credit Sales	Sundry creditors A/c
9	X	Sundry Debtors A/c
10	Y	Sundry Debtors A/c
11	Cash Sales	Sales A/c
12	Furniture	Fixed Assets
13	Weighing machine	Fixed Assets
14	Depreciation	Indirect Expenses
15	Rent	Indirect Expenses
16	Purchase Return	Purchase A/c
17	Bank Account	Bank Account
18	Sales Promotion Expenses	Indirect Expenses

Step 4 :

Gate way of Tally → Inventory Info First create stock groups for the following items under **'Primary'**

Oil

Soap

Rice

Creation of Unit of Measure

Oil - Ltrs

Soap - Nos

Rice - Kgs

Creation of Stock Items

Stock Item	**Stock Groups**
Coconut oil	Oil
Ordinary soaps	Soaps
Detergent Soaps	Soaps
Konaseema rice	Rice
Punjab Rice	Rice

Step 5 :

Gate way of Tally → Accounting Voucher

Date	Particulars		Function Key	Debit	Credit
1	Receipt Voucher		F6		
	Cash A/c	Dr		20,000	
	To Capital A/c				20,000
2	Purchase Voucher		F9		
	Purchase A/c	Dr		10,000	
	To Kerala Co. Ltd				10,000
3	Purchase Voucher		F9		
	Purchase A/c	Dr		25,000	
	To Hindustan Lever Ltd.				25,000
4	Purchase Voucher		F9		
	Purchase A/c	Dr		20,000	
	To Nima Washing Co.				20,000
5	Payment Voucher		F5		
	Purchase A/c	Dr		15,000	
	To Cash A/c				15,000
6	Purchase Voucher		F9		
	Purchase A/c	Dr		10,000	
	To Punjab Rice Ltd.				10,000
7	Sales Voucher		F8		
	X Ltd. A/c	Dr		24,000	
	To Sales A/c				24,000

8	Sales Voucher		F8		
	Y Ltd A/c	Dr		20,000	
	To Sales A/c				20,000
9	Receipt Voucher		F6		
	Cash A/c	Dr			
	To Sales A/c				
10	Payment Voucher		F5		
	Furniture A/c	Dr			
	To Cash A/c				
11	Receipt Voucher		F6		
	Cash A/c	Dr		25000	
	To Sales A/c				25000
12	Payment Voucher		F5		
	Weighing Machine	Dr		2000	
	To Cash A/c				2000
13	Journal Voucher				
	Depreciation A/c	Dr		200	
	To Weighing Machine				200
14	Kalarale Co. Ltd.	Dr		1000	
	To Purchase Returns A/c				1000
15	Payment Voucher		F5		
	Rent A/c	Dr		2000	
	To Bank.				2000
16	Payment Voucher		F5		
	Sales Promoter Exp. A/c	Dr		5000	
	To Cash A/c				5000
17	Receipt Voucher		F6		
	Bank A/c	Dr		20000	
	To X Co.				20000
18	Receipt Voucher		F6		
	Cash A/c	Dr		15000	
	To Y Ltd.				15000
19	Payment Voucher		F5		
	Kerala A/c	Dr		8000	
	To Bank Ltd.				8000
20	Payment Voucher		F5		
	Hindustan Ltd. A/c	Dr		25000	
	To Cash A/c				25000
21	Payment Voucher		F5		
	Nirma Washing Co. A/c	Dr		20000	
	To Bank				20000

Step 6 : Gateway of Tally Display → Cash/Fundsflow → Cash

ILLUSTRATION 12

Mr. Gupta started business with cash ₹ 3,00,000

Purchased 10 CTVs @ 20,000 each for cash.

Paid carriage on purchase ₹ 2000

Sold 05 CTVs 24,000 each for cash

Sold 05 CTVs @ 24,000 each to Shyam.

Paid salaries ₹ 2,000 and Rent ₹ 1,000

Prepare Cashflow Statement.

SOLUTION

Step 1 :

Give a Double click on Tally icon

Step 2 :

Create a Company by pressing Alt+F3 Button to select Company Information

Select Create Company or Hot Key character C from the key board. Fill All the Details and select type of a company as **Accounts with Inventory** and save it by pressing **Ctrl + A.**

Step 3 :

Gate Way of Tally → Accounts Info → Legers Single/Multiple Ledgers → Create

Gupta Capital	Capital
Purchases	Purchases
Carriage	Direct Expenses
Sales	Sales
Shyam	Sundry Debtor
Salaries	Indirect Expenses
Rent	Indirect Expenses

Step 4 :

Gatway of Tally → Accounting Voucher

Date	Particulars		Function Key	Debit	Credit
	Receipt Voucher		F6		
	Cash A/c	Dr		3,00,000	
	To Gupta Capital				3,00,000
	Payment Voucher				
	Purchase A/c	Dr		2,00,000	
	To Cash A/c				2,00,000
	Payment Voucher		F5		
	Carriage A/c	Dr		2,000	
	To Cash A/c				2,000
	Receipt Voucher		F6		
	Cash A/c	Dr		1,20,000	
	To Sales A/c				1,20,000
	Sales Voucher		F8		
	Shayam A/c	Dr		1,20,000	
	To Sales A/c				1,20,000

	Pavment Voucher	F5		
	Salaries A/c Dr		2,000	
	To Cash A/c			2,000
	Payment Voucher	F5		
	Rent A/c Dr		1,000	
	To Cash A/c			1,000

Step 5 :

Gateway of Tally → Display → Funds/Cash flow → Cash Flow

SHORT QUESTIONS WITH ANSWERS

Q. 1. What is Tally ?

Ans. Tally is the accounting Package created by Tally Solutions Ltd. Bangalore.

Q. 2. What are the important features of tally ?

Ans. It is user-friendly gives instant results, no codes to remember, flexible reports, interactive on line help. ODBC technology, permits to publish reports/documents on internet, web browser etc.

Q. 3. What is ODBC '?

Ans. Open Data Base Connectivity—to connect to other programs and exchange data dynamically.

Q. 4. What are the main steps to computerize the accounts of a company ?

Ans. 1. Creation of a company.

2. Ledger creations

3. Voucher entry

4. Viewing reports

Q. 5. What do you mean by hot keys/short keys in tally ?

Ans. Hot keys are the red colour Keys present in almost all the steps in windows which facilities quick commands.

Q. 6. How to create a company ?

Ans. Press <Alt + F3> and 'C' from the Gateway of Tally or 'C' from company Info.

Q. 7. What do you mean by base currency ?

Ans. Base currency is the currency of home country in which the companies maintain accounts and undergo transactions.

Q. 8. What is button bar ?

Ans. Button bar is the grey colour bar present on the right side of the screen which facilitates customization of reports, browse and take help and switching on different applications.

Q. 9. What are the compulsory fields on creation of Co. screen ?

Ans. Name, currency symbol, maintain, financial year.

Q. 10. What is Gateway of Tally ?

Ans. It is the blue colour screen, act as the gateway to enter into different applications such as Accounts Info, voucher entry, import of data, balance sheet, p&l a/c, ratio analysis, display, multi-accounting printing.

Q. 11. What are the frequently used keys under tally ?

Ans. Enter to log into the application highlighted and Esc to logout from the application currently working.

Q. 12. What is the difference between Shut Co. and Delete Co. ?

Ans. Shut Co. will close the currently used co. to he used later <Alt + Fl>. Delete Co. will erase the co. from the memory of the computer which cannot be retrieved later <Fl > <A> <Alt + D>.

Q. 13. How to change the period of the co. ?

Ans. <Alt + F2>, but it must correspond to the financial year of the co.

Q. 14. How to change the date of the co. ?

Ans. <F2> but it must correspond to the current period of the co.

Q. 15. What do you mean by features of Co. ?

Ans. <F11: Features> are used to activate applications like purchase and sales order, cost centers and cost categories, stock categories, VAT, TDS, etc.

Q. 16. How are the features are different from configuration ?

Ans. Features changes (F11: Features) affect only the current company, but configuration changes (F12: Configure) affect all the open companies.

Q. 17. What is the difference between accounts only and accounts with inventory ?

Ans. Inventory info option is deactivated when accounts only is selected under maintain field. Companies dealing with stock should select accounts with Inventory option to provide detailed stock ledger.

Q. 18. How to create ledger group ?

Ans. A, G, C under already existing ledger group.

Q. 19. Shortcut to create a ledger group ?

Ans. A, L, C

Q. 20. What are the pre defined ledger accounts ?

Ans. P&L a/c and cash a/c are created by default.

Q. 21. Grouping of accounts under tally means ?

Ans. Selecting an appropriate ledger group while creating the ledger account.

Q. 22. What are the primary voucher types ?

Ans. F4: Contra, F5: Payments, F6: Receipts, F7: Journal, F8: Sales, F9: Purchases.

Q. 23. Function of Reverse journal ?

Ans. It reverses the entry passed in it after a day or specified period.

Q. 24. Memorandum vouchers are ?

Ans. Reminders for the special transactions.

Q. 25. Optional vouchers can be created by ?

Ans. Marketing optional from the button bar at any voucher which can be optionally added into regular stream of voucher.

Q. 26. What are exceptional reports ?

Ans. Negative ledger, Negative stock over dues, Memorandum, Reverse journals and optional vouchers.

Q. 27. How to create a voucher type ?

Ans. Shortcut: AVC or IVC. The new voucher can be created only under the existing voucher type.

Q. 28. How to create and view petty cash book ?

Ans. 1. Create a ledger "Petty Cash" under cash in hand.

2. Enter the transactions in Receipts, payments and contra.

3. View the book by D, A, C, Enter, Petty Cash, Enter.

Q.29. Types of voucher Numbering ?

Ans. 1. Automatic 2. Manual 3. None at the voucher type creation/alteration screen.

Q. 30. How to view major reports ?

Ans.

Balance sheet	– B
P&La/c	– C
Ratio analysis	– R
Stock Summary	– S
Trial Balance	– D, T

<Alt + Fl> for detailed reports.

Q. 31. How to view reports of more than one company together ?

Ans. By clicking on new column button from the button bar and selecting the required company from the Gateway of Tally-List of Companies.

Q. 32. How to change the format of the report ?

Ans. Click on <F12: Configure> from the button bar and respond yes to the first prompt show vertical balance sheet or p&l a/c.

Q. 33. How to view BRS ?

Ans. Shortcut: D, A, C. B, Enter, Enter, F5: Reconcile-gave bank data <ctrl + A>, F5: Reconcile.

Q. 34. How to view the list of Dr's/Cr's ?

Ans. Either from Balance sheet or from list of ledgers by drill down facility.

Q. 35. How to alter a content of any report.

Ans. Highlight the account to be corrected press <enter> unless you reach the voucher entry-change the contents and accept.

If the error is commited while creating the ledger account then A, L, A change the contents and accept.

Q. 36. What is an Adult trial ?

Ans. Drilling down the report from highest level to the lowest, to check the errors.

Q. 37. What is a Tally Audit ?

Ans. This is available to the administrator to track if any unauthorized changes have taken place in the data following his previous review.

Display-statements of accounts

D, S, T

Q. 38. What is a Tally vault ?

Ans. It is used to keep an company data in encrypted form for additional security unless the password is given the company name would be shown in the form of asterisks (*) and the company will be identified by its number.

Q. 39. What is a Tally Locker ?

Ans. It is a mini vault like solid state device size (57 mm × 17 mm × 10 mm) available with the storage capacity of 16 MB, thumb sized. It is used as an external storage device.

Q. 40. What are the security measures under tally ?

Ans. 1. Use security control (password protection with administrator name)

2. Use tally audit feature (to trade unauthorized changes)

3. Tally Vault (to keep the company name and data in encrypted form)

Q. 41. What is an interest calculation option ?

Ans. It is available in simple and advanced mode, to be activated from F11: Features Then in the ledger creation you are asked whether you wish to activate interest calculation for the ledger, if get set the parameter then you will be able to calculate interest transaction wise

Q. 42. Short key for creation of new ledger a/c cost group during voucher entry ?

Ans. <Alt + C> in account field

Q. 43. Short key for involving calculator in voucher entry ?

Ans. <Alt + C> in amount field

Q. 44. Short key for deletion of a voucher ?

Ans. <Alt + D> in alternation mode.

Q. 45. Short key for deletion of ledger, group, cost cost center etc ?

Ans. <Alt + D> in alternation mode.

Q. 46. Short key for Insertion of a voucher during display.

Ans. <Alt + 1 >

Q. 47. Short key for duplication of voucher during display (on which cursor rests)?

Ans. <Alt + 2>

Q. 48. Short key to cancel a voucher during display.

Ans. <Alt + X>

Q. 49. Short key to repeat narration of last voucher ?

Ans. <Alt + R>

Q. 50. Short key to repeat narration of last voucher with some ledger account?

Ans. <Alt + R>

Q. 51. Short key for accepting any data or entry ?

Ans. <Ctrl + A>

Q. 52. Short key to exit the operations without confirmation?

Ans. <Ctrl + Q>

Q. 53. What are the restrictions to delete a ledger a/c ?

Ans. There must not be any voucher entered using that ledger a/c

Q. 54. List out the exceptional reports ?

Ans. Negative Stock, Negative Ledgers, Memorandum vouchers, Reversing journals, Optional vouchers, Post dated vouchers.

Q. 55. What is the use of Reversing journal ?

Ans. To enter any outstanding payments (liability) Ex. Outstanding salaries in the middle of the year

Q. 56. Which type of vouchers is used to make the entry of sales/purchase return ?

Ans. Credit note for sale return.

Debit note for purchase return.

Q. 57. Which type of vouchers is used to make the entry of transactions related to suspense payments?

Ans. Memo voucher.

Q. 58. How to display all the vouchers entered in a day ?

Ans. Gateway of Tally → Display → Day book.

Q. 59. What is sales return or rejections in note ?

Ans. When the customer sends back faulty goods to supplier, it is called Return or rejection in note.

Q. 60. What is the difference between purchase order and sales order?

Ans. When you want to buy the goods, you send the purchase order to suppliers and when the customers want to buy the goods they send sales order.

Q. 61. How can sales order and purchase order be activated and entered?

Ans. Sales orders and purchase orders can be activated through F11: Features and entered through 'Inventory vouchers'.

Q. 62. What is a stock group ?

Ans. It is a particular brand together so that extract stock of all items of that brand can be grouped under one head.

Q. 63. How to create units of measures ? Is it necessary ?

Ans. Gateway of tally → inventory info → units of measuring.

Shortcut: I, U, C. Yes it is necessary to create Unit of Measures.

Q. 64. What do you mean by Stock categories ? How to activate and create it?

Ans. It is a category where you group stock items by its nature or brand parallel to stock Group. It is to be activated from F11: Features. Shortcut to create categories is I O C.

Q. 65. Is it possible to maintain more than one Godown ? How.

Ans. Yes, it is to be activated through F11: Features and created through - I G C.

Q. 66. What is an invoice ?

Ans. When you sell the goods to customers, the bill you issue is called an invoice.

Q. 67. What is a Challan ?

Ans. It comprises delivery notes (sales challan), receipt note, rejection notes etc. It is a document which represents transactions of materials only affecting stock but not financial accounts.

Q. 68. Difference between Invoice and Challans ?

Ans. Challan—affects only inventory but not accounts.

Invoice—affects accounts also with the inventory.

Q. 69. Which report will show the financial position of the company ?

Ans. Balance Sheet.

QUESTIONS

OBJECTIVE TYPE

1. **Fill in the blanks :**

(*a*) .... is the most popular and widely accepted software.

(*b*) The basic types of computers are ....

(*c*) The basic components of a computer are ....

(*d*) Electronic Data Processing (EDP) is associated with ....

(*e*) Physically the main components of the computer are the ....

(*f*) The computer itself as a machine and related equipment used in an electronic data processing system are called ....

(*g*) Output unit of the computer turns out the ....

(*h*) Calculator performs all the necessary ....

(*i*) A machine which does the work of verification in punched card accounting is known as ....

(*j*) To get the fastest results in an electronic computer, input media used should be ....

(*k*) .... unit in a computer performs the functions of storage.

Ans. [(*a*) Tally; (*b*) digital computers and analog computers; (*c*) input unit, memory unit, logic unit, output unit and control unit; (*d*) electronic computers; (*e*) central processing unit; (*f*) hardware; (*g*) end product *i.e.* results; (*h*) calculation work; (*i*) verifier; (*j*) magnetic tape; (*k*) Memory]

2. **Which of the following statements are correct ?**

(*i*) The word computer comes from the word 'compute' which means to calculate.

(*ii*) The main purpose of TPS is to record, process, validate and store transactions.

(*iii*) Accounting software is not computer software.

(*iv*) Multi-user software can be operated at only one computer.

(*v*) The Gateway of Tally has four sections.

(*vi*) The process of preparing final accounts in Tally can broadly be classified into three steps.

Ans. [Correct : (*i*); (*ii*); (*v*)]

SHORT ANSWER TYPE

1. What is the role of Computer in Accounting functions ?
2. List out the advantages of using computers in Company's for its accounting functions.
3. Explain the term Computerised Accounting System.
4. Compare Manual and Computerised Accounting Systems.
5. Define the term Accounting Software.
6. Explain (1) Single user Software, and (2) Multi user Software.
7. Why Tally is the most popular package ?

LONG ANSWER TYPE

1. Discuss the role of Computerised Accounting System in an organisation.
2. Explain the features of good Computerised Accounting System.
3. Explain and discuss the features of Tally—an accounting software.
4. Discuss the steps of accounting process in Tally.
5. List the steps to be followed in creating a new company in Tally for accounting purposes.
6. Why do you think grouping of accounting heads is necessary ? Discuss the process of Grouping the accounting heads in Tally.
7. Discuss the process of creating

   (1) Single Ledger in Tally

   (2) Multiple Ledger in Tally.
8. Bring out Salient features of Tally as an accounting package.
9. "Accounting Softwares can be customised in accordance to the need of the organisation." Discuss.

CHAPTER 38

Government Accounting System

Accounting is a process of recording, classifying and summarising all the business transactions. Accounting is also meant for communicating the financial result and position to all stakeholders of the business. The accounting relating to organisations dealing in goods or services is termed as commercial accounting and it has been discussed in preceding chapters. This accounting is not similar or suitable to record the government activities for administration of the country. Therefore, this chapter is devoted for Government Accounting to record and administer the activities of the nation as a whole.

Meaning and Definition

Government accounting system refers to that accounting system which is specially designed for government, its various departments, offices and institutions. This system is the process of recording, classifying, summarising, analysing, communicating and interpretation of all financial transactions and other economic events of government involving the receipt, transfer, and disposition of government assets and liabilities etc.

Therefore, it may be treated as systematic process of recording of government revenues and expenditures. It is also concerned with the collection and utilisation of public funds and properties and to record all the revenues and expenditures of its different department and administrations.

> *"A system that is charged with identification, selection and analysis, measurement, estimation, processing, and communication of information of receipt, expenditure, assets, liabilities, costs and benefits and all other aspects that legitimately form part of fiscal management and is now the recognised handmaiden of fiscal policy."*
>
> ***—As per Shri Prem Chand***
>
> *"Government Accounting is the process of recording, analysing, classifying, summarising, communicating, and interpreting information about government in aggregate and in detail, reflecting all transactions involving the receipts, transfer, and disposition of government funds and property."*
>
> ***—As per Oshisami and Dean***

Features and Characteristics of Government Accounting

Government accounting is specially designed with unique characteristics for government and its various departments. Following are the main characteristics of government accounting system:

(i) **Unique Accounting System:** This is a unique accounting system specially designed to record revenues and expenditures of government institutions.

(ii) **Reporting of Collection and Utilisation of Public Funds:** The main objective of government and its various institutions is to provide public services to the society at large. Therefore, this accounting system also focuses on reporting the collection of public funds and its utilisation on public services.

(*iii*) **Rules and Regulations:** This accounting system is specially designed for reporting of collection and utilisation of public funds in accordance with the various rules and regulation framed by government from time to time like fiscal policies and budgets etc.

(*iv*) **Double Entry System:** The Government Accounting system is also based on the principles of double accounting principles to record all revenues and expenditures of government. It helps to record both effects (*i.e.*: Debit and Credit) of financial transactions of government.

(*v*) **Budgets and Control:** Annual budget is prepared by the government in which amount is allocated for government expenditure. Therefore, the government accounting is based on annual budget in order to monitor and control government expenditures.

(*vi*) **Fund Management:** All the projects of government for providing public services are executed through proper funds. These projects are funded by the government for its proper execution and timely completion. Therefore, government accounting helps to record and ascertain the results of every project by proper fund management.

(*vii*) **Auditing:** All the books of accounts of government departments are also audited by the Comptroller and Auditor General (C&AG) in order to prevent misuse and misappropriation of public funds.

Objectives of Government Accounting

Objectives of Government accounting are as follows :

1. Providing Information about Expenditure. The objective of government accounting is to provide information about the expenditure on various heads. It is very much desired because Parliament in case of the Central Government or the State Legislature in case of a state would like to know whether the amounts spent by the government on different activities are within the limits sanctioned by it or not.

2. Providing Information about Revenues. Government accounting provides information about the revenues of the government during the year. The revenues of the government can be tax revenues and non-tax revenues.

3. Providing Estimates. Government Accounting provides estimates as to whether the receipts are sufficient or not.

4. Comparison. Government Accounting helps in comparison of actual with estimated receipts and payments.

5. Determining Policies and Expenditure. Government Accounting helps in determining taxation policies and government expenditure on the basis of government accounts and budgets.

6. Providing Information about Loans and Deposits. Government accounting provides information about the loans given by the government to others and the loans and deposits which the government has to pay to its creditors along with their dates of repayment.

7. Information about Cash Availability. Government accounting provides information about the present availability of cash and expected availability of cash in the near future.

General Principles of Government Accounting

Following are the general principles in relation to government accounting:

(*i*) **Classification of Government Expenditures:** All the government expenditures are classified into heads (*i.e.*: major or minor) of different sectors like defence, health and construction etc. in order to maintain proper control over the utilisation of funds.

(*ii*) **Budgetary Controls:** Annual budget is forecasted by the government based on the final books of account of that year. Therefore, government accounting helps to maintain budgetary controls and to determine:

(*a*) The scope of different government activities and utilisation of funds; and

(*b*) The availability and proper collection of funds to complete all budgeted activities.

(*iii*) **Reporting of Activities:** The government accounting focuses on maintaining proper records and reporting of all government activities in order to maintain day to day administration of different activities and to report the results of annual accounts.

(*iv*) **Accounting Period:** The annual accounting of government activities is starts from 1st April and ends on 31st March.

(*v*) **Cash Basis of Accounting:** The Government Accounting is based on cash basis to record all the revenue and expenditures of different government activities unless it is specified otherwise by Comptroller and Auditor General of India (C&AG).

(*vi*) **Form of Government Accounts:** There are three different accounts are prepared in prepared in government accounting like Public Funds Account, Consolidated Fund Account, and Contingency Fund Account.

Difference between Government Accounting and Commercial Accounting

The accounting principles relating to commercial accounting are similarly applicable on government activities. However, there are certain features of government accounting which make it unique and different from general accounting principles as applicable on commercial accounting.

Following are the main differences between commercial and government accounting:

(*i*) **Meaning:** Government Accounting is designed to monitor the financial administration of activities of the government in the best possible way. It enables government to determine how little money it takes out of the pocket of tax payers in order to maintain its necessary activities at the proper standard of efficiency. While, the commercial accounting system is concerned with non-government organisations which are mainly concerned with the trade or manufacture and thereby to make profits.

(*ii*) **Objectives:** Government Accounting is concerned with the recording and reporting of collection and utilisation of public funds in order to provide best public services. While, Commercial Accounting is concerned with the non-government organisations engaged in trading and manufacturing to know the financial performance and position of business.

(*iii*) **Scope of Accounting:** The Scope of Government Accounting is mainly decided by the fiscal budget announced by the government. While, the scope of commercial accounting is decided by generally accepted accounting principles and standards applicable on commercial activities of non-government organisations.

(*iv*) **Basis of Accounting:** Generally, the Government Accounting is prepared on cash basis unless otherwise specified by Comptroller and Auditor's General (C&AG) on some specific matters. While, the commercial accounting is mainly based on accrual basis of accounting.

(*v*) **Accounting Concepts:** Various general accounting concepts are not applicable on government entities like matching concept where all expenditures relating to generated revenue should be reported in the same financial year. There is no relevance of these concepts in government accounting because government entities are not guided by profit motive and fiscal budgets are mainly used in government accounting to assist management and to provide the legal authority to levy taxes and make expenditure.

(*vi*) **Administration of Accounting:** There is Central and Operating Level of Accounting in order to administration and application of Government Accounting. While, there is no such central and operation level in case of commercial accounting.

(*vii*) **Accounting Rules and Provisions:** The accounting rules and provision relating to government accounting is framed by the concerned government in line with policies and budged proposed by the government. While, commercial accounting is mainly based on the Generally Accepted Accounting Principles (GAAP) and Accounting Standards applicable on concerned commercial activity.

(*viii*) **Users of Accounting Information:** The Government Accounting is mainly concerned with the reporting to the government regarding all the government activities like collection of revenue and utilisation of public funds. While, commercial accounting is concerned with the reporting of financial performance and position to various stakeholders.

(*ix*) **Audit of Accounting:** The books of accounts of government enterprises are audited by the recognised government department known as Comptroller and Auditor's General (C&AG). While, the books of accounts of commercial entities are audited by professional auditors

General Structure of the Financial Administration in India

The Constitution of India came into force on January 26, 1950 which declared India a Sovereign Socialist Secular Democratic Republic. The constitution is federal with a Union Government at the Centre, State Governments in the states and centrally administered union territories. The Union of India comprises 28 states, 6 centrally administered territories and one national capital region. The executive power of the union vests in the hands of the President and that of a state in the hands of a Governor. Every union territory is administered by the President through an administrator appointed by him. The initial responsibility for the administration of each department of government activities is on the head of the department concerned, who is controlled and guided in this respect by the government to which he is subject. In financial matters, each head of a department is thus responsible for the collection of revenue and for the control of expenditure relating to his department.

Government Accounting and Reporting in India

The Controller General of Accounts (CGA) is the prescribed accounting body of Indian Government which is mainly responsible for implementing effective accounting system for Government Activities. The Accounts of the Government Activities are controlled and maintained by the basic accounting units of Government Entities known as Pay and Account Offices.

These Pay and Account Offices are mainly responsible for managing all the financial transactions relating to various Government funds like Consolidated Fund, Contingency Fund, and Public Fund of India. All the information compiled by these Pay and Account Offices on monthly basis are provided to the Controller General of Accounts (CGA) for consolidation of monthly accounts. After consolidation of monthly accounts by Controller General of Accounts (CGA), a summarised report of all collection and utilisation of funds is also prepared for Finance Minister.

Roles and Responsibilities of Controller General of Accounts (CGA)

The primary role and responsibility of Controller General of Accounts (CGA) is to consolidate the monthly reports of Government Activities in order to summarise the report on fiscal deficit. He is also responsible for critical analysis of all Government activities including collection of revenue, utilisation of funds, management of borrowings, and report of deficit for the Finance Minister. He is also responsible for the preparation of Annual Appropriation and Union Finance Account presenting the consolidated report to the Indian Parliament. They also give advised on adoption of accounting procedures for newly launched Government schemes, programmes and activities.

Basic Structure of Government Accounts

The manner in which the Government Accounts have been kept is prescribed in the Constitution of India. These Accounts are divided in three main parts as follows:

1. **Consolidated Funds of India:** This fund is constituted under Article 266 (1) of the Constitution of India. It is sub-divided as follows:

   (*i*) **Revenue:** It deals with the proceeds of taxation, duties, and other heads classified as revenue such as irrigation, debt services and administrative services and expenditure. The net result of this part of Consolidated Fund represents either revenue deficit or revenue surplus for the year.

   (*ii*) **Capital:** It includes capital expenditure met usually from borrowed funds in order to increase the assets of a material character or of reducing recurring liabilities. As per Article

292 of the Constitution of India the Central Government can raise money by borrowing upon the security of the Consolidated Fund of India within limits prescribed by the Parliament. Similarly as per Article 293 of the Constitution of India, a State Government may borrow within the territory of India upon the security of the Consolidated Fund of the State within the limits prescribed by the State legislature.

Accounting for Central and State Government is done separately *i.e.*: Consolidated Fund of India is for the Central Government and Separate Consolidated Fund for each State and Union Territory.

2. **Public Fund of India:** This fund is constituted under Article 266 (2) of the Constitution of India. It includes the transactions relating to Debts (*i.e.,* Other than those include in Point-I stated above), Deposits, Advances, Remittances and Suspense. Even the above transactions relating to Union Territory Governments are also recorded in Public Fund of India because there is no separate Public Account in case of Union Territory Government.
3. **Contingency Fund of India:** This fund is constituted under Article 267 of the Constitution of India. This nature of this fund is like Imprest Account and records the transactions connected with the contingencies. This fund is also set up by the Union and State Government to meet the contingencies with authorisation of Parliament of India. At present, the corpus of Rs.500 Crores of this fund is held on behalf of President by the respective Secretary to the Government of India, Ministry of Finance, and Department of Economic Affairs.

The Comptroller and Auditor-General of India (CAG)

The Indian Constitution has recognised the Comptroller and Auditor-General as an independent statutory authority. Keeping in view the importance of a proper institutional framework for government accounting and auditing, the Constitution of India gives a special status to the Comptroller and Auditor-General and contains provisions to safeguard his independence. He is to discharge his duties of government accounting and audit without fear or favour. It is his duty to see, on behalf of the legislatures, that the expenses voted by them are not exceeded and that the money expended was legally available for the purpose for which it is meant.

As per Article 148 of the Constitution of India, the Comptroller and Auditor-General (*i.e.* C & AG) shall be appointed by the President and can be removed from the office only by the President on the like grounds as a judge of the Supreme Court. He can be removed only on the basis of proven misbehaviour or incapacity. He can be removed only through an order of the President after each house of Parliament has recommended the removal by a required majority.

Article 150 of the Constitution lays down that the accounts of the Union and of the States shall be maintained in such form as the President may, on the advice of the C & AG, prescribe.

Article 151 of the Constitution provides that the audit reports of the C & AG relating to the accounts of the Union/State Government shall be submitted to the President/Governor who shall cause them to be laid before the Parliament/State legislature.

Conditions of Service of the Comptroller and Auditor-General

The Comptroller and Auditor-General's (Duties, Powers and Conditions of Service) Act, 1971 as amended in 1976 provides as follows in regard to conditions of service of the C & AG :

"(*i*) The term of office of the Comptroller and Auditor-General shall be 6 years from the date on which he assumes office. But :

- (*a*) He shall vacate office on attaining the age of 65 years, if earlier than the expiry of the 6-year term ;
- (*b*) He may, at any time, resign his office, by writing under his hand, addressed to the President of India ;
- (*c*) He may be removed by impeachment.

(*ii*) His salary shall be equal to that of a judge of the Supreme Court.

(*iii*) On retirement he shall be eligible to an annual pension of ₹ 15,000.

(*iv*) In other matters, his conditions of service shall be determined by the Rules applicable to a member of the I.A.S. holding the rank of a Secretary to the Government of India.

(*v*) He shall be disqualified for any further Government 'office' after retirement so that he shall have no inducement to please the executive of the Union or the State.

(*vi*) The salaries etc. of the Auditor-General and his staff and the administrative expenses of his office shall be charged upon the revenue of India and shall, thus be non-votable."

Functions, Powers and Duties of the Comptroller and Auditor General (C&AG)

As per Article 149, 150, and 151 of the Constitution of India, Comptroller and Auditor General (C&AG) has following two main distinct functions:

(*i*) Compilation of Accounts;

(*ii*) Conduct of Audit of Government Entities.

Further, the Powers and duties of Comptroller and Auditor General (C&AG) in relation to accounts of the Union and State Government are provide in Article 150 of the Constitution of India and elaborated in Section 10 to 24 of Comptroller and Auditor General's Act, 1971.

Following are the Powers and Duties of Comptroller and Auditor General (C&AG):

(*i*) **Compilation of Accounts:** In order to prepare Comprehensive Accounts of Receipts and Expenditures of each Government (*i.e.*: Union and Various States), the Comptroller and Auditor General (C&AG) has to compile all the Accounts of the Union and each States. These Comprehensive Accounts are known as Finance Accounts and Comptroller and Auditor General (C&AG) has also to prepare annually and submit to the President a General Financial Statement incorporating a Summary of Accounts of the Union and all the States.

(*ii*) **Inspection of Accounts:** Comptroller and Auditor General (C&AG) is also empowered to inspect any Office of Accounts which is under control of the Union or State Government including the inspection of treasuries and offices responsible for keeping Initial and Subsidiary Accounts.

(*iii*) **Reporting to the President:** Comptroller and Auditor General (C&AG) also responsible for preparing and submitting to the President a General Financial Statement incorporating a Summary of the Accounts of the Union and all the States.

(*iv*) **Assistance to the Union and State Government:** Comptroller and Auditor General (C&AG) also responsible to assist the Union and every State Government by providing such information as they may require from time to time and such assistance in the preparation of their annual financial statements as they may ask for.

(*v*) **Audit of Government Activities:** It is a distinct function of the Comptroller and Auditor General (C&AG) to audit the various Government Activities. Following are the different duties of Comptroller and Auditor General (C&AG) with regards to audit of Government Activities:

- **Audit of Consolidated Fund:** Audit and Report on All Expenditure from the Consolidated Fund of India of Union and all the States to ascertain whether the money shown in the accounts as having been disbursed were legally available for and applicable to the services or purpose to which they have been applied and whether the expenditure confirms to the authority which governs it.
- **Audit of Contingency Fund and Public Account:** Audit and Report on all transactions of the Union and all the States relating to the Contingency Funds and Public Accounts.
- **Audit and Report on Accounts as Required by President:** Audit and Report on all Trading, Manufacturing Accounts, Balance Sheets, and Other Subsidiary Accounts kept by order of the President or the Governor of the State or of the Administrator of the Union Territory.
- **Audit and Report of Any Body or Authority Financed from Consolidated Fund:** Audit and Report on all receipts and payment of any body or authority if it is substantially

financed by grants or loans from the Consolidated Fund of India or any State /or Union Territory.

➢ **Audit and Report of Government Companies, Corporation, and Other Bodies or Authorities:** Audit and Report of Government Companies or Corporations or any other Bodies or Authorities in accordance with the Companies Act, 2013 or Any Other Relevant Legislation under which the Corporations or Bodies or Authorities has been set up.

(*vi*) **Certification:** As per Article 279 of the Constitution of India, the Comptroller and Auditor General (C&AG) also responsible to ascertain and certify the Net Proceeds of Any Tax and Duty.

Some Important Terms and Expressions of Government Finance

Following are some important terms and expression which are often used in government finance. These are discussed below:

(*i*) Demand for Grant. A basic principle of Government finance is that no expenditure can be incurred by any public authority without parliamentary sanction. For this the public authority has to request the parliament for such sanction. It is this request which is called Demand for Grant. The demand may be granted, refused or reduced. A refusal or reduction may jeopardise the legitimacy of the government in a parliamentary democracy, if it is taken as an expression of no-confidence in it.

(*ii*) Supplementary Grant. Normal grants are demanded at the time of presentation of the budget, but the amount so granted may be found inadequate at a later date. To meet the requirement expenditure a supplementary demand for grant may then be made. This may be explained citing an example : the amount granted for draught relief may be found inadequate due to prolonged failure of the monsoon, and then an additional grant may be asked for by the concerned ministry. If the amount is granted this is treated as a supplementary grant for drought relief.

(*iii*) Votable and non-votable items. Certain items of expenditure are charged to the consolidated fund or the Public Account. They are to be incurred regardless of legislature approval. These are called non-votable items. Other items are votable and expenditure thereon can be made only after the sanction of parliament. The government makes the demand for grants for these items of expenditure. These demand may be reduced or even rejected but in the case of non-votable items, it can at best be debated and nothing more than that.

(*iv*) Appropriation Act. Parliamentary or legislatory approval of budget proposal does not authorise the government to proceed with its expenditures immediately for which purpose an Appropriation Act has to be passed. This mean the executive branch of government has to be authorised through this Act to make the expenditures as per parliamentary approval. For this immediately after the presentation of the budget at both layers of government. Appropriation Bills are introduced and when a bill is passed, it becomes an act, the law enabling the government to make expenditure lawfully.

After the voting of the demands has been completed by the Legislature, an Appropriation in Bill is introduced in the Parliament or State Assembly to give legal effect to the demands so voted and to authorise the issue of moneys from the Consolidated Fund of India or the state to meet the grants made by the Legislature.

It may be noted that no money can be withdrawn from the consolidated fund until the Approprial Bill is passed by the Legislature. When the bill is passed by the Legislature, it becomes an Appropriation Act which authorises the issue of moneys from the consolidated fund for meeting the grants made by the Legislature.

(*v*) Vote on Account. When the voting of demands for expenditure for a particular financial year is not complete till the month of August, then it becomes necessary to make provision of grants before the beginning of the financial year. For making such a provision, a special estimate known as Vote on Account is presented which authorises the issue of money for various departments for meeting their financial requirements for three or four months before the complete provision for the grants will be made.

(*vi*) Mode of Classification of Services in the Central Budget. In central budget, services are first classified under different broad heads. After this services are sub-classified according to their essential natures. In the central budget, government services are classified into :

(*a*) General Services; (*b*) Social Services; (*c*) Economic Services, and (*d*) Grants-in-add and Contribution.

General services are further classified into :

(*a*) Administrative Services; (*b*) Defence Services, (*c*) Services of Debts, and (*d*) Fiscal Services.

Classification enhances the usefulness of the budgetary practice.

(*vii*) Local Government Accounting. Local government accounting is a sub-area of government accounting. There is a significant difference between business accounting and government accounting. Government accounting is basically a budget-driven accounting, and it is founded on the concept of "fund accounting."

The purpose of local government accounting is to recognize, measure, and report the financial transactions and events of local government entities. There are two types of local government entities : Urban local government entities and rural local government entities. The published accounts of local government entities in India generally comprises budgets and receipts and payments accounts. Efforts are now being made to improve the quality of local government accounting in India by introducing accrual based double entry accounting system.

(*viii*) Suspense Account in Government Accounting. The functions of Suspense Account in Government Accounting are as under :

(*a*) It is a control mechanism and it will ultimately get transferred to the Bank of the Government which is named in Government Accounting as Reserve Bank deposits.

(*b*) It is ultimately transferred to the regular accounts in the consolidated fund or the Pubic Account.

(*c*) When there is no other accounting head available suspense account acts to some extent as miscellaneous account.

(*ix*) Treasuries. All the States of India are divided into a number of districts. At the headquarter of each district there is a Government treasury with one or more sub-treasuries. The treasuries are the units of the fiscal system. These are the points at which the public accounts start. The Union Government and the State Governments have framed treasury rules in order to regulate the workings of treasuries. Generally, a treasury is divided into two sections, *viz.*, (*i*) for cash, stamps and opium under the charge of the treasurer ; and (*ii*) for all other accounts under the charge of the accountant. When any member of the public has to make payment to the government, he presents the money (*i.e.*, cash or stamps as directed by the Government) with a challan at a treasury and receives a receipt for the money paid by him. On the other hand, when one is to receive payment from the government, he presents a receipted bill or a cheque issued in his favour by a competent officer at a treasury and obtains payment.

The treasury is conducted by the Reserve Bank of India at every place where it has a branch or by the State Bank of India as its agent where the Reserve Bank of India has no office or branch of its own. The Central Government and the State Governments keep their own separate accounts with the Reserve Bank of India. All kinds of adjustments between the Central Government and different State Governments are adjusted by the Reserve Bank of India.

Functions of Treasury

The functions entrusted to the treasury in Government Accounting are :

(*a*) Collection of Money: Treasury is responsible for maintaining the receipt of money from the public and departmental offices for credit to government.

(*b*) Payment of Claims: It is also responsible for payment of claims against government on bills or cheques or other instruments presented by departmental drawing and disbursing officers or pensioners or other authorised to do so.

(*c*) Keeping Initials & Subsidiary Accounts: It keeps all the initials and subsidiary accounts of the receipts and payments occurring at them and rendering statements of such transactions to the Accountant General for detailed Compilation and Consolidation.

(*d*) **Acting as a Banker:** It is acting as a banker in respect of funds of Local Bodies, Zila Parishads, Panchayat and other Institutions etc. who keep their funds with the treasuries.

(*e*) **Acting as a Custodian:** It is also acting as a custodian for the custody of opium and other valuables because of the storing room facility provided at the treasuries including the custody of cash balances of the State Government and conducting cash business of Government at non-banking treasuries.

(*f*) **Compilation of Accounts:** Accounts are compiled in the lines o the budget. Initial Accounts are compiled by the treasury or departmental offices in some cases. Each treasury compiles all receipts and payments from day-to-day transactions for the Central Government and for the state each month. Details of the receipts and payments are available from these statements of treasuries prepared on monthly basis. These details are sent to the respective Accountant-General at the end of each month.

(*x*) **Public Accounts Committee (PAC).** The Parliament and each State Legislature set up a Public Accounts Committee for scrutinising the Appropriation Accounts and the report of the auditor thereon. The Committee also examines financial statements and the auditors' reports thereon of state corporations and other autonomous and semi-autonomous bodies.

Public Accounts Committee consists of opposition members of Parliament of both the Houses (*i.e.* Lok Sabha and Rajya Sabha) and in case of State Assemblies it consists of the members of the Legislative Assemblies. No member of the ruling party can be members of PAC It acts as a watchdog on the spending of public money. It examines that there had been no waste or extravagance of public funds and the money granted under budget allotment had been utilised within the scope of demand. It examines all reports on financial statements that are submitted to the Parliament and the President of India. This committee does not go into policies, objectives and how to go about them ; it is just doing post-mortem examination. The main function of the committee is to ascertain that the money granted by the Parliament or State Legislature has been spent by the Government within the scope of the demand. It is to ensure that grants should be spent on purposes which are set out in the detailed demand and the money recorded as spent against the grant must not be more than the amount granted. In brief, the aim of the committee is to see that high standard of public morality is maintained in all financial matters.

Public Accounts committee is not an executive body. It can only draw attention to irregularities and express its opinion thereon and records its findings and recommendations. This committee is assisted in its task by the Indian Audit and Accounts Department which furnishes the Appropriation Accounts and the Audit Reports thereon. Attention of the Committee is drawn through the Audit Reports to important financial irregularities which are noticed by the Indian Audit Department. Though scrutiny by the Public Accounts Committee is best in the nature of post mortum yet it helps to build public opinion about the government.

Accrual Basis of Accounting in Government of India

The government accounting system in India is predominantly cash basis accounting. The cash basis accounting is simple and easy to operate. But it has many limitations. One of the major limitations of cash basis accounting is that it fails to provide an effective mechanism for fixing accountability for performance. Another major limitation of cash basis accounting is that it does not keep an accurate track of assets and liabilities. Under cash basis accounting, it is easy to understate liabilities. In many countries, accrual accounting has replaced cash basis accounting in many areas of public sector accounting. Currently, there are initiatives underway in India to adopt accrual accounting as the foundation of government accounting. The Twelfth Finance Commission has recommended for adoption of accrual accounting in Government of India. The recommendation has been accepted and the Government of India has asked the Government Accounting Standards Advisory Board (GASAB) to draw a detailed road map and operational framework for implementation. Some pilot studies have been conducted in the Department of Post and certain units of

Central Public Works Departments besides initiated discussions with the Ministry of Railways and the Ministry of Defence in this regard. Accrual-based accounting is an important initiative to reform the system of accounts and financial reporting in the Government. A transition from cash to accrual-based accounting would make financial reporting more transparent and meaningful, leading to financial statements of government bodies reflecting the full economic impact of the decision taken. Through this reform central and state governments can demonstrate their commitment to achieving greater transparency and accountability, and also to producing better information for decision making which in term should lead to the better use of public resources.

BUDGETING FOR THE UNION BUDGET

The process, beginning with the budget presentation and ending with discussions and voting is long. The Constitutional and Parliamentary intricacies of the exercise are given below :

Document Details

The budget documents presented to Parliament comprise a lot of other things besides the finance minister's speech. These include :

- Annual Financial Statements
- Demands for Grants
- Appropriation Bill
- Finance Bill
- Memorandum explaining the provisions in the Finance Bill
- Macro-economic framework for the relevant financial Fiscal policy strategy statement for the financial year
- Medium term fiscal policy statement
- Expenditure budget volume-1
- Expenditure budget volume-2
- Receipts budget
- Budget at a glance
- Highlights of budget

Annual Financial Statement

This document shows the government's esitmates about what it expects to earn and spend during the year. These are shown under the three parts :

- Consolidated Fund
- Contingency Fund
- Public Account

Consolidated Fund

- **Article 266 :** Of the Constitution says Parliamentary approval is required to draw money from the Consolidated Fund.
- All earnings of the government, its borrowings and also its receipts from recoveries of loans that it grants from the Consolidated Fund.

Contingency Fund

- **Article 267 :** Of the Constitution which mandates that Parliamentary approval is required to draw money from the Consolidated Fund

- ₹ **500** ***crores.*** : The current corpus of the contingency Fund of India.
- Contingency Fund is an emergency pool of resources meant to meet urgent unforeseen expenditure.

Public Account

- Funds that the government holds in trusts such as provident funds, small savings collections, income of government set aside for expenditure on specific schemes are all kept in the public account.
- Public account funds do not belong to the government and have to be finally paid back to the persons/authorities who disposited them.
- Parliamentary authorisation for such payments is, therefore, not required.

Demand for Grants

- Of the Constitution that mandates that expenditure from the Consolidated Fund be voted by the Lok Sabha , are submitted in the form of demands for grants.
- Each department places demands for grants that are placed in the Lok Sabha along with the annual financial statement

Appropriation Bill

Article 114 (3)

- Of the Constitution that stipulates that no amount can be withdrawn from the Consolidated Fund without the enactment of a law. This is sought through the Appropriation Bill.

Finance Bill

Article 110

- Of the Constitution, under which Parliament has to pass a law to approve changes in direct taxes. Every year the government imposes new taxes, abolishes some old ones, changes regulations and alters some taxes. These are carried out by passing the Finance Bill.
- Parliament has to pass the Finance Bill within 75 days of its introduction.

What if it isn't passed within 75 days?

It is viewed as a vote of no confidence against the government

According to precedent.

- The speaker can call an all-party meeting
- Parliamentary affairs minister can reach out to the Opposition
- The speaker can put the bill to a voice vote without debate.

Money Bills

- Bills that exclusively contain provisions for imposition and abolition of taxes, for appropriation of money out of the Consolidated Fund, etc, are certified as Money Bills. They can be introduced only in Lok Sabha.
- Rajya Sabha cannot make amendments in a Money Bill passed by Lok Sabha, but can recommend amendments.
- Lok Sabha may accept or reject any or all recommandations of Rajya Sabha on a Money Bill. If it accepts recommendations, the Money Bill is deemed to have been passed by both houses. If it does not, the Bill is deemed to have been passed by both houses as it was passed by Lok Sabha. If Rajya Sabha fails to return a bill within in 14 days of receiving it, it is deemed to have been passed by both Houses.

QUESTIONS

OBJECTIVE TYPE

1. Mention the authorities responsible for maintaining accounts of–

(*i*) Post and Telegraph Offices; (*ii*) Railways;
(*iii*) Defence services; (*iv*) Accounts relating to transactions in the UK;
(*v*) Forest Department; (*vi*) Government Commercial Undertakings.

Ans. (*i*) Accountant General, Posts and Telegraphs
(*ii*) Railways Board
(*iii*) Military Accounts Department,
(*iv*) Accountant General, Common Wealth Relations Office
(*v*) Indian Audit and Accounts Department.
(*vi*) The accounts are maintained by the undertakings concerned.

SHORT/LONG ANSWER TYPE

1. Explain the difference between Government accounting and commercial accounting.
2. Give the general structure of the financial administration in India.
3. Explain the role of treasuries in relation to Government Accounting.
4. Explain the following terms :
   (*a*) Consolidated Fund (*b*) Contingency Fund
   (*c*) Public Accounts (*d*) Appropriations
5. Describe in detail compilation of Government accounts.
6. How is the Comptroller and Auditor-General of India helpful in the financial administration of the country ?
7. Give the various provisions as given in the Comptroller and Auditor-General's Act, 1971 in regard to conditions of service of C & AG.
8. Explain the powers and duties of the Comptroller and Auditor-General of India.
9. (*a*) What is the role of Public Accounts Committee in the Control of Public Expenditure ? Discuss.
   (*b*) What are the Appropriation Accounts and who prepares them ? Explain . **(*I.C.W.A. Final*)**
10. Explain, in brief, the system of financial administration in India.
11. Explain briefly the function of the Public Accounts Committee of the Parliament and the State Legislatures. What assistance is rendered to them by the Indian Audit and Accounts Department ?
12. Write short notes on the following :
    (*a*) Appropriation Act (*b*) Vote on Account
13. Describe the unique features of government accounting which make it desirable to treat it as a separate branch of accounting. **(*I.C.W.A. Final*)**
14. Write short notes on :
    (*i*) Public Account (*ii*) Contingency Fund. **(*I.C.W.A. Inter*)**
15. What are the main principles followed by the Government while allocating expenditure on a capital scheme between capital and revenue items. **(*C.A. Inter*)**
16. Describe briefly the Treasury System used for the primary record of Financial Transactions of the Government.
17. Who is the head of the Indian Audit and Accounts Department ? By whom is he appointed ? How are his salaries paid ? **(*I.C.W.A, Stage III*)**

18. Write short notes on : (*a*) Consolidated fund of India; (*b*) Contingency fund; (*c*) Appropriation Act; (*d*) The mode of classification of services in the Central Budget. ***(ICWA—Stage II)***

19. Write short notes :

(*a*) Supplementary Grant;
(*b*) Local Government Accounting;
(*c*) Public Accounts Committee;
(*d*) Structure of Government Accounts.

(ICWA—Stage II)

20. Write short notes on : (*a*) The application of double entry principle in Government accounts; (*b*) Accounting for commercial undertakings by Government departments; (*c*) Contingency Funds; and (*d*) Indian Audit and Accounts Department. ***(ICWA—Stage II)***

21. Write short notes on the following :

(*a*) Introduction of accrual basis accounting in Government of India, (*b*) Functions of Treasuries, (*c*) Demand for grant, (*d*) Votable and non-votable items. ***(ICWA—Stage II)***

22. Write short notes on the following :

(*a*) Appropriation Act; (*b*) Difference between Government and Commercial functions; (*c*) Principles of Government Accounting; (*d*) Demand for Grant. ***(ICWA—Stage II)***

23. What is the function of Suspense Account in Government Accounting ? ***(ICWA—Stage II)***

24. Write notes on the following :

(*a*) Finance Accounts of Central Government; (*b*) Supplementary Grant of Government Finance; (*c*) Public Accounts Committee; (*d*) Consolidated Fund. ***(ICWA—Stage II)***

25. Write short notes on :

(*a*) Treasury System (*b*) Votable and non-votable items. (*c*) Income and expenditure classifications of Central Government. ***(ICWA—Stage II)***

26. Write short notes on :

(*a*) Structure of Government Accounts. (*b*) Distinction between Government Accounts and Commercial Accounts. (*c*) Public Accounts Committee (*d*) Appropriation Act. ***(ICWA—Stage II)***

27. Write short notes on :

(*a*) Public Accounts Committee. (*b*) Purpose of Government Accounting and Commercial Accounting.

(ICWA—Final)

28. (*a*) What are the general principles of Government Accounting ? (*b*) State the basic structure in the form of Government Accounts. ***(ICWA—Final)***

29. Explain the structure of Government Accounts in India. ***(CA—PE-II)***

30. Discuss briefly the Budgeting Process for the Union Budget.